Lecture Notes in Computer Science　9730

Commenced Publication in 1973
Founding and Former Series Editors:
Gerhard Goos, Juris Hartmanis, and Jan van Leeuwen

Editorial Board

More information about this series at http://www.springer.com/series/7412

Aurélio Campilho · Fakhri Karray (Eds.)

Image Analysis and Recognition

13th International Conference, ICIAR 2016
in Memory of Mohamed Kamel
Póvoa de Varzim, Portugal, July 13–15, 2016
Proceedings

 Springer

Editors
Aurélio Campilho
University of Porto
Porto
Portugal

Fakhri Karray
University of Waterloo
Waterloo, ON
Canada

ISSN 0302-9743   ISSN 1611-3349   (electronic)
Lecture Notes in Computer Science
ISBN 978-3-319-41500-0   ISBN 978-3-319-41501-7   (eBook)
DOI 10.1007/978-3-319-41501-7

Library of Congress Control Number: 2016942533

LNCS Sublibrary: SL6 – Image Processing, Computer Vision, Pattern Recognition, and Graphics

Printed on acid-free paper

This Springer imprint is published by Springer Nature
The registered company is Springer International Publishing AG Switzerland

Preface

The 2016 International Conference on Image Analysis and Recognition (ICIAR 2016) along with these proceedings are dedicated to the memory of the founding chair of this conference, the late Mohamed Kamel, University Research Chair Professor at the University of Waterloo, Canada. Mohamed Kamel passed away peacefully on December 4, 2015. Mohamed was a friend, a research partner, and an enthusiast of this series of conferences, held periodically in Portugal and Canada, and which ran its 13th edition this year. Mohamed's passing was a great loss to our research community, and during this conference we organized in his honor, a special session dedicated to his memory and entitled: "Advances in Data Analytics and Pattern Recognition with Applications."

This series of annual conferences offers an opportunity for the participants to interact and present their latest research in theory, methodology, and applications of image analysis and recognition. ICIAR 2016, the International Conference on Image Analysis and Recognition, was held in Póvoa do Varzim, Portugal, July 13–15, 2016. ICIAR is organized by AIMI—Association for Image and Machine Intelligence—a not-for-profit organization registered in Ontario, Canada.

We received a total of 167 papers, 144 regular and 23 short papers, from 38 countries. Before the review process all the papers were checked for similarity using a comparison database of scholarly work. The review process was carried out by members of the Program Committee alongside other expert reviewers in the field of the conference. Each paper was reviewed by at least two reviewers, and checked by the conference chairs. A total of 89 papers (79 regular and 10 short) were finally accepted and appear in these proceedings. We would like to express our gratitude to the authors for their contribution, and we kindly thank the reviewers for the careful evaluation and feedback provided to the authors. It is this collective effort that resulted in the strong conference program and high-quality proceedings we are producing.

We were very pleased to include in our program, four outstanding keynote talks: "Computational Medicine: Towards Integrated Management of Cerebral Aneurysms" by Alexandro Frangi, University of Sheffield, UK; "Face Analysis for Intelligent Human–Computer Interaction" by Matti Pietikäinen, University of Oulu, Finland; "Novel Formulations of Large-Scale Image Retrieval" by Jiri Matas, Czech Technical University, Prague, Czech Republic; and "Sequence-Based Estimation of Multinomial Random Variables" by John Oommen, Carleton University, Ottawa, Canada. We would like to express our gratitude to the keynote speakers for accepting our invitation to share their vision and recent advances in their areas of expertise.

We would like to thank warmly Khaled Hammouda, the webmaster of the conference, for maintaining the website, interacting with the authors, and preparing the proceedings. We are also grateful to Springer's editorial staff, for supporting this publication in the LNCS series. We also would like to acknowledge the professional service of Viagens Abreu in taking care of the registration process and the special events of the conference.

Finally, we were very pleased to welcome all the participants to ICIAR 2016. For those who were not able to attend, we hope this publication provides a good insight into the research work presented at the conference, and we look forward to meeting you at the next ICIAR conference.

July 2016   Aurélio Campilho
                                                                      Fakhri Karray

Organization

General Chairs

Aurélio Campilho
University of Porto, Portugal
campilho@fe.up.pt

Fakhri Karray
University of Waterloo, Canada
karray@uwaterloo.ca

Conference Secretariat

Viagens Abreu SA
Porto, Portugal
congresses.porto@viagensabreu.pt

Webmaster

Khaled Hammouda
Waterloo, Ontario, Canada
khaledh@aimiconf.org

Supported by

AIMI – Association for Image and Machine Intelligence

Center for Biomedical Engineering Research
INESC TEC - INESC Technology and Science
Portugal

FEUP **FACULDADE DE ENGENHARIA**
UNIVERSIDADE DO PORTO

Department of Electrical and Computer Engineering
Faculty of Engineering
University of Porto
Portugal

CPAMI – Centre for Pattern Analysis and Machine Intelligence
University of Waterloo
Canada

Advisory Committee

M. Ahmadi	University of Windsor, Canada
P. Bhattacharya	Concordia University, Canada
T.D. Bui	Concordia University, Canada
M. Cheriet	University of Quebec, Canada
E. Dubois	University of Ottawa, Canada
Z. Duric	George Mason University, USA
G. Granlund	Linköping University, Sweden
L. Guan	Ryerson University, Canada
M. Haindl	Institute of Information Theory and Automation, Czech Republic
E. Hancock	The University of York, UK
J. Kovacevic	Carnegie Mellon University, USA
M. Kunt	Swiss Federal Institute of Technology (EPFL), Switzerland
K.N. Plataniotis	University of Toronto, Canada
A. Sanfeliu	Technical University of Catalonia, Spain
M. Shah	University of Central Florida, USA
M. Sid-Ahmed	University of Windsor, Canada
C.Y. Suen	Concordia University, Canada
A.N. Venetsanopoulos	University of Toronto, Canada
M. Viergever	University of Utrecht, The Netherlands
B. Vijayakumar	Carnegie Mellon University, USA
R. Ward	University of British Columbia, Canada
D. Zhang	The Hong Kong Polytechnic University, Hong Kong, SAR China

Program Committee

A. Abate	University of Salerno, Italy
J. Alba-Castro	University of Vigo, Spain
E. Alegre	University of Leon, Spain
L. Alexandre	University of Beira Interior, Portugal
H. Araújo	University of Coimbra, Portugal
E. Balaguer-Ballester	Bournmouth University, UK
T. Barata	Center for Earth and Space Research of University of Coimbra - CITEUC, Portugal
J. Barbosa	University of Porto, Portugal
J. Barron	University of Western Ontario, Canada
J. Batista	University of Coimbra, Portugal
A. Bharath	Imperial College, London, UK
J. Bioucas	University of Lisbon, Portugal
G. Bonnet-Loosli	Clermont Université, LIMOS, France
F. Camastra	University of Naples Parthenope, Italy
J. Cardoso	INESC TEC and University of Porto, Portugal
G. Carneiro	University of Adelaide, Australia
S. Choppin	Sheffield Hallam University, UK
M. Coimbra	University of Porto, Portugal
M. Correia	University of Porto, Portugal
S. Cruces	University of Seville, Spain
A. Dawoud	University of Southern Mississippi, USA
J. Debayle	Ecole Nationale Supérieure des Mines de Saint-Etienne (ENSM-SE), France
J. Dias	University of Coimbra, Portugal
G. Doretto	West Virginia University, USA
F. Dornaika	University of the Basque Country, Spain
M. El-Sakka	University of Western Ontario, Canada
J. Fernandez	CNB-CSIC, Spain
R. Fisher	University of Edinburgh, UK
G. Freeman	University of Waterloo, Canada
D. Frejlichowski	West Pomeranian University of Technology, Poland
G. Giacinto	University of Cagliari, Italy
G. Grossi	The University of Milan, Italy
L. Guan	Ryerson University, Canada
M. Haindl	Institute of Information Theory and Automation, Czech Republic
L. Heutte	Université de Rouen, France
C. Hong	The Hong Kong Polytechnic University, Hong Kong, SAR China
L. Igual	University of Barcelona, Spain
A. Khamis	CPAMI, University of Waterloo, Canada
Y. Kita	National Institute AIST, Japan
A. Kong	Nanyang Technological University, Singapore

J. Tavares	University of Porto, Portugal
L. Teixeira	University of Porto, Portugal
R. Torres	University of Campinas (UNICAMP), Brazil
A. Torsello	Università Ca' Foscari Venezia, Italy
A. Uhl	University of Salzburg, Austria
C. Veiga	IBIV - Sergas, Spain
M. Vento	Università di Salerno, Italy
Y. Voisin	Université de Bourgogne, France
E. Vrscay	University of Waterloo, Canada
Z. Wang	University of Waterloo, Canada
J. Weber	Université de Lorraine, France
M. Wirth	University of Guelph, Canada
J. Wu	University of Windsor, Canada
X. Xie	Swansea University, UK
J. Xue	University College London, UK
P. Yan	Philips Research, USA
P. Zemcik	Brno University of Technology, Czech Republic
Q. Zhang	Waseda University, Japan
H. Zhou	Queen's University Belfast, UK
R. Zwiggelaar	Aberystwyth University, UK

Additional Reviewers

R. Abdelmoula	University of Waterloo, Canada
R. Araujo	University of Waterloo, Canada
M. Ashraf	InnoVision Systems, Egypt
J. Avelino	Instituto Superior Tecnico, Portugal
A. Barkah	University of Waterloo, Canada
S. Bedawi	University of Waterloo, Canada
E. Bhullar	University of Saskatchewan, Canada
M. Camplani	University of Bristol, UK
C. Caridade	Polytechnic Institute of Coimbra, Portugal
C. Chen	West Virginia University, USA
M. Colic	North American University, USA
A. Cunha	University of Trás-os-Montes-e-Alto-Douro, Portugal
J. Cunha	University of Porto, Portugal
B. Dashtbozorg	Eindhoven University of Technology, The Netherlands
A. Dehban	Instituto Superior Tecnico, Portugal
A. Farahat	Hitachi America, Ltd., USA
L. Fernandez	University of León, Spain
J. Ferreira	University of Porto, Portugal
P. Ferreira	INESC TEC, Portugal
E. Fidalgo	University of Leon, Spain
M. Gangeh	University of Toronto, Canada
V. Gonzalez	The University of Edinburgh, UK
M. Hortas	University of Coruña, Spain

Contents

Image Enhancement and Restoration

Image Quality Assessment

Image Segmentation

Pattern Analysis and Recognition

Feature Extraction

Detection and Recognition

Matching

Motion and Tracking

3D Computer Vision

RGB-D Camera Applications

Visual Perception in Robotics

Biometrics

Biomedical Imaging

Brain Imaging

Cardiovascular Image Analysis

Image Analysis in Ophthalmology

Document Analysis

Applications

Obituaries

Advances in Data Analytics and Pattern Recognition with Applications

Adaptation Approaches in Unsupervised Learning: A Survey of the State-of-the-Art and Future Directions

JunHong Wang[1,2(✉)], YunQian Miao[3], Alaa Khamis[2,4], Fakhri Karray[2], and Jiye Liang[1]

[1] School of Computer and Information Technology,
Shanxi University, Taiyuan 030006, China
wjhwjh@sxu.edu.cn
[2] Department of Electrical and Computer Engineering,
University of Waterloo, Waterloo N2L 3G1, Canada
[3] NCR Canada Ltd., Waterloo N2V 1N3, Canada
[4] Engineering Science Department, Suez University, Suez, Egypt

Abstract. In real applications, data continuously evolve over time and change from one setting to another. This inspires the development of adaptive learning algorithms to deal with this data dynamics. Adaptation mechanisms for unsupervised learning have received an increasing amount of attention from researchers. This research activity has produced a lot of results in tackling some of the challenging problems of the adaptation process that are still open. This paper is a brief review of adaptation mechanisms in unsupervised learning focusing on approaches recently reported in the literature for adaptive clustering and novelty detection and discussing some future directions. Although these approaches have able to cope with different levels of data non-stationarity, there is a crucial need to extend these approaches to be able to handle large amount of data in distributed resource-limited environments.

Keywords: Domain adaptation · Unsupervised learning · Clustering · Novelty detection · Adaptation mechanisms

1 Introduction

In many real-world applications such as in speech recognition, finance and social media, data keep evolving and their properties changing from one domain to another. For example, in order to successfully develop automatic speech recognition (ASR) applications in real environments, it is crucial to take into account several mismatches between the testing and training requirement. These differences include speaker variabilities, environmental mismatches and language mismatches [1–3]. Another example is the Customers' buying preferences, which may vary over time, depending on the season, holidays, and availability.

© Springer International Publishing Switzerland 2016
A. Campilho and F. Karray (Eds.): ICIAR 2016, LNCS 9730, pp. 3–11, 2016.
DOI: 10.1007/978-3-319-41501-7_1

With the evolving of the concepts, the old learning model can not be suitable anymore. The changing of data distribution consequently affects the unsupervised learning model [4–6].

To address these difficulties, adaptation mechanisms for unsupervised learning are currently being extensively studied. The purpose of unsupervised learning is to extract valuable concepts or information from the data. The main tasks of unsupervised learning often include different adaptive clustering approaches and novelty detection (also often used as outlier detection or anomaly detection) [7–10].

This paper is organized as follows. Adaptive clustering approaches such as evolutionary spectral clustering techniques, self-organizing map, incremental clustering methods and clustering concept drift problem are outlined in Sect. 2. In Sect. 3, probabilistic-based novelty detection, neighborhood-based novelty detection, density ratio-based approach and the one-class SVM method are reviewed. Section 4 highlights the current and future research directions in the area. We conclude with a set of observations in Sect. 5.

2   Adaptive Clustering Approaches

According to the properties of unlabeled data, many different adaptive clustering approaches with different inspirations have been proposed. The following subsections describe some of these approaches.

2.1   Evolutionary Spectral Clustering Techniques

Evolving spectral graph describes a lot of real-world phenomena that evolve with time, such as social relationships, metabolic networks, etc. The object of the method is to discover the partitions of the evolving spectral graph such that the edges within a partition have high weight and the edges between these partitions have low weight. In [11], a kernel spectral clustering model with memory effect is proposed, which is an extension model of the Kernel Spectral Clustering (KSC). In [12], corresponds to a weighted kernel principal component analysis (PCA) approach based on least-squares SVM, a formulation for multi-way spectral clustering for evolving data is proposed. Most of the existing spectral clustering methods are effective and have already been used in many real areas such as pattern recognition, image analysis and speech recognition [13–16]. A challenge of the method of spectral clustering is how to change the models to process dynamic clustering of data in online resources application such as social networks.

2.2   Self-organizing Map

The self-organizing maps (SOM) have been commonly applied in the process of dealing with various problems, such as pattern recognition, feature extraction, image analysis [17,18]. SOM use the inherent property of local modeling and topology preservation of units that enhances interpretability of dynamics to deal with time-series prediction [19]. *Kohonen's* SOM is an efficient universal method, by projection into a lower dimension, which can be used to abstract of multivariate mean profiles [20]. In [21], self-organizing map is modified to incorporate long-term and short-term memory that enable discovering the occurrence of new clusters and exploring the properties of structural changes in data at the same time. However, as for unsupervised sequence processing in a common dynamic, a unified notation and a precise mathematical investigation and characterization of these models are needed.

2.3   Incremental Clustering Methods

Incremental clustering methods are designed with the ability to handle the dynamics in cluster results. For non-stationary data in many areas, online clustering is a huge challenge. Some online algorithms are attempting to suit for the dynamic datasets through some strategies. In [22], an incremental K-means is proposed based on K-means algorithm. An incremental algorithm is presented in [23], which deals with online topological mapping by relying on spectral clustering. Also, a similar approach for processing the problem of appearance-based localization in outdoor environments is given in [24,25]. Compared to the classical spectral clustering, the incremental approach does not need to save a huge and even growing data set, so many incremental algorithms have similar accuracy but with much lower computation costs.

2.4   Clustering Concept Drift Problem

Special emphasis is paid to concept drift problem in data stream mining. Data streams can be viewed as a series of data records. As the concepts and clusters in the data change with time, the underlying clusters may also change considerably with the time. Cao introduced a density-based method in an evolving data set for discovering arbitrary shape clusters [26]. In [27], a framework used to detect the drifting concepts based on N-Nodeset importance representative for categorical time-evolving data is proposed. In [28], a data labeling method is studied to detect the clusters of a time window from the concepts of the preceding window. Many algorithms for clustering time-evolving data have been applied in real-life data sets. For example, a clustering approach is proposed in [29] to analyze the clustering results of mining user profiles in the network.

2.5   Discussion

Clustering approaches do not need a prior knowledge of data distribution and can be used in incremental models. In addition, they can help in understanding the data distribution. However, some clustering-based techniques require a suitable similarity measure computation in a pairwise fashion between the data points and it is computationally expensive to calculate the similarity in high-dimensional data sets. Although the discussed approaches showed appealing success in making unsupervised learning algorithms adaptive to non-stationary data, the scalability of these algorithms is not well considered.

3   Novelty Detection

Novelty detection can be viewed as binary classification problems that identifies new-appeared instances in the test data that differ in certain respects from a collection of training data that contains only normal data. Because there exists a great deal of possible abnormal modes and some of them may be evolving continuously, it is impossible to model all the abnormal patterns [7, 8]. The following subsections describe some novelty detection techniques.

3.1   Probabilistic-Based Novelty Detection

Probabilistic-based methods for novelty detection are based on estimating the generative probability density function (PDF) of the normal data. There are many PDF estimation approaches used to produce models based on normal data. In [30], for the estimation of model parameters, a Gaussian Mixture Model is proposed to incorporate side information in the form of equivalence constraints into the model estimation procedure. Park et al. [31] provide theoretical support to this estimator by showing its asymptotic consistency on the minimum volume set of a probability density. Besides statistical methods, Breaban et al. [32] use projection pursuit for novelty detection by identifying subspaces of the original attribute space where abnormal data are present. Probabilistic-based approaches are mathematically well-formed and after the model has been constructed, only a minimal amount of information is required. However, the performance of probabilistic-based approaches is limited when the size of the training set is very small.

3.2   Neighborhood-Based Novelty Detection

The neighborhood-based methods analyze the k-nearest samples of data points, which assume potential novelties lie far away from their neighbors, while normal data lie near their neighborhoods. Zhang et al. propose in [33] a method for detection the outlier of objects using a new Local Distance-based Outlier Factor. In [34], the proposed approach combines a nearest neighbours data description (NNDD) and a structural risk minimisation (SRM) for the detection of novelty, namely NNDDSRM. Bay and Schwabacher [35] introduced the distance-based outlier detection algorithm called ORCA. Neighborhood-based approaches do not need a priori knowledge of the data distribution and share some common assumptions with probabilistic approaches. However, these approaches rely on the existence of suitable similar metrics to establish the similarity between two samples, even in high-dimensional data spaces.

3.3   Density Ratio-Based Approach

Density ratio-based estimation has attracted many interest due to its potential for solving many challenging problems, such as outlier detection, covariant shift adaptation and some others. The main idea of density ratio-based approach is to compare the densities of the test and reference data, and then identify the novel instances based on the ratio between these two densities. The estimation of density ratio can be done directly without estimating the density functions of test and reference data [5]. In [36], a locally adaptive method for density-ratio estimation is proposed, in which the density ratio between reference and new data is used to detection novelty. Song et al. [37] introduce the concept of relative novelty and modified the one-class SVM formulation to incorporate the reference densities as density ratios. Density ratio-based approach is very effective in detecting relative novelties, however, it is limited in identifying novelties that are very dissimilar to the reference data.

3.4   The One-Class SVM Method

SVMs are noted as a popular technique used to form decision boundaries that separate data into different classes. The original SVM is a network that is ideally suited for binary pattern classification of linearly separable data. A number of attempts have been performed to transfer the idea of using kernels to compute inner products to the domain of unsupervised learning. A one-class SVM for static novelty detection proposed in [38] is used to construct a normality model to characterize the distribution of energy by the vibration spectra obtained from a three-shaft engine. Also, a one-class SVM method is proposed in [37], which assumes that samples locating outside of the boundary are novel. The main challenge of these methods is how to choose the appropriate kernel function.

3.5   Discussion

Probabilistic-based and neighborhood-based methods use distance measure to discriminate between novel and normal data samples. Density ratio-based approach requires to compare the densities of the test and reference data, and detect the novelty based on the ratio between these two densities. Meanwhile, one-class SVM approach assumes that objects locating outside of the boundary are novel and build the model based on the boundary of normal data.

4   Future Directions

There are several promising directions for further research in adaptation mechanisms in unsupervised learning, which are mainly associated with the open challenges that need to be tackled for the effective operation of the approach.

(1) Simultaneous detection of evolving and emerging concepts in non-stationary data.

In dynamic data, there usually exist two types of novelties: evolving and emerging. Evolving novelties are characterized by relatively new aspects of existing concepts, while emerging novelties are represented by concepts which are very different from the previously seen ones. In real situations, many of the truly novel concepts do not perfectly fit under one of these two categories, and normally have both emerging and evolving aspects [5]. Therefore, how to recognize both emerging and evolving novelties is an important direction.

(2) Fast adaptive algorithms for personalized learning.

Recently, personalized learning has received a lot of attention [39]. Most of algorithms for unsupervised learning are in direct interaction with thousands and may be millions of system users. The variety of users and their needs generate a challenging aspect of non-stationarity in the data. For example, a speech recognition system trained on the Canadian accent exhibits a degraded performance when applied to users of other accents. This generates a pressing need from those users to adapt the recognition models to provide personalized decisions. This has to be done using a few training samples provided by the user over a short period of time. The state-of-the-art approaches for domain adaptation depend on retraining of the learned models for each new user which is extremely inefficient.

(3) Other promising directions include, but are not limited to, multi-source domain adaptation and incremental optimization. Multi-source domain adaptation. Some researches [40] focus on the multi-source domain adaptation problem where there is more than one source domain available together with only one target domain. A core issue of multi-source domain adaptation is how to select good sources and samples for the adaptation. Many methods about incremental clustering [24,25] have been studied. In incremental learning procedures, the optimization process should be investigated in order to avoid over-fitting problems.

5   Conclusion

The non-stationary aspects of the data represent a new challenge for many existing unsupervised learning algorithms in machine learning. This generates a pressing need to efficiently adapt the unsupervised learning models to the users and the changing environments in the real-world applications such as speech recognition, finance and social media. The paper has reviewed recent adaptation mechanisms in unsupervised learning such as adaptive clustering and novelty detection. The paper also highlighted some future directions in this area. Most of existing approaches are mainly designed on the basis of traditional centralized systems, which do not consider handling either the large amount of data in distributed environments or the efficiency issues in resource-limited environments.

Acknowledgement. The paper is dedicated to the late Professor Mohamed Kamel, founding director of Centre for Pattern Analysis and Machine Intelligence (CPAMI) who gave us the chance to work on this interesting area of research. This contribution was made possible by NPRP grant # 06-1220-1-233 from the Qatar National Research Fund (a member of Qatar Foundation). The statements made herein are solely the responsibility of the authors.

References

1. Chan, A., Gouvea, E., Singh, R., Mosur, R., Rosenfield, R., Sun, Y., Huggins-Daines, D.: (First Draft) Hieroglpyhs : Building speech applications using sphinx and related resources (2004)
2. Lee, C.H., Lin, C.H., Juang, B.H.: A study on speaker adaptation of the parameters of continuous density hidden Markov models. IEEE Trans. Sig. Process. **39**(4), 806–814 (1991)
3. Leggetter, C.J., Woodland, P.C.: Maximum likelihood linear regression for speaker adaptation of continuous density hidden Markov models. Comput. Speech Lang. **9**(2), 171–185 (1995)
4. Miao, Y.Q.: Adaptive learning algorithms for non-stationary data, Ph.D. thesis, University of Waterloo (2015)
5. Miao, Y.Q., Farahat, A.K., Kamel, M.S.: Detecting emerging and evolving novelties with locally adaptive density ratio estimation. Knowl. Inf. Syst., 1–29 (2016)
6. Farahat, A.K., Kamel, M.S.: Statistical semantics for enhancing document clustering. Knowl. Inf. Syst. **28**(2), 365–393 (2011)
7. Pimentel, M.A.F., Clifton, D.A., Clifton, L., Tarassenko, L.: A review of novelty detection. Sig. Process. **99**, 215–249 (2014)
8. Chandola, V., Banerjee, A., Kumar, V.: Anomaly detection: a survey. ACM Comput. Surv. (CSUR) **41**(3), 1–69 (2009)
9. Sayed-Mouchaweh, M., Lughofer, E.: Learning in Non-Stationary Environments: Methods and Applications. Springer, New York (2012)
10. Sugiyama, M., Kawanabe, M.: Machine Learning in Non-Stationary Environments: Introduction to Covariate Shift Adaptation (2012)
11. Chi, Y., Song, X., Zhou, D., Hino, K., Tseng, B.L.: Evolutionary spectral clustering by incorporating temporal smoothness. In: Proceedings of the 13th ACM SIGKDD International Conference on Knowledge Discovery and Data Mining, pp. 153–162 (2007)
12. Langone, R.: Clustering evolving data using kernel-based methods. Ph.D. thesis, KU Leuven (2014)
13. Langone, R., Alzate, C., Suykens, J.A.K.: Kernel spectral clustering with memory efect. Phy. A Stat. Mech. Appl. **392**(10), 2588–2606 (2013)
14. Alzate, C., Suykens, J.A.K.: Multiway spectral clustering with out-of-sample extensions through weighted kernel PCA. IEEE Trans. Pattern Anal. Mach. Intell. **32**(2), 335–347 (2010)
15. Chang, H., Yeung, D.Y.: Robust path-based spectral clustering. Pattern Recogn. **41**(1), 191–203 (2008)
16. Wang, L., Leckie, C., Kotagiri, R., Bezdek, J.: Approximate pairwise clustering for large data sets via sampling plus extension. Pattern Recogn. **44**(2), 222–235 (2011)
17. Cottrell, M., Fort, J.C., Pags, G.: Theoretical aspects of the SOM algorithm. Neurocomputing **21**(1), 119–138 (1998)

18. de Bodt, E., Verleysen, M., Cottrell, M.: Kohonen maps versus vector quantization for data analysis. In: ESANN, pp. 211–218 (1997)
19. Barreto, G.A.: Time series prediction with the self-organizing map: A review. In: Hitzler, P., Hammer, B. (eds.) Perspectives on Neural-Symbolic Integration, pp. 135–158. Springer, Berlin (2007)
20. Kohonen, T.: Self-Organizing Maps, 3rd edn. Springer, Berlin (2001)
21. Sarlin, P.: Self-organizing time map: an abstraction of temporal multivariate patterns. Neurocomputing **99**, 496–508 (2013)
22. Chakraborty, S., Nagwani, N.K.: Analysis and Study of Incremental K-Means Clustering Algorithm. In: Mantri, A., Nandi, S., Kumar, G., Kumar, S. (eds.) HPAGC 2011. CCIS, vol. 169, pp. 338–341. Springer, Heidelberg (2011)
23. Langone, R., Agudelo, O.M., De Moor, B., et al.: Incremental kernel spectral clustering for online learning of non-stationary data. Neurocomputing **139**, 246–260 (2014)
24. Valgren, C., Duckett, T., Lilienthal, A.: Incremental spectral clustering and its application to topological mapping. In: Proceedings of the IEEE International Conference on Robotics and Automation, pp. 4283–4288 (2007)
25. Valgren, C., Lilienthal, A.: Incremental spectral clustering and seasons: Appearance-based localization in outdoor environments. In: Robotics and Automation, ICRA, pp. 1856–1861 (2008)
26. Cao, F., Ester, M., Qian, W., Zhou, A.: Density-based clustering over an evolving data stream with noise. In: Proceedings of the Sixth SIAM International Conference on Data Mining (SDM), pp. 328–339 (2006)
27. Chen, H.L., Chen, M.S., Lin, S.C.: Catching the trend: a framework for clustering concept-drifting categorical data. IEEE Trans. Knowl. Data Eng. **21**(5), 652–665 (2009)
28. Cao, F.Y., Huang, Z.X., Liang, J.Y.: Trend analysis of categorical data streams with a concept change method. Inform. Sci. **276**, 160–173 (2007)
29. Nasraoui, O., Soliman, M., Saka, E., Badia, A., Germain, R.: A web usage mining framework for mining evolving user profiles in dynamic web sites. Trans. Knowl. Data Eng. **20**(2), 202–215 (2008)
30. Shental, N., Bar-Hillel, A., Hertz, T., et al.: Computing Gaussian mixture models with EM using equivalence constraints. Adv. Neural Inform. Process. Syst. (NIPS) **16**(8), 465–472 (2004)
31. Park, C., Huang, J.Z., Ding, Y.: A computable plug-in estimator of minimum volume sets for novelty detection. Oper. Res. **58**(5), 1469–1480 (2009)
32. Breaban, M., Luchian, H.: Outlier detection with nonlinear projection pursuit. Int. J. Comput. Commun. Control **8**(1), 30–36 (2013)
33. Zhang, K., Hutter, M., Jin, H.: A new local distance-based outlier detection approach for scattered real-word data. Adv. Knowl. Discov. Data Min. **5476**, 813–822 (2009)
34. Cabral, G.G., Oliveira, A.L.I., Cahu, C.B.G.: Combining nearest neighbor data description and structural risk minimization for one-class classification. Neural Comput. Appl. **18**(2), 175–183 (2009)
35. Bay, S.D., Schwabacher, M.: Mining distance-based outlier sinnear linear time with randomization, a simplep runing rule. In: Proceedings of the 9th ACM International Conference on Knowl edge Discovery and Data Mining (SIGKDD), pp. 29–38. ACM (2003)

36. Miao, Y.Q., Farahat, A.K., Kamel, M.S.: Locally adaptive density ratio for detecting novelty in twitter streams. In: The 6th International Workshop on Modeling Social Media (MSM) - Behavioral Analytics in Social Media, Big Data and the Web, pp. 799–804 (2015)
37. Song, L., Teo, C.H., Smola, A.J.: Relative novelty detection. In: International Conference on Artificial Intelligence and Statistics (AISTATS), pp. 536–543 (2009)
38. Scholkopf, B., Williamson, R.C., Smola, A.J., Shawe-Taylor, J., Platt, J.: Support vector method for novelty detection. Adv. Neural Inform. Process. Syst.(NIPS) **12**, 582–588 (1999)
39. Hattori, Y., Inoue, S., Masaki, T., Hirakawa, G., Sudo, O.: Gathering large scale human activity information using mobile sensor devices. In: Proceedings of the Second International Workshop on Network Traffic Control, Analysis and Applications, pp. 708–713 (2010)
40. Sun, S., Shi, H., Wu, Y.: A survey of multi-source domain adaptation. Inform. Fusion **24**, 84–92 (2015)

Semi-supervised Dictionary Learning Based on Hilbert-Schmidt Independence Criterion

Mehrdad J. Gangeh[1,2]([✉]), Safaa M.A. Bedawi[3], Ali Ghodsi[4],
and Fakhri Karray[3]

[1] Department of Medical Biophysics, University of Toronto, Toronto, Canada
mehrdad.gangeh@utoronto.ca
[2] Departments of Radiation Oncology, and Imaging Research - Physical Sciences,
Sunnybrook Health Sciences Center, Toronto, Canada
[3] Department of Electrical and Computer Engineering,
Center for Pattern Analysis and Machine Intelligence,
University of Waterloo, Waterloo, Canada
{sbedawi,karray}@uwaterloo.ca
[4] Department of Statistics and Actuarial Science,
University of Waterloo, Waterloo, Canada
aghodsib@uwaterloo.ca

Abstract. In this paper, a novel semi-supervised dictionary learning and sparse representation (SS-DLSR) is proposed. The proposed method benefits from the supervisory information by learning the dictionary in a space where the dependency between the data and class labels is maximized. This maximization is performed using Hilbert-Schmidt independence criterion (HSIC). On the other hand, the global distribution of the underlying manifolds were learned from the unlabeled data by minimizing the distances between the unlabeled data and the corresponding nearest labeled data in the space of the dictionary learned. The proposed SS-DLSR algorithm has closed-form solutions for both the dictionary and sparse coefficients, and therefore does not have to learn the two iteratively and alternately as is common in the literature of the DLSR. This makes the solution for the proposed algorithm very fast. The experiments confirm the improvement in classification performance on benchmark datasets by including the information from both labeled and unlabeled data, particularly when there are many unlabeled data.

1 Introduction

Dictionary learning and sparse representation (DLSR) is one of the most successful mathematical models, which has led to state-of-the-art results in various applications such as face recognition [1–3], image denoising [4], texture classification [5], and emotion recognition [6]. DLSR, however, was originally proposed in an unsupervised setting [7]. The main objective function in the optimization problem related to DLSR is to minimize the reconstruction error between the original signal and the reconstructed one in the space of learned dictionary without including the information on class labels into the learning process. To

© Springer International Publishing Switzerland 2016
A. Campilho and F. Karray (Eds.): ICIAR 2016, LNCS 9730, pp. 12–19, 2016.
DOI: 10.1007/978-3-319-41501-7_2

formally describe the original DLSR formulation, we suppose that there is a finite set of data samples denoted as $\mathbf{X} = [\mathbf{x}_1, ..., \mathbf{x}_n] \in \mathbb{R}^{d \times n}$, where d is the dimensionality of the data and n is the number of data samples. In original DLSR, the data is decomposed using a few dictionary atoms by optimizing the empirical cost function

$$L(\mathbf{X}, \mathbf{D}, \boldsymbol{\alpha}) = \sum_{i=1}^{n} l(\mathbf{x}_i, \mathbf{D}, \boldsymbol{\alpha}), \tag{1}$$

where $\mathbf{D} \in \mathbb{R}^{d \times k}$ is a dictionary of k atoms, $\boldsymbol{\alpha} \in \mathbb{R}^{k \times n}$ are the sparse coefficients and L, l are loss functions. In the literature of the DLSR, the reconstruction error, in mean-squared sense, between the original signal and the reconstructed signal is the most common loss function, which is usually regularized by the ℓ_1 norm to induce sparsity into the coefficients. Thus, the formulation in (1) can be written as

$$L(\mathbf{X}, \mathbf{D}, \boldsymbol{\alpha}) = \min_{\mathbf{D}, \boldsymbol{\alpha}} \sum_{i=1}^{n} \left(\tfrac{1}{2} \|\mathbf{x}_i - \mathbf{D}\boldsymbol{\alpha}_i\|_2^2 + \lambda \|\boldsymbol{\alpha}_i\|_1 \right), \tag{2}$$

where $\boldsymbol{\alpha}_i$ is the ith column of α. In order to avoid arbitrarily large values for $\mathbf{D}$ and consequently, arbitrarily small values for α, we need an additional constraint on the dictionary atoms to limit their ℓ_2 norm to be smaller than or equal to one. The complete optimization problem in (2) after adding this constraint is as follows:

$$L(\mathbf{X}, \mathbf{D}, \boldsymbol{\alpha}) = \min_{\mathbf{D}, \boldsymbol{\alpha}} \sum_{i=1}^{n} \left(\tfrac{1}{2} \|\mathbf{x}_i - \mathbf{D}\boldsymbol{\alpha}_i\|_2^2 + \lambda \|\boldsymbol{\alpha}_i\|_1 \right),$$
$$\text{s.t.} \quad \|\mathbf{d}_j\|_2^2 \leq 1 \quad \forall j = 1, ..., k. \tag{3}$$

The original DLSR formulation given in (3) is unsupervised as the category information has not been taken into consideration in the optimization problem. However, in a supervised learning paradigm, where the ultimate goal is the classification of the data, this setting may not lead to an optimal discriminative dictionary nor coefficients. A more recent attempt in the literature was to incorporate the class labels into the learning of the dictionary and/or coefficients (refer to [8] for a review). This modification resulted in a new category of DLSR, namely called supervised dictionary learning and sparse representation (S-DLSR). Improvements (some significant) over unsupervised DLSR have been reported in the literature for the classification tasks [3,9–11].

Although S-DLSR benefits from the side information available from category information to learn a more discriminative dictionary, unfortunately, gathering labeled data is often very expensive and time consuming. Most data available is unlabeled and the sample size of the labeled data is often very small, which has a hindering effect on the discriminative quality of the learned dictionary. Semi-supervised learning (SSL) methods can potentially boost the performance of a machine learning system by utilizing both supervisory information and global data distribution. Using a large amount of unlabeled data, which is usually easily accessible, can improve revealing the manifold global distribution [12], and compensate for the small sample size of labeled data [13].

In this paper, a semi-supervised dictionary learning and sparse representation (SS-DLSR) based on Hilbert-Schmidt independence criterion (HSIC) is proposed. The proposed SS-DLSR approach finds a dictionary based on two criteria: first, the maximization of the dependency between the labeled data and the corresponding category information, and second, minimization of the distances between the unlabeled data and their nearest labeled data. The first criterion guarantees finding the space of maximum discrimination based on the information in the category information and labeled data, whereas the second criterion, guarantees that the unlabeled data remain as close as possible to their nearest-neighbor labeled data. Therefore, the learned dictionary (the projection directions computed by using the aforementioned criteria) benefits from the discriminative power of the category information in the labeled data and proximity information of the unlabeled data as an indication of global manifold distribution. the sparse coefficients are subsequently computed in the space of learned dictionary using the formulation given in (3).

2 Semi-supervised Dictionary Learning and Sparse Representation

2.1 Problem Statement

Let $\mathbf{X} = [\mathbf{x}_1, ..., \mathbf{x}_n] \in \mathbb{R}^{d \times n}$ be n data samples with the dimensionality of d. There are n_l labeled and n_u unlabeled data samples, where $n = n_l + n_u$. Let $\{(\mathbf{x}_1, \mathbf{y}_1), ..., (\mathbf{x}_{n_l}, \mathbf{y}_{n_l})\}$ be the pair of labeled data $(\mathbf{X}_l \in \mathbb{R}^{d \times n_l})$ and the corresponding labels $(\mathbf{Y} \in \{0, 1\}^{c \times n_l}$, where c is the number of classes), and $\mathbf{X}_u = [\mathbf{x}_{n_l+1}, ..., \mathbf{x}_n] \in \mathbb{R}^{d \times n_u}$ be the unlabeled data samples. We would like to find a dictionary, which can be considered as a transformation, based on two criteria (1) maximizing the dependency between the labeled data $\mathbf{X}_l$ and the labels $\mathbf{Y}$, and (2) minimizing the distance between each unlabeled data with the nearest label data. The first criterion is to guarantee finding a discriminative dictionary using the labeled data, and the second criterion is to ensure the unlabeled data samples are mapped close to their neighboring labeled data and therefore, the global connectivity of data is maintained in the space of the learned dictionary.

The first criterion is implemented using the Hilbert-Schmidt independence criterion (HSIC), which will be explained in the next subsection followed by the design of the dictionary and sparse coefficients for the proposed semi-supervised method.

2.2 Hilbert-Schmidt Independence Criterion

HSIC is a kernel-based measure of independence between two random variables $\mathcal{X}$ and $\mathcal{Y}$ proposed first by Gretton *et al.* [14,15]. It is computed based on the Hilbert-Schmidt norm of cross covariance operators in reproducing kernel Hilbert spaces (RKHSs) [15].

Our focus here is the empirical HSIC, which is computed using a finite set of data samples. To this end, considering $\mathcal{Z} := \{(\mathbf{x}_1, \mathbf{y}_1,), ..., (\mathbf{x}_{n_l}, \mathbf{y}_{n_l})\} \subseteq \mathcal{X} \times \mathcal{Y}$ as n_l independent observations drawn from joint probability distribution $P_{\mathcal{X} \times \mathcal{Y}}$, the empirical HSIC is computed using

$$\mathrm{HSIC}(\mathcal{Z}) = \frac{1}{(n_l - 1)^2} \mathrm{tr}(\mathbf{KHBH}), \tag{4}$$

where tr is the trace operator, and $\mathbf{K}$, $\mathbf{B}$, $\mathbf{H} \in \mathbb{R}^{n_l \times n_l}$. $\mathbf{K}$ and $\mathbf{B}$ are kernels on the data and labels, respectively. $\mathbf{H} = \mathbf{I} - n_l^{-1} \mathbf{ee}^\top$, where $\mathbf{I}$ is an identity matrix, $\mathbf{e}$ is a vector of all ones and therefore, $\mathbf{H}$ is a centering matrix. Since the empirical HSIC given in (4) is a measure of dependency between $\mathcal{X}$ and $\mathcal{Y}$, in order to maximize this dependency, tr($\mathbf{KHBH}$) should be maximized.

2.3 Dictionary Learning

As mentioned in the problem statement (Subsect. 2.1), the dictionary is learned based on two criteria. In order to maximize the dependency between the labeled data and the corresponding labels, as shown in [11], the following optimization problem has to be solved:

$$\max_{\mathbf{D}} \quad \mathrm{tr}(\mathbf{D}^\top \mathbf{X}_l \mathbf{HBHX}_l^\top \mathbf{D}),$$
$$\mathrm{s.t.} \quad \mathbf{D}^\top \mathbf{D} = \mathbf{I} \tag{5}$$

where $\mathbf{H}$ is the centering matrix, $\mathbf{B}$ is a kernel on labels, and $\mathbf{D}$ is the dictionary to be learned. By a few manipulations on the objective function given in (5), it can be demonstrated that it is another form of empirical HSIC:

$$\max_{\mathbf{D}} \mathrm{tr}(\mathbf{D}^\top \mathbf{X}_l \mathbf{HBHX}_l^\top \mathbf{D})$$
$$= \max_{\mathbf{D}} \mathrm{tr}(\mathbf{X}_l^\top \mathbf{DD}^\top \mathbf{X}_l \mathbf{HBH})$$
$$= \max_{\mathbf{D}} \mathrm{tr}\left(\left[(\mathbf{D}^\top \mathbf{X}_l)^\top \mathbf{D}^\top \mathbf{X}_l\right] \mathbf{HBH}\right)$$
$$= \max_{\mathbf{D}} \mathrm{tr}(\mathbf{KHBH}), \tag{6}$$

where $\mathbf{K} = (\mathbf{D}^\top \mathbf{X}_l)^\top \mathbf{D}^\top \mathbf{X}_l$ is a linear kernel on the projected labeled data into the space of learned dictionary $\mathbf{D}$. As can be clearly observed from the last statement in (6), the objective function in (5) has the form of the empirical HSIC and thus, the dictionary $\mathbf{D}$ projects the labeled data to the space of maximum dependency with the corresponding labels.

The second criterion is to minimize the distances between the unlabeled data and the nearest neighbor labeled data in the space of the dictionary learned. In other words, considering $\mathbf{z} = \mathbf{D}^\top \mathbf{x}$ as a projected data sample to the space of the learned dictionary, we would like to:

$$\min_{\mathbf{D}} \frac{1}{2} \sum_{i=1}^{n_l} \sum_{j=1}^{n_u} w_{i,j} (\mathbf{z}_i - \mathbf{z}_j)^2, \tag{7}$$

where $w_{i,j}$ are the weights that define the proximity (neighborhood) of the unlabeled to labeled data. One way to define it is based one nearest neighbor, i.e., $w_{i,j} = 1$ if the jth unlabeled data is the nearest to the ith labeled data and $w_{i,j} = 0$ otherwise.

It can be shown [16] that the objective function given in (7) can be written in matrix form as follows:

$$\min_{\mathbf{D}} \frac{1}{2} \sum_{i=1}^{n_l} \sum_{j=1}^{n_u} w_{i,j} (\mathbf{z}_i - \mathbf{z}_j)^2 = \min_{\mathbf{D}} \ \text{tr}(\mathbf{ZLZ}^\top) = \min_{\mathbf{D}} \ \text{tr}(\mathbf{D}^\top \mathbf{XLX}^\top \mathbf{D}), \quad (8)$$

where $\mathbf{L}$ is the Laplacian of the graph made by the projected data points $\mathbf{Z} = [\mathbf{z}_1, ..., \mathbf{z}_n]$ in the space of learned dictionary, and is defined as $\mathbf{L} = \mathbf{Q} - \mathbf{W}$, where $\mathbf{W}(i,j) = w_{i,j}$ and $\mathbf{Q}$ is a diagonal matrix, where $q_{i,i} = \sum_j w_{i,j}$.

Combining the two objective functions given in (5) and 8, the overall optimization problem for the computation of the dictionary can be written as follows:

$$\max_{\mathbf{D}} \ \text{tr} \left[\mathbf{D}^\top \left((1 - \eta) \mathbf{X}_l \mathbf{HBHX}_l^\top - \eta \ \mathbf{XLX}^\top \right) \mathbf{D} \right],$$
$$\text{s.t.} \quad \mathbf{D}^\top \mathbf{D} = \mathbf{I} \quad (9)$$

where $0 \leq \eta \leq 1$ is a constant that determines the relative contributions of the two terms in the objective function. According to the Rayleigh-Ritz theorem [17], the solution for the optimization problem given in (9) is the corresponding eigenvectors of the largest eigenvalues of $\mathbf{\Phi} = (1 - \eta) \mathbf{X}_l \mathbf{HBHX}_l^\top - \eta \ \mathbf{XLX}^\top$.

2.4   Sparse Coefficients

After the computation of the dictionary using (9), the sparse coefficients can be computed using the formulation provided in (2), which is called *lasso* if the dictionary is known [18]. Although (2) can be solved using fast iterative methods, since the dictionary is orthogonal, as shown in [19,20], the sparse coefficients can be computed using soft-thresholding with the soft-thresholding operator $S_\lambda(.)$:

$$\alpha_{ij} = S_\lambda \left(\left[\mathbf{D}^\top \mathbf{x}_i \right]_j \right), \quad (10)$$

where $\alpha_{i,j}$ is the (i,j)th element of $\boldsymbol{\alpha}$ and $S_\lambda(t)$ is defined as follows:

$$S_\lambda(t) = \begin{cases} t - 0.5\lambda & \text{if } t > 0.5\lambda \\ t + 0.5\lambda & \text{if } t < -0.5\lambda \\ 0 & \text{otherwise} \end{cases} \quad (11)$$

3   Experiments and Results

To validate the proposed semi-supervised dictionary learning and sparse representation method (SS-DLSR), two benchmark datasets publicly available from

Table 1. The classification rate (%) of the proposed SS-DLSR algorithm on two benchmark datasets. The results were compared for various settings in the proposed algorithm including different relative contributions of the labeled and unlabeled data on dictionary learning (varying η), and different ratios of labeled to unlabeled data (varying $n_l/(n_l + n_u)$).

$\frac{n_l}{n_l+n_u}$	Sonar			Ionosphere		
	$\eta = 0$	$\eta = 1$	η^*	$\eta = 0$	$\eta = 1$	η^*
0.5	69.03	51.29	70.97	88.45	76.90	86.72
	±5.78	±6.62	±3.95	±2.82	±5.15	±3.90
0.3	66.45	51.94	68.71	85.34	74.83	85.69
	±7.40	±4.01	±8.54	±3.92	±4.16	±3.99
0.1	57.74	49.19	61.45	78.94	73.45	80.34
	±4.97	±5.55	±8.13	±5.50	±5.28	±6.81
0.05	53.55	50.97	55.65	72.07	68.45	74.66
	±5.98	±5.44	±8.20	±13.52	±13.28	±6.56

UCI machine learning repository[1] were used. The two datasets were the Sonar ($n = 208$, $d = 60$, and $c = 2$) and the Parkinsons ($n = 297$, $d = 13$, and $c = 2$) datasets.

The performance of the proposed SS-DLSR was evaluated for a fixed dictionary size ($k = 8$) and varying relative ratio of the labeled to unlabeled data $n_l/(n_l + n_u)$. To this end, 70 % of the data was randomly selected as the training set and 30 % as the test set. The training data was further divided to different ratios of labeled and unlabeled data as shown in Table 1 ($n_l/(n_l + n_u) = \{0.05, 0.1, 0.3, 0.5\}$). One nearest neighbor was used as the proximity measure between the unlabeled and labeled data to determine the matrix of weights in (7). The value of η for the computation of the dictionary in (9) was set to three different values, i.e., 0 (ignoring unlabeled data), 1 (ignoring labeled data), and η^* (the most discriminative dictionary corresponding to best classification performance). The sparse coefficients were computed for the labeled portion of the training data as well as for the test data. A support vector machine (SVM) with radial basis function (RBF) kernel was used for the classification of the data by submission of the sparse coefficients to the classifier as suggested in [21]. The SVM was tuned using 5-fold cross validation on the labeled portion of training data to find the optimal kernel width (γ^*) and optimal trade-off parameter (C^*). Subsequently, the SVM was trained on whole labeled data in the training set using the optimal γ^* and C^* values and tested on the test set. The experiments were repeated 10 times for different random split of the data to training and test sets. The performance is reported in terms of classifier accuracy (averaged over 10 runs) in Table 1.

---

[1] http://archive.ics.uci.edu/ml/.

From the results provided in Table 1, there are several immediate observations. First, by adding unlabeled data to the learning of the dictionary (the columns in Table 1 corresponding with η^*), the classification performance is increased, which means that the learned dictionary is more discriminative. This reveals that the proposed algorithm can effectively incorporate the information from both labeled and unlabeled data into the learning of the dictionary. Second, by decreasing the rate of labeled to unlabeled data $(n_l/(n_l + n_u))$, the gain in performance from adding unlabeled data is increased. In realistic settings, there usually exist many unlabeled data and only a small number of labeled data. The proposed SS-DLSR algorithm benefits more from the information provided by the unlabeled data in these situations as can be observed by comparing the column corresponding with η^* (including both the labeled and unlabeled data into the dictionary learning) and the column with $\eta = 0$ (including only labeled data into the dictionary learning).

4 Discussion and Conclusion

In this paper, a novel semi-supervised dictionary learning and sparse representation method was proposed. A discriminative dictionary was learned in the space of maximum dependency between the labeled data and class labels, where the connectivity of the data was maintained by minimizing the distances between the unlabeled data and the corresponding nearest labeled data. As can be seen from (9), the dictionary has a closed form solution. Also, by using soft-thresholding, the sparse coefficients can be computed using a closed-form solution as given in (10). The proposed SS-DLSR approach is, therefore, very fast. The effectiveness of the proposed method in learning from both supervisory information (based on labeled data) and graph connectivity information (based on unlabeled data) was demonstrated by experiments on two benchmark datasets from UCI machine learning repository.

Acknowledgment. The first author gratefully acknowledges the funding from the Natural Sciences and Engineering Research Council (NSERC) of Canada under Post-doctoral Fellowship (PDF-454649-2014).

References

1. Zhong, C., Sun, Z., Tan, T.: Robust 3D face recognition using learned visual codebook. In: IEEE Conference on Computer Vision and Pattern Recognition (CVPR), pp. 1–6 (2007)
2. Wright, J., Yang, A.Y., Ganesh, A., Sastry, S.S., Ma, Y.: Robust face recognition via sparse representation. IEEE Trans. Pattern Anal. Mach. Intell. **31**(2), 210–227 (2009)
3. Yang, M., Zhang, L., Feng, X., Zhang, D.: Fisher discrimination dictionary learning for sparse representation. In: 13th IEEE International Conference on Computer Vision (ICCV), pp. 543–550 (2011)

4. Mairal, J., Elad, M., Sapiro, G.: Sparse representation for color image restoration. IEEE Trans. Image Process. **17**(1), 53–69 (2008)
5. Gangeh, M.J., Ghodsi, A., Kamel, M.S.: Dictionary learning in texture classification. In: Kamel, M., Campilho, A. (eds.) ICIAR 2011, Part I. LNCS, vol. 6753, pp. 335–343. Springer, Heidelberg (2011)
6. Gangeh, M.J., Fewzee, P., Ghodsi, A., Kamel, M.S., Karray, F.: Multiview supervised dictionary learning in speech emotion recognition. IEEE/ACM Trans. Audio Speech Lang. Process. **22**(6), 1056–1068 (2014)
7. Elad, M.: Sparse and Redundant Representations: From Theory to Applications in Signal and Image Processing. Springer, New York (2010)
8. Gangeh, M.J., Farahat, A.K., Ghodsi, A., Kamel, M.S.: Supervised dictionary learning and sparse representation-a review. CoRR abs/1502.05928 (2015)
9. Mairal, J., Bach, F., Ponce, J., Sapiro, G., Zisserman, A.: Supervised dictionary learning. In: Advances in Neural Information Processing Systems (NIPS), pp. 1033–1040 (2008)
10. Wright, J., Ma, Y., Mairal, J., Sapiro, G., Huang, T.S., Yan, S.: Sparse representation for computer vision and pattern recognition. Proc. IEEE **98**(6), 1031–1044 (2010)
11. Gangeh, M.J., Ghodsi, A., Kamel, M.S.: Kernelized supervised dictionary learning. IEEE Trans. Sig. Process. **61**(19), 4753–4767 (2013)
12. Zhou, D., Bousquet, O., Lal, T.N., Weston, J., Schölkopf, B.: Learning with local and global consistency. In: Advances in Neural Information Processing Systems (NIPS), pp. 321–328 (2004)
13. Chapelle, O., Schölkopf, B.: Semi-supervised Learning. MIT Press, Cambridge (2006)
14. Gretton, A., Herbrich, R., Smola, A.J., Bousquet, O., Schölkopf, B.: Kernel methods for measuring independence. J. Mach. Learn. Res. **6**, 2075–2129 (2005)
15. Gretton, A., Bousquet, O., Smola, A.J., Schölkopf, B.: Measuring statistical dependence with hilbert-schmidt norms. In: Jain, S., Simon, H.U., Tomita, E. (eds.) ALT 2005. LNCS (LNAI), vol. 3734, pp. 63–77. Springer, Heidelberg (2005)
16. von Luxburg, U.: A tutorial on spectral clustering. Stat. Comput. **17**(4), 395–416 (2007)
17. Lütkepohl, H.: Handbook of Matrices. Wiley, New York (1996)
18. Tibshirani, R.: Regression shrinkage and selection via the lasso. J. R. Stat. Soc. Ser. B **58**(1), 267–288 (1996)
19. Donoho, D.L., Johnstone, I.M.: Adapting to unknown smoothness via wavelet shrinkage. J. Am. Stat. Assoc. **90**(432), 1200–1224 (1995)
20. Friedman, J., Hastie, T., Hofling, H., Tibshirani, R.: Pathwise coordinate optimization. Ann. Appl. Stat. **1**(2), 302–332 (2007)
21. Raina, R., Battle, A., Lee, H., Packer, B., Ng, A.Y.: Self-taught learning: transfer learning from unlabeled data. In: Proceedings of the 24th International Conference on Machine Learning (ICML), pp. 759–766 (2007)

Transferring and Compressing Convolutional Neural Networks for Face Representations

Jakob Grundström[1,2](✉), Jiandan Chen[2], Martin Georg Ljungqvist[2], and Kalle Åström[1]

[1] Centre for Mathematical Sciences, Lund University, Lund, Sweden
pi07jg8@student.lth.se, kalle@maths.lth.se
[2] Axis Communications, Lund, Sweden
{jiandan.chen,martin.ljungqvist}@axis.com

Abstract. In this work we have investigated face verification based on deep representations from Convolutional Neural Networks (CNNs) to find an accurate and compact face descriptor trained only on a restricted amount of face image data. Transfer learning by fine-tuning CNNs pre-trained on large-scale object recognition has been shown to be a suitable approach to counter a limited amount of target domain data. Using model compression we reduced the model complexity without significant loss in accuracy and made the feature extraction more feasible for real-time use and deployment on embedded systems and mobile devices. The compression resulted in a 9-fold reduction in number of parameters and a 5-fold speed-up in the average feature extraction time running on a desktop CPU. With continued training of the compressed model using a Siamese Network setup, it outperformed the larger model.

1 Introduction

In visual recognition it is rapidly becoming a standard practice to use deep representations composed of layer activations extracted from *Convolutional Neural Networks* (CNNs) as object descriptors, see [1,17]. CNNs are frequent top performers on complex image analysis tasks. However, one of the drawbacks of CNNs is that they require vast amounts of data for training in order to perform well. The CNNs used for this purpose are therefore often pre-trained on huge labeled datasets for generic object recognition containing a large set of object categories, from here on we call those CNNs *generic CNNs*.

Generic CNNs, such as [13,19], can be regarded as general-purpose feature extractors producing *generic object descriptors*, descriptors that may also constitute good representations for domains other than the *source domain*.

Even though a generic CNN usually perform well in domains other than those it was trained for, it still lacks specificity. In many cases the object representations can be further improved by adapting the CNN to the *target domain*, as done in [1] and which led to state of the art results on 16 visual recognition benchmarks.

© Springer International Publishing Switzerland 2016
A. Campilho and F. Karray (Eds.): ICIAR 2016, LNCS 9730, pp. 20–29, 2016.
DOI: 10.1007/978-3-319-41501-7_3

The process of transferring a generic CNN to a new data domain is often called *fine-tuning* and is a way to do transfer learning. Fine-tuning involves training a CNN structure initialized with weights from the pre-trained generic CNN and using data from the target domain.

To recognise subjects in images of arbitrary angle, position, lighting and other variables is a complex task which requires large CNNs with many layers for training. To evaluate a trained CNN model on unseen data the entire CNN structure is needed. This is much more time efficient than training. However, a real-time application in an embedded device with limited computational resources is still a challenge for CNNs with many layers. A way to handle this is *model compression* [4, 9] where a large CNN can be trained into a smaller model.

A popular application of machine learning is face verification; its purpose is to confirm or deny a claimed identity. In a pair-wise formulation the problem is to decide if two face images of previously unseen identities are of matching or non-matching identities.

In this work we have, firstly, investigated face verification based on deep representations extracted from CNNs to find an accurate and compact face descriptor using a restricted amount of face image training data exclusively from publicly available datasets. Secondly, we have reduced the computational demands of the CNN architectures by the use of model compression in order to produce a faster and less resource-demanding feature extractor.

2 Related Works

Solving challenging *face identification* problems has proven a successful strategy to produce accurate face descriptors [22, 24, 26]. In [22] multiple CNNs are trained on a face identification problem including 10 000 identities. According to the authors training on such a hard classification problem, with many identities and many examples per identity, is crucial for the success of a descriptor. The recent work of [18] takes large-scale training to its extreme and use a non-public training set including roughly 8 million persons. With only a limited amount of publicly available face image data, we instead investigate how competitive a face descriptor can be when pre-trained on large-scale generic object recognition and then fine-tuned using significantly less data from the target domain.

Our fine-tuning approach builds on a CNN architecture presented in [7] and use the pre-trained weights of the *CaffeNet* CNN [11], an architecture similar to the renowned AlexNet CNN [13]. A similar fine-tuning setup was previously used in [12] to transfer-learn a generic CNN to recognise Flickr image categories.

The central idea of model compression is that the function learned by a large and slow but accurate model can be approximated with a fast and compact model. The compact model contains fewer parameters and ideally allows for faster processing. In [4] this idea was applied to compress large ensembles of machine learning models into compact neural networks. The concept is further investigated in [9] but with focus on transfer learning of the generalization properties from a complex model to a simpler one. For a well-performing model on one-of-many classification task and given a training example, most class probabilities would be close to zero. To increase the influence of those small values (i.e. the *dark knowledge* that encode relative likelihoods of the incorrect classes) in the cross-entropy loss function the authors smoothed the class probabilities of the complex model and used those as softened targets for learning the simpler model. The results of [2] shows that deep neural networks many times can be compressed into shallow neural networks. The compressed nets matched the performance of deep architectures on both phoneme recognition and image recognition. The shallow models were trained by regressing the logits of the class probabilities with l_2-loss.

With a pair-wise training in a *Siamese Network* setup it is possible to also leverage similarity. Examples of this is training done using the *Contrastive Loss* [6,8,24]. A recent class of face verification algorithms employ both discriminative and similarity-based objectives. For instance [21,23] use a combination of classification and verification supervision and show great results in face verification. Another way to perform supervised learning with both similarity-based and discriminative objectives is described by [3], where the authors present a method for learning a cross-domain similarity by combining Contrastive Loss and cross-entropy loss. We apply this approach to face verification.

3   Method

The investigated approaches include: (1) using a generic CNN as a general-purpose feature extractor; (2) training a CNN from scratch exclusively on face recognition data; (3) fine-tuning a generic CNN with face recognition data; (4) transferring a fine-tuned generic CNN to a compressed CNN architecture with model compression; (5) transferring a fine-tuned generic CNN to a compressed CNN architecture with model compression and train it as a Siamese Network.

In (1) we used the pre-trained generic CNN directly without modification, using the weights of CaffeNet [11], and extracted its 4096-dimensional last hidden layer activations as face descriptors. For (2) a CNN was trained from scratch exclusively on face recognition data and with random initialization of the weights. The learning rates were increased compared to fine-tuning and the network was allowed to train for longer, but stopping on the same minimum learning rate. Here we used the same architecture as the fine-tuned model (3). The approaches (3–5) are described in detail in the following sections.

For all the reported face verification results we used an implementation of the *Joint Bayesian* classifier [5] applied on CNN descriptors projected into a 200-dimensional space through *Principal Component Analysis* (PCA). The dimension 200 was empirically chosen with the aim to create a both compact and accurate descriptor.

Fine-Tuning. The CNN architecture of the fine-tuning setup is based on CaffeNet [11] but with a dimensionality reduction layer to facilitate for a more compact descriptor. In summary we perform the following modifications:

- **Replace output layer** with a new fully connected layer with as many hidden units as identities in the fine-tuning dataset.
- **Adjust learning rates** to learn the new layers faster than the pre-trained layers. Like [12], we set the initial learning rate to 0.001 and decreasing with a step size of 10 000 iterations with a factor of 10.
- **Insert bottleneck layer.** A fully-connected layer with number of hidden units reduced to 1024 was inserted before the output layer.

The inserted layer and the replaced output layer were randomly initialized while the rest of the CNN was initialized with weights pre-trained on large-scale generic object recognition. The face descriptors are then extracted as the activations of the 1024-dimensional last hidden layer from the fine-tuned CNN.

Model Compression. Fine-tuning from pre-trained weights sets some architectural constraints on a CNN, for example layers initialized with pre-trained weights need to conform to the dimensions of the pre-trained model. Initializing the bottom CNN layers with pre-trained weights for instance implicates a certain input size, in our case $256 \times 256 \times 3$ dimensions which is considered large for typical face recognition applications. The fine-tuned CNN model may be overparameterized when transferring to a less complex problem, as we do when fine-tuning for face identification from generic object recognition.

Model compression presents a way to overcome these problems. Especially, we use it to train a compressed model with a more light-weight CNN architecture and with the input size reduced to $64 \times 64 \times 3$, or effectively $56 \times 56 \times 3$ because of the subcropping data augmentation we use. We apply model compression to the fine-tuned CNN (3).

Training. The model compression setup follows the idea of [2] and consists of a complex model (3), acting as a teacher, and a simple model with reduced complexity (4) (see Table 1). During training both models are given identical images as input but scaled to match the input sizes of each CNN. The smaller model is then learned by performing simultaneous regression and classification, as depicted in Fig. 1, while the parameters of the larger model $\tilde{\Theta}$ are freezed by setting the learning rate to zero. The regression uses the class log-probabilities from the complex model $\tilde{z}$ as targets and is formulated using the *Euclidean Loss* as follows

$$\mathcal{L}(\Theta) = \frac{1}{2N} \sum_{n=1}^{N} ||\tilde{z}^{(n)} - z^{(n)}||_2^2,$$ (1)

over a mini-batch of N images $\{\mathbf{I}_n : n \in [1, N]\}$ and where z denote the log-probabilities predicted by the compressed model with parameters Θ.

The classification objective for the compressed model is formulated as common practice for CNNs, with cross-entropy loss according to the class label $l^{(n)}$

$$\mathcal{L}(\Theta) = -\frac{1}{N} \sum_{n=1}^{N} \log(p_{l^{(n)}}^{(n)}),$$ (2)

where the probability $p_k^{(n)}$ for a class $k \in \{1, K\}$ of an input image $\mathbf{I}_n$ is computed from the class log-probabilities z using softmax as follows

$$p_k^{(n)} = \frac{\exp\left(z_k^{(n)}\right)}{\sum_{j=1}^{K} \exp\left(z_j^{(n)}\right)}. \tag{3}$$

The training was done in a three stage process gradually increasing the weight of the Euclidean Loss (in steps 10^{-9}, 10^{-6} and 10^{-3}) while keeping the classification loss at unit weight.

The architecture of the compressed model is inspired by [20], using consecutive convolutional layers with 3×3 kernels including ReLU-activation functions rather than larger kernels. The convolutional layers use 1 pixel padding such that the dimensions are preserved and the max-pooling use 2×2 kernels with a stride size of 2.

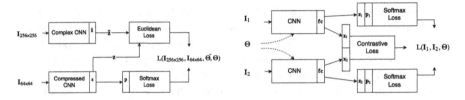

Fig. 1. Setups for model compression *(left)* and Siamese Network training *(right)*

The design (4–5) shown in Table 1 resulted in a compressed model with $6.7M$ parameters (not including bias parameters), which is close to a 9-fold reduction from the renowned AlexNet and the CaffeNet with their $60M$ parameters.

Siamese Network. To further improve the compressed model we turned to Siamese Network techniques (5) and adopted the pair-wise training setup using both identification and similarity illustrated in Fig. 1. A setup, in which we use a combination of softmax loss and contrastive loss, similar to [3]. The idea is to learn an embedding space for faces such that similar faces are pulled closer to each other and faces of different identities pushed away from each other if within a certain constant margin. This can be formulated mathematically with the *Contrastive Loss* function

$$\mathcal{L}(\Theta) = \frac{1}{2N} \sum_{n=1}^{N} y \|x_1^{(n)} - x_2^{(n)}\|_2^2 + \tag{4}$$
$$(1-y) \max(m - \|x_1^{(n)} - x_2^{(n)}\|_2, 0)^2,$$

with face embedding vectors x, a constant margin m and similarity $y \in \{0, 1\}$ [6,8].

Table 1. CNN architecture of the proposed compressed model

CNN layer	Kernel	Channels	Dimension	Parameters
Input (Subcropping)		3	56 × 56	
conv1 (relu)	3 × 3	32	56 × 56	864
conv2 (relu)	3 × 3	32	56 × 56	9216
pool1	2 × 2		28 × 28	
conv3 (relu)	3 × 3	64	28 × 28	18432
conv4 (relu)	3 × 3	64	28 × 28	36864
pool2	2 × 2		14 × 14	
conv5 (relu)	3 × 3	128	14 × 14	73728
conv6 (relu)	3 × 3	128	14 × 14	147456
pool3	2 × 2		7 × 7	
fc (dropout)		1024	1 × 1024	6422528
Total				6709088

The input to the training setup is a face image pair $(\mathbf{I}_1, \mathbf{I}_2)$ of matching or non-matching identities. The images are forward-passed through identical CNNs sharing the same parameters Θ producing embedding vectors (x_1, x_2) and the estimated class probabilities (p_1, p_2). The embedding vectors x are 256-dimensional linear projections of the 1024-dimensional feature layer and can be seen as a second output layer. The softmax loss is formulated according to the predicted class probabilities of the face identity output layer and labels of each pair-member respectively, while the contrastive loss is formulated using the embeddings (x_1, x_2) and the known binary similarity y.

Data. The training data used for CNN fine-tuning, model compression and for learning the Joint Bayesian is a combination of *FaceScrub* [15] and *MSRA-CFW* [25][1]. To avoid overlapping subjects w.r.t. the chosen evaluation dataset LFW [10] we applied blacklisting based on subject names. The dataset was expanded by data augmentation: adding noise, color augmentation and foveation. We balanced the subjects to have a minimum of 200 augmented samples per subject. The final dataset is based on 72 106 original images and were increased to 526 602 by data augmentation.

4   Results

The five presented approaches were all evaluated on the LFW benchmark [10] according to the *Unrestricted Labeled Outside Data* protocol. Figure 2 shows

---

[1] FaceScrub and MSRA-CFW were downloaded from individual URLs and many images failed to download or were corrupt. For MSRA-CFW we applied a haar-cascade face detector on the downloaded images and created weak annotations.

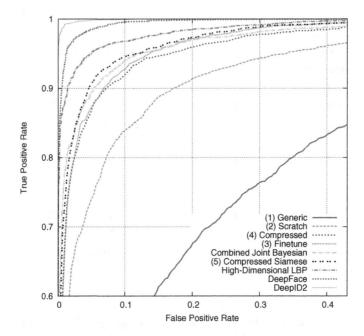

Fig. 2. Receiver-Operating-Characteristics (ROC) curves for the LFW face verification benchmark under the *Unrestricted Labeled Outside Data* protocol

the ROC curves of our approaches and also includes some of the referenced algorithms for comparison. In Table 2 we report the LFW scores as verification accuracy and standard deviation.

Using the generic CNN (1) as general purpose feature extractor gave worse results than training a CNN exclusively on a face image dataset of 777 subjects (2) (Sect. 3), the resulting LFW verification accuracies were 73.5 % and 86.8 % respectively. Fine-tuning a pre-trained CNN (3), transfer learning to the face domain, improved the results significantly and gave an accuracy of 91.6 %. Notably the results from (3) was transferred using model compression to a smaller, more efficient architecture (4) without significant loss in accuracy, 91.4 %.

With (5) the accuracy of the compressed model was improved by continued training using a Siamese Network setup with Contrastive Loss such that it outperformed the large fine-tuned CNN (3). This resulted in our best performing architecture with 92.9 % verification accuracy.

We performed a timing experiment extracting features from 1000 images with both the fine-tuned (3) and the compressed model architecture (4–5). The results were 191.46 ms and 37.72 ms respectively. This constitutes a 5.08-fold speed-up performing feature extraction using the compressed model.

Table 2. Verification accuracies and standard deviations of our five approaches on the LFW benchmark

CNN architecture	Verification accuracy (%)	Std.Dev. (%)
(1) Generic	73.5	1.45
(2) Scratch	86.8	1.59
(3) Fine-tune	91.6	1.24
(4) Compressed	91.4	1.68
(5) Compressed Siamese	92.9	1.42

5   Discussion

The results presented in Sect. 4 shows that good face verification accuracy can be achieved using a comparably small amount of labeled face data, 72 106 images, and with a reasonably compact face descriptor of 200 dimensions.

Our best performing descriptor (5) achieve verification accuracy on the LFW benchmark comparable to the *Combined Joint Bayesian* [5] (see Fig. 2), which use a similar amount of data, 99 773 images, and combines the score of 4 Joint Bayesian classifiers. Our approach uses only a single model and a more compact descriptor. Despite the successful applications of CNN-based transfer learning approaches in many visual tasks [1] we see that our results do not quite match the current state-of-the-art algorithms in face verification, which give accuracies up to 99.79 % on the LFW benchmark. Even so, it should be noted that most of the state-of-the-art algorithms use target domain data several magnitudes larger than the training set we used in this work.

Fine-tuning from a generic CNN provides a way to produce accurate descriptors also in the face recognition domain, even though the domain of face images intuitively is very distant from the domain of generic objects. Comparing the results of (2) and (3) we see that when limited amount of data is available in the target domain fine-tuning a generic CNN can improve generalization compared to training from scratch exclusively on data from the target domain.

Moreover, the benefits of the fine-tuning is transferred also to the compressed model. With model compression (4) the computational demands of the feature extraction could be significantly reduced with just a minor loss in accuracy.

Encouraging results from two very recent papers show that: state-of-the-art face verification can be achieved training a CNN model similar to but slightly deeper than (5) from scratch using more data [16], $2.6M$ images; model compression can be successfully applied also to compress state-of-the-art face verification algorithms [14]. Our results together with these two papers strengthen our hypothesis that fine-tuning combined with model compression makes it possible to achieve accuracy competitive to state-of-the-art in face verification using an efficient, compact model and less data.

6   Conclusion

Transfer learning by fine-tuning from generic CNNs has been shown to be a suitable approach when only a limited amount of data is available in the target domain. Our most accurate approach compares to face verification algorithms trained on a similar amount of data and with a more compact representation. However, the accuracy does not reach that of the state-of-the-art algorithms trained on target domain datasets of a significantly greater magnitude.

By using model compression we reduced the model complexity without significant loss in accuracy and produced a feature extractor more suitable for real-time use. The compression resulted in a 9-fold reduction in number of parameters and a 5-fold speed-up in the average feature extraction time on a quad-core CPU. Additionally, the compressed model gave higher accuracy than the larger model after continued training in a Siamese Network, 92.9 % on the LFW benchmark. This result suggests that model compression is a step towards deployment on platforms with less computational resources, such as embedded systems and mobile devices.

References

1. Azizpour, H., Razavian, A.S., Sullivan, J., Maki, A., Carlsson, S.: From generic to specific deep representations for visual recognition. CoRR abs/1406.5774 (2014). http://arxiv.org/abs/1406.5774
2. Ba, L.J., Caurana, R.: Do deep nets really need to be deep? CoRR abs/1312.6184 (2013). http://arxiv.org/abs/1312.6184
3. Bell, S., Bala, K.: Learning visual similarity for product design with convolutional neural networks. ACM Trans. Graph. **34**(4), 98:1–98:10 (2015). http://doi.acm.org/10.1145/2766959
4. Bucila, C., Caruana, R., Niculescu-Mizil, A.: Model compression. In: Proceedings of the Twelfth ACM SIGKDD International Conference on Knowledge Discovery and Data Mining, Philadelphia, PA, USA, 20–23 Aug 2006, pp. 535–541 (2006)
5. Chen, D., Cao, X., Wang, L., Wen, F., Sun, J.: Bayesian face revisited: a joint formulation. In: Fitzgibbon, A., Lazebnik, S., Perona, P., Sato, Y., Schmid, C. (eds.) ECCV 2012, Part III. LNCS, vol. 7574, pp. 566–579. Springer, Heidelberg (2012). http://dx.doi.org/10.1007/978-3-642-33712-3_41
6. Chopra, S., Hadsell, R., LeCun, Y.: Learning a similarity metric discriminatively, with application to face verification. In: 2005 IEEE Computer Society Conference on Computer Vision and Pattern Recognition, vol. 1, pp. 539–546 (2005)
7. Grundström, J.: Face verification and open-set identification for real-time video applications (2015). Student Paper
8. Hadsell, R., Chopra, S., LeCun, Y.: Dimensionality reduction by learning an invariant mapping. In: 2006 IEEE Computer Society Conference on Computer Vision and Pattern Recognition, vol. 2, pp. 1735–1742 (2006)
9. Hinton, G., Vinyals, O., Dean, J.: Distilling the knowledge in a neural network (2015). http://arxiv.org/abs/1503.02531
10. Huang, G.B., Ramesh, M., Berg, T., Learned-Miller, E.: Labeled faces in the wild: a database for studying face recognition in unconstrained environments. Technical report 07–49, University of Massachusetts, Amherst, October 2007

11. Jia, Y., Shelhamer, E., Donahue, J., Karayev, S., Long, J., Girshick, R., Guadarrama, S., Darrell, T.: Caffe: convolutional architecture for fast feature embedding (2014). arXiv preprint arXiv:1408.5093
12. Karayev, S., Hertzmann, A., Winnemoeller, H., Agarwala, A., Darrell, T.: Recognizing image style. CoRR abs/1311.3715 (2013). http://arxiv.org/abs/1311.3715
13. Krizhevsky, A., Sutskever, I., Hinton, G.E.: Imagenet classification with deep convolutional neural networks. In: Pereira, F., Burges, C., Bottou, L., Weinberger, K. (eds.) Advances in Neural Information Processing Systems 25, pp. 1097–1105. Curran Associates Inc. (2012). http://papers.nips.cc/paper/4824-imagenet-classification-with-deep-convolutional-neural-networks.pdf
14. Luo, P., Zhu, Z., Liu, Z., Wang, X., Tang, X.: Face model compression by distilling knowledge from neurons (2016). http://personal.ie.cuhk.edu.hk/~pluo/pdf/aaai16-face-model-compression.pdf
15. Ng, H., Winkler, S.: A data-driven approach to cleaning large face datasets. In: ICIP14, pp. 343–347 (2014)
16. Parkhi, O.M., Vedaldi, A., Zisserman, A.: Deep face recognition. In: British Machine Vision Conference (2015)
17. Razavian, A.S., Azizpour, H., Sullivan, J., Carlsson, S.: CNN features off-the-shelf: an astounding baseline for recognition. CoRR abs/1403.6382 (2014). http://arxiv.org/abs/1403.6382
18. Schroff, F., Kalenichenko, D., Philbin, J.: Facenet: a unified embedding for face recognition and clustering. CoRR abs/1503.03832 (2015). http://arxiv.org/abs/1503.03832
19. Sermanet, P., Eigen, D., Zhang, X., Mathieu, M., Fergus, R., LeCun, Y.: Overfeat: integrated recognition, localization and detection using convolutional networks. In: International Conference on Learning Representations (ICLR 2014). CBLS, April 2014. http://openreview.net/document/d332e77d-459a-4af8-b3ed-55ba
20. Simonyan, K., Zisserman, A.: Very deep convolutional networks for large-scale image recognition. CoRR abs/1409.1556 (2014). http://arxiv.org/abs/1409.1556
21. Sun, Y., Wang, X., Tang, X.: Deep Learning Face Representation by Joint Identification-Verification. Ph.D. thesis, arXiv (2014). http://arxiv.org/abs/1406.4773
22. Sun, Y., Wang, X., Tang, X.: Deep learning face representation from predicting 10,000 classes. In: Computer Vision and Pattern Recognition, pp. 1891–1898. IEEE (2014)
23. Sun, Y., Wang, X., Tang, X.: Deeply learned face representations are sparse, selective, and robust. CoRR abs/1412.1265 (2014). http://arxiv.org/abs/1412.1265
24. Taigman, Y., Yang, M., Ranzato, M., Wolf, L.: Deepface: closing the gap to human-level performance in face verification. In: Conference on Computer Vision and Pattern Recognition (CVPR) (2014)
25. Zhang, X., Zhang, L., Wang, X.J., Shum, H.Y.: Finding celebrities in billions of web images. IEEE Trans. Multimedia **14**(4), 995–1007 (2012)
26. Zhou, E., Cao, Z., Yin, Q.: Naive-deep face recognition: touching the limit of LFW benchmark or not? CoRR abs/1501.04690 (2015). http://arxiv.org/abs/1501.04690

Efficient Melanoma Detection
Using Texture-Based RSurf Features

Tomáš Majtner[(✉)], Sule Yildirim-Yayilgan, and Jon Yngve Hardeberg

Faculty of Computer Science and Media Technology,
NTNU Norwegian University of Science and Technology, Gjøvik, Norway
{tomas.majtner,sule.yildirim,jon.hardeberg}@ntnu.no

Abstract. Melanoma is the most dangerous form of skin cancer. It develops from the melanin-producing cells known as melanocytes. If melanoma is recognized and treated early, it is almost always curable. However, in early stages, melanomas are similar to benign lesions known as moles, which also originate from melanocytes. Therefore, much effort is put on the correct automated recognition of melanomas. Current computer-aided diagnosis relies on the use of various sets of colour and/or texture features. In this contribution, we present a fully automated melanoma recognition system, which employs a single set of texture-based RSurf features. The experimental evaluation demonstrates promising results and indicates strong discrimination power of these features for melanoma recognition tasks.

Keywords: Melanoma detection · Chan-Vese segmentation · RSurf features · k-NN classification · Benign lesion

1 Introduction

Malignant melanoma (Fig. 1), which is commonly referred to as melanoma, is the most serious type of skin cancer [1]. It develops in the melanocytes, the cells producing melanin, which gives skin its colour. The risk of melanoma has increasing trend in people under 40, especially women. The positive fact is that this form of cancer can be treated successfully, when it is detected and recognized early. However, the examination of a suspicious lesion is time-consuming and requires expert knowledge. It is therefore considered as a bottleneck in melanoma diagnosis and also provides a challenge for the automation of the recognition system. Therefore, precise melanoma recognition is still a topic that receives a lot of attention in this field. Many research groups are currently working on improving automated or semi-automated computer-aided diagnosis systems for melanoma diagnosis [2–7].

The entire process of automatic recognition of melanoma and benign lesion (Fig. 2) usually consists of several steps. First, the input image has to be pre-processed and lesion needs to be precisely segmented, thus the feature extraction will be applied only on the part of the image we want to examine. Subsequently, a classifier is needed to determine the proper class for an examined image.

© Springer International Publishing Switzerland 2016
A. Campilho and F. Karray (Eds.): ICIAR 2016, LNCS 9730, pp. 30–37, 2016.
DOI: 10.1007/978-3-319-41501-7_4

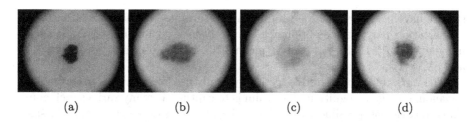

(a)   (b)   (c)   (d)

Fig. 1. Examples of melanoma lesions (a, b) and benign lesions (c, d) recognized by human expert. Images were acquired by a private dermatology practice in Pulheim, Germany and provided by Kajsa Møllersen.

In this paper, we introduce a fully automated recognition system, which takes raw input images from dermatoscope and classifies them either as melanoma or as benign lesions. The focus is put on feature extraction step of the classification process and our main objective is to develop a fast, efficient, well-defined, and easy to use solution for melanoma classification. The paper is organized as follows: in the next section we briefly introduce state-of-the-art in melanoma recognition. Subsequently, we focus on the description of our proposed solution. In the last sections, experimental evaluation with discussion about results is introduced together with the conclusion of our findings.

2   Related Work

All three essential steps of melanoma recognition, namely segmentation, feature extraction, and classification, were intensively studied during the last few years. An extensive overview of melanoma segmentation methods was presented by Silveira *et al.* [8]. In this comparison, different threshold methods together with adaptive method, gradient-based method, adaptive snakes method, level-set method, and others were considered. In their experiments, the best results were achieved by the use of an adaptive snake method and a level-set method. Another comparison of different segmentation methods were presented by Norton *et al.* [9]. Their study presented the best segmentation results for three-phase general border detection method presented in [9] and dermatologist-like method.

In 2012, Beuren *et al.* [10] presented a melanoma segmentation approach based on colour morphology. The authors demonstrated promising results when morphology techniques were used for segmentation in this domain. A different approach was used by Kropidłowski *et al.* [11], which employed histogram skin modelling. The authors concentrated on the correction of non-uniform image illumination caused by dermatoscope lighting and they presented segmentation results with mean sensitivity over 90 %.

To recognize the melanoma lesion, several rules were established for doctors, like the ABCD rule of dermoscopy or the 7-point checklist [12]. In automated diagnosis systems, colour-based features are commonly used [4], since colour is recognized as one of the key factors in melanoma recognition. However, several studies have been already done employing texture-based features [13,14]. In the classification part, various approaches have been used but most common ones include k-NN [5,13,15,16], fuzzy c-means [10], linear discriminant analysis [4], and SVM [17].

The works mentioned in this section typically use large number of features for melanoma image recognition. Their aim is to capture as many various melanoma characteristics as possible in the form of features. Subsequently, the classifier combine these features. Our proposed approach is different. We concentrate on a single set of well-defined texture-based features, which captures internal characteristics of the segmented object, namely melanoma. These features are fast to extract, which enable their usage in clinical practice.

3   Proposed Solution

In this section, we describe proposed methods for every step of melanoma classification. The pipeline, which we employed in our solution is shown in Fig. 2.

Fig. 2. The pipeline used in our automated melanoma recognition approach.

Image Preprocessing. The image preprocessing step starts with conversion of input RGB colour image to greyscale image. For this purpose, we separate three colour channels and calculate their entropy E defined as

$$E(I) = -\sum(p * \log_2 p),$$

where I is the examined image and p contains the histogram counts for every intensity value in I. Typically, the blue channel is the one with the highest entropy but in some cases it could also be another channel. This approach was chosen because the resulting greyscale image better captures the varying spatial distribution of the intensity values than weighted conversion from RGB to greyscale. In order to perform the classification more efficiently, we downsample each image by a factor of 2, from the original 1600×1200 pixels to 800×600 pixels.

Image Segmentation. After the preprocessing step, we concentrate on the image segmentation. For this task, we use a two stage Chan-Vese segmentation via graph cuts [18]. In the first stage, the intensity values of input image (Fig. 3 (a)) are normalized and the algorithm is used to detect the circular part capturing the skin (Fig. 3 (b)). In this stage, we eliminate the black background. In the second stage, the algorithm identifies the object inside the circular area

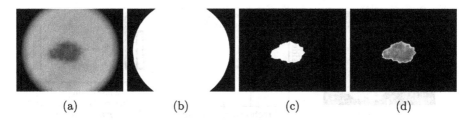

Fig. 3. (a) Melanoma image, (b) detected circular part capturing the skin, (c) mask of the segmented lesion, (d) unmasked melanoma image used for feature extraction.

segmented in the previous stage and creates a mask (Fig. 3 (c)). The output of this segmentation step is the pre-segmented image, which contains only the region corresponding to the examined lesion (Fig. 3 (d)).

Feature Extraction. The pre-segmented regions are subsequently used in the feature extraction step. For this task, we employed RSurf features, which were originally published for HEp-2 cells recognition [19]. The pre-segmented lesions and cell images have similar visual characteristics and RSurf features were shown as promising texture discriminator for cell images. For that reason, we naturally consider them also for extracting features from pre-segmented lesions.

The idea behind RSurf features is to divide the image into parallel sequences of intensity values from the upper-left corner to the bottom-right corner. In these intensity sequences, all the local maxima and minima are localized. Therefore, intensity values between two extreme points form either non-increasing or non-decreasing intensity sequences, which will be further referred to as *slopes*.

In general, we can sequentially scan the image and extract slopes in any direction. It was recommended in the original paper to scan the image in more directions to increase the robustness to rotational differences. This approach is also deliberately translational invariant, thus the ned object could be at any place in the image, which is advantageous for our purposes.

The set of all slopes are used to extract slope properties. Four characteristic functions $\Phi_1, ..., \Phi_4$ were originally designed for mapping each slope to a real value. The first function Φ_1 corresponds to the length of the slope, the second function Φ_2 returns the height difference between the highest and the lowest point of the slope, the third function Φ_3 defines the sum of all intensity values, which belong to the slope, and finally the fourth function Φ_4 corresponds to the number of sign changes of the second derivation of the slope. In the end, for each characteristic function, a normalized histogram of function values is built. The concatenation of histogram values from all characteristic functions forms the feature vector. The schematic visualization of the feature extraction step is given in Fig. 4.

Melanoma Classification. For the final classification and image class estimation, the weighted version of k-NN classifier is implemented using the MESSIF framework [20]. Here, the label for the query image is derived from the labels of its nearest neighbours, where each neighbour contributes with a different weight

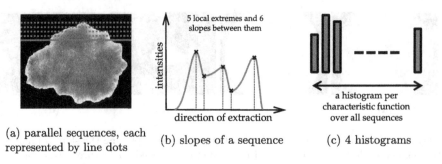

(a) parallel sequences, each represented by line dots

(b) slopes of a sequence

(c) 4 histograms

Fig. 4. The schematic visualization of the feature extraction step.

to the final decision. These weights depend on the distance between the query image and the neighbour. The nearest neighbour has therefore the highest impact on the final classification. In our tests presented in this paper, we set $k = 3$ and use leave-one-out cross-validation. Distances between feature vectors are computed using the L_1 metric. The concatenation of four histograms obtained in the feature extraction step we use as input to the classifier.

4   Experimental Evaluation

All the evaluations were performed on the dataset of 110 images, which includes 10 melanoma lesions and 100 benign lesions. Images were acquired from various patients between the years 2009 and 2012 by a private dermatology practice in Pulheim, Germany and provided by Kajsa Møllersen. All skin lesions were photographed prior to excision with a digital camera (Canon G10, Canon Inc., Tokyo, Japan) with an attached dermatoscope (DermLite FOTO, 3Gen LLC, California, USA). Excised lesions were examined by a dermatopathologist and the diagnostic was histopathologically confirmed. Examples are shown in Fig. 1.

One of the key innovations here is the use of RSurf features as texture discriminant for the recognition of melanoma lesions. These features are noise sensitive, therefore the use of Gaussian filter with small σ was suggested prior to the calculation to suppress the noise in the input image. Since stronger smoothing decreases the classification performance significantly, we performed a parametric study of the influence of Gaussian σ on the final classification. From the results presented in Fig. 5 we see, that the optimal choice is $\sigma = 0.5$.

Another important parameter is the number of histogram bins used for each characteristic function, which defines the feature vector length. For each characteristic function, the same number of bins is used. The feature vector is a concatenation of all histogram bins from all four characteristic functions. The parametric study in Fig. 6 shows the best results for a feature vector with 20 elements, which corresponds to five bins for each characteristic function.

In the slope extraction process, the number of used directions should be determined. For various combinations of directions, we obtained almost identical results, thus this parameter has no significant influence on the results. Therefore,

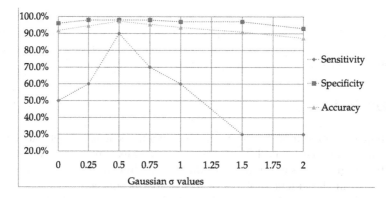

Fig. 5. The influence of Gaussian σ on the final classification.

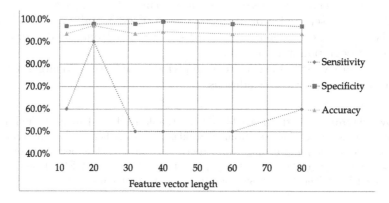

Fig. 6. The influence of various feature vector lengths on the final classification.

we decided to use the default option of $0°$, $45°$, $90°$, and $135°$, where $0°$ represents the horizontal direction.

The best results of our solution achieved for this dataset corresponds to the classification accuracy of 97.27 %, with sensitivity of 90 %, specificity of 98 %, and F_1 score of 0.86. The direct comparison of these results with the other approaches presented in the literature is difficult, since each research group performs tests on different image sets. However, when we look at the articles concentrating on feature extraction, we usually find classification accuracy close to 90 %, e.g. in [3–5,21]. Therefore, our results are promising and indicate that RSurf features are suitable for melanoma recognition.

As for the computation time, the most time consuming part of our entire solution is the image preprocessing part. The time to prepare one image for the feature extraction step varies from ∼0.6 s to ∼3.3 s on a single thread CPU with 2.6 GHz processor. The subsequent feature extraction and classification parts are significantly faster. Extracting all the features and building the feature space by pre-computing all the distances takes ∼22.3 s, which corresponds to ∼0.2 s per image. Also note that the feature space is formed only once at the beginning of the classification. The classification of a single preprocessed query image is therefore very fast and suitable for practical applications.

5   Conclusion

In this paper, we presented an automated melanoma recognition approach, which employs a set of texture-based RSurf features. These features were originally presented to recognize cells in fluorescence microscopy images. Here, we successfully employ them in the urgent problem of melanoma recognition.

The paper presents an entire system, which primarily consists of image pre-processing, image segmentation using a two stage Chan-Vese segmentation via graph cuts, feature extraction using RSurf features and melanoma classification using k-NN classifier. Presented solution achieved a classification accuracy of 97.27 %, with sensitivity of 90 % specificity of 98 %, and F_1 score of 0.86. With the very fast extraction time, RSurf features is a promising descriptor for melanoma recognition in clinical practice.

In the future, we will concentrate on applying these features in larger datasets that include also other skin conditions.

Acknowledgement. Authors would like to thank Herbert Kirchesch and Kajsa Møllersen for providing images, Roman Stoklasa for classifier implementation, and Marius Pedersen for proofreading this paper. This research has been supported by the Research Council of Norway through project no. 247689 "IQ-MED: Image Quality enhancement in MEDical diagnosis, monitoring and treatment".

References

1. Mermelstein, R.J., Riesenberg, L.A.: Changing knowledge and attitudes about skin cancer risk factors in adolescents. Health Psychol. **11**(6), 371 (1992)
2. Kassianos, A.P., Emery, J.D., Murchie, P., Walter, F.M.: Smartphone applications for melanoma detection by community, patient and generalist clinician users: a review. Br. J. Dermatol. **172**(6), 1507–1518 (2015)
3. Leachman, S.A., et al.: Methods of melanoma detection. In: Kaufman, H.L., Mehnert, J.M. (eds.) Melanoma. Cancer Treatment and Research, vol. 167, pp. 51–105. Springer, Heidelberg (2016)
4. Møllersen, K., Hardeberg, J.Y., Godtliebsen, F.: Divergence-based colour features for melanoma detection. In: Colour and Visual Computing Symposium, pp. 1–6. IEEE (2015)
5. Pennisi, A., Bloisi, D.D., Nardi, D., Giampetruzzi, A.R., Mondino, C., Facchiano, A.: Melanoma detection using delaunay triangulation. In: International Conference on Tools with Artificial Intelligence, pp. 791–798. IEEE (2015)
6. Santy, A., Joseph, R.: Segmentation methods for computer aided melanoma detection. In: Global Conference on Communication Technologies, pp. 490–493. IEEE (2015)

7. Stanganelli, I., Longo, C., Mazzoni, L., Magi, S., Medri, M., Lanzanova, G., Farnetani, F., Pellacani, G.: Integration of reflectance confocal microscopy in sequential dermoscopy follow-up improves melanoma detection accuracy. Br. J. Dermatol. **172**(2), 365–371 (2015)

8. Silveira, M., Nascimento, J.C., Marques, J.S., Marçal, A.R.S., Mendonça, T., Yamauchi, S., Maeda, J., Rozeira, J.: Comparison of segmentation methods for melanoma diagnosis in dermoscopy images. IEEE J. Sel. Top. Sign. Process. **3**(1), 35–45 (2009)

9. Norton, K.A., Iyatomi, H., Celebi, M.E., Ishizaki, S., Sawada, M., Suzaki, R., Kobayashi, K., Tanaka, M., Ogawa, K.: Three-phase general border detection method for dermoscopy images using non-uniform illumination correction. Skin Res. Technol. **18**(3), 290–300 (2012)

10. Beuren, A.T., Pinheiro, R.J., Facon, J.: Color approach of melanoma lesion segmentation. In: Systems, Signals and Image Processing, pp. 284–287. IEEE (2012)

11. Kropidłowski, K., Kociołek, M., Strzelecki, M., Czubiński, D.: Model based approach for melanoma segmentation. In: Chmielewski, L.J., Kozera, R., Shin, B.-S., Wojciechowski, K. (eds.) ICCVG 2014. LNCS, vol. 8671, pp. 347–355. Springer, Heidelberg (2014)

12. Argenziano, G., et al.: Dermoscopy of pigmented skin lesions: results of a consensus meeting via the internet. J. Am. Acad. Dermatol. **48**(5), 679–693 (2003)

13. Ballerini, L., Fisher, R.B., Aldridge, B., Rees, J.: A color and texture based hierarchical k-NN approach to the classification of non-melanoma skin lesions. In: Celebi, M.E., Schaefer, G. (eds.) Color Medical Image Analysis. LNCVB, vol. 6, pp. 63–86. Springer, Heidelberg (2013)

14. Barata, C., Ruela, M., Francisco, M., Mendonça, T., Marques, J.S.: Two systems for the detection of melanomas in dermoscopy images using texture and color features. IEEE Syst. J. **8**(3), 965–979 (2014)

15. Ballerini, L., Fisher, R.B., Aldridge, B., Rees, J.: Non-melanoma skin lesion classification using colour image data in a hierarchical k-NN classifier. In: International Symposium on Biomedical Imaging, pp. 358–361. IEEE (2012)

16. Glowacz, A., Glowacz, Z.: Recognition of images of finger skin with application of histogram, image filtration and k-NN classifier. Biocybernetics Biomed. Eng. **36**(1), 95–101 (2016). http://dx.doi.org/10.1016/j.bbe.2015.12.005. ISSN:0208-5216

17. Gilmore, S., Hofmann-Wellenhof, R., Soyer, H.P.: A support vector machine for decision support in melanoma recognition. Exp. Dermatol. **19**(9), 830–835 (2010)

18. Daněk, O., Matula, P., Maška, M., Kozubek, M.: Smooth Chan-Vese segmentation via graph cuts. Pattern Recogn. Lett. **33**(10), 1405–1410 (2012)

19. Majtner, T., Stoklasa, R., Svoboda, D.: RSurf-the efficient texture-based descriptor for fluorescence microscopy images of HEp-2 cells. In: 22nd International Conference on Pattern Recognition, pp. 1194–1199. IEEE (2014)

20. Batko, M., Novak, D., Zezula, P.: MESSIF: metric similarity search implementation framework. In: Thanos, C., Borri, F., Candela, L. (eds.) Digital Libraries: Research and Development. LNCS, vol. 4877, pp. 1–10. Springer, Heidelberg (2007)

21. Barata, C., Emre, C.M., Marques, J.S.: Melanoma detection algorithm based on feature fusion. In: Engineering in Medicine and Biology Society (EMBC), pp. 2653–2656. IEEE (2015)

High-Frequency Spectral Energy Map Estimation Based Gait Analysis System Using a Depth Camera for Pathology Detection

Didier Ndayikengurukiye and Max Mignotte[(✉)]

Département d'Informatique et de Recherche Opérationnelle (DIRO),
Université de Montréal, Montréal, QC, Canada
{ndayiked,mignotte}@iro.umontreal.ca

Abstract. This paper presents a new and simple gait analysis system, from a depth camera placed in front of a subject walking on a treadmill, capable of detecting a healthy gait from an impaired one. Our system relies on the fact that a normal or healthy walk typically exhibits a smooth motion (depth) signal, at each pixel with less high-frequency spectral energy content than an impaired or abnormal walk. Thus, the estimation of a map showing the location and the amplitude of the high-frequency spectral energy (HFSE), for each subject, allows clinicians to visually quantify and localize the different impaired body parts of the patient and to quickly detect a possible disease. Even if the HFSE maps obtained are clearly intuitive for a rapid clinical diagnosis, the proposed system makes an automatic classification between normal gaits and those who are not with success rates ranging from 88.23 % to 92.15 %.

Keywords: Gait analysis · Spectral energy · Map estimation · Pathology detection · Kinect

1 Introduction

The human gait movement is an essential and complex process of the human activity and also a remarkable example of collaborative interactions between the neurological, articular and musculoskeletal systems working effectively together. When everything is working properly, the healthy locomotor system produces a stable gait and a highly consistent, symmetric (nice) walking pattern [7,11].

This is why human gait impairment is often an important (and sometimes the first) clinical manifestation and indication of various medical disorders. In fact, abnormal or atypical gait can be caused by different factors, either orthopedic (hip injuries, bone malformations, etc.), muscular (weakness, dystrophy, fiber degeneration, etc.), neurological (Parkinson's disease, stroke [2], spinal stenosis, etc.) or neuropsychiatric (autism, schizophrenia, etc.). As a consequence, gait analysis is important (because possibly highly informative) and increasingly used nowadays for the diagnosis of many different types (and degrees) of diseases.

© Springer International Publishing Switzerland 2016
A. Campilho and F. Karray (Eds.): ICIAR 2016, LNCS 9730, pp. 38–45, 2016.
DOI: 10.1007/978-3-319-41501-7_5

In addition, it also exploited as a reliable and accurate indicator for early detection (and follow-up) of a wide range of pathologies.

In this field, the value of sophisticated, marker-based, video-based gait analysis is well established and have also proved their efficiency. Nevertheless, in order to be used, as an early (and fast) diagnostic tool, it is now important to design a reliable and accurate imaging system that is also inexpensive, non-invasive, fast, easy to set up and suitable for small room and daily clinical [3, 4, 15] (or home [6]) usage. This has now become possible thanks to the recent technological progress in depth sensor technology. In this paper, we focus on this kind of approach and introduce a new gait analysis system with the above mentioned advantages and characteristics over more sophisticated approaches. This new gait analysis system aims at distinguishing the healthy (human) gait from the impaired ones. In addition, our system localizes the affected body side of the patient and quantify the patients' gait pattern abnormality or alterations of a human subject. We hope this approach will be exploited, for example, as a good indicator or as a first interesting screening for a possible (orthopedic, muscular or neurological) disease, prior to a more thorough examination by a specialist doctor.

2   Previous Work

Current gait analysis systems can be performed with or without markers. Among the marker-based, gait analysis approaches, we can mention the sophisticated Vicon motion-tracking and capture system [1] which offers millimeter resolution of 3D spatial displacements. On one hand, this system is very accurate. On the other hand, the high cost of this system (which consists in real-time tracking multiple infrared red (IR) reflective markers with multiple IR cameras [14]), inhibits its widespread usage for routine clinical practices (since it requires lots of space, time, and expertise to be installed and used).

Therefore, marker-less systems are a promising alternative for clinical environments and are often regarded as easy-to-set-up, easy-to-use, and non-invasive. They are either based on stereo-vision [9], structured light [16], or time-of-flight (TOF) [8] technologies. Although low-cost, the setup and calibration procedure of these systems remain complex. Besides, stereo vision-based systems [10] are not guaranteed to work well if the patient's outfit lacks texture.

An interesting alternative is to use the recent Kinect^{TM} sensor which is based on structured light combined with machine learning technology and two other computer vision techniques; depth from focus and depth from stereo. The Kinect^{TM} is robust to texture-less surfaces, accurate and remains also compact and very affordable. This new sensor is able to real-time provide an image sequence where the value of each pixel is proportional to the inverse of the depth at each pixel location with a good accuracy. As interesting feature, the Kinect^{TM} camera is also capable to offer (*via* a machine learning subsystem) a real-time estimation of a set (of 20) 3D points representing the different joints of the human body (by selecting the skeleton *mode* of this sensor). This rough skeleton model was exploited by some authors [5, 6] in order to measure spatial-temporal gait variability (such as the stride duration, speed, etc.) and are compared to those obtained with the high-end Vicon MX system. They found that the Kinect was capable of providing accurate and robust results for some gait parameters, but further research is under way to see if these parameters can be subsequently used for a reliable gait analysis and classification system.

Amongst the existing gait analysis system which are based on a direct analysis of a depth map (related to a human walking session on a treadmill), and recorded by a Kinect^{TM}, as the system proposed in this work (see Fig. 1), we can cite the feasibility study proposed in [15] and tested on 6 subjects. In this work, the authors simply computed the mean of the obtained depth image sequence (over a gait cycle or a longer period) in order to compress the gait image sequence into a single image which was finally called a depth energy image (DEI). Through this DEI image, the authors were able to distinguish both visually and quantitatively (through the measurement of asymmetry indexes) an abnormal gait and more precisely possible asymmetries in the gait pattern (a symmetric walk generating a DEI exhibiting a symmetric silhouette, in terms of mean depth and conversely). In the same spirit, the authors in [3] propose to quantify the possible asymmetries between the two depth signals of the legs by first dividing each gait cycle in two sub-cycles (left and right steps), and by comparing these two sub-cycles, in terms of depth difference, after a rough spatial and temporal registration procedure. In fact, the two above-mentioned studies use (with many other studies) the notion of possible asymmetry between the depth signals of the legs or, more precisely, the amplitude difference between the right and left legs obtained by the two phases of the gait cycle, as main and relevant measure, for an abnormal or impaired human gait.

Nevertheless, this asymmetry measure should rather be computed, not directly on the pixel-wise depth signals (recorded by the depth sensor) but rather on some interesting features of this depth signal. In the case of an abnormal or impaired human gait, the depth signal exhibits, in time (and for some pixels, often located at the lower limbs), a continuous but (possibly locally) rugged, unsmooth depth signal or function describing in fact, an irregular leg motion (chaotic, unstable with

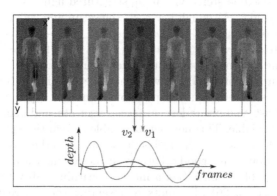

Fig. 1. Example of two depth signals for a gait cycle of an human subject: pixel on the hip (blue curve) and pixel on the thigh (orange curve). (Color figure online)

possible sharp transitions with even singularities in time like shock waves or discontinuities eventually sometimes caused by pain due to physical damage or without pain caused by neurological damage. In this case, the unsmooth behavior of the depth signal comprises some high-frequency harmonics that we can detect and eventually on which we can then compute some asymmetry indexes.

More precisely, in our application we have decided to quantify the atypical gait by exploiting asymmetry measures computed on a map exhibiting the high-frequency spectral (energy) content of the depth signal of each pixel as interesting and spectral more informative feature of the raw depth signal.

3   Data Description and Pre-processing

For the experiments, 17 (healthy) subjects (young male adults, 26.7 ± 3.8 years old, 179.1 ± 11.5 cm height and 75.5 ± 13.6 kg with no reported gait issues) were asked to walk normally on a treadmill (Life Fitness F3) with or without simulated length leg discrepancy (LLD). Every subject had to walk normally (group A), then with a 5 cm sole, impairing the normal walk, under the left foot (group B), then with the sole under the right foot (group C). After a habituation period of about 2 min, their normal speed was determined and their gait movement was simultaneously recorded using an inexpensive commercial Kinect^{TM} depth camera placed in front of the subject. The Kinect sensor outputs 30 depth maps per second (30 fps), with a resolution of 640 per 480 pixels and for all sequences, the same relative position and distance between the treadmill and the sensor were kept constant in order for the human subject to be located within the same image area. Therefore, the dataset contains 51 different video sequences of a human walk (of approximately 5 min long and containing around 180 gait cycles) with or without a simulated length leg discrepancy (LLD) issue which will be analyzed by our automatic gait analysis system. The institutional ethics review board approved the study.

Since the scene took place in a non-cluttered room where the treadmill is in the same position relatively to the camera, a silhouette extraction strategy (background and treadmill removal) can be easily defined as proposed in [12]. Finally, each sequence is filtered with $(3 \times 3 \times 3)$ median filter to reduce the noise level, while preserving the important image (sequence) features, i.e., spatial or depth discontinuities (see Fig. 2).

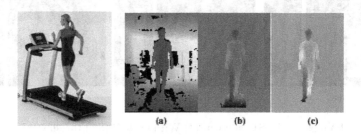

Fig. 2. Setup and pre-processing steps: (a) Original depth map, (b) After the background removal, (c) After the treadmill removal and contrast adjustment.

4   Proposed Model

Our model is based on the idea that, for a normal gait, the depth signal of each pixel of a human subject is smooth with little discontinuity. Conversely for a pathological gait (*i.e.*, associated to a possible pathology), the (pixel-wise) depth signal is not so smooth and exhibits some discontinuities which are in fact expressed by a greater amplitude of its high-frequency spectral energy.

Formally, let $s_p(t)$ be the depth signal of the pixel p. We compute the energy of the Fourier Transform of each pixel's depth signal to obtain $|S_p(\nu)|^2$. This energy spectrum is then high-pass filtered (by setting to zero all the energy values associated with frequencies that are less than a threshold τ, $\tau = 8$ obtained by trial and error in our case) in order to estimate the high-frequency spectral energy (HFSE) content at each location of the gait movement. In order to highlight some relevant features on this HFSE map, this one is then thresholded (by setting to zero all energy value below $\rho = 85$) in order to better localize the areas with a HFSE content (in terms of size, shape and difference between the left and right legs). In the case of a pathological gait, the unsmooth behavior of a depth signal comprises some high-frequency harmonics showing areas of high energy values that we can easily detect especially when this map is shown in pseudo colors (see Fig. 3). In addition, this allows the clinician to visually quantify and localize the different impaired body parts of the patient.

In order to now automatically classify a healthy gait from an impaired one, we extract three relevant features on this map at the lower limb level (between $1/2H$ and $1/4H$ with H the image height). These features are mainly based on the difference of the HFSE content between the left and right legs since visually, we can differentiate a healthy gait from an impaired one from the asymmetry between these two areas. To this end, we first calculate the axis of symmetry of the map (see the algorithm in Appendix) and let L and R be respectively the area occupied by the pixels whose energy values are non-zero and are located to the left (and right) of the axis of symmetry of the image of HFSE. The first

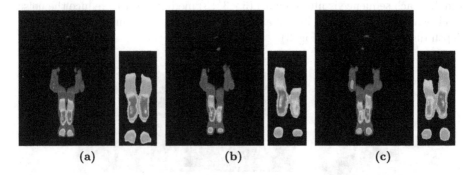

(a)   (b)   (c)

Fig. 3. HFSE maps for the S15 subject: (a) Without heel (and thresholded HFSE map at lower limbs) (b) Heel under left foot (and thresholded HFSE map at lower limbs) (c) Heel under right foot (and thresholded HFSE map at lower limbs).

considered feature is $\frac{L}{L+R}$, the second feature is $\frac{R}{L+R}$ and the third is $2 \times \frac{L}{R}$. We have normalized the first two features because the silhouettes of the subjects are usually not the same size. In addition, we have doubled the ratio to strengthen small differences between some ratio. These three features are used to train and test the Gaussian Naive Bayes (GNB), the k-Nearest Neighbors (k-NN), the Logistic Regression (LR) and the Support Vector Machine (SVM) classifiers.

5   Experimental Results

We performed experimentations on all 17 subjects and obtained 3 HFSE maps for each one. We treated these maps as it is shown by Fig. 3 for subject S15. As we can see, the classification of the maps in two categories (pathological or not) or in three categories (without heel, heel under left foot or heel under right foot) is easy for a human operator. Table 1 shows the value of the three features computed on the S15 thresholded HFSE map at lower limbs.

Finally, we did the classification using the Gaussian Naive Bayes (GNB), the k-Nearest Neighbors (k-NN), the Logistic Regression (LR) and Support Vector Machine (SVM) (with linear, polynomial[degree = 3], radial basis function[RBF] and sigmoid function as kernel function respectively) classifiers. We use the library from Pedregosa et al. [13] for all the four classifiers. Because we have a relatively small number of maps, we ordered the 51 maps randomly and we take one as a test set and the rest as training set. We repeat the process for all the maps and at the end we average the results (leave one cross-validation). Other experiments are made by dividing the 51 maps into k parts. Each of the k parts is taken as a test set and the k−1 others as training set. We also made the average of the results (k-fold cross-validation). The classification results are shown in Table 2 for the logistic regression and SVM models because we kept the classifiers giving the best performance (SVM best kernel: cubic polynomial).

Table 1. Features for the S15 subject

	Normalized left area $\frac{L}{L+R}$	Normalized right area $\frac{R}{L+R}$	Double ratio $2 \times \frac{L}{R}$
Without heel: A	0.52	0.48	2.16
Heel under left foot: B	0.62	0.38	3.29
Heel under right foot: C	0.42	0.58	1.44

Table 2. Classification success rate of 51 HFSE maps of 17 subjects in two classes (normal or not) and in three classes (A, B, C) for logistic regression (left) and support vector machine (right) (LOOCV: Leave one out cross-validation, k: k-fold cross-validation)

	2 classes	3 classes			2 classes	3 classes
LOOCV	90.20%	88.24%		LOOCV	92.16%	88.24%
$k = 5$	86.36%	88.36%		$k = 5$	88.36%	88.36%
$k = 4$	86.06%	88.46%		$k = 4$	84.62%	88.46%
$k = 3$	86.28%	88.24%		$k = 3$	66.67%	88.24%

6   Conclusion

In this paper, we have presented a new gait analysis system that is low cost, marker-less, non-invasive, simple to install and requiring a small room. The estimation of a map showing the location and the amplitude of the high-frequency spectral energy, obtained from each subject, allows the clinician to visually quantify and localize the different impaired body parts of the patient. We hope this approach will be exploited, for example, as a good indicator or as a first interesting screening for a possible (orthopedic, muscular or neurological) disease, prior to a more thorough examination by a specialist doctor. The proposed system is also capable to automatically classify between healthy patients and those who are not and to automatically localize the impaired body parts of the patient (right or left) with success rates ranging from 88.23 % to 92.15 % for SVM and 88.23 % to 90.19 % for logistic regression on test data.

A   Appendix: Algorithm

Estimation of the Asymmetry Indexes

I Thresholded high frequency spectral energy map (size: $height \times width$) of the depth signal of each pixel at lower limb (Input)

AI_j Asymmetry indexes of I ($j \in \{1, 2, 3\}$) (Output)

r Size of the search interval

G_I Gradient magnitude map of I

Vct   Vector of floats of size $height$

x_{sym} Column coordinate estimation of the longitudinal axis

Initialization : $G_I \leftarrow$ gradient magnitude map of I

1. Longitudinal Axis Estimation

▷ **for** *each* $i \in [0, \ldots, height]$ **do**
- grdMax $\leftarrow 0$
  for *each* $j \in [(width/2) - r, \ldots, (width/2) + r]$ **do**
    for *each* $m \in [0, \ldots, width/2]$ **do**
      grd $\leftarrow G_I[i][j - m] + G_I[i][j + m]$
      if (grd > grdMax) { pos $\leftarrow j$ grdMax $\leftarrow$ grd }

     Vct[i] $\leftarrow$ pos

▷ $x_{\text{sym}} \leftarrow$ median value of the vector elements Vct[]

2. Estimation of the Asymmetry Indexes

- $L, R \leftarrow$ Number of pixels located to the left (for L) and to the right (for R) of x_{sym} with a non-zero value

▷ $AI_1 \leftarrow L/L + R$ $AI_2 \leftarrow R/L + R$ $AI_3 \leftarrow 2L/R$

References

1. Motion capture systems from vicon. http://www.vicon.com/
2. Alexander, L.D., Black, S.E., Patterson, K.K., Gao, F., Danells, C.J., Mcllroy, W.E.: Association between gait asymmetry and brain lesion location in stroke patients. Stroke **40**(2), 537–544 (2009)
3. Auvinet, E., Multon, F., Meunier, J.: Lower limb movement asymmetry measurement with a depth camera. In: 2012 Annual International Conference of the IEEE Engineering in Medicine and Biology Society (EMBC), pp. 6793–6796, August 2012
4. Carse, B., Meadows, B., Bowers, R., Rowe, P.: Affordable clinical gait analysis: an assessment of the marker tracking accuracy of a new low-cost optical 3d motion analysis system. Physiotherapy **99**(4), 347–351 (2013). http://www.science direct.com/science/article/pii/S0031940613000266
5. Clark, R.A., Bower, K.J., Mentiplay, B.F., Paterson, K., Pua, Y.H.: Concurrent validity of the microsoft kinect for assessment of spatiotemporal gait variables. J. Biomech. **46**(15), 2722–2725 (2013)
6. Gabel, M., Gilad-Bachrach, R., Renshaw, E., Schuster, A.: Full body gait analysis with kinect. In: 2012 Annual International Conference of the IEEE Engineering in Medicine and Biology Society (EMBC), pp. 1964–1967. IEEE (2012)
7. Hamill, J., Bates, B., Knutzen, K.: Ground reaction force symmetry during walking and running. Res. Q. Exerc. Sport **55**(3), 289–293 (1984)
8. Hansard, M., Lee, S., Choi, O., Horaud, R.: Time-of-Flight Cameras. Springer, Heidelberg (2013)
9. Lazaros, N., Sirakoulis, G.C., Gasteratos, A.: Review of stereo vision algorithms: from software to hardware. Int. J. Optomechatronics **2**(4), 435–462 (2008)
10. Leu, A., Ristic-Durrant, D., Graser, A.: A robust markerless vision-based human gait analysis system. In: 2011 6th IEEE International Symposium on Applied Computational Intelligence and Informatics (SACI), pp. 415–420 (May 2011)
11. Loizeau, J., Allard, P., Duhaime, M., Landjerit, B.: Bilateral gait patterns in subjects fitted with a total hip prosthesis. Arch. Phys. Med. Rehab. **76**(6), 552–557 (1995)
12. Moevus, A., Mignotte, M., de Guise, J., Meunier, J.: Evaluating perceptual maps of asymmetries for gait symmetry quantification and pathology detection. In: 36th International Conference of the IEEE Engineering in Medicine and Biology Society, EMBC 2014, Chicago, Illinois, USA, August 2014
13. Pedregosa, F., Varoquaux, G., Gramfort, A., Michel, V., Thirion, B., Grisel, O., Blondel, M., Prettenhofer, P., Weiss, R., Dubourg, V., Vanderplas, J., Passos, A., Cournapeau, D., Brucher, M., Perrot, M., Duchesnay, É.: Scikit-learn: machine learning in python. J. Mach. Learn. Res. **12**, 2825–2830 (2011)
14. Potdevin, F., Gillet, C., Barbier, F., Coello, Y., Moretto, P.: The study of asymmetry in able-bodied gait with the concept of propulsion and brake. In: 9th Symposium on 3D Analysis of Human Movement, Valenciennes, France (2006)
15. Rougier, C., Auvinet, E., Meunier, J., Mignotte, M., de Guise, J.A.: Depth energy image for gait symmetry quantification. In: 2011 Annual International Conference of the IEEE Engineering in Medicine and Biology Society, EMBC, pp. 5136–5139. IEEE (2011)
16. Salvi, J., Pages, J., Batlle, J.: Pattern codification strategies in structured light systems. Pattern Recogn. **37**(4), 827–849 (2004)

Combining Low-Level Features of Offline Questionnaires for Handwriting Identification

Dirk Siegmund[✉], Tina Ebert, and Naser Damer

Fraunhofer Institute for Computer Graphics Research (IGD),
Fraunhoferstrasse 5, 64283 Darmstadt, Germany
{dirk.siegmund,tina.ebert,naser.damer}@igd.fraunhofer.de

Abstract. When using anonymous offline questionnaires for reviewing services or products it is often not guaranteed that a reviewer does this only once as intended. In this paper an applied combination of different features of handwritten characteristics and its fusion is presented to expose such manipulations. The presented approach covers the aspects of alignment normalization, segmentation, feature extraction, classification and fusion. Nine features from handwritten text, numbers and checkboxes are extracted and used to recognize hand-writer duplicates. The proposed method has been tested on a novel database containing pages of handwritten text produced by 1,734 writers. Furthermore we show that the unified biometric decision using a weighted sum combination rule can significantly improve writer identification performance even on low level features.

1 Introduction

Handwriting is a behavioral characteristic that is individual for every writer [2]. Therefore, handwriting identification has many applications, e.g. in security applications or forensics. One distinguishes between handwriting identification, which is a one-to-many comparison, and handwriting verification, that refers to a one-to-one comparison [16]. A specific scenario for the application of handwriting identification is the analysis of questionnaires. In certain surveys each person is allowed to fill out one questionnaire only, so the developed application needs to ensure that this demand is fulfilled. If someone submits more than one questionnaire this person is double enrolled, which needs to be detected and removed. This work focuses on the analysis of such questionnaires in an offline format. To our knowledge, there does not exist a database yet that yields complete questionnaires. Known handwriting databases like CEDAR [14], NIST [17] and CENPARMI [15] contain mostly isolated characters or single words that do not reflect unconstrained environments. The databases IAM [11], ICDAR 2013 [10] and the CVL dataset [8] contain large amounts of unconstrained handwritten English sentences but are limited by a small amount of writers (<350). Therefore, a novel database was created that contains handwritten texts and rating parts from actual review forms. From the samples of this new database different features were extracted. Most of the features get extracted from single words

© Springer International Publishing Switzerland 2016
A. Campilho and F. Karray (Eds.): ICIAR 2016, LNCS 9730, pp. 46–54, 2016.
DOI: 10.1007/978-3-319-41501-7_6

or lines, so a good segmentation process needs to be employed [5]. One way of doing this was described by Schomaker et al. [13] who used connected components as basic structure. There has already been a lot of research regarding the extraction of texture based and allographic features [1,12]. This work deals with the extraction of nine features of different types. To improve the outcome, all of these features were combined in a fusion process introduced by Damer et al. [6]. The results show the impact of the different features onto the identification process and how this can be used to identify double enrolled handwritings.

2   System Overview

The system presented in this paper consists of five parts: alignment normalization, segmentation, feature extraction, classification and fusion. Nine features are extracted from the handwriting elements: 'free text', 'date' and 'checkbox'. The features are mainly based on visible characteristics of the writing, such as: color, slant, word proportions and crosses. Furthermore local interest points in form of SURF Features getting used. The individual steps of the process are shown as program flow chart in Fig. 1.

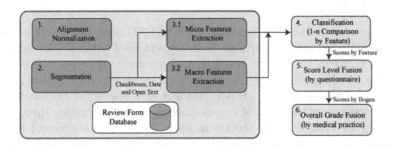

Fig. 1. Program flow chart.

(1) Alignment Normalization: The digitized questionnaires show an inconsistent alignment, due to the scanning process or mistake in the printing of the paper questionnaires. In order to correct the handwritten elements with respect to translation, rotation, and uniform scaling, an affine transformation matrix was calculated from the filled in questionnaire and the exemplar questionnaire. The approximated matrix of the affine transformation is used to correct the transformation with up to $5°$ of freedom in the target image.

(2) Segmentation: Artifacts that may have occurred due to the scanning process get removed using morphological closing. Background colors of the forms get removed using 'color thresholding'. Since areas for handwritten content are highlighted in a rectangular box, through which the contours of the binarized image can be recognized and extracted based on their geometric shape. The 'free text' field is not segmented into text lines or individual words, instead the whole

text area is used on the following steps. Where there are checkboxes, the detected rectangles get increased by a fixed pixel value. The surrounding rectangle (resp. underlying line) of the 'free text' and 'date' field get removed. To do this without cutting handwritten text that is crossing those lines, a horizontal and vertical color histogram from a image section of 1*5 pixel is used. When following the lines pixel by pixel the histogram differs where it comes through that a line gets intersected by handwritten text.

(3.1-3.2) Feature Extraction: Different features are extracted from the segmented and classified elements. A more detailed description of each feature follows in Sect. 4.

(4) Classification: For each feature type a questionnaire is compared with all other questionnaires (1-n comparison). The calculated similarity scores provide information about the similarity of handwriting in relation to each feature.

(5) Score Level Fusion: For each questionnaire the Similarity Scores are evaluated and merged as a result of the classification of each feature. The result gives information about which handwritings in the questionnaires are identical.

(6) Overall Grade Fusion: Detected, same handwritings (step 4) get filtered, based on their frequency of appearance.

3   Database

The here presented and used database contains 1,734 questionnaires with handwritings from 1,694 different writers. Five subjects filled out multiple (ten) questionnaires that can be used for evaluation of genuine comparisons. The various multi-page questionnaires were digitized with a scanner in high quality and collected as images in JPEG format. Arrangement and quantity of the handwritten elements depend on the type of questionnaires used. Altogether, there are 34 different types with different arrangements of free text fields, date fields and rating parts. Table 1 gives an overview of the used fields and the average amount of analyzed data per questionnaire. In total, the free text fields contain 36,813 words and 213,822 characters.

The language used in the review forms is German. The database contains handwritings of people of different ages and sex. Since the recording process was unconstrained, the handwritings were collected using different pens and blotting pads (Fig. 2).

Table 1. Total number of occurrences and average amount of data.

Field	Occurrences	Average amount of data
Free text	1,734	24.14 words
Date	1,734	6.24 digits
Checkboxes	12,521	7.23

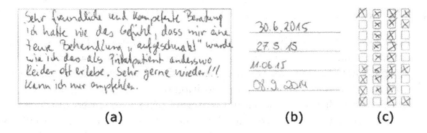

(a)   (b)   (c)

Fig. 2. Examples of the analyzed field types: (a) free text field, (b) date field and (c) checkboxes.

4   Feature Extraction

4.1   Writing Zones

In this work the 'free text' field was used to compute the height of the ascender and descender parts of single words which are determined by the upper and lower baseline (see Fig. 3c). These words get extracted using connected components, but since not all connected components form complete words, Hough Transformation was employed to connect single letters to words [9]. The separated words of each free text field are then examined and weighted according to their usability (long words are preferred). For the determination of the two baselines a procedure described by Mart et al. [12] was employed. First, a vertical projection p of the text line image is computed. Then, an ideal histogram $h_i(ub, lb)$ with variable position of the upper baseline ub and lower baseline lb is matched against the projection p by minimizing the square error

$$E(ub, lb) = \sum_i [h_i(ub, lb) - p_i]^2. \tag{1}$$

By analyzing the position of the two baselines only words consisting of the upper two zones are selected and their vertical projections are extracted as features.

4.2   Color Histogram

The calculation of a HSV color space histogram is used for comparing the color of the writing. The width of the histogram represents the distribution of colors while the height shows the frequency density.

4.3   Line Width

The line width is calculated by using the morphological operation 'erosion'. Different structural elements (rectangle, circle, triangle) were iteratively employed to erode the text by a factor of 1. After every single employment the ratio of remaining text elements gets calculated. The rate is summarized by a single value which represents the line thickness.

4.4 Checkboxes

To our knowledge there has been no research done yet about marks in checkboxes as a feature for handwriting identification. There are three properties that can be analyzed. First, the type of the mark can differ (two separate strokes or one connected line). Second, the length and position of the lines and their relation to one another is specific for an individual writer and third, the order of the strokes differs from writer to writer. To find the nonempty checkboxes all checkboxes were compared to an empty template using a correlation matrix. The box gets eliminated by employing a sliding window so that the crossmark only is left over. Using the Euclidean distance the outer corners of the crossmark are computed and the middle is found by another sliding window. These five keypoints (upper and lower left and right corners and the middle) are stored as a feature vector.

4.5 Digit Height

The height of the writing gets examined using the date field and here their digits in particular. For cropping the date from the background the morphological operator dilation is used to connect single elements. Then the contours of the text are getting calculated and written on a mask using topological structural analysis. The contours with an higher bounding rectangle than a certain threshold get used as mask on the original image of the date. The slope (see Fig. 3a) of the date gets removed calculating the minimum-area bounding rectangle of the text within the binarized image. The angle of the rotated bounding box is used to correct rotation of the cropped date. Single digits of the date get extracted using the number of white pixels within a bounding box of connected components in proportion to the width of a line (see Sect. 4.3). Height and aspect ratio of the digits get calculated using the enclosing bounding box.

4.6 Slant

Slant describes the obliqueness of the text or of the individual letters compared to the vertical axis (see Fig. 3b). The feature can vary both between handwritings of different people as well as within one word written by one person. For an automated handwriting comparison the calculation of the deviations have been implemented in two different ways. First the approach Bozinovic et al. [4] is used which is based on the calculation of an average angle of almost vertical elements on all text within the free text field. The second implementation [19] was carried out to eliminate identified weaknesses of individuals with untidy handwriting. It calculates means of horizontal and vertical projection histograms of the four 'most usable' classified single words of the 'free text' field (see Sect. 4.1). The individual words are then distorted by a likely minimum to a likely maximum angle. The angle with the highest deflection of the histogram is assumed to be at the correct angle.

4.7 SURF

The well known SURF features [3] have shown in many recent papers [7,18] the effectiveness of interest point based methods for writer identification. For each 'free text' field a set of interest points is extracted using the fast hessian detector. The kind of extracted feature points is specified using a library of 120 images. These feature were further processed within a bag of words approach.

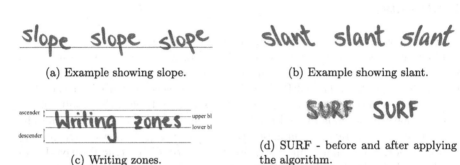

(a) Example showing slope.

(b) Example showing slant.

(c) Writing zones.

(d) SURF - before and after applying the algorithm.

Fig. 3. Examples of the different extracted features.

5 Fusion

In this work, the weighted sum combination rule is used to produce a fused unified biometric decision based on the provided decision scores from different features. As a first step for the fusion process, the scores from different biometric sources have to be normalized to a comparable range. Here, the min-max normalization is used and it can be formulated as,

$$S' = \frac{S - min\{S_k\}}{max\{S_k\} - min\{S_k\}} \tag{2}$$

Where $min\{S_k\}$ and $max\{S_k\}$ are the minimum and maximum value of scores existing in the training data of the corresponding biometric source and S' is the normalized score. Within the weighted sum score fusion, each biometric source must be given a weight that indicates its relevant effect on the fused decision such that more accurate sources will have larger effect. In this work, the Overlap Deviation Weighting (OLDW) proposed by Damer et al. [6] is used to control the effect of each biometric source in the final decision. Given the imposter scores S_k^I, the genuine scores S_k^G, the equal error rate EER and the score threshold at the equal error operating point T, the OLDW can be given as:

$$OLD_k = \sigma(\{S_k^I \mid S \geq T\} \cup \{S_k^G \mid S < T\}) \times EER \tag{3}$$

$$w_k = \frac{\frac{1}{OLD_k}}{\sum_{k=1}^{N} \frac{1}{OLD_k}} \tag{4}$$

Given the calculated weights, the fused score by the weighted sum rule F for N score sources is given as,

$$F = \sum_{k=1}^{N} w_k S_k, k = \{1, \ldots, N\} \tag{5}$$

6   Results

In the framework of this development a total of 1,734 questionnaires, based on 34 different questionnaire types were used. In order to evaluate the achieved results four test subjects had each filled in 10 questionnaires (4 times 10 Genuine, 1,694 Imposter). The EER (Equal-error-rate) was calculated for each feature separately in order to show their significance. In Table 2 the results of the different feature methods as well as their classification method are shown. The ROC (Receiver Operating Characteristics) curve in Fig. 4 shows their characteristic performance under different prioritization of TPR (True-Positive-Rate) and FPR (False-Positive-Rate). With an EER of 8.2 % and 10.7 % color histogram and SURF features performed best compared to all other features types (see Table 2). Local writing characteristics like slant or writing zones are not as distinctive as color or interest point. Although these properties are weaker than others the characteristics represented by them are important factors. While reading the slant of writing from the whole 'open text' field (using the approach by Bozinovic et al. [4]) resulted in a high error rate of 36.97 % while vertical histograms of single words showed only 24.7 % of EER. A reason for that could be that the slope of writing lines in the 'open text' field affects the distinctness negatively. The analysis of digits and crosses are not based on letters and thus complement the results to multi-modal characteristics. By fusing all scores of the extracted features an EER of 4.33 % have been achieved.

Table 2. Achieved scores of single and fused features.

Feature	Field	Classification metric	EER
Fusion			4.3 %
Color histogram	Open Text	Histogram Correlation	8.2 %
SURF	Open Text	Histogram Correlation	10.7 %
Slant hist.	Words	Distance btw. single values	24.7 %
Writing zones	Words	Histogram Correlation	30.1 %
Line width	Open Text	Distance btw. single values	30.2 %
Cross key points	Checkbox	Distance btw. single values	34.2 %
Digit height	Date Digits	Distance btw. single values	36.1 %
Slant	Open Text	Distance btw. single values	37.0 %
Digit aspect ratio	Date Digit	Distance btw. single values	40.0 %

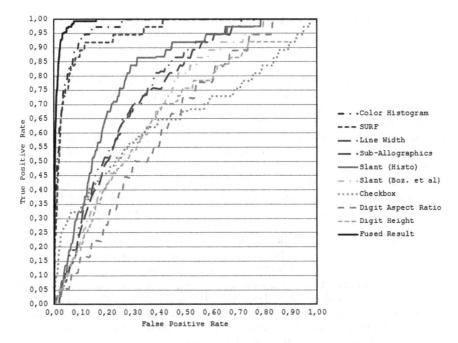

Fig. 4. ROC curve showing results by feature type. (Color figure online)

7 Conclusion

This work aimed at designing a high performing approach to apply handwriting duplicate checks. The work considered the scenario of hand written customer reviews. A novel and realistic database was collected to develop and evaluate this work. A number of different features were evaluated and combined into a unified fused approach. The proposed solution lead to a duplicate identification rate of 95.67 %.

References

1. Abdl, B., Mohammed, K., Hashim, S.Z.M.: Handwriting identication: a direction review. In: 2009 IEEE International Conference on Signal and Image Processing Applications (ICSIPA), pp. 459–463. IEEE (2009)
2. Arora, H., Lee, S., Srihari, S.N., Cha, S.H.: Individuality of handwriting. J. Forensic Sci. **47**(4), 1–17 (2002)
3. Bay, H., Tuytelaars, T., Van Gool, L.: Surf: speeded up robust features. In: Leonardis, A., Bischof, H., Pinz, A. (eds.) ECCV 2006, Part I. LNCS, vol. 3951, pp. 404–417. Springer, Heidelberg (2006)
4. Bozinovic, R.M., Srihari, S.N.: O-line cursive script word recognition. IEEE Trans. Pattern Anal. Mach. Intell. **11**(1), 68–83 (1989)
5. Cermeno, E., Mallor, S., Siguenza, J.A.: Offline handwriting segmentation for writer identification. In: 2014 International Symposium on Biometrics and Security Technologies (ISBAST), pp. 13–17. IEEE (2014)

6. Damer, N., Opel, A., Nouak, A.: Biometric source weighting in multibiometric fusion: towards a generalized and robust solution. In: 22nd European Signal Processing Conference, EUSIPCO 2014, Lisbon, Portugal, 1–5 September 2014, pp. 1382–1386 (2014)
7. Jain, R., Doermann, D.: Combining local features for offline writer identification. In: 2014 14th International Conference on Frontiers in Handwriting Recognition (ICFHR), pp. 583–588. IEEE (2014)
8. Kleber, F., Fiel, S., Diem, M., Sablatnig, R.: Cvl-database: An off-line database for writer retrieval, writer identication and word spotting. In: 2013 12th International Conference on Document Analysis and Recognition (ICDAR), pp. 560–564. IEEE (2013)
9. Likforman-Sulem, L., Hanimyan, A., Faure, C.: A hough based algorithm for extracting text lines in handwritten documents. In: Proceedings of the Third International Conference on Document Analysis and Recognition, 1995, vol. 2, pp. 774–777. IEEE (1995)
10. Louloudis, G., Gatos, B., Stamatopoulos, N., Papandreou, A.: Icdar 2013 competition on writer identication. In: 2013 12th International Conference on Document Analysis and Recognition (ICDAR), pp. 1397–1401, August 2013
11. Marti, U.V., Bunke, H.: The iam-database: an english sentence database for offline handwriting recognition. Int. J. Doc. Anal. Recogn. $5(1)$, 39–46 (2002)
12. Marti, U.V., Messerli, R., Bunke, H.: Writer identication using text line based features. In: Proceedings of Sixth International Conference on Document Analysis and Recognition, 2001, pp. 101–105. IEEE (2001)
13. Schomaker, L., Bulacu, M.: Automatic writer identication using connected-component contours and edge-based features of uppercase western script. IEEE Trans. Pattern Anal. Mach. Intell. $26(6)$, 787–798 (2004)
14. Siddiqi, I., Vincent, N.: Text independent writer recognition using redundant writing patterns with contour-based orientation and curvature features. Pattern Recogn. $43(11)$, 3853–3865 (2010)
15. Suen, C.Y., Nadal, C., Legault, R., Mai, T.A., Lam, L.: Computer recognition of unconstrained handwritten numerals. Proc. IEEE $80(7)$, 1162–1180 (1992)
16. Wang, D., Huang, Z., Lu, Y.: Text-independent writer recognition using modied texture and microstructure features. In: 2014 International Conference on Progress in Informatics and Computing (PIC), pp. 75–78. IEEE (2014)
17. Wilkinson, R.A., Geist, J., Janet, S., Grother, P., Burges, C.J., Creecy, R., Hammond, B., Hull, J.J., Larsen, N., Vogl, T.P., et al.: Therst census optical character recognition system conference, vol. 184. US Department of Commerce, National Institute of Standards and Technology (1992)
18. Wu, X., Tang, Y., Bu, W.: Offline text-independent writer identication based on scale invariant feature transform. IEEE Trans. Inf. Forensics Secur. $9(3)$, 526–536 (2014)
19. de Zeeuw, F.: Slant correction using histograms. Undergraduate thesis (2006). http://www.ai.rug.nl/axel/teaching/bachelorprojects/zeeuw_slantcorrection.pdf

Person Profiling Using Image and Facial Attributes Analyses on Unconstrained Images Retrieved from Online Sources

Elisabeth Wetzinger[(✉)], Michael Atanasov, and Martin Kampel

Computer Vision Lab, Vienna University of Technology,
Favoritenstrasse 9-11/183-2, 1040 Vienna, Austria
{elisabeth.wetzinger,michael.atanasov,martin.kampel}@tuwien.ac.at

Abstract. With the existence and growth of Social Network Services (SNS), they have become focus in data and image processing research and concerning their potential to describe persons based on online available information. In this paper we propose a novel approach for person profiling solely based on images for children and adolescents of age 10+. The application acquires pictures from search engines and SNS and performs image-based analysis focusing on facial attributes. Image analysis results using different image datasets are presented showing that image analytics faces challenges of its application unconstrained datasets, but has the potential to push SNS analytics to a new level of detail in people profiling. The applications aims at improving the target users' media literacy, raising their awareness for risks and consequences and at encouraging them in dealing responsibly with pictures online.

Keywords: Image analysis · Unconstrained image processing · Emotion recognition · Age estimation · Gender classification · Person profiling

1 Introduction

Social Network Services (SNS) analysis has become a research hot topic to analyse or visualise user behaviour or user networks, e.g. [4,5,29]. One objective is the recognition or description of persons or of relations between them based on information published online, e.g. [15]. In addition to text-based information, e.g. [6,23], also online images can be utilised, e.g. [3,24]. The unconstrained nature of images published online still bears challenges to image analysis algorithms [7]. To the best of the authors knowledge currently no approach exists which combines various algorithms for extracting facial attributes and synthesising the respective results to compose person descriptions from unconstrained images. Hence, the problem for the project "The Profiler" is stated as the development of a software framework, which combines person-related image-acquisition, the analysis of persons detected in the obtained images and the composition of the individual analysis outcomes to person profiles.

This paper introduces a novel approach aiming on describing individuals by using solely online available images. As image sources Google Custom Search

© Springer International Publishing Switzerland 2016
A. Campilho and F. Karray (Eds.): ICIAR 2016, LNCS 9730, pp. 55–62, 2016.
DOI: 10.1007/978-3-319-41501-7_7

Engine (GCSE) [17] and BING [25] as well as the SNSs Facebook [16], Twitter [30] and Instagram [18] are utilised. The acquired images are scanned for faces using the dlib face detector [8], which are then analysed for characteristic attributes (age, emotion, gender). Having selected reference face of the person, face recognition using a distance threshold is performed. Finally, a person description is created by synthesising the analytics results of all faces of the target person.

The remainder of this paper continues as follows: A brief overview about related work is given in Sect. 2. In Sect. 3 the architecture, workflow and image analysis implementation are presented. This is followed by first results of the proposed prototype in and their evaluation in Sect. 4. The paper concludes with a brief overview over future work (Sect. 5).

2 Related Work

The open source library OpenBR described by Klontz et al. [21] provides algorithms for face recognition, age and gender estimation. These are utilized for the proposed application. The library further implements the Spectrally Sampled Structural Subspaces Features (4SF) algorithm [20], which allows to specify different algorithms in every step of the analysis pipeline consisting of Detection, Normalisation, Representation, Extraction and Matching. Emotion recognition is based on the Facial Action Coding System (FACS) described by Ekman and Friesen [11]. FACS is a feature-based approach characterising affective facial features. Visible tensions of different facial muscles are assigned to Action Units. Combinations of activated AUs are then interpreted as emotions. The authors suggest an interpretation in their work [13] for the basic emotions *neutral, angry, scared, sad, happy, surprised, disgusted.*

With respect to describing persons based on information available online, Irani et al. calculate users' online social footprints and investigate on the reconstruction of a user's online social footprint based on textual information and prior knowledge either of a pseudonym or the person's name [19]. Based on a person's information utilised from one SNS, they show that up to 40 % of this person's profiles on other SNSs can be found. In [24] Mavridis et al. focus on context-assisted visual recognition and take into account the social context for SNS-based face recognition assuming a correlation between co-occurrences of faces in photos and the social relation of persons. They use photos taken with a camera or published on Facebook and meta-information (e.g. face labels). Face recognition is implemented based on the Viola Jones Facedetector [31] and Embedded Hidden Markov Models [26]. They show that utilising social information presuming a reliable seed for social information increases person recognition performance. PhaceBinder [3] aims at identifying people from photos taken with a mobile phone by combining face recognition technologies, tagged images and meta-information retrieved from SNS in a mobile app. Recognition accuracy is improved by limiting the search space prior to the analysis using gender information. In contrast to the proposed work, [3] build a database of annotated faces by crawling friend lists and the users' own photos uploaded in the SNS. Furthermore, they require at least four reference images per person for the face recognition and take into account gender information.

In contrast to these approaches, the proposed application utilises only information extracted by image analysis without any use of person-related meta information. Furthermore, it aims at creating person profiles based on the obtained results and their synthesis, which is novel compared to related work as the latter focus either on text-based data or combine image information with metadata. Further challenges in our approach, with respect to analytics accuracy, performance and profiling, result from the fact that target user group comprises children and adolescents from an age of 10 years onwards, from the utilisation of unconstrained image datasets found online and from providing the tool as a web-application.

3 Methodology

The architecture of the Profiler is designed using three layers: *presentation layer*, *service layer*, and *persistence layer*. The *presentation layer* includes the user interface and is implemented as a web application applying HTML5 and JavaScript using the AngularJS web application framework. The information transfer is secured with a SSL certificate. The underlying *service layer* contains a web server to serve the web application as well as the analysis logic and algorithms, which are implemented in Python and C++. To conduct the analysis steps the acquired images as well as the extracted information are cached temporarily. This is accomplished in the *persistence layer* using the HDD and a PostgreSQL database. A cleaning routine clears all related data from no longer active web sessions.

The central part of the Profiler is constituted of the analysis task, which is realised as pipeline consisting of three main processes Search & Acquisition, Preprocessing and Analysis & Synthesis (see Fig. 1).

Search & Acquisition. In this first step an image pool related to a target person is created using the person name as an input string. As basic image source for the acquisition process the Google Custom Search Engine [17] is integrated and in addition the Bing Search API serves as fallback option. They are utilised to download 30 publicly available images on the web related to the user-defined input string. In addition three SNSs are integrated as optional image sources:

- *Facebook:* Integration is based on the Facebook Graph API [16]. Users grant the Profiler application access to the images uploaded in their profile. The download starts with the profile directory.
- *Instagram:* Integrated using the Instagram API [18]. The application takes the Instagram username of the target person to find the public profile.
- *Twitter:* Integration is based on the Twitter API [30] using the Twitter account name as input query. .

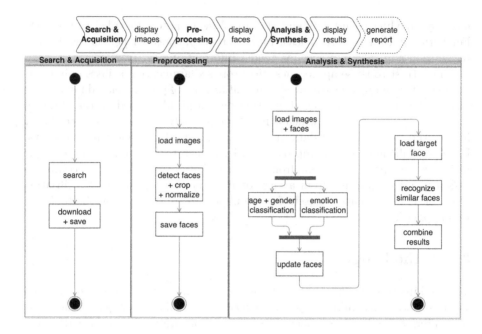

Fig. 1. Analysis pipeline of the profiler.

From each selected SNS a maximum of 25 images are utilised. All downloaded pictures are scaled proportionally to a limit of maximum 600 pixels width or height and served to the client.

Preprocessing. Prior to their analysis, the acquired images are normalised and scanned for faces. To perform the face detection and estimate their landmark points the dlib frontal face detector [8], and shape prediction [9] is integrated. All detected faces are cropped and the landmarks are used to rotate each face before it is stored for later analysis operations. If no is face detected, the respective image is discarded.

Analysis & Synthesis. On every detected face a detailed image analysis is performed compromising age and gender classification as well as emotion recognition. The estimated results of the analytics process are stored for every face allowing for alternative clusterings in the synthesis process later on.

Age & Gender Analysis. Age and gender estimation is implemented using the OpenBR framework [21]. For performance reasons parts of the age and gender estimation are executed in combination: Detection, Normalisation, Representation, and Extraction are the same for both estimations and therefore are performed once. The following Matching steps for age and gender classification are then processed in parallel.

Emotion Analysis. To classify a face's emotion the face tracker described by Saragih et al. [28] combined with the FACS [11] described in Sect. 2 is integrated. Following the localisation of key landmarks, such as mouth edges and eyebrows, visible facial muscle tensions are coded as activated Action Units (AU). To determine whether an AU is activated or not, the distances between the landmark points are measured, and combinations of activated AUs refer to specific emotions.

Synthesis. The image search for a person may be ambiguous as well as one image may show multiple faces. Furthermore, no reference dataset of the target person nor other individuals exist, which would be crucial to allow for face identification or verification. Therefore, the user is requested to select one reference face from within the detected faces representing the target person. Using this and a distance threshold the detected faces and their respective analytics results are grouped to distinguish between persons. The process of recognising similar faces is based on the OpenBR library [21] and classifies it as the target person if it lies within a distance threshold of 35 %.

Profile Visualisation and Report Generation. In a final step the aggregated information of each face recognised as belonging to the selected target person is displayed to the user. This visualisation includes the results of the classification algorithms as well as the regarding image source.

In addition, a PDF report is generated, which outlines the results and accumulates a profile consisting of following aggregated information: minimum, maximum and average age, the quantity of every predicted emotion, the respective quantity of faces estimated as male and female, the most frequent/dominant emotion. Further conclusions are made based on the obtained information: the resulting gender is based on a majority voting, the estimated age is based on the weighted average of all age estimations referring to the person. Additionally the total number of detected faces, which is recognised as the target person is presented per data source. This information is partly packed into text modules to generate a person profile report similar to a police record, which can be downloaded and printed.

4 Evaluation

The implemented image classification methods were evaluated on three face datasets: FERET Database [12], Adience collection of unfiltered faces for gender and age classification [10], and Extended Cohn-Kanade (CK+) [22]. The classifiers were tested separately, i.e. without the whole Profiler pipeline in order to gain isolated and valid results only focusing on the respective classifier.

The performance of the Profiler classifiers are evaluated individually for age, gender and emotion classification. Compared to related work, the analytics results of the Profiler perform as shown in Table 1: The age classification exhibits a less precise prediction with a deviation of 12.81 years. This is ascribed to the

Table 1. Comparison of gender, age, and emotion results.

Gender		
	Bekios-Calfa et al. [2]	The Profiler
Test set	FERET Database [12]	FERET Database [12]
Algorithm	Fisherfaces	4SF
# test images	199	352
Accuracy	93,33±2,33 %	88.92 %
Age		
	Fu et al. [14]	The Profiler
Test set	MORPH [27]	Adience [10]
Algorithm	ageing pattern subspace	4SF
# test images	8000	1808
Deviation	8.83 years	12.81 years
Emotion		
	Walecki et al. [32]	The Profiler
Test set	CK+ [22]	CK+ [22]
Algorithm	geometric	geometric
# test images	327	309
Accuracy	93.9 %	57.28 %

test set, which consists of *unconstrained* images, corresponding with the application field, being large in-the-wild images, of the Profiler. Further the labeled age data is given in discrete age classes. Emotion is classified as one of the following classes *neutral, angry, scared, sad, happy, surprised, disgusted*. Obtained emotion recognition results show a discrepancy to the results described in related work. This is an accepted compromise between accuracy and time consumption, since the execution of the classifiers must be feasible in for the end user acceptable time of less than 30 seconds. Further the accuracy of 93.9 % in emotion estimation of Walecki et al. [32] was only be reached under laboratory conditions (CK+ dataset). For unconstrained datasets the presented method shows an accuracy of 32.2 %.

Additionally, a comprehensive study evaluating the overall acceptance of the Profiler has been conducted and accepted for publication at NYRIS 2016 [1].

5   Conclusion

In this paper we presented a novel approach for person profiling based only on image-based information to improve childrens' and adolescents' media literacy. The proposed software prototype comprises search and acquisition of personal images from different online sources, preprocessing, analysis and synthesis of the found images and image-based information with respect to characteristic attributes. Based on the analytics results a personal profile is created, including the gender, estimated age and average emotion of the target person.

The evaluation shows that the application has the potential to add up significant information detail to person profiling based on online available data, but still faces challenges referring to image analysis on unconstrained datasets. Therefore future work includes the integration of further SNS and an extension of the age and emotion classifications. The latter is based on OpenBR and aims at increasing their accuracy and optimising computational costs. An extensive evaluation on the Profiler analytics is ongoing, including further testscenarios (e.g. usability, stress, security, analytics performance evaluations), larger testsets and testset adaptions. Finally, following related work the analytics process will be enriched by integrating meta information from SNS in order to generate more holistic profiles of individuals.

Acknowledgments. This research was partially funded by the Austrian Federal Ministry for Science, Research and Economy as part of the Sparkling Science project "The Profiler" (Grant NO. SPA 05/089).

References

1. Nyris13 (2016). http://www.hv.se/en/nyris13. Accessed Mar 2016
2. Bekios-Calfa, J., Buenaposada, J.M., Baumela, L.: Revisiting linear discriminant techniques in gender recognition. IEEE Trans. Pattern Anal. Mach. Intell. **33**(4), 858–864 (2011)
3. Bloess, M., Kim, H.N., Rawashdeh, M., El Saddik, A.: Knowing who you are and who you know: harnessing social networks to identify people via mobile devices. In: Li, S., El Saddik, A., Wang, M., Mei, T., Sebe, N., Yan, S., Hong, R., Gurrin, C. (eds.) MMM 2013, Part I. LNCS, vol. 7732, pp. 130–140. Springer, Heidelberg (2013)
4. Borgatti, S., Everett, M., Johnson, J.: Analyzing Social Networks. SAGE Publications, Thousand Oaks (2013)
5. Burt, R.S., Kilduff, M., Tasselli, S.: Social network analysis: foundations and frontiers on advantage. Ann. Rev. Psychol. **64**, 527–547 (2013)
6. Catanese, S., De Meo, P., Ferrara, E., Fiumara, G., Provetti, A.: Crawling facebook for social network analysis purposes, pp. 1–7 (2011)
7. Cheney, J., Klein, B., Jain, A.K., Klare, B.F.: Unconstrained face detection: state of the art baseline and challenges. In: 2015 International Conference on Biometrics (ICB), pp. 229–236. IEEE (2015)
8. dlib: dlib c++ library - face detection. http://dlib.net/face_detection_ex.cpp.html. Accessed Feb 2016
9. dlib: dlib c++ library - real-time face pose estimation. http://blog.dlib.net/2014/08/real-time-face-pose-estimation.html. Accessed Feb 2016
10. Eidinger, E., Enbar, R., Hassner, T.: Age and gender estimation of unltered faces. Trans. Inf. Forensic Secur. **9**(12), 2170–2179 (2014)
11. Ekman, P., Friesen, W.V.: Facial action coding system (1977)
12. Feret, C.: Facial image database. Image Group, Information Access Division, ITL, National Institute of Standards and Technology (2003)

13. Friesen, W.V., Ekman, P.: Emfacs-7: Emotional facial action coding system. Unpublished manuscript, University of California at San Francisco, vol. 2, p. 36 (1983)

14. Fu, Y., Guo, G., Huang, T.S.: Age synthesis and estimation via faces: a survey. IEEE Trans. Pattern Anal. Mach. Intell. **32**(11), 1955–1976 (2010)

15. Ghorab, M.R., Zhou, D., O'Connor, A., Wade, V.: Personalised Information retrieval: survey and classiffication. User Model. User Adap. Inter. **23**, 381–443 (2012)

16. Facebook Inc.: Facebook for developers. https://developers.facebook.com/docs/graph-api. Accessed Mar 2016

17. Google Inc.: Google custom search engine. https://cse.google.com/cse. Accessed Feb 2016

18. Instagram: Instagram developer documentation. https://www.instagram.com/developer/. Accessed Feb 2016

19. Irani, D., Webb, S., Li, K., Pu, C.: Large online social footprints an emerging threat. In: International Conference on Computational Science and Engineering, CSE 2009, vol. 3, pp. 271–276. IEEE (2009)

20. Klare, B.: Spectrally sampled structural subspace features (4sf). Michigan State University Technical report, MSU-CSE-11-16 (2011)

21. Klontz, J.C., Klare, B.F., Klum, S., Jain, A.K., Burge, M.J.: Open source biometric recognition. In: IEEE Sixth International Conference on Biometrics: Theory, Applications and Systems (BTAS), pp. 1–8. IEEE (2013)

22. Lucey, P., Cohn, J.F., Kanade, T., Saragih, J., Ambadar, Z., Matthews, I.: The extended cohnkanade dataset (ck+): a complete dataset for action unit and emotion specied expression. In: IEEE Computer Society Conference on Computer Vision and Pattern Recognition Workshops (CVPRW), pp. 94–101. IEEE (2010)

23. Malhotra, A., Totti, L., Meira, W., Kumaraguru, P., Almeida, V.: Studying user footprints in different online social networks. In: Proceedings of the 2012 IEEE/ACM International Conference on Advances in Social Networks Analysis and Mining, ASONAM 2012, pp. 1065–1070 (2012)

24. Mavridis, N., Kazmi, W., Toulis, P.: Friends with faces: how social networks can enhance face recognition and vice versa. In: Abraham, A., Hassanien, A.-E., Snáel, V. (eds.) Computational Social Network Analysis. Computer Communications and Networks. Springer, London (2010)

25. Microsoft: Bing developer guide. https://www.bing.com/dev. Accessed Mar 2016

26. Nefian, A.V., Hayes III, M.H.: Hidden markov models for face recognition. Choice **1**, 6 (1998)

27. Ricanek Jr., K., Tesafaye, T.: Morph: A longitudinal image database of normal adult age progression. In: 7th International Conference on Automatic Face and Gesture Recognition, pp. 341–345. IEEE (2006)

28. Saragih, J.M., Lucey, S., Cohn, J.F.: Face alignment through subspace constrained mean shifts. In: 2009 IEEE 12th International Conference on Computer Vision, pp. 1034–1041. IEEE (2009)

29. Scott, J.: Social Network Analysis. Sage, Thousand Oaks (2012)

30. Twitter: Rest apis twitter developers. https://dev.twitter.com/rest/public. Accessed Mar 2016

31. Viola, P., Jones, M.J.: Robust real time face detection. Int. J. Comput. Vis. **57**(2), 137–154 (2004)

32. Walecki, R., Rudovic, O., Pavlovic, V., Pantic, M.: Variable state latent conditional random fields for facial expression recognition and action unit detection. In: 11th IEEE International Conference and Workshops on Automatic Face and Gesture Recognition (FG), 2015, vol. 1, pp. 1–8. IEEE (2015)

Palm Print Identification and Verification Using a Genetic-Based Feature Extraction Technique

Joseph Shelton, John Jenkins, and Kaushik Roy[✉]

North Carolina A & T State University, 1601 East Market Street, Greensboro 27411, USA
{jashelt1,jmjenki1}@aggies.ncat.edu, kroy@ncat.edu

Abstract. In this paper, we investigate the performance of two feature extraction techniques on palm prints images. The first is the Local Binary Pattern (LBP) feature extraction technique. The second is the Genetic and Evolutionary Feature Extraction (GEFE) technique. A set of feature extractors are evolved by GEFE and the average and best performance of the extractors are compared to the best scheme of LBP. The techniques are tested on left hand, right hand and combined hand datasets. The results show varying performances between the extraction techniques, but the GEFE approach is promising.

1 Introduction

Biometric identification systems began in the 70s, when the first commercial system, known as Identimat, was developed [1]. Forty years later, fingerprint authorization is a standard identification system for laptops and mobile devices worldwide. Biometrics are being used for personal privacy, businesses, security and government. There are many different options of biometrics but they all come with their own issues. Accidents such as slicing or burns, and even diseases can distort an individual's fingerprint permanently [2]. Iris-based identification is also susceptible to disease-based failures [3]. There are ongoing investigations in regards to biometrics in order to make identification systems more efficient. With this in mind, it is necessary to consider other biometrics such as palm print.

In this paper, we present a genetic based feature extraction technique for palm print identification, which is a new attempt and necessary complement to the existing biometrics techniques proposed in Shelton et al. [4–8]. This technique is formally referred to as Genetic and Evolutionary Feature Extraction (GEFE), and it has been successfully applied on facial and iris datasets for identification [4–8]. GEFE is a hybrid of Genetic and Evolutionary Computations (GECs) & the Local Binary Patterns (LBP) feature extraction technique [9]. The LBP technique segments an entire biometric image into even sized regions and extracts features from each region. A GEC is designed to optimize LBP based feature extractors, where the region locations and dimensions are determined based on identification accuracy. GEFE has also been previously applied on facial and iris datasets and has outperformed the traditional feature extraction techniques [4–8].

In the remainder of this paper, Sect. 2 will present the methodology, which includes clarification on both LBP and GEFE techniques. Section 3 will explain the experiment performed and Sect. 4 will present our results, as we conclude with Sect. 5.

© Springer International Publishing Switzerland 2016
A. Campilho and F. Karray (Eds.): ICIAR 2016, LNCS 9730, pp. 63–68, 2016.
DOI: 10.1007/978-3-319-41501-7_8

2   Methodology

This section presents an explanation of the feature extraction techniques that we are experimenting with. The baseline approach is the standard LBP feature extraction approach. The presented approach is the GEFE approach.

2.1   Local Binary Patterns

The LBP feature extraction technique forms texture patterns from the pixel intensity vales of biometric images [9]. This method uses the texture patterns to create Feature Vectors (FVs) associated with the images. The LBP method can be applied to any uniquely textured data, such as facial and iris recognition. For biometric recognition, the first step is to split an image into even sized regions, as shown below in Fig. 1. A histogram is associated with each region, where the frequency of texture patterns are stored. A FV is formed from the concatenated histograms resulting from each region.

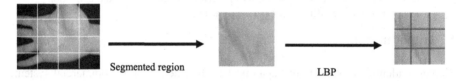

Segmented region   LBP

Fig. 1. Palm print segmented into regions for LBP

Texture patterns are measured by comparing pixel intensity values to one another within a region. More specifically, each pixel that is inclusively within a region will be compared with its nearest neighboring pixels. A pixel on the border of a region cannot be considered a center pixel since it does not have pixels within its region surrounding it entirely. Each texture pattern is represented as a binary string. Equations 1 and 2 show how a binary string can be extracted from a region on an image. The term $LBP(N_i, c)$, denotes the decimal value of a texture pattern for a neighborhood of pixels. The term c represents the pixel intensity value of the center pixel, N represents the set of neighboring pixel intensity values for c, and i represents the ith neighboring pixel of c. Equation 2 signifies the difference being taken between each neighboring pixel and the center pixel.

$$LBP(N_i, c) = \sum_{i=0}^{i-1} s(N_i, c)2^i \tag{1}$$

$$s(N_i, c) = \begin{cases} 0, & \text{if } N_i - c \leq 0 \\ 1, & \text{if } N_i - c > 0 \end{cases} \tag{2}$$

2.2   Genetic and Evolutionary Feature Extraction

GEFE, a technique proposed in Shelton et al., is a hybrid of a GEC with the LBP technique [4–8]. A GEC is a general problem solving technique based on simulated evolution

[10, 11]. A fitness function is used to compute the goodness of a solution and the best solutions procreate to create better solutions.

In the case of GEFE, each solution is a FE that is applied on a dataset of biometric images. The components of a FE are a set of widths and heights for all regions in a FE. In previous work, each region could have its own unique dimensions but in [4], it was shown that keeping all regions of a FE uniformly sized obtained a significantly better performance than allowing each region to have its own unique dimensions. Another component of a FE is that each region also has a unique location within the bounds of a biometric image. Each region also has a masking value, M_i, The masking value determines if a region will have features extracted from it. The purpose of this is for the fitness function.

The fitness, f_i, determines the goodness of a FE solution and its likelihood to procreate and create offspring FEs. An FE is applied on a dataset of biometric images. Each subject in the dataset has their images separated into a probe and gallery set and FVs are created. The Manhattan distance metric is used to get the similarity score between a probe and all the gallery FVs. The two FVs with the closest Manhattan distance are considered matches. The error rate, ε, is incremented if the closest matching gallery FV to the probe FV belong to different subjects. In addition, an effort is made to reduce the total number of regions necessary for extraction. Equation 3 shows the fitness formula, which is 10 times the number of errors added to the percent of patches used (the summation of all masking values over the total number of patches (n)). Both the number of errors and percentage of patches must be reduced to minimize the fitness.

$$f_i = 10\varepsilon + \frac{\sum_{j=0}^{n-1} m_{i,j}}{n} \tag{3}$$

3   Experiment

This research applied the LBP and GEFE techniques to palm print images taken from the CASIA-Palmprint image database [12]. CASIA-Palmprint consists of 5,502 palm print gray-scale images, captured from 312 subjects. For each subject, palm print images were collected from both left and right palms. We had a training set of 200 subjects to evolve feature extractors. This training set consisted of left hands only. Next, we had four test sets to apply both LBP and the feature extractors created by GEFE. Test set #1 consists of right hand palm prints only from the same individuals in the training set. Test set #2 consists of left hand palm prints from 100 different individuals. Test set #3 consists of right hand palm prints from 100 different individuals and test set #4 is a combination of set #2 and set #3, for a total of 200 individuals. We used eight samples per subject for all data sets.

GEFE used a Steady State Genetic Algorithm (SSGA) [13] with 2000 function evaluations with a population size of 20 candidates FEs. In SSGA, two parents are selected from the population to create an offspring. The offspring is then mutated and added to the next generation. Our best results occurred through a SSGA mutation rate of 0.1 and a mutation range of 0.7. For each dataset, the first image of each subject was used to develop a probe set while the remaining images of each subject were used to develop a gallery set.

4   Results

The identification accuracy results are shown below in Table 1. The palm print dataset used is denoted in the first column. In the second column, the feature extraction technique used is shown and in the third column, the average identification accuracy of GEFE is shown. The fourth column signifies the average number of regions used in the 30 best feature extractors from each GEFE run. In addition, for LBP, we split up the rows and columns from 1 by 1 to 15 by 15 and chose the best scheme for each test set. The best scheme and resulting number of regions is shown for LBP. The fifth and final column shows the accuracy of LBP as well as the best performing extractor from GEFE.

Table 1. Results of LBP vs GEFE for identification

Dataset	Methods	Average acc.	Avg. num regions	Best acc.
Training set	LBP	–	(1 * 4) = 4	95.45 %
	GEFE	97.5 %	17.09	98 %
Test set #1	LBP	–	(1 * 3) = 3	96 %
	GEFE	**94.78 %**	**17.09**	**96 %**
Test set #2	LBP	–	(1 * 5) = 5	97 %
	GEFE	**98.13 %**	**17.09**	**99 %**
Test set #3	LBP	–	(1 * 14) = 14	93 %
	GEFE	91.65 %	17.09	93 %
Test set #4	LBP	–	(1 * 15) = 15	94.5 %
	GEFE	**93.96 %**	**17.09**	**95 %**

The average performance shows a slightly inferior performance of GEFE when compared to LBP except for test set #2. The absolute best extractor from GEFE has an equal, if not greater, identification accuracy than LBP. However, the number of regions used by LBP is fewer than the number used by GEFE; this would result in smaller feature vectors in the case of LBP, and ultimately faster comparisons of vectors in a biometric system. However, there is promise for GEFE outperforming LBP on this dataset.

Figures 2, 3 and 4 denote the Cumulative Match Characteristic (CMC) curves of LBP and GEFE. In the case of test sets #1, 2 and 4, GEFE outperforms LBP. However, on test set #3, LBP has a better performance. Figure 5 shows the Receiver Operator Characteristic (ROC) curves for GEFE and LBP on all sets. For every test set, GEFE outperforms LBP. On test set #1, GEFE obtains a True Accept Rate (TAR) of 26.95 % at a False Accept Rate (FAR) of 0.00006 %. Test set #2 got a TAR of 37.85 % at a False Accept Rate (FAR) of 0 %. Test set #3 got a TAR of 29.88 % at a FAR of 0.0004 % and test set #4 obtained a TAR of 33.71 % at a FAR of 0.00007 %.

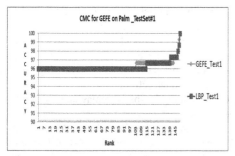

Fig. 2. CMC for GEFE on palm_Test#1

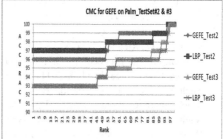

Fig. 3. CMC for GEFE on palm_Test#2 & 3

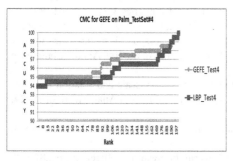

Fig. 4. CMC for GEFE on palm_Test#4

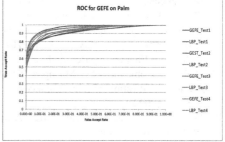

Fig. 5. ROC for GEFE on palm (Color figure online)

5   Conclusion and Future Work

The results show that GEFE outperform LBP in most aspects. Test set #3 shows LBP outperforming GEFE, but it is important to note that that set included right hands from different subjects then the training set. The identification accuracies were close as well as the verification accuracies, shown in the ROC curves. Future work will deal with applying a massive set of extractors evolved by GEFE towards mitigating replay attacks on a biometric system.

Acknowledgements.   This research is based upon work supported by the Science & Technology Center: Bio/Computational Evolution in Action Consortium (BEACON) and the Army Research Office (Contract No. W911NF-15-1-0524).

References

1. Jain, A., Flynn, P., Ross, A.A.: Handbook of Biometrics, pp. 90–95. Springer Science and Business Media, New York (2007)
2. Malčík, D., Drahanský, M.: Anatomy of biometric passports. J. Biomed. Biotechnol. **2012**, 1–8 (2012)

3. Aslam, T.M., Tan, S.Z., Dhillon, B.: Iris recognition in the presence of ocular disease. J. Roy. Soc. Interface **6**(34), 415–493 (2009)
4. Shelton, J., Dozier, G., Bryant, K., Smalls, L., Adams, J., Popplewell, K., Abegaz, T., Woodard, D., Ricanek, K.: Comparison of genetic-based feature extraction methods for facial recognition. In: Proceedings of the 2011 Midwest Artificial Intelligence and Cognitive Science Conference (MAICS-2011), April 16–17, Cincinnati (2011)
5. Shelton, J., Roy, K., O'Connor, B., Dozier, G.: Mitigating iris-based replay attacks. Int. J. Mach. Learn. Comput. (IJMLC) **4**(3), 204–209 (2014)
6. Shelton, J., Dozier, G., Bryant, K., Small, L., Adams, J., Popplewell, K., Abegaz, T., Woodard, D., Ricanek, K.: Genetic and evolutionary feature extraction via X-TOOLSS. In: The Proceedings of the 8th Annual International Conference on Genetic and Evolutionary Methods (GEM) (2011)
7. Roy, K., Shelton, J., O'Connor, B., Kamel, M.S.: Multibiometric system using fuzzy level set, and genetic and evolutionary feature extraction. IET Biometrics **4**(3), 151–161 (2015)
8. Shelton, J., Bryant, K., Abrams, S., Small, L., Adams, A., Leflore, D., Alford, A., Ricanek, K., Dozier, G.: Genetic and evolutionary biometric security: disposable feature extractors for mitigating biometric replay attacks. In: The 2012 Proceedings of the 10th Annual Conference on Systems Engineering Research (2012)
9. Ojala, T., Pietikainen, M., Maenpaa, T.: Multiresolution gray-scale and rotation invariant texture classification with local binary patterns. IEEE Trans. Pattern Anal. Mach. Intell. **24**, 971–987 (2002)
10. Fogel, L.J., Owens, A.J., Walsh, M.J.: Artificial Intelligence Through Simulated Evolution. Wiley, Hoboken (1966)
11. Kennedy, J., Eberhart, R., Shi, Y.: The Particle Swarm. In: Swarm Intelligence, pp. 287–325 (2001)
12. CASIA-Palmprint. http://biometrics.idealtest.org/
13. Davis, L.: Handbook of Genetic Algorithms. Van Nostrand Reinhold, New York (1991)

PCA-Based Face Recognition: Similarity Measures and Number of Eigenvectors

Sushma Niket Borade$^{(\boxtimes)}$ and Ratnadeep R. Deshmukh

Department of Computer Science and Information Technology,
Dr. Babasaheb Ambedkar Marathwada University,
Aurangabad 431004, India
sushma.borade@gmail.com,
rrdeshmukh.csit@bamu.ac.in

Abstract. This paper examines the performance of face recognition using Principal Component Analysis by (i) varying number of eigenvectors; and (ii) using different similarity measures for classification. We tested 15 similarity measures. ORL database is used for experimentation work which consists of 400 face images. We observed that changing similarity measure causes significant change in the performance. System showed best performance using following distance measures: Cosine, Correlation and City block. Using Cosine similarity measure, we needed to extract lesser images (30 %) in order to achieve cumulative recognition of 100 %. The performance of the system improved with the increasing number of eigenvectors (till roughly 30 % of eigenvectors). After that performance almost stabilized. Some of the worst performers are Standardized Euclidean, Weighted Modified SSE and Weighted Modified Manhattan.

Keywords: Biometrics · Face recognition · Principal component analysis · Distance measures

1 Introduction

There are many types of personal authentication systems and face recognition is one of the active research areas since last several decades. Several methods have been proposed to recognize faces [1–3]. There are two main categories of face recognition methods: feature-based and appearance-based [1]. Using appearance-based methods, a face image of size $N \times N$ pixels is represented by a vector in N^2 dimensional space. Practically, these spaces are too large to perform robust and fast recognition of faces. To solve this problem, dimensionality reduction is done using Principal Component Analysis (PCA) technique. In 1987, PCA was first used to represent face images by Sirovich and Kirby [4]. Turk and Pentland applied PCA to face recognition and presented eigenfaces method in 1991 [5]. We study the effect of 15 similarity measures on the performance of face recognition using PCA. Following characteristics are used to measure the system performance: area above cumulative match characteristics (CMC), rate of recognition and percent of images needed to extract to achieve cumulative recognition of 100 %.

© Springer International Publishing Switzerland 2016
A. Campilho and F. Karray (Eds.): ICIAR 2016, LNCS 9730, pp. 69–77, 2016.
DOI: 10.1007/978-3-319-41501-7_9

Organization of the paper is as follows: In Sect. 2, we present face recognition using PCA technique in detail. Various similarity measures are described in Sect. 3. In Sect. 4, experimental work and the results obtained are presented. Section 5 offers the conclusion.

2 Principal Component Analysis

We implemented face recognition using PCA as proposed by Turk and Pentland [5]. Let the gallery set of M face images be $\Gamma_1, \Gamma_2, ..., \Gamma_M$. The average face image of the whole set is defined by

$$\Psi = \frac{1}{M} \sum_{i=1}^{M} \Gamma_i \tag{1}$$

Each face image differs from the average face, Ψ, by the vector $\phi_i = \Gamma_i - \Psi$, where $i = 1$ to M. Find covariance matrix C as

$$C = AA^T, \text{ where matrix } A = [\phi_1 \phi_2 .. \phi_M]. \tag{2}$$

Matrix C is of size N^2 by N^2. It's computationally expensive to find its N^2 eigenvectors. Therefore form M by M matrix, $L = A^T A$ and get its M eigenvectors, v_i. The most significant M eigenvectors of C are found as:

$$u_l = \sum_{k=1}^{M} v_{lk} \phi_k, l = 1, \ldots, M \tag{3}$$

Now from these M eigenvectors, consider M' ($<M$) eigenvectors (with the highest M' eigenvalues). New probe image is projected into the facespace using operation:

$$w_k = u_k^T (\Gamma - \Psi) \tag{4}$$

for $k = 1, \ldots, M'$.

These values of w form projection vector $\Omega = [w_1, w_2, \ldots, w_{M'}]$. Probe image is then classified as belonging to closest face class by using some similarity measure.

3 Similarity Measures

Consider two feature vectors x and y of dimensions n each. The distances between these feature vectors can be calculated as [6–11]:

1. City block distance (or Manhattan distance):

$$d(x, y) = \sum_{i=1}^{n} |x_i - y_i| \tag{5}$$

2. Euclidean distance:

$$d(x,y) = \sqrt{\sum_{i=1}^{n} (x_i - y_i)^2} \qquad (6)$$

3. Squared Euclidean distance (Sum square error, SSE):

$$d(x,y) = \sum_{i=1}^{n} (x_i - y_i)^2. \qquad (7)$$

4. Mean square error (MSE):

$$d(x,y) = \frac{1}{n} \sum_{i=1}^{n} (x_i - y_i)^2 \qquad (8)$$

5. Cosine distance:

$$d(x,y) = -\frac{\sum_{i=1}^{n} x_i y_i}{\sqrt{\sum_{i=1}^{n} x_i^2 \sum_{i=1}^{n} y_i^2}} \qquad (9)$$

6. Mahalanobis distance:

$$d(x,y) = \sqrt{(x-y)S^{-1}(x-y)^t} \qquad (10)$$

where S is the covariance matrix of the distribution.

7. Standard Euclidean distance:

$$d(x,y) = \sqrt{(x-y)V^{-1}(x-y)^t} \qquad (11)$$

where V is the n by n diagonal matrix whose j^{th} diagonal element is $S(j)^2$, where S is the vector of standard deviations.

8. Minkowski distance:

$$d(x,y) = \left(\sum_{i=1}^{n} |x_i - y_i|^p\right)^{1/p}. \qquad (12)$$

where p is a scalar exponent and here $p > 0$.

9. Chebychev distance:

$$d(x,y) = max_i\{|x_i - y_i|\} \qquad (13)$$

10. Correlation distance:

$$d(x,y) = -\frac{n \sum_{i=1}^{n} x_i y_i - \sum_{i=1}^{n} x_i \sum_{i=1}^{n} y_i}{\sqrt{(n \sum_{i=1}^{n} x_i^2 - (\sum_{i=1}^{n} x_i)^2)(n \sum_{i=1}^{n} y_i^2 - (\sum_{i=1}^{n} y_i)^2)}} \qquad (14)$$

11. Canberra distance:

$$d(x,y) = \sum_{i=1}^{n} \frac{|x_i - y_i|}{|x_i| + |y_i|} \tag{15}$$

12. Modified SSE distance:

$$d(x,y) = \frac{\sum_{i=1}^{n}(x_i - y_i)^2}{\sum_{i=1}^{n} x_i^2 \sum_{i=1}^{n} y_i^2} \tag{16}$$

13. Modified Manhattan distance:

$$d(x,y) = \frac{\sum_{i=1}^{n} |x_i - y_i|}{\sum_{i=1}^{n} |x_i| \sum_{i=1}^{n} |y_i|} \tag{17}$$

14. Weighted Modified SSE distance:

$$d(x,y) = \frac{\sum_{i=1}^{n} z_i(x_i - y_i)^2}{\sum_{i=1}^{n} x_i^2 \sum_{i=1}^{n} y_i^2}, \quad z_i = \sqrt{1/\lambda_i} \tag{18}$$

where λ_i are eigenvalues.

15. Weighted Modified Manhattan distance:

$$d(x,y) = \frac{\sum_{i=1}^{n} z_i|x_i - y_i|}{\sum_{i=1}^{n} |x_i| \sum_{i=1}^{n} |y_i|}, \quad z_i = \sqrt{1/\lambda_i} \tag{19}$$

In this paper we perform identification task. CMC curve graphically represents the performance of the identification system. It is a plot of rank values on the X axis and probability of correct identification at or below that rank on the Y axis [10, 12].

4   Experiments and Results

We tested performance of the system using ORL face image database [13]. Face images are taken at the AT and T Laboratories between April 1992 and April 1994. ORL database contains images of 40 different persons, with 10 images per person. The face images are taken at different times by varying lighting, facial details and facial expressions. All face images are frontal with some pose variation. Each image is of size 112 × 92 pixels with 256 gray levels.

For experimental work, each face image is resized to 50 × 40 pixels. Training is done by considering first 5 images and testing is done considering remaining five images per person. This gave us gallery set of 200 images and probe set of 200 images. Experiments are implemented using MATLAB® R2013a. We used nearest mean rule in which we computed a template for each identity in the database. The closest identity is chosen as the match.

The experimental results with 15 similarity measures are listed in Tables 1, 2 and 3. The performance for face recognition is measured by calculating the area above cumulative match characteristic curve (CMCA). If CMCA is smaller, it indicates better recognition performance. We show how many images (in percents) should be extracted to get cumulative recognition rate between 80 to 100 %. If it is smaller, it implies that fewer images need to be extracted to get required cumulative recognition rate. We also find recognition rate that is achieved if the closest match is extracted from the system. If this first one recognition rate is more, it indicates better results. In Tables 1, 2 and 3, we used subscripts to mark the best results.

Table 1. Performance using 20 % of features (40).

Similarity measure	Rank (%) of images					CMCA	First 1 rec
	80	85	90	95	100	0–10000	
City block	1.62	3.09	4.56	13.75	50_4	401.25_4	166_4
Eucl; SSE; MSE	1.84	3.16	4.47	8.75	37.5_2	369.38_3	165_5
Cosine	0.94	2.5	4.06	8.75	30_1	336.25_1	170_1
Mahalanobis	3.90	5.83	13	30	60_5	583.13	151
Std Euclidean	2.31	4.23	10	18.75	67.5	510.63	161
Minkowski	1.84	3.16	4.47	8.75	37.5_2	369.38_3	165_5
Chebychev	4.74	6.25	9.38	20	72.5	516.25	134
Correlation	1.25	2.64	4.03	10	30_1	336.88_2	169_2
Canberra	4.17	6.11	12.5	30	92.5	623.75	148
Modified SSE	−2	3	7.5	23.75	90	531.88	169_2
ModManhattan	−0.8	3.33	8.5	16.25	47.5_3	431.25_5	168_3
WeigMod SSE	3.61	6.79	18.33	40	95	728.75	156
WeigMod Man	3.54	8.5	22.5	40	80	740.63	155

Table 2. Performance using 60 % of features (120).

Similarity measure	Rank (%) of images					CMCA	First 1 Rec
	80	85	90	95	100	0–10000	
City block	−0.21	1.88	3.96	9	35_2	344.38_3	173_1
Eucl; SSE;MSE	1.32	2.80	4.26	8.75	35_2	358.75_4	168_4
Cosine	0.88	2.35	3.82	7.5	30_1	325.63_2	171_3
Mahalanobis	16.25	26.5	38.75	67.5	92.5	1215.6	127
Std Euclidean	11	14.25	26.67	43.75	100	915.63	131
Minkowski	1.32	2.80	4.26	8.75	35_2	358.75_4	168_4
Chebychev	4.74	6.25	9.38	20	72.5_4	516.25	134
Correlation	0.74	2.21	3.68	6.25	30_1	322.5_1	172_2
Canberra	10	14.06	28.75	50	97.5	950	132
Modified SSE	0	4.17	8.5	21.25	82.5_5	536.25	166
ModManhattan	0.91	3.18	5.71	12.5	45_3	385.63_5	167_5
WeigMod SSE	11.5	21.67	35	62.5	95	1095.6	139
WeigMod Man	15	28.75	40	54.38	87.5	1123.8	114

Table 3. Performance using 90 % of features (180).

Similarity measure	Rank (%) of images					CMCA	First 1 rec
	80	85	90	95	100	0–10000	
City block	−1.25	1.25	3.75	9	35_2	340.63_3	175_1
Eucl; SSE; MSE	1.18	2.65	4.12	8.75	35_2	356.88_4	169_4
Cosine	0.88	2.35	3.82	6.25	30_1	323.13_1	171_3
Mahalanobis	9.46	12.5	25	34.17	77.5_5	838.13	97
Std Euclidean	27.5	34.5	45	60	100	1538.1	87
Minkowski	1.18	2.65	4.12	8.75	35_2	356.88_4	169_4
Chebychev	4.74	6.25	9.38	20	72.5_4	516.25	134
Correlation	0.63	2.19	3.75	6.67	30_1	323.75_2	172_2
Canberra	16.25	25.83	37.5	62.5	92.5	1212.5	110
Modified SSE	1.07	4.64	9.06	23.75	87.5	561.25	164
ModManhattan	1	3.5	6.67	15.83	57.5_3	422.5_5	166_5
WeigMod SSE	15	28.75	50	68.75	97.5	1323.8	124
WeigMod Man	28.13	36.67	50	65	90	1516.9	87

Table 4 reports the sorted similarity measures w.r.t the performance of the system using following characteristics: (i) recognition rate, (ii) overall recognition accuracy (i.e. CMCA), (iii) images (in percent) extracted to get 100 % cumulative identification.

Table 4. Sorted similarity measures with respect to the performance of the system.

No. of eigenvectors	First1	CMCA	Cum100
20 %	Cosine	Cosine	Cosine, Correlation
(40)	Correlation, Mod. SSE	Correlation	Euclidean
	Modified Manhattan	Euclidean	Modified Manhattan
60 %	City block	Correlation	Cosine, Correlation
(120)	Correlation	Cosine	City block, Eucl.
	Cosine	City block	Modified Manhattan
90 %	City block	Cosine	Cosine, Correlation
(180)	Correlation	Correlation	City block, Eucl.
	Cosine	City block	Modified Manhattan

The training set has 200 images (5 images per person). This produces 199 eigenvectors as there will be only $(M - 1)$ meaningful eigenvectors with remaining eigenvectors having associated eigenvalues of zero [5]. Figure 1 shows the variation in the system performance with number of eigenvectors for top 6 performers. We need to extract fewer images (30 %) to achieve 100 % cumulative recognition using Cosine distance measure if 10–90 % of eigenvectors are used and correlation if 30–90 % of eigenvectors are used. Performance with respect to rank increases till 10 % and 12 % of eigenvectors for Cosine and Correlation similarity measures respectively, and later it stabilizes.

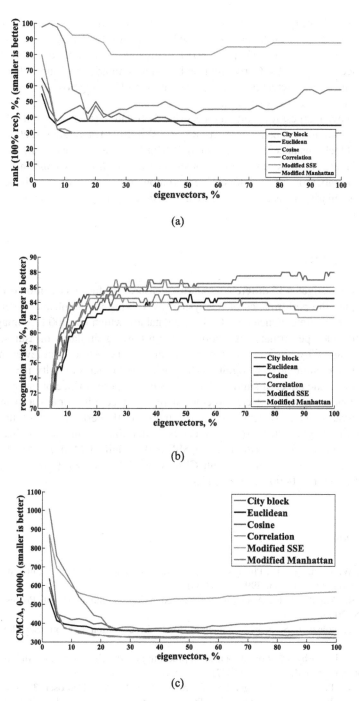

Fig. 1. Performance of the system with respect to number of eigenvectors (a) Cumulative 100 % recognition, (b) Recognition rate, (c) CMCA (Color figure online)

System achieved best performance using Cosine similarity measure (336.25–364.38) if 10–20 % of eigenvectors are used, 323.13 if 90 % of eigenvectors are used and Correlation (322.5–323.75) if 30–60 % of eigenvectors are used. For CMCA, top performance is shown by Correlation and Cosine similarity measures. Performance with these measures increases until approximately 30 % of eigenvectors are used, and then performance almost stabilizes.

We achieved largest recognition rates using Correlation (82.5–86 %) if 10–30 % of eigenvectors are used, Cosine distance (85–86 %) if 20–30 % of eigenvectors are used and City block distance (86–87.5 %) if 30–90 % of eigenvectors are used. Best recognition rate is achieved using City block measure. It shows increase in recognition rate with number of eigenvectors. The variation in the performance indicates that selecting similarity measure is a critical decision in designing a PCA-based face recognition.

5 Conclusions

This paper investigates 15 different similarity measures for face recognition using PCA. We examined the performance of the system by varying the number of eigenvectors. The experiments are conducted on ORL face database which has 400 face images. The best identification performance is reported using following similarity measures: Cosine, Correlation and City block. Using Cosine distance we need to extract fewer images to achieve 100 % cumulative recognition than using any other similarity measure. This research shows the effect of similarity measures on the performance of the system. It is observed that, as number of eigenvectors increased, recognition rates also increased. This observation is consistent with prior studies [10]. Performance of the system increased till roughly 30 % of eigenvectors. After that, it almost stabilized. Standardized Euclidean, Weighted Modified SSE and Weighted Modified Manhattan are worst performers to name a few with CMCA of (510.7–1538), (687.5–1323.8) and (734.4–1516.9) for 10–90 % of eigenvectors.

References

1. Zhao, W., Chellappa, R., Phillips, P.J., Rosenfeld, A.: Face recognition: a literature survey. ACM Comput. Surv. **35**, 399–458 (2003)
2. Jafri, R., Arabnia, H.R.: A survey of face recognition techniques. J. Inf. Process. Syst. **5**, 41–68 (2009)
3. Rao, A., Noushath, S.: Subspace methods for face recognition. Comput. Sci. Rev. **4**, 1–17 (2010)
4. Sirovich, L., Kirby, M.: Low-dimensional procedure for the characterization of human faces. J. Opt. Soc. Am. **4**, 519–524 (1987)
5. Turk, M., Pentland, A.P.: Eigenfaces for recognition. J. Cogn. Neurosci. **3**, 71–86 (1991)
6. Yambor, W., Draper, B.: Analyzing PCA-based face recognition algorithm: eigenvector selection and distance measures. In: Christensen, H., Phillips, J. (eds.) Empirical Evaluation Methods in Computer Vision, pp. 39–51. World Scientific Press, Singapore (2002)

7. Mathwork Help for Similarity Measures. http://www.mathworks.com/help/stats/pdist2.html
8. Perlibakas, V.: Distance measures for PCA-based face recognition. Pattern Recogn. Lett. **25**, 711–724 (2004)
9. Miller, P., Lyle, J.: The effect of distance measures on the recognition rates of PCA and LDA based facial recognition. In: Digital Image Processing. Clemson University, Clemson
10. Moon, H., Phillips, P.J.: Computational and performance aspects of PCA-based face recognition algorithms. Perception **30**, 303–321 (2001)
11. Borade, S.N., Deshmukh, R.R.: Effect of distance measures on the performance of face recognition using principal component analysis. In: Berretti, S. (ed.) Intelligent Systems Technologies and Applications, AISC, vol. 384, pp. 569–577. Springer, Heidelberg (2016)
12. Biometrics Testing and Statistics. www.biometrics.gov/documnets/biotestingandstats.pdf
13. ORL Face Database. http://www.cl.cam.ac.uk/research/dtg/attarchive/facedatabase.html

Image Enhancement and Restoration

Sinogram Restoration Using Confidence Maps to Reduce Metal Artifact in Computed Tomography

Louis Frédérique[1,3(✉)], Benoit Recur[2], Sylvain Genot[3],
Jean-Philippe Domenger[1], and Pascal Desbarats[1]

[1] LaBRI, University of Bordeaux, 351 Cours de la Libération, 33405 Talence, France
louis.frederique@labri.fr
[2] Inserm U1029 LAMC, University of Bordeaux,
Allée Geoffroy Saint-Hillaire, Bat. B2, 33600 Pessac, France
[3] Tomo Adour, Zone Europa, 5 Rue Johannes Kepler, 64000 Pau, France

Abstract. Metal artifact reduction (MAR) is a well-known problem and lots of studies have been performed during the last decades. The common standard methods for MAR consist of synthesizing missing projection data by using an interpolation or in-painting process. However, no method has been yet proposed to solve MAR problem when no sinogram is available. This paper proposes a novel MAR approach using confidence maps to restore an artifacted sinogram computed directly from the reconstructed image.

Keywords: Metal artifact reduction · Tomography · Confidence map · X-ray · Sinogram restoration

1 Introduction

In X-Ray computed tomography, presence of high density materials (such as metal implants) leads to the well-known metal artifacts in reconstructed image. It is characterized by a local hypo-signal and straight hyper-signal [1] and makes image analysis difficult to achieve. This observed phenomenon is due to high attenuations of the rays in high density materials.

Many different approaches have been proposed for metal artifact reduction (MAR) during the last decade. Currently, three kind of methods can be distinguished. In the most popular case, developed methods consider the artifact reduction as a missing data problem [2,7,8,13,14]. These methods are based on projection completion method. Missing data, represented by the metal traces in the sinogram, are replaced by synthetic data computed by interpolation or in-painting methods. They first suppress metal traces from the sinogram by making a difference between the original sinogram and the metal traces. Both methods obtain metal traces by segmentation of reconstructed image and forward-projection of this segmentation. The last stage consists of completing data by in-painting (for

© Springer International Publishing Switzerland 2016
A. Campilho and F. Karray (Eds.): ICIAR 2016, LNCS 9730, pp. 81–89, 2016.
DOI: 10.1007/978-3-319-41501-7_10

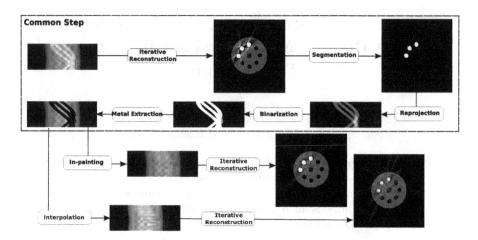

Fig. 1. Steps of method selected from the state of the art [2, 13] bringing out the common steps, in our case iterative reconstruction is performed with SART.

Chen et al.) or by interpolation (for Yu et al.). Figure 1 illustrates these methods bringing out the common steps. The second group of methods considers metal artifact reduction as a penalizing term in an iterative reconstruction method [3,11,12]. Such a method is based on local filtering assessing the coherence of a pixel with its neighborhood. Finally, the third group identifies metal directly in the sinogram and correct it before performing a reconstruction [4–6].

However, these methods start their process from the original projection data. In our context, only the reconstructed image is available due to clinical scanner usage. Thus, we focus our investigations on a solution based on the reconstructed image only. We propose an algorithm that reduces the artifact by restoring an artifacted sinogram computed from the reconstructed image. To identify these artifacts in projection space, we first compute confidence maps from image and generate their corresponding sinograms.

These maps represent hyper-signal and hypo-signal repartitions generated by metal artifact in the reconstructed image. In other words, each map is a representation of the amount of hyper or hypo-signal phenomenon that occurs during the initial acquisition/reconstruction process. They are obtained using an iterative reconstruction from a simulated acquisition of metal traces. The overall output function is a combination of these two maps, where negative and positive values represent the hypo-signal and the hyper-signal, respectively. In the following, we first detail and illustrate the proposed method. Finally, we discuss reconstruction result obtained by our method.

2 Sinogram Restoration Supervised by Confidence Maps

The proposed algorithm is based on a similar work-flow than in [2,13], except that the interpolation or in-painting part is replaced by a sinogram restoration.

Moreover, pixels that have to be corrected are selected according to two confidence maps computed from the sinogram of metal objects. These maps represent hyper-signal and hypo-signal generated by metal artifact. The values of each map correspond to the confidence of each reconstructed pixel.

Figure 2 and following sections illustrate the three algorithm steps, which are: (i) metal segmentation, (ii) confidence maps generation, and, (iii) artifact reduction using confidence maps.

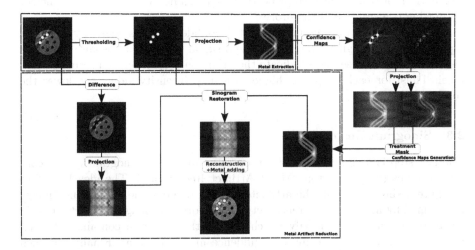

Fig. 2. Proposed method algorithm: each step is delimited on the image with a block

2.1 Metal Extraction

The goal of the first step is to extract metal from the image (cf. Fig. 2 step "Metal extraction"). To do this, a segmentation is performed to only keep metallic objects. Segmentation is done by applying a threshold T selected using method proposed by Prewitt et al. [10]. This threshold corresponds to the minimum between two local maxima in a smoothed histogram. Then, all values higher than T are considered as metal.

2.2 Confidence Maps Generation

The second step consists of reconstructing two images from a sinogram representing metal traces (cf. Fig. 2 step "Maps generation"). Image computed in the previous step is projected to provide a sinogram of these metal traces. Prior to computing the two confidence maps, we simulate a detector saturation at metal forward-projection positions by setting to 1 each pixel higher than a given threshold. Next, a bell function is added as background to avoid artifacts adding such as beam hardening and only permit to retrieve metal artifacts [9].

A first image is then obtained with an iterative process solving the linear system $S = AI_M$, where S represents the sinogram, I_M is the map we want to obtain and A corresponds the projection matrix. This process is defined by:

$$I_M^{k+1} = I_M^k + \lambda A^t(S - AI_M^k) \tag{1}$$

where A^t represents the retroprojection matrix and $\lambda \in \mathbb{R}_+^*$ is a coefficient optimizing convergence of the process.

We then obtain a representation of the confidence maps where hyper-signal represents values higher than 0 and hypo-signal represents absolute values of negative values. These maps indicate then the non-confidence of a reconstructed pixel. Thus, for each map, the higher the map intensity value, the lower the confidence.

2.3   Sinogram Restoration

The last step is a supervised restoration of an artifacted sinogram by the confidence maps (cf. Fig. 2 step "Metal Artifact Reduction"). The idea is to first compute a sinogram from the artifacted image without the metal. Such image is obtained by making a difference between the original image and metal image. Then, to estimate and identify which part of the sinogram contains artifacts, we compute a mask according to confidence map sinograms. Finally, for each pixel of metal image, we compute its trace in the sinogram in order to correct pixel's trajectory only. According to the works proposed by Liu et al. [6] pixel trajectory in a sinogram is defined by:

$$\rho = \sqrt{(x - x_c)^2 + (y - y_c)^2} + \sin(\arctan(\frac{y - y_c}{x - x_c}) + \theta) \tag{2}$$

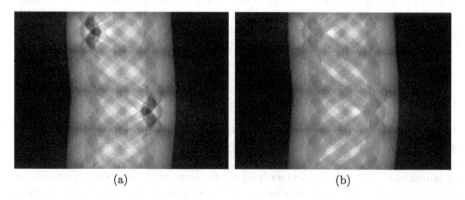

(a)   (b)

Fig. 3. Sinogram restoration step (a) sinogram computed from artifacted image (b) restored sinogram using pixel trajectory estimation.

where ρ represents detector position, (x, y) corresponds to pixel coordinates, (x_c, y_c) are center coordinates and θ corresponds to projection angle. The result of the restoration step is illustrated in Fig. 3.

3   Results and Discussion

In this section, we validate the proposed MAR method by an experimental study performed from the CT acquisition of a home-made phantom, which is a 3D printed cylinder of revolver like object, able to receive several metal rods. Figure 4(a) represents ground truth image obtained by acquiring *Kimagure* without metal rods and numerically adding them on the reconstructed image.

CT scanning of *Kimagure* was performed on a Siemens Somatom Open clinical scanner using helical geometry with the following parameters: voltage on X-ray source at 100 kV, tube current at 150 mA, pixel size at 0.1953 mm², slice thickness at 0.6 mm and the size of reconstructed CT image is 512×512 pixels.

Figure 4(d) illustrates the reconstruction of a slice of *Kimagure* containing hyper-signal (pointed by red circles) and hypo-signal (pointed by yellow circles) we want to reduce. Considering in our case that hyper-signal presence does not interfere with image analysis, our main goal is to reduce hypo-signal artifact.

The analysis is first based on the usage of PSNR and MSE metrics. Figure 4 illustrates the result from the presented method. Image Fig. 4(b) shows the reconstruction given by the clinical scanner. Image Fig. 4(c) is the image resulting from our proposed algorithm. PSNR and global MSE values are presented in Table 1 and Fig. 4(e) and (f) are local error images.

Table 1. PSNR and global MSE values for artifacted image and our result.

	Artifacted	Corrected
PSNR	23.47	22.82
Global MSE	292.42	339.50

If we compare the resulting values of PSNR and global MSE, we can notice that metrics values from our result are lower than artifacted values. This can indicate a non-artifact reduction, an artifact enhancement or a global intensity enhancement. By looking at local MSE images, we can see that some hyper-signal are enhanced very locally near metal rods which explains metrics values. However, most hyper and hypo-signal values between metal rods are well reduced and geometry seems to be well preserved and restored. Nevertheless, one of the remaining limitations of the proposed approach is the non-correction of some pixels around metal rods due to a lack of information in these areas.

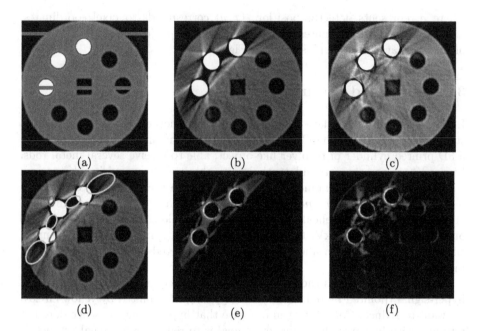

Fig. 4. Presentation of the result (a) Reference image without metal artifact and line profile indexes 150, 226, 254. (b) Artifacted image without correction, (c) Our method, (d) Original reconstruction without correction containing hyper-signal pointed by red circles and hypo-signal pointed by yellow circles, (e) and (f) MSE map values for each image. (Color figure online)

In order to complete phantom study, we develop now a profile analysis of the result. Horizontal profiles are extracted from reconstructed images along the lines shown in Fig. 4(a). Figure 5 shows intensity profiles at horizontal indexes 150, 226 and 254 (from top to bottom).

The analysis of the different profiles shows that image contrast is changed and pixel intensities are enhanced. Moreover, hypo-signal between metal rods and hyper-signal near metal are well reduced. Furthermore, we can also notice that globally, homogeneity is unchanged which reveals that no corruption has been added during the process. Meanwhile, we can observe that peaks are remaining, which indicate that some hyper-signal were enhanced instead of being reduced. We can also notice a slight geometry distortion of the middle square because of the difference between the profile 254 from position 240 to 270. By looking at profile 150, we can observe that hypo-signal positioned from 250 to 330 is going to be reduced because pixel intensities are higher than artifacted profile.

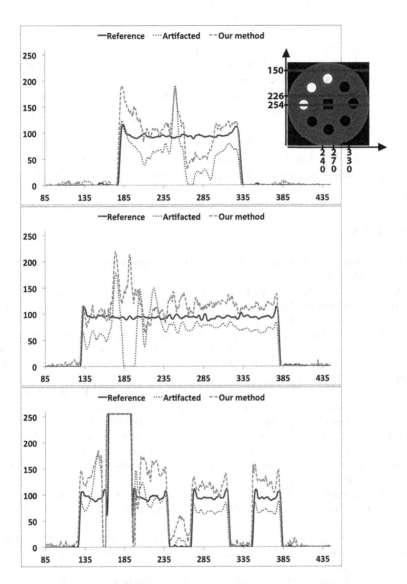

Fig. 5. Intensity profiles (and respective MSE value) along lines 150, 226, 254 according to horizontal pixel indexes, for the resulting images with the non metal artifacted image as reference profile.

4 Conclusion

In this paper we propose an algorithm to reduce metal artifacts from reconstructed images, without needing original projection data. Thanks to the confidence maps, we are able to restore an artifacted sinogram computed from the reconstructed image. Considering the results, our proposed method reduces significantly such degradations. However, due to a lack of information, some pixels are not corrected around metal rods.

Although the proposed algorithm demonstrates a good potential for metal artifact reduction, some improvements have to be done in the future. First, we have to improve artifact reduction in the sinogram by investigating a better artifact identification in the projection space, in order to reduce further remaining hyper and hypo-signals in reconstructed images. Second, we have to correct the slight distortion introduced during the process, to preserve perfectly original geometry.

References

1. Edward Boas, F., Fleischmann, D.: CT artifacts: causes and reduction techniques. Imaging Med. **4**(2), 229–240 (2012)
2. Chen, Y., Li, Y., Guo, H., Hu, Y., Luo, L., Yin, X., Gu, J., Christine, T.: CT metal artifact reduction method based on improved image segmentation and sinogram in-painting. Math. Probl. Eng. **2012** (2012)
3. De Man, B., Nuyts, J., Dupont, P., Marchal, G., Suetens, P.: Reduction of metal streak artifacts in X-ray computed tomography using a transmission maximum a posteriori algorithm. In: Nuclear Science Symposium, Conference Record, vol. 2, pp. 850–854. IEEE (1999)
4. Fernandez, J.-J., Laugks, U., Schaffer, M., Bäuerlein, F.J.B., Khoshouei, M., Baumeister, W., Lucic, V.: Removing contamination-induced reconstruction artifacts from cryo-electron tomograms. Biophys. J. **110**, 850 (2015)
5. Li, H., Noel, C., Haijian Chen, H., Li, H., Low, D., Moore, K., Klahr, P., Michalski, J., Gay, H.A., Thorstad, W., et al.: Clinical evaluation of a commercial orthopedic metal artifact reduction tool for CT simulations in radiation therapy. Med. Phys. **39**(12), 7507–7517 (2012)
6. Liu, J.J., Watt-Smith, S.R., Smith, S.M.: CT reconstruction using FBP with sinusoidal amendment for metal artefact reduction. In: DICTA, pp. 439–448. Citeseer (2003)
7. Meyer, E., Raupach, R., Lell, M., Schmidt, B., Kachelrieß, M.: Normalized metal artifact reduction (NMAR) in computed tomography. MED. PHYS. **37**(10), 5482–5493 (2010)
8. Meyer, E., Raupach, R., Lell, M., Schmidt, B., Kachelrieß, M.: Frequency split metal artifact reduction (FSMAR) in computed tomography. Med. Phys. **39**(4), 1904–1916 (2012)
9. Paziresh, M., Kingston, A., Myers, G., Latham, S., Sheppard, A.: Software X-ray beam hardening correction of cylindrical specimens. In: International Conference on Tomography of Materials and Structures, pp. 187–9190 (2013)
10. Prewitt, J., Mendelsohn, M.L.: The analysis of cell images*. Ann. N. Y. Acad. Sci. **128**(3), 1035–1053 (1966)

11. Snyder, D.L., O'Sullivan, J.A., Murphy, R.J., Politte, D.G., Whiting, B.R., Williamson, J.F.: Image reconstruction for transmission tomography when projection data are incomplete. Phys. Med. Biol. **51**(21), 5603 (2006)
12. Wang, G., Snyder, D.L., O'Sullivan, J., Vannier, M.W.: Iterative deblurring for CT metal artifact reduction. IEEE Trans. Med. Imaging **15**(5), 657–664 (1996)
13. Yu, H., Zeng, K., Bharkhada, D.K., Wang, G., Madsen, M.T., Saba, O., Policeni, B., Howard, M.A., Smoker, W.R.K.: A segmentation-based method for metal artifact reduction. Acad. Radiol. **14**(4), 495–504 (2007)
14. Zhang, Y., Yan, H., Jia, X., Yang, J., Jiang, S.B., Mou, X.: A hybrid metal artifact reduction algorithm for X-ray CT. Med. Phys. **40**(4), 041910 (2013)

Enhancement of a Turbulent Degraded Frame Using 2D-DTW Averaging

Rishaad Abdoola[✉] and Barend van Wyk

Department of Electrical Engineering, French South African Institute of Technology,
Tshwane University of Technology, Staatsartillerie Road, Pretoria 0001, South Africa
{AbdoolaR,vanwykB}@tut.ac.za

Abstract. Atmospheric turbulence causes objects in video sequences to appear blurred and waver slowly in a quasi-periodic fashion resulting in a loss of detail. A DTW (Dynamic Time Warping) averaging algorithm is presented to extract a single, geometrically improved and sharper frame from a sequence of frames using 2D-DTW. The extracted frame is shown to be sharper over utilizing simple temporal averaging by preserving edges and lines as well as being geometrically improved.

Keywords: Scintillation · Atmospheric turbulence · Dynamic Time Warping

1 Introduction

Atmospheric turbulence causes video sequences to appear blurred and waver in a quasi-periodic fashion causing problems in fields such as defense (surveillance and intelligence gathering) where detail in images is critical. Proposed hardware methods such as adaptive optics and DWFS (deconvolution from wavefront sensing) require complex devices and can be impractical. Image processing methods are more practical since improvements are implemented after the video is acquired and are independent of the cameras used for capture [1, 3–7, 11].

Numerous image processing methods have been proposed for the compensation of the blurring effects while fewer algorithms have been proposed for the correction of geometric distortions. In this paper the focus is placed on the extraction of a single corrected frame which can then be used for the restoration of the entire sequence. The 2D-DTW averaging algorithm is presented and its results are compared to the General Time-Averaging algorithm.

2 Visualizing Atmospheric Turbulence

Since atmospheric turbulence degraded images are not easily available, being able to simulate atmospheric effects would be advantageous. This also provides us with a set of ground truth sequences allowing us to compare the original sequences with the recovered sequences from the algorithms.

© Springer International Publishing Switzerland 2016
A. Campilho and F. Karray (Eds.): ICIAR 2016, LNCS 9730, pp. 90–100, 2016.
DOI: 10.1007/978-3-319-41501-7_11

A turbulence degraded sequence g can be modeled as

$$g(i,j,t) = D[x(i,j,t) * h(i,j,t),t] + \eta(i,j,t) \tag{1}$$

where $*$ denotes two-dimensional convolution, η denotes time-varying additive noise, D denotes the turbulence induced time-varying geometric distortion, h is the dispersive distortion component of the atmospheric turbulence and x is the original video [1]. The OTF (optical transfer function) to simulate the blurring effects can be modeled as

$$H(u,v) = e^{-\lambda(u^2+v^2)^{5/6}}, \tag{2}$$

where λ controls the severity of the blur [1]. The value of λ is varied between frames, within a range, to correctly simulate the time-varying effect of atmospheric blurring. Two methods were used to simulate the geometric distortions induced by atmospheric turbulence as summarized in Table 1. A detailed explanation of these methods can be found in [12].

Table 1. Simulating atmospheric turbulence

Simulation Algorithm
1. Use a 2-pass mesh warping algorithm to simulate the distortion effects. Alternatively, compute the motion fields from real turbulence degrade sequences.
2. Multiply each frame $X(u,v)$ in the sequence with the OTF described by (1), varying λ between frames.
3. Include the additive noise component in each frame.

3 General Algorithm

The general algorithm is based on similar methods, implemented in the literature, of correcting atmospheric turbulence [3, 5, 11]. The video sequence is corrected by applying image registration techniques to each frame with respect to a reference frame. This generates a sequence that is stable and geometrically correct. A reference frame is generated by either using a frame in the sequence with little geometric distortion and minimal blurring or, more practically, by temporally averaging a number of frames in the sequence. By viewing atmospheric turbulence as being quasi-periodic, averaging a number of frames would provide a reference frame that is geometrically correct, but blurred. For the purpose of registration, an optical flow algorithm as proposed by Lucas and Kanade [2] was implemented using a coarse-to-fine iterative strategy achieved through an image pyramid. An average of two levels of the pyramid was used for most of the sequences. The reference frames were generated by averaging the first N frames of the turbulence degraded sequences.

The algorithm performs well when no real motion is present in the sequence. The video sequence is stabilized, except for a few discontinuities caused by the optical flow calculations and/or the warping algorithm. When real motion is present in the scene the reference frame is degraded due to motion blur. Warping any frame towards the reference frame will cause further distortions and the restored sequence will be degraded to a greater extent than the turbulence sequence.

4   Dynamic Time Warping

DTW (Dynamic Time Warping) is a distance measure which allows for the non-linear mapping of one time signal to another. This is in contrast to non-warping distance measures that use points from the signals that occur at the same time to calculate the distance.

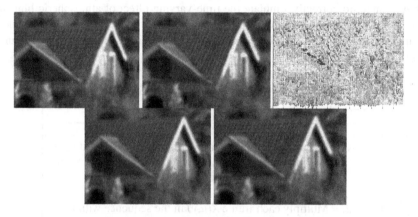

Fig. 1. (Top Left) Frame 1 and (Top centre) frame 7 of real sequence, (Top Right) flow field. (Bottom Left) time averaged frame and (Bottom Right) corrected frame. (Images courtesy of the CSIR, image distance 5 km)

Let $X = x1, x2... x_m$ and $Y = y1, y2... y_n$ be two time signals of length m and n respectively. The optimal alignment of these two time signals using DTW can be obtained using dynamic programming. Let T be an $m \times n$ distance matrix where $T(i,j) = |x_i - y_j|$. To obtain the DTW distance between X and Y, we need to find the optimal warping path through T i.e. the path that minimizes the sum of the cells it goes through. We can do this by backtracking through the matrix D where

$$D(i,j) = \min\left\{ \begin{array}{c} D(i,j-1) \\ D(i-1,j) \\ D(i-1,j-1) \end{array} \right\} + dist(x_i, y_j) \tag{3}$$

and $dist(x_i, y_j) = |x_i - y_j|$. While only three directions are searched from to create the next step in (6), many other possibilities exist for the selection of local constraints such as the Itakura [10] and Sakoe-Chiba [9] local constraints. The Sakoe-Chiba band constraint was used for the global constraints which define the search region for the optimal path as shown in Fig. 2.

Fig. 2. (Left) Sakoe-Chiba local constraints and (Right) Sakoe-Chiba global contraints used.

To use Dynamic Time Warping on the turbulence degraded frames each row from the images is treated as a time series.

4.1 Dynamic Time Warping Averaging

The temporal average of an image, $\bar{I}(x, y)$, for a sequence of N frames is defined as

$$\bar{I}(x, y) = \frac{1}{N} \sum_{t=1}^{N} I(x, y, t) \tag{4}$$

where t is the frame number. As can be seen from (7) each pixel, $\bar{I}(x_i, y_j, t_{k1})$ in an image is summed to the corresponding pixel in a different frame. If the images have been shifted or distorted the incorrect pixels will be summed as can be seen in Fig. 3 (Right). The final result will be an image that is degraded by a localized blur due to the temporal averaging. This is illustrated in Fig. 3 (Left).

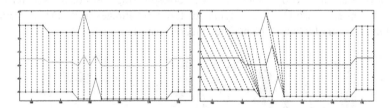

Fig. 3. (Left) Average of two signals from artificial image (average is shown as the centre signal), (Right) DTW average of two signals from artificial image (DTW average is shown as the centre signal). (Color figure online)

To obtain the dynamic time warping average [8] of two signals the correct pixel intensities from the corresponding frames need to be added and since we are also interested in averaging the location of the correct pixel intensities, the average of the time values needs to be determined as well.

Once both the average pixel intensities and the average temporal locations of the two signals are obtained the DTW-average signal is constructed. It can be seen in Fig. 3 (Right) that the DTW-averaged signal is edge preserving as opposed to the simple temporal averaging shown in Fig. 3 (Left). This allows us to average images while preserving their edges and avoiding the localized blur inherent in simple temporal averaging. To allow us to average more than two images the averaging is done in pairs [8] and the averaged time series at each level is then hierarchically combined to obtain the final average.

The difference between simple temporal averaging and DTW averaging of images can be illustrated on an artificially generated image of two squares. One of the squares in Fig. 4 (Centre Left) is shifted and the average is then calculated using temporal averaging and DTW-averaging. It can be seen that the DTW-averaging has preserved the edges of the square whereas the square in the temporal averaged image has become blurred.

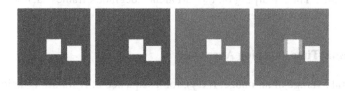

Fig. 4. (Left) Square image 1, (Centre Left) square image 2, (Centre Right) DTW-average of the two squares and (Right) temporal average of the two squares.

To determine the average of the two images in Fig. 4, each row of the first image was assumed to be matched to each row of the second image. This assumption however is not practical since in the case of turbulence the image becomes warped in both the vertical and horizontal directions. If the standard DTW-averaging algorithm is applied to the square image where there has been a shift in both directions the resulting output will be an image that has been further degraded due to the fact that the rows of the first image have been incorrectly matched to the corresponding rows of the second image (Fig. 5). In order to use DTW-averaging for turbulent images a 2D-DTW-averaging algorithm is required which is formulated and discussed in Sect. 4.2.

Fig. 5. (Left) Square image 1, (Centre Left) square image 2, (Centre Right) DTW-average and (Right) temporal average of two squares.

4.2 2D-Dynamic Time Warping

For the 2D-DTW we take each row, r, of the first image and calculate the DTW distance, $D(m,n)$, to all the rows of the second image to create the matrix D_{row} which consists of all the DTW distances between the two images.

$$D_{row} = \begin{bmatrix} D_{11} & D_{12} & D_{13} & \cdots & D_{1m} \\ D_{22} & D_{22} & D_{23} & \cdots & D_{1m} \\ D_{23} & D_{32} & D_{33} & \cdots & D_{3m} \\ \vdots & \vdots & \vdots & \vdots & \vdots \\ D_{m1} & D_{m2} & \cdots & D_{m(n-1)} & D_{mn} \end{bmatrix} \tag{5}$$

D_{row} can then be minimized using dynamic programming to obtain the optimal warp between the rows in the first and second images. Since the turbulence present in the sequences is quasi-periodic with a radius of δ pixels, we can reduce the search criteria between the rows of the image using the Sakoe-Chiba global constraints [9] to $r-\delta$ and $r+\delta$. The row matching is also done locally, by segmenting the image column wise, as the warping of the images can vary within the same row of an image.

Once we have obtained the optimal matching of the segmented rows we can use DTW-averaging to determine the average image. Figure 6 shows the 2D-DTW average algorithm applied to the same square images in Fig. 4 (Left) and (Centre Left).

Fig. 6. (Left) Square image 1, (Centre left) square image 2, (Centre right) 2D-DTW-average and (Right) temporal average of two frames.

The final algorithm can be outlined as follows:

2D-DTW averaging
1. Pair up the 2^n images from the sequence and find the 2D-DTW average as follows:
a. Determine the DTW distance between each segmented row, r, in Image A and its locally corresponding rows, $r-\delta$ to $r+\delta$, in Image B. δ is adjusted according to the level of turbulence present in the sequence.
b. Find the optimal warp for the segmented row using dynamic programming.
c. Find the DTW average between the optimally matched rows from step b.
2. Hierarchically combine each successive level by obtaining the 2D-DTW average until the final averaged image is obtained.

4.3   Dynamic Time Warping Using Phase Space

An alternate approach to adapting the DTW algorithm to two dimensions using the phase space was investigated and is presented. The Phase Space of a signal allows us to analyze a one-dimensional signal by representing the signal using its different phases. A new set of co-ordinates can be constructed for a signal by taking the time delay of the signal. Figure 7 shows the Henon series [13], S, as well as it's phase space or return map where the new co-ordinates of S were represented as $S(n) = [s(n), s(n + 1)]$.

Fig. 7.   Henon series and Henon return map.

In order to use the phase space representation for the turbulent images, the co-ordinates of each pixel (i,j) of the intensity images A and B could be represented as follows

$$S_A(i,j) = [A(i,j) \quad A(i,j+1) \quad A(i+1,j+1)]$$
$$S_B(i,j) = [B(i,j) \quad B(i,j+1) \quad B(i+1,j+1)]$$

(6)

Figure 8 shows the return maps for the same row of two turbulent frames. Applying the DTW algorithm to the phase spaces of the signals, we are able to match each pixel in row i of frame A to the correct pixel in row i of frame B. In order to calculate the distance between the points of the phase spaces we use the 1-norm distance. We also define the new co-ordinates of the phase space as the 8-neighbours of the pixel (i,j). By utilizing more information via the phase spaces, we are able to obtain a more accurate mapping of the columns, even if the rows of the images are not perfectly aligned. We still need to obtain a row mapping of the images in order to have a full shift map between the two images. This can be done by taking the shift maps of the columns of the images and warping Image A to Image B. We can then calculate the row shift map between Image B and the warped Image. This would require us to apply the DTW-Phase Space algorithm twice. Alternatively we could utilize the same method as described in Sect. 4.2. This would increase the computational complexity significantly.

The approach we take is to take each $S_B(i,j)$ window and determine the distance between this window and $S_A(i \pm \delta, j)$, where $\delta = (-N,..,N)$, represents the level of turbulent motion present in the sequence. We then take the minimum of these distances to be used in the distance matrix T. We also create an additional matrix T_v that is used to keep track of the δ which corresponds to the minimum distances selected for each $T(i,j)$. Therefore the minimum distance path through T is matched with T_v which is used to determine the row shifts of each pixel (i,j).

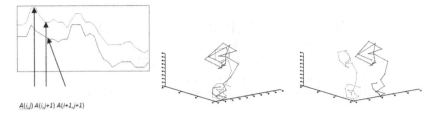

$A(i,j)$ $A(i,j+1)$ $A(i+1,j+1)$

Fig. 8. (Left) Co-ordinates, $S_A(i,j)$, of frame A in a turbulent sequence, (Centre) return maps for row i of image A and B and (Right) return maps shifted along one axis to view the signals more clearly. (Color figure online)

$$T(i,j) = \min\{\ dist(S_A(i \pm \delta), S_B(i,j))\ \}$$
$$Tv(i,j) = \delta_{\min}$$
(7)

This allows us to obtain both the horizontal and vertical shift maps simultaneously. Figure 9 shows an example of the shift maps between two warped Lena images.

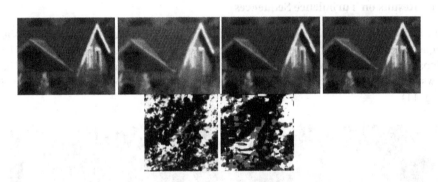

Fig. 9. (Top Left) Frame 1 and (Top Centre Left) frame 7 of real sequence, (Top Centre Right) frame 7 warped to frame 1 using elastic image registration, (Top Right) frame 7 warped to frame 1 using DTW-Phase space (Bottom Left). (Bottom Left) Shift map using elastic image registration and (Bottom Right) shift map using DTW-Phase space. (Images courtesy of the CSIR, Image distance 5 km)

5   Datasets and Results

The 2D-DTW averaged algorithm was applied to a simulated turbulence sequences as well as real turbulence-degraded sequences. Section 5.2 discusses the results of the 2D-DTW averaged images compared to the temporally averaged images based on the sharpness as well as the geometric correctness of the images compared to the original (Fig. 10).

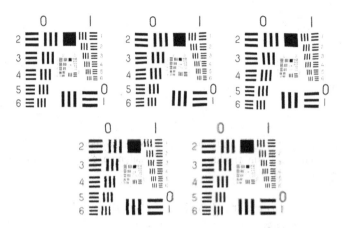

Fig. 10. (Tope Left) Original image, (Top Centre) frame 1 of warped testbar sequence, (Top Right) frame 2 of warped sequence, (Bottom Left) DTW-Phase space average of sequence and (Bottom Right) temporal average of sequence.

5.1 Results on Turbulence Sequences

The first sequence was generated by taking the real-turbulence field from a building site sequence and applying it to the testbar image using the method described in Sect. 2. The global constraint range was set to $\delta = 5$ for both the row search and pixel search. The rows were segmented to sub-rows of length equal to 30 pixels. 16 frames were averaged (Fig. 11).

Fig. 11. (Left) Real turbulence degraded frame 1, (Centre Left) real turbulence degraded frame 2, (Centre Right) DTW-Phase space average of sequence and (Right) temporal average of sequence. (Images courtesy of the CSIR, image distance 5 km)

The Building Site and Armscor sequences are real-turbulence degraded sequences. The global constraint range was set to $\delta = 5$ for both the row search and pixel search. The rows were segmented to sub-rows of length equal to 30 pixels. 8 frames were averaged (Fig. 12 and Table 2).

Table 2. MSE of the algorithms

Algorithms	Temporal average	DTW-phase space average
Testbar	5.0772	4.6869
Girl	3.5465	3.4267

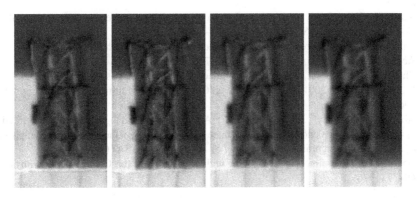

Fig. 12. (Left) Real turbulence degraded frame 1, (Centre Left) real turbulence degraded frame 2, (Centre Right) DTW-Phase space average of sequence and (Right) temporal average of sequence. (Images courtesy of the CSIR, image distance 7 km)

6   Conclusions and Future Work

A 2D-DTW averaging algorithm was presented to generate a geometrically improved and sharper frame from a sequence degraded by atmospheric turbulence. While it has shown the potential to correct and enhance turbulent sequences, a number of challenges still remain particularly in the adaptation from 1D-DTW to 2D-DTW.

References

1. Li, D., Mersereau, R.M., Frakes, D.H., Smith, M.J.T.: A new method for suppressing optical turbulence in video. In: Proceedings of European Signal Processing Conference (EUSIPCO 2005) (2005)
2. Lucas, B.D., Kanade, T.: An iterative image registration technique with an application to stereo vision (darpa). In: Proceedings of the 1981 DARPA Image Understanding Workshop, pp. 121–130, April 1981
3. Fraser, D., Thorpe, G., Lambert, A.: Atmospheric turbulence visualization with wide-area motion blur restoration. In: Optical Society of America, pp. 1751–1758 (1999)
4. Kopriva, I., Du, Q., Szu, H., Wasylkiwskyj, W.: Independent component analysis approach to image sharpening in the presence of atmospheric turbulence. Opt. Commun. **233**, 7–14 (2004). Elsevier
5. Frakes, D.H., Monaco, J.W., Smith, M.J.T.: Suppression of atmospheric turbulence in video using an adaptive control grid interpolation. In: Proceedings of the IEEE International Conference on Acoustics, Speech, and Signal Processing, pp. 1881–1884 (2001)
6. Li, D.: Restoration of atmospheric turbulence degraded video using kurtosis minimization and motion compensation. Ph.D. thesis, School of Electrical and Computer Engineering, Georgia Institute of Technology, May 2007
7. Tahtali, M., Fraser, D., Lambert, A.J.: Restoration of non-uniformly warped images using a typical frame as prototype. In: TENCON 2005-2005 IEEE Region 10, pp. 1382–1387 (2005)
8. Gupta, L., Molfese, D.L., Tammana, R., Simos, P.G.: Nonlinear alignment and averaging for estimating the evoked potential. IEEE Trans. Biomed. Eng. **43**(4), 348–356 (1996)

9. Sakoe, H., Chiba, S.: Dynamic programming optimization for spoken word recognition. IEEE Trans. Acoust. Speech Sig. Process. **26**, 623–625 (1980)
10. Itakura, F.: Minimum prediction residual principle applied to speech recognition. IEEE Trans. Acoust. Speech Sig. Process. **ASSP-23**, 52–72 (1975)
11. Zhao, W., Bogoni, L., Hansen, M.: Video enhancement by scintillation removal. In: Proceedings of the 2001 IEEE International Conference on Multimedia and Expo, pp. 393–396 (2001)
12. Abdoola, R., van Wyk, B.J., Monacelli, E.: A simple statistical algorithm for the correction of atmospheric turbulence degraded sequences. In: Proceeding of the 21st Annual Symposium of the Pattern Recognition Association of South Africa (PRASA) (2010)
13. Henon, M.: A two-dimensional mapping with a strange attractor. Commun. Math. Phys. **50**, 69–77 (1976)

Denoising Multi-view Images Using Non-local Means with Different Similarity Measures

Monagi H. Alkinani and Mahmoud R. El-Sakka$^{(\boxtimes)}$

Computer Science Department, University of Western Ontario,
London, ON N6A 5B7, Canada
{malkinan,melsakka}@uwo.ca

Abstract. We present a stereo image denoising algorithm. Our algorithm takes as an input a pair of noisy images of an object captured from two different directions (stereo images). We use either Maximum Difference or Singular Value Decomposition similarity metrics for identifying locations of similar searching windows in the input images. We adapt the Non-local Means algorithm for denoising collected patches from the searching windows. Experimental results show that our algorithm outperforms the original Non-local Means and our previous method Stereo images denoising using Non-local Means with Structural SIMilarity (S-SSIM), and it helps to estimate more accurate disparity maps at various noise levels.

Keywords: Non-local means · Patch-based image filtering · Stereo imaging · Structural similarity index · SVD · Additive noise reduction · Disparity map

1 Introduction

Digital images are often contaminated with undesired random additive noise during data acquisition, transmission or compression phases. Additive noise is generally modelled as:

$$v(x) = u(x) + n(x), x \in \Omega \tag{1}$$

where $v(x)$ is the noisy image, $u(x)$ is the noise-free image, $n(x)$ is the additive noise, and Ω denotes the set of all pixels in the image. If $n(x)$ is a Gaussian random process, then the noise is recognized as an additive Gaussian noise. This noise varies from being almost imperceptible to being very noticeable. Image denoising schemes attempt to estimate a new image that is closer to the noise-free image.

Patch-based image filtering is mainly a proximity operation dividing the noisy image into patches, or blocks, which are then manipulated separately in order to provide an estimate of the true pixel values based on similar patches located within a searching window. Such patch-based methods include Non-local Means

© Springer International Publishing Switzerland 2016
A. Campilho and F. Karray (Eds.): ICIAR 2016, LNCS 9730, pp. 101–109, 2016.
DOI: 10.1007/978-3-319-41501-7_12

(NL-Means) [1], K-means and Singular Value Decomposition (K-SVD) [2], and Block Matching 3D (BM3D) [3].

The NL-Means filter is a modified version of the pixel-based bilateral filter [4]. It preserves edges and blurs homogeneous areas by exploiting similarities among the various parts of the input image. Adapting the NL-Means filter for denoising stereo images would improve the extracted depth information from noisy stereo images.

A stereo imaging system uses two cameras located within the optical axes parallel and separated by distance. This system produces two or more images called multi-view images. The depth information can be extracted from these images by analyzing the differences between the images. Utilizing multi-view images is also widespread in video denoising [5,6]. Noisy stereo images often give disappointing depth information [7–9].

In this work, NL-Means is utilized for denoising stereo images. Our proposed method extends the NL-Means searching window to search the two images when seeking similar patches. In addition, we utilize the Maximum Difference (MD) and Singular Value Decomposition (SVD) similarity metrics. To improve the speed performance of our scheme, we bounded the utilized search windows to a fixed maximum size.

2   Previous Work

Zhang *et al.* showed that using multi-view images for image denoising has an outstanding benefit over using only one-view image [10], where a noisy pixel in multi-view images is estimated based on the corresponding pixels from all other images. In addition, they extended the idea of using patch-based PCA denoising from a single image to multi-view images denoising, where similar patches are collected locally and globally from the multiple images before applying the PCA algorithm. Maximum A Posteriori-Markov Random Field (MAP-MRF) is utilized by Heo *et al.* as a model for energy minimization in order to compute the disparity maps from multi-view image [11]. They proposed an algorithm that initially restores intensity difference by adapting NL-Means algorithm. Then, the dissimilarity of support pixel distributions are calculated, where mean square error (MSE) is utilized to group similar patches. In our previous work (S-SSIM) [12], we have adapted the NL-Means method for filtering stereo images in order to improve extracting the depth information disparity maps. Yet, our previous algorithm failed to achieve encouraging results when denoising stereo images with high noise level ($\sigma > 20$), because the structural similarity index is utilized. This is due to the fact that when the noise level increases, the structural similarity index would favor those patches with a similar noise pattern not the structure of the patches.

The rest of the paper is organized as follows. Section 3 describes the utilized methodology and the proposed method. In Sect. 4, we compare the performance of our proposed method with other denoising filters. Section 5 offers concluding comments, and future work.

3   Methodology

3.1   Patch Similarity Metric

Patch similarity measures assist similarity between patches within a searching window, based on the apparent differences. Patch-based denoising methods rely on accurate patch similarity measures. We proposed using two different similarity metrics: Maximum Difference or SVD-based similarity metrics. The maximum difference intends to find similarity between patches by computing the absolute maximum difference between reference patch and other patches. Meanwhile, SVD-based measure utilizes Singular Value Decomposition (SVD) to assist the similarity between patches [13]. SVD-based similarity metric consists of two stages: in the first stage, visual quality features are extracted from patches and their singular values are calculated, whereas in the second stage a machine learning scheme is utilized to identify the most discriminant features.

3.2   Non-local Means

The original NL-Means filter divides the input images into patches before filtering each patch separately. The similarity between patches in NL-Means is assessed based on the Euclidean and the luminance distances between patches. Patches with similar grey levels are assigned larger weights when averaging. Equation 2 is used to estimate a pixel i using NL-Means filter,

$$NLMeans\,[v]_i = \sum_{j \in I} \omega(i,j)\,[v]_j \tag{2}$$

where $[v]_i$ and $[v]_j$ are pixels intensities at location i and j, respectively, and $\omega(i,j)$ is a similarity measure between pixels i and j. The similarity weight, $\omega(i,j)$, satisfies the condition $0 \le \omega(i,j) \le 1$ and $\sum_j \omega(i,j) = 1$. It depends on the grey level similarity and the Euclidean distance between vectors $N\,[v]_i$ and $N\,[v]_j$, where $N\,[v]_k$ denotes a square neighbourhood of fixed size and centred at a pixel k. The weights are described as,

$$\omega(i,j) = \frac{1}{Z(i)} e^{-\frac{\|\left(N[v]_i\right) - \left(N[v]_j\right)\|^2}{h^2}} \tag{3}$$

where $Z(i)$ is a normalization factor and h is a filtering parameter set depending on the noise level. NL-Means filter preserves edges, regardless of their directions. The searching windows and patches size are determined based on the noise level. The size of the patches increases when the noise level is high.

3.3   The Proposed Method

We describe a new method for improving the process of denoising stereo images. The novelty of this method is the use of the NL-Means algorithm to denoise multi-view images by using either the maximum difference or SVD similarity measurements. Similar patches from left and right stereo images are used in order to increase the number of similar patches. In order to find similar patches, the reference patch is compared with other patches by using either MD or SVD-based similarity metrics. When there are similarities between the reference patch and the other patches, patches are grouped for weighted averaging process. Figure 1 shows an example of a collection of similar patches in a stereo image pair using our proposed method.

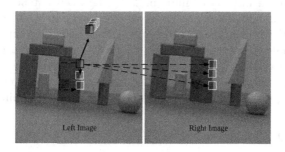

Fig. 1. Collecting similar patches from a stereo image: the patch with a black border is the reference patch, and the patches with white borders are similar patches

3.4 Algorithm Outline

Our algorithm is illustrated in Fig. 2. At each pixel k, the following procedure is performed:

1. Choose a fixed-size square patch "reference patch" $N\,[vl]_k$ centered at location k from the left image.
2. Use either MD or SVD-based similarity metrics to find the best match $N\,[vr]_q$ centered at location q for the reference patch within a bounded searching area in the right image and identify its window location.
3. Collect patches from the two windows and assign weights ω to each patch. Similar patches to the reference patch are assigned high weights. The weights are assigned as described in Eq. 3.
4. Calculate the weighted average of patches, in order to estimate the true pixel of the left image. The estimated value $NLMeans\,[vl]_i$, for a pixel i located in the left image is computed as described in Eq. 2.

4   Results

This section provides an experimental study for the performance of the proposed methods. We use a fixed 5×5 patch size and a fixed 9×9 searching window size. The fixed bounded searching area is used with the size $(-20, +20)$. Four stereo images are used in this experiment. The four images are grey-scale images, and they are shown in Fig. 3. MatLab is used for this experiment. The

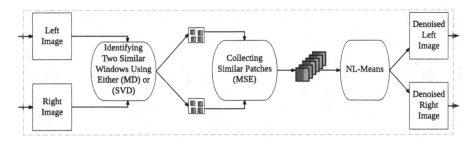

Fig. 2. A block diagram of the proposed denoising method for stereo image denoising

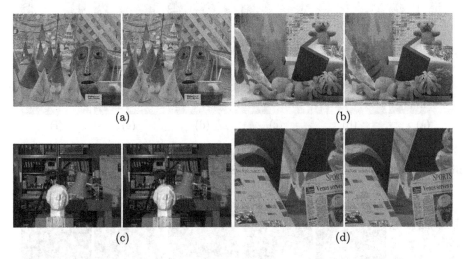

Fig. 3. The four used stereo images in the experiment: (a) *cones* images 450×375, (b) *teddy* images 450×375, (c) *tsukuba* images 384×288, and (d) *venus* images 434×383.

computers processor is Intel Core i7 (2.5 GHz). The methods are evaluated both qualitatively and quantitatively, respectively.

4.1 Qualitative Evaluation

The methods are perceptively evaluated in this section. Additive White Gaussian Noisy (AWGN) stereo images with ($\sigma = 40$) are chosen to perform this evaluation. Fragments of the four noisy grayscale stereo images and the corresponding estimates are shown in Fig. 4. Each column shows the results of the same denoising method when applied to different images. Figure 5 shows the disparity maps of these denoised images.

The fragments images in Fig. 4 show that our methods outperform other methods. Our methods preserve sharp edges; e.g., the newspaper edges in venus image. Homogeneous regions are smoothed properly by our methods; e.g., head

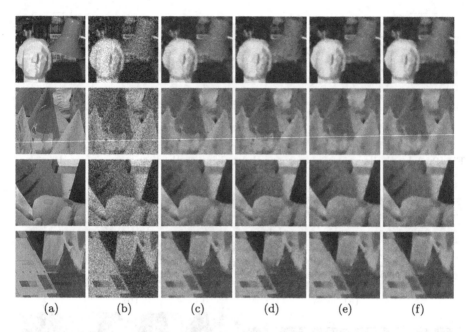

Fig. 4. Fragments of the noisy grayscale stereo images: (a) Original images, (b) AWGN images ($\sigma= 40$), (c) NLM, (d) S-SSIM, (e) S-MD* and (f) S-SVD*

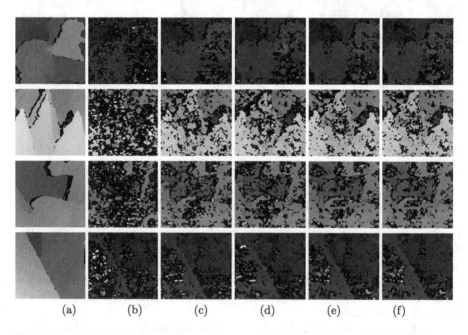

Fig. 5. Fragments of the disparity map images: (a) Original images, (b) AWGN images ($\sigma= 40$), (c) NLM, (d) S-SSIM, (e) S-MD* and (f) S-SVD*

and lamp in `tsukuba` image. The fragments of the disparity maps in Fig. 5 show that our methods outperform other methods. Our methods produce disparity maps with less errors; e.g., head and lamp in the disparity map of `tsukuba` image.

4.2   Quantitative Evaluation

Two image similarity metrics are used for the objective comparison between the results: (1) Mean SSIM (MSSIM) [14], and (2) peak signal-to-noise ratio (PSNR). The best result for SSIM is 1, while the PSNR has good results when its value is high. The experimental results of our proposed method are shown in Table 1, which compares the performance of our proposed methods (S-MD* and S-SVD*) with the original NL-Means and our previous method (S-SSIM). A bold font with a wavy under-bar highlights the highest values of SSIM, while the highest values of PSNR are highlighted with a bold font.

Figure 6 shows the performance of the methods on `tsukuba` image at various noise levels. The chart depicts that our methods are the preferable ones (from SSIM point of view). Our methods are preferable when they are used for denoising any of the four stereo images at any noise levels.

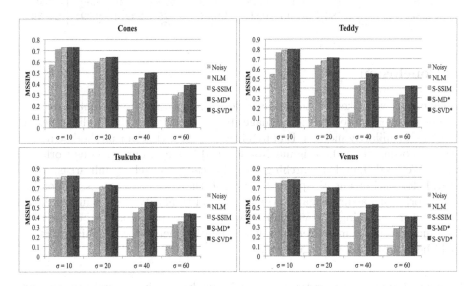

Fig. 6. The MSSIM performance of the denoising methods: NLM, S-SSIM, S-MD*, and S-SVD*, for the four stereo images at varies noise levels (σ).

Table 1. The performance of the denoising algorithms at various noise levels (σ).

	σ	$\sigma = 10$		$\sigma = 20$		$\sigma = 40$		$\sigma = 60$	
	Method	SSIM	PSNR	SSIM	PSNR	SSIM	PSNR	SSIM	PSNR
Cones	Noisy	0.572	25.06	0.353	21.13	0.165	15.91	0.097	12.91
	NLM	0.714	26.58	0.593	25.05	0.409	22.59	0.292	20.63
	S-SSIM	0.727	26.76	0.630	25.47	0.450	23.12	0.316	21.1
	S-MD*	0.728	26.79	0.639	25.57	0.491	23.67	0.382	22.24
	S-SVD*	0.729	**26.83**	0.640	**25.59**	0.496	**23.73**	0.387	**22.31**
Teddy	Noisy	0.543	25.68	0.317	21.42	0.147	16.16	0.087	13.19
	NLM	0.767	27.83	0.636	26.22	0.429	23.4	0.298	21.18
	S-SSIM	0.788	28.06	0.679	26.69	0.473	24.07	0.326	21.82
	S-MD*	0.796	**28.12**	0.710	**26.92**	0.547	**24.78**	0.417	23.1
	S-SVD*	0.795	28.11	0.709	26.89	0.546	**24.78**	0.419	**23.14**
Tsukuba	Noisy	0.588	25.63	0.367	21.67	0.183	16.79	0.106	13.82
	NLM	0.787	27.51	0.659	25.83	0.449	23.07	0.327	21.06
	S-SSIM	0.817	27.99	0.708	26.47	0.492	23.69	0.349	21.54
	S-MD*	0.821	28.02	0.727	**26.58**	0.551	**24.26**	0.431	22.65
	S-SVD*	0.821	**28.04**	0.724	26.53	0.552	24.25	0.431	**22.68**
Venus	Noisy	0.494	24.90	0.285	21.13	0.140	16.23	0.084	13.27
	NLM	0.748	26.74	0.614	25.44	0.399	22.88	0.280	20.94
	S-SSIM	0.767	26.93	0.650	25.81	0.436	23.56	0.300	21.54
	S-MD*	0.780	26.98	0.694	25.99	0.519	24.09	0.394	22.58
	S-SVD*	0.780	**26.99**	0.695	**26.00**	0.525	**24.14**	0.394	**22.59**

5   Conclusions

In this paper, we looked at stereo image denoising as a multi-view image denoising process. We restored the noisy images by using either maximum difference or SVD-based similarity metrics. Empirical results show that our method achieved better denoising than the original Non-local Means and our previous work (S-SSIM). We used bounded searching areas instead of searching full areas, as in S-SSIM, for optimizing its speed. We believe that our work opens a door for future work, such as investigating the traditional similarity metrics in Non-local Means when assigning the weights between similar patches. We believe that using more accurate measurements as a similarity metric for assigning weights would help improving our algorithm.

Acknowledgment. This research is partially funded by the Natural Sciences and Engineering Research Council of Canada (NSERC). This support is greatly appreciated. This research is also partially funded by the Cultural Bureau of Saudi Arabia in Canada. This support is greatly appreciated.

References

1. Buades, A., Coll, B., Morel, J.: A non-local algorithm for image denoising. In: IEEE Conference Computer Vision and Pattern Recognition, CVPR 2005, vol. 2, pp. 60–65 (2005)
2. Aharon, M., Elad, M., Bruckstein, A.: K-SVD: an algorithm for designing over-complete dictionaries for sparse representation. IEEE Trans. Sig. Process. **54**(11), 4311–4322 (2006)
3. Dabov, K., Foi, A., Katkovnik, V., Egiazarian, K.: Image denoising by sparse 3-D transform-domain collaborative filtering. IEEE Trans. Image Process. **16**(8), 2080–2095 (2007)
4. Tomasi, C., Manduchi, R.: Bilateral filtering for gray and color images. In: 1998 IEEE International Conference on Computer Vision, Bombay, India, pp. 839–846 (1998)
5. Bennett, E.P., McMillan, L.: Video enhancement using per-pixel virtual exposures. In: ACM SIGGRAPH 2005 Papers, New York, NY, USA, pp. 845–852 (2005)
6. Danielyan, A., Foi, A., Katkovnik, V., Egiazarian, K.: Image and video super-resolution via spatially adaptive block matching filtering. In: Proceedings of International Workshop on Local and Non-Local Approximation in Image Processing (LNLA) (2008)
7. Leclercq, P., Morris, J.: Robustness to noise of stereo matching. In: Proceedings 12th International Conference on Image Analysis and Processing, pp. 606–611 (2003)
8. Malik, A.S., Choi, T.S., Nisar, H.: Depth Map and 3D Imaging Applications: Algorithms and Technologies, 1st edn. IGI Global, Hershey (2011)
9. Samani, A., Winkler, J., Niranjan, M.: Automatic face recognition using stereo images. In: 2006 IEEE International Conference on Speech and Signal Processing, vol. 5, p. V (2006)
10. Zhang, L., Vaddadi, S., Jin, H., Nayar, S.K.: Multiple view image denoising. In: IEEE Conference on Computer Vision and Pattern Recognition, pp. 1542–1549 (2009)
11. Heo, Y.S., Lee, K.M., Lee, S.U.: Simultaneous depth reconstruction and restoration of noisy stereo images using non-local pixel distribution. In: IEEE Conference on Computer Vision and Pattern Recognition, pp. 1–8 (2007)
12. Alkinani, M.H., El-Sakka, M.R.: Non-local means for stereo image denoising using structural similarity. In: Kamel, M., Campilho, A. (eds.) Image Analysis and Recognition. LNCS, vol. 9164, pp. 51–59. Springer, Switzerland (2015)
13. Narwaria, M., Lin, W.: SVD-based quality metric for image and video using machine learning. IEEE Trans. Syst. Man Cybern. Part B Cybern. **42**(2), 347–364 (2012)
14. Wang, Z., Bovik, A., Sheikh, H., Simoncelli, E.: Image quality assessment: from error visibility to structural similarity. IEEE Trans. Image Process. **13**(4), 600–612 (2004)

Image Denoising Using Euler-Lagrange Equations for Function-Valued Mappings

Daniel Otero[1], Davide La Torre[1,2,3], and Edward R. Vrscay[1(✉)]

[1] Department of Applied Mathematics, Faculty of Mathematics,
University of Waterloo, Waterloo, ON N2L 3G1, Canada
{dotero,ervrscay}@uwaterloo.ca
[2] Department of Economics, Management,
and Quantitative Methods, University of Milan, Milan, Italy
davide.latorre@unimi.it
[3] Department of Applied Mathematics and Sciences,
Khalifa University, Abu Dhabi, UAE
davide.latorre@kustar.ac.ae

Abstract. In this paper, we consider a new method for representing complex images, e.g., hyperspectral images and video sequences, in terms of function-valued mappings (FVMs), also known as Banach-valued functions. At each (pixel) location x, the FVM image $u(x)$ is a *function*, as opposed to the traditional vector approach. We define the Fourier transform of an FVM as well as Euler-Lagrange conditions for functionals involving FVMs and then show how these results can be used to devise some FVM-based methods of denoising. We consider a very simple functional and present some numerical results.

1 Introduction

Vector-valued functions provide a quite natural representation for some types of images, for example, colour and hyperspectral (HS) images [4,11]. Furthermore, many efficient vector-based imaging tools have been introduced [2–4,7]. That being said, the vector-valued approach has some limitations when it comes to model the internal structure of certain complex data sets. For instance, let us consider a video sequence, which can be represented as a vector-valued function

$$u : \Omega \to \mathbb{R}^N. \tag{1}$$

Here, $\Omega \subset \mathbb{R}^2$ or $\mathbb{R}^3$ is the spatial domain, and each component u_i of the range of u, $1 \le i \le N$, is a time frame. Proposing a suitable space of functions as a suitable model for the temporal functions defined at each pixel of the video is not possible due to the finite dimensionality of the range of u. A similar situation exists in the case of HS images—here it is important to recall that the entries $u_i(x)$ comprising an HS image represent a discretization or sampling of the continuously-defined spectral function at x.

In this paper, to overcome the difficulty of modelling the internal structure of complex data sets using vector-valued functions, we propose to "unvectorize"

© Springer International Publishing Switzerland 2016
A. Campilho and F. Karray (Eds.): ICIAR 2016, LNCS 9730, pp. 110–119, 2016.
DOI: 10.1007/978-3-319-41501-7_13

them, i.e., consider the variable y in temporal or spectral space to be continuous as opposed to discrete. As a result, an image u is represented by a function-valued mapping (FVM). Briefly, an FVM is a mapping of the form:

$$u : X \to \mathcal{F}(Y), \tag{2}$$

where X is the support of the FVM (for digital images, the "pixel space") and $\mathcal{F}(Y)$ is a Banach space of either real- or complex-valued images supported on the set Y. In other words, at each $x \in X$, the "value" of the image function $u(x)$ is a *function* which belongs to a space $\mathcal{F}(Y)$ that is appropriate to the application. For example, an HS image could be represented as a FVM of the form,

$$u : X \subset \mathbb{R}^2 \to L^2(\mathbb{R}), \tag{3}$$

where $L^2(\mathbb{R})$ is the space of square-integrable functions supported on the real line, i.e., spectral functions with finite energy.

Of course, it remains to develop appropriate methods and tools which can operate on FVMs. In this paper, we define Fourier transforms and an Euler-Lagrange equation for FVMs which are then employed to denoise HS images.

It is important to mention that the FVM approach is not a novelty in other fields such as partial differential equations [20], harmonic analysis [15,17], statistics [1], and others [8]. Indeed, FVMs are known in the mathematical community as *Banach-valued functions*, the latter being studied mainly by analysts who have been interested in seeing if the classical results of real-valued functions still hold in the Banach-valued setting [6,8].

In imaging science, however, this methodology has been barely explored. Nevertheless, some contributions can be found which employ the concept of a function which assumes values in an infinite-dimensional Banach space. For example, in an effort to close the gap between the mathematical formalism of Banach-valued functions and practical applications in imaging, the authors in [14] use the FVM approach to provide a solid mathematical platform to describe and treat diffusion magnetic resonance images. Also, in [13], an analogue of FVMs is introduced, namely, measure-valued images, which are well suited for non-local image processing. As a matter of fact, non-local means denoising [5] and fractal image coding [12] are the two applications that are addressed in [13] using this measure-valued methodology.

Rather than introducing state-of-the-art algorithms for image denoising, the main purpose of this paper is to present the FVM approach as a mathematical framework that may offer interesting possibilities for the image processing community. That being said, we do present a couple of computational examples that illustrate both the novelty and the potential of FVMs.

2   Function-Valued Mappings

An FVM is a particular case of a mapping defined between two Banach spaces. Many definitions and properties that are valid in the real case can be extended without difficulties to this setting (see [1,6,8,16,20] for more details). In this section, we present a definition of the Fourier transform for FVMs, as well as an Euler-Lagrange equation for a certain type of functionals whose argument involve these kind of mappings.

2.1 Fourier Transform

In [17], Peetre provides perhaps one of the first generalizations of the Fourier transform for Banach-valued functions. In fact, for $p \in (1,2]$, Peetre proves that the Fourier transform is a bounded operator from $L^p(\mathbb{R}; Z)$ to $L^q(\mathbb{R}; Z)$, where q is the Hölder conjugate of p and Z is a Banach space. This result was extended further by Milman in [15]. Along these lines, in [18], as an application of the Bochner integral [1], the following definition of the Fourier transform is provided for Banach-valued functions that belong to $L^1(\mathbb{R}^n; H)$, where H is a separable Hilbert space:

$$U(\omega) := \int_{\mathbb{R}^n} e^{i\omega \cdot x} u(x)dx, \tag{4}$$

Note that in [18], the exponent of the complex exponential has a positive sign. Moreover, it is shown that $U(\omega)$ is well defined and that it is a bounded operator from $L^1(\mathbb{R}^n; H)$ to $L^\infty(\mathbb{R}^n; H)$. However, no definition of the inverse Fourier transform is presented.

The existing definitions of the Fourier transforms for Banach-valued functions provide the foundation for defining the Fourier transform of FVMs. In particular, we focus our attention on the elements of the space $L^1(\mathbb{R}^n; \mathcal{F}(Y))$; that is, the space of integrable FVMs.

Definition 1. *Let* $u \in L^1(\mathbb{R}^n; \mathcal{F}(Y))$, *where* $\mathcal{F}(Y)$ *is a complex-valued space. We define the Fourier transform of* u *as the integral*

$$\mathbf{F}(u)(\omega) := \int_{\mathbb{R}^n} e^{-i\omega \cdot x} u(x)dx, \tag{5}$$

where $\omega \in \mathbb{R}^n$. *In some cases, we will denote* $\mathbf{F}(u)(\omega)$ *as* $U(\omega)$ *as well.*

Theorem 1 [18]. $\mathbf{F}$ *is a bounded operator of the form*

$$\mathbf{F} : L^1(\mathbb{R}^n; \mathcal{F}(Y)) \to L^\infty(\mathbb{R}^n; \mathcal{F}(Y)). \tag{6}$$

Regarding the inverse transform, this operator is not well defined for all the elements that belong to $L^\infty(\mathbb{R}^n; \mathcal{F}(Y))$ since not all the FVMs of this space are in $L^1(\mathbb{R}^n; \mathcal{F}(Y))$. Given this, as is customary in harmonic analysis [9], we define this transform under the assumption that both u and U belong to $L^1(\mathbb{R}^n; \mathcal{F}(Y))$.

Definition 2. *If both* u *and* U *are elements of* $L^1(\mathbb{R}^n; \mathcal{F}(Y))$, *we define the inverse Fourier transform of* U *as*

$$\mathbf{F}^{-1}(U)(x) := \frac{1}{(2\pi)^n} \int_{\mathbb{R}^n} e^{i\omega \cdot x} U(\omega)d\omega. \tag{7}$$

Theorem 2 [16]. *If both u and U belong to $L^1(\mathbb{R}^n; \mathcal{F}(Y))$, then*

$$u(x) = \frac{1}{(2\pi)^n} \int_{\mathbb{R}^n} e^{i\omega \cdot x} U(\omega) d\omega. \tag{8}$$

It is clear that the operator $\mathbf{F}$ is linear, which is, of course, a consequence of the linearity of the integral of the Fourier transform. Let $\alpha, \beta \in \mathbb{C}$ and $u, v \in L^1(\mathbb{R}^n; \mathcal{F}(Y))$. We claim, without proof, that the following equality holds:

$$\mathbf{F}(\alpha u + \beta v) = \alpha \mathbf{F}(u) + \beta \mathbf{F}(v). \tag{9}$$

As expected, linearity also holds for the inverse operator $\mathbf{F}^{-1}$. Let $\alpha, \beta \in \mathbb{C}$ and $U, V \in L^1(\mathbb{R}^n; \mathcal{F}(Y))$. Then,

$$\mathbf{F}^{-1}(\alpha U + \beta V) = \alpha \mathbf{F}^{-1}(U) + \beta \mathbf{F}^{-1}(V). \tag{10}$$

As with the classical Fourier transform, in the FVM setting, we also have properties such as translation, scaling, modulation, differentiation with respect to x and integration. These are presented in the following theorems.

Theorem 3 [16]. *Let both $u \in L^1(\mathbb{R}^n; \mathcal{F}(Y))$. Also, let $\omega_0, x_0 \in \mathbb{R}^n$ and $a \in \mathbb{R}$, $a \neq 0$. Then, the following assertions hold:*

1. *Translation:* $\mathbf{F}(u(x - x_0))(\omega) = e^{-i\omega \cdot x_0} U(\omega)$.
2. *Modulation:* $\mathbf{F}(e^{-i\omega_0 \cdot x} u(x))(\omega) = U(\omega - \omega_0)$.
3. *Scaling:* $\mathbf{F}(u(ax))(\omega) = \frac{1}{|a|^n} U(\frac{\omega}{a})$.
4. *Integration:* $\int_{\mathbb{R}^n} u(x)\, dx = U(0)$.

Theorem 4 [16]. *Assume all $\frac{\partial^l u}{\partial x_j^l}$ and $(i\omega_j)^l U$ are elements of $L^1(\mathbb{R}^n; \mathcal{F}(Y))$ whenever $0 \le l \le k$. Then,*

$$\mathbf{F}\left(\frac{\partial^k u}{\partial x_j^k}\right)(\omega) = (i\omega_j)^k \mathbf{F}(u)(\omega). \tag{11}$$

2.2 The Euler-Lagrange Equation

We simply present the *Euler-Lagrange equation* of a given functional whose argument is a FVM of the form $u : X \subset \mathbb{R}^n \to \mathcal{F}(Y)$. In particular, we focus our attention on the following type of functionals:

$$I(u) = \int_X f(x, u(x), \nabla_x u(x)) dx, \tag{12}$$

where $f : X \times \mathcal{F}(Y) \times \mathcal{G}^n(Y) \to \mathbb{R}$ is a mapping that is Fréchet differentiable with respect to all of its arguments, and $\mathcal{G}^n(Y)$ is the Cartesian product of the range of $\nabla_x u$; that is, $\mathcal{G}^n(Y) = \mathcal{G}(Y) \times \cdots \times \mathcal{G}(Y)$, where $\frac{\partial u}{\partial x_i} : X \subset \mathbb{R}^n \to \mathcal{G}(Y)$. As expected, the solution of the Euler-Lagrange equation is a FVM that belongs to the set of stationary points of $I(u)$.

Theorem 5 [16]. *Let* (X, Σ, μ) *and* (Y, T, ν) *be finite measure spaces. Also, let* $u : X \subseteq \mathbb{R}^n \to \mathcal{F}(Y)$, $\frac{\partial u}{\partial x_i} : X \subset \mathbb{R}^n \to \mathcal{G}(Y)$, *and assume that the function*

$$\Phi(x) := f(x, u(x), \nabla_x u(x)) \tag{13}$$

is integrable over X. *In addition, suppose that the Fréchet derivatives of* $f :$ $X \times \mathcal{F}(Y) \times \mathcal{G}^n(Y) \to \mathbb{R}$ *with respect to all of its arguments are continuous. Define the functional* $I(u) : Z(\mathcal{F}(Y), \mathcal{G}(Y)) \to \mathbb{R}$ *as follows:*

$$I(u) := \int_X f(x, u(x), \nabla_x u(x)) dx, \tag{14}$$

where $Z(\mathcal{F}(Y), \mathcal{G}(Y))$ *is a Banach space of FVMs that depends on the function spaces* $\mathcal{F}(Y)$ *and* $\mathcal{G}(Y)$. *If* $u_0 : X \subset \mathbb{R}^n \to \mathcal{F}(Y)$ *is a stationary point of* $I(u)$, u_0 *is the solution of the equation*

$$\frac{\partial f}{\partial u}(u_0) - \nabla \cdot \frac{\partial f}{\partial \nabla_x u}(\nabla_x u_0) = 0. \tag{15}$$

where $\frac{\partial f}{\partial u} \in \mathcal{F}(Y)^*$ *and* $\frac{\partial f}{\partial \nabla_x u} \in \mathcal{G}^n(Y)^*$ *are the Fréchet derivatives of* f *with respect to* u *and* $\nabla_x u$ *respectively,* $\nabla \cdot$ *is the classical divergence operator, and* $\mathcal{F}(Y)^*$ *and* $\mathcal{G}(Y)^*$ *are the dual spaces of* $\mathcal{F}(Y)$ *and* $\mathcal{G}(Y)$ *respectively.*

We consider Eq. (15) as the Euler-Lagrange equation of the functional $I(u)$ defined in (14). As its classical counterpart, it is also a necessary condition for the solutions of the variational problem stated in the previous theorem. However, it is not a sufficient condition for the existence of such solutions. To determine if such solutions exist, the standard *sufficient conditions* from calculus of variations can be employed to such an end [20].

3   A Simple FVM-Based Denoising Method

In this section we describe one possible denoising method which employs a very simple functional to be minimized. Our motivation was to be able to use both the Euler-Lagrange equations as well as Fourier transforms to solve the minimization problem. We begin with the assumption that the HS images belong to $C^2(X; L^2(Y))$, where $X \subset \mathbb{R}^2$ and $Y \subset \mathbb{R}$. Of course, this is a quite strong—and "unrealistic"—requirement on the HS image in the spatial direction: piecewise $C^2(X; L^2(Y))$ would be more "realistic." Our assumption allows us to employ the formulation of the Euler-Lagrange equation presented earlier, where all derivatives are understood to be defined in the classical sense. Our regularity assumption, however, can be weakened by using the weak formulation of the Euler-Lagrange equation, which is beyond the scope of this conference paper.

Under this regularity assumption, we propose to recover a denoised reconstruction $\bar{u}$ of an HS image from a noisy observation f by minimizing the following functional $I : C^2(X; L^2(Y)) \to \mathbb{R}$:

$$\min_u \left\{ \frac{1}{2} \int_X \|\rho(u(x) - f(x))\|_2^2 \, dx + \int_X \|\nabla_x u(x)\|_2^2 \, dx \right\}. \tag{16}$$

The squared L^2 norm of the gradient—a kind of "elastic bending" term—is not an optimal norm in terms of denoising ability: An L^1 norm of the gradient (total variation) would be more effective. The squared L^2 norm was chosen because it yields a closed-form solution in terms of Fourier transforms.

Also note that we allow the regularization parameter $\rho = \rho(y)$ to be a function of the spectral parameter $y \in Y$, allowing denoising to be performed with different intensities across the spectral domain.

From Sect. 2.2, the Euler-Lagrange equation which corresponds to the functional in Eq. (16) is given by

$$\int_Y \left(\rho(u(x) - f(x)) - \frac{\partial^2 u(x)}{\partial x_1^2} - \frac{\partial^2 u(x)}{\partial x_2^2} \right) (y)\, dy = 0, \qquad (17)$$

Let us recall that the Euler-Lagrange equation states a necessary optimality condition for optimality. Among all possible solutions to Eq. (16) we consider a particular solution $\bar{u}$ such that

$$\left[\frac{\partial^2 \bar{u}(x)}{\partial x_1^2} + \frac{\partial^2 \bar{u}(x)}{\partial x_2^2} \right] (y) - [\rho(\bar{u}(x) - f(x)](y) = 0 \qquad (18)$$

for a.e. $x \in X$ and $y \in Y$. Such a $\bar{u}$ may be found by means of the Fourier transform. If we let $F(\omega) = \mathbf{F}\{f\}(\omega)$ denote the Fourier transform of f, then

$$\bar{u}(y) = \mathbf{F}^{-1} \left\{ \left[\frac{\rho(y)}{\|\omega\|_2^2 + \rho(y)} \right] F(\omega) \right\}. \qquad (19)$$

In the special case that $\rho(y) = \rho_0$, a constant, Eq. (19) becomes

$$\bar{u}(y) = \mathbf{F}^{-1} \left\{ \left[\frac{\rho_0}{\|\omega\|_2^2 + \rho_0} \right] F(\omega) \right\}, \qquad (20)$$

which is the classical low-pass filter result. Because of the simplicity of the model in (16), i.e., no coupling between spectral components with different y-values, the filtering in both (19) and (20) may be performed on each y-value independently. **Reversing the roles of the domains X and Y:** We may also consider HS images as mappings from the spectral domain $X \subset \mathbb{R}$ to the space $L^2(Y)$, where $Y \subset \mathbb{R}^2$. That is, associated with each spectral value $x \in X$ there is a 2D spatial image function $u(x)$. In this case, the relevant denoising functional is

$$\min_u \left\{ \frac{1}{2} \int_X \|\rho(u(x) - f(x))\|_2^2\, dx + \int_X \|u'(x)\|_2^2\, dx \right\}, \qquad (21)$$

where u' is the (classical) derivative of the FVM u (see [16] for details). The procedure described earlier also holds for this representation. In particular, if $\rho : Y \subset \mathbb{R}^2 \to \mathbb{R}$, a solution for the corresponding Euler-Lagrange equation has the same form as in Eq. (19), namely,

$$\bar{u}(y) = \mathbf{F}^{-1} \left\{ \left[\frac{\rho(y)}{\omega^2 + \rho(y)} \right] F(\omega) \right\}. \qquad (22)$$

4   Numerical Examples

In our experiments, we assume, for the sake of simplicity, that the power of the noise is constant over the entire HS data set. Also, we assume that the noise is Additive White Gaussian Noise (AWGN). In the discrete context, we consider HS images as 3-D data sets of size $M \times N \times P$; that is, a HS image is a collection of P bands or channels each one of size $M \times N$. Here we have employed two HS images, namely, *Indian Pines* and *Salinas-A*, the latter being a subset of the *Salinas* HS image—both of them can be downloaded from [10]. The sizes of the 3-D *Indian Pines* and *Salinas-A* data sets are $145 \times 145 \times 220$ and $83 \times 86 \times 224$, respectively. AWGN was added to these HS data (assumed to be noiseless). In all experiments, the Peak Signal-to-Noise Ratio (PSNR) before denoising was 30.103 dB.

As expected, we denoise HS images by means of either Eq. (19) or Eq. (22). Clearly, these equations yield continuous FVMs u, nevertheless, discrete approximations of such u can be obtained by means of the *fast Fourier transform*. This can be done easily by noticing that, in a discrete setting, Eq. (19) is equivalent to filtering each band of a noisy HS image independently, whereas Eq. (20) is analogous to denoising each spectral function in an independent fashion. In what follows, we refer to the filterings yielded by both Eq. (19) and Eq. (20) as the "SPATIAL" and "SPECTRAL" methods respectively. As expected, the strength of the denoising process for either each band or spectrum is determined by the function $\rho(y)$, which we obtained experimentally so that the performance of this approach is optimal in the Mean Squared Error (MSE) sense. Also, we consider the case in which ρ is constant across either the spatial or the spectral domains. Once again, we determine ρ experimentally for optimal performance w.r.t. the MSE.

Regarding measures of performance, we employed the Peak Signal-to-Noise Ratio (PSNR) and the Structural Similarity Index Measure (SSIM) [19]. For the latter, we computed the SSIM between the original and recovered HS images in both the spatial and spectral domains. In the spatial case, the SSIM is computed between bands, but in the spectral case the SSIM is computed between spectra. In each of these cases, an overall SSIM is obtained in the usual way—by simply averaging over all computed local SSIMs. A summary of the numerical results is shown in Table 1.

From these results, we observe that denoising with different intensities over either the spatial or spectral domains improves the performance of the proposed FVM approach. This should not be surprising since, in general, the PSNR is not constant across bands and spectra. Having a "regularizing function" $\rho(y)$ may therefore be deemed a good strategy for denoising purposes. Also, it is worthwhile to mention that changing the way in which HS images are represented has also an impact on the obtained reconstructions. Considering HS as FVMs that assign an image to each wavelength value seems to benefit the SPECTRAL denoising methodology. This may be due to the greater regularity that HS images tend to have throughout the spectral domain which, in turn, appears to validate, at least up to a certain extent, the choice of the space $C^2(X; L^2(Y))$

Table 1. Numerical results w.r.t. different image distances. The PSNR prior to denoising was 30.103 dB. The results presented in the second and fourth columns correspond to the cases in which the regularizing parameter is constant. The third and fifth columns show how the performance of the proposed methods is improved when the strength of the denoising process is allowed to vary across either the spatial or spectral domains.

	SPATIAL		SPECTRAL	
	ρ_0	$\rho(y)$	ρ_0	$\rho(y)$
SALINAS-A				
PSNR (dB)	33.1069	36.3229	34.1434	34.3676
SPATIAL SSIM	0.9008	0.9311	0.8125	0.8254
SPECTRAL SSIM	0.9872	0.9927	0.9874	0.9877
INDIAN PINES				
PSNR (dB)	31.5657	34.4031	33.1165	33.1600
SPATIAL SSIM	0.7368	0.8906	0.8035	0.8054
SPECTRAL SSIM	0.9873	0.9934	0.9906	0.9907

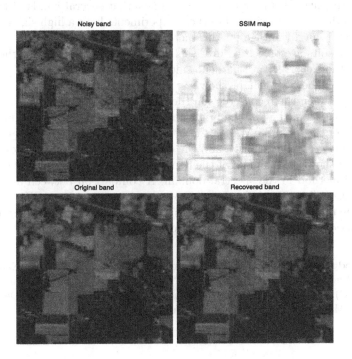

Fig. 1. Visual results for Band No. 23 of the *Indian Pines* image. **Top left:** Noisy band. **Bottom left:** Original (noiseless) band. **Bottom right:** Reconstructed (denoised) band. **Top right:** SSIM map between reconstructed (denoised) and original band.

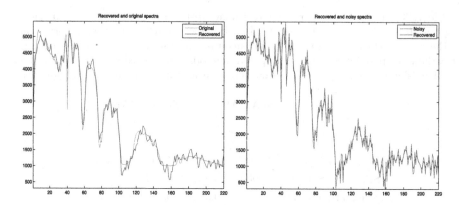

Fig. 2. Results of SPECTRAL denoising method for a particular spectral function of the *Indian Pines* image. **Left:** Original (noiseless) spectrum (green) and reconstructed spectrum (blue). **Right:** Noisy spectrum (red) and reconstructed spectrum (blue). (Color figure online)

as a reasonable model for HS images. Lastly, it can be noticed that the SPA-TIAL method employing the regularization function $\rho! : Y \subset \mathbb{R} \to \mathbb{R}$ yields the best performance. This may be due to the fact that several bands of the noisy HS images that were considered in these experiments have a high signal-to-noise ratio, which is an advantage for this method.

Visual results are presented in Figs. 1 and 2. Figure 1 shows how the SPEC-TRAL method carries out the denoising in the spatial domain—in this case, $\rho : \mathbb{R}^2 \to \mathbb{R}$. The SSIM map, shown at the top right of Fig. 1, illustrates the similarity between the reconstruction (denoised) and the original (noiseless) HS data for a particular band. The brightness in these maps is proportional to the magnitude of the local SSIM, i.e., the brighter a given location, the greater the similarity between the denoised and the original bands at that location [19].

Figure 2 shows an example of the denoising process performed by the afore-mentioned method in the spectral domain. A comparison between a particular reconstruction (blue) and the corresponding noisy spectrum (red) is shown on the left. On the right, the original spectrum (green) along with the corresponding reconstruction (blue) are shown for comparison.

Acknowledgements. This research has been supported in part by the Natural Sciences and Engineering Research Council of Canada (NSERC) in the form of a Discovery Grant (ERV). Financial support from the Faculty of Mathematics and the Department of Applied Mathematics (DO) is also gratefully acknowledged.

References

1. Aliprantis, C.D., Border, K.C.: Infinite Dimensional Analysis: A Hitchhiker's Guide. Springer, Heidelberg (2006)
2. Bach, F., Jenatton, R., Mairal, J., Obozinski, G.: Convex optimization with sparsity-inducing norms. In: Sra, S., Nowozin, S., Wright, S.J. (eds.) Optimization for Machine Learning, pp. 19–53. MIT Press, Massachusetts (2012)
3. Beck, A., Teboulle, M.: A fast iterative shrinkage-thresholding algorithm for linear inverse problems. SIAM J. Imaging Sci. Arch. **2**, 183–202 (2009)
4. Bresson, X., Chan, T.F.: Fast dual minimization of the vectorial total variation norm and applications to color image processing. Inverse Probl. Imaging **2**, 455–484 (2008)
5. Buades, A., Coll, B., Morel, J.-M.: A non-local algorithm for image denoising. In: Proceedings of the Conference on Computer Vision and Pattern Recognition, pp. 60–65. IEEE (2005)
6. Cartan, H., Cartan, H.P.: Differential Calculus. Hermann, Paris (1971)
7. Chambolle, A.: An algorithm for total variation minimization and applications. J. Math. Imaging Vis. **20**, 89–97 (2004)
8. Diestel, J., Uhl, J.J.: Vector Measures. American Mathematical Society, Providence (1977)
9. Folland, G.B.: A Course in Abstract Harmonic Analysis. CRC Press, Boca Raton (1995)
10. Grupo de Inteligencia Computacional de la Universidad del País Vasco, Hyperspectral Remote Sensing Scenes. http://www.ehu.eus/ccwintco/index.php
11. Martín-Herrero, J.: Anisotropic diffusion in the hypercube. IEEE Trans. Geosci. Remote Sens. **45**, 1386–1398 (2007)
12. Kunze, H., La Torre, D., Mendivil, F., Vrscay, E.R.: Fractal-Based Methods in Analysis. Springer Science & Business Media, Berlin (2011)
13. La Torre, D., Vrscay, E.R., Ebrahimi, M., Barnsley, M.F.: Measure-valued images associated fractal transforms, and the affine self-similarity of images. SIAM J. Imaging Sci. **2**, 470–507 (2009)
14. Michailovich, O., La Torre, D., Vrscay, E.R.: Function-valued mappings, total variation and compressed sensing for diffusion MRI. In: Campilho, A., Kamel, M. (eds.) ICIAR 2012, Part II. LNCS, vol. 7325, pp. 286–295. Springer, Heidelberg (2012)
15. Milman, M.: Complex interpolation and geometry of Banach spaces. Annali di Matematica Pura ed Applicata **136**, 317–328 (1984)
16. Otero, D.: Function-valued Mappings and SSIM-based Optimization in Imaging, Ph.D. thesis, University of Waterloo, Waterloo, ON, Canada (2015)
17. Peetre, J.: Sur la transformation de Fourier des fonctions à valeurs vectorielles. Rendicoti del Seminario Matematico della Università di Padova **42**, 15–26 (1969)
18. Thompson, H.: The Bochner Integral and an Application to Singular Integrals, M.Sc. thesis, Dalhousie University, Halifax, NS, Canada (2014)
19. Wang, Z., Bovik, A.C., Sheikh, H.R., Simoncelli, E.P.: Image quality assessment: From error visibility to structural similarity. IEEE Trans. Image Process. **13**, 600–612 (2004)
20. Zeidler, E.: Nonlinear Functional Analysis and its Applications. Springer, New York (1990)

Runtime Performance Enhancement of a Superpixel Based Saliency Detection Model

Qazi Aitezaz Ahmed[(⊠)] and Mahmood Akhtar

College of Electrical and Mechanical Engineering,
National University of Sciences and Technology (NUST), Islamabad, Pakistan
qazi14@yahoo.com, mahmood.akhtar@ceme.nust.edu.pk

Abstract. Reducing computational cost of image processing for various real time computer and robotic vision tasks, e.g. object recognition and tracking, adaptive compression, content aware image resizing, etc. remains a challenge. Saliency detection is often utilized as a pre-processing step for rapid, parallel, bottom-up processing of low level image features to compute saliency map. Subsequent higher level, complex computer vision tasks can then conveniently focus on identified salient locations for further image processing. Thus, saliency detection has successfully mitigated computational complexity of image processing tasks although processing speed enhancement still remains a desired goal. Recent fast and improved superpixel models are furnishing fresh incentive to employ them in saliency detection models to reduce computational complexity and enhance runtime speed. In this paper, we propose use of the superpixel extraction via energy driven sampling (SEEDS) algorithm to achieve processing speed enhancement in an existing saliency detection model. Evaluation results show that our modified model achieves over 60 % processing speed enhancement while maintaining accuracy comparable to the original model.

Keywords: Visual saliency · Superpixel · Over-segmentation · SEEDS

1 Introduction

Visual Saliency is a subset of the visual attention mechanism possessed by primates, including human beings, which exercises selective processing of visual stimulus to focus on relatively important and salient parts of the visual scene, leaving the rest un-processed. It thus enables the brain to cope with the massive influx of sensory visual data (10^8–10^9 bits per second), which is otherwise beyond the limited capacity of the brain to handle. Visual attention encompasses both an initial fast pre-attentive stage of bottom-up, low-level, saliency detection based on spontaneous, parallel processing of image data and feature cues (e.g. intensity, color, orientation etc.) and a second attentive stage which is relevance oriented, task dependent, top-down, memory assisted and voluntary selective gaze oriented image processing. The term 'visual saliency' is in fact synonymous to bottom-up saliency detection. Over the past two decades much research has been conducted to develop saliency detection models, mostly biologically inspired by the human visual system. Most of such models are of the bottom-up category, starting

© Springer International Publishing Switzerland 2016
A. Campilho and F. Karray (Eds.): ICIAR 2016, LNCS 9730, pp. 120–130, 2016.
DOI: 10.1007/978-3-319-41501-7_14

with the pioneering work by Itti *et al.* [1], which is the computational realization of an earlier model based on the renowned feature integration theory (FIT) of attention [2, 3].

The rapid advancement in mobile devices and affiliated computer vision applications spells out a compelling need for computationally efficient pre-processing saliency detection models. Such models furnish saliency map output which excels both in quality as well as processing speed and capability to achieve near real-time performance. This work contributes primarily towards identification and practical confirmation that front-end employment of superpixels in saliency detection models for image representation renders the models computationally efficient, robust and maximizes detection speed.

This paper is organized such that a brief outline of the various categories of bottom-up saliency detection models is presented in Sect. 2. However, for a detailed review readers may refer to [4–6]. Section 3 is dedicated to the review of our selected superpixel-based saliency detection model and Sect. 4 furnishes details of our proposed, alternate, modified superpixel-based saliency detection model. Finally, Sect. 5 presents our evaluation results and discussion, following by the conclusion.

2 General Categories of Saliency Detection Models

2.1 Cognitive Models

These models are based on the cognitive neuroscience theory of visual attention starting with the feature integration theory of attention [3]. The pioneer cognitive computational saliency detection model was proposed by Itti *et al.* [1] as shown in Fig. 1. It is a practical implementation of architecture proposed in [2]. Such models extract feature maps at multiple scales from an image based on inherent image feature attributes such as intensity, color, orientation, texture, motion etc. The feature maps are then summed across scales to compute the output master saliency map.

In the above shown model (Fig. 1), a 640×480 resolution input image is filtered with Gaussian pyramids to yield nine spatial scales of reduction. The center-surround feature maps for features of intensity (I), color (C) and orientation (O) are constructed and normalized. The intensity image I is obtained from RGB channels and a Gaussian pyramid I (σ) created where $\sigma \in [0...8]$. Six center-surround feature maps of intensity I(c, s) are computed. Four Gaussian Pyramids R (σ), B (σ), G (σ) and Y (σ) calculated from four color channels. Twelve feature maps for two double opponency color channels RG(c, s) and BY(c, s) are created. Also, 24 orientation feature maps O(c, s, θ) are obtained using Center-Surround. The 42 feature maps are summed across scale and normalized to create 3 conspicuity maps $\bar{I}, \bar{C}$ and $\bar{O}$. The three conspicuity maps are then combined linearly and again normalized to generate the final saliency map S.

2.2 Graphical Model

Graphical saliency detection models manage visual data as a graph within a probabilistic framework employing Markov chain or Hidden Markov model or Random Walker algorithms to calculate and establish the relations between graph's parameters. A

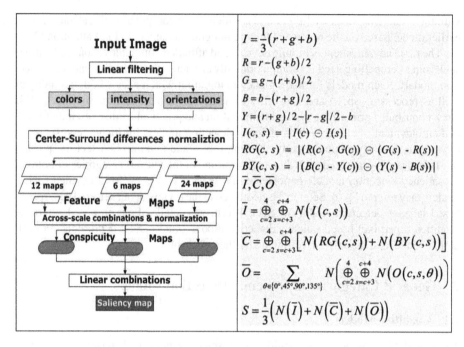

Fig. 1. Saliency detection model as presented by Itti *et al.* [1].

popular visual saliency model developed in this category is the graph based visual saliency model by Harel *et al.* [8].

2.3 Bayesian Models

The Bayesian model merges probabilistic statistical theory with the general principles established for cognitive models. The model handles the visual data (feature) as conditional probability based on available target information and computes saliency as posterior probability based on the Bayes' rule of statistical probability. Since all features are assumed to be independent or conditionally independent of each other in the probabilistic framework, the statistical probability is normally calculated as an entropy feature of the system. Saliency using natural statistics (SUN) by Zhang *et al.* [9] is a good example in this category.

2.4 Decision Theoretic Models

The decision theoretical models are error reducing feedback classification models that are applied to the field of saliency detection by selecting and defining visual data features. Such features are treated as classification parameters for deciding upon foreground and background classes to a scene which optimizes the said feedback and in essence fulfills the decision theoretic objective. Major work in this category of saliency detection models has been conducted by Gao and Vasconscelos *et al.* [10].

2.5   Spectral Analysis Models

Spectral Analysis Models are based on the premise that similar or uniform value features in spatial domain equal low level frequencies while sharp and dissimilar features in spatial domain are defined by high level frequencies in the frequency domain. Utilizing this fundamental concept Hou and Zhang [11] have proposed the first frequency domain model.

3   Superpixel Based Saliency Detection

The saliency detection model proposed by Liu *et al.* [12] falls in the category of cognitive models as it exploits the image color features and develops saliency maps after computing the image color histogram in CIEL*a*b* color space. It is comprised of three steps namely image simplification, computing superpixel similarity, and finally superpixel saliency through refined global contrast and spatial sparsity.

3.1   Image Simplification

The image simplification is executed firstly by converting the input image from RGB to CIEL*a*b* color space. The CIEL*a*b* image is then partitioned into approximately 200 superpixels, utilizing the simple linear iterative clustering (SLIC) algorithm [13]. The color quantization is then performed, where each color channel is quantized into q bins ($q = 16$). A Histogram of $q \times q \times q$ bins is created and q_{ck}, the mean color of each bin as well as the number of pixels falling in each bin are tabulated in table called Q. An m number of high-priority bins containing up to 95 % of image pixels are selected and the remaining low priority bins are merged with m bins that have closest similarity between their mean colors. The mean color q_{ck} of all m bins in Q table is recalculated and superpixel level histogram H_i is generated and normalized.

3.2   Superpixel Similarity

The inter-superpixel similarity, designated as $Sim\,(i, j)$, is defined as the product of their color similarity $Sim_c(i, j)$ and spatial similarity $Sim_d(i, j)$. The color similarity $Sim_c(i, j)$ is based on the intersection distance between the two superpixels Sp_i and Sp_j respective color histograms $H_i(k)$ and $H_j(k)$ as under

$$Sim_c(i,j) = \sum_{k=1}^{m} \min\{H_i(k), H_j(k)\} \tag{1}$$

$$Sim_d(i,j) = 1 - \frac{\left\| \mu_i - \mu_j \right\|}{d} \tag{2}$$

where d is the diagonal length of the image and μ_i and μ_j are the spatial centers of superpixels Sp_i and Sp_j. Finally, the inter-superpixel similarity is obtained as:

$$Sim(i,j) = Sim_c(i,j) * Sim_d(i,j) \tag{3}$$

3.3 Superpixel Saliency

Salient superpixels are relatively sparser than background superpixels with having more contrast. Therefore, in order to assess the saliency of superpixels the global contrast $GC(i)$ is first evaluated as under:

$$GC(i) = \sum_{j=1}^{n} W(i,j) \cdot \left\| mc_i - mc_j \right\| \tag{4}$$

where mc is the mean color of superpixels, and its weight $W(i, j)$ is defined as:

$$W(i,j) = \left| SP_j \right| \cdot Sim_d(i,j) \tag{5}$$

The normalized global contrast $NGC(i)$ measure for SP_i is calculated as follows

$$NGC(i) = \frac{GC(i) - GC_{min}}{GC_{max} - GC_{min}} \tag{6}$$

For each superpixel SP_i, the spatial spread $SS(i)$ of its color distribution would be

$$SS(i) = \frac{\sum_{j=1}^{n} Sim(i,j) \cdot D(j)}{\sum_{j=1}^{n} Sim(i,j)} \tag{7}$$

where $D(j)$ is the distance between the image center and the center of superpixel SP_j. An inverse normalization operation is performed on the spatial spread measures to obtain the normalized spatial sparsity $NSS(i)$ measure for each superpixel:

$$NSS(i) = \frac{SS(i) - SS_{max}}{SS_{min} - SS_{max}} \tag{8}$$

Since superpixels having higher inter-superpixel similarity would most probably have similar saliency value, therefore the normalized global contrast $NGC(i)$ and normalized spatial sparsity $NSS(i)$ measures are further refined to define $RGC(i)$ and $RSS(i)$ (as discussed in [12]) and the final saliency value $Sal(i)$ for each superpixel may then be computed as:

$$Sal(i) = RGC(i) \cdot RSS(i) \tag{9}$$

4   Proposed Model

The existing superpixel based saliency detection model [12] uses color histograms to compute color similarity of the superpixels. This model employs the simple linear iterative clustering (SLIC) algorithm [13] to generate superpixels. SLIC starts with partitioning an image into an initial regular grid of superpixels using localized k-means clustering and grows the superpixels by estimating each pixel distance to its cluster center localized nearby. It then updates the cluster centers. SLIC can produce superpixels at 5 Hz without GPU optimization.

We hypothesize and test herein that a relatively less time consuming approach for superpixel computation (and therefore for the superpixel based saliency detection) would employ superpixels extracted via energy driven sampling (SEEDS) algorithm [14]. The SEEDS process starts with an image partitioning into a grid of square superpixels. It uses Hill-Climbing to rapidly and continuously refine each superpixel by shifting blocks of pixels (and single pixels) at boundaries from one superpixel to another. It has been reported that SEEDS can achieve real time superpixel segmentation at 30 Hz and has superior performance in comparison to SLIC [15]. The superpixel saliency detection in general computes color histograms and SEEDS algorithm exploits those pre-computed histograms of superpixels to enhance runtime performance of the model in computing saliency maps. We therefore propose to modify the existing superpixel based saliency detection model by replacing the SLIC algorithm with the SEEDS algorithm.

4.1 Proposed Model Implementation

We implemented the existing superpixel based saliency detection model (Liu *et al.* [12]) locally in MATLAB as the author's original implementation was not accessible. We designate our above implementation as 'SP'. We also developed a modified version of 'SP' in MATLAB and designate herein as 'MSP'. The 'MSP' replaces SLIC algorithm with SEEDS algorithm for superpixel generation part of the superpixel based saliency

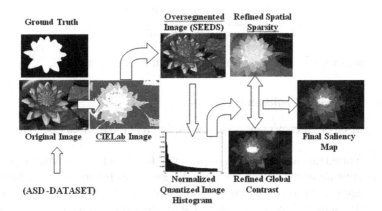

Fig. 2. Modified superpixel based saliency detection model 'MSP' utilizes the SEEDS algorithm as a preprocessing module for image simplification. It aims to enhance and improve the model's runtime speed whilst maintaining accuracy compatible with the original SP model. (Color figure online)

detection model as described in the previous section. A schematic diagram of 'MSP' is shown in Fig. 2.

For our evaluations, we also selected the following additional state-of-the-art saliency detection models: IK [1], CA [16], SR [11], GBVS [8], HC [17] and FT [18].

5   Experimental Testing and Evaluation of Results

We performed experimental testing with the ASD image dataset having 1000 images along with manually segmented salient object binary masks available online [18]. We conducted testing and evaluation of each saliency detection model against test criteria of Precision, Recall and F-measure. Precision and Recall are computed by comparison of the binary mask (M) and the ground-truth (G) such that $\dfrac{|M \cap G|}{|M|}$ represents precision and $\dfrac{|M \cap G|}{|G|}$ represents Recall. To plot different performance curves of precision versus recall (PR), the binary mask M is computed through a fixed thresholding t_f of the saliency map ranging from values 0 to 255 and their Precision and Recall scores are obtained. The procedure is repeated for all 1000 images in the ASD dataset and/the Precision and Recall values averaged and their PR curve plotted. Average Precision and Recall can be computed for adaptive threshold value T_a which is calculated as:

$$T_a = \frac{2}{WXH} \sum_{x=1}^{W} \sum_{y=1}^{H} S(x, y) \tag{10}$$

where W and H are the width and the height, respectively, of the Saliency map. S can also be binarized by using Otsu's method [7]. F-measure is the harmonic mean for precision and recall. It is a relatively better measure and can be computed as:

$$F_\beta = \frac{\left(1 + \beta^2\right) Precission \times Recall}{\beta^2 precision + Recall} \tag{11}$$

where the non-negative weight β^2 is usually chosen with a value of 0.3.

5.1   Benchmarking Results and Analysis

The comparison of saliency maps generated by different models (see Fig. 3) reveals the following.

A very blurred saliency map can be seen for the 'IK' model (row 3) which is probably due to an attribute of the model that severely downsizes the input image. Similarly, saliency maps generated by 'SR' model (row 5) present improper, non-uniform high-lighting of the salient objects once again due to downsizing of input images, but to a fixed resolution of 64 × 64 pixels. The 'CA' model (row 4) gives better visual results as compared to 'IK' and 'SR' models.

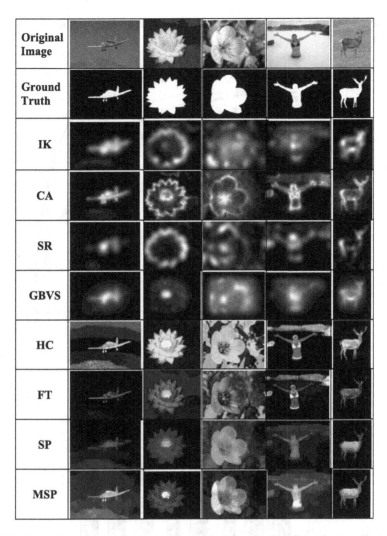

Fig. 3. Saliency maps of various saliency detection models (Color figure online)

The 'GBVS' model (row 6) saliency maps also shows salient object with ill-defined boundaries. The saliency maps generated by the 'HC' model (row 7) and 'FT' model (row 8) present salient objects with well-defined boundaries and also are uniformly highlighted.

The PR curves of different models (see Fig. 4) show that the 'SP' and 'MSP' demonstrate a high level of Precision at a selected range of Recall values i.e. Precision of 86 %–87 % at 0 %–60 % Recall values. It is clear that our proposed 'MSP' model exhibits the highest level of Precision (87 %) amongst all the selected saliency detection models. The proposed model surpasses the 'SP' model in the Recall value range of 0 %– 50 %. The PR curves for all other models ('IK', 'SR', 'GBVS' and 'CA') reflect low Precision versus Recall values which is in line with the previously discussed qualitative results, as shown in Fig. 3.

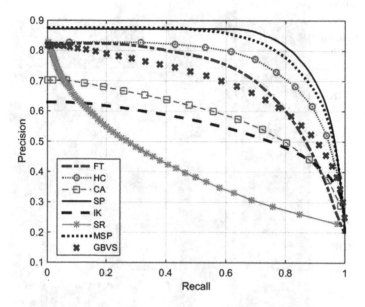

Fig. 4. PR curves of various saliency models

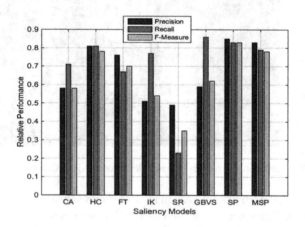

Fig. 5. Average Precision, Recall and F-measure values for different saliency models (Color figure online)

The summary of quantitative benchmarking results for various saliency models i.e., average Precision, Recall and F-measure values (see Fig. 5 and Table 1) substantiate the relatively low performance of 'IK', 'CA', 'SR' and 'GBVS' models as assessed in qualitative analysis of the saliency maps (Fig. 3). Clearly, the 'SP' model outperforms the 'HC' and 'FT' models with F-measure values of 83 %, 78 % and 70 % respectively.

Table 1. Summary of benchmarking evaluation results

Details	IK	CA	SR	GBVS	HC	FT	SP	MSP	Difference SP and MSP
F-measure (%)	54	58	35	62	78	70	83	78	5 %
Precision (%)	51	58	49	59	81	76	85	83	2 %
Recall (%)	77	72	23	86	82	67	83	79	4 %

5.2 SP Versus MSP Saliency Detection Performance Comparison

The saliency maps generated by the 'MSP' model (Fig. 3) reflect uniform highlighting of the salient objects as well as their sharply defined borders. On the other hand, the saliency maps produced by the 'SP' model indicate non-uniform highlighting of the salient object as well as ill-defined boundaries and edges. We also perform a runtime processing speed comparison between the existing 'SP' and our newly proposed 'MSP' models. It is heartening to note that the proposed 'MSP' model (employing the SEEDS over-segmentation model of [14]) has rendered saliency maps outputs at approximately 60 % faster speed (Table 2) than that of the existing 'SP' model, yet maintaining a comparable performance i.e., within 2–5 % tolerance range for average Precision, Recall and F-measure values (see Fig. 5 and Table 1). Also, the PR curve of 'MSP' model runs above that of the 'SP' model in the Recall value range 0–50 % (Fig. 4).

Table 2. Runtime processing speed comparison between the existing 'SP' and our newly proposed 'MSP' models

MSP (seconds) for 1000 images	SP (seconds) for 1000 images
12977	21075

MSP computation time reduced to $\dfrac{21075 - 12977}{12977} * 100\% = 62.4\%$ of SP time.

Consequently, speed of MSP is 60.3 % faster i.e., $100*((1/0.624)-1)$ %

6 Conclusion

This work has proposed a modification in the existing superpixel based saliency detection model. The performance of newly proposed modified superpixel based saliency detection model 'MSP' has been compared with a number of existing saliency detection models on standard ASD dataset containing 1000 images. It has been shown that the 'MSP' model (employing the SEEDS over-segmentation for superpixel generation) attains more than 60 % runtime speed enhancement over the existing state-of-the-art superpixel based saliency detection model at a comparable accuracy as computed using standard evaluation measures i.e., Precision, Recall and F-measure. Our work confirms that the recently developed SEEDS superpixel model holds great potential for rendering optimization of saliency detection models.

References

1. Itti, L., Koch, C., Niebur, E.: A model of saliency-based visual attention for rapid scene analysis. IEEE TPAMI **20**, 1254–1259 (1998)
2. Koch, C., Ullman, S.: Shifts in selective visual attention: towards the underlying neural circuitry. In: Vaina, L.M. (ed.) Matters of Intelligence, pp. 115–141. Springer, Heidelberg (1987)
3. Treisman, A.M., Gelade, G.: A feature-integration theory of attention. Cogn. Psychol. **12**, 97–136 (1980). 82
4. Borji, A., Itti, L.: State-of-the-art in visual attention modeling. IEEE TPAMI **35**(1), 185–207 (2013)
5. Borji, A., Sihite, D.N., Itti, L.: Salient object detection: a benchmark. In: Fitzgibbon, A., Lazebnik, S., Perona, P., Sato, Y., Schmid, C. (eds.) ECCV 2012, Part II. LNCS, vol. 7573, pp. 414–429. Springer, Heidelberg (2012)
6. Borji, A., Cheng, M.M., Jiang, H., Li, J.: Salient object detection: a survey (2014). arXiv preprint arXiv:1411.5878
7. Otsu, N.: A threshold selection method from gray-level histograms. IEEE Trans. Syst. Man Cybern. **9**(1), 62–66 (1979)
8. Harel, J., Koch, C., Perona, P.: Graph-based visual saliency. In: NIPS, pp. 545–552 (2007)
9. Zhang, L., Tong, M.H., Marks, T.K., Shan, H., Cottrell, G.W.: Sun: a Bayesian framework for saliency using natural statistics. J. Vis. **8**(7), 1–20 (2008). 32
10. Gao, D., Vasconcelos, N.: Discriminant saliency for visual recognition from clustered scenes. In: NIPS (2004)
11. Hou, X., Zhang, L.: Saliency detection: a spectral residual approach. In: CVPR, pp. 1–8 (2007)
12. Liu, Z., Meur, O., Luo, S.: Superpixel based saliency detection. In: International Workshop on Image and Audio Analysis for Multimedia Interactive services, pp. 1–4, July 2013
13. Achanta, R., Shaji, A., Smith, K., Lucchi, A., Fua, P., Susstrunk, S.: Slicsuperpixels compared to state-of-the-art superpixel methods. IEEE TPAMI **34**(11), 2274–2282 (2012)
14. Van den Bergh, M., Boix, X., Roig, G., de Capitani, B., Van Gool, L.: SEEDS: superpixels extracted via energy-driven sampling. In: Fitzgibbon, A., Lazebnik, S., Perona, P., Sato, Y., Schmid, C. (eds.) ECCV 2012, Part VII. LNCS, vol. 7578, pp. 13–26. Springer, Heidelberg (2012)
15. Zhua, H., Mengb, F., Cai, J., Lua, S.: Beyond Pixels: A Comprehensive Survey from Bottom-up to Semantic Image Segmentation and Cosegmentation, February 2015. arXiv: 1502.00717v
16. Goferman, J.S., Zelnik-Manor, L., Tal, A.: Context-aware saliency detection. In: CVPR, pp. 2376–2383 (2010)
17. Cheng, M.-M., Mitra, N.J., Huang, X., Torr, P.H.S., Hu, S.-M.: Global contrast based salient region detection. In: IEEE TPAMI (CVPR 2011) (2014)
18. Achanta, R., Hemami, S., Estrada, F. Susstrunk, S.: Frequency-tuned salient region detection. In: CVPR (2009)

Total Variation Minimization for Measure-Valued Images with Diffusion Spectrum Imaging as Motivation

Davide La Torre[1,2], Franklin Mendivil[3], Oleg Michailovich[4], and Edward R. Vrscay[5(⊠)]

[1] Department of Economics, Management, and Quantitative Methods,
University of Milan, Milan, Italy
davide.latorre@unimi.it
[2] Department of Applied Mathematics and Sciences,
Khalifa University, Abu Dhabi, UAE
davide.latorre@kustar.ac.ae
[3] Department of Mathematics and Statistics,
Acadia University, Wolfville, NS, Canada
franklin.mendivil@acadiau.ca
[4] Deparment of Electrical and Computer Engineering,
University of Waterloo, Waterloo, ON, Canada
olegm@uwaterloo.ca
[5] Deparment of Applied Mathematics, University of Waterloo,
Waterloo, ON, Canada
ervrscay@uwaterloo.ca

Abstract. In this paper, we present a notion of total variation for measure-valued images. Our motivation is Diffusion Spectrum Imaging (DSI) in which the diffusion at each voxel is characterized by a probability density function. We introduce a total variation denoising problem for measure-valued images. In the one-dimensional case, this problem (which involves the Monge-Kantorovich metric for measures) can be solved using cumulative distribution functions. In higher dimensions, more computationally expensive methods must be employed.

1 Introduction

Over the last few decades, Diffusion Magnetic Resonance Imaging (dMRI) has developed into an established tool of diagnostic medical imaging, which is nowadays used in a broad spectrum of clinical applications, including the diagnosis of oncological and neurodegenerative disorders [6]. In application to brain imaging, the advent of dMRI has made it possible to delineate the anatomical structure of white matter, thereby opening the possibility of quantitative exploration of *in vivo* connectivity of the brain by means of fibre tractography [1,3,7]. Naturally, the reliability and diagnostic value of such analysis depends on the quality of acquired diffusion data, which tend to be affected by various measurement artifacts, including noise [12].

© Springer International Publishing Switzerland 2016
A. Campilho and F. Karray (Eds.): ICIAR 2016, LNCS 9730, pp. 131–137, 2016.
DOI: 10.1007/978-3-319-41501-7_15

In a previous paper [10], we showed that *function-valued mappings* (FVM) provide a natural setting for a particular instance of dMRI known as *high angular resolution diffusion imaging* (HARDI), which excels in delineation of the orientational structure of crossing fibre bundles in the white matter of the brain. At each position/pixel $x \in \mathbb{R}^3$ and orientation $s \in \mathbb{S}^2 := \{u \in \mathbb{R}^3 \mid \|u\|_2 = 1\}$, HARDI provides a measurement which quantifies the apparent diffusivity of water molecules along the direction defined by s. Therefore, a HARDI signal u measured at position x, i.e., $u(x)$, can be assumed to be a square-integrable function supported over $\mathbb{S}^2$. In other words, the HARDI signal is considered to be an FVM, where $u : \mathbb{R}^3 \to \mathbb{L}_2(\mathbb{S}^2)$.

While useful for inferring the orientational characteristics of diffusion *in vivo*, the applicability of HARDI to estimation of microstructural characteristics of biological tissues remains limited. At the same time, much richer information can be obtained using a different variation of dMRI, known as *diffusion spectral imaging* (DSI) [15]. In fact, the latter allows estimation of the *ensemble averaged diffusion propagator* (EADP) $P(r)$–a probability measure that quantifies the likelihood of a water molecule to undergo displacement by $r \in \mathbb{R}^3$ in a given experimental time [13]. Moreover, considering the straightforward relation between DSI data and EADP through Fourier transformation, it is reasonable to assume that the datum of DSI measurements is equivalent to the datum of the estimates of EADP, which will be referred below to as *propagator signals*.

One could, in principle, also consider a propagator signal as a function-valued mapping. However, given the fact that the signal is, in fact, a probability density function, it may be beneficial to analyze and process it using mathematical methods that have been adopted for measures. In this paper, therefore, we consider propagator signals as *measure-valued mappings* (MVM): At each position/pixel/voxel x is associated a probability measure μ_x supported on $\mathbb{R}^3$, to be denoted as $\mu(x)$. Subsequently, to counteract the effect of both measurement and estimation noises, we then propose a novel *total variation* (TV) denoising method for MVMs. Of course, this requires a definition of total variation for measure-valued mappings which, in itself, is a nontrivial mathematical problem. Space limitations allow us only to outline our method below.

2   Measure-Valued Images

In what follows $X = [0,1]^n$, $n = 1, 2, 3$ will denote the "base space," i.e., the support of the images. $\mathbb{R}_g \subset \mathbb{R}_+^m$, $m = 1, 2, 3$, will denote a compact set of values that our image can assume at any $x \in X$. $\mathbb{B}$ will denote the Borel σ algebra on $\mathbb{R}_g$ and dx Lebesgue measure on X. Let $\mathcal{M}$ denote the set of all Borel probability measures on $\mathbb{R}_g$ and d_{MK} the Monge-Kantorovich metric (see [8]) on this set. That is, for $\alpha, \beta \in \mathcal{M}$,

$$d_{MK}(\alpha, \beta) = \sup_{\phi \in \mathrm{Lip}_1(\mathbb{R}_g)} \int_{\mathbb{R}_g} \phi(t) \, d(\alpha - \beta)(t), \tag{1}$$

where, as usual, $\mathrm{Lip}_1(\mathbb{R}_g) = \{f : \mathbb{R}_g \to \mathbb{R} : |f(x) - f(y)| \le \|x - y\|\}$. We can now define the following space of measure-valued images,

$$Y = \{\mu : X \to \mathcal{M}, \mu \text{ is Lebesgue integrable}\}, \tag{2}$$

with the following metric,

$$d_Y(\mu, \nu) = \int_X d_{MK}(\mu(x), \nu(x)) dx. \tag{3}$$

Note that d_Y is well defined since μ and ν are Lebesgue-integrable functions, d_{MK} is continuous and X is compact, which implies that the function $\xi(x) = d_{MK}(\mu(x), \nu(x))$ is integrable on X. It can be shown that the space (Y, d_Y) is complete (see [9]).

3   Total Variation

In image analysis, the notion of total variation or total variation regularization has applications in noise removal. The basic idea relies on the fact that signals with spurious detail have high total variation or, more mathematically, the integral of the absolute gradient of the signal is high. It is well known that the process of reducing the total variation of the signal removes unwanted detail whilst preserving important details such as edges (see [14]). The total variation (TV) of a differentiable greyscale image $f : X \subset \mathbb{R}^n \to \mathbb{R}$ is defined as follows

$$\|f\|_{TV} = \int_X \|\nabla f(x)\|_2 \, dx, \tag{4}$$

that is the integral of the $\|\cdot\|_2$ norm of the gradient. Other definitions of total variation are available in the literature–the reader is referred to [5] for an overview of many of the most recent ones.

In this section we introduce a notion of total variation for measure-valued images which, as usual, will involve derivatives. We define the *total variation* of $\mu \in Y$ to be

$$\|\mu\|_{TV} = \int_X \|D\mu\|_2 \, dx = \int_X \left(\sum_{i=1}^n |D_i \mu(x)|^2 \right)^{1/2} dx. \tag{5}$$

Here,

$$|D_i \mu(x)| := \sup_{\phi_i \in \mathrm{Lip}_1(\mathbb{R}_g)} \limsup_{h_i \to 0^+} \frac{1}{h_i} \int_{\mathbb{R}_g} \phi_i(t) \, d(\mu(x + \hat{e}_i h_i) - \mu(x)), \quad 1 \le i \le n,$$

are the analogues of the magnitudes of the directional derivative of μ at the point $x \in X$ in the directions of $\hat{e}_i$, the standard orthonormal basis vectors in $\mathbb{R}^n$. The TV norm in (5) may be used to define a *total variation distance* between μ and ν in Y as $\|\mu - \nu\|_{TV}$. A few additional comments are in order.

First, note that by taking the supremum over $\phi_i \in \text{Lip}_1(\mathbb{R}_g)$, we are using a Monge-Kantorovich-type norm on measures (see [8]) to compute the magnitude of the directional derivative. By taking the supremum over $\phi_i \in L^\infty(\mathbb{R}_g)$, the magnitude of the directional derivative is computed using the *variation norm* on measures.

Next, let $f : X \to \mathbb{R}$ be a differentiable function and $\mu(x) = \delta_{f(x)}$. Then for a direction $\hat{d} \in \mathbb{R}^n$ with $\|\hat{d}\| = 1$ and any $\phi \in \text{Lip}_1(\mathbb{R}_g)$,

$$\frac{1}{h} \int_{R_g} \phi(t) \, d(\mu(x + \hat{d}h) - \mu(x)) = \frac{\phi(f(x + \hat{d}h)) - \phi(f(x))}{h} \to \phi'(f(x)) \, \nabla f(x) \cdot \hat{d}.$$

(6)

Taking the supremum over $\phi \in \text{Lip}_1(\mathbb{R}_g)$, we obtain $|D_{\hat{d}}\mu(x)| = |\nabla f(x) \cdot \hat{d}|$ so that

$$\|\mu\|_{TV} = \int_X \left(\sum_i |\nabla f(x) \cdot \hat{e}_i|^2 \right)^{1/2} dx = \int_X \|\nabla f(x)\|_2 \, dx,$$

(7)

which agrees with the classical definition of TV for functions in Eq. (4). Our definition of total variation in (5) may therefore be viewed as a true extension of the classical definition to measure-valued mappings.

Finally, if $\mu(x)$ has a density $\rho_\mu(x, \cdot)$ for each $x \in X$, then a standard calculation shows that $D_{\hat{e}_i}\mu$ is a signed measure with density $\frac{\partial \rho_\mu}{\partial x_i}$. This is important for models where one fits data with a parametric form of $\mu(x)$ for each x.

4   The Inverse Problem and Total Variation Minimization

The total variation denoising problem for measure-valued images can now be formulated as follows: Given a noisy image $\tilde{\mu}$ (the "observed data") we seek a solution to the following optimization problem,

$$\min_{\mu \in Y} d_Y(\tilde{\mu}, \mu) + \lambda \|\nu\|_{TV},$$

(8)

where λ is a trade-off or regularization parameter.

We now show how to solve the optimization problem (8) practically in the special case that the pixel space $X = [0, 1]$ and the greyspace $\mathbb{R}_g = [0, 1]$. (Admittedly, this case is not very interesting from a practical perspective, but it does provide insight into some of the mathematical aspects of this problem. A discussion of the higher-dimensional situation $\mathbb{R}_g \subseteq \mathbb{R}^n$ for $n > 1$ would be much more complicated, requiring more space and details.) In this special case one can rely on the following characterization of the Monge-Kantorovich distance in terms of cumulative distribution functions. For more on the practical issue of computing the Monge-Kantorovich distance, see [11].

Theorem 1 [2,4]. *Let μ and ν two probability measures defined on $\mathbb{R}$ and $F_\mu(x) = \mu((-\infty, x])$ and $F_\nu(x) = \nu((-\infty, x])$ be the two corresponding cumulative distribution functions. Then*

$$d_{MK}(\mu, \nu) = \|F_\nu - F_\mu\|_1.$$

(9)

We now use this theorem to approximate the total variation integral $\|\mu\|_{TV}$ in (5) as follows: For a small, fixed value of $h \in \mathbb{R}$,

$$\|\mu\|_{TV} = \int_0^1 |D\mu(x)| \, dx \approx \int_0^1 \frac{\|F_{\mu(x+h)} - F_{\mu(x)}\|_1}{h} \, dx. \qquad (10)$$

The total variation minimization problem in (8) can now be reformulated as follows,

$$\min_{\mu \in Y} \int_0^1 \left[\|F_{\tilde{\mu}(x)} - F_{\mu(x)}\|_1 + \frac{\lambda}{h} \|F_{\mu(x+h)} - F_{\mu(x)}\|_1 \right] dx. \qquad (11)$$

It is worth noticing that the space Y is convex. It is also straightforward to show that the map $T : \mu \in Y \to \mathbb{R}_+$ (or $T : F \in Y \to \mathbb{R}_+$), defined as

$$TF := \int_0^1 \int_{\mathbb{R}_g} \left[|\tilde{F}(x,t) - F(x,t)| + \frac{\lambda}{h} |F(x+h,t) - F(x,t)| \right] dt \, dx, \qquad (12)$$

is convex. Equation (11) is therefore a convex minimization problem so that classical algorithms from convex programming can used to determine an optimal solution. Note also that if $\mu(x)$ has density $\rho_\mu(x, \cdot)$ for each $x \in X$, then from Theorem 1 above,

$$\|\mu\|_{TV} = \int_0^1 \int_{T \in \mathbb{R}_g} \left| \int_{-\infty}^T \frac{\partial \rho_\mu}{\partial x}(z,t) \, dt \right| dT \, dz. \qquad (13)$$

One way to solve Eq. (11) practically is to employ a finite subset of elements, $F_i \in Y$, $i = 1...n$. We now solve the minimization problem in (11) over the convex subset spanned by the F_i. Any function in this subset can be written as a convex combination of the F_i, that is,

$$F(x,t) = \sum_{i=1}^n \alpha_i F_i(x,t), \qquad (14)$$

where $\alpha_i \in [0,1]$, $\sum_{i=1}^n \alpha_i = 1$. The minimization problem in Eq. (11) can then be approximated by

$$\min \int_0^1 \int_{\mathbb{R}_g} \left(\left| \tilde{F}(x,t) - \sum_{i=1}^n \alpha_i F_i(x,t) \right| + \frac{\lambda}{h} \left| \sum_{i=1}^n \alpha_i (F_i(x+h,t) - F_i(x,t)) \right| \right) dt \, dx. \qquad (15)$$

An upper bound for the optimal value can be found by noticing that

$$\left| \tilde{F}(x,t) - \sum_{i=1}^n \alpha_i F_i(x,t) \right| + \frac{\lambda}{h} \left| \sum_{i=1}^n \alpha_i (F_i(x+h,t) - F_i(x,t)) \right|$$

$$= \left| \sum_{i=1}^n \alpha_i \tilde{F}(x,t) - \sum_{i=1}^n \alpha_i F_i(x,t) \right| + \frac{\lambda}{h} \left| \sum_{i=1}^n \alpha_i (F_i(x+h,t) - F_i(x,t)) \right|$$

$$\leq \sum_{i=1}^n \alpha_i \left(\left| \tilde{F}(x,t) - F_i(x,t) \right| + \frac{\lambda}{h} |F_i(x+h,t) - F_i(x,t)| \right) \qquad (16)$$

and then solving the linear programming model,

$$\min \sum_{i=1}^{n} \alpha_i \int_0^1 \int_{\mathbb{R}_g} \left(\left| \tilde{F}(x,t) - F_i(x,t) \right| + \frac{\lambda}{h} \left| F_i(x+h,t) - F_i(x,t) \right| \right), \quad (17)$$

subject to the constraint,

$$\sum_{i=1}^{n} \alpha_i = 1, \quad \alpha_i \in [0,1]. \quad (18)$$

A particularly simple choice has each F_i of the form

$$F(x,t) = \begin{cases} 0 & \text{if } t < \psi(x), \\ 1 & \text{if } t \geq \psi(x), \end{cases}$$

for some function $\psi : X \to \mathbb{R}_g$ (this corresponds to a point mass at $\psi(x)$ for each x). For instance, if $\{0 = t_0 < t_1 < \cdots < t_n = 1\}$ is a partition of $\mathbb{R}_g$, then $\psi_i(x) = t_i$ allows an estimation of the empirical CDF for $\tilde{F}$, though this approximation will be constant in x. Polynomial ψ give non-constant (in x) approximations and increasing the degree allows for arbitrarily close approximations.

The methods of this section can be generalized to higher dimensional X and $\mathbb{R}_g$, though $\dim(\mathbb{R}_g) > 1$ is more computationaly expensive. For direction fields in 2D, [4] provides an efficient computation of the Monge-Kantorovich distance on the circle. Research is ongoing for efficient computational algorithms for $\mathbb{S}^2$ and $\mathbb{R}^3$. Another alternative is to replace the Monge-Kantorovich metric on measures with another metric.

Acknowledgements. This work has also been supported in part by Discovery Grants from the Natural Sciences and Engineering Research Council of Canada (NSERC): FM (238549-2012) and ERV (Grant No. 106270-2012).

References

1. Basser, P.J., Mattiello, J., LeBihan, D.: MR diffusion tensor spectroscopy and imaging. Biophys. J. **66**(1), 259–267 (1994)
2. Brandt, J., Cabrelli, C., Molter, U.: An algorithm for the computation of the Hutchinson distance. Inform. Process. Lett. **40**, 113–117 (1991)
3. Bihan, D.L., Breton, E., Lallemand, D., Grenier, P., Cabanis, E., Laval-Jeantet, M.: MR imaging of intravoxel incoherent motions: application to diffusion and perfusion in neurological disorders. Radiology **161**, 401–407 (1986)
4. Cabrelli, C.A., Molter, U.M.: The Kantorovich metric for probability measures on the circle. J. Comput. Appl. Math. **57**, 345–361 (1995)
5. Goldluecke, B., Strekalovskiy, E., Cremers, D.: The natural vectorial total variation which arises from geometric measure theory. SIAM J. Imaging Sci. **5**(2), 537–563 (2012)
6. Johansen-Berg, H., Behrens, T.E.J.: Diffusion MRI: From Quantitative Measurements to In-Vivo Neuroanatomy, 1st edn. Academic, New York (2009)

7. Malcolm, J.G., Shenton, M.E., Rathi, Y.: Neural tractography using an unscented kalman filter. In: Prince, J.L., Pham, D.L., Myers, K.J. (eds.) IPMI 2009. LNCS, vol. 5636, pp. 126–138. Springer, Heidelberg (2009)
8. Kunze, H., La Torre, D., Mendivil, F., Vrscay, E.R.: Fractal-Based Methods in Analysis. Springer, Heidelberg (2012)
9. La Torre, D., Vrscay, E.R., Ebrahimi, A., Barnsley, M.: Measure-valued images, associated fractal transforms, and the affine self-similarity of images. SIAM J. Imaging Sci. **2**(2), 470–507 (2009)
10. Michailovich, O., La Torre, D., Vrscay, E.R.: Function-valued mappings, total variation and compressed sensing for diffusion MRI. In: Campilho, A., Kamel, M. (eds.) ICIAR 2012, Part II. LNCS, vol. 7325, pp. 286–295. Springer, Heidelberg (2012)
11. Mendivil, F.: Computing the Monge-Kantorovich distance. Comp. Appl. Math. (2016, to appear)
12. Brion, V., Poupon, C., Ri, O., Aja-Fernandez, S., Tristan-Vega, A., Mangin, J.F., Le Bihan, D., Poupon, F.: Noise correction for HARDI and HYDI data obtained with multi-channel coils and sum of squares reconstruction: An anisotropic extension of the LMMSE. Magn. Reson. Imaging **31**, 1360–1371 (2013)
13. Callahan, P.T.: Principles of Nuclear Magnetic Resonance Microscopy. Clarendon Press, Oxford (1991)
14. Strong, D., Chan, T.: Edge-preserving and scale-dependent properties of total variation regularization. Inverse Prob. **19**, 165–187 (2003)
15. Wedeen, V.J., Hagmann, P., Tseng, W.-Y., Reese, T.G., Weisskoff, R.M.: Mapping complex tissue architecture with diffusion spectrum magnetic resonance imaging. Magn. Reson. Med. **54**, 1377–1386 (2005)

Image Quality Assessment

Quality Assessment of Spectral Reproductions: The Camera's Perspective

Steven Le Moan[(✉)]

The Norwegian Colour and Visual Computing Laboratory,
NTNU in Gjøvik, Gjøvik, Norway
steven.lemoan@gmail.com

Abstract. This study introduces a computationally efficient framework to measure the difference between two reflectance spectra in terms of how an arbitrary RGB camera can distinguish between them under an arbitrary light source. Given one set of selected illuminants and one of selected camera models (red, green and blue sensors' spectral responses), results indicate that both sets can be reduced in order to alleviate the computational load of the task while losing little accuracy in measurements.

Keywords: Spectral reproduction · Spectral printing · Illuminant · Camera model

1 Introduction

Imagine looking at two paintings, seemingly identical under the light of day. One is an original, the other is a printed reproduction. Chances are, although they produce the same color sensation under that particular light, there exist other illuminants under which they appear different to the human eye. This is due to the fact that the reflectances of the original painting's pigments are almost impossible to reproduce exactly with common printing technologies and only an approximation can be obtained. As long as it allows for a good match under a standard illuminant such as CIED50 (daylight), this approximation is usually considered as acceptable [14]. Nevertheless, a variety of applications require that the reproduction matches the original under more than just one illuminant (replication of artwork, security printing, catalogues, camera calibration,...). For *spectral* reproduction (as opposed to *colorimetric*), the match between two reflectances is usually computed by means of a purely computational measure such as the Mean Square Error (MSE) [3]. Incidentally, the quality of a reproduction can only be assessed with respect to the application in which it will be used. For instance if the reproduced painting needs only to *look* like the original, the aim is then to mimic human perception. In that case, the MSE conveys very little meaning and a more perceptually-driven approach is needed [10].

This work was supported by the Research Council of Norway.

A. Campilho and F. Karray (Eds.): ICIAR 2016, LNCS 9730, pp. 141–147, 2016.
DOI: 10.1007/978-3-319-41501-7_16

If the goal is instead that both paintings should produce the same signal when captured by an RGB camera, quality needs to be measured in different terms. One approach is to check whether an arbitrary camera can distinguish between them under an arbitrary light source. If it cannot, then the reproduced painting is perfectly identical to the original as far as the camera is concerned. Similarly, applications pertaining to the calibration of RGB cameras with a printed color target (e.g. for jaundice detection in newborns [5]) also need to rely on such measure of *spectral fidelity* for reliability. There are however two main challenges underlying this approach: defining an "arbitrary light source" and an "arbitrary camera".

To overcome the first challenge, a method was recently introduced [10] to measure the perceived quality of a spectral reproduction in terms of perception and for a given set of more than 70 light sources of various kinds, in a manner that does not require to estimate and compare the color sensations produced under each of these sources. It was showed indeed that it is sufficient to compute the color sensation under one or two representative light source(s) to accurately measure the perceived difference between original and reproduction under any light from the set. As for the second challenge, Jiang *et al.* showed [7] that the spectral sensitivities of a group of 28 cameras can be well represented with only two sets of responses. Here I combine both methods to reduce the computational load of spectral fidelity assessment.

In the remainder of this paper, I first define a measure of spectral fidelity for a single-illuminant and single-camera configuration. I then tackle the problem of considering multiple illuminants and multiple cameras and demonstrate in particular that the results of the measure obtained from a set of 40 illuminants and 28 cameras can be well approximated by using only one representative illuminant and one representative camera.

2   A Measure of Spectral Image Quality for RGB Cameras

2.1   One Illuminant, One Camera

A spectral reproduction has perfect quality with respect to human perception if it is indistinguishable from the original under an arbitrary light source [10]. I propose to use the same definition for camera acquisition. Whereas human perception of color difference can be modeled by means of device-independent representations such as CIELAB or the more recent LAB2000HL [11], a camera needs only two stimuli to produce a different signal to distinguish between them. Whether two different radiances γ_1 and γ_2 will produce the same values in the camera's RGB space depend mostly on the spectral sensitivity of the camera's sensors, noted $\mathbf{S} = [\mathbf{r}, \mathbf{g}, \mathbf{b}]$ (where $\mathbf{r}$, $\mathbf{g}$ and $\mathbf{b}$ are column vectors of size N, representing respectively the sensor responses for its red, green and blue channels). The bit depth (precision) with which the stimulus is encoded, also plays an important role, however no significant difference was found between depths of 16 and 8 bits in these experiments. Most cameras working in this range, bit depth seems to not be an influential parameter here. If two input stimuli give the same RGB triplet, no matter how the RAW image (i.e. the direct response of the camera to the scene's radiance) is normalized to the final (typically sRGB) image, the discriminative information is lost during the acquisition process. On the other hand, when the produced signal are different, there is a way to distinguish between the two radiances with the camera. This is an all-or-nothing situation: either the camera can capture the discriminative information or not. Note that using some kind of distance measure (e.g. Euclidean) between RGB triplets in the camera's space could potentially give further indications as to the difference between them. However it would be difficult to assess the significance of such color differences without further information about how the RAW image would be further processed.

Assuming that γ_1 and γ_2 are the combination of a single light source **i** with two different reflectances $\mathbf{r_1}$ and $\mathbf{r_2}$ ($\gamma_1 = \mathbf{r_1} \odot \mathbf{i}$ and $\gamma_2 = \mathbf{r_2} \odot \mathbf{i}$, where $\odot$ denotes the entrywise product, also known as Hadamard product), and that $\mathbf{r_2}$ is a reproduction of $\mathbf{r_1}$, the colorimetric fidelity of the former with respect to the latter with respect to **i** is then either null or perfect (0 or 1). Note that this fidelity can alternatively be referred to as the *difference* between the two spectra. I define the *single Camera-measured Color Difference* (sCCD) between $\mathbf{r_1}$ and $\mathbf{r_2}$, under illuminant **i** and for camera σ as follows:

$$\mathrm{sCCD}_{\mathbf{i},\sigma}(\mathbf{r_1};\mathbf{r_2}) = f\left((\mathbf{r_1} \odot \mathbf{i})\,\mathbf{S}_\sigma; (\mathbf{r_2} \odot \mathbf{i})\,\mathbf{S}_\sigma\right) \tag{1}$$

where

$$f(x;y) = \begin{cases} 1, & \text{if } x = y. \\ 0, & \text{otherwise.} \end{cases} \tag{2}$$

and $\mathbf{r_1}$, $\mathbf{r_2}$ and **i** are row vectors of size N and $\mathbf{S}_\sigma$ is the set of spectral responses of camera σ.

2.2   Several Illuminants, Several Cameras

Given a set Θ of spectral power distributions of important light sources, and given a set Υ of spectral responses of different RGB cameras[1], I define the *multiple Camera-measured Spectral Difference* (mCSD) between $\mathbf{r_1}$ and $\mathbf{r_2}$ as the proportion of combinations illuminants/camera for which the reflectances are distinguishable:

$$\mathrm{mCSD}_{\Theta,\Upsilon}(\mathbf{r_1};\mathbf{r_2}) = \frac{1}{|\Upsilon|} \sum_{\sigma \in \Upsilon} \left[\frac{1}{|\Theta|} \sum_{\mathbf{i} \in \Theta} \mathrm{sCCD}_{\mathbf{i},\sigma}(\mathbf{r_1};\mathbf{r_2}) \right] \tag{3}$$

However, computing every single $\mathrm{sCCD}_{\mathbf{i},\sigma}(\mathbf{r_1};\mathbf{r_2})$ can represent a significant computational burden if many reflectances are to be compared, for instance when

---

[1] Note that this framework stands for cameras with any number of channels.

performing (or optimizing [12]) spectral gamut mapping for a whole multispectral image. In a previous work [10], it was demonstrated that Θ can be well represented by means of one or two representative illuminants when measuring spectral fidelity in terms of perception. Here, I propose a similar approach to approximate $\mathrm{mCSD}_{\Theta,\Upsilon}(\mathbf{r_1}; \mathbf{r_2})$ and suggest that both the illuminants and cameras sets can be reduced to improve the computational efficiency of the metric, such that:

$$\mathrm{mCSD}_{\Theta,\Upsilon}(\mathbf{r_1}; \mathbf{r_2}) \approx \mathrm{mCSD}_{\Theta',\Upsilon'}(\mathbf{r_1}; \mathbf{r_2}) = \frac{1}{|\Upsilon'|} \sum_{\sigma \in \Upsilon'} \left[\frac{1}{|\Theta'|} \sum_{i \in \Theta'} \mathrm{sCCD}_{i,\sigma}(\mathbf{r_1}; \mathbf{r_2}) \right]$$

$$(4)$$

where Υ' and Θ' are respectively the reduced (and representative) sets of cameras and illuminants, with $|\Upsilon'| << |\Upsilon|$ and/or $|\Theta'| << |\Theta|$.

In order to compute the reduced sets, two approach were considered: Principal Component Analysis (selection of the K components with highest eigenvalues) as well as the average of the set, as suggested recently in [8]. Note that in the case of Υ', these reduction methods are performed on the red, green and blue sets of sensitivity functions separately (i.e. the average of Υ would consist of three average functions). In the next section, $\mathrm{mCSD}_{\Theta,\Upsilon}(\mathbf{r_1}; \mathbf{r_2})$ and $\mathrm{mCSD}_{\Theta',\Upsilon'}$ are compared in different configurations.

3   Experimental Results

3.1   Data

These experiments were performed using the representative Standard Object Colour Spectra (SOCS) database [13] as testing data. For each reflectance in that database, two spectral reproductions were created [9]:

- The pseudo-inverse 31-channels reconstruction from a simulated 6-channel filter wheel camera.
- The reconstruction from the LabPQR interim connection space [4].

In both cases, training (respectively of the pseudo-inverse tranform and PQR basis), was performed using spectral measurements of the 1269 Munsell matte colour chips from the University of Joensuu's spectral database [6]

Additionally, I used a collection of 40 illuminants' spectral power distributions noted Θ_{All}, made of four equally-sized subgroups: 10 daylights (Θ_{Day}), 10 tungsten lights (Θ_{Tun}), 10 fluorescent lights (Θ_{Fluo}) and 10 LED lights (Θ_{LED}). These illuminants were selected randomly from the National Gallery's set [2] as well as from the University of Eastern Finland's daylights set [1] and the CIE standard illuminants. They were all normalized to have a maximal value of 1.

For modeling RGB cameras, I used the database of spectral sensitivities made available by Jiang et al. [7]. It consists of 28 cameras: 9 Canon, 10 Nikon and 9 of other brands. Two different bit depths were simulated (8 and 16 bits) by reducing the precision of the result of the application of these sensitivities to the radiances obtained from the aforementioned sets of reflectances and illuminants. Note that all computations were made in double precision. However, no significant changes were observed between results at these two depths.

3.2 Methodology

In order to evaluate how $mCSD_{\Theta',\Upsilon'}$ can approximate $mCSD_{\Theta,\Upsilon}(r_1; r_2)$, I computed the score given by each of them on every pair original/reproduction (original r_1 from SOCS and reproductions r_2 as described above) and measured the Pearson correlation coefficient ρ between the two sets of results. A high correlation means that the reduced set approximates well the full set for the application under consideration.

3.3 Results

Table 1 give the results obtained. I note K_σ and K_i the number of principal components extracted to represent Υ and Θ, respectively.

Table 1. Pearson's correlation coefficients ρ between $mCSD_{\Theta,\Upsilon}$ and $mCSD_{\Theta',\Upsilon'}$.

Υ' (V) Θ' (>)	PCA $K_i = 1$	PCA $K_i = 2$	PCA $K_i = 3$	Average i	All illuminants
PCA $K_\sigma = 1$	0.90	0.98	0.98	0.84	0.97
PCA $K_\sigma = 2$	0.97	0.99	0.98	0.95	0.98
PCA $K_\sigma = 3$	0.96	0.98	0.98	0.92	0.96
Average σ	0.90	0.98	0.98	0.95	0.95
All cameras	0.88	0.96	0.99	0.95	1

These results suggest that it is indeed possible to alleviate the tedious computation of $mCSD_{\Theta,\Upsilon}$ by drastically reducing the size of the sets of illuminants and camera sensitivities. Even reducing the size of both sets to one (i.e. one representative illuminant and one representative set of RGB spectral sensitivities) yields scores which are highly correlated ($\rho = 0.90$) to those of $mCSD_{\Theta,\Upsilon}$. Note, however, that the number of selected Principal Components influences the number of $sCCD_{i,\sigma}(r_1; r_2)$ values to compute an average of, with Eq. (4). If only one component is extracted from both sets for instance, the resulting score corresponds to a difference based on *one* representative camera and under *one* representative illuminant which, as described before, can either be 0 (the reflectances are distinguishable) or 1 (the reflectances are not distinguishable). This implies that the smaller the size of Θ' and Υ', the coarser the scale of possible spectral fidelity scores.

Interestingly, it seems easier to represent Υ than Θ as using the first PC of Υ and all of Θ yields a correlation of 0.97 versus 0.88 in the dual case (first PC of Θ and all of Υ). Also, note that increasing K_σ does not necessarily increase ρ

as the values for $K_\sigma = 3$ are systematically smaller than those for $K_\sigma = 2$. This suggests that, despite the fact that PCA permits to obtain results that correlate to a very large extent to those of mCSD$_{\Theta,\Upsilon}$, other dimensionality reduction approaches may be more appropriate to reduce the size of Υ in this context.

4   Conclusion and Future Work

I presented a computationally efficient framework to measure the difference between two reflectance spectra in terms of how an arbitrary RGB camera can distinguish between them under an arbitrary illuminant. Results indicate that it is not necessary to compute the signals produced by the reflectances in all the cameras RGB spaces and under all illuminants considered. Future work on this topic will include the investigation of other means to measure a camera's sensitivity to a difference between two radiances, particularly in the presence of noise. Other methods to reduce the dimensionality of the sets of cameras and illuminants should also be considered.

References

1. Daylight spectra, university of Eastern Finland (2016). http://cs.joensuu.fi/~spectral/databases/download/daylight.htm. Accessed 23 April 2016
2. Spectral power distribution curves, the national gallery (2016). http://research.ng-london.org.uk/scientific/spd/. Accessed 23 April 2016
3. Bakke, A.M., Farup, I., Hardeberg, J.Y.: Multispectral gamut mapping and visualization-a first attempt. In: SPIE, vol. 5667, pp. 193–200 (2005)
4. Derhak, M., Rosen, M.: Spectral colorimetry using LabPQR: an interim connection space. J. Imaging Sci. Tech. **50**(1), 53–63 (2006)
5. de Greef, L., Goel, M., Seo, M.J., Larson, E.C., Stout, J.W., Taylor, J.A., Patel, S.N.: Bilicam: using mobile phones to monitor newborn jaundice. In: Proceedings of the 2014 ACM International Joint Conference on Pervasive and Ubiquitous Computing, pp. 331–342. ACM (2014)
6. Hiltunen, J.: Munsell colors matt (spectrophotometer measured) (2016). https://www2.uef.fi/fi/spectral/munsell-colors-matt-spectrofotometer-measured. Accessed 23 April 2016
7. Jiang, J., Liu, D., Gu, J., Susstrunk, S.: What is the space of spectral sensitivity functions for digital color cameras?. In: 2013 IEEE Workshop on Applications of Computer Vision (WACV), pp. 168–179. IEEE (2013)
8. Le Moan, S., Blahová, J., Urban, P., Norberg, O.: Five dimensions for spectral colour management. J. Imaging Sci. Tech. **60** (2016). (To be published)
9. Le Moan, S., George, S., Pedersen, M., Blahová, J., Hardeberg, J.Y.: A database for spectral image quality. In: SPIE/IS&T Electronic Imaging, p. 93960 (2015)
10. Le Moan, S., Urban, P.: Image-difference prediction: from color to spectral. IEEE Trans. Image Process. **23**(5), 2058–2068 (2014)
11. Lissner, I., Urban, P.: Toward a unified color space for perception-based image processing. IEEE Trans. Image Process. **21**(3), 1153–1168 (2012)
12. Preiss, J., Fernandes, F., Urban, P.: Color-image quality assessment: from prediction to optimization. IEEE Trans. Image Process. **23**(3), 1366–1378 (2013)

13. Technical Committee ISO/TC 130, Graphic technology: ISO/TR 16066: Standard object colour spectra database for colour reproduction evaluation (SOCS). Technical report (2003)
14. Urban, P., Berns, R.S.: Paramer mismatch-based spectral gamut mapping. IEEE Trans. Image Process. **20**(6), 1599–1610 (2011)

An Image Database for Design and Evaluation of Visual Quality Metrics in Synthetic Scenarios

Christopher Haccius and Thorsten Herfet[✉]

Telecommunications Lab, Saarland University, 66123 Saarbrücken, Germany
{haccius,herfets}@nt.uni-saarland.de

Abstract. This paper presents a new image database which provides images for evaluation and design of visual quality assessment metrics. It contains 1688 images, 8 reference images, 7 types of distortions per reference image and 30 distortions per type and reference. The distortion types address image errors arising in visual compositions of real and synthetic content, thus provide a basis for visual quality assessment metrics targeting augmented and virtual reality content. In roughly 200 subjective experiments over 17.000 evaluations have been gathered and Mean Opinion Scores for the database have been obtained. The evaluation of several existing and widely used quality metrics on the proposed database is included in this paper. The database is freely available, reproducible and extendable for further scientific research.

Keywords: Synthetic Image Database · Subjective quality

1 Introduction

Subjective image quality assessment is essential in several areas of image processing and coding, where a person represents the final content consumer. The best way to obtain a measure of image quality is given by a subjective survey including numerous human assessors. This approach, however, is expensive with respect to time and money. Research has been dedicated to reduce the effort requirements for image evaluations, and algorithms have been designed to automatically predict visual quality. Existing quality metrics already offer good solutions for automatic image quality analysis. For design and evaluation of such metrics large subjectively evaluated datasets are essential.

Several image databases that are designed exactly for the purpose of design and evaluation of image quality metrics already exist (see Sect. 2). However image databases as well as image quality metrics have considered only image distortions that impact an image during capture or processing steps. With the advance of synthetic contents in augmented and virtual reality scenarios we observe a new class of image distortions. This novel distortions are due to errors occurring during the scene composition, before rendering.

In this paper we propose a novel image database that covers scene composition errors as well as capture and coding distortions. Our proposed database

© Springer International Publishing Switzerland 2016
A. Campilho and F. Karray (Eds.): ICIAR 2016, LNCS 9730, pp. 148–153, 2016.
DOI: 10.1007/978-3-319-41501-7_17

Table 1. Comparison of existing and our proposed Image Databases

	LIVE	TID	ESPL	SID
# of reference images	29	25	25	8
# of distortions	5	24	5	7
# of test images	1000	3000	525	1680
# of assessments	30.000	250.000	25.000	17.000
# of assessments per image	20–30	350	50	10
# of error assessments	100	1.000	200	300

was subjectively evaluated, and can serve as a solid foundation for metrics design and evaluation. An evaluation of existing metrics on our database shows that current metrics are not designed for scene composition errors, but correlate well to the capture and coding distortions we have included in our database.

2   Related Work

The first widely used image database with image distortions is the LIVE Image Quality Assessment Database developed by Sheikh et al. in 2004, with a second release published in 2005 [1]. The LIVE Database features a variety of photos distorted by compression artifacts, white noise of varying standard deviations, Gaussian blur with kernels of varying size and artifacts created by a fast fading Rayleigh channel. In 2008 Ponomarenko et al. created the Tampere Image Database (TID) which was updated in 2013, now including 3000 distorted images created from 25 reference images with 24 different distortion types [2]. The 24 different distortion types include different kinds of additive noise, quantization-, compression- and transmission errors, blurs, intensity shifts, contrast and saturation changes. With the growing demand for image quality assessments of synthetic image contents the ESPL Synthetic Image Database was created by Kundu et al. in 2014 and updated in 2015 [3]. The ESPL Database covers image distortions comparable to the distortions introduced in LIVE and TID, but different to LIVE and TID the ESPL database uses synthetic images from animated movies and computer games instead of photos as reference images.

Table 1 gives a direct comparison of the main characteristics between LIVE, TID, ESPL and our proposed SID. While our database has less per-image evaluations than the other databases, due to the finer granularity of distortion levels we have more user assessments than LIVE and ESPL for the analysis of the effect of a certain error type on a given reference image.

3   Proposal for a Novel Image Database

Novel scene compositions cause new kinds of image errors. Core to these new image distortions are errors created by misplaced or misaligned synthetic objects

Fig. 1. Images with synthetic content for generation of synthetic errors

in 3D scenes. This motivates the use of fully synthetic scenes as reference scenes. Fully synthetic scenes come with the benefit of a complete ground truth scene description in three spatial dimensions, allowing the modification of individual objects, which is a necessary requirement for the creation of synthetic image errors. In addition to that synthetic scenes can be used to generate further data like depth maps. Here we focus on image errors caused by object transformations, which are translation, rotation and scaling in 3D space. We therefore propose the use of eight synthetic scenes (shown in Fig. 1). All of these scenes are publicly available and may be modified and redistributed. Central elements of the scenes, e.g. the car, bowling ball or alarm clock, can be modified by affine 3D transformations to simulate possible scene composition errors.

The aforementioned databases have some image distortions in common. These are compression artifacts, blur and Gaussian noise. For comparison reasons among the existing and novel databases we include these distortions into our database as well. Hence, we propose to deteriorate the reference scenes by seven different error sources, which are JPEG and JPEG2000 compression artifacts, blurring, Gaussian noise, object translation, object rotation and object scaling. All images are rendered at the same size of 1920×1080 pixels, representing a realistic rendering resolution for many currently used applications. Each of the image distortions is defined by a set of parameters. For each scene and each distortion we apply 30 different parameter choices, which are normally distributed with mean μ chosen such that a parameter equal to μ results in no error. Exemplary, for translation $\mu = 0$ results in the reference image, for scaling $\mu = 1$ leads to a duplicate of the reference image. The whole dataset consists of 8 reference images + (8 scenes $\times$ 7 errors $\times$ 30 parameters) = 1688 images. For each error image the parameter choices are recorded in an 'info'-file, which is available both in text- and in Matlab format.

4   Image Evaluation

Distorted images can be evaluated subjectively and by machines. Subjective evaluations are time consuming, but important for the design and verification of automatic evaluation algorithms. In order to develop and test image quality metrics on our proposed database, subjective quality scores had to be assigned

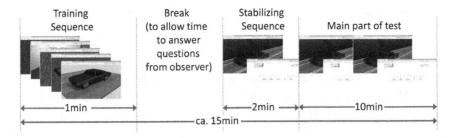

Fig. 2. Outline of experiment to gather assessor opinions

to the error images. Roughly 200 subjects have evaluated the images contained in our proposed database and from these evaluations MOS have been calculated.

Different ways to obtain assessor scores for information have been used and researched. Due to the number of test images and based on ITU recommendations [4] as well as a comparison conducted by Mantiuk et al. [5] we designed a single stimulus, hidden reference test which was made available over the internet. This internet-based test allowed access by many users all over the world, and at the same time enabled usage on display devices from smart phones to TV screens or projectors, thus covering a wide range of usage scenarios.

The structure of the experiment is outlined in Fig. 2. First, a training sequence presents the reference images to the assessor. In order to prohibit a direct relation between reference images and test images, user information (age, gender, kind of device used) are queried after the reference images are shown. In the second stage assessors go through a 2 min stabilizing sequence. This stabilizing sequence serves two purposes: First, assessors familiarize themselves with the task of image evaluations. Second, the range of image distortions (best and worst cases) are shown to the assessor to prevent cases where the lowest (or highest) score is assigned to an image, but a later observed worse (or better) image would require a more extreme score. The stabilizing sequence is followed by a 10 min main test sequence. Test images are presented iteratively for 3 s, followed by evaluation scales. The total experimental time therefore remains at roughly 15 min, which stays well inside the attention span of 30 min recommended by ITU-R BT.500-11.

For the MOS achieved in this experiment we calculated the least-square fit to an exponential curve as the ideal MOS based on the error parameter. Additionally, we have computed image quality scores using very different but widely used image quality metrics: Peak Signal to Noise Ratio (PSNR), Structural Similarity (SSIM) Index [6] and Visual Difference Predictor for High Dynamic Range Images (HDR-VDP-2) [7].

5   Evaluation and Conclusion

We have calculated rank correlations between the MOS scores obtained experimentally, our ideal MOS, PSNR metric, SSIM Index and HDR-VDP-2 Metric.

Table 2. Spearman-Correlation between MOS and existing metrics

	JPEG	Noise	Transformation	Classical	All
Ideal MOS	$\rho = 0.84$	$\rho = 0.88$	$\rho = 0.46$	$\rho = 0.81$	$\rho = 0.83$
PSNR	$\boldsymbol{\rho = 0.72}$	$\rho = 0.59$	$\rho = 0.31$	$\boldsymbol{\rho = 0.69}$	$\rho = 0.42$
SSIM	$\rho = 0.69$	$\boldsymbol{\rho = 0.64}$	$\boldsymbol{\rho = 0.36}$	$\rho = 0.67$	$\boldsymbol{\rho = 0.60}$
HDR-VDP 2	$\rho = 0.51$	$\rho = 0.56$	$\rho = 0.24$	$\rho = 0.52$	$\rho = 0.37$

Correlations are calculated for different error classes individually and for all distorted images together. Error classes are JPEG (including JPEG and JPEG2000), Noise (including Gaussian white noise and Gaussian blur), Transformation (including rotations, scalings and translations), Classical (superset of JPEG and Noise), and All (superset of all distortions). Table 2 gives Spearman's ρ [8] for the described correlations. The outperforming metric with respect to the calculated correlation measure for each error class is marked bold in both tables.

Three main observations can be made based on the analysis of our database and the corresponding MOS, PSNR, SSIM and HDR-VDP values. First, the correlation between MOS values and ideal MOS in Table 2 is significant enough to draw conclusions from the subjective experiments. Second, the correlation between MOS and ideal MOS is significantly smaller for the new transformation errors, which is intuitively clear as the mapping from three error parameters to a single error value does not necessarily correspond to the perceived error. Third, also for the analyzed quality metrics the correlation between MOS and computed quality in the correlation table is significantly smaller for transformation errors than for other error classes. Here, however, no error parameter is used, therefore the cause clearly are insufficient metrics. Figure 3 displays this observation for the PSNR metric: a visual evaluation already shows that PSNR and MOS are significantly more correlated for classical errors than for transformation errors.

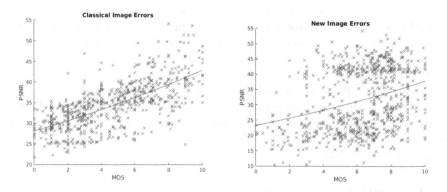

Fig. 3. PSNR vs MOS for Classical (left) and novel (right) Image errors

6   Access to SID2015 and Future Work

Our Synthetic Image Database is available for download from [9]. It contains all reference and test images accompanied by info-files which contain all necessary information to reproduce the images as well as the necessary synthetic sources. Additionally, we provide MOS scores for all images in a Matlab file.

A huge benefit of fully synthetic content over captured images is that further data can be produced. We provide Python scripts for Blender with our database that allow depth map and segmentation map rendering. We will continue subjective evaluations of the images and intend to update the database regularly with MOS values based on even more subjective tests. Furthermore, with the detailed descriptions of how to generate sample scenarios and distorted images, the database can be extended with further images and scenes that present interesting research scenarios for the research community.

The analysis of the available metrics and MOS data has shown that no tested metrics can cope with image distortions due to scene modifications before rendering. Addressing these and other novel image distortions which are becoming increasingly present due to new types of image contents will be an important task for future image quality assessment metrics.

References

1. Sheikh, H.R., Sabir, M.F., Bovik, A.C.: A statistical evaluation of recent full reference image quality assessment algorithms. IEEE Trans. Image Process. **15**(11), 3440–3451 (2006)
2. Ponomarenko, N., et al.: A new color image database TID2013: innovations and results. In: Blanc-Talon, J., Kasinski, A., Philips, W., Popescu, D., Scheunders, P. (eds.) ACIVS 2013. LNCS, vol. 8192, pp. 402–413. Springer, Heidelberg (2013)
3. Kundu, D., Evans, B.L.: Full-reference visual quality assessment for synthetic images: a subjective study. In: Proceedings of IEEE International Conference on Image Processing (2015)
4. International Telecommunication Union, Bt.500-11, methodology for the subjective assessment of the quality of television pictures. ITU-R Recommendation, BT (2002)
5. Mantiuk, R.K., Tomaszewska, A., Mantiuk, R.: Comparison of four subjective methods for image quality assessment. Comput. Graph. Forum **31**, 2478–2491 (2012). Wiley Online Library
6. Wang, Z., Bovik, A.C., Sheikh, H.R., Simoncelli, E.P.: Image quality assessment: from error visibility to structural similarity. IEEE Trans. Image Process. **13**(4), 600–612 (2004)
7. Mantiuk, R.K., Kim, K.J., Rempel, A.G., Heidrich, W.: HDR-VDP-2: a calibrated visual metric for visibility and quality predictions in all luminance conditions. ACM Trans. Graph. (TOG) **30**, 40 (2011). ACM
8. Spearman, C.: The proof and measurement of association between two things. Am. J. Psychol. **15**(1), 72–101 (1904)
9. Haccius, C., Herfet, T.: SSID-a synthetic image database (2016). http://www.nt.uni-saarland.de/SSID/. Accessed 29 Feb 2016

Perceptual Comparison of Multi-exposure High Dynamic Range and Single-Shot Camera RAW Photographs

Tomasz Sergej and Radosław Mantiuk[(✉)]

Faculty of Computer Science, West Pomeranian University of Technology,
Żołnierska 52, 71-210 Szczecin, Poland
rmantiuk@wi.zut.edu.pl

Abstract. In this paper we evaluate the perceptual fidelity of single-shot low dynamic range photographs of high dynamic range scenes. We argue that contemporary DSLR (digital single-lens reflex) cameras equipped with the high-end sensors are enough to capture full luminance range of the majority of typical scenes. The RGB images computed directly from the camera sensor data, called RAW images, retain the entire dynamic range of the sensor, however, they suffer from visible noise in dark regions. In this work we evaluate visibility of this noise in a perceptual experiment, in which people manually mark differences between a single-shot camera RAW image and a corresponding high quality image - the high dynamic range photograph created using the multi-exposure technique. We also show that the HDR-VDP-2 image quality metric can be efficiently applied to automatically detect noisy regions without the need for time-consuming experiments.

1 Introduction

A popular way to capture a photograph of a *high dynamic range* (HDR) scene using standard camera is to combine a number of photographs captured with different exposures [1]. This technique produces high quality HDR images, however it has a number of drawbacks. The photographed scene must be static and taken using tripod, otherwise ghosting and registration errors can appear. The multi-exposure technique suffers from the lens aberrations like flares or colour aberrations that distort the light signal coming from the scene [2].

The dynamic range of contemporary high end camera sensors is close to 13 f-stops. Interestingly, dynamic range of a typical natural scene is rarely greater than this range, so it is possible to capture these scenes with single-shot photographs. Even for more demanding scenes where dynamic range surpasses the capabilities of the camera sensor, it is perceptually acceptable to have small regions overexposed. For example we do not see details inside the small light bulb and do not expect that they will be seen in a photograph.

The essential problem of single-shot low dynamic range (LDR) photography of high dynamic scenes is noise visibility. To limit the overexposed areas to perceptually acceptable extent, the camera exposure parameters must be set to

© Springer International Publishing Switzerland 2016
A. Campilho and F. Karray (Eds.): ICIAR 2016, LNCS 9730, pp. 154–162, 2016.
DOI: 10.1007/978-3-319-41501-7_18

values that are inadequate to properly capture the scene's dark regions. As a result, in these dark areas the photon-shot noise dominates the signal, which is manifested by the perceptually visible noise (see an example in Fig. 1).

In this work we evaluate the visibility of this noise in the perceptual experiment, in which people manually mark local differences between a single-shot camera RAW image and a corresponding high quality image - the high dynamic range photograph created using the multi-exposure technique. As a results, we define the noise visibility for an average observer. Then, we test if the HDR-VDP-2 (high dynamic range visual difference predictor) image quality metric (IQM) [3] can be used to automatically detect the difference in noise visibility between RAW and HDR photographs. Difference maps created during the perceptual experiment are compared to the detection maps computed by HDR-VDP-2. This procedure, repeated for a number of scenes and observers, judges the efficiency of these objective metric in this very task. To the best of our knowledge, HDR-VDP-2 is the most reliable metric used to compare the high dynamic range images. However, in future work we plan to test other metrics like dynamic range independent IQM [4], or the Structural Similarity Index Metric [5].

The paper is organised in the following way. In Sect. 2 we briefly describe the multi-exposure HDR merging technique and the way in which we produced RGB photographs from the raw sensor data. Section 3 presents the perceptual experiment with local marking of the visible noise. In Sect. 4 we analyse the results of the experiment and compare the subjective results with the detection maps generated by the HDR-VDP-2 metric.

Fig. 1. Fragment of the Jewellery raw photograph (see the whole image in Fig. 3) with visible noise on the black card (left) and the same region cropped from the reference HDR photograph.

2   Background

2.1   Camera RAW

Digital camera sensors transform incoming photons into voltage output values. More precisely, these sensors are silicon-based integrated circuits including a dense matrix of photo-diodes that first convert photons into electric charge. Photons interact with silicon atoms generating electrons that are stored in a potential well. When the potential well is full, the pixel saturates, and no further electrons are stored. The number of photons impinging on the photo-diode during a given exposure time follows a Poisson distribution, as does the number of generated electrons stored in the potential well. The discrete nature of light that underlies this process results in the *photon shot noise*, which is visible in the regions of the sensor that captured an insufficient number of photons [6]. There are also other sources of the random noise generated during the camera acquisition process, like readout noise or thermal noise [7]. These sources additionally increase noise visibility and degrade the quality of photographs.

Most contemporary DSLR (digital single-lens reflex) cameras offer the ability to upload and store the raw sensor data as the CFA (colour-filter-array) image (called *Camera RAW*, or RAW). RAW advantage over the standard 8-bit RGB files is that it stores the luminance values with precision of the sensor photodiodes, which is 14-bit or more. Thus, the RAW images preserve higher dynamic range of the scene luminance. Contrary to the RGB photographs saved in e.g. JPEG format, the RAW data is not distorted by camera firmware, especially the noise is not reduced at the expense of decreasing the dynamic range.

2.2 Multi-exposure HDR Capture Technique

High dynamic range images can be captured using a sequence of LDR photographs of the same scene taken with different exposure using so called *multi-exposure technique* [1]. This technique allows to increase the dynamic range and to reduce the noise in an image. The goal of the method is to vary the exposure in order to control the light levels to be captured. By increasing the exposure time, low-light details will be represented well, at the cost of losing information in highly illuminated areas. On the other hand, decreasing exposure time will show the details in areas of high illumination. The sequence of photographs is then merged to create an HDR image containing the values approximately proportional to the luminance of a real scene. Under the assumption that the camera is perfectly linear, each photograph can be brought into the same domain by dividing each pixel by the exposure value and then merged by weighted addition.

In this work we used the multi-exposure technique to capture the reference high dynamic range images of the scene. For example for the Jewellery scene (see Sect. 3), we take 170 RAW photographs using all exposure time settings offered by the camera. Every exposure was captured 10 times to additionally reduce the noise. This conservative assumptions ensure proper representation of every scene region, no matter what it is dark or bright. As the RAW images are used for merging, the linear camera response function was assumed as the DSLR camera sensors are linear [8]. We applied a typical HDR merging technique based on the weighted summation of the pixel values from the consecutive frames. The box filter with 0.1 and 0.9 thresholds was used as the weighting function. We found this solution sufficient because a large number of captured photographs prevents inaccuracies.

We consider only the static scenes and stable camera position for the multi-exposure capture. Otherwise it would be necessary to compensate image misalignments [9], and remove ghosts and other artefacts from photographs [2].

2.3   HDR-VDP-2 Image Quality Metric

HDR-VDP-2 [3] is a perceptual metric that compares the reference (HDR image in our case) and test images (the camera raw image with potentially visible noise). It predicts the likelihood that the differences between the images are visible for average human observer. HDR-VDP-2 produces a *distortion map*, which tells how likely we will notice a difference between the two images. A unique feature of this metric is that it works with a full range of luminance values that can be found in the HDR images. Example detection maps generated by HDR-VDP-2 for Jewellery and Cathedral images are shown in Fig. 3 (bottom row).

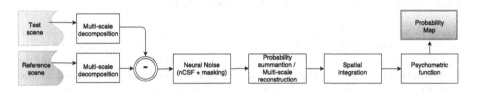

Fig. 2. The block-diagram of the HDR-VDP-2 operation.

The outline of the HDR-VDP-2 operation is presented in Fig. 2. During the multi-scale decomposition the reference and the test image is decomposed into four orientation bands and the maximum possible number of spatial frequency bands given the image resolution. This procedure uses the steerable pyramid to simulate the decomposition that is presumably made in the visual cortex. The differences in contrast detection are due to several sources of noise. HDR-VDP-2 modesl overall noise that affects detection in each band as the sum of the signal independent noise (neural CSF) and signal dependent noise (visual masking). All probabilities across all bands and orientations are summed to obtain the overall probability for all orientation and frequency selective mechanisms. The psychometric function is used to transform the contrast units after the probability summation and multi-scale reconstruction to yield the probability values. Larger patterns are easier to detect due to spatial integration which acts upon relatively large area. The spatially varying map is a result where every single pixel shows the probability of detecting a difference between images.

3   Experimental Evaluation

In the experiment, participants marked local differences between reference (HDR photographs) and test images (LDR photographs), creating a map of perceived noise caused by underexposure of the LDR photographs.

Stimuli. We captured a sequence of raw photographs of two high dynamic range scenes (see Fig. 3 (top row)). For the darkroom scene (we call it Jewellery), 90 photographs were taken at aperture f/16, ISO 100, and exposure time ranging from 1/4 to 68 s. For each exposure time we made 10 shots to further reduce the noise. For the scene Cathedral, 7 photographs were taken at aperture f/12, ISO 100, and exposure time ranging from 1 to 32 s.

Fig. 3. From left: the Jewellery and Cathedral high dynamic range photographs (the contrast domain local tone mapping [10] was used to visualise the scene details in the reproductions). The green squares depict fragments of the images evaluated in the perceptual experiment. Third and fourth image: detection maps generated by the HDR-VDP-2 metric for the Jewellery and Cathedral HDR scenes. Whiter pixels mean higher possibility of the perceivable differences. (Color figure online)

Our goal was to test a scenario where user takes an LDR photograph and wants to know whether there will be visible noise in the image. Therefore, the raw photograph chosen by the camera firmware as the best exposure was selected to be the test LDR photograph.

The HDR image was created using all shots from the Jewellery and Cathedral sequences. We replaced the under- and overexposed pixels with the minimum and maximum pixel values using the box filter (see details in Sect. 2). As we used only the raw photographs, the linear response function was assumed.

The raw images from the Canon 6D camera have resolution of 5472×3648 pixels. We did not reduce the image size because any low-pass filter could distort the noise visibility. Instead, only fragments of the full size photographs were evaluated by humans during experiment. These fragments of 900×900 pixel resolution are marked in Fig. 3 (top row) with green squares.

In the experiment we did not use the high dynamic range display, which would be the most suitable for perceptual evaluation of the high dynamic range scenes. However, we display the stimuli on the high quality LDR display with the brightness uniformity close to 1 %, and high accuracy of the colour reproduction (the sRGB colour profile was used). To avoid distortions that could be made by the tone mapping operator we apply only the linear tone mapping. For the scene Jewellery, we chose three levels of luminance: 10.10, 70.81, and 405.8 cd/m^2. The luminance of both the HDR and the LDR image of this scene was linearly scaled according to these values, i.e. all pixels of luminance equal to e.g. 70.81 cd/m^2 were set to 0.5 in the tone mapped image. The same procedure was repeated for the scene Cathedral, but for two different luminance levels: 62.36 and 764.28 cd/m^2. The aforementioned luminance values have been selected in such a way that the image fragments evaluated during experiment were correctly reproduced in at least one of the tone mapped images.

Procedure and Apparatus. We asked the participants to mark visible differences between the reference and test images. Observers used a custom brush-paint interface controlled by the computer mouse. The brush size could be reduced down to a single pixel. This procedure was repeated for every image fragment, resulting in 7 comparisons and finally 7 binary difference maps generated per observer. The experiment was performed in a darkened room. Images were displayed on 24 Eizo ColorEdge CG245W monitor with native resolution of 1920×1200 pixels. This display is equipped with the hardware colour calibration module and was calibrated before each experimental session to sRGB colour profile with the maximum luminance level increased to $200 \, \text{cd/m2}$. During the experiment, observers were sitting in front of the display at a distance of 65 cm (this distance was stabilised by a chin rest).

The photographs were taken using the Canon 6D camera with Canon EF 24-105 mm f/4L IS lens.

Participants. We repeated the experiment for 12 volunteer observers (age between 21 and 45 years (mean: 27.16, standard deviation: 7.71), 11 males and one female). They declared normal or corrected to normal vision and correct colour vision. The participants were aware that the image quality is evaluated, but they were naïve about the purpose of the experiment. While there were no time limitations to our study, the average subject finished in approximately 25 min.

3.1   Results

The goal of the experiment was to subjectively quantify the visibility of noise in the LDR photographs of the HDR scenes. The results were captured in the difference maps created by particular participants and then averaged over a number of observers.

Kendall Agreement. The experimental task of marking differences seems challenging, so the variation between observers is expected to be high. If the task turns out to be infeasible, we can expect to see little agreement in the difference maps produced by individual observers. To test the inter-observer agreement, we compute the Kendall rank correlation coefficient (or Kendall's tau (τ)), which is a statistic used to measure the association between two measured quantities. In our case, it assesses the similarity of the difference maps created by individual observers. As proposed by Čadík et al. [11], we used the τ value to assess whether participants marked similar areas for a given pair of test/reference images. The coefficient τ ranges from $\tau = -1/(o-1)$, which indicates no agreement between o observers, to $\tau = 1$ indicating that all observers responded the same.

We computed average coefficients $\bar{\tau}$ for each compared fragment. However, the results tend to be skewed toward very high values because most pixels did not contain any distortion and were consistently left unmarked by all observers. Therefore, we also compute a $\bar{\tau}_{masked}$, which considers only those pixels that were marked as distorted by at least two observers. We achieved $\bar{\tau}$ equal to 0.74 and $\bar{\tau}_{masked}$ to 0.28, averaged over all scenes. For comparison, in the similar experiment described in Čadíc et al. [11] and assumed as demonstrating a highly consistent outcome, the $\bar{\tau}$ and $\bar{\tau}_{masked}$ equaled to 0.78 and 0.41, respectively.

Difference Maps. Example difference maps created by two different observers are presented in Fig. 4 (top row). The black background shows untouched pixels while pixels marked by observer are drawn in grey, indicating the areas in the test image recognised as noisy by the human observer.

We averaged the difference maps over all observers to achieve the *reference difference maps*. These maps were binarised with the 0.5 threshold, i.e. the pixels marked by 50 % of observers were set to 1 and remaining pixels to 0. This thresholding gives reliable result during further statistical analysis, because it eliminates strong deviations in markings. Example reference difference maps are shown in Fig. 4 (bottom row). Please refer to supplementary material for the reference maps for all the images used during the experiment.

Fig. 4. From left: example difference map marked by the first observer, difference map created by the second observer, the reference difference map averaged over all observers and its binarised version with the 0.5 threshold. The maps correspond to the image fragments presented in Fig. 1.

4   Objective Noise Detection

Objective image quality metrics (IQMs) deliver quantitative assessment of the perceptual quality of images [12]. In this work we evaluate if the perceptual HDR-VDP-2 metric [3] can be used to detect perceivable noise in the camera raw images. More precisely, we assess whether the HDR-VDP-2 metric detects noise in a similar manner as human observers.

The key question is whether the HDR-VDP-2 generates the detection maps that are consistent with the reference difference maps achieved during the perceptual experiment. In the experiment, observers binary classified pixels that contained visible noise. The performance of such classification can be analysed using the receiver-operator-characteristic (ROC) [13]. More precisely, ROC captures the relation between the size of differences that were correctly marked by

HDR-VDP-2 (true positives), and the regions that do not contain the noise but were still marked (false positives). A larger area under the ROC curve (AUC) is assumed as better performance of HDR-VDP-2.

As a result of the perceptual experiment, we obtained the difference maps for 7 fragments of the evaluated raw photographs. These fragments were compared with the same regions cropped from the detection maps generated by HDR-VDP-2. The ROC plot for this comparison is presented in Fig. 5. The achieved AUC is equal to 0.68. This value is low as compared to the values typically reported for the HDR-VDP-2 metric. For example, Cadik et al. [14] reported AUC of 0.8 for the computer graphics artefact detection task, and Sergej et al. [15] AUC of 0.87 for the task of detection of the demosaicing artefacts. However, we obtained AUC value at an acceptable level and this lets us believe that the HDR-VDP-2 can reliably assess differences in the noise visibility between camera RAW and HDR images.

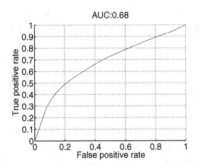

Fig. 5. Results of the ROC analysis for the HDR-VDP-2 metric.

5   Conclusions

In this work we attempt to evaluate the possibility of using a typical SLR camera with the low dynamic range sensor to capture a photograph of the high dynamic range scene. To do so, we merged sequences of the multi-exposure photographs of two example scenes into the high quality HDR images. Then, single-shot RAW images of the same scene were compared to this reference HDR. The perceptual experiment involving local marking the differences between images revealed that the RAW photographs are locally noisy and cannot be treated as a good reproduction of the high dynamic range scenes. The same findings have been confirmed by using the HDR-VDP-2 metric to compare the RAW image to the HDR reference.

Acknowledgements. The project was funded by the Polish National Science Centre (decision number DEC-2013/09/B/ST6/02270).

References

1. Mann, S., Picard, R.W.: On being undigital with digital cameras: Extending dynamic range by combining differently exposed pictures. In: Proceedings of IS&T, pp. 442–448 (1995)
2. Reinhard, E., Ward, G., Pattanaik, S., Debevec, P.: High Dynamic Range Imaging: Acquisition, Display, and Image-Based Lighting. Morgan Kaufmann Publishers Inc., San Francisco (2005)
3. Mantiuk, R., Kim, K.J., Rempel, A.G., Heidrich, W.: HDR-VDP-2: A calibrated visual metric for visibility and quality predictions in all luminance conditions. ACM Trans. Graph. **30**, 40:1–40:14 (2011)
4. Aydin, T.O., Mantiuk, R., Myszkowski, K., Seidel, H.P.: Dynamic range independent image quality assessment. In: ACM Transactions on Graphics (TOG), vol. 27, p. 69. ACM (2008)
5. Wang, Z., Bovik, A., Sheikh, H., Simoncelli, E.: Image quality assessment: From error visibility to structural similarity. IEEE Trans. Image Process. **13**, 600–612 (2004)
6. Foi, A., Trimeche, M., Katkovnik, V., Egiazarian, K.: Practical poissonian-gaussian noise modeling and fitting for single-image raw-data. IEEE Trans. Image Process. **17**, 1737–1754 (2008)
7. Kirk, K., Andersen, H.J.: Noise characterization of weighting schemes for combination of multiple exposures. In: Proceedings of the British Machine Vision Conference, pp. 115.1–115.10. BMVA Press (2006) doi:10.5244/C.20.115
8. Mantiuk, R., Krawczyk, G., Mantiuk, R., Seidel, H.P.: High dynamic range imaging pipeline: Perception-motivated representation of visual content. In: Human Vision and Electronic Imaging XII, Proceedings of the SPIE, vol. 6492 (2007)
9. Tomaszewska, A., Mantiuk, R.: Image registration for multi-exposure high dynamic range image acquisition. In: Proceedings of WSCG, pp. 49–56 (2007)
10. Mantiuk, R., Myszkowski, K., Seidel, H.P.: A perceptual framework for contrast processing of high dynamic range images. In: Proceedings of Applied Perception in Graphics and Visualization, pp. 87–94. ACM Press (2005)
11. Čadík, M., Herzog, R., Mantiuk, R., Myszkowski, K., Seidel, H.P.: New measurements reveal weaknesses of image quality metrics in evaluating graphics artifacts. ACM Trans. Graph. (TOG) **31**, 147 (2012)
12. Wang, Z., Bovik, A.: Modern Image Quality Assessment. Morgan & Claypool Publishers, New York (2006)
13. Baldi, P., Brunak, S., Chauvin, Y., Anderson, C.A.F., Nielsen, H.: Assessing the accuracy of prediction algorithms for classification: an overview. Bioinformatics **16**, 640–648 (2000)
14. Čadík, M., Herzog, R., Mantiuk, R., Mantiuk, R., Myszkowski, K., Seidel, H.P.: Learning to predict localized distortions in rendered images. Comput. Graph. Forum **32**, 401–410 (2013)
15. Sergej, T., Mantiuk, R.: Perceptual evaluation of demosaicing artefacts. In: Campilho, A., Kamel, M. (eds.) ICIAR 2014, Part I. LNCS, vol. 8814, pp. 38–45. Springer, Heidelberg (2014)

Objective Image Quality Measures of Degradation in Compressed Natural Images and their Comparison with Subjective Assessments

Alison K. Cheeseman[1,2], Ilona A. Kowalik-Urbaniak[1,3], and Edward R. Vrscay[1(✉)]

[1] Department of Applied Mathematics, Faculty of Mathematics, University of Waterloo, Waterloo, ON N2L 3G1, Canada
acheeseman@ece.utoronto.ca, ilona@clientoutlook.com, ervrscay@uwaterloo.ca
[2] The Edward S. Rogers Sr. Department of Electrical & Computer Engineering, University of Toronto, Toronto, ON M5S 3G4, Canada
[3] Client Outlook Inc., Waterloo, ON N2L 6B5, Canada

Abstract. This paper is concerned with the degradation produced in natural images by JPEG compression. Our study has been basically twofold: (i) To find relationships between the amount of compression-induced degradation in an image and its various statistical properties. The goal is to identify blocks that will exhibit lower/higher rates of degradation as the degree of compression increases. (ii) To compare the above *objective* characterizations with *subjective* assessments of observers.

The conclusions of our study are rather significant in several aspects. First of all, "bad" blocks, i.e., blocks exhibiting greater degrees of degradation visually, have among the lowest RMSEs of all blocks and among the medium-to-highest structural similarity (SSIM)-based errors. Secondly, the standard deviations of "bad" blocks are among the lowest of all blocks, suggesting a kind of "Weber law for compression," a consequence of contrast masking. Thirdly, "bad" blocks have medium-to-high high-frequency (HF) fractions as opposed to HF content.

1 Introduction

The study reported in this paper arose from a collaborative research program involving radiologists as well as a leading international developer of medical imaging software (AGFA Healthcare) [4]. Our goal has been to develop objective – as opposed to subjective – methods of assessing the degree to which medical images from various modalities and anatomical regions can be compressed before their diagnostic quality is compromised. There are two major motivations for this research: (1) To date, recommended compression ratios have been based on experiments in which radiologists subjectively assess the diagnostic quality of compressed images. Subjective experiments are labor-intensive and time-consuming (and therefore expensive). (2) Diagnostic quality is clearly related to visual quality. To date, however, radiologists have had to rely mostly on mean

© Springer International Publishing Switzerland 2016
A. Campilho and F. Karray (Eds.): ICIAR 2016, LNCS 9730, pp. 163–172, 2016.
DOI: 10.1007/978-3-319-41501-7_19

squared error (MSE) and its relative, PSNR, because of their prevalent use in the research literature. It is well known, however, that these measures provide poor assessments of visual quality. For this reason, it is necessary to examine whether more recent image fidelity measures, such as the structural similarity index (SSIM) [2], which are known to provide better assessments of visual quality, could be used in the assessment of diagnostic quality.

In [4], we examined the assessments of a number of image quality measures including SSIM and MSE/PSNR and how well they compared with subjective assessments of radiologists based on data collected in two experiments. Very briefly, SSIM provided the closest match to the radiologists' assessments whereas MSE and PSNR were observed to perform inconsistently.

Here it is important to mention that the above results were obtained from **global** analyses of the images, i.e., subjective assessments and objective measures of **entire images**. Generally, however, a radiologist will often judge a compressed image to be diagnostically unacceptable because of perceived degradations in certain regions or features. For this reason, we also pursued the much more ambitious problem of trying to predict which **local regions/features** of a medical image would demonstrate greater degrees of degradation, possibly the first to lose their diagnostic quality as the compression rate is increased.

Unfortunately, this aspect of the study was not conclusive. One problem was that much of our study at that time focussed on CT brain images which exhibit a rather low degree of variability in terms of structure, at least in the cortical region. Other regions of the body, e.g., the abdomen, which exhibit greater variability, did show some trends. This has led us to an examination of "natural images." e.g., the various (nonmedical) test images employed in the standard image processing literature.

As an illustration, in Fig. 1 below are plotted the degradations produced by JPEG compression of a subset (256) of all (4096) nonoverlapping 8×8 blocks of the standard 512×512 pixel, 8 bpp *Lena* image over the range of quality factors $100 \geq Q \geq 10$. Two different measures of degradation are shown in these plots: (a) MSE and (b) "DSSIM," a distance based on the SSIM measure, defined in Eq. (5) of Sect. 2. As expected, the degradation of blocks with respect to both measures generally increases as Q decreases. However, it is also quite clear that there is a great variation in the rates of degradation. Some blocks, which we shall refer to as "bad blocks", exhibit much higher rates of degradation than others, which we shall refer to as "good blocks."

There is an additional complication, however, in that blocks that are "bad" with respect to one measure, say, RMSE, are not necessarily "bad" with respect to the other. On the left of Fig. 2 are shown plots of the ordered measure pairs $(RMSE(Q), DSSIM(Q))$ for the selected 256 blocks over the range $100 \geq Q \geq 10$. On the right of this Figure is shown a plot of $RMSE$ vs $DSSIM$ errors for all 4096 8×8-pixel blocks of the $Q = 50$ JPEG-compressed *Lena* image. Both plots show that there is rather poor correlation between RMSE and DSSIM error measures. This, however, can be viewed quite positively: If MSE fails to detect "bad" blocks by characterizing them as "good", then DSSIM may

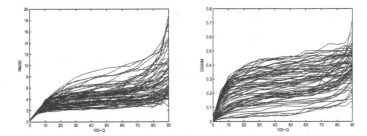

Fig. 1. Degradation vs. $Q' = 100 - Q$ for 256 8×8-pixel blocks of *Lena* image. **Left:** RMSE. **Right:** DSSIM. In both cases, the mean values are also plotted (in red). (Color figure online)

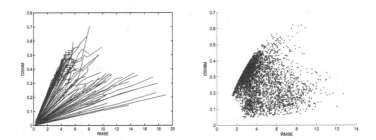

Fig. 2. Left: $RMSE(Q)$ vs. $DSSIM(Q)$ over the range $100 \geq Q \geq 10$ for the 256 8×8-pixel blocks of the *Lena* image. **Right:** $RMSE$ vs. $DSSIM$ errors for all 4096 blocks at $Q = 50$.

characterize them as "bad." In the end, these results must be compared with subjective assessments in order to verify that what is "bad" objectively is also "bad" visually. This is the subject of this preliminary study.

Some obvious questions arise from the above observations, e.g.,

1. What, if any, characteristics of blocks can be used to separate "bad" blocks from "good" blocks **for a given fidelity measure**? Previously we examined standard deviation, total variation, low- and high-frequency content.
2. What, if any, features can be used to characterize blocks that are "bad" with respect to one measure and "good" with respect to the other?
3. Which fidelity measure is **better visually**, i.e., which measure correponds better to human visual perception of degradation?

In our previous studies, none of the characteristics mentioned in Question 1 worked well. In this paper, we show that better indicators are (i) energy and (ii) high frequency **fraction** as opposed to **content**. We have also found that these indicators work equally well for JPEG2000 compression but this will have to be reported elsewhere.

2   Definitions of Important Quantities Used in This Paper

Here we let $\mathbf{x}, \mathbf{y} \in \mathbb{R}^{N \times N}$ denote two $N \times N$-dimensional image blocks, i.e., $\mathbf{x} = \{x_{ij}\}$ $1 \leq i, j \leq N$. In this study, $\mathbf{x}$ will usually represent a block of an uncompressed image and $\mathbf{y}$ the corresponding block of the compressed image. The mean squared error/distance (MSE) between $\mathbf{x}$ and $\mathbf{y}$ is given by

$$MSE(\mathbf{x}, \mathbf{y}) = \frac{1}{N^2} \sum_{i,j=1}^{N} (x_{ij} - y_{ij})^2 = \frac{1}{N^2} \|\mathbf{x} - \mathbf{y}\|_2^2, \tag{1}$$

where $\| \cdot \|_2$ denotes the usual Euclidean norm for $N \times N$ matrices. The root mean squared error/distance is

$$RMSE(\mathbf{x}, \mathbf{y}) = \sqrt{MSE(\mathbf{x}, \mathbf{y})} = \frac{1}{N} \|\mathbf{x} - \mathbf{y}\|_2. \tag{2}$$

Of course, $MSE(\mathbf{x}, \mathbf{y}) = 0$ if and only if $\mathbf{x} = \mathbf{y}$.

In this paper, the following form of the structural similarity index (SSIM) [2] between $\mathbf{x}$ and $\mathbf{y}$ is employed,

$$SSIM(\mathbf{x}, \mathbf{y}) = S_1(\mathbf{x}, \mathbf{y}) S_2(\mathbf{x}, \mathbf{y}) = \left[\frac{2\bar{\mathbf{x}}\bar{\mathbf{y}} + \epsilon_1}{\bar{\mathbf{x}}^2 + \bar{\mathbf{y}}^2 + \epsilon_1} \right] \left[\frac{2s_{\mathbf{xy}} + \epsilon_2}{s_{\mathbf{x}}^2 + s_{\mathbf{y}}^2 + \epsilon_2} \right], \tag{3}$$

where

$$\bar{\mathbf{x}} = \frac{1}{N^2} \sum_{i,j=1}^{N} x_{ij}, \quad s_{\mathbf{xy}} = \frac{1}{N^2 - 1} \sum_{i,j=1}^{N} (x_{ij} - \bar{\mathbf{x}})(y_{ij} - \bar{\mathbf{y}}), \quad s_{\mathbf{x}}^2 = s_{\mathbf{xx}}. \tag{4}$$

The small positive constants $\epsilon_1, \epsilon_2 \ll 1$ are added for numerical stability and can be adjusted to accommodate the perception of the human visual system (HVS).

Note that $-1 \leq SSIM(\mathbf{x}, \mathbf{y}) \leq 1$ and $SSIM(\mathbf{x}, \mathbf{y}) = 1$ if and only if $\mathbf{x} = \mathbf{y}$. $SSIM(\mathbf{x}, \mathbf{y})$ is a measure of the similarity between $\mathbf{x}$ and $\mathbf{y}$. In order to be able to make comparisons with the error measures, MSE and RMSE, it is convenient to define a SSIM-based error, or **dissimilarity measure**, as follows,

$$DSSIM(\mathbf{x}, \mathbf{y}) = \sqrt{1 - SSIM(\mathbf{x}, \mathbf{y})}. \tag{5}$$

Then $DSSIM(\mathbf{x}, \mathbf{y}) = 0$ if and only if $\mathbf{x} = \mathbf{y}$.

In the case that $\bar{\mathbf{x}} = \bar{\mathbf{y}}$, $S_1(\mathbf{x}, \mathbf{y}) = 1$. This is the case, or very nearly so, when $\mathbf{y}$ is a compressed version of $\mathbf{x}$. The DSSIM distance then becomes [1]

$$DSSIM(\mathbf{x}, \mathbf{y}) = \frac{1}{\sqrt{N^2 - 1}} \frac{\|\mathbf{x}_0 - \mathbf{y}_0\|_2}{\sqrt{s_{\mathbf{x}}^2 + s_{\mathbf{y}}^2 + \epsilon_2}}, \tag{6}$$

where $\mathbf{x}_0$ and $\mathbf{y}_0$ denote the zero-mean blocks,

$$\mathbf{x}_0 = \mathbf{x} - \bar{\mathbf{x}}\mathbf{1} \quad \mathbf{y}_0 = \mathbf{y} - \bar{\mathbf{x}}\mathbf{1}. \tag{7}$$

The $DSSIM(\mathbf{x}, \mathbf{y})$ distance in (6) is generated by a **weighted norm**. DSSIM is seen to penalize blocks $\mathbf{x}$ with lower variance.

Discrete Cosine Transform and JPEG Compression. We let c_{kl}, $0 \leq i, j \leq N - 1$, denote the coefficients of the standard DCT of $\mathbf{x} \in \mathbb{R}^{N \times N}$ [5]. Since this study is centered around JPEG compression, we consider the special case $N = 8$, where the DCT coeffients are conveniently arranged as an 8×8 array,

$$
\mathbf{c} = \begin{pmatrix} c_{00} & c_{01} & \cdots & c_{07} \\ c_{10} & c_{11} & \cdots & c_{17} \\ \vdots & \vdots & \ddots & \vdots \\ c_{70} & c_{71} & \cdots & c_{77} \end{pmatrix}. \tag{8}
$$

From Parseval's Theorem, $\|\mathbf{c}\|_2 = \|\mathbf{x}\|_2$. Now define the following counterdiagonal vectors of the DCT coefficients,

$$
\mathbf{d}_m = \{c_{kl}, \ k + l = m\}, \quad 0 \leq m \leq 14. \tag{9}
$$

We define the **low-** and **high-frequency content** of block $\mathbf{x}$ to be as follows,

$$
\|\mathbf{x}\|_{lc} = \left[\sum_{m=1}^{6} \|\mathbf{d}_m\|_2^2 \right]^{1/2}, \quad \|\mathbf{x}\|_{hc} = \left[\sum_{m=7}^{14} \|\mathbf{d}_m\|_2^2 \right]^{1/2}. \tag{10}
$$

Note that the DC coefficient $c_{00} = N\bar{\mathbf{x}}$ is omitted from the low-frequency content term since it is generally much greater in magnitude than the other DCT coefficients thereby masking their contributions. Moreover, c_{00} is virtually unchanged by compression. Also note that

$$
\|\mathbf{x}\|_{lc}^2 + \|\mathbf{x}\|_{hc}^2 = \|\mathbf{x}\|_2^2 - c_{00}^2 = \|\mathbf{x}_0\|_2^2 = (N^2 - 1)s_{\mathbf{x}}^2. \tag{11}
$$

We consider $\|\mathbf{x}_0\|_2$ to define the (reduced) energy of $\mathbf{x}$ and note that it is proportional to the standard deviation of $\mathbf{x}$. We also define the **low-** and **high-frequency fractions** of an image block $\mathbf{x}$ as follows,

$$
\|\mathbf{x}\|_{lf} = \frac{\|\mathbf{x}\|_{lc}}{\|\mathbf{x}_0\|_2} \quad \|\mathbf{x}\|_{hf} = \frac{\|\mathbf{x}\|_{hc}}{\|\mathbf{x}_0\|_2}. \tag{12}
$$

Note that by definition,

$$
\|\mathbf{x}\|_{lf}^2 + \|\mathbf{x}\|_{hf}^2 = 1. \tag{13}
$$

Equation (12) provides a more block-independent, hence compact, characterization of low- and high-frequency content than Eq. (10). A much better idea of the low-high frequency constitution of a block may be obtained by looking at the distribution of low-high fractions of blocks over the quarter circle $x^2 + y^2 = 1$, $0 \leq \theta \leq \frac{\pi}{2}$, as oppposed to low-high content over the first quadrant in $\mathbb{R}^2$.

Finally, because of space limitations, we omit a discussion of JPEG compression since it is a well-known procedure in image processing. The important idea of quantization of the DCT coefficients as determined by the quality factor

Q is discussed in many books, including [5]. Here we simply recall that JPEG compression exploits the fact that the magnitudes of coefficients in the counter-diagonals $\mathbf{d}_m$ generally decrease with m, being very small in the high-frequency region, i.e., $m \geq 7$. It essentially diminishes and, in many cases, removes, high-frequency DCT coefficients of low-magnitude.

3   Quantitative Measure of Compression-Induced Degradation of Image Blocks

We are primarily concerned with the RMSE and DSSIM distances between uncompressed and compressed (8×8-pixel) blocks and how they relate to various characteristics of the blocks, including standard deviation, total variation, frequency content and energy. For compactness of presentation, the presentation below is limited to the case of the *Lena* test image. The figures shown below are qualitatively quite similar to those obtained for many other standard "natural" test images, e.g., *Boat, San Francisco, Peppers*.

Because of space limitations, the figures below show degradation characteristics of subblocks of the *Lena* image compressed with JPEG at quality factor $Q = 50$. This represents a rather mid-range compression level which reveals general characteristics that are seen at both higher and lower compression rates.

In Fig. 3 are presented plots of RMSE and DSSIM errors between uncompressed and JPEG-compressed ($Q = 50$) blocks of the *Lena* test image vs. total variation (TV) of the uncompressed blocks. The left plot demonstrates a quite good correlation between RMSE and TV: blocks with low TV are "good" and those with high TV are "bad". Such a strong correlation is not observed for the DSSIM errors.

In Fig. 4 are shown plots of RMSE and DSSIM compression errors vs. the reduced energies/standard deviations $\|\mathbf{x}_0\|_2$ of the blocks. On the left, we see that blocks with the lowest energy exhibit lowest degradation in terms of RMSE, which is to be expected. The L^2 norms of the high-frequency bands $\mathbf{d}_m$ of these

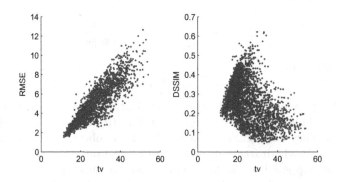

Fig. 3. RMSE and DSSIM distances between 4096 JPEG-compressed ($Q = 50$) and uncompressed 8×8-pixel blocks of *Lena* image vs. total variation of the blocks.

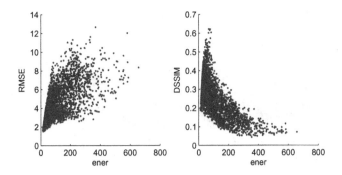

Fig. 4. RMSE and DSSIM distances between 4096 JPEG-compressed ($Q = 50$) and uncompressed 8×8-pixel blocks of *Lena* image vs. energy of the blocks.

blocks will be very small – as such, their removal by JPEG quantization will be virtually negligible. On the other hand, the DSSIM distances exhibit a roughly opposite behaviour – blocks with low energy exhibit a wide range of DSSIM errors, whereas blocks with high energy exhibit low DSSIM errors. This can be explained to a large extent by Eq. (6). These two plots provide a small possibility for separation of RMSE and DSSIM assessments of degradation.

In Fig. 5 are shown plots of RMSE and DSSIM compression errors vs. high-frequency content of the blocks, $\|\mathbf{x}\|_{hc}$ in Eq. (10). Plots of these errors vs low-frequency content, $\|\mathbf{x}\|_{lc}$ in Eq. (10), are virtually identical to the plots of errors vs. energy in Fig. 4 above since most of the energies of the blocks is contained in the low-frequency DCT coefficients.

The three sets of plots presented above show that there is a general correlation between RMSE and the characteristics of total variation (TV), energy (E) and high-frequency content (HC), with the last two being rather clear. Unfortunately, low RMSE does not necessarily imply that the degradations will not be noticed visually. The larger spread of DSSIM errors in the low TV, E and HC regimes

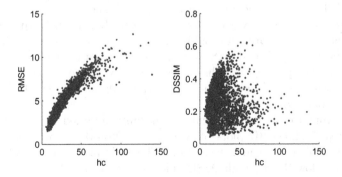

Fig. 5. RMSE and DSSIM distances between 4096 compressed and uncompressed 8×8-pixel blocks of *Lena* image vs. high-frequency content of the blocks.

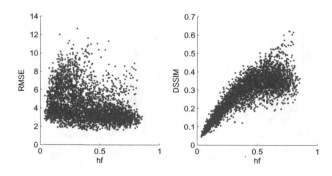

Fig. 6. RMSE and DSSIM distances between 4096 compressed and uncompressed 8×8-pixel blocks of *Lena* image vs. high-frequency fractions of the blocks.

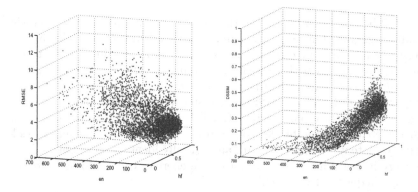

Fig. 7. RMSE and DSSIM distances between 4096 compressed and uncompressed 8×8-pixel blocks of *Lena* image vs. high-frequency fractions of the blocks.

indicates that not all blocks with low RMSE are necessarily visually equivalent, i.e., "good" in the sense of DSSIM.

Since JPEG compression generally removes higher-frequency DCT coefficients, it is natural to ask whether blocks with **higher high-frequency fractions**, as opposed to **content**, could exhibit greater **visual degradation**. In Fig. 6 are plotted RMSE and DSSIM compression errors vs. high-frequency fraction, Eq. (12). The plot at the right of this figure is very promising. It shows that that blocks with higher high-frequency fraction exhibit high DSSIM error but, for the most part, low RMSE.

Recall, from Fig. 4, the miniscule separability afforded by the energies of blocks. Figure 7 shows 3D plots of RMSE and DSSIM compression errors vs. both energy and high-frequency fraction. These 3D plots achieve a little more separability of low RMSE/high DSSIM blocks. Figures 4 and 6 represent projections of this 3D plot along in the "hf" and "en" directions, respectively.

4   Comparison with Subjective Evaluations

In order to determine whether the above exercise in separating RMSE and DSSIM assessments is valid visually, we have conducted a set of preliminary subjective experiments involving four individuals. Two images were used in this study, including the 512×512-pixel, 8 bpp *Lena* and *Peppers* images. Each image was JPEG-compressed at four different quality factors, $Q = 10, 15, 25$ and 35. This set of eight compressed images was presented to the subjects in random order several times. The subjects were asked to identify regions of the image that they assessed to be the most noticeably degraded, using an image viewer developed by Mr. Faerlin Pulido, at that time an undergraduate UW Computer Science student. The image viewer allowed the subject to toggle between the compressed image and the uncompressed original image. The subject was able to highlight rectangular regions of the image that he/she assessed as degraded. The coordinates of the blocks in these regions were then imported into MAT-LAB code for analysis. Our goal was to see how these subjectively-assessed "bad" blocks compared with blocks identified as "bad" by either DSSIM or RMSE. The results obtained by one subject for the *Lena* image compressed at $Q = 25$ are shown in Fig. 8. The results obtained from the other subjects are very similar to these results. Most noteworthy:

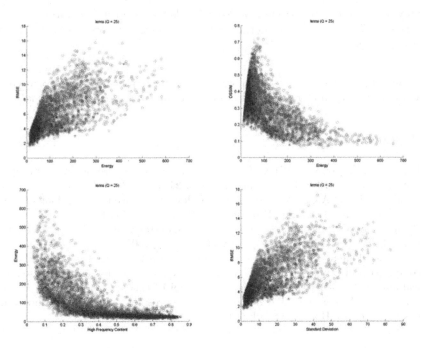

Fig. 8. Results of subjective analysis of JPEG-compressed *Lena* image at $Q = 25$. Red circles denote all 4096 8×8-pixel blocks of image. Blue dots indicate blocks identified by subject as degraded. (Color figure online)

1. The "bad" blocks identified by subjects as visually degraded had **low RMSE** errors and **medium-to-high DSSIM** errors.
2. The "bad blocks" corresponded to uncompressed blocks with **low energies** and **medium-to-high frequency fractions**.

Some interesting conclusions may be made from these features:

1. The fact that blocks with **low RMSE compression error were identified as "bad"** clearly implies that RMSE is **not** a good indicator of degradation.
2. The fact that "bad" blocks correspond to uncompressed blocks with low reduced energy/standard deviation, $\|\mathbf{x}_0\|_2$, indicates that a kind of **perceptual Weber law for compression** is at work here: For a given rate of compression distortions are more likely to be observed for blocks of lower variance. This is actually the principle of "contrast masking," see, e.g. [3].
3. The fact that "bad" blocks correspond to uncompressed blocks with medium-to-high frequency fraction is quite encouraging. It forces us to break away from the traditional RMSE-centered view that high frequency content is a sufficient criterion for the measurement of degradation.
4. The fact that "bad" blocks are characterized by medium-to-high DSSIM errors, as opposed to low RMSE errors, serves as strong evidence for the need for alternate image quality measures if visual quality is important.

Finally we mention that Comment No. 2 leads to the idea of a variance-based adaptive JPEG compression method which we have developed and which will be reported elsewhere.

Acknowledgements. This research was supported in part by a Discovery Grant (ERV) from the Natural Sciences and Engineering Research Council of Canada.

References

1. Brunet, D., Vrscay, E.R., Wang, Z.: On the mathematical properties of the structural similarity index. IEEE Trans. Image Process. **21**(4), 1488–1499 (2012)
2. Wang, Z., Bovik, A.C.: Mean squared error: love it or leave it? a new look at signal fidelity measures. IEEE Sig. Process. Mag. **26**(1), 98–117 (2009)
3. Wang, Z., et al.: Image quality assessment: from error visibility to structural similarity. IEEE Trans. Image Process. **13**(1), 600–612 (2004)
4. Kowalik-Urbaniak, I.A., et al.: The quest for "diagnostically lossless" medical image compression: a comparative study of objective quality metrics for compressedmedical images. In: SPIE Medical Imaging 2014. doi:10.1117/12:2043196
5. Rao, K.R., Hwang, J.J.: Techniques and Standards for Image, Video and Audio Coding. Prentice Hall, New York (1996)

Image Segmentation

Human Detection Based on Infrared Images in Forestry Environments

Ahmad Ostovar[✉], Thomas Hellström, and Ola Ringdahl

Department of Computing Science, Umeå University, Umeå, Sweden
{ahmado,thomash,ringdahl}@cs.umu.se

Abstract. It is essential to have a reliable system to detect humans in close range of forestry machines to stop cutting or carrying operations to prohibit any harm to humans. Due to the lighting conditions and high occlusion from the vegetation, human detection using RGB cameras is difficult. This paper introduces two human detection methods in forestry environments using a thermal camera; one shape-dependent and one shape-independent approach. Our segmentation algorithm estimates location of the human by extracting vertical and horizontal borders of regions of interest (ROIs). Based on segmentation results, features such as *ratio of height to width* and *location of the hottest spot* are extracted for the shape-dependent method. For the shape-independent method all extracted ROI are resized to the same size, then the pixel values (temperatures) are used as a set of features. The features from both methods are fed into different classifiers and the results are evaluated using *side-accuracy* and *side-efficiency*. The results show that by using shape-independent features, based on three consecutive frames, we reach a precision rate of 80 % and recall of 76 %.

Keywords: Human detection · Thermal images · Shape-dependent · Shape-independent · Side-accuracy · Side-efficiency

1 Introduction

Detecting presence of humans is crucial for both manned and autonomous forestry machines. Sometimes it is difficult for machine operators to detect humans due heavy occlusion and focus on other tasks, and it is valuable to have a reliable system that alerts the operator (or automatically stops the current operations) if humans are present close to the machine. For an autonomous machine, this functionality is even more important. In this paper, we present methods for detection of humans in forestry environments using a thermal camera. Whereas pixel values in images from an RGB camera represent color, pixel values in thermal images represent temperature. Using thermal images has both advantages and disadvantages compared with RGB images [1,2]. For example, shadows and lighting conditions do not affect the thermal images. On the other hand, the resolution of thermal images are often lower, and the texture of objects do not appear in thermal images.

© Springer International Publishing Switzerland 2016
A. Campilho and F. Karray (Eds.): ICIAR 2016, LNCS 9730, pp. 175–182, 2016.
DOI: 10.1007/978-3-319-41501-7_20

Similar to earlier works, regions of interest (ROIs) are first extracted by applying a segmentation method on thermal images such as thresholding based on pixel intensity, and then subject to human detection approach (shape-dependent or shape-independent) features for each ROI are generated [3–5]. Each ROI is then classified as containing or not containing a human by feeding the features into a classifier. We have developed and evaluated one shape-dependent and one shape-independent method. Shape-dependent methods are based on human characteristics [3,6] such as shape, height, length and location of the head [7,8]. Yasuno et al. [7] used the P-tile method for head detection. This method is based on the assumption that the object of interest covers a defined ratio of the image. As demonstrated by Bertozzi et al. [9] using lenient symmetry checks can filter out non-human objects by considering the assumption that humans are symmetrical objects. In our shape-dependent method, ratio of height to width and location of the hottest spot are used as features. Shape-independent methods typically use statistical characteristics of thermal images [1,5] as features. Fang et al. [5] used inertial similarity among ROIs to construct a set of features. Inertial of ROIs are based on the pixel brightness values and distance of a pixel to the center after size normalization. In our case all pixel values of the extracted ROIs are used as features.

The rest of the paper is organized as follows. After a description of image collection in Sect. 2, methods for extraction of regions of interest (ROIs) and the two proposed human detection methods are introduced in Sect. 3. The evaluation method is described in Sect. 4 and results are presented in Sect. 5 and discussed in Sect. 6.

2   Image Collection

For acquisition of data we used the *Optris PI200*[1] camera with spectral range of 7.5 to 13 μm. Images were collected at temperatures ranging from -10 to $+27\,°C$, with different amount of occlusion in forestry environments to simulate real working conditions. Furthermore, to consider changes in heat radiation [8] several persons walking and sitting at different distances from the camera and with different types of clothing were included. Totally 1135 thermal images were acquired[2] and then divided into 23 sets based on ambient temperature. Two sets were removed due to the amount of frames containing heavily occluded persons (more than 50 % of the human body). The reason for this occlusion was mainly that the snow was knee deep and all forestry objects were covered by snow, preventing human body heat radiation to reach the camera. In the remaining sets, 1042 thermal images were manually labeled such that if an image included a human, a region of interest was selected to cover the whole human body. 687 images included 754 humans and 355 of them contained only forestry objects and no humans.

---

[1] http://www.optris.com/thermal-imager-pi200, Optris Infrared Thermometers Products homepage, accessed 2015-11-15.

[2] https://archive.cs.umu.se/papers/2016-ThermalHumanDetection-AOstovar/, A selection of thermal images.

3 Human Detection

Detection of humans in the thermal images is done in two steps. In step one, regions of interest (ROIs) containing possible humans are identified. In step two, the ROIs are classified as human or non-human using two different methods, denoted *Shape-dependent* and *Shape-independent*, as described below.

3.1 Extracting Regions of Interest (ROIs)

To extract ROIs as rectangles in a thermal image, adaptive thresholds are first computed. Then vertical and horizontal borders are extracted. Given a thermal image tm, an initial threshold $t = \mu_{tm} + 2\sigma_{tm}$ is defined, where μ and σ are mean and standard deviation respectively, for all pixels in the image. Then an adaptive threshold $t_A = \mu_{tm>t} + \sigma_{tm>t}$ is computed, where μ and σ are computed for all pixels larger than t.

To define vertical borders of the ROIs, a vector $\mathbf{T}^{col}_{max}$ of max values for each column is created. Then, a binary vector $\mathbf{T}^{col}_{bin}$ is defined, with 1 for columns for which $\mathbf{T}^{col}_{max} > t_A$. In the next step, we detect crossings in $\mathbf{T}^{col}_{bin}$ from 0 to 1 and 1 to 0 to determine left and right borders of the ROIs.

The performed thresholding and also occlusion caused by objects or clothing, may result in regions of interest being split into several smaller segments (this problem has also been recognized in [8]). Therefore, segments are merged if the distance between them is smaller than half the size of the largest involved segment. Moreover, if within 80 pixel distance of a border, any value in $\mathbf{T}^{col}_{max}$ is greater than the average of $\mathbf{T}^{col}_{max}$, the border is extended to that point. The number of pixels which are considered for any extension possibility is not critical and varying this number would present similar results. Small segments are less likely to contain a nearby human and due to the low resolution of the thermal camera cannot be accurately detected. Therefore, segments smaller than five pixels are ignored. Horizontal borders are extracted in a similar way as the vertical borders, but only the part of the image that falls inside the generated vertical borders is considered in this operation. Figure 1 illustrates extracted ROIs in a thermal image including two humans.

The extracted ROIs are primarily used as input to the detection methods, but can in itself also be seen as a simple detection algorithm. Performance for this algorithm is presented in Sect. 5 and in Table 1.

3.2 Shape-Dependent Method

In this method, human characteristics including the ratio of height to width [3,6], and the location of the hottest spot (head) [7,8] in the ROI are extracted and used in a heuristically designed decision rule. To be classified as containing a human, the ratio of height to width must fall within the range of 0.8 to 1.8. These values are chosen as they are typical ratio for human in sitting and walking poses. A second requirement is that the hottest spot, presumable corresponding to the human head [7,10], is located in the upper third of the bounding box. Performance for this method is described in Sect. 5 and in Table 1.

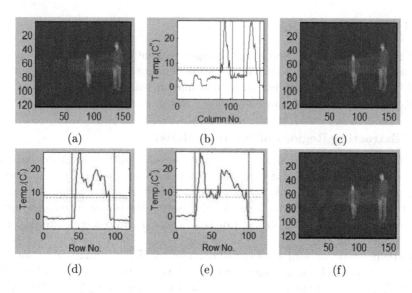

Fig. 1. Extracting ROIs. (a): A thermal image including two humans. (b): Vertical borders based on histogram of $\mathbf{T}_{max}^{col}$. (c): Vertical borders in thermal image. (d): Horizontal borders within the first vertical borders. (e): Horizontal borders within the second vertical borders. (f): Extracted ROIs. Red, green dashed and black lines are borders, adaptive threshold (t_A) and average of $\mathbf{T}_{max}^{col}$. (Color figure online)

3.3 Shape-Independent Method

In an initial step, the input ROI is resized to a fixed size of 25*35 pixels. These 875 pixels are input as features [1,5] to kNN, SVM and Naive Bayes classifiers. For kNN, k=5 is used. To further improve classification performance, the outcome of the three classifiers are fused by using majority voting. For each classifier, we combine classifications of three consecutive frames (frames 1 to 6 are considered) with majority voting. The assumption is that the location and poses of humans change slightly within consecutive frames, but the object of interest will still remain within the same extracted ROI. Images in the data set are collected with a rate of 10 Hz, thus, the maximum time difference between three consecutive frames is about 0.3 s. Performance for this method is presented in Sect. 5 and in Table 1.

4 Evaluation Method

To evaluate the developed algorithms, 21-fold cross validation has been used. Hence, classifiers are built using 20 data sets, and evaluated using the remaining set. The final performance values are the mean values from 21 such evaluations. Each extracted ROIs is compared with the ROIs that have been manually labeled as consisting a human. For a ROI to be regarded as correct it must overlap with a labeled ROI in the same image. Computation of overlap is based on the two concepts *side-accuracy* and *side-efficiency* as illustrated in Fig. 2, similar to performance indices introduced by Fang et al. [5]. Side-accuracy quantifies how much of the labeled ROI is covered by the extracted ROI, and is computed as the square root of the overlap area $S_{Overlap}$ divided by the area of the labeled ROI (S_{Human}). Side-efficiency quantifies how much of an extracted ROI is covered by the labeled ROI, and is defined as the square root of $S_{Overlap}$ divided by the area of extracted ROI (S_{ROI}). Both side-accuracy and efficiency are expressed as a percentage between 0 % and 100 %. In [11] it is suggested that both side-accuracy and side-efficiency should be greater than 50 % in order to avoid accepting ROIs that barely overlap a labeled ROI, and maybe do not even contain the object of interest in the overlap area.

Hence, an extracted ROI is regarded as a true positive (TP) if it overlaps a labeled ROI with both side-accuracy and efficiency greater than 50 %. Otherwise it is regarded as a false positive (FP). Also, an extracted ROI is considered as false positive if it is classified as human while there is no labeled ROI in the same image. If both side-accuracy and efficiency are greater than 50 % but the extracted ROI is classified as non-human then it is counted as false negative (FN). Performance is computed using precision and recall as defined in Eqs. 1 and 2. Precision represents the fraction of all extracted ROIs that are correct. Recall represents the fraction of all labeled ROIs that are extracted by the system.

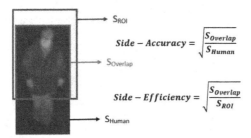

Fig. 2. Side-accuracy and efficiency definitions (adapted from [5]).

$$Precision = \frac{TP}{TP + FP} \tag{1}$$

$$Recall = \frac{TP}{TP + FN} \tag{2}$$

5 Experimental Results

In Table 1, cross-validated performance for four methods are presented and Table 2 demonstrates performance of shape-independent method based on different classifiers for one and three consecutive frames. The method for extraction

Table 1. Performance for algorithms for extraction of regions of interest (ROIs), the shape-dependent and the shape-independent method. Numbers in parentheses in the shape-independent method define the number of consecutive frames.

Performance	Precision	Recall
Extracted ROIs	59 %	84 %
Shape-dependent	79 %	38 %
Shape-independent (1)	80 %	74 %
Shape-independent (3)	80 %	76 %

Table 2. Performance of shape-independent method using SVM, kNN and Naive Bayes classifiers for one and three consecutive frames.

-	Shape-independent (1)		Shape-independent (3)	
Performance	Precision	Recall	Precision	Recall
SVM	80 %	75 %	82 %	79 %
kNN	80 %	70 %	80 %	73 %
Naive Bayes	75 %	65 %	75 %	66 %

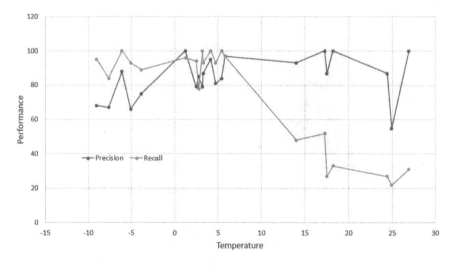

Fig. 3. Performance of shape-independent method based on ambient temperature. Recall is reduced in summer scenarios (higher temperatures than 10 °C) while precision shows more stability against higher temperatures. (Color figure online)

of ROIs is used to generate input for the detection methods, but has in itself a recall rate of 84 %, but only 59 % precision. This means that ROIs for 84 % of all humans are extracted, but also a lot of non-human ROIs are extracted. The shape-dependent method increases precision to 79 %, but the recall rate is reduced to 38 %. For the shape-independent method, precision is 80 % and recall 74 %. As presented in Table 2, the recall rate of the classifiers increased using three consecutive frames. Performance for the shape-independent method using three consecutive frames maintains the precision of 80 % and increases the recall to 76 %.

Performance is highly influenced by the ambient temperature. In Fig. 3, performance for the shape-independent method is plotted versus ambient temperature. Recall is reduced in summer scenarios with higher temperatures than 7 °C, while precision is roughly independent of temperature.

6   Summary and Discussion

The best results, precision 80 % and recall 76 % were achieved by the shape-independent method using three consecutive frames. This method uses majority voting combining a Naive Bayes classifier, kNN, and SVM. The performance for shape-dependent method was lower than for the shape-independent method. One reason for this could be that it is impossible to set parameters that cover all human poses. This was also noted by Fang et al. [5]. Considering three consecutive frames improved performance. It supports the hypothesis that small movements of a human between consecutive frames can be utilized to reduce the effect of occlusion and increase performance.

The ambient temperature and degree of occlusion directly affect performance of human detection using thermal images [2, 12]. For the 14 data sets with temperature below 7 °C, recall is above 80 % and precision above 60 % (see Fig. 3). In higher ambient temperature, objects other than humans produce additional bright areas in thermal images. These additional source of heat reduce the human detection performance based on pixel values of thermal images (shape-independent approach). Research by Nanda and Davis [3] report that to get 90 % recall rate in summer, the false discovery rate has to be raised to 100 %. Xu and Fujimura [12] detect humans in a winter scenarios and report a precision of 97.37 %, but with a recall rate no more than 35 %. The introduced shape-independent method showed satisfactory performance in temperatures below 7 °C. However, to be used in a safety system further improvements are necessary. We have considered to present performance for the shape-independent method using receiver operator characteristic (ROC) curve, but there are no suitable parameters to construct basis for the analysis. To enhance performance, additional features such as other morphological characteristics of humans [13], histograms of oriented gradient (HOG) [14] and inertial features [5] should be evaluated. Reconstruction of occluded humans using morphological approaches might also improve performance and should be investigated as possible extensions to the proposed methods.

Since the extracted ROIs are used as input to the other detection methods, their recall rate cannot exceed the 84 % recall rate of the extraction algorithm. To further improve performance, further development of the extraction algorithm should therefore also be considered.

References

1. Fang, Y., Yamada, K., Ninomiya, Y., Horn, B., Masaki, I.: Comparison between infrared-image-based and visible-image-based approaches for pedestrian detection. In: Proceedings of Intelligent Vehicles Symposium, 2003, pp. 505–510. IEEE (2003)
2. Gavrila, D., Giebel, J.: Shape-based pedestrian detection and tracking. In: Intelligent Vehicle Symposium, 2002, vol. 1, pp. 8–14, June 2002
3. Nanda, H., Davis, L.: Probabilistic template based pedestrian detection in infrared videos. In: Intelligent Vehicle Symposium, 2002, vol. 1, pp. 15–20. IEEE (2002)
4. Bertozzi, M., Broggi, A., Ghidoni, S., Meinecke, M.: A night vision module for the detection of distant pedestrians. In: Intelligent Vehicles Symposium, 2007, pp. 25–30. IEEE, June 2007
5. Fang, Y., Yamada, K., Ninomiya, Y., Horn, B., Masaki, I.: A shape-independent method for pedestrian detection with far-infrared images. IEEE Trans. Veh. Technol. **53**(6), 1679–1697 (2004)
6. Kancharla, T., Kharade, P., Gindi, S., Kutty, K., Vaidya, V.: Edge based segmentation for pedestrian detection using nir camera. In: 2011 International Conference on Image Information Processing (ICIIP), pp. 1–6 (2011)
7. Yasuno, M., Ryousuke, S., Yasuda, N., Aoki, M.: Pedestrian detection and tracking in far infrared images. In: Proceedings of Intelligent Transportation Systems, 2005, pp. 182–187. IEEE, September 2005
8. Xu, F., Liu, X., Fujimura, K.: Pedestrian detection and tracking with night vision. IEEE Trans. Intell. Transp. Syst. **6**(1), 63–71 (2005)
9. Bertozzi, M., Broggi, A., Fascioli, A., Graf, T., Meinecke, M.: Pedestrian detection for driver assistance using multiresolution infrared vision. IEEE Trans. Veh. Technol. **53**(6), 1666–1678 (2004)
10. Meis, U., Oberlander, M., Ritter, W.: Reinforcing the reliability of pedestrian detection in far-infrared sensing. In: Intelligent Vehicles Symposium, 2004, pp. 779–783. IEEE, June 2004
11. Wang, D., Posner, I., Newman, P.: What could move? finding cars, pedestrians and bicyclists in 3d laser data. In: 2012 IEEE International Conference on Robotics and Automation (ICRA), pp. 4038–4044, May 2012
12. Xu, F., Fujimura, K.: Pedestrian detection and tracking with night vision. In: Intelligent Vehicle Symposium, 2002, vol. 1, pp. 21–30. IEEE, June 2002
13. Bertozzi, M., Broggi, A., Grisleri, P., Graf, T., Meinecke, M.: Pedestrian detection and tracking with night vision. In: Proceedings of Intelligent Vehicles Symposium, 2003, pp. 662–667. IEEE (2003)
14. Suard, F., Rakotomamonjy, A., Bensrhair, A., Broggi, A.: Pedestrian detection using infrared images and histograms of oriented gradients. In: Intelligent Vehicles Symposium, 2006, pp. 206–212. IEEE, June 2006

Cell Segmentation Using Level Set Methods with a New Variance Term

Zuzana Bílková[1,2]([✉]), Jindřich Soukup[1,2], and Václav Kučera[1]

[1] Faculty of Mathematics and Physics,
Charles University in Prague, Prague, Czech Republic
[2] Institute of Information Theory an Automation of the ASCR,
Prague, Czech Republic
bilkova@utia.cas.cz

Abstract. We present a new method for segmentation of phase-contrast microscopic images of cells. The algorithm is based on the variational formulation of the level set method, i.e. minimizing of a functional, which describes the level set function. The functional is minimized by a gradient flow described by an evolutionary partial differential equation. The most significant new ideas are initialization using thresholding and the introduction of a new term based on local variance that speeds up convergence and achieves more accurate results. The proposed algorithm is applied on real data and compared with another algorithm. Our method yields an average gain in accuracy of 2 %.

Keywords: Segmentation · Level set method · Active contours · Phase contrast microscopy

1 Introduction

Live cell imaging captures crucial information of many biological processes with direct implication for human health [1]. The analysis of our microscopic images is used for the development of body implants, see [2]. The human body is very sensitive to foreign materials, unsuitable implants may cause immune reactions. Therefore, the biocompatibility or biotoxicity of various materials are studied.

The images we process come from experiments in vitro using cancer cells due to their resistance and easy laboratory preservation. The cells are scanned with a phase-contrast microscope at regular time intervals, in our case every 2 min. The images are analyzed to determine the rate of cell growth, which leads to the problem of segmentation of cells from the background.

The main goal is to find an efficient algorithm since the segmentation is usually performed manually, which is a tedious and time consuming work. Automatic segmentation is a complicated problem in itself and in our case there are several factors that make our task even more difficult. The microscopic images contain artifacts like halos, bright areas around the cell borders. The colour of the background is inconveniently similar to the colour of the cell interiors. The microscopic images also suffer from poor focus and impurities.

© Springer International Publishing Switzerland 2016
A. Campilho and F. Karray (Eds.): ICIAR 2016, LNCS 9730, pp. 183–190, 2016.
DOI: 10.1007/978-3-319-41501-7_21

There are various segmentation approaches in the literature, e.g. machine learning [3] or motion detection [2]. In this paper, we focus on the method of active contours, first introduced in [4], and its level set formulation proposed in [5]. We use the variational formulation by Li *et al.* [6] which does not need re-initialization. We introduce a new term into the formulation to improve the method for microscopic images and we propose an efficient initialization.

The remainder of this paper is organized as follows: the first part of Sect. 2 describes the variational formulation proposed by Li, in the second part we introduce our new term and propose a new initialization. In Sect. 3 we describe implementation. We validate our approach in Sect. 4 and conclude in Sect. 5.

2   Level Set Method

The level set method is a simple and versatile method for numerical analysis of the motion of a finite set of closed curves that divides the plane into exterior and interior regions, i.e. the background and the foreground.

A zero level set of a function ϕ is a set where the values of the function are equal to zero: $L_\phi(t) = \{(x, y) | \phi(t, x, y) = 0\}$. The main idea behind the level set method is that a curve can be seen as the implicitly given zero level set of a function in higher dimension. The goal is to capture and analyze the motion of the curve in time. Instead of moving the curve itself, we will be evolving the level set function.

2.1   Variational Formulation of the Level Set Method

In this section we describe the functional proposed by Li *et al.* [6]. An explicit energy functional $E(\phi)$ will be defined, so that the zero level curve of the minimizer ϕ captures the desired features in an image, in our case the cell edges.

The energy functional has two parts:

$$E(\phi) = E_m(\phi) + \mu P(\phi),$$

where $\mu > 0$ is a weighting parameter. The energy $E_m(\phi)$ depends on the image data, therefore it is called the external energy. The energy $P(\phi)$ is a function of ϕ only and is called the internal energy.

Internal Energy. In implementations of traditional level set methods, it is numerically important to maintain the level set function close to a signed distance function [7]. By definition, a signed distance function f must satisfy

$$|\nabla f(\mathbf{x}, t)| = 1 \quad \text{a.e. } \mathbf{x} \in \Omega, \forall t, \tag{1}$$

where $\Omega \subset \mathbb{R}^2$ is the image support.

One approach is a periodic re-initialization of the level set function. However, this technique has undesirable side-effects and it still remains a serious question when to apply the re-initialization process. Li *et al.* [6] introduced a new internal energy term that penalizes the deviation of the level set function from the signed distance function property (1):

$$P(\phi) = \int_\Omega \frac{1}{2} \left(|\nabla\phi| - 1\right)^2 dxdy. \tag{2}$$

Therefore, re-initialization is no longer necessary.

External Energy. Let I be an image. The edge indicator function is defined as $g = \frac{1}{1+|\nabla(G_\sigma * I)|^2}$, where G_σ is the Gaussian kernel with standard deviation σ and $*$ denotes convolution.

The external energy is defined as

$$E_m(\phi) = \lambda L(\phi) + \alpha A(\phi), \tag{3}$$

where $\lambda > 0$, α are constants and the terms $L(\phi)$ and $A(\phi)$ are

$$L(\phi) = \int_\Omega g\delta(\phi)|\nabla\phi|dxdy, \quad A(\phi) = \int_\Omega gH(-\phi)dxdy, \tag{4}$$

where δ is the delta distribution and H is the Heaviside function:

$$\int_{-\infty}^{\infty} \delta(x)dx = 1, \quad H(x) = \begin{cases} 1, & x \geq 0, \\ 0, & x < 0. \end{cases} \tag{5}$$

It is well known, [8], that the geometrical meaning of the energy $L(\phi)$ is the length of the zero level curve of the level set function ϕ and therefore adding it has a smoothing effect on the zero level curve. The energy functional $A(\phi)$ minimizes the area of the region inside the zero level curve and is proposed to speed up the curve evolution. In our case the initial contour will be placed outside the cells, therefore the coefficient α in (3) should be positive.

The total energy functional is defined by

$$E(\phi) = \mu P(\phi) + E_m(\phi) \tag{6}$$
$$= \mu \int_\Omega \frac{1}{2} \left(|\nabla\phi| - 1\right)^2 dxdy + \lambda \int_\Omega g\delta(\phi)|\nabla\phi|dxdy + \alpha \int_\Omega gH(-\phi)dxdy.$$

Gradient Flow Formulation. We seek the stationary solution of the energy functional E given by (6), which is computed using its Euler-Lagrange equation. The gradient flow that minimizes E is the following evolutionary equation:

$$\frac{\partial\phi}{\partial t} = -\frac{\partial E}{\partial \phi} = -E',$$

which is equivalent to solving the variational problem with the steepest-descent method.

To explicitly express the gradient flow we apply the Euler-Lagrange equation to the functional (6). The gradient flow is then defined by

$$\frac{\partial\phi}{\partial t} = \mu \left[\Delta\phi - \mathrm{div}\left(\frac{\nabla\phi}{|\nabla\phi|} \right) \right] + \lambda\delta(\phi)\mathrm{div}\left(g\frac{\nabla\phi}{|\nabla\phi|} \right) + \alpha g\delta(\phi). \tag{7}$$

2.2   New Variational Term in the Gradient Flow

To improve the accuracy and speed up the evolution we have incorporated a new term into the gradient flow (7).

Since our application is the segmentation of cell images, we can assume the images will have similar features. An image may contain undilated cells. A typical undilated cell is shown on the left of Fig. 1. The cell center is of a similar colour as the background and forms a visual edge inside the cell. As a consequence, a contour may form inside the cell, which is shown in the right image of Fig. 1.

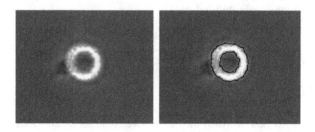

Fig. 1. Left image: image of an undilated cell. Right image: an undesired contour inside a cell that may form using Li's method.

To avoid the undesired interior contour, we introduce a new term to the gradient flow (7), which we call the variance term V. It is based on the assumption that the local variance of the background is significantly smaller than variance of the cells. The variance term uses the mean values of variance of areas currently assigned as background, denoted as v_1, and objects, denoted as v_2. Consequently, it drives the motion of the level set curve of ϕ towards one of them, depending on whether the variance of a point is more similar to either v_1 or v_2. The variance term is defined as

$$V(\phi) = \rho\delta(\phi)\left(-(Var - v_1)^2 + (Var - v_2)^2\right),\tag{8}$$

where $\rho > 0$ is a weighting parameter, Var is the variance of the image on a neighbourhood of a given point, v_1 is the mean exterior variance and v_2 is the mean interior variance. The delta distribution selects only the zero level curve from the domain of ϕ.

In contrast to Li's method, we do not use the edge indication function based on experimental results on our data.

The new gradient flow is then defined by

$$\frac{\delta\phi}{\delta t} = \mu\left[\triangle\phi - \operatorname{div}\left(\frac{\nabla\phi}{|\nabla\phi|}\right)\right] + \lambda\delta(\phi)\operatorname{div}\left(\frac{\nabla\phi}{|\nabla\phi|}\right) +$$
$$+ \alpha\delta(\phi) + \rho\delta(\phi)\left(-(Var - v_1)^2 + (Var - v_2)^2\right).\tag{9}$$

2.3   New Initialization of the Level Set Function by Variance

In the traditional level set formulation it is important to initialize the level set function ϕ as a signed distance function, [7]. Due to the new penalizing term (2) we can use more general functions in our formulation. The region based initialization proposed by Li *et al.* [6] is flexible for various applications.

As we process a sequence of images, a natural candidate for the initialization is the resulting level set function from the previous image. However, this method fails because the initial curve can partially lie inside a cell, which violates the assumption for the parameter of the area term (4).

Therefore we suggest a different approach. Our method utilizes the same property as when we introduced the variance term (8), i.e. the assumption that the background has significantly smaller variance than the cells. For each pixel we compute the variance of its neighborhood and then we use thresholding on the image of variance. This initialization provides fast convergence after a relatively small number of iterations (150 iterations for our images, cf. Sect. 4).

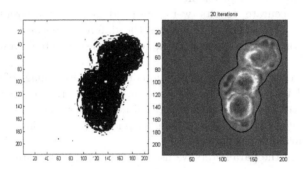

Fig. 2. Left image: initialization by thresholding the image of variance. Right image: a smooth curve after 20 iterations of our algorithm using the initialization by variance.

As an example, we use an image of a cell cluster. The first image in Fig. 2 shows the binary image obtained by thresholding. A method for optimizing the value of the threshold is described in Sect. 3.2. Although the initial level set function ϕ_0 has many zero level curves for only one cell cluster, due to the formulation of the gradient flow the small curves disappear after less than 20 iterations, see the second image in Fig. 2.

3   Implementation

3.1   Numerical Scheme

In practice, the delta distribution and the Heaviside function (5), $\delta(x) = H'(x)$, are numerically regularized [6]:

$$\delta_\epsilon(x) = \begin{cases} 0, & |x| > \epsilon, \\ \frac{1}{2\epsilon}\left[1 + \cos\left(\frac{\pi x}{\epsilon}\right)\right], & |x| \le \epsilon. \end{cases}$$

For all our experiments we set the parameter ϵ to 1, which is the pixel size.

The spatial derivatives are approximated by central differences. The time derivative is approximated by the forward difference with time step τ.

The level set function ϕ is discretized as $\phi_{i,j}^k$, where (i,j) is are space indexes and k is a time index. Then the level set evolution using the iterative gradient flow (9) can be written as the process:

$$\phi_{i,j}^{k+1} = \phi_{i,j}^k + \tau F(\phi_{i,j}^k),$$

where $F(\phi_{i,j}^k)$ is the approximation of the right hand side of (9).

3.2 Automatic Optimization of the Weighting Parameters

We used manual optimization of the parameters in our initial experiments. However, this method of optimizing can be tedious. Therefore, we tried several automatic methods of optimization in MATLAB to see whether the automatic methods are applicable to our problem.

The most accurate results were obtained by the trust-region-reflective method, see [9]. The method minimizes the difference between the results of the segmentation and the ground truth, i.e. images segmented manually by specialists.

We applied the automatic optimization only to the first image of the sequence and then used the resulting parameters for all of the remaining images. This process simulates the supposed use on real data, where only the ground truth of the first image is needed. The parameter ρ for our new variance term (8) was optimized separately.

The values of the parameters we used in our experiments are

$$\mu = 0.2, \ \lambda = 6.9913, \ \alpha = 0.33, \ \rho = 0.008, \ p = 2.0439, \qquad (10)$$

where the first four parameters are the weighting parameters in the gradient flow (9) and the last parameter is the threshold used in initialization by variance.

4   Results

Our images come from the Laboratory of Tissue Culture, University of South Bohemia in České Budějovice, Czech Republic.

The sequence we process has 2161 images. Images are taken in 2 min interval. Since we need manually segmented images from specialists as the ground truth and since it is time consuming to produce them, we chose 49 equidistantly distributed images from this sequence to analyze. The images were segmented by our algorithm and compared with results arising from the algorithm by Li et al., described in Sect. 2. We used our initialization by variance for both methods, which ensures convergence after 150 iterations for both algorithms. For Li's algorithm we used the same parameters specified in (10). We use the F_1 score for evaluation (the highest value being 1).

Table 1. Comparison of the mean values of F_1 scores of 49 images of our method, Li's method and our initialization – thresholding of the variance image.

F_1 score	Our algorithm	Li's algorithm	Our initialization
Original images	0.8901	0.8679	0.8415
Cropped images	0.8955	0.8720	0.8455

We computed the mean value of the F_1 scores of the 49 images for each algorithm and for the initialization by variance which is shown in Table 1. The threshold in the initialization by variance was chosen as the result of the automatic optimization (10). One problem of our images is embedded text at the corners of the images. We therefore evaluate the F_1 score also on cropped images without the text at the corners. Table 1 shows that our initialization by variance is already very efficient. The mean value of the F_1 score of our method is more than 2 % higher than Li's which is a considerable improvement taking into account the current high accuracy level and the inaccuracy of the manual segmentation.

Figure 3 demonstrates the robustness of our algorithm on one of the first images and on the last image of the sequence. There are isolated cell clusters on a background in the first image while the majority of the last image is covered with cells. The black curves represent the zero level set and separates the image into cells and background.

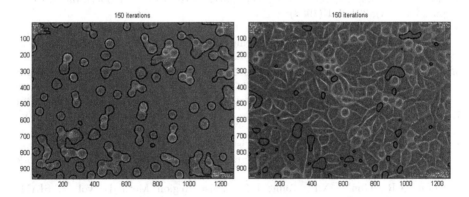

Fig. 3. Resulting segmentation of one of the first images of the sequence (left) and of the last image of the sequence (right).

5   Conclusion

In this paper we propose an improved variational level set method for segmentation of microscopic images of cells. A new term based on variance was incorporated into the functional and using the edge indicator function was omitted for our images. We also introduce an efficient region-based initialization. The results of the proposed algorithm are compared with the original method. We suppose that the method can be used generally for segmenting textures, e.g. grass from buildings or the sky.

Acknowledgements. The study was supported by the GAUK grant No. 914813/2013, the grant GAČR No. 13-29225S, the grant SVV-2015-260223 and the grant SVV-2016-260332. The authors would also like to thank the staff of the Working Place of Tissue Culture - Certified Laboratory at Nové Hrady for their assistance with the manual segmentation of the cells.

References

1. Li, F., Zhou, X., Zhao, H., Wong, S.T.C.: Cell segmentation using front vector flow guided active contours. In: Yang, G.-Z., Hawkes, D., Rueckert, D., Noble, A., Taylor, C. (eds.) MICCAI 2009, Part II. LNCS, vol. 5762, pp. 609–616. Springer, Heidelberg (2009)
2. Soukup, J., Císař, P., Šroubek, F.: Segmentation of time-lapse images with focus on microscopic images of cells. In: Petrosino, A. (ed.) ICIAP 2013, Part II. LNCS, vol. 8157, pp. 71–80. Springer, Heidelberg (2013)
3. Birkbeck, N., Sofka, M., Kohlberger, T., Zhang, J., Wetzl, J., Kaftan, J., Zhou, S.K.: Robust segmentation of challenging lungs in CT using multi-stage learning and level set optimization. In: Suzuki, K. (ed.) Computational Intelligence in Biomedical Imaging, pp. 185–208. Springer, New York (2014)
4. Kass, M., Witkin, A., Terzopoulos, D.: Snakes: active contour models. Int. J. Comput. Vis. **1**(4), 321–331 (1988)
5. Osher, S., Sethian, J.A.: Fronts propagating with curvature-dependent speed: algorithms based on Hamilton-Jacobi formulations. J. Comput. Phys. **79**(1), 12–49 (1988)
6. Li, C., Chenyang, X., Gui, C., Fox, M.D.: Level set evolution without re-initialization: a new variational formulation. In: IEEE Computer Society Conference on Computer Vision and Pattern Recognition, 2005. CVPR 2005, vol. 1, pp. 430–436. IEEE (2005)
7. Caselles, V., Kimmel, R., Sapiro, G.: Geodesic active contours. Int. J. Comput. Vis. **22**(1), 61–79 (1997)
8. Vemuri, B., Chen, Y.: Joint Image Registration and Segmentation. Geometric level set methods in imaging, vision, and graphics, pp. 251–269. Springer, New York (2003)
9. Conn, A.R., Gould, N.I., Toint, P.L.: Trust Region Methods, vol. 1. SIAM, Philadelphia (2000)

Video Object Segmentation Based on Superpixel Trajectories

Mohamed A. Abdelwahab[1,2(✉)], Moataz M. Abdelwahab[1], Hideaki Uchiyama[2],
Atsushi Shimada[2], and Rin-ichiro Taniguchi[2]

[1] Egypt Japan University of Science and Technology, Alexandria, Egypt
{mohamed.abdelwahab,moataz.abdelwahab}@ejust.edu.eg
[2] Kyushu University, Fukuoka, Japan
{uchiyama,atsushi,rin}@limu.ait.kyushu-u.ac.jp

Abstract. In this paper, a video object segmentation method utilizing the motion of superpixel centroids is proposed. Our method achieves the same advantages of methods based on clustering point trajectories, furthermore obtaining dense clustering labels from sparse ones becomes very easy. Simply for each superpixel the label of its centroid is propagated to all its entire pixels. In addition to the motion of superpixel centroids, histogram of oriented optical flow, HOOF, extracted from superpixels is used as a second feature. After segmenting each object, we distinguish between foreground objects and the background utilizing the obtained clustering results.

Keywords: Superpixel trajectory · Object segmentation · Affinity

1 Introduction

Video object segmentation has become an active research area in computer vision due to its usage in many applications such as action recognition, video indexing, video retrieval, and object tracking. However, it has many challenges due to the camera motion, occlusion, and changes in scale, and illumination.

In [1], spatial-temporal image described as a video matrix is decomposed into a low rank matrix and residual one representing the background and foreground objects respectively. To overcome the problem of camera motion, a frame transformation was used as a preprocessing step. However, this method fails to compensate the motion of the camera in case of a quick motion. In [2] objects are segmented based on analyzing local motion cues. Initially motion saliency maps are generated to represent fg/bg pixels. Then an appearance model is used iteratively in a refinement process. However in this method, a short term motion is only considered thus it cannot deal with objects having a discontinuity motion.

To overcome the problem of discontinuity of moving objects, [3–5] used long motion term. By this way objects can be detected even if they stop moving for a time. In these methods, long trajectories of sparse points are extracted. Then an affinity matrix is computed representing the motion distances between trajectories. However using sparse points needs a conversion from sparse to dense.

© Springer International Publishing Switzerland 2016
A. Campilho and F. Karray (Eds.): ICIAR 2016, LNCS 9730, pp. 191–197, 2016.
DOI: 10.1007/978-3-319-41501-7_22

Usually an energy minimization step is used for this conversion which is computational expensive.

In this paper, the proposed method produces dense clustering without any optimization step or complex affinity. Instead using the motion of point trajectories, we propose to use motion of the centroid of superpixel trajectories. This keeps the simplicity of the affinity computation furthermore sparse to dense label conversion becomes very easy. In addition of using long motion term, we propose to use HOOF extracted from superpixels as another motion cue. After that, we provide foreground segmentation by utilizing the object segmentation results.

This paper is organized as follows: Sect. 2 presents the proposed algorithm, the experimental results are reported and compared in Sects. 3 and 4 presents the conclusion.

2   The Proposed Algorithm

We propose a method based on two stages for object segmentation in video. In the first stage objects are segmented from each other, while distinguishing between foreground objects and the background is achieved in the second stage.

2.1   Object Segmentation

In this section the moving objects are segmented where each object has a unique cluster label. The detailed steps are explained as follows:

Extraction of superpixel trajectories: superpixel trajectories are extracted as mentioned in [6], where each video frame is partitioned into temporal consistent superpixels Sp_t^i, the superscript i indicates the spatial index and the subscript t represents the temporal index. A superpixel trajectory is represented by Tr_T^i, i.e. $Tr_T^i = [Sp_{t1}^i Sp_{t2}^i....Sp_{tn}^i]$ representing a superpixel trajectory i which exists at a period of time $T = t_1 : t_n$.

Affinity computation: in our method two motion cues are used to create the affinity matrix $\mathbf{W}$. The first one is long term motion modeled in [3] but here it is applied to the superpixel trajectory centroids, where motion distance, D^M, between two trajectories is taken as the maximum motion difference between them during their common time. By this way the algorithm can segment an object from the background even the object stops moving for a time. Since the direction of the motion is a discriminative feature, we use the histogram of oriented optical flow (HOOF) as a second motion cue. The $HOOF$ for superpixel Sp_t^i, and trajectory Tr_T^i are represented by $HOOF_t^i(b)$, and $HOOF_T^i(b)$ respectively, where b is the bin number. Let A, B represent two superpixel trajectories existing in time periods T_A, T_B respectively, $T_A \cap T_B > \Delta$, where $\Delta = 4$ [4]. The motion and HOOF distances are defined in (1), and (2) respectively.

$$D^M(A, B) = max_{t \in (T_A \cap T_B)} d_t^M(A, B)$$
$$where \; d_t^M(A, B) = (u_t^A - u_t^B)^2 + (v_t^A - v_t^B)^2 \tag{1}$$

$$D^{HOOF}(A, B) = \frac{1}{T_A \cap T_B} \sum_{\substack{b,t \\ t \in (T_A \cap T_B)}} \left| HOOF_{T_A}^A(b) - HOOF_{T_B}^B(b) \right| \qquad (2)$$

$$W(A, B) = exp(-D^M(A, B)/\lambda_M) \cdot exp(-D^{HOOF}(A, B)) \qquad (3)$$

u_t, v_t are velocity components in the x, y directions respectively i.e. $u_t = p_{t+\Delta} - p_t$, $v_t = q_{t+\Delta} - q_t$, where p, and q represent a spatial location of super-pixel centroid. The affinity $W(A, B)$ is calculated as in (3), where λ_M is a motion weight. In our method λ_M is selected to equal the maximum D^M i.e. it is adaptively changed based on the motion of the video.

Clustering: the clustering algorithm is applied to the affinity matrix **W** in the embedding space, where eigendecomposition of the normalized graph Laplacian **L** is used as

$$\mathbf{L} = \mathbf{D}^{-\frac{1}{2}}(\mathbf{D} - \mathbf{W})\mathbf{D}^{-\frac{1}{2}} = \mathbf{V}^T \Lambda \mathbf{V} \qquad (4)$$

D is a diagonal matrix with $d_{i,i} = \sum_j w_{i,j}$, **V** contains the eigenvectors, and Λ is a diagonal matrix that contains the eigenvalues. Only m eigenvectors are taken $[v_1, ... v_m]$ corresponding to smallest m eigenvalues, after neglecting first eigenvector v_0 [4].

In the embedding space, each trajectory is modeled using Gaussian Mixture Model GMM of K components, where K is the number of clusters. First K is initialized, in our experiments initial $K = 7$, then EM iterations algorithm is used to optimize the number of final clusters, where K is updated during the iterations [4].

Sparse to dense label conversion: the last step is to propagate the cluster labels from superpixel centroids to all pixels, simply for each superpixel, the entire pixels take the same cluster label as their centroid pixel. This is one of the advantages for using superpixel trajectories, that is no need for using appearance or motion models [4] to propagate labels to all pixels.

2.2 Foreground Object Detection

In this section, we propose a method for distinguishing between the foreground objects and the background. For each frame an initial motion saliency score is determined, similar to [7], for each superpixel depending on how the dominant motion of the superpixel, $Motion(Sp_t^i)$, is deviated from the frame dominant motion, $Motion(Fr_t)$. We assume the frame dominant motion is either static or translation. If the median of optical flow magnitudes <1 pixel, it is assumed a static. The dominant motions for a superpixel or a translated frame is defined as the mean of angles located in the $HOOF$ maximum bin.

For a superpixel, if the difference between $Motion(Sp_t^i)$ and $Motion(Fr_t)$ is greater than a threshold, the saliency of this superpixel, $Sal(Sp_t^i)$, equals the average of optical flow magnitudes of the superpixel dominant motion bin, otherwise it takes zero value. Then the superpixel saliency values are normalized for each frame. A refinement process is applied using the obtained clustering information. Here we use very simple way to avoid the complexity of the minimization methods [2,5]. Simply the saliency of each superpixel is updated using saliency of its trajectory and cluster as follows:

$$Sal(Sp_t^i) = average(Sal(Sp_t^i), Sal(Tr_T^i), Sal(Cluster_c)) \tag{5}$$

where the second term refers to the saliency of the trajectory i and the third term refers to the saliency of the superpixel cluster c, both of them are obtained by taking the average of their superpixel salienies. Figure 1 shows an example of saliency of a frame before and after refinement process. Foreground labels are obtained by thresholding the final saliency value.

3   Experimental Results

Two experiments were exploited to evaluate the proposed method. In experiment I, the proposed object segmentation is tested while the foreground detection is evaluated in the experiment II. In both experiments Berkeley Motion Segmentation dataset (BMS-26) [3] is used, it consists of 26 video sequences. Similarly to the [5], only the first 50 frames of each video is taken. In case the video has frames number less than 50 frames, the whole video frames are taken.

3.1   Evaluating Object Segmentation

To evaluate the segmentation results, a comparison to ground truth regions is performed. To do this a mapping reprocess is necessary, where each cluster in our segmentation is mapped into a ground label. This matching process is based on the maximum overlap between the cluster and ground regions. This means that multiple clusters may be assigned to the same ground region [3]. Five criteria are mentioned in [3,5] for evaluating any video segmentation scheme. They are defined as follows [5]: Density is the coverage percentage of labels on video sequence. Clustering error is defined as the percentage of wrong labels in total number of trajectory labels. Per region clustering error is defined as the average error of each region. Over segmentation parameter is adopted to evaluate the number of clusters to fit ground truth. Extracted objects is the number of

Table 1. Object segmentation comparison results for BMS dataset (50 frames).

Method	Density (%)	Clustering error (%)	Per region error (%)	Over-segmentation	Extracted objects
Proposed	78.10	3.85	22.51	2.75	24
Chen et al. [5]	5.36	1.93	23.80	1.08	30
Fragkiadaki et al. [8]	3.07	2.29	20.93	0.29	29
Brox et al. [3]	3.32	3.43	27.06	0.4	26

(a) Initial saliency

(b) Refined saliency

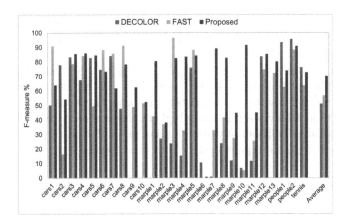

Fig. 1. Example of motion saliency refinement. (Color figure online)

Fig. 2. Object detection comparison results with DECOLOR [1] and FAST [2] methods for BMS dataset (50 frames). (Color figure online)

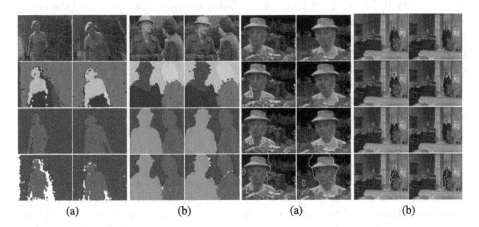

(a)   (b)   (a)   (b)

Fig. 3. Our video segmentation results, original frames in the 1st row, our segmentation 2nd row, the ground truth objects 3rd row, and the 4th row shows the segmentation results after mapped to the ground truth. (Color figure online)

Fig. 4. Sample frames comparison of foreground segmentation methods, original frames in the 1st row, DECOLOR method [1] 2nd row, FAST method [2] 3rd row, and the proposed method 4th row.

objects with less than 10 % wrong trajectory labels. These evaluating criteria are implemented in our code.

The input trajectories in our proposed method are not required to have full lengths. Short trajectories are removed (trajectories with length less than L_{min}). By varying the minimum length, L_{min}, the density is changed. As mentioned before, final cluster number is optimized by EM iterations, thus our proposed method is not very sensitive to the initial value of K.

Figure 3 shows frame samples of our segmentation results for Marple3, and Marple9 videos, using initial $K = 7, L_{min} = 20$. Table 1 compares our results to the related methods as reported in [5]. As clear from the table the segmentation results are comparable to other methods. Moreover, for density our method achieves significantly higher value compared to others. This high density is obtained without any optimization method, but simply by propagating cluster labels from superpixel centroids to other pixels.

3.2 Evaluating Foreground Object Detection

As mentioned before, our method does not only segment objects from each other but it separates between foreground objects and background. Our detection results are compared to the state of the art methods DECOLOR [1] and FAST [2]. We used their available codes and applied them to the 26 videos of BMS dataset. F-measure [5] is used for evaluating the detection results.

DECOLOR method depends on an image registration step, thus four videos (Cars9, Cars10, Marple1, and Marple13) failed in registration step and the code stopped running. Figure 4 shows a comparison of foreground detection for challenging videos, Marple4 and Marple11, where objects have a discontinuity moving. The proposed method shows better segmentation results in both videos compared to the [1, 2] methods.

A comparison for all videos in BMS dataset is shown in Fig. 2. It is clear that our detection method gives higher accuracy for many videos, in addition it achieves the highest average value.

4 Conclusion

A video object segmentation method using superpixel motion was presented. Moreover, a distinguishing between foreground objects and the background was introduced. Compared to traditional points trajectories methods, superpixel trajectories method has advanced by giving dense clustering while keeping simplicity of affinity computations. In the proposed method, the motion of superpixel centroids in addition to HOOF were used in clustering. The obtained clustering results were utilized in the foreground detection.

Acknowledgments. The authors would like to thank Egyptian Ministry of Higher Education (MoHE) and Egypt-Japan University of Science and Technology (E-JUST) for their support.

References

1. Zhou, X., Yang, C., Weichuan, Y.: Moving object detection by detecting contiguous outliers in the low-rank representation. IEEE Trans. Pattern Anal. Mach. Intell. **35**(3), 597–610 (2013)

2. Papazoglou, A., Ferrari, V.: Fast object segmentation in unconstrained video. In: Proceedings of the IEEE International Conference on Computer Vision (ICCV), pp. 1777–1784 (2013)
3. Brox, T., Malik, J.: Object segmentation by long term analysis of point trajectories. In: Daniilidis, K., Maragos, P., Paragios, N. (eds.) ECCV 2010, Part V. LNCS, vol. 6315, pp. 282–295. Springer, Heidelberg (2010)
4. Elqursh, A., Elgammal, A.: Online moving camera background subtraction. In: Fitzgibbon, A., Lazebnik, S., Perona, P., Sato, Y., Schmid, C. (eds.) ECCV 2012, Part VI. LNCS, vol. 7577, pp. 228–241. Springer, Heidelberg (2012)
5. Chen, L., Shen, J., Wang, W., Ni, B.: Video object segmentation via dense trajectories. IEEE Trans. Multimed. **17**(12), 2225–2234 (2015)
6. Chang, J., Wei, D., Fisher, J.: A video representation using temporal superpixels. In: Proceedings of the IEEE Conference on Computer Vision and Pattern Recognition (CVPR), pp. 2051–2058 (2013)
7. Faktor, A., Irani, M.: Video segmentation by non-local consensus voting. In: BMVC (2014)
8. Fragkiadaki, K., Zhang, G., Shi, J.: Video segmentation by tracing discontinuities in a trajectory embedding. In: IEEE Conference on Computer Vision and Pattern Recognition (CVPR), pp. 1846–1853 (2012)

Interactive 3D Segmentation of Lymphatic Valves in Confocal Microscopic Images

Jonathan-Lee Jones and Xianghua Xie[✉]

Department of Computer Science, Swansea University,
Singleton Park, Swansea, UK
x.xie@swansea.ac.uk
http://csvision.swan.ac.uk

Abstract. We present a novel method of segmentation of lymph valve leaflets from confocal microscopy studies. By using a user informed, layer based segmentation framework, we segment the outer boundary of the lymph valve in 3D from a series of confocal images. This boundary is then used to compute the surface structure of the vessel by providing a boundary constraint to a dual graph based on minimum surface segmentation. This segmentation creates a point cloud of voxels on the surface of the valve structure, we then apply an RBF interpolation to reconstruct it as a continuous surface.

1 Introduction

The lymphatic system is vital for maintaining healthy functionality in the body; fulfilling this task by the transport of fluids and immunological cells from and to the blood and interstitial spaces. The lymphatic system at its most basic is a system of pipes and valves to ensure unidirectional flow, but unlike the cardiovascular system it is not a pressurised closed system. Failure of the lymphatic system leading to lymphedema is a common complication in several disease states, and is a detrimental factor in recovery and improving quality of life in post operative patients. Texture analysis and deformable modelling, e.g. [12–14] may be applied to segment the vessel borders. The focus of this paper is to investigate the lymph valve structures, using computer imaging techniques to reconstruct the valve in 3D from *ex vivo* confocal microscopic image series. There has been little investigation of the lymphatic system in general, and even less on the valve structures. Segmenting the valves is a challenge, as they are small delicate structures and whereas finding the tip of the valve is relatively less ambiguous, the hinge region presents a significantly greater difficulty. Figure 1 provides example slices.

There is a great deal of interest in methods to find a minimal surface in 3D, Appleton [1] suggested, for example, a method of solving a continuous maxflow algorithm, whereas other methods have been put forward using geometric constraints [8], regional properties [4], and shape priors [9] to give but a few examples. Unlike in 2D segmentation, minimal surfaces must always be closed, with boundary constraints applied. They can be thought of like blowing a soap bubble, with the ring used to blow the bubble as the boundary constraining it,

© Springer International Publishing Switzerland 2016
A. Campilho and F. Karray (Eds.): ICIAR 2016, LNCS 9730, pp. 198–205, 2016.
DOI: 10.1007/978-3-319-41501-7_23

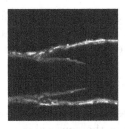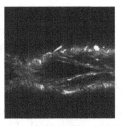

Fig. 1. Processed data showing the valve structure in a single data set. Notice how the shape and quality of the image changes from the slice on the periphery of the valve (right image) compared to a slice from the mid region (on the left).

and the bubble itself as the surface. By using an adaptation of our 2D method [6] into 3D, we can provide a boundary to meet the second constraint criteria required for minimal surface segmentation. This will be combined with the graph construction to provide segmentation of the surface as a whole. It is important when working in 3D to consider surfaces rather than direct shortest paths [2, 7, 10, 11] as it is a well known phenomenon that the shortest path between two points, does not necessarily correspond to a path on on the minimal surface between two closed shapes. We will apply interactive methods to allow expert knowledge to guide the difficult segmentation of the valve, and then use this user guided boundary to automatically segment the surface of the valve.

2   Proposed Method

Briefly, the proposed method first localise the outer boundaries of the lymph leaflets in 3D using an interactive segmentation method and then computes a complete 3D surface using a minimal surface algorithm. The user input is simplistic interaction by clicking a few points indicating a small number of points along the border. This interactive segmentation in 3D is an extension of our previous 2D method [6]. The user input is treated as a soft constraint, rather than a hard constraint, i.e. the segmentation does not necessarily pass the user points. This is achieved by finding a shortest path in a layered 3D graphs. The localised borders of the lymph leaflets are then used as boundary constraints for computing a minimal surface using a primal dual algorithm in discrete optimisation.

2.1   User Input

The user input is used to assist in labelling the root and tip of the valve. This is done using an adaptation of the imprecise user input which we have used previously in our 2D segmentation method [6]. User points are placed corresponding to the tip and the hinge points on the valve itself. These user points are used to find the valve boundary, which will be used to find the surface of the valve.

The segmentation forms a closed curve starting and finishing in the same point, circumscribing the boundary of the valve. This user input is effective but minimal and allows imprecision in user point placement which is desirable in 3D.

2.2   Graph Construction

In this graph, the 3D structure $\mathcal{I}$ is a representation made up from multiple layers $\mathcal{L}$ constructed from the sequential slices of the confocal series. The number of layers used is $2h$ where h is the number of slices in the confocal image series. The graph structure is made up of the slices s from s_1 to s_n, then the layers are replicated in reverse order (adding slices s_n to s_1), to construct a cube of twice the height of the original image stack. We construct a graph $G = (V, E)$, where V is the set of vertices, and E the set of weighted edges. For each voxel v, there exits an edge e to each of its neighbouring pixels on the same layer and to its neighbour in the subsequent layer. Therefore, a pair of neighbouring voxels $(p, q) \in V$ with a corresponding edge $e = (v_p, v_q)$ also have an edge to the corresponding point on the superseding layer $e = (v_{p_l}, v_{p_{l+1}})$, where l represents the current layer of the image. For each edge, we assign a weight w to build a weighted graph (V, E). These weights are calculated based on whether the edge is internal to a layer (w_i) or trans-layer (w_x). In order to be able to solve this problem in polynomial time, we enforce an order (as previously for the 2D method) moving through the image from l_1 to l_{2n} where n is the depth of the image cube, and layers l_1 to l_n represent moving through the images using the tip terminal point as a guide, then layers l_{n+1} to l_{2n} are returning using the hinge terminal point. This is done by ensuring that the inter-layer arcs are unidirectional. We use the user points as elastic soft constraints to help guide the segmentation.

User points are placed for both the ends of the valve (the tip and the hinge), and the source s is the tip point on layer 1 and sink t is set to the same point(as we need to create the full closed outline of the valve) but on layer l_{2n}, we also place user points on the ends of the valve for each layer to act as guide in the segmentation.

Edges of zero weight are not added from the start node s to each pixel in the first layer, and from the last layer $2n + 1$ to the terminal node t, making sure the first and the last user points elastic and not hard constraints, and all user points are treated equally.

If P is the set of pixels in the image, P_s is therefore the subset of pixels that also fall on the boundaries of our super pixels, and p_i and q_i are pixels in layer i giving v_{p_i} as the vertex p in layer i, we can define the set of nodes V as $V = \{s, t\} \cup \{p_i \in P_s \wedge 1 \leq i \leq k + 1\}$ and thusly the set of edges as,

$$
E = \begin{cases}
(s, v_{p_1}) | p \in P_s & \cup \\
(v_{p_{k+1}}, t) | p \in P_s & \cup \\
(v_{p_i}, v_{q_i}) | (p, q) \in N \wedge 1 \leq i \leq k + 1 & \cup \\
(v_{p_i}, v_{p_{i+1}}) | p \in P_s \wedge 1 \leq i \leq k + 1.
\end{cases}
\tag{1}
$$

2.3   Valve Boundary Detection

The first stage of our valve leaflet segmentation is to segment the boundary. Using the constructed graph G and manually labelled points for the apex and root of the valve, we assign weights to the edges in a similar manner as before. The edges on the directed layered graph are categorised as internal edges w_i within individual layers and inter-layer edges w_x. The weighting for these two types of edges is assigned differently. The internal edges are assigned weights based on edge features, i.e. boundary based edge weights similar to the 2D method are used, but not region based edge weights. The boundary based edge weights are calculated based on the magnitude of image gradients, i.e. using an edge detection function $g_e = 1/(1 + \nabla I)$ where I denotes the pre-processed image. Hence, for any given edge between neighbouring pixels (v_p, v_q), we assign a weight (w_e) according to

$$w_i((v_p, v_q)) := \frac{1}{2}||p - q||(g_e(p) + g_e(q)). \tag{2}$$

The attraction force imposed by user points is materialised through the inter-layer edge weights w_x. We apply distance transform to the user points in each layer of the graph, and the inter-layer edge weight is assigned as $w_x = d(v_{p_i}, v_{p_j})$ where d denotes the distance transform function. For layers l_1 to l_n we use the user points corresponding to the tip, and layers l_{n+1} to l_{2n} use the user points derived from the hinges. In this way, distance weighting produces iso-linear bands of weight around each user point, with increasing weight to go through to the next layer as the distance from the user point increases, favouring transition between layers as close as possible to the user point without straying too far from hard edges. In this way, finding the boundary of the valve becomes an energy minimisation problem similar to our previous 2D work [6].

The energy function for any curve C in our method is a combination of two terms, i.e. for any arc C between two points p_i and q_j, $C(p, q) = w_x + w_i$, where w_x can be written as $\alpha \sum_{i=1}^{k} ||C(s_i) - X_i||$, and w_i can be formulated as: $\beta \int_{0}^{L(C)} g(C(s))ds$. This is all providing that the points are treated as being in a sequential order, and that the interconnections between layers are uni-directional. The overall energy function can then be expressed as:

$$\mathcal{E}(C, s_1, ..., s_k) = \alpha \sum_{i=1}^{k} ||C(s_i) - X_i||$$

$$+ \beta \int_{0}^{L(C)} g(C(s))ds \quad s.t. s_i < s_j, \ \forall i < j. \tag{3}$$

where α and β are real constants used to weigh the effects of the edge based and distance based terms.

The first term in our cost equation is used to enforce the soft constraints placed by the user as a guideline to the terminal ends of the valve, and it penalises

Fig. 2. 3D Segmentation of the boundary of the valve leaflets.

the paths further away from these user points, helping the user control the segmentation. The second term is the boundary based data term that prefers the path passing through strong edges, the images are preprocessed to improve these images as described above. By using the layered graph construction, the minimisation of the energy function is achieved by finding the shortest path from the start point s to the end point t through the 3D graph.

As the graph will be very large, and therefore computationally expensive, the graph was constructed in segments. By using Dijkstra's algorithm, this allowed the points on the graph to be loaded in as needed, we operated on 10 layers at a time, as this provided a sufficient reduction in the size of graph. To further reduce the computational overheads, the image was automatically cropped to a tight box around the region of the valve, by using the manually input points to give a rough boundary, which was expanded in each direction to ensure the valve fitted within these confines in its entirety. Note, the inter-layer edges are unidirectional so that the path can not travel back to previously visited layers, to avoid making the segmentation problem NP hard. The results of this 3D segmentation, gave the boundary outline for the valve leaflet (see Fig. 2).

2.4   Valve Surface Segmentation

Once we obtain the boundary, the next stage is to calculate the point cloud for points on the surface of the valve. For this, the image stack was comprised of layers l_1 to l_n, where n is the number of slices in the series. Note this is a smaller graph than that is used for the border, as there is no need to have the $2n$ layers to ensure order in the user points. This is done using the voxel edge derived intensities for any given voxel v in the image stack, that are based on the edge map. A minimal surface segmentation performed using these weights, based on the method demonstrated in [5], with adapted cost functions.

The first stage is to construct a lattice framework to represent the 3D image. We first expand our original graph construction into a dual graph. From out planar primal graph, we define a dual graph by replacing each node with a facet, can connecting two nodes if their respective facets share an edge.

We can therefore define our lattice using the same connectivity used to construct the graph for boundary segmentation, namely with nodes being connected to their 8 neighbours on their layer, and immediate neighbour nodes on the layer above and below themselves. The lattice can be represented by set $P = (V, E, F, C)$ where the vertices $v \in V$, edges $e \in E \subseteq V \times V$, facets $f \in F \subseteq E \times E \times E \times E$ and cubes $c \in C \subseteq F \times F \times F \times F \times F \times F$, if we work with a 6 connected neighbourhood. For any given edge e_i we assign a weight w_i, with all weights being positive.

The minimum surface weight problem can therefore be defined as: $minQ(z) = \sum_i w_i z_i$, subject to $Bz = r$, where z is a positive vector indicating whether the facet is present in the minimal-weight surface. w_i is the weight of the facet, which corresponds to the weight of the edge in the 2D graph, and is defined as:

$$w_i = \alpha \sum_{i=1}^{k} ||C(s_i) - X_i|| + \beta \int_0^{L(C)} g(C(s))ds \tag{4}$$

and B is the incidence matrix boundary operator and r is a signed vector indicative of a closed contour. Once the problem is formulated, it can be resolve by using a Minimum-cost Circulation Flow Network (MCFN) based on work by Bitter *et al.* [3]. This can be formed in terms of the variable f:

$$\max_{f'} z_0^T f', s.t. C^T f' = 0, f' \leq \tilde{f} = w. \tag{5}$$

which requires the finding of the maximum divergence-free flow, passing through an initial surface z_0, which has the capacities given by the weights in the graph.

Once the MCFN has been solved, the results show facets that are to be included in the final solution. It is then a trivial task to deconstruct the dual lattice back to its primal roots and generate a node representing the centre of the volume indicated by the facet. These nodes will then be used to generate the final result by having a 3D RBF interpolation applied to them, to smooth outliers and provide a smooth surface which represents the valve itself.

3 Results

Our results were obtained from a data-set of five confocal series, from different lymph valves. These individual datasets each comprised of around 400 consecutive images of the lymph valve. These were used to construct the point cloud and surfaces. The point clouds represent voxels on the surface of the valve. Finding the surface for the valve is challenging, as the leaflets are very faint, and often merges into the wall, or exit the side of the frame. Some of the effects can be seen in the alternate views shown in Fig. 1. Furthermore, in order to obtain a coherent surface over these point clouds it is necessary to perform smoothing and RBF interpolation on the clouds. The results from the minimal surface segmentation are shown in Fig. 3, with a colour map applied to show the bands obtained from the RBF centres. The RBF centres for interpolation were taken at regular intervals (10 slices) through the image, as this provided an adequate smoothing to produce a surface, whilst keeping the computational overheads small so the operation is fast, and the resultant image manageable.

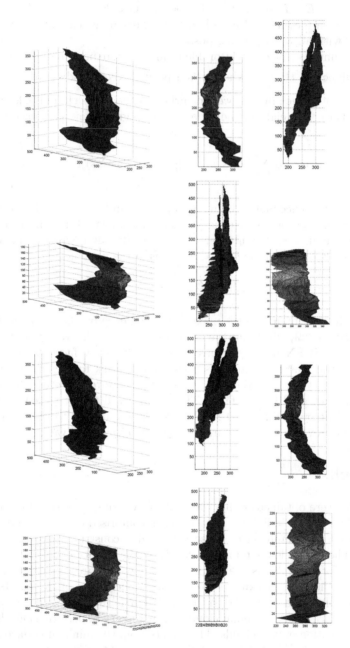

Fig. 3. 3D Segmentation results, showing the surface mapped over the point clouds. Coloured bands represent the regions used for the RBF interpolation. From left to right they are: an off centre view displaying the valve structure, X-Y, and X-Z planes, for each data-set. (Color figure online)

The proposed method achieved good segmentation of the lymph valves. By using user input to inform the boundary segmentation, we avoid the imaging problems inherent in the data of this type. Namely the nature of the images make identification of terminal regions of the valve exceedingly difficult, especially in the early and late stages. As can be seen in the second image in Fig. 1, it is almost impossible to discern where the valve starts and finishes in these regions, and even in the selected regions, where the valve can be seen, it differs greatly in shape as you move through the slices. The proposed method for boundary segmentation shows the versatility to allow the user to place guide points without the necessity for extreme precision, allowing for user input even in regions where this is difficult. The proposed method builds on our previous 2D work in [6] through the modification of the graph construction to allow for 3D segmentation. The poor quality of the images, coupled with the changing shape and irregularity of the valve made segmentation difficulty, but the proposed method manages to overcome these and provides a promising results.

References

1. Appleton, B., Talbot, H.: Globally minimal surfaces by continuous maximal flows. IEEE T-PAMI **28**(1), 106–118 (2006)
2. Armstrong, C.J., Barrett, W.A., Price, B.: Live surface. In: Volume Graphics (2006)
3. Bitter, I., Kaufman, A., Sato, M.: Penalized-distance volumetric skeleton algorithm. IEEE T-VCG **7**(3), 195–206 (2001)
4. Dou, X., Wu, X., Wahle, A., Sonka, M.: Globally optimal surface segmentation using regional properties of segmented objects. In: IEEE CVPR (2008)
5. Grady, L.: Minimal surfaces extend shortest path segmentation methods to 3D. IEEE T-PAMI **32**(2), 321–334 (2010)
6. Jones, J., Xie, X., Essa, E.: Combining region-based and imprecise boundary-based cues for interactive medical image segmentation. Int. J. Numer. Methods Biomed. Eng. **30**, 1649–1666 (2014)
7. Krueger, M., Delmas, P., Gimel'farb, G.: On 3D face feature segmentation using implicit surface active contours. In: International Conference on Image and Vision Computing, pp. 1–6 (2008)
8. Li, K., Wu, X., Chen, D., Sonka, M.: Globally optimal segmentation of interacting surfaces with geometric constraints. IEEE CVPR. **1**, 394–399 (2004)
9. Song, Q., Wu, X., Liu, Y., Sonka, M., Garvin, M.: Simultaneous searching of globally optimal interacting surfaces with shape priors. In: IEEE CVPR (2010)
10. Wagenknecht, G., Poll, A., Losacker, M., Blockx, I., Van der Linden, A.: A new combined live wire and active surface approach for volume-of-interest segmentation. In: IEEE Nuclear Science Symposium, pp. 3688–3692 (2009)
11. Wieclawek, W., Pietka, E.: Live-wire-based 3D segmentation method. In: IEEE EMBC, pp. 5645–5648 (2007)
12. Xie, X., Mirmehdi, M.: Texture exemplars for defect detection on random textures. In: Singh, S., Singh, M., Apte, C., Perner, P. (eds.) ICAPR 2005. LNCS, vol. 3687, pp. 404–413. Springer, Heidelberg (2005)
13. Xie, X., Mirmehdi, M.: Magnetostatic field for the active contour model: a study in convergence. In: BMVC, pp. 127–136 (2006)
14. Xie, X., Mirmehdi, M.: TEXEMS: Random Texture Representation and Analysis. In: Handbook of Texture Analysis. Chapter 4 (2008)

Automatic Nonlinear Filtering and Segmentation for Breast Ultrasound Images

Mohamed Elawady[1]([✉]), Ibrahim Sadek[2], Abd El Rahman Shabayek[3],
Gerard Pons[4], and Sergi Ganau[5]

[1] Universite Jean Monnet, CNRS, UMR 5516,
Laboratoire Hubert Curien, 42000 Saint-Etienne, France
`mohamed.elawady@univ-st-etienne.fr`
[2] Image and Pervasive Access Lab, CNRS UMI 2955, Singapore, Singapore
[3] Department of Computer Science, Faculty of Computers and Informatics,
Suez Canal University, Ismailia, Egypt
[4] Department of Computer Architecture and Technology,
University of Girona, Girona, Spain
[5] Radiology Department, UDIAT Centre Diagnostic, Sabadell, Spain

Abstract. Breast cancer is one of the leading causes of cancer death
among women worldwide. The proposed approach comprises three steps
as follows. Firstly, the image is preprocessed to remove speckle noise
while preserving important features of the image. Three methods are
investigated, i.e., Frost Filter, Detail Preserving Anisotropic Diffusion,
and Probabilistic Patch-Based Filter. Secondly, Normalized Cut or Quick
Shift is used to provide an initial segmentation map for breast lesions.
Thirdly, a postprocessing step is proposed to select the correct region
from a set of candidate regions. This approach is implemented on a
dataset containing 20 B-mode ultrasound images, acquired from UDIAT
Diagnostic Center of Sabadell, Spain. The overall system performance
is determined against the ground truth images. The best system performance is achieved through the following combinations: Frost Filter with
Quick Shift, Detail Preserving Anisotropic Diffusion with Normalized
Cut and Probabilistic Patch-Based with Normalized Cut.

Keywords: Breast cancer · Lesion segmentation · Ultrasound imaging ·
Speckle noise removal · Nonlinear filtering

1 Introduction

In 2012, breast cancer is ranked as the second most frequent cancer among
women worldwide. The breast cancer incidence and mortality have been raised
by more than 20 % and 14 % respectively, since the 2008 estimates [1,2]. Early
detection and diagnosis can significantly increase the breast cancer survival. Consequently, there is an insisting demand for developing accurate and affordable
computer aided diagnosis (CADx) systems. Mammography is the most widely
used imaging modality for predicting breast cancer in women. However, it introduces some limitations such as radiation risk, risk of false alarm, over-diagnosis or

© Springer International Publishing Switzerland 2016
A. Campilho and F. Karray (Eds.): ICIAR 2016, LNCS 9730, pp. 206–213, 2016.
DOI: 10.1007/978-3-319-41501-7_24

over-treatment, and limited sensitivity [3]. Fortunately, the introduction of ultrasound (US) medical imaging modality has helped to reduce these side effects. In general, breast ultrasound (BUS) imaging has advantages in terms of safety, cost, sensitivity, and accuracy over the conventional mammography. Although its own advantages, it requires professional radiologists. Therefore, radiologists are in need of CADx systems to help detect and analyze breast cancer. In the previous work, most of CADx systems consist of three main steps, i.e., preprocessing, feature extraction, classification [4,5].

Liu et al. [6] performed anisotropic diffusion filtering to eliminate speckle noise besides unsharp masking for edge enhancement. The filtered and enhanced image is fed into a Normalized Cut (NC) to get multiple small regions. Subsequently, alongside regions are merged into several bigger regions using region merging. Finally, potential lesions are extracted by morphological operations. Quan et al. [7] proposed to use region based NC instead of pixel based NC. In the first stage, a sigmoid filtering is applied to reinforce the differences between the ROI and the background, afterward the filtered image is divided into a group of over-segmented regions by a linear iterative clustering algorithm, where the over-segmented regions are treated as nodes rather than pixels. In the final step, the NC is applied to merge the over-segmented regions and to segment the ROI. A semi-automatic approach is introduced by Zhou et al. [8] to segment lesions in BUS images, Gaussian filter and histogram equalization are utilized to smooth and to enhance image contrast. Then, a pyramid mean shift filtering is applied to improve the homogeneity of the enhanced image. The final segmentation step is achieved, through NC and morphological operations.

This work contributes with (1) a comparative study on the most common preprocessing nonlinear techniques [9], and (2) a lesion isolation algorithm by means of Quick Shift. The paper is organized as follows. In Sect. 2, the fully automatic lesion extraction algorithm is introduced; in Sect. 3, the experimental results for proposed methods are shown and discussed. Finally, Sect. 4 concludes the work.

2 Framework

The ultrasound image contrast between the abnormality and the surrounding breast tissue is insufficient for direct lesion detection. This inherent difficulty in detection requires a considerable amount of processing to isolate candidate tumor regions. The process followed in this work can be summarized as follows: (a) the input images are preprocessed in Subsect. 2.1 to reduce the existing noise and to improve the contrast between the lesion and its surrounding, (b) the preprocessed images are segmented in Subsect. 2.2 to seek candidate lesions, and finally (c) the segmentation results are postprocessed in Subsect. 2.3 to remove any extra noisy regions. The suggested segmentation framework is presented in Fig. 1 and detailed in the following subsections.

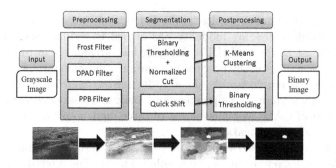

Fig. 1. The proposed framework used for lesion segmentation in BUS images.

2.1 Preprocessing

Noise reduction is a typical preprocessing step in BUS images to improve the results of later processing. Ultrasound imaging system is a coherent imaging system that produces images which suffer from speckle noise, primarily due to the interference of the returning wave at the transducer aperture [10], that degrades its quality. Several methods are used to eliminate speckle noise according to different mathematical models of the speckle phenomenon.

Frost Filter (FR). Frost et al. [11] proposed a local adaptive filter designed to despeckle images based on the local statistics. The noisy image is modeled as follows:

$$f(x,y) = [g(x,y) \cdot n(x,y)] * h(x,y), \tag{1}$$

where $f(x,y)$, $g(x,y)$, $n(x,y)$, and $h(x,y)$ denote noisy image, ideal noise-free image, noise, and impulse response in spatial coordinate (x,y), respectively. It relies upon three fundamental assumptions in its mathematical model: (1) Speckle noise is in direct proportion to the local grey level in any area, (2) The signal and the noise are statistically independent of each other, and (3) The sample mean and variance of a single pixel are equal to the mean and variance of the local area that is centered on that pixel.

Detail Preserving Anisotropic Diffusion (DPAD). Anisotropic diffusion technique was firstly introduced by Perona and Malik [12]. Speckle Reducing Anisotropic Diffusion (SRAD) filter was then proposed by Yu and Acton [13] to remove the speckle noise without removing significant parts of the image content, typically edges, lines or other details that are important for the interpretation of the image. Aja-Fernández and Alberola-López [14] has improved the speckle statistical properties estimation of [13]. The model equation is as follows:

$$I_p^{t+\triangle t} = I_p^t + \frac{\triangle t}{|\eta_p|} div[c(C_{p,t})\nabla I_p^t] \tag{2}$$

where I_p^t indicates the discrete image at p coordinate position. t represents the time step, and $|\eta_p|$ is the number of pixels in the window. ∇I_p^t indicates the gradient value, and $C_{p,t}$ represents the ratio between the local standard deviation and the local mean.

Probabilistic Patch-Based (PPB) Filter. Deledalle et al. [15] recently proposed a nonlocal means filter that performs a weighted average of the values of similar patches. These weights can be iteratively calculated based on both the similarity of noisy patches and their previous estimated similarity. The estimate value $\hat{f}_s^i(c)$ of the center pixel c at the patch s at ith iteration can be obtained by performing a weighted average w of all the pixels in the image,

$$\hat{f}_s^i(c) = \sum_t w(s,t) f_t(c), \qquad (3)$$

where $f_t(c)$ is the center pixel at the patch t. The iteration is repeated until there is no more change between two consecutive estimates.

2.2   Segmentation

Image segmentation is the process of partitioning the image into multiple segments (e.g. set of pixels or superpixels). The goal of segmentation is to isolate the lesion(s) from its surrounding pixels to put it into a more meaningful representation for doctors where normal and suspected regions are identified. In this work, Quick Shift is proposed as a robust fast segmentation step with significant effect in the breast cancer detection framework. The significance of our results is shown by comparing it to Normalized Cut which has been frequently used for the same purpose [6,16].

Quick Shift (QS). Quick Shift is based on an approximation of kernelized Mean-Shift. It is a local mode-seeking algorithm and is applied to the 5D space consisting of color information and image location. QS computes a hierarchical segmentation on multiple scales simultaneously and iteratively forms a tree of links to the nearest neighbor [17].

For each pixel (x,y), QS regards $(x,y,I(x,y))$ as a sample from a $d+2$ dimensional vector space. It then calculates the Parzen density estimate $P(x,y,I(x,y))$ with a Gaussian kernel [18]. Then QS constructs a tree connecting each image pixel (x,y) to its nearest neighbor $(x\prime,y\prime)$ which has greater density value where $(x',y') > (x,y) \Leftrightarrow P(x',y',I(x',y')) > P(x,y,I(x,y))$. Each pixel is connected to its closest higher density pixel.

Normalized Cut (NC). Normalized Cut is a graph partitioning problem based on a global criterion for segmentation that measures both the total similarity within the groups and the total dissimilarity between the different groups. It is based on a generalized eigenvalue problem used to optimize the NC criterion [19]. Gao et al. [16] proposed using NC after a boundary-detection function which combines texture and intensity information. Their algorithm defines a homogeneous patch for each pixel using the boundary map from the boundary-detection function.

2.3 Postprocessing

Lesion selection is a postprocessing step to find a correct lesion per image. The main reason of this step is choosing only one non-boundary region with the highest contrast value and the largest area among other candidate regions in global neighborhood. The eigenvectors of Normalized Cut segmentation are applied to k-means clustering method [20] to find lesion candidates across these different eigenvectors, while the Quick Shift easily selects the correct lesion by applying the gray-scale output to empirical binary thresholding.

3   Experiments and Discussion

A set of 20 breast B-mode ultrasound images [21] has been collected from different patients through UDIAT Diagnostic Center of Sabadell (Spain) with a Siemens ACUSON Sequoia C512 system 17L5 HD linear array transducer (8.5 MHz). Ground truth assessments are provided by an experienced radiologist to delineate any kind of lesion inside the images. For the proposed preprocessing algorithms, default parameter values of [FR, DPAD, PPB] are stably assigned, as stated in the very recent survey by Zhang et al. [9] to compare despeckle filters for breast ultrasound images. For the proposed segmentation methods, source codes of [QS[1], NC[2]] are publicly available. The parameters were empirically selected from half of the dataset. The second half was tested with these parameters. The reported results show that there is no need to further tune any of them and they can be directly applied to any new image. Values of the QS parameters (color/spatial ratio, kernel size, and maximum distance between pixels) are 0.8, 5 and 20 respectively. The input image of NC is empirically binarized after the preprocessing process, and its parameter (number of segments) is set to 4.

In order to evaluate the proposed methods quantitatively, three well-known statistical measures are used: Dice similarity coefficient, Jaccard similarity index (aka Area Overlap), and Sensitivity (aka True Positive Rate or Recall). Previous works [4–8] described different segmentation methods to discriminate bright lesions within BUS images. It should be noted that a fair comparison between methods is hard to make since results are based on different datasets. The proposed methods are implemented using MATLAB (R2014b, MathWorks Inc., MA) on a windows-based PC platform (Intel core i7-3630QM, 2.4 GHz and 8 GB

---

[1] http://www.vlfeat.org/overview/quickshift.html.
[2] http://www.timotheecour.com/software/ncut/ncut.html.

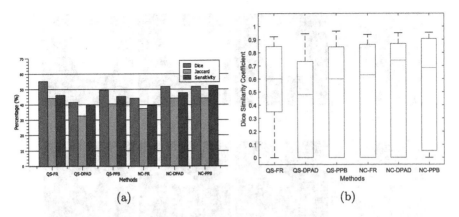

Fig. 2. Performance results across all proposed methods (segmentation [QS: Quick Shift and NC: Normalized Cut] and preprocessing [FR: Frost Filter, DPAD: Detail Preserving Anisotropic Diffusion and PPB: Probabilistic Patch-Based]): (a) Statistical metrics of Dice, Jaccard and Sensitivity measures calculated in average across all dataset images. (b) Box plot of Dice similarity coefficient. (Color figure online)

RAM). For 360×528 image, the run time of Quick Shift method (7.92 s) is $8\times$ faster than Normalized Cut method (65.51 s). Figure 2(a) shows analytical results of the proposed methods (segmentation, preprocessing). The following methods (Quick Shift with Frost Filter [QS-FR], Normalized Cut with Detail Preserving Anisotropic Diffusion [NC-DPAD] and Normalized Cut with Probabilistic Patch-Based [NC-PPB]) achieve best results among variant metrics (especially in Jaccard similarity coefficient) with slightly difference in comparison. Dice similarity coefficient shows superior achievement of [QS-FR] against other best candidates [NC-DPAD, NC-PPB], while the Sensitivity of NC-PPB is the best among others.

Figure 2(b) describes box plot of Dice Jaccard similarity coefficient for all proposed methods. [QS-FR] is less distributed among other methods (especially compared to the other candidates: [NC-DPAD, NC-PPB]), although the later methods achieve the best median results respectively. The failure cases exist in all methods due to the intensity similarity of surrounding tissues around the target lesion, leading to incorrect segmentation behavior without any prior knowledge while executing the preprocessing phase.

Figure 3 displays qualitative results of corrected lesion extraction for the best proposed methods [QS-FR, NC-DPAD, NC-PPB], such that similar acceptable outcomes are computed leading to decide the best method to be [QS-FR] as shown in the previously stated quantitative results. To sum up, QS needs a non-complex despeckle filter (FR) with efficient computation perspective to get a proper segmentation result.

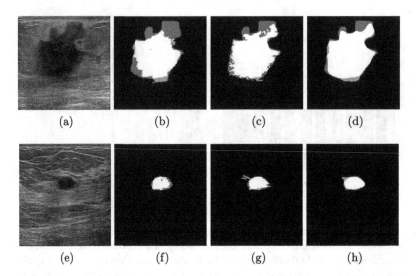

Fig. 3. Results of some successful lesion extraction for best proposed candidates. First column represents some of the input images. Second, third and fourth columns show the output results of [QS-FR, NC-DPAD, NC-PPB] respectively, in which white color is true segmented lesion, green color is false positive, red color is false negative and black color is true negative. (Color figure online)

4   Conclusion

In this paper, an automatic approach is proposed to detect breast lesions in ultrasound images. Three different filtering methods are analyzed for speckle noise reduction: FR, DPAD and PPB. NC and QS are used for breast lesions segmentation followed by a postprocessing step to select the correct candidate region from the output of segmentation step. The quantitative results are computed as average across all images such that our best performance is conducted through FR with QS, DPAD with NC and PPB with NC. The first combination is superior in terms of computational complexity, thereby it is a more preferable choice in real time applications. In the future, we would like to increase the dataset size and to use superpixel segmentation approaches to obtain more accurate and robust results.

References

1. Ferlay, J., Soerjomataram, I., Dikshit, R., Eser, S., Mathers, C., Rebelo, M., Parkin, D.M., Forman, D., Bray, F.: Cancer incidence and mortality worldwide: sources, methods and major patterns in GLOBOCAN 2012. Int. J. Cancer **136**(5), E359–E386 (2015)
2. Bray, F., Ren, J.S., Masuyer, E., Ferlay, J.: Global estimates of cancer prevalence for 27 sites in the adult population in 2008. Int. J. Cancer **132**(5), 1133–1145 (2013)

3. Heywang-Köbrunner, S.H., Hacker, A., Sedlacek, S.: Advantages and disadvantages of mammography screening. Breast Care **6**(3), 199–207 (2011)
4. Cheng, H., Shan, J., Ju, W., Guo, Y., Zhang, L.: Automated breast cancer detection and classification using ultrasound images: a survey. Pattern Recognit. **43**(1), 299–317 (2010)
5. Noble, J.A., Boukerroui, D.: Ultrasound image segmentation: a survey. IEEE Trans. Med. Imaging **25**(8), 987–1010 (2006)
6. Liu, X., Huo, Z., Zhang, J.: Automated segmentation of breast lesions in ultrasound images. In: 27th Annual International Conference of the Engineering in Medicine and Biology Society, IEEE-EMBS 2005, pp. 7433–7435. IEEE (2006)
7. Quan, L., Zhang, D., Yang, Y., Liu, Y., Qin, Q.: Segmentation of tumor ultrasound image via region-based ncut method. Wuhan Univ. J. Nat. Sci. **18**(4), 313–318 (2013)
8. Zhou, Z., Wu, W., Wu, S., Tsui, P.H., Lin, C.C., Zhang, L., Wang, T.: Semi-automatic breast ultrasound image segmentation based on mean shift and graph cuts. Ultrason. Imaging **36**(4), 256–276 (2014)
9. Zhang, J., Wang, C., Cheng, Y.: Comparison of despeckle filters for breast ultrasound images. Circuits Syst. Signal Process. **34**(1), 185–208 (2015)
10. Forouzanfar, M., Abrishami-Moghaddam, H.: Ultrasound Speckle Reduction in the Complex Wavelet Domain. In: Principles of Waveform Diversity and Design. SciTech Publishing an imprint of the IET, pp. 558–577 (2010)
11. Frost, V.S., Stiles, J.A., Shanmugan, K., Holtzman, J.: A model for radar images and its application to adaptive digital filtering of multiplicative noise. IEEE Trans. Pattern Anal. Mach. Intell. PAMI **4**(2), 157–166 (1982)
12. Perona, P., Malik, J.: Scale-space and edge detection using anisotropic diffusion. IEEE Trans. Pattern Anal. Mach. Intell. **12**, 629–639 (1990)
13. Yu, Y., Acton, S.: Speckle reducing anisotropic diffusion. IEEE Trans. Image Process. **11**, 1260–1270 (2002)
14. Aja-Fernández, S., Alberola-López, C.: On the estimation of the coefficient of variation for anisotropic diffusion speckle filtering. IEEE Trans. Image Process. **15**(9), 2694–2701 (2006)
15. Deledalle, C.A., Denis, L., Tupin, F.: Iterative weighted maximum likelihood denoising with probabilistic patch-based weights. IEEE Trans. Image Process. **18**(12), 2661–2672 (2009)
16. Gao, L., Yang, W., Liao, Z., Liu, X., Feng, Q., Chen, W.: Segmentation of ultrasonic breast tumors based on homogeneous patch. Med. Phys. **39**(6), 3299–3318 (2012)
17. Vedaldi, A., Soatto, S.: Quick shift and kernel methods for mode seeking. In: European Conference on Computer Vision (2008)
18. Parzen, E.: On estimation of a probability density function and mode. Ann. Math. Stat. **33**(3), 1065–1076 (1962)
19. Shi, J., Malik, J.: Normalized cuts and image segmentation. IEEE Trans. Pattern Anal. Mach. Intell. **22**(8), 888–905 (2000)
20. Vedaldi, A., Fulkerson, B.: VLFeat: an open and portable library of computer vision algorithms. In: Proceedings of the International Conference on Multimedia, pp. 1469–1472. ACM (2010)
21. Pons, G., Martí, J., Martí, R., Ganau, S., Vilanova, J.C., Noble, J.A.: Evaluating lesion segmentation on breast sonography as related to lesion type. J. Ultrasound Med. **32**(9), 1659–1670 (2013)

Pattern Analysis and Recognition

Phenotypic Integrated Framework
for Classification of ADHD Using fMRI

Atif Riaz$^{(\boxtimes)}$, Eduardo Alonso, and Greg Slabaugh

City University London, EC1V 0HB London, UK
{Atif.Riaz,E.Alonso,Gregory.Slabaugh.1}@city.ac.uk

Abstract. Attention Deficit Hyperactive Disorder (ADHD) is one of the most common disorders affecting young children, and its underlying mechanism is not completely understood. This paper proposes a phenotypic integrated machine learning framework to investigate functional connectivity alterations between ADHD and control subjects not diagnosed with ADHD, employing fMRI data. Our aim is to apply computational techniques to (1) automatically classify a person's fMRI signal as ADHD or control, (2) identify differences in functional connectivity of these two groups and (3) evaluate the importance of phenotypic information for classification. In the first stage of our framework, we determine the functional connectivity of brain regions by grouping brain activity using clustering algorithms. Next, we employ Elastic Net based feature selection to select the most discriminant features from the dense functional brain network and integrate phenotypic information. Finally, a support vector machine classifier is trained to classify ADHD subjects vs. control. The proposed framework was evaluated on a public dataset ADHD-200, and our classification results outperform the state-of-the-art on some subsets of the data.

Keywords: ADHD · Density clustering · Affinity propagation · Elastic net

1 Introduction

The brain can be envisioned as a large and complicated network controlling the complex systems of the body. While coordinating bodily function, the brain regions continuously share information, and regions exhibiting temporal correlation are said to be functionally connected. Research studies have shown that brain disorders such as Alzheimer's disease, epilepsy, ADHD can alter the functional connectivity of the brain network [1]. Accurate identification of altered functional connectivity induced by a particular disorder is thus an important task and may highlight the underlying mechanism of the disorder. Recently, resting state functional MRI (fMRI) has emerged as a promising neuroimaging tool to investigate functional activity of brain regions. In particular, fMRI has been employed to identify the connectivity alterations induced by disorders such as epilepsy, schizophrenia, and ADHD.

ADHD is one of the most common neurodevelopmental and mental disorders found in young children, affecting 5–10 % of children [2]. Like many other brain disorders, the mechanism underlying ADHD is still unknown [2]. ADHD has received significant research focus, including studies employing fMRI to investigate functional connectivity

© Springer International Publishing Switzerland 2016
A. Campilho and F. Karray (Eds.): ICIAR 2016, LNCS 9730, pp. 217–225, 2016.
DOI: 10.1007/978-3-319-41501-7_25

alterations in ADHD: [3] proposed a functional-anatomical discriminative region model for the identification of discriminant features and pattern classification of ADHD, and evaluated Elastic Net [4] based feature selection. Dey *et al.* [2] employed attributed graph distance measures for classification of ADHD, and similarly [1] investigated different graph based measures to assess their discriminative power. Tabas *et al.* [5] proposed a variant of Independent Component Analysis (ICA) to characterize the differences between control and patients, employing fMRI data. In [6] authors have applied a Bag of Words approach for classification of ADHD and achieved highest accuracy of 65 % on the Kennedy Krieger Institute (KKI) dataset. The studies show encouraging results, and demonstrate that machine learning techniques hold promise for the analysis of neuroimaging data.

In this paper, our motivation is to study functional connectivity alterations induced by ADHD. However, unlike previous work that relies on the image data alone, we integrate phenotypic data (such as age, gender, and IQ scores) in our machine learning framework to identify discriminant features to classify individuals as ADHD or non-ADHD (control). Our framework has several stages. In the first stage, the functional connectivity between brain regions is determined using the Affinity Propagation (AP) clustering algorithm [7]. Instead of requiring number of clusters in advance, AP takes a measure of similarity between data points and initial preference for each point for being cluster centroid. We propose a novel method to find these cluster centroids through a matrix derived from the Density Peaks (DP) algorithm by Rodriguez and Laio [8]. To our knowledge, this is the first paper to apply DP for classification of fMRI. Next, we select discriminant features through Elastic Net (EN), which combines shrinkage with grouped selection of variables. Finally we employ a support vector machine classifier to classify between control and ADHD. We demonstrate that the integrated phenotypic information in our framework improves performance.

This work makes several contributions. First, we propose a novel method to initialize the AP clustering algorithm by employing the Density Peaks approach. Second, we demonstrate the importance of phenotypic information for classification of control vs. ADHD based on functional connectivity between brain regions. In addition, our experimental results outperform the previous state-of-the-art for three test datasets of the publically available ADHD 200 data.

2   Data

The resting state fMRI data used in this study is from the NeuroBureau ADHD-200 competition [9]. The data consists of resting state functional MRI data as well as different phenotypic information for each subject. There was a global competition held for classification of ADHD subjects, and the consortium has provided training and an independent test dataset for each imaging site. For this study we employed datasets from four sites: Kennedy Krieger Institute (KKI), NeuroImage (NI), New York University Medical Center (NYU) and Peking University (Peking). All sites have a different number of subjects. Also, imaging sites have different scan parameters and equipment, which makes the dataset complex as well as diverse. This data has been pre-processed as part of the connectome project [10] and brain is parcellated into 90 regions using the Automated Anatomical Labelling [11] atlas. A more detailed description of the data and pre-processing steps appears in [9]. We have integrated phenotypic information of age, gender, verbal IQ, performance IQ and Full4 IQ, for all sites except from NeuroImage, for which phenotypic information is not available.

3   Methods

Our framework consists of the following modules: functional connectivity calculation, feature selection, phenotypic integration and classification. A block diagram of the methodological framework is presented in Fig. 1 and described below.

3.1   Dataset Balancing

In our study, datasets from two imaging sites are imbalanced, e.g. for Peking (61 Control vs. 24 ADHD) and for KKI (61 Control vs. 22 ADHD). This imbalance may hamper the performance of a classifier, which may overly focus on the majority class. One approach might be to apply random oversampling of the minority class or under sampling the majority class to balance the training dataset, but these strategies have been shown to have suboptimal performance [12]. Instead, we employ Synthetic Minority Over-sampling Technique (SMOTE) [13] to create synthetic minority samples. Consider $I_A \in I$, where I is the total set of individual subjects, and I_A is the set of minority ADHD subjects, and we denote an individual sample in I_A as x_i. We can synthesize additional minority subjects as

$$x_s = x_i + (\hat{x}_i - x_i) \times r \tag{1}$$

where $\hat{x}_i$ is a randomly chosen subject from K-nearest neighbours of $x_i \in I_A$, x_s is a synthetic subject and r is random number such that $r \in [0, 1]$.

3.2   Functional Connectivity

Functional connectivity can be estimated by correlation of time-domain signals [1, 2], as well as clustering [14]. We propose a hybrid framework which employs Affinity Propagation (AP) clustering [7] and the Density Peaks (DP) algorithm [8] for functional connectivity estimation.

   One of the most appealing properties of AP clustering is that it does not require an initial number of clusters. Instead, it takes a measure of similarity between data points. AP clustering is a message-passing algorithm where each data point is simultaneously considered as potential centroid and as being part of any cluster. Messages are passed between all data points until robust clusters and their centroids emerge. There are two kinds of messages passed between data points, namely responsibility and availability messages. The responsibility message $r(i,j)$ is sent from region i to a potential centroid candidate j, reflects the accumulated strength for how well suited region j is to serve as cluster centroid for region i, taking into consideration all other potential cluster centroids for the region. The availability message $a(i,j)$ is sent from a potential centroid candidate j to region i, and reflects the accumulated strength for how well suited it would be for region i to select region j as its centroid. Availability messages for all regions are initialized as

$$a(i,j) = 0 \tag{2}$$

and the responsibility is calculated as

$$r(i,j) = S(i,j) - \max_{j',j' \neq j}\{a(i,j') + S(i,j')\} \tag{3}$$

with the availability message as

$$a(i,j) = \min\left\{0, r(j,j) + \sum_{i',i' \neq \{i,j\}} \max\{0, r(i',j)\}\right\} \tag{4}$$

where S in Eq. 3 is the similarity measure between brain regions which is initialized as

$$S(i,j) = -\sqrt{\sum_{k=1}^{t}\left(\frac{(i_k - j_k)^2}{\sigma_k^2}\right)} \tag{5}$$

where σ_k is the standard deviation of kth dimension and t is the time points of regions. Instead of requiring an initial guess for number of clusters, the AP clustering algorithm requires a preference value p assigned for each region as the initial probability of being a cluster centroid. Selection of the preference value impacts the number of clusters produced [7, 14]. The value may be assigned to be median or minimum of similarities [7]. However, in this study we propose a novel method to initialize the preference value. We propose to estimate this initial strength for each region as being cluster centroid through the Density Peaks algorithm [8]. The density peak algorithm proposes that the cluster center can be identified as the points that have higher local density and are at larger distance from points with higher density. We initialize the preference for each region as

$$p(i) = \frac{\rho_i \delta_i - \min(\rho_i \delta_i)}{\max(\rho_i \delta_i) - \min(\rho_i \delta_i)} \times (N - 1) + c \tag{6}$$

where N is the number of brain regions ($N = 90$), $c = N/6$, ρ_i is the density of region i calculated as

$$\rho_i = \sum_{j}^{N} f(d_{ij} - d_c) \tag{7}$$

where d_c is a cut-off distance controlling the number of neighbors of i, and f is

$$f(x) = \begin{cases} 1, & if\ x<0 \\ 0, & otherwise \end{cases} \tag{8}$$

and δ_i is calculated as

$$\delta_i = \min_{j:\rho_j > \rho_i} d_{ij} \tag{9}$$

After initializing p, the availability and responsibility messages are updated, until robust clusters and their centroids emerge. From the AP clustering algorithm results, we construct a matrix M as

$$M_l(i,j) = \begin{cases} 1, & if\ i\ and\ j\ are\ in\ same\ cluster \\ 0, & otherwise \end{cases} \tag{10}$$

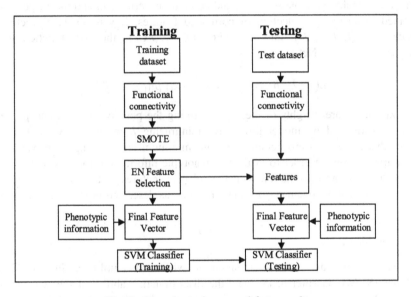

Fig. 1. Flowchart of proposed framework.

The cut-off distance d_c in Eq. 7 impacts clustering by varying the preference value computed in Eq. 6, yielding different clustering results. To address this issue, the AP clustering algorithm is run multiple times to yield multiple M matrices, with varying d_c so that the average number of neighbors is around 2 % to 8 % of the total number of points. Through these multiple runs of clustering, we produce K number of M matrices and calculate a functional connectivity matrix,

$$FC(i,j) = \frac{1}{K}\sum_{l=1}^{K} M_l(i,j) \tag{11}$$

This matrix represents the functional connectivity of a subject, such that each entry in $FC(i,j)$ represents an estimate of probability that the ith and j^{th} regions belong to the same functional connectivity. The constructed functional connectivity matrix of Eq. 11 has a dimensionality of 4005 ($90 \times 90/2$) unique features. The high dimension of the matrix may degrade the performance of classifier (the well known "curse of dimensionality" problem). Therefore, there is a need to select discriminant features.

3.3 Discriminant Feature Selection

The functional connectivity matrix may contain highly correlated features. We therefore investigate Elastic Net (EN) based feature selection [4] for extracting discriminant features. EN is an embedded based feature selection algorithm that encourages grouped selection of features and takes advantage of both lasso and ridge regression by combining their penalties in one single solution. Similar to lasso, the L_1 penalty is employed to enable variable selection and continuous shrinkage, and the L_2 penalty is combined to encourage selection of correlated features. If y is the label vector for subjects, $y_i \in (l_1, l_2, \ldots l_n)$, and $X = \{FC_1, FC_2, \ldots FC_n\}$, the cost function to be minimized by Elastic Net is

$$L(\lambda_1, \lambda_2, \beta) = ||y - X\beta||^2 + \lambda_1 ||\beta||_1 + \lambda_2 ||\beta||^2 \tag{12}$$

where λ_1 and λ_2 are weights of the terms forming the penalty function and β coefficients are estimated by model fitting. By minimizing L in Eq. 12, we extract the features that have non-zero coefficients with minimum error during cross validation using a training set. In order to evaluate phenotypic information for classification, we integrate phenotypic information with the selected features to formulate a combined feature set that can be evaluated for classification, as described in the next subsection.

3.4 Classification

The next step in our study is classification where we employ a Support Vector Machines (SVM) classifier to evaluate the discriminative ability of the selected features. SVM is a popular machine learning classifier and has been successfully evaluated in a number of neuroimaging studies (e.g., [14]). It seeks an optimal margin between the two classes (control and ADHD) during training, using labeled training data (1 for control, 2 for ADHD). The learned model is then employed for testing by presenting unseen testing data. The SVM classifier then predicts the label (control or ADHD) for each test subject.

4 Experimentation and Results

The proposed framework was evaluated on a dataset provided by the ADHD-200 consortium, and contains four categories of subjects: controls, ADHD-Combined, ADHD-Hyperactive/Impulsive, and ADHD-inattentive. Here we propose a binary classification problem: controls vs. ADHD, by combining all ADHD subtypes in one category, since we want to investigate differences and classification between control and ADHD.

We train the SVM classifier on training data employing selected features and phenotypic information as mentioned above. SMOTE was applied on Peking and KKI datasets to address the data imbalance issue described earlier. The trained SVM classifier was tested with independent test data provided for each individual site, and results are presented in Table 1, which also provides results with the results of competition teams (reported from NITRC [9]) and highest accuracy achieved by teams in individual imaging sites (data from [3]). It should be noted that parameters of our framework are held constant for all the datasets.

The results show that our framework outperforms the state-of-the-art in three (Peking, KKI and NYU) out of four imaging sites. Our framework performs well in different datasets despite of their diversity. Lower performance on the NI dataset might be due to the fewer number of training subjects and the lack of phenotyping information (unavailable for NI). In order to evaluate the importance of phenotyping information in our framework, we computed the results without integrating the phenotyping information. These results are presented in Table 2, which shows that phenotyping information provides better classification results for Peking and NYU.

For evaluation of our proposed novel methodology to initialize the AP clusters as discussed in Sect. 3.1, we compared our results with standard AP clustering results presented in Table 3.

Table 1. Comparison of our results with average results of competition teams [9] and highest accuracy achieved for individual site [3].

Name	Average accuracy [9]	Highest accuracy [3]	Our accuracy
Peking	51.0 %	58 %	**64.7 %**
KKI	43.1 %	81 %	**81.8 %**
NYU	32.3 %	56 %	**60.9 %**
NI	56.9 %	–	44.0 %

Table 2. Accuracy results with and without integrating phenotyping information.

Name	Accuracy with phenotyping	Accuracy without phenotyping
Peking	**64.7 %**	58.8 %
KKI	**81.8 %**	**81.8 %**
NYU	**60.9 %**	24.3 %

Table 3 shows that our proposed methodology is able to achieve better accuracy than AP clustering in all imaging sites.

Table 3. Comparison of our proposed methodology with AP results. Results show that our proposed methodology achieves better accuracy than AP clustering.

Name	Proposed methodology			AP clustering		
	Specificity	Sensitivity	Accuracy	Specificity	Sensitivity	Accuracy
Peking	**92.5 %**	**33.3 %**	**64.7 %**	81.4 %	**33.3 %**	58.8 %
KKI	75.0 %	**100.0 %**	**81.8 %**	87.5 %	33.3 %	72.7 %
NYU	**41.6 %**	**68.9 %**	**60.9 %**	41.6 %	62.0 %	56.1 %
NI	**42.8 %**	45.4 %	**44.0 %**	7.1 %	**63.6 %**	32.0 %

5   Conclusions

In this paper we have addressed the problem of identification of discriminant features between control and ADHD subjects for classification based upon fMRI data. Classification of neuroimaging data is considered a difficult task due to the high dimensionality of data. We have proposed a machine learning based framework for this problem and evaluated our method on four training and test datasets provided by NITRC. Our framework introduces a novel method for estimation of functional connectivity between brain regions. The brain is a complex network where a number of brain regions show coherent activity. Therefore, discriminant features might be highly correlated with other. Here, we employed Elastic Net for feature selection that encourages uncorrelated feature selection. In this work, we have evaluated importance of phenotypic information by integrating with selected features. Our results show that Elastic Net based feature selection integrated with phenotypic information may provide an important feature selection strategy. Our selected features and SVM classifier was able to outperform the state-of-the-art in classification accuracy on data from three institutions. In future work we will explore the clinical interpretation of the functional connectivity alterations produced in our framework, particularly in light of the phenotypic information.

References

1. dos Santos Siqueira, A., et al.: Abnormal functional resting-state networks in ADHD: graph theory and pattern recognition analysis of fMRI data. Biomed Res. Int. **2014**, 1–10 (2014)
2. Dey, S., Rao, A.R., Shah, M.: Attributed graph distance measure for automatic detection of attention deficit hyperactive disordered subjects. Front. Neural Circuits **8**, 64 (2014)
3. Nuñez-Garcia, M., Simpraga, S., Jurado, M.A., Garolera, M., Pueyo, R., Igual, L.: FADR: functional-anatomical discriminative regions for rest fMRI characterization. In: Zhou, L., Wang, L., Wang, Q., Shi, Y. (eds.) MLMI 2015. LNCS, vol. 9352, pp. 61–68. Springer, Heidelberg (2015)
4. Zou, H., Hastie, T.: Regularization and variable selection via the elastic net. J. Roy. Stat. Soc. Ser. B (Stat. Methodol) **67**(2), 301–320 (2005)

5. Tabas, A., Balaguer-Ballester, E., Igual, L.: Spatial discriminant ICA for RS-fMRI characterisation. In: Proceedings of 2014 International Workshop on Pattern Recognition in Neuroimaging, PRNI 2014, pp. 1–4 (2014)

6. Solmaz, B., Dey, S., Rao, A.R., Shah, M.: ADHD classification using bag of words approach on network features. In: SPIE Medical Imaging, pp. 83144T–83144T (2012)

7. Frey, B.J., Dueck, D.: Clustering by passing messages between data points. Science **315**(5814), 972–976 (2007)

8. Rodriguez, A., Laio, A.: Clustering by fast search and find of density peaks. Science **344**(6191), 1492–1496 (2014)

9. The ADHD-200 Sample. http://fcon_1000.projects.nitrc.org/indi/adhd200/

10. Preporcessed Connectome Project. http://neurobureau.projects.nitrc.org/ADHD200/Introduction.html

11. Tzourio-Mazoyer, N., et al.: Automated anatomical labeling of activations in SPM using a macroscopic anatomical parcellation of the MNI MRI single-subject brain. Neuroimage **15**(1), 273–289 (2002)

12. He, H., Garcia, E.A.: Learning from imbalanced data. Knowl. Data Eng. IEEE Trans. **21**(9), 1263–1284 (2009)

13. Chawla, N.V., et al.: SMOTE: synthetic minority over-sampling technique. J. Artif. Intell. Res. **16**, 321–357 (2002)

14. Rajpoot, K., et al.: Functional connectivity alterations in epilepsy from resting-state functional MRI. PLoS ONE **10**(8), e0134944 (2015)

Directional Local Binary Pattern
for Texture Analysis

Abuobayda M. Shabat and Jules-Raymond Tapamo[✉]

School of Engineering, Howard College Campus, University of KwaZulu-Natal,
Durban 4041, South Africa
abshabat@gmail.com, tapamoj@ukzn.ac.za

Abstract. In this paper, a new features method, the Directional Local
Binary Pattern (DLBP), is presented, with an objective to improve Local
Directional Pattern (LDP) for texture analysis. The idea of Directional
DLBP is inspired by the stability of the Kirsch mask directional responses
and the LBP neighboring concept. The result shows that Directional
Local Binary Pattern outperforms LDP and LBP.

Keywords: Texture features · Local Directional Pattern · Directional
Local Binary Pattern · Local Binary Pattern · Classification

1 Introduction

The main goal of texture analysis is to quantify the different qualities of an
image, such as smoothness, roughness, and bumpiness. This is modeled as a
spatial variation in pixel gray values. Texture represents a basic level of spatial
properties of a digital image, and can be defined as relationship between gray
levels in neighboring pixels [2]. Texture analysis has been applied in several areas,
including medical image analysis, biometrics, and security.

Gray Level Co-occurrence Matrix (GLCM) is one of the commonly used
textures based features extraction techniques. Haralick et al. [3] proposed it in
the early 1970s. It has since been used in many applications.

A study by Song et al. [12] used LBP operator to analyze textures of multi-
spectral images. The technique used achieved more than 4 % gain in the performance, compared to the popular GLCM method. Musci et al. [7] investigated the
use of Local phase quantization (LPQ) and LBP to characterize land-cover and
land-use. The result establishes that both LBP and LPQ outperform GLCM.

The successful application of the LBP inspired many scholars for further
research. Several adjustments of LBP have been proposed [1,8,10]. However,
LBP suffers from random noise, because it depends on neighboring pixels intensity. A more stable technique, based on Krisch masks, Local Directional Pattern
was recently presented by Jabid et al. [4]. LDP considers the edge response
values in eight directions around the pixels obtained from the Krisch gradient
operator rather than the raw pixel intensities like LBP. LDP has been applied

© Springer International Publishing Switzerland 2016
A. Campilho and F. Karray (Eds.): ICIAR 2016, LNCS 9730, pp. 226–233, 2016.
DOI: 10.1007/978-3-319-41501-7_26

in many areas, including texture classification [11], and facial expression interpretation [4]. One of the drawbacks of LDP is the number of significant bits, k,
considered after the generation of Kirsch mask responses. The choice $k = 3$, as
established in the literature is empirical. A careful investigation revealed that the
change in the value of k affects the performance of LDP. DLBP takes the best
of both LDP and Local Binary Pattern (LBP), by first computing the gradient
directional responses since it is more stable than the local neighboring following
LDP concept. And generates the code following the LBP concept.

2   Features Methods for Texture Analysis

Features extraction is one of the key processes in texture analysis. In this paper,
Local Binary Pattern (LBP), Local Directional Pattern (LDP) together with the
proposed Directional Local Binary Pattern (DLBP) are presented.

2.1   Local Binary Pattern

Local binary pattern introduced by Ojala et al. [8] is inspired by the general
definition of texture in the local neighbourhood. Given an image of size $R \times C$,
for each pixel $p = (x, y)$, where $0 \le x \le R$ and $0 \le y \le C$, the LBP code of p is
computed as

$$LBP_N(x, y) = \sum_{i=0}^{N-1} S(g_i - g_p)2^i \tag{1}$$

where g_p and g_i are the gray levels of pixel p and its ith neighbor, respectively;
and the function $S(x)$ is defined as

$$S(x) = \begin{cases} 1 & \text{if } x \ge 0 \\ 0 & \text{otherwise} \end{cases} \tag{2}$$

If for each pixel, N neighbors are considered, we can have 2^N distinct values
for the LBP code. It means a gray-scale image representing a texture can be
characterized using a 2^N-bin discrete distribution.

2.2   Local Directional Pattern

Local Directional Pattern (LDP) was introduced by Jabid et al. [4]. It has mostly
been used in face based biometrics and has received little attention from other
areas. LDP descriptors of an image are calculated using eight bit binary codes
generated from Kirsch masks application on each pixel of this image. Detailed
description of the three steps used to calculated LDP descriptors of an image I
is given below [5]:

1. **Computation of response values using Kirsch mask application:** for each pixel (x, y), Kirsch mask convolution response values, $(K_{M_0}(x, y), K_{M_1}(x, y) \ldots, K_{M_7}(x, y))$, are generated using Eq. 3 as

$$K_{M_q}(x, y) = \sum_{i=-1}^{1} \sum_{j=-1}^{1} M_q(i, j) \times I(x + i, y + j) \qquad (3)$$

where $K_{M_q}(x, y)$ represents the response value at direction M_q (see Fig. 1), for $q = 0, 1, \ldots, 7$. K_{M_q}, for $q = 0, 1, \ldots, 7$ are then allocated ranks based on their absolute values as shown in Fig. 2(b). In the rest of the text $K_{M_q} = m_q$

2. **Generation of LDP code:** assuming that k significant bits will be considered, from Kirsch mask convolution responses generated in the previous step set to 1 the corresponding bit positions of the k most significant responses, and leave other $(8 - k)$ bits to 0. This process is implemented by the function $S(x)$ defined in Eq. 2. The resulting LDP code of the pixel (x, y), $LDP_{x,y}(m_0, m_1, \ldots, m_7)$, can be derived as

$$LDP_{x,y}(m_0, m_1, \ldots, m_7) = \sum_{i=0}^{7} S(m_i - ms_k) \times 2^i \qquad (4)$$

where ms_k is the kth most significant response and $S(x)$ is defined in Eq. 2. Considering the Kirsch mask application on pixel (x, y) shown in Fig. 2, the LDP code for $k = 3$ is generated as follows:

$$\begin{bmatrix} -3 & -3 & 5 \\ -3 & 0 & 5 \\ -3 & -3 & 5 \end{bmatrix} \quad \begin{bmatrix} -3 & -3 & 5 \\ -3 & 0 & 5 \\ -3 & -3 & 5 \end{bmatrix} \quad \begin{bmatrix} -3 & 5 & 5 \\ -3 & 0 & 5 \\ -3 & -3 & -3 \end{bmatrix} \quad \begin{bmatrix} 5 & 5 & 5 \\ -3 & 0 & -3 \\ -3 & -3 & -3 \end{bmatrix}$$
$$M_0(\text{East}) \qquad M_1(\text{North East}) \qquad M_2(\text{North}) \qquad M_3(\text{North West})$$

$$\begin{bmatrix} 5 & 5 & -3 \\ 5 & 0 & -3 \\ -3 & -3 & -3 \end{bmatrix} \quad \begin{bmatrix} 5 & -3 & -3 \\ 5 & 0 & -3 \\ 5 & -3 & -3 \end{bmatrix} \quad \begin{bmatrix} -3 & -3 & -3 \\ 5 & 0 & -3 \\ 5 & 5 & -3 \end{bmatrix} \quad \begin{bmatrix} -3 & -3 & -3 \\ -3 & 0 & 5 \\ -3 & 5 & 5 \end{bmatrix}$$
$$M_4 \text{ (West)} \qquad M_5(\text{South West}) \qquad M_6(\text{South}) \qquad M_6(\text{South Est})$$

Fig. 1. Kirsch masks

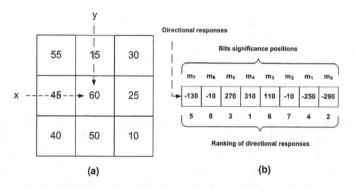

(a)   (b)

Fig. 2. Kirsch mask application response value of a pixel (x, y) with a gray value 60. (a) pixel (x, y) with the 8-neighborhood. (b) The middle row shows the directional response values, the row below represent the ranking of those responses. The ranking of responses is considered with the responses in absolute values.

- The response values are $(m_0, \ldots, m_7) = (-130, -10, 270, 310, 110, -10, -250, -290)$, and with $310, -280, 270$, being the largest values in absolute term, making m_4, m_0 and m_5 the most significant bits. $m_5 = 270$ is the 3th most significant directional response value.
- The LDP code, $LDP_{x,y}$, of the pixel (x, y) is then 49.

$$
\begin{aligned}
LDP_{x,y}(m_0, m_1, \ldots, m_7) &= \sum_{i=0}^{7} S(m_i - ms_k) \times 2^i \\
&= 0 \times 2^7 + 0 \times 2^6 + 1 \times 2^5 \\
&\quad + 1 \times 2^4 + 0 \times 2^3 + 0 \times 2^2 \\
&\quad + 0 \times 2^1 + 1 \times 2^0 \\
&= 49
\end{aligned}
$$

3. **Production of the LDP descriptor:** Given an image I of size $M \times N$, the LDP code of I, denoted by $LDP(I)$ is defined as

$$
LDP(I) = (LDP_{x,y})_{0 \leq x \leq M-1, 0 \leq y \leq N-1} \tag{5}
$$

LDP histogram can then be generated using Eq. 6, that is also called LDP descriptor. With $k = 3$, there are $56(=^8 C_3)$ distinct values generated and used to encode the image. The histogram H, with 56 bins, used to represent the image is generated using Eq. 6.

$$
H_i = \sum_{x=0}^{M-1} \sum_{y=0}^{N-1} p(LDP_{x,y}, C_i) \tag{6}
$$

where C_i is the ith LDP component, $i = 1, \ldots, ^8 C_3$ and p is defined as

$$
p(x, a) = \begin{cases} 1 & \text{if } x = 0 \\ 0 & \text{otherwise} \end{cases} \tag{7}
$$

Given a texture, T, and the number of significant bits k, a feature vector $ldb_{k,T}$ is generated and represented as

$$
ldp_{k,T} = (H_1, H_2, \ldots, H_{56}) \tag{8}
$$

2.3   Directional Local Binary Pattern

LDP proposed to solve the problem with LBP. In fact, LBP depends on neighboring pixels intensity which makes it unstable. Instead, LDP considers the edge response value in different directions. As it is well known, gradients are more stable than the gray levels. But the problem with LDP is to select the value of the number of significant bit k. The value k $= 3$ has widely been used in literature. Through our research, we established that the change in the value of the

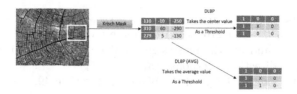

Fig. 3. The figure shows the computation of DLBP, by first calculating the eight directional edge responses and then generate the DLBP code in two different way, first, by using the center value as a threshold, secondly, using the average value as a threshold.

k affects performance. Our proposed method, Directional Local Binary Pattern (DLBP) takes the best of both LDP and LBP, by first computing the gradient directional responses since it is more stable than the local neighboring following LDP concept. And generates the code following the LBP concept.

The DLBP features are an eight binary code assigned to each pixel of an input window. DLBP descriptors are calculated in three steps:

1. Computation of Kirsch kernel application response values is similar to LDP.
2. In this step, two ways are proposed to generate DLBP code,
   (a) **Generation of DLBP code including the center pixel:** It is based on the values generated in the first step. For each pixel (x, y), its binary DLBP code can be generated by comparing the value, $v(x, y)$, to the response values $m_0, \ldots, m_7$. The DLBP code, $DLBP_{x,y}(m_0, \ldots, m_7)$, of the pixel (x, y) can then be calculated using Eq. 9.

$$DLBP_{x,y}(m_0, m_1, ..., m_7) = \sum_{i=0}^{7} S(m_i - v(x, y)) \times 2^i \qquad (9)$$

   (b) **Generation of the DLBP code, $DLBP(AVG)_{x,y}$, based on the average Kirsch mask application response values:** The average value is computed based on first step (see Eq. 10). This average is used as a threshold of $m_0, m_1, ..., m_7$. The DLBP code, $DLBP(AVG)_{x,y}$, of the pixel (x, y) for the directional response $(m_0, ..., m_7)$, is computed using Eq. 11.

$$AVG_{x,y} = \frac{\sum_{i=0}^{7} m_i + v(x, y)}{9} \qquad (10)$$

$$DLBP(AVG)_{x,y} = \sum_{i=0}^{7} S(m_i - AVG_{x,y}) \times 2^i \qquad (11)$$

Figure 3 shows an example of computation of DLBP code of a pixel.
3. The production of DLBP descriptor is similar to that of LDP descriptor using DLBP code generated in the previous step.

3   Experiments

3.1   Data Set

In our experiment, we gathered 3200 texture images from the Kylberg texture dataset [6]. These images are divided into 20 categories, each categories has 160 images. All the selected image have the size of 576 × 576. In Fig. 4 a sample of each category is shown. We used python-fortran framework to implement the proposed features using opencv and scikit-learn toolkit [9]. In this experiment, there are two main components in textural classification: Feature Extraction and Features Classification. During the features extraction stage all the proposed methods are calculated for each Image. In Features Classification, each image is classified according to the extracted features using 20 % as a test data set and the remains as a training data set.

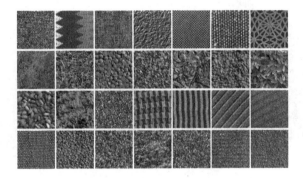

Fig. 4. The sample images of texture from Kylberg

3.2   Results and Discussion

In this section, a comparison between Local Directional Pattern, Local Binary Pattern and the presented method Directional Local Binary pattern.

The performance of LDP, LBP, DLBP and DLBP(AVG) will be compared using 6 different classifiers (K-neareast neighbor algorithm (k-NN), Support Vector Machine (SVM), Perceptron, Naive-Bayes (NB), Decision Tree (DT)) in different conditions.

Table 1 and Fig. 5 show the accuracies of LDP, LBP, DLBP and DLBP(AVG) using six different classifiers. Both DLBP and DLBP(AVG) methods are the best in performance using k-NN classifier. As the performance increases by 1 % compared to LDP and LBP. It can also be observed that the worst performances were achieved by LDP and LBP with accuracy of 93 %. For SVM classifier the three features methods LDP, DLBP and DLBP(AVG) performed equally, with an accuracy of 99 %, except LBP with accuracy of 98 %. With the DT classifier,

Table 1. Accuracies measures in % of LDP, LBP, DLBP and DLBP(AVG) using six different classifiers, $Gain_A$ is the gain when using average DLBP, and $Gain_C$ is the gain when using center DLBP

		Feature methods					
		DLBP	DLBP(AVG)	LDP	LBP	$Gain_C$	$Gain_A$
Classifiers	k-NN	94	94	93	93	+1	+1
	SVM	99	99	99	98	0	+1
	DT	94	94	88	87	+6	+7
	RF	73	78	78	70	+5	+8
	NB	90	90	86	86	+4	+4
	Perceptron	86	87	82	63	+5	+14

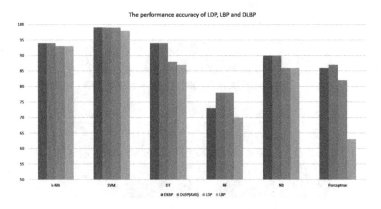

Fig. 5. The performance accuracy of LDP, LBP, DLBP and DLBP(AVG) using six different classifiers (Color figure online)

there was an increase by 6 % in the performance, as both DLBP and DLBP(AVG) performed very well (94 %), compared to LDP (88 %) and LBP (87 %). Using RF classifier, DLBP achieved the best performance with 78 %, yielding an increase of 5 %. Both NB and Perceptron Classifiers better accuracies using DBLP, with increases 6 % and 5 %, respectively. Table 1 shows that the best accuracies were achieved by DLBP(AVG) when using the Kylberg texture dataset. Improvements in performances range from 1 % to 5 %.

4   Conclusion

Directional Local Binary Pattern (DLBP) has been proposed, which enables users to select the number of significant bits for the coding features as it is done with LDP. DLBP builds on the strengths of both LDP (Local Directional Pattern) and Local Binary Pattern (LBP). It first computes the gradient directional responses since it is more stable than the local neighboring following LDP concept. It then generates the code following the LBP concept. The performances of LDP, LBP and DLBP were evaluated using Kylberg texture dataset of 3200 texture images using six different classifiers (K-neareast neighbor algorithm (KNN), Support Vector Machine (SVM), Perceptron, Naive-Bayes (NB), Adaboost, Decision Tree (DT)) in different conditions. Results show that DLBP outperforms the existing LDP and LBP.

References

1. Ahonen, T., Hadid, A., Pietikainen, M.: Face description with local binary patterns: application to face recognition. IEEE Trans. Pattern Anal. Mach. Intell. **28**(12), 2037–2041 (2006)
2. Burrascano, P., Fiori, S., Mongiardo, M.: A review of artificial neural networks applications in microwave computer-aided design (invited article). Int. J. RF Microw. Comput. Aided Eng. **9**(3), 158–174 (1999)
3. Haralick, R.M., Shanmugam, K., Dinstein, I.H.: Textural features for image classification. IEEE Trans. Syst. Man Cybern. SMC. **3**(6), 610–621 (1973)
4. Jabid, T., Kabir, M.H., Chae, O.: Local Directional Pattern (LDP) for face recognition. In: 2010 Digest of Technical Papers International Conference on Consumer Electronics (ICCE) (2010)
5. Jabid, T., Kabir, M.H., Chae, O.: Robust facial expression recognition based on local directional pattern. ETRI J. **32**(5), 784–794 (2010)
6. Kylberg, G.: Kylberg texture dataset v. 1.0 (2011)
7. Musci, M., Queiroz Feitosa, R., Costa, G.A., Fernandes Velloso, M.L.: Assessment of binary coding techniques for texture characterization in remote sensing imagery. Geosci. Remote Sens. Lett. IEEE **10**(6), 1607–1611 (2013)
8. Ojala, T., Pietikäinen, M., Mäenpää, T.: Multiresolution gray-scale and rotation invariant texture classification with local binary patterns. IEEE Trans. Pattern Anal. Mach. Intell. **24**(7), 971–987 (2002)
9. Pedregosa, F., Varoquaux, G., Gramfort, A., Michel, V., Thirion, B., Grisel, O., Blondel, M., Prettenhofer, P., Weiss, R., Dubourg, V., et al.: Scikit-learn: machine learning in Python. J. Mach. Learn. Res. **12**, 2825–2830 (2011)
10. Pietikäinen, M., Hadid, A., Zhao, G., Ahonen, T.: Computer Vision Using Local Binary Patterns. Computational Imaging and Vision, vol. 40. Springer, New York (2011)
11. Shabat, A.M., Tapamo, J.R.: A comparative study of local directional pattern for texture classification. In: 2014 World Symposium on Computer Applications & Research (WSCAR), pp. 1–7 (2014)
12. Song, C., Yang, F., Li, P.: Rotation invariant texture measured by local binary pattern for remote sensing image classification. In: 2010 Second International Workshop on Education Technology and Computer Science, pp. 3–6 (2010)

Kernel Likelihood Estimation for Superpixel Image Parsing

Hasan F. Ates$^{(\boxtimes)}$, Sercan Sunetci, and Kenan E. Ak

Department of Electrical and Electronics Engineering,
Isik University, Istanbul, Turkey
hasan.ates@isikun.edu.tr, {sercan.sunetci,kenan.ak}@isik.edu.tr

Abstract. In superpixel-based image parsing, the image is first segmented into visually consistent small regions, i.e. superpixels; then
superpixels are parsed into different categories. SuperParsing algorithm
provides an elegant nonparametric solution to this problem without any
need for classifier training. Superpixels are labeled based on the likelihood
ratios that are computed from class conditional density estimates of feature vectors. In this paper, local kernel density estimation is proposed to
improve the estimation of likelihood ratios and hence the labeling accuracy. By optimizing kernel bandwidths for each feature vector, feature
densities are better estimated especially when the set of training samples is sparse. The proposed method is tested on the SIFT Flow dataset
consisting of 2,688 images and 33 labels, and is shown to outperform
SuperParsing and some of its extended versions in terms of classification
accuracy.

Keywords: Image parsing · Image segmentation · Superpixel · Kernel
density estimation

1 Introduction

Scene and object classification are fundamental problems of computer vision with
significant body of work in literature. In the last ten years, due to the developments in machine learning and increase in computational capacity by parallel programming, complex supervised classification methods became applicable
and classification accuracies are significantly improved [1]. Superpixels recently
gained in importance in image segmentation and classification problems [2].
Superpixels represent a restricted form of region segmentation, balancing the
conflicting goals of reducing image complexity through pixel grouping while
avoiding undersegmentation [3] (see Fig. 1). There are several superpixel segmentation methods in literature [3–5]. These methods are differentiated from each
other in terms of their modeling constraints such as superpixel sizes, shapes and
regularity. The goal of superpixel based segmentation is to separate the image

H.F. Ates—This work is supported in part by TUBITAK project no: 115E307 and
by Isik University BAP project no: 14A205.

A. Campilho and F. Karray (Eds.): ICIAR 2016, LNCS 9730, pp. 234–242, 2016.
DOI: 10.1007/978-3-319-41501-7_27

Fig. 1. Superpixel segmentation

into visually meaningful atomic regions and obtain several segments that are consistent with object boundaries.

Being more flexible and consistent than pixel-based representation, super-pixel based segmentation have shown high success in classification and object detection algorithms [2]. For classification purposes, feature vectors are computed for each superpixel and classification is carried out at the superpixel level, instead of pixel-level. In superpixel-based object classification and image segmentation, in addition to standard features such as SIFT, different morphological and geometric features of superpixels are defined and used [6].

There are several image parsing/labeling methods proposed in literature; while some of them use pixel by pixel parsing [7], others use superpixel segments to parse images [8]. Most of these methods require a generative or discriminative model to be trained in advance for each class. Training is time-consuming and must be repeated if new training samples or new classes are added to the dataset. Recently nonparametric, data-driven approaches became popular [9]. There is no classifier training in these methods. Instead, for each test image, most similar training images are determined and directly used for labeling of the query image. SuperParsing [10] algorithm has this kind of architecture, uses superpixels for image labeling and requires no training, and it can easily scale to datasets with tens of thousands of images and hundreds of labels.

SuperParsing uses likelihood ratios computed from nonparametric class conditional feature densities that are estimated from the training set. Even though this approach gives successful results when the size of the dataset is medium to large, accurate estimation is not possible in the tails of the feature distribution where there are much fewer training samples especially for the under-represented, i.e. rare, classes of the dataset. As a result, there is a negative bias against these rare classes and the labeling accuracy is compromised. It is possible to balance the representation of classes in the training set by providing additional training samples for the rare classes [11]. However balancing the dataset to improve average class labeling accuracy generally reduces pixel-level accuracy.

In this paper we propose to improve likelihood estimation and overall parsing accuracy by using local kernel density estimation for class-conditional feature distributions. The bandwidths of Gaussian kernels are optimized for each feature vector in order to provide more accurate estimate of local feature densities. Estimation is carried out in adaptive local neighborhoods of feature vectors. The neighborhoods are determined according to the sparsity of training samples that belong to each class. The proposed method is tested on SIFT Flow dataset of 2,688 images and 33 labels, and substantially higher classification accuracy than SuperParsing is reported.

Section 2 summarizes the SuperParsing algorithm. Section 3 details kernel density estimation and its use in SuperParsing for improved likelihood computations. Section 4 provides and discusses the simulations results. Section 5 concludes the paper with ideas for future work.

2   SuperParsing Algorithm

In SuperParsing, first step for parsing a test image is to find a "retrieval subset" of training images. These images are used to compute the likelihood ratios and perform labeling at the superpixel level. A good retrieval set consists of images with a similar scene type, similar objects and spatial layout as the test image. In order to determine the retrieval set, scene-level matching is performed by using multiple global image descriptors (e.g. spatial pyramid [12], gist [13], tiny image [14], and color histogram).

Superpixels are used for labeling of test images based on the content of retrieval set. In [10], graph-based segmentation algorithm [5] is used for superpixel segmentation. 20 different superpixel features are used for labeling. These features include shape (e.g. superpixel area), location (e.g. superpixel mask), texture (e.g. texton/SIFT histograms), color (e.g. color histogram) descriptors of superpixels. These features are computed for each superpixel in the training set and stored together with their class labels. A class label is associated with a training superpixel if 50 % or more of the superpixel overlaps with the segment mask for that label.

2.1   Local Superpixel Labeling

Having segmented the test image, determined its retrieval set and extracted the features of all its superpixels, the final step is to compute a likelihood ratio score for each test superpixel and each class that is present in the retrieval set. Assuming that features are independent of each other, the log-likelihood ratio for each class c and superpixel s_i is:

$$L(s_i, c) = \log \frac{P(s_i|c)}{P(s_i|\bar{c})} = \sum_k \log \frac{P(f_i^k|c)}{P(f_i^k|\bar{c})} \tag{1}$$

where $\bar{c}$ is the set of all classes excluding c, and f_i^k is the feature vector of the kth type for s_i. The conditional densities $P(f_i^k|c)$, $P(f_i^k|\bar{c})$ are locally estimated in the neighborhood of f_i^k using labeled feature vectors from the retrieval set.

Specifically, if D is the set of all superpixels in the training set and N_i^k is the set of superpixels from the retrieval set within a local neighborhood of f_i^k, then

$$\frac{P(f_i^k|c)}{P(f_i^k|\bar{c})} = \frac{(n(c, N_i^k) + \epsilon)/n(c, D)}{(n(\bar{c}, N_i^k) + \epsilon)/n(\bar{c}, D)} = \frac{n(c, N_i^k) + \epsilon}{n(\bar{c}, N_i^k) + \epsilon} \times \frac{n(\bar{c}, D)}{n(c, D)} \qquad (2)$$

where $n(c, S)$ is the number of superpixels in set S with class label c, and ϵ is a small constant used to smooth likelihood counts. The set N_i^k contains retrieval set feature vectors whose L_2 distance from f_i^k is below a fixed threshold t_k. Note that the whole training set D is used to estimate $P(c)$ and $P(\bar{c})$, instead of just the retrieval set. At this point, labeling of the image can be obtained by simply assigning to each superpixel the class that maximizes Eq. (1).

3   Kernel Likelihood Estimation in SuperParsing

The data driven, nonparametric likelihood estimation in SuperParsing works well when the dataset is large enough so that there are enough training samples locally clustered around feature vectors of each superpixel in the test image. In that case, local counts of training samples from each class provide reliable measures of the class-conditional probabilities. However for rare classes, such as "door", "stair", that are under-represented in the database, the set of training samples is sparse, especially towards the tails of the distribution. It becomes even more problematic when we consider that training samples are obtained from a smaller retrieval subset of training images. Increasing the size of the feature neighborhood or the size of the retrieval set leads to matching with a higher number of unrelated samples and thus more noisy estimation of the likelihoods.

In this paper we propose to use kernel density estimation for more accurate modeling of local feature distributions. The size of the feature neighborhood is adaptively determined depending on the available set of training samples. Each sample contributes to the density estimate with a weight that is determined by a Gaussian kernel and the distance of the sample to the tested feature vector. In particular, assuming f^k is independent identically distributed (i.i.d), the probability $P(f^k)$ is given as:

$$P(f^k) = \frac{1}{Z} \sum_{j=1}^{|D|} \exp\left(-\frac{\|f^k - f_j^k\|^2}{\sigma_k^2}\right) \qquad (3)$$

where $|D|$ is the number of superpixels in the training set, σ_k is Gaussian kernel bandwidth and Z is an appropriate normalization factor. For each feature vector, the optimal bandwidth σ_k is estimated by the sskernel method of [15].

The optimized bandwidths are used for the estimation of $P(f^k|c)$ and $P(f^k|\bar{c})$ during computation of likelihoods (It turns out the optimal bandwidths for $P(f^k)$, $P(f^k|c)$ and $P(f^k|\bar{c})$ are the same in most cases). For the test superpixel s_i and its feature vector f_i^k, each training sample in its neighborhood is weighted by the kernel estimate as follows:

$$P(f_i^k|c) = \frac{1}{n(c,D)} \sum_{j=1}^{n(c,N_i^k)} \exp\left(-\frac{\|f_i^k - f_{c,j}^k\|^2}{\sigma_k^2}\right) \tag{4}$$

where $f_{c,j}^k$ are the neighboring vectors of class c. $P(f_i^k|\bar{c})$ is likewise defined.

The size of the neighborhood N_i^k is critical for correct estimation of the likelihood ratios. One choice is to use all samples in the retrieval set. However this creates over smoothed estimates of the conditional distributions. Instead we propose to select the T nearest neighbors of the test vector f_i^k, i.e. T samples with the lowest distance $\|f_i^k - f_j^k\|$.

However it is likely that T nearest neighbors will not contain samples from rare classes especially when the test vector is at the tails of the distribution $P(f^k|c)$. The proposed solution for this problem in the literature is to design a more balanced training set by introducing additional training samples for rare classes. It turns out that this solution improves average class-level accuracy but does not help much for the pixel-level accuracy. In this paper, in order to improve overall pixel-level accuracy, we propose to select an adaptive set of neighbors N_i^k for each test feature vector f_i^k. The procedure is as follows: we check the labels of T nearest neighbors in the set N_i^k; if all samples come from the same class or two different classes, then one sample $f_{c,j}^k$ with minimum distance $\|f_i^k - f_{c,j}^k\|$ is included into the set N_i^k for r additional class c. In this manner the neighborhood set is adaptively expanded when classes are under-represented.

4   Simulations and Discussions

In simulations, kernel-based estimation method is compared with original Super-Parsing and some of its modified versions. Success of algorithm is tested on SIFT Flow [9] dataset, which contains 2,688 images and 33 labels. This dataset includes scenery such as sea, coast, mountain, street, building. There are objects from 33 different semantic classes, such as sky, sea, tree, building, cars, at various densities. Dataset is separated into 2 subsets; 2.488 training images and 200 test images. In experiments overall pixel-level classification accuracy (i.e. correctly classified pixel percentage) and class-specific accuracies are compared.

The parameters of the algorithm are set as follows. The retrieval set size is 200 images, as in original SuperParsing. In graph-based segmentation method (GBS) [5], K controls superpixel color consistency and S determines the smallest superpixel size. In SuperParsing $K = 200$, $S = 100$. The nearest neighbor set size T is proportional to the average number of samples in the retrieval set. We test three alternatives: $(K = 300, S = 150, T = 20)$, $(K = 200, S = 100, T = 30)$, $(K = 400, S = 200, T = 15)$. The additional number of classes is set as $r = 4$.

We also look at two modifications of SuperParsing: Adaptive neighbor sets [11] and Multi-hypothesis SuperParsing [16]. In adaptive neighbor sets approach, each training sample in the set N_i^k is given a specific weight that is determined through extensive gradient-descent based optimization on the training set. In our

Table 1. Per-pixel labeling accuracy for SIFT Flow dataset

Method	Percentage accuracy	
	Baseline	MRF
SuperParsing1	74.11	76.20
SuperParsing2	74.08	75.80
Adaptive neighbor set	76.80	77.10
Multi-hypothesis	76.36	–
Kernel-based	76.64	77.50
Kernel + Multi-hypothesis	77.80	–

Table 2. Classification accuracies for different classes

Class	SuperParsing1	Kernel + Multi-hypothesis
crosswalk	**23.93**	14.73
staircase	12.07	**16.07**
door	10.07	**17.40**
grass	35.23	**46.37**
car	**51.32**	45.36
field	47.41	**70.47**
mountain	67.02	**73.70**
building	84.44	**89.01**
sky	91.23	**91.85**

multi-hypothesis approach, SuperParsing is run for multiple alternative super-pixel segmentations and log-likelihood estimates from all runs are combined at the pixel-level to improve labeling accuracy.

Table 1 gives the pixel-level labeling accuracies of the tested methods. The first column is for the baseline approach without any contextual modeling of superpixels. The second column is when Markov Random Field (MRF) model in [10] is used for contextual inference. The proposed kernel-based method is also incorporated into multi-hypothesis approach and named as Kernel + Multi-hypothesis on the table. Note that MRF version of multi-hypothesis approach is not developed yet. The parameter settings are as follows: SuperParsing1 ($K = 200$, $S = 100$), SuperParsing2 ($K = 300$, $S = 150$), Kernel-based ($K = 300$, $S = 150$), and Kernel + Multi-hypothesis (2 hypotheses with ($K = 300$, $S = 150$) and ($K = 400$, $S = 200$)).

Kernel-based method provides an improvement of more than 2 % over baseline SuperParsing and about 1.3 % when MRF is used. The performance is better than the adaptive neighbor set approach [11] with MRF model. Both methods use weighting of the training samples. However [11] fixes the descriptor weights

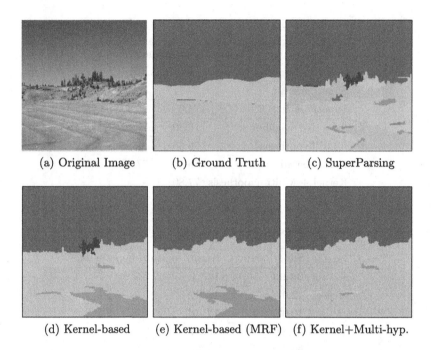

(a) Original Image   (b) Ground Truth   (c) SuperParsing

(d) Kernel-based   (e) Kernel-based (MRF)   (f) Kernel+Multi-hyp.

Fig. 2. Visual comparison (red: sky, green: mountain, light green: field, light orange: road, orange: sand) (Color figure online)

during the training phase; while in the proposed method weights are determined adaptively for each tested superpixel based on the distances between feature vectors. The bandwidth optimization needed for kernel-based estimation is much simpler and faster than the weight adaptation used in [11]. In addition, [11] uses flipped images in the training set and additional retrieval samples for rare classes to improve labeling accuracy.

When multi-hypothesis likelihood computation is combined with kernel-based method, pixel classification accuracy reaches to 77.80 %. We expect the accuracy to increase further when MRF contextual modeling is used in multi-hypothesis framework. Note that state-of-art results on SIFT Flow dataset, such as 81.7 % in [17], are produced by methods using advanced contextual models and classifiers, and therefore not included in Table 1.

At Table 2 accuracy percentages of some classes are compared for Kernel + Multi-hypothesis and for SuperParsing. As seen from the table, Kernel + Multi-hypothesis estimation improves the labeling accuracy of some medium-sized and small-sized classes, such as "grass" and "door". On the other hand, large-sized classes, such as "field", "building", "mountain", are also labeled with better accuracy, leading to an increase in overall pixel-level labeling accuracy.

At Fig. 2 labeling accuracies of the tested methods are compared visually. SuperParsing confuses "mountain" with "field" and "field' with "road". Kernel-based method has less visual error but confuses part of "field' with "sand".

Kernel with MRF and Kernel + Multi-hypothesis methods further improve the result of kernel-based method.

5 Conclusion

In this paper kernel density estimation and adaptive neighborhood selection are used to improve the classification performance of a nonparametric, data-driven image parsing algorithm. More accurate likelihood estimation combined with multi-hypothesis segmentation and MRF modeling achieves pixel-level accuracy that is competitive with state-of-art results that require advanced contextual modeling and extensive training.

As future work, we plan to incorporate more advanced contextual models into the framework to improve pixel-level and class average parsing accuracies. MRF framework will be implemented into the multi-hypothesis approach. The algorithm will also be tested on other larger datasets to evaluate the importance of accurate probability estimation. A more balanced training set will also be used to further improve labeling accuracy of rare classes in the dataset.

References

1. Van de Sande, K.E.A., Gevers, T., Snoek, C.G.M.: Evaluating color descriptors for object and scene recognition. IEEE Trans. Pattern Anal. Mach. Intell. **32**(9), 1582–1596 (2010)
2. Fulkerson, B., Vedaldi, A., Soatto, S.: Class segmentation and object localization with superpixel neighborhoods. In: IEEE 12th International Conference Computer Vision I (ICCV), pp. 670–677 (2009)
3. Achanta, R., et al.: SLIC superpixels compared to state-of-the-art superpixel methods. IEEE Trans. Pattern Anal. Mach. Intell. **34**(11), 2274–2282 (2012)
4. Vedaldi, A., Soatto, S.: Quick shift and kernel methods for mode seeking. In: Forsyth, D., Torr, P., Zisserman, A. (eds.) ECCV 2008, Part IV. LNCS, vol. 5305, pp. 705–718. Springer, Heidelberg (2008)
5. Felzenszwalb, P.F., Huttenlocher, D.P.: Efficient graph-based image segmentation. Int. J. Comput. Vis. **59**(2), 167–181 (2004)
6. Kluckner, S., Donoser, M., Bischof, H.: Super-pixel class segmentation in large-scale aerial imagery. In: Proceedings of Annual Workshop Austrian Association for Pattern Recognition (2010)
7. Shotton, J., Johnson, M., Cipolla, R.: Semantic texton forests for image categorization and segmentation. In: IEEE Conference on Computer Vision Pattern Recognition (CVPR) (2008)
8. Gould, S., Fulton, R., Koller, D.: Decomposing a scene into geometric and semantically consistent regions. In: ICCV (2009)
9. Liu, C., et al.: SIFT flow: dense correspondence across difference scenes. In: ECCV (2008)
10. Tighe, J., Lazebnik, S.: SuperParsing: scalable nonparametric image parsing with superpixels. Int. J. Comput. Vis. **101**(2), 329–349 (2013)
11. Eigen, D., Fergus, R.: Nonparametric image parsing using adaptive neighbor sets. In: CVPR, pp. 2799–2806 (2012)

12. Lazebnik, S., Schmid, C., Ponce, J.: Beyond bags of features: spatial pyramid matching for recognizing natural scene categories. In: CVPR (2006)
13. Oliva, A., Torralba, A.: Building the gist of a scene: the role of global image features in recognition. Vis. Percept. Progress Brain Res. **155**, 23–36 (2006)
14. Torralba, A., Fergus, R., Freeman, W.T.: 80 million tiny images: a large dataset for non-parametric object and scene recognition. IEEE Trans. Pattern Anal. Mach. Intell. **30**, 1958–1970 (2008)
15. Shimazaki, H., Shinomoto, S.: Kernel bandwidth optimization in spike rate estimation. J. Comput. Neurosci. **29**, 171–182 (2010)
16. Ak, K.E., Ates, H.F.: Scene segmentation and labeling using multi-hypothesis superpixels. In: Signal Processing and Communications Applications Conference (SIU), pp. 847–850 (2015)
17. George, M.: Image parsing with a wide range of classes and scene-level context. In: CVPR, pp. 3622–3630 (2015)

Multinomial Sequence Based Estimation Using Contiguous Subsequences of Length Three

B. John Oommen[1(✉)] and Sang-Woon Kim[2]

[1] Chancellor's Professor, School of Computer Science,
Carleton University, Ottawa K1S 5B6, Canada
oommen@scs.carleton.ca
[2] Department of Computer Engineering,
Myongji University, Yongin 17058, South Korea
kimsw@mju.ac.kr

Abstract. The Maximum Likelihood (ML) and Bayesian estimation paradigms work within the model that the data, from which the parameters are to be estimated, is treated as a *set* rather than as a *sequence*. The pioneering paper that dealt with the field of sequence-based estimation [2] involved utilizing both the information in the observations *and in their sequence of appearance*. The results of [2] introduced the concepts of Sequence Based Estimation (SBE) for the Binomial distribution, where the authors derived the corresponding MLE results when the samples are taken two-at-a-time, and then extended these for the cases when they are processed three-at-a-time, four-at-a-time etc. These results were generalized for the multinomial "two-at-a-time" scenario in [3]. This paper (This paper is dedicated to the memory of Dr. Mohamed Kamel, who was a close friend of the first author.) now further generalizes the results found in [3] for the multinomial case and for subsequences of length 3. The strategy used in [3] (and also here) involves a novel phenomenon called "Occlusion" that has not been reported in the field of estimation. The phenomenon can be described as follows: By occluding (hiding or concealing) certain observations, we map the estimation problem onto a lower-dimensional space, i.e., onto a binomial space. Once these occluded SBEs have been computed, the overall Multinomial SBE (MSBE) can be obtained by combining these lower-dimensional estimates. In each case, we formally prove and experimentally demonstrate the convergence of the corresponding estimates.

B. John Oommen is a *Fellow: IEEE* and *Fellow: IAPR*. The work was done while he was visiting at Myongji University, Yongin, Korea. He also holds an *Adjunct Professorship* with the Department of Information and Communication Technology, University of Agder, Grimstad, Norway. The work was partially supported by NSERC, the Natural Sciences and Engineering Research Council of Canada and a grant from the National Research Foundation of Korea. This work was also generously supported by the National Research Foundation of Korea funded by the Korean Government (NRF-2012R1A1A2041661).

© Springer International Publishing Switzerland 2016
A. Campilho and F. Karray (Eds.): ICIAR 2016, LNCS 9730, pp. 243–253, 2016.
DOI: 10.1007/978-3-319-41501-7_28

Keywords: Estimation using sequential information · Sequence based estimation · Estimation of multinomials · Fused estimation methods · Sequential information

1   Introduction

The theory of estimation has been studied for hundreds of years [5–7], and it has been the backbone for the learning (training) phase of statistical pattern recognition systems [1,8,9]. Traditionally, the ML and Bayesian estimation paradigms work within the model that the data, from which the parameters are to be estimated, is known, and that it is treated as a *set*. The position that we respectfully submit is that traditional ML and Bayesian methods ignore and discard[1] valuable *sequence*-based information. The goal of this paper is to "extract" and "utilize" the information contained in the observations when they are perceived *both as a set* and in *their sequence of appearance*. Put in a nutshell, this paper deals with the relatively new field of sequence-based estimation in which the goal is to estimate the parameters of a distribution by maximally "squeezing" out the *set*-based and *sequence*-based information latent in the observations.

The Maximum Likelihood (ML) and Bayesian estimation paradigms work within the model that the data, from which the parameters are to be estimated, is treated as a *set* rather than as a *sequence*. The pioneering paper that dealt with the field of Sequence-Based Estimation (SBE) [2] involved utilizing both the information in the observations *and in their sequence of appearance*. The question that this entails is the following: "Is there any information in the fact that in $\mathcal{X}$, x_i specifically precedes x_{i+1}?". Or in a more general case, "Is there any information in the fact that in $\mathcal{X}$, the **sequence** $x_i x_{i+1} \ldots x_{i+j}$ occurs $n_{i,i+1,\ldots i+j}$ times?". Our position, which we proved in [2] for binomial random variables[2], is that even though $\mathcal{X}$ is generated by an i.i.d. process, there is information in these pieces of sequential data which can be "maximally" utilized to yield the so-called family of SBEs.

If the MLE and any SBE of the parameter θ converge to the *same true, unknown, value*, what then is the advantage of having multiple estimates? The answer lies simply in the fact that although the traditional MLE and the SBEs converge *asymptotically* to the same value, they all have *completely different* values. This is all the more true because the information used in procuring each of these estimates is "orthogonal". Further, since the convergence properties of MLEs is asymptotic, one can glean and effectively utilize other information when the number of samples examined is "small".

The consequences of invoking SBEs are potentially many. If we are able to obtain reliable estimates of the parameters under investigation by utilizing the

---

[1] This information is, of course, traditionally used when we want to consider *dependence* information, as in the case of Markov models and n-gram statistics.

[2] The papers [2] and [3] explain the application of SBEs, and also about how we can fuse them to yield superior estimates. These aspects are not included here in the interest of space.

set-based *and* sequence-based information, this could potentially have advantages in all the fields where estimation is used.

The pioneering paper concerning SBEs [2] introduced its theory, experimental results and applications for the Binomial distribution, where the authors derived the corresponding MLE results when the samples are taken two-at-a-time, and then extended these for the cases when they are processed three-at-a-time, four-at-a-time etc. These results were generalized for the *multinomial* "two-at-a-time" scenario in [3].

This paper now further generalizes the latter results (those found in [3]) for the multinomial case and for subsequences of length 3. The results of the case when we deal with subsequences of length greater than 3 are currently being compiled. To the best of our knowledge, apart from our previous results of [2] and [4], all of these are novel to the field of estimation, learning and classification.

In the interest of space and brevity, the proofs of the theoretical results presented here are omitted. They are found in [4]. However, we add that all the theoretical results have been experimentally verified.

2   On Obtaining MSBEs Using Occluded SBEs

Informally speaking, the question of designing SBEs for multinomial random variables is, perhaps, "two orders of magnitude" more complex than that of designing them for binomial random variables[3] The reason for this is quite simple: For a vector of dimension d, there are $\binom{d}{2}$ possible pairs of binomial events, and it is no trivial task to generalize the expressions for the binomial SBEs (from [2]) to yield the corresponding multinomial SBE (MSBE). This, we believe, is the hurdle that we have encountered in this present paper, and its solution is the novel contribution.

How then have we proposed the solution to the problem even though we encounter $\binom{d}{2}$ possible pairs? Indeed, rather than consider the problem of computing the MSBE as a problem in its own right, we have shown how we can map this problem into a *linear* set of *Binomial* SBE (BSBE) problems. This is, as we shall see, achieved by effectively occluding (erasing, hiding or concealing) all the observations in the sequence other than the ones that are concerned in the specific binomial experiment. One can now procure corresponding BSBEs from these occluded sequences. The final MSBE result is now computed by effectively processing a sufficient set of such BSBEs, and combining them by means of a normalizing constraint. The details of all these aspects will be explained in the subsequent sections.

---

[3] The contents of this section is quite identical to the corresponding section in [3]. This is unavoidable because the notation is quite cumbersome. Besides, the fundamental theory of using "occlusion" is identical in both the papers. Unfortunately, it is futile to omit these concepts and to refer the reader to [3] - it will render the present paper to be quite incomprehensible.

2.1 Notation: MSBEs Using Pairs and Subsequences

Before we proceed with the theoretical and experimental results, it is necessary for us to formalize the notation that will be used[4].

Notation 1: To be consistent, we introduce the following notation.

- X is a multinomially distributed random variable, obeying the distribution S.
- $\mathcal{X} = \{x_1, x_2, \ldots, x_J\}$ is a realization of a sequence of occurrences of X, where each $x_i \in \mathcal{D}$.
- An index $a \in \mathcal{D}$ is said to be the unconstrained variable in any computation if all the other estimates $\{s_i\}$ are specified in terms of s_a, where $i \neq a$. It will soon be clear that in any computation there can only be *a single* unconstrained variable.
- $\mathcal{X}^{ab} = \{x_1, x_2, \ldots, x_{N_{ab}}\}$ is called the *Occluded* sequence of $\mathcal{X}$ (with N_{ab} items) with respect to a and b, if it is obtained from $\mathcal{X}$ by deleting the occurrences of all the elements except a and b. Whenever we refer to the sequence $\mathcal{X}^{ab} = \{x_1, x_2, \ldots, x_{N_{ab}}\}$, we always imply that the first variable (in this case a) is the unconstrained variable.
- Let $< j_1 j_2 \ldots, j_k >$ be the subsequence[5] examined in the *Occluded* sequence $\mathcal{X}^{ab}$, where each $j_m, (1 \leq m \leq k)$, is either a or b. Then[6]:
  - The BSBE, for s_a obtained by examining in $\mathcal{X}^{ab}$ the subsequence $< j_1 j_2 \ldots, j_k >$ will be given by $\widehat{q}_a\Big|_{<j_1 j_2 \ldots, j_k>}^{ab}$, where, as before, the first variable (in this case a) is the unconstrained variable.
  - Similarly, the BSBE, for s_b obtained by examining in $\mathcal{X}^{ab}$ the subsequence $< j_1 j_2 \ldots, j_k >$ will be given by $\widehat{q}_b\Big|_{<j_1 j_2 \ldots, j_k>}^{ab}$, where the first variable (in this case a) is the unconstrained variable.
- Consider the sequence $\mathcal{X}$ in which the index a is the unconstrained variable. Let $< j_1 j_2 \ldots, j_k >$ be the subsequence examined in the sequence $\mathcal{X}$, where each $j_m, (1 \leq m \leq k)$, is either a or '$*$', where each '$*$' is the *same* variable, say $c \in (\mathcal{D} - \{a\})$. Then:
  - The MSBE for s_a (where a is the unconstrained variable) obtained by examining in $\mathcal{X}$ the sequence $< j_1 j_2 \ldots, j_k >$ will be given by $\widehat{s}_a\Big|_{<j_1 j_2 \ldots, j_k>}^{a}$ where each j_i that is not a is replaced by a '$*$', and where each '$*$' is the *same* variable, say $c \in (\mathcal{D} - \{a\})$.
  - For any constrained variable b, the MSBE for s_b obtained by examining in $\mathcal{X}$ the sequence $< j_1 j_2 \ldots, j_k >$ will be given by $\widehat{s}_b\Big|_{<j_1 j_2 \ldots, j_k>}^{ab}$, where a is the unconstrained variable.

---

[4] We apologize for this cumbersome notation, but this is unavoidable considering the complexity of the problem and the ensuing analysis.

[5] For the present, we consider non-overlapping subsequences. We shall later extend this to overlapping sequences when we report the experimental results.

[6] The reader must take pains to differentiate between the q's and the s's, because the former refer to the BSBEs and the latter to the MSBEs.

– Trivially, for all a and b:

$$\sum_{b \neq a} \left. \widehat{s}_b \right|^{ab}_{<j_1 j_2 \ldots, j_k>} = 1 - \left. \widehat{s}_a \right|^{a}_{<j_1 j_2 \ldots, j_k>}.$$

□

A detailed example of Notation 1 is found in [3].

For any given a and b, if a is the unconstrained variable, we shall now derive the explicit form of $\left. \widehat{q}_a \right|^{ab}_{<j_1 j_2 \ldots, j_k>}$, $\left. \widehat{q}_b \right|^{ab}_{<j_1 j_2 \ldots, j_k>}$, $\left. \widehat{s}_a \right|^{a}_{<j_1 j_2 \ldots, j_k>}$, and $\left. \widehat{s}_b \right|^{ab}_{<j_1 j_2 \ldots, j_k>}$ for various subsequences $< j_1 j_2 \ldots, j_k >$.

By virtue of the Weak Law of Large Numbers, it is well known that the MLE converges with probability 1 and in the mean square sense to the true underlying parameter. Thus, all the estimates given in the following sections converge (w. p. 1, and in the mean square sense) to the true underlying value of the parameter.

2.2 The Fundamental Theorem of Fusing Occluded Estimates

Our first task is to formulate how we can compute the MSBEs by utilizing information gleaned by the *Binomial* SBEs (BSBEs) obtained from the set of $\binom{d}{2}$ occluded sequences. The theoretical basis for this is the following: Consider an occluded sequence, $\mathcal{X}^{ab}$, extracted from the original sequence, $\mathcal{X}$, by removing all the variables except a and b. In the sequence being examined, we choose one variable, say a to be the unconstrained variable. We shall first attempt to obtain BSBEs of the relative proportions of s_a and s_b, from $\mathcal{X}^{ab}$. Thereafter, we utilize the set of these relative proportions to compute the MSBEs of all the variables.

Theorem 1. *For every pair of indices, a and b, let $\mathcal{X}^{ab}$ be the Occluded sequence, extracted from the original sequence, $\mathcal{X}$, by removing all the variables except a and b. If we consider a to be the unconstrained variable, we define $q_a = \frac{s_a}{s_a + s_b}$ and $q_b = \frac{s_b}{s_a + s_b}$, where $q_a + q_b = 1$. Now let $\left. \widehat{q}_a \right|^{ab}_{\pi(a,b)} \neq 0$ and $\left. \widehat{q}_b \right|^{ab}_{\pi(a,b)} = 1 - \left. \widehat{q}_a \right|^{ab}_{\pi(a,b)}$ be the BSBEs of q_a and q_b respectively based on the occurrence[7] of any specific subsequence $\pi(a,b)$. Then, if c is a dummy variable[8] representing any of the variables, the MSBEs of s_a and s_b obtained by examining the occurrences[9] of $\pi(a,b)$ in every $\mathcal{X}^{ab}$ are:*

$$\left. \widehat{s}_a \right|^{a}_{\pi(a,b)} = \frac{1}{\sum_{\forall c} \rho_c}, \qquad and \qquad \left. \widehat{s}_b \right|^{ab}_{\pi(a,b)} = \frac{\left. \widehat{q}_b \right|^{ab}_{\pi(a,b)}}{\sum_{\forall c} \rho_c}, \tag{1}$$

---

[7] The issue of how BSBEs are obtained for specific instantiations of $\pi(a,b)$ is discussed in the subsequent sections.

[8] The fact that c is a dummy variable will not be repeated in the future invocations of this result.

[9] This, of course, makes sense only if $\forall c, \left. \widehat{q}_a \right|^{ac}_{\pi(a,c)} \neq 0$. This condition will not be explicitly stated in the future.

$$\text{where } \rho_a = 1 \text{ and } \forall c \neq a, \rho_c = \frac{\widehat{q_c}\Big|_{\pi(a,c)}^{ac}}{\widehat{q_a}\Big|_{\pi(a,c)}^{ac}}.$$

Proof. The proof of the result is omitted due to space considerations. It is in [4]. An example clarifying its use is also found in [3] and [4].   □

In [3], we had derived the explicit expressions for the MSBEs when the subsequences $\pi(a,b)$ are of length 2. We shall now generalize this for the case when the subsequences are of length greater than 2.

2.3   Computational Issues

In all the theoretical results that we shall prove, we shall deal with non-overlapping subsequences. Thus, the number of *non-overlapping* sequences of length two in $\mathcal{X}^{ab}$ is $\frac{N_{ab}}{2}$, and the number of *non-overlapping* sequences of length three in $\mathcal{X}^{ab}$ is $\frac{N_{ab}}{3}$ etc. In any sequence $\mathcal{X}^{ab}$, consider the contiguous sequences of length two (i.e., aa, ab, ba and bb). Since the elements of $\mathcal{X}$ are drawn independently and identically, the fact that two adjacent elements x_p and x_{p+1} in $\mathcal{X}^{ab}$ are a, is independent of the event that x_{p+1} and x_{p+2} can also assume the value of a. The pairwise event is thus, effectively, one of "drawing with replacement", and we can thus consider $N_{ab} - 1$ consecutive pairs in $\mathcal{X}^{ab}$. Observe that it would be statistically advantageous (since the number of occurrences obtained would be almost doubled) if all the overlapping $N_{ab} - 1$ subsequences of length 2 were considered, and where n_{aa}, n_{ab}, n_{ba} and n_{bb} were the number of occurrences of aa, ab, ba and bb respectively in these $N_{ab} - 1$ subsequences. Similarly, it would be advantageous to consider the overlapping $N_{ab} - 2$ subsequences of length 3 were considered etc. Indeed, we shall utilize *these* quantities in the experimental verification of our theoretical results.

3   MSBEs Using Three-at-a-Time Sequential Information

3.1   Theoretical Results

The following analytic results are true when the sequential information is processed three-at-a-time.

Theorem 2. *Let $q_a = \frac{s_a}{s_a + s_b}$ and $q_b = \frac{s_b}{s_a + s_b}$, where $q_a + q_b = 1$. Then, $\widehat{q_a}\Big|_{<aaa>}^{ab}$ and $\widehat{q_b}\Big|_{<aaa>}^{ab}$, the BSBEs of q_a and q_b obtained by examining the occurrences of $< aaa >$ in $\mathcal{X}^{ab}$ are:*

$$\widehat{q_a}\Big|_{<aaa>}^{ab} = \sqrt[3]{\frac{n_{aaa}}{N_{ab}/3}}, \qquad and \qquad \widehat{q_b}\Big|_{<aaa>}^{ab} = 1 - \sqrt[3]{\frac{n_{aaa}}{N_{ab}/3}}, \qquad (2)$$

where n_{aaa} is the number of occurrences of $< aaa >$ from among the $\frac{N_{ab}}{3}$ non-overlapping subsequences of length 3 in $\mathcal{X}^{ab}$. Consequently,

$$\left.\widehat{s}_a\right|^a_{<aaa>} = \frac{1}{\sum_{\forall c} \rho_c}, \qquad and \qquad \left.\widehat{s}_b\right|^{ab}_{<aaa>} = \frac{\left.\widehat{q}_b\right|^{ab}_{<aaa>}}{\sum_{\forall c} \rho_c}, \qquad (3)$$

where $\rho_a = 1$ and $\forall c \neq a, \rho_c = \frac{1 - \sqrt[3]{\frac{n_{aaa}}{N_{ac}/3}}}{\sqrt[3]{\frac{n_{aaa}}{N_{ac}/3}}}$.

Proof. The proof of the result is found in [4].   □

Theorem 3. *Let* $q_a = \frac{s_a}{s_a + s_b}$ *and* $q_b = \frac{s_b}{s_a + s_b}$, *where* $q_a + q_b = 1$. *Then,* $\left.\widehat{q}_a\right|^{ab}_{<bbb>}$ *and* $\left.\widehat{q}_b\right|^{ab}_{<bbb>}$, *the BSBEs of* q_a *and* q_b *obtained by examining the occurrences of* $< bbb >$ *in* $\mathcal{X}^{ab}$ *are:*

$$\left.\widehat{q}_a\right|^{ab}_{<bbb>} = 1 - \sqrt[3]{\frac{n_{bbb}}{N_{ab}/3}}, \qquad and \qquad \left.\widehat{q}_b\right|^{ab}_{<bbb>} = \sqrt[3]{\frac{n_{bbb}}{N_{ab}/3}}, \qquad (4)$$

where n_{bbb} is the number of occurrences of $< bbb >$ from among the $\frac{N_{ab}}{3}$ non-overlapping subsequences of length 3 in $\mathcal{X}^{ab}$. Consequently,

$$\left.\widehat{s}_a\right|^a_{<bbb>} = \frac{1}{\sum_{\forall c} \rho_c}, \qquad and \qquad \left.\widehat{s}_b\right|^{ab}_{<bbb>} = \frac{\left.\widehat{q}_b\right|^{ab}_{<bbb>}}{\sum_{\forall c} \rho_c}, \qquad (5)$$

where $\rho_a = 1$ and $\forall c \neq a, \rho_c = \frac{\sqrt[3]{\frac{n_{ccc}}{N_{ac}/3}}}{1 - \sqrt[3]{\frac{n_{ccc}}{N_{ac}/3}}}$.

Proof. The details are thus omitted. It is found in [4].   □

To simplify matters, we deal with the rest of the cases that involve three-at-a-time subsequences, by sub-dividing them into the cases when the subsequences contain *one* b, or *two* b's, which are then dealt with in a single theorem.

Theorem 4. *Let* $q_a = \frac{s_a}{s_a + s_b}$ *and* $q_b = \frac{s_b}{s_a + s_b}$, *where* $q_a + q_b = 1$. *Then,* $\left.\widehat{q}_a\right|^{ab}_{<uvw>}$, *the BSBE of* q_a *obtained by examining the occurrences of subsequences of length 3 of the form* $< uvw >$ *in* $\mathcal{X}^{ab}$ *of which only a single variable is* b, *can be computed as the real roots (if any) of the cubic equations given below for each such subsequence:*

1. $\left.\widehat{q}_a\right|^{ab}_{<baa>}$ *is the real root,* λ_a, *of* $\lambda^3 - \lambda^2 + \frac{n_{baa}}{N_{ab}/3} = 0$ *whose value is closest to* $\widehat{q}_a$;

2. $\left.\widehat{q}_a\right|^{ab}_{<aba>}$ *is the real root,* λ_a, *of* $\lambda^3 - \lambda^2 + \frac{n_{aba}}{N_{ab}/3} = 0$ *whose value is closest to* $\widehat{q}_a$;

3. $\widehat{q_a}\Big|^{ab}_{<aab>}$ is the real root, λ_a, of $\lambda^3 - \lambda^2 + \frac{n_{aab}}{N_{ab}/3} = 0$ whose value is closest to $\widehat{q_a}$;

where n_{baa}, n_{aba} and n_{aab} are the number of occurrences of $< baa >$, $< aba >$ and $< aab >$ respectively from among the $\frac{N_{ab}}{3}$ non-overlapping subsequences of length 3 in $\mathcal{X}^{ab}$. Similarly, $\widehat{q_b}\Big|^{ab}_{<uvw>} = \lambda_b = 1 - \lambda_a$. Finally, in each case,

$$\widehat{s_a}\Big|^{a}_{<uvw>} = \frac{1}{\sum_{\forall c} \rho_c}, \quad and \quad \widehat{s_b}\Big|^{ab}_{<uvw>} = \frac{\widehat{q_b}\Big|^{ab}_{<uvw>}}{\sum_{\forall c} \rho_c}, \qquad (6)$$

where $\rho_a = 1$ and $\forall c \neq a$, $\rho_c = \frac{\lambda_c}{\lambda_a}$.

Proof. The details of the proof are omitted here and are included in [4]. □

We now consider the scenario when the subsequence examined contains two b's. However, here, we first estimate the probability q_b using which infer the estimate of q_a. Indeed, the theorem mirrors the one above.

Theorem 5. *Let* $q_a = \frac{s_a}{s_a+s_b}$ *and* $q_b = \frac{s_b}{s_a+s_b}$, *where* $q_a+q_b = 1$. *Then,* $\widehat{q_b}\Big|^{ab}_{<uvw>}$, *the BSBE of* q_b *obtained by examining the occurrences of subsequences of length 3 of the form* $< uvw >$ *in* $\mathcal{X}^{ab}$ *of which* exactly *two variables are* b's, *can be computed as the real roots (if any) of the cubic equations given below for each such subsequence:*

1. $\widehat{q_b}\Big|^{ab}_{<abb>}$ is the real root, λ_b, of $\lambda^3 - \lambda^2 + \frac{n_{abb}}{N_{ab}/3} = 0$ whose value is closest to $\widehat{q_b}$;

2. $\widehat{q_b}\Big|^{ab}_{<bab>}$ is the real root, λ_b, of $\lambda^3 - \lambda^2 + \frac{n_{bab}}{N_{ab}/3} = 0$ whose value is closest to $\widehat{q_b}$;

3. $\widehat{q_b}\Big|^{ab}_{<bba>}$ is the real root, λ_b, of $\lambda^3 - \lambda^2 + \frac{n_{bba}}{N_{ab}/3} = 0$ whose value is closest to $\widehat{q_b}$;

where n_{abb}, n_{bab} and n_{bba} are the number of occurrences of $< abb >$, $< bab >$ and $< bba >$ respectively from among the $\frac{N_{ab}}{3}$ non-overlapping subsequences of length 3 in $\mathcal{X}^{ab}$. Similarly, $\widehat{q_a}\Big|^{ab}_{<uvw>} = \lambda_a = 1 - \lambda_b$. Finally, in each case,

$$\widehat{s_a}\Big|^{a}_{<uvw>} = \frac{1}{\sum_{\forall c} \rho_c}, \quad and \quad \widehat{s_b}\Big|^{ab}_{<uvw>} = \frac{\widehat{q_b}\Big|^{ab}_{<uvw>}}{\sum_{\forall c} \rho_c}, \qquad (7)$$

where $\rho_a = 1$ and $\forall c \neq a$, $\rho_c = \frac{\lambda_c}{\lambda_a}$.

Proof. This proof is similar to the proof of Theorem 4 (by merely replacing a by b and vice versa) and is not included to avoid repetition. □

3.2   Experimental Results: Sequences of Length Three

To justify and experimentally verify the claims of Sect. 3.1, we now present the results of our simulations on synthetic data for the cases studied in that subsection, namely for the case when the sequence is processed in subsequences of length three. As in the case of sequences of length 2, by virtue of the arguments of Sect. 2.3, we evaluate the *approximated* versions of the respective equations by considering the $N - 2$ overlapping sequences of length 3, and so the solutions are obtained by replacing the existing term, $N/3$, by $N - 2$ in Theorems 2 to 5.

As in the case of using pairwise sequences of symbols, the MSBE process for the estimation of the parameters for multinomial random variables was extensively tested for numerous distributions, but we merely cite one specific example. The case we report is when $d = 5$ and the true value of $S = [0.33\ 0.25\ 0.18\ 0.14\ 0.10]^T$. Here too, we have simultaneously tracked the progress of the "traditional" MLE computation using the identical data stream. Both the estimation methodologies were presented with random occurrences of the variables for $N = 390625$ (i.e., 5^8) time instances. As in [3,4], the criteria for the quality of the estimates were the values of E_{MLE}, the error of the MLE, and the error of the MSBE, E_{MSBE}, at time N.

In the case of the MSBE, the true underlying value of the estimates was computed using each of the estimates when the triples examined in every $\mathcal{X}^{ab}$ were $< aaa >$, $< bbb >$, $< baa >$, $< aba >$, $< aab >$, $< abb >$, $< bab >$ and $< bba >$. The results obtained are tabulated in [3,4] as a function of the number of samples processed. However, to demonstrate the true convergence properties of the estimates and to mitigate the sampling error, we report the values of the ensemble average of the errors in Table 1 taken over an ensemble of 100 experiments. From it one can observe the amazing convergence of every single estimate. For example, the traditional MLE, had the ensemble average error, E_{MLE}, of 0.1918 when only $N = 625$ symbols were processed. The error of the MSBE (when the subsequence examined was $< aaa >$) at that time was 0.2081. When $N = 390625$, the value of the E_{MLE} was exactly 0.1885, while the value of the E_{MSBE} was 0.1886 – demonstrating the power of the estimation strategy!

The same phenomenon can be observed for the other MSBEs, except that in some cases the estimates were much better for smaller values of N. One also observes that the error of the MLE and MSBE evaluated for a *single* experiment are not as smooth - especially when the number of samples processed is small[10]. But fortunately, things "average" out as time proceeds.

The estimated ensemble values of E_{MLE} and $E_{MSBE} \mid_{<aaa>}$ with N are plotted in [4]. From it we can see that after an initial transient phase, the two curves are *almost undistinguishable*. This same true for the values of E_{MSBE} estimated using the subsequences $< bbb >$, $< baa >$ etc. It is important to mention that the approximated values (using the $N - 2$ *overlapping* subsequences) also converge rapidly to the true values of S with a remarkable accuracy.

---

[10] In practice, this is augmented by the fact that the SBEs sometimes lead to complex solutions or to unrealistic solutions when the number of samples processed is too small.

Table 1. A table of the *ensemble* averages (taken over 100 experiments) of the error of the MLE, E_{MLE}, and the error of the MSBE, E_{MSBE}, at time N, when the triples examined in every $\mathcal{X}^{ab}$ were $< aaa >$, $< bbb >$, $< baa >$, $< aba >$, $< aab >$, $< abb >$, $< bab >$ and $< bba >$. Here $d = 5$ and $S = [0.33\ 0.25\ 0.18\ 0.14\ 0.10]^T$. The latter MSBEs were estimated by using the approximated results of Theorems 2 to 5 respectively involving the $N_{ab} - 2$ overlapping subsequences of length 3 (approximated using the issues discussed in Sect. 2.3).

N	E_{MLE}	E_{MSBE} $< aaa >$	E_{MSBE} $< bbb >$	E_{MSBE} $< baa >$	E_{MSBE} $< aba >$	E_{MSBE} $< aab >$	E_{MSBE} $< abb >$	E_{MSBE} $< bab >$	E_{MSBE} $< bba >$
5^2 (25)	0.1279	NaN	0.2955	NaN	NaN	NaN	NaN	NaN	NaN
5^3 (125)	0.1695	NaN	0.2305	0.2163	0.2014	0.2128	NaN	NaN	NaN
5^4 (625)	0.1875	0.1920	0.2110	0.2096	0.2025	0.2082	NaN	NaN	NaN
5^5 (3,125)	0.1886	0.1891	0.1973	0.1958	0.2027	0.1968	0.1925	NaN	0.1928
5^6 (15,625)	0.1883	0.1884	0.1937	0.1912	0.1984	0.1916	0.1905	0.1910	0.1905
5^7 (78,125)	0.1879	0.1880	0.1919	0.1881	0.1879	0.1880	0.1878	0.1882	0.1878
5^8 (390,625)	0.1879	0.1879	0.1895	0.1881	0.1882	0.1880	0.1883	0.1880	0.1883

4   Conclusions

In this paper, we have considered the problem of achieving Sequence Based Estimation (SBE) for multinomial distributions. Unlike traditional estimates, which ignore and discard valuable *sequence*-based information, SBEs "extract" the information contained in the observations when perceived as a *sequence*. The pioneering work in SBEs was presented in [2], and concerned Binomial distributions. Since then, the analysis for multinomial distributions was left open. The first step in solving the SBE problem for multinomial distributions was made in [3]. The strategy that we developed there involved a novel and previously-unreported phenomenon called "Occlusion" where by hiding (or concealing) certain observations, we mapped the original estimation problem onto a lower-dimensional binomial space. We have also shown how these consequent occluded SBEs could be fused to yield overall Multinomial SBE (MSBE). The results in [3] achieved this by only investigating the information found in pairs of symbols in the occluded sequence. In this paper, we have further generalized these results when we considered contiguous subsequences of length 3 in the occluded sequence, which was then fused to yield the overall MSBE. The theoretical results have been experimentally verified. The analytic and experimental results for the cases when the subsequences are of lengths greater than 3 will soon be published.

References

1. Fukunaga, K.: Introduction to Statistical Pattern Recognition. Academic Press, San Diego (1990)
2. Oommen, B.J., Kim, S.-W., Horn, G.: On the estimation of independent binomial random variables using occurrence and sequential information. Pattern Recogn. **40**, 3263–3276 (2007)

3. Oommen, B.J., Kim, S.-W.: Multinomial Sequence Based Estimation: The Case of Pairs of Contiguous Occurrences. In: To appear in the Proceedings of AI 2016, The 2016 Canadian Artificial Intelligence Conference, Victoria, Canada, This talk will be a Plenary/Keynote Talk at the Conference, May 2016
4. Oommen, B.J., Kim, S.-W.: Occlusion-based Estimation of Independent Multinomial Random Variables Using Occurrence and Sequential Information (To be submitted for Publication)
5. Ross, S.: Introduction to Probability Models, 2nd edn. Academic Press, San Diego (2002)
6. Shao, J.: Mathematical Statistics, 2nd edn. Springer, New York (2003)
7. Sprinthall, R.: Basic Statistical Analysis, 2nd edn. Allyn and Bacon, Boston (2002)
8. van der Heijden, F., Duin, R.P.W., de Ridder, D., Tax, D.M.J.: Classification, Parameter Estimation and State Estimation: An Engineering Approach using MATLAB. Wiley, England (2004)
9. Webb, A.: Statistical Pattern Recognition, 2nd edn. Wiley, New York (2002)

Feature Extraction

Rotation Tolerant Hand Pose Recognition Using Aggregation of Gradient Orientations

Pekka Sangi[✉], Matti Matilainen, and Olli Silvén

Center for Machine Vision and Signal Analysis,
University of Oulu, P.O.Box 4500, 90014 Oulu, Finland
psangi@ee.oulu.fi

Abstract. The visual recognition of hand poses is one of the central problems in the development of applications controlled by visual gestures. In this paper, a generic orientation histogram based technique is described and applied to the pose recognition from intensity images. The technique addresses the need for rotation tolerant recognition using an orientation normalization technique, where the uncertainty related to the reference point of normalization is also taken into account by cyclic filtering. To complement the scheme, the circularly symmetric composition of histogram aggregation regions is introduced and the rotation tolerance can be controlled by range selection. In the experiments, we provide results on the choice between the parameter values and make comparisons to the existing techniques, which show the potential of the approach.

Keywords: Gesture recognition · Feature extraction · Histograms of oriented gradients · Spatial binning

1 Introduction

Recognition of the poses of the human body and its parts is an important topic in the design of gesture based interfaces. In the recent 5–10 years, the development of depth sensors has lead to remarkable results in the field [16]. However, human vision can recognize poses without depth information. As this modality may not be available in some vision platforms or usable due to imaging conditions, computationally cheap recognition based on color or intensity images, addressed in this paper, remains an important topic. Different kinds of approaches have been considered in the previous work, e.g. template matching [2], contrast edge patterns [7], graph matching [10,17], finger tip detection [3], random forests [13], and neural networks [1]. The problem is challenging due to high-dimensionality of the hand structure, similarity of different hand parts, self-occlusions, and existence of non-relevant appearance variations [15].

In this work, we reconsider the analysis based on contrast edge patterns proposed in the early work by Freeman and Roth [7]. In their work, a single global orientation histogram was used. To avoid losing information on the location of

© Springer International Publishing Switzerland 2016
A. Campilho and F. Karray (Eds.): ICIAR 2016, LNCS 9730, pp. 257–267, 2016.
DOI: 10.1007/978-3-319-41501-7_29

specific gradient patterns, we derive histograms for multiple subregions as done in the HOG descriptor [4], which we adapt to our purpose. This choice is also supported by some earlier results in hand pose recognition. In [15], HOG is compared with Hu moments and shape context and shown to have favorable characteristics. Li and Wachs [10] integrate different descriptors with elastic graph matching (EGM), and HOG clearly outperforms other descriptors in their experiments.

One of the issues in hand pose recognition is managing varying in-plane rotation of the hand in the images to be recognized. One technique is to estimate the dominant orientation and compensate for it as done in [2]. However, this method is sensitive to the results of the orientation estimation. Alternative approaches are to generate rotated images during the training of the classifier and to use Fourier analysis combined with the polar representation [11]. As our contribution, we address the appearance change due to the in-plane rotation of the object by adapting an orientation normalization technique, which was originally used for keypoint descriptors [5,14]. To combine that with the spatial binning, we use a special circular organization for the subregions, where the orientation histograms are computed. In the following, we describe the approach in detail and consider efficacy of various design choices experimentally. Finally, we also make comparisons to some other hand pose recognition techniques.

2   Feature Computation

Our pose recognition system consists of feature vector computation and classification phases. The feature computation phase takes in the image patch to be recognized, and computes a set of base feature vectors via three steps, (1) gradient computation, (2) orientation normalization, and (3) aggregation. In the classification phase, this set is then used to construct feature vectors for the hypothetical rotations of the object, which are then used in distance evaluations.

2.1   Computation of Local Orientations

The first step in the processing pipeline is the evaluation of image gradients, which provides basic information on local orientations. Our choice is to compute the gradient magnitudes in the horizontal and vertical directions with the Sobel mask, which provides slightly better results than the differential mask $[-1, 0, +1]$. Moreover, we noted that the resolution of the patch should not be high. The gradient vectors are mapped to a polar representation (ϕ', v), where $\phi' \in [0°, 180°)$ encodes the orientation using the *double angle* scheme, which is insensitive to the reversion of the local contrast [7], and v is the vector magnitude. We adopt a convention that ϕ' refers to the tangential orientation as illustrated in Fig. 1(a).

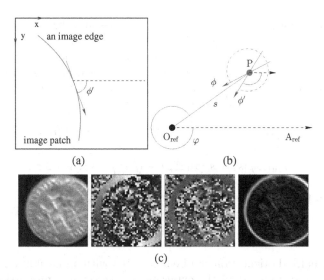

(a) (b)

(c)

Fig. 1. Representation of the local orientation. (a) The tangential direction which is used as a basis, (b) the normalization of the orientations according to a reference point. (c) An example of normalization: the analyzed patch, (double angle) gradient orientations ϕ', normalized gradient orientations ϕ, and gradient magnitude.

2.2 Orientation Normalization

In-plane orientation orientation of the hand (in a particular pose) can vary, which affects the angular component ϕ' of the polar representation. To get rid of this variation, we adapt an orientation normalization technique, which has been used to obtain rotation-invariant keypoint descriptors [5,14]. The idea is to normalize the orientation of a point according to the angular relationship of the point and the reference point (centroid of the keypoint area).

We adopt a polar representation for the image coordinates based on a reference point O_{ref}, which is the center of the image patch, and a reference axis A_{ref}, which points to the right from O_{ref}. Using these notions, locations P within the patch are represented by pairs (s, φ), where s is the distance from P to O_{ref} and $\varphi \in [0°, 360°)$ denotes the angle with respect to A_{ref}, as shown in Fig. 1(b). The local orientation, ϕ', is encoded similarly as the angle φ, namely, with respect to A_{ref}. Orientation normalization maps it to the angle

$$\phi = (\phi' - \varphi) \bmod M_\phi, \tag{1}$$

where the modulus M_ϕ is equal to $180°$. Figure 1(c) provides an example how orientation values become similar at the edges of a circular object.

One of the issues in the mapping is that we are uncertain about the location of the reference point O_{ref} used for normalization. We assume that the center of the image patch is the most suitable point for the task, but we can imagine that this might not be true due to potential errors in the determination of the patch area, for example.

To take this uncertainty into account, let us assume that the suitable reference point is within the disk D_{ref}, whose radius is u_{ref} and whose center point is at O_{ref}. Considering the reference point location as a random vector uniformly distributed over D_{ref}, the angular coordinate of a location P is a random variable, whose expected value is φ. By integration, we can show that the deviation $\Delta\varphi$ from the expectation is distributed as follows:

- If $s \leq u_{ref}$, then $\Delta\varphi \in [-180°, 180°]$ and the associated density is

$$p_{ru}(\Delta\varphi|s) \propto s\cos(\Delta\varphi) + \sqrt{u_{ref}^2 - s^2\sin^2(\Delta\varphi)}. \tag{2}$$

- If $s \geq u_{ref}$, then $\Delta\varphi \in [-a, a]$, where $a = \arcsin(u_{ref}/s)$, and

$$p_{ru}(\Delta\varphi|s) \propto 2\sqrt{u_{ref}^2 - s^2\sin^2(\Delta\varphi)}. \tag{3}$$

So, each normalized orientation can be associated with a distribution p_{ru}, which depends on the distance s. In the experiments, we set u_{ref} proportional to the square root of the image patch size.

2.3 Aggregation

In the aggregation step, a histogram based description for the patch is computed from normalized gradient information. The input to the step consists of tuples (s, φ, ϕ, v) and distributions p_{ru}. An aggregation region $\mathcal{A}$ is a subregion of the image patch, which is characterized by an orientation histogram computed over it. To do that, the bins of the histogram are established by selecting L points over the range $[0, M_\phi)$ so that adjacent points are separated by M_ϕ/L. The orientations ϕ computed over the image patch are quantized accordingly and the contribution of each $(s, \varphi) \in \mathcal{A}$ to the associated bin is a function of the gradient magnitude v. We use the magnitudes themselves as it is considered to be the best choice in [4].

It is computationally too complex to take into account the uncertainty distributions p_{ru} pixelwise in histogram computation. Therefore, we use an approach, where an average distribution, $\bar{p}_{ru}$, is computed over $\mathcal{A}$ first, using

$$\bar{p}_{ru}(\Delta\varphi|\mathcal{A}) \propto \sum_{p \in \mathcal{A}} p_{ru}(\Delta\varphi|s(\mathbf{p})), \tag{4}$$

where $s(\mathbf{p})$ denotes the distance s in $\mathbf{p} = [s, \varphi]$. The distribution $\bar{p}_{ru}$ is mapped to a filter mask, taking into account the double angle representation of the orientation, and orientation quantization. Then, the resulting mask is used to filter the original histogram cyclically. As fixed aggregation regions are used, the filter masks can be precomputed.

Finally, the magnitudes of the orientation histogram bins are normalized. Dalal and Triggs [4] note that the use of appropriate block normalization is important in HOG based detection, as gradient strengths vary very much due to

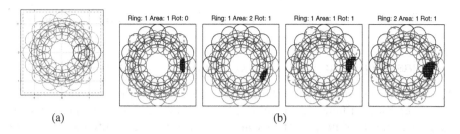

(a)   (b)

Fig. 2. Aggregation areas and sampling. (a) A spatial configuration which consists of 3 rings, 16 angles, and a fixed radius. The region to be classified is square shaped and the associated aggregation in zero orientation matches with the inner rectangle of the image. (b) Examples of sampling. Used pixels are within the rectangle which depends on the rotation considered.

local illumination variation and foreground-background contrast. Based on the results in [4], our choice is to use the L2 norm based scheme, where the histogram vector h is mapped to $h/\sqrt{\|h\|_2^2 + \epsilon^2}$, where $\epsilon > 0$ is a small constant. However, before that we emphasize stronger histogram bins h_i by mapping them to h_i^κ, where $\kappa \geq 1$ is a constant.

Normalization of the gradient orientations supports rotation tolerant classification. The selection of the aggregation regions takes us also towards this goal. The idea is to place the aggregation regions regularly around the reference point, and use several such rings (see Fig. 2(a)). For convenience, we use circular aggregation regions, which allows us to specify an aggregation ring m with a triplet (d_m, R_m, o_m), where d_m is the distance from the center point to the reference point, R_m is the radius $(d_m + R_m \leq \sqrt{2})$, and $o_m \in [0, 1)$ specifies the angular offset. For N angular places, the center point of the aggregation region $\mathcal{A}_{m,n}$ $(n \in \{0, 1, ..., N - 1\})$ is $(d_m, \alpha_{m,n})$, where $\alpha_{m,n} = 360°(n + o_m)/N$.

The locations of the aggregation regions suggest that the analyzed patch is effectively circular. However, using circular patches for the analysis may not be the best choice in practice as it omits the corners of the square patch. To avoid this, we adjust the representation so that the circular aggregation regions also cover the corners. Examples of the sampling are provided in Fig. 2(b).

Due to symmetricity, $\bar{p}_{ru}(\Delta\varphi|\mathcal{A})$ is approximately the same for all regions in a ring and the corresponding histogram filters can be shared. Separate filters must be computed for analyzed orientations when samplings in the ring depend on the orientation. We also adopt the convention that the number of angles, N, is a multiple of four as it reduces the number of different samplings that has to be done at the outer rings of the aggregation structure.

Finally, we note that during the run-time classification it may be necessary to limit the number of pixels sampled from each aggregation region $\mathcal{A}_{m,n}$, that is, to make sampling independent of the patch size. This can be done easily by drawing a random subset from the total set of pixels associated with $\mathcal{A}_{m,n}$. In addition, just one sampling is needed for each aggregation region of a ring m

when all regions are completely covered by the inner rectangle (e.g. the rings with the smallest radius in Fig. 2(a)).

3   Classification: Distance Evaluation and Training

As stated above, we constrain the number of aggregation regions in a ring, N, to be a multiple of four, that is, $N = 4N_s$. The value N_s is the number of samplings, which is used in the feature computation stage to compute the set of base feature vectors $\mathcal{V}$ ($|\mathcal{V}| = N_s$). Due to orientation normalization, feature vectors for the angular positions $n \in \{0, \ldots, N-1\}$ can be obtained by reorganizing the components of these base feature vectors. So, the feature vectors used by the classifier are specified by the pairs $(\mathcal{V}, n)$.

The basic operation is to match the test sample (encoded by the set $\mathcal{V}$) with the reference feature vectors r established during training. Matching is based on the evaluation of the distances

$$d(\mathcal{V}, r) = \min_{n \in \mathcal{N}} d((\mathcal{V}, n), r), \tag{5}$$

where $\mathcal{N} \subseteq \{0, \ldots, N-1\}$ is the set of angular positions considered. We assume that the in-plane angle takes values in a certain range during classification and matching is performed in the corresponding discrete positions.

During the training of the classifier, pose samples of certain class are provided for the system in an approximately fixed in-plane angle. The use of discrete angular positions can be compensated by rotating the training images slightly by some angles taken from the range $\pm 180°/N$. In addition, we use multiple patch sizes (shrunk, enlarged) for a training sample. So, multiple reference vectors r are obtained for each training sample. The shape of the object is also taken into account during training. Only the pixels which belong to the object area according to segmentation are allowed to vote during the feature vector computation.

4   Experiments

A prototype of the system described was developed in Matlab. For experiments, we use the datasets collected by J. Triesch for the studies summarized in [17]. The database has been utilized in many studies, e.g. [1,3,6,9,10,18], which motivates its usage in our work too. As the source for negative data, we exploit the indoor scene image dataset used in [12].

We experiment also with a proprietary dataset shot by us with an Intel RealSense F200 camera. Depth information provided by the camera is utilized in the collection of training and test data. Depth based segmentation enables the estimation of the bounding boxes for the hand regions, and it allows us to incorporate knowledge of the pose shape to the system during training as mentioned in Sect. 3. Each training image is also annotated by two keypoints, which allows rotating them to an approximately fixed in-plane angle. In our work, we use seven hand poses (Fig. 3), 20 images per pose for training (140 total), and 110 images for testing (770 total).

Fig. 3. The hand poses included in the proprietary dataset.

4.1 Feature Computation

In the first experiments, we consider options for feature computation (FC) in order to show the usefulness of some design ideas presented in Sect. 2 and to select the best options for classification. In our approach, we combine a nearest neighbor classifier with different FC configurations. In each case, the system is trained by a certain set of pose samples. During testing, the classifier outputs the closest pose class and associated distance for each test sample, which is either positive or negative. By varying the decision threshold used to detect the negative samples, we compute proportions of correct classifications and plot the associated curves. In the following, the results are presented by using the identified best configuration (see Table 1) as a reference in each case.

Table 1. Parameters of the default configuration.

Aggregation regions	80 ($M = 5, N = 16$)
- distance d_m	fixed ring distance 0.2
- radius R_m	fixed 0.3
- offset o_m	alternately 0/0.5
Histogram bin count L	12
Gradient operator	sobel
Ref. point uncertainty control	$\delta = 0.3$
Contrast normalization	L2, emphasis $\kappa = 2.5$
Sampling area	inner rectangle (no subsampling in ARs)
Rotation range	± 45 deg (± 2 ticks)

The experimental results of the feature computation are illustrated in Fig. 4. We use both datasets for training and testing here. The acronym 'd1' refers to the result with the Triesch database (original Triesch train/test split) and the label 'd2' refers to the result with our dataset.

(A) Image gradient operator. Our experimental result with different operators (difference $[-1, 0, +1]$ and the Sobel mask) is illustrated in Fig. 4(a). With the dataset 'd1', the performance of the operators is similar, whereas with 'd2' the Sobel operator provides slightly better results. Therefore, we have chosen to include the Sobel operator in our best configuration, whereas the simple difference mask is recommended in [4].

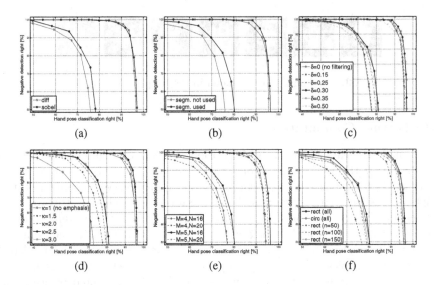

Fig. 4. Experimental comparison of feature computation settings: (a) Gradient operator. (b) Segmentation during training. (c) Reference point uncertainty control. (d) Contrast normalization of histograms. (e) Spatial configuration of aggregation regions (the number of rings and angles). (f) Sampling control. The right bunches of curves correspond to the results with the dataset 'd1' and the left ones to 'd2'. The black curves with circles correspond to the default configuration.

(B) Segmentation during training. The experimental result is shown in Fig. 4(b). In our work, we segmented the training samples of the dataset 'd1' manually. With both datasets, the result with segmentation is about 1–5% better than without it, so the segmentation should be used, if the background is not uniform in the training data.

(C) Reference point uncertainty. Associated filtering of the histograms is controlled with the variable δ and the result with different choices is shown in Fig. 4(c). We can observe that the performance can be improved by uncertainty based filtering and the best value for δ is about 0.3.

(D) Histogram normalization. It is emphasized in [4] that proper normalization of orientation histograms is important, which was also observed in our experiments. As discussed in Sect. 2.3, we propose a pre-emphasis technique, which is combined with the L2 normalization. The results obtained by varying the emphasis factor κ are illustrated in Fig. 4(d). For the dataset 'd1', the best results are obtained with $\kappa = 2.0$ and $\kappa = 2.5$ and with 'd2' the values are $\kappa = 2.5$ and $\kappa = 3.0$.

(E) Spatial configuration and sampling. According to some experimental work not discussed here, we noticed that appropriate choice for the aggregation region pattern is to use a fixed radius $d_m = d$, and fixed distance between the adjacent rings. In addition, the offset o_m alternates between the values 0 and 0.5. In Fig. 4(e), we compare the results with this scheme for some ring and angle counts.

It can be seen that the choice $M = 5$ and $N = 16$ provides relatively good results. Finally, Fig. 4(f) shows that using the inner rectangle as the sampling area can provide slightly better results than the circular window. In addition, the effect of reducing the number of pixels by subsampling is illustrated using the pixel counts $n \in \{50, 100, 150\}$.

We note a large difference in the performance with the datasets 'd1' and 'd2' in Fig. 4. This is partly explained by the fact that 67 % of the test images in 'd1' have uniform background, whereas the images of 'd2' are taken with varying backgrounds. If the background is changed to uniform, utilizing the available segmentation in 'd2', the rate of correct classification is increased by 5 %. So, the variability in the pose appearances also has significant impact on the accuracy.

4.2 Rotation Tolerance

In the feature computation experiments, the rotation range was ± 45 degrees, which requires evaluation for the integer angular positions within $[-2, +2]$ (mod 16). To show that the method is indeed rotation tolerant and study the sensitivity of the classification towards changes in the rotation range, we performed another test with the Triesch data. The classifier was trained as done above, but the test sets were generated by rotating the original images using the angles $\{0, 3, ..., 45\}$ degrees. The classifier was configured to use the rotation ranges $\pm n22.5$ degrees, where $n \in \{0, 1, 2, 3, 4\}$.

The results of the experiment are shown in Fig. 5. For a classifier with the range $\pm n22.5^{\circ}$, a critical rotation angle (CA) is $(n+1/2)22.5^{\circ}$. The first two plots show that the associated classifiers lose their performance gradually, when the test image rotations become greater than CA. If we consider the performance at the operating points on the diagonals, we can see that there is about 3 % drop in the performance, when the rotation range is increased from $\pm 0^{\circ}$ to $\pm 90^{\circ}$. Keeping also in the mind the distance evaluation effort required, the use of just the sufficient range is preferred.

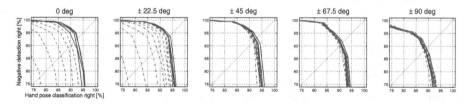

Fig. 5. Rotation tolerance experiment: classification results for five classifier rotation ranges. In each plot, the solid blue lines correspond to $\{0, 3, 6, 9\}$ degree rotations of the test images (i.e. the angle is below the critical angle (CA) of the ± 0 classifier), dashed magenta lines to rotations $\{12, 15, ..., 33\}$ (below CA of the ± 22.5 classifier) and dash-dotted red lines to rotations $\{36, 39, 42, 45\}$ (all below CAs of the three last classifiers). (Colour figure online)

4.3   Comparison to Other Methods

In the second set of experiments, we use a fixed setup for feature computation and consider the performance of our nearest neighbor classifier to the results provided in [18], where the Triesch database is also used. We neglect the negative detection performance and provide the best proportions of correct classifications. The comparison is provided for Just's protocol No. 2 [8, Appendix D] in Table 2, where 'light', 'dark', and 'complex' refer to different kinds of background. There are 119 training images (4 people) and 479 test images (16 people). The result for our method is provided for two ranges of rotation (RR).

Table 2. Comparison of the rates of correct classification.

Method	Light	Dark	Complex	Average
Just et al. [9]	92.8 %	92.8 %	81.3 %	89.0 %
Yao and Li [18]	93.6 %	94.3 %	90.0 %	92.6 %
Our (RR ±0°)	98.8 %	100.0 %	88.1 %	95.6 %
Our (RR ±45°)	98.8 %	99.4 %	86.3 %	94.8 %

Our method outperforms clearly (by 5.1–7.2 %) the other methods with uniform backgrounds even if we increase RR of testing. In the case of complex background, the performance of Yao's method is slightly better (by 1.9–3.7 %), but the average overall performance (about 95 %) is the best with our method. Interestingly, convolutional neural networks are applied to Triesch data by Barros et al. [1], who use 60 % of the data for training and 20 % for validation. They report 94 % F1 score at the best, whereas it is 97 % in our case obtained using only 8.4 % of the data for training.

5   Conclusion

In this work, we have developed a rotation tolerant approach to object recognition and applied it to the hand pose recognition task. Effectiveness of the approach is indicated by the experimental comparisons to other intensity image based methods. It should be noted that the method can give information on the in-plane angle of the hand, which may be useful in temporal gesture recognition. Future studies could include the development of weighting methods that would emphasize the relevant features of the hand poses, and substitution of the nearest neighbor classifier with a more advanced solution. This could provide improved means for addressing the appearance variations.

References

1. Barros, P., Magg, S., Weber, C., Wermter, S.: A multichannel convolutional neural network for hand posture recognition. In: Wermter, S., Weber, C., Duch, W., Honkela, T., Koprinkova-Hristova, P., Magg, S., Palm, G., Villa, A.E.P. (eds.) ICANN 2014. LNCS, vol. 8681, pp. 403–410. Springer, Heidelberg (2014)
2. Bastos, R., Sales Dias, M.: Skin color profile capture for scale and rotation invariant hand gesture recognition. In: Sales Dias, M., Gibet, S., Wanderley, M.M., Bastos, R. (eds.) GW 2007. LNCS (LNAI), vol. 5085, pp. 81–92. Springer, Heidelberg (2009)
3. Bhuyan, M., Neog, D., Kar, M.: Hand pose recognition using geometric features. In: Proceedings of National Conference on Communications (2011)
4. Dalal, N., Triggs, B.: Histograms of oriented gradients for human detection. In: Proceedings of CVPR (2005)
5. Fan, B., Wu, F., Hu, Z.: Aggregating gradient distributions into intensity orders: a novel local image descriptor. In: Proceedings of CVPR (2011)
6. Fang, Y., Cheng, J., Wang, J., Wang, K., Liu, J., Lu, H.: Hand posture recognition with co-training. In: Proceedings of ICPR (2008)
7. Freeman, W.T., Roth, M.: Orientation histograms for hand gesture recognition. In: IEEE International Workshop on Automatic Face and Gesture Recognition (1994)
8. Just, A.: Two-Handed Gestures for Human-Computer Interaction. Ph.D. Thesis, Ecole Polytechnique Fédérale de Lausanne (2006)
9. Just, A., Rodriguez, Y., Marcel, S.: Hand posture classification and recognition using the modified census transform. In: Proceedings of AFGR (2006)
10. Li, Y.T., Wachs, J.P.: HEGM: a hierarchical elastic graph matching for hand gesture recognition. Pattern Recogn. **47**, 80–88 (2014)
11. Liu, K., Skibbe, H., Schmidt, T., Blein, T., Palme, K., Brox, T., Ronneberger, O.: Rotation-invariant HOG descriptors using Fourier analysis in polar and spherical coordinates. Int. J. Comput. Vis. **106**(3), 342–364 (2014)
12. Quattoni, A., Torralba, A.: Recognizing indoor scenes. In: Proceedings of CVPR (2009)
13. Song, J., Sörös, G., Pece, F., Fanello, S.R., Izadi, S., Keskin, C., Hilliges, O.: In-air gestures around unmodified mobile devices. In: Proceedings of UIST, pp. 319–329 (2014)
14. Takacs, G., Chandrasekhar, V., Tsai, S., Chen, D., Grzeszczuk, R., Girod, B.: Fast computation of rotation-invariant image features by an approximate radial gradient transform. IEEE Trans. Image Process. **22**, 2970–2982 (2013)
15. Thippur, A., Ek, C.H., Kjellström, H.: Inferring hand pose: a comparative study of visual shape features. In: Proceedings of AFGR (2013)
16. Tompson, J., Stein, M., LeCun, Y., Perlin, K.: Real-time continuous pose recovery of human hands using convolutional networks. ACM Trans. Graph. **33**(5), Article No. 169, 169:1–169:10 (2014)
17. Triesch, J., von der Malsburg, C.: A system for person-independent hand posture recognition against complex backgrounds. IEEE Trans. PAMI **23**, 1449–1453 (2001)
18. Yao, Y., Li, C.T.: Hand posture recognition using SURF with adaptive boosting. In: Proceedings of BMVC (2012)

Extracting Lineage Information
from Hand-Drawn Ancient Maps

Ehab Essa[1], Xianghua Xie[2(✉)], Richard Turner[3], Matthew Stevens[3],
and Daniel Power[3]

[1] Department of Computer Science, Mansoura University, Mansoura, Egypt
[2] Department of Computer Science, Swansea University, Swansea, UK
x.xie@swansea.ac.uk
[3] Department of History and Classics, Swansea University, Swansea, UK
http://csvision.swan.ac.uk

Abstract. In this paper, we present an efficient segmentation technique
that extracts piecewise linear patterns from hand-drawn maps. The user
is only required to place the starting and end points and the method
is capable of extracting the route that connects the two, which closely
colocates with the hand-drawn map. It provides an effective approach to
interactively process and understand those historical maps. The proposed
method employs supervised learning to evaluate at every pixel location
the probability that such a lineage pattern exists, followed by shortest
path segmentation to extract the border of interest.

1 Introduction

This work is concerned with processing ancient hand-drawn Welsh Marcher lordships maps to extract piecewise lineage patterns that corresponds to lordship
boundaries. This system of landownership was established by the Norman kings
after their conquest of England in 1066 to protect their borders with Wales. It
reached its full extent after the English conquest of Wales in 1282. The basis
for any historical or geographical study of the Welsh Marches relies on William
Rees' four map sheets of South Wales and the Border in the Fourteenth Century
(Ordnance Survey, 1933). The challenge is to use these maps as the basis for
a geographical information systems, in which the extent and the ownership of
each Marcher lordship can be depicted throughout their individual histories.

Manual segmentation of the historical hand-drawn maps is a time-consuming,
tedious process, particularly when dealing with large maps. The maps are richly
annotated and textured, e.g. various map keys, texts and colouring, see Fig. 1
for an example. The delineation and separation of individual elements play an
important role in automated analysis and understanding of these maps. However,
automated segmentation of these maps is a non-trivial task. Image segmentation can be largely classified into automatic and user-aided or semi-automatic
approaches. In automatic segmentation methods, the segmented boundaries are
found without any user interaction. These methods are typically working by

A. Campilho and F. Karray (Eds.): ICIAR 2016, LNCS 9730, pp. 268–275, 2016.
DOI: 10.1007/978-3-319-41501-7_30

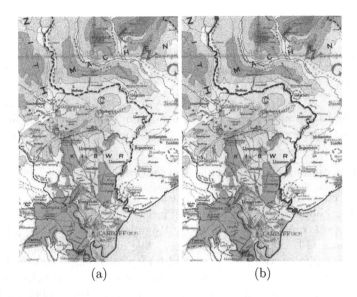

(a)   (b)

Fig. 1. An example of the South Wales lordship map. (a) original image. (b) final border of interest highlighted by blue. The two red dots are placed by the user and the path of interest is automated extracted. (Color figure online)

exploiting visual cues from the image, such as colour, texture, edge, and/or statistical distributions of those features as in [3,10,12–14,16]. However, in many cases they require high level knowledge to constrain the segmentation in order to cope with ambiguities in appearance, texture and shape. Semi-automatic segmentation methods introduce user interaction as an effective and efficient approach to transfer domain knowledge into the segmentation process. User can for example determine the region of interest, initialise the contour location [15,17], place some seed points on the object boundary [8,9] to guide the segmentation, or draw strokes inside and/or outside object of interest [1]. Generalising priors using learning techniques have been shown effective in many segmentation applications, e.g. [6].

In this paper, a semi-automatic segmentation method, with minimal user interaction, for extracting lineage patterns from ancient maps is proposed. The proposed method combines a machine learning method with a shortest path approach to delineate the boundaries of domains of marcher lords. Random forest classifier is used to generate a probability map of the potential location of the boundaries. A shortest path method based on the Dijkstra's algorithm is used to refine the segmentation between two seed points identified by the user. The proposed method is tested on the South Wales lordship maps in the fourteenth century as shown in Fig. 1(a) and achieves a promising results as in Fig. 1(b).

2   Proposed Method

Briefly, the proposed method first caries out pre-processing and feature extraction using histograms of orientated gradients (HoG) and histograms of intensities to highlight meaningful features for the boundary of interest. Next, random forest classifier is used to generate a probability map for the boundaries and suppress the background noise. The segmentation is then refined by finding the shortest path between user input seed points to obtain the final border.

2.1   Pre-processing and Feature Extraction

The images contains various features that are of no interest to us for extracting those lordship boundaries. The borders of interest are piecewise linear and have reasonably good contrast. We thus devise a simple pre-processing step to reduce certain amount of background ambiguities, while maintaining as much as possible for the boundaries. We use a thresholded map to enhance the original image and to produce a greyscale image for further processing. The map images are first binarised in order to reduce the interference from other symbols and topography details with the boundaries. The binary image is obtained by applying a thresholding on the three colour channels of the image (red, green and blue). Since the value of each colour channel varies between 0 to 255, we retrieve the index of image pixels between 70 and 170 of each channel and combine the result to produce the binary map. Figure 2 shows an example of such binary image on the left and the equivalent greyscale image on the right. The greyscale image is obtained by multiplying the binary image with the original image and used to extract the histogram of image intensity features which is a set of pixel greyscale value quantised into a finite number of bins.

The boundaries of interest are made of short line segments, i.e. piecewise linear. We employ histogram of oriented gradients (HoG) as the second set of visual features to represent and capture those patterns. HoG is one of the most successful image features in object detection e.g. human detection [4]. It measures the distribution of edge directions in local segments of an image. The HoG descriptor is achieved by dividing the image into non-overlapping small regions known as cells, to compute the histogram of gradient orientations for each region. The concatenation of these histograms are then produced to represent the image features. Each local histogram is also normalised within a larger region (with overlapping) to enhance the invariance to contrast and illumination variations. Here, to compute the direction of edges, image gradient is computed by convolving the image with derivative filters. Each pixel within the cell votes for one of the 9 histogram bins. The contrast normalisation is carried out based on L2-norm.

2.2   Boundary Evaluation

Next, we train a supervised classifier to evaluate every each pixel location for the possibility of containing one of those lineage patterns. Various machine learning

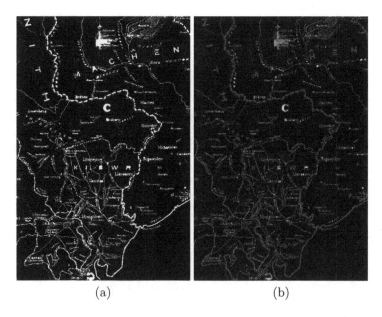

(a)   (b)

Fig. 2. Image pre-processing. (a) binary image. (b) greyscale image generated from the binary image and the original image. Feature extraction is carried out on the new greyscale image.

methods may be considered. Random Forest (RF) [2] is an ensemble-based classifier that combines a collection of decision trees to reduce the effect of overfitting and alleviate outlier problems to improve accuracy. RF is similar to bagging method in that it randomly samples training examples to train each decision tree separately. In addition, RF chooses a random subset of features attributes at each node to find the optimal tree splitting. In this work, we classify image pixels into two classes: boundary of the marcher lordship domains, and non-boundary.

In RF classification, a set of tress $r \in \{1, \cdots, R\}$ is trained separately on sub-sampling of the training examples. The testing of unseen parts of the map data is accomplished by introducing the unseen sample t to each decision tree starting from its root until it reaches the corresponding leaves and finally combines the predication result of each tree by computing the average predication of each class c:

$$P(c|v) = \frac{1}{R} \sum_{r=1}^{R} p_r(c|t). \tag{1}$$

Here, the number of trees R of the RF classifier sets to $R = 500$ and the number of attributes f randomly selected at each split is defined as $f = \sqrt{l}$, where l is the feature vector length.

The RF is trained on two features as aforementioned in Sect. 2.1, the histogram of the image intensity and HoG. These features extracted from a

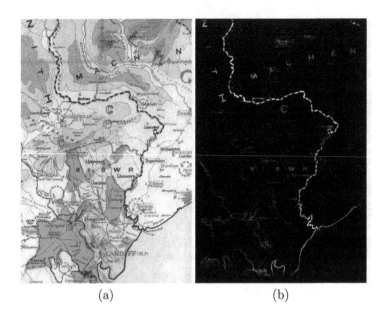

(a)   (b)

Fig. 3. The output of the RF classifier. (a) a binary classification result (highlighted by blue) superimposed on the original map. (b) the corresponding probabilistic map showing the possibility of each pixel in the map being considered as a pixel on the boundary of interest. The brighter the pixel the higher its probability. (Color figure online)

scanning window of size 128×128. An example binary classification result of the RF is shown in Fig. 3(a). The classifier can effectively highlight the border of interest. However, there are still some symbols that are misclassified, e.g. handwritten characters, which is inevitable.

2.3   Refinement Process Based on Shortest Path

Given that the boundaries of interest only contains a very small percentage of each entire map, eliminating the false positives while retaining high true positive rate is non-trivial. and may not be entirely plausible. In order to solve this problem, we proposed to use a shortest path algorithm based on Dijkstra's algorithm [5]. The proposed method finds the optimal path with minimum cost between two user points to refine the segmentation result. The cost function is defined using the probability values produced by the RF classifier. An example of the RF probability map is displayed in Fig. 3(b), where the brightness corresponds to the probability of the local region to be on the boundaries (i.e. bright white refers to high probability).

Shortest path is a combinatorial optimisation problem that working by finding the less costly solution of the problem from a finite set of all feasible solutions. The image is discretised to a graph $G(V, E)$, where V is a set of vertices represent

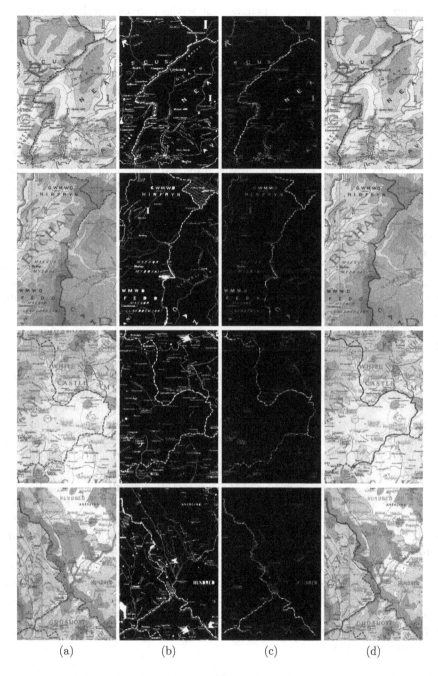

(a)   (b)   (c)   (d)

Fig. 4. Segmentation of the South Wales marcher lordship map. (a) original image. (b) binary image. (c) RF probability map. (d) the final border (blue) between two user points (red) superimposed on the original map. (Color figure online)

image pixels, and E is the set of edges. These edges are connecting vertices and also, carrying a weight value that reflects the cost of using this path.

There are several methods available using the shortest path algorithm, e.g. Intelligent Scissors [11] and Live Wire [7] which segment the image on the fly by following the user clicks. The costs of edges are usually defined based on the gradient magnitudes and orientation. However these methods are sensitive to background noise.

In this work, the Dijkstra's algorithm is used to find the path between two vertices in a graph where the total associated edge costs are minimised. Dijkstra's algorithm is a single-source algorithm that locates the shortest path from the source vertex to all other vertices in the graph with non-negative edge weights. The algorithm creates a shortest path tree starting from the source vertex and iteratively adding the vertex that has the lowest distance to the source. Each vertex is exploring its unvisited vertex neighbours and updating its assign distance value. As long as the algorithm does not reach the destination vertex, it keeps picking up unvisited vertex with the lowest distance value to be the new current vertex and it repeat these steps. The cost of each edge is defined as the negative log of the RF's probability value. Figure 1(b) shows the result of using the shortest path algorithm, cf. Fig. 3. This approach allows user to efficiently extract boundary of interest with just placing two points at a time.

3   Results

Here, we briefly summarise the evaluation that took place and the results we have achieved. The proposed method was tested on the South Wales marcher lordship map in the fourteenth century. The dimension of the image is 24401×16610 with resolution 600 dpi and bit depth 24. The map was recreated by William Rees and published by the Ordnance Survey in 1932. Due to the large size of the map, it is segmented to relatively small blocks for testing. The training of the RF classifier carries out on two blocks of the map of size 2000×2000.

Figure 4 shows some examples of the segmentation result. The boundaries of the domain marcher lord are drawn as a dash line. As illustrated in Fig. 4(b), the binary image removes some of the unrelated details that have the colour distribution differ from that of those boundaries. RF probability maps and the final border segmentation superimposed on the original maps are shown in columns (c) and (d). The proposed method successfully highlights the boundaries of interest. A full quantitative evaluation requires manual annotation of all the borders which is very time consuming. However, the qualitative results demonstrate the potential of the method to be applied to effectively extract lineages from those historic maps. This method serves as an important step in fully dissecting and tokenising those maps.

4   Conclusions and Future Work

We presented a semi-automatic segmentation method for Welsh marcher lordships map in order to delineate the boundaries of the marcher lord domains.

The proposed method extracts local features based HoG to train an RF classifier in order to produce a probability map of the boundary location. The segmentation is refined by using a shortest path algorithm based on Dijkstra's method to highlight the final border. The experimental results show promising performance of the proposed method. In the future work, we will extend the method to segment the map keys such as chief and lesser castles, and the other types of features.

References

1. Boykov, Y., Funka-Lea, G.: Graph cuts and efficient N-D image segmentation. IJCV **70**(1), 109–131 (2006)
2. Breiman, L.: Random forests. Mach. Learn. **5**(1), 5–32 (2001)
3. Comaniciu, D., Meer, P.: Mean shift: a robust approach toward feature space analysis. IEEE T-PAMI **24**(5), 603–619 (2002)
4. Dalal, N., Triggs, B.: Histograms of oriented gradients for human detection. CVPR. **1**, 886–893 (2005)
5. Dijkstra, E.: A note on two problems in connexion with graphs. Numer. Math. **1**(1), 269–271 (1959)
6. Essa, E., Xie, X., Sazonov, I., Nithiarasu, P., Smith, D.: Shape prior model for media-adventitia border segmentation in IVUS using graph cut. In: Menze, B.H., Langs, G., Lu, L., Montillo, A., Tu, Z., Criminisi, A. (eds.) MCV 2012. LNCS, vol. 7766, pp. 114–123. Springer, Heidelberg (2013)
7. Falcão, A.X., et al.: User-steered image segmentation paradigms: live wire and live lane. Graph. Models Image Process. **60**(4), 233–260 (1998)
8. Jones, J.-L., Essa, E., Xie, X., Smith, D.: Interactive segmentation of media-adventitia border in IVUS. In: Wilson, R., Hancock, E., Bors, A., Smith, W. (eds.) CAIP 2013, Part II. LNCS, vol. 8048, pp. 466–474. Springer, Heidelberg (2013)
9. Jones, J.L., Xie, X., Essa, E.: Combining region-based and imprecise boundary-based cues for interactive medical image segmentation. IJNMBE **30**(12), 1649–1666 (2014)
10. Malik, J., Belongie, S., Leung, T., Shi, J.: Contour and texture analysis for image segmentation. IJCV **43**(1), 7–27 (2001)
11. Mortensen, E.N., Barrett, W.A.: Interactive segmentation with intelligent scissors. Graph. Models Image Process. **60**(5), 349–384 (1998)
12. Rotem, O., Greenspan, H., Goldberger, J.: Combining region and edge cues for image segmentation in a probabilistic gaussian mixture framework. In: CVPR, pp. 1–8 (2007)
13. Shen, W., Wang, X., Wang, Y., Bai, X., Zhang, Z.: Deepcontour: a deep convolutional feature learned by positive-sharing loss for contour detection. In: CVPR, pp. 3982–3991 (2015)
14. Xie, X., Mirmehdi, M.: Texture exemplars for defect detection on random textures. In: Singh, S., Singh, M., Apte, C., Perner, P. (eds.) ICAPR 2005. LNCS, vol. 3687, pp. 404–413. Springer, Heidelberg (2005)
15. Xie, X., Mirmehdi, M.: Magnetostatic field for the active contour model: a study in convergence. In: BMVC, pp. 127–136 (2006)
16. Xie, X., Mirmehdi, M.: TEXEMS: random texture representation and analysis. In: Handbook of Texture Analysis, Chapter 4 (2008)
17. Yeo, S., Xie, X., Sazonov, I., Mirmehdi, M.: Geometric potential force for the deformable model. In: BMVC (2009)

Evaluation of Stochastic Gradient Descent Methods for Nonlinear Mapping of Hyperspectral Data

Evgeny Myasnikov[(✉)]

Samara State Aerospace University, Samara, Russia
`mevg@geosamara.ru`

Abstract. In this paper, we conducted a study of several gradient descent methods namely gradient descent, stochastic gradient descent, momentum method, and AdaGrad for nonlinear mapping of hyperspectral satellite images. The studied methods are compared in terms of both data mapping error and operation time. Two possible applications of the studied methods are considered. First application is the nonlinear dimensionality reduction of the hyperspectral images for the further classification. Another application is the visualization of the hyperspectral images in false colors. The study was carried out using well known hyperspectral satellite images.

Keywords: Hyperspectral image · Satellite image · Stochastic gradient descent · Momentum method · ADAGRAD · Nonlinear mapping

1 Introduction

High spectral resolution of hyperspectral satellite images offers many opportunities for the application of such images. But it also leads to the problems associated with the high spectral dimensionality of such images (usually the dimensionality of the space is of a few hundred). In this case it is reasonable to reduce the dimensionality of the spectral space. For this purpose linear dimensionality reduction techniques including Principal component analysis (PCA), Independent component analysis (ICA), and Projection pursuit are the most frequently used.

Nonlinear dimensionality reduction (NLDR) techniques are used less often. So Curvilinear component analysyis (CCA), and Curvilinear distance analysis (CDA) were used in [3,5] for dimensionality reduction of multispectral images. Another NLDR technique Locally linear embedding (LLE) was used in [4], and later LLE was combined with Laplacian Eigenmaps in [9]. Only a few attempts are made to use Nonlinear mapping algorithm (Sammon mapping) [8] for this purpose [6]. The main reasons for this can be considered a long run time and memory requirements of mapping algorithm.

This paper is devoted to the study of the effectiveness of stochastic gradient descent approaches for nonlinear mapping in the context of hyperspectral image analysis.

© Springer International Publishing Switzerland 2016
A. Campilho and F. Karray (Eds.): ICIAR 2016, LNCS 9730, pp. 276–283, 2016.
DOI: 10.1007/978-3-319-41501-7_31

The paper is organized as follows. The Sect. 2 briefly describes optimization methods used in the conducted study including base algorithm, stochastic gradient descent approach, momentum method, and the adaptive gradient algorithm. The Sect. 3 contains the description of the experimental study. Then the applications of the considered methods to the analysis of hyperspectral images are discussed. Finally, the conclusion is given.

2   Methods Used in the Study

2.1   Base Optimization Technique

Let N be the number of datapoints. Let $d_{i,j}$ be the distance between datapoints p_i and p_j in the multidimensional hyperspectral space, and $d^*_{i,j}$ be the distance between the same datapoints in the low-dimensional reduced space.

The data mapping error may be calculated using the following expression [8]:

$$\varepsilon = \frac{1}{\sum_{i,j=1;i<j}^{N} d_{i,j}} \cdot \sum_{i,j=1;i<j}^{N} \frac{(d_{i,j} - d^*_{i,j})^2}{d_{i,j}}. \tag{1}$$

The error (1) may be minimized by using a number of numerical techniques, but the method of gradient descent is the most widely used.

Let $Y(t)$ be a vector of parameters to be optimized at time t:

$$Y(t) = (y_1(t), ... y_N(t)). \tag{2}$$

Here $y_i, i = 1...N$ are coordinates of the datapoints $p_i, i = 1..N$ in a reduced space.

Using gradient descent algorithm involves changing many parameters (coordinates of objects in the output space) in compliance with the following expression

$$Y(t+1) = Y(t) - \alpha \cdot \bigtriangledown \varepsilon. \tag{3}$$

Here α is a coefficient (step size) of a gradient descent, $\bigtriangledown \varepsilon(t)$ is a gradient of the objective function:

$$\bigtriangledown \varepsilon = (\frac{\partial \epsilon}{\partial y_1}, ..., \frac{\partial \epsilon}{\partial y_N})^T. \tag{4}$$

Minimizing error (1) using a gradient descent is used quite often. It leads to the following simple recursive expression to search for the solution.

$$y_i(t+1) = y_i(t) + m \cdot \sum_{i,j=1;i\neq j}^{N} \frac{d_{i,j} - d^*_{i,j}}{d_{i,j} \cdot d^*_{i,j}} \cdot (y_i(t) - y_j(t)) \tag{5}$$

$$m = \frac{2 \cdot \alpha}{\sum_{i,j=1;i\neq j}^{N} d_{i,j}} \tag{6}$$

So the simple nonlinear mapping algorithm performs the initialization of low-dimensional coordinates $y_i(0)$, $i = 1..N$ followed by iterative refinement of points positions according to (5).

The computational complexity of one optimization step of the described procedure can be estimated as $O(N^2)$ (the computational complexity for the data mapping error is roughly the same) but it depends also on the dimensionality of low- and multidimensional spaces as distances in input and output spaces are used in (5).

To avoid recomputing the distances and to make the process independent on the high dimensionality of the spectral space we can precompute and store the distances between datapoints in the input multidimensional space. It requires $O(N^2)$ memory.

Thus, the method described above is indispensable for working with hyperspectral imaging because of the high computational complexity and memory requirements. To reduce the computational complexity of the method some other methods based on stochastic optimization are considered in the paper.

2.2   The Use of the Second Order Derivatives

The literature suggested many modifications of the gradient descent method (3). The most well-known algorithm is Newton's method, which takes into account the second order derivatives. In this case, the coordinates update is made in accordance with the following expression

$$Y(t+1) = Y(t) - H^{-1} \nabla \varepsilon \tag{7}$$

Here H^{-1} is Hessian matrix at step t. Unfortunately, Newton's method as presented is not applicable for minimization of functions containing a large number of variables. For this reason, the methods that take into account only the first order derivatives, or using information about an approximation of the second order are used to solve large-scale problems.

In particular, in the original paper [8] the following algorithm is proposed.

$$y_{i,j}(t+1) = y_{i,j}(t) - \frac{\partial \varepsilon}{\partial y_{i,j}} \bigg/ \frac{|\partial^2 \varepsilon|}{|\partial y_{i,j}^2|} \tag{8}$$

Here only the diagonal elements of the Hessian are used.

2.3   Nonlinear Mapping Using Stochastic Gradient Descent

The base version of the stochastic gradient descent assumes that a single random example is involved to approximate the gradient for each point at each iteration [6]:

$$y_i(t+1) = y_i(t) + m \cdot \frac{d_{i,j} - d_{i,j}^*}{d_{i,j} \cdot d_{i,j}^*} \cdot (y_i(t) - y_j(t)) \tag{9}$$

where j is a random example used to approximate the gradient at the iteration t of the optimization process.

The extension of this algorithm adopted in the present study (similar to [6]) is the use of small random subsamples (mini-batches) to approximate the gradient at each iteration:

$$y_i(t+1) = y_i(t) + m \cdot \sum_{j=1}^{L} \frac{d_{i,r_j} - d^*_{i,r_j}}{d_{i,r_j} \cdot d^*_{i,r_j}} \cdot (y_i(t) - y_{r_j}(t)) \tag{10}$$

Here r is a random subsample used to approximate the gradient at the iteration t of the optimization process, r_j is the j-th element of this subsample, L is the cardinality of subset r. With the above approach the size of subsamples defines the computational complexity of the algorithm per one iteration. For a subsets of size L the computational complexity is reduced to $O(LN)$.

2.4 Momentum Method

Momentum method [7] is further improvement of stochastic gradient descent. The main idea of the method is based on preserving the previous values of the gradient. It allows keeping the earlier direction of finding a solution to some extent.

$$Y(t+1) = Y(t) + \rho \cdot \triangle Y(t-1) - \alpha \cdot \triangledown \varepsilon \tag{11}$$

Here ρ determines the contribution of the previous step in a new value, $\triangle Y(t-1)$ is the vector of increments of the parameters obtained in the previous step.

2.5 Method of Adaptive Gradient

Method of adaptive gradient ADAGRAD [1] involves changing the parameters in accordance with the expression:

$$Y(t+1) = Y(t) - \frac{\alpha}{\sqrt{\sum_{\tau=1}^{t} diag^2(\triangledown \varepsilon)}} \cdot \triangledown \varepsilon \tag{12}$$

3 Experimental Results

To evaluate the algorithms several well-known hyperspectral images [2] were taken: Cuprite (512×614, 224 bands), Indian pines (145×145 220 bands, corrected), and others. To perform experiments in a reasonable time subsamples containing from 5000 to 10000 pixels were formed from the source images. Then, in the course of preliminary experiments the parameters of algorithms were evaluated.

During the comparison, the problem of two-(2D) and three-dimensional (3D) mapping was considered. This issue is important because 2D and 3D mappings allow you to perform visual analysis of hyperspectral images, and 3D mappings allow to synthesize the color representations of hyperspectral images (see Sect. 4.2 for further details). In all cases initialization in the low-dimensional space was done by projecting the datapoints from the hyperspectral space space to the first two (three) principal components. The results of the study are shown below (Intel Core i7 6500U @ 2.5 GHz).

Figure 1a shows the results for different methods and different values of step size. Figure 1b shows a comparison of the considered methods for a pair of test images, and two and three dimensional output spaces. As you can see, all the above methods provide a satisfactory solution to the problem. In all cases, the error decreases to quite small values. In most cases, the method of adaptive gradient (AdaGrad) demonstrates the best results among stochastic gradient methods, the method of moments (Momentum) shows consistent results in all cases.

It is worth noting that the base gradient descent algorithm (GD) uses the entire set of datapoints to compute the gradient at each iteration, and this algorithm has high computational time (per iteration). At the same time other algorithms use only a small subsets (minibatches) consisting of fifty objects.

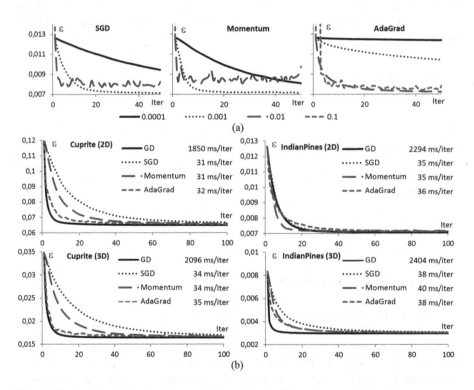

Fig. 1. Evaluation of stochastic gradient methods. Dependency of the data representation error (ε) on the number of iterations (Iter): for different values of parameter α (a), and for different optimization techniques (b)

Thus the complexity of the base gradient descent algorithm is $O(IN^2)$ versus $O(ILN)$ for stochastic gradient algorithms where I is the number of iterations, L is the number of datapoints in minibatch, N is the overall number of datapoints.

4 Applications of Nonlinear Mapping for Hyperspectral Image Analysis

Two different possible applications of the studied methods are considered in this paper. The first application is the dimensionality reduction of hyperspectral images for the further classification. The second application is the visualization of hyperspectral images.

4.1 Dimensionality Reduction of Hyperspectral Images Using Nonlinear Mapping

Due to the large amount of data and high dimensionality of spectral space some well-known classification methods (current implementations) cannot be used effectively for hyperspectral image classification. For this reason, researchers reduce the dimensionality of the spectral space. Principal component analysis is used most widely, and non-linear dimensionality reduction techniques remain poorly studied. This section presents the evaluation of some well-known classifiers for features obtained using a nonlinear dimensionality reduction of the spectral space. For comparison, classification results are shown for the extracted features using the principal component analysis technique. The following classifiers were used in evaluation: Bayes classifier (Bayes), k-nearest neighbors classifier (k-NN), and support vector machine (SVM). When performing experiments, the whole set of ground truth samples was divided into a training (60 percents) and a test (40 percents) subsets. The dimension of the reduced space ranged from 2 to 10 (SGD was used to reduce the dimensionality). The proportion of the correctly classified pixels of the test set (accuracy) was used as the assessment of the classification quality. The following Fig. 2 shows the results of the study.

In the experiments, in addition to the algorithm that minimizes the error (1), a modification of this algorithm that minimizes the following error (13) was also used.

$$\varepsilon_1 = \frac{1}{\sum_{i,j=1,i<j}^{N} d_{i,j}^2} \cdot \sum_{i,j=1,i<j}^{N} (d_{i,j} - d_{i,j}^*)^2 \tag{13}$$

It should be noted that the errors (1) and (13) are special cases of a more general form of expression for given μ and $\rho_{i,j}$

$$\varepsilon_0 = \mu \cdot \sum_{i,j=1,i<j}^{N} (\rho_{i,j} \cdot (d_{i,j} - d_{i,j}^*)^2) \tag{14}$$

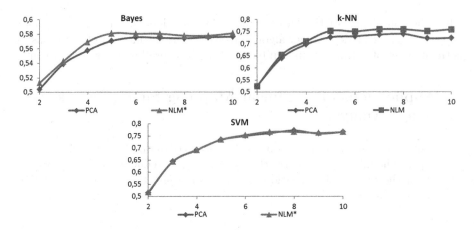

Fig. 2. Classification results. Dependency of the classification accuracy (Acc) on the dimensionality (Dim) of the reduced space

The choice of the error was made taking into account the resulting classification quality. In the first and the third case, a modification of the algorithm that minimizes the error (13) was used, and in the other case the method that minimizes (1) was used.

As it can be seen from the results of the experiments in the first and the second cases it was possible to obtain a visible increase in the quality of the classification using the nonlinear dimensionality reduction methods. In the third case, there were no significant differences.

4.2 Visualization of Hyperspectral Images Using Nonlinear Mapping

It is obvious that due to the high dimensionality of the spectral space direct visualization of hyperspectral images is impossible. For this reason, the visualization of hyperspectral imaging is performed, by selecting the displayed channels or by using a linear combination of channels of the original image or by performing the projection in the low-dimensional space, for example, using the principal component analysis Another approach is based on the nonlinear mapping and its main distinguishing feature is the fact that the distances between samples of the rendered image in the reduced low-dimensional space correspond (approximate) to the distances between pixels in the multidimensional spectral space. Visualization example of the Indian pines test image can be found in [6].

5 Conclusion

In this paper, we conducted a study of several gradient descent methods namely base gradient descent method, stochastic gradient descent method, momentum method, and AdaGrad for nonlinear mapping of hyperspectral images. The study showed that the momentum method and AdaGrad provide better results than the other considered methods. In addition two possible applications of the studied methods are considered in the paper. The first considered application is the nonlinear dimensionality reduction of the hyperspectral images for the further classification. It was demonstrated that nonlinear dimensionality reduction using considered methods provide better classification results compared to principal component analysis. Another application is the visualization of the hyperspectral images in false colors. The main distinguishing feature of such representation is the fact that the distances between samples of the rendered image correspond to the distances between samples in the multi-dimensional spectral space.

Acknowledgments. This work was financially supported by Russian Foundation for Basic Research, projects no. $15 - 07 - 01164 - a$, $16 - 37 - 00202$ mol_a.

References

1. Duchi, J., Hazan, E., Singer, Y.: Adaptive subgradient methods for online learning and stochastic optimization. J. Mach. Learn. Res. **12**, 2121–2159 (2011)
2. Hyperspectral Remote Sensing Scenes. http://www.ehu.eus/ccwintco/index.php?title=Hyperspectral_Remote_Sensing_Scenes
3. Journaux, L., Foucherot, I., Gouton, P.: Nonlinear reduction of multispectral images by curvilinear component analysis: application and optimization. In: International Conference on CSIMTA 2004 (2004)
4. Kim, D.H., Finkel, L.H.: Hyperspectral image processing using locally linear embedding. In: First International IEEE EMBS Conference on Neural Engineering, pp. 316–319 (2003)
5. Lennon, M., Mercier, G., Mouchot, M., Hubert-Moy, L.: Curvilinear component analysis for nonlinear dimensionality reduction of hyperspectral images. Proc. SPIE **4541**, 157–168 (2002)
6. Myasnikov, E.V.: Nonlinear mapping methods with adjustable computational complexity for hyperspectral image analysis. Proc. SPIE **9875**, 987508-1–987508-6 (2015)
7. Rumelhart, D.E., Hintont, G.E., Williams, R.J.: Learning representations by back-propagating errors. Nature **323**(6088), 533–536 (1986)
8. Sammon Jr., J.W.: A nonlinear mapping for data structure analysis. IEEE Trans. Comput. **C–18**(5), 401–409 (1969)
9. Shen-En, Q., Guangyi, C.: A new nonlinear dimensionality reduction method with application to hyperspectral image analysis. In: IEEE International Geoscience and Remote Sensing Symposium, pp. 270–273 (2007)

Automatic Selection of the Optimal Local Feature Detector

Bruno Ferrarini[1][(✉)], Shoaib Ehsan[1], Naveed Ur Rehman[2], Aleš Leonardis[3], and Klaus D. McDonald-Maier[1]

[1] School of Computer Science and Electronic Engineering, University of Essex, Colchester, UK
{bferra,sehsan,kdm}@essex.ac.uk
[2] Department of Electrical Engineering, COMSATS Institute of Information Technology, Islamabad, Pakistan
naveed.rehman@comsats.edu.pk
[3] School of Computer Science, University of Birmingham, Birmingham, UK
a.leonardis@cs.bham.ac.uk

Abstract. A large number of different local feature detectors have been proposed in the last few years. However, each feature detector has its own strengths and weaknesses that limit its use to a specific range of applications. In this paper is presented a tool capable of quickly analysing input images to determine which type and amount of transformation is applied to them and then selecting the optimal feature detector, which is expected to perform the best. The results show that the performance and the fast execution time render the proposed tool suitable for real-world vision applications.

Keywords: Feature detector · Repeatability · Performance evaluation

1 Introduction

Local feature detection is an important and challenging task in most vision applications. A large number of different approaches have been proposed so far [9]. All these techniques present various strengths and weaknesses, which make detectors' performance dependent on the application and, more generally, on the operating conditions, such as the transformation type and amount [4,8]. To overcome this problem, an obvious solution is to run multiple feature detectors so that the shortcomings of one detector are countered by the strengths of the other detectors. However, the computational demand of such an approach can be high and increases with the number of detectors employed. An alternative solution consists of a tool capable of automatically selecting the optimal feature detector to cope with any operating conditions as suggested in [9]. To the best of our knowledge, such idea has received none or little attention so far [5]. This paper aims to bridge this gap by proposing a tool which can determine the transformation type (T) and amount (A) of input images and then select the detector that is expected to perform the best under those particular operating conditions. The proposed approach requires to have a prior knowledge of

© Springer International Publishing Switzerland 2016
A. Campilho and F. Karray (Eds.): ICIAR 2016, LNCS 9730, pp. 284–289, 2016.
DOI: 10.1007/978-3-319-41501-7_32

how feature detectors perform under any of the considered operating conditions (T, A). So, in order to design an effective selection stage (Fig. 1), the evaluation framework proposed in [7] is utilized to characterize the performance of a set of feature detectors under varying transformation types and amounts. This performance characterization, as well as the results presented in this paper, are obtained with the image database available at [3]. This image database includes 539 scenes, which has been used for generating the datasets for three transformations, namely light reduction, JPEG compression and Gaussian blur. Each dataset has a reference image and several target images, which are obtained by the application of the same transformation to a reference image with increasing amounts. Considering that the JPEG and light reduction datasets include 13 target images and a blur dataset has 9 target images, the resulting number of operating conditions available in the image database [3] is 18865.

The rest of this paper is organized as follows. The proposed selection tool is introduced in Sect. 2 while its performance is discussed in Sect. 3. Finally, Sect. 4, draws conclusions and discusses the future directions for the automatic selection of the optimal feature detector.

2 The Automatic Selection Tool

The proposed system consists of four stages (Fig. 1). The first stage extracts global features from the input images, then the second and the third stages determine the type (T) and the amount (A) of transformation respectively. The last one selects the optimal detector, which is expected to obtain the highest repeatability. The following subsections describe those four stages of the proposed system and provide more details about the selection criterion of the optimal feature detector.

2.1 Global Feature Extraction

The first stage analyses the input pair of target and reference images and then builds a vector of three features: $F = [f_L, f_B, f_L]$. The component f_L is the light

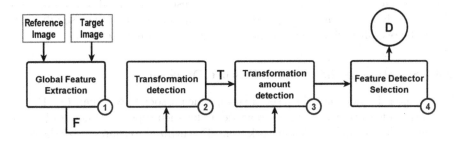

Fig. 1. The block diagram of the proposed automatic selection system; stage 1 extracts global features from input images, stage 2 and stage 3 determine the operation conditions, whereas the stage 4 selects the optimal feature detector.

reduction feature and is computed as the ratio between the mean of the image histogram of the target and the reference images: $f_L = h_t/h_r$. Hence, lower values of f_L correspond to higher amount of light reduction. The blur amount of an image is estimated with the perceptual blur metric proposed in [1]. The Gaussian Blur feature, f_B, is computed as the ratio of the perceptual blur indices of the target and reference images respectively: $f_B = b_t/b_r$. A high value of f_B corresponds to a relatively high level of blurring in the target image. The JPEG feature f_J is computed with the reference-less quality metric proposed in [10], which produces a quality index of an image by combining the blockiness and the zero-crossing rate of the image differential signal along vertical and horizontal lines. Higher the compression rate of a JPEG image, lower is the value of f_J.

2.2   Transformation Type Detection Stage

The transformation (T) is determined with a Support Vector Machine (SVM) classifier with a linear kernel function. The SVM has been trained utilizing a portion of the datasets [3] of 339 scenes chosen randomly. The related datasets for light changes, JPEG compression and Gaussian blur are employed to train the classifier. This results in a training set of 11865 feature vectors (13×339 for JPEG compression and light reduction, and 9×339 for blurring).

The overall accuracy of the prediction is above 99 %. Almost all the classification errors occur between blurred and JPEG compressed images at the lowest amounts of transformation (10–20 % of JPEG compression rate and 0.5–$1.0\,\sigma$ for Gaussian blur).

2.3   Transformation Amount Detection Stage

The third stage is composed of a set of SVMs, each specifically trained to predict the amount A of a single transformation type. So, once T is determined the corresponding SVM is activated to determine the transformation amount from the feature vector F.

The overall accuracy for light reduction is close to 100 % while the percentage of transformation amounts correctly classified by the JPEG and blur SVMs are just 75 % and 73 % respectively. However, the results presented in Sect. 3, show the relatively low accuracy of the JPEG and blur classifiers do not significantly affect the overall performance of the automatic selection system.

2.4   Selection of the Optimal Feature Detector

This stage is implemented as a set of rules, which associate each pair (T, A) with the optimal feature detector D to operate under such type and amount of transformation. The evaluation framework from [7] is utilized to characterize the set of feature detectors available at runtime for selection. Such characterization is carried out following the process described in [7] utilizing the training set (Sect. 2.2) of 339 datasets per transformation. First, the improved repeatability rate [2] is computed for each feature detector using the authors' original programs and the parameters values suggested by them. The average of the repeatability rates is computed across all the scene images that are undergone to the same type and amount of transformation. For example, the average repeatability of a detector at 20 % of JPEG compression is obtained as the mean of the repeatability scored with the 339 JPEG images compressed at 20 %.

Utilizing the outcomes of the performance characterization, the optimal feature detector for any operating condition is identified utilizing the highest average repeatability as a criterion. The resulting set of associations, $(T, A) \rightarrow D$, is utilized by the proposed tool at runtime to select of the most suitable feature detector for any given input target image.

3   Results and Discussion

This section presents the results of the comparison between the selection algorithm and several feature detectors working individually under varying uniform light reduction, Gaussian blur and JPEG compression. The evaluation criteria are the accuracy, which is measured by means of the gap between the average repeatability of the best detector and the optimal detector selected by the tool, and the execution time. The employed set of feature detectors represents a variety of different approaches [9] and includes the following: Edge-Based Region (EBR), Maximally Stable External Region (MSER), Intensity-Based Region (IBR), Salient Regions (SALIENT) Scale-invariant Feature Operator (SFOP), Speeded Up Robust Features (SURF). The scenes utilized for the tests are the remaining 200 scenes at [3], which are not included in the training set (Subsect. 2.2). Thus, 200 datasets each for light reduction, JPEG compression and blurring transformations have been utilized as a test set. As it is done for characterization of detectors' performance, the repeatability data are obtained using the original authors' programs and with the recommended control parameter values suggested by them.

Figure 2 shows a comparison of the average repeatability of the feature detectors working individually and the selection algorithm (red dotted line). Under JPEG compression, the accuracy of the selection is very high with a negligible gap error. Indeed, SURF performs the best under any transformation amount (Fig. 2c), so the accuracy of the selection depends only on the prediction of the transformation type, which is correct in more then 99 % of the cases. The automatic selection tool performs well also with light reduction as it can be appreciated from Fig. 2a where the red dotted line matches perfectly the SFOP's average curve up to 85 % and the SALIENT's curve at 90 % of light reduction (Fig. 2a). To the contrary, under Guassian blur some selection errors occurs as shown in Fig. 2d, where the gap between the average repeatability of the best detector and the one chosen as optimal by the selection tools is plotted. Between $1.5\,\sigma$ and $2.0\,\sigma$ (Fig. 2d) there is a dip of -1 %. In that range of blurring intensity the average curves of SURF and IBR intersect each other (Fig. 2b) and the wrong predictions of the transformation amount (A) causes some errors in the selection

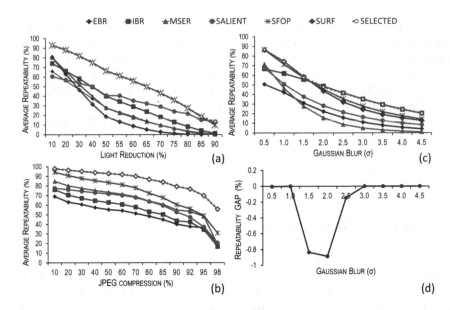

Fig. 2. Average repeatability curves of the proposed selection tool and feature detectors working individually for (a) light reduction, (b) Gaussian blur, (c) JPEG compression and (d) the average repeatability GAP between the proposed selection tool and feature detectors working individually under Gaussian blur.

of the optimal feature detector. Although, the probability that such classification error occurs is around 9 %, the resulting gap error is just −1 %. This is due to the little difference between the average repeatability values of SURF and IBR, which are close to each other at 1.5 σ (58.54 % vs 55.78 %) and at 2.0 σ (43.6 % vs 48.8 %).

A complete run of the proposed tool, from image loading to the detector selection, requires a time comparable to the fastest of the feature detectors considered: MSER. The hardware employed for the test is a laptop equipped with a i7-4710MQ CPU, 16 GB of RAM, and a SATA III SSD Hard drive and the test images have a resolution of 1080 × 717 pixels. MSER and IBR are available as binary executables and have a running time of 150 ms and 1.8 s respectively while the selection tool, which is a Matlab script, requires 170 ms to load images and select a detector. Hence, a system employing the proposed tool with those two feature detectors can extract features in 170 + 150 ms (when MSER is optimal) or 170 ms + 1.8 s (when IBR is optimal) while running both MSER and IBR with an image and select the best, would require always more than 1.9 s. Thus, the proposed system is equally or more efficient than running more feature detectors with the same image, in addition, it scales really well with the number of feature detectors employed.

4 Conclusions and Future Directions

The automatic tool for selecting the optimal feature detector proposed in this paper represents an attempt to achieve a fully adaptive feature detector system capable of coping with any operating condition. The proposed approach is based on the knowledge of the behaviour of detectors under different operating conditions, which are the transformation type T and the amount of such transformation, A. The next step towards a more robust automatic selection system is to consider the scene content as a part of the operating conditions as it is well known that a detector's performance depends also on that factor ([6,8]). Thus, modeling the scene content and designing a comprehensive evaluation framework that utilizes it together with the image transformation type and amount should, in our humble opinion, the direction to follow in order to achieve a robust selection tool.

References

1. Crete, F., Dolmiere, T., Ladret, P., Nicolas, M.: The blur effect: perception and estimation with a new no-reference perceptual blur metric. In: Electronic Imaging 2007, pp. 64920I–64920I. International Society for Optics and Photonics (2007)
2. Ehsan, S., Kanwal, N., Clark, A., McDonald-Maier, K.: Improved repeatability measures for evaluating performance of feature detectors. Electron. Lett. **46**(14), 998 (2010)
3. Ehsan, S., Clark, A.F., Ferrarini, B., McDonald-Maier, K.: JPEG, blur and uniform light changes image database. http://vase.essex.ac.uk/datasets/index.html
4. Ehsan, S., Clark, A.F., Ferrarini, B., Rehman, N.U., McDonald-Maier, K.D.: Assessing the performance bounds of local feature detectors: Taking inspiration from electronics design practices. In: 2015 International Conference on Systems, Signals and Image Processing (IWSSIP), pp. 166–169. IEEE (2015)
5. Ehsan, S., Clark, A.F., McDonald-Maier, K.D.: Rapid online analysis of local feature detectors and their complementarity. Sensors **13**(8), 10876–10907 (2013)
6. Ferrarini, B., Ehsan, S., Rehman, N.U., McDonald-Maier, K.D.: Performance characterization of image feature detectors in relation to the scene content utilizing a large image database. In: 2015 International Conference on Systems, Signals and Image Processing (IWSSIP), pp. 117–120. IEEE (2015)
7. Ferrarini, B., Ehsan, S., Rehman, N.U., McDonald-Maier, K.D.: Performance comparison of image feature detectors utilizing a large number of scenes. J. Electron. Imaging **25**(1), 010501 (2016)
8. Mikolajczyk, K., Tuytelaars, T., Schmid, C., Zisserman, A., Matas, J., Schaffalitzky, F., Kadir, T., Gool, L.V.: A comparison of affine region detectors. Int. J. Comput. Vis. **65**(1–2), 43–72 (2005)
9. Tuytelaars, T., Mikolajczyk, K.: Local invariant feature detectors: a survey. Found. Trends Comput. Graph. Vis. **3**(3), 177–280 (2008)
10. Wang, Z., Sheikh, H.R., Bovik, A.C.: No-reference perceptual quality assessment of jpeg compressed images. In: Proceedings of 2002 International Conference on Image Processing 2002, vol. 1, pp. 1-477. IEEE (2002)

Multiple Object Scene Description for the Visually Impaired Using Pre-trained Convolutional Neural Networks

Haikel Alhichri[✉], Bilel Bin Jdira, Yacoub bazi, and Naif Alajlan

Advanced Lab for Intelligent Systems' Research (ALISR), Department of Computer Engineering, College of Computer and Information Sciences, King Saud University, Po. Box 51178 Riyadh, 11543, Saudi Arabia
{hhichri,ybazi,najlan}@ksu.edu.sa

Abstract. This paper introduces a new method for multiple object scene description as part of a system to guide the visually impaired in an indoor environment. Here we are interested in a coarse scene description, where only the presence of certain objects is indicated regardless of its position in the scene. The proposed method is based on the extraction of powerful features using pre-trained convolutional neural networks (CNN), then training a Neural Network regression to predict the content of any unknown scene based on its CNN feature. We have found the CNN feature to be highly descriptive, even though it is trained on auxiliary data from a completely different domain.

The proposed methodology was assessed on four datasets representing different indoor environments. It achieves better results in terms of both accuracy and processing time when compared to state-of-the art.

Keywords: Visual impaired · Multiple object indoor scene description · Image multiple labeling · Convolutional neural networks (CNN) · NN regression

1 Introduction

Developing a method to increase the independent mobility of blind people is both important and challenging. Usually, blind people are only able to travel along routes that they have previously learned with the help of a sighted guide, white cane, or a guide-dog. In recent years, efforts have been made to develop devices that are able to detect nearby obstacles and give partial guidance instructions to blind people to enable them to move autonomously, even in unfamiliar environments [1, 2]. From the literature, one can deduce that the overwhelming majority of the contributions could be highlighted under one of the two categories confined to navigation (i.e., by allowing more freedom in terms of mobility, orientation, and obstacle avoidance) and recognition (i.e., by providing the blind person with information related to the nature of objects encountered in his/her context). Recently, multiple object scene description method is introduced as a solution towards recovering some sight function for a blind person by increasing his awareness of the objects present in the environment around him [1, 2]. A wearable

© Springer International Publishing Switzerland 2016
A. Campilho and F. Karray (Eds.): ICIAR 2016, LNCS 9730, pp. 290–295, 2016.
DOI: 10.1007/978-3-319-41501-7_33

computer vision system is used to capture and process images in order to recognize multiple objects in the scene.

In this paper, we propose to use pre-trained convolutional neural networks (CNN), as a tool to extract feature from the captured image. Then train a Neural Network to predict the content of any unknown scene based on its CNN feature. The paper shows that CNN feature are highly descriptive, and at the same time they have efficient computational costs.

The rest of the paper is organized as follows. In Sect. 2, we give a full description of the methodology, including the problem formulation, CNN theory, and appended Neural network regression layers. Section 3, presents the datasets and the experimental results. Finally, concluding remarks are given in Sect. 4.

2   Description of the Proposed Method

Problem Formulation. Let $\{\mathbf{I}_i, \mathbf{y}_i\}_{i=1}^{n}$ be a training set where $\mathbf{I}_i \in \mathcal{R}^{w \times h \times 3}$ is an image of size $w \times h \times 3$, and $\mathbf{y}_i \in \mathcal{R}^{1 \times c}$ is its corresponding "object indicator" vector of size c which is equal to number of objects of concern. Vector $\mathbf{y}_i$ is composed of a binary sequence where 1 indicated the presence of an object in the scene, while 0 indicated otherwise. Let us consider also $f_l^{\text{CNN}}, l = 1, \ldots, L$ be a CNN model with L layers pre-learned on a large amount of labeled auxiliary images from a different domain. Here f_l^{CNN} refers the output of the lth layer. Our aim is to develop a regression system that can map the test images $\{\mathbf{I}_i\}_{i=1}^{m}$ to binary vectors $\mathbf{y}_i$ (which indicates the presence or no presence of objects) based on the available training set as well the pre-learned CNN model.

Figure 1 gives an overview of the proposed framework, which is composed of a pre-trained CNN plus an appended fully-connected neural network which will be trained to perform the regression task. Unlike, other methods which try to train the whole combined network again (which would be computationally prohibitive for a single desktop computer), in this work, we only train the added NN.

Given the deep nature of CNN, one can extract features at different layers. In this work, we take the output of the hidden fully connected layers just before the last output layer (which is used to produce a classification result in the original CNN framework), to represent the training and test images as shown in Fig. 1. That is we feed each image $\mathbf{I}_i$ as input to the CNN and generate a feature representation vector $\mathbf{x}_i \in \mathcal{R}^D$ of dimension D at layer k, with $k = L - 1$. Regression is then performed by appending another neural network (NN) to the CNN, composed of two layers; one hidden layer (whose size is set as a parameter) and one output layer with has as many neurons as the objects we are trying to recognize. The appended NN is a fully connected meaning that every neuron in one layer is connected to all neurons in the next layer.

At test time, we feed each test CNN feature vector to this network and assume that output node j that has a predicted value larger than a given threshold (for example 0.5) indicates the presence of the object j.

To train the appended neural network we use the back propagation technique and minimize the following cost function: [3]:

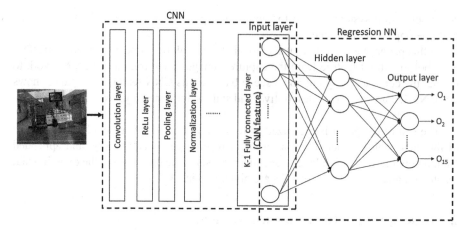

Fig. 1. Illustration of the proposed method consisting of a pre-trained CNN for feature extraction and an appended NN for regression.

$$\mathcal{L}_2\left(\theta_{DNN}\right) = \frac{1}{2n}\sum_{i=1}^{n}\sum_{k=1}^{c}||y_i - \theta_{DNN}\left(\mathbf{x}_i\right)||^2$$
$$+ \frac{\lambda}{2}\left(\sum_{l=1}^{H}||\mathbf{W}_l||_F^2 + \sum_{o=1}^{c}||\mathbf{W}_o||_F^2\right) \tag{1}$$

Where $\theta_{DNN}\left(\mathbf{x}_i\right)$ is the output of the NN for an input $\mathbf{x}_i$, $\mathbf{W}_l$ and $\mathbf{W}_o$ are the weights of the hidden layer and the output layer respectively, and H is the size of the hidden layer. The first term of (1) refers to the mean squared error between the estimated vector and the training labels, while the second term is again the weight decay penalty which helps in preventing overfitting.

The estimation of the vector of parameters $\theta_{DNN} = \left\{\mathbf{W}_l, \mathbf{W}_o\right\}$ of the NN starts by initializing the weights to small random values. Then the cost (1) is minimized with a min-batch gradient descent algorithm [4].

3   Experimental Results

Dataset Description. The images processed in this paper were acquired by means of a chest-mounted CMOS camera from the IDS Imaging Development Systems, model UI-1240LE-C-HQ with KOWA LM4NCL lens, carried by a wearable lightweight shield.

Four image datasets are collecting for evaluating the efficiency of the proposed image description method. The first two refer to two different buildings in the University of Trento, Italy, while the second two refer to the college of computer and information sciences building in the King Saud University (KSU), Saudi Arabia. Set 1 (University of Trento) accounts for a total of 131 images acquired in two separate daytimes (morning and evening), which was split into 61 training images (i.e., for training the NN model), and 70 for testing purposes. Set 2 (University of Trento) is composed of 130 images, divided into 58 training images, and 72 testing images. Set 3 (King Saud University) is composed of 320 images, divided into 161 training images, and 159 testing images. Finally Set 4 (King Saud University) is composed of 174 images, divided into 86 training images, and 88 testing images. It is noteworthy that the training images for all datasets were selected in such a way to cover all the predefined objects in the considered indoor environment.

As noted above, a list of objects of interest must be predefined. Thereupon, we have selected the objects deemed to be the most important ones in the considered indoor environments. Table 1, presents the list of objects considered in every set.

Table 1. List of objects considered in every set of images

Dataset	Number of objects	Objects considered
Set 1 (U of Trento)	15	External window, Board, Table, External door, Stair door, Access control reader, Office, Pillar, Display screen, People, ATM, Chairs, Bins, Internal door, and Elevator
Set 2 (U of Trento)	15	Stairs, Heater, Corridor, Board, Laboratories, Bins, Office, People, Pillar, Elevator, Reception, Chairs, Self-service, External door, and Display screen
Set 3 (KSU)	15	Pillar, Fire extinguisher/hose, Trash can, Chairs, External door, Hallway, Self service, Reception, Didactic service machine, Display screen, Board, Stairs, Elevator, Laboratory, Internal door
Set 4 (KSU)	15	Board, Fire extinguisher/hose, Trash cans, Chairs, External door, Didactic service machine, Self service, Reception, Cafeteria, Display screen, Pillar, Stairs, Elevator, Prayer room, Internal door

Preliminary Results. The efficiency of the proposed framework is expressed in terms of the well-known sensitivity (SEN) and specificity (SPE) accuracy measures defined in [2, 5]. They express the probability of correct detection of the presence and absence of an object, respectively.

$$\text{Sensitivity} = \frac{\textit{True Positives}}{\textit{True Positives} + \textit{False Negatives}}$$

$$\text{Specificity} = \frac{\textit{True} \text{ Negatives}}{\textit{True} \text{ Negatives} + \textit{False} \text{ Positives}}$$

Several pre-trained CNNs exist in the literature, including Caffe library models [6], ConvNet library models [7], Torch library [8], Neon library models [9], and others.

In this work, we selected the ImageNet library models, in particular the imagenet-matconvnet-vgg-vdp-16, imagenet-matconvnet-vgg-s, imagenet-matconvnet-vgg-m, imagenet-matconvnet-vgg-f models.

Table 2 presents comparison between the proposed method (pre-trained CNN + NN) and the state-of-the-art efficient method based on Compressive sensing and Gaussian process regression (CS + GP) [2], as well as the base method based on SURF feature matching also reported in [2]. To run these experiments, we used the *imagenet-matconvnet-vgg-vdp-16* pre-trained model, and we have set the parameters of the NN as follows: size of hidden layer 128, number of epochs 500, learning rate 0.01, drop rate 0.5. Also, note that any output node j that has a predicted value larger 0.25 indicates the presence of the object j.

Table 2. Comparison to state-of-the-art using the imagenet-matconvnet-vgg-vdp-16 model

		Set 1			Set 2			Set 3	Set 4
	Method:	CS+GP[2]	SURF+GP [2]	Proposed	CS+GP[2]	SURF+GP [2]	Proposed	Proposed	Proposed
Per object	1	98.57	83.33	100	83.33	98.57	85.71	87.5	94.29
	2	94.28	81.94	93.75	81.94	94.28	88.57	98.48	96
	3	85.71	100	95	100	85.71	100	95.24	82.61
	4	62.85	93.05	100	93.05	62.85	89.47	98.65	97.3
	5	88.57	90.27	92.86	90.27	88.57	65.38	86.21	88.89
	6	87.14	95.83	84.62	95.83	87.14	66.67	95.24	100
	7	91.42	79.16	100	79.16	91.42	94.44	78.57	100
	8	90	90.27	66.67	90.27	90	100	100	83.33
	9	97.14	93.05	100	93.05	97.14	87.5	71.43	100
	10	98.57	95.83	100	95.83	98.57	0	83.33	100
	11	90	93.05	100	93.05	90	71.43	91.3	0
	12	98.57	88.88	100	88.88	98.57	92	79.17	100
	13	100	93.05	71.43	93.05	100	92.86	100	100
	14	98.57	79.16	100	79.16	98.57	97.3	100	50
	15	95.71	100	100	100	95.71	100	100	92
Overall	SEN	77.72	71.16	**95.45**	71.16	77.72	**88.76**	**93.72**	**91.74**
	SPE	100	100	**92.89**	100	100	**88.19**	**96.61**	**94.53**
Time per scene		~2-3 s	60-90 s	<0.01 s	~2-3 s	60-90 s	<0.01 s	< 0.05 s	< 0.05 s

The results clearly show the significant superiority of the proposed method for both datasets. This is mainly due to the effectiveness of the image features extracted with the help of the pre-trained CNNs. Not only is the proposed method better in terms for accuracy but also in terms of execution time. Another advantage of the proposed method is the simplicity of the algorithm, since we don't need to have a dictionary of images for the objects compared to the state-of-the-art method in [1].

4   Conclusion

In this paper, we have presented a novel method for the coarse description of indoor scenes which can be used as a supporting solution towards a system for helping a blind person navigate in an indoor environment. The system makes the blind person aware of the presence/absence of a given set of objects in his environment. We have shown how we can effectively use convolutional neural networks to solve problem of multiple object scene description. Experimental results have shown significant improvement over state of the art, with reduced computational complexities.

References

1. Mekhalfi, M.L., Melgani, F., Bazi, Y., Alajlan, N.: Toward an assisted indoor scene perception for blind people with image multilabeling strategies. Expert Syst. Appl. **42**(6), 2907–2918 (2015)
2. Mekhalfi, M.L., Melgani, F., Bazi, Y., Alajlan, N.: A compressive sensing approach to describe indoor scenes for blind people. IEEE Trans. Circuits Syst. Video Technol. **25**(7), 1246–1257 (2015)
3. Bengio, Y., Courville, A., Vincent, P.: Representation learning: a review and new perspectives. IEEE Trans. Pattern Anal. Mach. Intell. **35**(8), 1798–1828 (2013)
4. Schmidhuber, J.: Deep learning in neural networks: an overview. Neural Netw. **61**, 85–117 (2015)
5. Razavi, N., Gall, J., Van Gool, L.: Scalable multi-class object detection. In: Proceedings of the 2011 IEEE Conference on Computer Vision and Pattern Recognition, Colorado Springs, USA, pp. 1505–1512 (2011)
6. Caffe | Deep Learning Framework. http://caffe.berkeleyvision.org/. Accessed 09 Mar 2016
7. ConvNet: Deep Convolutional Networks. http://libccv.org/doc/doc-convnet/. Accessed 09 Mar 2016
8. Torch | Scientific computing for LuaJIT. http://torch.ch/. Accessed 09 Mar 2016
9. Nervana Neon - Scalable Deep Learning library. http://www.nersc.gov/users/data-analytics/data-analytics/neon-scalable-deep-learning-library/. Accessed 09 Mar 2016

Detection and Recognition

Effective Comparison Features
for Pedestrian Detection

Kang-Kook Kong, Jong-Woo Lee, and Ki-Sang Hong[✉]

Image Information Processing Laboratory, POSTECH,
San 31 Hyoja-Dong, Pohang 790-784, Republic of Korea
{mjkkk,ljw0610,hongks}@postech.ac.kr

Abstract. For real applications of pedestrian detection, both detection speed and detection accuracy are important. In this paper we propose a detector based on effective comparison features (ECFs) for simultaneously improving detection accuracy and speed. ECFs are defined as the features helping to improve actual performance. Using only these ECFs as feature candidates for the split nodes of decision trees, our detector can achieve accurate results. As an additional benefit, detection speed is improved by earlier rejection of negative samples. Experiments are conducted using well-known benchmark datasets for pedestrian detection. The experimental results of our ECF detector show that our detection speed is 1–2 orders of magnitude faster than the speed of state-of-the-art algorithms, with comparable detection accuracy.

Keywords: Pedestrian detection · AdaBoost · Aggregated channel features · Effective comparison features

1 Introduction

For pedestrian detection, aggregated channel features (ACFs) [5] are among the best of the features proposed to date in terms of detection accuracy and feature computation speed. To improve the detection accuracy of ACFs, filtering-based features have been proposed, including locally decorrelated channel features (LDCFs) [12] and filtered channel features (FCFs) [18]. However, although they offer state-of-the-art accuracy, the filtering time required to construct numerous channels weakens the advantage of the high speed of ACFs. To address this problem, we revisit aggregated channel comparison features (ACCFs) [11], which have the most promising detection speed among ACF-based features, as an alternative because they do not require a filtering operation to compute channels, unlike LDCFs or FCFs.

ACCFs incorporate an operation by which ACFs are compared after being obtained. This operation is widely used in 3D or 2D object detection [8,9,17], keypoint descriptors [3], face alignment [7], and human pose estimation [14] and is equivalent to the operation of the self-similarity features described in [2]. These ACCFs exhibit better accuracy than ACFs while maintaining a high detection speed. However, to be one of the best features in terms of detection accuracy

© Springer International Publishing Switzerland 2016
A. Campilho and F. Karray (Eds.): ICIAR 2016, LNCS 9730, pp. 299–308, 2016.
DOI: 10.1007/978-3-319-41501-7_34

and speed, ACCFs still need further improvement in terms of accuracy when compared with LDCFs and FCFs.

In our paper, effective comparison features (ECFs) are proposed to improve the detection accuracy and speed of the original ACCFs [11]. Our detector is derived from the ECFs, which contribute to the improvement of detection performance. Experiments are conducted using well-known benchmark datasets for pedestrian detection. Compared with other ACF-based features such as LDCFs and FCFs, our ECFs improve the detection speed by approximately 8 times over LDCFs and by approximately 40 times over FCFs. Moreover, the achieved accuracy is comparable to that of state-of-the-art algorithms.

2   ECFs

2.1   Baseline Features

Before explaining ECFs specifically, we briefly review ACCFs [11] and their baseline ACFs [5]. ACFs consist of 10 channels suitable for pedestrian detection: 3 color channels (LUV), 1 gradient magnitude channel, and 6 gradient orientation channels. The channel pyramid computation for multi-scale pedestrian detection is fast because of the usage of the near-scale invariance of HOG [6]. Based on these channels, an aggregation operation is added to improve feature stability and increase detection speed. More specifically, the dimension of each channel of ACF is 512 for a 128×64 pedestrian window size with a 4×4 aggregation region. After obtaining ACFs, ACCFs perform a comparison operation between them to further improve the detection performance. The ith ACCF, $g(i)$, is defined as

$$g(i) = g^c_{pq} = f^c_p - f^c_q, \tag{1}$$

where f^c_p and f^c_q $[c = 1, 2, \cdots, 10, p, q = 1, \cdots, 512 \ (p \neq q)]$ are the pth and qth features that belong to the cth channel of the ACFs, respectively. The number of all the possible feature combinations of ACCF is $\binom{512}{2} \times 10$. A set of all possible ACCFs, G, can be defined as

$$G = \left\{ g(i) \right\}, \quad i = 1, \cdots, \binom{512}{2} \times 10. \tag{2}$$

A naive method for improving the detection accuracy of an ACCF detector is to increase the quantity of feature candidates for the optimal features of split nodes. However the accuracy improvement by a moderate increase in the number of feature candidates is not significant [11]. Besides, in the extreme case where all possible ACCFs are used as feature candidates, it is inefficient and almost impossible to search the full feature space because the number of all possible feature combinations, $|G| = \binom{512}{2} \times 10$, is so huge.

2.2 Proposed Method

ECFs. In contrast to the naive method, our proposed method is to improve the quality of the feature candidates. We define the features that contribute to the improvement of detection performance as ECFs. The effectiveness of each ACCF is measured by the relative importance [1,10]. Given K strong classifiers $\{H_M^k\}_{k=1}^K$ each of which consists of M weak classifiers (decision trees) with J split nodes, the relative importance of the ith feature, $v(i; H_M^1, \cdots, H_M^K)$, can be defined as

$$v(i; H_M^1, \cdots, H_M^K) = \sum_{k=1}^{K} \sum_{m=1}^{M} \sum_{j=1}^{J} \tau_{k,m,j} I\big(\eta(h_m^k, j) = i\big), \tag{3}$$

where $\tau_{k,m,j}$ denotes the improvement (importance) at the jth split node of the mth weak classifier belonging to the kth strong classifier h_m^k, $I(\cdot)$ represents the indication function, and $\eta(h, j)$ returns the selected feature at the jth split node of the weak classifier h. In the case where $\tau_{k,m,j} = 1$, the relative importance of each feature is the summation over all split nodes of all weak classifiers in all strong classifiers for which the feature was selected as the splitting feature. This summation of the relative importance is equivalent to the frequency of each feature used in the split nodes of the learned classifiers. Therefore the relative importance can be reasonable measurement of effectiveness under the assumption that ECFs will be selected many times as features of split nodes.

It is almost impossible to consider all ACCFs at a time, but it is possible to consider a small subset of them several times in multiple strong classifiers.

Algorithm 1. Mining step of ECFs

Data: The pairs of the training samples and their labels, $\{(x_n, y_n)\}_{n=1}^N$
Input: The set of all possible ACCFs G, The relative importance $V = \{v(i)\}_{i=1}^{|G|}$
Output: The set of ECFs G^*

1 initialization: $v(i) \leftarrow 0$ for all i
2 **for** $k \leftarrow 1$ **to** K **do**
3   initialization: $w_{m=1,n} \leftarrow \frac{1}{N}$ for all n
4   **for** $m \leftarrow 1$ **to** M **do**
5   generate S feature candidates from G randomly
6   find the optimal weak classifier h_m
7   **for** $j \leftarrow 1$ **to** J **do**
8   find the optimal feature $g(i^*)$ corresponding to the jth node of h_m
9               $v(i^*) \leftarrow v(i^*) + \tau_{k,m,j}$
10   computation: $e_m = \frac{\sum_{n=1}^N w_{m,n} I(y_n \neq h_m(x_n))}{\sum_{n=1}^N w_{m,n}}$
11   computation: $\beta_m = \frac{1}{2} \log \frac{1-e_m}{e_m}$
12   update: $w_{m+1,n} = \exp(-y_n H_m(x_n))$, where $H_m = \sum_{t=1}^m \beta_t h_t$

13 return: $G^* = \{g(i) \mid v(i) > \theta\}$

Algorithm 2. Retraining step of the final detector

Data: The pairs of the training samples and their labels, $\{(x_n, y_n)\}_{n=1}^N$
Input: The set of ECFs G^*
Output: The final detector H_M
1 initialization: $w_{m=1,n} \leftarrow \frac{1}{N}$ for all n
2 **for** $m \leftarrow 1$ **to** M **do**
3   generate $|G^*|/R$ feature candidates from G^* randomly
4   find the optimal weak classifier h_m
5   computation: $e_m = \frac{\sum_{n=1}^N w_{m,n} I(y_n \neq h_m(x_n))}{\sum_{n=1}^N w_{m,n}}$
6   computation: $\beta_m = \frac{1}{2} \log \frac{1-e_m}{e_m}$
7   update: $w_{m+1,n} = \exp(-y_n H_m(x_n))$, where $H_m = \sum_{t=1}^m \beta_t h_t$
8 return: $H_M = \sum_{m=1}^M \beta_m h_m$

By repeating the training procedures several times to learn multiple strong classifiers, ECFs can be mined from the statistics of the selected features in these classifiers' split nodes. The final strong classifier is retrained using these ECFs only. Therefore, our ECF detector is learned from two steps, which are the mining step (Algorithm 1) of ECFs, and the retraining step (Algorithm 2) of the final classifier using mined ECFs.

Mining Step. Our goal for the mining step is to extract the set of ECFs from the set of all possible ACCFs using the pairs of the training samples and their labels, (x_n, y_n) $(n = 1, 2, \cdots, N)$. In Algorithm 1, the ith relative importance, $v(i)$, represents the effectiveness of the ith ACCF, $g(i)$. Initially, the relative importance of all features, $\{v(i)\}_{i=1}^{|G|}$, is set to zero. The training procedures for multiple strong classifiers are repeated K times. In each training procedure, the training sample weights, $w_{m=1,n}$, are initially set uniformly, and the subprocedures for learning the weak classifier are repeated M times to obtain M weak classifiers. At the mth iteration, the optimal weak classifier is selected to minimize the error, e_m, among the S feature candidates randomly generated from the set of all possible ACCFs, G. For the optimal feature, $g(i^*)$, of the split nodes of the optimal weak classifier, the corresponding i^*th relative importance, $v(i^*)$, increases by $\tau_{k,m,j}$. Each iteration in the subprocedure is terminated after computing the voting weight, β_m, and updating the training sample weights, $w_{m+1,n}$.

Retraining Step. The retraining step of the final detector is the same as the overall training procedure for the original ACCF detector; the difference is in the part of feature candidate generation, where candidates are randomly generated from a set of ECFs instead of the set of all possible ACCFs, G. The set of ECFs, G^*, is defined as

$$G^* = \Big\{ g(i) \,|\, v(i) > \theta \Big\}, \tag{4}$$

where $v(i)$ is the ith relative importance of the ith ACCF obtained from the mining step and θ is a thresholding parameter for feature effectiveness. If θ is a negative number, $G^* = G$, i.e., all ACCFs are considered to be ECFs, whereas if $\theta = \infty$, no ACCFs are considered as ECFs and G^* is an empty set. In the experiments, θ is set to a proper positive number to generate T feature candidates ($T = 10{,}240$ in our experiments).

Detection Speed. In our ECF detector, the subset of ECFs is used as a list of candidates for the optimal features of the split nodes. As an additional benefit, detection speed is improved. Each weak classifier of the ECF detector is stronger than that of the original ACCF detector because it is based on the ECFs. These lead to earlier rejection of negative samples, resulting in a faster detection speed than that of the original ACCF detector.

3   Experimental Results

Recent algorithm proposals have their own ideas for improving detection accuracy and provide the recommended parameter settings of the training phase to further improve the detection accuracy for the CalTech testing dataset [12,18]. The typical parameter settings are of a bigger model size than the 64×32 object window, with more bootstrapping rounds and augmented positive and negative samples. We follow the experimental settings. By default, our model has an 128×64 object window. For the CalTech testing dataset, each weak classifier is a depth-5 decision tree and 4,096 weak classifiers are learned through RealBoost with 5 bootstrapping rounds (32-512-1024-2048-4096) using the CalTech+ training dataset. For the INRIA testing dataset, each weak classifier is a depth-2 or -3 decision tree and 2,048 weak classifiers are learned through DiscreteBoost with 4 bootstrapping rounds (32-128-512-2048) using the INRIA training dataset. In our ECF detector, we use the settings $\tau_{k,m,j} = 1$; $S = 1{,}000$; and $K = 8$ in the mining step (Algorithm 1) and $R = 16$ in the retraining step (Algorithm 2).

3.1   Performance of ECFs

Experiments are conducted to show the effectiveness of our ECFs. The results are summarized in Table 1 for the CalTech testing dataset and in Table 2 for the INRIA testing dataset. We consider the effects of bootstrapping round and model size for ACFs and ACCFs (Table 1, group 1). The use of more bootstrapping rounds reduces the miss rate by 2.4%, from 29.8% to 27.4%, in the ACF detectors. Thus, 5 bootstrapping rounds are used to train detectors by default. Compared with an ACF detector, an ACCF detector reduces the miss rate by 2.2%, from 27.4% to 25.2%. The result of the CalTech testing dataset (Table 1, group 1) and that of the INRIA testing dataset (Table 2, group 1) demonstrate that the comparison operation makes an important contribution to the improvement of the detection accuracy. Further improvement of the detection accuracy of ACCFs is possible using a bigger model size, where the miss rate is reduced

Table 1. Accuracy [log-average miss rate (MR %)] and speed (frames per second) comparison for the CalTech testing dataset. The CalTech+ training dataset is used.

Features	Bootstrapping round	Model size	Depth	MR (%)	Speed (fps)
ACF	64-256-1024-4096	64 × 32	5	29.8	21.8
ACF	32-512-1024-2048-4096	64 × 32	5	27.4	16.4
ACCF	32-512-1024-2048-4096	64 × 32	5	25.2	10.2
ACCF	32-512-1024-2048-4096	128 × 64	5	22.4	10.8
ECF	32-512-1024-2048-4096	128 × 64	5	**19.5**	**17.7**
LDCF	32-512-1024-2048-4096	64 × 32	5	24.8	5.3
LDCF	32-512-1024-2048-4096	128 × 64	5	20.7	1.7
FCF	32-512-1024-2048-4096	128 × 64	5	18.5	0.4

Table 2. Accuracy [log-average miss rate (MR %)] and speed (frames per second) comparison for the INRIA testing dataset. The INRIA training dataset is used.

Features	Bootstrapping round	Model size	Depth	MR (%)	Speed (fps)
ACF	32-128-512-2048	128 × 64	2	18.1	37.2
ACF	32-128-512-2048	128 × 64	3	16.1	37.1
ACCF	32-128-512-2048	128 × 64	2	15.3	37.2
ACCF	32-128-512-2048	128 × 64	3	13.9	37.3
ECF	32-128-512-2048	128 × 64	2	12.9	40.0
ECF	32-128-512-2048	128 × 64	3	**12.0**	**39.8**
LDCF	32-128-512-2048	128 × 64	2	15.8	4.6
LDCF	32-128-512-2048	128 × 64	3	13.8	4.7

by 2.8 %, from 25.2 % to 22.4 %. Thus, a 128 × 64 model size is used to train detectors by default.

We observe the detection accuracy and detection speed of ECFs. Compared with the ACCF detector, the ECF detector reduces the miss rate by 2.9 %, from 22.4 % to 19.5 % (Table 1). This result shows that the most frequently used features in multiple strong classifiers can be regarded as ECFs and that the mining step of these ECFs is necessary to improve the detection accuracy. One interesting point is in the results of detection speed. In most cases, the detection speed decreases as the detection accuracy increases because more computations are required to improve the accuracy. However, in ECFs, the detection speed is enhanced from 10.8 fps to 17.7 fps and the detection accuracy is improved. This can be explained by fast rejection.

The detector can reject unpromising object windows earlier when using ECFs than when using ACCFs, as shown in Fig. 1. Given a test image, one detector tests approximately 100,000 candidate windows. For the same candidate windows, the ECF detector needs approximately 100 weak classifiers to reject most

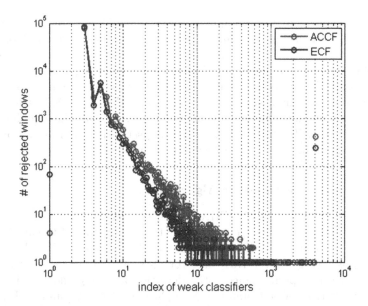

Fig. 1. The number of rejected windows at each weak classifier of ACCFs and ECFs. (Color figure online)

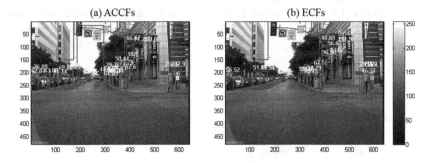

Fig. 2. Detection results of (a) ACCF and (b) ECF detectors for a given image of CalTech dataset.

candidate windows, whereas the ACCF detector needs more weak classifiers. For the test image, the detection results of ACCFs and ECFs are shown in Figs. 2a and b, respectively. In contrast to the ACCF detector, the ECF detector yields results with lesser false positives. The tendencies of the detection accuracy and speed are also observed in the INRIA testing dataset (Table 2). In the case in which depth-3 decision trees are used, the ECF detector reduces the miss rate by 1.9 % from 13.9 % to 12.0 % and improves the detection speed from 37.3 fps to 39.8 fps.

We compare the accuracy and speed of our ECFs with those of LDCFs [12] and FCFs [18] (Table 1, group 2). LDCFs and FCFs can be regarded as the modified features of ACFs for improving their detection accuracy. These detectors give the-state-of-the-art accuracy but are somewhat slow because of the filtering time required to construct numerous channels. More specifically, 40 filters are used in LDCFs and 490 or 610 filters are used in FCFs. In contrast to these detectors, our ECF detector does not require a filtering operation. Consequently, our ECF detector is approximately 8 times faster than an LDCF detector and approximately 40 times faster than an FCF detector while having the similar detection accuracy. For the INRIA testing dataset (Table 2, group 2), our ECF detector is approximately 8 times faster than the LDCF detector.

3.2   Comparison with Other Algorithms

For the CalTech (Fig. 3) and INRIA testing dataset (Fig. 4), we compare the detection accuracy of our ECF detector with that of the state-of-the-art detectors reported in the Caltech Pedestrian Detection Benchmark [4]. For the CalTech testing dataset (Fig. 3), our ECF detector does not exhibit the best accuracy but offers excellent performance if the detection accuracy and speed are considered together. Because CompAct-Deep [2], DeepParts [15] and CCF [16] are based on deep architectures, they cannot to be easily compared with our detector directly. However, it may be difficult to obtain a high detection speed because they are CNN-based approaches. Compared with the detector using Checkerboards of FCFs [18], our detector is approximately 40 times faster with minor loss of accuracy, as shown in Table 1. For the INRIA testing dataset (Fig. 4), our ECF detector is almost top-ranked. In fact, the SpatialPooling [13] that gives the

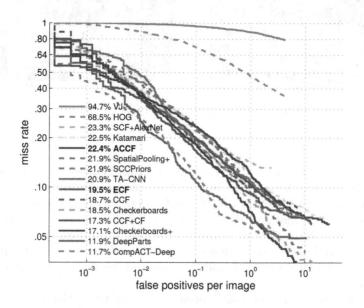

Fig. 3. CalTech dataset. (Color figure online)

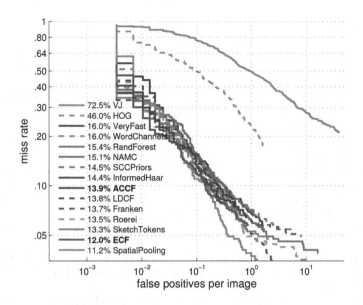

Fig. 4. INRIA dataset. (Color figure online)

best accuracy is based on ACFs and spatially pooled covariance and LBP features. Thus, this detector may have difficult in obtaining a high detection speed. Therefore our ECFs may be the best features from the viewpoints of detection accuracy and speed.

4   Conclusions

We have proposed ECFs as a means of improving the detection accuracy and speed of the original ACCFs. ECFs, among all possible ACCFs, can be mined from the effectiveness analyzing statistics of selected features of multiple learned classifiers. Compared with other ACF-based features such as LDCFs and FCFs, our ECFs improve the detection speed by approximately 8 times over LDCFs and approximately 40 times over FCFs. Moreover the achieved accuracy is comparable to that of state-of-the-art algorithms, other than CNN-based approaches, when using the CalTech and INRIA testing datasets. Because our ECFs are fast and accurate, our features can be applied to numerous areas requiring a high detection speed or low computational power. As another application, such as an object-proposal method, our ECF detector can take the role of obtaining pedestrian candidate windows for other detectors requiring heavy computation power.

Acknowledgments. This work was supported by the National Research Foundation of Korea (NRF) grant funded by the Korea government (MEST) (No. 2011-0016669).

References

1. Breiman, L., Ihaka, R.: Nonlinear discriminant analysis via scaling and ace technical report. Univ. California, Berkeley (1984)
2. Cai, Z., Saberian, M., Vasconcelos, N.: Learning complexity-aware cascades for deep pedestrian detection. In: Proceedings of the IEEE International Conference on Computer Vision, pp. 3361–3369 (2015)
3. Calonder, M., Lepetit, V., Strecha, C., Fua, P.: BRIEF: binary robust independent elementary features. In: Daniilidis, K., Maragos, P., Paragios, N. (eds.) ECCV 2010, Part IV. LNCS, vol. 6314, pp. 778–792. Springer, Heidelberg (2010)
4. Dollár, P.: Caltech Pedestrian Detection Benchmark. http://www.vision.caltech.edu/Image_Datasets/CaltechPedestrians/
5. Dollár, P., Appel, R., Belongie, S., Perona, P.: Fast feature pyramids for object detection. IEEE Trans. Pattern Anal. Mach. Intell. **36**(8), 1532–1545 (2014)
6. Dollár, P., Belongie, S., Perona, P.: The fastest pedestrian detector in the west. In: BMVC, vol. 2, p. 7. Citeseer (2010)
7. Dollár, P., Welinder, P., Perona, P.: Cascaded pose regression. In: 2010 IEEE Conference on Computer Vision and Pattern Recognition (CVPR), pp. 1078–1085. IEEE (2010)
8. Drost, B., Ulrich, M., Navab, N., Ilic, S.: Model globally, match locally: efficient and robust 3d object recognition. In: 2010 IEEE Conference on Computer Vision and Pattern Recognition (CVPR), pp. 998–1005. IEEE (2010)
9. Gall, J., Yao, A., Razavi, N., Van Gool, L., Lempitsky, V.: Hough forests for object detection, tracking, and action recognition. IEEE Trans. Pattern Anal. Mach. Intell. **33**(11), 2188–2202 (2011)
10. Hastie, T., Tibshirani, R., Friedman, J., Hastie, T., Friedman, J., Tibshirani, R.: The Elements of Statistical Learning, vol. 2. Springer, New York (2009)
11. Kong, K.K., Hong, K.S.: Design of coupled strong classifiers in adaboost framework and its application to pedestrian detection. Pattern Recogn. Lett. **68**, 63–69 (2015)
12. Nam, W., Dollar, P., Han, J.H.: Local decorrelation for improved pedestrian detection. In: Advances in Neural Information Processing Systems, pp. 424–432 (2014)
13. Paisitkriangkrai, S., Shen, C., van den Hengel, A.: Strengthening the effectiveness of pedestrian detection with spatially pooled features. In: Fleet, D., Pajdla, T., Schiele, B., Tuytelaars, T. (eds.) ECCV 2014, Part IV. LNCS, vol. 8692, pp. 546–561. Springer, Heidelberg (2014)
14. Shotton, J., Girshick, R., Fitzgibbon, A., Sharp, T., Cook, M., Finocchio, M., Moore, R., Kohli, P., Criminisi, A., Kipman, A., et al.: Efficient human pose estimation from single depth images. IEEE Trans. Pattern Anal. Mach. Intell. **35**(12), 2821–2840 (2013)
15. Tian, Y., Luo, P., Wang, X., Tang, X.: Deep learning strong parts for pedestrian detection. In: Proceedings of IEEE International Conference on Computer Vision (2015)
16. Yang, B., Yan, J., Li, S.: Convolutional channel features. In: Proceedings of IEEE International Conference on Computer Vision (2015)
17. Yuan, J., Luo, J., Wu, Y.: Mining compositional features for boosting. In: IEEE Conference on Computer Vision and Pattern Recognition, CVPR 2008, pp. 1–8. IEEE (2008)
18. Zhang, S., Benenson, R., Schiele, B.: Filtered channel features for pedestrian detection. In: 2015 IEEE Conference on Computer Vision and Pattern Recognition (CVPR), pp. 1751–1760. IEEE (2015)

Counting People in Crowded Scenes via Detection and Regression Fusion

Cemil Zalluhoglu$^{(\boxtimes)}$ and Nazli Ikizler-Cinbis

Department of Computer Engineering, Hacettepe University, Ankara, Turkey
{cemil,nazli}@cs.hacettepe.edu.tr

Abstract. It is particularly important for surveillance systems to track the number of people in crowded scenes. In this paper, we look into this problem of counting people in crowded scenes and propose a framework that fuses information coming from detection, tracking and region regression together. For counting by regression, we propose to use region covariance features in the form of Sigma Sets in conjunction with interest point features. Experimental results on two benchmark datasets demonstrate that using region covariance features for the purpose of people counting yields effective results. Moreover, our results indicate that fusing detection and regression is beneficial for more accurate people counting in crowded scenes.

Keywords: People counting · Regression · Detection · Region covariance

1 Introduction

Crowd size estimation is a crucial task in visual surveillance. Knowing the size and distribution of people can provide valuable information for crowd control and public space design. Also, real-time estimation of crowd size is significantly important for safety control, and serves as an important tool to prevent overcrowding problems like congestion, delay and security related abnormalities such as fighting and rioting. Counting people in public spaces is a challenging problem due to severe occlusions, scene perspective distortion, cluttered background, poor and complex illumination.

In recent years, significant progress has been made in people counting. Loy *et al.* [1] provide an extensive review on this topic. The taxonomy of current approaches are generally divided into three main categories; counting by detection, counting by clustering and counting by regression. For *counting by detection, monolithic detection approaches* [2,3] rely on full-body detectors trained on different types of features such as Haar wavelets, edgelets, HOGs, etc. Monolithic detection methods get high accuracy results if the crowd is sparse [3,4]. *Part-based detection methods* [5] are used for handling the partial occlusion problem, where several different part detectors are used for finding people in occlusions. *Shape matching based methods* [6,7] describe shape prototypes for

© Springer International Publishing Switzerland 2016
A. Campilho and F. Karray (Eds.): ICIAR 2016, LNCS 9730, pp. 309–317, 2016.
DOI: 10.1007/978-3-319-41501-7_35

detecting pedestrians. In *counting by clustering*, the patterns of coherent motion in crowd is discovered by means of clustering [8,9] over tracklets.

Third class of approaches relies on *regression* for counting. Such approaches estimate crowd size using holistic and local description of crowd patterns instead of detection and tracking. In general, counting by regression methods have three main components: feature representation, geometric correction, regression modeling. Total edge pixels and histogram of edge orientation are examples of structure-based features [1], whereas gray-level co-occurrence matrix (GLCM) [10], local binary pattern (LBP) and HOG [2] features are examples for the texture features that are being used. In these approaches, several regression models, including ridge regression (RR) [11], multi output ridge regression (MORR) [12], cumulative attribute ridge regression (CA-RR) [13] gaussian process regression (GPR) have been utilized.

In this paper, we propose a framework that combines detection and regression with the aim of estimating better person counts. During regression, we propose to make use of region covariance features in conjunction with interest point based features. For more efficient usage of region covariances, we use Sigma Sets [14], which use Cholesky decomposition to carry region covariance matrices to Euclidean space. We test our proposed framework on Mall and PETS 2009 datasets and our experimental results show that the region covariance representation based on Sigma Sets provide promising performance in person counting. Furthermore, our results demonstrate that it is possible to obtain more accurate person counting estimates when detection and regression are used in conjunction in a unified framework.

2   Proposed Method

In person counting, the aim is the return the total number of people in video frames. More formally, given a video $\mathcal{X} = \{x_1, x_2, x_3, \ldots x_n\}$, our objective is to

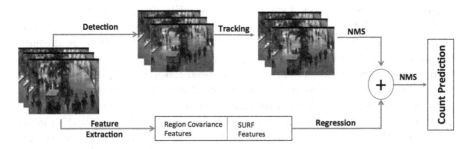

Fig. 1. Our proposed people counting framework combines detection and regression for people counting. In the detection pipeline, we make use of tracking in between frames to locate people that go undetected between frames. For regression we propose to use region covariance features in the form of Sigma Sets together with SURF features for obtaining better count estimates.

learn a mapping $\mathcal{F} : \mathcal{X} \to \mathcal{C}$ where $\mathcal{C}$ is the count of people of the corresponding video $\mathcal{X}$. In this work, we present a unified framework that combines detection and regression for estimating this mapping $\mathcal{F}$. In this framework, we further use tracking to identify undetected regions between frames, *i.e.* to fill the holes that go undetected between frames in detection. Our overall architecture is illustrated in Fig. 1.

2.1   Detection

For detecting people, we use two different detectors. First one is the upper body detector proposed by [15]. This method uses a sliding window approach, where each window is subdivided into patches which are described by Histogram of Gradients (HOG). After generating these patches a linear SVM is used for classification. By using upper body detection we aimed to find people whose lower part of the body does not appear due to occlusions. We apply this detector on foreground regions obtained after background subtraction.

The other detector that we utilize is a state-of-the-art person detection Fast R-CNN [16]. This method is suitable for detecting sparse crowds. Fast R-CNN method takes whole image (video frame) and a batch of object proposal regions as an input. This convolutional network processes entire image with several convolutional and pooling layers to obtain a convolutional feature map. Region of interest (ROI) pooling layer is used to extract fixed-length feature vector for

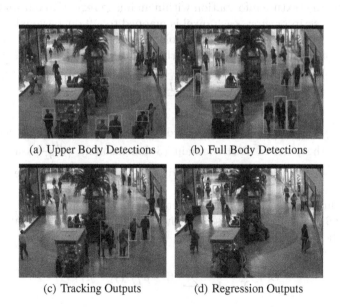

(a) Upper Body Detections   (b) Full Body Detections

(c) Tracking Outputs   (d) Regression Outputs

Fig. 2. Sample outputs from each of the components of our proposed framework. The upper body (a) and full body detections (b) are tracked in time to locate missing detections between frames (c). Those detections are then fused with the regression outputs (d) to get the final count estimation.

each proposed region. These vectors are then used as an input of fully connected layer. There are two outputs of the fully connected layer. First one is softmax probabilities that represent probability of K object classes and background class totally K+1 categories and the other one is bounding box positions of people which we use in our proposed method.

Sample detection results are given in Fig. 2. After getting the detection outputs from both the upper body and the full body detectors, we apply non-maximum suppression technique on these results to avoid counting the same person twice on that frame.

In order to locate people that go undetected between frames, we also make use of a tracker. For this purpose, we use Meanshift tracker [17], and track each person bounding box, which are output from detection phase. We apply this tracking procedure five frames forward and five frames backward in time. In this way, we are able to locate people who stay stationary in a few frames or those that cannot be found by the detector.

2.2   Regression

For regression, we propose to use Region Covariance [18] features, together with SURF (Speeded-up Robust Features) [19]. In this section, we first describe the details of this feature extraction, and then the training phase.

Region Covariance features: Region covariance descriptor [18] is widely used for encoding the texture information within an image region. In our implementation of this descriptor, first, each pixel is mapped to a 9-dimensional vector that consists of the x-y coordinates, RGB color intensities and the first and second derivatives of intensity. More formally, the feature vector f is identified as

$$f(x,y) = \begin{bmatrix} x & y & I(x,y) & \left|\frac{\partial I(x,y)}{\partial x}\right| & \left|\frac{\partial I(x,y)}{\partial y}\right| & \left|\frac{\partial^2 I(x,y)}{\partial x^2}\right| & \left|\frac{\partial^2 I(x,y)}{\partial y^2}\right| \end{bmatrix}^T \tag{1}$$

where, (x y) denotes the x and y coordinates of the pixel, I(x,y) denotes the intensity of the pixel in RGB domain (3-dimensional), $\left|\frac{\partial I(x,y)}{\partial x}\right|$ and $\left|\frac{\partial I(x,y)}{\partial y}\right|$ represent the first order derivatives, and $\left|\frac{\partial^2 I(x,y)}{\partial x^2}\right|$ and $\left|\frac{\partial^2 I(x,y)}{\partial y^2}\right|$ are the second order derivatives.

Given this 9-dimensional feature vector, an image region can be represented with a 9×9 covariance matrix C of the feature points f_i that fall into that region, such that

$$C = \frac{1}{N-1} \sum_{i=1}^{N} (f_i - \mu_f)^*(f_i - \mu_f)^T \tag{2}$$

where μ is the mean of the feature vectors f_i, N is the total number of feature points and * denotes the complex conjugation.

While the covariance matrix provides important discriminative information about a region, one important drawback of using this covariance matrix as is, is that, the covariance matrices lie in Riemannian manifold and they cannot be compared using regular similarity measures. The similarity measures defined [18] for their comparison are time-consuming, which is prohibitive for use in person counting problem, because of the excessive amount of processing required for each frame.

An alternative has been proposed by Hong et al. [14], which makes use of the fact that every covariance matrix has a unique Cholesky decomposition, and use this decomposition to define a feature vector that is based on the covariance matrices and at the same time, lie on Euclidean space. Their proposed region descriptor called Sigma Set is defined as $S = \{s_i\}$ and each Sigma point s_i is calculated as

$$s_i = \{\beta L_1, \ldots, \beta L_d, (-\beta L_1), \ldots, (-\beta L_d)\} \tag{3}$$

where L_i is the i-th column of L which is the lower triangular matrix obtained via Cholesky decomposition of the covariance matrix $C = LL^T$ [14]. β is a scalar, which is taken $\beta = \sqrt{2}$ in our experiments. In order to efficiently use the discriminative properties of region covariances, we use the Sigma Set as the first part of our feature vector.

Speeded Up Robust Features (SURF): SURF [19] descriptor is commonly used in object detection and recognition tasks. First, the interest points are detected by SURF, where Hessian-matrix approximation computed by using integral images is used. Then, SURF descriptors, which are based on sum of Haar wavelet component responses are extracted around the detected interest points. We observe that interest points keep valuable information about distribution of crowd.

After the extraction of each of the aforementioned features, region covariances (aka. Sigma Sets) and SURF features of each region are concatenated in order to form our proposed region representation for person counting.

Training: For training the regression method, we use L2-regularized L2-loss Support Vector Regression (SVR). While constructing the training data, there are excessively many possible regions that can be used as negative samples, i.e.the regions that do not include any person. For this reason, while sampling the negative examples for training, we use the same amount of positive and negative samples. For choosing the parameters of SVR, we apply five-fold cross validation.

In the process of combining detection and regression outputs, we apply non-maxima suppression (NMS) to the combined responses in each frame. The result of this NMS step gives us the final count of the people in that particular frame.

3   Experiments

3.1   Experimental Setup

In our experiments, we have used two benchmark datasets for people counting, namely PETS 2009 [20] and the Mall datasets [12]. Statistics and properties of

Table 1. Properties of dataset: N_f = number of frames, FPS = frame per second, R = Resolution, C = Colour, Loc= Location, S = Shadows, Ref = Reflections, Loi = Loitering, CrS = Crowd size (min and max number of people), T_p = total number of people in dataset

DataSet	N_f	FPS	R	C	Loc	S	Ref	Loi	CrS
Mall	2000	< 2	640 × 480	RGB	Indoor	Yes	Yes	Yes	13–53
Pets2009	1505	~ 7	768 × 576	RGB	Outdoor	Yes	No	No	0 42

these datasets are presented in Table 1. PETS 2009 dataset has been collected for testing many surveillance tasks including object tracking, crowd counting and event recognition. For people counting problem, this dataset has 460 video frames within two sequences (13–57,13–59). Mall dataset was collected from a publicly accessible webcam in a shopping mall and is more challenging than the previous established benchmark datasets due to severe occlusion, varying illumination circumstances at different times of the day and perspective distortion caused by the camera.

The feature vectors are extracted from each region of each frame of the video using sliding window method. As a common practice, we perform perspective scaling while deciding the region size. This is needed due to the perspective distortion that make far people appear more smaller than people who are closer to the camera.

We compare our result on different settings of datasets, as used in the literature. On Mall dataset, firstly we use same training/testing splits as in [21]. Second setting includes first 800 frames as training and remaining as testing [13]. For Pets 2009 dataset, we use same settings as in [20]. Five-fold cross validation is applied in each experiment.

The performance of our method is evaluated via two standard measures that are commonly used for evaluating people counting. These are Mean Absolute Error (MAE) and Mean Relative Error (MRE) measures, which are defined as

$$MAE = \frac{1}{N} \sum_i^N |y_i - \widehat{y_i}| \qquad MRE = \frac{1}{N} \sum_i^N \frac{|y_i - \widehat{y_i}|}{y_i}$$

where N is the total number of frames in video, y_i is estimated count number and $\widehat{y_i}$ is the ground truth number of people in i-th frame.

3.2 Experimental Results

We first compare our method to the detection-only and regression-only counterparts on the Mall dataset. For this purpose, we implement the following baselines: (1) Regression with SURF features only, (2) Regression with Region Covariance features only, (3) Detection and Tracking, and the combination of these three approaches.

Table 2. Comparison of the baseline methods and our proposed method on the Mall dataset.

Method	MAE	MRE
SURF Regression	23.45	74.77
Detection + Tracking	17.56	56.21
Region Covariance Regression	11.72	38.77
SURF + Detection + Tracking	18.11	56.58
Region Covariance + Detection + Tracking	9.48	32.63
Region Covariance + SURF Regression	8.12	25.16
Proposed Method	**3.71**	**12.49**

Table 3. Comparison of other methods and our proposed method

Mall dataset				Pets 2009 dataset			
Dataset	Method	MAE	MRE	Dataset	Method	MAE	MRE
Mall	Ryan et al. [21]	2.58	8.52	Pets2009	Chan et al. [20]	2.30	8.36
	Cavazza et al. [24]	2.63	8.74	(13–57)	Cavazza et al. [24]	2.29	8.12
	Proposed Method	3.71	12.49		Albiol et al. [25]	2.80	12.60
					Proposed Method	2.50	13.61
Mall	Chen et al. [13]	3.43	10.50	(13–59)	Chan et al. [20]	1.65	4.09
	Liaw et al. [23]	3.91	12.10		Cavazza et al. [24]	1.56	3.32
	Saunders et al. [11]	3.59	11.00		Albiol et al. [25]	3.86	24.90
	Chan et al. [22]	3.72	11.50		Proposed Method	1.85	5.73
	Cavazza et al. [24]	3.36	16.42				
	Proposed Method	3.56	11.31				

Table 2 shows the comparison of these baselines and our proposed method. We observe that regression based only on SURF features produce inferior results, whereas regression using region covariance features produce much lower error rates, hence better predictions. We also observe that people counting based solely on detection and tracking yields comparably worse results than covariance-based people counting. In the second part of Table 2, the combination of detection and regression approaches are presented. As it can be seen, the combination of detection with regression yields significant improvement. The best error rates are obtained with our proposed framework which fuses regression and detection together, over joint representations of region covariance and SURF features.

Next, we compare our method with previous studies in the literature on the Mall and Pets 2009 datasets in Table 3. The upper rows of this table include experimental results using the same training/testing split of [21] and the second part of the table include results using the settings of [13]. All these studies use same feature set; size (area and perimeter length), shape (perimeter orientation histogram), edges (edge orientation histogram), keypoints (SURF and FAST keypoints) and textures (contrast, homogeneity, energy, entropy). The studies differ in terms of their regression method; GPR in [22], CA-RR in [13], RFR in [23], RR in [11] and HLR in [24].

Table 3 demonstrates that our proposed method yields comparable results to the existing literature on people counting. As discussed above, existing work require more features and more complex regressors. On the contrary, we have achieved comparable performance by using two features (region covariance and SURF) and standard off-the-shelf SVR regressor. As opposed to pure counting techniques, our method additionally finds the location of people, which is a plus.

4   Conclusion

In this work, we propose a framework that integrates standard regression and detection techniques in a unified framework for people counting. By using region covariance features in the form of Sigma Sets in regression, we observe that significant performance gains are obtainable. Further performance boost is achieved when SURF and region covariance features are used in combination. Our experiments also show that fusing detection and regression produce effective results for person counting. One of the advantages of our approach is to be able to output the location estimates of the people, together with the predicted counts. Future work includes investigation of new representative features and·inclusion of deep learning architectures into our unified framework.

References

1. Loy, C.C., Chen, K., Gong, S., Xiang, T.: Crowd counting and profiling: methodology and evaluation. In: Modeling, Simulation and Visual Analysis of Crowds, pp. 347–382. Springer, New York (2013)
2. Dalal, N., Triggs, B.: Histograms of oriented gradients for human detection. In: IEEE Computer Society Conference on Computer Vision and Pattern Recognition, CVPR 2005 (2005)
3. Leibe, B., Seemann, E., Schiele, B.: Pedestrian detection in crowded scenes. In: IEEE Computer Society Conference on Computer Vision and Pattern Recognition, CVPR 2005 (2005)
4. Dollar, P., Wojek, C., Schiele, B., Perona, P.: Pedestrian detection: an evaluation of the state of the art. IEEE Trans. Pattern Anal. Mach. Intell. **34**(4), 743–761 (2012)
5. Felzenszwalb, P.F., Girshick, R.B., McAllester, D., Ramanan, D.: Object detection with discriminatively trained part-based models. IEEE Trans. Pattern Anal. Mach. Intell. **32**(9), 1627–1645 (2010)
6. Zhao, T., Nevatia, R., Wu, B.: Segmentation and tracking of multiple humans in crowded environments. IEEE Trans. Pattern Anal. Mach. Intell. **30**(7), 1198–1211 (2008)
7. Ge, W., Collins, R.T.: Marked point processes for crowd counting. In: IEEE Computer Society Conference on Computer Vision and Pattern Recognition, CVPR 2009 (2009)

8. Rabaud, V., Belongie, S.: Counting crowded moving objects. In: IEEE Computer Society Conference on Computer Vision and Pattern Recognition, CVPR 2006 (2006)
9. Brostow, G.J., Cipolla, R.: Unsupervised bayesian detection of independent motion in crowds. In: IEEE Computer Society Conference on Computer Vision and Pattern Recognition, CVPR 2006 (2006)
10. Haralick, R.M., Shanmugam, K., Dinstein, I.H.: Textural features for image classification. IEEE Trans. Syst. Man Cybern. $3(6)$, 610–621 (1973)
11. Saunders, C., Gammerman, A., Vovk, V.: Ridge regression learning algorithm in dual variables. In: Proceedings of the 15th International Conference on Machine Learning, ICML 1998 (1998)
12. Chen, K., Loy, C.C., Gong, S., Xiang, T.: Feature mining for localised crowd counting. In: BMVC 2012 (2012)
13. Chen, K., Gong, S., Xiang, T., Loy, C.: Cumulative attribute space for age and crowd density estimation. In: Proceedings of the IEEE Conference on Computer Vision and Pattern Recognition (2013)
14. Hong, X., Chang, H., Shan, S., Chen, X., Gao, W.: Sigma set: a small second order statistical region descriptor. In: Computer Vision and Pattern Recognition, CVPR 2009 (2009)
15. Eichner, M., Ferrari, V.: Calvin upper-body detector (2012). http://groups.inf.ed.ac.uk/calvin/calvinupperbodydetector/
16. Girshick, R.: Fast r-cnn. In: International Conference on Computer Vision (ICCV) (2015)
17. Comaniciu, D., Ramesh, V., Meer, P.: Kernel-based object tracking. IEEE Trans. Pattern Anal. Mach. Intell. $25(5)$, 564–577 (2003)
18. Tuzel, O., Porikli, F., Meer, P.: Region covariance: a fast descriptor for detection and classification. In: Leonardis, A., Bischof, H., Pinz, A. (eds.) ECCV 2006. LNCS, vol. 3952, pp. 589–600. Springer, Heidelberg (2006)
19. Bay, H., Ess, A., Tuytelaars, T., Van Gool, L.: Speeded-up robust features (surf). Comput. Vis. Image Underst. $110(3)$, 346–359 (2008)
20. Chan, A.B., Morrow, M., Vasconcelos, N.: Analysis of crowded scenes using holistic properties. In: Performance Evaluation of Tracking and Surveillance Workshop at CVPR (2009)
21. Ryan, D., Denman, S., Sridharan, S., Fookes, C.: An evaluation of crowd counting methods, features and regression models. Comput. Vis. Image Underst. 130, 1–17 (2015)
22. Chan, A.B., Liang, Z.-S.J., Vasconcelos, N.: Privacy preserving crowd monitoring: counting people without people models or tracking. In: IEEE Conference on Computer Vision and Pattern Recognition, CVPR 2008 (2008)
23. Criminisi, A., Shotton, J., Konukoglu, E.: Decision forests for classification, regression, density estimation, manifold learning and semi-supervised learning. Microsoft Research, Technical report. MSR-TR-2011-114, October 2011
24. Cavazza, J., Murino, V.: People counting by huber loss regression. In: The IEEE International Conference on Computer Vision (ICCV) Workshops (2015)
25. Albiol, A., Silla, M.J., Albiol, A., Mossi, J.M.: Video analysis using corner motion statistics. In: Proceedings of the IEEE International Workshop on Performance Evaluation of Tracking and Surveillance (2009)

Multi-graph Based Salient Object Detection

Idir Filali[1], Mohand Said Allili[2(✉)], and Nadjia Benblidia[1]

[1] LRDSI Laboratory, University of Blida 1, Blida, Algeria
inf_tyg@yahoo.fr, benblidia@yahoo.com
[2] LARIVIA Laboratory, Universite du Quebec en Outaouis, Gatineau, QC, Canada
mohandsaid.allili@uqo.ca

Abstract. We propose a multi-layer graph based approach for salient object detection in natural images. Starting from a set of multi-scale image decomposition using superpixels, we propose an objective function optimized on a multi-layer graph structure to diffuse saliency from image borders to salient objects. After isolating the object kernel, we enhance the accuracy of our saliency maps through an objectness-like based refinement approach. Beside its simplicity, our algorithm yields very accurate salient objects with clear boundaries. Experiments have shown that our approach outperforms several recent methods dealing with salient object detection.

Keywords: Multi-layer graphs · Multi-scale segmentation · Salient object detection

1 Introduction

Saliency detection aims to localize most informative objects or regions in images. Saliency detection methods rely either on a local or global contrast estimation. Local contrast based methods [9] assume that regions which stand out from their neighborhoods have high saliency values. These methods are more suitable to highlight salient object boundaries instead of the entire objects. Global contrast based methods [1,12] express rarity of regions in terms of global statistics compared to the overall image. They are better at highlighting entire salient regions. However, they are less accurate to detect large-sized objects due to the fact the object statistics dominate the global statistics of the image.

Recently, several methods have proposed to combine local and global contrasts to overcome the aforementioned limitations. Among proposed techniques, graph-based methods have emerged as an excellent tool for salient object detection [8,11]. In addition to the simplicity they provide for combining several image cues, graphs are efficient in encoding spatial priors such as object contiguity and location. For example, [11] propose a graph-based method to detect salient objects far from the image border. In [4,5], random walk models are used to extract salient objects on graphs. However, since the graphs are built of the image lattice, these methods incur a huge computation time. To circumvent this limitation, [11] use superpixels instead of pixels and propose to calculate saliency

© Springer International Publishing Switzerland 2016
A. Campilho and F. Karray (Eds.): ICIAR 2016, LNCS 9730, pp. 318–324, 2016.
DOI: 10.1007/978-3-319-41501-7_36

based on graphs. Furthermore, to make use of multi-resolution image information, [8] use global contrast and spatial contiguity to generate initial saliency maps. Then, a region merging procedure with dynamic scale control is used to generate the so-called *saliency trees*. This method highlights salient object regions with well-defined boundaries. Similarly, [10] propose a hierarchical model to estimate saliency maps at different image resolutions. These maps are then combined using a weighted color distance. This method yields a good saliency maps, but may assign high saliency values to isolated background regions. Note that the majority of graph-based methods use the image borders to extract the background. One major limitation of these methods is that they can not deal efficiently with variable object scale as the graph construction highly depends on the initial (arbitrary) segmentation scale. Some parts of the salient object can then be confounded with the background in case of over/under segmentation. A multi layered graph based method can provide a solution to this problem.

In this paper we propose a multi-layerd graph ranking approach for salient object detection. Starting from a multi-scale image decomposition of the image into superpixels, each layer of the graph will be constructed on superpixels of a given segmentation scale. The image saliency is obtained by optimizing an objective function on the graph, which detects the location of coarse and fine parts of salient objects. We also propose a window based refinement process which narrows the object localization and enhances the overall contrast of the object with the immediate background. Experiments on the standard MSRA 5000 dataset containing complex scenes have demonstrated that our approach outperforms several recent state-of-the art methods.

This paper is organized as follows: Sect. 2 presents our algorithm for multigraph salient object detection. Section 3 presents some experimental results validating our approach. We then end the paper with a conclusion.

2 Graph Ranking for Saliency Detection

Our saliency method is composed of two main phases. In the first phase, we propagate the information of the image border to have an approximate location of the salient object. In the second phase, a refinement process is performed inside a bounding box containing the object to better locate its boundaries. These steps are explained as follows:

2.1 Multi-layer Graph for Saliency Detection

Our method is based on a multi-layered graph structure where each layer contains segmentation of a given scale. The segmentations are obtained using the SLIC algorithm [2]. For L resolutions, we define the following superpixel sets: $\Omega_1, \Omega_2, \ldots, \Omega_L$ where each set $\Omega_\ell, \ell \in \{1, 2, ..., L\}$, contains n_ℓ superpixels which constitute the nodes of the ℓ-th layer of the graph (see Fig. 1).

We choose experimentally three resolutions $L = 3$, with $n_1 = 150$, $n_2 = 500$ and $n_3 = 1000$. Each node represented by one segment is connected to each of his direct neighbors located on the same layer as well as its indirect neighbors on the others layers with which it intersects or shares a boundary. We consider the following minimization to propagate the ranking from each node to the remaining nodes of the image:

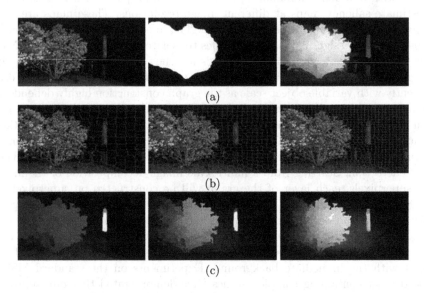

(a)

(b)

(c)

Fig. 1. Comparison between obtained saliency maps using single-layer and multi-layer graphs. (a) represents, from left to right, the original image, the ground truth and the saliency map generated by the multi-layered graph. (b) represents, from left to right, the segmentation of the image into 150, 500 and 1000 superpixels, respectively. (c) represents, from left to right, saliency maps generated by a single-layer graph using each segmentation of the same column in (b).

$$\mathbf{f}^* = \arg\min_{\mathbf{f}} \left[\left(\sum_{\ell=1}^{L} \sum_{i,j=1}^{n_\ell} w_{ij}^{(\ell)} \left(f_i^{(\ell)} / \sqrt{d_i^{(\ell)}} - f_j^{(\ell)} / \sqrt{d_j^{(\ell)}} \right)^2 + \lambda \sum_{i=1}^{n_\ell} (f_i^{(\ell)} - y_i^{(\ell)})^2 \right) \right.$$
$$\left. + \sum_{\ell=1}^{L-1} \sum_{m=\ell+1}^{L} \left(\sum_{i=1}^{n_\ell} \sum_{j=1}^{n_m} w_{ij}^{(\ell,m)} \left(f_i^{(\ell)} / \sqrt{\tilde{d}_i^{(\ell)}} - f_j^{(m)} / \sqrt{\tilde{d}_j^{(m)}} \right)^2 \right) \right], \qquad (1)$$

where $d_i^{(\ell)} = \sum_{k=1}^{n_\ell} w_{ik}^{(\ell)}$, $\tilde{d}_i^{(\ell)} = \sum_{m=1,m\neq\ell}^{L} \sum_{k=1}^{n_m} w_{ik}^{(\ell,m)}$ and $w_{ik}^{(\ell,m)} = e^{-\alpha.\|c_{\ell i} - c_{mk}\|}$ is the weight between superpixels $r_i^{(\ell)}$ and $r_i^{(m)}$ situated in the levels Ω_ℓ and Ω_m, respectively, with α a constant that controls the sensitivity of the weight set experimentally to 10 and $c_{\ell i}$ represents the mean color vector of $r_i^{(\ell)}$.

We note that $y^{(\ell)} = [y_1^{(\ell)}, y_2^{(\ell)}, \ldots, y_n^{(\ell)}]$ is the indicator vector in which $y_i^{(\ell)} = 1$ if a region $r_i^{(\ell)}$ in the layer ℓ is a query and $y_i^{(\ell)} = 0$, otherwise. Following the work [15], the queries are made of the superpixels of the four borders in each layer. Note also that $f = \bigcup_{\ell=1}^{L} f^{(\ell)}$ where $f^{(\ell)} = \{f_1^{(\ell)}, f_2^{(\ell)}, \ldots, f_{n_\ell}^{(\ell)}\}$ represent the ranking of regions at the ℓ-th level and λ is a regularization constant set experimentally to 0.99. Let $D_i^{(\ell)} = \tilde{d}_i^{(\ell)} + d_i^{(\ell)}$, $W = [W^{\ell,m}]$, with ℓ and m, $(\ell, m) \in (\{1, 2, \ldots, L\})^2$ are the line and column numbers respectively and $W^{\ell,m} = [W_{ij}^{\ell,m}]$, $i \in \{1, 2, \ldots, n_\ell\}$ and $j \in \{1, 2, \ldots, n_m\}$. The minimization of the equation Eq. (1) is done as follows: $\mathbf{f}^* = (\mathbf{I} - \gamma \mathbf{L})^{-1}\mathbf{y}$, where $\gamma = 1/(1+\lambda)$ and $\mathbf{L}$ is the Laplacian matrix given by: $\mathbf{L} = \mathbf{D}^{-1/2}\mathbf{W}\mathbf{D}^{1/2}$, where D is a diagonal matrix $\mathbf{D} = \mathrm{diag}[D_1^{(1)}, \ldots, D_{n_1}^{(1)}, \ldots, \ldots, D_1^{(L)}, \ldots, D_{n_L}^{(L)}]$.

We perform a propagation process from each of the four borders of the image (top, down, left and right) by considering the regions located on them are queries. We then obtain four saliency maps (S_T, S_D, S_L, S_R) that are combined as follows: $\mathbf{S} = \mathbf{S}_T \circ \mathbf{S}_D \circ \mathbf{S}_R \circ \mathbf{S}_L$, where $\circ$ designates the Hadamard product between matrices. We then perform a second propagation process from the most salient elements extracted from $\mathbf{S}$ (the kernel of the object) to the rest of the image. This is achieved by a proper initialization of Eq. (1), then the saliency value at the superpixel $r_i^{(\ell)}$ is computed as follows: $s_i^{(\ell)} = 1 - f_i^{(\ell)}$. We then obtain a second saliency map S_2.

2.2 Window Based Saliency Refinement

For more accurate saliency estimation, we narrow the saliency area to a restricted space that is more likely to contain the salient object (i.e., objectness-like measure [3]). For this purpose, we define a window initialized to the borders of the image and progressively reduced to fit tightly to the area containing the salient object with high plausibility. The optimal adjustment os the window is entirely guided by S_2 as it is shown in Eq. (2). Let x_0 and y_0 be the height and the width of the image. The window extent is defined as $\mathcal{X} = [\delta_1, x_0 - \delta_2]$ for the abscissas axis and $\mathcal{Y} = [\delta_3, y_0 - \delta_4]$ for the ordinates axis, with δ_1, δ_2, δ_3 and δ_4:

$$(\delta_1, \delta_2, \delta_3, \delta_4) = \arg \max_{\delta_1, \delta_2, \delta_3, \delta_4} \left\{ \sum_{x \notin \mathcal{X}} \sum_{y \notin \mathcal{Y}} S(x, y) \right\} \leq \eta * \sum_{x=1}^{x_0} \sum_{y=1}^{y_0} S(x, y). \quad (2)$$

where η is a threshold set experimentally (usually $\eta = 0.99$). Equation (2) aims to define a window that contains most salient parts of the image and discard the background with weak saliency percentage compared to the over all image. We perform a second multi-layer graph based saliency detection process in the inner part of the window by minimizing Eq. (1) (see Fig. 2 for illustration).

3 Experimental Results

The performance of the proposed model is evaluated quantitatively on a widely used MSRA dataset [7] which contains 5,000 images with their ground truth.

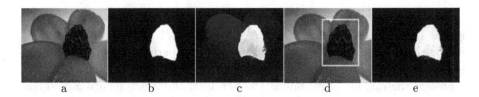

Fig. 2. Examples of window-based refinement: (a) The input image, (b) the ground truth, (c) saliency map obtained using Eq. (1), (d) Window position Eq. (2), (e) saliency map obtained using window refinement process.

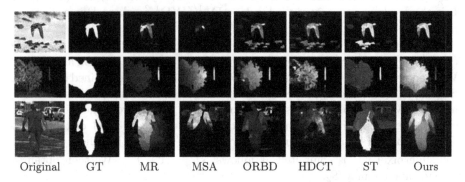

Original   GT   MR   MSA   ORBD   HDCT   ST   Ours

Fig. 3. Visual comparison between our method and five state of the arts approaches.

We compare our multi graph based manifold ranking (MMR) and our window based refinement (WMMR) with five state of the art saliency detection methods: ST [8], MSA [13], ORBD [14], HDCT [6] and MR [11]. Figure 3 shows some examples that compare our method to those of the state of the art. We evaluate the performance of our method using the PR (precision-recall) curve, the ROC (receiver operating characteristic) curve, the AUC (Area Under ROC Curve) and MAE (Mean absolute error) scores. The *F-Measure* is the weighted harmonic sum of the *precision* and *recall* computed as follows:

$$F_\nu = \frac{(1+\nu) \times precision \times recall}{\nu \times precision + recall},$$ (3)

where we set $\nu = 0.3$ for all the compared methods. The curves are obtained by binarizing the saliency map using thresholds in the range from 1 and 254. Figure 4a shows the *precision/recall* comparison of our method with five state of the art methods. Figure 4b shows the *true positive/false positive* comparison one and Table 1 shows a quantitative comparison of the best average *F-measure* with its corresponding *precision* and *recall* values, AUC and MAE measures obtained on all saliency maps generated on the MSRA dataset by each compared method. The best values is returned by our WMMR method in all measures. The results demonstrate clearly the performance of our method with regard to the compared ones. We can note also that our method has obtained a better quality for saliency maps where objects are more contrasted with the background and have clearer boundaries.

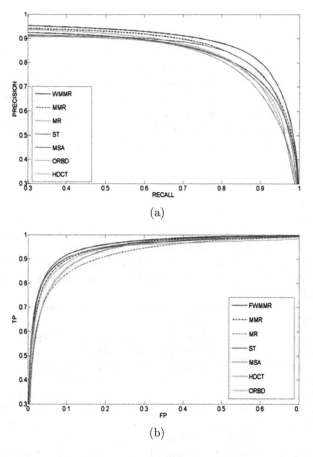

(a)

(b)

Fig. 4. Comparative results between our method and five state-of-the-art saliency detection methods on the MSRA dataset. (Color figure online)

Table 1. Quantitative comparison between our approach and five state of the art saliency detection methods

	WMMR	MMR	MR	ST	MSA	ORBD	HDCT
Precision (%)	**88.85**	87.82	86.10	86.90	85.75	85.48	86.61
Recall (%)	**76.70**	75.94	71.11	76.52	73.65	73.48	73.12
F-Measure (%)	**85.71**	84.76	82.11	84.26	82.62	82.37	83.08
AUC (%)	**85.66**	85.44	82.80	85.35	80.75	83.57	85.55
MAE (%)	**11.01**	13.28	12.86	12.88	14.61	11.04	14.22

4 Conclusion

We have presented a multi-layer graph based algorithm for salient object detection. Our method is able to accurately localize fine and coarse parts of salient objects. It also uses a refinement process using an objectness-like measure narrowing the salient object search. Experimental results have demonstrated that our method outperforms recent sate-of-the-art methods. Our salient objects are generally more emphasized and the backgrounds are more efficiently discarded, which make our results more suitable to applications such as object segmentation and selective object recognition.

References

1. Achanta, R., Hemami, S., Estrada, F., Susstrunk, S.: Frequency-tuned salient region detection. In: IEEE CVPR, pp. 1597–1604 (2009)
2. Achanta, R., Shaji, A., Smith, K., Lucchi, A., Fua, P., Sösstrunk, S.: SLIC superpixels compared to state-of-the-art superpixel methods. IEEE TPAMI 34(11), 2274–2282 (2012)
3. Alexe, B., Deselaers, T., Ferrari, V.: Measuring the objectness of image windows. IEEE TPAMI 34(11), 2189–2202 (2012)
4. Gopalakrishnan, V., Hu, Y., Rajan, D.: Random walks on graphs for salient object detection in images. IEEE TIP 19(12), 3232–3242 (2010)
5. Jiang, B., Zhang, L., Lu, H., Yang, C., Yang, M.-H.: Saliency detection via absorbing Markov chain. In: IEEE ICCV, pp. 1665–1672 (2013)
6. Kim, J., Han, D., Tai, Y.W., Kim, J.: Salient region detection via high-dimensional color transform and local spatial support. IEEE TIP 25(1), 9–23 (2016)
7. Liu, T., Yuan, Z., Sun, J., Wang, J., Zheng, N., Tang, X., Shum, H.: Learning to detect a salient object. IEEE TPAMI 33(2), 353–367 (2011)
8. Liu, Z., Zou, W., Le Meur, O.: Saliency tree: a novel saliency detection framework. IEEE TIP 23(5), 1937–1952 (2014)
9. Seo, H.J., Milanfar, P.: Static and space-time visual saliency detection by self-resemblance. In: IEEE CVPR Workshops, vol. 9(12), pp. 45–52 (2009)
10. Yan, Q., Xu, L., Shi, J., Jia, J.: Hierarchical saliency detection. In: IEEE CVPR, pp. 1155–1162 (2013)
11. Yang, C., Zhang, L., Lu, H., Ruan, X.: Saliency detection via graph-based manifold ranking. In: IEEE CVPR, pp. 3166–3173 (2013)
12. Zhang, L., Gu, Z., Li, H.: SDSP: a novel saliency detection method by combining simple priors. In: IEEE ICIP, pp. 171–175 (2013)
13. Zhu, L., Klein, D.A., Frintrop, S., Cao, Z., Cremers, A.B.: A multi-size superpixel approach for salient object detection based on multivariate normal distribution estimation. IEEE TIP 23(12), 5094–5107 (2014)
14. Zhu, W., Liang, S., Wei, Y., Sun, J.: Saliency optimization from robust background detection. In: IEEE CVPR, pp. 2814–2821 (2014)
15. Zhou, D., Bousquet, O., Lal, T., Weston, J., Scholkopf, B.: Learning with local and global consistency. NIPS (2003)

Analysis of Temporal Coherence in Videos for Action Recognition

Adel Saleh[1(✉)], Mohamed Abdel-Nasser[1], Farhan Akram[1],
Miguel Angel Garcia[2], and Domenec Puig[1]

[1] Department of Computer Engineering and Mathematics,
Rovira i Virgili University, Tarragona, Spain
{adelsalehali.alraimi,domenec.puig}@urv.cat
[2] Department of Electronic and Communications Technology,
Autonomous University of Madrid, Madrid, Spain
miguelangel.garcia@uam.es

Abstract. This paper proposes an approach to improve the performance of activity recognition methods by analyzing the coherence of the frames in the input videos and then modeling the evolution of the coherent frames, which constitute a sub-sequence, to learn a representation for the videos. The proposed method consist of three steps: coherence analysis, representation leaning and classification. Using two state-of-the-art datasets (Hollywood2 and HMDB51), we demonstrate that learning the evolution of subsequences in lieu of frames, improves the recognition results and makes actions classification faster.

1   Introduction

Recognizing human activity is a core operation of several applications, such as surveillance systems and human-computer interaction. Thus, the performance of these applications mainly depends on the accuracy of human activity recognition systems. Recently, several approaches have been proposed to improve the performance of human action recognition in videos. These approaches can be categorized in three main trends [21]. The first trend includes the use of hand-crafted descriptors, such as local spatio-temporal descriptors [4,6,7]. The second trend includes the use of convolutional neural networks (CNNs) where they learn image representations instead of extracting hand-crafted descriptors. CNNs were proposed as a tool for action recognition in [3]. A motion capturing method that uses a two-stream CNN was proposed in [12]. Tran et al. [16] proposed effective and compact features using 3D CNN model. The third trend utilizes the temporal structure of videos. Recently, recurrent neural networks have been used to learn action representation. Yue-Hei Ng et al. [22] explored several convolutional temporal feature pooling architectures. In addition, they proposed a method to model the videos as an ordered sequence of frames using a recurrent neural network. They use long short-term memory (LSTM) cells that are connected to the output of the underlying CNN. Moreover, Srivastava et al. [14] used multilayer LSTM networks to learn representations of video sequences. This method was

© Springer International Publishing Switzerland 2016
A. Campilho and F. Karray (Eds.): ICIAR 2016, LNCS 9730, pp. 325–332, 2016.
DOI: 10.1007/978-3-319-41501-7_37

tested using two type of input sequences: patches of image pixels and high-level representations of video frames extracted using a pre-trained convolutional net.

Although, several approaches have been proposed to improve the performance of activity recognition, they did not achieve good accuracy. To improve the performance of activity recognition methods, in this paper we analyse the coherence of the frames in each input video and then model the evolution of the coherent frames to learn a representation of the whole video. We exploit the fact that high-level visual signals change slowly over time. The coherence analysis divides each video into a series of coherent subsequences. Our work is similar to [2], however our novelty is that we model the evolution of the coherent frames in each video. We show that learning the evolution of sub-sequences instead of frames, improves the recognition results and makes actions classification faster.

The rest of the paper is organized as follows. In Sect. 2 we explain the steps of the proposed method. Section 3 includes the experimental results and discussion. Finally, the conclusion and some lines of future work are given in Sect. 4.

2   Proposed Method

Figure 1 shows steps of the proposed method. In the first step, we extract descriptors from each frame and then analyze the coherence of frames of the input video. This step divides each video into subsequences. Then, each subsequence is encoded using one Fisher vector. In the second step, we input the Fisher vectors [9] to the ranking machine used in [2] to get a representation of the input video. We used the learned representation to discriminate between actions in the third step of the proposed method.

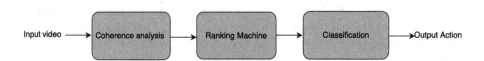

Fig. 1. Proposed method.

2.1   Coherence Analysis

To find the coherent frames, we compute dense HOG descriptors for each frame in the input video $H = [h_1, h_2, ..., h_n]$ where n indicates the number of frames of the input video. Assume that h_t and h_{t+1} are HOG descriptors of each pair of consecutive frames, we calculate the correlation between them. Thus, we compute a correlation vector for each video, $C = [c_1, c_2, ..., c_{n-1}]$. To examine the coherence of two consecutive frames, we apply the following hard threshold:

$$C'(t) = \begin{cases} 1 & C(t) \geq c_{th} \\ 0 & C(t) < c_{th} \end{cases} \qquad (1)$$

In this equation, c_{th} is the mean of the correlation vector C, '1' indicates that the two frames are coherent and they belong to the same subsequence (see Fig. 2). In turn, '0' indicates that the two frames do not belong to the same subsequence. We compute one Fisher vector for each subsequence instead of computing one Fisher vector for each frame, thus reducing the complexity of the problem because it reduces the number of samples that we input to the ranking machine.

In this paper, we used the HOG descriptor and the correlation metric for coherence analysis, however any other descriptor and similarity metric can be employed to perform that task.

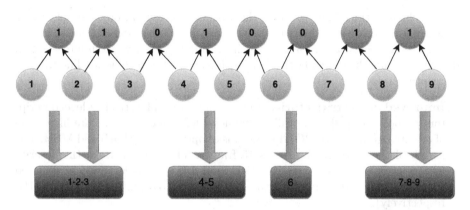

Fig. 2. Illustration of the coherence Analysis. Yellow circles include the frame number, green circles show the similarity indicator, and each red rectangle represents one subsequence (coherent frames). (color figure online)

2.2   Temporal Representation Using a Ranking Machine

To learn a temporal representation of the subsequences we use the ranking machine proposed in [2]. In this method, each frame in the input video is represented by a vector x, which includes local descriptors. If the input video consists of n frames, we can then consider the video as a sequence of n vectors (X). This sequence is then smoothed using a *time varying mean* method to suppress abrupt action changes in videos. The time varying mean method works as follows: $m_t = \frac{1}{t} \sum_{i=1}^{t} x_i$. The unit vector of m_t can be computed as follows: $v_t = \frac{m_t}{\|m_t\|}$. Note that v_t only contains information about the direction; therefore, this approach guaranties a smooth output. The smoothed vectors are then sent to the ranking machine to compute the final representation of the input video.

The ranking machine is an optimization problem in which we find a value of parameter u such that: $\forall i, j, i \succ j \iff t_i \succ t_j \iff v_i \succ v_j \iff u^T v_i \succ u^T v_j$. It optimizes the following objective [2]:

$$\underset{u}{\arg\min} \quad \frac{1}{2}\|u\|^2 + C \sum_{\forall i,j,v_i \succ v_j} \epsilon_{ij}$$

$$s.t. \quad u^T(v_{t_i} - v_{t_j}) \geq 1 - \epsilon_{ij}$$

$$\epsilon_{ij} \geq 0 \tag{2}$$

If ψ learns the order of vectors v_t then the score of v_{t+1} is greater than the score of v_t, where the score of v_t is defined as $\psi(v_t, u) = u^T v_t$.

2.3 Classification Step and the Utilized Descriptors

In the classification step, we send the learned representation of input videos to a support vector machine with one-against-all strategy to classify them. To calculate the vector x for each frame in an input video, we compute a set of descriptors and then encode them using Fisher vector technique. The utilized descriptors are:

- **Improved dense trajectories.** In this paper we exploit the low-level descriptors proposed in [18]. The utilized low-level feature descriptors are histogram of oriented gradients (HOG), histograms of optical flow (HOF) and MBH. The length of the used trajectories is 15 frames. The dimensions of the descriptors were 96 for HOG, 108 for HOF, and 192 for MBH (we concatenated the horizontal and vertical motion boundary histogram, MBHx and MBHy, respectively).
- **Gradient and optical flow histograms.** According to [19], HOG and HOF descriptors show good performance on a challenging datasets compared to the classical descriptors of activity recognition. Unlike HOG descriptor that captures information about the appearance, HOF captures the local motion information. The proposed method computed the HOG and HOF descriptors using the settings of [18]. To calculate HOG, the proposed method computed gradient magnitude responses in the horizontal and vertical directions. To calculate HOF, optical flow displacement vectors in horizontal and vertical directions were determined. Then, for each response the magnitude is quantized in a number of orientations. For HOG descriptor, orientations were quantized into 8 bins, whilst they were quantized into 9 bins for HOF [7]. We used the L2-norm to normalize the descriptors. The dimensions of HOG and HOF were 96 ($2 \times 2 \times 3 \times 8$) and 108 ($2 \times 2 \times 3 \times 9$), respectively.
- **Motion boundary histograms (MBH) descriptor [1].** Wang et al. [17] showed the robustness of MBH against camera and background motion. The intuition behind MBH is computing oriented gradients over the vertical and the horizontal optical flow displacements. Indeed, information related to motion changes in the boundaries is attained using the flow difference, while information with constant scene from the camera is discarded.

3   Experimental Results and Discussion

3.1   Datasets

We used two state-of-the-art datasets to evaluate the proposed method: HMDB51 and Hollywood2.

HMDB51 is a generic action classification dataset [5]. The videos of this dataset were collected from YouTube and some movies. It contains around 6670 videos, which were further grouped into 51 action classes in which each class contains around 100 videos. To measure the performance of the proposed method, we used three training and testing splits and then the average accuracy over them was computed.

Hollywood2 dataset was collected from 69 Hollywood movies [8]. It contains 1,707 videos, which were grouped into 12 action classes. The training set contains 823 videos whilst the testing one contains 884 videos.

3.2   Results

Table 1 shows the performance of the proposed method with the two state-of-the-art datasets. It achieves a recognition rate of 70.2 with Hollywood2 dataset, beating the state-of-art methods. It also outperforms fresh deep learning approaches, such as [11,15]. The reason of these results is the suppression of the redundant information which is achieved with the coherence analysis. In other words, we suppress unnecessary information via computing one Fisher vector for each subsequence. The proposed method works better than the baseline of [2] (see Table 2) in the case of slow actions, since it makes the input sequences more generalized and lightens the unnecessary details. Our method outperforms the baseline of [2] in the case of slow actions with less dramatic changes as in the following cases: AnswerPhone, SitDown and SitUp.

In the case of HMDB51 dataset, we achieve a recognition rate of 55.33 whilst the baseline of [2] achieves a rate of 55.54. The main reason of these results is the difficulty of the recognition of some videos and the high variation within several classes. Table 3 shows the performance of the proposed method with 12 randomly

Table 1. Comparison of the performance of the proposed method with the related works using HMDB51 and Hollywood2. We show the mAP rate for Hollywood2 and HMDB51 datasets.

Method	HMB51	Hollywood2
Two-stream ConvNe [13]	**59.40**	-
VideoDarwin [2] (with out data augmentation)	55.54	69.71
Composite LSTM Mode [14]	44.00	-
Kinematic of the Trajectories [10]	58.20	-
Coherence Analysis	40.55	65.00
Coherence Analysis+ VideoDarwin (with out data augmentation)	55.3	**70.20**

Table 2. Analysis of the performance of the proposed method with the baseline of [2] with Hollywood2 dataset (each entity shows one-against-all accuracy).

Action	Baseline of[2]	Proposed
AnswerPhone	0.39	**0.41**
DriveCar	0.96	0.96
Eat	0.74	0.73
FightPerson	0.84	0.86
GetOutCar	0.74	0.72
HandShake	0.55	0.52
HugPerson	0.53	0.53
Kiss	0.63	0.63
Run	0.89	0.89
SitDown	0.80	**0.82**
SitUp	0.45	**0.50**
StandUp	0.83	**0.85**

Table 3. Analysis of the performance the proposed method with the baseline of [2] with HMDB51 dataset (each entity shows one-against-all accuracy).

Action	Baseline of [2]	Proposed
Brush hair	0.89	**0.91**
Cartwheel	0.52	0.52
Chew	0.39	**0.47**
Clap	0.84	**0.86**
Climb	0.52	0.52
Climbs tairs	0.62	**0.67**
Dive	0.53	0.50
Dribble	0.56	**0.57**
Drink	0.42	**0.44**
Eat	0.37	0.33
Fall floor	0.32	0.29
Kick	0.23	0.21

selected actions from 51 classes. We achieve better recognition with 'brush hair', 'clap', 'climbs tair', 'dribble' and 'drink'. All these actions are also slow. We notice that the available datasets lack of diversity. Consequently, the trained models are suffering from overfitting, thus training datasets should be collected in the cross category style mentioned in [20] to generalize actions and avoid over-fitting. In fact, the results of [13] are better than the ones of the proposed method because we do not use data augmentation, in order to demonstrate the effectiveness of the proposed method. Indeed, the CNN model proposed in [13] has a good performance because it represents a higher level semantic concept, but it has a high time complexity and requires complicated training passes. In turn, the proposed method is faster. The model of [13] took approximately one day for one temporal CNN on a system consisting of four *NVIDIA Titan cards* (it took 3.1 times the aforementioned training time on a single GPU). In the contrary, our approach took approximately 14 h on Core i7 2.5 GHz CPU with 16 GB RAM. This indicates that the proposed method obtains comparable results with a small training time.

4   Conclusion and Future Work

In this paper we analyzed the coherence of the frames in each video and then modeled the evolution of the coherent frames to learn a representation for the video. The learned representation improved the description of the videos, yielding good recognition rates. The future work will focus on the use of CNN features with the proposed method to further improve the recognition rate.

Acknowledgment. This work was partly supported by Universitat Rovira i Virgili, Spain, and Hodeidah University, Yemen.

References

1. Dalal, N., Triggs, B., Schmid, C.: Human detection using oriented histograms of flow and appearance. In: Leonardis, A., Bischof, H., Pinz, A. (eds.) ECCV 2006. LNCS, vol. 3952, pp. 428–441. Springer, Heidelberg (2006)
2. Fernando, B., Gavves, E., Oramas, J., Ghodrati, A., Tuytelaars, T.: Modeling video evolution for action recognition. In: IEEE Conference on Computer Vision and Pattern Recognition (2015)
3. Karpathy, A., Toderici, G., Shetty, S., Leung, T., Sukthankar, R., Fei-Fei, L.: Large-scale video classification with convolutional neural networks. In: Proceedings of the IEEE conference on Computer Vision and Pattern Recognition, pp. 1725–1732 (2014)
4. Klaser, A., Marszałek, M., Schmid, C.: A spatio-temporal descriptor based on 3D-gradients. In: BMVC 2008–19th British Machine Vision Conference, pp. 275:1–275:10. British Machine Vision Association (2008)
5. Kuehne, H., Jhuang, H., Garrote, E., Poggio, T., Serre, T.: HMDB: a large video database for human motion recognition. In: Proceedings of the International Conference on Computer Vision (ICCV) (2011)
6. Laptev, I.: On space-time interest points. Int. J. Comput. Vis. **64**(2–3), 107–123 (2005)
7. Laptev, I., Marszałek, M., Schmid, C., Rozenfeld, B.: Learning realistic human actions from movies. In: IEEE Conference on Computer Vision and Pattern Recognition, pp. 1–8. IEEE (2008)

8. Laptev, I., Marszałek, M., Schmid, C., Rozenfeld, B.: Learning realistic human actions from movies. In: Conference on Computer Vision & Pattern Recognition. http://lear.inrialpes.fr/pubs/2008/LMSR08

9. Oneata, D., Verbeek, J., Schmid, C.: Action and event recognition with fisher vectors on a compact feature set. In: Proceedings of the IEEE International Conference on Computer Vision, pp. 1817–1824 (2013)

10. Saleh, A., Garcia, M.A., Akram, F., Abdel-Nasser, M., Puig, D.: Exploiting the kinematic of the trajectories of the local descriptors to improve human action recognition (2016)

11. Sharma, S., Kiros, R., Salakhutdinov, R.: Action recognition using visual attention. CoRR abs/1511.04119 (2015). http://arxiv.org/abs/1511.04119

12. Simonyan, K., Zisserman, A.: Two-stream convolutional networks for action recognition in videos. In: Advances in Neural Information Processing Systems, pp. 568–576 (2014)

13. Simonyan, K., Zisserman, A.: Two-stream convolutional networks for action recognition in videos. CoRR abs/1406.2199 (2014). http://arxiv.org/abs/1406.2199

14. Srivastava, N., Mansimov, E., Salakhutdinov, R.: Unsupervised learning of video representations using lstms. arXiv preprint arXiv:1502.04681 (2015)

15. Srivastava, N., Mansimov, E., Salakhutdinov, R.: Unsupervised learning of video representations using lstms. CoRR abs/1502.04681 (2015). http://arxiv.org/abs/1502.04681

16. Tran, D., Bourdev, L.D., Fergus, R., Torresani, L., Paluri, M.: C3D: generic features for video analysis. CoRR abs/1412.0767 (2014). http://arxiv.org/abs/1412.0767

17. Wang, H., Kläser, A., Schmid, C., Liu, C.L.: Action recognition by dense trajectories. In: IEEE Conference on Computer Vision and Pattern Recognition (CVPR), pp. 3169–3176. IEEE (2011)

18. Wang, H., Schmid, C.: Action recognition with improved trajectories. In: IEEE International Conference on Computer Vision (ICCV), pp. 3551–3558. IEEE (2013)

19. Wang, H., Ullah, M.M., Klaser, A., Laptev, I., Schmid, C.: Evaluation of local spatio-temporal features for action recognition. In: BMVC 2009-British Machine Vision Conference, pp. 124.1–124.11. BMVA Press (2009)

20. Wang, X., Farhadi, A., Gupta, A.: Actions ~ transformations. CoRRabs/1512.00795 (2015). http://arxiv.org/abs/1512.00795

21. Wang, X., Farhadi, A., Gupta, A.: Actions ~ transformations (2015)

22. Ng, J.Y.-H., Hausknecht, M., Vijayanarasimhan, S., Vinyals, O., Monga, R., Toderici, G.: Beyond short snippets: Deep networks for video classification. In: Proceedings of the IEEE Conference on Computer Vision and Pattern Recognition, pp. 4694–4702 (2015)

Effectiveness of Camouflage Make-Up Patterns Against Face Detection Algorithms

Vojtěch Frič[✉]

Department of Computer Science and Engineering, Faculty of Applied Sciences,
University of West Bohemia, Plzeň, Czech Republic
fricv@kiv.zcu.cz

Abstract. The goal of this research was to evaluate which make-up patterns are effective in disrupting face detection algorithms. Three free or open source implementations of various face detection algorithms were selected. These were at first tested on an unaltered dataset. The dataset was then augmented with different make-up patterns. The patterns were chosen arbitrarily with the goal to disrupt the detection algorithms. The results show that the selected patterns decrease the accuracy of the face detection algorithms by about 10 %.

Keywords: Face detection · Make-up camouflage · Object detection · Computer vision

1 Introduction

In 2010 Adam Harvey released the project [1] focused on personal privacy. The goal of his project was to develop make-up patterns and fashion designs that would help to disrupt the performance of face detection algorithms. In context of this article, the face detection is a process of locating a face or multiple faces in an image. The face recognition is understood as a process of assigning a label from a known set to a face. The detection task can be seen as the first step in the recognition process because the face has to be located before it is labelled.

As it would be infeasible to create an original dataset containing enough data, I have decided to generate the make-up dataset using an already available dataset. This approach enables to gather significant amount of data already prepared for testing. The downside of this approach is that it can not substitute the real data recorded with a digital camera. The presented augmentation algorithm does not model any artefacts that would otherwise form during digital photography.

2 Libraries and Algorithms Tested

The following list itemizes the libraries used during the testing of the effectiveness of the make-up against the face detection.

© Springer International Publishing Switzerland 2016
A. Campilho and F. Karray (Eds.): ICIAR 2016, LNCS 9730, pp. 333–340, 2016.
DOI: 10.1007/978-3-319-41501-7_38

2.1 CCV

The CCV (v0.7) library implements the SURF-Cascade Detection (SCD) algorithm based on [2]. The algorithm is derived from the Viola-Jones face detector [3] but it uses SURF features instead of Haar features. The classification step is also different. SCD employs linear regression instead of decision trees and different convergence criterion during the training phase. The provided detector was trained on the AFLW dataset [4].

2.2 OpenCV

The OpenCV (v3.0.0) library uses a Haar Feature-based cascade classifier. The implemented object detector has been initially proposed by Paul Viola [3] and improved by Rainer Lienhart [5]. In my tests, I have used the tree-based 20×20 gentle adaboost frontal face detector created by Rainer Lienhart[1] provided together with the library source code.

2.3 dlib

The dlib (v18.17) library implements the algorithm from [6]. The provided detector was trained on Labeled Faces in the Wild dataset [7]. In contrast to other tested algorithms, the dlib's detector was trained on frontal upright, frontal rotated and side looking faces. This fact preclude the direct comparison of particular results of each library, as the default detector in dlib is trained on a broader spectrum of face positions.

3 Face Masking Algorithm

3.1 Prerequisites

The masking algorithm requires three source images and the target image. First, it requires an image of a face with neutral facial expression which is then used to extract the necessary landmarks for further processing. This image is then used as a universal canvas for each pattern. Second, a grayscale alpha mask is used to remove unwanted areas from the source template in the final composition. The alpha mask follows for a common approach where the black colour represents total transparency, white colour represents total opaqueness, and intermediate shades of gray represent partial transparency. The third image is the pattern to superimpose onto the face.

The canvas image is required to contain only a single upright face. No restrictions are placed on the number of faces in the target image. The algorithm does not perform any colour corrections between the source image and the target image. This was intentionally left out because the motivation for this algorithm was to superimpose uniform colour patterns on the faces. The colour correction process can be easily added as it is the last step when superimposing the source onto the target face.

---

[1] File haarcascade_frontalface_alt2.xml.

3.2   Approximate Alignment

The first step is to detect facial landmarks in the canvas image. The face detector uses the Histogram of Oriented Gradients (HOG) features combined with a linear classifier, an image pyramid, and sliding window detection scheme. The pose estimator was created using implementation from the paper [8] available in *dlib* library. The pose estimator returns 68 landmarks, such as the corners of the mouth, the eyebrows, the eyes, and so forth (see Fig. 1a).

Next step is the alignment of the detected target face. The alignment is performed by finding an affine transform from detected landmarks to reference landmarks on the canvas face. During the alignment phase, the target image is also scaled and cropped in order to extract a rectangular image containing only the face. The affine transform is then applied to the detected target landmarks thus providing aligned landmarks without the need to run the landmark detection on the aligned target image. Those steps are performed for each face detected in the target image. The result of this step is a set of rectangular images containing aligned upright faces.

The algorithm gives more accurate results if the canvas face has similar orientation to the target face. This is because the landmark detection algorithm always returns an outline of the whole head rather than the facial area only. If the head of the subject in the target image is tilted or turned to the side, the source template with similar attitude provides better results with fewer artefacts. In the experiments, faces with different yaw rotations were used. The appropriate source face is selected by measuring the absolute distance between the corresponding aligned landmarks. The source face with the lowest score is then used in the next step. The score is calculated as a Euclidean distance of the corresponding landmarks:

$$score = \sum_{i=1}^{68} \left(\mathbf{X}_i - \mathbf{Y}_i \right)^2 . \tag{1}$$

The target face can be rotated arbitrarily (as long as it is detected by the HOG detector). When the face is partially turned to the side, the perspective projection also affects the landmarks. To better align the source image, the projection transform between the canvas image and the target image is estimated. This transform is then used to transform the aligned source image and the aligned source landmarks in a way similar to the alignment step. This helps to adjust the source image before the final composition. Although the morphing step can morph arbitrary images if the amount of movement is minimized, the morphing provides results with fewer geometric artefacts.

The transformed source face could be used in the final composition after these steps were performed. However, the resulting image would look very unnatural due to the different shape of the facial features in the source and target image. This discrepancy can lead to obscuring parts of the target face. To reduce the effect of different shapes of facial features, the last step taken is to morph the source face to the target face.

The Beier-Neely morphing algorithm [9] was used to morph the faces. This algorithm works by transforming key lines from one image to another. Each line then affects pixels in its vicinity. The effect of the line on the pixels is controlled by a set of parameters. This morphing algorithm has one major limitation. The source and target image need to be of the same size. The presented algorithm solves this problem by extracting aligned face images of a uniform size. The control lines are defined using the detected landmarks. The performance of the morphing algorithm is affected by the number of pixels in the morphed image and the number of the control lines. Thus, to improve the performance of the algorithm, a reduced number of control lines was used (see Fig. 1b). During the experiments, it was found that upsampled images provide better-looking results. This is due to the morphed image is downsampled during composing of the final image, an appropriate interpolation can reduce the aliasing artifacts produced by morphing.

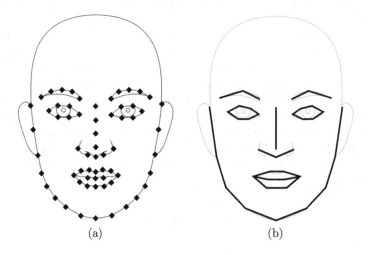

(a)   (b)

Fig. 1. Face with detected landmarks and control lines displayed

4   Experiments and Results

I have written a simple program for each of the selected libraries. My test programs were based on the provided demo source code by the authors of the libraries. For OpenCV, the image was converted to grayscale and its histogram was equalized. No preprocessing was done for other libraries.

All algorithms were first tested on the unaltered FDDB dataset [10]. The dataset contains annotations for 5171 faces in a set of 2845 images selected from the Faces in the Wild data set [11]. Each of the augmented datasets was tested again, with the same program.

4.1   Tested Patterns

5 patterns were tested in total. The patterns were in black and white colour in order to disrupt the detectors more. Black and white are not usual colours on human face. Also, the black and white colours are not affected by converting the image to grayscale. This means that the test score should not be affected by colour manipulation in the preprocessing steps.

Asymmetry. This pattern (Fig. 2a) is a triangular shape on the left cheek of the subject. The goal of this pattern is to disrupt the symmetry of the face. The effect of this pattern is diminished if the subject is looking to the left and shows more of the right side of his or her head.

Block Patterns. Two similar block patterns were tested (Fig. 2b and c). The first consists of roughly rectangular regions under the eyes, the other adds another two blocks above the eyes. The idea behind this pattern is that it creates a pattern which is not present in a human face. However, as this pattern is symmetrical it might be less of a challenge for the detection algorithms looking for symmetry in a human face.

Nose Pattern. This pattern (Fig. 2d) is roughly triangular shape starting on the forehead and continuing down to the tip of the nose. This pattern covers the bridge of the nose. It should be most effective against Viola-Jones face detectors [3] such as the one implemented in OpenCV framework.

Inverted Triangles. This pattern (Fig. 2e) consists of two triangles on the cheeks. Each triangle is filled with solid colour and the bottom side border has a thick line with colour opposite to the inside colour. This pattern was taken from the CVDazzle webpage [1].

4.2   Detection Evaluation

Two types of scores are presented in the FDDB dataset — discrete and continuous. The discrete one assigns the score of 1 if the ratio of the intersection of a detected region to an annotated face region is greater than 0.5, and 0 otherwise. The continuous type uses the overlap ratio itself as the score. The annotations are provided as a list of ellipses where every face region is represented as a 6-tuple:

$$(r_a, r_b, \Theta, c_x, c_y, s),$$

where r_a and r_b refer to the half-length of the major and minor axes; Θ is the angle between the major axis and the horizontal axis; and c_x and c_y are the x and y coordinates of the centre; and $s \in \{-\infty, \infty\}$ is a confidence score associated with the detection of this elliptical region.

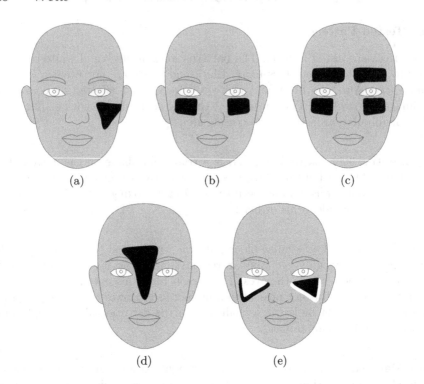

(a)   (b)   (c)

(d)   (e)

Fig. 2. Faces with different patterns

I have selected different scoring scheme to accommodate for different regions returned by different detectors. The score is calculated as follows:

$$dist(d, a) = \|d_c, a_c\|^2, \tag{2}$$

$$S(d, a) = \begin{cases} 1 & \text{if } dist < r_b, \\ 0 & \text{if } otherwise, \end{cases} \tag{3}$$

where d_c and a_c are detection and annotation centres; $dist(\cdot, \cdot)$ is the Euclidean distance of those centres; r_b is the minor axis radius of an annotation ellipse; and $S(\cdot, \cdot)$ is the final score of the detection.

Each implementation was first tested on the original dataset and then on the augmented dataset. A number of statistics was recorded for each run:

- t_p — number of correctly identified faces,
- f_p — number of detected areas which are not face,
- f_n — number of missed faces.

Those values were then used to calculate the *accuracy* for each run. Detailed results are in Table 1. The *accuracy* is calculated as

$$accuracy = \frac{t_p}{t_p + f_n + f_p}. \tag{4}$$

Table 1. Accuracy of detection (higher is better)

	dlib	CCV	OpenCV
Original	**0.760**	**0.710**	**0.593**
Assymetry	0.692	0.658	0.473
Blocks	0.703	0.673	0.501
Blocks2	**0.627**	**0.644**	0.363
Nose	0.679	0.651	**0.310**
Triangles	0.675	0.660	0.470

5 Conclusion

The results clearly show that the make-up patterns do affect the face detection algorithms. The hypothesis presented by Adam Harvey holds. The most affected detector is the one implemented in the OpenCV framework. This corresponds to the motivation presented in CV Dazzle which targeted the OpenCV framework specifically. All tested patterns disrupt the accuracy of the algorithms to similar degree. The only exception is the pattern with two blocks (Fig. 2c) which has the biggest impact on *dlib* and *CCV* libraries. The biggest impact on the *OpenCV* implementation has the nose pattern.

Acknowledgements. This research work has been partly supported by the project SGS-2013-029 of the Czech Ministry of Education, Youth and Sports.

References

1. Harvey, A.: CV Dazzle: Camouage from face detection (2010). https://cvdazzle. com
2. Li, J., Zhang, Y.: Learning SURF cascade for fast and accurate object detection. In: 2013 IEEE Conference on Computer Vision and Pattern Recognition (CVPR), pp. 3468–3475, June 2013
3. Viola, P., Jones, M.: Rapid object detection using a boosted cascade of simple features. In: CVPR 2001, pp. 511–518 (2001)
4. Köstinger, M., et al.: Annotated facial landmarks in the wild: a largescale, real-world database for facial landmark localization. In: 2011 IEEE International Conference on Computer Vision Workshops (ICCV Workshops), pp. 2144–2151. IEEE (2011)
5. Lienhart, R., Maydt, J.: An extended set of haar-like features for rapid object detection. In: Proceedings of the 2002 International Conference on Image Processing, vol. 1, pp. I–900. IEEE (2002)
6. Dalal, N., Triggs, B.: Histograms of oriented gradients for human detection. In: IEEE Computer Society Conference on Computer Vision and Pattern Recognition, CVPR 2005, vol. 1, pp. 886–893. IEEE (2005)

7. Huang, G.B., et al.: Labeled Faces in the Wild: A Database for Studying Face Recognition in Unconstrained Environments. Technical report 07-49. University of Massachusetts, Amherst, October 2007

8. Kazemi, V., Sullivan, J.: One millisecond face alignment with an ensemble of regression trees. In: Proceedings of the 2014 IEEE Conference on Computer Vision and Pattern Recognition, pp. 1867–1874 (2014)

9. Beier, T., Neely, S.: Feature-based Image Metamorphosis. SIGGRAPH Comput. Graph. **26**(2), 35–42 (1992). ISSN: 0097–8930

10. Jain, V., Learned-Miller, E.: FDDB: A Benchmark for Face Detection in Unconstrained Settings. Technical report UM-CS-2010-009. University of Massachusetts, Amherst (2010)

11. Berg, T.L., et al.: Who's in the picture. Adv. Neural Inf. Process. Syst. **17**, 137–144 (2005)

A Comparative Study of Vision-Based Traffic Signs Recognition Methods

Nadra Ben Romdhane[1,2(✉)], Hazar Mliki[1], Rabii El Beji[2], and Mohamed Hammami[1]

[1] MIRACL-FS, Sfax University, Rte Sokra Km 3, BP 802 3018 Sfax, Tunisia
nadrabenromdhane@yahoo.fr, mliki.hazar@gmail.com,
mohamed.hammami@fss.rnu.tn
[2] National Engineering School of Gabes, Gabes, Tunisia
Rabi3elbeji@yahoo.fr

Abstract. Traffic signs recognition is an important component in driver assistance systems as it helps driving under safety regulations. The aim of this work is to propose a vision based traffic sign recognition. In the recognition process, we detect the potential traffic signs regions using monocular color based segmentation. Afterwards, we identify the traffic sign class using its HoG features and the SVM classifier. As shown experimentally, compared to leading methods from the literature under complex conditions, our method has a higher efficiency.

Keywords: Traffic sign detection · Traffic sign recognition · SVM classifier

1 Introduction

Automatic traffic sign recognition (TSR) is an important task for an Advanced Driver Assistance System (ADAS). In fact, some higher-end car models already offer such system [1]. The traffic signs colors and pictogram make them easily perceived and interpreted. Therefore, they raise driving safety by warning against danger and difficulties around the drivers and help them with their navigation by providing useful information. However, recognizing traffic signs in out-door context is still a challenging problem as it has to overcome weather conditions, traffic sign appearance variation and real-time processing constraint.

Actually, the traffic sign recognition performs on two steps: detection and classification of Traffic Sign Detection. In the detection step, the image is segmented relying on the visual key of traffic signs features such as color [2, 3] and shape [4]. Once the candidate traffic sign regions have been detected, a classifying step is performed to make the decision to keep or reject a candidate region of traffic sign. To ensure a prominent classification, there are training-based methods [5, 6] and model-based methods [7].

In our work, we have defined the appropriate methods to use in the proposed solution for traffic sign detection and classification. For the detection step, we opted for a color based method since it provides a faster focusing on the potential areas of traffic signs. In fact, similar objects to the traffic signs shapes may coexist in the background like windows, mail boxes and cars. Besides, methods based on shapes require robust edge detection algorithm which is not an easy task with a not head-on viewing angle or with

© Springer International Publishing Switzerland 2016
A. Campilho and F. Karray (Eds.): ICIAR 2016, LNCS 9730, pp. 341–348, 2016.
DOI: 10.1007/978-3-319-41501-7_39

low resolution traffic sign capture. For classification step, we used an SVM classifier thanks to its performance in statistical learning theory and robustness already proved in TSR topic.

The remainder of this paper is organized as follows: Sect. 2 presents the proposed method. Section 3 discusses a set of extensive experimental evaluations and compares the performance of our method with existing methods. Section 4 summarizes the main contributions of the present work and highlights its perspectives.

2   Our Proposed Traffic Sign Recognition

In our context of study, we are interested to recognize danger and prohibitory traffic signs since they constitute the important cause of accident-prone situations. The proposed method for traffic sign recognition performs on two steps: detection and classification (Fig. 1).

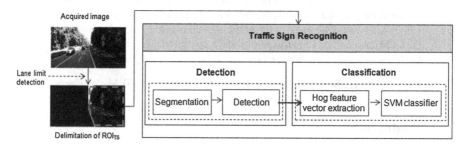

Fig. 1. The proposed traffic sign recognition process

2.1   Traffic Sign Detection

This step aims to find out the potential road signs regions. Therefore, we delimited the ROI_{TS} by applying our proposed algorithm for lane limit detection proposed in [8]. Then, relying on the detected lane limits in the near region (ROI_r and ROI_l) (Fig. 2(a)), we used the right lane limit and the vanishing line (Hz) to draw a quadrilateral on the right side of the image (Fig. 2(b)). This quadrilateral is considered as our new Region of Interest (ROI_{TS}). Applying a thresholding on each of HSV component, we segmented the TS appearing on the ROI_{TS} (Fig. 2(c)). Then, we apply a closed morphology

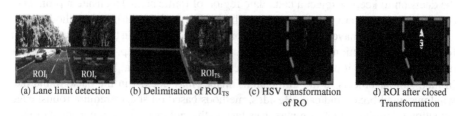

| (a) Lane limit detection | (b) Delimitation of ROI_{TS} | (c) HSV transformation of RO | d) ROI after closed Transformation |

Fig. 2. Traffic sign detection

operation to have more compact areas of interests and eliminate interruptions (Fig. 2(d)). Next, a bounding box characteristic (height, width, area) is calculated for all potential regions. A several constraint rules based on shape properties [9] are applied to each potential region in order to eliminate regions that cannot be TS. These regions are going to be the input of the next classifying step.

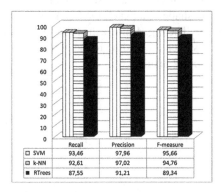

	Recall	Precision	F-measure
□ SVM	93,46	97,96	95,66
□ k-NN	92,61	97,02	94,76
■ RTrees	87,55	91,21	89,34

Fig. 3. Comparative results of different classifiers

2.2 Traffic Sign Classification

The classification of potential traffic sign regions is a key step since it helps to make a decision to keep or reject a potential traffic sign. To ensure a prominent classification, we applied the Histogram of Oriented Gradients (HOG) operator to extract the HOG feature vector [10]. In our proposed method, each of potential TS region is normalized to 32×32 pixels. Then, the region is divided into 12×12 non-overlapping local regions. The HOG features are extracted from each local region. Histograms of edge gradients with 9 orientations are calculated from each 4×4 local cells. The gradient at each pixel is discretized into one of 9 orientation bins, and each pixel "votes" for the orientation of its gradient. Then, this vector is used as the input for an SVM classifier [11].

3 Performance Evaluation of Our Proposed Method

In order to evaluate the performance of the proposed method, we carried out a series of experiments on the "German Traffic Sign Detection Benchmark (GTSDB)" [12].

3.1 Validation of the Used HOG Descriptor Block Size and SVM Classifier

In order to justify our choice of the block size of HOG descriptor and the SVM classifier, we conducted two series of experiments on images taken from the GTSDB.

Firstly, we tested the effectiveness of different HOG descriptor block sizes to choose the adequate size. Secondly, we conducted a comparative study of the SVM classifier with the most common classifiers used in the literature: k-NN (k-Nearest Neighbor) [20] and RTrees (Random Trees) [21].

In order to have a descriptor with the same size for all the images, we scaled each one to a fixed size of 32 × 32 pixels, taking into consideration the height/width ratio of the panel. As the selected descriptor is a global descriptor, we must determine the size distribution of HOG blocks that gives the best results in terms of classification. Since we seek to characterize the shape of a panel, the block size must be square and ranges from 4 × 4 to 32 × 32 pixels. The Fig. 4 shows the ROC curves we obtained for different block sizes using SVM classifier. According to the obtained curves, the block size that gives the best results is 12 × 12 pixels.

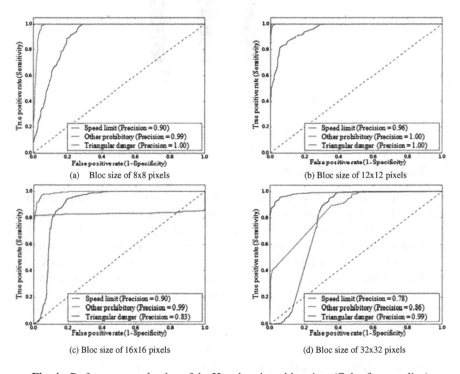

Fig. 4. Performance evaluation of the Hog descriptor bloc sizes (Color figure online)

In order to select the best classifier, we made a comparison between SVM, k-NN, and RTrees classifiers using the 12 × 12 bloc size HOG descriptor. The results of which are shown in Fig. 3. As illustrated, SVM classifier gave the highest recall, precision and F-measure rates.

3.2   Evaluation of the Traffic Sign Recognition

In this section, we evaluate the performance of our method with the most known ones in the literature in order to demonstrate the advantages of our proposed techniques. For this evaluation, we proceeded in three steps. We applied a qualitative evaluation, a quantitative evaluation and we analyzed the processing time.

Qualitative Evaluation. For this evaluation, we compared our solution with the method proposed by Long et al. [6] (Method A) and Jack and Majid [19] (method B) which have proved their performance in real time environment condition. We have implemented both of them according to their corresponding manuscript. We illustrate in Fig. 5 the recognition results of the two methods on some images illustrating different conditions. The first line indicates the different environment conditions; the second line illustrates the original images; and the following lines illustrate successively the TS recognition results obtained by our proposed method, Method A and Method B.

* SL: Speed Limit sign, TD: Triangular danger sign, P: Prohibitory sign.

Fig. 5. Qualitative performance evaluation of the three methods

The different methods give good detection and classification results in normal conditions where the texture of the TS is clearly discriminated from the texture of the background (Fig. 5(a)). They also give good results in the case of faded and furthest TS during a foggy day (Fig. 5(e)). Furthermore, they overcome the most challenging problems of intense illumination, strong shadow and complex Background where we have a multiple occluded TS (Fig. 5(c)). Our results are better than those obtained with Method A, since we identify TS in frames presenting a combination of strong shadow, intense illumination and complex background (Fig. 5(b)). Unlike our method and Method A, Method B succeeds to recognize TS in cloudy day with complex background where TS are furthest and blurred. Nevertheless, the detection and classification fail for the three methods in some critical situations such as the presence of intense rain, and confusion of the TS texture with the background (Fig. 5(f)).

Quantitative Evaluation. In order to further evaluate our traffic sign recognition method, we first compared its performance with Method A and B in terms of Recall, Precision and F-measure [14]. The performance measure of the three methods is given in Fig. 6. Compared to the Method A, we note that our method gave an average improvement of 2.53 % in the Recall rate, 3.56 % in the Precision rate, and 3.12 % in the F-measure rate. Regarding the Method B, it overcomes our method with a gain of 1.08 % in the Recall rate, 7.93 % of Precision rate and 4.78 % in the F-measure rate.

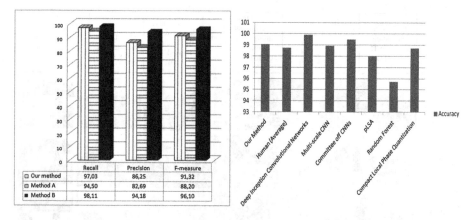

Fig. 6. Comparative performance evaluation of the three methods

Fig. 7. Comparative performance evaluation of traffic signs recognition methods

Afterword, we compared our method with recent works on the GTSDB dataset: Human (Average) [13], Deep Inception Convolutional Networks [15], Multi-scale CNN [5], Committee off CNNs [5], pLSA [16], Random Forest [17] and Compact Local Phase Quantization [18]. The obtained results (Fig. 7) show that our method provides a competitive result which is comparable with most of these previous works. In fact, we record a 99.05 % of TS recognition accuracy.

4   Conclusion

In this paper, we presented our traffic sign recognition method and compared its performance with respect to most recent methods. The experimental evaluation showed that, with our method, we can recognize traffic signs in most of constraining situations. We demonstrated its performance through a qualitative and quantitative evaluation on the GTSDB. Our method gave an average Recall rate of 97.03 %, Precision rate of 86.25 %, F-measure rate of 91.32 %, and an accuracy rate of 99.05 % on the GTSDB database. These results show the efficiency of our proposed method while maintaining a timing that is acceptable for real-time applications.

Encouraged by the promising performance of our method, we are currently examining how to compute the depth distance between the recognized traffic sign and the vehicle carrying the stereovision. Such step has an important impact on further stages such as geometrical discarding, tracking and measuring the remaining distance to a curved lane portion.

References

1. Toyota Safety Sense (Online). http://www.toyota.com
2. Berkaya, S.K., Gunduz, H., Ozsen, O., Akinlar, C., Gunal, S.: On circular traffic sign detection and recognition. J. Expert Syst. Appl. **48**, 67–75 (2016)
3. Han, Y., Virupakshappa, K., Oruklu, E.: Robust traffic sign recognition with feature extraction and k-NN classification methods. In: International Conference on Electro/Information Technology, pp. 484–488 (2015)
4. Malik, Z., Siddiqi, I.: Detection and recognition of traffic signs from road scene images. In: Frontiers of Information Technology (FIT), pp. 330–335 (2014)
5. Sermanet, P., LeCun, Y.: Traffic sign recognition with multi-scale convolutional networks. In: The International Joint Conference on Neural Networks, pp. 2809–2813 (2011)
6. Chen, L., Li, Q., Li, M., Mao, Q.: Traffic sign detection and recognition for intelligent vehicle. In: IEEE Intelligent Vehicles Symposium (IV) (2011)
7. Peker, A.U., Tosun, O., Akin, H.L., Acarman, T.: Fusion of map matching and traffic sign recognition. In: Proceedings of the Intelligent Vehicles Symposium, pp. 867–872 (2014)
8. Ben Romdhane, N., Hammami, M., Ben-Abdallah, H.: A lane detection and tracking method for driver assistance system. In: Knowledge-Based and Intelligent Information and Engineering Systems, Germany, pp. 407–417 (2011)
9. Andrey, V., Kang Hyun, J.: Automatic detection and recognition of traffic signs using geometric structure analysis. In: SICE-ICASE, pp. 1451–1456 (2006)
10. Felzenszwalb, P., McAllester, D., Ramanan, D.: A discriminatively trained, multiscale, deformable part model. In: Computer Vision and Pattern Recognition, pp. 1–8 (2008)
11. Vapnik, V.N.: Statistical Learning Theory. Wiley, New York (1998)
12. Stallkamp, J., Schlipsing, M., Salmen, J., Igel, C.: The German traffic sign recognition benchmark: a multi-class classification competition. In: Proceedings of the IJCNN, pp. 1453–1460 (2011)
13. Menze, M., Geiger, A.: Object scene flow for autonomous vehicles. In: Conference on Computer Vision and Pattern Recognition (CVPR) (2015)
14. David, O., Dursun, D.: Advanced Data Mining Techniques, 1st edn, p. 138. Springer, Heidelberg (2008)
15. Aly, S., Deguchi, D., Murase, H.: Blur-invariant traffic sign recognition using compact local phase quantization. In: 16th International IEEE Annual Conference on Intelligent Transportation Systems (2013)
16. Haloi, M.: A novel pLSA based traffic signs classification system. In: APMediaCast (2015)
17. Zaklouta, F., Stanciulescu, B., Hamdoun, O.: Traffic sign classification using Kd-trees and random forests. In: International Joint Conference on Neural Networks, pp. 2151–2155 (2011)
18. Haloi, M.: Traffic sign classification using deep inception based convolutional networks. CoRR (2015)

19. Jack, G., Majid, M.: Real-time detection and recognition of road traffic signs. IEEE Trans. Intell. Transp. Syst. **13**(4), 1498–1506 (2012)
20. Zaklouta, F., Stanciulescu, B.: Warning traffic sign recognition using a HOG-based K-d tree. In: Proceedings of IEEE Intelligent Vehicles Symposium (IV), pp. 1019–1024 (2011)
21. Greenhalgh, J., Mirmehdi, M.: Traffic sign recognition using MSER and random forests. In: Proceedings of 20th European Signal Processing Conference (EUSIPCO), pp. 1935–1939 (2012)

A Copy-Move Detection Algorithm Using Binary Gradient Contours

Andrey Kuznetsov[1,2(✉)] and Vladislav Myasnikov[1,2]

[1] Samara National Research University (SNRU), Samara, Russia
kuznetsoff.andrey@gmail.com, vmyas@geosamara.ru
[2] Image Processing Systems Institute of the Russian Academy
of Sciences (IPSI RAS), Samara, Russia

Abstract. Nowadays copy-move attack is one of the most obvious ways of digital image forgery in order to hide the information contained in images. Copy-move process consists of copying the fragment from one place of an image, changing it and pasting it to another place of the same image. However, only a few existing studies reached high detection accuracy for a narrow range of transform parameters. In this paper, we propose a copy-move detection algorithm that uses features based on binary gradient contours that are robust to contrast enhancement, additive noise and JPEG compression. The proposed solution showed high detection accuracy and the results are supported by conducted experiments for wide ranges of transform parameters. A comparison of features based on binary gradient contours and based on various forms of local binary patterns showed a significant 20–30 % difference in detection accuracy, corresponding to an improvement with the proposed solution.

Keywords: Copy-move detection · Transformed duplicate · Forgery · Local binary pattern · Binary gradient contours · k-d tree

1 Introduction

Nowadays, digital images play an important role in different spheres of human society. At present, digital image usage is great. They are often used to prove various facts or events. However, we cannot be sure that these data has not been altered by people with malicious intent.

Statistics indicate that users uploaded over 300 million digital images a day using Facebook social network in 2015 [1]. It should be noted that a huge number of web applications (Instagram, Twitter, Flickr, etc.) process a comparable to Facebook traffic of digital images. It is evident that such a huge amount of data will not be missed by attackers, because people firstly analyze information as it is, and then express criticism over it. Digital images may be easily changed by attackers to hide data and provide forgeries to the end users. Created forgeries can be used in compromising form and cause serious political and economic consequences if fake data is not detected. That is the problem that led to a rapid development of forgery detection algorithms.

One of the most frequently used image forgery method is copying a fragment from one place of an image and paste it to another place of the same image. Such attacks are

A. Campilho and F. Karray (Eds.): ICIAR 2016, LNCS 9730, pp. 349–357, 2016.
DOI: 10.1007/978-3-319-41501-7_40

called copy-move attacks, and the copied regions are called *duplicates*. Different transforms can be applied to a duplicate before paste: affine transform, contrast enhancement, additive noise, and others. In this paper we detect duplicates transformed using contrast enhancement, additive noise and JPEG compression.

Currently, there is a large number of papers on development of algorithms for transformed and plain duplicates detection: a common step for all these algorithms is creating features that are robust to duplicate's transform and are calculated for every sliding window position [2–4]. Among invariant features used are the keypoint-based SIFT [5] and SURF [6] and the block-based DCT [7], FMT [8], PCA [9], SVD [10] and Zernike moments [11]. We have already proposed an algorithm for plain copy-move detection based on hash function calculation in a sliding window in 2014 [12]. That solution showed high efficiency and low computational complexity.

The proposed algorithm refers to an intensity-based group of copy-move detection algorithms (all the existing groups are presented in [2]). One way of calculating local intensity characteristics is to use local binary patterns (LBP). LBP has already been used for copy-move detection [13, 14], but in [15] it has been shown that LBP are sensitive to additive noise, and there should be applied invariant to transform LBP modifications.

In this paper, we propose a new algorithm for copy-move detection using features based on binary gradient contours (BGC), proposed by Fernández et al. [16] for texture classification. BGC are an LBP modification that allows high-precision detection of transformed duplicates for a wide range of transform parameters.

2 Local Binary Pattern

LBP [17, 18] is a well-known and commonly used local feature in pattern recognition. In practice, LBP operator combines statistical and structural properties of texture analysis, and enables to construct descriptors of digital images. To calculate LBP, a 3×3 window is usually used: 8 values are compared with the central pixel and a sequence of 8 bits is assigned to the center pixel (Fig. 1). Larger neighborhoods of central pixels can be used to calculate LBP code: P stands for the number of pixels adjacent to the central, R stands for the neighborhood radius.

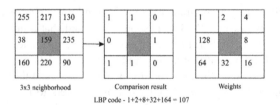

3x3 neighborhood   Comparison result   Weights

LBP code - 1+2+8+32+164 = 107

Fig. 1. Base LBP version

Let us also define P pixels located on a circle of radius R $f_i = f(x_i, y_i), i = \overline{0, P-1}$ that are adjacent to the central pixel $f_c = f(x_c, y_c)$. *LBP code* is defined as follows:

$$LBP_{P,R}(x_c, y_c) = \sum_{i=0}^{P-1} I(f_i \geq f_c) \cdot 2^i, \text{ where } I(n) = \begin{cases} 1, n = true, \\ 0, n = false, \end{cases} \tag{1}$$

A strict code mapping (1) leads to a one-to-one transform of a binary sequence to an integer value. For example, for $P = 8$ we have 256 different LBP codes. As described in [17], such transform is robust to contrast enhancement and intensity variation ranges can be specified explicitly [19]. However basic LBP algorithm is sensitive to additive noise [15], so it can be hardly used in copy-move detection tasks. To solve this problem, researchers developed LBP modifications that are more robust to transforms and are used for texture classification. Later in this paper we show comparison with existing LBP-based algorithms: uniform LBP – *ULBP* [20], local ternary pattern – *LTP* [21], uniform LTP – *ULTP* [21], full LBP [22] – *Full_LBP*, rotation invariant uniform LBP [18] – *RIU* and robust LBP [15] – *RLBP*.

3 Binary Gradient Contours

BGC were proposed by Fernández et al. [16]. BGC belong to the class of descriptors based on pairwise comparison of pixel values selected in a clockwise order from a neighborhood using some pre-defined route. It is obvious that the number of different methods of BGC construction depends on the number of different routes for the neighborhood. Three ways of BGC calculation were proposed [16], which will be denoted later as *BGC_1*, *BGC_2* and *BGC_3*.

The first two methods use one route for the whole neighborhood of the central pixel to generate the code. The first method is described by the following sequence $\{0, 1, 2, 3, 4, 5, 6, 7, 0\}$, where '0' denotes to the index of the upper left pixel in the neighborhood. In this case the BGC code is calculated as follows:

$$BGC^1(x_c, y_c) = \sum_{i=0}^{7} I\left(f_i - f_{(i+1)\bmod 8} \geq 0\right) \cdot 2^i. \tag{2}$$

The second method is based on the route of the form $\{0, 3, 6, 1, 4, 7, 2, 5, 0\}$. In this case the BGC code is calculated as follows:

$$BGC^2(x_c, y_c) = \sum_{i=0}^{7} I\left(f_{3i\bmod 8} - f_{3(i+1)\bmod 8} \geq 0\right) \cdot 2^i. \tag{3}$$

Both methods generate $2^8 - 1$ different code values.

The third method of BGC code calculation is different from the previous ones. It is based on two different routes – $\{1, 3, 7, 5, 1\}$ and $\{0, 2, 4, 6, 0\}$. Every route usage leads to $2^4 - 1$ different codes and the whole BGC code is calculated as follows:

$$BGC^3(x_c, y_c) = (2^4 - 1) \cdot \sum_{i=0}^{3} I(f_{2i} - f_{2(i+1)\mathrm{mod}8} \geq 0) \cdot 2^i$$

$$+ \sum_{i=0}^{3} I(f_{2i+1} - f_{(2i+3)\mathrm{mod}8} \geq 0) \cdot 2^i - 2^4. \tag{4}$$

4 Copy-Move Detection Algorithm

In this section the copy-move detection algorithm description is presented. The algorithm consists of three main steps:

1. Features calculation (using LBP modifications and BGC).
2. Nearest features search.
3. Detection errors reduce.

4.1 Features Calculation

Let $W_{k,l}$ be a processing window with size $M_1 \times M_2$ for an image f. Let $s \in \mathbf{N}$ be a window shift ($s = 1$ for a sliding window). The number of processing window positions is calculated as follows:

$$L = \left(\left\lfloor \frac{N_1 - M_1}{s} \right\rfloor + 1 \right) \cdot \left(\left\lfloor \frac{N_2 - M_2}{s} \right\rfloor + 1 \right).$$

Let us suppose further that for each pixel $f(x_c, y_c) \in W_{k,l}$, where $x_c \in [k+1, k+M_1 - 1]$, $y_c \in [l+1, l+M_2 - 1]$ the pattern code $t(x_c, y_c) \in \mathbf{N}^+$, $\mathbf{N}^+ \equiv \mathbf{N} \cup \{0\}$ is calculated. The number of different codes $Q \in \mathbf{N}$ depends on the selected pattern. The values $t(x_c, y_c)$ for every processing window position are used to calculate a Q-dimensional feature $\mathbf{h} \in \mathbf{R}^Q$ using histogram of pattern codes. Features are then placed in the matrix $\mathbf{M}^{L \times Q} = [\mathbf{h}_0, \ldots, \mathbf{h}_{L-1}]^T$.

4.2 Nearest Features Search

The obvious way to find the nearest features is a pairwise comparison of all vectors, but this solution is computationally inefficient. In order to reduce the computational complexity of the nearest vectors search significantly, we use one of the binary search tree structures – *k-d tree*.

The matrix data $\mathbf{M}^{L \times Q}$ is used for the tree generation and its applying. As a software implementation we used *createns* function implemented in Matlab R2015b. The Euclidean distance was chosen as the distance measure, and the number of nearest neighbors K was set to 10. The matrix of features' indexes $\mathbf{D}^{L \times K}$ is created after the tree applying. Its elements $d_{ij} = \arg\left(\mathbf{h}_{d_{ij}}\right), d_{ij} \in \mathbf{N}^+_{[0,L-1]}/\{i\}$ correspond to the indexes of features that are nearest to $\mathbf{h}_i$.

4.3 Filtering Step

The last step is meant for filtering the results of nearest features search and leads to reduction false detected and missed duplicates. During $\mathbf{D}^{L \times K}$ analysis, we select only pairs of features $\left(\mathbf{h}_i, \mathbf{h}_j\right)$, which meet the following conditions:

1. $\forall i \in [0, L-1], j \in [0, Q-1], \left\|\mathbf{h}_i - \mathbf{h}_{d_{ij}}\right\| \leq 0.1$, where $\|\bullet\|$ is a Euclid norm;
2. $\forall i \in [0, L-1], j \in [0, Q-1], d\left(\mathbf{h}_i, \mathbf{h}_{d_{ij}}\right) \geq 10$, where $d\left(\mathbf{h}_i, \mathbf{h}_j\right)$ is a distance between $\mathbf{h}_i$ and $\mathbf{h}_j$.

For each pair of features that meet these constraints we calculate the difference between the corresponding processing windows coordinates and their frequency. The most frequently occurred features are marked as copy-move detected regions in the result image.

5 Experiments

To carry out research we used a standard PC (Intel Core i5-3470 3.2 GHz, 8 GB RAM). We then selected 10 grayscale images with size 512×512 and created their forgeries using a self-developed automatic copy-move generation procedure. Using the developed forgery generation procedure, we created 1200 forgeries: 120 images for each of the 10 initial images (40 images for each transform type), which were further analyzed using the detection algorithm (Sect. 4). This procedure allows to control the size of duplicates and the values of transform parameters. We generated forgeries using the following transforms:

1. Contrast enhancement (multiplicative coefficient range $a \in [0.2, 0.9]$, additive coefficient range $b \in [5, 30]$).
2. Gaussian ($\sigma < 0.01$) and impulse noise ($p < 0.05$).
3. JPEG compression (quality range $q \in [50, 90]$).

Figure 2 shows examples of forgeries.

To estimate detection accuracy of the proposed algorithm, we used $F1$ score value, which considered both the precision Pr and the recall Rc to compute the score:

$$F1 = 2 \cdot \frac{Pr \cdot Rc}{Pr + Rc}. \tag{5}$$

Conducted research showed that LBP and LTP, ULBP and ULTP showed similar results in all experiments, so we display $F1$ values only for LTP and ULTP further.

We can see from Fig. 3 that $F1$ reaches high values for all ranges of contrast enhancement parameters when using BGC-based features (last three bars in the chart).

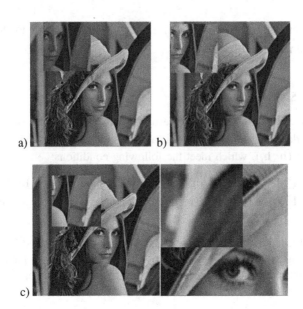

Fig. 2. Images with duplicates transformed using: (a) contrast enhancement, (b) additive noise and (c) JPEG compression

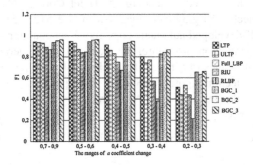

Fig. 3. A comparison of *F1* values among BGC-based and LBP-based features for contrast enhancement

Using LBP-based features for copy-move detection leads to a fast decline of *F1* value for reducing the value of multiplicative coefficient of contrast enhancement.

The chart in Fig. 4 shows that *F1* reaches high values for large values of σ^2 when BGC-based features are used. If we use other LBP-based features for copy-move detection, the *F1* value is extremely low. The only exception is for *LTP* usage – it provides very close to BGC result (nearly 60 %).

We can see from Fig. 5 that *F1* values are also higher for BGC-based features when duplicates are transformed by JPEG compression. When the value of compression quality *q* decreases, only BGC-based features using the second and the third methods lead to high *F1* values and can be used for copy-move detection.

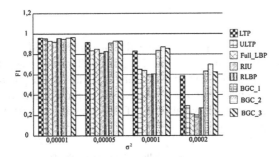

Fig. 4. A comparison of *F1* values among BGC-based and LBP-based features for additive noise

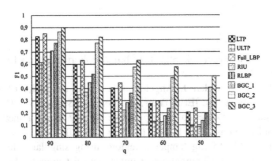

Fig. 5. A comparison of *F1* values among BGC-based and LBP-based features for JPEG compression

The proposed solution shows higher or equal Precision and Recall values in comparison with SIFT and DCT features. We used the same dataset of 1200 images for comparison. Table 1 shows average detection accuracy of transformed duplicates (JPEG and Gaussian noise) using SIFT, DCT and BGC_3 features. It can be seen that the proposed solution provides better detection accuracy values. At the same time, BGC features have lower computational complexity than DCT and SIFT features.

Table 1. A comparison of Precision and Recall values for SIFT, DCT and BGC_3 features usage.

	Contrast enhancement		JPEG compression		Gaussian noise	
	Pr	*Rc*	*Pr*	*Rc*	*Pr*	*Rc*
SIFT	0.85	0.7	0.8	0.6	0.67	0.5
DCT	0.82	0.74	0.74	0.62	0.65	0.6
BGC_3	**0.92**	**0.86**	**0.85**	**0.62**	**0.77**	**0.65**

6 Conclusion

In this paper we proposed a copy-move detection algorithm based on the usage of BGC features. The developed solution showed 20–30 % difference in accuracy in comparison with LBP-based features when wide ranges of transform parameters are used. Further we will carry out research in affine-transformed duplicates detection. We will also analyze combinations of several types of BGC-based and LBP-based features to raise detection accuracy more.

Acknowledgements. This work was financially supported by the Russian Scientific Foundation (RSF), grant no. 14-31-00014 "Establishment of a Laboratory of Advanced Technology for Earth Remote Sensing".

References

1. The Top 20 Valuable Facebook Statistics. http://zephoria.com/top-15-valuable-facebook-statistics
2. Christlein, V., Riess, C., Jordan, J., Angelopoulou, E.: An evaluation of popular copy-move forgery detection approaches. IEEE Trans. Inf. Forensic Secur. **7**(6), 1841–1854 (2012)
3. Mahdian, B., Saic, S.: Detection of copy-move forgery using a method based on blur moment invariants. Forensic Sci. Int. **171**(2), 180–189 (2007)
4. Kang, X., Wei, S.: Identifying tampered regions using singular value decomposition in digital image forensics. In: International Conference on Computer Science and Software Engineering, vol. 3, pp. 926–930. IEEE Press, New York (2008)
5. Huang, H., Guo, W., Zhang, Y.: Detection of copy-move forgery in digital images using SIFT algorithm. In: Pacific-Asia Workshop on Computational Intelligence and Industrial Application 2008,vol. 2, pp. 272–276 (2008)
6. Shivakumar, B.L., Baboo, S.: Detection of region duplication forgery in digital images using SURF. Int. J. Comput. Sci. Issues **8**(4), 199–205 (2011)
7. Fridrich, J., Soukal, D., Lukas, J.: Detection of copy-move forgery in digital images. http://www.ws.binghamton.edu/fridrich/Research/copymove.pdf
8. Bayram, S., Sencar, H., Memon, H.: An efficient and robust method for detecting copy-move forgery. In: IEEE International Conference on Acoustics, Speech, and Signal Processing 2009, pp. 1053–1056 (2009)
9. Popescu, A., Farid, H.: Exposing digital forgeries by detecting duplicated image regions. http://www.ists.dartmouth.edu/library/102.pdf
10. Kang, X., Wei, S.: Identifying tampered regions using singular value decomposition in digital image forensics. In: International Conference on Computer Science and Software Engineering 2008, vol. 3, pp. 926–930 (2008)
11. Ryu, S.-J., Lee, M.-J., Lee, H.-K.: Detection of copy-rotate-move forgery using Zernike moments. In: Böhme, R., Fong, P.W., Safavi-Naini, R. (eds.) IH 2010. LNCS, vol. 6387, pp. 51–65. Springer, Heidelberg (2010)
12. Vladimirovich, K.A., Valerievich, M.V.: A fast plain copy-move detection algorithm based on structural pattern and 2D Rabin-Karp rolling hash. In: Campilho, A., Kamel, M. (eds.) ICIAR 2014, Part I. LNCS, vol. 8814, pp. 461–468. Springer, Heidelberg (2014)
13. Li, L., Li, S., Zhu, H.: An efficient scheme for detection copy-move forged images by local binary patterns. J. Inf. Hiding Multimed. Sig. Process. **4**(1), 46–56 (2013)

14. Davarzani, R., Yaghmaie, K., Mozaffari, S., Tapak, M.: Copy-move forgery detection using multi-resolution local binary patterns. Forensic Sci. Int. **231**(1–3), 61–72 (2013)
15. Ren, J., Jiang, X., Yuan, J.: Noise-resistant local binary pattern with an embedded error-correction mechanism. IEEE Trans. Image Process. **22**(10), 4049–4060 (2013)
16. Fernández, A., Álvarez, M.X., Bianconi, F.: Image classification with binary gradient contours. Opt. Lasers Eng. **49**(9–10), 1177–1184 (2011)
17. Wang, L., He, D.-C.: Texture classification using texture spectrum. Pattern Recogn. **23**(8), 905–910 (1990)
18. Ojala, T., Pietikinen, M., Menp, T.: Multiresolution grayscale and rotation invariant texture classification with local binary patterns. IEEE Trans. Pattern Anal. Mach. Intell. **24**(7), 971–987 (2002)
19. Myasnikov, V.: A local order transform of digital images. Comput. Opt. **39**(3), 397–405 (2015). (in Russian)
20. Arasteh, S., Hung, C.-C.: Color and texture image segmentation using uniform local binary patterns. Mach. Graph. Vis. **15**(3–4), 265–274 (2006)
21. Tan, X., Triggs, B.: Enhanced local texture feature sets for face recognition under difficult lighting conditions. IEEE Trans. Image Process. **19**(6), 1635–1650 (2010)
22. Guo, Z.H., Zhang, D.: A completed modeling of local binary pattern operator for texture classification. IEEE Trans. Image Process. **19**(6), 1657–1663 (2010)

Object Detection and Localization Using Deep Convolutional Networks with Softmax Activation and Multi-class Log Loss

AbdulWahab Kabani and Mahmoud R. El-Sakka[⊠]

Department of Computer Science, The University of Western Ontario,
London, ON, Canada
{akabani5,melsakka}@uwo.ca

Abstract. We introduce a deep neural network that can be used to localize and detect a region of interest (ROI) in an image. We show how this network helped us extract ROIs when working on two separate problems: a whale recognition problem and a heart volume estimation problem. In the former problem, we used this network to localize the head of the whale while in the later we used it to localize the heart left ventricle from MRI images. Most localization networks regress a bounding box around the region of interest. Unlike these architecture, we treat the problem as a classification problem where each pixel in the image is a separate class. The network is trained on images along with masks which indicate where the object is in the image. We treat the problem as a multi-class classification. Therefore, the last layer has a softmax activation. Furthermore, during training, the mutli-class log loss is minimized just like any classification task.

Keywords: Localization · Detection · Recognition · Artificial neural networks · Deep learning · Convolutional neural network · Image classification

1 Introduction

A Convolutional Neural Network (convnet or CNN) is a special type of neural network that contains some layers with restricted connectivity. Such networks were introduced a long time ago [5] and achieved excellent results on the famous MNIST data set [9]. However, it took them few years to outperform the state of the art methods in visual recognition challenges. Currently, CNNs can produce the state of the art performance in many classification tasks. Such a success is driven by the availability of large training data sets [3,13], powerful hardware, regularization techniques such as Dropout [7,17], initialization methods [6], ReLU activations [10], and data augmentation. Since 2012, many networks that can perform classification were introduced [8,15,18].

Typically, CNNs have been used for classification tasks. However, they can also be used for detection and localization [4,12,14,16,19]. A common way to

© Springer International Publishing Switzerland 2016
A. Campilho and F. Karray (Eds.): ICIAR 2016, LNCS 9730, pp. 358–366, 2016.
DOI: 10.1007/978-3-319-41501-7_41

localize an object in the image is to treat the problem as a regression task. In this setting, a bounding box center (or top left corner) is regressed along with the height and width of the bounding box. In this paper, we propose an architecture that treats the problem as a classification task. Pixels are classified as to whether they are inside the bounding box or not. The network is trained on the images and on masks. The mask of one image has the same size as the image and indicates where the bounding box is (or the pixels that belong to the target object are). We experiment with two types of images: right whale aerial images and heart MRI images.

The localization we describe in this paper helped us improve the classification performance on these data sets. In general, we find localization to be very helpful when the number of training images is very small. This is because localizing a region of interest reduces the number of degrees of freedom by removing background pixels that are unrelated to the classification task. This also reduces the amount of time needed for training the classifier. Furthermore, removing background pixels and training a classifier to classify only the region of interest is very important when the amount of RAM in the GPU card is limited. Image subsampling can be used to reduce the size of the image in order to fit it in the GPU RAM. However, subsampling may not be suitable in images where the region of interest (ROI) is very small with respect to the image size. This is because image subsampling may shrink the ROI to a point where it is difficult for the classifier to learn useful features. On the other hand, localization can reduce the input image size by extracting the ROI and removing the unrelated background pixels.

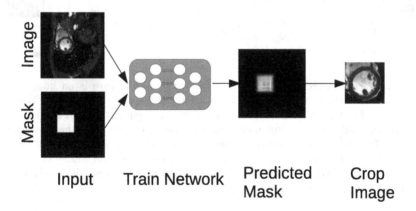

Fig. 1. Model overview: A set of training images along with masks are used to train the network. Once the network is trained, it can be used to predict a mask which identifies the location of the region of interest. Finally, this predicted mask is thresholded (using otsu [11]) and used to crop the image.

Figure 1 shows an overview of the method. Training images and corresponding masks are used to train a neural network. Once the network is trained, the network can be used to predict masks. Once the predicted mask is thresholded, it can be used to find the region of interest in the original image. In Sect. 2, we introduce the architecture of the network. We describe how we trained the network in Sect. 3. In Sect. 4, we present our experimentation with two data sets: a north american right whale data set and short axis heart MRI data set. We conclude our work in Sect. 5.

2   Architecture

The architecture of the localization network (shown in Fig. 2) is similar to many classification networks. The main difference is the last layer, which is a flattened 2D mask predicted by the network. The training images along with their corresponding masks are re-sized to a certain size. In general, we resize the images by taking the mean of the width and height of images in the data set. We resized the images to 128×128 and 112×224 for the MRI images and the whale images, respectively. The input image and the corresponding mask should have the same size. Furthermore, the last layer is a fully connected with $height \times width$ neurons. Reshaping the output layer to 2D produces the predicted masks. The network parameters are summarized in Table 1.

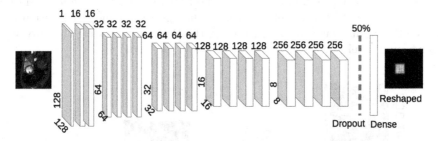

Fig. 2. Localization architecture: The input of the architecture is an image of size 128×128 for the Heart MRI images (described in this Figure.) Note that for the whale images (not shown in this Figure), we used a different input size 112×224. Besides the difference in input size, the number of layers and other parameters are the same for both data sets. In this figure, the output of the network is a layer with $128 \times 128 = 16384$ possible classes. The output layer is simply a flattened mask and reshaping this layer gives us back the predicted mask. The pixels with the highest intensities represent the location of the region of interest.

Each convolutional layer is followed by ReLU activation [10]. The output layer has a softmax activation to ensure that the sum of all pixels in the predicted mask is 1 and that the value of one pixel is between 0 and 1. Maxpooling is used to detect features at different scales. The network is regularized with a 50 % dropout rate.

The most important layer in this network is probably the output layer. It is crucial to design the network such that the number of parameters in the last

Table 1. Localization network architecture: this tables shows the type of layer, the kernel size, shape of the layer, and the number of parameters in each layer.

No	Type	kernel	Shape	Parameters
1	Convolution	(7,7)	(16, 128, 128)	800
2	Convolution	(7,7)	(16, 128, 128)	12,560
3	MaxPooling	_	(16, 64, 64)	0
4	Convolution	(5,5)	(32, 64, 64)	12,832
5	Convolution	(5,5)	(32, 64, 64)	25,632
6	Convolution	(5,5)	(32, 64, 64)	25,632
7	Convolution	(5,5)	(32, 64, 64)	25,632
8	MaxPooling	_	(32, 32, 32)	0
9	Convolution	(5,5)	(64, 32, 32)	51,264
10	Convolution	(5,5)	(64, 32, 32)	102,464
11	Convolution	(5,5)	(64, 32, 32)	102,464
12	Convolution	(5,5)	(64, 32, 32)	102,464
13	MaxPooling	_	(64, 16, 16)	0
14	Convolution	(5,5)	(128, 16, 16)	204,928
15	Convolution	(5,5)	(128, 16, 16)	409,728
16	Convolution	(5,5)	(128, 16, 16)	409,728
17	Convolution	(5,5)	(128, 16, 16)	409,728
18	MaxPooling	_	(128, 8, 16)	0
19	Convolution	(5,5)	(256, 8, 8)	819,456
20	Convolution	(5,5)	(256, 8, 8)	1,638,656
21	MaxPooling	_	(256, 4, 4)	0
23	Flatten	_	4096	0
24	Dropout	_	4096	0
25	Dense	_	16384	67,125,248

layer is as large as possible but also appropriate for the GPU RAM available. Since the output layer is fully connected, it has the largest number of parameters in the network. It is important to make sure that the number of pixels in the input image and the input mask equals the number of units in the output layer.

3   Training and Localizing

The network is trained on two types of images: north atlantic whale images [2] and heart MRI images [1]. We minimize the mutli-class logloss (categorical cross-entropy). Initially, the learning rate is set at a relatively high value 0.01 and gradually reduced if the validation loss does not improve. Because the last layer in the network is a softmax layer, the pixels of the predicted mask are probabilities.

Therefore, it is crucial that pixels of the input mask are also probabilities (sum up to 1 and their range is between 0 and 1). Therefore, we standardize each pixel in the input mask by Eq. 1:

$$y_{ij} = \frac{pixel_{ij}}{\sum_{i=1}^{H} \sum_{j=1}^{W} pixel_{ij}} \tag{1}$$

where y_{ij} is the normalized pixel value such that $y_{ij} \in [0, 1]$ and $\sum_{i=1}^{H} \sum_{j=1}^{W} y_{ij} = 1$, $pixel_{ij}$ is the pixel value at row i and column j.

Once the training is complete, the output layer is reshaped to have a 2D shape. Then, this reshaped layer (our predicted mask) can be thresholded using otsu. The image is thresholded as shown in Eq. 2:

$$I(i,j)_{thresholded} = \begin{cases} 1, & \text{if } I(i,j) \geq threshold_{Otsu} \\ 0, & \text{otherwise,} \end{cases} \tag{2}$$

Then, the predicted mask is resized back to the original size of the image. Finally, the predicted mask can be used to extract the region of interest from the original image.

During training, the images are transformed in order to alleviate overfitting. These transformations are summarized in Table 2.

Table 2. Data augmentation: Random transformations along with parameters. These transformations are applied randomly to each image before sending it to the GPU. Important note: the same transformation should be applied to both the image and corresponding mask.

Transformation	Parameters
Horizontal Flip	Randomness = 50 %
Vertical Flip	Randomness = 50 %
Horizontal Shift	Up to 20 % of width
Vertical Shift	Up to 20 % of height
Gaussian Blurring	Up to $\sigma = 1$

It is very important to note that the same transformation should be applied to both the image and corresponding mask. Otherwise, the network will never converge and the training will fail. It is worth mentioning that the network can also learn the object scale if there is a variation in scale in the training data. If there is no scale variation in the training data and scale learning is desired, the training images and masks can be transformed to simulate scale variations.

4   Experiments

All experiments were ran on a laptop with GTX980M graphics with 4 GB RAM. Training the localizer takes around 160 s per epoch (around 4.5 h to train 100 epochs).

Figure 3 shows the multi-class logarithmic loss (also known as categorical cross-entropy) progress while training for both the training and validation images. The equation for this metric is:

$$logloss = -\frac{1}{n}\sum_{i=1}^{N}\sum_{j=1}^{M} y_{ij}log(p_{ij}) \tag{3}$$

where N is the number of images in the data set, M is the number of pixels in the mask. y_{ij} is a pixel in the true input mask i. y_{ij} has a 0 value if it corresponds to the background and a higher value if it is inside the ROI. p_{ij} is the corresponding predicted pixel value.

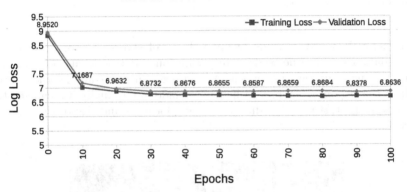

Fig. 3. The loss curves when training the network to localize the left ventricle in heart MRI images. Since the validation and training losses are very close to each other, increasing the capacity of the network is likely to improve results at the expense of longer training time. (Color figure online)

Since the validation and training losses are very close to each other, increasing the capacity of the network is likely to improve results at the expense of longer training time. It is worth mentioning that using an architecture similar to the Oxford Visual Geometry Group (VGG) net [15] can usually lead to better results at the expense of time. The VGG [15] architecture is a very deep network with small kernel sizes and it is usually used for classification. Modifying our network architecture to be similar to VGG can lead to better results at the expense of longer training times. Since localization is usually a preprocessing step before classification, we opted for an architecture that can converge fast and produce good results within a decent amount of training time. If better localization results are desired, the network can be made deeper with smaller kernel sizes.

It may be difficult to understand how good the localizer is by analyzing the log loss progress. The lower the loss, the better the localizer. However, it may not be clear how good the localizer is. Figure 4 shows how the performance

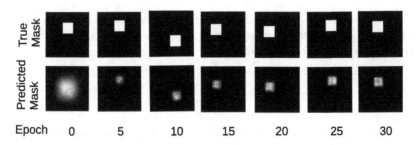

Fig. 4. This figure shows how the network performance in tracking the location of the left ventricle improves as it is being trained. The same image is shown across different epochs. Due to data augmentation, the true (and predicted) location of the left ventricle changes. At epoch 0, the network predicts the location of the left ventricle to be in the middle of the image. Later, the network gradually becomes capable at predicting the location of the left ventricle.

of the network improves while training. Figure 4 shows only one image from the validation set but due to data augmentation, the true location of region of interest changes during each epoch. At the beginning of training, the network predicts the region of interest to be in the middle. Gradually, we can see that the network is starting to predict the correct location and size of the region of interest.

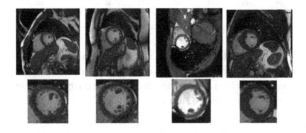

Fig. 5. A random sample of MRI images showing the heart. In the lower row, the left ventricle is localized and cropped.

Figures 5 and 6 show the result of localizing the left ventricle in MRI images and the right whale heads in right whale images. The performance of this network seems to be very robust. When scanning the validation set for wrong localization, we could not find any examples where the network completely returned the wrong region of interest. However, for the MRI images, we did notice that when the left ventricle is very small and at end-systole, some regions of interest were larger than they should be.

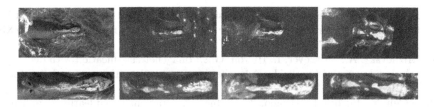

Fig. 6. A random sample of right whale images along with the resulting head crops. These head crops can be passed to a right whale classifier to recognize the whale.

5   Conclusion

We introduced a network that can be used to localize a region of interest. Unlike many localization networks, we do not regress a bounding box. Instead, the network is trained using the training images and the corresponding masks. The network predicts a mask, which is then thresholded and used to extract the region of interest from the original image. It is worth mentioning that this network can learn a region of interest of any shape (rectangle, triangle, circle, etc.). It can also be used for supervised segmentation of an arbitrary shaped object.

Acknowledgements. This research is partially funded by the Natural Sciences and Engineering Research Council of Canada (NSERC). This support is greatly appreciated. We would also like to thank kaggle, the National Oceanic Atmospheric Administration Fisheries for providing the whale data set. We would also like to thank Booz Allen Hamilton, and the National Heart, Lung, and Blood Institute (NHLBI) for providing the MRI images.

References

1. Data science bowl cardiac challenge data. https://www.kaggle.com/c/second-annual-data-science-bowl. (Accessed on 19 March 2016)
2. Right whale recognition. https://www.kaggle.com/c/noaa-right-whale-recognition. (Accessed on 19 January 2016)
3. Deng, J., Dong, W., Socher, R., Li, L.J., Li, K., Fei-Fei, L.: Imagenet: a large-scale hierarchical image database. In: IEEE Conference on Computer Vision and Pattern Recognition, CVPR 2009, pp. 248–255. IEEE (2009)
4. Erhan, D., Szegedy, C., Toshev, A., Anguelov, D.: Scalable object detection using deep neural networks. In: Proceedings of the IEEE Conference on Computer Vision and Pattern Recognition, pp. 2147–2154 (2014)
5. Fukushima, K.: Neocognitron: a self-organizing neural network model for a mechanism of pattern recognition unaffected by shift in position. Biol. Cybern. **36**(4), 193–202 (1980)
6. Glorot, X., Bengio, Y.: Understanding the difficulty of training deep feedforward neural networks. In: International Conference on Artificial Intelligence and Statistics, pp. 249–256 (2010)

7. Hinton, G.E., Srivastava, N., Krizhevsky, A., Sutskever, I., Salakhutdinov, R.R.: Improving neural networks by preventing co-adaptation of feature detectors. arXiv preprint arXiv:1207.0580 (2012)

8. Krizhevsky, A., Sutskever, I., Hinton, G.E.: Imagenet classification with deep convolutional neural networks. In: Advances in neural information processing systems, pp. 1097–1105 (2012)

9. LeCun, Y., Bottou, L., Bengio, Y., Haffner, P.: Gradient-based learning applied to document recognition. Proc. IEEE **86**(11), 2278–2324 (1998)

10. Nair, V., Hinton, G.E.: Rectified linear units improve restricted boltzmann machines. In: Proceedings of the 27th International Conference on Machine Learning (ICML 2010), pp. 807–814 (2010)

11. Otsu, N.: A threshold selection method from gray-level histograms. Automatica **11**(285–296), 23–27 (1975)

12. Szegedy, C., Toshev, A., Erhan, D.: Deep neural networks for object detection. In: Advances in Neural Information Processing Systems, pp. 2553–2561 (2013)

13. Russakovsky, O., Deng, J., Su, H., Krause, J., Satheesh, S., Ma, S., Huang, Z., Karpathy, A., Khosla, A., Bernstein, M., et al.: Imagenet large scale visual recognition challenge. Int. J. Comput. Vis. **115**(3), 211–252 (2015)

14. Sermanet, P., Eigen, D., Zhang, X., Mathieu, M., Fergus, R., LeCun, Y.: Overfeat: Integrated recognition, localization and detection using convolutional networks. arXiv:1312.6229 (2013)

15. Simonyan, K., Zisserman, A.: Very deep convolutional networks for large-scale image recognition. arXiv preprint arXiv:1409.1556 (2014)

16. Song, H.O., Girshick, R., Jegelka, S., Mairal, J., Harchaoui, Z., Darrell, T.: On learning to localize objects with minimal supervision. arXiv preprint arXiv:1403.1024 (2014)

17. Srivastava, N., Hinton, G., Krizhevsky, A., Sutskever, I., Salakhutdinov, R.: Dropout: a simple way to prevent neural networks from overfitting. J. Mach. Learn. Res. **15**(1), 1929–1958 (2014)

18. Szegedy, C., Liu, W., Jia, Y., Sermanet, P., Reed, S., Anguelov, D., Erhan, D., Vanhoucke, V., Rabinovich, A.: Going deeper with convolutions. arXiv preprint arXiv:1409.4842 (2014)

19. Szegedy, C., Toshev, A., Erhan, D.: Deep neural networks for object detection. In: Advances in Neural Information Processing Systems, pp. 2553–2561 (2013)

Clustering-Based Abnormal Event Detection: Experimental Comparison for Similarity Measures' Efficiency

Najla Bouarada Ghrab[1](✉), Emna Fendri[2], and Mohamed Hammami[2]

[1] Miracl-ISIMS, Sfax University, Sakiet Ezzit, Sfax, Tunisia
najla.bouarada@yahoo.fr
[2] Miracl-FS, Sfax University, Road Sokra, Sfax, Tunisia
fendri.msf@gnet.tn, Mohamed.Hammami@fss.rnu.tn

Abstract. The detection of abnormal events is a major challenge in video surveillance systems. In most of the cases, it is based on the analysis of the trajectories of moving objects in a controlled scene. The existing works rely on two phases. Firstly, they extract normal/abnormal clusters from saved trajectories through an unsupervised clustering algorithm. In the second phase, they consider a new detected trajectory and classify it as either normal or abnormal. In both phases, they need to compute similarity between trajectories. Thus, measuring such a similarity is a critical step while analyzing trajectories since it affects the quality of further applications such as clustering and classification. Despite the differences of the measured distances, authors claim the performance of the adopted distance. In this paper, we present a comparative experimental study on the efficiency of four distances widely used as trajectories' similarity measure. Particularly, we examine the impact of the use of these distances on the quality of trajectory clustering. The experimental results demonstrate that the Longest Common SubSequence (LCSS) distance is the most accurate and efficient for the clustering task even in the case of different sampling rates and noise.

Keywords: Event detection · Normal event · Abnormal event · Trajectory · Unsupervised clustering · Similarity measure

1 Introduction

Video surveillance has become the most adopted solution facing the increased rates of delinquency, crime and terrorism over the last decade. Typically, multiple video camera's streams are displayed in a central monitoring room to be controlled by security personnel. However, due to fatigue, distraction and interruptions, manual monitoring may be inefficient. Automating this task through intelligent systems has become a very significant research topic which aims to automatically detect and recognize events from the video streams. Dealing with event detection, many researchers [1,2] have been interested in classifying events

© Springer International Publishing Switzerland 2016
A. Campilho and F. Karray (Eds.): ICIAR 2016, LNCS 9730, pp. 367–374, 2016.
DOI: 10.1007/978-3-319-41501-7_42

as either normal or abnormal. An event can be defined by the trajectory of any detected moving object. For instance, an abnormal event detection consists in an abnormal trajectory detection. This is a challenging task because we can hardly specify abnormality in an explicit manner (*i.e.* abnormal scenarios). Therefore, most of the proposed approaches [3,4] identified firstly normal trajectories (*i.e.* normal events) and then considered the rest of trajectories as abnormal ones. Typically, they proceed by an unsupervised clustering of a set of learned trajectories to distinguish between normal and abnormal trajectories. Once clusters are extracted, a new trajectory is classified as normal or abnormal according to the cluster to which it belongs to or it is close to. In order to either carry out an event clustering or a new event classification, we need to measure the similarity between pairs of events (*i.e.* trajectories). In the literature, different distances are proposed to compute similarity between two trajectories [5–7]. According to the trajectories' representations, we classify the proposed distances into three categories: (a) Similarity measures based on geometric shapes [8]: the trajectories are considered as a geometric shape, (b) Similarity measures based on time series [5,6]: the trajectories are defined as an ordered sequence of positions over the time. Measuring the similarity between pairs of trajectories is effected between sequences of sampled vectors by ignoring the time component. This category is the most used for trajectories' clustering for an abnormal event detection, and (c) Spatio-temporal similarity measures [9]: The trajectories are defined through the spatial and temporal components and probably other dynamic characteristics like speed, direction and curvature.

The quality of the clustering approach depends on the performance of the adopted distance. In the literature, none of the distances has been judged as the best for trajectories' clustering. In this paper, we present a comparative study on the accuracy and the effectiveness of trajectories' similarity measures in a clustering-based approach for an abnormal event detection. The remaining of this paper is organized as follows. In Sect. 2, we present the generic process adopted for an abnormal event detection. Section 3 provides an overview of the recent state of art concerning trajectories' similarities. The experimental observations regarding the efficiency of the compared similarity measures are described in Sect. 4, and in Sect. 5 our major conclusions are drawn.

2   Trajectory Classification: The Generic Process

Classifying a trajectory as normal or abnormal generally involves two phases as presented in Fig. 1: an offline phase to extract models of clusters and an online phase to classify a new trajectory.

The offline phase aims to learn normal trajectory patterns and includes two steps: trajectories' clustering and clusters' modeling. The first step addresses two main issues: the definition of a similarity measure and the clustering or grouping algorithm. Since normal events appear frequently and dominate data and abnormal ones appear rarely [10], large clusters are considered as clusters of normal trajectories (*i.e.* normal events) and the others as clusters of abnormal trajectories

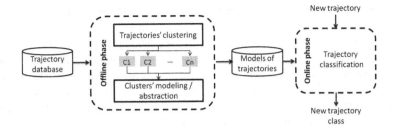

Fig. 1. Trajectory classification process

(*i.e.* abnormal events). The second step of the offline phase consists in modeling clusters of normal trajectories to prepare the database of models. A cluster's model is a compact representation of a cluster partition. It can be minimally specified by the centroid of the cluster [11] or extended with an envelope [12].

The online phase tends to classify a new trajectory as normal or abnormal. This phase is achieved by computing the distances between the new trajectory (to be classified) and the clusters' models of normal trajectories. Therefore, the new trajectory is associated to the cluster which model is the nearest. In the two phases (offline and online), the similarity measure represents a critical element to decide about the efficiency of the process. In the next section, we present an overview of the similarity measures used in the literature.

3   Similarity Measures for Trajectories

In this section, we are interested in the similarity measures based on time series. Thus, trajectory T of a moving object, given by Eq. 1, is defined as an ordered series of time stamped positions in two-dimensional Euclidean space [5].

$$T = [(t_1, s_1), (t_2, s_2), ..., (t_n, s_n)] \tag{1}$$

where s_i represents the coordinates recorded by tracking the object at the timestamp t_i, and n is the number of timestamps defined as the length of a trajectory.

Trajectories in the trajectory database are obtained from tracking of moving objects. So, they may be of different lengths and/or of different sampling rates (which leads to a local time shift into trajectories) and may contain noise. The accuracy of a similarity measure depends on the quality of the trajectory. Similarity measures can be applied either on trajectories as they were already registered (called raw representation) or on preprocessed trajectories. Preprocessing can unify the size of trajectories or offer new representations to trajectories by reducing their dimensionality without any change of their fundamental characteristics. Many trajectories' distances functions are proposed in the literature and the most widely used are: Euclidean distance, Dynamic Time Warping (DTW), Longest Common SubSequence (LCSS), Edit Distance on Real Sequences (EDR), Edit Distance with Real Penality (ERP) and Hausdorff distance (HD). In this work, we are interested in comparing four similarity distances: DTW, LCSS, EDR and HD. In fact, the chosen similarity measures operate on raw trajectories and do not require any preprocessing. The Euclidean distance is not included in this comparison because it needs a preprocessing step. In our study, we referred to and relied on the following assumption: Let $Rest(T_1)$ be the last $N-1$ points in T_1 and $Rest(T_2)$ be the last $M-1$ points in T_2, where N is the length of T_1 and M is the length of T_2.

Dynamic Time Warping (DTW): DTW [13] measures the distances between two trajectories by searching all possible point combinations. It aims to optimize matching between the two trajectories by distorting them temporally in order to minimize their distance. It allows them to be stretched or compressed. It can handle local time shifting by duplicating the previous element of the trajectories. This distance, defined by Eq. 2, can be computed between trajectories of different lengths but it cannot handle noise. In [14], the authors use the DTW distance to identify similar trajectories that are invariant under translation, scaling and rotational transformations.

$$DTW(T_1, T_2) = \begin{cases} 0 & \text{if } n=m=0 \\ \infty & \text{if } n=0 \text{ or } m=0 \\ dist(t_1,t_2) + min \left\{ \begin{array}{l} DTW(Rest(T_1),Rest(T_2)), \\ DTW(Rest(T_1),T_2), \\ DTW(T_1,Rest(T_2)) \end{array} \right\} & \text{otherwise} \end{cases} \quad (2)$$

Longest Common SubSequence (LCSS): The LCSS distance [6] compares two trajectories by counting the maximum number of matched points in the two trajectories. It can handle local time shifting and different lengths of trajectories by enabling them to be stretched. Moreover, it deals with trajectories that contain noise by enabling some points of the trajectories to be not matched. The LCSS distance is used in [15] to find hierarchical clusters of similar trajectories. In [16], the LCSS distance is used to measure the similarity between trajectories of different lengths to group trajectories into routes. Clustering is performed with the spectral algorithm. The LCSS between two trajectories is given by Eq. 3.

$$LCSS_{\delta,\epsilon}(T_1, T_2) = \begin{cases} 0 & \text{if } n=0 \text{ or } m=0 \\ 1 + LCSS_{\delta,\epsilon}(Rest(T_1), Rest(T_2)) & \text{if } |t_{1x,n}-t_{2x,m}|<\epsilon \text{ and} \\ & |t_{1y,n}-t_{2y,m}|<\epsilon \text{ and } |n-m|\leq\delta \\ max \left\{ \begin{array}{l} LCSS_{\delta,\epsilon}(Rest(T_1),T_2), \\ LCSS_{\delta,\epsilon}(T_1,Rest(T_2)) \end{array} \right\} & otherwise \end{cases}$$

$$(3)$$

where δ allows the stretching of the trajectories in time and ϵ is the matching threshold. The $LCSS_{\delta,\epsilon}$ computes the number of similar points between the two trajectories based on the values of δ and ϵ. The distance function is defined by Eq. 4:

$$D_{LCSS} = 1 - LCSS_{\delta,\epsilon}(T_1, T_2)/min(n, m) \tag{4}$$

Edit Distance on Real Sequences (EDR): EDR [5] is based on the Edit Distance. It seeks the minimum number of edit operations required to change one trajectory into another. It assigns penalties to the gaps between two matched sub-trajectories according to the length of gaps. This distance, given by Eq. 5, can handle local time shift, different lengths of trajectories and it is not sensible to noise. In [2], the authors compute the similarity of trajectories and use the spectral clustering algorithm for trajectory clustering.

$$EDR(T_1, T_2) = \begin{cases} n & \text{if } m = 0 \\ m & \text{if } n = 0 \\ min \left\{ \begin{array}{l} EDR(Rest(T_1), Rest(T_2)) + subcost, \\ EDR(Rest(T_1), T_2) + 1, \\ EDR(T_1, Rest(T_2)) + 1 \end{array} \right\} & otherwise \end{cases} \tag{5}$$

where $subcost = 0$ if $match(r_1, s_1) = true$ and $subcost = 1$ otherwise. $match$ (r_1, s_1) is true if and only if $|t_{1,x} - t_{2,x}| < \epsilon$ and $|t_{1,y} - t_{2,y}| < \epsilon$, where ϵ is the matching threshold.

Hausdorff Distance (HD): HD [8] corresponds to the maximum deviation between two trajectories. It is defined as the maximum of the minimum Euclidean distances between each point of one trajectory to another. The HD was used in [17] to group trajectories according to their spatial proximity. The one-side or the directed Hausdorff distance is defined by Eq. 6:

$$\widetilde{\delta}_H(T_1, T_2) = max_{t_1 \in T_1} \, min_{t_2 \in T_2} \, d(t_1, t_2) \tag{6}$$

where $d(t_1, t_2)$ is the Euclidean distance between two points. And the (bidirectional) Hausdorff distance between T_1 and T_2 is defined by Eq. 7:

$$\delta_H(T_1, T_2) = max(\widetilde{\delta}_H(T_1, T_2), \widetilde{\delta}_H(T_2, T_1)) \tag{7}$$

4   Experiments and Results

Due to the absence of benchmark datasets for trajectories' clustering, where the ground-truth distance between any pair of trajectories is known in advance, the evaluation of the effectiveness of different similarity measures objectively is a challenging task. In addition, trajectories' distances computation is not an end but rather the input of further applications. Therefore, this section includes the experiments that aim to evaluate four distances in the context of trajectories' clustering. A synthetic database created by Anjum et al. [18] that contains 100 trajectories is used in this evaluation. The trajectories are of different lengths and are split in 8 clusters.

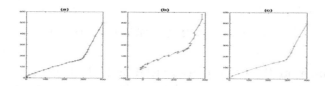

Fig. 2. Example of trajectory and its transformations: (a) raw trajectory, (b) trajectory with noise, and (c) trajectory with local time shift.

In this study, the agglomerative hierarchical clustering (CAH) [21] was performed to evaluate the four distances. This algorithm can group trajectories even if the number of clusters is unknown. It can also be used with any valid measure of distance even if the trajectories are of different lengths and in the presence of noise. Specifically, we computed the Leave One Out rate [19] and the Correct Clustering Rate (CCR) [20] with raw trajectories and trajectories with two transformations: adding noise and with a local time shift. Figure 2 shows an example of raw trajectory and its transformations.

The rates Leave One Out and CCR with the four distances while operating on raw trajectories are shown in Table 1. Although rates of Leave One Out are almost similar, by examining the CCR values, we note that LCSS has a better result compared to the other distances. The accuracy of the distance function based Longest Common Subsequence depends on the determination of the values for ϵ and δ. We tested the algorithm with different values of δ and we concluded that if a value is greater than 20–30 %, the length of trajectories does not improve the results. For the value of ϵ, we used an adaptive value to the compared trajectories. This value is equal to the maximum of the standard deviation of the two trajectories multiplied by 0.2. The same value of ϵ is used for EDR.

Table 1. Clustering results with raw trajectories.

Rates \ Distances	DTW	LCSS	EDR	HD
Leave One Out	0.98	0.99	0.97	0.97
CCR	0.70	0.89	0.75	0.74

The second experiment aimed to evaluate the quality of clustering in the presence of noise in trajectories. The results, provided in Table 2, confirm that the DTW is very sensitive to noise; nevertheless the LCSS distance is even better.

Another experiment that aims to evaluate the impact of local time shift on the quality of clustering was carried out. The results, presented in Table 3, show that unlike the LCSS distance, the other distances are sensitive to a local time shift.

Table 2. Clustering results with trajectories by adding noise.

Rates \ Distances	DTW	LCSS	EDR	HD
Leave One Out	0.97	0.98	0.98	0.97
CCR	0.62	0.90	0.75	0.92

Table 3. Clustering results with trajectories with local time shift.

Rates \ Distances	DTW	LCSS	EDR	HD
Leave One Out	0.96	0.99	0.96	0.94
CCR	0.63	0.90	0.74	0.61

As shown in the three tables, we can notice that the LCSS distance gives the best rates for trajectories clustering even in the presence of noise or with a local time shift. The results of the other distances are not satisfactory. Indeed, our experiments confirm that the DTW distance is sensitive to noise. Although the EDR is not sensitive to the local time shift and noise, the results show that the LCSS is the best. For the HD, it only uses one pairwise points to measure similarity, which cannot distinguish trajectories in the same path with opposite directions.

5   Conclusion

In this paper, we were interested in abnormal trajectories' detection. The majority of proposed approaches rely on trajectories' classification. Thus, we first presented the generic process involving an offline phase of trajectories' clustering followed by a real time phase for a new trajectory classification. Since both phases require computing similarity distances between pairs of trajectories, we proposed to evaluate the effectiveness of the four most used distances. The results of three series of experiments conclude on the quality of LCSS and the sensitivity of the DTW, EDR and HD to noise and local time shift.

References

1. Wang, T., Chen, J., Snoussi, H.: Online detection of abnormal events in video streams. J. Electr. Comput. Eng. **2013**, 12 (2013)
2. Zhou, Y., Yan, S., Huang, T.S.: Detecting anomaly in videos from trajectory similarity analysis. In: IEEE International conference on multimedia and expo, pp. 1087–1090. IEEE, Beijing (2007)
3. Makris, D., Ellis, T.: Learning semantic scene models from observing activity in visual surveillance. IEEE Trans. Syst. Man Cybern. B Cybern. **35**, 397–408 (2005)

4. Ivanov, I., Dufaux, F., Ha, T.M., Ebrahimi, T.: Towards generic detection of unusual events in video surveillance. In: Sixth IEEE International Conference on Advanced Video and Signal Based Surveillance, pp. 61–66. IEEE, Genova (2009)

5. Chen, L., Ozsu, M.T., Oria, V.: Robust and fast similarity search for moving object trajectories. In: Proceedings of the 2005 ACM SIGMOD International Conference on Management of Data, pp. 491–502. ACM, Baltimore Maryland (2005)

6. Vlachos, M., Gunopulos, D., Kollios, G.: Discovering similar multidimensional trajectories. In: Proceedings 18th International Conference on Data Engineering, pp. 673–684. IEEE, San Jose (2002)

7. Sankararaman, S., Agarwal, P.K., Mlhave, T., Boedihardjo, A. P.: Computing similarity between a pair of trajectories. In: CoRR (2013)

8. Alt, H., Guibas, L.J.: Discrete geometric shapes: matching, interpolation, and approximation. Handbook of Computational Geometry, Technical report (1996)

9. van Kreveld, M., Luo, J.: The definition and computation of trajectory and subtrajectory similarity. In: 15th Annual ACM International Symposium on Advances in Geographic Information Systems, pp. 44:1–44:4. ACM, New York (2007)

10. Jiang, F., Yuan, J., Tsaftaris, S., Katsaggelos, A.: Anomalous video event detection using spatiotemporal context. Comput. Vis. Image Underst. **115**, 323–333 (2011)

11. Melo, J., Naftel, A., Bernardino, A., Santos-Victor, J.: Detection and classification of highway lanes using vehicle motion trajectories. IEEE Trans. Intell. Transp. Syst. **7**, 188–200 (2006)

12. Junejo, I.N., Javed, O., Shah, M.: Multi feature path modeling for video surveillance. In: Proceedings of the 17th International Conference on Pattern Recognition, pp. 716–719. IEEE (2004)

13. Berndt, D.J., Clifford, J.: Using dynamic time warping to find patterns in time series. In: KDD Workshop (1994), pp. 359–370 (1994)

14. Vlachos, M., Gunopulos, D., Das, G.: Rotation invariant distance measures for trajectories. In: Proceedings of the Tenth ACM SIGKDD International Conference on Knowledge Discovery and Data Mining, pp. 707–712 (2004)

15. Buzan, D., Sclaroff, S., Kollios, G.: Extraction and clustering of motion trajectories in video. In: 17th International Conference on Pattern Recognition, pp. 521–524. IEEE (2004)

16. Morris, B., Trivedi, M.: Trajectory learning for activity understanding: Unsupervised, multilevel, and long-term adaptive approach.J. IEEE Trans. Pattern Anal. Mach. Intell. **33**(11), 2287–2301 (2011)

17. Junejo, I., Foroosh, H.: Trajectory rectification and path modeling for video surveillance. In: 11th International Conference on Computer Vision, pp. 1–7 (2007)

18. Anjum, N., Cavallaro, A.: Multifeature object trajectory clustering for video analysis. IEEE Trans. Circ. Syst. Video Tech. **18**, 1555–1564 (2008)

19. Keogh, E., Kasetty, S.: On the need for time series data mining benchmarks: a survey and empirical demonstration. Data Min. Knowl. Disc. **7**, 349–371 (2003)

20. Zhang, Z., Huang, K., Tan, T.: Comparison of similarity measures for trajectory clustering in outdoor surveillance scenes. In: 18th International Conference on Pattern Recognition, pp. 1135–1138. IEEE, Hong Kong (2006)

21. Duda, R.O., Hart, P.E., Stork, D.G.: Pattern Classification. Wiley-Interscience, Hoboken (2001)

Matching

Improved DSP Matching with RPCA
for Dense Correspondences

Fanhuai Shi[(✉)] and Yanli Zhang

Department of Control Science & Engineering, Tongji University, Shanghai, China
fhshi@tongji.edu.cn

Abstract. The Deformable Spatial Pyramid (DSP) matching method is popular for dense matching of images with different scenes but sharing similar semantic content, which achieves high matching accuracy. However, the warped image generated by DSP is not smooth, which mainly results from the noisy flow field by DSP. We observed the flow field could be decomposed into a low-rank term and a sparse term. Meanwhile, Robust Principle Component Analysis (RPCA) is capable of recovering the low-rank component from an observation with sparse noises. So, in this paper we propose to use RPCA to deal with the non-smoothness in DSP by recovering the low-rank term from the flow field. Experiments on VGG and LMO datasets verify that our approach obtains smoother warped image and gains higher matching accuracy than the DSP.

Keywords: Scene correspondences · DSP matching · RPCA · Low-rank matrix

1 Introduction

Dense correspondence between images across scenes is a new problem in computer vision, which focuses on images with different scenes but sharing similar semantic content. This new field has brought many interesting applications [1–4]. The main challenges for this problem are the serious intra-class variations, such as appearance and background difference. To address these, Kim *et al.* [5] proposes a deformable spatial pyramid (DSP) matching method by regularizing match consistency at multiple spatial levels, which obtains higher matching quality. As shown in Fig. 1(c), the warped images keep the geometrical structure of query image and the colour information of example image. Nevertheless, the generated warped image is not smooth.

To find out what causes this non-smoothness, we investigate the flow fields generated by DSP. Flow field is referred as the pixel displacements from the query image to the example image. Method in paper [6] is followed to visualize the flow fields where hue and saturation represent the orientation and the magnitude of each flow vector respectively. As showed in Fig. 1(d), the flow fields are structure-regular globally except for certain uniformly distributed noises which make the warped images unsmooth. A second order derivative of each flow field is further implemented to investigate the displacement changes of neighboring pixels, which is visualized in Fig. 1(e) in grey colors where white represents the zero value.

© Springer International Publishing Switzerland 2016
A. Campilho and F. Karray (Eds.): ICIAR 2016, LNCS 9730, pp. 377–384, 2016.
DOI: 10.1007/978-3-319-41501-7_43

(a)   (b)   (c)   (d)   (e)

Fig. 1. Examples of DSP method. First two columns: source image pair to match. Third column: generated image by warping the second image to the first one using the estimated correspondences by DSP. Forth column: the estimated flow field. Fifth column: second order derivative image of each flow field.

As shown in Fig. 1(e), the second order derivative of each point in the flow fields is very close to 0 except for certain grey values, which indicates the changes of neighboring pixels' displacements are very similar. Moreover, similar displacement changes reveal flow field substantially has a low rank. Besides, comparing Fig. 1(d), (e), we find pixels whose flow vector's second order derivatives are in grey colors are exactly those randomly distributed noises, which inspires us to decompose the flow field into a low-rank term and a sparse term (see Fig. 2). Furthermore, Robust Principle Component Analysis (RPCA) [7] is popular for recovering the low-rank component from certain observation by solving the convex program. Motivated by this, we use RPCA to recover the low-rank term from the flow field generated by DSP. Afterward, the obtained low-rank term is taken as the final flow field while densely matching images.

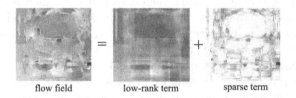

flow field   low-rank term   sparse term

Fig. 2. Example of flow field decomposing.

To validate the idea, a variety of qualitative and quantitative experiments are conducted. The proposed approach is also compared with DSP on two different datasets: VGG and LMO. Experiments show that our method obtains smoother warped image and higher matching accuracy than DSP.

2 Related Work

Researches on densely matching images from different scenes but sharing similar semantic content are mainly based on two frameworks: SIFT flow [8] and Deformable Spatial Pyramid (DSP) matching [5].

SIFT flow adopts the computational framework of optical flow to build the correspondences by matching dense SIFT descriptors instead of pixels, which is capable of producing dense pixel-to-pixel correspondences but lacks invariance to scale changes. To overcome this weakness, lots of methods are proposed. Such as, Hassner et al. [9] raise a Scale-Less SIFT method by extracting dense sift features at multiple scales. Qiu et al. [10] present a Scale-Space SIFT Flow method by adding a scale factor in the energy function and optimizing the scale field and flow field using an iterative framework. Tau and Hassner [11] propose a propagation based method by propagating the scales of sparse interest points to its neighbors.

Different with the pixel-level operation of SIFT flow, DSP regularizes match consistency at multiple spatial levels by building a pyramid graph. This spatial model makes DSP more robust to image variations, which motivates many researchers to work based on the framework of DSP. Such as, Hsu et al. [12] combines DSP with adaptive feature selection and dynamic neighborhood construction, which outperforms many previous works. However, the adaptive feature selection is very time consuming. Hur et al. [13] propose a Generalized Deformable Spatial Pyramid (GDSP) matching method by taking rotations and scales into account. This GDSP effectively preserves the geometry information of objects. However, it gains no obvious improvement on matching genetic scene images.

3 Approach

3.1 RPCA Theory Review

Suppose that there is a matrix $D \in R$ and it can be decomposed as $D = A + E$ where A has low rank and E is sparse. RPCA theory is proposed to recover A and E from D by solving the following objective function:

$$\min_{A,E} \quad \|A\|_* + \gamma\|E\|_1$$
$$subject\ to \quad D = A + E \tag{1}$$

Here, $\|A\|_*$ represents the nuclear norm of matrix A and E_1 the L_1 norm of matrix E.

However, this is an NP-hard problem. Inspired by Matrix Rank Minimization theory [14] and Compressed Sensing [15], RPCA exploits the Principal Component Pursuit to estimate the optimal solution by minimizing the weighted combination of a nuclear norm and a L_1 norm:

$$\min_{A,E} \quad \|A\|_* + \gamma \|E\|_1$$
$$\text{subject to} \quad D = A + E \tag{2}$$

Here, $\|A\|_*$ represents the nuclear norm of matrix A and E_1 the L_1 norm of matrix E.

As discussed in [7], the low-rank matrix can be efficiently recovered using convex optimization under broad conditions, such as the presence of gross errors and outlying observations. Even when the sparse matrix is relatively dense, the low-rank matrix also can be recovered if the weight constant is chosen appropriately [16].

3.2   Improved DSP with RPCA

To establish correspondences across scenes, DSP uses a spatial pyramid graph model which includes two layers: a grid-cell layer and a pixel-level layer. In the model, each grid cell is defined as a node and neighboring nodes within the same level or across adjacent levels are connected except for nodes in pixel-level layer which are only connected to their father nodes in order to improve computational efficiency.

So in the pixel-level layer, DSP only imposes smoothness constraint between each pixel and its father node without regulating smoothness between neighboring pixels. As a consequence, pixels having same father node are matched to the location where their father node is matched. Yet, nearby pixels are not necessarily matched to nearby locations, which mainly resulting in those noises in the flow field making the warped image unsmooth, as illustrated in Fig. 1(c). Actually, neighboring pixels should have similar displacements, which is the essence of entailing a smoothness constraint between neighboring nodes [5, 8].

As discussed in Sect. 1, if ignoring these noises, the flow field is globally structure-regular. Regular structures naturally have very low intrinsic dimensionality [17]. In mathematics, the regular-structured component is essentially low-rank. It is verified by conducting the second order derivative of the flow field in Sect. 1. Thus, we are inspired to use the RPCA to recover the regular-structured term in the flow field and take it as the final correspondence between images.

Let w be the flow field between one image pair by DSP and $w(p) = (u(p), v(p))$ ($u \in U, v \in V$) denotes the flow vector of the pixel at $p = (x, y)$. RPCA is then implemented on U and V respectively. Our optimization objectives are defined as:

$$\min_{U_0,E_X} \quad rank(U_0) + \gamma \|E_X\|_0$$
$$\text{subject to} \quad U = U_0 + E_X \tag{3}$$

and

$$\min_{V_0,E_Y} \quad rank(V_0) + \gamma \|E_Y\|_0$$
$$\text{subject to} \quad V = V_0 + E_Y \tag{4}$$

Here, E_X and E_Y are the sparse terms. The objectives are further relaxed by the convex optimization as:

$$\min_{U_0,E_X} \quad \|U_0\|_* + \gamma\|E_X\|_1$$
$$subject\ to \quad U = U_0 + E_X$$
(5)

and

$$\min_{U_0,E_X} \quad \|V_0\|_* + \gamma\|E_Y\|_1$$
$$subject\ to \quad V = V_0 + E_Y$$
(6)

Figure 3 shows some examples by DSP and our approach respectively. The warped images generated by our approach are obviously smoother than ones by DSP.

Fig. 3. Examples of different methods. First row: image pairs to match. Second and third rows: results by DSP and our approach respectively, where the left is the warped image from the second to the first while the right is the flow field.

4 Experiments

4.1 Datasets and Metrics

To the best of our knowledge, there are no standard database and criterion for evaluating the quality of densely matching images across scenes. So we follow the evaluation methods in [9]. That is, the matching accuracy is estimated on two different tasks: object matching and scene matching using existing VGG [18] and LabelMe Outdoor (LMO) [3] datasets respectively.

Object Matching. VGG dataset is used for this task which has 8 different sets. Images in each set have 5 specific variations and all have the ground truth correspondences. To estimate the corresponding accuracy, we use the ratio of correct (RoC) matches metric and follow the setting in [12] that matching is considered correct if the corresponding location falls within T pixels from the ground truth. T is set as 0.005 of the image dimension. Besides, label transfer accuracy (LT-ACC) and intersection over union (IoU) metrics are also used to estimate label transfer accuracy. For each set in VGG, 20 pairs of images are randomly picked used for the experiments.

Scene Matching. LMO dataset is used for this task. Images in it are mostly outdoor scenes and are annotated. As DSP does, we randomly split the dataset into two parts where one is used as query images while the other is used as example images. In theory matching can be implemented on any image pairs. However, the correspondences will be meaningless if the image pair share no similar local structures. To avoid this, for each query image, its nearest example image is first searched using GIST [3], and the correspondences are then built between them. To measure the matching quality, label transfer accuracy (LT-ACC) metric is used by counting how many pixels are correctly labelled based on the ground truth while transferring the class label of each pixel in the example image to its corresponding pixel in the query image.

4.2 Implementation Details

DSP extracts SIFT descriptors of 16×16 patch size using the VLFeat library and sets the constant weight α as 0.005. To compare with it, we maintain the same parameters. For the parameter γ in RPCA (see formula (6)), through lots of experiments, we find when γ is set as 0.03, the result is fine mostly. So γ is fixed as 0.03.

4.3 Quantitative Result

Table 1 shows mean scores of our approach and DSP under different metrics. For the RoC metric, our approach outperforms DSP by about 10 points, which benefits from the key essence of the proposed approach that it is designed to improve the corresponding location accuracy. Besides, our approach gains about 1 point and 2 points under LT-ACC and IoU respectively. For LT-ACC and IoU, the accuracy is estimated by only counting how many pixels are correctly labelled as background or foreground. So it is not suitable for determining whether corresponding locations are precise, which is the main reason that our results under LT-ACC and IoU are not obviously improved compared with DSP.

Table 1. Quantitative results

Approach	Dataset			
	VGG			LMO
	RoC	LT-ACC	IoU	LT-ACC
DSP(%)	76.07	77.27	68.67	73.18
Ours(%)	86.89	78.25	70.72	74.24

4.4 Qualitative Result

To further exhibit the ability, our approach is applied to scene parsing [3] using LMO dataset. A couple of visual comparisons with DSP are illustrated in Fig. 4. We see the reshaped instances by DSP are unsmooth and fractured. Especially, DSP fails to recover contours of the objects. In contrast, our approach obtains more visually meaningful correspondences and correspondences in object regions are much smoother.

Fig. 4. Examples of different methods. First row: image pairs to match. Second and third rows: results by DSP and our approach separately, where the left is the warped image from the second image to the first one according to the correspondences, while the right is the label transferred image on which pixel labels are marked by colors, denoting one of the classes in the LMO dataset as shown in the last column. (Color figure online)

5 Conclusion and Future Work

In this paper, a RPCA-based approach is proposed to improve the existing DSP method. As discussed, the warped image by DSP is unsmooth. By exploring the flow field generated by DSP, we find the flow field can be decomposed into an addiction of a low-rank component and a sparse component, which inspires us to use RPCA to refine the flow field. Experiments show that our approach generates the much smoother warped images and it explicitly improves the performance of DSP, which is significantly important for computer vision tasks, such as image retrieval, and video depth estimation etc. Though our approach is primarily designed for DSP, it provides a new way to improve the matching quality for image matching and could be further applied to other advanced methods.

Acknowledgement. This work is supported in part by National Natural Science Foundation of China under Grant No. 61175014, and the Fundamental Research Funds for the Central Universities of China.

References

1. Barnes, C., Shechtman, E., Goldman, D.B., Finkelstein, A.: The generalized patchmatch correspondence algorithm. In: Daniilidis, K., Maragos, P., Paragios, N. (eds.) ECCV 2010, Part III. LNCS, vol. 6313, pp. 29–43. Springer, Heidelberg (2010)

2. HaCohen, Y., Shechtman, E., Goldman, D.B., Lischinski, D.: Non-rigid dense correspondence with applications for image enhancement. ACM SIGGRAPH **30**(4), 70:1–70:9 (2011)

3. Liu, C., Yuen, J., Torralba, A.: Nonparametric scene parsing via label transfer. IEEE Trans. Pattern Anal. Mach. Intell. (PAMI) **33**, 2368–2382 (2011)

4. Karsch, K., Liu, C., Kang, S.B.: Depth extraction from video using non-parametric sampling. In: Fitzgibbon, A., Lazebnik, S., Perona, P., Sato, Y., Schmid, C. (eds.) ECCV 2012, Part V. LNCS, vol. 7576, pp. 775–788. Springer, Heidelberg (2012)

5. Kim, J., Liu, C., Sha, F., Grauman, K.: Deformable spatial pyramid matching for fast dense correspondences. In: Proceedings of the IEEE Conference on Computer Vision and Pattern Recognition (CVPR), pp. 2307–2314 (2013)

6. Baker, S., Scharstein, D., Lewis, J., Roth, S., Black, M.J., Szeliski, R.: A database and evaluation methodology for optical flow. Int. J. Comput. Vis. (ICCV) **92**(1), 1–31 (2007)

7. Candès, E.J., Li, X., Ma, Y., Wright, J.: Robust principal component analysis? J. ACM **58**(3), 11:1–11:30 (2011)

8. Liu, C., Yuen, J., Torralba, A.: Sift flow: dense correspondence across scenes and its applications. IEEE Trans. Pattern Anal. Mach. Intell. (PAMI) **33**(5), 978–994 (2011)

9. Hassner, T., Mayzels, V., Zelnik-Manor, L.: On sifts and their scales. In: IEEE Conference on Computer Vision and Pattern Recognition (CVPR), pp. 1522–1528 (2012)

10. Qiu, W., Wang, X., Bai, X., Yuille, A.L., Tu, Z.: Scale-space SIFT flow. In: Applications of Computer Vision (WACV), pp. 1112–1119 (2014)

11. Tau, M., Hassner, T.: Dense correspondences across scenes and scales. IEEE Trans. Pattern Anal. Mach. Intell. (PAMI) **38**(5), 875–888 (2016)

12. Hsu, K.J., Lin, Y.Y., Chuang, Y.Y.: Robust image alignment with multiple feature descriptors and matching-guided neighborhoods. In: IEEE Conference on Computer Vision and Pattern Recognition (CVPR), pp. 1921–1930 (2015)

13. Hur, J., Lim, H., Park, C., Ahn, S.C.: Generalized deformable spatial pyramid: geometry-preserving dense correspondence estimation. In: IEEE Conference on Computer Vision and Pattern Recognition (CVPR), pp. 1392–1400 (2015)

14. Natarajan, B.K.: Sparse approximate solutions to linear systems. SIAM J. Comput. **24**(2), 227–234 (1995)

15. Candès, E.J., Romberg, J., Tao, T.: Robust uncertainty principles: exact signal reconstruction from highly incomplete frequency information. IEEE Trans. Inf. Theor. **52**(2), 489–509 (2006)

16. Ganesh, A., Wright, J., Li, X., Candes, E.J., Ma, Y.: Dense error correction for low-rank matrixes via principal component pursuit. In: Information Theory Proceedings (ISIT), pp. 1513–1517 (2010)

17. Liang, X., Ren, X., Zhang, Z., Ma, Y.: Repairing sparse low-rank texture. In: Fitzgibbon, A., Lazebnik, S., Perona, P., Sato, Y., Schmid, C. (eds.) ECCV 2012, Part V. LNCS, vol. 7576, pp. 482–495. Springer, Heidelberg (2012)

18. Mikolajczyk, K., Schmid, C.: A performance evaluation of local descriptors. IEEE Trans. Pattern Anal. Mach. Intell. (PAMI) **27**(10), 1615–1630 (2005)

An Approach to Improve Accuracy
of Photo–to–Sketch Matching

Georgy Kukharev[1], Yuri Matveev[2(✉)], and Paweł Forczmański[1]

[1] West Pomeranian University of Technology, 71-210 Szczecin, Poland
{gkukharev,pforczmanski}@wi.zut.edu.pl
[2] ITMO University, 197101 Saint Petersburg, Russia
matveev@mail.ifmo.ru

Abstract. The problem of automatically matching sketches to facial photos is discussed. The idea presented is based on generating a population of sketches which imitates sketches generated from verbal descriptions provided by a virtual group of witnesses in forensic practice. Structures of benchmark photo–sketch databases are presented that are intended to model and implement a face photo retrieval by a given sketch. A new component of these databases is a population of sketches that represents each separate class of original photos. In this case, the original sketch is transformed into such population and then within this population we find a sketch that is similar to the given sketch. We demonstrate results of experiments based on proposed methods for photo to sketch matching on CUFS and CUFSF databases.

Keywords: Facial photo · Sketch · Photo–to–sketch matching

1 Introduction

An analysis of publications on sketch–based face recognition revealed its high complexity and low performance [1,2]. This fact is due to the following reasons. The first one is related to low quality of sketches, drawn by artists or generated in criminalistics systems. The second one is related to immature technology (ideas, methods and practice) of photo–sketch matching and also lack of experience in such matching. The third one is due to a lack of publicly available benchmark databases of sketches and flaws in these databases. We have to note that the last reason is fundamental and inhibits the development of methods of photo–sketch matching. A baseline framework for photo–sketch matching was presented in [3]. Few solutions for above listed problems are shown in [4–6].

The idea presented in this paper is based on the assumption that as we do not know *apriori* an original photo, we have to increase the representativeness of a sketch database. This can be made by generating a population of sketches which imitates sketches created according to verbal descriptions of group of L witnesses in a criminal investigation (be referred to as Forensic Sketch).

© Springer International Publishing Switzerland 2016
A. Campilho and F. Karray (Eds.): ICIAR 2016, LNCS 9730, pp. 385–393, 2016.
DOI: 10.1007/978-3-319-41501-7_44

Two methods of generating such populations are presented in [4]. In the first one, a given sketch is modified L times by changing facial parameters and shifting an image within facial area. Sketches generated in such a way form the population of the first type (Population 1). The second method implements a procedure of cumulative averaging of sketches from Population 1 and sketches generated in such a way form the population of the second type (Population 2). Both methods can be applied to any photos, for example to mug-shots or ordinary photos.

The examples of generated sketches from Populations 1 and 2 are shown in Fig. 1, where a sketch from Population 1 has visible changes in the width and height of the face area and a sketch from Population 2 has visible changes in all parameters of the original model with additionally blurred edges of facial primitives and textures.

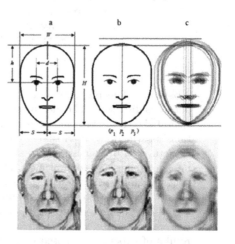

Fig. 1. A given sketch (a), sketches from Population 1 (b) and Population 2 (c), and their models

The main parameters of a face model are following: W – face width; H – face height; S – distance to the facial symmetry axis; h – distance to the eyes line; d – distance between centers of eyes.

The algorithm for generating Population 1 is following. We form $L > 2$ new sketches from a given sketch by geometrical changes in a facial area. We assume that the facial area occupies no less than 80 % of the whole image. For every $l = 1, 2, ..., L$ we define three parameters p_1, p_2 and p_3. Parameters p_1 and p_2 determine changes in H and W of the given sketch (or facial image) which in turn change h and d. The parameter p_3 determines changes in S. We calculate parameters p_i using a generator of random numbers and mapping this values into the interval $\pm a$ so that:

$$\forall i \in \{1, 2, 3\} \; p_i = sgn\left(r_i^{(n)}\right)\left[ar_i^{(u)}\right], \tag{1}$$

where $r^{(n)}$ and $r^{(u)}$ - normally and uniformly distributed random numbers, respectively; sgn - sign of the number, $[.]$ - integer part of the value, and a - scale factor, that varies from 1 to A, A - maximum extent of changes. The parameter a can be related, for example, with the number of pixels that correspond to the changes (increase or decrease) in the central part of a face or position of an eyes line or a face symmetry axis.

We have to note the following:

1. The modification of sketches and their representation in the form of Population 1 emulate the acquisition of new data from a group of witnesses. Such a solution allows to construct better presentation of a sketch from available data and to enhance the accuracy of photo-to-sketch matching.
2. The comparison may be performed with an average (for the whole population) sketch or with each sketch from a population, for example, on the basis of majoritarian mechanisms or mixtures of experts [7].
3. The transformation of sketches of Population 1 to sketches of Population 2 improves the similarity in photo–sketch pairs. The marked effect in conjunction with the mechanisms mentioned in previous item leads to further enhancement of the accuracy of photo–sketch matching.

In matching sketches from Populations 1 and 2 with the given sketch we were focused on the subjective similarity of these sketches. We observed a significant decrease of Structural SIMilarity index (SSIM) [8,9] for sketches from Population 1 (case of inaccurate given parameters) and an increase for sketches from Population 2, see Fig. 2. As we expected, the SSIM index for sketches from Population 1 changes randomly, while for Population 2 the SSIM index increases incrementally with increasing the sketch index (the number of averaged sketches from Population 1).

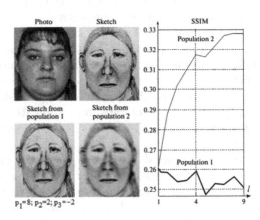

Fig. 2. Original photo, composite forensic sketch (http://prikol.i.ua/view/474038), sketches from Populations 1 and 2, and corresponding values of the SSIM index

These observations are based on experiments on CUHK Face Sketch and CUHK Face Sketch FERET databases [10,11], and also on open access databases of sketches and corresponding photos. These observations also confirm that using sketches from Populations 1 and 2 can improve the accuracy of photo–sketch matching. As shown in [12], the accuracy of photo–sketch matching depends directly on the number of sketches per original photo.

2   Structure of "Photo–Sketch" Databases

To develop methods of photo–sketch matching for the task of sketch–based photo retrieval we can use publicly available CUHK databases [10,11]: Face Sketch database (CUFS) and Face Sketch FERET database (CUFSF), where each class consists of an original photo and a corresponding sketch. However, in CUHK databases there are only sketches which were generated automatically from original photos (Viewed Sketch) and then corrected manually by artists (Artist Sketch). Moreover, collections of photos in these databases are very small. For practical applications such collections of sketches are insufficient due to two reasons. The first one is related to the fact that CUHK databases don't contain any needed metadata. The second one is related to the fact that anthropometric face alignment, implemented in CUHK databases, is practically unattainable in real–life scenarios. This is due to the fact that we do not know in advance how the original photo looks like. Thus parameters of the face photo are unknown, and we do not know if it corresponds to the given verbal description and to the generated sketch based on it. That is why in this paper we discuss a method of generating populations of sketches that have to be added to available databases as their extension in order to overcome above problems. Each class (subject) in a new database consists of Photo (P), Viewed Sketch (VS), Artist Sketch (AS) and Forensic Sketch (FS), respectively.

Let us note that if original sketches AS and FS are not available, subsets of sketches from Populations 1 and 2 can be generated from VS as their approximation. In this case such a modification (produced by a method from [4]) imitates gathering new data from a group of witnesses. Even with sketches from Population 1 we can solve the task of photo–sketch matching effectively enough. The transformation of data from Population 1 into Population 2 increases the similarity in photo–sketch pairs and the accuracy of photo–sketch matching correspondingly.

Geometric facial features in sketches (width and height, symmetry, shift, etc.) change to some extent only and a range of changes may depend on various factors. In case of VS, changes in geometric facial features depend only on one constant - the distance between centers of eyes in the original photo. However, in case of a single original photo and a corresponding single sketch VS it may be insufficient to build a representative class of sketches in Populations 1 and 2. In order to overcome this limitation, a database has to contain multiple images for each class, taking into account parameter d, as shown in Table 1.

Table 1. A structure of an extended database with Populations 1 and 2

Class k	Distance between the center of the eyes (d)				
	d_1	d_2	d_3		d_L
	P_1	P_2	P_3		P_L
	VS_1	VS_2	VS_3	...	VS_L
	AS_1	AS_2	AS_3		AS_L
	FS_1	FS_2	FS_3		FS_L
	Population 1	Population 1	Population 1		Population 1
	Population 2	Population 2	Population 2		Population 2

Let us consider an example how to create sketches for the extended database. In Fig. 3 the original photo (FERET database, class no. 91), three sketches from Population 1 (upper row) and three sketches from Population 2 (lower row) are presented. Given sketches are the result of changing in the parameter $d = \{45, 46, 47\}$ and 9 randomly chosen values of p_1, p_2, p_3 for each d. Then, sketches from Population 1 were used to create sketches of Population 2. Figure 3 presents sketches from Populations 1 and 2 with the highest value of SSIM with the original photo. Sketches with the highest SSIM have one common feature – an equal distance between centers of the eyes ($d = 44$).

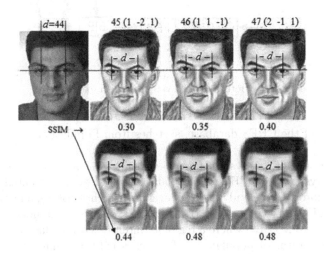

Fig. 3. Results of sketch-photo matching

The first and the most important conclusion is that irrespective to sizes of an original photo and generated sketches (Population 1), it is possible to find their matching by altering the distance between centers of eyes and using SSIM as a similarity criterion. The same can be applied to sketches from Population 2. The second conclusion is that SSIM depends not only on exact equality of distances between centers of the eyes, but obviously also on a texture of a sketch. For such cases, an extended photo–sketch database contains an extra information, important for recognition.

3 Experiments

3.1 Experiments on CUFS Database

Based on 100 original sketches from the CUFS database we generated new subsets of sketches of Populations 1 and 2, with $A = 3$. Using both original and generated data we conducted three experiments with the same subset of photos (used as references), but with different subsets of sketches: original sketches from

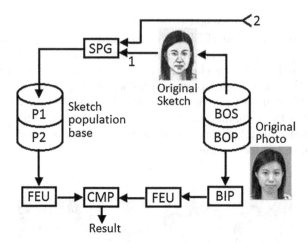

Fig. 4. Structure of the system used in experiments

the test part of the CUFS database; sketches from Population 1; sketches from Population 2.

The structure of the system for experiments is shown in Fig. 4. The main parts of the system are CUHK/CUFS databases that are represented by a block of original photos (BOP) and a block of original sketches (BOS); a feature extraction unit (FEU) and a comparator (CMP). The system was extended with a block of image processing (BIP) where a region of interest within a face is selected and blurred; a generator of populations of sketches (SPG); a database that stores sketches of Populations 1 and 2. The input 2 is a source of new populations of sketches generated by an external generator.

In the first experiment on matching original sketches from the CUHK database with original photos we used a simple schema to compare features extracted directly from original sketches and photos. In second and the third experiments original photos are preprocessed before feature extraction (region of interest within a face is selected and blurred) and Populations 1 and 2 of sketches instead of a single original sketch are used. The aim of experiments was to search an original photo (P) in the CUFS database by a given sketch (S) and evaluate this search accuracy numerically/qualitatively.

The dimensions of original photos and sketches (gray–scale images) are 250×200 pixels. A feature extraction procedure is based on the two-dimensional discrete cosine transform (2D DCT) of original images (photos and sketches). To represent the images we used values starting from the upper–left corner of the spectral matrix of order g, which are selected by the "zigzag" method [7]. In this case a model of a facial area is described by $g(g+1)/2$ spectral components.

The accuracy of retrieval (Retrieval Rate–RR) is calculated as the ratio of R correctly found photos to a total number of K search attempts and is expressed in percents. Therefore $RR = \frac{R}{K}100\,\%$ where K is the maximum number of search attempts that is equal to the number of photo–sketch pairs [13]. The classifier is implemented basing on the criterion of minimum distance (CMD) in the L_1 metric with rank $= 1$ [14]. The task of classification of sketch S_j is reduces to calculation of distances:

$$dis(k) = distance(P_k, S_j), \ \forall k \ and \ \forall j \leq K. \tag{2}$$

Index k corresponds to the minimum value of $dis(k)$ that defines the maximum of proximity (or similarity) measure between a sketch S_j and a photo P_k in a database. The result of retrieval is considered correct if $j \equiv k$.

At a priori unknown value of g, in each experiment there is a variational task on selecting the "best value of g". To solve it we have performed 40 attempts to search for $10 \leq g \leq 50$. The number of selected spectral components in this case was in the range from 55 to 1275.

Dynamics of RR for original sketches and photos is presented by the curve a in Fig. 5. The accuracy of photo retrieval by the given sketch (or sketch classification) increases with increasing the value g, and reaches maximum of only $\approx 83\,\%$, in spite of original photo–sketch pairs have a significant level of SSIM.

In this scenario, every original sketch from the CUFS database is represented by L additional sketches in Populations 1 and 2. Thus, each original photo taken from the FERET database is compared with L sketches from every class. In this case the classification of a sketch $S(j,l)$ is reduces to the calculation of all distances:

$$dis(k,l) = distance(P_k, S_{j,l}), \ \forall k, \forall l \leq L \ and \ \forall j \leq K. \tag{3}$$

Index k, that corresponds to the minimal value of $dis(k,l)$, defines the maximum of a similarity measure between a sketch $S_{j,l}$ and a photo P_k among all photos in a database. As earlier, the result of retrieval is true if $j \equiv k$.

Dynamics of the RR for sketches from Population 1 is represented by the curve b in Fig. 5. It should be noted, that results are worse than we expected, taking into consideration properties of sketches from Population 1. Dynamics of the RR for sketches from Population 2 is represented by the curve c in Fig. 5. In comparison with the curve "a" this result is higher on average by $30\,\%$. Moreover, $RR = 100\,\%$ is already achieved at $g = 35$. This high value of RR is mainly the result of the following factors: specific properties of sketches from Population 2; using the area of interest in original photos and sketches; blurring the selected face area in an original photo (an averaging filter with a window of size 5×5 or 7×7). The first factor

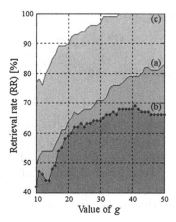

Fig. 5. Results of face photo retrieval with different populations of sketches

contributed approximately 20 %, while the second and the third ones added together approximately 10 % to the observed increase.

The in–depth analysis of the results unveils that a modification of original images in first two experiments makes it possible to increase the recognition rate up to 10 %. Only within the third experiment (where we used sketches from Population 2) the desirable result with the recognition rate up to 100 % has been achieved. Experimentally we have proved that the usage of sketches from Populations 1 and 2 with $A \in \{5, 7, 10\}$ gives RR reduced by 5–10 % on average. It is caused by lack of additional anthropometric alignment of original sketches and photos. Unfortunately, such an alignment, as practice shows, is not always possible due to the unavailability of original photos.

3.2   Experiments on FERET and CUFSF Databases

To investigate influence of anthropometric alignment on the accuracy of photo–sketch matching we have built and used our own database that contains 220 photo-sketch pairs from the CUFSF database harmonized by facial geometric parameters using reference points defined in the CUFSF database. Each image in a pair represents a selected facial area of 160×128 pixels in gray scale. The alignment was performed automatically using the express method presented in [7].

Table 2. Results of photo–sketch matching on the CUFSF database

Popul. no.	Measure	Rank of the result of classification for $g = 21$									
		1	2	3	4	5	6	7	8	9	10
1	no	168	20	11	9	6	1	1	1	1	2
	%	76.4	9.1	5	4.1	2.7	0.45	0.45	0.45	0.45	0.9
Cumulative sum [%]			85.4	90.5	94.6	97.3	97.75	98.2	98.65	**99.1**	100
2	no	190	13	8	4	3	0	0	0	1	1
	%	86.4	5.9	3.6	1.8	1.4	0	0	0	0.45	0.45
Cumulative sum [%]			92.3	95.9	97.7	**99.1**	99.1	99.1	99.1	99.55	100

Further, from this initial database of sketches new sketches of Population 1 with the parameter $A \leq 3$ and from them sketches of Population 2 have been generated. Face photo retrieval based on sketches from Population 2 has been done. We calculated a rank of correct classification and a cumulative sum of results up to $rank = 10$. The results are summarized in Table 2 and they are better than ones presented in [15] and competitive to ones presented recently in [16].

4   Conclusions

Evaluating the results we can note that the accuracy of matching photos from the FERET database with sketches from the CUFSF database (which were transformed into sketches of Population 2) is equal to 86.4 % for rank 1 and more than 99 % for rank 5. Such high accuracy is related to both quality of original sketches from CUFS and CUFSF databases, and proposed solutions with new populations of sketches.

Acknowledgments. This work was partially financially supported by the Government of the Russian Federation, Grant 074-U01.

References

1. Klare, B.F., Li, Z., Jain, A.K.: Matching forensic sketches to mug shot photos. IEEE T. Pattern Anal. **33**(3), 639–718 (2011). 646
2. Hu, H., Klare, B., Bonnen, K., Jain, A.K.: Matching composite sketches to face photos: a component-based approach. IEEE Trans. Info Forens. Secur. **8**(3), 191–204 (2013)
3. Klum, S., Klare, B., Han, H., Jain, A.K.: Sketch based face recognition: forensic vs. composite sketches. In: Proceedings of ICB, pp. 1–8 (2013)
4. Kukharev, G., Buda, K., Shchegoleva, N.: Sketch generation from photo to create test databases. Przeglad Elektrotechniczny (Electrical Review) **9**(2), 97–100 (2014)
5. Kukharev, G., Buda, K., Shchegoleva, N.: Methods of face photo-sketch comparison. Pattern Recogn. Image Anal. **24**(1), 102–113 (2014)
6. Bobulski, J., Kubanek, M.: Person identification system using sketch of the suspect. OPT APPL **4**(42), 865–873 (2012)
7. Hitrov, M.V.: Methods of Facial Image Processing, Recognition in Biometrics, 388 p. SPb, Politechnika (2013). (in Russian)
8. Wang, Z., Bovik, A.C.: A universal image quality index. IEEE Signal Proc. Let. **9**(3), 81–84 (2002)
9. Wang, Z., Bovik, A.C., Sheikh, H.R., Simoncelli, E.P.: Image quality assessment: From error measurement to structural similarity. IEEE T. Image Process **13**(1), 1–14 (2004)
10. CUHK Face Sketch Database (CUFS). http://mmlab.ie.cuhk.edu.hk/archive/facesketch.html
11. CUHK Face Sketch FERET Database. http://mmlab.ie.cuhk.edu.hk/cufsf
12. Zhang, Y., Ellyson, S., Zone, A., Gangam, P., Sullins, J., McCullough, C., Canavan, S., Yin, L.: Recognizing face sketches by a large number of human subjects: a perception-based study for facial distinctiveness. In: Proceedings of the FG 2011, Santa Barbara, California, March 21–25, pp. 707–712 (2011)
13. Phillips, P.J., Moon, H., Rizvi, S.A., Rauss, P.J.: The FERET evaluation. In: Wechsler, H., Phillips, P.J., Bruce, V., Soulie, F.F., Huang, T.S. (eds.) Face Recognition: From Theory to Applications. Springer, Berlin (1998)
14. Li, S.Z., Jain, A. (eds.): Handbook of Face Recognition. Springer, London (2011)
15. Tang, X., Wang, X.: Face sketch recognition. IEEE T. Circ. Syst. Vid. **14**(1), 50–57 (2004)
16. Peng, C., Gao, X., Wang, N., Li, J. Graphical Representation for Heterogeneous Face Recognition, arXiv preprint arXiv:1503.00488 (2015)

Motion and Tracking

Bio-inspired Boosting for Moving Objects Segmentation

Isabel Martins[1,2(✉)], Pedro Carvalho[2,3], Luís Corte-Real[3,4], and José Luis Alba-Castro[1]

[1] University of Vigo, Vigo, Spain
[2] School of Engineering, Polytechnic Institute of Porto, Porto, Portugal
`mis@isep.ipp.pt`
[3] INESC TEC, Porto, Portugal
[4] Faculty of Engineering, University of Porto, Porto, Portugal

Abstract. Developing robust and universal methods for unsupervised segmentation of moving objects in video sequences has proved to be a hard and challenging task. State-of-the-art methods show good performance in a wide range of situations, but systematically fail when facing more challenging scenarios. Lately, a number of image processing modules inspired in biological models of the human visual system have been explored in different areas of application. This paper proposes a bio-inspired boosting method to address the problem of unsupervised segmentation of moving objects in video that shows the ability to overcome some of the limitations of widely used state-of-the-art methods. An exhaustive set of experiments was conducted and a detailed analysis of the results, using different metrics, revealed that this boosting is more significant when challenging scenarios are faced and state-of-the-art methods tend to fail.

Keywords: Bio-inspired motion detection · Video segmentation

1 Introduction

Segmentation of moving objects in video sequences is a fundamental step in many computer vision applications. Therefore, the identification of changing or moving areas in a video is a crucial step. Despite the large number of methods proposed in the literature to address the unsupervised segmentation of moving objects, none has been able to fully deal with complex and challenging scenarios that include poor lighting conditions, sudden illumination changes, shadows and parasitic background motion.

Comprehensive reviews of background subtraction (BS) approaches have been presented in [1, 2]. Although they provide an overview of existing methods, the results reported by different authors have not been computed on a common dataset, making it hard to establish fair comparisons. Also, many datasets do not contain a balanced set of videos presenting real application challenges. Moreover, metrics used to evaluate the average algorithms' performance do not reveal how they perform frame by frame. Recent research has shown that methods appear to be complementary in nature, with the best-performing methods being beaten by combining several of them [3].

Recently, a considerable number of image processing modules inspired in biological models of the human visual system have been explored [4–6]. The ultimate goal is to copy the recognition capability of the human visual system. The image processing

© Springer International Publishing Switzerland 2016
A. Campilho and F. Karray (Eds.): ICIAR 2016, LNCS 9730, pp. 397–406, 2016.
DOI: 10.1007/978-3-319-41501-7_45

occurring at the level of the human retina allows not only noise and illumination variation removal, but also static and dynamic contours enhancement. Hence, this approach can be used for illumination normalization and motion detection.

This paper proposes a new scheme to address the problem of unsupervised segmentation of moving objects, which exploits the fusion of information obtained from two inherently different approaches: a bio-inspired motion detection method, using low-level information from the modeling of the human visual system, and a BS algorithm based on pixel color information. The biologically inspired model of the human retina presented in [6] has been adopted for the former. Experiments were performed with several BS algorithms showing that our method consistently improves the results, particularly in complex situations, where the BS algorithms critically fail.

The paper is organized as follows. Section 2 introduces the bio-inspired model of the retina that motivated our proposal. Section 3 presents the bio-inspired motion segmentation method. The experimental setup and the obtained results are presented in Sects. 4 and 5, respectively. Final conclusions are presented in Sect. 6.

2   The Retina Model

Figure 1 presents the global architecture of the adopted retina model [6] as a combination of low-level processing modules. Basically, it is a layered model with: (1) photoreceptors, where local contrast is enhanced; (2) outer plexiform layer (OPL), where the non-separable spatio-temporal filtering removes spatio-temporal noise and enhances spatial high-frequency contours while reducing or removing the mean luminance; (3) inner plexiform layer (IPL), with two channels: the parvocellular (Parvo) channel, dedicated to spatial analysis enhancing static contours contrast, and the magnocellular (Magno) channel that enhances moving contours and removes static ones.

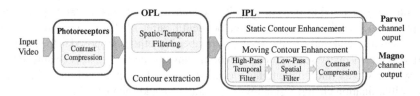

Fig. 1. The retina model proposed in [6].

As our goal is to extract the regions with moving contours, we will focus on the Magno channel output. A temporal effect is introduced on its output signal. This effect is modeled by a first order high-pass temporal filter, with transfer function given by (1), where τ is the temporal constant of the filter. This filter enhances changed areas. Its output is smoothed by a spatial low-pass filter. Finally, local contrast compression enhances the resulting contour information.

$$A(z) = b\frac{1 - z^{-1}}{1 - bz^{-1}} \quad \text{with} \quad b = e^{-1/\tau} \tag{1}$$

The Magno channel output signal magnitude is dependent on the velocity of the moving areas, with high response for fast moving areas and null response for static regions. The response of the filter is also stronger for moving contours perpendicular to the motion direction. The tuning of the temporal constant allows the adjustment of the response to temporal changes in the scene. A low value allows the enhancement of only fast changes whereas a higher value allows the enhancement of slower changes. It affects not only the response to the contours of moving objects, but also to parasitic background motion. The response decays with time leading to fuzzy contours.

3   Bio-inspired Hybrid Segmentation Method

The proposed bio-inspired hybrid segmentation, represented in Fig. 2, merges information from two inherently different approaches: (1) the bio-inspired motion segmentation that identifies regions of motion; (2) a BS method, based on pixel color information, that extracts the silhouettes of the moving objects. The final foreground mask, called *HybridMask*, is obtained by merging the outputs of the two modules.

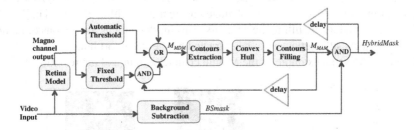

Fig. 2. Block diagram of the bio-inspired hybrid segmentation method

The bio-inspired motion segmentation consists of the segmentation of the Magno channel output signal of the retina model, which allows the detection of transient events (motion, changes) with reduced noise errors even in difficult lighting conditions. It is a low spatial frequency signal that gives a coarse representation of contours enabling motion blobs to be reliably extracted.

The high-pass temporal filter of the Magno channel introduces a temporal effect on the output signal, clearly visible as a trace left by the moving objects. This parameter can be set up in the configuration of the model, allowing tuning of the retina model to the characteristics of the input video sequence. However, in all the experiments reported, the default value (2.0) was used. The variable delay introduced by the filter depends on the value of its temporal constant. Hence, if the range of the apparent velocities of the objects is known in advance, a delay can be introduced in the BS module to compensate for this delay. However, experimental results have shown that, with the temporal constant used, a null delay provides good results.

The Magno segmentation process leads to the definition of the Magno Moving Areas Mask, M_{MAM}. The process can be summarized as follows. Let M be the Magno channel output signal. In the absence of moving objects, its magnitude is very low, corresponding to residual noise. In the presence of moving objects, the magnitude of M takes higher values in the neighborhood of moving contours. First, a Magno Motion Detection Mask, M_{MDM}, is created according to:

$$M_{MDM}(x,y,t) = \begin{cases} 1, & \text{if } (M(x,y,t) > T_{Var} \quad or \quad HybridMask(x,y,t-1) = 1 \\ & or(M(x,y,t) > T_{Low} \quad and \quad M_{MAM}(x,y,t-1) = 1)) \\ 0, & otherwise \end{cases} \quad (2)$$

T_{Var} is a dynamically changing global threshold, taking the value of 2.5 standard deviations of the magnitude of the Magno channel output signal. To get temporally stable regions of motion, the M_{MDM} is connected to the previous M_{MAM} by adding pixels with a value above a fixed value T_{Low} (experimentally set to 15.0) that were set in the previous M_{MAM}. The Magno segmentation fails to detect still foreground objects as it relies on motion information. To avoid loosing stopped foreground objects, pixels that were set in the previous *HybridMask* are also added to the M_{MDM}.

Finally, to create the M_{MAM} from the M_{MDM}, a connected component analysis is performed to extract the exterior closed contours. To avoid highly non-convex blobs, the convex hull of these contours is calculated using the algorithm presented in [8]. The final M_{MAM} is obtained by filling the contours. This mask contains the regions of motion where the objects silhouettes are to be extracted by the BS algorithm.

Figure 3 shows an example of the Magno channel output and the resulting M_{MAM}.

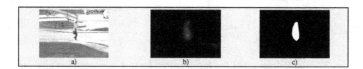

Fig. 3. (a) Input frame, (b) Magno channel output (M), (c) Magno Moving Areas Mask (M_{MAM})

As stated before, the Magno channel output signal gives a fuzzy representation of contours. This allows the extraction of temporally stable motion blobs, but not the precise contours of the objects. Thus, a pixel-level BS algorithm based on pixel color information is needed to extract these contours. Experiments were performed with several state-of-the-art BS algorithms, reported in [3]. However, other algorithms could be used in this module. The fact that GMM is widely used, and that finding the best parameter set for a particular application is not a trivial task, often leads to the use of the default parameters. For this reason, we decided to include it in our experiments using those settings. For each input frame, the foreground mask resulting from the BS algorithm is referred to as *BSmask*.

The fusion step combines the complementary information resulting from the two approaches to enhance overall detection accuracy. The Magno segmentation produces spatially and temporally coherent regions due to the spatio-temporal integration performed by the retina. These results are robust to spatio-temporal noise, global illumination changes and soft shadows, but the masks tend to be larger than the objects due to the fuzziness of the contours. On the other hand, BS algorithms perform well in extracting the silhouettes of foreground objects in a large number of situations, but are less robust. Their performance is also highly dependent on the correct tuning of the parameters. The fusion step uses the regions provided by the Magno channel segmentation to focus the foreground detection. The final foreground mask, *HybridMask*, is created according to:

$$HybridMask(x, y, t) = \begin{cases} 1, & \text{if } M_{MAM}(x, y, t) = 1 \quad and \quad BS_{mask}(x, y, t) = 1 \\ 0, & \text{otherwise} \end{cases} \tag{3}$$

4 Experimental Setup

An exhaustive set of experiments was conducted to evaluate the performance of the proposed method compared with the base BS method. Only one set of parameters was used for all the videos. The default parameter set was used for the setup of the retina model (available in OpenCV). The bio-inspired motion segmentation module is running with no configurable parameters. For evaluation purposes, several alternatives were used as BS method: MOG2, refers to the masks outputted by MOG2, available in OpenCV, using default parameters; GMM [7], KNN [7], AMBER [11], CwisarDH [12], Spectral360 [13], SuBSENSE [14] and FTSG [15] refer to the computed masks made available in the CDnet site [9]. These masks were generated with the parameters adjusted to maximize overall performance.

The experiments were conducted on the complete set of videos of the CDnet 2014 Dataset [9]. Evaluation was performed using the ground truth (GT) segmentation provided along with the videos. Each mask can have 5 labels: *Moving*, corresponding to foreground pixels; *Static*, corresponding to background pixels; *Shadow* corresponding to moving shadows; *Non-ROI* corresponding to regions outside the ROI; *Unknown* corresponding to pixels whose status is unclear.

The following seven metrics are often used to rank BS methods [3, 10]: Recall (Re), Specificity (Sp), False Positive Rate (FPR), False Negative Rate (FNR), Percentage of Wrong Classifications (PWC), Precision (Pr) and F-measure. We assessed the proposed and base methods over each video by computing these metrics, followed by a category-average and an overall-average metric. In our comparisons, the F-measure was used as an indicator of performance since, as reported in [3, 10], it correlates most strongly with the rankings produced by evaluation algorithms.

Considering the image segmentation as a partition, a metric based on the normalized symmetric distance between partitions, d_{sym}, was proposed in [16]. This metric has shown to be consistent with the subjective evaluation that a human observer would make and can provide an error value for each of the frames.

These complementary metrics allowed us to evaluate the improvement achieved by the proposed method, and identify failures. When computing the metrics, pixels classified as *Shadow* are considered as *Static* and pixels classified as *Non-ROI* or *Unknown* are discarded.

5   Analysis of Results and Discussion

Table 1 shows the average values for the first set of metrics across all categories for the overall set of videos. The proposed bio-inspired boosting method consistently outperforms the base method. As expected, as the base BS algorithm quality improves, the boosting achieved by the fusion with the bio-inspired motion segmentation is lower. However, for the eight algorithms tested, the overall measures improve using the hybrid method even if, for some categories, there is some marginal decrease in performance. There are also some scenarios where we should not expect to achieve improvements with the proposed method, like in the intermittent object motion category. Table 2 shows the average F-measure for each category. Mind that the best methods are complex algorithms that already combine different approaches.

Table 1. Overall results across all categories.

Method	Re	Sp	FPR	FNR	PWC	Pr	F-measure
MOG2	0.535	0.979	0.021	0.464	3.836	0.508	0.430
Hybrid-MOG2	**0.542**	**0.972**	**0.011**	**0.457**	**2.910**	**0.670**	**0.515**
GMM	0.660	0.971	0.028	0.339	4.052	0.611	0.568
Hybrid-GMM	**0.669**	**0.972**	**0.028**	**0.331**	**4.026**	**0.623**	**0.579**
KNN	0.662	0.980	0.020	0.338	3.363	0.675	0.596
Hybrid-KNN	**0.670**	**0.980**	**0.019**	**0.329**	**3.314**	**0.687**	**0.607**
AMBER	0.722	0.963	0.020	0.278	2.808	0.712	0.666
Hybrid-AMBER	**0.720**	**0.965**	**0.018**	**0.279**	**2.647**	**0.724**	**0.673**
Spectral360	0.748	0.951	0.015	0.252	2.370	0.718	0.690
Hybrid- Spectral360	**0.741**	**0.952**	**0.014**	**0.258**	**2.283**	**0.729**	**0.694**
CwisarDH	0.681	0.977	0.006	0.319	1.536	0.775	0.706
Hybrid-CwisarDH	**0.687**	**0.978**	**0.005**	**0.312**	**1.475**	**0.787**	**0.742**
SuBSENSE	0.806	0.974	0.009	0.194	1.663	0.752	0.742
Hybrid-SuBSENSE	**0.802**	**0.975**	**0.008**	**0.198**	**1.615**	**0.759**	**0.745**
FTSG	0.786	0.975	0.007	0.214	1.272	0.775	0.746
Hybrid-FTSG	**0.785**	**0.976**	**0.007**	**0.215**	**1.247**	**0.781**	**0.750**

The evaluation of the results using the partition distance metric, d_{sym}, computed frame by frame, gives us a new insight about the performance of the bio-inspired method compared to the base ones. Unlike the F-measure, this is an error measure and, therefore, a lower value means higher quality. To illustrate, Table 3 shows the average F-measure and average d_{sym} for the video *streetCornerAtNight* from the *Night Videos* category, one of the most difficult categories [3]. This video consists of traffic scenes captured at night and the main challenge is to deal with low-visibility of vehicles and their very strong headlights that cause halos and reflections on the street. The learning of the background and foreground detection by the BS methods critically fail in these scenes. However, the retina model processing acts on the input frame for illumination normalization, strongly attenuating variations of illumination. Figure 4, on the left, shows the evolution of the d_{sym} metric from frame 800 to frame 2999 for different base algorithms alone and with boosting. As illustrated, all the algorithms tend to fail in the same frames, corresponding to the most difficult situations, and in these frames the bio-inspired segmentation achieves a significant improvement in the quality of the segmentation. Figure 4, on the right, illustrates the evolution of the F-measure from frame 956 to frame 998, where the d_{sym} shows the first peak (shadowed region). It is clear that the d_{sym} results are consistent with the F-measure results.

Table 2. Average % of improvement in F-measure for each category and across all categories.

Category	MOG2	GMM	KNN	AMBER	Spectral360	CwisarDH	SuBSENSE	FTSG
badWeather	16.09	1.71	1.67	-0.11	-0.25	0.48	0.06	-0.04
baseline	11.23	1.10	0.79	0.50	-0.04	0.72	-0.11	-0.11
cameraJitter	20.87	0.64	0.73	0.04	-0.23	0.63	0.05	0.13
dynamicBackground	89.64	2.11	1.60	0.18	-0.20	1.20	0.04	-0.09
intermittentObjectMotion	-2.60	0.20	-0.71	0.06	-0.41	0.55	-0.85	0.61
lowFrameRate	5.69	1.17	1.88	1.46	-0.01	2.81	-0.11	1.46
nightVideos	18.95	8.30	8.48	11.39	8.12	7.74	6.09	2.55
PTZ	17.49	2.76	2.98	1.56	3.45	4.04	0.28	1.69
shadow	9.43	1.70	2.47	0.63	0.27	0.74	-0.09	0.04
thermal	0.26	1.08	0.82	0.12	-0.32	0.75	0.23	0.32
turbulence	84.59	0.56	0.59	0.02	0.04	0.00	0.03	0.08
Overall	**19.79**	**1.76**	**1.76**	**0.97**	**0.64**	**1.40**	**0.39**	**0.45**

Table 3. Average F-measure and average d_{sym} for video *streetCornerAtNight*.

Frame # 800-2999		MOG2	GMM	KNN	AMBER	Spectral360	CwisarDH	SuBSENSE	FTSG
F-measure	BS only	0.174	0.336	0.349	0.395	0.445	0.350	0.604	0.568
	Hybrid	**0.306**	**0.453**	**0.447**	**0.465**	**0.550**	**0.481**	**0.618**	**0.606**
d_{sym}	BS only	0.034	0.021	0.020	0.018	0.019	0.021	0.013	0.014
	Hybrid	**0.021**	**0.016**	**0.016**	**0.015**	**0.015**	**0.016**	**0.012**	**0.013**

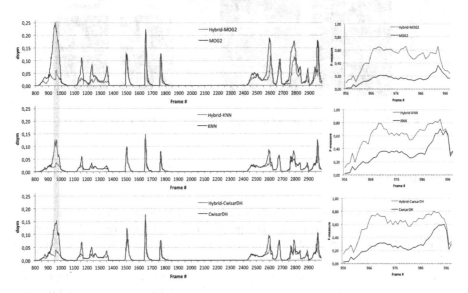

Fig. 4. Left: Evolution of d_{sym} from frame 800 to frame 2999. Right: Evolution of F-measure from frame 956 to frame 998 (shadowed region) of video *streetCornerAtNight*. (Color figure online)

Table 4 reports some of the results obtained for the video *copyMachine* from the *Shadow* category, an indoor scene with very noticeable shadows. The hybrid segmentation shows to be much less sensitive to shadows, failing only on very hard shadows.

Figure 5 shows the original frame, the GT, the *BSmasks* and the *HybridMasks* for frame 968 of the video *streetCornerAtNight*, on the left, and frames 2778 and 2816 of the video *copyMachine*, on the right.

Table 4. Average F-measure and average d_{sym} for video *copyMachine*.

Frame # 500-3399	MOG2	Hybrid-MOG2	KNN	Hybrid-KNN	AMBER	Hybrid-AMBER	CwisarDH	Hybrid-CwisarDH
F-measure	0.506	**0.522**	0.623	**0.653**	0.658	**0.678**	0.878	**0.895**
d_{sym}	0.062	**0.058**	0.056	**0.051**	0.054	**0.050**	0.032	**0.029**

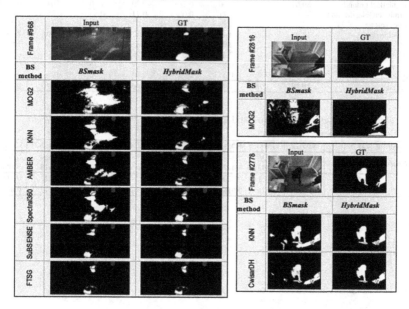

Fig. 5. Foreground masks. Left: video *streetCornerAtNight*. Right: video *copyMachine*.

6   Conclusions

This paper proposes a bio-inspired hybrid method for the unsupervised segmentation of moving objects in video sequences. The proposed method improves well-known and widely used state-of-the-art algorithms in complex situations where these fail. The fusion of the BS method with the proposed bio-inspired motion segmentation greatly reduces the number of false positives. Hence, the combination of the two approaches boosts overall detection accuracy. A detailed analysis of the results, using complementary types of metrics, has revealed that these improvements are more significant when the BS method faces more difficult scenarios, like challenging illumination conditions or shadows, and fails. It must be highlighted that all the experiments in all the testing scenarios were run with the same set of parameters. After the detailed analysis of the results and the identification of the scenarios where the proposed method significantly boosts the segmentation, future work will concentrate in finding the best set of parameters to apply in each situation and automatically adjust them in real time.

Acknowledgements. Work supported by the Galician Regional Government under agreement for funding the Atlantic Research Center for Information and Communication Technologies (AtlantTIC) and research contract GRC2014/024 (Modalidade: Grupos de Referencia Competitiva 2014) and project "TEC4 Growth - Pervasive Intelligence, Enhancers and Proofs of Concept with Industrial Impact/NORTE-01-0145-FEDER-000020", financed by the North Portugal Regional Operational Programme (NORTE 2020), under the PORTUGAL 2020 Partnership Agreement, and through the European Regional Development Fund (ERDF).

References

1. Bouwmans, T.: Traditional and recent approaches in background modeling for foreground detection: an overview. Comput. Sci. Rev. **11**, 31–66 (2014)
2. Elhabian, S.Y., El-Sayed, K.M., Ahmed, S.H.: Moving object detection in spatial domain using background removal techniques — state-of-art. Recent Patents Comput. Sci. **1**, 32–54 (2008)
3. Wang, Y., Jodoin, P.-M., Porikli, F., Konrad, J., Benezeth, Y., Ishwar, P.: CDnet 2014: an expanded change detection benchmark dataset. In: Proceedings of IEEE Workshop on Change Detection (CDW-2014) at CVPRW-2014, pp. 387–394 (2014)
4. Itti, L., Koch, C., Niebur, E.: A model of saliency-based visual attention for rapid scene analysis. IEEE Trans. Pattern Anal. Mach. Intell. **20**(11), 1254–1259 (1998)
5. Reinhard, E., Devlin, K.: Dynamic range reduction inspired by photoreceptor physiology. IEEE Trans. Visual. Comput. Graph. **11**, 13–24 (2005)
6. Benoit, A., Caplier, A., Durette, B., Herault, J.: Using human visual system modeling for bio-inspired low level image processing. Comput. Vis. Image Underst. **114**(7), 758–773 (2010)
7. Zivkovic, Z., van der Heijden, F.: Efficient adaptive density estimation per image pixel for the task of background subtraction. Pattern Recogn. Lett. **27**(7), 773–780 (2006)
8. Sklansky, J.: Finding the convex hull of a simple polygon. Pattern Recogn. Lett. **1**, 79–83 (1982)
9. ChangeDetection.NET (CDNET). http://www.changedetection.net
10. Goyette, N., Jodoin, P., Porikli, F., Konrad, J., Ishwar, P.: Changedetection.net: a new change detection benchmark dataset. In: Proceedings of IEEE Workshop on Change Detection (CDW-2012), at CVPRW-2012 (2012)
11. Wang, B., Dudek, P.: A fast self-tuning background subtraction algorithm. In: Proceedings of IEEE Workshop on Change Detection (CDW-2014), at CVPRW-2014 (2014)
12. Gregorio, M.D., Giordano, M.: Change detection with weightless neural networks. In: Proceedings of IEEE Workshop on Change Detection (CDW-2014), at CVPRW-2014 (2014)
13. Sedky, M., Moniri, M., Chibelushi, C.C.: Spectral-360: a physical-based technique for change detection. In: Proceedings of IEEE Workshop on Change Detection (CDW-2014), at CVPRW-2014 (2014)
14. St-Charles, P.-L., Bilodeau, G.-A., Bergevin, R.: Flexible background subtraction with self-balanced local sensitivity. In: Proceedings of IEEE Workshop on Change Detection (CDW-2014), at CVPRW-2014 (2014)

15. Wang, R., Bunyak, F., Seetharaman, G., Palaniappan, K.: Static and moving object detection using flux tensor with split gaussian models. In: Proceedings of IEEE Workshop on Change Detection (CDW-2014), at CVPRW-2014 (2014)
16. Cardoso, J.S., Corte-Real, L.: Toward a generic evaluation of image segmentation. IEEE Trans. Image Process. **14**(11), 1773–1782 (2005)

A Lightweight Face Tracking System for Video Surveillance

Andrei Oleinik[✉]

ITMO University, St. Petersburg, Russia
andrey_oleynik@niuitmo.ru

Abstract. This paper deals with the problem of multiple face tracking for video surveillance systems. Although a considerable number of
object tracking approaches have been developed, the video surveillance
scenario allows additional assumptions on the tracker's operational environment. Based on these assumptions, the tracking system including a
face detector and a tracking subsystem is presented. The tracking algorithm is based on computationally inexpensive Binary Robust Independent Elementary Features (BRIEF). The implemented tracking system
was tested on two video sequences. The experiments showed a significant
improvement of processing rate over a detector-based system along with
a reasonable tracking quality.

Keywords: Object tracking · Face tracking · Computer vision · Binary
descriptors · Video surveillance

1 Introduction

Visual object tracking is a challenging and practically significant problem of
computer vision. Development of compact and powerful video processing hardware is gradually expanding tracking systems' application area, which includes
video surveillance, traffic monitoring, robotics, audiovisual applications [1].

At this point, many object tracking algorithms have been developed. Surveys
on the problem are provided in [2,3] and experimental comparative studies of
existing trackers are carried out in [4,5].

This paper deals with multiple face tracking for video surveillance systems.
Several challenges are related to this problem. First, the *drifting problem* emerges
due to the tracking error accumulation. Moreover, mismatch errors are possible,
when the tracker confuses faces with intersecting trajectories. Finally, repeating
detection of new faces may cause a substantial degradation of processing rate.

On the other hand, advantage can be taken of the specific operating conditions of surveillance cameras. For example, it is reasonable to consider faces
as rigid objects and employ a set of simple and computationally cheap features
to construct a face representation. Furthermore, a face detector can not only
find new faces in the camera's field of view but also correct tracking errors. Utilization of tracking methods removes the necessity to run the detector on every
frame, significantly improving the operating rate.

© Springer International Publishing Switzerland 2016
A. Campilho and F. Karray (Eds.): ICIAR 2016, LNCS 9730, pp. 407–414, 2016.
DOI: 10.1007/978-3-319-41501-7_46

This paper presents a fast and simple multiple face tracking system comprised of a face detector and a tracking subsystem. The tracking algorithm uses binary descriptors. So far, various descriptor-based tracking approaches have been proposed [6–9]. In this paper, Binary Robust Independent Elementary Features (BRIEF) [10] are employed. The key feature of BRIEF is its outstanding computational efficiency. In contrast to [11], BRIEF does not require special hardware (such as high performance graphic processors) for a high-speed implementation.

An approach utilizing BRIEF has been proposed [8]. There, static and dynamic dictionaries are used. In contrast, the proposed method applies BRIEF solely for estimation of faces' inter-frame translation without such dictionaries.

2   Methods

2.1   Problem Statement

In general case, the multiple object tracking problem is stated as follows. For every video frame and for every object (e.g. face, car, person) the tracker provides: the object's *location* (e.g. bounding box, ellipse, centroid), the object's *identifier* and, optionally, the *confidence level*. In this paper, a rectangular bounding box is used as a location. Hereinafter, a set of locations with the same identifier is referred as *track*. Depending on the specific case, the assignment of a new track to an occluded object can be considered as an error or not. Some authors have developed models that can handle lost objects [12]. In the presented method, an occluded object always acquires a new identifier. If needed, simple face recognition methods can be applied to join the tracks.

The considered face tracking scenario is a special case of the outlined above object tracking problem. Thus, additional assumptions can be introduced:

- The position and the orientation of the surveillance camera are fixed, its focus distance and field of view are constant and known;
- There are no significant non-linear distortions of video frames;
- The maximum motion speed of faces does not exceed some given value;
- Deviation of each face from the frontal pose is insignificant.

These assumptions make possible the usage of simple and computationally inexpensive tracking methods. For example, this case does not require rotation invariant face feature representation. Moreover, the limitations on the maximum face movement speed make it possible to bound face search region.

2.2   System Structure Overview

Figure 1 presents the system comprised of two basic subsystems: detector and tracker. The detector processes only a relatively small fraction of frames while a computationally inexpensive approach is used to handle the rest frames.

Remark. Hereinafter, the term "tracker" denotes the subsystem that is used solely to maintain tracks, while the term "tracking system" stands for the combination of the detector and the tracker.

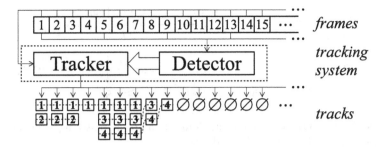

Fig. 1. Tracking system structure. Note that new tracks are created only on those frames that are processed by the detector. The tracker evaluates locations of the faces on the rest of the frames. A track can be terminated on an arbitrary frame.

The structure is *flexible* as the tracker is independent of the detection algorithm. Moreover, the right choice of the proportion of frames processed by the detector helps to reach the trade-off between the tracking quality and speed. Furthermore, the detector corrects the tracks, mitigating the drifting problem.

Here, the face detector based on cascade classifiers [13] was used. In general, any face detector can be used, for example one of those described in [14].

The tracker performs three basic functions: *tracks initialization and updating, tracks termination* and *inter-frame tracks maintenance*. While termination and maintenance of the tracks are performed on each frame, initialization and updating are carried out solely on those frames that are processed by the detector.

Tracks Initialization and Updating. First, the tracker estimates new locations of the tracked faces and terminates outdated tracks (see details below). After that, the detected faces are used to create new tracks and update the existing ones. Locations of the detected faces are compared with the existing tracks. As a result, a weighted bipartite graph is constructed (Fig. 2). Edges connect only those detection-track pairs whose overlap exceeds a predefined threshold. Then, the matching with the maximum number of edges and the minimum total cost is found as the solution of *minimum cost flow* problem [15]. This approach allows resolution of ambiguous matches (e.g., when paths of two faces cross). Then, locations of the tracks assigned to detections are corrected. The remaining detected faces are used to create tracks, while the rest tracks are not modified.

Tracks Termination. In order to prevent tracks from drifting, it is crucial to timely terminate them. To control the error accumulation, the concept of *cumulative score* C_k is introduced. On the k-th frame the *confidence score* $c_k \in (0, 1]$ is known (Sect. 2.3). Thus, C_k is defined as $C_k = \prod_{g=0}^{G} c_{k-g}$. Here, $G \geq 0$ is the age of the track since its last update or initialization. When C_k drops below a predefined threshold, the track is terminated. When the track is initialized or updated, c_k is set to 1. This approach not only suppresses tracks drifting, but also maintains them if the corresponding faces are not detected.

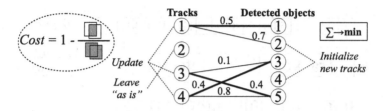

Fig. 2. Detections to tracks assignment. Note that a greedy matching algorithm would choose the edges with the costs 0.1 and 0.8.

Inter-frame Tracks Maintenance. The evaluation of the face's location on the next frame is an important component of the tracker's functionality. A tracking method based on binary descriptors is discussed in the Sect. 2.3.

2.3   Face Tracking Using Binary Descriptors

Since the face's position on the previous frame is known, the tracker computes its location on the current frame and estimates c_k. Here, *binary descriptors* are used in order to accomplish this task. Binary descriptors are local features computed in a set of *keypoints* found by a *keypoint detector*. The Hamming distance is used as a difference metric. FAST [16] keypoint detector was employed and BRIEF [10] descriptors were used. This approach leads to the following procedure:

1. In the face region of the previous frame, the keypoints are found and the descriptors are computed;
2. Based on the imposed assumptions (Sect. 2.1), the face region is extended (Fig. 3). In the extended region, keypoints and descriptors are retrieved;
3. A pairwise comparison of the descriptors from the previous and current frames is carried out. The pairs with the Hamming distance below a predefined threshold T_H are retained and used for the further computation;
4. A new location of the face is estimated (see details below).

After the descriptors comparison is performed, a set of matches is formed: $(p_n, p'_n, w_n); n = 1 \ldots N$. Here $p_n = (x_n, y_n)$, $p'_n = (x'_n, y'_n)$ — the keypoints' coordinates on the previous and current frames respectively. The weights $w_n \in [w_{min}, 1]$ are obtained from the corresponding Hamming distance values, where a zero distance leads to $w_n = 1$ and the T_H value is converted to $w_n = w_{min}$.

Taking into account the assumptions stated in Sect. 2.1, only two components are included into the *motion model*: a *shift* $(\delta x, \delta y)$ and a *uniform scale s*. The problem of these parameters estimation is reduced to the following minimization problem: $\theta = (\delta x, \delta y, s) = \arg \min_{\theta} L_w(\theta)$, where

$$L_w(\theta) = \sum_{n=1}^{N} w_n \| f(p_n, \theta) - p'_n \|^2, \quad f(p, \theta) = s \cdot p + (\delta x, \delta y). \tag{1}$$

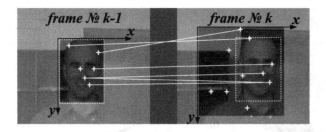

Fig. 3. Descriptors matching.

Since the coordinate transformation $f(p, \theta)$ is a linear function, θ may be obtained analytically as the solution of a system of *three* linear equations [17]. Once θ is estimated, the new location of the face is known.

The *confidence level* c_k is evaluated as follows (α is used to adjust the sensitivity of c_k to the matching error):

$$c_k = \left(1 + \alpha \cdot \min_\theta L_w(\theta) \right)^{-1}. \tag{2}$$

Since the motion model has only three degrees of freedom, the computational procedure is simple and stable. However, due to the usage of simple features many incorrect matches (i.e. *outliers*, see Fig. 3) may appear. Possible ways of dealing with this problem include setting a low (i.e. strict) threshold T_{H}, modification of weights w_n (e.g. based on distances of keypoints from the face region center) and utilization of outliers detection methods such as RANSAC [17].

3   Experimental Results

The aim of the experiments was to evaluate the system's computational efficiency and the tracking quality. The proposed solution was expected to dramatically increase the processing rate without any significant loss of the tracking quality.

The code was written in C++ using OpenCV [18] and LEMON [19] libraries. The re-trained cascade detector from OpenCV library was used.

Unfortunately, the majority of existing object tracking benchmarks have been developed for vehicle or person tracking scenarios [20,21] and thus inappropriate for the considered case. Two 352×288 records were used for evaluation (Fig. 4 (a)). *Video 1* is the part of SPEVI dataset [22]. *Video 2* is a grayscale video surveillance record. ViPER-GT [23] was used for ground truth creation.

The processing rate gain achieved by the usage of the tracker depends on the proportion of the frames processed by the detector (see Fig. 1). The higher the number of processed frames on a single detector run (*detector running period*, denoted by T_{det}), the higher the overall processing rate. The experimental relation between the average frame *processing time* and T_{det} is shown on Fig. 4 (b). Overall, the experimental results show a substantial (three-time or four-time) processing rate gain as compared with the baseline.

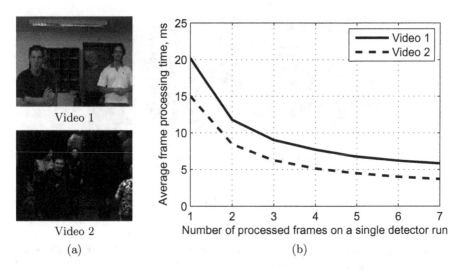

Video 1

Video 2

(a)   (b)

Fig. 4. Evaluation recordings (a) and the experimental relation between average frame processing time and $\mathcal{T}_{\text{det}}$ (b). Test video records include: motinas_multi_face_frontal sequence from SPEVI dataset (Video 1) and the surveillance recording (Video 2).

In order to estimate the system's tracking quality, *Multiple Object Tracking Accuracy* (MOTA) and *Multiple Object Tracking Precision* (MOTP) metrics [24] were adopted. MOTA is based on the tracker's *miss rate* (*miss*), *false positive rate* (*fp*) and *mismatch error rate* (*mme*). The developed system was compared with the baseline implementation, which runs the face detector on every frame (*Baseline*). The results of the comparison are presented in Table 1.

The bigger $\mathcal{T}_{\text{det}}$, the smaller is the total number of tracked objects. Essentially, this means higher *miss* along with lower *fp* and *mme*. In the extreme case, no objects are tracked (*miss* = 100 %, *fp* = *mme* = 0 %). Thus the aggregate metrics MOTA and MOTP should be used to assess overall tracking quality.

Although the degradation of MOTA is observed, it is on the acceptable level. It can be seen that the main problem is the growth of the miss rate as the $\mathcal{T}_{\text{det}}$ value increases. To avoid this problem, it is crucial to use a robust face detector: an undetected face is missed on the next $\mathcal{T}_{\text{det}} - 1$ frames.

Table 1. Experimentally estimated tracking quality.

Test video	Tested system	miss, %	fp, %	mme, %	MOTA	MOTP
Video 1	Baseline	8,40	0,57	0,19	0,91	0,29
	Tracking system, $\mathcal{T}_{\text{det}} = 3$	11,0	0,83	0,4	0,88	0,21
	Tracking system, $\mathcal{T}_{\text{det}} = 5$	13,0	0,35	0,28	0,86	0,20
Video 2	Baseline	29,0	1,4	0,46	0,70	0,25
	Tracking system, $\mathcal{T}_{\text{det}} = 3$	32,0	2,0	0,64	0,65	0,15
	Tracking system, $\mathcal{T}_{\text{det}} = 5$	36,0	1,5	0,40	0,62	0,15

Note that the tracking system has a better MOTP than the baseline (in contrast to MOTA, smaller MOTP is better). MOTP depends on multiple factors such as the quality of the ground truth and the number of detections. Faces missed by the tracking system are likely to deteriorate MOTP of the baseline. Thus, it can be considered sufficiently low for all compared implementations.

4   Conclusions

In this paper, a face tracking system for video surveillance is presented. Its structure is very simple and flexible. The tracker subsystem is based on computationally inexpensive BRIEF binary descriptors and FAST keypoint detector.

The fact that the system is developed under the particular assumptions does not mean that it will inexorably fail if these conditions are violated. Further research and experiments may discover the full potential of the approach.

The experiments have shown a significant (four-fold) improvement of the processing rate over the baseline along with reasonable tracking quality. Consequently, various face detectors can be integrated into the presented system to create a fully functional high-speed multiple face tracking solution.

The algorithm is easy to implement and optimize, so it may be applied not only in full-scale video surveillance systems, but in embedded solutions integrated into surveillance cameras.

Acknowledgements. This work was partially financially supported by the Government of the Russian Federation, Grant 074-U01. The author expresses his sincere appreciation to Professor Georgy Kukharev, his scientific adviser; Yuri Matveev, Head of SIS Department; and Aleksandr Melnikov for their critical remarks and advice that significantly improved this paper.

References

1. Melnikov, A., Akhunzyanov, R., Kudashev, O., Luckyanets, E.: Audiovisual liveness detection. In: Murino, V., Puppo, E. (eds.) ICIAP 2015. LNCS, vol. 9280, pp. 643–652. Springer, Heidelberg (2015)
2. Yilmaz, A., Javed, O., Shah, M.: Object tracking: a survey. ACM Comput. Surv. **38**(4), 1–45 (2006)
3. Yang, H., Shao, L., Zheng, F., Wang, L., Song, Z.: Recent advances and trends in visual tracking: a review. Neurocomputing **74**(18), 3823–3831 (2011)
4. Smeulders, A.W.M., Chu, D.M., Cucchiara, R., Calderara, S., Dehghan, A., Shah, M.: Visual tracking: an experimental survey. IEEE Trans. Pattern Anal. Mach. Intell. **36**(7), 1442–1468 (2014)
5. Kristan, M., Matas, J., et al.: The visual object tracking VOT2015 challenge results. In: IEEE International Conference on Computer Vision Workshops, pp. 1–23 (2015)
6. Ta, D.N., Chen, W.C., Gelfand, N., Pulli, K.: SURFTrac: efficient tracking and continuous object recognition using local feature descriptors. In: IEEE Conference on Computer Vision and Pattern Recognition (CVPR), pp. 2937–2944. IEEE (2009)

7. Bilinski, P., Bremond, F., Kaaniche, M.B.: Multiple object tracking with occlusions using HOG descriptors and multi resolution images. In: 3rd International Conference on Crime Detection and Prevention (ICDP), pp. 1–6. IET (2009)

8. Minnehan, B., Spang, H., Savakis, A.E.: Robust and efficient tracker using dictionary of binary descriptors and locality constraints. In: Bebis, G., et al. (eds.) ISVC 2014, Part I. LNCS, vol. 8887, pp. 589–598. Springer, Heidelberg (2014)

9. Panti, B., Monteiro, P., Pereira, F., Ascenso, J.: Descriptor-based adaptive tracking-by-detection for visual sensor networks. In: IEEE International Conference on Multimedia & Expo Workshops (ICMEW), pp. 1–6. IEEE (2015)

10. Calonder, M., Lepetit, V., Strecha, C., Fua, P.: BRIEF: binary robust independent elementary features. In: Daniilidis, K., Maragos, P., Paragios, N. (eds.) ECCV 2010, Part IV. LNCS, vol. 6314, pp. 778–792. Springer, Heidelberg (2010)

11. Ishii, I., Ichida, T., Gu, Q., Takaki, T.: 500-fps face tracking system. J. Real-Time Image Process. 8(4), 379–388 (2013)

12. Pinho, R.R., Tavares, J.M.R.S.: Tracking features in image sequences with Kalman filtering, global optimization, Mahalanobis distance and a management model. Comput. Model. Eng. Sci. 46(1), 51–76 (2009)

13. Viola, P., Jones, M.: Rapid object detection using a boosted cascade of simple features. In: IEEE Computer Society Conference on Computer Vision and Pattern Recognition (CVPR), vol. 1, pp. 511–518. IEEE (2001)

14. Kukharev, G., Kamenskaya, E., Matveev, Y., Shchegoleva, N.: Methods of Facial Images Processing and Recognition in Biometrics (in Russian). Politechnika, Saint-Petersburg (2013)

15. Ahuja, R.K., Magnanti, T.L., Orlin, J.B.: Network Flows: Theory, Algorithms, and Applications, 1st edn. Prentice Hall, Upper Saddle River (1993)

16. Rosten, E., Drummond, T.W.: Machine learning for high-speed corner detection. In: Leonardis, A., Bischof, H., Pinz, A. (eds.) ECCV 2006, Part I. LNCS, vol. 3951, pp. 430–443. Springer, Heidelberg (2006)

17. Szeliski, R.: Computer Vision: Algorithms and Applications. Texts in Computer Science, 1st edn. Springer, London (2011)

18. OpenCV (open source computer vision library). http://opencv.org/

19. LEMON graph library. https://lemon.cs.elte.hu/trac/lemon

20. Li, L., Nawaz, T., Ferryman, J.: PETS 2015: datasets and challenge. In: 12th IEEE International Conference on Advanced Video and Signal Based Surveillance (AVSS), pp. 1–6. IEEE (2015)

21. Collins, R., Zhou, X., Teh, S.K.: An open source tracking testbed and evaluation web site. In: IEEE International Workshop on Performance Evaluation of Tracking and Surveillance (PETS 2005), vol. 2, p. 35 (2005)

22. Maggio, E., Piccardo, E., Regazzoni, C., Cavallaro, A.: Particle PHD filtering for multi-target visual tracking. In: IEEE International Conference on Acoustics, Speech and Signal Processing (ICASSP), vol. 1, pp. 1101–1104. IEEE (2007)

23. Doermann, D., Mihalcik, D.: Tools and techniques for video performance evaluation. In: 15th International Conference on Pattern Recognition, 2000. Proceedings, vol. 4, pp. 167–170 (2000)

24. Bernardin, K., Stiefelhagen, R.: Evaluating multiple object tracking performance: the CLEAR MOT metrics. EURASIP J. Image Video Process. 2008, 1–10 (2008)

Single Droplet Tracking in Jet Flow

Gokhan Alcan, Morteza Ghorbani, Ali Kosar, and Mustafa Unel[✉]

Faculty of Engineering and Natural Sciences, Sabanci University, Istanbul, Turkey
{gokhanalcan,morteza,kosara,munel}@sabanciuniv.edu

Abstract. Fluid systems such as the multiphase flow and the jet flow usually involve droplets and/or bubbles whose morphological properties can provide important clues about the underlying phenomena. In this paper, we develop a new visual tracking method to track the evolution of single droplets in the jet flow. Shape and motion features of the detected droplets are fused and Bhattacharyya distance is employed to find the closest droplet among possible candidates in consecutive frames. Shapes of the droplets are not assumed to be circles or ellipses during segmentation process, which utilizes morphological operations and thresholding. The evolution of single droplets in the jet flow were monitored via Particle Shadow Sizing (PSS) technique where they were tracked with 86 % average accuracy and 15 fps real-time performance.

Keywords: Jet flow · Droplet · Bubble · Morphology · Segmentation · Tracking · Bhattacharyya distance

1 Introduction

Understanding of several physical phenomena in experimental studies of biology, chemistry and medicine generally depends on the analysis of observed small entities' behaviour. These entities can be bubbles, droplets, cells or deliberately included tracer particles. Growth or shrink of the observed surfaces, abnormal motion of the tracer particles, interactions of monitored entities, size and shape characteristics of the bubbles and the droplets can provide remarkable clues about the underlying phenomena in several biomedical, chemical and microfluidic applications.

To extract the flow characteristics and to be able to manipulate small sized particles such as bubbles and droplets in several microfluidic applications, kinetical and structural information about these entities are required. Recently, droplet-based microfluidic systems aim to localize and track the droplets throughout the flow to extract their unique features [1–3]. Also, several microfluidic systems utilize advanced visualization technologies and employ state-of-the-art computer vision algorithms to understand the physics related to the performed experiments [4].

Improvements in visualization technology enabled to develop advanced measurement techniques to investigate entities in microfluidics. Particle Image Velocimetry (PIV) is a commonly used measurement technique that provides

© Springer International Publishing Switzerland 2016
A. Campilho and F. Karray (Eds.): ICIAR 2016, LNCS 9730, pp. 415–422, 2016.
DOI: 10.1007/978-3-319-41501-7_47

instantaneous velocity fields of the micro particles (seedings), which reflect the light and enable to monitor the flow [5,6]. Laser Doppler Anemometry (LDA) is another advanced measurement technique that utilizes well-known Doppler shift effect in laser beam to measure the velocity of gas or fluid flows [7]. Unlike PIV, LDA transmitting probe is targeted to a single point in gas or fluid flow. Phase Doppler Anemometry (PDA) is an extension of LDA, where unlike LDA three receiving probes measure the scattered angle of the particle to obtain coarse structural information about investigated particles [8]. Finally, Particle Shadow Sizing (PSS) is a whole field optical imaging technique, which can provide both velocity fields and shapes of particles in multiphase flows. Unlike other methods, the light source is located on the optical axis of the high speed camera and particle shadows are monitored [9].

In addition to advanced visualization technology, several micro particles, bubbles and droplets tracking algorithms have been implemented in various visualization systems to investigate the characteristics of the flow. Cheng and Burkhardt [10] developed a bubble contour tracking system with the assumption of circular shape. Okawa et al. [11] employed the bubble shape function to track the rising bubbles in a pipe. In addition to shape/contour modeling based tracking methods, Jüngst et al. [12] proposed a label free tracking for long term observation of lipid droplets throughout the cells by Coherent Anti-Stokes Raman Scattering (CARS) microscopy. Basu [13] also presented a time-resolve analysis of droplets via droplet morphology and velocimetry (DMV), which includes several preprocessing steps to distinguish foreground from background and correlation steps. Different from these methods, matching based tracking was proposed by Qian et al. [14] that utilizes genetic algorithms. The method can distinguish similar sized and shaped bubbles in even kinetic occlusion cases as well. Xue et al. [15] presented a tracking and 3D reconstruction method using stereo vision by matching correspondences of bubble distinct features from different half views.

In this paper, we develop a new vision based tracking method to track the evolution of the droplets in jet flow which can be easily adapted to several biomedical applications. Shape and motion features of detected droplets are used along with Bhattacharyya distance [16] to locate the tracked droplet(s) among candidate droplets in consecutive frames. Instead of assuming circular or elliptical boundaries, droplet boundaries are employed as they are, and the evolution of a single droplet in jet flow was tracked with the average accuracy of 86.01 %.

The organization of this paper is as follows: Sect. 2 presents the proposed approach in two steps as droplet segmentation and droplet tracking. Results are provided and discussed in Sect. 3. Finally, Sect. 4 concludes the paper with some remarks and indicates possible future directions.

2   Proposed Approach

Interactions of droplets (split, merge, stick or occlusions) during the flow, undesired illumination problems and dramatic morphological changes of the droplets can lead to decrease in the accuracy of detection and tracking. Despite the existence of advanced flow measurement techniques, robust computer vision solutions are still needed to overcome these issues. Proposed approach aims to tackle some of these problems and can be implemented in two stages as segmentation of droplets individually, and tracking of preselected single droplet in upcoming video frames.

2.1   Droplet Segmentation

Since Particle Shadow Sizing (PSS) technique is preferred as the most effective way to visualize spherical multiphase structures such as bubbles and droplets, sufficient contrast should be ensured to segment the droplet shadows. To increase the distinguishability, a stretching operation [17] is employed, which provides better histogram scale with rough uniform distribution (Fig. 1(b)).

To eliminate the noise and sharpen the edges of droplets, an appropriately selected circular structuring element is employed and morphological opening operation [18] is applied to contrast adjusted images (Fig. 1(c)). Morphologically open image is thresholded by an optimum level determined by Otsu's [19] method (Fig. 1(d)). Due to simultaneous illumination changes, thresholding may cause some gaps in shadow images that can be compensated by image filling [20] operations (Fig. 1(e)).

Finally, Connected Component Analysis (CCA) [21] is utilized to extract droplets' structural properties such as center of mass coordinates (C_x,C_y), perimeter and area that are used in tracking process.

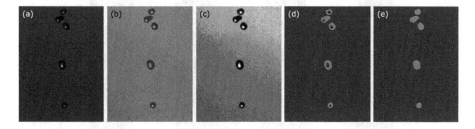

Fig. 1. (a) Original image, (b) Contrast stretching, (c) Morphological opening (d) Thresholding, and (e) Image filling

2.2   Droplet Tracking

Tracking starts with the selection of a target bubble/droplet in the segmented image. Since droplets can be monitored in at most 10 upcoming frames, they were generally selected in the frames where they first appeared. However, any detected droplet can be selected as the target droplet.

Selected droplet is represented by an object feature vector that includes both morphological and motion characteristics and can be constructed as follows:

$$Obj = (C_x, \ C_y, \ p, \ A, \ E, \ T) \tag{1}$$

where C_x and C_y are the center of mass coordinates, p is the perimeter, A is the area and E is the eccentricity of selected droplet. T is the thinness ratio [22] which can be calculated as:

$$T = \frac{4\pi A}{p^2} \qquad (2)$$

Feature vectors of each segmented droplet regions are calculated in consecutive frames by using (1). Droplet vertical center of mass is directly related to the velocity of the droplet against gravitational force, which could be assumed as slightly changing for a single droplet.

Preselected droplet feature vector (Tar) is compared with each feature vector (Obj) of single droplets in the next frame and Bhattacharyya distance [16] is employed to find the similarity between two feature vectors.

Bhattacharyya distance can be calculated as

$$D_B(Obj, Tar) = \frac{1}{4}ln\left(\frac{1}{4}\left(\frac{\sigma_{Obj}^2}{\sigma_{Tar}^2} + \frac{\sigma_{Tar}^2}{\sigma_{Obj}^2} + 2\right)\right) + \frac{1}{4}\left(\frac{(\mu_{Obj} - \mu_{Tar})^2}{\sigma_{Obj}^2 + \sigma_{Tar}^2}\right) \qquad (3)$$

where $D_B(Obj, Tar)$ is the Bhattacharyya distance between the object feature vector (Obj) and the target feature vector (Tar), σ_{Obj}^2 and σ_{Tar}^2 are variances, μ_{Obj} and μ_{Tar} are means of the object and target feature vectors, respectively. Minimum Bhattacharyya distance between these vectors would designate the targeted droplet (Fig. 2).

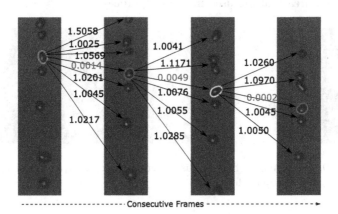

Fig. 2. Minimum Bhattacharyya distances between the target and single droplets

Bhattacharyya distance is usually employed to find most probable distribution of selected different features. Mahalanobis distance could also be used to measure the similarity; however it is a particular case of Bhattacharyya distance where standard deviations of the distributions are assumed to be the same. Thus, Bhattacharyya distance is more reliable than Mahalanobis distance.

By considering the flow direction, abnormal traveled distance are penalized via increasing the corresponding D_B (Algorithm 1). In our case, downward flow with slightly changing speed is considered. For different scenarios, a priori knowledge about the flow could be employed as well.

Algorithm 1. Single Droplet Tracking

    Construct Object feature vector via segmentation
    Initialization:
        IsTracked=true;
        d=maximum possible travel distance;
        maxDB=maximum Bhattacharyya distance to go on tracking;
    while IsTracked == true **do**
        Segment the next frame
        Construct the object feature vectors of each single droplet regions
        Order the segmented regions vertically ascending
        Calculate each of $D_B(Obj, Tar)$
        if (Tar(2)-Obj(2) < 0) || (|Tar(2)-Obj(2)| > d)
            Penalize: Increase D_B by 1
        endif
        Select the target droplet according to minimum D_B
        if $(\min(D_B) > maxDB)$
            End of tracking: IsTracked = false
        else
            Tar ← Obj
        endif
    end

---

3 Results and Discussion

The images are obtained from a Particle Shadow Sizing (PSS) system that monitors the jet flow. Around 850 shadow images are acquired and processed in the tracking algorithm. As can be seen from Table 1, minimum Bhattacharyya distances during single droplet tracking are below 0.05 with 86 % average accuracy and around 15 fps real-time tracking performance in MATLAB environment, which shows that proposed tracking method performs quite well.

Out of nearly 336 visible droplets, 5 representative droplets are analyzed here. In order to show the changes of the droplets, tracked droplets are extracted and the cropped sub-images of the tracked droplets' contours are depicted in Fig. 3. Circumference, area, thinness ratio and eccentricity information about these droplets are presented in Fig. 4.

Droplet 1 preserved its elliptical shape and just its orientation was changed during the flow. Droplet 2 and 3 underwent some dramatic changes due to their spring motion. Droplet 4 and 5 are disturbed by other droplets and their shapes and motion were changed dramatically.

Table 1. Tracking performances

Accuracy percentage	Total droplet number	Bhattacharyya distances	
		Average	Standart deviation
86.01	336	0.0460	0.4768

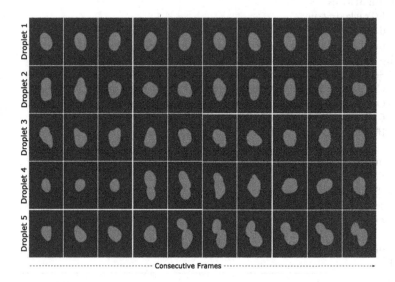

Fig. 3. Tracked droplets' contours

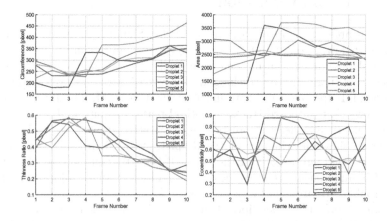

Fig. 4. Structural features of tracked droplets (Color figure online)

There may exist several slightly changing droplets in a fluid flow which may not be easily tracked even by human eyes. Assumption of circular or elliptical shapes may also fail due to dramatic changes during the fluid flow. Finally, interactions with other droplets may lead to merge, split and stick which also complicates to track the target. However, based on above examples, it is more likely that the proposed approach can handle these situations.

4   Conclusion and Future Directions

We have now presented a new visual single droplet tracking algorithm in a fluid flow. Particle Shadow Sizing (PSS) technique is utilized to monitor the droplets because of its capability of the whole field structural monitoring. Our single droplet tracking algorithm segments the droplet regions from shadow images and extract their morphological information. In upcoming frames, structural and motion information of individually detected droplets are fused and Bhattacharyya distance is employed to choose the closest candidate droplet regions. Since droplets' shapes are not assumed to be circular or elliptical, morphological changes of droplets during their evolution can be investigated.

Our tracking algorithm could achieve real time performance with 15 fps in MATLAB environment and single droplets were tracked with 86 % accuracy.

As a future work, multiple droplet tracking method will be developed to investigate the interactions between particles, bubbles and droplets with high accuracy and less execution time.

Acknowledgments. This work was supported by TUBITAK (The Scientific and Technological Research Council of Turkey) under Grant No 113S092. Equipment utilization support from Sabanci University Nanotechnology Research and Applications Center (SUNUM) is gratefully acknowledged.

References

1. Teh, S.Y., Lin, R., Hung, L.H., Lee, A.P.: Droplet microfluidics. Lab Chip 8(2), 198–220 (2008)
2. Joensson, H.N., Uhlén, M., Svahn, H.A.: Droplet size based separation by deterministic lateral displacement separating droplets by cell-induced shrinking. Lab Chip 11(7), 1305–1310 (2011)
3. Can, Z., Chen, F., Bao, N., He, H., Xu, P., Jana, S., Jung, S., Lian, H., Lu, C.: Droplet sorting based on the number of encapsulated particles using a solenoid valve. Lab Chip 13(1), 171–178 (2013)
4. Alcan, G., Ghorbani, M., Kosar, A., Unel, M.: Vision based cone angle estimation of bubbly cavitating flow and analysis of scattered bubbles using micro imaging techniques. Industrial Electronics Society, IECON 2015-41st Annual Conference of the IEEE (2015)
5. Prasad, A.K.: Particle image velocimetry. Curr. Sci. Bangalore 79(1), 51–60 (2000)
6. Brossard, C., Monnier, J.C., Barricau, P., Vandernoot, F.X., Le Sant, Y., Champagnat, F., Le Besnerais, G.: Principles and applications of particle image velocimetry. AerospaceLab 1, 1–11 (2009)

7. Durst, F., Melling, A., Whitelaw, J.H.: Principles and practice of laser-Doppler anemometry. NASA STI/Recon Technical Report A 76, 47019 (1976)
8. Bachalo, W.D., Houser, M.J.: Phase/Doppler spray analyzer for simultaneous measurements of drop size and velocity distributions. Opt. Eng. **23**(5), 235583–235583 (1984)
9. Estevadeordal, J., Goss, L.: PIV with LED: particle shadow velocimetry (PSV). In: 43rd AIAA Aerospace Sciences Meeting and Exhibit, Meeting Papers, pp. 12355–12364 (2005)
10. Cheng, D.C., Burkhardt, H.: Bubble tracking in image sequences. Int. J. Therm. Sci. **42**(7), 647–655 (2003)
11. Okawa, T., Suzuki, Y., Kataoka, I., Aritomi, M., Mori, M.: Numerical implementation of interfacial drag force for one-dimensional, two-way bubble tracking method. J. Nucl. Sci. Technol. **37**(4), 387–396 (2000)
12. Jngst, C., Winterhalder, M.J., Zumbusch, A.: Fast and long term lipid droplet tracking with CARS microscopy. J. Biophotonics **4**(6), 435–441 (2011)
13. Basu, A.S.: Droplet morphometry and velocimetry (DMV): a video processing software for time-resolved, label-free tracking of droplet parameters. Lab Chip **13**(10), 1892–1901 (2013)
14. Qian, X., Zhu, H., Yu, X., Chen, G.: Genetic algorithm based bubble matching and tracking in aerated water flows. Intell. Control Autom. **3**, 2146–2148 (2004)
15. Xue, T., Qu, L., Wu, B.: Matching and 3-D reconstruction of multibubbles based on virtual stereo vision. IEEE Trans. Instrum. Measur. **63**(6), 1639–1647 (2014)
16. Kailath, T.: The divergence and Bhattacharyya distance measures in signal selection. IEEE Trans. Commun. Technol. **15**(1), 52–60 (1967)
17. Gonzales, R.C., Woods, R.E., Eddins, S.L.: Digital Image Processing Using MAT-LAB. Pearson Prentice Hall, Upper Saddle River (2004)
18. Haralick, R.M., Sternberg, S.R., Zhuang, X.: Image analysis using mathematical morphology. IEEE Trans. Pattern Anal. Mach. Intell. **4**, 532–550 (1987)
19. Otsu, N.: A threshold selection method from gray-level histograms. Automatica **11**, 285–296 (1975)
20. Soille, P.: Morphological Image Analysis: Principles and Applications. Springer, Heidelberg (2013)
21. Haralick, R.M., Shapiro, L.G.: Computer and Robot Vision. Addison-Wesley Longman Publishing Co., Boston (1991)
22. Wu, Q., Merchant, F., Castleman, K.: Microscope Image Processing. Academic press, Boston (2010)

Video Based Group Tracking and Management

Américo Pereira[1,2(✉)], Alexandra Familiar[1,2], Bruno Moreira[1,2],
Teresa Terroso[1,4], Pedro Carvalho[1,3], and Luís Côrte-Real[1,2]

[1] INESC TEC, Porto, Portugal
americo.j.pereira@inesctec.pt
[2] Faculty of Engineering, University of Porto, Porto, Portugal
[3] School of Engineering, Polytechnic Institute of Porto, Porto, Portugal
[4] The School of Management and Industrial Studies,
Polytechnic Institute of Porto, Vila do Conde, Portugal

Abstract. Tracking objects in video is a very challenging research topic, particularly when people in groups are tracked, with partial and full occlusions and group dynamics being common difficulties. Hence, its necessary to deal with group tracking, formation and separation, while assuring the overall consistency of the individuals. This paper proposes enhancements to a group management and tracking algorithm that receives information of the persons in the scene, detects the existing groups and keeps track of the persons that belong to it. Since input information for group management algorithms is typically provided by a tracking algorithm and it is affected by noise, mechanisms for handling such noisy input tracking information were also successfully included. Performed experiments demonstrated that the described algorithm outperformed state-of-the-art approaches.

Keywords: Video · Groups · Tracking · Management

1 Introduction

Video object tracking has been an increasingly growing area of research, mainly in video-surveillance scenarios, but with applications in many other areas. In nearly all of these scenarios we can have groups of people. Due to the proximity of people in groups, its hard to understand the movement of each individual, and traditional detection and tracking algorithms tend to be less effective on these scenarios. Occlusions, unpredictable movements and merging/splitting of groups are just some associated problems. Group analysis and tracking can brings advantages, such as predicting the position of the persons in the group even under heavy occlusion. However, it also adds several challenges, including: the number of occlusions; temporal changes in the group structure; different individual trajectories within the group. An important challenge is the group definition itself. Correctly defining a group is a critical step for subsequent group handling.

© Springer International Publishing Switzerland 2016
A. Campilho and F. Karray (Eds.): ICIAR 2016, LNCS 9730, pp. 423–430, 2016.
DOI: 10.1007/978-3-319-41501-7_48

This paper proposes enhancements to a group tracking and management algorithm with the main focus of increasing robustness. This translates into a new algorithm that, as the base one, receives individual tracks as input and assists in the detection, creation and management of groups but enables increased performance, especially in the presence of tracking errors. Results show that it outperforms state-of-the-art proposals, as well as the original proposal, even when introducing common tracking errors on the input data.

The remaining of this paper is structured as follows. A brief literature review is presented in Sect. 2. The proposed algorithm enhancements are presented in Sect. 3 along with a description of experiments that were performed. The datasets and metrics used for testing and evaluation are described in Sect. 4. Finally, the conclusions and observations, as well as future work is presented in Sect. 5.

2   Group Concepts and Tracking

Detection is typically the basis of any tracking system since it is responsible for obtaining representations of objects of interest to be tracked. A survey of recent algorithms dedicated to person detection is present on [1,2]. For a more in-depth study of the underlying principles, techniques and algorithms related to video object tracking, the reader is referred to some of the many existing surveys. Aggarwal and Ryoo [3] provided a recent update to their previous surveys describing a vast number of publications with a special focus on the interpretation of human motion. Another survey was presented by Smeulders et al. [4], where a set of nineteen tracking algorithms were thoroughly evaluated and experimented.

The concept of group is viewed socially as a set of people who are in spacial proximity and interact with one another with a common goal [5]. While this is a good principle, it's not enough to identify a group. Other factors, such as size, duration, velocity and structure are also fundamental in defining and managing groups. When considering a group tracking scenario, three entities can be defined: person, group and crowd. An entity is considered to be a crowd when there is a set of people dense enough, that it becomes impossible to distinguish between individuals [6]. Some authors proposed treating a group as a set of individual entities [7] when individual segmentation is possible and see the group as a single entity [8], otherwise. Work related to group tracking is present in [9] in which the counting of pedestrians moving in groups is addressed. The estimation of the number of people present in a group is based on projection information, enabled by accurate camera calibration information. The approach presented in [10] creates a framework that includes both detection and tracking for individuals and groups with sharing of information between them. The authors used a Decentralized Particle Filter [11] to model individuals with a position and speed; for groups, a match was made between the groups and the individuals in it. In [12], the authors focused on group tracking and behaviour recognition in long sequences. The proposal started by segmenting the people in the scene, detecting the blobs, following the several objects, grouping them in more complex entities and using that information to detect events. A common problem when dealing with groups is the need to handle the exit and re-entering in the scene of its members. This adds the difficulty of deciding whether it should be considered the same group or not. In [13], a re-acquisition process was proposed using a descriptor based in co-variance matrices to model the group and deal with these situations.

3   Group Management and Tracking

3.1   Base Algorithm

The proposed solution is an evolution of the state-of-the-art algorithm described in [12] and was assessed under the same conditions. The inputs of the base algorithm are intended to be the results from a people tracking algorithm, which are first filtered in order to reduce errors. The algorithm uses a metric named Group (In)Coherence (GI) [12], which represents the probability of a set of people being a group. It is defined as the average of distance between individuals ($\bar{d}$), standard deviation of speed (σ_{speed}) and direction (σ_{dir}), each weighted differently (see Eq. 1).

$$GI = w_1 \cdot \bar{d} + w_2 \cdot \sigma_{speed} + w_3 \cdot \sigma_{dir} \; . \tag{1}$$

These values are measured over a time window T; a common value of T is 20 frames, since its sufficient time for trajectories to be long enough without adding too much delay to the system. The weights w_1, w_2, w_3 were normalized.

The algorithm consists of 4 phases: creation, update, split/merge and termination. In the creation step, trajectories of objects are analysed through the T time window and a group is created if objects are close to each other and the associated GI is valid. The update step consists on validating the GI of a group through the time window. The split step is responsible for splitting a object/objects that consistently move away from their group, resulting in a two groups. As the name suggests, the merge step is responsible for merging two groups if they are linked. Finally, the termination step erases empty groups and groups without new physical objects for a long period of time.

Identification (ID) management is performed by considering that the group ID is given by the set of people in the group. Finally, a group termination module is employed to delete any objects that have not been present in the scene for an extended period of time, which include both people and groups.

3.2   Proposed Enhancements

The base algorithm uses GI as the metric for group classification decision. The authors proposed the following weights: $w_1 = 0.7$, $w_2 = 0.15$ and $w_3 = 0.15$, which reflects the importance of the average distance between people. While using the GI criterion with a single threshold provides good results, it may cause unnecessary fragmentations. We propose several changes so that the robustness and performance of the base algorithm is augmented.

Hysteresis. We argue that using hysteresis can reduce the number of fragmentations and propose two different threshold values for the splitting and merging events, as they should only happen when the algorithm is fairly confident, even if that delays the decisions. Merge events should only happen when $GI < t_{min}$ and, likewise, splitting events should only happen when $GI > t_{max}$, where t_{min} and t_{max} represent the hysteresis thresholds values. This avoids unwanted jitter in the decisions caused by excessive splitting or premature grouping.

Average Speed. Instantaneous speed and direction represent the most immediate movement, but are noisy and often suffer from inconsistencies derived from tracking errors [12]. We propose the use of the average speed $s_{i,k}^*$ (Eq. 2) in the previous t frames, for the calculation of the speed deviation.

$$s_{i,k}^* = \frac{1}{T} \sum_{t=1}^{T} \sqrt{(P_{x,i,k} - P_{x,i,k-t})^2 + (P_{y,i,k} - P_{y,i,k-t})^2} \,, \tag{2}$$

where $P_{x,i,k}$ $P_{y,i,k}$ are the X and Y coordinates of person i in frame k. Experiments show that generally a value of 5 for T is sufficient to obtain good results.

Group Elements Distance. When a group grows, individual distances will tend to increase; but the average distance, used in the base algorithm, can remain similar (see Fig. 1a). To address this, we propose the use of distance d^*:

$$d^* = (0.75 \times \bar{d}_{center} + 0.25 \times d_{closest2}) \,, \tag{3}$$

where $\bar{d}_{center}$ is the average distance of members to the group centroid, $d_{closest2}$ is the average distance to the closest two persons. The weights were empirically determined.

Angle and Direction of Movement. The direction has been used to assess the type of movement, but in cases such as Fig. 1b where the movement is only present in one direction, it may contribute to a wrong decision in the original GI formula as the direction displacement might not suffice. Even though the two represented persons are splitting, this only happens in a single axis. Equation 4 represents how the group is spreading from their movement angle. Equation 5 represents the smallest angle between the person and the group.

$$\theta_{deviation} = \sqrt{\frac{1}{N} \sum_{i=1}^{N} (\theta_{min}(i))^2} \,, \tag{4}$$

$$\theta_{min} = min(|max(\theta_i, \bar{\theta}) - min(\theta_i, \bar{\theta}) + 180|, |\theta_i - \bar{\theta}|) \,, \tag{5}$$

where θ_i is the angle of movement of the person i and $\bar{\theta}$ is the mean angle of a group. We argue that the use of σ_{dir} to characterize the group movement is not

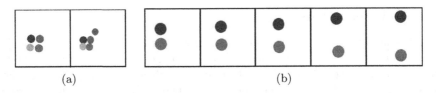

(a)   (b)

Fig. 1. Example of scenarios. (a) Two situations that have similar average distances and the base algorithm may fail and merge all persons. (b) Simulated movement of people splitting in one axis.

enough and, as such, we propose the addition of a weighted contribution of the group spreading angle (see Eq. 6).

$$\sigma^*_{dir} = 0.75 \times \sigma_{dir} + 0.25 \times \theta_{deviation} \; , \tag{6}$$

where σ_{dir} is the direction deviation used in GI. The weights were determined empirically.

Non-Linear Evaluation. The previous proposed enhancements are alternative components for the calculation of GI (Eq. 1). However, we argue that it is necessary to go further and change the way GI is used. We propose a non-linear formulation of GI, depending on the group motion (Eq. 7).

$$GI = \begin{cases} 0.85 \times d^* + 0.10 \times \sigma^*_{speed} + 0.05 \times \sigma^*_{dir} \text{ if } \bar{s} < 0.2 \\ 0.60 \times d^* + 0.15 \times \sigma^*_{speed} + 0.25 \times \sigma^*_{dir} \text{ if } \bar{s} > 0.75 \\ 0.75 \times d^* + 0.15 \times \sigma^*_{speed} + 0.10 \times \sigma^*_{dir} \text{ otherwise} \; , \end{cases} \tag{7}$$

where $\bar{s}$ is the normalized average speed of the group and σ^*_{speed} is the standard deviation of speed between entities, calculated using the speed formula s^*_i. These presented weights were obtained empirically for each type of motion.

4   Results

Group tracking data can be obtained from well known datasets such as CAVIAR [14] or BIWI [15], they have annotated data for both individuals and groups. However, these datasets miss some specific group evolution situations. One dataset that contains prominent group social interactions and annotated data is the Friends Meet dataset [16], used in different proposals on the literature. As such, we performed the evaluation of both the base algorithm and the proposed changes using the subset of 13 sequences from the Friends Meet Dataset depicting real scenarios. These sequences contain interesting and difficult group situations and have associated reference information for objective assessment. The evaluation was two-fold: without and with noise. The following Subsect. 4.1 describes the noise addition process and its importance. Next the results are presented and discussed in Subsect. 4.2.

4.1   Addition of Noise

State-of-the-art group management algorithms are often assessed using noise
free tracking data. While this has several challenges by itself, we also analyse
the algorithms with noisy data resulting in a significantly challenging task. For
the latter, we added typical tracking errors to the reference data, as characterized
in [4]: localization errors (type I); false positives (type II); false negatives (type
III). Three increasingly levels of noise were implemented, adding tracking errors
of the three types. The levels represent the quantity of noise added, resulting in
more difficult tracking data as the noise increases. To simulate errors of type I,
we performed random perturbations on the localization and size of bounding
boxes. By doing this we create a jitter in the localization of the detections and
subsequently degrade the ability to track them. False positives were simulated by
randomly adding bounding boxes with typical size and position and an associated
identification across the videos. For the errors of type III, portions of existing
tracks were randomly selected and cut from the data as a way to simulate miss
detections. For all these perturbations, uniform distributions were used.

4.2   Proposal Evaluation

Traditionally, metrics such as precision and recall have been used in detection
and tracking, but are not sufficient for evaluating groups; hence other metrics are
needed. Track Fragmentation (TF) [17] is used to capture the number of discontinuities in the group trajectory when compared to the ground truth. Another
useful metric is the Group Detection Success Rate (GDSR) [10], which represents the success hit rate of detecting groups. Therefore, the results of the algorithms were evaluated using precision, recall, GDSR and TF* $(TF^* = 1 - TF)$.
Figure 2a depicts the effect of noise in the initial algorithm. Before the addition
of noise (first bar of the columns), the metrics are above 90 % and the average
fragmentation is 0.59. The fragmentation occurs because the GI value fluctuates
around the threshold value. In the presence of tracking errors, the performance

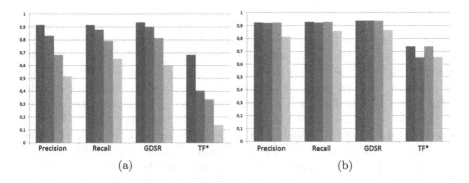

Fig. 2. Performance comparison of the initial algorithm in (a) and proposed algorithm
in (b). The bars represent, from left to right, no noise and increasing levels of noise.

drastically degrades with the increase of the noise intensity. With this its noticeable that the base algorithm fails to handle severe errors. Figure 2b depicts the average results of the proposed algorithm with the increase of noise. The comparison clearly shows that our proposal achieves better performance. An additional experiment was performed, comparing the initial algorithm [12], the proposed algorithm and the state-of-the-art algorithm $DEEPER - JIGT$ [10]. Since for the latter only GDSR values were available, the comparison was made using this metric. Our proposal obtained the best results of 93 %, while the initial algorithm and $DEEPER - JIGT$ obtained 81 % and 88.46 %, respectively. Its noticeable that the proposed algorithm modifications enable better performance, namely in the presence of noise inputs.

5   Conclusion

Object tracking in video is an unsolved problem, with proposals tending to focus on specific applications. In particular, tracking and management of groups has received significant less attention from the research community, and proposals still lack maturity and sufficient robustness.

This paper presents a group tracking and management algorithm that is an evolution of a state-of-the-art algorithm. Enhancements to the GI metric are proposed so that noisy tracking data and group dynamics have less impact in the decision criteria, resulting in a better group management. Evaluation was performed using well known sequences. The algorithms were tested in the same conditions and the addition of noise for the tracking data was also performed in order to simulate the effects of tracking in a real and uncontrolled scenario. The results show that the proposed method outperforms state-of-the-art algorithms, namely in the presence of noisy inputs.

The experiments reported show that our proposal enables a better and more robust performance and has the potential to be improved. Next steps will primarily include the preparation of additional realistic datasets and exhaustive experiments to improve the parametrization. Information about the scene, known a priori or automatically extracted, could also be used for an automatic adaptation of the parameters. For an even more in-depth and demanding assessment, the proposed algorithm should be integrated in a real people tracking algorithm and promote the exchange of information between them.

Acknowledgment. This work was partially funded by Project "TEC4Growth - Pervasive Intelligence, Enhancers and Proofs of Concept with Industrial Impact/NORTE-01-0145-FEDER-000020", financed by the North Portugal Regional Operational Programme (NORTE 2020), under the PORTUGAL 2020 Partnership Agreement, and through the European Regional Development Fund (ERDF).

References

1. Dollar, P., Wojek, C., Schiele, B., Perona, P.: Pedestrian detection: an evaluation of the state of the art. IEEE Trans. Pattern Anal. Mach. Intell. **34**(4), 743–761 (2012)
2. Nguyen, D.T., Li, W., Ogunbona, P.O.: Human detection from images and videos: a survey. Pattern Recogn. **51**, 148–175 (2016)
3. Aggarwal, J.R., Ryoo, M.S.: Human activity analysis: a review. ACM Comput. Surv. **43**, 16:1–16:43 (2011)
4. Smeulders, A.W., Chu, D.M., Cucchiara, R., Calderara, S., Dehghan, A., Shah, M.: Visual tracking: an experimental survey. IEEE Trans. Pattern Anal. Mach. Intell. **36**(7), 1442–1468 (2014)
5. Gauquelin, M., Gauquelin, F.: Dicionário de Psicologia: as idéias, as obras, os homens. Centre d'Étude et de Promotion de la Lecture, Paris (1987)
6. Junior, S.J., et al.: Crowd analysis using computer vision techniques. IEEE Signal Process. Mag. **27**(5), 66–77 (2010)
7. Kong, D., Gray, D., Tao, H.: A viewpoint invariant approach for crowd counting in Pattern Recognition. In: 18th International Conference on ICPR 2006, vol. 3, pp. 1187–1190. IEEE (2006)
8. Ali, S., Shah, M.: A lagrangian particle dynamics approach for crowdow segmentation and stability analysis. In: IEEE Conference on Computer Vision and Pattern Recognition, CVPR 2007, pp. 1–6. IEEE (2007)
9. Kilambi, P., Ribnick, E., Joshi, A.J., Masoud, O., Papanikolopoulos, N.: Estimating pedestrian counts in groups. Comput. Vis. Image Underst. **110**(1), 43–59 (2008)
10. Bazzani, L., Cristani, M., Murino, V.: Decentralized particle filter for joint individual-group tracking. In: IEEE Conference on. Computer Vision and Pattern Recognition (CVPR), pp. 1886–1893. IEEE (2012)
11. Chen, T., Schon, T.B., Ohlsson, H., Ljung, L.: Decentralized particle filter with arbitrary state decomposition. IEEE Trans. Signal Process. **59**(2), 465–478 (2011)
12. Gárate, C., Zaidenberg, S., Badie, J., Brémond, F., et al.: Group tracking and behavior recognition in long video surveillance sequences. In: International Conference on Computer Vision Theory and Applications (VISAPP), vol. 2. IEEE (2014)
13. Bak, S., Corvee, E., Bremond, F., Thonnat, M.: Multiple-shot human re-identification by mean Riemannian covariance grid. In: 8th IEEE International Conference on Advanced Video and Signal-Based Surveillance (AVSS), pp. 179–184. IEEE (2011)
14. Caviar dataset. http://homepages.inf.ed.ac.uk/rbf/CAVIARDATA1/. (Accessed on 08 February 2015)
15. Biwi dataset. http://www.vision.ee.ethz.ch/datasets/index.en.html. (Accessed on 09 February 2015)
16. Friends meet dataset. http://www.iit.it/en/datasets-and-code/datasets/fmdataset.html. (Accessed on 09 February 2015)
17. Yin, F., Makris, D., Velastin, S.A.: Performance evaluation of object tracking algorithms. In: IEEE International Workshop on Performance Evaluation of Tracking and Surveillance, Rio De Janeiro (2007)

3D Computer Vision

Calibration of Shared Flat Refractive Stereo Systems

Tim Dolereit[1,2]($\boxtimes$) and Uwe Freiherr von Lukas[1]

[1] Fraunhofer Institute for Computer Graphics Research IGD,
Joachim-Jungius-Str. 11, 18059 Rostock, Germany
tim.dolereit@igd-r.fraunhofer.de
[2] Institute for Computer Science, University of Rostock,
Albert-Einstein-Str. 22, 18059 Rostock, Germany

Abstract. The calibration of underwater camera systems differs significantly from calibration in air due to the refraction of light. In this paper, we present a calibration approach for a shared flat refractive stereo system that is based on virtual object points. We propose a sampling strategy in combination with an efficiently solvable set of equations for the calibration of the refractive parameters. Due to the independence of calibration targets of known dimensions, the approach can be realized by using stereo correspondences alone.

Keywords: Underwater camera calibration · Underwater imaging · 3D reconstruction

1 Introduction

Computer vision tasks that have to be performed underwater face significantly different challenges than those performed in air. Many approaches, such as camera calibration, are founded on the pinhole camera model which is invalid underwater due to refraction of light [9]. Therefore, beneficial measures like the reprojection error become inefficient, since refractive forward projection is computationally expensive [1]. A camera in the presence of a planar refractive interface is termed *flat refractive system* by Treibitz et al. [9]. Motivated by Agrawal et al. [1], such a system is composed of an axis and layers (see left of Fig. 1). The axis is the interface normal through the center of projection of the camera. The layers are fixed to the camera and their thickness is measured along the axis. An Interfaces is the physical boundary of a layer where refraction happens.

We propose the term *shared flat refractive stereo system* for the case of a second camera that is located behind the same interface system like in the left of Fig. 1. The refractive parameters are the orientation (denoted by angle δ in 2D) between the axis N and the optical axis A_l of the master camera as well as the layer thicknesses. The calibration processes are termed *axis determination* and *recovery of layer thickness* in the following. The pose of the slave camera is known relative to the master camera and does not count to the refractive parameters.

© Springer International Publishing Switzerland 2016
A. Campilho and F. Karray (Eds.): ICIAR 2016, LNCS 9730, pp. 433–442, 2016.
DOI: 10.1007/978-3-319-41501-7_49

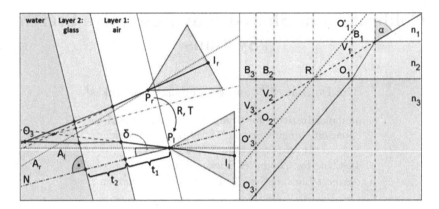

Fig. 1. Left: Refractive parameters δ, t_1 and t_2 of a shared flat refractive stereo system. Right: Magnification of the refraction area for one camera. (Color figure online)

In this work, we propose an approach for the calibration of a shared flat refractive stereo system with known refractive indices of all participating media, known glass layer thickness and a stereo camera that is calibrated for its intrinsic and relative extrinsic parameters in advance. Our contributions for the calibration of refractive parameters of a shared flat refractive stereo system are:

- the formulation of a simple set of equations that can be solved efficiently for recovery of the air layer thickness,
- a combination with a hypothesis testing strategy for axis determination that is independent of the reprojection error,
- tests on simulated and real data that show that refractive calibration can be performed from stereo correspondences alone.

2   Related Work

In the literature on underwater camera calibration refractive effects are usually supposed to be absorbed by the conventional camera parameters [8] or are handled by modeling them explicitly. Absorption is insufficient and only approximately valid in the case of an interface that is perpendicular to the image sensor. When refraction is modeled explicitly, it is possible to trace rays physically correct. Treibitz et al. [9] propose an approach for calibration of a flat refractive system that is restricted to an interface perpendicular to the image sensor. Bräuer-Burchardt et al. [2] have the same restriction for their approach for calibration of a flat refractive stereo system (no shared interface).

The setup in this work is a stereo camera with an arbitrary pose to the interface system. A valid approach is to place a known pattern onto the interface and use some kind of pose estimation from 3D-2D point correspondences algorithm as in [10]. However, it is not always possible to focus the camera on the interface and the scene simultaneously. The most common approach is to use a known calibration pattern in water [1,4].

There is only a small number of approaches that are independent of calibration targets. Sedlazeck and Koch [7] present an approach for calibration of a flat refractive stereo system from stereo correspondences. An initialization of all the parameters is necessary and optimization is performed in nested loops. Kang et al. [5] propose a method for calibration of a flat refractive system with multiple layers. A special calibration target is not needed but a restriction is that at least three refractive interfaces are necessary.

The approach most similar to ours is the one of Chen and Yang [3]. They propose an approach for calibration of a flat refractive stereo system (no shared interface) with multiple layers. The authors conclude that the estimation of multiple layers should be avoided. In contrast to Chen and Yang [3], our approach simultaneously provides a novel error measure which makes the calibration independent of the reprojection error, while being still very accurate. We do not use structured light for generation of stereo correspondences and utilize a lower number of features.

3   Virtual Object Points

The proposed approach is based on virtual object points at a location that can be non-ambiguously related to the corresponding real object point. This location (V_3) is the intersection of the interface normal through the real object point (O_3) and the backwards extended incident ray (dashed black line in Fig. 1). In the following, it will be shown how this leads to some useful simplifications in a shared flat refractive stereo system.

3.1   Relation to Real Object Points

The right side of Fig. 1 shows a magnified section of the refractions in the left side of the figure and is representative for both cameras. By ignoring the thickness of the glass layer at first, the relation

$$\frac{\overline{B_3V_3}}{\overline{B_3O_3'}} = \frac{\cos\alpha}{\sqrt{\left(\frac{n_3}{n_1}\right)^2 - \sin^2\alpha}} \tag{1}$$

can be derived by trigonometry in right-angled triangles (here triangle $B_3O_3'R$). This is constructed by the refracted ray (solid blue) that is shifted in parallel (dashed blue) to pass point R on the second refractive interface. As can be seen, the point O_3' does not coincide with the real object point O_3, resulting in an offset of distance $\overline{O_3O_3'}$. As the points O_1, O_1', O_3 and O_3' form a parallelogram, this offset is equal to the distance $\overline{O_1O_1'}$. For the sake of distinguishability of the following derivations, the triangle RB_2O_2, that is equal to the triangle RO_1O_1' is constructed. By construction, the offset distance

$$\overline{O_3O_3'} = \overline{O_1O_1'} = \overline{B_2O_2}. \tag{2}$$

Similarly to Eq. 1 and with some additional rearranging, the relation

$$\overline{B_2O_2} = \frac{\overline{B_2V_2} * \sqrt{\left(\frac{n_3}{n_1}\right)^2 - \sin^2 \alpha}}{\cos \alpha} \tag{3}$$

can be derived. The distance $\overline{B_2V_2}$ is equal to $\overline{O_1V_1}$ by construction and with a known glass layer thickness that is equal to distance $\overline{B_1O_1}$,

$$\overline{B_2V_2} = \overline{O_1V_1} = \overline{B_1O_1} - \overline{B_1V_1}. \tag{4}$$

The relation

$$\overline{B_1V_1} = \frac{\overline{B_1O_1} * \cos \alpha}{\sqrt{\left(\frac{n_2}{n_1}\right)^2 - \sin^2 \alpha}} \tag{5}$$

can again be derived similarly to Eq. 1 with some additional rearranging.

The application of Eqs. 1 to 5 results in the final formulation of a model for the relation between the location of the virtual and the real object point. It is possible to compute the distance to the real object by

$$\overline{B_3O_3} = \frac{\overline{B_3V_3} * \sqrt{\left(\frac{n_3}{n_1}\right)^2 - \sin^2 \alpha}}{\cos \alpha} + \overline{O_3O'_3}, \tag{6}$$

if the distance to the virtual point $\overline{B_3V_3}$, the glass layer thickness $\overline{B_1O_1}$ and the angle of incidence α are known.

3.2 Computation

A ray through the center of projection (P_l, P_r) can be computed for every pixel (I_l, I_r). As refraction happens in a plane, a plane of refraction is formed by each ray and the interface normal (axis). The computation of the virtual object points can be realized by the intersection of each plane of refraction with the opposite ray belonging to a pair of corresponding pixels. The intersection can be performed as long as both planes do not coincide.

4 Calibration of Refractive Parameters

The processes of *axis determination* and *recovery of layer thickness* are realized simultaneously by a hypothesis testing strategy. The recovery of the air layer thickness t_1 for one hypothetical axis (dashed blue) is schematically shown in Fig. 2a–c. With this axis, the two virtual object points V_l and V_R can be computed as proposed in Sect. 3.2. A maximal distance can be computed for both these points by placing the interface at the center of projection of the closer camera (Fig. 2a). The application of Eq. 6 to both virtual object points has to result in the same real object point O.

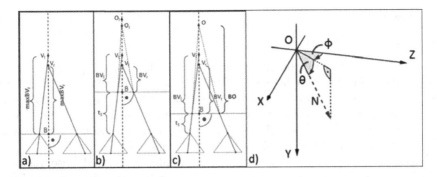

Fig. 2. (a) Virtual object points and their maximal distance. (b) Wrong placement of the refractive interface. (c) Correct placement. (d) Parametrization of the angle range for hypothetical axes in the camera coordinate system (X: left, Y: down, Z: look at). (Color figure online)

For the sake of readability, $\dfrac{\sqrt{\left(\frac{n_3}{n_1}\right)^2 - \sin^2\alpha}}{\cos\alpha}$ is substituted by Z, the number subscripts in Eq. 6 are now omitted and replaced by subscript l for left and r for right, respectively:

$$\overline{BO_l} = \overline{BV_l} * Z_l + \overline{OO_l'} = (maxBV_l - t_1) * Z_l + \overline{OO_l'}, \qquad (7)$$

$$\overline{BO_r} = \overline{BV_r} * Z_r + \overline{OO_r'} = (maxBV_r - t_1) * Z_r + \overline{OO_r'}. \qquad (8)$$

As $\overline{BO_l}$ has to be equal to $\overline{BO_r}$, we get

$$(maxBV_l - t_1) * Z_l + \overline{OO_l'} = (maxBV_r - t_1) * Z_r + \overline{OO_r'} \qquad (9)$$

and some rearranging results in

$$(Z_l - Z_r) * t_1 = maxBV_l * Z_l - maxBV_r * Z_r + \overline{OO_l'} - \overline{OO_r'}. \qquad (10)$$

As can be seen, the application of Eq. 10 on every stereo correspondence results in a linear system of the shape $Ax = b$ with $x = t_1$ and can be solved for the air layer thickness straight forward.

This has to be done for every hypothetical axis. The following error measure based on Eqs. 7 and 8 is minimized to determine the best fitting axis:

$$Err = \sum_{i=1}^{n} \left| \overline{BO_{li}} - \overline{BO_{ri}} \right|^2. \qquad (11)$$

The range of hypothetical axes is represented by the angles ϕ and θ in the camera coordinate system as shown in Fig. 2d. Both are bounded by 45 degrees in positive and negative direction. This value is to a certain extent arbitrary, but also appropriate as larger angles can result in ray directions parallel to and also away from the interface, depending on the camera's field of view. This range is sampled in full 1 degree steps in a first iteration and the angle combination with the minimal error is determined. In further iterations, this can be refined on its decimals in positive and negative direction.

5   Results

5.1   Simulated Test Data

The simulated test setup consists of two cameras that converge to get a maximally overlapping area at a distance of 20 cm in water. At this distance, 3D points are placed in a regular grid of dimension 19×10 to fill both views equally. Both cameras are placed 10 cm away from the interface and both are pointing down. The angles are $\phi = -8.5°$ and $\theta = -35°$. The separation between both cameras amounts to 10 cm and the interface thickness is equal to 1 cm.

To check the stability of our algorithms, normally distributed noise was generated. The noise is added in both stereo-views to the true pixel values of the computed image points. For every noise level, 100 iterations were performed and four error measures where computed and averaged (Fig. 3). The angle error is the difference between the true axis and the determined one in degrees, the layer thickness error is the difference between the true air layer thickness and the determined one in percent, the 3D distance error is the Euclidean distance between the true 3D points and the points that have been reconstructed after calibration and the reprojection error is self-explanatory. The results are overall satisfactory.

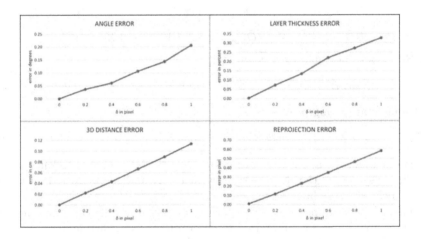

Fig. 3. Resulting errors from simulated test data.

In Fig. 4 the error plot of the tested hypothetical axes is shown for the maximal noise level. As can be seen, the minimum can be determined reliably. Therefore, the simple hypothesis testing strategy is sufficient.

5.2   Real Test Data

Two cameras are placed outside of an aquarium in a configuration similar to the simulated setup (see top left of Fig. 5). The scene contains objects at a distance of 20 to 40 cm in water.

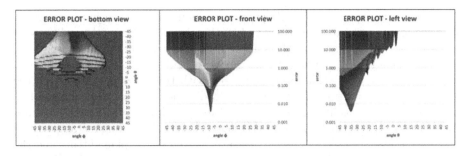

Fig. 4. Plot of the approximate errors of the hypothesis testing strategy for simulated test data with the highest level of noise. The green areas indicate invalid hypothetical axes. The minimum is still clearly detectable.

Fig. 5. Top left: Real imaging setup. Middle left: Acquisition of ground truth data. Bottom left: Scene with checker pattern. Right: Scene and SIFT features.

Four different calibration strategies are compared. The first one is the disregard of refractive effects by stereo calibration in air and ignoring refraction completely. The second one is the absorption of refractive effects by stereo calibration in water. The third one is our refractive calibration with the aid of a checker pattern for simplification of feature detection and correspondence determination. This is realized by a single image like the one in the bottom left of Fig. 5. The fourth one is our refractive calibration from scene stereo correspondences that are determined by the SIFT algorithm [6] (see right of Fig. 5). Since a brute force matching is likely to result in correspondences that are unreliable, the number is reduced by filtering. Nevertheless, this does not guarantee absolutely reliable correspondences. Hence, the refractive calibration is performed iteratively by randomly selecting 30 different correspondences. Every iteration responds with an error value (Eq. 11). Since the computation is quite fast, 1000 iterations are processed and the calibration with the overall smallest error is chosen.

To be able to compare the results, an image of a checker pattern placed onto the interface was taken (see middle left of Fig. 5). The result of the application of a pose estimation from 3D-2D point correspondences algorithm is supposed to serve to a certain amount as ground truth data for the refractive calibration, however, there is no measure of its accuracy. For every calibration strategy, the 3D point cloud corresponding to the image of a reference checker pattern in water is reconstructed. These are compared with the 3D point cloud from the ground truth calibration and the Euclidean distance between the single points is measured. The results are presented in Table 1. Additionally, length measurements along the four sides and the two diagonals of the bounding rectangle of the checker corners are used as quality measure, as well as the plane fitting and the reprojection error. Both of our refractive calibrations outperform the disregard and absorption strategy significantly. Nevertheless, the error values of the calibration from scene correspondences is significantly larger which indicates that the simple feature selection approach should be improved. With the additional features from the checker pattern, the reprojection error is even smaller than that of the ground truth data.

Table 1. Different error measures that are used for the quality testing of the 3D reconstructed point clouds after calibration by the strategies DIS - disregard, ABS - absorption, EST - pose estimation (ground truth), CAL - own refractive calibration (with checker features) and SCN - own (from scene correspondences alone).

Error measure		DIS	ABS	EST	CAL	SCN
3D distance error	$X - MAX(cm)$	0.733	1.747	REF	0.040	0.095
	$X - MEAN(cm)$	0.636	1.666	REF	0.035	0.060
	$Y - MAX(cm)$	3.423	5.219	REF	0.153	0.224
	$Y - MEAN(cm)$	3.040	4.991	REF	0.141	0.136
	$Z - MAX(cm)$	4.780	1.554	REF	0.062	0.655
	$Z - MEAN(cm)$	4.190	1.281	REF	0.048	0.452
	$3D - MEAN(cm)$	5.216	5.417	REF	0.153	0.476
Length measurement error	$\overline{AB}(cm)$	0.186	0.045	0.052	0.047	0.004
	$\overline{AB}(\%)$	2.065	0.501	0.578	0.525	0.048
	$\overline{CD}(cm)$	0.152	0.057	0.057	0.058	0.040
	$\overline{CD}(\%)$	1.691	0.634	0.631	0.644	0.450
	$\overline{AC}(cm)$	0.013	0.018	0.026	0.006	0.025
	$\overline{AC}(\%)$	0.224	0.307	0.427	0.097	0.416
	$\overline{BD}(cm)$	0.046	0.016	0.026	0.014	0.070
	$\overline{BD}(\%)$	0.766	0.274	0.440	0.239	1.163
	$\overline{AD}(cm)$	0.230	0.067	0.068	0.053	0.078
	$\overline{AD}(\%)$	2.128	0.619	0.633	0.490	0.718
	$\overline{BC}(cm)$	0.019	0.017	0.051	0.046	0.006
	$\overline{BC}(\%)$	0.176	0.158	0.471	0.423	0.060
Plane fitting error	$MEAN(cm)$	0.082	0.042	0.023	0.024	0.041
Reprojection error	$LEFT - MEAN(pixel)$	3.301	0.665	0.152	0.069	0.217
	$RIGHT - MEAN(pixel)$	3.237	0.674	0.154	0.073	0.234

6   Conclusions and Future Work

In this work, an approach for the calibration of the refractive parameters of a shared flat refractive stereo system is proposed. The formulated equations can be solved efficiently and simultaneously provide a novel error measure that can be readily utilized. This error measure is used in a hypothesis testing strategy and makes the calibration independent of the computationally expensive refractive reprojection error. It is shown that our approach works on simulated and real image data. Special calibration targets are not necessary since the refractive calibration can be performed on stereo correspondences alone. Nevertheless, easily detectable features like checker pattern corners improve the overall quality.

The future work should contain a more mature feature selection strategy to improve the results of the refractive calibration from scene correspondences alone. The chosen setup with a very steep angle of the cameras to the interface is representative but not very general. First experiments show, that the accuracy of our approaches improves with lower angles.

Acknowledgments. This research has been supported by the German Federal State of Mecklenburg-Western Pomerania and the European Social Fund under grant ESF/IV-BM-B35-0006/12.

References

1. Agrawal, A., Ramalingam, S., Taguchi, Y., Chari, V.: A theory of multi-layer flat refractive geometry. In: 2012 IEEE Conference on Computer Vision and Pattern Recognition (CVPR), pp. 3346–3353 (2012)
2. Bräuer-Burchardt, C., Kühmstedt, P., Notni, G.: Combination of air- and water-calibration for a fringe projection based underwater 3D-scanner. In: Effenberg, A.O., Azzopardi, G., Petkov, N. (eds.) CAIP 2015. LNCS, vol. 9257, pp. 49–60. Springer, Heidelberg (2015). doi:10.1007/978-3-319-23117-4_5
3. Chen, X., Yang, Y.-H.: Two-view camera housing parameters calibration for multi-layer flat refractive interface. In: 2014 IEEE Conference on Computer Vision and Pattern Recognition (CVPR), pp. 524–531 (2014)
4. Gedge, J., Gong, M., Yang, Y.-H.: Refractive epipolar geometry for underwater stereo matching. In: 2011 Canadian Conference on Computer and Robot Vision (CRV), pp. 146–152. IEEE (2011)
5. Kang, L., Wu, L., Wei, Y., Yang, Z.: Theory of multi-level refractive geometry. Electron. Lett. **51**(9), 688–690 (2015)
6. Lowe, D.G.: Object recognition from local scale-invariant features. In: The Proceedings of the Seventh IEEE International Conference on Computer Vision, vol. 2, pp. 1150–1157 (1999)
7. Sedlazeck, A., Koch, R.: Calibration of housing parameters for underwater stereo-camera rigs. In: Proceedings of the British Machine Vision Conference, pp. 118.1–118.11. BMVA Press (2011)
8. Shortis, M.: Calibration techniques for accurate measurements by underwater camera systems. Sensors **15**(12), 30810–30826 (2015)

9. Treibitz, T., Schechner, Y.Y., Kunz, C., Singh, H.: Flat refractive geometry. IEEE Trans. Pattern Anal. Mach. Intell. **34**(1), 51–65 (2012)
10. Yamashita, A., Higuchi, H., Kaneko, T., Kawata, Y.: Three dimensional measurement of object's surface in water using the light stripe projection method. In: Proceedings of 2004 IEEE International Conference on Robotics and Automation, ICRA 2004, vol. 3, pp. 2736–2741. IEEE (2004)

3D Structured Light Scanner on the Smartphone

Tomislav Pribanić[1], Tomislav Petković[1], Matea Đonlić[1(✉)], Vincent Angladon[2], and Simone Gasparini[2]

[1] Faculty of Electrical Engineering and Computing, University of Zagreb, Zagreb, Croatia
{tomislav.pribanic,tomislav.petkovic.jr,matea.donlic}@fer.hr
[2] University of Toulouse, IRIT-INP, Toulouse, France
{vincent.angladon,simone.gasparini}@irit.fr

Abstract. In the recent years turning smartphones into 3D reconstruction devices has been greatly investigated. Different 3D reconstruction concepts have been proposed, and one of the most popular is based on IR projection of a pseudor-andom dots (speckle) pattern. We demonstrate our idea how a pseudorandom dots pattern can be used and we also present an active approach applying a structured light (SL) scanning on the smartphone. SL has a number of advantages compared to other 3D reconstruction concepts and likewise our smartphone implementation inherits the same advantages compared to other smartphone based solutions. The shown qualitative and quantitative results demonstrate the comparable outcome with the standard type SL scanner.

Keywords: Smartphone · 3D reconstruction · Structured light · Pseudorandom dots pattern

1 Introduction

Apple's iPhone started the era of modern smartphones in 2007. Other smartphone models soon followed causing the recognition of a smartphone as a visual computing powerhouse. A modern smartphone has a high-speed multi-core CPU, a 3D graphic processor, a DSP for image and video processing, a high resolution camera, a high quality color display, and quite impressive local storage capabilities. Therefore, turning a smartphone into a powerful 3D reconstruction device opens additional application and research avenues which are beyond a simple gadget, e.g. reverse engineering (digitiza-tion of complex, free-form surfaces), object recognition, 3D map building, biometrics, clothing design, and others.

3D surface reconstruction methods applicable to smartphones may be categorized into passive and active methods. Most common passive 3D reconstruction solutions require the user to go around the object carefully taking a relatively large number of images [1, 2] that are processed in a SLAM pipeline to extract a 3D shape. Image processing of such approaches (e.g. extracting image features and matching them across the images) is a central part and it is to a large extent typically done in the cloud requiring a network connection to upload the acquired images. On the other hand, complete on board smartphone solutions heavily rely on the additional sensors such as accelerometer

© Springer International Publishing Switzerland 2016
A. Campilho and F. Karray (Eds.): ICIAR 2016, LNCS 9730, pp. 443–450, 2016.
DOI: 10.1007/978-3-319-41501-7_50

and gyroscope [3]. Alternatively, the shape from silhouettes has also been proposed, still creating relatively coarse 3D models of small-scale objects [4].

In the context of active stereo, there are solutions proposing the photometric stereo where the smartphone screen is conveniently used as a light source, however, as noted by the authors themselves, a dark environment is required [5, 6]. Somewhat more robust solution, but at the expense of using an extra smartphone, is proposed in [7]. They used a pair of smartphones which collaborate as master and slave: the slave was illuminating the scene using the flash from appropriate viewing points while the master recorded images of the object. Considering such approaches, it becomes apparent that the lack of an appropriate light source on the smartphone is a substantial obstacle for implementing any form of active stereo. Project Tango by Google is perhaps one of the most well-known examples where, in order to overcome that obstacle, a custom made IR projector and IR camera are installed in a smartphone [8]. Unfortunately, added IR projector may be used only for 3D depth sensing and not much beyond. Finally, some of the more recent work proposed the use of a laser line projector attached to a smartphone [9]. Although conceptually simple, such solution, similarly to all single line laser approaches, requires many images for 3D surface reconstruction making it necessary to have an effective 3D registration tool to combine single line reconstructions. The authors in [9] impose a constraint that a marker has to be visible and tracked throughout the frames.

To the best of our knowledge no smartphone-based solution considered a well-established and powerful concept for 3D shape acquisition, a structured light (SL) strategy [10]. Briefly, the SL concept involves the use of a camera-projector pair where a pattern, designed to contain a certain code, is projected and the corresponding code is then identified on the camera image(s). Through found camera-projector pixels correspondences a triangulation of 3D points is carried out. During this work we have identified a number of commercially available smartphones [11], which have an embedded pico projector. In particular we have used the Samsung Galaxy Beam smartphone [12]. Our main contribution is demonstration how such smartphones can be successfully turned into very efficient 3D scanning devices. Interestingly, Samsung (including other manufactures as well) have not considered the use of a camera-projector pair for SL scanning, since apparently smartphone's camera and pico projector typically do not share a common field of view (FOV). To redirect light rays, complex configurations of mirrors have been extensively used in all kinds of imaging systems [13]. As an additional contribution we propose the use of a simple adapter with a first surface mirror which, as will be shown, neatly resolves the FOV issue. We demonstrate the use of the proposed system using one of the most popular and robust SL scanning strategies: multiple phase shifting (MPS) [14]. We also show the implementation of a pseudorandom dots pattern for projection, basically the same type of pattern has been used in the first version of globally popular Microsoft Kinect for Xbox 360 (Kinect v1).

2 Method

We first describe the used hardware in Subsect. 2.1, then the imaging geometry in Subsect. 2.2, and finally, we describe the used SL approach in Subsect. 2.3.

2.1 Hardware Components

Figure 1 shows the Samsung Galaxy Beam smartphone which has a 5 MP camera and a 15 lm DLP projector. Unfortunately, camera and projector have no common FOV. To overcome this difficulty we propose using a small re-attachable adapter with a first surface mirror as shown in Fig. 2. This allows defining the geometrical and computational framework for the 3D surface scanning between a camera and a projector, as described below.

Fig. 1. Samsung Galaxy Beam: a camera and an embedded pico projector comprise an angle of 90°, having no common FOV.

Fig. 2. Smartphone on a tripod with the deflection adapter for projector attached. Note the mirror image of the projector, i.e. a virtual projector.

2.2 Camera-Projector Imaging Geometry

Figure 3 represents a cross-section view of a smartphone positioned sideways and upgraded with a first surface planar mirror placed in the front of the projector. Smartphone's projector P_R (real) and camera C have their respective FOVs denoted with green lines which evidently do not intersect. We are interested in reconstructing a point A which is within camera's FOV, but not within the projector's FOV. The red dashed line joining the projector P_R and the point A represents a hypothetical pattern projection on A which obviously cannot happen due to insufficient FOV of the projector. However, consider a planar mirror positioned at an angle α with respect to the optical axis of the projector P_R as shown in Fig. 3. This will create a virtual projector P_V on the opposite side of a mirror, which can project a SL pattern on the point A with the corresponding projector coordinate p. In addition, the effect of mirroring will provide a mirror image A_m of the point A, which is not visible to the virtual projector P_V. The real projector P_R can be related to the point A_m through a pattern projection with the corresponding projector coordinate p_m.

Without loss of generality, let us assume that the world frame axes x_w and y_w coincide with the mirror edges, as shown in Fig. 3, and with the third axis z_w defined by the right hand rule. This allows expressing a simple spatial position relationship between A and A_m, i.e. they differ only in the sign of y_w coordinate. Similarly, optical centers P_R of the real projector and P_V of the virtual projector differ only in the sign of y_w coordinate.

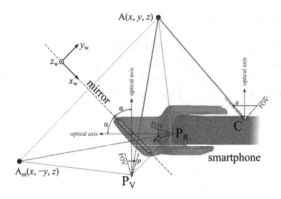

Fig. 3. Representation of 3D structured light scanner comprised of smartphone embedded camera and projector, and a planar first surface mirror (see text for more details).

The described imaging geometry can be calibrated using any standard calibration technique for 3D scanner (camera/projector) calibration. In particular, we have adopted an approach from [15].

2.3 3D Reconstruction Using Structured Light

The basic principle of SL approach is summarized as follows: a projector projects a certain number of images on the object of interest. The projected images have a particular structure, a code, which is decoded in the acquired camera images. 3D position is triangulated from the decoded SL code.

Among more than a dozen different SL patterns we have chosen one of the time multiplexing strategies, a well-known phase shifting (PS) method [10]. PS consists of projecting a number ($N \geq 3$) of periodic sine patterns, shifted by some period amount. The patterns are sequentially projected with a projector on the object of interest, are recorded by the camera, and are then processed in order to compute a wrapped phase map. Due to the periodic nature of sine patterns, the wrapped phase map does not provide a unique code, rather it is said that the code is wrapped within $[-\pi, +\pi]$ interval. One way to unwrap the wrapped phase map and recover the SL code is to project additional PS patterns having a different number of periods compared to the first set. Such multiple phase shifting (MPS) procedure provides two wrapped values φ_{w1} and φ_{w2}. Computing the unwrapped phase Φ_{UW} from the φ_{w1} and φ_{w2} and extracting the SL code can be done in number of different ways; we have followed the algorithm described in [14]. In brief, the algorithm in [14] emphasizes the fact that the unwrapped phase can be computed using either of φ_{R1} and φ_{R2} as:

$$\Phi_{UW} = k_1 \cdot \lambda_1 + \varphi_{R1} = k_2 \cdot \lambda_2 + \varphi_{R2} \tag{1}$$

where λ_1 and λ_2 are wavelengths corresponding to the number of periods of the first and second sine pattern. Parameters k_1 and k_2 are integers of full sine periods needed to reach the same unwrapped value using the estimated wrapped values φ_{R1} and φ_{R2}. Values φ_{R1}

and φ_{R2} are normalized such that $\varphi_{R1} \in [0, \lambda_1]$ and $\varphi_{R2} \in [0, \lambda_2]$. In a nutshell, the algorithm of [14] computes first all feasible pairs of (k_1, k_2) given some chosen values for λ_1 and λ_2. Next, it chooses a specific pair (k_1, k_2) that yields the smallest discrepancy when computing the unwrapped phase Φ_{UW} using Eq. (1).

Multiple-shot methods (like PS method) produce superior reconstruction than single-shot methods in terms of resolution and accuracy but have a substantially longer acquisition times and are mostly unsuitable for dynamic scenes without using an expensive high-speed hardware. To tackle this issue, we also describe our proposal, based on the projection of a Kinect-like pseudorandom dots pattern, for extracting a depth map from a single shot. During the scanning procedure, a single image of the pseudorandom dots pattern is continuously projected using smartphone's projector and a deflection adapter, and a video sequence of the illuminated moving object is acquired using smartphone's camera. Then, each frame of the captured video sequence is matched with the reference image of the pseudorandom dots pattern. Due to limited space we omit here details how to extract SL code from a random dots pattern, instead we refer the interested reader to one alternative such as [16].

3   Results

3.1   Application Example: On the Construction of a Shoe Insole

To demonstrate the applicability of the proposed smartphone scanner we have examined one practical application. During a shoe insole production it is customary to ask an individual to step in a special type of foam, leaving his/her imprint of the sole (foot, Fig. 4(a)). Next, the imprint is 3D scanned and, if needed, modified by the physician before it is carved out by a CAM milling machine. We note that a general purpose SL scanner or even a particularly designed foot scanner is normally used to scan such imprint (Fig. 4(b, c)). Therefore we have scanned the same imprint using a type of SL scanner as shown in Fig. 4(c) and using our 3D smartphone scanner. Due to a typically higher demand for precision and accuracy in such applications, in this particular experiment we have used the MPS method [14].

Table 1. Absolute mean distances (expressed in millimeters) between two corresponding points (nearest neighbor) from the various registered views.

	View 1	View 2	View 3	View 4	View 5
Smartphone to standard scanner (mm)	0.57	0.54	0.50	0.67	0.57
Standard scanner to smartphone (mm)	0.53	0.51	0.52	0.62	0.61

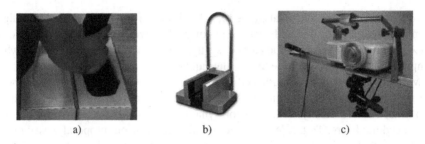

Fig. 4. (a) Taking patient's sole imprint. (b) Example of specially designed foot scanner; may be used only for foot scanning. (c) Standard scanner consisting of industrial camera and projector fastened on a tripod; may be used as a general purpose scanning device.

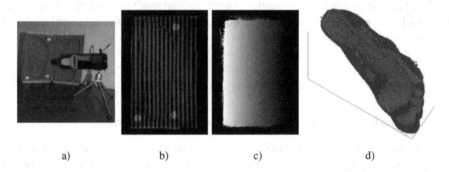

Fig. 5. (a) The proposed 3D system during 3D scanning. (b) Projected sine pattern during MPS. (c) Recovered unwrapped phase map. (d) Shape of the foot sole. Two clouds of points, red and blue, initially reconstructed from two different types of scanners and afterwards registered in the common coordinate system. Both clouds successfully overlap. (Color figure online)

We have compared the 3D point clouds of the proposed method and a standard scanner. For a qualitative comparison, Fig. 5(d) strongly suggests that two clouds of points overlap nicely, after being registered to the same coordinate system. In addition, to provide a quantitative measure of agreement between registered point clouds, we provide the absolute mean distance between corresponding points from the various registered views at the final stage of the registration process. We have considered two cases: first when the smartphone scanner point cloud was registered to the standard scanner and second when the standard scanner point cloud was registered to the smartphone scanner (Table 1). Figures in the table strongly indicate that the 3D output of two types of scanners is basically the same.

3.2 Moving Female Face

Projecting a more than one pattern, as explained in the previous section, typically requires an object to be still. To show feasibility of our solution for moving objects too, we demonstrate solution of projecting a single image pattern. For this experiment we have recorded a female moving her head under the proposed pseudorandom dots pattern. Figure 6 shows four selected frames from this recording. The input sequence only contains images with the pseudorandom dots pattern making it impossible to retrieve a speckle-free texture.

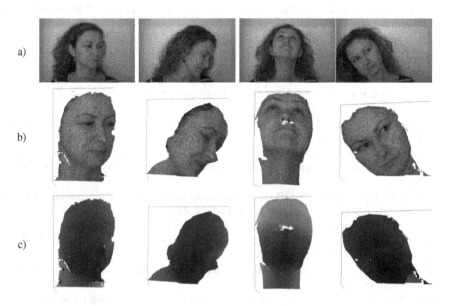

Fig. 6. Four frames from a movie of a moving female face. 3D reconstruction was performed using the pseudorandom dots pattern. Rows contain: (a) input frames; (b) textured 3D surface where input image is used as texture; (c) 3D surface textured as depth map.

4 Discussion and Conclusion

The shown results clearly demonstrate that a smartphone with an embedded pico projector can be turned into a very powerful 3D SL scanner. We have successfully implemented one of MPS variants. We note that PS is generally regarded as state of the art strategy when it comes to the highest demands in 3D SL scanning of static objects. In addition, acknowledging in recent years an increasing number of widely affordable 3D devices based on projecting laser speckle pattern, such as Kinect v1, we have also presented an approach using a pseudorandom dots pattern on a smartphone. Since it projects a single pattern, such algorithm is capable of scanning moving object too, as shown on Fig. 6, in the case of moving female model.

One of the everlasting challenges in SL is constructing a so called hybrid pattern [17]. The hybrid pattern is expected to be suitable for reconstruction of both static and moving objects within the same captured frame where a different (de)coding is applied depending on object movement thus allowing higher quality 3D data for static objects. Inspired by some of the latest research in that respect [18, 19], our future work will be directed towards the design and implementation of hybrid patterns on the proposed smartphone system.

Acknowledgment. This work has been supported in parts by the Croatian Science Foundation's funding of the project IP-11-2013-3717. We also acknowledge the support of Croatian-French Program "Cogito", Hubert Curien partnership, funding the project "Three-dimensional reconstruction using smartphone".

References

1. 123D Catch. http://www.123dapp.com/catch. Accessed Nov 2015
2. Trnio. http://www.trnio.com. Accessed Nov 2015
3. Tanskanen, P., Kolev, K., Meier, L., Camposeco, F., Saurer, O., Pollefeys, M.: Live metric 3D reconstruction on mobile phones. In: IEEE ICCV 2013, pp. 65–72 (2013)
4. Hartl, A., Gruber, L., Arth, C., Hauswiesner, S., Schmalstieg, D.: Rapid reconstruction of small objects on mobile phones. In: IEEE Conference on CVPR Workshops 2011, pp. 20–27 (2011)
5. Wang, C., Bao, M., Shen, T.: 3D model reconstruction algorithm and implementation based on the mobile device. J. Theor. Appl. Inf. Technol. **46**(1), 255–262 (2012)
6. Trimensional. http://www.trimensional.com. Accessed Nov 2015
7. Won, J.H., Lee, M.H., Park, I.K.: Active 3D shape acquisition using smartphones. In: IEEE Conference on CVPR Workshops 2012, pp. 29–34 (2012)
8. Project Tango. https://www.ifixit.com/Teardown/Project+Tango+Teardown/23835. Accessed Nov 2015
9. Slossberg, R., Wetzler, A., Kimmel, R.: Freehand laser scanning using mobile phone. In: Proceeding of the British Machine Vision Conference, pp. 88.1–88.10 (2015)
10. Salvi, J., Fernandez, S., Pribanić, T., LLado, X.: A state of the art in structured light patterns for surface profilometry. Pattern Recogn. **43**, 2666–2680 (2010)
11. List of projector phones. https://en.wikipedia.org/wiki/Projector_phone. Accessed Nov 2015
12. Samsung Galaxy Beam. http://www.samsung.com/global/microsite/galaxybeam/feature.html. Accessed Nov 2015
13. Reshetouski, I., Ihrke, I.: Mirrors in computer graphics, computer vision and time-of-flight imaging. In: Grzegorzek, M., Theobalt, C., Koch, R., Kolb, A. (eds.) Time-of-Flight and Depth Imaging. LNCS, vol. 8200, pp. 77–104. Springer, Heidelberg (2013)
14. Pribanić, T., Mrvoš, S., Salvi, J.: Efficient multiple phase shift patterns for dense 3D acquisition in structured light scanning. Image Vis. Comput. **28**, 1255–1266 (2010)
15. Zhang, Z.: A flexible new technique for camera calibration. IEEE Trans. PAMI **22**(11), 1330–1334 (2000)
16. McIlroy, P., Izadi, S., Fitzgibbon, A.: Kinectrack: Agile 6-DoF tracking using a projected dot pattern. In: International Symposium on Mixed and Augmented Reality, pp. 23–29 (2012)
17. Ishii, I., Yamamoto, K., Doi, K., Tsuji, T.: High-speed 3D image acquisition using coded structured light projection. In: IEEE/RSJ International Conference on Intelligent Robots and Systems, pp. 925–930 (2007)
18. Zhang, Y., Xiong, Z., Yang, Z., Wu, F.: Real-time scalable depth sensing with hybrid structured light illumination. IEEE Trans. Image Process. **23**, 97–109 (2014)
19. Petković, T., Pribanić, T., Đonlić, M.: The self-equalizing De Bruijn sequence for 3D profilometry. In: Proceeding of the British Machine Vision Conference, pp. 155.1–155.11 (2015)

Stereo and Active-Sensor Data Fusion for Improved Stereo Block Matching

Stefan-Daniel Suvei[1(✉)], Leon Bodenhagen[1], Lilita Kiforenko[1],
Peter Christiansen[2], Rasmus N. Jørgensen[2], Anders G. Buch[1],
and Norbert Krüger[1]

[1] University of Southern Denmark, 5230 Odense M, Denmark
{stdasu,lebo,lilita,anbu,norbert}@mmmi.sdu.dk
[2] Aarhus University, 8200 Aarhus N, Denmark
{pech,rnj}@eng.au.dk

Abstract. This paper proposes an algorithm which uses the depth information acquired from an active sensor as guidance for a block matching stereo algorithm. In the proposed implementation, the disparity search interval used for the block matching is reduced around the depth values obtained from the active sensor, which leads to an improved matching quality and denser disparity maps and point clouds. The performance of the proposed method is evaluated by carrying out a series of experiments on 3 different data sets obtained from different robotic systems. We demonstrate with experimental results that the disparity estimation is improved and denser disparity maps are generated.

1 Introduction

Due to the popularity increase of autonomous robots and the fact that 3D sensors are widely available, 3D scene reconstruction has become an important research area, because it has the potential of enabling robots to perform accurate and complex tasks.

3D scene reconstruction can be performed using only one sensor in it's most basic form, or multiple sensors for increased field of view and completeness of the scene. In principle there are two main approaches for 3D reconstruction with multiple sensors. One is to use multiple active sensors (e.g. structured light, LIDAR) or multiple stereo cameras that have partially overlapping fields of view. For example, in [1] multiple structured-light based sensors are used with an algorithm that takes the correlation between the sensors into account. In [2] a modified ICP algorithm is used to fuse the point clouds generated by multiple overhead stereo cameras. Using the known sensor extrinsics, the search space for the closest points between two different point clouds is reduced. This approach has the advantage of working with only one data type, but it can lead to incomplete results due to the sensor's limitations.

The second approach is to use different types of sensors and fuse their data cues - e.g. active sensors with stereo cameras. This has the advantage of combining sensors with complementary properties - active 3D sensors are precise but

© Springer International Publishing Switzerland 2016
A. Campilho and F. Karray (Eds.): ICIAR 2016, LNCS 9730, pp. 451–461, 2016.
DOI: 10.1007/978-3-319-41501-7_51

can be sensitive to infrared light (Carmine) or are very sparse (LIDAR), while stereo is of high resolution, but can be noisy in textureless areas. The fusion of active and passive sensors has been investigated before in the literature and two main fusion options can be identified: *a posteriori* and *a priori*. As presented in [3–6], the *a posteriori* fusion method is improving the final result of the vision system by combining the disparity maps of the passive and active sensors. The fusion is done either directly at the object level [3,6] or by constructing a cost map [4,5], where the two types of sensor have different weights according to the level of trust in each specific region.

In the *a priori* fusion technique the depth information from the active sensor is integrated into the stereo matching algorithm, such that it actually guides the stereo computation. An example of this principle is shown in [7], where the data and smoothness costs of the energy minimization function used for the global stereo matching algorithm are determined using the Kinect depth information. Similarly, in [8] the stereo computation is sped up by using the LIDAR depth data to limit the disparity search space of the stereo matching process.

Similar to [7,8], in this paper we propose an *a priori* method which improves the stereo matching process by limiting the disparity search range around the depth value obtained from the active sensor. In this way the active sensor is

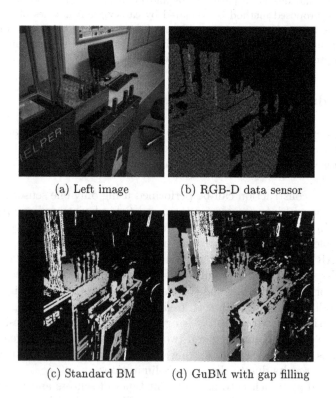

(a) Left image   (b) RGB-D data sensor

(c) Standard BM   (d) GuBM with gap filling

Fig. 1. Comparison results of disparity maps

actually guiding the stereo process, leading to a better matching quality and a denser disparity map (as shown in Fig. 1d). However, in contrast to [7,8], we focus on a local stereo matching algorithm - more precisely block matching - because it requires less memory and computation time and also it scales well for large images. The performance of the proposed method is evaluated by carrying out a series of experiments on 3 different data sets obtained from 3 different robotic systems - two with RGB-D data sensors and one with a LIDAR.

2   Methodology

Assuming that the stereo camera calibration has been performed beforehand, the algorithm can be split into three main steps: (1) Data preprocessing, (2) Data registration, and (3) Stereo correspondence with data fusion.

We note that the first two steps are performed only once for each system. The following paragraphs describe the three steps in more detail.

2.1   Data Preprocessing

In this initial step a pair of stereo images is rectified and an initial point cloud of a test scene is computed. Additionally, a point cloud representing the same scene but from the active sensor is generated and the points which are outside the field of view of the camera are filtered out by using a pass-through filter.

2.2   Data Registration

To apply the necessary geometric transformations between the two data sets, the sensors need to be calibrated. Due to the fact that the tests were performed on different platforms which had to have the freedom of changing the active sensor's placement for varied experimental possibilities, a definitive external calibration between the stereo cameras and the active sensors could not be performed. However, as a work around this issue, the data is registered using the modified ICP implementation from the Covis library [9]. The algorithm uses the point clouds from **Step 1** and applies RANSAC to best fit them. This is a preprocessing step which is performed once for each platform and it gives a refined transformation that can be used to register the two data sets.

2.3   Stereo Correspondence with Data Fusion

Given a pair of stereo images, the depth information can be computed by either optimizing a global cost minimization function (global stereo matching) or by using small surrounding areas of the pixels (local stereo matching).

Block Matching: One of the most popular local stereo algorithms is Block Matching (BM), where the depth information is computed by determining the pixel-distances of similar pixel-regions in the stereo images pair. In essence, the disparity of a pixel is computed by defining a reference block of neighboring pixels in the left image, and then searching for the most similar block in the right image, which will reference the corresponding matching pixel. Because the images are rectified beforehand, pixel-features in the left image will be in the same pixel rows in the right image. This restricts the search to only horizontal lines. We can therefore define LB (Left Block) and RB (Right Block) as the small blocks around the point $P_l(u, v)$ in the left image, and $P_r(u, v - d)$ in the right image, where d is the disparity value that needs to be identified.

If we assume that the block size is $(2n+1) \times (2n+1)$ pixels and that both i and $j \in [-n, n]$, then $LB(u+i, v+j)$ represents the intensity of $P_l(u+i, v+j)$, where $P_l \in LB$ and $RB(u+i, v+j+d)$ represents the intensity of $P_r(u+i, v+j+d)$ with $P_r \in RB$. The similarity of the two blocks can then be determined by using the sum of absolute differences (SAD), as follows:

$$SAD(u, v, d) = \sum_{i=-n}^{n} \sum_{j=-n}^{n} |LB(u+i, v+j) - RB(u+i, v+j+d)| \quad (1)$$

where $d \in D$. D represents the disparity interval which is typically set for the entire image and it is the one that limits the actual disparity search. Identifying the most similar block means minimizing (1) : $d_S = argmin_d SAD(u, v, d)$. By computing the d_S values for all the matching stereo pixels, a disparity map is built which essentially contains all the depth information regarding the scene.

Using this principle, the correspondence problem is transformed into a 1D search problem which guarantees to find the solution (i.e. best-matching block). However, because the similarity check is done for all the pixels, the computation load is high and it increases with the image resolution.

Fusion Algorithm: Choosing the disparity interval D is crucial, because it directly influences the computation of the stereo matching process - a small interval will make the algorithm skip some matching pixels, while a too large interval will increase the computation time and increase the risk of having wrong matches. We therefore propose the use of the depth information from the active sensors to limit D around an expected value for each pixel. An important step in doing this is to efficiently transform the depth data from the structured light sensor or the LIDAR into a dense disparity range. This is done through a remapping process. With the transformation from **Step 2**, each $\mathbf{p} \in \mathbb{R}^3$ from the active sensor's point cloud is mapped to the left image coordinate system. The depth ranges are transformed into disparities by using the corresponding image displacements available from the stereo camera calibration process as follows:

$$d_L = Bf/Z \quad (2)$$

where B is the baseline, f is the focal length and Z is the depth value. The resulting Sensor Disparity Map (SDM) can be observed in Fig. 2a. Because the

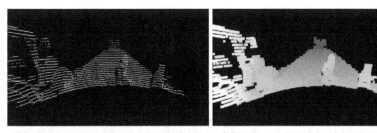

(a) Original SDM for SAFE LIDAR   (b) Dilated SDM for SAFE LIDAR

Fig. 2. The active sensor's original and dilated disparity map

depth measurements of the active sensors can be of low resolution (especially in the LIDAR's case), the SDM can be sparse. To compensate for this, a morphological dilation operator is applied. A rectangular structuring element of size 3×3 pixels is used, with a number of 11 iterations for LIDAR and only 2 for the structured light sensor. These values were chosen such that the dilated regions around the original points would barely overlap (see Fig. 2b).

Using the SDM and the d_L values, we can now perform Guided Block Matching (GuBM). First, D becomes $D = [d_L - R, d_L + R]$, where R is a constant fixed at the beginning of the algorithm with the purpose of limiting the disparity range around d_L. Secondly, to add extra weight to d_L, we use a Gaussian operator to modify (1) as follows:

$$SAD(u, v, d, d_L) = \sum_{i=-n}^{n} \sum_{j=-n}^{n} \frac{|LB(u+i, v+j) - RB(u+i, v+j+d)|}{exp\left(-\frac{(d-d_L)^2}{2\sigma^2}\right)} \quad (3)$$

hence the value of d that minimizes (3) will be biased towards d_L. We note that σ was empirically fixed to 500. In areas where no value for d_L available, d_L is set to equal d, ensuring that the denominator in (3) reduces to 1.

Missing data caused by occlusions, textureless areas or even light conditions will still generate empty regions in the Stereo Disparity Map (StDM). These situations can be accounted for by applying Guided Block Matching with gap Filling (GuBM-F), in which we consider $StDM(P(u, v))$ as the disparity value computed for pixel $P(u, v)$ after GuBM and $SDM(P(u, v))$ as the disparity value for the same pixel, but in the dilated Sensor Disparity Map, then the final stereo disparity value d_S is computed as follows (the resulting dense disparity map is shown in Fig. 1d):

$$d_S = \begin{cases} StDM(P(u, v)), & \text{if } StDM(P(u, v)) > 0 \\ SDM(P(u, v)), & \text{if } StDM(P(u, v)) = 0 \text{ and } SDM(P(u, v)) > 0 \\ 0, & \text{otherwise} \end{cases} \quad (4)$$

3   Results

The proposed algorithm was tested on three different platforms, as follows:

Agricultural Robot Platform: The SAFE platform [10] is a multi-sensor platform, consisting of a stereo camera, a LIDAR sensor, a thermal camera, an RGB camera and a radar. The platform is used in outdoor environments on autonomous tractors to ensure safety of the system, but also for the possible humans in the field. For our algorithm, only the stereo camera and LIDAR inputs are used. The LIDAR is a Velodyne HDL-32E sensor which rotates at a frequency of 10 Hz. Using 32 horizontal scan beams and a horizontal field of view of 360°, it can record 700.000 points/second. The stereo system uses two Point Grey Flea3 cameras, which operate at 15 Hz and output images with a 1920 × 1080 pixels resolution.

Industrial Robot Platform: The scope of the ACAT project [11] is to make industrial robotic systems understand and use information created for humans. The vision platform of the system consists of a Carmine sensor and a stereo camera. The PrimeSense Carmine sensor is a 3D sensor with a horizontal field of view of 57.5°, running at 10 Hz. The stereo camera consists of two AVT Pike F-421C cameras operating at 30 Hz and 1024 × 1024 pixels resolution.

Welfare Robot Platform: The Care-O-Bot [12] is a welfare robotics platform targeting various tasks within the home environment. The robot is equipped with a PrimeSense Carmine sensor and a stereo system, comprised of two AVT Prosilica GC2450 cameras, which operate at 15 fps and output images with a resolution of 2448 × 2050 pixels.

The proposed algorithm has been tested on 3 different data sets by using and accordingly modifying the block matching implementation available from the OpenCV library [13]. The stereo cameras have been calibrated beforehand using the Matlab Stereo Calibration Toolbox [14].

To preserve as much detail as possible (i.e. sharper disparity edges), a SAD window size of 9 (3 × 3 block) is used for all test runs. Additionally, we apply a simple speckle filter with a window size of 100 pixels and a range of 32 pixels to filter out the speckle noise. However, since the purpose is to show the advantage of reducing the disparity range D, no other refinements are applied on the data. Figure 3 shows a comparison between the result of the standard block matching method (BM), the semi-global block matching (SGBM) and the guided one, where $R = 50$. Comparing the results of the standard BM (Fig. 3, row 2) with the GuBM results (Fig. 3, row 4), we notice that some of the errors caused by the lack of texture, repetitive structures or sun-light influence in the standard BM are decreased by using the reduced disparity range. Additionally, by using the gap filling improvement in GuBM-F, we can generate disparity maps that are comparable in density with those generated with SGBM.

To test the time performance of GuBM, 30 runs (10 for BM, SGBM and GuBM each) have been performed on each of the three data sets, on an Intel

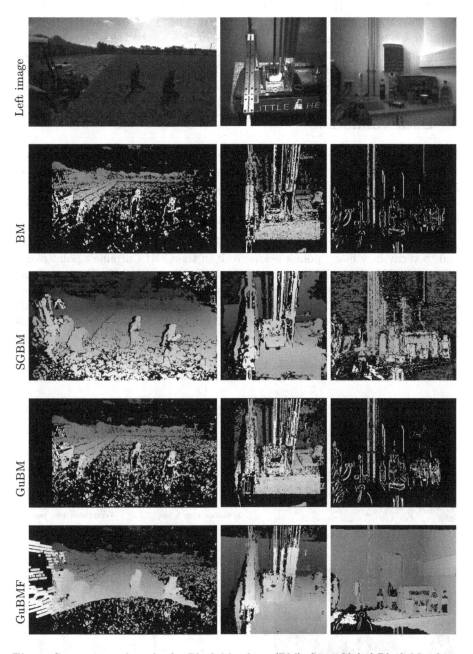

Fig. 3. Comparison of results for Block Matching (BM), Semi Global Block Matching (SGBM), Guided Block Matching (GuBM) and Guided Block Matching with gap filling (GuBM-F). First column shows the result for the SAFE data set, the second one for the ACAT data set and the third one for the COB data.

Core i5-4210U, 1.7 GHz (64 bit) machine. On average, the BM has run times of 1.57 s (SAFE), 4.286 s (COB) and 0.729 s (ACAT). The results show that the introduction of (3) alongside the disparity reduction interval slows down the performance of GuBM, generating run times of 2.476 s (SAFE), 5.862 s (COB) and 1.067 s (ACAT). Compared to SGBM, GuBM is much faster, SGBM generating run times of 4.390 s (SAFE), 10.450 s (COB) and 1.916 s (ACAT).

4   Data Validation

In this section we perform a few tests in order to quantify the level of improvement achieved by the proposed algorithm. The idea is to verify the level of accuracy as well as the number of extra points added by the fusion method, compared to the standard block matching and the standard active sensor point cloud. For this reason, we consider the following two test cases:

***Carmine* Test:** The calibration plate in Fig. 4a is used to define a test plane and to verify how many points belong to it in the COB Carmine's point cloud, the standard block matching point cloud and the proposed method's point cloud. The first step is to bring the three point clouds in the same reference coordinate system and to delete the unnecessary points around the plate. Next, we identify and verify the *inlier* percentage for each situation. We consider an inlier a point that verifies the plane's equation:

$$a \cdot X + b \cdot Y + c \cdot Z + d < Limit \tag{5}$$

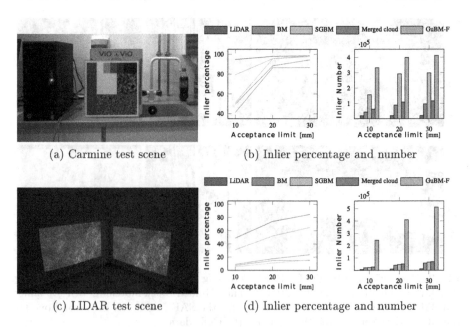

(a) Carmine test scene   (b) Inlier percentage and number

(c) LIDAR test scene   (d) Inlier percentage and number

Fig. 4. Scene and inlier analysis for the Carmine and LIDAR tests (Color figure online)

where a, b, c and d are the test plane's coefficients and X, Y and Z are the point's coordinates. However, because the sensors have different levels of accuracy, we consider three different inlier acceptance limits for the plane fitting test: 10 mm, 20 mm and 30 mm.

Table 1 (Carmine block) contains the statistical analysis of the point distribution for each test and acceptance limit case. Figure 4b shows how the *inlier* percentage is affected by the used method and by the change of the acceptance limit. Given that the RGB-D data sensor acts as "ground truth" and is the one guiding the stereo correspondence algorithm, our method can not achieve that level of accuracy. However, the two figures show that for all three of the acceptance limits, the GuBM-F presents a significant improvement of the *inlier* percentage and number compared to the standard BM method, SGBM or even the Merged Cloud - which is the merging of the resulting point cloud of the standard BM with the Carmine one.

LIDAR Test: For this test we use the same procedure as for the *Carmine* test, but here the LIDAR and stereo camera of the SAFE platform were pointed towards a wall which had a projected image on it (see Fig. 4c). Because the purpose is to demonstrate that the stereo process can be guided towards a good result by the LIDAR depth data, we chose a particularly difficult case for stereo, where the light condition is poor, the overall wall surface is textureless and the pattern of the projected image is repetitive. The results are shown in Table 1 (LIDAR block) and Fig. 4d. This test shows that the GuBM-F offers an improved result over the standard BM, SGBM and the Merged Cloud methods, both in *inlier* numbers, but also in the *inlier* percentage, even though the initial stereo data is noisy. Perhaps most interesting is the difference in completeness and accuracy when compared to SGBM. Given the difficulty of the test case, SGBM finds very few correct matches, GuBM-F performing roughly 5 times better, in terms of *inlier* percentage.

Table 1. *Carmine* and *LIDAR* tests analysis

Acceptance limit	Data	Carmine test					LIDAR test				
		Carmine	BM	SGBM	Merged Cloud	GuBM-F	LIDAR	BM	SGBM	Merged Cloud	GuBM-F
0.01	Number of points	19794	103251	304838	123045	417292	13108	279421	416023	292529	786474
	Number of inliers	18752	42723	155938	61475	330948	6400	19898	22042	26298	243961
	Inlier percentage	94.7	41.3	51.1	49.7	79.3	48.8	7.2	5.2	8.9	31
	Mean distance	0.0031	0.0058	0.0040	0.0050	0.0035	0.0046	0.0050	0.0050	0.0049	0.0049
0.02	Number of points	19794	103251	304838	123045	417292	13108	279421	416023	292529	786474
	Number of inliers	19387	89399	291428	108786	399178	9712	41550	45938	51262	410195
	Inlier percentage	97.9	86.5	95.6	88.4	95.6	74	14.8	11.04	17.5	52.1
	Mean distance	0.0029	0.0105	0.0089	0.0093	0.0053	0.0079	0.0100	0.010	0.0096	0.0090
0.03	Number of points	19794	103251	304838	123045	417292	13108	279421	416023	292529	786474
	Number of inliers	19511	96718	297757	116229	410943	11094	58165	65253	69259	511169
	Inlier percentage	98.5	86.6	97.6	94.4	98.4	84.6	14.8	15.68	23.6	64.9
	Mean distance	0.0036	0.0115	0.0093	0.0102	0.0058	0.0092	0.0149	0.0150	0.0140	0.0119

5   Conclusion

In this paper we present an *a priori* fusion method which improves a local stereo matching algorithm by using the depth information provided by an active sensor (Carmine or LIDAR) to guide the stereo correspondence process by limiting the disparity search interval.

Two sets of experiments have been conducted with the purpose of quantifying the level of improvement over the standard Block Matching and Semi Global Block Matching algorithm. The run-time comparison shows that GuBM-F is on average 46 % slower than BM due to the complexity of the Gaussian operator computation. However, it is 43 % faster than SGBM. The statistical analysis reveals that the resulting point cloud of the GuBM-F method is much denser (i.e. bigger number of inliers) than the one computed using BM, SGBM or even the Merged Cloud, but also more accurate (i.e. bigger inlier percentage and a smaller mean distance). This means that the resulting point cloud of GuBM-F is a more accurate representation of the scene, which is a useful feat for a wide variety of robotic tasks.

Acknowledgement. This work was supported by the projects Patient@home and SAFE Perception which are funded by the Danish Innovation Fond.

References

1. Wang, J., Zhang, C., Zhu, W., Zhang, Z., Xiong, Z., Chou, P.A.: 3D scene reconstruction by multiple structured-light based commodity depth cameras. In: IEEE International Conference on Acoustics, Speech and Signal Processing, pp. 5429–5432 (2012)
2. Zhu, M.X., Scharfenberger, C., Wong, A., Clausi, D.A.: Simultaneous scene reconstruction and auto-calibration using constrained iterative closest point for 3D depth sensor array. In: 12th Conference on Computer and Robot Vision, pp. 39–45 (2015)
3. Gurram, P., Rhody, H., Kerekes, J., Lach, S., Saber, E.: 3D scene reconstruction through a fusion of passive video and lidar imagery. In: 36th IEEE Applied Imagery Pattern Recognition Workshop, pp. 133–138 (2007)
4. Moghadam, P., Wijesoma, W.S., Feng, D.J.: Improving path planning and mapping based on stereo vision and lidar. In: 10th International Conference on Control, Automation, Robotics and Vision, pp. 384–389 (2008)
5. Reina, G., Milella, A., Halft, W., Worst, R.: Lidar and stereo imagery integration for safe navigation in outdoor settings. In: IEEE International Symposium on Safety, Security, and Rescue Robotics, pp. 1–6 (2013)
6. Zhang, F., Clarke, D., Knoll, A.: Vehicle detection based on lidar and camera fusion. In: IEEE 17th International Conference on Intelligent Transportation Systems, pp. 1620–1625 (2014)
7. Somanath, G., Cohen, S., Price, B., Kambhamettu, C.: Stereo+kinect for high resolution stereo correspondences. In: International Conference on 3D Vision, pp. 9–16 (2013)
8. Badino, H., Huber, D., Kanade, T.: Integrating lidar into stereo for fast and improved disparity computation. In: International Conference on 3D Imaging, Modeling, Processing, Visualization and Transmission, pp. 405–412 (2011)

9. SDU University: Covis library (2007). http://covis.sdu.dk/
10. SDU Robotics: Safe - safe perception and behavior in autonomous agricultural machines (2014). http://caro.sdu.dk/index.php/projects/projectslist?view=project&task=show&id=20
11. Acat project (2013). http://www.acat-project.eu/
12. Graf, B., Reiser, U., Hägele, M., Mauz, K., Klein, P.: Robotic home assistant care-o-bot 3 - product vision and innovation platform. In: IEEE Workshop on Advanced Robotics and its Social Impacts, pp. 139–144 (2009)
13. Bradski, G.: Dr. Dobb's Journal of Software Tools (2000)
14. MathWorks: Matlab stereo calibration app (2013). http://se.mathworks.com/help/vision/ug/stereo-camera-calibrator-app.html

Dense Lightfield Disparity Estimation Using Total Variation Regularization

Nuno Barroso Monteiro[1,2(✉)], João Pedro Barreto[2], and José Gaspar[1]

[1] Institute for Systems and Robotics, University of Lisbon, Lisbon, Portugal
{nmonteiro,jag}@isr.tecnico.ulisboa.pt
[2] Institute for Systems and Robotics, University of Coimbra, Coimbra, Portugal
jpbar@isr.uc.pt

Abstract. Plenoptic cameras make a trade-off between spatial and angular resolution. The knowledge of the disparity map allows to improve the resolution of these cameras using superresolution techniques. Nonetheless, the disparity map is often unknown and must be recovered from the lightfield captured. Hence, we focus on improving the disparity estimation from the structure tensor analysis of the epipolar plane images obtained from the lightfield. Using an hypercube representation, we formalize a data fusion problem with total variation regularization using the Alternating Direction Method of Multipliers. Assuming periodic boundary conditions allowed us to integrate the full 4D lightfield efficiently using the frequency domain. We applied this methodology to a synthetic dataset. The disparity estimations are more accurate than those of the structure tensor.

Keywords: Lightfield · Disparity · Denoising · ADMM · Total variation

1 Introduction

The plenoptic cameras allow to capture the direction and contribution of each ray to the total amount of light captured on an image. These cameras sample the plenoptic function.

The original 7D plenoptic function can be simplified into a 4D lightfield, the lumigraph $L(u, v, x, y)$ [7]. The lightfield is parameterized describing a ray by its intersection with two planes. In this parameterization a light ray intersects the first plane at coordinates (u, v) and then intersects a second plane at (x, y). The first pair of coordinates define the location of the ray and the second pair of coordinates allows to define the direction of the ray.

The image sensors are flat, therefore, this 4D space must be mapped into a 2D space, limiting the spatial and angular resolution [6]. Superresolution techniques are useful to overcome this limitation. These techniques can be applied if the images are shifted by sub-pixel amounts between successive images [8] or if there is *a priori* knowledge of the camera geometry to obtain this sub-pixel accuracy [5]. In plenoptic cameras we do not know the correspondence between

A. Campilho and F. Karray (Eds.): ICIAR 2016, LNCS 9730, pp. 462–469, 2016.
DOI: 10.1007/978-3-319-41501-7_52

the image views since the depth map, and consequently the disparity map, of the scene is unknown. Therefore, the knowledge of the disparity map is a requirement for superresolution techniques. In this work, we will focus on improving and recovering the disparity map from the lightfield captured.

2   Related Work

The problem of depth or disparity estimation is widely studied in computer vision. In the recent years, with the appearance of commercial versions this subject has been studied more intensively in plenoptic cameras.

Adelson and Wang [1] applied their lenticular array setup to estimate depth using the different views provided by the sensor by observing the vertical and horizontal parallax between the different views. Other strategies consider that the object becomes blurred according to their distance from the plane of focus [9]. More recent approaches, estimate depth from the epipolar plane images (EPI) obtained from the lightfield using the structure tensor analysis [4,13,15]. In these images, points in space are projected onto lines which can be more robustly detected than point correspondences.

Wanner et al. [15] proposed a global optimization framework that is based on the regularization and integration of the disparity maps obtained from the EPIs. This framework can be preceded of a labeling scheme to impose visibility constraints that imply a discretization of the disparity values. This step is computationally expensive and the discretization reduces the accuracy of the disparity estimation. Hence, Wanner et al. [13] considered a more efficient approach by performing a fast denoising scheme of a disparity estimation that combines the disparities obtained from two slices with orthogonal directions according to the coherence measurement of the structure tensor. In this method, the occlusion is handled by merging the information of horizontal and vertical EPIs. Although the results are good, the allowed disparity range is small and the occlusion boundaries are noisy. Diebold et al. [4] proposed a method that allows to extend the allowed disparity range using a refocusing scheme. The refocus of the EPIs to virtual depth layers allows to accommodate the orientation of the lines in the EPIs to the allowed disparity range. The results are then integrated into a global disparity map using a metric for occlusion handling that is based on a coherence measurement.

In this work, we propose a variational method to regularize and integrate the 2D EPIs of the full 4D lightfield without the discretization of the disparity values. This approach is computed efficiently by considering periodic boundary conditions that allows us to use Fast Fourier Transforms (FFTs).

3   Disparity Estimation from Lumigraph

Let us consider the 4D lightfield or lumigraph introduced in Sect. 1. The lumigraph $L\left(u,v,x,y\right)$ maps an intensity value to the light ray whose direction is defined by the intersection with the main lens plane at (u,v) and the image

Fig. 1. Epipolar plane images obtained from slicing and stacking the sequence of view-point images at position A and B for the *Still* dataset [14].

plane at (x, y) where u,v are the viewpoint coordinates, and x,y are the image coordinates.

The sampling of the lightfield and the configuration of the plenoptic camera satisfies the conditions presented by Bolles et al. [3] for constructing an EPI (Fig. 1). In the EPI, a point in space is projected onto a line with a slope $\Delta x/\Delta u$ proportional to its disparity. Considering the geometry defined by the EPI, the disparity d of a point in space is given by $d = f/z = \Delta x/\Delta u$, where z is the depth of the point, and f is the distance between the main lens plane and the image plane. To compute the slopes of the lines in the EPIs, we will use the structure tensor analysis similarly to Diebold et al. [4] and Wanner et al. [13].

4   Disparity Estimation Regularization

The EPI analysis allows to retrieve disparity information from a static scene for each pixel. The approaches used, normally, depend on gradient computations that increase the noise of the original image. Therefore, denoising using regularization is a useful approach to obtain a more accurate disparity estimation.

Let us consider the lumigraph $\mathbf{L} \in \mathbb{R}^{n_u \times n_v \times n_x \times n_y}$, where n_u,n_v are the horizontal and vertical angular resolutions, and n_x,n_y, are the horizontal and vertical spatial resolutions. For each ray in the lumigraph we can assign a disparity value performing an analysis of the EPIs. Therefore, the disparity values have the same dimensionality of the lumigraph, i.e., $\mathbf{D} \in \mathbb{R}^{n_u \times n_v \times n_x \times n_y}$.

Let us consider an alternative representation for the disparity structure, an hypercube $\mathbf{H}$. The hypercube is a set of datacubes $\mathbf{C}_{v_k}(u, x, y) = \mathrm{D}(u, v_k, x, y)$ that are obtained fixing one of the angular coordinates. These datacubes $\mathbf{C}_{(.)}$ consist on a vertical stack of the disparity observations obtained from the EPIs (Fig. 2). Another observation of the hypercube can be obtained by fixing u. Although they represent the same object, the disparity observations may differ due to the nature of the structure tensor.

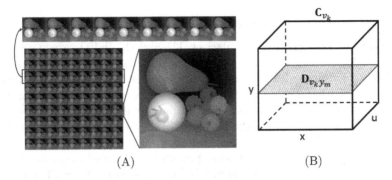

(A)   (B)

Fig. 2. Disparity hypercube representation. (A) Hypercube and datacube (green) represented as matrices, and image (blue) as viewed from a given viewpoint. (B) Datacube structure for fixed $v = v_k$. (Color figure online)

For an easier notation, let us consider that the disparity observations from a datacube $\mathbf{C}_{v_k}$ can be represented as a two-dimensional matrix, where each line corresponds to the disparity retrieved from each of the pixels of the EPI, lexicographically ordered (Fig. 2). Let the matrix representing the observed disparity be $\mathbf{Y}_{v_k} \in \mathbb{R}^{n_y \times (n_x \times n_u)}$. Assuming that our observations are only affected by i.i.d. additive noise $\mathbf{W}_{v_k} \in \mathbb{R}^{n_y \times (n_x \times n_u)}$, we can model our disparity observations as $\mathbf{Y}_{v_k} = \mathbf{Z}_{v_k} + \mathbf{W}_{v_k}$, where $\mathbf{Z}_{v_k} \in \mathbb{R}^{n_y \times (n_x \times n_u)}$ are the real disparities from the datacube. For simplicity, we assume that the boundary conditions are periodic. This allows to compute convolutions and matrix inversions using FFTs. The previous observation model can be generalized for the hypercube $\mathbf{H}$ by including the datacubes $\mathbf{C}_{v_k}, k = 1, \ldots, n_v$ (Fig. 2).

$$\mathbf{Y}_v = \mathbf{M}_v \mathbf{Z} + \mathbf{W}_v \tag{1}$$

with $\mathbf{Y}_v, \mathbf{Z}, \mathbf{W}_v \in \mathbb{R}^{(n_y \times n_v) \times (n_x \times n_u)}$ resulting from the vertical stacking of the matrices $\mathbf{Y}_{v_k}$, $\mathbf{Z}_{v_k}$, and $\mathbf{W}_{v_k}$ for $k = 1, \ldots, n_v$, respectively. $\mathbf{M}_v \in \mathbb{R}^{(n_y \times n_v) \times (n_y \times n_v)}$ correspond to a uniform subsampling of $\mathbf{Z}$. This allows to include disparity observations from several viewpoints while considering the same virtual camera motion to obtain the EPIs. Similarly, we can obtain the observation model for the hypercube observation obtained by fixing u, $\mathbf{Y}_u = \mathbf{Z}^T \mathbf{M}_u^T + \mathbf{W}_u$.

These structures (Fig. 2) represent a repeating sequence of disparity images that differ in a small number of pixels due to the different viewpoint coordinates. Since we obtain natural like images we propose to apply an isotropic total variation regularizer proposed by Rudin et al. [11] to promote sharp discontinuities at edges. This type of regularizer has already been used in the context of lightfield analysis [13]. This leads to an optimization problem that is similar to the one presented by Simões et al. [12] in the context of hyperspectral cameras superresolution:

$$\hat{\mathbf{Z}} = \arg\min_{\mathbf{Z}} \frac{1}{2} \|\mathbf{Y}_v - \mathbf{M}_v \mathbf{Z}\|_F^2 + \frac{\lambda_u}{2} \|\mathbf{Y}_u^T - \mathbf{M}_u \mathbf{Z}\|_F^2 + \lambda_r \mathrm{TV}(\mathbf{Z}\mathbf{D}_h, \mathbf{Z}\mathbf{D}_v) \tag{2}$$

where $\|\cdot\|_F = \sqrt{tr\left[(\cdot)(\cdot)^T\right]}$ corresponds to the Frobenius norm, TV corresponds to the isotropic total variation regularizer [11], and $\mathbf{D}_h$ and $\mathbf{D}_v$ are matrices that allow to compute the horizontal and vertical discrete differences considering periodic boundary conditions, respectively. In this optimization problem, the first two terms are data-fitting terms while the last term is the regularizer. The data terms should explain the observed disparities considering the observation models for $\mathbf{Y}_v$ and $\mathbf{Y}_u$. The weights λ_u and λ_r allows to control the contribution of each of the terms.

The solution for this optimization problem is obtained using an Alternating Direction Method of Multipliers (ADMM) instance, the Split Augmented Lagrangian Shrinkage Algorithm (SALSA) [2]. Thus, the optimization variable $\mathbf{Z}$ is split into auxiliary variables using the variable splitting technique. The optimization problem (2) is now defined by:

$$\hat{\mathbf{Z}} = \arg\min_{\mathbf{Z}} \tfrac{1}{2}\left\|\mathbf{Y}_v - \mathbf{M}_v\mathbf{V}_1\right\|_F^2 + \tfrac{\lambda_u}{2}\left\|\mathbf{Y}_u^T - \mathbf{M}_u\mathbf{V}_2\right\|_F^2 + \lambda_r\mathrm{TV}\left(\mathbf{V}_3,\mathbf{V}_4\right)$$
$$\text{subject to} \quad \mathbf{V}_1 = \mathbf{Z}, \quad \mathbf{V}_2 = \mathbf{Z}, \quad \mathbf{V}_3 = \mathbf{Z}\mathbf{D}_h, \quad \mathbf{V}_4 = \mathbf{Z}\mathbf{D}_v \tag{3}$$

Considering $f(\mathbf{V}) = \tfrac{1}{2}\left\|\mathbf{Y}_v - \mathbf{M}_v\mathbf{V}_1\right\|_F^2 + \tfrac{\lambda_u}{2}\left\|\mathbf{Y}_u^T - \mathbf{M}_u\mathbf{V}_2\right\|_F^2 + \lambda_r\mathrm{TV}$ $(\mathbf{V}_3,\mathbf{V}_4)$, $\mathbf{V} = \left[\mathbf{V}_1^T\ \mathbf{V}_2^T\ \mathbf{V}_3^T\ \mathbf{V}_4^T\right]^T$, and $\mathbf{G} = \left[\mathbf{I}\ \mathbf{I}\ \mathbf{D}_h^T\ \mathbf{D}_v^T\right]^T$, the problem has the following Augmented Lagrangian [10]:

$$\mathcal{L}(\mathbf{Z},\mathbf{V},\mathbf{A}) = f(\mathbf{V}) + \frac{\mu}{2}\left\|\mathbf{G}\mathbf{Z}^T - \mathbf{V} - \mathbf{A}\right\|_F^2 \tag{4}$$

where μ is a positive constant called the penalty parameter. Now, we are able to apply SALSA. Considering as input the observations $\mathbf{Y}_v$ and $\mathbf{Y}_u$, the parameters λ_u, λ_r and μ, and the initializations for $\mathbf{V}^{(0)}$ and $\mathbf{A}^{(0)}$, we will solve the following optimizations at each iteration k until a stopping criterion is satisfied:

$$\mathbf{Z}^{(k+1)} = \arg\min_{\mathbf{Z}} \mathcal{L}(\mathbf{Z},\mathbf{V}^{(k)},\mathbf{A}^{(k)})$$
$$\mathbf{V}^{(k+1)} = \arg\min_{\mathbf{V}} \mathcal{L}(\mathbf{Z}^{(k+1)},\mathbf{V},\mathbf{A}^{(k)}) \tag{5}$$

The algorithm described above has a matrix $\mathbf{G}$ with full column rank (due to the presence of identity matrix $\mathbf{I}$), and the function $f(\cdot)$ is a sum of closed, proper, and convex functions. Therefore, the conditions for the convergence of SALSA established in [2] are met.

5   Experimental Results

The methodology described in the previous sections was applied to the *Still* synthetic dataset provided by the HCI Heidelberg Group [14] (Fig. 2). The results of the regularization with one and two data terms are compared with the disparity estimates from the structure tensor. The ground truth provided with the synthetic dataset is used to determine the PSNR values. Since the ground truth

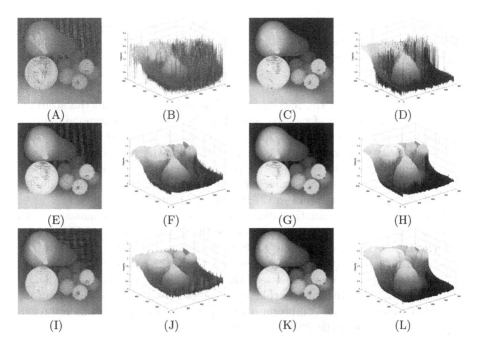

(A)   (B)   (C)   (D)

(E)   (F)   (G)   (H)

(I)   (J)   (K)   (L)

Fig. 3. Disparity estimation using the structure tensor analysis (top) and after regularization with one (middle) and two data terms (bottom). The columns correspond to the disparity estimates using a 2D representation (1st and 3rd columns) and a 3D representation (2nd and 4th columns) to highlight the noise. Peripheral viewpoints are depicted on the 1st and 2nd columns. Central viewpoints are depicted on the 3rd and 4th columns.

values correspond to depth measurements and our values are disparity measurements, we converted the depth ground truth to disparity. The results are depicted in Fig. 3.

The structure tensor analysis was performed assuming an equal contribution for each of the color channels. Also, the smoothing of the image and the components of the structure tensor was obtained by applying Gaussian distributions with standard deviation 0.8 and 3.2, respectively. To compute the derivatives we considered the 3×3 Sobel mask. For the optimization problem, we consider an equal contribution for each of the data terms ($\lambda_u = 1$), and the penalty parameter μ to be fixed and equal to 1 since it only affects the convergence speed and not the convergence. The parameter λ_r was fine tuned by performing a denoising of the disparity ground truth and selecting the one that provides the highest PSNR.

From Fig. 3, we can see that the hypercube obtained from the structure tensor analysis presents a noticeable decay on accuracy in the peripheral viewpoints. Focusing on a specific viewpoint (peripheral or central), we can conclude that the depth accuracy also depends on the region of the image. The disparity estimates are less accurate on homogeneous regions, which in the EPI represent regions of constant intensity between the lines that we want to detect. A small change of intensity in these regions lead to disparity estimates that change rapidly and have high variability. This is more noticeable on the 3D representation of the disparity estimates (Fig. 3B and D).

The hypercube after the regularization has reduced noise and the accuracy remains almost the same from the central to the peripheral viewpoints, which confirms the statement of Sect. 4. Indeed, if we compare the 3D representations of the disparity estimates we can see that the noise is significantly reduced. This is confirmed by the increased PSNR after regularization (from 8.65 dB to 10.76 dB). The noise can be further reduced by considering the additional data term of the optimization problem (2) (PSNR of 11.00 dB).

Furthermore, the formulation allows to select specific disparity measurements for each of the observations of the hypercube through the matrices $\mathbf{M}_v$ and $\mathbf{M}_u$. Therefore, we performed the same analysis but now considering only the disparity observations with higher coherence values from each hypercube observation. In this scenario, a compromise between the two hypercube observations will only occur for disparities with similar coherence values between the two observations instead of achieving this compromise for all disparities. Hence, this approach leads to an increase in the PSNR value for 11.38 dB.

6   Conclusions

In this work, we formalize a data fusion problem which uses the full 4D lightfield. The optimization problem was solved by resorting to an ADMM instance that provides good results with few iterations. Furthermore, we considered simplifications to the boundary conditions that allowed to use FFTs in the computations. Therefore, the algorithm is computationally efficient. This methodology was applied to a synthetic dataset and allows to obtain estimates that are more accurate and robust to noise. The results are improved when we consider only the disparities with higher coherence values in each of the hypercube observations.

The formulation for the data fusion problem can still be improved. In the formulation, we are considering the full 4D lightfield information for the disparities but we are not considering blurring in the observation models. Additionally, the initial disparity estimations can also be improved. The disparity observations were obtained from the structure tensor analysis of the EPIs, but we did not consider refocusing or occlusion handling [4] to improve the disparity observations.

Acknowledgments. We would like to thank Prof. José Bioucas-Dias for the discussions that allowed us to improve our work. This work has been supported by the Portuguese Foundation for Science and Technology (FCT) project [UID / EEA / 50009 / 2013] and by the CMU-Portugal Project Augmented Human Assistance (AHA) [CMUP-ERI / HCI / 0046 / 2013]. Nuno Barroso Monteiro is funded by FCT PhD grant PD/BD/105778/2014.

References

1. Adelson, E.H., Wang, J.Y.A.: Single lens stereo with a plenoptic camera. IEEE Trans. Pattern Anal. Mach. Intell. **2**, 99–106 (1992)
2. Afonso, M.V., Bioucas-Dias, J.M., Figueiredo, M.A.: An augmented lagrangian approach to the constrained optimization formulation of imaging inverse problems. IEEE Trans. Image Process. **20**(3), 681–695 (2011)
3. Bolles, R.C., Baker, H.H., Marimont, D.H.: Epipolar-plane image analysis: an approach to determining structure from motion. Int. J. Comput. Vis. **1**(1), 7–55 (1987)
4. Diebold, M., Goldluecke, B.: Epipolar plane image refocusing for improved depth estimation and occlusion handling (2013)
5. Georgiev, T., Lumsdaine, A.: Superresolution with plenoptic camera 2.0. Adobe Systems Incorporated, Technical report (2009)
6. Georgiev, T., Zheng, K.C., Curless, B., Salesin, D., Nayar, S., Intwala, C.: Spatio-angular resolution tradeoffs in integral photography. In: Rendering Techniques 2006, pp. 263–272 (2006)
7. Gortler, S.J., Grzeszczuk, R., Szeliski, R., Cohen, M.F.: The lumigraph. In: Proceedings of the 23rd Annual Conference on Computer Graphics and Interactive Techniques, pp. 43–54. ACM (1996)
8. Ng, M.K., Yau, A.C.: Super-resolution image restoration from blurred low-resolution images. J. Math. Imaging Vis. **23**(3), 367–378 (2005)
9. Ng, R., Levoy, M., Brédif, M., Duval, G., Horowitz, M., Hanrahan, P.: Light field photography with a hand-held plenoptic camera. Comput. Sci. Tech. Rep. CSTR **2**(11), 1–11 (2005)
10. Nocedal, J., Wright, S.: Numerical Optimization. Springer, New York (2006)
11. Rudin, L.I., Osher, S., Fatemi, E.: Nonlinear total variation based noise removal algorithms. Phys. D: Nonlinear Phenom. **60**(1), 259–268 (1992)
12. Simões, M., Bioucas-Dias, J., Almeida, L.B., Chanussot, J.: A convex formulation for hyperspectral image superresolution via subspace-based regularization. IEEE Trans. Geosci. Remote Sens. **53**(6), 3373–3388 (2015)
13. Wanner, S., Goldluecke, B.: Variational light field analysis for disparity estimation and super-resolution. IEEE Trans. Pattern Anal. Mach. Intell. **36**(3), 606–619 (2014)
14. Wanner, S., Meister, S., Goldluecke, B.: Datasets and benchmarks for densely sampled 4d light fields. In: VMV, pp. 225–226. Citeseer (2013)
15. Wanner, S., Straehle, C., Goldluecke, B.: Globally consistent multi-label assignment on the ray space of 4d light fields. In: Proceedings of the IEEE Conference on Computer Vision and Pattern Recognition, pp. 1011–1018 (2013)

Target Position and Speed Estimation Using LiDAR

Enes Dayangac$^{(\boxtimes)}$, Florian Baumann, Josep Aulinas, and Matthias Zobel

ADASENS Automotive GmbH, Oberhof 13, 88138 Weissensberg, Germany
{enes.dayangac,florian.baumann,josep.aulinas,matthias.zobel}@adasens.com
http://www.adasens.com

Abstract. In this paper, an efficient and reliable framework to estimate the position and speed of moving vehicles is proposed. The method fuses LiDAR data with image based object detection algorithm output. LiDAR sensors deliver 3D point clouds with a positioning accuracy of up to two centimeters. 2D object data leads to a significant reduction of the search space. Outliers removal techniques are applied to the reduced 3D point cloud for a more reliable representation of the data. Furthermore, a multi-hypothesis Kalman filter is implemented to determine the target object's speed. The accuracy of the position and velocity estimation is verified through real data and simulation. Additionally, the proposed framework is real-time capable and suitable for embedded-vision related applications.

Keywords: LiDAR · Velodyne · Kalman filter · Multi-hypotheses · 3D point cloud · Sensor fusion · Distance · Speed estimation

1 Introduction

The automotive industry integrates varieties of peripheral sensors into advanced driver assistance systems (ADAS), e.g., ultrasonic sensors, camera sensors, mid and long range radar and LiDAR. Redundancy in the data can be exploited by sensor fusion, leading to an accurate observation of the state of the vehicle and its surroundings.

LiDAR technology is advancing and provides a full line of sensors capable of delivering accurate real-time 3D data up to 2.2 million points per second. However, it is challenging to process the resulting point cloud to retrieve relevant information in real time. Also, LiDAR is incapable of sensing visual cues such as lines, color, and brightness differences e.g. for the identification of traffic lights, brake lights, turning signals or signs. Unlike LiDAR, camera systems are able to detect and recognize objects such as traffic signs, pedestrians, or vehicles.

In this paper, a framework is presented where the distance to the target object and the target speed can be reliably estimated by integrating the data collected from LiDAR and camera sensors. 2D object detection and tracking systems are deployed to detect objects in the camera data and reduce the search space in the

© Springer International Publishing Switzerland 2016
A. Campilho and F. Karray (Eds.): ICIAR 2016, LNCS 9730, pp. 470–477, 2016.
DOI: 10.1007/978-3-319-41501-7_53

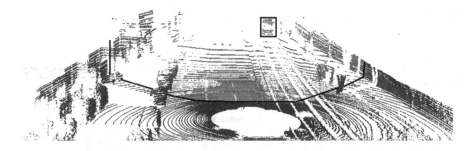

Fig. 1. A LiDAR 3D point cloud is illustrated. In the 2D image (from the KITTI data [1], 2011-09-26, drive 001 image sequence), the object is detected and overlapped with 3D data to reduce the search space. The bold line indicates the camera field of view and the box represents the vehicle in the point cloud.

3D point cloud (see Fig. 1). Along with outlier removal, filtering techniques are implemented to estimate the target speed accurately. The framework is tailored for vehicle detection. Also, it is applicable to any kind of target objects such as pedestrians, cyclists, or vehicles to enhance ADAS, e.g., forward collision warning, crossing traffic detection, or advanced emergency braking.

This paper is structured as follows. Section 2 reviews related work and Sect. 3 presents the proposed approach including fundamentals. Experimental results are shown in Sect. 4 and conclusions are drawn in Sect. 5.

2   Related Work

Distance and speed estimation with LiDAR sensors and the combination with an object detection system is a challenging research area in computer vision. Regarding the automotive industry and autonomous driving scenarios, LiDAR systems are becoming the next generation of driver assistance systems [2,3] and have high potential for achieving outstanding results.

Most of the research combines several redundant techniques to obtain a more accurate and robust system. For instance, Mählisch et al. propose a sensor fusion framework between video and LiDAR data, used to improve vehicle detection [4]. Premebida et al. propose a LiDAR and vision based approach for pedestrian and vehicle detection and tracking [5]. Ogawa et al. propose a system for pedestrian tracking and detection [6], solely using an in-vehicle LiDAR sensor. Mählisch et al. combine LiDAR, video and ESP data for vehicle tracking to enhance adaptive cruise control [7].

In comparison to these approaches, we propose a framework that combines LiDAR data with an object detection system. The contribution of this paper is to reduce the complexity in 3D data for a robust estimation of an object's distance and speed. According to the best of our knowledge, this approach has not yet been investigated.

3   Robust and Accurate Estimation

An overview of our proposed method is illustrated in Fig. 2. The general architecture can be divided into three parts: data association, outlier removal and
estimation.

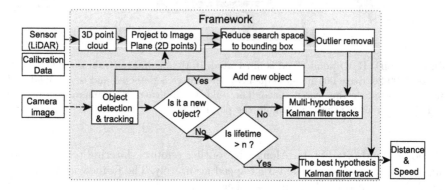

Fig. 2. Proposed framework system architecture.

3.1   Data Association

3D Mapping: 3D information is given by LiDAR, which provides a set of 3D
data points. The 3D points $X_i = [x, y, z]^T$, $i \in \mathbb{N}$, $i \leq n$ where i is the point index
and n the number of points in the cloud with respect to the LiDAR coordinate
system. These points are transformed first to the camera coordinate system and
then to the image coordinate system. In order to compute these transformations,
each 3D point $X_i' = [x, y, z, 1]^T$ is represented as an homogeneous point. Let
$T_{4 \times 4}$ be the homogeneous transformation matrix from the LiDAR to the camera
coordinate system and $P_{3 \times 4}$ is the 10 degrees of freedom camera projection
matrix. The pinhole camera model [8] is used for mapping from LiDAR to image
plane in Eq. 1.

$$x_i = PTX_i' \tag{1}$$

Search Space Reduction: There are millions of unstructured points in LiDAR
data. Thus, it is costly to process LiDAR points such as filtering out the points
on the ground plane or segmenting objects to generate target hypotheses. For
real time processing, it is required to reduce the search space. In our method,
the points are filtered in the camera scene. Additionally, the output bounding
box from the object detection and tracking is used to decrease the search space.
Using this reduced search space, the indices of 3D points are associated to a
bounding box representing an object.

Data: 3D points $X_i = [x, y, z]^T$ per bounding box
Result: mean(inliers)
$\mu = \text{mean}(X_i)$; $\sigma = \text{standardDeviation}(X_i)$
$[bin1, bin2] = \text{kMeans}(x, z, \|X_i\|)$
Choose the bin having larger number of points, bin $= \max(bin1, bin2)$
while *not at end of the bin* **do**
$\qquad$ get next point X_j from the bin
$\qquad k = \frac{\|X_j - \mu\|}{\sigma}$
$\qquad$ **if** $k < threshold$ **then**
$\qquad\qquad$ | set X_j as inlier
$\qquad$ **end**
end

Algorithm 1. Outliers removal based on k-Means clustering and the ratio of absolute deviation to standard deviation.

3.2 Outlier Removal

In the 3D points belonging to an object, the outliers exist due to the following issues: The cluttered backgrounds happens at the edge of the detected bounding boxes, or the occlusion causes foreground outliers (see Fig. 3). Another issue is that target objects, such as vehicles, have glass windows where LiDAR 3D points becomes inaccurate in positioning. Finally, the detected bounding boxes can be imprecise, bigger or smaller. Therefore, a smaller Region of Interest (ROI) is considered to represent the object in detected bounding boxes. Consequently, a k-Means clustering algorithm [9] is applied and the ratio of absolute deviation to standard deviation is checked to determine outliers as shown in Algorithm 1.

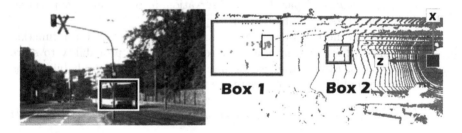

Fig. 3. Left: The box represents the detection of an object which is partially occluded by a traffic light (from KITTI data [1] 2011-09-26, drive 001 image sequence). Right: Top view LiDAR point cloud. The detected object is represented by Box 1 which has a cluttered background due to imprecise object detection. In Box 2, outliers exist due to occlusion.

3.3 Estimation

In this framework, the object detection and tracking algorithms detect and track an object over a number of frames. The algorithms locate the object and assigns an identification number to the same object through out an image sequence. The approach relies on these algorithms with the assumption of having a lower false alarm rate in urban environments. Using the identification number and detection, the corresponding 3D points are chosen. Based on the 3D points belonging to the object, the goal is to measure the object's position and speed accurately.

Kalman Filter: An extended four-state Kalman filter [10] is designed using a constant velocity model. The main requirement for the filter is to produce reliable estimations of position and speed of target vehicles. Therefore, the state vector consists of: Longitudinal distance z and lateral offset x of the target vehicle w.r.t. the ego vehicle coordinate system, relative speed $\dot{z}$ in Z-direction and $\dot{x}$ in X-direction between target and ego vehicles.

Distance observations from LiDAR are used as measurements in order to update the states. All these steps are standard and commonly used for generic object tracking in moving scenarios. The filter is required to be designed and parametrized to converge to the actual values quickly. Besides, the speed of such convergence is highly influenced by state vector initialization.

Multiple Tracks: Implementing several filters with different initial hypotheses might improve convergence time, which is critical in object detection for automotive applications. Therefore, multi-hypotheses Kalman filter tracks are initialized when a new target object is detected. That is, for each target object, multiple Kalman filters $\{K_0, K_1, K_2, ... , K_m\}$ are initialized at initial speeds v_i. The subscript m is the total number of filters and v_i ranges between values $V_{range} = [V_{min}, V_{max}]$ using a step value $\Delta v = \frac{|V_{max} - V_{min}|}{m}$.

If there is a target object having the position $p_{current}$, we can simply use the speed hypothesis and predict the next position $p_{current}$ using the formula $p_{next} = p_{current} + v_i dt$. Compared to the observation, incorrect speed hypotheses will yield bigger errors in the Kalman filter prediction.

As soon as the lifetime of an object is bigger than n, the error function $f_{error}(x, z)$ in Eq. 2 is taken into account to compute the probability to score all the filter tracks. After n frames, the filter with the highest probability (the smallest state error) is used to estimate the trajectory.

$$f_{error}(x, z) = |x_{prediction} - x_{observation}| + |z_{prediction} - z_{observation}| \quad (2)$$

A Kalman filter's complexity is $O(n^2)$ and adding additional filters for multiple tracks increases the complexity linearly. Thus, n and V_{range} can be chosen arbitrarily depending on the application.

4   Experiments

In this section, evaluation results are presented. For the evaluation, a series of experiments are conducted using both real sensor data and synthetic data in order to assess the performance. The filter state error for different hypotheses and their run-time performances are measured. Also, average position and speed errors are explored using a varying number of hypotheses and lifetime while tuning the observation noise level.

For the sensor data, the LiDAR operates at 10 Hz and generates over one million points per second. Also, a simulation script is set up to generate synthetic data with Gaussian noise. Additionally, the proposed algorithms run on a single core of an Intel i7-2630QM CPU at 2.00 GHz.

Table 1. Average run-time per target object ($V_{range} = [-30, 30]$ m/s, $\Delta v = 0.25$).

Data association	62.50 ms
Outlier removal	0.37 ms
Estimation	1.94 ms

Experimental Results: The run-time performances are inspected on real sensor data deploying 240 hypotheses per target object according to Sect. 3. The run-time results are presented in Table 1 where data association, outlier removal and estimation take 62.50 ms, 0.37 ms and 1.94 ms respectively.

The different initial hypotheses were enforced to improve the convergence time for more accurate estimation in Sect. 3.3. In Fig. 4 (left), some of the hypotheses are chosen and shown where initial speeds are $v_1 = -30$, $v_2 = -18.75$, $v_3 = -7.5$, $v_4 = 0.25$, $v_5 = 3.75$ m/s. It is clear that the filter state error f_{error} differs according to given initial speeds. In Fig. 4 (left), v_4 is a better estimation which converges faster than others, whereas v_1 has the biggest state error between observation and estimation. The number of hypotheses vs. FPS (Frames per Seconds) graph is drawn in Fig. 4 (right), where more hypotheses mean fewer FPS.

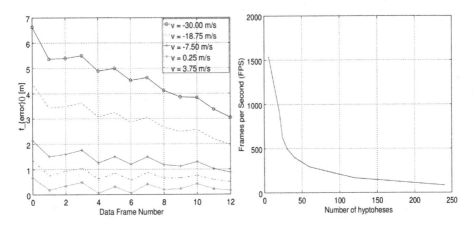

Fig. 4. Left: Different hypotheses yield varying state error f_{error} over data frame number where real relative speed is around 0 m/s. Right: FPS vs. Number of hypotheses.

Tracking an object with multiple hypotheses and the estimation with the highest probability is used for updating the target position and speed. The chosen lifetime for multiple hypotheses affects the error according to the simulation in Fig. 5. Also, larger number of hypotheses decrease the average position and speed error as shown in Fig. 6. However there is only small difference between 60, 120 and 240 hypotheses.

In the experiments using the real data, selected 3D points that belong to a target object have an average standard deviation of $\sigma_z = 0.15\,\text{m}$ in longitudinal distance. The average standard deviation in all directions is 0.6 m. According to this, the position estimation is in the range of 0.1 – 0.3 m accuracy in Fig. 5.

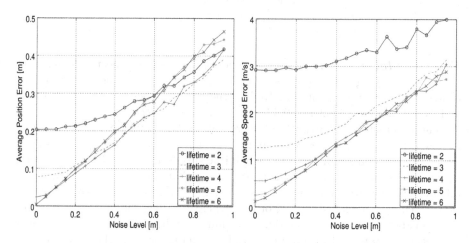

Fig. 5. Average system error using different target lifetimes and noise levels with 240 hypotheses.

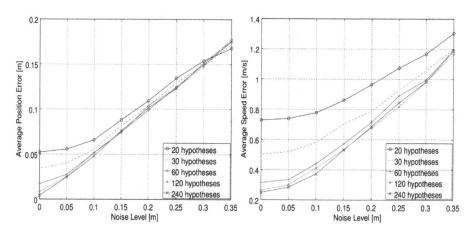

Fig. 6. Average system error using different number of hypotheses and noise levels at lifetime = 5.

5   Conclusions

A sensor fusion strategy is presented to estimate the position and the speed of target objects from LiDAR data. The 3D search space is massively reduced by assuming that 3D points that belong to a target object will be reprojected within the 2D object bounding box on the image plane. Let the noise level be 0.2 m in Fig. 6, the experimental results demonstrate that position and speed can be estimated with an accuracy of up to 0.1 m and 0.7 m/s. Furthermore, our approach produces consistent estimates after five frames. Future work should focus on optimizing the data association stage, which is currently the main bottleneck of our proposed method. The remaining stages of this approach, e.g., outlier removal, filtering, position and distance computation, are proven to be real-time suitable for embedded-vision purposes in ADAS applications.

References

1. Geiger, A., Lenz, P., Stiller, C., Urtasun, R.: Vision meets robotics: The kitti dataset. Int. J. Robot. Res. (IJRR) (2013)
2. Rasshofer, R., Gresser, K.: Automotive radar and lidar systems for next generation driver assistance functions. Adv. Radio Sci. **3**(B.4), 205–209 (2005)
3. Ghring, D., Wang, M., Schnrmacher, M., Ganjineh, T.: Radar/lidar sensor fusion for car-following on highways. In: Automation, Robotics and Applications (ICARA), pp. 1838–1845 (2011)
4. Mählisch, M., Schweiger, R., Ritter, W., Dietmayer, K.: Sensorfusion using spatio-temporal aligned video and lidar for improved vehicle detection. In: IEEE Intelligent Vehicles Symposium (2006)
5. Premebida, C., Monteiro, G., Nunes, U., Peixoto, P.: A lidar and vision-based approach for pedestrian and vehicle detection and tracking. In: Intelligent Transportation Systems Conference (ITSC), pp. 1044–1049. IEEE (2007)
6. Ogawa, T., Sakai, H., Suzuki, Y., Takagi, K., Morikawa, K.: Pedestrian detection and tracking using in-vehicle lidar for automotive application. In: Intelligent Vehicles Symposium, pp. 734–739. IEEE (2011)
7. Mählisch, M., Hering, R., Ritter, W., Dietmayer, K.: Heterogeneous fusion of video, lidar and esp data for automotive acc vehicle tracking. In: Multisensor Fusion and Integration for Intelligent Systems, pp. 139–144. IEEE (2006)
8. Hartley, R., Zisserman, A.: Multiple View Geometry in Computer Vision, 2nd edn. Cambridge University Press, New York (2003)
9. Duda, R.O., Hart, P.E., Stork, D.G.: Pattern Classification, 2nd edn. Wiley-Interscience, New York (2000)
10. Kalman, R.E.: A new approach to linear filtering and prediction problems. J. Basic Eng. **82**(1), 35–45 (1960)

RGB-D Camera Applications

Combining 3D Shape and Color for 3D Object Recognition

Susana Brandão[1]([✉]), João P. Costeira[1], and Manuela Veloso[2]

[1] Instituto Superior Técnico, Lisboa, Portugal
susana.brandao@tecnico.ulisboa.pt, jpc@isr.ist.utl.pt
[2] Carnegie Mellon University, Pittsburgh, USA
mmv@cs.cmu.edu

Abstract. We present new results in object recognition based on color and 3D shape obtained from 3D cameras. Namely, we further exploit diffusion processes to represent shape and the use of color/texture as a perturbation to the diffusion process. Diffusion processes are an effective tool to replace shortest path distances in the characterization of 3D shapes. They also provide effective means for the seamlessly representation of color and shape, mainly because they provide information both the color and on their distribution over surfaces. While there have been different approaches for incorporating color information in the diffusion process, this is the first work that explores different parameterizations of color and their impact on recognition tasks. We present results using very challenging datasets, where we propose to recognize different instances of the same object class assuming a very limited a-priori knowledge on each individual object.

1 Introduction

We here exploit the use of diffusion processes to represent color and texture information associated with a 3D surface such as the partial view obtained by a RGB+D camera. Our objective is to further improve on the Partial View Heat Kernel descriptor (PVHK), previously introduced in [3], and that represents shapes using diffusion processes as surrogates for distance and that represents color and shape by directing associating RGB data to position.

The PVHK descriptor represents partial views as an organized set of distances between a point at surface center and those in the surface boundary, as showed in the topmost example in Fig. 1. To ensure that the set of distances is resilient to noise, distances are represented by the result of a diffusion process as represented in the example at the bottom of Fig. 1. In the example we simulate the process by which temperature initially concentrated on a single reference

S. Brandão—This research is partially supported by the NSF under award NSF IIS-1012733, a student fellowship from the FCT within the CMU-Portugal dual degree program and from the FCT under strategy grant FCT [UID/EEA/50009/2013]. The views and conclusions contained herein are those of the authors only.

A. Campilho and F. Karray (Eds.): ICIAR 2016, LNCS 9730, pp. 481–489, 2016.
DOI: 10.1007/978-3-319-41501-7_54

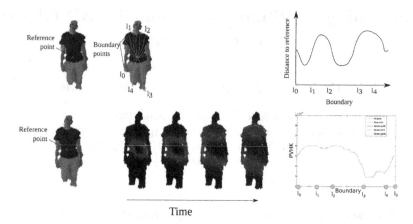

Fig. 1. Representing partial views from distances to a reference point. At the top, we use the shortest path distance between a reference point and the boundary. At the bottom, we use heat diffusion has a surrogate. The reference point now becomes a heat source, and as time passes temperature propagates from the source to the rest of the object. When heat reaches the boundary, the temperature there will depend on the distance to the source. (Color figure online)

point spreads over the surface. The idea is that at each time instant the temperature at each point depends on an average of all the paths that lead to the reference point. Thus temperature is more robust to the presence of holes, common in RGB-D active cameras.

In [3], and for the first time, was proposed a descriptor that directly associates color to position in the 3D shape using weights affecting the diffusion rate at each point, making it faster in some parts of the surface and slower in others. We illustrate the impact of adding appearance information to the descriptor by considering a person in the same position, wearing the same clothes but with different colors, as in Fig. 2.

Fig. 2. Impact of different colors and their distribution on the partial view descriptor. Different colors now represent different heat propagation rates, changing the temperature at the boundary for object with the same shape. (Color figure online)

This paper focuses on the map between RGB information, in $\mathbb{R}^3$, into scalar weights, assessing the impact on recognition tasks of different scalar functions. We carry the recognition task using a nearest neighbor classifier and a set of a-priori labeled partial views. As the performance of such classifier depends on the number of partial views in the dataset, we here also study how good is the color extention of PVHK at generalizing to new descriptors, not present in the library of known partial views.

2 Related Work

As far as we are aware, only diffusion based representations have been proposed to jointly represent color and 3D shape ensuring that color is directly mapped into the 3D position, i.e., so that a change in the texture position would lead to a change in the descriptor. The photometric heat kernel [5], directly associates appearance to 3D coordinates by representing each point in the surface by its physical coordinates plus RGB values. Each point was described using diffusion processes in the R^6 space, however the representation changed with the color gradient, not absolute value, i.e., a white wall becomes equivalent to a blue wall.

Other RGB-D descriptors lose the correlation between the color/texture and the 3D position. Namely those introduced in [2,7], resort to extending ad-hoc the descriptor dimension to include some color/texture descriptor on the extra dimensions, without associating appearance features with positions in the object.

Furthermore, from the diffusion based approaches, the C-PVHK heat kernel was the first to introduce a weighted scheme. A similar approach was later used in [1] for complete 3D shapes. However, they do not explicit the exact mapping between RGB values and color. Finally, we note that the PVHK as been used in different contexts for object recognition from multiple views of different objects, [4,8] showing its potential for applications with RGB+D cameras.

3 Joint Representation of Color and Texture

In the following, we review the formalism to simulate heat diffusing on surfaces represented by meshes such as those returned by RGB-D sensors.

3.1 Heat Kernel

Formally, the temperature diffusion over a surface, as the one in Fig. 3 defined by a set of vertices $V = \{v_1, v_2, ..., v_{N_V}\}$, with coordinates $\{\bar{x}_1, \bar{x}_2, ..., \bar{x}_{N_V}\}$ together with a set of edges $E = \{e_1 = (v_l, v_k), e_2, ..., e_{N_E}\}$, is described by Eq. 1:

$$L\bar{T}(t) = -\partial_t \bar{T}(t),\qquad(1)$$

Fig. 3. Example of the mesh structure, where the dots represent vertices and lines connecting the dots correspond to edges.

where $L \in \mathbb{R}^{N_v \times N_v}$, is a discrete Laplace-Beltrami operator, and $\bar{T}(t) \in \mathbb{R}^{N_v}$ is a vector containing the temperatures over all vertices in the surface at instant t. In this work, we use a distance based representation of L, where L is a weighted graph Laplacian where the weight of each edge is the inverse of its length:

$$L\bar{T}(t) = (D - W)\,\bar{T}(t),$$ (2)

$$[W]_{v_i,v_j} = \begin{cases} 1/\|\bar{x}_{v_i} - \bar{x}_{v_j}\|^2, & \text{iff} \quad e_l = (v_j, v_i) \in E \\ 0, & \text{otherwise} \end{cases},$$ (3)

and where D is a diagonal matrix with entries $D_{ii} = \sum_{j=1}^{N}[W]_{ij}$.

The heat kernel, $k(v_j, v_s, t)$ is the solution of Eq. 1 at time instant t and vertex v_j when the initial temperature $\bar{T}(0)$, is zero everywhere except at source vertex v_s, i.e., $\bar{T}(0) : [\bar{T}(0)]_i = 1$, iff $i = v_s$, 0 otherwise.

The above initial value problem has a closed form solution, Eq. 4, in terms of the Laplace-Beltrami operator's eigenvectors, ϕ_i, and eigenvalues, λ_i:

$$k(v_j, v_s, t) = \sum_{i=1}^{N} e^{-\lambda_i t}[\bar{\phi}_i]_{v_j}[\bar{\phi}_i]_{v_s},$$ (4)

where $[\bar{\phi}_i]_{v_j}$ is the value of $\bar{\phi}_i$ at the vertex v_j.

Equation 4 contains information on the complete surface through the eigenvalues and eigenvectors of L, i.e., even when v_j and v_s are fixed points on the object surface, the descriptors changes if L changes.

3.2 Heat Kernel for RGB-D Representation

The color PVHK, C-PVHK, requires a slight modification of the heat equation. The heat equation represents surfaces with the same diffusion rate on all points. By using different rates at different points, [3] showed that objects with the same geometry and different color/texture had different descriptors, even thought when the colors were the same, only distributed differently over the object. Thus, to differentiate objects on both appearance and geometry, we relate appearance with diffusion rate and rewrite the heat equation in Eq. 1 as:

$$C^{-1}L\bar{T}(t) = -\partial_t\bar{T}(t)$$ (5)

where C is a diagonal matrix, whose element $[C]_{v,v}$ is any scalar associated with color, or texture, at vertex v.

The solution to the non-homogeneous problem in Eq. 5 is identical to the solution to the homogeneous problem in Eq. 1, but the eigenvalues, λ_i^c, and eigenvectors $\bar{\phi}_i^c$ are now the solution of the generalized eigenvalue problem $L\bar{\phi}_i^c = C\bar{\phi}_i^c\lambda_i^c$. With the same previous initial condition, the heat kernel at $t = t_s$ then becomes:

$$k^c(v_j, v_s, t_s) = \sum_{i=1}^{30} [\bar{\phi}_i^c]_{v_j} \exp(-\lambda_i^c t_s)[\bar{\phi}_i^c]_{v_s}[C]_{v_s,v_s}. \qquad (6)$$

Furthermore, we consider that heat reaches the boundary for $t_s = 1/\lambda_2$ and that the reference point is the center of mass of the partial view in the depth image, as in [4,8]. As for all objects we have seen, we observe $\exp(\lambda_i/\lambda_2) < 10^{-4}$ for all $i > 30$ we use only the first 30 eigenvalues and eigenvectors while computing this descriptor. Algorithm 1 represents the overall algorithm for computing the C-PVHK descriptor of a single partial view.

Input: Vertices X in the camera coordinate system, mesh M, Boundary vertices
    $B = \{v_{b1}, v_{b2}, ..., v_{bM}\}$ and a diagonal matrix representing color C
Output: C-PVHK descriptor, $\bar{z} \in \mathbb{R}^M$.
FIND SOURCE POSITION:
$v_s \leftarrow \text{findCentralPoint}(X)$
COMPUTE LAPLACE-BELTRAMI OPERATOR:
$L \leftarrow \text{computeLaplaceBeltrami}(M, X)$ (from Eq. 2)
ESTIMATE GENERALIZED EIGENVALUES AND EIGENVECTORS:
$\{\bar{\phi}_i, \lambda_i, i = 1, ..., 30\} \leftarrow \text{generalizedEigenvectors}(L, C)$
COMPUTE TIME AT WHICH HEAT REACHES THE BOUNDARY:
$t_s \leftarrow 1/\lambda_2$
COMPUTE TEMPERATURE AT BOUNDARY:
$\bar{z} : [\bar{z}]_i \leftarrow k(v_{bj}, v_s, t_s)$ (from Eq. 6)

Algorithm 1. Computing the C-PVHK descriptor

4   Assessing the Impact of Color Parameterization

We here show how the color extension of the partial view heat kernel allows to disambiguate different instances within four different classes of small real objects.

We evaluate the use of color by comparing the performance of C-PVHK with that of PVHK. We thus experiment different maps from the RGB values, provided by the sensor, to the scalar $[C]_{v,v}$. This map can take many forms, and we could think of especially tailored maps for any given library. Here we are interested in understanding the impact of simple parameters with impact on recognition, namely: (a) the map co-domain, i.e., we will analyse if there is any benefit on having $[C]_{v,v}$ taking values only on the interval [0.01,10] vs smaller intervals; (b) the size of the object library, i.e., consider the impact of using more or less partial views on the object library.

4.1   Object Library

We used all instances of four different objects from a publicly available RGB-D dataset [6]. We selected objects with different shapes, presenting significant changes in color and texture, as showed in Fig. 4. In particular, we used: all the food cans, the cereal boxes, the instant noodles packages, and the shampoo packages.

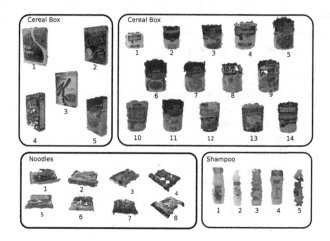

Fig. 4. Objects in Library-II, composed of 32 objects divided in four classes.

We considered libraries with 35, 20, 15, 10 and 5 partial views per object. These partial views were equally distributed over the angle θ. All the other partial views were used for testing.

4.2   Recognition Results

We evaluate the performance of both descriptors over 16 different experiments, covering four different scalar functions $[C]_{v,v} = c(v) : \mathbb{R}^3 \rightarrow \mathbb{R}$, and four different library sizes. The scalar functions we tested were: $c_1(v) = (h(v) + 1/2) \times 2$, $c_2(v) = (h(v) + 10^{-3}) \times 2$, $c_3(v) = (h(v) + 5) \times 2$, $c_4(v) = (h(v) + 1/2) \times 10$, where $h(v)$ is the hue value of the pixel. Their co-domains differ in the lower and upper bounds, as well as range.

Furthermore, and following [4,8], we use the Modified Hausdorff distance to assess the similarity between two descriptors. Classification follows a nearest neighbor approach.

Precision for different mapping functions, aggregated by object class

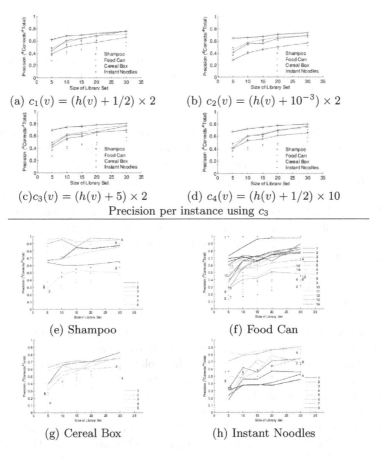

(a) $c_1(v) = (h(v) + 1/2) \times 2$ (b) $c_2(v) = (h(v) + 10^{-3}) \times 2$

(c) $c_3(v) = (h(v) + 5) \times 2$ (d) $c_4(v) = (h(v) + 1/2) \times 10$

Precision per instance using c_3

(e) Shampoo   (f) Food Can

(g) Cereal Box   (h) Instant Noodles

Fig. 5. Precision for different scalar functions and object classes and instances. Dots correspond to results with PVHK (no-color), lines correspond to results using C-PVHK. (Color figure online)

The assessment is made by first looking into recognition results in a aggregated fashion, i.e., combining precision results of all the instances of each class, as presented in Fig. 5 (a)–(d). Then, to provide more insight on the reasons that lead to false classification, we use the mapping function with better results, and look into the the precision results of each instance individually, in Fig. 5 (e)–(f)

In all the experiments, the increase of library size and the use of color clearly improved precision results. However, results also hint to no direct relation between the range of values of $c(v)$ and precision. However, c_3, which takes vales in the interval $[10, 12]$ performs better for smaller datasets, in particular when compared with c_2, which can take values very close to zero. Results also show that not all objects are sensitive to the library size, e.g., instances of the shampoo

(a) Instant Noodles 1   (b) Instant Noodles 6

Fig. 6. Examples of partial views from two objects in the instant noodles library. (a) is the object with label 1 in Fig. 4 and in Fig. 5(d), and (b) is the object with label 6.

class present similar precisions regardless of library size. This is expected has they have less features, i.e., are more symmetric, than other objects.

The class with worst precision was the *Instant Noodle* class. When looking into the results instances we see that the object with the label 1 is considerably worst than all other objects. In Fig. 6(a), we show different partial views of this object and, when comparing with instances of the same class with higher precision, Fig. 6(b), we notice a large variance in shape between viewing angles. Thus, our guess is that adding color to the representation of objects whose shapes change considerably only harms recognition.

5   Conclusion

In this paper we have tested the impact of different scalar functions on the recognition of observations obtained with an RGB-D camera.

Our experiments show that, by indexing color to the geometry, we improve recognition results. We also show that unless the $[C]_{v,v}$ takes very small values, all mappings behave similarly. Finally, we concluded that the number of partial views in the object library is of utmost importance for recognition.

We also showed that misclassification rates are higher when the object shapes varies extraordinarily between viewing angles due the object reflectivity properties that make it difficult to the RGB-D sensor to reconstruct the object surface. In shapes that were not particularly affected, precision was significantly higher.

References

1. Abdelrahman, M., Farag, A., Swanson, D., El-Melegy, M.: Heat diffusion over weighted manifolds: A new descriptor for textured 3D non-rigid shapes. In: CVPR (2015)
2. Blum, M., Springenberg, J.T., Wülfing, J., Riedmiller, R.: A learned feature descriptor for object recognition in RGB-D data. In: ICRA (2012)
3. Brandão, S., Costeira, J.P., Veloso, M.V.: The partial view heat kernel descriptor for 3D object representation. In: ICRA (2014)
4. Brandão, S., Veloso, M., Costeira, J.P.: Multiple hypotheses for object class disambiguation from multiple observations. In: 2nd International Conference on 3D Vision, 3DV 2014, Tokyo, Japan, December 8–11, 2014 (2014)
5. Kovnatsky, A., Bronstein, M.M., Bronstein, A.M., Kimmel, R.: Photometric heat kernel signatures

6. Lai, K., Bo, L., Ren, X., Fox, D.: A large-scale hierarchical multi-view RGB-D object dataset. In: ICRA, May 2011
7. Lai, K., Bo, L., Ren, X., Fox, D.: Sparse distance learning for object recognition combining RGB and depth information. In: ICRA (2011)
8. Ribeiro, F., Brandão, S., Costeira, J.P., Veloso, M.: Global localization by soft object recognition from 3D partial views. In: IROS (2015)

Privacy-Preserving Fall Detection in Healthcare Using Shape and Motion Features from Low-Resolution RGB-D Videos

Irene Yu-Hua Gu$^{(\boxtimes)}$, Durga Priya Kumar, and Yixiao Yun

Department of Signals and Systems, Chalmers University of Technology,
41296 Gothenburg, Sweden
{irenegu,yixiao}@chalmers.se, durga@student.chalmers.se

Abstract. This paper addresses the issue on fall detection in healthcare using RGB-D videos. Privacy is often a major concern in video-based detection and analysis methods. We propose a video-based fall detection scheme with privacy preserving awareness. First, a set of features is defined and extracted, including local shape and shape dynamic features from object contours in depth video frames, and global appearance and motion features from HOG and HOGOF in RGB video frames. A sequence of time-dependent features is then formed by a sliding window averaging of features along the temporal direction, and use this as the input of a SVM classifier for fall detection. Separate tests were conducted on a large dataset for examining the fall detection performance with privacy-preserving awareness. These include testing the fall detection scheme that solely uses depth videos, solely uses RGB videos in different resolution, as well as the influence of individual features and feature fusion to the detection performance. Our test results show that both the dynamic shape features from depth videos and motion (HOGOF) features from low-resolution RGB videos may preserve the privacy meanwhile yield good performance (91.88 % and 97.5 % detection, with false alarm $\leq$ 1.25 %). Further, our results show that the proposed scheme is able to discriminate highly confused classes of activities (falling versus lying down) with excellent performance. Our study indicates that methods based on depth or low-resolution RGB videos may still provide effective technologies for the healthcare, without impact personnel privacy.

Keywords: Fall detection · Dynamic shape feature · Motion feature · HOG of Optical Flow · RGB-D videos · Healthcare · Privacy-preserving video analysis

1 Introduction

E-healthcare and m-healthcare have drawn increasing interest lately. A wide spread availability or usage of wearable devices, sensors and wireless data transfer provides new opportunities to employ technologies for healthcare. There is also

© Springer International Publishing Switzerland 2016
A. Campilho and F. Karray (Eds.): ICIAR 2016, LNCS 9730, pp. 490–499, 2016.
DOI: 10.1007/978-3-319-41501-7_55

a growing need for healthcare due to the aging population in many developed countries in the world. Many elderly people often live alone at home [1]. Statistics show that falling is one of the most fatal problems for them, that could cause bone fracture and other serious health issues [2]. It is often difficult for themselves to seek help immediately after the fall, especially when severe injuries occur. There is an increasing need for automatic systems that detect falls and timely trigger alarm for emergency medical attention. Many existing solutions employ wearable devices with motion sensors, such as accelerometers and gyroscopes [2]. Despite reasonable results from these wearables, they suffer from issues such as synchronization, battery life and uncomfortableness. Meanwhile, monitoring by visual sensors has the advantage of non-invasive and less-disturbing however there is a concern on privacy issue.

Much effort was made to detect human falls in videos. One way is to analyze the 2D bounding boxes containing the target person in each image frame. Debard et al. [3] extract four features from the bounding box to describe a fall, including aspect ratio, torso angle, center speed and head speed. A SVM classifier is used to detect falls using these features. Charfi et al. [4] define 14 features based on the bounding box such as height and width, aspect ratio, and centroid coordinates of the box. Transforms (Fourier, wavelets) are applied to these features before fall detection through SVM and AdaBoost classification. The main drawback is insufficient description of the shape or motion by solely using the rigid bounding box, and the performance is also heavily dependent on view angles. Another commonly adopted strategy is to represent the fall in 3D settings. Auvinet et al. [5] reconstruct a 3D volume of the person from 8 cameras based on camera calibration, and a fall is indicated if a large portion of the body volume is found near the ground for a certain period of time. Mastorakis et al. [6] measure the velocity of target person based on the contraction or expansion of the width, height and depth of the 3D bounding box, and detect a fall by thresholding the velocity. Stone and Skubic [7] model the vertical state of a 3D object in each depth image frames, and segment the time series in on-ground state from those in vertical state. An ensemble of decision trees is then used to compute a confidence that a fall occurs before an on-ground state. It is worth noting the trade-off between the performance and complexity in 3D modeling or multi-camera methods.

In this paper, we propose a novel human fall detection scheme using RGB-D videos. The main novelties of the paper include: (a) the proposed scheme treats all camera view videos in a same way; (b) we define time-dependent feature vectors from RGB and depth videos separately for each activity; (c) we conduct privacy-preserving studies by separately evaluating the detection performance using component features from RBG videos of different resolutions and from D-videos. In the proposed method, the foreground object (human) is first detected by differencing 2 RGB frames, followed by using SURF keypoints to mark the boundary for the rectangular bounding box. For each individual video frame, we then use the depth video for extracting local shape and shape dynamic features from estimated object contours, and use the RGB video for extracting global appearance and motion features from HOG and HOGOF (HOG of

Optical Flow). A time-dependent feature vector is then formed from these features by using a short sliding window averaging, and the result is used as the input of a soft-margin SVM classifier. We have conducted a set of tests on using features from depth videos and from different spatial-resolution RGB videos, and on using individual types of features for fall detection, for the evaluation of the effectiveness of the proposed scheme as well as their related privacy issue.

The remainder of the paper is organized as follows. Section 2 gives the big picture of the proposed scheme. Section 3 describes the proposed methods in detail. Section 4 shows some test results on a large RGB-D video dataset. Finally, the conclusion is given in Sect. 5.

2   The Proposed Scheme: The Big Picture

As shown in Fig. 1, the proposed fall detection scheme consists of several main blocks: (i) characterize local shape and shape dynamic features from the object contours in depth video frames; (ii) characterize global appearance and motion features from RGB video frames; (iii) formulate a sequence of time-dependent feature vectors and apply feature fusion; (iv) detect falls through using a binary C-SVM classifier. Tests on the proposed scheme also contains several steps. This includes fall detection from: (a) using individual features from depth videos; (b) using individual features from different-resolution RGB videos; and (c) using fused features. The key steps are are detailed in the next section.

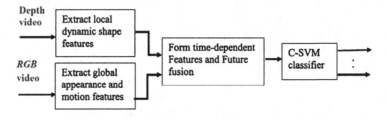

Fig. 1. Block diagram of the proposed scheme for fall detection.

3   Proposed Fall Detection Scheme

In this section, the steps of formulating a sequence of time-dependent feature vectors is described. First, in Sects. 3.1 and 3.2, we describe how features are defined on individual frames of depth videos and RGB videos. We then describe the method for obtaining a sequence of time-dependent features in Sect. 3.3.

3.1   Motion and Appearance Features from using RGB Images

A foreground moving object (human) is detected by using the difference image from two consecutive RGB video frames. SURF keypoint detector [8] is applied

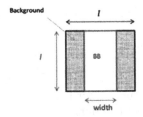

Fig. 2. The object aspect ratio is kept by filling the extra width area with background pixels before the normalization.

to detect interest points in the difference image from which the object bounding box (sized $w \times h$) is formed. The bounding box is then normalized to a fixed size of $l \times l$, where object aspect ratio is kept by filling the extra width area with background pixels (see Fig. 2) before normalizing the bounding box (BB) [11].

For each frame, the normalized box is used for extracting two types of features from the RGB video. For jth frame, these two types of feature vectors are:

$$\mathbf{f}_{RBG}^{j} = [\mathbf{f}_{HOG}^{j}, \ \mathbf{f}_{HOGOF}^{j}] \tag{1}$$

where HOG (Histogram of Oriented Gradients) feature vector is computed by using the method in [9], and HOGOF (HOG of Optical Flow) vector is computed using a pair of normalized bounding boxes between jth and $(j-1)$th frames (see Fig. 3 for HOGOF computation).

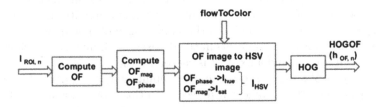

Fig. 3. Computing HOGOF: first, optical flow (OF) is computed, followed by computing the magnitudes OF_{mag} and phases OF_{phase}. The OF image is then converted to HSV image where I_{sat} and I_{hue} are the saturation and hue images, and color-coded by the MATLAB function flowtoColor(), resulting in I_{HSV} image in RGB color space. Finally, HOG features are extracted.

The basic idea is that the spatial appearance of object is described by HOG features, while the temporal-directional motions (described by the optical flow) over all pixels are then described by the spatial distribution, forming the spatio-temporal feature HOGOF.

3.2   Dynamic Shape from Object Contours using Depth Images

In each depth video frame, a contour of object (human) is estimated by morphological operations. An object bounding box is then set as the tight rectangular box to the contour. Several inflection points (8 in our tests) of the contour are detected and used for forming the feature vector. A shape feature vector for jth frame of depth video is defined as:

$$\mathbf{f}_{Depth}^j = [\mathbf{f}_s^j,\ \mathbf{f}_{sd}^j] \tag{2}$$

where $\mathbf{f}_s^j$ is the 2D shape feature vector formed by using several extrema (set to be 8 in our tests) in the object contour,

$$\mathbf{f}_s^j = \left[\mathbf{g}^j, \{\mathbf{E}_i^j\}_{i=1}^8, \{d_i^j\}_{i=1}^8, \theta^j, AR^j, Ecc^j\right]^T \tag{3}$$

where $\mathbf{g}^j$ is the contour centroid coordinates, $\mathbf{E}_i^j$ are the coordinates of extrema, d_i^j is the distance from the extrema to the centroid, θ^j and AR^j are the orientation and aspect ratio of the box (before resizing), and Ecc^j is the eccentricity, all in jth frame. Further, shape dynamic feature vector is defined as:

$$\mathbf{f}_{sd}^j = \left[\{\nabla d_i^j\}_{i=1}^8,\ \{k_i^j\}_{i=1}^8,\ k_g^j\right]^T \tag{4}$$

where $\nabla d_i^j = \eta(d_i^j - d_i^{j-1})$, η is the frame rate, $k_i = \eta\,\mathrm{dist}[\mathbf{E}_i^j, \mathbf{E}_i^{j-1}]$, and $k_g^j = \eta\,\mathrm{dist}[\mathbf{g}^j, \mathbf{g}^{j-1}]$ are the instantaneous velocity of extrema points and the centroids between jth and $(j-1)$th frames, and $\mathrm{dist}(\cdot,\cdot)$ is the Euclidean distance.

3.3   Formulating a Time-Dependent Sequence of Feature Vectors

To obtain a time-dependent sequence of feature vectors, the following method is adopted. Since the total number of frames is different for different *video events* (i.e., the segment of video that contains the human activity of interest), the following steps are applied to obtain the same length of time-dependent feature vector sequence for all *video events* in the dataset. Assuming that a video event consists of *len* frames, and a fixed M is chosen for the number of time-dependent feature vectors. We use a short non-overlapping sliding window of size $W = len/M$ to compute the average feature vector in this short time interval followed by feature normalization, as depicted in Fig. 4. This results in a time-dependent sequence of feature vectors with a fixed size M along the temporal direction.

We then stack these M vectors into the columns of the feature matrix $\mathbf{F}$. For example, the time-dependent HOG matrix corresponding to $\mathbf{f}_{HOG}^j$ in (1) is formed as follows:

$$\mathbf{F}_{HOG} = [\,\bar{\mathbf{f}}_{HOG}^1, \bar{\mathbf{f}}_{HOG}^2, \cdots, \bar{\mathbf{f}}_{HOG}^M] \tag{5}$$

where $\bar{\mathbf{f}}_{HOG}^j = \frac{1}{W}\sum_{i=1}^W \mathbf{f}_{HOG}^{(j-1)W+i}$. For other feature vectors in (1) and (2), the same method is applied to form the corresponding time-dependent feature matrix. Finally, a simple feature-level fusion is applied by concatenating all feature matrices into an augmented feature matrix as follows:

$$\mathbf{F} = [\mathbf{F}_{RGB},\ \mathbf{F}_{Depth}] \tag{6}$$

where $\mathbf{F}_{RGB}$ and $\mathbf{F}_{Depth}$ are the time-dependent component feature matrices corresponding to the feature vectors in (1) and (2).

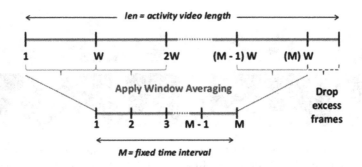

Fig. 4. Temporal window averaging for computing $\mathbf{F}$ in (5): for each video event of length len, a time-dependent $\mathbf{F}$, consisting of M-columns of time-dependent feature vectors, is computed by a non-overlapping sliding window (length $W = \text{round}(len/M)$) for obtaining the averaging feature vector $\bar{\mathbf{f}}^j = \frac{1}{W} \sum_{i=1}^{W} \mathbf{f}^{(j-1)W+i}, j = 1, \cdots, M$.

3.4 Fall Detection using a Binary C-SVM Classifier

We formulate the fall detection as a binary classification problem which distinguishes the fall from other activities. That is, all remaining activities are treated as one negative class. Since the activity *lying down* is the most confusion video event to the *fall* event, we focus on using 2 sets of video events, falls and lying down, for our tests without loss of generality or impact the results. We use a C-SVM for the classification. C-SVM is formulated as the constrained optimization problem that maximizes the margins,

$$\min \left(\frac{1}{2} \|\mathbf{w}\|^2 + C \sum_{i=1}^{N} \xi_i \right)$$
$$\text{s.t.:} \quad y_i(\langle \mathbf{w}, \Phi(\mathbf{x}_i) \rangle + b) \geq 1 - \xi_i, \tag{7}$$
$$\xi_i \geq 0$$

where $\langle \cdot, \cdot \rangle$ is the inner product, $\mathbf{w}$ is the weight vector, b is a bias, $C > 0$ is a regularization parameter, ξ_i is a slack variable, and $K(\mathbf{x}_i, \mathbf{x}_j) = <\Phi(\mathbf{x}_i), \Phi(\mathbf{x}_j)>$ is a kernel function. Given a training set $\mathcal{X} = \{(\mathbf{x}_k, y_k)\}_{k=1}^{N}$, where $\mathbf{x}_k$ is the feature vector of kth video defined in (6), $y_i \in \{+1, -1\}$ is the corresponding class label, and N is the total number of videos in the training set. A binary C-SVM classifier with RBF kernel [10] is trained for 2 classes of video activities (*fall* and *lying down*). For each feature $\mathbf{x} = \mathbf{F}$ from a test video, its class label $\hat{y} = \text{sgn}(a)$. A fall is detected if $\hat{y} = \text{sgn}(a) = +1$.

4   Experimental Results

4.1   Dataset and Setup

A RGB-D video dataset was made in our university campus from a *Kinect* sensor. A total of 20 participants was involved. We chose *lying down* as the negative class as it is visually the most confusing activity to falls. The video frame rate is 20

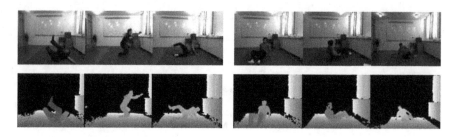

Fig. 5. Keyframes from the RGB-D video dataset on *falls* and *lying downs*. Columns 1–3: falls; Columns 4–6: lying down. Row-1: from RGB videos; Row-2: from depth videos.

frames/sec, and the image size is 640×480 pixels. Each video is approximated 10 seconds long. There are 400 RGB videos and 400 depth videos in *each* of the fall and lying down activities. We partition the dataset into 80 % for training and 20 % for testing. Figure 5 shows several video frames from falling and lying down.

The SURF thresholds for RGB and depth images were set to 50 and 1000, respectively. For HOG features, bounding boxes are then partitioned into cells of 8×8 pixels, and 9 (unsigned) bins were used for the histogram. Blocks were formed by grouping 2×2 adjacent cells with 50 % overlap. HOGOF features were extracted based on the code in [12,13]. $M = 10$ was chosen for time-dependent **F** before the training. A C-SVM classifier with RBF kernels was employed [14], where C and γ were optimized by grid search and 10-fold cross-validation.

4.2   Results and Evaluation

Three case-studies were conducted to separately examine the performance. They are detailed as follows.

Case Study-1: Performance Comparison by using Different Resolution Objects. To study the impact of image resolution to the performance of fall detection, tests were conducted on using objects with different sizes. Since the classifier uses the feature vector in the bounding box area, these results are associated with those from using different image resolution. Table 1 shows the results on the testset. Observing the table, one can see that, despite the bounding box size reduced to half in each direction (equivalent to reducing the image area to $1/4$ while keeping a fixed l value), or less than 100 pixels for the human body if we assume the average aspect ratio of human is approximately $1/3$. This is encouraging since one may significant reduce the video spatial resolution to protect the privacy or identity of the person being monitored, without much impact on the fall detection performance.

Table 1. Performance comparison: results on the *testset* from using different normalized bounding box sizes. In all tests, the classifier was trained by 80 % videos, and then tests on the remaining 20 % videos. The normalized window size was $l \times l$ for both RGB and depth videos, where the full feature **F** in (6) was extracted.

Bounding box size (l)	Detection rate (%)	False alarm (%)
16	97.50	1.25
24	97.50	1.25
32	97.50	2.25

Case Study-2: Performance Comparison from Separately using Features from Depth Videos and RGB Videos. Observing that depth videos do not show clear personnel identity, this case study is designed to compare the detection performance by purely using features from depth videos, and from different types of features in RGB videos. The results are shown in Table 2.

Table 2. Performance comparison: results on the *testset* by using features in depth videos and different types of features in RGB videos. In all tests, the classifier was trained by 80 % videos, and tests on the remaining 20 % videos. Window size was $l = 32$.

Feature used in (6)	Detection rate (%)	False alarm (%)
$\mathbf{F}_{\text{Depth}}$	91.88	0.00
$\mathbf{F}_{\text{RGB}} = (\mathbf{F}_{\text{HOGOF}}, \mathbf{F}_{\text{HOG}})$	(96.88, 96.88)	(1.25, 2.50)
$\mathbf{F}$	97.50	2.50

Observing the results in the table, one can observe that using features solely from depth videos has yielded rather high (91.88 %) detection, although it is still somewhat below the results from using features in RGB videos. This is still encouraging, as depth videos reveal little personnel identity hence it is very useful if privacy becomes a major concern. One can also observe that solely using $\mathbf{F}_{\text{HOGOF}}$ (without $\mathbf{F}_{\text{HOG}}$) in RGB videos seems to be sufficient under the test scenarios. This is not surprising, as $\mathbf{F}_{\text{HOGOF}}$ is the spatial-temporal characterization of object, while $\mathbf{F}_{\text{HOG}}$ is the spatial appearance characterization of object. Simplifying $\mathbf{F}_{\text{RGB}}$ may significantly reduce the computation. Finally, feature fusion has led to slightly enhanced performance.

Case Study-3: Performance Comparison from using Different Number of Training Videos. To obtain an idea on how many videos would be sufficient for training the classifier, we have conducted tests by using the classifier trained from different number of videos. Table 3 shows the fall detection results on the *testset* by using the classifier trained from 80 % and 50 % partitions of the entire video set (400 RGB videos + 400 depth videos). From the results in Table 3,

Table 3. Performance on the *testset* where the classifier was trained by different number of videos. In all tests, $\mathbf{F}$ in (6) is the feature, and $l = 32$ is the normalized window size.

# training videos (N_{Depth}, N_{RGB})	Detection rate (%)	False alarm (%)
(200,200)	95.25	5.00
(320,320)	97.50	2.50

one can see that using a large number of training videos is still beneficial to enhance the performance, especially for the confusion activities such as fall and lying down.

5 Conclusion

The proposed fall detection scheme characterizes human falls by measuring the local dynamic shape from depth videos, and global dynamic appearances from HOG and HOGOF in RGB videos, and by forming time-dependent feature matrix for each video activity. Our study, different from many other work, has put more emphasis on privacy-preserving issues in fall detection by separately evaluating the performance related to using depth videos and RGB videos separately, by seeking effective *time-dependent* features from videos, and by focusing on two activities (falls and lying down) that are most difficult to be distinguished by a classifier. Our test results show that the feature fusion is effective in obtaining high detection with low false alarms. Test results also show that using the proposed time-dependent feature matrix from depth videos provides a good tradeoff between the fall detection performance (91.88 % detection rate) and the personnel privacy. Further, our test results show that the fall detection performance is not very sensitive by using features from different image resolution RGB-videos, hence, indicating the possibility of employing low resolution RBG-videos for preserving the personnel privacy without significantly impact the performance. Results also show that HOGOF features are sufficient for distinguishing falls from lying downs in RBG-videos. Future work will be conducted on more extensive tests over a range of parameters and their tradeoff on the performance and the privacy.

References

1. United Nations: "World Population Ageing 2013," Population Division, Department of Economic and Social Affairs (DESA), United Nations, pp. 1–95 (2013)
2. Mubashir, M., Shao, L., Seed, L.: A survey on fall detection: principles and approaches. Neurocomputing **100**, 144–152 (2013)
3. Debard, G., et al.: Camera-based fall detection on real world data. In: International Workshop on Theoretical Foundations of Computer Vision, pp. 356–375 (2012)

4. Charfi, I., et al.: Optimized spatio-temporal descriptors for real-time fall detection: comparison of support vector machine and Adaboost-based classification. J. Electron. Imaging **22**(4), 1–17 (2013)
5. Auvinet, E., et al.: Fall detection with multiple cameras: an occlusion-resistant method based on 3-D silhouette vertical distribution. IEEE Trans. Inf. Technol. Biomed. **15**(2), 290–300 (2011)
6. Mastorakis, G., Makris, D.: Fall detection system using Kinects infrared sensor. J. Real-Time Image Process. **9**(4), 635–646 (2014)
7. Stone, E.E., Skubic, M.: Fall detection in homes of older adults using the Microsoft Kinect. IEEE J. Biomed. Health Inf. **19**(1), 290–301 (2015)
8. Bay, H., Tuytelaars, T., Gool, L.V.: Speeded-up robust features (SURF). Comput. Vis. Image Underst. **10**(3), 346–359 (2008)
9. Dadal, N., Triggs, B.: Histograms of oriented gradients for human detection. In: IEEE Conference on CVPR, vol. 1, pp. 886–893 (2005)
10. Cristianini, N., Shawe-Taylor, J.: An Introduction to Support Vector Machines. Cambridge University Press, New York (2000)
11. Yun, Y., Gu, I.Y.H.: Human fall detection via shape analysis on Riemannian manifolds with applications to elderly care. In: IEEE International Conference on ICIP, pp. 3280–3284 (2015)
12. Liu, C.: Beyond pixels: exploring new representations and applications for motion analysis. Doctoral thesis, MIT, USA (2009)
13. Baker, S., et al.: A database and evaluation methodology for optical flow. Technical report, Microsoft Research, MSR-TR-2009-179 (2009)
14. Chang, C.C., Lin, C.J.: LIBSVM: a library for support vector machines. ACM Trans. Intell. Syst. Technol. **2**(3), 27:1–27:27 (2011)

Visual Perception in Robotics

Proprioceptive Visual Tracking of a Humanoid Robot Head Motion

João Peixoto[1]([✉]), Vitor Santos[1,2], and Filipe Silva[1,2]

[1] Universidade de Aveiro, Aveiro, Portugal
{joao.peixoto,vitor,fmsilva}@ua.pt
[2] Institute for Electronics Engineering and Informatics of Aveiro - IEETA,
Aveiro, Portugal

Abstract. This paper addresses the problem of measuring a humanoid robot head motion by fusing inertial and visual data. In this work, a model of a humanoid robot head, including a camera and inertial sensors, is moved on the tip of an industrial robot which is used as ground truth for angular position and velocity. Visual features are extracted from the camera images and used to calculate angular displacement and velocity of the camera, which is fused with angular velocities from a gyroscope and fed into a Kalman Filter. The results are quite interesting for two different scenarios and with very distinct illumination conditions. Additionally, errors are introduced artificially into the data to emulate situations of noisy sensors, and the system still performs very well.

Keywords: Kalman filter · SURF · Inertial sensor · Humanoid balance

1 Introduction

Humanoid robot balance is a relevant and complex problem despite the continuous progresses done by the research community in the field. The electromechanical limitations and flaws of the structures and actuators make the problem even harder by forbidding the existence of reliable models. Hence, to control these robots, a rich set of sensors, both proprioceptive and exteroceptive, are required. For balance measurement, and ultimately its control, force and/or inertial sensors are usually combined, but the trend may be pushed further, and the combination of more sensors altogether promises more robust and effective representations of the robot internal state, and its state on the environment.

In that line, this paper presents a method for combining inertial and visual data to measure, and later control, humanoid robot motion, namely at the level of the head, where cameras are normally placed, along possibly with inertial sensors. Combining such data may be presented as a challenging task, however it may be very valuable in several contexts, including motion learning. This sensorial merging can increase the robustness of the information since various sensors will feed data into a single model. This work was developed for PHUA (Project Humanoid at the University of Aveiro) with the intention of aiding the progress made to date to this project [1].

© Springer International Publishing Switzerland 2016
A. Campilho and F. Karray (Eds.): ICIAR 2016, LNCS 9730, pp. 503–511, 2016.
DOI: 10.1007/978-3-319-41501-7_56

The method presented in this paper is based on the Kalman Filter tool, which will combine both sets of data (visual and inertial) into a single representation that describes the movement of the robot, namely its head. The line of focus of this research is to monitor especially the angular position of the robot's head relatively to the gravity vector.

2   Related Work

The creation of visual-inertial systems has been a complex field of study for some time. Many researchers use this approach in order to improve data that inertial systems can't achieve alone. Commonly, visual-inertial systems are used to enhance odometry [2] and in aiding navigation [3]. This kind of data merging has been also applied to humanoid platforms in ego-motion estimation [4]. Often, this approaches use Extended Kalman Filter (EKF) needing complex formulas in order to describe the systems and the relation between sets of data. Commonly, these research activities are based on experiments, lacking a robust ground truth in order to compare the results to. This paper aims to simplify the problem in order to understand how simplistic a model can be and yet create a functional system with improved data, relying on a ground truth, in order to objectively compare the results with and without the merging of different types of data.

3   Experimental Setup

For this paper, we used a trustworthy tool in order to obtain a reliable ground truth, as well as repeatable experiments. This can be accomplished with an industrial manipulator. The manipulator used is a FANUC 200iB, which presents a high repeatability ($\pm 0.10\,\text{mm}$), and has six degrees of freedom. For this fact we are able to perform and reproduce testing trials with high repeatability rates as well as acquiring extremely reliable data from its end-effector. In this case we aimed to obtain the orientation of the FANUC end-effector. The software was developed in language C++ in the environment ROS [5] (Robotic Operating System) and makes use of ROS Topics and Bags (Fig. 1).

Fig. 1. Experimental setup (left) and a detailed view of the components (right)

4 Proposed Approach

4.1 Kalman Filter

The Kalman Filter is a powerful statistic tool created by Rudolf Kalman based on linear algebra, which intends to estimate the value of a set of state variables. In order to do that, the filter does an estimation of the values that it is expecting, based on a given model that describes the behavior of the system.

The first thing needed to implement the Kalman Filter is to define the state variables. In this case we will use angular position and velocity as state variables, since we obtain them directly from the sensors and they can describe fairly well the behavior of the system $(x_k = [\theta_k; \dot{\theta}_k]^T)$.

Now, it is important to define the model that describes the behavior of the humanoid. This is not a simple task, since we don't know what kind of behavior it will have. If we assume that the robot is in angular motion with constant acceleration, we just need to assume that the acceleration is the process noise, otherwise we need to calculate it using the previously known angular velocities. This way, we can use an overall model for any behavior of the robot:

$$\theta_k = \theta_{k-1} + \dot{\theta}_{k-1}\Delta t + \frac{1}{2}\ddot{\theta}_{k-1}\Delta t^2 \tag{1}$$

$$\dot{\theta}_k = \dot{\theta}_{k-1} + \ddot{\theta}_{k-1}\Delta t \tag{2}$$

$$\ddot{\theta}_k = \ddot{\theta}_{k-1} = 0 \tag{3}$$

$$
\begin{bmatrix} \theta_{x_k} \\ \theta_{y_k} \\ \theta_{z_k} \\ \dot{\theta}_{x_k} \\ \dot{\theta}_{y_k} \\ \dot{\theta}_{z_k} \end{bmatrix}
=
\begin{bmatrix}
1 & 0 & 0 & \Delta t & 0 & 0 \\
0 & 1 & 0 & 0 & \Delta t & 0 \\
0 & 0 & 1 & 0 & 0 & \Delta t \\
0 & 0 & 0 & 1 & 0 & 0 \\
0 & 0 & 0 & 0 & 1 & 0 \\
0 & 0 & 0 & 0 & 0 & 1
\end{bmatrix}
\begin{bmatrix} \theta_{x_{k-1}} \\ \theta_{x_{k-1}} \\ \theta_{z_{k-1}} \\ \dot{\theta}_{x_{k-1}} \\ \dot{\theta}_{y_{k-1}} \\ \dot{\theta}_{z_{k-1}} \end{bmatrix}
+
\begin{bmatrix}
\frac{\Delta t^2}{2} & 0 & 0 \\
0 & \frac{\Delta t^2}{2} & 0 \\
0 & 0 & \frac{\Delta t^2}{2} \\
\Delta t & 0 & 0 \\
0 & \Delta t & 0 \\
0 & 0 & \Delta t
\end{bmatrix}
\begin{bmatrix} \frac{\dot{\theta}_{x_{k-1}} - \dot{\theta}_{x_{k-2}}}{\Delta t_{k-1}} \\ \frac{\dot{\theta}_{y_{k-1}} - \dot{\theta}_{y_{k-2}}}{\Delta t_{k-1}} \\ \frac{\dot{\theta}_{z_{k-1}} - \dot{\theta}_{z_{k-2}}}{\Delta t_{k-1}} \end{bmatrix}
\tag{4}
$$

θ is the angular position
$\dot{\theta}$ is the angular velocity
$\ddot{\theta}$ is the angular acceleration
Δt is a temporal iteration.

Regarding the measurements, we just need to add as many as we need and then relate them to the state variable matrix. In this case, we have a defined number of outputs from the sensors, which are the angular position and velocities for the three axis and a variable number of outputs from the camera, resulting in Eq. (5). It is possible to obtain more than one measurement from the image, therefore we present formula (5) using n measurements. In these experiments, the camera was aligned with the y axis of the sensor, as we can observe in Fig. 2.

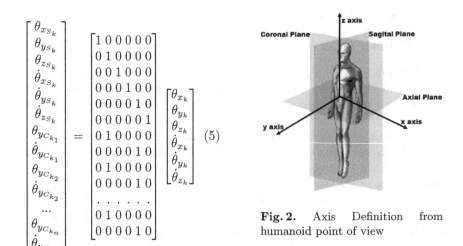

$$
\begin{bmatrix}
\theta_{x_{S_k}} \\
\theta_{y_{S_k}} \\
\theta_{z_{S_k}} \\
\dot{\theta}_{x_{S_k}} \\
\dot{\theta}_{y_{S_k}} \\
\dot{\theta}_{z_{S_k}} \\
\theta_{y_{C_{k_1}}} \\
\dot{\theta}_{y_{C_{k_1}}} \\
\theta_{y_{C_{k_2}}} \\
\dot{\theta}_{y_{C_{k_2}}} \\
\cdots \\
\theta_{y_{C_{k_n}}} \\
\dot{\theta}_{y_{C_{k_n}}}
\end{bmatrix}
=
\begin{bmatrix}
1 & 0 & 0 & 0 & 0 & 0 \\
0 & 1 & 0 & 0 & 0 & 0 \\
0 & 0 & 1 & 0 & 0 & 0 \\
0 & 0 & 0 & 1 & 0 & 0 \\
0 & 0 & 0 & 0 & 1 & 0 \\
0 & 0 & 0 & 0 & 0 & 1 \\
0 & 1 & 0 & 0 & 0 & 0 \\
0 & 0 & 0 & 0 & 1 & 0 \\
0 & 1 & 0 & 0 & 0 & 0 \\
0 & 0 & 0 & 0 & 1 & 0 \\
\cdots & \cdots & \cdots & \cdots & \cdots & \cdots \\
0 & 1 & 0 & 0 & 0 & 0 \\
0 & 0 & 0 & 0 & 1 & 0
\end{bmatrix}
\begin{bmatrix}
\theta_{x_k} \\
\theta_{y_k} \\
\theta_{z_k} \\
\dot{\theta}_{x_k} \\
\dot{\theta}_{y_k} \\
\dot{\theta}_{z_k}
\end{bmatrix}
\quad (5)
$$

Fig. 2. Axis Definition from humanoid point of view

The subscript S stands for values measured from the inertial sensor
The subscript C stands for values measured from the camera.

4.2 Visual Tracking

When it comes to visual tracking, one of the most common and intuitive ways to analyze an image is to perceive certain image regions (blobs) that can describe an object which the robot can identify. However, it is not always possible to use these global methods, since there aren't always images simple enough to apply this method to. As a result, there is the need to find a method which may be used in more diverse situations.

An alternative way to work with an image is to try to extract some points (features) that may show special properties such as being invariant to scale and position. These are know as local features since they are calculated in key points instead of global methods as those based in blob analysis. There are many different approaches for these local descriptors, and for the work in this paper the features of choice was SURF.

The idea of this method is to keep track of some relevant features in a given image and extract information regarding the transformation between sets of features, frame by frame.

Features are associated to pixels and are most relevant as a group. After finding the SURF features with a specific detection algorithm [6], it is necessary to extract them [6,7] (extracted features are known as descriptors).

Descriptors save the information relative to a point (in the case of SURF a $n \times 128$ vector, where n is the number of features and 128 is used to describe the quality of the point in relation to its surroundings [6]). Having the extracted features, we need to compare the features [8,9] existing in $frame_i$ and $frame_{i-1}$ in order to find the ones that match, i.e., that exist in both frames. The next step consists of calculating the transformation [10,11] that occurred from $frame_{i-1}$ to $frame_i$, and extract the rotation component.

This extracted rotation ($\Delta\theta_{B_i}$) will be the base value to calculate the orientation of the camera. This method allows to obtain a value for θ and $\dot{\theta}$, (6) and (7), yielding for each frame, a single measurement of angular position and velocity.

$$\dot{\theta}_i = \frac{\Delta\theta_{B_i}}{t_i - t_{i-1}} \tag{6}$$

$$\theta_i = \theta_{i-1} + \dot{\theta}_i(t_i - t_{i-1}) \tag{7}$$

We can easily deduce from Eq. (7) that $\theta_i = \theta_{i-1} + \Delta\theta_{B_i}$. This implies that if the time of acquisition of each frame is unknown, we can still know the orientation of the camera, although we can't perceive its angular velocity. If the time of acquisition is known, we can obtain both the angular position and velocity (which is the best case scenario).

In Figs. 3 and 4 we can observe two consecutive frames with a portion of the features found (red cross) and features matched (blue asterisk). For visualization purposes, only a fraction (about 1/10) of the actual features is represented.

Fig. 3. Detected and Matched Features - frame 32 - first experiment (Color figure online)

Fig. 4. Detected and Matched Features - frame 33 - first experiment (Color figure online)

5   Results

The experiment consists of the rotation of the set of camera and inertial sensors around the *y-axis* describing a semi-circle with $r = 150\,\text{mm}$ and $\alpha \in [0; \pi]$, using two different backgrounds and illuminations. The *base image frame* (the image frame with $\alpha = \frac{\pi}{2}$) from each experiment is presented in Figs. 5 and 6. We can observe that experiment one was done under much brighter illumination conditions and has more suitable objects for blob extraction, however blob extraction was not applied in any of the experiments, being used only the feature extraction

Fig. 5. Base frame from experiment one (good light)   **Fig. 6.** Base frame from experiment two (poor light)

method to determine θ and $\dot{\theta}$, thus we can compare equal sets of data that went under the same calculations.

The results of the experiments are shown in Table 1. These are the comparison between the values obtained from the algorithms and the values obtained from the FANUC robot, using formula (8), which essentially describes the average of the absolute difference between two sets of data:

$$res = \frac{\sum_{t=1}^{n} |F_t - d_t|}{n} \quad (8)$$

res mean error (displayed on tables)
F_t Ground truth from FANUC at instant t
d_t data measured or predicted
n number of measurements.

The raw data obtained from the experiment is the one that comes from the sensors, in which we get θ_x, θ_y, θ_z, $\dot{\theta}_x$, $\dot{\theta}_y$ and $\dot{\theta}_z$. The ground truth data (obtained from the FANUC) is only θ_x, θ_y and θ_z. The experiment was performed in such a way that there was only rotation around y, which will simplify the analysis

Table 1. Results from two different experiments without and with noise added to the measurements. The numbers represent the mean error when compared to the ground truth provided by the FANUC robot.

	Exp1	Exp2	Exp1 (noise)	Exp2 (noise)
Inertial	1.58°	2.80°	8.82°	8.73°
Visual	2.26°	4.68°	2.26°	4.68°
Inertial Kalman ($\ddot{\theta}=0$)	1.56°	2.52°	5.03°	4.35°
Visual Kalman ($\ddot{\theta}=0$)	2.42°	6.16°	2.43°	3.80°
Both Kalman ($\ddot{\theta}=0$)	1.09°	2.43°	2.15°	2.47°
Inertial Kalman ($\ddot{\theta}\neq0$)	1.49°	2.57°	4.86°	3.87°
Visual Kalman ($\ddot{\theta}\neq0$)	1.96°	3.79°	1.99°	2.86°
Both Kalman ($\ddot{\theta}\neq0$)	1.00°	2.49°	2.08°	2.37°

and will prove the concept for 3D rotation. Therefore, we will need to compare the rotation obtained from the FANUC in y axis to the rotations obtained from the sensors, camera and merged data.

In Table 1, *"Inertial"* is the comparison between the FANUC robot and sensor data (raw), *"Visual"* is the average of the comparisons between the data obtained from the visual data (one or multiple feature tracking) and the ground truth, *"Inertial and Visual Kalman"* is the inertial and visual data processed by the Kalman Filter (no merging), *"Both Kalman"* is the merged data submitted to the Kalman process, whilst $\ddot\theta = 0$ and $\ddot\theta \neq 0$ refers to the comparison of data submitted to Kalman Filter process with $\ddot\theta_k = 0$ and $\ddot\theta_k = \frac{\dot\theta_{k-1} - \dot\theta_{k-2}}{t_{k-1} - t_{k-2}}$ respectively.

Figures 7 and 8 present the the ground truth, inertial, visual and combined data in **Exp1 (noise)** and **Exp2 (noise)** where the Kalman filter including both inertial and visual performed nearly as good as the ground truth.

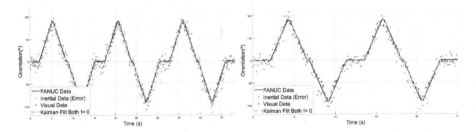

Fig. 7. All data from **Exp1 (Noise)** (Color figure online)   **Fig. 8.** All data from **Exp2 (Noise)** (Color figure online)

As we can verify in Table 1, the inertial data obtained in **Exp1** is very reliable, which almost excludes the need to use other data in order to improve it, since we may be actually distorting its good results. If we apply the inertial data into a Kalman Filter, it improves, but it in a negligible manner. This may be explained by the fact that the model used in the Kalman Filter is not describing the movement of the robot but rather the general laws of motion regarding angular displacement. The visual data is worst than the inertial data, however, when we apply this data (only) into a Kalman Filter, the output of the filter has a great increase in accuracy. The results are better when we calculate $\ddot\theta$. As it was expected, joining inertial and visual data into a single Kalman Filter improves the accuracy of result, surpassing the individual accuracy of each.

In experiment **Exp2** the results are not so promising. The sensors data is slightly poorer and the visual data is much worst, as it was expected, since the captured images weren't as good as in the first experiment. The deficiency in illumination greatly influences the experiment (Figs. 5 and 6). Despite that, the conclusions are similar to the ones obtained in **Exp1**.

In order to understand how this technique behaves in less accurate data, noise was added to the sensor data (to each value was added a normal distributed random number in the range $[-10°; 10°]$) and the exact same calculations were repeated.

At this point, the sensor data is highly inaccurate and no good conclusion may be taken from it in order to perceive the robot orientation.

The visual results may be better, but aren't still accurate enough to use due to a lack of measurements in time (each frame takes around 0.3 s in order to be taken and processed as the sensor data is more than 3 times faster). In experiment one, we can see that the usage of vision data improves greatly the accuracy of the Kalman Filter data. Calculating the acceleration during the Kalman Filter process improves slightly the output results.

Remember that the model used in Kalman Filter plays a role in guessing the state variable matrix value. The model used does not predict the movement of the robot, since we don't know what the robot will do, but even so, it can greatly improve the results when a large error occurs, thus proving the power of this tool.

The same conclusion may be taken from **Exp2 with noise**. In this case, since the visual data isn't as good as in **Exp1 with noise**, the output from the Kalman Filter isn't as good either.

It is also important to notice that *"Visual"* and *"Visual Kalman"* have the same rate of data acquisition (about 3 Hz), whilst all the others have the same acquisition rate as *"Inertial"* (about 10 Hz). This is relevant because, even though *"Visual"* data may have a smaller error, it also has less measurements per second than *"Both Kalman"*, which may affect the response of the humanoid.

6   Conclusions and Future Perspectives

This paper studies the effect of merging visual and inertial data with a Kalman Filter to measure a robot angular position and velocity. The trials were successful, proving that it is possible to use different sources of measurements in order to merge and improve them into an overall set of state variables that describe the behavior of the object of study, as shown in Sect. 5. The Kalman Filter works better when we try to deduce the angular acceleration at every iteration, however, not doing so does not present itself as a big loss in accuracy.

When the data is highly unreliable (inertial data with error), we can use subsets of external data (visual data) that isn't fully reliable by itself, but may help in filtering the noise in the initial data.

In conclusion, this approach was validated by the results and the next step is to try to implement this method in a real-life situation with real-time calculations. There is a problem that must be solved in order to accomplish this, which is the synchronization of the inertial and visual data when being processed by the Kalman Filter. In this work, all the image related calculations were made and then fed into the filter. In real-time experiments, the time that the image needs in order to be processed may be a challenge when trying to implement the filter. Some modifications to the system may be of need.

References

1. Santos, V., Moreira, R., Silva, F.: Mechatronic design of a new humanoid robot with hybrid parallel actuation. Int. J. Adv. Robot. Syst. **9** (2012)
2. Comport, A.I., Malis, E., Rives, P.: Accurate quadrifocal tracking for robust 3D visual odometry. In: Proceedings - IEEE International Conference on Robotics and Automation (2007)
3. Weiss, S., Achtelik, M.W., Lynen, S., Chli, M., Siegwart, R.: Real-time onboard visual-inertial state estimation and self-calibration of MAVs in unknown environments. In: Proceedings - IEEE International Conference on Robotics and Automation (2012)
4. Tsotsos, K., Pretto, A., Soatto, S.: Visual-inertial ego-motion estimation for humanoid platforms. In: IEEE-RAS International Conference on Humanoid Robots (2012)
5. Quigley, M., Conley, K., Gerkey, B., FAust, J., Foote, T., Leibs, J., Berger, E., Wheeler, R., Mg, A.: ROS: an open-source Robot Operating System. ICRA, 3 (Figure 1) (2009)
6. Bay, H., Ess, A., Tuytelaars, T., Van Gool, L.: Speeded-up robust features (SURF). Comput. Vis. Image Underst. **110**(3), 346–359 (2008)
7. Bradski, G., Kaehler, A.: Learning OpenCV: Computer Vision with the OpenCV Library, vol. 1 (2008)
8. Lowe, D.G.: Distinctive image features from scale-invariant keypoints. Int. J. Comput. Vis. **60**(2), 91–110 (2004)
9. Muja, M., Lowe, D.G.: Fast approximate nearest neighbors with automatic algorithm configuration. In: International Conference on Computer Vision Theory and Applications (VISApp 2009) (2009)
10. Hartley, R., Zisserman, A.: Multiple view geometry in computer vision (2004)
11. Torr, P.H.S., Zisserman, A.: MLESAC: a new robust estimator with application to estimating image geometry. Comput. Vis. Image Underst. **78**(1), 138–156 (2000)

A Hybrid Top-Down Bottom-Up Approach for the Detection of Cuboid Shaped Objects

Rafael Arrais[1(✉)], Miguel Oliveira[1,2], César Toscano[1], and Germano Veiga[1]

[1] INESC TEC - Instituto de Engenharia de Sistemas e Computadores, Tecnologia e Ciência, R. Dr. Roberto Frias, 465, 4200 Porto, Portugal
{rafael.arrais,germano.veiga.pt}@ieee.org, ctoscano@inesctec.pt
[2] IEETA - Instituto de Engenharia Electrónica e Telemática de Aveiro, Aveiro, Portugal
m.riem.oliveira@gmail.com

Abstract. While bottom-up approaches to object recognition are simple to design and implement, they do not yield the same performance as top-down approaches. On the other hand, it is not trivial to obtain a moderate number of plausible hypotheses to be efficiently verified by top-down approaches. To address these shortcomings, we propose a hybrid top-down bottom-up approach to object recognition where a bottom-up procedure that generates a set of hypothesis based on data is combined with a top-down process for evaluating those hypotheses. We use the recognition of rectangular cuboid shaped objects from 3D point cloud data as a benchmark problem for our research. Results obtained using this approach demonstrate promising recognition performances.

Keywords: Bottom-up processing · Top-down processing · Visual perception · Object recognition · Point cloud processing

1 Introduction

Visual perception may be defined as the process through which the visual sensory inputs received in the retina are conveyed and processed in order to create an understanding or gain some insight from the received stimuli. In other words, perception is the process of perceiving something with the senses. Over the last decades, several researchers have studied perception, in an attempt to characterize the process and describe the mechanisms that it comprises. In 1970, Richard Gregory stated that perception is organized as a top-down processing mechanism, in the sense that past experiences affect the way we perceive novel stimuli [1]. He argued that a perceptual hypothesis was created in the brain to explain the received stimulus, and that this hypothesis was conditioned by prior knowledge [2]. On the other hand, James Gibson opposed that perception is not subject to hypothesis, rather it is a data-driven process that is triggered by the sensorial stimuli and the information flows in a single direction, that is, perception is a bottom-up process [3,4]. Gibson argued that there is enough information in our environment to make sense of the world in a direct way.

© Springer International Publishing Switzerland 2016
A. Campilho and F. Karray (Eds.): ICIAR 2016, LNCS 9730, pp. 512–520, 2016.
DOI: 10.1007/978-3-319-41501-7_57

One important aspect of this discussion is that the top-down processing theory is capable of explaining phenomena such as optical illusions (e.g. see Charlie Chaplin's hollow head[1], or the Necker cube[2]), attributing them to the formation of incorrect hypothesis. Although Gibson discarded these arguments by stating that optical illusions are artificial examples not encountered in our normal visual environments, the fact is that there are clear indications that at least some form of (partial) top-down processing takes place, even if interleaved with bottom-up processing [5].

Despite the fact that some works still use a pure bottom-up approach (e.g., see [6]), the fact is that over the past years, several computer vision algorithms proposed for visual perception have come to incorporate some form of top-down mechanism (e.g., see [7,8]). While top-down approaches are in general more straightforward to design and implement, several works have shown that the integration of top-down processing increases the performance of recognition systems, in particular when dealing with occlusions [9]. On the other hand, it is not trivial to generate the set of hypothesis to be verified by top-down approaches, in particular because this set has to be small (i.e., only a moderate number of hypotheses can be verified in reasonable time) and contain plausible hypothesis (i.e. hypothesis should have a high probability of being true). This problem has been identified by some authors. For example, the work from [10] proposes to use semantics in order to restrict the hypothesis space.

In this paper, we propose a hybrid top-down bottom-up approach to object recognition. Note that we do not refer to a dual top-down bottom-up configuration as in [11], where a cognitive architecture was proposed in which a top-down pathway across layers is used, creating effectively a bidirectional processing architecture with feedback. Unlike in the previous case, our approach uses a bottom-up, data driven design to generate a set of hypothesis for object locations which are later evaluated in a top-down fashion. We refer to this as a hybrid approach, and expect that it may somehow embrace the best of both worlds, by addressing the shortcomings of both the bottom-up as well as the top-down approaches. The generation of hypothesis is an efficient bottom up process, that creates only a small set of plausible hypothesis. Also, because the hypothesis are evaluated using a top-down approach, the accuracy of recognition is very good.

We use the recognition of rectangular cuboid shaped objects from 3D point cloud data, as a benchmark problem for our research. A cuboid is a convex polyhedron bounded by six quadrilateral faces. A rectangular cuboid, in particular, is a cuboid in which each of the faces is a rectangle, which means that each pair of adjacent faces meet in a 90 degree angle. The motivation to use this geometry as a case study comes from the fact that boxes are used in many industrial applications as the prevailing option for packaging, storage and transportation. Therefore, the importance of detecting cuboid shape objects could have a significant impact on industrial applications, such as the automatic detection of packages or the monitoring of stocks in automated warehouses.

---

[1] https://youtu.be/QbKw0_v2clo.
[2] https://en.wikipedia.org/wiki/Necker_cube.

There are some previous works on the detection of cuboid-shaped objects. In [12], a sequential scene analysis system which detects geometric primitives including cuboids from range data is presented. This work was later extended in [13]. In [14] a box-like object detection algorithm is proposed. This approach is a pure bottom-up approach since it uses edges detected in the image to trigger the search for the boxes. The novelty of this work is to attempt a hybrid bottom-up top-down approach.

The remainder of this paper is organized as follows: Sect. 2 describes the proposed algorithm, Sect. 3 provides results and Sect. 4 some conclusions.

2   Proposed Approach

This section describes the hybrid strategy that blends bottom-up data driven hypothesis generation with top-down hypothesis validation to detect cuboid shaped objects from 3D data. First, in Sect. 2.1, we describe the generation of hypotheses and then, in Sect. 2.2, we detail the evaluation of those hypotheses.

2.1   Bottom-Up Generation of Primary Face Hypotheses

The first step of the process is to generate a hypothesis for the location of one of the faces of the cuboid. We refer to this as the primary face of the cuboid. The objective is to find sets of points which could belong to the primary face of a cuboid object. A Random Sample Consensus (RANSAC) procedure is used to extract, from the point cloud, a list of points that belong to a plane. We then assume that this plane contains the primary face of the cuboid. As the faces of the cuboid are planar, the RANSAC procedure uses a plane model, defined by the Hessian formulation $p_x \cdot x + p_y \cdot y + p_z \cdot z + d = 0$, where $\mathbf{p} = \{p_x, p_y p_z\}$ is the vector containing the normal direction of the plane. The RANSAC plane estimation procedure receives one parameter as input, which defines the maximum distance to the plane, under which a point from the point cloud is considered an inlier of the RANSAC plane. This parameter, the distance threshold t_d can be adjusted to produce better results for a given scenario. The effect of the distance threshold on the overall performance of the approach will be addressed in Sect. 3.

In order to obtain a connected set of points from the RANSAC inliers, these are clustered using an Euclidean clustering mechanism[3] and the largest cluster is selected. These selected points span across a volume defined by t_d. Therefore, it is necessary to project the points into the RANSAC plane so that it is possible to address the estimation of the primary face's bounding rectangle in $\mathbb{R}^2$ space. The next step in the procedure is to estimate the pose and dimensions of the primary face bounding polygon, by computing the vertices of a rectangle defined in the plane detected by the RANSAC procedure. For any given point cloud, several primary face searches are executed. For each detected primary face, the points belonging to the largest cluster, i.e., the points which are assumed to belong

---

[3] pointclouds.org/documentation/tutorials/cluster_extraction.php.

to the primary face, are removed from the point cloud that is used, resulting in a smaller input data for the next search. The cascade iterative search is finished when a specified percentage of points from the original point cloud is reached, indicating that a considerable amount of points were already selected as candidates for primary faces of cuboids. It should be noted that for a specific cuboid, multiple faces can be selected as primary faces by this approach, as shown in Fig. 1.

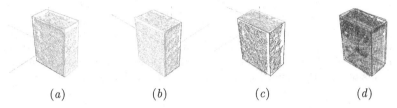

(a) $\qquad$ (b) $\qquad$ (c) $\qquad$ (d)

Fig. 1. Multiple planes found by RANSAC selected as primary face. In this point cloud, three planes were selected as primary faces. Images (a), (b) and (c) show different cuboid faces being selected as primary (represented as yellow). Green, cyan, red and purple represent edges and points belonging to adjacent faces; Image (d) represent the final validated cuboids, for each primary face. (Color figure online)

2.2   Top-Down Evaluation of Adjacent Faces

In the previous section we have addressed the mechanisms used to generate a hypothesis of a primary face, including the support plane as well as the primary face bounding rectangle. With this information and with the prior knowledge of the configuration of a cuboid shaped object, it is possible to infer each of the four candidate adjacent faces. Let $\mathbf{p} = \{p_x, p_y, p_z\}$ be the unit vector normal to the plane that contains the primary face, and $\mathbf{v}^{(i)} = \{v_x, v_y, v_z\}^{(i)}$ the ith vertice of the polygon (rectangle) that defines the primary face. The normal vector of the plane that contains the adjacent face $\mathbf{a}^{(i)} = \{a_x, a_y, a_z\}^{(i)}$ is given by:

$$\mathbf{a}^{(i)} = \mathbf{p} \times \mathbf{e}^{(i)}, \tag{1}$$

where $\times$ denotes the external product between two vectors, and $\mathbf{e}^{(i)}$ the edge through which the ith face is adjacent to the primary face, defined as:

$$\mathbf{e}^{(i)} = \left\{ v_x^{(i+1)} - v_x^{(i)}, v_y^{(i+1)} - v_y^{(i)}, v_z^{(i+1)} - v_z^{(i)} \right\}. \tag{2}$$

The plane $\pi^{(i)}$ that contains the ith adjacent face is represented in the Hessian form $\pi^{(i)} : a_x^{(i)} \cdot x + a_y^{(i)} \cdot y + a_z^{(i)} \cdot z + d^{(i)} = 0$, where $d^{(i)}$ is given by:

$$d^{(i)} = -\left(a_x^{(i)} \cdot v_x^{(i)} + a_y^{(i)} \cdot v_y^{(i)} + a_z^{(i)} \cdot v_z^{(i)} \right). \tag{3}$$

Figure 2 (a) illustrates the mechanism used to infer $\mathbf{a}^{(i)}$.

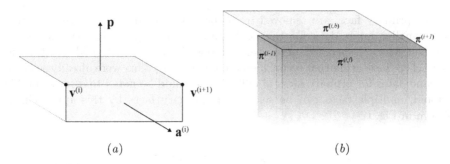

Fig. 2. Top-down evaluation of adjacent faces: (a) illustration of the mechanism used to estimate the adjacent faces (shown in green) starting from the primary face hypothesis (shown in yellow); (b) procedure for selecting the 3D points that belong to the adjacent face (points outside the defined volume are filtered). (Color figure online)

The procedures described previously determine a set of four adjacent faces for each primary face hypothesis. We now focus on how to decide if the adjacent faces are supported by observations, i.e., by points from the input point cloud. To do that, we propose to assess if a point is an observation of a given adjacent face. The mechanism is composed of two different filters which remove points from the input point cloud, followed by an Euclidean clustering of the remaining points. The first filter compares the normal estimated for each point[4] in the input point cloud $\mathcal{I}$ with the normal estimated for the adjacent face (see Eq. 1). Let $\alpha^{(i,k)}$ be the angle between the estimated normal for each point $\mathcal{I}^{(k)}$ and the normal $\mathbf{a}^{(i)}$ to the ith adjacent face plane. Then the point cloud after filtering ($\mathcal{P}$) is given by:

$$\mathcal{P} = \left\{ \mathcal{I}^{(k)} \in \mathcal{I} \mid \alpha^{(i,k)} < t_a, \forall k \in [0, n[\right\}, \tag{4}$$

where t_a is the angle threshold, and n the number of points in $\mathcal{I}$.

The second filter assesses which of the points from the input point cloud $\mathcal{I}$ are inside a volume defined around the adjacent face. To do this, we use the signed distance between a point $\mathbf{x}_0 = \{x_0, y_0, z_0\}$ and a plane $\pi : a{\cdot}x + b{\cdot}y + c{\cdot}z + d = 0$, defined as:

$$f(\mathbf{x}_0, \pi) = \frac{a \cdot x_0 + b \cdot y_0 + c \cdot z_0 + d}{\sqrt{a^2 + b^2 + c^2}}, \tag{5}$$

where $f(\cdot)$ is the function that computes the signed distance. The volume that is used to check if the input point cloud points are close to the ith adjacent face is bounded by five planes. Note that, to define a volume, we would need six planes. However, the sixth plane (i.e., the plane that contains the face opposite to the primary face) is not known in advance because the height or depth of the cuboid has not yet been estimated. Therefore, for a given adjacent face i, we define an infinite volume unbounded from one side, by using five planes.

---

[4] pointclouds.org/documentation/tutorials/normal_estimation.php.

Let 1 be a list that contains the five planes as follows: the plane that contains the primary face, $\pi^{(p)}$; the plane that is *behind* the adjacent face $\pi^{(i,b)}$: $a_x^{(i)}$ · $x + a_y^{(i)}$ · $y + a_z^{(i)}$ · $z + d^{(i)} - \Delta = 0$; the plane in front on the adjacent face, $\pi^{(i,f)}$: $a_x^{(i)}$ · $x + a_y^{(i)}$ · $y + a_z^{(i)}$ · $z + d^{(i)} + \Delta = 0$; the plane to the *left* of the adjacent face $\pi^{(i-1)}$; and the plane to the *right* of the adjacent face, $\pi^{(i+1)}$. Note that Δ is a parameter that defines the maximum distance between a point and the plane that contains the adjacent face. Thus, the list of planes for the *ith* adjacent face is defined as $\mathbf{1}^{(i)} = \{\pi^{(p)}, \pi^{(i,b)}, \pi^{(i,f)}, \pi^{(i-1)}, \pi^{(i+1)}\}$. For a given adjacent face i, the points from the input point cloud $\mathcal{I}^{(k)}$ that are inside the volume are given by:

$$\mathcal{P} = \left\{\mathcal{I}^{(k)} \in \mathcal{I} \mid f\big(\mathcal{I}^{(k)}, l^{(i,j)}\big) \cdot f\big(\mathbf{q}^{(i)}, l^{(i,j)}\big) \geq 0, \forall k \in [0, n[, \wedge \forall j \in [0, 5[\right\}, \quad (6)$$

where $l^{(i,j)}$ is the jth index plane of list $\mathbf{1}^{(i)}$, and $\mathbf{q}^{(i)}$ is a point defined beforehand that is surely inside the volume, for example:

$$\mathbf{q}^{(i)} = \left\{\frac{v_x^{(i)} + v_x^{(i+1)}}{2}, \frac{v_y^{(i)} + v_y^{(i+1)}}{2}, \frac{v_z^{(i)} + v_z^{(i+1)}}{2}\right\}. \quad (7)$$

After filtering the points, it is necessary to estimate the value of the height h for the adjacent face. Let $\mathcal{S}$ be the point cloud obtained after executing the filters defined in Eqs. (4) and (6). The value of h is estimated by finding the point $\mathcal{S}^{(k)}$ with the largest perpendicular distance to the plane that contains the primary face.

$$h = \max\left(f\big(\mathcal{S}^{(k)}, \pi^{(p)}\big)\right), \forall k \in [0, m[, \quad (8)$$

where m is the number of points in $\mathcal{S}$. When there is sufficient evidence that the face is observed in the data, we refer to the face as a valid face. The process of validating an adjacent face is the following: let the ratio between the number of points and the area of the *ith* adjacent face be denoted as $r^{(i)}$. If $r^{(i)} > t_{ppa}$ then the adjacent face is validated, where t_{ppa} is the points per area threshold parameter. The impact of this parameter on the overall performance of the procedure will be analyzed in Sect. 3.

The previous lines described the validation of the four adjacent faces for a given primary face hypothesis. To assess if the cuboid hypothesis initially determined by the RANSAC search of the primary face, we propose the following test: if one or more adjacent faces are validated, the cuboid hypothesis is accepted. Otherwise, the hypothesis is rejected.

3   Results

In this section we present quantitative results that evaluate the capability to successfully detect cuboid shaped objects from 3D data using the proposed hybrid top-down bottom-up approach.

In order to test our approach, a large-scale multi-view object dataset of common objects was used [15]. The RGB-D object dataset is composed by both RGB and depth images with a resolution of 640 × 480, containing 300 distinct objects, organized into 51 categories. The 250,000 object views that compose the dataset were obtained by spinning objects placed on a turntable at constant speed. The cameras were placed at about one meter from the objects, with varying heights and angles.

To evaluate the impact of the threshold parameters presented in Sect. 2, we conducted several tests by defining a range of values for each parameter. The distance threshold, t_d and the maximum distance to the plane parameter, Δ, varied simultaneously, ranging from 0.005 to 0.01 m in six equally spaced values. The adjacent face points per area threshold, t_{ppa}, also varied in six equally spaced values, ranging from 1×10^3 to 250×10^3 points per square meter. The angle threshold, t_a, was set to a fixed value of 30 degrees.

For each combination of parameters, 100 recognition tests were conducted. A test consists in presenting to the detection algorithm a segmented object point cloud from the dataset described above, and to compare the results given by the algorithm against predefined ground truth data. Half of the experiments were conducted on objects that are cuboid shaped objects (e.g. cereal box, cell phone and sponge) and half assessed non-cuboid shaped objects of the dataset (e.g. onion, banana and light bulb). A total of 36 experiments were performed representing all the possible combinations of parameters. The resultant ROC curve is displayed in Fig. 3.

As expected, the obtained ROC curve shows a trade-off between the true positive rate and the false positive rate. A good compromise could be to select the set of parameter values that achieve 0.80 true positive rate and about 0.12 false positive rate.

Figure 4 displays some images with the result of the proposed algorithm. In Figs. 4 (a) and (b) correct detections are shown, while in Figs. 4 (c) and (d) show examples of typical failures, i.e., shortcomings of the proposed approach.

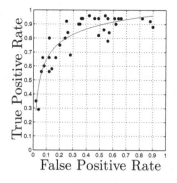

Fig. 3. ROC curve showing the recognition performance of the proposed approach.

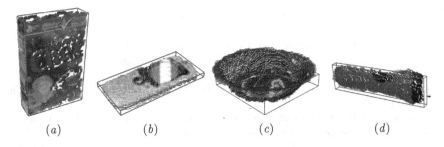

Fig. 4. Recognition of cuboid-shaped objects from 3D data: (*a*) and (*b*) correct recognitions of a cereal box and a cell phone, respectively; (*c*) false recognition of a bowl as a cuboid-shaped object, the bottom part was selected as the primary face and the side of the bowl was eligible for an adjacent face, due to a poor selection of the Δ parameter; (*d*) incorrect recognition of a flashlight, the visible side was selected as primary face due to a low value of t_{ppa}.

4   Conclusions

This paper proposes a hybrid top-down bottom-up approach to object recognition. This design option was taken to address some of the shortcomings of both bottom-up as well as top-down approaches. Results show that it is possible to successfully detected cuboid shaped objects using a bottom-up procedure to generate a set of hypothesis based on data, and a top-down process for evaluating the previously generated hypothesis, and that interesting recognition and false alarm rates can be achieved.

Future work will focus on devising different processes for validating the cuboid hypothesis. In addition, we want to look into mechanisms for handling occlusions as well as for extending the proposed hybrid approach to the detection of objects with different shapes.

Acknowledgments. This work has been supported by the "Fundação para a Ciência e Tecnologia" (Portuguese Foundation for Science and Technology) under grant agreements SFRH/BPD/109651/2015 and National Funds within projects UID/EEA/50014/2013 and UID/CEC/00127/2013. This work was also financed by the ERDF "European Regional Development Fund through the Operational Programme for Competitiveness and Internationalisation - COMPETE 2020 Programme within project POCI-01-0145-FEDER-006961 and project " NORTE -01 -0145 -FEDER-000020", financed by the North Portugal Regional Operational Programme (NORTE 2020, under the PORTUGAL 2020 Partnership Agreement). Finally, this work was also funded by the European Union's Seventh Framework Programme under grant n° 610917 (STAMINA).

References

1. Gregory, R.: The Intelligent Eye. ERIC, New York (1970)
2. Gregory, R.: Concepts and Mechanisms of Perception. Charles Scribner Sons, New York (1974)
3. Gibson, J.: The Senses Considered as Perceptual Systems. Houghton Mifflin, Boston (1966)
4. Gibson, J.: A theory of direct visual perception, Vision and Mind: selected readings in the philosophy of perception, pp. 77–90 (2002)
5. Neisser, U.: Cognition and reality: Principles and implications of cognitive psychology. WH Freeman/Times Books/Henry Holt & Co (1976)
6. Nasse, F., Grzeszick, R., Fink, G.A.: Toward object recognition with proto-objects and proto-scenes. In: 2014 International Conference on Computer Vision Theory and Applications (VISAPP), vol. 2, pp. 284–291 (2014)
7. Buso, V., Gonzalez-Diaz, I., Benois-Pineau, J.: Object recognition with top-down visual attention modeling for behavioral studies. In: 2015 IEEE International Conference on Image Processing (ICIP), pp. 4431–4435 (2015)
8. Hejrati, M., Ramanan, D.: Analysis by synthesis: 3D object recognition by object reconstruction. In: 2014 IEEE Conference on Computer Vision and Pattern Recognition (CVPR), pp. 2449–2456 (2014)
9. Kunze, L., Burbridge, C., Alberti, M., Thippur, A., Folkesson, J., Jensfelt, P., Hawes, N.: Combining top-down spatial reasoning and bottom-up object class recognition for scene understanding. In: 2014 IEEE/RSJ International Conference on Intelligent Robots and Systems (IROS 2014), pp. 2910–2915 (2014)
10. Hwang, S.J., Sha, F., Grauman, K.: Sharing features between objects and their attributes. In: 2011 IEEE Conference on Computer Vision and Pattern Recognition (CVPR), pp. 1761–1768 (2011)
11. Principe, J., Chalasani, R.: Cognitive architectures for sensory processing. Proc. IEEE **102**(4), 514–525 (2014)
12. Hager, G.D., Wegbreit, B.: Scene parsing using a prior world model. Int. J. Robot. Res. **30**(12), 1477–1507 (2011)
13. Brucker, M., Leonard, S., Bodenmliller, T., Hager, G.: Sequential scene parsing using range and intensity information. In: 2012 IEEE International Conference on Robotics and Automation (ICRA), pp. 5417–5424 (2012)
14. Chen, C., Aggarwal, J.: Recognition of box-like objects by fusing cues of shape and edges. In: 19th International Conference on Pattern Recognition, ICPR 2008, pp. 1–5 (2008)
15. Lai, K., Bo, L., Ren, X., Fox, D.: A large-scale hierarchical multi-view rgb-d object dataset. In: 2011 IEEE International Conference on Robotics and Automation (ICRA), pp. 1817–1824. IEEE (2011)

The Impact of Convergence Cameras in a Stereoscopic System for AUVs

João Aguiar, Andry Maykol Pinto[(✉)], Nuno A. Cruz, and Anibal C. Matos

INESTEC and Faculdade de Engenharia da Universidade do Porto,
Rua Dr. Roberto Frias, s/n, 4200-465 Porto, Portugal
{ee10018,andry.pinto,nacruz,anibal}@fe.up.pt

Abstract. Underwater imaging is being increasingly helpful for the autonomous robots to reconstruct and map the marine environments which is fundamental for searching for pipelines or wreckages in depth waters. In this context, the accuracy of the information obtained from the environment is of extremely importance. This work presents a study about the accuracy of a reconfigurable stereo vision system while determining a dense disparity estimation for underwater imaging. The idea is to explore the advantage of this kind of system for underwater autonomous vehicles (AUV) since varying parameters like the baseline and the pose of the cameras make possible to extract accurate 3D information at different distances between the AUV and the scene. Therefore, the impact of these parameters is analyzed using a metric error of the point cloud acquired by a stereoscopic system. Furthermore, results obtained directly from an underwater environment proved that a reconfigurable stereo system can have some advantages for autonomous vehicles since, in some trials, the error was reduced by 0.05 m for distances between 1.125 and 2.675 m.

Keywords: Underwater perception · Stereoscopic · Convergence cameras · Autonomous underwater vehicle

1 Introduction

Several researchers are developing novel vision systems for perceiving the aquatic environment using the UAVs (autonomous underwater vehicles). The idea beyond this effort is to enhance the ability of these vehicles to understand and to navigate in harsh environments, especially, for operating close to man-made structures and the sea-floor. Nonetheless, the perceptual information is not collected as easily as expected by underwater robotic applications due to severe conditions related with the light propagation in deep waters. These conditions affect the accuracy and the detail with the environment is perceived which is quite relevant for mapping underwater structures, obstacle avoidance and precise location for docking.

Nowadays, there are technological solutions already available for robotic applications such as the Sound Navigation and Ranging (SONAR), that calculates the distance using sound waves. Although the SONAR evidencing

© Springer International Publishing Switzerland 2016
A. Campilho and F. Karray (Eds.): ICIAR 2016, LNCS 9730, pp. 521–529, 2016.
DOI: 10.1007/978-3-319-41501-7_58

significant advantages for greater distances, the multiple reflections of the sound waves often result in a noisy sensor data for smaller distances. Therefore, vision-based systems enhance the capabilities of AUVs by complementing the sensor information available from the SONAR. In this context, the stereoscopic systems are suitable vision-based sensors since they are a cost-effective solutions and provide rich information of texture; however, their effectiveness depends on the visibility of the scene and is affected by suspensoids, backscattering and light absorption. Conventional stereoscopic systems for underwater environments often resort to small baselines and to a pre-defined camera poses (usually, parallel configurations) which may not be the most flexible approach for measuring 3D information for an autonomous vehicle because the objects of interest could have different relative distances to the UAV which influences the accuracy of the sensor data that is possible to be retrieved.

This paper introduces the concept of a Reconfigurable stereoscopic system based on SElf-adjusting cameras (RSECam) that converge or diverge according to the average distance to the scene. Besides this novel concept, the research provides also a preliminary study about the effect of the baseline and the pose of cameras in the performance of the system, by analyzing the accuracy of the point cloud that is obtained on underwater scenarios.

A set of experiments are conducted as a proof-of-concept for the RSECam. These validations provide a practical and quantitative analysis of the perceptual system in a real water tank, with several distinct objects at different ranges and including two different baselines (11 cm and 29 cm).

Therefore, contributions of this article include:

- A novel concept of a Reconfigurable stereoscopic system based on SElf-adjusting cameras (RSECam);
- A study about the impact of convergence cameras, in metric units, for the proposed underwater stereoscopic system;
- Qualitative evaluations for a proof-of-concept of the RSECam: have mainly considered realistic scenarios.

The article is organized as follows: Sect. 2 presents a brief review of systems that perceive distance information from the underwater environment. Section 3 shows the concept of the RSECam technique. Afterwards, Sect. 4 presents more practical results for the proof-of-concept. The experiments showed that reconfigurable stereoscopic configurations based on convergence cameras increase, in some cases, the accuracy of the 3D information when compared to conventional stereoscopic systems (with parallel or pre-determined configurations).

Finally, Sect. 5 presents the most important conclusions of this research.

2   Related Works

Intelligent and autonomous robotic vehicles have been developed with advanced visual systems [10] and they are capable to perform tasks that would otherwise be too dangerous, expensive or even impossible to achieve. The most often used sensors for underwater applications are the acoustic sensors due to the advantages of the sound propagation in water. Acoustic sensors are used in several applications like, for example, obstacle detection [4]. The work [12] presents an experimentally study of capabilities and limitations of underwater localization methods based on a robotic fish equipped with small, low-power sounder (buzzer) and microphones. In this experience, the authors achieved an underwater localization resolution of 20 cm over a range of 10 m. Other sensors used in range measurement are the LiDAR (Light Detection And Ranging) sensors despite of the light attenuation and absorption problems when submerged [3]. They are very useful for small and accurate distances and several investigators are already trying to decrease the undesirable backscattering problem [11]. LiDAR sensors can be separated in two different groups: the ones that work with triangulation and those that use ToF (time of flight). The former have higher resolution (less than 1 mm) than ToF but only for short ranges (less than 1 m). The latter are better for distances greater than 2.5 m and they have a 5 mm range precision for 8 m distances. In the case of [6] and considering a range of 10 m, the prototype based in ToF technology achieved a precision of 30 mm (Jerlov Type III). They also presented some 3D reconstructions on-the-fly. The LiDAR-based techniques are discussed with detail in [7]. Another possible approach for distance measurement the visual triangulation which can be grouped in active or passive techniques. The first needs a light source like a laser [8] or even structured light [5]. Two cameras are used at least for the second approach in order to determine the 3D information from the scene. The work presented in [1] concludes that structured light can be used in underwater environments and authors reported good results for a 3D reconstruction in low turbidity waters. However the solution presented in the research requires a projector and a structure capable of protecting both the camera and the projector itself when submerging the rig in water. The presence of a projector in this kind of system makes the range measurement easier due to the fact that it normally projects a well-defined pattern however, the power required by the projector device is substantial which reduces the autonomy of the robotic vehicle. Passive techniques require a minimum number of cameras of two to successfully measure the distance of a certain object within the scene and through a stereo correspondence - features captured on the left camera are found in the right camera and then, the disparity (difference between right and left pixels) can be determined. The biggest disadvantage of this technique is related to underwater imaging. Some image preprocessing algorithms are being created to mitigate some of the issues, for instance, the backscattering problem [13]. However, these methods usually affect the distance that is measured to the objects, for instance, the research [13] presented an average error of 28 cm for an object at 246 cm due to the presence of scattering. Two different cameras were used in [12] for underwater ranging measurement. This solution presented good results since the average error was about 10 % for distances under 5 m. Finally, the research presented in [13] demonstrates a similar comparison and the influence of the baseline distance is also studied. As can be noticed, the range error increases with the distance of the cameras to the object and, in this particular case, the results were obtained with 50 cm of baseline and considering distances greater than 10 m.

Currently, the limited visual perception capability of AUVs restricts the use these vehicles in purely autonomous operations with a medium complexity. Therefore, it becomes crucial the development of vision-based methods for understanding the sea-floor to allow a more efficient use of such robotic systems in real environments [9].

3   The Reconfigurable Stereoscopic System Based on SElf-adjusting Cameras (RSECam)

This research presents the concept of a Reconfigurable stereoscopic system based on SElf-adjusting cameras (RSECam). In its essence, the RSECam adjusts the pose of the cameras to rearrange the configuration of the stereo rig, for achieving a more accurate 3D measures when compared to conventional solutions.

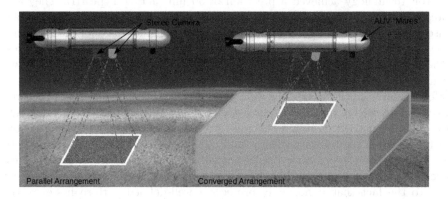

Fig. 1. The concept of RSECam.

The system should adjust the configuration of its camera according to the distance between the vision sensor to the scene. This changes the region where the two cameras' fields of view converge or intersect, often called by stereo window. Thus, the stereo window is modified by converging or diverging the cameras based on the rule that nearing objects lead to higher convergence angle values. The convergence is the angle formed by the cameras[1] and it is sometimes called by "toe-in". Moreover, the convergence point determines where the object appears in relation to the stereo window. Figure 1 presents the concept and the example of a practical application of the stereoscopic system that is proposed in this paper. Closer the convergence point means that the horopter[2] gets closer

---

[1] For simplicity, this paper assumes that a stereo rig is formed by 2 cameras.
[2] Horopter is the range of depth values within which objects can be measured by the stereo vision.

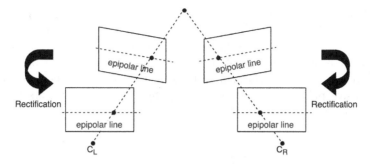

Fig. 2. The rectification process for convergence of the cameras.

and shrinks the depth range and obviously the area or volume. Thus, the resolution of depth estimation should improve in theory. The RSECam could be extremely relevant for applications where the distance to the scene is constantly changing, like the AUV (autonomous underwater vehicles).

Considering a parallel stereo rig, the distance to an object can be determined through a triangulation' principle and can be approximated by: $Z(x,y) = f.\beta/disp(x,y)$, where f is the focal length, β is the baseline and $disp(x,y)$ is the disparity between corresponding points (x,y). Although the parallel configuration denotes a particular case for the stereoscopy and it is difficult to be achieved in real life applications due to mechanical misalignments of cameras, the large majority of stereoscopic sensors resort to this kind of configuration. Besides that, the extraction of 3D information from converged cameras can be as simpler as the parallel cameras by considering properties of the epipolar constraint, since the possible locations of a point that is seen in one image is a line on the conjugated image. Thus, a rectification process can be performed which defines a transformation of each image plane in the way that pairs of conjugate epipolar lines become collinear and parallel to one of the image axes, see Fig. 2. This is intrinsically related to the extrinsic configuration of the stereo rig (mutual position and orientation).

A reliable extrinsic calibration is crucial for range measurements using the RSECam concept since these parameters are extremely important for the rectification procedure of converged cameras (a more detailed justification is presented in [2]). Obliviously, new extrinsic parameters are required when the pose of cameras is modified. Therefore, this paper proposes a quadratic approximation of discretized and manually obtained extrinsic configurations. This quadratic approximation adjusts automatically the extrinsic configuration that is currently used by the RSECam, where a set of conventional calibrations (using the chessboard method) are conducted for different convergence angles. Thus, a set of translation matrices and the angular values can be modeled as a function of the convergence angle which is constrained by a maximum and minimum distance to the targets. Besides the advantages of the RSECam that were already discussed in this paper, the concept is translated into a substantial increase of the mechanical complexity when compared to a conventional stereo sensors. In addition, the downside of converged cameras is related with a distortion effect caused by the two views (called the "keystone effect") and with mechanical tolerances and calibration errors. Therefore, a set of experiments must be conducted to evaluate the principles that support the RSECam concept before a complex and expensive prototyping of a setup that fulfill the requirements needed by AUVs (to be properly installed).

4   Results

A set of comprehensive experiments were conducted as part of this research in order to analyze the proposed RSECam. These experiments provide a preliminary study about the accuracy that could be expected from a self-reconfigurable stereo sensor under realistic underwater scenarios. The major goal is to validate the concept of the RSECam, which means to conduct a proof-of-concept regarding the dynamic convergence of cameras according to the average distance to a target (9×9 neighbors are considered). Therefore, the accuracy of the system is evaluated using the point cloud as a function of some factors such as the convergence angle (pose of cameras) and the baseline.

A simple but effective setup was developed for these trials: a stereo rig installed outside of a water tank with an acrylic window. This configuration is composed of two Mako-125C cameras with a 6 mm lens, two stepper motors and one micro-controller. Each camera is supported by a base that is attached to a stepper motor and, moreover, the baseline of cameras could be modified by a horizontal slide. The micro-controller is responsible for controlling motors and, consequently, to converge or diverge the cameras according to the desired pose. The setup of the hardware and a diagram of the process that originates the point cloud is depicted in Fig. 3. First, the cameras configuration is defined and extrinsic parameters are obtained. Then, images are rectified, the stereo correspondence is performed and the disparity is converted to 3D points. The dynamic configuration of the RSECam is obtained by a quadratic interpolation

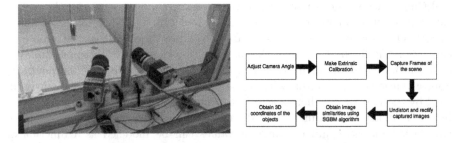

Fig. 3. The setup of the RSECam: a proof-of-concept (on the left). The architecture for extracting 3D information from the RSECam (on the right).

of the extrinsic parameters that were obtained by manual calibration procedures from a set of 4 convergence angles (−1.1, 6.3, 12.3 and 16.8 degrees).

A set of objects were placed inside the water tank at known distances: 1.125 m, 2.125 m, 2.625 m and 3.125 m. The distance error was analyzed in four distinct convergence angles (0°, 4°, 11° and 19.7°) and two baselines 0.11 m and 0.19 m: Fig. 4(a) and (b), respectively.

As expected, the error increases with the distance to a target. Figure 4(a) represents the results for a 0.11 m of baseline and it shows that the object at higher distance could only be seen for a convergence angle between 0° and 4°.

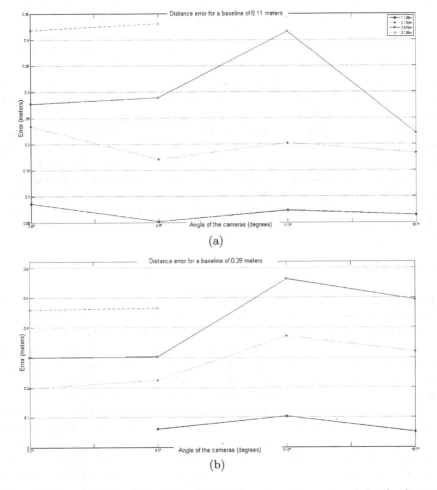

(a)

(b)

Fig. 4. The average error (in metric units) of 20 surrounding measures for the distance between the target to the stereo sensor as a function of the converged angle: considering a baseline of 0.11 m and 0.29 m, respectively. The absence of data represents objects outside the field of view of the sensor for that specific convergence angle. (Color figure online)

In general, the error evolution for the two closest objects demonstrate a consistent and significant decay for higher convergence angular values. The object at 2.625 m showed a high error for an angle of 11° which could be interpreted as an outlier since this error reduced to 0.22 m when the angle was 19.7° (following the same error profile as the trial with the target at 2.125 m). This outlier could be motivated by the keystoning effect, the difficulty in calibrating underwater stereo sensors and errors on the extrinsic parameters caused by a poor interpolation of the calibration samples (6.3° and 12.3°).

The trials conducted with a baseline value of 0.29 m follow a profile similar to Fig. 4(a) however, with a higher average error. Figure 4(b) demonstrates that the best convergence angle was 19.7° for the closest object and about 4° for objects at 2.125 m and 2.675 m. An increase of error (up to 0.25 m) was also verified in the 11° (for objects at 2.675 m) which decreases for a convergence angle of 19.7°. This can be justified by the increase of the baseline and the difficulties in calibrating the stereo system in underwater. Please noticed that object at larger distance cannot produce a relevant discussion since it goes outside the field of view of the sensor for half of the experiments. Additional trials contemplating more convergence angles must be conducted in the future.

Therefore, the results conducted in this research prove that the simultaneously manipulating of both the convergence and the interaxial gives control over the depth and the placement of objects within that 3D space which can improve the accuracy of 3D information retrieved from the environment. This could lead to significant advances for the navigation of AUVs however, more detailed experiments should be performed before the installation of a such sensor on a realistic robotic platform.

5   Conclusion

This paper presented a Reconfigurable stereoscopic system based on SElf-adjusting cameras (RSECam) which is a stereo system that converges or diverges the cameras according to the average distance to the scene. A preliminary study presents the impact of modifying the convergence point (by changing the pose of the cameras and the baseline) on the quality of the information. A set of experiments were conducted as a proof-of-concept and to quantify if the self-adjusting capability represents any advantage when compared to conventional stereoscopic systems. The results obtained from realistic underwater sequences proved that the accuracy of the 3D process was improved in some convergence angles. This is more evident for smaller distances (to the target) and for a stereo configuration with small baseline values since the error of the distance measured was decreased up to 0.10 m. This means that a vision sensor based on the RSECam will outperform conventional stereoscopic systems based on pre-defined configurations of the cameras.

For future activities, the RSECam technique will be tested in other realistic scenarios and, in addition, a navigation methodology will be developed to provide helpful and complementarity information for close range operations of AUVs.

Acknowledgments. This work is financed by the ERDF through COMPETE 2020 Programme within project "POCI-01-0145-FEDER-006961", and by National Funds through the FCT Portuguese Foundation for Science and Technology as part of project UID/EEA/50014/2013. Additionally, by the project "NORTE-01-0145-FEDER-000036" is financed by the NORTE 2020, and a H2020 project, under grant agreement No. 692427.

References

1. Bruno, F., Bianco, G., Muzzupappa, M., Barone, S., Razionale, A.: Experimentation of structured light and stereo vision for underwater 3D reconstruction. J. Photogramm. Remote Sens. **66**(4), 508–518 (2011)
2. Fusiello, A., Trucco, E., Verri, A.: A compact algorithm for rectification of stereo pairs. Mach. Vis. Appl. **12**(1), 16–22 (2000)
3. Jaffe, J.S.: Computer modeling and the design of optimal underwater imaging systems. IEEE J. Ocean. Eng. **15**(2), 101–111 (1990)
4. Li, J.-H., Lee, M.-J., Lee, W.-S., Kim, J.-T., Kang, H.-J., Suh, J.-H.: Real time obstacle detection in a water tank environment and its experimental study. In: IEEE/OES Autonomous Underwater Vehicles (AUV), pp. 1–5. IEEE (2014)
5. Massot-Campos, M., Oliver-Codina, G.: Underwater laser-based structured light system for one-shot 3D reconstruction. In: IEEE Sensors, pp. 1138–1141. IEEE (2014)
6. McLeod, D., Jacobson, J., Hardy, M., Embry, C.: Autonomous inspection using an underwater 3D LiDAR. In: IEEE Oceans-San Diego, p. 18. IEEE (2013)
7. Moroni, D., Pascali, M.A., Reggiannini, M., Salvetti, O.: Underwater scene understanding by optical and acoustic data integration. In: Proceedings of Meetings on Acoustics, pp. 70–85. Acoustical Society of America (2014)
8. Muljowidodo, K., Rasyid, M.A., SaptoAdi, N., Budiyono, A.: Vision based distance measurement system using single laser pointer design for underwater vehicle. Indian J. Mar. Sci. **38**(3), 324–331 (2009)
9. Pinto, A.M., Correia, M.V., Moreira, A.P., Costa, P.G.: Unsupervised flow-based motion analysis for an autonomous moving system. Image Vis. Comput. **32**(6–7), 391–404 (2014)
10. Pinto, A.M., Moreira, A.P., Costa, P.G.: An architecture for visual motion perception of a surveillance-based autonomous robot. In: IEEE International Conference on Autonomous Robot Systems and Competitions (ICARSC), pp. 205–211. IEEE (2014)
11. Rumbaugh, L.K., Bollt, E.M., Jemison, W.D., Li, Y.: A 532 nm chaotic LiDAR transmitter for high resolution underwater ranging and imaging. In: IEEE Oceans-San Diego, pp. 1–6. IEEE (2013)
12. Shatara, S., Tan, X., Mbemmo, E., Gingery, N., Henneberger, S.: Experimental investigation on underwater acoustic ranging for small robotic fish. In: IEEE International Conference on Robotics and Automation, pp. 712–717. IEEE (2008)
13. Zheng, B., Zheng, H., Zhao, L., Gu, Y., Sun, L., Sun, Y.: Underwater 3D target positioning by inhomogeneous illumination based on binocular stereo vision. In: IEEE Oceans, p. 14. IEEE (2012)

Biometrics

Gender Recognition from Face Images Using a Fusion of SVM Classifiers

George Azzopardi[1], Antonio Greco[2(✉)], and Mario Vento[2]

[1] University of Malta, Msida, Malta
george.azzopardi@um.edu.mt
[2] University of Salerno, Fisciano, Italy
{agreco,mvento}@unisa.it

Abstract. The recognition of gender from face images is an important application, especially in the fields of security, marketing and intelligent user interfaces. We propose an approach to gender recognition from faces by fusing the decisions of SVM classifiers. Each classifier is trained with different types of features, namely HOG (shape), LBP (texture) and raw pixel values. For the latter features we use an SVM with a linear kernel and for the two former ones we use SVMs with histogram intersection kernels. We come to a decision by fusing the three classifiers with a majority vote. We demonstrate the effectiveness of our approach on a new dataset that we extract from FERET. We achieve an accuracy of 92.6 %, which outperforms the commercial products Face++ and Luxand.

Keywords: Gender recognition · HOG · LBP · Histogram intersection

1 Introduction

In the last few years the identification of certain demographic attributes, such as gender, age and race, has involved various research areas, including computer vision. Here we concentrate on the automatic gender recognition problem from face images. Such a system has various applications. Examples include behaviour adaptation of intelligent user interfaces and adaptive advertising billboards. A system that stores the gender of each customer could help to collect demographic statistics in order to evaluate the effectiveness of the marketing strategies. Furthermore, video surveillance systems could first use gender identification in order to reduce the search space in their database, yielding a much more efficient retrieval process.

The gender recognition task seems to be effortless for humans. In fact, an individual is able to distinguish a male from a female by simply observing the face [1]. It also seems that the visual system of our brains has developed neurons that are selective for faces [2]. The detection of the facial features, such as beard or mustache, eyes, earrings, make-up among others, could be very challenging for a computer vision algorithm. These problems are mainly due to the variations in pose, facial expressions, occlusions, and changes in illumination. Other challenges

© Springer International Publishing Switzerland 2016
A. Campilho and F. Karray (Eds.): ICIAR 2016, LNCS 9730, pp. 533–538, 2016.
DOI: 10.1007/978-3-319-41501-7_59

include the intra-variation within the two classes due to age and racial features. Nevertheless, most of the methods [3–5] perform gender recognition by using only features that are extracted from faces.

A typical facial gender recognition algorithm carries out four steps: (i) face detection; (ii) pre-processing; (iii) feature extraction; and (iv) binary classification. Most of the approaches use the Viola-Jones algorithm [6] for face detection and the Support Vector Machine [7] for classification. The main difference lies in the type of features extracted from faces. The most used features for gender recognition are the pixel intensity values, the Local Binary Pattern (LBP) descriptor and the fiducial distances. The latter are the distances between specific facial points (e.g. eye corners, face contour, tip of the nose) and have been widely used in recent years for face recognition [5,8].

The pixel intensity values, also called raw features, can be directly used to train a binary classifier for gender recognition. Sometimes, the raw feature extraction is carried out after a pre-processing step, in order to deal with pose (face alignment) and brightness variations (histogram equalization). Techniques such as principal component analysis (PCA) have also been used to reduce the dimensionality of the feature vectors [3,9,10].

The histograms of LBP features [11] in the face region are often used as discriminative feature vectors for gender classification [12]. Other methods that combine LBP and shape features were proposed in [4,13], where pixel intensity values were also considered.

A different approach is based on the search of the facial landmarks, the so-called fiducial points, and their mutual spatial arrangement. These points could be labeled by hand or using predefined masks like the Active Shape Model (ASM) [14]. The distances between these fiducial points are used as discriminant features for gender recognition [8]. Deep learning and convolutional neural networks have also been proposed for the localization of facial landmarks [5].

The contribution of our work is two-fold. First, we take the majority vote from the output of three SVM classifiers that are configured with different types of features, namely HOG [15], LBP and raw pixels. We demonstrate that shape, texture and raw features are orthogonal to each other as we achieve considerable higher accuracy when combining them. Second, we evaluate our method on a subset of the FERET [16], a standard benchmark dataset for face recognition, which we collected specifically for gender recognition purposes. We made it publicly available with the name GENDER-FERET [17], thus our results are reproducible and can be compared with new approaches.

2   Method

Figure 1 shows the architecture of the proposed method. First we perform face detection using the Viola-Jones algorithm [6]. Then we crop the detected face and resize it to 128×128 pixels. We transform the image into a ($128 \times 128 =$) 16384-element feature vector and divide each element by 255 so that all dimensions have the same range of [0,1].

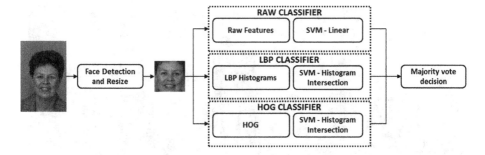

Fig. 1. Architecture of the proposed method

We apply the LBP descriptor [11] to the entire image by comparing the intensity value of each pixel with a 3×3 neighbourhood. We use a spatial tiling of 3×3 and generate a 256-element L2-normalized histogram for each tile. Finally, we merge the nine histograms to form a $(256 \times 9 =)$ 2304-element vector for each image. We use the LBP histogram-based descriptors with an SVM classifier characterized by a histogram intersection kernel.

As to the HOG descriptor we first compute the gradient and angle of every pixel by considering the responses of first-order partial derivatives of a 2D Gaussian function with a $\sigma = 1$. Then we sample blocks of 32×32 pixels that overlap by 50 % and for each block we use a spatial tiling of 2×2. For each tile we compute the L2-normalized weighted histogram of 9 bins (in intervals of $20°$), clip the normalized values at 0.2 and normalize again. Considering we use face images of size 128×128 pixels, the HOG descriptor results in a (7 blocks $\times$ 7 blocks $\times$ 4 tiles $\times$ 9 bins $=$) 1764-element vector. Similar to the LBP-based descriptor, since this descriptor is based on histograms, we train an SVM classifier with a histogram intersection kernel.

The result of each classifier is a pair of probabilities that a given image has a male or a female face. In order to come up with a decision we sum the three male probabilities and the three female probabilities and if the total male probability is greater than the total female probability then we label the given face image to be a male otherwise a female.

3 Evaluation

Despite the effort of the Benchmarking Facial Image Analysis Technologies (BeFIT) [18], there is not yet a standard dataset for the evaluation of gender recognition algorithms. Most of the available datasets are designed for face detection and recognition. FERET [16] is among the most important benchmark datasets for face recognition, but it does not provide gender annotations. For this reason, we extracted a subset of FERET by choosing only the frontal images, without variations in pose, but with different expressions, backgrounds and illumination conditions, as shown with some examples in Fig. 2. The dataset is balanced, so we

Fig. 2. Examples of faces in the GENDER-FERET dataset. The bounding boxes indicate the faces detected by Viola-Jones [6]. The images in the last column are (top) the average male face and (bottom) the average female face of this dataset.

Table 1. Experimental results. The first 5 columns show the combination of features that we use. Every set of features is combined with an SVM classifier whose type of kernel, Linear or Histogram Intersection (H.Int) is specified underneath. The last five columns show the results in terms of male (M) and female (F) true positives (TP) and false positives (FP), along with accuracy.

Raw (Linear)	LBP (Linear)	HOG (Linear)	LBP (H.Int)	HOG (H.Int)	M (TP)	F (TP)	M (FP)	F (FP)	Accuracy (%)
✓					208	209	28	27	88.3
	✓				205	201	31	35	86.0
		✓			204	209	32	27	87.5
✓	✓				215	212	21	24	90.5
✓		✓			212	214	24	22	90.3
	✓	✓			212	211	24	25	89.6
✓	✓	✓			215	214	21	22	90.9
			✓		189	213	47	23	85.2
				✓	208	217	28	19	90.0
✓			✓		212	214	24	22	90.3
✓				✓	219	215	17	21	91.9
			✓	✓	212	220	24	16	91.5
✓			✓	✓	217	220	19	16	**92.6**
Face++ [19]					233	190	3	46	89.6
Luxand [20]					235	186	1	50	89.2

have the same number of male and female images (473 m, 473 f). Then we selected 50 % of the images to form a training set (237 m, 237 f) and the remaining 50 % to form a test set (236 m, 236 f). The face of a person is either in the training or in the test set, but not in both. Different variations in expression, facial features, background and illumination were also considered in both sets. We call the newly formed dataset GENDER-FERET and make it publicly available [17]. We use the accuracy rate as a performance measurement on the test set.

As shown in Table 1, the accuracy is above 85 % using any combination of feature or classifier. The classifier that relies on only raw pixel values achieves 88.3 % of accuracy, which is better than both the LBP- and the HOG-based classifiers. Performance significantly increases when we combine the decisions of different classifiers. Using only linear SVMs the highest accuracy that we achieve is 90.9 %, while the best accuracy (92.6 %) is achieved using histogram intersection kernel for both the LBP and HOG classifiers.

Since there are no standard datasets for the gender recognition algorithms, the comparison with the results published in other studies is infeasible. For a more realistic comparison on the same test set, we apply the commercial libraries, namely Face++ [19] and Luxand [20]. In Table 1 we also report the results of these commercial methods, which are substantially lower than the performance achieved by our method.

4   Discussion and Conclusion

We propose a method for gender recognition from face images using a fusion of SVM classifiers. The method has been evaluated on the new GENDER-FERET dataset, which includes variations in expressions, facial features, background and illumination. The experimental results show that by taking the majority vote of three SVM classifiers we are able to significantly improve the performance of gender recognition from face images. The result suggests that the HOG-, LBP-, and pixel-based descriptors, which essentially describe the properties of shape, texture and intensity distribution, are complementary features. By using the majority vote rule, we can exploit the abilities of the three classifiers, and come to a more certain decision.

The confusion matrices reported in Table 1 show that our method has a good generalization ability, while Face++ and Luxand seem to be specialized in the recognition of males. It is important to note that we could not train the Face++ and Luxand algorithms on the same training set that we used to configure our system. This is because only the preconfigured versions of these algorithms are available. In future work we will use larger and heterogeneous datasets in order to evaluate the generalization ability of the classifier and to compare the performance of the proposed method in even more challenging situations.

References

1. Marquardt Beauty Analysis. Face variations by sex (2014). http://www.beautyanalysis.com/beauty-and-you/face-variations/face-variations-sex/
2. Perrett, D.I., Rolls, E.T., Caan, W.: Visual neurones responsive to faces in the monkey temporal cortex. Exp. Brain Res. **47**(3), 329–342 (1982)
3. Moghaddam, B., Yang, M.-H.: Learning gender with support faces. IEEE Trans. Pattern Anal. Mach. Intell. **24**(5), 707–711 (2002)

4. Alexandre, L.A.: Gender recognition: a multiscale decision fusion approach. Pattern Recognit. Lett. **31**(11), 1422–1427 (2010)

5. Sun, Y., Wang, X., Tang, X.: Deep convolutional network cascade for facial point detection. In: Proceedings of the IEEE Conference on Computer Vision and Pattern Recognition, pp. 3476–3483 (2013)

6. Viola, P., Jones, M.J.: Robust real-time face detection. Int. J. Comput. Vis. **57**(2), 137–154 (2004)

7. Cortes, C., Vapnik, V.: Support-vector networks. Mach. Learn. **20**(3), 273–297 (1995)

8. Brunelli, R., Poggio, T.: Face recognition: features versus templates. IEEE Trans. Pattern Anal. Mach. Intell. **10**, 1042–1052 (1993)

9. Baluja, S., Rowley, H.A.: Boosting sex identification performance. Int. J. Comput. Vis. **71**(1), 111–119 (2007)

10. Yang, J., Zhang, D., Frangi, A.F., Yang, J.-Y.: Two-dimensional PCA: a new approach to appearance-based face representation and recognition. IEEE Trans. Pattern Anal. Mach. Intell. **26**(1), 131–137 (2004)

11. Ojala, T., Pietikäinen, M., Mäenpää, T.: Multiresolution gray-scale and rotation invariant texture classification with local binary patterns. IEEE Trans. Pattern Anal. Mach. Intell. **24**(7), 971–987 (2002)

12. Lian, H.-C., Lu, B.-L.: Multi-view gender classification using local binary patterns and support vector machines. In: Wang, J., Yi, Z., Żurada, J.M., Lu, B.-L., Yin, H. (eds.) ISNN 2006. LNCS, vol. 3972, pp. 202–209. Springer, Heidelberg (2006)

13. Tapia, J.E., Perez, C.A.: Gender classification based on fusion of different spatial scale features selected by mutual information from histogram of LBP, intensity, shape. IEEE Trans. Inf. Forensics Secur. **8**(3), 488–499 (2013)

14. Milborrow, S., Nicolls, F.: Locating facial features with an extended active shape model. In: Forsyth, D., Torr, P., Zisserman, A. (eds.) ECCV 2008, Part IV. LNCS, vol. 5305, pp. 504–513. Springer, Heidelberg (2008)

15. Dalal, N., Triggs, B.: Histograms of oriented gradients for human detection. In: IEEE Computer Society Conference on Computer Vision and Pattern Recognition, 2005. CVPR 2005, vol. 1, pp. 886–893. IEEE (2005)

16. Phillips, P.J., Moon, H., Rizvi, S.A., Rauss, P.J.: The FERET evaluation methodology for face-recognition algorithms. IEEE Trans. Pattern Anal. Mach. Intell. **22**(10), 1090–1104 (2000)

17. Mivia Lab University of Salerno. Gender-FERET dataset (2016). http://mivia.unisa.it/database/gender-feret.zip

18. Karlsruhe Insitute of Technology. Befit - benchmarking facial image analysis technologies (2011). http://fipa.cs.kit.edu/412.php

19. Face++. Leading face recognition on cloud (2014). http://www.faceplusplus.com/

20. Luxand. Facial feature detection technologies (2015). https://www.luxand.com/

Kinship Verification from Faces via Similarity Metric Based Convolutional Neural Network

Lei Li[1], Xiaoyi Feng[1], Xiaoting Wu[1], Zhaoqiang Xia[1],
and Abdenour Hadid[1,2(✉)]

[1] School of Electronics and Information, Northwestern Polytechnical University,
Xi'an 710129, Shaanxi, China
[2] Center for Machine Vision Research (CMVS), University of Oulu, Oulu, Finland
`hadid@ee.oulu.fi`

Abstract. The ability to automatically determine whether two persons
are from the same family or not is referred to as Kinship (or family) verification. This is a recent and challenging research topic in computer vision.
We propose in this paper a novel approach to kinship verification from
facial images. Our solution uses similarity metric based convolutional
neural networks. The system is trained using Siamese architecture specific constraints. Extensive experiments on the benchmark KinFaceW-I
& II kinship face datasets showed promising results compared to many
state-of-the-art methods.

Keywords: Kinship verification · Similarity metric learning · Convolutional neural networks · Siamese architecture

1 Introduction

Verifying whether two persons are from the same family or not is termed kinship
(or family) verification. Automatic kinship verification aims at deriving computational models to determine whether two persons belong to the same family or
not based only on patterns such as faces, voices and gaits. The inputs of such a
system can be two faces (Face A and Face B) and the expected output is a decision whether Person A is a family member (father, sister, mother, brother etc.)
of Person B or not. Such an application can be useful e.g. for finding missing
children, image annotation, and social media comprehension [14,16]. Although
a DNA test is the most accurate mean for kinship verification, it unfortunately
cannot be used in many scenarios such as in video surveillance.

In the literature of biometrics, it has been rarely looked into kinship verification as a soft biometric modality. We focus our work on face patterns and explore
if a query face belongs to a certain group of people sharing some similarities in
facial appearance. Due to genetic similarities, there is indeed facial resemblance
among family members. We limit our definition of family to immediate members
such as parents and siblings. As shown in Fig. 1, face-based family verification
is a very challenging problem as it not only encounters all variations as in face

© Springer International Publishing Switzerland 2016
A. Campilho and F. Karray (Eds.): ICIAR 2016, LNCS 9730, pp. 539–548, 2016.
DOI: 10.1007/978-3-319-41501-7_60

Parents   Children | Parents   Children

Positive examples | Negative examples

Fig. 1. Examples of image pairs of positive and negative kinship relationships

recognition problems (such as illumination changes, pose variations, blur and low resolution images) but has also to deal with other factors such as mixed ethnicities, effects of aging, multiple age groups and unbalanced number of members that naturally exist in a family.

The few existing works on kinship verification basically share similar facial representations as in face recognition. This includes for instance the use of LBP (Local Binary Patterns), LPQ (Local Phase Quantization) and HOG (Histograms Of Gradients) features as inputs to SVMs (Support Vector Machines) for classification [2,8]. Such approaches work well under some limited image variations (in terms of illumination, image resolution, blur etc.) but tend to suffer under unconstrained settings or to generalize to unseen data.

However, the very recent developments in machine learning suggest that enhanced performance can be obtained using learned features e.g. based on deep learning methods [5,13,15] instead of hand-crafted features e.g. LBP, LPQ and HOG.

In this present work, we introduce a novel approach to kinship verification from facial images using deep learning. Instead of using Mahalanobis distance learning on different objective functions and constraints as in previous works, we propose the use of a deep learning architecture to better capture the non-linearity relationship between the image pairs of the same family [15]. We build our novel solution using a Convolutional Neural Network (CNN) and the Siamese architecture [1] to extract highly discriminative multi-scale features and to derive a new similarity metric. We report our preliminary experimental investigations on the benchmark KinFaceW-I & II kinship face datasets showing very promising performance compared to state-of-the-art methods.

2   Related Work

Kinship verification is a relatively new research topic which has already attracted a significant number of works in the recent years. For instance, among the first works, Fang *et al.* [2] proposed an approach based on facial attributes such as skin, hair and eye color, and facial geometry. The reported experimental results on a small dataset showed that the color information may play a key role in kinship verification.

Xia *et al.* [14] proposed a method based on transfer subspace learning to reduce image differences in kinship pairs caused by different age stages. The method was only evaluated on image pairs collected under constrained settings (e.g. limited illumination changes). To cope with this limitation, Zhou *et al.* [16] presented a scheme using Gabor-based Gradient Orientation Pyramid descriptors to model the facial information for unconstrained kinship verification.

More recently, Lu *et al.* [9] introduced a new approach for kinship verification using metric learning and a combination of different local features. The metric learning was used for mapping the face images into a new space where image pairs with kinship relationship are located close to each other while image pairs without kinship relationship are put far from each other. Experiments on several kinship face databases have been reported, showing promising results.

In the recent few years, deep learning has become a very appealing approach to automatically learn highly discriminative features from large amount of data and build robust classifiers. This resulted in remarkable performance improvements in many computer vision and pattern recognition tasks including object recognition, action analysis, and face verification. Many architectures of deep learning have been proposed in the literature e.g. [3,4,12] and implementation platforms have been made available for research purposes.

In this work, we propose a novel approach to kinship verification from facial images using similarity metric based convolutional neural networks (SMCNN). Our approach is partially inspired by the work of Yan *et al.* [15] which proposed a metric learning method based on deep neural networks for the task of face verification. However, different from the work of Yan *et al.* which considered hand-crafted features as inputs to the deep neural network, our approach explores automatically learned features for kinship verification.

3   Proposed Approach

Our proposed approach using similarity metric based convolutional neural networks (SMCNN) for kinship verification is illustrated in Fig. 2. The basic idea is inspired by the work of Chopra *et al.* [1] on deep learning of face verification. The novelties in our approach include (i) the connection between the first and the second convolutional layers aiming at eliminating the redundant information generated by the symmetrical structure in SMCNN, and (ii) inspired by the discriminative deep metric learning method in [15], we restrain the specific distance between the image pair in the cost function of the Siamese architecture in order to better distinguish image pairs of kinship versus non kinship relationships.

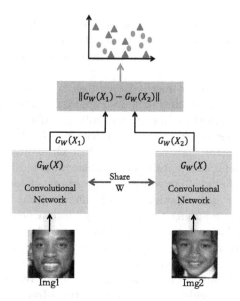

Fig. 2. The framework of our proposed approach using similarity metric based convolutional neural networks (SMCNN) for kinship verification. An image pair is first fed into two identical convolutional neural networks. The L_1 norm between their outputs is then computed. Finally, a decision is made based a learned threshold.

3.1   Convolutional Neural Networks

As can be seen from Fig. 2, the SMCNN architecture consists of two identical convolutional neural networks. Each of them contains 8 layers (see Fig. 3): 4 convolutional layers, 3 pooling layers and a full connection layer. The connection orders of these layers are as follows: $C_1 - P_2 - C_3 - P_4 - C_5 - P_6 - C_7 - F_8$, where C_t is the convolutional layer, P_t denotes a pooling (sub-sampling) layer, and F_t represents a full connection layer. t is the layer index. In our proposed

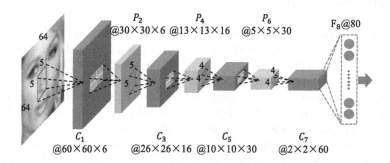

Fig. 3. The architecture of the Convolutional Neural Network in SMCNN. The dark green represents the convolutional layers, shallow green represents the subsampling layers and last blue layer is the full connection layer. (Color figure online)

Table 1. Parameters of the convolutional neural network.

Layers	C_1	P_2	C_3	P_4	C_5	P_6	C_7	F_8
Input-number	1	6	6	16	16	30	30	60
Out-number	6	6	16	16	30	30	60	80
Filter-size	5×5	2×2	5×5	2×2	4×4	2×2	4×4	2×2

approach, the pooling layer is carrying the sub-sampling operation. The detailed parameters of each layer are given in Table 1.

3.2 The Cost Function of SMCNN

Let x_i and x_j denote the gray-scale input images (i.e. corresponding to the gray-scale images of $Img1$ and $Img2$ in Fig. 2), and y the label of the image pair (x_i, x_j). $y = 1$ if the image pair has a kinship relationship (referred to as positive pair) and $y = -1$ otherwise (referred to as negative pair). W represents the weights of the convolutional neural network. $G_W(x_i)$ and $G_W(x_j)$ represent the features given by the convolutional neural network. The distance between $G_W(x_i)$ and $G_W(x_j)$ is measured by L_1 norm, which is defined as:

$$D_G(x_i, x_j) = \|G_W(x_i) - G_W(x_j)\|_1 \tag{1}$$

The distance $D_G(x_i, x_j)$ should be smaller for positive image pairs and larger for negative image pairs. In [4], two thresholds have been used for classification. If $D_G(x_i, x_j)$ is smaller than a pre-defined threshold τ_1 then $D_G(x_i, x_j)$ belongs to a positive pair. Otherwise, if $D_G(x_i, x_j)$ is larger than a threshold $\tau_2(\tau_1 < \tau_2)$, then $D_G(x_i, x_j)$ belongs to a negative pair.

For simplicity of the classification scheme using the two convolutional neural networks, the thresholds τ_1 and τ_2 can be combined into one threshold τ so that τ is larger than 1 and:

$$y(\tau - D_G(x_i, x_j)) > 1 \tag{2}$$

where $\tau_1 = \tau - 1$ and $\tau_2 = \tau + 1$. The cost function of SMCNN can be formulated as follows:

$$\begin{aligned} \arg\min_{G} J &= J_1 + J_2 \\ &= \sum_{i,j} f(1 - y(\tau - D_G(x_i, x_j))) \\ &+ \frac{\lambda}{2}(\|W\|_{\mathbb{F}}^2 + \|b\|_{\mathbb{F}}^2) \end{aligned} \tag{3}$$

where $f(t) = \frac{1}{\beta}log(1 + exp(\beta t))$ is the generalized logistic loss [10], β is a sharpness parameter, operation $\|M\|_{\mathbb{F}}$ denotes the Frobenius norm of the matrix M, and λ is a regularization parameter.

To minimize the cost function in Eq. 3, sub-gradient descent algorithm is adopted in the convolutional neural network. W_t denotes the weighting parameters in t layer, and b_t represents the bias term. Based on the principle of backpropagation, the key idea is to calculate the error term δ_F in the full connection layer. So, the error term of SMCNN is:

$$\delta = y \cdot f'(u) \cdot sign(c) \tag{4}$$

where y is the label of the image pair ($y = 1$ or $y = -1$), $u = 1 - y(-D_G(x_i, x_j))$, $c = abs(G_W(x_i) - G_W(x_j))$ and $sign$ is the sign function which is an approximation of the partial derivative c in abs function, as illustrated in Eq. 5:

$$sign(c) = \begin{cases} -1 & , & c < 0 \\ 0 & , & c = 0 \\ +1 & , & c > 0 \end{cases} \tag{5}$$

The error term of the full connection layer in the convolutional neural network can be calculated as follows:

$$\begin{aligned} \delta_{F_i} &= \delta \odot s'(F_8(x_i)) \\ \delta_{F_j} &= -\delta \odot s'(F_8(x_j)) \end{aligned} \tag{6}$$

where $F_8(x_i)$ is the output of the full connection layer, the symbol s' is the partial derivative of activation function used in the full connection layer, the '$\odot$' denotes the element-wise product operator. After computing the error term δ_F of the full connection layer, the partial derivative of W_t and b_t can be computed by backpropagation [1]. Then, gradient descent algorithm can be used to update the corresponding parameters as follows:

$$\begin{aligned} W_t &= W_t - \rho \cdot \frac{\partial J}{\partial W} \\ b_t &= b_t - \rho \cdot \frac{\partial J}{\partial b} \end{aligned} \tag{7}$$

Where ρ is a learning rate which is set in our experiments to $\rho = 0.001$.

3.3   Implementation

Used Toolbox: We used the deep learning toolbox called "DeepLearnToolbox" [11]. DeepLearnToolbox does not contain a ready framework for SMCNN. So, we made changes to build the SMCNN. The changes are mainly related to two aspects. First, we changed the connection between the first convolutional layer and the second convolutional layer. Second, we changed the activation function from *sigmoid* to *tanh*.

Partial Connection: To extract different (hopefully complementary) features and keep the number of connections within reasonable bounds, the partial connection scheme is adopted between the first convolutional layer and the third convolutional layer, as illustrated in Table 2.

Table 2. Connection scheme between layers C_1 and C_3.

		C3															
		1	2	3	4	5	6	7	8	9	10	11	12	13	14	15	16
C1	1	√				√	√	√			√	√	√	√		√	√
	2	√	√			√	√	√			√	√	√	√			√
	3	√	√	√				√	√	√			√		√	√	√
	4		√	√	√			√	√	√	√			√		√	√
	5			√	√	√			√	√	√	√		√	√		√
	6				√	√	√			√	√	√	√		√	√	√

Activation Function: We use the *tanh* function as the activation function in SMCNN. The *tanh* function and its derivative are computed as follows:

$$s(z) = tanh(z) = \frac{exp(z) - exp(-z)}{exp(z) + exp(-z)}$$
$$s'(z) = tanh'(z) = 1 - tanh^2(z)$$

(8)

Parameter Initialization: We randomly initialized the weights W_t and the bias term b_t based on *Gaussian* distribution, with mean value of 0 and standard deviation of 0.05.

4   Experimental Analysis

To evaluate the performance of our proposed approach SMCNN, we experimented with the publicly available benchmark datasets KinFaceW [7]. KinFaceW datasets contain KinFaceW-I as well as KinFaceW-II and include four kinship relationships: Father-Son (FS), Father-Daughter(FD), Mother-Son (MS) and Mother-Daughter (MD). The number of kinship pair relations in KinFaceW-I is 156, 134, 116, 127 for FS, FD, MS and MD, respectively. In KinFaceW-II, there are in total 250 kinship pair relations. Based on the webpage of KinFaceW, we use the pre-specified training/testing split, which was generated randomly and independently for 5-folds. Four folds are used for training while the remaining fold is used for testing.

Given the fact that the size of the database is not big enough to optimally estimate all the parameters in SMCNN, we first used all the training samples to build a basic model. Then, we perform fine-tuning on the basic model based on the image pairs in different relations. During the fine-tuning step, we set the number of fine-tuning iterations to 20, 50, 100 and 200 to prevent over fitting. The intermediate representations in the convolutional layers of the MS relationship model are shown in Fig. 4.

To gain insight into the performance of our approach, we compared our results against those of related methods including DMML [15], MNRML [9] and the Similarity Measure (SM) [6]. The obtained results are shown in Table 3 while the ROC curves of our method are illustrated in Fig. 5.

  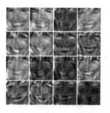

Fig. 4. Input of the networks and outputs of the layers in SMCNN. Images are for input image (left), first convolutional result (middle), and third convolutional result (right), respectively.

Table 3. Compare the fine-tuning results with the others (Accuracy: %).

Method	KinFaceW-I				KinFaceW-II			
	FD	FS	MD	MS	FD	FS	MD	MS
DMML 2014 [15]	74.5	69.5	69.5	**75.5**	78.5	**76.5**	78.5	**79.5**
MNRML 2014 [9]	72.5	66.5	66.2	72.0	76.9	74.3	77.4	77.6
SM 2015 [6]	66.1	62.2	64.3	70.0	74.9	71.0	76.9	76.4
Proposed SMCNN	**75.0**	**75.0**	72.2	68.7	**79.0**	75.0	**85.0**	78.0

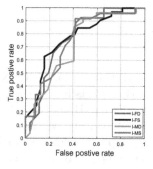 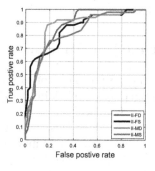

Fig. 5. The ROC curves of different kinship relationships obtained on KinFaceW-I (left) and KinFaceW-II (right). There are four different colors which represent different kinship relationships: red (FS), black (FS), green (MS) and pink (MD). (Color figure online)

As can be seen from Table 3, our proposed approach compares favorably against the related methods in the state-of-the-art. On KinFaceW-I, our approach yields in the best performance for all kinship relationships except for MS relationship for which the best results are obtained with DMML 2014 [15]. On KinFaceW-II, our proposed approach gives the best results in two cases (FD and MD) while DMML 2014 [15] yields in slightly better results in two other cases (FS and MS). Note that our approach outperforms MNRML 2014 [9] and SM 2015 [6] methods in all cases and for both KinFaceW-I and KinFaceW-II.

We can notice from Table 3 that the results on KinFaceW-II are better than those on KinFaceW-I. The reason is that the images in KinFaceW-II are cropped from the same pictures and hence sharing similar environment, such as illuminate intensity and chrominance. However, KinFaceW-I is collected from different pictures in uncontrolled environments.

5 Conclusion

In this paper, a novel method for kinship verification from facial images is introduced. It uses Similarity Metric based Convolutional Neural Network (SMCNN). The experimental results on benchmark datasets KinFaceW-I & II achieved promising results which compare favorably against those results of related methods in the state-of-the-art.

As a future work, we plan to evaluate our methodology on several other databases and also on other face related classification tasks such as face verification, age estimation and gender classification. It is finally worth noting that one can expect much better results with deep learning when a large number of training images are available for training. So, it is of great interest to re-evaluate the performance of our method when re-training our models on larger databases.

Acknowledgments. The financial support of the Academy of Finland, Infotech Oulu, Nokia Foundation, the Northwestern Polytechnical University, and the Shaanxi Province is acknowledged.

References

1. Chopra, S., Hadsell, R., Lecun, Y.: Learning a similarity metric discriminatively, with application to face verification. In: IEEE Computer Society Conference on Computer Vision and Pattern Recognition, 2005. CVPR 2005, vol. 1, pp. 539–546 (2005)
2. Fang, R., Tang, K.D., Snavely, N., Chen, T.: Towards computational models of kinship verification. In: Proceedings/ICIP. International Conference on Image Processing, pp. 1577–1580 (2010)
3. Hinton, G.E., Osindero, S., Teh, Y.W.: A fast learning algorithm for deep belief nets. Neural Comput. **18**(7), 1527–1554 (2006)
4. Huang, G., Lee, H., Learned-Miller, E.: Learning hierarchical representations for face verification with convolutional deep belief networks. In: 2012 IEEE Conference on Computer Vision and Pattern Recognition (CVPR), pp. 2518–2525, June 2012
5. Khalil-Hani, M., Sung, L.S.: A convolutional neural network approach for face verification. In: 2014 International Conference on High Performance Computing & Simulation (HPCS), pp. 707–714 (2014)
6. Kou, L., Zhou, X., Xu, M., Shang, Y.: Learning a genetic measure for kinship verification using facial images. Math. Prob. Eng. 2015, 1–5 (2015)
7. Lu, J., Zhou, X., Tan, Y.P., Shang, Y., Zhou, J.: Neighborhood repulsed metric learning for kinship verification. In: 2012 IEEE Conference on Computer Vision and Pattern Recognition (CVPR), pp. 2594–2601 (2012)

8. Lu, J., Hu, J., Liong, V.E., Zhou, X., Bottino, A., Ul Islam, I., Figueiredo Vieira, T., Qin, X., Tan, X., Chen, S.: The FG 2015 kinship verification in the wild evaluation. In: 2015 11th IEEE International Conference and Workshops on Automatic Face and Gesture Recognition (FG) (2015)

9. Lu, J., Zhou, X., Tan, Y.P., Shang, Y., Zhou, J.: Neighborhood repulsed metric learning for kinship verification. IEEE Trans. Pattern Anal. Mach. Intell. **36**(2), 331–345 (2014)

10. Mignon, A.: PCCA: a new approach for distance learning from sparse pairwise constraints. In: 2012 IEEE Conference on Computer Vision and Pattern Recognition, pp. 2666–2672 (2012)

11. Palm, R.B.: Prediction as a candidate for learning deep hierarchical models of data (2012)

12. Shuiwang, J., Ming, Y., Kai, Y.: 3D convolutional neural networks for human action recognition. IEEE Trans. Pattern Anal. Mach. Intell. **35**(1), 221–231 (2013)

13. Taigman, Y., Yang, M., Ranzato, M., Wolf, L.: Deepface: closing the gap to human-level performance in face verification. In: 2014 IEEE Conference on Computer Vision and Pattern Recognition (CVPR), pp. 1701–1708 (2014)

14. Xia, S., Shao, M., Luo, J., Fu, Y.: Understanding kin relationships in a photo. IEEE Trans. Multimed. **14**(4), 1046–1056 (2012)

15. Yan, H., Lu, J., Deng, W., Zhou, X.: Discriminative multimetric learning for kinship verification. IEEE Trans. Inf. Forensics Secur. **9**(7), 1169–1178 (2014)

16. Zhou, X., Lu, J., Hu, J., Shang, Y.: Gabor-based gradient orientation pyramid for kinship verification under uncontrolled environments. In: ACM International Conference on Multimedia, pp. 725–728 (2012)

Combination of Topological and Local Shape Features for Writer's Gender, Handedness and Age Classification

Nesrine Bouadjenek$^{(\boxtimes)}$, Hassiba Nemmour, and Youcef Chibani

Laboratoire d'Ingénierie des Systèmes Intelligents et Communicants (LISIC), Faculty of Electronics and Computer Sciences, University of Sciences and Technology Houari Boumediene (USTHB) Algiers, Algiers, Algeria
{nbouadjenek,hnemmour,ychibani}@usthb.dz

Abstract. In this work, writer's gender, handedness and age range prediction is addressed through automatic analysis of handwritten sentences. Three SVM-based predictors associated to different data features are developed. Then, a Fuzzy MIN-MAX combination rule is proposed to aggregate robust prediction from individual systems. Experiments are carried on two public Arabic and English datasets. Results in terms of prediction accuracy demonstrate the usefulness of the proposed algorithm, which provides a gain between 1 % and 10 % over both individual systems and classical combination rules. Moreover, it is much more relevant than various state of the art methods.

Keywords: Fuzzy MIN-MAX · Handwriting recognition · Soft-biometrics · SVM

1 Introduction

Handwriting recognition is widely used as a biometric tool for personal identification. Recently, some research works showed that it can be used for predicting soft-biometric traits such as the writer's gender, handedness, ethnicity and age range. This kind of information is useful in forensic identification of anonymous author writing as well as when attributing historical documents. Up to now, there are only few studies that addressed handwriting-based soft-biometrics prediction. The first work was developed in 2001 by Cha et al., [1], who proposed to classify US population into sub-categories related to the gender, the age range and ethnicity. Then, some works were developed using well-known classifiers such as SVM, GMM, Linear discriminant analysis and random forest [2–5]. Recall that SVM-based prediction constitutes one of the best systems. However, its performance depends on data features that are used. In previous works, several directional, textural, structural and gradient features were employed to generate pertinent features from handwritten text [6–9]. Results reported on various datasets, indicate that there is no method that can outperform all the others.

© Springer International Publishing Switzerland 2016
A. Campilho and F. Karray (Eds.): ICIAR 2016, LNCS 9730, pp. 549–557, 2016.
DOI: 10.1007/978-3-319-41501-7_61

For this reason, Liwicki, et al., [3] propose to combine classifiers trained on different features. The combination step was restricted to classical rules such as MAX, MIN and Average. To get a more effective combination, the present work proposes a new Fuzzy MIN-MAX algorithm for improving writer's gender, handedness and age range prediction. First, three SVM predictor trained on different features are developed. Considered features are pixel density, pixel distribution and the Histogram Of Template (HOT). Afterwards, SVM outputs are expressed as membership degrees that are combined through the Fuzzy MIN-MAX algorithm to aggregate a robust prediction. Experimental analysis is carried on public Arabic and English handwritten datasets.

The rest of this paper is arranged as: Sect. 2 describes proposed prediction systems. Section 3 presents the proposed Fuzzy MIN-MAX combination. Section 4 details experimental results while the last section reports the main conclusions of this work.

2   SVM-Based Soft-Biometrics System

Soft-biometrics prediction system is composed of two main steps that are feature generation and classification (Fig. 1). As SVM is currently one of the best classifiers, efforts are focused on the use of robust features. In an earlier work, a set of locally computed, orientation, texture and topological features were investigated [8–10]. Obtained results for gender, handedness and age range prediction showed that even though there are some features that outperform the others, there is no one that gives the best results for all soft-biometrics traits. Consequently, combining multiple SVM associated to different features is a fruitful way for improving the prediction accuracy. Presently, three SVM trained on pixel density, pixel distribution and HOT features are developed. Considered features are briefly described in what follows.

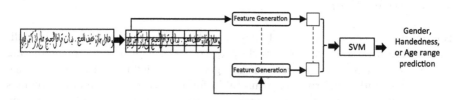

Fig. 1. Soft-biometrics prediction system.

2.1   Topological Features

Two grid-based features, namely, pixel density and pixel distribution are used to highlight topological properties of handwritten data. The density is obtained by considering the ratio between the number of pixels that belong to the text and the cell's size. As reported in [8,11], within a given cell, the distribution is based on four measures that are: Heights of the left and the right parts of the stroke and widths of the upper and lower parts of the stroke.

2.2 Histogram of Template

Histogram Of Template (HOT) was recently introduced for human detection [12] to stroke orientations within images. Presently, we investigate its applicability for describing local orientations in handwritten texts. As shown in Fig. 2, 20 templates are used to highlight positional relationships between three neighboring pixels. For each template if the three pixels satisfy a logical function, we say that the pixel P meets the template and then a histogram for pixels meeting the different templates is established. This constitutes the Histogram of Template "HOT" that is obtained according to two logical functions. Using the first function (Eq. 1), a pixel P meets a given template if it has higher gray level value than the two other pixels in the considered template. On the other hand, the second logical function utilizes gradient values (Eq. 2). For all templates, the sum of gradient magnitudes of the three pixels are computed. Then, the histogram of templates is established by assigning the pixel P to the template that has the largest sum.

$$I(P) > I(P1)\&I(P) > I(P2) \tag{1}$$

$$Template_k\{mag(P) + mag(P1) + mag(P2)\} == \\ max_i(Template_i\{mag(P) + mag(P1) + mag(P2)\}) \tag{2}$$

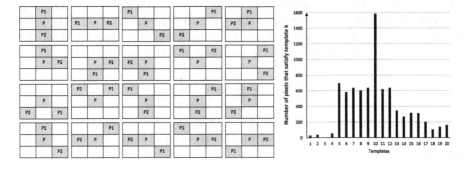

Fig. 2. Example of histogram with 20 orientation templates.

3 Fuzzy MIN-MAX Algorithm

In soft-biometrics prediction, combination efforts were limited to average, maximum and minimum rules. Results reported in [3] evince an improvement about 3 % in the overall accuracy. Nevertheless, various combination approaches combine these rules to develop more precise decisions. For instance, minimum and maximum rules are associated to classifier membership degrees to elaborate the well-known Sugeno's Fuzzy Integral [13]. On the other hand, Lu and Ito showed that combined MIN-MAX rules can achieve a robust modular classifier combination [14]. To take advantage from the flexibility and effectiveness of Fuzzy logic operators, we propose a Fuzzy MIN-MAX algorithm for combining soft-biometrics predictors. As shown in Fig. 3, this method combines membership

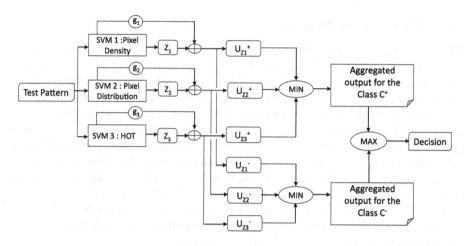

Fig. 3. Flowchart of the Fuzzy MIN-MAX combination.

degrees derived from SVM output according to pertinence information expressed through Fuzzy measures.

For each test sample, SVM outputs are transformed into membership degrees in the two classes of interest according to the steps of Algorithm 2. Then, SVM evidence in each class is obtained as the maximal agreement between the membership degree and the SVM reliability in this class. For each SVM Z_i, the reliability is expressed through Fuzzy measures $g(Z_i)$ as follows:

$$g(Z_i) = \alpha \frac{1 + exp(t_i)}{\sum_{i=1}^{N}[1 + exp(t_i)]} \tag{3}$$

t_i: The training accuracy of the SVM Z_i in the considered class.
α : User defined parameter that controls the relevance of Fuzzy measure, it scales in $]0.1,1]$.

Algorithme 1. Fuzzy class membership model

If $Z_i \geq 1$ then $\begin{cases} h_+(Z_i) = Z_i/MaxVal \\ h_-(Z_i) = 0 \end{cases}$

Else
{

If $Z_i \leq -1$ then $\begin{cases} h_+(Z_i) = 0 \\ h_-(Z_i) = Z_i/MaxVal \end{cases}$

Else

$\begin{cases} h_+(Z_i) = (1 + Z_i)/2 \\ h_-(Z_i) = (1 - Z_i)/2 \end{cases}$

}

Note that, $MaxVal$ corresponds to the maximal value of all SVM outputs. Then, the Fuzzy MIN-MAX combination described in Algorithm 2, is applied to aggregate a robust prediction.

Algorithme 2. Fuzzy MIN-MAX combination

For each test pattern do:

1. Calculate prediction decisions in the two classes as follows:
   - Generate predictor outputs Z_i, $i = 1, \ldots, N$ (N: number of predictors or SVM)
   - Transform each output into membership degrees in positive and negative classes $h^+(Z_i)$, $h^-(Z_i)$, according to Algorithm 1.
   - The decision in each class is such as:

$$U_{Z_i^+} = MAX(h^+(Z_i), G^+(Z_i))$$

$$U_{Z_i^-} = MAX(h^-(Z_i), G^-(Z_i))$$

2. Evaluate aggregated decisions in positive and negative classes as :

$$C^+ = MIN(U_{Z_i^+})_{i=1:N}$$
$$C^- = MIN(U_{Z_i^-})_{i=1:N}$$

3. Assign the test pattern to the class with the highest decision:

$$Decision = MAX(C^+, C^-)$$

---

4   Experimental Results

Proposed combination method is evaluated on corpuses extracted from two public datasets, collected in a multi-script unconstrained writing environment. These datasets, namely, IAM[1] and KHATT[2] contain handwritten sentences, in English and Arabic languages, respectively. Three corpuses were selected to perform soft-biometrics prediction. For IAM dataset, there are 165 samples for gender, 20 samples for handedness and 84 samples for age predictions, while for KHATT dataset, there are 90 samples for gender, 84 samples for handedness and 90 samples for age predictions. Also, considered age ranges are "25–34 years" / "35–56 years" for IAM dataset and "16 to 25 years" / "26 to 50 years" for KHATT dataset. As for most of classification and data mining tasks, 2/3 of samples were used for the training step while the remaining 1/3 were used for testing the system. Figure 4 shows samples from IAM and KHATT datasets.

In all experiments, features were locally calculated by applying a uniform grid on text images, then the optimal grid size was selected based on the best

---

[1] http://www.iam.unibe.ch/fki.
[2] http://khatt.ideas2serve.net.

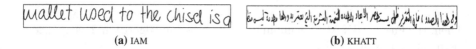

(a) IAM   (b) KHATT

Fig. 4. Samples extracted from IAM and KHATT datasets.

classification accuracy. Here for space considerations, we only present the best results that were subsequently employed in the combination step.

Tables 1 and 2 summarize the results of individual and combined systems, obtained for gender, handedness and age range prediction. Note that for gender prediction, there is no descriptor that outperforms the others whatever the dataset. Furthermore, the performance of the Fuzzy MIN-MAX algorithm is assessed comparatively to Max and Mean rules. As reported, the proposed algorithm outperforms the other rules. Compared to individual systems, the Fuzzy MIN-MAX provides an improvement that varies between 1 % and 2.75 %.

For handedness prediction, IAM scores are high because of the reduced number of data (20 samples for each class). For this reason, the performance reaches 90 % with all features. However with the Fuzzy MIN-MAX algorithm the performance is improved to 100 %. Regarding KHATT corpus, the best prediction accuracy that is 80.36 % is obtained using pixel distribution, As can be seen,

Table 1. Soft-biometrics prediction results for individual systems (%).

Soft-biometrics	Dataset	Pixel density	Pixel distribution	HOT
Gender	IAM	**73.63**	70.90	71.82
	KHATT	71.11	73.33	**75.56**
Handedness	IAM	90.00	90.00	90.00
	KHATT	76.78	**80.36**	75.00
Age	IAM	**73.21**	71.42	69.64
	KHATT	**76.67**	72.22	71.11

Table 2. Soft-biometrics prediction results for combined systems (%).

Soft-biometrics	Dataset	Max	Mean	Fuzzy MIN-MAX
Gender	IAM	72.73	71.82	**76.36**
	KHATT	63.33	68.89	**76.67**
Handedness	IAM	80.00	80.00	**100.00**
	KHATT	75.00	78.57	**91.07**
Age	IAM	65.24	64.23	**80.00**
	KHATT	70.00	75.56	**78.89**

Table 3. State of the art results.

Soft Biometrics	Reference	Dataset	Features	Classifier	Classifica-tion Rate (%)
Gender	[6]	QUWI	Direction+ curvature+ Turtuosity+ Chaine code	Kernel discriminant analysis	73.70
	[9]	IAM	Histogram of Oriented Gradients	SVM	75.45
		KHATT	′′	′′	68.89
	Proposed	IAM	Fuzzy MIN-MAX algorithm		76.36
		KHATT	′′		76.67
Handedness	[5]	QUWI	Direction+ curvature+ Turtuosity+ Chaine code	KNN	70.00
	[3]	IAM	Mean[GMM (Off-line+On-line)]		86.64
	[9]	IAM	Histogram of Oriented Gradients	SVM	100.00
	Proposed	IAM	Fuzzy MIN-MAX algorithm		100.00
		KHATT	′′		91.07
Age	[6]	QUWI	Direction+curvature +Turtuosity	Random Forest	62.40
	[9]	IAM	Histogram of Oriented Gradients	SVM	73.21
		KHATT	′′	′′	67.78
	Proposed	IAM	Fuzzy MIN-MAX algorithm		80.00
		KHATT	′′		78.89

the proposed algorithm also outperforms the other combination rules. It gives an improvement that reaches 10 % for both datasets.

Unlike all previous results, for the age prediction task, pixel density outperforms other features with a gain of 1.79 % with IAM and 4.45 % for the KHATT corpus. Furthermore, when combining these systems, the classification scores are improved once again using the Fuzzy MIN-MAX algorithm to 80.00 % for IAM and 78.89 % for KHATT corpus.

5   Discussion and Conclusion

This work is focused on automatic prediction of soft-biometric traits, namely, gender, handedness and age range, from handwritten sentences analysis. First, three SVM predictors associated to different data features are developed. Then, a Fuzzy MIN-MAX algorithm is proposed to aggregate a robust prediction. Experiments were performed on Arabic and English datasets. The Fuzzy MIN-MAX combination was evaluated comparatively to individual systems as well as to classical combination rules. In addition, some state of the art results are reported in Table 3. The main inferences can be summarized as follows:

- The inspection along all datasets, reveals that the three SVM predictors provide satisfactory performance but there is no descriptor that allows the best discriminative power. Thereby, SVM combination is necessary.
- Although results reported in Table 3 are obtained for different private datasets, the examination of feature generation and classification methods, highlights the superiority of the proposed approach, which gives a gain between 1 % and 10 % in the prediction accuracy. Indeed, the Fuzzy MIN-MAX combination rectifies misclassifications by exploiting at best complementary information between individual systems.

To improve again our results, we intend in a future work, to investigate new classification schemes such as Convolutional Neural Networks (CNN). Also, it would be interesting to develop a multiclass prediction of various soft-biometrics traits.

References

1. Cha, S.H., Srihari, S.N.: A priori algorithm for sub-category classification analysis of handwriting. In: IEEE (ed.), Document Analysis and Recognition, pp. 1022–1025, september 2001
2. Bandi, K.R., Srihari, S.N.: Writer demographic classification using bagging and boosting. In: Proceedings of International Graphonomics Society Conference, pp. 133–137 (2005)
3. Liwicki, M., Schlapbach, A., Loretan, P., Bunke, H.: Automatic detection of gender and handedness from on-line handwriting. In: Conference of the International Graphonomics Society, pp. 179–183 (2007)
4. Liwicki, M., Schlapbach, A., Bunke, H.: Automatic gender detection using on-line and off-line information. Pattern Anal. Appl. **14**, 87–92 (2011)
5. Al-Maadeed, S., Ferjani, F., Elloumi, S., Hassaine, A.: Automatic handedness detection from off-line handwriting. In: 2013 7th IEEE GCC Conference and Exhibition (GCC), pp. 119–124, November 2013
6. Al-Maadeed, S., Hassaine, A.: Automatic prediction of age, gender, and nationality in offline handwriting. EURASIP J. Image Vid. Process **2014**(1), 1–10 (2014). http://jivp.eurasipjournals.springeropen.com/articles/10.1186/1687-5281-2014-10
7. Siddiqi, I., Djeddi, C., Raza, A., Souici-meslati, L.: Automatic analysis of handwriting for gender classification. Pattern Anal. Appl. **18**(4), 887–899 (2015)

8. Bouadjenek, N., Nemmour, H., Chibani, Y.: Local descriptors to improve off-line handwriting-based gender prediction. In: 2014 6th International Conference of Soft Computing and Pattern Recognition (SoCPaR), pp. 43–47, August 2014

9. Bouadjenek, N., Nemmour, H., Chibani, Y.: Histogram of oriented gradients for writer's gender, handedness and age prediction. In: 2015 International Symposium on Innovations in Intelligent SysTems and Applications (INISTA), pp. 220–224, September 2015

10. Bouadjenek, N., Nemmour, H., Chibani, Y.: Age, gender and handedness prediction from handwriting using gradient features. In: 2015 13th International Conference on Document Analysis and Recognition (ICDAR), pp. 1116–1120, August 2015

11. Bertolini, D., Oliveira, L.S., Justino, E., Sabourin, R.: Reducing forgeries in writer-independent off-line signature verification through ensemble of classifiers. Pattern Recogn. **43**(1), 387–396 (2010)

12. Shaopeng Tang, S., Goto: histogram of template for human detection. In: 2010 IEEE International Conference on Acoustics Speech and Signal Processing (ICASSP), pp. 2186–2189, March 2010

13. Cho, S.-B., Kim, J.H.: Combining multiple neural networks by fuzzy integral for robust classification. IEEE Trans. Syst. Man Cybern. **25**(2), 380–384 (1995)

14. Bao-Liang, L., Ito, M.: Task decomposition and module combination based on class relations: a modular neural network for pattern classification. IEEE Trans. Neural Netw. **10**(5), 1244–1256 (1999)

Hybrid Off-Line Handwritten Signature Verification Based on Artificial Immune Systems and Support Vector Machines

Yasmine Serdouk$^{(\boxtimes)}$, Hassiba Nemmour, and Youcef Chibani

Laboratoire D'Ingénierie des Systèmes Intelligents Et Communicants (LISIC),
University of Sciences and Technology Houari Boumediene (USTHB),
Bab Ezzouar El-Alia BP. 32, 16111 Algiers, Algeria
{yserdouk,hnemmour,ychibani}@usthb.dz

Abstract. This paper proposes a new handwritten signature verification method based on a combination of an artificial immune algorithm with SVM. In a first step, the Artificial Immune Recognition System (AIRS) is trained to develop a set of representative data (memory cells) of both genuine and forged signature classes. Usually, to classify a questioned signature, dissimilarities are calculated with respect to all memory cells and handled according to the k Nearest Neighbor rule. Presently, we propose the training of these dissimilarities by a Support Vector Machine (SVM) classifier to get a more discriminating decision. Histogram of oriented gradients is used for feature generation. Experiments conducted on two standard datasets reveal that the proposed system provides a significant accuracy improvement compared to the conventional AIRS.

Keywords: Artificial immune recognition system · Handwritten signature verification · HOG · SVM

1 Introduction

The authentication of individuals based on their handwritten signatures is required in various life domains like official contracts, banking or financial transactions. Thereby, Signature Verification Systems (SVS) are developed to allow an automatic and robust identity verification. Roughly, there are two approaches for developing an SVS. The first is based on on-line dynamic signatures while the second approach is dedicated for off-line signatures that are previously affixed on paper documents. Also, the verification process can be addressed either as writer-dependent or writer-independent [1]. In the case of writer-dependent, a specific verification system is developed for each person to authenticate its genuine signatures. Furthermore, the writer-independent verification develops one generic system for all persons, which aims to detect genuine signatures without giving information about the writer identity.

During the past years, various signature verification systems were developed based on Dynamic Time Warping, neural networks, Hidden Markov Models and

© Springer International Publishing Switzerland 2016
A. Campilho and F. Karray (Eds.): ICIAR 2016, LNCS 9730, pp. 558–565, 2016.
DOI: 10.1007/978-3-319-41501-7_62

SVM [2]. Currently, SVM is the most commonly used classifier since it can significantly outperform the others [3]. However, verification scores reported in literature still require improvement, which lets the development of efficient verification methods an ongoing research topic. Recently, inspired from the human immune system, the Artificial Immune Recognition System (AIRS) introduced by Watkins [4] provided interesting performance in various pattern recognition tasks, such as thyroid diagnosis [5] and fault detection [6]. In earlier works, we have successfully employed the AIRS for writer-dependent off-line signature verification [7–10]. Basically, AIRS imitates some functions of the natural immune system. It adopts a supervised learning process to create new data, called memory cells that represent all classes. Then, k Nearest Neighbor (kNN) is used to classify test data. Experiments showed that AIRS suffers from two major drawbacks. First, since a specific AIRS is trained for each writer, user-defined parameters need a careful experimental tuning. Thereby, extensive tests are performed to reach the best selection. Second, the kNN success depends on the pertinence of memory cells produced by the AIRS training.

To overcome the AIRS shortcomings, this work proposes a hybrid verification system that combines AIRS with SVM. More precisely, AIRS is trained to develop a set of memory cells that describe both genuine and forged signatures for a given writer. Then, a new training set is created by substituting original signature features by their dissimilarities with respect to all memory cells. Finally, SVM is used to automatically separate between genuine and forged dissimilarities. For feature generation, a Histogram of Oriented Gradients (HOG) that is calculated by applying a uniform grid over signature images is employed. The rest of this paper is organized as follows: Sect. 2 presents the proposed hybrid verification system. Experiments are presented and discussed in Sect. 3. Finally, the main conclusions are given in the last section.

2   Proposed Hybrid Signature Verification System

The proposed system is devoted for solving the writer-dependent off-line handwritten signature verification. The aim is to automatically separate genuine signatures from skilled forgeries. For a clearer explanation of the hybrid verification system, we briefly review the AIRS theory. Then, the steps required for performing the hybrid verification are introduced. In addition, to make the paper self-contained, HOG features are presented.

2.1   Artificial Immune Recognition System

The Artificial Immune Recognition System (AIRS) is a supervised learning algorithm inspired by the natural immune system [4]. It employs immune mechanisms as antibodies (B-Cells) to recognize dangerous invaders, known as antigens. Each training or test sample is named antigen while the system units are called B-Cells. Similar B-Cells are represented by Artificial Recognition Balls (ARBs) that compete with each other for a fixed resources number. The AIRS algorithm is summarized through the following steps [4].

(a) Initialization. In this step data are normalized, such that Euclidian distance scales in the range [0–1]. Then, an Affinity Threshold (AT) is computed from the whole training data according to the following equation:

$$AT = \frac{\sum_{i=1}^{n-1} \sum_{j=i+1}^{n} affinity(ag_i, ag_j)}{n(n-1)/2}. \tag{1}$$

ag_i represents the feature vector of the ith antigen (training sample). *Affinity* is the Euclidian distance while n is the total number of training samples.

AT is used in the condition of a memory cell replacement. The initialization step is achieved by seeding of initial Memory Cells (MC) pool and initial ARBs pool. In other words, for each class of interest (two classes in our case), at least one training sample is randomly selected to be used as prototype of its class in the MC and ARB pools.

(b) Training Process. The training of each antigen (training sample) is a one-shot process that is described in what follows:

- **MC-Match identification:** the ARB having the highest stimulation to the antigen, called MC-Match, is selected. The stimulation ST is defined as:

$$ST(ag_i, MC) = 1 - affinity(ag_i, MC). \tag{2}$$

- **ARBs generation and resources competition:** generate a set of randomly mutated clones (ARBs) from MC-Match. Then, a competition between these clones is carried according to their stimulation levels.
- **MC-Candidate selection:** the ARB with the highest stimulation is selected. This clone is called Memory Cell candidate (MC-Candidate).
- **MC pool update:** MC-Candidate will replace or will be added to the population of memory cells based on a comparison with MC-match.

(c) Classification. Evolved MC pool is used by a kNN classification to assign unknown data into the right class.

More details about the AIRS training are given in [5]. Note that in the classical AIRS, several set-up parameters need to be experimentally tuned for each writer (see Table 1). Moreover, the decision effectiveness depends on the kNN performance. In order to get a more robust signature verification while using the same parameters for all writers, we propose a hybrid verification system, in which the kNN classification is substituted by a support vector decision.

Table 1. AIRS parameters description.

Parameter	Definition
Mutation rate	Mutation probability of an ARB
Clonal rate	Controls the number of generated mutated clones
Affinity threshold scalar	Used in the MC-Candidate and MC-Match comparison
Stimulation threshold	Stopping threshold
Resources number	Limits the number of mutated clones in the ARBs pool

2.2 Proposed Verification System

The proposed hybrid signature verification is performed according to the following steps (see Fig. 1).

- Train AIRS according to steps reported in Subsect. 2.1.
- Develop new training and testing sets by substituting signature features by their dissimilarities with respect to all memory cells in the MC Pool.
- Train SVM on the new training dissimilarity set to separate genuine dissimilarities from forged dissimilarities.
- Incorporate the dissimilarity vector of each questioned signature into the support vector decision to decide if it is a genuine or a forged signature.

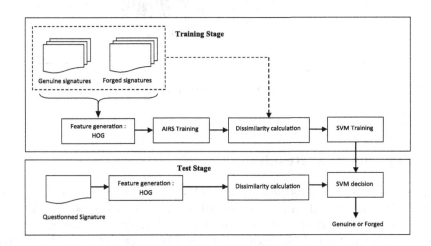

Fig. 1. Proposed hybrid signature verification system.

2.3 Histogram of Oriented Gradients (HOG)

HOG is computed on a dense grid applied over images as shown in Fig. 2. Each cell will have its own histogram calculated according to the following steps [11].

– For each pixel $P(x, y)$, calculate horizontal and vertical gradients as:

$$g_x(x, y) = P(x + 1, y) - P(x - 1, y) . \tag{3}$$

$$g_y(x, y) = P(x, y + 1) - P(x, y - 1) . \tag{4}$$

– Then, gradient magnitude and phase are obtained as follows:

$$M(x, y) = \sqrt{g_x(x, y)^2 + g_y(x, y)^2} . \tag{5}$$

$$\varphi(x, y) = arctan\left(\frac{g_x(x, y)}{g_y(x, y)}\right) . \tag{6}$$

– Construct the cell histogram of gradients by accumulating magnitudes with orientations. Accumulation is done with respect to the Freeman code.

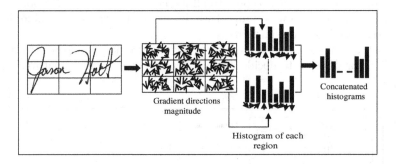

Fig. 2. HOG computation flowchart.

3   Experimental Results

The proposed signature verification system is evaluated using two publicly available off-line signature datasets, namely, MCYT-75 and GPDS-300. The MCYT-75 corpus[1] contains 75 signers from four different Spanish sites. For each signer, there are 15 genuine and 15 forged signatures. The GPDS-300 corpus[2], collected by the Grupo de Procesado Digital de Senales, contains 300 writers represented by 24 genuine and 30 forged signatures. Performance evaluation is carried using three error types that are the False Rejection Rate (FRR), the False Acceptance Rate (FAR) and the Average Error Rate (AER).

---

[1] MCYT dataset is available on: http://atvs.ii.uam.es/mcyt75so.html/.
[2] GPDS dataset is available on: http://www.gpds.ulpgc.es/download/.

Experiments were repeated 5 times by changing the training and test sets. Consequently, the average results are presented in this paper. Moreover, according to the protocol reported in [12], the training stage utilizes 10 genuine and 10 forged signatures that are randomly selected from datasets while the remaining signatures are used in the test stage. Presently, AIRS is implemented using the same set-up parameters for all writers. Nevertheless, since the kNN performance is strongly dependent on the number of neighbors, we tried to select the k value allowing the best AER on training data. As shown in Fig. 3 for both datasets, the best accuracy is obtained when considering one neighbor with an AER about 36%. From this outcome, we infer that kNN classification cannot deal with the variability information offered by the evolved memory cells. Consequently, to improve the AIRS classifier, the proposed system performs a second training round that takes advantage from both training set and memory cells to achieve a more robust verification. Table 2 reports error rates using AIRS and the proposed hybrid system.

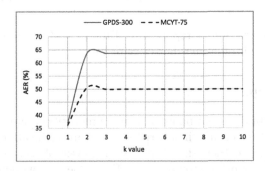

Fig. 3. AER variations according to the k values for AIRS-based verification.

Table 2. Signature verification results obtained for AIRS and the proposed system.

Dataset	Methodology	FAR (%)	FRR(%)	AER (%)
MCYT-75	AIRS	46.13	26.29	36.21
	Proposed system	**20.26**	**21.43**	**20.85**
GPDS-300	AIRS	49.43	15.54	37.12
	Proposed system	**08.41**	**28.10**	**15.58**

As expected, performance of the proposed system exceeds that of classical AIRS. Indeed, for the two datasets and unlike the conventional AIRS, the proposed system provides lower FAR than FRR, which reflects its ability to favor the reduction of false acceptance errors. In addition, compared to the classical AIRS, our proposed system allows a significant improvement in AER values with a gain about 15% for MCYT-75 and 21% for GPDS-300. So, the gap between the two systems grows with the number of writers. Furthermore, compared to

Table 3. MCYT-75 state-of-the-art.

References	Classifier	#Genuine signatures	AER (%)
[13]	Variability measure	10	22.13
[14]	Degree of authenticity	9	21.61
	Proposed system	**10**	**20.85**

Table 4. GPDS-300 state-of-the-art.

References	Classifier	#Genuine signatures	AER (%)
[12]	SVM	10	23.03
[12]	SVM	10	21.52
[12]	SVM	10	15.35
[15]	MLP	24	13.76
	Proposed system	**10**	**15.58**

some state-of-the-art results reported in Tables 3 and 4, the proposed system provides similar and sometimes better error rates.

4 Conclusion

In this paper, hybrid system based on combining artificial immune system with SVM is proposed for off-line handwritten signature verification. This proposed system aims to strengthen the classification power of conventional AIRS by incorporating a support vector decision. Experiments conducted on two public datasets, showed the effectiveness of the proposed algorithm, even if it uses the same selection of AIRS parameters. Precisely, it outperforms the classical AIRS with a gain of 15.36 % for MCYT-75 and with 21.54 % for GPDS-300, in the AER results. Moreover, the comparison with the state-of-the-art confirms the efficiency of the proposed system. To complete the present work, we plan to associate the proposed system with more effective data features in order to further improve the verification scores.

References

1. Bertolini, D., Oliveira, L.S., Justino, E., Sabourin, R.: Reducing forgeries in writer-independent off-line signature verification through ensemble of classifiers. J. Pattern Recogn. **43**, 387–396 (2010)
2. Impedovo, D., Modugno, R., Pirlo, G., Stasolla, E.: Handwritten signature verification by multiple reference sets. In: 11th International Conference on Frontiers in Handwriting Recognition, pp. 19–21. Montréal, Canada (2008)
3. Justino, E.J.R., Bortolozzi, F., Sabourin, R.: A comparison of SVM and HMM classifiers in off-line signature verification. J. Pattern Recogn. Lett. **26**, 1377–1385 (2005)

4. Watkins, A.B.: AIRS: A resource limited artificial immune classifier. Master's Thesis at the Mississippi State University, USA (2001)
5. Kodaz, H., Ozsen, S., Arslan, A., Günes, S.: Medical application of information gain based artificial immune recognition system (AIRS): diagnosis of thyroid disease. J. Expert Syst. Appl. **36**, 3086–3092 (2009)
6. Laurentys, C.A., Palhares, R.M., Caminhas, W.M.: A novel artificial immune system for fault behavior detection. J. Expert Syst. Appl. **38**, 6957–6966 (2011)
7. Nemmour, H., Chibani, Y.: Off-line signature verification using artificial immune recognition system. In: 10th International Conference on Electronics Computer and Computation, pp. 164–167. Ankara (2013)
8. Serdouk, Y., Nemmour, H., Chibani, Y.: Topological and textural features for off-line signature verification based on artificial immune algorithm. In: 6th International Conference on Soft Computing and Pattern Recognition, Tunis, pp. 118–122 (2014)
9. Serdouk, Y., Nemmour, H., Chibani, Y.: New off-line handwritten signature verification method based on artificial immune recognition system. J. Expert Syst. Appl. **51**, 186–194 (2016)
10. Serdouk, Y., Nemmour, H., Chibani, Y.: An improved artificial immune recognition system for off-line handwritten signature verification. In: 13th International Conference on Document Analysis and Recognition, Tunis, pp. 196–200 (2015)
11. Dalal, N., Triggs, B.: Histograms of orientated gradients for human detection. In: IEEE Computer Society Conference on Computer Vision and Pattern Recognition, San Diego, CA, USA, pp. 886–893 (2005)
12. Ferrer, M.A., Vargas, J.F., Morales, A., Ordonez, A.: Robustness of off-line signature verification based on gray level features. IEEE Trans. Inf. Forensics Secur. **7**, 966–977 (2012)
13. Alonso-Fernandez, F., Fairhurst, M.C., Fierrez, J., Ortega-Garcia, J.: Automatic measures for predicting performance in off-line signature. In: IEEE International Conference on Image Processing, San Antonio, TX, pp. 369–372 (2007)
14. Prakash, H.N., Guru, D.S.: Geometric centroids and their relative distances for off-line signature verification. In: 10th International Conference on Document Analysis and Recognition, Barcelona, pp. 121–125 (2009)
15. Kumar, R., Sharma, J.D., Chanda, B.: Writer-independent off-line signature verification using surroundedness feature. J. Pattern Recogn. Lett. **33**, 301–308 (2012)

Selection of User-Dependent Cohorts Using Bezier Curve for Person Identification

Jogendra Garain$^{(\boxtimes)}$, Ravi Kant Kumar$^{(\boxtimes)}$,
Dakshina Ranjan Kisku$^{(\boxtimes)}$, and Goutam Sanyal$^{(\boxtimes)}$

Department of Computer Science and Engineering, National Institute
of Technology Durgapur, Durgapur 713209, West Bengal, India
jogs.cse@gmail.com, vit.ravikant@gmail.com,
drkisku@gmail.com, nitgsanyal@gmail.com

Abstract. The traditional biometric systems can be strengthened further with exploiting the concept of cohort selection to achieve the high demands of the organizations for a robust automated person identification system. To accomplish this task the researchers are being motivated towards developing robust biometric systems using cohort selection. This paper proposes a novel user-dependent cohort selection method using Bezier curve. It makes use of invariant SIFT descriptor to generate matching pair points between a pair of face images. Further for each subject, considering all the imposter scores as control points, a Bezier curve of degree n is plotted by applying De Casteljau algorithm. As long as the imposter scores represent the control points in the curve, a cohort subset is formed by considering the points determined to be far from the Bezier curve. In order to obtain the normalized cohort scores, T-norm cohort normalization technique is applied. The normalized scores are then used in recognition. The experiment is conducted on FEI face database. This novel cohort selection method achieves superior performance that validates its efficiency.

Keywords: Bezier curve · SIFT descriptor · Imposter scores · Control point · Biometric system · Cohort subset · Normalization technique

1 Introduction

Due to variations in facial expressions, pose, illuminations, environments and sensing devices used to capture the face images, the performance of a face recognition system can vary a lot. Therefore, to minimize the effects of these factors could decrease the overall non-matching errors and achieve high throughput. Since the applications of this domain are used in very high security areas, therefore the performance cannot be compromised with the design of biometric systems. In order to fulfill the demands of cent percent accuracy, many researchers are utilizing cohort selection concept to develop the robust biometric systems. A cohort set generally contains scores which are basically imposter scores obtained as matching score by comparing a query template with the false (non-matched) template. Amin Merati et al. in [1] have exploited cohort selection technique which can be added as positive accelerator to the traditional biometric system to perform better with 50 % reduction in computational cost. The authors

© Springer International Publishing Switzerland 2016
A. Campilho and F. Karray (Eds.): ICIAR 2016, LNCS 9730, pp. 566–572, 2016.
DOI: 10.1007/978-3-319-41501-7_63

in [2] have also stated that the cohorts having high and low matching scores hold distinct features to classify the subjects effectively. To extend the works done in [1, 2] and achieve robustness, it needs to determine the points which are located far from the curve and they are considered as the members of the cohort subset. In the prior work [3], the authors of this paper have used Max-Min-Centroid-Cluster method for cohort selection which trims down the computational cost to $2/5^{th}$ of the total cost if the whole set of faces are used as cohort set. The biometric systems not using cohort, work faster but Tistarelli et al. [5] and Aggarwal et al. [6] stated that the performance can be increased by applying cohort selection. Auckenthaler et al. [7] have explained cohort and score normalization based on Bayes' theorem which has been applied to enrich the performance of a speaker verification system and Tulyakov et al. [8] added that combination of two score normalization techniques can further improve the accuracy of a biometric system.

In the proposed work, SIFT matching [4] is applied to get the matching points between two faces. Moreover, the matching scores can be used to decide the cohort scores to be included in the cohort set. The proposed algorithm is tested on FEI face database [10] and achieves high recognition accuracy.

The paper is organized as follows. Section 2 discusses cohort selection method. Experimental results are given in Sect. 3 and concluding remarks are made in the last section.

2 Cohort Selection

Let, there be n number of subjects $\{S_i,\ i = 1,\ 2,...,\ n\}$ which are enrolled in the system's database and each subject has only one face sample. So for each query template there will be a genuine score (g) and $n-1$ imposter scores or cohort scores (δ). Considering these cohort scores as control points, plot a Bezier curve (B) of degree $n-2$ using De Casteljau algorithm [9]. The mathematical representation of a Bezier curve of degree n, controlled by $n + 1$ number of cohort scores (δ), is shown in Eq. (1).

$$B(t) = \sum_{i=0}^{n} b_i^n(t) \cdot \delta_{i+1},\ \ 0 \le t \le 1 \tag{1}$$

where $b_i^n = \binom{n}{i}.t^i.(1 - t)^{n-i}$ is the Bernstein basis polynomial of degree n.

The curve will pass through the dense area where the control points have a value closer to the mean of all the values, shown in Fig. 2. Therefore the points are as much far from the curve as discriminative from the others. So these points are selected as cohort in the subset which helps to normalize the matching score between query template and claimed template at the time of authentication. Though the points with zero values may be far are not considered due to not having any effect on the normalized score. However Bezier curve always passes through the starting and ending control points. So the distances from these two points to the curve are always zero. For this constraint our proposed algorithm selects the starting control point if the score value is greater than zero. The algorithm written below and the flow chart given in Fig. 1, depict the proposed work and exhibit how cohort scores can be selected.

Algorithm 1. Bezier-Cohorts

Input: Set of cohort scores $S = \{\delta_1, \delta_2, ..., \delta_{n-1}\}, n \rightarrow$ no of enrolled template, $\delta_i \rightarrow$ cohort score of ith Subject.

Output: Cohort Subset $\{C_S\}$

1. Plot a Bezier curve using De Casteljau algorithm considering all δ_i as control points.

2. Find the Euclidean distances (d_i) of each control point δ_i from the curve.

3. Calculate the mean (μ) of all distances $(d_i), i = 1, 2, ..., n-1$.

4. If $\delta_1 > 0, C_S = \{\delta_1\}$ *otherwise* $C_S = \{\phi\}, \phi \rightarrow NULL$

5. $C_S = \{C_S \cup \delta_i\}$ where $d_i > \mu, i = 2, 3, ..., n-1$.

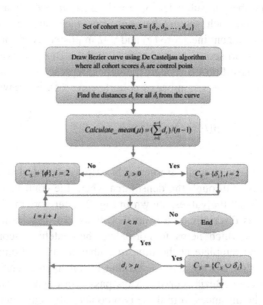

Fig. 1. Flow chart of the proposed method.

Figure 2 gives a view of how the points are selected for a subject in the cohort set. In the figure it is clearly visible that 23 cohort have been selected for Subject 1. Figure 3 plots the number of cohorts for each and every enrolled face. After getting the cohort subset the scores are normalized using T-norm as shown in Eq. (2).

$$S_{T-norm}(Normalized\_Score) = \frac{g - \mu}{\sigma}. \tag{2}$$

where g = genuine score, μ = mean and σ = Standard deviation.

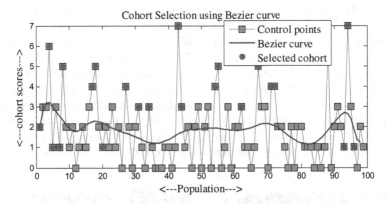

Fig. 2. Cohort selection for a subject using Bezier curve

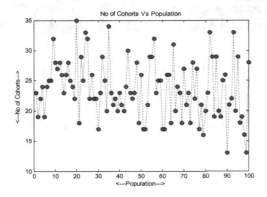

Fig. 3. Number of cohorts per enrolled subject.

3   Experimental Setup and Results

The FEI face database [10] comprises of Brazilian face images captured between June 2005 and March 2006 at the Artificial Intelligence Laboratory of FEI in São Bernardo do Campo, São Paulo, Brazil. This database contains a total of 2800 images where each of 200 individuals have 14 different face profiles which have a rotation variation up to 180 degrees. All are colour images with white and uniform background. Each image is 640 × 480 pixels in size but scale might differ up to 10 %. Additionally a subset of 400 face images of 200 individuals captured in controlled environment is provided. Here each individual has one neutral and one smiling face image cropped to 360 × 260 pixels in size. Among these 100 neutral and 100 smiling faces of first 100 individuals are used as enrolled and training datasets respectively in our experiment. For testing, we have taken 100 low quality (captured at poor lighting condition) faces, the 14th instance from the FEI database, of the same 100 individuals and cropped to the same size 360 × 260 pixels. Few sample face images with three instances are shown in Fig. 4(a). The selection of face image of one subject and corresponding non-matched cohort faces selected using our proposed algorithm is shown in Fig. 4(b). The performance of this novel cohort selection method is reached up to 98.55 % accuracy for verification and 96.5 % for identification. Both verification and identification accuracies are determined on the dataset prepared for evaluation which is satisfactory and can lead to implement a future model. The ROC curve is shown in Fig. 5(a) which represents the trade-off between False Rejection Rate (FAR) and False Acceptance Rate (FRR) and this curve is determined when cohort selection is not applied. On the other hand, when cohort selection is applied, a ROC curve is determined to represent the performance of the proposed algorithm in terms of FRR and FAR shown in Fig. 5(b).

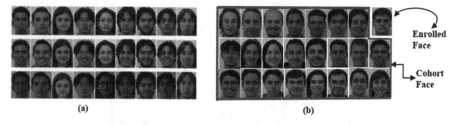

Fig. 4. (a) Sample faces from FEI database are shown. (b) Enrolled face and the corresponding cohort faces are shown.

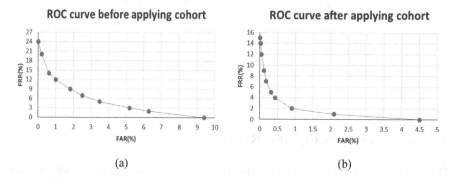

Fig. 5. (a) Receiver operating characteristics (ROC) curve before applying cohort selection (b) Receiver operating characteristics (ROC) curve after applying cohort selection

Table 1. Performance chart.

Cohort selection	FAR (%)	FRR (%)	EER (%)	GAR (%)	Accuracy (%)
Before applying	5.2	3	4.1	97	95.9
After applying	0.9	2	1.45	98	98.55

The effects of cohort selection in terms of FAR, FRR, EER, GAR and overall accuracy have been given in Table 1.

4 Conclusion

In the existing literatures, cohorts are being selected from enrolled identity, however in the proposed work, cohort subsets are constructed from training set. The number of cohorts in the selected subset is not considered as a constant number. Thus it varies from 13 to 35. It is the evidence of cutting the computational cost along with performance enhancement. If the stored database is not too heavy then all templates can be used as cohort. However for a large database cohort subset selection is necessary to avoid additional computations. All faces chosen for experiment are frontal faces so this work can be enhanced by taking faces of different pose and expression to make the system more robust. Other biometric traits can also be used to this methodology.

References

1. Merati, A., Poh, N., Kittler, J.: User-specific cohort selection and score normalization for biometric systems. IEEE Trans. Inf. Forensics Secur. **7**(4), 1270–1277 (2012)
2. Merati, A., Poh, N., Kittler, J.: Extracting discriminative information from cohort models. In: Proceedings of 4th IEEE International Conference on Biometrics: Theory Applications and Systems (BTAS), pp. 1–6 (2010)
3. Garain, J., Kumar, R.K., Sanyal, G., Kisku, D.R.: Cohort selection of specific user using max-min-centroid-cluster (mmcc) method to enhance the performance of a biometric system. Int. J. Secur. Appl. **9**(6), 263–270 (2015)
4. Lowe, D.G.: Distinctive image features from scale-invariant key points. Int. J. Comput. Vis. **60**(2), 91–110 (2004)
5. Tistarelli, M., Sun, Y., Poh, N.: On the use of discriminative cohort score normalization for unconstrained face recognition. IEEE Trans. Inf. Forensics Secur. **9**(12), 2063–2075 (2014)
6. Aggarwal, G., Ratha, N.K., Bolle, R.M.: Biometric verification: looking beyond raw similarity scores. In: Proceedings of Computer Vision and Pattern Recognition Workshop, p. 31 (2006)
7. Auckenthaler, R., Carey, M., Thomas, H.L.: Score normalization for text-independent speaker verification systems. Digit. Signal Proc. **10**, 42–54 (2000)
8. Tulyakov, S., Zhang, Z., Govindaraju, V.: Comparison of combination methods utilizing T-normalization and second best score model. In: Proceedings of the IEEE Conference on Computer Vision and Pattern Recognition Workshop, pp. 1–5 (2008)

9. De Faget, P., De Casteljau, D.F.D.: Outillage methodes calcul. Enveloppe Soleau 40.040, Institute National de la Propriete Industrielle, Paris (1959)
10. Thomaz, C.E., Giraldi, G.A.: A new ranking method for principal components analysis and its application to face image analysis. Image Vis. Comput. **28**(6), 902–913 (2010)

Biomedical Imaging

Bag of Visual Words Approach for Bleeding Detection in Wireless Capsule Endoscopy Images

Indu Joshi[1], Sunil Kumar[2(✉)], and Isabel N. Figueiredo[3]

[1] Department of Computer Science and Engineering,
National Institute of Technology, Delhi, India
[2] Department of Applied Sciences, National Institute of Technology, Delhi, India
skumar.iitd@gmail.com
[3] CMUC, Department of Mathematics, University of Coimbra, Coimbra, Portugal

Abstract. Wireless Capsule Endoscopy(WCE) is a revolutionary technique for visualizing patient's entire digestive tract. But, the analysis of a huge number of images produced during an examination of a patient is hindering the application of WCE. In this direction, we automated the process of bleeding detection in WCE images based on improved Bag of Visual Words (BoVW). Two feature integration schemes have been explored. Experimental results show that the best classification performance is obtained using integration of SIFT and uniform LBP features. The highest classification accuracy achieved is **95.06 %** for a visual vocabulary of length 100. Results reveal that the proposed methodology is discriminating enough to classify bleeding images.

Keywords: Wireless capsule endoscopy · Bag-of-Visual-Words · SIFT · Local binary pattern · Computer-aided diagnosis

1 Introduction

Traditional endoscopy is used to examine various gastrointestinal (GI) related diseases. But it is a very painful technique, also it cannot be used to view the small intestine completely. WCE is an alternate to traditional endoscopy. It is a new-age medical technology which eliminates a patient's pain and enables to view the entire small intestine. US Food and Drug Administration (FDA) approved WCE in 2001. In WCE, a capsule whose size is that of a multivitamin tablet is swallowed by a patient. The capsule then moves towards the GI tract of patient and captures an eight hour long video with a speed of 2 frames per second. It generates approximately 56000 images in this process. These images are transmitted wirelessly to a recording device attached to the waist of patient. After the whole examination these images are then downloaded to a computer and analysed by the medical doctors.

This technique looks very promising in detecting various diseases of GI tract like bleeding, ulcer, polyps, tumors etc. But, it has a major issue that it requires a lot of time of medical doctors to analyse those huge number of images, also it might be the case that some abnormal images may be overlooked by the

© Springer International Publishing Switzerland 2016
A. Campilho and F. Karray (Eds.): ICIAR 2016, LNCS 9730, pp. 575–582, 2016.
DOI: 10.1007/978-3-319-41501-7_64

medical doctors due to oversight. Also, some abnormalities cannot be seen by the naked eyes because of their size and distribution. This motivates us to automate the process of reliably analysing the abnormalities in the GI tract to assist the doctors in decision making.

In this work, we are particularly interested in detecting bleeding (See Fig. 1) in WCE images. Some attempts have already been made in literature to automate the process of bleeding detection in WCE images. Without being exhaustive we mention some of the state of art works here. Li and Meng [1] have exploited colour features of WCE images. They have used chromaticity moments which are calculated in HSI colour space using discrete Tchebichef polynomials as basis function. Lv *et al.* [2] have used spatial pyramids over illumination invariant colour histograms. Figueiredo *et al.* [3] have utilized the second component of CIE lab colour space along with image segmentation and enhancement techniques to segregate the potential bleeding region, and have proposed their own bleeding detectors using eigenvalue of Hessian and Laplacian of enhanced image. Cui *et al.* [4] have proposed six colour features in HSI colour space to classify bleeding and normal WCE images. Pan *et al.* [5] have extracted colour texture features in RGB and HSI colour space and have used probabilistic neural network classifier to classify bleeding images.

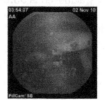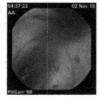

Fig. 1. Examples of bleeding frames.

BoVW is a very popular approach for image classification inspired by models used in natural language processing. It has been successfully used in various image processing techniques targeted for medical applications [6–9]. An improved BoVW approach has been proposed in [9] for polyp detection in WCE images. To the best of our knowledge, in literature, BoVW has not been utilized for bleeding detection in WCE images. In this work, images are represented as histogram of features. We have explored two different strategies for bag of words representation of features. K-means clustering is sensitive to the initial center choices and sometimes can lead to bad clusters, so to reduce the chances of poor clustering we have used K-means++ algorithm [10] to quantize the training features. Also, unlike traditional bag of words approach where complete image is divided into non-overlapping blocks, we have taken only those square patches which lie in the neighbourhood of key points detected using Scale Invariant Feature Transform (SIFT). Experimental results show that the proposed method is very promising in bleeding detection in WCE images.

The rest of the paper consists of Sect. 2, where the proposed methodology is described; Sect. 3, where the experimental results are reported; Sect. 4, where conclusions and future research directions are discussed.

2 Methodology

In this section, we describe the proposed method for the classification of WCE images with bleeding using BoVW approach. BoVW framework gives an efficient representation of features. Therefore, for this reason we have used bag of words paradigm for representing image features.

2.1 Bag of Visual Words

Bag of Visual Words is a technique through which an image is represented as a collection of local features. In this technique, local features are extracted from all the images of the training set. Clustering over these features is used to generate the visual vocabulary. The resulting cluster centres serve as the visual words. For every testing image, features are extracted and assigned to the nearest visual word. The normalised histogram of these quantized features serves as the feature vector of the image. The dimensionality of the histogram is same as the size of the visual dictionary.

2.2 Feature Extraction and BoVW Representation

Each WCE image is represented by features around key points, since key points contain a lot of local information and thus features around neighbourhood of these points can represent the image well. SIFT is being used as key point detector and a patch of 8×8 is extracted around the key point.

Approach I: Keeping in mind the state of art; SIFT [11], local binary pattern (LBP) [12] and uniform LBP [13] features are extracted from the image. 128 dimensional SIFT and 10 dimensional uniform LBP (with parameters $p = 8$, $r = 1$, where p represents pixel points and r represents the radius) features around key points were integrated to make a 138 dimensional feature vector of the image. SIFT and LBP features were integrated likewise. The feature vectors originating from training images are clustered through K-means++ and visual vocabulary/dictionary is found out (see Fig. 2). The histogram corresponding to dictionary serves as the final feature vector of the image that is given as an input to the SVM for classification.

Approach II: SIFT features and uniform LBP features are clustered individually and two separate visual vocabulary are obtained through K-means++ clustering. The two histograms obtained are then integrated to form a final histogram which serves as the final feature vector of the image. Similarly, we obtained the final feature vector of the image using SIFT and LBP features (see Fig. 3). These are then send to the SVM for classification.

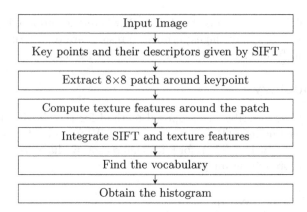

Fig. 2. Flowchart depicting Approach I.

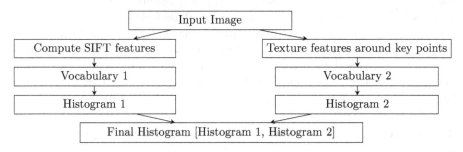

Fig. 3. Flowchart depicting Approach II.

3   Experimental Results and Discussion

This section describes various experiments performed in order to evaluate the discrimination ability of the method. We have used 912 images out of which 456 images are normal images and 456 images have bleeding. The images had a resolution of 576 × 576. To make the dataset representative enough, frames were collected from 10 different patients' WCE video segments. These videos were recorded at the Department of Gastroenterology in the University Hospital of Coimbra, Portugal and obtained with the capsule PillCam SB, manufactured by Given Imaging, Yoqneam, Israel. In order to avoid over-fitting, we have used 4-fold cross validation in all experiments. We have used RBF kernel for classification through SVM. Optimal parameters for classification are found using grid search approach [14]. In all the experiments, we have used vlfeat [15] for clustering and libSVM [14] for classification. To assess the classification of WCE images by SVM, we use a standard performance measure, accuracy, which is defined as follows

$$Accuracy = \frac{Number\ of\ correct\ predictions}{Number\ of\ positives + Number\ of\ negatives}.$$

Table 1. Classification accuracy achieved using Approach I.

Vocabulary size	SIFT	SIFT + unif. LBP	SIFT + LBP
50	91.23 %	90.35 %	92.76 %
100	91.89 %	**95.06 %**	**94.52 %**
150	**93.86 %**	94.52 %	89.91 %
200	93.20 %	90.79 %	93.97 %

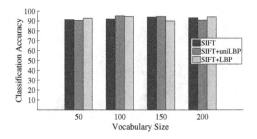

Fig. 4. Classification accuracy achieved using Approach I. (Color figure online)

3.1 Experiment 1

In this section, we evaluate the performance of Approach I. We first evaluate the performance of SIFT features alone. The results are reported in Table 1, and indicate that SIFT features alone are good to discriminate between bleeding and normal images. We next evaluate the performance of SIFT + LBP and SIFT + uniform LBP. The results are listed in Table 1 and Fig. 4. From the same we observe that SIFT + uniform LBP achieves the highest classification accuracy of **95.06 %** which is convincing because uniform LBP provides textural information. SIFT + LBP performs quite well but not good as SIFT + uniform LBP which could be attributed to the fact that the textural features in bleeding images are less discriminating. The high dimensionality of SIFT + LBP compared to SIFT + Uniform LBP brings some redundancy in feature vector contributing to lower accuracy as compared to SIFT + uniform LBP.

3.2 Experiment 2

In this section we evaluate the performance of Approach II for bleeding detection in WCE images. The results are given in Table 2 using combination of SIFT + LBP features and also of SIFT + uniform LBP features. A comparison of both the approaches is given in Figs. 4 and 5. Results in Figs. 5 and 6 indicate that Approach I outperforms Approach II. Hence Approach I is a better integration scheme over Approach II. Also, the results clearly reveal the fact that textural features in bleeding images are not discriminating enough because when LBP and uniform LBP features are individually clustered and concatenated with SIFT features, they don't contribute much towards the classification.

Table 2. Classification accuracy obtained using Approach II.

Vocabulary size	SIFT + LBP	SIFT + unif. LBP
50	**93.86%**	**92.65 %**
100	90.57 %	90.35 %
150	89.58 %	88.71 %
200	89.69 %	89.58 %

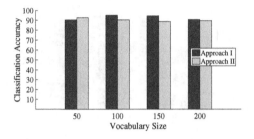

Fig. 5. Comparison of Approach I and Approach II with SIFT + LBP features. (Color figure online)

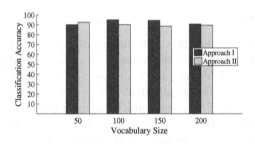

Fig. 6. Comparison of Approach I and Approach II with SIFT + uniform LBP features. (Color figure online)

3.3 Experiment 3

In thirst for further improving the classification accuracy, we tried to introduce the concept of multi-resolution analysis in the classification of bleeding images. We have explored multi-resolution analysis using uniform LBP with three different parameters ($p = 8, r = 1$; $p = 16, r = 3$; $p = 24, r = 5$). However for this, we needed to extract patches of larger sizes; so we extract patches with two different sizes 24×24 and 32×32. Approach I has been used for bag of words representation of image features, as the same has been found better in our previous experiments. The results are reported in Table 3 and Fig. 7. They show that introducing multi-resolution analysis using large sized image patches contributes nothing, rather introduces redundancy and adversely affects the

Table 3. Classification accuracy obtained using multi-resolution analysis through uniform LBP

Vocabulary size	24×24 patch	32×32 patch
50	87.28 %	92.87 %
100	**93.42 %**	91.45 %
150	88.82 %	91.29 %
200	89.47 %	**93.53 %**

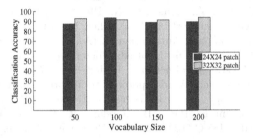

Fig. 7. Classification accuracy obtained using multi-resolution analysis (Color figure online)

discrimination ability of SIFT features. We can very easily conclude that image patches of larger sizes are not able to capture local information of the image well.

4   Conclusions

We have considered BoVW based two different approaches for bleeding detection in WCE images. In first approach, SIFT and texture features are integrated together and then clustering is performed while in second approach, features are clustered individually and then integration is done. In our experiments we have observed that Approach I is better than Approach II. We have obtained an accuracy of **95.06 %** using Approach I which confirms the discriminative ability of the same. The proposed idea may be further improved by considering some colour features and integrating them with SIFT and uniform LBP features.

Acknowledgement. This work was supported in part by CMUC – UID/MAT/00324/ 2013, funded by FCT/MCTES (Portugal) and co-funded by the European Regional Development Fund through the Partnership Agreement PT2020.

References

1. Li, B., Meng, M.Q.H.: Computer-aided detection of bleeding regions for capsule endoscopy images. IEEE Trans. Biomed. Eng. **56**(4), 1032–1039 (2009)
2. Lv, G., Yan, G., Wang, Z.: Bleeding detection in wireless capsule endoscopy images based on color invariants and spatial pyramids using support vector machines. In: Engineering in Medicine and Biology Society, pp. 6643–6646 (2011)
3. Figueiredo, I.N., Kumar, S., Leal, C., Figueiredo, P.N.: Computer-assisted bleeding detection in wireless capsule endoscopy images. Comput. Methods Biomech. Biomed. Eng. Imaging Vis. **1**(4), 198–210 (2013)
4. Cui, L., Hu, C., Zou, Y., Meng, M.Q.H.: Bleeding detection in wireless capsule endoscopy images by support vector classifier. In: 2010 IEEE International Conference on Information and Automation (ICIA), pp. 1746–1751 (2010)
5. Pan, G., Yan, G., Qiu, X., Cui, J.: Bleeding detection in wireless capsule endoscopy based on probabilistic neural network. J. Med. Syst. **35**(6), 1477–1484 (2011)
6. Hwang, S.: Bag-of-Visual-Words approach to abnormal image detection in wireless capsule endoscopy videos. In: Bebis, G., Boyle, R., Parvin, B., Koracin, D., Wang, S., Kyungnam, K., Benes, B., Moreland, K., Borst, C., DiVerdi, S., Yi-Jen, C., Ming, J. (eds.) ISVC 2011, Part II. LNCS, vol. 6939, pp. 320–327. Springer, Heidelberg (2011)
7. Aman, J.M., Yao, J., Summers, R.M.: Content-based image retrieval on ct colonography using rotation and scale invariant features and Bag-of-Words model. In: Biomedical Imaging: From Nano to Macro, pp. 1357–1360 (2010)
8. Caicedo, J.C., Cruz, A., Gonzalez, F.A.: Histopathology image classification using bag of features and kernel functions. In: Combi, C., Shahar, Y., Abu-Hanna, A. (eds.) AIME 2009. LNCS, vol. 5651, pp. 126–135. Springer, Heidelberg (2009)
9. Yuan, Y., Li, B., Meng, M.H.: Improved bag of feature for automatic polyp detection in wireless capsule endoscopy images. IEEE Trans. Autom. Sci. Eng. (99), 1–7 (2015)
10. Arthur, D., Vassilvitskii, S.: K-means++: The advantages of careful seeding. In: Proceedings of the Eighteenth Annual ACM-SIAM Symposium on Discrete Algorithms, pp. 1027–1035 (2007)
11. Lowe, D.G.: Distinctive image features from scale-invariant keypoints. Int. J. Comput. Vis. **60**(2), 91–110 (2004)
12. Ojala, T., Pietikainen, M., Harwood, D.: A comparative study of texture measures with classification based on featured distributions. Pattern Recogn. **29**(1), 51–59 (1996)
13. Ojala, T., Pietikainen, M., Maenpaa, T.: Multiresolution gray-scale and rotation invariant texture classification with local binary patterns. IEEE Trans. Pattern Anal. Mach. Intell. **24**(7), 971–987 (2002)
14. Chang, C.C., Lin, C.J.: LIBSVM: a library for support vector machines. ACM Trans. Intell. Syst. Technol. 2, 27:1–27:27 (2011). http://www.csie.ntu.edu.tw/~cjlin/libsvm
15. Vedaldi, A., Fulkerson, B.: VLFeat: an open and portable library of computer vision algorithms (2008). http://www.vlfeat.org/

Central Medialness Adaptive Strategy for 3D Lung Nodule Segmentation in Thoracic CT Images

Luis Gonçalves[1,2], Jorge Novo[3(✉)], and Aurélio Campilho[1,2]

[1] INESC TEC - INESC Technology and Science, Porto, Portugal
{up201306966,campilho}@fe.up.pt
[2] Faculdade de Engenharia, Universidade Do Porto, Porto, Portugal
[3] Department of Computer Science, University of A Coruña, A Coruña, Spain
jnovo@udc.es

Abstract. In this paper, a Hessian-based strategy, based on the central medialness adaptive principle, was adapted and proposed in a multiscale approach for the 3D segmentation of pulmonary nodules in chest CT scans. This proposal is compared with another well stated Hessian based strategy of the literature, for nodule extraction, in order to demonstrate its accuracy.

Several scans from the Lung Image Database Consortium and Image Database Resource Initiative (LIDC-IDRI) database were employed in the test and validation procedure. The scans include a large and heterogeneous set of 569 solid and mostly solid nodules with a large variability in the nodule characteristics and image conditions. The results demonstrated that the proposal offers correct results, similar to the performance of the radiologists, providing accurate nodule segmentations that perform the desirable scenario for a posterior analysis and the eventual lung cancer diagnosis.

Keywords: Computer-aided diagnosis · Thoracic CT imaging · Lung cancer · Pulmonary nodule segmentation · Hessian-based approaches

1 Introduction and Previous Work

Nowadays, from all the different pathologies, lung cancer is one of the most dangerous diseases in the world. As reference, in the United States the total number of deaths regarding lung cancer is higher than the sum of colon, breast and prostate cancers all together [1], situation that can be extrapolated to any other developed country. This makes the early detection and diagnosis a crucial task to maximize the chances of survival.

From all the possibilities, the Computed Tomography (CT) of the thorax is widely employed for the analysis and diagnose of numerous lung diseases. It represents the most common imaging modality for detecting and diagnosing pulmonary nodules. Computer-aided diagnosis (CAD) systems for lung cancer were proposed. There is a large variability of strategies that can be generally organized

© Springer International Publishing Switzerland 2016
A. Campilho and F. Karray (Eds.): ICIAR 2016, LNCS 9730, pp. 583–590, 2016.
DOI: 10.1007/978-3-319-41501-7_65

in 5 main steps: lung parenchyma extraction, nodule candidates identification, nodules detection, benign/malignant categorization and the corresponding lung cancer diagnosis. In this CAD scheme, nodule segmentation is a crucial and complex task that has to provide the entire nodule region for a posterior analysis to determine its malignancy.

Over the years, different methodologies were presented to segment lung nodules. Among the different proposals we can find a large and heterogeneous set of possibilities. Most of the approaches begin from a previous detection of the nodule followed by different strategies to obtain a detailed nodule contour. These strategies include thresholding, region growing, clustering or deformable models. Many proposals are also combined with image pre-processing in order to enhance the input image quality and facilitate the posterior nodule segmentation. We selected some representative works of the state-of-the-art nodule segmentation.

Armato et al. [2] used multiple gray-level thresholds in the segmented lung parenchyma to extract nodule like structures, followed by nearby segment grouping and further refinement to obtain the final nodule segmentations. Setio et al. [3] employed a multistage process with thresholding and morphological operations to obtain the nodule region. Gu et al. [4] implemented a "click and grow" algorithm that begins with a manual seed selection followed by region growing based on intensity similarity. Multiple "click and grow" are generated and finally a voting process defines the final segmentation. Zhang et al. [5] applied an improved fuzzy C-means to, first, detect the centroids of the clusters and, second, achieve the nodule segmentation. Regarding deformable models, [6] used template matching to extract the nodule on PET images and then utilized an active contour model for further precise nodule segmentation. Chen et al. [7] employed a front surface propagation to distinguish the nodule volume from the pulmonary blood vessels. Zhao et al. [8] combined self-generating neural networks and particle swarm optimization for nodule segmentation and preserve the integrity in cavitary nodule segmentations.

Despite the fact that many approaches already exist, the task of pulmonary nodule segmentation in CT images still represents a challenging issue as nodules usually present large variability regarding the nodule properties like shape, texture or intensity characteristics, among others. They also can be connected to anatomic structures like blood vessels or pleural walls that complicates the identification of the entire nodule contour. The CT scans can also have a large variability on imaging conditions, including the manufacture noisy artifacts or poor image definition.

2   Methodology

From all the methodologies, we focus in one of the most relevant and referenced works, proposed by Murphy et al. [9]. This method computes the Curvedness (CV) and Shape Index (SI), two local image features, from the Hessian matrix that are thresholded to identify and extract the nodule region. In this paper, we propose a new approach for lung nodule segmentation that employs a Hessian-based strategy. In particular, the central adaptive medialness principle, that we previously used in the lung nodule candidate detection [10], is applied for the lung nodule segmentation task.

Both strategies have an image enhancement step that calculates the 3D Hessian matrix at each voxel and computes the corresponding eigenvalues at every voxel, which are combined to identify and segment the lung nodules. As we focus this study on lung nodule segmentation, we start from the detected nodule. Figure 1 illustrates the general scheme of the nodule segmentation process. As shown, the input phase is a multiscale smoothing to reduce the levels of noise and ease the nodule segmentation. After that, the 3D Hessian matrix and the corresponding eigenvalues are computed and further combined to finally generate the segmentation mask of the entire nodule.

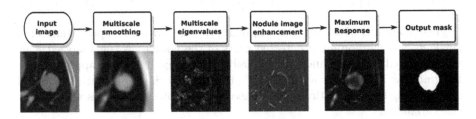

Fig. 1. Nodule segmentation process. Different phases to obtain the final segmentation mask.

As the nodules present a large variability in terms of size, we constructed a multi-scale method, integrating the analysis for a range of σ's. Having the Gaussian second order derivative of an image I with scale σ at a voxel x as:

$$\frac{\partial^2 I_\sigma}{\partial x^2} = I(x) * \frac{\partial^2 G(\sigma, x)}{\partial x^2} \tag{1}$$

The Hessian matrix with the partial derivatives at the voxel $x = (x_1, x_2, x_3)$ is obtained

$$H(I)_\sigma = \begin{bmatrix} \frac{\partial^2 I}{\partial x_1{}^2} & \frac{\partial^2 I}{\partial x_1 \partial x_2} & \frac{\partial^2 I}{\partial x_1 \partial x_3} \\ \frac{\partial^2 I}{\partial x_2 \partial x_1} & \frac{\partial^2 I}{\partial x_2{}^2} & \frac{\partial^2 I}{\partial x_2 \partial x_3} \\ \frac{\partial^2 I}{\partial x_3 \partial x_1} & \frac{\partial^2 I}{\partial x_3 \partial x_2} & \frac{\partial^2 I}{\partial x_3{}^2} \end{bmatrix} \tag{2}$$

From this $H(I)_\sigma$ the method calculates the eigenvalues: $|\lambda_1| \leq |\lambda_2| \leq |\lambda_3|$. Nodule enhancement methods combine the eigenvalues based on SI and CV [9] and the central adaptive medialness [11] to extract the 3D nodule region. The final response, $V(x)$, is calculated as the maximum response at each voxel x over the range of n σ's to guarantee that nodules with a large variability in size are correctly segmented:

$$V(x) = \max_{\sigma_1 \leq \sigma_j \leq \sigma_n} V_{\sigma_j}(x) \tag{3}$$

2.1   Shape Index and Curvedness Approach

In [9], the authors down-sample the image. Then, they apply a Gaussian filter ($\sigma = 1$) to reduce the noise influence. After obtaining the principal curvatures with $\sigma = 1$, the method derives SI and CV using the maximum (λ_3) and minimum (λ_1) eigenvalues of the Hessian matrix. Finally, the nodule segmentation masks are constructed by thresholding both SI and CV. The pixels that satisfy both criteria are considered as the final segmentation V^{SI-CV} as:

$$SI = \tfrac{2}{\pi} arctan\left(\tfrac{\lambda_3+\lambda_1}{\lambda_3-\lambda_1}\right) \qquad CV = \sqrt{\lambda_3^2 + \lambda_1^2} \qquad V^{SI-CV} = SI \cup CV \tag{4}$$

The main drawback of the original proposal was the application of a single σ. The method often detected parts of the nodule, as the analyzed scale was not fitted to the nodule size, specially for large nodules. Our approach is to integrate the results over a range of σ's instead of a single one with the aim of guaranteeing that the entire nodule region is segmented in nodules with a large size variability.

2.2   Central Adaptive Medialness Approach

The central adaptive medialness strategy is inspired by the work in [11]. Originally, the method was proposed for the detection of 3D tubular structures, being successfully applied in 3D lung vessel segmentation in chest CT scans. It was the winner of the VESSEL12 challenge [12]. This method, given a pixel p and a σ, uses λ_1, λ_2 and λ_3 as:

$$V^{med}(\sigma, p) \begin{cases} 0 & \lambda_1 + \lambda_2 + \lambda_3 \geq 0 \\ -\tfrac{\lambda_2}{\lambda_3} * (\lambda_2 + \lambda_3) & otherwise \end{cases} \tag{5}$$

Generally, the method is only applied where the sum of the eigenvalues is less than 0, that is, for bright objects. In this case, we use the two largest eigenvalues to measure the structure strength, and their ratio is applied to correct the deviation from the center of the target structure.

This strategy has as main advantage a higher robustness with respect to noise, a desired property in this complex domain. Having this in mind, we previously applied this strategy in lung nodule candidate generation [10], achieving promising results. In this case, we adapt it to lung nodule segmentation to evaluate if it maintains its robustness and correct performance.

3   Results

The nodules evaluated in this work were taken from the LIDC-IDRI lung image database [13]. Only solid or mostly solid nodules that were annotated by 4 experienced radiologists were considered. A total number of 569 nodules from about

700 images were taken, being 336 small, 90 medium and 143 large nodules. The sizes were established as indicated in Table 1. A large variability is included as no other restriction regarding image conditions or nodule characteristics were introduced.

Regarding the methods, a range of σ's large enough to cover all the nodule sizes was used, being between 0.5 and 3.5, with increasing steps of 0.5. Thus, small nodules (about $3\,mm$) to large nodules (about $50\,mm$–$60\,mm$) can be identified and successfully segmented. Moreover, thresholds of $SI = 0.4$, $CV = 0.005$ and $V^{med} = 0.1$ were applied in each measures.

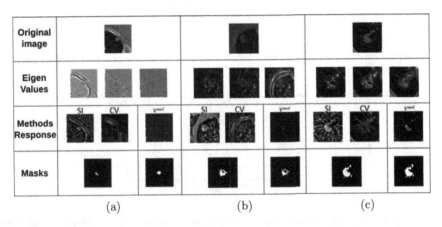

Fig. 2. Stages of the segmentation process for a particular σ. The columns of Methods Response and Masks give the result for all σ's. (a) Medium, juxtapleural nodule. (b) Large, juxtapleural nodule, crossed by an airway. (c) Large, lobulated nodule.

Figure 2 shows the partial results that are obtained after each stage of the segmentation process in three difficult representative segmentations. Although the process is performed in the entire 3D CT image, 2D representative slices are represented. These results show the input image, the 3 eigenvalues (λ_1, λ_2 and λ_3) derived from the Hessian matrix, the results for V^{med}, CV and SI, and the final results for each one of the methods.

Generally, both strategies offer good segmentation in nodules with a well defined region, even in cases with an irregular and complex contours. A couple of difficult segmentations are illustrated in Fig. 2b and c for a large juxtapleural nodule crossed by an airway and for a large lobulated nodule. Even in these hard conditions the two methods can produce good results on most of the nodules.

The central adaptive medialness strategy offers more robust results specially when the boundary of the nodules is not well defined. An example of that can be seen in Fig. 2a, where the SI and CV fails. In this case, the variation of intensities happens from the top left corner to the bottom right corner, so the method enhances most of the lung and the nodule, although the far end of the nodule is brighter than the rest. When performing the threshold operation, only that

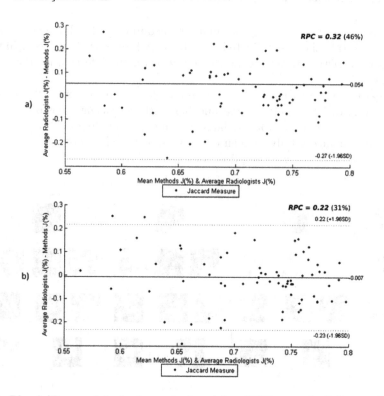

Fig. 3. Bland-Altman plots for large sized nodules. RPC, reproducibility coefficient. RPC=1.96SD. SD, standard deviation. (a) *SI* and *CV* adapted method. (b) central adaptive medialness method.

brighter part is preserved instead of the entire nodule. On the contrary, the central adaptive medialness strategy is capable to enhance blob like structures with low response in the remaining lung, providing a correct nodule segmentation.

3.1   Segmentation Agreement

Additionally, we analyzed the automatic segmentations and the manual segmentations of the radiologists in an agreement study to further evaluate the performance of the proposed approaches. For this purpose we used the Jaccard index defined by:

$$Jaccard = \frac{A \cap B}{A \cup B} \tag{6}$$

where A and B represent the areas of the segmentations to be compared. The Jaccard index tends to one for largely similar segmentations, as the intersection is practically the same as the union. On the contrary, with a low level of agreement the Jaccard index tends to zero.

We measured the agreement between the radiologists segmentations and also compared the segmentations of each method against the radiologists', resulting

Table 1. Bland-Altman study results. Mean of the difference between the mean Jaccard value of the radiologists and the mean Jaccard value of the methods segmentations.

Nodules	Volume (mm^3)	SI and CV	Central ad. med.
Small	<500	0.03	−0.05
Medium	≥500–1000	0.0027	−0.033
Big	>1000	0.054	−0.007

in three Jaccard values for the radiologists (one radiologist with respect to the other three) and four Jaccard values for each method (the method against each of the four radiologists). The results were averaged for each radiologist and method as the radiologists segmentations are anonymous so it is impossible to link annotations of the same specialist over the different analyzed scans.

These mean Jaccard indexes were analyzed using the Bland-Altman method [14], to evaluate the agreement between metrics for the different methods. In the Bland Altman plots, the vertical axis represents the difference between the mean Jaccard value of the radiologists segmentations and the mean Jaccard values of the automatic methods. The horizontal axis is their Mean Value. For illustration purposes we illustrate in Fig. 3 the Bland-Altman plots for big nodules, also calculated for small and medium nodules. The nodules were divided by size according to the ranges presented in Table 1. The global Mean Difference for every Bland-Altman study is presented in Table 1. The central adaptive medialness method presents in general a lower absolute value, indicating that it agrees more with the radiologists than the SI and CV does. Thus, the central adaptive medialness strategy offers sensitively a better behaviour for the nodule segmentation task, providing results more similar to the ones that are provided by the radiologists.

4   Conclusions

In this paper, we propose a multiscale approach for lung nodule segmentation in chest CT images. This method uses a Hessian-based strategy, the central medialness adaptive principle, to extract the 3D nodule volume. This strategy was originally formulated for 3D tubular detection, demonstrating its suitability in vessel extraction in chest CT scans and now providing its accurateness in nodule segmentation. This proposal was compared with another well stated Hessian-based strategy, the SI and CV method proposed in [9], one of the most popular and cited works for lung nodule extraction. We adapted and improved the SI and CV method for nodule segmentation to work under the same conditions as our proposal.

Both approaches were tested with 569 solid and mostly solid nodules presenting a large variability in characteristics. The results demonstrated that the central medialness adaptive approach provides accurate results, outperforming the results of the improved SI and CV method, specially in nodules with not very clear contours as juxtapleural nodules and working more similar to the radiologists performance, as the agreement segmentation study showed.

Acknowledgments. This work is financed by project NORTE-01-0145-FEDER-000016 by the North Portugal Regional Operational Programme (NORTE 2020), under the PORTUGAL 2020 Partnership Agreement, and through the European Regional Development Fund (ERDF); and through the FCT – Fundação para a Ciência e a Tecnologia (Portuguese Foundation for Science and Technology) within the grant contract SFRH/BPD/85663/2012 (J. Novo).

References

1. Greenlee, R.T., Murray, T., Bolden, S., Wingo, P.A.: Cancer statistics. CA Cancer J. Clin. **2000**(50), 7–33 (2000)
2. Armato, S.G., Giger, M.L., MacMahon, H.: Automated detection of lung nodules in ct scans: preliminary results. Med. Phys. **28**(8), 1552–1561 (2001)
3. Setio, A.A.A., Jacobs, C., Gelderblom, J., van Ginneken, B.: Automatic detection of large pulmonary solid nodules in thoracic CT images. Med. Phys. **42**(10), 5642–5653 (2015)
4. Gu, Y., Kumar, V., Hall, L.O., Goldgof, D.B., et al.: Automated delineation of lung tumors from CT images using a single click ensemble segmentation approach. Pattern Recogn. **46**(3), 692–702 (2013)
5. Zhang, X., Zhang, C., Tang, W., Wei, Z.: Medical image segmentation using improved fcm. Sci. China Inf. Sci. **55**(5), 1052–1061 (2012)
6. Qiang, Y., Zhang, X., Ji, G., Zhao, J.: Measuring agreement in method comparison studies. J. Comput. Theoret. Nanosci. **12**, 1972–1976 (2015)
7. Chen, B., Kitasaka, T., Honma, H., Takabatake, H., et al.: Automatic segmentation of pulmonary blood vessels and nodules basedon local intensity structure analysis and surface propagation in 3D chest CT images. Int. J. Comput. Assist. Radiol. Surg. **2010**, 465–482 (2012)
8. Zhao, J., Ji, G., Xia, Y., Zhang, X.: Cavitary nodule segmentation in computed tomography images based on self-generating neural networks and particle swarm optimisation. Int. J. Bio-Inspired Comput. **7**(1), 62–67 (2015)
9. Murphy, K., van Ginneken, B., Schilham, A.M.R., et al.: A large-scale evaluation of automatic pulmonary nodule detection in chest CT using local image features and k-nearest-neighbour classification. Med. Image Anal. **13**, 757–770 (2009)
10. Novo, J., Gonçalves, L., Mendonça, A.M., Campilho, A.: 3D lung nodule candidates detection in multiple scales. In: MVA 2015-IAPR International Conference on Machine Vision Applications, pp. 61–64 (2015)
11. Krissian, K., Malandain, G., Ayache, N., Vaillant, R., Trousset, Y.: Model-based detection of tubular structures in 3d images. Comput. Vis. Image Underst. **80**(2), 130–171 (2000)
12. Rudyanto, R.D., Kerkstra, S., van Rikxoort, E.M., et al.: Comparing algorithms for automated vessel segmentation in computed tomography scans of the lung: the VESSEL12 study. Med. Image Anal. **18**(7), 1217–1232 (2014)
13. Armato, S.G., McLennan, G., Bidaut, L., et al.: The lung image database consortium (LIDC) and image database resource initiative (IDRI): a completed reference database of lung nodules on CT scans. Med. Phys. **38**, 915–931 (2011)
14. Bland, J.M., Altman, D.G.: Measuring agreement in method comparison studies. Stat. Methods Med. Res. **8**(2), 135–160 (1999)

A Self-learning Tumor Segmentation Method on DCE-MRI Images

Szabolcs Urbán[1(✉)], László Ruskó[2], and Antal Nagy[1]

[1] Department of Image Processing and Computer Graphics,
University of Szeged, Szeged, Hungary
{urbansz,nagya}@inf.u-szeged.hu
[2] GE Hungary Healthcare Division, Szeged, Hungary
laszlo.rusko@ge.com

Abstract. Tumor segmentation is a challenging, but substantial task in diagnosis, treatment planning and monitoring. This paper presents a self-learning technique to segment lesions on clinical 3D MRI images. The method is self-learning and iterative: instead of creating a model from manually segmented tumors it learns a given individual tumor in an iterative way without user interaction in the learning cycles. Based on a manually defined region of interest the presented iterative approach first learns the tumor features from the initial region using Random Forest classifier, then in each subsequent cycle it updates the previously learned model automatically. The method was evaluated on liver DCE-MRI images using manually defined tumor segmentation as reference. The algorithm was tested for various types of liver tumors. The presented results showed good correlation with the reference using absolute volume difference and DICE similarity measurements which gave 7.8 % and 88 % average results respectively.

Keywords: Tumor · Segmentation · Self-learning · MRI

1 Introduction

Tumor segmentation is an important task of oncology because the location and the change of the volume of the lesions plays crucial role in therapeutic decisions. The more accurate the tumor quantification the more reliable is the evaluation of the therapy's effectiveness. Manual tumor contouring is very time-consuming and can introduce large inter- and intraoperator variability. It is a challenging task due to the large variation in localization, shape, size, and intensity heterogeneity of the lesions. There is a need for computer assisted tools which make this process more accurate, efficient, and reproducible.

In the literature there are various supervised learning-based tumor segmentation methods, which use previously learned model to segment a given individual tumor. Among others Tang et al. published a method based on single contrast MR images [10]. Geremia et al. proposed a method using multi-modal MR images [4].

© Springer International Publishing Switzerland 2016
A. Campilho and F. Karray (Eds.): ICIAR 2016, LNCS 9730, pp. 591–598, 2016.
DOI: 10.1007/978-3-319-41501-7_66

However these methods need a large amount of labeled data, which can be expensive and requires significant amounts of time.

Active learning (AL) methods use machine learning algorithm in combination with user interactions, especially asks the user to label voxels from uncertainty regions (is it tumor or not). Top et al. formulated 3D interactive image segmentation in an AL framework using Random Walker classifier [11]. Zhou et al. presented an iterative AL method based on conditional random field algorithm, using color and location information with user guidance. The evaluation of their method was made on 2D color images and on one case which contained five slices of a CT image [12]. A stroke segmentation method was presented using AL method with features from multiple images with the Random Forest classifier. They gave back the most uncertain voxels to the user for labeling [3]. These methods strongly rely on user interaction which is usually time-consuming and considers previous contouring experiences.

Bauer et al. [1] proposed a method which integrated quick manual corrections into a fully automatic segmentation method for brain tumor images. Therefore the method uses both previously learned model and user interactions. Su et al. published a segmentation method which first uses a knowledge-based Fuzzy-C means clustering (with six classes including healthy and tumorous tissues) and then an SVM- based AL method to segment brain tumors on multi-modal MRI images [9]. They did not take into account manual labels, but used a Mahalanobis-based distance in each class to actively select the training examples. This method specified for brain tumors using multi-modality MRI images.

In this work we propose a method which is a special variant of an AL algorithm: it learns the tumorous voxels in an iterative way without any seed points from the user. On one hand the method generates automatically the labels for both the tumorous and background voxels in contrast to a typical AL algorithm, which incorporates user-defined labels. On the other hand it does not learn a model based on a previous training phase involving a large database: it learns a model from the actually segmented region of interest (ROI). The user has to provide a ROI and after each iteration the user can indicate if additional iteration is necessary or not. The method is not specialized to any type of anatomy or tumor, however in this work we focused on liver tumors.

2   The Proposed Method

The proposed method consists of two main steps. First, an initial region is extracted from the user-defined ROI. Then, Random Forest-based iterative learning process is applied to generate a sequence of contours from which the user can select the one that fits the user's expectations.

2.1   Feature Selection

The method is based on four main image features: intensity, geodesic distance from the initial region, patch-based similarity and spherical coordinates inside the ROI.

Intensity: In order to reduce noise, anisotropic diffusion filter [6] was applied to the MRI images. Then the intensities were normalized to the [0,1000] range.

Geodesic Distance Map: The gradient magnitude of the image contains information about the boundary of the tumor and other structures in the region. In order to take this information into account this information geodesic distance map was used based on the Fast Marching algorithm [8]. It produces a distance map which contains distances from a given seed region incorporating the gradient magnitude image in its speed function.

Patch-Based Similarity: Similarity of image patches within one image can help to extract the distinctive structure in a local neighbourhood. For this purpose the modality independent neighbourhood descriptor (MIND) was used which published by Heinrich et al. [5]. It was originally proposed for registration and it can be calculated using the following equations:

$$MIND(I, x, r) = \frac{1}{n} exp\left(- \frac{D_p(I, x, x + r)}{V(I, x)} \right) \tag{1}$$

$$D_p(I, x_1, x_2) = \sum_{p \in P} (I(x_1 + p) - I(x_2 + p))^2 \tag{2}$$

$$V(I, x) = \frac{1}{6} \sum_{n \in N} D_p(I, x, x + n) \tag{3}$$

In this work the searching region (R) defined as the six-neighbourhood weighted by the spacing between voxels. The metric is used in the following way: the similarity is calculated for each voxel as the sum of absolute differences between descriptors of a given voxel and the mean descriptor calculated from the automatically generated initial region.

Spherical Coordinates: We defined θ as the counterclockwise angle in the x-y plane from the positive x-axis, ϕ as the elevation angle from the x-y plane and r as the distance from the origin to a specified point. Therefore the conversation equations were the followings:

$$r = \sqrt{x^2 + y^2 + z^2} \tag{4}$$

$$\theta = tan^{-1}(y/x) \tag{5}$$

$$\phi = tan^{-1}(z/\sqrt{(x^2 + y^2)}) \tag{6}$$

In experiments using the Cartesian coordinates (x,y,z) the learned model always contained "straight cuts" in all directions which is not characteristic for tumor. However, using spherical coordinates these sharp borders disappeared.

2.2   Classifier

The applied classifier was Random Forest, which is an ensemble machine learning algorithm introduced in [2]. During prediction each voxel is classified based on the votes of various decision trees. The used implementation was the Random Jungle 2.0 [7]. The number of trees was set to 100, the maximum depth of trees set to the used number of features. The motivation to use this learning algorithm was that it has the capability to learn a model on the training images with relatively high accuracy. In this work we strongly rely on this, because the train and test samples were also used from the same ROI.

2.3 Layer by Layer Learning

In general a tumor and its surrounding can be inhomogeneous and complex. In order to handle these difficulties a layer by layer learning process is constructed (See Fig. 1). In each iteration three different regions were defined to constrain the learning process inside the ROI:

1. *tumorous region*, which represents the actual tumor segmentation (foreground samples, green contour);
2. *neutral region*, which is just outside of the previous region, it contains either foreground or background samples (between the green and the blue contour)
3. *background region*, which is the whole region outside of the neutral region (background samples, outside the blue contour)

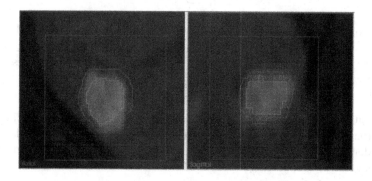

Fig. 1. The used layers: foreground samples (inside green contour), background samples (outside the blue contour) and the neutral region (between foreground and background samples) in a ROI (red). (Color figure online)

2.4 Self-learning Cycle

The main part of the proposed method is the iterative self-learning algorithm. To learn the model of an individual tumor, both the training and the test set is selected from the voxels of the ROI. In this way the algorithm can be used to segment different types of tumors in various environments.

The overview of the algorithm is shown in Fig. 2. A learning cycle is constructed which can learn the tumorous voxels in an iterative way. Two sets of features were defined for the two Random Forest classification steps. The first set of features consists of intensity, similarity and geodesic distance map, considering the similar voxels and the edges with the distance from the center. Consequently, the initial region can be expanded in a homogeneous region to generate more foreground samples. The second set of the features consists of intensity, similarity and spherical coordinates. As a result it can classify voxels into foreground even if the region contains ambiguous image information based on the shape of the actual tumor segmentation.

One iteration consists of two parts: (1) train and test using the first set of features; (2) train and test using the second set of features. In each test parts only the 3D largest connected component of the positive samples are considered as the result.

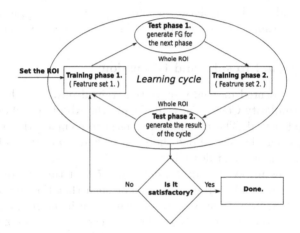

Fig. 2. The overview of the method.

We use the presumption that the manually defined ROI is set around the tumorous region therefore its central part contains a region from the whole tumor. In the first iteration the positive (tumor) samples are defined as the central region of the selected ROI. Then, the $i+1$-th iteration uses the result of the i-th iteration as foreground. In cases when the border of the tumor is well separable from its background the learning process stops at the border. However, in cases when there is a very weak boundary the actual contour can be stopped by the user when the method approximates the tumor boundary. Furthermore, when the tumor has an inner and an outer part both can be segmented using the proposed method. First, the inner part can be segmented, then the user can indicate that there is an outer region with different characteristics. In this case the method adds a new layer to the actual result as foreground samples. This way the learning process proceeds and it can segment the whole tumor. Such cases will be presented in the next section.

3   Results

In this section we demonstrate our experimental results applying the proposed method to DCE-MRI images to segment tumors inside the liver.

3.1   Data

The method was evaluated using 17 dynamic contrast enhanced (DCE)-MRI images of the liver, which are frequently used in clinical liver imaging. They were acquired with a 1.5 Tesla MRI scanner using the Liver Acquisition with Volume Acquisition (LAVA) protocol using 3 dimensional spoiled gradient echo pulse sequences. In this study the slice thickness was 5 mm in each case. Images were acquired in three phases following contrast administration: arterial phase, portal phase, and a delayed phase. In most cases the portal phase image was used because the tumors have the most visible contours in this image.

3.2   Experimental Results and Discussion

Tumors were segmented manually by a well trained physician. For the evaluation the Dice Similarity Coefficient (DICE) and the Absolute Volume Difference (AVD) were calculated. The first metric is used to compare the overlap of two segmentation, while the second one shows the difference of two volumes, which is important in tumor quantification.

The test exams involved a total number of 17 liver tumors. In each case an ROI was defined manually around the tumor such that the tumor was in the middle of the ROI. The iterations were executed until the result best approximated the tumor visually. The achieved best results for each tumor was involved in the evaluation. According to the error metrics DICE was 88 % (STD: 2 %) and AVD was 7.8 % (STD 5 %) in average, which shows that the results correlate well with the reference segmentation (see Table 1).

Table 1. Experimental results

Cases	1	2	3	4	5	6	7	8	9	10	11	12	13	14	15	16	17
DICE (%)	85	90	85	89	92	91	85	87	87	89	93	91	87	85	85	91	85
AVD (%)	8.2	3.7	4.2	6.7	9.7	15.1	0.6	11.2	1.7	8.9	7.3	1.4	16.9	1.4	11.5	11.9	12.3

To best of our knowledge this is the first method using self-learning cycle. Therefore the achieved results were compared with the most similar approach [9]. Our method achieved 90 % True Positive Rate (TPR) in average for whole tumor segmentation, while they achieved 88.4 %, 86.3 % and 82.5 % TPR on different regions of tumors using multiparamteric brain MRI images.

3.3   Segmentation of Regions Inside Tumor

The proposed method can handle tumors with different appearance. Three different tumor types is demonstrated: homogeneous tumor, heterogeneous with unclear boundary and heterogeneous with ring. In case of a mostly homogeneous tumor (see Fig. 3a) the method segmented the tumor in four iterations producing a very similar contour to the ground truth segmentation (DICE: 91 %, AVD: 15 %). In this case the arterial phase of the LAVA image was used therefore the tumor characteristics are different then on third phase LAVA images, which were used in cases b and c. A tumor with an inner structure and an outer ring can be seen on Fig. 3b. First the inner structure was segmented and then the whole tumor including the outer ring after five iterations. The achieved result correlate well with the shown manual contour: DICE was 87 % and AVD was 1.7 %. A tumor with an unclear boundary is shown in Fig. 3c. It contains an inner darker structure and a fuzzy boundary. First, the inner part is segmented and finally the whole tumor in a total of six iterations. According to the error metrics DICE was 89 % and AVD was 6.7 % in the case of whole tumor.

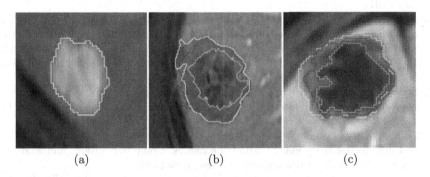

(a)   (b)   (c)

Fig. 3. Segmentation of 3 different cases: full segmentation (red), segmentation of the inner part (cyan), reference segmentation (yellow). (Color figure online)

4   Conclusions

A new, self-learning tumor segmentation algorithm is introduced to facilitate the tumor segmentation task. To the best of our knowledge, this is the first work that shows its usability of such a method for general tumor segmentation. Experiments with even complex, challenging liver tumors showed that it can segment significantly different types of tumors with high precision. Furthermore not just the whole tumor, but its internal parts can be delineated. According to the evaluation the presented method allows the user stopping the learning process in order to achieve tumor contours with 88 % DICE in average. In the future, the usability of the method shall be confirmed by more extensive clinical study, including publicly available brain tumor MRI images.

Acknowledgements. We would like to thank to Department of Radiology, University of Szeged providing the input images, especially for Dr. O. Urbán for creating the reference tumor contours.

This work was supported by Analitic Healthcare Quality User Information Program of the National Research, Development and Innovation Fund, Hungarian Government, Grant VKSZ_12-1-2013-0012.

References

1. Bauer, S., Porz, N., Meier, R., Pica, A., Slotboom, J., Wiest, R., Reyes, M.: Interactive segmentation of MR images from brain tumor patients. In: 2014 IEEE 11th International Symposium on Biomedical Imaging (ISBI), pp. 862–865, April 2014
2. Breiman, L.: Random forests. Mach. Learn. **45**(1), 5–32 (2001)
3. Chyzhyk, D., Dacosta-Aguayo, R., Matar, M., Graa, M.: An active learning approach for stroke lesion segmentation on multimodal MRI data. Neurocomputing **150, Part A**, 26–36 (2015)
4. Geremia, E., Menze, B.H., Ayache, N.: Spatially adaptive random forests. In: 2013 IEEE 10th International Symposium on Biomedical Imaging (ISBI), pp. 1344–1347, April 2013
5. Heinrich, M.P., Jenkinson, M., Bhushan, M., Matin, T., Gleeson, F.V., Brady, S.M., Schnabel, J.A.: Mind: modality independent neighbourhood descriptor for multi-modal deformable registration. Med. Image Anal. **16**(7), 1423–1435 (2012)
6. Perona, P., Malik, J.: Scale-space and edge detection using anisotropic diffusion. IEEE Trans. Pattern Anal. Mach. Intell. **12**(7), 629–639 (1990)
7. Schwarz, D.F., Knig, I.R., Ziegler, A.: On safari to random jungle: a fast implementation of random forests for high-dimensional data. Bioinformatics **26**(14), 1752–1758 (2010)
8. Sethian, J.A.: Level Set Methods and Fast Marching Methods: Evolving Interfaces in Computational Geometry, Fluid Mechanics, Computer Vision, and Materials Science. Cambridge Universtiy Press, New York (1999)
9. Su, P., Xue, Z., Chi, L., Yang, J., Wong, S.: Support vector machine (SVM) active learning for automated glioblastoma segmentation. In: 2012 9th IEEE International Symposium on Biomedical Imaging (ISBI), pp. 598–601 (2012)
10. Tang, H., Lu, H., Liu, W., Tao, X.: Tumor segmentation from single contrast MR images of human brain. In: 2015 IEEE 12th International Symposium on Biomedical Imaging (ISBI), pp. 46–49, April 2015
11. Top, A., Hamarneh, G., Abugharbieh, R.: Active learning for interactive 3D image segmentation. In: Fichtinger, G., Martel, A., Peters, T. (eds.) MICCAI 2011, Part III. LNCS, vol. 6893, pp. 603–610. Springer, Heidelberg (2011)
12. Zhou, L., Qiao, Y., Li, Y., He, X., Yang, J.: Interactive segmentation based on iterative learning for multiple-feature fusion. Neurocomputing **135**, 240–252 (2014)

Morphological Separation of Clustered Nuclei in Histological Images

Shereen Fouad[1(✉)], Gabriel Landini[1], David Randell[1], and Antony Galton[2]

[1] School of Dentistry,University of Birmingham, Birmingham, UK
{s.a.fouad,g.landini,d.a.randell}@bham.ac.uk
[2] Department of Computer Science,University of Exeter, Exeter, UK
a.p.galton@exeter.ac.uk
http://www.birmingham.ac.ukz, http://www.exeter.ac.uk

Abstract. Automated nuclear segmentation is essential in the analysis of most microscopy images. This paper presents a novel concavity-based method for the separation of clusters of nuclei in binary images. A heuristic rule, based on object size, is used to infer the existence of merged regions. Concavity extrema detected along the merged-cluster boundary are used to guide the separation of overlapping regions. Inner split contours of multiple concavities along the nuclear boundary are estimated via a series of morphological procedures. The algorithm was evaluated on images of H400 cells in monolayer cultures and compares favourably with the state-of-art watershed method commonly used to separate overlapping nuclei.

Keywords: Histological images · Nuclear segmentation · Concavity analysis · Mathematical morphology

1 Introduction and Related Work

Automated nuclear segmentation plays an important role in computer-assisted analysis of histopathological images. Improving the quality and accuracy of nuclear segmentation has become an increasingly important topic, for which numerous analytical procedures have been proposed. One main challenge is the separation of clusters of overlapping nuclei. These often appear as irregular shapes resulting from an overlap of the 3D extent of nuclei on 2D image projections. An additional complication is that the overlapping nucleus boundaries are often indistinct and make the algorithmic separation a non-trivial challenge. This is especially relevant for the diagnosis of many diseases, including cancer, where identifying and characterising cellular abnormalities play an important role. There has been extensive, well-focused research by various groups on the splitting of nuclear clusters; a review paper [1] addresses recent advances and current challenges with respect to this problem. The well-known watershed algorithm [2,3] has been used to address region separation by creating unique 'basins' where nuclei are defined by the ridges bounding the basins. Although this

© The Author(s) 2016
A. Campilho and F. Karray (Eds.): ICIAR 2016, LNCS 9730, pp. 599–607, 2016.
DOI: 10.1007/978-3-319-41501-7_67

can result in successful separation in some images, there are well-documented problems with over- and under-segmentation in cells/nuclei that overlap, particularly when the boundary gradients at the overlaps are weak. Other methods use measures of concavity of the cluster contour to find the nuclei [4–6] or use ellipse-fitting to infer the overlapping nuclei, one drawback being that the performance tends to be sensitive to fluctuations of the contours. Also, most methods detect but do not split clusters into individual nuclei segments in the 2D image. While it might not be possible to resolve this in all cases, such splittings are often necessary for extracting additional features (object counting, computing spatial relations) which are operationally useful even when derived from segmentations that include some mis-assigned pixels. Other methods [7–9] employ iterative split-line algorithms to generate inner edges, and use concavity points to construct edge-path graphs. From these, the possible combinations of lines linking every pair of concavity points are computed and the shortest set of lines satisfying certain conditions is generated at the final splitting step. The split-lines are generated subject to the conditions that they yield sub-contours with acceptable nuclear sizes and do not intersect with other lines. While this can produce reasonable results in simple cases, it often fails in complex configurations, for a number of reasons: (a) from all the possible combinations of split-lines it is difficult to identify which point pairs to link; (b) the number of split combinations increases dramatically with the number of concavity points, becoming computationally costly and slow; (c) object separation uses straight lines along the inferred boundaries, while real nuclear boundaries are curved; (d) iterative separation usually leads to over-segmentation, as illustrated later.

Here we propose a new method for the detection and separation of individual nuclei in clusters based on the geometrical characteristics of the cluster boundary, particularly contour curvature; this approach overcomes several limitations mentioned earlier. The expected positions and shapes of individual candidate nuclei are estimated and followed by a series of morphological operations that separate the cluster into individual nuclear regions. The validity and effectiveness of the proposed framework was assessed through a series of experiments on images of clumped nuclei.

2   The Proposed Algorithm

We investigated cluster separation on images of monolayers of H400 cells (an oral cancer cell line) grown on glass and captured at ×20 magnification (inter-pixel distance is $0.34\,\mu m$) stained with Haematoxylin. These are typical conditions used in a variety of gene expression analyses. The haematoxylin (blue/violet) dye is primarily taken up by nucleic acids (therefore highlighting nuclei). Often eosin (pink dye) is used as a counter-stain, staining proteins in the intra- and extra-cellular compartments. A typical analysis of these cultures starts with a standard image pre-processing step such as colour deconvolution to unmix the dyes (if more than one is used) in order to facilitate extraction of the objects of interest. Nucleus segmentation is best performed on the Haematoxylin channel image owing to its aforementioned affinity to nucleic acids. Following this, a global thresholding method is applied to obtain a binary image of the nuclei where any clustered groups of nuclei would require separation. In the experiments described later, however, we work on a manually segmented 'gold standard' set of nuclear images. All imaging procedures were implemented on the popular ImageJ platform [10].

2.1   Identifying Potential Nuclei Clusters

This initial step extracts the boundaries of potential nuclear clusters R in the binary image I_1 representing the nuclei when the area of R is larger than some empirically determined value. This is followed by a concavity analysis (explained in the next section), where identified concavity points S serve as the input to the following region-splitting algorithm. Large regions with no concavity points imply lack of overlap, in which case region-splitting is not required; whereas the presence of one or more concavity points indicates contours that potentially enclose two or more nuclei.

2.2   Concavity Point Detection

This step detects the most dominant set of concavity points in a region boundary. Concavity points represent junctions where overlapping occurs and they are used here to guide the subsequent separation steps. A closed region R is defined by an ordered set of N boundary points, say $R = \{p_i | i \in \{1...N\}\}$. A point p_i corresponds to the ith boundary point and p_{i+1} and p_{i-1} are the next and previous boundary points, respectively. Determining concavity/convexity in a boundary relies on the mathematical property of two dimensional vectors defined along the periphery of the closed-loop region R. A two-dimensional vector V_1 is defined between points p_{i-1} and p_i, and a second one, V_2, is defined between points p_{i+1} and p_i. The cross product $V_1 \times V_2$ characterizes the boundary curvature. If the boundary points are ordered in the clockwise direction, then a point $p_i \in R$ belongs to a *concave segment* if $V_1 \times V_2 \leq 0$. To reduce the sensitivity of the algorithm to small fluctuations and noise, a tolerance value gap representing the length of the vectors is introduced. Similarly to the approach in [7], the most dominant concavity point is then selected from each detected concave segment, based on the angle between contour points. The selected point s corresponds to the deepest indentation between two overlapping nuclei, minimising the angle $Angle(p_i) = \pi - \arccos\left(\frac{(p_i - p_{i-gap}) \cdot (p_{i+gap} - p_i)}{\|p_i - p_{i-gap}\| \|p_{i+gap} - p_i\|}\right)$ between the vectors. The final list of concavity points, S, is passed as an input to the following splitting algorithm.

2.3   Region-Splitting Algorithm

The presence of a single concavity point $(s_1 \in S)$ in the cluster boundary indicates a potential overlap of two individual nuclei. In this special case, the algorithm creates a 4-connected[1] split-line that links s_1 to the midpoint, p_i, where i corresponds to the middle position of the opposite convex boundary. It is worthwhile mentioning that other splitting procedures such as the watershed separation would fail to produce split-lines in these cases.

On the other hand, two or more concavity points along the boundary imply potential overlap between multiple nuclei. The proposed model takes as input a region of clustered nuclei with multiple detected concavity points and returns the optimal inner separating boundaries. The whole process is summarized in Fig. 1 (using a synthetic cluster region)[2] and it consists of the following steps:

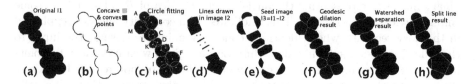

Fig. 1. Illustration of our method from (a) to (f) for splitting nuclei clusters with multiple concavity points. Figures (g) and (h) show the results of the watershed [2,3] and split-line methods [7–9], respectively.

1. Convex Contour Extraction. This step extracts the coordinates and number of pixels located on convex segments between each consecutive pair of concavity points (see Fig. 1(b)). For robustness, the algorithm only considers convex segments that are large enough to fit a candidate cell. A given value θ_1 serves as a threshold for detecting effective convex regions.

2. Circle Fitting. Least-squares fitting [11] is used to compute the best fitting circles to the set of points in each of the convex segments, and each circle corresponds now to a candidate individual nucleus, as shown in Fig. 1(c). With each circle crl with centre $c \in \check{C}$ and radius rad is associated a pair of consecutive concavity points, $s_n, s_{n+1} \in S$, located on the cluster boundary. The circles are inspected and modified before nuclear separation takes place, as follows. The algorithm constrains the radii to be less than an empirically determined threshold θ_2, estimated in advance, which corresponds to the maximum radius of a real nucleus, then it replaces radii larger than this with this threshold value. As for circle centres in $\check{C}$, on rare occasions they might be located outside the clustered nuclear region R. The algorithm corrects this by recursively shifting the circle centre coordinates, in small increments, towards their corresponding convex segments until it is repositioned inside R. To do this, the recursive shift checks the intensity value of a centre point in image I_1.

3. Estimating Candidate Nuclei. The circle centres provide an a priori estimation of the expected position of the nuclei in the cluster. We noted that

---

[1] Our binary image objects are 8-connected in a 4-connected background.
[2] Boundaries in Fig. 1(b) are thickened for display purposes.

clusters are likely to have regions with two closely opposing convex segments. The procedure described so far would yield two partially overlapping circular zones with adjacent centres, see Fig. 1(c). Intuitively, however, an observer with a range of possible nuclear sizes and shapes in mind would conclude that opposing segments are likely to correspond to only one rounded object, not two. To resolve this, the algorithm checks the pairwise distance between all the assigned centres. Consider a circle crl_a, with centre c_a, radius rad_a and concavity points (s_a, s_{a+1}). To find whether another centre c_b (located in circle crl_b with radius rad_b and concavity points (s_b, s_{b+1})) is inside the circle crl_a, we measure the Euclidean distance $\check{D}$ between c_a and c_b. Point c_b is inside crl_a if $\check{D} \leq rad_a$. Accordingly, the status of centre c_b with respect to c_a is set to Binary Centres (**BC**) if ($\check{D} \leq rad_a$ and $(s_a, s_{a+1}) \neq (s_b, s_{b+1})$), implying their close proximity, representing a single candidate object. This is shown in Fig. 1(c) in blob pairs [L,C] and [J,E].

It might be argued, however, that nuclear boundaries often take the form of ellipses rather than circles, while the procedure above aims to detect nearby centres of overlapping circles. In other words, the distance between the two centres c_a and c_b might be larger than the radius rad_a in the case of elliptical candidate nuclei. This situation, illustrated in blob pair [K, D] in Fig. 1(c), is not detected by our algorithm so far, and would lead to an incorrect separation into two assumed circular objects instead of a single elliptical object. To provide a viable segmentation of overlapping elliptical objects, the algorithm introduces a correction factor, namely $\check{O}$, that is multiplied by the radius rad_a. This factor increases the distance span that is to be compared with $\check{D}$, thereby allowing for the detection of elliptical objects. Accordingly, $\forall (c_a, c_b) \in \check{C}$, the status of centre c_b with respect to c_a is assigned as **BC** if ($\check{D} \leq rad_a \times \check{O}$ and $(s_a, s_{a+1}) \neq (s_b, s_{b+1})$), otherwise, it is assigned as **SC** (Single Centre), as shown in blobs M, A, B, F, G, H, I in Fig. 1(c). Note that, if the status of c_b is deemed to be **BC** with respect to c_a, then the algorithm imposes the same **BC** relation on c_a, and saves the concavity information of both centres.

4. Morphological Operations for Cluster Splitting. This step produces the final inner edges to separate the overlapping nuclei by means of a series of mathematical morphology operations [12]. The idea revolves around geodesic dilations, without merging, of seeds representing single regions belonging uniquely to each candidate object. This principle is similar to the well-known watershed separation method (natively available in ImageJ [10]), but while that method uses the ultimate eroded points as seeds (often leading to over-segmentation) our approach uses much larger seeds derived from the regions containing convex segments and estimated centres of regions. This avoids the over-segmentation typical of the watershed method. The seed image is created as follows. On a new blank binary image I_2, a preliminary set of line segments is drawn. Their positions depend on the status of the candidate object centres (each of which is located between a pair of concavity points as described earlier). If a centre is labelled as **BC** with respect to another (i.e., together representing a single candidate nucleus), the algorithm retrieves the concavity information relative to both centres and draws two lines, each linking one of the two pairs of associated concavity points from the opposite sides of the boundary. The order of linking these is given by the encoding order in the cluster boundary. Furthermore, if a centre is labelled as SC (i.e., representing a single candidate object) then two lines are drawn, linking the circle centre to each of the surrounding concavity points. Some of the resulting lines, as illustrated in Fig. 1(d), might create closed polygons, which are then filled. This is followed by subtracting the image I_2 from the original image I_1, yielding a seed image I_3, which retains some parts of the original cluster, as seen in Fig. 1(e). Since each segmented sub-region (seed) is now unique to a detected object in the cluster, these can then be conditionally dilated to form individual nuclear objects by means of a geodesic dilation operation, without merging, of the seed image I_3, inside the original image I_1 which acts as a mask. The dilation progresses with two restrictions, one being the mask extent of the original cluster and the other a logical operation that prevents pixels connected to different seeds from merging. The geodesic dilation of seed I_3 with respect to the mask I_1 is defined as $D_{(I_1)}(I_3) = (I_3 \oplus B) \cap I_1$, where $\oplus$ denotes the dilation of I_3 with the structure element B, and $\cap$ performs a pixel-wise logical AND (intersection) between the dilated image and the mask I_1. The final segmentation result is depicted in Fig. 1(f). The separation results of the watershed [2,3] and iterative split-line methods [7–9] are shown in Fig. 1(g) and (h), yielding under- and over- segmentation, respectively.

3　Experiments and Evaluation

Our proposed method was tested using four large monolayer images of H400 cells. A total of 2610 nuclei were hand-drawn by one of us to produce a gold-standard set, which was used to obtain another set of binary images.[3] Among these, a total of 497 nuclei formed 203 clusters with various degrees of complexity in their fused boundaries. Potential clusters were processed when their area was larger than 1600 pixels[2] and contained concavity points. The optimal range of parameter values were initially chosen before applying to the tested images. The optimal values of gap and $\check{O}$ depended on the geometry and size of the cluster, so they were tested at values of $\{5, 10, 15\}$ and $\{2, 3\}$, respectively. Those were the values that generated regions with the highest circularity and within the optimal nuclear area. The thresholds θ_1 and θ_2 were constrained to be larger than 20 and less than 20 pixels, respectively. The qualitative results shown in Fig. 2 (upper row) demonstrate the ability of our algorithm to resolve complex clusters (with four or more overlapping nuclei) while avoiding over- and under-segmentation. The procedure can generate contours close to actual nucleus boundaries. The lower rows of Fig. 2 show the superiority of our approach over the watershed separation, which generates spurious edges in some simple configurations.

---

[3] Hand-segmented nuclei regions were filled in white and the background in black. As a result, nuclei with overlapping boundaries will appear in clusters and the ones with separated boundaries will appear individually.

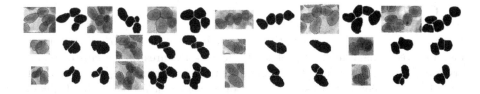

Fig. 2. First row: image pairs correspond to the gold-standard and the result of our splitting method. Second and third rows: triplets (left to right) show the gold-standard, our splitting method result and the watershed result.

Quantitative results (summarized in Table 1) were obtained using three different measures. Our segmentation result was compared visually with the gold-standard to estimate the *True Positive Rate* $TPR = \frac{TP}{TP+FN}$ and the *Positive Predictive Value* $PPV = \frac{TP}{TP+FP}$, where the True Positives (TP), False Positives (FP), and False Negatives (FN) are the numbers of correctly detected nuclei, incorrectly detected nuclei, and undetected nuclei, respectively. The third measure was given by the *Jaccard Index* (JI), which is defined as the ratio $JI = \frac{|\breve{G} \cap I|}{|\breve{G} \cup I|}$ between the pixel-counts of the intersection and union of the gold-standard segmented image $\breve{G}$ and the test segmentation I. The JI ranges from 0 (no overlap between the images) to 1 (complete congruence). Note that the line-of-sight 2D projections of the gold-standard images show inferred overlapping nuclear boundaries which cannot be separated and represented in a single binary image. The JI match of $\breve{G}$ and I is measured as follows. Using standard morphological operations we (i) extract the symmetric difference of the filled overlapping regions with respect to their filled intersections ('lenses') to generate a set of 'lunes'; (ii) separate the lunes into their component parts by a morphological erosion, (iii) apply a binary dilation without merging operation to the separated lune parts within a mask image (the merged filled nuclear profiles). The split-line generated in each of the lens-like regions approximates their medial-axis transform. Overall, the proposed method outperforms the classical watershed in terms of TPR, PPV and JI. During the experiments, we observed that the algorithm preserves the ellipticity of the reconstructed nuclear regions, and in particular it outperforms watershed segmentation in clusters that lack prominent 'necks'; it is, however, sensitive to the *gap* and $\breve{O}$ parameters.

Table 1. Quantitative results: performance evaluation of the proposed splitting method compared to the watershed method in terms of TPR, PPV and JI.

Segmentation algorithm	TPR	PPV	JI
The proposed model	0.98	0.98	0.74
The watershed model	0.95	0.97	0.69

4   Conclusion

We presented a novel mathematical morphology-based algorithm for separating clustered binary nuclear profiles. Concavity features of the cluster boundary are extracted and guide the subsequent region-splitting steps. Optimal split boundaries are computed using a series of morphological operations. Unlike in iterative split-line models, our non-iterative algorithm provides separation while avoiding over-segmentation. Qualitative and quantitative results tested on hand-segmented datasets of images of H400 cells verify that the segmentation accuracy of the proposed method outperforms the watershed separation approach.

Acknowledgments. The research reported in this paper was supported by the Engineering and Physical Sciences Research Council (EPSRC), UK through funding under grant EP/M023869/1 "Novel context-based segmentation algorithms for intelligent microscopy".

References

1. Irshad, H., Veillard, A., Roux, L., Racoceanu, D.: Methods for nuclei detection, segmentation, and classification in digital histopathology: a review-current status and future potential. Biomed. Eng. **7**, 97–114 (2014)
2. Beucher, S., Lantuejoul, C.: Use of watersheds in contour detection. In: Proceedings of the International Workshop on Image Processing, Real-Time Edge and Motion Detection/Estimation, CCETT/IRISA, pp. 17–21 (1979)
3. Gran, V., Mewes, A.U.J., Alcaniz, M., Kikinis, R., Warfield, S.K.: Improved watershed transform for medical image segmentation using prior information. IEEE Trans. Med. Imag. **23**(4), 447–458 (2004)
4. Bai, X., Sun, C., Zhou, F.: Splitting touching cells based on concave points and ellipse fitting. Pattern Recog. **42**(11), 2434–2446 (2009)
5. Plissiti, M.E., Louka, E., Nikou, C.: Splitting of overlapping nuclei guided by robust combinations of concavity points. In: SPIE 9034, Medical Imaging 2014: Image Processing, 903431 (2014)
6. Zafari, S., Eerola, T., Sampo, J., Kalviainen, H., Haario, H.: Segmentation of overlapping elliptical objects in silhouette images. IEEE Trans. Image Process. **24**(12), 5942–5952 (2015)

7. Fatakdawala, H., Basavanhally, A., Jun, X., Bhanot, G., Ganesan, S., Feldman, M., Tomaszewski, J., Madabhushi, A.: Expectation maximization driven geodesic active contour with overlap resolution (EMaGACOR): application to lymphocyte segmentation on breast cancer histopathology. In: Ninth IEEE International Conference on Bioinformatics and BioEngineering, pp. 69–76 (2009)

8. Kong, H., Gurcan, M., Belkacem-Boussaid, K.: Partitioning histopathological images: an integrated framework for supervised color-texture segmentation and cell splitting. IEEE Trans. Med. Imaging **30**(9), 1661–1677 (2011)

9. Latorre, A., Alonso-Nanclares, L., Muelas, S., Peña, J.M., Defelipe, J.: Segmentation of neuronal nuclei based on clump splitting and a two-step binarization of images. Expert Syst. Appl. **40**(16), 6521–6530 (2013)

10. Rasband, W.S. (1997-2016) ImageJ, U.S. National Institutes ofHealth, Bethesda, Maryland, USA. http://imagej.nih.gov/ij/

11. Pratt, V.: Direct least-squares fitting of algebraic surfaces. In: Stone, M.C. (ed.) 14th Annual Conference on Computer Graphics and Interactive Techniques, pp. 145–152. ACM, New York (1987)

12. Dougherty, E.: Mathematical Morphology in Image Processing. CRC Press, Boca Raton (1992)

Fitting of Breast Data Using Free Form Deformation Technique

Hooshiar Zolfagharnasab[✉], Jaime S. Cardoso, and Hélder P. Oliveira

INESC TEC and Faculdade de Engenheira, Universidade do Porto, Porto, Portugal
{hzab,jaime.cardoso,helder.f.oliveira}@inesctec.pt
http://www.inesctec.pt/

Abstract. Nowadays, breast cancer has become the most common cancer amongst females. As long as breast is assumed to be a feminine symbol, any imposed deformation of surgical procedures can affect the patients' quality of life. However, using a planning tool which is based on parametric modeling, not only improves surgeons' skills in order to perform surgeries with better cosmetic outcomes, but also increases the interaction between surgeons and patients during the decision for necessary procedures. In the current research, a methodology of parametric modeling, called Free-Form Deformation (FFD) is studied. Finally, confirmed by a quantitative analysis, we proposed two simplified versions of FFD methodology to increase model similarity to input data and decrease required fitting time.

Keywords: Parametric modeling · Free-form deformation · Breast cancer · Planing tool

1 Introduction

Accounting for almost 29 % of all newly diagnosed cancers in 2015 (excluding cancers of the skin), breast cancer is the most frequent cancer among women [1]. Since surgery is performed as the most common treatment, breast deformation is taken place consequently due to tissue removal. It is clear that the imposed breast deformation is strongly dependent upon the amount of removed tissue. Normally, two types of surgeries are considered: mastectomy in which the whole breast is removed, and lumpectomy, also called as Breast Cancer Conservative Treatment (BCCT), in which the tumor together with a thin layer of healthy surrounding tissue are removed [2]. Despite differences between the amount of removed tissue, survival rate of both surgeries are almost the same; therefore, since BCCT

H. Zolfagharnasab—This work was funded by the Project "NanoSTIMA: Macro–to–Nano Human Sensing: Towards Integrated Multimodal Health Monitoring and Analytics/NORTE–01–0145–FEDER–000016" financed by the North Portugal Regional Operational Programme (NORTE 2020), under the PORTUGAL 2020 Partnership Agreement, and through the European Regional Development Fund (ERDF), and also by Fundação para a Ciência e a Tecnologia (FCT) within PhD grant number SFRH/BD/97698/2013.

A. Campilho and F. Karray (Eds.): ICIAR 2016, LNCS 9730, pp. 608–615, 2016.
DOI: 10.1007/978-3-319-41501-7_68

requires less tissue to be removed, final aesthetic outcome is expected to be more satisfactory to the patients [3].

Not only the success of a surgery, but also the satisfactory aesthetic outcome is assumed to be important in a patient's point of view. Therefore, providing a tool to increase the interaction between patients and surgeons can be an interesting framework to assist surgeons in planning surgeries with better cosmetic outcomes. As the aforementioned tool is equipped to use mathematical formulated models, it can generate different post-surgical breast shapes. Free-Form Deformation (FFD), is an example of the approaches used in parametric modeling; however, it has not generally been used for breast data. In this paper, a comparative study is presented to apply the FFD methodology in 3D breast data. Our principal contribution is focused on simplifying FFD methodology to produce better fitting results, in meaningful time. It should be noted that the original FFD designed to be used in closed objects, which is not the case of the data that we are using.

2   Related Works

Parametric modeling is the process of transforming specific data to mathematical models; however, in the mathematical scope, it is called fitting instead of modeling. The method proposed by Ruiz et al. [4] is an example that creates a fitted surface to the input data by satisfying the Nyquist-Shannon criteria. Then, the minimization problem (which is defined based on the residual distance between the surface and the input data) is solved by the Gauss-Newton iterative method to approach the surface to the data iteratively. Highlighting the application of parametric modeling of human body, Weiss et al. [5] fitted the parameters of SPACE (Shape Completion and Animation for PEople) predefined models to depth data and image silhouettes of human body. In their work, they fitted each scanned body data to the closest predefined model.

The idea of using parametric models for breast surgery planning purposes was inspired from the research carried out by Oliveira et al. [6], in which they benefited from Three-Dimensional (3D) models acquired with a low-cost device instead of the most common used Two-Dimensional (2D) HD images, to assess breast aesthetic outcome after BCCT. Now, the idea behind the presented work in this paper is to develop a parametric model to be incorporated in a planning tool based on 3D information.

In the following, more detail of the FFD approach, that is the basis of this work will be presented, using the work of Bardinet et al. [7].

2.1   Free-Form Deformation

The methodology proposed in [7] uses an algorithm to perform parametric fitting in two steps. In the first step, it fits a superquadratic to input data by changing parameters of the superellipsoid in order to minimize the Euclidean distance (also called error distance) between the input data and the superellipsoid.

Since there might not be a specific set of parameters to fit the quadric model to the data completely, such a problem can be categorized as a least-square issue. The second step is proceeded by initiating a 3D parallelepipedic grid of points, called grid of control points, that surrounds the fitted superellipsoid (Fig. 1).

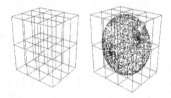

Fig. 1. Left: Superellipsoid surrounded by control grid, Right: Control grid

The dimensions and orientation of the grid are defined by radial parameters of the superellipsoid. Containing $(l + 1)(m + 1)(n + 1)$ points, the grid is linked to the fitted superellipsoid using a tensor product of tri-variants Bernstein's polynomials:

$$X = \sum_{i=0}^{l}\sum_{j=0}^{m}\sum_{k=0}^{n} C_l^i C_m^j C_n^k (1 - s)^{l-i} s^i (1 - t)^{m-j} t^j .(1 - u)^{n-k} u^k P_{ijk} \qquad (1)$$

The parametric model is defined as X, and P is a matrix containing the points of the control grid. Besides, s, t, and u are used to denote local coordinate of each model point regarding to its corresponding control point. Compacting the summations, Eq. 1 can be rewritten, as:

$$X = BP \qquad (2)$$

where B is called the deformation matrix. Considering δX as the displacement field between input data and superellipsoid, Eq. 2 can be rewritten regarding to linear equation system:

$$\delta X = B\delta P \qquad (3)$$

The superellipsoid is then deformed through relocating the control points of the grid. Within iterative steps, the points on the superellipsoid are approached to the input data by solving the following minimization equation:

$$min_p ||BP - X||^2 := min_{\delta P} ||B\delta P - \delta X||^2 + \alpha \sum_{j=1}^{NP}\sum_{j'} ||P_j - P_{j'}||^2 \qquad (4)$$

In the second term, j' corresponds to the neighbors of P in the position of j and NP stands for the number of control points. In other words, the second term is an internal energy corresponding to the insertion of a zero-length springs between control points, that is being regularized by the weight of α. The equation can be solved using Singular Value Decomposition (SVD) of the matrix B.

3   Moving Towards Better and Faster Breast Fitting Using FFD

A preliminary analysis of the FFD approach (Sect. 2.1) on 3D data which contain an open side demonstrated a disadvantage. An issue called Redundant Bent Layer (RBL) affected the performance of modeling negatively by increasing distance amongst the model and input data. The misalignments of the RBL points (depicted in Fig. 2) is the main reason of the decrease in the similarity between parametric model and input data. RBL occurs when both closed sides of the initial model (both hemispheres of the fitted superellipsoid) are pulled to the closed side of breast data. Since the control points are arranged in a 3D formation, the two pulled sides of the initial model cannot be overlaid completely. Therefore, a gap is imposed between two sides of deformed model. This gap is responsible for producing wrong fitted surface which increases the distance between parametric model and input data. In order to eliminate the RBL on the parametric model, two solutions can be taken into consideration by modifying either the initial model, or the arrangement of the control points.

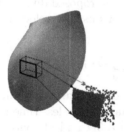

Fig. 2. Cross section view of a parametric model of a breast using algorithm of [7]: Segmentation of the cube will result in a part of breast model together RBL which is located in back of the modeled breast.

3.1   Modifying the Initial Model

The Achilles heel of the RBL is the definition of the initial model; therefore, replacing it with an open-sided object could overcome the issue. Two initial models are proposed in this paper: a finite boundary plane and a superquadric model based on a superparaboloid similar to the one proposed in [8].

The first solution suggests in using a finite boundary plane to fulfills both the requirements of using an open-sidedness and flexibility (in any direction) whilst the second solution suggests using a superparaboloid which was previously introduced in [8]. It not only aims to satisfy the requirement of open-sidedness of the initial model, but also performs the fitting process with less iterations, since the primitive shape is similar to the objects (breast) to fit. Finally, it is recommended to set up both suggested initial models to be orthogonal to the largest principle direction of data. This assures that the model is initiated in a correct place where can overlay the input data completely. For this purpose we used a Principle Component Analysis (PCA) approach.

3.2   Modifying the Arrangement of Control Points

Previously discussed, the FFD carries out the deformation of the initial model by relocating the control points. In [7], it was suggested to use control points arranged in a 3D grid. As discussed before, referring to an open-side breast data, the control points located in the open-side of the model provide a circumstance in which RBL has emerged. Additionally, their participation in the calculating new location of model points imposes additional computation (and time) costs to the algorithm. Therefore, we propose to remove ineffective control points by reducing the dimensions of the control grid from 3D to 2D.

Dimension reduction should be carried out with regard to the presentation of input data. In other words, the dimension in which less data is presented, can be a suitable candidate to be removed. Common methodologies to perform PCA can lead to obtain the best removal candidate. Assuming the third dimension as the candidate of removal, the proposed dimension reduction of control points simplifies the nested summations used to relocate control points in Eq. 1:

$$X_{new} = \sum_{i=0}^{l} \sum_{j=0}^{m} C_l^i C_m^j (1-s)^{l-i} s^i (1-t)^{m-j} t^j . P_{ij} \tag{5}$$

X_{new} denotes the points of the parametric model. The less control points are considered in the computation, the less time is required for fitting. Figure 3 shows the difference between a 3D grid of control points (originally suggested by the authors in [7]) and proposed 2D grid.

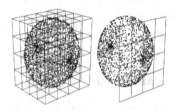

Fig. 3. Left: 3D cube of control points, Right: 2D grid of control points with initial model of superellipsoid. The dimension which is removed has been identified by PCA to contain less presented data.

4   Implementation and Results

The original methodology discussed in [7] together with proposed methodologies were implemented using C++ and Mathworks Matlab R2015a respectively, and evaluated on a 3.40 GHz machine equipped with 8 GB of memory.

The iterative modality of the studied algorithms, requires to define a stop criterion. Such criterion is defined in relation to the Euclidean distance between the models being generated in each two consecutive steps. Furthermore, as far as the average distance between two consecutive generated model exceeds 1.50 mm, the algorithm continues iterative fitting.

Two metrics are considered for the evaluation of the explained methodologies; distance error and computation time. Distance error stands for the average of Euclidean distance between the input data and the generated parametric model. Not only Euclidean, but also Hausdorff distance is calculated. The smaller the distance error is, the more similar the two sets will be. Besides, the computation time is also a key advantage in comparisons. Expectedly, faster methodologies are more preferable.

The evaluated dataset includes 70 breast models. Each 3D model in the dataset was obtained by scanning a patient with Microsoft Kinect, and reconstructing it via the 3D reconstruction algorithm proposed in [9]. Table 1 presents the results obtained by the different methodologies in terms of average fitting errors (Euclidean and Hausdorff) together with standard deviation. It is important to notice that bi-directional distances (from model to data and from data to model) are reported, since there might be differences in the quantity of points between the two comparing pointclouds. Also, the average number of required iterations to reach to stop criterion are reported. Inasmuch as superparaboloid methodologies have been implemented in a different compiler, time comparison cannot lead to mere deduction; however, comparison can be carried out with respect to the number of iterations, since it is compiler independent. Beside the numerical analysis, visual comparisons are depicted in Fig. 4.

The smallest average Euclidean error from parametric model to input data was 1.21 mm which is obtained by the superellipsoid and a 2D FFD. The methodology of using a plane with a 2D FFD takes the second rank with average Euclidean error of 1.25 mm, and finally the superellipsoid with 3D FFD stands in the third rank by obtaining an error of 1.31 mm. With respect to the error from input data to model, the smallest distance error was obtained by using methodology of superellipsoid deformed by a 3D FFD with an error of 1.70 mm. And in the following rank, superparaboloid deformed by 3D FFD, stands with the error of 2.28 mm. Third rank belongs to the methodology which uses a superellipsoid and a 2D FFD presenting an error of 2.71 mm. A brief look to the Table 1 and the requirements of the fitting stage reveals that the methodologies based on FFD superellipsoid and plane generate more precise parametric models than superparaboloid. Considering Model to Ground-truth Euclidean distance, the suggested improvement of 2D arrangement of control points surpasses other method since it eliminates the RBL phenomena. With a small gap, the methodology of using plane with 2D FFD stands in the second rank since using plane as the

Table 1. Reported results to compare proposed methodologies of FFD

	Methodology		Euclidean (M→GT) (mm)	Euclidean (GT→M) (mm)	Hausdorff (M→GT) (mm)	Hausdorff (GT→M) (mm)	Time (s)	Mean No. Itr
MATLAB	Superparaboloid + FFD (3D)	μ	1.57	2.28	11.02	26.28	1955	3.60
		σ	0.25	0.48	3.93	7.84	273	
	Superparaboloid + FFD (2D)	μ	1.60	3.03	7.14	29.62	324	10.42
		σ	0.25	0.81	1.76	7.62	41	
C++	Superellipsoid + FFD (3D)	μ	**1.31**	1.70	7.63	13.43	3001	10.42
		σ	0.08	0.25	1.52	4.83	1445	
	Superellipsoid + FFD (2D)	μ	**1.21**	2.71	5.62	24.27	64	5.33
		σ	0.11	0.52	1.33	7.49	21	
	Plane (2D) + FFD (2D)	μ	**1.25**	2.78	6.27	23.67	45	3.83
		σ	0.11	0.52	1.71	8.23	24	

initial model cannot present the boundaries of breast better than superellipsoid. On the other hand, methodologies using superparaboloid generate parametric models with more distance errors. Although using predefined initial model can accelerate the convergence, the shrinkage of the parametric model in the boundaries emerges additional distance error. Such shrinkage is visible in generated models depicted in Fig. 4-e and f. Also, investigating the arrangement of the control points admits the advantage of using 2D grid instead of 3D. Eliminating increscent control points leads to both the increase of the efficiency of remained control points and decreasing time complexity of algorithm. Additionally, the proposed improvement presented in this paper demonstrated smaller error in comparison to the original methodology and also in fitting time.

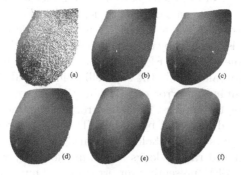

Fig. 4. Visual comparison of performed experiments on same input data; (a) original patient breast; (b) Plane + FFD (2D); (c) Superellipsoid + FFD (2D); (d) Superellipsoid + FFD (3D); (e) Superparaboloid + FFD (2D); (f) Superparaboloid + FFD (3D)

5 Conclusion

Put all together, parametric modeling is a technique which converts input data into a mathematical model. Mentioning the importance of a parametric modeling in a planning tool, methodologies of FFD have been studied in this paper and two improvements were proposed to enhance it; improvement of the initial model and modification of control points arrangements. Quantitative analysis indicated the proposed approach improves the performance of FFD methodology by decreasing the average distance error. Visual analysis accompanied with quantitative results indicate that the proposed methodologies suffer from model shrinkage in the boundaries. Since the mentioned shrinkage is responsible for the increase of distance between input data and model, possible future work will be concentrated to generate parametric models with less shrinkage which leads to less distance error.

References

1. American Cancer Society: Breast cancer facts and figures 2015–2016. In: American Cancer Society (ACS) (2015)
2. Oliveira, H.P., Cardoso, J.S., Magalhães, A., Cardoso, M.J.: Methods for the aesthetic evaluation of breast cancer conservation treatment: a technological review. Current Med. Imaging Rev. 9(1), 32–46 (2013)
3. Cardoso, M.J., Oliveira, H., Cardoso, J.: Assessing cosmetic results after breast conserving surgery. J. Surg. Oncol. 110(1), 37–44 (2014)
4. Ruiz, O., Arroyave, S., Acosta, D.: Fitting of analytic surfaces to noisy point clouds. Am. J. Comput. Math. 3(1), 18–26 (2013)
5. Weiss, A., Hirshberg, D., Black, M.J.: Home 3D body scans from noisy image and range data. In: IEEE International Conference on Computer Vision, pp. 1951–1958 (2011)
6. Oliveira, H.P., Cardoso, J.S., Magalhaes, A.T., Cardoso, M.J.: A 3D low-cost solution for the aesthetic evaluation of breast cancer conservative treatment. Comput. Methods Biomech. Biomed. Eng. Imaging Vis. 2(2), 90–106 (2014)
7. Bardinet, E., Cohen, L.D., Ayache, N., Smith, S., Siebert, J.P., Oehler, S., Ju, X., Ray, A.K.: A parametric deformable model to fit unstructured 3D data. Comput. Vis. Image Underst. 71(1), 39–54 (1998)
8. Pernes, D., Cardoso, J.S., Oliveira, H.P.: Fitting of superquadrics for breast modelling by geometric distance minimization. In: 8th IEEE International Conference on Bioinformatics and Biomedicine, pp. 293–296 (2014)
9. Costa, P., Monteiro, J.P., Zolfagharnasab, H., Oliveira, H.P.: Tessellation-based coarse registration method for 3D reconstruction of the female torso. In: 8th IEEE International Conference on Bioinformatics and Biomedicine, pp. 301–306 (2014)

Domain Adaptive Classification for Compensating Variability in Histopathological Whole Slide Images

Michael Gadermayr[1](✉), Martin Strauch[1], Barbara Mara Klinkhammer[2],
Sonja Djudjaj[2], Peter Boor[2], and Dorit Merhof[1]

[1] Aachen Center for Biomedical Image Analysis, Visualization and Exploration
(ACTIVE), Institute of Imaging and Computer Vision,
RWTH Aachen University, Aachen, Germany
michael.gadermayr@lfb.rwth-aachen.de

[2] Institute of Pathology, University Hospital Aachen, RWTH Aachen University,
Aachen, Germany

Abstract. Histopathological whole slide images of the same organ stained with the same dye exhibit substantial inter-slide variation due to the manual preparation and staining process as well as due to inter-individual variability. In order to improve the generalization ability of a classification model on data from kidney pathology, we investigate a domain adaptation approach where a classifier trained on data from the source domain is presented a small number of user-labeled samples from the target domain. Domain adaptation resulted in improved classification performance, especially when combined with an interactive labeling procedure.

1 Motivation

Clinical routine and research in pathology require to annotate large numbers of microscopic images from whole slide scanners. Here, we focus on an application scenario from kidney pathology where the objects of interest are the so-called glomeruli (Fig. 1) that are responsible for blood filtration. Automated classification of image patches to detect the presence of a glomerulus would facilitate the work of pathologists who currently count and segment glomeruli manually for diagnostic as well as research purposes.

However, variations, such as different staining intensity and thickness of the kidney slices lead to qualitative differences between whole slide images (Fig. 1), even if all images show kidneys stained with the same dye and originating from the same scanner. As these variations have effects on color, texture and morphology [1], they can reduce the generalization ability of a classifier trained on a source domain image to a target domain image. Although variability in color can be compensated by means of stain-normalization [2], variations concerning texture and morphology cannot be compensated effectively. Recently, supervised approaches for glomerulus detection based on HOG features [3] as well

© Springer International Publishing Switzerland 2016
A. Campilho and F. Karray (Eds.): ICIAR 2016, LNCS 9730, pp. 616–622, 2016.
DOI: 10.1007/978-3-319-41501-7_69

as several color and texture features [4] have been proposed. These approaches assume, however, similar feature distributions for source (training data) and target domain images.

Here, we explore the application of domain adaptation [5,6] to the task of discriminating between glomerulus and non-glomerulus regions (patches) in whole slide images. Domain adaptation generally addresses the problem of varying marginal distributions of the samples in the source domain and the target domain, which is referred to as domain change. The goal is to adapt the source to the target domain distribution which can be performed on classifier or image representation level [5].

Pathological cases can exhibit strong differences with respect to the normal case [1]. This study focuses on domain changes in non-pathological cases as they can occur due to changes in recording parameters [5,6]. Although considerable effort is spent on keeping the recording parameters constant, manual sample preparation leads to inter-slide variations that can be considered as domain changes.

We specifically focus on the efficient representation-level domain adaptation technique proposed in [6] that allows interactive labeling, aiming to quantify the impact of the active-learning component. Interactiveness in this context means that the target domain label data is acquired selectively during the domain adaptation process. This can be performed effectively in the considered application scenario as label data is per se not available beforehand for a new whole slide image and have to be acquired interactively. For image representation, the focus is on efficient and discriminative texture descriptors [3,7,8] which are robust to illumination changes [9] and color intensity.

In our experiments, domain adaptation by allowing the user to label a small number of image patches from the target domain greatly improved classification accuracy with respect to learning on source or target domain data alone. Whereas non-interactive domain adaptation delivered only slight improvements, superior outcomes were obtained with the interactive labeling scheme where the user is presented target domain samples for which the label is most uncertain.

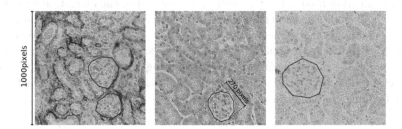

Fig. 1. Patches from histopathological whole slide images of a mouse kidney exhibiting the typical variability between experiments. The glomeruli are outlined in red. (Color figure online)

2   Experimental Study

In this experimental study, the focus is on the discrimination between glomerulus and non-glomerulus patches in whole slide image data [3,4]. In the mammalian kidney, the glomerulus is the first segment of a nephron, a microscopical functional unit of the kidney. The glomerulus consists of a tuft of small blood vessels (capillaries), where blood is filtered and urine is produced. Several kidney diseases affect and damage the glomeruli, which results in a loss of the filter function. The diagnosis, and thereby the decision on adequate treatment is currently based on renal biopsies. Due to clinical needs there is a strong research focus on renal diseases and specifically on the analysis of glomerular damage. In both biopsies of human patients and kidney tissue of experimental animals, identification (and counting) of glomeruli is an essential first step in histopathological analysis. Since such manual identification and quantification of morphological glomerular alterations is extremely time consuming, supporting automated glomeruli detection would extremely facilitate the analyses of glomerular diseases in both clinical and experimental settings.

2.1   Domain Adaptive Classification

We investigated an interactive domain adaptation approach [6] which is based on three repetitive stages: *query+*, *reweighting* and *query-*. Prior to each iteration, the classification model is trained based on the available labeled training data. The aim of the *query+* stage is to select new (target domain) data which, when correctly labeled, helps to improve the classifier's decision boundaries. The authors proposed a criterion based on uncertainty (i.e. the distance between a data point and the decision boundary) and diversity. Specifically, the u most uncertain target domain samples are clustered into k clusters. Finally, the most uncertain sample per cluster is selected to be manually classified by the user. In the *reweighting* stage, the source domain feature weights are adjusted according to their fit with the new data based on the mean cosine-angle similarity [6]. In order to remove misleading data, source domain training samples which are misclassified by the current classification model, are removed (*query-* stage) in each iteration and are no longer considered. Although the proposed method contains an (interactive) active learning component (specifically the *query+* stage), the method can also be effectively utilized in a non-interactive way by adding randomly selected samples in the *query+* stage instead of specific ones. By evaluating this method with and without interaction, not only the effect of domain adaptation, but also the impact of the active learning component can be estimated.

2.2   Image Representations

The effectiveness of texture classification strongly depends on image representation. Therefore, three different well known image representations from the literature were applied, namely Histograms of Oriented Gradients [3] (HOG), Multi-resolution Local Binary Patterns [7] (LBP) and Fisher Vectors [8] (FV).

In case of HOG, the RHOG derivative [3], which is based on concatenation of several single histograms, was applied. LBP was deployed with the standard circular eight pixel neighborhood with a radius of one and two pixels. FV were combined with SIFT low level features, sampled densely at each third pixel position. All methods were applied separately to the three color channels. Finally, the feature vectors were L^2 normalized.

2.3 Image Data

The whole slide images were obtained from resected mice kidneys which show high similarities to human ones. Kidneys were fixed in methyl Carnoy's solution and embedded in paraffin, 1-μm sections were stained and processed as previously described [10]. Immunohistochemistry against α-SMA (alpha smooth muscle actin) was performed using a mouse-anti-α-SMA antibody (clone 1A4, Dako). Nuclei were counterstained with methyl green. Whole slides were digitalized with a NanoZoomer 2.0HT digital slide scanner (Hamamatsu) and a 20× objective lens. Image data is collected from eight whole slide images (with 53248 × 40704 pixels) of non-pathologic tissue exhibiting distinct inter-slide variability as shown in Fig. 1.

2.4 Evaluation Protocol

In order to eliminate bias due to unbalanced class distributions as well as further post-processing, in this study we focus on the classification task (of extracted image patches) instead of the detection task (of glomeruli on a whole slide image). The classification accuracy obtained with balanced training data indicates how well detection can be performed without having to deal with biases. Consequently, from each whole slide image one distinct data set consisting of two classes (glomerulus and non-glomerulus patches) is built. Overall, eight data sets (one per whole slide image) are created where each data set consists of between 100 and 150 glomerulus patches (the number is limited by the number of glomeruli) as well as exactly 1000 non-glomerulus patches.

The classification policy allows a repeated selection of splits (consisting of training and evaluation subsets) to increase the validity. Two different experiments are performed. The first one (Exp$_1$) is based on training data from one single whole slide image (i.e. one data set) and evaluation is performed on another data set. In this case, in one random split 100 images (50 per class) are used for training, 50 (25 per class) for adaptation and 50 (25 per class) for evaluation. The second experiment (Exp$_2$) is based on a large training data set from seven different whole slide images (leaving only the evaluation data set out). In that case, 700 patches are utilized for training in each individual random split, and again 50 are selected for adaptation and 50 for evaluation. As training and evaluation sets are always distinct, there is no need for any further restriction to avoid biases. Experiments are repeated for all combinations of training and evaluation sets (Exp$_1$) and for the eight different evaluation sets (Exp$_2$), respectively. Finally, mean classification accuracies and standard deviations are reported.

For classification, the efficient linear C-SVM is utilized in order to keep execution time low and thereby to avoid waiting periods during interaction. The classifier's c-value as well as the parameters u and k are evaluated during cross-validation. Runtime measurements are performed on an Intel Core i7-6700K architecture with 4.00 GHz clock frequency. The method is implemented in Matlab/MEX based on parallel processing.

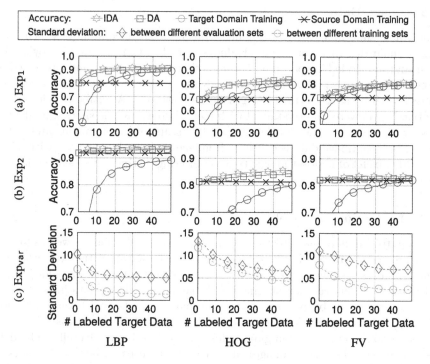

Fig. 2. Mean accuracies for training based on one data set (Exp$_1$) and based on all available training data (Exp$_2$) and standard deviations with varying training data (Exp$_{var}$).

2.5   Results

In Fig. 2, the obtained accuracies for Exp$_1$ (a), Exp$_2$ (b) as well as the standard deviations (c) for Exp$_1$ are illustrated. Figure 2(a) shows the results of Exp$_1$ for variable amounts of labeled target domain data (horizontal axis) and for the different classifier trainings (see legend). Considering all three image representations (LBP, HOG, FV; see Sect. 2.2), distinct and consistent improvements were obtained with interactive domain adaptation (IDA). Improvements with non-interactive domain adaptation (DA) were slightly lower, especially if little target domain data was available. Training with target domain data alone required much more labeled data to achieve reasonable outcomes, and the classification rates of IDA could not be reached even with 50 labeled images. Considering the different image representations, LBP performed best, resulting in a maximum accuracy above 90%. With 10 labeled images, the average accuracy of LBP increased from 80% to 90%. Similar improvements by labeling could be obtained with the other image representations.

In Fig. 2(b), the results of Exp_2 are presented. In case of the more diverse training data (Exp_2), outcomes could be generally improved. Nevertheless, IDA based on few labeled target domain images still led to enhancements in combination with all image representations. DA only slightly improved the outcomes in this setting.

Figure 2(c) shows the standard deviations of accuracies based on different evaluation sets (upper data points) and based on different training data sets (lower data points) in case of IDA (from Exp_1). It can be observed that both standard deviations noticeably decreased with increasing labeled target domain data. This was especially the case for the deviation of different training data sets. If sufficient target domain data was available (approx. 15 samples in case of LBP), variations due to the source domain training data almost disappeared.

The computation time in case of seven training data sets (corresponding to Exp_2) for one interactive iteration was between 0.15 and 0.55 s (0.15 s with HOG, 0.23 s with LBP and 0.55 s with FV). Due to the smaller amount of training data, computation times were significantly lower for Exp_1.

3   Discussion and Conclusion

We investigated interactive and non-interactive domain adaptation for histopathological image classification and showed that especially interactive domain adaptation has a positive effect on the classification performance in both experimental settings. Regarding the three image representations, we noticed that LBP performed best on average. The impact of domain adaptation was especially pronounced in case of Exp_1 with little training data showing low variability. On training data with high variability (Exp_2), IDA still outperformed target domain training, however to a lesser extent. Comparing the outcomes of Exp_1 and Exp_2, we notice that a low variability in the training data (Exp_1) cannot be completely compensated by domain adaptation, as the by far best performances are obtained by combining IDA with highly variable training data.

The computational effort between two interactive steps was quite low (e.g. 0.23 s in case of LBP), which allows a continuous user interaction without any waiting periods.

In summary, we notice that especially the interactive domain adaptive classification approach can be effectively applied to histopathological whole slide images. While the user interactions lead to slightly increased time consumption compared to fully automated systems, this is compensated by improved classification accuracies that also reduce the time requirements for post-hoc correction of the results.

References

1. Fioretto, P., Mauer, M.: Histopathology of diabetic nephropathy. Semin. Nephrol. **27**(2), 195–207 (2007)
2. Macenko, M., Niethammer, M., Marron, J.S., Borland, D., Woosley, J.T., Guan,X., Schmitt, C., Thomas, N.E.: A method for normalizing histology slides for quantitative analysis. In: Proceedings of ISBI 2009, pp. 1107–1110 (2009)
3. Kato, T., Relator, R., Ngouv, H., Hirohashi, Y., Takaki, O., Kakimoto, T., Okada, K.: Segmental hog: new descriptor for glomerulus detection in kidneymicroscopy image. BMC Bioinform. **16**(1), 316 (2015)
4. Herve, N., Servais, A., Thervet, E., Olivo-Marin, J.C., Meas-Yedid, V.: Statistical color texture descriptors for histological images analysis. In: Proceedings of ISBI 2011, pp. 724–727 (2011)
5. Jhuo, I.H., Liu, D., Lee, D.T., Chang, S.F.: Robust visual domain adaptation with low-rank reconstruction. In: Proceedings of CVPR 2012
6. Persello, C.: Interactive domain adaptation for the classification of remote sensing images using active learning. IEEE Trans. Geosci. Remote Sens. **10**(4), 736–740 (2013)
7. Ojala, T., Pietikäinen, M., Mäenpää, T.: Multiresolution Gray-Scale and rotation invariant texture classification with local binary patterns. IEEE Trans. Pattern Anal. Mach. Intell. **24**(7), 971–987 (2002)
8. Sánchez, J., Perronnin, F., Mensink, T., Verbeek, J.J.: Image classification with the fisher vector: theory and practice. Int. J. Comput. Vis. **105**(3), 222–245 (2013)
9. Wang, J.G., Li, J., Yau, W.Y., Sung, E.: Boosting dense SIFT descriptors and shape contexts of face images for gender recognition. In: Proceedings of CVPR 2010, pp. 96–102 (2010)
10. Boor, P., Bábíčková, J., Steegh, F.: Role of platelet-derived growth factor-cc in capillary rarefaction in renal fibrosis. Am. J. Pathol. **185**(8), 2132–2142 (2015)

Comparison of Flow Cytometry and Image-Based Screening for Cell Cycle Analysis

Damian J. Matuszewski[1,2(✉)], Ida-Maria Sintorn[1,2], Jordi Carreras Puigvert[1,3], and Carolina Wählby[1,2]

[1] Science for Life Laboratory, Uppsala, Sweden
[2] Department of Information Technology, Centre for Image Analysis, Uppsala University, Uppsala, Sweden
`damian.matuszewski@it.uu.se`
[3] Division of Translational Medicine and Chemical Biology, Department of Medical Biochemistry and Biophysics, Karolinska Institutet, Stockholm, Sweden

Abstract. Quantitative cell state measurements can provide a wealth of information about mechanism of action of chemical compounds and gene functionality. Here we present a comparison of cell cycle disruption measurements from commonly used flow cytometry (generating one-dimensional signal data) and bioimaging (producing two-dimensional image data). Our results show high correlation between the two approaches indicating that image-based screening can be used as an alternative to flow cytometry. Furthermore, we discuss the benefits of image informatics over conventional single-signal flow cytometry.

Keywords: Quantitative microscopy · DNA content histogram

1 Introduction

Optical microscopy is one of the most widely used techniques in cell and tissue research. As every form of cytologic instrumentation it represents a compromise between information content, fluorescence sensitivity, and acquisition speed. Conventional fluorescence microscopy provides high content information for the cost of low acquisition speed. Development of precise robotics has resulted in the creation of automated image-based high-content screening (IBHCS) systems. These systems are capable of imaging multiple stains of large numbers of cell populations in a short period of time [1]. Given that the samples are typically placed in microwell plates, containing up to 1536 wells per plate, this represents a perfect setting for high-throughput approaches. Consequently, the bottleneck has moved to analyzing the images: extracting information and interpreting the vast amount of generated data.

On the other hand, commonly used flow cytometry (FC) constitutes the opposite trade-off, with much higher single cell throughput (in the range of tens of thousands of analyzed cells per second) and information content reduced to a single or a handful of signals per cell. In a typical FC experiment hundreds of

© Springer International Publishing Switzerland 2016
A. Campilho and F. Karray (Eds.): ICIAR 2016, LNCS 9730, pp. 623–630, 2016.
DOI: 10.1007/978-3-319-41501-7_70

thousands of cells are analyzed. This allows for analysis of cell populations and drawing robust conclusions about their distributions and dynamics. However, it does not allow for analyzing signal distributions or patterns within cells or how cells interact or spatially organize themselves. Additionally, despite the large analysis capacity per sample, numerous replicates require more preparation time, larger volumes, and higher initial cell numbers, thereby making FC an overall mid-throughput approach.

In this paper we present a comparative case study of two approaches for cell cycle analysis: FC and IBHCS. Similar image based approaches were presented in [2,3]. Here we quantitatively compare FC and IBHCS using automatic gate selection.

2   Materials and Methods

We used two different cell lines (lung cancer A549 and colon epithelial non-transformed CCD841) exposed to 5 different treatments: Dimethyl Sulfoxide (DMSO), Aphidicolin, Nocodazole, NaCl and Cisplatin. The cell lines were obtained from ATCC and maintained in Dulbecco's Modified Eagle Medium (Invitrogen) supplemented with 10 % fetal bovine serum (Invitrogen) and 1 % penicillin/streptomycin (Invitrogen), at 37 °C and 5 % CO_2. NaCl and Cisplatin formulated in 0.9 % NaCl were purchased from Hospira; Aphidicolin and Nocodazole were purchased from Sigma-Aldrich and dissolved in DMSO from Merck.

2.1   Image-Based Screening

An illustration of the workflow in the IBHCS is shown in Fig. 1A. A549 and CCD841 cells were seeded 24 h prior to exposure to the compounds at a density of 1000 and 2500 cells per well respectively in imaging 384-well plates (Falcon). The cells were then exposed to the vehicle (DMSO or NaCl), $0.16 \mu M$–$0.5 \mu M$ of Aphidicolin, $0.16 \mu M$–$0.5 \mu M$ of Nocodazole, and $1.6 \mu M$–$5 \mu M$ of Cisplatin for 24 h. Directly after, the cells were fixed in 4 % paraformaldehyde (PFA) in PBS (Santa Cruz) for 15 min, and 2 µg/ml Hoechst 33342 (Sigma-Aldrich) in Phosphate Buffered Saline (PBS) (Invitrogen) was added for 15 min to stain the DNA. Subsequently, the cells were imaged with an ImageXpress (Molecular Devices) high-throughput microscope. At this point, the sample preparation has typically taken approximately 3.5 h, with minimal volumes used given the microwell plate format. Next, CellProfiler [4] was used to segment the cell nuclei by Gaussian smoothing followed by Otsu thresholding and watershed segmentation to split clustered nuclei based on intensity. Too small and too large objects were excluded. This commonly used segmentation approach provided good results (see Fig. 2), unaffected by small illumination variations between images. No background correction was necessary as the illumination field was even in this dataset. Finally, the total DNA content (integrated intensity of the DNA stain) was measured per nucleus. The CellProfiler processing pipelines

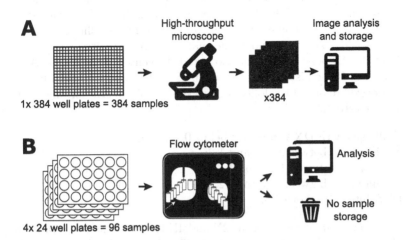

Fig. 1. Workflow diagram of the image-based screening (A) and flow cytometry (B).

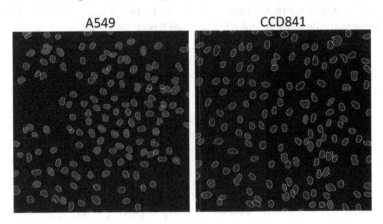

Fig. 2. Segmentation results for the negative controls of the two analyzed cell lines. White lines represent the outline of the cell segmentation results obtained with Cell-Profiler. The simple approach of Gaussian smoothing followed by Otsu thresholding and watershed segmentation gave satisfactory results.

(with all the parameters used) and sample images can be found at http://www.cb.uu.se/~damian/IBS-FC_comparison/.

The negative control histograms for DNA content analysis typically present two peaks that can be used to estimate the distribution of cells in different cell cycle phases, as shown in Fig. 3. The higher peak to the left (2N) corresponds to the normal amount of DNA, whereas the smaller peak to the right (4N) corresponds to the double amount of the DNA present in the nucleus after DNA replication during mitosis. The pooled histogram from all negative control wells for each cell line was analyzed to determine the integrated intensity values corresponding to the centers of the 2N and 4N sub-populations. These values were then applied as input parameters to define a search range for the exact 2N and 4N DNA peaks for each well and to normalize DNA intensity, such that the maximum of the 2N peak corresponds to 1 and the center of the 4N DNA peak corresponds to 2. If the histogram is normalized in this way, the individual cells can be categorized to one of the following five sub-populations according to DNA content as suggested in [3]:

- sub-2N all cells with DNA intensity below 0.75,
- 2N DNA intensity between 0.75 and 1.25,
- S DNA intensity between 1.25 and 1.75,
- 4N DNA intensity between 1.75 and 2.5,
- >4N DNA intensity above 2.5.

In order to avoid multiple peaks at 2N and 4N locations the histograms were smoothed with a Gaussian filter ($\sigma = 1.5$). The data analysis described here was performed with PopulationProfiler, a light-weight screening data analysis tool developed at Centre for Image Analysis, Uppsala University [5]. The DNA content measurements and the software are freely available [6].

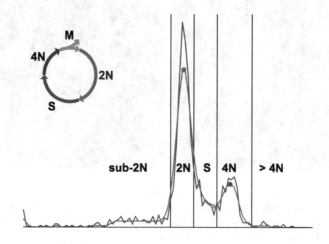

Fig. 3. Identification of the cell cycle sub-populations based on DNA content. The blue and red lines show data before and after smoothing, respectively. The red, blue and green dots on the histogram mark respectively the 2N peak, the 4N peak and the local minimum between them. The circular diagram in the top left corner illustrates transitions between the cell cycle phases: 2N (Gap 1), S (DNA synthesis), 4N (Gap 2) and M (Mitosis). (Color figure online)

2.2 Flow Cytometry

An illustration of the FC workflow is shown in Fig. 1B. FC collects single cell measurements in real time, as compared to IBHCS where image analysis has to be applied after the data has been collected. A549 and CCD841 cells were seeded in 24 well plates (Greiner) at a density of 50.000 and 75.000 cells per well, respectively. After 24 h, the cells were exposed to the corresponding concentrations of the aforementioned compounds for 24 h. Next, the cells were trypsinized, collected into 1.5 ml Eppendorf tubes to be pelleted by centrifugation, and washed once with PBS. Subsequently the cells were lysed in Vindelv's PI solution containing propidium iodide (PI), Tris, NaCl, Tergitol-type NP-40 and RNase (all from Sigma-Aldrich). The cells were then incubated for 1 h at 4 °C in the dark, to allow for the staining of the DNA, and subsequently analyzed by FC using a Beckman Coulter Navios. At this point, the sample preparation and analysis has typically taken 5 to 6 h. In the case of a FC capable of analyzing samples in 96 well plate format this time may be shorter. The analysis of the data was done with the Beckman Coulter Kaluza software. It is to be noted at this point that this procedure is intended to maintain the nuclei intact, and it is to be emphasized that after the described steps, there is a large loss of cells mainly due to the trypsinization and washing steps. Upon initial acquisition of the samples, a size exclusion gating was applied to ensure single cell population measurements by excluding cell debris and cell doublets. Next, gates corresponding to different cell cycle phases were set using the negative control (DMSO) as reference. The gates were left unaltered for the rest of the samples.

3   Results

Figure 4A presents a table with Pearson's correlation coefficients between normalized cell cycle subpopulation distribution vectors found with IBHCS and FC. Each value corresponds to a crosswise pair of different drug-dose combinations. Figure 4B and C show tables with corresponding calculations but in these cases comparing results within IBHCS and FC respectively. For print clarity Fig. 4 shows results for pooled data from multiple runs of the same experiments. There were two replicates for each drug-dose combination in FC and three in IBHCS. Similar results were obtained when individual experiment runs were investigated. Figure 5 shows the mean contribution of the three main cell cycle subpopulations (2N, S and 4N) measured in % with the two methods.

For each table in Fig. 4, the background color is scaled so that white corresponds to low correlation and dark red to high. A characteristic "cross" pattern corresponding to low correlation caused by high response to Nocodazole (a drug affecting cell cycle by arresting cells in the 4N phase) is visible in all three tables. This demonstrates that both approaches provide similar results and can be successfully used for cell cycle analysis. The diagonal in Fig. 4A presents the Pearson's correlation coefficient between corresponding drug-dose combinations as outcomes from the two analysis approaches. In most cases it is above 90 %. The lowest correlation on the diagonal is observed for the two doses of Nocodazole. This corresponds to the biggest differences between IBHCS and FC percentages of 4N subpopulations in Fig. 5. We believe the cause for this is the very low cell count in IBHCS (below 400 for this particular treatment). For all

A FLOW CYTOMETRY

IMAGE-BASED SCREENING	No Cells	DMSO	Noc 0.16	Noc 0.5	Aph 0.16	Aph 0.5	NaCl	Cisplatin 1.6	Cisplatin 5
DMSO-Noc	2449	0.97	0.01	0.07	0.90	0.62	0.97	0.93	0.56
DMSO-Aph	4108	0.98	-0.01	0.04	0.92	0.64	0.98	0.94	0.58
Noc 0.16	353	0.13	0.86	0.84	0.24	0.04	0.12	0.25	0.06
Noc 0.5	337	0.17	0.77	0.75	0.28	0.11	0.16	0.28	0.13
Aph 0.16	2332	0.72	0.44	0.49	0.90	0.86	0.72	0.87	0.86
Aph 0.5	2103	0.52	0.20	0.25	0.75	0.92	0.53	0.68	0.93
NaCl	2777	0.97	-0.01	0.05	0.91	0.64	0.98	0.94	0.58
Cisplatin 1.6	2162	0.90	0.29	0.35	0.97	0.80	0.90	0.97	0.77
Cisplatin 5	1671	0.63	0.53	0.59	0.87	0.89	0.64	0.82	0.90

B IMAGE-BASED SCREENING

IMAGE-BASED SCREENING	DMSO-Noc	DMSO-Aph	Noc 0.16	Noc 0.5	Aph 0.16	Aph 0.5	NaCl	Cisplatin 1.6	Cisplatin 5
DMSO-Noc	1.00	1.00	0.28	0.35	0.79	0.59	1.00	0.93	0.68
DMSO-Aph	1.00	1.00	0.23	0.31	0.78	0.60	1.00	0.93	0.68
Noc 0.16	0.28	0.23	1.00	0.98	0.49	0.20	0.25	0.42	0.49
Noc 0.5	0.35	0.31	0.98	1.00	0.57	0.33	0.32	0.48	0.54
Aph 0.16	0.79	0.78	0.49	0.57	1.00	0.89	0.79	0.95	0.98
Aph 0.5	0.59	0.60	0.20	0.33	0.89	1.00	0.60	0.77	0.89
NaCl	1.00	1.00	0.25	0.32	0.79	0.60	1.00	0.93	0.68
Cisplatin 1.6	0.93	0.93	0.42	0.48	0.95	0.77	0.93	1.00	0.90
Cisplatin 5	0.68	0.68	0.49	0.54	0.98	0.89	0.68	0.90	1.00

C

FLOW CYTOMETRY	No Cells	DMSO	Noc 0.16	Noc 0.5	Aph 0.16	Aph 0.5	NaCl	Cisplatin 1.6	Cisplatin 5
DMSO	19142	1.00	-0.05	0.01	0.93	0.65	1.00	0.96	0.58
Noc 0.16	11784	-0.05	1.00	1.00	0.20	0.17	-0.06	0.16	0.21
Noc 0.5	10518	0.01	1.00	1.00	0.27	0.25	0.00	0.23	0.29
Aph 0.16	9997	0.93	0.20	0.27	1.00	0.86	0.93	0.99	0.82
Aph 0.5	10519	0.65	0.17	0.25	0.86	1.00	0.65	0.81	1.00
NaCl	17480	1.00	-0.06	0.00	0.93	0.65	1.00	0.96	0.59
Cisplatin 1.6	14115	0.96	0.16	0.23	0.99	0.81	0.96	1.00	0.76
Cisplatin 5	9196	0.58	0.21	0.29	0.82	1.00	0.59	0.76	1.00

0.0 — 1.0

Fig. 4. Pearson's correlation coefficients of normalized cell cycle subpopulation vectors - image-based screening vs. flow cytometry (A), image-based screening vs. image-based screening (B), and flow cytometry vs. flow cytometry (C). Various treatments: Aphidicolin (Aph), Nocodazole (Noc), NaCl and Cisplatin were applied to cell line A549. The drug dose is stated by the name (in μM). Dark background indicates high correlation. (Color figure online)

analyzed drug-dose combinations the cell count in IBHCS was much lower than in FC (see Fig. 4). Nevertheless, even in the least populous case of Nocodazole, it was still sufficient to observe significant drug response (low correlation between Nocodazole and negative controls, as seen in Fig. 4B). This shows that less cells suffice to perform cell cycle analysis using IBHCS.

Comparing Fig. 4B and C it can be observed that while the overall correlation pattern is very similar, the individual values can be quite different, especially in the case of correlations between Nocodazole and other treatments. In this case FC always shows lower correlation value than IBHCS. Again we believe that the reason for this is the low cell count and the fact that the gating is not exactly the same in the two approaches and also that the strong effect of Nocodazole on the cell cycle manifests in different ways.

4   Conclusions

FC is frequently chosen for cell cycle analysis. However, it is often more time consuming than IBHCS, especially if many treatments are to be tested, and leads to irretrievable loss of the analyzed sample. This makes discrimination

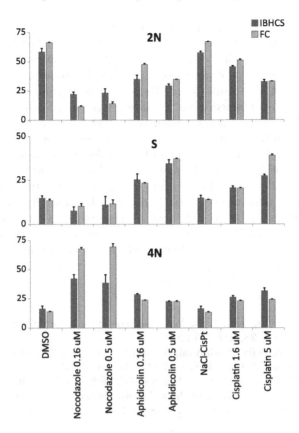

Fig. 5. Comparison between IBHCS and FC measures of the contribution (in %) of the three main cell cycle subpopulations (2N, S and 4N) for various tested treatments. The standard deviation was calculated for three and two replicates of IBHCS and FC respectively.

between true signals and artifacts, and tracing errors in the analysis very difficult. On the other hand, IBHCS preserves raw data in the form of images, so that potential artifacts can be revealed by visual analysis. Furthermore, original biological samples can be re-imaged at a higher resolution, potentially revealing additional information. This contributes to reproducible measurements and possibility of further morphological analysis of intensity distribution in the nucleus or of other stains/compartments for interesting treatments. That is, IBHCS allows measuring a multitude of morphological features as well as comprehensive texture analysis of cells directly from images.

The sample preparation procedures for FC often lead to loss of cultured cells due to trypsinization, a treatment that may also have variable effect on cells in different phases of the cell cycle. As a consequence, this approach requires much larger amounts of cells and results may be skewed. IBHCS utilizes the biological sample more efficiently. However, new FCs that require a lower cell number are becoming available [7]. In the near future we will observe more systems that merge the strengths of microscopy with those of FC. In fact the first multispectral image FCs, instruments that combine the speed and sample size of FC with the resolution and sensitivity of microscopy, are already commercially available [8].

Comparison of the results from the presented image-based DNA content analysis with those obtained using FC shows high correlation between the two approaches. The Pearson's correlation coefficient for corresponding results is above 75 % for all tested drug-dose combinations and above 90 % in more than 66 % of cases. The lowest correlation is observed for the two doses of Nocodazole (86 % and 75 % for 1.6 and 5 μM respectively). This, we believe, is caused by the low number of cells in the IBHCS analysis (these are the two least populated samples), as well as by the fact that Nocodazole has a strong effect on the cell cycle. Since the gating in the two approaches is not done in exactly the same manner, the effect manifests in different ways (some cells classified as 4N in FC would be considered as > 4N in IBHCS) which also affects the correlation.

References

1. Zanella, F., Lorens, J.B., Link, W.: High content screening: seeing is believing. Trends Biotechnol. **28**, 237–245 (2010)
2. Gasparri, F., Cappella, P., Galvani, A.: Multiparametric cell cycle analysis by automated microscopy. J. Biomol. Screen. **11**, 586–598 (2006)
3. Chan, G.K.Y., Kleinheinz, T.L., Peterson, D., Moffat, J.G.: A simple high-content cell cycle assay reveals frequent discrepancies between cell number and ATP and MTS proliferation assays. PLoS ONE **8**, e63583 (2013). doi:10.1371/journal.pone.0063583
4. Carpenter, A.E., Jones, T.R., Lamprecht, M.R., Clarke, C., Kang, I.H., Friman, O., et al.: Cell Profiler: image analysis software for identifying and quantifying cell phenotypes. Genome Biol. **7**, R100 (2006). doi:10.1186/gb-2006-7-10-r100
5. Matuszewski, D.J., Wählby, C., Puigvert, J.C., Sintorn, I.M.: PopulationProfiler: a tool for population analysis and visualization of image-based cell screening data. PLOS ONE **11**, e0151554 (2016). doi:10.1371/journal.pone.0151554
6. Matuszewski, D.J., Wählby, C., Puigvert, J.C., Sintorn, I.M.: PopulationProfiler site. http://cb.uu.se/~damian/PopulationProfiler.html
7. Black, C.B., Duensing, T.D., Trinkle, L.S., Dunlay, R.T.: Cell-based screening using high-throughput flow cytometry. Assay Drug Dev. Technol. **9**, 13–20 (2011)
8. Amnis Corporation. https://amnis.com/flowsight.html. Accessed 25 Feb 2016

Brain Imaging

Improving QuickBundles to Extract Anatomically Coherent White Matter Fiber-Bundles

Francesco Cauteruccio[1], Claudio Stamile[2], Giorgio Terracina[1],
Domenico Ursino[3(✉)], and Dominique Sappey-Marinier[2]

[1] DEMACS, University of Calabria, Rende, Italy
{cauteruccio,terracina}@mat.unical.it
[2] CREATIS, CNRS UMR5220, INSERM U1044, Université de Lyon,
Université Lyon 1, INSA-Lyon, Lyon, France
stamile@creatis.insa-lyon.fr, dominique.sappey-marinier@univ-lyon1.fr
[3] DIIES, University Mediterranea of Reggio Calabria, Reggio Calabria, Italy
ursino@unirc.it

Abstract. The construction of White Matter (WM) fiber-bundles has been largely investigated in the literature. Indeed, both manual and automatic approaches for isolating and extracting WM fiber-bundles have been proposed in the past. Each family of approaches has its pros and cons. One of the most known automatic approaches is QuickBundles (QB). Undoubtedly, the main feature of this approach is its quickness. However, due to its way of proceeding, QB could return anatomically incoherent fiber-bundles. In this paper, we propose an approach that integrates QB with a string-based fiber representation to overcome this problem. We also present the results of some experiments conceived to compare our approach with QB.

1 Introduction

In the past, White Matter (WM) fiber-bundles have been largely investigated from several viewpoints. Different papers (e.g., [5]) show how the analysis of WM structures is important to better understand and predict how the effects caused by certain neurodegenerative pathologies, such as multiple sclerosis, affect the brain, causing motor disability [12] and other symptoms. Furthermore, [7] shows how fiber-bundles extraction is used in neurosurgical planning to help the surgeon during an operation. WM fiber-bundles could be extracted with the support of expert neuroanatomists, who manually delineate the regions of interest [11]. However, this way of proceeding is time consuming and operator dependent, avoiding the possibility to analyze data derived from the analysis of large cohorts.

To overcome such limitations, different automatic algorithms for isolating and extracting WM fiber-bundles have been proposed in the literature [6,16]. We can group them in two categories, namely: (i) atlas-based algorithms [16], which

© Springer International Publishing Switzerland 2016
A. Campilho and F. Karray (Eds.): ICIAR 2016, LNCS 9730, pp. 633–641, 2016.
DOI: 10.1007/978-3-319-41501-7_71

need an a priori knowledge about the location of certain WM brain regions, and
(ii) algorithms that do not need a priori knowledge [6]. Atlas-based approaches
are very simple and fast. They are based on the registration of pre-labeled WM
fiber-bundles atlases on the subject's image. However, these approaches suffer
of different limitations, e.g., only the fiber-bundles specified in the WM atlases
can be extracted, and the quality of the extracted fibers depends on the algorithm used to register the atlases. Interestingly, these approaches could integrate
enhancing techniques, such as clustering [16], which are supervised and tuned
by experts through some parameters.

The approaches that do not need a priori knowledge are based on the formalization of particular similarity and proximity measures in $\mathbb{R}^3$ aimed to: *(i)*
group in the same subset those fibers having the same structure; *(ii)* maximize
the discrimination of fibers having different forms. Among them, *QuickBundles*
(QB) [6] is, probably, the most famous one. Due to its simplicity, QB showed
good results in terms of fiber-bundle extraction and execution time. However, as
a side effect, the pure unsupervised approach used by it could lead to the extraction of anatomically incoherent regions. Indeed, the process of fiber generation
adopted by QB does not take prior information from neuroanatomists into consideration. Nevertheless, this last information could play a key role for obtaining
more satisfying results. As a consequence, this limitation could generate a bias
in real applications, where anatomical information is important for analysis.

In this paper, we propose an approach that integrates QB with a string-based
fiber representation in such a way as to extract anatomically homogeneous WM
fiber-bundles. Given a set $F = \{f_1, f_2, \ldots, f_n\}$ of WM fibers to cluster and a set
$M = \{m_1, m_2, \ldots, m_k\}$ of models, our approach consists of the following steps:
(i) application of a string-based fiber representation formalism to construct the
set T (resp., V) of the strings corresponding to F (resp., M); *(ii)* construction
of a matrix D such that $D[i, j]$ indicates the dissimilarity degree between the
string corresponding to f_i and the one associated with m_j; *(iii)* assignment of
each fiber of F to at most one model of M on the basis of D in such a way as
to produce a set $B = \{b_1, b_2, \ldots, b_k\}$ of WM fiber-bundles; interestingly, at this
stage, it is not possible to distinguish symmetrical structures; *(iv)* application
of QB to each bundle of B for overcoming this limitation. We conducted an
experimental campaign to compare the performance of our approach with that
of QB. As will be clear below, obtained results are very encouraging.

This paper is organized as follows: in Sect. 2, we present QB and the string-
based fiber representation. In Sect. 3, we provide a technical description of the
proposed approach. In Sect. 4, we illustrate the experimental campaign conducted to evaluate it. Finally, in Sect. 5, we draw our conclusion and delineate
some possible future developments of this research.

2 Preliminaries

QuickBundles. QuickBundles (QB, for short) [6] is an efficient unsupervised algorithm to cluster WM fiber-bundles. The idea behind it is simple. At each iteration, a given fiber of the tractography could be assigned to a pre-existing cluster

or it could generate a new cluster. Initially, the first fiber is simply assigned to a first cluster containing only it. As for the other fibers, the assignment of a fiber to a cluster is performed according to a given threshold θ. If the distance between the current fiber and the centroid of at least one cluster is less than θ, the fiber is assigned to the cluster corresponding to the minimum distance. Otherwise, if there does not exist any cluster whose centroid has a distance from the current fiber less than θ, a new cluster is created and the fiber is assigned to it. This process is repeated until all the fibers in the tractography are assigned to a cluster. In order to measure the distance between two fibers, a new metric, called Minimum Average Direct Flip (MDF), is introduced. Differently from most classical clustering algorithms, like K-Means, in QB there is no re-assignment or updating step. So, when a fiber is assigned to one cluster, it is not possible for that fiber to change its cluster.

String-Based Fiber Representation. In our application scenario, involved fibers are translated into strings and they represent multi-view data. As a consequence, the one-to-one matching assumption used in classical string-based distance metrics (like the Levenshtein distance [10]) is weak and the corresponding metric could not work properly. The Semi-Blind Edit Distance (SBED, for short) [4,14] was conceived to overcome this assumption and to allow the computation of the minimum edit distance between two strings, provided that finding the optimal matching schema, under a set of constraints, is part of the problem. It can be summarized as follows.

Let $\langle \bar{s}_1, \bar{s}_2 \rangle$ be an alignment (in classical terms) for s_1 and s_2, let $M_{\langle \pi_1, \pi_2, \chi \rangle}$ be a $\langle \pi_1, \pi_2, \chi \rangle$-matching schema with constraints χ. We say that $\langle \bar{s}_1, \bar{s}_2 \rangle$ has a match at j if either: *(i)* $\bar{s}_1[j] \in \Pi_1, \bar{s}_2[j] \in \Pi_2$ and $\bar{s}_1[j] = \bar{s}_2[j]$, or *(ii)* $\bar{s}_1[j]$ and $\bar{s}_2[j]$ match, according to $M_{\langle \pi_1, \pi_2, \chi \rangle}$. The *distance* between $\bar{s}_1$ and $\bar{s}_2$ under $M_{\langle \pi_1, \pi_2, \chi \rangle}$ is the number of positions at which $\langle \bar{s}_1, \bar{s}_2 \rangle$ does not have a match.

Given two integers π_1 and π_2, such that $0 < \pi_1 \leq |\Pi_2|$ and $0 < \pi_2 \leq |\Pi_1|$, the $\langle \pi_1, \pi_2, \chi \rangle$-edit distance between s_1 and s_2 ($\mathcal{L}_{\langle \pi_1, \pi_2, \chi \rangle}(s_1, s_2)$ for short) is the minimum edit distance that can be obtained according to any $\langle \pi_1, \pi_2, \chi \rangle$-matching schema and over any string alignment $\langle \bar{s}_1, \bar{s}_2 \rangle$ of s_1 and s_2.[1]

As an example, let $s_1 =$ AAABCCDCAA and $s_2 =$ EEFGHGGFHH, which determines $\Pi_1 = \{$A,B,C,D$\}$ and $\Pi_2 = \{$E,F,G,H$\}$. For $\pi_1 = \pi_2 = 1$ and the constraint $\chi = \{\langle$A,E$\rangle\}$, the best alignment gives $\mathcal{L}_{\langle 1,1,\chi \rangle}(s_1, s_2) = 5$ with the optimal matching schema $\{$A$\}$-$\{$H$\}$, $\{$B$\}$-$\{$E$\}$, $\{$C$\}$-$\{$F$\}$, and $\{$D$\}$-$\{$G$\}$.

To the best of our knowledge, there is no approach in the literature facing the same problem handled by SBED, even if there are some variants. In fact, several approaches have been proposed to carry out the computation of the similarity of parameterized strings, i.e., strings where some of the symbols act as parameters that can be properly substituted at no cost (see, [1,2,8,9]).

---

[1] The interested reader can find all details about SBED and algorithms for its computation in [4,14].

3   Technical Description of the Proposed Approach

Our approach joins together QB and SBED and aims at overcoming the main problem of the former by using the latter. Its first ingredient is a WM fiber-bundle reference model, which must represent an approximate shape of the fiber-bundle to extract. It could be obtained in two different ways, namely: *(i)* by exploiting a spline curve to draw the profile of the fiber-bundle of interest, or *(ii)* by importing the mean-line profile of the fiber-bundle of interest from an atlas of pre-labeled fiber-bundles. Both kinds of models can be constructed either by a generic user or with the support of an expert one. In this paper the first approach has been adopted; indeed, models of interest were manually delineated as described in [14]. The second ingredient of our approach is a fiber representation formalism allowing fibers to be mapped on strings. Actually, a bijective mapping is needed. For this purpose, let $F = \{f_1, f_2, \ldots, f_n\}$ be a set of fibers. Here, a generic fiber $f_i \in F$ is defined as a sequence $f_i = (v_1, v_2, \ldots, v_m)$ of voxels in the three-dimensional space. Due to lack of space, in the following, we consider the case in which all the fibers of F have the same number m of voxels. However, we point out that this is not a hard condition for our approach. Indeed, as shown in [14], our SBED metric can be applied also to strings having different dimensions. A color can be associated with each voxel $v_r \in f_i$, derived from its orientation in the space. Thus, a fiber $f_i \in F$ can be represented by using colors in the RGB color space. By discretizing the RGB space, we define a map $\Psi : RGB \rightarrow \Sigma$, where $\Sigma \subset \mathbb{N}_0$ and $|\Sigma| = s$. With the support of this map, a generic fiber f_i can now be expressed as a string in Σ^m.

Once the two main ingredients of our approach have been defined, it is possible to describe it. Specifically, let $F = \{f_1, f_2, \ldots, f_n\}$ be a set of WM fibers to cluster and let $M = \{m_1, m_2, \ldots, m_k\}$ be the set of models. Our approach consists of the following steps:

– Construction of the set $T = \{t_1, t_2, \ldots, t_n\}$ of the strings corresponding to F and of the set $V = \{v_1, v_2, \ldots, v_k\}$ of the strings corresponding to M. For this purpose, the fiber representation formalism described above is applied.
– Construction of a $n \times k$ matrix D. The element $D[i, j]$ of D indicates the dissimilarity degree computed by applying SBED on the string t_i, associated with f_i, and the string v_j, associated with m_j.
– Assignment of each fiber of F to at most one model of M as follows: *(i)* for each row i of D, let μ be the minimum value of this row and let j_μ be the corresponding column; *(ii)* if μ is lesser than a certain threshold Th then f_i is assigned to m_{j_μ}; otherwise, f_i is not assigned to any model.
– At the end of this step, we have a set $B = \{b_1, b_2, \ldots, b_k\}$ of WM fiber-bundles, one for each model of M. However, these bundles have a weak point. Indeed, the assignment approach described above is incapable of distinguishing among symmetrical structures [14]. To overcome this limitation, for each bundle $b_l \in B$, we apply QB to it. QB returns the same bundle b_l, if it does not have a symmetrical structure. Otherwise, QB may split b_l into a set $CS = \{C_1, C_2, \ldots, C_q\}$ of clusters. Let v_l be the element of V associated

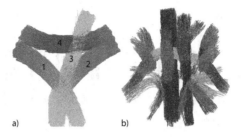

Fig. 1. The two phantoms used in our experimental campaign

with b_l. We construct a set $DS = \{d_1, d_2, \ldots, d_q\}$ of distances. The generic element d_α, $1 \leq \alpha \leq q$ of DS is equal to the average SBED between the strings corresponding to the fibers of $C_\alpha \in CS$ and v_l. Let d_μ be the minimum value of DS. Then the fibers of C_μ are assigned to b_l. Consider now $\overline{CS} = CS - \{C_\mu\}$. For each $C_\beta \in \overline{CS}$, we compute the set $\overline{DS}_\beta = \{d_1, d_2, \ldots, d_{k-1}\}$ of the average distances between the strings corresponding to the fibers of C_β and the strings of $V - \{v_l\}$. Let d_ν be the minimum of $\overline{DS}_\beta$. Then the fibers of C_β are assigned to b_ν.

4   Experimental Campaign

Our experimental campaign consisted of two phases. The former was devoted to tune our approach. The latter aimed to compare it with the classical QB. In both cases we exploited simulated diffusion phantoms, as well as some classical performance measures, namely, Precision, Recall, F-Measure and Overall [13].

Phase 1: Parameter Tuning. As for this phase, the input dataset consisted of the virtual phantom shown in Fig. 1(a) and created by Phantomas [3]. In order to obtain the ground truth, experts segmented this phantom manually into 4 fiber-bundles, which are numbered in Fig. 1(a). In order to reconstruct the WM fibers, probabilistic streamline tractography was performed using MRTrix [15] based on the fiber orientation density (FOD) information contained in the phantom. To find the best value of the input parameter Th, we considered different values of it ranging from 0.20 to 0.50. The corresponding values of Precision, Recall, F-Measure and Overall for the four models are reported in Fig. 2. From the analysis of this figure, we can observe that, from $Th = 0.20$ to $Th = 0.36$, an increase of Th leads to an increase of at least one between Precision and Recall and to an increase of both F-Measure and Overall, which (we recall) are parameters combining Precision and Recall. Starting from $Th = 0.36$ no further increase of the values of performance measures can be observed in any model, and our approach shows a stable behavior. As a consequence, we chose to set Th to the middle of this range and we set it to 0.44.

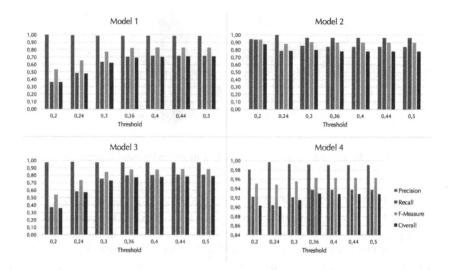

Fig. 2. Variation of the four performance measures against the threshold Th for each model of the phantom of Fig. 1(a)

Phase 2: Comparison with the Classical QB. After having tuned Th, we applied the classical QB on the previous phantom to compare the performance of our approach (with $Th = 0.44$) with that of QB. The obtained results are reported in Table 1. From the analysis of this table we can observe that our approach shows a much higher average Precision, a slightly lower average Recall, a higher average F-Measure and a much higher average Overall than QB.

To obtain a (possible) confirmation of this result, we applied both our approach, with $Th = 0.44$, and QB on a second phantom shown in Fig. 1(b). This consisted of a virtual diffusion MR phantom that accurately simulates the brain complexity with the fiber geometry used in the 2nd HARDI Reconstruction Challenge (ISBI 2013). Data were generated by means of Phantomas [3]. To obtain the ground truth, experts segmented all the fiber-bundles in the phantom manually. At the end of this task, they defined the approximate shapes of

Table 1. Performance values obtained by our approach and QB when applied on the phantom of Fig. 1(a)

Model	Our approach				QB			
	Precision	Recall	F-Measure	Overall	Precision	Recall	F-Measure	Overal
1	0.99	0.72	0.83	0.71	0.96	1.00	0.98	0.95
2	0.84	0.96	0.90	0.78	0.54	0.77	0.64	0.12
3	0.97	0.81	0.88	0.78	0.54	0.77	0.64	0.12
4	0.99	0.94	0.96	0.93	1.00	0.93	0.96	0.93
Avg values	0.95	0.85	0.89	0.80	0.76	0.87	0.80	0.54

Table 2. Performance values obtained by our approach and QB when applied on the phantom of Fig. 1(b)

Model	Our approach				QB			
	Precision	Recall	F-Measure	Overall	Precision	Recall	F-Measure	Overal
1	0.94	0.71	0.81	0.67	0.91	0.70	0.79	0.63
2	0.90	0.64	0.75	0.57	0.33	0.71	0.45	−0.76
3	0.78	0.41	0.54	0.29	0.31	0.75	0.44	−0.90
4	0.89	0.69	0.77	0.60	0.85	0.75	0.80	0.62
5	0.77	0.57	0.66	0.40	0.80	0.78	0.79	0.58
6	0.96	0.68	0.79	0.65	0.29	0.79	0.43	−1.13
7	0.94	0.29	0.45	0.27	0.14	0.82	0.24	−4.33
8	0.68	0.33	0.45	0.18	0.13	0.91	0.23	−4.96
Avg values	0.86	0.54	0.63	0.45	0.47	0.78	0.52	−1.28

these fiber-bundles; in particular, they identified 17 models. Numbering these models in Fig. 1(b) was not possible due to the 3D nature of this image.

Because of its fully unsupervised nature, QB was capable of extracting just 8 out of the 17 fiber-bundles of the phantom. Our approach, instead, extracted all the 17 fiber bundles. As a consequence, a comparison between our approach and QB was possible only for the 8 models detected by QB. Obtained results are reported in Table 2.

From the analysis of this table we can observe that QB generally shows a higher value of Recall than our approach (this can be observed in 7 out of 8 models), but lower values of Precision (which were much lower in 5 cases, lower in 2 cases and slightly higher in only 1 case). As for the combined parameters F-Measure and Overall, our approach shows better results than QB in 6 out of 8 cases. Finally, if we consider the average values of these measures, we obtain that our approach shows a better Precision, a better F-Measure, a better Overall and a worse Recall than QB.

As previously pointed out, this difference of behavior is due to the nature of the structures extracted by QB. In fact, the fiber-bundles obtained by QB are not isolated but they are merged with other structures that are spatially near to them (even if they present a completely different anatomical meaning). By contrast, the fiber-bundles obtained by our approach are "purer", since they contain only anatomically uniform fibers, corresponding to the fiber bundles of our interest. In support of this reasoning, it is well known that, in this application field, Precision is much more important than Recall.

5   Conclusion

In this paper, we have proposed an approach that integrates QuickBundle with a string-based fiber representation for extracting anatomically coherent WM fiber-bundles. Our approach overcomes the main problem of QB, i.e., the possibility that it returns anatomically incoherent fiber clusters, in which the desired fiber-bundles are not isolated but merged with other structures spatially near to them (even if they present a completely different anatomical meaning). This paper must not be considered as an ending point of our research efforts. Indeed, several developments are possible. First of all, we plan to extend our experiments from phantoms to real cases. After this, we would like to further improve QB in such a way as to correct fiber assignments to clusters when these assignments appear uncorrect in a second time. Finally, we will work on the SBED constraint optimizations in such a way as to define an approach that allows the discovery of the best constrains for improving the extraction of specific WM fiber-bundles.

References

1. Apostolico, A., Erdős, P.L., Lewenstein, M.: Parameterized matching with mismatches. J. Discrete Algorithms **5**(1), 135–140 (2007)
2. Baker, B.S.: Parameterized pattern matching: algorithms and applications. J. Comput. Syst. Sci. **52**(1), 28–42 (1996)
3. Caruyer, E., Daducci, A., Descoteaux, M., Houde, J.-C., Thiran, J.: Phantomas: a flexible software library to simulate diffusion mr phantom. In: ISMRM (2014)
4. Cauteruccio, F., Stamile, C., Terracina, G., Ursino, D., Sappey-Mariniery, D.: An automated string-based approach to white matter fiber-bundles clustering. In: IJCNN, pp. 1–8 (2015)
5. Colby, J.B., Soderberg, L., Lebel, C., Dinov, I.D., Thompson, P.M., Sowell, E.R.: Along-tract statistics allow for enhanced tractography analysis. Neuroimage **59**(4), 3227–3242 (2012)
6. Garyfallidis, E., Brett, M., Correia, M.M., Williams, G.B., Nimmo-Smith, I.: Quickbundles, a method for tractography simplification. Front. Neurosci. **6**, 175 (2012)
7. Golby, A.J., Kindlmann, G., Norton, I., Yarmarkovich, A., Pieper, S., Kikinis, R.: Interactive diffusion tensor tractography visualization for neurosurgical planning. Neurosurgery **68**(2), 496–505 (2011)
8. Greco, G., Terracina, G.: Frequency-based similarity for parameterized sequences: formal framework, algorithms, and applications. Inf. Sci. **237**, 176–195 (2013)
9. Hazay, C., Lewenstein, M., Sokol, D.: Approximate parameterized matching. ACM Trans. Algorithms (TALG) **3**(3), 29 (2007)
10. Levenshtein, V.: Binary codes capable of correcting deletions, insertions, and reversals. Sov. Phys.-Dokl. **10**(8), 707–710 (1966)
11. Mårtensson, J., Nilsson, M., Ståhlberg, F., Sundgren, P.C., Nilsson, C., van Westen, D., Larsson, E.-M., Lätt, J.: Spatial analysis of diffusion tensor tractography statistics along the inferior fronto-occipital fasciculus with application in progressive supranuclear palsy. MAGMA **26**(6), 527–537 (2013)
12. Pantano, P., Mainero, C., Iannetti, G.D., Caramia, F., Di Legge, S., Piattella, M.C., Pozzilli, C., Bozzao, L., Lenzi, G.L.: Contribution of corticospinal tract damage to cortical motor reorganization after a single clinical attack of multiple sclerosis. Neuroimage **17**(4), 1837–1843 (2002)
13. Powers, D.: Evaluation: From precision, recall and f-factor to roc, informedness, markedness & correlation. Technical report, Adelaide, Australia (2007)

14. Stamile, C., Cauteruccio, F., Terracina, G., Ursino, D., Kocevar, G., Sappey-Marinier, D.: A model-guided string-based approach to white matter fiber-bundles extraction. In: Guo, Y., Friston, K., Aldo, F., Hill, S., Peng, H. (eds.) BIH 2015. LNCS, vol. 9250, pp. 135–144. Springer, Heidelberg (2015)

15. Tournier, J.D., Calamante, F., Connelly, A.: MRtrix: diffusion tractography in crossing fiber regions. Int. J. Imaging Syst. Technol. **22**, 53–66 (2012)

16. Zhang, S., Correia, S., Laidlaw, D.H.: Identifying white-matter fiber bundles in dti data using an automated proximity-based fiber-clustering method. IEEE Trans. Vis. Comput. Graph. **14**(5), 1044–1053 (2008)

Automatic Rating of Perivascular Spaces in Brain MRI Using Bag of Visual Words

Víctor González-Castro[1](✉), María del C. Valdés Hernández[1],
Paul A. Armitage[2], and Joanna M. Wardlaw[1]

[1] Department of Neuroimaging Sciences, Centre for Clinical Brain Sciences,
University of Edinburgh, Edinburgh, UK
victor.gonzalez@ed.ac.uk

[2] Department of Cardiovascular Sciences, University of Sheffield, Sheffield, UK

Abstract. Perivascular spaces (PVS), if enlarged and visible in magnetic resonance imaging (MRI), relate to poor cognition, depression in older age, Parkinson's disease, inflammation, hypertension and cerebral small vessel disease. In this paper we present a fully automatic method to rate the burden of PVS in the basal ganglia (BG) region using structural brain MRI. We used a Support Vector Machine classifier and described the BG following the bag of visual words (BoW) model. The latter was evaluated using a) Scale Invariant Feature Transform (SIFT) descriptors of points extracted from a dense sampling and b) textons, as local descriptors. BoW using SIFT yielded a global accuracy of 82.34 %, whereas using textons it yielded 79.61 %.

Keywords: Brain MRI · Perivascular spaces · Bag of visual words · SIFT · SVM

1 Introduction

Perivascular spaces (PVS) are fluid-containing spaces that surround the walls of the brain small arteries, veins and capillaries. They are normally microscopic. When enlarged, they are seen in T2-weighted (T2W) brain MRI as round or linear structures with intensities close to the cerebrospinal fluid (CSF) and with less than 3 mm diameter in cross section. An increase of enlarged PVS has been associated with worse cognition, depression at older ages, Parkinson's disease, inflammation, hypertension and cerebral small vessel disease in the form of lacunar stroke and vascular dementia [7]. They are increasingly recognised as an important component of the brain's circulation and fluid drainage pathways. Therefore, quantifying the PVS has a huge interest [1,9,13].

Manual quantifications (i.e. segmentations) of PVS are very time consuming, and the existent automatic methods present serious limitations, due to the overlap in PVS shape, intensity, location and size with these of lacunes [13]. Recently, Wang et al. presented a method based on thresholding T2-weighted (T2W) images acquired using a 1.5T MRI scanner to quantify PVS in the basal

© Springer International Publishing Switzerland 2016
A. Campilho and F. Karray (Eds.): ICIAR 2016, LNCS 9730, pp. 642–649, 2016.
DOI: 10.1007/978-3-319-41501-7_72

ganglia with good results [15], but it required manual intervention. Cai et al. also developed an automatic method to quantify PVS, but using high resolution 7T MRI scans [1], which still have limited applicability for clinical use.

As an alternative to quantitative measurements, several similar visual rating scales have been proposed in recent years. Potter et al. reviewed their ambiguities and combined their strengths to develop a more comprehensive scale which proved to be robust [7]. However, as any visual recognition process, it is subject to observer bias and relatively insensitive to subtle changes. An automatic PVS rating method (e.g. replicating the visual rating scale using image processing and pattern recognition) could overcome these and the drawbacks of the existent segmentation methods.

The application of pattern recognition and machine learning for segmenting brain structures or lesions has been already explored [4]. Chen et al. proposed a framework based on multiple instance learning to distinguish between absent/mild vs. moderate/severe SVD in computer tomography (CT) scans which achieved approximately 75 % accuracy [2]. However, to the best of our knowledge, there are not similar methods that deal with the PVS burden (i.e. replicating the PVS visual rating scale).

In this paper we propose an automatic method to rate PVS in the basal ganglia from structural T2-weighted MRI. The images are described following the bag of visual words (BoW) model [10] and classified using support vector machine (SVM) [14]. We used dense-SIFT [5] as local descriptors. Given the wide use of textons as descriptors for pattern recognition applications in medical imaging [3], these were also evaluated and compared against dense-SIFT.

The paper is organised as follows: In Sect. 2 the dataset and the proposed method are explained. Section 3 introduces the experimental setup, results and discussion and, finally, the conclusions are presented in Sect. 4.

2 Materials and Methods

2.1 Imaging Data

We used data from 264 patients who gave written consent to participate on a study of stroke mechanisms [12]. Brain MRI was conducted on a 1.5 tesla GE Signa LX clinical scanner (General Electric, Milwaukee, WI), equipped with a self-shielding gradient set and 8-channel-phased array heal coil following the protocol described in [12]. For our classification we used the T2W images (TE/TR = 147/9002 milliseconds, field of view 240×240 mm, acquisition matrix 256×256, slice thickness 5 mm, 1 mm inter-slice gap and voxel size $0.94 \times 0.94 \times 6.5$ mm).

2.2 PVS Visual Rating Scale

PVS were assessed using the visual rating scale developed by Potter et al. [7]. It rates the PVS separately in three major anatomical brain regions, i.e. midbrain, basal ganglia (BG) and centrum semiovale (CS) using T2W MRI, assigning 0 (no EPVS), 1 (mild; 1–10 EPVS), 2 (moderate; 11–20 EPVS), 3 (frequent; 21–40 EPVS) or 4 (severe; >40 EPVS)[1]. Examples of each rating for the BG region are shown in Fig. 1. In this paper, we will focus only on the PVS in the BG, since moderate to severe PVS in this region is considered a marker of cerebral SVD, associated with cognitive decline [11], vascular dementia and stroke [8].

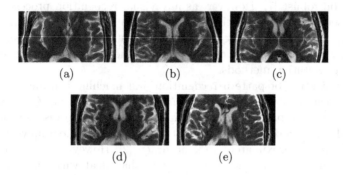

(a)   (b)   (c)

(d)   (e)

Fig. 1. Example for the EPVS ratings in the BG 0 to 4 ((a) to (e), respectively).

2.3 Pre-processing

The intracranial volume and cerebrospinal fluid (CSF) were segmented automatically using optiBET [6] and FSL-FAST [16]. All subcortical structures were segmented automatically using other tools from the same FMRIB Software Library (FSL) on a pipeline described in [12]. For our classifier, we choose the axial slice with the highest number of PVS containing at least one characteristic BG structure, following the indications from Wang et al. [15]. As first approximation, from the slices that contained BG structures, we selected those in which the total area of these structures was more than 5 % the area of the intracranial volume.

On each of the slices initially selected, a polygon enclosing the BG, internal and external capsules and thalami was automatically drawn by joining anatomical points in the insular cortex, the closest points to them in the lateral ventricles (frontal and occipital horns) and the intercept of the genu of the corpus callosum with the septum; and subtracting from it the region occupied by the CSF. These steps are illustrated in Fig. 2.

From this subset of slices, the slice where our classifier operated was selected after applying contrast-limited adaptive histogram equalisation (CLAHE) [17] to the polygonal region and thresholding it to 0.43 times the maximum intensity level [13,15] (Fig. 2(d)). Further, we counted the number of hyperintense blobs with area between 3 and 15 times the in-plane voxel dimensions [15].

---

[1] More details about this visual rating scale can be found at http://www.sbirc.ed.ac.uk/documents/epvs-rating-scale-user-guide.pdf.

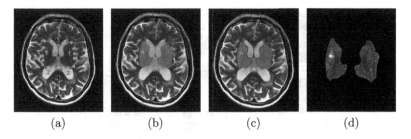

(a)   (b)   (c)   (d)

Fig. 2. Steps of the BG segmentation: (a) Detection of the vertices in the insular cortex
(1), lateral ventricles (2) and genu (3); (b) creation of the polygon; (c) subtraction of
the CSF from the BG polygonal region and (d) segmented BG region

Although this procedure overestimates the number of PVS in the presence of
other features of SVD markers (e.g. small lesions and lacunes) [13], it provides
a good estimate of the axial slice with more PVS.

2.4   Description of the Basal Ganglia Region

The extracted and histogram-equalised BG region is described following the bag
of visual words (BoW) model [10]. Each region is represented as a function of
the frequency of appearance of certain visual elements, called visual words. The
set of visual words is called dictionary.

First of all, a set of images is used to build the dictionary. From each image
we define a dense grid to extract a set of keypoints. These may also be sampled
randomly or using detectors of salient points [5]. Thereafter, each patch (i.e.
small region) around the selected keypoints is characterised, typically by means
of any descriptor that retrieves information about how the intensities of the pixels
are distributed. After that, these descriptors (i.e. one per patch) are clustered
into k groups, each one having a prototype vector which is called visual word
(i.e. the dictionary has k visual words). In this work we have used the k-means
clustering method.

Once the dictionary is built, each image of the dataset is described through a
process called "image representation": First, the same selection and description
of the keypoints is carried out. Then, we consider the visual word in the dictionary with the closest distance (e.g. euclidean) to a keypoint descriptor to be
representative of that keypoint. The histogram of the visual words representative
of all keypoints is used as the final image descriptor. This process is represented
in Fig. 3.

In this work, the keypoints have been described using the Scale Invariant
Feature Transform (SIFT) [5], which consists of two different parts: keypoint
detector and keypoint descriptor. We are extracting the points from a dense
grid, so we only consider the keypoint descriptor. Basically, SIFT descriptors
are based on histograms of oriented gradients computed from the intensities of
the regions that result from dividing a square window around the keypoints into
4×4 sub-windows. More details about SIFT can be found in [5].

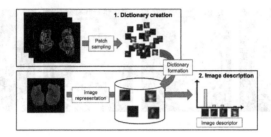

Fig. 3. Schematic representation of the bag of visual words description process.

3   Experiments and Results

3.1   Experiments

Our sample is formed by 264 datasets of MRI structural scans and their corresponding visual rating scores. The latter were made by an experienced neuroradiologist (Table 1). Since a "moderate to severe" rating of PVS in the basal ganglia is a marker of SVD [11], we dichotomised the PVS scores into 0 (PVS scores 0-1) and 1 (PVS scores 2-4), as per [8]. This resulted in 133 and 131 datasets with classes 0 (negative) and 1 (positive), respectively.

Table 1. Distribution of the visual ratings in the dataset.

PVS rating	0	1	2	3	4	TOTAL
Num. images	5	128	68	44	19	264

The data was divided into training and test sets using a random stratified split: 70 % for the training set and 30 % for the test set. All the images in the training set were used to build the BoW dictionary. Afterwards, this dictionary was used to represent the images of both sets, as it was explained in Sect. 2.4. We used different number k of visual words in the dictionary to assess their impact on the classification.

We used the SIFT descriptors [5] of keypoints located on a dense grid as local descriptors, i.e. called dense-SIFT. As, to the best of our knowledge, this is the first work that attempts to automatically rate the PVS burden of the brain, we cannot compare its performance against any other computational approach. Therefore, we provide a comparison of the results obtained from using dense-SIFT descriptors with those obtained from textons using the raw intensities of the regions [3]. In both cases, the keypoints of the dense sampling were separated by 1 pixel and the region around them was a 8×8 square.

Finally, a Support Vector Machine (SVM) with a Radial Basis Function (RBF) kernel (i.e. $K(\mathbf{x}, \mathbf{x}') = \exp(-\gamma \|\mathbf{x} - \mathbf{x}'\|^2)$), was trained using the training set and then the descriptors of the images in the test set were classified.

This process (i.e. set division, dictionary creation, image representation and classification) was repeated 10 times. The results presented in this paper are the average of these 10 iterations.

3.2 Results and Discussion

The results of the experiments have been measured in terms of accuracy, as the dataset is quite balanced (133 negative and 131 positive elements), using the visual ratings as ground truth. Table 2 shows the best results using the BoW descriptors based on dense-SIFT and textons with the number k of visual words in the dictionary, regularization parameter C of the SVM and γ of the RBF kernel.

Table 2. Overall accuracy and its standard deviation along the 10 iterations (std); TNR and TPR of the SVM classification of the BoW descriptors based on SIFT and textons. The parameters k, C and γ these results were obtained with are also provided.

	k	C	γ	Accuracy (%)	TNR (%)	TPR (%)	std.
Dense-SIFT	1250	1	10^{-3}	82.34	80.77	83.95	3.93
Textons	500	75	10^{-5}	79.61	83.85	75.26	5.20

The best accuracy obtained by dense-SIFT (82.34 %) – achieved with $k = 1250$ words in the visual dictionary, $C = 1$ and $\gamma = 0.001$ – is higher than that obtained by the textons (79.61 %) ($k = 500$, $C = 75$ and $\gamma = 10^{-5}$). Moreover, the true positive rate (TPR) (i.e. the images with moderate to severe PVS correctly classified) was higher than the true negative rate (TNR) with the dense-SIFT whereas with the textons the TPR was lower than the TNR. Despite the accuracy being influenced by the number of visual words k the behaviour of TNR with respect to TPR was not influenced by k (Fig. 4).

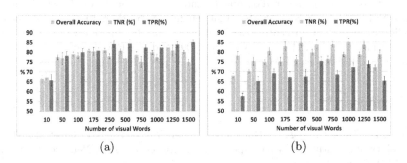

(a)   (b)

Fig. 4. Global accuracies, TNR and TPR with their corresponding Standard Errors, with different number of visual words using dense SIFT (a) and textons (b).

We could cite as a limitation of our approach the use of a single slice instead of using the whole volume. However, we based this decision on a clinically proven visual rating scale [7] and validated guidelines [15]. In addition, the big slice thickness (5 mm) compared to the size of the PVS (1 to 5 mm diameter) makes it implausible to use a 3D approach to characterise these structures.

4   Conclusion

In this paper we present an automatic method to rate the burden of PVS in the BG (one of the markers of small vessel disease) on brain MRI into (a) none or mild and (b) moderate to severe. The BG region is described by means of a bag of visual words (BoW) model using SIFT as descriptors of keypoints sampled from a dense grid (i.e. dense-SIFT). We have compared dense-SIFT with textons to illustrate the validity of our SVM classification approach.

The proposed dense-SIFT-based method achieves an accuracy of 82.34 %, a higher balance between the accuracies in the detections of both classes and more accuracy in the detection of the brains with moderate to severe PVS than textons. This is the first time that this type of automatic rating is carried out so 82.34 % is a promising starting point. A next step will be to evaluate this approach against the output from other methods that quantify PVS [1,13,15] and to see if it works in other brain regions such as centrum semiovale.

A limitation of this work may be the fact that the ground truth we are using is a visual (and, therefore, subjective) rating. However, the visual rating scale has shown a high inter-rater reliability in previous works [7] so this should not affect the validity of the results shown in this paper too much. Future work should compare the inter-rater agreement with the performance of our method using the ratings from a second rater on this sample, not available at the moment. In addition, we could use other keypoint sampling methods and different local descriptors in the BoW, and use information from all candidate BG slices.

Acknowledgements. We would like to thank Dr. Stephen Makin (patient recuitment), study participants, radiographers and staff at the Brain Research Imaging Centre Edinburgh, a SINAPSE (Scottish Imaging Network A Platform for Scientific Excellence) collaboration centre, the Wellcome Trust for funding the primary study that provided the data (Ref. No. 088134/Z/09) and the Row Fogo Charitable Trust (Grants Nos. R35865 and R43412).

References

1. Cai, K., Tain, R., Das, S., Damen, F.C., Sui, Y., Valyi-Nagy, T., et al.: The feasibility of quantitative MRI of perivascular spaces at 7T. J. Neurosci. Meth. **256**, 151–156 (2015)
2. Chen, L., et al.: Identification of cerebral small vessel disease using multiple instancelearning. In: Navab, N., Hornegger, J., Wells, W.M., Frangi, A.F. (eds.) MICCAI 2015. LNCS, vol. 9349, pp. 523–530. Springer, New York (2015)

3. Gangeh, M.J., Sørensen, L., Shaker, S.B., Kamel, M.S., de Bruijne, M., Loog, M.: A texton-based approach for the classification of lung parenchyma in CT images. In: Jiang, T., Navab, N., Pluim, J.P.W., Viergever, M.A. (eds.) MICCAI 2010, Part III. LNCS, vol. 6363, pp. 595–602. Springer, Heidelberg (2010)
4. Ithapu, V., Singh, V., Lindner, C., Austin, B.P., Hinrichs, C., Carlsson, C.M., Bendlin, B.B., Johnson, S.C.: Extracting and summarizing white matter hyperintensities using supervised segmentation methods in Alzheimer's disease risk and aging studies. Hum. Brain Mapp. **35**(8), 4219–4235 (2014)
5. Lowe, D.G.: Object recognition from local scale-invariant features. In: The Proceedings of the Seventh IEEE International Conference on Computer Vision, 1999, vol. 2, pp. 1150–1157 (1999)
6. Lutkenhoff, E.S., Rosenberg, M., Chiang, J., Zhang, K., Pickard, J.D., Owen, A.M., Monti, M.M.: Optimized brain extraction for pathological brains (optiBET). PLoS One **9**(12), e115551 (2014)
7. Potter, G.M., Chappell, F.M., Morris, Z., Wardlaw, J.M.: Cerebral perivascular spaces visible on magnetic resonance imaging: development of a qualitative rating scale and its observer reliability. Cerebrovasc. Dis. **39**(3–4), 224–231 (2015)
8. Potter, G.M., Doubal, F.N., Jackson, C.A., Chappell, F.M., Sudlow, C.L., Dennis, M.S., Wardlaw, J.M.: Enlarged perivascular spaces and cerebral small vessel disease. Int. J. Stroke **10**(3), 376–381 (2015)
9. Ramirez, J., Berezuk, C., McNeely, A.A., Scott, C.J.M., Gao, F., Black, S.E.: Visible Virchow-Robin spaces on magnetic resonance imaging of Alzheimer's disease patients and normal elderly from the Sunnybrook Dementia Study. J. Alzheimers Dis. **43**(2), 415–424 (2015)
10. Sivic, J., Zisserman, A.: Video google: a text retrieval approach to object matching in videos. In: Proceedings of Ninth IEEE International Conference on Computer Vision, 2003, vol. 2, pp. 1470–1477 (2003)
11. Staals, J., Makin, S.D.J., Doubal, F.N., Dennis, M.S., Wardlaw, J.M.: Stroke subtype, vascular risk factors, and total MRI brain small-vessel disease burden. Neurology **83**(14), 1228–1234 (2014)
12. Valdés Hernández, M.D.C., Armitage, P.A., Thrippleton, M.J., Chappell, F., Sandeman, E., Muñoz Maniega, S., Shuler, K., Wardlaw, J.M.: Rationale, design and methodology of the image analysis protocol forstudies of patients with cerebral small vessel disease and mild stroke. Brain Behav. **5**(12), e00415 (2015)
13. Valdés Hernández, M.D.C., Piper, R.J., Wang, X., Deary, I.J., Wardlaw, J.M.: Towards the automatic computational assessment of enlargedperivascular spaces on brain magnetic resonance images: a systematic review. J. Magn. Reson. Imaging **38**(4), 774–785 (2013)
14. Vapnik, V.: The Nature of Statistical Learning Theory, 2nd edn. Springer, Heidelberg (1995)
15. Wang, X., Valdés Hernández, M.D.C., Doubal, F., Chappell, F.M., Piper, R.J., Deary, I.J., Wardlaw, J.M.: Development and initial evaluation of asemi-automatic approach to assess perivascular spaces on conventionalmagnetic resonance images. J. Neurosci. Meth. **257**, 34–44 (2016)
16. Zhang, Y., Brady, M., Smith, S.: Segmentation of brain MR images through a hidden Markov random field model and the expectation-maximization algorithm. IEEE Trans. Med. Imaging **20**(1), 45–57 (2001)
17. Zuiderveld, K.: Contrast limited adaptive histogram equalization. In: Paul, S.H. (ed.) Graphics Gems IV, pp. 474–485. Academic Press Professional Inc., London (1994)

White Matter Fiber-Bundle Analysis Using Non-negative Tensor Factorization

Claudio Stamile[1,2], François Cotton[1,4], Frederik Maes[3],
Dominique Sappey-Marinier[1,5], and Sabine Van Huffel[2,6(✉)]

[1] CREATIS, CNRS UMR5220, INSERM U1044, Université de Lyon,
Université Lyon 1, INSA-Lyon, Lyon, France
stamile@creatis.insa-lyon.fr
[2] Department of Electrical Engineering (ESAT), STADIUS,
KU Leuven, Leuven, Belgium
Sabine.VanHuffel@esat.kuleuven.be
[3] Department of Electrical Engineering (ESAT), PSI,
KU Leuven, Leuven, Belgium
[4] Service de Radiologie, Centre Hospitalier Lyon-Sud, Hospices Civils de Lyon,
Pierre-Bénite, France
[5] CERMEP - Imagerie du Vivant, Université de Lyon, Bron, France
[6] iMinds Medical Information Technologies, Leuven, Belgium

Abstract. With the development of advanced image acquisition and processing techniques providing better biomarkers for the characterization of brain diseases, the automatic analysis of biomedical imaging constitutes a critical point. In particular, analysis of complex data structure is a challenge for better understanding complex brain pathologies like multiple sclerosis (MS).

In this work, we describe a new fully automated method based on non-negative tensor factorization (NTF) to analyze white matter (WM) fiber-bundles. This method allows to extract, from a WM fiber-bundle, the set of fibers affected by the pathology, discriminating fibers affected by the pathological from the healthy fibers.

Our method was validated on simulated data and also applied on real MS patients. Results show the high precision level of our method to extract fibers affected by the pathological process.

Keywords: Non-negative tensor factorization · White matter · Multiple sclerosis · DTI · Tractography

1 Introduction

In the last decade, the interest in new methods to analyze white matter (WM) fiber-bundles increased. Different papers [3,7,14] suggest how the analysis of WM structures using diffusion tensor imaging (DTI) information is a powerful tool to better investigate neurodegenerative processes. All those methods were largely applied to characterize WM structure affected by the pathology [3,7] and also to understand the brain development mechanisms [14].

© Springer International Publishing Switzerland 2016
A. Campilho and F. Karray (Eds.): ICIAR 2016, LNCS 9730, pp. 650–657, 2016.
DOI: 10.1007/978-3-319-41501-7_73

From a methodological point of view, all these techniques present different limitations. In [3,7] the authors show a first semi-automated method to analyze the mean signal profile along the WM structure. Unfortunately both methods are not fully automated, in particular, the extraction of the fiber-bundles of interest should be performed manually by a neurologist. This manual step drastically reduces the possibility to apply the method to large datasets. A first example of a fully automated method is described in [14]. In this paper the authors described a pipeline that allows to extract and study how the signal changes along different WM fiber-bundles. If the method performs a fully automated analysis, it still analyzes the mean signal profile of the fiber-bundle. The simple mean analysis of the signal reduces the sensitivity of the method to detect the presence of "abnormal" regions [10] especially when those changes are relatively small like relapsing remitting (RR) form of multiple sclerosis (MS). Furthermore, this approach does not allow to distinguish which set of fibers within the bundle are affected by the pathology and which are not. As ulterior point, all the methods previously described do not allow to analyze multiple diffusion maps at the same time, reducing the capability to exploit complementary information.

In order to overcome all these limitations, in this paper a new fully automated method is presented. Major contribution is given by the original application of non-negative tensor factorization (NTF) to analyze WM fiber-bundles. Compared to the other techniques, NTF allows to have a global view of the fiber-bundle allowing to better characterize the subset of fibers affected by the pathology. Moreover, due to the adaptability of NTF, complementary information derived from multiple diffusion maps could be used at the same time.

Tests on simulated and real data show the capability of our method to distinguish between fibers affected by the pathological process and fibers belonging to normal tissue.

This paper is structured as follows. In Sect. 2, we provide a detailed description of our approach. In Sect. 3, we present our experimental campaign. Finally, in Sect. 4, we draw our conclusions.

2   Materials and Methods

2.1   Data Acquisition and Protocol

Five relapsing-remitting (RR) MS patients (4 women and 1 man, mean ($\pm$SD) age: 36.8 ± 9.5 years; media disease duration: 4.24y; max 16.5y) (median Expanded Disability Status Scale (EDSS) = 2.5, range = $[0; 4]$) and one healthy control (HC) subject (age: 24y) were included in this study. Inclusion criteria specified that studied patients were diagnosed as RR MS if they present at least one new Gadolinium-enhancing lesion during the six months preceding study enrollment. The DTI image set consisted of the acquisition of 60 contiguous 2 mm-thick slices parallel to the bi-commissural plane (AC-PC), and were acquired using a 2D Echo-Planar Imaging (EPI) sequence (TE/TR = $60/8210$ ms, FOV = $224 \times 224 \times 120$ mm^3) with 32 gradient directions (b = $1000 \frac{s}{mm^2}$). The nominal voxel size at acquisition ($2 \times 2 \times 2$ mm^3) was interpolated to $0.875 \times 0.875 \times 2$ mm^3 after reconstruction.

2.2 Processing and Fiber-Bundle Extraction

Diffusion data of each subject are processed in order to compute the tensor model using the FDT module of FSL. The obtained tensor image is then non-rigidly co-registered to the Illinois Institute of Technology (IIT) atlas [13] using the DTI ToolKit (DTI-TK) [15]. The resulting tensor image is then used to compute 6 diffusion metric maps: fractional anisotropy (FA), mean diffusivity (MD), radial diffusivity (λ_r) and the three eigenvalues of diffusion tensor (λ_1, λ_2, λ_3). Probabilistic streamline tractography was performed using MRTrix [12] based on the fiber orientation density (FOD) information of IIT Atlas. From the atlas, twenty fiber bundles were extracted using 20 ROIs of the JHU atlas [5] as seed and mask. Fibers within each of the 20 bundles are then reordered according to common start/end point. For each fiber-bundle, a classical K-Means algorithm [6] is performed to generate two different clusters, R_1 for the starting points and R_2 for the ending points. Fiber points are then reordered from R_1 to R_2 and fibers that did not link the two clusters (broken fibers) are automatically removed. As final post-processing step each fiber is resampled with the same number $c = 100$ of points (also called nodes). Fiber-bundles processed with the previous described pipeline could be formalized as a set $Z = \{f_1, f_2, \ldots, f_n\}$ composed of n fibers $f_i = \{p_1, \ldots, p_c\}$ where $p_q = (x_q, y_q, z_q) \mid 1 \leq q \leq c$. The coordinate p_q is used to extract the voxel's value of one of the m diffusion maps in the corresponding location of f_i. With this formalization it is possible to analyze the changes of each diffusion map along each fiber belonging to a bundle.

2.3 Tensor Construction

Application of a tensor model to analyze brain data is a recent trend in signal processing. More in detail, a tensor model was successfully applied to event related potential (ERP) analysis [16] but also to tumor tissue type differentiation based on magnetic resonance spectroscopic imaging [4]. In this work tensor factorization is applied on diffusion data.

Starting from a fiber-bundle we create a tensor $\mathcal{X} \in \mathbb{R}^{c \times n \times m}$ (Fig. 1). Where c is the number of cross-sections of each fiber, n is the number of fibers within the bundle and m is the number of diffusion maps that we want to use. Following this tensor formalization, an element $x_{i,j,k} \in \mathcal{X}$ represents the value in the $i-th$ cross-section of the $j-th$ fiber of the bundle, extracted from the $k-th$ modality. This tensor formalization give us the possibility to analyze, at the same time, local and global aspects of a fiber-bundle. Local information could be obtained by analyzing $x_{:,j,k}$ which represents the values of the $k-th$ modality extracted along all the cross-sections of the $j-th$ fiber. We can also obtain global information of the fiber-bundle by analyzing $x_{i,:,k}$ which represents the values on the entire $i-th$ cross-section extracted from the $k-th$ modality (Fig. 1).

With this formalization it is easy to see how cross-section based methods, like the two described in [10,11], are special cases of the tensor-based model. In this paper we use C to denote the cross-sectional component, F to denote the

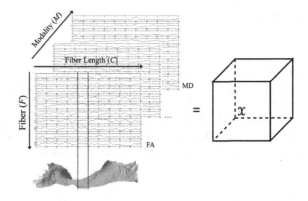

Fig. 1. Tensor representation of WM fiber-bundle

fiber-wise component and M to denote the modality component of the tensor $\mathcal{X}$ representing a fiber-bundle.

2.4   Non-negative CPD Analysis

The non-negative canonical polyadic decomposition (NCPD) decomposition factorizes [2] a tensor into a sum of positive component rank-one tensors. For example, given a third-order tensor $T \in \mathbb{R}^{i \times j \times k}$ we wish to write it as:

$$T \approx [\![ABC]\!] = \sum_{r=1}^{R} a_r \circ b_r \circ c_r \qquad A, B, C \geq 0 \qquad (1)$$

where $A = [a_1, \ldots, a_R] \in \mathbb{R}_+^{i \times R}$, $B = [b_1, \ldots, b_R] \in \mathbb{R}_+^{j \times R}$, $C = [c_1, \ldots, c_R] \in \mathbb{R}_+^{k \times R}$ are non-negative factor matrices. R is the rank, defined as the number of rank-one terms and "$\circ$" represent the outer product.

In our case, in order to compute the CPD of the tensor $\mathcal{X}$ built starting from a fiber-bundle, the solution of the following optimization problem is required:

$$[C^*, F^*, M^*] = \min_{C, F, M \geq 0} \left\| \mathcal{X} - \sum_{i=1}^{R} C(:, i) \circ F(:, i) \circ M(:, i) \right\|_2^2 + \alpha \|Vec(F)\|_1 \qquad (2)$$

where C, F and M are the aftermentioned cross-section, fibers and modality matrices and α is the parameter that control the sparsity imposed by using l_1-norm regularization. In this work the optimization problem 2 with non-negativity constraints is solved using the structured data fusion method [9] available in Tensorlab [8]. As last step, in order to associate at each fiber one of the three classes of tissues, the k-means++ algorithm [1] is applied on the fiber component (F^*) obtained from the NCPD.

3   Experiments

3.1   Simulated Data

30 different "pathological" variations were simulated on the control subject's diffusion maps. All the variations were generated along 3 different fiber-bundles, namely, cortico-spinal tract (CST), superior longitudinal fasciculi (SLF), and inferior longitudinal fasciculi (IFO). Small spherical regions of radius r were randomly selected along the WM fiber-bundles. The voxel's eigenvalues inside each region were changed according to the following equations:

$$\lambda_2^* = \lambda_2 + \rho * (\lambda_1 - \lambda_2) \quad \lambda_3^* = \lambda_3 + \rho * (\lambda_1 - \lambda_3)$$

and all diffusion metrics were recomputed according to the new value of λ_2^* and λ_3^*. In order to simulate small variations, we performed the tests using $r = 2$ and $\rho = 0.2$. Along each fiber-bundle 2 or 3 regions were randomly selected to put the signal changes. To quantify the quality of the delineation of the fibers containing the simulated variations, the True Positive (TP), True Negative (TN), False Positive (FP) and False Negative (FN) fractions were used to compute the performance measurements used in this work. More in detail we focus our attention on the precision ($P_r = \frac{TP}{TP+FP}$), recall ($R_e = \frac{TP}{TP+FN}$) and F-Measure ($M_e = \frac{2*TP}{2*TP+FP+FN}$). Since multiple test were performed, for each of the three diffusion metrics, mean ($\overline{P_r}$, $\overline{R_e}$, $\overline{M_e}$) and standard deviation (σP_r, σR_e, σM_e) were computed.

Rank of $R = 3$ was selected for NCPD. This value was chosen based on the presence of 3 main regions: *(i)* healthy tissue, *(ii)* "pathological" tissue, *(iii)* voxels with partial volume effect. Automatic rank selection is still an open problem and needs to be explored through further research.

Different tests were performed using different diffusion metrics at the same time ("λ_2, λ_3", "$FA, MD, \lambda_2, \lambda_3$" and "$FA, MD$"). Moreover, in order to find the best value of the regularization weight α, tests were performed with different values. The α-interval ($0 < \alpha \le 0.8$) was divided into 30 steps. We reported the results for certain values of α in Table 1. Best results were obtained using $\alpha = 0.1388$ and using λ_2, λ_3 as features. Worst performances were obtained using $\alpha = 0.6898$ and $\lambda_2, \lambda_3, FA, MD$ as features. We can also see how the regularization parameter α strongly influences the quality of the delineation. Indeed, high values of α show a degradation in the detection performances. Similar behavior is also visible for small values of α. The best results were visible in the range going from $\alpha = 0.0561$ to $\alpha = 0.1939$. Despite the high values of precision, the proposed method shows low performances in term of recall. Indeed, the method seems to underestimate the subset of fibers really affected by the pathological process.

3.2   Application on Multiple Sclerosis Patients

The proposed method was also applied on real data. More in detail, the CST and SLF of two MS subjects from the dataset described in Sect. 2.1 were selected.

Table 1. Changes in mean ($\overline{P_r}$, $\overline{R_e}$, $\overline{M_e}$) and standard deviation (σP_r, σR_e, σM_e) of precision, recall and F-Measure according to regularization parameter (α) and different features.

| | λ_2, λ_3 | | | | | | FA, MD, λ_2, λ_3 | | | | | | FA, MD | | | | | |
α	$\overline{P_r}$	σP_r	$\overline{R_e}$	σR_e	$\overline{M_s}$	σM_s	$\overline{P_r}$	σP_r	$\overline{R_e}$	σR_e	$\overline{M_s}$	σM_s	$\overline{P_r}$	σP_r	$\overline{R_e}$	σR_e	$\overline{M_s}$	σM_s
0.0561	0.66	0.17	0.48	0.16	0.53	0.15	0.65	0.20	0.38	0.19	0.44	0.18	0.61	0.19	0.39	0.15	0.44	0.13
0.0837	0.66	0.19	0.41	0.18	0.48	0.19	0.69	0.17	0.41	0.22	0.47	0.19	0.61	0.18	0.40	0.09	0.47	0.10
0.1112	0.64	0.19	0.47	0.17	0.51	0.16	0.66	0.16	0.37	0.20	0.43	0.18	0.60	0.18	0.38	0.10	0.45	0.11
0.1388	**0.67**	**0.16**	**0.42**	**0.18**	**0.49**	**0.16**	0.69	0.17	0.40	0.20	0.47	0.18	0.61	0.19	0.39	0.09	0.46	0.09
0.1663	0.67	0.19	0.41	0.20	0.47	0.19	0.68	0.16	0.34	0.21	0.41	0.21	0.60	0.18	0.43	0.10	0.48	0.09
0.1939	0.65	0.19	0.44	0.18	0.50	0.15	0.69	0.18	0.36	0.20	0.44	0.19	0.59	0.18	0.37	0.11	0.44	0.10
0.2490	0.65	0.16	0.35	0.18	0.42	0.18	0.66	0.17	0.37	0.20	0.44	0.19	0.60	0.19	0.36	0.13	0.43	0.11
0.5520	0.67	0.18	0.42	0.16	0.48	0.12	0.63	0.16	0.39	0.24	0.43	0.21	0.60	0.17	0.41	0.18	0.46	0.16
0.6898	0.64	0.16	0.41	0.22	0.46	0.19	0.60	0.18	0.30	0.20	0.34	0.18	0.62	0.18	0.43	0.18	0.47	0.15
0.7449	0.63	0.19	0.37	0.16	0.44	0.17	0.58	0.19	0.42	0.21	0.44	0.19	0.61	0.19	0.37	0.17	0.42	0.15

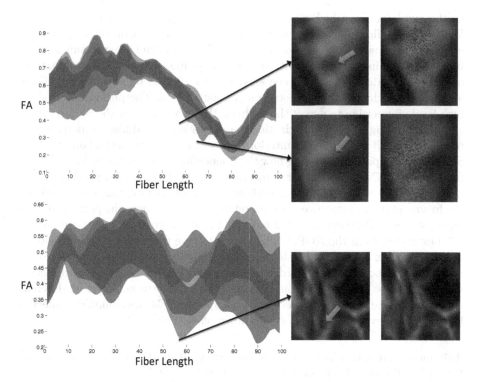

Fig. 2. Application of tensor factorization on two fiber-bundles in two MS patients. On top CST of the first subject. On left, the mean signal profile of FA along each set of fibers shows that the red fibers have change the FA signal in two regions corresponding to MS lesions (right figures). On the bottom plot, the mean FA signal along fibers belonging to SLF on the second MS patient. The red fiber-bundle show a large change in the regions affected by the pathology due to the presence of MS lesion (right figure).

Using the results obtained in the previous section, we used as regularization parameter $\alpha = 0.1388$ and λ_2, λ_3 as features. Results of the application are shown in Fig. 2. The application on the MS patients, shows the capability of our method to detect subsets of fibers within the bundle affected by the pathological event. The quality of the fiber-bundle extraction is also confirmed by the analysis of the mean FA signal [14]. The mean signal profile shows along each subset of fibers, how in certain cross-sections a change in the signal, appears. It is possibile to see how, for one fiber-bundle a negative-peak in the FA signal is present in certain cross-sections. This behavior is not confirmed by the other fiber-bundles. Indeed, for the other two classes of fibers the mean FA profile does not show cross-sections where the signal drastically changes.

4   Conclusion

In this work we described a new fully automated pipeline capable to analyze WM fiber-bundles. The major contribution is the application of NTF to WM analysis. We showed how a tensor-based model is a powerful tool to analyze fiber-bundles taking into account multi diffusion maps information. The capability of our method to distinguish between sets of fibers affected by pathological effects and set of healthy fibers was tested on simulated data. The performances show high level of precision to detect those fibers. We also show how the performances change according to the regularization parameter and the diffusion metrics used to analyze the fiber-bundle. As ulterior step, we applied our method on CST and SLF of two MS patients showing how the fibers affected by the pathological event pass through WM regions affected by real damage. We exploited partially NTF, since we focus our attention to the differentiation of fibers within the bundle. In the future we plan to improve our method in order to increase the performance in terms of recall. Moreover, we plan to exploit also the cross-sectional component (C^*) extracted from the NCPD. The idea is to give more complete information about the region along the fiber-bundle affected by the presence of MS. Moreover, we will extend our method in order to analyze longitudinal data, more in detail, we will increase the order of our tensor to analyze data acquired at different time points. The goal is to underline how a specific WM fiber-bundle is affected longitudinally by the presence of pathologic phenomena.

Acknowledgement. This research was supported by ERC Advanced Grant, #339804 BIOTENSORS and EU MC ITN TRANSACT 2012 #316679.

References

1. Arthur, D., Vassilvitskii, S.: k-means++: The advantages of careful seeding. In: Proceedings of the Eighteenth Annual ACM-SIAM Symposium on Discrete Algorithms, pp. 1027–1035 (2007)
2. Cichocki, A., Zdunek, R., Phan, A.H., Amari, S.I.: Nonnegative Matrix and Tensor Factorizations: Applications to Exploratory Multi-way Data Analysis and Blind Source Separation. Wiley, Chichester (2009)

3. Colby, J.B., Soderberg, L., Lebel, C., Dinov, I.D., Thompson, P.M., Sowell, E.R.: Along-tract statistics allow for enhanced tractography analysis. Neuroimage **59**(4), 3227–3242 (2012)

4. Halandur Nagaraja, B., Sima, D., Sauwen, N., Himmelreich, U., De Lathauwer, L., Van Huffel, S.: Tensor based tumor tissue type differentiation using magnetic resonance spectroscopic imaging. In: Annual International Conference of the IEEE, EMBC, pp. 7003–7006 (2015)

5. Hua, K., Zhang, J., Wakana, S., Jiang, H., Li, X., Reich, D.S., Calabresi, P.A., Pekar, J.J., van Zijl, P.C.M., Mori, S.: Tract probability maps in stereotaxic spaces: analyses of white matter anatomy and tract-specific quantification. Neuroimage **39**(1), 336–347 (2008)

6. MacQueen, J.: Some methods for classification and analysis of multivariate observations. In: Proceedings of the Fifth Berkeley Symposium on Mathematical Statistics and Probability, vol. 1, pp. 281–297 (1967)

7. Mårtensson, J., Nilsson, M., Ståhlberg, F., Sundgren, P.C., Nilsson, C., van Westen, D., Larsson, E.-M., Lätt, J.: Spatial analysis of diffusion tensor tractography statistics along the inferior fronto-occipital fasciculus with application in progressive supranuclear palsy. MAGMA **26**(6), 527–537 (2013)

8. Sorber, L., Van Barel, M., De Lathauwer, L.: Tensorlab v2.0, January 2014

9. Sorber, L., Van Barel, M., De Lathauwer, L.: Structured data fusion. Sel. Top. Sig. Process. **9**(4), 586–600 (2015)

10. Stamile, C., Kocevar, G., Cotton, F., Durand-Dubief, F., Hannoun, S., Frindel, C., Rousseau, D., Sappey-Marinier, D.: Detection of longitudinal dti changes in multiple sclerosis patients based on sensitive WM fiber modeling. In: ISMRM, May-June 2015, Toronto, Canada (2015)

11. Stamile, C., Kocevar, G., Cotton, F., Durand-Dubief, F., Hannoun, S., Frindel, C., Rousseau, D., Sappey-Marinier, D.: A longitudinal model for variations detection in white matter fiber-bundles. In: IWSSIP, pp. 57–60 (2015)

12. Tournier, J.D., Calamante, F., Connelly, A.: MRtrix: diffusion tractography in crossing fiber regions. Int. J. Imaging Syst. Technol. **22**, 53–66 (2012)

13. Varentsova, A., Zhang, S., Arfanakis, K.: Development of a high angular resolution diffusion imaging human brain template. Neuroimage **91**, 177–186 (2014)

14. Yeatman, J.D., Dougherty, R.F., Myall, N.J., Wandell, B.A., Feldman, H.M.: Tract profiles of white matter properties: automating fiber-tract quantification. PLoS One **7**(11), e49790 (2012)

15. Zhang, H., Yushkevich, P.A., Alexander, D.C., Gee, J.C.: Deformable registration of diffusion tensor MR images with explicit orientation optimization. Med. Image Anal. **10**(5), 764–785 (2006)

16. Zink, R., Hunyadi, B., Van Huffel, S., De Vos, M.: Tensor-based classification of auditory mobile BCI without subject-specific calibration phase. J. Neural Eng. **13**(2), 026005 (2016)

Cardiovascular Image Analysis

A Flexible 2D-3D Parametric Image Registration Algorithm for Cardiac MRI

L.W. Lorraine Ma and Mehran Ebrahimi[✉]

Faculty of Science, University of Ontario Institute of Technology,
2000 Simcoe Street North, Oshawa, ON L1H 7K4, Canada
{lok.ma,mehran.ebrahimi}@uoit.ca

Abstract. We propose a mathematical formulation aimed at parametric intensity-based registration of a deformed 3D volume to a 2D slice. The approach is flexible and can accommodate various regularization schemes, similarity measures, and optimizers. We evaluate the framework on 2D-3D registration experiments of *in vivo* cardiac magnetic resonance imaging (MRI) aimed at image-guided surgery applications that use of real-time MRI as a visualization tool. An affine transformation is used to demonstrate this parametric model. Target registration error, Jaccard and Dice indices are used to validate the algorithm and demonstrate the accuracy of the registration scheme on both simulated and clinical data.

Keywords: Image registration · Inverse problems · 2D to 3D alignment · Cardiac MRI · Optimization · Multi-level · Multi-resolution

1 Introduction

Cardiovascular disease is the leading cause of death globally, claiming more lives than cancer and chronic lower respiratory disease combined [1]. In Canada, cardiovascular disease is responsible for approximately 1 in every 3 deaths, with a quarter of those deaths resulting from myocardial infarction [2].

Ventricular arrhythmias commonly occur in patients with previous myocardial infarction due to myocardial scarring, which can disrupt electrical activity in the heart. Arrhythmias in the ventricles are potentially life-threatening because they can render the heart unable to effectively circulate blood through the body, and are associated with increased risk of sudden cardiac death [3,4].

Treatment options include catheter ablation, removing or isolating anatomic structure responsible for abnormal propagation of electrical impulses. X-ray fluoroscopy is traditionally used to guide cardiac catheterization procedures. However, because of its poor soft tissue contrast and the ionizing radiation involved, real-time magnetic resonance imaging (MRI) has been proposed as an alternative [5–7]. With superior soft tissue contrast, real-time MRI used during cardiovascular procedures would better capture anatomical features of the heart.

Real-time MRI provides live positional updates during intervention in 2D, but the tradeoff between image quality and acquisition time means that 2D real-time

© Springer International Publishing Switzerland 2016
A. Campilho and F. Karray (Eds.): ICIAR 2016, LNCS 9730, pp. 661–671, 2016.
DOI: 10.1007/978-3-319-41501-7_74

MRI lacks in image quality compared to high-quality 3D MRI volumes acquired prior to intervention. Ideally, one would register the 3D prior images to 2D real-time images, combining the advantages of both to obtain high-quality images that account for small amounts of motion, such as motion due to respiration, in real time.

In this paper, we propose a mathematical framework to align high-resolution 3D MR images to noisier 2D real-time MR images. While previous work in the area focused on rigid body transformation [7–9], we extend the model to affine parametric registration and investigate ill-posedness of the registration as an inverse problem.

A general mathematical model is introduced in Sect. 2. The discretization of the model is covered in Sect. 3, followed by a Gauss-Newton optimization strategy described in Sect. 4. Computational experiments and results on both simulated and real 2D-3D data will be presented in Sect. 5. Finally, Sect. 6 is dedicated to discussion and conclusions.

2   Mathematical Model

Consider the registration problem of a 3D template image $\mathcal{T}$ to a 2D reference image $\mathcal{R}$, where $\mathcal{R}$ is a realization of $\mathcal{T}$ deformed via a transformations y and sliced at a certain location, e.g. z. The reference and template images are represented by mappings $\mathcal{R} : \Omega \subset \mathbb{R}^2 \to \mathbb{R}$ and $\mathcal{T} : \Omega \times \mathcal{Z} \subset \mathbb{R}^3 \to \mathbb{R}$ of compact support. Considering a slice location z, the goal is to find the transformation $y : \mathbb{R}^3 \to \mathbb{R}^3$ such that $\mathcal{L}_z(\mathcal{T}[y])$ is similar to $\mathcal{R}$, in which $\mathcal{T}[y]$ is the transformed template image and $\mathcal{L}_z : \mathrm{L}^2(\Omega \times \mathcal{Z}) \to \mathrm{L}^2(\Omega)$ is the slicing operator at level $z \in \mathcal{Z} \subset \mathbb{R}$, where $\mathcal{L}_z(\mathcal{T}(x^1, x^2, x^3)) := \mathcal{T}(x^1, x^2, z)$ for $(x^1, x^2, x^3) \in \mathbb{R}^3$. A formulation of the 2D-3D image registration of a template image $\mathcal{T}$ to a reference image $\mathcal{R}$ can be written as the following problem.

2D-3D Image Registration Problem: Given two images $\mathcal{R} : \Omega \subset \mathbb{R}^2 \to \mathbb{R}$ and $\mathcal{T} : \Omega \times \mathcal{Z} \subset \mathbb{R}^3 \to \mathbb{R}$ and an arbitrary given slice location $z \in \mathbb{R}$, find a transformation $y : \mathbb{R}^3 \to \mathbb{R}^3$ that minimize the objective functional

$$\mathcal{J}[y] := \mathcal{D}[\mathcal{L}_z(\mathcal{T}[y]), \mathcal{R}] + \mathcal{S}[y - y^{\mathrm{ref}}].$$

Here, $\mathcal{D}$ is a distance that measures the dissimilarity of $\mathcal{L}_z(\mathcal{T}[y])$ and $\mathcal{R}$, and $\mathcal{S}$ is a regularization expression on the transformation y that penalizes transformations "away" from y^{ref}.

2.1   Parametric 2D-3D Registration

It is possible that y can be parametrized via parameters w. For example if y is an affine transformation, the transformation on a point $x = (x^1, x^2, x^3)$ can be expressed as

$$y(w; x) = \begin{pmatrix} w_1 & w_2 & w_3 \\ w_5 & w_6 & w_7 \\ w_9 & w_{10} & w_{11} \end{pmatrix} \begin{pmatrix} x^1 \\ x^2 \\ x^3 \end{pmatrix} + \begin{pmatrix} w_4 \\ w_8 \\ w_{12} \end{pmatrix}.$$

In general, for the parametric registration problem we equivalently aim to minimize

$$J[w] := \mathcal{D}[\mathcal{L}_z(\mathcal{T}[y(w)]), \mathcal{R}] + \mathcal{S}[w - w^{\text{ref}}]. \tag{1}$$

Here we assume sum of squared distances (SSD) is the dissimilarity measure $\mathcal{D}$

$$\mathcal{D}[\mathcal{L}_z(\mathcal{T}), \mathcal{R}] = \mathcal{D}^{\text{SSD}}[\mathcal{L}_z(\mathcal{T}), \mathcal{R}] := \frac{1}{2} \int_\Omega (\mathcal{L}_z(\mathcal{T}(x)) - \mathcal{R}(x))^2 \, dx.$$

Furthermore, the regularization functional $\mathcal{S}$ can be defined as

$$\mathcal{S}[w - w^{\text{ref}}] := \frac{1}{2} \times (w - w^{\text{ref}})^T \mathbf{M} (w - w^{\text{ref}})$$

for a symmetric positive definite weight matrix $\mathbf{M}$ that acts as a regularizer (see [10,11]).

If no regularization is imposed on w, for any pair of given images $\mathcal{R}$ and $\mathcal{T}$ the above model is ill-posed. Therefore, to yield a unique w, we require a regularizer $\mathcal{S}$ independent of the input images. The following theorem proves this claim.

Theorem 1. *Consider a given z. Any two affine transformations w^A and w^B that satisfy the following conditions yield $\mathcal{L}_z(\mathcal{T}[y(w^A; x)]) = \mathcal{L}_z(\mathcal{T}[y(w^B; x)])$:*

$$\begin{pmatrix} w_1^A \\ w_5^A \\ w_9^A \end{pmatrix} = \begin{pmatrix} w_1^B \\ w_5^B \\ w_9^B \end{pmatrix}, \begin{pmatrix} w_2^A \\ w_6^A \\ w_{10}^A \end{pmatrix} = \begin{pmatrix} w_2^B \\ w_6^B \\ w_{10}^B \end{pmatrix}, \begin{pmatrix} w_3^A - w_3^B \\ w_7^A - w_7^B \\ w_{11}^A - w_{11}^B \end{pmatrix} z + \begin{pmatrix} w_4^A - w_4^B \\ w_8^A - w_8^B \\ w_{12}^A - w_{12}^B \end{pmatrix} = \begin{pmatrix} 0 \\ 0 \\ 0 \end{pmatrix}.$$

Proof. Note that for any given z and w

$$\mathcal{L}_z[\mathcal{T}[y(w; x)]] = \mathcal{L}_z \left[\mathcal{T} \left[\begin{pmatrix} w_1 & w_2 & w_3 \\ w_5 & w_6 & w_7 \\ w_9 & w_{10} & w_{11} \end{pmatrix} \begin{pmatrix} x^1 \\ x^2 \\ x^3 \end{pmatrix} + \begin{pmatrix} w_4 \\ w_8 \\ w_{12} \end{pmatrix} \right] \right]$$

$$= \mathcal{T} \left[\begin{pmatrix} w_1 & w_2 & w_3 \\ w_5 & w_6 & w_7 \\ w_9 & w_{10} & w_{11} \end{pmatrix} \begin{pmatrix} x^1 \\ x^2 \\ z \end{pmatrix} + \begin{pmatrix} w_4 \\ w_8 \\ w_{12} \end{pmatrix} \right].$$

Now consider w^A and w^B that for any x^1, x^2

$$\begin{pmatrix} w_1^A & w_2^A & w_3^A \\ w_5^A & w_6^A & w_7^A \\ w_9^A & w_{10}^A & w_{11}^A \end{pmatrix} \begin{pmatrix} x^1 \\ x^2 \\ z \end{pmatrix} + \begin{pmatrix} w_4^A \\ w_8^A \\ w_{12}^A \end{pmatrix} = \begin{pmatrix} w_1^B & w_2^B & w_3^B \\ w_5^B & w_6^B & w_7^B \\ w_9^B & w_{10}^B & w_{11}^B \end{pmatrix} \begin{pmatrix} x^1 \\ x^2 \\ z \end{pmatrix} + \begin{pmatrix} w_4^B \\ w_8^B \\ w_{12}^B \end{pmatrix}.$$

Therefore for any x^1, x^2

$$\begin{pmatrix} w_1^A - w_1^B \\ w_5^A - w_5^B \\ w_9^A - w_9^B \end{pmatrix} x^1 + \begin{pmatrix} w_2^A - w_2^B \\ w_6^A - w_6^B \\ w_{10}^A - w_{10}^B \end{pmatrix} x^2 = - \left[\begin{pmatrix} w_3^A - w_3^B \\ w_7^A - w_7^B \\ w_{11}^A - w_{11}^B \end{pmatrix} z + \begin{pmatrix} w_4^A - w_4^B \\ w_8^A - w_8^B \\ w_{12}^A - w_{12}^B \end{pmatrix} \right].$$

Equating the right-hand-side and left-hand-side to zero completes the proof.

This suggests that if no regularization is imposed, the first two columns of w^A and w^B have to match. In addition, for any given third columns of w^A and w^B, a given z, and a given fourth column of w^A, we can always compute the fourth column of w^B that yields the same sliced result. This suggests that if we impose no regularization, the parameters of w have to be reduced to 9 instead of 12. In practice, since we typically have information about the reference w^{ref}, we impose regularization and keep the number of parameters as 12 in the parametric affine case.

Furthermore, regardless of how many parameters we choose for w, the registration problem may be ill-posed in theory due to the intensities of images $\mathcal{R}$ and $\mathcal{T}$. For example, if $\mathcal{R}$ is image of a disk in 2D and $\mathcal{T}$ is image of a sphere in 3D, the problem yields infinitely many solutions since infinitely many cross-sections of a sphere can yield a disk. Due to the structure of the employed input images, this does not happen in practice. That being said, we regularize the affine transformation w in all cases.

3   Discretization

Here we apply a discretize-then-optimize paradigm (see [12] and the FAIR software [11] for details) to minimize the functional in Eq. (1). Assuming that Ω, or equivalently each slice of the image, is discretized into n pixels and $\mathcal{Z}$ into l pixels, we can define discretized grids x_R and x_T respectively relating to $\mathcal{R}$ and $\mathcal{T}$ such that $x_R = [x_k^1, x_k^2]_{k=1,\ldots,n}$ and $x_T = [x_j^1, x_j^2, x_j^3]_{j=1,\ldots,n \times l}$. Expressions $\mathbf{x}_R$ and $\mathbf{x}_T$ denote discretizations of Ω and $\Omega \times \mathcal{Z}$ respectively. Throughout this paper, it is assumed that cell-centered-discretized images R, T respectively contains n and nl pixels. Furthermore, $\mathbf{y} \approx y(w; \mathbf{x}_T)$, $\mathbf{w} = w$, $R \approx \mathcal{R}(\mathbf{x}_R)$, and $T \approx \mathcal{T}(\mathbf{x}_T)$ each corresponding to a discretization. Table 1 summarizes size of the corresponding discrete variables throughout this manuscript. Discretization of the operators $\mathcal{D}, \mathcal{S}$ are represented by D, S (see [11]). For a given z, the discretization of the operator $\mathcal{L}_z$, denoted by L_z can be computed as

$$L_z = I_{n \times nl} := I_{n \times n} \otimes [\overbrace{0,\ldots,0, \underbrace{1}_{\lceil l(z+\omega)/2\omega \rceil\text{-th component}}, 0,\ldots,0}^{1 \times l \text{ size}}]$$

in which we have assumed $\mathcal{Z}$ is the interval $(-\omega, \omega)$. The discretized problem is now to minimize the functional

$$J[\mathbf{w}] := D[L_z(T(\mathbf{y}(\mathbf{w}))), R] + S(\mathbf{w} - \mathbf{w}^{\text{ref}}).$$

4   Optimization

We compute the derivative and Hessian of J denoted by dJ and H_J respectively in a Gauss-Newton approach described in Algorithm 1 [13]. For simplicity, we allow ourselves to interchangeably refer to derivatives of real-valued functions as Jacobians as well. Hessian and Jacobian of the regularization S are denoted respectively as dS and H_S. To proceed, we represent the Jacobian of the objective function J as $dJ := \frac{\partial J}{\partial \mathbf{w}}$. Now define $L := L_z(T(\mathbf{y}(\mathbf{w})))$ and $r := L - R$. Choosing the SSD distance measure and defining $\Psi(r) := \frac{1}{2}r^T r = D[L_z(T(\mathbf{y}(\mathbf{w}))), R]$ yields $J[\mathbf{w}] = \Psi + S(\mathbf{w} - \mathbf{w}^{\text{ref}})$. Hence using the chain-rule

$$
\begin{aligned}
\frac{\partial J}{\partial \mathbf{w}} &= \left(\frac{\partial \Psi}{\partial r}\right)\left(\frac{\partial r}{\partial L}\right)\left(\frac{\partial L}{\partial T}\right)\left(\frac{\partial T}{\partial \mathbf{y}}\right)\left(\frac{\partial \mathbf{y}}{\partial \mathbf{w}}\right) + \left(\frac{\partial S}{\partial \mathbf{w}}\right) \\
&= r^T \times I_{n\times n} \times I_{n\times nl} \times dT \times d\mathbf{y} + dS \\
&= r^T \times I_{n\times n} \times I_{n\times nl} \times dT \times d\mathbf{y} + (\mathbf{w} - \mathbf{w}^{\text{ref}})^T \mathbf{M}
\end{aligned}
$$

in which $dT := \frac{\partial T}{\partial \mathbf{y}}$ represents the derivative of the interpolant and $d\mathbf{y} := \frac{\partial \mathbf{y}}{\partial \mathbf{w}}$ is the derivative of the transformation $\mathbf{y}$ with respect to $\mathbf{w}$. Derivatives $d\mathbf{y}$ and dT are both available in FAIR [11]. Finally, the Hessian of J denoted by H_J can be approximated as

$$
H_J = d^2\Psi + H_S \approx dr^T dr + H_S = dr^T dr + \mathbf{M},
$$

where

$$
dr = \left(\frac{\partial r}{\partial L}\right)\left(\frac{\partial L}{\partial T}\right)\left(\frac{\partial T}{\partial \mathbf{y}}\right)\left(\frac{\partial \mathbf{y}}{\partial \mathbf{w}}\right) = I_{n\times n} \times I_{n\times nl} \times dT \times d\mathbf{y} = I_{n\times nl} \times dT \times d\mathbf{y}.
$$

In practice, to speed up the computations, matrix-free implementation of the algorithm can be applied. We also consider different discrete representations of the image registration problem, and address the discrete problems sequentially in the so-called multi-level approach. Starting with the coarsest and thus most

Table 1. Sizes of discrete variables. n and l correspond to the number of pixels in each slice and the number of slices in the discretization, respectively.

Variable(s)	Size
R, L, r	$n \times 1$
T	$nl \times 1$
$\mathbf{x}_R$	$2n \times 1$
$\mathbf{x}_T, \mathbf{y}$	$3nl \times 1$
$\mathbf{w}, \mathbf{w}^{\text{ref}}$	12×1
S, J, Ψ	1×1
dT	$nl \times 3nl$
$d\mathbf{y}$	$3nl \times 12$
dr	$n \times 12$
dJ, dS	1×12
$H_J, H_S, \mathbf{M}$	12×12

inexpensive problem, a solution is computed, which then serves as a starting guess for the next finer discretization. This procedure has several advantages. It adds additional regularization to the registration problem (more weight is given to more important structure), it is very efficient (typically, most of the work is done on the computationally inexpensive coarse representations, and only a refinement is required on the costly finest representation), it preserves the optimization character of the problem and thus allows the use of established schemes for line searches and stopping. The use of this technique leads to optimal schemes in the sense that only a fixed number of arithmetic operations is expected for every data point and prevents the optimization problem from being trapped in a local minimum.

Algorithm 1. Minimizing $J[\mathbf{w}]$ using Gauss-Newton Approach

---

Initialize $[\mathbf{w}] \leftarrow [\mathbf{w}_0]$.
while not converged **do**
    Evaluate H_J and dJ at $[\mathbf{w}]$.
    Solve the descent direction from the linear equation $H_J[\delta\mathbf{w}] = -dJ^T$.
    Find a positive scalar step-size $\mathbf{s}$ using a line-search scheme.
    Update $[\mathbf{w}] \leftarrow [\mathbf{w}] + \mathbf{s}[\delta\mathbf{w}]$.
end while

---

5 Experiments and Results

5.1 Data

3D pre-procedural and 2D real-time cardiac MRI were acquired from 6 volunteers using a 1.5T MRI scanner (GE Healthcare, Waukesha, WI).

Prior 3D (cine) images: Each pre-procedural 3D volume consists of a stack of short-axis slices of the heart with a resolution of $1.37 \times 1.37 \times 8\,\mathrm{mm}^3$ and a field of view (FOV) of $350 \times 350\,\mathrm{mm}^2$. The images were acquired at end-expiration breath-hold during the end-diastolic cardiac phase with an electrocardiogram (ECG) gated GE FIESTA pulse sequence.

Real-time images: 2D real-time images were aquired at the same slice locations as in the pre-procedural scans, but under free-breathing conditions. The images were obtained with a fast spiral balanced steady state free precession sequence at a frame rate of 8 fps, an in-plane resolution of $2.2 \times 2.2\,\mathrm{mm}^2$, slice thickness 8 mm, and a FOV of $350 \times 350\,\mathrm{mm}^2$. The images were also ECG-gated, and only end-diastole phase images were used in the following experiments.

5.2   Controlled 3D to 2D Experiments on Cardiac MRI

Controlled experiments were performed where the 2D reference image was a slice of the 3D cine volume transformed with a known affine transformation. In this example, 2D-3D registration was performed between the original 3D volume and the generated reference image where $n = 128 \times 128$, $l = 12$, $\Omega = (-175, 175) \times (-175, 175) \, \text{mm}^2$, $\mathcal{Z} = (-48, 48) \, \text{mm}$. Also, we assume the regularizer $\mathbf{M}$ is a diagonal 12×12 matrix with unit entries on the main diagonal except for locations 3, 7, and 11 where entries are 10^6, i.e., large. This regularizer ensures the third column of the computed $\mathbf{w}$ to be $[0, 0, 1]^T$ in practice; see Theorem 1. Linear interpolation and an Armijo line search [13] were

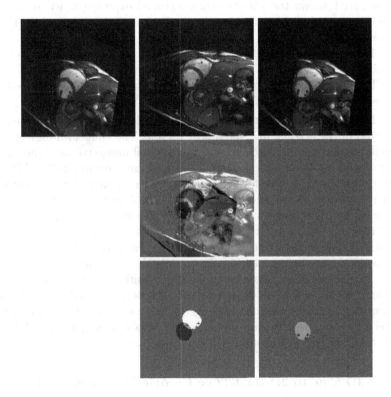

Fig. 1. Results of registration between a 3D image and a 2D cine image in a controlled experiment. (a) Reference image R. (b), (c) Template slice L before and after registration. (d), (e) Difference between the reference image and template slice $(L - R)$ before and after registration. (f) Segmentation masks showing left ventricle overlap before registration, with out-of-plane reference image landmarks projected onto image ($\times$) and in-plane template image landmarks ($+$). (g) Segmentation masks showing left ventricle overlap after registration, with out-of-plane reference image landmarks projected onto image ($\times$) and in-plane template image landmarks ($+$).

Table 2. Jaccard indices and Dice coefficients of left ventricle overlap before and after registration in the controlled experiment described above.

	Jaccard	Dice	TRE (mm)
Before registration	0.05	0.10	43.2 ± 4.3
After registration	1.00	1.00	1.8 ± 0.1

used in the multi-level Gauss-Newton optimization framework with a stopping criteria of 100 fixed iterations that was tuned to yield satisfactory results for our experiments.

Figure 1 shows the results of a controlled experiment where the reference image was produced by transforming a 3D cine volume with arbitrarily selected parameters $\mathbf{w} = [w_1, w_2, ..., w_{12}] = [1.2, 0.2, -0.1, 23\,\text{mm}, -0.2, 1, 0.1, -41\,\text{mm}, 0, 0.1, 0.9, -15\,\text{mm}]$ and then slicing with L_z, where the slicing operation was applied at location $z = -4\,\text{mm}$.

The Dice similarity coefficient and Jaccard index used are defined as:
$\text{Dice}(A, B) = \frac{2|A \cap B|}{|A| + |B|}$ and $\text{Jaccard}(A, B) = \frac{|A \cap B|}{|A \cup B|}$.

The left ventricle and landmarks in the left ventricle were manually segmented in the original 3D cine image volume. The endocardium of the left ventricle was outlined for each slice in the original image volume, and the in-plane segmentations stacked to produce a 3D segmentation mask. The 3D segmentation mask was then transformed using transformation parameters obtained from the registration, i.e., $\mathbf{w}$, and then sliced at $z = -4\,\text{mm}$ to obtain $L = L_z(T(\mathbf{y}(\mathbf{w})))$. Jaccard and Dice indices were then computed between the projected masks of the reference image and the slice described above. The target registration error (TRE) before registration was obtained by measuring the l^2-normed distance between the landmark locations in the initially transformed volume and in the template image. Landmark locations in the initially transformed volume (from which the 2D reference slice is taken) can be computed using the manually selected landmark locations and the initial transformation, which are known. The TRE after registration was similarly obtained from landmark locations in the template image transformed with $\mathbf{w}$, see Table 2.

5.3   3D Cine to 2D Real-Time Cardiac MRI Registration

Experiments were performed where a 2D real-time image was taken to be the reference image. 2D-3D registration was performed between a 3D cine image volume and the real-time reference image with the same parameters as in the controlled experiment, with the exception that there is no initial transformation applied on the reference image.

The real-time and cine cardiac MRI are already rather aligned initially in the z-direction so performing registration between images from different slices would be a better indicator of how well the algorithm works to move things in the z-direction. By choosing the slicing operation at location $z = -36\,\text{mm}$, the initial

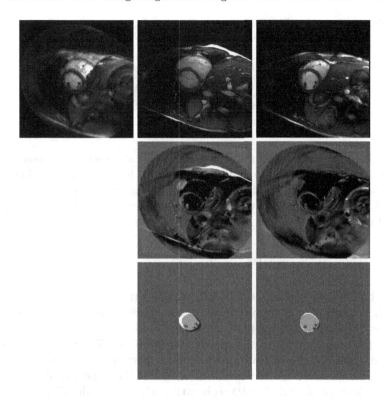

Fig. 2. Results of registration between a 3D cine image and a 2D real-time image on the same subject as in the controlled experiment, with an initial misalignment of approximately 32 mm in the z-direction (through the image plane). (a) Reference image R. (b), (c) Template slice L before and after registration. (d), (e) Difference between the reference image and template slice $(L - R)$ before and after registration. (f) Segmentation masks showing left ventricle overlap before registration, with in-plane reference image landmarks ($\times$) and out-of-plane template image landmarks projected onto image ($+$). (g) Segmentation masks showing left ventricle overlap after registration, with in-plane reference image landmarks ($\times$) and out-of-plane template image landmarks projected onto image ($+$).

template slice was geometrically positioned approximately 32 mm away from the location of the reference image (at $z_0 = -4$ mm). To register the images, the registration algorithm must now produce a result that translates the 3D template image approximately 32 mm in the z-direction, along with appropriate alignments in the x-, y-directions. To validate registration results, the left ventricle in each of the 2D real-time images was segmented by an expert. Results including projected left ventricle overlap before and after registration are shown in Fig. 2. Jaccard and Dice indices were again computed between the projected masks of the 2D real-time image and a slice of the 3D mask transformed using parameters

Table 3. Jaccard indices and Dice coefficients of left ventricle overlap before and after registration between a 3D cine image and 2D real-time image, described above.

	Jaccard	Dice	TRE (mm)
Before registration	0.67	0.80	32.8 ± 0.3
After registration	0.87	0.93	4.5 ± 0.1

obtained from the registration. The TRE was also computed assuming that z_0, the z-coordinate location of the 2D reference image, is known. The l^2-normed distances of the landmarks in the reference image and template images before and after registration were used to compute the TREs. The results are shown in Table 3.

6   Discussion and Conclusion

In the previous section, it was demonstrated that the algorithm performs very well in controlled experiments where the reference image is a transformed and sliced version of the template image, and also where the initial misalignment due to translation alone was approximately 50 mm. The presented example was a nominal instance of several experiments performed over a range of parameters. We can conclude that between images of the same modality, the proposed multi-level parametric 2D-3D registration scheme can align images well for misalignments within reasonable limits encountered in clinical applications, such as motion due to respiration. The left ventricle overlap between the 3D cine volume and a 2D real-time image in the previous section aligned well after registration, as quantified by the Jaccard and Dice indices. The registration algorithm corrected the large z-direction translation and produced a resulting image with structural features in the heart very similar to those in the reference image as shown in Fig. 2. It is worth noting that, the regions outside the heart may not look as similar due to large motion of surrounding organs such as the lungs and diaphragm. For images of two different acquisition types – real-time and prior cine, the registration algorithm improved alignment. For multi-modality experiments where intensities differ more drastically, one can consider using other dissimilarity measures and/or optimizers [11,14] that can fit well within the context of the general proposed model.

Acknowledgments. This research was supported in part by a Natural Sciences and Engineering Research Council of Canada (NSERC) Discovery Grant for M. Ebrahimi. We would like to thank Drs. Graham Wright and Robert Xu of Sunnybrook Research Institute, Toronto, Canada, for valuable discussions and providing the MR data.

References

1. Mozaffarian, D., et al.: Heart disease and stroke statistics - 2015 update: a report from the american heart association. Circulation **131**, e29–e322 (2015)
2. The Public Health Agency of Canada: Tracking Heart Disease and Stroke in Canada (2009)
3. Koplan, B.A., Stevenson, W.G.: Ventricular tachycardia and sudden cardiac death. Mayo. Clin. Proc. **84**, 289–297 (2009)
4. Kokolis, S., Clark, L.T., Kokolis, R., Kassotis, J.: Ventricular arrhythmias and sudden cardiac death. Prog. Cardiovasc. Dis. **48**, 426–444 (2006)
5. Lardo, A.C.: Real-time magnetic resonance imaging: diagnostic and interventional applications. Pediatr. Cardiol. **21**, 80–98 (2000)
6. Rhode, K.S., Hill, D.L.G., Edwards, P.J., et al.: Registration and tracking to integrate X-Ray and MR images in an XMR facility. IEEE Trans. Med. Imag. **22**, 1369–1378 (2003)
7. Xu, R., Wright, G.A.: Registration of real-time and prior imaging data with applications to MR guided cardiac interventions. In: Camara, O., Mansi, T., Pop, M., Rhode, K., Sermesant, M., Young, A. (eds.) STACOM 2014. LNCS, vol. 8896, pp. 265–274. Springer, Heidelberg (2015)
8. Smolíková, R., Wachowiak, M.P., Drangova, M.: Registration of fast cine cardiac MR slices to 3D preprocedural images: toward real time registration for MRI-guided procedures. In: Proceedings of the SPIE 5370, Medical Imaging 2004: Image Processing, pp. 1195–1205. SPIE, Bellingham (2004)
9. Smolíková-Wachowiak, R., Wachowiak, M.P., Fenster, A., Drangova, M.: Registration of two-dimensional cardiac images to preprocedural three-dimensional images for interventional applications. J. Magn. Reson. Im. **22**, 219–228 (2005)
10. Modersitzki, J.: Numerical Methods for Image Registration. Oxford U. Press, Oxford (2004)
11. Modersitzki, J.: FAIR: Flexible Algorithms for Image Registration. SIAM, Philadelphia (2009)
12. Haber, E., Modersitzki, J.: A multilevel method for image registration. SIAM J. Sci. Comput. **27**, 1594–1607 (2006)
13. Nocedal, J., Wright, S.J.: Numerical Optimization, 2nd edn. Springer, New York (2006)
14. Goshtasby, A.: 2-D and 3-D Image Registration. Wiley Press, New York (2005)

Sparse-View CT Reconstruction Using Curvelet and TV-Based Regularization

Ali Pour Yazdanpanah$^{(\boxtimes)}$ and Emma E. Regentova

Electrical and Computer Engineering Department, University of Nevada,
Las Vegas 89154, USA
`pouryazd@unlv.nevada.edu`

Abstract. The reconstruction from sparse-view projections is one of important problems in computed tomography limited by the availability or feasibility of a large number of projections. Total variation (TV) approaches have been introduced to improve the reconstruction quality by smoothing the variation between neighboring pixels. However, the TV-based methods for images with textures or complex shapes may generate artifacts and cause loss of details. Here, we propose a new regularization model for CT reconstruction by combining regularization methods based on TV and the curvelet transform. Combining curvelet regularizer, which is optimally sparse with better directional sensitivity than wavelet transforms with TV on the other hand will give us a unique regularization model that leads to the improvement of the reconstruction quality. The split-Bregman (augmented Lagrangian) approach has been used as a solver which makes it easy to incorporate multiple regularization terms including the one based on the multiresolution transformation, in our case curvelet transform, into optimization framework. We compare our method with the methods using only TV, wavelet, and curvelet as the regularization terms on the test phantom images. The results show that there are benefits in using the proposed combined curvelet and TV regularizer in the sparse view CT reconstruction.

Keywords: Computed tomography · Sparse-view reconstruction · Curvelet · Total variation

1 Introduction

Computed Tomography (CT) is used as a common tool for medical diagnostics, non-destructive testing, airport baggage screening and etc. For medical, security or industrial applications of CT a limited number of views is an option for whether reducing the radiation dose or screening time, and obviously cost of operation. In applications such as non-destructive testing or inspection of a large object, like a turbine or a cargo container one angular view can take up to a few minutes for only one slice. Furthermore some views could be simply unavailable due to the system configuration. Also in recent years, radiation exposure concerns in medical CT applications have increased [1].

© Springer International Publishing Switzerland 2016
A. Campilho and F. Karray (Eds.): ICIAR 2016, LNCS 9730, pp. 672–677, 2016.
DOI: 10.1007/978-3-319-41501-7_75

The total variation regularization have been widely used in the area of image denoising and restoration [2,3], sparse-view CT reconstruction, and interior tomography [4–6]. Recently, Candes, proposed an efficient sparsifying transform named curvelet transform [7]. Curvelet, unlike wavelets, has better directional sensitivity, better l_1-norm sparsity and does not generate the staircase-type noise. These features make curvelet transform very suitable for sparse-view CT reconstruction.

In this paper, we propose a new optimization model for CT reconstruction by combining two recently-developed regularization methods based on total variation and the curvelet transform. The split-Bregman is an efficient solver [8–10] used in our CT reconstruction framework. One of the advantages which make it useful for the proposed framework is that it allows for incorporating extra regularization terms.

The paper is organized as follows. In Sect. 2, the proposed regularization model for computed tomography system is formulated and the optimization problem is solved. Results are demonstrated in Sect. 3. Conclusions are drawn in Sect. 4.

2 Materials and Methods

A computed tomography system can be defined as a linear equation in two different scenarios: noise-free Eq. (1) and noisy Eq. (2) cases:

$$A\mathrm{x} = b. \tag{1}$$

$$A\mathrm{x} + n = b. \tag{2}$$

where $b \in R^N$ is the projection data, $\mathrm{x} \in R^M$ is the reconstruction image, $A \in R^{N \times M}$ is the system geometry matrix, and n is the approximation of the interference of noise, error, and other factors present in a practical imaging process. Assuming noise and given the sparse-view model, the reconstruction problem is ill-posed for minimizing the least-squares function. Therefore, the following cost function with a regularization term has been considered.

$$\underset{\mathrm{x}}{\text{minimize}} \ |\phi(\mathrm{x})|_1 \quad \text{subject to} \quad \|b - A\mathrm{x}\|_2^2 \leq \sigma \tag{3}$$

where ϕ is a sparsifying transform and σ is an upper bound of the uncertainty in the projections (b). Here l_1-norm denoted by $|.|_1$ and l_2-norm by $\|.\|_2$. The constrained optimization in Eq. (3) is equivalent to the following unconstrained optimization problem [9,11]:

$$\underset{\mathrm{x}}{\text{minimize}} \ |\phi(\mathrm{x})|_1 + \lambda \|b - A\mathrm{x}\|_2^2 \tag{4}$$

where $\lambda > 0$ is a balancing constant which relies on the sparsity of the underlying image x under linear transformation. Considering the problem, the sparsifying term $\phi(\mathrm{x})$ can include different regularizers. In this study, we proposed and formulate the optimization problem using a combination of both total variation and curvelet regularizers. In our CT reconstruction approach:

$$|\phi(\mathbf{x})|_1 = \alpha_{TV}(|\nabla_x(\mathbf{x})|_1 + |\nabla_y(\mathbf{x})|_1) + \alpha_C|C(\mathbf{x})|_1 \tag{5}$$

where ∇ is the discrete gradient operator and C is the curvelet transform and constants α_{TV} and α_C are the weighting parameters stressing the TV and curvelet terms. Total variation is ideally suited if the reconstructed data are piecewise constant throughout the image [12]. Recently, curvelet regularization has been used for de-noising, and for more general applications like solving the inverse problem [7,13]. By taking advantage of a sparsity constraint in the curvelet domain, the curvelet regularization can also be considered as a sparsifying transform ϕ.

The proposed optimization problem has both l_1 and l_2-norm terms that complicates finding the solution in a closed-form. The split-Bregman framework [9] is adopted in this paper. In the split-Bregman framework, l_1 and l_2-norm terms will split into Bregman update steps and an unconstrained optimization problem. Our proposed optimization problem:

$$\hat{\mathbf{x}} = \underset{\mathbf{x}}{\operatorname{argmin}} |\phi(\mathbf{x})|_1 + \lambda\|b - A\mathbf{x}\|_2^2 \tag{6}$$

is solved by iterating over the following Eqs. (7–13):

$$\mathbf{x}^{(i+1)} = \underset{\mathbf{x}}{\operatorname{argmin}} \frac{\lambda}{2}\|b - A\mathbf{x}\|_2^2 + \frac{\mu}{2}\|p_{TV,x}^{(i)} - \nabla_x(\mathbf{x}) - v_{TV,x}^{(i)}\|_2^2 +$$
$$\frac{\mu}{2}\|p_{TV,y}^{(i)} - \nabla_y(\mathbf{x}) - v_{TV,y}^{(i)}\|_2^2 + \frac{\mu}{2}\|p_C^{(i)} - C(\mathbf{x}) - v_C^{(i)}\|_2^2 \tag{7}$$

$$p_{TV,x}^{(i+1)} = \underset{p}{\operatorname{argmin}} |p|_1 + \frac{\mu}{2}\|p - \nabla_x(\mathbf{x}^{(i+1)}) - v_{TV,x}^{(i)}\|_2^2 \tag{8}$$

$$p_{TV,y}^{(i+1)} = \underset{p}{\operatorname{argmin}} |p|_1 + \frac{\mu}{2}\|p - \nabla_y(\mathbf{x}^{(i+1)}) - v_{TV,y}^{(i)}\|_2^2 \tag{9}$$

$$p_C^{(i+1)} = \underset{p}{\operatorname{argmin}} |p|_1 + \frac{\mu}{2}\|p - C(\mathbf{x}^{(i+1)}) - v_C^{(i)}\|_2^2 \tag{10}$$

$$v_{TV,x}^{(i+1)} = v_{TV,x}^{(i)} + (\nabla_x(\mathbf{x}^{(i+1)}) - p_{TV,x}^{(i+1)}) \tag{11}$$

$$v_{TV,y}^{(i+1)} = v_{TV,y}^{(i)} + (\nabla_y(\mathbf{x}^{(i+1)}) - p_{TV,y}^{(i+1)}) \tag{12}$$

$$v_C^{(i+1)} = v_C^{(i)} + (C(\mathbf{x}^{(i+1)}) - p_C^{(i+1)}) \tag{13}$$

The general solution for the sub-problem Eq. (7), requires finding the roots of its derivatives:

$$A^\dagger(b - A\mathbf{x}) + \frac{\mu}{\lambda}\phi^\dagger(p^{(i)} - \phi(\mathbf{x}) - v^{(i)}) = 0 \tag{14}$$

This can be rewritten as:

$$(A^\dagger A + \frac{\mu}{\lambda}\phi^\dagger\phi)\mathrm{x} = A^\dagger b + \frac{\mu}{\lambda}\phi^\dagger(p^{(i)} - v^{(i)}) \tag{15}$$

where $\phi^\dagger, A^\dagger$ are the backward sparsifying transformation and the back projector, respectively. However, the normal inversion cannot be obtained, because $\phi^\dagger\phi \neq I$ and A is not a square matrix, so the conjugate gradient method [14] was chosen as a solution for Eq. (15). The solution for p in Eqs. (8, 9, and 10) can be found using a shrinkage operator as follows:

$$p^{(i+1)} = shrink(\phi(\mathrm{x}) + v^{(i)}, \frac{1}{\mu}) \tag{16}$$

$$shrink(k, t) = \frac{k}{|k|}max(|k| - t, 0) \tag{17}$$

where t is a threshold and k is each of the coefficients for the point-wise shrinkage operator.

3   Results

We evaluate the proposed method on two sets simulated data under fan-beam geometry: the SheppLogan phantom [15] and the head phantom which is built

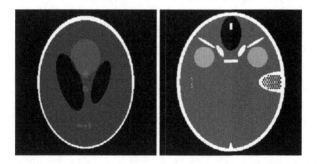

Fig. 1. Left: SheppLogan phantom, Right: FORBILD head phantom.

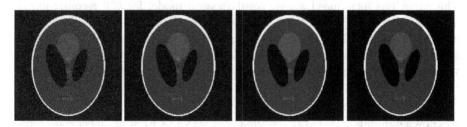

Fig. 2. Left to right: SheppLogan phantom reconstruction result using wavelet, curvelet, TV, and the proposed curvelet + TV based methods.

based on the work of the FORBILD group [16] (Fig. 1). Both of the simulated data have the size of 256×256 pixels and simulated with only 100 equally spaced projections. We have reconstructed these phantoms using four different methods: TV-based regularization (TV), wavelet-based regularization (wavelet), curvelet-based regularization (curvelet) and the proposed, i.e., curvelet + TV. Figures 2 and 3 show the comparison between the outcomes of the methods for SheppLogan and FORBILD phantoms. The peak signal-to-noise ratio (PSNR) was calculated to objectively evaluate the test data in Table 1.

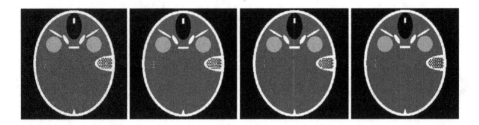

Fig. 3. Left to right: FORBILD head phantom reconstruction result using wavelet, curvelet, TV, and the proposed curvelet + TV based methods.

Table 1. PSNR (dB) values for all the methods in our experiment

Method	SheppLogan	FORBILD
Wavelet	19.2	22.0
Curvelet	26.6	28.7
TV	31.4	29.6
Proposed	37.7	36.2

4   Conclusions

The paper has introduced a new regularization model for CT reconstruction. The proposed and formulated regularization model is based on TV and the curvelet transform. The performance of proposed optimization problem in both subjective quality and PSNR is higher than that for the reference methods. The visible artifacts are greatly reduced and the improvement in objective quality ranges from 7 to 14 dB.

Acknowledgments. This work was supported by NASA EPSCoR under cooperative agreement No. NNX10AR89A.

References

1. Brenner, D.J.J., Hall, E.J.: Computed tomography: an increasing source of radiation exposure. N. Engl. J. Med. **357**(22), 2277–2284 (2007)
2. Oliveira, J.P., Bioucas-Dias, J.M., Figueiredo, M.A.T.: Adaptive total variation image deblurring: a majorization-minimization approach. Sig. Process. **89**, 1683–1693 (2009)
3. Beck, A., Teboulle, M.: Fast gradient-based algorithms for constrained total variation image denoising and deblurring problems. IEEE Trans. Image Process. **18**(11), 2419–2434 (2009)
4. Sidky, E.Y., Pan, X.: Image reconstruction in circular cone-beam computed tomography by constrained, total-variation minimization. Phys. Med. Biol. **53**(17), 4777–4807 (2008)
5. Herman, G.T., Davidi, R.: On image reconstruction from a small number of projections. Inv. Probl. **24**(4), 45011–45028 (2008)
6. Yang, J., Yu, H., Jiang, M., Wang, G.: High-order total variation minimization for interior tomography. Inv. Probl. **26**(3), 035013 (2010)
7. Starck, J.L., Candes, E.J., Donoho, D.L.: The curvelet transform for image denoising. IEEE Trans. Image Process. **11**(6), 670–684 (2002)
8. Tai, X.C., Wu, C.: Augmented Lagrangian method, dual methods and split Bregman iteration for ROF model. In: Tai, X.-C., Mørken, K., Lysaker, M., Lie, K.-A. (eds.) Scale Space Variational Methods in Computer Vision. LNCS, vol. 5567, pp. 502–513. Springer, Berlin (2009)
9. Goldstein, T., Osher, S.: The split Bregman method for L1 regular-ized problems. SIAM J. Imaging Sci. **2**(2), 323–343 (2009)
10. Aelterman, J., Luong, H.Q., Goossens, B., Piurica, A., Philips, W.: Augmented Lagrangian based reconstruction of non-uniformly sub-Nyquist sampled MRI data. Sig. Process. **91**(12), 2731–2742 (2011)
11. Vandeghinste, B., Goossens, B., Holen, R.V., Vanhove, C., Pizurica, A., Vandenberghe, S., Staelens, S.: Iterative CT reconstruction using shearlet-based regularization. IEEE Trans. Nucl. Sci. **60**(5), 3305–3317 (2013)
12. Afonso, M.V., Bioucas-Dias, J.M., Figueiredo, M.A.T.: An augmented lagrangian approach to the constrained optimization formulation of imaging inverse problems. IEEE Trans. Image Process. **20**(3), 681–695 (2011)
13. Wu, H., Maier, A., Hornegger, J.: Iterative CT reconstruction using curvelet-based regularization. In: Meinzer, H.-P., Deserno, T.M., Handels, H., Tolxdorff, T. (eds.) Bildverarbeitung für die Medizin. Springer, Heidelberg (2013)
14. Hestenes, M.R., Stiefel, E.: Methods of conjugate gradients for solving linear systems. J. Res. Nat. Bureau Stand. **49**(6), 409–436 (1952)
15. Shepp, L.A., Logan, B.F.: Reconstructing interior head tissue from X-ray transmissions. IEEE Trans. Nucl. Sci. **21**(1), 228–236 (1974)
16. FORBILD group. http://www.imp.uni-erlangen.de/phantoms/head/head.html

Estimating Ejection Fraction and Left Ventricle Volume Using Deep Convolutional Networks

AbdulWahab Kabani and Mahmoud R. El-Sakka$^{(\boxtimes)}$

Department of Computer Science, The University of Western Ontario,
London, ON, Canada
{akabani5,melsakka}@uwo.ca

Abstract. We present a fully automated method to estimate the ejection fraction, the end-systolic and end-diastolic volumes from cardiac MRI images. These values can be manually measured by a cardiologist but the process is slow and time consuming. The method is based on localizing the left ventricle of the image. Then, the slices are cleaned, re-ordered, and preprocessed using the DICOM meta fields. The end-systolic and end-diastolic images for each slice are identified. Finally, the end-systolic and end-diastolic images are passed to a neural network to estimate the volumes.

Keywords: Localization · Detection · Cardiac MRI · Left ventricle · Automatic ejection fraction estimation

1 Introduction

Cardiologists can assess cardiac function by analyzing the end-systolic and end-diastolic volumes, and ejection fraction. These values can be manually measured by a cardiologist but the process is slow and time consuming. We introduce an automated method that can estimate these values. We developed our method on a data set with 700 training studies and tested it on 440 testing studies. The data set is compiled by the National Institutes of Health and Children's National Medical Center [1].

In general, left ventricle volume can be estimated by detecting it and segmenting its cavity [3,7,9,10]. Once the cavity (the blood pool) is segmented, the volume can be calculated by summing up the sub-volumes of all slices according to simpson's rule.

In this paper, we take a slightly different approach and estimate the volume using a convolutional neural network. A Convolutional Neural Network (convnet or CNN) is a special type of neural network that contains some layers with restricted connectivity. CNNs have been producing excellent results on many classification tasks. This is all thanks to the availability of large training data sets [2,14], powerful hardware, regularization techniques such as Dropout [6,16], initialization methods [4], ReLU activations [12], and data augmentation. Since 2012, many networks that can perform classification were introduced [8,15,17].

© Springer International Publishing Switzerland 2016
A. Campilho and F. Karray (Eds.): ICIAR 2016, LNCS 9730, pp. 678–686, 2016.
DOI: 10.1007/978-3-319-41501-7_76

In general, CNNs can produce excellent results on many classification tasks if large amounts of training data is available. However, this requirement can be alleviated if the data is cleaned, standardized, and transformed such that to minimize viewpoint variance. The total size of the data set described in this paper is 1140 studies (700 training studies and 440 testing studies). On this data set with only 700 training studies, we were able to estimate the volume with around $+/- 15$ ml error. Furthermore, we were able to estimate the ejection fraction with $+/- 5\%$ error. The ejection fraction is one of the most important cardiac measurements since it describes how good the heart is in pumping blood.

First, we localize the left ventricle (Sect. 2). Then, the data is preprocessed, cleaned and standardized (Sect. 3). Finally, the volume of the left ventricle is estimated (Sect. 4). In Sect. 5, we present the results. We conclude our work in Sect. 6.

2   Left Ventricle Localization

For each patient, there are 8–16 short axis views (slices). These views show cross-sections of the left ventricle at different levels. Each slice contains around 30 images spanning the cardiac cycle (one heartbeat). The end-diastolic volume is the volume when the left ventricle is fully expanded while the end-systolic volume is when the left ventricle is contracted. To estimate these two volumes, for each slice, we need to identify the image with the largest blood pool area (end-diastole) and the one with the smallest area (end-systole).

In order to do that, we first localize the left ventricle and crop the image to get rid of the background pixels. We train a localization network on the training images and on the corresponding masks. The masks indicate where the left ventricle is in the image. Figure 1 shows the summary of the localization.

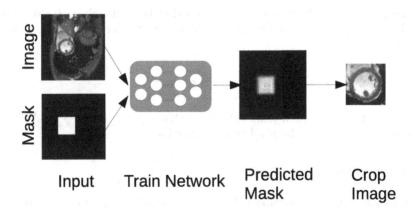

Fig. 1. Model Overview: A set of training images along with masks are used to train the network. Once the network is trained, it can be used to predict a mask which identifies the location of the region of interest. Finally, this predicted mask is thresholded (using Otsu [13]) and used to crop the image.

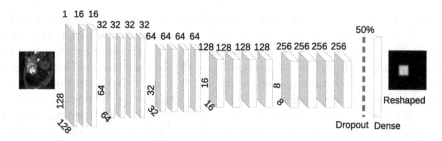

Fig. 2. Localization architecture: The input of the architecture is an image of size 128×128. In this figure, the output of the network is a layer with $128 \times 128 = 16384$ possible classes. The output layer is simply a flattened mask and reshaping this layer gives us back the predicted mask. The pixels with the highest intensities represent the location of the region of interest.

The architecture of the localization network (shown in Fig. 2) is similar to many classification networks. The image goes through many convolutional and maxpooling layers. The output layer has $h \times w$ number of units where h and w are the dimensions of the input image. Reshaping the output layer produces the predicted mask. Once thresholded, the predicted mask can be used to predict the location of the left ventricle. In the predicted mask, the pixels with high intensity values correspond to where the network predicts the left ventricle to be whereas pixels with values close to 0 correspond to background pixels.

Each convolutional layer is followed by ReLU activation [12]. The output layer has a softmax activation to ensure that the sum of all pixels in the predicted mask is 1 and that the value of one pixel is between 0 and 1. Maxpooling is used to detect features at different scales. The network is regularized with a 50% dropout rate.

The pixels of the input mask are supposed to be probabilities (sum up to 1 and their range is between 0 and 1). Therefore, we standardize each pixel in the input mask by Eq. 1:

$$y_{ij} = \frac{pixel_{ij}}{\sum_{i=1}^{H} \sum_{j=1}^{W} pixel_{ij}} \tag{1}$$

where y_{ij} is the normalized pixel value such that $y_{ij} \in [0,1]$ and $\sum_{i=1}^{H} \sum_{j=1}^{W} y_{ij}$ sums up to 1, $pixel_{ij}$ is the pixel value at row i and column j.

3   Preprocessing

Once the left ventricle is localized (Fig. 3), the meta fields are used to standarize and clean the data. First, we re-size all images using the pixel spacing and slice location meta fields. The images in this data set have different pixel spacing. This ensures that all images sizes are measured in the same units despite the difference in pixel spacing. Equations 2 and 3 ensure that the volume of the blood pool inside the left ventricle is directly proportional its area inside the image.

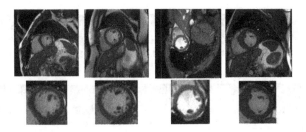

Fig. 3. A random sample of MRI images showing the heart. In the lower row, the left ventricle is localized and cropped.

$$w_{new} = w_{old} \times p_w \times \frac{\sqrt{\Delta s}}{\sqrt{10}} \tag{2}$$

$$h_{new} = h_{old} \times p_h \times \frac{\sqrt{\Delta s}}{\sqrt{10}} \tag{3}$$

where w_{old} is the old image width, w_{new} is the new image width, h_{old} is the old image height, h_{new} is the new image height, respectively. p_w and p_h are the pixel spacing for the width and height. Δs is the slice height. Since most slice heights in the data set are 10 mm, we normalize each equation by $\sqrt{10}$.

Before passing the slices to the neural network to estimate the volume, the slices needs to be standarized. Many slices are in arbitrary order in the study. Therefore, we use the meta field *slicelocation* to sort all slices. This sorted almost all slices from the top of the heart to the bottom. However, since the field *slicelocation* is based on an unkown reference point, for some studies the slices were reversed (from the bottom of the heart to the top). Therefore, we trained a small neural network (Fig. 4) to predict the slice location. We mainly use this network

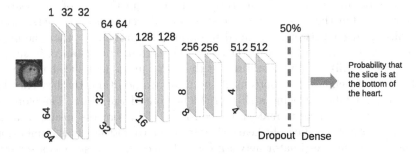

Fig. 4. Slice Localizer Network: this network outputs a probability that a certain image in a slice is located at the bottom (or base) of the heart. In other words, if the image is of a slice at the base of the heart, the network will output a high probability. If the image is showing a slice near the top of the heart, the network will output a low probability.

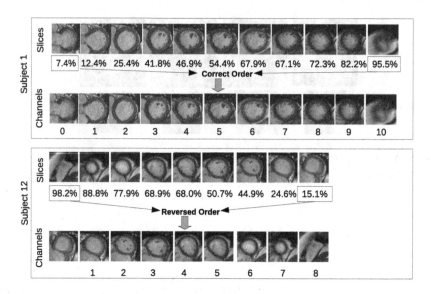

Fig. 5. Ordering the Slices: this figure shows the end-diastolic image from each slice in subjects 1 and 12. The slices of subject 1 are in the correct order (from the top of the heart to the bottom). On the other hand, the slices of subject 12 are in reverse order. The slice localizer is trained to output the probability that the image is showing the top of the heart or the bottom. For instance, in subject 12, the slice localizer network states that the image in the first slice has a 98.2 % of being in the bottom of the heart. In addition, the last slice has a 15.1 % probability of being a slice in the bottom of the heart. Therefore, we should reverse the slices to make them consistent. This process ensures that for all subjects, the slices show the heart from top to bottom.

to predict the top and bottom slices of the heart, if these appear to be in the wrong order, we reverse them.

Figure 5 shows the end-diastolic image from each slice in subjects 1 and 12. The slices of subject 1 are in the correct order (from the top of the heart to the bottom). On the other hand, the slices of subject 12 are in reverse order. The slice localizer network is trained to output the probability that the image represent a slice at the top of the heart or the bottom. For instance, in subject 12, the slice localizer network states that the image in the first slice has a 98.2 % probability of being in the bottom of the heart. In addition, the last slice has a 15.1 % probability of being a slice in the bottom of the heart. Therefore, we should reverse the slices to make them consistent. This process ensures that for all subjects, the slices show the heart slices from top to bottom. This is important because the volume estimator network (Sect. 4) accepts each slice as a separate channel and expects the slices to be ordered and consistent.

4   Volume Estimation

In Sect. 2, we localized the left ventricle in the image. After that (in Sect. 3), the images were re-sized using the pixel spacing meta field in the DICOM files to ensure that the left ventricle cavity area is consistent across all images. Furthermore, a slice localization network was used to predict the slice location. The slices were ordered so that they are consistent before passing them to the volume estimation network.

The end systole and end diastole for each slice are defined as the images with the smallest and largest blood pool, respectively. Therefore, for each slice, we threshold the images and the end systolic and end diastolic images are chosen to be the ones with the smallest and largest white pixels in one slice, respectively. The end systolic and end diastolic images from each slice form the channels of the input we pass to the volume estimation architecture.

As shown in Fig. 6, the input to the network is a set of images with size 96×96 pixels. The input has 36 channels (18 channels are for the diastole images and 18 channels for the systole images). In other words, we extract 1 systole image and 1 diastole image from each slice (a slice is a set of 30 images representing one heartbeat). We assume that the maximum number of slices possible is 18. After that, the input is passed through multiple sets of convolutional layers and maxpooling (8 convolutional layers & 1 maxpooling; 8 convolutional layers & 1 maxpooling; 4 convolutional layers & 1 maxpooling; 4 convolutional layers & 1 maxpooling; 2 convolutional layers & 1 maxpooling). The convolutional kernel size is (5,5). The activation for all convolutional layer is leaky

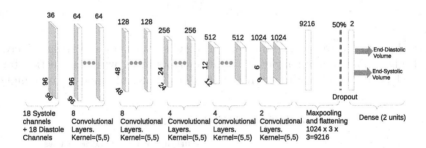

Fig. 6. Volume Estimation Architecture: the input to the network is a set of images with size 96×96 pixels. The input has 36 channels (18 channels are for the diastole images and 18 channels for the systole images). In other words, we extract 1 systole image and 1 diastole image from each slice (a slice is a set of 30 images representing one heartbeat). We assume that the maximum number of slices possible is 18. After that, the input is passed through multiple sets of convolutional layers and maxpooling (8 convolutional layers & 1 maxpooling; 8 convolutional layers & 1 maxpooling; 4 convolutional layers & 1 maxpooling; 4 convolutional layers & 1 maxpooling; 2 convolutional layers & 1 maxpooling). The convolutional kernel size is (5,5). The network is regularized with dropout. The output layer contains 2 output units: one unit returns the predicted end diastole volume and the other returns the predicted end systole volume.

rectification (with leakiness $=0.1$) [5,11]. The network is regularized with dropout. The output layer contains 2 output units: one unit returns the predicted end diastole volume and the other returns the predicted end systole volume. We optimize the root mean square error between the true volumes and the predicted volumes.

In addition to regularizing the network with dropout, we augment the data by performing random transformations. These transformations include randomly rotating the input between -20 and 20 degrees. We also perform random horizontal and vertical flipping. Finally, we perform random Gaussian blurring (up to $\sigma = 1.0$).

5   Results

The model was trained on a laptop with the graphics card GTX980M (4 GB dedicated RAM). Figure 7 shows the training and validation loss while training. The gap between the training loss and the validation loss remains almost the same throughout training. After 100 epochs, the validation error drops from 40 ml to around 15 ml. Each epoch takes around 4 min to complete (total training time is 6.7 h). On the other hand, predicting the volumes is done in real time.

The ejection fraction is probably the most important quantity since it measures the fraction of outbound blood pumped from the heart with each heartbeat. In general, low ejection fraction is an indication of heart problems. This quantity can be calculated as shown in Eq. 4

$$EF = 100 \times \frac{(V_D - V_S)}{V_D} \tag{4}$$

where V_D and V_S are the end diastolic and end systolic volumes, respectively.

Table 1 shows a summary of the volume errors along with the ejection fraction. The end diastolic volume error in milliliter (15.82 ml) appears to be higher

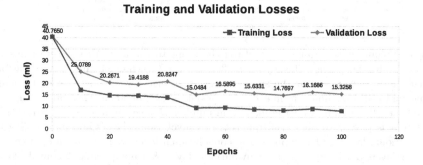

Fig. 7. Training and Validation Loss: the figure shows how the training and validation loss (error) improves over the course of training. The loss (or the error) is measured in milliliter (ml).

Table 1. Errors Summary - the table displays a summary of the volume errors in milliliter and as a percentage. In addition, the ejection fraction error is shown. Abbreviations: ESV is the End Systolic Volume error. EDV is the End Diastolic Volume error. EF is the Ejection Fraction error.

EDV(ml)	ESV(ml)	EDV(%)	ESV(%)	EF(%)
15.82	11.16	17.67	20.49	5.64

than the end systolic volume error (11.16 ml). However, when normalizing the errors by the true volume, we can see that the end diastolic percentage error (17.67 %) is better than the end systolic percentage error (20.49 %). Finally, the ejection fraction error is on average 5.64 %.

6   Conclusion

We described a model based on deep learning that can estimate the volume of the left ventricle. First, the left ventricle is localized. Then, the slice location is predicted and the slices of the study are ordered and preprocessed. After that, we identify the end systolic and end diastolic images for each slice. The end systolic and end diastolic images for each slice are stacked together and passed to a network that can estimate the end diastolic and end systolic volumes.

Acknowledgements. This research is partially funded by the Natural Sciences and Engineering Research Council of Canada (NSERC). This support is greatly appreciated. We would also like to thank kaggle, Booz Allen Hamilton, and the National Heart, Lung, and Blood Institute (NHLBI) for providing the MRI images.

References

1. Data science bowl cardiac challenge data. https://www.kaggle.com/c/second-annual-data-science-bowl. Accessed 19 Mar 2016
2. Deng, J., Dong, W., Socher, R., Li, L.J., Li, K., Fei-Fei, L.: Imagenet: a large-scale hierarchical image database. In: 2009 IEEE Conference on Computer Vision and Pattern Recognition. CVPR 2009, pp. 248–255. IEEE (2009)
3. Germano, G., Kiat, H., Kavanagh, P.B., Moriel, M., Mazzanti, M., Su, H.T., Train, K.F.V., Berman, D.S.: Automatic quantification of ejection fraction from gated myocardial perfusion spect. J. Nucl. Med. **36**(11), 2138 (1995)
4. Glorot, X., Bengio, Y.: Understanding the difficulty of training deep feedforward neural networks. In: International Conference on Artificial Intelligence and Statistics, pp. 249–256 (2010)
5. Graham, B.: Spatially-sparse convolutional neural networks. arXiv preprint (2014). arXiv:1409.6070
6. Hinton, G.E., Srivastava, N., Krizhevsky, A., Sutskever, I., Salakhutdinov, R.R.: Improving neural networks by preventing co-adaptation of feature detectors (2012). arXiv:1207.0580

7. Kaus, M.R., von Berg, J., Weese, J., Niessen, W., Pekar, V.: Automated segmentation of the left ventricle in cardiac MRI. Med. Image Anal. **8**(3), 245–254 (2004)
8. Krizhevsky, A., Sutskever, I., Hinton, G.E.: Imagenet classification with deep convolutional neural networks. In: Advances in Neural Information Processing Systems, pp. 1097–1105 (2012)
9. Lin, X., Cowan, B.R., Young, A.A.: Automated detection of left ventricle in 4D MR images: experience from a large study. In: Larsen, R., Nielsen, M., Sporring, J. (eds.) MICCAI 2006. LNCS, vol. 4190, pp. 728–735. Springer, Heidelberg (2006)
10. Lynch, M., Ghita, O., Whelan, P.F.: Automatic segmentation of the left ventricle cavity and myocardium in MRI data. Comput. Biol. Med. **36**(4), 389–407 (2006)
11. Maas, A.L., Hannun, A.Y., Ng, A.Y.: Rectifier nonlinearities improve neural network acoustic models. In: Proceedings of ICML, vol. 30 (2013)
12. Nair, V., Hinton, G.E.: Rectified linear units improve restricted Boltzmann machines. In: Proceedings of the 27th International Conference on Machine Learning (ICML-10), pp. 807–814 (2010)
13. Otsu, N.: A threshold selection method from gray-level histograms. Automatica **11**(285–296), 23–27 (1975)
14. Russakovsky, O., Deng, J., Su, H., Krause, J., Satheesh, S., Ma, S., Huang, Z., Karpathy, A., Khosla, A., Bernstein, M., et al.: Imagenet large scale visual recognition challenge. Int. J. Comput. Vis. **115**(3), 211–252 (2015)
15. Simonyan, K., Zisserman, A.: Very deep convolutional networks for large-scale image recognition (2014). arXiv:1409.1556
16. Srivastava, N., Hinton, G., Krizhevsky, A., Sutskever, I., Salakhutdinov, R.: Dropout: a simple way to prevent neural networks from overfitting. J. Mach. Learn. Res. **15**(1), 1929–1958 (2014)
17. Szegedy, C., Liu, W., Jia, Y., Sermanet, P., Reed, S., Anguelov, D., Erhan, D., Vanhoucke, V., Rabinovich, A.: Going deeper with convolutions (2014). arXiv:1409.4842

A Hybrid Model for Extracting the Aortic Valve in 3D Computerized Tomography and Its Application to Calculate a New Calcium Score Index

Laura Torío[✉], César Veiga, María Fernández, Victor Jiménez, Emilio Paredes, Pablo Pazos, Francisco Calvo, and Andrés Íñiguez

Cardiología, Instituto de Investigación Biomédica (IBI), Hospital Álvaro Cunqueiro, Vigo, Spain
Laura.Torio.Rodriguez@sergas.es

Abstract. In this paper a new scheme for automatic segmentation of the Aortic Valve in 3D computed tomography image sequences is presented. The algorithm is based on a new approach that uses a combination of Region Growing and Mathematical Morphology techniques in a hybrid framework. The output of the algorithm is used to assess the Aortic Valve Calcium Score in a new way that calculates the Agatston Score separately in both Sinuses and Leaflets, deriving a new index based on their ratios. Aortic Valve borders and leaflets identification is still a challenging task, and commonly based on intensive user interaction that limits its applicability. In this paper a fast and accurate model-free, automated method for segmenting and extracting morphological parameters with Score Calcium calculation is presented. Results of the proposed method are also provided showing a high correlation with the expected values.

Keywords: Aortic Valve (AoV) · Computed Tomography (CT) · Medical image segmentation · Region growing · Aortic root · Leaflets · Valsalva sinuses

1 Introduction

Heart related diseases represent the leading cause of death globally and it is expected to increase over the years [1]. According to American Heart Association statistics cardiovascular disease is responsible for more than 17.3 million deaths per year and it is projected to grow to more than 23.6 million by 2030. Moreover, the primary cause of cardiovascular morbidity and mortality among heart diseases in Europe is Cardiovascular Arterial Disease (CAD) [3]. It is caused by the buildup of calcium on cardiac structures as coronary arteries or several valves including the aortic valve. Therefore, the deployment of accurate, portable and real-time evaluation techniques such as automatic interpretation of images that strengthen research and diagnostic for cardiovascular diseases is increasingly needed and interesting due to his public health relevance worldwide [2, 4].

Specifically Calcific or Calcified Aortic Valve Disease (CAVD) is a slow and continuous progressive disease ranging from mild thickening of the valve without obstruction of blood flow, known as aortic sclerosis, to severe calcification with impaired

© Springer International Publishing Switzerland 2016
A. Campilho and F. Karray (Eds.): ICIAR 2016, LNCS 9730, pp. 687–694, 2016.
DOI: 10.1007/978-3-319-41501-7_77

mobility of veils, or aortic stenosis [5, 6]. Although aortic valve calcium score from MDCT (Multidetector row computed tomography) images has been assessed by different ways, a total valvular Agatston score (AGS) is generally calculated. As well, the calcium mass score located within the aortic valve structures or the mean aortic valve calcification (AVC) score allow to study the influence and to determine the degree of the aortic valve calcification [7]. Along with prosthesis misplacement, and/or annulus-prosthesis size mismatch, heavily calcified cusps are an important predictor to identify patients prone to develop for example significant post-implant paravalvular aortic regurgitation (PAR) or to avoid post-interventional paravalvular leakage (PVL) [8].

In this scenario, the development of computer vision tools, pattern recognition and image processing techniques and computer-assisted diagnosis (CAD) schemes, applied to automate analysis process in cardiology to improve usefulness of CT sequences are of great interest.

The purpose of this study was to assess the anatomy of the aortic root noninvasively from MDCT images, additionally getting the amount and distribution of calcification of the native aortic valve using a scoring system analogous to the Agatston calcium scoring of coronary arteries. This paper is organized in five sections. Number 2 offers an overview of previous work on modeling and segmentation of cardiac structures and on calcium quantifying methods, which includes some mathematical and software features. The new algorithm for patient-specific valve segmentation and quantification model is described in Sect. 3. Number 4 introduces some experiments and applications results, concluding with Sect. 5.

2   Background

2.1   Imaging the Aortic Valve Anatomy

Since the first characterization sketches of the aortic valve were made by Leonardo da Vinci in 1513 until nowadays, the aortic valve has been of great interest to the scientific communities. Particularly its geometry was considered too rigid to accommodate the dimensional variability observed in normally functioning valves. However, currently a morphologically realistic 3D reconstruction of the aortic valve can be easily obtained from several imaging modalities such as ultrasounds, magnetic resonances or CT, by using advanced image-processing techniques. Leaflets can also be measured especially by MRI and echocardiography, because by CT it is complicated to capture their movement (Fig. 1).

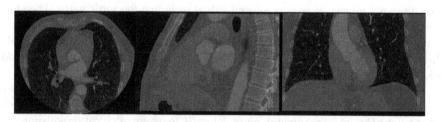

Fig. 1. General MDCT cardiac image: axial, coronal and sagittal views.

2.2 Mathematical Morphology and Region Growing for Automatic Segmentation

Image-processing techniques derive from Mathematical Morphology (MM), a theory from late sixties that aims to analyze the shape and form of objects based on set theory, topology, lattice algebra, random functions, etc. [9]. Based on logical operations (AND, OR, and modifications) operated on binarized images, MM provides image filters tools for performing tasks as noise reduction or edge detection. In addition, morphological filters are specially suited to the extraction or suppression of image structures and most are designed using some knowledge about the shape and geometrical properties of the image objects, as well as create erosions and dilations of the segmented result [10] (Fig. 2).

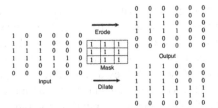

Fig. 2. Patch binarized of an image showing the mask for erode and dilate operation results.

Regarding image segmentation, some region growing based techniques are used. This is a region-based method where an initial set of small areas is iteratively merged according to similarity constraints. RG examines an initial set of "seed points" and determines whether the pixel neighbors should be added to the region increasing its size [11]. Region Growing offers several advantages over conventional segmentation techniques like gradient and Laplacian methods. The borders of regions found by region growing are perfectly thin, since we only add pixels to the exterior of our region, and connected.

2.3 Aortic Valve Calcium Score Assessment

There are several ways to assess aortic valve calcium score using MDCT [7]. For quantitative assessment of aortic valve calcification a total valvular Agatston score (AGS) is generally calculated. The Agatston score dates back into the 1980s and is a measure of calcium generally used for Coronary Calcification studies [13]. Nowadays it is very useful also for Aortic Valve calcification measures, using a weighted value assigned to the highest density of calcification on the aortic valve [12]. Density is measured in Hounsfield Units and scored of 1 for 130–199 HU, 2 for 200–299 HU, 3 for 300–399 HU, and 4 for 400 HU and greater. This weighted score is multiplied by the AoV calcified area in pixels and the calcium score obtained for each tomographic slice is then summed up to give the total aortic valve calcium score (AVCS).

Other studies [7] have determined the degree of valve calcification through the calcium mass score located within the aortic valve structures, considering mass score more reproducible than volume and AGS score specially when performed in contrast enhanced scans. Ewe et al. [7] quantified aortic valve calcification in cubic millimeters from MDCT studies instead of using the AGS score. And Haensig et al. [15] calculated the mean AVC as AGS and demonstrated that there was a significant association between the AVC and PAR, suggesting that the preoperative AVC can identify patient risk to develop significant post-implant PAR.

3   Aortic Valve Segmentation

The ability to identify and quantify three-dimensional (3D) morphological parameters of the aortic valve apparatus from cardiological images as well as image-based morphological assessment for surgical interventions constitute a valuable tool in diagnosis, treatment and follow-up of patients with aortic valve related diseases, so there is a considerable need to develop a standardized frameworks for 3D valve segmentation and shape representation. This section describes the new method for automatic segmentation of the aortic root based on morphological mathematics, region growing methods, and its implementation using python modules and libraries. To provide a high level of usability we use SimpleITK as a cross-language programming interface to the open-source Insight Toolkit (ITK) that facilitates rapid prototyping and use of ITK's algorithms from an interactive interpreter. Some other python libraries as scipy or numpy have been used.

3.1   A New Method for Three Dimensional (3D) Segmentation

The method for automatic identification of the AoV apparatus is based on several image-processing techniques. Once the Volume of Interest (VoI) is identified, a seed within the structure is selected manually or previously set. This seed evolves towards the aortic-valve sinuses as showed in Fig. 3. Similarly to identify the blood within the valve, the segmented borders correspond to the "lumen" of the structure. Then, by a dilate-erode operation, the AoV structure is divided into two differentiated parts, the one that correspond to the leaflets that falls within the inner valve, and the Valsalva sinuses that lies on the dilation of the segmented structure. Once the structure is identified, the Agatston score is computed within the VOI and the separated index are calculated and provided as a result.

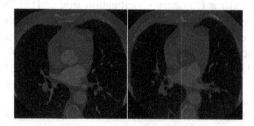

Fig. 3. Two-dimensional slices of the study showing the AoV identification by the evolution of the region growing algorithm from an initial seed point.

3.2   Algorithm Implementation

The first step of the algorithm reads the DICOM image series as a 3D image from where the automatic segmentation will be extracted. A Volume of Interest (VoI) is set by selecting the range of the study that contains aortic root region. It can be performed both by entering a user input range or previously automatically established. Next step is to set a seed point within the valve region, with adjustable radius, which will allow the algorithm to segment pixels connected to it.

The AoV identification algorithm is based on a region growing technique that extracts a connected set of pixels whose intensities are consistent with the pixel statistics of a seed point located on the AoV geometrical center corresponding to blood. The pixels connected to this seed point whose values are within the confidence interval are grouped, controlling the width of the confidence interval by the 'multiplier' variable. After this initial segmentation, the mean and variance are re-calculated using all the previous segmented pixels. The segmentation is then recalculated and the process is repeated for the specified number of iterations. The lower and upper thresholds are restricted to lie within the valid numeric limits of the input data pixel type. Also, the limits may be adjusted to contain the seed point's intensity. The algorithm was implemented setting parameters number of iterations and multiplier to 1 and 3 respectively. Figure 4 shows obtained images, corresponding to aortic valve borders and leaflets respectively. It is about masking original CT image with aortic valve segmentation label so that result image contains only our volume of interest AoV region not just as a simple label but containing real intensity values from CT.

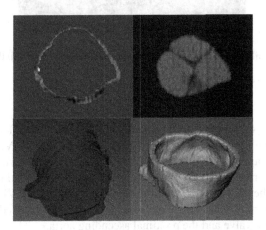

Fig. 4. Aortic valve structures and 3D reconstructions extracted from CT.

Once these desired images are obtained, an additional step based on MM filter is implemented, namely the extraction of the sinuses wall. The Erode filter allows obtaining the surrounding region the segmented lumen in the AoV. For this purpose, a kernel of 3×3 was used in the dilation process. The segmented result of step 1 is subtracted to the result of this step in order to get the ribbon (Valsalva sinuses). Figure 4 shows the result of this ribbon containing the Original CT Hounsfield units on this area.

3.3   Application of the Proposed Methodology for AoV Agatston Score Assessment (Rational Calcium Score)

This section covers the main reason to need not only a labeled mask but also a mask with the original Hounsfield units. These values are needed to generate a detection range to classify image pixels according to their intensities, corresponding to calcification levels of the aortic root, similar to the aortic-valve calcium scoring (AVCS) but in a separate way (Sinuses and Leaflets). Significant differences regarding to the degree of calcification and its distribution was found between the outer and inner parts of the valve, so we decide to compare a separated calcium quantification in each one to obtain a relation index. They are obtained as the total amount of the calcification present in borders or sinus (Assinus), and the one within the aortic valve corresponding to the leaflets (Asleaflets). Then the AVCS relation is compared for the entire valve as a Rational Calcium Score. Threshold for leaflet calcium detection is set at 450 HU for non-contrast scans, however the greatest discriminatory value for contrast scan images was seen at 650 HU [14] (Fig. 5).

$$\text{Rational Calcium Score } = \text{Asleaflets}/\text{Assinus}$$

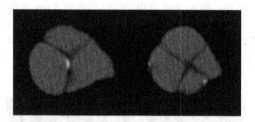

Fig. 5.   Different calcified valves segmented and quantified with the model.

4   Results

Data from 4 patients, enrolled at the University of Vigo Meixoeiro Hospitals (Vigo, ES), undergoing clinically indicated CT imaging for assessment of TAVI were considered. The protocol was approved by the local Institutional Review Board (Comité Ético de Galicia), and informed consent from all participants was obtained. Studies were performed using the LightSpeed VCT from GE Medical Systems KVP 120. Images were acquired with 0.6 mm thick scan. Each acquired sequence covered the whole heart, including the aortic valve and the proximal ascending aorta.

The above described method was coded in python, using ITK, scipy and numpy libraries, in order to evaluate the performance. As previously mentioned the image segmentation is based on region growing techniques, appropriately adjusting parameters as multiplier to define a confidence interval wide enough to capture 99 % of samples in the segment, and the number of iterations.

The final scope of this work was to assess the impact of the amount of calcification in the native aortic valve an algorithm that account the number of voxels within the Agatson Score was coded. The calcium score index was calculated considering pixel weigh by its intensity levels according to an X-factor (weighting factor between 1 and 4 based on set ranges for the value of the largest intensity pixel in the plaque), getting a measure analogous to the Agatston score to quantify the amount of calcium plaque present in the walls of the coronary arteries but for aortic root.

Table 1 shows results of the four patients analyzed. The first and the second column contain the number of images in the study and the VoI Size, third and fourth give the Agatston Score on sinus and leaflets respectively, and the last column provide values of the new index introduced in this paper.

Table 1. Summary of results of the experiments.

	N° slices	VOI size	Sinus AS	Leaflets As	Sinus/Leaflets As
Case 1	280	$40 \times 40 \times 40$	117	386	0.303
Case 2	280	$40 \times 40 \times 40$	85	629	0.135
Case 3	280	$40 \times 40 \times 40$	132	206	0.303
Case 4	280	$40 \times 40 \times 40$	185	529	0.135

5   Conclusions

MSCT plays an important role for preoperative patient screening. It allows for detailed anatomic assessment and for accurate detection, localization and quantification of AoV calcification. In this study, using a novel approach for AoV identification based on RG, and dilate filters from the Mathematical Morphology field the AoV structured is isolated into separate parts (Valsalva Sinuses and leaflets). Once the structure is identified the assessment of the Calcium is a simple task through a new index (Rational Calcium Score) is calculated.

This work integrates pattern recognition techniques to automatically delineate and quantitatively describe aortic geometry in CT image sequences, a challenging task that has been explored only to a limited extent. Although the algorithm was tested only on 4 patients, good results were obtained showing a high correlation between returned score values and the expected ones; also it is projected to increase testing cases shortly. The proposed technique appears promising for clinical application since the new score gives useful information to assess a disease diagnosis of the patient helping the assessment and posterior treatment.

References

1. Lozano, R., Naghavi, M., Foreman, K., et al.: Global and regional mortality from 235 causes of death for 20 age groups in 1990 and 2010 a systematic analysis for the global burden of disease study 2010. Lancet **380**, 2095–2128 (2010)
2. Freeman, R.V., Otto, C.M.: Spectrum of calcific aortic valve disease pathogenesis, disease progression, and treatment strategies. Circulation **111**, 3316–3326 (2005)
3. Villines, T.C., et al.: Prevalence and severity of coronary artery disease and adverse events among symptomatic patients with coronary artery calcification scores of zero undergoing coronary computed tomography angiography. J. Am. Coll. Cardiol. **58**, 2533–2540 (2011)

4. Budoff, M.J.: Interpreting the coronary-artery calcium score. N. Engl. J. Med. **2012**(366), 1550–1551 (2012)
5. Otto, C.M., Lind, B.K., Kitzman, D.W., et al.: Association of aortic-valve sclerosis with cardiovascular mortality and morbidity in the elderly. N. Engl. J. Med. **341**, 142 (1999)
6. Stewart, B.F., Siscovick, D., Lind, B.K., et al.: Clinical factors associated with calcific aortic valve disease. cardiovascular health study. J. Am. Coll. Cardiol. **29**, 630–634 (1997)
7. Colli, A., Gallo, M., Bernabeu, E., D'Onofrio, A., Tarzia, V., Gerosa, G.: Aortic valve calcium scoring is a predictor of paravalvular aortic regurgitation after transcatheter aortic valve implantation. Ann. Cardiothorac. Surg. **1**(2), 156–159 (2012)
8. Sinning, J.M., Werner, N., Nickenig, G., Grube, E.: Next-generation transcatheter heart valves: current trials in Europe and the USA. Methodist Debakey Cardiovasc. J. **8**, 9–12 (2012)
9. Serra, J.: Image Analysis and Mathematical Morphology. Academic Press, London (1982)
10. Soille, P.: Morphological Image Analysis: Principles and Applications. Springer, Heidelberg (1999)
11. Adams, R., Bischof, L.: Seeded region growing. IEEE Trans. Pattern Anal. Mach. Intell. **16**(6), 641–647 (1994)
12. Agatston, A.S., Janowitz, W.R., Hildner, F.J., Zusmer, N.R., Viamonte Jr., M., Detrano, R.: Quantification of coronary artery calcium using ultrafast computed tomography. J. Am. Coll. Cardiol. **15**, 827–832 (1990)
13. Hoffmann, U., Brady, T.J., Muller, J.: Cardiology patient page. Use of new imaging techniques to screen for coronary artery disease. Circulation **108**(8), e50–e53 (2003)
14. Jilaihawi, H., Makkar, R.R., Kashif, M., Okuyama, K., Chakravarty, T., Shiota, T., Fontana, G.P.: A revised methodology for aortic-valvar complex calcium quantification for transcatheter aortic valve implantation. Eur. Heart J. Cardiovasc. Imaging **4**, 3–7 (2014)
15. Haensig, M., Lehmkuhl, L., Rastan, A.J.: Aortic valve calcium scoring is a predictor of significant paravalvular aortic insufficiency in transapical-aortic valve implantation. Eur. J. Cardiothorac. Surg. **41**, 1234–1241 (2012)

Image Analysis in Ophthalmology

Automatic Optic Disc and Fovea Detection in Retinal Images Using Super-Elliptical Convergence Index Filters

Behdad Dashtbozorg[1]([⊠]), Jiong Zhang[1], Fan Huang[1],
and Bart M. ter Haar Romeny[1,2]

[1] Department of Biomedical Engineering, Eindhoven University of Technology,
Eindhoven, The Netherlands
{B.Dasht.Bozorg,J.Zhang1,F.Huang,B.M.TerHaarRomeny}@tue.nl
[2] Sino-Dutch School for Biomedical and Information Engineering,
Northeastern University, Shenyang, China

Abstract. This paper presents an automatic optic disc (OD) and fovea detection technique using an innovative super-elliptical filter (SEF). This filter is suitable for the detection of semi-elliptical convex shapes and as such it performs well for the OD localization. Furthermore, we introduce a setup for the simultaneous localization of the OD and fovea, in which the detection result of one landmark facilitates the detection of the other one. The evaluation is performed on 1200 images of the MESSIDOR dataset containing both normal and pathological cases of diabetic retinopathy (DR) and macular edema (ME). The proposed approach achieves success rates of 99.75 % and 98.87 % for the OD and fovea detection, respectively and outperforms or equals all known similar methods.

Keywords: Retina · Fovea · Optic disc · Convergence index filter · Diabetic retinopathy

1 Introduction

The detection of the optic disc (OD) in retinal images is a prerequisite step toward the automatic measurement of signs associated with several retinal diseases. The shape and appearance of the OD are useful for the glaucoma detection and analysis of white lesions related to diabetic retinopathy (DR). The OD is also a point of interest for retinal measurements, such as the distance between the fovea and the OD, which can be used for the estimation of macula location. In addition, the OD location is required to determine protocolized regions of interest for the assessment of signs related to vascular changes, such as fractal dimension, central retinal artery/vein equivalent and central artery-to-vein diameter ratio [11].

On the other hand, the macula is a key region in the screening for DR and other retinal pathologies such as macular edema (ME) and age-related macular degeneration (AMD). Since the macula is essential for sharp central vision,

© Springer International Publishing Switzerland 2016
A. Campilho and F. Karray (Eds.): ICIAR 2016, LNCS 9730, pp. 697–706, 2016.
DOI: 10.1007/978-3-319-41501-7_78

the locations of lesions, such as microaneurysms, hemorrhages and drusen with respect to the center of macula (fovea) are important for disease classification and grading. Hence, accurate automatic detection of the OD and fovea is a crucial step for automatic computer-aided diagnosis.

In literature, two types of criteria have been widely used for the OD detection. Conventional approaches are based on the analysis of pixel intensity features since the OD is usually the brightest region in a retinal fundus image [6,9,13,14]. Alternatively, methods are developed that exploit the features related to the vasculature and nerve fiber pattern [5,22], since the OD is the entry and exit point of the nerves and blood vessels. There are also OD detection techniques that combine the information from the vascular tree with the intensity features [4,15].

Most fovea detection methods are operated in two stages. In the first stage, the OD center is detected and a region of interest is defined using the known average distance between the fovea and the OD location. In the second stage, the fovea location is obtained by exploiting the visual appearance of the fovea in that region. Yu et al. [21] used the vascular arches to find a region of interest where the fovea location is obtained by selecting the lowest response of a template matching. In the method proposed by Giachetti et al. [9], the center of symmetry of bright and dark regions is localized based on a radial symmetry transform of vessel-inpainted images. Then the final OD and fovea locations are obtained by using a vascular density estimator. Gegundez et al. [8] introduced a method for fovea detection by defining a region of interest with respect to the OD location and the vascular tree. After vessels removal and image smoothing, the fovea center is obtained using multi-thresholding and feature extraction techniques. In the method introduced by Kao et al. [10], firstly the OD is localized by a template matching technique with adaptive Gaussian templates. Then by searching the non-vascular region, the line connecting the OD center and the fovea is determined, and finally the fovea is detected by matching the fovea template around the center of this line. The recent method presented by Aquino [3] uses both the visual and the anatomical features for the fovea detection. Then a specific type of morphological processing is employed to improve the localization of the fovea.

There are two major contributions in this paper: First, we propose a new convergence index filter, called super-elliptical filter (SEF), suitable for the detection of any semi-elliptical convex shape. Second, we introduce a setup of paired SEF filters (PSEF) which is used for the simultaneous detection of optic disc and fovea in fundus images.

The rest of this paper is organized as follows. In Sect. 2, the convergence index filters as well as the proposed super-elliptical filter are introduced. Section 3 presents our approach for the OD and fovea detection. Experimental results are shown in Sect. 4. Finally, Sect. 5 summarizes the conclusion.

2   Super-Elliptical Convergence Index Filter

The convergence index (CI) filters are suitable for the detection of convex shapes and objects with a limited range of sizes regardless of their contrast with respect to the background. The CI filters evaluate the convergence degree of gradient vectors within a local area (support region) towards a pixel of interest [12].

Given an input image $I(x,y)$, for each pixel with spatial coordinates (x,y), the convergence index (CI) is defined by

$$CI(x,y) = \frac{1}{M} \sum_{(\theta_i,m) \in G} \cos\left(\varphi\left(x,y,\theta_i,m\right)\right), \tag{1}$$

where M is the number of points in the filter support region G, and $\varphi\left(x,y,\theta_i,m\right)$ is the orientation angle of the gradient vector at the polar coordinate (θ_i,m) with respect to the line, with direction i, that connects (θ_i,m) to (x,y). The angular difference φ, is given by

$$\varphi(x,y,\theta_i,m) = \theta_i - \alpha(x,y,\theta_i,m),$$

$$\alpha\left(x,y,\theta_i,m\right) = \tan^{-1}\left(\frac{\frac{\partial}{\partial x}I(x+m\times\sin(\theta_i),y+m\times\cos(\theta_i))}{\frac{\partial}{\partial y}I(x+m\times\sin(\theta_i),y+m\times\cos(\theta_i))}\right), \tag{2}$$

where α is the image gradient orientation within the convergence filter support region. As shown in Fig. 1(a), the support region polar coordinates are denoted by the radial coordinate m, the distance from point of interest (x,y) in pixel, and angular coordinate θ_i which is sampled with N equally spaced radial lines ($\theta_i = \frac{2\pi}{N}(i-1)$, $i \in \{1,...,N\}$). The set of radial lines are emerging from the point where the filter is being applied to, and equally distributed over a circular region centred at the point of interest (x,y).

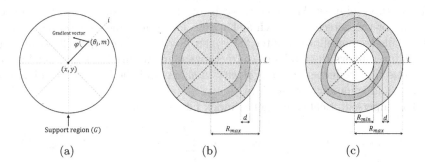

(a)   (b)   (c)

Fig. 1. (a) Schematics of the convergence index filter; (b) Adaptive ring filter and (c) sliding band filter, where the support region lines are depicted with dashed lines and the support region is specified in blue. (Color figure online)

Several CI filters have been proposed according to the way how the support region G [12] is defined. Among different CI filters, the adaptive ring filter (ARF) [19] and the sliding band filter (SBF) [17] are more suitable for the OD detection, since they can be parameterized to use a narrow band and ignore the gradients information at the center of the OD, reducing the vascular interference. The ARF shown in Fig. 1(b) has a ring-shaped region of support and its radius changes adaptively. The response of the ARF is obtained via:

$$ARF(x,y) = \max_{0 \leq r \leq R_{max}} \frac{1}{N \times d} \sum_{i=1}^{N} \sum_{m=r}^{r+d} \cos\left(\varphi(x,y,\theta_i,m)\right), \qquad (3)$$

where N is the number of support region lines as described previously, d corresponds to the width of the ring (band), and R_{max} represents the outer limit of the band.

The SBF support region shown in Fig. 1(c) is a band of fixed width with varying radius in each direction, where the maximization of the convergence index at each point is obtained by:

$$SBF(x,y) = \frac{1}{N} \sum_{i=1}^{N} \left[\max_{R_{min} \leq r \leq R_{max}} \sum_{m=r}^{r+d} \cos\left(\varphi(x,y,\theta_i,m)\right) \right], \qquad (4)$$

where R_{min} and R_{max} represent the inner and outer sliding band limits, respectively. The SBF has a more generic formulation compared to the ARF, which makes it more desirable for OD segmentation [6].

Since the shape of an OD sometimes differs from an expected rounded convex region, the ARF may fail in the detection of OD. On the other hand, the SBF is too generic and its result can easily be affected by the presence of vessels near the OD boundary.

In general the OD appears as a super-elliptical shape [18]. If a 2-fold symmetrical semi-rounded convex shape is elongated diametrically, its equi-contours become super-ellipses. We refer to such an object as a super-elliptical convex region. For the detection of such a shape we introduce a new convergence index filter, called super-elliptical filter (SEF), see Fig. 2(a). The super-elliptical band in this filter allows the model to characterize a larger variety of shapes whilst at the same time reducing the irregularity in shape and the interference of vessels by its 2-fold symmetry constraints.

The super-elliptical convergence index filter is defined by

$$
\begin{aligned}
SEF(x,y) = \frac{1}{N} \max_{1 \leq j \leq N/4} & \left[\max_{R_{min} \leq r \leq R_{max}} \frac{1}{2d} \sum_{m=r}^{r+d} \left(\cos(\varphi_{(j,m)}) + \cos(\varphi_{(j+\frac{N}{2},m)}) \right) \right. \\
& + \max_{R_{min} \leq r \leq R_{max}} \frac{1}{2d} \sum_{m=r}^{r+d} \left(\cos(\varphi_{(j+\frac{N}{4},m)}) + \cos(\varphi_{(j+\frac{3N}{4},m)}) \right) \\
& + \sum_{i=1}^{N/4-1} \max_{R_{min} \leq r \leq R_{max}} \frac{1}{4d} \sum_{m=r}^{r+d} \left(\cos(\varphi_{(j+i,m)}) + \cos(\varphi_{(j-i+\frac{N}{2},m)}) \right. \\
& \left. \left. + \cos(\varphi_{(j+i+\frac{N}{2},m)}) + \cos(\varphi_{(j-i+N,m)}) \right) \right],
\end{aligned}
\qquad (5)
$$

where N is the number of support region radial lines and d corresponds to the width of the band, which can move between R_{min} and R_{max}. To simplify

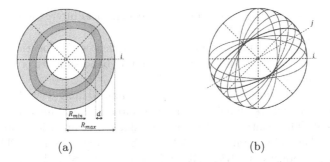

(a)   (b)

Fig. 2. (a) Schematics of the proposed super elliptical convergence index filter; (b) Possible super-ellipse orientations, where j represents the index of ellipse axis angle.

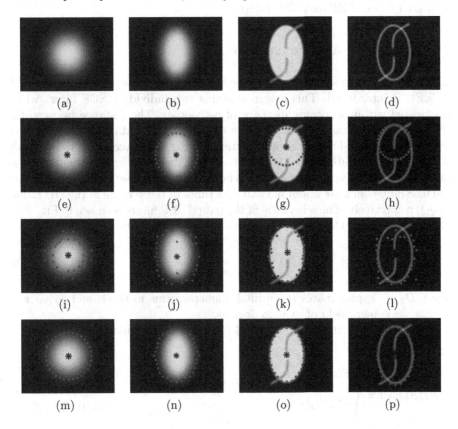

Fig. 3. (a–d) Phantom images; Maximum filter response (blue or green star) and corresponding band support points (red dots) of (e–h) ARF, (i–l) SBF and (m–p) SEF filters ($N = 32$, $d = 6$ px, $R_{min} = 50$ and $R_{max} = 90$ px). (Color figure online)

the equation, we used $\varphi_{(i,m)}$ instead of $\varphi(x, y, \theta_i, m)$ which represents the angle between the gradient vector at point (i, m) and the direction that is currently being analyzed. Figure 2(a) shows the SEF filter design schematics. In order to consider the possible orientations of the super-elliptical filter, the parameter j is introduced as illustrated in Fig. 2(b).

The maximum response of the SEF filter indicates the location of interest, the OD center in our case, and the corresponding band support points represent the shape of the detected object.

Figure 3(a)–(d) show different sample phantom images with background intensity of zero, where different gray-tone circular and elliptical objects are superimposed. The contrast between each shape's boundaries and the background is weakened by adding noise followed by Gaussian blurring. The location of maximum responses of ARF, SBF and the proposed SEF filters, and the corresponding support points are shown in Fig. 3. As we can see in this figure, the SEF filter gives the most accurate location and the best shape representation compared to the ARF and SBF filters.

3   Optic Disc and Fovea Detection

Here a setup for the simultaneous detection of OD and fovea, called paired SEF (PSEF), is introduced. This design contains two individual SEF filters which are located within a specific distance of each other. The distance between the SEF filters is constrained in accordance to the vertical and horizontal distances between the OD and the fovea, as illustrated in Fig. 4(a). According to the study of [20], the average diameter of the human optic disc is 1.85 mm. The horizontal and vertical distances from the fovea center to the optic disc center are 4.90 mm and 0.58 mm, which are about 5.3 and 0.58 times of the average of the OD radius (r_{OD}), respectively. The schematic of the paired SEF filters is shown in Fig. 4(b). The average of the OD radius in pixels can be estimated by

$$r_{OD} = 0.03 \left(\frac{D_{FOV}}{\tan(\phi_{FOV}/2)} \right), \tag{6}$$

where D_{FOV} approximates the retinal diameter value in pixels and ϕ_{FOV} represents the camera field of view in degrees.

The response of the PSEF for pixel (x, y) can be formulated as

$$PSEF(x,y) = \begin{cases} SEF_{OD}(x,y) + \displaystyle\max_{\substack{x-5.5\times r_{OD}\leq p\leq x-5\times r_{OD} \\ y-r_{OD}\leq q\leq y+0.5\times r_{OD}}} SEF_{FC}(p,q) & \text{if } x \geqslant \frac{M}{2} \\ SEF_{OD}(x,y) + \displaystyle\max_{\substack{x+5.0\times r_{OD}\leq p\leq x+5.5\times r_{OD} \\ y-r_{OD}\leq q\leq y+0.5\times r_{OD}}} SEF_{FC}(p,q) & \text{if } x < \frac{M}{2} \end{cases}$$

$$\tag{7}$$

where $p, q \in \mathbb{N}$, the $SEF_{OD}(x,y)$ and the $SEF_{FC}(p,q)$ are the pair of filters for the detection of OD and fovea centralis and M represents the width of the input image. If $x \geqslant M/2$, the fovea is on the left side of the OD; otherwise the fovea is on the right side. For the $SEF_{OD}(x,y)$ filter, the inner and outer limits of the support region are set as $0.8r_{OD}$ and $1.2r_{OD}$ while these limits for the $SEF_{FC}(p,q)$ filter are set as $0.5r_{OD}$ and $1r_{OD}$. The number of radial lines, N, is set to an optimal value of 32 for both filters and the band widths of $0.1r_{OD}$

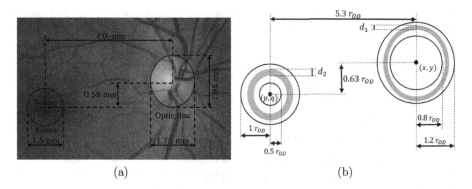

(a)   (b)

Fig. 4. (a) Schematics of dimensions and positions of OD and fovea; (b) PSEF setup.

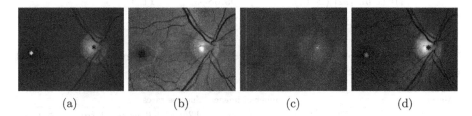

(a)   (b)   (c)   (d)

Fig. 5. (a) Original color fundus image with manually annotated OD (black star) and fovea (white star); (b) Normalized green channel; (c) PSEF response; (d) Maximum response of PSEF indicating the OD location (red star) and the corresponding detected fovea (green star). (Color figure online)

and $0.2r_{OD}$ are used for the $SEF_{OD}(x,y)$ and the $SEF_{FC}(p,q)$, respectively. Note that the SEF_{FC} filter is applied on the inverted green channel since the fovea usually appears darker than the background in retinal fundus images.

For the OD and fovea detection, the normalization technique proposed by Foracchia et al. [7] is employed to obtain an image with uniform distribution for both illumination and contrast. The normalized image is shown in Fig. 5(b). Figure 5(c) gives the filtered image by applying the PSEF filter defined in (7). Finally, the location of OD is obtained by finding the coordinate of the maximum filter response and the corresponding point (p,q) represents the location of fovea as shown in Fig. 5(d).

4   Results

The proposed method is validated on the images of the MESSIDOR dataset [1], since it is the only dataset with publicly available ground truth for both the OD and the fovea centers. This dataset includes 1200 retinal fundus color images acquired from a Topcon non-mydriatic retinograph with 45° field of view. The images have resolutions of 1440×960, 2240×1488, or 2304×1536 pixels. The manually delimited OD boundaries for all 1200 images and the annotations of fovea centers for 1136 images are provided by the University of Huelva which are publicly available [2].

Table 1. Success rate of the proposed approach for OD detection on all 1200 images of MESSIDOR dataset compared with other methods.

Methods	Success rates	Number of fails
PSEF (proposed)	**99.75 %**	**3**
Marin *et al.* [14] (2015)	99.75 %	3
Dashtbozorg *et al.* [6] (2015)	99.83 %	2
Bekkers *et al.* [5] (2014)	99.50 %	6
Giachetti *et al.* [9] (2013)	99.67 %	4
Mendonça *et al.* [15] (2013)	99.75 %	3
Aquino *et al.* [4] (2012)	98.83 %	14
Yu *et al.* [22] (2012)	99.08 %	11
Lu *et al.* [13] (2011)	99.75 %	3

Table 2. Success rate of the proposed approach for fovea detection on the MESSIDOR dataset compared with other methods.

Methods	Number of images	Success rates			
		$0.25r_{OD}$	$0.5r_{OD}$	$1r_{OD}$	$2r_{OD}$
PSEF (proposed)	1200	66.50 %	93.75 %	**98.87 %**	99.58 %
Kao *et al.* [10] (2014)	1200	-	-	97.80 %	-
Gegundez-Arias *et al.* [8] (2013)	1200	**93.92 %**	96.08 %	96.92 %	97.83 %
Yu *et al.* [21] (2011)	1200	-	95.00 %	-	-
Niemeijer *et al.* [8,16] (2009)	1200	93.50 %	**96.83 %**	97.92 %	-
PSEF (proposed)	1136	69.19 %	**95.86 %**	99.65 %	99.91 %
Aquino [3] (2014)	1136	**83.01 %**	91.28 %	98.24 %	99.56 %
Giachetti *et al.* [9] (2013)	1136	-	-	99.1 %	-
Gegundez-Arias *et al.* [3,8] (2013)	1136	76.23 %	93.84 %	98.24 %	99.30 %

For the evaluation of the OD localization technique, a detected position is considered correct if it is inside the manually annotated OD boundary. Table 1 summarizes the results for the OD detection, where the PSEF approach provides similar or better performance than most of the state-of-the-art methods. Our results are comparable to those obtained by the OD detection methods presented by Marin *et al.* [14], Mendonça *et al.* [15] and Lu *et al.* [13]. These methods as well as our approach fail to detect the OD in only 3 cases out of 1200 images, while the method proposed by Dashtbozorg *et al.* [6] fails in only 2 images. Nevertheless, our proposed approach does not require any previous segmentation for the initialization of OD location and the time requirement for the OD and fovea detection on one image is about 2.4 s.

For the evaluation of the fovea detection, an obtained fovea location is considered correct if the Euclidean distance to the location of the manually annotated fovea is less than the OD radius (r_{OD}). For further evaluation, three additional distances are also included as criteria. These distances are $0.25r_{OD}$, $0.5r_{OD}$ and $2r_{OD}$ which are also used by Gegundez-Arias et al. [8] and Aquino [3]. We analyze the performance of our fovea detection results on 1136 images to compare with the results reported in [3,8,9], and we also repeat the experiment for the whole set to compare with other methods where all the 1200 images have been used [10,16,21]. As shown in Table 2, the PSEF approach achieves a success rate of 98.87 % for the distance less than $1r_{OD}$ which is higher than ones reported by Kao et al. [10], Niemeijer et al. [16], and Gegundez-Arias et al. [8] for all 1200 images. For the set of 1136 images, we obtain a success rate of 99.65 % which is relevantly higher than those achieved by Aquino [3], Giachetti et al. [9], and Gegundez-Arias et al. [8]. The results presented in Table 2 demonstrate that better performance is achieved by the proposed approach for fovea detection compared to other methods.

5   Conclusion

In this paper we have presented an automatic OD and fovea detection technique using a proposed super-elliptical filter (SEF). This filter is suitable for the detection of semi-elliptical convex regions. Compared with the SBF, the SEF is less irregular and it is more tolerant to the presence of vessels and other interfering structures. Furthermore, the PSEF setup is proposed for the simultaneous detection of OD and fovea. The PSEF is constructed by considering a pair of SEF filters located within a specific spatial constraint, which is based on the average distance of OD and fovea in the human eye. Compared with other techniques, the proposed method does not require retinal blood vessel extraction and it is robust to imaging artifacts and different types of retinal lesions. The results on the MESSIDOR dataset show a similar performance compared to other recently published OD localization approaches and the presented method outperforms the state-of-the-art methods approaches for fovea detection.

Acknowledgments. The work is part of the Hé Programme of Innovation Cooperation, which is financed by the Netherlands Organization for Scientific Research (NWO), dossier No. 629.001.003.

References

1. MESSIDOR: Methods for Evaluating Segmentation and Indexing techniques Dedicated to Retinal Ophthalmology (2004). http://messidor.crihan.fr
2. Expert system for early automated detection of DR by analysis of digital retinal images project website (2012). http://www.uhu.es/retinopathy/muestras2.php
3. Aquino, A.: Establishing the macular grading grid by means of fovea centre detection using anatomical-based and visual-based features. Comput. Biol. Med. **55**, 61–73 (2014)
4. Aquino, A., Gegundez, M.E., Marin, D.: Automated optic disc detection in retinal images of patients with diabetic retinopathy and risk of macular edema. Int. J. Biol. Life Sci. **8**(2), 87–92 (2012)

5. Bekkers, E., Duits, R., Romeny, B.H.: Optic nerve head detection via group correlations in multi-orientation transforms. In: Campilho, A., Kamel, M. (eds.) ICIAR 2014, Part II. LNCS, vol. 8815, pp. 293–302. Springer, Heidelberg (2014)

6. Dashtbozorg, B., Mendonça, A.M., Campilho, A.: Optic disc segmentation using the sliding band filter. Comput. Biol. Med. **56**, 1–12 (2015)

7. Foracchia, M., Grisan, E., Ruggeri, A.: Luminosity and contrast normalization in retinal images. Med. Image Anal. **9**(3), 179–190 (2005)

8. Gegundez-Arias, M.E., Marin, D., Bravo, J.M., Suero, A.: Locating the fovea center position in digital fundus images using thresholding and feature extraction techniques. Comput. Med. Imaging Graph. **37**(5), 386–393 (2013)

9. Giachetti, A., Ballerini, L., Trucco, E., Wilson, P.J.: The use of radial symmetry to localize retinal landmarks. Comput. Med. Imaging Graph. **37**(5), 369–376 (2013)

10. Kao, E.F., Lin, P.C., Chou, M.C., Jaw, T.S., Liu, G.C.: Automated detection of fovea in fundus images based on vessel-free zone and adaptive Gaussian template. Comput. Methods Prog. Biomed. **117**(2), 92–103 (2014)

11. Knudtson, M.D., Lee, K.E., Hubbard, L.D., Wong, T.Y., Klein, R., Klein, B.E.: Revised formulas for summarizing retinal vessel diameters. Curr. Eye Res. **27**(3), 143–149 (2003)

12. Kobatake, H., Hashimoto, S.: Convergence index filter for vector fields. IEEE Trans. Image Process. **8**(8), 1029–1038 (1999)

13. Lu, S.: Accurate and efficient optic disc detection and segmentation by a circular transformation. IEEE Trans. Med. Imaging **30**(12), 2126–2133 (2011)

14. Marin, D., Gegundez-Arias, M.E., Suero, A., Bravo, J.M.: Obtaining optic disc center and pixel region by automatic thresholding methods on morphologically processed fundus images. Comput. Methods Prog. Biomed. **118**(2), 173–185 (2015)

15. Mendonça, A.M., Sousa, A., Mendonça, L., Campilho, A.: Automatic localization of the optic disc by combining vascular and intensity information. Comput. Med. Imaging Graph. **37**(5), 409–417 (2013)

16. Niemeijer, M., Abràmoff, M.D., Van Ginneken, B.: Fast detection of the optic disc and fovea in color fundus photographs. Med. Image Anal. **13**(6), 859–870 (2009)

17. Pereira, C.S., Fernandes, H., Mendonça, A.M., Campilho, A.C.: Detection of lung nodule candidates in chest radiographs. In: Martí, J., Benedí, J.M., Mendonça, A.M., Serrat, J. (eds.) IbPRIA 2007. LNCS, vol. 4478, pp. 170–177. Springer, Heidelberg (2007)

18. Quigley, H.A., Brown, A.E., Morrison, J.D., Drance, S.M.: The size and shape of the optic disc in normal human eyes. Arch. Ophthalmol. **108**(1), 51–57 (1990)

19. Wei, J., Hagihara, Y., Kobatake, H.: Detection of cancerous tumors on chest x-ray images-candidate detection filter and its evaluation. In: IEEE International Conference on Image Processing, vol. 3, pp. 397–401 (1999)

20. Williams, T., Wilkinson, J.: Position of the fovea centralis with respect to the optic nerve head. Optom. Vis. Sci. **69**(5), 369–377 (1992)

21. Yu, H., Barriga, S., Agurto, C., Echegaray, S., Pattichis, M., Zamora, G., Bauman, W., Soliz, P.: Fast localization of optic disc and fovea in retinal images for eye disease screening. In: SPIE Medical Imaging, p. 796317. International Society for Optics and Photonics (2011)

22. Yu, H., Barriga, E.S., Agurto, C., Echegaray, S., Pattichis, M.S., Bauman, W., Soliz, P.: Fast localization and segmentation of optic disk in retinal images using directional matched filtering and level sets. IEEE Trans. Inf. Technol. Biomed. **16**(4), 644–657 (2012)

Age-Related Macular Degeneration Detection and Stage Classification Using Choroidal OCT Images

Jingjing Deng[1], Xianghua Xie[1(✉)], Louise Terry[2], Ashley Wood[2], Nick White[2], Tom H. Margrain[2], and Rachel V. North[2]

[1] Department of Computer Science, Swansea University, Singleton Park, Swansea SA2 8PP, UK
{csjd,x.xie}@swansea.ac.uk
[2] School of Optometry and Vision Sciences, Cardiff University Cathays, Cardiff CF24 4HQ, UK
http://csvision.swan.ac.uk

Abstract. Age-Related Macular Degeneration (AMD) is a progressive eye disease which damages the retina and causes visual impairment. Detecting those in the early stages at most risk of progression will allow more timely treatment and preserve sight. In this paper, we propose a machine learning based method to detect AMD and distinguish the different stages using choroidal images obtained from optical coherence tomography (OCT). We extract texture features using a Gabor filter bank and non-linear energy transformation. Then the histogram based feature descriptors are used to train the random forests, Support Vector Machine (SVM) and neural networks, which are tested on our choroid OCT image dataset with 21 participants. The experimental results show the feasibility of our method.

Keywords: AMD diseases classification · Choroidal OCT image · Texture analysis

1 Introduction

Age-Related Macular Degeneration is the leading cause of sight loss and visual impairment among older adults (above 55 years) [5]. It affects the outer retinal layers, particularly the photoreceptors, retinal pigment epithelium (RPE) and choroid, leading to central vision loss. The exact cause of AMD is still not fully understood, but is known to be multifactorial, with increasing age being the most consistent factor [1]. The condition can be clinically categorised into three stages. An early stage, where vision is relatively unaffected, that may progress to one of two advanced stages: dry (atrophic) AMD or wet (neovascular) AMD. In both end stages, the choroid is affected. The wet AMD subtype is characterised by growth of new blood vessels from the choroid into the retina, forming a choroidal neovascular membrane (CNVM). These vessels are prone to leakage

© Springer International Publishing Switzerland 2016
A. Campilho and F. Karray (Eds.): ICIAR 2016, LNCS 9730, pp. 707–715, 2016.
DOI: 10.1007/978-3-319-41501-7_79

causing oedema, haemorrhage, and in some cases pigment epithelial detachments (PED). These changes result in sudden and severe loss of central vision. The dry AMD subtype represents an atrophy of the RPE retina, and loss of choroidal vasculature. Currently, optical coherence tomography (OCT) imaging of the retina is the gold standard diagnostic technique for this condition. However, advances in OCT now allow us to visualise the deeper structures, including the choroid. Histology has shown these choroidal vessels to have changed substantially in advanced AMD [19]. Detecting these changes in *vivo* particularly in early disease may improve detection of AMD, prior to retinal damage.

To detect textural changes to the vasculature in these images, machine learning and pattern recognition techniques, such as random forests, SVM and neural networks, can be applied. These machine learning algorithms have been shown effective in various classification problem, for example, distinguishing different human conversational scenarios [7], segmenting the region of interest in OCT and IVUS images [9,13]. Random forests [4] is an ensemble learning method, it grows a number of decision trees independently using the subsets which are randomly sampled from the complete training set with replacement. During the classification stage, the testing sample walks through each decision tree by evaluating its features at non-leaf node, and finally reaches a leaf node at the bottom, which votes the class with largest proposition of training samples it holds. The random forests combine all voting results from individual decision trees, and assigns the most voted class to the testing sample. SVM [6] separates the samples by mapping the feature into high dimensional space and finding the separation hyper-planes for different classes. The testing sample is represented in the high dimensional space using the same mapping function, and its class is determined by the region it falls on, which is bounded by the hyper-planes. Neural networks [11] consider the supervised classification as a function fitting problem given the input feature as argument, and the prediction as function value. Then the unknown function can be learned by approximating with one or more layers of interconnected neurons organised hierarchically. Recently, deep neural networks have shown great learning capacity and higher accuracy compared with the traditional learning methods in almost all aspects of pattern recognition [17].

Koprowski et al. [14] proposed a method to classify choroidal OCT images into pre-defined clinical conditions by extracting high level features, such as number of detected objects, and average position of the centre of gravity, from low level texture information. Whereas, in this paper we present a method using the low level texture features not only to detect disease, but also to categorise into broadly defined AMD disease stages instead of specific clinical conditions. The rest of this paper is organised as follows. Section 2 provides the details of the OCT image acquisition procedure, Sect. 3 presents our proposed method including feature extraction, and classifier training. The experimental results are illustrated and discussed in Sect. 4. Section 5 concludes the work, and presents the future plan.

2   Data

Participants were recruited with dry AMD (n = 7, Age = 80.00 ± 9.95) and wet AMD (n = 7, Age = 82.00 ± 4.43), along with a group of healthy age-similar controls (n = 7, Age = 68.85 ± 6.64). In order to avoid any bias which may be introduced by having a predominant class, we imaged 7 participants for each class. All participants underwent long-wavelength OCT imaging using a 1060 nm light source. This wavelength penetrates deeper into the retina and choroid, allowing visualization of the deeper structures, and also benefits from reduced intraocular scattering caused by media opacities such as cataract [18]. Firstly, the length of the participants eyes were measured, and then followed by 20° × 20° (512 × 512 × 1024) volume scan, This is approximately 10.3 mm wide given a mean axial eye length of 24.46 mm. The images were scaled laterally using the measured axial eye length of each patient, the scan angle and assumed refractive index of the ocular media.

All OCT images were collected by a single trained operator (AW), and classified by three experienced, masked observers into three groups: normal, dry AMD, and wet AMD. The classifications were based on the retinal appearance

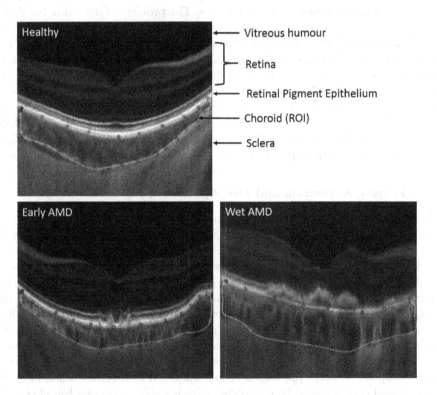

Fig. 1. Three example OCT images representing the 3 classification groups used as ground truth. The green contours were labelled manually highlighting the choroid regions of interest (ROI). (Color figure online)

and Age-Related Eye Disease Study definitions of disease progression [2]. This was taken as ground truth. For each image, 100 slices of the choroid regions were labelled, 20 of which were randomly selected and used in training and testing. For the control group, 20 slices out of 512 for each participant were randomly chosen. Thus, we had a total of 420 images in total with the choroidal region labelled as a closed contour. Figure 1 shows examples of OCT images from each groups.

3   Method

In this paper, we proposed a machine learning-based method to detect AMD and distinguish the different stages using choroidal OCT imaging. To our knowledge, this is the first work testing the feasibility of classifying AMD by choroidal appearance in OCT images. At the dry stage of AMD the first sign includes the accumulating of drusen between retina and Bruch's membrane. The choroid is affected in the progression to both Wet & Dry subtypes, either as the source of new blood vessels that invade the retina (Wet) or through a progressive loss of vasculature (Dry). These pathological processes affect the textural appearance of choroid sections on the OCT image. The problem of detecting the AMD and distinguishing different stages can be approached as a texture classification problem. However, the changes of texture appearance are subtle, and often not noticeable. To tackle this problem, Gabor filtering followed by an energy transformation was employed to detect frequency information of the input images within different scales and orientations. The histogram of energy responses were used to form the feature descriptors for pre-labelled choroid regions. Given the ground truth of AMD stage, a set of classifiers were trained in a supervised fashion, which will be used for AMD classification. The flowchart shown in Fig. 2 illustrates the steps from preprocessing, to feature extraction, to classification.

3.1   Feature Extraction and Descriptors

Gabor filters have been widely used in texture analysis [10,20], especially in surface defects detection [3,15,16,22] and image segmentation [8,21], due to its capacity of representing the frequency and orientation information which is fairly similar to the human visual perception. In our case, we used 2D Gabor filter which could be defined by a complex sinusoid multiplied by a Gaussian function. For images, the Gabor responses can be computed by convolving the image matrix with the Gabor filter matrix which is simply obtained by sampling at discrete coordinates from the continuous Gabor function. To compute the feature image in multi-scales, we filtered the image using a Gabor filter bank first, and then applied an energy transformation proposed by Jain et al. [12] to the responses, where the responses are subjected to a bounded non-linearity (Eq. 1), and then followed by convolving with a square averaging kernel (Eq. 2).

$$\psi(g) = tanh(\alpha g) = \frac{1 - e^{-2\alpha g}}{1 + e^{-2\alpha g}} \tag{1}$$

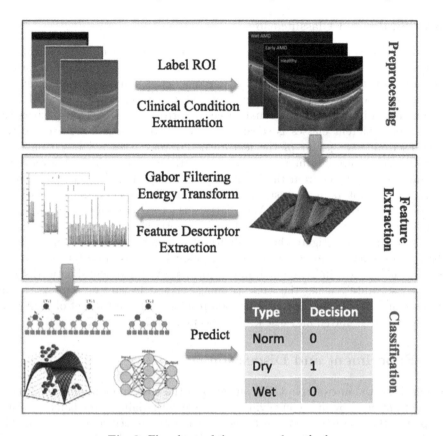

Fig. 2. Flowchart of the proposed method.

$$\mathcal{E}(C_x, C_y) = \frac{1}{S^2} \sum_{(a,b) \in W_{C_x C_y}} | \psi(g(a,b)) | \qquad (2)$$

where g is Gabor function, $W_{C_x C_y}$ is the averaging window with size of $S \times S$ pixels, and centred at (C_x, C_y) image coordinate.

The labelled choroid layers varied greatly in shape thickness and appearance between individuals, as illustrated in Fig. 1. In (dry) AMD we initially expected the choroid, and consequently its texture, to be affected locally. Examining the small patches from the labelled region is not a reasonable way to diagnose the disease, as considerable amount of patches will have quite similar feature pattern, which to some extent introduces a large amount of noise to the training stage. Instead of considering local features, the histogram of the texture energy of the labelled choroid region are computed as the feature descriptors. As the feature image is bounded within $[0, 1]$ (Eqs. 1 and 2), the histogram can be computed without any further normalisation. The feature descriptors were formed by concatenating histograms of the energy image of different scales and orientations consistently.

3.2 Supervised Classification

Random forests and SVM are traditional data-driven discriminative models for supervised classification problems. The feature descriptors were designed for representing the distributions of edges at different scales and orientations. Random forests treat each feature as an independent component, whereas SVM finds the manifold in higher dimensional space by correlating the features, where the data from different classes is separable. These two classifiers are used to test the discriminative power of the feature descriptors extracted based on lower level image texture information. Neural networks can learn the high level representations of features from the inputs hierarchically, and then generalize more abstract descriptors in an unsupervised fashion. The supervised classification is carried out by stacking the SoftMax layer on the top, and back-propagating the prediction error back to the lower layers to optimize the weights of neurons. It was used to investigate the possibility of generalizing higher representation based on the hand crafted feature descriptors, where it is important in the case of modelling across individuals. Random forests, SVM and neural networks were trained separately using the same training set and feature descriptors during the learning procedure. The classification results on the testing set of individual classifiers are reported and discussed in Sect. 4.

4 Experiment and Discussion

Figure 3 shows an example OCT image, and the corresponding energy feature images obtained by first convolving the image with Gabor filter bank and then applying the non-linear energy transformation, as described in Sect. 3.1. The Gabor filter bank is created from the initial 39 by 39 pixels 2D Gabor filter with 5 levels of scale and 8 orientations (every 45 degrees). The top row of Fig. 2(b) shows the energy responses from different orientations of the first scale, and the bottom row is obtained from the last scale. It clearly shows that the Gabor filter bank detects the edge of different orientation from fine level to coarse level. We extracted the histogram of the energy feature images for the labelled choroid region with 11 bins, and then concatenated the histograms across scales and orientations, which forms a feature descriptor vector with 440 components. Then, a random forests with 50 decision trees, an SVM with radial basis function kernel, and a shallow neural networks with one hidden layer and 360 neurons were trained and tested using the feature descriptors independently.

To carry out the classification, 10-fold cross validation was adopted, that is, the whole dataset was evenly partitioned into ten randomly sampled subsets across different patients, and one subset was retained for testing, the remaining 9 subsets were used to train the classifier. Tables 1, 2 and 3 show the confusion matrices of random forests, SVM and neural networks, and the average of 94.7 %, 97.1 %, and 84.7 % were achieved respectively. A significant accuracy difference was found between neural networks and other two classifiers. The neural network is suitable for learning the hierarchical representation of the features from the raw image patches such as conventional photographs which have relatively high

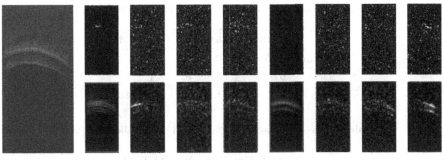

(a) OCT Image   (b) Energy feature images from different scales and orientations

Fig. 3. (a) shows the original OCT image; (b) shows the energy feature images obtained by filtering the original image with different scales and orientations of Gabor filters. The Gabor filters are applied to the whole image first as shown in figures, and then only the choroid sections which were manually labelled beforehand are used in the study.

intensity contrast. In our case, we employed the Gabor filter bank to detect the edge based feature, and then used histograms to generalise it. Using such feature descriptors, the discriminative models trained by finding the separation boundary should outperform the generalization model. Furthermore, 2-Fold cross validation was carried out, and the results are reported in Table 4. We observed the decrease of average accuracy of all classifiers, especially random forest, which is caused by reducing the proposition of the training set. However, the results strongly suggest that it is feasible to detect AMD pathological changing the choroid and distinguish different stages of disease by examining the image texture of the choroid.

Table 1. Confusion matrix of 10-Fold random forests (%).

	Normal	Dry AMD	Wet AMD
Normal	99.0 ± 2.5	3.5	0.3
Dry	0.7	87.0 ± 9.1	1.6
Wet	0.3	9.5	98.1 ± 4.2

Table 2. Confusion matrix of 10-Fold SVM (%).

	Normal	Dry AMD	Wet AMD
Normal	96.5 ± 4.8	0.0	1.9
Dry	0.0	97.4 ± 4.5	0.7
Wet	3.5	2.6	97.4 ± 3.9

Table 3. Confusion matrix of 10-Fold neural networks (%).

	Normal	Dry AMD	Wet AMD
Normal	86.5 ± 9.3	7.3	5.1
Dry	6.6	80.8 ± 10.2	8.1
Wet	6.9	11.9	86.8 ± 8.3

Table 4. Classification results of 2-Fold cross validation (%).

	Normal	Dry AMD	Wet AMD	Ave.
R.F.	95.4	80.0	90.8	88.7
SVM	95.3	93.1	94.7	94.4
N.N.	80.3	73.1	81.0	78.1

5   Conclusion

In this paper, we have presented a machine learning-based method to detect and distinguish different stages of AMD using choroidal OCT imaging. The experimental results show the feasibility of the proposed method, where a computer-aided AMD classification system can be built. However, a larger dataset is necessary to account for large within-group variation, particularly in the early disease stage. This will be addressed in our future work.

References

1. Ambati, J., Fowler, B.J.: Mechanisms of age-related macular degeneration. Neuron **75**(1), 26–39 (2012)
2. AREDS: The age-related eye disease study system for classifying age-related macular degeneration from stereoscopic color fundus photographs: the age-related eye disease study report number 6. Am. J. Ophthalmol. **132**(5), pp. 668–681 (2001)
3. Bodnarova, A., Bennamoun, M., Latham, S.: Optimal Gabor filters for textile flaw detection. Pattern Recogn. **35**(12), 2973–2991 (2002)
4. Breiman, L.: Random forests. Mach. Learn. **45**(1), 5–32 (2001)
5. Bunce, C., Zekite, A., Walton, S., Rees, A., Patel, P.: Certifications for sight impairment due to age related macular degeneration in England. Public Health **129**(2), 138–142 (2015)
6. Cortes, C., Vapnik, V.: Support-vector networks. Mach. Learn. **20**(3), 273–297 (1995)
7. Deng, J., Xie, X., Daubney, B.: A bag of words approach to subject specific 3D human pose interaction classification with random decision forests. Graph. Models **76**(3), 162–171 (2014)
8. Dunn, D., Higgins, W.E.: Optimal Gabor filters for texture segmentation. IEEE Trans. Image Process. **4**(7), 947–964 (1995)

9. Essa, E., Xie, X., Jones, J.L.: Minimum S-excess graph for segmenting and tracking multiple borders with HMM. In: Navab, N., Hornegger, J., Wells, W.M., Frangi, A.F. (eds.) Medical Image Computing and Computer-Assisted Intervention–MICCAI 2015. LNCS, vol. 9350, pp. 28–35. Springer, Switzerland (2015)

10. Grigorescu, S.E., Petkov, N., Kruizinga, P.: Comparison of texture features based on Gabor filters. IEEE Trans. Image Process. **11**(10), 1160–1167 (2002)

11. Hinton, G.E., Salakhutdinov, R.R.: Reducing the dimensionality of data with neural networks. Science **313**(5786), 504–507 (2006)

12. Jain, A.K., Farrokhnia, F.: Unsupervised texture segmentation using Gabor filters. In: IEEE International Conference on Systems, Man and Cybernetics, pp. 14–19 (1990)

13. Jones, J.L., Xie, X., Essa, E.: Combining region-based and imprecise boundary-based cues for interactive medical image segmentation. Int. J. Numer. Methods Biomed. Eng. **30**(12), 1649–1666 (2014)

14. Koprowski, R., Teper, S., Wróbel, Z., Wylegala, E.: Automatic analysis of selected choroidal diseases in OCT images of the eye fundus. Biomed. Eng. Online **12**(1), 117 (2013)

15. Kumar, A., Pang, G.K.: Defect detection in textured materials using Gabor filters. IEEE Trans. Indus. Appl. **38**(2), 425–440 (2002)

16. Kumar, A., Pang, G.K.: Defect detection in textured materials using optimized filters. IEEE Trans. Syst. Man Cybern. Part B Cybern. **32**(5), 553–570 (2002)

17. LeCun, Y., Bengio, Y., Hinton, G.E.: Deep learning. Nature **521**(7553), 436–444 (2015)

18. Povazay, B., Bizheva, K., Hermann, B., Unterhuber, A., Sattmann, H., Fercher, A., Drexler, W., Schubert, C., Ahnelt, P., Mei, M., et al.: Enhanced visualization of choroidal vessels using ultrahigh resolution ophthalmic OCT at 1050 nm. Opt. Express **11**(17), 1980–1986 (2003)

19. Spraul, C.W., Lang, G.E., Grossniklaus, H.E., Lang, G.K.: Histologic and morphometric analysis of the choroid, Bruch's membrane, and retinal pigment epithelium in postmortem eyes with age-related macular degeneration and histologic examination of surgically excised choroidal neovascular membranes. Surv. ophthalmol. **44**, S10–S32 (1999)

20. Xie, X.: A review of recent advances in surface defect detection using texture analysis techniques. ELCVIA Electron. Lett. Comput. Vis. Image Anal. **7**(3) (2008)

21. Xie, X., Mirmehdi, M.: Colour image segmentation using texems. Ann. BMVA **1**(6), 1–10 (2007)

22. Xie, X., Mirmehdi, M.: TEXEMS: texture exemplars for defect detection on random textured surfaces. IEEE Trans. Pattern Anal. Mach. Intell. **29**(8), 1454–1464 (2007)

3D Retinal Vessel Tree Segmentation and Reconstruction with OCT Images

Joaquim de Moura[1], Jorge Novo[1(✉)], Marcos Ortega[1], and Pablo Charlón[2]

[1] Departamento de Computación, Universidade da Coruña, A Coruña, Spain
{joaquim.demoura,jnovo,mortega}@udc.es, pcharlon@sgoc.es
[2] Instituto Oftalmológico Victoria de Rojas, A Coruña, Spain

Abstract. Detection and analysis of the arterio-venular tree of the retina is a relevant issue, providing useful information in procedures such as the diagnosis of different pathologies. Classical approaches for vessel extraction make use of 2D acquisition paradigms and, therefore, obtain a limited representation of the vascular structure. This paper proposes a new methodology for the automatic 3D segmentation and reconstruction of the retinal arterio-venular tree in Optical Coherence Tomography (OCT) images. The methodology takes advantage of different image analysis techniques to initially segment the vessel tree and estimate its calibers along it. Then, the corresponding depth for the entire vessel tree is obtained. Finally, with all this information, the method performs the 3D reconstruction of the entire vessel tree.

The test and validation procedure employed 196 OCT histological images with the corresponding near infrared reflectance retinographies. The methodology showed promising results, demonstrating its accuracy in a complex domain, providing a coherent 3D vessel tree reconstruction that can be posteriorly analyzed in different medical diagnostic processes.

Keywords: Computer-aided diagnosis · Retinal imaging · OCT · Vessel tree · 3D segmentation

1 Introduction and Previous Work

Nowadays, eye fundus is widely used in many analysis and diagnostic processes. Hence, the study of retinal images provide the specialists useful information that can be of a great utility to obtain accurate diagnosis in a large variability of pathologies. In that sense, Computer-Aided Diagnostic (CAD) systems in the ophthalmology field have widely spread over the years, as they facilitate specialists work, increasing their productivity and helping to establish preventive and therapeutic strategies.

The automatic detection and extraction of relevant structures of the retina help to significantly improve the procedure of clinical assessment. From all of them, the arterio-venular tree is of particular relevance. Retinal microcirculation is the easiest and less invasive way to access to the circulatory system in human body. Moreover, different studies established retinal vessel caliber as a relevant

© Springer International Publishing Switzerland 2016
A. Campilho and F. Karray (Eds.): ICIAR 2016, LNCS 9730, pp. 716–726, 2016.
DOI: 10.1007/978-3-319-41501-7_80

parameter in the evaluation of diabetic patients [1]. Smith *et al.* [2] indicated that small structural vessel changes in the retina can anticipate the development of severe hypertension. Some studies [3] also established calculations on the retinal microcirculation as possible biomarkers for cerebrovascular disease, or others [4,5] that related the retinal vessels calibers to cardiovascular illnesses events. Besides the medical field, the retinal vessel tree was also applied with other purposes as, for example, the identification in biometric systems [6], similar to fingerprints or other biometric traits.

Given the relevance of this structure, many authors have faced this task over the years, proposing different methodologies for retinal vessel tree extraction. Classical acquisitions methods such as angiography or retinography depict vessel structure as a 2D projection of the real 3D layout. Thus, the vast majority of the approaches present in the literature are proposed in 2D representing partial information of the vasculature. Some representative examples are here presented. Yong *et al.* [7] proposed an adaptative threshold to localize and segment the vessels. Edge detectors were also employed, as in the work of Xiaolin *et al.* [8], where Canny was employed to detect the vessels and modified with a with a bilateral filter to remove the noise. Mendonça and Campilho [9] introduced an approach based on the combination of vessel centerline extraction and region growing to fill the resultant extracted vessels. Wavelet transform also demonstrated its utility in the problem, as Nayak *et al.* [10] indicated, being used in a method that extracts the vessel tree for diabetic retinopathy patients. Graph-cuts were also employed, as Chen *et al.* [11] proposed, in an automatic and unsupervised system was constructed using graph-cuts to identify the blood vessels. Artificial Neural Networks (ANNs) were commonly used in medical imaging methodologies, given their potential and robustness to provide accurate results in significantly adverse conditions. They were also used in this problem, as Chen *et al.* [12] implemented, where the method inputs image patches to the ANNs that differentiates the vessels from the rest of the retina.

In recent years with the appearance and popularization of the Optical Coherence Tomography (OCT) depth information in the retina can be analyzed, including presence and location of vessels. Some studies have been presented to undertake this task although most of them still present 2D projections of the vessel tree for this new modality. Guimaraes *et al.* [13] employed the OCT fundus images to locate the depth of the vessels, enclosed in the study of abnormal retinal vascular patterns. Pilch *et al.* [14] employed an statistical shape model created with a set of vessels that were manually segmented and used in a training phase. The model is then employed to segment the contours in axial direction. Wu *et al.* [15] designed a method using Coherent Point Drift to segment the retinal vessel point sets, that are posteriorly used as landmarks for image registration.

For that reason, in this work, we propose a 3D segmentation and reconstruction of the arterio-venular tree of the retina, taking advantage of the Optical Coherence Tomography (OCT) images that provide depth information in the eye fundus. Thus, it offers a complete set of characteristics of the vasculature that can permit to proceed with more reliable analysis and diagnostic processes involving the retinal microcirculation analysis.

2   Methodology

The input images of the method are obtained by the OCT technique that offers the near infrared reflectance retinographies and the corresponding histological sections. This technique permits to obtain tomographic images of the biological tissue with high resolution, performing consecutive measurements over the retina. Thus, these images compose the 3D visualization of the eye fundus of the patient. In Fig. 1 we can see an example of the OCT image of a patient. The input images include the selection of the region of interest (ROI), that indicates the part of the retinography corresponding with the histological sections, containing relevant structures to be analyzed, in particular in our case, the retinal vessels.

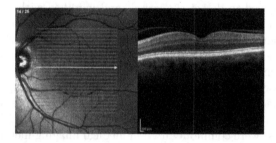

Fig. 1. Example of near infrared reflectance retinography and histological section.

The methodology firstly extracts the vessel tree in the near infrared reflectance retinography, constructs a list of segments and corrects possible mistakes at the intersections. Then, the method estimates the diameter at each point of the vessels. Posteriorly, these segments and diameters are mapped in the histological sections to search for the z coordinate, that is, the depth at the points. Finally, with all this information, the 3D reconstruction of the vessel tree is achieved, interpolating with splines all the segments to obtain a smoother representation. Next subsection details each step.

2.1   2D Vessel Detection

Firstly, we segment the vessels in the 2D retinography, given its simplicity and well-established techniques. A segmentation based in morphological operators is applied [16] to obtain an initial representation of vessels. Segmentation approaches in 2D can not be directly used for reconstruction as they typically present cumulative errors due to misrepresentation of edges. Thus, a centerline-based approach is needed to correct deviations in the structure. The main idea is to have segments representing the approximate central line of vessels in order to get coordinates and to detect characteristic points (mainly bifurcations and crossings). This is computed by applying the approach proposed in [6] that exploits the idea that vessels can be thought of as creases (ridges or valleys) when images are seen as landscapes, curvature level curves are employed to calculate the creases (crest and valley lines). Among the different definitions of a crease, this work uses the one that is based on level set extrinsic curvature or LSEC, given its invariant properties. This method provides the vessel tree segmentation that is going to be the kernel structure to construct the entire 3D segmentation.

Creaseness measurement does not return a 1-pixel width segment as there are degrees of creaseness along the vessel. Hence, we label all the pixels with a tracking process that is going to check across the entire crease image, guaranteeing that all the pixels belong to any particular segment. At the end, we have a skeleton vessel tree structure where all the vessels are represented by one-pixel width segment with an initial and final point. Small segments are removed as they are obtained from other structures different to vessels or even noise in the image. Figure 2(a),(b) and (c) shows an example of vessel and segment extraction.

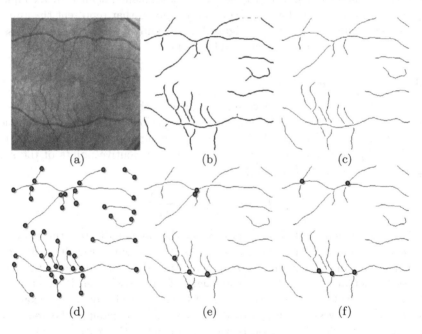

Fig. 2. Example of the methodology in the 2D vessel tree extraction and refinement.(a) Input retinography.(b) 2D Vessel tree extraction.(c) Resultant Segments.(d) Entire set of end points.(e) Corrected bifurcations.(f) Corrected crossings.

2.2 Intersections Reconstruction

The main drawback of the crease method is the loss of vessel connectivity mainly in the intersection points as in these regions the direction of the crease can not be established as it can seen in Fig. 2. In order to correct miscalculations, a further analysis for those regions was designed to reconstruct the intersections. All the end points of the segments were analyzed for being distinguished as: real ends, bifurcations or crossings.

Bifurcations. When an end point is significantly close to any point of another segment. The method calculates for each end point its closest distance to any other segment, and defines a threshold to filter those that are at a distance we consider that belongs to a bifurcation. In that case, the end point is connected to the segment by interpolation of the continuity of its own segment.

Crossings. In this case, it is represented by a couple of end points that are close to other segment. If both end points are inside of a given threshold, a continuity among them is considered. Both points are again connected by interpolation joining in a single segment that crosses the other one.

The rest of the points are considered correct end points. This way, we have correctly characterized all the vessels in a set of segments, defined by a couple of begin and end points, and a list of consecutive pixels that represent the approximated center line of the vessel. Figure 2(d),(e) and (f) illustrates a process of end points analysis and intersection refinement.

2.3 Caliber Estimation

We also need to estimate the vessel caliber at each point of the segments, in order to correctly represent its appearance in the posterior 3D reconstruction. The orientation of each pixel is used in this estimation. An orientation θ is calculated by means of the angle between two consecutive points of the same segment $P_1(x_1, y_1)$ and $P_2(x_2, y_2)$ as:

$$\theta = arctan\left(\frac{y_2 - y_1}{x_2 - x_1}\right) \tag{1}$$

The perpendicular of this orientation at the point indicates, therefore, the directions to compute the caliber of the vessel, as shown in Fig. 3(a). Hence, in both perpendicular directions we search for the edges that delimits the limits of vessel, calculating r_1 and r_2 as the length of the vessel in each direction. We search in both sides as the central point of the segment is not always exactly in the center of the vessel as Fig. 3(b) illustrates with an example. Therefore, the computed diameter, $d = r_1 + r_2$, is better adjusted to the real scenario.

2.4 Vessel Mapping in the Histological Sections

The next phase is the estimation of the vessel depth, z, at all the detected points of the vessel tree. This can be analyzed in the OCT scans, where we can compute the exact depth in the retina where vessels are located.

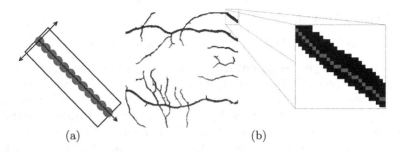

Fig. 3. Diameter estimation. (a) Representation of the analyzed direction at each point of a segment. (b) Example with the segments overlapping the vessels.

In the OCT images, the retinal vessels are visualized as structures that block the transmission of light and leave a shadow, as presented in Fig. 4(a), with a width proportional to the vessel diameter, in the corresponding histological section where they are placed. As we know each histological section corresponds to a band in the 2D image, consequently we detect the intersection of this band in the 2D retinography with the detected segments. Then, these intersection points, and the corresponding diameters, are mapped in the histological section, constructing a rectangle with a width corresponding to the associated $r_1 + r_2$. This way, we identify the projection zone of the vessel, that is, the region that corresponds to the vessel shadow, as shown in Fig. 4(b). In this projection zone, we can identify the location of the vessel which represents the depth z where the vessel is placed.

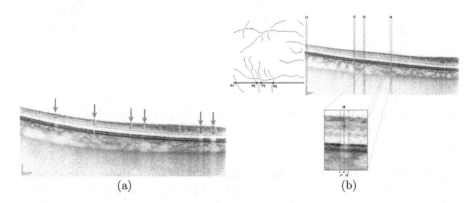

Fig. 4. Vessel mapping in the histological sections. (a) Example of shadow projection of a set of vessels. (b) Example of mapping performed and construction of the associated rectangles covering the projection zones.

2.5   Depth Vessel Estimation

We obtain the corresponding z, depth, at each vessel point in 3 consecutive steps.

ILM and RPE layers segmentation. Firstly, we delimit the region where the vessel could be placed inside the projection zone to reduce the search space. The region of interest is delimited between the retinal layers Inner Limitant Membrane (ILM), the first intraretinal layer, and the Retinal Pigment Epithelium (RPE), formed by pigmented cells at the external part of the retina.

Canny edge detector is applied to find the limits of the layers considering that ILM and RPE contain the clearest edges due to the highest contrast of intensities of these layers. Then, in order to gain information, we apply the gradient to this image in horizontal direction, deriving strongest detections and guaranteeing a correct acquisition of both layers. Finally, the upper connected line of this detected edges corresponds to the limits of the ILM layer. The lower connected lines delimit de RPE layer, as shown in Fig. 5(a).

Vessel region detection. Each vessel is searched for within both layers, appearing as a small elliptic region with darker intensities due to its particular reflectance properties compared to retinal layers. Therefore, darkest neighbourhood inside the region of interest is identified as the center of the vessel, as illustrated in Fig. 5(b). Before that, a mean filter with a window of 3×3 is applied to smooth the ROI and avoid noisy detections.

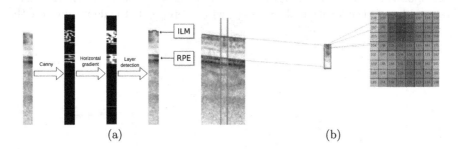

Fig. 5. Vessel detection in the histological sections. (a) Detection of ILM and RPE layers. (b) Detection of the vessel in the search region.

Depth calculation. After vessel location in OCT scans, their depth values z can be obtained. This is achieved by taking RPE layer lower limit as baseline and computing the height of the vessel center related to the baseline:

$$z = |C_v - P_i| \tag{2}$$

where z is the distance that measure the depth value, C_v indicates the y coordinate of the center of the detected vessel in the histological image, and P_i indicates the y coordinate of the lower limit of the RPE layer.

2.6 3D Reconstruction

Having all the vessel information gathered, the 3D reconstruction of the arterio-venular tree can be performed at this stage. Each vessel is represented as a segment S, where each point P_i of the segment S is represented by its spatial coordinates (x, y, z) and the diameter d. In order to get an smoother representation, an spline interpolation is applied to the set of points of S connecting them in a curve.

With all the curves of the segments, and given that the vessels are tubular structures, the 3D reconstruction is implemented as tubular shapes centered in the segment points P_i of the constructed curves and with diameter d, indicating the caliber at this point of the vessel. This procedure is applied to all the interpolated curves of all the segments obtaining, therefore, the final 3D vessel tree reconstruction. Figure 6 presents a 3D representation of a crossing and a bifurcation.

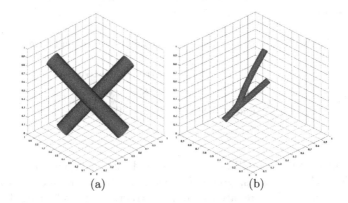

(a)   (b)

Fig. 6. Examples of 3D reconstructions. (a) A crossing. (b) A bifurcation.

3 Results

The proposed methodology was tested with a set of 196 OCT histological images that were taken with a confocal scanning laser ophtalmoscope, a CIRRUS™ HD-OCT–Carl Zeiss Meditec, that also provides the near infrared reflectance retinographies. The scans are centered in the macula, from both left and right eyes of healthy patients, and with a resolution of 1520×496 pixels. Different tests have been designed to validate key steps of the methodology versus manual annotations of an expert.

Crossings and bifurcations. First of all, we analyzed the intersection reconstruction module. A total of 17 crossings and 26 bifurcations were manually annotated by a clinician expert and it was calculated the amount of them correctly identified and included by the intersection module. According to that, a percentage of success rate is shown in Table 1 as the ratio between them.

Table 1. Results obtained at different stages of the methodology.

	Correction of crossings	Correction of bifurcations	Vessel mapping in OCT	Depth calculation
correctly processed	15	22	525	641
Test set size	17	26	607	704
Success rate (%)	88,23	84,61	86,49	91,05

Caliber estimation. In this case, we randomly selected 20 segments and for each segment 10 random points, summing a total of 200 points. Corresponding diameters at the selected points were also manually annotated by the clinician expert to compare with the method. At each point, the corresponding error is calculated as $d_e - d_c$ and the relative error as $\frac{d_e - d_c}{d_e}$, where d_e is the expected diameter and d_c is the diameter obtained by the method. Table 2 exposes the obtained results.

Table 2. Results obtained at the caliber estimation phase.

	Error	Relative error
Global mean	0,1800	0,0425
Global standard deviation	0,3186	0,0752

Vessels mapping in OCT. We also tested the accuracy of the mapping method. For all the images, points P_e belonging to the projection zone I_e in the OCT histological section are randomly extracted. By evaluating if the point P_e is contained in the projection zone I_c calculated by the proposed method a

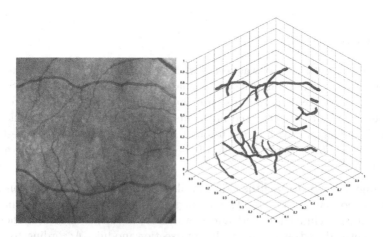

Fig. 7. 3D reconstruction of the vessel tree in a selected region of interest.

success rate can again be obtained. This was evaluated in a set of 607 mapped points. The results are shown in Table 1.

Depth calculation. We manually segmented the vessel region in the histological sections and defined as gold standard a success if the detection provided by the methodology falls in the manual detection. Table 1 shows the success rate in the analyzed images with a set of 704 annotated vessels, demonstrating that this strategy is robust in detecting the vessel location.

We finally include in Fig. 7 the 3D reconstruction of a vessel tree to show the capabilities of the method and the potential of the 3D extraction and reconstruction of the arterio-venular tree with respect to classical 2D identifications in further analysis and diagnostic and other applications.

4 Conclusions

In this paper, we propose a new methodology for 3D retinal vessel tree segmentation using OCT images that permits to obtain and represent the 3D model of a complex structure as is the vasculature of the eye. 3D segmentation approaches, instead of classical 2D ones, offer more information for the analysis of the retinal microcirculation, proven to be key for early assessment of several prevalent conditions such as hypertension, diabetes or cardiovascular risk.

The proposed methodology offers a complete analysis including a 2D retinography vasculature extraction, caliber estimation, mapping with the corresponding OCT histological sections and estimation of the depth coordinate, deriving the set of (x, y, z) coordinates and diameter d of the entire arterio-venous tree. The methodology was tested with 196 OCT histological sections and the corresponding near infrared reflectance retinographies, testing the different steps of the method, and providing promising results.

Future works plan to improve the phases of the method, in order to increase the success rates that were achieved. Moreover, a more complete validation is planned to do to strengthen the conclusions here reached. Finally, the methodology is planned for being expanded with the automatic classification of artery and vein, providing further information for analysis and diagnostic processes.

Acknowledgments. This work is supported by the Instituto de Salud Carlos III of the Spanish Government and FEDER funds of the European Union through thePI14/02161 and theDTS15/00153 research projects.

References

1. Klein, R., Klein, B., Moss, S., et al.: Retinal vascular caliber in persons with type 2 diabetes: the Wisconsin Epidemiological Study of Diabetic Retinopathy: XX. Ophthalmol. J. **113**(9), 1488–1498 (2006)
2. Smith, W., Wang, J.J., Wong, T.Y., et al.: Retinal arteriolar narrowing is associated with 5-year incident severe hypertension: The blue mountains eye study. Hypertens. J. **44**(4), 442–447 (2004)

3. De Jong, F.J., Ikram, M.K., Witteman, J.C., et al.: Retinal vessel diameters and the role of inflammation in cerebrovascular disease. Ann. Neurol. J. **61**(5), 491–495 (2007)
4. Sun, C., Liew, G., Wang, J.J., et al.: Retinal vascular caliber, blood pressure, and cardiovascular risk factors in an Asian population: the Singapore malay eye study. Invest. Ophthalmol. Vis. Sci. J. **49**(5), 1784–1790 (2008)
5. Wong, T.Y.: Quantitative retinal venular caliber and risk of cardiovascular disease in older persons. Arch. Intern. Med. J. **166**(21), 2388–2394 (2006)
6. Ortega, M., Penedo, M.G., Rouco, J., et al.: Personal verification based on extraction and characterisation of retinal feature points. J. Vis. Lang. Comput. **20**(2), 80–90 (2009)
7. Yong, Y., Yuan, Z., Shuying, H., et al.: Effective combined algorithms for retinal blood vessels extraction. Adv. Inf. Sci. Serv. Sci. J. **4**(3), 263–269 (2012)
8. Xiaolin, S., Zhenhua, C., Chuang, M., et al.: Retinal vessel tracking using bilateral filter based on canny method. In: International Conference on Audio, Language and Image Processing, pp. 1678–1682 (2010)
9. Mendonça, A.M., Campilho, A.: Segmentation of retinal blood vessels by combining the detection of centerlines and morphological reconstruction. IEEE Trans. Med. Imag. **25**(9), 1200–1213 (2006)
10. Nayak, C.: Retinal blood vessel segmentation algorithm for diabetic retinopathy using wavelet: a survey. Int. J. Recent Innovation Trends Comput. Commun. **3**(3), 927–930 (2013)
11. Chen, X., Niemeijer, M., Zhang, L., et al.: Three-dimensional segmentation of fluid-associated abnormalities in retinal OCT: probability constrained graph-search-graph-cut. IEEE Trans. Med. Imag. **31**(8), 1521–1531 (2012)
12. Ding, C., Xia, Y., Li, Y.: Supervised Segmentation of Vasculature in Retinal Images Using Neural Networks. In: IEEE International Conference on Orange Technologies, pp. 49–52 (2014)
13. Guimaraes, P., Rodrigues, P., Bernardes, R., Serranho, P.: 3D blood vessels segmentation from optical coherence tomography. Acta Ophthalmologica **90** (2012). doi:10.1111/j.1755-3768.2012.2712.x
14. Pilch, M., Wenner, Y., Strohmayr, E., et al.: Automated segmentation of retinal blood vessels in spectral domain optical coherence tomography scans. Biomed. Opt. Express **3**(7), 1478–1491 (2012)
15. Wu, J., Gerendas, B., Waldstein, S., et al.: Stable registration of pathological 3D-OCT scans using retinal vessels. In: Proceedings of the Ophthalmic Medical Image Analysis First International Workshop, OMIA 2014, Held in Conjunction with MICCAI 2014, pp. 1–8 (2014)
16. Calvo, D., Ortega, M., Penedo, M.G., Rouco, J.: Automatic detection and characterisation of retinal vessel tree bifurcations and crossovers in eye fundus images. Comput. Methods Programs Biomed. **103**, 28–38 (2011)

Segmentation of Retinal Blood Vessels Based on Ultimate Elongation Opening

Wonder A.L. Alves[1,2]($\boxtimes$), Charles F. Gobber[1], Sidnei A. Araújo[1], and Ronaldo F. Hashimoto[2]

[1] Informatics and Knowledge Management Graduate Program,
Universidade Nove de Julho, São Paulo, SP, Brazil
wonder@uninove.br
[2] Department of Computer Science, Institute of Mathematics and Statistics,
University of São Paulo, São Paulo, SP, Brazil

Abstract. This paper proposes a method for segmentation of retinal blood vessels based on ultimate attribute opening (UAO). The proposed approach analyzes the space of numerical residues generated by UAO in order to select the residues extracted from elongated regions by means of an elongation shape descriptor. Thus, the residues extracted are used to define the ultimate elongation opening. Experimental results, using the public datasets DRIVE and STARE show that the proposed approach is fast, simple and comparable to other methods found in the literature.

Keywords: Elongation descriptor · Ultimate opening · Retina image · Blood vessels segmentation

1 Introduction

The segmentation of blood vessels network is an initial and important task in the retinal image analysis process, through which it is possible to identify signs of hypertension, diabetes, arteriosclerosis and cardiovascular diseases [1,2].

In the last decades, many methods were proposed to automatic segmentation of blood vessels network in retinal image [1–7]. These methods were tested in public datasets and evaluated quantitatively by comparison with manual segmentations using ROC (receiver operating characteristic) analysis.

In this paper, we propose an approach for segmentation of retinal blood vessels based on ultimate attribute opening (UAO). In this sense, we analyse the space of numerical residues generated by UAO in order to select the residues extracted of elongated regions using an elongation shape descriptor. Thus, the extracted residues are used to define the ultimate elongation opening (UEO), as shown in Sect. 2. Experimental results using the public datasets DRIVE [1] and STARE [2], described in Sect. 3, show that the proposed approach is fast, simple and comparable to other methods with the same objective found in the literature. Finally, we present our conclusions in Sect. 4.

© Springer International Publishing Switzerland 2016
A. Campilho and F. Karray (Eds.): ICIAR 2016, LNCS 9730, pp. 727–733, 2016.
DOI: 10.1007/978-3-319-41501-7_81

2   Proposed Method

Firstly, we observed that many existing methods use the green channel from the RGB retinal image, since it reveal the best contrast in the blood vessel network [1,2]. Thus, let f a green channel image defined on domain $\mathcal{D} \subset \mathbb{Z}^2$ and co-domain $\mathbb{K} = \{0, 1, ..., 2^{\text{bits}} - 1\}$. However, the image f contains many contrasting regions that do not coincide with regions of blood vessels, then to eliminate these undesirable artifacts of f and, at the same time, preserving the regions of blood vessels, it is applied the residual operator closing top-hat $\varphi_{\mathcal{B}}^{TH}$ by Structural Element (SE) disk $\mathcal{B}$ with correspondent radius to at least half thickness major vessel, that is, 7 pixels considering the dataset images from DRIVE and STARE. In this manner, regions of blood vessels are erased through a closing $\varphi_{\mathcal{B}}(f)$ and then they are restored through of the difference with the reference image f (see more details in [8]), as shown in Fig. 1.

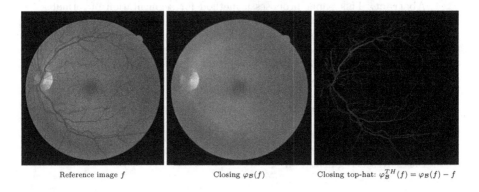

Reference image f · · · · · Closing $\varphi_{\mathcal{B}}(f)$ · · · · · Closing top-hat: $\varphi_{\mathcal{B}}^{TH}(f) = \varphi_{\mathcal{B}}(f) - f$

Fig. 1. Illustration showing an example of preprocessing step.

In the sequence, we apply in the image $\varphi_{\mathcal{B}}^{TH}(f)$ a residual operator based on UAO [9], that is a powerful multi-scale operator based on contrasts extracted from an increasing family of attribute openings $\{\gamma_i^\kappa : i \in \mathcal{I}\}$ indexed by set $\mathcal{I} = \{0, 1, ..., \mathcal{I}_{MAX}\}$. More precisely, the UAO $\mathcal{R}^\theta$ is defined for any image f as follows:

$$\mathcal{R}^\theta(f) = \sup_{i \in \mathcal{I}} \{r_i(f) : r_i(f) = \gamma_i^\kappa(f) - \gamma_{i+1}^\kappa(f)\}. \tag{1}$$

As shown in [10], an increasing family of attribute openings $\{\gamma_i^\kappa : i \in \mathcal{I}\}$ can be obtained through a sequence of pruned trees $(\mathcal{T}_f^0, \mathcal{T}_f^1, ..., \mathcal{T}_f^{\mathcal{I}_{MAX}})$ from structure of the max-tree [11] $\mathcal{T}_f$ constructed by the image f. Then, the i-th residue $r_i(f)$ can be obtained from the nodes $\mathcal{N}r(i) = \mathcal{T}_f^i \backslash \mathcal{T}_f^{i+1}$, i.e.,

$$r_{\mathcal{T}_f^i}(C) = \begin{cases} \texttt{level}(C) - \texttt{level}(\texttt{parent}(C)), & \text{if } \texttt{parent}(C) \notin \mathcal{N}r(i), \\ \texttt{level}(C) - \texttt{level}(\texttt{parent}(C)) \\ \quad + \; r_{\mathcal{T}_f^i}(\texttt{parent}(C)), & \text{otherwise,} \end{cases} \tag{2}$$

where `level` and `parent` are functions that represent the gray level and the parent node of C in $\mathcal{T}_f$. Thus,

$$\forall p \in \mathcal{D}, [r_i(f)](p) = \begin{cases} r_{\mathcal{T}_f^i}(\mathcal{SC}(\mathcal{T}_f^i, p)), & \text{if } \mathcal{SC}(\mathcal{T}_f^i, p) \in \mathcal{N}r(i), \\ 0, & \text{otherwise,} \end{cases} \quad (3)$$

where $\mathcal{SC}(\mathcal{T}_f^i, p)$ the smallest connected component (CC) or node containing $p \in \mathcal{D}$ in the tree $\mathcal{T}_f$. Those facts lead to efficient algorithms for computing UAO and its variations [12,13].

Based on these considerations, we analyse the space of numerical residues r_i generated by UAO in order to select the residues extracted of elongated regions using elongation shape descriptor Ω defined for all node $C \in \mathcal{N}r(i)$, as follows:

$$\Omega(C) = \begin{cases} \text{desirable,} & \text{if } \dfrac{1}{\pi \, \text{SemiMajorAxis}(C)^2/(4 \, \text{Area}(C))} \le \alpha, \\ \text{undesirable,} & \text{otherwise.} \end{cases} \quad (4)$$

where Area(C) is the area of CC C and SemiMajorAxis(C) is the length of semi-major axis of the best fitting ellipse on C computed by central moments. Other ways to obtain the elongation shape descriptor can be found at [5,14]. Thus, the elongation residues is defined for all pixel $p \in \mathcal{D}$, as follows:

$$[r_i^{\Omega}(f)](p) = \begin{cases} r_{\mathcal{T}_f^i}(\mathcal{SC}(\mathcal{T}_f^i, p)), & \text{if } \mathcal{SC}(\mathcal{T}_f^i, p) \in \mathcal{N}r(i) \text{ and } \exists C \in \mathcal{N}r(i) \\ & \text{such that } \Omega(C) \text{is desirable,} \\ 0, & \text{otherwise,} \end{cases} \quad (5)$$

and thus we defined the UEO as follows: $\mathcal{R}^{\Omega}(f) = \sup\{r_i^{\Omega}(f) : i \in \mathcal{I}\}$. The UEO is an example of shape ultimate opening that can be found at [15,16]. Figure 2 shows an example of the application of UEO.

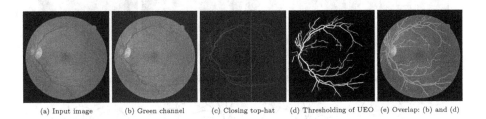

(a) Input image   (b) Green channel   (c) Closing top-hat   (d) Thresholding of UEO   (e) Overlap: (b) and (d)

Fig. 2. Application of ultimate elongation opening.

3   Results and Experiments

To evaluate the performance of the proposed method we used the images from public datasets *Digital Retinal Images for Vessel Extraction* (DRIVE) and *Structured Analysis of the Retina* (STARE). The DRIVE dataset is composed by 40

RGB color images, including seven with some pathology. The images were randomly chosen from a triage program for diabetic retinopathy detection in the Netherlands. They were acquired by a Canon CR5 3CCD camera, with a resolution of 768×584 pixels, with 8 bit depth by channel of color. The 40 images were divided into two sets of 20 images, one for training and other for testing phase. For each image of the training set it is provided a manually segmented image while for test set two images manually segmented are provided for each image [1]. The database STARE is composed by 20 RGB color images, among which ten present some pathology. These images were captured by a TopCon TRV-50 camera with a resolution of 700×605, with 8 bit depth by channel of color. For each image of this dataset two manually segmented images are provided [2]. In both

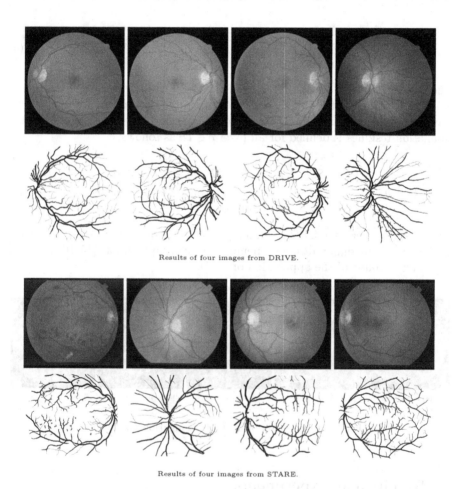

Results of four images from DRIVE.

Results of four images from STARE.

Fig. 3. Results of segmentations of four images extracted from each dataset. Note that, the black pixels indicate true positives, white indicate true negatives, blue indicate false positives and red indicate false negatives. (Color figure online)

databases the manual segmentations were conducted by experts. We employed the following performance measures: sensitivity, specificity and accuracy [2]. The sensitivity ($\frac{TP}{TP+FN}$) evaluates the rate of true positives; the specificity ($\frac{TN}{TN+FP}$) evaluates the rate of true negatives (TN) and the accuracy ($\frac{TP+TN}{TP+TN+FP+FN}$) evaluates the rate of pixels correctly classified. Note that, TP, TN, FP and FN are the amounts of true positives, true negatives, false positives and false negatives, respectively. Figure 3 presents four results of segmentations of blood vessels in retinal images (with or without pathologies) extracted for each dataset (DRIVE and STARE).

From Fig. 3, we can see that the majority of blood vessels were extracted properly, although there is the presence of small noise and extremely fine blood vessels that were lost. It is noteworthy that all the images were segmented using the same parameters. Comparative results of different approaches, including the approach proposed in this paper, are presented in Table 1. Analyzing the results one can see that the proposed approach is comparable to other approaches from the literature, even using only one attribute to describe the blood vessels. It is important to highlight that if we consider a set of attributes extracted from the node in $\mathcal{N}r(i)$, we can build classifiers whose results tend to be much better.

Table 1. Comparison of different approaches for segmentation of blood vessels in the images of DRIVE and STARE datasets.

The results for images of DRIVE dataset			
Method	Sensitivity	Specificity	Accuracy
According to Expert	0, 7761	0, 9725	0, 9473
[3]	0, 7344	0, 9764	0, 9452
[2]	0, 7193	0, 9773	0, 9441
Proposed Approach	0, 6902	0, 9800	0, 9429
[4]	0, 6793	0, 9801	0, 9416
[5]	0, 6924	0, 9779	0, 9413
[6]	–	–	0, 9258
[7]	0, 6478	0, 9625	0, 9222
The results for images of STARE dataset			
Method	Sensitivity	Specificity	Accuracy
According to Expert	0, 8949	0, 9390	0, 9354
[7]	–	–	0, 9513
[5]	0, 7149	0, 9749	0, 9471
Proposed Approach	0, 6835	0, 9739	0, 9460
[3]	0, 6996	0, 9730	0, 9440
[1]	0, 6751	0, 9567	0, 9267

4   Conclusion

In this paper was presented an application of UAO in a problem of segmentation of retinal blood vessels. The proposed approach analyzes the space of numerical residues generated by UAO in order to select the residues extracted of elongated regions through elongation shape descriptor. Thus, the residues extracted of elongation regions are used to define the UEO. From the performed experiments, we conclude that even using a single attribute, the proposed approach is comparable to other approaches from the literature, in terms of results. With respect to time processing, the proposed approach took, in average, 0.95 s to segment an image on a computer with a processor $i7$ with 8 GB of RAM. In the future works, we intend to improve the accuracy of this method by increasing the number of attributes extracted from $\mathcal{N}r(i)$ and using a more robust classifier.

Acknowledgments. The authors would like to thank UNINOVE and FAPESP São Paulo Research Foundation (Process 2016/02547-5) by financial support.

References

1. Hoover, A., Kouznetsova, V., Goldbaum, M.: Locating blood vessels in retinal images by piecewise threshold probing of a matched filter response. IEEE Trans. Med. Imaging **19**, 203–210 (2000)
2. Staal, J., Abramoff, M., Niemeijer, M., Viergever, M., van Ginneken, B.: Ridge based vessel segmentation in color images of the retina. IEEE Trans. Med. Imaging **23**, 501–509 (2004)
3. Mendona, A., Campilho, A.: Segmentation of retinal blood vessels by combining the detection of centerlines and morphological reconstruction. IEEE Trans. Med. Imaging **25**, 1200–1213 (2006)
4. Niemeijer, M., Staal, J., Van Ginneken, B., Loog, M., Abramoff, M.D.: Comparative study of retinal vessel segmentation methods on a new publicly available database (2004)
5. Xu, Y., Géraud, T., Najman, L.: Two applications of shape-based morphology: blood vessels segmentation and a generalization of constrained connectivity. In: Hendriks, C.L.L., Borgefors, G., Strand, R. (eds.) ISMM 2013. LNCS, vol. 7883, pp. 390–401. Springer, Heidelberg (2013)
6. Al-Diri, B., Hunter, A., Steel, D.: An active contour model for segmenting and measuring retinal vessels. IEEE Trans. Med. Imaging **28**, 1488–1497 (2009)
7. Jiang, X., Mojon, D.: Adaptive local thresholding by verification-based multi-threshold probing with application to vessel detection in retinal images. IEEE Trans. Pattern Anal. Mach. Intell. **25**, 131–137 (2003)
8. Soille, P.: Morphological Image Analysis: Principles and Applications. Springer-Verlag New York Inc., Secaucus (2003)
9. Retornaz, T., Marcotegui, B.: Scene text localization based on the ultimate opening. In: Proceedings of the 8th International Symposium on Mathematical Morphology and its Applications to Image and Signal Processing, ISMM 2008, pp. 177–188 (2007)

10. Alves, W.A.L., Morimitsu, A., Hashimoto, R.F.: Scale-space representation based on levelings through hierarchies of level sets. In: Benediktsson, J.A., Chanussot, J., Najman, L., Talbot, H. (eds.) Mathematical Morphology and Its Applications to Signal and Image Processing. LNCS, vol. 9082, pp. 265–276. Springer, Heidelberg (2015)
11. Salembier, P., Oliveras, A., Garrido, L.: Anti-extensive connected operators for image and sequence processing. IEEE Trans. Image Process. **7**, 555–570 (1998)
12. Fabrizio, J., Marcotegui, B.: Fast implementation of the ultimate opening. In: Proceedings of the 9th International Symposium on Mathematical Morphology, pp. 272–281 (2009)
13. Alves, W.A.L., Hashimoto, R.: Ultimate grain filter. In: 2014 IEEE International Conference on Image Processing (ICIP), Paris, France, pp. 2953–2957 (2014)
14. Serna, A., Marcotegui, B., Decencière, E., Baldeweck, T., Pena, A.M., Brizion, S.: Segmentation of elongated objects using attribute profiles and area stability: application to melanocyte segmentation in engineered skin. Pattern Recogn. Lett. **47**, 172–182 (2014). Advances in Mathematical Morphology
15. Hernandez, J., Marcotegui, B.: Shape ultimate attribute opening. Image Vis. Comput. **29**, 533–545 (2011)
16. Alves, W.A.L., Morimitsu, A., Castro, J.S., Hashimoto, R.F.: Extraction of numerical residues in families of levelings. In: Conference on Graphics, Patterns and Images (SIBGRAPI), vol. 26 (2013)

Document Analysis

ISauvola: Improved Sauvola's Algorithm for Document Image Binarization

Zineb Hadjadj[1,2(✉)], Abdelkrim Meziane[2], Yazid Cherfa[1], Mohamed Cheriet[3], and Insaf Setitra[2]

[1] University of Blida, Blida, Algeria
hadjadj_zineb@yahoo.fr, cherfa_yazid@yahoo.fr
[2] Research Center in Scientific and Technical Information (CERIST), Algiers, Algeria
{ameziane, isetitra}@mail.cerist.dz
[3] École de Technologie Supérieure, Montreal, QC, Canada
mohamed.cheriet@etsmtl.ca

Abstract. Binarization of historical documents is difficult and is still an open area of research. In this paper, a new binarization technique for document images is presented. The proposed technique is based on the most commonly used binarization method: Sauvola's, which performs relatively well on classical documents, however, three main defects remain: the window parameter of Sauvola's formula does not fit automatically to the image content, is not robust to low contrasts, and not invariant with respect to contrast inversion. Thus on documents such as magazines, the content may not be retrieved correctly. In this paper we use the image contrast that is defined by the local image minimum and maximum in combination with the computed Sauvola's binarization step to guarantee good quality binarization for both low and correctly contrasted objects inside a single document, without adjusting manually the user-defined parameters to the document content.

1 Introduction

1.1 Overview

One critical step of the analysis is to identify and retrieve foreground and background objects correctly; however it is not easy to binarize and find the best thresholds because of change of illumination or noise presumed issues.

For document images of a good quality, global thresholding [1–3] is capable of extracting the document text efficiently. But for document images suffering from different types of document degradation, adaptive thresholding, which estimates a local threshold for each document image pixel [4–8], is usually capable of producing much better binarization results.

Some binarization methods try to incorporate global or local approaches, like [9–12, 16]. Certain methods also have incorporated background estimation and normalization steps, like [11–13]. The image edges that can usually be detected around the text stroke boundary is also used in certain binarization methods, like [13–15].

© Springer International Publishing Switzerland 2016
A. Campilho and F. Karray (Eds.): ICIAR 2016, LNCS 9730, pp. 737–745, 2016.
DOI: 10.1007/978-3-319-41501-7_82

Because Sauvola's binarization is widely used in practice and gives good results on document images, this paper focuses on that particular method.

1.2   Sauvola's Algorithm and Issues

Sauvola's method [5] takes a grayscale image as input. Since most of document images are color images, converting color to grayscale images is required [17].

From the grayscale image, Sauvola proposed to compute a threshold at each pixel using:

$$T = m \times \left[1 + k \times \left(\frac{s}{R} - 1 \right) \right] \tag{1}$$

where k is a user-defined parameter, m and s are respectively the mean and the local standard deviation computed in a window of size ω centered on the current pixel and R is the dynamic range of standard deviation ($R = 128$ with 8-bit gray level images). The size of the window used to compute m and s remains user-defined in the original paper.

The main advantages of Sauvola's method is that it performs relatively well on noisy and blurred documents [18] and its computational efficiency.

Due to the binarization formula (1), the user must provide two parameters $(\omega; k)$. Some techniques have been proposed to estimate them. [19] state that $\omega = 14$ and $k = 0.34$ is the best compromise for show-through removal and object retrieval quality in classical documents. [20] based the parameter research on Optical Character Recognition (OCR) result quality and found $\omega = 60$ and $k = 0.4$. [5, 18] used $\omega = 15$ and $k = 0.5$. Adjusting those free parameters usually requires an a priori knowledge on the set of documents to get the best results. Therefore there is no consensus in the research community regarding those parameter values.

In [21], a learning framework for the optimization of the binarization methods is introduced, which is designed to determine the optimal parameter values for a document image.

Sauvola's method suffers from different limitations among the following ones [22].

- *Missing low-contrast objects.*
- *Keeping textured text as is.*
- *Handling badly various object sizes.*
- *Spatial object interference.*

In the remainder of this paper, we present a method to overcome one of the four limitations of Sauvola's binarization mentioned previously, which is the *Missing of low-contrast objects.*

The rest of the paper is structured as follows. In Sect. 2 we first expose the general principle of the proposed method. In Sect. 3 we present some results of the proposed method applied to real documents and compare them to other methods' results. We conclude on the achievements of this work in Sect. 4.

2 Proposed Method

An improvement of Sauvola's algorithm is introduced in this section. This results in a three-step process: (1) An initialization map is extracted from the document image to identify high-probability text pixels; (2) Sauvola's algorithm is applied on the input document image; and, finally, (3) To produce the final binarization, we just have to detect in sauvola's binarization image the set of pixels overlapping with each text pixel of the initialization map.

In the next subsection, an initial binarization is estimated using the image contrast.

2.1 Step 1: Initialization Step

At this step, we use an initialization approach that is based on image contrast to identify high-probability text pixels. The used initialization first constructs a contrast image, evaluated by the local maximum and minimum, and then detects the high contrast image pixels which usually lie around the text stroke boundary.

- Contrast Image Construction

In the proposed technique, the used image contrast (Fig. 1(b)) is calculated based on the local image maximum and minimum [15] as follows:

$$D(x, y) = \frac{f_{max}(x, y) - f_{min}(x, y)}{f_{max}(x, y) + f_{min}(x, y) + \epsilon}, \qquad (2)$$

where $f_{max}(x, y)$ and $f_{min}(x, y)$ refer to the maximum and the minimum image intensities within a local neighborhood window. In the implemented system, the local neighborhood window is a 3×3 square window. The term ϵ is a positive and very small number, which is added in case the local maximum is equal to 0.

The image contrast in (2) minimizes the image background and brightness variation properly. In particular, the numerator captures the local image difference that is similar to the traditional image gradient. The denominator (the normalization term) is used to avoid an artifact of uneven background and lowers the effect of the image contrast and brightness variation [15].

- High Contrast Pixels Detection

The purpose of the contrast image construction is to detect the desired high contrast image pixels lying around the text stroke boundary. As described in the last subsection, the constructed contrast image has a clear bimodal pattern where the image contrast around the text stroke boundary varies within a small range but is obviously much larger compared with the image contrast within the document background. We therefore detect the desired high contrast image pixels by using Otsu's global thresholding method (Fig. 1(c)).

Fig. 1. High contrast pixel detection: (a) input image, (b) image contrast, (c) high contrast image pixels and (d) is (c) after morphological opening operation

To remove the small objects, we use the morphological open binary image operator[1] (Fig. 1(d)). As can be seen in Fig. 1(d) some faint characters or low contrasted text pixels was suppressed but this issue will be solved at the third step.

2.2   Step 2: Sauvola's Binarization Step

At this step, Sauvola's thresholding described in Sect. 1.2 is performed on the input document image.

In our experiments, we found that the value of R in Eq. (1) has a very small effect on the binarization quality while the values of k and window size affect it significantly. Low contrasted objects may be considered as textured background or show-through artifacts due to the threshold formula and may be removed or partially retrieved. A low value of k parameter can help retrieving low-contrasted objects but since it is set for the whole document, it also alters other parts of the result: correctly contrasted objects are thicker in that case, possibly causing unintended connections between components. This is due to the fact that background noise and artifacts are usually poorly contrasted and are retrieved as objects.

The size of the window is an important parameter to get good results, too low a value may lead to broken characters and/or characters with holes whereas too large a value may lead to bold characters. Its size must depend on the contents of the document.

An optimal combination of k and ω will produce a good binary image. In our experiments we choose a low value for k parameter to detect all the text pixels (low and correctly contrasted) and a low value for ω parameter to reduce the overlapping between characters.

2.3   Step 3: Sequential Combination

At this step, we use a sequential combination between the contrast image and Sauvola's binarization image to obtain the final binary result.

---

[1] Numerically, this is done by using the function **bwareaopen** of Matlab.

The sequential combination consist in detecting in Sauvola binarization image the set of pixels overlapping with each text pixel of the high contrast image as described in Algorithm 1.

Algorithm 1. Step 3: Sequential combination between the high contrast image and Sauvola's binarization image.

Require: The high contrast image I_C (constructed at step 1) and Sauvola binarization image I_S (constructed at step 2)

Ensure: The final binary result I_B

1: **for** all pixel p in I_C: **do**

2: **if** $I_C(p)$=true **then** //p is part of an object in I_C

3: Detect the set of pixels overlapping with p in I_S.

4: **end if**

5: **end for**

6: Store the new binary result to I_B.

The proposed method described was implemented in Matlab; the results are presented and discussed in the following section.

3   Experiments and Discussion

The described method has been tested on the document images used in the Document Image Binarization Contests (DIBCO) that suffer from different types of document degradation. We also compare our method with other well-known binarization methods including Sauvola's thresholding method [5].

Multiple tests performed on document images have demonstrated that the following parameters: $\omega = 15 \times 15$, $R = 128$ as recommended in [5] and $k = 0.01$ give the best binarization results. A low value of k parameter can help retrieving low-contrasted objects, since it is set for the whole document, it also alters other parts of the result: lot of background noise and artifacts are retrieved as objects but our proposed sequential combination (the third step) can suppress the noise efficiently because it suppresses the contrast of the document background through the normalization as described in Sect. 2.1

The binarization results in Figures below show the superior performance of the proposed thresholding technique.

Figure 2(a) illustrates a faint characters degraded document image. Our binarization technique first constructs a contrast image by the local image maximum and minimum and then extracts the high contrast image (Fig. 2(b)) which is used to suppress the background noise and artifacts. Then Sauvola's algorithm is applied on the input image (Fig. 2(c)) to detect all the text pixels (low and correctly contrasted). After that, we combine sequentially between the two results by detecting in Sauvola binarization image the set of pixels overlapping with each text pixel of the high contrast image to produce the final binarization. As can be seen in Fig. 2(f) (the final result) the faint characters are reasonably well detected by using our method. On the other hand,

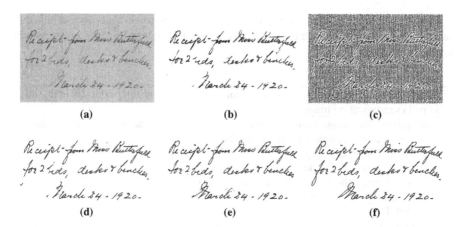

Fig. 2. Image HW2 from the DIBCO'11 test dataset: (a) input image, (b) high contrast image, (c) binarization result obtained using Sauvola's method, (d) Su's method (ranked 2nd in DIBCO'11), (e) Howe's method (ranked 3rd in DIBCO'11) and (f) the result of the proposed method

Fig. 3. Image H12 from the HDIBCO'12 test dataset: (a) input image, (b) binarization results obtained using Sauvola's method, (c) Lelore's method (ranked 2nd in H-DIBCO'12) and (d) the proposed method

Sauvola's method produces a lot of noise due to the variation within the document background, Su's method and Howe's method cannot detect some weak characters .

Figure 4(a) illustrates a bleed-through degraded document image, as can be seen in Fig. 4(c) the bleed-through is reasonably well removed by using our method. The proposed method can suppress more noise than Sauvola's method because it suppresses the contrast of the document background through the normalization in the initialization step. As a comparison, Sauvola's method simply classifies dark background pixels as the text pixels improperly.

Figures 3(a) and 5(a) illustrate a faint characters degraded document image. Figure 5 shows that the proposed technique is tolerant to the variations in document contrast and able to binarize faint characters and badly illuminated image with little background noise where some other methods may either introduce a certain amount of noise or fail to detect the document text with a low image contrast shown in Fig. 3(c).

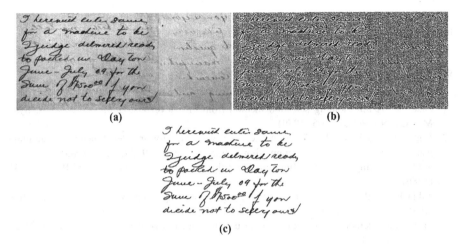

Fig. 4. Image HW4 from the DIBCO'13 test dataset: (a) input image, (b) binarization results obtained using Sauvola's method and (c) the proposed method

Fig. 5. Image H04 from the HDIBCO'10 test dataset: (a) input image, (b) Sauvola's method and (c) the proposed method

Figures 2, 3, 4 and 5 further show four document binarization examples. As shown, our proposed method extracts the text properly from document images that suffer from different types of degradation. On the other hand, Sauvola's method often produces a certain amount of noise due to the variation within the background.

4 Conclusion and Future Prospects

This paper presents an efficient historical document image binarization technique that is efficient against different types of document degradation such as faint characters and uneven illumination. The proposed technique makes use of Sauvola's algorithm and the image contrast that is evaluated based on the local minimum and maximum. Such a combined method leads, as shown in the experiments, to high accuracy when applied to historical document images, with a variety of degradations. The proposed method succeeds indeed to capture low and correctly contrasted objects inside a single document. However, the performance of our binarization method is limited in case of both small and large objects in a same document; Sauvola's method fails to retrieve all objects correctly because its window parameter is defined for an image as a whole. In future work we will focus on handling various object sizes.

References

1. Otsu, N.: A thresholding selection method from gray-level histogram. IEEE Trans. Syst. Man Cybern. **9**(1), 62–66 (1979)
2. Kapur, J.N., Sahoo, P.K., Wong, A.K.C.: A new method for gray-level picture thresholding using the entropy of the histogram. Graph. Image Process. **29**, 273–285 (1985)
3. Kittler, J., Illingworth, J.: Minimum error thresholding. Pattern Recognit. **19**(1), 41–47 (1986)
4. Niblack, W.: An Introduction to Digital Image Processing. Prentice Hall, Englewood Cliffs (1986)
5. Sauvola, J., Pietikainen, M.: Adaptive document image binarization. Pattern Recognit. **33**(2), 225–236 (2000)
6. Bernsen, J.: Dynamic thresholding of grey-level images. In: Proceedings of the Eighth International Conference on Pattern Recognition, Paris, France, pp. 1251–1255, October 1986
7. Wolf, C., Jolion, J.M.: Extraction and recognition of artificial text in multimedia documents. Pattern Anal. Appl. **6**(4), 309–326 (2003)
8. Feng, M.L., Tan, Y.P.: Contrast adaptive binarization of low quality document images. IEICE Electron. Express **1**(16), 501–506 (2004)
9. Kim, I.K., Jung, D.W., Park, R.H.: Document image binarization based on topographic analysis using a water flow model. Pattern Recogn. **35**(1), 265–277 (2002)
10. Gatos, B., Pratikakis, I., Perantonis, S.J.: Adaptive degraded document image binarization. Pattern Recogn. **39**(3), 317–327 (2006)
11. Lu, S., Su, B., Tan, C.L.: Document image binarization using background estimation and stroke edges. Int. J. Doc. Anal. Recogn. **13**(4), 303–314 (2010)
12. Ntirogiannis, K., Gatos, B., Pratikakis, I.: A combined approach for the binarization of handwritten document images. Pattern Recogn. Lett. - Spec. Issue Front. Handwrit. Process. **35**, 3–15 (2012). doi:10.1016/j.patrec.2012.09.026
13. Moghaddam, R.F., Cheriet, M.: RSLDI: restoration of singlesided low-quality document images. Pattern Recogn. **42**(12), 3355–3364 (2009)
14. Howe, N.: Document binarization with automatic parameter tuning. Int. J. Doc. Anal. Recogn. **16**, 247–258 (2012)
15. Su, B., Lu, S., Tan, C.L.: Binarization of historical handwritten document images using local maximum and minimum filter. In: International Workshop on Document Analysis Systems, pp. 159–165, June 2010
16. Hadjadj, Z., Meziane, A., Cheriet, M., Cherfa, Y.: An active contour based method for image binarization: application to degraded historical document images. In: ICFHR 2014, Crete, Greece, pp. 655–660 (2014). doi:10.1109/ICFHR.2014.115
17. Moghaddam, R.F., Cheriet, M.: A multi-scale framework for adaptive binarization of degraded document images. Pattern Recogn. **43**(6), 2186–2198 (2010)
18. Sezgin, M., Sankur, B.: Survey over image thresholding techniques and quantitative performance evaluation. J. Electron. Imaging **13**, 146–165 (2004)
19. Badekas, E., Papamarkos, N.: Automatic evaluation of document binarization results. In: Sanfeliu, A., Cortés, M.L. (eds.) CIARP 2005. LNCS, vol. 3773, pp. 1005–1014. Springer, Heidelberg (2005)

20. Rangoni, Y., Shafait, F., Breuel, T.M.: OCR based thresholding. In: Proceedings of IAPR Conference on Machine Vision Applications, pp. 98–101 (2009)
21. Cheriet, M., Moghaddam, R.F., Hedjam, R.: A learning framework for the optimization and automation of document binarization methods. Comput. Vis. Image Underst. (CVIU) **117** (3), 269–280 (2013)
22. Lazzara, G., Géraud, T.: Efficient multiscale Sauvola's binarization. Int. J. Doc. Anal. Recogn. **17**(2), 105–123 (2014)

Recognition of Handwritten Arabic Words with Dropout Applied in MDLSTM

Rania Maalej[1(✉)], Najiba Tagougui[2,3], and Monji Kherallah[4]

[1] Research Group on Intelligent Machines, National School of Engineers of Sfax,
University of Sfax, Sfax, Tunisia
rania.mlj@gmail.com
[2] Higher Institute of Management of Gabes, Gabes, Tunisia
najiba.tagougui@isggb.rnu.tn
[3] Faculty of Computer Science and Information Technology, Al Baha University, Al Bahah,
Kingdom of Saudi Arabia
[4] Faculty of Sciences, University of Sfax, Sfax, Tunisia
monji.kherallah@enis.rnu.tn

Abstract. Offline handwriting recognition is the ability to decode an intelligible handwritten input from paper documents into digitized format readable by machines. This field remains an on-going research problem especially for Arabic Script due to its cursive appearance, the variety of writers and the diversity of styles. In this paper we focus on the Intelligent Words Recognition system based on MDLSTM, on which a dropout technique is applied during training stage. This technique prevents our system against overfitting and improves the recognition rate. To evaluate our system we use IFN/ENIT database.

Keywords: RNN · LSTM · MDLSTM · Dropout · Offline Arabic handwritten recognition

1 Introduction

In offline handwriting recognition, researchers have usually extracted a sequence of features from the input image either manually or automatically then they use a classifier such as a Hidden Markov Model (HMM) or a Neural Network (NN) to classify got features. But the trend is toward combining those two sequential and visual aspects, in order to get a generic system robust to distortion, scale and rotation. The most successful system in this Holistic approach is based on Recurrent Neural Networks (RNN), Long Short Term Memory (LSTM) and Connectionist Temporal Classification (CTC). For example, a powerful system [1] based on Multidimensional Long Short Term Memory (MDLSTM) and CTC is successfully applied to recognize offline Arabic Handwriting script. This system is tested by a large database "IFN/ENIT" [2]. But with the huge number of parameters, overfitting can occur. In order to protect the network against this problem, dropout is applied. This technique consists in temporarily removing some units from the network. Those removed units are randomly selected only during the training

© Springer International Publishing Switzerland 2016
A. Campilho and F. Karray (Eds.): ICIAR 2016, LNCS 9730, pp. 746–752, 2016.
DOI: 10.1007/978-3-319-41501-7_83

stage. With such regularization method, we can improve network performance and the error rate is significantly reduced.

This paper is organised as follows. Section 2 presents relevant previous works. Section 3 describes our contribution and in Sect. 4 we report on experiment results. Finally, conclusions and futures work are presented in Sect. 5.

2   Related Work

The traditional procedure of recognition is based on six steps Image Acquisition, Pre-processing, Segmentation, Features Extraction, Classification and Post Processing. The Features Extraction stage requires considerable time and expertise because they must be redesigned for each alphabet. To overcome this complex step, a system trained on pixel data is proposed. This kind of system, which is subsumed into Holistic approaches, has the same difficulty degree to recognize several languages. And, the main interest of using those raw images in training is the ability to learn both the visual and the sequential aspect of cursive handwriting at the same time.

Lately, most of the works done are based on HMM [3] or on hybridization of HMM with neural networks [4]. Although HMM's success, it has several drawbacks among which we can mention the poor discrimination and the lack of power to manage the long-term dependencies in sequences because they follow a first-order equation.

The suitable solution adapted by some researchers was the use of Recurrent Neural Networks RNN [5]. In fact, RNNs prove its efficiency for modeling times series. They can be trained discriminatively and they do not require a prior knowledge of data.

On the other hand, RNN suffer from the vanishing gradient and the burden of exploding. Those problems can be solved with a particular node called the Long Short-Term Memory, this node holds better results either in speech recognition [6] or in online handwriting recognition [7]. For the latter field, Bidirectional LSTM was proposed because it provides the possibility to integrate context in both sides of each given letter in the input sequence. This architecture is not the right choice for offline handwriting recognition because the input data is no longer one-dimensional, so we opt for applying the MDLSTM.

The concept of Multidimensional Long Short Term Memory (MDLSTM) [8, 9] is to combine a Multi-Dimensional Recurrent Neural Network (MDRNN) with the LSTM nodes. MDRNN is a recurrent network on which a single recurrent connection is replaced by many connections to represent all spatio-temporal dimensions of input data.

Due to the large number of hidden layers and the huge number of parameters, over-fitting can occur on MDLSTM network. This drawback can be corrected by using dropout [9]. This technique was successfully applied with several types of deep neural networks [10–12] and it shows a significant improvement for a recognition rate (see Table 1). It was also successfully used in RNN, specifically in BLSTM and it has shown its effectiveness by reducing label error by more than 8 % on ADAB Dataset for online Arabic handwriting recognition [13].

Table 1. Error recognition rate reduced with dropout

Authors	Network	Dataset	Error rate reduction w/dropout
Srivastava et al. [10]	CNN	CIFAR-10	37 %
Miao and Metze [11]	DNN	TIMIT	11,6 %
Zhang et al. [12]	DNN	LVCSR	12,3 %
Maalej et al. [13]	BLSTM	ADAB	8,12 %

3   System Overview

In this section, we present the architecture of our offline Arabic handwriting recognition system based on MDLSTM and CTC and on which the dropout technique is applied during training stage.

MDLSTM is a robust method that allows a flexible modeling of this multidimensional context by providing recurrent connections for every spatio-temporal dimensions existing in the input data. These connections make MDLSTM strong against local distortion in image input (e.g. rotation, shears ...). The issue of this approach is how to get one-dimensional label sequences from the two-dimensional images. The proposed solution is to push data through a hierarchy of MDLSTM layers as well as sub-samples windows added after each level to incrementally collapse the two-dimensional images into one-dimensional sequences to be finally labelled by the output layers.

Output layers are based especially on the CTC method [14]. This technique involves a Softmax layer to compute the probability distribution for each step throughout the input sequence.

This distribution covers the 120 Target labels incremented by one extra blank symbol to represent a non-output. So, in total, the size of this Softmax layer achieves 121.

At every timestep the network chooses to emit a label or not. All these decisions define a distribution over alignments between the input and target sequences. Afterwards, and due to forward-backward algorithm, CTC sum over all possible alignments and finally it normalizes the probability of the target sequence given the input sequence [1]. Thus CTC is the best choice for unsegmented cursive handwriting recognition.

The architecture of our proposed network contains 28 layers, three of which are hidden and fully connected. As we can see in Fig. 1, these hidden layers are composed by respectively 2, 10 and 50 LSTM units [15]. This node has the advantage of temporarily saving information.

Concerning the Dropout technique, it is applied only in feed-forward connections after some MDLSTM layers, more precisely, before sub-sample layers which not fully-connected. The selection of those layers is carefully done to not affect the recurrent connections in order to keep the RNN's ability to model long input sequences (see Fig. 1). Dropout layers return the same input except dropped nodes that return null. In our system, 50 % of nodes are randomly dropped.

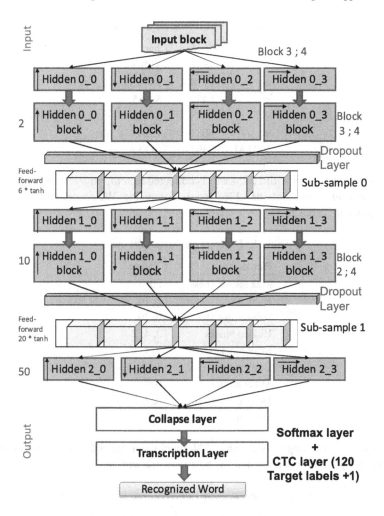

Fig. 1. Architecture of proposed recognition system.

4   Experiments Results

To validate our system, we use IFN/ENIT [2] Database, with 32492 images of Arabic words written by more than 1000 writers. Those words are 937 Tunisian town/village names. IFN/ENIT Database is divided in 5 sets (see Table 2) and it was successfully used by more than 50 research groups [16–18] as well in Offline Arabic handwriting recognition competition in ICDAR 2009 [19].

Table 2. The IFN/ENIT database

Sets	Words	Characters
a	6537	51984
b	6710	53862
c	6477	52155
d	6735	54166
e	6033	45169
TOTAL	32492	257336

We train our system with 19724 words collected in *seta*, *set b* and *setc*, however we use *set d* and *set e*, that contains 12768 words, for testing. We fix network's parameters as mentioned in Table 3.

Table 3. Different parameters for training

Parameters	Values
Max tests no best	20
Hidden size	2, 10, 50
Sub-sample size	6, 20
Hidden blocks	3, 4; 2, 4
Input blocks	3, 4
Learn rate	1e-4
Momentum	0.9
Dropout layer Size	6, 20
Dropout percentage	50 %

Our network training finished after 224 epochs in total and it takes more than 96 h (see Fig. 2). In 218th epoch we find the best network with least label error.

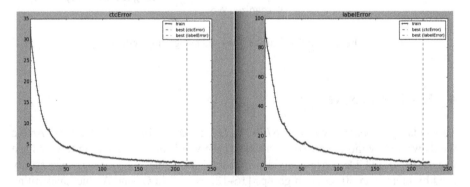

Fig. 2. Label Error and CTC Error during 224 epochs for training

Label error is a Levenshtein distance [20], this string metric measures the difference between two words. It is equal to the minimum number of characters that must be deleted, inserted or substituted to change one sequence into the other.

After training, we test our best obtained network with *set d* and *set e*. We get an impressive label error rate which does not exceed 12,09 % compared to 16,97 % obtained with the same architecture without dropout, and 16,30 % obtained with CDBN approach (See Table 4).

Table 4. Label error recognition rate comparison using the IFN/ENIT database with no features extraction

Authors	Approach	(LER)
Present work	MDLSTM w/CTC w/dropout	12,09 %
Graves [22]	MDLSTM w/CTC	16,97 %
Elleuch et al. [21]	CDBN	16,30 %

5 Conclusion

In this manuscript, we propose a new offline Arabic handwriting recognition system based on MDLSTM with CTC and on which dropout technique is applied in some hidden layers. This architecture makes our system able to recognize an unsegmented input data in the form of raw pixel. We notice that this MDLSTM's regularization, using dropout, significantly improves the offline Arabic handwriting recognition. Our contribution is to add two dropout layers, on which 50 % of nodes are dropped. This choice has successfully decreased label error rate by more than 4,88 %.

Acknowledgment. We would like to express our great appreciation to Mr. Alex Graves for making RNNLIB library as an open source available on internet [22].

References

1. Graves, A.: Offline Arabic handwriting recognition with multidimensional recurrent neural networks. In: Märgner, V., El Abed, H. (eds.) Guide to OCR for Arabic Scripts, pp. 297–313. Springer, London (2012)
2. Pechwitz, M., Maddouri, S.S., Märgner, V., Ellouze, N., Amiri, H.: IFN/ENIT-database of handwritten Arabic words. In: Proceedings of CIFED, vol. 2, pp. 127–136, October 2002
3. Pechwitz, M., Maergner, V.: HMM based approach for handwritten Arabic word recognition using the IFN/ENIT-database, p. 890. IEEE, August 2003
4. Dreuw, P., Doetsch, P., Plahl, C., Ney, H.: Hierarchical hybrid MLP/HMM or rather MLP features for a discriminatively trained gaussian HMM: a comparison for offline handwriting recognition. In: 2011 18th IEEE International Conference on Image Processing (ICIP), pp. 3541–3544. IEEE, September 2011
5. Graves, A., Liwicki, M., Bunke, H., Schmidhuber, J., Fernández, S.: Unconstrained on-line handwriting recognition with recurrent neural networks. In: Advances in Neural Information Processing Systems, pp. 577–584 (2008)

6. Graves, A., Mohamed, A.R., Hinton, G.: Speech recognition with deep recurrent neural networks. In: 2013 IEEE International Conference on Acoustics, Speech and Signal Processing (ICASSP), pp. 6645–6649. IEEE, May 2013

7. Kozielski, M., Doetsch, P., Ney, H.: Improvements in RWTH's system for off-line handwriting recognition. In: 2013 12th International Conference on Document Analysis and Recognition (ICDAR), pp. 935–939. IEEE, August 2013

8. Graves, A.: Supervised Sequence Labelling, pp. 5–13. Springer, Berlin (2012)

9. Hinton, G.E., Srivastava, N., Krizhevsky, A., Sutskever, I., Salakhutdinov, R.R.: Improving neural networks by preventing co-adaptation of feature detectors (2012). arXiv preprint arXiv: 1207.0580

10. Srivastava, N., Hinton, G., Krizhevsky, A., Sutskever, I., Salakhutdinov, R.: Dropout: a simple way to prevent neural networks from overfitting. J. Mach. Learn. Res. **15**(1), 1929–1958 (2014)

11. Miao, Y., Metze, F.: Improving low-resource CD-DNN-HMM using dropout and multilingual DNN training (2013)

12. Zhang, S., Bao, Y., Zhou, P., Jiang, H., Dai, L.: Improving deep neural networks for LVCSR using dropout and shrinking structure. In: 2014 IEEE International Conference on Acoustics, Speech and Signal Processing (ICASSP), pp. 6849–6853. IEEE, May 2014

13. Maalej, R.,Tagougui, N., Kherallah, M.: Online Arabic handwriting recognition with dropout applied in deep recurrent neural networks. In: 2016 12th IAPR International Workshop on Document Analysis Systems (DAS), pp. 418–421. IEEE, April 2016

14. Graves, A., Fernández, S., Gomez, F., Schmidhuber, J.: Connectionist temporal classification: labelling unsegmented sequence data with recurrent neural networks. In: Proceedings of the 23rd International Conference on Machine Learning, pp. 369–376. ACM, June 2006

15. Hochreiter, S., Schmidhuber, J.: Long short-term memory. Neural Comput. **9**(8), 1735–1780 (1997)

16. Kessentini, Y., Paquet, T., Hamadou, A.B.: Off-line handwritten word recognition using multi-stream hidden Markov models. Pattern Recogn. Lett. **31**(1), 60–70 (2010)

17. AlKhateeb, J.H., Ren, J., Jiang, J., Al-Muhtaseb, H.: Offline handwritten Arabic cursive text recognition using hidden markov models and re-ranking. Pattern Recogn. Lett. **32**(8), 1081–1088 (2011)

18. Pechwitz, M., El Abed, H., Märgner, V.: Handwritten Arabic word recognition using the IFN/ENIT-database. In: Märgner, V., El Abed, H. (eds.) Guide to OCR for Arabic Scripts, pp. 169–213. Springer, London (2012)

19. El Abed, H., Märgner, V.: ICDAR 2009-Arabic handwriting recognition competition. Int. J. Doc. Anal. Recogn. (IJDAR) **14**(1), 3–13 (2011)

20. Levenshtein, V.I.: Binary codes capable of correcting deletions, insertions, and reversals. In: Soviet physics Doklady, vol. 10, no. 8, pp. 707–710, February 1966

21. Elleuch, M., Tagougui, N., Kherallah, M.: Deep learning for feature extraction of Arabic handwritten script. In: Azzopardi, G., Petkov, N. (eds.) CAIP 2015. LNCS, vol. 9257, pp. 371–382. Springer, Heidelberg (2015). doi:10.1007/978-3-319-23117-4_32

22. Graves, A.: Rnnlib: a recurrent neural network library for sequence learning problems (2008). http://sourceforge.net/projects/rnnl/

Direct Unsupervised Text Line Extraction from Colored Historical Manuscript Images Using DCT

Asim Baig[1]([⊠]), Somaya Al-Maadeed[1], Ahmed Bouridane[2],
and Mohamed Cheriet[3]

[1] Qatar University, Doha, Qatar
{asim.baig,s_alali}@qu.edu.qa
[2] Northumbria University, Newcastle upon Tyne, UK
ahmed.bouridane@northumbria.ac.uk
[3] École de technologie supérieure, Montreal, Canada
mohamed.cheriet@etsmtl.ca

Abstract. Extracting lines of text from a manuscript is an important preprocessing step in many digital paleography applications. These extracted lines play a fundamental part in the identification of the author and/or age of the manuscript. In this paper we present an unsupervised approach to text line extraction in historical manuscripts that can be applied directly to a color manuscript image. Each of the red, green and blue channels are processed separately by applying DCT on them individually. One of the key advantages of this approach is that it can be applied directly to the manuscript image without any preprocessing, training or tuning steps. Extensive testing on complex Arabic handwritten manuscripts shows the effectiveness of the proposed approach.

Keywords: Text line extraction · Segmentation · DCT · Historical manuscripts · Color image processing

1 Introduction

A large number of ancient and historical manuscripts are being scanned and digitized in order to be preserved for future generation. Researchers in the field of paleography are greatly interested in being able to analyzing these ancient documents. Automatic detection of text lines in these documents can be of great benefit to them. Automatic text line detection is considered to be a key preprocessing step in many digital paleographic applications such as Content Based Image Retrieval (CBIR) [1], manuscript author identification [2] and manuscripts age detection [3] to name a few. Reliable and quick extraction of text lines can improve the accuracy of these applications.

Text line extraction is a difficult problem to solve; it becomes even more difficult due to the complexity inherent in historical manuscripts. Handwritten, ancient and historical manuscripts are generally faded with dirt marks, smudges, wrinkling, tears and other such types of noise. In addition, the irregular structure of these documents poses additional challenge to the extraction of text lines [4, 5]. To make matters worse

© Springer International Publishing Switzerland 2016
A. Campilho and F. Karray (Eds.): ICIAR 2016, LNCS 9730, pp. 753–762, 2016.
DOI: 10.1007/978-3-319-41501-7_84

these manuscripts contain text on page margins which is written in arcs, square blocks and other more complex designs. Figure 1 shows some examples of more complex historical documents.

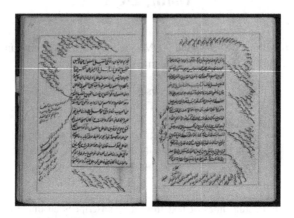

Fig. 1. Examples of complex historical manuscripts

It is no surprise therefore that a lot of effort has gone into the search for an effective and reliable text line extraction algorithm. Sulem et al. in [6] provides one of the most detailed survey of techniques for text line segmentation in historical images of its time. Most approaches in literature tend to have a pre-processing step of some sort to make text line extraction easy. In [7], dynamic programming is used to compute the path of minimum cost between two consecutive lines in a binary image. This approach has played a fundamental part in applications such as automatic transcription and ground truth creation [8, 9]. Text line extraction schemes can also be categorized based on the type of approaches used. Bulacu et al. in [10] utilized the horizontal projection profile of black pixel changes on order to obtain the line separation. Similar approach is used by Marti and Bunke in [11] where they post process the horizontal projections based on connected components in the document image. It is interesting to note that quite a few approaches also use Hough transform in order to attempt to detect straight lines in historical manuscripts images [12, 13]. Another approach used in quite a few algorithms [14] is the smearing method, which generates black line blocks by filling in white spaces between black pixels. In recent years seam carving approaches have attracted a lot of attention. It does make sense to use these approaches since the main focus of text line extraction is to find the seam between the two lines of text. In [15] the authors evaluate an energy map in such a way that the gaps between lines generate low energy values. They tend solve the problem of detecting the path of minimum energy. Similarly, Asi et al. work directly on grayscale images by constructing a distance transform and using it to detect medial seams of the text lines and seams separating two text lines [16]. Another set of successful text line extraction approaches [17] utilize steerable filters in order solve the issue to close cluster writing, fluctuating and cross cutting lines. Shin Hyunkyung in [18] also uses DCT for color images in order to segment text lines quickly. In this paper we also present a novel approach to text line extraction in historical manuscript images using Discrete Cosine Transform (DCT), just like the approach presented by Shin in [18] but the similarities between his and our approach ends there. He uses DC three primary AC coefficients from a DC block to generate a grayscale image and then uses a direct Markov Model to estimate the periodicity of the text thereby extracting text lines. Whereas, in the proposed approach DCT is applied to each channel separately and each channel is filtered according to a threshold set on the values of DCT coefficients. This allows the approach to be more flexible, fast and robust.

The rest of the paper is structured as follows. Section 2 outlines the proposed approach with Sect. 3 discussing the database used, experimental setup and results obtained. Section 4 provides the conclusion with references provided at the end.

2 The Proposed Approach

Discrete Cosine Transform (DCT) is basically a technique to convert any signal into elementary frequency components i.e. a sum of cosine functions oscillating at different frequencies. The most common form of DCT used for image processing is the blocked DCT where the DCT is applied separately to 8 × 8 blocks of the image. The proposed approach uses blocked DCT on overlapping 8 × 8 blocks of the image. It is interesting to look at the 8 × 8 block processed via DCT and understand its structure as it helps to appreciate the proposed approach better.

It is common knowledge that the result of blocked DCT is an 8 × 8 array of transform coefficients. Top most element of this 8 × 8 array i.e. (0,0) element is called the DC or zero frequency component. The values with increasing horizontal and vertical indices represent higher vertical and horizontal frequencies. Further information about DCT and its workings can be found in [19–22]. The DC component is basically the average value of all the pixels in the block being processed. Figure 2 shows how the coefficients are represented in the 8 × 8 block and how each frequency range is distributed within the block. This structure of DCT coefficients is particularly useful in image and video compression but it also provide some interesting insights when evaluated in reference to images of written text.

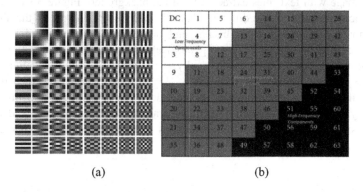

(a)   (b)

Fig. 2. (a) The representation of frequency coefficients in 8 × 8 Block of DCT, (b) The frequency range distribution in the 8 × 8 block of DCT

Ideally any written text whether it is a handwritten manuscript, a printed newspaper or a typeset document is the presence of dark text on a consistent light background. Even though the text in the very old handwritten manuscripts tends to fade over time and the background does not remain as consistent or light but the contrast is still there and the background is still comparatively lighter than the text in the foreground. This means that if DCT is applied to a block of image consisting of only background pixels, the DC component will be very high. As mentioned above the DC component is purely the average of all the pixel values in the block. Similarly, if the DCT is applied to a block of pixels containing written text as well, the DC component will have a lower value. However, the issue may arise due to the presence of degradation or noise (such as smudges, spills or fingerprints) similar to the written word in the image.

In addition, a block consisting of pixels only belonging to the background will have higher values for the low and medium frequency ranges and smaller values or even zeros for high frequency components. This is due to the fact that background tends generally to be smooth and of consistent color thus generating low and medium frequencies. Similarly, a block consisting of pixels from the text part of the document will have higher values for high frequency components and lower values for low and medium frequency components. It therefore makes sense to threshold the DCT response of the manuscript image in order to extract text lines from the background and noise.

This above mentioned approach is utilized in the proposed algorithm. In order to make sure that the algorithm works seamlessly with a multitude of manuscripts and under a variety of conditions a reliable adaptive threshold needs to be established. This threshold is established by calculating the average of the values in each 8×8 DCT block. The averaging process normalizes the values so that a single threshold is able to work for a diverse selection of manuscripts. The threshold is set at a low value such that any score below the threshold is set to 1 (one) and scores above the threshold are set to 0 (zero). This type of threshold process generates a binary image with ones around the written content and zeros elsewhere. This binary image is used to extract the text lines from the background.

As mentioned earlier, this threshold is applied to each channel separately i.e. R, G and B channels are extracted from the colored image and DCT based threshold applied to each channel. The three processed channels are then concatenated to generate a colored image with text lines extracted from the background. Figure 3 shows the text line extraction results for the different channels and the final output of the algorithm.

It should be noted that the background border around each word in the final output is created by applying the morphological operation of dilation with a 10 pixel disk size, which was evaluated empirically. This border is useful to delimit the text lines thus making them easier to process. This disk size can be tuned to reduce or increase the border. Increasing the dilation disk size will merge the line borders effectively tuning the algorithm to extract paragraphs instead of lines and reducing the disk size can allow for extraction of lines written very close together and even assist in word extraction.

Fig. 3. (a) Original Image, (b) Final output of the proposed algorithm, (c) Processed Red Channel, (d) Processed Green Channel, (e) Processed Blue Channel (Color figure online)

3 Results and Discussion

The biggest issue in attempting to evaluate the performance of these types of algorithms is the lack of any standardized matrix. One approach is to execute the proposed approach over a large database of diverse set of images and evaluate the performance subjectively. This subjective analysis can later be enhanced by evaluating the approach

Table 1. Subjective results for proposed algorithm

Sr. no.	Committee member	Total pages evaluated	Good	OK	Bad
1.	Domain expert	7169	6308 *(87.99 %)*	683 *(9.54 %)*	178 *(2.4 %)*
2.	Image processing expert		6030 *(84.11 %)*	912 *(12.72 %)*	227 *(3.166 %)*
3.	Grad student		6457 *(90.06 %)*	597 *(8.32 %)*	115 *(1.604 %)*

Table 2. Some interesting and informative results

Sr. No.	Input Image	Output Image	Discussion
1.			The proposed approach is able to not only extact text lines from the main body of the page but also the comments written in diagonal and curved writing around the borders
2.			The proposed algoithm is not effected by direction of the written text.

against a standard benchmark dataset. In this paper we perform only subjective evaluation of the performance with benchmark testing planned for future.

The proposed algorithm is tested over 7000 images of pages from historical Arabic handwritten manuscripts ranging from 1st Century to 14th Century. These manuscripts were collected by Qatar University in collaboration with Islamic History Museum Qatar and Qatar National Library under the project funded by Qatar National Foundation. In addition, the proposed algorithm is also evaluated over some complex document images acquired from the internet in order to showcase its diversity. Subjective analysis of the results was performed by a committee consisting of three members (domain expert, image processing expert and grad student). They marked

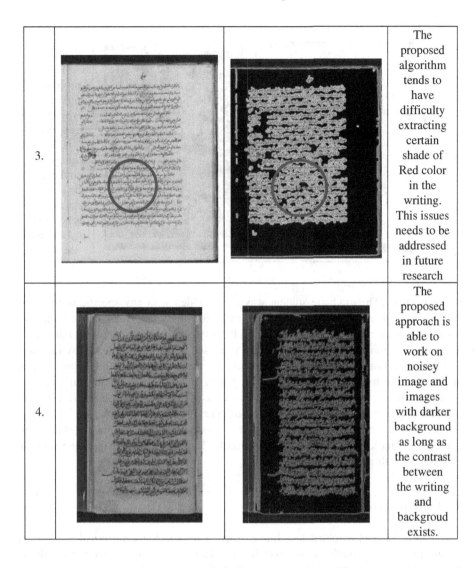

| 3. | | | The proposed algorithm tends to have difficulty extracting certain shade of Red color in the writing. This issues needs to be addressed in future research |
| 4. | | | The proposed approach is able to work on noisey image and images with darker background as long as the contrast between the writing and backgroud exists. |

each image as good, OK or bad depending upon whether they thought the text lines were extracted properly or not. Table 1 provides the subjective results.

This committee to analyse the results was designed with a specific ideas in mind. The domain expert was selected to represent the end users of the proposed system while the image processing expert was selected to represent the developers and the graduate student represents the layman. The domain expert was evaluating text line extraction from the perspective of being able to use it in further analysis. The main focus for him was on clear separation between the lines and complete line extraction without any words missing or incomplete. On the other hand the Image Processing Expert evaluated the results from the development prospective. His main focus was on existence of noise in the image and availability of clear demarkation (black area

5.	 	A limitation of the proposed approach is when the degardation in the image is similar to the written text as well as being in and around the text.

between lines). The graduate student was not provided with any specific instructions and was tasks to evaluate the outputs on how he felt about each image. The subjective results are interesting in that they do vary a bit between different evaluators but overall they are quite consistent and show that the proposed approach is able to provide good text line extraction from the development and use perspective. A voting approach may also provide an interesting insight into the quality of text line extraction. In future we plan to evaluate the proposed approach against a standard benchmark dataset and compared it against the state of the art algorithms.

A few of the more interesting results are discussed in Table 2 to highlight the pros, cons and limitations of the proposed approach. The limitations of the algorithm are highlighted with a red circle in the results.

4 Conclusions

This paper presents a robust text line extraction approach for historical manuscript images that works directly on the color images. The approach is based on thresholding blocked DCT coefficients separately on Red, Green and Blue color channels. The presented approach performs effectively irrespective of the direction and type of written text. Extensive testing of the algorithm was performed on a large dataset and results evaluated subjectively to show the effectiveness of this approach. Future research should focus on resolving this issue of different text color word segmentation and effect of different size dilation disks on algorithm performance. In addition, a voting approach should also be tried for subjective testing and the proposed algorithm should be compared against the state of the art algorithms on a standard benchmark dataset.

Acknowledgement. This publication was made possible by NPRP grant # NPRP NPRP7-442-1-082 from the Qatar National Research Fund (a member of Qatar Foundation). The statements made herein are solely the responsibility of the authors.

References

1. Shahab, S.A., Al-Khatib, W.G., Mahmoud, S.A.: Computer Aided Indexing of Historical Manuscripts. In: International Conference on Computer Graphics, Imaging and Visualisation, Sydney, 2006, pp. 287–295. doi:10.1109/CGIV.2006.31

2. Fiel, S., Hollaus, F., Gau, M., Sablatnig, R.: Writer identification on historical Glagolitic documents. In: SPIE Proceedings on Document Recognition and Retrieval XXI, p. 902102 (2013). doi:10.1117/12.2042338

3. He, S., Sammara, P., Burgers, J., Schomaker, L.: Towards style-based dating of historical documents. In: 14th International Conference on Frontiers in Handwriting Recognition (ICFHR), Heraklion, pp. 265–270 (2014). doi:10.1109/ICFHR.2014.52

4. Antonacopoulos, A., Clausner, C., Papadopoulous, C., Pletschacher, S.: Historical document layout analysis competition. In: IEEE International Conference on Document Analysis and Recognition (ICDAR), pp. 1516–1520 (2011)

5. Antonacopoulos, A., Clausner, C., Papadopoulous, C., Pletschacher, S.: ICDAR 2013 competition on Historical Newspaper Layout Analysis (HNLA 2013). In: IEEE International Conference on Document Analysis and Recognition (ICDAR), pp. 1454–1458 (2013)

6. Sulem, L.L., Zahour, A., Taconet, B.: Text line segmentation of historical documents: a survey. Int. J. Doc. Anal. Recogn. (IJDAR) 9(2–4), 123–138 (2007). doi:10.1007/s10032-006-0023-z

7. Liwicki, M., Indermuhle, E., Bunke, H.: On-line handwritten text line detection using dynamic programming. In: International Conference on Document Analysis and Recognition, vol. 1, pp. 447–451 (2007)

8. Fischer, A., Wuthrich, M., Liwicki, M., Frinken, V., Bunke, H., Viehhauser, G., Stolz, M.: Automatic transcription of handwritten medieval documents. In: International Conference on Virtual Systems and Multimedia, pp. 137–142 (2009)

9. Fischer, A., Indermühle, E., Bunke, H., Viehhauser, G., Stolz, M.: Ground truth creation for handwriting recognition in historical documents. In: IAPR International Workshop on Document Analysis Systems, pp. 3–10 (2010)

10. Bulacu, M., van Koert, R., Schomaker, L., van der Zant, T.: Layout analysis of handwritten historical documents for searching the archive of the cabinet of the Dutch Queen. In: International Conference on Document Analysis and Recognition, pp. 357–361 (2007)

11. Marti, U.V., Bunke, H.: Using a statistical language model to improve the performance of an HMM-based cursive handwriting recognition system. Int. J. Pattern Recogn. Artif. Intell. **15** (01), 65–90 (2001)

12. Louloudis, G., Gatos, B., Pratikakis, I., Halatsis, C.: Text line detection in handwritten documents. Pattern Recogn. **41**(12), 3758–3772 (2008)

13. Likforman-Sulem, L., Hanimyan, A., Faure, C.: A Hough based algorithm for extracting text lines in handwritten documents. In: International Conference on Document Analysis and Recognition, vol. 2, pp. 774–777 (1995)

14. Nikolaou, N., Makridis, M., Gatos, B., Stamatopoulos, N., Papamarkos, N.: Segmentation of historical machine-printed documents using adaptive run length smoothing and skeleton segmentation paths. Image Vis. Comput. **28**(4), 590–604 (2010)

15. Arvanitopoulos, N., Susstrunk, S.: Seam carving for text line extraction on color and grayscale historical manuscripts. In: Proceedings of International Conference on Frontiers in Handwriting Recognition, ICFHR, pp. 726–731, December 2014

16. Arvanitopoulos, N., Susstrunk, S.: Seam carving for text line extraction on color and grayscale historical manuscripts. In: Proceedings of International Conference on Frontiers in Handwriting Recognition, ICFHR, pp. 726–731, December 2014

17. Alaql, O., Lu, C.C.: Text line extraction for historical document images using steerable directional filters. In: 2014 International Conference on Audio, Language and Image Processing (ICALIP), Shanghai, 2014, pp. 312–317. doi:10.1109/ICALIP.2014.7009807

18. Shin, H.K.: Fast text line segmentation model based on DCT for color image. Korean Inf. Process. Soc. Trans. **17D**(6), 463–470 (2010). doi:10.3745/KIPSTD.2010.17D.6.463

19. Ahmed, N., Natarajan, T., Rao, K.R.: Discrete Cosine Transform. IEEE Trans. Comput. **C-32**, 90–93 (1974)

20. Strang, G.: The Discrete Cosine Transform. SIAM Rev. **41**(1), 135–147 (1999)

21. Hung, A.C., Meng, T.H.-Y.: A comparison of fast DCT algorithms. Multimed. Syst. **2**(5), 204–217 (1994)

22. Haque, M.A.: A two-dimensional fast cosine transform. IEEE Trans. Acoust. Speech Signal Process. **ASSP-33**, 1532–1539 (1985)

Applications

Applications

Time Series Analysis of Garment Distributions via Street Webcam

Sen Jia, Thomas Lansdall-Welfare, and Nello Cristianini[(✉)]

Intelligent Systems Laboratory, University of Bristol, Bristol, UK
{sen.jia,thomas.lansdall-welfare,nello.cristianini}@bris.ac.uk

Abstract. The discovery of patterns and events in the physical world by analysis of multiple streams of sensor data can provide benefit to society in more than just surveillance applications by focusing on automated means for social scientists, anthropologists and marketing experts to detect macroscopic trends and changes in the general population. This goal complements analogous efforts in documenting trends in the digital world, such as those in social media monitoring. In this paper we show how the contents of a street webcam, processed with state-of-the-art deep networks, can provide information about patterns in clothing and their relation to weather information. In particular, we analyze a large time series of street webcam images, using a deep network trained for garment detection, and demonstrate how the garment distribution over time significantly correlates to weather and temporal patterns. Finally, we additionally provide a new and improved labelled dataset of garments for training and benchmarking purposes, reporting 58.19 % overall accuracy on the ACS test set, the best performance yet obtained.

1 Introduction

The idea of observing collective behaviour on a large scale goes back to at least the 1930s in the social sciences [12], where the general goal was to record and study social habits, the spread of fashions, and even the (anonymous) opinions of the masses. Indeed, the study of how certain habits and behaviours arise and spread has continued to be of great interest to marketing and social sciences alike.

While classical tools were not much different than those of anthropology, involving interviews, observations and questionnaires, it has recently become possible to access the aspects of collective behaviour that are online. For example, the analysis of Twitter content has been used to detect large-scale mood shifts [9], as well as detecting phenomena such as flu outbreaks [8]. Major shifts in culture have also been detected in book content [11] and in musical styles [10] by data-driven approaches. However, observing collective behaviour in the physical world requires a different approach, one which can take advantage of the widespread distribution of cameras and other physical sensors within our society. While anonymous observation of collective behaviour certainly has implications for

A. Campilho and F. Karray (Eds.): ICIAR 2016, LNCS 9730, pp. 765–773, 2016.
DOI: 10.1007/978-3-319-41501-7_85

Table 1. A training set created by merging garment categories from the ACS and Fashionista datasets is used to train a garment classifier.

ACS category	# Images	Fashionista category	# Images	Merged training set	Total
blouses	896	blouse	13,808	blouse	14,704
cloak	7,061	–	0	cloak	7,061
coat	9,061	coat	4,738	coat	13,799
jacket	9,366	hoodie, jacket, cardigan	23,879	jacket	33,245
long dress	10,090	–	0	long dress	10,090
polo shirt, sport shirt	780	–	0	sports shirt	780
robe	5,799	–	0	robe	5,799
shirt	1,425	–	0	shirt	1,425
short dress	4,285	romper, dress	36,035	short dress	40,320
suit, suit of clothes	6,054	blazer	12,651	suit	18,705
sweater	5,209	sweater	8,934	sweater	14,143
jersey, T-shirt, tee shirt	1,426	t-shirt, shirt	28,950	T-shirt	30,376
undergarment, upper body	5,538	bra	757	undergarment	6,295
uniform	3,353	–	0	uniform	3,353
vest, waistcoat	750	vest	6,959	vest	7,709
total training images	71,093		136,711		207,804

mass surveillance, it can also shed light on interesting trends that might be found in various aspects of society.

Previous work has used this idea to monitor activity in smart cities [1], using sensor meta-data and semantic annotations of street camera and microphones to detect changes. A further study [13] used webcams to detect events in New York, such as a parade, by fusing information from visual (CCTV) and social (Twitter) sensors in the same location. In those approaches the emphasis is on the combination and modelling of multiples streams of sensor data, including cameras and social media content, to detect any interesting patterns or violations thereof.

In this paper, we show how recent advances in deep learning applied to computer vision, combined with webcam data freely available on the web, can be used in a similar way to reveal patterns in what people are wearing, and how this relates to the temporal and weather patterns in the same location. More specifically, we train a Convolutional Neural Network (CNN) [7] on a new, combined and annotated dataset of clothing images generated from the "Apparel

Classification with Style" (ACS) [2] and "Fashionista" [14] datasets, achieving a new record of 58.19 % on the ACS test set. We used this classifier to find garments items in 243,470 images taken on the street in New York over 420 days before analyzing patterns of pedestrian flow and choice of clothing relative to the time and the local weather.

Our approach further exemplifies the opportunities for a new sort of mass observation, one which can discover large-scale patterns in society by combining multiple sources of information, including webcams, social media, sensor data, and more. This can (and should) be done without the need to use any personal data, if automated anonymisation techniques are used and the data is aggregated, as performed in this study.

This paper makes the following contributions:

1. We compiled a new training set for garment classification that we show achieves state-of-the-art performance when combined with deep learning networks,
2. We analyze real-world images from a street webcam in Williamsburg, New York, showing that there are trends in the pedestrian flow and what people are wearing based upon the time of year,
3. We show that the choice of garments found in the images can be partially explained by the local weather.

2   Methods and Data

2.1   Garment Training Data

In order to train a classifier that can recognise instances of different garments within images, we first created a training set by merging together two of the most popular, publicly available datasets for garment classification, namely the ACS [2] and Fashionista [14] datasets. Fashionista contains 158,235 images collected from the "Chictopia.com" fashion website, organized into 53 garment categories by users when they upload images, while the ACS dataset contains 88,951 garments images organized into 15 garment categories crawled from the web based upon ImageNet [3]. The ACS dataset is provided split into a training set containing 71,093 images, which we use here, and a separate test set containing 17,858 images which we hold out to use to validate our garment classifier in Sect. 2.2.

Using the 15 garment categories provided by the ACS dataset, we manually selected the closest corresponding categories from the Fashionista dataset, as shown in Table 1, allowing us to merge the data into a single training set. To ensure that there was no intersection between our newly created merged training set and the ACS test data set, we performed the following test. We pre-processed each training image, following the procedure in [2], by resizing the largest side to 320 pixels and normalising the image histogram. Each training image was then compared to each test image using a pixel comparison, finding that there was no intersection between the two datasets.

2.2   Training a Convolutional Neural Network

Typically, the identification of garments within images requires accurate pose estimation in order to extract what a person is wearing [15]. However, this approach is often prohibitively expensive for real-world applications. We take a deep learning approach to garment classification, implementing a convolutional neural network using the AlexNet [7] network in Caffe [6], a popular deep learning library.

Following the procedure of AlexNet [7], we first augmented the training set using multiple-crop and horizontal flips. Using a batch size of 128, we trained the network for 450,000 iterations with a dynamic learning rate starting at 0.01 and scaling 10 times smaller every 100,000 iterations. We take the final snapshot of the classifier after the last iteration as the garment classifier for the experiments in this paper.

We tested the garment classifier on the ACS test set which we held out from the training set, and was found to have zero intersection with the merged training set detailed in Table 1. We found that the overall accuracy of the classifier was a state-of-the-art 58.19 % on the ACS test set, a new record for garment classification.

3   Experiments

Once we had a trained garment classifier, we wished to demonstrate on real-world data that the combination of advances in computer vision and freely available webcam data can reveal patterns in real-world trends, such as what people are wearing, and how it relates to the time of day, week and year along with weather patterns in the same location.

3.1   Styleblaster Webcam

Styleblaster is a real-time fashion website that captures images of people walking past a street webcam in Williamsburg, New York during daylight hours (between 7 a.m. and 8 p.m.). The images are uploaded to the website and annotated with a timestamp of when the image was taken. Importantly for this study, the webcam captures an image for every person that walks past the camera without applying any discrimination or filtering, enabling us to study the hourly and daily pedestrian traffic in the area, as well as the fashion trends over time.

For this study, we analyzed 243,470 images from Styleblaster dated between October 2012 and May 2015. We found that occasionally the webcam would capture an empty image (one not containing a person) due to background noise such as roadworks, snowdrifts or changes in illumination. To remove these images from those we analyzed, we applied a person detection algorithm using the fast R-CNN deep network [5] based upon [4]. This process removed 51,299 images, leaving us with 192,171 images containing a person for our analysis.

3.2 Pedestrian Flow Analysis

The webcam images from Styleblaster capture every person it detects walking past on the street without discrimination. This allowed us to analyze the pedestrian flow on the street by counting how many people were detected each hour and on each day, as shown in Fig. 1.

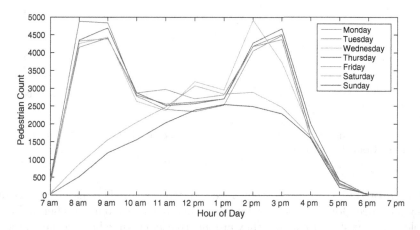

Fig. 1. Total pedestrian count for each hour of the day, separated by day of the week. A clear separation between weekdays and weekends can be seen, with weekdays exhibiting peaks of pedestrian activity between 8 a.m. and 10 a.m., and again between 2 p.m. and 4 p.m. (Color figure online)

We can see that during weekdays there are two main peaks of activity, one in the morning between 8 a.m. and 10 a.m. and one in the early afternoon between 2 p.m. and 4 p.m. During the weekends, there are no distinguished peaks of activity however, with a gradual increase in pedestrians until just after midday before tailing off again. This suggests that we are detecting people travelling to and from work or school during the weekdays, as the peaks are not found during the weekend.

3.3 Garment Distribution

We further analyzed the distribution of what people are wearing at different times of the year by applying the garment classifier detailed in Sect. 2.2 to the person bounding box in each of the 192,171 Styleblaster images that contained a person. For each image, we obtained a label and a confidence in the prediction, thresholding the results so that we only consider labels that have a confidence over 0.5, resulting in a total of 36,883 garment detections.

While we report an accuracy across all 15 garment categories, four categories ("blouses", "sports shirt", "shirt" and "vest") received too few positive predictions to meaningfully study the variation in their distribution. We believe that

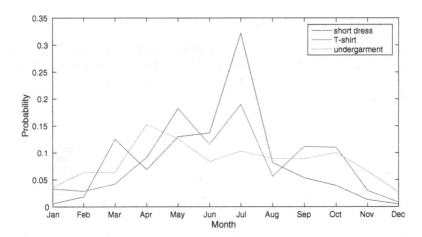

Fig. 2. Conditional probability of each month given that a specific garment was detected. (Color figure online)

for each of these categories, they received too few predictions either because they have been found to be difficult to classify, both with our classifier and in [2] ("blouses", "vest") or because they are incorrectly classified as another category due to their visual similarity (i.e. "sports shirt" is misclassified as "T-shirt" and "shirt" is misclassified as "jacket").

For the remaining 11 garment categories, we calculated the conditional probability of each month given we have detected a garment, displayed in Figs. 2 and 3 for readability. We can see that there are generally two trends that the garments follow, either peaking in the summer months, for example "short dress", "T-shirt" and "undergarments"[1] or exhibiting a trough during the summer, as found for most of the rest of the garment types.

3.4   Garment Weather Patterns

We further studied the relationship between the garment distributions and the local weather at that time. We obtained temperature and precipitation data for the closest weather station to Williamsburg, New York from the "National Centers for Environmental Information" website[2] for each day that we had images from Styleblaster, resulting in maximum temperature and precipitation time series similar to those for each garment category. Maximum temperature was used due to the images being taken during the daytime, when the maximum temperature for the day is typically reached. We then used multi-dimensional scaling (MDS) to embed the data in a space based upon the similarity of the

---

[1] We use the label "undergarment" from the ACS dataset for this category, however it more generally refers to more revealing clothing including tank tops, corsets, spandex sportswear etc., along with actual undergarments.

[2] http://www.ncdc.noaa.gov/.

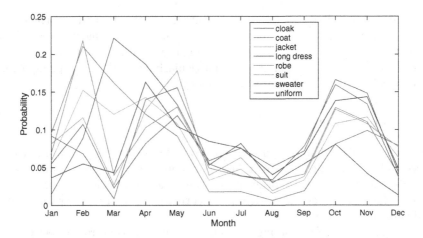

Fig. 3. Conditional probability of each month given that a specific garment was detected. (Color figure online)

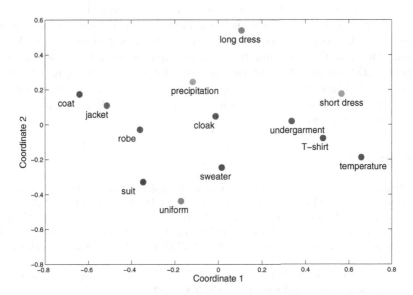

Fig. 4. Visualization showing the similarity of the garment categories with the local daily maximum temperature and precipitation using multi-dimensional scaling. (Color figure online)

time series' while preserving distances as much as possible, resulting in a dimensionality reduction of the data.

In Fig. 4 we visualize the first two Eigenvectors from MDS, with the geometric distance indicating the correlation between the different garment categories and the weather information. We found that "T-shirt", "undergarment" and "short dress" are all close to the temperature, indicating that they correlate well with the maximum daily temperature, while the other garment categories are more distant, with "coat" and "jacket" being the furthest from temperature. No garment categories were found to be particularly related to the precipitation, with "cloak" being the closest garment category.

4   Conclusions

This study shows that computer vision tools based on deep networks can be successfully· be applied to street images coming from a webcam, in order to identify garments worn by pedestrians, and generate a time series of garment types. This time series shows significant correlations with weather information and time information.

The possibility of extracting semantic-level information from street cameras opens the possibility of large-scale observation of trends and fashions, which can complement analogous efforts in observation of media content. However it also creates the potential for abuse if it was applied at the individual level. All of our experiments were aimed at observing collective and average behaviour only.

It is easy to imagine a software infrastructure observing hundreds of webcams, as well as other types of web sensors, trying to detect changes, trends, and events. This would surely qualify as an example of Mass Observation to the social scientists of the 1930s, whose goal was stated as the study and recording of the social habits of ordinary people, within an anthropological perspective. The implications of this infrastructure need to be carefully assessed in light of ethical considerations.

References

1. Albakour, M.-D., Macdonald, C., Ounis, I.: Using sensor metadata streams to identify topics of local events in the city. In: SIGIR 2015, pp. 711–714 (2015)
2. Bossard, L., Dantone, M., Leistner, C., Wengert, C., Quack, T., Van Gool, L.: Apparel classification with style. In: Lee, K.M., Matsushita, Y., Rehg, J.M., Hu, Z. (eds.) ACCV 2012, Part IV. LNCS, vol. 7727, pp. 321–335. Springer, Heidelberg (2013)
3. Deng, J., Dong, W., Socher, R., Li, L.-J., Li, K., Fei-Fei, L.: ImageNet : a large-scale hierarchical image database. In: CVPR 2009 (2009)
4. Girshick, R., Donahue, J., Darrell, T., Malik, J.: Rich feature hierarchies for accurate object detection and semantic segmentation. In: CVPR 2014 (2014)
5. Girshick, R.B.: Fast R-CNN. CoRR, abs/1504.08083 (2015)
6. Jia, Y., Shelhamer, E., Donahue, J., Karayev, S., Long, J., Girshick, R., Guadarrama, S., Darrell, T.: Caffe: convolutional architecture for fast feature embedding. arXiv preprint 2014. arXiv:1408.5093
7. Krizhevsky, A., Sutskever, I., Hinton, G.E.: Imagenet classification with deep convolutional neural networks. NIPS 25, 1097–1105 (2012)
8. Lampos, V., De Bie, T., Cristianini, N.: Flu detector - tracking epidemics on Twitter. In: Balcázar, J.L., Bonchi, F., Gionis, A., Sebag, M. (eds.) ECML PKDD 2010, Part III. LNCS, vol. 6323, pp. 599–602. Springer, Heidelberg (2010)

9. Lansdall-Welfare, T., Lampos, V., Cristianini, N.: Effects of the recession on public mood in the UK. In: WWW 2012 Companion, pp. 1221–1226 (2012)
10. Mauch, M., MacCallum, R.M., Levy, M., Leroi, A.M.: The evolution of popular music: USA 1960–2010. R. Soc. Open Sci. **2**(5), 150081 (2015)
11. Michel, J.-B., Shen, Y.K., Aiden, A.P., Veres, A., Gray, M.K., Pickett, J.P., Hoiberg, D., Clancy, D., Norvig, P., Orwant, J., et al.: Quantitative analysis of culture using millions of digitized books. Science **331**(6014), 176–182 (2011)
12. Moran, J.: Mass-observation, market research, the birth of the focus group, 1937–1997. J. Br. Stud. **47**, 827–851 (2008)
13. Wang, Y., Kankanhalli, M.S.: Tweeting cameras for event detection. In: WWW 2015, pp. 1231–1241 (2015)
14. Yamaguchi, K.: Parsing clothing in fashion photographs. In: CVPR 2012, pp. 3570–3577 (2012)
15. Yamaguchi, K., Kiapour, M., Berg, T.: Paper doll parsing: retrieving similar styles to parse clothing items. In: ICCV 2013, pp. 3519–3526 (2013)

Automatic System for Zebrafish Counting in Fish Facility Tanks

Francisco J. Silvério[1](✉), Ana C. Certal[2], Carlos Mão de Ferro[2],
Joana F. Monteiro[2], José Almeida Cruz[2], Ricardo Ribeiro[2],
and João Nuno Silva[1]

[1] INESC-ID Lisboa, Instituto Superior Técnico, Universidade de Lisboa,
Lisbon, Portugal
fjsilverio@hotmail.com, joao.n.silva@inesc-id.pt
[2] Champalimaud Centre for the Unknown, Lisbon, Portugal
{ana.certal,carlos.maodeferro,joana.monteiro,jose.cruz,
ricardo.ribeiro}@neuro.fchampalimaud.org

Abstract. In this project we propose a computer vision method, based
on background subtraction, to estimate the number of zebrafish inside
a tank. We addressed questions related to the best choice of parameters
to run the algorithm, namely the threshold blob area for fish detection
and the reference area from which a blob area in a threshed frame may
be considered as one or multiple fish. Empirical results obtained after
several tests show that the method can successfully estimate, within a
margin of error, the number of zebrafish (fries or adults) inside fish tanks
proving that adaptive background subtraction is extremely effective for
blob isolation and fish counting.

Keywords: Computer vision · Zebrafish counting · Background
subtraction · Hu moments · Image processing

1 Introduction

Zebrafish (*danio rerio*) is a small freshwater fish that is widely used as an animal model in biomedical research [2]. Research laboratories around the world
require a huge number of individuals to perform a great variety of experiments.
Those fish are breed and maintained in big fish facilities managing hundreds to
thousands fish tanks. Usually these tanks are standardized containers (from 3 to
8 L for instance) which may host up to dozens of animals each.

Obtaining an up to date count of the total number of animals in a fish facility is an essential task, performed by human technicians who manually extract
animals with the help of small fish nets. This manual counting process requires
a significant amount of time and is error prone. Moreover, handling animals for
counting induces significant stress, with all the harmful consequences that may
cause to the animals and, consequently, affect the scientific experiments they are
involved in.

© Springer International Publishing Switzerland 2016
A. Campilho and F. Karray (Eds.): ICIAR 2016, LNCS 9730, pp. 774–782, 2016.
DOI: 10.1007/978-3-319-41501-7_86

Finding a noninvasive automatic procedure to obtain the precise number of zebrafish in facilities tanks, avoiding all the disadvantages of manual counting, is a long sought goal of fish facilities managers.

Today there are many examples of complex applications of computer vision techniques such as: optical character recognition, machine inspection, 3D model building, medical imaging, face detection, visual authentication and people tracking [12]. Some of the previous applications make use of techniques such as background subtraction which have particular interest in this article. Background subtraction is specially relevant when, for example, the need for isolating moving regions in a sequence of images arises. In fish counting, since images are two-dimensional, the main difficulties to overcome are: regions where fish overlap, mirroring effect, i.e., fish reflections on the tanks sides and, mainly, fish shoaling. In this paper, we propose an experimental setup for video collection and a technique for fish counting that combines background subtraction, blob counting and mirror compensation (Sect. 3). Our main achievements were: building a full prototype of a counting device, counting the number of fish in a tank with a maximum error margin of 15 % of the real fish value inside it given by manual counting and ensuring that all the procedures regarding the recording of the videos do not cause stress to the animals (noninvasive technique).

2   Related Work

Currently, the problem of counting objects using computer vision relies on different techniques. Y.H. Toh et al. [13] presents a method for counting feeder fish using image processing techniques where background and noise are filtered and blobs are counted to give a counting estimate.

Another approach [7] suggests the development of algorithms which allow the recognition of fish in the images and track the locations of individual fish from frame to frame to determine if overlapping is most likely to happen in future frames. The background is adjusted according to images with no fish which are used to calculate a histogram for the pixel amplitude used to define thresholds to be set and then isolate regions containing fish.

Alternatively, canny edge detection algorithm is used combined with a coral-blackening background process [4]. Video is recorded in a coral reef environment, which represents a much more complex background than, for instance, the one presented in Y.H. Toh et al. [13] project. In this case, the Zernike moment [9] of every individual blob is calculated having in consideration a standard predefined fish template. In order to identify different fish species and count them in every frame, a set of orthogonal Zernike moments are chosen and applied due to their rotational, translational and scale invariant properties.

Sub-processing systems consisting of texture and colour analysis are considered [11], as well as fish detection and fish tracking. The analysis of the statistical moments of the grey-level histogram is the chosen approach to describe mathematically the image texture (e.g. brightness and smoothness). In colour analysis hue, saturation and pixels values are compared to predefined threshold to decide which color one region has in a frame. Gaussian Mixture Model (GMM) [11] which allows dealing with multi-modal backgrounds and Adaptive Poisson Mixture Model variant are also used [1], as mixture-based algorithms. Despite the great relevance of the aforementioned references, the most significant contributions for this project are: the original work developed by Zivkovic [14] and Heijden [15] regarding the use of GMMs in background subtraction and the use of Hu moments developed by M.-K. Hu [8].

Despite being extremely relevant and sharing some techniques, the previously described methods show significant differences comparing to our work since environment parameters such as image background and fish feature are not the same. As a consequence, the need for the development of a different algorithm for this specific application emerged.

3   Implementation

This work includes the development of a full prototype of a counting device and it can be found in Fig. 1.

Videos were recorded at Champalimaud Centre for the Unknown Fish Facility and were processed offline. Fish were raised and maintained at the Champalimaud Fish Platform according to Martins et al. (2016) and manipulated by staff accredited for animal experimentation by the Portuguese Veterinary Agency (DGAV) [10].

Fig. 1. Zebrafish Recording Setup (left: on at the Fish Facility, right: in standby mode). (Color figure online)

The container was designed to achieve a parallelepiped structure, made of acrylic, and covered, inside, in blue musgami paper (waterproof). Moreover, given the different physical patterns exhibited by the zebrafish, it was thought that a clean blue environment could bring good image contrast and quality, representing an advantage for video processing. In this way the background subtraction algorithm can rapidly stabilize and, more effectively, allow the detection of fish in the foreground. There are several holes carved on the bottom of the container which are intended to fix each aquarium to it making sure that the distance to the camera is always constant and it does not influence the algorithm output. Blue LEDs [3] are fixed to a moving piece that was designed to fit on the top of each tank, at exactly the same place, that maintains the same light intensity per area in each aquarium since its distance to the tank is always constant.

In this setup, it can be seen in Fig. 1, that there is specific hardware selected for both video recording and user interaction. In this way, to record the videos, a Raspberry Pi 2, Model B [5] is used with an integrated camera [6]. On the front side of the container there is a fixed touch screen which transforms the container into an interactive setup for the user, representing an all-in-one recording system.

3.1   Estimating the Number of the Fish

Background Subtraction with GMMs. Regarding video properties, it is relevant to state that each frame has a size of 640 × 480 and is acquired at a frame rate of 25 Hz. Each frame is initially cropped so that the tank can be the only region of interest in it. Then, an algorithm of background subtraction is applied to the frame with the tank.

This background subtraction uses a GMM background subtraction scheme [14,15] that automatically selects specific components, for each pixel in the image. This makes the differentiation between what is considered as background (blue environment) and foreground (fish moving between successive frames) possible. This technique allows adaptability during frame variation to guarantee that the background is consistently subtracted and only foreground variations are able to be identified. The resulting black and white image, where black represents the background and white the fish (blobs from now on), is eroded and dilated to remove tiny white blobs and obtain a clean background subtracted frame to analyse.

Blob Counting. After the dilation, a routine for blob contours detection occurs as well as the calculation of each blob pixel area (inside the contour). In case a blob has an area larger than a given threshold (different for fries and adult fish), it may represent fish or multiple fish together in a big blob.

Each detected blob contour larger than the threshold is counted representing the first counting approximation. Afterwards, the decision whether a blob represents a fish or multiple fish is made taking into consideration testing of videos previously performed (different from the ones used to extract results from the counting algorithm). These videos contain only one fish (fries, or adults, in each genotype) and are used to register the average area (reference area from now on) that the fish assumes during a five minute video (7500 frames). Then, each blob area is divided by the reference area multiplied by two (the reference is two fish overlapping) giving a correction number for the counting done so far. Different reference areas, bigger or lower than the calculated in the tests, are applied as the number of fish increases in the tank. In fact, after testing it was possible to build intervals with typical average areas that specific amounts of fish represent and, this way, if a frame has a total blob area in one of this intervals, a specific reference area is used.

It is understandable that, for instance, if the number of fish is 35 (maximum number of fish per tank in this project), a blob with the same size as a case where there are 25 fish may represent more fish. This justifies why the reference area used to divide the blob area by is lower than twice the reference area calculated in the tests. The reference area is decreased by 100 pixel for each area interval. At the first interval (fish number <10 or 15) the reference area is twice the reference area given by the tests and keeps decreasing 100 pixel until the last interval (the fourth, fish number >30).

In cases where shoaling at the bottom of the tank is detected (by checking if the total blob area in the bottom of the tank is equal or higher than 90 % of the total blob area detected in the frame) the reference area used is half the reference area given by the tests because higher compensation needs to be done.

Mirrored Counting Compensation. In the recorded videos two areas containing fish mirroring can be detected: the right side of the tank and the upper part (water surface). Near these regions fish are reflected like in a mirror which may lead to count some fish twice. Thus, the method used for mirror compensation is calculating each Hu moment for each blob based on M.-K. Hu [8] work that presents a theory of two-dimensional moment invariants for planar geometric figures.

In that technique, absolute orthogonal invariants are derived which are used in our project to get the pattern identification of similar shape independent of size, position and orientation. Hence and since a reflected fish is similar in size and has opposite orientation comparing to the original fish, it is possible to identify which fish is producing a reflection and to compensate this counting by subtracting the number of mirrored fish to the overall counting that was made until this step.

4   Results and Discussion

In this project, fish with different genotypes were recorded: wild type zebrafish from strains AB and TU, mutant Nacre zebrafish and transgenic fish from multiple lines with TU and Nacre background. From this point, we will assume that fish are divided into four different categories with different genotype and age: AB/TU fries (30-day old), adults AB/TU (3-month old), Nacre fries (30-day old) and adults Nacre (3-month old). For each of these categories, we collected videos from tanks containing schools of 13 different sizes: 5, 7, 10, 12, 15, 17, 20, 22, 25, 27, 30, 32 and 35 fish. The only exception is AB/TU fries category since the maximum number of fish available in tanks with this features was 27 by the time recording occurred. For each different category and school size we collected 20 videos of 40 s each, thus totalling 200 videos for AB/TU fries and 260 for each of the remaining categories.

Table 1. Average fish count error for each number of fish in the different categories after 20 samples.

	Number of fish in the tank												
Fish Category	**5**	**7**	**10**	**12**	**15**	**17**	**20**	**22**	**25**	**27**	**30**	**32**	**35**
AB/TU fries	4%	13%	7%	10%	4%	9%	7%	9%	4%	3%			
Nacre fries	14%	12%	15%	6%	8%	6%	11%	3%	4%	5%	1%	8%	4%
Nacre Adults	21%	13%	18%	12%	29%	6%	9%	20%	9%	11%	7%	3%	4%
AB/TU Adults	0%	6%	5%	3%	9%	11%	14%	3%	5%	24%	15%	12%	29%

After applying the described counting algorithm to those 40 s videos, we obtained the results in Table 1 where acceptable average errors are indicated in green and not acceptable in red. Let us denote the estimated number of fish detected in each frame of a video by: f_m^n, $n = 1, ..., N$ and $m = 1, ..., M$, where N and M are the number of videos and number of frames per video, respectively. The number of fish is given by: $\hat{F}_n = median(f_1^n, f_2^n, ..., f_M^n)$. Consequently, the error in a video and the average error for N sample videos, can be, respectively, calculated by:

$$e_n = \frac{|\hat{F}_n - K_n|}{K_n} \qquad\qquad \bar{e} = \frac{\sum_{n=1}^N e_n}{N}$$

where K_n represents the real number of fish, which is known *a priori*. Regarding fries' category, we can see that the highest error observed was 15 %, for Nacre fries in a 10 fish tank. In the adult fish category, there were certain fish quantities which did not meet the acceptable margin. For instance, in the videos with 15 Nacre adults fish the average error is 29 % which means that approximately 5 fish were not detected, in average, in those videos which is far from the real value. This is due to the significant high number of videos where shoaling occurred. An example can be seen in Fig. 2(a) where a frame from a video with 22 AB/TU adult zebrafish shoaling lead to wrong counting and another (with the same number, genotype and age), (b), where fish are distributed across the frame during the video leading to a good result. In Fig. 2 we can see by the analysis of the histograms for (a) and (b) that for videos where shoaling occurs, the percentage of total blob area detected in each frame is significantly lower than the case where shoaling does not occur. Thus, it is understandable that if there is less blob area in a frame than it should, it will lead to unacceptable results. In particular fish shoal in the bottom of the tank and it is extremely difficult for the algorithm to output correct counts. This occurs for videos with few or many fish because fish are closely together in multiple layers behind each other. In Fig. 3, we can see how the fish count per frame varies within individual videos for fish in the different categories. It can be seen that the algorithm outputs a number within the error margin in early frames and maintains the

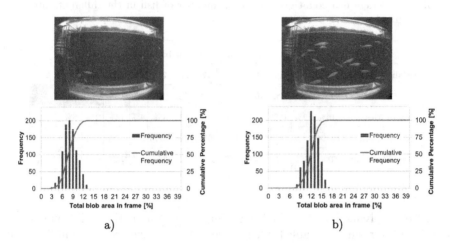

Fig. 2. Frequency and cumulative frequency histogram for a video with 22 fish. (a) with shoaling, (b) without shoaling.

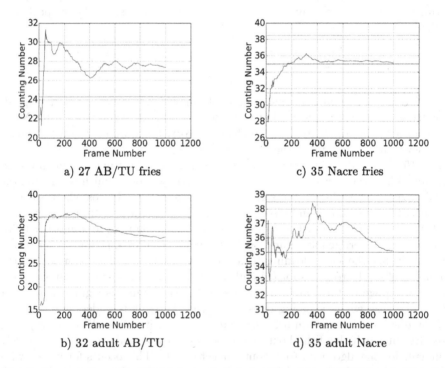

Fig. 3. Computed number of fish in tank during a 40 s video (1000 frames). The red lines represent the acceptable error margin and the green line is the real fish number in the tank. (Color figure online)

error margin until 1000 frames. Nacre zebrafish tend to reflect more the light, resulting in bigger blobs for single fish, when comparing to the AB/TU, since these are darker, which explains the multiple peaks in Fig. 3(d). These peaks are not so evident in Nacre fries due to their small dimensions which, in the end, compensates the reflection.

5   Conclusion and Future Work

We presented a noninvasive technique for zebrafish count in fish facility tanks. The algorithm showed very good results in fries categories, where the average error was always in the acceptable margin defined at the beginning of the project. However, fish shoaling is a problem that deeply affects the algorithm performance and in these cases unacceptable counting numbers are calculated. In our project, some adult fish numbers did not meet the acceptable margin due to the previous limitation. Nevertheless, we could conclude that in cases where shoaling does not occur, this algorithm also presents good results for adult zebrafish. In case a product was developed using our technique, since we can identify shoaling, we could also ignore those frames while counting and automatically put the program in standby until no shoaling was detected. As future work, this algorithm could be implemented with two cameras: one as the one used in this project, another recording on top of the tank (to give the shoal depth) and applying our algorithm. Another interesting and useful approach would be to use background subtraction with features detection and extraction algorithms to identify, in each tank, for instance, how many males or females exist.

Acknowledgments. This work was supported by national funds through Fundação para a Ciência e a Tecnologia (FCT) with reference UID/CEC/50021/2013.

References

1. Boom, B.J., et al.: A research tool for long-term and continuous analysis of fish assemblage in coral-reefs using underwater camera footage. Ecol. Inf. 1–23 (2014)
2. Egan, R.J., et al.: Understanding behavioral and physiological phenotypes of stress and anxiety in zebrafish. Behav. Brain Res. **205**(1), 38–44 (2009)
3. EGLO: 92065 | LED STRIPES-FLEX. http://www.eglo.com/eglo_global/Produ cts/Main-Collections/Interior-Lighting/LED-STRIPES-FLEX/92065
4. Fabic, J.N., Turla, I.E., Capacillo, J.A., David, L.T., Naval, P.C.: Fish population estimation and species classification from underwater video sequences using blob counting and shape analysis, pp. 1–6. IEEE, March 2013
5. Foundation, P.: Raspberry Pi 2, Model B. https://www.adafruit.com/pdfs/rasp berrypi2modelb.pdf
6. Foundation, P.: Raspberry Pi Camera. https://www.raspberrypi.org/documenta tion/hardware/camera.md
7. Khanfar, H., et al.: Automatic fish counting in underwater video. In: 66th Gulf and Caribbean Fisheries Institute, pp. 1–9, November 2013

8. Hu, M.-K.: Visual pattern recognition by moment invariants. IEEE Trans. Inf. Theor. **8**(2), 179–187 (1962)
9. Qader, H.A., Ramli, A.R., Al-haddad, S.: Fingerprint recognition using zernike moments (2006)
10. Martins, S., et al.: Toward an Integrated Zebrafish Health Management Program Supporting Cancer and Neuroscience Research (2016)
11. Spampinato, C., et al.: Detecting, tracking and counting fish in low quality unconstrained underwater videos. In: Proceedings of 3rd International Conference on Computer Vision Theory and Applications (VISAPP), pp. 514–519 (2008)
12. Szeliski, R.: Computer Vision: Algorithms and Applications. Texts in Computer Science. Springer, London (2011)
13. Toh, Y.H., Ng, T.M., Liew, B.K.: Automated fish counting using image processing, pp. 1–5. IEEE, December 2009
14. Zivkovic, Z.: Improved adaptive Gaussian mixture model for background subtraction, vol.2, pp. 28–31. IEEE (2004)
15. Zivkovic, Z., van der Heijden, F.: Efficient adaptive density estimation per image pixel for the task of background subtraction. Pattern Recognit. Lett. **27**(7), 773–780 (2006)

A Lightweight Mobile System for Crop Disease Diagnosis

Punnarai Siricharoen[✉], Bryan Scotney, Philip Morrow, and Gerard Parr

School of Computing and Information Engineering, University of Ulster, Coleraine, UK
siricharoen-p@email.ulster.ac.uk,
{bw.scotney,pj.morrow,gp.parr}@ulster.ac.uk

Abstract. This paper presents a low-complexity mobile application for automatically diagnosing crop diseases in the field. In an initial pre-processing stage,
the system leverages the capability of a smartphone device and basic image
processing algorithms to obtain consistent leaf orientation and to remove the
background. A number of different features are then extracted from the leaf,
including texture, colour and shape features. Nine lightweight sub-features are
combined and implemented as a feature descriptor for this mobile environment.
The system is applied to six wheat leaf types: non-disease, yellow rust, Septoria,
brown rust, powdery mildew and tan spots, which are commonly occurring wheat
diseases worldwide. The standalone application demonstrates the possibilities for
disease diagnosis under realistic circumstances, with disease/non-disease detection accuracy of approximately 88 %, and can provide a possible disease type
within a few seconds of image acquisition.

Keywords: Mobile standalone application · Crop disease · Texture · Shape ·
SVM

1 Introduction

Intelligent Decision Support Systems (DSSs) for crop monitoring have been developed
worldwide for efficient crop disease and pest management [1, 2]. The systems employ
an integrated approach and provide an interactive interface for users to request information to help with crop management. The outputs of the system help to estimate disease
risks and provide options for disease control [3]. Many previous studies [4, 5] have
proposed frameworks that integrate imaging techniques as a part of the system based on
recent cloud technology for preliminary screening of visible diseases in the field. Users
can access crop information or request basic disease detection from a server back to their
smartphone. In our work, we propose a lightweight but efficient mobile automated
system based on imaging techniques and show the potential of the standalone version
for real-time diagnosis of crop diseases. This alternative to using a client-server interaction eliminates the delay and transfer time required, especially when users are
uploading image data.

In a general framework, the basic imaging procedure includes pre-processing to
enhance the image quality and consistency, leaf and disease segmentation, feature
extraction and disease classification. Leaf segmentation is essential especially when a
cluttered background is captured. Sophisticated techniques have been developed for leaf

© Springer International Publishing Switzerland 2016
A. Campilho and F. Karray (Eds.): ICIAR 2016, LNCS 9730, pp. 783–791, 2016.
DOI: 10.1007/978-3-319-41501-7_87

segmentation [6]. Our system leverages the programmable smartphone device to automatically eliminate background. For feature extraction, previous studies have demonstrated that the combination of different features, particularly texture, colour and shape features, effectively represent disease characteristics. Work on fusion of features from images acquired under controlled conditions has been undertaken [5, 7, 8]. Our system analytically selects nine sub-features from the three feature sets which are low-complexity and have the potential to characterise disease patterns. Ultimately, our system can provide users with information on whether crops are infected (disease/non-disease) and can also provide information on the possible disease to support crop management.

2   System Overview

Our lightweight mobile application system is illustrated in Fig. 1. The application enables users to capture and/or upload an image (see Fig. 2(a)). If the user selects to upload a photo, only one main leaf is required for the automated classification. The user is required to semi-manually prepare the leaf image. Firstly, the user can call *Auto-rotate* to instigate an automated rotation system to adjust the leaf horizontally; otherwise, the user can manually rotate the leaf clockwise (CW) or counterclockwise (CCW). Then the image background can be removed using a cropping function. If the user has a leaf sample in hand, they can capture the leaf image in the overlay template displayed in a capture screen (see Fig. 2(g)). This approach enables the leaf to have consistent orientation and for the background to be removed automatically. The user can also alter the leaf shape template to correspond to different plants. Once the user calls the *Identify* function, a leaf will be processed for three main feature sets, including colour, texture and shape features. For colour and texture features, the *Cr* colour component (from YCbCr) is used. The co-occurrence matrix is constructed from this component and then three main features - local homogeneity, correlation and entropy of the leaf texture - are computed from the matrix; a global contrast is also included as another texture feature. The same colour component is extracted for basic statistical information, such as mean, standard deviation and skewness. For disease shapes, disease regions are segmented from a leaf using binary thresholding. The segmented disease patches are computed for elongatedness and hydraulic radius properties. In total, nine sub-features from three feature sets are generated to form a feature descriptor for training a binary classification model using a Support Vector Machine (SVM-2 in Fig. 1). This model can differentiate disease from non-disease. After the non-disease leaves are filtered out, only disease feature descriptors are learned for our multiclass model (SVM-5 in Fig. 1) to classify five different diseases, including brown rust (BR), Septoria (ST), yellow rust (YR), powdery mildew (PM), and Tan spots (TS). The application can identify whether the leaf is a diseased or non-diseased leaf; if it is a diseased leaf, the system displays the possible disease type in a small caption (see Fig. 2(f) and (h)) as guidance for the user so that they can apply suitable techniques for controlling the disease.

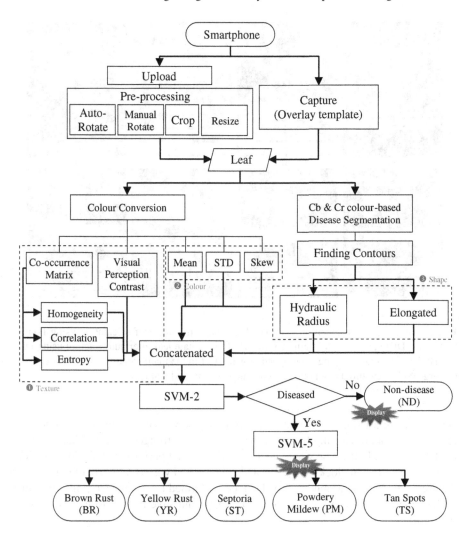

Fig. 1. Mobile system flow for monitoring wheat disease

3 Semi-automated Pre-processing

Leaf rotation and background removal are important for accurate disease classification. Pre-processing requires user participation only when the user needs to upload an image. Previous research [9] has demonstrated the potential for using a 2-D Discrete Fourier transform (DFT) in detecting global frequency where wheat leaf veins are strongly aligned in a particular direction (corresponding to the orientation of the leaf edge itself). The resulting Fourier spectrum represents a spectrum line that is orthogonal to the leaf orientation. The Fourier transform of an image is implemented in our mobile system; Fig. 2(b) shows a thresholded Fourier spectrum (in white); then the spectrum line is

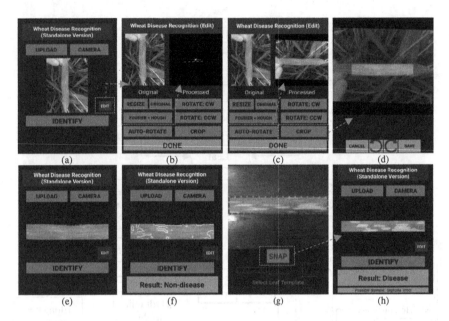

Fig. 2. Targeted leaf acquisition (a) upload an image (b) find leaf orientation using Fourier transform (DFT) and Hough line transform (HLT) (c) rotate leaf after auto-rotating using DFT and HLT (d) manual cropping (e) cropped targeted leaf in the main menu (f) identified leaf type (g) targeted leaf captured in an overlay template (h) identified leaf type

detected using a Hough line transform (HLT) as shown with the red-dotted line. The leaf is rotated automatically based on the angle of the strongest detected line from the HLT (Fig. 2(c)). In the case where DFT and HLT cannot perform well for leaf rotation, we provide a manual clockwise (CW) and counterclockwise (CCW) rotation menu for the user. Finally, background removal can be performed by using a *Crop* interface that enables the user to crop the leaf area (Fig. 2(d)) and save it back to the main menu (Fig. 2(e)).

4   Feature Extraction

The extracted leaf region from pre-processing (or from a captured image) is considered for feature extraction. Figure 3 shows six different disease patches each from a different wheat leaf. It can be seen that non-disease has a homogeneous greenish texture, whereas areas of disease are inhomogeneous in colour distribution and shape. The three main feature sets include texture, colour and shape features which have been demonstrated to best-represent disease patterns [7, 8]. Theoretically, non-disease can be filtered out from the group using texture and colour characteristics. Shape can be used to distinguish striped disease (YR) and the random shape of Septoria (ST) compared to spotty diseases (BR, TS and PM). A number of features were gathered with the choice of features motivated by previous work [5–8]. Nine sub-features which will be described in the following sections were selected based on computational efficiency and individual feature accuracies.

Fig. 3. Different disease patches (a) Non-disease (ND) (b) Brown rust (BR) (c) Yellow rust or stripe rust (YR) (d) Septoria (ST) (e) Tan spots (TS) (f) Powdery mildew (PM)

4.1 Texture Features

The co-occurrence matrix is commonly used to represent spatial relationships of pairs of intensity levels in an image (such as levels i and j that are separated by distance d and direction θ) [10]. We select three main textural features that are derived from the co-occurrence matrix: local homogeneity, a local linear-dependency measure using correlation, and entropy (which represents pattern complexity).

Another textural feature proposed by Tamura et al. [11] is a contrast feature that is based on human visual perception. Tamura contrast considers a global variation of intensity levels and polarization of distribution of high and low intensity areas in an image. The mixture of two components, global variation (or standard deviation, σ) and polarization (or kurtosis, α_4) is used to define the Tamura contrast:

$$F_{con} = \sigma / (\alpha_4)^{1/4} \tag{1}$$

4.2 Colour Features

Basic measures of statistical information in an image are derived from a histogram of intensity values; these are straightforward to compute and include mean (μ), standard deviation (σ) and skewness. Skewness measures asymmetry of the intensity histogram, which can be negative or positive depending on whether the distribution "leans to the left" or "to the right" of the mean value, respectively. Skewness (F_{skew}) can be computed as

$$F_{skew} = \sigma^{-3} \sum_{i=1}^{N} (i - \mu)^3 h(i) \tag{2}$$

where $h(i)$ is a histogram of intensity i. For both texture and colour features, we empirically selected the Cr colour component (from YCbCr) as a colour representation for the application.

4.3 Shape Features

Disease segmentation is required to extract the disease areas from the main leaf. Otsu thresholding is applied to Cb and Cr colour components of the leaf image, as it has been shown in previous work that these combined colour components for disease segmentation are robust to different lighting conditions [9]. Then the contours of individual disease patches are extracted based on border following algorithms to find connected components of a binary disease image [12]. Figure 2(f) and (h) show the detected contours (white circle) of non-disease and Septoria diseased leaves. Each contour is processed for two shape features, elongatedness and hydraulic radius. Elongatedness of a diseased patch is based on the ratio of its principal major axis (L_m)and principal minor axis (L_n) and is useful in separating striped disease, such as yellow rust (YR), from other spotty diseases (BR, PM, TS). If a leaf contains N diseased patches, the average value of the N elongatedness values is used to represent the degree of elongatedness degree of that disease:

$$F_{Elong} = \frac{1}{N} \sum_{i=1}^{N} \frac{L_{m,i}}{L_{n,i}} \tag{3}$$

Hydraulic radius (F_{HR}) is used to measure the complexity of a diseased shape and is a ratio of perimeter (P_d) to disease area (A_d).

$$F_{HR} = \frac{1}{N} \sum_{i=1}^{N} \frac{A_{d,i}}{P_{d,i}} \tag{4}$$

5 SVM Classification

Nine sub-features (4 textures, 3 colours, and 2 shapes) are combined as a feature descriptor of a leaf and are then used for training a binary classification model (disease/non-disease) using a Support Vector Machine (SVM-2) to filter out non-disease leaves. SVM is applied in the lightweight application as it has been shown to obtain high accuracy and good generalization with economical computation [13]. After the leaf is classified as a diseased leaf, the same descriptors are then used for training a multiclass classification using SVM-5 to provide the user with the possible disease presented in the leaf (a linear kernel is selected empirically for SVM-2 and SVM-5).

6 Experimentation and Results

Our diseased and non-diseased leaf datasets are acquired from various sources including high quality images from the Food and Environment Research Agency (UK FERA) [2], from photographs taken of crops at a farm near Coleraine, Northern Ireland, and from a range of internet sources. The images vary in quality, size and lighting conditions. In preparation, the targeted leaf in each image was segmented manually from the background, as only one main leaf in an image is used for model learning. The proposed system is implemented on a Samsung Galaxy A3 smartphone using OpenCV4Android and libSVM on Android [13]. A total of 610 leaf images are used for learning in the smartphone system, using a 5-fold cross-validation scheme.

The results in Table 1 show the binary classification performance in identifying diseased and non-diseased leaves. The accuracy in detecting disease has high precision at around 92 % and recall at approximately 93 %, corresponding values for non-disease are approximately 65 % and 61 %, respectively. One possible impact on the performance of non-disease detection is due to the imbalanced nature of the data between non-disease images (~100) and disease images (~500). The performance of the classifier is much lower on the class with the small sample size (non-disease class). Although techniques for learning from imbalanced data can be employed, such as synthetic data generation and subsampling methods [14], because of our small dataset, only the original images are used in the experimentation. In addition, there is considerable variation of image quality and size between the datasets used. Overall, disease/non-disease classification accuracy is approximately 88 %.

Table 1. Performance measure of Disease vs. Non-disease plant patterns

	#Image	Precision (%)	Recall (%)	Avg. Acc. (%)
Disease (D)	505	91.98	93.07	87.54
Non-disease (ND)	105	64.65	60.95	

Although some disease types are obvious in their visual appearance, in practice the uncontrolled images have a high degree of variation, which is important for accurately computing colour distribution, overall textures or shapes. Our experimental results based on nine lightweight features and an SVM linear kernel can detect five different diseases, as exhibited in the confusion matrix in Fig. 4(a), which shows the true positive rate of disease identification. Brown rust and Septoria show the highest true positive rates. Figure 4(b)–(e) shows examples of diseased and non-disease leaves. The non-disease, powdery mildew and Septoria diseased leaves in Fig. 4(b), (c) and (d), respectively are correctly identified. The detected diseased regions are shown with white boundaries. Yellow rust and tan spots have a very low true positive rate, and both tend to be incorrectly classified as Septoria disease. All three diseases including yellow rust, tan spots and Septoria diseases have similar colour distributions, which are mainly yellow and brown. Also, when the severity of disease is high, the disease patches tend to connect to each other, which impacts negatively on the disease segmentation. When all the diseased regions connects, this can result in a random shape similar to Septoria disease, as shown in Fig. 4(e); hence yellow rust is frequently misclassified as Septoria.

We have demonstrated an independent system for lightweight mobile plant disease monitoring that requires low computational effort, taking less than 4 s to detect each disease. The user is simply required to crop an image to select a wheat leaf and the image is processed locally, whereas for the other similar work [5], the user is required to select a particular diseased region in a leaf and the cropped image is sent for processing at the remote server. In addition, non-disease leaf identification which is important for the farmers' early decision in crop management is considered in our application but is omitted in most previous work [5, 7, 8]. The presence of disease is detected with a

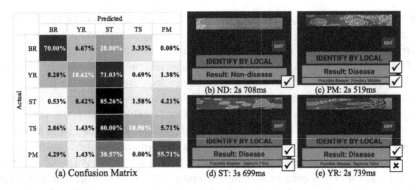

Fig. 4. (a) Confusion matrix and % true positive rate for each of the disease (b)–(e) Screen display results of different disease types (Non-disease (ND), Powdery Mildew (PM), Septoria (ST), and Yellow rust (YR)) from Samsung Galaxy A3 with corresponding response time of the image size 2448 × 326 pixels.

promising accuracy in our work, although there are a number of false positives (a non-disease detected as a disease). In this stage of our work, for any particular disease detected, the user is required to seek expert advice. Our application size is less than 5 MB, but the OpenCV manager application (21 MB) is also required.

The system developed considers disease shape, overall texture and colour information inside the leaves regardless of the type or the shape of the leaf itself. Whilst the application is currently targeted at wheat diseases, it could be extended to other plants in the large-scale with similar disease characteristics and integrated with an intelligent decision support system to improve accuracy in classifying a particular disease.

Acknowledgement. I would like to thank Dr. David Gibson, University of Bristol who provided the FERA labelled images and the IU-ATC (EPSRC) for partially funding the project.

References

1. Gent, D.H., De Wolf, E., Pethybridge, S.J.: Perceptions of risk, risk aversion, and barriers to adoption of decision support systems and integrated pest management: an introduction. Am. Phytopathol. Soc. **101**, 640–643 (2013)
2. FERA: UK Food and environment research agency. http://www.cropmonitor.co.uk/
3. Lucas, J.A.: Plant Pathology and Plant Pathogens. Blackwell Science, Hoboken (1988)
4. Prasad, S., Peddoju, S.K., Ghosh, D.: AgroMobile: a cloud-based framework for agriculturists on mobile platform. Int. J. Adv. Sci. Technol. **59**, 41–52 (2013)
5. Xia, Y.: Intelligent diagnose system of wheat diseases based on android phone. J. Inf. Comput. Sci. **12**, 6845–6852 (2015)
6. Gibson, D., Burghardt, T., Campbell, N., Canagarajah, N.: Towards automating visual in-field monitoring of crop health. In: IEEE International Conference on Image Processing, pp. 3906–3910 (2015)
7. Tian, Y., Zhao, C., Lu, S., Guo, X.: SVM-based Multiple classifier system for recognition of wheat leaf diseases. In: Conference on Dependable Computing, Yichang, China, pp. 2–6 (2010)

8. Sarayloo, Z., Asemani, D.: Designing a classifier for automatic detection of fungal diseases in wheat plant. In: 23rd Iranian Conference on Electrical Engineering, pp. 1193–1197 (2015)

9. Siricharoen, P., Scotney, B., Morrow, P., Parr, G.: Automated wheat disease classification under controlled and uncontrolled image acquisition. In: International Conference on Image Analysis and Recognition, pp. 456–464 (2015)

10. Haralick, R.M., Shanmugam, K., Its'shak, D.: Textural features for image classification. IEEE Trans. Syst. Man Cybern. **3**, 613–621 (1973)

11. Tamura, H., Mori, S., Yamawaki, T.: Textural features corresponding to visual perception. IEEE Trans. Syst. Man Cybern. **8**, 460–473 (1978)

12. Suzuki, S., Abe, K.: Topological structural analysis of digitized binary images by border following. Comput. Vis. Graph. Image Process. **30**, 32–46 (1985)

13. Hsu, C.-W., Chang, C.-C., Lin, C.-J.: A practical guide to support vector classification. https://www.csie.ntu.edu.tw/~cjlin/libsvm/

14. He, H., Garcia, E.A.: Learning from imbalanced data. IEEE Trans. Knowl. Data Eng. **21**, 1263–1284 (2009)

Automatic Cattle Identification Using Graph Matching Based on Local Invariant Features

Fernando C. Monteiro[✉]

Polytechnic Institute of Bragança, Bragança, Portugal
`monteiro@ipb.pt`

Abstract. Cattle muzzle classification can be considered as a biometric identifier important to animal traceability systems to ensure the integrity of the food chain. This paper presents a muzzle-based classification system that combines local invariant features with graph matching. The proposed approach consists of three phases; namely feature extraction, graph matching, and matching refinement. The experimental results showed that our approach is superior than existing works as ours achieves an all correct identification for the tested images. In addition, the results proved that our proposed method achieved this high accuracy even if the testing images are rotated in various angles.

1 Introduction

Cattle identification and traceability plays an important role for disease control, vaccination management and also for maintaining consumer confidence in farm produce. Today's animal identification is based on ear notching, branding and RFID tags. These markers, however, may be lost and cannot prevent fraud in trade. The approach for beef cattle identification should be guaranteed to be permanent, difficult to faked, easy to acquire, inexpensive, accurate and humane [4]. The use of biometric identification methods is less prone to errors and frauds and should be explored.

The muzzle patterns or nose print of cattle are the uneven patterns on the surface of the skin of the nose. As fingerprints are unique to human beings, the ridges and valleys of each cow's muzzle form a pattern that is likewise unique to that animal as shown by Baranov et al. in their seminal paper [3].

In this paper, a new muzzle-based cattle identification method was proposed. This method consists of three steps: feature extraction, graph matching, and matching refinement. In the first step, the Scale Invariant Feature Transform (SIFT) technique [7] was used to extract local invariant features. In the second step, a graph matching technique that preserves structural information was used to reduce the features and to find the highest matching score images. In the matching refinement phase, the Maximum Likelihood Estimation SAmple Consensus (MLESAC) algorithm is used to estimate the inliers and to exclude the mismatched features. The animal identity is then assigned according to the highest similarity score between the tested image and the training one.

© Springer International Publishing Switzerland 2016
A. Campilho and F. Karray (Eds.): ICIAR 2016, LNCS 9730, pp. 792–800, 2016.
DOI: 10.1007/978-3-319-41501-7_88

The remainder of this paper is organized as follows: Sect. 2, describes the used materials and the proposed method. In Sect. 3, we present the results and the discussion of the findings. Finally, conclusions are drawn in Sect. 4.

2 Materials and Methods

This section explains about the data, previous methods and the proposed method for cattle identification based on digital muzzle photo data.

2.1 Data Acquisition

Several authors have used muzzle pattern through lifted ink prints on a piece of paper for the cattle identification [4,8]. However, the data capturing requires special skills (e.g. controlling the animal and getting the pattern on a paper), and the difficulties of the wet condition of the cattle nose and the cattle nervous feeling leading to smeared and motion blurred muzzle print [8]. Using muzzle photos to recognize animals by their muzzle pattern enables the identification from a distant point of view. Thus, the animal will not be stressed or affected in its natural behaviour.

The images have been collected from 15 animals with 5 muzzle images each. In Fig. 1 is shown a sample of muzzle images captured from three animals. Four of the collected muzzle photos of each individual are used as the training data and the rest is used as the testing data.

Fig. 1. A sample of images collected from three different animals.

2.2 Previous Methods

Noviyanto and Arymurthy [8] proposed a method for cattle identification using muzzle ink printed pattern. They convert the lifted on paper data into digital images using a scanner. Features from muzzle patterns are extracted with the SIFT technique. These features are used in a matching process based on the Euclidean distance and the number of matched features or matching score will be used as a measure of pattern similarity. They also proposed a matching refinement technique that uses the difference in orientation for every pair of matched points to exclude mismatched features.

Awad et al. [2] used SIFT to detect the interesting feature points for image matching. The muzzle image corresponding to the SIFT feature vector that has the shortest Euclidean distance to the input feature vector is considered as the most similar one. At the end of the matching process, the Random Sample Consensus (RANSAC) algorithm is used to remove the mismatched features, and ensure the robustness of the similarity score.

Tharwat et al. [9] used the Local Binary Patterns (LBP) technique to extract local features which are invariant to rotation and changes in the images (colour, texture, and pixel intensity). They also used Linear Discriminant Analysis to discriminate between different classes.

Ahmed et al. [1] used the Speeded-Up Robust Features (SURF) feature point's information obtained from a set of reference images. In the training phase, the SURF features are stored in matrices that represent the descriptors of each image. After that, two different classifiers are used, namely, Support Vector Machine classifier and minimum Euclidean distance to find image matching.

2.3   Local Invariant Feature Detection

In our muzzle pattern recognition approach, both a training and a test image are represented as graphs using representative features, where graph matching finds the pattern and its corresponding features by minimizing the distance between the two graphs. Since graph matching is a NP problem, a reduced set of relatively sparse salient features can be selected and their proper relations can be used to build the associated graph descriptor.

In the last years, SIFT features proved to perform well in face recognition and object detection. These features are based on the appearance of the object at particular interest points and are invariant to image scale and rotation [7]. They are also robust to changes in illumination and occlusion which are very important characteristics in the case of images acquired in an uncontrolled environment.

SIFT generates attributes representing the neighbour texture around the feature points of the image. To ensure scale invariance, SIFT uses a cascading filtering approach where each pixel is compared against neighbouring pixels in three scales to detect the local maxima and minima using the Difference of Gaussians. If the pixel is maximum or minimum off all neighbouring pixels, it is considered to be a potential feature. Following on, the detected feature is examined to determine the stability for each feature accordingly with their contrast and edge parameters. The features with low contrast and unstable locations along edges are rejected. The resulting set of points is then used to create the feature vectors.

SIFT features are obtained from a set of reference images and stored in a database. For image matching, the features of a test image is compared to this database. Previous works [7] usually used Euclidean distance to find candidate matching. However this approach does not preserve the point neighbouring structure of the features. In our work, to resolve the issue, we proposed to build an attributed graph from the SIFT features and then use graph matching to find its corresponding features in the reference image by minimizing the distortions of the two matching graphs.

2.4   Graph Matching

We define an attributed graph as a graph $G = (V, E, A)$ where V represents a set of nodes, E, the edges between nodes, and A, attributes. Each node $v_i \in V$ or edge $e_{ij} \in E$ has an associated attribute $a_i \in A$ or $a_{ij} \in A$. In feature correspondence problems, a node attribute a_i usually describes a locally extracted feature i in an image, and an edge attribute a_{ij} represents the relationship between two features i and j in the image.

Let $G = (V, E, A)$ and $G' = (V', E', A')$ be two attributed graphs. The objective of graph matching is to determine the correct correspondences between V and V' that best preserves the attributes between edges $e_{ij} \in E$ and $e_{i'j'} \in E'$. For each pair of edges $e_{ij} \in E$ and $e_{i'j'} \in E'$ there is an affinity or similarity $w_{ii';jj'} = f(a_{ij}, a_{i'j'})$ that measures the mutual consistency of attributes between the pairs of nodes.

For a pairwise edge similarity $w_{ii';jj'} \in \mathbb{R}_0^+$ between two matches (i, i') and (j, j'), we adopt the symmetric transfer error (STE) used in [5]. Given the two matches, the transfer error of (j, j') with respect to (i, i') is computed based on the homography transformation $\mathrm{T}_{ii'}$ and denoted by $d_{jj'|ii'}$ and formulated as

$$d_{jj'|ii'} = \| x_{j'} - \mathrm{T}_{ii'}(x_j) \|. \tag{1}$$

The lower the value of the transfer error the better the homography transfers the feature points v_j to that of feature $v_{j'}$. $(d_{jj'|ii'} + d_{j'j|i'i})/2$ represents the symmetric version of (i, i'). Thus, the STE similarity measure is given by

$$w_{ii';jj'} = \max\left(0, \alpha - \frac{d_{jj'|ii'} + d_{j'j|i'i} + d_{ii'|jj'} + d_{i'i|j'j}}{4}\right). \tag{2}$$

This measure is invariant to scale and deformation changes in the images. As in [5] we set $\alpha = 50$.

A solution of graph matching is defined as a subset of possible correspondences represented with an assignment binary matrix $\mathbf{X} \in \{0, 1\}^{n \times n'}$, where n denotes the number of nodes in each graph, such that $\mathbf{X}_{ii'} = 1$ implies that node v_i corresponds to node $v_{i'}$, e.g. feature i in image I is matched to feature i' in image I', and $\mathbf{X}_{ii'} = 0$ otherwise. The graph matching problem can be formulated as an integer quadratic program (IQP) [6], generally expressed as finding the indicator vector $\mathbf{x}^*$ that maximizes the quadratic score function as follows

$$\begin{aligned} \mathbf{x}^* &= \arg\max\left(\mathbf{x}^T \mathbf{W} \mathbf{x}\right) \\ s.t. \quad &\mathbf{x} \in \{0, 1\}^{n \times n'}, \quad \mathbf{X} \mathbf{1}_{n' \times 1} \leq \mathbf{1}_{n \times 1}, \quad \mathbf{X}^T \mathbf{1}_{n \times 1} \leq \mathbf{1}_{n' \times 1} \end{aligned} \tag{3}$$

where the constraints refer to the one-to-one matching from G to G'. $\mathbf{1}_{n \times 1}$ denotes an all-ones vector.

In general, no efficient algorithm exists that can guarantee the optimal restrictions since this IQP is NP-hard, and it becomes necessary to use an approximate solution [6]. Continuous relaxation of the IQP are among the most successful methods for non-bipartite graph matching. By dropping the two way matching constraints and relaxing integer constraints from Eq. 3, the original IQP could be approximated to a continuous problem as

$$\widetilde{\mathbf{x}}^* = \arg\max\left(\widetilde{\mathbf{x}}^T \mathbf{W} \widetilde{\mathbf{x}}\right), \qquad s.t. \qquad \widetilde{\mathbf{x}} \in [0,1]^{nn'} \tag{4}$$

whose solution is obtained by the eigenvector associated with the largest eigenvalue of $\mathbf{W}$. Assuming that the solution of the relaxed problem is close to the optimal discrete solution, the final solution is obtained by incorporating the matching constraints. As the graph matching module, we employed the reweighted random walk matching (RRWM) algorithm proposed by Cho and Lee [5]. The Hungarian algorithm is adopted for the final discretization.

2.5 Matching Refinement

Torr and Zisserman [10] proposed MLESAC (Maximum Likelihood Estimation SAmple Consensus) which is a generalization of the RANSAC estimator. The main idea is to evaluate the quality of the consensus set calculating its likelihood rather than just the number of inliers. Instead of using heurist measures, the MLESAC evaluates the likelihood of the model hypothesis. It estimates the ratio of valid correspondences and is solved by an expectation maximization algorithm.

3   Experimental Results

The muzzle images are captured in different illumination, rotation, quality levels and distance from the animal. Previous works standardized the set of muzzle images in orientation and scale [4]. In our work the images were used without any preprocessing operation. In every muzzle image, a rectangle region centred on the minimum line between the nostrils is taken as the region of interest (ROI). The illustration of the ROI is shown in Fig. 2.

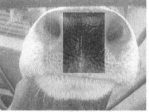

Fig. 2. Highlighted rectangle region is the ROI of the muzzle image.

The dataset was randomly divided into training and testing dataset. During the training phase, to prove that our proposed method was robust against rotation we increased the training dataset by rotating the images 20 degrees to each side, building a training dataset of 180 images (15 animals × 4 images × 3 orientations = 180 images).

3.1   Graph Matching Results

An attributed graph is constructed from the obtained SIFT features to each test image. The RRWM algorithm is then applied to obtain the maximum matching score accordingly to Eq. 3, normalized by the random walk step of RRWM. Figure 3 shown the score encoded in *jet* colour map with the minimum score represented by blue colour and the maximum score represented by the red colour.

Fig. 3. Matching similarity score encoded in the *jet* colour map. (Colour figure online)

From Fig. 4 we can see that there are misclassified matching features. To obtain a final matching score between two images we refined the graph matching result, using the MLESAC algorithm, in order to detect the inlier features that follows the same affine geometric transform, excluding the mismatched features.

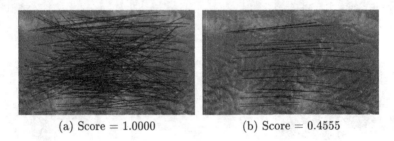

(a) Score = 1.0000   (b) Score = 0.4555

Fig. 4. Matching refinement by detecting affine transformation. (a) Graph matching detected features. (b) Refined matching features with the same affine transformation.

Our similarity score was used to find the training image with the highest score and should not be mistakenly used as the probability that an animal is identified. A high score is obtained when the majority of the matches follow the same affine transformation, increasing the probability that it is the same animal.

3.2   Robustness to Rotation

From the results of Fig. 5, it can be seen that even when the input images are rotated with different angles, our proposed method gives a high identification score. This proves that our method is robust against rotations in the image. This is a very important feature for animal identification system as it is very difficult to take accurate images from moving animals.

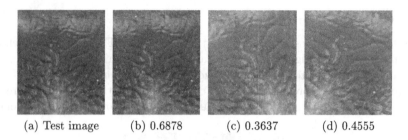

(a) Test image   (b) 0.6878   (c) 0.3637   (d) 0.4555

Fig. 5. Samples of rotated muzzle images in different angles. (a) Testing image. (b) Another image of the same animal. (c) Image (b) rotated 20 ° left. (d) Image (b) rotated 20 ° right. At the bottom, the matching similarity score with the testing image.

3.3 Identification Results

After the refinement graph matching process, the training image with the highest score is considered as the recognized animal. Some examples of graph matching refinement are shown in Fig. 6.

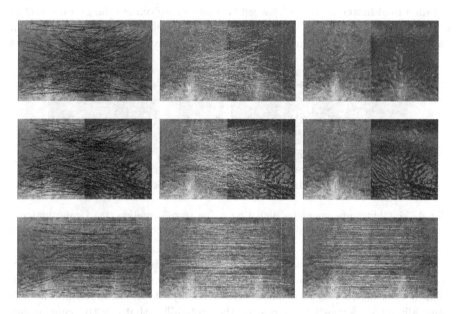

Fig. 6. Graph matching feature correspondence between animal 9 and animals 1, 5 and 9. Left: Feature matching similarity. Centre: Matching features. Right: Refined results.

The average score results obtained between five randomized animals are summarized in Table 1. The scores obtained between testing and training images of the same animal are always higher than the ones obtained with other animal images, even with image rotation. This is true for all the 15 tested animals.

Table 1. Matching averaged scores obtained between five animals.

Animal	Cattle 1	Cattle 5	Cattle 9	Cattle 12	Cattle 15
Cattle 1	**0.5116**	0.0376	0.0264	0.0220	0.0187
Cattle 5	0.0227	**0.2817**	0.0143	0.0220	0.0194
Cattle 9	0.0271	0.0190	**0.7292**	0.0197	0.0184
Cattle 12	0.0487	0.0245	0.0325	**0.4832**	0.0256
Cattle 15	0.0152	0.0127	0.0111	0.0101	**0.5412**

4 Conclusion

This paper proposed a cattle identification approach that uses muzzle images local invariant features as input to graph matching. The proposed method is robust from three perspectives. First, it uses the robustness of the SIFT features to image scale, shift, and rotation. Second, it uses a graph matching technique that preserves the node structure of the features. And third, it uses the MLESAC algorithm as a robust outlier detector for refining the graph matching results and ensure the robustness of the matching process. The results proved that our method achieved good results even if the images are rotated in several angles.

References

1. Ahmed, S., Gaber, T., Tharwat, A., Hassanien, A.E., Snael, V.: Muzzle-based cattle identification using speed up robust feature approach. In: International Conference on Intelligent Networking and Collaborative Systems, pp. 99–104 (2015)
2. Awad, A., Zawbaa, H., Mahmoud, H., Nabi, E., Fayed, R., Hassanien, A.: A robust cattle identification scheme using muzzle print images. In: Federated Conference on Computer Science and Information Systems, pp. 529–534 (2013)
3. Baranov, A.S., Graml, R., Pirchner, F., Schmid, D.O.: Breed differences and intrabreed genetic variability of dermatoglyphic pattern of cattle. J. Anim. Breed. Genet. **110**(1–6), 385–392 (1993)
4. Barry, B., Gonzales-Barron, U., McDonnell, K., Butler, F., Ward, S.: Using muzzle pattern recognition as a biometric approach for cattle identification. Trans. ASABE **50**(3), 1073–1080 (2007)
5. Cho, M., Lee, J., Lee, K.M.: Reweighted random walks for graph matching. In: Maragos, P., Paragios, N., Daniilidis, K. (eds.) ECCV 2010, Part V. LNCS, vol. 6315, pp. 492–505. Springer, Heidelberg (2010)
6. Cour, T., Srinivasan, P., Shi, J.: Balanced graph matching. Adv. Neural Inform. Process. Syst. **19**, 313–320 (2007)
7. Lowe, D.G.: Distinctive image features from scale-invariant keypoints. Int. J. Comput. Vision **60**(2), 91–110 (2004)
8. Noviyanto, A., Arymurthy, A.M.: Beef cattle identification based on muzzle pattern using a matching refinement technique in the SIFT method. Comput. Electron. Agric. **99**, 77–84 (2013)

9. Tharwat, A., Gaber, T., Hassanien, A.E.: Cattle identification based on muzzle images using gabor features and SVM classifier. In: Hassanien, A.E., Tolba, M.F., Taher Azar, A. (eds.) AMLTA 2014. CCIS, vol. 488, pp. 236–247. Springer, Heidelberg (2014)
10. Torr, P.H.S., Zisserman, A.: MLESAC: A new robust estimator with application to estimating image geometry. CVIU **78**(1), 138–156 (2000)

An Intelligent Vision-Based System Applied to Visual Quality Inspection of Beans

P.A. Belan, S.A. Araújo[(⊠)], and W.A.L. Alves

Informatics and Knowledge Management Graduate Program,
Universidade Nove de Julho - UNINOVE, São Paulo, SP, Brazil
{belan, saraujo, wonder}@uninove.br

Abstract. In this work it is proposed an intelligent vision-based system for automatic classification of beans most consumed in Brazil. The system is able to classify the grains contained in a sample according to their skin colors, and is composed by three modules: image acquisition and pre-processing; segmentation of grains and classification of grains. In the conducted experiments, we used an apparatus controlled by a PC that includes a conveyor belt, an image acquisition chamber and a camera, to simulate an industrial line of production. The results obtained in the performed experiments indicate that the proposed system could be applied to visual quality inspection of beans produced in Brazil, since one of the steps in this process is the measurement of the mixture contained in a sample, taking into account the skin color of grains, for determining the predominant class of product and, consequently, its market price.

Keywords: Beans · Computer vision · Quality inspection

1 Introduction

The use of computational tools in agriculture has increased in the last years and there are many examples in the literature where the efforts are focused on developing computational systems for agricultural tasks such as: visual quality inspection of fruits and vegetables [1–5] and analysis of seeds and grains [6–12].

Bean is one of the most agricultural products consumed in Brazil and is present in the daily diet of the Brazilian people. Currently, the country is the largest producer of beans and the product consumption per person reaches 19 kilos per year, on average. As most food products, its visual properties are very important to help the choice of consumers. In Brazil, the quality inspection of beans is conducted manually following a set of standards and procedures of the Brazilian Ministry of Agriculture, Livestock and Supply – BMALS [13]. This procedure is basically done as follows: a sample of 250 g is extracted from a batch of beans; from this sample, the foreign matter and impurities are separated using a circular sieve with holes of 5 mm of diameter and finally, a visual inspection of the sample (after extraction of foreign matter and impurities) is performed to determine the group, class and type of the product [13]. The group refers to the botanical species (I-*Phaseolus vulgaris* or II-*Vigna unguiculata*), the class identifies the beans according to their skin colors (Black, White, or Mixed Colors), independent of the group, and the type is related to defects found in the sample, such as broken, moldy,

A. Campilho and F. Karray (Eds.): ICIAR 2016, LNCS 9730, pp. 801–809, 2016.
DOI: 10.1007/978-3-319-41501-7_89

burned, crushed, damaged by insects (chopped), sprouted, wrinkled, stained, discolored and damaged by various other causes [11, 13].

The main problems assigned to manual inspection processes, including visual quality inspection of beans, are the inconvenience of time consuming, high cost, parallax errors and the difficulty of standardization of results [6]. Moreover, according to Patil et al. [12], the human detection capabilities can be affected by environment and personal factors. In this context, computational systems can be applied in these processes aiming to reduce operating costs and standardize results, providing competitive advantages for companies. In the case of Brazilian beans, a computer vision system (CVS) that counts automatically the number of grains of different classes and subclasses, taking into account their skin colors, is a very useful tool to determine the predominant class of product and, consequently, its market price.

Although we have a range of works in the literature dealing with analysis and classification of seeds and grains, there are only a few papers [6–12] addressing the development of systems for automatic classification of beans. The works [6–11] demonstrate the need and the importance of computational systems focused on visual inspection of beans. However, it is possible to observe in these works a severe limitation: the spacing required between grains in the samples to be analyzed, in order to facilitate the segmentation process. This occurs because it is a great challenge for a CVS to identify the edges of each grain when they are very close or glued to each other. The problem is that this limitation hinders the applicability of such systems in industrial processes, considering that an additional equipment to make the arrangement of grains/seeds in each sample to be analyzed is needed. In addition, these works do not consider beans produced and consumed in Brazil.

The limitation aforementioned was overcome by Araujo et al., [11], which proposed a robust correlation-based granulometry module for segmentation of grains and conducted several experiments considering most consumed Brazilian beans. However, the drawback of the system proposed in [11] is the time consumption.

In this work, we present an Intelligent Vision-based System for automatic classification of Brazilian beans aiming to improve the time consumption of the CVS proposed in [11], with similar accuracy. The proposed system employs the Wateshed Transform (WT) [14] with refinement heuristics for segmenting the grains and a Multilayer Perceptron neural network for classifying them.

2 Materials and Methods

The system proposed in this paper was implemented in C/C ++ using the library for Image Processing and Computer Vision OpenCV[1]. In the conducted experiments, we used the same apparatus showed in [11], which is controlled by a PC and is composed by a conveyor belt, an image acquisition chamber and a camera, and aims to simulate an industrial line of production. In addition, as in [11], we consider only the most consumed Brazilian beans (carioca, mulatto and black). The objectives in the performed

---

[1] Available at http://opencv.org/.

experiments were: i) evaluating the accuracy of developed system for classification of beans, based on their skin colors and ii) measuring the computational time spent by the system for analyzing an image, considering the same three datasets (DS) proposed by Araujo et al. [11] in their sampling mode experiments and named here as DS1, DS2 and DS3. In the acquisition of images from DS3 Araujo et al. [11] consider the same mixture of grains of DS1, but using grains extracted from different batches of beans.

In summary, we evaluated 300 images, each one containing 100 mixed grains, as described in Table 1. Each dataset contain 100 images, divided into 10 subsets, according to the mixture of grains black, mulatto and carioca. Thus, in all analyzed images there are 30,000 grains of beans. Our results (success rate of classification and computational cost) were compared with results achieved in [11].

Table 1. Mixture of grains in the images from DS1, DS2 and DS3.

Subset	Number of images in the Subset	Number of carioca grains in each image		Number of mulatto grains in each image		Number of black grains in each image	
		DS1, DS3	DS2	DS1, DS3	DS2	DS1, DS3	DS2
1	10	100	20	0	20	0	60
2	10	95	20	5	60	0	20
3	10	95	60	0	20	5	20
4	10	90	40	5	40	5	20
5	10	85	40	10	20	5	40
6	10	85	20	5	40	10	40
7	10	80	30	10	30	10	40
8	10	85	30	15	40	0	30
9	10	85	40	0	30	15	30
10	10	70	34	15	33	15	33

3 Proposed Intelligent Vision-Based System

The proposed system is composed by three modules, which are explained in detail in the following subsections.

3.1 Image Acquisition and Pre-processing

The input of proposed system is a RGB color image (I) with 800×600 pixels (Fig. 1). The first step is to convert this image to CIELab color space, which facilitates the extraction of background, since it separates the information of chromaticity and luminance. In the sequence, using appropriate thresholds (i.e. t_L, t_a and t_b) for color components L, a and b (Eq. 1), the image I is binarized, as showed in Fig. 2.

$$b(x,y) = \begin{cases} 0, & \text{if } I(x,y).L < = t_L \text{ and } I(x,y).a < = t_a \text{ and } I(x,y).b < = t_b \\ 1, & \text{Otherwise} \end{cases} \quad (1)$$

where: $I(x, y).L$, $I(x, y).a$ and $I(x, y).b$ are the color components of pixel (x, y) from image I in the CIELab color space and b is the binarized image. Unfortunately, it is not easy to define automatically the thresholds t_L, t_a and t_b.

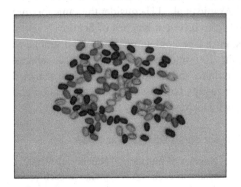

Fig. 1. Input image. (Color figure online)

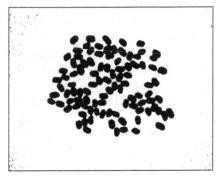

Fig. 2. Binarized image.

Finally, to eliminate the remaining noise in the image b, a mathematical morphology operation of erosion, with a square structuring element (2×2), is employed generating the image showed in the Fig. 3, in which the regions without grains are discarded to accelerate the processing time of the next module.

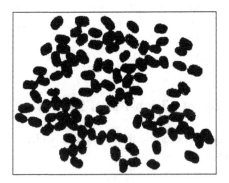

Fig. 3. Final result of pre-processing module.

3.2 Segmentation of Grains

In this module, the well-known region-based segmentation approach called Watershed Transform (WT) [14] is used to segment the grains, as showed in Fig. 4. Generally, WT suffers with the problem of over-segmentation, especially if the image to be segmented is corrupted with different kinds of noise. For overcoming this problem we applied the erosion in the binarized image, as explained before. In addition, grains (connected components – CCs) can be erroneously merged or splitted. Thus, for improving the segmentation by WT, we employed additional operations of merging and splitting using heuristic information (i.e. average size of CCs, center of CCs, distance between the centers of CCs and orientation of CCs). The merger of two CCs (grains) is made when the distance between their centers is smaller than the average size of a grain. In the other hand, the splitting of a CC is applied when its area is at least twice the average size of a grain. This procedure employs as heuristics the center, orientation and size of CC to split it up to 5 grains. Examples of these operations are showed in Fig. 5, which illustrates two cases of merging, where the grains are connected by a black line and one case of splitting where two grains are separated by a white line. Unfortunately, these operations do not totally avoid the existence of false positive and false negative cases.

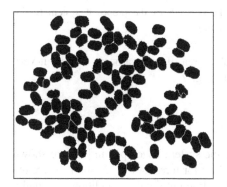

Fig. 4. Output of segmentation by WT.

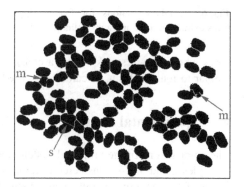

Fig. 5. Improved segmentation with the use of merging (m) and splitting (s).

3.3   Classification of Grains

In this last module, the proposed system maps out each segmented grain to one of the three classes of beans, that is, carioca (C), mulatto (M) or black (B), as showed in Fig. 7, using a Multilayer Perceptron neural network (MLP-ANN) with the following architecture: 6 neurons in the input layer, two hidden layers with 30 and 45 neurons and only one neuron in the output layer to indicate the class of grain. Other configuration parameters were: stop criteria = number of epochs (500) or error 10^{-5} and learning rate = 0·05.

The vector of features used for classification task is composed by average values of 6 color components of pixels belonging to each grain (extracted form input image), considering RGB and CIELab color spaces. To accelerate the operations of features extraction and classification, only the pixels over 10 radial lines (defined experimentally) from the center of a grain were considered, as showed in Fig. 6. Although it may seem easy the classification of grains, some mistakes can occur because there are many

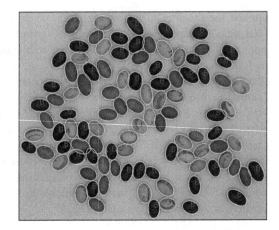

Fig. 6. Radial projections for features extraction. (Color figure online)

Fig. 7. Final result of the proposed system (Color figure online)

cases where brown streaks cover a considerable area of carioca bean, making it very similar to mulatto bean, as can be observed in Fig. 7.

4 Experimental Results

The comparisons of the proposed system and the system developed in [11] are shown in Tables 2 and 3. We considered different values for thresholds t_L, t_a and t_b, since the images from the three datasets were acquired in different lighting conditions. Actually, they are very important for the success of last two modules. In the Table 3, the dataset well as the used thresholds t_L, t_a and t_b, are placed in the first column. The following columns present, respectively, the subset and the amount of grains carioca, black and mulatto; the amount of true positives (TP), false positives (FP) and of false negative (FN) cases in the segmentation of grains and, finally, the success rates in segmentation and classification tasks.

The results presented in Table 3 show the high success rates of the proposed system with small numbers of FP and FN cases for DS1. Actually, the system has achieved the best results for this dataset. For DS2, the system present the worst classification success hate (98·64 %). Probably, it occurred because the images of DS2 are darkest than images from two other datasets. With respect to DS3, the proposed system has achieved high success rate in the classification task, but it shows the worst result with respect to segmentation. In this dataset, only 9,480 out of 10,000 grains were correctly segmented.

As can be seen in Table 3, the proposed system was able to detect correctly 97·39 % of grains in all 300 analyzed images. Although this rate is lower than that one developed by Araújo et al. [11], the proposed system is about 18 times faster than the their system, as demonstrated in Table 2. With respect to classification task, the system proposed in this work classified correctly 28,966 out of 29,217 grains detected by segmentation module (99·14 %), following the high rates described in [11]. In

Table 2. Comparison of computational cost for processing a sample image (800 × 600 pixels).

Module	Time (in seconds) spent by the system developed in Araújo et al. [11]	Time (in seconds) spent by the proposed system (s)
Image acquisition and pre-processing	6	0.1
Segmentation of grains	11	0.8
Classification of grains	1	0.1
Total	18	1.0

Table 3. Results of proposed intelligent vision-based system for DS1, DS2 and DS3.

	subset	Segmentation of grains				Classification
		TP	FN	FP	Success rate (%)	Success rate (%)
DS1 $t_L=45$, $t_a=5$ and $t_b=20$	1	997	3	1	99.70	99.60
	2	1000	0	0	100.00	99.60
	3	1000	0	2	100.00	99.80
	4	996	4	2	99.60	99.40
	5	998	2	1	99.80	99.50
	6	1000	0	0	100.00	100.00
	7	1000	0	3	100.00	99.70
	8	993	7	2	99.30	99.10
	9	995	5	0	99.50	99.50
	10	995	5	0	99.50	99.50
	Subtotal	**9,974**	**26**	**11**	**99.70**	**99.57**
DS2 $t_L=35$, $t_a=10$ and $t_b=22$	1	982	18	1	98.20	98.27
	2	973	27	16	97.30	98.89
	3	971	29	22	97.10	99.30
	4	983	17	11	98.30	99.40
	5	977	23	12	97.70	98.89
	6	966	34	14	96.60	97.96
	7	976	24	3	97.60	97.85
	8	985	15	4	98.50	98.89
	9	977	23	11	97.70	98.79
	10	973	27	9	97.30	98.17
	Subtotal	**9,763**	**237**	**103**	**97.60**	**98.64**
DS3 $t_L=30$, $t_a=8$ and $t_b=20$	1	951	49	42	95.10	99.30
	2	928	72	63	92.80	99.09
	3	940	60	50	94.00	98.99
	4	898	102	89	89.80	98.68
	5	940	60	55	94.00	99.50
	6	960	40	39	96.00	99.90
	7	944	56	52	94.40	99.60
	8	970	30	19	97.00	98.89
	9	972	28	24	97.20	99.60
	10	977	23	10	97.70	98.68
	Subtotal	**9,480**	**520**	**443**	**94.80**	**99.22**
	Total	**29,217**	**783**	**557**	**97.39**	**99.14**

summary, even though the success rates of proposed system were not better than those ones achieved in [11], it outperforms the systems presented in [6, 9], and represents a good alternative for online beans inspection, especially because its speed in processing a sample image.

5   Conclusions and Future Works

The overall success rates of proposed vision-based system in the segmentation (97·39 %) and classification (99·14 %) tasks indicate that it could be used as part of visual quality inspection process of Brazilian beans, for determining the class of the product. In addition, it could be used in online inspection of beans, especially because its speed. However, it is clear that improvements are necessary to make the system more robust. In future works we intend to improve it, in order to minimize the errors in the segmentation task and conduct experiments in continuous mode (online inspection).

Acknowledgments. The authors would like to thank UNINOVE, FAPESP–São Paulo Research Foundation by financial support (#2014/09194-5) and CNPq–Brazilian National Research Council for the scholarship granted to S. A. Araújo (#311971/2015-6).

References

1. Liu, J., Yang, W.W., Wang, Y., Rababah, T.M., Walker, L.T.: Optimizing machine vision based applications in agricultural products by artificial neural network. Int. J. of Food Eng. **7**(3), 1–23 (2011)
2. Savakar, D.G.: Identification and classification of bulk fruits images using artificial neural networks. Int. J. Eng. Innovative Tech. **1**(3), 36–40 (2012)
3. Rodríguez-Pulido, F.J., Gordillo, B., González-Miret, M.L., Heredia, F.J.: Analysis of food appearance properties by computer vision applying ellipsoids to colour data. Comput. Electron. Agric. **99**, 108–115 (2013)
4. Stegmayer, G., Milone, D.H., Garran, S., Burdyn, L.: Automatic recognition of quarantine citrus diseases. Expert Syst. Appl. **40**(9), 3512–3517 (2013)
5. Gómez-Sanchis, J., Martín-Guerrero, J.D., Soria-Olivas, E., Martínez-Sober, M., Magda-lena-Benedito, R., Blasco, J.: Detecting rottenness caused by Penicillium genus fungi in citrus fruits using machine learning techniques. Expert Syst. Appl. **39**(1), 780–785 (2012)
6. Kiliç, K., Boyacl, I.H., Köksel, H., Küsmenoglu, I.A.: Classification system for beans using computer vision system and artificial neural networks. J. Food Eng. **78**(3), 897–904 (2007)
7. Aguilera, J.M., Cipriano, A., Eraña, M., Lillo, I., Mery, D., Soto A. Computer Vision for Quality Control in Latin American Food Industry: a Case Study, In: Proc. of Int. Conf. on Comp.Vision, Rio de Janeiro (2007) 1–11
8. Venora, G., Grillo, O., Ravalli, C., Cremonini, R.: Tuscany beans landraces, on-line identification from seeds inspection by image analysis and linear discriminant analysis. Agrochimica **51**(4–5), 254–268 (2007)
9. Venora, G., Grillo, O., Ravalli, C., Cremonini, R.: Identification of Italian landraces of bean (Phaseolus vulgaris L.) using an image analysis system. Sci. Hortic. **121**(4), 410–418 (2009)

10. Laurent, B., Ousman, B., Dzudie, T., Carl, M.F.M., Emmanuel, T.: Digital camera images processing of hard-to-cook beans. J. Eng. Tech. Res. **2**(9), 177–188 (2010)
11. Araújo, S.A., Pessota, J.H., Kim, H.Y.: Beans quality inspection using correlation-based granulometry. Eng. Appl. Artif. Intell. **40**, 84–94 (2015)
12. Patil, N.K., Yadahalli, R.M., Pujari, J.: Comparison between HSV and YCbCr color model color-texture based classification of the food grains. Int. J. Comput. Appl. **34**(4), 51–57 (2011)
13. BMALS–Brazilian Ministry of Agriculture, Livestock and Supply. Law n° 6·305, Decree n° 93·563, of 11/11/86, normative instruction n° 12. http://extranet.agricultura.gov.br/sislegis/action/detalhaAto.do?method=consultarLegislacaoFederal. Accessed April 2011
14. Najman, L., Talbot, H.: Mathematical Morphology: From Theory to Applications. Wiley, Hoboken (2010)

Obituaries

Remembering the ICIAR Founding Chair: Mohamed Kamel

Aurélio Campilho

ICIAR Chair, Professor Faculty of Engineering,
University of Porto, Porto, Portugal

The ICIAR (International Conference on Image Analysis and Recognition) community mourns the loss of our esteemed ICIAR founding chair, the late Dr. Mohamed Kamel, who passed peacefully away in December, 2015.

Dr. Mohamed Kamel conceived the ICIAR series of conferences as an opportunity for cooperation among researchers in Portugal and Canada, together with many authors coming from other countries, in the field of Image Analysis and Recognition. From 2004, the conference was organized annually, in several locations that *"share in common the blue of the sea* (quoting Mohamed)", such as Póvoa do Varzim and Vilamoura in Portugal, or Halifax and Burnaby in Canada.

ICIAR will continue to be held in different venues as certainly Mohamed would wish. This will maintain his memory and legate alive.

In 1989, almost thirty years ago, I was fortunate to know Mohamed in a conference in Spain. His pioneering work and outstanding scientific contributions were an inspiring reference for all in the Image Analysis and Recognition community. I was extremely honored to cooperate with Mohamed in several activities, and in particular to co-chair the ICIAR conferences and co-edit twelve Springer LNCS proceedings.

© Springer International Publishing Switzerland 2016
A. Campilho and F. Karray (Eds.): ICIAR 2016, LNCS 9730, pp. 813–814, 2016.
DOI: 10.1007/978-3-319-41501-7

Professor Mohamed Kamel visited many times Portugal, spent six months at FEUP - Faculty of Engineering, University of Porto as a Visiting Professor. He was part of the Advisory Committee of the Department of Electrical and Computer Engineering from FEUP. I and members of my research group were honored to interact with Mohamed during these three decades and this tight collaboration resulted in several co-authorship publications.

But most importantly, Mohamed was a close friend. He will be much missed.

Remembering an IEEE Pioneer: Mohamed Kamel

Fakhri Karray

University Research Chair Professor,
Department of Electrical and Computer Engineering,
University of Waterloo, Waterloo, Canada

The pattern recognition and intelligent systems community mourns the passing of one of its pioneers and leading researchers, the late Dr. Mohamed Kamel, a University Research Chair Professor in Cooperative Intelligent Systems at the University of Waterloo. Dr. Kamel passed peacefully the evening of December 4, 2015. Dr. Kamel joined the faculty of Engineering at the University of Waterloo in 1985. Since 2004, he was affiliated with the department of Electrical and Computer Engineering as Canada Research Chair and later as University Research Chair professor. He retired in the summer of 2015 and was named Professor Emeritus.

Professor Kamel has been a pioneer in the fields of Pattern Recognition and Intelligent Systems. His contributions to the practice, research and education in these fields have been truly remarkable and outstanding. They earned him international recognition and honors including: Fellow of the Royal Society of Canada, Life IEEE fellow, EIC fellow, CAE fellow, IAPR fellow, IEEE Canada McNaughton Award, membership of editorial boards of international journals and several best paper awards.

This article is provided with permission from Autosoft Journal.

© Springer International Publishing Switzerland 2016
A. Campilho and F. Karray (Eds.): ICIAR 2016, LNCS 9730, pp. 815–816, 2016.
DOI: 10.1007/978-3-319-41501-7

Dr. Kamel's work, publications and professional activities have benefited and influenced faculty members and students in Electrical and Computer Engineering, Systems Design Engineering and Computer Science Departments. His graduates (more than 90 PhD and M.Sc candidates) are successful professionals and making excellent contributions in academia and industry throughout the world.

Dr. Kamel has cooperated with many professors from many departments at the University and was a co-founding member of the Center for Pattern Analysis and Machine Intelligence (CPAMI), which he directed till his passing. Dr. Kamel was very collegial, cooperative, supportive of others and has mentored several junior faculty members. He has also cooperated with many researchers around the globe such as in the US, Portugal, Egypt, Hong Kong, to name a few.

In 1986, Kamel co-founded Virtek Vision International with Tom King, Andrew Wong and Bob Nally. Virtek commercialized research developed in the Pattern Analysis and Machine Intelligence Laboratory and was acquired by Gerber Technology in 2008. Professor Kamel served on its board and as Chair of Virtek's Technology Advisory Group.

He will be sorely missed by his former students, colleagues at the University and friends from around the world and by the research community at large. The passing of Dr. Kamel is a major loss to all those who have known him and to the global scientific community. A memorial event will be held at the University of Waterloo to honor the life and achievements of Dr. Mohamed Kamel.

Author Index

Printed in the United States
By Bookmasters

Foreword

Welcome to the proceedings of the 2016 edition of the European Conference on Computer Vision held in Amsterdam! It is safe to say that the European Conference on Computer Vision is one of the top conferences in computer vision. It is good to reiterate the history of the conference to see the broad base the conference has built in its 13 editions. First held in 1990 in Antibes (France), it was followed by subsequent conferences in Santa Margherita Ligure (Italy) in 1992, Stockholm (Sweden) in 1994, Cambridge (UK) in 1996, Freiburg (Germany) in 1998, Dublin (Ireland) in 2000, Copenhagen (Denmark) in 2002, Prague (Czech Republic) in 2004, Graz (Austria) in 2006, Marseille (France) in 2008, Heraklion (Greece) in 2010, Florence (Italy) in 2012, and Zürich (Switzerland) in 2014.

For the 14th edition, many people worked hard to provide attendees with a most warm welcome while enjoying the best science. The Program Committee, Bastian Leibe, Jiri Matas, Nicu Sebe, and Max Welling, did an excellent job. Apart from the scientific program, the workshops were selected and handled by Hervé Jégou and Gang Hua, and the tutorials by Jacob Verbeek and Rita Cucchiara. Thanks for the great job. The coordination with the subsequent ACM Multimedia offered an opportunity to expand the tutorials with an additional invited session, offered by the University of Amsterdam and organized together with the help of ACM Multimedia.

Of the many people who worked hard as local organizers, we would like to single out Martine de Wit of the UvA Conference Office, who delicately and efficiently organized the main body. Also the local organizers Hamdi Dibeklioglu, Efstratios Gavves, Jan van Gemert, Thomas Mensink, and Mihir Jain had their hands full. As a venue, we chose the Royal Theatre Carré located on the canals of the Amstel River in downtown Amsterdam. Space in Amsterdam is sparse, so it was a little tighter than usual. The university lent us their downtown campuses for the tutorials and the workshops. A relatively new thing was the industry and the sponsors for which Ronald Poppe and Peter de With did a great job, while Andy Bagdanov and John Schavemaker arranged the demos. Michael Wilkinson took care to make Yom Kippur as comfortable as possible for those for whom it is an important day. We thank Marc Pollefeys, Alberto del Bimbo, and Virginie Mes for their advice and help behind the scenes. We thank all the anonymous volunteers for their hard and precise work. We also thank our generous sponsors. Their support is an essential part of the program. It is good to see such a level of industrial interest in what our community is doing!

Amsterdam does not need any introduction. Please emerge yourself but do not drown in it, have a nice time.

October 2016

Theo Gevers
Arnold Smeulders

website always up to date. Finally, the preparation of these proceedings would not have been possible without the diligent effort of the publication chairs, Albert Ali Salah and Robby Tan, and of Anna Kramer from Springer.

October 2016

Bastian Leibe
Jiri Matas
Nicu Sebe
Max Welling

Preface

Welcome to the proceedings of the 2016 European Conference on Computer Vision (ECCV 2016) held in Amsterdam, The Netherlands. We are delighted to present this volume reflecting a strong and exciting program, the result of an extensive review process. In total, we received 1,561 paper submissions. Of these, 81 violated the ECCV submission guidelines or did not pass the plagiarism test and were rejected without review. We employed the iThenticate software (www.ithenticate.com) for plagiarism detection. Of the remaining papers, 415 were accepted (26.6 %): 342 as posters (22.6 %), 45 as spotlights (2.9 %), and 28 as oral presentations (1.8 %). The spotlights – short, five-minute podium presentations – are novel to ECCV and were introduced after their success at the CVPR 2016 conference. All orals and spotlights are presented as posters as well. The selection process was a combined effort of four program co-chairs (PCs), 74 area chairs (ACs), 1,086 Program Committee members, and 77 additional reviewers.

As PCs, we were primarily responsible for the design and execution of the review process. Beyond administrative rejections, we were involved in acceptance decisions only in the very few cases where the ACs were not able to agree on a decision. PCs, as is customary in the field, were not allowed to co-author a submission. General co-chairs and other co-organizers played no role in the review process, were permitted to submit papers, and were treated as any other author.

Acceptance decisions were made by two independent ACs. There were 74 ACs, selected by the PCs according to their technical expertise, experience, and geographical diversity (41 from European, five from Asian, two from Australian, and 26 from North American institutions). The ACs were aided by 1,086 Program Committee members to whom papers were assigned for reviewing. There were 77 additional reviewers, each supervised by a Program Committee member. The Program Committee was selected from committees of previous ECCV, ICCV, and CVPR conferences and was extended on the basis of suggestions from the ACs and the PCs. Having a large pool of Program Committee members for reviewing allowed us to match expertise while bounding reviewer loads. Typically five papers, but never more than eight, were assigned to a Program Committee member. Graduate students had a maximum of four papers to review.

The ECCV 2016 review process was in principle double-blind. Authors did not know reviewer identities, nor the ACs handling their paper(s). However, anonymity becomes difficult to maintain as more and more submissions appear concurrently on arXiv.org. This was not against the ECCV 2016 double submission rules, which followed the practice of other major computer vision conferences in the recent past. The existence of arXiv publications, mostly not peer-reviewed, raises difficult problems with the assessment of unpublished, concurrent, and prior art, content overlap, plagiarism, and self-plagiarism. Moreover, it undermines the anonymity of submissions. We found that not all cases can be covered by a simple set of rules. Almost all controversies during the review process were related to the arXiv issue. Most of the reviewer inquiries were resolved by giving the benefit of the doubt to ECCV authors. However, the problem will have to be discussed by the community so that consensus is found on how to handle the issues brought by publishing on arXiv.

Particular attention was paid to handling conflicts of interest. Conflicts of interest between ACs, Program Committee members, and papers were identified based on the authorship of ECCV 2016 submissions, on the home institutions, and on previous collaborations of all researchers involved. To find institutional conflicts, all authors, Program Committee members, and ACs were asked to list the Internet domains of their current institutions. To find collaborators, the Researcher.cc database (http://researcher.cc/), funded by the Computer Vision Foundation, was used to find any co-authored papers in the period 2012–2016. We pre-assigned approximately 100 papers to each AC, based on affinity scores from the Toronto Paper Matching System. ACs then bid on these, indicating their level of expertise. Based on these bids, and conflicts of interest, approximately 40 papers were assigned to each AC. The ACs then suggested seven reviewers from the pool of Program Committee members for each paper, in ranked order, from which three were chosen automatically by CMT (Microsofts Academic Conference Management Service), taking load balancing and conflicts of interest into account.

The initial reviewing period was five weeks long, after which reviewers provided reviews with preliminary recommendations. With the generous help of several last-minute reviewers, each paper received three reviews. Submissions with all three reviews suggesting rejection were independently checked by two ACs and if they agreed, the manuscript was rejected at this stage ("early rejects"). In total, 334 manuscripts (22.5 %) were early-rejected, reducing the average AC load to about 30.

Authors of the remaining submissions were then given the opportunity to rebut the reviews, primarily to identify factual errors. Following this, reviewers and ACs discussed papers at length, after which reviewers finalized their reviews and gave a final recommendation to the ACs. Each manuscript was evaluated independently by two ACs who were not aware of each others, identities. In most of the cases, after extensive discussions, the two ACs arrived at a common decision, which was always adhered to by the PCs. In the very few borderline cases where an agreement was not reached, the PCs acted as tie-breakers. Owing to the rapid expansion of the field, which led to an unexpectedly large increase in the number of submissions, the size of the venue became a limiting factor and a hard upper bound on the number of accepted papers had to be imposed. We were able to increase the limit by replacing one oral session by a poster session. Nevertheless, this forced the PCs to reject some borderline papers that could otherwise have been accepted.

We want to thank everyone involved in making the ECCV 2016 possible. First and foremost, the success of ECCV 2016 depended on the quality of papers submitted by the authors, and on the very hard work of the ACs, the Program Committee members, and the additional reviewers. We are particularly grateful to Rene Vidal for his continuous support and sharing experience from organizing ICCV 2015, to Laurent Charlin for the use of the Toronto Paper Matching System, to Ari Kobren for the use of the Researcher.cc tools, to the Computer Vision Foundation (CVF) for facilitating the use of the iThenticate plagiarism detection software, and to Gloria Zen and Radu-Laurentiu Vieriu for setting up CMT and managing the various tools involved. We also owe a debt of gratitude for the support of the Amsterdam local organizers, especially Hamdi Dibeklioglu for keeping the

Organization

General Chairs

Theo Gevers   University of Amsterdam, The Netherlands
Arnold Smeulders   University of Amsterdam, The Netherlands

Program Committee Co-chairs

Bastian Leibe   RWTH Aachen, Germany
Jiri Matas   Czech Technical University, Czech Republic
Nicu Sebe   University of Trento, Italy
Max Welling   University of Amsterdam, The Netherlands

Honorary Chair

Jan Koenderink   Delft University of Technology, The Netherlands
     and KU Leuven, Belgium

Advisory Program Chair

Luc van Gool   ETH Zurich, Switzerland

Advisory Workshop Chair

Josef Kittler   University of Surrey, UK

Advisory Conference Chair

Alberto del Bimbo   University of Florence, Italy

Local Arrangements Chairs

Hamdi Dibeklioglu   Delft University of Technology, The Netherlands
Efstratios Gavves   University of Amsterdam, The Netherlands
Jan van Gemert   Delft University of Technology, The Netherlands
Thomas Mensink   University of Amsterdam, The Netherlands
Michael Wilkinson   University of Groningen, The Netherlands

Workshop Chairs

Hervé Jégou   Facebook AI Research, USA
Gang Hua   Microsoft Research Asia, China

Tutorial Chairs

Jacob Verbeek   Inria Grenoble, France
Rita Cucchiara   University of Modena and Reggio Emilia, Italy

Poster Chairs

Jasper Uijlings   University of Edinburgh, UK
Roberto Valenti   Sightcorp, The Netherlands

Publication Chairs

Albert Ali Salah   Boğaziçi University, Turkey
Robby T. Tan   Yale-NUS College and National University
                                   of Singapore, Singapore

Video Chair

Mihir Jain   University of Amsterdam, The Netherlands

Demo Chairs

John Schavemaker   Twnkls, The Netherlands
Andy Bagdanov   University of Florence, Italy

Social Media Chair

Efstratios Gavves   University of Amsterdam, The Netherlands

Industrial Liaison Chairs

Ronald Poppe   Utrecht University, The Netherlands
Peter de With   Eindhoven University of Technology, The Netherlands

Conference Coordinator, Accommodation, and Finance

Conference Office
Martine de Wit   University of Amsterdam, The Netherlands
Melanie Venverloo   University of Amsterdam, The Netherlands
Niels Klein   University of Amsterdam, The Netherlands

Area Chairs

Radhakrishna Achanta	Ecole Polytechnique Fédérale de Lausanne, Switzerland
Antonis Argyros	FORTH and University of Crete, Greece
Michael Bronstein	Universitá della Svizzera Italiana, Switzerland
Gabriel Brostow	University College London, UK
Thomas Brox	University of Freiburg, Germany
Barbara Caputo	Sapienza University of Rome, Italy
Miguel Carreira-Perpinan	University of California, Merced, USA
Ondra Chum	Czech Technical University, Czech Republic
Daniel Cremers	Technical University of Munich, Germany
Rita Cucchiara	University of Modena and Reggio Emilia, Italy
Trevor Darrell	University of California, Berkeley, USA
Andrew Davison	Imperial College London, UK
Fernando de la Torre	Carnegie Mellon University, USA
Piotr Dollar	Facebook AI Research, USA
Vittorio Ferrari	University of Edinburgh, UK
Charless Fowlkes	University of California, Irvine, USA
Jan-Michael Frahm	University of North Carolina at Chapel Hill, USA
Mario Fritz	Max Planck Institute, Germany
Pascal Fua	Ecole Polytechnique Fédérale de Lausanne, Switzerland
Juergen Gall	University of Bonn, Germany
Peter Gehler	University of Tübingen — Max Planck Institute, Germany
Andreas Geiger	Max Planck Institute, Germany
Ross Girshick	Facebook AI Research, USA
Kristen Grauman	University of Texas at Austin, USA
Abhinav Gupta	Carnegie Mellon University, USA
Hervé Jégou	Facebook AI Research, USA
Fredrik Kahl	Lund University, Sweden
Iasonas Kokkinos	Ecole Centrale Paris, France
Philipp Krähenbühl	University of California, Berkeley, USA
Pawan Kumar	University of Oxford, UK
Christoph Lampert	Institute of Science and Technology Austria, Austria
Hugo Larochelle	Université de Sherbrooke, Canada
Neil Lawrence	University of Sheffield, UK
Svetlana Lazebnik	University of Illinois at Urbana-Champaign, USA
Honglak Lee	Stanford University, USA
Kyoung Mu Lee	Seoul National University, Republic of Korea
Vincent Lepetit	Graz University of Technology, Austria
Hongdong Li	Australian National University, Australia
Julien Mairal	Inria, France
Yasuyuki Matsushita	Osaka University, Japan
Nassir Navab	Technical University of Munich, Germany

Sebastian Nowozin	Microsoft Research, Cambridge, UK
Tomas Pajdla	Czech Technical University, Czech Republic
Maja Pantic	Imperial College London, UK
Devi Parikh	Virginia Tech, USA
Thomas Pock	Graz University of Technology, Austria
Elisa Ricci	FBK Technologies of Vision, Italy
Bodo Rosenhahn	Leibniz-University of Hannover, Germany
Stefan Roth	Technical University of Darmstadt, Germany
Carsten Rother	Technical University of Dresden, Germany
Silvio Savarese	Stanford University, USA
Bernt Schiele	Max Planck Institute, Germany
Konrad Schindler	ETH Zürich, Switzerland
Cordelia Schmid	Inria, France
Cristian Sminchisescu	Lund University, Sweden
Noah Snavely	Cornell University, USA
Sabine Süsstrunk	Ecole Polytechnique Fédérale de Lausanne, Switzerland
Qi Tian	University of Texas at San Antonio, USA
Antonio Torralba	Massachusetts Institute of Technology, USA
Zhuowen Tu	University of California, San Diego, USA
Raquel Urtasun	University of Toronto, Canada
Joost van de Weijer	Universitat Autònoma de Barcelona, Spain
Laurens van der Maaten	Facebook AI Research, USA
Nuno Vasconcelos	University of California, San Diego, USA
Andrea Vedaldi	University of Oxford, UK
Xiaogang Wang	Chinese University of Hong Kong, Hong Kong, SAR China
Jingdong Wang	Microsoft Research Asia, China
Lior Wolf	Tel Aviv University, Israel
Ying Wu	Northwestern University, USA
Dong Xu	University of Sydney, Australia
Shuicheng Yan	National University of Singapore, Singapore
MingHsuan Yang	University of California, Merced, USA
Ramin Zabih	Cornell NYC Tech, USA
Larry Zitnick	Facebook AI Research, USA

Technical Program Committee

Austin Abrams	Pulkit Agrawal	Andrea Albarelli
Supreeth Achar	Jorgen Ahlberg	Alexandra Albu
Tameem Adel	Haizhou Ai	Saad Ali
Khurrum Aftab	Zeynep Akata	Daniel Aliaga
Lourdes Agapito	Ijaz Akhter	Marina Alterman
Sameer Agarwal	Karteek Alahari	Hani Altwaijry
Aishwarya Agrawal	Xavier Alameda-Pineda	Jose M. Alvarez

Mitsuru Ambai
Mohamed Amer
Senjian An
Cosmin Ancuti
Juan Andrade-Cetto
Marco Andreetto
Elli Angelopoulou
Relja Arandjelovic
Helder Araujo
Pablo Arbelaez
Chetan Arora
Carlos Arteta
Kalle Astroem
Nikolay Atanasov
Vassilis Athitsos
Mathieu Aubry
Yannis Avrithis
Hossein Azizpour
Artem Babenko
Andrew Bagdanov
Yuval Bahat
Xiang Bai
Lamberto Ballan
Arunava Banerjee
Adrian Barbu
Nick Barnes
Peter Barnum
Jonathan Barron
Adrien Bartoli
Dhruv Batra
Eduardo
    Bayro-Corrochano
Jean-Charles Bazin
Paul Beardsley
Vasileios Belagiannis
Ismail Ben Ayed
Boulbaba Benamor
Abhijit Bendale
Rodrigo Benenson
Fabian Benitez-Quiroz
Ohad Ben-Shahar
Dana Berman
Lucas Beyer
Subhabrata Bhattacharya
Binod Bhattarai
Arnav Bhavsar

Simone Bianco
Hakan Bilen
Horst Bischof
Tom Bishop
Arijit Biswas
Soma Biswas
Marten Bjoerkman
Volker Blanz
Federica Bogo
Xavier Boix
Piotr Bojanowski
Terrance Boult
Katie Bouman
Thierry Bouwmans
Edmond Boyer
Yuri Boykov
Hakan Boyraz
Steven Branson
Mathieu Bredif
Francois Bremond
Stefan Breuers
Michael Brown
Marcus Brubaker
Luc Brun
Andrei Bursuc
Zoya Bylinskii
Daniel Cabrini Hauagge
Deng Cai
Jianfei Cai
Simone Calderara
Neill Campbell
Octavia Camps
Liangliang Cao
Xiaochun Cao
Xun Cao
Gustavo Carneiro
Dan Casas
Tom Cashman
Umberto Castellani
Carlos Castillo
Andrea Cavallaro
Jan Cech
Ayan Chakrabarti
Rudrasis Chakraborty
Krzysztof Chalupka
Tat-Jen Cham

Antoni Chan
Manmohan Chandraker
Sharat Chandran
Hong Chang
Hyun Sung Chang
Jason Chang
Ju Yong Chang
Xiaojun Chang
Yu-Wei Chao
Visesh Chari
Rizwan Chaudhry
Rama Chellappa
Bo Chen
Chao Chen
Chao-Yeh Chen
Chu-Song Chen
Hwann-Tzong Chen
Lin Chen
Mei Chen
Terrence Chen
Xilin Chen
Yunjin Chen
Guang Chen
Qifeng Chen
Xinlei Chen
Jian Cheng
Ming-Ming Cheng
Anoop Cherian
Guilhem Cheron
Dmitry Chetverikov
Liang-Tien Chia
Naoki Chiba
Tat-Jun Chin
Margarita Chli
Minsu Cho
Sunghyun Cho
TaeEun Choe
Jongmoo Choi
Seungjin Choi
Wongun Choi
Wen-Sheng Chu
Yung-Yu Chuang
Albert Chung
Gokberk Cinbis
Arridhana Ciptadi
Javier Civera

James Clark
Brian Clipp
Michael Cogswell
Taco Cohen
Toby Collins
John Collomosse
Camille Couprie
David Crandall
Marco Cristani
James Crowley
Jinshi Cui
Yin Cui
Jifeng Dai
Qieyun Dai
Shengyang Dai
Yuchao Dai
Zhenwen Dai
Dima Damen
Kristin Dana
Kostas Danilidiis
Mohamed Daoudi
Larry Davis
Teofilo de Campos
Marleen de Bruijne
Koichiro Deguchi
Alessio Del Bue
Luca del Pero
Antoine Deleforge
Hervé Delingette
David Demirdjian
Jia Deng
Joachim Denzler
Konstantinos Derpanis
Frederic Devernay
Hamdi Dibeklioglu
Santosh Kumar Divvala
Carl Doersch
Weisheng Dong
Jian Dong
Gianfranco Doretto
Alexey Dosovitskiy
Matthijs Douze
Bruce Draper
Tom Drummond
Shichuan Du
Jean-Luc Dugelay

Enrique Dunn
Zoran Duric
Pinar Duygulu
Alexei Efros
Carl Henrik Ek
Jan-Olof Eklundh
Jayan Eledath
Ehsan Elhamifar
Ian Endres
Aykut Erdem
Anders Eriksson
Sergio Escalera
Victor Escorcia
Francisco Estrada
Bin Fan
Quanfu Fan
Chen Fang
Tian Fang
Masoud Faraki
Ali Farhadi
Giovanni Farinella
Ryan Farrell
Raanan Fattal
Michael Felsberg
Jiashi Feng
Michele Fenzi
Andras Ferencz
Basura Fernando
Sanja Fidler
Mario Figueiredo
Michael Firman
Robert Fisher
John Fisher III
Alexander Fix
Boris Flach
Matt Flagg
Francois Fleuret
Wolfgang Foerstner
David Fofi
Gianluca Foresti
Per-Erik Forssen
David Fouhey
Jean-Sebastien Franco
Friedrich Fraundorfer
Oren Freifeld
Simone Frintrop

Huazhu Fu
Yun Fu
Jan Funke
Brian Funt
Ryo Furukawa
Yasutaka Furukawa
Andrea Fusiello
David Gallup
Chuang Gan
Junbin Gao
Jochen Gast
Stratis Gavves
Xin Geng
Bogdan Georgescu
David Geronimo
Bernard Ghanem
Riccardo Gherardi
Golnaz Ghiasi
Soumya Ghosh
Andrew Gilbert
Ioannis Gkioulekas
Georgia Gkioxari
Guy Godin
Roland Goecke
Boqing Gong
Shaogang Gong
Yunchao Gong
German Gonzalez
Jordi Gonzalez
Paulo Gotardo
Stephen Gould
Venu M. Govindu
Helmut Grabner
Etienne Grossmann
Chunhui Gu
David Gu
Sergio Guadarrama
Li Guan
Matthieu Guillaumin
Jean-Yves Guillemaut
Guodong Guo
Ruiqi Guo
Yanwen Guo
Saurabh Gupta
Pierre Gurdjos
Diego Gutierrez

Abner Guzman Rivera
Christian Haene
Niels Haering
Ralf Haeusler
David Hall
Peter Hall
Onur Hamsici
Dongfeng Han
Mei Han
Xufeng Han
Yahong Han
Ankur Handa
Kenji Hara
Tatsuya Harada
Mehrtash Harandi
Bharath Hariharan
Tal Hassner
Soren Hauberg
Michal Havlena
Tamir Hazan
Junfeng He
Kaiming He
Lei He
Ran He
Xuming He
Zhihai He
Felix Heide
Janne Heikkila
Jared Heinly
Mattias Heinrich
Pierre Hellier
Stephane Herbin
Isabelle Herlin
Alexander Hermans
Anders Heyden
Adrian Hilton
Vaclav Hlavac
Minh Hoai
Judy Hoffman
Steven Hoi
Derek Hoiem
Seunghoon Hong
Byung-Woo Hong
Anthony Hoogs
Yedid Hoshen
Winston Hsu

Changbo Hu
Wenze Hu
Zhe Hu
Gang Hua
Dong Huang
Gary Huang
Heng Huang
Jia-Bin Huang
Kaiqi Huang
Qingming Huang
Rui Huang
Xinyu Huang
Weilin Huang
Zhiwu Huang
Ahmad Humayun
Mohamed Hussein
Wonjun Hwang
Juan Iglesias
Nazli Ikizler-Cinbis
Evren Imre
Eldar Insafutdinov
Catalin Ionescu
Go Irie
Hossam Isack
Phillip Isola
Hamid Izadinia
Nathan Jacobs
Varadarajan Jagannadan
Aastha Jain
Suyog Jain
Varun Jampani
Jeremy Jancsary
C.V. Jawahar
Dinesh Jayaraman
Ian Jermyn
Hueihan Jhuang
Hui Ji
Qiang Ji
Jiaya Jia
Kui Jia
Yangqing Jia
Hao Jiang
Tingting Jiang
Yu-Gang Jiang
Zhuolin Jiang
Alexis Joly

Shantanu Joshi
Frederic Jurie
Achuta Kadambi
Samuel Kadoury
Yannis Kalantidis
Amit Kale
Sebastian Kaltwang
Joni-Kristian Kamarainen
George Kamberov
Chandra Kambhamettu
Martin Kampel
Kenichi Kanatani
Atul Kanaujia
Melih Kandemir
Zhuoliang Kang
Mohan Kankanhalli
Abhishek Kar
Leonid Karlinsky
Andrej Karpathy
Zoltan Kato
Rei Kawakami
Kristian Kersting
Margret Keuper
Nima Khademi Kalantari
Sameh Khamis
Fahad Khan
Aditya Khosla
Hadi Kiapour
Edward Kim
Gunhee Kim
Hansung Kim
Jae-Hak Kim
Kihwan Kim
Seon Joo Kim
Tae Hyun Kim
Tae-Kyun Kim
Vladimir Kim
Benjamin Kimia
Akisato Kimura
Durk Kingma
Thomas Kipf
Kris Kitani
Martin Kleinsteuber
Laurent Kneip
Kevin Koeser
Effrosyni Kokiopoulou

Piotr Koniusz
Theodora Kontogianni
Sanjeev Koppal
Dimitrios Kosmopoulos
Adriana Kovashka
Adarsh Kowdle
Michael Kramp
Josip Krapac
Jonathan Krause
Pavel Krsek
Hilde Kuehne
Shiro Kumano
Avinash Kumar
Sebastian Kurtek
Kyros Kutulakos
Suha Kwak
In So Kweon
Roland Kwitt
Junghyun Kwon
Junseok Kwon
Jan Kybic
Jorma Laaksonen
Alexander Ladikos
Florent Lafarge
Pierre-Yves Laffont
Wei-Sheng Lai
Jean-Francois Lalonde
Michael Langer
Oswald Lanz
Agata Lapedriza
Ivan Laptev
Diane Larlus
Christoph Lassner
Olivier Le Meur
Laura Leal-Taixé
Joon-Young Lee
Seungkyu Lee
Chen-Yu Lee
Andreas Lehrmann
Ido Leichter
Frank Lenzen
Matt Leotta
Stefan Leutenegger
Baoxin Li
Chunming Li
Dingzeyu Li

Fuxin Li
Hao Li
Houqiang Li
Qi Li
Stan Li
Wu-Jun Li
Xirong Li
Xuelong Li
Yi Li
Yongjie Li
Wei Li
Wen Li
Yeqing Li
Yujia Li
Wang Liang
Shengcai Liao
Jongwoo Lim
Joseph Lim
Di Lin
Weiyao Lin
Yen-Yu Lin
Min Lin
Liang Lin
Haibin Ling
Jim Little
Buyu Liu
Miaomiao Liu
Risheng Liu
Si Liu
Wanquan Liu
Yebin Liu
Ziwei Liu
Zhen Liu
Sifei Liu
Marcus Liwicki
Roberto Lopez-Sastre
Javier Lorenzo
Christos Louizos
Manolis Lourakis
Brian Lovell
Chen-Change Loy
Cewu Lu
Huchuan Lu
Jiwen Lu
Le Lu
Yijuan Lu

Canyi Lu
Jiebo Luo
Ping Luo
Siwei Lyu
Zhigang Ma
Chao Ma
Oisin Mac Aodha
John MacCormick
Vijay Mahadevan
Dhruv Mahajan
Aravindh Mahendran
Mohammed Mahoor
Michael Maire
Subhransu Maji
Aditi Majumder
Atsuto Maki
Yasushi Makihara
Alexandros Makris
Mateusz Malinowski
Clement Mallet
Arun Mallya
Dixit Mandar
Junhua Mao
Dmitrii Marin
Elisabeta Marinoiu
Renaud Marlet
Ricardo Martin
Aleix Martinez
Jonathan Masci
David Masip
Diana Mateus
Markus Mathias
Iain Matthews
Kevin Matzen
Bruce Maxwell
Stephen Maybank
Scott McCloskey
Ted Meeds
Christopher Mei
Tao Mei
Xue Mei
Jason Meltzer
Heydi Mendez
Thomas Mensink
Michele Merler
Domingo Mery

Ajmal Mian
Tomer Michaeli
Ondrej Miksik
Anton Milan
Erik Miller
Gregor Miller
Majid Mirmehdi
Ishan Misra
Anurag Mittal
Daisuke Miyazaki
Hossein Mobahi
Pascal Monasse
Sandino Morales
Vlad Morariu
Philippos Mordohai
Francesc Moreno-Noguer
Greg Mori
Bryan Morse
Roozbeh Mottaghi
Yadong Mu
Yasuhiro Mukaigawa
Lopamudra Mukherjee
Joseph Mundy
Mario Munich
Ana Murillo
Vittorio Murino
Naila Murray
Damien Muselet
Sobhan Naderi Parizi
Hajime Nagahara
Nikhil Naik
P.J. Narayanan
Fabian Nater
Jan Neumann
Ram Nevatia
Shawn Newsam
Bingbing Ni
Juan Carlos Niebles
Jifeng Ning
Ko Nishino
Masashi Nishiyama
Shohei Nobuhara
Ifeoma Nwogu
Peter Ochs
Jean-Marc Odobez
Francesca Odone

Iason Oikonomidis
Takeshi Oishi
Takahiro Okabe
Takayuki Okatani
Carl Olsson
Vicente Ordonez
Ivan Oseledets
Magnus Oskarsson
Martin R. Oswald
Matthew O'Toole
Wanli Ouyang
Andrew Owens
Mustafa Ozuysal
Jason Pacheco
Manohar Paluri
Gang Pan
Jinshan Pan
Yannis Panagakis
Sharath Pankanti
George Papandreou
Hyun Soo Park
In Kyu Park
Jaesik Park
Seyoung Park
Omkar Parkhi
Ioannis Patras
Viorica Patraucean
Genevieve Patterson
Vladimir Pavlovic
Kim Pedersen
Robert Peharz
Shmuel Peleg
Marcello Pelillo
Otavio Penatti
Xavier Pennec
Federico Pernici
Adrian Peter
Stavros Petridis
Vladimir Petrovic
Tomas Pfister
Justus Piater
Pedro Pinheiro
Bernardo Pires
Fiora Pirri
Leonid Pishchulin
Daniel Pizarro

Robert Pless
Tobias Pltz
Yair Poleg
Gerard Pons-Moll
Jordi Pont-Tuset
Ronald Poppe
Andrea Prati
Jan Prokaj
Daniel Prusa
Nicolas Pugeault
Guido Pusiol
Guo-Jun Qi
Gang Qian
Yu Qiao
Novi Quadrianto
Julian Quiroga
Andrew Rabinovich
Rahul Raguram
Srikumar Ramalingam
Deva Ramanan
Narayanan Ramanathan
Vignesh Ramanathan
Sebastian Ramos
Rene Ranftl
Anand Rangarajan
Avinash Ravichandran
Ramin Raziperchikolaei
Carlo Regazzoni
Christian Reinbacher
Michal Reinstein
Emonet Remi
Fabio Remondino
Shaoqing Ren
Zhile Ren
Jerome Revaud
Hayko Riemenschneider
Tobias Ritschel
Mariano Rivera
Patrick Rives
Antonio Robles-Kelly
Jason Rock
Erik Rodner
Emanuele Rodola
Mikel Rodriguez
Antonio
    Rodriguez Sanchez

Gregory Rogez
Marcus Rohrbach
Javier Romero
Matteo Ronchi
German Ros
Charles Rosenberg
Guy Rosman
Arun Ross
Paolo Rota
Samuel Rota Bulò
Peter Roth
Volker Roth
Brandon Rothrock
Anastasios Roussos
Amit Roy-Chowdhury
Ognjen Rudovic
Daniel Rueckert
Christian Rupprecht
Olga Russakovsky
Bryan Russell
Emmanuel Sabu
Fereshteh Sadeghi
Hideo Saito
Babak Saleh
Mathieu Salzmann
Dimitris Samaras
Conrad Sanderson
Enver Sangineto
Aswin Sankaranarayanan
Imari Sato
Yoichi Sato
Shin'ichi Satoh
Torsten Sattler
Bogdan Savchynskyy
Yann Savoye
Arman Savran
Harpreet Sawhney
Davide Scaramuzza
Walter Scheirer
Frank Schmidt
Uwe Schmidt
Dirk Schnieders
Johannes Schönberger
Florian Schroff
Samuel Schulter
William Schwartz

Alexander Schwing
Stan Sclaroff
Nicu Sebe
Ari Seff
Anita Sellent
Giuseppe Serra
Laura Sevilla-Lara
Shishir Shah
Greg Shakhnarovich
Qi Shan
Shiguang Shan
Jing Shao
Ling Shao
Xiaowei Shao
Roman Shapovalov
Nataliya Shapovalova
Ali Sharif Razavian
Gaurav Sharma
Pramod Sharma
Viktoriia Sharmanska
Eli Shechtman
Alexander Shekhovtsov
Evan Shelhamer
Chunhua Shen
Jianbing Shen
Li Shen
Xiaoyong Shen
Wei Shen
Yu Sheng
Jianping Shi
Qinfeng Shi
Yonggang Shi
Baoguang Shi
Kevin Shih
Nobutaka Shimada
Ilan Shimshoni
Koichi Shinoda
Takaaki Shiratori
Jamie Shotton
Matthew Shreve
Abhinav Shrivastava
Nitesh Shroff
Leonid Sigal
Nathan Silberman
Tomas Simon
Edgar Simo-Serra

Dheeraj Singaraju
Gautam Singh
Maneesh Singh
Richa Singh
Saurabh Singh
Vikas Singh
Sudipta Sinha
Josef Sivic
Greg Slabaugh
William Smith
Patrick Snape
Jan Sochman
Kihyuk Sohn
Hyun Oh Song
Jingkuan Song
Qi Song
Shuran Song
Xuan Song
Yale Song
Yi-Zhe Song
Alexander
    Sorkine Hornung
Humberto Sossa
Aristeidis Sotiras
Richard Souvenir
Anuj Srivastava
Nitish Srivastava
Michael Stark
Bjorn Stenger
Rainer Stiefelhagen
Martin Storath
Joerg Stueckler
Hang Su
Hao Su
Jingyong Su
Shuochen Su
Yu Su
Ramanathan Subramanian
Yusuke Sugano
Akihiro Sugimoto
Libin Sun
Min Sun
Qing Sun
Yi Sun
Chen Sun
Deqing Sun

Ganesh Sundaramoorthi
Jinli Suo
Supasorn Suwajanakorn
Tomas Svoboda
Chris Sweeney
Paul Swoboda
Raza Syed Hussain
Christian Szegedy
Yuichi Taguchi
Yu-Wing Tai
Hugues Talbot
Toru Tamaki
Mingkui Tan
Robby Tan
Xiaoyang Tan
Masayuki Tanaka
Meng Tang
Siyu Tang
Ran Tao
Dacheng Tao
Makarand Tapaswi
Jean-Philippe Tarel
Camillo Taylor
Christian Theobalt
Diego Thomas
Rajat Thomas
Xinmei Tian
Yonglong Tian
YingLi Tian
Yonghong Tian
Kinh Tieu
Joseph Tighe
Radu Timofte
Massimo Tistarelli
Sinisa Todorovic
Giorgos Tolias
Federico Tombari
Akihiko Torii
Andrea Torsello
Du Tran
Quoc-Huy Tran
Rudolph Triebel
Roberto Tron
Leonardo Trujillo
Eduard Trulls
Tomasz Trzcinski

Yi-Hsuan Tsai
Gavriil Tsechpenakis
Chourmouzios Tsiotsios
Stavros Tsogkas
Kewei Tu
Shubham Tulsiani
Tony Tung
Pavan Turaga
Matthew Turk
Tinne Tuytelaars
Oncel Tuzel
Georgios Tzimiropoulos
Norimichi Ukita
Osman Ulusoy
Martin Urschler
Arash Vahdat
Michel Valstar
Ernest Valveny
Jan van Gemert
Kiran Varanasi
Mayank Vatsa
Javier Vazquez-Corral
Ramakrishna Vedantam
Ashok Veeraraghavan
Olga Veksler
Jakob Verbeek
Francisco Vicente
Rene Vidal
Jordi Vitria
Max Vladymyrov
Christoph Vogel
Carl Vondrick
Sven Wachsmuth
Toshikazu Wada
Catherine Wah
Jacob Walker
Xiaolong Wang
Wei Wang
Limin Wang
Liang Wang
Hua Wang
Lijun Wang
Naiyan Wang
Xinggang Wang
Yining Wang
Baoyuan Wang

Chaohui Wang
Gang Wang
Heng Wang
Lei Wang
Linwei Wang
Liwei Wang
Ping Wang
Qi Wang
Qian Wang
Shenlong Wang
Song Wang
Tao Wang
Yang Wang
Yu-Chiang Frank Wang
Zhaowen Wang
Simon Warfield
Yichen Wei
Philippe Weinzaepfel
Longyin Wen
Tomas Werner
Aaron Wetzler
Yonatan Wexler
Michael Wilber
Kyle Wilson
Thomas Windheuser
David Wipf
Paul Wohlhart
Christian Wolf
Kwan-Yee Kenneth Wong
John Wright
Jiajun Wu
Jianxin Wu
Tianfu Wu
Yang Wu
Yi Wu
Zheng Wu
Stefanie Wuhrer
Jonas Wulff
Rolf Wurtz
Lu Xia
Tao Xiang
Yu Xiang
Lei Xiao
Yang Xiao
Tong Xiao
Wenxuan Xie

Lingxi Xie
Pengtao Xie
Saining Xie
Yuchen Xie
Junliang Xing
Bo Xiong
Fei Xiong
Jia Xu
Yong Xu
Tianfan Xue
Toshihiko Yamasaki
Takayoshi Yamashita
Junjie Yan
Rong Yan
Yan Yan
Keiji Yanai
Jian Yang
Jianchao Yang
Jiaolong Yang
Jie Yang
Jimei Yang
Michael Ying Yang
Ming Yang
Ruiduo Yang
Yi Yang
Angela Yao
Cong Yao
Jian Yao
Jianhua Yao
Jinwei Ye
Shuai Yi
Alper Yilmaz
Lijun Yin
Zhaozheng Yin

Xianghua Ying
Kuk-Jin Yoon
Chong You
Aron Yu
Felix Yu
Fisher Yu
Lap-Fai Yu
Stella Yu
Jing Yuan
Junsong Yuan
Lu Yuan
Xiao-Tong Yuan
Alan Yuille
Xenophon Zabulis
Stefanos Zafeiriou
Sergey Zagoruyko
Amir Zamir
Andrei Zanfir
Mihai Zanfir
Lihi Zelnik-Manor
Xingyu Zeng
Josiane Zerubia
Changshui Zhang
Cheng Zhang
Guofeng Zhang
Jianguo Zhang
Junping Zhang
Ning Zhang
Quanshi Zhang
Shaoting Zhang
Tianzhu Zhang
Xiaoqun Zhang
Yinda Zhang
Yu Zhang

Shiliang Zhang
Lei Zhang
Xiaoqin Zhang
Shanshan Zhang
Ting Zhang
Bin Zhao
Rui Zhao
Yibiao Zhao
Enliang Zheng
Wenming Zheng
Yinqiang Zheng
Yuanjie Zheng
Yin Zheng
Wei-Shi Zheng
Liang Zheng
Dingfu Zhou
Wengang Zhou
Tinghui Zhou
Bolei Zhou
Feng Zhou
Huiyu Zhou
Jun Zhou
Kevin Zhou
Kun Zhou
Xiaowei Zhou
Zihan Zhou
Jun Zhu
Jun-Yan Zhu
Zhenyao Zhu
Zeeshan Zia
Henning Zimmer
Karel Zimmermann
Wangmeng Zuo

Additional Reviewers

Felix Achilles
Sarah Adel Bargal
Hessam Bagherinezhad
Qinxun Bai
Gedas Bertasius
Michal Busta
Erik Bylow
Marinella Cadoni

Dan Andrei Calian
Lilian Calvet
Federico Camposeco
Olivier Canevet
Anirban Chakraborty
Yu-Wei Chao
Sotirios Chatzis
Tatjana Chavdarova

Jimmy Chen
Melissa Cote
Berkan Demirel
Zhiwei Deng
Guy Gilboa
Albert Gordo
Daniel Gordon
Ankur Gupta

Kun He
Yang He
Daniel Holtmann-Rice
Xun Huang
Liang Hui
Drew Jaegle
Cijo Jose
Marco Karrer
Mehran Khodabandeh
Anna Khoreva
Hyo-Jin Kim
Theodora Kontogianni
Pengpeng Liang
Shugao Ma
Ludovic Magerand
Francesco Malapelle
Julio Marco
Vlad Morariu

Rajitha Navarathna
Junhyuk Oh
Federico Perazzi
Marcel Piotraschke
Srivignesh Rajendran
Joe Redmon
Helge Rhodin
Anna Rohrbach
Beatrice Rossi
Wolfgang Roth
Pietro Salvagnini
Hosnieh Sattar
Ana Serrano
Zhixin Shu
Sven Sickert
Jakub Simanek
Ramprakash Srinivasan
Oren Tadmor

Xin Tao
Lucas Teixeira
Mårten Wädenback
Qing Wang
Yaser Yacoob
Takayoshi Yamashita
Huiyuan Yang
Ryo Yonetani
Sejong Yoon
Shaodi You
Xu Zhan
Jianming Zhang
Richard Zhang
Xiaoqun Zhang
Xu Zhang
Zheng Zhang

Contents – Part III

Image and Video Processing

Poster Session 4

Poster Session 3 (Continued)

Reflection Symmetry Detection via Appearance of Structure Descriptor

Ibragim R. Atadjanov and Seungkyu Lee[(✉)]

Department of Computer Engineering,
Kyung Hee University, Seoul, Republic of Korea
ibragim.atadjanov@gmail.com, seungkyu@khu.ac.kr

Abstract. Symmetry in visual data represents repeated patterns or shapes that is easily found in natural and human-made objects. Symmetry pattern on an object works as a salient visual feature attracting human attention and letting the object to be easily recognized. Most existing symmetry detection methods are based on sparsely detected local features describing the appearance of their neighborhood, which have difficulty in capturing object structure mostly supported by edges and contours. In this work, we propose a new reflection symmetry detection method extracting robust 4-dimensional Appearance of Structure descriptors based on a set of outstanding neighbourhood edge segments in multiple scales. Our experimental evaluations on multiple public symmetry detection datasets show promising reflection symmetry detection results on challenging real world and synthetic images.

Keywords: Symmetry detection · Structure · Feature · Reflection

1 Introduction

An object with repeated patterns in balance such as rotation and bilateral reflection symmetry can be easily recognized out of background. Symmetry pattern on an object works as a salient visual feature attracting human attention. Various types of symmetry (rotation, reflection, translation, etc.) are mathematically defined and represented by a set of similar patterns located under certain repetition rules. Symmetry is omnipresent in real world objects such as snow crystal, face, flower, butterfly, and most of human-made objects such as buildings, cars, clothes, etc. Symmetry has been studied in computer vision as a discriminative visual clue in object recognition, shape matching and scene understanding [1]. Reflection symmetry is the most common and essential type that can be found almost everywhere in the surroundings. However, reflection symmetry detection from real world images is not a trivial task due to image noises, partial occlusion, perspective distortion and the lack of robust features to support the symmetry. Many researchers have devoted to practical and robust reflection symmetry detection method under various challenging environments as extensively summarized in [2]. Most of symmetry detection methods are based on sparsely detected

© Springer International Publishing AG 2016
B. Leibe et al. (Eds.): ECCV 2016, Part III, LNCS 9907, pp. 3–18, 2016.
DOI: 10.1007/978-3-319-46487-9_1

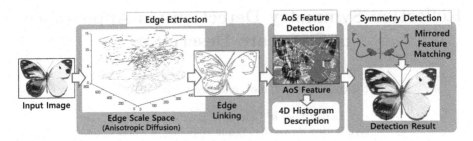

Fig. 1. Proposed reflection symmetry detection method using our appearance of structure (AoS) feature

feature points describing respective local neighborhood. Marola [3] introduces an algebraic technique for detecting a planar bilateral symmetry in Euclidean space. They fit polynomials to input image and detect bilateral symmetry on those fitted polynomials. Prasad and Yegnanarayana [4] propose gradient vector flow and symmetry saliency map for bilateral symmetry detection. They use edge gradients in order to be robust to illumination change. Mitra et al. [5] define general regularity in 3D geometry based on a region based matching. In order to figure out potential regularity, they rigidly transform (rotation, reflection, etc.) a matched key point to the other building meaningful transformation clusters. The feature based methods such as Loy and Eklundh [6] find symmetry matches based on sparse key points like SIFT. They show fast and robust symmetry detection performance with real world images. However appearance based features frequently cannot be detected from low-textured objects and as a result symmetry pattern cannot be detected neither. In such sparse feature point based symmetry detection method, the quality of the extracted feature is critical in the performance of symmetry detection. Feature detection and description are essential in many computer vision tasks including symmetry detection. Symmetry detection methods based on sparse appearance features such as SIFT [7], MSER [8], Scale and Affine Invariant Interest Point [9] are incompetent when symmetric objects have limited amount of textures or show significant changes in intensity across repeated patterns. On the other hand, symmetry of an object is frequently represented by the shape of edge structure very well. In many cases, structure of an object is the most critical and visually salient aspect attracting human attention more. Butterfly in Fig. 1 is a good example, where patterns on the wings hardly support the symmetry of the butterfly, yet we easily recognize the reflection symmetry structure based on the overall silhouette of the butterfly supported by its boundaries.

Mikolajczyk et al. [10] propose an edge-based feature for shape recognition. The feature is defined by multiple neighbour edges and estimated in scale invariant manner similar to SIFT. Atadjanov and Lee [11] propose Scale Invariant Structure Feature that also finds set of edges with extremum curvature responses. Unlike [10], they construct scale space in 1-dimensional domain describing edge signature. They claim that using isotropic filtering in 2D image is not suitable for edge based key points that are anisotropically localized in image. Zitnick [12] develop image binary patch descriptor based on the location, orientation and length of edges. Edge Foci Interest Point [13] describes structure at the point roughly equidistant from neighbour edges with orientations perpendicular to the point. For wide-baseline correspondence task, Meltzer and Soatto [14] construct edge descriptor as a list of histogram of gradient orientations computed on each anchor point on the edge describing its region in the corresponding scale. They describe the edge by gradient orientations of local regions aligned to the edge. Therefore, the descriptor is not invariant to illumination change. Guan et al. [15] propose a 3-dimensional histogram descriptor for image matching that is computed from line segment votes lying on the local region of the key point. The volume of the region is calculated based on the scale where the feature point is detected. Histogram collects weights calculated for each line segment around the key point having similar orientation and location information. Therefore, the method is capable of building a structure feature reflecting local shape around the key point.

We observe that the symmetry pattern can be represented and detected better by incorporating structure description rather than just depending on texture and appearance descriptors. Overall symmetry shape can be described better by its global structure and local appearance provides strength of the symmetryness on it. Structure based methods produce significant amount of false matches due to the absence of description ability of local neighbourhood even though they detect more true positive symmetry patterns. In this paper, we propose a generalized Appearance of Structure (AoS) feature for reflection symmetry detection. Our appearance of structure feature finds key points with extreme curvature responses on edge line segments extracting structure information and describes local appearance represented by edges and contours. We propose to build 4-dimensional histogram for the description of the appearance of structure feature that accumulates neighbour edge points around the feature point and investigate their orientation, location and curvature encoding both local structure and appearance. Finally, we apply our appearance of structure feature for reflection symmetry detection. We perform extensive experimental evaluations qualitatively and quantitatively on two public symmetry detection datasets. We also perform an analytical evaluation based on human perception on the true symmetry axes.

2   Edge Extraction

Our appearance of structure feature point is localized on an edge and describes local structure supported by edge segments around it. Therefore, the performance of our feature point detection and description is highly dependent upon edge extraction result. Extracting clean, clear and correct edges is not a trivial task. An edge can be observed in multiple scales. But we hope to find an optimal scale in which edge becomes most salient and is able to describe local appearance. We adapt the anisotropic diffusion for scale space construction suggested by Liu et al. [16]. The authors claim that the scale of an edge can be chosen as the scale where the gradient magnitude becomes local maximum. We denote gradient of intensity and its marginals as ∇I and I_x, I_y and find maximum ∇I of edge points over multiple scales. Instead of zero-crossing detection, we find a local maxima of transformed gradient, $\nabla \tilde{I}_t$ defined as follows [16].

$$\nabla \tilde{I}_t = sign(\nabla I_t)(1 - \frac{\nabla I_t}{max(abs(\nabla I_t))}) \tag{1}$$

where ∇I_t is derivative of spatial gradient on a scale. The second-moment matrix of 3D Harris takes the following format.

$$M = \begin{pmatrix} I_x^2 & I_x I_y & I_x \nabla \tilde{I}_t \\ I_x I_y & I_y^2 & I_y \nabla \tilde{I}_t \\ I_x \nabla \tilde{I}_t & I_y \nabla \tilde{I}_t & \nabla \tilde{I}_t^2 \end{pmatrix} \tag{2}$$

Eigenvalues of the matrix M measure the changes in the principal directions [17], defining the 3D-Harris response R.

$$R = det(M) - ktrace3(M) = \lambda1 \cdot \lambda2 \cdot \lambda3 - k(\lambda1 + \lambda2 + \lambda3) \tag{3}$$

R gets negative value on an edge point, since edge has single big eigenvalue in general [17]. Therefore, the optimal scale $s(x, y)$ of an edge point location (x, y) can be chosen using the following formulation [16].

$$s(x, y) = arg \max_t |R(x, y, t)|, R(x, y, t) < 0. \tag{4}$$

In order to let nearby edges have similar scales, we propagate chosen scale to its neighbour and connect the edges as illustrated in the edge extraction step in Fig. 1. Left image shows all edges in all scales in 3-dimensional plot and right image shows the edge propagation result.

3   AoS Feature Point Detection

For each edge point e_i (Fig. 2(a)), we define its neighborhood with edge segment $\{e_i', e_i''\}$ inside the circle whose radius equals to the scale s_i of the edge point. We calculate curvature γ_i and orientation ϕ_i for each edge point as follows. The curvature γ_i of an edge point is calculated based on the orientation change between vectors $\overrightarrow{e_i' e_i}$ and $\overrightarrow{e_i e_i''}$.

$$\gamma_i = \gamma(e_i) = \arctan \frac{y_{e_i''} - y_{e_i}}{x_{e_i''} - x_{e_i}} - \arctan \frac{y_{e_i} - y_{e_i'}}{x_{e_i} - x_{e_i'}} \tag{5}$$

where (x_{e_i}, y_{e_i}), $(x_{e_i'}, y_{e_i'})$ and $(x_{e_i''}, y_{e_i''})$ are coordinates of ith edge point and its edge segment's endpoints, e_i' and e_i'', respectively. $|\gamma_i|$ is the approximation for curvature at e_i edge point.

The orientation ϕ_i of an edge point is the orientation of the vector $\overrightarrow{z_i e_i}$ starting at the center point z_i of the line segment $\overline{e_i' e_i''}$ and going through the edge point e_i.

$$\phi(e_i) = \arctan \frac{y_{e_i''} - y_{e_i'}}{x_{e_i''} - x_{e_i'}} - \frac{\gamma}{|\gamma|} * \pi/2 \tag{6}$$

Now, we select key points from edge points that have local maximum curvature above a threshold value. These outstanding points are robustly detected from geometrical distortions, however, edges having circular shape show similar curvature values over a series of consecutive points yielding multiple nearby key points from small local region. Considering both key point density and the number of key points to conduct symmetry detection task with maximum performance, we choose all such key points for our symmetry detection. Let e_i^p, e_i and e_i^n be three consecutive edge points on a edge segment. We choose e_i as a key point if it satisfies the following two conditions.

$$Cond(e_i) = \{|\gamma_i| + \epsilon > |\gamma_i^p|, |\gamma_i| + \epsilon > |\gamma_i^n|\} \tag{7}$$

where ϵ is error tolerance for the key point selection. This allows us to select edge point with slightly lower curvature value than its two neighbours. In other words, we choose a point having local maxima curvature by the precision of ϵ to be robust to the errors in curvature calculation caused by discrete pixel locations in an image. Note that the orientation that we have calculated at this step is for each selected edge point. In the following subsection, we will develop our appearance of structure key point description based on these edge points and its orientation further for better description.

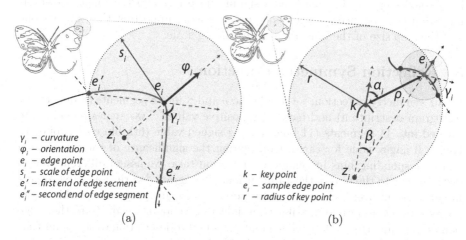

Fig. 2. (a) The orientation and curvature of an edge point based on its neighborhood edge segment. (b) Calculation of 4D Histogram bins for each key point. ρ_i - geometrical distance between locations of key point k and edge point e_i. α_i - angle between orientation of key point k and vector starting at key point going through edge point $\overrightarrow{(k, e_i)}$. β_i - angle between orientations of key point k and edge point e_i. γ_i - curvature of edge point e_i.

4   AoS Feature Point Description

Local regional neighborhood of key point is proportional to the scale of the key point. Therefore we describe key point based on the shape structure within the corresponding scale. In other words edge points detected in the previous step within the circle boundary describes the key point. The radius of the circle is proportional to the scale of the key point. To this purpose, we collect edge points within the circle boundary with the scale not less than the scale of key point. We obtain the orientation $\phi(k)$ of key point k using similar method used in [7]. In our case, we collect orientations of edge points rather than all neighbourhood pixels in the SIFT.

Our key point descriptor is built from the responses of 4-dimensional histogram of weighted votes from all edge points inside its neighborhood region encoding the appearance of edges and contours. With each edge point, 4 parameter values (ρ, $\angle\alpha$, $\angle\beta$, γ) are defined as shown in Fig. 2(b). ρ is the distance between key point k and edge point e_i. $\angle\alpha$ is the angle between key point orientation ϕ and the line $\overline{k, e_i}$ connecting the key point k with edge point e_i. $\angle\beta$ is the angle between key point ϕ and edge point orientations ϕ_i. γ is the angle representing the curvature of sample edge point e_i. These 4 dimensions describe the structure such as relative location and shape of each edge point inside the regional neighborhood collectively. A set of four parameter values from an edge point make one vote in the 4-dimensional histogram. In order to let our descriptor be invariant to scale and rotation in the voting step, distance ρ is normalized by the scale radius r of the key point and two angle values ($\angle\alpha$ and $\angle\beta$) are calculated respective to the orientation phi of the key point. Two angle dimensions have equal step size in their bins assigning no priority in the range. However, regarding the distance ρ, closer edge point is more important than farther one and the step size of the bins are assigned in log scale.

5   Reflection Symmetry Detection

In our symmetry detection, we divide the ρ and γ into 8 segments (8 bins in the histogram description) and have only positive values. Two angles α and β are divided into 11 segments (11 bins) having signed value (6th bin corresponds to having 0 angle value for each). Considering the significance of each dimension and corresponding bins in symmetry detection task, we assign different weight distributions to the bins of the 4-dimensional histogram description. First, α gets uniform weight over its bins because we do not have any preference in this angle. ρ gets zero mean normal distributed weight to give lower weight to farther edge points assuming that a closer edge point gives better description to key point that is located at the origin of the 4-dimensional descriptor. γ gets normal distributed weight with the mean at the maximum value of it to give higher weight to the edge point with higher curvature. β is the angle difference between key point and edge point orientations. It gets zero mean normal distributed weight to give higher weight to smaller angle difference. Finally, we get the following histogram weight function with an edge point.

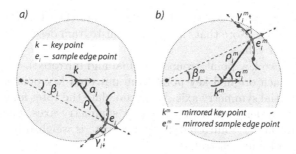

Fig. 3. Key point mirroring example. (a) Original key point. (b) Mirrored key point

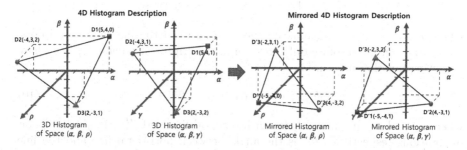

Fig. 4. Histogram description mirroring example with two 3-dimensional parameter spaces: Three edge points (D1, D2, D3) are accumulated in the histogram. Mirrored histogram description is created by flipping β and α values.

$$w(e_i) = \frac{s_i}{S} \cdot \exp(-\frac{b_\rho^2(\rho_i)}{2\sigma_\rho^2}) \exp(-\frac{b_\beta^2(\beta_i)}{2\sigma_\beta^2}) \exp(-\frac{(b_\gamma(\gamma_i) - b_\gamma(\gamma_{max}))^2}{2\sigma_\gamma^2}) \quad (8)$$

where e_i is i^{th} edge point inside the local regional neighborhood of key point, b_ρ, b_β and b_γ are binning function of each dimension with edge point e_i, S is scaling factor based on all σ values and the radius of local regional neighborhood of key point. s_i is scale of ith edge point. ρ_i, β_i and γ_i are 3 parameter values. σ_ρ, σ_β, and σ_γ can be decided proportional to the maximum allowed range of each dimension.

Based on the extracted structure key points and their 4-dimensional description, we perform reflection symmetry detection in an image. Reflection symmetry pattern can be found by matching a key point descriptor with mirrored key points. In order to find mirrored matches, we create a set of all flipped key points. Figure 3(b) is an example of mirrored key point of an original key point shown in Fig. 3(a). For each mirrored key point, we have to update its description to reflect the flipped structure of the pattern. ρ in the description does not change in the mirroring step. Two angles ($\angle\alpha$ and $\angle\beta$) get opposite signed values. For γ we use its absolute value in the description and there is no change in this value. Figure 4 gives an example of mirrored histogram description in the two 3-dimensional parameter spaces, (α, β, ρ) and (α, β, γ). In this example, we assume that the key point collects three edge points (D1, D2, D3) as accumulated in the histogram. Note that the mirrored histogram description is obtained by flipping β and α values.

Based on the two key point groups (original and mirrored), we detect top K best matches of each original key point from mirrored key points. Each match vote for one potential symmetry axis. We accumulate the votes for each potential symmetry axis in order to find the strongest symmetry axes. Each match (i^{th} original key point and j^{th} mirrored key point) vote is weighed by the following function consists of four constraints.

$$W_{ij} = \begin{cases} F_{ij}\Phi_{ij}S_{ij}D_{ij}, & \text{if } \Phi_{ij} > 0 \\ 0, & \text{otherwise} \end{cases} \qquad (9)$$

where $F_{ij} = 1 - fd_{ij}$ is similarity measure between the matched descriptors. fd_{ij} is the sum of absolute differences of all descriptor elements. Φ_{ij} is a phase weighting function used in [3].

$$\Phi_{ij} = 1 - \cos(\alpha_i + \alpha_j - 2\theta_{ij}) \qquad (10)$$

where α_i and α_j are angles between horizontal line and i^{th} and j^{th} key point orientations respectively. θ_{ij} is the angle between horizontal line and the line connecting i^{th} and j^{th} key points. S_{ij} is scale constraint.

$$S_{ij} = \exp(\frac{-|s_i - s_j|}{\sigma(s_i + s_j)})^2 \qquad (11)$$

where s_i, s_j are scales of ith and j^{th} key points. Finally, D_{ij} is distance constraint.

$$D_{ij} = \exp(\frac{-d_{ij}^2}{2\sigma_d^2}) \qquad (12)$$

where d_{ij} is geometric distance between i^{th} and j^{th} key points. F_{ij}, S_{ij}, and D_{ij} are adopted from [6]. In order to accumulate votes and detect final reflection axis, we transform all potential symmetry axes into Hough space with the calculated symmetry weights of the matches supporting respective axis. In the Hough space, the point (axis) with maximum accumulated weight value has been chosen as a candidate reflection symmetry axis.

6   Experimental Results

We evaluate our reflection symmetry detection method in three ways: (1) quantitative evaluation on two symmetry detection public datasets distributed in symmetry detection competitions at CVPR 2011 [18] and CVPR 2013 [19] workshops, (2) qualitative comparison to the most recent results in [11], and (3) analytic evaluation based on human perception. In our experiments, we use 8, 11, 11, 8 bins for ρ, α, β, and γ, respectively. The radius of neighbourhood at each

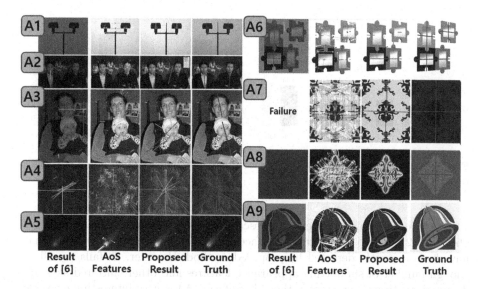

Fig. 5. Experimental results on CVPR'11 workshop dataset [18]. Proposed method is compared to Loy and Eklundh [6] that is the most well performing prior method reported on the dataset. Second column show our dominant appearance of structure features.

key point is set to 5 times of key point scale, which is selected empirically. In symmetry pattern matching, we choose top 10 best matches for each key point. We limit the number of detected axes at most 5 for single symmetry detection and 10 for multiple symmetry detection. For our first and second evaluations, we count the number of true and false positives of each method following the suggested decision rule in [19] counting true positive detection if angle deviation of detected axis is smaller than 10 degree and the center point of the axis is located within one fifth of the length of ground truth axis. In our third analytic evaluation, symmetry detection rate is re-evaluated by human evaluators.

6.1 Quantitative Evaluation on Two Public Datasets

Figure 5 shows reflection symmetry detection results on CVPR 2011 workshop dataset [18] which contains various real and synthetic images with single and multiple symmetry axes. Loy et al. [6] is the most well performing reported method on the dataset. We compare our method with it quantitatively and qualitatively. CVPR 2011 workshop dataset [18] contains total 258 images in 4 categories: (1) 79 real images with single symmetry, (2) 85 real images with multiple symmetries, (3) 55 synthetic images single symmetry, and (4) 39 synthetic images with multiple symmetries. A1 in Fig. 5 contains one global symmetry and two local symmetries. Proposed method successfully detects all tree symmetry axes while [6] detects only global symmetry axis. A1 is almost no textured image but has very clear boundaries that helps proposed method using appearance of

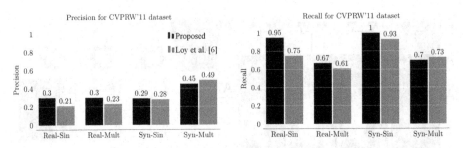

Fig. 6. Precision and recall rates of proposed and Loy and Eklundh [6] on CVPR'11 workshop dataset [18]

structure feature to extract enough descriptors even with small local symmetry objects. A2 has two clear symmetry faces mostly supported face contours that have been correctly detected by proposed method. However, [6] fails to collect enough number of supporting appearance features and other cluttered axes are detected as stronger symmetry than those faces. A4 is very interesting example in which several our detections look better than given ground truth. Diagonal symmetry axes in the ground truth do not reflect the concentric ellipses, while our detected axes find those unexpected but correct symmetry axes. In fact, this observation (correct detections that are not listed in given ground truth or mistakenly presented) has brought our further performance evaluation and analysis based on human perception that is presented in the next subsection. A5 has almost no texture to support the symmetry object except the contour of the object. That's why only our method detects the symmetry axis. A6 has symmetry axes on the skewed patterns where our method detects more correct axes than [6]. However, the skewed shape of the objects in A6 make our method difficult to find complete axes. As our feature groups edge segments on the local regional area, skewed local contour pairs become weak supports for the symmetry axes. With less textured synthetic images such as A7, A8, and A9, [6] frequently fails with only few number of detected feature points. Especially, A7 has less than 10 SIFT features and [6] gives no result image. Figure 6 shows corresponding precision and recall results calculated with all default parameters and settings. Except multiple - synthetic image category, proposed method performs better in both precision and recall rates.

CVPR 2013 workshop dataset [19] contains 121 real world images with single (75 images) and multiple (46 images) symmetry subgroups. Figure 7 shows selected detection results compared to [6] and Fig. 8 shows precision-recall curves compared to four previous methods [6,20–22] appeared in the competition. In B1 in Fig. 7, proposed method detects longer and complete symmetry axis because contours and edges support the symmetry of the object more than local appearances. The handles of the bag in B1 that are correctly detected only by our method clearly show this fact. B2 is a nature image with many random edge segments on the tree. In such nature images, it is very difficult to extract clean symmetry edges and proposed method only detect partial symmetry axis of the

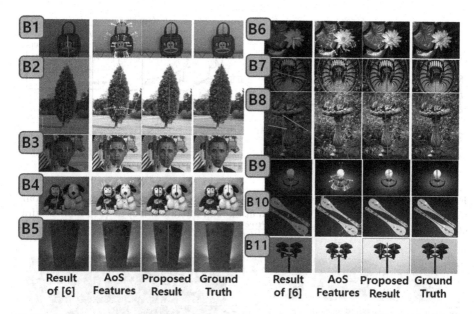

| Result of [6] | AoS Features | Proposed Result | Ground Truth | Result of [6] | AoS Features | Proposed Result | Ground Truth |

Fig. 7. Experimental results on CVPR'13 workshop dataset [19]. Second column images show our dominant feature points.

tree. In B3, B4, and B5, proposed method detects more complete symmetry axes supported by the contour of objects while [6] fails to find complete axes due to the lack of enough number of SIFT feature points to support them. B6 and B8 are nature images with occlusions and background clutters. Background clutters always cause a problem in grouping true supporting feature point pairs. As a result, our method detects more false symmetry axes with them than other images. Usually clutters consist of set of short edges with random scale factor that is almost not probable that they build a long connected edge in our scale propagation step. We can exclude such edges with smaller length than its scale or by putting a threshold on the connected edge length. B7 and B9 are good for both methods as they have clean and enough texture and structure features. B10 has two symmetric objects and proposed method detects one of them correctly.

Figure 8 illustrates precision-recall curves for single and multiple datasets of CVPR 2013 workshop dataset [19] compared to four prior methods (Loy and Eklundh [6], Michaelsen et al. [20], Patraucean et al. [21], and Kondra et al. [22]). For both single and multiple symmetry datasets, proposed method outperforms all previous methods in almost all region of the curves. Especially in the single symmetry result, proposed method shows very high recall values proving that our method gives few number of false negative detections. In other words, we detect most expected ground truth symmetry axes.

We also compare proposed method with the most recent reflection symmetry detection results reported in [11] that uses structure only feature based on edge segments (Fig. 9). In C1, [11] detects the most complete axis, however, proposed

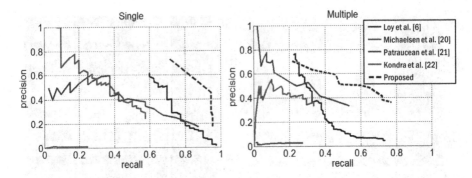

Fig. 8. Precision-Recall curves on CVPR13 workshop dataset [19] compared to four prior methods (Loy et al. [6], Michaelsen et al. [20], Patraucean et al. [21], and Kondra et al. [22]) $*Precision = \frac{true.positive}{true.positive+false.positive}$, $Recall = \frac{true.positive}{true.positive+false.negative}$

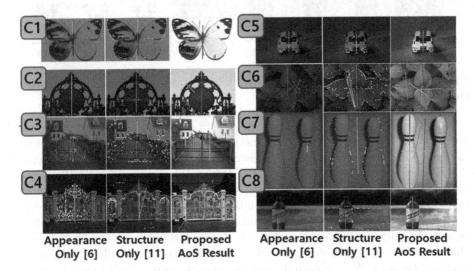

Fig. 9. Comparison with structure only [11] and appearance only [6] reflection symmetry detection methods with our appearance of structure (AoS) reflection symmetry detection

method finds slightly better axis location in its detected angle based on the support of local appearance. In C5, C7 and C8, proposed method finds more complete axes (C5, C7) or more number of correct axes (C7, C8).

Figure 10 illustrates sample images where our method fails. These images are mostly nature images with background clutters or small foreground images. F1 and F4 have both cluttered background and small symmetry object. In F1, [6] successfully detects symmetry axis. F2 and F5 have small or unclear symmetry objects to extract enough number of features to support true symmetry axes. Note that the detected axis in F2 is not listed in the ground truth, however it is meaningful axis based on the similar shape of the two airplanes.

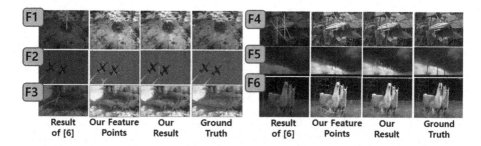

Fig. 10. Failure cases with nature background clutters or small foreground objects

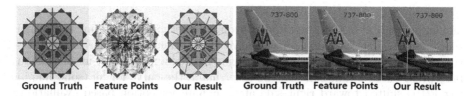

Fig. 11. Example for potential symmetry axes that are missed in ground truth but detected by proposed method

6.2   Evaluation Based on Human Perception

As we already have observed in several experimental results (Fig. 5 A4, Fig. 10 F2), complete labeling of all true reflection symmetry axes is hardly possible. Figure 11 shows two such examples where potential true symmetry axes are detected by proposed method but are not listed in the ground truth. Ground truth of two public datasets [18,19] do not contain complete potential symmetry axes and we easily can find missing but outstanding reflection symmetry axis. Our observation is that the quantitative evaluation on the predetermined ground truth can be unfair for every methods.

Therefore we perform a new evaluation test based on human perception on the single symmetry dataset of [19]. First we run reflection symmetry methods on the dataset finding out top 10 potential symmetry axes for each image. After that we let 20 human evaluators decide if each detected axis is true symmetry axis without prior knowledge on given ground truth. If more than half of votes are collected from the evaluators, we conclude that human sees that it is a true symmetry axis. If both ground truth and human evaluation say that it is true symmetry axis, we count it as real true positive axis. If human evaluation says that it is a true symmetry axis but not listed in the given ground truth, we count it as neither true positive nor false positive in the evaluation. If multiple axes are detected and decided as true symmetry axes from the single corresponding ground truth in the list, we count only once for them as true positive. In Fig. 12, we show new precision and recall curves for [6] and proposed method based on human perception evaluation. Compared to original curves appeared in Fig. 8,

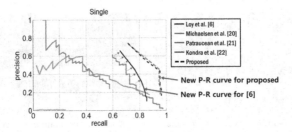

Fig. 12. New precision and recall curves based on human perception evaluation are overlayed on the original curves appeared in Fig. 8

human perception based evaluation of proposed method (dashed line in Fig. 12) shows almost identical curve. As we have already mentioned, our method has very few number of false positives resulting in limited improvement in this human perception based evaluation. On the other hand, the curve for [6] (solid line in Fig. 12) is shifted toward right side after human perception based evaluation. This indicates that there are false positive detections in this method which are counted as true symmetry axes by human evaluators. We believe that this human perception based evaluation is more meaningful if we expect to use detected symmetry patterns as visually salient features for object characterization.

Alternatively, we can count all symmetry axes decided by human evaluators as true positives totally ignoring given ground truth. However in this case, we have a problem in counting the number of true positive axes, because multiple detected axes can be found from one real symmetry axis due to noise or other challenging conditions. This problem involves another human perception based decision if two nearby detected axes are actually from single true symmetry axis or not.

7   Conclusion

In this paper we propose new appearance of structure (AoS) feature based reflection symmetry detection method. Extensive evaluation on two public datasets show promising results of our method. Proposed method finds robust and outstanding edge feature points and builds an appearance of structure descriptor capturing local appearance of edges and contours. We have observed that synthetic images and manmade objects collect stronger supports for reflection symmetry due to their clean and precise shapes. Nature images with cluttered background contain many random edge segments that distract capturing underlying reflection symmetry pattern. We also have seen that a small sized symmetry object can be found well with our method.

References

1. Park, M., Lee, S., Chen, P.C., Kashyap, S., Butt, A., Liu, Y.: Performance evaluation of state-of-the-art discrete symmetry detection algorithms. In: IEEE Conference on Computer Vision and Pattern Recognition, pp. 1–8, June 2008
2. Lee, S., Liu, Y.: Curved glide-reflection symmetry detection. IEEE Trans. Pattern Anal. Mach. Intell. **34**, 266–278 (2012)
3. Marola, G.: A technique for finding the symmetry axes of implicit polynomial curves under perspective projection. IEEE Trans. Pattern Anal. Mach. Intell. **27**, 465–470 (2005)
4. Prasad, V., Yegnanarayana, B.: Finding axes of symmetry from potential fields. IEEE Trans. Image Process. **13**, 1559–1566 (2004)
5. Mitra, N.J., Guibas, L., Pauly, M.: Partial and approximate symmetry detection for 3D geometry. ACM Trans. Graph. (SIGGRAPH) **25**, 560–568 (2006)
6. Loy, G., Eklundh, J.-O.: Detecting symmetry and symmetric constellations of features. In: Leonardis, A., Bischof, H., Pinz, A. (eds.) ECCV 2006. LNCS, vol. 3952, pp. 508–521. Springer, Heidelberg (2006)
7. Lowe, D.: Distinctive image features from scale-invariant keypoints. Int. J. Comput. Vis. **60**, 91–110 (2004)
8. Matas, J., Chum, O., Urban, M., Pajdla, T.: Robust wide baseline stereo from maximally stable extremal regions. In: Proceedings of the British Machine Vision Conference, pp. 36.1-36.10. BMVA Press (2002)
9. Mikolajczyk, K., Schmid, C.: Scale and affine invariant interest point detectors. Int. J. Comput. Vis. **60**, 63–86 (2004)
10. Mikolajczyk, K., Zisserman, A., Schmid, C.: Shape recognition with edge-based features. In: Proceedings of the British Machine Vision Conference, pp. 79.1–79.10. BMVA Press (2003)
11. Atadjanov, I., Lee, S.: Bilateral symmetry detection based on scale invariant structure feature. In: IEEE International Conference on Image Processing, pp. 3447–3451, September 2015
12. Zitnick, C.L.: Binary coherent edge descriptors. In: Daniilidis, K., Maragos, P., Paragios, N. (eds.) ECCV 2010, Part II. LNCS, vol. 6312, pp. 170–182. Springer, Heidelberg (2010)
13. Zitnick, C.L., Ramnath, K.: Edge foci interest points. In: IEEE International Conference on Computer Vision, pp. 359–366, November 2011
14. Meltzer, J., Soatto, S.: Edge descriptors for robust wide-baseline correspondence. In: IEEE Conference on Computer Vision and Pattern Recognition, pp. 1–8, June 2008
15. Guan, W., You, S.: Robust image matching with line context. In: Proceedings of the British Machine Vision Conference. BMVA Press (2013)
16. Liu, X.M., Wang, C., Yao, H., Zhang, L.: The scale of edges. In: IEEE Conference on Computer Vision and Pattern Recognition, pp. 462–469, June 2012
17. Harris, C., Stephens, M.: A combined corner and edge detector. In: Proceedings of the Alvey Vision Conference, pp. 23.1–23.6. Alvety Vision Club (1988)
18. Rauschert, I., Liu, J., Brockelhurst, K., Kashyap, S., Liu, Y.: Symmetry detection competition: a summary of how the competition is carried out. In: IEEE Conference on Computer Vision and Pattern Recognition Workshop, Symmetry Detection Real World Images, pp. 1–66, June 2011

19. Liu, J., Slota, G., Zheng, G., Wu, Z., Park, M., Lee, S., Rauschert, I., Liu, Y.: Symmetry detection from realworld images competition 2013: summary and results. In: IEEE Conference on Computer Vision and Pattern Recognition Workshops, pp. 200–205, June 2013
20. Michaelsen, E., Muench, D., Arens, M.: Recognition of symmetry structure by use of gestalt algebra. In: IEEE Conference on Computer Vision and Pattern Recognition Workshops, pp. 206–210, June 2013
21. Patraucean, V., von Gioi, R., Ovsjanikov, M.: Detection of mirror-symmetric image patches. In: IEEE Conference on Computer Vision and Pattern Recognition Workshops, pp. 211–216, June 2013
22. Kondra, S., Petrosino, A., Iodice, S.: Multi-scale kernel operators for reflection and rotation symmetry: further achievements. In: IEEE Conference on Computer Vision and Pattern Recognition Workshops, pp. 217–222, June 2013

Faceless Person Recognition:
Privacy Implications in Social Media

Seong Joon Oh[✉], Rodrigo Benenson, Mario Fritz, and Bernt Schiele

Max-Planck Institute for Informatics, Saarbrücken, Germany
{joon,benenson,mfritz,schiele}@mpi-inf.mpg.de

Abstract. As we shift more of our lives into the virtual domain, the volume of data shared on the web keeps increasing and presents a threat to our privacy. This works contributes to the understanding of privacy implications of such data sharing by analysing how well people are recognisable in social media data. To facilitate a systematic study we define a number of scenarios considering factors such as how many heads of a person are tagged and if those heads are obfuscated or not. We propose a robust person recognition system that can handle large variations in pose and clothing, and can be trained with few training samples. Our results indicate that a handful of images is enough to threaten users' privacy, even in the presence of obfuscation. We show detailed experimental results, and discuss their implications.

Keywords: Privacy · Person recognition · Social media

1 Introduction

With the growth of the internet, more and more people share and disseminate large amounts of personal data be it on webpages, in social networks, or through personal communication. The steadily growing computation power, advances in

Person A training samples.   Is this person A ?

Fig. 1. An illustration of one of the scenarios considered: can a vision system recognise that the person in the right image is the same as the tagged person in the left images, even when the head is obfuscated?

Electronic supplementary material The online version of this chapter (doi:10.1007/978-3-319-46487-9_2) contains supplementary material, which is available to authorized users.

© Springer International Publishing AG 2016
B. Leibe et al. (Eds.): ECCV 2016, Part III, LNCS 9907, pp. 19–35, 2016.
DOI: 10.1007/978-3-319-46487-9_2

machine learning, and the growth of the internet economy, have created strong revenue streams and a thriving industry built on monetising user data. It is clear that visual data contains private information, yet the privacy implications of this data dissemination are unclear, even for computer vision experts. We are aiming for a transparent and quantifiable understanding of the loss in privacy incurred by sharing personal data online, both for the uploader and other users who appear in the data.

In this work, we investigate the privacy implications of disseminating photos of people through social media. Although social media data allows to identify a person via different data types (timeline, geolocation, language, user profile, etc.) [1], we focus on the pixel content of an image. We want to know how well a vision system can recognise a person in social photos (using the image content only), and how well users can control their privacy when limiting the number of tagged images or when adding varying degrees of obfuscation (see Fig. 1) to their heads.

An important component to extract maximal information out of visual data in social networks is to fuse different data and provide a joint analysis. We propose our new Faceless Person Recogniser (described in Sect. 5), which not only reasons about individual images, but uses graph inference to deduce identities in a group of non-tagged images. We study the performance of our system on multiple privacy sensitive user scenarios (described in Sect. 3), analyse the main results in Sect. 6, and discuss implications and future work in Sect. 7. Since we focus on the image content itself, our results are a lower-bound on the privacy loss resulting from sharing such images.

Our contributions are:

– We discuss dimensions that affect the privacy of online photos, and define a set of scenarios to study the question of privacy loss when social media images are aggregated and processed by a vision system.
– We propose our new Faceless Person Recogniser, which uses convnet features in a graphical model for joint inference over identities.
– We study the interplay and effectiveness of obfuscation techniques with regard of our vision system.

2 Related Work

Nowadays, essentially all online activities can be potentially used to identify an internet user [1]. Privacy of users in social network is a well studied topic in the security community [1–4]. There are works which consider the relationship between privacy and photo sharing activities [5,6], yet they do not perform quantitative studies.

Camera Recognition. Some works have shown that it is possible to identify the camera taking the photos (and thus link photos and events via the photographer), either from the file itself [7] or from recognisable sensing noise [8,9]. In this work we focus exclusively on the image content, and leave the exploitation of image content together with other forms of privacy cues (e.g. additional meta-data from the social network) for future work.

Image Types. Most previous work on person recognition in images has focused either on face images [10] (mainly frontal head) or on the surveillance scenario [11,12], where the full body is visible, usually in low resolution. Like other areas of computer vision, the last years have seen a shift from classifiers based on hand-crafted features and metric learning approaches [13–19] towards methods based on deep learning [20–27]. Different from face recognition and surveillance scenarios, the social network images studied here tend to show a diverse range of poses, activities, points of view, scenes (indoors, outdoors), and illumination. This increased diversity makes recognition more challenging and only a handful of works have addressed explicitly this scenario [28–30]. We construct our experiments on top of the recently introduced PIPA dataset [29], discussed in Sect. 4.

Recognition Tasks. The notion of "person recognition" encompasses multiple related problems [31]. Typical "person recognition" considers a few training samples over many different identities, and a large test set. It is thus akin to fine grained categorization. When only one training sample is available and many test images (typical for face recognition and surveillance scenarios [10,12,32]), the problem is usually named "re-identification", and it becomes akin to metric learning or ranking problems. Other related tasks are, for example, face clustering [26,33], finding important people [34], or associating names in text to faces in images [35,36]. In this work we focus on person recognition with on average 10 training samples per identity (and hundreds of identities), as in typical social network scenario.

Cues. Given a rough bounding box locating a person, different cues can be used to recognise a person. Much work has focused on the face itself ([20–27,37] to name a few recent ones). Pose-independent descriptors have been explored for the body region [28–30,38,39]. Various other cues have been explored, for example: attributes classification [40,41], social context [42,43], relative camera positions [44], space-time priors [45], and photo-album priors [46]. In this work, we build upon [30] which fuses multiple convnet cues from head, body, and the full scene. As we will discuss in the following sections, we will also indirectly use photo-album information.

Identify Obfuscation. Some previous works have considered the challenges of detection and recognition under obfuscation (e.g. see Fig. 1). Recently, [47] quantified the decrease in Facebook face detection accuracy with respect to different types of obfuscation, e.g. blur, blacking-out, swirl, and dark spots. However, on principle, obfuscation patterns can expose faces at a higher risk of detection by a fine-tuned detector (e.g. blur detector). Unlike their work, we consider the *identification* problem with a system *adapted* to obfuscation patterns. Similarly, a few other works studied face recognition under blur [48,49]. However, to the best of our knowledge, we are the first to consider person recognition under head obfuscation using a trainable system that leverages full-body cues.

3   Privacy Scenarios

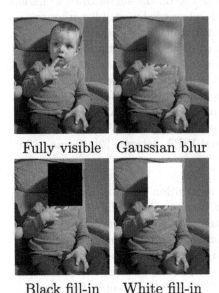

Fully visible   Gaussian blur

Black fill-in   White fill-in

Fig. 2. Obfuscation types considered.

We consider a hypothetical social photo sharing service user. The user has a set of photos of herself and others in her account. Some of these photos have identity tags and the others do not have such identity tags. We assume that all heads on the test photos have been detected, either by an automatic detection system, or because a user is querying the identity of a specific head. Note that we do not assume that the faces are visible nor that persons are in a frontal-upstanding pose. A "tag" is an association between a given head and a unique identifier linked to a specific identity (social media user profile).

Goal. The task of our recognition system is to identify a person of interest (marked via its head bounding box), by leveraging all the photos available (both with and without identity tags). In this work, we want to explore how effective different strategies are to protect the user identity.

We consider four different dimensions that affect how hard or easy it is to recognise a user:

Number of Tagged Heads. We vary the number of tagged images available per identity. The more tagged images available, the easier it should be to recognise someone in new photos. In the experiments of Sects. 5 and 6 we consider that 1~10 tagged images are available per person.

Obfuscation Type. Users concerned with their privacy might take protective measures by blurring or masking their heads. Other than the fully visible case (non-obfuscated), we consider three other obfuscations types, shown in Fig. 2. We consider both black and white, since [47] showed that commercial systems might react differently to these. The blurring parameters are chosen to resemble the YouTube face blur feature.

Amount of Obfuscation. Depending on the user's activities (and her friends posting photos of her), not all photos might be obfuscated. We consider a variable fraction of these.

Domain Shift. For the recognition task, there is a difference if all photos belong to the same event, where the appearance of people change little; or if the set of photos without tags correspond to a different event than the ones with identity tags. Recognising a person when the clothing, context, and illumination have changed ("across events") is more challenging than when they have not ("within events").

Table 1. Privacy scenarios considered. Each row in the table can be applied for the "across events" and "within events" case, and over different obfuscation types. See text Sect. 3. The obfuscation fraction indicates $^{\text{tagged}}/_{\text{non-tagged}}$ heads. Bold abbreviations are reused in follow-up figures. In scenario S_1^τ, $\tau \in \{1.25,\ 2.5,\ 5,\ 10\}$.

Abbreviation	Brief description	Amount of tagged heads	Amount of obfuscated heads
S_0	Privacy indifferent	100 %	0 %
$\mathbf{S_1^\tau}$	Some of my images are tagged	τ instances	0 %
$\mathbf{S_2}$	One non-tagged head is obfuscated	10 instances	0 %/1 instance
$\mathbf{S_3}$	All my heads are obfuscated	10 instances	100 %
S_3'	All tagged heads are obfuscated	10 instances	100 %/0 %
S_3''	All non-tagged heads are obfuscated	10 instances	0 %/100 %

Based on these four dimensions, we discuss a set of scenarios, summarised in Table 1. Clearly, these only cover a subset of all possible combinations along the mentioned four dimensions. However, we argue that this subset covers important and relevant aspects for our exploration on privacy implications.

Scenario S_0. Here all heads are fully visible and tagged. Since all heads are tagged, the user is fully identifiable. This is the classic case without any privacy.

Scenario S_1. There is no obfuscation but not all images are tagged. This is the scenario commonly considered for person recognition, e.g. [28–30]. Unless otherwise specified we use S_1^{10}, where an average of 10 instances of the person are tagged (average across all identities). This is a common scenario for social media users, where some pictures are tagged, but many are not.

Scenario S_2. Here the user has all of her heads visible, except for the one non-tagged head being queried. This would model the case where the user wants to conceal her identity in one particular published photo.

Scenario S_3. The user aims at protecting her identity by obfuscating all her heads (using any obfuscation type, see Fig. 2). Both tagged and non-tagged heads are obfuscated. This scenario models a privacy concerned user. Note that the body is still visible and thus usable to recognise the user.

Scenarios S_3' & S_3''. These consider the case of a user that inconsistently uses the obfuscation tactic to protect her identity. Albeit on the surface these seems like different scenarios, if the visual information of the heads cannot be propagated from/to the tagged/non-tagged heads, then these are functionally equivalent to S_3.

Each of these scenarios can be applied for the "across/within events" dimension. In the following sections we will build a system able to recognise persons across these different scenarios, and quantify the effect of each dimension on the recognition capabilities (and thus their implication on privacy). For our system, the tagged heads become training data, while the non-tagged heads are used as test data.

4   Experimental Setup

We investigate the scenarios proposed in Sect. 3 through a set of controlled experiments on a recently introduced social media dataset: PIPA (People In Photo Albums) [29]. In this section, we project the scenarios in Sect. 3 onto specific aspects of the PIPA dataset, describing how much realism can be achieved and what are possible limitations.

PIPA Dataset. The PIPA dataset [29] consists of annotated social media photos on Flickr. It contains ~40k images over ~2k identities, and captures subjects appearing in diverse social groups (e.g. friends, colleagues, family) and events (e.g. conference, vacation, wedding). Compared to previous social media datasets, such as [28] (~600 images, 32 identities), PIPA presents a leap both in size and diversity. The heads are annotated with a bounding box and an identity tag. The individuals appear in diverse poses, point of view, activities, sceneries, and thus cover an interesting slice of the real world. See examples in [29,30], as well as Figs. 1 and 10.

One possible limitation of the dataset, is that only repeating identities have been annotated (i.e. a subset of all persons appearing in the images). However, with a test set covering ~13k instances over ~600 identities (~20 instances/identity), it still presents a large enough set of identities to enable an interesting study and derive relevant conclusions. We believe PIPA is currently the best public dataset for studying questions regarding privacy in social media photos.

Albums. From the Flickr website, each photo is associated with an album identifier. The ~13k test instances are grouped in ~8k photos belonging to ~350 albums. We use the photo album information indirectly during our graph inference (Sect. 5.3).

Protocol. The PIPA dataset defines train, validation, and test partitions (~17k, ~5k, ~8k photos respectively), each containing disjoint sets of identities [29]. The train partition is used for convnet training. The validation data is used for component-wise evaluation of our system, and the test set for drawing final conclusions. The validation and test partitions are further divided into $split_0$ and $split_1$. Each $split_{0/1}$ contains half of the instances for each identity in the validation and test sets (~10 instances/identity per split, on average).

Splits. When instantiating the scenarios from Sect. 3, the tagged faces are all part of $split_0$. In S_1, S_2, and S_3, $split_1$ is never tagged. The task of our Faceless Person Recognition System is to recognise every query instance from $split_1$, possibly leveraging other non-tagged instances in $split_1$.

Domain Shift. Other than the one split defined in [29,30] proposed additional splits with increasing recognition difficulty. We use the "Original" split as a good proxy for the "within events" case, and the "Day" split for "across events". In the day split, $split_0$ and $split_1$ contain images of a given person across different days.

5 Faceless Recognition System

In this section, we introduce the Faceless Recognition System to study the effectiveness of privacy protective measures in Sect. 3. We choose to build our own baseline system, as opposed to using an existing system as in [47], for adaptibility of the system to obfuscation and reproducibility for future research.

Our system does joint recognition employing a conditional random field (CRF) model. CRF often used for joint recognition problems in computer vision [42,43,50,51]. It enables the communication of information across instances, strengthening weak individual cues. Our CRF model is formulated as follows:

$$\underset{Y}{\arg\max} \; \frac{1}{|V|} \sum_{i \in V} \phi_\theta(Y_i|X_i) + \frac{\alpha}{|E|} \sum_{(i,j) \in E} 1_{[Y_i=Y_j]} \psi_{\widetilde{\theta}}(X_i, X_j) \qquad (1)$$

with observations X_i, identities Y_i and unary potentials $\phi_\theta(Y_i|X_i)$ defined on each node $i \in V$ (detailed in Sect. 5.1) as well as pairwise potentials $\psi_{\widetilde{\theta}}(X_i, X_j)$ defined on each edge $(i, j) \in E$ (detailed in Sect. 5.2). $1_{[\cdot]}$ is the indicator function, and $\alpha > 0$ controls the unary-pairwise balance.

Unary. We build our unary ϕ_θ upon a state of the art, publicly available person recognition system, `naeil` [30]. The system was shown to be robust to decreasing number of tagged examples. It uses not only the face but also context (e.g. body and scene) as cues. Here, we also explore its robustness to obfuscation, see Sect. 5.1.

Pairwise. By adding pairwise terms over the unaries, we expect that the system to propagate predictions across nodes (instances). When a unary prediction is weak (e.g. obfuscated head), the system aggregates information from connected nodes with possibly stronger predictions (e.g. visible face), and thus deduce the query identity. Our pairwise term $\psi_{\widetilde{\theta}}$ is a siamese network build on top of the unary features, see Sect. 5.2.

Experiments on the validation set indicate that, for all scenarios, the performance improves with increasing values of α, and reaches the plateau around $\alpha = 10^2$. We use this value for all the experiments and analysis.

In the rest of the section, we provide a detailed description of the different parts and evaluate our system component-wise.

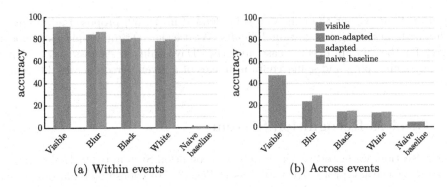

(a) Within events   (b) Across events

Fig. 3. Impact of head obfuscation on our unary term. Compared to visible (unobfuscated) case, it struggles on obfuscations (blur, black, and white); nonetheless, it is still far better than the naive baseline classifier that blindly predicts the most popular class. "Adapted" means CNN models are trained for the corresponding obfuscation type. (Color figure Online)

5.1 Single Person Recognition

We build our single person recogniser (the unary potential ϕ_θ of the CRF model) upon the state of the art person recognition system `naeil` [30].

First, 17 AlexNet [52] cues are extracted and concatenated from multiple regions (head, body, and scene) defined relative to the ground truth head boxes. We then train per-identity logistic regression models on top of the resulting 4096×17 dimensional feature vector, which constitute the $\phi_\theta(\cdot|X_i)$ vector.

The AlexNet models are trained on the PIPA train set, while the logistic regression weights are trained on the tagged examples (split$_0$). For each obfuscation case, we also train new AlexNet models over obfuscated images (referred to as "adapted" in Fig. 3). We assume that at test time the obfuscation can be easily detected, and the appropriate model is used. We always use the "adapted" model unless otherwise stated.

Figures 3 and 4 evaluate our unary term over the PIPA validation set, under different obfuscation, within/across events, and with varying number of training tags. In the following, we discuss our main findings on how single person recognition is affected by these measures.

Adapted Models Are Effective for Blur. When comparing "adapted" to "non-adapted" in Fig. 3, we see that adaptation of the convnet models is overall positive. It makes minor differences for black or white fill-in, but provides a good boost in recognition accuracy for the blur case, especially in the across events case (5+ percent points gain).

Robustness to Obfuscation. After applying black obfuscation in the within events case, our unary performs only slightly worse (from "visible" 91.5 % to "black adapted" 80.9 %). This is 80 times better than a naive baseline classifier (1.04 %)

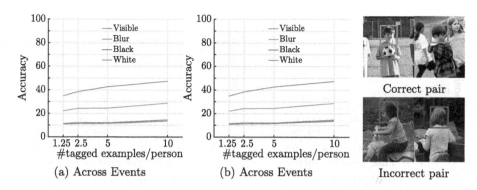

Fig. 4. Single person recogniser at different tag rates.

Fig. 5. Matching in social media

that blindly predicts the most popular class. In the across events case, the "visible" performance drops from 47.4 % to 14.7 %, after black obfuscation, which is still more than 3 times accurate than the naive baseline (4.65 %).

Black and White Fill-In Have Similar Effects. [47] suggests that white fill-in confuses a detection system more than does the black. In our recognition setting, black and white fill-in have similar effects: 80.9 % and 79.6 % respectively, for within events, adapted case (see Fig. 3). Thus, we omit the experiments for white fill-in obfuscation in the next sections.

The System Is Robust to Small Number of Tags. As shown in Fig. 4 the single person recogniser is robust to a small number of identity tags. For example, in the within events, visible case, it performs at 69.9 % accuracy even at 1.25 instances/identity tag rate, while using 10 instances/identity it achieves 91.5 %.

5.2 Person Pair Matching

In this section, we introduce a method for predicting matches between a pair of persons based on head and body cues. This is the pairwise term in our CRF formulation (Eq. 1). Note that person pair matching in social media context is challenging due to clothing changes and varying poses (see Fig. 5).

We build a Siamese neural network to compute the match probability $\psi_{\tilde{\theta}}(X_i, X_j)$. A pair of instances are given as input, whose head and body features are then computed using the single person recogniser (Sect. 5.1), resulting in a $2 \times (2 \times 4096)$ dimensional feature vector. These features are passed through three fully connected layers with ReLU activations with a binary prediction at the end (match, no-match).

We first train the siamese network on the PIPA train set, and then fine-tune it over $split_0$, the set of tagged samples. We train three types of models: one for visible pairs, one for obfuscated pairs, and one for mixed pairs. Like for the unary

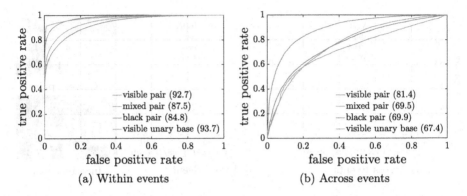

(a) Within events   (b) Across events

Fig. 6. Person pair matching on the set of pairs in photo albums. The numbers in parentheses are the equal error rates (EER). The "visible unary base" refers to the baseline where only unaries are used to determine match.

term, we assume that obfuscation is detected at test time, so that the appropriate model is used. Further details can be found in the supplementary materials.

Evaluation. Figure 6 shows the matching performance. We evaluate on the set of pairs within albums (used for graph inference in Sect. 5.3). The performance is evaluated in the equal error rate (EER), the accuracy at the score threshold where false positive and false negative rates meet. The three obfuscation type models are evaluated on the corresponding obfuscation pairs.

Fine-Tuning on split$_0$ is Crucial. By fine-tuning on the tagged examples of query identities, matching performance improves significantly. For the visible pair model, EER improves from 79.1 % to 92.7 % in the within events setting, and from 74.5 % to 81.4 % in across events.

Unary Baseline. In order to evaluate whether the matching network has learned to predict match better than its initialisation model, we consider the unary baseline. See "visible unary base" in Fig. 6. It first compares the unary prediction (argmax) for a given pair, and then determines its confidence using the prediction entropies. See supplementary materials for more detail.

The unary baseline performs marginally better than the visible pair model under the within events: 93.7 % versus 92.7 %. Under the across events, on the other hand, the visible pair model beats the baseline by a large margin: 81.4 % versus 67.4 % (Fig. 6). In practice, the system has no information whether the query image is from within or across events. The system thus uses the pairwise trained model (visible pair model), which performs better on average.

General Comments. The matching network performs better under the within events setting than across events, and better for the visible pairs than for mixed or black pairs. See Fig. 6.

5.3   Graph Inference

Given the unaries from Sect. 5.1 and pairwise from Sect. 5.2, we perform a joint inference to perform more robust recognition. The graph inference is implemented via PyStruct [53]. The results of the joint inference (for the black obfuscation case) are presented in Fig. 7, and discussed in the next paragraphs.

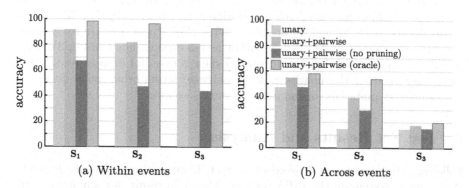

(a) Within events   (b) Across events

Fig. 7. Validation performance of the CRF joint inference in three scenarios, S_1, S_2, and S_3 (see Sect. 3), under black fill-in obfuscation. After graph pruning, joint inference provides a gain over the unary in all scenarios.

Across-Album Edge Pruning. We introduce some graph pruning strategies which make the inference tractable and more robust to noisy predictions. Some of the scenarios considered (e.g. S_2) require running inference for each instance in the test set (∼6k for within events). In order to lower down the computational cost from days to hours, we prune all edges across albums. The resulting graph only has fully connected cliques within albums. The across-album edge pruning reduces the number of edges by two orders of magnitude.

Negative Edge Pruning. As can be seen in Fig. 7, simply adding pairwise terms ("unary+pairwise (no pruning)") can hurt the unaries only performance. This happens because many pairwise terms are erroneous. This can be mitigated by only selecting confident (high quality, low recall) predictions from $\psi_{\widehat{\theta}}$. We found that selecting positive pairs $\psi_{\widehat{\theta}}(X_i, X_j) \geq 0.5$ works best (any threshold in the range [0.4, 0.7] works equally fine). These are the "unary+pairwise" results in Fig. 7, which show an improvement over the unary case, especially for the across events setting. The main gain is observed for S_2 (one obfuscated head) across events, where the pairwise term brings a jump from 15 % to 39 %.

Oracle Pairwise. To put in context the gains from the graph inference, we build an oracle case that assumes perfect pairwise potentials ($\psi_{\widehat{\theta}}(X_i, X_j) = 1_{[Y_i=Y_j]}$, where $1_{[\cdot]}$ is the indicator function and Y are the ground truth identities). We do not perform negative edge pruning here. The unaries are the same as for the other cases in Fig. 7. We can see that the "unary+pairwise" results are within

70 %+ of the oracle case "(oracle)", indicating that the pairwise potential $\psi_{\widetilde{\theta}}$ is rather strong. The cases where the oracle perform poorly (e.g. S_3 across events), indicate that stronger unaries or better graph inference is needed. Finally, even if no negative edge is pruned, adding oracle pairwise improves the performance, indicating that negative edge pruning is needed only when pairwise is imperfect.

Recognition Rates Are Far from Chance Level. After graph inference, all scenarios in the within event case reach recognition rates above 80 % (Fig. 7a). When across events, both S_1 and S_2 are above 35 % (Fig. 7b). These are recognition far above the chance level (1 %/5 % within/across events, shown in Fig. 3). Only S_3 (all user heads with black obfuscation) show a dreadful drop in recognition rate, where neither the unaries nor the pairwise terms bring much help. See supplementary materials for more details in this section.

6   Test Set Results and Analysis

Following the experimental protocol in Sect. 4, we now evaluate our Faceless Recognition System on the PIPA test set. The main results are summarised in Figs. 8 and 9. We observe the same trends as the validation set results discussed in Sect. 5. Figure 10 shows some qualitative results over the test set. We organize the results along the same privacy sensitive dimensions that we defined in Sect. 3 in order to build our study scenarios.

Amount of Tagged Heads. Figure 8 shows that even with only 1.25 tagged photos per person on average, the system can recognise users far better than chance level (naive baseline; best guess before looking at the image). Even with such little amount of training data, the system predicts 56.8 % of the instances correctly within events and 31.9 % across events; which is 73× and 16× higher than chance level, respectively. We see that even few tags provide a threat for privacy and thus users concerned with their privacy should avoid having (any of) their photos tagged.

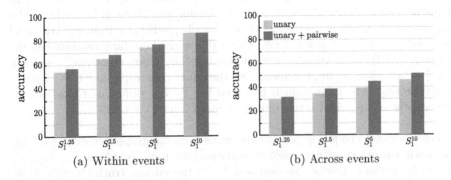

(a) Within events   (b) Across events

Fig. 8. Impact of number of tagged examples: $S_1^{1.25}$, $S_1^{2.5}$, S_1^5, and S_1^{10}.

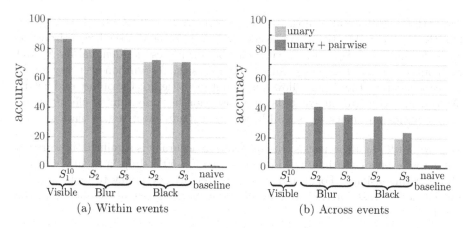

(a) Within events   (b) Across events

Fig. 9. Co-recognition results for scenarios S_1^{10}, S_2, and S_3 with black fill-in and Gaussian blur obfuscations (white fill-in match black results). (Color figure Online)

Fig. 10. Examples of queries in across events setting, not identified using only tagged (red boxes) samples, but successfully identified by the Faceless Recognition System via joint prediction of the query and non-tagged (white boxes) examples. A subset of both tagged and non-tagged examples are shown; there are ~10 tagged and non-tagged examples originally. Non-tagged examples are ordered in the match score against the query (closest match on the left). (Color figure online)

Obfuscation Type. For both scenario S_2 and S_3, Fig. 9 (and the results from Sect. 5.1) indicates the same privacy protection ranking for the different obfuscation types. From higher protection to lower protection, we have Black ≈ White > Blur > Visible. Albeit blurring does provide some protection, the machine learning algorithm still extracts useful information from that region. When our full Faceless Recognition System is in use, one can see that (Fig. 9) obfuscation helps, but only to a limited degree: e.g. 86.4 % (S_1) to 71.3 % (S_3) under within events and 51.1 % (S_1) to 23.9 % (S_3) under across events.

Amount of Obfuscation. We cover three scenarios: every head fully visible (S_1), only the test head obfuscated (S_2), and every head fully obfuscated (S_3). Figure 9 shows that within events obfuscating either one (S_2) or all (S_3) heads is not very effective, compared to the across events case, where one can see larger drops for $S_1 \rightarrow S_2$ and $S_2 \rightarrow S_3$. Notice that unary performances are identical for S_2 and S_3 in all settings, but using the full system raises the recognition accuracy for S_2 (since seeing the other heads allow to rule-out identities for the obfuscated head). We conclude that within events head obfuscation has only limited effectiveness, across events only blacking out all heads seems truly effective (S_3 black).

Domain Shift. In all scenarios, the recognition accuracy is significantly worse in the across events case than within events (about $\sim$50 % drop in accuracy across all other dimensions). For a user, it is a better privacy policy to make sure no tagged heads exist for the same event, than blacking out all his heads in the event.

7   Discussion and Conclusion

Within the limitation of any study based on public data, we believe the results presented here are a fresh view on the capabilities of machine learning to enable person recognition in social media under adversarial condition. From a privacy perspective, the results presented here should raise concern. We show that, when using state of the art techniques, blurring a head has limited effect. We also show that only a handful of tagged heads are enough to enable recognition, even across different events (different day, clothes, poses, point of view). In the most aggressive scenario considered (all user heads blacked-out, tagged images from a different event), the recognition accuracy of our system is 12× higher than chance level. It is very probable that undisclosed systems similar to the ones described here already operate online. We believe it is the responsibility of the computer vision community to quantify, and disseminate the privacy implications of the images users share online. This work is a first step in this direction. We conclude by discussing some future challenges and directions on privacy implications of social visual media.

Lower Bound on Privacy Threat. The current results focused singularly on the photo content itself and therefore a lower bound of the privacy implication of posting such photos. It remains as future work to explore an integrated system that will also exploit the images' meta-data (timestamp, geolocation, camera identifier, related user comments, etc.). In the context of the era of "selfie" photos, meta-data can be as effective as head tags. Younger users also tend to cross-post across multiple social media, and make a larger use of video (e.g. Vine). Using these data-form will require developing new techniques.

Training and Test Data Bounds. The performance of recent techniques of feature learning and inference are strongly coupled with the amount of available training data. Person recognition systems like [20, 26, 27] all rely on undisclosed training data in the order of millions of training samples. Similarly, the evaluation of privacy issues in social networks requires access to sensitive data, which is often not available to the public research community (for good reasons [1]). The used PIPA dataset [29] serves as good proxy, but has its limitations. It is an emerging challenge to keep representative data in the public domain in order to model privacy implications of social media and keep up with the rapidly evolving technology that is enabled by such sources.

From Analysing to Enabling. In this work, we focus on the analysis aspect of person recognition in social media. In the future, one would like to translate such analyses to actionable systems that enable users to control their privacy while still enabling communication via visual media exchanges.

Acknowledgements. This research was supported by the German Research Foundation (DFG CRC 1223).

References

1. Narayanan, A., Shmatikov, V.: Myths and fallacies of personally identifiable information. Commun. ACM **53**(6), 24–26 (2010)
2. Narayanan, A., Shmatikov, V.: De-anonymizing social networks. In: IEEE Symposium on Security and Privacy (2009)
3. Zheleva, E., Getoor, L.: To join or not to join: the illusion of privacy in social networks with mixed public and private user profiles. In: International Conference on World Wide Web (2009)
4. Mislove, A., Viswanath, B., Gummadi, K.P., Druschel, P.: You are who you know: inferring user profiles in online social networks. In: International Conference on Web Search and Data Mining (2010)
5. Ahern, S., Eckles, D., Good, N.S., King, S., Naaman, M., Nair, R.: Over-exposed? Privacy patterns and considerations in online and mobile photo sharing. In: Proceedings of the SIGCHI Conference on Human Factors in Computing Systems (2007)
6. Besmer, A., Richter Lipford, H.: Moving beyond untagging: photo privacy in a tagged world. In: Proceedings of the SIGCHI Conference on Human Factors in Computing Systems, pp. 1563–1572. ACM (2010)
7. Kee, E., Johnson, M.K., Farid, H.: Digital image authentication from JPEG headers. Trans. Inf. Forensics Secur. **6**(3), 1066–1075 (2011)
8. Dirik, A.E., Sencar, H.T., Memon, N.: Digital single lens reflex camera identification from traces of sensor dust. Trans. Inf. Forensics Secur. **3**, 539–552 (2008)
9. Chen, M., Fridrich, J., Goljan, M., Lukáš, J.: Determining image origin and integrity using sensor noise. Trans. Inf. Forensics Secur. **3**, 74–90 (2008)
10. Huang, G.B., Ramesh, M., Berg, T., Learned-Miller, E.: Labeled faces in the wild: a database for studying face recognition in unconstrained environments. Technical report, UMass (2007)
11. Benfold, B., Reid, I.: Guiding visual surveillance by tracking human attention. In: BMVC (2009)
12. Bedagkar-Gala, A., Shah, S.K.: A survey of approaches and trends in person re-identification. Image Vis. Comput. **32**, 270–286 (2014)
13. Guillaumin, M., Verbeek, J., Schmid, C.: Is that you? Metric learning approaches for face identification. In: ICCV (2009)

14. Chen, D., Cao, X., Wen, F., Sun, J.: Blessing of dimensionality: high-dimensional feature and its efficient compression for face verification. In: CVPR (2013)

15. Cao, X., Wipf, D., Wen, F., Duan, G.: A practical transfer learning algorithm for face verification. In: ICCV (2013)

16. Lu, C., Tang, X.: Surpassing human-level face verification performance on lfw with gaussianface. arXiv (2014)

17. Li, W., Wang, X.: Locally aligned feature transforms across views. In: CVPR (2013)

18. Zhao, R., Ouyang, W., Wang, X.: Person re-identification by salience matching. In: ICCV (2013)

19. Bak, S., Kumar, R., Bremond, F.: Brownian descriptor: a rich meta-feature for appearance matching. In: WACV (2014)

20. Taigman, Y., Yang, M., Ranzato, M., Wolf, L.: Deepface: closing the gap to human-level performance in face verification. In: CVPR (2014)

21. Li, W., Zhao, R., Xiao, T., Wang, X.: DeepReID: deep filter pairing neural network for person re-identification. In: CVPR (2014)

22. Yi, D., Lei, Z., Li, S.Z.: Deep metric learning for practical person re-identification. In: ICPR (2014)

23. Hu, Y., Yi, D., Liao, S., Lei, Z., Li, S.Z.: Cross dataset person re-identification. In: Shan, S., Jawahar, C.V., Jawahar, C.V. (eds.) ACCV 2014 Workshops. LNCS, vol. 9010, pp. 650–664. Springer, Heidelberg (2015)

24. Zhou, E., Cao, Z., Yin, Q.: Naive-deep face recognition: touching the limit of lfw benchmark or not? arXiv (2015)

25. Parkhi, O.M., Vedaldi, A., Zisserman, A.: Deep face recognition. BMVC 1(3), 6 (2015)

26. Schroff, F., Kalenichenko, D., Philbin, J.: Facenet: a unified embedding for face recognition and clustering. In: CVPR (2015)

27. Sun, Y., Wang, X., Tang, X.: Deeply learned face representations are sparse, selective, and robust. In: CVPR (2015)

28. Gallagher, A., Chen, T.: Clothing cosegmentation for recognizing people. In: CVPR (2008)

29. Zhang, N., Paluri, M., Taigman, Y., Fergus, R., Bourdev, L.: Beyond frontal faces: improving person recognition using multiple cues. In: CVPR (2015)

30. Oh, S.J., Benenson, R., Fritz, M., Schiele, B.: Person recognition in personal photo collections. In: ICCV (2015)

31. Gong, S., Cristani, M., Yan, S., Loy, C.C. (eds.): Person Re-identification. Springer, Heidelberg (2014)

32. Wu, L., Shen, C., van den Hengel, A.: Personnet: person re-identification with deep convolutional neural networks. In: arXiv (2016)

33. Cui, J., Wen, F., Xiao, R., Tian, Y., Tang, X.: Easyalbum: an interactive photo annotation system based on face clustering and re-ranking. In: SIGCHI (2007)

34. Mathialagan, C.S., Gallagher, A.C., Batra, D.: VIP: finding important people in images. In: CVPR (2015)

35. Everingham, M., Sivic, J., Zisserman, A.: Hello! My name is... buffy-automatic naming of characters in TV video. In: BMVC (2006)

36. Everingham, M., Sivic, J., Zisserman, A.: Taking the bite out of automated naming of characters in TV video. IVC 27, 545–559 (2009)

37. Ding, C., Tao, D.: A comprehensive survey on pose-invariant face recognition. In: arXiv (2015)

38. Cheng, D.S., Cristani, M., Stoppa, M., Bazzani, L., Murino, V.: Custom pictorial structures for re-identification. In: BMVC (2011)

39. Gandhi, V., Ronfard, R.: Detecting and naming actors in movies using generative appearance models. In: CVPR (2013)
40. Kumar, N., Berg, A.C., Belhumeur, P.N., Nayar, S.K.: Attribute and simile classifiers for face verification. In: CVPR (2009)
41. Layne, R., Hospedales, T.M., Gong, S., Mary, Q.: Person re-identification by attributes. In: BMVC (2012)
42. Gallagher, A.C., Chen, T.: Using group prior to identify people in consumer images. In: CVPR (2007)
43. Stone, Z., Zickler, T., Darrell, T.: Autotagging facebook: social network context improves photo annotation. In: CVPR Workshops (2008)
44. Garg, R., Seitz, S.M., Ramanan, D., Snavely, N.: Where's waldo: matching people in images of crowds. In: CVPR (2011)
45. Lin, D., Kapoor, A., Hua, G., Baker, S.: Joint people, event, and location recognition in personal photo collections using cross-domain context. In: Daniilidis, K., Maragos, P., Paragios, N. (eds.) ECCV 2010, Part I. LNCS, vol. 6311, pp. 243–256. Springer, Heidelberg (2010)
46. Shi, J., Liao, R., Jia, J.: Codel: a human co-detection and labeling framework. In: ICCV (2013)
47. Wilber, M.J., Shmatikov, V., Belongie, S.J.: Can we still avoid automatic face detection? arXiv (2016)
48. Gopalan, R., Taheri, S., Turaga, P., Chellappa, R.: A blur-robust descriptor with applications to face recognition. PAMI **34**, 1220–1226 (2012)
49. Punnappurath, A., Rajagopalan, A.N., Taheri, S., Chellappa, R., Seetharaman, G.: Face recognition across non-uniform motion blur, illumination, and pose. IEEE Trans. Image Process. **24**, 2067–2082 (2015)
50. Vu, T., Osokin, A., Laptev, I.: Context-aware CNNs for person head detection. In: International Conference on Computer Vision (ICCV) (2015)
51. Hayder, Z., He, X., Salzmann, M.: Structural kernel learning for large scale multiclass object co-detection. In: 2015 IEEE International Conference on Computer Vision (ICCV), pp. 2632–2640. IEEE (2015)
52. Krizhevsky, A., Sutskever, I., Hinton, G.E.: Imagenet classification with deep convolutional neural networks. In: NIPS (2012)
53. Müller, A.C., Behnke, S.: PyStruct – learning structured prediction in python. J. Mach. Learn. Res. **15**, 2055–2060 (2014)

Segmental Spatiotemporal CNNs
for Fine-Grained Action Segmentation

Colin Lea[✉], Austin Reiter, René Vidal, and Gregory D. Hager

Johns Hopkins University, Baltimore, USA
clea1@jhu.edu, {areiter,hager}@cs.jhu.edu, rvidal@cis.jhu.edu

Abstract. Joint segmentation and classification of fine-grained actions is important for applications of human-robot interaction, video surveillance, and human skill evaluation. However, despite substantial recent progress in large-scale action classification, the performance of state-of-the-art fine-grained action recognition approaches remains low. We propose a model for action segmentation which combines low-level spatiotemporal features with a high-level segmental classifier. Our spatiotemporal CNN is comprised of a spatial component that represents relationships between objects and a temporal component that uses large 1D convolutional filters to capture how object relationships change across time. These features are used in tandem with a semi-Markov model that captures transitions from one action to another. We introduce an efficient constrained segmental inference algorithm for this model that is orders of magnitude faster than the current approach. We highlight the effectiveness of our Segmental Spatiotemporal CNN on cooking and surgical action datasets for which we observe substantially improved performance relative to recent baseline methods.

1 Introduction

New spatiotemporal feature representations [1,2] and massive datasets like ActivityNet [3] has catalyzed progress towards large-scale action recognition in recent years. In the large-scale case, the goal is to classify diverse actions like skiing and basketball, so it is often advantageous to capture contextual cues like the background appearance. In contrast, despite active development on fine-grained action recognition (e.g. [4–8]) progress has been comparatively modest. Many of these models do not capture the nuances necessary for recognizing fine-grained actions such as subtle changes in object location.

In this paper we provide a methodology built around the idea of modeling object states, their relationships, and how they change over time. Our goal is to temporally segment a video and to classify each of its constituent actions. We target goal-driven activities performed in a situated environment, like a kitchen, where a static camera captures a user who performs dozens of actions. For concreteness, refer to the sub-sequence depicted in Fig. 1: A user places a tomato onto a cutting board, cuts it with a knife, and places it into a salad bowl. This is part of a much longer salad preparation sequence. There are many

© Springer International Publishing AG 2016
B. Leibe et al. (Eds.): ECCV 2016, Part III, LNCS 9907, pp. 36–52, 2016.
DOI: 10.1007/978-3-319-46487-9_3

applications of this task including in industrial manufacturing [9,10], surgical training [11–13], and general human activity analysis (e.g. cooking, sports) [4,6, 14–17].

We introduce a Spatiotemporal CNN (ST-CNN) which encodes low-level visual information and a semi-Markov model that captures high-level temporal information. The spatial component of the ST-CNN is a variation on VGG [18] designed for fine-grained tasks which encodes object state, location, and inter-object relationships. Our network is smaller than models like VGG [18] and AlexNet [19] and induces more spatial invariance. This model diverges from recent fine-grained models which typically use holistic approaches to model the scene.

The temporal component of the ST-CNN captures how object relationships change over the course of an action. In the tomato cutting example the `cut` action changes the tomato's state from *whole* to *diced* and the `place` action requires moving the tomato from location *cutting board* to *bowl*. Each action is represented as a linear combination of shared temporal convolutional filters. The probability of an action at any given time is computed using 1D convolutions over the spatial activations. These filters are on the order of 10 s long and explicitly capture mid-range motion patterns.

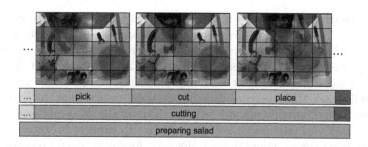

Fig. 1. Our model encodes object relationships and how these relationships change temporally. (top) Latent *hand* and *tomato* regions are highlighted in different colors on images from the 50 Salads dataset. (bottom) We evaluate on multiple label granularities that model fine-grained or coarse-grained actions. (Color figure online)

The segmental component jointly segments and classifies actions using a Semi-Markov Conditional Random Field [20] that encodes pairwise transitions between action segments. This model offers two benefits over traditional time series models like linear chain Conditional Random Fields (CRFs) and Recurrent Neural Networks. Features are computed segment-wise, as opposed to per-frame, and we condition the action at each segment on the previous segment instead of the previous frame. Traditionally these models have higher computational complexity than their frame-wise alternatives. In this work we introduce a new constrained inference algorithm that is one to three order of magnitude faster than the common inference technique.

Despite a large number of action recognition datasets in the computer vision community, few are sufficient for modeling fine-grained segmentation and classification. We apply our approach to two datasets: University of Dundee 50 Salads [21], which is in the cooking domain, and the JHU-ISI Surgical Assessment Working Set (JIGSAWS) [11], which is in the surgical robotics domain. Both of these datasets have reasonable amounts of data, interesting task granularity, and realistic task variability. On these datasets, our model substantially outperforms popular methods such as Dense Trajectories, spatial Convolutional Neural Networks, and LSTM-based Recurrent Neural Networks.

In summary, our contributions are:

- We develop a Spatiotemporal CNN that captures object relationships and how relationships change over time.
- We introduce an efficient algorithm for segmental inference that is one to three orders of magnitude faster than the common approach.
- We substantially outperform recent methods for fine-grained recognition on two challenging datasets.

2   Related Work

Holistic Features: Holistic methods using spatiotemporal features with a bag of words representation are standard for large-scale [1, 22–24] and fine-grained [4–6, 23, 25] action analysis. The typical baseline represents a given clip using Improved Dense Trajectories (IDT) [1] with a histogram of dictionary elements [4] or a Fisher Vector encoding [1]. Dense Trajectories concatenate HOG, HOF, and MBH texture descriptors along optical flow trajectories to characterize small spatiotemporal patches. Empirically they perform well on large-scale tasks, in part because of their ability to capture background detail (e.g. sport arena versus mountaintop). However, for fine-grained tasks the image background is often constant so it is more important to model objects and their relationships. These are typically not modeled in holistic approaches. Furthermore, the typical image patch size for IDT (neighborhood = 32px, cell size = 2px) is too small to extract high-level object information.

Large-Scale Action Classification: While recent work has extended CNN models to video [2, 24, 26–30], often results are only superior when concatenated with IDT features [24, 28, 29]. These models improve over holistic methods by encoding spatial and temporal relationships within an image. Several papers (e.g. [2, 26, 30]) have proposed models to fuse spatial and temporal techniques. While each achieve state of the art, their models are only marginally better than IDT baselines. Our approach is similar in that we propose a spatiotemporal CNN, but our temporal filters are applied in 1D and are much longer in duration.

From Large-Scale Detection to Fine-Grained Segmentation: Despite success in classification, large-scale approaches are inadequate for tasks like action localization and detection which are more similar to fine-grained segmentation. In the 2015 THUMOS large-scale action recognition challenge[1], the top team fused IDT and CNN approaches to achieve 70 % mAP on classification. However, the top method only achieves 18 % (overlap $\geq$0.5) for localization. Heilbron *et al.* [3] found similar results on ActivityNet with 11.9 % (overlap $\geq$0.2). This suggests that important methodological changes are necessary for identifying and localizing actions regardless of fine-grained or large-scale.

Moving to fine-grained recognition, recent work has combined holistic methods with human pose or object detection. On MPII Cooking Rohrbach *et al.* [4] combine IDT with pose features to get a detection score of 34.5 % compared to 29.5 % without pose features. Cheron *et al.* [7] show that if temporal segmentation on MPII is known then CNN-based pose features achieve 71.4 % mAP. While this performance is comparatively high, classification is a much easier problem than detection. Object-centric methods (e.g. [5,6,8]), first detect the identity and location of objects in an image. Ni *et al.* [8] achieve 54.3 % mAP on MPII Cooking and 79 % on the ICPR 2012 Kitchen Scene Context-based Gesture Recognition dataset. While performance is state of the art, their method requires learning object models from a large number of manual annotations. In our work we learn a latent object representation without object annotations. Lastly, on Georgia Tech Egocentric Activities Li *et al.* [6] use object, egocentric, and hand features to achieve 66.8 % accuracy for action classification versus an IDT baseline of 39.8 %. Their features are similar to IDT but they use a recent hand-detection method to find the regions of most importance in each image.

Temporal Models: Several papers have used Conditional Random Fields for action segmentation and classification (e.g. [13,23,31,32]). CRFs offer a principled approach for combining multiple energy terms like segment-wise unaries and pairwise action transitions. Most of these approaches have been applied to simpler activities like recognizing *walking* versus *bending* versus *drawing* [31]. In each of the listed cases, segments are modeled with histograms of holistic features. In our work segments are modeled using spatiotemporal CNN activations.

Recently, there has been significant interest in Recurrent Neural Networks (RNNs), specifically those using Long Short Term Memory (LSTM) (e.g. [30,33,34]). LSTM implicitly learns how latent states transition between actions through the use of gating mechanisms. While their performance is often impressive, they are blackbox models that are hard to interpret. In contrast, the temporal component of our CNN explicitly learns how latent states transition and is easy to interpret and visualize. It is more similar to those in speech recognition (e.g. [35,36]) which learn phonemes using 1D convolutional filters or in robotics which learn sensor-based action primitives [37]. For completeness we compare our model with LSTM.

3   Spatiotemporal Model

In this section we introduce the spatial and temporal components of our ST-CNN. The input is a video including a color image and a motion image

---

[1] THUMOS Challenge: http://www.thumos.info/.

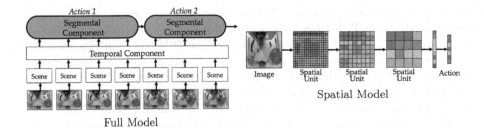

Full Model   Spatial Model

Fig. 2. (left) Our model contains three components. The spatial, temporal, and segmental units encode object relationships, how those relationships change, and how actions transition from one to another. (right) The spatial component of our model.

for each frame. The output is a vector of action probabilities at every frame. Figure 2 (left) depicts the full Segmental Spatiotemporal model.

3.1   Spatial Component

In this section, we introduce a CNN topology, inspired by VGG [18], that by construction captures object state and location in fine-grained actions. First we introduce the mathematical framework, as depicted in Fig. 2 (right), and then highlight differences between our approach and other CNNs. For a recent introduction to CNNs see [38].

For each timestep t there is an image pair $I_t = \{I_t^c, I_t^m\}$ where I_t^c is a color image and I_t^m is a Motion History Image [39]. The motion image captures when an object has moved into or out of a region and is computed by taking the difference between frames across a 2 second window. Other work (e.g. [27]) has shown success using optical flow as a motion image. We found that optical flow was insufficient for capturing small hand motions and was noisy due to the video compression.

The input is decomposed into an $N \times N$ grid of non-overlapping regions indexed by $i \in \{1, \ldots, R\}$. For each region, feature vector r_i, encodes object location and state and is computed by applying a series of spatial convolutional units over that part of the image. Each spatial unit, indexed by $l \in \{1, \ldots, L\}$, consists of a convolution layer with F_l filters of size 3×3, a Rectified Linear Unit (ReLU), and 3×3 max pooling. In Fig. 2 (right), each colored block in the third spatial unit corresponds to a feature vector r_i in that region.

A fully connected layer with F_{fc} states captures relationships between regions and their corresponding objects. For example, a state may produce a high score for *tomato* in the region with the cutting board and *knife* in the region next to it. Let $r \in \mathbb{R}^{R \cdot F_L}$ be the concatenation of all features $\{r_i\}_{i=1}^R$ and $h \in \mathbb{R}^{F_{fc}}$ be the fully connected states. The state is a function of weight matrix $W^{(0)}$ and biases $b^{(0)}$:[2]

---

[2] For notational clarity we denote all weight matrices as $W^{(\cdot)}$ and bias vectors $b^{(\cdot)}$ to reduce the number of variables.

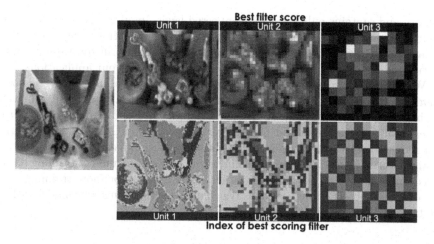

Fig. 3. The user is chopping vegetables. The top images show the best filter activations after each convolutional unit from the CNN. The activations around the cutting board and bowl are high (yellow) whereas in unimportant regions are low (black/red). The bottom images indicate which filter gave the highest activation for each region. Each color corresponds to a different filter index. (Color figure online)

$$h = \text{ReLU}(W^{(0)}r + b^{(0)}) \tag{1}$$

Ideally, the spatial and temporal components of our CNN should be trained jointly, however, this requires an exhorbitant amount of GPU memory, so the spatial model is trained and then the temporal model is trained. As such, we train the spatial component with auxiliary labels, z. We define z_t to be the ground truth action label for each timestep and compute the probability, $\hat{z}_t$, of that frame being each action using the softmax function:

$$\hat{z}_t = \text{softmax}(W^{(1)}h + b^{(1)}) \tag{2}$$

Note, that $\hat{z}_t$ is computed solely for training purposes. The input to the temporal component is the latent activations h_t.

Figure 3 shows example CNN activations after each spatial unit. The top row shows the sum of all filter activations after that layer and the bottom row shows the color corresponding to the best scoring filter at that location. We find that these filters are similar to mid-level object detectors. Notice the relevant objects in the image and the regions corresponding to the action all have high activations and different best-scoring filters.

Relationships to Other CNNs: Our network is inspired by models like VGG and AlexNet but differs in important ways. Like VGG, we employ a sequence of spatial units with common parameters like filter size. However, we found that using two consecutive convolution layers in each spatial unit has negligible impact on performance. Normalization layers, like in AlexNet, did not improve performance either. Overall our network is shallower, has fewer spatial regions, and contains only one fully connected layer. In addition, common data-augmentation techniques like image rotation and translation have a negative impact on our performance. These augmentations tend to introduce unwanted spatial and rotational invariances which are important for our applications.

We performed cross validation using one to seven spatial units and grid sizes from 1×1 to 9×9 and found three spatial units with a 3×3 grid achieved the best results. By contrast, for image classification, deep networks tend to use at least four spatial units and have larger grid counts. VGG uses a 7×7 grid and Alexnet uses a 12×12 grid. A low spatial resolution naturally induces more spatial invariance which is useful when there is limited amounts of training data. To contrast, if the grid resolution is larger, there needs to be more training data to capture all object configurations. We compare performance our model with a pre-trained VGG network in the results.

3.2   Temporal Component

Temporal convolutional filters capture how the scene changes over the course of an action. These filters capture properties like the scene configuration at the beginning or end of an action and different ways users perform the same action.

For time t and video duration T let $H = \{h_t\}_{t=1}^T$ be the set of spatial features and $y_t \in \{1, \ldots, C\}$ be an action label. For convenience we define $H_{t:t+d}$ to be a sequence of features from time t to $t+d-1$. We learn F_e temporal filters $W^{(2)} = \{W_1^{(2)}, \ldots, W_{F_e}^{(2)}\}$ with biases $b^{(2)} = \{b_1^{(2)}, \ldots, b_{F_e}^{(2)}\}$ shared across actions. Each filter is of duration d such that $W_i^{(2)} \in \mathbb{R}^{F_{fc} \times d}$. The activation for the i-th filter at time t is given by a 1D convolution between the spatial features $H_{t:t+d}$ and the temporal filters using a ReLU non-linearity:

$$a_{t,i} = \text{ReLU}(W_i^{(2)} * H_{t:t+d} + b_i^{(2)}) = \text{ReLU}(\sum_{t'=0}^{d-1} W_{i,t'}^{(2)} H_{t+t'} + b_i^{(2)}) \qquad (3)$$

A score vector $s_t \in \mathbb{R}^C$ is a function of weight vectors $W^{(3)} \in \mathbb{R}^{F_e \times C}$ and biases $b^{(3)}$ with the softmax function:

$$s_t = \text{softmax}(W^{(3)} a_t + b^{(3)}) \qquad (4)$$

We choose filter lengths that span 10 s of video. This is much larger than those used in related work (e.g. [2,30]). Qualitatively we find these filters capture states, transitions between states, and attributes like action duration. In principle we could create a deep temporal model. In preliminary experiments we found that multiple layers did not improve performance, however, it is worth further exploration.

3.3   Learning

We learn parameters $W = \{W^0, W^1, W^2, W^3\}$, $b = \{b^0, b^1, b^2, b^3\}$, and the spatial convolutional filters with the cross entropy loss function. We minimize the spatial network and temporal networks independently using ADAM [40], a recent method for stochastic optimization. Dropout regularization was used on fully connected layers.

Parameters such as grid size, number of filters, and non-linearity functions were chosen using cross validation. We use $F = \{64, 96, 128\}$ filters in the three corresponding spatial units and $F_{fc} = 256$ fully connected states. We used Keras [41], a library of deep learning tools, to implement our model.

4   Segmental Model

We jointly segment and classify actions with a constrained variation on the Semi-Markov CRF (SM-CRF) [20] using the activations from the spatiotemporal CNN and a pairwise term that captures action-to-action transitions between segments.

Let tuple $P_j = (y_j, t_j, d_j)$ be the jth action segment where y_j is the action label, t_j is the start time, and d_j is the segment duration. There is a sequence of M segments $P = \{P_1, \ldots, P_M\}$ for $0 < M \leq T$ such that the start of segment j coincides with the end of the previous segment $t_j = t_{j-1} + d_{j-1}$ and the durations sum to the total time $\sum_{i=1}^{M} d_i = T$. Given scores $S = \{s_1, \ldots, s_T\}$ we infer segments P that maximize the energy $E(S, P)$ for the whole video using segment function $f(\cdot)$:

$$E(S, P) = \sum_{j=1}^{M} f(S, y_{j-1}, y_j, t_j, d_j) \tag{5}$$

This model is a Conditional Random Field where $\Pr(P|S) \propto \exp(E(S, P))$. Our segment function contains transition matrix $A \in \mathbb{R}^{C \times C}$ and the sum of spatiotemporal CNN scores across a segment:

$$f(S, y_{j-1}, y_j, t_j, d_j) = A_{y_{j-1}, y_j} + \sum_{t=t_j}^{t_j + d_j - 1} S_t^{y_j} \tag{6}$$

Each element A_{y_{j-1}, y_j} of our pairwise term models the probability of transitioning from action y_{j-1} at segment $j - 1$ to y_j at segment j. A is given by the log probabilities computed directly from the training data.

4.1   Segmental Inference

The inference method proposed by Sarawagi and Cohen [20], and rediscovered by Pirsiavash and Ramanan [23] for Segmental Regular Grammars, solves the following discrete optimization problem:

$$P^* = \underset{P_1, \ldots, P_M}{\arg\max} \; E(S, P) \quad s.t. \sum_{i=1}^{M} d_i = T \quad \text{and} \quad 0 < M \leq T \tag{7}$$

Sarawagi and Cohen introduced an algorithm, which we refer to as Segmental Viterbi, that extends the traditional Viterbi method to the problem of joint segmentation and classification. The optimal labeling is computed by recursively computing the best score, $V_{t,c}$, for each time step t and class c where t corresponds to the ending time for a segment with duration d:

$$V_{t,c} = \max_{\substack{d \in \{1...D\} \\ c' \in \mathcal{Y}/c}} V_{t-d,c'} + f(S, c', c, t, d) \tag{8}$$

Their forward pass using our energy is shown in Algorithm 1. The optimal labels are recovered by backtracking through the matrix.

Their approach is inherently frame-wise: for each frame, they compute scores for all possible segment durations, current labels, and previous labels. In the naive case this results in an algorithm of complexity $O(T^2C^2)$ because the segments can be of arbitrary length. If the maximum segment duration, D, is bounded then complexity is reduced to $O(TDC^2)$.

We introduce an algorithm that is inherently segmental which is applicable for a broad range of energy functions so long as the energy is decomposable across frames in each segment. For each segment, we maximize over the start times, current labels, and previous labels. Instead of optimizing over segment durations, we optimize over the number of segments in a sequence. This can be computed efficiently formulating it as a constrained optimization problem where K is an upper bound on the number of segments:

$$P^* = \arg\max_{P_1,...,P_M} E(S, P) \quad s.t. \quad 0 < M \leq K \tag{9}$$

In all cases, we set K based on the maximum number of segments in the training split. The best score for the kth segment starting at time t is given by $\bar{V}_{t,c}^k$. The recursive update is

$$\bar{V}_{t,c}^k = \max_{c' \in \mathcal{Y}} \bar{V}_{t-1,c'}^{k'} + A_{c',c} + S_{t,c} \tag{10}$$

where, if staying in the same segment ($c = c'$), then $k' = k$ and $A_{c',c} = 0$, otherwise $k' = k - 1$ and $A_{c',c}$ is the pairwise term.

The forward pass for our method is shown in Algorithm 2. Similar to Segmental Viterbi, the optimal labeling is found by backtracking through $\bar{V}$.

Algorithm 1. Seg. Viterbi [20]	Algorithm 2. Our algorithm
for $t = 1 : T$ **do**	**for** $k = 1 : K$ **do**
for $c = 1 : C$ **do**	**for** $c = 1 : C$ **do**
$v_{cur} = V_{t-1,c}$	**for** $t = 1 : T$ **do**
$v_{prev} = \max_{c' \in \mathcal{Y}/c} \bar{V}_{t-1,c'}^{k-1} + A_{c',c}$	$v_{cur} = \bar{V}_{t-1,c}^k$
$V_{t,c} = \max(v_{cur}, v_{prev}) + S_t^c$	$v_{prev} = \max_{c' \in \mathcal{Y}/c} \bar{V}_{t-1,c'}^{k-1} + A_{c',c}$
	$\bar{V}_{t,c}^k = \max(v_{cur}, v_{prev}) + S_t^c$

The complexity of our algorithm is $O(KTC^2)$. Assuming $K < D$ our solution is $\frac{D}{K}$ times more efficient than Segmental Viterbi. Clearly it becomes more efficient as the ratio of the number of segments K to the maximum segment duration D decreases. In most practical applications, K is much smaller than D. In the evaluated datasets there is a speedup of one to three orders of magnitude. Note, however, our method requires more memory than Segmental Viterbi. Ours has space complexity $O(KTC)$ whereas Segmental Viterbi has $O(TC)$. Typically $K << T$ so the increase in memory is easily manageable on any modern computer.

5   Experimental Setup

Historically, most action recognition datasets were developed for classifying individual actions using pre-trimmed clips. Recent datasets for fine-grained recognition have been developed to classify many actions, however they often contain too few users or an insufficient amount of data to learn complex models. MPII Cooking [4] has a larger number of videos but some actions are rarely performed. Specifically, seven actions are performed fewer than ten times each. Furthermore there is gratuitous use of a background class because it was labeled for (sparse) action detection instead of (dense) action segmentation. Georgia Tech Egocentric Activities [42] has 28 videos across seven tasks. Unfortunately, the actions in each task are independent thus there are only three videos to train on and one for evaluation. Furthermore the complexities of egocentric video are beyond the scope of this work. We use datasets from the ubiquitous computing and surgical robotics communities which contain many instances of each action.

University of Dundee 50 Salads: Stein and McKenna introduced 50 Salads [21] for evaluating fine-grained action recognition in the cooking domain. We believe this dataset provides great value to the computer vision community due to the large number of action instances per class, the high quality labels, plethora of data, and multi-modal sensors (RGB, depth, and accelerometers).

This dataset includes 50 instances of salad preparation where each of the 25 users makes a salad in two different trials. Videos are annotated at four levels of granularity. The coarsest level ("high") consists of labels *cut and mix ingredients*, *prepare dressing*, and *serve salad*. At the second tier ("mid") there are 17 fine-grained actions like *add vinegar*, *cut tomato*, *mix dressing*, *peel cucumber*, *place cheese into bowl*, and *serve salad*. At the finest level ("low") there are 51 actions indicating the start, middle, and end of the previous 17 actions. For each granularity there is also a *background* class.

A fourth granularity ("eval"), suggested by [21], consolidates some object-specific actions like *cutting a tomato* and *cutting a cucumber* into object-agnostic actions like *cutting*. Actions include *add dressing*, *add oil*, *add pepper*, *cut*, *mix dressing*, *mix ingredients*, *peel*, *place*, *serve salad on plate*, and *background*. These labels coincide with the tools instrumented with accelerometers.

JHU-ISI Gesture and Skill Assessment Working Set (JIGSAWS): JIGSAWS [11] was developed for recognizing actions in robotic surgery training tasks like suturing, needle passing, and knot tying. In this work we evaluate using the suturing task which includes 39 trials of synchronized video and robot kinematics data collected from a daVinci medical robot. The video is captured from an overhead endoscopic camera and depicts two tools and the training task apparatus. The suturing task consists of 10 fine-grained actions such as *insert needle into skin*, *tie a knot*, *transfer needle between tools*, and *drop needle at finish*. Videos last about two minutes and contain 15 to 37 action instances per video. Users perform low-level actions in significantly different orders. We evaluate using Leave One User Out as suggested in [11]. Most prior work on this dataset focuses on the kinematics data which consists of positions, velocities, and robot joint information. We compare against [13] who provide video-only results. Their approach uses holistic features with a Markov Semi-Markov CRF.

Metrics: We evaluate on segmental and frame-wise metrics as suggested by [37] for the 50 Salads dataset. The first measures segment *cohesion* and the latter captures overall *coverage*.

The segmental metric evaluates the ordering of actions but not the specific timings. The motivation is that in many applications there is high uncertainty in the location of temporal boundaries. For example, different annotators may have different interpretations of when an action starts or ends. As such, the precise location of temporal boundaries may be inconsequential. This score, $A_{edit}(P, P^*)$, is computed using the Levenshtein distance which is a function of segment insertions, deletions, and substitutions [43]. Let the ground truth segments be $P = \{P_1, \ldots, P_M\}$ and predicted segments be $P^* = \{P_1^*, \ldots, P_N^*\}$. The number of edits is normalized by the maximum of M and N. For clarity we show the score $(1 - A_{edit}(P, P^*)) \times 100$ which is from 0 to 100.

Frame-wise accuracy measures the percentage of correct frames in a sequence. Let $y = \{y_1, \ldots, y_T\}$ be the true labels and $y^* = \{y_1^*, \ldots, y_T^*\}$ be the predicted labels. The score is a function of each frame: $A_{acc}(y, y^*) = \frac{1}{T} \sum_{t=1}^{T} \mathbf{1}(y_t = y_t^*)$.

We also include action classification results which assume temporal segmentation is known. These use the accuracy metric applied to segments instead of individual frames.

Baselines: We evaluate two spatial baselines on both datasets using Improved Dense Trajectories and a pre-trained VGG network, and one temporal baseline using a Recurrent Neural Network with LSTM. For the classification results, the (known) start and end times are fed into the segmental model to predict each class.

The Dense Trajectory (IDT) baseline is comparable to Rohrbach *et al.* [4] on the MPII dataset. We extract IDT, create a KMeans dictionary ($k = 2000$), and aggregate the dictionary elements into a locally normalized histogram with a sliding window of 30 frames. We only use one feature type, HOG, because it outperformed all other feature types or their combination. This may be due to the large dimensionality of IDT and relatively low number of samples from our training sets. Note that it took 18 h to compute IDT features on 50 Salads compared to less than 5 h for the CNN features using a Nvidia Titan X graphics card.

Table 1. 50 salads

Spatial models	Edit	Accuracy
VGG	7.58	38.30
IDT	16.77	54.28
S-CNN	**24.10**	**66.64**
Spatiotemporal	Edit	Accuracy
S-CNN + LSTM	58.84	66.30
ST-CNN	60.98	71.37
ST-CNN + Seg	**62.06**	**72.00**

Table 2. JIGSAWS

Spatial models	Edit	Accuracy
VGG	**24.29**	45.91
IDT	8.45	53.92
S-CNN	20.10	**67.25**
Spatiotemporal	Edit	Accuracy
[13] STIPS+CRF	-	71.78
S-CNN + LSTM	54.07	68.37
ST-CNN	59.89	71.21
ST-CNN + Seg	**66.56**	**74.22**

Table 3. 50 salads granularity analysis

Labels	Classes	Edit	Acc.	Classif.
Low	52	29.30	44.13	39.67
Mid	18	48.94	58.06	63.49
Eval	10	66.44	72.71	86.63
High	4	83.2	92.43	95.14

Table 4. Speedup analysis

Labels	Dur	#Segs	Speedup
Low	2289	65	35×
Mid	3100	25	124×
Eval	3100	24	129×
High	11423	6	1902×
JIGSAWS	1107	37	30×

For our spatial-only results, we classify the action at each time step with a linear Support Vector Machine using the features from IDT, VGG, or our spatial CNN. These results highlight how effective each model is at representing the scene and are not meant to be state of the art. The CNN baseline uses the VGG network [18] pretrained on Imagenet. We use the activations from FC6, the first of VGG's three fully connected layers, as the features at each frame.

In addition we compare our temporal model to a Recurrent Neural Network with LSTM using our spatial CNN as input. The LSTM baseline was implemented in Keras and uses one LSTM layer with 64 latent states.

6 Results and Discussion

Tables 1 and 2 show performance using Dense Trajectories (IDT), VGG, LSTM, and our models. S-CNN, ST-CNN, and ST-CNN + Seg refer to the spatial, spatiotemporal, and segmental components of our model. These 50 Salads results are on the "eval" granularity. Our full model has 27.8 % better accuracy on 50 Salads and 37.6 % better accuracy on JIGSAWS relative to the IDT baseline. Figure 4 shows example predictions using each component of our model.

Spatial Model: Our results are consistent with the claim that holistic methods like IDT are insufficient for fine-grained action segmentation. Interestingly, we

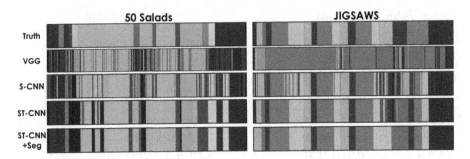

Fig. 4. The plots on top depict the ground truth action predictions for a given video. Each color corresponds to a different class label. Subsequent rows show predictions using VGG, S-CNN, ST-CNN, and ST-CNN + Seg. (Color figure online)

also see that the VGG results are also relatively poor which could be due to the data augmentation to train the model. While our results are still insufficient for many practical applications the accuracy of our spatial model is at least 12 % better than IDT and 21 % better than VGG on both datasets. Note that the edit score is very low for all of these models. This is not surprising because each model only uses local temporal information which results in many oscillations in predictions, as shown in Fig. 4.

Many actions in 50 Salads, like cutting, require capturing small hand motions. We visualized IDT[3] and found it does not detect many tracklets for these actions. In contrast, when the user performs actions like placing ingredients in the bowl, IDT generates thousands of tracklets. Even though the IDT features are normalized we find this is still problematic. We visualized our method, for example as shown in Fig. 3, and qualitatively found it is better at capturing details necessary for finer motions.

Temporal Model: The spatiotemporal model (ST-CNN) outperforms the spatial model (S-CNN) on both datasets. The effect on edit score is substantial and likely due to the large temporal filters. Aside from modeling temporal evolution these have a byproduct of smoothing out predictions. By visualizing these features we see they tend to capture different phases of an action like the start or finish. In contrast, while LSTM substantially improves edit score over the spatial model it has a negligible impact on accuracy. LSTM is capable of learning how actions transition across time, however, it does not appear that it sufficiently captures this information. Due to the complex nature of this method, we were not able to visualize the internal parameters in a meaningful way.

Segmental Model: The segmental model provides a notable improvement on JIGSAWS but only a modest improvement on 50 Salads. By visualizing the results we see that the segmental model helps in some cases and hurts in others. For example, when the predictions oscillate (like in Fig. 4 (right)) the segmental model provides a large improvement. However, sometimes the model smooths

---

[3] Visualization was performed using the public software from Wang and Schmid [1].

over actions that are short in duration. Future work should look at incorporating additional cues such as duration to better model each action class.

Action Granularity: Table 3 shows performance on all four action granularities from 50 Salads using our full model. Columns 3 and 4 show scores for segmental and frame-wise metrics on the action segmentation task and the last shows action classification accuracies which assume temporal segmentation is known. While performance decreases as the number of classes increases, results degrade sublinearly with each additional class. Some errors at the finer levels are likely due to temporal shifts in the predictions. Given the high accuracy at the courser levels, future work should look at modeling finer granularities using by modeling actions hierarchically.

Other Results: Lea *et al.* [37] showed results using the instrumented kitchen tools on 50 Salads. Their model achieves an edit score of 58.46 % and accuracy of 81.75 %. They also achieve state of the art performance on JIGSAWS with 78.91 % edit and 83.45 % accuracy. Note we do not expect to achieve as high performance from video. These results used domain-specific sensors which are well suited to each application but may not be practical for real-world deployment. To contrast, video is much more practical for deployment but is more complicated to model.

Our classification accuracy on JIGSAWS is 90.47 %. This is notably higher than the state of the art [12] which achieves 81.17 % using a video-based linear dynamical system model and also better than their hybrid approach using video and kinematics which achieves 86.56 %. For joint segmentation and classification the improvement over the state of the art [13] is modest. These surgical actions can be recognized well using position and velocity information [37], thus our ability to capture object relationships may be less important on this dataset.

Speedup: Table 4 shows the speedup of our inference algorithm compared to Segmental Viterbi on all 50 Salads and JIGSAWS label sets. One practical implication is that our algorithm scales readily to full-length videos. On 50 Salads, Segmental Viterbi takes 2 h to compute high-level predictions for all trials compared to a mere 4 s using ours.

7   Conclusion

In this paper we introduced a segmental spatiotemporal CNN that substantially outperforms popular methods like Dense Trajectories, pre-trained spatial CNNs, and temporal models like Recurrent Neural Networks with LSTM. Furthermore, our approach takes less time to compute features than IDT, less time to train than LSTM, and performs inference more efficiently than traditional Segmental methods. We hope the insights from our discussions are useful for highlighting the nuances of fine-grained action recognition.

Acknowledgements. This work was funded in part by grants NIH R01HD87133-01, ONR N000141310116, and an Intuitive Surgical Research Grant.

References

1. Wang, H., Schmid, C.: Action recognition with improved trajectories. In: IEEE International Conference on Computer Vision (ICCV) (2013)
2. Sun, L., Jia, K., Yeung, D.Y., Shi, B.: Human action recognition using factorized spatio-temporal convolutional networks. In: IEEE International Conference on Computer Vision (ICCV) (2015)
3. Caba Heilbron, F., Escorcia, V., Ghanem, B., Carlos Niebles, J.: ActivityNet: a large-scale video benchmark for human activity understanding. In: IEEE Conference on Computer Vision and Pattern Recognition (CVPR) (2015)
4. Rohrbach, M., Rohrbach, A., Regneri, M., Amin, S., Andriluka, M., Pinkal, M., Schiele, B.: Recognizing fine-grained and composite activities using hand-centric features and script data. Int. J. Comput. Vis. (IJCV) **119**, 346–373 (2015)
5. Fathi, A., Rehg, J.M.: Modeling actions through state changes. In: IEEE Conference on Computer Vision and Pattern Recognition (CVPR) (2013)
6. Li, Y., Ye, Z., Rehg, J.M.: Delving into egocentric actions. In: IEEE Conference on Computer Vision and Pattern Recognition (CVPR) (2015)
7. Cheron, G., Laptev, I., Schmid, C.: P-CNN: pose-based CNN features for action recognition. In: IEEE International Conference on Computer Vision (ICCV) (2015)
8. Ni, B., Paramathayalan, V.R., Moulin, P.: Multiple granularity analysis for fine-grained action detection. In: IEEE Conference on Computer Vision and Pattern Recognition (CVPR) (2014)
9. Vo, N.N., Bobick, A.F.: From stochastic grammar to Bayes network: probabilistic parsing of complex activity. In: IEEE Conference on Computer Vision and Pattern Recognition (CVPR) (2014)
10. Hawkins, K.P., Bansal, S., Vo, N.N., Bobick, A.F.: Anticipating human actions for collaboration in the presence of task and sensor uncertainty. In: IEEE International Conference on Robotics and Automation (ICRA) (2014)
11. Gao, Y., Vedula, S.S., Reiley, C.E., Ahmidi, N., Varadarajan, B., Lin, H.C., Tao, L., Zappella, L., Béjar, B., Yuh, D.D., et al.: JHU-ISI gesture and skill assessment working set (JIGSAWS): a surgical activity dataset for human motion modeling. In: MICCAI Workshop: Modeling and Monitoring of Computer Assisted Interventions (M2CAI) (2014)
12. Zappella, L., Haro, B.B., Hager, G.D., Vidal, R.: Surgical gesture classification from video and kinematic data. Med. Image Anal. **17**, 732–745 (2013)
13. Tao, L., Zappella, L., Hager, G.D., Vidal, R.: Surgical gesture segmentation and recognition. In: Medical Image Computing and Computer Assisted Intervention (MICCAI), pp. 339–346 (2013)
14. Lei, J., Ren, X., Fox, D.: Fine-grained kitchen activity recognition using RGB-D. In: ACM Conference on Ubiquitous Computing (UbiComp) (2012)
15. Morariu, V.I., Davis, L.S.: Multi-agent event recognition in structured scenarios. In: IEEE Conference on Computer Vision and Pattern Recognition (CVPR) (2011)
16. Koppula, H.S., Gupta, R., Saxena, A.: Learning human activities and object affordances from RGB-D videos. Intl. J. Robot. Res. (IJRR) **32**(8), 951–970 (2013)
17. van Kasteren, T., Englebienne, G., Kröse, B.J.: Activity recognition using semi-Markov models on real world smart home datasets. J. Ambient Intell. Smart Environ. **2**, 311–325 (2010)
18. Simonyan, K., Zisserman, A.: Very deep convolutional networks for large-scale image recognition. In: International Conference Learning Representations (ICLR) (2015)

19. Krizhevsky, A., Sutskever, I., Hinton, G.E.: ImageNet classification with deep convolutional neural networks. In: Pereira, F., Burges, C., Bottou, L., Weinberger, K. (eds.) Advances in Neural Information Processing Systems (NIPS) (2012)
20. Sarawagi, S., Cohen, W.W.: Semi-Markov conditional random fields for information extraction. In: Advances in Neural Information Processing Systems (NIPS) (2004)
21. Stein, S., McKenna, S.J.: Combining embedded accelerometers with computer vision for recognizing food preparation activities. In: ACM Conference on Ubiquitous Computing (UbiComp) (2013)
22. Wang, H., Kläser, A., Schmid, C., Liu, C.L.: Action recognition by dense trajectories. In: IEEE Conference on Computer Vision and Pattern Recognition (CVPR) (2011)
23. Pirsiavash, H., Ramanan, D.: Parsing videos of actions with segmental grammars. In: IEEE Conference on Computer Vision and Pattern Recognition (CVPR) (2014)
24. Jain, M., van Gemert, J.C., Snoek, C.G.M.: What do 15,000 object categories tell us about classifying and localizing actions? In: IEEE Conference on Computer Vision and Pattern Recognition (CVPR) (2015)
25. Pishchulin, L., Andriluka, M., Schiele, B.: Fine-grained activity recognition with holistic and pose based features. In: German Conference on Pattern Recognition (GCPR) (2014)
26. Karpathy, A., Toderici, G., Shetty, S., Leung, T., Sukthankar, R., Fei-Fei, L.: Large-scale video classification with convolutional neural networks. In: IEEE Conference on Computer Vision and Pattern Recognition (CVPR) (2014)
27. Simonyan, K., Zisserman, A.: Two-stream convolutional networks for action recognition in videos. In: Advances in Neural Information Processing Systems (NIPS), pp. 568–576 (2014)
28. Tran, D., Bourdev, L., Fergus, R., Torresani, L., Paluri, M.: Learning spatiotemporal features with 3D convolutional networks. In: The IEEE International Conference on Computer Vision (ICCV) (2015)
29. Peng, X., Schmid, C.: Encoding feature maps of cnns for action recognition. In: CVPR, THUMOS Challenge 2015 Workshop (2015)
30. Ng, J.Y., Hausknecht, M.J., Vijayanarasimhan, S., Vinyals, O., Monga, R., Toderici, G.: Beyond short snippets: deep networks for video classification. In: IEEE Conference on Computer Vision and Pattern Recognition (CVPR) (2015)
31. Shi, Q., Cheng, L., Wang, L., Smola, A.: Human action segmentation and recognition using discriminative semi-Markov models. Intl. J. Comput. Vis. (IJCV) **93**, 22–32 (2011)
32. Tang, K., Fei-Fei, L., Koller, D.: Learning latent temporal structure for complex event detection. In: IEEE Conference on Computer Vision and Pattern Recognition (CVPR) (2012)
33. Vinyals, O., Toshev, A., Bengio, S., Erhan, D.: Show and tell: a neural image caption generator. In: IEEE Conference on Computer Vision and Pattern Recognition (CVPR) (2015)
34. Donahue, J., Hendricks, L.A., Guadarrama, S., Rohrbach, M., Venugopalan, S., Saenko, K., Darrell, T.: Long-term recurrent convolutional networks for visual recognition and description. In: IEEE Conference on Computer Vision and Pattern Recognition (CVPR) (2015)
35. Hannun, A.Y., Case, C., Casper, J., Catanzaro, B.C., Diamos, G., Elsen, E., Prenger, R., Satheesh, S., Sengupta, S., Coates, A., Ng, A.Y.: Deep speech: scaling up end-to-end speech recognition. CoRR abs/1412.5567 (2014)

36. Abdel-Hamid, O., Deng, L., Yu, D.: Exploring convolutional neural network structures and optimization techniques for speech recognition. In: INTERSPEECH International Speech Communication Association (2013)
37. Lea, C., Vidal, R., Hager, G.D.: Learning convolutional action primitives for fine-grained action recognition. In: IEEE International Conference on Robotics and Automation (ICRA) (2016)
38. Ian Goodfellow, Y.B., Courville, A.: Deep Learning. MIT Press (2016, in preparation). http://www.deeplearningbook.org/
39. Davis, J., Bobick, A.: The representation and recognition of action using temporal templates. In: IEEE Conference on Computer Vision and Pattern Recognition (CVPR) (1997)
40. Kingma, D.P., Ba, J.: Adam: a method for stochastic optimization. In: International Conference Learning Representations (ICLR) (2014)
41. Chollet, F.: Keras (2015). https://github.com/fchollet/keras
42. Fathi, A., Farhadi, A., Rehg, J.M.: Understanding egocentric activities. In: IEEE International Conference on Computer Vision (ICCV) (2011)
43. Navarro, G.: A guided tour to approximate string matching. ACM Comput. Surv. **33**, 31–88 (2001)

Structure from Motion on a Sphere

Jonathan Ventura[✉]

Department of Computer Science,
University of Colorado Colorado Springs, Colorado Springs, USA
jventura@uccs.edu

Abstract. We describe a special case of structure from motion where the camera rotates on a sphere. The camera's optical axis lies perpendicular to the sphere's surface. In this case, the camera's pose is minimally represented by three rotation parameters. From analysis of the epipolar geometry we derive a novel and efficient solution for the essential matrix relating two images, requiring only three point correspondences in the minimal case. We apply this solver in a structure-from-motion pipeline that aggregates pairwise relations by rotation averaging followed by bundle adjustment with an inverse depth parameterization. Our methods enable scene modeling with an outward-facing camera and object scanning with an inward-facing camera.

1 Introduction

Accurate visual 3D reconstruction is highly dependent on establishing sufficient baseline between images so that the translation between them can be reliably estimated and 3D points can be accurately triangulated. However, we have found that, in practice, it is difficult for an untrained user to capture image sequences with sufficient baseline; typically, the natural inclination is to rotate the camera instead of translating it, which causes the structure-from-motion system to fail.

In this work, we instead specifically target camera rotation as the basis for structure from motion. The critical assumption here is that the camera rotates at some fixed distance from the origin, with its optical axis aligned with the ray between the origin and the camera center. We call this "spherical motion."

The camera could be pointing inward or outward. An example of an inward-facing camera would be object scanning setups such as a turntable or spherical gantry. An example of an outward-facing camera would be a typical user capturing a panorama – the user holds the camera away from their body at a fixed distance while rotating.

In either case, the global scale of the 3d reconstruction is unknown, as is always the case in pure monocular structure-from-motion. The global scale is determined by the radius of the sphere, which we arbitrarily set to unit length. However, what is interesting about this particular case of camera motion is that the relative scale between camera pairs is known, because the radius of the sphere is fixed. This is a distinct advantage over general monocular camera motion estimation, where the relative scale of the translation between camera

© Springer International Publishing AG 2016
B. Leibe et al. (Eds.): ECCV 2016, Part III, LNCS 9907, pp. 53–68, 2016.
DOI: 10.1007/978-3-319-46487-9_4

pairs must be determined by point triangulation and scale propagation, which is highly susceptible to scale drift. With spherical camera motion, we can directly compose relative pose estimates to determine the complete camera trajectory without needing to propagate scale. A second advantage is that the relative pose between cameras is fully determined by three rotational degrees of freedom and so can be estimated from three point correspondences as opposed to the five correspondences needed in the general case.

In this paper, after a survey of related work (Sect. 2), we analyze the geometry of spherical camera motion (Sect. 3) and derive efficient solvers for the essential matrix (Sect. 4). We integrate these solvers into a complete structure-from-motion pipeline (Sect. 5) and present an evaluation of our methods on synthetic and real data (Sect. 6) followed by conclusions and future work (Sect. 7).

2   Related Work

A particular problem of interest in geometric computer vision is inferring the essential matrix relating two images from point correspondences, especially from a minimal set of correspondences [14]. Minimal solutions are useful for application in a random sample consensus (RANSAC) [6] loop to robustly estimate the motion parameters and separate inliers from outliers. Nistér [17] derived an efficient minimal solution from five point correspondences and Stewénius et al. [26] later improved the accuracy of this method. In this work, we derive a solution for the essential matrix from at least three correspondences which applies when the camera undergoes spherical motion.

Several previous works have considered solutions for monocular relative pose given circular motion or single-axis rotation as observed with a turntable [7,11, 16] or a non-holonomic vehicle [23]. In this work we derive a spherical motion solver which allows three rotational degrees of freedom and thus requires three point correspondences in the minimal case.

Also closely related are the works by Peleg and Ben-Ezra [19] and Shum and Szeliski [24] on stereo or multi-perspective panoramas. In these works, an outward-facing camera is spun on a circular path and images are captured at regular intervals. They demonstrated that by careful sampling of the images, stereo cylindrical panoramas can be created and used for either surround-view stereo viewing or 3D stereo reconstruction. These works use either controlled capture on a turntable [24] or manifold mosaicing [20] to obtain the positions of the images in the sequence, whereas we develop an automatic, accurate structure-from-motion pipeline which applies to both circular and spherical motion image sequences.

Structure-from-motion refers to simultaneously estimating camera poses and 3D scene geometry from an image sequence or collection. For example, Pollefeys et al. describe a pipeline for visual modeling with a handheld camera [21], and Snavely et al. developed a structure-from-motion system from unstructured internet image collections [25]. Most related to the present work is the 1DSfM approach of Wilson and Snavely [28], where the camera orientations are first estimated using a robust global rotation averaging approach [2] and then the camera translations are estimated separately. In our approach, the camera's position is directly determined by its orientation, so the second translation estimation step is not needed.

3   The Geometry of Spherical Camera Motion

In this section we give expressions for the absolute and relative pose matrices induced by spherical motion and derive the form of the essential matrix.

3.1   Camera Extrinsics

Inward-Facing Camera. For an inward-facing camera, the 3×4 camera extrinsics matrix P can be expressed using a 3×3 rotation matrix R and a 3×1 vector $\mathbf{z}$:

$$P_{in} = [R \mid \mathbf{z}], \tag{1}$$

where $\mathbf{z} = [0\ 0\ 1]^\top$.

Outward-Facing Camera. For an outward-facing camera, the translation direction is reversed:

$$P_{out} = [R \mid -\mathbf{z}]. \tag{2}$$

3.2   Relative Pose

Given two inward-facing cameras with extrinsics $P_1 = [R_1 \mid \mathbf{z}]$ and $P_2 = [R_2 \mid \mathbf{z}]$, we can now derive the relative pose $[R \mid \mathbf{t}_{in}]$ between them. The relative rotation is

$$R = R_2 R_1^\top. \tag{3}$$

and the relative translation is

$$\mathbf{t}_{in} = \mathbf{z} - \mathbf{r}_3 \tag{4}$$

where $\mathbf{r}_3$ denotes the third column of R.

For outward-facing cameras with relative pose $[R \mid \mathbf{t}_{out}]$, the rotation is the same and the translation direction is reversed:

$$\mathbf{t}_{out} = \mathbf{r}_3 - \mathbf{z}. \tag{5}$$

3.3   Essential Matrix

The essential matrix E relates corresponding camera normalized (i.e. calibrated) homogeneous points $\mathbf{u}$ and $\mathbf{v}$ in two images such that

$$\mathbf{v}^\top E \mathbf{u} = 0. \tag{6}$$

If the two images have relative pose $[\mathsf{R}|\mathbf{t}]$ then

$$\mathsf{E} = [\mathbf{t}]_\times \mathsf{R}, \tag{7}$$

where $[\mathbf{a}]_\times$ is the skew-symmetric matrix such that $[\mathbf{a}]_\times \mathbf{b} = \mathbf{a} \times \mathbf{b} \; \forall \; \mathbf{b}$.

Plugging in the relative pose expressions given above, the essential matrices for inward- and outward-facing cameras are

$$\mathsf{E}_{in} = [\mathbf{z} - \mathbf{r}_3]_\times \mathsf{R} \tag{8}$$

and

$$\mathsf{E}_{out} = [\mathbf{r}_3 - \mathbf{z}]_\times \mathsf{R}. \tag{9}$$

Note that $\mathsf{E}_{in} = -\mathsf{E}_{out}$. Since the essential matrix is only defined up to scale, the essential matrix for inward- and outward-facing cameras underoing the same relative rotation is equivalent.

4   Solving for the Essential Matrix

Here we characterize the essential matrix relating cameras undergoing spherical motion and derive a solution for all possible essential matrices arising from at least three correspondences between two images.

In general, the essential matrix has five degrees of freedom [9], corresponding to three rotational degrees of freedom and two translational, since in the general case the translation is only defined up to scale. However, the special form of essential matrix for spherical motion derived above is determined completely by three rotational degrees of freedom. This implies that we can solve for the essential matrix using only three correspondences, as opposed to the five correspondences needed in the general case [17].

The essential matrix for spherical motion has a special form and can be fully described by six parameters $e_1, \ldots, e_6$:

$$\mathsf{E} = \begin{bmatrix} e_1 & e_2 & e_3 \\ e_2 & -e_1 & e_4 \\ e_5 & e_6 & 0 \end{bmatrix} \tag{10}$$

This can be derived using the fact that, since R is orthonormal, each column can be expressed as a cross product of the other two.

4.1   Finding the Nullspace

Given $n \geq 3$ corresponding image points $\mathbf{u}_1, \ldots, \mathbf{u}_n$ and $\mathbf{v}_1, \ldots, \mathbf{v}_n$, we have n epipolar constraint equations of the form

$$\mathbf{v}_i^\top \mathsf{E} \mathbf{u}_i = 0. \tag{11}$$

We re-arrange and stack the epipolar constraints to form a linear system on the parameters:

$$
\begin{bmatrix}
u_{11}v_{11} - u_{12}v_{12} & u_{11}v_{12} + u_{12}v_{11} & u_{13}v_{11} & u_{13}v_{12} & u_{11}v_{13} & u_{12}v_{13} \\
\vdots & \vdots & \vdots & \vdots & \vdots & \vdots \\
u_{n1}v_{n1} - u_{n2}v_{n2} & u_{n1}v_{n2} + u_{n2}v_{n1} & u_{n3}v_{n1} & u_{n3}v_{n2} & u_{n1}v_{n3} & u_{n2}v_{n3}
\end{bmatrix}
\begin{bmatrix}
e_1 \\ e_2 \\ e_3 \\ e_4 \\ e_5 \\ e_6
\end{bmatrix} = 0
$$

(12)

where u_{ij} denotes the j-th element of $\mathbf{u}_i$.

We now find three 6×1 vectors $\mathbf{b}_1, \mathbf{b}_2, \mathbf{b}_3$ spanning the right nullspace of the $n \times 6$ matrix on the left-hand side of Eq. 12. The essential matrix must be of the form

$$
\mathsf{E} =
\begin{bmatrix}
b_{11}x + b_{21}y + b_{31}z & b_{12}x + b_{22}y + b_{32}z & b_{13}x + b_{23}y + b_{33}z \\
b_{12}x + b_{22}y + b_{32}z & -b_{11}x - b_{21}y - b_{31}z & b_{14}x + b_{24}y + b_{34}z \\
b_{15}x + b_{25}y + b_{35}z & b_{16}x + b_{26}y + b_{36}z & 0
\end{bmatrix}
$$

(13)

for some scalars x, y, z. Here b_{ij} denotes the j-th element of vector b_i.

Any choice of scalars x, y, z will produce a solution for E which satisfies the epipolar constraints. However, a second requirement is that the matrix must satisfy the properties of an essential matrix; namely, that it is rank two and that both non-zero singular values are equal [5]. These properties lead to non-linear constraints which are solved in the following subsection.

4.2 Applying Non-linear Constraints

The requirements on the singular values of the essential matrix are enforced by the following cubic constraints [5]:

$$
\mathsf{E}\mathsf{E}^\top\mathsf{E} - \frac{1}{2}\text{trace}(\mathsf{E}\mathsf{E}^\top)\mathsf{E} = 0.
$$

(14)

This 3×3 matrix equation gives a system of nine cubic constraints in x, y, z. Since the essential matrix is only determined up to scale, we let $z = 1$.

Using a symbolic math toolbox, we found that this system has rank six, and that the second and third rows of the system form a linearly independent set of six equations.

We separate these six equations into a 6×10 matrix A of coefficients and a vector $\mathbf{m}$ of 10 monomials such that

$$
\mathbf{A}\mathbf{m} = \mathbf{0}
$$

(15)

where

$$
\mathbf{m} = \begin{bmatrix} x^3 & x^2y & xy^2 & y^3 & x^2 & xy & y^2 & x & y & 1 \end{bmatrix}^\top .
$$

(16)

4.3 Solution Using the Action Matrix Method

The action matrix method has been established as a general tool to solve systems of polynomial equations arising from geometric computer vision problems [13]. Briefly, once we have found a Gröbner basis [3,4] for the system of polynomial equations, we can derive a transformation from the coefficient matrix to an action matrix whose eigenvalues and eigenvectors contain the solutions.

Using the Macaulay2 algebraic geometry software system, we determined that Eq. 15 has at most four solutions. By ordering the monomials in $\mathbf{m}$ using graded reverse lexicographic ordering and running Gauss-Jordan elimination on A, we immediately arrive at a Gröbner basis for the ideal I generated by the six polynomial equations, since this leaves only four monomials that are not divisible by any of the leading monomials in the equations. These monomials form a basis for the quotient ring $\mathbb{C}[x, y]/I$ and are the same basis monomials reported by Macaulay2.

Let G be the 6×4 matrix such that $\begin{bmatrix} \mathsf{I}_6 & \mathsf{G} \end{bmatrix}$ is the result of running Gauss-Jordan elimination on A. Now we have

$$\begin{bmatrix} \mathsf{I}_6 & \mathsf{G} \end{bmatrix} \mathbf{m} = \mathbf{0} \tag{17}$$

which implies that

$$x^3 + G_{11}y^2 + G_{12}x + G_{13}y + G_{14} = 0 \tag{18}$$

$$x^2 y + G_{21}y^2 + G_{22}x + G_{23}y + G_{24} = 0 \tag{19}$$

$$xy^2 + G_{31}y^2 + G_{32}x + G_{33}y + G_{34} = 0 \tag{20}$$

$$y^3 + G_{41}y^2 + G_{42}x + G_{43}y + G_{44} = 0 \tag{21}$$

$$x^2 + G_{51}y^2 + G_{52}x + G_{53}y + G_{54} = 0 \tag{22}$$

$$xy + G_{61}y^2 + G_{62}x + G_{63}y + G_{64} = 0. \tag{23}$$

Using Eqs. 20, 22 and 23 we can define a 4×4 matrix A_x as

$$\mathsf{A}_x = \begin{bmatrix} -G_{31} & -G_{32} & -G_{33} & -G_{34} \\ -G_{51} & -G_{52} & -G_{53} & -G_{54} \\ -G_{61} & -G_{62} & -G_{63} & -G_{64} \\ 0 & 1 & 0 & 0 \end{bmatrix} \tag{24}$$

so that

$$\mathsf{A}_x \begin{bmatrix} y^2 \\ x \\ y \\ 1 \end{bmatrix} = x \begin{bmatrix} y^2 \\ x \\ y \\ 1 \end{bmatrix}. \tag{25}$$

Thus the eigenvalues of A_x are solutions for x, and the eigenvectors contain corresponding solutions for y. A_x is the "action matrix" for x and $y^2, x, y, 1$ are the basis monomials.

Once we have found up to four real-valued solutions for x and y by eigen-decomposition of A_x, we apply them in Eq. 13 to produce four solutions for the essential matrix E.

4.4   Solution by Reduction to Single Polynomial

A possibly faster method to find solutions for x and y would be to use the characteristic polynomial of A_x to find its eigenvalues:

$$|A_x - xI_3| = 0. \tag{26}$$

This involves computing the determinant of a 4×4 matrix of polynomials in y. We found that a slight speedup is possible by transforming the problem to instead use a 3×3 symbolic determinant.

First, we define $\mathbf{m}'$ which is a reordering the monomials in $\mathbf{m}$:

$$\mathbf{m}' = \begin{bmatrix} x^3 & x^2y & xy^2 & y^3 & y^2 & y & x^2 & xy & x & 1 \end{bmatrix}^\top. \tag{27}$$

The system of equations $A\mathbf{m} = \mathbf{0}$ from Eq. 15 is rewritten using this new ordering. We form a reordered matrix of coefficients A' such that

$$A'\mathbf{m}' = \mathbf{0}. \tag{28}$$

Let G' be the 6×4 matrix such that $\begin{bmatrix} I_6 & G' \end{bmatrix}$ is the result of running Gauss-Jordan elimination on A'. Now we have

$$\begin{bmatrix} I_6 & G' \end{bmatrix} \mathbf{m}' = \mathbf{0} \tag{29}$$

which implies that

$$x^3 + G'_{11}x^2 + G'_{12}xy + G'_{13}x + G'_{14} = 0 \tag{30}$$

$$x^2y + G'_{21}x^2 + G'_{22}xy + G'_{23}x + G'_{24} = 0 \tag{31}$$

$$xy^2 + G'_{31}x^2 + G'_{32}xy + G'_{33}x + G'_{34} = 0 \tag{32}$$

$$y^3 + G'_{41}x^2 + G'_{42}xy + G'_{43}x + G'_{44} = 0 \tag{33}$$

$$y^2 + G'_{51}x^2 + G'_{52}xy + G'_{53}x + G'_{54} = 0 \tag{34}$$

$$y + G'_{61}x^2 + G'_{62}xy + G'_{63}x + G'_{64} = 0. \tag{35}$$

Using Eqs. 33, 34 and 35 we can define a 3×3 matrix $B(y)$ as

$$B(y) = \begin{bmatrix} G'_{41} & G'_{43} + G'_{42}y & G'_{44} + y^3 \\ G'_{51} & G'_{53} + G'_{52}y & G'_{54} + y^2 \\ G'_{61} & G'_{63} + G'_{62}y & G'_{64} + y \end{bmatrix} \tag{36}$$

so that

$$B(y) \begin{bmatrix} x^2 \\ x \\ 1 \end{bmatrix} = \mathbf{0}. \tag{37}$$

Because $B(y)$ has a null vector, its determinant must be equal to zero, leading to a quartic polynomial $\langle n \rangle$ in y:

$$\langle n \rangle \equiv |B(y)| = 0. \tag{38}$$

The quartic polynomial $\langle n \rangle$ can be solved in closed-form using Ferrari's method. Once we have four solutions for y, the corresponding solutions for x are found by finding a null vector of $B(y)$. Then the solutions for x and y are used to produce solutions for the essential matrix using Eq. 13.

4.5 Decomposition of the Essential Matrix

Once we have a solution for the essential matrix, we need to decompose it into a rotation and translation to find the relative pose. The decomposition follows the normal procedure for extracting a "twisted pair" of solutions [9], giving two solutions for the rotation, R_a and R_b, and one solution for the translation direction $\hat{t}$ which is only determined up to scale.

Let $E \sim USV^\top$ be the singular value decomposition of E where U and V are chosen such that $|U| > 0$ and $|V| > 0$. Define matrix D as

$$D = \begin{bmatrix} 0 & 1 & 0 \\ -1 & 0 & 0 \\ 0 & 0 & 1 \end{bmatrix}. \tag{39}$$

Then $R_a = UDV^\top$ and $R_b = UD^\top V^\top$. The solution for the translation direction is $\hat{t} = [U_{13} \; U_{23} \; U_{33}]^\top$.

Only one of the rotations is consistent with spherical motion. Let t_a and t_b be corresponding translation vectors for rotation solutions R_a and R_b, respectively, determined by Eq. 4 if the cameras are inward-facing or Eq. 5 if the cameras are outward-facing. We can choose the correct relative pose solution by choosing the rotation whose corresponding translation is closest to the translation solution t.

Specifically, we define scores s_a and s_b according to the absolute value of the normalized dot product between t_a or t_b and $\hat{t}$:

$$s_a = \frac{|t_a \cdot \hat{t}|}{||t_a||}, s_b = \frac{|t_b \cdot \hat{t}|}{||t_b||}. \tag{40}$$

The solution with higher score is chosen as the correct relative pose:

$$[R| \; t] = \begin{cases} [R_a| \; t_a] & \text{if } s_a > s_b, \\ [R_b| \; t_b] & \text{otherwise.} \end{cases} \tag{41}$$

5 An Integrated Structure from Motion Pipeline

The algorithms described in Sect. 4 enable us to solve for the relative pose between two cameras from a minimal or overdetermined set of image correspondences. The minimal solver is useful for random sample consensus (RANSAC) [6] where we compute relative pose hypotheses from randomly sampled minimal sets of correspondences and accept the hypothesis with the highest number of inliers.

In this section we describe an integrated structure-from-motion pipeline which uses our novel solvers to recover the camera trajectory from a spherical motion image sequence by aggregating pairwise relationships and produce a 3D point cloud reconstruction of the scene.

The input to the pipeline is a sequence of images captured by an inward- or outward-facing camera undergoing spherical motion. We assume the camera is pre-calibrated so that its intrinsic parameters including focal length, principal point, and radial and tangential distortion coefficients are known.

5.1   Feature Tracking and Relative Pose Estimation

We first use feature detection and tracking to establish image correspondences between neighboring images in the sequence. Between each successive pair of images in the sequence, we apply one of our spherical motion solvers from Sect. 4 in a Preemptive RANSAC loop [18] in order to robustly estimate the essential matrix and find a consensus set of inliers. To test inliers we threshold the Sampson error [9] between the epipolar line and the image point in the second image. Outlier feature tracks are removed from consideration in successive frames.

Either minimal solver gives at most four solutions for the essential matrix from three correspondences. We choose the essential matrix with lowest error on a fourth randomly sampled correspondence. Finally, the decomposition of the essential matrix gives two possible rotations R_a and R_b which are disambiguated using the score function described in Sect. 4.5.

5.2   Loop Closure

After processing the images in sequence, we detect loop closures by matching features between non-neighboring images. Each feature in image i is matched to its nearest neighbor in image j. The set of putative matches between images i and j are then filtered using Preemptive RANSAC with one of our minimal solvers, and the resulting relative pose is recorded if the number of inliers exceeds a threshold.

5.3   Global Pose Estimation by Rotation Averaging

At this point, we have a set of estimated rotations R_{ij} between images i and j in the sequence. Now we can apply rotation averaging [8] to produce a global estimate of all camera orientations. Specifically, we use the robust L1 rotation averaging method of Chatterjee and Madhav Govindu [2]. Since the translation of each camera is fully determined by the camera's rotation, this effectively produces an estimate of all camera poses.

5.4   Inverse Depth Bundle Adjustment

Finally, we refine the camera pose estimates using bundle adjustment. The output of the previous steps is an estimated pose $[R_i|t_i]$ for each camera and features matches between images. The feature matches are aggregated into feature tracks across multiple images.

The rotation R_i of each camera is parameterized by a 3×1 vector r_i where $R_i = \exp_{SO(3)}(r_i)$. Since the translation is vector is fixed, we do not need to explicitly parameterize it.

We found that, especially with an outward-facing camera, the traditional methods of algebraic triangulation and bundle adjustment over 3D point locations are unstable because of the small baselines involved. Instead, we use an inverse depth parameterization which extends the work of Yu and Gallup [29].

Each 3D point $\mathbf{x}_j$ has a designated reference camera with index n_j so that

$$\mathbf{x}_j = \mathsf{R}_{n_j}^\top (w_j \mathbf{u}_{n_j,j} - \mathbf{t}_{n_j}) \tag{42}$$

where $\mathbf{u}_{n_j,j}$ is the observation of point j in camera n_j and w_j is the inverse depth of point j. We set the reference camera of each point to be the first camera which observed it in the image sequence.

The output of global rotation averaging gives an initialization for the camera rotations. To initialize the 3D points, we first linearly solve for w_j using all observations of the point. Then we use non-linear optimization over all rotation and inverse depth parameters to minimize the total robustified re-projection error

$$\sum_{(i,j)\in\mathcal{V}} h(\|\pi(\mathbf{u}_{i,j}) - \pi(\mathsf{R}_i\mathbf{x}_j + \mathbf{t}_i)\|^2) \tag{43}$$

where $\pi(\mathbf{u})$ is the perspective projection function $\pi([x\ y\ z]^\top) = [x/z\ y/z]^\top$ and $(i,j) \in \mathcal{V}$ if camera i observes point j. $h(\cdot)$ is the Huber cost function which robustifies the minimization against outlier measurements [10].

6   Evaluation

6.1   Essential Matrix Solvers

In this section we evaluate the speed and accuracy of our novel essential matrix solvers and compare them against the state-of-the-art five-point solution by Stewénius et al. [26] for general camera motion. We will refer to our action matrix solution from Sect. 4.3 as **Spherical** and our polynomial solution from Sect. 4.4 as **SphericalPoly**, and we will refer to the five-point solution as **Stewénius**. We use the implementation of **Stewénius** provided in the OpenGV library [12].

Random Problem Generation. To make synthetic data for our tests, we generate random spherical motion problems using the following scheme. First we generate a random rotation of the desired magnitude θ and calculate the first and second camera poses according to this relative rotation, so that both cameras lie on the unit sphere. Then we randomly generate 3D points within a range of distances from the first camera; we use a distance range of $[0.25\ 0.75]$ for inward-facing cameras and $[4\ 8]$ for outward-facing cameras. Each 3D point is projected into both cameras using a focal length of 600 and Gaussian noise is added to the point observations with standard deviation of σ pixels.

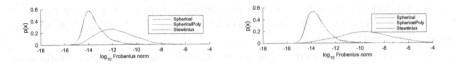

Fig. 1. Kernel density plots for numerical error of minimal solvers with ideal observations and inward-facing cameras (*top*) and outward-facing cameras (*bottom*).

Timing. We calculated the average computation for our solvers over 10 000 randomly generated problems. The testing was performed on a 2.6 GHz Intel Core i5 with optimized code written in C++. **Spherical** and **SphericalPoly** takes 6.9 μs and 6.4 μs on average, respectively. **Stewénius** takes 98 μs; however, the implementation in OpenGV is not optimized for speed.

Numerical Accuracy. We tested the numerical accuracy of the solvers with ideal, zero-noise observations. We generated 1000 random problems with a rotation of $\theta = 1$ degrees and $\sigma = 0$ pixels using both the inward- and outward-facing configuration. We then ran each solver on the problem sets and calculated the Frobenius norm of the error between estimated and true essential matrix. To test the minimal configuration, our solvers used three correspondences for estimation with a fourth for disambiguation and **Stewénius** used five corresponces for estimation with a sixth for disambiguation. The results are plotted in Fig. 1.

Our spherical solvers are almost equivalent to each other in numerical accuracy and are two to four orders of magnitude more accurate than **Stewénius** for spherical camera motion estimation.

Noise. We tested the robustness of the solvers to varying levels of added noise in the image observations. We generated 1000 random problems with a rotation of $\theta = 1$ degrees and $\sigma = 0, 1, \ldots, 10$ pixels using both the inward- and outward-facing configuration. We then ran each solver on the problem sets and calculated the angular error $\|\log_{SO(3)}(R_{\text{true}} \cdot R_{\text{estimate}}^{\top})\|$. For a fair comparison on noisy data, each solver used five correspondences for estimation. The results are plotted in Fig. 2.

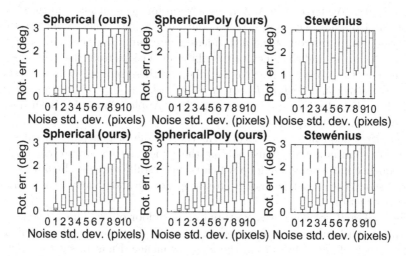

Fig. 2. Box plots for angular error of minimal solvers with noisy observations and inward-facing cameras (*top*) and outward-facing cameras (*bottom*).

Again, both of our solvers are about equivalent in terms of accuracy and outperform **Stewénius** for spherical motion estimation with noisy correspondences.

6.2   Structure-from-Motion Pipeline

We tested the entire proposed structure-from-motion pipeline on several image sequences captured with both inward- and outward-facing configurations. We describe here the details of our implementation and show the resulting 3D reconstructions.

Implementation Details. In our experiments we apply the Oriented FAST and Robust BRIEF (ORB) feature detector [22] and Kanade-Lucas-Tomasi (KLT) feature tracker [15,27]. The KLT tracker uses sub-pixel refinement which is especially helpful for a handheld, outward-facing camera where baseline the between images might be small relative to the scene depth. We use an threshold of 2 pixels for both RANSAC inlier testing and the Huber cost function.

For efficiency, in our experiments we only detect loop closures with the first frame in the sequence. We detect loop closures by iterating through the sequence backward from the last frame and stop when the number of inliers is below the threshold. Feature matches are chosen as the nearest neighbor in Hamming distance between ORB descriptors. A loop closure is accepted if it has at least 100 inliers.

The pipeline was implemented in C++ using OpenCV for image processing functions and Ceres [1] for non-linear optimization. We set a minimum inverse depth of 0.01; points at this distance are essentially points at infinity.

Video Tests. We tested our system on several image sequences captured both indoors and outside with inward- and outward-facing camera configurations. While the general motion of the test videos is circular, they were captured with a handheld camera and thus inevitably exhibit deviations from the circular path. A circular motion solver similar to [23] failed on these sequences in our tests.

For the *street* and *bookshelf* sequences, we used a Sony $\alpha5100$ camera with 16 mm lens. For the *face* sequence we used an Apple iPhone 5s. Both devices were set to record 1080p video.

The *street* sequence was captured in the middle of a neighborhood street corner. We spun in a circle while holding the camera in our outstretched hands. This sequence has a complete loop which is successfully detected by our system. Figure 3 shows the reduction in drift after loop closure and a view of the complete 3D reconstruction.

The *bookshelf* sequence was captured in an indoor office. This sequence was also capture with outward-facing configuration but does not complete a full loop and has much closer objects than the *street* sequence. Figure 3 shows a view of the 3D reconstruction.

Fig. 3. *Top left*: Estimated camera centers from the *street* sequence before loop closure. *Bottom left*: Camera centers after rotation avergaging and bundle adjustment. *Middle*: 3D reconstruction of the *street* sequence. The red dots are camera centers and the blue dots are reconstructed scene points. *Right*: 3D reconstruction of the *bookshelf* sequence. (Color figure online)

The *face* sequence was captured by holding the iPhone in an outstretched hand with the lens pointed at the user's shoulder. Rotating the arm produces inward-facing spherical motion which was used to capture a scan of the user's face. Figure 4 shows a sample image and the 3D reconstruction.

To further illustrate the accuracy of these reconstructions, we selected image pairs from each sequence and performed stereo rectification using the recovered relative pose. We used block matching to produce disparity maps as shown in Figs. 4 and 5.

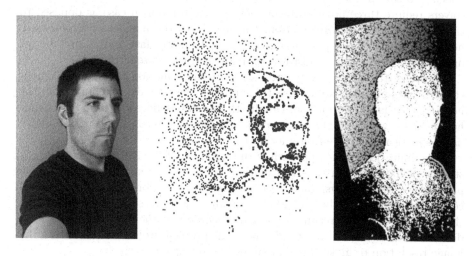

Fig. 4. *Left*: Image from the *face* sequence. *Middle*: 3D reconstruction of the *face* sequence. The red dots are camera centers and the blue dots are reconstructed scene points. *Right*: Disparity map from a rectified stereo pair from the *face* sequence. (Color figure online)

Fig. 5. Disparity maps from from the *street* and *bookshelf* sequences.

7 Conclusions and Future Work

In this work we analyzed the geometry of spherical camera motion. We introduced two solvers for the essential matrix arising from spherical motion. The solvers require three point correspondences in the minimal case as opposed to the five needed for general motion, which reduces the number of hypothesese needed for random sample consensus. The solvers are fast and exhibit better numerical accuracy and robustness to noise than the state-of-the-art.

By integrating these solvers into a structure-from-motion pipeline, we demonstrated that spherical motion greatly simplifies the problem by eliminating the need for translation estimation. Despite the small baselines captured by a hand-held camera, we found that accurate and large-scale reconstruction is possible using spherical structure-from-motion.

One limitation of the approach is the rigidness of the spherical motion constraint; deviations from spherical motion will cause the structure-from-motion pipeline to fail. The system is less sensitive to deviations from the spherical constraint when the sphere's radius is small relative to scene depth; however, the precision of the 3D reconstruction also degrades as the radius-to-depth ratio decreases. One possible way to alleviate this problem would be to increase the image resolution to make the parallax detectable again.

Future work includes more exploration of the potential applications of spherical structure-from-motion for user-friendly scene modeling and object scanning.

Acknowledgments. This material is based upon work supported by the National Science Foundation under Grant No. 1464420.

References

1. Agarwal, S., Mierle, K., et al.: Ceres solver. http://ceres-solver.org
2. Chatterjee, A., Madhav Govindu, V.: Efficient and robust large-scale rotation averaging. In: IEEE International Conference on Computer Vision (ICCV) (2013)
3. Cox, D.A., Little, J., O'shea, D.: Using Algebraic Geometry, 2nd edn. Springer, New York (2005)
4. Cox, D.A., Little, J., O'shea, D.: Ideals, Varieties, and Algorithms, 3rd edn. Springer, New York (2007)
5. Faugeras, O.: Three-Dimensional Computer Vision: A Geometric Viewpoint. MIT Press, Cambridge (1993)
6. Fischler, M.A., Bolles, R.C.: Random sample consensus: a paradigm for model fitting with applications to image analysis and automated cartography. Commun. ACM **24**(6), 381–395 (1981)
7. Fitzgibbon, A.W., Cross, G., Zisserman, A.: Automatic 3D model construction for turn-table sequences. In: Koch, R., Van Gool, L. (eds.) SMILE 1998. LNCS, vol. 1506, pp. 155–170. Springer, Heidelberg (1998)
8. Hartley, R., Trumpf, J., Dai, Y., Li, H.: Rotation averaging. Int. J. Comput. Vis. **103**(3), 267–305 (2013)
9. Hartley, R., Zisserman, A.: Multiple View Geometry in Computer Vision. Cambridge University Press, Cambridge (2003)
10. Huber, P.J.: Robust estimation of a location parameter. Ann. Math. Stat. **35**(1), 73–101 (1964)
11. Jiang, G., Quan, L., Tsui, H.T.: Circular motion geometry using minimal data. IEEE Trans. Pattern Anal. Mach. Intell. **26**(6), 721–731 (2004)
12. Kneip, L., Furgale, P.: OpenGV: a unified and generalized approach to real-time calibrated geometric vision. In: 2014 IEEE International Conference on Robotics and Automation (ICRA) (2014)
13. Kukelova, Z., Bujnak, M., Pajdla, T.: Automatic generator of minimal problem solvers. In: Forsyth, D., Torr, P., Zisserman, A. (eds.) ECCV 2008, Part III. LNCS, vol. 5304, pp. 302–315. Springer, Heidelberg (2008)
14. Longuet-Higgins, H.C.: A computer algorithm for reconstructing a scene from two projections. In: Readings in Computer Vision: Issues, Problems, Principles, and Paradigms, pp. 61–62 (1987)
15. Lucas, B.D., Kanade, T.: An iterative image registration technique with an application to stereo vision. In: IJCAI, pp. 674–679 (1981)
16. Mendonça, P.R.S., Wong, K.Y.K., Cipolla, R.: Epipolar geometry from profiles under circular motion. IEEE Trans. Pattern Anal. Mach. Intell. **23**(6), 604–616 (2001)
17. Nister, D.: An efficient solution to the five-point relative pose problem. IEEE Trans. Pattern Anal. Mach. Intell. **26**(6), 756–770 (2004)
18. Nister, D.: Preemptive RANSAC for live structure and motion estimation. In: Ninth IEEE International Conference on Computer Vision, Proceedings (2003)
19. Peleg, S., Ben-Ezra, M.: Stereo panorama with a single camera. In: IEEE Computer Society Conference on Computer Vision and Pattern Recognition (1999)
20. Peleg, S., Herman, J.: Panoramic mosaics by manifold projection. In: 1997 IEEE Computer Society Conference on Computer Vision and Pattern Recognition, Proceedings (1997)
21. Pollefeys, M., Van Gool, L., Vergauwen, M., Verbiest, F., Cornelis, K., Tops, J., Koch, R.: Visual modeling with a hand-held camera. Int. J. Comput. Vision **59**(3), 207–232 (2004)

22. Rublee, E., Rabaud, V., Konolige, K., Bradski, G.: ORB: an efficient alternative to SIFT or SURF. In: 2011 IEEE International Conference on Computer Vision (ICCV) (2011)
23. Scaramuzza, D., Fraundorfer, F., Siegwart, R.: Real-time monocular visual odometry for on-road vehicles with 1-point ransac. In: IEEE International Conference on Robotics and Automation, ICRA 2009, pp. 4293–4299 (2009)
24. Shum, H.Y., Szeliski, R.: Stereo reconstruction from multiperspective panoramas. In: The Proceedings of the Seventh IEEE International Conference on Computer Vision (1999)
25. Snavely, N., Seitz, S.M., Szeliski, R.: Photo tourism: exploring photo collections in 3D. ACM Trans. Graph. (TOG) **25**, 835–846 (2006). ACM
26. Stewénius, H., Engels, C., Nistér, D.: Recent developments on direct relative orientation. ISPRS J. Photogramm. Remote Sens. **60**(4), 284–294 (2006)
27. Tomasi, C., Kanade, T.: Detection and tracking of point features. Technical report, CMU-CS-91-132, School of Computer Science, Carnegie Mellon University, Pittsburgh (1991)
28. Wilson, K., Snavely, N.: Robust global translations with 1DSfM. In: Fleet, D., Pajdla, T., Schiele, B., Tuytelaars, T. (eds.) ECCV 2014, Part III. LNCS, vol. 8691, pp. 61–75. Springer, Heidelberg (2014)
29. Yu, F., Gallup, D.: 3D reconstruction from accidental motion. In: 27th IEEE Conference on Computer Vision and Pattern Recognition (2014)

Evaluation of LBP and Deep Texture Descriptors with a New Robustness Benchmark

Li Liu[1]([⊠]), Paul Fieguth[2], Xiaogang Wang[3],
Matti Pietikäinen[4], and Dewen Hu[5]

[1] College of Information System and Management,
National University of Defense Technology, Changsha, China
liuli_nudt@nudt.edu.cn
[2] Department of Systems Design Engineering,
University of Waterloo, Waterloo, Canada
pfieguth@uwaterloo.ca
[3] Department of Electronic Engineering,
Chinese University of HongKong, Shatin, China
xgwang@ee.cuhk.edu.hk
[4] The Center for Machine Vision Research,
University of Oulu, Oulu, Finland
mkp@ee.oulu.fi
[5] College of Mechatronics and Automation,
National University of Defense Technology, Changsha, China
dwhu@nudt.edu.cn

Abstract. In recent years, a wide variety of different texture descriptors has been proposed, including many LBP variants. New types of descriptors based on multistage convolutional networks and deep learning have also emerged. In different papers the performance comparison of the proposed methods to earlier approaches is mainly done with some well-known texture datasets, with differing classifiers and testing protocols, and often not using the best sets of parameter values and multiple scales for the comparative methods. Very important aspects such as computational complexity and effects of poor image quality are often neglected.

In this paper, we propose a new extensive benchmark (RoTeB) for measuring the robustness of texture operators against different classification challenges, including changes in rotation, scale, illumination, viewpoint, number of classes, different types of image degradation, and computational complexity. Fourteen datasets from the eight most commonly used texture sources are used in the benchmark. An extensive evaluation of the recent most promising LBP variants and some non-LBP descriptors based on deep convolutional networks is carried out. The best overall performance is obtained for the Median Robust Extended Local Binary Pattern (MRELBP) feature. For textures with very large appearance variations, Fisher vector pooling of deep Convolutional Neural Networks is clearly the best, but at the cost of very high computational complexity. The sensitivity to image degradations and computational complexity are among the key problems for most of the methods considered.

Keywords: Local binary pattern · Deep learning · Performance evaluation · Texture classification

© Springer International Publishing AG 2016
B. Leibe et al. (Eds.): ECCV 2016, Part III, LNCS 9907, pp. 69–86, 2016.
DOI: 10.1007/978-3-319-46487-9_5

1 Introduction

Texture is a ubiquitous and fundamental characteristic of the appearance of virtually all natural surfaces. Texture classification plays an important role in the fields of computer vision and pattern recognition, including biomedical image analysis, industrial inspection, analysis of satellite or aerial imagery, document image analysis, face analysis and biometrics, object recognition, material recognition and content based image retrieval.

The texture classification problem is conventionally divided into two subproblems of feature extraction and classification. It is generally agreed that the extraction of powerful texture features is of greater importance to the overall success of a texture classification strategy and, consequently, most research focuses on the feature extraction part, with extensive surveys [1,2]. Nevertheless it remains a challenge to design texture features which are computationally efficient, highly discriminative and effective, and robust to the imaging environment, including changes in illumination, rotation, view point, scaling, occlusion, and noise level.

A texture image or region obeys some statistical properties and exhibits repeated structures. Therefore, dense orderless statistical distribution of local texture features have been dominating the texture recognition literature since 1990s. The study of texture recognition has inspired many of the early representations of images. The idea of representing texture using the statistics of local features have led to the development of "textons" [3,4], the popular "Bag-of-Words (BoW)" models [5–9] and their variants such as the Fisher Vector [10]. Within the BoW framework, texture images are represented as histograms by pooling over a discrete vocabulary of discriminative and robust local features [4,6]. Important local texture descriptors include filter banks such as Gabor wavelets [11], LM filters [4], MR8 filters [6], raw pixel intensity-based features such as Local Binary Pattern (LBP) [5], Patch descriptors [8], random features [9], sparse descriptors such as SPIN [7], SIFT [1] and RIFT [7], and others [1,2]. Alternatives to simple histogram pooling have been proposed, such as Fisher Vectors (FVs) [12].

LBP [2,5] has emerged as one of the most prominent texture features and a great many new variants continue to be proposed. LBP's strengths include avoiding the time consuming discrete vocabulary pretraining stage in the BoW framework, its overall computational simplicity, its monotonic gray-scale invariance, its flexibility, and ease of implementation.

Recently, methods based on deep convolutional networks have emerged as a promising alternative to conventional "manually designed" features such as LBP. Important examples includes FV-CNN [13,14], obtained by Fisher Vector pooling of a Convolutional Neural Network (CNN) filter bank pretrained on large-scale datasets such as ImageNet, ScatNet (Scattering Convolution Networks) [15,16], PCANet [17] and RandNet [17]. When comparing these to LBP, only basic single resolution LBP methods have been normally considered [18] and no systematic performance evaluation has been carried out.

However, there has been a proliferation of LBP-related methods, so any comparison against a relatively small set cannot be considered an exhaustive investigation against the LBP strategy. Furthermore recent LBP studies show that the use of multi-scale information, for example, can significantly improve the performance of LBP variants, therefore it is highly pertinent to perform a more comprehensive performance evaluation and fair comparison of LBP approaches against novel challengers from the deep learning domain. The tests performed in this paper seek to explore and assess four criteria:

Computational complexity is an important factor in designing computer vision systems systems for real-world applications, particularly for portable computing systems (*e.g.*, smart phones, smart glasses) with strict low power constraints. Many papers emphasize primarily recognition accuracy, where we feel the need to balance this perspective with computational complexity as well.

Multiscale variations have been proposed for most LBP variations in their respective original works, but usually limited to three scales. Since the spatial support of a texture descriptor influences its classification performance, for fair comparison we propose to implement multiscale and rotational-invariant formulations of *each* LBP method up to nine scales, following the multiscale analysis approach proposed by Ojala *et al.* [5].

A large number of texture classes is one aspect complicating many texture analysis problems, together with the associated dynamics within a class (intra-class variations), such as variations in periodicity, directionality and randomness, and the external dynamics due to changes in the imaging conditions including variations in illumination, rotation, view point, scaling, occlusion and noise. Despite this complexity, most existing LBP variants have been evaluated only on small texture datasets with a relatively small number of texture classes, such as certain popular benchmark Outex test suites [5]. Experimental results based on datasets with small intraclass variations can be misleading; there are more challenging texture datasets with many texture classes or large intraclass variations, such as UIUC [7], UMD [19], CUReT [8] and KTHTIPS2b [20], DTD [21], ALOT [22] and Outex_TC40 [23], however, the performance of many LBP variants in these more challenging datasets is unknown. There is therefore significant value in performing a large scale empirical study on such challenging texture datasets.

Robustness to poor image quality, due to noise, image blurring and random image corruption, is usually neglected in the performance evaluation of texture operators. However any feature which performs only under idealized circumstances is almost guaranteed to disappoint in practice, therefore we are proposing an ensemble of robustness tests to better assess the generalizability of a given strategy away from its training setting. Noise can be severe in many medical (ultrasound, radiography), astronomical, and infrared images. The two main limitations in image accuracy are blur and noise, both of which we will test.

The main contributions of this paper are to propose a new challenging benchmark for a fair evaluation of different descriptors in texture classification, presenting a performance evaluation of the most promising LBP variants, and comparing to recent well-known texture features based on deep convolutional networks. In order to establish a common software platform and a collection of datasets for easy evaluation, we plan to make both the source code and datasets available on the Web.

2   Local Binary Pattern Methods Under Comparison

Local Binary Pattern (LBP). The original LBP [24] characterizes the spatial structure of a local image texture pattern by thresholding a 3×3 square neighborhood with the value of the center pixel and considering only the sign information to form a local binary pattern. A circular symmetric neighborhood is suggested, where locations that do not fall exactly at the center of a pixel are interpolated [5]. The LBP operator was extended to multiscale analysis to allow any radius and number of pixels in the neighborhood. A rotation invariant version $LBP_{r,p}^{ri}$ of $LBP_{r,p}$ was obtained by grouping together those LBPs that are actually rotated versions of the same pattern. Observing that some LBP patterns occur more frequently than others, the *uniform* LBP $LBP_{r,p}^{u2}$ preserves only these frequent patterns, grouping all remaining ones. $LBP_{r,p}^{riu2}$ is the combination of $LBP_{r,p}^{ri}$ and $LBP_{r,p}^{u2}$ [5].

Median Binary Pattern (MBP). Instead of using only the gray value of the center pixel for thresholding, MBP uses the local median. MBP also codes the value of the center pixel, resulting in a doubling in the number of LBP bins.

Local Ternary Pattern (LTP). LTP was proposed by Tan and Triggs in [25] to tackle the image noise in uniform regions. Instead of binary code, the pixel difference is encoded by three values according to a threshold T. LTP is capable of encoding pixel similarity modulo noise using the simple rule that any two pixels within some range of intensity are considered similar, but no longer strictly invariant to gray scale transformations.

Noise Resistant Local Binary Pattern (NRLBP). In a similar strategy to LTP, Ren *et al.* [26] proposed to encode small pixel difference as an uncertain bit, and then to determine its value based on the other bits of the LBP code. The main idea of NRLBP is to allow multiple LBP patterns to be generated at one pixel position, however NRLBP requires a lookup table of size 3^p for p neighboring pixels, which limits the neighborhood size.

Novel Extended Local Binary Pattern (NELBP). NELBP [27] is designed to make better use of the nonuniform patterns instead of discarding them. NELBP classifies and combines the "nonuniform" local patterns based on analyzing their structure and occurrence probability.

Local Binary Pattern Variance (LBPV). Guo *et al.* [28] proposed LBPV to incorporate local contrast information by utilizing the variance as a locally adaptive weight to adjust the contribution of each LBP code. LBPV avoids the quantization pretraining used in [5].

Noise Tolerant Local Binary Pattern (NTLBP). With similar motivations as NELBP [27], Fathi and Naghsh-Nilchi [29] proposed NTLBP that not only

Table 1. Summary of texture datasets used in our experimental evaluation. $\Theta_1 = \{5°, 10°, 15°, 30°, 45°, 60°, 75°, 90°\}$, $\Theta_2 = \{0°, 5°, 10°, 15°, 30°, 45°, 60°, 75°, 90°\}$

Texture Dataset	Texture Classes	Sample Size (pixels)	# Images /Class	# Train /Class	# Test /Class	# Images in Total	Train/Test Predefined?	Instances Categories?	Description
Outex_TC10	24	128 × 128	180	20	160	4320	Yes	Instances	rotation changes (0° angle for training and angles in Θ_1 for testing)
Outex_TC12_000	24	128 × 128	200	20	180	4800	Yes	Instances	illumination variations, rotation changes
Outex_TC12_001	24	128 × 128	200	20	180	4800	Yes	Instances	(0° angle for training and angles in Θ_2 for testing)
CUReT	61	200 × 200	46	46	92	5612	No	Instances	illumination changes, small rotations, shadowing, pose changes
Brodatz	111	215 × 215	9	3	6	999	No	Instances	lack of intraclass variations
BrodatzRot	111	128 × 128	9	3	6	999	No	Instances	rotation changes, lack of intraclass variations
UIUC	25	320 × 240	40	20	20	1000	No	Instances	strong scale, rotation and viewpoint changes, nonrigid deformations
UMD	25	320 × 240	40	20	20	1000	No	Instances	strong scale, rotation and viewpoint changes
KTH-TIPS2b	11	200 × 200	432	324	108	4752	Yes	Categories	illumination changes, small rotation changes, large scale changes
DTD	47	Not Fixed	120	80	40	5640	Yes	Categories	Attribute-based class, many texture categories per class
ALOT	250	384 × 256	100	50	50	25000	No	Instances	strong illumination changes, large number of classes, rotation changes
Outex_TC40_A	294	128 × 128	180	80	100	52920	Yes	Instances	rotation changes, large number of classes
Outex_TC40_B	294	128 × 128	180	80	100	52920	Yes	Instances	illumination changes, rotation changes, large number of classes
Outex_TC40_C	294	128 × 128	180	80	100	52920	Yes	Instances	illumination changes, rotation changes, large number of classes

Datasets for Noise Robustness Evaluation						
Texture Dataset	Texture Classes	Sample Size (pixels)	# Images /Class	# Train Images in Total	# Test Images in Total	Description
Outex_TC11n	24	128 × 128	20	480 (20 * 24)	480 (20 * 24)	Training: illuminants (inca), Rotations (0°)
Outex_TC23n	68	128 × 128	20	1360 (20 * 68)	1360 (20 * 68)	Testing: Training images injected with Gaussian Noise
Outex_TC11b	24	128 × 128	20	480 (20 * 24)	480 (20 * 24)	Training: illuminants (inca), Rotations (0°)
Outex_TC23b	68	128 × 128	20	1360 (20 * 68)	1360 (20 * 68)	Testing: Training images blurred by Gaussian PSF
Outex_TC11s	24	128 × 128	20	480 (20 * 24)	480 (20 * 24)	Training: illuminants (inca), Rotations (0°)
Outex_TC23s	68	128 × 128	20	1360 (20 * 68)	1360 (20 * 68)	Testing: Training images injected with Salt-and-Pepper
Outex_TC11c	24	128 × 128	20	480 (20 * 24)	480 (20 * 24)	Training: illuminants (inca), Rotations (0°)
Outex_TC23c	68	128 × 128	20	1360 (20 * 68)	1360 (20 * 68)	Testing: Training images with Random Pixel Corruption

uses nonuniform patterns but also tolerates noise by using a circular majority voting filter and a scheme to regroup the nonuniform LBP patterns into several different classes.

Pairwise Rotation Invariant Cooccurrence Local Binary Pattern (PRICoLBP). Borrowing from Gray Level Cooccurrence Matrices (GLCM) [30], Qi et al. [31] proposed PRICoLBP to encapsulating the joint probability of pairs of LBPs at relative displacements. PRICoLBP incorporates two types of context: spatial cooccurrence and orientation cooccurrence. The method aims to preserve the relative angle between the orientations of individual features. The length of the feature vector may limit the applicability of PRICoLBP.

Multiscale Joint encoding of Local Binary Pattern (MSJLBP). Instead of considering cooccurrences of LBPs at different locations as in PRICoLBP [31], MSJLBP [32] was proposed to jointly encode the pairwise information of LBPs at the same centered location but from two different scales.

Completed Local Binary Pattern (CLBP). CLBP was proposed by Guo et al. [33] to combine multiple LBP type features (CLBP_S, CLBP_M and CLBP_C) via joint histogramming for texture classification. The image local differences between a center pixel and its neighbors are decomposed into two complementary components: the signs and the magnitudes (CLBP_S and CLBP_M). The center pixels, representing image gray level, were also regarded to have discriminative information and are converted into a binary code by global thresholding.

discriminative Completed Local Binary Pattern (disCLBP). Guo et al. [34] proposed a three-layered learning model, estimating the optimal pattern subset of interest by simultaneously considering the robustness, discriminative power and representation capability of features. This model is generalized and can be integrated with existing LBP variants such as conventional LBP, rotation invariant patterns, CLBP and LTP to derive new image features.

Table 2. Classification results (%) for various LBP variants on the Outex_TC10 and Outex_TC12 (Outex_TC12_000 and Outex_TC12_001) test suites as a function of neighborhood size (the number scales used for multiscale analysis). For each method, the highest classification accuracies are highlighted in bold for each dataset. LEP filtering support is 65 × 65. Some results (○) are not provided for efficiency reasons.

Test Suite		Outex_TC10 (Rotation Invariance)									Outex_TC12 (Illumination and Rotation Invariance)								
No.	Method	3×3	5×5	7×7	9×9	11×11	13×13	15×15	17×17	19×19	3×3	5×5	7×7	9×9	11×11	13×13	15×15	17×17	19×19
1	LBP^{riu2}	84.71	93.44	97.21	98.91	99.01	99.38	99.56	99.66	**99.69**	64.97	82.07	86.79	89.64	89.12	89.72	90.81	91.39	**92.14**
2	MBP^{riu2}	80.21	87.40	89.92	92.47	94.24	94.90	95.16	95.21	**95.29**	63.18	73.01	79.71	83.66	84.57	85.09	85.69	86.22	**86.69**
3	LTP^{riu2}	92.94	97.14	98.54	99.32	99.53	99.74	99.84	99.84	**99.92**	73.59	86.46	90.88	92.08	92.35	92.78	93.25	93.77	**94.28**
4	$NRLBP^{riu2}$	89.79	93.78	96.67	97.01	**98.07**	97.81	95.60	95.05	93.44	71.35	83.00	87.05	88.92	89.57	**90.20**	88.78	87.48	86.76
5	NELBP	83.52	93.88	97.08	98.70	98.88	98.93	99.48	99.53	**99.64**	69.02	85.34	88.72	89.91	89.59	90.10	91.30	92.15	**93.55**
6	NTLBP	84.24	91.88	96.15	98.10	98.88	99.19	**99.35**	99.32	99.24	67.06	82.21	88.28	91.61	92.71	93.63	94.88	**95.27**	95.23
7	$PRICoLBP_g$	—	—	—	—	—	**94.48**	—	—	—	—	—	—	—	—	**92.53**	—	—	—
8	MSJLBP	—	—	**96.67**	—	—	—	—	—	—	—	—	**95.47**	—	—	—	—	—	—
9	$disCLBP$	89.30	97.47	98.93	99.79	**99.95**	○	○	○	○	75.22	89.80	94.40	96.00	**96.10**	○	○	○	○
10	LEP	—	—	—	—	—	—	—	—	**81.90**	—	—	—	—	—	—	—	—	**81.46**
11	CLBP	96.72	98.67	99.35	99.45	99.51	99.51	99.51	99.53	**99.58**	91.54	94.48	95.67	**95.78**	95.49	95.39	95.43	95.43	95.42
12	ELBP	96.41	99.38	99.66	**99.71**	99.71	99.66	99.64	99.56	99.53	92.08	97.37	**97.57**	97.08	96.52	96.10	96.06	96.05	96.03
13	BRINT	91.88	96.95	98.52	99.04	99.32	99.32	99.30	**99.40**	99.35	87.48	94.29	96.28	97.16	97.29	97.53	97.71	97.96	**98.13**
14	MRELBP	—	**98.44**	—	99.69	—	99.79	—	**99.82**	—	—	**96.24**	—	99.03	—	99.56	—	**99.57**	—
15	$LBPV^{riu2}$	91.30	94.35	97.24	98.49	98.93	99.22	**99.27**	99.14	99.11	76.88	86.76	92.72	93.34	93.92	93.81	93.92	**94.03**	94.00
16	CLBPHF	87.42	94.61	98.20	99.01	99.56	99.69	**99.71**	99.71	99.69	78.39	90.29	93.34	94.10	94.07	94.07	94.39	94.61	**94.80**
17	LBPD	—	—	**98.78**	—	—	—	—	—	—	—	—	**96.67**	—	—	—	—	—	—
18	RILPQ	—	—	—	—	—	**99.58**	—	—	—	—	—	—	—	—	**97.43**	—	—	—

Extended Local Binary Pattern (ELBP). ELBP is proposed by Liu *et al.* [35] to combine several LBP–related features: pixel intensities and differences from local patches. The intensity-based features consider the intensity of the central pixel (CI) and those of its neighbors (NI); differences are computed by radius and by angle. ELBP reflects the combination of radial differences (RD) and two intensities.

Binary Rotation Invariant and Noise Tolerant Texture descriptor (BRINT). Similar to CLBP [33] and ELBP [35], BRINT [36] combines three individual descriptors BRINT_S, BRINT_M and BRINT_C. Unlike CLBP and ELBP, where only rotation invariant uniform patterns are considered, BRINT uses all of the rotation invariant patterns. In BRINT, pixels are sampled in a circular neighborhood, but keeping the number of bins in a single-scale LBP histogram constant and small, such that arbitrarily large circular neighborhoods can be sampled and compactly encoded. BRINT has low feature dimensionality and noise robustness.

Median Robust Extended Local Binary Pattern (MRELBP). In order to jointly capture microtexture and macrotexture information, Liu *et al.* [37] built on the NI, RD and CI of ELBP [35] but with nonlocal–median pixel sampling, significantly outperforming ELBP, especially in situations of noise, image blurring and random image corruption. Moreover, MRELBP is fast to compute and has much lower feature dimensionality.

Completed Local Binary Pattern Histogram Fourier Features (CLBPHF). Ahonen *et al.* [38] proposed the LBP Histogram Fourier features (LBPHF) to achieve rotation invariance globally by first computing a uniform LBP histogram over the whole image, and then constructing rotationally invariant features from the DFT transform of the histogram. Later in [39], LBPHF is combined CLBP [33] to further improve its distinctiveness and results CLBPHF.

Local Energy Pattern (LEP). Zhang *et al.* [40] proposed LEP for texture classification, where multiscale and multiorientation Gaussian-like second order derivative filters are used to filter the original image. LEP encodes the relationship among different feature channels using an N-nary coding scheme, rather than binary. One downside of the LEP is that pretraining is required.

Local Binary Pattern Difference (LBPD). Covariance Matrices capture correlation among elementary features of pixels over an image region. Ordinary LBP features cannot be used as elementary features, since they are not numerical variables in Euclidean spaces. To address this problem, Hong *et al.* [41] developed COV-LBP. First the LBPD, a Euclidean space variant, was proposed, reflecting how far one LBP lies from the LBP mean of a given image region. Secondly, the covariance was found of a bank of discriminative features, including LBPD.

Rotation Invariant Local Phase Quantization (RILPQ). LPQ [42] is generated by quantizing the Fourier transform phase in local neighborhoods, such that histograms of LPQ labels computed within local regions are used as a texture descriptor similar to LBP, leading to a tolerance to image blur. LPQ was generalized with a rotation invariant extension to RILPQ [43].

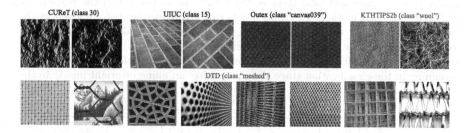

Fig. 1. Datasets such as CUReT, UIUC and Outex addressed the problem of instance-level identification. KTH-TIPS2b addressed the problem of category-level material recognition. The DTD dataset addresses a very different problem of category-level attribute recognition, *i.e.* describing a pattern using intuitive attributes. In DTD, many visually very different texture categories appear in the same attribute class, which makes the classification problem very challenging.

2.1 Recent Non-LBP Deep Learning Approaches

FV-CNN. Deep convolutional neural networks (CNN) have demonstrated their power as a universal representation for recognition. However, global CNN activations lack geometric invariance, which limits their robustness for recognizing highly variable images. Cimpoi *et al.* [13,14] propose an effective texture descriptor FV-CNN, obtained by first extracting CNN features from convolutional layers for an texture image at multiple scale levels, and then performing orderless Fisher Vector pooling of these features.

ScatNet. Despite significant progress, there is still little insight into the internal operation and behavior of deep CNN models. Arguably one instance that has led to a clear mathematical justification is the multistage architectures of ConvNet [13,44], and specifically in the wavelet convolutional scattering network (Scat-Net) [15,16] where the convolutional filters are predefined as wavelets, hence no learning process is needed. ScatNet has been extended to achieve rotation and scale invariance [45].

PCANet and **RandNet.** Motivated by ScatNet, Chan *et al.* [17] proposed a simple deep learning network, PCANet, based on cascaded / multistage principal component analysis (PCA), binary hashing, and histogram pooling. The authors also introduced RandNet, a simple variation of PCANet, which shares the same topology as PCANet, but in which the cascaded filters are randomly selected, not learned.

Table 3. Performance comparison for LBP variants tested on a number of texture datasets in terms of classification scores (%) and computational complexity (including feature extraction time and feature dimensionality). All results in Part I are obtained with a NNC classifier, with the exception of SVM for the DTD results. Results for PCANet and RandNet on DTD are also obtained with SVM. For each dataset, the highest score is shadowed, and those scores which are within 1 % of the highest are boldfaced. For each method, the total number of highlighted scores are given in the "# Bold" column. In the "Time" column, the reported time does not include the extra training time for those methods labeled with (⋆). The (⋄) label in the LBPD method means that although LBPD has low feature dimensionality, it is pretty time consuming in the classification stage since it requires an affine invariant metric in the NNC classification.

No.	Method / # Classes	Outex_TC10 (24)	Outex_TC12 (24)	CUReT (61)	Brodatz (111)	BrodatzRot (111)	UMD (25)	UIUC (25)	KTHTIPS2b (11)	DTD (47)	ALOT (250)	Outex_TC40A (294)	Outex_TC40LBC (294)	# Bold	Feature Extraction Time (ms)	Feature Dimension	Outex_TC23a σ=5 (68)	Outex_TC23b σ=1 (68)	Outex_TC23c ρ=15% (68)	Outex_TC23c υ=20% (68)
	Part I: Evaluation the performance of representative LBP methods.																			
1	MRELBP [37]	99.82	99.58	97.10	90.86	81.92	98.66	94.73	68.98	44.89	97.28	96.20	78.97	6	416.6	800	79.2	85.8	99.9	96.9
2	CLBP [33]	99.45	95.78	97.33	92.34	84.35	98.62	95.75	64.18	42.63	96.74	96.98	65.49	7	127.9	3552	5.6	36.1	2.9	2.9
3	ELBP [35]	99.66	97.57	96.60	93.24	85.92	98.93	94.61	64.84	39.80	97.21	96.18	67.70	6	114.6	2200	3.3	19.7	1.5	4.4
4	CLBPHF [39]	99.69	94.80	97.05	91.95	82.07	97.24	92.55	68.10	50.21	96.30	96.42	69.63	5	256.2	4580	17.5	39.1	2.9	1.5
5	disCLBP [34]	99.95	96.10	96.98	93.18	83.77	97.53	94.24	63.83	44.47	95.01	97.54	74.00	4	(⋆)585.8	7796	12.3	27.1	4.4	2.6
6	LTP^{riu2} [25]	99.92	94.28	96.33	92.41	83.51	96.66	93.27	63.45	41.45	94.60	96.85	69.14	4	231.8	420	7.7	24.3	3.5	2.9
7	BRINT [36]	99.35	98.13	97.02	90.83	78.77	97.44	93.30	66.67	45.35	96.13	96.24	81.85	3	248.8	1296	27.4	59.1	1.5	1.6
8	LBP^{riu2} [5]	99.69	92.14	97.03	90.70	79.22	96.15	88.36	62.69	37.09	94.15	94.83	71.72	2	87.2	210	8.4	16.6	1.5	1.5
9	NELBP [27]	99.64	93.55	96.85	90.19	80.08	95.55	88.29	62.39	39.93	95.20	95.39	74.87	2	91.3	273	10.3	17.8	1.5	1.5
10	MSJLBP [32]	96.67	95.47	97.20	92.94	79.11	96.53	83.00	65.51	43.14	95.65	88.59	60.09	2	854.6	3540	4.9	14.8	3.5	2.7
11	NTLBP [29]	99.32	95.27	96.11	89.31	80.25	95.72	88.13	61.30	38.24	94.47	91.70	69.49	1	332.3	3540	9.0	21.7	4.7	3.7
12	PRICoLBP$_g$ [31]	94.48	92.53	96.25	92.94	77.00	95.39	80.38	61.17	44.53	54.38	89.56	64.16	1	380.4	4580	5.6	19.6	2.1	1.5
13	LBPV^{riu2} [28]	99.27	93.92	95.85	87.63	75.80	93.79	81.98	59.03	36.21	91.87	92.88	73.20	1	350.7	158	15.4	15.6	1.5	2.6
14	RILPQ [43]	99.58	97.43	93.41	92.15	79.59	97.49	91.17	58.75	42.70	94.85	90.76	69.33	1	44.8	256	56.5	53.9	1.5	2.6
15	LBPD [41]	98.78	96.67	94.23	89.74	74.79	92.99	90.98	63.47	35.86	92.82	89.96	60.60	0	(⋄)54.2	289	14.8	40.2	2.9	2.6
16	NRLBP^{riu2} [26]	98.07	89.57	94.00	87.42	75.77	93.32	81.10	58.61	37.77	87.86	89.93	61.34	0	356.9	50	9.1	20.3	2.9	5.3
17	LEP [40]	81.90	81.46	88.31	82.64	61.41	91.75	81.80	63.13	38.67	89.67	74.97	56.07	0	(⋆)1088.9	520	76.8	100.0	1.8	5.6
18	MBP^{riu2} [46]	95.29	86.69	92.09	87.25	74.57	92.41	80.89	61.49	27.73	88.23	84.90	45.46	0	215.6	420	5.2	13.5	2.5	2.6
	Part II: comparing MRELBP with deep convolutional network based approaches.																			
1	MRELBP (SVM) [37]	99.97	99.77	99.02	93.12	85.06	99.36	96.88	77.91	44.89	99.08	97.15	77.79	5	416.6	800	70.5	69.8	99.1	95.5
2	FV-VGGVD (SVM) [13]	80.0	82.3	99.0	98.7	92.1	99.0	99.8	88.2	72.3	99.5	93.7	71.6	8	(⋆)2655.4	65536	71.5	83.6	5.2	9.5
3	FV-VGGM (SVM) [13]	72.8	77.5	98.7	98.6	88.2	99.0	99.7	79.9	66.8	99.4	92.6	56.8	7	(⋆)358.8	65536	43.9	65.7	1.5	4.9
4	FV-AlexNet (SVM) [13]	99.69	99.06	99.66	84.46	75.08	98.40	96.15	68.92	35.72	98.03	94.07	77.93	5	10883.7	596	31.3	53.0	1.5	1.5
5	ScatNet (PCA) [16]	67.3	72.3	98.4	98.2	83.1	99.7	99.1	77.9	62.9	99.1	90.4	51.8	1	(⋆)238.6	32768	46.0	63.6	5.0	8.6
6	ScatNet (NNC) [16]	98.59	98.10	95.51	83.03	73.72	93.36	88.64	63.53	26.53	85.27	87.55	72.45	0	10883.7	596	45.3	41.9	1.5	2.9
7	PCANet [17] (NNC)	39.87	45.53	92.03	90.89	37.21	90.50	57.70	59.43	41.44	88.35	59.49	44.39	0	(⋆)711.8	2048	50.7	51.9	1.5	1.5
8	PCANet^{riu2} [17] (NNC)	35.36	40.88	81.48	85.76	29.96	85.67	49.80	52.15	30.11	79.77	33.25	21.80	0	(⋆)725.6	80	43.9	36.8	1.5	2.6
9	RandNet [17] (NNC)	47.43	52.45	90.87	91.14	40.84	90.87	56.57	60.67	36.66	86.94	65.28	42.55	0	711.8	2048	6.2	27.7	1.5	1.5
10	RandNet^{riu2} [17] (NNC)	43.54	45.70	80.46	85.59	30.78	87.40	48.20	56.90	26.51	73.51	45.14	25.96	0	725.6	80	5.9	20.6	1.5	1.5

Table 4. Classification scores (%) in the context of additive Gaussian noise and Gaussian blurring.

Robust to	Gaussian noise		Gaussian blur							
Dataset (Outex_)	TC11n	TC23n	TC11b				TC23b			
No Method	$\sigma = 5$	$\sigma = 5$	$\sigma = 0.5$	$\sigma = 0.75$	$\sigma = 1$	$\sigma = 1.25$	$\sigma = 0.5$	$\sigma = 0.75$	$\sigma = 1$	$\sigma = 1.25$
1 MRELBP [37]	**91.5**	**79.2**	**100.0**	**100.0**	**93.8**	75.4	99.9	**97.9**	85.8	61.8
2 CLBP [33]	11.9	5.6	98.8	74.8	49.6	23.1	86.6	55.4	36.1	21.2
3 ELBP [35]	9.4	3.3	98.3	71.5	38.5	21.5	86.2	39.9	19.7	11.0
4 CLBPHF [39]	20.6	17.5	99.6	81.3	47.9	29.4	85.4	59.2	39.1	25.1
5 disCLBP [34]	25.2	12.3	100.0	70.2	39.4	20.8	95.6	51.0	27.1	14.1
6 LTP^{riu2} [25]	13.7	7.7	96.9	58.3	27.3	13.7	77.3	43.1	24.3	13.3
7 BRINT [36]	*61.9*	*27.4*	*100.0*	*97.1*	*80.4*	*44.6*	*100.0*	*79.5*	*59.1*	*39.1*
8 LBP^{riu2} [5]	17.7	8.4	94.2	46.5	24.6	12.7	72.4	30.3	16.6	9.7
9 NELBP [27]	19.2	10.3	94.0	47.7	28.3	17.1	73.3	32.0	17.8	10.5
10 MSJLBP [32]	17.7	4.9	96.0	46.0	26.0	11.9	74.9	28.9	14.8	8.9
11 NTLBP [29]	24.0	9.0	96.3	49.0	33.1	19.4	80.1	35.7	21.7	14.1
12 PRICoLBP$_g$ [31]	15.4	5.6	98.1	50.0	26.5	14.4	81.1	32.5	19.6	11.3
13 LBPV^{riu2} [28]	27.1	15.4	96.9	52.1	22.3	17.1	73.9	34.3	15.6	8.3
14 RILPQ [43]	*82.9*	*56.5*	*100.0*	*99.2*	*76.7*	*45.8*	*100.0*	*76.0*	*53.9*	*37.2*
15 LBPD [41]	24.6	14.8	99.4	85.8	65.2	45.4	87.7	56.0	40.2	30.6
16 NRLBP^{riu2} [26]	21.7	9.1	93.3	46.0	20.0	9.2	63.2	36.3	20.3	8.8
17 LEP [40]	**91.9**	**76.8**	**100.0**	**100.0**	**100.0**	**100.0**	**100.0**	**100.0**	**100.0**	**99.8**
18 MBP^{riu2} [46]	12.1	5.2	85.4	29.0	18.5	11.9	58.7	22.5	13.5	10.6
19 FV-VGGVD (SVM) [13]	**93.1**	71.5	**100.0**	**100.0**	**96.5**	**89.8**	99.6	**94.1**	**83.1**	**71.8**
20 FV-VGGM (SVM) [13]	81.5	43.9	100.0	99.0	87.3	60.8	96.5	87.7	65.7	42.4
21 ScatNet (PCA) [16]	60.2	31.3	100.0	94.8	80.0	64.6	97.7	72.4	53.0	41.1
22 FV-AlexNet (SVM) [13]	81.5	46.0	100.0	98.8	87.7	60.4	97.1	82.8	63.6	43.4
23 ScatNet (NNC) [16]	77.1	45.3	100.0	91.7	68.5	40.2	92.7	60.4	41.9	24.0
24 PCANet [17]	74.0	50.7	100.0	100.0	86.0	56.9	100.0	99.2	51.9	31.0
25 PCANet^{riu2} [17]	62.7	43.9	100.0	88.8	52.5	32.5	100.0	64.6	36.8	25.7
26 RandNet [17]	15.3	6.2	100.0	78.1	56.5	37.4	96.2	40.4	27.7	19.4
27 RandNet^{riu2} [17]	14.8	5.9	97.8	64.2	42.1	33.3	81.1	37.2	20.6	18.9

3 Experimental Setup

We conducted experiments on the *fourteen* texture datasets shown in Table 1. These datasets are derived from the eight most commonly used texture sources: Outex [23], CUReT [8], Brodatz [47], UIUC [7], UMD [19], KTHTIPS2b [20], ALOT [22] and DTD [21]. The experimental setup on the three test suites **Outex_TC10**, **Outex_TC12_000** and **Outex_TC12_001**, which were designated by Ojala *et al.* [5] for rotation and illumination invariant texture classification, was kept exactly as in [5].

Following Ojala *et al.* we created **Outex_TC40_A**, **Outex_TC40_B** and **Outex_TC40_C** [5] for large-scale texture classification. Each dataset contains 294 texture classes, with training data acquired under illuminant "inca" and rotations $0°$, $30°$, $45°$ and $60°$, and tested with rotations $5°$, $10°$, $15°$, $75°$ and $90°$. The test images in **A** are from illumination "inca", the same as the training images, and thus simpler than datasets **B** and **C**, with testing data from illumination types "Horizon" and "TL84", respectively.

For **CUReT**, we use the same subset of images as in [8,9]. For **Brodatz** [47] we use the same dataset as [1,7,48]. The **BrodatzRot** dataset is generated from Brodatz by rotating each sample at a random angle, helping to test rotation invariance. The challenging **UIUC** dataset [7] contains images with strong scale, rotation and viewpoint changes in uncontrolled illumination environment. The **UMD** dataset [19] is similar to UIUC with higher resolution images but exhibits less nonrigid deformations and stronger illumination changes. We resize images in ALOT to obtain lower resolution (384×256). ALOT is challenging as it represents a significantly larger number of classes (250) compared to UIUC and UMD (25) and has very strong illumination changes (8 levels of illumination), albeit with less dramatic viewpoint changes.

Generalizing the texture recognition problem to a recognition of surface material, **KTH-TIPS2b** [20] has four physical samples for each class, imaged under 3 viewing angles, 4 illuminants, and 9 different scales. A quite different database, **DTD** contains textures in the wild, collected from the web and organized according to a list of 47 attribute categories inspired from human perception, with a single category containing rather different textures, as shown in Fig. 1. This dataset aims at supporting real-world applications where the recognition of texture properties is a key component.

To evaluate the robustness with respect to random noise, we considered Gaussian noise, image blurring, salt-and-pepper noise, and random pixel corruption, the same noise types tested in [49]. We use only the noise-free texture images for training and test on the noisy data, as summarized in Table 1. The test suites are based on Outex_TC11n and Outex_TC23n, which have 24 and 68 texture classes, respectively. The noise parameters include Gaussian noise standard deviation σ, Gaussian blur standard deviation σ, Salt-and-Pepper noise density ρ, and pixel corruption density v.

Implementation Details. For the evaluated methods, we use the original source code if it is publicly available, and for the remainder we have developed our own implementation. To ensure fair comparisons, the parameters of each method are fixed across all the datasets, since it is difficult and undesirable to tune the parameters of each method for each evaluation. In most cases we use the default parameters suggested in the original papers. For ScatNet, we used the same feature presented in [15]. For PCANet and RandNet, we used the parameter settings suggested for texture classification in [17].

For most of the tested LBP methods, multiscale variations had been proposed in the original work, but usually limited to three scales. Since the spatial support of a texture descriptor influences its classification performance, for fair comparison we implemented multiscale and rotational invariant formulations of *each* LBP method up to nine scales, following the multiscale analysis approach proposed by Ojala *et al.* [5], representing a texture image by concatenating histograms from multiple scales.

Each texture sample is preprocessed, normalized to zero mean and unit standard deviation. For CUReT Brodatz, BrodatzRot, UIUC, UMD and ALOT, half of the class samples were selected at random for training and the remaining half for testing, and all results are reported over 100 random partitionings of training and testing sets. For KTHTIPS2b, we follow the training and testing scheme of [50]: training on three samples and testing on the remainder. For DTD, we follow Cimpoi et al. [13,21], where 80 images per class were randomly selected as training and the rest 40 as testing. All results for DTD are reported over 10 random partitionings of training and testing sets, following [13]. There have been some proposals to use more sophisticated classifiers, such as support vector machines (SVM), SVM ensembles, decision trees, or random forests. However, in this work our focus was on the distinctiveness and robustness of various LBP variants, rather than on the impact of the classifier. Therefore, unless otherwise stated, we limit our study to using the nearest neighbor classifier (NNC) and keep the other components as similar as possible.

4   Experimental Results

4.1   Overall Results

Table 2 evaluates the multiscale and rotational-invariant formulations of each LBP method up to nine scales. We can observe a general trend of performance increase with neighborhood size, with most LBP methods achieving a best performance beyond three scales, clearly indicating the necessity of using larger areas of spatial support for LBP feature extraction. Based on the results in Table 2, in our following experiments we use that neighborhood size which gives the highest score for each LBP method.

The main results for RoTeB are summarized in Table 3, including a comprehensive evaluation of all methods on fourteen benchmark datasets with varying difficulty, computation complexity comparison (including feature extraction time and feature dimensionality), with detailed noise robustness evaluation presented in Tables 4 and 5.

The most robust method is MRELBP [37] which gives the best overall performance, considering the trade off between classification accuracy, computational complexity and robustness to several types of noise. Generally MRELBP even performs better than the recent well-known deep convolutional networks based approach — ScatNet [45]. Keep in mind that the expensive computational cost of ScatNet is a severe drawback. The MRELBP benefits from its sampling scheme the spatial domain spanned by which is much larger than by many other LBP variants. This is likely to result in better discrimination capability. More importantly, instead of applying the standard thresholding to the raw pixel values, MRELBP applies it to the local medians, which works surprisingly robustly.

For the noise-free results of Table 3, we can clearly observe the best performing methods as CLBP [33], ELBP [35], MRELBP [37], CLBPHF [39], ScatNet (PCA) [15,16] and FV-CNN [13]. Among these six methods, clearly the feature extraction time of ScatNet is much more longer than others and represents a significant drawback. The feature dimensionality of CLBP, ELBP, and CLBPHF are relatively high, with the FV-CNN at an extremely high feature dimension. A serious shortcoming of PCANet and RandNet is their lack of rotation invariance.

If the textures have very large within-class appearance variations, due to view and scale variations and combined texture categories as in DTD, then the FV-CNN methods cleraly perform the best. Nevertheless, from the Outex results it can be observed that FV-CNN is relatively weak on rotation invariance, despite FV-CNN methods using data augmentation to explore multiscale information. Moreover, FV-CNN is computationally expensive, making it unfeasible to run in real-time embedded systems with low-power constraints. Interestingly, CLBPHF [39] works rather well for DTD, perhaps because it is more insensitive to large texture appearance variations than the other LBP descriptors. The 50.21 % of CLBPHF on DTD is much higher than the scores given by MR8, LM filters and Patch features, close to 52.3 % of BoW encoding of SIFT features reported in [14].

Finally, from Table 3, the best scores on datasets Outex_TC10, Outex_TC12 and CUReT are 99.95 %, 99.58 % and 99.66, nearly perfect scores even with simple NNC classification. Especially for Outex_TC10, thirteen methods give scores higher than 99 %, leaving essentially no room for improvement. Because of that saturation, and because most LBP variants have not been evaluated in recognizing a large number of texture classes, we prepared the new Outex_TC40 benchmark test suite with 294 texture classes, where the results are significantly more spread out.

4.2 Noise Robustness

Noise robustness results are shown in Tables 4 and 5. The training images were all noise free which makes the problem very hard. From Table 3 the overall best results (without noise) were given by CLBP, CLBPHF, ELBP, MRELBP, ScatNet (PCA) and FV-CNN, however with the exception of MRELBP, all of them perform poorly in noisy situations, especially when the noise level is high. The results in both tables are consistently strong: MRELBP has exceptional noise tolerance that could not be matched by any of the other tested methods, clearly driven by the nonlinear, regional medians captured by MRELBP.

From the random noise and blur tests of Table 4 the best performing methods are LEP, MRELBP and FV-CNN, due to the filtering built into each of these methods. Although RILPQ is specifically designed to address image blur, it is outperformed by LEP, MRELBP and FV-CNN in that context.

Table 5 presents the results for salt-and-pepper noise and random pixel corruption respectively. As the noise level increases, with few exceptions the performance of most of the LBP methods reduces to random classification. MRELBP stands out exceptionally clearly, performing very well (above 90 %) up to 30 % random pixel corruption, difficult noise levels where MRELBP offers strong performance, but where not a single other method delivers acceptable results.

Table 5. Classification scores (%) in the context of random salt and pepper noise with density ρ and randomly corrupted pixels. In the latter case we corrupted a certain percentage of randomly chosen pixels from each of the images, replacing their values with independent samples from a uniform distribution. The corrupted pixels are randomly chosen for each test image, with the locations unknown to the algorithm.

		Salt and Pepper Noise										Random Corrupted Pixels									
		Outex_TC11s (24 classes)					Outex_TC23s (68 classes)					Outex_TC11c (24 classes)					Outex_TC23c (68 classes)				
		Noise Density ρ					Noise Density ρ					Percentage of corrupted pixels v					Percentage of corrupted pixels v				
No.	Method	5%	15%	30%	40%	50%	5%	15%	30%	40%	50%	5%	10%	20%	30%	40%	5%	10%	20%	30%	40%
1	MRELBP [37]	100.0	100.0	100.0	85.8	50.2	100.0	99.9	94.0	54.6	19.2	100.0	100.0	100.0	99.6	90.6	99.6	99.2	96.9	89.8	57.5
2	CLBP [33]	17.3	8.3	4.2	4.2	4.2	7.6	2.9	1.5	1.6	1.5	61.9	26.5	4.2	4.2	4.2	28.7	5.7	2.9	3.0	2.9
3	ELBP [35]	40.4	4.6	4.2	4.2	4.2	16.2	1.5	1.5	1.5	1.5	60.6	31.9	13.1	7.1	4.2	25.4	11.3	4.4	2.9	2.9
4	CLBPHF [39]	14.4	4.2	4.2	4.2	4.2	6.0	2.9	1.6	1.4	1.5	50.0	11.9	4.2	4.2	4.2	23.2	3.4	1.5	0.3	1.5
5	disCLBP [34]	11.0	8.3	8.3	8.3	8.3	5.1	4.4	2.9	1.5	1.5	57.5	24.6	4.4	4.2	4.2	21.5	5.8	2.6	1.5	1.5
6	LTP^{riu2} [25]	9.0	6.3	8.3	8.3	8.3	4.3	3.5	2.9	2.9	2.9	60.0	23.3	4.4	4.2	4.2	21.1	6.6	2.9	2.6	2.9
7	BRINT [36]	30.8	7.1	6.0	4.4	4.2	15.9	1.5	1.5	1.3	1.5	89.0	53.5	17.5	7.3	4.2	62.1	20.4	1.6	1.5	1.5
8	LBP^{riu2} [5]	31.7	4.2	4.2	4.2	4.2	11.8	1.5	1.5	1.5	1.5	51.5	8.3	4.2	4.2	4.2	21.3	6.0	1.5	1.5	1.5
9	NELBP [27]	27.3	4.2	4.2	4.2	4.2	12.2	1.5	1.5	1.5	1.5	51.5	11.3	4.2	4.2	4.2	25.3	5.6	1.5	1.5	1.5
10	MSJLBP [32]	14.2	8.3	4.4	4.2	4.2	7.1	3.5	1.5	1.5	1.5	32.3	16.7	7.5	4.2	4.2	14.4	5.6	2.7	1.7	1.2
11	NTLBP [29]	74.4	22.1	4.8	5.0	6.3	40.5	4.7	3.8	2.6	2.7	82.5	45.6	11.9	4.2	4.2	49.8	22.9	3.7	1.5	1.5
12	PRICoLBP$_g$ [31]	9.6	5.2	4.2	4.2	4.2	4.2	2.1	1.5	1.5	1.5	31.7	10.0	4.2	4.2	4.2	9.0	3.0	1.5	1.5	1.5
13	LBPV^{riu2} [28]	4.6	4.2	4.2	4.2	4.2	2.8	1.5	1.5	1.5	1.5	17.7	5.0	4.2	4.2	4.2	4.0	1.5	1.5	1.5	1.5
14	RILPQ [43]	15.0	4.2	4.2	4.2	4.2	3.2	1.5	1.5	1.5	1.5	62.7	37.7	11.7	7.5	5.4	27.9	8.7	2.6	2.0	1.6
15	LBPD [41]	25.2	8.3	4.2	4.2	5.0	10.3	2.9	1.5	1.5	0.1	32.3	18.1	7.1	4.2	4.2	12.5	6.5	2.6	1.5	1.5
16	NRLBP^{riu2} [26]	8.8	8.1	8.3	4.2	4.2	2.1	2.9	2.6	1.5	1.5	72.5	41.3	21.9	12.7	7.7	25.1	10.1	5.3	2.6	1.5
17	LEP [40]	14.0	5.0	4.6	4.0	4.2	10.1	1.8	1.7	1.4	1.5	86.5	64.0	24.2	12.3	7.1	65.8	28.4	5.6	2.7	1.5
18	MBP^{riu2} [46]	31.0	8.3	4.2	4.2	4.2	17.0	2.5	1.5	1.5	1.5	45.0	18.8	8.1	4.2	4.2	23.5	8.0	2.6	1.6	1.5
19	FV-VGGVD (SVM) [13]	21.0	12.1	6.0	6.5	4.2	10.3	5.2	2.3	1.5	1.8	63.5	51.5	23.1	11.7	10.0	34.3	19.1	9.5	4.4	2.8
20	FV-VGGM (SVM) [13]	6.2	5.6	3.1	4.2	3.8	2.	1.5	3.5	1.8	2.1	34.4	15.8	12.1	9.2	13.3	10.4	7.8	4.9	5.2	5.0
21	ScatNet (PCA) [16]	4.6	4.2	4.2	4.2	4.2	1.4	1.5	1.5	1.5	1.5	29.2	12.1	5.2	4.2	4.2	3.5	1.5	1.5	1.5	1.5
22	FV-AlexNet (SVM) [13]	10.4	6.7	6.6	4.2	4.2	2.8	5.0	4.3	3.1	1.5	44.8	29.2	11.2	9.0	6.0	13.5	7.0	8.6	4.1	2.8
23	ScatNet (NNC) [16]	4.2	4.2	4.2	4.2	4.2	1.5	1.5	1.5	1.5	1.5	56.0	9.8	4.2	4.2	4.2	14.6	3.2	2.9	1.7	1.5
24	PCANet [17]	14.6	6.7	4.4	4.4	4.8	1.6	1.5	1.5	1.5	1.5	70.6	32.5	11.9	10.4	7.7	19.1	5.1	1.5	1.5	1.5
25	PCANet^{riu2} [17]	4.8	4.4	4.6	4.6	4.0	2.4	1.5	1.5	1.5	1.5	49.2	20.2	6.5	5.4	4.8	19.9	6.2	2.6	1.6	1.4
26	RandNet [17]	4.8	4.2	4.2	4.2	4.2	1.5	1.5	1.5	1.5	1.4	10.7	4.9	4.2	4.2	4.2	3.4	1.7	1.5	1.5	1.5
27	RandNet^{riu2} [17]	4.2	4.2	4.2	4.2	4.3	1.5	1.5	1.5	1.5	1.5	11.5	4.2	4.0	4.7	5.5	2.6	1.7	1.5	1.5	1.5

4.3 Computational Complexity

Feature extraction time and dimensionality (Table 3) are two key factors determining the computational cost of LBP methods. The stated computation times are the average time spent by each method to generate its multiscale features. All of the methods were implemented in MATLAB 2010b on 2.9 GHz Intel quad core CPU with 16 GB RAM. The feature extraction time was measured as the average over 480 images of size 128×128. Note that the reported time does not include the training time for those methods labeled with $(\star)$ in Table 3. The reported feature dimensionality is the final dimensionality of each method given to the NNC classifier.

ScatNet is the most computationally expensive method for feature extraction, followed by FV-VGGVD. Its time cost for feature extraction is 125 times that of LBP^{riu2} and 26 times of MRELBP. Compared with LBP^{riu2}, most of the remaining methods do not introduce much computation overhead at the feature extraction stage. In terms of feature dimensionality, FV-CNN is extreme,

Table 6. Summary of various LBP methods used in our experimental study. Different schemes for parameters (r, p) are defined. Scheme 1: $(1, 8), (2, 16), (r, 24)$ for $3 \leq r \leq 9$; Scheme 2: $(r, 8), r = 1, \cdots, 9$; Scheme 3: $(1, 8), (r, 24)$ for $2 \leq r \leq 9$; Scheme 4: $(2, 8)$; Scheme 5: $(1, 8), (3, 8)$ and $(5, 8)$; Scheme 6: $(r, 8), r = 2, 4, 6, 8$. "Partial" in the "Noise Robust?" column means "robust to random Gaussian white noise and blur but highly sensitive to salt and pepper and random pixel corruption". Those with $(\star)$ in the "Optimal Operator Size" column represent the size of the receptive field, meaning much larger input image size is required. In the "Relative Performance" column, we consider the classification performance of LBP as baseline and use ★ and X to represent better and worse than baseline respectively.

No.	Method	(r, p) Scheme	Encoding Scheme	Needs Training?	Optimal Operator Size	Feature Extraction	Feature Dimension	Noise Robust?	Rotation Invariant?	Monotonic Illumination Invariant?	Relative Performance
1	LBP^{riu2}	Scheme 1	riu2		19×19	Very fast	210	No	Yes	Yes	Baseline
2	MRELBP	Scheme 6	riu2		17×17	Fast	800	Yes	Yes	Yes	★★★
3	CLBP	Scheme 1	riu2		9×9	Fast	3552	No	Yes	Yes	★★
4	ELBP	Scheme 1	riu2		7×7	Fast	2200	No	Yes	Yes	★★
5	CLBPHF	Scheme 1	u2		19×19	Fast	4580	Partial	Yes	Yes	★★
6	disCLBP	Scheme 1	Reported	✓	11×11	Moderate	7796	No	Yes	Yes	★
7	LTP^{riu2}	Scheme 1	riu2		19×19	Fast	420	No	Yes	No	★
8	BRINT	Scheme 3	ri		19×19	Fast	1296	Partial	Yes	Yes	★
9	NELBP	Scheme 1	Reported		19×19	Very fast	273	No	Yes	Yes	Similar
10	MSJLBP	Scheme 5	Reported		7×7	Moderate	3540	No	Somewhat	Yes	X
11	NTLBP	Scheme 1	Reported		17×17	Fast	388	No	Yes	Yes	X
12	$PRICoLBP_g$	Scheme 4	Reported		13×13	Fast	3540	No	Somewhat	Yes	X
13	$LBPV^{riu2}_{r,p}$	Scheme 1	riu2		15×15	Moderate	158	No	Yes	Yes	X
14	RILPQ	PreFiltering	Original		13×13	Fast	256	Partial	Yes	Yes	★
15	LBPD	PreFiltering	Original		7×7	Fast	289	Partial	Yes	Yes	X
16	$NRLBP^{riu2}$	Scheme 2	riu2		11×11	Fast	50	No	Yes	No	XX
17	LEP	PreFiltering	ri	✓	32×32	Fast	520	Partial	No	No	XX
18	MBP^{riu2}	Scheme 1	riu2		19×19	Fast	420	No	Yes	No	XX
19	PCANet	Multistage filtering, binarizing	Original	✓	5×5	Moderate	2048	Partial	No	No	XXX
20	$PCANet^{riu2}$		riu2	✓	5×5	Moderate	80	Partial	No	No	XXX
21	RandNet		Original	✓	5×5	Moderate	2048	No	No	No	XXX
22	$RandNet^{riu2}$		riu2		5×5	Moderate	80	No	No	No	XXX
23	ScatNet	Repeating filtering, nonlinear, pooling	N/A		32×32	Very slow	596	Partial	Yes	Yes	★★
24	AlexNet+FV		N/A	✓	$163 \times 163(\star)$	Moderate	32768	Partial	No	No	★★★
25	VGG-M+FV		N/A	✓	$139 \times 139(\star)$	Moderate	65536	Partial	No	No	★★★
26	VGG-VD+FV		N/A	✓	$252 \times 252(\star)$	Slow	65536	Partial	No	No	★★★

with the dimensionality of *dis*CLBP, CLBPHF, CLBP, PRICoLBP, MSJLBP, PCANet and RandNet also relatively high.

We provide Table 6 to summarize the properties of all evaluated methods including recommended operator size, feature dimensionality, robustness to image variations, tolerance of image noise and computational complexity. In order to establish a common software platform and a collection of datasets for easy evaluation, we plan to make both the source code and datasets available online.

5   Conclusions

A total of 27 methods were applied to 14 datasets, designed to test and stress an exceptional range of class types, image sizes, and disturbance invariance. The best overall performance is obtained for the MRELBP when distinctiveness, robustness and computational complexity are all taken into consideration. If the textures have very large within-class appearance variations, the FV-CNN methods clearly perform the best, however at a cost of high computational complexity. The problem of very high computational complexity should be solved to make them useful, especially in real-time embedded systems with low-power constraints. Furthermore, excellent results are obtained with FV-CNN for most test sets, but lack some robustness to noise and rotations. The role of FV is important and should be considered also with LBP methods in future studies.

In general, both micro- and macro-structures are important for texture description, since most LBP variants achieve their best performance beyond three scales, and a combination of multiple complementary texture descriptors turns out to be more powerful than a single descriptor. In general, LBP noise robustness improves when a prefiltering step is involved; however it does not necessarily guarantee good discriminability (*e.g.* LEP) and robustness to other noise types (*e.g.* salt and pepper).

It is possible that a classic CNN network could learn how to explore the properties of textured images more efficiently when trained on a very large texture dataset (similar to *ImageNet*). Unfortunately, to the best of our knowledge, such a database does not exist. We believe that a truly important question is to determine what makes a ***good large scale*** texture dataset. We have started to build such a dataset.

Based on our study, the work on CNNs for texture recognition mainly focuses on the domain transferability of CNNs. For texture, it is possible that simple networks might be enough to achieve similar or better results on texture datasets. Instead of devoting to design more and more complex networks, we feel that designing simple and efficient networks is important for problems such as mobile computing. Therefore, in the future, it would also be of great interest to study how to utilize effective LBP type computations with deep learning architectures.

Acknowledgments. This work has been supported by the National Natural Science Foundation of China under contract number 61202336 and by the Open Project Program of the National Laboratory of Pattern Recognition.

84   L. Liu et al.

References

1. Zhang, J., Marszalek, M., Lazebnik, S., Schmid, C.: Local features and kernels for classification of texture and object categories: a comprehensive study. Int. J. Comput. Vis. **73**(2), 213–238 (2007)
2. Pietikäinen, M., Hadid, A., Zhao, G., Ahonen, T.: Computer Vision Using Local Binary Patterns. Springer, London (2011)
3. Julesz, B., Bergen, J.: Textons, the fundamental elements in preattentive vision and perception of textures. Bell Syst. Tech. J. **62**(6), 1619–1645 (1983)
4. Leung, T., Malik, J.: Representing and recognizing the visual appearance of materials using three-dimensional textons. Int. J. Comput. Vis. **43**(1), 29–44 (2001)
5. Ojala, T., Pietikäinen, M., Mäenpää, T.: Multiresolution gray-scale and rotation invariant texture classification with local binary patterns. IEEE Trans. Pattern Anal. Mach. Intell. **24**(7), 971–987 (2002)
6. Varma, M., Zisserman, A.: A statistical approach to texture classification from single images. Int. J. Comput. Vis. **62**(1–2), 61–81 (2005)
7. Lazebnik, S., Schmid, C., Ponce, J.: A sparse texture representation using local affine regions. IEEE Trans. Pattern Anal. Mach. Intell. **27**(8), 1265–1278 (2005)
8. Varma, M., Zisserman, A.: A statistical approach to material classification using image patches. IEEE Trans. Pattern Anal. Mach. Intell. **31**(11), 2032–2047 (2009)
9. Liu, L., Fieguth, P.: Texture classification from random features. IEEE Trans. Pattern Anal. Mach. Intell. **34**(3), 574–586 (2012)
10. Sanchez, J., Perronnin, F., Mensink, T., Verbeek, J.: Image classification with the fisher vector: theory and practice. Int. J. Comput. Vis. **105**(3), 222–245 (2013)
11. Manjunath, B., Ma, W.: Texture features for browsing and retrieval of image data. IEEE Trans. Pattern Anal. Mach. Intell. **18**(8), 837–842 (1996)
12. Perronnin, F., Sánchez, J., Mensink, T.: Improving the fisher kernel for large-scale image classification. In: Daniilidis, K., Maragos, P., Paragios, N. (eds.) ECCV 2010. LNCS, vol. 6314, pp. 143–156. Springer, Heidelberg (2010). doi:10.1007/978-3-642-15561-1_11
13. Cimpoi, M., Maji, S., Vedaldi, A.: Deep filter banks for texture recognition and segmentation. In: IEEE Conference on Computer Vision and Pattern Recognition (CVPR), pp. 3828–3836, June 2015
14. Cimpoi, M., Maji, S., Kokkinos, I., Vedaldi, A.: Deep filter banks for texture recognition, description, and segmentation. Int. J. Comput. Vis. **118**(1), 65–94 (2016)
15. Sifre, L., Mallat, S.: Combined scattering for rotation invariant texture analysis. In: Proceedings of the European Symposium Artificial Neural Networks, April 2012
16. Bruna, J., Mallat, S.: Invariant scattering convolution networks. IEEE Trans. Pattern Anal. Mach. Intell. **35**(8), 1872–1886 (2013)
17. Chan, T., Jia, K., Gao, S., Lu, J., Zeng, Z., Ma, Y.: PCANet: a simple deep learning baseline for image classification? IEEE Trans. Image Process. **24**(12), 5017–5032 (2015)
18. Fernández, A., Álvarez, M., Bianconi, F.: Texture description through histograms of equivalent patterns. J. Math. Imaging Vis. **45**(1), 76–102 (2013)
19. Xu, Y., Yang, X., Ling, H., Ji, H.: A new texture descriptor using multifractal analysis in multiorientation wavelet pyramid. In: IEEE Conference on Computer Vision and Pattern Recognition (CVPR), pp. 161–168 (2010)
20. Mallikarjuna, P., Fritz, M., Targhi, A., Hayman, E., Caputo, B., Eklundh, J.O.: The kth-tips and kth-tips2 databases. http://www.nada.kth.se/cvap/databases/kth-tips/

21. Cimpoi, M., Maji, S., Kokkinos, I., Mohamed, S., Vedaldi, A.: Describing textures in the wild. In: IEEE Conference on Computer Vision and Pattern Recognition (CVPR), June 2014
22. Burghouts, G., Geusebroek, J.: Material specific adaptation of color invariant features. Pattern Recogn. Lett. **30**(3), 306–313 (2009)
23. Ojala, T., Mäenpää, T., Pietikänen, M., Viertola, J., Kyllonen, J., Huovinen, S.: Outex-new framework for empirical evaluation of texture analysis algorithms. In: Proceedings of the 16th International Conference Pattern Recognition, pp. 701–706 (2002)
24. Ojala, T., Pietikäinen, M., Harwood, D.: A comparative study of texture measures with classification based on feature distributions. Pattern Recogn. **29**(1), 51–59 (1996)
25. Tan, X., Triggs, B.: Enhanced local texture feature sets for face recognition under difficult lighting conditions. IEEE Trans. Image Process. **19**(6), 1635–1650 (2010)
26. Ren, J., Jiang, X., Yuan, J.: Noise-resistant local binary pattern with an embedded error-correction mechanism. IEEE Trans. Image Process. **22**(10), 4049–4060 (2013)
27. Zhou, H., Wang, R., Wang, C.: A novel extended local-binary-pattern operator for texture analysis. Inform. Sci. **178**(22), 4314–4325 (2008)
28. Guo, Z., Zhang, L., Zhang, D.: Rotation invariant texture classification using LBP variance (LBPV) with global matching. Pattern Recognit. **43**(3), 706–719 (2010)
29. Fathi, A., Naghsh-Nilchi, A.: Noise tolerant local binary pattern operator for efficient texture analysis. Pattern Recognit. Lett. **33**(9), 1093–1100 (2012)
30. Haralick, R., Shanmugam, K., Dinstein, I.: Textural features for image classification. IEEE Trans. Syst. Man Cybern. **3**(6), 610–621 (1973)
31. Qi, X., Xiao, R., Li, C., Qiao, Y., Guo, J., Tang, X.: Pairwise rotation invariant co-occurrence local binary pattern. IEEE Trans. Pattern Anal. Mach. Intell. **36**(11), 2199–2213 (2014)
32. Qi, X., Qiao, Y., Li, C., Guo, J.J.: Multiscale joint encoding of local binary patterns for texture and material classification. In: Proceedings of British Machine Vision Conference (BMVC) (2013)
33. Guo, Z., Zhang, L., Zhang, D.: A completed modeling of local binary pattern operator for texture classification. IEEE Trans. Image Process. **9**(16), 1657–1663 (2010)
34. Guo, Y., Zhao, G., Pietikäinen, M.: Discriminative features for texture description. Pattern Recognit. **45**(10), 3834–3843 (2012)
35. Liu, L., Zhao, L., Long, Y., Kuang, G., Fieguth, P.: Extended local binary patterns for texture classification. Image Vis. Comput. **30**(2), 86–99 (2012)
36. Liu, L., Long, Y., Fieguth, P., Lao, S., Zhao, G.: BRINT: binary rotation invariant and noise tolerant texture classification. IEEE Trans. Image Process. **23**(7), 3071–3084 (2014)
37. Liu, L., Lao, S., Fieguth, P., Guo, Y., Wang, X., Pietikainen, M.: Median robust extended local binary pattern for texture classification. IEEE Trans. Image Process. **25**(3), 1368–1381 (2016)
38. Ahonen, T., Matas, J., He, C., Pietikäinen, M.: Rotation invariant image description with local binary pattern histogram fourier features. In: Salberg, A.-B., Hardeberg, J.Y., Jenssen, R. (eds.) SCIA 2009. LNCS, vol. 5575, pp. 61–70. Springer, Heidelberg (2009)
39. Zhao, Y., Ahonen, T., Matas, J., Pietikäinen, M.: Rotation invariant image and video description with local binary pattern features. IEEE Trans. Image Process. **21**(4), 1465–1477 (2012)

40. Zhang, J., Liang, J., Zhao, H.: Local energy pattern for texture classification using self-adaptive quantization thresholds. IEEE Trans. Image Process. **22**(1), 31–42 (2013)
41. Hong, X., Zhao, G., Pietikainen, M., Chen, X.: Combining LBP difference and feature correlation for texture description. IEEE Trans. Image Process. **23**(6), 2557–2568 (2014)
42. Ojansivu, V., Heikkilä, J.: Blur insensitive texture classification using local phase quantization. In: Elmoataz, A., Lezoray, O., Nouboud, F., Mammass, D. (eds.) ICISP 2008. LNCS, vol. 5099, pp. 236–243. Springer, Heidelberg (2008). doi:10.1007/978-3-540-69905-7_27
43. Ojansivu, V., Rahtu, E., Heikkilä, J.: Rotation invariant local phase quantization for blur insensitive texture analysis. In: IEEE International Conference on Pattern Recognition (ICPR), pp. 1–4 (2008)
44. Krizhevsky, A., Ilya, S., Hinton, G.: Imagenet classification with deep convolutional neural networks. In: Advances in Neural Information Processing Systems, pp. 1097–1105 (2012)
45. Sifre, L., Mallat, S.: Rotation, scaling and deformation invariant scattering for texture discrimination. In: IEEE Conference on Computer Vision and Pattern Recognition (CVPR), pp. 1233–1240, June 2013
46. Hafiane, A., Seetharaman, G., Zavidovique, B.: Median binary pattern for textures classification. In: Proceedings of the 4th International Conference on Image Analysis and Recognition, pp. 387–398 (2007)
47. Brodatz, P.: Textures: A Photographic Album for Artists and Designers. Dover Publications, New York (1966)
48. Liu, L., Fieguth, P., Kuang, G., Clausi, D.: Sorted random projections for robust rotation invariant texture classification. Pattern Recogn. **45**(6), 2405–2418 (2012)
49. Wright, J., Yang, A., Ganesh, A., Sastry, S., Ma, Y.: Robust face recognition via sparse representation. IEEE Trans. Pattern Anal. Mach. Intell. **31**(2), 210–227 (2009)
50. Caputo, B., Hayman, E., Mallikarjuna, P.: Class-specific material categorization. In: Internaltional Conference on Computer Vision (ICCV), pp. 1597–1604 (2005)

MS-Celeb-1M: A Dataset and Benchmark
for Large-Scale Face Recognition

Yandong Guo[(⊠)], Lei Zhang, Yuxiao Hu, Xiaodong He, and Jianfeng Gao

Microsoft Research, Redmond, WA, USA
{yandong.guo,leizhang,yuxiao.hu,xiaohe,jfgao}@microsoft.com

Abstract. In this paper, we design a benchmark task and provide the associated datasets for recognizing face images and link them to corresponding entity keys in a knowledge base. More specifically, we propose a benchmark task to recognize one million celebrities from their face images, by using all the possibly collected face images of this individual on the web as training data. The rich information provided by the knowledge base helps to conduct disambiguation and improve the recognition accuracy, and contributes to various real-world applications, such as image captioning and news video analysis. Associated with this task, we design and provide concrete measurement set, evaluation protocol, as well as training data. We also present in details our experiment setup and report promising baseline results. Our benchmark task could lead to one of the largest classification problems in computer vision. To the best of our knowledge, our training dataset, which contains 10M images in version 1, is the largest publicly available one in the world.

Keywords: Face recognition · Large scale · Benchmark · Training data · Celebrity recognition · Knowledge base

1 Introduction

In this paper, we design a benchmark task as to recognize one million celebrities from their face images and identify them by linking to the unique entity keys in a knowledge base. We also construct associated datasets to train and test for this benchmark task. Our paper is mainly to close the following two gaps in current face recognition, as reported in [1]. First, there has not been enough effort in determining the identity of a person from a face image with disambiguation, especially at the web scale. The current face identification task mainly focuses on finding similar images (in terms of certain types of distance metric) for the input image, rather than answering questions such as "who is in the image?" and "if it is Anne in the image, which Anne?". This lacks an important step of "recognizing". The second gap is about the scale. The publicly available datasets are much smaller than that being used privately in industry, such as Facebook [2,3] and Google [4], as summarized in Table 1. Though the research in face recognition highly desires large datasets consisting of many distinct people, such

© Springer International Publishing AG 2016
B. Leibe et al. (Eds.): ECCV 2016, Part III, LNCS 9907, pp. 87–102, 2016.
DOI: 10.1007/978-3-319-46487-9_6

large dataset is not easily or publicly accessible to most researchers. This greatly limits the contributions from research groups, especially in academia.

Our benchmark task has the following properties. First, we define our face recognition as to determine the identity of a person from his/her face images. More specifically, we introduce a **knowledge base** into face recognition, since the recent advance in knowledge bases has demonstrated incredible capability of providing accurate identifiers and rich properties for celebrities. Examples include Satori knowledge graph in Microsoft and "freebase" in [5]. Our face recognition task is demonstrated in Fig. 1.

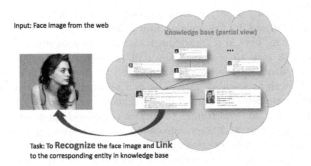

Fig. 1. An example of our face recognition task. Our task is to recognize the face in the image and then link this face with the corresponding entity key in the knowledge base. By recognizing the left image to be "Anne Hathaway" and linking to the entity key, we know she is an American actress born in 1982, who has played Mia Thermopolis in The Princess Diaries, not the other Anne Hathaway who was the wife of William Shakespeare. Input image is from the web. (Image resource: http://www.hdwallpapers. in/anne_hathaway_2-wallpapers.html, retrieved by image.bing.com.)

Linking the image with an entity key in the knowledge base, rather than an isolated string for a person's name naturally solves the disambiguation issue in the traditional face recognition task. Moreover, the linked entity key is associated with rich and comprehensive property information in the knowledge base, which makes our task more similar to human behavior compared with traditional face identification, since retrieving the individual's name as well as the associated information naturally takes place when humans are viewing a face image. The rich information makes our face recognition task practical and beneficial to many real applications, including image search, ranking, caption generation, image deep understanding, etc.

Second, our benchmark task targets at recognizing **celebrities**. Recognizing celebrities, rather than a pre-selected private group of people, represents public interest and could be directly applied to a wide range of real scenarios. Moreover, only with popular celebrities, we can leverage the existing information (e.g. name, profession) in the knowledge base and the information on the web to build a large-scale dataset which is publicly available for training, measurement, and re-distributing under certain licenses. The security department may have many labeled face images for criminal identification, but the data can not be publicly shared.

Third, we select **one million** celebrities from freebase and provide their associated entity keys, and encourage researchers to build recognizers to identify each people entity. Considering each entity as one class may lead to, to the best of our knowledge, the largest classification problem in computer vision. The clear definition and mutually exclusiveness of these classes are supported by the unique entity keys and their associated properties provided by the knowledge base, since in our dataset, there are a significant amount of celebrities having same/similar names. This is different from generic image classification, where to obtain a large number of exclusive classes with clear definition itself is a challenging and open problem [6].

The large scale of our problem naturally introduces the following attractive challenges. With the increased number of classes, the inter-class variance tends to decrease. There are celebrities look very similar to each other (or even twins) in our one-million list. Moreover, large intra-class variance is introduced by popular celebrities with millions of images available, as well as celebrities with very large appearance variation (e.g., due to age, makeups, or even sex reassignment surgery).

In order to evaluate the performance of our benchmark task, we provide concrete measurement set and evaluation protocol. Our measurement set consists of images for a subset of celebrities in our one-million celebrity list. The celebrities are selected in a way that, our measurement set mainly focuses on popular celebrities to represent the interest of real application and users, while the measurement set still maintains enough (about 25 %) tail celebrities to encourage the performance on celebrity coverage. We manually label images for these celebrities carefully. The correctness of our labeling is ensured by deep research on the web content, consensus verification, and multiple iterations of carefully review. In order to make our measurement more challenging, we blend a set of distractor images with this set of carefully labeled images. The distractor images are images of other celebrities or ordinary people on the web, which are mainly used to hide the celebrities we select in the measurement.

Along with this challenging yet attractive large scale benchmark task proposed, we also provide a very large training dataset to facilitate the task. The training dataset contains about 10M images for 100K top celebrities selected from our one-million celebrity list in terms of their web appearance frequency. Our training data is, to the best of our knowledge, the largest publicly available one in the world, as shown in Table 1. We plan to further extend the size in the near future. For each of the image in our training data, we provide the thumbnail of the original image and cropped face region from the original image (with/without alignment). This is to maximize the convenience for the researchers to investigate using this data.

With this training data, we trained a convolutional deep neural network with the classification setup (by considering each entity as one class). The experimental results show that without extra effort in fine-tuning the model structure, we recognize 44.2 % of the images in the measurement set with the precision 95 % (hard case, details provided in Sect. 4). We provide the details of our experiment setup and experimental results to serve as a very promising baseline in Sect. 4.

Contribution Summary. Our contribution in this paper is summarized as follows.

- We design a benchmark task: to recognize one million celebrities from their face images, and link to their corresponding entity keys in freebase [5].
- We provide the following datasets,[1]
  - One million celebrities selected from freebase with corresponding entity keys , and a snapshot for freebase data dumps;
  - Manually labeled measurement set with carefully designed evaluation protocol;
  - A large scale training dataset, with face region cropped and aligned (to the best of our knowledge, the largest publicly available one).
- We provide promising baseline performance with our training data to inspire more research effort on this task.

Our benchmark task could lead to a very large scale classification problem in computer vision with meaningful real applications. This benefits people in experimenting different recognition models (especially fine-grained neural network) with the given training/testing data. Moreover, we encourage people to bring in more outside data and evaluate experimental results in a separate track.

2   Related Works

Typically, there are two types of tasks for face recognition. One is very well-studied, called face verification, which is to determine whether two given face images belong to the same person. Face verification has been heavily investigated. One of the most widely used measurement sets for verification is Labeled Faces in the Wild (LFW) in [7,8], which provides 3000 matched face image pairs and 3000 mismatched face image pairs, and allows researchers to report verification accuracy with different settings. The best performance on LFW datasets has been frequently updated in the past several years. Especially, with the "unrestricted, labeled outside data" setting, multiple research groups have claimed higher accuracy than human performance for verification task on LFW [4,9].

Recently, the interest in the other type of face recognition task, face identification, has greatly increased [3,9–11]. For typical face identification problems, two sets of face images are given, called gallery set and query set. Then the task is, for a given face image in the query set, to find the most similar faces in the gallery image set. When the gallery image set only has a very limited number (say, less than five) of face images for each individual, the most effective solution is still to learn a generic feature which can tell whether or not two face images

---

[1] Instructions and download links: http://msceleb.org.

are the same person, which is essentially still the problem of face verification. Currently, the MegaFace in [11] might be one of the most difficult face identification benchmarks. The difficulty of MegaFace mainly comes from the up-to one million distractors blended in the gallery image set. Note that the query set in MegaFace are selected from images from FaceScrub [12] and FG-NET [13], which contains 530 and 82 persons respectively.

Several datasets have been published to facilitate the training for the face verification and identification tasks. Examples include LFW [7,8], Youtube Face Database (YFD) [14], CelebFaces+ [15], and CASIA-WebFace [16]. In LFW, 13000 images of faces were collected from the web, and then carefully labeled with celebrities' names. The YFD contains 3425 videos of 1595 different people. The CelebFace+ dataset contains 202, 599 face images of 10, 177 celebrities. People in CelebFaces+ and LFW are claimed to be mutually exclusive. The CASIA-WebFace [16] is currently the largest dataset which is publicly available, with about 10K celebrities, and 500K images. A quick summary is listed in Table 1.

Table 1. Face recognition datasets

Dataset	Available	People	Images
IJB-A [17]	Public	500	5712
LFW [7,8]	Public	5K	13K
YFD [14]	Public	1595	3425 videos
CelebFaces [15]	Public	10K	202K
CASIA-WebFace [16]	Public	10K	500K
Ours	**Public**	100K	about 10M
Facebook	Private	4K	4400K
Google	Private	8M	100-200M

As shown in Table 1, our training dataset is considerably larger than the publicly available datasets. Another uniqueness of our training dataset is that our dataset focuses on facilitating our celebrity recognition task, so our dataset needs to cover as many popular celebrities as possible, and have to solve the data disambiguation problem to collect right images for each celebrity. On the other hand, the existing datasets are mainly used to train a generalizable face feature, and celebrity coverage is not a major concern for these datasets. Therefore, for the typical existing dataset, if a name string corresponds to multiple celebrities (e.g., Mike Smith) and would lead to ambiguous image search result, these celebrities are usually removed from the datasets to help the precision of the collected training data [18].

3   Benchmark Construction

Our benchmark task is to recognize one million celebrities from their face images, and link to their corresponding entity keys in the knowledge base. Here we describe how we construct this task in details.

3.1   One Million Celebrity List

We select one million celebrities to recognize from a knowledge graph called freebase [5], where each entity is identified by a unique key (called machine identifier, MID in freebase) and associated with rich properties. We require that the entities we select are human beings in the real world and have/had public attentions.

The first step is to select a subset of entities (from freebase [5]) which correspond to real people using the criteria in [1]. In freebase, there are more than 50 million topics capsulated in about 2 billion triplets. Note that we don't include any person if his/her facial appearance is unknown or not clearly defined.

The second step is to rank all the entities in the above subset according to the frequency of their occurrence on the web [1]. We select the top one million entities to form our celebrity list and provide their entity keys (MID) in freebase. We concern the public attention (popularity on the web) for two reasons. First, we want to align our benchmark task with the interest of real applications. For applications like image search, image annotations and deep understanding, and image caption generation, the recognition of popular celebrities would be more attractive to most of the users than ordinary people. Second, we include popular celebrities so that we have better chance to obtain multiple authority images for each of them to enable our training, testing, and re-distributing under certain licenses.

We present the distribution of the one million celebrities in different aspects including profession, nationality, age, and gender. In our one million celebrity list, we include persons with more than 2000 different professions (Fig. 2(a)), and come from more than 200 distinct countries/regions (Fig. 2(b)), which introduces a great diversity to our data. We cover all the major races in the world (Caucasian, Mongoloid, and Negroid). Moreover, as shown in Fig. 2(c), we cover a large range of ages in our list. Though we do not manually select celebrities to make the profession (or gender, nationality, age) distribution uniform, the diversity (gender, age, profession, race, nationality) of our celebrity list is guaranteed by the large scale of our dataset. This is different from [17], in which there are about 500 subjects so the manual balancing over gender distribution is inevitable.

Note that our property statistics are limited to the availability of freebase information. Some celebrities in our one million list do not have complete properties. If a certain celebrity does not have property A available in freebase, we do not include this celebrity for the statistic calculation of the property A.

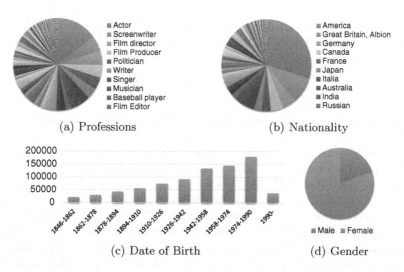

(a) Professions   (b) Nationality

(c) Date of Birth   (d) Gender

Fig. 2. Distribution of the properties of the celebrities in our one-million list in different aspects. The large scale of our dataset naturally introduces great diversity. As shown in (a) and (b), we include persons with more than 2000 different professions, and come from more than 200 distinct countries/regions. The figure (c) demonstrates that we don't include celebrities who were born before 1846 (long time before the first roll-film specialized camera "Kodak" was invented [19]) and covers celebrities of a large variance of age. In (d), we notice that we have more females than males in our one-million celebrity list. This might be correlated with the profession distribution in our list.

3.2   Celebrity Selection for Measurement

In order to evaluate the recognition performance on the one million celebrities obtained in the last subsection, we build up a measurement set which includes a set of carefully labeled images blended with another set of randomly selected face images as distractors. The measurement set construction is described in details in the following subsections, while the evaluation protocol is described in Sect. 4.

For the labeled images, we sample a subset of celebrities[2] from the one-million celebrity list due to limited labeling resource. The sampling weight is designed in a way that, our measurement set mainly focuses on top celebrities (rank among the top in the occurrence frequency list) to represent the interest of real applications and users, yet maintain a certain amount of tail celebrities (celebrities not mentioned frequently on the web, e.g., from 1 to 10 times in total) to guarantee the measurement coverage over the one-million list.

---

[2] Currently there are 1500. We will increase the number of celebrities in our measurement set in the future.

More specifically, let f_i denote the number of documents mentioned the ith celebrity on the web. Following the method in [1], we set the probability for the ith celebrity to get selected to be proportional to f_i', defined as,

$$f_i' = f_i^{\frac{1}{\sqrt{5}}},$$ (1)

where the exponent $1/\sqrt{5}$ is obtained empirically to include more celebrities with small f.

Though it seems to be a natural solution, we do not set the sampling weights to be proportional to f_i, since this option will make our measurement set barely contain any celebrities from the bottom 90 % in our one-million list (ordered by f_i). The reason is that the distribution of f is very long-tailed. More than 90 % of the celebrities have f smaller than 30, while the top celebrities have f larger than one million. We need to include sufficient number of tail celebrities to encourage researchers to work on the hard cases to improve the performance from the perspective of recognition coverage. This is the reason that we applied the adjustment in (1).

With the sampling weight f' in (1) applied, our measurement set still mainly focuses on the most popular celebrities, while about 25 % of the celebrities in our measurement set come from the bottom 90 % in our one-million celebrity list (ordered by f). If we do not apply the adjustment in (1), but just use f as the sampling weight, less than 10 % of the celebrities in the measurement set come from the bottom 90 % in our one-million celebrity list.

Since the list of the celebrities in our measurement set is not exposed[3], and our measurement set contains 25 % of the celebrities in our measurement set come from the bottom 90 %, researchers need to include as many celebrities as possible (not only the popular ones) from our one-million list to improve the performance of coverage. This pushes the scale of our task to be very large.

3.3   Labeling for Measurement

After we have the set of celebrities for measurement, we provide two images for each of the celebrity. The correctness of our image labeling is ensured by deep research on the web content, multiple iterations of carefully review, and very rigorous consensus verification. Details are listed as follows.

Scraping. Scraping provides image candidates for each of the celebrities selected for the measurement set. Though in the end we provide only two images per celebrity for evaluation, we scraped about 30 images per celebrities. During the scraping procedure, we applied different search queries, including the celebrity's name, name plus profession, and names in other languages (if available). The advantages of introducing multiple variations of the query used for each celebrity is that with multiple queries, we have better chance to capture the images which

---

[3] We publish images for 500 celebrities, called development set, while hold the rest 1000 for grand challenges.

are truly about the given celebrity. Moreover, the variation of the query and scraping multiple images also brings in the diversity to the images for the given celebrity. Especially for the famous celebrities, the top one image returned by search engine is typically his/her representative image (frontal facial image with high quality), which is relatively easier to recognize, compared with the other images returned by the search engine. We increase the scraping depth so that we have more diverse images to be recognized for each of the celebrity.

Fig. 3. Labeling GUI for "Chuck Palhniuk". (partial view) As shown in the figure, in the upper right corner, a representative image and a short description is provided. For a given image candidate, judge can label as "not for this celebrity" (red), "yes for this celebrity" (green), or "broken image" (dark gray). (Color figure online)

Label. Labeling picks up the images which are truly about the given celebrity. As shown in Fig. 3, for each given celebrity, we (all the authors) manually label **all** the scraped image candidates to be truly about this celebrity or not. Extreme cautious was applied. We have access to the page which contains the scraped image to be labeled. Whenever needed, the judge (the authors) is asked to visit the original page with the scraped image and read the page content to guide his/her labeling. The rich information on the original page benefits the quality of the labeling, especially for a lot of the hard cases. Each of the image-celebrity entity pair was judged by at least two persons. Whenever there is a conflict, the two judges review together and provide the final decision based on verbal discussion. In total, we have about 30K images labeled, spent hundreds of hours.

In our measurement set, we select two images for each of the celebrity to keep the evaluation cost low. We have two subset (each of them have the same celebrity list), described as follows.

– **Random set**
The image in this subset is randomly selected from the labeled images. One image per celebrity. This set reveals how many celebrities are truly covered by the models to be tested.
– **Hard set**
The image in this subset is the one (from the labeled images) which is the most different from any images in the training dataset. One image per celebrity. This set is to evaluate the generalization ability of the model.

Then, we blend the labeled images with images from other celebrities or ordinary people. The evaluation protocol is introduced in details in the next section.

4   Celebrity Recognition

In this section, we set up the evaluation protocol for our benchmark task. More-over, in order to facilitate the researchers to work on this problem, we provide a training dataset which is encouraged (optional) to use. We also present the baseline performance obtained by using our provided training data. We also encourage researchers to train with outside data and evaluate in a separate track.

4.1   Evaluation Protocol

We evaluate the performance of our proposed recognition task in terms of pre-cision and coverage (defined in the following subsection) using the settings described as follows.

Setup. We setup our evaluation protocol as follows. For a model to be tested, we collect the model prediction for both the labeled image and distractors in the measurement set. Note that we don't expose which images in the measurement are labeled ones or which are distractors. This setup avoids human labeling to the measurement set, and encourages researchers to build a recognizer which could robustly distinguish one million (as many as possible) people faces, rather than focusing merely on a small group of people.

Moreover, during the training procedure, if the researcher leverages outside data for training, we do not require participants to exclude celebrities in our measurement from the training data set. Our measurement still evaluate the generalization ability of our recognition model, due to the following reasons. There are one million celebrities to be recognized in our task, and there are mil-lions of images for some popular celebrities on the web. It is practically impos-sible to include all the images for every celebrity in the list. On the other hand, according to Sect. 4.2, the images in our measurement set is typically not the representative images for the given celebrity (e.g., the top one searching result). Therefore the chance to include the measurement images in the training set is relatively low, as long as the celebrity list in the measurement set is hidden. This is different from most of the existing face recognition benchmark tasks, in which the measurement set is published and targeted on a small group of people. For these traditional benchmark tasks, the evaluation generalization ability relies on manually excluding the images (from the training set) of all the persons in the measurement set (This is mainly based on the integrity of the participants).

Evaluation Metric. In the measurement set, we have n images, denoted by $\{x_i\}_{i=1}^n$. The first m images $\{x_i | i = 1, 2, 3, ..., m\}$ are the labeled images for our selected celebrities, while the rest $\{x_i | i = m + 1, ..., n\}$ are distractors. Note that we hide the order of the images in the measurement set.

For the ith image, let $g(x_i)$ denote the ground truth label (entity key obtained by labeling). For any model to be tested, we assume the model to output

$\{\hat{g}(x_i), c(x_i)\}$ as the predicted entity key of the ith image, and its corresponding prediction confidence. We allow the model to perform rejection. That is, if $c(x_i) < t$, where t is a preset threshold, the recognition result for image x_i will be ignored. We define the precision with the threshold t as,

$$P(t) = \frac{|\{x_i|\hat{g}(x_i) = g(x_i) \wedge c(x_i) \geq t, i = 1, 2, ..., m\}|}{|\{x_i|c(x_i) \geq t, i = 1, 2, ..., m\}|}, \quad (2)$$

where the nominator is the number of the images of which the prediction is correct (and confidence score is larger than the threshold). The denominator is the number of images (within the set $\{x_i\}_{i=1}^m$) which the model does have prediction (not reject to recognize).

The coverage in our protocol is defined as

$$C(t) = \frac{|\{x_i|c(x_i) \geq t, i = 1, 2, ..., m\}|}{m} \quad (3)$$

For each given t, a pair of precision $P(t)$ and coverage $C(t)$ can be obtained for the model to be tested. The precision $P(t)$ is a function of $C(t)$. Our major evaluation metric is the maximum of the coverage satisfying the condition of precision, $P(t) \geq P_{min}$. The value of P_{min} is 0.95 in our current setup. Other metrics and analysis/discussions are also welcomed to report. The reason that we prefer a fixed high precision and measure the corresponding coverage is because in many real applications high precision is usually more desirable and of greater value.

4.2 Training Dataset

In order to facilitate the above face recognition task we provide a large training dataset. This training dataset is prepared by the following two steps. First, we select the top 100K entities from our one-million celebrity list in terms of their web appearance frequency. Then, we retrieve approximately 100 images per celebrity from popular search engines.

We do not provide training images for the entire one-million celebrity list for the following considerations. First, limited by time and resource, we can only manage to prepare a dataset of top 100K celebrities as a v1 dataset to facilitate the participants to quickly get started. We will continuously extend the dataset to cover more celebrities in the future. Moreover, as shown in the experimental results in the next subsection, this dataset is already very promising to use. Our training dataset covers about 75 % of celebrities in our measurement set, which implies that the upper bound of recognition recall rate based on the provided training data cannot exceed 75 %. Therefore, we also encourage the participants, especially who are passionate to break this 75 % upper bound to treat the dataset development as one of the key problems in this challenge, and bring in outside data to get higher recognition recall rate and compare experimental results in a separate track. Especially, we encourage people label their data with entity keys

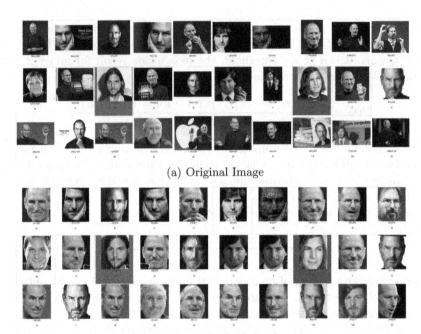

(a) Original Image

(b) Aligned Face Image

Fig. 4. Examples (subset) of the training images for the celebrity with entity key m.06y3r (Steve Jobs). The image marked with a green rectangle is claimed to be Steve Jobs when he was in high school. The image marked with a red rectangle is considered as a noise sample in our dataset, since it is synthesized by combining one image of Steve Jobs and one image of Ashton Kutcher, who is the actor in the movie "Jobs". (Color figure online)

in the freebase snapshot we provided and publish, so that different dataset could be easily united to facilitate collaboration.

On example in our training dataset is shown in Fig. 4. As shown in the figures, same celebrity may look very differently in different images. In Fig. 4, we see images for Steve Jobs (m.06y3r) when he was about 20/30 years old, as well as images when he was about 50 years old. The image at row 2, column 8 (in green rectangle) in Fig. 4 is claimed to be Steve Jobs when he was in high school. Notice that the image at row 2, column 3 in Fig. 4, marked with red rectangle is considered as a noise sample in our dataset, since this image was synthesized by combining one image of Steve Jobs and one image of Ashton Kutcher, who is the actor in the movie "Jobs".

As we have mentioned, we do not manually remove the noise in this training data set. This is partially because to prepare training data of this size is beyond the scale of manually labeling. In addition, we have observed that the state-of-the-art deep neural network learning algorithm can tolerate a certain level of noise in the training data. Though for a small percentage of celebrities their image search result is far from perfect, more data especially more individuals covered by the training data could still be of great value to the face recognition research, which is also reported in [18]. Moreover, we believe that data cleaning, noisy label removal, and learning with noisy data are all good and real problems that are worth of dedicated research efforts. Therefore, we leave this problem open and do not limit the use of outside training data.

4.3   Baseline

There are typically two categories of methods to recognize people from face images. One is template-based. For methods in this category, a gallery set which contains multiple images for the targeted group of people is pre-built. Then, for the given image in the query set, the most similar image(s) in the gallery set (according to some certain metrics or in pre-learned feature space) is retrieved, and the annotation of this/these similar images are used to estimate the identity of the given query image. When the gallery is not very large, this category of methods is very convenient for adding/removing entities in the gallery since the face feature representation could be learned in advance. However, when the gallery is large, a complicated index needs to be built to shorten the retrieval time. In this case, the flexibility of adding/removing entities for the methods in this category vanishes. Moreover, the accuracy of the template-based methods highly relies on the annotation accuracy in the gallery set. When there are many people in the targeted group, accurate annotation is beyond human effort and could be a very challenging problem itself.

We choose the second category, which is a model-based method. More specifically, we model our problem as a classification problem and consider each celebrity as a class.

In our experiment, we trained a deep neural network following the network structure in [20]. Training a deep neural network for 100K celebrities is not a trivial task. If we directly train the model from scratch, it is hard to see the model starts to converge even after a long run due to the large number of categories. To address this problem, we started from training a small model for 500 celebrities, which have the largest numbers of images for each celebrity. In addition, we used the pre-trained model from [20] to initialize this small model. This step is optional, but we observed that it helps the training process converge faster. After 50,000 iterations, we stopped to train this model, and used it as a pre-trained model to initialize the full model of 100K celebrities. After 250,000 iterations, with learning rate decreased from the initial value 0.01 to 0.001 and 0.0001 after 100,000 and 200,000 iterations, the training loss decrease becomes very slow and indiscernible. Then we stopped the training and used the last model snapshot to evaluate the performance of celebrity recognition on our measurement set. The experimental results (on the published 500 celebrities) are shown in Fig. 5 and Table 2.

The promising results can be attributed to the deep neural network capability and the high quality of image search results thanks for years of improvement in image search engines. However, the curves also shows that the task is indeed very challenge. To achieve both high precision and high recall, a great amount

Table 2. Experimental results on the 500 published celebrities

	Coverage@Precision 99 %	Coverage@Precision 95 %
Hard Set	0.052	0.442
Random Set	0.606	0.728

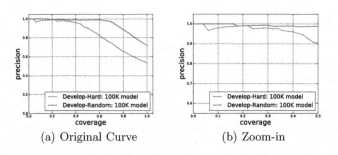

(a) Original Curve   (b) Zoom-in

Fig. 5. Precision-coverage curve with our baseline model

of research efforts need to be spent on data collection, cleaning, learning algorithm, and model generalization, which are valuable problems to computer vision researchers.

5   Discussion and Future Work

In this paper, we have defined a benchmark task which is to recognize one million celebrities in the world from their face images, and link the face to a corresponding entity key in a knowledge base. Our face recognition has the property of disambiguation, and close to the human behavior in recognizing images. We also provide concrete measurement set for people to evaluate the model performance easily, and provide, to the best of our knowledge, the largest training dataset to facilitate research in the area.

Beyond face recognition, our datasets could inspire other research topics. For example, people could adopt one of the cutting-edge unsupervised/semi-supervised clustering algorithms [21–24] on our training dataset, and/or develop new algorithms which can accurately locate and remove outliers in a large, real dataset. Another interesting topic is the to build estimators to predict a person's properties from his/her face images. For example, the images in our training dataset are associated with entity keys in knowledge base, of which the gender information (or other properties) could be easily retrieved. People could train a robust gender classifier for the face images in the wild based on this large scale training data. We look forward to exciting research inspired by our training dataset and benchmark task.

References

1. Guo, Y., Zhang, L., Hu, Y., He, X., Gao, J.: MS-Celeb-1M: challenge of recognizing one million celebrities in the real world. In: IS&T International Symposium on Electronic Imaging (2016)
2. Taigman, Y., Yang, M., Ranzato, M., Wolf, L.: DeepFace: closing the gap to human-level performance in face verification. In: Proceedings of IEEE Computer Society Conference on Computer Vision and Pattern Recognition (CVPR), June 2014
3. Taigman, Y., Yang, M., Ranzato, M., Wolf, L.: Web-scale training for face identification. In: Proceedings of IEEE Computer Society Conference on Computer Vision and Pattern Recognition (CVPR), pp. 2746–2754. IEEE (2015)
4. Schroff, F., Kalenichenko, D., Philbin, J.: FaceNet: a unified embedding for face recognition and clustering. In: Proceedings of IEEE Computer Society Conference on Computer Vision and Pattern Recognition (CVPR), June 2015
5. Google: Freebase data dumps (2015). https://developers.google.com/freebase/data
6. Russakovsky, O., Deng, J., Su, H., Krause, J., Satheesh, S., Ma, S., Huang, Z., Karpathy, A., Khosla, A., Bernstein, M., Berg, A.C., Fei-Fei, L.: ImageNet large scale visual recognition challenge. Int. J. Comput. Vis. (IJCV) **115**(3), 211–252 (2015)
7. Huang, G.B., Ramesh, M., Berg, T., Learned-Miller, E.: Labeled faces in the wild: a database for studying face recognition in unconstrained environments. Technical report 07–49, University of Massachusetts, Amherst, October 2007
8. Huang, G.B., Learned-Miller, E.: Labeled faces in the wild: updates and new reporting procedures. Technical report UM-CS-2014-003, University of Massachusetts, Amherst, May 2014
9. Sun, Y., Wang, X., Tang, X.: DeepID3: face recognition with very deep neural networks. arXiv preprint arXiv:1502.00873 (2014)
10. Fan, H., Yang, M., Cao, Z., Jiang, Y., Yin, Q.: Learning compact face representation: packing a face into an int32. In: Proceedings of ACM International Conference on Multimedia, pp. 933–936. ACM (2014)
11. Kemelmacher-Shlizerman, I., Seitz, S., Miller, D., Brossard, E.: The MegaFace Benchmark: 1 Million Faces for Recognition at Scale. ArXiv e-prints (2015)
12. Ng, H.W., Winkler, S.: A data-driven approach to cleaning large face datasets. In: Proceedings of IEEE International Conference on Image Processing (ICIP), October 2014
13. Panis, G., Lanitis, A.: An overview of research activities in facial age estimation using the FG-NET aging database. In: Agapito, L., Bronstein, M.M., Rother, C. (eds.) ECCV 2014 Workshops. LNCS, vol. 8926, pp. 737–750. Springer, Heidelberg (2015)
14. Wolf, L., Hassner, T., Maoz, I.: Face recognition in unconstrained videos with matched background similarity. In: Proceedings of IEEE Computer Society Conference on Computer Vision and Pattern Recognition (CVPR) (2011)
15. Sun, Y., Wang, X., Tang, X.: Deep learning face representation from predicting 10,000 classes. In: Proceedings of IEEE Computer Society Conference on Computer Vision and Pattern Recognition (CVPR), June 2014
16. Yi, D., Lei, Z., Liao, S., Li, S.Z.: Learning face representation from scratch. arXiv preprint arXiv:1411.7923 (2014)

17. Klare, B.F., Klein, B., Taborsky, E., Blanton, A., Cheney, J., Allen, K., Grother, P., Mah, A., Jain, A.K.: Pushing the frontiers of unconstrained face detection and recognition: IARPA Janus benchmark A. In: Proceedings of IEEE Computer Society Conference on Computer Vision and Pattern Recognition (CVPR), June 2015
18. Parkhi, O.M., Vedaldi, A., Zisserman, A.: Deep face recognition. In: Proceedings of the British Machine Vision Conference (BMVC) (2015)
19. Eastman, G.: Camera. US Patent 388850 A (1888)
20. Krizhevsky, A., Sutskever, I., Hinton, G.E.: Imagenet classification with deep convolutional neural networks. In: Advances in Neural Information Processing Systems (NIPS), pp. 1097–1105. MIT Press (2012)
21. Ng, A.Y., Jordan, M.I., Weiss, Y.: On spectral clustering: analysis and an algorithm. In: Advances in Neural Information Processing Systems (NIPS), pp. 849–856. MIT Press (2001)
22. Belkin, M., Niyogi, P.: Semi-supervised learning on Riemannian manifolds. J. Mach. Learn. $\mathbf{56}$(1–3), 209–239 (2004)
23. Zhu, X., Ghahramani, Z., Lafferty, J.: Semi-supervised learning using gaussian fields and harmonic functions. In: Proceedings of International Conference on Machine Learning, pp. 912–919 (2003)
24. Zhou, D., Bousquet, O., Lal, T.N., Weston, J., Schlkopf, B.: Learning with local and global consistency. In: Advances in Neural Information Processing Systems (NIPS), pp. 321–328. MIT Press (2004)

Hierarchical Beta Process with Gaussian Process Prior for Hyperspectral Image Super Resolution

Naveed Akhtar[1]($\boxtimes$), Faisal Shafait[2], and Ajmal Mian[1]

[1] School of Computer Science and Software Engineering,
The University of Western Australia, 35 Stirling Highway,
6009 Crawley, WA, Australia
naveed.akhtar@research.uwa.edu.au, ajmal.mian@uwa.edu.au
[2] School of Electrical Engineering and Computer Science,
National University of Sciences and Technology, H-12, Islamabad, Pakistan
faisal.shafait@seecs.edu.pk

Abstract. Hyperspectral cameras acquire precise spectral information, however, their resolution is very low due to hardware constraints. We propose an image fusion based hyperspectral super resolution approach that employes a Bayesian representation model. The proposed model accounts for spectral smoothness and spatial consistency of the representation by using Gaussian Processes and a spatial kernel in a hierarchical formulation of the Beta Process. The model is employed by our approach to first infer Gaussian Processes for the spectra present in the hyperspectral image. Then, it is used to estimate the activity level of the inferred processes in a sparse representation of a high resolution image of the same scene. Finally, we use the model to compute multiple sparse codes of the high resolution image, that are merged with the samples of the Gaussian Processes for an accurate estimate of the high resolution hyperspectral image. We perform experiments with remotely sensed and ground-based hyperspectral images to establish the effectiveness of our approach.

Keywords: Hyperspectral · Super-resolution · Beta/Gaussian Process

1 Introduction

Spectral characteristics of materials are considered vital in remote sensing, medical imaging and forensics [1–6]. Recently, they have also shown improved performance in various computer vision tasks, e.g. recognition [7–9], document analysis [10,11], tracking [12], pedestrian detection [13] and segmentation [14]. Hyperspectral imaging is an emerging modality that can efficiently obtain high-fidelity spectral representations of a scene. Nevertheless, the low resolution of contemporary hyperspectral cameras is currently a bottleneck in its ubiquitous use [4,15,16].

Reflectance spectra are characterized by their intensity distributions over continuous wavelength ranges. Hence, hyperspectral cameras integrate scene

B. Leibe et al. (Eds.): ECCV 2016, Part III, LNCS 9907, pp. 103–120, 2016.
DOI: 10.1007/978-3-319-46487-9_7

radiance with hundreds of spectrally sharp bases, thereby requiring longer exposures. This results in a reduced resolution image. Moreover, it is not straightforward to use high resolution sensors in hyperspectral cameras because they

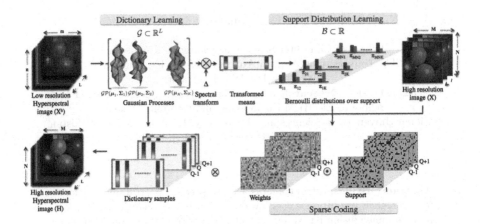

Fig. 1. Schematics: Using the proposed model, a set of Gaussian Processes ($\mathcal{GP}$s) is
inferred for the spectra in hyperspectral image. The means of the $\mathcal{GP}$s are transformed
according to the spectral channels of a high resolution image **X** of the same scene.
The transformed means and **X** are used to compute a set $\mathcal{B}$ of Bernoulli distributions,
signifying the activity level of $\mathcal{GP}$s in the sparse codes of **X**. Multiple sparse codes of
X are computed using the proposed model, each satisfying $\mathcal{B}$. The computed codes are
used with the samples of $\mathcal{GP}$s to estimate the high resolution hyperspectral image.

further reduce the photon density that is already confined by the spectral filters. These constraints make hyperspectral image super resolution a particularly
interesting research problem [17].

Currently, the resolution of the cameras that perform a gross quantization
of the scene radiance (e.g. RGB and RGB-NIR), is orders of magnitude higher
than that of hyperspectral cameras [4]. We collectively term the images acquired
by these cameras as the *multi-spectral* images. In this work, we propose to take
advantage of the high resolution of a multi-spectral image by merging its spatial
patterns with the samples of Gaussian Processes [18], learned to represent the
hyperspectral image of the same scene. Gaussian Processes provide an excellent
tool for modeling natural spectra [19] because they can easily incorporate the
regularly occurring smoothness of spectra. To learn the Gaussian Processes,
we propose a novel Bayesian representation model. Our model also incorporates
spatial consistency in the representation by employing a kernel in the hierarchical
formulation of the Beta Process [20]. We provide a detailed Markov Chain Monte
Carlo (MCMC) analysis [21] for the Bayesian inference using our model.

Employing the proposed model, we develop an approach for hyperspectral
image super resolution, shown in Fig. 1. The approach first uses the model to
infer Gaussian Processes to represent the low resolution hyperspectral image.
Then, the mean parameters of the processes are transformed to match the spectral quantization of the high resolution multi-spectral image. The model is then

employed with the transformed means and the multi-spectral image to infer a set of Bernoulli distributions. These distributions record the activity level of the Gaussian Processes in the representation of the multi-spectral image. Exploiting these distributions, the model is later applied to infer a set of sparse codes for the multi-spectral image, that are used with the samples of the Gaussian Processes to obtain a high resolution hyperspectral image. Experiments on remotely sensed and ground-based hyperspectral images show that our approach obtains higher fidelity super resolution images as compared to the state-of-the-art approaches.

2   Related Work

Hyperspectral imaging has been used in remote sensing for over three decades [22]. However, hyperspectral instruments installed in contemporary remote sensing platforms still lack in spatial resolution [5,16]. High cost of replacing these instruments and hardware limitations have motivated significant research in signal processing based resolution enhancement of remote sensing imagery [16]. Pan-sharpening [23] is one of the common techniques used for this purpose. It fuses a pan-chromatic high resolution image with a hyperspectral image to improve its spatial resolution. Wavelet based pan-sharpening [24], Intensity-Hue-Saturation transform based methods [25,26] and pan-sharpening with principal component analysis [27] are a few representative examples of this category.

Whereas sharp spatial patterns are apparent in pan-sharpened images, the resulting images often suffer from significant spectral distortions [28]. This can be attributed to the spectral limitations of the pan-chromatic images [29]. Therefore, [30] and [31] fused multi-spectral images with hyperspectral images. They used hyperspectral unmixing [32] for the image fusion. However, these methods assume relatively small difference between the spectral resolutions of the images being fused. Moreover, they also under-perform when the imaged scenes are highly mixed [33]. For such cases, their performance have been improved by Zurita-Milla et al. [34] by employing a sliding window technique.

Recently, matrix factorization based approaches have consistently shown state-of-the-art performance in hyperspectral image super resolution. These approaches are divided into three categories based on their underlying assumptions. The methods in the **first category** [4,16,17,33] assume that only the spectral transform between the images being fused is known beforehand. Kawakami et al. [4] factored a hyperspectral image and an RGB image into their respective bases and used the sparse codes of the RGB image with the basis of the hyperspectral image. Huang et al. [33] applied a similar approach to remote sensing imagery, using singular value decomposition to learn the bases, whereas a sparsity controlled approach was employed in [17] for non-negative matrix factorization. Motivated by the success of Bayesian matrix factorization in RGB and gray scale image super resolution [35], Akhtar et al. [16] developed a Bayesian approach for hyperspectral image super resolution.

The approaches in the **second category** [36–40] additionally assume priori knowledge of the spatial transform between the images. Lanaras et al. [36,37] formulated hyperspectral image super resolution as a coupled unmixing problem and proposed a matrix factorization algorithm to solve it. Their approach exploits the physical constraints generally followed by the spectral signatures. Wycoff et al. [38] proposed to use the ADMM algorithm [41] for the factorization procedure. A variational based approach is also proposed by Wei et al. [39] for the same purpose. In [40], Yokoya et al. exploited the coupling between the images being fused and developed a coupled matrix factorization technique for hyperspectral image super resolution. They also noted that in practice, it is challenging to obtain an accurate estimate of the spatial transform between the images being fused. Nevertheless, accurate transform is generally assumed and exploited by the approaches in this category. The methods in the **third category** [29] assume availability of high resolution hyperspectral training data. This implicitly imposes both of the above assumptions in addition to the requirement that abundant training data is available despite hardware limitations.

Overall, the least restrictive methods are those belonging to the first category, in which our approach also falls. Akhtar et al. [16] have established the usefulness of Bayesian sparse representation for hyperspectral image super resolution. Nevertheless, their approach has two major limitations. That is, it neither considers the spectral smoothness nor the spatial consistency of the representation of the nearby image pixels. In this paper, we address these limitations by (1) employing Gaussian Processes for the spectral signatures to incorporate smoothness into their representation; and (2) enforcing spatial consistency of the representation with a suitable kernel in the hierarchical formulation of the Beta Process.

3   Problem Formulation

Let us denote an acquired hyperspectral image with L spectral bands by $\mathbf{X}^h \in \mathbb{R}^{m \times n \times L}$. Let $\mathbf{X} \in \mathbb{R}^{M \times N \times l}$ be the high resolution image of the same scene obtained by a multi-spectral sensor. We aim at estimating a high resolution hyperspectral image $\mathbf{H} \in \mathbb{R}^{M \times N \times L}$ by merging $\mathbf{X}$ with $\mathbf{X}^h$. The two available images are considered to be linear mappings of the target image. Formally, $\mathbf{X}^h = \boldsymbol{\Omega}^h(\mathbf{H})$ and $\mathbf{X} = \boldsymbol{\Omega}(\mathbf{H})$, where $\boldsymbol{\Omega}^h : \mathbb{R}^{M \times N \times L} \to \mathbb{R}^{m \times n \times L}$ and $\boldsymbol{\Omega} : \mathbb{R}^{M \times N \times L} \to \mathbb{R}^{M \times N \times l}$. Moreover, we consider $M \gg m, N \gg n$ and $L \gg l$, to appropriately model the practical conditions. We neither assume prior knowledge of the spatial transform between the images being fused nor the availability of high resolution hyperspectral training data. Following [4,16,17,33,37], we assume aligned $\mathbf{X}$ and $\mathbf{X}^h$. In practice, accurate alignment is possible using beam-splitting mechanism [13].

We denote the number of pure spectral signatures (a.k.a endmembers) in an imaged scene by K and the kth signature by $\boldsymbol{\psi}_k \in \mathbb{R}^L$. These signatures represent the reflectances of spectrally distinct materials in the scene Let $\boldsymbol{\Psi} \in \mathbb{R}^{L \times K}$ be the matrix comprising these spectral signatures. Thus, a pixel $\mathbf{x}^h \in \mathbb{R}^L$ of the hyperspectral image can be represented as $\mathbf{x}^h = \boldsymbol{\Psi} \boldsymbol{\alpha}$, where $\boldsymbol{\alpha} \in \mathbb{R}^K$ is a coefficient vector. A pixel of the multi-spectral image can similarly be represented as $\mathbf{x} = \widetilde{\boldsymbol{\Psi}} \boldsymbol{\beta}$, where $\widetilde{\boldsymbol{\Psi}} \in \mathbb{R}^{l \times K}$ is obtained by transforming $\boldsymbol{\Psi}$, such that $\widetilde{\boldsymbol{\Psi}} = \boldsymbol{\Delta} \boldsymbol{\Psi}$. Following the literature (see Sect. 2), we assume *a priori* knowledge of the spectral transformation operator $\boldsymbol{\Delta} \in \mathbb{R}^{l \times L}$. Since the exact value of K is generally unknown, we allow for $K > L$. Hence, we expect the coefficient vectors $\boldsymbol{\alpha}$ and $\boldsymbol{\beta}$ to be sparse. Adopting the naming conventions from the sparse representation literature [42], we refer to $\boldsymbol{\Psi}$ and $\widetilde{\boldsymbol{\Psi}}$ as *dictionaries*; to their columns as *dictionary atoms*; and the vectors $\boldsymbol{\alpha}$ and $\boldsymbol{\beta}$ as *sparse codes*.

4 Proposed Approach

Our approach utilizes a hierarchical Bayesian sparse representation model, that we propose to represent hyperspectral images. The model is used to infer an ensemble of dictionaries for the hyperspectral image in the form of Gaussian Processes ($\mathcal{GP}$s) [18]. $\mathcal{GP}$s are particularly well-suited for forming dictionaries for hyperspectral images because they can easily incorporate the relative smoothness of the natural spectra with appropriate kernels. The approach transforms the mean parameters of the $\mathcal{GP}$s and uses them with the multi-spectral image $\mathbf{X}$ to estimate the activity level of the $\mathcal{GP}$s in the sparse representation of $\mathbf{X}$. We again utilize the proposed model for this estimation. Lastly, the model is used to learn multiple sparse codes of $\mathbf{X}$ that are combined with the samples from the $\mathcal{GP}$s to compute the high resolution hyperspectral image. The proposed approach is summarized in Fig. 1.

4.1 Dictionary Learning

Below, we describe the proposed representation model and its Bayesian inference process that results in the learning of the $\mathcal{GP}$s (i.e. dictionary atoms). Other stages of our approach also exploit the same model, with minor variations in the inference process. We explain those variations in Sects. 4.2 and 4.3.

Representation model: We model the ith pixel of a hyperspectral image as $\mathbf{x}_i^h = \boldsymbol{\Psi}\boldsymbol{\alpha}_i + \boldsymbol{\epsilon}_i^h$, where $\boldsymbol{\epsilon}_i^h \in \mathbb{R}^L$ represents noise. The following hierarchical Bayesian representation model is proposed to compute the probability distributions over the dictionary atoms and the sparse codes:

$$\mathbf{x}_i^h = \boldsymbol{\Psi}\boldsymbol{\alpha}_i + \boldsymbol{\epsilon}_i^h \tag{1}$$

$$\boldsymbol{\psi}_k \sim \mathcal{GP}(\boldsymbol{\psi}_k|\mathbf{0}, \boldsymbol{\Sigma}_k) \qquad z_{ik} \sim \text{Bern}(z_{ik}|\pi_{ik})$$

$$\boldsymbol{\Sigma}_k(\theta_a, \theta_b) = \frac{1}{\eta_k}\exp\left(\frac{-|\theta_b - \theta_a|}{\eta_o}\right) \qquad \pi_{ik} = \mathbf{e}^{\text{T}}(\boldsymbol{\kappa} \odot \boldsymbol{\Xi}_{ik})\mathbf{e}$$

$$\boldsymbol{\Xi}_{ik}(q,r) \sim \text{Beta}\left(\boldsymbol{\Xi}_{ik}(q,r)|e_o\rho_k, f_o(1-\rho_k)\right)$$

$$\eta_k \sim \text{Gam}(\eta_k|a_o, b_o)$$

$$\alpha_{ik} = w_{ik}z_{ik} \qquad \rho_k \sim \text{Beta}\left(\rho_k\Big|\frac{g_o}{K}, \frac{h_o(K-1)}{K}\right)$$

$$w_{ik} \sim \mathcal{N}(w_{ik}|0, \lambda_w^{-1}) \qquad \boldsymbol{\epsilon}_i^h \sim \mathcal{N}(\boldsymbol{\epsilon}_i^h|\mathbf{0}, \lambda_\epsilon^{-1}\mathbf{I}_L)$$

$$\lambda_w \sim \text{Gam}(\lambda_w|c_o, d_o) \qquad \lambda_\epsilon \sim \text{Gam}(\lambda_\epsilon|k_o, l_o).$$

In the above expressions, $\mathcal{N}$, Gam, Bern and Beta respectively denote the Normal, Gamma, Bernoulli and the Beta probability distributions. The symbol

$\odot$ denotes the element-wise product and the subscript 'o' signifies the hyper-parameters of the distributions whose values remain fixed during the inference process (discussed below). For reading convenience, we explain the remaining symbols along the relevant discussion on the representation model.

In the proposed model, we let the kth dictionary atom ψ_k to be a sample drawn from a Gaussian Process. We define the kernel of a Gaussian Process, i.e. $\Sigma_k \in \mathbb{R}^{L \times L}$, such that it promotes high correlations between the adjacent coefficients of ψ_k. Recall that, ψ_k signifies a spectral signature in our formulation. Thus, the kernel incorporates the relative smoothness of the spectra in the proposed model. In the given definition of the kernel, θ_t denotes the wavelength at the tth channel of the image, whereas $|.|$ represents the absolute value. Such an exponential form of the kernel is common for Gaussian Processes [18]. However, we also include an additional scaling parameter η_k in the kernel to allow it to adjust to the observed data. The value of this parameter is automatically inferred in our approach. We place a non-informative Gamma prior over η_k; such that $\text{Gam}(\eta_k | a_o, b_o) = \frac{b_o^{a_o} \eta_k^{(a_o - 1)}}{\Gamma(a_o)} \exp(-b_o \eta_k)$, where $\Gamma(.)$ is the well-known Gamma function. The remaining model also utilizes the same functional form of the Gamma prior. In our approach, the value of η_o is fixed to $1/L$.

We compute the kth coefficient α_{ik} of α_i as the product of a sample w_{ik} from a Normal distribution, with precision λ_w; and a sample $z_{ik} \in \{0, 1\}$ from a Bernoulli distribution, with parameter $0 \leq \pi_{ik} \leq 1$. Thus, according to our model, a pixel x_i^h selects the kth dictionary atom in its representation with a probability π_{ik}. This statistical modeling of α_i is inspired by the weighted Beta-Bernoulli Process [43]. Zhou et al. [43] showed that Bernoulli priors over the support of α_i, with conjugate Beta priors, successfully capture the intrinsic sparsity of the signal. On the other hand, Normal priors (over w_{ik}) take care of the coefficient weights. For a similar situation, Akhtar et al. [16] directly placed a Beta probability prior over the Bernoulli distribution parameter. However, their approach neither forces the atoms of the dictionary nor the sparse codes to be similar for the nearby pixels in the image. To enforce this spatial consistency in the representation model, we compute π_{ik} as a weighted sum of the samples from a Beta probability distribution. In our approach, these Beta distribution samples signify the probabilities of selection of ψ_k in the representations of the nearby pixels of x_i^h. Hence, ψ_k has more chances to get selected for x_i^h, if that dictionary atom is also used in the representations of the nearby pixels of x_i^h.

Concretely, we let $\pi_{ik} = \mathbf{e}^{\text{T}}(\kappa \odot \Xi_{ik})\mathbf{e}$, where $\mathbf{e} \in \mathbb{R}^P$ is a vector of 1s; $\kappa \in \mathbb{R}^{P \times P}$ is the spatial kernel and $\Xi_{ik} \in \mathbb{R}^{P \times P}$ comprises the samples of a Beta probability distribution. Here, P is the size of the image patch that contains the neighborhood pixels centered around x_i^h. We compute a coefficient of κ at index (q, r) as $\kappa(q, r) = \exp(-\|\mathcal{I}_i - \mathcal{I}_j\|_2 / \sigma_o)$, where $\mathcal{I}_t$ denotes the index of the tth pixel in the image and σ_o decides the kernel width. We sample $\Xi_{ik}(q, r)$ from a Beta distribution and, keeping in view the physical significance of these samples, we place a second Beta prior over the parameter ρ_k of the distribution. The second prior plays the same role in our model that is played by the Beta prior in the model employed by Akhtar et al. [16]. However, the resulting stochastic process uses $\mathcal{GP}$ as the base measure in our model, instead of a Multi-variate Gaussian, as in [16]. We also note that the notion of hierarchical construction of the Beta Process was first introduced by Thibaux and Jordan [20]. However, our model differs from their proposal, as they did not use a kernel for computing π_{ik} and employed a Normal distribution as the base measure.

Following the literature [4,16] we consider white noise in our model. In Eq. 1, the covariance matrix of the noise distribution is denoted as $\lambda_\epsilon^{-1}\mathbf{I}_L$, where $\mathbf{I}_L \in \mathbb{R}^{L \times L}$ is the identity matrix. We place a Gamma prior over the noise precision λ_ϵ. This allows a Bayesian model to automatically adjust to the noise level of the observed data [43].

Inference: We perform Markov Chain Monte Carlo (MCMC) analysis [21] to infer the posterior probability distributions over the dictionary atoms and the sparse codes using our model. Below, we derive the expressions of the probability distributions that are sampled sequentially to perform the MCMC analysis. The sampling process is carried out iteratively.

Sampling ψ_k: For brevity, let us denote the contribution of ψ_k to $\mathbf{x}_i^h$ as $\mathbf{x}_{i_{\psi_k}}^h = \mathbf{x}_i^h - \mathbf{\Psi}(\mathbf{w}_i \odot \mathbf{z}_i) + \psi_k(w_{ik}z_{ik})$, where $\mathbf{w}_i, \mathbf{z}_i \in \mathbb{R}^K$ are the vectors formed by concatenating w_{ik} and z_{ik}, $\forall k$. According to our model, the posterior probability distribution over ψ_k can be expressed as:

$$p(\psi_k|-) \propto \prod_{i=1}^{mn} \mathcal{N}(\mathbf{x}_{i_{\psi_k}}^h | \psi_k(w_{ik}z_{ik}), \lambda_\epsilon^{-1}\mathbf{I}_L)\mathcal{GP}(\psi_k|\mathbf{0}, \mathbf{\Sigma}_k).$$

Exploiting the linear Gaussian model [44], it can be shown that $\mathcal{GP}(\psi_k|\boldsymbol{\mu}_k, \widehat{\mathbf{\Sigma}}_k)$ must be used to sample this posterior probability distribution, where

$$\widehat{\mathbf{\Sigma}}_k = \left(\mathbf{\Sigma}_k^{-1} + \lambda_\epsilon \sum_{i=1}^{mn}(w_{ik}z_{ik})^2\right)^{-1}, \quad \boldsymbol{\mu}_k = \lambda_\epsilon \widehat{\mathbf{\Sigma}}_k \sum_{i=1}^{mn}(w_{ik}z_{ik})\mathbf{x}_{i_{\psi_k}}^h.$$

Sampling η_k: According to the proposed model, the posterior probability distribution over η_k can be written as $p(\eta_k|-) \propto \mathcal{GP}\left(\mathbf{\Psi}|\mathbf{0}, \frac{1}{\eta_k}\widetilde{\mathbf{\Sigma}}_k\right) \mathrm{Gam}(\eta_k|a_o, b_o)$, where $\mathbf{0}$ is a vector of zeros in $\mathbb{R}^L$ and $\widetilde{\mathbf{\Sigma}}_k = \exp(-|\theta_b - \theta_a|/\eta_o)$. The right hand side of the proportionality can be further be expanded into the following expression: $\frac{b_o^{a_o}\left(\sqrt[L]{2\pi}\right)^{-1}\eta_k^{a_o-1}}{\Gamma(a_o)\sqrt{\det\left(\frac{1}{\eta_k}\widetilde{\mathbf{\Sigma}}_k\right)}} \exp\left\{-\frac{\eta_k}{2}\psi_k^{\mathrm{T}}\widetilde{\mathbf{\Sigma}}_k\psi_k - b_o\eta_k\right\}$, which is proportional to the Gamma probability distribution $\mathrm{Gam}\left(\eta_k|a_o + \frac{L}{2}, b_o + \frac{1}{2}\psi_k^{\mathrm{T}}\widetilde{\mathbf{\Sigma}}_k\psi_k\right)$, that we use to sample η_k.

Sampling w_{ik}: The posterior distribution over w_{ik} has the functional form $p(w_{ik}|-) \propto \mathcal{N}(\mathbf{x}_{i_{\psi_k}}^h | \psi_k(w_{ik}z_{ik}), \lambda_\epsilon^{-1}\mathbf{I}_L)\mathcal{N}(w_{ik}|0, \lambda_w^{-1})$. Again, making the use of the linear Gaussian model, w_{ik} can be sampled from $\mathcal{N}(w_{ik}|\mu_w, \widehat{\lambda}_w^{-1})$, where $\widehat{\lambda}_w = \lambda_w + \lambda_\epsilon z_{ik}^2 \psi_k^{\mathrm{T}}\psi_k$ and $\mu_w = z_{ik}\psi^{\mathrm{T}}\mathbf{x}_{i_{\psi_k}}^h \lambda_\epsilon/\lambda_w$.

Sampling λ_w: According to our model, the posterior over λ_w can be written as: $p(\lambda_w|-) \propto \prod_{i=1}^{mn} \mathcal{N}(\mathbf{w}_i|\mathbf{0}, \lambda_w^{-1}\mathbf{I}_K)\text{Gam}(\lambda_w|c_o, d_o)$. Hence, employing the conjugacy between the Normal and the Gamma distributions, we sample λ_w from $\text{Gam}(\lambda_w|\frac{Kmn}{2} + c_o, \frac{1}{2}\sum_{i=1}^{mn}\mathbf{w}_i^\mathsf{T}\mathbf{w}_i + d_o)$.

Sampling z_{ik}: We can write $p(z_{ik}|-) \propto \mathcal{N}(\mathbf{x}_{i_{\psi_k}}^h|\boldsymbol{\psi}_k(w_{ik}z_{ik}), \lambda_\epsilon^{-1}\mathbf{I}_L)\text{Bern}(z_{ik}|\pi_{ik})$. From here, it is easy to show that z_{ik} must be sampled from the Bernoulli distribution: $\text{Bern}\left(z_{ik}|\frac{\gamma}{1-\pi_{ik}+\gamma}\right)$, where $\gamma = \exp\left(-\frac{\lambda_\epsilon}{2}(\boldsymbol{\psi}_k^\mathsf{T}\boldsymbol{\psi}_k w_{ik}^2 - 2w_{ik}\mathbf{x}_{i_{\psi_k}}^{h\mathsf{T}}\boldsymbol{\psi}_k)\right)$.

Sampling $\Xi_{ik}(q, r)$: Let $\Xi_{ik}(q, r) = \xi_{ik}$ and $\pi_{ik}^{\sim(q,r)} = \pi_{ik} - \kappa(q,r)\xi_{ik}$. Using these notations, we can express the posterior distribution over $\Xi_{ik}(q, r)$ as:

$$p(\xi_{ik}|-) \propto \text{Beta}\left(\xi_{ik}|e_o\rho_k, f_o(1 - \rho_k)\right) \prod_{q,r\in\{1,\dots,P\}} \text{Bern}\left(z_{ik}|\kappa(q,r)\xi_{ik} + \pi_{ik}^{\sim(q,r)}\right).$$

This distribution can not be directly sampled. However, considering its functional form, it is possible to associate the popularity of the kth dictionary atom to the pixels in the neighborhood $\aleph$ of $\mathbf{x}_i^h$ as:

$$\xi_{ik} \sim \text{Beta}\left(\xi_{ik}\Big|e_o\rho_k + \sum_{\{j:(p,q)\in\aleph\}} z_{jk}, f_o(1 - \rho_k) + \sum_{\{j:(p,q)\in\aleph\}}(1 - z_{jk})\right).$$

We use the above distribution as the proposal distribution $\mathcal{Q}$ in the Metropolis Hastings (MH) algorithm [45] and in step τ of MH algorithm, we draw $\xi_{ik}^* \sim \mathcal{Q}(\xi_{ik}|\xi_{ik}^\tau)$, where ξ_{ik}^τ is the current ξ_{ik}, and accept the sample with a probability:

$$\varrho = \min\left\{1, \frac{p(\xi_{ik}^*)\mathcal{Q}(\xi_{ik}^\tau|\xi_{ik}^*)}{p(\xi_{ik}^\tau)\mathcal{Q}(\xi_{ik}^*|\xi_{ik}^\tau)}\right\}$$

It can be shown that the fraction in the brackets can be analytically computed as follows:

$$\left(\frac{\xi_{ik}^\tau}{\xi_{ik}^*}\right)^{\sum_{\{j:(p,q)\in\aleph\}}z_{jk}} \left(\frac{1-\xi_{ik}^\tau}{1-\xi_{ik}^*}\right)^{\sum_{\{j:(p,q)\in\aleph\}}(1-z_{jk})} \prod_{\{j:(p,q)\in\aleph\}}\left(1+\frac{\Upsilon}{\xi_{ik}^\tau}\right)^{z_{jk}}\left(1-\frac{\Upsilon}{1-\xi_{ik}^\tau}\right)^{1-z_{jk}},$$

where $\Upsilon = \kappa(p,q)(\xi_{ik}^* - \xi_{ik}^\tau)$.

Sampling ρ_k: The posterior on ρ_k can be expressed as:

$$p(\rho_k|-) \propto \text{Beta}\left(\rho_k|g_o/K, h_o(K-1)/K\right)\prod_{i=1}^{mn}\text{Beta}\left(\xi_{ik}|e_o\rho_k, f_o(1-\rho_k)\right).$$

For analytical simplification, we let $e_o = f_o = 1$. By expanding the expressions for the distributions and neglecting the constant terms, we can show that $\forall i \in \{1,\dots,mn\}$:

$$p(\rho_k|-) \propto \frac{\rho_k^{\left(\frac{g_o}{K}-1\right)}(1-\rho_k)^{\left(\frac{h_o(K-1)}{K}-1\right)}}{(\Gamma(\rho_k)\Gamma(1-\rho_k))^{mn}}\left(\frac{\xi_{ik}}{1-\xi_{ik}}\right)^{\rho_k mn}.$$

Here, the term depending on ξ_{ik} can be simplified to $\exp\left(\rho_k \sum_{i=1}^{mn} \log \frac{\xi_{ik}}{1-\xi_{ik}}\right)$. Therefore, following Zhou et al. [46], we use slice sampling algorithm [47] to sample ρ_k from the following exponential distribution:

$$\rho_k \sim \text{Exp}\left(\sum_{i=1}^{mn} \log \frac{\xi_{ik}}{1-\xi_{ik}}\right) \mathcal{R}(\varsigma, \upsilon, \omega),$$

where $\mathcal{R}(\varsigma, \upsilon, \omega)$ is the range of ρ_k and $\upsilon \sim \text{Unif}(0, (1-\rho_k)^{\left(\frac{h_o(K-1)}{K}-1\right)})$, $\varsigma \sim \text{Unif}(0, \rho_k^{\left(\frac{q_o}{K}-1\right)})$ and $\omega \sim \text{Unif}(0, \sin^{mn}(\pi\rho_k))$. Here, Unif denotes the uniform distribution. We restrict $0 < \rho_k < 1$ and exploit the fact that $\Gamma(\rho_k)\Gamma(1-\rho_k) \propto 1/\sin(\pi\rho_k)$ [48] to arrive at the expression for sampling ω.

Sampling λ_ϵ: We have $p(\lambda_\epsilon|-) \propto \prod_{i=1}^{mn} \mathcal{N}(\mathbf{x}_i^h | \boldsymbol{\Psi}(\mathbf{w}_i \odot \mathbf{z}_i), \lambda_\epsilon^{-1}\mathbf{I}_L)\text{Gam}(\lambda_\epsilon|k_o, l_o)$. Again, by employing the conjugacy of the probability distributions we can sample λ_ϵ from $\text{Gam}\left(\lambda_\epsilon | \frac{Lmn}{2} + k_o, \frac{1}{2}\sum_{i=1}^{mn} ||\mathbf{x}_i^h - \boldsymbol{\Psi}(\mathbf{w}_i \odot \mathbf{z}_i)||_2^2 + l_o\right)$, where $||.||_2$ denotes the vector ℓ-2 norm.

4.2 Support Distribution Learning

Once the inference is complete, we get a set $\mathcal{G} \subset \mathbb{R}^L$ of K Gaussian Processes, where each process represents a probability distribution over a dictionary atom. Probability distributions over other model parameters (e.g. z_{ik}) are also inferred as by-products, however they are not required by our approach. We transform the means of the $\mathcal{GP}$s using the spectral transformation operator $\boldsymbol{\Delta}$ and use them to represent the high resolution multi-spectral image $\mathbf{X}$. To learn the representation, we again use the proposed model. However, during inference, instead of sampling for the dictionary atoms, we keep them fixed to the transformed means of the $\mathcal{GP}$s. For our model, this implies $\eta_k \to \infty$. Therefore, we also do not sample for η_k. These modifications in the sampling process effectively reduce our dictionary learning process to a sparse coding process. We defer further discussion on sparse coding to Sect. 4.3. Here, we are interested in the set $\mathcal{B} \subset \mathbb{R}$ of $K \times MN$ Bernoulli distributions (i.e. parameters $\pi_{ik}, \forall i, k$) computed by the inference process. This set contains K distributions for each pixel of $\mathbf{X}$ that determines the support (indices of non-zero elements) of the sparse codes for that pixel. Since the basis vectors for the sparse codes are the transformed means of the $\mathcal{GP}$s, $\mathcal{B}$ encodes the activity level of the $\mathcal{GP}$s in the sparse representation of $\mathbf{X}$. We store $\mathcal{B}$ to later exploit it in an accurate reconstruction of the high resolution hyperspectral image.

We emphasize that the association of K Bernoulli distributions with a single pixel in our approach is different from the affiliation of K such distributions with the complete image, used by Akhtar et al. [16]. Our approach computes more distributions to promote spatial consistency in the representations.

4.3   Sparse Coding

Let us briefly consider the sparse coding process for a pixel $\mathbf{x}$ of $\mathbf{X}$, discussed in the previous section. That process computes the codes $\boldsymbol{\beta}$ of $\mathbf{x}$, such that their support follows the Bernoulli distributions in $\mathcal{B}$. Let $\mathbf{z} \in \mathbb{R}^K$ be the binary vector indexing that support. It is easy to imagine that sampling the same distributions in $\mathcal{B}$ multiple times, can often result in different $\mathbf{z}$. Being a sample of the *learned* Bernoulli distributions, each such $\mathbf{z}$ is a useful support of the sparse codes for our approach. This entails the existence of multiple useful sparse codes and hence, multiple useful reconstructions of $\mathbf{x}$ in our probabilistic settings.

Let $\widetilde{\boldsymbol{\Psi}}$ denote the dictionary formed by the transformed means of the $\mathcal{GP}$s. We can write, $\widetilde{\mathbf{x}} = \widetilde{\boldsymbol{\Psi}}(\mathbf{w} \odot \mathbf{z})$, where $\boldsymbol{\beta} = \mathbf{w} \odot \mathbf{z}$ and $\widetilde{\mathbf{x}}$ is the reconstructed $\mathbf{x}$. We propose the following lemma regarding $\widetilde{\mathbf{x}}$:

Lemma 1. $\left\| \mathbb{E}\left[\widetilde{\mathbf{x}}\right] - \mathbf{x} \right\|_2^2 \leq \left\| \widetilde{\mathbf{x}} - \mathbf{x} \right\|_2^2$, *where* $\mathbb{E}[.]$ *is the expectation operator.*

Proof: We can write $\left\| \mathbb{E}\left[\widetilde{\mathbf{x}}\right] - \mathbf{x} \right\|_2^2 = \left\| \widetilde{\boldsymbol{\Psi}} \mathbb{E}\left[\boldsymbol{\beta}\right] - \mathbf{x} \right\|_2^2$. Since $\boldsymbol{\beta} = \mathbf{w} \odot \mathbf{z}$ and multiple $\mathbf{z}$ exist, we can exploit the conditional expectation of the discrete random variables to write $\mathbb{E}\left[\boldsymbol{\beta}\right] = \mathbb{E}\left[\mathbb{E}[\boldsymbol{\beta}|\mathbf{z}]\right]$ [49]. From the results in [16], we already know that $\mathbb{E}\left[\mathbb{E}[\boldsymbol{\beta}|\mathbf{z}]\right] = \boldsymbol{\beta}_{opt}$, where $\boldsymbol{\beta}_{opt}$ is the optimal $\boldsymbol{\beta}$ with respect to the squared error. Since, $\mathbb{E}\left[\widetilde{\mathbf{x}}\right] = \widetilde{\boldsymbol{\Psi}} \boldsymbol{\beta}_{opt}$ and $\widetilde{\mathbf{x}} = \widetilde{\boldsymbol{\Psi}} \boldsymbol{\beta}$, where $\boldsymbol{\beta}$ is not guaranteed to be optimal, $\left\| \mathbb{E}\left[\widetilde{\mathbf{x}}\right] - \mathbf{x} \right\|_2^2 \leq \left\| \widetilde{\mathbf{x}} - \mathbf{x} \right\|_2^2$.

Lemma 1 shows that the expected value of multiple reconstructions of $\mathbf{x}$ can be superior to its single reconstruction. Moreover, by using $\widetilde{\boldsymbol{\Psi}} = \boldsymbol{\Delta\Psi}$ in the above proof, we can extend this result to show that $\left\| \mathbb{E}[\widetilde{\mathbf{h}}] - \mathbf{h} \right\|_2^2 \leq \left\| \widetilde{\mathbf{h}} - \mathbf{h} \right\|_2^2$, where $\mathbf{h}$ and $\widetilde{\mathbf{h}}$ denote the pixels of the target high resolution hyperspectral image and its reconstruction, respectively. To exploit this finding, we adopted the following strategy for the reconstruction of the super resolution image $\mathbf{H}$. First, we compute Q sparse codes for $\mathbf{X}$ using our model. For these computations, we fixed both $\widetilde{\boldsymbol{\Psi}}$ and $\mathcal{B}$ during the Bayesian inference. Since the sparse codes in Sect. 4.2 were also computed using the same $\mathcal{B}$ and $\widetilde{\boldsymbol{\Psi}}$, we also use them in the upcoming computations. Second, we draw $Q + 1$ samples from the already inferred Gaussian Processes and use them with the available $Q + 1$ sparse codes to construct the same number of reconstructions of $\mathbf{H}$. Finally, we estimate the expected value of these $Q + 1$ reconstructions by computing their mean. Note that, the reconstructions are performed pixel-wise in our approach, where pixels represent natural spectra. In light of Lemma 1 and the above discussion, the mean reconstructed pixels are smoothened spectra with minimum squared error with respect to the ground-truth pixels.

5   Experiments

We have evaluated our approach on both remote sensing and ground-based hyperspectral images. For the evaluation metrics, we used the Root Mean Squared

Error (RMSE) [16] and the Spectral Angle Mapper (Sam) [50]. We mainly compare our approach to the Matrix Factorization based approach (MF) [4], the Spatial-Spectral Fusion Method (SSFM) [33], the Generalized Simultaneous OMP based method (GSOMP) [17] and the Bayesian Sparse Representation approach (BSR) [16]. These are the state-of-the-art approaches in the first category of the hyperspectral super-resolution techniques (see Sect. 2) to which our approach also belongs. We note that few approaches from the second and the third category have recently reported impressive results [29,37,40]. However, those results are obtained by exploiting additional prior knowledge, which is not always available (and hence, not assumed in this work).

In our experiments, we used the author-provided implementations for GSOMP and BSR, with the parameter values reported for the same data sets in [16,17]. Due to the unavailability of public codes for MF and SSFM, we implemented these approaches using the SPAMS library [51], that is well-know for its accuracy. The parameter values of these approaches were carefully optimized such that the achieved results were the same or better than the previously reported best results for these approaches on common images. We defer the discussion on the parameter settings of our approach to Sect. 6. We follow a common evaluation protocol [4,16,17] that considers an available hyperspectral image as the ground truth and constructs a low resolution hyperspectral image by averaging 32×32 disjoint blocks of the ground truth. A high resolution multi-spectral image is constructed by spectral transformation of the ground truth, with a known transformation operator Δ.

Table 1. Benchmarking on remote sensing images: The results are in the range of 8 bit images. The best results are given in bold in green cells. The second best values are in blue cells. Image names are according to the source data set.

	AVIRIS data set							
Image	SC01		SC02		SC03		SC04	
Method	RMSE	Sam	RMSE	Sam	RMSE	Sam	RMSE	Sam
MF [4]	1.32	1.85	1.55	1.60	1.62	1.51	2.73	2.49
SSFM [33]	1.35	1.68	1.56	1.59	1.77	1.59	2.68	2.31
GSOMP [17]	1.30	1.39	1.52	1.63	1.79	1.80	1.54	2.05
BSR [16]	1.21	1.33	1.54	1.61	1.46	1.58	1.62	1.77
Proposed	**0.92**	**1.26**	**1.32**	**1.47**	**1.11**	**1.35**	**1.36**	**1.54**

For the remote sensing images, we used a data set provided by NASA[1], that contains four hyperspectral images collected by the airborne sensor AVIRIS [52]. These $512 \times 512 \times 224$ images are acquired in the wavelength range 370–2500 nm, over Cuprite mines in Nevada, US. Due to water absorptions and low signal-to-noise ratio, we removed 36 channels from the images, corresponding to the

---

[1] Download link: ftp://popo.jpl.nasa.gov/pub/free_data/f970619t01p02r02c_rfl.tar.

wavelengths 370, 380, 1330 to 1430, 1780 to 1970, 2490 and 2500 nm. The resulting images are considered as the ground truth. We constructed a high resolution multi-spectral image by selecting six bands of the ground truth, corresponding to the wavelengths 480, 560, 660, 830, 1650 and 2220 nm. These bands roughly correspond to the visible and mid-infrared wavelength channels of NASA-Landsat 7 satellite. Thus, the spectral transform $\Delta \in \mathbb{R}^{6 \times 188}$ is a binary matrix in this experiment, similar to [16,17,33].

Comparison of performance on the remote sensing images is summarized in Table 1. The results are computed using the 8-bit intensity range. As visible in the table, a considerable improvement in the results is achieved by our approach. On average, the RMSE values for our approach are ~18 % better than the previous lowest values. Similarly, the average gain in the spectral angle mapper values is ~9 %. This gain can be attributed to the spectral smoothness and the spatial consistency of the images reconstructed by our approach, which are common attributes of remote sensing hyperspectral images. In Fig. 2, we compare the reconstructions of two randomly selected contiguous pixels of image SC01 by BSR [16] and our approach. BSR showed the second best results on this image. Our approach not only reconstructs each pixel better due to the spectral smoothness, but also due to the similarities between the adjacent pixels. The angles (in $\mathbb{R}^{188}$) between the shown ground truth pixels is 1.26°. For our approach, this angle is 1.28°, whereas for BSR, its value is 3.23°. We also show examples of the reconstructed spectral images for SC01 by our approach and BSR in Fig. 3.

For the ground-based images, we evaluated our approach on hyperspectral images of everyday objects from the CAVE database [53] and the images of indoor and outdoor scenes from the Harvard database [54]. The $512 \times 512 \times 31$ images of the CAVE database are acquired using tunable filters over the

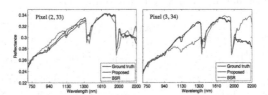

Fig. 2. Effect of spectral smoothness and spatial consistency: Two contiguous ground truth pixels for SC01 are shown along their estimates with BSR [16] and our approach.

wavelength range 400–700 nm. The fixed focal length of the sensor has resulted in a blur for the first two spectral bands of the images. We removed these bands in our experiments to avoid any bias in the results. The remaining images are considered as the ground truth. The use of tunable filters in the Harvard database has resulted in spatial distortions in some images with moving objects (e.g. grass, trees). We also avoid these images in our experiments for a fair evaluation. Following [16,17] we used the top-left 1024×1024 spatial patches as the ground truth for this database.

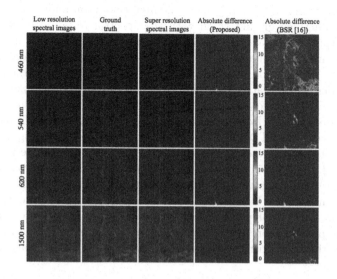

Fig. 3. Spectral images for SC01 at 460, 540, 620 and 1500 nm: The 512×512 reconstructions of the ground truth are shown along the used 16×16 low resolution images. Absolute differences between the reconstructions and the ground truth are also shown. The absolute difference images for BSR [16] are included for comparison.

Table 2. Benchmarking on ground-based images: CMF [40] and TDGU [29] (in red) are included for *reference only* as these approaches belong to different categories.

Image	CAVE database [53]									
	Balloons		Beads		Cloth		Pompos		CD	
Method	RMSE	Sam	RMSE	Sam	RMSE	Sam	RMSE	Sam	RMSE	Sam
MF [4] (Cat. 1)	2.3	8.0	8.2	14.9	6.0	7.9	4.3	10.7	7.9	14.9
SSFM [33] (Cat. 1)	2.4	8.4	8.9	15.3	7.6	8.2	4.3	11.9	8.1	16.4
GSOMP [17] (Cat. 1)	2.3	8.1	6.3	14.1	4.2	5.2	4.4	**10.0**	7.5	18.7
BSR [16] (Cat. 1)	2.1	7.9	5.9	14.2	4.0	5.9	4.1	11.1	5.4	12.9
Proposed (Cat. 1)	**1.9**	**7.6**	**5.8**	**13.7**	**3.7**	**5.0**	**3.9**	10.1	**5.3**	**10.6**
CMF [40] (Cat. 2)	2.9	4.3	7.2	7.5	5.2	4.5	3.5	3.6	6.1	7.0
TDGU [29] (Cat. 3)	1.6	-	6.9	-	-	-	-	-	3.5	-

Image	Harvard database [54]									
	Img h0		Img c2		Img d3		Img b5		Img b2	
Method	RMSE	Sam	RMSE	Sam	RMSE	Sam	RMSE	Sam	RMSE	Sam
MF [4] (Cat. 1)	2.6	2.7	2.9	2.6	1.8	3.3	2.4	2.5	2.1	3.0
SSFM [33] (Cat. 1)	3.1	2.8	3.2	2.8	2.1	3.6	2.3	2.9	2.3	3.1
GSOMP [17] (Cat. 1)	3.3	2.9	2.8	**1.9**	1.7	3.2	0.9	2.2	1.6	2.7
BSR [16] (Cat. 1)	2.4	2.9	2.6	2.2	**1.3**	3.2	0.9	2.2	**1.1**	2.5
Proposed (Cat. 1)	**2.2**	**2.5**	**2.4**	**1.9**	1.4	**3.0**	**0.8**	**2.1**	**1.1**	**2.3**
CMF [40] (Cat. 2)	2.3	2.4	2.4	2.0	1.4	3.0	1.6	2.1	1.7	2.1
TDGU [29] (Cat. 3)	-	-	-	-	-	-	0.7	-	-	-

Following [4,16,17] we constructed the high resolution multi-spectral images by transforming the ground truth with the spectral response of Nikon D700 camera (http://www.maxmax.com/spectral_response.htm). In Table 2, we show the results on five commonly used benchmarking images of each database. For reference, we also include results of representative methods from the remaining two categories of the matrix factorization based hyperspectral super-resolution techniques. The results of Coupled Matrix Factorization (CMF) [40] based approach are directly taken from [37], whereas the performance of the Training Data Guided Up-sampling (TDGU) method are taken from [29]. In Fig. 4, we show examples of the super resolution spectral images. Although the performance of the proposed approach is generally better than the existing approaches in the same category, the improvements in the results are not as significant as for the remote sensing images. In our opinion, the lower spectral resolution and larger variations in the spatial patterns in the ground-based images are the reasons behind this phenomenon. Nevertheless, our approach is generally able to perform better than the existing approaches on the ground-based images as well.

6   Discussion on Parameters

In all the experiments we used the value 10^{-6} for $a_o, b_o, c_o, d_o, k_o, l_o$ and 1 for e_o and f_o. The values of g_o and h_o were adjusted to give a parabolic probability density function of the Beta distributions, for which $g_o/K \approx h_o(K-1)/K$. We used $\eta_o = 1/L$ and the spatial kernel width was set to 2 for the Harvard database and 1 for the remaining data sets. This resulted in $P = 5$ and $P = 3$ respectively. Except for P, our model is fairly insensitive to small perturbations in the parameter values, which is a common observation for Bayesian models [16]. The reported results are sensitive to the value of P because the considered low

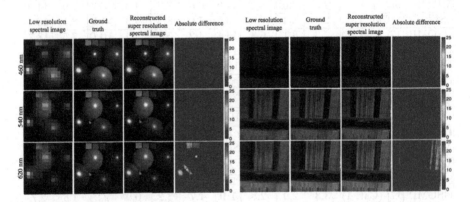

Fig. 4. Spectral reconstruction at 460, 540 and 620 nm: The used 16×16 low resolution images are shown along the reconstructions and the 512×512 ground truth. Absolute differences between the reconstructions and the ground truth are also given. (Left) 'Balloons' from the CAVE database [53]. (Right) 'Img h0' form the Harvard database [54].

resolution hyperspectral images have very small spatial dimensions. Keeping in view the spatial dimensions of the images, we used $K = 100$ for the Harvard database and 10 for the remaining data sets.

We initialized λ_ϵ to 10^6, λ_w to 10^3, η_k to $10^{-3}, \forall k$ and π_{ik} to $10^{-3}, \forall i, k$. These initial values were selected considering the physical significance of the parameters in our model. Nevertheless, the approach is generally insensitive to these initial values. To learn the Gaussian Processes, we initialized the dictionary with random samples of Multi-variate Gaussians and initialized the spare codes by allowing half of them to have value 1. For sparse coding, we used the LASSO solver of the SPAMS library [51] to initialize the sparse codes. In our experiments, we processed the images as 2×2 overlapping patches.

We used 500 sampling iterations for dictionary learning and 300 and 100 iterations respectively for learning the Bernoulli distributions in $\mathcal{B}$ and sparse coding. Fewer iterations were enough in the later stages because fewer probability distributions were required to be sampled in those stages. We computed the codes 25 time, i.e. $Q = 25$ in our experiments.

7   Conclusion

We proposed a Bayesian approach for hyperspectral super resolution that fuses a high resolution multi-spectral image with a hyperspectral image. It utilizes a Bayesian sparse representation model that places Gaussian Process priors on the dictionary and uses a kernel to promote spatial consistency in the representation. We also derived inference equations for the proposed model. The model is used for inferring Gaussian Processes for the dictionary atoms, estimating their popularity in the representation of the multi-spectral image and computing multiple sparse codes of that image. The sparse codes of the multi-spectral image are used with the samples of the Gaussian Processes to finally estimate the super resolution image. We tested our approach on remote sensing and ground-based images. Our results show that the approach is useful for both types of images.

Acknowledgment. Supported by ARC Discovery Grant DP110102399.

References

1. Edelman, G., Gaston, E., Van Leeuwen, T., Cullen, P., Aalders, M.: Hyperspectral imaging for non-contact analysis of forensic traces. Forensic Sci. Intl. **223**(1), 28–39 (2012)
2. Lu, G., Fei, B.: Medical hyperspectral imaging: a review. J. Biomed. Opt. **19**(1), 010901 (2014)
3. Zhou, Y., Chang, H., Barner, K., Spellman, P., Parvin, B.: Classification of histology sections via multispectral convolutional sparse coding. In: CVPR, June 2014
4. Kawakami, R., Wright, J., Tai, Y.W., Matsushita, Y., Ben-Ezra, M., Ikeuchi, K.: High-resolution hyperspectral imaging via matrix factorization. In: CVPR, pp. 2329–2336, June 2011

5. Dias, J.B., Plaza, A., Valls, G.C., Scheunders, P., Nasrabadi, N., Chanussot, J.: Hyperspectral remote sensing data analysis and future challenges. IEEE Geosci. Remote Sens. Mag. **1**(2), 6–36 (2013)
6. Charles, A., Olshausen, B., Rozell, C.: Learning sparse codes for hyperspectral imagery. IEEE J. Sel. Top. Signal Process. **5**(5), 963–978 (2011)
7. Zhang, D., Zuo, W., Yue, F.: A comparative study of palmprint recognition algorithms. ACM Comput. Surv. **44**(1), 2:1–2:37 (2012)
8. Uzair, M., Mahmood, A., Mian, A.: Hyperspectral face recognition using 3D-DCT and partial least squares. In: Proceedings British Machine Vision Conference 2013 (BMVC), pp. 57.1–57.10 (2013)
9. Di, W., Zhang, L., Zhang, D., Pan, Q.: Studies on hyperspectral face recognition in visible spectrum with feature band selection. IEEE Trans. Syst. Man Cybern. Part A: Syst. Hum. **40**(6), 1354–1361 (2010)
10. Khan, Z., Shafait, F., Mian, A.: Automatic ink mismatch detection for forensic document analysis. Pattern Recogn. **48**(11), 3615–3626 (2015)
11. Kim, S.J., Deng, F., Brown, M.S.: Visual enhancement of old documents with hyperspectral imaging. Pattern Recogn. **44**(7), 1461–1469 (2011)
12. Nguyen, H.V., Banerjee, A., Chellappa, R.: Tracking via object reflectance using a hyperspectral video camera. In: CVPRW, pp. 44–51, June 2010
13. Hwang, S., Park, J., Kim, N., Choi, Y., So Kweon, I.: Multispectral pedestrian detection: benchmark dataset and baseline. In: IEEE Conference on Computer Vision and Pattern Recognition, June 2015
14. Tarabalka, Y., Chanussot, J., Benediktsson, J.A.: Segmentation and classification of hyperspectral images using minimum spanning forest grown from automatically selected markers. IEEE Trans. Syst., Man, Cybern., Syst. **40**(5), 1267–1279 (2010)
15. Chen, C., Li, Y., Liu, W., Huang, J.: Image fusion with local spectral consistency and dynamic gradient sparsity. In: CVPR, June 2014
16. Akhtar, N., Shafait, F., Mian, A.: Bayesian sparse representation for hyperspectral image super resolution. In: IEEE Conference on Computer Vision and Pattern Recognition, June 2015
17. Akhtar, N., Shafait, F., Mian, A.: Sparse Spatio-Spectral Representation for Hyperspectral Image Super-Resolution. In: Fleet, D., Pajdla, T., Schiele, B., Tuytelaars, T. (eds.) ECCV 2014. LNCS, vol. 8695, pp. 63–78. Springer, Heidelberg (2014). doi:10.1007/978-3-319-10584-0_5
18. Rasmussen, C.E.: Gaussian processes for machine learning. Citeseer (2006)
19. Dobigeon, N., Tourneret, J.Y., Richard, C., Bermudez, J., Mclaughlin, S., Hero, A.O.: Nonlinear unmixing of hyperspectral images: models and algorithms. IEEE Signal Process. Mag. **31**(1), 82–94 (2014)
20. Thibaux, R., Jordan, M.I.: Hierarchical beta processes and the Indian buffet process. In: International Conference on Artificial Intelligence and Statistics, pp. 564–571 (2007)
21. Bishop, C.M.: Pattern Recognition and Machine Learning (Information Science and Statistics). Springer, Secaucus (2006)
22. Solomon, J., Rock, B.: Imaging spectrometry for earth remote sensing. Science **228**(4704), 1147–1152 (1985)
23. Alparone, L., Wald, L., Chanussot, J., Thomas, C., Gamba, P., Bruce, L.: Comparison of pansharpening algorithms: outcome of the 2006 GRS-S data-fusion contest. IEEE Trans. Geosci. Remote Sens. **45**(10), 3012–3021 (2007)
24. Nunez, J., Otazu, X., Fors, O., Prades, A., Pala, V., Arbiol, R.: Multiresolution-based image fusion with additive wavelet decomposition. IEEE Trans. Geosci. Remote Sens. **37**(3), 1204–1211 (1999)

25. Haydn, R., Dalke, G.W., Henkel, J., Bare, J.E.: Application of the IHS color transform to the processing of multisensor data and image enhancement. In: Proceedings of the International Symposium on Remote Sensing of Environment (1982)
26. Carper, W.J., Lilles, T.M., Kiefer, R.W.: The use of intensity-hue-saturation transformations for merging SOPT panchromatic and multispectral image data. Photogram. Eng. Remote Sens. **56**(4), 457–467 (1990)
27. Shah, V.P., Younan, N.H., King, R.L.: An efficient pan-sharpening method via a combined adaptive PCA approach and contourlets. IEEE Trans. Geosci. Remote Sens. **46**(5), 1323–1335 (2008)
28. Cetin, M., Musaoglu, N.: Merging hyperspectral and panchromatic image data: qualitative and quantitative analysis. Int. J. Remote Sens. **30**(7), 1779–1804 (2009)
29. Kwon, H., Tai, Y.W.: RGB-guided hyperspectral image upsampling. In: International Conference on Computer Vision (2015)
30. Zhukov, B., Oertel, D., Lanzl, F., Reinhackel, G.: Unmixing-based multisensor multiresolution image fusion. IEEE Trans. Geosci. Remote Sens. **37**(3), 1212–1226 (1999)
31. Minghelli-Roman, A., Polidori, L., Mathieu-Blanc, S., Loubersac, L., Cauneau, F.: Spatial resolution improvement by merging MERIS-ETM images for coastal water monitoring. IEEE Geosci. Remote Sens. Lett. **3**(2), 227–231 (2006)
32. Keshava, N., Mustard, J.: Spectral unmixing. IEEE Signal Process. Mag. **19**(1), 44–57 (2002)
33. Huang, B., Song, H., Cui, H., Peng, J., Xu, Z.: Spatial and spectral image fusion using sparse matrix factorization. IEEE Trans. Geosci. Remote Sens. **52**(3), 1693–1704 (2014)
34. Zurita-Milla, R., Clevers, J.G., Schaepman, M.E.: Unmixing-based Landsat TM and MERIS FR data fusion. IEEE Trans. Geosci. Remote Sens. **5**(3), 453–457 (2008)
35. He, L., Qi, H., Zaretzki, R.: Beta process joint dictionary learning for coupled feature spaces with application to single image super-resolution. In: 2013 IEEE Conference on Computer Vision and Pattern Recognition (CVPR), pp. 345–352, June 2013
36. Lanaras, C., Baltsavias, E., Schindler, K.: Advances in hyperspectral and multispectral image fusion and spectral unmixing. ISPRS – Intl. Arch. Photogrammetry, Remote Sens. Spat. Inf. Sci. **3**, W3 (2015)
37. Lanaras, C.A., Baltsavias, E., Schindler, K.: Hyperspectral super-resolution by coupled spectral unmixing. In: International Conference on Computer Vision (2015)
38. Wycoff, E., Chan, T.H., Jia, K., Ma, W.K., Ma, Y.: A non-negative sparse promoting algorithm for high resolution hyperspectral imaging. In: ICASSP, pp. 1409–1413, May 2013
39. Wei, Q., Bioucas-Dias, J., Dobigeon, N., Tourneret, J.Y.: Hyperspectral and multispectral image fusion based on a sparse representation. IEEE Trans. Geosci. Remote Sens. **53**(7), 3658–3668 (2015)
40. Yokoya, N., Yairi, T., Iwasaki, A.: Coupled nonnegative matrix factorization unmixing for hyperspectral and multispectral data fusion. IEEE Trans. Geosci. Remote Sens. **50**(2), 528–537 (2012)
41. Boyd, S., Parikh, N., Chu, E., Peleato, B., Eckstein, J.: Distributed optimization and statistical learning via the alternating direction method of multipliers. Found. Trends Mach. Learn. **3**(1), 1–122 (2011)
42. Rubinstein, R., Bruckstein, A., Elad, M.: Dictionaries for sparse representation modeling. Proc. IEEE **98**(6), 1045–1057 (2010)

43. Zhou, M., Chen, H., Paisley, J., Ren, L., Li, L., Xing, Z., Dunson, D., Sapiro, G., Carin, L.: Nonparametric Bayesian dictionary learning for analysis of noisy and incomplete images. IEEE Trans. Image Process. **21**(1), 130–144 (2012)

44. Roweis, S., Ghahramani, Z.: A unifying review of linear Gaussian models. Neural Comput. **11**(2), 305–345 (1999)

45. Hastings, W.K.: Monte Carlo sampling methods using Markov chains and their applications. Biometrika **57**(1), 97–109 (1970)

46. Zhou, M., Yang, H., Sapiro, G., Dunson, D.B., Carin, L.: Dependent hierarchical beta process for image interpolation and denoising. In: International Conference on Artificial Intelligence and Statistics, pp. 883–891 (2011)

47. Damien, P., Wakefield, J., Walker, S.: Gibbs sampling for Bayesian non-conjugate and hierarchical models by using auxiliary variables. J. Roy. Stat. Soc. Ser. B Stat. Methodol. **61**, 331–344 (1999)

48. Havil, J.: Gamma: Exploring Euler's Constant. The Mathematical Intelligence **27**(1), 86–88 (2005)

49. Ross, S.M.: Introduction to Probability Models. Academic Press, San Diego (2014)

50. Yuhas, R.H., Goetz, A.F., Boardman, J.W.: Discrimination among semi-arid landscape endmembers using the spectral angle mapper (SAM) algorithm. In: Summaries of the Third Annual JPL Airborne Geoscience Workshop, vol. 1, pp. 147–149. JPL Publication, Pasadena (1992)

51. Mairal, J., Bach, F., Ponce, J., Sapiro, G.: Online learning for matrix factorization and sparse coding. J. Mach. Learning Res. **11**, 19–60 (2010)

52. Green, R.O., Eastwood, M.L., Sarture, C.M., Chrien, T.G., Aronsson, M., Chippendale, B.J., Faust, J.A., Pavri, B.E., Chovit, C.J., Solis, M., Olah, M.R., Williams, O.: Imaging spectroscopy and the airborne visible/infrared imaging spectrometer (AVIRIS). Remote Sens. Environ. **65**(3), 227–248 (1998)

53. Yasuma, F., Mitsunaga, T., Iso, D., Nayar, S.: Generalized assorted pixel camera: post-capture control of resolution, dynamic range and spectrum. Technical report, Dept. of Comp. Sci., Columbia University, CUCS-061-08, November 2008

54. Chakrabarti, A., Zickler, T.: Statistics of real-world hyperspectral images. In: CVPR, pp. 193–200, June 2011

A 4D Light-Field Dataset and CNN Architectures for Material Recognition

Ting-Chun Wang[1]([✉]), Jun-Yan Zhu[1], Ebi Hiroaki[2], Manmohan Chandraker[2], Alexei A. Efros[1], and Ravi Ramamoorthi[2]

[1] University of California, Berkeley, USA
{tcwang0509,junyanz,efros}@berkeley.edu
[2] University of California, San Diego, USA
hebi@eng.ucsd.edu, {mkchandraker,ravir}@cs.ucsd.edu

Abstract. We introduce a new light-field dataset of materials, and take advantage of the recent success of deep learning to perform material recognition on the 4D light-field. Our dataset contains 12 material categories, each with 100 images taken with a Lytro Illum, from which we extract about 30,000 patches in total. To the best of our knowledge, this is the first mid-size dataset for light-field images. Our main goal is to investigate whether the additional information in a light-field (such as multiple sub-aperture views and view-dependent reflectance effects) can aid material recognition. Since recognition networks have not been trained on 4D images before, we propose and compare several novel CNN architectures to train on light-field images. In our experiments, the best performing CNN architecture achieves a 7% boost compared with 2D image classification (70% → 77%). These results constitute important baselines that can spur further research in the use of CNNs for light-field applications. Upon publication, our dataset also enables other novel applications of light-fields, including object detection, image segmentation and view interpolation.

Keywords: Light-field · Material recognition · Convolutional neural network

1 Introduction

Materials affect how we perceive objects in our daily life. For example, we would not expect to feel the same when we sit on a wooden or leather chair. However, differentiating materials in an image is difficult since their appearance depends on the confounding effects of object shape and lighting. A more robust way to determine the material type is using the surface reflectance or the bidirectional reflectance distribution function (BRDF). However, measuring the reflectance is hard. Previous works use gonioreflectometers to recover the reflectance, which is cumbersome, and does not easily apply to spatially-varying BRDFs or Bidirectional Texture Functions (BTFs) [8,24].

© Springer International Publishing AG 2016
B. Leibe et al. (Eds.): ECCV 2016, Part III, LNCS 9907, pp. 121–138, 2016.
DOI: 10.1007/978-3-319-46487-9_8

An alternative to directly measuring the reflectance, is to consider multiple views of a point at once. By doing so, material recognition can be improved as demonstrated by Zhang et al. [38]. We exploit the multi-views in a light-field representation instead. Light-field cameras have recently become available and are able to capture multiple viewpoints in a single shot. We can therefore obtain the intensity variation under different viewing angles with minimal effort. Therefore, one of the main goals of this paper is to investigate whether 4D light-field information improves the performance of material recognition over 2D images. We adopt the popular convolutional neural network (CNN) framework to perform material classification in this work. However, there are two key challenges: First, all previous light-field datasets include only a few images, so they are not large enough to apply the data-hungry deep learning approaches. Second, CNN architectures have previously not been adapted to 4D light-fields; Thus, novel architectures must be developed to perform deep learning with light-field inputs. Our contributions are shown in Fig. 1 and summarized below:

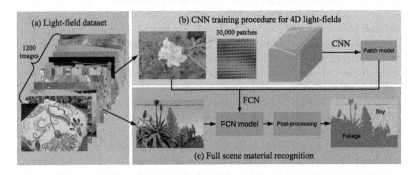

Fig. 1. Overview of our system and contributions. (a) We collect a new light-field dataset, which contains 1200 images labeled with 12 material classes. (b) Using (microlens) light-field patches extracted from this dataset, we train a CNN by modifying previous 2D models to take in 4D inputs. (c) Finally, we convert the patch model to an FCN model by fine-tuning on full images, and perform full scene material segmentation.

(1) We introduce the first mid-size light-field image dataset (Sect. 3). Our dataset contains 12 classes, each with 100 images labeled with per pixel ground truth (Fig. 2). We then extract 30,000 patches from these images. Although we use this dataset for material recognition, it is not limited to this purpose and can be used for other light-field related applications. Upon publication, the dataset will be released publicly.

(2) We investigate several novel CNN architectures specifically designed for 4D light-field inputs (Sect. 4). Since no recognition CNN has been trained on light-fields before, we implement different architectures to work on 4D data (Figs. 4 and 5). Instead of training a new network from scratch, we reuse the spatial filters from previous 2D models, while adding new angular filters into the network architecture. We also find directly training a fully convolutional

network (FCN) very unstable, and thus train on extracted patches first and fine-tune on full images afterwards. The proposed architectures are not limited to material recognition, and may be used for other light-field based tasks as well.

(3) Using our best-performing architecture, we achieve about 6–7% boost compared with single 2D image material classification, increasing the accuracy from 70 % to 77 % on extracted patches and 74 % to 80 % on full images (Sect. 5). These act as important baselines for future work in light-field based material recognition.

2   Related Work

Light-field datasets: The most popular dataset is the one introduced by Wanner et al. [35], which contains 7 synthetic scenes and 5 real images captured using a gantry. Another well-known one is the Stanford light-field archive [1], which provides around 20 light-fields sampled using a camera array, a gantry and a light-field microscope. The synthetic light-field archive by Marwah et al. [23] contains 5 camera light-fields and 13 display light-fields. Other datasets contain fewer than ten images [13,15,33,34] or are only suitable for particular purposes [17,27]. Clearly, there is a lack of large light-field datasets in prior works. In this work, we use the Lytro Illum camera to build a dataset with 1200 light-field images.

Material databases: The early work on material recognition was primarily on classifying instance-level textures, such as the CUReT database [8] and the more diversified KTH-TIPS [4,10] database. Recently, the Describable Textures Dataset (DTD) [5] features real-world material images. Some work on computer-generated synthetic datasets has also been introduced [18,36].

For category-level material databases, the most well-known is the Flickr Material Database (FMD) [29], which contains ten categories with 100 images in each category. Subsequently, Bell et al. [2] released OpenSurfaces which contains over 20,000 real-world scenes labeled with both materials and objects. More recently, the Materials in Context Database (MINC) [3] brought the data size to an even larger scale with 3 million patches classified into 23 materials. However, these datasets are all limited to 2D, and thus unsuitable for investigating the advantages of using multiple views. Although our dataset is not as large as the MINC dataset, it is the first mid-size 4D light-field dataset, and is an important step towards other learning based light-field research. Zhang et al. [38] also propose a reflectance disk dataset which captures intensities of different viewing angles for 20 materials. However, their dataset lacks the spatial information, and is much smaller compared to our dataset.

Material recognition: Material recognition methods can mainly be classified into two categories. The first one recognizes materials based on the object reflectance [7,20,21,38]. Most work of this type requires the scene geometry or illumination to be known, or requires special measurement of the BRDF beforehand.

The other body of work extracts features directly from the image appearance, and is thus more flexible and can work on real-world images. Liu et al. [19] propose a model to combine low- and mid-level features using a Bayesian generative framework. Hu et al. [12] extend the Kernel descriptors with variances of gradient orientations and magnitudes to handle materials. Schwartz and Nishino [28] introduce visual material traits and explicitly avoid object-specific information during classification. Qi et al. [26] introduce a pairwise transform invariant feature and apply it to perform material recognition. Cimpoi et al. [5] propose a framework based on neural network descriptors and improved Fisher vectors (IFV). Recently, Cimpoi et al. [6] combine object descriptors and texture descriptors to achieve state-of-the-art results on FMD. However, none of these methods are applicable to the 4D case. In this work, we implement different methods to deal with this dimensionality change from 2D to 4D.

Convolutional neural networks: Convolutional neural networks (CNNs) have proven to be successful in modern vision tasks such as detection and recognition, and are now the state-of-the art methods in most of these problems. Since the work by Krizhevsky et al. [16] (a.k.a. AlexNet), in recent years many advanced architectures have been introduced, including GoogLeNet [32] and VGG [30]. For per-pixel segmentation, Farabet et al. [9] employ a multi-scale CNN to make class predictions at every pixel in a segmentation. A sliding window approach is adopted by Oquab et al. [25] to localize patch classification of objects. Recently, a fully convolutional framework [22] has been proposed to generate dense predictions from an image directly.

Multi-image CNNs: For CNNs trained on multiple image inputs, Yoon et al. [37] train a super-resolution network on light-field images; however, their goal is different from a high-level recognition task. Besides, only a couple of images instead of the full light-fields are sent into the network at a time, so the entire potential of the data is not exploited. Su et al. [31] propose a "view-pooling" framework to combine multiple views of an object to perform object recognition. In their architecture, convolutional maps independently extracted from each view are maxpooled across all views. However, we find this does not work well in the light-field case. Rather, we demonstrate that it is advantageous to exploit the structure of light-fields in combining views much earlier in the network. This also has the advantage that memory usage is reduced. In this work, to ease the training of 4D light-fields, we initialize the weights with pre-trained 2D image models. We investigate different ways to map the 4D light-field onto the 2D CNN architecture, which has not been explored in previous work, and may be beneficial to learning-based methods for other light-field tasks in the future.

3   The Light-Field Material Dataset

While the Internet is abundant with 2D data, light-field images are rarely available online. Therefore, we capture the images ourselves using the Lytro Illum camera. There are 12 classes in our dataset: fabric, foliage, fur, glass, leather, metal, plastic, paper, sky, stone, water, and wood. Each class has 100 images labeled with material types. Compared with FMD [29], we add two more classes, fur and sky. We believe these two classes are very common in natural scenes, and cannot be easily classified into any of the ten categories in FMD.

The images in our dataset are acquired by different authors, in different locations (e.g. shops, campus, national parks), under different viewpoints and lighting conditions, and using different camera parameters (exposure, ISO, etc.). The spatial resolution of the images is 376×541, and the angular resolution is 14×14. Since the pixel size of the Lytro camera is small ($1.4 \mu m$), one problem we encountered is that the images are often too dark to be usable. Water is also a particularly challenging class to capture, since the corresponding scenes usually entail large motions. Overall, of the 1448 acquired images, we retain 1200 not deemed too repetitive, dim or blurred. We then manually classified and labeled the images with per pixel material category using the *Quick Selection Tool* of Photoshop. For each material region, we manually draw the boundary along the region. We check the segmentation results, and further refine the boundaries until we obtain final accurate annotation.

In Fig. 2 we show some example images for each category of the dataset. Then, in Fig. 3a we show example light-field images, where each block of pixels shows different viewpoints of a 3D point. We then demonstrate the benefits of using light-fields: from the 2D images alone, it is difficult to separate sky from blue paper due to their similar appearances; However, with the aid from light-field images, it becomes much easier since paper has different reflectance from different viewpoints while sky does not. Next, in Fig. 3b we print out a photo of a pillow, and take a picture of the printed photo. We then test both 2D and light-field models on the picture. It is observed that the 2D model predicts the material as fabric since it assumes it sees a pillow, while the light-field model correctly identifies the material as paper.

Finally, to classify a point in an image, we must decide the amount of surrounding context to include, that is, determine the patch size. Intuitively, using small patches will lead to better spatial resolution for full scene material segmentation, but large patches contain more context, often resulting in better performance. Bell et al. [3] choose the patch scale as 23.3 % of the smaller image length, although they find that scale 32 % has the best performance. Since our images are usually taken closer to the objects, we use 34 % of the smaller image length as the patch size, which generates about 30,000 patches of size 128×128. This is roughly 2500 patches in each class. The patch centers are separated by at least half the patch size; also, the target material type occupies at least half the patch. Throughout our experiments, we use an angular resolution of 7×7. We randomly select 70 % of the dataset as training set and the rest as test set. Patches from the same image are either all in training or in test set, to ensure that no similar patches appear in both training and test sets.

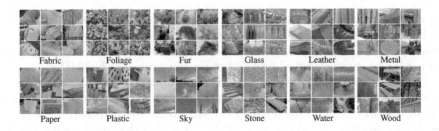

| Fabric | Foliage | Fur | Glass | Leather | Metal |
| Paper | Plastic | Sky | Stone | Water | Wood |

Fig. 2. Example images in our dataset. Each class contains 100 images.

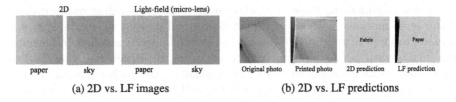

(a) 2D vs. LF images   (b) 2D vs. LF predictions

Fig. 3. Example benefits of using light-field images. (a) From the 2D images, it is difficult to distinguish between paper and sky. However, with the light-field images it becomes much easier. (b) We print out a picture of a pillow, and test both 2D and light-field models on the picture. The 2D model, without any reflectance information, predicts the material as fabric, while the light-field model correctly identifies the material as paper.

4   CNN Architectures for 4D Light-Fields

We now consider the problem of material recognition on our 4D light-field dataset and draw contrasts with recognition using 2D images. We train a Convolutional Neural Network for this patch classification problem. Formally, our CNN is a function f that takes a light-field image R as input and outputs a confidence score p_k for each material class k. The actual output of f depends on the parameters θ of the network that are tuned during training, i.e., $p_k = f(R; \theta)$. We adopt the softmax loss, which means the final loss for a training instance is $-\log(e^{p_t}/(\sum_{i=1}^{k} e^{p_i}))$, where t is the true label. At test time, we apply the softmax function on the output p_k, where the results can be seen as the predicted probability per class.

We use the network architecture of the recent VGG-16 model [30], a 16-layer model, as it performs the best on our dataset when using 2D images. We initialize the weights using the MINC VGG model [3], the state-of-the-art 2D material recognition model, and then fine-tune it on our dataset.

The biggest challenge, however, is we have 4D data instead of 2D. In other words, we need to find good representations for 4D light-field images that are compatible with 2D CNN models. We thus implement a number of different architectures and report their performance. The results may be used as baselines, and might be useful for designing other learning-based methods for light-fields in

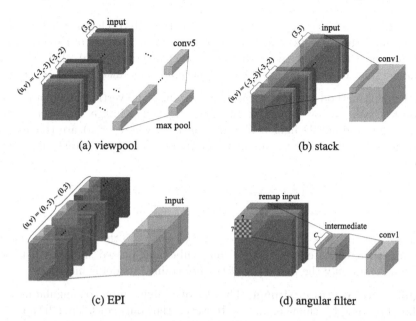

Fig. 4. Different CNN architectures for 4D light-field inputs. The RGB colors represent the RGB channels, while (u, v) denotes different angular coordinates (from $(-3, -3)$ to $(3, 3)$ in our experiments). (a) After each view is passed through the convolutional part, they are max pooled and combined into one view, and then sent to the fully connected part. (b) All views are stacked across the RGB channels to form the input. (c) The inputs are the horizontal and vertical EPIs concatenated together (only vertical ones are shown in the figure). (d) A 7×7 angular filter is first applied on the remap image. The intermediate output is then passed to the rest of the network. (Color figure online)

the future. In our implementation, the best performing methods (angular filter and 4D filter) achieve 77 % classification accuracy on the extracted patches, which is 7 % higher than using 2D images only. Details of each architecture are described below.

2D average. First and the simplest, we input each image independently and average the results across different views. This, however, definitely does not exploit the implicit information inside light-field images. It is also time consuming, where the time complexity grows linearly with angular size.

Viewpool. Second, we leverage the recent "viewpool" method proposed in [31] (Fig. 4a). First, each view is passed through the convolutional part of the network separately. Next, they are aggregated at a max view-pooling layer, and then sent through the remaining (fully-connected) part of the network. This method combines information from different views at a higher level; however, max pooling only selects one input, so still only one view is chosen at each pixel. Also, since all views need to be passed through the first part of the network, the memory consumption becomes extremely large.

Stack. Here, we stack all different views across their RGB channels before feeding them into the network, and change only the input channel of the first layer while leaving the rest of the architecture unchanged (Fig. 4b). This has the advantage that all views are combined earlier and thus takes far less memory.

EPI. For this method, we first extract the horizontal and vertical epipolar images (EPIs) for each row or column of the input light-field image. In other words, suppose the original 4D light-field is $L(x, y, u, v)$, where (x, y) are the spatial coordinates and (u, v) are the angular coordinates. We then extract 2D images from L by

$$
\begin{aligned}
L(x, y = y_i, u, v = 0) \quad &\forall i = 1, ..., h_s \\
L(x = x_j, y, u = 0, v) \quad &\forall j = 1, ..., w_s
\end{aligned}
\tag{1}
$$

where $(u, v) = (0, 0)$ is the central view and (h_s, w_s) are the spatial size. These EPIs are then concatenated into a long cube and passed into the network (Fig. 4c). Again only the first layer of the pre-trained model is modified.

Angular filter on remap image. The idea of applying filters on angular images was first proposed by Zhang et al. [38]. However, they only considered 2D angular images, while in our case we have 4D light-field images. Also, by incorporating the filters into the neural network, we can let the network learn the filters instead of manually designing them, which should achieve better performance.

For this method, we use the remap image instead of the standard image as input. A remap image replaces each pixel in a traditional 2D image with a block of angular pixels $h_a \times w_a$ from different views, where (h_a, w_a) are the angular size. The remap image is thus of size $(h_a \times h_s) \times (w_a \times w_s)$. It is also similar to the raw micro-lens image the Lytro camera captures; the only difference is that we eliminate the boundary viewpoints where the viewing angles are very oblique.

Before sending the remap image into the pre-trained network, we apply on it an angular filter of size $h_a \times w_a$ with stride h_a, w_a and output channel number C (Fig. 4d). After passing this layer, the image reduces to the same spatial size as the original 2D input. Specifically, let this layer be termed I (intermediate), then the output of this layer for each spatial coordinate (x, y) and channel j is

$$
\ell^j(x, y) = g\Big(\sum_{i=r,g,b} \sum_{u,v} w_i^j(u, v) L^i(x, y, u, v) \Big) \quad \forall j = 1, ..., C
\tag{2}
$$

where L is the input (RGB) light-field, i, j are the channels for input light-field and layer I, $w_i^j(u, v)$ are the weights of the angular filter, and g is the rectified linear unit (ReLU). Afterwards, ℓ^j is passed into the pre-trained network.

4D filter. Finally, since the light-field has a 4D structure, it becomes intuitive to apply a 4D filter to train the network. However, directly applying a 4D filter is problematic due to several reasons. First, a 4D filter contains far more parameters than a 2D filter. Even the smallest 4D filter ($3 \times 3 \times 3 \times 3$) contains the same number of parameters as a 9×9 2D filter. This is expensive in terms of

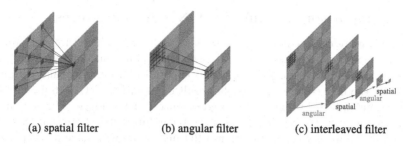

(a) spatial filter   (b) angular filter   (c) interleaved filter

Fig. 5. (a) New spatial and (b) angular filters on a remap light-field image. The pooling feature is also implemented in a similar way. (c) By interleaving the angular and spatial filters (or vice versa), we mimic the structure of a 4D filter.

both computation and memory. Second, a 4D filter is not present in any pre-trained network, so we need to train it from scratch, which means we cannot take advantage of the pre-trained model.

Our solution is to decompose a 4D filter into two consecutive 2D filters, a spatial filter and an angular filter, implemented on a remap image as shown in Fig. 5. The new spatial filter is similar to a traditional 2D filter, except that since we now work on "blocks" of pixels, it takes only one pixel from each block as input (Fig. 5a). This can be considered as a kind of "stride", but instead of stride in the output domain (where the filter itself moves), we have stride in the input domain (where the input moves while the filter stays). The angular filter, on the other hand, convolves an internal block normally just as a traditional 2D filter, but does not work across the block boundaries (Fig. 5b). By interleaving these two types of filters, we can approximate the effect of a 4D filter while not sacrificing the advantages stated above (Fig. 5c). The corresponding pooling structures are also implemented in the same way. To use the pre-trained models, the parameters from the original spatial filters are copied to the new spatial filters, while the angular filters are inserted between them and trained from scratch.

5   Experimental Results

The various architectures in Sect. 4 are trained end-to-end using back-propagation. To ease the training of 4D light-fields, we initialize the weights with pre-trained 2D image models. The optimization is done with Stochastic Gradient Descent (SGD) using the Caffe toolbox [14]. The inputs are patches of spatial resolution 128×128 and angular resolution 7×7. To bring the spatial resolution to the normal size of 256×256 for VGG, we add a deconvolution layer at the beginning. We use a basic learning rate of 10^{-4}, while the layers that are modified or newly added use 10 times the basic learning rate. Below, we present a detailed performance comparison between different scenarios.

5.1   Comparison of Different CNN Architectures

We first compare the prediction accuracies for different architectures introduced in the previous section. Each method is tested 5 times on different randomly divided training and test sets to compute the performance average and variance. In Table 1, the first column (2D) is the result of the MINC VGG-16 model fine-tuned on our dataset, using only a single (central view) image. The remaining columns summarize the results of the other 4D architectures. Note that these 4D methods use more data as input than a 2D image; we will make a comparison where the methods take in an equal number of pixels in Sect. 5.3, and the results are still similar.

As predicted, averaging results from each view (2D avg) is only slightly better than using a 2D image alone. Next, the viewpool method actually performs slightly worse than using a 2D input; this indicates that the method is not suitable for light-fields, where the viewpoint changes are usually very small. The stack method and the EPI method achieve somewhat better performance, improving upon 2D inputs by 2–3%. The angular filter method achieves significant improvement over other methods; compared to using 2D input, it obtains about 7% gain. This shows the advantages of using light-fields rather than 2D images, as well as the importance of choosing the appropriate representation. The 4D filter method achieves approximately the same performance as the angular filter method. However, the angular filter method consumes much less memory, so it will be used as the primary comparison method in the following. The performance of each material class for the angular filter method is detailed in Table 2.

Table 1. Classification accuracy (average and variance) for different architectures. The 2D average method is only slightly better than using a single 2D image; the viewpool method actually performs slightly worse. The stack method and the EPI method both achieve better results. Finally, the angular filter method and the 4D filter method obtain the highest accuracy.

Architecture	2D	2D avg	viewpool	stack	EPI	angular	4D
Accuracy (%)	$70.2_{\pm 1.0}$	$70.5_{\pm 0.9}$	$70.0_{\pm 1.0}$	$72.8_{\pm 1.1}$	$72.3_{\pm 1.0}$	$\mathbf{77.0_{\pm 1.1}}$	$\mathbf{77.0_{\pm 1.1}}$

Table 2. Patch accuracy by category for the angular filter method.

Fabric: 65.5%	Foliage: 92.5%	Fur: 77.9%	Glass: 65.2%
Leather: 91.1%	Metal: 73.5%	Paper: 60.4%	Plastic: 50.0%
Sky: 98.2%	Stone: 87.1%	Water: 92.0%	Wood: 72.6%

To further test the angular filter method, we compare performances by varying three parameters: the filter location, the filter size, and the number of output channels of the angular filter. First, we apply the angular filter at different layers of the VGG-16 network, and compare their performance. The classification accuracies when the filter is applied on layer 1 and layer 2 are 76.6 % and 73.7 %, respectively. Compared with applying it on the input directly (77.8 %), we can see that the performance is better when we combine different views earlier. This also agrees with our findings on the viewpool method and 4D method. Next, we decompose the 7 × 7 angular filter into smaller filters. The accuracies for three consecutive 3 × 3 filters and a 5 × 5 filter followed by a 3 × 3 filter are 74.8 % and 73.6 %, respectively. It can be seen that making the filters smaller does not help improve the performance. One reason might be that in contrast to the spatial domain, where the object location is not important, in the angular domain the location actually matters (e.g. the upper-left pixel has a different meaning from the lower-right pixel), so a larger filter can better capture this information. Finally, we vary the number of output channels of the angular filter. Since the filter is directly applied on the light-field input, this can be considered as a "compression" of the input light-field. The fewer channels we output, the more compression we achieve using these filters. We test the number from 3 (all views compressed into one view) to 147 (no compression is made), and show the results in Table 3. It can be seen that the performance has a peak at 64 channels. We hypothesize that with fewer channels, the output might not be descriptive enough to capture variations in our data, but a much larger number of channels leads to overfitting due to the resulting increase in number of parameters.

Table 3. Number of output channels of the angular filter architecture. As we can see, using more channels increases the performance up to some point (64 channels), then the performance begins to drop, probably due to overfitting. This may also be related to light-field compression, where we do not need the entire 49×3 input channels and can represent them in fewer channels for certain purposes.

Number of channels	3	16	32	64	128	147
Accuracy	71.6 %	74.8 %	76.7 %	**77.8 %**	73.6 %	72.8 %

5.2   Comparison Between 2D and Light-Field Results

The confusion matrices for both 2D and light-field methods (using the angular filter method) are shown in Fig. 6, and a graphical comparison is shown in Fig. 7a. Relative to 2D images, using light-fields achieves the highest performance boost on leather, paper and wood, with absolute gains of over 10 %. This is probably because the appearances of these materials are determined by complex effects such as subsurface scattering or inter-reflections, and multiple views help in disambiguating these effects. Among all the 12 materials, only the performance for glass drops. This is probably because the appearance of glass is often dependent on the scene rather than on the material itself. Figure 8 shows some examples that are misclassified using 2D inputs but predicted correctly using light-fields, and vice versa. We observe that light-fields perform the best when the object information is missing or vague, necessitating reliance only on local texture or reflectance. On the other hand, the 2D method often generates reasonable results if the object category in the patch is clear.

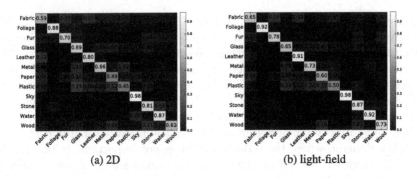

(a) 2D   (b) light-field

Fig. 6. Confusion matrix comparison between 2D and light-field results.

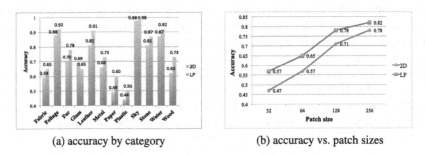

(a) accuracy by category   (b) accuracy vs. patch sizes

Fig. 7. Prediction accuracy comparison for using 2D and light-field inputs. (a) We first show the accuracies for each category. It can be seen that using light-fields achieves the highest performance boost on leather, paper and wood, obtaining absolute gains of over 10 %. On the other hand, only the performance of glass drops. (b) Next, we vary the input patch size and test the performance again. It can be seen that as the patch size becomes smaller, the gain steadily increases.

Next, we change the patch size for both methods, and test their accuracies to see the effect of patch size on performance gain. We tried patch sizes 32, 64, 128 and 256 (Fig. 7b). It is observed that as we shrink the patch size from 128, the absolute gain steadily increases, from 7 % to 10 %. If we look at the relative gain, it is growing even more rapidly, from about 10 % at size 128 to 20 % at size 32. At size 256 the absolute gain becomes smaller. A possibility is that at this scale, the object in the patch usually becomes apparent, and this information begins to dominate over the reflectance information. Therefore, the benefits of light-fields are most pronounced when using small patches. As the patch becomes smaller and smaller, it becomes harder and harder to recognize the object, so only local texture and reflectance information is available. Also note that although increasing the patch size will lead to better accuracy, it will also reduce the output resolution for full scene classification, so it is a tradeoff and not always better. Finally, while we have shown a significant increase in accuracy from 2D to 4D material recognition, once the dataset is published, our approach can still be improved by future advances that better exploit the full structure of 4D light-field data.

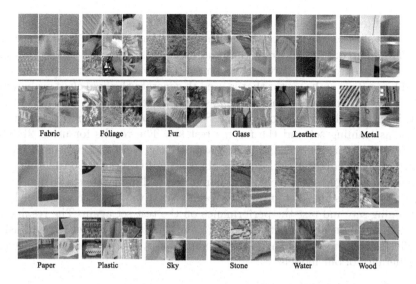

Fig. 8. Prediction result discrepancy between 2D and light-field inputs. The first 3×3 grids show example patches that are predicted correctly using LF inputs, but misclassified using 2D inputs. The second grids show the opposite situation, where 2D models output the correct class but LF models fail. We found that the LF model performs the best when the object information is missing or vague, so we can only rely on the local texture, viewpoint change or reflectance information.

5.3 Comparison Between Spatial/angular Resolution

Since light-field images contain more views, which results in an effectively larger number of pixels than 2D images, we also perform an experiment where the two inputs have the same number of pixels. Specifically, we extract the light-field image with a spatial resolution of 128×128 and an angular resolution of 4×4, and downsample the image in the spatial resolution by a factor of 4. This results in a light-field image of the same size as an original 2D image. The classification results for using original 2D input and this downsampled light-field are 70.7 % and 75.2 % respectively. Comparing with the original light-field results (77.8 %), we observe that reducing the spatial resolution lowers the prediction accuracy, but it still outperforms 2D inputs by a significant amount.

5.4 Results on Other Datasets

Finally, to demonstrate the generality of our model, we test it on other datasets. Since no light-field material datasets are available, we test on the synthesized BTF database [36]. The database captures a large number of different viewing and lighting directions on 84 instances evenly classified into 7 materials. From the database we can render arbitrary views by interpolation on the real captured data. We thus render light-field images and evaluate our model on these rendered images.

First, directly applying our model on the BTF database already achieves 65.2 % classification accuracy (for the materials that overlap). Next, since the BTF database contains different material categories from our dataset, we use our models to extract the 4096-dimensional output of the penultimate fully connected layer. This is the vector that is used to generate the final class probability in the network, and acts as a feature descriptor of the original input. We then use this feature descriptor to train an SVM. We pick two-thirds of the BTF dataset as training set and the rest as test set. The results for using 2D and light-field inputs are 59.8 % and 63.7 % respectively. Note that light-field inputs achieve about 4 % better performance than using 2D inputs. Considering that the rendered images may not look similar to the real images taken with a Lytro camera, this is a somewhat surprising result. Next, we fine-tune our models on the training set, and test the performance on the test set again. The results for using 2D and light-field inputs are 67.7 % and 73.0 % respectively. Again using light-fields achieves more than 5 % performance boost. These results demonstrate the generality of our models.

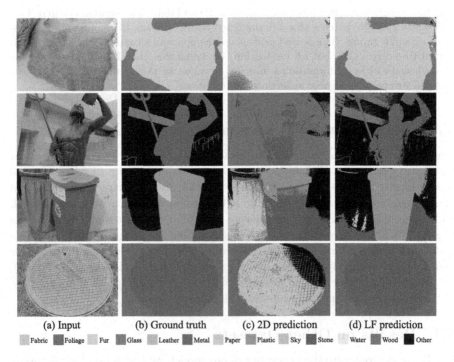

(a) Input   (b) Ground truth   (c) 2D prediction   (d) LF prediction

Fabric   Foliage   Fur   Glass   Leather   Metal   Paper   Plastic   Sky   Stone   Water   Wood   Other

Fig. 9. Full scene material classification examples. Bottom: legend for material colors. Compared with using 2D inputs, we can see that our light-field method produces more accurate prediction results. (Color figure online)

5.5   Full Scene Material Segmentation

Finally, we convert our patch model to a fully convolutional model and test it on an entire image to perform material segmentation. We do not directly train a fully convolutional network (FCN) since we find it very unstable and the training loss seldom converges. Instead, we first train our model on image patches as described previously, convert it to a fully convolutional model, and then fine-tune it on entire images. To train on a full image, we add another material class to include all other materials that do not fall into any of the 12 classes in our dataset. We repeat this process for both our models of patch size 256 and 128 to get two corresponding FCN models, and combine their results by averaging their output probability maps. Finally, as the probability map is low-resolution due to the network stride, we use edge-aware upsampling [11] to upsample the probability map to the same size as the original image. The per pixel accuracy for FCN prediction before and after the guided filter is 77.0 % and 79.9 %, respectively. The corresponding accuracies for 2D models are 70.1 % and 73.7 %, after we apply the same procedure. Note that our method still retains 6–7% boost compared with 2D models. Example results for both methods are shown in Fig. 9.

6   Conclusion

We introduce a new light-field dataset in this work. Our dataset is the first one acquired with the Lytro Illum camera, and contains 1200 images, which is much larger than all previous datasets. Since light-fields can capture different views, they implicitly contain the reflectance information, which should be helpful when classifying materials. In view of this, we exploit the recent success in deep learning approaches, and train a CNN on this dataset to perform material recognition. To utilize the pre-trained 2D models, we implement a number of different architectures to adapt them to light-fields, and propose a "decomposed" 4D filter. These architectures provide insights to light-field researchers interested in adopting CNNs, and may also be generalized to other tasks involving light-fields in the future. Our experimental results demonstrate that we can benefit from using 4D light-field images, obtaining an absolute gain of about 7 % in classification accuracy compared with using a single view alone. Finally, although we utilize this dataset for material recognition, it can also spur research towards other applications that combine learning techniques and light-field imagery.

Acknowledgements. This work was funded in part by ONR grant N00014152013, NSF grant IIS-1617234, Draper Lab, a Google Research Award, support by Nokia, Samsung and Sony to the UC San Diego Center for Visual Computing, and a GPU donation from NVIDIA.

References

1. Adams, A., Levoy, M., Vaish, V., Wilburn, B., Joshi, N.: Stanford light field archive. http://lightfield.stanford.edu/
2. Bell, S., Upchurch, P., Snavely, N., Bala, K.: Opensurfaces: a richly annotated catalog of surface appearance. ACM Trans. Graph. (TOG) **32**(4), 111 (2013)
3. Bell, S., Upchurch, P., Snavely, N., Bala, K.: Material recognition in the wild with the materials in context database. In: Proceedings of the IEEE Conference on Computer Vision and Pattern Recognition (CVPR) (2015)
4. Caputo, B., Hayman, E., Mallikarjuna, P.: Class-specific material categorisation. In: Proceedings of the IEEE International Conference on Computer Vision (ICCV) (2005)
5. Cimpoi, M., Maji, S., Kokkinos, I., Mohamed, S., Vedaldi, A.: Describing textures in the wild. In: Proceedings of the IEEE Conference on Computer Vision and Pattern Recognition (CVPR) (2014)
6. Cimpoi, M., Maji, S., Vedaldi, A.: Deep filter banks for texture recognition and segmentation. In: Proceedings of the IEEE Conference on Computer Vision and Pattern Recognition (CVPR) (2015)
7. Cula, O.G., Dana, K.J.: 3D texture recognition using bidirectional feature histograms. Int. J. Comput. Vis. **59**(1), 33–60 (2004)
8. Dana, K.J., Van Ginneken, B., Nayar, S.K., Koenderink, J.J.: Reflectance and texture of real-world surfaces. ACM Trans. Graph. (TOG) **18**(1), 1–34 (1999)
9. Farabet, C., Couprie, C., Najman, L., LeCun, Y.: Learning hierarchical features for scene labeling. IEEE Trans. Pattern Anal. Mach. Intell. (PAMI) **35**(8), 1915–1929 (2013)
10. Hayman, E., Caputo, B., Fritz, M., Eklundh, J.-O.: On the significance of real-world conditions for material classification. In: Pajdla, T., Matas, J. (eds.) ECCV 2004. LNCS, vol. 3024, pp. 253–266. Springer, Heidelberg (2004). doi:10.1007/978-3-540-24673-2_21
11. He, K., Sun, J., Tang, X.: Guided image filtering. In: Daniilidis, K., Maragos, P., Paragios, N. (eds.) ECCV 2010. LNCS, vol. 6311, pp. 1–14. Springer, Heidelberg (2010). doi:10.1007/978-3-642-15549-9_1
12. Hu, D., Bo, L., Ren, X.: Toward robust material recognition for everyday objects. In: BMVC (2011)
13. Jarabo, A., Masia, B., Bousseau, A., Pellacini, F., Gutierrez, D.: How do people edit light fields? ACM Trans. Graph. (TOG) **33**(4), 146:1–146:10 (2014)
14. Jia, Y., Shelhamer, E., Donahue, J., Karayev, S., Long, J., Girshick, R., Guadarrama, S., Darrell, T.: Caffe: convolutional architecture for fast feature embedding. In: Proceedings of the ACM International Conference on Multimedia (2014)
15. Kim, C., Zimmer, H., Pritch, Y., Sorkine-Hornung, A., Gross, M.H.: Scene reconstruction from high spatio-angular resolution light fields. ACM Trans. Graph. (TOG) **32**(4), 73 (2013)
16. Krizhevsky, A., Sutskever, I., Hinton, G.E.: Imagenet classification with deep convolutional neural networks. In: Advances in Neural Information Processing Systems (2012)
17. Li, N., Ye, J., Ji, Y., Ling, H., Yu, J.: Saliency detection on light field. In: Proceedings of the IEEE Conference on Computer Vision and Pattern Recognition (CVPR) (2014)

18. Li, W., Fritz, M.: Recognizing materials from virtual examples. In: Fitzgibbon, A., Lazebnik, S., Perona, P., Sato, Y., Schmid, C. (eds.) ECCV 2012. LNCS, vol. 7575, pp. 345–358. Springer, Heidelberg (2012). doi:10.1007/978-3-642-33765-9_25
19. Liu, C., Sharan, L., Adelson, E.H., Rosenholtz, R.: Exploring features in a bayesian framework for material recognition. In: Proceedings of the IEEE Conference on Computer Vision and Pattern Recognition (CVPR) (2010)
20. Liu, C., Gu, J.: Discriminative illumination: per-pixel classification of raw materials based on optimal projections of spectral BRDF. IEEE Trans. Pattern Anal. Mach. Intell. (PAMI) **36**(1), 86–98 (2014)
21. Lombardi, S., Nishino, K.: Single image multimaterial estimation. In: Proceedings of the IEEE Conference on Computer Vision and Pattern Recognition (CVPR) (2012)
22. Long, J., Shelhamer, E., Darrell, T.: Fully convolutional networks for semantic segmentation. In: Proceedings of the IEEE Conference on Computer Vision and Pattern Recognition (CVPR) (2015)
23. Marwah, K., Wetzstein, G., Bando, Y., Raskar, R.: Compressive light field photography using overcomplete dictionaries and optimized projections. ACM Trans. Graph. (TOG) **32**(4), 1–11 (2013)
24. Nicodemus, F.E., Richmond, J.C., Hsia, J.J., Ginsberg, I.W., Limperis, T.: Geometrical considerations and nomenclature for reflectance, vol. 160. US Department of Commerce, National Bureau of Standards Washington, DC, USA (1977)
25. Oquab, M., Bottou, L., Laptev, I., Sivic, J.: Learning and transferring mid-level image representations using convolutional neural networks. In: Proceedings of the IEEE Conference on Computer Vision and Pattern Recognition (CVPR) (2014)
26. Qi, X., Xiao, R., Li, C.G., Qiao, Y., Guo, J., Tang, X.: Pairwise rotation invariant co-occurrence local binary pattern. IEEE Trans. Pattern Anal. Mach. Intell. (PAMI) **36**(11), 2199–2213 (2014)
27. Raghavendra, R., Raja, K.B., Busch, C.: Exploring the usefulness of light field cameras for biometrics: an empirical study on face and iris recognition. IEEE Trans. Inf. Forensics Secur. **11**(5), 922–936 (2016)
28. Schwartz, G., Nishino, K.: Visual material traits: Recognizing per-pixel material context. In: Proceedings of the IEEE International Conference on Computer Vision (ICCV) Workshops (2013)
29. Sharan, L., Rosenholtz, R., Adelson, E.: Material perception: what can you see in a brief glance? J. Vis. **9**(8), 784–784 (2009)
30. Simonyan, K., Zisserman, A.: Very deep convolutional networks for large-scale image recognition. arXiv preprint arXiv:1409.1556 (2014)
31. Su, H., Maji, S., Kalogerakis, E., Learned-Miller, E.: Multi-view convolutional neural networks for 3d shape recognition. In: Proceedings of the IEEE International Conference on Computer Vision (ICCV) (2015)
32. Szegedy, C., Liu, W., Jia, Y., Sermanet, P., Reed, S., Anguelov, D., Erhan, D., Vanhoucke, V., Rabinovich, A.: Going deeper with convolutions. In: Proceedings of the IEEE Conference on Computer Vision and Pattern Recognition (CVPR) (2015)
33. Tao, M.W., Hadap, S., Malik, J., Ramamoorthi, R.: Depth from combining defocus and correspondence using light-field cameras. In: Proceedings of the IEEE International Conference on Computer Vision (ICCV) (2013)
34. Wang, T.C., Efros, A., Ramamoorthi, R.: Occlusion-aware depth estimation using light-field cameras. In: Proceedings of the IEEE International Conference on Computer Vision (ICCV) (2015)

35. Wanner, S., Meister, S., Goldlücke, B.: Datasets and benchmarks for densely sampled 4D light fields. In: Annual Workshop on Vision, Modeling and Visualization, pp. 225–226 (2013)
36. Weinmann, M., Gall, J., Klein, R.: Material classification based on training data synthesized using a BTF database. In: Fleet, D., Pajdla, T., Schiele, B., Tuytelaars, T. (eds.) ECCV 2014. LNCS, vol. 8691, pp. 156–171. Springer, Heidelberg (2014). doi:10.1007/978-3-319-10578-9_11
37. Yoon, Y., Jeon, H.G., Yoo, D., Lee, J.Y., Kweon, I.: Learning a deep convolutional network for light-field image super-resolution. In: Proceedings of the IEEE International Conference on Computer Vision (ICCV) Workshops (2015)
38. Zhang, H., Dana, K., Nishino, K.: Reflectance hashing for material recognition. In: Proceedings of the IEEE Conference on Computer Vision and Pattern Recognition (CVPR) (2015)

Graph-Based Consistent Matching
for Structure-from-Motion

Tianwei Shen, Siyu Zhu, Tian Fang$^{(\boxtimes)}$, Runze Zhang, and Long Quan

Department of Computer Science and Engineering,
Hong Kong University of Science and Technology, Hong Kong, China
{tshenaa,szhu,tianft,rzhangaj,quan}@cse.ust.hk

Abstract. Pairwise image matching of unordered image collections greatly affects the efficiency and accuracy of Structure-from-Motion (SfM). Insufficient match pairs may result in disconnected structures or incomplete components, while costly redundant pairs containing erroneous ones may lead to folded and superimposed structures. This paper presents a graph-based image matching method that tackles the issues of completeness, efficiency and consistency in a unified framework. Our approach starts by chaining all but singleton images using a visual-similarity-based minimum spanning tree. Then the minimum spanning tree is incrementally expanded to form locally consistent strong triplets. Finally, a global community-based graph algorithm is introduced to strengthen the global consistency by reinforcing potentially large connected components. We demonstrate the superior performance of our method in terms of accuracy and efficiency on both benchmark and Internet datasets. Our method also performs remarkably well on the challenging datasets of highly ambiguous and duplicated scenes.

Keywords: Structure-from-Motion · Image matching · Loop consistency

1 Introduction

Image matching is a computationally expensive step in 3D reconstruction, especially for large-scale unordered image datasets. Due to the large number of high-dimensional feature descriptors in an image, the naive quadratic matching scheme imposes a heavy computational burden on large-scale high-resolution 3D reconstruction [35]. Tremendous progress has been achieved either on reducing the cost of feature matching [19] or image indexing techniques [15,22] to pre-compute a subset of match candidates. Modern large-scale Structure-from-Motion (SfM) systems [1,12] usually use vocabulary tree [22] to choose the visually similar match pairs, which decreases the complexity of pairwise image matching from $O(n^2)$ to $O(kn)$ with respect to the number of images.

Electronic supplementary material The online version of this chapter (doi:10.1007/978-3-319-46487-9_9) contains supplementary material, which is available to authorized users.

© Springer International Publishing AG 2016
B. Leibe et al. (Eds.): ECCV 2016, Part III, LNCS 9907, pp. 139–155, 2016.
DOI: 10.1007/978-3-319-46487-9_9

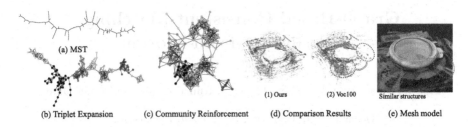

Fig. 1. Pipeline of the matching framework. (a) The minimum spanning tree (MST); (b) The triplet expansion process; (c) The final match graph after component merging, with different colors representing different communities; (d) Comparison of the proposed method with image retrieval techniques (see Sect. 5 for details); (e) The reference mesh model. (Color figure online)

However, two problems remain to be solved. One major drawback of the image indexing techniques is that the number of retrieved items k for a query image is hard to determine. Many previous works have adopted an empirical similarity threshold or a fixed retrieved number, which ignores the global connectivity of the image collection. Sometimes post-processing steps, such as query expansion [1,4], are also needed to prevent the missing of true positive matches. As a result, the actual number of matches is still large to ensure the completeness and accuracy of 3D reconstruction.

On the other hand, large-scale image datasets often contain ambiguous scenes due to symmetric and repetitive textured patterns. These repetitive yet distinct patterns are not only visually similar, but can also pass the two-view geometric verification and form erroneous epipolar geometry. The false match pairs can collapse the SfM results and lead to folded or superimposed structures. Due to the existence of ambiguous patterns, adding more yet potentially incorrect pairwise matches may severely hurts the performance of SfM. Therefore, a sufficient and consistent subset of matches is superior to a redundant matching set that may contain false matches, which somewhat contradicts with the principle of mining as much connectivity as possible. Moreover, since it is difficult to filter out the wrong epipolar geometry and relative poses during camera pose estimation, a consistent match graph is crucial to the success of 3D reconstruction.

In this paper, we propose a matching algorithm that efficiently generates a sparse match graph spanning the whole image dataset, while simultaneously filters out inconsistent matches which pass the two-view geometric verification. Our method jointly discovers the connectivity pattern of the scene and achieves a good trade-off between computational efficiency and sufficient image connectivity in a consistent manner. The consistency of the matching set is guaranteed by enforcing *loop consistency* [33] both locally and globally along the successive steps.

As our main contribution, we propose the first unified framework, to the best of our knowledge, that jointly conducts efficient pairwise image matching and solves the SfM ambiguity problem. This novel matching algorithm significantly accelerates the matching process without sacrificing the accuracy of SfM models. Moreover, it is capable of handling extremely ambiguous scenes with loop consistency checking.

2   Related Work

2.1   Image Retrieval Techniques for 3D Reconstruction

To avoid the costly exhaustive match, image retrieval has been extensively employed as a pre-processing step for large-scale SfM. Vocabulary tree [22] is the most widely used technique to rank the database images given a query image. Several later methods [3,13,23] incorporate geometric cues to improve the retrieval performance for 3D reconstruction. Query expansion [4] is a popular technique to increase the recall of retrieval results. Lou et al. [16] employ relevance feedback and entropy minimization to explore the connectivity between images as quickly as possible. As an example of exhaustive matching techniques, preemptive matching proposed by Wu [31] argues that features at a larger pyramid scale tend to be more stable. Therefore, by matching a small subset of local descriptors in an image, we can decide whether to continue the full putative feature matching. Recently, Schönberger et al. [25] compare these matching techniques and propose a learning-based method to predict whether a pair of images have overlapping regions. Zhou et al. [34] propose a multi-image matching algorithm based on loop consistency [33] and low-rank modeling. Most of these works have focused on improving the performance of image retrieval in terms of precision and recall. Little attention has been paid on the actual effect of increased recall on the final results of SfM. As we have demonstrated in Sect. 5, in large-scale urban scenes, more matches do not necessarily guarantee a better reconstruction.

2.2   Optimization of the Viewing Graph

Another line of works is to reduce the geometric computation by optimizing the match graph (also known as the viewing graph). Snavely et al. [26] propose a efficient SfM pipeline by computing a skeletal image set that approximates the accuracy of the full set in terms of covariance. Havlena et al. [9] also relies on image indexing techniques and selects a minimal connected dominating set of the image collection. The images in the reduced set form atomic 3D model and are incrementally merged into a connected model, similar to [10]. Recently, Sweeney et al. [28] propose a viewing graph optimization method that achieves excellent accuracy while remaining efficient for the SfM process. It is similar to our work in that they enforce loop consistency in the viewing graph, while we check loop consistency in the matching process.

All of the above methods accelerate the reconstruction process but either start from a time-consuming full match graph, or use vocabulary tree to initialize the match graph whose candidate number is difficult to choose. Instead, we concentrate on the optimization of the match graph and come up with an efficient match graph construction method without altering either incremental or global SfM pipelines.

2.3 Ambiguous Structures

Identification and removal of erroneous epipolar geometry is a recent research focus for SfM. Zach et al. [32] use the supplementary information in the third view which does not exist in the two-view relation to infer the correctness of two-view geometry. Their subsequent work [33] exploits loop consistency to infer incorrect geometric transformations, which forms the basis of our work. However, this formulation has strong assumptions on the statistical independence of erroneous matches, thus it will fail on highly ambiguous scenes where similar but distinct patterns become norms instead of outliers. Roberts et al. [24] sample a minimal configuration (a spanning tree of the match graph) to infer data associations based on the missing correspondence cue [32] and the timestamp cue. This is based on the assumption that the time and sequence information are correlated, which is generally not satisfied in unordered datasets. Jiang et al. [14] also sample a spanning tree from a relatively complete pairwise match graph, and iteratively replace problematic edges in a greedy way. Wilson et al. [29] analyse disambiguation on a visibility graph encoding relations of cameras and points. This method identifies bad tracks based on the observation that bad tracks in urban scenes connect two or more clusters of useful tracks. Heinly et al. [11] use a post-processing step which first splits the camera graph and then leverages conflicting observations to identify duplicated structures. The set of camera subgraphs that are free from conflict are then merged into a correct reconstruction.

Instead, the proposed method solves the ambiguity problem jointly with the efficient construction of a robust and consistent match graph, without modifying the SfM pipeline. We argue that the origin of ambiguity comes from a faulty matching process, thus the early detection of erroneous edges in the match graph would be beneficial to the later geometric computation. This generic matching framework is orthogonal to and can be combined with the other disambiguation methods.

3 Problem Formulation

In this section, we introduce a couple of basic building blocks of the graph-based matching algorithm and a set of criteria that needs to be satisfied. The inputs of the method are a set of images $\mathcal{I} = \{I_i\}$ and their corresponding feature points. The matching method is based on the analysis of the underlying graph encoding pairwise matches and epipolar geometry. We denote the undirected match graph as $G = (\mathcal{V}, \mathcal{E})$ where each vertex $v_i \in \mathcal{V}$ corresponds to an image $I_i \in \mathcal{I}$. Two vertices v_i and v_j are connected by an edge $e_{ij} \in \mathcal{E}$ if their corresponding images have more than S_I inliers after epipolar geometric verification. Each edge e_{ij} is associated with the epipolar geometry and relative motion between an image pair computed using five-point algorithm [21]. The initial edge set $\mathcal{E}$ is empty and we aim to incrementally build the match graph. We ensure that the running time of all the graph algorithms used in the method is an order of magnitude lower than the image matching operation.

Let T_{ij} be an abstract geometric relation associated with the edge e_{ij}, e.g. T_{ij} can be the relative rotation R_{ij} computed from feature correspondences. We further require that this geometric relation can be chained, denoted by $\circ$, and satisfies $T_{ij} \circ T_{ji} = \mathbb{I}(\forall i, j)$ where $\mathbb{I}$ denotes the identity map. Then in a consistent yet noisy setting, the discrepancy should be small between the identity map and the chained transformation on a closed loop. We first consider the minimum configuration of closed loops and give the following definition for the weakly consistent match graph.

Definition 1 *(Weak Consistency). A match graph $G = (\mathcal{V}, \mathcal{E})$ is **weakly** $(\epsilon, \mathcal{E})$-**consistent**, if the pairwise geometric relations T_{ij}, T_{jk}, T_{ki} of any 3-length loop (i, j, k) with respect to the edge set $\mathcal{E}$ satisfy the following loop consistency constraint*

$$d(T_{ij} \circ T_{jk} \circ T_{ki}, \mathbb{I}) \leq \epsilon \\ \forall (i, j, k), e_{ij} \in \mathcal{E}, e_{jk} \in \mathcal{E}, e_{ki} \in \mathcal{E} \tag{1}$$

where the distance function $d(\widetilde{T}, \mathbb{I})$ measures the discrepancy between the chained motion $\widetilde{T}$ and the identity map $\mathbb{I}$. The above definition does not capture all essences of a consistent match graph because some erroneous matches may only manifest themselves in longer loops. Therefore, we refine this notion by defining *strong consistency*:

Definition 2 *(Strong Consistency). A match graph $G = (\mathcal{V}, \mathcal{E})$ is **strongly** $(\epsilon, \mathcal{E})$-**consistent** if for any loop $(n_0, n_1, \ldots, n_{m-1})$ of length m with respect to the edge set $\mathcal{E}$, the following condition holds*

$$d((\textstyle\prod_{i=0}^{m-2} T_{n_i n_{i+1}}) \circ T_{n_{m-1} n_0}, \mathbb{I}) \leq \epsilon \\ \forall (n_0, n_1, \ldots, n_{m-1}), e_{n_0 n_1} \in \mathcal{E}, e_{n_1 n_2} \in \mathcal{E}, \ldots, e_{n_{m-1} n_0} \in \mathcal{E}, \tag{2}$$

where $\prod$ denotes the chaining of a set of geometric transformations with $\circ$ operator.

To find a consistent match graph, we need to balance the following three performance criteria:

(1) *Completeness.* The match graph should span as many as images to guarantee the completeness of 3D models. This criterion corresponds to minimizing the number of connected components in G.

(2) *Efficiency.* The time complexity of the match graph construction should depend on the underlying connectivity pattern of the image collection.

(3) *Consistency.* The edges should be both robust meaning that each of them contains a large number of inlier feature matches, and consistent measured by ϵ (the smaller the better) and $|\mathcal{E}|$ (the larger the better) in Definitions 1 and 2. This criterion may contradict with *efficiency*, hence we need to find a good trade-off between them.

Algorithm 1. Online Minimum Spanning Tree

Input: The match graph $G = (\mathcal{V}, \mathcal{E})$ with empty edge set $\mathcal{E} = \emptyset$, the singleton rejection threshold S_R, the match inlier threshold $S_I^\star$, an array recording the failure time ft[] $\leftarrow 0$

Output: A minimum spanning tree or forest of G

1: **for** $v \in \mathcal{V}$ **do**
2:     MAKE-SET(v)
3: **end for**
4: **for** e_{ij} ordered by $w(e_{ij})$, increasing **do**
5:     **if** UNION-FIND(i) $\neq$ UNION-FIND(j) & ft[i] $< S_R$ & ft[j] $< S_R$ **then**
6:         Verify whether (i, j) is a true match using a strict inlier threshold $S_I^\star$
7:         **if** (i, j) matches **then**
8:             UNION(i, j)
9:         **else**
10:             ft[i]++; ft[j]++;
11:         **end if**
12:     **end if**
13: **end for**

---

4   Graph-Based Consistent Matching

The proposed method can be decomposed into three steps illustrated in Fig. 1: (a) match graph initialization, (b) graph expansion by strong triplets and (c) community-based graph reinforcement. The purpose of *match graph initialization* is to minimize the number of connected components and discard singleton images in the match graph (*completeness*). The *expansion* and *reinforcement* steps are successively applied to efficiently explore the scene structure (*efficiency*), while weak and strong consistency are iteratively verified along the process (*consistency*). The three steps are detailed in the following sections.

4.1   Match Graph Initialization

Criterion (1) can be separately accomplished by quickly chaining the views in an image collection. To achieve this goal, we try to find a *minimum spanning tree* of the match graph. This seems impossible since we do not have the connectivity information before computing feature correspondences and epipolar geometry. However, similarity scores and rank information given by the vocabulary tree parameterizes a *priori* match graph. We can modify Kruskal's algorithm to get an online version of minimum spanning tree algorithm for the ongoing match graph.

If the image collection contains singleton views or separated scenes, the initialization process may be unreasonably long since it needs to explore every possible edge to join the singleton image. To increase the stability of the tree structure and cope with singleton images, we consider the mutually-connected edge weight. We query the i-th image with respect to the other images in the dataset and get the rank list $Rank_i$. The rank of image j in $Rank_i$ is denoted as

$Rank_i(j)$. The edge weight $w(e_{ij})$ of node i and node j is defined as the quadratic mean of $Rank_i(j)$ and $Rank_j(i)$, namely $w(e_{ij}) = \sqrt{\frac{Rank_i^2(j)+Rank_j^2(i)}{2}}$. Since quadratic mean is greater or equal to other mean metrics, such as arithmetic mean ($\frac{x_1+x_2}{2}$) or harmonic mean ($\sqrt{x_1 x_2}$), it can be viewed as a worst-case metric to penalize more severely on the edge weight if either of $Rank_i(j)$ or $Rank_j(i)$ is large.

The algorithm first orders the edge set by weights in increasing order and then probes (feature correspondences and geometric verification) the most probable pair that can join two disjoint sets using the union-find data structure. If it succeeds, the two disjoint sets are merged; otherwise it proceeds to the next best probable edge that connects two components. If an image has been involved in S_R failed tests, it is regarded as a singleton image and discarded from the dataset.

The tree match graph seems to be fragile since it contains no loop for consistency checking. To get the most robust initial match pairs, a stricter inlier threshold $S_I^\star (= 40)$ is applied in the match verification. It is assumed that in self-similar environments true positive matches have larger similarity responses compared to false positive ones, even for highly ambiguous scenes (as shown in Fig. 4(a)). Therefore, the tree edges are consistent in nature due to the greedy property of the online minimum spanning tree algorithm. Since our aim is to get a consistent matching set that generates accurate and complete SfM models, we assume that the matching algorithm in the following sections operates on a connected component of the image collection. This *online minimum spanning tree* algorithm is described in Algorithm 1.

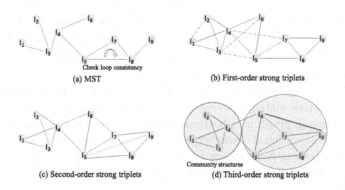

Fig. 2. Illustration of the tree expansion step up to third-order strong triplets. (a) The minimum spanning tree; (b) First-order strong triplets are selected by traversing the minimum spanning tree and checking loop consistency of two adjacent edges. The dashed red lines represents either unmatched image pairs or inconsistent weak triplets, while the solid red lines are verified edges; (c) Second-order strong triplets (marked by solid green lines) built upon the first-order ones; (d) The partial match graph after the expansion step. The community structures are further utilized for checking strong consistency. (Color figure Online)

4.2   Graph Expansion by Strong Triplets

We now consider the trade-off between *efficiency* and *consistency*. Intuitively, strong consistency (Definition 2) is much harder to satisfy because the enumeration of all loops in a graph costs exponential time. Weak consistency (Definition 1) would be relatively easy to achieve, although the time complexity of verifying all 3-length loops is $O(n^3)$ in the worst cases, which is unacceptable for large-scale datasets. Therefore, we aim to exactly satisfy weak consistency with respect to the match graph and approximately guarantee strong consistency on this graph.

We refer to 3-length loops as *strong triplets*, which differs from *weak triplets* that do not form closed loops. The number of strong triplets depends on the structure of the scene dataset, which is agnostic to the matching algorithm. To get a consistent match graph, ideally we want as many strong triplets as possible. Since the adjacent match pairs are the most likely to compose strong triplets, we propose a greedy tree expansion method to grow the match graph from weak triplets.

After connecting different views with a spanning tree, we get a weakly-connected match graph. Two adjacent edges with a common vertex induce a weak triplet and once the two end points get connected it becomes a strong triplet. The detection of all weak triplets can be done efficiently by traversing two steps starting from each node. The first-order strong triplets are formed by traversing the minimum spanning tree, while the second-order strong triplets are built upon the first-order ones and the tree, so on and so forth. The gain of exploring local connectivity diminishes as the triplet expansion process iterates. Therefore, the match graph is expanded up to the third-order strong triplets mainly for the efficiency concern. Figure 2 illustrates the match graph expansion process. Specifically, the pairwise rotation R_{ij} is used as the surrogate for the abstract relative geometric relation T_{ij} in Definitions 1 and 2. The distance function $d(\widetilde{R}, \mathbb{I})$ between the chained rotation $\widetilde{R}$ and $\mathbb{I}$ is defined as the rotation angle of $\widetilde{R}$ as $d(\widetilde{R}, \mathbb{I}) = \theta(\widetilde{R}) = \arccos(\frac{\mathrm{Tr}(\widetilde{R})-1}{2})$.

Different from the methods in [18,33] that uses explicit Bayesian inference to remove inconsistent matches after getting a complete match graph, we generate a consistent match graph in a bottom-up way, thus preventing the interference of good and bad matches. However, since this step only addresses local loops consistency with length 3, the error may accumulate along the longer sequence and cause motion drifts in the SfM model. We further address this issue in the next section.

4.3   Community-Based Graph Reinforcement

The expanded match graph robustly estimates the local structures of scenes and generates a consistent matching set enforced by strong triplets. Although this simplified match graph suffices to generate a consistent reconstruction, it has two major drawbacks. First, in this match graph, only strong triplets get verified and the consistency of longer loops (*strong consistency*) is neglected. Second, this

Algorithm 2. Component Merging Algorithm

Input: The intermediate match graph after triplet expansion $G_t = (\mathcal{V}, \mathcal{E}_t)$, community-wise match number S_C, loop discrepancy threshold θ

Output: The final match graph $G_f = (\mathcal{V}, \mathcal{E}_f)$

1: Compute structures on G_t and split $\mathcal{V}$ into m communities $\{\mathcal{V}_1, \ldots, \mathcal{V}_m\}$
2: Create the candidate matching set Φ
3: Rank Φ in decreasing order by edge weights
4: Reserve the first $\frac{S_c m(m-1)}{2}$ elements of Φ to get Φ'
5: **for** each image pair $(i, j) \in \Phi'$ **do**
6:     Match (i, j) and compute the relative rotation R_{ij}
7:     Find the shortest path of length l between (i, j) using *Breath-First-Search* algorithm
8:     Compute the chained rotation R_c and the discrepancy angle $\theta_c = \arccos(\frac{\mathrm{Tr}(R_c)-1}{2})$
9:     **if** $\theta_c < \theta/\sqrt{l}$ **then**
10:         $\mathcal{E}_t = \mathcal{E}_t \cup (i, j)$
11:     **end if**
12: **end for**
13: Iterate 1-12 if the stopping criterion does not satisfy
14: $\mathcal{E}_f = \mathcal{E}_t$

---

match graph, without closed-loop structures at a global scale, does not reflect the genuine pose graph of the dataset. Because this matching algorithm starts with a tree structure, the match graph after the triplet completion stage would roughly preserve this skeletal structure.

To tackle the above weaknesses, we propose a component merging algorithm inspired by techniques in community detection. *Community detection* [7] is widely used in the analysis of complex networks. It aims to divide a graph into groups with denser connections inside and sparser connections outside. This allows us to attain a coarse-grained description of the match graph and detect higher-level connectivity. The intra-connectivity within groups is strong enough since it contains consistent strong triplets, while the inter-connectivity in longer loops is left to be detected and verified.

Let A_{ij} be an element of the adjacent matrix of a general graph where $A_{ij} = 1$ if i and j are connected and $A_{ij} = 0$ otherwise. The degree d_i of a node i is the number of other nodes that connects to it, denoted as $d_i = \sum_j A_{ij}$. If the graph is randomized without a significant community structure, the probability of an edge existing between node i and node j is $\frac{d_i d_j}{2m}$, where $m = \frac{1}{2} \sum_{ij} A_{ij}$ is the total number of edges in G. Suppose that the match graph is structured such that the node i belongs to a community V_p and the node j belongs to a community V_q, then the modularity [20] Q measures the difference of the fraction of intra-community connections between a graph and the random graph:

$$Q = \frac{1}{2m} \sum_{ij} (A_{ij} - \frac{d_i d_j}{2m}) \delta(V_p, V_q) \tag{3}$$

Table 1. Reconstruction accuracy of three small datasets [27] with ground-truth. The absolute camera location errors c_{err} and camera rotation errors R_{err} are measured in meters and degrees respectively. The *#matches* for our method is showed as *the number of consistent matches / the number of total attempted matches*.

	fountain-P11			Herz-Jesu-P25			Castle-P30		
	#matches	c_{err}	R_{err}	#matches	c_{err}	R_{err}	#matches	c_{err}	R_{err}
Ours	52/55	0.019	0.414	155/231	0.030	0.399	112/283	0.220	0.476
Full match	55	0.016	0.407	300	0.028	0.389	435	0.167	0.513

Table 2. Running time and re-projection error for different methods. The meaning of the first row: *Dataset*, the name of the scene; *#views*, the number of cameras; *#Rviews*, the number of successfully registered cameras, with F meaning that the reconstruction fails; *#UM/#TM*, the number of useful matches which pass geometric verification and loop consistency verification / the number of total attempted matches; *M+GV*, the running time of matching and geometric verification; *GO*, the running time of graph operations including loop consistency verification, community detection, etc.; *Total time*, the total running time of the proposed matching algorithm; *Speedup*, the speedup factor of our matching algorithm w.r.t *Voc100*; *ReprojError*, mean re-projection error (in pixels) of resulted SfM models; The running time of vocabulary tree is not documented since both methods depend on it. The matching time of *Voc25* is not recorded as well since it has roughly the same number of matches as that of the graph-based matching method.

Dataset	#views	#Rviews			#matches				Running Time					ReprojError		
		Ours	Voc25	Voc100	Ours		Voc25	Voc100	Ours			Voc100	Speedup	Ours	Voc25	Voc100
					#UM	#TM			M+GV	GO	Total time					
SportsArena	157	151	F	F	529	2621	2654	9554	8.8 min	0.1 min	8.9 min	29.4 min	3.3x	0.736	F	F
TempleOfHeaven	341	341	F	F	2795	2901	4483	18466	14.2 min	0.2 min	14.4 min	68.0 min	4.7x	0.544	F	F
NotreDame	699	675	685	687	11765	15729	12142	45280	0.98 hrs	0.7 min	0.99 hrs	2.76 hrs	2.8x	0.654	0.705	0.672
TreviFountain	1906	1906	1906	1906	27182	30187	33821	124925	1.87 hrs	2.1min	1.90 hrs	7.10 hrs	3.9x	**0.568**	0.693	0.602
Colosseum	2006	1980	1999	2006	26723	32653	35130	143439	2.72 hrs	2.3 min	2.76 hrs	11.23 hrs	4.1x	**0.466**	0.615	0.489

where $\delta(i,j) = 1$ if $i = j$ and 0 otherwise. If every node is itself a community, the modularity is zero. In practice, a value larger than 0.3 indicates that the graph has a significant community structure. After the triplet expansion step, the community structure on the match graph manifests the sparse connections between communities that may yields incomplete SfM models due to insufficient tracks and wide baseline. In this case, even though the match graph is connected as a whole, SfM may still fail into separated models. We aim to find the community structure of the match graph and reinforce intra-community connectivity visual similarity cues.

To avoid defeating the purpose of speeding up the pairwise matching, we choose a fast greedy approach to estimate the community structure [5]. This hierarchical algorithm starts with each node being a sole community and iteratively joins separate communities whose amalgamation results in the largest increase in Q. Specifically, we use the weighted graph with the edge weight being the number of fundamental matrix inliers F_{inlier} between an image pair, which helps identify weak connections. Therefore, A_{ij} of the match graph in Eq. 3 is defined as

$$A_{ij} = \begin{cases} F_{inlier} & i \, and \, j \, are \, connected \\ 0 & otherwise \end{cases} \tag{4}$$

The match graph is merged into a single community after $n-1$ such joins. The modularity Q has a single peak over the generation of the dendrogram [5] which indicates the most significant community structure. We take the vertex partition when the modularity reaches the peak. Hence the number of communities depends upon the connectivity pattern of the match graph.

After getting the community structure of the intermediate match graph, image pairs across groups constitutes a candidate list $\Phi = \{(i,j)|i \in \mathcal{V}_p, j \in \mathcal{V}_q, p = [1, \ldots, m], q = [1, \ldots, m], p \neq q\}$ for matching and geometric verification. For a match graph with n nodes, if the community detection algorithm generates m groups of roughly equal size, the scale of the candidate matching set is $O((\frac{n}{m})^2)$, which is still quadratic in the number of images. To reduce the cost of matching, we rank the candidate list by quadratic mean of $Rank_i(j)$ and $Rank_j(i)$, and only match the most probable S_C community-wise pairs. Thus the candidate list is pruned to a smaller matching set Φ' of size $\frac{S_C m(m-1)}{2}$, which only depends on the number of communities. This component merging process is iterative and stops if the number of communities does not change.

The issue with *strong consistency* is taken care of during the graph reinforcement stage. Intuitively it can be only achieved approximately since verifying all loops is computationally intractable. As is observed in several previous studies [6,18], random errors accumulated in the longer loops affect the effectiveness of loop consistency checking. As a result, the verification process further simplifies to checking the strong consistency with respect to the shortest loop that contains the new edge. For an image pair (I_i, I_j), we use breath-first-search algorithm to find the shortest path in the match graph. Together with the direct link between I_i and I_j, they form the shortest loop. The loop consistency of this cycle is verified with a discrepancy threshold weighted by the cycle length [6]. The full component merging algorithm is given in Algorithm 2.

5   Experiments

Implementation. We used SiftGPU [30] to extract and match SIFT [17] features. To compute similarity scores and rank information, we implemented a multi-threaded version of the vocabulary tree algorithm [22] to ensure the cost of image retrieval is significantly lower than that of the matching process. The vocabulary tree has a depth of 6 and a branching factor of 8 with tf-idf weighting and min-distance metric. We used 7-point algorithms embedded in RANSAC [8] to compute the fundamental matrix of image pairs for geometric verification. We obtained the SfM models using a standard incremental SfM pipeline using [2] as the underlying bundle adjustment solver. All experiments were running on a multi-core PC with Intel(R) Core(TM) i7-4770K processors and 32 GB main

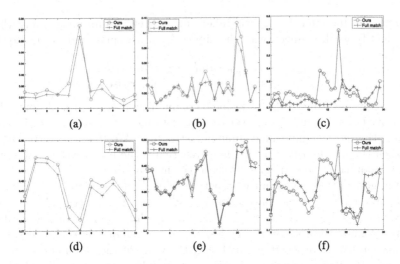

(a)   (b)   (c)

(d)   (e)   (f)

Fig. 3. Per-camera absolute location errors of (a) *fountain-P11* (b) *Herz-Jesu-P25* (c) *Castle-P30* and the corresponding per-camera orientation errors (d)(e)(f). Our method achieves the same level of accuracy as that of the full match, despite the fact that the number of matches is much smaller than the full match.

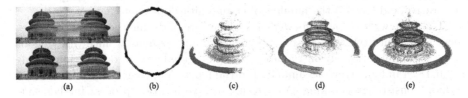

(a)   (b)   (c)   (d)   (e)

Fig. 4. Disambiguation performance of different methods on the highly ambiguous *TempleOfHeaven* dataset. (a) The true-positive feature correspondences (top: the front-front match) and the false-positive feature correspondences (bottom: the front-back match) of *TempleOfHeaven*. After geometric verification using fundamental matrix, the erroneous false-positive match has much fewer inliers (246) than that of the true-positive match (2349); (b) The match graph of our method; (c) The SfM models using *Voc100* as input; (d) The SfM models using [33] applied on *Voc100* as input; (e) The correct SfM model using the consistent matching method.

memory. We used the same set of parameters for all experiments with pairwise inlier number $S_I = 20$, singleton rejection threshold $S_R = 20$, community-wise match number $S_C = 30$ and loop discrepancy threshold $\theta_c = 2°$.

Datasets. We tested the algorithm on three types of datasets, namely the benchmark datasets, the Internet datasets, and the ambiguous datasets. First, the datasets *fountain-P11*, *Herz-Jesu-P25*, and *Castle-P30* were obtained from the well-known benchmark datasets [27] with the ground-truth camera calibrations. Further, we tested the scalability and efficiency of the method on relatively large Internet datasets from [1], namely *NotreDame*, *TreviFountain* and *Colosseum*.

Fig. 5. 3D Reconstruction models and their corresponding match graphs for Rome16 K [1] datasets. From left to right: *Colosseum*, *TreviFountain*, *NotreDame*. The corresponding match graphs show the community partition using different colors. (Color figure online)

Finally, we show our method has superior performance on ambiguous datasets which are *Cup*, *Books*, *Desk*, *ForbiddenCity*, *Indoor*. We also introduce two more highly ambiguous datasets, namely *SportsArena* (Fig. 1) and *TempleOfHeaven* (Fig. 4).

Accuracy Evaluation. We conducted experiments on multi-view benchmark datasets [27] to evaluate accuracy. We fix the SfM pipeline and use the full matching and the graph-based matching results as inputs respectively. The reconstruction accuracy is measured by the error of absolute camera location c_{err} and the absolute error of camera orientation R_{err}, in meters and degrees respectively. We do not conduct comparison with image retrieval techniques because the datasets are too small and candidate lists for vocabulary tree are hard to choose. The experiment results (see Table 1 and Fig. 3) show that the graph-based method is adaptive to the complexity of the datasets and achieves the same level of accuracy as that of the full match.

Scalability and Efficiency. Next, we tested the scalability and time efficiency of the method on Internet datasets [1]. For comparison the matching set containing top-100 candidates per image, denoted as *Voc100*, is retrieved and matched. We ensure that this fixed number is enough for reconstruction and all failure cases of *Voc100* are not caused by insufficient matches. A smaller matching set *Voc25*, composed of top-25 candidates per image, is also retrieved and compared. The aim is to test the effectiveness of the proposed method. *Voc25* roughly contains the same number of matches as the consistent matching set but does not necessarily guarantee complete SfM results. We measure the re-projection error of SfM results with different matching inputs. The comparison result (see Table 2) shows that the graph-based matching algorithm significantly accelerates the matching process, with speedup factors ranging from 3.3 for *SportArena*, to 4.7 for *TempleOfHeaven* compared with *Voc100*. The overhead introduced by various graph operations is negligible compared to the cost of pairwise image

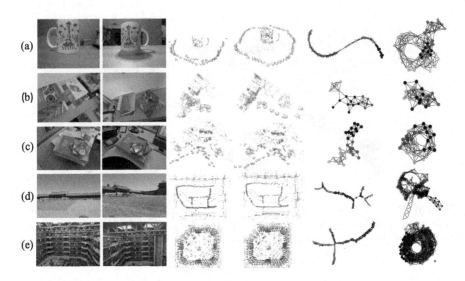

Fig. 6. Experiment results on ambiguous datasets from previous works [14,24]. From left to right: the first two columns - two views of an ambiguous scene; 3rd column - the SfM model using full match; 4th column - the SfM model using consistent matching; 5th column - the match graph after triplet expansion; 6th column - the match graph after component merging (different colors represents different communities). From top to bottom: (a) *Cup* (b) *Books* (c) *Desk* (d) *ForbiddenCity* (e) *Indoor*. (Color figure online)

matching, as is shown in the GO column of Table 2. The re-projection error of the SfM models with the consistent matching set is systematically smaller. We also found that the community-based graph reinforcement step is crucial in the success of large-scale reconstructions since the local consistency achieved by triplet expansion fails to detect the community-level connectivity. Please refer to the supplementary materials for more details.

Redundancy and Disambiguation. We then used ambiguous datasets to demonstrate how erroneous matches can ruin the final SfM result. *Temple-OfHeaven* dataset is composed of 341 rotationally symmetric images, which is a failure case of Jiang et al. [14]. In this extremely symmetric dataset, even the front views and the back views would match and form a reasonable epipolar geometry (see Fig. 4(a)).

The 3D reconstruction with *Voc100* and *Voc25* of the *TempleOfHeaven* dataset both yielded folded structures. The same went for the *SportsArena* dataset, in which *Voc100* generated a 3D reconstruction with superimposed structures (see Fig. 1) and the reconstruction of *Voc25* contained erroneous registrations of camera poses. All these cases failed because the methods mentioned above ignore the structure of the scene and lack geometric consistency checking. In contrast, the proposed matching method progressively explores the connectivity from the local to the whole and check consistency along the path. Figure 4(b)

Fig. 7. A failure case. (a) Two views from a self-similar scene; (b) The SfM model using full match; (c) The SfM model using the consistent matching algorithm; (d) The correct SfM model solely using the skeletal tree match graph as input.

visualizes the final match graph which greatly resembles the actual scene. We also tried the iterative version [18] of removing erroneous match pairs using Bayesian inference proposed by Zach et al. [33] on *TempleOfHeaven*. Although it removed 3575 out of 18466 match pairs, the obtained matching set still failed to render a correct reconstruction. We also applied this method on Internet datasets to filter the matches. But it was generally infeasible for large-scale datasets since a single iteration would take more than 8 h on *Voc100* of the *TreviFountain* dataset, due to the fact that the inference on Bayesian networks is generally NP-hard.

We further tested our matching algorithm on several ambiguous datasets from previous works [14,24] and the results are showed in Fig. 6. Solely by optimizing the input match graph, our consistent matching yields efficient and correct camera pose registrations compared with the exhaustive matching method.

Limitations. The current loop consistency checking is solely based on pairwise rotation, making it difficult to detect the inconsistency in datasets with pure translation motion, such as *Street* dataset (see Fig. 7). Thus it is possible to extend our algorithm to check the chained pose consistency, namely using displacements on a fixed scale as the surrogate relative transformation to verify loop consistency.

6   Conclusions

In this paper, we present a unified image matching framework using greedy graph expansion and community detection to discover both local and inter-community consistent match pairs. Our method significantly reduces the number of image pairs for matching without degrading the quality of subsequent SfM pipeline, and improves the robustness of SfM in scenes with ambiguous structures.

Our approach provides a sufficient and consistent image matching set as the input of SfM. This matching framework does not assume knowing any global motion information, nor incorporate translation or other scale-dependent constraints into the loop consistency checking. Hence, our future work is to combine the components in SfM, e.g. track selection and global pose registration, to further optimize 3D reconstruction.

Acknowledgement. The authors would like to thank all the anonymous reviewers for their constructive feedbacks. This work is supported by Hong Kong RGC 16208614, T22-603/15N, Hong Kong ITC PSKL12EG02, and China 973 program, 2012CB316300.

References

1. Agarwal, S., Furukawa, Y., Snavely, N., Simon, I., Curless, B., Seitz, S.M., Szeliski, R.: Building rome in a day. Commun. ACM **54**(10), 105–112 (2011)
2. Agarwal, S., Mierle, K., et al.: Ceres solver. http://ceres-solver.org
3. Chum, O., Matas, J.: Large-scale discovery of spatially related images. PAMI **32**(2), 371–377 (2010)
4. Chum, O., Mikulik, A., Perdoch, M., Matas, J.: Total recall ii: query expansion revisited. In: CVPR, pp. 889–896 (2011)
5. Clauset, A., Newman, M.E., Moore, C.: Finding community structure in very large networks. Phys. Rev. E **70**(6), 066111 (2004)
6. Enqvist, O., Kahl, F., Olsson, C.: Non-sequential structure from motion. In: ICCV Workshops, pp. 264–271 (2011)
7. Fortunato, S.: Community detection in graphs. Phys. Rep. **486**(3), 75–174 (2010)
8. Hartley, R., Zisserman, A.: Multiple View Geometry in Computer Vision. Cambridge University Press, New York (2003)
9. Havlena, M., Torii, A., Pajdla, T.: Efficient structure from motion by graph optimization. In: Daniilidis, K., Maragos, P., Paragios, N. (eds.) ECCV 2010. LNCS, vol. 6312, pp. 100–113. Springer, Heidelberg (2010). doi:10.1007/978-3-642-15552-9_8
10. Havlena, M., Torii, A., Knopp, J., Pajdla, T.: Randomized structure from motion based on atomic 3d models from camera triplets. In: CVPR, pp. 2874–2881 (2009)
11. Heinly, J., Dunn, E., Frahm, J.-M.: Correcting for duplicate scene structure in sparse 3D reconstruction. In: Fleet, D., Pajdla, T., Schiele, B., Tuytelaars, T. (eds.) ECCV 2014. LNCS, vol. 8692, pp. 780–795. Springer, Heidelberg (2014). doi:10.1007/978-3-319-10593-2_51
12. Heinly, J., Schonberger, J.L., Dunn, E., Frahm, J.M.: Reconstructing the world* in six days*(as captured by the yahoo 100 million image dataset). In: CVPR, pp. 3287–3295 (2015)
13. Jegou, H., Douze, M., Schmid, C.: Hamming embedding and weak geometric consistency for large scale image search. In: Forsyth, D., Torr, P., Zisserman, A. (eds.) ECCV 2008. LNCS, vol. 5302, pp. 304–317. Springer, Heidelberg (2008). doi:10.1007/978-3-540-88682-2_24
14. Jiang, N., Tan, P., Cheong, L.F.: Seeing double without confusion: structure-from-motion in highly ambiguous scenes. In: CVPR, pp. 1458–1465 (2012)
15. Kulis, B., Grauman, K.: Kernelized locality-sensitive hashing for scalable image search. In: ICCV, pp. 2130–2137 (2009)
16. Lou, Y., Snavely, N., Gehrke, J.: MatchMiner: efficient spanning structure mining in large image collections. In: Fitzgibbon, A., Lazebnik, S., Perona, P., Sato, Y., Schmid, C. (eds.) ECCV 2012. LNCS, vol. 7573, pp. 45–58. Springer, Heidelberg (2012)
17. Lowe, D.G.: Distinctive image features from scale-invariant keypoints. IJCV **60**(2), 91–110 (2004)
18. Moulon, P., Monasse, P., Marlet, R.: Global fusion of relative motions for robust, accurate and scalable structure from motion. In: ICCV, pp. 3248–3255 (2013)

19. Muja, M., Lowe, D.G.: Fast approximate nearest neighbors with automatic algorithm configuration. VISAPP **1**, 331–340 (2009)
20. Newman, M.E., Girvan, M.: Finding and evaluating community structure in networks. Phys. Rev. E **69**(2), 026113 (2004)
21. Nistér, D.: An efficient solution to the five-point relative pose problem. PAMI **26**(6), 756–770 (2004)
22. Nister, D., Stewenius, H.: Scalable recognition with a vocabulary tree. In: CVPR, pp. 2161–2168 (2006)
23. Philbin, J., Chum, O., Isard, M., Sivic, J., Zisserman, A.: Object retrieval with large vocabularies and fast spatial matching. In: CVPR, pp. 1–8 (2007)
24. Roberts, R., Sinha, S.N., Szeliski, R., Steedly, D.: Structure from motion for scenes with large duplicate structures. In: CVPR, pp. 3137–3144 (2011)
25. Schönberger, J.L., Berg, A.C., Frahm, J.M.: Paige: pairwise image geometry encoding for improved efficiency in structure-from-motion. In: CVPR, pp. 1009–1018 (2015)
26. Snavely, N., Seitz, S.M., Szeliski, R.: Skeletal graphs for efficient structure from motion. In: CVPR (2008)
27. Strecha, C., von Hansen, W., Gool, L.V., Fua, P., Thoennessen, U.: On benchmarking camera calibration and multi-view stereo for high resolution imagery. In: CVPR, pp. 1–8 (2008)
28. Sweeney, C., Sattler, T., Hollerer, T., Turk, M., Pollefeys, M.: Optimizing the viewing graph for structure-from-motion. In: ICCV, pp. 801–809 (2015)
29. Wilson, K., Snavely, N.: Network principles for sfm: disambiguating repeated structures with local context. In: ICCV, pp. 513–520 (2013)
30. Wu, C.: Siftgpu: A gpu implementation of scale invariant feature transform (sift) (2007)
31. Wu, C.: Towards linear-time incremental structure from motion. In: 3DV, pp. 127–134 (2013)
32. Zach, C., Irschara, A., Bischof, H.: What can missing correspondences tell us about 3d structure and motion? In: CVPR, pp. 1–8 (2008)
33. Zach, C., Klopschitz, M., Pollefeys, M.: Disambiguating visual relations using loop constraints. In: CVPR, pp. 1426–1433 (2010)
34. Zhou, X., Zhu, M., Daniilidis, K.: Multi-image matching via fast alternating minimization. In: CVPR, pp. 4032–4040 (2015)
35. Zhu, S., Fang, T., Xiao, J., Quan, L.: Local readjustment for high-resolution 3d reconstruction. In: CVPR, pp. 3938–3945 (2014)

All-Around Depth from Small Motion
with a Spherical Panoramic Camera

Sunghoon Im[(⊠)], Hyowon Ha, François Rameau, Hae-Gon Jeon,
Gyeongmin Choe, and In So Kweon

Korea Advanced Institute of Science and Technology (KAIST),
Daejeon, Republic of Korea
{shim,hwha,frameau,hgjeon,gmchoe}@rcv.kaist.ac.kr,
iskweon77@kaist.ac.kr

Abstract. With the growing use of head-mounted displays for virtual
reality (VR), generating 3D contents for these devices becomes an important topic in computer vision. For capturing full 360 degree panoramas
in a single shot, the Spherical Panoramic Camera (SPC) are gaining in
popularity. However, estimating depth from a SPC remains a challenging problem. In this paper, we propose a practical method that generates
all-around dense depth map using a narrow-baseline video clip captured
by a SPC. While existing methods for depth from small motion rely on
perspective cameras, we introduce a new bundle adjustment approach
tailored for SPC that minimizes the re-projection error directly on the
unit sphere. It enables to estimate approximate metric camera poses
and 3D points. Additionally, we present a novel dense matching method
called sphere sweeping algorithm. This allows us to take advantage of the
overlapping regions between the cameras. To validate the effectiveness
of the proposed method, we evaluate our approach on both synthetic
and real-world data. As an example of the applications, we also present
stereoscopic panorama images generated from our depth results.

Keywords: Structure from Motion (SfM) · Small motion · Stereoscopic
panorama · Spherical Panoramic Camera

1 Introduction

For virtual reality (VR) purpose, monoscopic 360° videos are currently the most
commonly filmed contents. Major electronic companies are constantly launching
new VR head-mounted displays [1–3] to further immerse users into VR contents.
For capturing 360° scenes, cheap and compact Spherical Panoramic Cameras
(SPC) equipped with two fisheye lenses, are gaining in popularity.

Only two types of omnidirectional imaging sensor have the ability to capture
a full 360° image. The first possibility is to employ a panoramic catadioptric
camera [4,5]. A catadioptric camera is the association of a perspective camera
with a convex mirror whose shapes are conic, spherical, parabolic or hyperbolic.
This layout requires complex optics which incurs a loss of resolution. However,

© Springer International Publishing AG 2016
B. Leibe et al. (Eds.): ECCV 2016, Part III, LNCS 9907, pp. 156–172, 2016.
DOI: 10.1007/978-3-319-46487-9_10

Fig. 1. Spherical panoramic cameras (Ricoh Theta S, Samsung Gear 360 and LG 360)

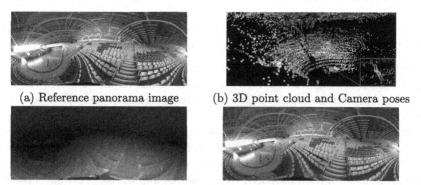

(a) Reference panorama image   (b) 3D point cloud and Camera poses

(c) Our depth result from small motion (d) Anaglyph panorama image using (c)

Fig. 2. Stereoscopic panorama generation from small motion.

such type of camera can be cost-effective since a single camera is sufficient to cover the whole scene [6,7]. The second type of spherical sensors are called polydioptric cameras, with such sensors, images captured from multiple cameras are stitched to form a single spherical image. This bulky architecture allows to obtain a high resolution panoramic image, but is relatively expensive. To balance the advantage of the cost efficiency and image quality, some companies have recently released spherical panoramic cameras (SPCs) [8–10] (see Fig. 1). The SPC consists of two fisheye cameras (covering a field of view of 200° each) staring at opposite directions.

Several 3D reconstruction algorithms [11,12] involving omnidirectional cameras have been developed for VR applications. However, these methods are effective only when the input images contain large motions. For the practical uses, one interesting research direction is depth estimation from a small-motion video clip captured by off-the-shelf cameras, such as DSLRs or mobile phone cameras [13–15]. Although these approaches achieve competitive results, they have not been applied to spherical sensors.

In this paper, we present an accurate dense 3D reconstruction algorithm using small baseline image sequences captured by a SPC as shown in Fig. 2. To achieve this, we design a novel bundle adjustment which minimizes the residuals directly on the unit sphere and estimates approximated-metric depth as well as camera poses; this approach is presented in Sect. 3.2. In order to estimate the all-around depth map, we propose a novel sphere sweeping algorithm in Sect. 3.3. This approach utilizes both the frontal and rear cameras for taking advantage of overlapping regions. The qualitative and quantitative results in Sect. 4 demonstrate that the proposed framework generates highly accurate depth of the entire surrounding scene. Using the accurate depth map, we also show realistic 3D panoramas which are suitable for VR devices (Sect. 4.4).

2   Related Work

The related work can be divided in two categories: the 3D reconstruction from small baseline images and the depth estimation from fisheye cameras.

Structure from Small Motion. Structure from Small Motion (SfSM) have recently been spotlighted [13–17]. These approaches require 2 steps; the camera poses estimation and the dense 3D reconstruction. A simplified version of this framework has been presented in [16] where the dense 3D reconstruction is computed using a sequence of images captured by a linearly moving DSLR camera mounted on a rail. To do so, the authors developed an approach inspired by light-field cameras. The 3D reconstruction method designed for unstructured small motions have been proposed by Yu and Gallup in [13]. This novel method relies on the small angle approximation and inverse depth computation. Therefore, their bundle adjustment is initialized with zero motion and random depths. After bundle adjustment, the dense depth map is computed using a plane sweeping algorithm [18] and a MRF optimization. Other improvements of this method have been developed, for instance, in [14], Im *et al.* designed a new bundle adjustment for rolling shutter cameras. More recently, Ha *et al.* [15] presented a framework for uncalibrated SfSM and proposed a plane sweeping stereo with a robust measure based on the variance of pixel intensity.

3D Reconstruction Using Fisheye Cameras. Although omnidirectional cameras have been extensively used for sparse 3D reconstruction and SLAM [11, 19–23], estimating the dense depth map from the fisheye cameras remains a challenging problem. For this particular problem, Li [24] presented a fisheye stereo method, where the author reformulated a conventional stereo matching scheme for binocular spherical stereo system using the unified spherical model. Kim and Hilton [25] also proposed a stereo matching method for a fisheye stereo camera, where a continuous depth map is obtained from a partial differential equation optimization. Meanwhile, Hane *et al.* [12] presented a real-time plane-sweeping algorithm which is suitable for images acquired with fisheye cameras.

In this paper, we combine these two concepts for SPCs. This configuration is more challenging than the previous methods due to the sensor characteristics. Thus, the ultimate goal of this work is to estimate an accurate and dense depth map using a unified optimization framework designed for weakly overlapping dual fisheye camera system. We show the details of our method in the next section.

3   All-Around Depth from Small Motion

To capture our dataset we used a Ricoh Theta S (see Fig. 1(a)). This sensor is a consumer device which has the advantage to be cheap and compact. Each fisheye camera has a field of view of approximatively 200°. Therefore, a small overlapping region is still available, this extra information is taken into consideration in our technique in order to obtain a better estimation of the depth at the boundary regions of the image. Another advantage of using this dual fisheye sensor is that the both images are captured simultaneously on the same imaging sensor thanks to a clever design involving mirrors and prisms (see Fig. 4). Thus, the images are always acquired simultaneous without requiring an external electronic trigger.

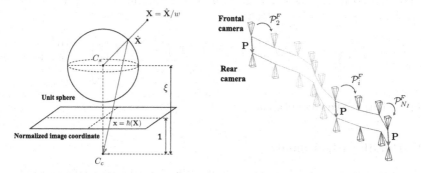

(a) Unified omnidirectional camera model   (b) Camera extrinsic parameterization

Fig. 3. Illustration on bundle adjustment variables

The goal of the proposed method is to estimate an all-around dense depth map from a 360° spherical video clip with small viewpoint variations for realistic stereoscopic applications. Our method consists of two steps: (1) a bundle adjustment (BA) for camera pose estimation along with a sparse 3D reconstruction, and (2) a sphere sweep stereo for dense depth map estimation. Our method differs from the prior works [13–15] by its adaptation to the unified spherical camera model making our approach very versatile (compatible with any single viewpoint camera). Furthermore, we propose a novel formulation of the dense matching which takes overlapping regions into consideration. The details of these techniques are explained in the following sections.

3.1   Unified Omnidirectional Camera Model

The spherical model allows us to represent the projection of any single view-point cameras thanks to a stereographic projection model [26–29]. Indeed, the image formation process for any central camera can be expressed by a double projection on a unit sphere (see Fig. 3). Firstly, the 3D point $\mathbf{X}(X, Y, Z)$ is projected on a camera-centered unit sphere $\hat{\mathbf{X}} = \mathbf{X}/\|\mathbf{X}\|$. Then, the point $\hat{\mathbf{X}}(\hat{X}, \hat{Y}, \hat{Z})$ is projected onto the image plane at the pixel coordinates $\mathbf{u}(u, v, 1)$. The distance between the unit sphere center C_s and the shifted camera center C_c is defined as ξ, which maps the radial distortion on the image. According to [29], the projection $\hbar(\mathbf{X})$ of a 3D point onto the normalized image coordinates $\mathbf{x}(x, y, 1)$ can be expressed as follows:

$$\mathbf{x} = \mathbf{K}^{-1}\mathbf{u} = \hbar(\mathbf{X}) = \begin{bmatrix} X/(Z + \|\mathbf{X}\|\xi) \\ Y/(Z + \|\mathbf{X}\|\xi) \\ 1 \end{bmatrix}, \tag{1}$$

where $\mathbf{K}$ is the intrinsic matrix that contains the focal lengths f_x, f_y, the skew parameter α and the principal point coordinates c_x, c_y. The back-projection from the normalized image coordinates to the world coordinates is also an essential relationship which can be written as:

$$\mathbf{X} = \hbar^{-1}(\mathbf{x}, w) = \frac{1}{w} \left(\frac{\xi + \sqrt{1 + (1 - \xi^2)(x^2 + y^2)}}{x^2 + y^2 + 1} \begin{bmatrix} x \\ y \\ 1 \end{bmatrix} - \begin{bmatrix} 0 \\ 0 \\ \xi \end{bmatrix} \right), \tag{2}$$

where w is the inverse depth such that $w = \frac{1}{\|\mathbf{X}\|}$.

3.2   Bundle Adjustment

In this section, we introduce our bundle adjustment tailored for a SPC consisting of two fisheye cameras looking at opposite directions. The input of our approach is a short video clip where each frame is a concatenated image of the two simultaneous fisheye camera images, the average image of an input clip is shown in Fig. 4(a). For the sake of convenience, we consider the left and right images separately, and name them, respectively, frontal and rear camera.

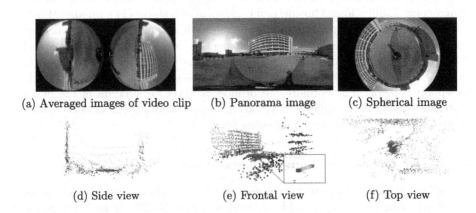

(a) Averaged images of video clip   (b) Panorama image   (c) Spherical image

(d) Side view   (e) Frontal view   (f) Top view

Fig. 4. The 3D point cloud and camera poses from our bundle adjustment

As explored in the prior works, the use of the inverse depth representation is known to be effective in regularizing the scales of the variables in the optimization. To utilize it in our case, we design a cost function (re-projection error) for the bundle adjustment to be computed on the unit sphere instead of in the image domain. This particularity is motivated by two major observations. Firstly, the spherical model takes into account the non-linear resolution induced by the fisheye lenses (the re-projection error is uniformly mapped on the sphere, which is not the case in the image domain). Secondly, the transformation from the unit sphere to the image coordinates yields strong non-linearity in the cost function which is not recommended for small motion bundle adjustment (hardly converges with a high-order model).

The j-th feature point lying on the sphere of the first camera is noted $\hat{\mathbf{X}}_{1j}$. Its corresponding 3D coordinates can be computed by back-projection using the inverse depth ($w_j \in \mathbf{W}$): $\mathbf{X}_j = \frac{\hat{\mathbf{X}}_{1j}}{w_j}$. Then, the projection of this 3D point onto the unit sphere of the i-th camera is calculated using the extrinsic camera matrix parameterized by a rotation vector $\mathbf{r}_i$ and a translation vector $\mathbf{t}_i$. This rigid transformation is followed by a normalization on the sphere: $\langle \mathbf{X} \rangle = \frac{\mathbf{X}}{\|\mathbf{X}\|}$.

By considering the frontal camera (F) and the rear camera (R) are fixed in a rigid body, our bundle adjustment is designed to refine the extrinsic parameters for the frontal camera images and the 3D coordinates of both features captured in the frontal and rear camera images by minimizing all the re-projection errors as:

$$\underset{\mathbf{r},\mathbf{t},\mathbf{W}^F,\mathbf{W}^R}{\text{argmin}} \sum_{i=1}^{N_I} \left(\sum_{j=1}^{N_F} \|\hat{\mathbf{X}}_{ij}^F - \langle \mathcal{P}_i^F \begin{bmatrix} \mathbf{X}_j^F \\ 1 \end{bmatrix} \rangle \|_{\text{H}} + \sum_{j=1}^{N_R} \|\hat{\mathbf{X}}_{ij}^R - \langle \mathcal{P}_i^R \begin{bmatrix} \mathbf{X}_j^R \\ 1 \end{bmatrix} \rangle \|_{\text{H}} \right), \quad (3)$$

where i and j stand for the image index and the feature index, N_I the number of frames, N_F and N_R the numbers of features in the frontal and rear camera images, $\hat{\mathbf{X}}_{ij}^F$ and $\hat{\mathbf{X}}_{ij}^R$ the unit sphere coordinates of the j-th feature for the i-th image, and $\| \cdot \|_{\text{H}}$ the Huber loss function with a scaling factor set as the focal length. The rigid motion matrices $\mathcal{P}_i^F$ and $\mathcal{P}_i^R$ are all expressed in a single referential coordinates system thanks to the 3×4 extrinsic calibration matrix $\mathbf{P}$ (between the frontal camera to the rear camera):

$$\mathcal{P}_i^F = [\mathcal{R}(\mathbf{r}_i)|\mathbf{t}_i], \; \mathcal{P}_i^R = \mathbf{P} \begin{bmatrix} \mathcal{P}_i^F \\ m \end{bmatrix} \begin{bmatrix} \mathbf{P} \\ m \end{bmatrix}^{-1}, \; m = \begin{bmatrix} 0 \; 0 \; 0 \; 1 \end{bmatrix}, \quad (4)$$

where the function $\mathcal{R}$ transforms the Rodrigues rotation angles into their rotation matrix. For the initialization of the bundle adjustment parameters, all the rotation and translation vectors are set to zero which is a reasonable assumption for small motion 3D reconstruction [13–15]. The metric-scale extrinsic matrix $\mathbf{P}$ are pre-calibrated and our bundle adjustment takes advantage of the sensor parameters. This helps to estimate the rigid transformation between the frontal and the rear camera. Consequently, our BA is designed to embrace all inter-frame poses of both cameras in one optimization framework. Therefore, the reconstructed 3D structure and poses are estimated with an approximate metric scale (the scale may not be perfectly metric, but close to it). Thus, we can set the initial depth for all features as 10 m or 100 m for indoor or outdoor scene, respectively.

To find the feature correspondences for the frontal camera, we extract Harris corner features [30] from the first image. We filter out the features on the boundary pixels which has low image resolution and can cause inaccurate feature matching. By using a Kanade-Lucas-Tomashi (KLT) algorithm [31], these features are then tracked in the other images to find their correspondences, and tracked back to the first image to filter outliers by their bidirectional error. The points having an error larger than 0.1 pixel are discarded. The same process is done for the rear camera images. To solve the minimization problem, we use the Ceres solver [32] to optimize our bundle adjustment which uses Huber loss function to be robust to outliers.

3.3 Sphere Sweeping Algorithm

With the camera extrinsic parameters estimated from the previous section, our goal is to estimate dense depth maps for both fisheye images. The plane sweeping algorithm [18] is a powerful method for dense matching between multiview images. The main idea is to back-project the images onto successive virtual planes, perpendicular to the z-axis, and find the depth of the plane that has the highest photo consistency for each pixel. Hane et $al.$ [12] adapt the plane sweeping algorithm to the fisheye camera model. Their idea is to adapt the planar homography on the unit sphere, which involves a systematic transformation between the sphere and the image plane.

Though the plane sweeping approach using fisheye camera can estimate a large field of view depth map, the accuracy can be lower especially for image boundary pixels due to their low spatial resolution [12]. A SPC can compensate this resolution issue by using the overlapping region between the rear and the frontal camera. To achieve this goal, we propose a new dense matching algorithm suitable for SPCs, called sphere sweeping (Fig. 5). Instead of using virtual planes, we utilize virtual spheres centered at the reference camera. It lets us utilize the

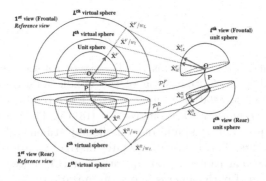

Fig. 5. Illustration on the sphere sweeping algorithm

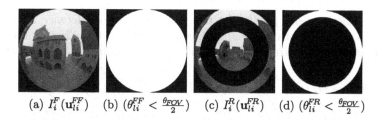

(a) $I_i^F(\mathbf{u}_{li}^{FF})$ (b) $(\theta_{li}^{FF} < \frac{\theta_{FOV}}{2})$ (c) $I_i^R(\mathbf{u}_{li}^{FR})$ (d) $(\theta_{li}^{FR} < \frac{\theta_{FOV}}{2})$

Fig. 6. Examples of warped image and visibility ($i = 1$, $l = 0$). (a) Warped image from frontal to frontal. (b) Visibility mask of (a). (c) Warped image from rear to frontal image. (d) Visibility mask of (c).

color consistency of the overlapping region, which ensures a better estimation of the boundary depths.

Basically, our sphere sweeping algorithm back-projects the image pixel $\mathbf{u}$ in the reference image onto a virtual sphere $\mathbf{S}$, and then projects them onto the other images to obtain color intensity profiles $\mathcal{I}$. An important idea is that we can use two simultaneous virtual spheres centered at the frontal and rear cameras, respectively, and utilize them together for dense matching. When the l-th virtual spheres have an inverse radius (depth) w_l, the back-projections of $\mathbf{u}^F$ and $\mathbf{u}^R$ onto the frontal and rear camera's virtual spheres are described respectively as:

$$\mathbf{S}_l^F = \hbar^{-1}(\mathbf{K}_F^{-1}\mathbf{u}^F, w_l), \ \mathbf{S}_l^R = \hbar^{-1}(\mathbf{K}_R^{-1}\mathbf{u}^R, w_l) \tag{5}$$

Now, we can consider four possible cases of projections: frontal-to-frontal (FF), frontal-to-rear (FR), rear-to-frontal (RF), and rear-to-rear (RR). The projections of the frontal and rear camera's spheres onto an i-th frontal camera image are computed by:

$$\mathbf{u}_{li}^{FF} = \mathbf{K}_F\hbar(\mathcal{P}_i^F \begin{bmatrix} \mathbf{S}_l^F \\ 1 \end{bmatrix}), \ \mathbf{u}_{li}^{RF} = \mathbf{K}_F\hbar(\mathcal{P}_i^F \begin{bmatrix} \mathbf{P} \\ \mathbf{m} \end{bmatrix}^{-1} \begin{bmatrix} \mathbf{S}_l^R \\ 1 \end{bmatrix}) \tag{6}$$

And the projections onto the i-th rear camera image are computed by:

$$\mathbf{u}_{li}^{FR} = \mathbf{K}_R\hbar(\mathbf{P} \begin{bmatrix} \mathcal{P}_i^F \\ \mathbf{m} \end{bmatrix} \begin{bmatrix} \mathbf{S}_l^F \\ 1 \end{bmatrix}), \ \mathbf{u}_{li}^{RR} = \mathbf{K}_R\hbar(\mathbf{P} \begin{bmatrix} \mathcal{P}_i^F \\ \mathbf{m} \end{bmatrix} \begin{bmatrix} \mathbf{P} \\ \mathbf{m} \end{bmatrix}^{-1} \begin{bmatrix} \mathbf{S}_l^R \\ 1 \end{bmatrix}) \tag{7}$$

Since each camera has a certain Field-Of-View (FOV), the projected image coordinates should be selectively used depending on whether they are in the field of view or not. For this reason, we measure the angle between the camera's principal axis and the ray direction for each projection using the following formulations:

$$\theta_{li}^{FF} = \cos^{-1}([0\ 0\ 1]\ \langle\mathcal{P}_i^F \begin{bmatrix} \mathbf{S}_l^F \\ 1 \end{bmatrix}\rangle), \quad \theta_{li}^{FR} = \cos^{-1}([0\ 0\ 1]\ \langle\mathbf{P} \begin{bmatrix} \mathcal{P}_i^F \\ \mathbf{m} \end{bmatrix} \begin{bmatrix} \mathbf{S}_l^F \\ 1 \end{bmatrix}\rangle), \tag{8}$$

$$\theta_{li}^{RF} = \cos^{-1}([0\ 0\ 1]\ \langle\mathcal{P}_i^F \begin{bmatrix} \mathbf{P} \\ \mathbf{m} \end{bmatrix}^{-1} \begin{bmatrix} \mathbf{S}_l^R \\ 1 \end{bmatrix}\rangle), \quad \theta_{li}^{RR} = \cos^{-1}([0\ 0\ 1]\ \langle\mathbf{P} \begin{bmatrix} \mathcal{P}_i^F \\ \mathbf{m} \end{bmatrix} \begin{bmatrix} \mathbf{P} \\ \mathbf{m} \end{bmatrix}^{-1} \begin{bmatrix} \mathbf{S}_l^R \\ 1 \end{bmatrix}\rangle). \tag{9}$$

Finally, the intensity profiles for the j-th pixel in the reference frontal and rear images w.r.t. the l-th inverse depth can be obtained by collecting the image intensities for all the corresponding visible projected points:

$$\mathcal{I}_{lj}^{FF} = \{I_i^F(\mathbf{u}_{lij}^{FF})|\theta_{lij}^{FF} < \frac{\theta_{FOV}}{2}\}, \; \mathcal{I}_{lj}^{FR} = \{I_i^R(\mathbf{u}_{lij}^{FR})|\theta_{lij}^{FR} < \frac{\theta_{FOV}}{2}\}, \qquad (10)$$

$$\mathcal{I}_{lj}^{RF} = \{I_i^F(\mathbf{u}_{lij}^{RF})|\theta_{lij}^{RF} < \frac{\theta_{FOV}}{2}\}, \; \mathcal{I}_{lj}^{RR} = \{I_i^R(\mathbf{u}_{lij}^{RR})|\theta_{lij}^{RR} < \frac{\theta_{FOV}}{2}\}. \qquad (11)$$

where $i = \{1, \cdots, N_i\}$ and θ_{FOV} is the field-of-view angle ($200°$ in our paper). A Bicubic interpolation is used for calculating the sub-pixel intensities. Figure 6 shows the examples of warped image and masks of reference image.

Our matching cost is formulated as a weighted sum of variances of two intensity profiles. The effectiveness of the variance as a matching cost for small motion case has been demonstrated in [15]. For the frontal and rear cameras, our matching costs are respectively:

$$V_{lj}^F = \mathrm{Var}(\mathcal{I}_{lj}^{FF}) + \lambda \mathrm{Var}(\mathcal{I}_{lj}^{FR}), \qquad (12)$$

$$V_{lj}^R = \mathrm{Var}(\mathcal{I}_{lj}^{RR}) + \lambda \mathrm{Var}(\mathcal{I}_{lj}^{RF}), \qquad (13)$$

where $\mathrm{Var}(\cdot)$ is the variance function and λ is a weight for balancing the two variance values from the opposite side images. These costs are stacked over all the inverse depth candidates $w_1, \cdots, w_L$ to build cost volumes $\mathbf{V}^F$ and $\mathbf{V}^R$ for the frontal and rear camera, respectively.

Initial depth maps are extracted from $\mathbf{V}^F$ and $\mathbf{V}^R$ via Winner-Takes-All(WTA) method. For each of the frontal and rear camera's cost volumes, we compute a confidence map as $\mathbf{C} = 1 - \min(\mathbf{V})/\mathrm{median}(\mathbf{V})$ to remove outliers having confidence values under a certain threshold (<0.01). Finally, the depth maps are refined via a tree-based aggregation method proposed in [33]. It helps improving the quality of the results without masking out any depth on the untextured region.

4   Experimental Results

We assess our method with both synthetic and real-world datasets. In Sect. 4.2, a large series of synthetic experiments is conducted with both to quantitatively measure the accuracy of our method with respect to the baseline magnitude and the number of images. A comparison of our method against the conventional

Table 1. Re-projection error percentage w.r.t. the number of iteration.

# of iteration	Initial	1	2	3	4
Proposed	100 %	**48.7 %**	**7.9 %**	**4.4 %**	**3.8 %**
Standard	100 %	74.3 %	67.8 %	64.4 %	61.6 %

Table 2. The average reconstructed scale value

Checkerboard size	10 cm	5 cm	2 cm
1st trial	13.9 cm	5.1 cm	3.3 cm
2nd trial	10.9 cm	7.7 cm	1.9 cm
3rd trial	9.5 cm	6.1 cm	2.5 cm

plane sweeping with real images is provided in Sect. 4.3. These tests underline the high versatility of the proposed method with real-world data. We implemented our method using both MATLAB and C++. A computer equipped with an Intel i7 3.4 GHz and 16 GB was used for the computations. The proposed algorithm takes about 10 min for a 30 frames (540 × 960) sequence. Among all the computation steps, the dense matching is clearly the most time-consuming. But, it is expected that a GPU parallelization could significantly increase the speed of the overall algorithm [12,34]. The algorithm for feature extraction, tracking and bundle adjustment takes about 1 min. The intrinsic and extrinsic parameters are pre-calibrated by using [35–37].

4.1 Validation for the Convergence and Scale Estimation

To demonstrate the effectiveness of the proposed BA in terms of convergence, we conduct multiple experiments against its conventional counter-part (BA on the image domain). Specifically, we measure the re-projection errors of both technique at every iteration. Table 1 shows re-projection error percentage (average over 20 datasets) with respect to the number of iteration. It is clear that the standard BA on the image domain does not converge at all, whereas, the proposed BA always converges well. It is because the double projection process (world to sphere and sphere to image) tends to generate singularities which induces many local minimum in the cost function.

As the proposed bundle adjustment is designed to approximately estimate the metric scale, we conduct a quantitative evaluation method to estimate the accuracy of the reconstructed scale obtained by our approach. To measure the scale, we use 3 types of calibration checkerboard (2, 5, 10 cm) with 3 different backgrounds and average the scale of the squares on the checkerboard. The reconstructed scale may not be perfectly metric scale since the baseline between two fisheye cameras is very small, but it is close to the metric as shown in Table 2, which could not be accomplished using previous pinhole-based SfSM methods [13–15]. We also measure the reconstructed scale values in Fig. 10(f), the height of the reconstructed bookshelf is 2 m, which in reality is 2.1 m.

4.2 Synthetic Datasets

For quantitative evaluation, we rendered synthetic image sequences for both frontal and rear camera (with ground-truth depth maps) via Blender^{TM}.

The synthetic dataset consists of a pair of 30 images with a resolution of 480×960 and a 200° field of view. The two cameras are oriented at opposite directions in order to imitate the image sequences acquired from our spherical panoramic camera. We use the depth map robustness measure ($R3$) [14, 15, 38], which is the percentage of pixels that have less than 3 label differences from the depth map ground-truth[1] (see Fig. 8).

We performed experiments to evaluate the effect of the baseline magnitude and the number of images on the resulting depth maps. We firstly compute the R measures for baselines over the minimum depth value of the scene (Baseline = Min.depth $\times 10^b$) where $b = -3.5, -3.3, \ldots, -1.1$. In Fig. 8(a), the R measure underlines that the proposed method achieves stable performances when the baseline b is larger than -1.5.

Next, Fig. 8(b) reports the performances of the proposed method according to the number of images used with a fixed baseline $b = -1.5$. We can observe that better performances are achieved with a greater number of images, however, the performance gain ratio is reduced as the number of images increases. The experiment shows that utilizing 20 images is a good trade-off between the performance gain and the burden of dense depth reconstruction for the proposed method. The example result and error map are shown in Fig. 7.

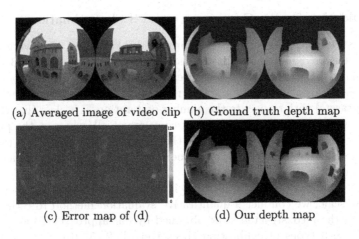

(a) Averaged image of video clip   (b) Ground truth depth map

(c) Error map of (d)   (d) Our depth map

Fig. 7. Our depth map and error map. (128 labels, 480×960, FOV: 200)

4.3   Real-World Datasets

In this subsection, we demonstrate the performances of the proposed algorithm on various indoor and outdoor scenes captured by a Ricoh Theta S with video mode. For the real-world experiments, we use 1 second video clips for indoor scenes and uniformly sampled 30 images from 3 seconds video clips for outdoor datasets since the minimum depth in outdoor is usually larger than indoor scenes. The datasets were captured from various users with different motions.

---

[1] We convert ground-truth depth to the quantized sweeping labels.

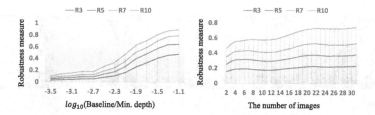

Fig. 8. Quantitative evaluation on the magnitude of baseline (left) and the number of images used (right).

To generate our panoramic images, we do not apply the standard approach which consists in the back-projection of both images on a common unit sphere. This approach is prone to parallax errors since the translation between the cameras is neglected. Instead, we project our dense 3D reconstruction on a unique sphere (located in between the two cameras) in order to create a synthetic spherical view which ensures a perfect stitching. This method preserves the structure of the scene by using all the intrinsic and extrinsic parameters (Fig. 10, 2nd row). Panorama depth maps are obtained by applying the similar process. As shown in Fig. 10 (4th row), the proposed method shows promising results regardless of the environment.

We also compare our sphere sweeping method with the conventional plane sweeping method using our hardware setup. The warped images via conventional homography-based method [12] are flipped on the boundary region where the FOV is larger than 180°, so the depth maps estimated with these flipped images in Fig. 9(b) contain significant artifacts on the image boundary. Figure 9(c) and (d) show that the sphere sweeping method outperforms the competing method.

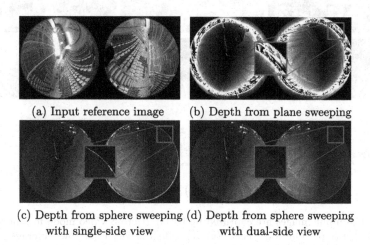

(a) Input reference image   (b) Depth from plane sweeping

(c) Depth from sphere sweeping (d) Depth from sphere sweeping
    with single-side view   with dual-side view

Fig. 9. Comparison on dense matching method.

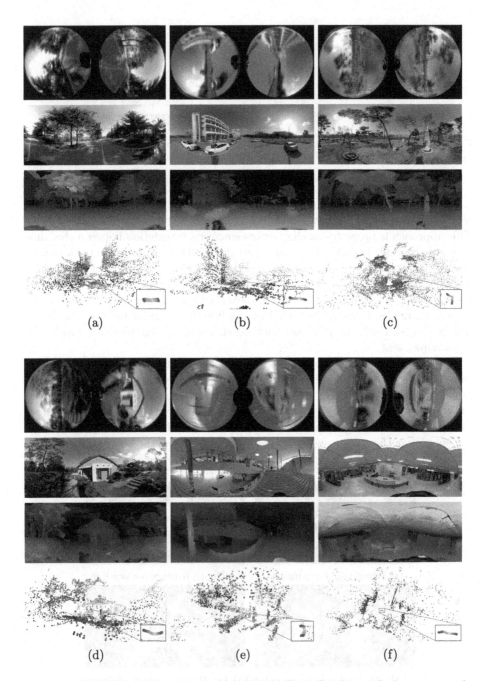

Fig. 10. The input images are captured by Ricoh Theta S video mode for one second (30 frames). (a)–(d) Outdoor scene. (e)–(f) Indoor scene. First row: Averaged image of video clip. Second row: Panorama images. Third row: Our depth map from small motion. Fourth row: Sparse 3D and Camera poses.

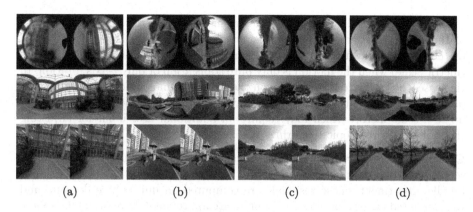

(a)   (b)   (c)   (d)

Fig. 11. VR applications. Top: Averaged images of video clip, Middle: Anaglyph panoramic images(red-cyan), Bottom: Stereoscopic VR images.

Especially, the depth map (Fig. 9(d)) obtained with our strategy using overlapping regions shows better performance than that of single-side view.

4.4 Applications

Since our method can reconstruct accurate 3D of the surrounding environment, it can deliver a 360 degree 3D visual experience using a head-mounted display [1–3]. Many approaches propose to generate anaglyph panoramas [39] and stereoscopic images [40,41], to produce VR contents in a cost effective way. In this subsection, we show the anaglyph panorama and the 360° stereoscopic images as applications.

In order to create a convincing 3D effect, we generate two synthetic views with the desired baseline (typically 5 to 7.5 cm to mimic the human binocular vision). The computation of such synthetic images is one again based on the dense 3D structure of the scene (as discussed in the previous section). The resulting anaglyphs and stereoscopic panoramas are available in Fig. 11. The 3D effect obtained with our method is realistic thanks to our accurate depth map computation approach.

5   Conclusion and Discussion

Discussion. In contrast to the prior SfSM BA methods [13–15] designed for pinhole cameras, our BA uses usual rotation representation, instead of the small-angle approximated matrix. Indeed, it has been demonstrated that spherical sensors are particularly robust to motion ambiguity while small magnitude motions are performed [42]. With this observation, the proposed BA may have the potential to be generalized to any type of motion. However, our method cannot handle large rotations due to the limitation of the feature tracking algorithm. This could be an interesting direction to pursue this work further.

Furthermore, we have noticed some degenerated cases throughout the course of the study. First, the estimated camera poses and the 3D points cannot be matched with the camera extrinsic parameters between frontal and rear cameras (metric scale) when the motion is only pure translation or only z-axis rotation. In this case, the estimated depth map on the fisheye cannot produce a well-aligned panorama depth. If the two cameras have zero baseline, the reconstruction is up to a scale factor, which may require an additional user input for adjusting the scale for stereoscopic rendering.

Conclusion. We have proposed a practical 3D reconstruction method for stereoscopic panorama from small motion with SPC. We achieved this by utilizing our bundle adjustment whose residuals are computed on unit sphere domain, and the estimated camera pose and 3D points are approximately metric. Our sphere sweeping algorithm enables to compute all-around dense depth maps, minimizing the loss of spatial resolution. With the estimated all-around image and depth map, we have shown practical utilities by introducing 360° stereoscopic and anaglyph images as VR contents.

Acknowledgement. This work was supported by the National Research Foundation of Korea (NRF) grant funded by the Korea government (MSIP) (No. 2010-0028680). Sunghoon Im and Hae-Gon Jeon were partially supported by Global Ph.D. Fellowship Program through the National Research Foundation of Korea (NRF) funded by the Ministry of Education (NRF-2016907531, NRF-2015034617).

References

1. Oculus. https://www.oculus.com/
2. Gear vr. http://www.samsung.com/global/galaxy/wearables/gear-vr/
3. Google cardboard. https://www.google.com/get/cardboard/
4. Nayar, S.K.: Catadioptric omnidirectional camera. In: IEEE Computer Vision and Pattern Recognition (CVPR) (1997)
5. Gaspar, J., Winters, N., Santos-Victor, J.: Vision-based navigation and environmental representations with an omnidirectional camera. IEEE Trans. Robot. Autom. **16**(6), 890–898 (2000)
6. Kang, S.B., Szeliski, R.: 3-d scene data recovery using omnidirectional multibaseline stereo. Intl. J. Comput. Vis. (IJCV) **25**(2), 167–183 (1997)
7. Lytro immerge. https://www.lytro.com/immerge/
8. Ricoh 360 cam. https://theta360.com/en/
9. Gear 360. http://www.samsung.com/global/galaxy/gear-360/
10. Lg 360 cam. http://www.lgcorp.com/news/innoProduct1.dev/
11. Caruso, D., Engel, J., Cremers, D.: Large-scale direct slam for omnidirectional cameras. In: IEEE/RSJ International Conference on Intelligent Robots and Systems (IROS) (2015)
12. Hane, C., Heng, L., Lee, G.H., Sizov, A., Pollefeys, M.: Real-time direct dense matching on fisheye images using plane-sweeping stereo. In: Proceedings of International Conference on 3D Vision (3DV) (2014)
13. Yu, F., Gallup, D.: 3d reconstruction from accidental motion. In: IEEE Computer Vision and Pattern Recognition (CVPR) (2014)

14. Im, S., Ha, H., Choe, G., Jeon, H.G., Joo, K., Kweon, I.S.: High quality structure from small motion for rolling shutter cameras. In: IEEE International Conference on Computer Vision (ICCV) (2015)
15. Ha, H., Im, S., Park, J., Jeon, H.G., Kweon, I.S.: High-quality depth from uncalibrated small motion clip. In: IEEE Computer Vision and Pattern Recognition (CVPR) (2016)
16. Kim, C., Zimmer, H., Pritch, Y., Sorkine-Hornung, A., Gross, M.: Scene reconstruction from high spatio-angular resolution light fields. Proc. SIGGRAPH **32**(4), 73:1–73:12 (2013)
17. Joshi, N., Zitnick, C.L.: Micro-baseline stereo. Technical report, MSR-TR-2014-73, Microsoft Research (2014)
18. Collins, R.T.: A space-sweep approach to true multi-image matching. In: IEEE Computer Vision and Pattern Recognition (CVPR) (1996)
19. Micusik, B., Pajdla, T.: Structure from motion with wide circular field of view cameras. IEEE Trans. Pattern Anal. Mach. Intell. (TPAMI) **28**(7), 1135–1149 (2006)
20. Sturm, P., Ramalingam, S., Tardif, J.P., Gasparini, S., Barreto, J.: Camera models and fundamental concepts used in geometric computer vision. Found. Trends Comput. Graph. Vis. **6**(1–2), 1–183 (2011)
21. Schonbein, M., Geiger, A.: Omnidirectional 3d reconstruction in augmented manhattan worlds. In: IEEE/RSJ International Conference on Intelligent Robots and Systems (IROS) (2014)
22. Mičušík, B., Pajdla, T.: Autocalibration & 3d reconstruction with non-central catadioptric cameras. In: IEEE Computer Vision and Pattern Recognition (CVPR) (2004)
23. Bunschoten, R., Kröse, B.: Robust scene reconstruction from an omnidirectional vision system. IEEE Trans. Robot. Autom. **19**(2), 351–357 (2003)
24. Li, S.: Binocular spherical stereo. IEEE Trans. Intell. Transp. Syst. **9**(4), 589–600 (2008)
25. Kim, H., Hilton, A.: 3d scene reconstruction from multiple spherical stereo pairs. Intl. J. Comput. Vis. (IJCV) **104**(1), 94–116 (2013)
26. Geyer, C., Daniilidis, K.: A unifying theory for central panoramic systems and practical implications. In: Vernon, D. (ed.) ECCV 2000. LNCS, vol. 1843, pp. 445–461. Springer, Heidelberg (2000). doi:10.1007/3-540-45053-X_29
27. Ying, X., Hu, Z.: Can we consider central catadioptric cameras and fisheye cameras within a unified imaging model. In: Pajdla, T., Matas, J. (eds.) ECCV 2004. LNCS, vol. 3021, pp. 442–455. Springer, Heidelberg (2004). doi:10.1007/978-3-540-24670-1_34
28. Courbon, J., Mezouar, Y., Eck, L., Martinet, P.: A generic fisheye camera model for robotic applications. In: IEEE/RSJ International Conference on Intelligent Robots and Systems (IROS) (2007)
29. Barreto, J.P.: A unifying geometric representation for central projection systems. Comput. Vis. Image Underst. (CVIU) **103**(3), 208–217 (2006)
30. Harris, C., Stephens, M.: A combined corner and edge detector. In: Alvey Vision Conference, vol. 15, p. 50 (1988)
31. Lucas, B.D., Kanade, T., et al.: An iterative image registration technique with an application to stereo vision. IJCAI **81**, 674–679 (1981)
32. Agarwal, S., Mierle, K., et al.: Ceres solver. http://ceres-solver.org
33. Yang, Q.: A non-local cost aggregation method for stereo matching. In: IEEE Computer Vision and Pattern Recognition (CVPR) (2012)

34. Gallup, D., Frahm, J.M., Mordohai, P., Yang, Q., Pollefeys, M.: Real-time plane-sweeping stereo with multiple sweeping directions. In: IEEE Computer Vision and Pattern Recognition (CVPR) (2007)

35. Mei, C., Rives, P.: Single view point omnidirectional camera calibration from planar grids. In: IEEE International Conference on Robotics and Automation (ICRA) (2007)

36. Lébraly, P., Deymier, C., Ait-Aider, O., Royer, E., Dhome, M.: Flexible extrinsic calibration of non-overlapping cameras using a planar mirror: application to vision-based robotics. In: IEEE/RSJ International Conference on Intelligent Robots and Systems (IROS) (2010)

37. Lébraly, P., Royer, E., Ait-Aider, O., Dhome, M.: Calibration of non-overlapping cameras - application to vision-based robotics. In: Proceedings of British Machine Vision Conference (BMVC) (2010)

38. Scharstein, D., Szeliski, R.: A taxonomy and evaluation of dense two-frame stereo correspondence algorithms. Intl. J. Comput. Vis. (IJCV) **47**(1–3), 7–42 (2002)

39. Ideses, I., Yaroslavsky, L.: Three methods that improve the visual quality of colour anaglyphs. J. Opt. A: Pure Appl. Opt. **7**(12), 755 (2005)

40. Peleg, S., Ben-Ezra, M., Pritch, Y.: Omnistereo: panoramic stereo imaging. IEEE Trans. Pattern Anal. Mach. Intell. (TPAMI) **23**(3), 279–290 (2001)

41. Richardt, C., Pritch, Y., Zimmer, H., Sorkine-Hornung, A.: Megastereo: constructing high-resolution stereo panoramas. In: IEEE Computer Vision and Pattern Recognition (CVPR) (2013)

42. Gluckman, J., Nayar, S.K.: Ego-motion and omnidirectional cameras. In: IEEE International Conference on Computer Vision (ICCV) (1998)

On Volumetric Shape Reconstruction from Implicit Forms

Li Wang$^{(\boxtimes)}$, Franck Hétroy-Wheeler, and Edmond Boyer

Univ. Grenoble Alpes & Inria & CNRS, LJK, 38000 Grenoble, France
{li.wang,franck.hetroy,edmond.boyer}@inria.fr

Abstract. In this paper we report on the evaluation of volumetric shape reconstruction methods that consider as input implicit forms in 3D. Many visual applications build implicit representations of shapes that are converted into explicit shape representations using geometric tools such as the Marching Cubes algorithm. This is the case with image based reconstructions that produce point clouds from which implicit functions are computed, with for instance a Poisson reconstruction approach. While the Marching Cubes method is a versatile solution with proven efficiency, alternative solutions exist with different and complementary properties that are of interest for shape modeling. In this paper, we propose a novel strategy that builds on Centroidal Voronoi Tessellations (CVTs). These tessellations provide volumetric and surface representations with strong regularities in addition to provably more accurate approximations of the implicit forms considered. In order to compare the existing strategies, we present an extensive evaluation that analyzes various properties of the main strategies for implicit to explicit volumetric conversions: Marching cubes, Delaunay refinement and CVTs, including accuracy and shape quality of the resulting shape mesh.

1 Introduction

Visual computing applications usually consider explicit representations for 3D shapes, in the form of surface or volume meshes in general. This is true for most visualization applications and also for applications that require local neighboring information within the shape or on its surface, as often the case with shape optimization or shape deformation applications for example. In order to generate such explicit representations from visual observations many methods consider as input an implicit representation that identifies the shape as being a region $\mathcal{V}$ within an observation domain $\Omega \in \mathbb{R}^3$. Such implicit representation is typically given as a scalar function $f : \Omega \to \mathbb{R}$ which takes different values inside and outside $\mathcal{V}$, for instance an indicator function or a distance function in 3D. These implicit representations f are often encountered in reconstruction applications that consider point clouds, as obtained with for instance stereo, multi-stereo and depth scanning apparatus, e.g. [18,24] (see Fig. 1). They can also be built directly from image primitives, for instance the implicit visual hull form, e.g. [15] with image silhouettes. The conversion then from implicit to explicit representations

© Springer International Publishing AG 2016
B. Leibe et al. (Eds.): ECCV 2016, Part III, LNCS 9907, pp. 173–188, 2016.
DOI: 10.1007/978-3-319-46487-9_11

Fig. 1. The Gargoyle multi-view point cloud and the associated Poisson reconstructions with Marching Cubes and CVT. Distances to the implicit form are color encoded on the right, from low (blue) to high (red). (Color figure online)

usually consists in the polyhedrization of the region $\mathcal{V}$, where both the resulting polyhedral volume and the associated polygonal surface approximations are potentially considered by vision and graphics applications *e.g.* [1,19,40]. In this paper we report on a novel approach to solve for this important conversion step and we provide a comparative study of the main strategies available.

Existing approaches for such 3D implicit form conversions into volumetric tessellations can be roughly divided into two categories. A first category, that includes the Marching Cubes method [31] and its extensions, adopts a fixed-grid strategy where the observation domain Ω is discretized into cells that are traditionally cubic. Inside and outside cells are identified with respect to the input implicit function and the boundary cells can be further polygonized into a triangle mesh approximating the shape surface. This strategy is efficient and fast and has been very widely used in vision and graphics applications over the last decades. However the 3D shape discretization into cubic cells with constrained orientations produces a poor shape tessellation which can result in surface approximations with elongated or small triangles. Thus, an additional re-meshing step is consequently often required. In addition, attaching the grid to Ω makes the tessellation changing with any shape transformation, even rigid. A second category of approaches, such as [36] with the Delaunay tetrahedrization, discretizes instead the inside region $\mathcal{V}$. These approaches usually provide better shape tessellations which are as well independent of rigid shape transformations and hence plausibly better suited for dynamic scene modeling. Still, they require expert control to monitor the cell refinement step that is performed. Moreover, as the boundary of a tetrahedral structure can present non manifold parts it is difficult to guarantee a correct topology for the boundary mesh approximating the surface. In this paper, we explore a different strategy that also belongs to the second category and discretizes $\mathcal{V}$ instead of Ω. The approach builds on Centroidal Voronoi Tessellations (CVTs) that provide regular shape tessellations which boundaries are obtained by clipping frontier cells with the given implicit boundary form. In contrast to Delaunay-based methods, the boundary surface of the output volume is, by construction, manifold and the approach has only a few parameters.

In order to highlight the main features of the proposed CVT approach, including its limitations, we propose in this paper a comprehensive evaluation that compares all methods with respect to consistent criteria: the topology correctness of the produced volumetric model; The accuracy with respect to the input implicit form; The quality of the volumetric tessellation; And the computation times. The main result of this evaluation is that the CVT approach provably outperforms the other strategies in terms of accuracy and cell regularity, however to the price of higher computation times with respect to Marching Cubes. To summarize, our main contribution is twofold:

1. We introduce a CVT approach to polyhedrize implicit shape representations and provide a practical algorithm for that purpose.
2. We present a qualitative and quantitative comparison of Marching Cubes-, Delaunay- and CVT-based strategies to produce volume and surface shape approximations.

These contributions are detailed in Sects. 3 and 4 respectively, after a presentation of related works in Sect. 2.

2   Related Work

As mentioned earlier methods for the polyhedrization of implicit forms fall into two main categories: first, *Eulerian* methods that consider a grid discretizing the observation domain Ω and second *Lagrangian* methods which perform a discretization of the shape volume $\mathcal{V}$.

Eulerian Strategies Originally designed for isosurface extraction, *i.e.* estimating the implicit surface defined by $\{x \in \Omega, f(x) = cst\}$, the Marching cubes (MC) algorithm introduced in [31] is the most prominent approach in this category as a result of its efficiency and versatility of applications. It considers a regular cubical grid that partitions Ω, where Ω is typically a bounding box. For each cube within the grid that intersects the shape, the algorithm determines the intersection faces by linearly interpolating, along cube edges, the f values at the cube vertices. Many methods have then been proposed that adapt this strategy to sharp features, *e.g.* [23], or to resolve topological ambiguities induced by the original method, see [33] for a survey. Other methods have also proposed more complex interpolation schemes [17,26] to better locate surface points along cube edges. To speed up computations, which may be slow since the complexity is cubic with respect to the grid size, several authors have suggested to replace the grid by an adaptive structure such as an octree, *e.g.* [21]. Marching Cubes methods focus on the polygonization of the shape boundary surface and not on the volumetric tessellations which is irregular by construction: interior cells are cubic while boundary cells are not. Extensions to other subdivision schemes including tetrahedral, octahedral and hexahedral subdivisions, *e.g.* [6,8,37] have also been proposed that provide more isotropic polyhedral cells. However the discretization grid in these schemes is still fixed.

Lagrangian Strategies. Instead of subdividing Ω, approaches in this category tessellate the shape volume. The interest is first to reduce the complexity, which allows for better accuracies than MC at similar resolutions. This can be an important feature when modeling large scenes, *e.g.* [24]. Second, attaching the subdivision to the shape eases the implementation of kinematic models that can be defined over volumetric representations. This can help modeling dynamic scenes as in [1]. In this category, shape tetrahedrization is widely used to generate a volumetric tessellation. For example, the isosurface stuffing algorithm from [25] creates a regular tetrahedrization from a body-centered cubic (BCC) grid. As for the Marching cubes approaches described above, the resulting tessellation depends however on the orientation of the grid. The Delaunay refinement technique, as in [36], also generates Delaunay tetrahedrizations with guarantees on tetrahedron shapes. However, degenerate tetrahedra, typically slivers, can still appear, although their number can be reduced by global [2] or local [38] optimization techniques.

Centroidal Voronoi Tessellations (CVTs) are a special type of Voronoi tessellations with regular Voronoi cells [39]. Such tessellations are known to be optimal quantizers [13] and their cells, mostly truncated octahedra, are more isotropic than cubes or tetrahedra. Consequently, CVTs have been used to discretize 2D and 3D shapes in many scientific domains [14]. While methods have been proposed to clip a CVT to a surface mesh [27,39,41], to the best of our knowledge, none is able yet to handle implicit forms. We introduce therefore in the next section a new clipping method for CVTs.

Surface Reconstruction. We focus in this paper on methods for the polyhedrization of implicit forms however it is worth mentioning approaches that reconstruct the zero-set surface of an implicit form, see *e.g.* [3] for a review. Approaches in this category focus on surface tessellation where we consider volumetric tessellations.

Evaluation. In the literature, 2D and 3D shape reconstruction techniques are mostly evaluated according to the *quality* of the constructed cells. This is indeed crucial for applications such as Finite Element Modeling. Quality is usually defined with respect to the shape of the cell [16]. In some cases the quality metrics reflect the fact that the cell should stay away from degenerate configurations. For instance, tetrahedra with at least one small angle are usually to be avoided [10]. In other cases, an ideal shape is defined, and the quality metrics are defined as distance to this ideal. This is the case with CVTs, for which the ideal cell shape is known to be a truncated octahedron as mentioned in [13]. In this work, the dimensionless second moment of a polytope is introduced and can be used as a measure of the regularity of a CVT cell [39]. Metrics have also been proposed for other types of cells, such as hexahedra [16], as well as algebraically for general cells [22].

A few works have investigated the geometric accuracy of a given reconstruction. Geometric accuracy can be defined as a distance between the boundaries of the given input form and of the volumetric reconstruction obtained. *Metro* [12], introduced in the context of mesh simplification, is a common tool to evaluate the distance between two triangulated surfaces. More recently and focusing on surface reconstruction, Berger et al. [4] have recently introduced better metrics based on discrete differential geometry concepts in order to quantitatively evaluate distances between an implicit surface and a surface mesh. We build on this work for accuracy evaluation.

In Sect. 4, we compare the shape tessellations obtained with Marching Cubes, Delaunay refinement and CVT approaches using both shape quality and geometric accuracy criteria. We also discuss the theoretical guarantees given by each approach, as well as their computation times.

3   CVT for Implicit Forms

Centroidal Voronoi Tessellations are used in shape modeling to discretize 2D and 3D shapes into polygonal and polyhedral cells, respectively, centered around points called *sites* and distributed inside the shapes. CVT cells optimally partition the input domain in the sense of k-means clusters minimizing a variance or quantification error [14]. To this purpose, CVT algorithms alternatively re-estimate site locations and their associated cells, in an iterative manner. Approaches exist that compute CVTs given explicit forms for shapes, usually meshes as in [27,39,41]. We consider here the case of shapes defined by implicit forms in 3D and also, more specifically, implicit forms obtained from point clouds, a frequent case when modeling shapes with visual observations.

3.1   Background

Given a finite set of n points $X = \{x_i\}_{i=1}^n$ in $\mathbb{R}^3$, called *sites*, the *Voronoi cell* or *Voronoi region* Ω_i of x_i is defined as follows:

$$\Omega_i = \{x \in \mathbb{R}^3 \mid \|x - x_i\| \leq \|x - x_j\|, \ \forall j \neq i\},$$

where $\|.\|$ denotes the Euclidean distance. The partition of $\mathbb{R}^3$ into Voronoi cells is called a *Voronoi tessellation*. A *clipped Voronoi tessellation* is then the intersection between the Voronoi tessellation and a volume $\mathcal{V} \in \mathbb{R}^3$ and a *centroidal Voronoi tessellation* (CVT) is a special type of clipped Voronoi tessellation where the site of each Voronoi cell Ω_i is also its center of mass or centroid, *i.e.*:

$$x_i = \frac{\int_{\Omega_i} x \, dx}{\int_{\Omega_i} dx}.$$

This property ensures that CVTs are local minima of the quantization error $E : \mathbb{R}^{3n} \to \mathbb{R}$ below, also called the CVT energy function or the distortion [14].

$$E(X) = \sum_{i=1}^n E_i(X) = \sum_{i=1}^n \int_{\Omega_i} \|x - x_i\|^2 \, dx. \tag{1}$$

3.2   Algorithm Overview

Our CVT algorithm considers as input an implicit function $f : \Omega \to \mathbb{R}$ defined over a domain $\Omega \in \mathbb{R}^3$ and such that $f(x) = 0$ on the boundary surface $\mathcal{S}$ of a shape $\mathcal{V}$. In the case of an indicator function, f has zero values outside $\mathcal{V}$ and the value 1 inside. The algorithm takes also as input the number of sites-cells n and follows the traditional CVT scheme below:

1. Initialization: find initial positions for the n sites inside $\mathcal{V}$.
2. Clipping: compute the Voronoi tessellation of the sites, then restrict it to $\mathcal{V}$ by computing its intersection with $\mathcal{S}$.
3. Optimization: update the position of the sites by minimizing the CVT energy function (1).

Steps 2 and 3 are iterated several times where the number of iterations is a user-defined parameter. Any initialization can, in principle, be applied here. In our experiments, the sites are randomly positioned inside $\mathcal{V}$. At the first iteration, the cells of the clipped Voronoi tessellation constructed after step 2 are not uniform nor regular (see Fig. 3(a)) and do not minimize the CVT energy (1). Step 3 optimizes therefore the site locations in order to minimize E. In the literature, the two main strategies for such minimization are Lloyd's gradient descent method and the L-BFGS quasi-Newton method [30]. In our approach, we choose the latter since it is known to be faster [30]. As shown in Fig. 3(b), once convergence is reached, the clipped Voronoi cells are almost uniform and regularly spaced. Besides, they yield a better approximation of the shape $\mathcal{V}$, as shown in Sect. 4.

3.3   Clipping

In order to clip a Voronoi tessellation with the implicit function f describing the shape $\mathcal{V}$, we introduce an algorithm that consists of the following main steps (see Fig. 2):

1. Given the unbounded Voronoi tessellation $\bigcup_i \Omega_i$ of the sites $\{x_i\}$, identify which cells Ω_i intersect the implicit surface $\mathcal{S}$ bounding $\mathcal{V}$.

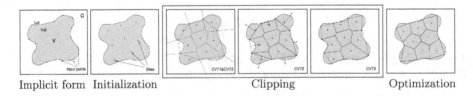

Implicit form   Initialization   Clipping   Optimization

Fig. 2. The different steps of the CVT algorithm. The clipping and optimization steps are iterated until the sites are stabilized.

(a)   (b)

Fig. 3. Voronoi tessellations of a torus with and without optimization. (a) A clipped Voronoi tessellation with random initial positions for the sites. (b) Clipped CVT after optimization.

2. For each of these boundary cells Ω_j,
   (a) Compute the intersection between the edges of Ω_j and $\mathcal{S}$, this intersection being represented as a set of points P_j (red dots in Fig. 2 CVT1 & CVT2).
   (b) Build the boundary clipped Voronoi cell Ω'_j as the convex hull of the intersection points in P_j and the vertices of Ω_j that are inside $\mathcal{V}$ (CVT1 in Fig. 2 CVT1 & CVT2).
   (c) (CVT-2 only) Add to each boundary cell the point at the intersection between $\mathcal{S}$ and the ray along the normal to Ω'_j. Rebuild Ω'_j by connecting it with other intersection points of P_j (CVT2 in Fig. 2).

Step 1 is carried out by first converting infinite Voronoi cells into finite cells using a bounding surface around $\mathcal{V}$ and second by detecting boundary cells as cells with at least one vertex outside $\mathcal{V}$. Step 2 is discussed below.

Intersections of Ω_j with $\mathcal{S}$. Boundary cells are convex polytopes composed of bounded polygons and segments. We first interpolate f values along segments to find their intersections with f. To this purpose, several strategies can be considered depending on the information available on f. When both function values and derivatives are available, Hermite interpolation can be used, as advocated in [17]. It provides fast and accurate interpolated values as long as the local approximation is valid. When only function values are available, linear interpolation, with for instance the false position algorithm, can be used to iteratively locate the intersection. In any cases, the bisection method can be applied. It is slower than the previous strategies but more robust. A combination of the bisection and Hermite methods can also be considered to first reduce the search space so that the Hermite approximation becomes more valid. Note that polyhedrization approaches are independent of the interpolation scheme and can all consider any of them. For the purpose of evaluation, and without loss of generality, we use the bisection method with all approaches in the comparisons presented in the evaluation Sect. 4.

Convex hull. Once the edge intersection points are determined, the clipped Voronoi cell is computed as the convex hull of the intersection points and the cell vertices inside the surface. Since Voronoi cells are convex, this is guaranteed to provide a boundary surface with a correct topology (see CVT1 & CVT2 in Fig. 2).

Sharp features. Sharp features, in case they occur, are not preserved by default by the clipping algorithm CVT1 (see Fig. 4 (a) for instance). This also true for Marching Cubes and Delaunay strategies for which specific solutions have been proposed, *e.g.* [23] and [11] respectively. CVT easily adapts to sharp features when identified as a list of points that can be simply assigned to their closest sites before the convex hull computation. This is a nice feature of the CVT strategy that is flexible and allows for such additional points without significantly increasing the complexity (only slightly modifying the convex hull computation) and while keeping the topological guarantees. This would be difficult to implement with the Marching Cubes or Delaunay strategies without fundamentally modifying the associated algorithms. Figure 4 (b) shows an example of such a reconstruction.

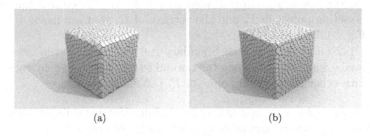

(a)   (b)

Fig. 4. Tessellations of the characteristic function of a cube: (a) CVT1 algorithm without additional points. (b) CVT2 algorithm with sharp feature points added.

4   Evaluation

In order to compare the different strategies for shape modeling mentioned different criteria can be considered. As emphasized in [32] for a similar evaluation, a given method will easily favor one of these criteria at the cost of the others, depending on the targeted application. In this work, our target is the reconstruction from implicit functions. This includes theoretical guarantees, the accuracy of the approximation with respect to the input implicit boundary surface, the quality of the resulting cells, and the time complexity.

4.1   Methodology

Methods. The four different methods we compare are the following:

- MC: the implementation of the Marching Cubes algorithm with topological guarantees [28];

– CGAL: the CGAL [7] implementation of the Delaunay tetrahedrization based algorithm, which uses the Delaunay refinement technique followed by mesh optimization to remove degenerated tetrahedra [20];

– CVT1[1]: a first proposed implementation of the clipped CVT algorithm, *i.e.* only Voronoi edge intersections with the surface are considered as surface points (see Sect. 3.3);

– CVT2(see footnote 1): an extension of CVT1 where an additional point which is the intersection between the surface and a ray estimated by boundary clipped Voronoi cell is added. (see Sect. 3.3).

To compare shape tessellations on a fair basis, similar resolutions, *i.e.* cell numbers, are required. While the resolution is easily imposed with CVT, which can be an advantage when similar shape discretizations are required, it is less easy with MC and space discretizations. In practice, we first compute the Marching Cubes tessellation. We then use $\sqrt{3}/2$ times the length of a cube as the targeted radius of a tetrahedron's circumsphere for the Delaunay tetrahedrization approach, in order for the size of this circumsphere to be similar to the size of the cube's circumsphere. For the CVT approaches, we simply sample randomly as many sites as the number of cubes inside the shape.

Data. Methods are first evaluated on a set of 97 object meshes, from the Princeton Segmentation Benchmark [9], for statistical comparisons on the accuracy (see Fig. 6). We next consider point clouds obtained from vision reconstructions and from which implicit forms are built. The DANCER (Fig. 5) was obtained with a multiview system followed by a Poisson implicit function estimation [7]. GARGOYLE (Fig. 1) was obtained with [4] and the three other shapes, KNEEL-INGLADY, AQUARIUS and SKULL, were obtained with [18] followed by the same Poisson estimation [7] (other implicit function estimation could be considered). DANCER's MC results are extracted from $50 \times 50 \times 50$ and $100 \times 100 \times 100$ voxel grid for different resolution tests. Others' MC results are from $100 \times 100 \times 100$ voxel grid.

4.2   Theoretical Guarantees

Two theoretical guarantees are in practice often required: the manifoldness of the output volumetric mesh and the topological correctness with respect to the input form. A k-manifold is a k-dimensional object which is locally homeomorphic to a k-dimensional disk. A k-manifold allows for non ambiguous definitions of geometrical quantities such as the local geodesic neighborhood of any point, which is critical in many shape processing applications. It allows for instance to smooth and deform shapes in a consistent way. Topological correctness is the fact that input and output shapes present the same topology, for example the same number of components. This is an important property when considering properties over sets of shapes.

---

[1] Source code will be released.

The original Marching Cubes algorithm [31] is known to produce surface meshes which can be non-manifold and which topology can differ from the input implicit surface. Many methods have been proposed to solve for non-manifoldness and topological ambiguities, see [33] for a survey. 2D Delaunay triangulations are known to be, under some sampling assumptions, good geometrical and topological approximations of the input shape [5]. This has been used for instance in order to robustly model surfaces evolving over time [35]. However, this is not the case in higher dimensions [34]. Thus, an additional post-processing step, such as [29], is required to guarantee manifoldness in the case of Delaunay tetrahedrizations. In contrast, a 3D CVT is manifold by construction: it is composed of convex 3D cells and on its surface every edge which is generated by the intersection of a bisector of CVT and the implicit surface is shared by exactly 2 faces because it belongs to a bisector.

4.3   Accuracy

The accuracy measures how close the estimated shape approximation is to the implicit form. To this aim we compare shape surfaces. The geometric similarity between two surfaces can be defined in several ways. Following the evaluation in [4], we consider distances between shapes in both directions and the following metrics:

- *Dmean*: the mean of distances between the input shape and the reconstructed surface in both directions;
- *Drms*: the root-mean-square (RMS) of these distances;
- *Nmean*: the mean angle deviation;
- *Nrms*: the RMS angle deviation.

Distances are estimated at points regularly distributed on both shapes and by searching for the closest point on the other shape in the facet normal directions. The same principle applies for normal angles that are estimated between closest points in the evaluation sets on both the input and the reconstructed surfaces. In order to build regular evaluation point sets, we use a particle system to sample implicit surfaces [4], and we compute 2D CVTs on the reconstructed boundary surface to generate sample points regularly distributed on both surfaces. Using a particle system and 2D CVTs to regularly distribute evaluation points on the surface ensures that we do not estimate distances between two discretizations of the input implicit surface at different scales, as can be the case with *Metro* [12].

4.4   Shape Quality

Besides the accuracy of the approximation, tessellations can also be compared with respect to the cell shape properties. Compactness, that ensures regularity, is for instance desirable for, *e.g.*, local discrete operations on shapes such as deformations or quantification optimality. We first assess cell regularity for the Marching Cubes and CVT approaches (Delaunay tetrahedra are not compact by construction). For Delaunay tetrahedrizations, we compare them to CVTs using the dual tetrahedrizations of CVTs and boundary triangle quality metrics. Dual tetrahedrizations are computed by projecting the sites of the boundary Voronoi cells on the surface and then optimizing their position as in [41].

Cell regularity. Marching Cubes-generated tessellations are mostly made of cubes, however the boundary cells may be very irregular. In order to assess cell regularity, following [39] we use the criterion G_3 for polytopes referred to as the *dimensionless second moment* of the cell by Conway and Sloane [13]. The definition of G_3 for a cell Ω is:

$$G_3(\Omega) = \frac{\int_\Omega \|x - \hat{x}\|^2 \, dx}{3Vol(\Omega)^{5/3}}$$

where $\hat{x}$ is the centroid of the cell and $Vol(\Omega)$ its volume. $G_3(\Omega)$ reflects how far Ω is from the optimal quantizer in three dimensions. Hence, this criterion intuitively accounts for the compactness of the cell.

Tetrahedron quality. We use four standard quality metrics for tetrahedra [41]:

- VQ_1: minimum dihedral angle of the tetrahedron;
- VQ_2: maximum dihedral angle;
- VQ_3: radius-ratio, defined as $\frac{3r_i}{r_c}$, where r_i and r_c are the radii of the inscribed and circumscribed spheres, respectively;
- VQ_4: meshing quality, defined as $\frac{12\sqrt[3]{9V^2}}{\sum l_{i,j}^2}$, where V is the volume of the tetrahedron and $l_{i,j}$ is the length of an edge i, j of the tetrahedron.

Boundary triangle quality. Four similar criteria are used for boundary triangles:

- SQ_1: minimum angle of the triangle;
- SQ_2: maximum angle;
- SQ_3: radius-ratio, defined as $\frac{2r_i}{r_c}$, where r_i and r_c are the radii of the inscribed and circumscribed circles, respectively;
- SQ_4: meshing quality, defined as $\frac{4\sqrt{3S}}{\sum l_{i,j}^2}$ where S is the area of the triangle and $l_{i,j}$ is the length of an edge i, j of the triangle.

4.5 Results and Discussion

Accuracy. We first compare methods on a set of various shapes: 97 meshes taken from the Princeton Benchmark [9]. These meshes belong to 5 different categories and the algorithms have been run with a fixed resolution for a given category, which can however vary over categories: 50^3, 80^3 and 100^3 for the Marching Cubes. The number of sites for CVT is taken as the number of inner cubes with MC, this for each mesh. Results in Fig. 6 show method rankings with respect the accuracy criteria defined previously. It demonstrates that CVT approaches are statistically significantly better than MC and Delaunay.

Accuracy quantitative have also been conducted on the mentioned vision datasets (see Table 2). Additionally, qualitative results are color-coded in Fig. 1 and Fig. 5. In these experiments, 10 iterations are performed for both Delaunay tetrahedrization and CVT approaches. CGAL failed to compute a tetrahedrization on the GARGOYLE and SKULL datasets (the process was stopped after 18 h of computation). These results show that CVT2 performs better than other approaches on all our experiments. On point datasets that describe smooth shapes (DANCER and GARGOYLE), CVT1 performs better than Marching Cubes even without the optimization step.

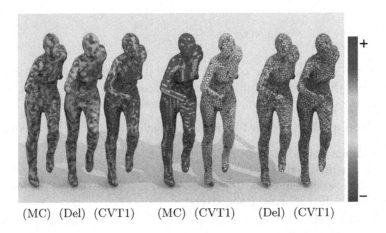

(MC) (Del) (CVT1)   (MC) (CVT1)   (Del) (CVT1)

Fig. 5. Accuracy (left), cell regularity (middle) and tetrahedron quality (right) of 3D implicit form tessellations with MC, Delaunay refinement (Del) and CVT1.

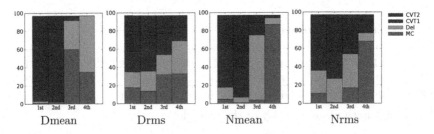

Dmean   Drms   Nmean   Nrms

Fig. 6. Accuracy rankings on 100 meshes from the Princeton Benchmark [9]. Implicit forms were obtained using Poisson reconstructions [7] and accuracies measured on samples obtained using the particle system approach [4].

Shape Quality. Table 2 shows the maximum $Gmax$ and the mean $Gmean$ values of the cell regularity $G_3(\Omega)$ over all cells of Marching Cubes and CVTs tessellations. These results show the benefit of optimizing site positions to generate more regular cells. The mean tetrahedron and boundary triangle quality measures are given in Table 3. According to our experiments, the CVT approach gives better results than the Delaunay tetrahedrization for all of them.

Table 1. Computational time (s) for each experiment.

Method	DANCERLOW	DANCER	AQUARIUS	KNEELINGLADY	GARGOYLE	SKULL
MC	0.1	0.6	1.6	1.1	1.3	1.9
CGAL (10 it.)	1036	1052	162	198	-	-
CVT1 (0 it.)	0.4	1.4	7.2	7.4	9.1	18
CVT1 (10 it.)	4.9	25	135	123	160	342
CVT2 (10 it.)	5.1	25	136	125	165	363

Table 2. Accuracy and regularity results on the datasets. (Dmean, Drms, Gmax, Gmean) $\times 10^{-2}$.

Dataset (nb of sites)	Method	Dmean	Drms	Nmean	Nrms	Gmax	Gmean	CVT2
DANCER LOW (2365)	MC	27.16	29.72	1.31	1.41	3210	19.30	
	CGAL (10 it.)	27.12	29.72	1.30	1.41	-	-	
	CVT1 (0 it.)	27.14	29.67	1.31	1.41	1647	11.00	
	CVT1 (10 it.)	27.13	29.66	1.30	1.41	11.84	8.18	
	CVT2 (10 it.)	27.05	29.64	1.30	1.41	11.84	8.15	
DANCER (14474)	MC	22.10	25.46	1.14	1.25	5999	14.49	
	CGAL (10 it.)	21.72	25.11	1.14	1.25	-	-	
	CVT1 (0 it.)	21.86	25.41	1.13	1.25	75.85	9.75	
	CVT1 (10 it.)	21.76	25.25	1.12	1.24	9.82	8.07	
	CVT2 (10 it.)	21.16	25.29	1.12	1.24	9.82	8.03	
AQUARIUS (64588)	MC	21.64	23.99	1.32	1.42	29825	12.17	
	CGAL (10 it.)	21.65	23.99	1.32	1.42	-	-	
	CVT1 (10 it.)	21.83	24.14	1.33	1.42	13.17	8.16	
	CVT2 (10 it.)	21.59	23.94	1.31	1.41	13.02	8.15	
KNEELING LADY (73150)	MC	2.55	3.98	0.40	0.63	5870	11.80	
	CGAL (10 it.)	2.60	3.83	0.40	0.63	-	-	
	CVT1 (10 it.)	2.58	4.00	0.40	0.63	19.05	8.16	
	CVT2 (10 it.)	2.50	3.93	0.39	0.62	19.05	8.15	
GARGOYLE (106497)	MC	0.38	0.54	0.20	0.29	54467	12.65	
	CVT1 (10 it.)	0.38	0.54	0.19	0.28	10.20	8.02	
	CVT2 (10 it.)	0.37	0.53	0.19	0.28	10.19	8.00	
SKULL (225034)	MC	7.12	9.76	0.82	1.00	82716	11.26	
	CVT1 (10 it.)	7.15	9.81	0.83	1.00	17.87	8.07	
	CVT2 (10 it.)	7.07	9.67	0.82	1.00	17.56	8.06	

Table 3. Mean tetrahedron quality measures over all cells of the tessellation and mean triangle quality measures over all boundary triangles of the tessellation (best result in bold).

Dataset	Method	$\overline{VQ_1}$	$\overline{VQ_2}$	$\overline{VQ_3}$	$\overline{VQ_4}$	$\overline{SQ_1}$	$\overline{SQ_2}$	$\overline{SQ_3}$	$\overline{SQ_4}$
DANCER	CGAL (10 it.)	50.75	96.48	0.84	0.90	47.92	75.13	0.93	0.94
	CVT1 (10 it.)	**51.32**	**95.49**	**0.85**	**0.91**	**52.56**	**69.23**	**0.97**	**0.97**
AQUARIUS	CGAL (10 it.)	51.35	95.89	0.83	0.90	47.73	75.37	0.92	0.94
	CVT1 (10 it.)	**51.55**	**95.33**	**0.84**	**0.92**	**52.56**	**69.23**	**0.97**	**0.97**
KNEELING LADY	CGAL (10 it.)	51.54	95.71	0.83	0.90	48.32	74.59	0.93	0.94
	CVT1 (10 it.)	**51.63**	**95.16**	**0.84**	**0.92**	**50.95**	**71.27**	**0.96**	**0.96**

Computation Times. Timings are shown in Table 1. CGAL fails to compute a tetrahedrization for the GARGOYLE and the SKULL datasets. The Marching Cubes algorithm is the fastest of the four tested methods, as a result of the increased complexity of Delaunay and Voronoi tessellation computations. It has to be mentioned that most of the computation time of CVT approach lies in the 3D Delaunay triangulation (dual of CVT) which is costly and cannot be avoided (it takes about 70 % of the CVT computation time en average). The CVT approach performs anyway always faster than the Delaunay tetrahedrization.

5   Conclusion

We have presented a comparison of different strategies to convert an implicit form in 3D into an explicit shape representation. This includes a new strategy that uses Centroidal Voronoi Tessellations to build a 3D mesh composed of convex Voronoi cells around a pre-defined number of sites. The evaluation shows that CVTs provide the most accurate and the most regular shape tessellations when compared to Marching Cubes and Delaunay refinement strategies. As such, CVTs are a good alternative to Marching cubes, in particular when modeling dynamic scenes for which accuracy, regularity and invariance to rigid transformation are desirable properties of shape tessellation. Delaunay refinement, while providing boundary surfaces with *good* triangles does not outperform CVTs nor Marching cubes in any case. Finally, Marching cubes is always the fastest strategy, hence a solution for applications requiring fast solutions, though less accurate and regular than CVTs.

References

1. Allain, B., Franco, J.S., Boyer, E.: An efficient volumetric framework for shape tracking. In: Proceedings of the IEEE Conference on Computer Vision and Pattern Recognition, pp. 268–276. IEEE (2015)

2. Alliez, P., Cohen-Steiner, D., Yvinec, M., Desbrun, M.: Variational tetrahedral meshing. In: ACM Transactions on Graphics (TOG), vol. 24, pp. 617–625. ACM (2005)
3. de Araujo, B., Lopes, D.S., Jepp, P., Jorge, J.A., Wyvill, B.: A survey on implicit surface polygonization. ACM Comput. Surv. (CSUR) **47**(4), 60 (2015)
4. Berger, M., Levine, J.A., Nonato, L.G., Taubin, G., Silva, C.T.: A benchmark for surface reconstruction. ACM Trans. Graph. (TOG) **32**(2), 20 (2013)
5. Boissonnat, J.D., Oudot, S.: Provably good sampling and meshing of surfaces. Graph. Models **67**(5), 405–451 (2005)
6. Carr, H., Theußl, T., Möller, T.: Isosurfaces on optimal regular samples. In: ACM International Conference Proceeding Series, vol. 40, pp. 39–48. Citeseer (2003)
7. CGAL: Computational Geometry Algorithms Library. http://www.cgal.org/
8. Chan, S.L., Purisima, E.O.: A new tetrahedral tesselation scheme for isosurface generation. Comput. Graph. **22**(1), 83–90 (1998)
9. Chen, X., Golovinskiy, A., Funkhouser, T.: A benchmark for 3d mesh segmentation. In: ACM Transactions on Graphics (TOG), vol. 28, p. 73. ACM (2009)
10. Cheng, S.W., Dey, T.K., Edelsbrunner, H., Facello, M.A., Teng, S.H.: Silver exudation. J. ACM (JACM) **47**(5), 883–904 (2000)
11. Cheng, S.W., Dey, T.K., Ramos, E.A.: Delaunay refinement for piecewise smooth complexes. Discrete Comput. Geom. **43**(1), 121–166 (2010)
12. Cignoni, P., Rocchini, C., Scopigno, R.: Metro: measuring error on simplified surfaces. In: Computer Graphics Forum, vol. 17, pp. 167–174. Wiley Online Library (1998)
13. Conway, J., Sloane, N.: Voronoi regions of lattices, second moments of polytopes, and quantization. IEEE Trans. Inf. Theor. **28**(2), 211–226 (1982)
14. Du, Q., Faber, V., Gunzburger, M.: Centroidal voronoi tessellations: applications and algorithms. SIAM Rev. **41**(4), 637–676 (1999)
15. Esteban, C.H., Schmitt, F.: Silhouette and stereo fusion for 3d object modeling. Comput. Vis. Image Underst. **96**(3), 367–392 (2004)
16. Field, D.A.: Qualitative measures for initial meshes. Int. J. Numer. Meth. Eng. **47**(4), 887–906 (2000)
17. Fuhrmann, S., Kazhdan, M., Goesele, M.: Accurate isosurface interpolation with hermite data. In: 2015 International Conference on 3D Vision (3DV), pp. 256–263. IEEE (2015)
18. Furukawa, Y., Ponce, J.: Accurate, dense, and robust multiview stereopsis. IEEE Trans. Pattern Anal. Mach. Intell. **32**(8), 1362–1376 (2010)
19. Huang, C.H., Allain, B., Franco, J.S., Navab, N., Ilic, S., Boyer, E.: Volumetric 3d tracking by detection. In: Proceedings of the IEEE Conference on Computer Vision and Pattern Recognition. IEEE (2016)
20. Jamin, C., Alliez, P., Yvinec, M., Boissonnat, J.D.: Cgalmesh: a generic framework for delaunay mesh generation. ACM Trans. Math. Softw. (TOMS) **41**(4), 23 (2015)
21. Kazhdan, M., Klein, A., Dalal, K., Hoppe, H.: Unconstrained isosurface extraction on arbitrary octrees. In: Symposium on Geometry Processing, vol. 7, pp. 256–263 (2007)
22. Knupp, P.M.: Algebraic mesh quality metrics. SIAM J. Sci. Comput. **23**(1), 193–218 (2001)
23. Kobbelt, L.P., Botsch, M., Schwanecke, U., Seidel, H.P.: Feature sensitive surface extraction from volume data. In: Proceedings of the 28th Annual Conference on Computer Graphics and Interactive Techniques, pp. 57–66. ACM (2001)

24. Labatut, P., Pons, J.P., Keriven, R.: Robust and efficient surface reconstruction from range data. In: Computer Graphics Forum, vol. 28, pp. 2275–2290. Wiley Online Library (2009)

25. Labelle, F., Shewchuk, J.R.: Isosurface stuffing: fast tetrahedral meshes with good dihedral angles. In: ACM Transactions on Graphics (TOG), vol. 26, p. 57. ACM (2007)

26. Lempitsky, V.: Surface extraction from binary volumes with higher-order smoothness. In: Proceedings of the IEEE Conference on Computer Vision and Pattern Recognition, pp. 1197–1204. IEEE (2010)

27. Lévy, B.: Restricted voronoi diagrams for (re)-meshing surfaces and volumes. In: 8th International Conference on Curves and Surfaces, vol. 6, p. 14 (2014)

28. Lewiner, T., Lopes, H., Vieira, A.W., Tavares, G.: Efficient implementation of marching cubes' cases with topological guarantees. J. Graph. Tools 8(2), 1–15 (2003)

29. Lhuillier, M.: 2-manifold tests for 3d delaunay triangulation-based surface reconstruction. J. Math. Imag. Vis. 51(1), 98–105 (2015)

30. Liu, Y., Wang, W., Lévy, B., Sun, F., Yan, D.M., Lu, L., Yang, C.: On centroidal voronoi tessellation energy smoothness and fast computation. ACM Trans. Graph. (ToG) 28(4), 101 (2009)

31. Lorensen, W.E., Cline, H.E.: Marching cubes: a high resolution 3d surface construction algorithm. In: ACM Siggraph Computer Graphics, vol. 21, pp. 163–169. ACM (1987)

32. Meyer, M., Kirby, R.M., Whitaker, R.: Topology, accuracy, and quality of isosurface meshes using dynamic particles. IEEE Trans. Vis. Comput. Graph. 13(6), 1704–1711 (2007)

33. Newman, T.S., Yi, H.: A survey of the marching cubes algorithm. Comput. Graph. 30(5), 854–879 (2006)

34. Oudot, S.Y.: On the topology of the restricted delaunay triangulation and witness complex in higher dimensions. arXiv preprint arXiv:0803.1296 (2008)

35. Pons, J.P., Boissonnat, J.D.: Delaunay deformable models: topology-adaptive meshes based on the restricted delaunay triangulation. In: 2007 IEEE Conference on Computer Vision and Pattern Recognition, pp. 1–8. IEEE (2007)

36. Shewchuk, J.R.: Tetrahedral mesh generation by delaunay refinement. In: Proceedings of the Fourteenth Annual Symposium on Computational Geometry, pp. 86–95. ACM (1998)

37. Sinha, S.N., Mordohai, P., Pollefeys, M.: Multi-view stereo via graph cuts on the dual of an adaptive tetrahedral mesh. In: 2007 IEEE 11th International Conference on Computer Vision, pp. 1–8. IEEE (2007)

38. Tournois, J., Wormser, C., Alliez, P., Desbrun, M.: Interleaving delaunay refinement and optimization for practical isotropic tetrahedron mesh generation. ACM Trans. Graph. 28(3), 75:1–75:9 (2009)

39. Wang, L., Hétroy-Wheeler, F., Boyer, E.: A hierarchical approach for regular centroidal voronoi tessellations. In: Computer Graphics Forum, vol. 35, pp. 152–165. Wiley Online Library (2016)

40. Wu, Z., Song, S., Khosla, A., Yu, F., Zhang, L., Tang, X., Xiao, J.: 3d shapenets: a deep representation for volumetric shapes. In: Proceedings of the IEEE Conference on Computer Vision and Pattern Recognition, pp. 1912–1920. IEEE (2015)

41. Yan, D.M., Wang, W., Lévy, B., Liu, Y.: Efficient computation of clipped voronoi diagram for mesh generation. Comput. Aided Des. 45(4), 843–852 (2013)

Multi-attributed Graph Matching
with Multi-layer Random Walks

Han-Mu Park and Kuk-Jin Yoon$^{(\boxtimes)}$

Gwangju Institute of Science and Technology, Gwangju, Korea
{hanmu,kjyoon}@gist.ac.kr

Abstract. This paper addresses the multi-attributed graph matching problem considering multiple attributes jointly while preserving the characteristics of each attribute. Since most of conventional graph matching algorithms integrate multiple attributes to construct a single attribute in an oversimplified way, the information from multiple attributes are not often fully exploited. In order to solve this problem, we propose a novel multi-layer graph structure that can preserve the particularities of each attribute in separated layers. Then, we also propose a multi-attributed graph matching algorithm based on the random walk centrality for the proposed multi-layer graph structure. We compare the proposed algorithm with other state-of-the-art graph matching algorithms based on the single-layer structure using synthetic and real datasets, and prove the superior performance of the proposed multi-layer graph structure and matching algorithm.

Keywords: Graph matching · Multi-layer structure · Multiple attributes

1 Introduction

Graph structure has been widely adopted to model various problems in computer vision such as categorization [1,2], detection and tracking [3–5], and shape matching [6–8], because a graph can effectively reduce the ambiguity caused by various deformations and outliers thanks to the structured information. A graph structure consists of a set of vertices, edges, and attributes. Here, attributes are associated values with vertices or edges belonging to the graph. In a feature point matching application, for example, feature points can be defined as vertices, and the pairwise relations between feature points can be established as edges. Then, vertex attributes describe the appearances of feature points such as color and gradient information [9,10], and edge attributes describe geometric relations between pairs of feature points such as angle and distance [1,8–12]. Since an attribute assigns distinctiveness to each of vertices or edges, the definition of attributes enormously affects matching performance.

Multiple attributes are often employed simultaneously because a single attribute is not capable of representing the complex properties of image contents in general. Most of graph matching algorithms [1,4,6,8–10,12] integrate

© Springer International Publishing AG 2016
B. Leibe et al. (Eds.): ECCV 2016, Part III, LNCS 9907, pp. 189–204, 2016.
DOI: 10.1007/978-3-319-46487-9_12

multiple attributes to construct a single attribute, and there are two common ways of attribute integration: attribute-level and affinity-level integration. The attribute-level integration combines multiple attributes at an attribute description step in order to establish a new attribute containing the whole information of multiple attributes. After that, affinity values of matching candidates are computed by using the integrated attributes. An example for this type of integration is Histogram-Attributed Relational Graph (HARG) proposed by Cho *et al.* [1]. In HARG representation, each edge is defined with the log-polar histogram that is constructed by concatenating a log-distance histogram and a polar-angle histogram. On the other hand, the affinity-level integration is performed at an affinity computation step. Firstly, each of affinity values is computed for each attribute, then multiple affinity values are integrated to construct a unified affinity value. For example, Zhou *et al.* [10] and Yan *et al.* [9] define two types of affinity based on the differences in distance and angle between vertices, and then linearly integrate the values to construct affinity between matching candidates. However, the problem is that, although integrations are performed at various stages, information from multiple attributes are not fully exploited in most cases; because the integration process is likely to oversimplify the characteristics of attributes.

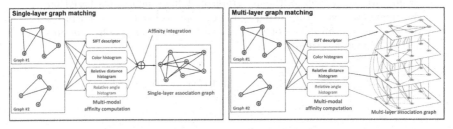

(a) Single-layer graph matching with multiple attributes

(b) Multi-layer graph matching with multiple attributes (proposed)

Fig. 1. Two types of formulation for graph matching problems with multiple attributes. (a) The multiple attributes are integrated, and then an affinity matrix is constructed. (b) The multiple attributes are separately represented, and affinity matrices are constructed for multiple layers that are linked to one another (rank-4 tensor form).

In this paper, we propose a multi-layer graph matching algorithm that considers multiple attributes jointly while preserving the characteristics of each attribute. The main contribution of this paper is twofold. First, we propose a multi-layer structure to represent the multiple attributes as described in Fig. 1. The proposed structure consists of multiple layers in which each layer represents a single attribute and multiple layers are closely linked to one another. While the single-layer structure can lose important information during the attribute integration process, the proposed structure can preserve the characteristics of each attribute in multiple separated layers. Second, we propose a novel multi-attributed graph matching algorithm based on the random walk centrality concept for the proposed multi-layer graph structure. To obtain centrality values of matching candidates, the random walkers traverse the multi-layer association graph according to the transition probability that is derived from pairwise attributes.

The rest of this paper is organized as follows. First, Sect. 2 gives an overview of related works. Section 3 provides explanations on the problem formulation and the proposed multi-layer structure. Then, we explain details of the proposed matching algorithm in Sect. 4. Finally, experimental results are presented in Sect. 5.

2   Related Works

The multi-layer network structure has been studied in the field of network theory for several decades [13] to represent complicated relations in the natural environment. The network consists of multiple layers that describe various aspects of relations and are closely connected to each other. In order to analyze multi-layer networks, several diagnostics have been proposed in previous researches [13], such as vertex degree and path. Especially, *centrality* is one of the most frequently used concepts, and is employed to identify the importance of each vertex (*e.g.* degree or sum of distances from other vertices). In order to compute the centrality for each vertex, random walk-based methods have attracted appreciable interest as in [13–16], because it is intuitive and easy to interpret various centrality concepts. For example, PageRank [15] employs the random walk centrality to measure the ranks of webpages. Each random walker moves along contained hyperlinks, then the stationary distribution of the walkers on the webpage network is defined as their ranks. Moreover, Domenico *et al.* [17] and Solé-Ribalta *et al.* [16] proposed its generalized versions for an undirected multiplex network structure. In these algorithms, random walkers can move from any vertex to any other vertices in different layers with given transition probabilities.

Interestingly, Cho *et al.* [11] provided a connection between the concept of random walk centrality and graph matching problems, which is called Reweighted Random Walk Matching (RRWM). In order to formulate the graph matching problem, they employed an association graph structure. As described in Fig. 1(a), each of possible matching candidates is defined as the vertex of the association graph, and the pairwise relation between two matches is described as an edge. Then, similarly to the random walk centrality computation process, random walkers traverse the association graph along the edges. Finally, the correct correspondences can be obtained from the stationary distribution of the walkers. They presented that the random walk view of a graph matching problem has the same form with a classical spectral graph matching formulation [6,8,12].

Our work is inspired by the random walk centrality measure for the multi-layer structure and RRWM for graph matching. Based on these, we propose a multi-layer association graph structure for multiple attributes, and then identify trustful correspondences based on the random walk centrality concept.

3   Multi-layer Graph Structure

In this section, we propose a multi-layer graph structure to consider multiple attributes while preserving their characteristics independently. First, we introduce single-layer graph matching formulations for conventional graph structures, and then generalize the formulation for the multi-layer graph structure.

3.1   Single-Layer Graph Matching Problem

In single-layer graph matching problems, an attributed graph $\mathcal{G}$ is defined as $\mathcal{G}(\mathcal{V}, \mathcal{E}, \mathcal{A})$, where $\mathcal{V}$ and $\mathcal{E}$ represent vertices and edges respectively, and $\mathcal{A}$ is a set of single-type attributes that describe vertices and edges. Most applications need multiple attributes to describe complex properties. Nonetheless, the single-layer structure can handle the cases, because multiple attributes can be regarded as a single-type attribute by various integration methods [1,4,6,8–10,12] as described in Fig. 1(a).

In order to define a correspondence problem for given two graphs $\mathcal{G}^P$ and $\mathcal{G}^Q$, Lawler's quadratic assignment problem (QAP) formulation [8,10–12] is widely employed, which consists of an assignment matrix $\mathbf{X}$ and an affinity matrix $\mathbf{W}$. $\mathbf{X}$ is an $N^P \times N^Q$ matrix, where N^P and N^Q are numbers of vertices in $\mathcal{G}^P$ and $\mathcal{G}^Q$ respectively, and represents possible correspondences. Each element of the matrix, $\mathbf{X}_{i;a}$, is a binary value indicating the correspondence relation between $v_i^P \in \mathcal{V}^P$ and $v_a^Q \in \mathcal{V}^Q$. For example, $\mathbf{X}_{i;a} = 1$ when v_i^P is matched with v_a^Q, and $\mathbf{X}_{i;a} = 0$ otherwise. On the other hand, $\mathbf{W}$ is an $N^P N^Q \times N^P N^Q$ matrix that describes structural information of matching candidates. A non-diagonal elements of the matrix, $\mathbf{W}_{ia;jb}$, indicates a *pairwise affinity* between two matching candidates (v_i^P, v_a^Q) and (v_j^P, v_b^Q), and each diagonal element, $\mathbf{W}_{ia;ia}$, indicates a *unary affinity* of a matching candidate (v_i^P, v_a^Q). Then, a graph matching problem can be formulated as a QAP as follows:

$$\hat{\mathbf{x}} = arg \max_{\mathbf{x}}(\mathbf{x}^\top \mathbf{W} \mathbf{x}),$$

$$s.t. \quad \mathbf{x} \in \{0,1\}^{N^P N^Q}, \quad \forall i \sum_{a=1}^{N^Q} \mathbf{x}_{ia} \le 1, \quad \forall a \sum_{i=1}^{N^P} \mathbf{x}_{ia} \le 1, \tag{1}$$

where $\mathbf{x}$ is an $N^P N^Q$ dimensional vector that is originated from $\mathbf{X}$ by columnwise vectorization, and the inequality constraints represent the one-to-one matching constraint between $\mathcal{G}^P$ and $\mathcal{G}^Q$. Since the QAP is an NP-hard problem, efficient algorithms which guarantee an optimal solution are unknown. For this reason, recent researches [8,10–12,18] have aimed at finding an approximated solution by relaxing the constraints in various ways.

As mentioned earlier, Cho *et al.* [11] presented the viewpoint which interprets the single-layer graph matching problem as a random walk centrality computation problem by constructing a single-layer association graph $\mathcal{G}^S(\mathcal{V}^S, \mathcal{E}^S, \mathcal{A}^S)$. In this viewpoint, each matching candidate (v_i^P, v_a^Q) is considered as a node $v_{ia}^S \in \mathcal{V}^S$, and a relation between two vertices v_{ia}^S and v_{jb}^S is considered as an edge $e_{ia;jb}^{S} \in \mathcal{E}^{S}$. Their attributes $a_{ia;jb}^{S} \in \mathcal{A}^{S}$ are defined from the affinity values $\mathbf{W}_{ia;jb}$. Because these attributes do not directly reflect the node-to-node transition probability, the probabilistic transformation process for the association graph is required to describe the traversal of random walkers. For this purpose, Cho *et al.* [11] proposed an affinity preserving normalization method that adopts a concept of absorbing Markov chain. First, the maximum degree d_{max} is computed as Eq. (2) to preserve the original relations among affinity values while constructing the probabilistic network. Then, $\mathbf{W}$ is normalized by using d_{max} as following:

$$\widetilde{\mathbf{W}} = \tfrac{1}{d_{max}}\mathbf{W}, \quad s.t. \quad d_{max} = \max_i \mathbf{d}_i = \max_i \textstyle\sum_k \mathbf{W}_{ik}. \tag{2}$$

In order to describe the centrality value of each vertex, a distribution vector of random walkers $\mathbf{x}$ is defined as an $N^P N^Q$ dimensional vector. Then, all of the random walkers simultaneously and iteratively traverse the network based on the transition probability defined in $\widetilde{\mathbf{W}}$ until reaching to the stationary distribution $\bar{\mathbf{x}}$. Finally, the optimal solution $\hat{\mathbf{x}}$ can be obtained from $\bar{\mathbf{x}}$ by adopting any discretization methods such as Hungarian algorithm [19].

3.2 Multi-layer Graph Matching Problem

In this section, we propose a multi-layer association graph structure to jointly describe multiple attributes while preserving characteristics of each attribute. The proposed multi-layer association graph $\mathcal{G}^{M}(\mathcal{V}^{M}, \mathcal{E}^{M}, \mathcal{L}^{M}, \mathcal{A}^{M})$ is inspired from the multiplex network structure [13,16,17] that is frequently adopted to describe the complex networks which have multiple types of connections, such as social network. The multiplex network structure consists of multiple layers that share an index set of nodes (*e.g.* the IDs of people in a social network), and the relations between the nodes are independently defined for each layer. Each node can be connected to other nodes through two types of links: *intra-layer* and *inter-layer* links. The *intra-layer* links indicate the connection between two nodes in the same layer, and the *inter-layer* links indicate the connection between two nodes in different layers.

Similarly, the proposed association graph $\mathcal{G}^{M}$ consists of multiple layers that share the same index set of matching candidates as described in Fig. 1(b). Each vertex $v_{ia}^{\alpha} \in \mathcal{V}^{M}$ is distinguished from other vertices according to the layer index (*e.g.* $v_{ia}^{\alpha} \neq v_{ia}^{\beta}$, where $\alpha, \beta \in \mathcal{L}^{M}$ are layer indices when $\mathcal{L}^{M}$ denotes a set of layer indices). Each edge $e_{ia;jb}^{\alpha;\beta} \in \mathcal{E}^{M}$ should be represented with the layer indices because the vertices are identified by not only the vertex indices but also the layer indices. Similarly to the multiplex network structure, the *intra-layer* edges $e_{ia;jb}^{\alpha;\alpha}$ are defined for the connections between the vertices in the same layer, and the *inter-layer* edges $e_{ia;ia}^{\alpha;\beta}$ are defined for the connections between the same-indexed vertices in different layers.

According to the definition of multi-layer association graph structure, the affinity information can be represented as a rank-4 tensor $\mathbf{\Pi}$. Each element of the tensor, $\mathbf{\Pi}_{ia;jb}^{\alpha;\beta}$, describes an affinity value between two matching candidates v_{ia}^{α}

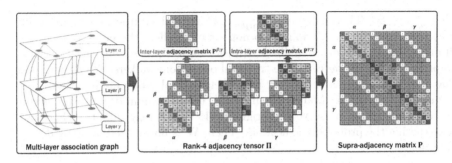

Fig. 2. Supra-adjacency matrix $\mathbf{P}$ constructed from the multi-layer association graph $\mathcal{G}^M$ and the adjacency tensor $\mathbf{\Pi}$

to v_{jb}^{β}. Similarly, the assignment information can be also represented as a rank-2 tensor $\mathbf{T}$. Because the high-rank tensor form is hard to understand intuitively, an unfolding method that converts the high-rank tensor to a lower rank matrix is frequently adopted [16,20–22]. For example, an $N^P N^Q \times L$ dimensional rank-2 assignment tensor (matrix) $\mathbf{T}$ can be unfolded to an $N^P N^Q L \times 1$ dimensional rank-1 assignment tensor (vector) $\mathbf{t}$, where L is the number of layers. In the same manner, $\mathbf{\Pi}$ can be also unfolded to an $N^P N^Q L \times N^P N^Q L$ dimensional rank-2 tensor $\mathbf{P}$. This flattened matrix $\mathbf{P}$ is called *supra-adjacency matrix* [16,20,21], which consists of two types of block adjacency matrices as illustrated in Fig. 2. The detailed information about the block matrix construction is presented in Sect. 3.3. Finally, the multi-attributed graph matching problem can be formulated as

$$\hat{\mathbf{t}} = arg\max_{\mathbf{t}}\left(\mathbf{t}^{\top}\mathbf{P}\mathbf{t}\right),$$

$$s.t. \begin{cases} \mathbf{t} \in \{0,1\}^{N^P N^Q L}, \\ \forall i \sum_{\alpha=1}^{L}\sum_{a=1}^{N^Q} \mathbf{t}_{ia}^{\alpha} \le 1, \quad \forall a \sum_{\alpha=1}^{L}\sum_{i=1}^{N^P} \mathbf{t}_{ia}^{\alpha} \le 1, \end{cases} \tag{3}$$

where the one-to-one constraints are adopted to the layer-wise integrated solution because matching candidates (vertices) $\mathcal{V}^M$ are shared across all layers. In Sect. 4, we propose a novel graph matching algorithm to solve this problem.

3.3   Supra-Transition Matrix Construction

The *supra-adjacency matrix* consists of two types of block matrices: intra-layer and inter-layer adjacency matrix. The intra-layer adjacency matrix $\mathbf{P}^{\alpha;\alpha}$ describes the edges between vertices in the same layer, and the inter-layer adjacency matrix $\mathbf{P}^{\alpha;\beta}$ describes the edges between vertices in different layers. Each of block matrices is constructed according to the definitions of proposed multi-layer graph structure. Then, the *supra-adjacency matrix* $\mathbf{P}$ can be expressed by arranging the block matrices according to their layer index as following:

$$P = \begin{pmatrix} P^{\alpha;\alpha} & P^{\beta;\alpha} & \dots & P^{\omega;\alpha} \\ P^{\alpha;\beta} & P^{\beta;\beta} & \dots & P^{\omega;\beta} \\ \vdots & \vdots & \ddots & \vdots \\ P^{\alpha;\omega} & P^{\beta;\omega} & \dots & P^{\omega;\omega} \end{pmatrix}. \tag{4}$$

In order to apply the random walk centrality concept, P should be converted into a transition matrix $\widetilde{P}$ that describes the transition probabilities of all vertices. Since P consists of multiple types of layers that contain distinctive characteristics (e.g. different scales), the stochastic normalization of whole matrix is a difficult process. Fortunately, however, thanks to the block structure of the *supra-adjacency matrix*, the separate normalization of each block matrix can be applied. Therefore, we first adopt block-wise normalization for the affinity scaling to get P', and then construct the *supra-transition matrix* $\widetilde{P}$ by applying the affinity preserving normalization [11] again as follows:

$$\widetilde{P} = \frac{1}{d_{max}} P' = \frac{1}{d_{max}} \begin{pmatrix} \widetilde{P}^{\alpha;\alpha} & \widetilde{P}^{\beta;\alpha} & \dots & \widetilde{P}^{\omega;\alpha} \\ \widetilde{P}^{\alpha;\beta} & \widetilde{P}^{\beta;\beta} & \dots & \widetilde{P}^{\omega;\beta} \\ \vdots & \vdots & \ddots & \vdots \\ \widetilde{P}^{\alpha;\omega} & \widetilde{P}^{\beta;\omega} & \dots & \widetilde{P}^{\omega;\omega} \end{pmatrix}, \tag{5}$$

$$s.t. \quad d_{max} = \max_i d_i = \max_i \sum_k P'_{ik},$$

where $\widetilde{P}^{\alpha;\alpha}$ and $\widetilde{P}^{\alpha;\beta}$ are intra-layer and inter-layer transition matrices. The details about the stochastic normalization methods for each type of block matrices are presented in following subsections.

Intra-layer Transition Matrix Construction. Each intra-layer adjacency matrix $P^{\alpha;\alpha}$ is constructed based on the definition of an affinity value for each attribute. Since the intra-layer connections are only defined for the vertices of the same layer, the intra-layer transition matrix $\widetilde{P}^{\alpha;\alpha}$ can be constructed by using conventional affinity preserving normalization methods [11] as follows:

$$\widetilde{P}^{\alpha;\alpha} = \frac{1}{d^{\alpha}_{max}} P^{\alpha;\alpha}, \quad s.t. \quad d^{\alpha}_{max} = \max_i d^{\alpha}_i = \max_i \sum_k P^{\alpha;\alpha}_{ik}. \tag{6}$$

Inter-layer Transition Matrix Construction. The affinity values of inter-layer connections are uniformly set to 1 because the relative importance of the edges is unknown. Therefore, the inter-layer adjacency matrix $P^{\alpha;\beta}$ can be initially defined as an $N^P N^Q \times N^P N^Q$ all-ones matrix. Then, the row-wise probabilistic normalization is applied to construct the inter-layer transition matrix $\widetilde{P}^{\alpha;\beta}$. However, since the proposed multi-layer graph structure does not consider the inter-layer connections between vertices that have different indices, non-diagonal elements should be set to zero in the normalization process. Moreover, each layer should have the same transition probability because the relative importance of the layers is also unknown without any prior knowledge. Finally, the inter-layer transition matrix $\widetilde{\mathbf{P}}^{\alpha;\beta}$ can be defined as follows:

$$\widetilde{\mathbf{P}}^{\alpha;\beta} = \frac{1}{N^P N^Q L} \mathbf{P}^{\alpha;\beta} = \frac{1}{N^P N^Q L} \mathbf{I}_{N^P N^Q}, \tag{7}$$

where $\mathbf{I}_{N^P N^Q}$ denotes an $N^P N^Q \times N^P N^Q$ identity matrix. Unfortunately, the above uniform transition probability distribution can decrease the distinctiveness among matching candidates in practical environments. To handle this problem, we employ an assumption that strongly connected vertices with others have more valuable and reliable information to propagate than other vertices. The assumption is reasonable because true correspondences usually organize a strongly connected cluster in practical graph matching applications. Moreover, this assumption is one of the theoretical bases of the spectral matching scheme [8], which is frequently adopted in recent graph matching researches. Based on the assumption, we can design a weight vector using the degrees of intra-layer connections for computing relative importance among vertices. Then, the reinforced inter-layer transition matrix can be defined as follows:

$$\widetilde{\mathbf{P}}^{\alpha;\beta} = \mathrm{diag}\left(\frac{\mathbf{d}^\alpha}{d_{max}^\alpha}\right) \circ \left(\frac{1}{N^P N^Q L} \mathbf{P}^{\alpha;\beta}\right), \tag{8}$$

where $\mathrm{diag}\left(\mathbf{d}^\alpha / d_{max}^\alpha\right)$ is a diagonal matrix that describes the normalized degrees of the vertices, and the operator $\circ$ indicates the Hadamard product.

3.4   Advantages Against the Single-Layer Structure

The main difference between the proposed multi-layer structure $\widetilde{\mathbf{P}}$ and the integrated single-layer structure $\widetilde{\mathbf{W}}$ is in how the relations between multiple attributes are described. While $\widetilde{\mathbf{W}}$ describes the relations between multiple attributes at the affinity definition level, $\widetilde{\mathbf{P}}$ describes it in the multi-layer structure. By embedding the relations in the multi-layer structure, the proposed structure achieves two advantages against the single-layer structure. First, $\widetilde{\mathbf{P}}$ provides a probabilistic viewpoint of multi-attributed graph matching problems. Generalizing the single-attributed (or integrated-attributed) graph matching problem to the multi-attributed problem is difficult because of the complex relations among multiple attributes. In this sense, the probabilistic viewpoint of the multi-layer network can provide an efficient way to solve the complicated problem. Second, $\widetilde{\mathbf{P}}$ can adaptively describe various combinations of multiple attributes. Of course, $\widetilde{\mathbf{W}}$ may be appropriately designed to deal with a specific type of the problem by using various methods such as machine learning. However, the specially designed $\widetilde{\mathbf{W}}$ does not guarantee satisfactory performance for other types of the problem. On the other hand, $\widetilde{\mathbf{P}}$ can adaptively describe the relation between attribute pairs using the transition probability that is iteratively adjusted during the proposed matching process. In Sect. 4, we propose a multi-layer graph matching algorithm that takes these advantages into account based on the proposed structure.

4   Multi-layer Random Walk Graph Matching Algorithm

The proposed framework for computing random walk centrality of vertices is rather similar to the general random walk framework. In the framework, a random walker starts a traversal from any arbitrary node and then randomly moves to the new node according to the transition probability of given network. Suppose the current distribution of random walkers is given as t_k, then the next distribution t_{k+1} can be obtained by multiplying the transition matrix $\widetilde{P}$ as follows:

$$t_{k+1}^\top = t_k^\top \widetilde{P}. \tag{9}$$

When the distribution t_{k+1} is equal to t_k after the iterative traversal, t_k is called stationary distribution $\bar{t}$. Because $\bar{t}$ should not be changed by the transition, $\bar{t}$ has to satisfy the following equation,

$$\lambda \bar{t}^\top = \bar{t}^\top \widetilde{P}. \tag{10}$$

Since $\bar{t}$ is a non-negative vector and $\widetilde{P}$ is irreducible, λ is the maximal eigenvalue of $\widetilde{P}$ and $\bar{t}$ is a normalized eigenvector of $\widetilde{P}$ corresponding to λ according to the Perron-Frobenius theorem. Finally, the normalized eigenvector (the stationary distribution $\bar{t}$) can be obtained by iteratively updating the vector based on the power iteration method [8, 11] as follows:

$$t_{k+1}^\top = \frac{1}{\left\| t_k^\top \widetilde{P} \right\|_2} t_k^\top \widetilde{P}. \tag{11}$$

By generalizing this basic random walk framework, we propose the novel multi-layer graph matching algorithm as described in Algorithm 1. Initially, a uniform distribution vector t_0 and a *supra-transition matrix* $\widetilde{P}$ are generated. Then, for each iteration step, a next distribution vector $\bar{t}$ is computed by multiplying the previous distribution t and the transition matrix $\widetilde{P}$. The update is repeated until the distribution vector $\bar{t}$ reaches to the stationary state.

To encourage the matching constraints in Eq. (3.2), the proposed algorithm employed a reweighting process in the middle of iteration steps similarly to the single-layer random walk graph matching algorithm [11]. Random walkers traverse according to the transition probability during the iteration steps, however, the traversal does not consider about the matching constraints. By applying the reweighting process [11] controlled by the reweighting factor θ, random walkers can jump to the constrained nodes regardless of the transition probability. The reweighting process consists of two steps: *inflation* and *bistochastic normalization*. The purpose of our *inflation* procedure is to filter out unreliable matching candidates, which is indicated in Line 9 of Algorithm 1. During the *inflation* step, the large assignment values are amplified, and the small assignment values are attenuated. Line 10 of Algorithm 1 indicates a *bistochastic normalization* step using the Sinkhorn method [23], which encourages the one-to-one matching constraint by transforming the assignment matrix to the bistochastic matrix. During this normalization step, the assignment distribution vector is transformed to an

---

Algorithm 1. Multi-layer Random Walk Graph Matching

Input: Multi-layer affinity tensor $\mathbf{\Pi}$, reweight factor θ, inflation factor ρ, minimum
　　　　layer importance value τ
Output: Assignment vector $\hat{\mathbf{t}}$
　1: (*Initialization*)
　2: Generate an uniform assignment vector $\mathbf{t}_0$
　3: Generate a multi-layer transition matrix $\widetilde{\mathbf{P}}$ from $\mathbf{\Pi}$
　4: **repeat**
　5:　　(*Calculate the next distribution*)
　6:　　$\bar{\mathbf{t}}^{\top} \leftarrow \mathbf{t}^{\top}\widetilde{\mathbf{P}}$
　7:　　**for** $\alpha = 1$ **to** L
　8:　　　(*Reweighting random walks for each layer* [11])
　9:　　　$\mathbf{u}^{\alpha} \leftarrow \exp(\rho \cdot \bar{\mathbf{t}}^{\alpha}/\max(\bar{\mathbf{t}}^{\alpha}))$
　10:　　　Bistochastic normalize $\mathbf{u}^{\alpha}$ by using the Sinkhorn method [23]
　11:　　　(*Compute layer importance*)
　12:　　　$\mathbf{s}^{\alpha} \leftarrow \mathrm{sum}(\mathrm{intersect}(\mathbf{u}^{\alpha}, \bar{\mathbf{t}}^{\alpha}))$
　13:　　**end**
　14:　Normalize the layer importance vector $\mathbf{s}$ into the interval $[\tau, 1]$
　15:　(*Gathering reweighted distribution with layer strength*)
　16:　$\mathbf{u}^{temp} \leftarrow \sum_{\alpha} \mathbf{s}^{\alpha}\mathbf{u}^{\alpha}$
　17:　(*Diffusing reweighted distribution to whole layer*)
　18:　$\forall \alpha \; \mathbf{u}^{\alpha} \leftarrow \mathbf{u}^{temp}$
　19:　(*Update information of reweighted jump*)
　20:　$\mathbf{t} \leftarrow \theta\bar{\mathbf{t}} + (1-\theta)\mathbf{u}$
　21: **until** $\mathbf{t}$ converges
　22: (*Integrate the assignment vector*)
　23: $\hat{\mathbf{t}} \leftarrow \sum_{\alpha} \mathbf{t}^{\alpha}$
　24: Discretize the assignment vector $\hat{\mathbf{t}}$

---

assignment matrix, and then the rows and columns of the matrix are alternatively normalized until converges. As a result, the contradictions among the
matching candidates in the assignment distribution could be removed. These
steps are separately applied for each layer to preserve the distinctiveness of multiple layers.

After the reweighting process, the reweighted distribution vectors $\mathbf{u}$ should
be integrated to prevent a contradiction among the layers. One of the possible methods is gathering the distribution vectors according to any predefined
priority of layers at once, and then propagating again to each layer. However,
it is difficult to decide the most important layer without any prior knowledge,
because the attributes have various characteristics hard to compare with each
other. For that reason, we empirically define a layer importance measure as the
intersection of reweighted distribution and current assignment distribution. The
proposed measure is based on the observation that the large difference between
the current assignment distribution and the reweighted distribution means that
the reweighting process causes large information loss. Our extensive experiments
with this measure show the meaningful performance enhancement. After calculating each layer importance value, the importance vector $\mathbf{s}$ is normalized into

the interval $[\tau, 1]$, where τ is a minimum importance value. At the end of iteration steps, the reweighted distribution is integrated with the current assignment distribution to generate the biased assignment distribution (reweighting jump in [11]). Finally, the converged distribution vector $\mathbf{t}$ is discretized to obtain a binary solution $\hat{\mathbf{t}}$ by using Greedy mapping [8] or Hungarian method [19].

5   Experimental Results

In order to evaluate the proposed algorithm, we perform experiments with the synthetic dataset and the WILLOW object class dataset[1] [1]. We compare our algorithm with the widely used graph matching algorithms including Reweighted Random Walk Matching (RRWM) [11], Factorized Graph Matching (FGM) [10], Spectral Matching (SM) [8], Max Pooling Matching (MPM) [18], Graduated Assignment Graph Matching (GAGM) [24], and Integer Projected Fixed Points matching (IPFP) [25]. In all experiments, we fix the reweighting factor θ to 0.2, the inflation factor ρ to 30, and the minimum layer importance value τ to 0.1. Moreover, the parameters of other algorithms are also fixed to those given in the original papers. Our evaluation framework is based on the open MATLAB programs of [11], and the source codes of other matching methods are obtained from the authors.

5.1   Performance Evaluation for Synthetic Dataset

In this experiment, we generate a pair of synthetic graphs which contain outliers and deformations in similar manners represented in [11,12]. We first define an initial graph $^0\mathcal{G}$ which has several types of attributes $^0\mathcal{A}$. To reflect the characteristics according to attribute types, we randomly assign affinity values with different variances for each layer. Then we generate two graphs $^1\mathcal{G}$ and $^2\mathcal{G}$ with small attribute deformation based on a Gaussian function $\mathcal{N}(0, \epsilon^2)$ and randomly defined outliers v_{out}. The affinity matrix $\mathbf{W}^\alpha$ of layer α is defined by $\exp(-|^1a_{ij}^\alpha - ^2a_{ab}^\alpha|_2/\sigma^2)$, where $^1a_{ij}^\alpha$ and $^2a_{ab}^\alpha$ are edge attributes that are normalized into the interval $[0,1]$, and σ^2 is a scaling factor which is set to 0.3. For the attribute integration of single-layer graph matching methods, we aggregate the normalized affinity matrices from multiple layers by summing them.

Table 1. Parameter setting for the synthetic graph matching experiments

Experiments	Varied parameter	Fixed parameters
Deformation	$\epsilon = 0 \sim 0.3$	$N_{att} = 5, 10,\ N_{out} = 2,\ N_{in} = 10,\ \sigma^2 = 0.3$
Outlier	$N_{out} = 0 \sim 10$	$N_{att} = 5, 10,\ N_{in} = 10,\ \epsilon = 0.1,\ \sigma^2 = 0.3$
Attributes	$N_{att} = 4 \sim 20$	$N_{out} = 2,\ N_{in} = 10,\ \epsilon = 0.2,\ \sigma^2 = 0.3$

---

[1] http://www.di.ens.fr/willow/research/graphlearning/.

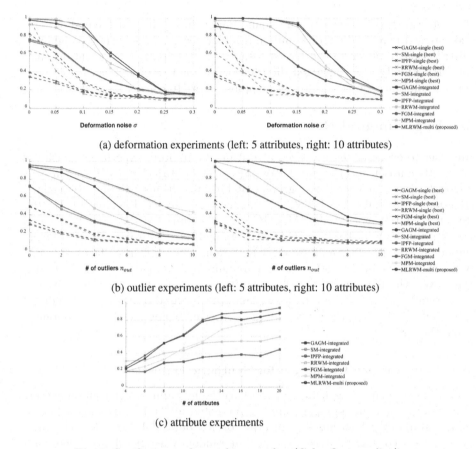

(a) deformation experiments (left: 5 attributes, right: 10 attributes)

(b) outlier experiments (left: 5 attributes, right: 10 attributes)

(c) attribute experiments

Fig. 3. Synthetic graph matching results. (Color figure online)

Then, we design three experiments by changing parameters: the magnitude of deformation ϵ, the number of outliers n_{out}, and the number of attributes n_{att}. First, in the deformation experiment, the magnitude of deformation ϵ is varied and other variables are fixed. Similarly, in the outlier experiment, only the number of outliers n_{out} is changed. In the last experiment, both parameters, ϵ and n_{out}, are fixed and the number of attributes n_{att} is varied. For all experiments, the number of inliers n_{in} is fixed to 10, and each test is iterated 100 times. Details of the parameters are represented in Table 1.

As shown in Fig. 3, the proposed algorithm, Multi-Layer Random Walk Matching (MLRWM-multi), shows comparable performance with other methods under deformation.[2] However, 'MPM-integrated' and 'FGM-intgrated' yield bet-

---

[2] '-single', '-integrated', and '-multi' represent the results obtained by using a single affinity using a single attribute, an integrated affinity using multiple attribute, and the multiple affinity using multiple attributes (proposed), respectively. Among the many '-single' results for each method, only the best result is shown for comparison.

ter performance than ours in the outlier and attribute experiments. Since MPM selects correspondences that have the maximum affinity values, this method is highly robust against the variation caused by outliers. On the other hand, 'MPM-integrated' is relatively weak for the attribute deformation as shown in Fig. 3(a). In addition, when the portion of outliers is small, the proposed method is still better than 'MPM-integrated' and the others except 'FGM-integrated' as shown in Fig. 3(c). In contrast with MPM, 'FGM-integrated' shows superior performance in all of the synthetic graph matching experiments. These results are caused by the experimental design that does not consider the credibility of attributes. In order to reflect practical environments, the credibility of each attribute should be considered because each attribute has different powers of description for various applications. Although we took account of this issue by adopting different variances of affinity values, it is not enough to effectively reflect realistic scenarios. Furthermore, since our algorithm defines the layer importance by observing characteristics of real images as mentioned in Sect. 4, the importance value could be inaccurately estimated in this experiment. For that reason, our method yields the relatively declined performance than 'FGM-integrated'. However, the proposed method outperforms 'FGM-integrated' in a realistic scenario; because real data generally contains both unreliable and reliable attributes whereas synthetic images contain either reliable attributes or unreliable attributes. Details are represented in Sect. 5.2.

5.2   Performance Evaluation for WILLOW Dataset

In this experiment, we evaluate the proposed algorithm with graphs which are constructed from general images in the WILLOW object class dataset [1]. The dataset consists of five categories (*face, motorbike, car, duck, winebottle*), and all images are manually annotated. In oder to construct a graph, we extract interest points by using the Hessian detector [26]. Among the extracted features, 10 nearest points from the annotated points are selected as inliers. Outliers are randomly selected from the rest of interest points. To define the multi-attribute problem, we use four types of attributes: SIFT descriptor [27], color histogram in RGB color space, relative distance histogram, and relative angle histogram which are the parts of HARG [1]. Edge attributes are defined by concatenating descriptors (or histograms) of two vertices. Exceptionally, the relative angle- and distance- histogram layers define edge attributes by following the definition of HARG for better matching performance. To compute the pairwise affinity value between two attribute vectors, we adopt the normalized Hamming distance measure [1]. Because the attributes have different scales according to the definitions, we normalize the affinity matrices by $(\mathbf{W}/\max(\mathbf{W}))$ before integrating the layers. Finally, the integrated affinity matrices are constructed by summing the normalized affinity matrices.

Based on the above criteria, we generate 100 pairs of graphs for each category and evaluate the performance of matching algorithms. As shown in Table 2 and Fig. 4, our algorithm shows robust performance in all categories except the *face* category. Especially, the proposed method outperforms FGM in most of the

Table 2. Performance on the WILLOW dataset [1]. Red and blue bold numbers denote the best and the second-best performance in each category.

	face					*motorbike*					*car*				
	Desc	ColH	RdiH	RAnH	**Multi**	Desc	ColH	RdiH	RAnH	**Multi**	Desc	ColH	RdiH	RAnH	**Multi**
GAGM [24]	57.75	8.85	16.62	54.22	67.48	17.32	7.22	11.20	50.92	43.08	19.72	7.32	11.32	47.13	42.62
SM [8]	57.85	8.73	16.70	54.72	67.23	17.23	7.25	11.65	51.55	43.13	19.92	7.22	11.70	47.77	42.72
IPFP [25]	57.53	8.70	16.83	56.62	68.22	17.35	7.27	11.32	52.82	42.75	19.82	7.28	12.73	48.60	42.22
RRWM [11]	58.22	8.67	20.37	56.40	73.88	17.20	7.22	13.07	**53.10**	51.20	19.80	7.18	13.70	48.53	48.77
FGM [10]	58.13	8.17	20.32	61.27	**76.80**	17.60	7.00	14.97	43.13	38.03	20.28	6.88	12.80	38.65	35.88
MPM [18]	58.70	9.17	16.10	58.80	**80.15**	17.45	7.23	10.73	51.77	52.53	19.97	7.15	12.43	46.82	**48.78**
Proposed	-	-	-	-	70.55	-	-	-	-	54.23	-	-	-	-	50.92
	duck					*winebottle*					Average				
	Desc	ColH	RdiH	RAnH	**Multi**	Desc	ColH	RdiH	RAnH	**Multi**	Desc	ColH	RdiH	RAnH	**Multi**
GAGM [24]	16.95	7.25	13.28	44.13	37.97	23.50	6.98	12.35	54.23	44.10	27.05	7.52	12.95	50.13	47.05
SM [8]	17.02	7.43	13.18	44.32	38.12	23.35	7.07	12.83	54.92	44.13	27.07	7.54	13.21	50.65	47.07
IPFP [25]	16.83	7.03	13.73	**46.33**	37.87	23.47	7.18	13.92	55.13	44.58	27.00	7.49	13.71	51.90	47.13
RRWM [11]	17.25	7.38	16.12	46.30	45.42	23.72	7.27	15.57	54.33	51.93	27.24	7.54	15.76	51.73	54.24
FGM [10]	16.68	7.35	15.90	37.58	34.12	24.38	7.18	16.15	50.03	45.33	27.42	7.32	16.03	46.13	46.03
MPM [18]	16.62	7.10	13.72	43.95	44.03	24.05	7.05	11.18	**55.70**	52.27	27.36	7.54	12.83	51.41	**55.55**
Proposed	-	-	-	-	**47.33**	-	-	-	-	55.32	-	-	-	-	55.67

(a) WILLOW-*face*: MLRWM(10/10), RRWM(8/10), MPM(7/10), SM(7/10)

(b) WILLOW-*motorbike*: MLRWM(10/10), RRWM(10/10), MPM(7/10), SM(5/10)

(c) WILLOW-*car*: MLRWM(9/10), RRWM(8/10), MPM(6/10), SM(3/10)

(d) WILLOW-*duck*: MLRWM(9/10), RRWM(7/10), MPM(2/10), SM(5/10)

(e) WILLOW-*winebottle*: MLRWM(9/10), RRWM(8/10), MPM(8/10), SM(6/10)

Fig. 4. Qualitative comparison of feature graph matching results for all categories in the WILLOW dataset. The blue lines indicate true correspondences, and the red lines indicate false correspondences or outliers. From top to bottom: each of object categories in the WILLOW dataset. From left to right: graph matching algorithms – MLRWM(proposed), RRWM [11], MPM [18], SM [8]. (Color figure online)

categories unlike the synthetic graph matching experiments. This proves the superiority of the proposed multi-layer graph structure and matching algorithm for multiple attributes. Our algorithm presents relatively lower performance for the *face* category (but still comparable to others) because the failure case of the layer importance estimation is occurred more frequently than other categories. In those cases, the uniform layer importance shows better performance in our additional experiments. Since our current layer importance estimation approach does not use any prior knowledge, we expect that it is possible to improve the estimation accuracy by using the additional information or techniques such as machine learning algorithm. We will focus on this issue in the future to improve the proposed algorithm.

6   Conclusion

In this paper, we have presented a novel multi-attributed graph matching algorithm based on the multi-layer structure. We first designed a multi-layer structure to consider multiple attributes jointly while preserving the characteristics of each attribute in separated layers. Based on the proposed structure, we also proposed the novel multi-attributed graph matching algorithm by adopting the random walk centrality concept. In our extensive experiments, the proposed graph matching algorithm showed the better performance than the state-of-the-art algorithms based on the single-layer graph structure.

Acknowledgments. This work was supported by the National Research Foundation of Korea (NRF) grant funded by the Korea government (MSIP) (No. NRF-2015R1A2A1A01005455).

References

1. Cho, M., Alahari, K., Ponce, J.: Learning graphs to match. In: Proceedings of IEEE International Conference on Computer Vision (2013)
2. Duchenne, O., Joulin, A., Ponce, J.: A graph-matching kernel for object categorization. In: Proceedings of IEEE International Conference on Computer Vision (2011)
3. Chen, H.T., Lin, H.H., Liu, T.L.: Multi-object tracking using dynamical graph matching. In: Proceedings of IEEE Conference on Computer Vision and Pattern Recognition (2001)
4. Gomila, C., Meyer, F.: Graph-based object tracking. In: Proceedings of IEEE International Conference on Image Processing (2003)
5. Xiao, J., Cheng, H., Sawhney, H., Han, F.: Vehicle detection and tracking in wide field-of-view aerial video. In: Proceedings of IEEE Conference on Computer Vision and Pattern Recognition (2010)
6. Duchenne, O., Bach, F., Kweon, I.S., Ponce, J.: A tensor-based algorithm for high-order graph matching. IEEE Trans. Pattern Anal. Mach. Intell. **33**(12), 2383–2395 (2011)

7. Huang, Q.X., Zhang, G.X., Gao, L., Hu, S.M., Butscher, A., Guibas, L.: An optimization approach for extracting and encoding consistent maps in a shape collection. ACM Trans. Graph. **31**(6), 167 (2012)
8. Leordeanu, M., Hebert, M.: A spectral technique for correspondence problems using pairwise constraints. In: Proceedings of IEEE International Conference on Computer Vision (2005)
9. Yan, J., Wang, J., Zha, H., Yang, X., Chu, S.: Consistency-driven alternating optimization for multi-graph matching: a unified approach. In: IEEE Transactions on Image Processing (2014)
10. Zhou, F., De la Torre, F.: Factorized graph matching. In: Proceedings of IEEE Conference on Computer Vision and Pattern Recognition (2012)
11. Cho, M., Lee, J., Lee, K.M.: Reweighted random walks for graph matching. In: Maragos, P., Paragios, N., Daniilidis, K. (eds.) ECCV 2010, Part V. LNCS, vol. 6315, pp. 492–505. Springer, Heidelberg (2010)
12. Cour, T., Srinivasan, P., Shi, J.: Balanced graph matching. In: Proceedings of Advances in Neural Information Processing Systems (2006)
13. Kivelä, M., Arenas, A., Barthelemy, M., Gleeson, J.P., Moreno, Y., Porter, M.A.: Multilayer networks. J. Complex Netw. **2**(3), 203–271 (2014)
14. Noh, J.D., Rieger, H.: Random walks on complex networks. Phys. Rev. Lett. **92**(11), 118–701 (2004)
15. Page, L., Brin, S., Motwani, R., Winograd, T.: The pagerank citation ranking: bringing order to the web. Technical report, Stanford InfoLab (1999)
16. Solé-Ribalta, A., De Domenico, M., Gómez, S., Arenas, A.: Random walk centrality in interconnected multilayer networks. arXiv preprint (2015). arXiv:1506.07165
17. De Domenico, M., Solé-Ribalta, A., Omodei, E., Gómez, S., Arenas, A.: Centrality in interconnected multilayer networks. arXiv preprint (2013). arXiv:1311.2906
18. Cho, M., Sun, J., Duchenne, O., Ponce, J.: Finding matches in a haystack: a max-pooling strategy for graph matching in the presence of outliers. In: Proceedings of IEEE Conference on Computer Vision and Pattern Recognition (2014)
19. Munkres, J.: Algorithms for the assignment and transportation problems. J. Soc. Ind. Appl. Math. **5**(1), 32–38 (1957)
20. De Domenico, M., Solé, A., Gómez, S., Arenas, A.: Random walks on multiplex networks. arXiv preprint (2013). arXiv:1306.0519
21. Gomez, S., Diaz-Guilera, A., Gomez-Gardeñes, J., Perez-Vicente, C.J., Moreno, Y., Arenas, A.: Diffusion dynamics on multiplex networks. Phys. Rev. Lett. **110**(2), 028701 (2013)
22. Kolda, T.G., Bader, B.W.: Tensor decompositions and applications. Soc. Ind. Appl. Math. Rev. **51**(3), 455–500 (2009)
23. Sinkhorn, R.: A relationship between arbitrary positive matrices and doubly stochastic matrices. Ann. Math. Stat. **35**, 876–879 (1964)
24. Gold, S., Rangarajan, A.: A graduated assignment algorithm for graph matching. IEEE Trans. Pattern Anal. Mach. Intell. **18**(4), 377–388 (1996)
25. Leordeanu, M., Hebert, M., Sukthankar, R.: An integer projected fixed point method for graph matching and map inference. In: Proceedings of Advances in Neural Information Processing Systems (2009)
26. Murphy, K.P.: Machine Learning: A Probabilistic Perspective. MIT Press, Cambridge (2012)
27. Lowe, D.G.: Distinctive image features from scale-invariant keypoints. Int. J. Comput. Vis. **60**(2), 91–110 (2004)

Deep Learning of Local RGB-D Patches for 3D Object Detection and 6D Pose Estimation

Wadim Kehl[1]([✉]), Fausto Milletari[1], Federico Tombari[1,2], Slobodan Ilic[1,3], and Nassir Navab[1]

[1] Technical University of Munich, Munich, Germany
wadimkehl@gmail.com
[2] University of Bologna, Bologna, Italy
[3] Siemens AG, Munich, Germany

Abstract. We present a 3D object detection method that uses regressed descriptors of locally-sampled RGB-D patches for 6D vote casting. For regression, we employ a convolutional auto-encoder that has been trained on a large collection of random local patches. During testing, scene patch descriptors are matched against a database of synthetic model view patches and cast 6D object votes which are subsequently filtered to refined hypotheses. We evaluate on three datasets to show that our method generalizes well to previously unseen input data, delivers robust detection results that compete with and surpass the state-of-the-art while being scalable in the number of objects.

1 Introduction

Object detection and pose estimation are of primary importance for tasks such as robotic manipulation, scene understanding and augmented reality, and have been the focus of intense research in recent years. The availability of low-cost RGB-D sensors enabled the development of novel methods that can infer scale and pose of the object more accurately even in presence of occlusions and clutter.

Fig. 1. Results of our voting-based approach that uses auto-encoder descriptors of local RGB-D patches for 6-DoF pose hypotheses generation. (Left) Cast votes from each patch indicating object centroids, colored with their confidence. (Middle) Segmentation map obtained after vote filtering. (Right) Final detections after pose refinement.

© Springer International Publishing AG 2016
B. Leibe et al. (Eds.): ECCV 2016, Part III, LNCS 9907, pp. 205–220, 2016.
DOI: 10.1007/978-3-319-46487-9_13

Methods such as Hinterstoisser et al. and related [14, 18, 27] detect objects in the scene by employing templates generated from synthetic views and matching them efficiently against the scene. While these holistic methods are implemented to be very fast at a low FP-rate, their recall drops quickly in presence of occlusion or substantial noise. Differently, descriptor-based approaches [2, 13, 23] rely on robust schemes for correspondence grouping and hypothesis verification to withstand occlusion and clutter, but are computationally intensive. Other methods like Brachmann et al. [5] and Tejani et al. [30] follow a local approach where small RGB-D patches vote for object pose hypotheses in a 6D space. Although such methods are not taking global context into account, they proved to be robust towards occlusion and the presence of noise artifacts since they infer the object pose using only its parts. Their implementations are based on classical Random Forests where the chosen features to represent the data can strongly influence the amount of votes that need to be cast to accomplish the task and, consequently, the required computational effort.

Recently, convolutional neural networks (CNNs) have shown to outperform state-of-the-art approaches in many computer vision tasks by leveraging the CNNs' abilities of automatically learning features from raw data. CNNs are capable of representing images in an abstract, hierarchical fashion and once a suitable network architecture is defined and the corresponding model is trained, CNNs can cope with a large variety of object appearances and classes.

Recent methods performing 3D object detection and pose estimation successfully demonstrated the use of CNNs on data acquired through RGB-D sensors such as depth or normals. For example, [11, 12] make use of features produced by a network to perform classification of region proposals via SVMs. A noteworthy work is Wohlhart et al. [32], that demonstrates the applicability of CNNs for descriptor learning of RGB-D views. This work uses a holistic approach and delivers impressive results in terms of object retrieval and pose estimation, although can not be directly applied to object detection in clutter since a precise object localization would be needed. Nonetheless, it does hint towards replacing hand-crafted features with learned ones for this task.

Our work is inspired by [32] and we demonstrate that neural networks coupled with a local voting-based approach can be used to perform reliable 3D object detection and pose estimation under clutter and occlusion. To this end, we deeply learn descriptive features from local RGB-D patches and use them afterwards to create hypotheses in the 6D pose space, similar to [5, 30].

In practice, we train a convolutional autoencoder (CAE) [22] from scratch using random patches from RGB-D images with the goal of descriptor regression. With this network we create codebooks from synthetic patches sampled from object views where each codebook entry holds a local 6D pose vote. In the detection phase we sample patches in the input image on a regular grid, compute their descriptors and match them against codebooks with an approximate k-NN search. Matching returns a number of candidate votes which are cast only if their matching score surpasses a threshold (see a schematic in Fig. 2).

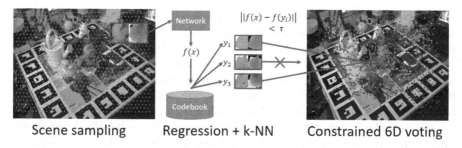

Scene sampling   Regression + k-NN   Constrained 6D voting

Fig. 2. Illustration of the voting. We densely sample the scene to extract scale-invariant RGB-D patches. These are fed into a network to regress features for a subsequent k-NN search in a codebook of pre-computed synthetic local object patches. The retrieved neighbors then cast 6D votes if their feature distance is smaller than a threshold τ.

We will show that our method allows for training on real data, efficient matching between synthetic and real patches and that it generalizes well to unseen data with an extremely high recall. Furthermore, we avoid explicit background learning and scale well with the number of objects in the database.

2   Related Work

There has recently been an intense research activity in the field of 3D object detection, with many methods proposed in literature traditionally subdivided into feature-based and template-based. As for the first class, earlier approaches relied on features [4,20] directly detected on the RGB image and then back-projected to 3D [19,25]. With the introduction of 3D descriptors [28,31], approaches replaced image features with features directly computed on the 3D point cloud [23], and introduced robust schemes for filtering wrong 3D correspondences and for hypothesis verification [2,6,13]. They can handle occlusion and are scalable in the number of models, thanks to the use of approximate nearest neighbor schemes for feature matching [24] yielding sub-linear complexity. Nevertheless, they are limited when matching surfaces of poor informative shape and tend to report non real-time run-times.

On the other hand, template-based approaches are often very robust to clutter but scale linearly with the number of models. LineMOD [15] performed robust 3D object detection by matching templates extracted from rendered views of 3D models and embedding quantized image contours and normal orientations. Successively, [27] optimized the matching via a cascaded classification scheme, achieving a run-time increase by a factor of 10. Improvements in efficiency are also achieved by the two-stage cascaded detection method in [7] and by the hashing matching approach tailored to LineMOD templates proposed in [18]. Other recent approaches [3,10,21] build discriminative models based on such representations using SVM or boosting applied to training data.

Recently, another category of methods has emerged based on *learning* RGB-D representations, which are successively classified or matched at test time.

[5,30] use random forest-based voting schemes on local patches to detect and estimate 3D poses. While the former regresses object coordinates and conducts a
subsequent energy-based pose estimation, the latter bases its voting on a scale-
invariant LineMOD-inspired patch representation and returns location and pose
simultaneously. Recently, CNNs have also been employed [11,12,32] to learn
RGB-D features. The main limitations of this category of methods is that, being
based on discriminative classifiers, they usually require to learn the background
as a negative class, thus making their performance dataset-specific. Instead, we
train neural networks in an unsupervised fashion and use them as a plug-in
replacement for methods based on local features.

3   Methodology

In this section, we first give a description of how we sample local RGB-D patches
of the given target objects and the scene while ensuring scale-invariance and
suitability as a neural network input. Secondly, we describe the employed neural
networks in more detail. Finally, we present our voting and filtering approach
which efficiently detects objects in real scenes using a trained network and a
codebook of regressed descriptors from synthetic patches.

3.1   Local Patch Representation

Our method follows an established paradigm for voting via local information.
Given an object appearance, the idea is to separate it into its local parts and
let them vote independently [5,8,26,30]. While most approaches rely on hand-
crafted features for describing these local patches, we tackle the issue by regressing them with a neural network.

To represent an object locally, we render it from many viewpoints equidistantly sampled on an icosahedron (similar to [15]), and densely extract a set
of scale-independent RGB-D patches from each view. To sample invariantly to
scale, we take depth z at the patch center point and compute the patch pixel
size such that the patch corresponds to a fixed metric size m (here: 5 cm) via

$$patch_{size} = \frac{m}{z} \cdot f \qquad (1)$$

with f being the focal length of the rendering camera. After patch extraction,
we de-mean the depth values with z and clamp them to $\pm m$ to confine the patch
locally not only along x and y, but also along z. Finally, we normalize color and
depth to $[-1, 1]$ and resize the patches to 32×32. See Fig. 3 for an exemplary
synthetic view together with sampled local patches.

An important advantage of using local patches as in the proposed framework
is that it avoids the problematic aspect of background modeling. Indeed, for
what concerns discriminative approaches based on learning a background and a
foreground class, a generic background appearance can hardly be modeled, and
recent approaches based on discriminative classifiers such as CNNs deploy scene

 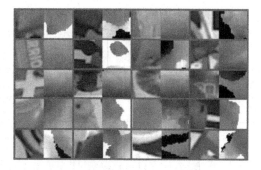

Fig. 3. Left: For each synthetic view, we sample scale-invariant RGB-D patches $\mathbf{y}_i$ of a fixed metric size on a dense grid. Their associated regressed features $f(\mathbf{y}_i)$ and local votes $v(\mathbf{y}_i)$ are stored into a codebook. Right: Examples from the approx. 1.5 million random patches taken from the LineMOD dataset for autoencoder training.

data for training, thus becoming extremely dataset-specific and necessitating refinement strategies such as hard negative mining. Also, both [5,32] model a supporting plane to achieve improved results, with the latter even introducing real images intertwined with synthetic renderings into the training to force the CNN to abstract from real background. Our method instead does not need to model the background at all.

3.2 Network Training

Since we want the network to produce discriminative features for the provided input RGB-D patches, we need to bootstrap suitable filters and weights for the intermediate layers of the network. Instead of relying on pre-trained, publicly available networks, we decided to train from scratch due to multiple reasons:

1. Not many works have incorporated depth as an additional channel in networks and most remark that special care has to be taken to cope with, among others, sensor noise and depth 'holes' which we can control with our data.
2. We are one of the first to focus on local RGB-D patches of small-scale objects. There are no pre-trained networks that have been so far learned on such data, and it is unclear how well other networks that were learned on RGB-D data can generalize to our specific problem at hand.
3. To robustly train deep architectures, a high amount of training samples is needed. By using patches from real scenes, we can easily create a huge training dataset which is specialized to our task, thus enhancing the discriminative power of our network.

Note that other works usually train a CNN on a classification problem and then use a 'beheaded' version of the network for other tasks (e.g. [9]). Here, we cannot simply convert our problem into a feasible classification task because of the sheer amount of training samples that range in the millions.

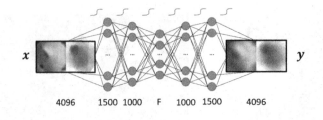

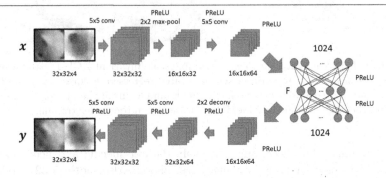

Fig. 4. Depiction of the employed AE (top) and CAE (bottom) architectures. For both, we have the compressing feature layer with dimensionality F.

Although we could assign each sample to the object class it belongs to, this would bias the feature training and hence, counter the learning of a generalized patch feature representation, independent of object affiliations. It is important to point out that also [32] aimed for feature learning, but with a different goal. Indeed, they enforce distance similarity of feature space and object pose space, while we instead strive for a compact representation of our local input patches, independent of the objects' poses.

We teach the network regression on a large variety of input data by randomly sampling local patches from the LineMOD dataset [15], amounting to around 1.5 million total samples. Furthermore, these samples were augmented such that each image got randomly flipped and its color channels permutated. Our network aims to learn a mapping from the high-dimensional patch space to a much lower feature space of dimensionality F, and we employ a traditional autoencoder (AE) and a convolutional autoencoder (CAE) to accomplish this task.

Autoencoders minimize a reconstruction error $||x - y||$ between an input patch x and a regressed output patch y while the inner-most compression layer condenses the data into F values. We use these F values as our descriptor since they represent the most informative compact encoding of the input patch. Our architectures can be seen in Fig. 4. For the AE we use two encoding and decoding layers which are all connected with tanh activations. For the CAE we employ multiple layers of 5×5 convolutions and PReLUs (Parametrized Rectified Linear Unit) before a single fully-connected encoding/decoding layer, and use a deconvolution with learned 2×2 kernels for upscaling before proceeding back again with 5×5 convolutions and PReLUs. Note that we conduct one max-pool operation after the first convolutions to introduce a small shift-invariance.

3.3   Constrained Voting

A problem that is often encountered in regression tasks is the unpredictability of output values in the case of noisy or unseen, ill-conditioned input data. This is especially true for CNNs as a deep cascade of non-linear functions composed of many parameters. In our case, this can be caused by e.g., unseen object parts, general background appearance or sensor noise in color or depth. If we were to simply regress the translational and rotational parts, we would be prone to this input sensitivity. Furthermore, this approach would always cast votes at each image sampling position, increasing the complexity of sifting through the voting space afterwards. Instead, we render an object from many views and store local patches $\mathbf{y}$ of this synthetic data in a database, as seen in Fig. 3. For each $\mathbf{y}$, we compute its feature $f(\mathbf{y}) \in \mathbb{R}^F$ and store it together with a local vote $(t_x, t_y, t_z, \alpha, \beta, \gamma)$ describing the patch 3D center point offset to the object centroid and the rotation with respect to the local object coordinate frame. This serves as an object-dependent codebook.

During testing, we take each sampled 3D scene point $\mathbf{s} = (s_x, s_y, s_z)$ with associated patch $\mathbf{x}$, compute its deep-regressed feature $f(\mathbf{x})$ and retrieve k (approximate) nearest neighbors $\mathbf{y}_1, ..., \mathbf{y}_k$. Each neighbor casts then a global vote $v(\mathbf{s}, \mathbf{y}) = (t_x + s_x, t_y + s_y, t_z + t_y, \alpha, \beta, \gamma)$ with an associated weight $w(v) = e^{-||f(\mathbf{x}) - f(\mathbf{y})||}$ based on the feature distance.

Notably, this approach is flexible enough to provide three main practical advantages. First, we can vary k in order to steer the amount of possible vote candidates per sampling position. Together with a joint codebook for all objects, we can retrieve the nearest neighbors with sub-linear complexity, enabling scalability. Secondly, we can define a threshold τ on the nearest neighbor distance, so that retrieved neighbors will only vote if they hold a certain confidence. This reduces the amount of votes cast over scene parts that do not resemble any of the codebook patches. Furthermore, if noise sensitivity perturbs our regressed

Fig. 5. Casting the constrained votes for $k = 10$ with a varying distance threshold (left to right): $\tau = 15$, $\tau = 7$, $\tau = 5$. The projected vote centroids v_i are colored according to their scaled weight $w(v_i)/\tau$. It can be seen that many votes accumulate confidently around the true object centroid for differently chosen thresholds.

feature, it is more likely to be hindered from vote casting. Lastly and of significance, it is assured that each vote is numerically correct because it is unaffected by noise in the input data, given that the feature matching was reliable. See Fig. 5 for a visualization of the constrained voting.

Vote Filtering. Casting votes can lead to a very crowded vote space that requires refinement in order to keep detection computationally feasible. We thus employ a three-stage filtering: in the first stage we subdivide the image plane into a 2D grid (here: cell size of 5×5 pixels) and throw each vote into the cell the projected centroid points to. We suppress all cells that hold less than k votes and extract local maxima after bilinear filtering over the accumulated weights of the cells. Each local mode collects the votes from its direct cell neighbors and performs mean shift with a flat kernel, first in translational and then in quaternion space (here: kernel sizes 2.5 cm and 7 degrees). This filtering is computationally very efficient and removes most spurious votes with non-agreeing centroids, while retaining plausible hypotheses, as can be seen in Fig. 6. Furthermore, the retrieved neighbors of each hypotheses' constituting votes hold synthetic foreground information that can be quickly accumulated to create meaningful segmentation maps (see Fig. 1 for an example on another sequence).

Fig. 6. Starting with thousands of votes (left) we run our filtering to retrieve intermediate local maxima (middle) that are further verified and accepted (right).

4   Evaluation

4.1   Reconstruction Quality

To evaluate the performance of the networks, we trained AEs and CAEs with feature layer dimensions $F \in \{32, 64, 128, 256\}$. We implemented our networks with Caffe [17] and trained each with an NVIDIA Titan X with a batch size of 500. The learning rate was fixed to 10^{-5} and we ran 100,000 iterations for each network. The only exception was the 256-dim AE, which we trained for 200,000 iterations for convergence due to its higher number of parameters.

For a visual impression of the results, we present the reconstruction quality side-by-side of AEs and CAEs on six random RGB-D patches in Fig. 7. Note that

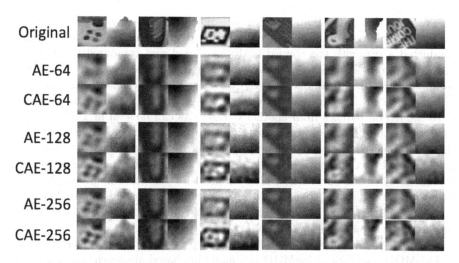

Fig. 7. RGB-D patch reconstruction comparison between our AE and CAE for a given feature dimensionality F. Clearly, the AE and CAE focus on different qualities and both networks increase the reconstruction fidelity with a wider compression layer.

these patches are test samples from another dataset and thus have not been part of the training, i.e. the networks are reconstructing previously unseen data.

It is apparent that the CAEs put more emphasis on different image properties than their AE pendants. The AE reconstructions focus more on color and are more afflicted by noise since weights of neighboring pixels are trained in an uncorrelated fashion in this architecture. The CAE patches instead recover the spatial structure better at the cost of color fidelity. This can be especially seen for the 64-dimensional CAE where the remaining $1.56\% = (64/4096)$ of the input information forced the network to resort to grayscale in order to preserve image structure. It can be objectively stated that the convolutional reconstructions for 128 dimensions are usually closer to their input in visual terms. Subsequently, at dimensionality 256 the CAE results are consistently of higher fidelity both in terms of structure and color/texture.

4.2   Multi-instance Dataset from Tejani et al.

We evaluated our approach on the dataset of Tejani et al. [30]. Upon inspection, the dataset showed problems with the ground truth annotation, which has been confirmed by the authors via personal communication. We thus re-annotated the dataset by ICP and visual inspection of each single frame. The authors then supplied us with their recomputed scores of the method in [30] on such corrected version of the dataset, which they are also going to publish on their website. To evaluate against the authors' method (LC-HF), we follow their protocol and extract the $N = 5$ strongest modes in the voting space and subsequently verify each via ICP and depth/normal checks to suppress false positives.

We used this dataset first to evaluate how different networks and feature dimensions influence the final detection result. To this end, we fixed $k = 3$ and conducted a run with the trained CAEs, AEs and also compared to PCA[1] as means for dimensionality reduction. Since different dimensions and methods lead to different feature distances we set $\tau = \infty$ for this experiment, i.e. votes are unconstrained. Note that we already show here generalization since the networks were trained on patches from another dataset. As can be seen in Table 1, PCA provides a good baseline performance that surpasses even the CAE at 32 dimensions, although this mainly stems from a high precision since vote centroids rarely agreed. In turn, both networks supplied similar behavior and we reached a peak at 128 with our CAE, which we fixed for further evaluation. We also found $\tau = 10$ and a sampling step of 8 pixels to provide a good balance between accuracy and runtime. For a more in-depth self comparison, we kindly refer the reader to the supplementary material.

For this evaluation we also supply numbers from the original implementation of LineMOD [14]. Since LineMOD is a matching-based approach, we evaluated such that each template having a similarity score larger than 0.8 is taken into the same verification described above. It is evident that LineMOD fares very well on most sequences since the amount of occlusion is low. It only showed problems where objects sometimes are partially outside the image plane (e.g. 'joystick','coffe'), have many occluders and thus a smaller recall ('milk') or where the planar 'juice' object decreased the precision by occasional misdetections in the table. Not surprisingly, LineMOD outperforms the other two methods largely for the small 'camera' since it searches the entire specified scale space whereas LC-HF and our method both rely on local depth for scale inference. Although our local voting does detect instances in the table as well, there is rarely an agreeing centroid that survives the filtering stage and our method is by far more robust to larger occlusions and partial views. We are thus overtaking the other methods in 'coffe' and 'joystick'. The 'milk' object is difficult to handle with local methods since it is uniformly colored and symmetric, defying a reliable accumulation of vote centroids. Although the 'joystick' is mostly black, its geometry allows us to recover the pose very reliably. All in all, we outperform the state-of-the art in holistic matching slightly while clearly improving over the state-of-the-art in local-based detection by significant 9.6 % on this challenging dataset. Detailed numbers are given in Tables 2 and 3. Unfortunately, runtimes for LC-HF are not provided by the authors.

Table 1. F1-scores on the Tejani dataset using PCA, AE and CAE for patch descriptor regression with a varying dimension F. We highlight the best method for a given F. Note that the number for CAE-128 deviates from Table 3 since here we set $\tau = \infty$.

F	32	64	128	256	F	32	64	128	256	F	32	64	128	256
PCA	0.33	0.43	0.46	0.47	AE	**0.43**	**0.63**	0.65	0.66	CAE	0.32	0.58	**0.70**	**0.69**

---

[1] Due to computational constraints we took only 1 million patches for PCA training.

4.3   LineMOD Dataset

We evaluated our method on the benchmark of [15] in two different ways. To compare to a whole set of related work that followed the original evaluation protocol, we remove the last stage of vote filtering and take the $N = 100$ most confident votes for the final hypotheses to decide for the best hypothesis and use the factor $k_m = 0.1$ in their proposed error measure. To evaluate against Tejani et al. we instead follow their protocol and extract the $N = 5$ strongest modes in the voting space and choose $k_m = 0.15$. Since the dataset provides one object ground truth per sequence, we use only the codebook that is associated to that object for retrieving the nearest neighbors. Two objects, namely 'cup' and 'bowl', are missing their meshed models which we manually created. For either

Fig. 8. Scene sampling, vote maps and detection output for two objects on the Tejani dataset. Red sample points were skipped due to missing depth values. (Color figure online)

Table 2. Average runtime on [30]. Note that the feature regression is done on the GPU.

Stage	Runtime (ms)
Scene sampling	0.03
CNN regression	477.3
k-NN &voting	61.4
Vote filtering	1.6
Verification	130.5
Total	670.8

Table 3. F1-scores for each sequence on the re-annotated version of [30]. Note that we show the updated LC-HF scores provided by the authors.

Sequence	LineMOD	LC-HF	Our approach
Camera (377)	**0.589**	0.394	0.383
Coffee (501)	0.942	0.891	**0.972**
Joystick (838)	0.846	0.549	**0.892**
Juice (556)	0.595	**0.883**	0.866
Milk (288)	**0.558**	0.397	0.463
Shampoo (604)	**0.922**	0.792	0.910
Total (3164)	0.740	0.651	**0.747**

protocol we eventually verify each hypothesis via a fast projective ICP followed by a depth and normal check. Results are given in Tables 4 and 5 (Fig. 8).

Table 4. Detection rate for each sequence of [15] using the original protocol.

	ape	bvise	bowl	cam	can	cat	cup	driller	duck	eggb	glue	holep	iron	lamp	phone
Us	**96.9**	94.1	**99.9**	97.7	95.2	97.4	**99.6**	96.2	**97.3**	99.9	78.6	96.8	**98.7**	96.2	92.8
[15]	95.8	98.7	**99.9**	97.5	95.4	**99.3**	97.1	93.6	95.9	99.8	91.8	95.9	97.5	97.7	93.3
[18]	96.1	92.8	99.3	97.8	92.8	98.9	96.2	**98.2**	94.1	99.9	96.8	95.7	96.5	98.4	93.3
[27]	95.0	98.9	99.7	**98.2**	**96.3**	99.1	97.5	94.3	94.2	99.8	96.3	**97.5**	98.4	97.9	**95.3**
[16]	93.9	**99.8**	98.8	95.5	95.9	98.2	99.5	94.1	94.3	**100**	**98.0**	88.0	97.0	88.8	89.4

Table 5. F1-scores for each sequence of [15]. Note that these LineMOD scores are supplied from Tejani et al. with their evaluation since [15] does not provide them. It is evident that our method performs by far better than the two competitors.

	ape	bvise	bowl	cam	can	cat	cup	driller	duck	eggb	glue	holep	iron	lamp	phone
Us	**98.1**	94.8	100	**93.4**	**82.6**	**98.1**	99.9	**96.5**	**97.9**	100	**74.1**	**97.9**	91.0	**98.2**	**84.9**
[15]	53.3	84.6	-	64.0	51.2	65.6	-	69.1	58.0	86.0	43.8	51.6	68.3	67.5	56.3
[30]	85.5	**96.1**	-	71.8	70.9	88.8	-	90.5	90.7	74.0	67.8	87.5	73.5	92.1	72.8

We compute the precision average over the 13 objects also used in [5] and report 95.2 %. We are thus between their plane-trained model with an average of 98.3 % and their noise-trained model of 92.6 % on pure synthetic data. We fare relatively well with our detections and can position ourselves nicely between the other state-of-the-art approaches. We could observe that we have a near-perfect recall for each object and that our network regresses reliable features allowing to match between synthetic and real local patches. We regard this to be the most important finding of our work since achieving high precision on a dataset can be usually fine-tuned. Nonetheless, the recall for the 'glue' is rather low since it is thin and thus occasionally missed by our sampling. Based on the overall observation, our comparison of the F1-scores with [30] gives further proof of the soundness of our method. We can present excellent numbers and also show some qualitative results of the votes and detections in Fig. 9.

4.4   Challenge Dataset

Lastly, we also evaluated on the 'Challenge' dataset used in [1] containing 35 objects in 39 tabletop sequences with varying amounts of occlusion. The related work usually combines many different cues and descriptors together with elaborate verification schemes to achieve their results. We use this dataset to convey three aspects: we can reliably detect multiple objects undergoing many levels of occlusion while attaining acceptable detection results, we show again generalization on unseen data and that we accomplish this at low runtimes. We present

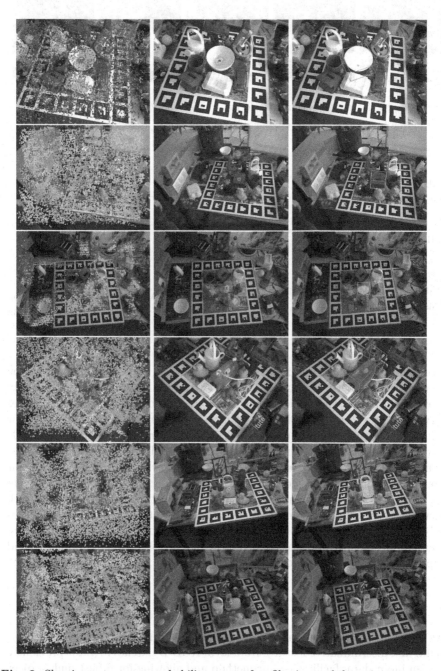

Fig. 9. Showing vote maps, probability maps after filtering and detection output on some frames for different objects on the LineMOD dataset.

Fig. 10. Detection output on selected frames from the 'Challenge' dataset.

Table 6. Precision, recall and F1-scores on the 'Challenge' dataset.

Method	Precision	Recall	F1-score
GHV [1]	1.00	0.998	0.999
Tang [29]	0.987	0.902	0.943
Xie [33]	1.00	0.998	0.999
Aldoma [2]	0.998	0.998	0.997
Our approach	0.941	0.973	0.956

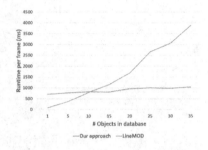

Fig. 11. Average runtime per frame on the 'Challenge' dataset with a changing amount of objects in the database.

a comparison of our method and related methods in Table 6 together with the average runtime per frame in Fig. 11. Since we do not employ a computationally heavy verification the precision of our method is the lowest due to false positives surviving the checks. Nonetheless, we have a surprisingly high recall with our feature regression and voting scheme that brings our F1-score into a favorable position. It is important to note here that the related works employ a combination of local and global shape descriptors often directly processing the 3D point cloud, exploiting different color, texture and geometrical cues and this taking up to 10–20 s per frame. Instead, although our method does not attain such accuracy, it still provides higher efficiency thanks to the use of RGB-D patches only, as well as good scalability with the number of objects due to our discrete sampling (leading to an upper bound on the number of retrieved candidates) and approximate nearest-neighbor retrieval relying on sub-linear methods (Fig. 10).

5   Conclusion

We showed that convolutional auto-encoders have the ability to regress meaningful and discriminative features from local RGB-D patches even for previously unseen input data, facilitating our method and allowing for robust multi-object and multi-instance detection under various levels of occlusion. Furthermore, our vote casting is inherently scalable and the introduced filtering stage allows to suppress many spurious votes. One main observation is that CAEs can abstract enough to reliably match between real and synthetic data. It is still unclear how a more refined training can further increase the results since different architectures have a tremendous impact on the network's performance. A proper in-depth analysis is promising and demands future work.

Acknowledgments. The authors would like to thank Toyota Motor Corporation for supporting and funding this work.

References

1. Aldoma, A., Tombari, F., Di Stefano, L., Vincze, M.: A global hypothesis verification framework for 3D object recognition in clutter. TPAMI **38**(7), 1383–1396 (2015)
2. Aldoma, A., Tombari, F., Prankl, J., Richtsfeld, A., Di Stefano, L., Vincze, M.: Multimodal cue integration through hypotheses verification for RGB-D object recognition and 6DOF pose estimation. In: ICRA (2013)
3. Aubry, M., Maturana, D., Efros, A., Russell, B., Sivic, J.: Seeing 3D chairs : exemplar part-based 2D–3D alignment using a large dataset of CAD models. In: CVPR (2014)
4. Bay, H., Tuytelaars, T., Gool, L.: SURF: speeded up robust features. In: Leonardis, A., Bischof, H., Pinz, A. (eds.) ECCV 2006. LNCS, vol. 3951, pp. 404–417. Springer, Heidelberg (2006). doi:10.1007/11744023_32
5. Brachmann, E., Krull, A., Michel, F., Gumhold, S., Shotton, J., Rother, C.: Learning 6D object pose estimation using 3D object coordinates. In: Fleet, D., Pajdla, T., Schiele, B., Tuytelaars, T. (eds.) ECCV 2014. LNCS, vol. 8690, pp. 536–551. Springer, Heidelberg (2014). doi:10.1007/978-3-319-10605-2_35
6. Buch, A.G., Yang, Y., Krüger, N., Petersen, H.G. In search of inliers: 3D correspondence by local and global voting. In: CVPR (2014)
7. Cai, H., Werner, T., Matas, J.: Fast detection of multiple textureless 3-D objects. In: Chen, M., Leibe, B., Neumann, B. (eds.) ICVS 2013. LNCS, vol. 7963, pp. 103–112. Springer, Heidelberg (2013). doi:10.1007/978-3-642-39402-7_11
8. Gall, J., Yao, A., Razavi, N., Van Gool, L., Lempitsky, V.: Hough forests for object detection, tracking, and action recognition. TPAMI **33**(11), 2188–2202 (2011)
9. Girshick, R., Donahue, J., Darrell, T., Berkeley, U.C., Malik, J.: Rich feature hierarchies for accurate object detection and semantic segmentation. In: CVPR (2014)
10. Gu, C., Ren, X.: Discriminative mixture-of-templates for viewpoint classification. In: Daniilidis, K., Maragos, P., Paragios, N. (eds.) ECCV 2010. LNCS, vol. 6315, pp. 408–421. Springer, Heidelberg (2010). doi:10.1007/978-3-642-15555-0_30
11. Gupta, S., Girshick, R., Arbeláez, P., Malik, J.: Learning rich features from RGB-D images for object detection and segmentation. In: CVPR (2014)
12. Gupta, S., Arbelaez, P., Girshick, R., Malik, J.: Aligning 3D models to RGB-D images of cluttered scenes. In: CVPR (2015)
13. Hao, Q., Cai, R., Li, Z., Zhang, L., Pang, Y., Wu, F., Rui, Y.: Efficient 2D-to-3D correspondence filtering for scalable 3D object recognition. In: CVPR (2013)
14. Hinterstoisser, S., Cagniart, C., Ilic, S., Sturm, P., Navab, N., Fua, P., Lepetit, V.: Gradient response maps for real-time detection of textureless objects. TPAMI **34**(5), 879–888 (2012)

15. Hinterstoisser, S., Lepetit, V., Ilic, S., Holzer, S., Bradski, G., Konolige, K., Navab, N.: Model based training, detection and pose estimation of texture-less 3D objects in heavily cluttered scenes. In: Lee, K.M., Matsushita, Y., Rehg, J.M., Hu, Z. (eds.) ACCV 2012. LNCS, vol. 7724, pp. 548–562. Springer, Heidelberg (2013). doi:10.1007/978-3-642-37331-2_42

16. Hodan, T., Zabulis, X., Lourakis, M., Obdrzalek, S., Matas, J.: Detection and fine 3D pose estimation of textureless objects in RGB-D images. In: IROS (2015)

17. Jia, Y., Shelhamer, E., Donahue, J., Karayev, S., Long, J., Girshick, R., Guadarrama, S., Darrell, T.: Caffe: convolutional architecture for fast feature embedding, Technical report (2014). http://arxiv.org/abs/1408.5093

18. Kehl, W., Tombari, F., Navab, N., Ilic, S., Lepetit, V.: Hashmod: a hashing method for scalable 3D object detection. In: BMVC (2015)

19. Lowe, D.G.: Local feature view clustering for 3D object recognition. In: CVPR (2001)

20. Lowe, D.G.: Distinctive image features from scale-invariant keypoints. IJCV **60**(2), 91–110 (2004)

21. Malisiewicz, T., Gupta, A., Efros, A.: Ensemble of exemplar-SVMs for object detection and beyond. In: ICCV (2011)

22. Masci, J., Meier, U., Cireşan, D., Schmidhuber, J.: Stacked convolutional auto-encoders for hierarchical feature extraction. In: Honkela, T., Duch, W., Girolami, M., Kaski, S. (eds.) ICANN 2011. LNCS, vol. 6791, pp. 52–59. Springer, Heidelberg (2011). doi:10.1007/978-3-642-21735-7_7

23. Mian, A., Bennamoun, M., Owens, R.: On the repeatability and quality of keypoints for local feature-based 3D object retrieval from cluttered scenes. IJCV **89**, 348–361 (2009)

24. Muja, M., Lowe, D.: Scalable nearest neighbour methods for high dimensional data. TPAMI **36**(11), 2227–2240 (2014)

25. Pauwels, K., Rubio, L., Diaz, J., Ros, E.: Real-time model-based rigid object pose estimation and tracking combining dense and sparse visual cues. In: CVPR (2013)

26. Pepik, B., Gehler, P., Stark, M., Schiele, B.: 3D2Pm3D deformable part models. In: ECCV (2012)

27. Rios-Cabrera, R., Tuytelaars, T.: Discriminatively trained templates for 3D object detection: a real time scalable approach. In: ICCV (2013)

28. Rusu, R.B., Holzbach, A., Blodow, N., Beetz, M.: Fast geometric point labeling using conditional random fields. In: IROS (2009)

29. Tang, J., Miller, S., Singh, A., Abbeel, P.: A textured object recognition pipeline for color and depth image data. In: ICRA (2011)

30. Tejani, A., Tang, D., Kouskouridas, R., Kim, T.-K.: Latent-class hough forests for 3D object detection and pose estimation. In: Fleet, D., Pajdla, T., Schiele, B., Tuytelaars, T. (eds.) ECCV 2014. LNCS, vol. 8694, pp. 462–477. Springer, Heidelberg (2014). doi:10.1007/978-3-319-10599-4_30

31. Tombari, F., Salti, S., Stefano, L.: Unique signatures of histograms for local surface description. In: Daniilidis, K., Maragos, P., Paragios, N. (eds.) ECCV 2010. LNCS, vol. 6313, pp. 356–369. Springer, Heidelberg (2010). doi:10.1007/978-3-642-15558-1_26

32. Wohlhart, P., Lepetit, V.: Learning descriptors for object recognition and 3D pose estimation. In: CVPR (2015)

33. Xie, Z., Singh, A., Uang, J., Narayan, K.S., Abbeel, P.: Multimodal blending for high-accuracy instance recognition. In: IROS (2013)

A Neural Approach to Blind Motion Deblurring

Ayan Chakrabarti$^{(\boxtimes)}$

Toyota Technological Institute at Chicago, Chicago, USA
`ayanc@ttic.edu`

Abstract. We present a new method for blind motion deblurring that uses a neural network trained to compute estimates of sharp image patches from observations that are blurred by an unknown motion kernel. Instead of regressing directly to patch intensities, this network learns to predict the complex Fourier coefficients of a deconvolution filter to be applied to the input patch for restoration. For inference, we apply the network independently to all overlapping patches in the observed image, and average its outputs to form an initial estimate of the sharp image. We then explicitly estimate a single global blur kernel by relating this estimate to the observed image, and finally perform non-blind deconvolution with this kernel. Our method exhibits accuracy and robustness close to state-of-the-art iterative methods, while being much faster when parallelized on GPU hardware.

Keywords: Blind deconvolution · Motion deblurring · Deep learning

1 Introduction

Photographs captured with long exposure times using hand-held cameras are often degraded by blur due to camera shake. The ability to reverse this degradation and recover a sharp image is attractive to photographers, since it allows rescuing an otherwise acceptable photograph. Moreover, if this ability is *consistent* and can be relied upon post-acquisition, it gives photographers more flexibility at the time of capture, for example, in terms of shooting with a zoom-lens without a tripod, or trading off exposure time with ISO in low-light settings. Beginning with the seminal work of Fergus *et al.* [7], the last decade has seen considerable progress [3,4,10,13,14,19,20] in the development of effective blind motion deblurring methods that seek to estimate camera motion in terms of the induced blur kernel, and then reverse its effect. This progress has been helped by the development of principled evaluation on standard benchmarks [12,19], that measure performance over a large and diverse set of images.

Some deblurring algorithms [3,20] emphasize efficiency, and use inexpensive processing of image features to quickly estimate the motion kernel. Despite their

---

Electronic supplementary material The online version of this chapter (doi:10. 1007/978-3-319-46487-9_14) contains supplementary material, which is available to authorized users.

© Springer International Publishing AG 2016
B. Leibe et al. (Eds.): ECCV 2016, Part III, LNCS 9907, pp. 221–235, 2016.
DOI: 10.1007/978-3-319-46487-9_14

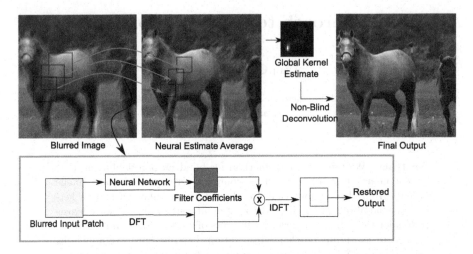

Fig. 1. Neural Blind Deconvolution. Our method uses a neural network trained for per-patch blind deconvolution. Given an input patch blurred by an unknown motion blur kernel, this network predicts the Fourier coefficients of a filter to be applied to that input for restoration. For inference, we apply this network independently on all overlapping patches in the input image, and compose their outputs to form an initial estimate of the sharp image. We then infer a single global blur kernel that relates the input to this initial estimate, and use that kernel for non-blind deconvolution.

speed, these methods can yield remarkably accurate kernel estimates and achieve high-quality restoration for many images, making them a practically useful post-processing tool for photographers. However, due to their reliance on relatively simple heuristics, they also have poor outlier performance and can fail on a significant fraction of blurred images. Other methods are iterative—they reason with parametric prior models for natural images and motion kernels, and use these priors to successively improve the algorithm's estimate of the sharp image and the motion kernel. The two most successful deblurring algorithms fall [14,19] in this category, and while they are able to outperform previous methods by a significant margin, they also have orders of magnitude longer running times.

In this work, we explore whether discriminatively trained neural networks can match the performance of traditional methods that use generative natural image priors, and do so without multiple iterative refinements. Our work is motivated by recent successes in the use of neural networks for other image restoration tasks (*e.g.*, [2,5,16,21]). This includes methods [16,21] for *non-blind* deconvolution, *i.e.*, restoring a blurred image when the blur kernel is known. While the estimation problem in blind deconvolution is significantly more ill-posed than the non-blind case, these works provide insight into the design process of neural architectures for deconvolution.

Hradiš *et al.* [9] explored the use of neural networks for blind deconvolution on images of text. Since text images are highly structured—two-tone with thin sparse contours—a standard feed-forward architecture was able to achieve successful restoration. Meanwhile, Sun *et al.* [18] considered a version of the problem with restrictions on motion blur types, and were able to successfully train a neural network to identify the blur in an observed natural image patch from among a small discrete set of oriented box blur kernels of various lengths. Recently, Schuler *et al.* [17] tackled the general blind motion deblurring problem using a neural architecture designed to mimic the computational steps of traditional iterative deblurring methods. They designed learnable layers to carry out extraction of salient local image features and kernel estimation based on these features, and stacked multiple copies of these layers to enable iterative refinement. Remarkably, they were able to train this multi-stage network with relative success. However, while their initial results are very encouraging, their current performance still significantly lags behind the state of the art [14,19]—especially when the unknown blur kernel is large.

In this paper, we propose a new approach for blind deconvolution of natural images degraded by arbitrary motion blur kernels due to camera shake. At the core of our algorithm is a neural network trained to restore individual image patches. This network differs from previous architectures in two significant ways:

1. Rather than formulate the prediction task as blur kernel estimation through iterative refinement (as in [17]), or as direct regression to deblurred intensity values (as in [2,5,16,21]), we train our network to output the complex Fourier coefficients of a *deconvolution* filter to be applied to the input patch.
2. We use a multi-resolution frequency decomposition to encode the input patch, and limit the connectivity of initial network layers based on locality in frequency (analogous to convolutional layers that are limited by locality in space). This leads to a significant reduction in the number of weights to be learned during training, which proves crucial since it allows us to successfully train a network that operates on large patches, and therefore can reason about large blur kernels (*e.g.*, in comparison to [17]).

For whole image restoration, the network is independently applied to every overlapping patch in the input image, and its outputs are composed to form an initial estimate of the latent sharp image. Despite reasoning with patches independently and not sharing information about a common global motion kernel, we find that this procedure by itself performs surprisingly well. We show that these results can be further improved by using the restored image to compute a global blur kernel estimate, which is finally used for non-blind deconvolution. Evaluation on a standard benchmark [19] demonstrates that our approach is competitive when considering accuracy, robustness, and running time.

2   Patch-Wise Neural Deconvolution

Let $y[n]$ be the observed image of a scene blurred due to camera motion, and $x[n]$ the corresponding latent sharp image that we wish to estimate, with $n \in$

$\mathbb{Z}^2$ indexing pixel location. The degradation due to blur can be approximately modeled as convolution with an unknown blur kernel k:

$$y[n] = (x * k)[n] + \epsilon[n], \quad k[n] \geq 0, \sum_n k[n] = 1, \tag{1}$$

where $*$ denotes convolution, and $\epsilon[n]$ is i.i.d. Gaussian noise.

As shown in Fig. 1, the central component of our algorithm is a neural network that carries out restoration locally on individual patches in $y[n]$. Formally, our goal is to design a network that is able to recover the sharp intensity values $x_p = \{x[n] : n \in p\}$ of a patch p, given as input a larger patch $y_{p+} = \{x[n] : n \in p^+\}$, $p^+ \supset p$ from the observed image. The larger input is necessary since values in $x_p[n]$, especially near the boundaries of p, can depend on those outside $y_p[n]$. In practice, we choose p^+ to be of size 65×65, with its central 33×33 patch corresponding to p. In this section, we describe our formulation of the prediction task for this network, its architecture and connectivity, and our approach to training it.

2.1 Restoration by Predicting Deconvolution Filter Coefficients

As depicted in Fig. 1, the output of our network are the complex discrete Fourier transform (DFT) coefficients $G_{p+}[z] \in \mathbb{C}$ of a deconvolution filter, where z indexes two-dimensional spatial frequencies in the DFT. This filter is then applied DFT $Y_{p+}[z]$ of the input patch $y_{p+}[n]$:

$$\hat{X}_{p+}[z] = G_{p+}[z] \times Y_{p+}[z]. \tag{2}$$

Our estimate $\hat{x}_p[n]$ of the sharp image patch is computed by taking the inverse discrete Fourier transform (IDFT) of $\hat{X}_{p+}[z]$, and then cropping out the central patch $p \subset p^+$. Since $x[n]$ and $y[n]$ are both real valued and k is unit sum, we assume that $G_{p+}[z] = G_{p+}^*[-z]$, and $G_{p+}[0] = 1$. Therefore, the network only needs to output $(|p^+| - 1)/2$ unique complex numbers to characterize G_{p+}, where $|p^+|$ is the number of pixels in p^+.

Our training objective is that the output coefficients $G_{p+}[z]$ be optimal with respect to the quality of the final sharp intensities $\hat{x}_p[n]$. Specifically, the loss function for the network is defined as the mean square error (MSE) between the predicted and true sharp intensity values $\hat{x}_p[n]$ and $x_p[n]$:

$$L(\hat{x}_p, x_p) = \frac{1}{|p|} \sum_{n \in p} (\hat{x}_p[n] - x_p[n])^2. \tag{3}$$

Note both the IDFT and the filtering in (2) are linear operations, and therefore it is trivial to back-propagate the gradients of (3) to the outputs $G_{p+}[z]$, and subsequently to all layers within the network.

Motivation. As with any neural-network based method, the validation of the design choices in our approach ultimately has to be empirical. However, we attempt to provide the reader with some insight into our motivation for making these choices. We begin by considering the differences between predicting deconvolution filter coefficients and regressing directly to pixel intensities $x_p[n]$, as was done in most prior neural restoration methods [2,5,16,21]. Indeed, since we use the predicted coefficients to estimate $x_p[n]$ and define our loss with respect to the latter, our overall formulation *can* be interpreted as a regression to $x_p[n]$. However, our approach enforces a specific parametric form being enforced on the learned mapping from $y_{p+}[n]$ to $x_p[n]$. In other words, the notion that the sharp and blurred image patches are related by convolution is "baked-in" to the network's architecture. Additionally, providing $Y_{p+}[z]$ separately at the output alleviates the need for the layers within our network to retain a linear encoding of the input patch all the way to the output.

Another alternative formulation could have been to set-up the network to predict the blur kernel k itself like in [17], which also encodes the convolutional relationship between the network's input and output. However, remember that our network works on local patches independently. For many patches, inferring the blur kernel may be impossible from local information alone—for example, a patch with only a vertical edge would have no content in horizontal frequencies, making it impossible to infer the horizontal structure of the kernel. But in these cases, it would still be possible to compute an optimal deconvolution filter and restored image patch (in our example, the horizontal frequency values of $G_{p+}[z]$ would not matter). Moreover, our goal is to recover the restored image patch and estimating the kernel solves only a part of the problem, since non-blind deconvolution is not trivial. In contrast, our predicted deconvolution filter can be directly applied for restoration, and because it is trained with respect to restoration quality, the network learns to generate these predictions by reasoning both about the unknown kernel and sharp image content.

It may be helpful to consider what the optimal values of $G_{p+}[z]$ should be. One interpretation for these values can be derived from Wiener deconvolution [1], in which ideal restoration is achieved by applying a filter using (2) with coefficients given by

$$G_{p+}[z] = \left(|K[z]|^2 S_{p+}[z] + \sigma_\epsilon^2 \right)^{-1} K^*[z] S_{p+}[z]. \tag{4}$$

Here, $K[z]$ is the DFT of the kernel k, and $S_{p+}[z]$ is the spectral profile of $x_{p+}[n]$ (*i.e.*, a DFT of its auto-correlation function). Note that in blind deconvolution, both $S_{p+}[z]$ and $K[z]$ are unknown and iterative algorithms can be interpreted as explicitly estimating these quantities through sequential refinement. In contrast, our network is discriminatively trained to directly predict the ratio in (4).

2.2   Network Architecture

Our network needs to work with large input patches in order to successfully handle large blur kernels. This presents a challenge in terms of the number of

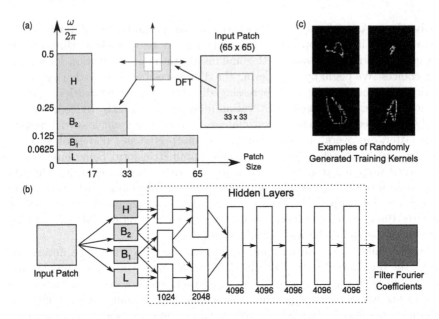

Fig. 2. Network Architecture. (a) To limit the number of weights in the network, we use a multi-resolution decomposition to encode the input patch into four "bands", containing low-pass (L), band-pass (B_1, B_2), and high-pass H frequency components. Higher frequencies are sampled at a coarser resolution, and computed from a smaller patch centered on the input. (b) Our network regresses from this input encoding to the complex Fourier coefficients of a restoration filter, and contains seven hidden layers (each followed by a ReLU activation). The connectivity of the initial layers is limited to adjacent frequency bands. (c) Our network is trained with randomly generated synthetic motion blur kernels of different sizes.

weights to be learned and the feasibility of training since, as observed by [21] and by us in our own experiments, the traditional strategy of making the initial layers convolutional with limited support performs poorly for deconvolution. This why the networks for blind deconvolution in [16,21] have either used only fully connected layers [16], or large oriented on-dimensional convolutional layers [21].

We adopt a novel approach to parameterizing the input patch and defining the connectivity of the initial layers in our network. Specifically, we use a multi-resolution decomposition strategy (illustrated in Fig. 2 (a)) where higher spatial frequencies are sampled with lower resolution. We compute DFTs at three different levels, corresponding to patches of three different sizes ($17 \times 17, 33 \times 33$, and 65×65) centered on the input patch, and from each retain the coefficients corresponding to $4 < \max |z| \le 8$. Here, $\max |z|$ represents the larger magnitude of the two components (horizontal and vertical) of the frequency indices in z.

This decomposition gives us 104 independent complex coefficients (or 208 scalars) from each DFT level that we group into "bands". Note that the indices z correspond to different spatial frequencies ω for different sized DFTs, with coefficients from the smaller-size DFTs representing a coarser sampling in the frequency domain. Therefore, the three bands above correspond to high- and band-pass components of the input patch. We also construct a low-pass band by including the coefficients corresponding to $\max |z| \leq 4$ from the largest (*i.e.*, , 65×65) decomposition. This band only has 81 scalar components (40 complex coefficients and a scalar DC coefficient). As suggested in [11], we apply a de-correlating linear transform to the coefficients of each band, based on their empirical covariance on input patches in the training set.

Note that our decomposition also entails a dimensionality reduction—the total number of coefficients in the four bands is lower than the size of the input patch. Such a reduction may have been problematic if the network were directly regressing to patch intensities. However, we find this approximate representation suffices for our task of predicting filter coefficients, since the full input patch $y_{p^+}[n]$ (in the form of its DFT) is separately provided to (2) for the computation of the final output $\hat{x}_p[n]$.

As depicted in Fig. 2 (b), we use a feed-forward network architecture with seven hidden layers to predict the coefficients $G_{p^+}[z]$ from our encoding of the observed blurry input patch. Units in the first layer are only connected to input coefficients from pairs of adjacent frequency bands—with groups of 1024 units connected to each pair. Note that these groups do not share weights. We adopt a similar strategy for the next layer, connecting units to pairs of adjacent groups from the first layer. Each group in this layer has 2048 units. Restricting connectivity in this way, based on locality in frequency, reduces the number of weights in our network, while still allowing good prediction in practice. This is not entirely surprising, since many iterative algorithms (including [14,19]) also divide the inference task into sequential coarse-to-fine reasoning at individual scales. All remaining layers in our network are fully connected with 4096 units each. Units in all hidden layers have ReLU activations [15].

2.3 Training

Our network was trained on a synthetic dataset that is entirely disjoint from the evaluation benchmark [19]. This was constructed by extracting sharp image patches from images in the Pascal VOC 2012 dataset [6], blurring them with synthetically generated kernels, and adding Gaussian noise. We set the noise standard deviation to 1 % to match the noise level in the benchmark [19].

The synthetic motion kernels were generated by randomly sampling six points in a limited size grid (we generate an equal number of kernels from grid sizes of 8×8, 16×16, and 24×24), fitting a spline through these points, and setting the kernel values at each pixel on this spline to a value sampled from a Gaussian distribution with mean one and standard deviation of half. We then clipped these values to be positive, and normalized the kernel to be unit sum.

There is an inherent phase ambiguity in blind deconvolution—one can apply equal but opposite translations to the blur kernel and sharp image estimates to come up with equally plausible explanations for an observation. While this ambiguity need not be resolved globally, we need our local $G_{p^+}[z]$ estimates in overlapping patches to have consistent phase. Therefore, we ensured that the training kernels have a "canonical" translation by centering them so that each kernel's center of mass (weighted by kernel values) is at the center of the window. Figure 2 (c) shows some of the kernels generated using this approach.

We constructed separate training and validation sets with different sharp patches and randomly generated kernels. We used about 520,000 and 3,000 image patches and 100,000 and 3,000 kernels for the training and validation sets respectively. While we extracted multiple patches from the same image, we ensured that the training and validation patches were drawn from different images. To minimize disk access, we loaded the entire set of sharp patches and kernels into memory. Training data was generated on the fly by selecting random pairs of patches and kernels, and convolving the two to create the input patch. We also used rotated and mirrored versions of the sharp patches. This gave us a near inexhaustible supply of training data. Validation data was also generated on the fly, but we always chose the same pairs of patches and kernels to ensure that validation error could be compared across iterations.

We used stochastic gradient descent for minimizing the loss function (3), with a batch-size of 512 and a momentum value of 0.9. We trained the network for a total of 1.8 million iterations, which took about 3 days using an NVIDIA Titan X GPU. We used a learning rate of 32 (higher rates caused gradients to explode) for the first 800 k iterations, at which point validation error began to plateau. For the remaining iterations, we dropped the rate by a factor of $\sqrt{2}$ every 100 k iterations. We kept track of the validation error across iterations, and at the end of training, used the weights that yielded the lowest value of that error.

3   Whole Image Restoration

Given an observed blurry image $y[n]$, we consider all overlapping patches y_{p+} in the image, and use our trained network to compute estimates $\hat{x}_p$ of their latent sharp versions. We then combines these restored patches to form an initial an estimate $x_N[n]$ of the sharp image, by setting $x_N[n]$ to the average of its estimates $\hat{x}_p[n]$ from all patches $p \ni n$ that contain it, using a Hanning window to weight the contributions from different patches.

While this feed-forward and purely local procedure achieves reasonable restoration, we have so far not taken into account the fact that the entire image has been blurred by the same motion kernel. To do so, we compute an estimate of the global kernel $k[n]$, by relating the observed image $y[n]$ to our neural-average estimate $x_N[n]$. Formally, we estimate this kernel $k[n]$ as

$$k = \arg \min \sum_i \|(k * (f_i * x_N)) - (f_i * y)\|^2, \tag{5}$$

subject to the constraint that $k[n] > 0$ and $\sum_n k[n] = 1$. We do not assume that the size of the kernel is known, and always estimate $k[n]$ within a fixed-size support (51×51 as is standard for the benchmark [19]). Here, $f_i[n]$ are various derivative filters (we use first and second order derivatives at 8 orientations). Like in [19], we only let strong gradients participate in the estimation process by setting values of $(f_i * x_N)$ to zero except those at the two percent pixel locations with the highest magnitudes.

This approach to estimating a global kernel from an estimate of the latent sharp image is fairly standard. But while it is typically used repeatedly within an iterative procedure that refines the estimates of the sharp image as well (e.g., in [14,19]), we estimate the kernel only once from the neural average output.

We adopt a relatively simple and fast approach to optimizing (5) under the positivity and unit sum constraints on k. Specifically, we minimize $L1$ regularized versions of the objective:

$$k_\lambda = \arg\min \sum_i \|(k * (f_i * x_N)) - (f_i * y)\|^2 + \lambda \sum_n |k[n]|, \qquad (6)$$

for a small range of values for the regularization weight λ. This optimization, for each value of λ, can be done very efficiently in the Fourier domain using half-quadratic splitting [8]. We clip each kernel estimate $k_\lambda[n]$ to be positive, set very small or isolated values to zero, and normalize the result to be unit sum. We then pick the kernel $k_\lambda[n]$ which yields the lowest value of the original un-regularized cost in (5). Given this estimate of the global kernel, we use EPLL [22]—a state-of-the-art *non-blind* deconvolution algorithm—to deconvolve $y[n]$ and arrive at our final estimate of the sharp image $x[n]$.

4 Experiments

We evaluate our approach on the benchmark dataset of Sun *et al.* [19], which consists of 640 blurred images generated from 80 high quality natural images, and 8 real motion blur kernels acquired by Levin *et al.* [12]. We begin by analyzing patch-wise predictions from our neural network, and then compare the performance of our overall algorithm to the state of the art.

4.1 Local Network Predictions

Figure 3 illustrates the typical behavior of our trained neural network on individual patches. All patches in the figure are taken from the same image from [19], which means that they were all blurred by the same kernel (the kernel, and its Fourier coefficients, are also shown). However, we see that the predicted restoration filter coefficients are qualitatively different across these patches.

While some of this variation is due to the fact that the network is reasoning with these patches independently, remember from Sect. 2.1 that we expect the ideal restoration filter to vary based on image content. The predicted filters in Fig. 3 can be understood in that context as attempting to amplify different subsets of the frequencies attenuated by the blur kernel, based on which frequencies the network believes were present in the original image. Comparing the Fourier coefficients of the ground truth sharp patch to our restored outputs, we see that our network restores many frequency components attenuated in the observed patch, without amplifying noise.

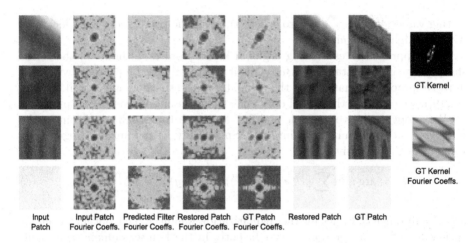

GT Kernel

GT Kernel
Fourier Coeffs.

Input   Input Patch   Predicted Filter Restored Patch   GT Patch   Restored Patch   GT Patch
Patch   Fourier Coeffs. Fourier Coeffs.   Fourier Coeffs. Fourier Coeffs.

Fig. 3. Examples of per-patch restoration using our network. Shown here are different patches extracted from a blurred image from [19]. For each patch, we show the observed blurry patch in the spatial domain, its DFT coefficients $Y[z]$ (in terms of log-magnitude), the predicted filter coefficients $G[z]$ from our network, the DFT of the resulting restored patch $X[z]$, and the restored patch in the spatial domain. As comparison, we also show the ground truth sharp image patch and its DFT, as well as the common ground truth kernel of the network and its DFT.

These examples also validate our decision to estimate a restoration filter instead of the blur kernel from individual patches. Most patches have no content in entire ranges of frequencies even in their ground-truth sharp versions (most notably, the patch in the last row that is nearly flat), which makes estimating the corresponding frequency components of the kernel impossible. However, we are still able to restore these patches since that just requires identifying that those frequency components are absent.

Looking at the restored patches in the spatial domain, we note that while they are sharper than the input, they still have a lot of high-frequency information missing. However, remember that even our direct neural estimate $x_N[n]$ of the sharp image is composed by averaging estimates from multiple patches at each pixel (see Fig. 1, and the supplementary material for examples of these estimates). Moreover, our final estimates are computed by fitting a global kernel estimate to these locally restored outputs, benefiting from the fact that correctly restored frequencies in all patches are coherent with the same (true) blur kernel.

4.2 Performance Evaluation

Next, we evaluate our overall method and compare it to several recent algorithms [3,4,10,13,14,17,19,20] on the Sun *et al.* benchmark [19]. Deblurring quality is measured in terms of the MSE between the estimated and the ground truth sharp image, ignoring a fifty pixel wide boundary on all sides in the latter, and after finding the crop of the restored estimate that aligns best with this

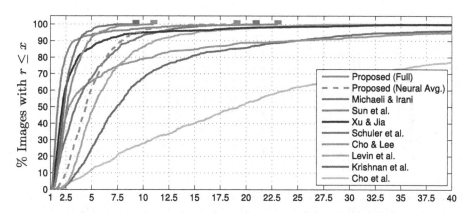

Fig. 4. Cumulative distributions of the error ratio r for different methods on the Sun *et al.* [19] benchmark. These errors were computed after using EPLL [22] for blind deconvolution using the global kernel estimates from each algorithm. The only exception is the "neural average" version of our method, where the errors correspond to those of our initial estimates computed by directly averaging per-patch neural network outputs, without reasoning about a global kernel.

Table 1. Quantiles of error-ratio r and success rate ($r \leq 5$), along with kernel estimation time for different methods

Method	Mean	95 %-ile	Max	Success rate	Time
(Neural avg.)	4.92	9.39	19.11	61 %	
Proposed	3.01	5.76	11.04	92 %	65s (GPU)
Michaeli and Irani [14]	2.57	4.49	9.31	96 %	91 min (CPU)
Sun et al. [19]	2.38	5.98	23.07	93 %	38 min (CPU)
Xu and Jia [20]	3.63	9.97	65.33	86 %	25s (CPU)
Schuler et al. [17]	4.53	11.21	20.96	67 %	22s (CPU)
Cho and Lee [3]	8.69	40.59	111.19	66 %	1s (CPU)
Levin et al. [13]	6.56	15.13	40.87	47 %	4 min (CPU)
Krishnan et al. [10]	11.65	34.93	133.21	25 %	3 min (CPU)
Cho et al. [4]	28.13	89.67	164.94	12 %	1 min (CPU)

ground truth. Performance on the benchmark is evaluated [14,19] using quantiles of the *error ratio* r between the MSE of the estimated image and that of the deconvolving the observed image with the ground truth kernel using EPLL [22]. Results with $r \leq 5$ are considered to correspond to "successful" restoration [14].

Figure 4 shows the cumulative distribution of the error-ratio for all methods on the benchmark. We also report specific quantiles of the error ratio—mean, and outlier performance in terms of 95 %-ile and maximum value—as well as the success rate of each method in Table 1. The results for [14,17] were provided by their authors, while those for all other methods are from [19]. Results for all methods were obtained using EPLL for blind-deconvolution based on their kernel estimates, and are therefore directly comparable to those of our overall

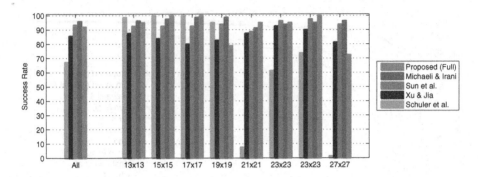

Fig. 5. Success rates of different methods, evaluated over the entire Sun *et al.* [19] dataset, and separately over images blurred with each of the 8 kernels. The kernels are sorted according to size (noted on the x-axis).

method. We also report the performance of our initial estimates from just the direct neural averaging step in Fig. 4 and Table 1, which did not involve any global kernel estimation or the use of non-blind deconvolution with EPLL.

The performance of the full version of our method performs is close to that of the two state-of-the-art methods of Michaeli and Irani [14] and Sun *et al.* [19]. While our mean errors are higher than those of both and [14,19], we have a near identical success rate and better outlier performance than [19]. Note that our method outperforms the remaining algorithms by a significant margin on all metrics. The best amongst these is the efficient approach of Xu and Jia [20] which is able to perform well on many individual images, but has higher errors and succeeds less often on average than our approach and that of [14,19]. Figure 5 compares the success rate of different methods over individual kernels in the benchmark, to study the effect of kernel size. We see that the previous neural approach of [17] suffers a sharp drop in accuracy for larger kernel sizes. In contrast, our method's performance is more consistent across the whole range of kernels in [19] (albeit, our worst performance *is* with the largest kernel).

In addition to accuracy, Table 1 also reports the running time for kernel estimation for all methods. We see that while our method has nearly comparable performance to the two state-of-the-art methods [14,19], it offers a significant advantage over them in terms of speed. A MATLAB implementation of our method takes a total of only 65 s for kernel estimation using an NVIDIA Titan X GPU. The majority of this time, 45 s, is taken to compute the initial neural-average estimate x_N. On the other hand, [14,19] take 91 min and 38 min respectively, using the MATLAB/C implementations of these methods provided by their authors on an I-7 3.3 GHz CPU with 6 cores.

While [14,19]'s running times could potentially be improved if they are reimplemented to use a GPU, their ability to benefit from parallelism is limited by the fact that both are iterative techniques whose computations are largely sequential (in fact, we only saw speed-ups of 1.4X and 3.5X in [14,19], respectively, when going from one to six CPU cores). In contrast, our method maps naturally to parallel architectures and is able to fully saturate the available cores on a

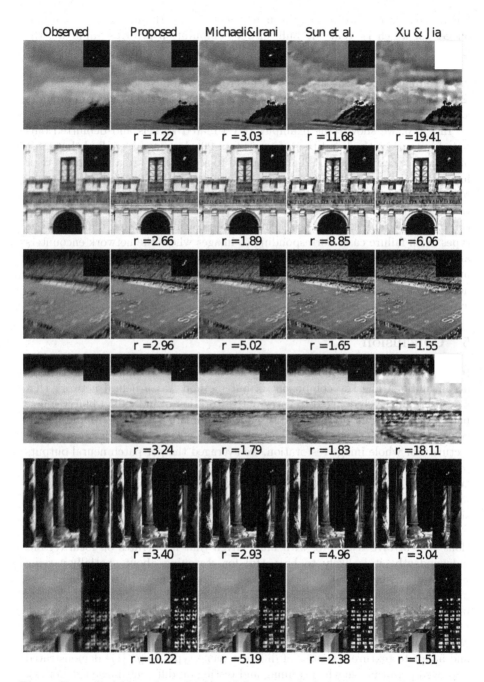

Fig. 6. Example deblurred results from different methods. The estimated kernels are shown inset, with the ground truth kernel shown with the observed images in the first column. This figure is best viewed in the electronic version.

GPU. Batched forward passes through a neural network are especially efficient on GPUs, which is what the bulk of our computation involves—applying the local network *independently* and in-parallel on all patches in the input image.

Some methods in Table 1 are able to use simpler heuristics or priors to achieve lower running times. But these are far less robust and have lower success rates—[20] has the best performance amongst this set. Our method therefore provides a new and practically useful trade-off between reliability and speed.

In Fig. 6, we show some examples of estimated kernels and deblurred outputs from our method and those from [14,19,20]. In general, we find that most of the failure cases of [14,19,20] correspond to scenes that are a poor fit to their hand-crafted generative image priors—*e.g.*, most of [19,20]'s failure cases correspond to images that lack well-separated strong edges. Our discriminatively trained neural network derives its implicit priors automatically from the statistics of the training set, and is relatively more consistent across different scene types, with failure cases corresponding to images where the network encounters ambiguous textures that it can't generalize to. We refer the reader to the supplementary material and our project website at http://www.ttic.edu/chakrabarti/ndeblur for more results. The MATLAB implementation of our method, along with trained network weights, is also available at the latter.

5   Conclusion

In this paper, we introduced a neural network-based method for blind image deconvolution. The key component of our method was a neural network that was discriminatively trained to carry out restoration of individual blurry image patches. We used intuitions from a frequency-domain view of non-blind deconvolution to formulate the prediction task for the network and to design its architecture. For whole image restoration, we averaged the per-patch neural outputs to form an initial estimate of the sharp image, and then estimated a global blur kernel from this estimate. Our approach was found to yield comparable performance to state-of-the-art iterative blind deblurring methods, while offering significant advantages in terms of speed.

We believe that our network can serve as a building block for other applications that involve reasoning with blur. Given that it operates on local regions independently, it is likely to be useful for reasoning about spatially-varying blur—*e.g.*, arising out of defocus and subject motion. We are also interested in exploring architectures and pooling strategies that allow efficient sharing of information across patches. We expect that such sharing can be used to communicate information about a common blur kernel, to exploit "internal" statistics of the image (which forms the basis of the method of [14]), and also to identify and adapt to texture statistics of different scene types (*e.g.*, [17] demonstrated improved performance when training and testing on different image categories).

Acknowledgments. The author was supported by a gift from Adobe Systems, and by the donation of a Titan X GPU from NVIDIA Corporation that was used for this research.

References

1. Brown, R.G., Hwang, P.Y.: Introduction to Random Signals and Applied Kalman Filtering, 3rd edn. Wiley, New York (1996)
2. Burger, H.C., Schuler, C.J., Harmeling, S.: Image denoising: can plain neural networks compete with BM3D? In: Proceedings of CVPR (2012)
3. Cho, S., Lee, S.: Fast motion deblurring. In: SIGGRAPH (2009)
4. Cho, T.S., Paris, S., Horn, B.K., Freeman, W.T.: Blur kernel estimation using the radon transform. In: Proceedings of CVPR (2011)
5. Eigen, D., Krishnan, D., Fergus, R.: Restoring an image taken through a window covered with dirt or rain. In: Proceedings of ICCV (2013)
6. Everingham, M., Eslami, S.A., Van Gool, L., Williams, C.K., Winn, J., Zisserman, A.: The pascal visual object classes challenge: a retrospective. IJCV **111**(1), 98–136 (2014)
7. Fergus, R., Singh, B., Hertzmann, A., Roweis, S.T., Freeman, W.T.: Removing camera shake from a single photograph. In: SIGGRAPH (2006)
8. Geman, D., Yang, C.: Nonlinear image recovery with half-quadratic regularization. Trans. Imag. Proc. **4**, 932–946 (1995)
9. Hradiš, M., Kotera, J., Zemcík, P., Šroubek, F.: Convolutional neural networks for direct text deblurring. In: Proceedings of BMVC (2015)
10. Krishnan, D., Tay, T., Fergus, R.: Blind deconvolution using a normalized sparsity measure. In: Proceedings of CVPR. IEEE (2011)
11. LeCun, Y., Bottou, L., Orr, G.B., Müller, K.-R.: Efficient backprop. In: Orr, G.B., Müller, K.-R. (eds.) Neural Networks: Tricks of the Trade. LNCS, vol. 1524, pp. 9–50. Springer, Heidelberg (1998). doi:10.1007/3-540-49430-8_2
12. Levin, A., Weiss, Y., Durand, F., Freeman, W.T.: Understanding and evaluating blind deconvolution algorithms. In: Proceedings of CVPR (2009)
13. Levin, A., Weiss, Y., Durand, F., Freeman, W.T.: Efficient marginal likelihood optimization in blind deconvolution. In: Proceedings of CVPR (2011)
14. Michaeli, T., Irani, M.: Blind deblurring using internal patch recurrence. In: Fleet, D., Pajdla, T., Schiele, B., Tuytelaars, T. (eds.) ECCV 2014. LNCS, vol. 8691, pp. 783–798. Springer, Heidelberg (2014). doi:10.1007/978-3-319-10578-9_51
15. Nair, V., Hinton, G.E.: Rectified linear units improve restricted boltzmann machines. In: Proceedings of ICML (2010)
16. Schuler, C.J., Burger, H.C., Harmeling, S., Scholkopf, B.: A machine learning approach for non-blind image deconvolution. In: Proceedings of CVPR (2013)
17. Schuler, C.J., Hirsch, M., Harmeling, S., Schölkopf, B.: Learning to deblur. In: PAMI (2015)
18. Sun, J., Cao, W., Xu, Z., Ponce, J.: Learning a convolutional neural network for non-uniform motion blur removal. In: Proceedings of CVPR (2015)
19. Sun, L., Cho, S., Wang, J., Hays, J.: Edge-based blur kernel estimation using patch priors. In: Proceedings of ICCP (2013)
20. Xu, L., Jia, J.: Two-phase kernel estimation for robust motion deblurring. In: Daniilidis, K., Maragos, P., Paragios, N. (eds.) ECCV 2010. LNCS, vol. 6311, pp. 157–170. Springer, Heidelberg (2010). doi:10.1007/978-3-642-15549-9_12
21. Xu, L., Ren, J.S., Liu, C., Jia, J.: Deep convolutional neural network for image deconvolution. In: NIPS (2014)
22. Zoran, D., Weiss, Y.: From learning models of natural image patches to whole image restoration. In: Proceedings of ICCV (2011)

Joint Face Representation Adaptation
and Clustering in Videos

Zhanpeng Zhang[1], Ping Luo[1,2], Chen Change Loy[1,2], and Xiaoou Tang[1,2(✉)]

[1] Department of Information Engineering,
The Chinese University of Hong Kong, Hong Kong, China
`zhzhanp@gmail.com, xtang@ie.cuhk.edu.hk`
[2] Shenzhen Key Lab of Comp. Vis. & Pat. Rec.,
Shenzhen Institutes of Advanced Technology, CAS, Shenzhen, China

Abstract. Clustering faces in movies or videos is extremely challenging since characters' appearance can vary drastically under different scenes. In addition, the various cinematic styles make it difficult to learn a universal face representation for all videos. Unlike previous methods that assume fixed handcrafted features for face clustering, in this work, we formulate a joint face representation adaptation and clustering approach in a deep learning framework. The proposed method allows face representation to gradually adapt from an external source domain to a target video domain. The adaptation of deep representation is achieved without any strong supervision but through iteratively discovered weak pairwise identity constraints derived from potentially noisy face clustering result. Experiments on three benchmark video datasets demonstrate that our approach generates character clusters with high purity compared to existing video face clustering methods, which are either based on deep face representation (without adaptation) or carefully engineered features.

Keywords: Convolutional network · Transfer learning · Face clustering · Face recognition

1 Introduction

Face clustering in videos aims at grouping detected faces into different subsets according to different characters. It is a popular research topic [1–5] due to its wide spectrum of applications, *e.g.* video summarization, content-based retrieval, story segmentation, and character interaction analysis. It can be even exploited as a tool for collecting large-scale dataset for face recognition [4].

Clustering faces in videos is challenging. As shown in Fig. 1, the appearance of a character can vary drastically under different scenes as the story progresses. The viewing angles and lighting also vary widely due to the rich cinematic techniques, such as different shots (*e.g.* deep focus, follow shot), variety of lighting techniques, and aesthetics. In many cases, the face is blur due to fast motion or occluded due to interactions between characters. The blurring and occlusion are more severe for fantasy and action movies, *i.e. Harry Potter* series.

© Springer International Publishing AG 2016
B. Leibe et al. (Eds.): ECCV 2016, Part III, LNCS 9907, pp. 236–251, 2016.
DOI: 10.1007/978-3-319-46487-9_15

Fig. 1. Faces at different time of the movie *Harry Potter*. Face clustering in videos is challenging due to the various appearance changes as the story progresses.

Conventional techniques that assume fixed handcrafted features [2,4] may fail in the cases as shown in Fig. 1. Specifically, handcrafted features are susceptible to large appearance, illumination, and viewpoint variations, and therefore cannot cope with drastic appearance changes. Deep learning approaches have achieved substantial advances for face representation learning [6–8]. These methods could arguably provide a more robust representation to our problem. However, two issues hinder a direct application of deep learning approaches. Firstly, contemporary deep models [6–8] for face recognition are trained with web images or photos from personal albums. These models overfit to the training data distributions thus will not be directly generalizable to clustering faces in different videos with different cinematic styles. Secondly, faces detected in videos usually do not come with identity labels[1]. Hence, we cannot adopt the popular transfer learning approach [11] to adapt these models for our desired videos.

In the absence of precise face annotations, we need to provide deep models with the new capability of learning from weak and noisy supervisions to achieve model adaptation for unseen videos. To this end, we formulate a novel deep learning framework that jointly performs representation adaptation and face clustering in a target video. On one hand, deep representation adaptation provides robust features that permit for better face clustering under unconstrained variations. On the other hand, the clustering results, in return, provide weak pairwise constraints (whether two faces should/should not be assigned to the same cluster) for learning more robust deep representation.

We note that pairwise constraints derived from face tracks (*i.e.* detection or tracking result of face image subsequences) have been used in previous studies to improve video face clustering [3–5]. In particular, faces appearing in the same frame unlikely belong to the same person while any two faces in the same face track should belong to the same person. Our approach differs to these studies in that we not only exploit such static constraints. Our method also

---

[1] Unless we perform joint matching of visual appearance with video's script [9,10]. However, an accurate visual-script matching is still far from addressed. This option is beyond the scope of this study.

takes advantage of weak dynamic constraints obtained from joint clustering. How to carefully utilize such noisy constraints is challenging and we show that our approach is capable of forming a positive and alternating feedback loop between representation adaptation and clustering.

Contributions: (1) We formulate the video face clustering in a novel deep learning framework. An alternating feedback loop between representation adaptation and clustering is proposed to adapt the deep model from a source domain to a target video domain. To our knowledge, this is the first attempt to introduce deep learning for video face clustering. (2) Different from existing methods that construct static pairwise constraints from the face trajectories, we iteratively discover inter and intra person constraints that allow us to better adapt the face representation in the target video. Experiments on three benchmark video datasets show that the proposed method significantly outperforms existing state-of-the-art methods [2,4,12]. In addition, we apply the adapted representation for face verification in the target video. The results demonstrate the superiority of our method compared to deep face representation without adaptation [7]. Code will be released to provide details of our algorithm[2].

2   Related Work

Traditional face clustering methods [13–16] are usually purely data-driven and unsupervised. In particular, these algorithms mainly focus on clustering the photo albums. How to find a good distance metric between faces or effective subspace for face representation is the key point for these algorithms. For example, Zhu *et al.* [14] propose a rank-order distance that measures similarity between two faces using their neighboring information. Fitzgibbon and Zisserman [17] develop a joint manifold distance (JMD) that measures the distance between two subspaces. Each subspace is invariant to a desired group of transformations. In addition, there are also techniques that utilize the user interaction [18], extra information on the web [19] and prior knowledge of family photo albums [20] to improve the performance. Another line of work on clustering employs linear classification cost as a clustering criterion, such as DIFFRAC discriminative clustering framework [21].

Recently, clustering face in videos has attracted more attention. Existing algorithms aim at exploiting the inherent pairwise constraints obtained from the face tracks for better clustering performance. Cinbis *et al.* [3] learn a cast-specific metric, adapted to the people appearing in a particular video, such that pairs of faces within a track are close and faces appearing together in a video frame are far form each other. More recently, Xiao *et al.* [2] introduce subspace clustering to solve this problem, and design a weighted block-sparse regularizer to incorporate the pairwise constraints. These algorithms usually employ handcrafted feature thus the representation effectiveness is limited. For example, the algorithm in [2] extracts SIFT descriptor from the detected facial landmarks. It cannot deal with

---

[2] http://mmlab.ie.cuhk.edu.hk/projects/DeepFaceClustering/index.html.

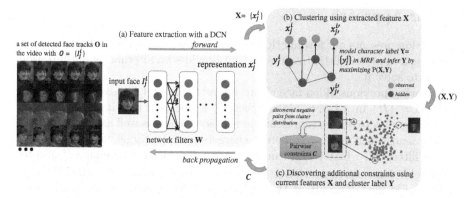

Fig. 2. Illustration of the proposed framework. We propose an alternating feedback loop between representation adaptation (a) and clustering (b). In each loop, the DCN extracts face representation (a) by which we perform face clustering in an MRF (b). After that, we discover new negative pairs and add them to the pairwise constraints for DCN adaptation (c). The deep face representation is gradually adapted from an external source domain (e.g., a large-scale face photo dataset) to a target video domain.

Fig. 3. The pairwise identity constraints set initialized by the face tracks.

profile faces. In addition, in these works, the constraints extracted from the face tracks are sparse and not updated in the clustering process. It may fail to provide enough information to guide the clustering. To mitigate this problem, Wu *et al.* [4] augment the constraints by a local smoothness assumption before clustering. Different from these studies, we gain richer guidance by iteratively generating constraints based on the clustering process.

In addition to the inherent pairwise constraint, recent works on video face clustering also incorporate contextual information [1]. For example, clothing [22], speech [23], gender [12], video editing style [24], and cluster proportion prior [25] are employed as additional cues to link faces of the same person. While additional context may introduce uncertainty and its availability will limit the application scenario, in this work, we focus on adapting better face representation via dynamic clustering constraints, which are robust and readily obtainable.

3 Our Approach

This section presents our formulation of joint face representation adaptation and clustering as a probabilistic framework, and provides an alternating optimization method to solve it.

Following previous video face clustering methods [2,4,5], given a set of face tracks $\mathbf{O} = \{I_j^i\}$ in a target video, where I_j^i is the j-th face image of the i-th track, our goal is to obtain representation of face images as well as to partition all the face images according to different characters of the target video. We define a set of filters $\mathbf{W}$, which transform the raw pixels of each face image I_j^i into its high-level hidden representation $\mathbf{x}_j^i$ in a Deep Convolutional Network (DCN), as shown in Fig. 2(a). The filters $\mathbf{W}$ are initialized by training on external large-scale face dataset (see Sect. 3.3). To guide the clustering process, we also define a set of pairwise identity constraints $\mathbf{C} = \{c(I_j^i, I_{j'}^{i'})\}$ for any pair of face images:

$$c(I_j^i, I_{j'}^{i'}) = \begin{cases} 1 & I_j^i \text{ and } I_{j'}^{i'} \text{ belong to the same identity,} \\ -1 & I_j^i \text{ and } I_{j'}^{i'} \text{ belong to different identities,} \\ 0 & \text{not defined.} \end{cases} \quad (1)$$

Note that different from previous studies [3–5], the identity constraints $\mathbf{C}$ will be updated iteratively instead of kept static. As shown in Fig. 3, at the very beginning, we initialize the identity constraints (denoted as $\mathbf{C}_0$) by assuming all the face images in the same track have the same identity, $i.e.$ $c(I_j^i, I_{j'}^{i'}) = 1$, $i = i'$. In addition, for faces in partially or fully overlapped face tracks ($e.g.$ faces appearing in the same frame of the video), their identities should be exclusive. Thus, we define $c(I_j^i, I_{j'}^{i'}) = -1$. The constraints between the remaining face pairs are undefined, $i.e.$ $c(I_j^i, I_{j'}^{i'}) = 0$.

Then we define a set of cluster labels $\mathbf{Y} = \{y_j^i\}$, where $y_j^i = \ell$ and $\ell \in \{1, 2, ..., K\}$, indicating the corresponding face image I_j^i belongs to which one of the K characters, as shown in Fig. 2(b). To this end, the clusters and face representation can be obtained by maximizing a posteriori probability (MAP)

$$\mathbf{X}^*, \mathbf{Y}^*, \mathbf{W}^* = \arg\max_{\mathbf{X}, \mathbf{Y}, \mathbf{W}} p(\mathbf{X}, \mathbf{Y}, \mathbf{W} | \mathbf{O}, \mathbf{C}), \quad (2)$$

where $\mathbf{O} = \{I_j^i\}$ and $\mathbf{X} = \{\mathbf{x}_j^i\}$. $\mathbf{C}$ is the dynamic identity constraint. By factorization, Eq. (2) is proportional to $p(\mathbf{C}|\mathbf{O}, \mathbf{W})P(\mathbf{C}|\mathbf{X}, \mathbf{Y}, \mathbf{O}, \mathbf{W})p(\mathbf{X}, \mathbf{Y}|\mathbf{O}, W)$ $P(\mathbf{W}|\mathbf{O})$. Note that the image set $\mathbf{O}$ is given and fixed, then we can remove it in the last term. Here we also make the following assumptions: (1) the update of constraints $\mathbf{C}$ is independent to $\mathbf{W}$, $i.e.$ $P(\mathbf{C}|\mathbf{X}, \mathbf{Y}, \mathbf{O}, \mathbf{W}) = P(\mathbf{C}|\mathbf{X}, \mathbf{Y})$; (2) $\mathbf{O}$ is independent to the inference process of $\mathbf{Y}$ because $\mathbf{Y}$ is inferred from $\mathbf{X}$, $i.e.$ $p(\mathbf{X}, \mathbf{Y}|\mathbf{O}, W) = p(\mathbf{X}, \mathbf{Y}|\mathbf{W})$; (3) inference of the cluster label $\mathbf{Y}$ is independent to $\mathbf{W}$, $i.e.$ $p(\mathbf{X}, \mathbf{Y}|\mathbf{W}) = p(\mathbf{X}, \mathbf{Y})$. Then we have

$$p(\mathbf{X}, \mathbf{Y}, \mathbf{W} | \mathbf{O}, \mathbf{C}) \propto p(\mathbf{C}|\mathbf{O}, \mathbf{W})p(\mathbf{C}|\mathbf{X}, \mathbf{Y})p(\mathbf{X}, \mathbf{Y})p(\mathbf{W}), \quad (3)$$

where the first term $p(\mathbf{C}|\mathbf{O}, \mathbf{W})$ solves filters $\mathbf{W}$ of the DCN by using the pairwise identity constraints as supervision. This can be implemented by imposing a contrastive loss in the DCN training process (see Sect. 3.3 for details). As a result, the hidden representation $\mathbf{X}$ can be obtained using the learned filters $\mathbf{W}$. The second term $p(\mathbf{C}|\mathbf{X}, \mathbf{Y})$ updates these constraints leveraging $\mathbf{X}$ and the estimated character labels $\mathbf{Y}$, as discussed in Sect. 3.2. The forth term $p(\mathbf{W})$ regularizes the network filters.

In Eq. (3), the third term $p(\mathbf{X}, \mathbf{Y})$ infers the character label $\mathbf{Y}$ given the hidden representation $\mathbf{X}$. Motivated by the fact that if two face images are close in the space of the hidden representation, the character labels are likely to be the same, we establish the relation between face pairs by Markov Random Field (MRF), where each node represents a character label y_j^i and each edge represents the relation between the character labels. For each node y_j^i, we associate it with the observed variable $\mathbf{x}_j^i$. Then we have

$$p(\mathbf{X}, \mathbf{Y}) = p(\mathbf{X}|\mathbf{Y})p(\mathbf{Y}) \propto \prod_{i,j} \Phi(\mathbf{x}_j^i|y_j^i) \prod_{i,j} \prod_{i',j' \in \mathcal{N}_j^i} \Psi(y_j^i, y_{j'}^{i'}), \qquad (4)$$

where $\Phi(\cdot)$ and $\Psi(\cdot)$ are the unary and pairwise term, respectively. $\mathcal{N}_j^i$ signifies a set of face images, which are the neighbors of y_j^i and defined by the representation similarity.

The parameters of Eq. (3) are optimized by alternating between the following three steps as illustrated in Fig. 2, (1) fix the filter $\mathbf{W}$ of DCN, obtain the current face representation $\mathbf{X}$, and infer character labels $\mathbf{Y}$ by optimizing MRF as defined in Eq. (4), (2) update the identity constraints $\mathbf{C}$ given $\mathbf{X}$ and the inferred character labels $\mathbf{Y}$, and (3) update the hidden face representation using $\mathbf{W}$ by minimizing the contrastive loss of the identity constraints, corresponding to maximizing $p(\mathbf{C}|\mathbf{O}, \mathbf{W})p(\mathbf{W})$. This optimization process is conducted for $T = 3$ iterations in our implementation. We will describe these three steps in Sects. 3.1, 3.2, and 3.3 respectively.

3.1   Inferring Character Labels

Given the current face representation $\mathbf{X}$, we infer the character labels $\mathbf{Y}$ by maximizing the joint probability $p(\mathbf{X}, \mathbf{Y})$. We employ the Gaussian distribution to model the unary term $\Phi(\cdot)$ in Eq. (4)

$$\Phi(\mathbf{x}_j^i|y_j^i = \ell) \sim \mathcal{N}(\mathbf{x}_j^i|\mu_\ell, \Sigma_\ell), \qquad (5)$$

where μ_ℓ and Σ_ℓ denote the mean vector and covariance matrix of the ℓ-th character, which are obtained and updated in the inference process. For the pairwise term $\Psi(\cdot)$ in Eq. (4), it is defined as

$$\Psi(y_j^i, y_{j'}^{i'}) = \exp\left\{ \alpha v(\mathbf{x}_j^i, \mathbf{x}_{j'}^{i'}) \cdot \left(\mathbf{1}(y_j^i, y_{j'}^{i'}) - \mathbf{1}(v(\mathbf{x}_j^i, \mathbf{x}_{j'}^{i'}) > 0) \right) \right\}, \qquad (6)$$

where $\mathbf{1}(\cdot)$ is an indicator function and α is a trade-off coefficient updated in the inference process. Furthermore, $v(\cdot, \cdot)$ is a pre-computed function that encodes the relation between any pair of face images $\mathbf{x}_j^i$ and $\mathbf{x}_{j'}^{i'}$. Similar to [4], positive relation (*i.e.* $v(\cdot,\cdot) > 0$) means that the face images are likely from the same character. Otherwise, they belong to different characters. Specifically, the computation of v is a combination of two cues: (1) the similarity between appearances of a pair of face images and (2) the pairwise spatial and temporal constraints of the face images. For instance, face images within a face track belong to the same character, while face images appearing in the same frame belong to different characters. Intuitively, Eq. (6) encourages face images with positive relation to be the same character. For example, if $v(\mathbf{x}_j^i, \mathbf{x}_{j'}^{i'}) > 0$ and $y_j^i = y_{j'}^{i'}$, we have $\Psi(y_j^i, y_{j'}^{i'}) = 1$. However, if $v(\mathbf{x}_j^i, \mathbf{x}_{j'}^{i'}) > 0$ but $y_j^i \neq y_{j'}^{i'}$, we have $\Psi(y_j^i, y_{j'}^{i'}) < 1$, indicating the character label assignment is violating the pairwise constraints.

To solve Eq. (4), we employ the simulated field algorithm [26], which is a classic technique for MRF optimization. To present the main steps of our work clearly, we provide the details of this algorithm and the computation of $v(\cdot,\cdot)$ in the *supplementary material*.

3.2   Dynamic Pairwise Identity Constraints

Different from previous methods [2,4,12], where the identity constraints between a pair of face images are fixed after initialized at the very beginning, the identity constraints $\mathbf{C}$ in our approach is updated iteratively in the adaptation process to obtain additional supervision to adapt the face representation. In particular, after inferring the character labels $\mathbf{Y}$ in Sect. 3.1, we compute the confidence value that measures the possibility of a face pair from different characters, *i.e.* negative pair. After that, we append pairs with high confidence to the current set of pairwise constraints $\mathbf{C}$. The negative pair generation process is motivated by the facts that: diverse clusters contain large noise, while clusters with high purity are compact; and faces from the same character are likely to be close in the representation space. Specifically, for the face pairs in each cluster, we define the confidence Q by

$$Q(i_\ell, i_\ell') = \frac{1}{1 + \gamma e^{-trace(\Sigma_\ell)D_{i_\ell,i_\ell'}}} \tag{7}$$

where i_ℓ and i_ℓ' denote the faces in cluster ℓ. $trace(\Sigma_\ell)$ is the trace of the covariance matrix, which describes the variations within the cluster. $D_{i_\ell,i_\ell'}$ is the L2-distance between the faces in the learned face representation space $\mathbf{X}$. γ is a scale factor for normalization. In this case, face pairs in diverse clusters with large distances will have high confidence. In our implementation, face pairs with confidence value $Q(i_\ell, i_\ell') > 0.5$ are selected as additional negative pairs.

3.3   Face Representation Adaptation

Pre-training DCN. The network filter $\mathbf{W}$ is initialized by pre-training DCN to classify massive identities as discussed in DeepID2+ [7]. We adopt its network architecture due to its exceptional performance in face recognition.

Specifically, DCN takes face image of size 55×47 as input. It has four successive convolution layers followed by one fully connected layer. Each convolution layer contains learnable filters and is followed by a 2×2 max-pooling layer and Rectified Linear Units (ReLUs) [27] as the activation function. The number of feature map generated by each convolution layer is 128, and the dimension of the face representation generated by the final fully connected layer is 512. Similar to [7], our DCN is pre-trained on CelebFace [28], with around $290,000$ faces images from $12,000$ identities. The training process is conducted by back-prorogation using both the identification and verification loss functions.

Fine-tuning Face Representation by C. After updating the identity constraints **C** in Sect. 3.2, we update the hidden face representation by backpropagating the constraint information to the DCN. In particular, given a constraint in **C**, we minimize a contrastive loss function [7], $E_c(\mathbf{x}_j^i, \mathbf{x}_{j'}^{i'})$, which is defined as

$$E_c = \begin{cases} \frac{1}{2} \parallel \mathbf{x}_j^i - \mathbf{x}_{j'}^{i'} \parallel_2^2, & c(I_j^i, I_{j'}^{i'}) = 1, \\ \frac{1}{2} \max(0, \tau - \parallel \mathbf{x}_j^i - \mathbf{x}_{j'}^{i'} \parallel_2^2), & c(I_j^i, I_{j'}^{i'}) = -1, \end{cases} \tag{8}$$

where τ is the margin between different identities. Eq. (8) encourages face images of the same character to be close and that of the different characters to be far away from each other.

To facilitate representation adaptation, beside E_c, we fine-tune DCN by backpropagating the errors of the MRF defined in Sect. 3.1. We take the negative logarithm of Eq. (4), drop the constant terms, and obtain $\frac{1}{2} \sum_{i,j} \sum_{\ell=1}^{K} \mathbf{1}(y_j^i = \ell)\left(\ln |\Sigma_\ell| + (\mathbf{x}_j^i - \mu_\ell)^{\mathsf{T}} \Sigma_\ell^{-1}(\mathbf{x}_j^i - \mu_\ell)\right)$. Note that in the step of representation adaptation, we update network filters **W** while keeping the remaining parameters fixed, such as **Y**, Σ, and μ. Therefore, minimizing the above function is equivalent to optimize **W**, such that the distance between each face image and its corresponding cluster center is minimized. We define this loss function as below

$$E_{MRF} = \frac{1}{2} \sum_{\ell=1}^{K} \mathbf{1}(y_j^i = \ell) \parallel x_j^i - \mu_\ell \parallel_2^2 . \tag{9}$$

By minimizing Eq. (9), the representation naturally reduces the intra-personal variations.

Combining Eqs. (8) and (9), the training process is conducted by backpropagation using stochastic gradient descent (SGD) [29]. Algorithm 1 shows the entire pipeline of the proposed joint face representation adaptation and clustering.

4   Experiments

4.1   Datasets

Experiments are conducted on three publicly available face clustering datasets: Accio [30], BF0502 [31] and Notting-Hill [32]. The Accio dataset is collected from

---

Algorithm 1. Joint face representation adaptation and clustering with dynamic constraints

---

Input:
  Face tracks $\mathbf{O} = \{\mathbf{I}_j^i\}$, character number K of the target video.
Output:
  Character labels $\mathbf{Y}$ and filters $\mathbf{W}$ of the DCN.
1: Generate a set of initial pairwise constraints, denoted as $\mathbf{C}_0$, using the face tracks $\mathbf{O}$ as introduced at the beginning of Sect. 3.
2: Pre-train the filters $\mathbf{W}$ of DCN with an external face dataset as discussed in Sect. 3.3.
3: Fine-tune filters $\mathbf{W}$ of DCN with $\mathbf{C}_0$ as discussed in Sect. 3.3.
4: **for** $t = 1$ to T **do**
5:    Generate the face representation $\mathbf{x}_j^i$ for each face image I_j^i.
6:    Infer the corresponding character label y_j^i with fixed $\mathbf{W}$ by maximizing Eq. (4) (Sect. 3.1).
7:    Discover additional negative face pairs $\mathbf{C}_t$ and append them to the pairwise identity constraints $\mathbf{C}$ (Sect. 3.2).
8:    Fine-tune the face representation by minimizing Eqs. (8) and (9) using back-propagation on the DCN (Sect. 3.3).
9: **end for**

---

the eight *"Harry Potter"* movies and we use the first instalment of this series in our experiment (denoted as Accio-1 in the following text). Accio-1 contains multiple challenges, such as a large number of dark scenes and many tracks with non-frontal faces. In addition, the number of the faces of each character is unbalanced (e.g., there are 51,620 faces of the character *"Harry Potter"*, while 4,843 faces for *"Albus Dumbledore"*). In particular, there are 36 characters, 3,243 tracks, and 166,885 faces in the test movie. The face tracks are obtained by tracking-by-detection using a particle filter [30]. BF0502 [31] is collected from the TV series "Buffy the Vampire Slayer". Following the protocol of other face video clustering studies [2, 4, 12], we evaluate on 6 main casts including 17,337 faces in 229 face tracks. The dataset Notting-Hill is gathered from the movie *"Notting Hill"*. It includes faces of 5 main casts, with 4,660 faces in 76 tracks.

4.2 Evaluation Criteria and Baselines

The clustering performance is measured in two different ways. In the first one, we evaluate how the algorithm balances the precision and recall. In particular, we employ the *B-cubed precision and recall* [1, 33] to compute one series of score pairs for the tested methods given different numbers of clusters. Specifically, the B-cubed precision is the fraction of face pairs assigned to a cluster with matching identity labels. The B-cubed recall is the average fraction of face pairs belonging to the groundtruth identity assigned to the same cluster [15]. To combine the precision and recall, we use the F_1-score (the harmonic mean of these two metrics).

Table 1. B-cubed precision (P), recall (R), and F_1-score (F) with different iterations (T) of the proposed method on the Accio-1 [30] dataset, with cluster number $K = 36$.

T=1			T=2			T=3			T=4		
P	R	F	P	R	F	P	R	F	P	R	F
0.63	0.30	0.41	0.68	0.32	0.44	0.69	0.35	0.46	0.67	0.33	0.44

Table 2. B-cubed precision (P), recall (R), and F_1-score (F) of different methods on the Accio-1 [30] (Harry Potter) dataset.

Methods	#cluster=40			#cluster=50			#cluster=60			#cluster=120			#cluster=240		
	P	R	F	P	R	F	P	R	F	P	R	F	P	R	F
K-means	.246	.114	.156	.262	.105	.150	.289	.089	.136	.321	.059	.100	.379	.044	.079
K-means-DeepID2$^+$	.543	.201	.293	.574	.181	.275	.581	.155	.244	.594	.099	.169	.612	.074	.132
DIFFRAC [21]	.307	.109	.160	.326	.080	.129	.338	.089	.141	.336	.057	.098	.347	.032	.059
DIFFRAC-DeepID2$^+$	.557	.213	.301	.586	.181	.277	.607	.160	.253	.622	.120	.201	.620	.068	.122
WBSLRR [2]	.296	.153	.202	.322	.117	.172	.346	.092	.145	.354	.087	.140	.384	.033	.061
WBSLRR-DeepID2$^+$	.502	.206	.292	.533	.184	.274	.551	.161	.249	.599	.114	.192	.637	.054	.100
HMRF [4]	.272	.128	.174	.295	.101	.151	.303	.093	.142	.342	.067	.112	.403	.041	.074
HMRF-Fisher	.583	.234	.334	.591	.184	.281	.604	.176	.273	.667	.127	.213	.712	.086	.154
HMRF-DeepID2$^+$	.599	.230	.332	.616	.211	.314	.621	.174	.272	.644	.128	.214	.669	.075	.135
DeepID2$^+ \cdot C_0$	.655	.253	.365	.676	.238	.352	.684	.192	.300	.713	.155	.255	.785	.132	.226
DeepID2$^+ \cdot C_0 \cdot$Intra	.657	.312	.423	.685	.286	.404	.698	.229	.345	.735	.201	.316	.781	.158	.263
Full model	**.711**	**.352**	**.471**	**.739**	**.312**	**.439**	**.768**	**.242**	**.368**	**.779**	**.203**	**.322**	**.841**	**.172**	**.286**

For the second evaluation metric, we use *accuracy* computed from a confusion matrix, which is derived by the best match between the cluster labels and groundtruth identities. The best match is obtained by using the Hungarian method [34]. This evaluation metric is widely employed in current video face clustering methods [2, 4, 12, 25].

We compare the proposed method with the following classic and state-of-the-art approaches: (1) K-means [35]; (2) Unsupervised Logistic Discriminant Metric Learning (ULDML) [3]; (3) Penalized Probabilistic Clustering (PPC) [36]; (4) DIFFRAC [21] discriminative clustering; (5) HMRF-based clustering [4]; (6) Weighted Block-Sparse Low Rank Representation (WBSLRR) method [2]; (7) Multi-cue Augmented Face Clustering (McAFC) [12]. The latter three recent approaches are specifically designed for face clustering in videos.

4.3 Experiments on Accio-1 (Harry Potter) [30]

Effects of the Iterations in the Adaptation Process. The evaluation is first conducted on the Accio-1 dataset [30]. Firstly, to demonstrate the effectiveness of the alternating adaptation process, we report the performance in different iterations in Table 1. Given that there are 36 characters in this movie, we set the cluster number $K = 36$ here. It is observed that the performance increases and it converges when $T = 3$. This demonstrates the benefits of the alternating adaptation process.

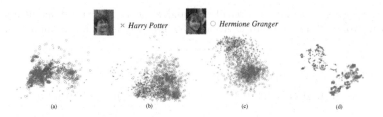

Fig. 4. Visualization of different characters' face representation in a chapter of the movie *"Harry Potter"*. (a)–(c): projecting different representations to a 2D space by PCA: (a) raw pixel value, (b) DeepID2$^+$, and (c) our adapted representation. (d): projecting the adapted representation to a 2D space by t-SNE [38].

Performance of Different Variants and Competitors. To verify other components of the proposed method, we further test different variants of our method, as well as other existing models:

- DeepID2$^+ \cdot \mathbf{C}_0$: We perform clustering with fixed DCN filters $\mathbf{W}$ and pairwise constraints set $\mathbf{C}_0$. That means we do not perform representation adaptation after training the network on the face photo dataset and initial pairwise constraints. This variant corresponds to the typical transfer learning strategy [11] adopted in most deep learning studies. Since our network structure and pre-training data are identical to that of [7], We use the notation DeepID2$^+$.
- DeepID2$^+ \cdot \mathbf{C}_0 \cdot$Intra: We finetune DCN filters $\mathbf{W}$ only with the intra person constraints (Eq. (9)) but not the inter person constraints (Eq. (8)).
- "HMRF$^+$" and "HMRF-DeepID2$^+$": Since HMRF [4] only uses the raw pixel value or handcrafted features, for fair comparison, we also use the DCN representation initially trained on the face photo dataset for this method. Similar notation scheme is used for K-means [35], DIFFRAC [21] and WBSLRR [2] algorithms, and Fisher Vector [37] representation.

We report the B-cubed precision and recall, as well as the F_1-score of different methods in Table 2. It is observed that:

- As the cluster number increases, the precision increases while the recall decreases. This is intuitive since larger number of clusters decreases the cluster size and improves the cluster purity.
- This dataset is very challenging. For example, the K-means [35] only achieved 0.379 in precision even the cluster number is nearly six times of the identities.
- The DCN representation improves the performance substantially (e.g., the DIFFRAC [21], HMRF [4], and WBSLRR [2] method have 0.2–0.3 improvements in terms of precision when employing the DCN representation).
- The proposed method (*i.e.* full model) performs the best, and the comparison on different variants of the proposed method demonstrates the superiority of the alternating adaptation process (e.g., the performance of full model is better than that of "DeepID2$^+ \cdot \mathbf{C}_0$").

Fig. 5. Example results in different clusters generated by the proposed method on Accio-1 [30]. Face pairs in red rectangles are incorrectly assigned to a same cluster. (Color figure online)

- Interestingly, by comparing "DeepID2$^+$·$\mathbf{C}_0$" and "DeepID2$^+$·$\mathbf{C}_0$·Intra", we can observe obvious improvement on recall, but the precision can hardly increase. This is because using only the intra person constraints can decrease the distances between the faces of the same character, but can not provide discriminative information directly to correct the wrong pairs in the cluster. Thus, both intra- and inter-person constraints are important for discriminative face clustering.

Representation Visualization. Figure 4 visualizes different representations by projecting them to a 2D space. Firstly, in Fig. 4(a, b and c), we project the representations by PCA. We can observe that for the original pixel values, the representations are severely overlapped. By pre-training DCN with face dataset and adapting the representation, we can gradually obtain more discriminative representation. After that, we use the t-SNE [38] dimensionality reduction and Fig. 4(d) shows that the characters can be almost linearly separated. This demonstrates the effectiveness of the adapted face representation.

Example Results. Figure 5 shows some clustering examples, where each bank except the right bottom one denotes a cluster. It is observed that each cluster covers a character's faces in different head pose, lighting conditions, and expressions. This demonstrates the effectiveness of the adapted face representation. We also show some failed cases indicated by the red rectangles, where each pair with different characters is incorrectly partitioned in the same cluster. These faces fail mainly because of the unbalanced face number of the identity (*e.g.* , some characters just appear in a few shots) and some extreme lighting conditions.

4.4 Experiments on BF0502 [31] and Notting Hill [32]

We report the accuracy of our method and other competitors in Figs. 6 and 7. Following previous research [2,4,12], each algorithm is repeated for 30 times, and the mean accuracy and standard deviation are reported. The results of the competitors are gathered from the literatures [2,4,12]. Figure 6 shows that our method achieves substantial improvement compared to the best competitor (from 62.76 % to 92.13 %), demonstrating the superiority of our method.

Methods	Accuracy(%)
K-means	39.31 ± 4.51
ULDML [3]	41.62 ± 0.00
PPC [36]	78.88±5.15
HMRF [4]	50.30 ± 2.73
WBSLRR [2]	62.76 ±1.10
Our method	**92.13 ±0.90**

Fig. 6. Left: Clustering accuracies of the state-of-the-art methods and our method on the BF0502 [31] dataset. Right: Example clustering results. Each row denotes a cluster.

Methods	Accuracy(%)
K-means	69.16 ± 3.22
ULDML [3]	73.18 ± 8.66
PPC [36]	78.88±5.15
HMRF [4]	84.39 ± 1.47
CMVFC [39]	93.42 ± 0.00
McAFC [12]	96.05 ±0.39
WBSLRR [2]	96.29 ±0.00
Our method	**99.04 ±0.20**

Fig. 7. Left: Clustering accuracies of the state-of-the-art methods and ours on the Notting Hill [32] dataset. Right: Example clustering results. Each row denotes a cluster.

4.5   Computational Cost

Training a high-capacity DCN from scratch is time consuming due to the large amount of training data. However, given the DCN pre-trained on a large face dataset, for a new target video, we only need to perform representation adaptation. Table 3 shows the running time of our algorithm on the videos. In particular, the DCN adaptation in Table 3 is the time that we use to train the DCN with a Nvidia Titan GPU and the total time additionally includes the computation cost of other steps (*i.e.* inferring the character label $\mathbf{Y}$ in Sect. 3.1 and updating the constraints in Sect. 3.2). It is observed that the time cost is feasible in many applications, where face clustering can be performed off-line.

4.6   Application to Face Verification

To further demonstrate the effectiveness of the adapted face representation, we perform face verification on the Accio-1 dataset [30]. To evaluate the representation directly, for each face pair, we calculate the L2 distance of the representation

Table 3. Running time for the Accio-1 [30] (Harry Potter), BF0502 [31], and Notting Hill [32] dataset (in minutes).

Accio-1		BF0502		Notting Hill	
DCN adaptation	Total	DCN adaptation	Total	DCN adaptation	Total
13.8	30.3	2.2	5.3	0.5	1.4

to measure the pairwise similarity, instead of training a joint Bayesian model as in [7]. If the distance is larger than a threshold, the face pair is regarded as negative (*i.e.* different identities). The threshold is determined by 1,000 validation face pairs (500 positive and 500 negative samples) randomly chosen from Accio-1 [30] dataset. Evaluation is performed on another 1,000 randomly chosen face pairs (500 positive and 500 negative samples) from this dataset. The validation and test faces are exclusive in terms of scenes and identities. Similar to Sect. 4.3, we compare the performance among different representations, including (1) DeepID2$^+$, (2) DeepID2$^+$·C_0, and (3) full model. Figure 8 shows the Receiver Operating Characteristic Comparison (ROC). It is evident that representation adapted by the proposed method outperforms the original deep representation and can handle different cinematic styles better.

Fig. 8. (a): ROC of face verification on Accio-1 [30] dataset. The number in the legend indicates the verification accuracy. (b) and (c): negative and positive pairs failed to be matched by DeepID2+ [7] but successfully matched after adaptation by our approach.

5   Conclusion

In this work, we have presented a novel deep learning framework for joint face representation adaptation and clustering in videos. In the absence of precise face annotations on the target video, we propose a feedback loop in which the deep representation provides robust features for face clustering, and the clustering results provide weak pairwise constraints for learning more suitable deep representation with respect to the target video. Experiments on three benchmark video datasets demonstrate the superiority of the proposed method when compared to the state-of-the-art video clustering methods that either use handcrafted features or deep face representation (without adaptation). The effectiveness of the adapted face representation is further demonstrated by a face verification experiment.

Acknowledgments. This work is partially supported by SenseTime Group Limited, the Hong Kong Innovation and Technology Support Programme, the General Research Fund sponsored by the Research Grants Council of the Kong Kong SAR (CUHK 416312), the External Cooperation Program of BIC, Chinese Academy of Sciences (No. 172644KYSB20150019), the Science and Technology Planning Project of Guangdong Province (2015B010129013, 2014B050505017), and the National Natural Science Foundation of China (61503366, 61472410; Corresponding author is Ping Luo).

References

1. Zhang, L., Kalashnikov, D.V., Mehrotra, S.: A unified framework for context assisted face clustering. In: ACM Conference on International Conference on Multimedia Retrieval (2013)
2. Xiao, S., Tan, M., Xu, D.: Weighted block-sparse low rank representation for face clustering in videos. In: Fleet, D., Pajdla, T., Schiele, B., Tuytelaars, T. (eds.) ECCV 2014. LNCS, vol. 8694, pp. 123–138. Springer, Heidelberg (2014). doi:10.1007/978-3-319-10599-4_9
3. Cinbis, R., Verbeek, J., Schmid, C.: Unsupervised metric learning for face identification in tv video. In: ICCV (2011)
4. Wu, B., Zhang, Y., Hu, B.G., Ji, Q.: Constrained clustering and its application to face clustering in videos. In: CVPR (2013)
5. Wu, B., Lyu, S., Hu, B., Ji, Q.: Simultaneous clustering and tracklet linking for multi-face tracking in videos. In: ICCV (2013)
6. Taigman, Y., Yang, M., Ranzato, M., Wolf, L.: DeepFace: closing the gap to human-level performance in face verification. In: CVPR (2014)
7. Sun, Y., Wang, X., Tang, X.: Deeply learned face representations are sparse, selective, and robust. In: CVPR (2015)
8. Schroff, F., Kalenichenko, D., Philbin, J.: FaceNet: a unified embedding for face recognition and clustering. In: CVPR (2015)
9. Ding, L., Yilmaz, A.: Learning relations among movie characters: a social network perspective. In: Daniilidis, K., Maragos, P., Paragios, N. (eds.) ECCV 2010. LNCS, vol. 6314, pp. 410–423. Springer, Heidelberg (2010). doi:10.1007/978-3-642-15561-1_30
10. Tapaswi, M., Bauml, M., Stiefelhagen, R.: Improved weak labels using contextual cues for person identification in videos. In: FG (2015)
11. Yosinski, J., Clune, J., Bengio, Y., Lipson, H.: How transferable are features in deep neural networks? In: NIPS (2014)
12. Zhou, C., Zhang, C., Fu, H., Wang, R., Cao, X.: Multi-cue augmented face clustering. In: ACM Multimedia Conference (2015)
13. Li, Z., Tang, X.: Bayesian face recognition using support vector machine and face clustering. In: CVPR (2004)
14. Zhu, C., Wen, F., Sun, J.: A rank-order distance based clustering algorithm for face tagging. In: CVPR (2011)
15. Otto, C., Klare, B., Jain, A.: An efficient approach for clustering face images. In: International Conference on Biometrics (2015)
16. Cao, X., Zhang, C., Fu, H., Liu, S., Zhang, H.: Diversity-induced multi-view subspace clustering. In: CVPR (2015)
17. Fitzgibbon, A., Zisserman, A.: Joint manifold distance: a new approach to appearance based clustering. In: CVPR (2003)

18. Tian, Y., Liu, W., Xiao, R., Wen, F., Tang, X.: A face annotation framework with partial clustering and interactive labeling. In: CVPR (2007)
19. Berg, T., Berg, A., Edwards, J., Maire, M., White, R., Teh, Y.W., Learned-Miller, E., Forsyth, D.: Names and faces in the news. In: CVPR (2004)
20. Xia, S., Pan, H., Qin, A.: Face clustering in photo album. In: ICPR (2014)
21. Bach, F.R., Harchaoui, Z.: Diffrac: a discriminative and flexible framework for clustering. In: NIPS, pp. 49–56 (2008)
22. El-Khoury, E., Senac, C., Joly, P.: Face-and-clothing based people clustering in video content. In: ACM International Conference on Multimedia Information Retrieval (2010)
23. Paul, G., Elie, K., Sylvain, M., Jean-Marc, O., Paul, D.: A conditional random field approach for audio-visual people diarization. In: ICASSP (2014)
24. Tapaswi, M., Parkhi, O.M., Rahtu, E., Sommerlade, E., Stiefelhagen, R., Zisserman, A.: Total cluster: a person agnostic clustering method for broadcast videos. In: Proceedings of Indian Conference on Computer Vision Graphics and Image Processing (2014)
25. Tang, Z., Zhang, Y., Li, Z., Lu, H.: Face clustering in videos with proportion prior. In: IJCAI (2015)
26. Celeux, G., Forbes, F., Peyrard, N.: EM procedures using mean field-like approximations for markov model-based image segmentation. Pattern Recogn. **36**(1), 131–144 (2003)
27. Nair, V., Hinton, G.E.: Rectified linear units improve restricted boltzmann machines. In: ICML (2010)
28. Sun, Y., Wang, X., Tang, X.: Deep learning face representation from predicting 10,000 classes. In: CVPR (2014)
29. Krizhevsky, A., Sutskever, I., Hinton, G.E.: Imagenet classification with deep convolutional neural networks. In: NIPS (2012)
30. Ghaleb, E., Tapaswi, M., Al-Halah, Z., Ekenel, H.K., Stiefelhagen, R.: Accio: a data set for face track retrieval in movies across age. In: ACM International Conference on Multimedia Retrieval (2015)
31. Everingham, M., Sivic, J., Zisserman, A.: Hello! my name is.. buffy -automatic naming of characters in TV video. In: BMVC (2006)
32. Zhang, Y., Xu, C., Lu, H., Huang, Y.: Character identification in feature-length films using global face-name matching. IEEE Trans. Multimedia **11**(7), 1276–1288 (2009)
33. Amigó, E., Gonzalo, J., Artiles, J., Verdejo, F.: A comparison of extrinsic clustering evaluation metrics based on formal constraints. Inf. Retrieval **12**(4), 461–486 (2009)
34. Kuhn, H.W.: The hungarian method for the assignment problem. Naval Res. Logistics Q. **2**(1–2), 83–97 (1955)
35. Bishop, C.M.: Pattern Recognition and Machine Learning. Springer, New York (2006)
36. Lu, Z., Leen, T.K.: Penalized probabilistic clustering. Neural Comput. **19**(6), 1528–1567 (2007)
37. Parkhi, O., Simonyan, K., Vedaldi, A., Zisserman, A.: A compact and discriminative face track descriptor. In: CVPR, pp. 1693–1700 (2014)
38. Van der Maaten, L., Hinton, G.: Visualizing data using t-sne. J. Mach. Learn. Res. **9**, 2579–2605 (2008)
39. Cao, X., Zhang, C., Zhou, C., Fu, H., Foroosh, H.: Constrained multi-view video face clustering. IEEE Trans. Image Process. **24**(11), 4381–4393 (2015)

Uncovering Symmetries in Polynomial Systems

Viktor Larsson$^{(\boxtimes)}$ and Kalle Åström

Lund University, Lund, Sweden
{viktorl,kalle}@maths.lth.se

Abstract. In this paper we study symmetries in polynomial equation systems and how they can be integrated into the action matrix method. The main contribution is a generalization of the partial p-fold symmetry and we provide new theoretical insights as to why these methods work. We show several examples of how to use this symmetry to construct more compact polynomial solvers. As a second contribution we present a simple and automatic method for finding these symmetries for a given problem. Finally we show two examples where these symmetries occur in real applications.

1 Introduction

Polynomial systems have become an integral part of Computer Vision due to their ability to encode many geometric constraints. Polynomial solvers have been successfully used for many minimal problem such as absolute pose estimation [1–3], relative pose estimation [4–6] and homography estimation [7,8]. They have also been used for some some non-minimal problem such as PnP [9,10].

One technique for constructing polynomial solvers is the so called *action matrix* method. The method reduces the polynomial system to an eigenvalue problem for which there exist good numerical methods. For a brief introduction to polynomial solvers in Computer Vision we recommend Byröd et al. [11].

In [12] Ask et al. considers polynomial systems, where the degree of each monomial has the same remainder modulo p. This introduces a p-fold symmetry into the solution set. By taking this symmetry into account they construct smaller and more stable polynomial solvers. This work was later extended by Kuang et al. [13] to polynomial systems where this symmetry only exists in a subset of the variables. This type of symmetry has been used in [1,9,14–16].

In this paper we generalize the symmetry from [12,13] and provide new theoretical insight as to why these methods work. We show that if the system has these symmetries the action matrix can be chosen block diagonal and by considering only a single block we can construct more compact solvers.

In [17] Corless et al. also use symmetries in the action matrix method. Their approach is based on studying the group structure of the symmetry using tools from linear representation theory. While the paper present theory for symmetries

Electronic supplementary material The online version of this chapter (doi:10.1007/978-3-319-46487-9_16) contains supplementary material, which is available to authorized users.

B. Leibe et al. (Eds.): ECCV 2016, Part III, LNCS 9907, pp. 252–267, 2016.
DOI: 10.1007/978-3-319-46487-9_16

of general group structure and show a few examples with integer or rational coefficients it is not clear how to directly apply it to build polynomial solvers for types of problems encountered in Computer Vision. In contrast the theory developed in this paper classifies the symmetry based on the monomial structure in the equations. This allows the method to integrate naturally into the standard methods for building polynomial solvers.

The main contributions in this paper are:

- We generalize the partial p-fold symmetry studied in [12,13] and show how to exploit this symmetry to construct more compact polynomial solvers.
- We present a simple and automatic method for finding these symmetries in polynomial systems.
- We show two examples where these symmetries occur in the polynomial systems from real applications.

1.1 Background and Notation

The set of all polynomials over $\mathbb{C}$ is denoted $\mathbb{C}[X]$. The solutions $V \subset \mathbb{C}^n$ to a set of polynomial equations $f_i(x) = 0$, $i = 1, 2, \ldots n$ is called an *affine variety*. The set of all polynomial combinations of f_i, i.e. $I = \{\sum_i h_i(x)f_i(x) \mid h_i \in \mathbb{C}[X]\}$ defines an ideal in the polynomial ring $\mathbb{C}[X]$. For an ideal I we can define the quotient ring $\mathbb{C}[X]/I$, which consists of equivalence classes with respect to I, i.e. two elements are equivalent if their difference lies in I. From algebraic geometry it is well known that if the set of solutions to a system is finite then the corresponding quotient ring $\mathbb{C}[X]/I$ is a finite dimensional vectorspace. For an introduction to algebraic geometry we recommend [18].

Throughout the paper we use the multi-index notation for monomials, i.e.

$$x^\alpha = x^{(\alpha_1,\ldots,\alpha_n)} = \prod_k x_k^{\alpha_k}, \quad \text{so e.g.} \quad x^{(2,0,1)} = x_1^2 x_3.$$

2 Symmetries in Polynomial Equation Systems

We start with a simple example.

Example 1. Consider the following system of polynomial equations

$$\begin{cases} x^2 + y - 2 = 0, \\ x^2 y^2 - 1 = 0. \end{cases} \tag{1}$$

The system has six solutions given by

$$(\pm 1, 1), \ (\pm\varphi, -\varphi^{-1}), \ (\pm\varphi^{-1}, \varphi) \quad \text{where} \quad \varphi = \frac{1 + \sqrt{5}}{2}. \tag{2}$$

Since each monomial has the x-variable raised to an even power, we can for any solution flip the sign of x and get another solution. This type of symmetry was studied in [12,13] and is characterized in the following definition.

Definition 1. *The polynomial $f(x, y)$ has a **partial p-fold symmetry** in x if the sum of the exponents for x of each monomial has the same remainder q modulo p, i.e.*

$$f(x, y) = \sum_k a_k x^{\alpha_k} y^{\beta_k} \implies q \equiv \mathbb{1}^T \alpha_k \bmod p \quad \forall k. \tag{3}$$

In [13] it was shown that if we have a system of polynomials with this property the solution set will also have a p-fold symmetry. More specifically if $\mathcal{V}$ is the set of solutions then

$$(x, y) \in \mathcal{V} \implies (e^{2\pi i \frac{k}{p}} x, y) \in \mathcal{V} \quad k = 0, 1, 2, ..., p - 1. \tag{4}$$

Example 2. The polynomial system

$$\begin{cases} x^3 - 1 = 0, \\ xy - 1 = 0 \end{cases} \tag{5}$$

has three solutions given by

$$\mathcal{V} = \{(1, 1), \quad (\frac{1 + i\sqrt{3}}{2}, \frac{1 - i\sqrt{3}}{2}), \quad (\frac{1 - i\sqrt{3}}{2}, \frac{1 + i\sqrt{3}}{2})\}. \tag{6}$$

While this system does not have any partial p-fold symmetries, the solution set has the following property

$$(x, y) \in \mathcal{V} \implies (e^{2\pi i \frac{1}{3}} x, e^{2\pi i \frac{2}{3}} y) \in \mathcal{V}, \tag{7}$$

which is similar to that in (4). In this work we consider a generalization of the partial p-fold symmetry characterized by the following definition.

Definition 2. *The polynomial $f(x)$ has a **weighted p-fold symmetry** with weights $c \in \mathbb{Z}_p^n$ if the c-weighted sum of the exponents for x of each monomial has the same remainder q modulo p, i.e.*

$$f(x) = \sum_k a_k x^{\alpha_k} \implies q \equiv c^T \alpha_k \bmod p \quad \forall k. \tag{8}$$

Example 3. Below are three examples

$$\begin{array}{lll} f_1(x, y) = x^3 - x^2 y^2 + y^3, & p = 3, & c = (2, 1), \\ f_2(x, y) = x^5 + x^3 y + x, & p = 4, & c = (1, 2), \\ f_3(x, y, z) = x + y^2 + yz - 1, & p = 2, & c = (0, 1, 1). \end{array}$$

Note that the vector c is not unique, e.g. for the first polynomial $c = (1, 2)$ would also work. If p is not prime then for any factor of p we also have a symmetry, e.g. the polynomial f_2 also has a 2-fold symmetry. From the last example it becomes clear that the partial p-fold symmetry from [13] is a special case of the weighted symmetry where the weights are binary, corresponding to the symmetry variables.

Similarly to (4) we will see that for any polynomial equation system with c-weighted p-fold symmetry, the solution set has a corresponding symmetry. For any vector $c \in \mathbb{Z}_p^n$ we define the matrix

$$
D_p^c = \text{diag}\left(\left\{\exp(2\pi i \frac{c_k}{p})\right\}_{k=1}^n \right). \tag{9}
$$

Definition 3. *A set $V \subset \mathbb{C}^n$ has a **c-weighted p-fold symmetry** if and only if it is stable under D_p^c, i.e.*

$$
D_p^c V \subset V. \tag{10}
$$

The following two theorems are directly adapted from Kuang et al. [13] where they are proved for regular partial p-fold symmetry.

Theorem 1. *Let $f_i(x) = 0, i = 1, 2, ..., m$ be a polynomial system and denote the set of solutions $V \subset \mathbb{C}^n$. If each f_i has a c-weighted p-fold symmetry then so does the set of solutions V.*

Proof. Take any $x \in V$. Consider some f_i and let q be the remainder from Definition 2. Let x^β be any monomial from f_i and consider the effect of D_p^c,

$$
(D_p^c x)^\beta = \prod_k (e^{2\pi i \frac{c_k}{p}} x_k)^{\beta_k} = \prod_k e^{2\pi i \frac{c_k \beta_k}{p}} x_k^{\beta_k} = e^{2\pi i \frac{c^T \beta}{p}} x^\beta = e^{2\pi i \frac{q}{p}} x^\beta. \tag{11}
$$

Then if $f_i(x) = \sum_k a_k x^{\alpha_k}$ we have

$$
f_i(D_p^c x) = \sum_k a_k (D_p^c x)^{\alpha_k} = \sum_k a_k e^{2\pi i \frac{q}{p}} x^{\alpha_k} = e^{2\pi i \frac{q}{p}} f_i(x) = 0, \tag{12}
$$

and since this holds for any $i = 1, 2, \ldots, m$ we must have that $D_p^c x \in V$. □

Theorem 2. *Let $f_i(x) = 0, i = 1, 2, ..., m$ be a polynomial system where the solution set V has a c-weighted p-fold symmetry. Then there exist an equivalent system where each polynomial has c-weighted p-fold symmetry.*

Proof. Let $x \in V$. Then for any f_i we have

$$
f_i\left((D_p^c)^k x\right) = 0, \quad k = 0, 1, 2, ..., p - 1. \tag{13}
$$

Decompose f_i into $f_i(x) = g_0(x) + g_1(x) + ... + g_{p-1}(x)$ such that each monomial in g_q has the c-weighted remainder q modulo p, i.e.

$$
g_q(x) = \sum_k a_k x^{\gamma_k} \implies c^T \gamma_k \equiv q \bmod p. \tag{14}
$$

Then if we denote $\omega = e^{2\pi i \frac{1}{p}}$ we have

$$
f_i(x) = g_0(x) + g_1(x) + ... + g_{p-1}(x), \tag{15}
$$

$$
f_i(D_p^c x) = g_0(x) + \omega g_1(x) + ... + \omega^{p-1} g_{p-1}(x), \tag{16}
$$

$$
\cdots
$$

$$
f_i((D_p^c)^{p-1} x) = g_0(x) + \omega^{p-1} g_1(x) + ... + \omega g_{p-1}(x). \tag{17}
$$

Since each $f_i((D_p^c)^k \boldsymbol{x}) = 0$ we can rewrite this as

$$
\begin{bmatrix}
1 & 1 & 1 & \cdots & 1 \\
1 & \omega & \omega^2 & \cdots & \omega^{p-1} \\
\vdots & \vdots & \vdots & \ddots & \vdots \\
1 & \omega^{p-1} & \omega^{p-2} & \cdots & \omega
\end{bmatrix}
\begin{bmatrix}
g_0(\boldsymbol{x}) \\
g_1(\boldsymbol{x}) \\
g_2(\boldsymbol{x}) \\
\vdots \\
g_{p-1}(\boldsymbol{x})
\end{bmatrix}
= \boldsymbol{0}. \tag{18}
$$

Since the matrix is non-singular we must have $g_k(\boldsymbol{x}) = 0$ for $k = 0, 1, 2, \ldots, p-1$. By definition each g_k will have a c-weighted p-fold symmetry and by replacing each equation $f_i(\boldsymbol{x}) = 0$ by the equations $\{g_k(\boldsymbol{x}) = 0\}_{k=0}^{p-1}$ it is clear that we get an equivalent system where each polynomial has the correct symmetry. □

Corollary 1. *Take any polynomial $f \in I = \langle f_1, f_2, \ldots, f_m \rangle$ where each f_i has c-weighted p-fold symmetry and decompose*

$$
f(\boldsymbol{x}) = g_0(\boldsymbol{x}) + g_1(\boldsymbol{x}) + \ldots + g_{p-1}(\boldsymbol{x}), \tag{19}
$$

such that each monomial in g_q has the c-weighted remainder q modulo p, then each component g_q is a polynomial in I.

Proof. This is a consequence of the proof of the previous theorem. □

Theorem 3. *Let $f_i(\boldsymbol{x}) = 0$, $i = 1, 2, \ldots, m$ be a polynomial system with c-weighted p-fold symmetry and $\mathcal{B}$ be a monomial (linear) basis for $\mathbb{C}[X]/I$. Let $\mathcal{B}_q \subset \mathcal{B}$ be the set of basis monomials with c-weighted exponent remainder q modulo p. Then any element $[h(\boldsymbol{x})] \in \mathbb{C}[X]/I$ where $h(\boldsymbol{x})$ has a c-weighted symmetry can be expressed in the quotient ring as a linear combination of the basis elements with the same remainder, i.e.*

$$
[h(\boldsymbol{x})] \in [\text{span } \mathcal{B}_q] \tag{20}
$$

for some q.

Proof. Since $\mathcal{B}$ is a linear basis for $\mathbb{C}[X]/I$ there exist coefficients a_k such that

$$
[h(\boldsymbol{x})] = \left[\sum_k a_k b_k(\boldsymbol{x}) \right] \quad \text{where} \quad b_k \in \mathcal{B}. \tag{21}
$$

Since the ideal vanishes on $\mathcal{V}$ we have

$$
h(\boldsymbol{x}) = \sum_k a_k b_k(\boldsymbol{x}) \quad \boldsymbol{x} \in \mathcal{V}. \tag{22}
$$

But this means that $(h(\boldsymbol{x}) - \sum_k a_k b_k(\boldsymbol{x})) \in I$ and from Corollary 1 we know that we can split this into p terms with different c-weighted remainders, which all belong to I. In particular if $h(\boldsymbol{x})$ has c-weighted remainder q we have,

$$
h(\boldsymbol{x}) = \sum_{b_k \in \mathcal{B}_q} a_k b_k(\boldsymbol{x}) \quad \boldsymbol{x} \in \mathcal{V}, \tag{23}
$$

which is sufficient to show $[h(\boldsymbol{x})] = \left[\sum_{b_k \in \mathcal{B}_q} a_k b_k(\boldsymbol{x})\right]$ since the elements in $\mathbb{C}[X]/I$ are uniquely determined by their values on $\mathcal{V}$.   □

Corollary 2. *For any action polynomial $a(\boldsymbol{x}) \in \mathbb{C}[X]$ with $\boldsymbol{c}$-weighted remainder zero the corresponding action matrix becomes block diagonal.*

Proof. If $a(\boldsymbol{x})$ has $\boldsymbol{c}$-weighted remainder zero then all polynomials in $a(\boldsymbol{x})\mathcal{B}_q$ will have remainder q. From Theorem 3 we get $[a(\boldsymbol{x})\mathcal{B}_q] \subset [\text{span } \mathcal{B}_q]$ and the result follows.

2.1   Solving Equation Systems with Symmetries

Once the symmetries have been identified they can be used to construct more compact polynomial solvers. From Corollary 2 we know that if we choose our action polynomial $a(\boldsymbol{x}) \in \mathbb{C}[X]$ to be invariant with respect to the symmetry the corresponding action matrix will be block diagonal. The idea is then to only consider a single block of the matrix, i.e. we only consider the action of $a(\boldsymbol{x})$ on a subset of the basis monomials $\mathcal{B}$. Next we show two concrete examples where we construct the partial action matrix and use it to recover the solutions.

Example 4. Consider again the system in Example 1,

$$\begin{cases} x^2 + y - 2 = 0, \\ x^2 y^2 - 1 = 0. \end{cases} \tag{24}$$

We saw earlier that this system has six solutions and a 2-fold partial symmetry in the x variable, or equivalently a $(1,0)$-weighted 2-fold symmetry. For this system the quotient ring $\mathbb{C}[X]/I$ is spanned by the monomials

$$\mathcal{B} = \{1, \ x, \ y, \ xy, \ y^2, \ xy^2\}. \tag{25}$$

We can group these into two sets, based on their $(1,0)$-weighted remainder modulo 2,

$$\mathcal{B}_0 = \{1, \ y, \ y^2\} \quad \text{and} \quad \mathcal{B}_1 = \{x, \ xy, \ xy^2\}. \tag{26}$$

Now instead of working with the entire basis $\mathcal{B}$ we will only consider the subset $\mathcal{B}_0$. If we choose x^2 to be our action polynomial (note that this has $(1,0)$-remainder zero) we have the following multiplication maps [1]

$$T_{x^2}[1] = x^2 = 2 - y, \quad T_{x^2}[y] = x^2 y, \quad T_{x^2}[y^2] = x^2 y^2 = 1. \tag{27}$$

Since one of the monomials was not in the span of $\mathcal{B}_0$ we need to generate more equations. Multiplying the first equation by y we get

$$x^2 y + y^2 - 2y = 0 \implies T_{x^2}[y] = x^2 y = 2y - y^2 \in \text{span } \mathcal{B}_0. \tag{28}$$

---

[1] $T_\alpha : \mathbb{C}[X]/I \to \mathbb{C}[X]/I$ is the linear map corresponding to multiplication by $\alpha(\boldsymbol{x})$.

Finally we can construct our action matrix,

$$\begin{bmatrix} 0 & 0 & 1 \\ -1 & 2 & 0 \\ 0 & -1 & 2 \end{bmatrix} \begin{bmatrix} y^2 \\ y \\ 1 \end{bmatrix} = x^2 \begin{bmatrix} y^2 \\ y \\ 1 \end{bmatrix}. \tag{29}$$

Even though the system has six solutions we only have to solve a 3×3 eigenvalue problem. From each eigenvector we can construct two solutions with different signs for x.

Next we show a similar example but where the equation system has multiple symmetries.

Example 5. Consider the equation system

$$\begin{cases} x^2 + y^2 - 2 = 0, \\ xy^2 - x = 0. \end{cases} \tag{30}$$

This system has a 2-fold partial symmetry in the x variable and 2-fold partial symmetry in y, or equivalently two 2-fold symmetries with weights $c_1 = (1,0)$ and $c_2 = (0,1)$. The equation system has six solutions and a basis for the quotient ring $\mathbb{C}[X]/I$ is given by

$$\mathcal{B} = \{1, \ x, \ y, \ xy, \ y^2, \ y^3\}. \tag{31}$$

Grouping the basis monomials based on their c_k-weighted remainders modulo 2:

$$\mathcal{B}_{0,0} = \{1, \ y^2\}, \ \mathcal{B}_{0,1} = \{y, \ y^3\}, \ \mathcal{B}_{1,0} = \{x\}, \ \mathcal{B}_{1,1} = \{xy\}. \tag{32}$$

Let us choose to work with $\mathcal{B}_{0,0}$. By multiplying the second equation with x we get that all the monomials in the system have the same remainder as our monomial basis,

$$\begin{cases} x^2 + y^2 - 2 = 0, \\ x^2y^2 - x^2 = 0. \end{cases} \tag{33}$$

Choosing again the action polynomial as x^2 we get the following multiplications

$$T_{x^2}[1] = x^2 = 2 - y^2 \in \text{span } \mathcal{B}_{0,0}, \quad T_{x^2}[y^2] = x^2y^2 = x^2 = 2 - y^2 \in \text{span } \mathcal{B}_{0,0}, \tag{34}$$

which allows us to construct a 2×2 action matrix

$$\begin{bmatrix} -1 & 2 \\ -1 & 2 \end{bmatrix} \begin{bmatrix} y^2 \\ 1 \end{bmatrix} = x^2 \begin{bmatrix} y^2 \\ 1 \end{bmatrix}. \tag{35}$$

This matrix has eigenvalues 0 and 1 with corresponding eigenvectors $\begin{pmatrix} 2 \\ 1 \end{pmatrix}, \begin{pmatrix} 1 \\ 1 \end{pmatrix}$. The two eigenpairs give us the following possibilities

$$\begin{cases} y^2 = 2 \\ x^2 = 0 \end{cases} \quad \text{and} \quad \begin{cases} y^2 = 1 \\ x^2 = 1 \end{cases}. \tag{36}$$

The first eigenvector gives two solutions $(0, \sqrt{2})$ and $(0, -\sqrt{2})$ and the second gives four solutions $(1, \pm 1)$, $(-1, \pm 1)$. In this example we chose the basis $\mathcal{B}_{0,0}$ but we could also have used $\mathcal{B}_{0,1}$ to recover the solutions. However the other two choices would not have allowed us to recover the complete solution set.

3   Revealing Hidden Symmetries

In the previous section we have studied symmetries which depend on the exponents of the monomials. These properties are however not preserved under a linear change of variables and for some problems there can exist weighted symmetries which only appear after a change of variables.

Example 6. For $\alpha \in (-\sqrt{2}, \sqrt{2})$ consider the following family of polynomial systems

$$\begin{cases} x^2 + y^2 = 1 \\ x + y = \alpha \end{cases}.$$ (37)

Clearly the solution set is stable under the transform which switches x and y since the equation system is unchanged. But in this formulation the system does not have any weighted p-fold symmetries. Performing a change of variables

$$\begin{cases} \hat{x} = x + y \\ \hat{y} = x - y \end{cases} \implies \begin{cases} \frac{1}{2}\hat{x}^2 + \frac{1}{2}\hat{y}^2 = 1 \\ \hat{x} = \alpha \end{cases}$$ (38)

reveals a 2-fold symmetry in the $\hat{y}$ variable.

The previous example showed a polynomial system which was invariant to a specific linear transform. After a change of variables the symmetry was transformed into a weighted p-fold symmetry as in Sect. 2. The following theorem shows that under some weak assumptions this can be done in general.

Theorem 4. *Let $f_i(x) = 0$, $i = 1, 2, \ldots, m$ be a polynomial system with a finite number of solutions. If there exist an invertible matrix $A \neq I$ such that the solution set $\mathcal{V} = \{x \mid f(x) = 0\} \subset \mathbb{C}^n$ is stable under A, then the polynomial system exhibits a c-weighted p-fold symmetry after a linear change of variables.*

Proof. We start by noting that we can without loss of generality assume that span $\mathcal{V} = \mathbb{C}^n$. If this does not hold it will be sufficient to consider the restriction of A to the span of $\mathcal{V}$, i.e. $A_{|\mathcal{V}} : \text{span } \mathcal{V} \to \text{span } \mathcal{V}$.

Since $\mathcal{V}$ is finite and A injective we have that $A\mathcal{V} = \mathcal{V}$. This means that A acts as a permutation on the elements of $\mathcal{V}$. It follows that there must exist $p \in \mathbb{N}$ such that

$$A^p s = s \quad \forall s \in \mathcal{V},$$ (39)

since there are only a finite number of possible permutations. This implies

$$A^p = I,$$ (40)

since the elements of $\mathcal{V}$ span $\mathbb{C}^n$. This is a sufficient condition for A to be diagonalizable and that the eigenvalues of A are p:th roots of unity, i.e. $\lambda_k = e^{2\pi i \frac{c_k}{p}}$. Let S be the matrix which diagonalizes A, then

$$A = SDS^{-1} = S\mathrm{diag}\left(\{e^{2\pi i \frac{c_k}{p}}\}_{k=1}^n\right)S^{-1}. \tag{41}$$

Note that by definition $D = D_p^c$ for $c = (c_1, c_2, \ldots, c_n) \in \mathbb{Z}_p^n$ and if we perform the change of variables $\hat{x} = S^{-1}x$ the solution set instead becomes stable under D_p^c and thus the system has a c-weighted p-fold symmetry. $\qquad \square$

If the system has multiple symmetry matrices we can use all of them if we are able to diagonalize them simultaneously. It is a well-known fact from linear algebra that a set of diagonalizable matrices can be simultaneously diagonalized if and only if they commute.

4   Finding Symmetries in Practice

Unless there is some problem specific knowledge it can be difficult to find the change of variables which reveals the symmetry. In this section we present a simple and automatic method for determining if a given problem has any symmetries of the type presented in this paper.

Assume that we are given a family of polynomial systems $\{f_i(x, a) = 0\}$, which depends on some data $a \in \mathbb{C}^m$, i.e. for fix a each $f_i(x, a)$ is polynomial in x. To find the symmetries we do the following:

1. Take some instance $a^0 \in \mathbb{C}^m$ and solve the problem $\{f_i(x, a^0) = 0\}$ using any method. This can for example be accomplished by selecting some a^0 where the solutions are known, or by using some numerical solver (e.g. PHCPack [19]). Denote the solutions s_k^0, $k = 1, 2, \ldots, N$.
2. Next we generate a sequence of polynomial systems by updating data in small increments, $a^{t+1} = a^t + \epsilon$. For each solution s_k^0 we generate a *solution trajectory* by tracking the solution using non-linear refinement methods (e.g. Newton-Raphson). So to find s_k^{t+1} we solve $\{f_i(x, a^{t+1}) = 0\}$ by starting non-linear refinement at s_k^t. This is repeated until the matrices

$$S_k = \begin{bmatrix} s_k^0 \ s_k^1 \ \ldots \ s_k^t \end{bmatrix} \in \mathbb{C}^{n \times t}, \quad k = 1, 2, \ldots, N \tag{42}$$

are all of full rank and $t > n$.
3. For each pair, $i \neq j$, we try to find a matrix $A_{ij} \in \mathbb{C}^{n \times n}$ such that

$$A_{ij}S_i = S_j. \tag{43}$$

Since the system is overdetermined and the solution matrices S_i might have some small errors we solve (43) in a least square sense. If the residuals are sufficiently close to zero, we add the matrix A_{ij} to a list of possible symmetry matrices.
4. For each matrix A_{ij} we check if the solution set is stable, i.e. if for each k there exist $\ell \neq k$ such that $A_{ij}S_k = S_\ell$. The matrices which satisfy this are the symmetry matrices.
5. Finally we generate new instances and check if the symmetry matrices work.

5   Weak Perspective-n-Points

In this section we show a practical example where we can construct a more compact polynomial solver by exploiting a symmetry in the problem. We consider the problem of estimating a weak perspective camera (also known as scaled orthographic camera) from n 2D-3D point correspondences. We find the pose which minimizes the squared reprojection error. By eliminating the translation and performing a change of variables the problem can be reduced to (see supplementary material)

$$\min_{s,R} \left\| R \operatorname{diag}(a_1, a_2, a_3) - \begin{bmatrix} b_{11} & b_{12} & b_{13} \\ b_{21} & b_{22} & b_{23} \end{bmatrix} \right\|_F^2 \quad \text{s.t.} \quad RR^T = s^2 I_2, \quad (44)$$

where $a_1 \geq a_2 \geq a_3 \geq 0$.

5.1   Parameterizing the Constraints

We use the unconstrained quaternion parametrization of the scaled 2×3 rotation,

$$R(q) = \begin{bmatrix} q_1^2 + q_2^2 - q_3^2 - q_4^2 & 2(q_2 q_3 - q_1 q_4) & 2(q_1 q_3 + q_2 q_4) \\ 2(q_1 q_4 + q_2 q_3) & q_1^2 - q_2^2 + q_3^2 - q_4^2 & 2(q_3 q_4 - q_1 q_2) \end{bmatrix}, \quad (45)$$

where $q = (q_1, q_2, q_3, q_4)$ and $\|q\|_2 = s$. In this parametrization the problem in (44) becomes unconstrained and the cost function

$$f(q) = \|R(q)A - B\|_F^2. \quad (46)$$

is a quartic polynomial in the elements of q. Since each element in $R(q)$ is of degree two we have that $f(q)$ only contains monomials of degrees $0, 2$ and 4.

We find the optimal pose by studying the first-order necessary conditions for (46). Since the problem is now unconstrained in the unscaled quaternion representation we simply solve for the critical points, i.e.

$$g(q) = \nabla_q f(q) = 0. \quad (47)$$

Since $f(q)$ only contains even terms, this equation system $g(q) = 0$ can only contain odd terms (degree 1 or 3). Thus we can directly see that the equation system will have at least a two-fold symmetry. This symmetry correspond to the sign ambiguity of the quaternion representation, i.e. $R(q) = R(-q)$.

5.2   Additional Symmetries in the Solutions

The quaternion parametrization is inherently ambiguous since the sign of the quaternion does not matter. But it turns out that there is a further ambiguity which comes from the fact that the third row of the rotation matrix is ignored. By studying (45) we can see that $R(q_1, q_2, q_3, q_4) = R(iq_4, iq_3, -iq_2, -iq_1)$ holds for all $q \in \mathbb{C}^4$. For the full 3×3 rotation matrix this corresponds to changing sign of the third row. Together these ambiguities introduce a four-fold symmetry into the solution set which can be described by the matrices

$$A_1 = \begin{pmatrix} -1 & 0 & 0 & 0 \\ 0 & -1 & 0 & 0 \\ 0 & 0 & -1 & 0 \\ 0 & 0 & 0 & -1 \end{pmatrix} \quad \text{and} \quad A_2 = \begin{pmatrix} 0 & 0 & 0 & i \\ 0 & 0 & i & 0 \\ 0 & -i & 0 & 0 \\ -i & 0 & 0 & 0 \end{pmatrix}. \tag{48}$$

To diagonalize the matrices we perform the change of variables,

$$\hat{q} = \frac{1}{\sqrt{2}} \begin{bmatrix} 0 & -i & -i & 0 \\ -1 & 0 & 0 & 1 \\ i & 0 & 0 & i \\ 0 & -1 & 1 & 0 \end{bmatrix} q. \tag{49}$$

In these new variables the rotation matrix becomes

$$R(\hat{q}) = \begin{bmatrix} \hat{q}_1^2 - \hat{q}_2^2 - \hat{q}_3^2 + \hat{q}_4^2 & -i\hat{q}_1^2 - i\hat{q}_2^2 + i\hat{q}_3^2 + i\hat{q}_4^2 & 2(\hat{q}_1\hat{q}_2 + 2\hat{q}_3\hat{q}_4) \\ -i\hat{q}_1^2 + i\hat{q}_2^2 - i\hat{q}_3^2 + i\hat{q}_4^2 & -\hat{q}_1^2 - \hat{q}_2^2 - \hat{q}_3^2 - \hat{q}_4^2 & 2i(\hat{q}_3\hat{q}_4 - \hat{q}_1\hat{q}_2) \end{bmatrix}. \tag{50}$$

Note that the only mixed terms are $\hat{q}_1\hat{q}_2$ and $\hat{q}_3\hat{q}_4$. This leads to one 2-fold symmetry in $(\hat{q}_1, \hat{q}_2)$ and one 2-fold symmetry in $(\hat{q}_3, \hat{q}_4)$.

5.3   Constructing a Polynomial Solver

By studying the problem in Macaulay2 [20] and Maple [21] we find that the system has 33 solutions. Ignoring the trivial solution, the rest of the solutions can be grouped into eight groups of four solutions. Using the method from Sect. 2.1 we constructed a polynomial solver. We used the following eight basis monomials,

$$\mathcal{B}_{0,0} = \{\hat{q}_1\hat{q}_2, \ \hat{q}_2^2, \ \hat{q}_3^2\hat{q}_4^2, \ \hat{q}_3^2, \ \hat{q}_3\hat{q}_4^3, \ \hat{q}_3\hat{q}_4, \ \hat{q}_4^4, \ \hat{q}_4^2\}, \tag{51}$$

which have the weighted remainder zero for both symmetries. For our action polynomial we used $a(\hat{q}) = \hat{q}_1\hat{q}_2$, which also has zero remainder.

5.4   Experimental Evaluation

In this section we experimentally evaluate the polynomial solver from the previous section. Using the same method we also constructed a solver which only uses the partial 2-fold symmetry present in the original formulation. For comparison we also used the automatic method from Kukelova et al. [22] to generate a polynomial solver. This solver does not take any symmetry into account. The

Table 1. Size of the elimination template and action matrix for the three solvers.

	2x2-sym	2-sym	Kukelova et al. [22]
Elimination template	104 × 90	234 × 276	243 × 276
Action matrix	8 × 8	16 × 16	33 × 33

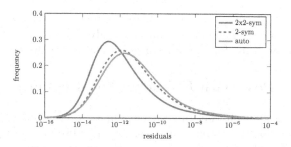

Fig. 1. Histogram over the residuals for 1000 random instances.

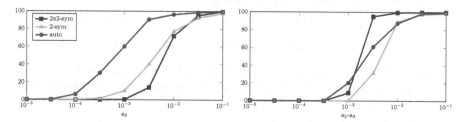

Fig. 2. Percentage of successful instances (all residuals smaller than 10^{-6}) when the structure is close to planar, i.e. $a_3 \approx 0$ (Left) and when there are two almost equal singular values, i.e. $a_2 \approx a_3$. (Right)

sizes of the elimination templates and action matrices for the three methods can be seen in Table 1.

We evaluated the three solvers on synthetic instances. Figure 1 shows the distribution of the residuals over 1000 random instances. The automatically generated solver and the solver using only the partial 2-fold symmetry has very similar performance, while the solver utilizing the full symmetry performs slightly better. The average runtimes for the instances were 11.2 ms for the 2-sym solver and 2.7 ms for the 2x2-sym solver. For the automatically generated solver the average runtime was 2.1 s.[2]

Degeneracies. Under some conditions the problem changes nature and the polynomial solvers break down. For this problem we empirically found that this happens when either the structure is planar ($a_3 = 0$) or if two of the singular values are equal ($a_1 = a_2$ or $a_2 = a_3$). Close to these configurations the solvers become numerically unstable. We compare the performance of the polynomial solver on random instances close to these degeneracies. We generated random instances where the third singular value approached zero and instances where $|a_2 - a_3|$ approached zero. Figure 2 shows the percentage of successful instances

---

[2] The large runtime is due to use of the MATLAB function `rref` for performing the elimination. In principal this could replaced by a faster implementation, which most likely would yield runtimes similar to the 2-sym solver.

(defined as all residuals less than 10^{-6}) as we approach the degenerate configurations. For the planar degeneracy the automatically generated solver has slightly better performance while for the other degeneracy the results are comparable.

6   Absolute Pose with Unknown Focal Length

In this section we show another practical example, where symmetry occurs naturally in the polynomial systems. We consider the absolute pose problem with unknown focal length. The problem has 7 degrees of freedom and requires at least 3.5 points to be determined. We consider the (almost) minimal problem of estimation from four 2D-3D point correspondences.

The normalized image points x_k should satisfy the projection equations

$$\lambda_k x_k = \lambda_k \left(x_k \ y_k \ f \right)^T = R X_k + t, \quad k = 1, 2, 3, 4. \tag{52}$$

This means that the four vectors $\lambda_1 x_1, \lambda_2 x_2, \lambda_3 x_3$ and $\lambda_4 x_4$ differ only by a rigid transformation from the 3D points X_k. We form the vectors from the first point to the others, i.e.

$$V = \left[(X_2 - X_1), (X_3 - X_1), (X_4 - X_1) \right], \tag{53}$$

$$v = \left[(\lambda_2 x_2 - \lambda_1 x_1), (\lambda_3 x_3 - \lambda_1 x_1), (\lambda_4 x_4 - \lambda_1 x_1) \right]. \tag{54}$$

Since rigid transformations preserve lengths and angles we must have

$$V^T V = v^T v, \tag{55}$$

which gives six independent equations in the five unknowns: $f, \lambda_1, \lambda_2, \lambda_3$ and λ_4.

In this formulation the problem has two 2-fold symmetries, corresponding to the sign ambiguities in the focal length and the projective depths λ_k. Together these introduce a four-fold symmetry in the solution set.

Since the problem is overconstrained we cannot use all equations from (55). Using Macaulay2 [20] we found that if we discard one of the off-diagonal equations ($V_i^T V_j = v_i^T v_j$) the remaining system has 40 solutions. However if we discard one of the diagonal equations ($\|V_i\|^2 = \|v_i\|^2$) we get 24 solutions. By exploiting the symmetry we only have to find 10 and 6 of these solutions respectively.

Using the method from Sect. 2.1 we construct a polynomial solver for the case with 24 solutions. The solver uses both symmetries and only has to find 6 solutions. We used $a(x) = \lambda_1 \lambda_2$ as our action polynomial and as our monomial basis we used

$$\mathcal{B}_{0,0} = \{1, \ \lambda_1 \lambda_4, \ \lambda_2 \lambda_4, \ \lambda_3^2, \ \lambda_3 \lambda_4, \ \lambda_4^2\}. \tag{56}$$

The elimination template is of size 139×185 and the resulting action matrix is 6×6. Note that neither the action polynomial nor the monomial basis contain the focal length f. However this does not pose any problem, as once the lengths λ_i are recovered the equations in (55) reduce to a second degree polynomial in f which can be easily solved. Figure 3 show two examples where we have applied the solver to pose estimation problems from real images.

Fig. 3. Examples of pose estimation from real images.

6.1 Experimental Evaluation

We compare the polynomial solver with the most accurate solvers from Bujnak [23] based on the ratio and distance constraints (denoted `Best-Ratio` and `Best-Dist`). We also compare with the more recent method from Zheng et al. [10] (denoted `Zheng` in the experiments). In 2015 Wu [2] presented another minimal solver for this problem. We do not include a comparison with this method since we were unable to find any implementation, but in their paper the performance is similar to that of [10]. For the experiment we generated 3D points uniformly in the box $[-2, 2] \times [-2, 2] \times [4, 8]$ in the camera's coordinate system. The cameras were then randomly generated with focal length $f = 1000$. Figure 4 shows the reprojection error for 1000 random instances, both with and without random noise added to the image coordinates. We can see that the solver has comparable performance to current state-of-the-art methods. The average runtimes for the four methods were 149 ms (`Best-Dist`), 4.44 ms (`Best-Ratio`), 4.65 ms (`Zheng`) and 3.90 ms for our solver.

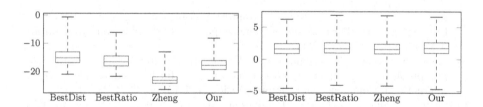

Fig. 4. The squared reprojection error for 1000 random instances. If there are multiple solutions we take the smallest error. *Left:* No noise added. *Right:* Gaussian noise with 5 px standard deviation added to the image points.

7 Conclusions

In this paper we have presented new techniques for using symmetry in the action matrix method. The theory relies on a generalization of the partial p-fold symmetry from [13]. However in contrast to [13] our method allows us to handle multiple independent symmetries, resulting in even more compact polynomial solvers. Furthermore, we have shown that these symmetries are not restricted to theoretical examples, but occur in real problems from Computer Vision.

Acknowledgments. This work has been funded by the Swedish Research Council (grant no. 2012-4213), the Strategic Research Area ELLIIT and by the Wallenberg Autonomous Systems Program.

References

1. Haner, S., Åström, K.: Absolute pose for cameras under flat refractive interfaces. In: Proceedings of the IEEE Conference on Computer Vision and Pattern Recognition (CVPR), pp. 1428–1436 (2015)
2. Wu, C.: P3.5p: pose estimation with unknown focal length. In: Proceedings of the IEEE Conference on Computer Vision and Pattern Recognition (CVPR), pp. 2440–2448 (2015)
3. Albl, C., Kukelova, Z., Pajdla, T.: R6p-rolling shutter absolute camera pose. In: Proceedings of the IEEE Conference on Computer Vision and Pattern Recognition (CVPR), pp. 2292–2300(2015)
4. Stewénius, H., Nistér, D., Oskarsson, M., Åström, K.: Solutions to minimal generalized relative pose problems. In: Workshop on Omnidirectional Vision (OMNIVIS), vol. 1, p. 3(2005)
5. Nistér, D.: An efficient solution to the five-point relative pose problem. IEEE Trans. Pattern Anal. Mach. Intell. (PAMI) **26**(6), 756–770 (2004)
6. Kuang, Y., Solem, J.E., Kahl, F., Åström, K.: Minimal solvers for relative pose with a single unknown radial distortion. In: Proceedings of the IEEE Conference on Computer Vision and Pattern Recognition (CVPR), pp. 33–40. IEEE (2014)
7. Kukelova, Z., Heller, J., Bujnak, M., Pajdla, T.: Radial distortion homography. In: Proceedings of the IEEE Conference on Computer Vision and Pattern Recognition (CVPR), pp. 639–647 (2015)
8. Brown, M., Hartley, R.I., Nistér, D.: Minimal solutions for panoramic stitching. In: Proceedings of the IEEE Conference on Computer Vision and Pattern Recognition (CVPR), pp. 1–8. IEEE (2007)
9. Zheng, Y., Kuang, Y., Sugimoto, S., Åström, K., Okutomi, M.: Revisiting the pnp problem: a fast, general and optimal solution. In: Proceedings of the IEEE International Conference on Computer Vision (ICCV), pp. 2344–2351 (2013)
10. Zheng, Y., Sugimoto, S., Sato, I., Okutomi, M.: A general and simple method for camera pose and focal length determination. In: Proceedings of the IEEE Conference on Computer Vision and Pattern Recognition (CVPR), pp. 430–437 (2014)
11. Byröd, M., Josephson, K., Åström, K.: Fast and stable polynomial equation solving and its application to computer vision. Int. J. Comput. Vision (IJCV) **84**(3), 237–256 (2009)
12. Ask, E., Kuang, Y., Åström, K.: Exploiting p-fold symmetries for faster polynomial equation solving. In: Proceedings of the International Conference on Pattern Recognition (ICPR), pp. 3232–3235. IEEE (2012)
13. Kuang, Y., Zheng, Y., Åström, K.: Partial symmetry in polynomial systems and its applications in computer vision. In: The IEEE Conference on Computer Vision and Pattern Recognition (CVPR), June 2014

14. Kneip, L., Li, H., Seo, Y.: UPnP: an optimal $O(n)$ solution to the absolute pose problem with universal applicability. In: Fleet, D., Pajdla, T., Schiele, B., Tuytelaars, T. (eds.) ECCV 2014. LNCS, vol. 8689, pp. 127–142. Springer, Heidelberg (2014). doi:10.1007/978-3-319-10590-1_9
15. Ask, E., Enqvist, O., Kahl, F.: Optimal geometric fitting under the truncated l2-norm. In: Proceedings of the IEEE Conference on Computer Vision and Pattern Recognition (CVPR), pp. 1722–1729 (2013)
16. Enqvist, O., Ask, E., Kahl, F., Åström, K.: Tractable algorithms for robust model estimation. Int. J. Comput. Vision (IJCV) **112**(1), 115–129 (2015)
17. Corless, R.M., Gatermann, K., Kotsireas, I.S.: Using symmetries in the eigenvalue method for polynomial systems. J. Symbolic Comput. **44**(11), 1536–1550 (2009)
18. Cox, D.A., Little, J., O'Shea, D.: Ideals, Varieties, and Algorithms: An Introduction to Computational Algebraic Geometry and Commutative Algebra, 3/e (Undergraduate Texts in Mathematics). Springer-Verlag New York Inc, Secaucus (2007)
19. Verschelde, J.: Algorithm 795: phcpack: a general-purpose solver for polynomial systems by homotopy continuation. ACM Trans. Math. Softw. (TOMS) **25**(2), 251–276 (1999)
20. Grayson, D.R., Stillman, M.E.: Macaulay2, a software system for research in algebraic geometry. http://www.math.uiuc.edu/Macaulay2/
21. Monagan, M.B., Geddes, K.O., Heal, K.M., Labahn, G., Vorkoetter, S.M., McCarron, J., DeMarco, P.: Maple 10 Programming Guide. Maplesoft, Waterloo ON, Canada (2005)
22. Kukelova, Z., Bujnak, M., Pajdla, T.: Automatic generator of minimal problem solvers. In: Forsyth, D., Torr, P., Zisserman, A. (eds.) ECCV 2008. LNCS, vol. 5304, pp. 302–315. Springer, Heidelberg (2008). doi:10.1007/978-3-540-88690-7_23
23. Bujnák, M.: Algebraic solutions to absolute pose problems. Ph.D. thesis (2012)

ATGV-Net: Accurate Depth Super-Resolution

Gernot Riegler[(✉)], Matthias Rüther, and Horst Bischof

Institute for Computer Graphics and Vision, Graz University of Technology,
Graz, Austria
{riegler,ruether,bischof}@icg.tugraz.at

Abstract. In this work we present a novel approach for single depth map super-resolution. Modern consumer depth sensors, especially Time-of-Flight sensors, produce dense depth measurements, but are affected by noise and have a low lateral resolution. We propose a method that combines the benefits of recent advances in machine learning based single image super-resolution, *i.e.* deep convolutional networks, with a variational method to recover accurate high-resolution depth maps. In particular, we integrate a variational method that models the piecewise affine structures apparent in depth data via an anisotropic total generalized variation regularization term on top of a deep network. We call our method *ATGV-Net* and train it end-to-end by unrolling the optimization procedure of the variational method. To train deep networks, a large corpus of training data with accurate ground-truth is required. We demonstrate that it is feasible to train our method solely on synthetic data that we generate in large quantities for this task. Our evaluations show that we achieve state-of-the-art results on three different benchmarks, as well as on a challenging Time-of-Flight dataset, all without utilizing an additional intensity image as guidance.

Keywords: Deep networks · Variational methods · Depth super-resolution

1 Introduction

Over the last decade depth sensors have entered the mass market which substantially improved in package size, energy consumption and price. This made depth data an interesting and important auxiliary input for computer vision tasks, for example in pose estimation [14,35], or scene understanding [16]. However, current sensors are limited by physical and manufacturing constraints. Hence, depth outputs are affected by degenerations due to noise, quantization and missing values, and typically have a low resolution.

To alleviate the use of depth data, recent methods focus on increasing the spatial resolution of the acquired depth maps. A common approach to

Electronic supplementary material The online version of this chapter (doi:10.1007/978-3-319-46487-9_17) contains supplementary material, which is available to authorized users.

© Springer International Publishing AG 2016

B. Leibe et al. (Eds.): ECCV 2016, Part III, LNCS 9907, pp. 268–284, 2016.
DOI: 10.1007/978-3-319-46487-9_17

tackle this problem is to utilize a high-resolution intensity image as guidance [12,25,29]. These methods are motivated by the statistical co-occurrences of edges in intensity images and discontinuities in depth. In practical scenarios, however, a depth sensor is not always accompanied by an additional camera and the depth map has to be projected to the guidance image, which is also problematic due to noisy depth measurements. Therefore, approaches that solely rely on the depth input for super-resolution are becoming popular [1,13,20].

In contrast to super-resolution methods for depth data, machine learning based methods for natural images [11,33,36,37] are advancing rapidly and achieve impressive results on standard benchmarks. Those methods learn a mapping from a low-resolution input space to a plausible and visually pleasing high-resolution output space. The inference is performed for small, overlapping patches of the image independently, and are then averaged for the final output. This is not optimal for depth data, as it is characterised by textureless, piecewise affine regions that have sharp depth discontinuities. In contrast, variational methods are especially suited for this task, because the aforementioned prior information can be exploited in the model's regularization term. A prominent example is the total generalized variation (TGV) [3] that is for example utilized in [12].

In this work we propose a method that combines the advantages of datadriven methods and energy minimization models by combining a deep convolutional network with a powerful variational model to compute an accurate high-resolution output from a single low-resolution depth map input. Deep networks recently demonstrated impressive capabilities in single-image super resolution [22]. We utilize a similar architecture for our network, but instead of just producing the refined depth map as output, we design the network to additionally predict the locations of the depth discontinuities in the high-resolution output space. Both outputs are then used as input for a variational model to refine the high-resolution estimate. The variational model uses an anisotropic TGV pairwise regularization that is weighted by the network output. To integrate the variational method into our network and learn the joint model end-to-end, we unroll all computation steps of the primal-dual optimization scheme [5] that is used for inference with layers of a deep network. Therefore, we name our method *ATGV-Net*. Finally, we deal with the problem of obtaining accurate ground-truth data for training. The training of deep networks requires a large corpus of data. We demonstrate that we can train our model entirely on synthetic depth data that we generate in large quantities and obtain state-of-the-art results on four different benchmark datasets.

Our contributions can be summarized as follows: (i) We integrate a variational model with anisotropic TGV regularization into a deep network by unrolling the optimization steps of the primal-dual algorithm [5] and train the whole model end-to-end (see Sect. 3). (ii) We demonstrate that our joint model can be trained entirely on synthetic data for single depth map super-resolution (see Sect. 4.1). (iii) Finally, we show that our method improves upon state-of-the-art results on four different benchmark datasets (see Sects. 4.2, 4.3 and 4.4).

2   Related Work

Depth Super-Resolution. In general, the work on super-resolution is roughly divided in approaches that use a series of aligned images to produce a high-resolution output, and single image super-resolution, *i.e.* approaches that use only one low-resolution image as input. We focus in this related work on the latter as our method falls into this category.

Natural images often contain repetitive structures and therefore, a patch might be visible on different scales within the same image. Glasner *et al.* [15] exploit this knowledge in their seminal work. For each image patch they search similar patches across various scales in the image and combine them for a high-resolution estimate. A similar idea is employed for depth data by Hornáček *et al.* [20], but instead of reasoning about 2D patches, they reason in terms of patches containing 3D points. The 3D points of the depth map patch can be translated and rotated with six degree of freedom to find related patches within the same depth map. Aodha *et al.* [1] search for similar patches not within the same image, but in an ancillary database and they formulate a Markov Random Field (MRF) that enforces smooth transition between the candidate high-resolution patches.

More recently, machine learning approaches have become popular for single image super-resolution. They achieve higher accuracy and are at the same time more efficient in testing, because they do not rely on a computational intensive patch search. Sparse coding approaches [40,42] learn dictionaries for the low- and high-resolution domains that are coupled via a common encoding. To increase the inference speed, Timofte *et al.* [36] replace the ℓ_1 norm in the sparse coding step with the ℓ_2 norm, which can be solved in closed form and replace a single dictionary by man smaller sub-dictionaries to improve accuracy. In [33], Schulter *et al.* substitute the flat code-book of sparse coding methods with a random regression forest. A test patch traverses the trees of the forest and each leaf node stores regression coefficients to predict a high-resolution estimate. Deep learning based approaches recently showed very good results for single image super-resolution, too. Dong *et al.* [11] train a convolutional network of three layers. The input to the network is the bilinear upsampled low-resolution image and the network is trained with the Euclidean loss on the network output and the corresponding ground-truth high-resolution image. This idea was substantially improved by Kim *et al.* [22]. They train a deep network with up to 20 convolutional layers with filters of size 3×3 and therefore, increasing the receptive field to 41×41 pixel from 15×15 pixels of the network in [11]. Further, the network does not output directly the high-resolution estimate, but the residual to the pre-processed input image, aiding training of the very deep networks [19].

These learning based methods have mainly been applied to color images, where a huge amount of training data can be easily obtained. In contrast, large datasets with dense, accurate depth maps have only very recently become available, *e.g.* [17]. Therefore, most methods for depth map super-resolution are not based on machine learning, but utilize a high-resolution intensity image as guidance. One of the first works in this direction is by Diebel and Thrun [9].

They apply a MRF for the upsampling task and weight their smoothness term according to the gradients of the guidance image. Yang et al. [41] propose an approach based on a bilateral filter that is iteratively applied to estimate a high-resolution output map. Park et al. [29] present a least-squares method, that incorporates edge aware weighting schemes in the regularization term of their formulation. A more recent approach of Ferstl et al. [12] utilizes a variational framework for image guided depth upsampling, where they also use the total generalized variation [3] as regularization term. One of the few machine learning based approaches for depth map super-resolution is by Kwon et al. [25]. They collect their own training data using KinectFusion [21] and facilitate sparse coding with an additional multi-scale approach and an advanced edge weighting term, that emphasizes intensity edges corresponding to depth discontinuities. Ferstl et al. [13] use sparse coding with dictionaries trained on the 31 synthetic depth maps of [1] to predict the depth discontinuities in the high-resolution domain from the low-resolution depth data. Those edge estimates are then used in an anisotropic diffusion tensor of their regularization term.

Deep Network Integration of Energy Minimization Methods. Energy minimization methods, such as Markov Random Fields (MRFs), or variational methods have a wide range of applications in computer vision. They consist of unary terms, for example the class likelihood of a pixel for semantic segmentation, or the depth value in depth super-resolution, and pairwise terms, which measure the dependencies on neighbouring pixels. Recently, the integration of those models into deep networks gained a lot of attention, as deep networks jointly trained with energy minimization methods achieve excellent results. For example, Tompson et al. [38] propose the joint training of a convolutional network and a MRF for human pose estimation. The MRF is realized by very large convolutional filters to model the pairwise interactions between joints and can be interpreted as one iteration of loopy belief propagation. In [8,34] the authors show how to compute the derivative with respect to the mean field approximation [24] in MRFs. This allows end-to-end learning and improves results for instance in semantic segmentation. Similarly, Zheng et al. [43] show that the computation steps of the mean field approximation can be modeled by operations of a convolutional network and unroll the iterations on top of their network.

While the latter approaches for semantic segmentation are designed for a discrete label space, the variational approach by Ranftl and Pock [31] has a continuous output space. They show that the gradient of a loss function can be back-propagated through the energy functional of a variational method by implicit differentiation, if the functional is smooth enough. This approach has been extended for depth denoising and upsampling by Riegler et al. [32]. Recently, Ochs et al. [28] propose a technique that allows the back-propagation through non-smooth energy functionals using Bregman proximity functions [6], but did not demonstrate the use in combination with deep networks.

Our approach utilizes a variational method on top of a deep network, but instead of implicitly differentiating the energy functional as in [31,32] we unroll every step of an exact optimization scheme [5], in the spirit of [10]. This has two major advantages: First, we can incorporate stronger pairwise regularization terms and second, the optimization gets more robust, allowing the successful training of deeper networks. This is similar to [43], but instead of the mean field approximation, we unroll the steps of the primal-dual algorithm by Chambolle and Pock [5], which converges to the global optimal solution of the convex energy functional. For parametrizing the variational method we use a 10 layer deep network of 3×3 convolutions, and train on the residual similarly to [22]. Additionally, we train the network to predict the depth discontinuities in the high-resolution output space. This output is used to weight the pairwise regularization term of the variational part. Finally, we demonstrate that we can train a deep network for this task by rendering synthetic depth maps in large quantities with a ray-caster running on the GPU.

3   ATGV-Net

In this section we describe our method that takes a single low-resolution, probably noisy depth map as input and computes a high-resolution output. We first introduce the notation used throughout this work and then detail our variational model, how we integrate it on top of a deep network and finally the network itself.

In the remainder of this work we denote the low-resolution depth map input as $s_k^{(\mathrm{lr})} \in \mathbb{R}^{M \times N}$. Further, for training we assume that we have for each input sample an accurate, high-resolution ground-truth depth map $t_k \in \mathbb{R}^{\rho M \times \rho N}$, where $\rho > 1$ is the given upsampling factor. The only preprocessing step in our method is a bilinear upsampling of the low-resolution input depth map $s_k^{(\mathrm{lr})}$ to the size of the ground-truth target depth map. We denote this mid-level representation of the input as $s_k \in \mathbb{R}^{\rho M \times \rho N}$.

Given a training set $\{(s_k, t_k)\}_{k=1}^{K}$ of K training pairs we follow [31,32] and formulate the training task as the following bi-level optimization problem:

$$\min_{w} \frac{1}{K} \sum_{k=1}^{K} L(u^*(f(w, s_k)), t_k) \tag{HL}$$

$$\text{s.t.} \quad u^*(f(w, s_k)) = \arg\min_{u} E(u; f(w, s_k)). \tag{LL}$$

This optimization problem has an intuitive interpretation: In the higher-level problem (HL) we want to minimize some weights w, such that the minimizer u^* of the energy functional E in the lower-level problem (LL), which is parameterized by a learnable function f, achieves a low loss L over all training samples. We provide more details on the energy functional and on the parametrization in Sects. 3.1 and 3.2, respectively. For the loss we only impose the restriction that we can compute the gradient with respect to u^*. For the remainder of this work we will use the Euclidean loss:

$$L(u^*(f(w, s_k)), t_k) = \|u^*(f(w, s_k)) - t_k\|_2^2. \tag{1}$$

The authors of [31,32] have proven that the bi-level optimization problem can be solved by implicit differentiation, if certain assumptions for the energy functional

Fig. 1. Our model consists of a deep convolutional network with $L = 10$ layers (blue rectangles) that predicts a first high-resolution depth map and depth discontinuities. The output of the network is then feed to an unrolled primal-dual optimization algorithm (red rectangles) realized by operations in a deep network that further refines the result. This enables us to train the joint model end-to-end. Best viewed magnified in the electronic version.

E hold. Namely, E has to be strongly convex, twice differentiable with respect to u and once differentiable with respect to f. Further, the gradient of f has to be computable with respect to w. The last constraint is satisfied by construction since the parametrization f is realized by a deep network. However, the first constraints drastically limit the choice of energy functionals and therefore, the authors of [31,32] had to design smooth approximations. In the following we show that this constraints can be eliminated by unrolling the optimization steps of the lower-level problem (LL) on top of a deep network, similar to [43].

3.1 Unrolling the Optimization

For the energy functional we have the requirement that it should refine the initial high-resolution depth estimate. Therefore, we use a $\text{TGV}_2\text{-}\ell_2$ variational model [3] that favors the piecewise affine surfaces apparent in depth maps. In addition, we incorporate an anisotropic diffusion tensor [30,39] into the regularization and name our model *ATGV-Net*. The optimization of the energy functional in conjunction with a guidance intensity image already provides good results for depth super-resolution [13]. In the following we demonstrate, how we can significantly improve the model by parametrizing the energy functional by a deep network and learn it end-to-end by unrolling the optimization procedure.

In general, our energy functional consists of a pairwise regularization term R and an ℓ_2 data term:

$$E(u; f(w, s_k)) = R(u, h(w_h, s_k)) + \frac{e^{w_\lambda}}{2} \|u - g(w_g, s_k)\|_2^2. \qquad (2)$$

The functional is parameterized by a function $f(w, s_k) = [h(w_h, s_k), w_\lambda, g(w_g, s_k)]^T$ that has learnable weights w and takes the mid-resolution depth map s_k as input. The functions h and g are realized as a single deep network and described in Sect. 3.2. The parameter w_λ controls the trade-off between data and regularization term and is also learned. We take the exponential of w_λ to ensure convexity of the energy functional. For the pairwise regularization term we utilize the total generalized variation (TGV) [3] of second order that favors piecewise affine solutions and is therefore ideal for depth maps:

$$R(u, h(w_h, s_k)) = \min_v \alpha_1 \|T(h(w_h, s_k))(\nabla_u u - v)\|_1 + \alpha_0 \|\nabla_v v\|_1, \qquad (3)$$

where α_0 and α_1 are user defined parameters. In the regularization term, an anisotropic diffusion tensor T enforces a low degree of smoothness across depth discontinuities and vice versa, more smoothness in homogeneous regions. This anisotropic diffusion tensor is based on the Nagel-Enkelmann operator [27]:

$$T(h(w_h, s_k)) = \exp(-\beta \|h(w_h, s_k)\|_2^\gamma)nn^T + n_\perp n_\perp^T, \tag{4}$$

with β and γ being adjustable parameters weighting the magnitude and sharpness of the tensor. The gradient normal of h is given by

$$n = \frac{h(w_h, s_k)}{\|h(w_h, s_k)\|_2}, \quad n_\perp \cdot n = 0. \tag{5}$$

To optimize this energy functional we chose the first-order primal-dual algorithm by Chambolle and Pock [5], as it guarantees fast convergence. To apply the optimization algorithm, we first reformulate Eq. (2) as saddle-point problem with dual variables p, q as

$$\min_{u,v} \max_{p,q} \alpha_1 \langle T(h(w_h, s_k))(\nabla_u u - v), p \rangle + \alpha_0 \langle \nabla_v v, q \rangle + \frac{e^{w_\lambda}}{2} \|u - g(w_g, s_k)\|_2^2 \tag{6}$$

$$\text{s.t. } p \in \{p \in \mathbb{R}^{2 \times \rho M \times \rho N} \mid \|p_{:,i,j}\|_2 \le 1\}, q \in \{q \in \mathbb{R}^{4 \times \rho M \times \rho N} \mid \|q_{:,i,j}\|_2 \le 1\}, \tag{7}$$

where ∇_u and ∇_v denote operators in the discrete setting that compute the forward differences of u and v. A single iteration of the optimization procedure to obtain u^* is then given by:

$$p^{n+1} = \text{proj}(p^n + \sigma_p \alpha_1 (T(h(w_h, s_k))(\nabla_u \bar{u}^n - \bar{v}^n))) \tag{8}$$

$$q^{n+1} = \text{proj}(q^n + \sigma_q \alpha_0 \nabla_v \bar{v}^n) \tag{9}$$

$$u^{n+1} = \frac{u^n + \tau_u(\alpha_1 \nabla_u^T T(h(w_h, s_k))p^{n+1} + e^{w_\lambda} g(w_g, s_k))}{1 + \tau_u e^{w_\lambda}} \tag{10}$$

$$v^{n+1} = v^n + \tau_v(\alpha_0 \nabla_v^T q^{n+1} + \alpha_1 T(h(w_h, s_k))p^{n+1}) \tag{11}$$

$$\bar{u}^{n+1} = u^{n+1} + \theta(u^{n+1} - u^n) \tag{12}$$

$$\bar{v}^{n+1} = v^{n+1} + \theta(v^{n+1} - v^n), \tag{13}$$

with $u^0 = g(w_g, s_k)$, $v^0, p^0, q^0 = 0$, $\sigma_p, \sigma_q, \tau_u, \tau_v > 0$, $\theta \in [0, 1]$, and $\text{proj}(p) = \frac{p}{\max(1, \|p\|_2)}$ is the point-wise projection to the unit hyper-sphere:

The key observations are: (i) The single computation steps in this optimization algorithm can be realized by operations of a deep network, i.e. individual network layers, and (ii) given a fixed number of iterations, the algorithm can be unrolled like a recurrent neural network, similar to [43]. This allows us to use the back-propagation algorithm to train the optimization procedure, i.e. all hyper-parameters, jointly with the parametrization, i.e. the deep network. See Fig. 1 for a visualization of the concept. In the following we detail how the individual computation steps are realised within our model. We provide a graphical

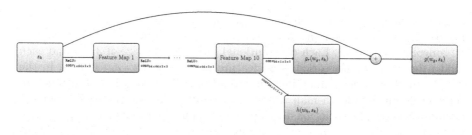

Fig. 2. Overview of our deep network architecture. Our network consists of 10 convolutional layers with 3×3 filters and 64 feature maps in the hidden layers (blue rectangles). The input to the network (green rectangle) is the mid-resolution depth map and the output is (i) the residual that after adding to the mid-resolution input produces the high-resolution estimate $g(w_g, s_k)$ and (ii) the estimates of the depth discontinuities in the high-resolution output $h(w_h, s_k)$ (red rectangles). Best viewed magnified in the electronic version.

representation of a single iteration of the optimization procedure in terms of deep network operations in the supplemental material.

Dual Update. The gradient ascent of the dual variables in Eqs. (8) and (9) consists of scalar multiplication, point-wise addition and multiplication, the gradient operators ∇_u, ∇_v, and the projection. The scalar multiplication and the point-wise operations are trivial operations and are implemented in most deep learning frameworks. The ∇-operator is basically a convolution with two filters, $\nabla_x = [-1, 1]$ and $\nabla_y = [-1, 1]^T$. Therefore, it can be implemented with a standard convolutional layer that has fixed filter coefficients. Additionally, we have to ensure a reflecting padding of the layer input, *i.e.* Neumann boundary conditions. Finally, the proj-operator is a composition of a point-wise division, a max-operator and the ℓ_2 norm. We implemented the max-operator as shifted ReLU, and the ℓ_2 norm as custom layer.

Primal Update. The gradient descent of the primal variables in Eqs. (10) and (11) consists of similar operations as the dual update, and therefore, can be implemented with the same building blocks. Additional operators are ∇_u^T, ∇_v^T. These operators are defined as $\nabla^T p = \nabla_x p_x + \nabla_y p_y$. From this definition we can see that this operation can again be implemented with a convolutional layer that has fixed filter coefficients. However, we have to ensure a negative symmetric padding of the layer input, *i.e.* Dirichlet boundary conditions.

Over-Relaxation. The over-relaxation step of the primal variables in Eqs. (12) and (13) can be simplified to a weighted sum of two terms, *i.e.* $\bar{u} = (1+\theta)u^{n+1} - \theta u^n$ and $\bar{v} = (1+\theta)v^{n+1} - \theta v^n$.

3.2   Parametrization

After we have described the variational model and how to integrate it on top of a deep network, we now detail the parametrization functions $h(w_h, s_k)$ and

$g(w_g, s_k)$. Inspired by the recent success in single image super-resolution for color images [22], we implement $g(w_g, s_k)$ as a deep convolutional neural network with 10 convolutional layers. Each convolutional filter has the size of 3×3 and each hidden layer of the network has 64 feature maps. As $g(w_g, s_k)$ is used in the data term of our energy functional it should provide a good initial estimate of the high-resolution depth map. However, the output of this network is not the estimate of the high-resolution depth map itself, but the residual $g_r(w_g, s_k)$, such that $g(w_g, s_k) = g_r(w_g, s_k) + s_k$. Learning the residual instead of the full output aids the training procedure of the network [22], and has been applied before in other super-resolution methods [33, 36, 37].

The parameterization function $h(w_h, s_k)$ is used for weighting the pairwise regularization term. As we argued before, the regularization should be small near depth discontinuities and high in smooth areas. Therefore, we implemented $h(w_h, s_k)$ as an additional network output of size $2 \times \rho M \times \rho N$ and train it to estimate the gradient of the high-resolution target ∇t_k. This method has two benefits: First, we get more accurate estimates for the depth discontinuities than what we would get from the gradient of the high-resolution estimate $g(w_g, s_k)$. Secondly, the joint training of both objectives in a single deep network improves the performance of both tasks, because the weights w_h and w_g share the majority of parameters and only the parameters of the last layer, the output, differ. A graphical depiction of our deep network parametrization is shown in Fig. 2.

3.3 Training

In the previous sections we presented the description of our model. In this section we detail how we train it given a large set of training samples $\{(s_k, t_k)\}_{k=1}^{K}$. The training procedure is two-fold: In a first step we initialize the deep convolutional network, i.e. the functions g and h. Therefore, we train the network by mini-batch gradient descent with momentum term on the following loss function:

$$L_p(\{(s_k, t_k)\}_{k=1}^{K}) = \frac{1}{K} \sum_{k=1}^{K} \|g(w_g, s_k) - t_k\|_2^2 + \|h(w_h, s_k) - \nabla t_k\|_2^2. \quad (14)$$

In the following evaluations we set the learning rate to 0.001 and the momentum parameter to 0.9 for the initializing of the network. With this setting we train the network for 30 epochs on non-overlapping patches of size 32×32 pixel.

In the second step of the training procedure we add the unrolled primal-dual optimization algorithm as introduced in Sect. 3.1 on top of the network. Then, we train the joint model end-to-end on the Euclidean loss stated in Eq. (1) with mini-batch gradient descent. We set the learning rate to 0.001 and the momentum parameter 0.9 to train the whole model for 5 epochs on non-overlapping patches of size 128×128 pixel. In contrast to the method of implicit differentiation [31, 32], our method is still robust if we use a high learning rate, and as a consequence converges in fewer training iterations. Further, it enables us to optimize the parameter w_λ, as well ass all hyper-parameters of the optimization procedure.

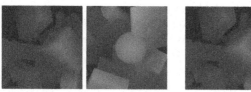
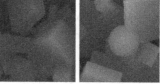

(a) rendered high-resolution ground-truth   (b) corresponding mid-resolution input

Fig. 3. Examples of our generated depth maps. (a) visualizes the high-resolution ground-truth data. By resampling those depth maps with a scale factor ρ and adding depth dependent noise we create the low-resolution input. (b) shows the mid-resolution input, which is the bilinear upsampled low-resolution data. Best viewed magnified in the electronic version.

4   Evaluation

In this section we present an exhaustive experimental evaluation of the proposed *ATGV-Net*. First, we show how we generate a huge amount of training data with accurate ground-truth needed to train the deep network. Then, we demonstrate evaluation results on four standard benchmark datasets for depth map super-resolution: Following [1,13,20], we evaluate our method on the noise-free Middlebury disparity maps *Teddy, Cones, Tsukuba* and *Venus*. Additionally, we show results for the Laserscan dataset as proposed in [1]. In a second evaluation we compare our results on the noisy Middlebury 2007 dataset as proposed in [29] and finally, we demonstrate the real-world applicability of our method on the challenging ToFMark dataset [12].

We set the initial parameters of our model to $\alpha_1 = 17$, $\alpha_0 = 1.2$ for the regularization term, $\beta = 9$, $\gamma = 0.85$ for the anisotropic diffusion tensor, and $w_\lambda = 0.01$ for all experiments. Further, we fix the number of iterations of the primal-dual algorithm to 10.

4.1   Training Data

One challenge in training very deep networks is the need for a huge amount of training data. In [1,13] the authors use a small set, *i.e.* 31 depth maps, of synthetic rendered images for training and in [32] the authors trained and tested their method on the synthetic New Tsukuba dataset [26]. Only very recently larger datasets with accurate depth maps have been released [17], or have been added to existing benchmarks [4]. In our method we also make use of synthetically rendered data, but produce them in a much larger quantity.

For this purpose we implemented a ray-caster [2] that runs on the GPU and enables us to generate thousands of synthetic depth maps of high quality in a few minutes. For each image we randomly place between 24 and 42 rectangular cuboids and up to 3 spheres in a predefined volume. Further, we randomly scale and rotate each solid to achieve an infinitely number of possible constellations. Then, we place a virtual camera at the origin of the coordinate system and cast

Table 1. Results on the noise-free Middlebury and Laserscan data. We report the error as root mean squared error (RMSE) in pixel disparity for the Middlebury data and in *mm* for the Laserscan data, respectively. We highlight the best result in boldface and the second best in italic.

	×2				×4				×4		
	Cones	Teddy	Tsukuba	Venus	Cones	Teddy	Tsukuba	Venus	Scan21	Scan30	Scan42
NN	4.3772	3.2596	9.7968	2.1408	6.1236	4.5168	13.3248	2.9432	0.0177	0.0163	0.0396
Bicubic	3.8392	2.7668	8.3648	1.8192	4.9544	3.5744	10.6960	2.3504	0.0132	0.0125	0.0326
Diebel and Thrun [9]	2.9588	2.1060	6.4208	1.3624	4.5624	3.2040	8.7840	1.9408	–	–	–
Ferstl et al. [12]	2.8240	2.1408	7.0592	1.2840	3.6372	2.5068	10.0128	1.4624	–	–	–
Zeyde et al. [42]	2.7680	1.9616	6.1936	1.3200	3.8468	2.7812	8.7632	1.7592	0.0100	0.0093	0.0246
Timofte et al. [36]	2.7872	1.9816	6.1280	1.3328	3.0256	3.0256	9.6304	1.9616	0.0106	0.0101	0.0264
Aodha et al. [1]	4.5076	3.2988	9.6192	2.2088	6.0168	4.1036	13.3328	2.6920	0.0175	0.0170	0.0452
Hornáček et al. [20]	3.9744	3.1640	9.2832	2.0592	5.5944	4.7828	11.6352	3.6008	0.0205	0.0179	0.0299
Ferstl et al. [13]	2.4988	1.7588	5.6064	1.1464	3.7336	2.6680	7.8416	1.8096	0.0085	0.0083	0.0190
CNN only	1.0275	*0.8201*	*2.3610*	*0.2266*	3.0015	1.5330	*6.4361*	0.4219	*0.0083*	*0.0082*	*0.0120*
CNN + ATGV-L2	*1.0145*	0.8374	**2.3197**	0.2720	*2.9832*	*1.5175*	**6.4223**	*0.4124*	0.0084	0.0083	0.0120
ATGV-Net	**1.0021**	**0.8155**	2.3846	**0.1991**	**2.9293**	**1.5029**	6.6327	**0.3764**	**0.0081**	**0.0081**	**0.0117**

a ray for each pixel of the camera image. For each ray we compute the distance between the image plane and the closest surface it hits, or in the case it does not hit any surface, we return a maximum distance value for the background. In Fig. 3 we illustrate two random examples of the more than 40,000 depth maps that we have generated with this method.

Given this generated depth maps as noise free ground-truth, we create the low-resolution depth maps $s_k^{(\mathrm{lr})} = \downarrow_\rho t_k$ for the network training by resampling the generated ground-truth depth maps t_k by the scale factor of ρ that is used in the evaluation. Depending on the dataset, we additionally add depth-dependent noise $\eta(s_k^{(\mathrm{lr})})$ to the low-resolution depth map. Finally, we upsample this low-resolution, probably noisy depth maps with bilinear interpolation to obtain our mid-level representation $s_k = \uparrow_\rho (s_k^{(\mathrm{lr})} + \eta(s_k^{(\mathrm{lr})}))$.

4.2 Clean Middlebury and Laserscan

In this first experiment we evaluate the performance of our proposed method on the images *Teddy*, *Cones*, *Tsukuba* and *Venus* of the Middlebury dataset as in [1,13,20]. The disparity is interpreted as depth and we test upsampling factors of ×2 and ×4. Additionally, we evaluate on the Laserscan dataset images *Scan21*, *Scan30* and *Scan42* with an upsampling factor of ×4 as in [1,13]. We compare our results to simple upsamling methods, such as nearest neighbor and bicubic upsampling, as well as to state-of-the-art depth upsampling methods that rely on an additional guidance image as input [9,12]. Further, we show the results of recent sparse coding based approaches for single image super-resolution [36,42], two approaches based on a Markov Random Field [1,20] and a recent variational approach that uses sparse coding to estimate edge priors [13]. To demonstrate the effect of our variational model on top of the deep network, we show the results of the high-resolution estimates of the network only (CNN only), the results, where we add the variational model, but without joint training (CNN + ATGV-L2), and the results after end-to-end training (*ATGV-Net*).

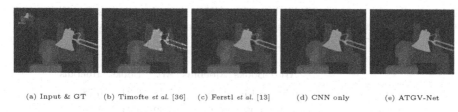

(a) Input & GT   (b) Timofte *et al.* [36]   (c) Ferstl *et al.* [13]   (d) CNN only   (e) ATGV-Net

Fig. 4. Qualitative results for the noise-free Middlebury image *Tsukuba*, $\rho = 4$. (a) depicts the ground-truth and the input data. (b) and (c) show the results of state-of-the-art methods. (d) and (e) present the results of the deep network only and our proposed model trained end-to-end. Best viewed magnified in the electronic version.

The results in terms of the root mean squared error (RMSE) are summarized in Table 1.[1] We can clearly see that the deep network already achieves a significant performance improvement compared to the other methods on both datasets and upsampling factors. Interestingly, we obtain even better results as the methods [9,12] that utilize an additional guidance image for the upsampling. This is especially pronounced in test samples with structures that are well simulated in the training data, such as *Venus*. Further, the variational model on top of the network slightly increases the performance and training the whole model end-to-end gives the overall best results. One exception is the *Tsukuba* sample, where the results get slightly worse after end-to-end training. An explanation might be that fine, elongated structures, *e.g.* near at the lamp of *Tsukuba*, are not well represented in the training data. In the qualitative results, see Fig. 4, we can further observe that the deep network with 10 layers achieves already very good results with sharper depth discontinuities compared to other methods. However, the improvement of the variational model on top of the deep network is hardly visible. This becomes more apparent in the next experiment.

4.3 Noisy Middlebury

In this experiment we evaluate our method on the Middlebury disparity maps *Art*, *Books* and *Moebius* with added depth dependent Gaussian noise to simulate the acquisition process of a Time-of-Flight sensor, as proposed by Park *et al.* [29]. Therefore, we add to our low-resolution synthetic training data $s_k^{(lr)}$ depth dependent Gaussian noise of the form $\eta(x) = \mathcal{N}(0, \sigma s_k^{(lr)}(x)^{-1})$, with $\sigma = 651$. Exemplar training images are depicted in Fig. 3. We report quantitative results in Table 2 and visualize qualitative results in Fig. 5.

We again compare our method to simple upsampling methods, such as nearest neighbor and bilinear interpolation. We compare our proposed method to other approaches that utilize an additional intensity image as guidance. Those methods include the Markov Random Field based approach in [9], the bilateral filtering with cost volume in [41], the guided image filter in [18], the noise-aware bilateral filter in [7], the non-local means filter in [29] and the variational model in [12].

---

[1] Note that we present our results over the full disparity range $[0, 255]$, as opposed to *e.g.* [13], where the disparities are scaled to a narrower range.

Table 2. Results on noisy Middlebury data. We report the error as RMSE in pixel disparity and highlight the best result in boldface and the second best in italic.

	×2			×4		
	Art	Books	Moebius	Art	Books	Moebius
NN	6.55	6.16	6.59	7.48	6.31	6.78
Bilinear	4.58	3.95	4.20	5.62	4.31	4.56
Yang et al. [41]	3.01	1.87	1.92	4.02	2.38	2.42
He et al. [18]	3.55	2.37	2.48	4.41	2.74	2.83
Diebel and Thrun [9]	3.49	2.06	2.13	4.51	3.00	3.11
Chan et al. [7]	3.44	2.09	2.08	4.46	2.77	2.76
Park et al. [29]	3.76	1.95	1.96	4.56	2.61	2.51
Ferstl et al. [12]	3.19	1.52	1.47	4.06	*2.21*	*2.03*
CNN only	2.02	1.27	1.50	3.55	2.41	2.68
CNN + ATGV-L2	*1.93*	*1.14*	*1.37*	*3.40*	2.24	2.51
ATGV-Net	**1.84**	**1.13**	**1.24**	**2.98**	**1.72**	**1.95**

To evaluate the influence of the variational model on top of the deep network, we report the results of the network only (CNN only), results with the variational model on top of the network, but without joint training (CNN + ATGV-L2), and the results after end-to-end training (ATGV-Net).

From the quantitative results in Table 2 we observe that the *CNN only* already performs better than state-of-the-art methods that utilize an additional guidance input for most images and upsampling factors. Further, the variational model on top of the deep network slightly improves the results, but end-to-end training of the whole model results in significant improvement. This improvement of *ATGV-Net* over the network only is also apparent in the qualitative results (Fig. 5). We observe less noise in homogeneous areas in the *ATGV-Net* estimates, especially in the background, compared to the *CNN only* estimates. The results of [12] look also very sharp, but produce errors near depth discontinuities and in-between fine structures. In contrast, our method preserves those finer structures. We refer to the supplemental material for additional qualitative results, as well as quantitative results in terms of mean absolute error (MAE).

4.4   ToFMark

In our final experiment we evaluate our method on the challenging ToFMark dataset [12]. This dataset consists of three time-of-flight (ToF) depth maps of three different scenes. For each scene there exists an accurate high-resolution structured-light scan as ground-truth. The ToF depth maps have a resolution of 120×160 pixel and the target resolution, given by the guidance intensity image (that we do not use in our method) is 610×810 pixel. This corresponds to an upsampling factor of approximately $\rho = 5$. As the target high-resolution depth-map is given in the camera coordinate system of the structured light scanner, we prepare our training data accordingly. We project our high-resolution synthetic

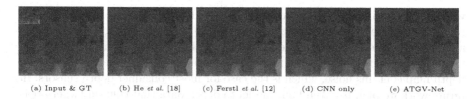

(a) Input & GT   (b) He *et al.* [18]   (c) Ferstl *et al.* [12]   (d) CNN only   (e) ATGV-Net

Fig. 5. Qualitative results for the noisy Middlebury image *Moebius*, $\rho = 4$. (a) depicts the ground-truth and the input data. (b) and (c) show the results of state-of-the-art methods. (d) and (e) present the results of the deep network only and our proposed model trained end-to-end. Best viewed magnified in the electronic version.

Table 3. Results on real Time-of-Flight data from the ToFMark benchmark dataset. We report the error as RMSE in *mm* and highlight the best result in boldface and the second best in italic.

	Books	Devil	Shark
NN	30.46	27.53	38.21
Bilinear	29.11	25.34	36.34
Kopf *et al.* [23]	27.82	24.30	34.79
He *et al.* [18]	27.11	23.45	33.26
Ferstl *et al.* [12]	**24.00**	*23.19*	*29.89*
ATGV-Net	*24.67*	**21.74**	**28.51**

training depth maps to the ToF coordinate system using the provided projection matrix. In the low-resolution depth maps we add depth dependent noise and back project the remaining points to the target camera coordinate system. This yields a very sparse depth map that we subsequently inpaint with bilinear interpolation to obtain our final mid-resolution training inputs.

We compare our results to simple nearest neighbour and bilinear interpolation, and three state-of-the-art depth map super-resolution methods that utilize an additional guidance image as input. The quantitative results are shown in Table 3 as RMSE in *mm*. Please see the supplemental material for qualitative results. Even on this difficult dataset we are at least on par with state-of-the-art methods that utilize an additional intensity image as guidance input.

5   Conclusion

We presented a combination of a deep convolutional network with a variational model for single depth map super-resolution. We designed the convolutional network to compute the high-resolution depth map, as well as the depth discontinuities. The network output was utilized in our variational model to further refine the result. By unrolling the optimization procedure of the variational model, we were able to optimize the joint model end-to-end, which lead to improved accuracy. Further, we demonstrated the feasibility to train our method on a massive amount of synthetic generated depth data and obtain state-of-the-art results on four different benchmarks. Our model is especially useful if the low-resolution depth map contains noise, which is the case for most consumer depth sensors. In future work we plan to extend our model to depth data that contain larger areas of missing pixels, *e.g.* from structured light sensors. This is straight-forward by setting $w_\lambda = 0$ for areas where depth measurements are missing.

Acknowledgment. This work was supported by *Infineon Technologies Austria AG* and the Austrian Research Promotion Agency under the *FIT-IT Bridge* program, project #838513 (TOFUSION).

References

1. Aodha, O.M., Campbell, N.D., Nair, A., Brostow, G.J.: Patch based synthesis for single depth image super-resolution. In: European Conference on Computer Vision (ECCV) (2012)
2. Apple, A.: Some techniques for shading machine renderings of solids. In: Proceedings of the April 30–May 2 1968, Spring Joint Computer Conference (1968)
3. Bredies, K., Kunisch, K., Pock, T.: Total generalized variation. SIAM J. Imaging Sci. **3**(3), 492–526 (2010)
4. Butler, D.J., Wulff, J., Stanley, G.B., Black, M.J.: A naturalistic open source movie for optical flow evaluation. In: European Conference on Computer Vision (ECCV) (2012)
5. Chambolle, A., Pock, T.: A first-order primal-dual algorithm for convex problems with applications to imaging. J. Math. Imaging Vis. **40**(1), 120–145 (2011)
6. Chambolle, A., Pock, T.: On the ergodic convergence rates of a first-order primal-dual algorithm. Math. Program. **159**, 253–287 (2016)
7. Chan, D., Buisman, H., Theobalt, C., Thrun, S.: A noise-aware filter for real-time depth upsampling. In: European Conference on Computer Vision Workshops (ECCVW) (2008)
8. Chen, L.C., Schwing, A.G., Yuille, A.L., Urtasun, R.: Learning deep structured models. In: Proceedings of the International Conference on Machine Learning (ICML) (2015)
9. Diebel, J., Thrun, S.: An application of Markov random fields to range sensing. In: Proceedings of Conference on Neural Information Processing Systems (NIPS) (2005)
10. Domke, J.: Generic methods for optimization-based modeling. In: Proceedings of the International Conference on Artificial Intelligence and Statistics (AISTATS) (2012)
11. Dong, C., Loy, C.C., He, K., Tang, X.: Learning a deep convolutional network for image super-resolution. In: Fleet, D., Pajdla, T., Schiele, B., Tuytelaars, T. (eds.) ECCV 2014, Part IV. LNCS, vol. 8692, pp. 184–199. Springer, Heidelberg (2014)
12. Ferstl, D., Reinbacher, C., Ranftl, R., Rüther, M., Bischof, H.: Image guided depth upsampling using anisotropic total generalized variation. In: IEEE International Conference on Computer Vision (ICCV) (2013)

13. Ferstl, D., Rüther, M., Bischof, H.: Variational depth superresolution using example-based edge representations. In: IEEE International Conference on Computer Vision (ICCV) (2015)
14. Girshick, R., Shotton, J., Kohli, P., Criminisi, A., Fitzgibbon, A.W.: Efficient regression of general-activity human poses from depth images. In: IEEE International Conference on Computer Vision (ICCV) (2011)
15. Glasner, D., Bagon, S., Irani, M.: Super-resolution from single image. In: IEEE International Conference on Computer Vision (ICCV) (2009)
16. Gupta, S., Girshick, R., Arbeláez, P., Malik, J.: Learning rich features from RGB-D images for object detection and segmentation. In: Fleet, D., Pajdla, T., Schiele, B., Tuytelaars, T. (eds.) ECCV 2014, Part VII. LNCS, vol. 8695, pp. 345–360. Springer, Heidelberg (2014)
17. Handa, A., Patraucean, V., Badrinarayanan, V., Stent, S., Cipolla, R.: Understanding real world indoor scenes with synthetic data. In: IEEE Conference on Computer Vision and Pattern Recognition (CVPR) (2016)
18. He, K., Sun, J., Tang, X.: Guided image filtering. In: Daniilidis, K., Maragos, P., Paragios, N. (eds.) ECCV 2010, Part I. LNCS, vol. 6311, pp. 1–14. Springer, Heidelberg (2010)
19. He, K., Zhang, X., Ren, S., Sun, J.: Deep residual learning for image recognition. In: IEEE Conference on Computer Vision and Pattern Recognition (CVPR) (2016)
20. Hornáček, M., Rhemann, C., Gelautz, M., Rother, C.: Depth super resolution by rigid body self-similarity in 3D. In: IEEE Conference on Computer Vision and Pattern Recognition (CVPR) (2013)
21. Izadi, S., Kim, D., Hilliges, O., Molyneaux, D., Newcombe, R., Kohli, P., Shotton, J., Hodges, S., Freeman, D., Davison, A., Fitzgibbon, A.: KinectFusion: real-time 3D reconstruction and interaction using a moving depth camera. In: ACM Symposium on User Interface Software and Technology (2011)
22. Kim, J., Lee, J.K., Lee, K.M.: Accurate image super-resolution using very deep convolutional networks. In: IEEE Conference on Computer Vision and Pattern Recognition (CVPR) (2016)
23. Kopf, J., Cohen, M.F., Lischinski, D., Uyttendaele, M.: Joint bilateral upsampling. ACM Trans. Graph. (TOG) 26(3), 96 (2007)
24. Krähenbühl, P., Koltun, V.: Efficient inference in fully connected CRFs with gaussian edge potentials. In: Proceedings of Conference on Neural Information Processing Systems (NIPS) (2012)
25. Kwon, H., Tai, Y.W., Lin, S.: Data-driven depth map refinement via multi-scale spare representations. In: IEEE Conference on Computer Vision and Pattern Recognition (CVPR) (2015)
26. Martull, S., Peris, M., Fukui, K.: Realistic CG stereo image dataset with ground truth disparity maps. In: International Conference on Pattern Recognition Workshops (ICPRW) (2012)
27. Nagel, H.H., Enkelmann, W.: An investigation of smoothness constraints for the estimation of displacement vector fields from image sequences. IEEE Trans. Pattern Anal. Mach. Intell. (TPAMI) 8(5), 565–593 (1986)
28. Ochs, P., Ranftl, R., Brox, T., Pock, T.: Bilevel optimization with nonsmooth lower level problems. In: Aujol, J.-F., Nikolova, M., Papadakis, N. (eds.) SSVM 2015. LNCS, vol. 9087, pp. 654–665. Springer, Heidelberg (2015)
29. Park, J., Kim, H., Tai, Y.W., Brown, M.S., Kweon, I.S.: High quality depth map upsampling for 3D-TOF cameras. In: IEEE International Conference on Computer Vision (ICCV) (2011)

30. Ranftl, R., Gehrig, S., Pock, T., Bischof, H.: Pushing the limits of stereo using variational stereo estimation. In: IEEE Intelligent Vehicles Symposium (2012)

31. Ranftl, R., Pock, T.: A deep variational model for image segmentation. In: Jiang, X., Hornegger, J., Koch, R. (eds.) GCPR 2014. LNCS, vol. 8753, pp. 107–118. Springer, Heidelberg (2014)

32. Riegler, G., Ranftl, R., Rüther, M., Bischof, H.: Joint training of an convolutional neural net and a global regression model. In: Proceedings of the British Machine Vision Conference (BMVC) (2015)

33. Schulter, S., Leistner, C., Bischof, H.: Fast and accurate image upscaling with super-resolution forests. In: IEEE Conference on Computer Vision and Pattern Recognition (CVPR) (2015)

34. Schwing, A.G., Urtasun, R.: Fully Connected Deep Structured Networks. arXiv preprint arXiv:1503.02351 (2015)

35. Shotton, J., Fitzgibbon, A., Cook, M., Sharp, T., Finocchio, M., Moore, R., Kipman, A., Blake, A.: Real-time human pose recognition in parts from single depth images. In: Cipolla, R., Battiato, S., Farinella, G.M. (eds.) Machine Learning for Computer Vision. SCI, vol. 411, pp. 125–141. Springer, Heidelberg (2013)

36. Timofte, R., Smet, V.D., Gool, L.V.: Anchored neighborhood regression for fast example-based super-resolution. In: IEEE International Conference on Computer Vision (ICCV) (2013)

37. Timofte, R., De Smet, V., Van Gool, L.: A+: adjusted anchored neighborhood regression for fast super-resolution. In: Cremers, D., Reid, I., Saito, H., Yang, M.-H. (eds.) ACCV 2014. LNCS, vol. 9006, pp. 111–126. Springer, Heidelberg (2015)

38. Tompson, J., Jain, A., LeCun, Y., Bregler, C.: Joint training of a convolutional network and a graphical model for human pose estimation. In: Proceedings of Conference on Neural Information Processing Systems (NIPS) (2014)

39. Werlberger, M., Trobin, W., Pock, T., Wedel, A., Cremers, D., Bischof, H.: Anisotropic Huber-L1 optical flow. In: Proceedings of the British Machine Vision Conference (BMVC) (2009)

40. Yang, J., Wright, J., Huang, T.S., Ma, Y.: Image super-resolution via sparse representation. IEEE Trans. Image Process. **19**(11), 2861–2873 (2010)

41. Yang, Q., Yang, R., Davis, J., Nistér, D.: Spatial-depth super resolution for range images. In: IEEE Conference on Computer Vision and Pattern Recognition (CVPR) (2007)

42. Zeyde, R., Elad, M., Protter, M.: On single image scale-up using sparse-representations. In: Boissonnat, J.-D., Chenin, P., Cohen, A., Gout, C., Lyche, T., Mazure, M.-L., Schumaker, L. (eds.) Curves and Surfaces 2011. LNCS, vol. 6920, pp. 711–730. Springer, Heidelberg (2012)

43. Zheng, S., Jayasumana, S., Romera-Paredes, B., Vineet, V., Su, Z., Du, D., Huang, C., Torr, P.: Conditional random fields as recurrent neural networks. In: IEEE International Conference on Computer Vision (ICCV) (2015)

Indoor-Outdoor 3D Reconstruction Alignment

Andrea Cohen[1](✉), Johannes L. Schönberger[1](✉), Pablo Speciale[1],
Torsten Sattler[1], Jan-Michael Frahm[2], and Marc Pollefeys[1,3]

[1] ETH Zürich, Zürich, Switzerland
{acohen,jsch}@inf.ethz.ch
[2] UNC Chapel Hill, Chapel Hill, USA
[3] Microsoft, Redmond, USA

Abstract. Structure-from-Motion can achieve accurate reconstructions
of urban scenes. However, reconstructing the inside and the outside of a
building into a single model is very challenging due to the lack of visual
overlap and the change of lighting conditions between the two scenes.
We propose a solution to align disconnected indoor and outdoor models
of the same building into a single 3D model. Our approach leverages
semantic information, specifically window detections, in multiple scenes
to obtain candidate matches from which an alignment hypothesis can
be computed. To determine the best alignment, we propose a novel cost
function that takes both the number of window matches and the intersection of the aligned models into account. We evaluate our solution on
multiple challenging datasets.

1 Introduction

Recent progress in the area of 3D reconstruction enables the generation of large-
scale [12] and detailed outdoor models [25], as well as accurate indoor reconstructions [9] and their floor-plans [2,19]. The resulting 3D models are useful for
a wide range of applications, from virtual tourism [16,27], visualization of apart-
ments for real estate [19], cultural heritage [7,23,29], and image-based localization [18,30], to real-time camera pose tracking on mobile devices for Augmented
Reality [22], and autonomous navigation [20]. Ideally, a single joint reconstruction of the interior and exterior is desirable as it would, for example, enable a user
to seamlessly enter buildings in a virtual city model rather than only exploring
the outside. Similarly, a combined model would allow autonomous robots to easily transition between the indoor and outdoor world. However, state-of-the-art
approaches often fail to reconstruct both parts into a single 3D model.

Obtaining a joint indoor-outdoor model is hard for multiple reasons: on the
one hand, the indoor and outdoor parts of a scene typically exhibit a weak
connection through a limited number of visual observations such as doorways or

Electronic supplementary material The online version of this chapter (doi:10.
1007/978-3-319-46487-9_18) contains supplementary material, which is available to
authorized users.

© Springer International Publishing AG 2016
B. Leibe et al. (Eds.): ECCV 2016, Part III, LNCS 9907, pp. 285–300, 2016.
DOI: 10.1007/978-3-319-46487-9_18

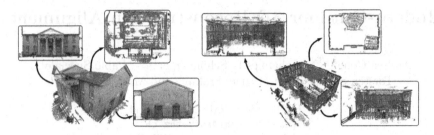

Fig. 1. The proposed method aligns disconnected Structure-from-Motion reconstructions of the inside and outside to produce a single 3D model of a building. Our approach also handles incomplete reconstructions and multiple indoor models (*c.f.* right model)

windows. As a result, great care must be taken when capturing data to ensure enough visual overlap for feature matching and to prevent the models from being disconnected [28]. This problem is often aggravated by the fact that there can be a strong change in illumination in transition areas. In practice, Structure-from-Motion (SfM) models disconnect quite often, even when an experienced user carefully takes images of a single outdoor scene [4]. It is, thus, very hard to connect indoor and outdoor scenes through feature matches reliably for most practical applications. On the other hand, even if we capture enough imagery to visually connect indoors and outdoors, *e.g.* by recording a video sequence, the connections are usually rather weak. Consequently, it is hard to prevent drift between the two models. Additionally, indoor reconstructions are often incomplete and disconnected, *e.g.* when some rooms are not accessible. This makes the alignment problem even harder, since several indoor models have to be aligned to one or more outdoor models for which the relative scale is also unknown. For the case of incomplete models, the solution might be ambiguous even for humans without prior knowledge of the building.

In this paper, we propose an alignment algorithm that exploits scene semantics to establish correspondences between indoor and outdoor models. More precisely, we exploit the fact that the windows of a building can be seen both from the inside and the outside. Towards this goal, we apply semantic classifiers to detect windows in the indoor and outdoor scenes. A single match between an indoor and outdoor window determines an alignment hypothesis (scale, rotation, translation) between the two models. All hypotheses are inspected and grossly wrong alignments are detected and discarded using a measure of intersection of the two models. Plausible alignments are then further refined using additional window matches. Our approach is robust to noisy window detections and is able to align disconnected indoor and outdoor models (*c.f.* Fig. 1). Furthermore, our method can handle both multiple and/or incomplete indoor or outdoor models.

Concretely, we make the following contributions: we present a novel approach for aligning indoor and outdoor reconstructions of a building by detecting and aligning windows in both models. We propose a novel quality metric for the resulting alignment based on detecting intersections between the two models.

We exploit multi-view redundancy to ensure robustness to noisy window detections. As a result, our proposed algorithm is able to tackle the challenging problem of joining indoor and outdoor models of a building into a single reconstruction. In addition, our method works purely on sparse point clouds and does not require any dense geometry. We demonstrate the practical applicability of our approach on multiple challenging datasets.

2 Related Work

There is a clear trend of using higher level (semantic) information for both sparse and dense 3D reconstruction: Ceylan *et al.* [3] and Cohen *et al.* [6] actively detect and exploit symmetries and repetitions to improve the quality of SfM reconstructions. Häne *et al.* [11] and Savinov *et al.* [24] combine semantic image classification and dense 3D reconstruction, showing that jointly optimizing over the labels and the shape of the 3D model improves the results for both. All these methods use a higher level understanding of the scene to optimize the reconstruction results. In contrast, we use semantic information to enable reconstruction in the first place by aligning indoor and outdoor models that cannot be related by low-level feature matches alone.

Indoor reconstruction approaches usually exploit Manhattan world assumptions to obtain clean, dense 3D models from streams of photos [9,29]. Given a set of panoramas as input, Cabral and Furukawa [2] determine for each pixel whether it belongs to the floor, wall, or ceiling. Given these structural classifications, they estimate a piecewise planar floor plan and create a compact, textured mesh from the generated plan. While the previous approaches operate on densely sampled images, Liu *et al.* [19] estimate the layout of each room from a sparse set of photos. Prior knowledge of the floor plan and semantic classification is then used to align the individual rooms. Recently, Ikehata *et al.* [13] showed that parsing the structure of the scene can significantly aid the indoor reconstruction process. They reason about the semantic relation between different scene parts and the structure of the rooms and use this knowledge during reconstruction.

Martin *et al.* [21] and Cohen *et al.* [4] consider the problem of aligning visually disconnected 3D models without using traditional feature matches. Martin *et al.* determine the room layout of individual 3D models by solving a jigsaw puzzle problem, utilizing annotated floor plans and the temporal flow of crowds between rooms. Cohen *et al.* reason about the spatial arrangement of individual sub-models to obtain a closed model of the outside of a single building. Their method is based on determining potential connection points between the models and detecting free-space violations using semantic information. The two approaches solely focus on indoor [21] and outdoor reconstructions [4], respectively. In contrast, our approach addresses the problem of linking previously disconnected indoor and outdoor models. In addition, we also show that indoor models can help to connect partial outdoor models and vice-versa.

Strecha *et al.* [28] reconstruct both the outside and the inside of a historic castle. In contrast to our method, which does not constrain the capture setup,

Strecha *et al.* heavily constrain the capture to be able to reconstruct the whole scene as a single model. In particular, they very carefully take images with high visual overlap between indoors and outdoors to prevent the reconstruction from disconnecting into multiple sub-models. Often, this is impractical or even impossible. Hence, our approach is specifically designed to handle separate models.

Simultaneously to our work, Koch *et al.* [14] also developed a method to tackle the problem of indoor-outdoor model alignment using 3D line matching. 3D lines are detected using the original images and the reconstructed (separate) models. The models are then aligned using the transformation that matches the highest number of line segments. The method assumes that the 3D line segments found are mostly located on windows and doors, indirectly matching these structures between both models without explicitly using semantics, as opposed to our method. In addition, they also need to know the scale of both models in advance and they only deal with one indoor and one outdoor model. Our method overcomes these limitations. Both works are complementary, since our method's results could be used as input for [14] which would act as a refinement step.

3   Method Overview

Given separate indoor and outdoor models, we propose to align the inside and outside of a building through semantic information. Specifically, as windows are visible both from inside and outside, we use window detections to generate correspondences between the two models, which are then used to compute the alignment between the models. This approach naturally extends to room-to-room registrations by detecting and aligning doors. However, similarly to [19], we found that door detection performs poorly. In this paper, we thus focus on indoor-to-outdoor alignments via window detections.

In the following, we provide an overview of our algorithm, as illustrated in Fig. 2, before presenting algorithmic details in the next sections. As input, our method uses sparse SfM models of the indoor and outdoor scenes, as well as the images used to generate them.

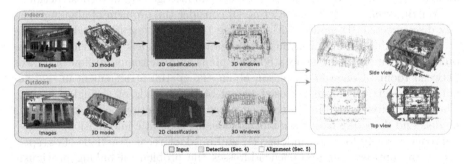

Fig. 2. Given SfM reconstructions of indoors and outdoors together with their input images, we leverage per-pixel semantic classification to detect windows in 3D. These windows are then used to compute a registration between both scenes that maximizes the number of aligned windows while avoiding that the models intersect each other

Window Detection. First, we apply a per-pixel classifier to detect windows in all input images. For each image, we employ a façade parsing approach on the rectified images, similar to Cohen *et al.* [5], to obtain the 2D rectangles that most likely correspond to the actual windows seen in the photos. Next, we use the known camera poses and the sparse 3D scene points to estimate the 3D planes containing the windows. Leveraging the SfM points, we estimate 3D window positions for each image individually. We then detect overlapping 3D windows and compute consensus window positions. Using all images in the reconstruction also allows us to handle occlusions more robustly, *e.g.*, due to vegetation in front of a façade. Section 4 describes this process in more detail.

Model Alignment. Given 3D window detections for the indoor and outdoor models, we next register the disjoint models based on window correspondences. Computing the alignment boils down to finding a similarity transformation between the models, which can be computed from three point correspondences in the general case and from two point matches if the gravity direction is known. One potential approach would be to simply obtain point correspondences by aligning the centers of gravity of the windows and apply RANSAC [8] to estimate the transformation. However, the appearance of a window can change dramatically when viewed from the inside and the outside, *e.g.*, due to illumination changes or by actually looking through the window. As such, we need to consider each pair of indoor and outdoor windows, which means RANSAC-based approaches quickly become infeasible. Consider a simple case, where 20 windows are detected for the outdoor model and 3 windows are detected for a partial indoor reconstruction of a corner room. There are 1140 (resp. 190) potential combinations to draw 3-(resp. 2)-tuples of window matches. Out of all these configurations, exactly one is correct, leading to inlier ratios below 1 %.

In order to avoid the combinatorial growth in complexity, we exploit the width and height of the 3D window detections to estimate a similarity transformation from a single window correspondence. Using a single match allows us to exhaustively generate the set of all possible alignment configurations. In the previous example, there are 60 potential combinations, out of which 3 are correct. The obtained alignments are then ranked based on the fact that the indoor models must not intersect with the outdoor model by enforcing free-space constraints. Alignments that violate this constraint are discarded. Otherwise, we determine the window support of the transformation, *i.e.*, the number of correctly aligned indoor-outdoor window detections, and refine the best alignment in an iterative procedure. Section 5 provides details on the alignment process.

Handling Ambiguities Due to Symmetries. Given a reconstruction of a single floor in a multi-story building, it can be impossible to determine to which floor the model belongs if the windows are symmetric between floors[1]. We thus determine the number of floors and estimate the best alignment per floor, enabling a user to choose a transformation and hence resolve the ambiguity.

---

[1] Again, detecting doors could resolve these ambiguities for the ground floor, but it would still remain for other floors.

4 Window Detection

In this section, we describe our window extraction approach (*c.f.* Fig. 3). Our approach leverages a pre-trained per-pixel classifier to detect windows in all of the images used to reconstruct the indoor and outdoor models. The labels for image i are fed into a façade parsing algorithm to obtain a set $\mathcal{W}_{2D}(i)$ of 2D window detections, where each window $w \in \mathcal{W}_{2D}(i)$ is defined by its four corners. For each 2D window, we obtain a corresponding 3D window by projecting it onto a 3D plane estimated using the sparse SfM points. As shown in Fig. 3, these individual window projections are not necessarily consistent between images. We thus use all individual window projections to compute a consensus set $\mathcal{W}_{3D}$ of 3D windows that is consistent across all images of a model. This window detection pipeline is applied separately on each indoor and outdoor model.

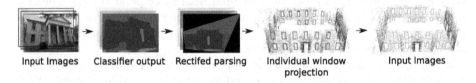

Input Images   Classifier output   Rectifed parsing   Individual window   Input Images
                                                               projection

Fig. 3. The proposed 3D window detection pipeline

Image Classification. We use the supervised learning method of Ladický *et al.* [17] to obtain a pixel-wise semantic classification of the images used for reconstruction. Since we found that a classifier trained on indoor images performs poorly on photos taken on the outside and vice-versa, we train two separate classifiers. For training the indoor classifier, we use the annotated datasets provided by [19]. To train the outdoor classifier, we use the eTrims dataset [15]. The classification scores can then be used in a façade parsing algorithm to obtain the best scoring set of windows per image.

Natural Frame Estimation. To simplify the subsequent steps of our procedure, we align each 3D model into a canonical coordinate system. We choose the coordinate system that is aligned to the façade directions of the building. To achieve this, we determine the main axes of each model by estimating the vanishing points in each input image. The vanishing points then vote for the three coordinate directions. Next, we align the coordinate system of each 3D model with the x-y-z-axes, such that the vertical axis is aligned with z and walls are mostly aligned with the x or y direction under a Manhattan world assumption.

Image Rectification and Façade Parsing. Following most works on indoor reconstruction [9, 13, 29], we use the Manhattan world assumption. This assumption is not strictly necessary, but simplifies and robustifies further processing and allows us to restrict our search for window planes to those parallel to the x-z and y-z planes. We therefore rectify all images w.r.t. x- and y-aligned planes to synthesize fronto-parallel images of the walls (*c.f.* step 3 in Fig. 3). The façade parsing algorithm presented in Cohen *et al.* [5] is then used to extract the set $\mathcal{W}_{2D}(i)$ of 2D windows for image i by obtaining the four corner vertices of the rectangles corresponding to window detections in the rectified image. For outdoor models, this method also provides the number of floors detected per image. As discussed in Sect. 3, knowing the number of floors for a building enables our alignment approach to generate multiple plausible hypotheses if the indoor model only covers a single floor. Additionally, assuming that all windows on the same floor have the same height, façade parsing can better handle incomplete window labellings (e.g., due to occlusion). It requires < 1 s per image and provides better results compared to directly extracting windows from the semantic labels.

Individual Window Projection. Let $\mathcal{W}_{2D}(i) = \{w_1^i, \ldots, w_n^i\}$ be the set of 2D windows detected in the previous step for image i, and let $P^i = \{p_0^i, \ldots, p_m^i\}$ be the set of 3D SfM points that are visible in image i. We extract the subset $P'^i \subset P^i$ of points whose projections in the image fall inside any of the detected 2D windows w_j^i, $j = 1, \ldots, n$. We then use P'^i to estimate the window plane π as the best fitting plane parallel to either the x-z or y-z plane. The normal of the plane π is chosen to agree with the direction to which image i was rectified for the window extraction. All windows w_j^i are then projected onto π to obtain a set of 3D windows $\mathcal{W}_{3D}(i) = \{W_j^i\}_{j=1,\ldots,n}$ for image i.

Window Grouping and Consensus. Given the sets of 3D windows $\mathcal{W}_{3D}(i)$ detected for each *individual* image i, we next group the overlapping 3D windows from *all* images into clusters C. All 3D windows from the same cluster are then used to estimate a single 3D consensus window (*c.f.* the last two stages in Fig. 3).

First, we cluster all 3D windows that overlap and are on the same plane (up to a threshold computed as 20 % of the average window length). To decide whether two windows W_i and W_j overlap, we intersect their areas in the common plane. We use an agglomerative clustering approach, *i.e.*, we initialize the clustering procedure by creating a separate cluster C for each window W_j^i in each image and then iteratively merge clusters. Two clusters C_s and C_t, $s \neq t$, are merged if there exist two overlapping windows $W_j^i \in C_s$ and $W_l^k \in C_t$, $i \neq k$. Once all overlapping clusters are merged, we compute a consensus window $W(C)$ for each cluster C: first, we determine the bounding box B containing all windows in the cluster, *i.e.*, $W_j^i \subseteq B$ for all $W_j^i \in C$. Next, for each image i observing a window $W_j^i \in C$, we project its per-pixel classifier scores onto B to accumulate the scores. We then compute $W(C)$ as the rectangle inside the bounding box that maximizes the sum of window scores minus wall scores in B. The computation of such a rectangle is known as the *maximum sum rectangular sub-matrix problem* and can be optimally computed using a 2D version of Kadane's algorithm [1]. The output is the set of consensus windows $\mathcal{W}_{3D} = \{W(C)\}$ for each sub-model.

5   Model Alignment

The goal of the alignment procedure is to transform the initially disjoint indoor and outdoor models into a common reference frame. Since traditional feature correspondences are not available, we instead employ window-to-window matches to facilitate the alignment. We utilize the fact that a single window correspondence defines a similarity transformation that registers one indoor against one outdoor model. This allows us to exhaustively evaluate all potential matches rather than having to rely on appearance to establish correspondences. This is important since the appearance of a window can change quite drastically between indoors and outdoors[2] or might even be completely different, e.g., due to closed shutters or partial occlusion. A natural way to define the best alignment is to find the transformation that explains the largest number of window correspondences. However, the transformation maximizing the number of inlier matches is not necessarily plausible. For example, it does not guarantee that an indoor model does not protrude from the outside of the building. In this section, we introduce and discuss a quality metric that takes both the number of inliers and the intersection between the models into account.

The input to our alignment procedure are sets $\mathcal{M}_{in}$ and $\mathcal{M}_{out}$ of axis-aligned indoor and outdoor models, respectively, as well as the consensus windows $\mathcal{W}_{3D}$ detected in the previous step. The output is a set of ranked configurations of aligned models $\mathcal{K}_s = \{(\mathcal{C}_i, e_i) \mid e_i < e_{i+1}\}$, where the energy e_i measures the cost of a configuration $\mathcal{C}_i$ and a lower energy denotes a better configuration. A configuration $\mathcal{C}_i$ relates two or more models through a set of window-to-window correspondences $\mathcal{C}_i = \{(W_a(m_j), W_b(m_k)), \ldots \mid j \neq k \}$. A single correspondence $(W_a(m_j), W_b(m_k))$ relates model m_j to m_k and defines a 3D similarity transformation $\mathbf{T}_{jk}$. The alignment procedure repeatedly searches for unique optimal configurations by minimizing the objective function

$$\underset{\mathcal{C}}{\text{minimize}} \quad e = E_W(\mathcal{C}, \mathcal{W}_{3D}) + E_I(\mathcal{C}, \mathcal{M}_{in}, \mathcal{M}_{out})$$
$$\text{subject to} \quad E_I(\mathcal{C}, \mathcal{M}_{in}, \mathcal{M}_{out}) < \lambda \tag{1}$$

The term E_W measures the cost of the window alignment between the models, i.e., how well the estimated transformations align the windows. Likewise, the term E_I measures the cost of the model alignment in terms of the intersection of the models and λ defines the maximum intersection allowed. We solve this constrained optimization problem through exhaustive search in the space of possible configurations. For N windows in each of the M models, the number of possible configurations is $O(N^M)$. As the number of windows and models is typically relatively small, exhaustive search is feasible. A window-to-window correspondence $(W_a(m_j), W_b(m_k))$ relates the 3D consensus window W_a detected in an indoor model m_j to the 3D consensus window W_b in an outdoor model m_k. The correspondence also defines a relative 3D similarity $\mathbf{T}_{jk}$ transforming coordinates in model m_j into the coordinate frame of model m_k. Section 5.1 describes the process of establishing these correspondences and then chaining them to form a configuration $\mathcal{C}$. Section 5.2 defines the terms of E_W and E_I used to rank the set of configurations $\mathcal{K}$.

---

[2] We noticed that the indoor classifier sometimes splits a window into multiple parts while the outdoor classifier usually detects the whole window. This is due to the indoor images typically being taken closer to the windows, such that the frames appear larger, as well as the stronger contrast against the outdoor illumination.

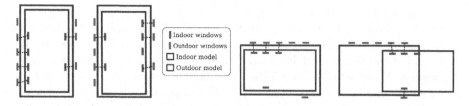

Fig. 4. (Left) Window term example. The alignment on the left has a lower cost than the one on the right. (Right) Intersection term example. Both alignments have the same E_W. The solution on the left is chosen since E_I is lower

5.1 Correspondence Search

For correspondence search, we exhaustively explore all possible configurations $\mathcal{C}_i$. We only consider window-to-window matches between indoor and outdoor models. We start by generating all unique pairwise window combinations between every unique pair of indoor and outdoor models. This initial set of combinations determines alignments between pairs of models. To handle the case of multiple indoor and outdoor models, we then generate all unique combinations of the initial set of combinations and repeat this process until all possible configurations are explored. The resulting set $\mathcal{K}$ contains the entire space of configurations aligning the models through chains of correspondences. Each correspondence in a configuration defines a relative 3D similarity that can be used to align the corresponding models into a common reference frame. For each correspondence $(W_a(m_j), W_b(m_k))$, we estimate its associated similarity transformation $\mathbf{T}_{jk}$ from the four corresponding 3D window corners in $W_a(m_j)$ and $W_b(m_k)$. To handle noisy window detections more robustly, we exploit the fact that the windows are already axis-aligned, *i.e.*, the rotations around the x- and y-axes are already fixed. Hence, we first estimate a 2D similarity transformation in the x-y plane and then independently infer the z-translation. This comes with two main benefits: first, the 2D window locations are usually less accurate than their estimated vertical plane. As a result, we obtain more robust orientation alignment around the z-axis. Second, a single window correspondence provides us with redundant observations for both the scale and z-translation estimation. To estimate the scale, we can use either the vertical or horizontal length of the window frames. For the z-translation, either the top or bottom side of the window frame. Generating these multiple possible alignments per window correspondence enables us to handle partial occlusions of windows more robustly, *e.g.*, caused by furniture or curtains. Chaining similarities using the recurrence relation $\mathbf{T}_{jkl} = \mathbf{T}_{kl} \cdot \mathbf{T}_{jk}$ enables us to transform any model's m_j coordinate system into any other model's m_k coordinate system, if they are within the same configuration $\mathcal{C}$. For each configuration, we align their contained models and windows into a single reference frame.

At this point, each $\mathbf{T}_{jk}$ is determined from a single window correspondence. However, a correct transformation chain is expected to put all corresponding windows in a configuration close to each other in 3D space. Hence, we look for these additional window correspondences in a densification step through mutual nearest neighbor search in 3D space. For two windows $(W_a(m_j), W_b(m_k))$ to be mutual nearest neighbors, their centroids must be mutually closest in 3D space and the distance must be smaller than a fraction $\alpha = 0.25$ of their average window frame lengths. In addition, we enforce consistent orientation with a maximum angular distance of $\beta = 20°$. This densification procedure usually extends configurations by additional window correspondences. We then refine the initial alignments between models by estimating the similarity transformations from all window correspondences. The densification might lead to duplicate configurations in $\mathcal{K}$ containing the exact same correspondences. We prune these duplicates to reduce the computational cost in the following steps.

We apply the proposed correspondence search in an iterative manner, *i.e.*, we repeatedly densify the correspondences, prune duplicates, re-estimate similarities using the densified correspondences, and align the models using the refined similarities. This iterative refinement strategy terminates if the densification finds no additional correspondences.

5.2   Configuration Evaluation

Given the set of unordered configurations, the next step is to determine whether they are plausible and to rank the plausible ones based on their quality. As defined in Eq. (1), we propose the energy $E_W + E_I$ to jointly model the quality of the window alignments E_W (window term) and the amount of model intersection E_I (intersection term). In the following, we define and discuss both terms.

Window Term. Intuitively, a good alignment explains as many window alignments as possible, similar to inlier counting in RANSAC. Given a configuration $\mathcal{C}_i$ and the set of 3D consensus windows $\mathcal{W}_{3D}$, we define the window term as

$$E_W(\mathcal{C}_i, \mathcal{W}_{3D}) = |\mathcal{W}_{3D}| - 2 \cdot |\mathcal{C}_i| \ . \tag{2}$$

Thus, the window term counts the number windows that do not have a correspondence. A configuration with a higher number of explained window correspondences thus results in lower energy (*c.f.* Fig. 4(left)).

Intersection Term. The window term reflects positive evidence for the quality of an alignment. However, it is not sufficient on its own, as illustrated in Fig. 4(right). The two configurations explain the same number of window matches, but the one to the right is clearly implausible as the indoor model intersects the outer hull of the building. We thus use a second term that determines the amount of intersection by measuring the amount of free-space violations between the aligned models. Intuitively, none of the 3D points in one reconstruction should be positioned in between a 3D point from another model and the cameras observing this second point. We thus create a 3D voxel grid for each model spanning the entire reconstruction including cameras and points, using a resolution of 200^3 voxels. A voxel is marked as free space if it is intersected by a viewing ray from one of the cameras to a sparse 3D point. The intersection ratio

γ_{jk} between two aligned models m_j and m_k is then defined as the fraction of the sparse 3D points in model m_j that lie within a free-space voxel of m_k. The voxel grids can be efficiently pre-computed before the alignment procedure in the respective coordinate frames of the original models. Then, the intersection is computed by transforming the sparse points into the respective coordinate frame of the voxel grid of the other model. The energy term is defined as the maximum intersection of any combination of models in the configuration $\mathcal{C}_i$

$$E_I(\mathcal{C}_i) = \min\{1 - \epsilon, \max\{\gamma_{jk} \ \forall \ m_j \in \mathcal{C}_i, m_k \in \mathcal{C}\}\}. \tag{3}$$

Here $\epsilon > 0$ is a small constant chosen to ensure that $E_I \in [0, 1)$. Ideally, no 3D point in a model should violate the free-space of another model. However, this is rarely the case in practice due to noise and outliers in the reconstruction. Thus, we allow a certain amount of intersection by setting $\lambda = 0.05$, *i.e.*, less than 5 % of all points in a model are allowed to violate the free-space constraint. All configurations containing two models with an intersection ratio of λ or more are discarded (*c.f.* Eq. 1) during correspondence search.

Discussion. By definition $E_I(\mathcal{C}_i) \in [0, 1)$. Consequently, a configuration $\mathcal{C}_i$ with one more window correspondence than another configuration $\mathcal{C}_j$ will always have a lower energy. This implies that the intersection term only acts as negative evidence towards implausible configurations and it does not fully assess the quality of a configuration: scaling an indoor model such that it completely fits into the hull of a building results in no free-space violation. However, this configuration is only correct if the indoor model actually fills the whole space. If, on the other hand, the indoor model only contains part of the indoor scene, *e.g.* a single room, there is a high chance that this configuration will not have any window match, resulting in a high energy which denotes a bad configuration. Alignment might be good.

6   Experimental Evaluation

In this section, we evaluate the accuracy and robustness of our proposed alignment approach. We provide both qualitative and quantitative results by showing different visualizations and comparing our estimated alignments with ground

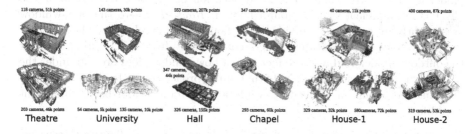

Fig. 5. Datasets used for experimental evaluation. We report the number of cameras and *sparse* points in each model. Dense point clouds are shown for visualization only

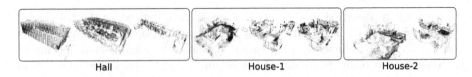

Fig. 6. Window detections obtained as described in Sect. 4

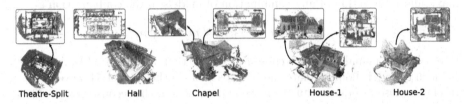

Fig. 7. Alignments between indoor and outdoor models computed by our approach

truth. In addition, we present and discuss failure cases of our approach. In the following, we first introduce the datasets.

Datasets. We collected a diverse set of six datasets (Fig. 5), spanning the possible input scenarios of our approach: (1) single indoor and single outdoor model (*Theatre, House-1, Chapel*), (2) multiple indoor models and single outdoor model (*University, House-2*), and (3) single indoor and multiple outdoor models (*Theatre-Split*). All buildings have multiple floors and we use a state-of-the-art SfM pipeline [25, 26] to reconstruct the models from photos taken with a single calibrated camera. Each of the datasets presents different challenges for our algorithm that we evaluate in the following sections.

Qualitative Evaluation. Figures 1 and 7 show the best alignments produced by our proposed algorithm. We show dense models computed from the SfM output using PMVS [10] for better visualization, with the aligned models colored in red and blue. Despite the noisy window detections, we obtain the correct alignments for most datasets. These results demonstrate that our approach is able to estimate alignments that are accurate enough to pass visual inspection. There are, however, problems with the house datasets. In *House-2*, the indoor model is slightly too small. The noisy location of the detected windows also affects the alignment of the ground floor in *House-1*, where the bow-window area slightly intersects the outside of the house. This is related to the fact that the appearance of the datasets differs considerably from the training data for the outdoor model, and also the fact that a bow-window does not fall under the Manhattan-world assumption. Note that our approach correctly aligns the small, disconnected rooms in *University*, while a pure room layout-based alignment would fail.

Quantitative Evaluation. To quantitatively evaluate the alignment accuracy, we generate ground truth as follows: we manually label window corners in indoor and outdoor images for the *Theatre, University, House-2* and *Hall* datasets. The technique described in Sect. 4 is then used to obtain the 3D coordinates for each window. Next, we manually select correspondences between indoor and outdoor windows to estimate a ground truth similarity transformation using least-squares. The absolute scale of the reconstruction is determined by measurement of the real-world window sizes. Using this ground truth alignment, we determine the quality of our alignments by calculating the positional error of the aligned sparse 3D points produced by our method. With a mean error of ≈ 0.05 m (*Theatre*), ≈ 0.42 m (*University*), ≈ 0.19 m (*Hall*) and ≈ 0.54 m (*House-2*, which results in an inaccurate alignment), the indoor and outdoor models are accurately aligned to a degree that is already difficult to notice by visual inspection. Note that the sizes of *University, Hall* and *House-2* are 36×25 m, 40×16 m and 9×9.5 m, resulting in an error of less than 1 % of the dataset's size for the success cases, and only 5 % for the failure case.

In addition, we also removed images from the outdoor reconstruction for *Theatre*. As a result, SfM splits this model into back and front façade models. We call this dataset *Theatre-Split*. Figure 7 shows that our approach successfully connects the outdoor models through the indoors. We manually labelled corresponding cameras, and obtain an average camera pose error of ≈ 0.16 m with a median of ≈ 0.05 m. Beyond the quantitative evaluation, the *Theatre-Split* dataset is a very interesting scenario, demonstrating additional applications of our method. For example, it is often impossible to create full models for individual houses in a connected building block or occlusions prevent feature matches around the corners of buildings [4]. Our approach enables the creation of full building models even in these cases.

Windows Evaluation. Figure 6 shows the 3D window detections obtained with the approach described in Sect. 4 for a selection of datasets. Many window detections are noisy, especially indoors, where many windows are either missing (inside of *Hall*) or their shape, size, or location is inaccurate (*House-1* and *House-2*). In addition, there are a few false-detections due to noisy SfM points. Despite the large number of windows detected in some cases, our approach generates the ranked alignments for all datasets in under one minute. This can be attributed to our proposed combinatorial correspondence search scheme (Sect. 5.1). In our experiments, we were able to detect, on average, 73.9 % of all indoor and 66 % of all outdoor windows. Even for detection rates as low as 45 %, our approach still works.

6.1 Discussion

Even though our approach is robust to noisy and missing window detections, it fails if there are no common windows between two models or if the detected number of windows is very small and their shape is too inaccurate. Possible reasons for missing or corrupt window detections include occlusion, incorrect labeling by our semantic classifier, a lack of 3D points preventing the estimation of the 3D window locations, *etc.* This results in different windows sizes for indoor and outdoor models, which in turn leads to wrong scale estimates. This is especially problematic if the number of common windows is small. *House-2* depicts one such case, in which we are not able to infer the correct scale of the interior model. If there are enough common windows, our approach is rather robust against such cases, since it is likely that at least one of the window matches leads to a correct scale estimate. In addition, our proposed similarity estimation can handle partial occlusions. Further robustness could be gained by considering indoor-indoor and outdoor-outdoor alignments, *e.g.*, using techniques similar to [4,21]. Another potential failure may arise in the presence of many noisy points in the reconstructions. A correct alignment could potentially violate the intersection constraint.

Similar to most vision-based reconstruction systems, our approach is vulnerable to multiple symmetry effects. First, along the vertical direction, where a room placement would be plausible on multiple floors. We obtain valid room placements on all three floors for the *University* and on two floors for the *Hall* dataset. With prior knowledge, a human could manually select the correct floor from the set of top-ranked configurations. Second, rotational symmetry, as depicted by the *Chapel* dataset. Even though the alignment shown in Fig. 7 looks visually plausible, it is actually off by a 180° rotation around the z-axis. Our approach finds the rotated alignment as the best solution due to window occlusions on one side of the outdoor model. Given an alignment computed with the proposed method, we could use an approach similar to [6] to detect symmetry planes for either the inside or outside model. The symmetry planes can then be used to hypothesize additional rotationally symmetric alignments, while the intersection constraint would rule out any invalid configurations. Last, if the task is to align a small room to a building with many rooms and windows, our approach will generate many plausible room placements. Choosing the best alignment is impossible without prior knowledge of the building layout.

7   Conclusion

We are among the first to tackle the problem of indoor-outdoor alignment. Our insight is to use semantic features (windows) to bridge the appearance gap in the alignment. This insight is potentially more broadly applicable, e.g., aerial-ground image alignment. We qualitatively and quantitatively showed the efficacy of our method on six challenging datasets. Our method handles disjoint reconstructions that might have been acquired at different times, thus giving more flexibility to the data acquisition stage for 3D reconstruction. Our results provide a valuable baseline for this difficult and important problem. In the future, we would like to explore other semantic cues such as doors, elevators, or staircases, in order to disambiguate across floors and symmetric configurations.

Acknowledgements. This project was funded by the CTI Switzerland grant #17136.1 Geometric and Semantic Structuring of 3D point clouds, and the European Union's Horizon 2020 research and innovation programme under grant agreement #637221.

References

1. Bentley, J.: Programming pearls: algorithm design techniques. ACM Commun. **27**(9), 856–873 (1984)
2. Cabral, R., Furukawa, Y.: Piecewise planar and compact floorplan reconstruction from images. In: CVPR (2014)
3. Ceylan, D., Mitra, N.J., Zheng, Y., Pauly, M.: Coupled Structure-from-motion and 3D symmetry detection for urban facades. ACM Trans. Graph. **33**(1), 2:1–2:15 (2013)
4. Cohen, A., Sattler, T., Pollefeys, M.: Merging the unmatchable: stitching visually disconnected SfM models. In: ICCV (2015)
5. Cohen, A., Schwing, A.G., Pollefeys, M.: Efficient structured parsing of facades using dynamic programming. In: CVPR (2014)
6. Cohen, A., Zach, C., Sinha, S., Pollefeys, M.: Discovering and exploiting 3D symmetries in structure from motion. In: CVPR (2012)
7. Cosmas, J., Itegaki, T., Green, D., Joseph, N., Gool, L.V., Zalesny, A., Vanrintel, D., Leberl, F., Grabner, M., Schindler, K., Karner, K., Gervautz, M., Hynst, S., Waelkens, M., Vergauwen, M., Pollefeys, M., Cornelis, K., Vereenooghe, T., Sablatnig, R., Kampel, M., Axell, P., Meyns, E.: Providing multimedia tools for recording, reconstruction, visualisation and database storage/access of archaeological excavations. In: VAST (2003)
8. Fischler, M., Bolles, R.: Random sample consensus: a paradigm for model fitting with applications to image analysis and automated cartography. Commun. ACM **24**(6), 381–395 (1981)
9. Furukawa, Y., Curless, B., Seitz, S.M., Szeliski, R.: Reconstructing building interiors from images. In: ICCV (2009)
10. Furukawa, Y., Ponce, J.: Accurate, dense, and robust multi-view stereopsis. PAMI **32**(8), 1362–1376 (2010)
11. Häne, C., Zach, C., Cohen, A., Angst, R., Pollefeys, M.: Joint 3D scene reconstruction and class segmentation. In: CVPR (2013)
12. Heinly, J., Schönberger, J.L., Dunn, E., Frahm, J.M.: Reconstructing the world* in six days *(As captured by the Yahoo 100 million image dataset). In: CVPR (2015)
13. Ikehata, S., Yan, H., Furukawa, Y.: Structured indoor modeling. In: ICCV (2015)
14. Koch, T., Korner, M., Fraundorfer, F.: Automatic alignment of indoor and outdoor building models using 3D line segments. In: CVPR Workshops (2016)
15. Korč, F., Förstner, W.: eTRIMS image database for interpreting images of man-made scenes. Technical report TR-IGG-P-2009-01, Dept. of Photogrammetry, University of Bonn. http://www.ipb.uni-bonn.de/projects/etrims_db/
16. Kushal, A., Self, B., Furukawa, Y., Gallup, D., Hernandez, C., Curless, B., Seitz, S.: Photo tours. In: 3DIMPVT (2012)
17. Ladický, L., Russell, C., Kohli, P., Torr, P.: Associative hierarchical random fields. PAMI **36**(6), 1056–1077 (2014)
18. Li, Y., Snavely, N., Huttenlocher, D., Fua, P.: Worldwide pose estimation using 3D Point clouds. In: Fitzgibbon, A., Lazebnik, S., Perona, P., Sato, Y., Schmid, C. (eds.) ECCV 2012. LNCS, vol. 7572, pp. 15–29. Springer, Heidelberg (2012). doi:10.1007/978-3-642-33718-5_2
19. Liu, C., Schwing, A.G., Kundu, K., Urtasun, R., Fidler, S.: Rent3D: floor-plan priors for monocular layout estimation. In: CVPR (2015)
20. Lynen, S., Sattler, T., Bosse, M., Hesch, J., Pollefeys, M., Siegwart, R.: Get out of my lab: large-scale, real-time visual-inertial localization. In: RSS (2015)

21. Martin-Brualla, R., He, Y., Russell, B.C., Seitz, S.M.: The 3D jigsaw puzzle: mapping large indoor spaces. In: Fleet, D., Pajdla, T., Schiele, B., Tuytelaars, T. (eds.) ECCV 2014. LNCS, vol. 8691, pp. 1–16. Springer, Heidelberg (2014). doi:10.1007/978-3-319-10578-9_1

22. Middelberg, S., Sattler, T., Untzelmann, O., Kobbelt, L.: Scalable 6-DOF localization on mobile devices. In: Fleet, D., Pajdla, T., Schiele, B., Tuytelaars, T. (eds.) ECCV 2014. LNCS, vol. 8690, pp. 268–283. Springer, Heidelberg (2014). doi:10.1007/978-3-319-10605-2_18

23. Russell, B.C., Martin-Brualla, R., Butler, D.J., Seitz, S.M., Zettlemoyer, L.: 3D Wikipedia: using online text to automatically label and navigate reconstructed geometry. In: SIGGRAPH Asia (2013)

24. Savinov, N., Ladicky, L., Häne, C., Pollefeys, M.: Discrete optimization of ray potentials for semantic 3D reconstruction. In: CVPR (2015)

25. Schönberger, J.L., Radenovic, F., Chum, O., Frahm, J.M.: From single image query to detailed 3D reconstruction. In: CVPR (2015)

26. Schönberger, J.L., Frahm, J.M.: Structure-from-motion revisited. In: CVPR (2016)

27. Snavely, N., Garg, R., Seitz, S.M., Szeliski, R.: Finding paths through the world's photos. In: SIGGRAPH (2008)

28. Strecha, C., Krull, M., Betschart, S.: The chillon project: aerial/terrestrial and indoor integration. Technical report, Pix4D. https://pix4d.com/chillon/

29. Xiao, J., Furukawa, Y.: Reconstructing the world's museums. In: ECCV (2012)

30. Zeisl, B., Sattler, T., Pollefeys, M.: Camera pose voting for large-scale image-based localization. In: ICCV (2015)

The Unreasonable Effectiveness of Noisy Data for Fine-Grained Recognition

Jonathan Krause[1(✉)], Benjamin Sapp[2], Andrew Howard[2], Howard Zhou[2],
Alexander Toshev[2], Tom Duerig[2], James Philbin[2], and Li Fei-Fei[1]

[1] Stanford University, Stanford, USA
{jkrause,feifeili}@cs.stanford.edu
[2] Google, Mountain View, USA
benjamin.sapp@gmail.com, howarda@google.com, howardzhou@google.com,
toshev@google.com, tduerig@google.com, philbinj@gmail.com

Abstract. Current approaches for fine-grained recognition do the following: First, recruit experts to annotate a dataset of images, optionally also collecting more structured data in the form of part annotations and bounding boxes. Second, train a model utilizing this data. Toward the goal of solving fine-grained recognition, we introduce an alternative approach, leveraging free, noisy data from the web and simple, generic methods of recognition. This approach has benefits in both performance and scalability. We demonstrate its efficacy on four fine-grained datasets, greatly exceeding existing state of the art without the manual collection of even a single label, and furthermore show first results at scaling to more than 10,000 fine-grained categories. Quantitatively, we achieve top-1 accuracies of 92.3 % on CUB-200-2011, 85.4 % on Birdsnap, 93.4 % on FGVC-Aircraft, and 80.8 % on Stanford Dogs without using their annotated training sets. We compare our approach to an active learning approach for expanding fine-grained datasets.

1 Introduction

Fine-grained recognition refers to the task of distinguishing very similar categories, such as breeds of dogs [27,36], species of birds [4,5,57,59], or models of cars [30,69]. Since its inception, great progress has been made, with accuracies on the popular CUB-200-2011 bird dataset [59] steadily increasing from 10.3 % [59] to 84.6 % [68].

The predominant approach in fine-grained recognition today consists of two steps. First, a dataset is collected. Since fine-grained recognition is a task inherently difficult for humans, this typically requires either recruiting a team of experts [37,57] or extensive crowd-sourcing pipelines [4,30]. Second, a method

---

Work done while J. Krause was interning at Google.

Electronic supplementary material The online version of this chapter (doi:10. 1007/978-3-319-46487-9_19) contains supplementary material, which is available to authorized users.

© Springer International Publishing AG 2016
B. Leibe et al. (Eds.): ECCV 2016, Part III, LNCS 9907, pp. 301–320, 2016.
DOI: 10.1007/978-3-319-46487-9_19

Fig. 1. There are more than 14,000 species of birds in the world. In this work we show that using noisy data from publicly-available online sources can not only improve recognition of categories in today's datasets, but also scale to very large numbers of fine-grained categories, which is extremely expensive with the traditional approach of manually collecting labels for fine-grained datasets. Here we show 4,225 of the 10,982 categories recognized in this work.

for recognition is trained using these expert-annotated labels, possibly also requiring additional annotations in the form of parts, attributes, or relationships [5,26,35,74]. While methods following this approach have shown some success [5,28,35,74], their performance and scalability is constrained by the paucity of data available due to these limitations. With this traditional approach it is prohibitive to scale up to all 14,000 species of birds in the world (Fig. 1), 278,000 species of butterflies and moths, or 941,000 species of insects [24].

In this paper, we show that it is possible to train effective models of fine-grained recognition using noisy data from the web and simple, generic methods of recognition [53,54]. We demonstrate recognition abilities greatly exceeding current state of the art methods, achieving top-1 accuracies of 92.3 % on CUB-200-2011 [59], 85.4 % on Birdsnap [4], 93.4 % on FGVC-Aircraft [37], and 80.8 % on Stanford Dogs [27] *without using a single manually-annotated training label from the respective datasets*. On CUB, this is nearly at the level of human experts [6,57]. Building upon this, we scale up the number of fine-grained classes recognized, reporting first results on over 10,000 species of birds and 14,000 species of butterflies and moths.

The rest of this paper proceeds as follows: After an overview of related work in Sect. 2, we provide an analysis of publicly-available noisy data for fine-grained recognition in Sect. 3, analyzing its quantity and quality. We describe a more traditional active learning approach for obtaining larger quantities of fine-grained data in Sect. 4, which serves as a comparison to purely using noisy data. We present extensive experiments in Sect. 5, and conclude with discussion in Sect. 6.

2   Related Work

Fine-Grained Recognition. The majority of research in fine-grained recognition has focused on developing improved models for classification [1,3,5,7–9,14, 16,18,20–22,28,29,35,36,40,41,48–50,65,67,68,70–72,74–77]. While these works have made great progress in modeling fine-grained categories given the limited data available, very few works have considered the impact of that data [57,67,68]. Xu et al. [68] augment datasets annotated with category labels and parts with web images in a multiple instance learning framework, and Xie et al. [67] do multitask training, where one task uses a ground truth fine-grained dataset and the other does not require fine-grained labels. While both of these methods have shown that augmenting fine-grained datasets with additional data can help, in our work we present results which completely forgo the use of any curated ground truth dataset. In one experiment hinting at the use of noisy data, Van Horn et al. [57] show the possibility of learning 40 bird classes from Flickr images. Our work validates and extends this idea, using similar intuition to significantly improve performance on existing fine-grained datasets and scale fine-grained recognition to over ten thousand categories, which we believe is necessary in order to fully explore the research direction.

Considerable work has also gone into the challenging task of curating fine-grained datasets [4,27,30,31,57–59,64,69] and developing interactive methods for recognition with a human in the loop [6,60–62]. While these works have demonstrated effective strategies for collecting images of fine-grained categories, their scalability is ultimately limited by the requirement of manual annotation. Our work provides an alternative to these approaches.

Learning from Noisy Data. Our work is also inspired by methods that propose to learn from web data [10,11,15,19,34,44] or reason about label noise [38,42,51,57,66]. Works that use web data typically focus on detection and classification of a set of coarse-grained categories, but have not yet examined the fine-grained setting. Methods that reason about label noise have been divided in their results: some have shown that reasoning about label noise can have a substantial effect on recognition performance [65], while others demonstrate little change from reducing the noise level or having a noise-aware model [42,51,57]. In our work, we demonstrate that noisy data can be surprisingly effective for fine-grained recognition, providing evidence in support of the latter hypothesis.

3   Noisy Fine-Grained Data

In this section we provide an analysis of the imagery publicly available for fine-grained recognition, which we collect via web search.[1] We describe its quantity, distribution, and levels of noise, reporting each on multiple fine-grained domains.

---

[1] Google image search: http://images.google.com.

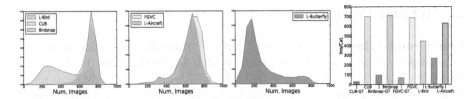

Fig. 2. Distributions of the number of images per category available via image search for the categories in CUB, Birdsnap, and L-Bird (far left), FGVC and L-Aircraft (middle left), and L-Butterfly (middle right). At far right we aggregate and plot the average number of images per category in each dataset in addition to the training sets of each curated dataset we consider, denoted CUB-GT, Birdsnap-GT, and FGVC-GT.

3.1 Categories

We consider four domains of fine-grained categories: birds, aircraft, Lepidoptera (a taxonomic order including butterflies and moths), and dogs. For birds and Lepidoptera, we obtained lists of fine-grained categories from Wikipedia, resulting in 10,982 species of birds and 14,553 species of Lepidoptera, denoted L-Bird ("Large Bird") and L-Butterfly. For aircraft, we assembled a list of 409 types of aircraft by hand (including aircraft in the FGVC-Aircraft [37] dataset, abbreviated FGVC). For dogs, we combine the 120 dog breeds in Stanford Dogs [27] with 395 other categories to obtain the 515-category L-Dog. We evaluate on two other fine-grained datasets in addition to FGVC and Stanford Dogs: CUB-200-2011 [59] and Birdsnap [4], for a total of four evaluation datasets. CUB and Birdsnap include 200 and 500 species of common birds, respectively, FGVC has 100 aircraft variants, and Stanford Dogs contains 120 breeds of dogs. In this section we focus our analysis on the categories in L-Bird, L-Butterfly, and L-Aircraft in addition to the categories in their evaluation datasets.

3.2 Images from the Web

We obtain imagery via Google image search results, using all returned images as images for a given category. For L-Bird and L-Butterfly, queries are for the scientific name of the category, and for L-Aircraft and L-Dog queries are simply for the category name (*e.g.* "Boeing 737-200" or "Pembroke Welsh Corgi").

Quantifying the Data. How much fine-grained data is available? In Fig. 2 we plot distributions of the number of images retrieved for each category and report aggregates across each set of categories. We note several trends: Categories in existing datasets, which are typically common within their fine-grained domain, have more images per category than the long-tail of categories present in the larger L-Bird, L-Aircraft, or L-Butterfly, with the effect most pronounced in L-Bird and L-Butterfly. Further, domains of fine-grained categories have substantially different distributions, *i.e.* L-Bird and L-Aircraft have more images

Fig. 3. Examples of cross-domain noise for birds, butterflies, airplanes, and dogs. Images are generally of related categories that are outside the domain of interest, *e.g.* a map of a bird's typical habitat or a t-shirt containing the silhouette of a dog.

per category than L-Butterfly. This makes sense – fine-grained categories and domains of categories that are more common and have a larger enthusiast base will have more imagery since more photos are taken of them. We also note that results tend to be limited to roughly 800 images per category, even for the most common categories, which is likely a restriction placed on public search results.

Most striking is the large difference between the number of images available via web search and in existing fine-grained datasets: even Birdsnap, which has an average of 94.8 images per category, contains only 13 % as many images as can be obtained with a simple image search. Though their labels are noisy, web searches unveil an order of magnitude more data which can be used to learn fine-grained categories.

In total, for all four datasets, we obtained 9.8 million images for 26,458 categories, requiring 151.8 GB of disk space. All urls will be released.

Noise. Though large amounts of imagery are freely available for fine-grained categories, focusing only on scale ignores a key issue: *noise*. We consider two types of label noise, which we call *cross-domain* noise and *cross-category* noise. We define cross-domain noise to be the portion of images that are not of any category in the same fine-grained domain, *i.e.* for birds, it is the fraction of images that do not contain a bird (examples in Fig. 3). In contrast, *cross-category* noise is the portion of images that have the wrong label within a fine-grained domain, *i.e.* an image of a bird with the wrong species label.

To quantify levels of cross-domain noise, we manually label a 1,000 image sample from each set of search results, with results in Fig. 4. Although levels of noise are not too high for any set of categories (max. 34.2 % for L-Butterfly), we notice an interesting correlation: cross-domain noise decreases moderately as the number of images per category (Fig. 2) increases. We hypothesize that categories with many search results have a corresponding large pool of images to draw results from, and thus actual search results will tend to be higher-precision.

In contrast to cross-domain noise, cross-category noise is much harder to quantify, since doing so effectively requires ground truth fine-grained labels of query results. To examine cross-category noise from at least one vantage point,

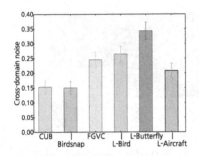

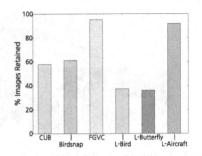

Fig. 4. The cross-domain noise in search results for each domain.

Fig. 5. The percentage of images retained after filtering.

we show the confusion matrix of given versus predicted labels on 30 categories in the CUB [59] test set and their web images in Fig. 6, left and right, which we generate via a classifier trained on the CUB training set, acting as a noisy proxy for ground truth labels. In these confusion matrices, cross-category noise is reflected as a strong off-diagonal pattern, while cross-domain noise would manifest as a diffuse pattern of noise, since images not of the same domain are an equally bad fit to all categories. Based on this interpretation, the web images show a moderate amount more cross-category noise than the clean CUB test set, though the general confusion pattern is similar.

We propose a simple, yet effective strategy to reduce the effects of cross-category noise: exclude images that appear in search results for more than one category. This approach, which we refer to as *filtering*, specifically targets images for which there is explicit ambiguity in the category label (examples in Fig. 7). As we demonstrate experimentally, filtering can improve results while reducing training time via the use of a more compact training set – we show the portion of images kept after filtering in Fig. 5. Agreeing with intuition, filtering removes more images when there are more categories. Anecdotally, we have also tried a few techniques to combat cross-domain noise, but initial experiments did not see any improvement in recognition so we do not expand upon them here. While reducing cross-domain noise should be beneficial, we believe that it is not as important as cross-category noise in fine-grained recognition due to the absence of out-of-domain classes during testing.

4   Data via Active Learning

In this section we briefly describe an active learning-based approach for collecting large quantities of fine-grained data. Active learning and other human-in-the-loop systems have previously been used to create datasets in a more cost-efficient way than manual annotation [12,46,73], and our goal is to compare this more traditional approach with simply using noisy data, particularly when considering the application of fine-grained recognition. In this paper, we apply active learning to the 120 dog breeds in the Stanford Dogs [27] dataset.

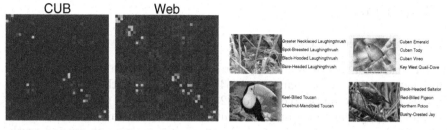

Fig. 6. Confusion matrices of the predicted label (column) given the provided label (row) for 30 CUB categories on the CUB test set (left) and search results for CUB categories (right). For visualization purposes we remove the diagonal.

Fig. 7. Examples of images removed via ltering and the categories whose results they appeared in. Some share similar names (left examples), while others share similar locations (right examples).

Our system for active learning begins by training a classifier on a seed set of input images and labels (*i.e.* the Stanford Dogs training set), then proceeds by iteratively picking a set of images to annotate, obtaining labels with human annotators, and re-training the classifier. We use a convolutional neural network [25,32,53] for the classifier, and now describe the key steps of sample selection and human annotation in more detail.

Sample Selection. There are many possible criterion for sample selection [46]. We employ confidence-based sampling: For each category c, we select the $b\hat{P}(c)$ images with the top class scores $f_c(x)$ as determined by our current model, where $\hat{P}(c)$ is a desired prior distribution over classes, b is a budget on the number of images to annotate, and $f_c(x)$ is the output of the classifier. The intuition is as follows: even when $f_c(x)$ is large, false positives still occur quite frequently – in Fig. 8 left, observe that the false positive rate is about 20 % at the highest confidence range, which might have a large impact on the model. This contrasts with approaches that focus sampling in uncertain regions [2,17,33,39]. We find that images sampled with uncertainty criteria are typically ambiguous and difficult or even impossible for both models *and* humans to annotate correctly, as demonstrated in Fig. 8 bottom row: unconfident samples are often heavily occluded, at unusual viewpoints, or of mixed, ambiguous breeds, making it unlikely that they can be annotated effectively. This strategy is similar to the "expected model change" sampling criteria [47], but done for each class independently.

Human Annotation. Our interface for human annotation of the selected images is shown in Fig. 9. Careful construction of the interface, including the addition of both positive and negative examples, as well as hidden "gold standard" images for immediate feedback, improves annotation accuracy considerably (see Supplementary Material for quantitative results). Final category decisions are made via majority vote of three annotators.

5   Experiments

5.1   Implementation Details

The base classifier we use in all noisy data experiments is the Inception-v3 convolutional neural network architecture [54], which is among the state of the art methods for generic object recognition [23,43,52]. Learning rate schedules are determined by performance on a holdout subset of the training data, which is 10 % of the training data for control experiments training on ground truth datasets, or 1 % when training on the larger noisy web data. Unless otherwise noted, all recognition results use as input a single crop in the center of the image.

Our active learning comparison uses the Yahoo Flickr Creative Commons 100M dataset [55] as its pool of unlabeled images, which we first pre-filter with a binary dog classifier and localizer [53], resulting in 1.71 million candidate dogs. We perform up to two rounds of active learning, with a sampling budget B of 10× the original dataset size per round[2]. For experiments on Stanford Dogs, we use the CNN of [25], which is pre-trained on a version of ILSVRC [13,43] with dog data removed, since Stanford Dogs is a subset of ILSVRC training data.

Fig. 8. Left: Classifier confidence versus false positive rate on 100,000 randomly sampled from Flickr images (YFCC100M [55]) with dog detections. Even the most confident images have a 20 % false positive rate. **Right:** Samples from Flickr. Rectangles below images denote correct (green), incorrect (red), or ambiguous (yellow). **Top row:** Samples with high confidence for class "Pug" from YFCC100M. **Bottom row:** Samples with low confidence score for class "Pug". (Color figure online)

Fig. 9. Our tool for binary annotation of fine-grained categories. Instructional positive images are provided in the upper left and negatives are provided in the lower left.

---

[2] To be released.

Table 1. Comparison of data source used during training with recognition performance, given in terms of Top-1 accuracy. "CUB-GT" indicates training only on the ground truth CUB training set, "Web (raw)" trains on all search results for CUB categories, and "Web (filtered)" applies filtering between categories within a domain (birds). L-Bird denotes training first on L-Bird, then fine-tuning on the subset of categories under evaluation (*i.e.* the filtered web images), and L-Bird + CUB-GT indicates training on L-Bird, then fine-tuning on Web (filtered), and finally fine-tuning again on CUB-GT. Similar notation is used for the other datasets. "(MC)" indicates using multiple crops at test time (see text for details). We note that only the rows with "-GT" make use of the ground truth training set; all other rows rely solely on noisy web imagery.

Training data	Acc.	Dataset	Training data	Acc.	Dataset
CUB-GT	84.4	CUB [59]	FGVC-GT	88.1	FGVC [37]
Web (raw)	87.7		Web (raw)	90.7	
Web (filtered)	89.0		Web (filtered)	91.1	
L-Bird	91.9		L-Aircraft	90.9	
L-Bird(MC)	92.3		L-Aircraft(MC)	93.4	
L-Bird + CUB-GT	92.2		L-Aircraft + FGVC-GT	94.5	
L-Bird + CUB-GT(MC)	92.8		L-Aircraft + FGVC-GT(MC)	95.9	
Birdsnap-GT	78.2	Birdsnap [4]	Stanford-GT	80.6	Stanford Dogs [27]
Web (raw)	76.1		Web (raw)	78.5	
Web (filtered)	78.2		Web (filtered)	78.4	
L-Bird	82.8		L-Dog	78.4	
L-Bird(MC)	85.4		L-Dog(MC)	80.8	
L-Bird + Birdsnap-GT	83.9		L-Dog + Stanford-GT	84.0	
L-Bird + Birdsnap-GT(MC)	85.4		L-Dog + Stanford-GT(MC)	85.9	

5.2   Removing Ground Truth from Web Images

One subtle point to be cautious about when using web images is the risk of inadvertently including images from ground truth test sets in the web training data. To deal with this concern, we performed an aggressive deduplication procedure with all ground truth test sets and their corresponding web images. This process follows Wang *et al.* [63], which is a state of the art method for learning a similarity metric between images. We tuned this procedure for high near-duplicate recall, manually verifying its quality. More details are included in the Supplementary Material.

5.3   Main Results

We present our main recognition results in Table 1, where we compare performance when the training set consists of either the ground truth training set, raw web images of the categories in the corresponding evaluation dataset, web images after applying our filtering strategy, all web images of a particular domain, or all images including even the ground truth training set.

On CUB-200-2011 [59], the smallest dataset we consider, even using raw search results as training data results in a better model than the annotated training set, with filtering further improving results by 1.3 %. For Birdsnap [4], the largest of the ground truth datasets we evaluate on, raw data mildly under-performs using the ground truth training set, though filtering improves results to be on par. On both CUB and Birdsnap, training first on the very large set of categories in L-Bird results in dramatic improvements, improving performance on CUB further by 2.9 % and on Birdsnap by 4.6 %. This is an important point: even if the end task consists of classifying only a small number of categories, training with more fine-grained categories yields significantly more effective net-works. This can also be thought of as a form of transfer learning within the same fine-grained domain, allowing features learned on a related task to be use-ful for the final classification problem. When permitted access to the annotated ground truth training sets for additional fine-tuning and domain transfer, results increase by another 0.3 % on CUB and 1.1 % on Birdsnap.

For the aircraft categories in FGVC, results are largely similar but weaker in magnitude. Training on raw web data results in a significant gain of 2.6 % compared to using the curated training set, and filtering, which did not affect the size of the training set much (Fig. 5), changes results only slightly in a positive direction. Counterintuitively, pre-training on a larger set of aircraft does not improve results on FGVC. Our hypothesis for the difference between birds and aircraft in this regard is this: since there are many more species of birds in L-Bird than there are aircraft in L-Aircraft (10,982 vs. 409), not only is the training size of L-Bird larger, but each training example provides stronger information because it distinguishes between a larger set of mutually-exclusive categories. Nonetheless, when access to the curated training set is available for fine-tuning, performance dramatically increases to 94.5 %. On Stanford Dogs we see results similar to FGVC, though for dogs we happen to see a mild loss when comparing to the ground truth training set, not much difference with filtering or using L-Dog, and a large boost from adding in the ground truth training set.

An additional factor that can influence performance of web models is domain shift – if images in the ground truth test set have very different visual properties compared to web images, performance will naturally differ. Similarly, if category names or definitions within a dataset are even mildly off, web-based methods will be at a disadvantage without access to the ground truth training set. Adding the ground truth training data fixes this domain shift, making web-trained models quickly recover, with a particularly large gain if the network has already learned a good representation, matching the pattern of results for Stanford Dogs.

Limits of Web-Trained Models. To push our models to their limits, we additionally evaluate using 144 image crops at test time, averaging predic-tions across each crop, denoted "(MC)" in Table 1. This brings results up to 92.3 %/92.8 % on CUB (without/with CUB training data), 85.4 %/85.4 % on Birdsnap, 93.4 %/95.9 % on FGVC, and 80.8 %/85.9 % on Stanford Dogs. We note that this is close to human expert performance on CUB, which is estimated to be between 93 % [6] and 95.6 % [57].

Table 2. Comparison with prior work on CUB-200-2011 [59]. We only include methods which use no annotations at test time. Here "GT" refers to using Ground Truth category labels in the training set of CUB, "BBox" indicates using bounding boxes, and "Parts" additionally uses part annotations.

Method	Training annotations	Acc.
Alignments [21]	GT	53.6
PDD [50]	GT + BB + Parts	60.6
PB R-CNN [74]	GT + BB + Parts	73.9
Weak Sup. [77]	GT	75.0
PN-DCN [5]	GT + BB + Parts	75.7
Two-Level [65]	GT	77.9
Consensus [48]	GT + BB + Parts	78.3
NAC [49]	GT	81.0
FG-Without [29]	GT + BB	82.0
STN [26]	GT	84.1
Bilinear [35]	GT	84.1
Augmenting [68]	GT + BB + Parts + Web	84.6
Noisy Data + CNN [54]	Web	92.3

Comparison with Prior Work. We compare our results to prior work on CUB, the most competitive fine-grained dataset, in Table 2. While even our baseline model using only ground truth data from Table 1 was at state of the art levels, by forgoing the CUB training set and only training using noisy data from the web, our models greatly outperform all prior work. On FGVC, which is more recent and fewer works have evaluated on, the best prior performing method we are aware of is the Bilinear CNN model of Lin *et al.* [35], which has accuracy 84.1 % (ours is 93.4 % without FGVC training data, 95.9 % with), and on Birdsnap, which is even more recent, the best performing method we are aware of that uses no extra annotations during test time is the original 66.6 % by Berg *et al.* [4] (ours is 85.4 %). On Stanford Dogs, the most competitive related work is [45], which uses an attention-based recurrent neural network to achieve 76.8 % (ours is 80.8 % without ground truth training data, 85.9 % with).

We identify two key reasons for these large improvements: The first is the use of a strong generic classifier [54]. A number of prior works have identified the importance of having well-trained CNNs as components in their systems for fine-grained recognition [5,26,29,35,74], which our work provides strong evidence for. On all four evaluation datasets, our CNN of choice [54], trained on the ground truth training set alone and without any architectural modifications, performs at levels at or above the previous state-of-the-art. The second reason for improvement is the large utility of noisy web data for fine-grained recognition, which is the focus of this work.

We finally remind the reader that our work focuses on the application-level problem of recognizing a given set of fine-grained categories, which might not come with their own expert-annotated training images. The use of existing test sets serves to provide an accurate measure of performance and put our work in a larger context, but results may not be strictly comparable with prior work that operates within a single given dataset.

Comparison with Active Learning. We compare using noisy web data with a more traditional active learning-based approach (Sect. 4) under several different settings in Table 3. We first verify the efficacy of active learning itself: when training the network from scratch (*i.e.* no fine-tuning), active learning improves performance by up to 15.6 %, and when fine-tuning, results still improve by 1.5 %.

How does active learning compare to using web data? Purely using filtered web data compares favorably to non-fine-tuned active learning methods (4.4 % better), though lags behind the fine-tuned models somewhat. To better compare the active learning and noisy web data, we factor out the difference in scale by performing an experiment with subsampled active learning data, setting it to be the same size as the filtered web data. Surprisingly, performance is very similar, with only a 0.4 % advantage for the cleaner, annotated active learning data, highlighting the effectiveness of noisy web data despite the lack of manual annotation. If we furthermore augment the filtered web images with the Stanford Dogs training set, which the active learning method notably used both as training data and its seed set of images, performance improves to even be slightly better than the manually-annotated active learning data (0.5 % improvement).

Table 3. Active learning-based results on Stanford Dogs [27], presented in terms of top-1 accuracy. Methods with "(scratch)" indicate training from scratch and "(ft)" indicates fine-tuning from a network pre-trained on ILSVRC, with web models also fine-tuned. "subsample" refers to downsampling the active learning data to be the same size as the filtered web images. Note that Stanford-GT is a subset of active learning data, which is denoted "A.L." .

Training Procedure	Acc.
Stanford-GT (scratch)	58.4
A.L., one round (scratch)	65.8
A.L., two rounds (scratch)	74.0
Stanford-GT (ft)	80.6
A.L., one round (ft)	81.6
A.L., one round (ft, subsample)	78.8
A.L., two rounds (ft)	82.1
Web (filtered)	78.4
Web (filtered) + Stanford-GT	82.6

These experiments indicate that, while more traditional active learning-based approaches towards expanding datasets are effective ways to improve recognition performance given a suitable budget, simply using noisy images retrieved from the web can be nearly as good, if not better. As web images require no manual annotation and are openly available, we believe this is strong evidence for their use in solving fine-grained recognition.

Very Large-Scale Fine-Grained Recognition. A key advantage of using noisy data is the ability to scale to large numbers of fine-grained classes. However, this poses a challenge for evaluation – it is infeasible to manually annotate images with one of the 10,982 categories in L-Bird, 14,553 categories in L-Butterfly, and would even be very time-consuming to annotate images with the 409 categories in L-Aircraft. Therefore, we turn to an approximate evaluation, establishing a rough estimate on true performance. Specifically, we query Flickr for up to 25 images of each category, keeping only those images whose title strictly contains the name of each category, and aggressively deduplicate these images with our training set in order to ensure a fair evaluation. Although this is not a perfect evaluation set, and is thus an area where annotation of fine-grained datasets is particularly valuable [57], we find that it is remarkably clean on the surface: based on a 1,000-image estimate, we measure the cross-domain noise of L-Bird at only 1 %, L-Butterfly at 2.3 %, and L-Aircraft at 4.5 %. An independent evaluation [57] further measures all sources of noise combined to be only 16 % when searching for bird species. In total, this yields 42,115 testing images for L-Bird, 42,046 for L-Butterfly, and 3,131 for L-Aircraft.

Fig. 10. Classification results on very large-scale fine-grained recognition. From top to bottom, depicted are examples of categories in L-Bird, L-Butterfly, and L-Aircraft, along with their category name. The first examples in each row are correctly predicted by our models, while the last two examples in each row are errors, with our prediction in grey and correct category (according to Flickr metadata) printed below.

Given the difficulty and noise, performance is surprisingly high: On L-Bird top-1 accuracy is 73.1 %/75.8 % (1/144 crops), for L-Butterfly it is 65.9 %/68.1 %, and for L-Aircraft it is 72.7 %/77.5 %. Corresponding mAP numbers, which are better suited for handling class imbalance, are 61.9, 54.8, and 70.5, reported for the single crop setting. We show qualitative results in Fig. 10. These categories span multiple continents in space (birds, butterflies) and decades in time (aircraft), demonstrating the breadth of categories in the world that can be recognized using only public sources of noisy fine-grained data. To the best of our knowledge, these results represent the largest number of fine-grained categories distinguished by any single system to date.

How Much Data is Really Necessary? In order to better understand the utility of noisy web data for fine-grained recognition, we perform a control experiment on the web data for CUB. Using the filtered web images as a base, we train models using progressively larger subsets of the results as training data, taking the top ranked images across categories for each experiment. Performance versus the amount of training data is shown in Fig. 11. Surprisingly, relatively few web images are required to do as well as training on the CUB training set, and adding more noisy web images always helps, even when at the limit of search results. Based on this analysis, we estimate that one noisy web image for CUB categories is "worth" 0.507 ground truth training images [56].

Error Analysis. Given the high performance of these models, what room is left for improvement? In Fig. 12 we show the taxonomic distribution of the remaining errors on L-Bird. The vast majority of errors (74.3 %) are made between very similar classes at the genus level, indicating that most of the remaining errors are indeed between extremely similar categories, and only very few errors (7.4 %)

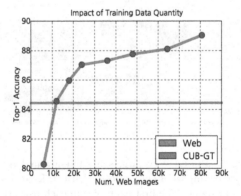

Fig. 11. Number of web images used for training vs. performance on CUB-200-2011 [59]. We vary the amount of web training data in multiples of the CUB training set size (5,994 images). Also shown is performance when training on the ground truth CUB training set (CUB-GT).

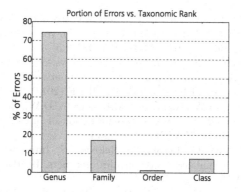

Fig. 12. The errors on L-Bird that fall in each taxonomic rank, represented as a portion of all errors made. For each error made, we calculate the taxonomic rank of the least common ancestor of the predicted and test category.

are made between dissimilar classes, whose least common ancestor is the "Aves" (*i.e.* Bird) taxonomic class. This suggests that most errors still made by the models are fairly reasonable, corroborating the qualitative results of Fig. 10.

6 Discussion

In this work we have demonstrated the utility of noisy data toward solving the problem of fine-grained recognition. We found that the combination of a generic classification model and web data, filtered with a simple strategy, was surprisingly effective at discriminating fine-grained categories. This approach performs favorably when compared to a more traditional active learning method for expanding datasets, but is even more scalable, which we demonstrated experimentally on up to 14,553 fine-grained categories. One potential limitation of the approach is the availability of imagery for categories either not found or not described in the public domain, for which an alternative method such as active learning may be better suited. Another limitation is the current focus on classification, which may be problematic if applications arise where multiple objects are present or localization is otherwise required. Nonetheless, with these insights on the unreasonable effectiveness of noisy data, we are optimistic for applications of fine-grained recognition in the near future.

Acknowledgments. We thank Gal Chechik, Chuck Rosenberg, Zhen Li, Timnit Gebru, Vignesh Ramanathan, Oliver Groth, and the anonymous reviewers for valuable feedback.

References

1. Angelova, A., Zhu, S., Lin, Y.: Image segmentation for large-scale subcategory flower recognition. In: Workshop on Applications of Computer Vision (WACV), pp. 39–45. IEEE (2013)

2. Balcan, M.-F., Broder, A., Zhang, T.: Margin based active learning. In: Bshouty, N.H., Gentile, C. (eds.) COLT 2007. LNCS (LNAI), vol. 4539, pp. 35–50. Springer, Heidelberg (2007). doi:10.1007/978-3-540-72927-3_5

3. Berg, T., Belhumeur, P.N.: Poof: Part-based one-vs.-one features for fine-grained categorization, face verification, and attribute estimation. In: Computer Vision and Pattern Recognition (CVPR), pp. 955–962. IEEE (2013)

4. Berg, T., Liu, J., Lee, S.W., Alexander, M.L., Jacobs, D.W., Belhumeur, P.N.: Bird-snap: large-scale fine-grained visual categorization of birds. In: Computer Vision and Pattern Recognition (CVPR), June 2014

5. Branson, S., Van Horn, G., Perona, P., Belongie, S.: Improved bird species recognition using pose normalized deep convolutional nets. In: British Machine Vision Conference (BMVC) (2014)

6. Branson, S., Van Horn, G., Wah, C., Perona, P., Belongie, S.: The ignorant led by the blind: a hybrid human-machine vision system for fine-grained categorization. Int. J. Comput. Vision (IJCV), 1–27 (2014)

7. Chai, Y., Lempitsky, V., Zisserman, A.: Bicos: A bi-level co-segmentation method for image classification. In: International Conference on Computer Vision (ICCV). IEEE (2011)

8. Chai, Y., Lempitsky, V., Zisserman, A.: Symbiotic segmentation and part localization for fine-grained categorization. In: International Conference on Computer Vision (ICCV), pp. 321–328. IEEE (2013)

9. Chai, Y., Rahtu, E., Lempitsky, V., Gool, L., Zisserman, A.: TriCoS: a tri-level class-discriminative co-segmentation method for image classification. In: Fitzgibbon, A., Lazebnik, S., Perona, P., Sato, Y., Schmid, C. (eds.) ECCV 2012. LNCS, vol. 7572, pp. 794–807. Springer, Heidelberg (2012). doi:10.1007/978-3-642-33718-5_57

10. Chen, X., Gupta, A.: Webly supervised learning of convolutional networks. In: International Conference on Computer Vision (ICCV). IEEE (2015)

11. Chen, X., Shrivastava, A., Gupta, A.: Neil: Extracting visual knowledge from web data. In: International Conference on Computer Vision (ICCV), pp. 1409–1416. IEEE (2013)

12. Collins, B., Deng, J., Li, K., Fei-Fei, L.: Towards scalable dataset construction: an active learning approach. In: Forsyth, D., Torr, P., Zisserman, A. (eds.) ECCV 2008. LNCS, vol. 5302, pp. 86–98. Springer, Heidelberg (2008). doi:10.1007/978-3-540-88682-2_8

13. Deng, J., Dong, W., Socher, R., Li, L.J., Li, K., Fei-Fei, L.: ImageNet: a large-scale hierarchical image database. In: Computer Vision and Pattern Recognition (CVPR) (2009)

14. Deng, J., Krause, J., Fei-Fei, L.: Fine-grained crowdsourcing for fine-grained recognition. In: Computer Vision and Pattern Recognition (CVPR), pp. 580–587 (2013)

15. Divvala, S.K., Farhadi, A., Guestrin, C.: Learning everything about anything: webly-supervised visual concept learning. In: Computer Vision and Pattern Recognition (CVPR), pp. 3270–3277. IEEE (2014)

16. Duan, K., Parikh, D., Crandall, D., Grauman, K.: Discovering localized attributes for fine-grained recognition. In: Computer Vision and Pattern Recognition (CVPR), pp. 3474–3481. IEEE

17. Erkan, A.N.: Semi-supervised learning via generalized maximum entropy. Ph.D. thesis, New York University (2010)

18. Farrell, R., Oza, O., Zhang, N., Morariu, V.I., Darrell, T., Davis, L.S.: Birdlets: Subordinate categorization using volumetric primitives and pose-normalized appearance. In: International Conference on Computer Vision (ICCV), pp. 161–168. IEEE (2011)
19. Fergus, R., Fei-Fei, L., Perona, P., Zisserman, A.: Learning object categories from internet image searches. Proc. IEEE **98**(8), 1453–1466 (2010)
20. Gavves, E., Fernando, B., Snoek, C.G., Smeulders, A.W., Tuytelaars, T.: Fine-grained categorization by alignments. In: International Conference on Computer Vision (ICCV), pp. 1713–1720. IEEE
21. Gavves, E., Fernando, B., Snoek, C.G., Smeulders, A.W., Tuytelaars, T.: Local alignments for fine-grained categorization. Int. J. Comput. Vision (IJCV), 1–22 (2014)
22. Goering, C., Rodner, E., Freytag, A., Denzler, J.: Nonparametric part transfer for fine-grained recognition. In: Computer Vision and Pattern Recognition (CVPR), pp. 2489–2496. IEEE (2014)
23. He, K., Zhang, X., Ren, S., Sun, J.: Deep residual learning for image recognition. In: Computer Vision and Pattern Recognition (CVPR). IEEE (2016)
24. Hinchliff, C.E., Smith, S.A., Allman, J.F., Burleigh, J.G., Chaudhary, R., Coghill, L.M., Crandall, K.A., Deng, J., Drew, B.T., Gazis, R., Gude, K., Hibbett, D.S., Katz, L.A., Laughinghouse, H.D., McTavish, E.J., Midford, P.E., Owen, C.L., Ree, R.H., Rees, J.A., Soltis, D.E., Williams, T., Cranston, K.A.: Synthesis of phylogeny and taxonomy into a comprehensive tree of life. Proc. Nat. Acad. Sci. (2015). http://www.pnas.org/content/early/2015/09/16/1423041112.abstract
25. Ioffe, S., Szegedy, C.: Batch normalization: accelerating deep network training by reducing internal covariate shift. In: International Conference on Machine Learning (ICML) (2015)
26. Jaderberg, M., Simonyan, K., Zisserman, A., Kavukcuoglu, K.: Spatial transformer networks. In: Neural Information Processing Systems (NIPS) (2015)
27. Khosla, A., Jayadevaprakash, N., Yao, B., Fei-Fei, L.: Novel dataset for fine-grained image categorization. In: First Workshop on Fine-Grained Visual Categorization, Conference on Computer Vision and Pattern Recognition (CVPR), Colorado Springs, CO, June 2011
28. Krause, J., Gebru, T., Deng, J., Li, L.J., Fei-Fei, L.: Learning features and parts for fine-grained recognition. In: International Conference on Pattern Recognition (ICPR), Stockholm, Sweden, August 2014
29. Krause, J., Jin, H., Yang, J., Fei-Fei, L.: Fine-grained recognition without part annotations. In: Conference on Computer Vision and Pattern Recognition (CVPR). IEEE
30. Krause, J., Stark, M., Deng, J., Fei-Fei, L.: 3d object representations for fine-grained categorization. In: 4th International IEEE Workshop on 3D Representation and Recognition (3dRR-13). IEEE (2013)
31. Kumar, N., Belhumeur, P.N., Biswas, A., Jacobs, D.W., Kress, W.J., Lopez, I.C., Soares, J.V.: Leafsnap: a computer vision system for automatic plant species identification. In: Fitzgibbon, A., Lazebnik, S., Perona, P., Sato, Y., Schmid, C. (eds.) European Conference on Computer Vision (ECCV), vol. 7573, pp. 502–516. Springer, Heidelberg (2012)
32. LeCun, Y., Bottou, L., Bengio, Y., Haffner, P.: Gradient-based learning applied to document recognition. Proc. IEEE **86**(11), 2278–2324 (1998)
33. Lewis, D.D., Catlett, J.: Heterogeneous uncertainty sampling for supervised learning. In: International Conference on Machine Learning (ICML), pp. 148–156 (1994)
34. Li, L.J., Fei-Fei, L.: Optimol: automatic online picture collection via incremental model learning. Int. J. Comput. Vision (IJCV) **88**(2), 147–168 (2010)

35. Lin, T.Y., RoyChowdhury, A., Maji, S.: Bilinear cnn models for fine-grained visual recognition. In: International Conference on Computer Vision (ICCV). IEEE
36. Liu, J., Kanazawa, A., Jacobs, D., Belhumeur, P.: Dog breed classification using part localization. In: Fitzgibbon, A., Lazebnik, S., Perona, P., Sato, Y., Schmid, C. (eds.) ECCV 2012. LNCS, vol. 7572, pp. 172–185. Springer, Heidelberg (2012). doi:10.1007/978-3-642-33718-5_13
37. Maji, S., Kannala, J., Rahtu, E., Blaschko, M., Vedaldi, A.: Fine-grained visual classification of aircraft. Technical report (2013)
38. Mnih, V., Hinton, G.E.: Learning to label aerial images from noisy data. In: International Conference on Machine Learning (ICML), pp. 567–574 (2012)
39. Mozafari, B., Sarkar, P., Franklin, M., Jordan, M., Madden, S.: Scaling up crowdsourcing to very large datasets: a case for active learning. Proc. VLDB Endowment 8(2), 125–136 (2014)
40. Nilsback, M.E., Zisserman, A.: A visual vocabulary for flower classification. In: Computer Vision and Pattern Recognition (CVPR), vol. 2, pp. 1447–1454. IEEE (2006)
41. Pu, J., Jiang, Y.-G., Wang, J., Xue, X.: Which looks like which: exploring interclass relationships in fine-grained visual categorization. In: Fleet, D., Pajdla, T., Schiele, B., Tuytelaars, T. (eds.) ECCV 2014. LNCS, vol. 8691, pp. 425–440. Springer, Heidelberg (2014). doi:10.1007/978-3-319-10578-9_28
42. Reed, S., Lee, H., Anguelov, D., Szegedy, C., Erhan, D., Rabinovich, A.: Training deep neural networks on noisy labels with bootstrapping (2014). arXiv preprint arXiv:1412.6596
43. Russakovsky, O., Deng, J., Su, H., Krause, J., Satheesh, S., Ma, S., Huang, Z., Karpathy, A., Khosla, A., Bernstein, M., Berg, A.C., Fei-Fei, L.: ImageNet large scale visual recognition challenge. Int. J. Comput. Vision (IJCV), 1–42, April 2015
44. Schroff, F., Criminisi, A., Zisserman, A.: Harvesting image databases from the web. Pattern Anal. Mach. Intell. (PAMI) 33(4), 754–766 (2011)
45. Sermanet, P., Frome, A., Real, E.: Attention for fine-grained categorization (2014). arXiv preprint arXiv:1412.7054
46. Settles, B.: Active learning literature survey. Univ. Wis. Madison 52(55–66), 11 (2010)
47. Settles, B., Craven, M., Ray, S.: Multiple-instance active learning. In: Advances in Neural Information Processing Systems (NIPS), pp. 1289–1296 (2008)
48. Shih, K.J., Mallya, A., Singh, S., Hoiem, D.: Part localization using multi-proposal consensus for fine-grained categorization. In: British Machine Vision Conference (BMVC) (2015)
49. Simon, M., Rodner, E.: Neural activation constellations: unsupervised part model discovery with convolutional networks. In: ICCV (2015)
50. Simon, M., Rodner, E., Denzler, J.: Part detector discovery in deep convolutional neural networks. In: Asian Conference on Computer Vision (ACCV), vol. 2, pp.162–177 (2014)
51. Sukhbaatar, S., Fergus, R.: Learning from noisy labels with deep neural networks (2014). arXiv preprint arXiv:1406.2080
52. Szegedy, C., Ioffe, S., Vanhoucke, V.: Inception-v4, inception-resnet and the impact of residual connections on learning (2016). arXiv preprint arXiv:1602.07261
53. Szegedy, C., Liu, W., Jia, Y., Sermanet, P., Reed, S., Anguelov, D., Erhan, D., Vanhoucke, V., Rabinovich, A.: Going deeper with convolutions. In: Computer Vision and Pattern Recognition (CVPR) (2015)

54. Szegedy, C., Vanhoucke, V., Ioffe, S., Shlens, J., Wojna, Z.: Rethinking the inception architecture for computer vision. In: Computer Vision and Pattern Recognition (CVPR). IEEE (2016)
55. Thomee, B., Shamma, D.A., Friedland, G., Elizalde, B., Ni, K., Poland, D., Borth, D., Li, L.J.: The new data and new challenges in multimedia research (2015). arXiv preprint arXiv:1503.01817
56. Torralba, A., Efros, A., et al.: Unbiased look at dataset bias. In: Computer Vision and Pattern Recognition (CVPR), pp. 1521–1528. IEEE (2011)
57. Van Horn, G., Branson, S., Farrell, R., Haber, S., Barry, J., Ipeirotis, P., Perona, P., Belongie, S.: Building a bird recognition app. and large scale dataset with citizen scientists: the fine print in fine-grained dataset collection. In: Computer Vision and Pattern Recognition (CVPR). IEEE (2015)
58. Vedaldi, A., Mahendran, S., Tsogkas, S., Maji, S., Girshick, B., Kannala, J., Rahtu, E., Kokkinos, I., Blaschko, M.B., Weiss, D., Taskar, B., Simonyan, K., Saphra, N., Mohamed, S.: Understanding objects in detail with fine-grained attributes. In: Computer Vision and Pattern Recognition (CVPR) (2014)
59. Wah, C., Branson, S., Welinder, P., Perona, P., Belongie, S.: The Caltech-UCSD Birds-200-2011 dataset. Technical report CNS-TR-2011-001, California Institute of Technology (2011)
60. Wah, C., Belongie, S.: Attribute-based detection of unfamiliar classes with humans in the loop. In: Computer Vision and Pattern Recognition (CVPR), pp. 779–786. IEEE (2013)
61. Wah, C., Branson, S., Perona, P., Belongie, S.: Multiclass recognition and part localization with humans in the loop. In: International Conference on Computer Vision (ICCV), pp. 2524–2531. IEEE (2011)
62. Wah, C., Horn, G., Branson, S., Maji, S., Perona, P., Belongie, S.: Similarity comparisons for interactive fine-grained categorization. In: Computer Vision and Pattern Recognition (CVPR) (2014)
63. Wang, J., Song, Y., Leung, T., Rosenberg, C., Wang, J., Philbin, J., Chen, B., Wu, Y.: Learning fine-grained image similarity with deep ranking. In: Proceedings of the IEEE Conference on Computer Vision and Pattern Recognition, pp. 1386–1393 (2014)
64. Welinder, P., Branson, S., Mita, T., Wah, C., Schroff, F., Belongie, S., Perona, P.: Caltech-UCSD Birds 200. Technical report CNS-TR-2010-001, California Institute of Technology (2010)
65. Xiao, T., Xu, Y., Yang, K., Zhang, J., Peng, Y., Zhang, Z.: The application of two-level attention models in deep convolutional neural network for fine-grained image classification. In: Computer Vision and Pattern Recognition (CVPR). IEEE
66. Xiao, T., Xia, T., Yang, Y., Huang, C., Wang, X.: Learning from massive noisy labeled data for image classification. In: Computer Vision and Pattern Recognition (CVPR). IEEE
67. Xie, S., Yang, T., Wang, X., Lin, Y.: Hyper-class augmented and regularized deep learning for fine-grained image classification. In: Computer Vision and Pattern Recognition (CVPR). IEEE
68. Xu, Z., Huang, S., Zhang, Y., Tao, D.: Augmenting strong supervision using web data for fine-grained categorization. In: International Conference on Computer Vision (ICCV) (2015)
69. Yang, L., Luo, P., Loy, C.C., Tang, X.: A large-scale car dataset for fine-grained categorization and verification. In: Computer Vision and Pattern Recognition (CVPR). IEEE

70. Yang, S., Bo, L., Wang, J., Shapiro, L.G.: Unsupervised template learning for fine-grained object recognition. In: Advances in Neural Information Processing Systems (NIPS), pp. 3122–3130 (2012)
71. Yao, B., Bradski, G., Fei-Fei, L.: A codebook-free and annotation-free approach for fine-grained image categorization. In: Computer Vision and Pattern Recognition (CVPR), pp. 3466–3473. IEEE (2012)
72. Yao, B., Khosla, A., Fei-Fei, L.: Combining randomization and discrimination for fine-grained image categorization. In: Computer Vision and Pattern Recognition (CVPR), pp. 1577–1584. IEEE (2011)
73. Yu, F., Zhang, Y., Song, S., Seff, A., Xiao, J.: Construction of a large-scale image dataset using deep learning with humans in the loop (2015). arXiv preprint arXiv:1506.03365
74. Zhang, N., Donahue, J., Girshick, R., Darrell, T.: Part-based r-cnns for fine-grained category detection. In: Fleet, D., Pajdla, T., Schiele, B., Tuytelaars, T. (eds.) ECCV 2014. LNCS, vol. 8689, pp. 834–849. Springer, Heidelberg (2014). doi:10.1007/978-3-319-10590-1_54
75. Zhang, N., Farrell, R., Darrell, T.: Pose pooling kernels for sub-category recognition. In: Computer Vision and Pattern Recognition (CVPR), pp. 3665–3672. IEEE (2012)
76. Zhang, N., Farrell, R., Iandola, F., Darrell, T.: Deformable part descriptors for fine-grained recognition and attribute prediction. In: International Conference on Computer Vision (ICCV), pp. 729–736. IEEE (2013)
77. Zhang, Y., Wei, X-S., Wu, J., Cai, J., Lu, J., Nguyen, V.A., Do, M.N.: Weakly supervised fine-grained image categorization (2015). arXiv preprint arXiv:1504.04943

A Simple Hierarchical Pooling Data Structure for Loop Closure

Xiaohan Fei$^{(\boxtimes)}$, Konstantine Tsotsos, and Stefano Soatto

UCLA Vision Lab, University of California, Los Angeles, USA
{feixh,ktsotsos,soatto}@cs.ucla.edu

Abstract. We propose a data structure obtained by hierarchically pooling Bag-of-Words (BoW) descriptors during a sequence of views that achieves average speedups in large-scale loop closure applications ranging from 2 to 20 times on benchmark datasets. Although simple, the method works as well as sophisticated agglomerative schemes at a fraction of the cost with minimal loss of performance.

Keywords: Loop closure · Hierarchical pooling · Bag-of-words · Descriptor aggregation

1 Introduction

We tackle the problem of *loop closure* in vision-based navigation. This is a particular classification task whereby a training set of images is indexed by location, and given a test image one wants to query the database to decide whether the former is present in the latter, and if so return the indexed location. This is closely related to *scene recognition*, where the focus is on a particular instance, as opposed to an object class (we want to determine whether we are at particular intersection in a given city, not whether we are at *some* intersection of *some* urban area). As such, test images are only subject to *nuisance variability* due to viewpoint, illumination and partial occlusion from moving objects, but otherwise there is no *intrinsic* (intra-class) variability.

The state-of-the-art for image retrieval is based on convolutional neural network (CNN) architectures, trained to marginalize nuisance and intrinsic variability. In a discriminatively trained network, the compositionality property afforded by linear convolutions, while critical to model intra-class variability, is unhelpful for loop closure, as there is no intrinsic variability. At the same time, a CNN does not respect the topology of data space at higher levels of the hierarchy, since filters at any given layer are supported on the entire feature map of the previous layer. In loop closure, locality is key, and while one could retrieve from the feature map the locations that correspond to active units, this requires some effort [26].

Given the critical importance of loop closure in location services ranging from smartphones to autonomous vehicles, we focus on its peculiarities, and attempt to harvest some of the components of neural networks to improve the state-of-the-art. Stripped of the linear convolutions (we do not need to model intrinsic

© Springer International Publishing AG 2016
B. Leibe et al. (Eds.): ECCV 2016, Part III, LNCS 9907, pp. 321–337, 2016.
DOI: 10.1007/978-3-319-46487-9_20

variability) and ReLu, what we have left is a *hierarchical spatially pooled data structure built upon local photometric descriptors* [11,18]. There are no filters, and no learning other than the trivial pooling of local descriptors. Motivated by this intuition, we propose a new hierarchical representation for loop closure, detailed in Sect. 2.

Loop closure is also closely related to location, or "place," recognition [6,33,35] and large-scale visual search [5,13,21], but with some important restrictions.

First, both previous data (training images) and current (test, or query) data are usually available as time-indexed sequences, even if they are captured by different agents, and training images may be aggregated into a "map" [14] or reduced to a collection of "keyframes" [20]. Second, as a binary classification task (at each instant of time, a loop closure is either detected or not), the cost of missed detections and false alarms are highly asymmetric: We pay a high price for declaring a loop closure that isn't, but there is minor harm in missing one, as temporal continuity affords many second chances in subsequent images. This is unlike large-scale image retrieval, where we wish to find what we are looking for (few missed detections, or high recall) even if we have to wade through some irrelevant hits (many false alarms, or low precision).

Like image retrieval, however, the challenge with loop closure is scaling. In navigation applications, it may be hours before we return to a previously seen portion of the scene. Therefore, we have to store, and search through, hundreds of thousands to millions of images. Our goal in this paper is to *design a hierarchical data structure that helps speed up matching by leveraging on the two domain-specific constraints above:* temporal adjacency, and high precision.

Assuming continuous trajectories, the first translates to proximity in pose space $SE(3)$ (position and orientation). For the second, the best trade-off with missed detections can be achieved by testing every datum in the training set via *linear search accelerated via an inverted index.* Our goal is to achieve similar performance at a fraction of the cost compared to inverted index search. This cannot be achieved in a worst-case setting. What matters instead is *average performance* trading off precision with computational cost. We evaluate such average performance empirically on the *KITTI* [9], *Oxford* [6] and *TUM RGB-D* [29] datasets, as well as demonstrate extensions to general image retrieval on the *ukbench* [21] and *INRIA Holidays* [13] datasets. To demonstrate scalability, we also evaluate our algorithm on augmented datasets with around 40 K images.

We propose a simple data structure based on hierarchical pooling of location likelihoods – in the form of sample distributions of BoW descriptors – with respect to the topology of pose space. In practice, this means simply constructing BoW descriptors, that represent the likelihood of the locations that generated them, and pooling them temporally in a fine-to-coarse fashion, either by averaging, summing, or taking the index-wise maximum.

While averaging likelihoods may seem counter-productive, in Sect. 2 we show it makes sense in the context of the classical theories of sampling and anti-aliasing. In Sect. 3 we show that, despite its simplicity, it works as well as sophisticated agglomerative schemes at a fraction of the effort.

1.1 Related Work

Loop closure is a key component in robotic mapping (SLAM) [37], autonomous driving, location services on hand-held devices, and for wearables such as virtual reality displays. Loop closure methods can be roughly divided into 3 categories: appearance-only, map-only and methods in between. Appearance-only methods [6] are essentially large-scale image retrieval algorithms, influenced by [21] and more in general the literature of BoW object recognition and categorization [27]. Map-only methods [15] use the data (images, but most often range sensors) to infer the configuration of points in 3D space, and then seek to match subsets of these points, often using variants of ICP [4] as a building block. These methods do not scale beyond a few hundreds of thousands of points, or thousands of keyframes, and are often limited to what is referred to as "short-term" loop closure [15], necessary for instances when complete loss of visual reference occurs while tracking. There are also a variety of map-to-image and image-to-map [25] methods that show great promise, but have yet to prove scalability to the point where the map spans tens if not hundreds of kilometers [6].

For scalability, the most common choice is to combine quantized local descriptors into a BoW and then use an inverted index. FAB-MAP [6] extends the basic setup by learning a generative model of the visual words using a Chow-Liu tree to model the probability of co-occurrence of visual words. FAB-MAP 2.0 scales further by exploiting sparsity to make the inverted index retrieval architecture more efficient. Starting from [8], SIFT or SURF descriptors were replaced by more efficient binary descriptors such as BRIEF [3] and ORB [23] to achieve comparable precision and recall to FAB-MAP 2.0 with an order of magnitude speed increase. Several recent mapping and localization systems adopt it as a module, including [17] and ORB-SLAM [19].

In addition to the specific loop closure literature, general ideas from spatial data structures and agglomerative clustering [31] are also relevant to this work, including k-d trees [24], dual trees and decision trees [10], as well as data structures used for retrieval such as pyramid matching [12] and its spatial version [16]. In more general terms, this work also relates to visual navigation and mapping, structure-from-motion, and location recognition, including the use of global descriptors [33].

Our method can be considered appearance-only, but it is loosely informed by geometry, in the sense that the scene domain (pose space) provides the topology with respect to which we pool descriptors. Also closely related to our approach are [32,34], which present techniques for merging only pairs of BoWs; in [5] queries are expanded by using retrieved and verified images, which is orthogonal to and can be viewed as a *query-end* version of our method.

2   Methodology

Since our focus is on a spatial structure that facilitates accelerated loop closure queries, we integrate components from recent state-of-the-art methods within our data structure and adopt such methods as a baseline, against which we compare our method. Specifically, we adopt [19] as a baseline, consisting of a BoW where each word is an element of a dictionary of descriptors obtained off-line by hierarchical k-means clustering, with each word weighted by its inverse document frequency. FAST detectors [22] and BRIEF descriptors [3] are employed, and TF-IDF [1,2,27] is used to weigh the BoW relative to the inverse document frequency. This standard pipeline, with different clustering procedures to generate the dictionary and different features, comprises most basic large-scale retrieval systems, including appearance-only loop closure. However, the number of false alarms in large-scale settings is crippling, so temporal consistency and geometric verification are typically used as correction mechanisms.

2.1   Hierarchical Testing

Construction of Hierarchy. Our data structure can be interpreted as a hierarchical version of TF-IDF. To illustrate the method, we first assume that every frame is a "keyframe" and therefore we have a time-series of BoWs, obtained as described above, and organized into a linear structure or *un-oriented list*, as we wish to retrieve frames regardless of the direction of traversal. Each node is associated with a histogram, in the form of a BoW, representing the likelihood of a pose $g(t) \in SE(3)$ (position $T(t) \in \mathbb{R}^3$ and orientation $R(t) \in SO(3)$) given the data (the image at time t, $I(t)$): $h^t \doteq \mathrm{BoW}(t) \sim p(I(t)|g(t))$, where the equivalence is up to normalization, and the density function is approximated with a histogram with N bins, equal to the size of the dictionary.

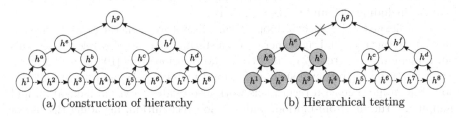

(a) Construction of hierarchy   (b) Hierarchical testing

Fig. 1. (a) **Construction of hierarchy** for an 8-long sequence of (key) frames and constant branching factor of 2. Dashed lines indicate temporal order. (b) **Hierarchical testing**: If h^e does not score higher than the threshold, the whole sub-tree rooted at h^e (shaded) will not be searched. In the case of sum- or max-pooling, this would *not* introduce loss of precision compared to searching only the lowest level nodes.

We now construct a second level, or "layer", of the data structure, simply by pooling adjacent histograms (Fig. 1a). This is repeated for higher layers until either a maximum depth is reached, or until a single root node is left. Several standard choices for the pooling operation are available which allow us to trade off between precision and cost (Sect. 3). Suppose h^p is the parent histogram which has child histograms $\{h^k\}, k = 1, 2 \ldots K$. Both h^p and $h^k \in \mathbb{R}^N$. Mean- or average-pooling refers to $h^p = \frac{1}{K}\sum_{k=1}^{K} h^k$, sum-pooling refers to $h^p = \sum_{k=1}^{K} h^k$, and max-pooling refers to $h_i^p = \max_k\{h_i^k\}$, where $i = 1, 2 \ldots N$. Once we have constructed the hierarchy for database histograms, raw histograms are used as queries for loop closure detection.

Query Processing. Similarities between pooled and query histograms are computed using the *intersection kernel* [30], that is the area of the intersection of the two histograms. Thus, if h^q (a query histogram) has bin values $h_1^q, \ldots, h_N^q$, and similarly for h^p, we have that

$$\mathbb{I}(h^q, h^p) = \sum_{i=1}^{N} \min\{h_i^q, h_i^p\} \tag{1}$$

The intersection kernel is related to many divergence functions [36] as well as to metrics used in optimal transport problems.

Sum- and max-pooling operators have the following upper bound property when intersection kernel is applied: For a query histogram h^q, a parent histogram h^p and its child h^k in the database,

$$\mathbb{I}(h^q, h^p) > \mathbb{I}(h^q, h^k) \tag{2}$$

therefore if $\mathbb{I}(h^q, h^p) < \tau$, $\mathbb{I}(h^q, h^k) < \tau$ must hold.

Since our goal is to search for the closest match, or at least for all matches that exceed a threshold $\tau > 0$ (we seek large values of $\mathbb{I}$), if $\mathbb{I}(h^q, h^p) < \tau$, the chance of any of h^p's descendants exceeding the threshold is rare (or impossible, in the case of max- or sum-pooling as shown by the upper bound property), therefore we stop searching the sub-tree rooted at h^p (Fig. 1b).

Therefore, search in a hierarchical TF-IDF setting simply boils down to *greedy breadth-first search, while maintaining an inverted index for each layer.* If only one layer is used, this reduces to standard linear search using an inverted index.

A key point is that with sum- or max-pooling, the proposed method *has exactly the same precision-recall behavior as standard inverted index search* while still achieving a substantial speedup. With mean-pooling, a large speedup can be achieved with only a minimal loss of precision (Sect. 3).

Different trees with different depths and different branching factors can be constructed, trading off expected risk and computation time, characterized empirically in Sect. 3.4. In addition to a fixed depth and branching factor, one could devise more clever schemes to determine the topology of the tree, discussed in Sect. 2.2. However, we find that the benefit is limited compared to the straightforward fixed-topology architecture.

2.2 Keyframes and Adaptive Tree Topology

So far we have assumed that the time-series of data $\{h^t\}_{t=1}^{T}$ is sampled regularly (at constant time or space intervals), but it can also be sampled adaptively, by exploiting statistics of the data stream to decide which samples, or *keyframes*, to use. The data structure above does not change, since all that is required is a topology or adjacency structure to construct the tree.

Adaptive (sub)-sampling can be done in many ways, and there are a wide variety of standard heuristics for selecting keyframes. Our goal here is not to determine the best method for selecting keyframes, but to focus on the data structure regardless of the sub-sampling mechanism. Consequently, we limit ourselves to constructing it either on the raw time series, or on any subsampling of it, as generated by standard keyframe selection methods.

Just like selecting keyframes, building the hierarchy can be understood as a form of (sub)-sampling. Regardless of whether subsampling is regular (as in building the tree above) or adaptive (as in selecting keyframes), classical sampling theory [28] suggests that what should be stored at the samples is *not* the value of the function, but the local average relative to the topology of the domain where the data are defined (*anti-aliasing*). This lends credence to the use of mean-pooling, which initially may seem counter-intuitive since our goal is to maintain high precision.

In our case, the domain is time, or the order of keyframes, as a proxy of location in $SE(3)$. The range of the data is the space of likelihood functions, approximated by histograms h^t. Therefore, anti-aliasing simply reduces to averaging neighboring histograms. The study of the optimal averaging, both in terms of support and weights, is beyond our scope here, where for mean-pooling we simply average nearest neighbors in the tree topology relative to a uniform prior. We do not delve into considering more sophisticated anti-aliasing schemes, since we have found that simple topologies yield attractive precision-computational cost trade-off, which is unlikely to be significantly disrupted by fine-tuning the weights.

The practice of averaging likelihood functions as a way of anti-aliasing descriptors has also been recently shown by [7] in the context of pooling local descriptors for correspondences in wide-baseline matching. Our method can be considered an extension (or special case) where the correspondence and pooling are performed in time, and the descriptors are histograms of visual words, a mid-level representation, rather than histograms of gradient orientation, the result of low-level processing.

While the choice of heuristics for keyframe selection has no effect on our method, which can be applied to the raw time series or to the sequence of keyframes, the same (adaptive sampling) heuristics used to (down)-sample keyframes from the regularly sampled images could be used to aggregate nodes at one level into parents one level above. This would give rise to trees having different levels of connectivity at different layers, and indeed potentially at each node.

We have found that, in practice, these heuristics fail to yield significant performance improvements when compared to trees with fixed topology having constant splitting factors that match the average of their adaptive counter-part. Representative experiments are shown in Sect. 3.4.

3 Evaluation

The most important evaluation for the proposed method is to test performance in-the-loop when incorporated into a real system (ORB-SLAM [19], in this case), discussed in Sect. 3.2 where we find a 65 % reduction in mean query time with no loss in localization performance and no missed loop closures relative to the baseline. We investigate query-time reduction and precision-recall behavior while varying vocabulary size and tree topology in Sects. 3.3 and 3.4, respectively. In Sect. 3.5 we augment standard datasets to explore various test-time scenarios, and Sect. 3.6 presents a generalization of our method to other image retrieval tasks. Sect. 3.1 discusses the datasets and methodology used throughout the evaluation.

3.1 Datasets and Methodology for Loop Closure

We perform experiments using the common loop closure datasets of *KITTI*, *Oxford City Centre*, and *Oxford New College* [6,9]. The *KITTI* dataset consists of several sequences on the order of 1000 stereo pairs in length. To provide additional experimental evaluation at large scale, we augment *KITTI* by concatenating all sequences, to form the *concatenated KITTI* dataset consisting of approx. 40 K images. For all sequences we construct the data structure using all frames unless otherwise noted, in which case we adopt the keyframe selection strategy of our baseline (Sect. 3.2).

Unless otherwise stated, we build the hierarchical data structure using the left stereo images of the sequences (when stereo is available) and evaluate loop closure correctness using the provided ground truth poses. The evaluation protocol is as follows: traverse the sequence and insert BoW of images into the database incrementally, while using each image to query the database before it is added. Two images are regarded as a correct match if they were taken within 15 meters of each other. To avoid trivial matches, we prevent the query from matching temporally adjacent images. This evaluation protocol mimics loop closure in a practical SLAM system, which we test in Sect. 3.2.

To evaluate matching, missed detection and false alarms are traded off by an arbitrary choice of threshold, as in any detection algorithm. Since the threshold affects the average query time (we can make that quite short by choosing a threshold that yields no false alarms while rejecting every hypothesis) we must come to a reasonable choice. Unless otherwise stated, we adopt the following policy: We generate precision-recall curves on *KITTI* 00. Then, we select the smallest threshold that yields zero false alarms and use it on other sequences. Of course, that may yield a non-zero false alarm rate in datasets that are not used in setting the threshold, but this (as is customary) can be handled by verification steps afterwards. This is a limitation inherent to the choice of image representation, in this case Bag-of-Words, and not a sensitivity that our hierarchical data structure is designed to circumvent.

3.2 In-the-loop with the Baseline

We use components of ORB-SLAM [19], made available by the authors, as the baseline for our experiments. We use this as a *black box* and implement our hierarchy atop its single-layer inverted index architecture for performing image queries. As a result, we also inherit some of the limitations of its components (e.g. keyframe selection, discriminability of quantized descriptors and BoW representations, sensitivity to matching threshold selection), which are common to the majority of SLAM systems.

We first show that when using ORB-SLAM *as is*, with no change in thresholds or tuning, a significant reduction in image query time can be achieved simply by applying our max-pooling hierarchy, which by construction achieves identical precision-recall performance to the original system, missing no loop closures that may be critical to pose-graph optimization algorithms. In Fig. 2b, we compare the trajectories estimated by ORB-SLAM with and without our max-pooling hierarchy on *KITTI*. Errors relative to ground truth are similar (within 1σ of each other over multiple trials); mean query times are reduced by 65 % (2.04 ms from 5.80 ms). No loop closures are missed by our max-pooling method that would not be missed without our data structure, confirming that improvement in speed comes at no loss of classification performance. In Fig. 2a we show this speedup holds with increasing scale by showing query times for the *concatenated KITTI* dataset for different vocabulary sizes (Sect. 3.3) and various pooling strategies using the methodology of Sect. 3.5.

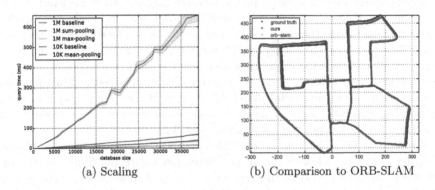

(a) Scaling   (b) Comparison to ORB-SLAM

Fig. 2. (a) **Scaling:** Timings for concatenated *KITTI* sequences (approx. 40 K images) with 1 M and 10 K vocabularies. (b) Comparison to **ORB-SLAM** with and without our data structure. Multiple trials yield nearly identical trajectories with and without our data structure, with no loop closures missed while achieving a 2–3x speedup.

3.3 Varying Vocabulary Size

Some may argue that a speedup could be easily gained by just using a larger vocabulary. It is true that with a larger vocabulary, each visual word is associated with a much smaller list of documents in the inverted index system which leads to shorter query time. However, the vocabulary size should be determined by the performance of the specific task as well as the volume of the data and a larger vocabulary is not always better. A larger vocabulary has finer division of feature space compared to a smaller vocabulary but is also more sensitive to quantization errors (two slightly different images may have completely different histograms). In this case, mean-pooling may not be ideal as shown in Figs. 4c and d. However, sum/max-pooling can still be applied to gain further speedup while maintaining same precision-recall as shown in Fig. 3c and d, and also on augmented dataset as shown in Fig. 2a.

3.4 Varying Tree Topology

Variable Depth and Branching Factor. Figure 3 shows timings of the baseline and our algorithm with different topologies and pooling schemes at the same threshold on two of the *KITTI* sequences with many loop closures. Only time to query the database is counted, time for feature extraction and descriptor quantization are excluded. Figure 4a and b show precision-recall curves for the mean-pooling variants. We use $d_i b_j$-X to denote a hierarchy with i layers, a branching factor of j and pooling strategy X. Note that for baseline and our proposed algorithm with configuration $d_2 b_4$-mean and $d_2 b_8$-mean, the precision-recall curves are nearly identical, while our approach is 2–5 times faster. For configuration $d_2 b_{16}$-mean, while its performance is slightly worse, it achieves *an order of magnitude speedup* relative to the baseline.

As mentioned in Sect. 2.1, sum/max-pooling have *exactly the same precision-recall behavior* as the baseline. In these two datasets, sum/max-pooling are slightly slower than inverted index search. Since both of these operations rapidly reduce sparsity in the histograms, we expect slower performance relative to mean-pooling. However, sum/max-pooling have their advantages when a much larger vocabulary is used as shown in Sect. 3.3.

Adaptive Domain-Based Clustering. In addition to the baseline algorithm, we generate a second baseline by applying the same algorithm to keyframes, rather than to all stored images. In principle, the heuristics involved in the selection of keyframes could be propagated to all nodes of the data structure, as discussed in Sect. 2.2. However, our experiments indicate that this yields minor benefits compared to simple averaging. The second row of Table 2a shows average time-cost rate[1] for searching via an inverted index among keyframes, which is worse than searching in a simple hierarchy built on raw images, as shown in the second row of Table 1c. A simple regular sampling strategy on top of keyframes can speedup searching by a large margin as shown in Table 2a.

---

[1] Time-cost rate is defined as the increase of query time per thousand (1 k) images in the database. Average time-cost rate is the average of time-cost rates computed for all sequences in each dataset.

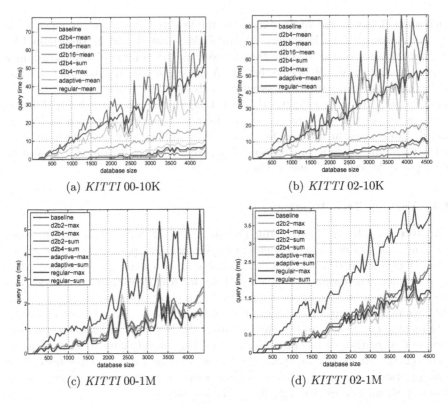

(a) *KITTI* 00-10K

(b) *KITTI* 02-10K

(c) *KITTI* 00-1M

(d) *KITTI* 02-1M

Fig. 3. Timings of baseline and proposed algorithm with different topologies and pooling strategies on *KITTI* dataset 00 and 02 using *all* frames. $d_i b_j$ -X: a hierarchy with i layers, a branching factor of j and pooling strategy X. Adaptive sampling: spectral clustering in $SE(3)$. Regular sampling: sampling at the average rate of adaptive sampling scheme. Baseline: inverted index search. Two different vocabulary sizes (10 K and 1 M) are considered.

Instead of a fixed topology of the data structure, corresponding to regular grouping, we can consider adaptive grouping based on a variety of criteria. Adaptive sampling, or grouping, based on *geometry* includes performing spectral clustering in $SE(3)$. Curves in Fig. 3 indicate that adaptive sampling achieves marginal improvements compared to regular sampling at a constant rate equal to the average of the adaptive sampling rate. Similarly, parallax-based sampling, based on clustering only the translational component of pose, also yields underwhelming improvements. We do, however, expect adaptive sampling to win in some cases, as it has in a number of smaller-scale experiments we conducted with different motion characteristics from smooth driving, for instance the *TUM RGB-D* dataset (Fig. 5) [29].

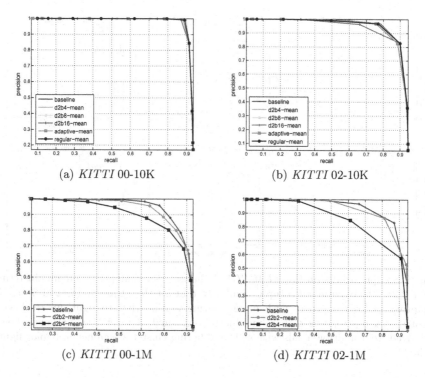

Fig. 4. Precision-recall curves of baseline and proposed algorithm with different topologies on *KITTI* dataset 00 and 02 using *all* frames. Two different vocabulary sizes (10 K and 1 M) are considered. Notations have the same meanings as in Fig. 3.

3.5 Quantifying Speedup Using Synthetic Ground-Truth

Depending on the particular query image, our method could reduce or increase search time relative to the mean. The former occurs when correspondence fails early allowing us to rule out subsequent tests at finer scales. However, in the worst-case we may end up performing more comparisons than inverted index search when the test reaches the finest scale too often. In practice, what matters is that our algorithm shortens test time *on average* during long sequences. Since most *KITTI* sequences contain few or no loop closures, we generate synthetic positive and negative queries as follows: For sequences 01 to 21, we generate positive queries by sampling the right stereo images of each sequence (slightly different from the left images from which we constructed the database), and generate negative queries by sampling images from sequence 00. For the *Oxford* datasets, we construct the database using odd-numbered images, generate positive queries from the even-numbered images, and negative queries again from *KITTI* 00.

Overall performance is measured by combining both sets of queries. Of course, even in the negative case our algorithm could find erroneous correspondences, which are then labeled as false alarms. Similarly, we may find no correspondence in

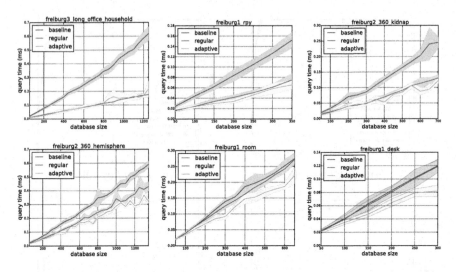

Fig. 5. Sample results on the *TUM RGB-D* dataset using adaptive domain clustering (Sect. 2.2). The experiment setup is similar to that for the *Oxford* dataset in Sect. 3.5. Adaptive (yellow) improves with more exciting motion (left to right, up to down). Limited speedup relative to baseline due to very small dataset size. Variance shown is derived from multiple trials with sightly differing cluster assignments. (Color figure online)

the former case (missed detection). We use average time-cost rate to evaluate how the searching algorithm scales with size of the database. Table 1 reports experiment results on raw *KITTI*. Table 2 reports average speedup when keyframe selection is applied on both *KITTI* and *Oxford*. Figure 2a shows linear scaling of average query time on the much larger *concatenated KITTI*. Practical deployment on even larger datasets typically comes with context (*e.g.* GPS or odometry) that limits the data volume.

3.6 Experiments in Image Retrieval Tasks

Although our approach is geared towards the loop closure scenario, its usage is not restricted to it. A hierarchical structure of this form could be built on top of any histogram-based representation of images where some proxy of topology is available. In more general settings when a temporal stream of images is unavailable, extra labeling information, such as geotags, class labels, or textual annotations could be used. A hierarchy can be constructed using affinity between these alternate forms of metadata, provided that affinity implies proximity in the solution space. We test this using two publicly available image retrieval benchmarks: *ukbench* [21] and *INRIA Holidays* [13].

ukbench[2] consists of 2550 groups of 4 images each (10200 total). Each group contains the same object under different viewpoint, rotation, scale and lighting

---

[2] http://vis.uky.edu/~stewe/ukbench/.

Table 1. Average time-cost rate and speedup over 21 sequences of *KITTI* using *all* frames. 1st col: grouping strategies. 2nd col: pooling operations. 3rd col: average time-cost rate, which describes how the query time increases per 1 k images inserted into the database. In 1a, b and c, a 10 K vocabulary is used; in 1d, a 1 M vocabulary is used.

(a) positive queries; KITTI - 10K

structure	pooling	rate(ms/1k)	speedup
inverted index	N/A	10.07	1.00
hierarchical	mean	**0.69**	**14.59**
	sum	8.70	1.16
	max	6.65	1.52

(b) negative queries; KITTI - 10K

structure	pooling	rate(ms/1k)	speedup
inverted index	N/A	9.86	1.00
hierarchical	mean	**0.34**	**29.00**
	sum	6.28	1.57
	max	5.04	1.96

(c) overall; KITTI - 10K

structure	pooling	rate(ms/1k)	speedup
inverted index	N/A	9.88	1.00
hierarchical	mean	**0.38**	**26.00**
	sum	7.92	1.25
	max	6.06	1.63

(d) overall; KITTI - 1M

structure	pooling	rate(ms/1k)	speedup
inverted index	N/A	0.64	1.00
hierarchical	mean	N/A	N/A
	sum	**0.30**	**2.13**
	max	**0.30**	**2.13**

Table 2. A comparison of search in flat and hierarchical structure on *KITTI* and *Oxford* dataset. Notations have the same meanings as in Table 1 except that 3rd column describes average time-cost rate over the 21 *KITTI keyframe* sequences and all 4 sequences in the *Oxford* dataset respectively. The keyframes are generated by running ORB-SLAM.

(a) overall; KITTI - 10K

structure	pooling	rate(ms/1k)	speedup
inverted index	N/A	8.97	1.00
hierarchical	mean	**0.88**	**10.14**
	sum	7.87	1.14
	max	6.00	1.50

(b) overall; Oxford - 10K

structure	pooling	rate(ms/1k)	speedup
inverted index	N/A	6.98	1.00
hierarchical	mean	**1.61**	**4.34**
	sum	4.71	1.48
	max	4.20	1.66

conditions. We use the same evaluation protocol provided by the author: Count how many of 4 images are top-4 when using a query image from that set of four images. We use pre-computed visual words provided by the authors, which are quantized SIFT descriptors using a 1 M vocabulary.

INRIA Holidays[3] contains 500 image groups (1491 total), each of which represents a distinct scene under different rotations, viewpoint and illumination changes, blurring, etc. Performance is measured by mean average precision (mAP) averaged over all 500 queries. We use the 4.5 million SIFT descriptors and 100 K vocabulary provided by the authors.

The baseline remains to search using an inverted index system. We use a three-layer hierarchy with the original histograms at the bottom layer. At the second layer, histograms belonging to the same object/scene are pooled (pooling

---

[3] https://lear.inrialpes.fr/~jegou/data.php.

Table 3. A comparison of search in flat and hierarchical structure on *ukbench* and *INRIA Holidays*. 1st col: grouping strategies. 2nd col: pooling operations. 3rd col: average query time. *ukbench* takes average number of top-4 retrieved images as score. *INRIA Holidays* takes mAP as evaluation metric.

(a) ukbench

structure	pooling	time(ms)	speedup	score
inverted index	N/A	1.47	1.00	2.72
Random hierarchical	mean	0.38	3.87	2.80
	sum	**0.37**	**3.97**	**2.83**
	max	0.39	3.77	2.82
Greedy affinity hierarchical	mean	0.38	3.87	2.80
	sum	0.38	3.87	**2.83**
	max	**0.37**	**3.97**	2.82

(b) INRIA Holidays

structure	pooling	time(ms)	speedup	mAP
inverted index	N/A	9.11	1.00	0.56
Random hierarchical	mean	**5.57**	**1.63**	0.58
	sum	6.19	1.47	**0.63**
	max	6.24	1.46	0.62
Greedy affinity hierarchical	mean	5.58	**1.63**	0.57
	sum	6.82	1.34	**0.63**
	max	6.53	1.40	0.62

based on prior information available about the data and problem space). At the top layer, we compare two different strategies to build the hierarchy: Random grouping and greedy affinity grouping. Random grouping: We randomly group every N histograms from the second layer. Greedy affinity grouping: We greedily group every N histograms based on their nearest neighbors in affinity (which is the histogram intersection score). In each setup, we also compare the different choices of pooling operators. Tables 3a and b show results on the *ukbench* and *INRIA Holidays* datasets with $N = 16$.

In these image retrieval tasks, we *completely discard the threshold and only search down those nodes which have top 10 highest scores*. Thus even for sum/max-pooling, the precision-recall behavior should be different from the baseline. All hierarchical approaches, regardless of pooling operation and grouping scheme, are faster than the baseline. The observation that speedup is available even for the random grouping scheme shows that the speedup does not just hinge on grouping similar images, though grouping similar images can boost the speedup further as we have shown in previous experiments on the driving data. We also notice improved score/mAP in these two experiments, likely due to the grouping of histograms of the same object/scene at the second layer of our hierarchy and the top-4 scoring mechanism imposed by the benchmark.

4   Discussion

We have presented a hierarchical data structure consisting of pooled local descriptors representing the likelihood of locations given the images they generate, while maintaining an inverted index at each level of the data structure. While mean-pooling of histograms may seem counter-productive, it is a sensible choice when considered an anti-aliasing procedure in the context of classical sampling theory, where the data structure, as well as keyframes, are tasked with *down-sampling* the native rate. We have compared several pooling strategies, and found that mean-pooling provides the most speedup at a small cost to performance; sum-pooling has the upper-bound property and accelerates search to a reasonable degree without loss of performance; and max-pooling shares the same property with sum-pooling but exhibits a larger speedup due better approximating the nodes below it.

For simplicity, we chose a fixed topology (depth and branching factor) and studied the resulting performance empirically. We have found that sophisticated heuristics do not improve performance enough to justify the added complexity. We have benchmarked our scheme on public datasets, where we have shown that even a shallow tree can significantly cut down on test time with minimal impact to precision, which is the main goal of loop closure.

Acknowledgements. This work was supported by AFRL FA8650-11-1-7156, ONR N00014-15-1-2261 and ARO W911NF-15-1-0564.

References

1. Aizawa, A.: An information-theoretic perspective of tf-idf measures. Inf. Process. Manage. **39**(1), 45–65 (2003)
2. Blei, D.M., Ng, A.Y., Jordan, M.I.: Latent dirichlet allocation. J. Mach. Learn. Res. **3**, 993–1022 (2003)
3. Calonder, M., Lepetit, V., Strecha, C., Fua, P.: BRIEF: binary robust independent elementary features. In: Daniilidis, K., Maragos, P., Paragios, N. (eds.) ECCV 2010. LNCS, vol. 6314, pp. 778–792. Springer, Heidelberg (2010). doi:10.1007/978-3-642-15561-1_56
4. Chetverikov, D., Svirko, D., Stepanov, D., Krsek, P.: The trimmed iterative closest point algorithm. In: 2002 IEEE International Conference on Pattern Recognition (ICPR), vol. 3, pp. 545–548. IEEE (2002)
5. Chum, O., Philbin, J., Sivic, J., Isard, M., Zisserman, A.: Total recall: automatic query expansion with a generative feature model for object retrieval. In: 2007 IEEE International Conference on Computer Vision (ICCV), pp. 1–8. IEEE (2007)
6. Cummins, M., Newman, P.: Highly scalable appearance-only slam-fab-map. 2.0. In: Robotics: Science and Systems, Seattle, USA, vol. 5 (2009)
7. Dong, J., Soatto, S.: Domain size pooling in local descriptors: Dsp-sift. In: 2015 IEEE Conference on Computer Vision and Pattern Recognition (CVPR) (2015)
8. Galvez-Lopez, D., Tardos, J.D.: Real-time loop detection with bags of binary words. In: 2011 IEEE/RSJ 2015 IEEE Conference on Intelligent Robots and Systems (IROS), pp. 51–58. IEEE (2011)
9. Geiger, A., Lenz, P., Stiller, C., Urtasun, R.: Vision meets robotics: the kitti dataset. Intl. J. of Robotics Res., 0278364913491297 (2013)
10. Geman, D., Jedynak, B.: An active testing model for tracking roads in satellite images. IEEE Trans. Pattern Anal. Mach. Intell. **18**(1), 1–14 (1996)
11. Girshick, R., Iandola, F., Darrell, T., Malik, J.: Deformable part models are convolutional neural networks (2014). arXiv preprint arXiv:1409.5403
12. Grauman, K., Darrell, T.: The pyramid match kernel: Discriminative classification with sets of image features. In: 2015 IEEE International Conference on Computer Vision (ICCV), vol. 2, pp. 1458–1465. IEEE (2005)
13. Jegou, H., Douze, M., Schmid, C.: Hamming embedding and weak geometric consistency for large scale image search. In: Forsyth, D., Torr, P., Zisserman, A. (eds.) ECCV 2008. LNCS, vol. 5302, pp. 304–317. Springer, Heidelberg (2008). doi:10.1007/978-3-540-88682-2_24

14. Jones, E., Soatto, S.: Visual-inertial navigation, localization and mapping: a scalable real-time large-scale approach. Intl. J. of Robotics Res. (2011)

15. Klein, G., Murray, D.: Parallel tracking and mapping for small AR workspaces. In: Proceedings of the 2007 6th IEEE and ACM International Symposium on Mixed and Augmented Reality, pp. 1–10. IEEE Computer Society (2007)

16. Lazebnik, S., Schmid, C., Ponce, J.: Beyond bags of features: spatial pyramid matching for recognizing natural scene categories. In: 2006 IEEE Conference on Computer Vision and Pattern Recognition (CVPR), vol. 2, pp. 2169–2178. IEEE (2006)

17. Lim, H., Lim, J., Kim, H.J.: Real-time 6-d of monocular visual slam in a large-scale environment. In: 2014 IEEE International Conference on Robotics and Automation (ICRA), pp. 1532–1539. IEEE (2014)

18. Mahendran, A., Vedaldi, A.: Understanding deep image representations by inverting them. In: 2015 IEEE Conference on Computer Vision and Pattern Recognition (CVPR), pp. 5188–5196. IEEE (2015)

19. Mur-Artal, R., Montiel, J., Tardos, J.D.: Orb-slam: a versatile and accurate monocular slam system. IEEE Trans. Rob. **31**(5), 1147–1163 (2015)

20. Newcombe, R.A., Davison, A.J.: Live dense reconstruction with a single moving camera. In: 2010 IEEE Conference on Computer Vision and Pattern Recognition (CVPR), pp. 1498–1505. IEEE (2010)

21. Nister, D., Stewenius, H.: Scalable recognition with a vocabulary tree. In: 2006 IEEE Conference on Computer Vision and Pattern Recognition (CVPR), vol. 2, pp. 2161–2168. IEEE (2006)

22. Rosten, E., Drummond, T.: Machine learning for high-speed corner detection. In: Leonardis, A., Bischof, H., Pinz, A. (eds.) ECCV 2006. LNCS, vol. 3951, pp. 430–443. Springer, Heidelberg (2006). doi:10.1007/11744023_34

23. Rublee, E., Rabaud, V., Konolige, K., Bradski, G.: Orb: an efficient alternative to sift or surf. In: 2011 IEEE International Conference on Computer Vision (ICCV), pp. 2564–2571. IEEE (2011)

24. Samet, H.: The design and analysis of spatial data structures, vol. 85. Addison-Wesley, Reading (1990)

25. Sattler, T., Leibe, B., Kobbelt, L.: Fast image-based localization using direct 2d-to-3d matching. In: 2011 IEEE International Conference on Computer Vision (ICCV), pp. 667–674. IEEE (2011)

26. Simonyan, K., Vedaldi, A., Zisserman, A.: Deep inside convolutional networks: visualising image classification models and saliency maps. In: Workshop at International Conference on Learning Representations (2014)

27. Sivic, J., Zisserman, A.: Video google: a text retrieval approach to object matching in videos. In: 2003 IEEE International Conference on Computer Vision (ICCV), pp. 1470–1477. IEEE (2003)

28. Smale, S., Zhou, D.X.: Shannon sampling ii: connections to learning theory. Appl. Comput. Harmonic Anal. **19**(3), 285–302 (2005)

29. Sturm, J., Engelhard, N., Endres, F., Burgard, W., Cremers, D.: A benchmark for the evaluation of rgb-d slam systems. In: 2012 IEEE/RSJ International Conference on Intelligent Robot Systems (IROS) (2012)

30. Swain, M.J., Ballard, D.H.: Color indexing. Intl. J. Comput. Vis. **7**(1), 11–32 (1991)

31. Tishby, N., Pereira, F.C., Bialek, W.: The information bottleneck method. In: Proceedings of the Allerton Conference (2000)

32. Torii, A., Sivic, J., Pajdla, T.: Visual localization by linear combination of image descriptors. In: 2011 IEEE International Conference on Computer Vision Workshops (ICCV Workshops), pp. 102–109. IEEE (2011)

33. Torralba, A., Murphy, K.P., Freeman, W.T., Rubin, M.A.: Context-based vision system for place and object recognition. In: 2003 IEEE International Conference on Computer Vision (ICCV), pp. 273–280. IEEE (2003)
34. Turcot, P., Lowe, D.G.: Better matching with fewer features: The selection of useful features in large database recognition problems. In: 2009 IEEE International Conference on Computer Vision Workshops (ICCV Workshops), pp. 2109–2116. IEEE (2009)
35. Ulrich, I., Nourbakhsh, I.: Appearance-based place recognition for topological localization. In: 2000 IEEE International Conference on Robotics and Automation (ICRA), vol. 2, pp. 1023–1029. IEEE (2000)
36. Vasconcelos, N.: On the efficient evaluation of probabilistic similarity functions for image retrieval. IEEE Trans. Inf. Theory $50(7)$, 1482–1496 (2004)
37. Williams, B., Cummins, M., Neira, J., Newman, P., Reid, I., Tardós, J.: A comparison of loop closing techniques in monocular slam. Rob. Auton. Syst. $57(12)$, 1188–1197 (2009)

A Versatile Approach for Solving PnP, PnPf, and PnPfr Problems

Gaku Nakano[✉]

Central Research Labs, NEC Corporation, Kawasaki, Japan
g-nakano@cq.jp.nec.com

Abstract. This paper proposes a versatile approach for solving three kinds of absolute camera pose estimation problem: PnP problem for calibrated cameras, PnPf problem for cameras with unknown focal length, and PnPfr problem for cameras with unknown focal length and unknown radial distortion. This is not only the first least squares solution to PnPfr problem, but also the first approach formulating three problems in the same theoretical manner. We show that all problems have a common subproblem represented as multivariate polynomial equations. Solving these equations by Gröbner basis method, we derive a linear form for the remaining parameters of each problem. Finally, we apply root polishing to strictly satisfy the original KKT condition. The proposed PnP and PnPf solvers have comparable performance to the state-of-the-art methods on synthetic distortion-free data. Moreover, the novel PnPfr solver gives the best result on distorted point data and demonstrates real image rectification against significant distortion.

Keywords: Absolute camera pose estimation · PnP Problem · Focal Length · Radial distortion

1 Introduction

Camera parameter estimation from n pairs of 2D-3D point correspondence in a single image has been a fundamental problem in computer vision and photogrammetry community. The camera parameters consist of two kinds of parameters. One is the extrinsic parameters which determine the position and the orientation of the camera, i.e., 3D rotation and translation. The other is the intrinsic parameters which are optical properties of the camera unaffected by the extrinsic parameters, i.e., focal length, skew, principal point, aspect ratio, lens distortion, etc. The name of the parameter estimation problem is different depending on unknown parameters: Perspective-n-Point (PnP) problem when the extrinsic parameters are unknown and all the intrinsic parameters are calibrated in advance, PnPf problem for partially calibrated cameras when only focal length is known, PnPfr problem when radial distortion of the lens is additionally unknown.

Electronic supplementary material The online version of this chapter (doi:10.1007/978-3-319-46487-9_21) contains supplementary material, which is available to authorized users.

© Springer International Publishing AG 2016
B. Leibe et al. (Eds.): ECCV 2016, Part III, LNCS 9907, pp. 338–352, 2016.
DOI: 10.1007/978-3-319-46487-9_21

It is well discussed that $n = 3$ is the minimal number of the points required to solve PnP problem [1–3]. The trend of the latest PnP solvers is to find the global optimal solution for $n \geq 3$ case in linear complexity $O(n)$ without considering planar or non-planar scene. The first $O(n)$ method is EPnP [4], but it does not assure the global optimality. Hesch and Roumeliotis [5] proposed Direct Least Square method (DLS) which finds all stationary points of the first optimality condition, also known as the Karush–Kuhn–Tucker (KKT) condition, by solving a system of nonlinear multivariate polynomial equations. The DLS approach has been improved for more stability and efficiency [6, 7], and extended to generalized camera model which has multiple focal points [8]. However, applications of PnP problem are limited due to the strict assumption that the intrinsic parameters are never changed during shooting a scene. Prior full calibration is mandatory, but it is difficult for cameras having a zoom lens.

PnPf problem deals with a relaxed assumption where the intrinsic parameters are known except for focal length. Since principal point, skew, and aspect ratio are invariant to zoom change, focal length is the only varying parameter. Moreover, for recent digital cameras, we can assume that zero skew (square pixels), one aspect ratio (parallel mount of lens and camera), and principal point is at the image center (center aligned lens and camera). P4Pf [9–11] and PnPf [12–14] solvers have been proposed, which use $n = 4$ for the minimal case and $n \geq 4$ for the least square case, respectively. Kanaeva et al. [14] extended EPnP to PnPf problem by improving EPnP's drawbacks, and pointed out that Zheng et al.'s PnPf solver [13] sometimes fails to calculate focal length on real data. However, PnPf problem's assumption ignores the fact that lens distortion is also changeable according to zoom variation. Similarly to PnP problem, complete prior lens distortion correction is difficult for zooming cameras. Therefore, PnPf solvers can handle only slight zoom change where lens distortion can be ignored or approximated by fixed parameters.

To deal with lens distortion, P4Pfr [15, 16] and P5Pfr [17] solvers have been developed. They modeled radial lens distortion by Fitzgibbon's division model [18] for simple formulations. Kukelova et al. [17] showed that the three-parameter division model is practically sufficient for 3D shape reconstruction from real images even with significant distortion. Since these solvers are designed for the minimal case, they cannot improve the parameter accuracy for n points without a costly reprojection error minimization. Addition to the P4Pfr and P5Pfr solvers, some methods correcting lens distortion from a single image have been proposed [19, 20]. However, those methods are not sufficiently fast for real-time applications, such as Visual SLAM and augmented reality.

This paper proposes three solvers for PnP, PnPf, and PnPfr problems which are derived from the same theoretical formulation. Inspired by Kukelova et al.'s P5Pfr solver [17], the key is to find a common subproblem among the three problems. The common subproblem is expressed by only a part of the extrinsic parameters, therefore, this subproblem can be solved by Gröbner basis method similarly to the existing PnP solvers [6–8]. Regarding the solutions of the common subproblem as known parameters, we show that estimation of the remaining parameters can be formulated as a linear problem. This part slightly differs

Table 1. Comparison of PnP, PnPf, and PnPfr problems. Numbers marked with † and * indicate the case of the one- and the three-parameter division model for radial distortion, respectively. This paper discusses only the latter case

Parameters	PnP	PnPf	PnPfr
Rotation	✓	✓	✓
Translation	✓	✓	✓
Focal length		✓	✓
Radial distortion			✓
# of parameters	6	7	$8^†$, 10^*
Required points	3	4	$4^†$, 5^*

depending on each problem but can be solved in the same manner. Finally, for easy implementation of root polishing, we derive new equations without Lagrange multipliers, which are equivalent to the original KKT condition. This is an extension of Nakano's approach for PnP problem [7].

Synthetic data experiments show that the proposed PnP and PnPf solvers have the same accuracy and efficiency as the state-of-the-art methods on PnP and PnPf problems without lens distortion. For lens distortion data, the proposed PnPfr solver is the only method that is able to improve the parameter accuracy with increasing the number of the points. Moreover, we show that the PnPfr solver successfully corrects significant lens distortion on real images taken by an ultra-wide zoom camera.

2 Problem Formulation

This section describes mathematical formulations of PnP, PnPf, and PnPfr problems. In this paper, we assume the standard pinhole camera model for the projection between 2D-3D point correspondences and the three-parameter division model for radial distortion [17].

The projection of a 3D point $\mathbf{p}_i = [x_i, y_i, z_i]^\mathsf{T}$ onto a 2D image point $\mathbf{m}_i = [u_i, v_i, w_i]^\mathsf{T}$ represented by the homogeneous coordinates can be written as

$$\mathbf{m}_i \sim \mathsf{K}(\mathsf{R}\mathbf{p}_i + \mathbf{t}), \tag{1}$$

where $\sim$ denotes equality up to scale, R is a 3×3 rotation matrix, $\mathbf{t} = [t_x, t_y, t_z]^\mathsf{T}$ is a translation vector, and $\mathsf{K} = diag([1, 1, f^{-1}])$ is the calibration matrix of the camera with focal length f. As mentioned in Sect. 1, we assume zero skew, one aspect ratio, and principal point corresponding to the image center.

The common unknowns among PnP, PnPf, and PnPfr problems are the extrinsic parameters, R and $\mathbf{t}$. The homogeneous term w_i and intrinsic parameters to be estimated are different in each problem. In PnP problem, $w_i = 1$ and f is known. In PnPf problem, $w_i = 1$ but f is unknown. In PnPfr problem, f is also unknown and $w_i = 1 + \mathbf{k}^\mathsf{T}\mathbf{d}_i$, where $\mathbf{d}_i = [u_i^2 + v_i^2, (u_i^2 + v_i^2)^2, (u_i^2 + v_i^2)^3]^\mathsf{T}$ and $\mathbf{k} = [k_1, k_2, k_3]^\mathsf{T}$ is a 3×1 vector containing the unknown radial distortion coefficients.

Note that the image coordinates u_i and v_i represent undistorted points in PnP and PnPf problems but distorted points in PnPfr problem. Hereafter, for simple notations, this paper does not distinguish the description of distorted or undistorted points.

Now we formulate PnPfr problem. PnP and PnPf problems can be similarly derived by regarding f or $\mathbf{k}$ as the knowns. Given n point correspondences, PnPfr problem can be written as a constrained nonlinear optimization,

$$\min_{\mathbf{R},\mathbf{t},f,\mathbf{k}} \sum_{i=1}^{n} \left\| [\mathbf{m}_i]_\times \mathrm{K}(\mathrm{R}\mathbf{p}_i + \mathbf{t}) \right\|^2 \tag{2}$$
$$\text{s.t.} \quad \mathrm{R}^\mathsf{T}\mathrm{R} = \mathrm{I}, \quad det(\mathrm{R}) = 1,$$

where $[\ ]_\times$ denotes a matrix representation of the vector cross product, i.e.,

$$[\mathbf{m}_i]_\times = \begin{bmatrix} 0 & -w_i & v_i \\ w_i & 0 & -u_i \\ -v_i & u_i & 0 \end{bmatrix}. \tag{3}$$

This operator is introduced to eliminate the scale ambiguity of Eq. (1).

In Eq. (2), the total number of the unknowns is 10, of which three from R, three from $\mathbf{t}$, one from f, and three from $\mathbf{k}$. Since $[\mathbf{m}_i]_\times$ is of rank two, Eq. (1) gives us two equations for each point correspondences. Therefore, Eq. (2) can be solved by $n \geq 5$ point correspondence. PnP and PnPf problems are also solvable because they have totally six and seven unknowns, which are less than 10, respectively. Table 1 summarizes the unknown parameters and the number of the unknowns in each problem.

3   Proposed Method

This section describes the derivation of the proposed method. We begin with an overview of the key idea, which divides the least squares problem into two subproblems. Then, we derive efficient solutions to the subproblems based on Gröbner basis method and a linear method, respectively. Finally, we introduce a root polishing technique to satisfy the KKT condition of the original problem.

3.1   Overview

Define three row vectors $\mathbf{a}_i^\mathsf{T}$, $\mathbf{b}_i^\mathsf{T}$, and $\mathbf{c}_i^\mathsf{T}$ corresponding to the first, second and third row of $[\mathbf{m}_i]_\times$, respectively. Note that those terms contain the unknown radial distortion $\mathbf{k}$ in w_i. By introducing them into Eq. (2), the cost function can be rewritten by

$$\min_{\mathbf{R},\mathbf{t},f,\mathbf{k}} \sum_{i=1}^{n} \left\| [\mathbf{m}_i]_\times \mathbf{q}_i \right\|^2 = \sum_{i=1}^{n} (\mathbf{a}_i^\mathsf{T}\mathbf{q}_i)^2 + (\mathbf{b}_i^\mathsf{T}\mathbf{q}_i)^2 + (\mathbf{c}_i^\mathsf{T}\mathbf{q}_i)^2, \tag{4}$$

where $\mathbf{q}_i = \mathrm{K}(\mathrm{R}\mathbf{p}_i + \mathbf{t})$. The rotation matrix constraints are omitted here.

Interpreting Eq. (4) from the point of view of algebraic geometry, the two vectors, $\mathbf{m}_i$ and $\mathbf{q}_i$, are collinear without noise in data. In other words, minimizing Eq. (4) with noisy data is equivalent to finding the optimal parameters so that the three terms are closed to zeros. Therefore, if we minimized each term as an independent subproblem and obtained solutions from them, we can expect that one of the solutions is closed to the global optimum. This is the key idea of the proposed method.

Let us move on how to build the subproblems. Expanding $\mathbf{a}_i^\mathsf{T}\mathbf{q}_i$, $\mathbf{b}_i^\mathsf{T}\mathbf{q}_i$ and $\mathbf{c}_i^\mathsf{T}\mathbf{q}_i$, we obtain

$$\mathbf{a}_i^\mathsf{T}\mathbf{q}_i = -w_i(\mathbf{r}_2^\mathsf{T}\mathbf{p}_i + t_y) + v_i f^{-1}(\mathbf{r}_3^\mathsf{T}\mathbf{p}_i + t_z), \tag{5}$$

$$\mathbf{b}_i^\mathsf{T}\mathbf{q}_i = w_i(\mathbf{r}_1^\mathsf{T}\mathbf{p}_i + t_x) - u_i f^{-1}(\mathbf{r}_3^\mathsf{T}\mathbf{p}_i + t_z), \tag{6}$$

$$\mathbf{c}_i^\mathsf{T}\mathbf{q}_i = -v_i(\mathbf{r}_1^\mathsf{T}\mathbf{p}_i + t_x) + u_i(\mathbf{r}_2^\mathsf{T}\mathbf{p}_i + t_y), \tag{7}$$

where $\mathbf{r}_j$ denotes the j-th row of $\mathbf{R}$. Interestingly, Eq. (7) does not have w_i, a function of $\mathbf{k}$, and is expressed by only a part of the extrinsic parameters, $\mathbf{r}_1$, $\mathbf{r}_2$, t_x, and t_y whereas Eqs. (5) and (6) consist of all the unknown parameters.

Thus, we can define the first subproblem by

$$\min_{\mathbf{r}_1,\mathbf{r}_2,t_x,t_y} \sum_{i=1}^{n}(\mathbf{c}_i^\mathsf{T}\mathbf{q}_i)^2 \tag{8}$$
$$\text{s.t.} \quad \|\mathbf{r}_1\|^2 = 1, \quad \|\mathbf{r}_1\|^2 - \|\mathbf{r}_2\|^2 = 0, \quad \mathbf{r}_1^\mathsf{T}\mathbf{r}_2 = 0.$$

There seems to be eight unknowns in Eq. (8). However, actual degrees of freedom is five due to the three constraints for $\mathbf{r}_1$ and $\mathbf{r}_2$. Therefore, Eq. (8) can be solved by $n \geq 5$ point correspondences. After finding $\mathbf{r}_1$ and $\mathbf{r}_2$, we can recover $\mathbf{R}$ by calculating the third row, $\mathbf{r}_3 = \mathbf{r}_1 \times \mathbf{r}_2$.

Plugging $\mathbf{R}$, t_x, and t_y into Eqs. (5) and (6), we still have five unknowns, t_z, f, and $\mathbf{k}$. Since the rotation matrix has been already estimated, the remaining unknowns do not have any constraints.

Therefore, we can build the second subproblem as

$$\min_{t_z,f,\mathbf{k}} \sum_{i=1}^{n}(\mathbf{a}_i^\mathsf{T}\mathbf{q}_i)^2 + (\mathbf{b}_i^\mathsf{T}\mathbf{q}_i)^2. \tag{9}$$

Given $n \geq 5$ point correspondences, we can solve Eq. (9) because $2n$ equations are available for the five unknowns.

The estimated parameters from the above two subproblems are not the optimal solution to the original problem, Eq. (4). Therefore, we finally refine the parameters by conducting a root polishing to get more accuracy and optimality.

From Sects. 3.2 to 3.4, we will discuss the details of specific methods for each step.

3.2 Solving the First Subproblem

From Eq. (7), the cost function of Eq. (8) can be rewritten by

$$\min_{\mathbf{r}_1,\mathbf{r}_2,t_x,t_y} \sum_{i=1}^{n}(\mathbf{c}_i^\mathsf{T}\mathbf{q}_i)^2 = \left\|A\hat{\mathbf{r}} + B\hat{\mathbf{t}}\right\|^2, \tag{10}$$

where

$$A = \begin{bmatrix} -v_1\mathbf{p}_1^\mathsf{T} & u_1\mathbf{p}_1^\mathsf{T} \\ \vdots & \vdots \\ -v_n\mathbf{p}_n^\mathsf{T} & u_n\mathbf{p}_n^\mathsf{T} \end{bmatrix}, \quad B = \begin{bmatrix} -v_1 & u_1 \\ \vdots & \vdots \\ -v_n & u_n \end{bmatrix}, \quad \hat{\mathbf{r}} = \begin{bmatrix} \mathbf{r}_1 \\ \mathbf{r}_2 \end{bmatrix}, \quad \hat{\mathbf{t}} = \begin{bmatrix} t_x \\ t_y \end{bmatrix}. \tag{11}$$

Since there are no constraints about $\hat{\mathbf{t}}$, we can express $\hat{\mathbf{t}}$ as a function of $\hat{\mathbf{r}}$, i.e.,

$$\hat{\mathbf{t}} = -(B^\mathsf{T}B)^{-1}B^\mathsf{T}A\hat{\mathbf{r}}. \tag{12}$$

Substituting this into Eq. (10), we obtain a new constrained problem as follows:

$$\min_{\mathbf{r}_1,\mathbf{r}_2} \hat{\mathbf{r}}^\mathsf{T}M\hat{\mathbf{r}} \\ \text{s.t. } \left\|\mathbf{r}_1\right\|^2 = 1, \quad \left\|\mathbf{r}_1\right\|^2 - \left\|\mathbf{r}_2\right\|^2 = 0, \quad \mathbf{r}_1^\mathsf{T}\mathbf{r}_2 = 0, \tag{13}$$

where

$$M = A^\mathsf{T}A - A^\mathsf{T}B(B^\mathsf{T}B)^{-1}B^\mathsf{T}A. \tag{14}$$

Since Eq. (13) has a similar form in the existing PnP solvers [6–8], we can use same Gröbner basis technique for solving the optimal $\hat{\mathbf{r}}$. If we introduce a quaternion based parameterization for representing the rotation matrix as in [6,8], we obtain up to 40 solutions, which is exactly the same number of the solutions to [6–8]. However, there is a sign ambiguity for $\mathbf{r}_1$ and $\mathbf{r}_2$, that means $-\mathbf{r}_1$ and $-\mathbf{r}_2$ also give the minimum error with satisfying the constraints. Therefore, the number of the solutions is actually 20, not 40. Any quaternion based parameterizations cannot distinguish the sign ambiguity of $\pm\hat{\mathbf{r}}$ because quaternion has a sign ambiguity in itself. To obtain 20 solutions by Gröbner basis method, we need to derive new equations independent to the norm definition of $\mathbf{r}_1$ and $\mathbf{r}_2$.

Let M_{ij} be a (i,j) entry of 3×3 block matrix which partitions the 6×6 matrix M into 2×2 blocks. The Lagrange function of Eq. (13) can be written by

$$L = \mathbf{r}_1^\mathsf{T}M_{11}\mathbf{r}_1 + 2\mathbf{r}_1^\mathsf{T}M_{12}\mathbf{r}_2 + \mathbf{r}_2^\mathsf{T}M_{22}\mathbf{r}_2 \\ + \lambda_1(1 - \left\|\mathbf{r}_1\right\|^2) + \lambda_2(\left\|\mathbf{r}_1\right\|^2 - \left\|\mathbf{r}_2\right\|^2) + 2\lambda_3\mathbf{r}_1^\mathsf{T}\mathbf{r}_2, \tag{15}$$

where λ_i is a Lagrange multiplier and the multiplier 2 for λ_3 is merely for convenience. The KKT condition of Eq. (15) is given by

$$\frac{\partial L}{\partial \mathbf{r}_1} = M_{11}\mathbf{r}_1 + M_{12}\mathbf{r}_2 + (\lambda_2 - \lambda_1)\mathbf{r}_1 + \lambda_3 \mathbf{r}_2 = \mathbf{0}, \tag{16}$$

$$\frac{\partial L}{\partial \mathbf{r}_2} = M_{22}\mathbf{r}_2 + M_{12}^\mathsf{T}\mathbf{r}_1 - \lambda_2 \mathbf{r}_2 + \lambda_3 \mathbf{r}_1 = \mathbf{0}, \tag{17}$$

$$\frac{\partial L}{\partial \lambda_1} = 1 - \|\mathbf{r}_1\|^2 = 0, \tag{18}$$

$$\frac{\partial L}{\partial \lambda_2} = \|\mathbf{r}_1\|^2 - \|\mathbf{r}_2\|^2 = 0, \tag{19}$$

$$\frac{\partial L}{\partial \lambda_3} = \mathbf{r}_1^\mathsf{T}\mathbf{r}_2 = 0, \tag{20}$$

Multiplying $[\mathbf{r}_1]_\times$ and $[\mathbf{r}_2]_\times$ to Eqs. (16) and (17), respectively, we obtain

$$[\mathbf{r}_1]_\times (M_{11}\mathbf{r}_1 + M_{12}\mathbf{r}_2) + \lambda_3 [\mathbf{r}_1]_\times \mathbf{r}_2 = \mathbf{0}, \tag{21}$$

$$[\mathbf{r}_2]_\times (M_{22}\mathbf{r}_2 + M_{12}^\mathsf{T}\mathbf{r}_1) + \lambda_3 [\mathbf{r}_2]_\times \mathbf{r}_1 = \mathbf{0}. \tag{22}$$

Using the relation $[\mathbf{r}_1]_\times \mathbf{r}_2 = -[\mathbf{r}_2]_\times \mathbf{r}_1$, we can eliminate λ_3 by adding Eqs. (21) and (22). Thus, we obtain

$$[\mathbf{r}_1]_\times (M_{11}\mathbf{r}_1 + M_{12}\mathbf{r}_2) + [\mathbf{r}_2]_\times (M_{22}\mathbf{r}_2 + M_{12}^\mathsf{T}\mathbf{r}_1) = \mathbf{0}. \tag{23}$$

Moreover, multiplying $\mathbf{r}_2^\mathsf{T}$ and $\mathbf{r}_1^\mathsf{T}$ to Eqs. (16) and (17), respectively, we obtain

$$\mathbf{r}_2^\mathsf{T}(M_{11}\mathbf{r}_1 + M_{12}\mathbf{r}_2) + \lambda_3 \|\mathbf{r}_2\|^2 = 0, \tag{24}$$

$$\mathbf{r}_1^\mathsf{T}(M_{22}\mathbf{r}_2 + M_{12}^\mathsf{T}\mathbf{r}_1) + \lambda_3 \|\mathbf{r}_1\|^2 = 0. \tag{25}$$

Since the norm of $\mathbf{r}_1$ and $\mathbf{r}_2$ are equal to each other as in Eq. (19), we can also eliminate λ_3 by subtracting Eq. (24) from Eq. (25),

$$\mathbf{r}_2^\mathsf{T}(M_{11}\mathbf{r}_1 + M_{12}\mathbf{r}_2) - \mathbf{r}_1^\mathsf{T}(M_{22}\mathbf{r}_2 + M_{12}^\mathsf{T}\mathbf{r}_1) = 0. \tag{26}$$

It should be noted that Eqs. (23) and (26) hold for any types of normalization of $\mathbf{r}_1$ as long as the other constraints, Eqs. (19) and (20), are satisfied. Hence, instead of Eq. (18), we can use a linear constraint for eliminating the sign ambiguity of $\mathbf{r}_1$ and $\mathbf{r}_2$, e.g., $r_{11} = 1$ or $r_{11} + r_{12} + r_{13} = 1$, where r_{ij} is the (i, j) element of R. Therefore, we can obtain $\mathbf{r}_1$ and $\mathbf{r}_2$ by solving Eqs. (19), (20), (23), and (26) together with the new linear constraint for $\mathbf{r}_1$.

Since the above equations can be represented by a system of nonlinear polynomial equations, the solution can be obtained by using Gröbner basis method. A simple way is to use an automatic generator of Gröbner basis solvers developed by Kukelova et al. [21]. In our case, the automatic generator gives a 105×125 template matrix for Gauss-Jordan elimination and a 20×20 action matrix for the eigenvalue computation. We obtained a further optimized 97×117 template matrix by sorting all equations before starting necessary equation extraction in the automatic solver. This solver gives at most 20 pairs of $\mathbf{r}_1$ and $\mathbf{r}_2$, from which we can recover $\hat{\mathbf{t}}$ by Eq. (12) and two rotation matrices by considering the sign ambiguity:

$$R = \begin{bmatrix} \mathbf{r}_1^{\mathsf{T}} \\ \mathbf{r}_2^{\mathsf{T}} \\ (\mathbf{r}_1 \times \mathbf{r}_2)^{\mathsf{T}} \end{bmatrix}, \quad R = \begin{bmatrix} -\mathbf{r}_1^{\mathsf{T}} \\ -\mathbf{r}_2^{\mathsf{T}} \\ (\mathbf{r}_1 \times \mathbf{r}_2)^{\mathsf{T}} \end{bmatrix}. \tag{27}$$

An example code for the automatic generator of this subproblem is shown in Appendix A in the supplemental material.

3.3 Solving the Second Subproblem

The solution to the second subproblem slightly differs on PnP, PnPf, PnPfr problems. Due to limitations of space, we show a solution to PnPfr problem only. Solutions to PnP and PnPf problems are described in Appendix B in the supplemental material.

Regarding R, t_x, and t_y from Sect. 3.2 as known parameters, we can rewrite Eq. (9) as

$$\min_{t_z, f, \mathbf{k}} \sum_{i=1}^{n} \left\| \begin{bmatrix} \mathbf{a}_i^{\mathsf{T}} \\ \mathbf{b}_i^{\mathsf{T}} \end{bmatrix} \mathbf{q}_i \right\|^2 = \|L\mathbf{x} + \mathbf{g}\|^2, \tag{28}$$

where

$$L = \begin{bmatrix} v_1 & v_1 z_1^c & -y_1^c \mathbf{d}_1^{\mathsf{T}} \\ -u_1 & -u_1 z_1^c & x_1^c \mathbf{d}_1^{\mathsf{T}} \\ & \vdots & \\ v_n & v_n z_1^c & -y_n^c \mathbf{d}_n^{\mathsf{T}} \\ -u_n & -u_n z_1^c & x_n^c \mathbf{d}_n^{\mathsf{T}} \end{bmatrix}, \quad \mathbf{x} = \begin{bmatrix} f^{-1} t_z \\ f^{-1} \\ \mathbf{k} \end{bmatrix}, \quad \mathbf{g} = \begin{bmatrix} -y_1^c \\ x_1^c \\ \vdots \\ -y_n^c \\ x_n^c \end{bmatrix}, \tag{29}$$

$$x_i^c = \mathbf{r}_1^{\mathsf{T}} \mathbf{p}_i + t_x, \quad y_i^c = \mathbf{r}_2^{\mathsf{T}} \mathbf{p}_i + t_y, \quad z_i^c = \mathbf{r}_3^{\mathsf{T}} \mathbf{p}_i.$$

This is a linear form for the unknown vector $\mathbf{x}$, therefore, the solution can be obtained by solving a normal equation $\mathbf{x} = -(L^{\mathsf{T}}L)^{-1}L^{\mathsf{T}}\mathbf{g}$. Then, t_z can be recovered by dividing the first element by the second element in $\mathbf{x}$.

3.4 Root Polishing

As a result from Sects. 3.2 and 3.3, we can obtain all the unknown parameters. However, these parameters are not the optimal solution because the subproblems are kinds of approximation of the original problem. In order to increase the accuracy and optimality, we introduce a root polishing technique so that the parameters strictly satisfies the KKT condition.

Let us recall the original PnPfr problem, Eq. (4). Since $\mathbf{a}_i$, $\mathbf{b}_i$, and $\mathbf{c}_i$ are linearly independent, we can equivalently rewrite the cost function of Eq. (4) as

$$\min_{R, \mathbf{t}, f, \mathbf{k}} \sum_{i=1}^{n} (\mathbf{a}_i^{\mathsf{T}} \mathbf{q}_i)^2 + (\mathbf{b}_i^{\mathsf{T}} \mathbf{q}_i)^2 = \|C_{(f, \mathbf{k})}\mathbf{r} + D_{(f, \mathbf{k})}\mathbf{t}\|^2, \tag{30}$$

where $C_{(f,k)}$ and $D_{(f,k)}$ are $n \times 9$ and $n \times 3$ coefficient matrices containing the unknowns f and k, respectively. Due to limitations of space, we describe the details of the formulation in Appendix C in the supplemental material.

Similarly to the first subproblem in Sect. 3.2, we can express t as a function of the other unknowns,

$$t_{(r,f,k)} = -(D^T D)^{-1} D^T C r. \tag{31}$$

Here, we omitted the subscript (f, k) of C and D for simple notations. Then, plugging Eq. (31) into Eq. (30), we obtain a new constrained problem

$$\begin{aligned} \min_{r,f,k} \quad & r^T G_{(f,k)} r \\ \text{s.t.} \quad & R^T R = I, \quad det(R) = 1, \end{aligned} \tag{32}$$

where

$$G_{(f,k)} = C^T C - C^T D (D^T D)^{-1} D^T C. \tag{33}$$

Root polishing is performed to find the optimal solution of Eq. (32), a constrained problem, with initial guess from the first and the second subproblems. A typical and easy way to solve Eq. (32) is convert the constrained problem into an unconstrained problem by expressing the rotation matrix with Euler angle or Cayley transform. However, those representations cannot be uniquely determined in the singularity case, which often happens in real camera motions. Alternative way is to solve new equations, which are equivalent to the original KKT condition without any Lagrange multipliers. Introducing Nakano's approach [7] for PnP problem, we obtain such new equations as follows:

$$R^T mat(Gr) - mat(Gr)^T R = 0_{3\times3}, \tag{34}$$

$$mat(Gr) R^T - R \, mat(Gr)^T = 0_{3\times3}, \tag{35}$$

$$R^T R - I = 0_{3\times3}, \tag{36}$$

$$det(R) - 1 = 0, \tag{37}$$

$$\frac{\partial}{\partial f} r^T Gr = 0, \tag{38}$$

$$\frac{\partial}{\partial k} r^T Gr = 0_{3\times1}. \tag{39}$$

Here, $mat(\ )$ is a reshaping operator from a 9×1 vector to a 3×3 square matrix. As Nakano proved in [7], the above equations hold for any types of rotation parameterization instead of Eqs. (36) and (37), e.g., quaternion.

We can solve the system of nonlinear equations, Eq. (34) through Eq. (39), by a simple Gauss-Newton method. An important thing to note here is that numerical differentiation is required in the Gauss-Newton iteration for PnPfr problem because $G_{(f,k)}$, Eq. (33), cannot be analytically represented by the two unknonws, f and k. On the other hand, in the case of PnP and PnPf problems, we can compute C and D without the unknowns and do not need to update G

in the iteration. The details of the formulation are also described in Appendix C in the supplemental material. This procedure takes less than 10 iterations in almost all cases as long as we have tested. After the convergence, we can recover t according to Eq. (31).

4   Experiments on Synthetic Data

Using synthetic data, we have evaluated the proposed PnP, PnPf and PnPfr solvers on accuracy with respect to varying the number of the points n and varying zero-mean Gaussian noise with standard deviation σ on image points. All tests were executed on Core i7-6700 with 16GB RAM on MATLAB 2015b.

In this section, we call our PnP, PnPf, and PnPfr solvers as VPnP, VPnPf, and VPnPfr. The proposed solvers were compared with the following existing methods; EPnP+GN [4], OPnP [6], UPnP [8] for PnP problem, and DLT [22], GPnPf+GN [13], EPnPfR [14][1] for PnPf and PnPfr problems. We used the original MATLAB code available on the web except for UPnP written in C++.

Due to limitations of space, we will discuss non-planar scene only. However, the conclusion and the tendency of the methods would not change if tested with planar scene. We generated randomly distributed 3D points in the x-, y-, and z-range of $[-2, 2] \times [-2, 2] \times [4, 8]$. Then, those points are projected onto a virtual camera with image resolution 640×480 [pixels], focal length 800 [pixels], principal point at the coordinate $[320, 240]$. For evaluating VPnPfr, we distorted image points by small radial distortion $[k_1, k_2, k_3] = [-0.1, 0, 0]$, and compared with the conventional PnPf solvers assuming zero distortion. In the case of PnPf and PnPfr problems, as suggested in [15], we scaled image points with a factor of $2/\max(width, height)$ so that all points have normalized coordinates between ± 1. The ground-truth rotation and translation of the camera are randomly generated. We measured the relative error of estimated parameters except for the rotation matrix. The rotation error was the absolute error given by $\max_{k \in \{1,2,3\}} \cos^{-1}(\mathbf{r}_k^\mathsf{T} \mathbf{r}_{k,true})$ [degrees], where $\mathbf{r}_k$ and $\mathbf{r}_{k,true}$ are k-th column of the estimated and the ground-truth rotation matrices, respectively. We performed 500 independent trials for each test.

4.1   Accuracy w.r.t. Varying Number of Points

We configured $6 \leq n \leq 100$ and $\sigma = 2$ in this experiment. The reason for starting by $n = 6$ is that DLT and EPnP+GN cannot work on $n = 5$. Figure 1 shows the median errors of PnP, PnPf, and PnPfr solvers.

In the case of PnP and PnPf problems (top and middle in Fig. 1), most of the solvers except for DLT have same performance. This result shows that the proposed approach, which sequentially solves subproblems, gives globally optimal solution as the existing methods do.

---

[1] EPnPfR is not a method for PnPfr problem but an extension of EPnP to PnPf problem. Although the meaning of "fR" is not mentioned in the paper, it is inferred "focal length" and "Regularization" for EPnP.

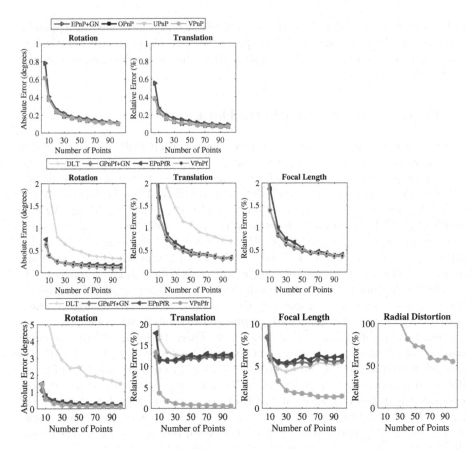

Fig. 1. Median error w.r.t. varying number of points ($6 \leq n \leq 100$) with fixed image noise ($\sigma = 2$). *Top*: PnP problem. *Middle*: PnPf problem. *Bottom*: PnPfr problem

As shown in the bottom plots in Fig. 1, VPnPfr outperforms the other methods in the case of distorted image points. Interestingly, the existing PnPf solvers cannot improve the accuracy of translation and focal length with increasing n, whereas the rotation error becomes lower. The result of the intrinsic parameters implies that VPnPfr requires $n \geq 100$ for focal length and radial distortion estimation to converge the optimal solution on $\sigma = 2$.

4.2 Accuracy w.r.t. Varying Image Noise

In the next experiment, we have studied the accuracy with respect to varying $1 \leq \sigma \leq 5$ in the case of fixed $n = 20$. The median errors of PnP, PnPf, and PnPfr solvers are shown on top, middle, and bottom, in Fig. 2, respectively.

Similarly to the previous experiment in Sect. 4.1, our VPnP and VPnPf have comparable performance to the state-of-the-art solvers in PnP and PnPf problems. In addition to that, we can also observe an interesting result in the case of PnPfr problem.

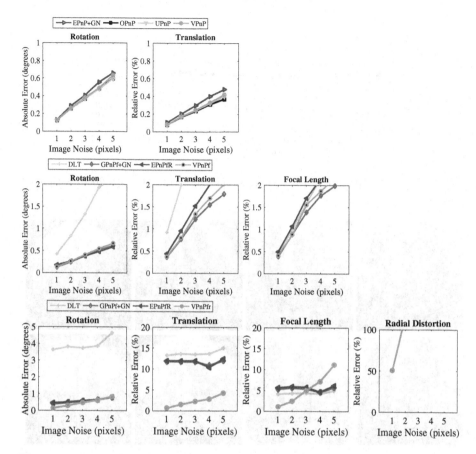

Fig. 2. Median error w.r.t. varying image noise ($1 \leq \sigma \leq 5$) with fixed number of points ($n = 20$). *Top*: PnP problem. *Middle*: PnPf problem. *Bottom*: PnPfr problem

As the image noise increases, focal length estimation of VPnPfr becomes worse than that of PnPf solvers, which assume zero distortion. The image noise seems to affect translation rather than focal length for PnPf solvers. From this, if we need only focal length, PnPf solvers might be more suitable than VPnPfr when the image points have potentially large errors. However, VPnPfr is still the best method for estimating the intrinsic and extrinsic parameter simultaneously.

4.3 Computational Time w.r.t. Varying Number of Points

We measured the computational time with $6 \leq n \leq 2000$ and $\sigma = 2$. Figure 3 shows the average time. Note that UPnP is a mex implementation.

The proposed VPnP and VPnPf take less than 3 ms which is sufficiently fast for real-time applications. Moreover, these runtime increases moderately, almost in $O(1)$, even in the thousands of the points. This is the fastest for large number of points, $n \geq 400$. In contrast, the runtime of VPnPfr grows $O(n)$. The solver

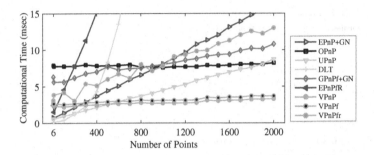

Fig. 3. Computational time w.r.t. varying number of points ($6 \leq n \leq 2000$) with fixed image noise ($\sigma = 2$)

Fig. 4. Results of the proposed PnPfr solver on real images. *Top*: Original images with small (1st column, 58° HFOV) to significant (4th column, 118° HFOV) distortion. *Bottom*: Undistorted images corresponding to the original images on the top row

for the first subproblem is completely same, therefore, the difference is caused by the root polishing. In the current implementation, updating the matrix G is required in every Gauss-Newton iteration for VPnPfr, but only once for VPnP and VPnPf as shown in Appendix C in the supplemental material. We can expect that the runtime of VPnPfr becomes closed to that of VPnP and VPnPf if we introduce a more optimized implementation on the root polishing.

5   Experiments on Real Data

We have tested the proposed PnPfr solver to remove lens distortion on real images. We mounted an ultra-wide vari-focal lens, TAMRON 12VM412ASIR, on a USB 3.0 camera, iDS UI-3370CP-C-HQ. The focal length of the lens is manually changeable from 4.0 mm to 12 mm. This is equivalent to the horizontal field of view from 58° to 118° for the camera. To obtain 2D-3D point correspondences for calculating the camera parameters, we took a single image of a 6×9 checkerboard pattern for each scene and detected corners by libcbdetect [23].

Figure 4 shows the original distorted and the undistorted images on the top and the bottom rows, respectively. Straight lines of buildings and brick patterns on the road are successfully corrected even with a significant distortion.

6 Conclusions

In this paper, we have proposed a versatile approach for solving PnP, PnPf, and PnPfr problems from $n \geq 5$ point correspondences. The proposed PnPfr solver is the first method for PnPfr problem in the least-squares sense. Based on the derivation of the PnPfr solver, we also have formulated PnP and PnPf solvers in the same theoretical manner, which can be implemented with slight changes from the PnPfr solver. By evaluating the proposed methods on synthetic data, we have shown that the PnP and PnPf solvers have the same performance with the-state-of-the-art methods for undistorted points. Moreover, the PnP and PnPf solvers are the fastest for large point set, $n \geq 400$. On a real image experiment using an ultra-wide zoom camera, the novel PnPfr solver have corrected significant lens distortion corresponding to 118° HFOV. Future works of the PnPfr solver are to improve the runtime of root polishing and accuracy of the distortion coefficients for high image noise.

References

1. Fischler, M.A., Bolles, R.C.: Random sample consensus: a paradigm for model fitting with applications to image analysis and automated cartography. Commun. ACM **24**(6), 381–395 (1981)
2. Haralick, B.M., Lee, C.N., Ottenberg, K., Nölle, M.: Review and analysis of solutions of the three point perspective pose estimation problem. Int. J. Comput. Vis. **13**(3), 331–356 (1994)
3. Wu, Y., Hu, Z.: PnP problem revisited. J. Math. Imaging Vis. **24**(1), 131–141 (2006)
4. Lepetit, V., Moreno-Noguer, F., Fua, P.: EPnP: an accurate o(n) solution to the PnP problem. Int. J. Comput. Vis. **81**(2), 155–166 (2009)
5. Hesch, J.A., Roumeliotis, S.I.: A direct least-squares (dls) method for PnP. In: 2011 IEEE International Conference on Computer Vision (ICCV), pp. 383–390. IEEE (2011)
6. Zheng, Y., Kuang, Y., Sugimoto, S., Astrom, K., Okutomi, M.: Revisiting the PnP problem: a fast, general and optimal solution. In: 2013 IEEE International Conference on Computer Vision (ICCV), pp. 2344–2351. IEEE (2013)
7. Nakano, G.: Globally optimal DLS method for PnP problem with cayley parameterization. In: Proceedings of the British Machine Vision Conference (BMVC), pp. 78.1-78.11. BMVA Press, September 2015
8. Kneip, L., Li, H., Seo, Y.: UPnP: an optimal $O(n)$ solution to the absolute pose problem with universal applicability. In: Fleet, D., Pajdla, T., Schiele, B., Tuytelaars, T. (eds.) ECCV 2014. LNCS, vol. 8689, pp. 127–142. Springer, Heidelberg (2014). doi:10.1007/978-3-319-10590-1_9

9. Abidi, M.A., Chandra, T.: A new efficient and direct solution for pose estimation using quadrangular targets: algorithm and evaluation. IEEE Trans. Pattern Anal. Mach. Intell. **17**(5), 534–538 (1995)

10. Bujnak, M., Kukelova, Z., Pajdla, T.: A general solution to the p. 4p problem for camera with unknown focal length. In: IEEE Conference on Computer Vision and Pattern Recognition CVPR 2008, pp. 1–8. IEEE (2008)

11. Wu, C.: P3.5p: Pose estimation with unknown focal length. In: Proceedings of the IEEE Conference on Computer Vision and Pattern Recognition, pp. 2440–2448 (2015)

12. Penate-Sanchez, A., Andrade-Cetto, J., Moreno-Noguer, F.: Exhaustive linearization for robust camera pose and focal length estimation. IEEE Trans. Pattern Anal. Mach. Intell. **35**(10), 2387–2400 (2013)

13. Zheng, Y., Sugimoto, S., Sato, I., Okutomi, M.: A general and simple method for camera pose and focal length determination. In: Proceedings of the IEEE Conference on Computer Vision and Pattern Recognition, pp. 430–437 (2014)

14. Kanaeva, E., Gurevich, L., Vakhitov, A.: Camera pose and focal length estimation using regularized distance constraints. In: Proceedings of the British Machine Vision Conference (BMVC), pp. 162.1–162.12. BMVA Press, September 2015

15. Josephson, K., Byrod, M.: Pose estimation with radial distortion and unknown focal length. In: IEEE Conference on Computer Vision and Pattern Recognition, CVPR 2009, pp. 2419–2426. IEEE (2009)

16. Bujnak, M., Kukelova, Z., Pajdla, T.: New efficient solution to the absolute pose problem for camera with unknown focal length and radial distortion. In: Kimmel, R., Klette, R., Sugimoto, A. (eds.) ACCV 2010. LNCS, vol. 6492, pp. 11–24. Springer, Heidelberg (2011). doi:10.1007/978-3-642-19315-6_2

17. Kukelova, Z., Bujnak, M., Pajdla, T.: Real-time solution to the absolute pose problem with unknown radial distortion and focal length. In: Proceedings of the IEEE International Conference on Computer Vision, pp. 2816–2823 (2013)

18. Fitzgibbon, A.W.: Simultaneous linear estimation of multiple view geometry and lens distortion. In: Proceedings of the 2001 IEEE Computer Society Conference on Computer Vision and Pattern Recognition, CVPR 2001, vol. 1, pp. I–125. IEEE (2001)

19. Bukhari, F., Dailey, M.N.: Automatic radial distortion estimation from a single image. J. Themat. Imaging Vis. **45**(1), 31–45 (2013)

20. Wildenauer, H., Micusik, B.: Closed form solution for radial distortion estimation from a single vanishing point. In: Proceedings of the British Machine Vision Conference (BMVC), BMVA Press (2013)

21. Kukelova, Z., Bujnak, M., Pajdla, T.: Automatic generator of minimal problem solvers. In: Forsyth, D., Torr, P., Zisserman, A. (eds.) ECCV 2008. LNCS, vol. 5304, pp. 302–315. Springer, Heidelberg (2008). doi:10.1007/978-3-540-88690-7_23

22. Hartley, R.I., Zisserman, A.: Multiple View Geometry in Computer Vision, 2nd edn. Cambridge University Press, Cambridge (2004). ISBN 0521540518

23. Geiger, A., Moosmann, F., Car, O., Schuster, B.: Automatic camera and range sensor calibration using a single shot. In: International Conference on Robotics and Automation (ICRA), St. Paul, USA, May 2012

Depth Map Super-Resolution by Deep Multi-Scale Guidance

Tak-Wai Hui[1], Chen Change Loy[1,2]($\boxtimes$), and Xiaoou Tang[1,2]

[1] Department of Information Engineering,
The Chinese University of Hong Kong, Sha Tin, Hong Kong
{twhui,ccloy,xtang}@ie.cuhk.edu.hk
[2] Shenzhen Institutes of Advanced Technology,
Chinese Academy of Sciences, Shenzhen, China

Abstract. Depth boundaries often lose sharpness when upsampling from low-resolution (LR) depth maps especially at large upscaling factors. We present a new method to address the problem of depth map super resolution in which a high-resolution (HR) depth map is inferred from a LR depth map and an additional HR intensity image of the same scene. We propose a Multi-Scale Guided convolutional network (MSG-Net) for depth map super resolution. MSG-Net complements LR depth features with HR intensity features using a multi-scale fusion strategy. Such a multi-scale guidance allows the network to better adapt for upsampling of both fine- and large-scale structures. Specifically, the rich hierarchical HR intensity features at different levels progressively resolve ambiguity in depth map upsampling. Moreover, we employ a high-frequency domain training method to not only reduce training time but also facilitate the fusion of depth and intensity features. With the multi-scale guidance, MSG-Net achieves state-of-art performance for depth map upsampling.

1 Introduction

The use of depth information of a scene is essential in many applications such as autonomous navigation, 3D reconstruction, human-computer interaction and virtual reality. The introduction of low-cost depth camera facilitates the use of depth information in our daily life. However, the resolution of depth maps which is provided in a low-cost depth camera is generally very limited. To facilitate the use of depth data, we often need to address an upsampling problem in which the corresponding high-resolution (HR) depth map is recovered from a given low-resolution (LR) depth map.

Depth map super-resolution is a non-trivial task. Specifically, fine structures in HR image are either lost or severely distorted (depending on the scale factor used) in LR image because they cannot be fully represented by the limited spatial resolution. A brute-force upsampling of LR image simply causes those structures which are supposed to have sharp boundaries become blurred in the upsampled image. Ambiguity in super-resolving the severely distorted fine structures often

© Springer International Publishing AG 2016
B. Leibe et al. (Eds.): ECCV 2016, Part III, LNCS 9907, pp. 353–369, 2016.
DOI: 10.1007/978-3-319-46487-9_22

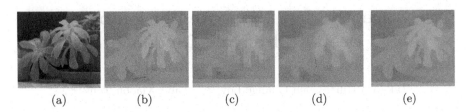

(a)	(b)	(c)	(d)	(e)

Fig. 1. Ambiguity in upsampling depth map. (a) Color image. (b) Ground truth. (c) (Enlarged) LR depth map downsampled by a factor of 8. Results for upsampling: (d) SRCNN [11], (e) Our solution without ambiguity problem.

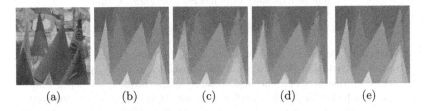

(a)	(b)	(c)	(d)	(e)

Fig. 2. Over-texture transfer in depth map refinement and upsampling using intensity guidance. (a) Color image. (b) Ground truth. (c) Refinement of (b) using (a) by Guided Filtering [8] ($r = 4, \epsilon = 0.01^2$). Results of using (a) to guide the 2× upsampling of (b): (d) Ferstl *et al.* [4], (e) Our solution.

exists, especially for the case of single-image upsampling. Figure 1(c–d) demonstrates the upsampling ambiguity problem.

To address the aforementioned problem, a corresponding intensity image[1] is often used to guide the upsampling process [1–7] or enhance the low-quality depth maps [8–10]. This is due to the fact that a correspondence between an intensity edge and a depth edge can be most likely established. Since the intensity image is at a higher resolution, its intensity discontinuities can be used to locate the associated depth discontinuities in a higher resolution. Although there could be an exception that an intensity edge does not correspond to a depth edge or vice versa, this correspondence assumption has been used widely in the literature.

One would encounter issues too in exploiting the intensity guidance. Specifically, suppose we have a perfectly registered pair of depth map D and intensity image Y possessing the *same* resolution. It is not straight forward to use Y to guide the refinement of D or the upsampling of LR D. The variation of depth structures in D may not be consistent with that of the intensity structures in Y as they are different in nature. Using image-guided filtering, features in intensity images are often over-transferred to the depth image at the boundaries between textured and homogeneous regions. Figure 2(c–d) illustrates two examples for the over-texture transferring problem. Our proposed method that complements D with only consistent structures from Y can avoid this problem (Fig. 2(e)).

---

[1] Intensity image represents either a color or grayscale image. We only study grayscale image in this paper.

In this paper, we present a novel end-to-end upsampling network, a Multi-Scale Guided convolutional network (MSG-Net), which learns HR features in the intensity branch and complements the LR depth structures in the depth branch to overcome the aforementioned problems. MSG-Net is appealing in that it allows the network to learn rich hierarchical features at different levels. This in turn makes the network to better adapt for upsampling of both fine- and large-scale structures. At each level, the upsampling of LR depth features is closely guided by the associated HR intensity features possessing the same resolution. The integrated multi-scale guidance progressively resolves ambiguity in depth map upsampling. We further present a high-frequency training approach to reduce training time and facilitate the fusion of depth and intensity features. Note that unlike existing super-resolution networks [11,12] that require pre-upsampling of input image by a conventional method such as bicubic interpolation *outside* the network. Our approach learns upsampling kernels *inside* a network to fully explore the upsampling ability of a CNN. We show that such a multi-scale upsampling method uses a more effective way to upscale LR images, while capable of exploiting the guidance from HR intensity features seamlessly.

Contributions: (1) We propose a new framework to address the problem of depth map upsampling by complementing a LR depth map with the corresponding HR intensity image using a convolutional neural network in a multi-scale guidance architecture (MSG-Net). To the best of our knowledge, no prior studies have proposed this idea for CNN before. (2) With the introduction of multi-scale upsampling architecture, our compact single-image upsampling network (MS-Net) in which no guidance from HR intensity image is present already outperforms most of the state-of-the-art methods requiring guidance from HR intensity image. (3) We discuss detailed steps to enable both MSG-Net and MS-Net to perform image-wise upsampling and end-to-end training.

2   Related Work

There is a variety of methods to perform image super resolution in the literature. Here, we categorize them into four groups:

Local methods are based on filtering. Yang *et al.* used the joint bilateral filter [1] to weight the degree of smoothing in each depth patch by considering the color similarity between the center pixel and its neighborhood [13]. Liu *et al.* designed the upsampling weights using geodesic distances [14]. With the use of image segmentation, Lu *et al.* developed a smoothing method to reconstruct depth structures within each segment [6].

Global methods formulate depth upsampling as an optimization problem where a large cost is given to a pixel in depth map if neighboring depth pixels have similar color in the associated intensity image but different depth values. Diebel *et al.* proposed Markov Random Field (MRF) formulation, which consists of a data term from LR depth map and a smoothness term from the corresponding HR intensity image for depth upsampling [15]. Park *et al.* utilized nonlocal means filtering in which intensity features are acted as weights in depth regularization [2]. Ferstl *et al.* used an anisotropic diffusion tensor to regularize depth upsampling [4]. Yang *et al.* developed an adaptive color-guided auto regression model for depth recovery [5]. Aodha *et al.* especially focused on single-image upsampling as MRF labeling problem [16].

Dictionary methods exploit the relationship between a paired LR and HR depth patches through sparse coding. Yang *et al.* sought the coefficients of this representation to generate HR output [17]. Timofte *et al.* improved sparse-coding method by introducing the anchored neighborhood regression [18]. Ferstl *et al.* proposed to learn a dictionary of edge priors for an anisotropic guidance [19]. Li *et al.* proposed a joint examples-based upsampling method [20]. Kwon *et al.* formulated an upscaling problem which consists of scale-dependent dictionaries and TV regularization [7].

CNN-based methods are in distinction to dictionary-based approaches in that CNN do not explicitly learn dictionaries. With the motivation from convolutional dictionaries [21], Osendorfer *et al.* presented a convolutional sparse coding method for super-resolving images [22]. Wang *et al.* developed a cascade of sparse coding based networks (CSCN) [12] that are constructed by using modules from the network for the learned iterative shrinkage and thresholding algorithm (LISTA) [21]. However, their decoder uses sparse code to infer a HR patch separately. All the recovered patches are required to put back to the corresponding positions in HR image. Dong *et al.* proposed an end-to-end super-resolution convolutional neural network (SRCNN) to achieve image restoration [11].

Comparing to the above methods, our CNNs exhibit several advantages. We do not explicitly formulate an optimization problem as the global methods [2,4,5,15] or design a fixed filter as the local methods [6,13,14] because CNN can be trained to address the upsampling problem. In contrast to the dictionary methods [7,19], our networks are self-regularized. No extra regularization on the upsampled image is necessary outside the network. In distinction to other single-image super resolution CNNs [11,12,22], our networks do not use a single *fixed* (non-trainable) upsampling operator. More importantly, our MSG-Net is specifically designed for image-guided depth upsampling. Rich hierarchical features in the HR intensity image are learned to guide the upsampling of the LR depth map progressively in multiple levels towards the desired HR depth map. The multi-scale fusion architecture in turn enables MSG-Net to achieve high-quality upsampling performance especially at large upscaling factors.

Our work is related to the multi-scale CNNs for semantic segmentation (FCN) [23], inferring images of chairs [24], optical flow generation (FlowNet) [25] and holistically-nested edge detection (HED) [26]. Our network architecture differs from theirs significantly. An upsampling network is used in [24]. A downsampling network is used in HED. A downsampling sub-network followed by an upsampling sub-network is used in FlowNet and FCN. We use an upsampling (depth) branch in parallel with a downsampling (intensity) branch. This network architecture has not been studied yet. In common to [23–25], we use multiple backwards convolutions for upsampling. But we do not use feed-fowarding and unpooling. All the above networks do not use deep supervision except HED.

3   Intensity-Guided Depth Map Upsampling

Suppose we have a LR depth map D_l which is down-sampled from its HR counterpart D_h. Additionally, a corresponding HR intensity image Y_h of the same scene is available. Our goal is to recover D_h using D_l and Y_h.

We first present some insights about the upsampling architecture. These motivate us on the design of our proposed upsampling CNNs.

Spectral Decomposition. We have observed that simple upsampling operator like bicubic interpolation performs very well in smooth region, but sharpness is lost along edges. Unlike SRCNN [11] and CSCN [12], we do not enlarge D_l using a *fixed* upsampling operator and then *refine* the enlarged D_l afterwards. To achieve optimal upsampling, we believe that different spectral components of D_l need to be upsampled using different strategies because a single upsampling operator is unlikely to be suitable for upsampling of all kinds of structures.

Multi-scale Upsampling. Multi-scale representation has played an important role in the success of addressing low-level problems like motion-depth fusion [27], optical flow generation [23] and depth map recovery [7]. Different structures in an image have different scales. A multi-scale upsampling CNN that allows the use of scale-dependent upsampling kernels can greatly improve the quality of the recovered HR image especially at large upscaling factors.

3.1   Formulation

We design MSG-Net to upsample a LR image D_l not in a single level but progressively in multiple levels to a desired HR image $\widehat{D}_h$ with multi-scale guidance from the corresponding HR intensity image Y_h. We upsample D_l in m levels for the upscaling factor 2^m. Figure 3 shows an overview of the network architecture. It consists of five stages, namely feature extraction (each for Y- and D-branches), downsampling, upsampling, fusion and reconstruction. We will discuss the details of each stage in this section.

Overview. It is not possible to determine the absolute depth value of a pixel from an intensity patch alone as it is an ill-posed problem. Flat intensity patches (regardless of what intensity values they possess) do not contribute much improvement in depth super resolution. Therefore, we complement depth features with the associated intensity features in *high-frequency domain*. In other words, we perform an **early spectral decomposition** of D_l: $D_l = l(D_l) + h(D_l)$. By using the high-frequency (h) components of both Y and D images as the inputs, this gives room for the network to focus on structured features for joint upsampling and filtering. This in turn improves the upsampling performance greatly. We have also experienced a reduction in the convergence time if the network are trained in high-frequency domain. We obtain the high-frequency

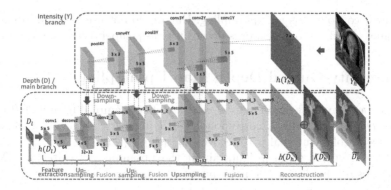

Fig. 3. The architecture of MSG-Net. For the ease of representation, only an upsampling CNN with upscaling factor 8 is presented. There are three multi-scale upsampling levels. Each level consists of an upsampling and a fusion stage.

components of D_l, D_h, and Y_h by applying a low-pass filter $\mathbf{W}_l$ to them as follows:

$$h(D_l) = D_l - \mathbf{W}_l * D_l, \tag{1.1}$$

$$h(D_h) = D_h - (\mathbf{W}_l * D_l)^{\uparrow D_h}, \tag{1.2}$$

$$h(Y_h) = Y_h - \mathbf{W}_l * Y_h, \tag{1.3}$$

where $(I_l)^{\uparrow D_h}$ performs a bicubic upsampling on I_l to the same resolution as D_h.

Suppose the upscaling factor is $s = 2^m$, then there are M layers (including m upsampling levels) in the main branch and $2m$ layers in the Y branch. MSG-Net can be expressed as follows:

$$F_1^Y = \sigma(\mathbf{W}_{c(1)}^Y * h(Y_h) + \mathbf{b}_1^Y), \text{ (feature extraction)} \tag{2.1}$$

$$F_j^Y = \sigma(\mathbf{W}_{c(j)}^Y * F_{j-1}^Y + \mathbf{b}_j^Y), \text{ (post-feature extraction)} \tag{2.2}$$

$$F_{2j'}^Y = maxpool(F_{2j'-1}^Y), \text{ (downsampling)} \tag{2.3}$$

$$F_1 = \sigma(\mathbf{W}_{c(1)} * h(D_l) + \mathbf{b}_1), \text{ (feature extraction)} \tag{2.4}$$

$$F_k = \sigma\left(\mathbf{W}_{d(k)} \star F_{k-1} + \mathbf{b}_k\right), \text{ (upsampling)} \tag{2.5}$$

$$F_{k+1} = \sigma\left(\mathbf{W}_{c(k+1)} * \left(F_{2(m+1-k/3)}^Y, F_k\right) + \mathbf{b}_{k+1}\right), \text{ (fusion)} \tag{2.6}$$

$$F_{k+2+k'} = \sigma\left(\mathbf{W}_{c(k+2+k')} * F_{k+1+k'} + \mathbf{b}_{k+2+k'}\right), k' \in \{0, 1\} \text{ (post-fusion)} \tag{2.7}$$

$$F_M = h(\widetilde{D_h}) = \mathbf{W}_{c(M)} * F_{M-1} + \mathbf{b}_M, \text{ (reconstruction)} \tag{2.8}$$

$$\widetilde{D_h} = h(\widetilde{D_h}) + (\mathbf{W}_l * D_l)^{\uparrow \widetilde{D_h}}, \text{ (post-reconstruction)} \tag{2.9}$$

where $j = \{2, 3, 5, \ldots, 2m - 1\}$, $j' = \{4, 6, \ldots, 2m\}$, $k = \{2, 5, \ldots, 3m - 1\}$ and $M = 3(m + 1)$. The operators $*$ and $\star$ represent convolution and backwards convolution respectively. Vectors (or blobs) having superscript Y in (2) belongs to HR intensity (Y) branch of MSG-Net. $\mathbf{W}_{c(i)/d(i)}$ is a kernel (subscripts c and

d stand for convolution and deconvolution respectively) of size $n_{i-1} \times f_i \times f_i \times n_i$ (n_{i-1} and n_i are the numbers of feature maps in the $(i-1)^{th}$ and i^{th} layers, respectively) and $\mathbf{b}_i$ is a n_i-dimensional bias vector (it is a scalar in the top layer). Each layer is followed by an activation function for non-linear mapping except the top layer. We use parametric rectified linear unit (PReLU) [28] as the activation function (σ) due to its generalization and improvement in model fitting, where $\sigma(y) = \max(0, y) + a \min(0, y)$ and a is a learnable slope coefficient for negative y.

Denote F as our overall network architecture for MSG-Net and $\Theta = \{\mathbf{W}, \mathbf{b}, \mathbf{a}\}$ as the network parameters controlling the forward process, we train our network by minimizing the mean squared error (MSE) for N training samples as follows:

$$L(\Theta) = \frac{1}{N} \sum\nolimits_{i=1}^{N} ||F(h(Y_{h(i)}), h(D_{l(i)}); \Theta) - h(D_{h(i)})||^2. \qquad (3)$$

The loss is minimized using stochastic gradient descent.

Feature Extraction. MSG-Net first decomposes a LR high-frequency depth map $h(D_l)$ and the associated HR high-frequency image $h(Y_h)$ into different spectral components (sub-bands) at the bottom layer and the first two layers of the D- and Y-branches respectively. This facilitates the network to learn for scale-dependent and spectral-dependent upsampling operators afterwards.

Multi-scale Upsampling. We perform upsampling in m levels. Backwards convolution (or so-called deconvolution) (**deconv**) in the ith layer is used to upsample the sub-bands $F_{i-1} = \{f_{(i-1,j)}, j = 1, \ldots, n_{i-1}\}$ in the $(i-1)^{th}$ layer. Each **deconv** layer has a set of trainable kernels $\mathbf{W}_{d(i)} = \{\mathbf{w}_{d(i,j)}, j = 1, \ldots, n_i\}$ such that $\mathbf{w}_{d(i,j)} = \{w_{d(i,j,k)}, k = 1, \ldots, n_{i-1}\}$ and $w_{d(i,j,k)}$ is a $f_i \times f_i$ filter. **Deconv** recovers the jth HR sub-band in the ith layer by utilizing the dependency across all LR sub-bands in the $(i-1)^{th}$ layer as follows:

$$f_{(i,j)} = \sum\nolimits_{k=1}^{n_{i-1}} w_{d(i,j,k)} \star f_{(i-1,k)} + b_{(i,j)}. \qquad (4)$$

More specifically, each element in a HR sub-band is constructed by element-wise summation of a corresponding set of enlarged blocks of pixels across all the LR sub-bands in the previous layer. Suppose a stride s is used, each enlarged block of pixels is centered in a 2D regular grid with length s.

Fischer et al. [25] and Long et al. [23] proposed to feed-forward and concatenate feature maps from lower layers. MSG-Net uses a more effective design. We directly enlarge feature maps which originate from the previous layer without feed-forwarding. Unlike the "unpooling + convolution" (**uconv**) layer introduced by Dosovitskiy et al. [24], our upsampling uses backwards convolution in which it diffuses a set of feature maps to another set of larger feature maps. The diffusion is governed by the learned **deconv** filters but not simply filling zeros. More importantly, **uconv**s are used in their networks to facilitate the transformation from a high-level representation generated by multiple fully-connected (FC) layers to two images but not to upsample a given LR image.

To compromise both computational efficiency and upsampling accuracy, we set f_i for $\mathbf{W}_{d(i)}$ to be $2s + 1$. Having such a kernel size ensures that all the inter-pixels between the demultiplexed pixels in each feature map are completely covered by **deconv** filter $\mathbf{W}_d$. We observed that $\mathbf{W}_d$ with a size larger than $(2s + 1) \times (2s + 1)$ does not bring significant improvement.

Downsampling. The associated HR intensity image Y_h posses the same resolution as HR depth map D_h. In our design, D_l is progressively upsampled by a factor of 2 in a multi-scale manner. In order to match the size of the feature maps for D and Y, we progressively downsample the feature maps extracted from $h(Y_h)$ in the reverse pace by a convolution followed by a 3×3 maximum pooling with stride $= 2$. Downsampling of feature maps in Y-branch can also be achieved by using a 3×3 convolution with stride $= 2$. The resulting CNN performs slightly poorer than the one using pooling.

Fusion. The upsampled feature maps F_k are complemented with the corresponding feature maps $F^Y_{2(m+1-k/3)}$ in Y-branch possessing the same resolution. The fusion kernel $\mathbf{W}_{c(k+1)}$ in (2.6) constructs a new set of sub-bands by fusing the local features in the vicinity defined by $\mathbf{W}_{c(k+1)}$ across all the sub-bands of F_i and $F^Y_{2(m+1-k/3)}$. As intensity features in Y_h may not be consistent with depth structures in D_h, a post-fusion layer is introduced to learn a better coupling. An extra post-fusion layer is included for an enhanced fusion before reconstruction.

Reconstruction. The enlarged feature maps from the previous upsampling levels are generally "dense" in nature. Due to spectral decomposition, the energy (i.e. intensity) of each pixel in an image is distributed across different spectral components. Reconstruction layer combines n_{M-1} upsampled sub-bands and recovers a HR image. Finally, we convert the recovered HR $h(\widetilde{D_h})$ from high-frequency domain back to an ordinary HR depth map $\widetilde{D_h}$ by a post-reconstruction step in (2.9). This is achieved by using the upsampled low-frequency image $(\mathbf{W}_l * D_l)^{\uparrow \widetilde{D_h}}$ in (1.2) as the missed low-frequency component for $\widetilde{D_h}$.

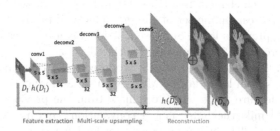

Fig. 4. The network architecture of MS-Net for single-image super resolution. For the ease of representation, only a 8× upsampling CNN is presented.

3.2 A Special Case: Single-Image Upsampling

Removing the (intensity) guidance branch and fusion stages of MSG-Net, it reduces to a compact multi-scale network (MS-Net) for super-resolving images by sacrificing some upsampling accuracy. Figure 4 illustrates its network architecture. MS-Net is used for single-image super resolution. It consists of three stages, namely feature extraction, multi-scale upsampling and reconstruction. For an upscaling factor $s = 2^m$, there are only $(m + 2)$ layers. MS-Net can be expressed as follows:

$$F_1 = \sigma(\mathbf{W}_{c(1)} * h(D_l) + \mathbf{b}_1), \text{ (feature extraction)} \tag{5.1}$$

$$F_i = \sigma(\mathbf{W}_{d(i)} \star F_{i-1} + \mathbf{b}_i), i = 2, ..., M - 1, \text{ (upsampling)} \tag{5.2}$$

$$F_M = h(\widetilde{D_h}) = \mathbf{W}_{c(M)} * F_{M-1} + b_M, \text{ (reconstruction)} \tag{5.3}$$

$$\widetilde{D_h} = h(\widetilde{D_h}) + (\mathbf{W}_l * D_l)^{\uparrow \widetilde{D_h}}. \text{ (post-reconstruction)} \tag{5.4}$$

Denote F as our overall network architecture for MS-Net and $\Theta = \{\mathbf{W}, \mathbf{b}, \mathbf{a}\}$ as the network parameters controlling the forward process, we train our network by minimizing the mean squared error (MSE) for N training samples as follows:

$$L(\Theta) = \frac{1}{N} \sum_{i=1}^{N} ||F\left(h\left(D_{l(i)}\right); \Theta\right) - h\left(D_{h(i)}\right)||^2. \tag{6}$$

The loss is also minimized using stochastic gradient descent.

SS-Net vs MS-Net: Comparing the number of **deconv** parameters in the network using a single large-stride **deconv** layer (SS-Net) with that in a multi-scale small-stride **deconv** network (MS-Net), the number of **deconv** parameters for the latter one is indeed lower. Suppose all **deconv** layers in MS-Net have $s = 2$, then there are only $25 \sum_{i=2}^{m+1} n_{i-1}n_i$ kernel parameters. If they all have the same number of feature maps i.e. $n_1 = n_2 = ... = n$, then there are $25\,mn^2$ kernel parameters. For SS-Net, there are $(2^{m+1} + 1)^2 n^2$ kernel parameters.

4 Experiments

4.1 Training Details

We collected 58 RGBD images from MPI Sintel depth dataset [29], and 34 RGBD images (6, 10 and 18 images are from 2001, 2006 and 2014 datasets respectively) from Middlebury dataset [30–32]. We used 82 images for training and 10 images for validation. We augmented the training data by a 90°-rotation. The training and testing RGBD data were normalized to the range $[0, 1]$.

Instead of using large-size images for training, sub-images were generated from them by dividing each image into a regular grid of small overlapping patches. This training approach does not reduce the performance of CNN but it leads to a reduction in training time [23]. We performed a regular sampling on the raw images with stride = $\{22, 21, 20, 24^2\}$ for the scale = $\{2, 4, 8, 16\}$ respectively. We excluded patches without depth information due to occlusion. There were roughly $190,000$ training sub-images. To synthesize LR depth samples $\{D_l\}$, we first filtered each full-resolution sub-image by a 2D Gaussian kernel and then downsampled it by the given scaling factor. The LR/HR patches $\{D_l\}/\{D_h\}$ (and $\{Y_h\}$) were prepared to have sizes $20^2/39^2$, $16^2/63^2$, $12^2/95^2$, $8^2/127^2$ for the upscaling factors $2, 4, 8, 16$, respectively. We do not prefer to use a set of large-size sub-images for training upsampling networks with large upscaling factors (e.g. $8\times, 16\times$). We have experienced that using them cannot improve the training accuracy significantly. Moreover, this increases the computation time and memory burden for training.

It is possible to train MS-Net (but not MSG-Net) without padding as SRCNN [11] to reduce memory usage and training time. We have to pad zeros for convolution layers in MSG-Net so that the dimension of the feature maps in the intensity branch can match that in the depth branch. We need to crop the resulted feature maps after performing backwards convolution so that the reconstructed HR depth map $\widetilde{D_h}$ is close to the desired resolution[3]. For consistency, we trained all our CNNs except SRCNN and its variant with a padding scheme.

We built our networks on top of the *caffe* CNN implementation [33]. CNNs were trained with smaller base learning rates for large upscaling factors. Base learning rates varied from $3e-3$ to $6e-5$ for MSG-Net and $4e-3$ to $4e-4$ for MS-Net. We chose momentum to be 0.9. Unlike SRCNN [11], we used stepwise decrease (5 steps with learning rate multiplier $\gamma = 0.8$) as the learning policy because we experienced that a lower learning rate usage in the later part of training process can reduce fluctuation in the convergence curve. We trained each MS-Net and MSG-Net for $5e+5$ iterations. We set the network parameters: $\mathbf{W}_l = \frac{1}{9}I_3$, $f_1^Y = 7, n_1^Y = 49, n_1 = 64$ and $(f_i = 5, n_i = 32)$ for other layers. We initialized all the filter weights and bias values as PReLU networks [28].

We trained a specific network for each upscaling factor $s \in \{2, 4, 8, 16\}$. We adopted the following pre-training and fine-tuning scheme for MSG-Net: (1) we pre-trained the Y- and D- branches for a $2\times$ MSG-Net separately, (2) we transfered the first two layers of them (D-branch: {conv1, deconv2} and Y-branch: {conv1Y, conv2Y}) to a plain $2\times$ MSG-Net and then fine-tuned it. For training MSG-Net with other upsampling factors ($2^m, m > 1$), we transfered all the layers except the last four layers in the D-branch from the network trained with upsampling factor 2^{m-1} to a plain network and then fine-tuned it. We trained SRCNNs for different upscaling factors using the same strategy as recommended by the authors [11]. We also modified SRCNN by replacing the activation functions from ReLU to PReLU. We name this variant as SRCNN2.

---

[2] For training $16\times$ MSG-Net, we reduced the amount of training samples by about 35% using stride = 24 (instead of 19) in order to fulfill the blob-size limit in caffe.

[3] As we used odd-size **deconv** kernels, both the horizontal and vertical dimension of each feature map is one pixel lesser than the ideal one.

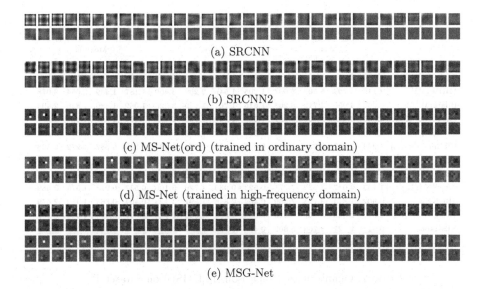

(a) SRCNN

(b) SRCNN2

(c) MS-Net(ord) (trained in ordinary domain)

(d) MS-Net (trained in high-frequency domain)

(e) MSG-Net

Fig. 5. Visualization of the bottom-layer kernels for five CNNs trained for 8× upsampling. Their kernel sizes are: 9 × 9 for SRCNN and SRCNN2, 5 × 5 for MS-Net, 7 × 7 (Top: Y-branch), 5 × 5 (Bottom: D-branch) for MSG-Net.

4.2 Analysis of the Learned Kernels

The bottom-layer filters of SRCNN which is trained for depth map upsampling are different than the one trained for image super resolution [11]. As shown in Fig. 5a, we can recognize some flattened edge-like and Laplacian filters. The filters near the right of second row are completely flat (or so-called "dead" filters). Figure 5b visualizes the filters of the trained SRCNN2. In comparison to SRCNN, SRCNN2 has sharper edge-like filters and fewer "dead" filters.

We trained MS-Net in two approaches: using ordinary and high-frequency (i.e. with early spectral decomposition) domains. As shown in Fig. 5c and d, we can recognize simple gradient operators such as horizontal, vertical and diagonal filters for both of the cases. When MS-Net is trained in ordinary domain, it first decomposes the components of LR depth map into a complete spectrum and performs spectral upsampling subsequently. By training MS-Net in high-frequency domain, all the bottom-layer kernels become high-pass filters. Similar patterned filters (bottom of Fig. 5e) are present in the first layer of the D-branch of MSG-Net as well. For the Y-branch, the learned filters (top of Fig. 5e) contain both textured and low-varying filters.

4.3 Results

We provide both quantitative and qualitative evaluations on our image-guided upsampling CNN (MSG-Net) and single-image upsampling CNN (MS-Net) to the state-of-the-art methods. We report upsampling performance in terms of

Table 1. Quantitative comparison (in RMSE) on dataset A.

	Art				Books				Moebius			
	2×	4×	8×	16×	2×	4×	8×	16×	2×	4×	8×	16×
Bilinear	2.834	4.147	5.995	8.928	1.119	1.673	2.394	3.525	1.016	1.499	2.198	3.179
MRFs [15]	3.119	3.794	5.503	8.657	1.205	1.546	2.209	3.400	1.187	1.439	2.054	3.078
Bilateral [13]	4.066	4.056	4.712	8.268	1.615	1.701	1.949	3.325	1.069	1.386	1.820	2.494
Park et al. [2]	2.833	3.498	4.165	6.262	1.088	1.530	1.994	2.760	1.064	1.349	1.804	2.377
Guided [8]	2.934	3.788	4.974	7.876	1.162	1.572	2.097	3.186	1.095	1.434	1.878	2.851
Kiechle et al. [3]	1.246	2.007	3.231	<u>5.744</u>	0.652	0.918	1.274	1.927	0.640	0.887	1.272	2.128
Ferstl et al. [4]	3.032	3.785	4.787	7.102	1.290	1.603	1.992	2.941	1.129	1.458	1.914	2.630
Lu et al. [6]	-	-	5.798	7.648	-	-	2.728	3.549	-	-	2.422	3.118
SRCNN [11]	1.133	2.017	3.829	7.271	0.523	0.935	1.726	3.100	0.537	0.913	1.579	2.689
SRCNN2	0.902	1.874	3.704	7.309	0.464	0.846	1.591	3.123	0.454	0.864	1.482	2.679
Wang et al. [12]	1.670	2.525	3.957	6.226	0.668	1.098	1.646	2.428	0.641	0.979	1.459	2.202
MS-Net	<u>0.813</u>	<u>1.627</u>	<u>2.769</u>	5.802	<u>0.417</u>	<u>0.724</u>	<u>1.072</u>	<u>1.802</u>	<u>0.413</u>	<u>0.741</u>	<u>1.138</u>	<u>1.910</u>
MSG-Net	**0.663**	**1.474**	**2.455**	**4.574**	**0.373**	**0.667**	**1.029**	**1.601**	**0.357**	**0.661**	**1.015**	**1.633**

Table 2. Quantitative comparison (in RMSE) on dataset B.

	Dolls[a]				Laundry				Reindeer			
	2×	4×	8×	16×	2×	4×	8×	16×	2×	4×	8×	16×
Bicubic	0.914	1.305	1.855	2.625	1.614	2.408	3.452	5.095	1.938	2.809	3.986	5.823
Park et al. [2]	0.963	1.301	1.745	2.412	1.552	2.132	2.770	4.158	1.834	2.407	2.987	4.294
Aodha et al.	-	1.977	-	-	-	2.969	-	-	-	3.178	-	-
CLMF0 [34]	0.990	1.271	1.878	2.291	1.689	2.312	3.084	4.312	1.955	2.690	3.417	4.674
CLMF1 [34]	0.972	1.267	1.707	2.232	1.689	2.512	2.892	4.302	1.948	2.699	3.331	4.774
Ferstl et al. [4]	1.118	1.355	1.859	3.574	1.989	2.511	3.757	6.407	2.407	2.712	3.789	7.271
Kiechle et al. [3]	0.696	0.921	1.259	<u>1.736</u>	0.746	1.212	2.077	3.621	0.920	1.559	2.583	4.644
AP [5]	1.147	1.350	1.646	2.323	1.715	2.255	2.848	4.656	1.803	2.431	2.949	4.088
SRCNN [11]	0.581	0.946	1.518	2.445	0.635	1.176	2.430	4.579	0.765	1.499	2.864	5.249
SRCNN2	0.473	0.881	1.461	2.422	0.506	1.084	2.314	4.601	0.603	1.352	2.740	5.330
Wang et al. [12]	0.670	0.989	1.445	2.107	1.039	1.630	2.466	3.834	1.252	1.914	2.878	4.526
MS-Net	<u>0.437</u>	<u>0.740</u>	<u>1.166</u>	1.832	<u>0.475</u>	<u>0.883</u>	<u>1.618</u>	<u>3.385</u>	<u>0.556</u>	<u>1.107</u>	<u>1.972</u>	<u>3.921</u>
MSG-Net	**0.345**	**0.690**	**1.051**	**1.597**	**0.371**	**0.787**	**1.514**	**2.629**	**0.424**	**0.984**	**1.757**	**2.919**

[a] We excluded 9 pixels for calculating RMSE as they are not filled in the ground truth.

root mean squared error (RMSE). We evaluate our methods on the hole-filled Middlebury RGBD datasets. We denote them as A [4], B [5] and C [19]. The RMSE values in Tables[4] 1, 2 and 3 for the compared methods are computed using the upsampled depth maps provided by Ferstl et al. [4], Yang et al. [5] and Ferstl et al. [19] respectively, except the evaluations for Kiechle et al. [3] and Wang et al. [12] (code packages provided by the authors), Lu et al. [6] (upsampled depth maps provided by the authors) and SRCNN(2) (trained by ourself). The best RMSE for each evaluation is in bold, whereas the second best one is underlined. Since the ground-truths are quantized to 8-bit, we convert all recovered HR

---

[4] Evaluations of several upscaling factors are not available from the authors.

Table 3. Quantitative comparison (in RMSE) on dataset C.

	Tsukuba			Venus			Teddy			Cones		
	2×	4×	8×	2×	4×	8×	2×	4×	8×	2×	4×	8×
Park et al. [2]	6.61	9.75	15.1	1.27	1.8	2.99	3.73	4.89	7.15	4.0	5.64	7.73
Li et al. [20]	8.29	11.9	15.84	2.29	3.55	5.76	2.78	4.92	7.24	3.24	6.34	8.9
Ferstl et al. [4]	7.2	10.3	17.2	2.15	2.52	4.04	2.71	3.3	5.39	3.5	4.45	7.14
Kiechle et al. [3]	3.48	5.95	10.9	0.8	1.17	1.76	1.28	2.94	2.76	1.7	4.17	5.11
Kwon et al. [7][a]	_2.31_	_5.56_	_5.67_	_0.53_	_1.14_	_1.68_	_0.83_	_1.80_	**2.19**	_0.92_	_2.13_	**2.37**
MSG-Net[b]	**1.143**	**2.233**	**3.649**	**0.142**	**0.329**	**0.762**	**0.695**	**1.307**	_2.275_	**0.807**	**1.772**	_2.748_
Aodha et al. [16]	8.993	12.39	-	2.175	2.597	-	3.233	4.030	-	4.262	5.740	-
Timofte et al. [18]	9.135	12.09	-	2.099	2.331	-	3.253	3.718	-	4.257	5.490	-
Kiechle et al. [3]	3.653	6.212	10.08	0.607	0.819	1.169	1.198	1.822	2.370	1.465	2.974	_4.516_
Ferstl et al. [19]	5.254	7.352	-	1.108	1.742	-	1.694	2.595	-	2.185	3.498	-
Lu et al. [6]	-	10.29	13.77	-	1.734	2.134	-	2.723	3.468	-	3.985	5.344
SRCNN [11]	3.275	7.939	11.28	0.456	0.789	1.706	1.170	1.985	3.252	1.484	3.585	5.180
SRCNN2	2.796	7.178	11.20	0.315	0.718	1.593	0.947	1.891	3.136	1.183	3.439	5.171
Wang et al. [12]	3.979	6.281	_9.589_	0.828	1.191	1.786	1.368	2.026	3.015	1.856	3.078	4.865
MS-Net	_2.472_	_4.996_	9.986	_0.259_	_0.422_	_0.881_	_0.822_	_1.533_	_2.874_	_1.100_	_2.770_	5.217
MSG-Net	**1.848**	**4.292**	**8.428**	**0.142**	**0.346**	**1.040**	**0.713**	**1.485**	**2.760**	**0.905**	**2.595**	**4.229**

[a]The reported values in the top-half of Table 3 are obtained from their supplementary material. Please note that depth maps for [7] are initialized using Park et al. [2].
[b]We used the RMSE calculation suggested by [7]: (1) Depth maps are normalized, (2) compute the absolute difference and convert it to uint8 and (3) calculate RMSE.

depth maps in the same data type in order to have a fair evaluation. Following [6,7,19], we performed evaluation on dataset C only up to 8× due to the low resolution ($< 450 \times 375$) of the ground-truths.

As shown in the three tables, our single-image upsampling CNN (MS-Net) achieves state-of-the-art performance. SRCNN2 performs better than the original SRCNN due to the use of PReLU as the activation function. Although MS-Net and SRCNN(2) are both designed for single-image super resolution, MS-Net outperforms SRCNN(2). This is because MS-Net performs image upsampling but not image refinement as SRCNN(2). MS-Net (and also MSG-Net) are trained to learn different upsampling operators for different spectral components of LR depth map. They are not constrained only to a fixed non-trainable upsampling operator. The upsampling performance is further improved when MSG-Net upsamples LR depth map with the guidance from HR intensity image of the same scene. This in turn allows MSG-Net to outperform MS-Net. Figure 6 shows 8× upsampled depth maps for different methods. It is observed that HR depth boundaries reconstructed by MSG-Net are sharper than the compared methods. The evaluations suggest that multi-scale guidance has played an important role in the success of depth map super resolution in MSG-Net.

The Role of Guidance. We evaluate several variants of MSG-Net at upscaling factor 8: (1) MS(woG)-Net (without Y-branch), (2) MSG(2,4)-Nets (Intensity-guidance only applied at deconv(2,4) respectively) and (3) MSG-Net(ord)

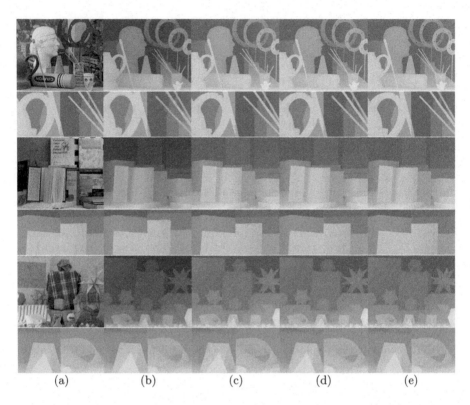

(a)   (b)   (c)   (d)   (e)

Fig. 6. Upsampled depth maps for dataset *A*. (a) Color image and ground-truth depth patches. Upsampled results from (b) Ferstl *et al.* [4], (c) Kiechle *et al.* [3], (d) SRCNN [11], and (e) MSG-Net.

(trained in ordinary domain). As summarized in Table 4, MSG-Net outperforms the others. Comparing to the partially guided variants MSG(2, 4)-Nets, MS(woG)-Net loses some upsampling performance due to the absence of guidance branch.

Table 4. RMSE for different variants of MSG-Net with upscaling factor 8.

	Art	Reindeer	Cones
MS(woG)-Net	2.596	1.801	4.667
MSG(2)-Net	2.510	1.866	4.514
MSG(4)-Net	2.574	1.788	4.249
MSG-Net(ord)	3.110	2.386	5.105
SSG-Net	2.770	1.954	4.517
MSG-Net	**2.455**	**1.757**	**4.229**

Table 5. Computation time (sec).

	2×	4×	8×	16×
MS-Net	0.211	0.221	0.247	0.277
MSG-Net	0.247	0.296	0.326	0.368

Fig. 7. Convergence curves.

The Role of Multi-scale Upsampling. We consider the single-scale variant of MSG-Net: SSG-Net (deconv4 uses stride $= 8$, conv3Y - pool4Y in Y-branch and deconv2 - conv3_2 in D-branch are removed). As shown in Table 4, SSG-Net performs poorer than MSG-Net. This suggests that multi-scale architecture is necessary in guided upsampling.

Training in Frequency-Domain. As presented in Table 4 and Fig. 7, MSG-Net not only performs better than its ordinary-domain trained counterpart MSG-Net(ord) in upsampling accuracy but it also converges faster. The difference in the speed of convergence is more obvious between MS-Net and MS-Net(ord). This verifies our motivation in earlier section that using high-frequency domain can facilitate depth-intensity fusion and reduce training time.

Timings. We summarize the computation time for upscaling different LR depth maps *Art* to their full resolution (1376×1088) using MS-Net and MSG-Net in Table 5. Upsamplings were performed in MATLAB with a TITAN X GPU.

5   Conclusion

We have presented a new framework to address the problem of depth map upsampling by using a multi-scale guided convolutional neural network (MSG-Net). A LR depth map is progressively upsampled with the guidance of the associated HR intensity image. Using such a design, MSG-Net achieves state-of-the-art performance for super-resolving depth maps. We have also studied a special case of it for multi-scale single-image super resolution (MS-Net) without guidance. Although sacrificing some upsampling performance, MS-Net in turn has a compact network architecture and it still achieves good performance.

Acknowledgment. This work is partially supported by SenseTime Group Limited.

References

1. Kopf, J., Cohen, M., Lischinski, D., Uyttendaele, M.: Joint bilateral upsampling. ToG **26**(3), Article No. 96 (2007)
2. Park, J., Kim, H., Tai, Y.W., Brown, M., Kweon, I.: High quality depth map upsampling for 3D-TOF cameras. In: ICCV, pp. 1623–1630 (2011)
3. Kiechle, M., Hawe, S., Kleinsteuber, M.: A joint intensity and depth co-sparse analysis model for depth map super-resolution. In: ICCV, pp. 1545–1552 (2013)
4. Ferstl, D., Reinbacher, C., Ranftl, R., Rüther, M., Bischof, H.: Image guided depth upsampling using anisotropic total generalized variation. In: ICCV, pp. 993–1000 (2013)
5. Yang, J., Ye, X., Li, K., Hou, C., Wang, Y.: Color-guided depth recovery from RGB-D data using an adaptive autoregressive model. TIP **23**(8), 3962–3969 (2014)
6. Lu, J., Forsyth, D.: Sparse depth super resolution. In: CVPR, pp. 2245–2253 (2015)
7. Kwon, H., Tai, Y.W., Lin, S.: Data-driven depth map refinement via multi-scale sparse representation. In: CVPR, pp. 159–167 (2015)
8. He, K., Sun, J., Tang, X.: Guided image filtering. PAMI **35**(6), 1397–1409 (2013)

9. Hui, T.W., Ngan, K.: Depth enhancement using RGB-D guided filtering. In: ICIP, pp. 3832–3836 (2014)

10. Shen, X., Zhou, C., Xu, L., Jia, J.: Mutual-structure for joint filtering. In: ICCV, pp. 3406–3414 (2015)

11. Dong, C., Loy, C., He, K., Tang, X.: Image super-resolution using deep convolutional networks. PAMI **38**(2), 295–307 (2015)

12. Wang, Z., Liu, D., Yang, J., Han, W., Huang, T.: Deep networks for image super-resolution with sparse prior. In: ICCV, pp. 370–378 (2015)

13. Yang, Q., Yang, R., Davis, J., Nistér, D.: Spatial-depth super resolution for range images. In: CVPR (2007)

14. Liu, M.Y., Tuzel, O., Taguchi, Y.: Joint geodesic upsampling of depth images. In: CVPR, pp. 169–176 (2013)

15. Diebel, J., Thrun, S.: An application of Markov random fields to range sensing. In: NIPS (2005)

16. Mac Aodha, O., Campbell, N.D.F., Nair, A., Brostow, G.J.: Patch based synthesis for single depth image super-resolution. In: Fitzgibbon, A., Lazebnik, S., Perona, P., Sato, Y., Schmid, C. (eds.) ECCV 2012. LNCS, vol. 7574, pp. 71–84. Springer, Heidelberg (2012). doi:10.1007/978-3-642-33712-3_6

17. Yang, J., Wright, J., Huang, T., Ma, Y.: Image super-resolution via sparse representation. TIP **11**(9), 2861–2873 (2010)

18. Timofte, R., Smet, V.D., Gool, L.V.: Anchored neighborhood regression for fast example-based super-resolution. In: ICCV, pp. 1920–1927 (2013)

19. Ferstl, D., Ruether, M., Bischof, H.: Variational depth superresolution using example-based edge representations. In: ICCV, pp. 513–521 (2015)

20. Li, Y., Xue, T., Sun, L., Liu, J.: Joint example-based depth map super-resolution. In: ICME, pp. 152–157 (2012)

21. Gregor, K., LeCun, Y.: Learning fast approximations of sparse coding. In: ICML, pp. 399–406 (2010)

22. Osendorfer, C., Soyer, H., Smagt, P.: Image super-resolution with fast approximate convolutional sparse coding. In: Loo, C.K., Yap, K.S., Wong, K.W., Beng Jin, A.T., Huang, K. (eds.) ICONIP 2014. LNCS, vol. 8836, pp. 250–257. Springer, Heidelberg (2014). doi:10.1007/978-3-319-12643-2_31

23. Long, J., Shelhamer, E., Darrell, T.: Fully convolutional networks for semantic segmentation. In: CVPR, pp. 3431–3440 (2015)

24. Dosovitskiy, A., Springenberg, J.T., Brox, T.: Learning to generate chairs with convolutional neural networks. In: CVPR, pp. 1538–1546 (2015)

25. Fischer, P., Dosovitskiy, A., Ilg, E., Häusser, P., Hazirbas, C., Golkov, V., Smagt, P., Cremers, D., Brox, T.: FlowNet: learning optical flow with convolutional networks. In: ICCV, pp. 2758–2766 (2015)

26. Xie, S., Tu, Z.: Holistically-nested edge detection. In: ICCV, pp. 1395–1403 (2015)

27. Hui, T.W., Ngan, K.: Motion-depth: RGB-D depth map enhancement with motion and depth in complement. In: CVPR, pp. 3962–3969 (2014)

28. He, K., Zhang, X., Ren, S., Sun, J.: Delving deep into rectifiers: surpassing human-level performance on imagenet classification. In: ICCV, pp. 1026–1034 (2015)

29. Butler, D.J., Wulff, J., Stanley, G.B., Black, M.J.: A naturalistic open source movie for optical flow evaluation. In: Fitzgibbon, A., Lazebnik, S., Perona, P., Sato, Y., Schmid, C. (eds.) ECCV 2012. LNCS, vol. 7577, pp. 611–625. Springer, Heidelberg (2012). doi:10.1007/978-3-642-33783-3_44

30. Scharstein, D., Szeliski, R.: A taxonomy and evaluation of dense two-frame stereo correspondence algorithms. IJCV **47**(1), 7–42 (2002)

31. Scharstein, D., Pal, C.: Learning conditional random fields for stereo. In: CVPR (2007)
32. Scharstein, D., Hirschmüller, H., Kitajima, Y., Krathwohl, G., Nešić, N., Wang, X., Westling, P.: High-resolution stereo datasets with subpixel-accurate ground truth. In: Jiang, X., Hornegger, J., Koch, R. (eds.) GCPR 2014. LNCS, vol. 8753, pp. 31–42. Springer, Heidelberg (2014). doi:10.1007/978-3-319-11752-2_3
33. Jia, Y., Shelhamer, E., Donahue, J., Karayev, S., Long, J., Girshick, R., Guadarrama, S., Darrell, T.: Caffe: convolutional architecture for fast feature embedding. arXiv preprint arXiv:1408.5093 (2014)
34. Lu, J., Shi, K., Min, D., Lin, L., Do, M.N.: Cross-based local multipoint filtering. In: CVPR, pp. 430–437 (2012)

SEAGULL: Seam-Guided Local Alignment for Parallax-Tolerant Image Stitching

Kaimo Lin[1,2(✉)], Nianjuan Jiang[2], Loong-Fah Cheong[1], Minh Do[2], and Jiangbo Lu[2]

[1] National University of Singapore, Singapore, Singapore
linkaimo1990@gmail.com
[2] Advanced Digital Sciences Center, Singapore, Singapore
Nianjuan.jiang@adsc.com.sg

Abstract. Image stitching with large parallax is a challenging problem. Global alignment usually introduces noticeable artifacts. A common strategy is to perform partial alignment to facilitate the search for a good seam for stitching. Different from existing approaches where the seam estimation process is performed sequentially after alignment, we explicitly use the estimated seam to guide the process of optimizing local alignment so that the seam quality gets improved over each iteration. Furthermore, a novel structure-preserving warping method is introduced to preserve salient curve and line structures during the warping. These measures substantially improve the effectiveness of our method in dealing with a wide range of challenging images with large parallax.

1 Introduction

Traditional image stitching techniques estimate a global 2D transformation (e.g. homography transformation) to align the input images [3, 22, 23]. The underlying assumption is that the images are taken at a fixed viewpoint or the scene is roughly planar. Violation of these assumptions will result in visual artifacts such as ghosting or misalignment that cannot be accounted for by a global 2D transformation. Such misalignment between the warped image and the reference image is referred to as parallax, and in this paper, we primarily want to address the problem of image stitching under large parallax.

For images with *small* parallax, some spatially-varying warping methods [19,20,25] combined with advanced image composition techniques like seam cutting [2,15] and multi-band blending [4] usually suffice. However, when the images are taken from different viewpoints and the scene contains non-planar or discontinuous surfaces (often the case when the images are taken casually by users), most existing methods fail to produce satisfactory stitching results due to the presence of *large* parallax [26]. For images with large parallax, global alignment,

---

Electronic supplementary material The online version of this chapter (doi:10.1007/978-3-319-46487-9_23) contains supplementary material, which is available to authorized users.

B. Leibe et al. (Eds.): ECCV 2016, Part III, LNCS 9907, pp. 370–385, 2016.
DOI: 10.1007/978-3-319-46487-9_23

Fig. 1. Comparison of global alignment and our seam-guided local alignment. Left: Input images. Middle: Stitching result by APAP [25] (all features are used). Right: Stitching result by our method (only features around the final stitching seam are used).

as an over-simplified model to account for the underlying camera-scene geometry, cannot produce visually plausible stitching results (see Fig. 1). Instead, one only needs to find an alignment model that will produce good seams to stitch two images. The desiderata of a good seam is that it should either pass through non-salient homogeneous regions or salient regions if the latter are well-aligned locally. Therefore, the problem boils down to finding such a parallax-free local region for stitching. Recent works [11,26] propose different strategies to select a subset of sparse feature matches that will facilitate finding such local regions for stitching. In these works, when the current alignment hypothesis is not satisfactory, a new set of features will be selected to generate an alternative alignment. This means the location of the current seam and its alignment quality are *not* used in any way to influence the new feature selection. Without exploiting the current results to decide or guide the next attempts, these existing methods have a few limitations: (1) the quality of a new seam might indeed be worse than the previous one; (2) if the scene in view is complex, then indeed one might have to generate a large number of alignment hypotheses before hitting upon a satisfactory one; and (3) it is non-trivial to decide the threshold setting that can be effectively used in all images for terminating the hypothesis generation process.

In this paper, we propose a *seam-guided local alignment (SEAGULL)* scheme for image stitching in the presence of large parallax. As its name suggests, we iteratively look for a good local alignment by performing seam-guided feature reweighting. Specifically, we weight the feature matches according to their current alignment errors (*i.e.*, the distance between two matching features after alignment) and their distances to the current estimated seam. This scheme stems from our observation that treating all the feature matches uniformly is usually not desirable in the presence of large parallax. For instance, methods [20,25] that aim at global alignment across the entire overlapping region often suffer from noticeable local distortions due to parallax or misalignment at the estimated seam. It follows that feature matches with large misalignment or far away from the current estimated seam should be weighted down when computing the image alignment refinement (see Fig. 1 Right). Another motivation of our iterative alignment refinement scheme is that the current alignment does provide useful information to guide the search for a better seam. Generally, at least some parts of the estimated seam pass through well-aligned parallax-free regions. We stand a much better chance to obtain an improved seam by locally perturbing the current seam rather than trying out an entirely new one. This is a much more effective strategy to deal with scenes with large and complex parallax.

To overcome the local minima problem of the iterative seam refinement, we generate multiple initial alignment hypotheses from subsets of feature matches obtained by a *superpixel-based feature grouping* method. Each alignment hypothesis is then further refined by our seam-guided local alignment process. The optimized local alignment with the best stitching quality will be selected as the final stitching result. Our feature grouping method usually generates a small set of alignment hypotheses for optimization, yet because of the refinement process, these hypotheses are usually sufficient for obtaining a good stitching result.

The second contribution of our paper stems from the following observation. Many image alignment methods based on a subset of sparse feature matches do not have adequate control of the warping in image regions containing few features selected for alignment estimation. This results in noticeable distortion of the salient scene structures (e.g. lines and curves) in those regions. Even for regions with selected features, if these features contain certain amount of parallax, the warping may still suffer from unpleasant distortion in the aforementioned salient structures. Thus we propose a novel *structure-preserving warping* method that can effectively preserve curve and line structures during warping. We augment the basic CPW [20] framework with a new non-local structure-preserving term, so that similarity transformation constraints are enforced on the detected curve and line structures in the image, as well as on local mesh grids. Unlike the approach of [5,7,13,14], our non-local structure-preserving term introduces a sparse linear system and can be easily integrated into many other mesh-based warping methods [20,21]. [18] also introduces a line-preserving term in video stitching task. However, ours is more general and can also preserve curve structures.

2   Related Work

Image stitching is a well studied topic, yet stitching images with large parallax is still fraught with difficulties. A comprehensive survey can be found in [22]. Here, we briefly review related works from different perspectives.

Homography-Based Methods. Early methods [3,23] employ only one single homography to align two images. These methods can generate good stitching results if the images are taken from the same viewpoint or the scenes are roughly planar. However, these assumptions can be easily violated in practice when parallax exists. Although advanced composition methods (e.g. multi-band blending [4], seam cut [15]) can be used to alleviate the problem to some extent, artifacts still remain especially when parallax is large. Gao *et al.* [10] used a dual-homography model to stitch images and obtained good results when the scene can be roughly modeled by two dominant planes.

Spatially-Varying Warps. Spatially-varying warping methods [19,20,25] are introduced to handle images with parallax. Combined with advanced composition techniques, these methods can be very effective for generating visually plausible stitching results for images with small parallax. In particular, Lin *et al.* [19] estimated a smoothly varying affine field to align the images. Zaragoza *et al.* [25] proposed to use as-projective-as-possible warps to interpolate a smoothly varying projective stitching field. Li *et al.* [16] developed a dual-feature warping model for image alignment, using both the sparse feature matches and line correspondences. However, their method needs to predetermine line correspondences, which is a difficult task for images with large parallax. Also, for line structures without correspondences, this method cannot guarantee their straightness after warping. Our method, on the other hand, can preserve all curve and line structures effectively as long as they are detected.

Shape-Preserving Methods. Shape preserving warping methods mainly aim at generating natural-looking stitching results given a particular alignment model. Chang *et al.* [6] proposed a Shape-Preserving Half-Perspective (SPHP) warp that can smoothly transit from a projective transformation in the overlapping region into a similarity transformation in the non-overlapping region, with the latter aiming to counteract the unnatural perspective arising from the strange viewpoint (e.g. excessive tilting) associated with the projective transformation. Lin *et al.* [17] also proposed a warping model that combines two stitching fields (homography and global similarity) to generate natural-looking panoramas. These methods do not explicitly handle parallax.

Seam-Driven Stitching Methods. While the existing spatially-varying methods have been demonstrated to work well on images with moderate parallax, Zhang and Liu [26] argued that they may fail on images with large parallax. Gao *et al.* [11] posited that there is no need to employ all the feature matches in estimating the warping model, so long as the ultimate objective is to generate visually plausible results. Zhang and Liu [26] used this observation and proposed a hybrid transformation model to handle images with large parallax. They combined homography warp and content-preserving warp (CPW) [20] to align images. A randomized feature selection algorithm is developed to hypothesize homography candidates that may lead to good stitching seams. As its name suggests, warping hypotheses are searched for in a randomized fashion, in which the current pass does not use the alignment knowledge gained from the previous iterations. Our method, on the other hand, iteratively refines the warping model by adjusting feature weights according to their distances to a particular seam.

3   Stitching Algorithm

In this section, we will first briefly introduce our stitching pipeline before introducing the details of each step. For clarity of exposition, we take the two-image stitching case as an example. We keep the reference image fixed and warp the

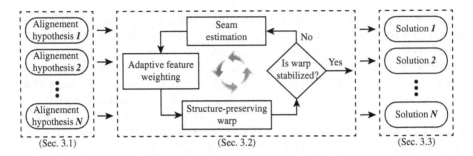

Fig. 2. The pipeline of our stitching algorithm.

target image. Stitching multiple images can be easily extended from this pipeline by adding one image at a time. As shown in Fig. 2, our stitching pipeline takes in multiple local alignment hypotheses as input, and applies seam-guided local alignment on each of these hypotheses to obtain locally optimal stitching. The final stitching is selected as the one with the best stitching seam quality.

3.1 Alignment Hypotheses Generation

For images with large parallax, it is shown that finding a local alignment that facilitates a seamless stitch is more effective in practice [11,26]. In this paper, we propose multiple alignment hypotheses to locate a good seam for stitching. Our goal is to generate a small set of hypotheses that are representative and distinctive from each other. To that end, we use a superpixel-based feature grouping method. Specifically, we first use SIFT [24] to obtain an initial set of feature matches. Then, we over-segment the target image using the method in [1]. Our goal is to partition the superpixels that contain features into several representative superpixel groups. Before the grouping, we first remove those outlier features in each superpixel by performing homography fitting with RANSAC [9].

In the grouping process, only superpixels that contain features are used. At the very beginning, all the superpixels are labeled as 'ungrouped'. In each iteration, we initialize a superpixel group S_i with the ungrouped superpixel that has the largest number of features. Then, we check all the neighboring ungrouped superpixels of S_i and add them to the group one by one if the homography fitting error of the new group is less than 5 pixels[1]. The growing process terminates when no more neighboring superpixels of S_i can be added. We repeat the above process in the remaining ungrouped superpixels until all the superpixels have been assigned to a group. Given these superpixel groups, we also perform a merging step to further reduce the group number. Specifically, we merge two superpixel groups if the homography fitting error of the newly merged group is also smaller than 5 pixels. This merging step starts from the group with the largest number of features, and tries to merge all the other groups to it

---

[1] Unless otherwise noted, all the constant parameters in our algorithm are set for an image resolution of around 720p.

in descending order of group size. We repeat this process for the remaining unmerged groups until no more groups can be merged. Finally, we use features in each resulting superpixel group to estimate a local homography. Each warped target image is regarded as a local alignment hypthesis.

To avoid only generating local homography hypotheses which could be biased, we further enrich the hypothesis set by combining different superpixel groups to produce extra alignment hypotheses. The total number of such combinations is given by $C_k^2 + C_k^3 + \ldots + C_k^k$, where k is the number of the groups (usually $k = 1 \sim 4$).

3.2 Seam-Guided Local Alignment

Our seam-guided local alignment optimizes each alignment hypothesis by iterating over the following three steps. Firstly, feature matches are weighted according to their current alignment errors and distances to the current estimated seam. Then, the target image is warped by a novel structure-preserving warping method. Finally, a stitching seam is estimated based on 'colored edge images'. The iteration terminates when there is little change of the mesh vertice locations compared to the previous iteration (average change less than one pixel) or the iteration number exceeds 5. For a reasonably good alignment hypothesis, this process usually terminates in $2 \sim 3$ iterations. Otherwise, we will just terminate those bad cases early by setting the hard limit of 5 iterations for run-time efficiency. Upon iteration termination, the final stitching seam quality is recorded.

Adaptive Feature Weighting. In each iteration, we compute a weight for each feature match using the following expression:

$$w = \lambda \left(e^{-\frac{d_m^2}{2\sigma_m^2}} + \epsilon \right), \tag{1}$$

where the terms in the bracket depend on the current alignment error of the feature and λ depends on the distance of the feature to the current seam. Specifically, d_m is the distance between the feature in the warped target image and its correspondence in the reference image. The terms $\epsilon = 0.01$ and $\sigma_m = 10$ are constants. λ is set to 1.5 if $d_s \leq 20$ (d_s is the shortest distance from the feature to the current seam), and 0.1 otherwise. In the first iteration when the seam has not been estimated, all d_s are set to zero.

Structure-Preserving Warp. We use a $m \times n$ grid mesh to represent the target image. Image warping is achieved by texture mapping using the coordinates of mesh vertices after deformation. Our proposed structure-preserving warp consists of a feature term and two structure-preserving terms. Different from CPW [20], our structure-preserving terms include both local and non-local similarity constraints. The total energy function is given by the following:

$$E(\hat{V}) = \lambda_1 E_f(\hat{V}) + \lambda_2 E_{ls}(\hat{V}) + \lambda_3 E_{cs}(\hat{V}), \tag{2}$$

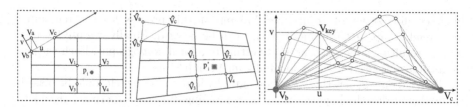

Fig. 3. Structure-preserving warp. Please refer to the text for details (Color figure online).

where $\hat{V}$ are the unknown coordinates of mesh vertices to be estimated. The feature term, local and non-local structure terms are denoted by $E_f(\hat{V})$, $E_{ls}(\hat{V})$, and $E_{cs}(\hat{V})$ respectively. The constant λ_1, λ_2, and λ_3 are the associated weights for these three terms ($\lambda_1 = 5$, $\lambda_2 = 1$, and $\lambda_3 = 10$ in our implementation). All these terms will form a sparse linear system which can be easily minimized.

Feature Term. The feature term is defined the same way as the data term in CPW [20]. As shown in Fig. 3 left, each feature point p_i can be represented by the 2D bilinear interpolation of the four vertices ($V_k, k = 1, \ldots, 4$) of its enclosing grid cell. To align p_i to its matched location p_i' (green square in Fig. 3 middle) after deformation, we define the feature term as:

$$E_f(\hat{V}) = \sum_i w_i \| \sum_{k=1}^4 c_k \hat{V}_k - p_i' \|^2, \tag{3}$$

where $\hat{V}$ contains the unknown mesh vertices. The bilinear coefficients ($c_k, k = 1, \ldots, 4$) are used to determine the location of p_i after warping. The feature weight w_i for p_i will be updated during iterations as given in Eq. 1.

Structure-Preserving Terms. Our structure-preserving terms are defined on both local and non-local similarity transformation constraints. According to [20], in a triangle consisting of three vertices, the coordinates (u, v) for a vertex V_a in the local coordinate system defined by the other two vertices V_b and V_c is given by

$$V_a = V_b + u(V_c - V_b) + vR_{90}(V_c - V_b), R_{90} = \begin{bmatrix} 0 & 1 \\ -1 & 0 \end{bmatrix}. \tag{4}$$

For a triangle that undergoes a similarity transformation, the new vertex $\hat{V}_a$ can still be represented by $\hat{V}_b$ and $\hat{V}_c$ using the same local coordinates (u, v) computed from its initial shape. Hence, one can minimize the following cost to encourage similarity transformation on a given triangle,

$$C_{tri} = \| \hat{V}_a - (\hat{V}_b + u(\hat{V}_c - \hat{V}_b) + vR_{90}(\hat{V}_c - \hat{V}_b)) \|^2. \tag{5}$$

Locally, as shown in Fig. 3 left, each grid cell can be divided into two triangles. We sum up C_{tri} defined over all the triangles in the grid mesh to compute our local similarity term E_{ls}. This local similarity constraint is also used in [20] to maintain spatial smoothness of the warping. However, it does not provide sufficient constraints on salient structures larger than the size of the mesh cells. Therefore, we explicitly extract contours, and use triangles defined on each of the contours to compute a set of non-local similarity constraints. Specifically, we first extract contours from the target image using OpenCV's contour detection function. For contours with branching nodes, we break them at these nodes and collect the sub-contours as curve segments. Otherwise, each contour is a curve segment. Curve segments with a length shorter than 20 pixels will be discarded. Then we uniformly sample key points (green curve in Fig. 3 right) along each curve and define a set of triangles formed by the two endpoints (red points in Fig. 3 right) and each key point. The non-local similarity term is thus given by

$$E_{cs}(\hat{V}) = \sum_{i=1}^{N_c} \sum_{j=1}^{N_k} \|\hat{V}_{key}^{i,j} - (\hat{V}_b^i + u(\hat{V}_c^i - \hat{V}_b^i) + vR_{90}(\hat{V}_c^i - \hat{V}_b^i))\|^2, \qquad (6)$$

where N_c is the total number of curve segments and N_k is the number of key points on each curve segment i. The curve vertices $\hat{V}_{key}^{i,j}$, $\hat{V}_b^i$, and $\hat{V}_c^i$ can be represented by the mesh vertices using bilinear interpolation just like the feature term. Note that the non-local structure-preserving term is also valid for line structures. Therefore, we also employ a line detector [12] to detect line segments in the target image and add them to the current curve set.

Seam Estimation. To apply the seam cut technique [15], one first computes a difference map between the reference image and the target image in the overlapping region. The difference map is usually obtained by calculating either the color difference of the pixels or the Canny edge map difference [26]. The pixel color difference approach has more discriminatory power compared to the Canny edge map approach, whereas the latter has stronger robustness against illumination changes. We combine the strength of both by retaining pixel colors that are near the extracted Canny edges, and refer to this representation as the 'colored edge image'. Specifically, we expand the edge map mask by 1 pixel on either side of the edge and retain the original color of the pixels on the expanded edge mask, with other pixels' colors set to black. Our stitching seam is obtained by applying the seam cut technique [15] on the 'colored edge images'.

3.3   Stitching Seam Quality Assessment

Since SEAGULL targets on local alignment and can preserve salient scene structures during the warp, we only need to evaluate the alignment quality along the final stitching seam. Specifically, for each pixel p_i on the final stitching seam, we first define a 15×15 local patch (in pixels) centered at p_i. Then we compute the ZNCC score between the local patch in the target image and that in the reference image. The seam quality is then defined as follows:

Fig. 4. Our dataset used in this paper.

$$Q_{seam}(p) = \frac{1}{N} \sum_{i}^{N} (1.0 - \frac{ZNCC(p_i) + 1}{2}), \tag{7}$$

where N is the total number of pixels on the seam, excluding the ones that are not on the colored edge masks.

4   Experiments

We demonstrate the effectiveness of SEAGULL in two aspects. Firstly, we conduct several experiments to validate the design of the individual components in SEAGULL, specifically, the alignment hypothesis generation, the seam-guided local alignment optimization, and the structure-preserving warping method. Secondly, we compare the overall performance of SEAGULL with two state-of-the-art stitching methods, APAP [25] and Zhang and Liu's method [26]. We evaluate the methods over two datasets: the first comprises of 24 pairs of images taken by us using mobile phones with challenging parallax variation (Fig. 4), and the second uses the images from Zhang and Liu's published dataset, which can be found on their project website. To suppress the intensity difference along the estimated seam, we apply the method from [8] to all the final stitching results.

4.1   Homography Hypothesis Evaluation

We compare the alignment hypothesis generation method in SEAGULL with that in [11,26], in which [11] is based on homography fitting with RANSAC [9], and [26] is based on randomized feature selection (for more details, refer to [26]). The experiment is conducted on our own dataset of 24 pairs of images. We use the same threshold for homography fitting errors in all three methods. For [26], the iteration terminates when the average penalty value of all the features is larger than a threshold. However, the value of the threshold is not reported in [26] and we find it quite tricky to set a universally appropriate value. If the value is too small, many features may not have the chance to be selected in the whole process. If the value is too large, each feature may be selected multiple times and the algorithm may generate many redundant homography hypotheses.

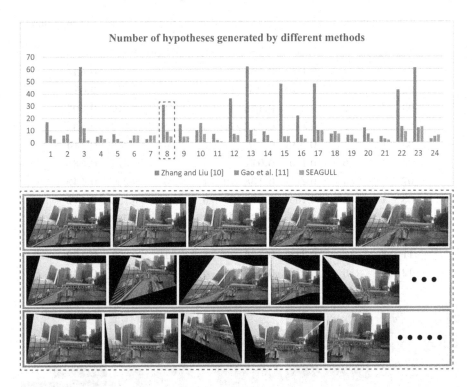

Fig. 5. Comparison of different hypothesis generation methods. The last three rows show example alignment hypotheses produced by SEAGULL, [11,26] respectively.

In the presence of large and complex parallax, any feature may contribute to the search of a good stitching seam. Our goal is to try as many features as possible while keeping the number of hypotheses small. Therefore, we choose a different termination condition whereby the algorithm of [26] is terminated if more than 80 % of the features have been selected at least once in the previous iterations.

Figure 5 shows the comparison results. The top graph shows the number of alignment hypotheses generated by the respective methods. Since [26] contains randomness in seed selection, we run the algorithm ten times and record the mean values. As can be seen from the graph, in most of the cases, SEAGULL generates the smallest set of alignment hypotheses. [26] usually generates more hypotheses than the other two methods. The reason is that its homography fitting process in each iteration will terminate immediately when one candidate feature can not be added to the current group regardless of the other unchecked nearest neighbors. This premature termination results in many small feature groups, given that there are inevitable feature mismatches. The bottom figure shows some alignment hypotheses generated by these methods on the image pair *No.8*. We can see that all of our results are fairly good for further optimization. However, some results from [11,26] are clearly unsuitable for stitching.

Table 1. Stitching seam quality before and after seam-guided local optimization.

No.	Homo	Opti	Before	After	No.	Homo	Opti	Before	After
01	1	1	0.186	**0.148**	13	3	3	0.094	**0.045**
02	1	1	**0.059**	0.061	14	1	1	0.117	**0.074**
03	1	2	0.227	**0.135**	15	4	4	0.319	**0.205**
04	2	2	0.326	**0.217**	16	3	1	0.163	**0.138**
05	1	1	**0.333**	0.387	17	1	4	0.338	**0.114**
06	4	6	0.150	**0.072**	18	4	1	0.374	**0.336**
07	1	4	0.275	**0.168**	19	1	3	0.206	**0.142**
08	1	3	0.166	**0.072**	20	3	1	0.192	**0.170**
09	5	1	0.189	**0.066**	21	2	2	**0.164**	0.179
10	4	4	0.265	**0.195**	22	1	3	0.172	**0.080**
11	1	1	0.288	**0.256**	23	8	10	0.206	**0.159**
12	6	6	0.273	**0.265**	24	4	1	0.326	**0.148**

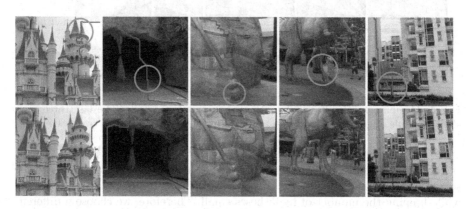

Fig. 6. Comparison of with and without our seam-guided local optimization. Top: Results without optimization. Bottom: Results with optimization.

4.2   Seam-Guided Local Optimization Evaluation

To demonstrate the effectiveness of our seam-guided local optimization, we compare the final stitching seam quality with and without the optimization part. The experiment is also conducted on our own dataset. For each example, we take the alignment hypothesis that leads to the best stitching result after local optimization, and apply seam estimation on both alignments before and after the local optimization. We compare the respective seam quality in Table 1. Particularly, stitching seam quality with and without the local optimization is listed in columns '**After**' and '**Before**', respectively. A smaller value usually indicates noticeable visually improved seam quality. As we can see, in most of the cases, the seam quality improves after our seam-guided local optimization. In some

Fig. 7. Evaluations of our weighting scheme and non-local structure-preserving term. Left: CPW [20] with equally weighted features. Middle: CPW [20] with seam-guided weighted features. Right: Our structure-preserving warp.

examples (i.e. 02, 05, and 21), the two stitching results share similar seam quality and are all visually plausible. Figure 6 provides a visual comparison of stitching results with a difference in seam quality larger than 0.05. We can see that our seam-guided local optimization clearly improves the seam quality. Besides the seam quality comparison, we also record the index of the alignment hypothesis that leads to the best stitching with and without the optimization process. Column **'Homo'** in Table 1 indicates the index of the alignment hypothesis that produces the best stitching result without our local optimization. Column **'Opti'** indicates the index of the best alignment hypothesis with the optimization. Interestingly, the homography hypothesis with the best stitching quality at the beginning does not always lead to the best stitching result after optimization.

4.3   Structure-Preserving Warp Evaluation

Our structure-preserving warp effectively preserves salient curve and line structures during image warping while facilitating good local alignment around the estimated seam. An example using CPW [20] with equally weighted feature matches is shown in Fig. 7 left. Since the detected feature matches may contain wrong pairs and the parallax is too large for 2D global alignment, salient curve and line structures are severely distorted during the warp. Using global homography fitting to remove the mismatches is not a good practice for images with large parallax, since it may also accidentally discard many correct ones. Figure 7 middle shows the warping result by augmenting CPW with our weighted feature matches. We can see that our seam-guided weighting scheme has effectively removed most of the local distortions while facilitating the alignment around the estimated seam. Figure 7 right shows the result of our warping method. It further preserves extracted curve and line structures across the entire image region.

Fig. 8. Comparison with APAP [25]. Top: APAP's results. Bottom: SEAGULL's results (Color figure online).

4.4 Comparison with APAP [25]

We use the source code provided by the authors to obtain image alignment by APAP method [25], after which we apply our seam estimation for fair comparison. All the results are generated using default parameters. Some of the comparison results are given in Fig. 8. APAP tries to align as many feature matches as possible in the entire overlapping region without explicitly preserving salient scene structures. It suffers from local distortions in both overlapping and non-overlapping regions (green rectangle regions in Fig. 8) caused by feature matches with large parallax. Furthermore, as the APAP warp is decoupled from the seam estimation process, such local distortion can have negative impact on seam estimation. The estimated seam may accidentally pass through these distorted regions and generate broken structures (green circle regions in Fig. 8). Our adaptive feature weighting explicitly avoids using feature matches with large parallax or far away from the estimated seam of interest to minimize the undesired local distortions. Together with our novel structure-preserving warp, our final stitching results are visually much more appealing for the given examples.

4.5 Comparison with Zhang and Liu's Method [26]

Zhang and Liu's method [26] is currently the state-of-the-art for parallax-tolerant image stitching. Since the source code is not available, we only test our method on the datasets released by the authors. In most cases, SEAGULL generates visually comparable stitching results, and produces noticeably better ones on some examples. The complete comparison can be found in the supplementary material. Here we show examples with noticeable improvements to demonstrate the advantages of SEAGULL. In Zhang and Liu's method, the best homography is selected from various rough alignment candidates. Therefore, the final stitching seam without any further optimization may still be contaminated by large misalignment (Fig. 9 row 1), even though the stitching quality as a whole might seem acceptable. Furthermore, since salient scene structures like curves or lines are not explicitly preserved by their method, they are found distorted in some stitching results (Fig. 9 row 2–4). In comparison, our structure-preserving warp does not produce such artifacts on these examples.

Fig. 9. Comparison with Zhang and Liu's method [26]. Left: Zhang and Liu's results. Right: SEAGULL's results.

4.6 Discussion

All our experiments are performed on a desktop computer with an Intel i7 CPU and 32 GB memory. For each alignment hypothesis, the seam-guided local alignment process takes about $3 \sim 4$ s. The proposed algorithm usually takes less than one minute to find the best stitching result without code optimization. Since the optimization for each alignment hypothesis is independent from one another, our method can be readily parallelized for better runtime. Our method could fail if the parallax is too large in the periphery of the overlapping region, or these local regions consist of rich salient structures but few feature matches.

5   Conclusions

In this paper, we propose a seam-guided local alignment method for large parallax image stitching. We closely couple the local alignment computation and the seam estimation via adaptive feature weighting. Salient curve and line structures are explicitly preserved during the warping by enforcing both local and non-local similarity constraints. Our superpixel-based feature grouping method effectively reduces the number of alignment hypotheses while still discovering good initial alignments for later optimization. The proposed method is evaluated on a variety of image pairs with large parallax and outperforms state-of-the-art stitching methods in terms of effectiveness and robustness.

Acknowledgements. This work was supported by the Singapore PSF grant 1321202075 and the HCCS research grant at the ADSC from Singapore's Agency for Science, Technology and Research (A*STAR) (This work was partly done when Kaimo was interning in ADSC.).

References

1. Achanta, R., Shaji, A., Smith, K., Lucchi, A., Fua, P., Susstrunk, S.: SLIC super-pixels compared to state-of-the-art superpixel methods. IEEE Trans. Pattern Anal. Mach. Intell. **34**(11), 2274–2282 (2012)
2. Agarwala, A., Dontcheva, M., Agrawala, M., Drucker, S., Colburn, A., Curless, B., Salesin, D., Cohen, M.: Interactive digital photomontage. ACM Trans. Graph. **23**(3), 294–302 (2004)
3. Brown, M., Lowe, D.G.: Automatic panoramic image stitching using invariant features. Int. J. Comput. Vis. (IJCV) **74**(1), 59–73 (2007)
4. Burt, P.J., Adelson, E.H.: A multiresolution spline with application to image mosaics. ACM Trans. Graph. **2**(4), 217–236 (1983)
5. Carroll, R., Agarwala, A., Agrawala, M.: Image warps for artistic perspective manipulation. ACM Trans. Graph. **29**(4), 127:1–127:9 (2010)
6. Chang, C.H., Sato, Y., Chuang, Y.Y.: Shape-preserving half-projective warps for image stitching. In: Proceedings of CVPR (2014)
7. Chang, C.H., Chuang, Y.Y.: A line-structure-preserving approach to image resizing. In: Proceedings of CVPR, pp. 1075–1082 (2012)
8. Farbman, Z., Hoffer, G., Lipman, Y., Cohen-Or, D., Lischinski, D.: Coordinates for instant image cloning. ACM Trans. Graph. **28**(3), 67:1–67:9 (2009)
9. Fischler, M.A., Bolles, R.C.: Random sample consensus: a paradigm for model fitting with applications to image analysis and automated cartography. Commun. ACM **24**(6), 381–395 (1981)
10. Gao, J., Kim, S.J., Brown, M.S.: Constructing image panoramas using dual-homography warping. In: Proceedings of CVPR (2011)
11. Gao, J., Li, Y., Chin, T.J., Brown, M.S.: Seam-driven image stitching. In: Euro-graphics, pp. 45–48 (2013)
12. von Gioi, R.G., Jakubowicz, J., Morel, J.M., Randall, G.: LSD: a fast line segment detector with a false detection control. IEEE Trans. Pattern Anal. Mach. Intell. **32**(4), 722–732 (2010)
13. He, K., Chang, H., Sun, J.: Rectangling panoramic images via warping. ACM Trans. Graph. **32**(4), 79:1–79:10 (2013)
14. Krähenbühl, P., Lang, M., Hornung, A., Gross, M.: A system for retargeting of streaming video. ACM Trans. Graph. **28**(5), 126:1–126:10 (2009)
15. Kwatra, V., Schödl, A., Essa, I., Turk, G., Bobick, A.: Graphcut textures: image and video synthesis using graph cuts. ACM Trans. Graph. **22**(3), 277–286 (2003)
16. Li, S., Yuan, L., Sun, J., Quan, L.: Dual-feature warping-based motion model estimation. In: Proceedings of ICCV, pp. 4283–4291 (2015)
17. Lin, C.C., Pankanti, S.U., Ramamurthy, K.N., Aravkin, A.Y.: Adaptive as-natural-as-possible image stitching. In: Proceedings of CVPR (2015)
18. Lin, K., Liu, S., Cheong, L.F., Zeng, B.: Seamless video stitching with hand-held camera inputs. Comput. Graph. Forum **35**(2), 479–487 (2016)
19. Lin, W.Y., Liu, S., Matsushita, Y., Ng, T.T., Cheong, L.F.: Smoothly varying affine stitching. In: Proceedings of CVPR (2011)

20. Liu, F., Gleicher, M., Jin, H., Agarwala, A.: Content-preserving warps for 3D video stabilization. ACM Trans. Graph. (Proc. SIGGRAPH) **28**(3), 44:1–44:9 (2009)
21. Liu, S., Yuan, L., Tan, P., Sun, J.: Bundled camera paths for video stabilization. ACM Trans. Graph. (TOG) **32**(4), 78:1–78:10 (2013)
22. Szeliski, R.: Image alignment and stitching: a tutorial. Found. Trends. Comput. Graph. Vis. **2**(1), 1–104 (2006)
23. Szeliski, R., Shum, H.-Y.: Creating full view panoramic image mosaics and environment maps. In: Proceedings of the 24th Annual Conference on Computer Graphics and Interactive Techniques, SIGGRAPH 1997, pp. 251–258 (1997)
24. Wu, C.: SiftGPU: a GPU implementation of scale invariant feature transform (SIFT) (2007). http://cs.unc.edu/ccwu/siftgpu
25. Zaragoza, J., Chin, T.J., Brown, M.S., Suter, D.: As-projective-as-possible image stitching with moving DLT. In: Proceedings of CVPR (2013)
26. Zhang, F., Liu, F.: Parallax-tolerant image stitching. In: Proceedings of CVPR (2014)

Grid Loss: Detecting Occluded Faces

Michael Opitz[(⊠)], Georg Waltner, Georg Poier, Horst Possegger,
and Horst Bischof

Institute for Computer Graphics and Vision,
Graz University of Technology,
Graz, Austria
michael.opitz@icg.tugraz.at

Abstract. Detection of partially occluded objects is a challenging computer vision problem. Standard Convolutional Neural Network (CNN) detectors fail if parts of the detection window are occluded, since not every sub-part of the window is discriminative on its own. To address this issue, we propose a novel loss layer for CNNs, named *grid loss*, which minimizes the error rate on sub-blocks of a convolution layer independently rather than over the whole feature map. This results in parts being more discriminative on their own, enabling the detector to recover if the detection window is partially occluded. By mapping our loss layer back to a regular fully connected layer, no additional computational cost is incurred at runtime compared to standard CNNs. We demonstrate our method for face detection on several public face detection benchmarks and show that our method outperforms regular CNNs, is suitable for realtime applications and achieves state-of-the-art performance.

Keywords: Object detection · CNN · Face detection

1 Introduction

We focus on single-class object detection and in particular address the problem of face detection. Several applications for face detection, such as surveillance or robotics, impose realtime requirements and rely on detectors which are fast, accurate and have low memory overhead. Traditionally, the most prominent approaches have been based on boosting [1–7] and Deformable Parts Models (DPMs) [3,8]. More recently, following the success of deep learning for computer vision, e.g. [9], methods based on Convolutional Neural Networks (CNNs) have been applied to single-class object detection tasks, e.g. [10–13].

Electronic supplementary material The online version of this chapter (doi:10. 1007/978-3-319-46487-9_24) contains supplementary material, which is available to authorized users.

B. Leibe et al. (Eds.): ECCV 2016, Part III, LNCS 9907, pp. 386–402, 2016.
DOI: 10.1007/978-3-319-46487-9_24

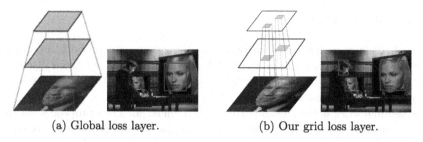

(a) Global loss layer.   (b) Our grid loss layer.

Fig. 1. Schematic overview of (a) standard global loss and (b) the proposed grid loss with an illustrative example on FDDB.

One of the most challenging problems in the context of object detection is handling partial occlusions. Since the occluder might have arbitrary appearance, occluded objects have significant intra-class variation. Therefore, collecting large datasets capturing the huge variability of occluded objects, which is required for training large CNNs, is expensive. The main question we address in this paper is: How can we train a CNN to detect occluded objects?

In standard CNNs not every sub-part of the detection template is discriminative alone (i.e. able to distinguish faces from background), resulting in missed faces if parts of the detection template are occluded. Our main contribution is to address this issue by introducing a novel loss layer for CNNs, named *grid loss*, which is illustrated in Fig. 1. This layer divides the convolution layer into spatial blocks and optimizes the hinge loss on each of these blocks separately. This results in several independent detectors which are discriminative on their own. If one part of the window is occluded, only a subset of these detectors gets confused, whereas the remaining ones will still make correct predictions.

By requiring parts to be already discriminative on their own, we encourage the CNN to learn features suitable for classifying parts of an object. If we would train a loss over the full face, the CNN might solve this classification problem by just learning features which detect a subset of discriminative regions, e.g. eyes. We divide our window into sub-parts and some of these parts do not contain such highly prototypical regions. Thus, the CNN has to also learn discriminative representations for other parts corresponding to e.g. nose or mouth. We find that CNNs trained with grid loss develop more diverse and independent features compared to CNNs trained with a regular loss.

After training we map our grid loss layer back to a regular fully connected layer. Hence, no additional runtime cost is incurred by our method.

As we show in our experiments, grid loss significantly improves over using a regular linear layer on top of a convolution layer without imposing additional computational cost at runtime. We evaluate our method on publicly available face detection datasets [14–16] and show that it compares favorably to state-of-the-art methods. Additionally, we present a detailed parameter evaluation providing further insights into our method, which shows that grid loss especially benefits detection of occluded faces and reduces overfitting by efficiently combining several spatially independent detectors.

2   Related Work

Since there is a multitude of work in the area of face detection, a complete discussion of all papers is out of scope of this work. Hence, we focus our discussion only on seminal work and closely related approaches in the field and refer to [17] for a more complete survey.

A seminal work is the method of Viola and Jones [5]. They propose a realtime detector using a cascade of simple decision stumps. These classifiers are based on area-difference features computed over differently sized rectangles. To accelerate feature computation, they employ integral images for computing rectangular areas in constant time, independent of the rectangle size.

Modern boosting based detectors use linear classifiers on SURF based features [18], exemplars [19], and leverage landmark information with shape-indexed features for classification [20]. Other boosting based detectors compute integral images on oriented gradient features as well as LUV channels and use shallow boosted decision trees [3] or constrain the features on the feature channels to be block sized [21]. Additionally, [7] proposes CNN features for the boosting framework.

Another family of detectors are DPM [8] based detectors, which learn root and part templates. The responses of these templates are combined with a deformation model to compute a confidence score. Extensions to DPMs have been proposed which handle occlusions [22], improve runtime speed [23] and leverage manually annotated part positions in a tree structure [16].

Further, there are complimentary approaches improving existing detectors by domain adaption techniques [24]; and exemplar based methods using retrieval techniques to detect and align faces [25,26].

Recently, CNNs became increasingly popular due to their success in recognition and detection problems, e.g. [9,27]. They successively apply convolution filters followed by non-linear activation functions. Early work in this area applies a small number of convolution filters followed by sum or average pooling on the image [28–30]. More recent work leverages a larger number of filters which are pre-trained on large datasets, e.g. ILSVRC [31], and fine-tuned on face datasets. These approaches are capable of detecting faces in multiple orientations and poses, e.g. [10]. Furthermore, [12] uses a coarse-to-fine neural network cascade to efficiently detect faces in realtime. Successive networks in the cascade have a larger number of parameters and use previous features of the cascade as inputs. [32] propose a large dataset with attribute annotated faces to learn 5 face attribute CNNs for predicting hair, eye, nose, mouth and beard attributes (e.g. black hair vs. blond hair vs. bald hair). Classifier responses are used to re-rank object proposals, which are then classified by a CNN as face vs. non-face.

In contrast to recent CNN based approaches for face detection [10,12,32], we exploit the benefits of part-based models with our grid loss layer by efficiently combining several spatially independent networks to improve detection performance and increase robustness to partial occlusions. Compared to [32], our method does not require additional face-specific attribute annotations and is more generally applicable to other object detection problems. Furthermore, our method is suitable for realtime applications.

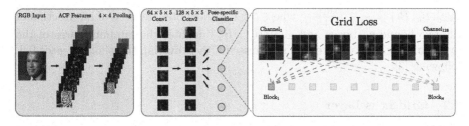

Fig. 2. Overview of our method: our detection CNN builds upon Aggregate Channel Features (ACF) [2]. For each window, after pooling, we apply successive convolution filters to the input channels. To distinguish faces from non-faces we use pose-specific classifiers. Instead of minimizing the loss over the last full convolution map, we divide the map into small blocks and minimize a loss function on each of these blocks independently. We train our CNN end-to-end with backpropagation.

3   Grid Loss for CNNs

We design the architecture of our detector based on the following key requirements for holistic detectors: We want to achieve realtime performance to process video-stream data and achieve state-of-the-art accuracy. To this end, we use the network architecture as illustrated in Fig. 2. Our method detects faces using a sliding window, similar to [33]. We apply two convolution layers on top of the input features as detailed in Sect. 3.1. In Sect. 3.2, we introduce our grid loss layer to obtain highly accurate part-based pose-specific classifiers. Finally, in Sect. 3.3 we propose a regressor to refine face positions and skip several intermediate octave levels to improve runtime performance even further.

3.1   Neural Network Architecture

The architecture of our CNN consists of two 5×5 convolution layers (see Fig. 2). Each convolution layer is followed by a Rectified Linear Unit (ReLU) activation. To normalize responses across layers, we use a Local Contrast Normalization (LCN) layer in between the two convolution layers. Further, we apply a small amount of dropout [34] of 0.1 after the last convolution layer. We initialize the weights randomly with a Gaussian of zero mean and 0.01 standard deviation. Each unit in the output layer corresponds to a specific face pose, which is trained discriminatively against the background class. We define the final confidence for a detection window as the maximum confidence over all output layer units.

In contrast to other CNN detectors, mainly for speed reasons, we use Aggregate Channel Features (ACF) [2] as low-level inputs to our network. For face detection we subsample the ACF pyramid by a factor of 4, reducing the computational cost of the successive convolution layers.

At runtime, we apply the CNN detector in a sliding window fashion densely over the feature pyramid at several scales. After detection, we perform Non Maxima Suppression (NMS) of two bounding boxes B_a and B_b using the overlap score

$o_{\text{NMS}}(B_a, B_b) = \frac{|B_a \cap B_b|}{\min(|B_a|, |B_b|)}$, where $|B_a \cap B_b|$ denotes the area of intersection of the two bounding boxes and $\min(|B_a|, |B_b|)$ denotes the minimum area of the two bounding boxes. Boxes are suppressed if their overlap threshold exceeds 0.3, following [3].

3.2 Grid Loss Layer

CNN detection templates can have non-discriminative sub-parts, which produce negative median responses over the positive training set (see Fig. 3a). To achieve an overall positive prediction for a given positive training sample, they heavily rely on certain sub-parts of a feature map to make a strong positive prediction. However, if these parts are occluded, the prediction of the detector is negatively influenced. To tackle this problem, we propose to divide the convolution layers into small $n \times n$ blocks and optimize the hinge loss for each of these blocks separately. This results in a detector where sub-parts are discriminative (see Fig. 3b). If a part of an input face is occluded, a subset of these detectors will still have non-occluded face parts as inputs. More formally, let $\boldsymbol{x}$ denote a vectorized $f \times r \times c$ dimensional tensor which represents the last convolution layer map, where f denotes the number of filters, r denotes the number of rows and c the number of columns of the feature map. We divide $\boldsymbol{x}$ into small $f \times n \times n$ non-overlapping blocks $\boldsymbol{f}_i$, $i = 1 \ldots N$, with $N = \lceil \frac{r}{n} \rceil \cdot \lceil \frac{c}{n} \rceil$. To train our layer, we use the hinge loss

$$l(\boldsymbol{\theta}) = \sum_{i=1}^{N} \max(0, m - y \cdot (\boldsymbol{w}_i^\top \boldsymbol{f}_i + b_i)), \tag{1}$$

where $\boldsymbol{\theta} = [\boldsymbol{w}_1, \boldsymbol{w}_2, \ldots, \boldsymbol{w}_N, b_1, b_2, \ldots, b_N]$, m is the margin, $y \in \{-1, 1\}$ denotes the class label, $\boldsymbol{w}_i$ and b_i are the weight vector and bias for block i, respectively. In all our experiments we set m to $\frac{1}{N}$, since each of the N classifiers is responsible to push a given sample by $\frac{1}{N}$ farther away from the separating hyperplane.

Since some of the part classifiers might correspond to less discriminative face parts, we need to weight the outputs of different independent detectors correctly.

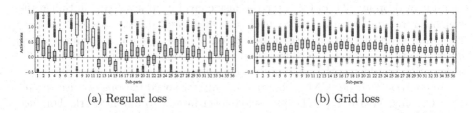

(a) Regular loss   (b) Grid loss

Fig. 3. Boxplot of 2×2 part activations on the positive training set (i.e. by dividing the detection template into non-overlapping parts, as in Fig. 2). Activations trained by regular loss functions can have parts with negative median response. We mark parts whose 25 % percentile is smaller than 0 (red) and parts which have significant positive median activations compared to other parts (yellow).(Color figure online)

Therefore, we combine this local per-block loss with a global hinge loss which shares parameters with the local classifiers. We concatenate the parameters $\boldsymbol{w} = [\boldsymbol{w}_1, \boldsymbol{w}_2, \ldots, \boldsymbol{w}_N]$ and set $b = \sum_i b_i$. Our final loss function is defined as

$$ l(\boldsymbol{\theta}) = \max(0, 1 - y \cdot (\boldsymbol{w}^\top \boldsymbol{x} + b)) + \lambda \cdot \sum_{i=1}^{N} \max(0, m - y \cdot (\boldsymbol{w}_i^\top \boldsymbol{f}_i + b_i)), \quad (2) $$

where λ weights the individual part detectors vs. the holistic detector and is empirically set to 1 in our experiments (see Sect. 4.3). To optimize this loss we use Stochastic Gradient Descent (SGD) with momentum. Since the weights $\boldsymbol{w}$ are shared between the global and local classifiers and b is a sum of existing parameters, the number of additional parameters is only $N - 1$ compared to a regular classification layer. However, at runtime no additional computational cost occurs, since we concatenate the local weight vectors to form a global weight vector and sum the local biases to obtain a global bias.

During training, the holistic loss backpropagates an error for misclassified samples to the hidden layers. Also, if certain parts are misclassifying a given sample, the part loss backpropagates an additional error signal to the hidden layers. However, for part detectors which are already discriminative enough to classify this sample correctly, no additional part error signal is backpropagated. In this way error signals of less discriminative parts are strengthened during training, encouraging the CNN to focus on making weak parts stronger rather than strengthening already discriminative parts (see Fig. 3b). This can also be observed when a sample is correctly classified by the holistic detector, but is misclassified by some part detectors. In this case only an error signal from the part classifiers is backpropagated, resulting in the part detectors becoming more discriminative. By training a CNN this way, the influence of several strong distinguished parts decreases, since they cannot backpropagate as many errors as non-discriminative parts, resulting in a more uniform activation pattern across parts, as seen in Fig. 3. With more uniform activations, even if some parts fail due to occlusions, the detector can recover. We experimentally confirm robustness to occlusions of our method in Sect. 4.4.

Regularization Effect. Good features are highly discriminative and decorrelated, so that they are complementary if they are composed. Another benefit of grid loss is that it reduces correlation of feature maps compared to standard loss layers, which we experimentally show in Sect. 4.5. We accredit this to the fact that the loss encourages parts to be discriminative. For a holistic detector a CNN might rely on a few mid-level features to classify a window as face or background. In contrast to that, with grid loss the CNN has to learn mid-level features which can distinguish each face part from the background, resulting in a more diverse set of mid-level features. More diverse features result in activations which are decorrelated. Another interpretation of our method is, that we perform efficient model averaging of several part-based detectors with a shared feature representation, which reduces overfitting. We show in Sect. 4.6 that with a smaller training set size the performance difference to standard loss functions increases compared to grid loss.

Deeply Supervised Nets. The output layer of a neural network has a higher chance of discriminating between background and foreground windows if its features are discriminative. Previous works [19,35] improve the discriminativeness of their feature layers for object classification by applying a softmax or hinge loss on top of their hidden layers. Inspired by this success we replace the standard loss with our grid loss and apply it on top of our hidden layers. As our experiments show (Sect. 4.1), this further improves the performance without sacrificing speed, since these auxiliary loss layers are removed in the classification step.

3.3 Refinement of Detection Windows

Sliding window detectors can make mislocalization errors, causing high confidence predictions to miss the face by a small margin. This results in highly confident false positive predictions. To correct these errors, we apply a regressor to refine the location of the face. Further, we empirically observe that our CNN with the proposed grid loss is able to detect faces which are slightly smaller or bigger than the sliding window. Tree based detectors use an image pyramid with 8 intermediate scales per octave. Applying several convolutions on top of all these scales is computationally expensive. Based on our observation, we propose to omit several of these intermediate scales and rely on the regressor to refine the face location. Details of this regressor CNN are provided in the supplementary material.

Evaluation protocols for face detection use the PASCAL VOC overlap criterion to assess the performance. For two faces F_a and F_b, the overlap o_{voc} is defined as

$$o_{\text{voc}}(F_a, F_b) = \frac{|F_a \cap F_b|}{|F_a \cup F_b|}, \tag{3}$$

where $|F_a \cap F_b|$ denotes the intersection and $|F_a \cup F_b|$ denotes the union of two face representations, i.e. ellipses or bounding boxes.

For ellipse predictions, the parameters major and minor axis length, center coordinates and orientation impact the PASCAL overlap criteria differently. For example, a difference of 1 radiant in orientation changes the overlap of two ellipses more than a change of 1 pixel in major axis length. To account for these differences, we compare minimizing the standard Sum of Squares Error (SSE) error with maximizing the PASCAL overlap criteria in Eq. (3) directly. We compute the gradient entries g_i, $i = 1, \ldots, 5$, of the loss function numerically by central differences:

$$g_i(\boldsymbol{r}) \approx \frac{o_{\text{voc}}(\boldsymbol{r} + \epsilon_i \cdot \boldsymbol{a}_i, \boldsymbol{y}) - o_{\text{voc}}(\boldsymbol{r} - \epsilon_i \cdot \boldsymbol{a}_i, \boldsymbol{y})}{2 \cdot \epsilon_i}, \tag{4}$$

where $\boldsymbol{r}$ denotes the regressor predictions for the ellipse parameters, $\boldsymbol{y}$ denotes the ground truth parameters, $\boldsymbol{a}_i$ denotes the i-th standard basis vector where only the i-th entry is nonzero and set to 1 and ϵ_i is the step size. Since the input size of this network is 40×40 pixels, we use a patch size of 40×40 pixels to rasterize both the ground truth ellipse and the predicted ellipse. Furthermore, we choose ϵ_i big enough so that the rasterization changes at least by 1 pixel.

4   Evaluation

We collect 15,106 samples from the Annotated Facial Landmarks in the Wild (AFLW) [36] dataset to train our detector on 80×80 pixel windows in which 60×60 faces are visible. Similar to [3], we group faces into 5 discrete poses by yaw angle and constrain faces to have pitch and roll between -22 and $+22$ degrees. Further following [3], we create rotated versions of each pose by rotating images by $35°$. We discard grayscale training images, since ACFs are color based. Finally, we mirror faces and add them to the appropriate pose-group to augment the dataset.

We set the ACF pre-smoothing radius to 1, the subsampling factor to 4 and the post-smoothing parameter to 0. Since we shrink the feature maps by a factor of 4, our CNN is trained on 20×20 input patches consisting of 10 channels.

For training we first randomly subsample 10,000 negative examples from the non-person images of the PASCAL VOC dataset [37]. To estimate convergence of SGD in training, we use 20 % of the data as validation set and the remaining 80 % as training set. The detector is bootstrapped by collecting 10,000 negative patches in each bootstrapping iteration. After 3 iterations of bootstrapping, no hard negatives are detected.

Our regressor uses input patches of twice the size of our detector to capture finer details of the face. Since no post-smoothing is used, we reuse the feature pyramid of the detector and crop windows from one octave lower than they are detected.

We evaluate our method on three challenging public datasets: Face Detection Data Set and Benchmark (FDDB) [14], Annotated Faces in the Wild (AFW) [16] and PASCAL Faces [15]. FDDB consists of 2,845 images with 5,171 faces and uses ellipse annotations. PASCAL Faces is extracted from 851 PASCAL VOC images and has 1,635 faces and AFW consists of 205 images with 545 faces. Both AFW and PASCAL Faces use bounding box annotations.

4.1   Grid Loss Benefits

To show the effectiveness of our grid loss layer we run experiments on FDDB [14] using the neural network architecture described in Sect. 3.1 under the evaluation protocol described in [14]. For these experiments we do not use our regressor to exclude its influence on the results and apply the network densely across all 8 intermediate scales per octave (i.e. we do not perform layer skipping or location refinement). We compare standard logistic loss, hinge loss and our grid loss at a false positive count of 50, 100, 284 (which corresponds to ≈ 0.1 False Positives Per Image (FPPI)) and 500 samples. Further, during training we apply grid loss

Table 1. True positive rates of logistic (L), hinge (H), grid + logistic (G+L), grid + hinge (G+H), grid hidden + hinge (G-h+H) and grid hidden + logistic (G-h+L) loss functions on FDDB at a false positive (FP) count of 50, 100, 284 and 500. **Best** and <u>second best</u> results are highlighted.

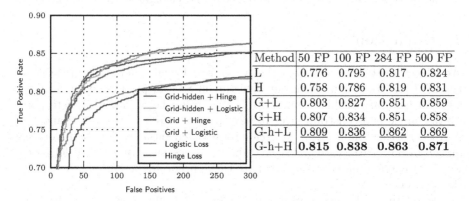

Method	50 FP	100 FP	284 FP	500 FP
L	0.776	0.795	0.817	0.824
H	0.758	0.786	0.819	0.831
G+L	0.803	0.827	0.851	0.859
G+H	0.807	0.834	0.851	0.858
G-h+L	<u>0.809</u>	<u>0.836</u>	<u>0.862</u>	<u>0.869</u>
G-h+H	**0.815**	**0.838**	**0.863**	**0.871**

to our hidden layers to improve the discriminativeness of our feature maps. In Table 1 we see that our grid loss performs significantly better than standard hinge or logistic loss, improving true positive rate by 3.2 % at 0.1 FPPI. Further, similar to the findings of [19,35] our grid loss also benefits from auxiliary loss layers on top of hidden layers during training and additionally improves the true positive rate over the baseline by about 1 %.

4.2 Block Size

To evaluate the performance of our layer with regard to the block size, we train several models with different blocks of size $n = 2^{\{1,2,3,4\}}$ in the output and hidden layer. We constrain the block size of the hidden layers to be the same as the block size of the output layers. Results are shown in Table 2. Our layer works best with small blocks of size 2 and degrades gracefully with larger blocks. In particular, if the size is increased to 16 the method corresponds to a standard CNN regularized with the method proposed in [35,38] and thus, the grid loss layer does not show additional benefits.

4.3 Weighting Parameter

To evaluate the impact of the weighting parameter λ, we conduct experiments comparing the true positive rate of our method at a false positive count of 284 (≈ 0.1 FPPI) with block sizes of $2^{\{1,2,3,4\}}$ and $\lambda = \{5, 1, 0.1, 0.05, 0.01, 0.005, 0.001\}$.

Figure 4 shows that our method performs best with $\lambda \approx 1$ and smaller blocks of size 2 or 4. The performance of our method stays stable until λ is varied more than one order of magnitude. As λ decreases, the network converges to the performance of a regular CNN trained on hinge loss.

Table 2. Comparison of different block sizes on FDDB.

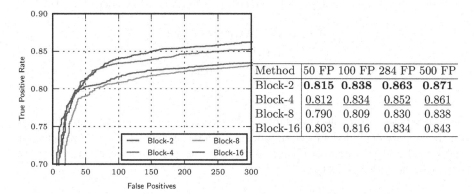

Method	50 FP	100 FP	284 FP	500 FP
Block-2	**0.815**	**0.838**	**0.863**	**0.871**
Block-4	<u>0.812</u>	<u>0.834</u>	<u>0.852</u>	<u>0.861</u>
Block-8	0.790	0.809	0.830	0.838
Block-16	0.803	0.816	0.834	0.843

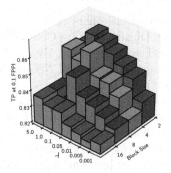

Fig. 4. Evaluation of the weighting parameter λ.

4.4   Robustness to Occlusions

To show that grid loss helps to detect faces with occlusions, we run an experiment on the Caltech Occluded Faces in the Wild (COFW) dataset [39]. The original purpose of the COFW dataset is to test facial landmark localization under occlusions. It consists of 1,852 faces with occlusion annotations for landmarks. We split the dataset into 329 heavily occluded faces with $\geq 30\%$ of all landmarks occluded (COFW-HO) and 1,523 less occluded faces (COFW-LO). Since this dataset is proposed for landmark localization, the images do not contain a large background variation.

For a fair evaluation, we measure the FPPI on FDDB, which has a more realistic background variation for the task of face detection. We report here the true positive rate on COFW at 0.1 FPPI on FDDB. This evalution ensures that the detectors achieve a low false positive rate in a realistic detection setting and still detect occluded faces.

We evaluate both, the grid loss detector and the hinge loss detector on this dataset. The performance difference between these two detectors should increase on the occluded subset of COFW, since grid loss is beneficial for detecting

Table 3. True Positive Rate on COFW Heavily Occluded (COFW-HO) and Less Occluded (LO) subsets of a grid loss detector (G) and a hinge loss detector (H).

Method	COFW-HO	COFW-LO
G	**0.979**	**0.998**
H	0.909	0.982

occluded faces. In Table 3 we indeed observe that the performance difference on the heavily occluded subset significantly increases from 1.6 % to 7 % between the two detectors, demonstrating the favourable performance of grid loss for detecting occluded objects.

4.5   Effect on Correlation of Features

With grid loss we train several classifiers operating on spatially independent image parts simultaneously. During training CNNs develop discriminative features which are suitable to classify an image. By dividing the input image into several parts with different appearance, the CNN has to learn features suitable to classify each of these face parts individually.

Since parts which are located on the mouth-region of a face do not contain e.g. an eye, the CNN has to develop features to detect a mouth for this specific part detector. In contrast to that, with standard loss functions the CNN operates on the full detection window. To classify a given sample as positive, a CNN might solve this classification problem by just learning features which e.g. detect eyes. Hence, by operating on the full detection window, only a smaller set of mid-level features is required compared to CNNs trained on both, the full detection window and sub-parts.

Therefore, with our method, we encourage CNNs to learn more diverse features. More diverse features result in less correlated feature activations, since for a given sample different feature channels should be active for different mid-level features. To measure this, we train a CNN with and without grid loss. For all spatial coordinates of the last 12×12 convolution layer, we compute a 128×128 dimensional normalized correlation matrix. We sum the absolute values of the off-diagonal elements of the correlation matrices. A higher number indicates more correlated features and is less desirable. As we see in Table 4 our grid loss detector learns significantly less correlated features.

Table 4. Grid loss reduces correlation in feature maps.

Method	Correlation
Grid loss	**225.96**
Hinge loss	22500.25

4.6   Training Set Size

Regularization methods should improve performance of machine learning methods especially when the available training data set is small. The performance gap between a method without regularization to a method with regularization should increase with a smaller amount of training data. To test the effectiveness of our grid loss as regularization method, we subsample the positive training samples by a factor of 0.75–0.01 and compare the performance to a standard CNN trained on hinge loss, a CNN trained with hinge loss on both the output and hidden layers [35,38], and a CNN where we apply grid loss on both hidden layers and the output layer. To assess the performance of each model, we compare the true positive rate at a false positive count of 284 ($\approx$ 0.1 FPPI). In Table 5 we see that our grid loss indeed acts as a regularizer. The performance gap between our method and standard CNNs increases from 3.2 % to 10.2 % as the training set gets smaller. Further, we observe that grid loss benefits from the method of [35,38], since by applying grid loss on top of the hidden layers, the performance gap increases even more.

Table 5. Impact of training on a sub-set (i.e. 0.75–0.01) of the positive training set on FDDB at 0.1 FPPI using the hinge loss (H), hinge loss on hidden layers (H-h) and our grid loss (G) and grid loss on hidden layers (G-h).

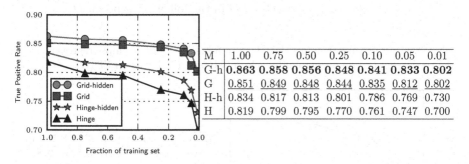

M	1.00	0.75	0.50	0.25	0.10	0.05	0.01
G-h	**0.863**	**0.858**	**0.856**	**0.848**	**0.841**	**0.833**	**0.802**
G	0.851	0.849	0.848	0.844	0.835	0.812	0.802
H-h	0.834	0.817	0.813	0.801	0.786	0.769	0.730
H	0.819	0.799	0.795	0.770	0.761	0.747	0.700

4.7   Ellipse Regressor and Layer Skipping

We compare the impact of an ellipse regressor trained on the PASCAL overlap criterion with a regressor trained on the SSE loss. We evaluate the impact on the FDDB dataset using the continuous evaluation protocol [14], which weighs matches of ground truth and prediction with their soft PASCAL overlap score. In Table 6 we see that minimizing the numerical overlap performs barely better than minimizing the SSE loss in the parameter space of the ellipse (i.e. 0.1 % to 0.2 %). We hypothesize that this is caused by inconsistent annotations in our training set.

Further, we compare our model with and without an ellipse regressor using different image pyramid sizes. We evaluate the performance on the FDDB

Table 6. Continuous evaluation of the two proposed ellipse loss functions: numerical PASCAL VOC overlap (NUM) and SSE on FDDB.

Method	50 FP	100 FP	284 FP	500 FP	1000 FP
NUM (D)	**0.680**	**0.690**	**0.702**	**0.708**	**0.714**
SSE (D)	0.679	0.688	0.700	0.706	0.713

dataset under the discrete evaluation protocol. In Table 7 we see that regressing ellipses improves the true positive rate by about 1 %. But more importantly, using a regressor to refine the face positions allows us to use fewer intermediate scales in our image pyramid without significant loss in accuracy. This greatly improves runtime performance of our detector by a factor of 3–4 (see Sect. 4.10).

4.8 Building a Highly Accurate Detector

Grid loss can also be used to improve the detection performance of deeper networks, yielding highly accurate detections. To this end, following [40], we replace each 5 × 5 convolution layer with two 3 × 3 layers, doubling the number of layers from 2 to 4. After the first convolution layer we apply LCN. Further, we increase the number of convolution filters in our layers to 64, 256, 512 and 512, respectively. We denote this detector *Big* in the following experiments.

Table 7. Effect of numerical loss (NUM), SSE loss (SSE) and no ellipse regressor (w/o) applied densely (D) on all pyramid levels or skipping (S) layers on FDDB.

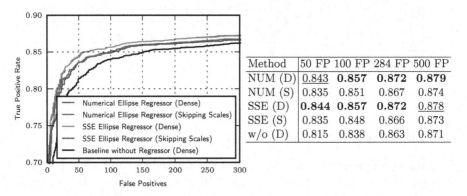

Method	50 FP	100 FP	284 FP	500 FP
NUM (D)	0.843	**0.857**	**0.872**	**0.879**
NUM (S)	0.835	0.851	0.867	0.874
SSE (D)	**0.844**	**0.857**	**0.872**	0.878
SSE (S)	0.835	0.848	0.866	0.873
w/o (D)	0.815	0.838	0.863	0.871

4.9 Comparison to the State-of-the-Art

We compare our detector to the state-of-the-art on the FDDB dataset [14], the AFW dataset [16] and PASCAL Faces dataset [15], see Figs. 5, 6 and 7. For evaluation on AFW and PASCAL Faces we use the evaluation toolbox provided by [3]. For evaluation on FDDB we use the original evaluation tool provided by [14]. We report the accuracy of our small fast model and our large model. On FDDB our fast network combined with our regressor retrieves 86.7 % of all faces at a false positive count of 284, which corresponds to about 0.1 FPPI on this dataset. With our larger model we can improve the true positive rate to 89.4 % at 0.1 FPPI, outperforming the state-of-the-art by 0.7 %. In our supplementary material we show that when we combine AlexNet with our method, we can increase the true positive rate to 90.1 %. On PASCAL Faces and AFW we outperform the state-of-the-art by 1.38 % and 1.45 % Average Precision (AP) respectively.

4.10 Computational Efficiency

We implemented our method with Theano [41] and Python and ran our experiments on a desktop machine with a NVIDIA GTX 770 and a 3.20 GHz Intel Core i5 CPU. Our small dense model needs about 200 ms (GPU) to run on images with a size of 640 × 480 pixels. With skipping intermediate scales our network runs in about 50 ms (GPU) on the same computer using non-optimized Python code. On the CPU our small network runs in about 170 ms with layer skipping,

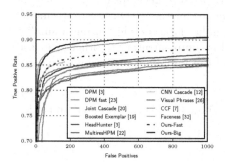

Fig. 5. Discrete evaluation on the FDDB [14] dataset.

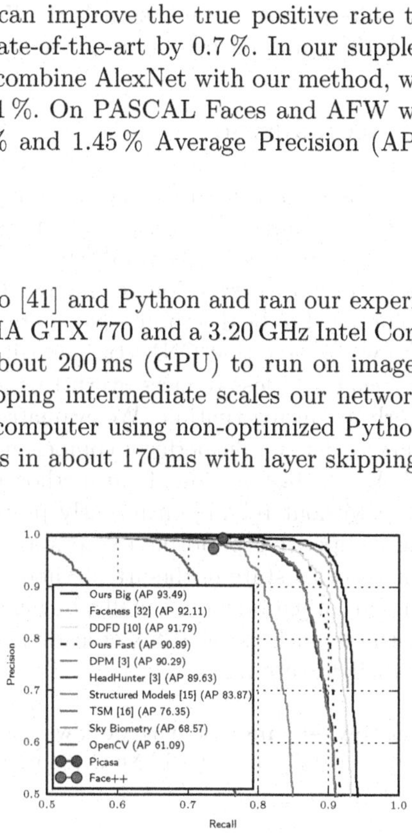

Fig. 6. Evaluation on the PASCAL Faces [15] dataset.

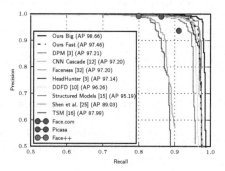

Fig. 7. Our method outperforms state-of-the-art methods on AFW [16].

achieving competitive runtime performance compared to fast tree based methods, e.g. [3,21], while outperforming them in accuracy. Note that we do not rely on speedup techniques such as image patchwork [42,43], decomposing convolution filters into separable kernels [44,45], or cascades [12]. Combining our method with these approaches can improve the runtime performance even more.

5   Conclusion

We presented a novel loss layer named grid loss, which improves the detection accuracy compared to regular softmax and hinge loss layers by dividing the last convolution layer into several part detectors. This results in a detector which is more robust to occlusions compared to standard CNNs, since each detector is encouraged to be discriminative on its own. Further, in our experimental evaluation we observe that CNNs trained with grid loss develop less correlated features and that grid loss reduces overfitting. Our method does not add any additional overhead during runtime. We evaluated our detector on face detection tasks and showed that we outperform competing methods on FDDB, PASCAL Faces and AFW. The fast version of our method runs at 20 FPS on standard desktop hardware without relying on recently proposed speedup mechanisms, while achieving competitive performance to state-of-the-art methods. Our accurate model outperforms state-of-the-art methods on public datasets while using a smaller amount of parameters. Finally, our method is complementary to other proposed methods, such as the CNN cascade [12] and can improve the discriminativeness of their feature maps.

Acknowledgements. This work was supported by the Austrian Research Promotion Agency (FFG) project DIANGO (840824).

References

1. Benenson, R., Mathias, M., Tuytelaars, T., Van Gool, L.: Seeking the Strongest Rigid Detector. In: Proceedings of the CVPR (2013)
2. Dollár, P., Appel, R., Belongie, S., Perona, P.: Fast feature pyramids for object detection. PAMI **36**(8), 1532–1545 (2014)
3. Mathias, M., Benenson, R., Pedersoli, M., Gool, L.: Face detection without bells and whistles. In: Fleet, D., Pajdla, T., Schiele, B., Tuytelaars, T. (eds.) ECCV 2014. LNCS, vol. 8692, pp. 720–735. Springer, Heidelberg (2014). doi:10.1007/978-3-319-10593-2_47
4. Schulter, S., Leistner, C., Wohlhart, P., Roth, P.M., Bischof, H.: Accurate object detection with joint classification-regression random forests. In: Proceedings of the CVPR (2014)
5. Viola, P., Jones, M.J.: Robust real-time face detection. IJCV **57**(2), 137–154 (2004)
6. Zhang, S., Benenson, R., Schiele, B.: Filtered channel features for pedestrian detection. In: Proceedings of the CVPR (2015)
7. Yang, B., Yan, J., Lei, Z., Li, S.Z.: Convolutional channel features. In: Proceedings of the ICCV (2015)

8. Felzenszwalb, P.F., Girshick, R.B., McAllester, D., Ramanan, D.: Object detection with discriminatively trained part-based models. PAMI **32**(9), 1627–1645 (2010)
9. Krizhevsky, A., Sutskever, I., Hinton, G.E.: ImageNet classification with deep convolutional neural networks. In: NIPS (2012)
10. Farfade, S.S., Saberian, M., Li, L.J.: Multi-view face detection using deep convolutional neural networks. In: Proceedings of the ICMR (2015)
11. Hosang, J., Omran, M., Benenson, R., Schiele, B.: Taking a deeper look at pedestrians. In: Proceedings of the CVPR (2015)
12. Li, H., Lin, Z., Shen, X., Brandt, J., Hua, G.: A convolutional neural network cascade for face detection. In: Proceedings of the CVPR (2015)
13. Sermanet, P., Kavukcuoglu, K., Chintala, S., LeCun, Y.: Pedestrian detection with unsupervised multi-stage feature learning. In: Proceedings of the CVPR (2013)
14. Jain, V., Learned-Miller, E.: FDDB: A benchmark for face detection in unconstrained settings. Technical report UM-CS-2010-009, University of Massachusetts, Amherst (2010)
15. Yan, J., Zhang, X., Lei, Z., Li, S.Z.: Face detection by structural models. IVC **32**(10), 790–799 (2014)
16. Zhu, X., Ramanan, D.: Face detection, pose estimation and landmark estimation in the wild. In: Proceedings of the CVPR (2012)
17. Zafeiriou, S., Zhang, C., Zhang, Z.: A survey on face detection in the wild: past present and future. CVIU **138**, 1–24 (2015)
18. Li, J., Zhang, Y.: Learning surf cascade for fast and accurate object detection. In: Proceedings of the CVPR (2013)
19. Li, H., Lin, Z., Brandt, J., Shen, X., Hua, G.: Efficient boosted exemplar-based face detection. In: Proceedings of the CVPR (2014)
20. Chen, D., Ren, S., Wei, Y., Cao, X., Sun, J.: Joint cascade face detection and alignment. In: Fleet, D., Pajdla, T., Schiele, B., Tuytelaars, T. (eds.) ECCV 2014. LNCS, vol. 8694, pp. 109–122. Springer, Heidelberg (2014). doi:10.1007/978-3-319-10599-4_8
21. Yang, B., Yan, J., Lei, Z., Li, S.Z.: Aggregate channel features for multi-view face detection. In: Proceedings of the IJCB (2014)
22. Ghiasi, G., Fowlkes, C.C.: Occlusion coherence: localizing occluded faces with a hierarchical deformable part model. In: Proceedings of the CVPR (2014)
23. Yan, J., Lei, Z., Wen, L., Li, S.: The fastest deformable part model for object detection. In: Proceedings of the CVPR (2014)
24. Li, H., Hua, G., Lin, Z., Brandt, J., Yang, J.: Probabilistic elastic part model for unsupervised face detector adaptation. In: Proceedings of the ICCV (2013)
25. Shen, X., Lin, Z., Brandt, J., Wu, Y.: Detecting and aligning faces by image retrieval. In: Proceedings of the CVPR (2013)
26. Kumar, V., Namboodiri, A.M., Jawahar, C.V.: Visual phrases for exemplar face detection. In: Proceedings of the ICCV (2015)
27. Girshick, R., Donahue, J., Darrell, T., Malik, J.: Rich feature hierarchies for accurate object detection and semantic segmentation. In: Proceedings of the CVPR (2014)
28. Garcia, C., Delakis, M.: Convolutional face finder: a neural architecture for fast and robust face detection. PAMI **26**(11), 1408–1423 (2004)
29. Rowley, H., Baluja, S., Kanade, T., et al.: Neural network-based face detection. PAMI **20**(1), 23–38 (1998)
30. Vaillant, R., Monrocq, C., LeCun, Y.: Original approach for the localisation of objects in images. IEEE Proc. Vis., Image Sig. Proces. **141**(4), 245–250 (1994)

31. Russakovsky, O., Deng, J., Su, H., Krause, J., Satheesh, S., Ma, S., Huang, Z., Karpathy, A., Khosla, A., Bernstein, M., Berg, A.C., Fei-Fei, L.: ImageNet large scale visual recognition challenge, IJCV, pp. 1–42 (2015)
32. Yang, S., Luo, P., Loy, C.C., Tang, X.: From facial parts responses to face detection: a deep learning approach. In: Proceedings of the ICCV (2015)
33. Sermanet, P., Eigen, D., Zhang, X., Mathieu, M., Fergus, R., LeCun, Y.: OverFeat: integrated recognition, localization and detection using convolutional networks. In: Proceedings of the ICLR (2014)
34. Srivastava, N., Hinton, G., Krizhevsky, A., Sutskever, I., Salakhutdinov, R.: Dropout: a simple way to prevent neural networks from overfitting. JMLR **15**(1), 1929–1958 (2014)
35. Szegedy, C., Liu, W., Jia, Y., Sermanet, P., Reed, S., Anguelov, D., Erhan, D., Vanhoucke, V., Rabinovich, A.: Going deeper with convolutions. In: Proceedings of the CVPR (2015)
36. Köstinger, M., Wohlhart, P., Roth, P.M., Bischof, H.: Annotated Facial Landmarks in the Wild: A large-scale, real-world database for facial landmark localization. In: Proceedings of the BeFIT (in conj. with ICCV) (2011)
37. Everingham, M., Eslami, S.M.A., Van Gool, L., Williams, C.K.I., Winn, J., Zisserman, A.: The Pascal visual object classes challenge: a retrospective. IJCV **111**(1), 98–136 (2015)
38. Lee, C.Y., Xie, S., Gallagher, P., Zhang, Z., Tu, Z.: Deeply-supervised nets. In: Proceedings of the AISTATS (2015)
39. Burgos-Artizzu, X., Perona, P., Dollár, P.: Robust face landmark estimation under occlusion. In: Proceedings of the ICCV (2013)
40. Simonyan, K., Zisserman, A.: Very deep convolutional networks for large-scale image recognition. In: Proceedings of the ICLR (2015)
41. Bastien, F., Lamblin, P., Pascanu, R., Bergstra, J., Goodfellow, I.J., Bergeron, A., Bouchard, N., Bengio, Y.: Theano: new features and speed improvements. In: Proceedings of the NIPS Deep Learning Workshop (2012)
42. Dubout, C., Fleuret, F.: Exact acceleration of linear object detectors. In: Fitzgibbon, A., Lazebnik, S., Perona, P., Sato, Y., Schmid, C. (eds.) ECCV 2012. LNCS, vol. 7574, pp. 301–311. Springer, Heidelberg (2012). doi:10.1007/978-3-642-33712-3_22
43. Girshick, R., Iandola, F., Darrell, T., Malik, J.: Deformable part models are convolutional neural networks. In: Proceedings of the CVPR (2015)
44. Jaderberg, M., Vedaldi, A., Zisserman, A.: Speeding up convolutional neural networks with low rank expansions. In: Proceedings of the BMVC (2014)
45. Zhang, X., Zou, J., He, K., Sun, J.: Accelerating very deep convolutional networks for classification and detection (2015). arXiv:abs/1505.06798

Large-Scale R-CNN with Classifier Adaptive Quantization

Ryota Hinami$^{(\boxtimes)}$ and Shin'ichi Satoh

National Institute of Informatics, The University of Tokyo, Tokyo, Japan
{hinami,satoh}@nii.ac.jp

Abstract. This paper extends R-CNN, a state-of-the-art object detection method, to larger scales. To apply R-CNN to a large database storing thousands to millions of images, the SVM classification of millions to billions of DCNN features extracted from object proposals is indispensable, which imposes unrealistic computational and memory costs. Our method dramatically narrows down the number of object proposals by using an inverted index and efficiently searches by using residual vector quantization (RVQ). Instead of k-means that has been used in inverted indices, we present a novel quantization method designed for linear classification wherein the quantization error is re-defined for linear classification. It approximates the error as the empirical error with pre-defined multiple exemplar classifiers and captures the variance and common attributes of object category classifiers effectively. Experimental results show that our method achieves comparable performance to that of applying R-CNN to all images while achieving a 250 times speed-up and 180 times memory reduction. Moreover, our approach significantly outperforms the state-of-the-art large-scale category detection method, with about a 40~58 % increase in top-K precision. Scalability is also validated, and we demonstrate that our method can process 100 K images in 0.13 s while retaining precision.

Keywords: Image retrieval · Object detection · Image indexing

1 Introduction

With the explosive increase in multimedia data in recent years, there is a growing demand for information retrieval from large image/video databases. Large-scale object retrieval is a well-researched task that is used in many applications. Its purpose is to retrieve specific objects in a large image database as quickly as possible (i.e., immediately). Most of the existing object retrieval methods exploit the bag-of-visual-words (BoVW) model, where objects are retrieved using local descriptor matching. This approach is suited to specific objects (e.g., buildings, logos), but not to objects of generic *categories* (e.g., cat, bicycle), because

Electronic supplementary material The online version of this chapter (doi:10. 1007/978-3-319-46487-9_25) contains supplementary material, which is available to authorized users.

© Springer International Publishing AG 2016
B. Leibe et al. (Eds.): ECCV 2016, Part III, LNCS 9907, pp. 403–419, 2016.
DOI: 10.1007/978-3-319-46487-9_25

local descriptor matching cannot capture the variation within a category well enough. A popular object categorization is based on the deformable part model (DPM) [1,2], which uses HOG features instead of local descriptors to better describe object appearances in combination with SVM. R-CNN [3] extends the DPM by using convolutional neural network (CNN) features and achieves a significant improvement in accuracy. However, performing immediate object category detection on a large image database has not been tried until quite recently.

Recently, Aytar and Zisserman [4] attempted a large-scale object category detection. Unlike the traditional sliding window approach, their method achieved immediate detection throughout a large scale dataset. They developed a sparse representation of a HOG classifier and a new mid-level image representation using a vocabulary of *classifier patches* and performed fast retrieval using an inverted file index. Although this method achieved immediate retrievals on large-scale image datasets, its accuracy was significantly lower than that of the original sliding window-based approach. Moreover, because the performance of object category detection has significantly improved recently, this method still has a large performance gap compared with state-of-the-art object category detection. Most of the other work on accelerating object detection such as [5–9] assume that images are unknown (pre-processing of images is not permitted) and their runtime grows linearly with the number of images, namely the method that can process 150 images per second takes over 10 min to detect objects from 100 K images, which is far from large-scale immediate object detection. Although other studies [10,11] have focused on fast object retrieval and detection simultaneously, both methods are based on BoVW models designed for specific object retrieval and are thus not suitted to object category detection.

The performance of object category detection has dramatically increased in the past few years. Previously, the sliding window-based method with a HOG-based classifier such as DPM [1,2] was widely used. Recently though, R-CNN [3] and its enhancements [12–14] have shown significant performance boosts over conventional methods. The key ideas of R-CNN are (1) limiting candidates by using object proposal instead of the exhaustive search with sliding window, and (2) exploiting features learned by a DCNN, which results in high classification accuracy even with linear SVM. Our objective is to apply R-CNN to all images in a large database immediately. However, this is a very difficult problem even if pre-processing using a database is permitted, because the number of object proposals grows to the millions or even billions if the database stores thousands to millions of images. That is, to apply R-CNN to a large database, we must classify millions to billions of high-dimensional vectors with linear SVM, which imposes high computational and memory costs.

Litayem et al. [15] accelerated the prediction phase of linear SVM by using locality sensitive hashing (LSH) [16]. LSH compresses the original high-dimensional vectors into small binary codes. A linear SVM classifier is then approximated by using the Hamming distance between the hashed data and the hashed hyperplane of the classifier, which can be computed extremely quickly. Although it achieves both high levels of compactness and computational efficiency, it assumes that all features x are L_2-normalized ($\|x\| = 1$), and thus,

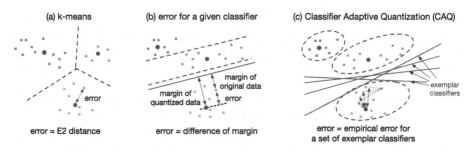

Fig. 1. An intuitive illustration of the difference in the quantization error between (a) the error defined by k-means and (b) the error in terms of a given classifier. (c) illustrates the error of CAQ, where red arrows indicate the error for each exemplar classifier (the error of CAQ is the sum of these).

information on the original unnormalized feature is lost. Although many work have investigated the scalable SVM such as [17], most of them focus on the acceleration of the training phase and there is few work that focus on the acceleration of the prediction (testing) phase.

Recent progress in approximate nearest neighbor (ANN) searches has made it possible to handle billions of vectors efficiently. Several approaches have been studied for selecting nearest neighbor candidates from large amounts of vectors quickly, including tree-based indexing (e.g., k-d tree [18] and FLANN [19]), and hashing represented by LSH [16]. Product quantization (PQ) [20] is a widely used approach to compress vectors into very short code so that all vectors can be stored in memory. PQ divides the feature space into a Cartesian product of subspaces that are quantized independently, which permits much finer quantization with an efficient learning procedure. PQ also permits efficient distance computations with a table lookup. Moreover, it has been shown to be more accurate than hashing-based methods such as spectral hashing [21] and hamming embedding [22].

An inverted index is another useful technique to avoid brute-force scans in large-scale searches. Inverted indices are built upon codewords learned from large datasets, and each codeword stores a list of data. This allows immediate access to a list of vectors close to any query vector and enables one to reduce the search time significantly over that of an exhaustive scan. The effectiveness of an inverted index for image retrieval was first demonstrated by Sivic and Zisserman in [23]. Jegou et al. in [20] also exploited an inverted index wherein the inverted list stores PQ-compressed data instead of the image IDs and performed well on billion-scale ANN searches. Most recent ANN search methods are based on this system, which is called IVFADC and combines an inverted index with coarse quantization and reranking based on compact code.

An inverted multi-index (IMI) [24,25] is the current state-of-the-art indexing method of ANN searches; it is used instead of normal inverted indices. IMI achieves much finer subdivisions of the search space by constructing an inverted index using PQ. However, in our case, we find IMI does not improve the performance or even worse than IVFADC (k-means) in some cases (discussed in Sect. 4.4). Therefore, we use the standard inverted index and explore another novel quantizer suited to our task that improves performance without using IMI.

In this paper, we extend R-CNN to larger scales by incorporating state-of-the-art ANN search techniques (IVFADC). Our method narrows down a huge amount of feature vectors extracted from object proposals by using an inverted index and efficiently applies linear SVM by using fast distance computation with compressed code. We use residual vector quantization (RVQ) [26,27] to compress data instead of PQ because RVQ achieves significantly better performance than PQ does at a similar cost in our task.

In addition, we present a novel quantizer designed for linear classification to improve the performance of the inverted index. Most inverted indices methods utilize k-means, wherein the quantization error is defined as the Euclidean distance between a data point and its assigned codeword, and learns the codebook that minimizes the error. Although it is effective in a ANN search whose objective is to find the closest vector in Euclidean space, it is not suited to our task. We therefore re-define the quantization distortion that adapts a large-scale linear classification task. The basic idea is to define the quantization error as the difference in classification score before and after quantization as in Figure 1 (b). However, this error depends on the classification boundary which, as indicated by the red line in Fig. 1, is defined by each object category we want to detect, and is unknown in advance. We therefore prepare *exemplar classifiers*, a set of category classifiers trained beforehand and approximate the quantization distortion by their empirical error. This is equivalent to k-means with another metric that can capture the variation and essence of object classifiers, as shown in Fig. 1 (c). We demonstrate that this quantization, called Classifier Adaptive Quantization (CAQ), is more effective than k-means in our task. It even outperforms IMI that is a state-of-the-art ANN search. We demonstrate our method—index inversion by CAQ and RVQ compression—can perform object detection immediately from a large database (takes 0.12 second from 100 K images) while retaining the high accuracy of R-CNN, and thereby demonstrating that ANN search techniques are extremely effective at immediate large-scale object category detection.

Contributions. Our contributions are as follows: (1) a large-scale R-CNN architecture using the state-of-the-art techniques of an ANN search. It achieves excellent memory and computational efficiency while retaining the high level of accuracy of R-CNN, which itself outperforms a recent state-of-the-art large-scale object detection method by 40∼58 % in top-K precision; (2) classifier adaptive quantization, a novel quantization method for linear classification that performs better than traditional k-means in large-scale object detection tasks. To the best of our knowledge, no quantizations has been designed for linear classification.

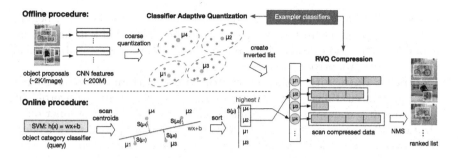

Fig. 2. Architecture of the proposed method.

2 Overview of Large-Scale R-CNN

In this section, we briefly overview our method. Our objective is to apply R-CNN [3] to all images in a large database immediately. R-CNN consists of the following steps: (i) detect object proposals by using a selective search; (ii) extract CNN features from the object proposals; (iii) apply SVM to the extracted features. In our setting, because the image database is given in advance, steps (i) and (ii) can be done offline. Therefore, our main focus is step (iii), i.e., applying SVM to a large amount of vectors efficiently.

The database consists of N images and around 2000 object proposals are detected in each image (n_i proposals from the ith image). $v_{i,j}$ ($i = 1, ..., N$, $j = 1, ..., n_i$) is a D-dimensional DCNN feature vector ($D = 4096$ in our case) extracted from each object proposal. SVM computes the classification score $S(v_{i,j}) = w \cdot v_{i,j} - b$, where w and b represent the hyperplane and bias of the SVM classifier. Since the total number of $v_{i,j}$s is very large in a large database, computing the classification score for all vectors entails a huge number of computations and takes up a huge amount of memory. However, we can solve this problem by using an inverted index and reranking based on compact code.

2.1 Offline Procedure

Fig. 2 is an overview of our method. Our approach can be divided into offline and online procedures. The offline procedure is performed as follows:

1. **Detect proposal objects and Extract features:** We follow a similar procedure to that of R-CNN. Object proposals are first detected in a selective search [28], entailing around 2000 proposals per image. Around $2000 \times N$ proposals are thus obtained from the image datasets. DCNN features are then extracted from each proposal.
2. **Construct an inverted index:** To avoid an exhaustive search, we construct an inverted index. We use a structure similar to the one proposed in [20]. Feature vectors $v_{i,j}$ are quantized coarsely into k clusters represented by k codewords $c(1), ..., c(k)$ (k-means is used in [20]). An inverted index is then

constructed with k lists $L_1, ..., L_k$, where each list L_i stores data that belongs to the corresponding cluster with a codeword $c(i)$. Instead of k-means, we use a novel quantization designed for linear classification (see Sect. 3). We call this Classifier Adaptive Quantization (CAQ).

3. **Compress data with residual vector quantization:** To reduce memory and computational costs, feature vectors are stored in an inverted file structure after compressing them into small codes. We take a product quantization (PQ)-based approach [20]. Although it is mainly used for Euclidean distance approximations, it can be easily extended to approximations of inner products. We tested various compression method and found that residual vector quantization (RVQ) [26,27] has significantly better performance than PQ or optimized product quantization (OPQ) that is used in IVFADC and IMI. Figure 3 shows a comparison of object detection performance with compressed features. It also indicates the number of sub-codebooks M should be large enough (M=32 to 128) to achieve sufficient object detection performance with compressed codes.

RVQ learns multiple sub-codebooks one by one by minimizing the error greedily. The first sub-codebook is learned by performing k-means on original vectors. The second sub-codebook is learned by performing k-means on residual vectors with respect to the assigned codewords of the first sub-codebook, which is a similar process to the residual encoding used in IVFADC. This process is repeated until all sub-codebooks are learned. RVQ is also related to additive quantization (AQ), where the vector is approximated by the sum of codewords from different codebooks. However, encoding of AQ using such and such a method becomes too slow as the number of codebooks grows, and this makes it impossible to compress a large number of high-dimensional CNN features. Therefore, we decided to use RVQ with M=64.

We do not encode the residual vector with respect to the coarse quantizer as in IVFADC [20] because we found that residual encoding does not improve performance. This suggested that the quantization of CNN features has to be extremely fine in order to achieve reasonable performance (M=64), and therefore, the effect of coarse quantization is more limited than in the original IVFADC (M=~16 is used).

2.2 Online Procedure

Next, we describe the online procedure of the proposed architecture. We assume that an SVM classifier $h(x) = w_q \cdot x + b_q$ is given as query. We scan an inverted file structure by using the following procedure:

1. **Scan the codewords of the coarse quantizer:** Query SVM is applied to codewords of an inverted index; i.e., a classification score $S(c(i)) = w_q \cdot c(i) + b_q$ is computed for each codeword $c(i)(i = 1, ..., k)$.
2. **Scan the data in list with the highest score:** The codewords with l highest score $c(i_1), c(i_2), ..., c(i_l)$ are selected, and their corresponding inverted

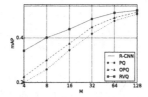

Fig. 3. Comparison of data compression methods on the PASCAL VOC 2007 object detection task. R-CNN calculates detection scores for all object proposals by applying SVM to the original DCNN features. The detection procedures of PQ, OPQ, and RVQ are also based on R-CNN, but approximate the SVM score by using compressed codes.

lists $L_{i_1}, L_{i_2}, ..., L_{i_l}$ are scanned. The inner product $w_q \cdot v$ is approximated by the inner product between the query and RVQ-compressed data, i.e., $w_q \cdot v \sim w_q \cdot \sum_{m=1}^{M} c_m(i_m) \sim \sum_{m=1}^{M} w_q \cdot c_m(i_m)$, where $c_m(i_m)$ is the i_mth codeword of the mth sub-codebook assigned to v. This can be computed very quickly using a pre-computed distance table. The table is created in a manner similar to the asymmetric distance computation (ADC) in [20]

3. **Perform non-maximum suppression and output results:** The scanned candidates are sorted in the order of the computed score, and a ranked list is output after non-maximum suppression (NMS). NMS rejects regions that overlap with a higher scoring region and have an intersection-over-union (IoU) value of > 0.3. Note that if only the top-K scoring objects have to be detected, NMS is applied to only the top-ranked regions.

3   Classifier Adaptive Quantization

3.1   Quantization Distortion for Linear Classifier

In this section, we describe a quantization method suited to linear classification. K-means is a popular vector quantization method that is optimal for some tasks including a nearest neighbor search by minimizing the quantization distortion. It defines the quantization distortion as:

$$E = \frac{1}{n} \sum_x \|x - c(i_x)\|^2, \tag{1}$$

where $\| \cdot \|$ denotes the l_2-norm, n is the total number of data samples, i_x is a codeword ID assigned to data x, and the i_xth codeword is denoted as $c(i_x)$. K-means learns the codebook minimizing this distortion.

Although k-means is suitable for nearest neighbor searches wherein the error is defined by the distance between a query and a data point in a Euclidean space, we assert that it is not optimal for linear classification. In our case, through the quantization process, the classifier score of the original data is approximated by the score of the quantized data. Therefore, it is natural that the quantization error is defined by the difference in the classifier score before and after quantization, as illustrated in Fig. 1. Here, we denote the hypothesis of a certain linear SVM classifier as $h(x) = w \cdot x + b$. We can define the quantization distortion for this classifier as follows:

$$E = \frac{1}{n} \sum_x \| w \cdot x - w \cdot c(i_x) \|^2, \tag{2}$$

where the bias b is canceled by taking the difference and does not affect the quantization distortion at all. Although this distortion can be defined if the classifier is known in advance, the classifier is often given as a query in a retrieval task, and hence would be unknown before it is given. We thus modify this quantization distortion to be able to deal with unknown classifiers.

We prepare a set of SVM classifiers trained on a variety of categories ($180 \sim 2000$ classifiers in our case). We call them *exemplar classifiers*. We approximate the distortion for any query classifier by the empirical error of these exemplar classifiers. We assume they capture common attributes in any category of classifiers, as well as their variance. The training of exemplar classifiers is detailed in Sect. 4.1. Let us denote the hyperplanes of exemplar classifiers as $\{w^{(1)}, w^{(2)}, ..., w^{(n_w)}\}$, $w^{(i)} \in \mathbb{R}^D$, where n_w is the number of exemplar classifiers, and these form the rows of a matrix $W \in \mathbb{R}^{n_w \times D}$. We define the empirical distortion of exemplar classifiers as follows:

$$E = \frac{1}{n} \sum_x \| Wx - Wc(i_x) \|^2, \tag{3}$$

which is the distortion of the *classifier adaptive quantization* (CAQ) we present. By minimizing E, we can expect reasonable performance for all possible object classifiers. Furthermore, we use it below to formulate the encoding and codebook learning.

3.2   Encoding and Codebook Learning

In this section, we formulate the encoding and codebook learning of CAQ and show that they can be performed by revising the k-means algorithm with little additional cost. First, let us consider the task of encoding, i.e., finding the codeword assigned to a data sample x. An assignment i_x that minimizes the coding error is obtained by solving the following equation:

$$i_x = \arg\min_i \| Wx - Wc(i) \|^2, \tag{4}$$

which is equivalent to doing a nearest neighbor search to data projected by W.

Next, let us show how to learn a codebook that minimizes the distortion in Eq. (3). Similarly to k-means, we take an alternating optimization strategy wherein the codebook and assignment are optimized alternately. The minimization over the assignment i with a fixed codebook is performed by solving Eq. (4).

The following equation is used to update a codebook given an assignment:

$$c(i) = \arg\min_{c(i)} \sum_{x \in N_i} \|Wx - Wc(i)\|^2, \tag{5}$$

where N_i is the set of data samples assigned to codeword $c(i)$. If $c(i)$ is the centroid of the cluster ($c(i) = \frac{1}{n_i} \sum_{x \in N_i} x$, where n_i is the size of N_i), Eq. (5) is satisfied. From Eqs. (4) and (5), we can see that this problem is equivalent to the k-means if data samples are Wx and codewords are $Wc(i)$. Therefore, assignments can be obtained simply by applying k-means in the subspace into which the data samples are projected by W, which is equivalent to the k-means with Mahalanobis distance. Since the codewords are defined in a data space, they can be obtained as the centroids of the data assigned to each cluster.

CAQ is based on the simple k-means algorithm, which has two merits. Firstly, we can make use of the rich literature on k-means and distributed implementations, e.g., clustering with large datasets and vocabularies can be efficiently performed using fast k-means such as [29]. Secondly, CAQ is easily incorporated into other systems based on k-means, such as joint inverted indexing [30]. Note that although W can be generated with other metric learning approaches, we at least confirmed that CAQ outperformed the Mahalanobis metrics. This is true because the CAQ metric considers the bias of the object category classifier while the Mahalanobis metric considers only the distribution of the data.

4   Experiments

4.1   Datasets and Implementation Details

We used the popular PASCAL VOC 2007 detection dataset to evaluate our method. The test set consisted of 4952 images from 20 different categories. In addition, the validation set of ILSVRC 2011 and 2012 [31] (100K images in total) were used as distractors in the large-scale experiments. A previous study [4] also used these distractors to evaluate large-scale category detection.

Our implementation was based on R-CNN. We used the same network as R-CNN, which was pre-trained for ImageNet classification and fine-tuned for PASCAL VOC object detection. We used 4096-dimensional fc7 feature vectors. Different from R-CNN, our method is designed for large-scale data, as explained in Sect. 2; data is accessed through an inverted index and each inverted list stores data compressed by RVQ. To learn the codebook, we used randomly selected regions detected with a selective search. We used 500000 samples to learn a codebook for coarse quantization (an inverted index) and 100000 samples for the quantization of the data compressions (PQ, OPQ and RVQ). PQ, OPQ, and RVQ set K=256 as the size of the sub-codebook (8 bits assigned per sub-codebook) in all experiments, while k=4096 and 16384 are used for coarse quantization. We used hard negative mining to train the SVMs used in the test phase (the same training algorithm and hyper-parameters as in the original R-CNN).

The training and validation parts of the PASCAL VOC 2007 (5011 images in total) were used to train the SVMs and learn the codebooks.

In addition, we prepared exemplar classifiers for CAQ. Here, we describe how we constructed these exemplar classifiers W. The training set of the ILSVRC 2014 detection datasets, which has 200 categories, was used to train detectors. This set is completely separated from the test datasets. We constructed four sets of exemplar classifiers, W_{180}, W_{200}, W_{1800}, and W_{2000}. W_{200} was formed from 200 classifiers trained on 200 categories of the ILSVRC training set. W_{180} excluded the 20 categories corresponding to PASCAL VOC from these 200 categories. W_{2000} and W_{1800} were constructed from 200 and 180 categories of ILSVRC; ten detectors were constructed from each category. For each category, 10 sets of 500 positive samples were randomly selected from the training set of ILSVRC and they formed 10 detectors (one detector per set). W_{200} and W_{2000} were not used in most of our experiments in order to strictly reproduce the situation that the query is completely unknown during training.

In addition to these four sets, we used *eigen queries* as exemplar classifiers (introduced in [32]). We generated eigen queries from W_{1800}. Here, we performed eigenvalue decomposition on the covariance matrix of W_{1800} and selected eigen-vectors corresponding to the largest d eigen values to be eigen queries that were the principal components of W_{1800}.

4.2   Comparison with R-CNN

We first demonstrate that our method compares well with R-CNN on the PASCAL VOC 2007 dataset. We compared R-CNN with three versions of our method: (i) an exhaustive search where all feature vectors compressed by RVQ are scanned (referred to as RVQ), (ii) a non-exhaustive search where an inverted index is constructed by CAQ and inverted lists store the original 4096-dimensional vectors (referred to as CAQIVF + original), and (iii) a non-exhaustive search where inverted lists store RVQ-compressed vectors (referred to as CAQIVF + RVQ). $M=64$ (64 bytes code) was used in RVQ, and $k=16384$ and $l=64$ were used in the inverted file retrieval. We used W_{1800} as the exemplar classifiers for CAQ. Note that *R-CNN* which is used as baseline in this paper corresponds to an exhaustive search to the original 4096-dimensional vectors, and other settings (e.g., feature extraction are done offline) are the same as our method.

Table 1 shows the average precision on PASCAL VOC 2007 for our three versions and R-CNN as a baseline. Our methods compare well with R-CNN; even the non-exhaustive retrieval RVQ compression (CAQIVF + RVQ) achieved a mAP of 50.1 %, while R-CNN obtained a mAP of 54.2 %. Next, we evaluated the efficiency. Table 2 lists the number of code comparisons, timings, and amount of memory used. The number of code comparisons and the timings are the means over PASCAL's 20 categories. The results for CAQIVF + RVQ show the first scan for codewords of the inverted index and the second scan for compressed vectors separately. RVQ achieved a 90× speed-up and 256× memory reduction compared with R-CNN, which demonstrates the efficiency of RVQ compression.

CAQIVF + RVQ reduced the number of comparisons from about 10M to 42K, including both codewords and compressed data, which led to a 250× faster (and 180× memory efficient) search compared with R-CNN. An inverted index is more effective on a larger database, as we show later in Sect. 4.6. Note that the timings in Table 2 exclude the NMS processing, because it depends on the way of evaluation. We found that NMS takes 0.1 s to detect all objects on PASCAL VOC 2007 and takes ~10 ms to detect the top-100 scored objects. It should be noted that our method is compatible with Fast and Faster R-CNN and offline processing time for feature extraction can be reduced by using these methods.

Table 1. Comparison of our method with R-CNN on PASCAL VOC 2007 (%). M=64, k=16384, and l=64 were used for our methods.

VOC 2007	aero	bike	bird	boat	bott	bus	car	cat	chair	cow	table	dog	horse	mbik	pers	plant	sheep	sofa	train	tv	mAP
R-CNN	64.3	69.6	50.1	41.9	32.1	62.6	70.9	60.9	32.7	58.5	46.2	56.1	60.4	67.2	54.1	31.5	52.8	48.9	57.8	64.8	54.2
RVQ(Exhaustive)	62.8	66.6	46.5	38.0	29.0	62.2	68.5	59.5	26.1	54.8	45.3	49.9	56.3	66.0	53.1	28.5	52.9	45.5	52.2	62.3	51.3
CAQIVF+original	61.1	67.8	48.3	40.0	32.5	62.4	67.9	57.9	28.6	57.1	44.9	55.3	58.4	66.4	47.9	30.8	53.4	47.5	56.1	64.4	52.4
CAQIVF+RVQ	60.3	65.6	44.9	36.7	28.9	60.7	66.9	56.8	25.0	53.0	45.7	49.1	55.5	65.6	47.0	27.2	52.4	44.9	50.9	61.8	50.0

4.3   Evaluation of CAQ

In this section, we make a detailed evaluation of CAQ. We constructed an inverted file structure by using coarse quantization with CAQ. For pure evaluations of the performance of CAQ as a quantizer of an inverted index, we measured the recall without RVQ re-ranking. Recall is defined as the number of relevant objects in a list returned by the inverted index divided by the total number of ground truth objects. The performance of k-means was also measured as a baseline. To investigate the effect of exemplar classifiers, we tested four different cases: W_{180}, W_{200}, W_{1800}, and W_{2000}. We also used eigen queries as exemplar classifiers while varying the number of eigenvectors d.

   Figure 4(a), (b) show the recall as a function of the list length, i.e., the number of codes returned by an inverted index. We used codebook sizes of k=16384 in (a) and k=4096 in (b) and varied l, the number of lists to be scanned, from 1 to 128. All our methods using CAQ outperformed k-means, which demonstrates the superiority of CAQ over k-means as an inverted index of this task. The performance on W_{200} (W_{2000}) was higher than on W_{180} (W_{1800}). This indicates that the accuracy depends on whether exemplar classifiers include the same category as the query. In addition, W_{1800} (W_{2000}) was higher than W_{180} (W_{1800}). It appears that exemplar classifiers with a larger number of classes can better capture the essence of the category classifier. The eigen queries method with $d = 180$ was inferior to W_{1800}, but superior to W_{180} in most case, especially with a larger list length. The results of eigen queries for various d are shown in Fig. 4(c). The highest recall was on $d = 100, 200$, although the value is not so sensitive to changing d. Although accuracy of the eigen queries was not so good, it can reduce the computational cost of encoding and learning the codebook, an effect that stands out when the number of exemplar classifiers is large.

Table 2. Number of code comparisons, search time, and memory consumption in PASCAL VOC 2007 test (4952 images). The accuracy of the corresponding methods are shown in Table 1. The times were measured on a single core.

Method	Comparisons	Search time	Memory
R-CNN	9927228	6258.5 ms	163 GB
RVQ	9927228	69.5 ms	0.64 GB
CAQIVF + original	41892	518.0 ms	163 GB
CAQIVF + RVQ			
inverted index	16384	15.0 ms	0.27 GB
compressed	25508	6.5 ms	0.64 GB
total	41892	24.5 ms	0.91 GB

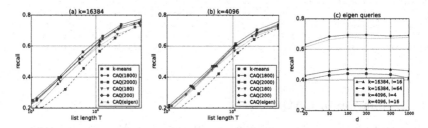

Fig. 4. Evaluation of CAQ on PASCAL VOC 2007. (a), (b): Recall as a function of the candidate list length. CAQ (eigen) used eigen queries with d=180. The codebook size is k=16384 in (a) and k=4096 in (b). (c): using eigen queries as exemplar classifiers while varying their number d from 20 to 1000.

4.4   Comparison of Object Detection Performance

In this section, we compare the object detection performances of various indexing methods. We measured mAP and changed the inverted index as follows: CAQ with various exemplar classifiers, k-means, and IMI [24,25] using PQ and OPQ. IMI was adapted for our task by changing the order of the priority queue to the score of the linear classifier. IMI was constructed using PQ and OPQ with two sub-codebooks. We performed RVQ-based re-ranking and NMS on a list of candidates returned by the inverted index to evaluate the performance of the overall object detection pipeline.

Figure 5 shows the performance comparisons for codebook sizes (sub-codebook sizes in IMI) of k=16384 in (a) and k=4096 in (b). CAQ outperformed k-means, IMI (PQ), and IMI (OPQ) in most cases. Note that IMI was inferior to even the k-means-based inverted index with larger list length despite that it has been shown to outperform IVFADC (k-means) in ANN searches. This implies that a finer partition is not always a good thing, which has a different nature from that of a nearest neighbor search. In our task, relevant regions sometimes have lower scores than irrelevant regions do because the classifier

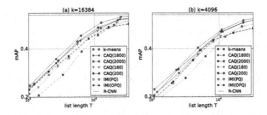

Fig. 5. Object detection performance of CAQ, k-means, and IMI with PQ and OPQ on PASCAL VOC 2007. The figure plots mAP as a function of the candidate list length. The codebook size is k=16384 in (a) and k=4096 in (b).

(SVM + CNN feature) is not perfect, due to the so-called semantic gap [33]. By coarse quantization, in our case, regions with similar appearances tend to be clustered together and relevant regions with lower scores can be detected together along with other many relevant regions with higher scores. Conversely, isolated regions (not similar to relevant objects) that have high scores but are irrelevant can be excluded by the inverted index. We consider these are the reasons that a coarser inverted index sometimes outperformed a finer one. Thus, we consider that a moderate-grained quantizer in which objects of similar categories belong to the same cluster is the best as an inverted index used in this task. From this perspective, CAQ is certainly reasonable because it exploits the response to the various object classifiers, and thus, objects that are semantically close in terms of object category tend to belong to the same cluster. This seems to be the reason that the CAQ-based inverted index outperformed the k-means one and IMI.

4.5   Comparison with State-of-the-art Methods

To show the superiority of our method over the previous ones, we compared it with [4], a recently proposed method of large-scale category detection. We also compared it with Video Google [23], which is based on the bag-of-visual-words (BoVW) method. Following [4], we used the top-k precision (k=10, 50, and 100) to evaluate them. We evaluated RVQ, CAQIVF + original, and CAQIVF + RVQ using the same settings as in Sect. 4.2. NMS was applied to the top-scored regions until the number of candidates reached 100.

Table 3 shows the precisions of the top 10, 50, and 100 ranked detections on PASCAL 2007. Included are the results from [4] (FS + HOG-SC and FS + RR + HOG-SC) and for Video Google (also reported in [4]). FS + HOG-SC uses an inverted index and re-ranking that re-evaluates candidates using the original HOG classifier template. FS + RR + HOG-SC adds a second re-ranking stage similar to what is done in NMS. Video Google was tested with two different vocabulary sizes, 10K and 200K. The results show that our method significantly outperforms [4] and Video Google. Compared with FS + RR + HOG-SC, CAQIVF + RVQ increases by 57.5 %, 53.0 %, and 40.0 % on PR@100, PR@50 and PR@10 in mean precision of 20 categories. There are mainly two reasons for this significance performance boost: 1) R-CNN was more accurate than DPM, 2) the proposed method was comparable in accuracy to the R-CNN due to its used of state-of-the-art ANN search techniques and CAQ, while [4] performed far worse than the original DPM. The search time was also shorter. CAQIVF + RVQ can processed the PASCAL VOC 2007 testset in 38.2 ms including the processing time of NMS, while [4] reported that FS + RR + HOG-SC takes 1.3 s. Note that although these timings were not measured in completely the same experimental environment, both methods were evaluated using a single core. Moreover, we can see, by comparing the R-CNN with CAQIVF + original or by comparing RVQ with CAQIVF + RVQ, that a non-exhaustive search does not decrease performance at all. Rather, CAQIVF + RVQ outperformed RVQ. This indicates an inverted index is especially effective in retrieval tasks that only need to detect top-ranked objects.

Table 3. Comparison with previous methods on PASCAL VOC 2007(%). Mean values of top 10, 50, and 100 precisions over 20 categories are shown. The search times of our methods include the time taken by the whole procedure including the NMS re-ranking. Our versions used M=64, k=16384, and l=64. Although times of FS + HOG-SC and FS + RR + HOG-SC reported in [4] are also shown in brackets for reference, they are not directly comparable because the experimental environment was different.

Method	PR@10	PR@50	PR@100	Search time
R-CNN	96.5	90.8	87.0	6.2 s
RVQ	91.0	89.8	82.9	77.4 ms
CAQIVF + original	97.0	90.9	85.2	529.9 ms
CAQIVF + RVQ	93.5	89.8	85.0	29.1 ms
FS + HOG-SC [4]	45.9	28.9	22.0	(1.2 s)
FS + RR + HOG-SC [4]	53.5	36.8	27.5	(1.3 s)
Video Google 10K [23]	25.8	14.8	10.2	-
Video Google 200K [23]	32.9	17.4	11.1	-

4.6   Large-Scale Experiments

To investigate the scalability of our method, we added 100 K distractors from the ILSVRC 2011/2012 validation sets to the PASCAL VOC 2007 dataset (105K images in total). Since we do not have reliable ground truth for the ILSVRC validation set, we performed a manual evaluation similar to what is done in [4]. In these experiments, we extracted features using the Fast R-CNN framework [13], an accelerated version of R-CNN, to speed-up feature extraction. We used the VGG-16 network [34] distributed by one of the authors of [13]. It was trained for detection on PASCAL VOC 2007 and used 4096-dimensional fc6 features. SVM was also trained on these features. We used the CAQIVF + RVQ with the parameters of M=64, k=16384, and l=16 in this experiment.

Table 4 shows the results for PASCAL VOC 2007 alone and the combined set. We can see that the performance is not affected by the distractors. Moreover, the search time was only 130 ms while the exhaustive search of RVQ took 2.7 s.

Table 4. Large-scale experiments with 100 K added distractors. k=16384, l=16, and M=64 were used.

Datasets	PR@10	PR@50	PR@100	Search time	Memory
PASCAL (5K)	94.0	87.6	81.1	29.1 ms	0.91 GB
PASCAL+ILSVRC (105K)	91.0	88.0	81.2	129.6 ms	13.61 GB

5   Conclusion

This paper introduced large-scale R-CNN. The proposed method achieved immediate and accurate object category detection from a large image database by combining the state-of-the-art object detection method and state-of-the-art nearest neighbor search. Our experiments demonstrated that this method performed comparably to the original R-CNN on PASCAL VOC 2007 in terms of accuracy, but with a 250 times speed-up and 180 times memory reduction. Moreover, it significantly outperformed the state-of-the-art large-scale category detection method, and its accuracy and search speed were not affected by the addition of 100 K distractors.

We also presented classifier adaptive quantization (CAQ), whose quantization distortion is defined on the basis of the linear classification score to further improve the performance of our large-scale R-CNN. We confirmed that performance significantly increased as a result of using CAQ as an inverted index instead of k-means and that it also outperformed an inverted multi-index.

References

1. Felzenszwalb, P., Mcallester, D., Ramanan, D., Irvine, U.C.: A discriminatively trained, multiscale, deformable part model. In: CVPR (2008)
2. Felzenszwalb, P.F., Girshick, R.B., McAllester, D., Ramanan, D.: Object detection with discriminatively trained part-based models. PAMI **32**(9), 1627–1645 (2010)
3. Girshick, R., Donahue, J., Darrell, T., Berkeley, U.C., Malik, J.: Rich feature hierarchies for accurate object detection and semantic segmentation. In: CVPR (2014)
4. Aytar, Y., Zisserman, A.: Immediate, scalable object category detection. In: CVPR (2014)
5. Dean, T., Ruzon, M.A., Segal, M., Shlens, J., Vijayanarasimhan, S., Yagnik, J.: Fast, accurate detection of 100,000 object classes on a single machine. In: CVPR (2013)
6. Sadeghi, M.A., Forsyth, D.: 30Hz object detection with DPM V5. In: Fleet, D., Pajdla, T., Schiele, B., Tuytelaars, T. (eds.) ECCV 2014, Part I. LNCS, vol. 8689, pp. 65–79. Springer, Heidelberg (2014)

7. Girshick, R.: Fast R-CNN (2015)
8. Ren, S., He, K., Girshick, R., Sun, J.: Faster R-CNN: towards real-time object detection with region proposal networks. In: NIPS, pp. 1–10 (2015)
9. Redmon, J., Girshick, R., Farhadi, A.: You only look once: unified, real-time object detection. In: CVPR (2015)
10. Lampert, C.H.: Detecting objects in large image collections and videos by efficient subimage retrieval. In: ICCV (2009)
11. Shen, X., Lin, Z., Brandt, J., Avidan, S., Wu, Y.: Object retrieval and localization with spatially-constrained similarity measure and k -NN re-ranking. In: CVPR (2012)
12. He, K., Zhang, X., Ren, S., Sun, J.:Spatial pyramid pooling in deep convolutional networks for visual recognition. In: ECCV (2014)
13. Girshick, R.: Fast R-CNN. In: ICCV (2015)
14. Ouyang, W., Wang, X., Zeng, X., Qiu, S., Luo, P., Tian, Y., Li, H., Yang, S.,Wang, Z., Loy, C.c., Tang, X.: DeepID-Net : Deformable deep convolutional neural networks forobject detection. In: CVPR (2015)
15. Litayem, S., Joly, A., Boujemaa, N.: Hash-Based Support Vector Machines Approximation for Large Scale Prediction. In: BMVC. (2012)
16. Andoni, A., Indyk, P.: Near-optimal hashing algorithms for approximate nearest neighbor in high dimensions. In: FOCS, vol. 51, pp. 459–468 (2006)
17. Akata, Z., Perronnin, F., Harchaoui, Z., Schmid, C.: Good practice in large-scale learning for image classification. IEEE Trans. Pattern Anal. Mach. Intell. **36**(3), 507–520 (2014)
18. Silpa-anan, C., Hartley, R.: Optimised KD -trees for fast image descriptor matching. In: CVPR (2008)
19. Muja, M., Lowe, D.G.: Fast approximate nearest neighbors with automatic algorithmic configuration. In: VISApp. (2009)
20. Jégou, H., Douze, M., Schmid, C.: Product quantization for nearest neighbor search. PAMI **33**(1), 117–128 (2011)
21. Weiss, Y., Torralba, A., Fergus, R.: Spectral hashing. In: NIPS (2009)
22. Jegou, H., Douze, M., Schmid, C.: Hamming embedding and weak geometric consistency for large scale image search. In: ECCV (2008)
23. Sivic, J., Zisserman, A.: Video Google: a text retrieval approach to object matching in videos. In: ICCV (2003)
24. Babenko, A., Lempitsky, V.: The inverted multi-index. In: CVPR (2012)
25. Babenko, A., Lempitsky, V.: The inverted multi-index. PAMI **37**(6), 1247–1260 (2015)
26. Chen, Y., Guan, T., Wang, C.: Approximate nearest neighbor search by residual vector quantization. Sensors **10**(12), 11259–11273 (2010)
27. Juang, B.H., Gray Jr., A.H.: Multiple stage vector quantization for speech coding. In: IEEE International Conference on Acoustics, Speech, and Signal Processing, ICASSP 1982. vol. 7, pp. 597–600. IEEE (1982)
28. Uijlings, J.R., van de Sande, K.E., Gevers, T., Smeulders, A.W.: Selective search for object recognition. IJCV **104**(2), 154–171 (2013)
29. Philbin, J., Chum, O., Isard, M., Sivic, J., Zisserman, A.: Object retrieval with large vocabularies and fast spatial matching. In: CVPR (2007)
30. Xia, Y., He, K., Wen, F., Sun, J.: Joint inverted indexing. In: ICCV (2013)
31. Deng, J., Berg, A., Satheesh, S., Su, H., Khosla, A., Fei-Fei, L.: Imagenet large scale visual recognition competition 2012 (ILSVRC 2012) (2012)

32. Raval, N., Tonge, R.V., Jawahar, C.V.: Image retrieval using eigen queries. In: Lee, K.M., Matsushita, Y., Rehg, J.M., Hu, Z. (eds.) ACCV 2012, Part II. LNCS, vol. 7725, pp. 461–474. Springer, Heidelberg (2013)
33. Smeulders, A., Worring, M.: Content-based image retrieval at the end of the early years. PAMI **22**(12), 1–32 (2000)
34. Simonyan, K., Zisserman, A.: Very Deep Convolutional Networks for Large-Scale Image Recognition. In: ICLR (2015)

Face Detection with End-to-End Integration of a ConvNet and a 3D Model

Yunzhu Li[1], Benyuan Sun[1], Tianfu Wu[2(✉)], and Yizhou Wang[1(✉)]

[1] Nat'l Engineering Laboratory for Video Technology,
Key Laboratory of Machine Perception (MoE),
Cooperative Medianet Innovation Center,
Shanghai Sch'l of EECS, Peking University, Beijing 100871, China
{leo.liyunzhu,sunbenyuan,Yizhou.Wang}@pku.edu.cn
[2] Department of ECE and the Visual Narrative Cluster,
North Carolina State University, Raleigh, USA
tianfu_wu@ncsu.edu

Abstract. This paper presents a method for face detection in the wild, which integrates a ConvNet and a 3D mean face model in an end-to-end multi-task discriminative learning framework. The 3D mean face model is predefined and fixed (e.g., we used the one provided in the AFLW dataset). The ConvNet consists of two components: (i) The face proposal component computes face bounding box proposals via estimating facial key-points and the 3D transformation (rotation and translation) parameters for each predicted key-point w.r.t. the 3D mean face model. (ii) The face verification component computes detection results by pruning and refining proposals based on facial key-points based configuration pooling. The proposed method addresses two issues in adapting state-of-the-art generic object detection ConvNets (e.g., faster R-CNN) for face detection: (i) One is to eliminate the heuristic design of predefined anchor boxes in the region proposals network (RPN) by exploiting a 3D mean face model. (ii) The other is to replace the generic RoI (Region-of-Interest) pooling layer with a configuration pooling layer to respect underlying object structures. The multi-task loss consists of three terms: the classification Softmax loss and the location smooth l_1-losses of both the facial key-points and the face bounding boxes. In experiments, our ConvNet is trained on the AFLW dataset only and tested on the FDDB benchmark with fine-tuning and on the AFW benchmark without fine-tuning. The proposed method obtains very competitive state-of-the-art performance in the two benchmarks.

Keywords: Face detection · Face 3D model · ConvNet · Deep learning · Multi-task learning

---

Y. Li and B. Sun contributed equally to this work and are joint first authors.

© Springer International Publishing AG 2016
B. Leibe et al. (Eds.): ECCV 2016, Part III, LNCS 9907, pp. 420–436, 2016.
DOI: 10.1007/978-3-319-46487-9_26

1   Introduction

1.1   Motivation and Objective

Face detection has been used as a core module in a wide spectrum of applications such as surveillance, mobile communication and human-computer interaction. It is arguably one of the most successful applications of computer vision. Face detection in the wild continues to play an important role in the era of visual big data (e.g., images and videos on the web and in social media). However, it remains a challenging problem in computer vision due to the large appearance variations caused by nuisance variabilities including viewpoints, occlusion, facial expression, resolution, illumination and cosmetics, etc.

It has been a long history that computer vision researchers study how to learn a better representation for unconstrained faces [12,34,40]. Recently, together with large-scale annotated image datasets such as the ImageNet [8], deep ConvNets [21,22] have made significant progress in generic object detection [14,16,32], as well as in face detection [23,30]. The success is generally considered to be due to the region proposal methods and region-based ConvNets (R-CNN) [15]. The two factors used to be addressed separately (e.g., the popular combination of the Selective Search [37] and R-CNNs pretrained on the ImageNet), and now they are integrated through introducing the region proposal networks (RPNs) as done in the faster-RCNN [32] or are merged into a single pipeline for speeding up the detection as done in [26,31]. In R-CNNs, one key layer is the so-called RoI (Region-of-Interest) pooling layer [14], which divides a valid RoI (e.g., an object bounding box proposal) evenly into a grid with a fixed spatial extent (e.g., 7×7) and then uses max-pooling to convert the features inside the RoI into a small feature map. In this paper, we are interested in adapting state-of-the-art ConvNets of generic object detection (e.g., the faster R-CNN [32]) for face detection by overcoming the following two limitations:

Fig. 1. Some example results in the FDDB face benchmark [19] computed by the proposed method. For each testing image, we show the detection results (left) and the corresponding heat map of facial key-points with the legend shown in the right most column. (Best viewed in color) (Color figure online)

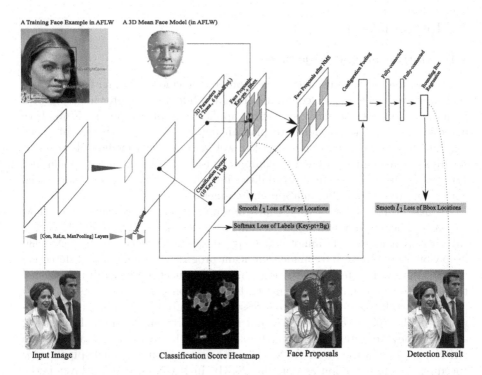

A Training Face Example in AFLW   A 3D Mean Face Model (in AFLW)

Input Image   Classification Score Heatmap   Face Proposals   Detection Result

Fig. 2. Illustration of the proposed method of an end-to-end integration of a ConvNet and a 3D model for face detection (Top), and some intermediate and the final detection results for an input testing image (Bottom). See the legend for the classification score heat map in Fig. 1. The 3D mean face model is predefined and fixed in both training and testing. The key idea of the proposed method is to learn a ConvNet to estimate the 3D transformation parameters (rotation and translation) w.r.t. the 3D mean face model to generate accurate face proposals and predict the face key points. The proposed ConvNet is trained in a multi-task discriminative training framework consisting of the classification Softmax loss and the location smooth l_1-losses [14] of both the facial key-points and the face bounding boxes. It is surprisingly simple w.r.t. its competitive state-of-the-art performance compared to the other methods in the popular FDDB benchmark [19] and the AFW benchmark [41]. See text for details. (Color figure online)

(i) RPNs need to predefine a number of anchor boxes (with different aspect ratios and sizes), which requires potentially tedious parameter tuning in training and is sensitive to the (unknown) distribution of the aspect ratios and sizes of the object instances in a random testing image.

(ii) The RoI pooling layer in R-CNNs is predefined and generic to all object categories without exploiting the underlying object structural configurations, which either are available from the annotations in the training dataset (e.g., the facial landmark annotations in the AFLW dataset [20]) as done in [41] or can be pursued during learning (such as the deformable part-based models [10,30]).

To address the two above issues in learning ConvNets for face detection, we propose to integrate a ConvNet and a 3D mean face model in an end-to-end multi-task discriminative learning framework. Figure 1 shows some results of the proposed method.

1.2 Method Overview

Figure 2 illustrates the proposed method. We use 10 facial key-points in this paper, including "LeftEyeLeftCorner", "RightEyeRightCorner", "LeftEar", "NoseLeft", "NoseRight", "RightEar", "MouthLeftCorner", "MouthRight-Corner", "ChinCenter", "CenterBetweenEyes" (see an example image in the left-top of Fig. 2). The 3D mean face model is then represented by the corresponding ten 3D facial key-points. The architecture of our ConvNet is straight-forward when taking into account a 3D model (see Sect. 3.2 for details).

The key idea is to learn a ConvNet to (i) estimate the 3D transformation parameters (rotation and translation) w.r.t. the 3D mean face model for each detected facial key-point so that we can generate face bounding box proposals and (ii) predict facial key-points for each face instance more accurately. Leveraging the 3D mean face model is able to "kill two birds with one stone": Firstly, we can eliminate the manually heuristic design of anchor boxes in RPNs. Secondly, instead of using the generic RoI pooling, we devise a "configuration pooling" layer so as to respect the object structural configurations in a meaningful and principled way. In other words, we propose to learn to compute the proposals in a straight-forward top-down manner, instead of to design the bottom-up heuristic and then learn related regression parameters. To do so, we assume a 3D mean face model is available and facial key-points are annotated in the training dataset. Thanks to many excellent existing work in collecting and annotating face datasets, we can easily obtain both for faces nowadays. In learning, we have multiple types of losses involved in the objective loss function, including classification Softmax loss and location smooth l_1-loss [14] of facial key-points, and location smooth l_1-loss of face bounding boxes respectively, so we formulate the learning of the proposed ConvNet under the multi-task discriminative deep learning framework (see Sect. 3.3).

In summary, we provide a clean and straight-forward solution for end-to-end integration of a ConvNet and a 3D model for face detection[1]. In addition to the competitive performance w.r.t the state-of-the-art face detection methods on the FDDB and AFW benchmarks, the proposed method is surprisingly simple and it is able to detect challenging faces (e.g., small, blurry, heavily occluded and extreme poses).

Potentially, the proposed method can be utilized to learn to detect other rigid or semi-rigid object categories (such as cars) if the required information (such as the 3D model and key-point/part annotation) are provided in training.

---

[1] We use the open source deep learning package, MXNet [5], in our implementation. The full source code is released at https://github.com/tfwu/FaceDetection-ConvNet-3D.

2   Related Work

There are a tremendous amount of existing works on face detection or generic object detection. We refer to [40] for a more thorough survey on face detection. We discuss some of the most relevant ones in this section.

In human/animal vision, how the brain distills a representation of objects from retinal input is one of the central challenges for systems neuroscience, and many works have been focused on the ecologically important class of objects–faces. Studies using fMRI experiments in the macaque reveal that faces are represented by a system of six discrete, strongly interconnected regions which illustrates hierarchical information processing in the brain [12], as well as some other results [34]. These findings provide some biologically-plausible evidences for supporting the usage of deep learning based approaches in face detection and analysis.

The seminal work of Viola and Jones [38] made face detection by a computer vision system feasible in real world applications, which trained a cascade of AdaBoost classifiers using Haar wavelet features. Many works followed this direction with different extensions proposed in four aspects: appearance features (beside Haar) including Histogram of Oriented Gradients (HOG) [7], Aggregate Channel Features (ACF) [9], Local Binary Pattern (LBP) features [1] and SURF [3], etc.; detector structures (beside cascade) including the the scalar tree [11] and the width-first-search tree [18], etc.; strong classifier learning (beside AdaBoost) including RealBoost [33] and GentleBoost [13], ect; weak classifier learning (beside stump function) including the histogram method [25] and the joint binarizations of Haar-like feature [28], etc.

Most of the recent face detectors are based on the deformable part-based model (DPM) [10,27,41] with HOG features used, where a face is represented by a collection of parts defined based on either facial landmarks or heuristic pursuit as done in the original DPM. [27] showed that a properly trained vanilla DPM can yield significant improvement for face detection.

More recent advances in deep learning [21,22] further boosted the face detection performance by learning more discriminative features from large-scale raw data, going beyond those handcrafted ones. In the FDDB benchmark, most of the face detectors with top performance are based on ConvNets [23,30], combining with cascade [23] and more explicit structure [39].

3D information has been exploited in learning object models in different ways. Some works [29,35] used a mixture of 3D view based templates by dividing the view sphere into a number of sectors. [17,24] utilized 3D models in extracting features and inferring the object pose hypothesis based on EM or DP. [36] used a 3D face model for aligning faces in learning ConvNets for face recognition. Our work resembles [2] in exploiting 3D model in face detection, which obtained very good performance in the FDDB benchmark. [2] computes meaningful 3D pose candidates by image-based regression from detected face key-points with traditional handcrafted features, and verifies the 3D pose candidates by a parameter sensitive classifier based on difference features relative to the 3D pose. Our work integrates a ConvNet and a 3D model in an end-to-end multi-task discriminative learning fashion, which is more straightforward and simpler compared to [2].

Our Contributions. The proposed method contributes to face detection in three aspects.

(i) It presents a simple yet effective method to integrate a ConvNet and a 3D model in an end-to-end learning with multi-task loss used for face detection in the wild.

(ii) It addresses two limitations in adapting the state-of-the-art faster RCNN [32] for face detection: eliminating the heuristic design of anchor boxes by leveraging a 3D model, and replacing the generic and predefined *RoI pooling* with a *configuration pooling* which exploits the underlying object structural configurations.

(iii) It obtains very competitive state-of-the-art performance in the FDDB [19] and AFW [41] benchmarks.

Paper Organization. The remainder of this paper is organized as follows. Section 3 presents the method of face detection using a 3D model and details of our ConvNet including its architecture and training procedure. Section 4 presents details of experimental settings and shows the experimental results in the FDDB and AFW benchmarks. Section 5 first concludes this paper and then discuss some on-going and future work to extend the proposed work.

3   The Proposed Method

In this section, we introduce the notations and present details of the proposed method.

3.1   3D Mean Face Model and Face Representation

In this paper, a 3D mean face model is represented by a collection of n 3D key-points in the form of (x, y, z) and then is denoted by a $n \times 3$ matrix, $F^{(3)}$. Usually, each key-point has its own semantic name. We use the 3D mean face model in the AFLW dataset [20] which consists of 21 key-points. We select 10 key-points as stated above.

A face, denoted by f, is presented by its 3D transformation parameters, Θ, for rotation and translation, and a collection of 2D key-points, $F^{(2)}$, in the form of (x, y) (with the number being less than or equal to n). Hence, $f = (\Theta, F^{(2)})$. The 3D transformation parameters Θ are defined by,

$$\Theta = (\mu, s, A^{(3)}), \tag{1}$$

where μ represents a 2D translation (dx, dy), s a scaling factor, and $A^{(3)}$ a 3×3 rotation matrix. We can compute the predicted 2D key-points by,

$$\hat{F}^{(2)} = \mu + s \cdot \pi(A^{(3)} \cdot F^{(3)}), \tag{2}$$

where $\pi()$ projects a 3D key-point to a 2D one, that is, $\pi : \mathbb{R}^3 \to \mathbb{R}^2$ and $\pi(x, y, z) = (x, y)$. Due to the projection $\pi()$, we only need 8 parameters out of the original 12 parameters. Let $A^{(2)}$ denote a 2×3 matrix, which is composed by the top two rows of $A^{(3)}$. We can re-produce the predicted 2D key-points by,

$$\hat{F}^{(2)} = \mu + A^{(2)} \cdot F^{(3)} \tag{3}$$

which makes it easy to implement the computation of back-propagation in training our ConvNet.

Note that we use the first sector in a 4-sector X-Y coordinate system to define all the positions, that is, the origin point $(0, 0)$ is defined by the left-bottom corner in an image lattice.

In face datasets, faces are usually annotated with bounding boxes. In the FDDB benchmark [19], however, faces are annotated with ellipses and detection performance are evaluated based on ellipses. Given a set of predicted 2D key-points $\hat{F}^{(2)}$, we can compute proposals in both ellipse form and bounding box form.

Computing a Face Ellipse and a Face Bounding Box based on a set of Predicted 2D Key-Points. For a given $\hat{F}^{(2)}$, we first predict the position of the top of head by,

$$\begin{pmatrix} x \\ y \end{pmatrix}_{\text{TopOfHead}} = 2 \times \begin{pmatrix} x \\ y \end{pmatrix}_{\text{CenterBetweenEyes}} - \begin{pmatrix} x \\ y \end{pmatrix}_{\text{ChinCenter}}.$$

Based on the keypoints of a face proposal, we can compute its ellipse and bounding box.

Face Ellipse. We first compute the outer rectangle. We use as one axis the line segment between the top-of-the-head key-point and the chin key-point, and then compute the minimum rectangle, usually a rotated rectangle, which covers all the key-points. Then, we can compute the ellipse using the two edges of the (rotated) rectangle as the major and minor axes respectively.

Face Bounding Box. We compute a face bounding box by the minimum upright rectangle which covers all the key-points, which is also adopted in the FDDB benchmark [19].

3.2   The Architecture of Our ConvNet

As illustrated in Fig. 2, the architecture of our ConvNet consists of:

(i) *Convolution, ReLu and MaxPooling Layers.* We adopt the VGG [4] design in our experiments which has shown superior performance in a series of tasks. There are 5 groups and each group has 3 convolution and ReLu consecutive layers followed by a MaxPooling layer except for the 5th group. The spatial extent of the final feature map is of 16 times smaller than that of an input image due to the sub-sampling.

(ii) *An Upsampling Layer.* Since we will measure the location difference between the input facial key-points and the predicted ones, we add an upsampling layer to compensate the sub-sampling effects in previous layers. It is implemented by deconvolution. We upsample the feature maps to 8 times bigger in size (i.e., the upsampled feature maps are still quarter size of an input image) considering the trade-off between key-point location accuracy, memory consumption and computation efficiency.

(iii) *A Facial Key-point Label Prediction Layer.* There are 11 labels (10 facial key-points and 1 background class). It is used to compute the classification Softmax loss based on the input in training.

(iv) *A 3D Transformation Parameter Estimation Layer.* This is the key observation in this paper. Originally, there are 12 parameters in total consisting of 2D translation, scaling and 3×3 rotation matrix. Since we focus on the 2D projected key-points, we only need to account for 8 parameters (see the derivation above).

(v) *A Face Proposal Layer.* At each position, based on the 3D mean face model and the estimated 3D transformation parameters, we can compute a face proposal consisting of 10 predicted facial key-points and the corresponding face bounding box. *The score of a face proposal* is the sum of *log* probabilities of the 10 predicted facial key-points. The predicated key-points will be used to compute the smooth l_1 loss [14] w.r.t. the ground-truth key-points. We apply the non-maximum suppression (NMS) to the face proposals in which the overlap between two bounding boxes a and b is computed by $\frac{|a \cap b|}{|b|}$ (where $| \cdot |$ represents the area of a bounding box), instead of the traditional intersection-over-union, accounting for the fact that it is rarely observed that one face is inside another one.

(vi) *A Configuration Pooling Layer.* After NMS, for each face proposal, we pool the features based on the predicted 10 facial key-points. Here, for simplicity, we use all the 10 key-points without considering the invisibilities of certain key-points in different face examples.

(vii) *A Face Bounding Box Regression Layer.* It is used to further refine face bounding boxes in the spirit similar to the method [14]. Based on the configuration pooling, we add two fully-connected layers to implement the regression. It is used to compute the smooth l_1 loss of face bounding boxes.

Denote by ω all the parameters in our ConvNet, which will be estimated through multi-task discriminative end-to-end learning.

3.3 The End-to-End Training

Input Data. Denote by $C = \{0, 1, \cdots, 10\}$ as the key-point labels where $\ell = 0$ represents the background class. We use the image-centric sampling trick as done in [14,32]. Without loss of generality, considering a training image with only one face appeared, we have its bounding box, $B = (x, y, w, h)$ and m 2D key-points $(m \leq 10)$, $\{(\mathbf{x}_i, \ell_i)_{i=1}^{m}\}$ where $\mathbf{x}_i = (x_i, y_i)$ is the 2D position of the ith key-point and $\ell_i \geq 1 \in C$. We randomly sample m locations outside the face bounding box B as the background class, $\{(\mathbf{x}_i, \ell_i)_{i=m+1}^{2m}\}$ (where $\ell_i = 0, \forall i > m$). Note that in our ConvNet, we use the coordinate of the upsampled feature map which is half size along both axes of the original input. All the key-points and bounding boxes are defined accordingly based on ground-truth annotation.

The Classification Softmax Loss of Key-point Labels. At each position $\mathbf{x}_i$, our ConvNet outputs a discrete probability distribution, $p^{\mathbf{x}_i} = (p_0^{\mathbf{x}_i}, p_1^{\mathbf{x}_i}, \cdots, p_{10}^{\mathbf{x}_i})$, over the 11 classes, which is computed by the Softmax over the 11 scores as usual [21]. Then, we have the loss,

$$\mathcal{L}_{cls}(\omega) = -\frac{1}{2m} \sum_{i=1}^{2m} \log(p_{\ell_i}^{\mathbf{x}_i}) \tag{4}$$

The Smooth l_1 Loss of Key-point Locations. At each key-point location $\mathbf{x}_i$ ($\ell_i \geq 1$), we compute a face proposal based on the estimated 3D parameters and the 3D mean face, denoted by $\{(\hat{\mathbf{x}}_j^{(i)}, \hat{\ell}_j^{(i)})_{j=1}^{10}\}$ the predicted 10 keypoints. So, for each key-point location $\mathbf{x}_i$, we will have m predicted locations, denoted by $\hat{\mathbf{x}}_{i,j}$ ($j = 1, \cdots, m$). We follow the definition in [14] to compute the smooth l_1 loss for each axis individually.

$$\mathcal{L}_{loc}^{pt}(\omega) = \frac{1}{m^2} \sum_{i=1}^{m} \sum_{j=1}^{m} \sum_{t \in \{x,y\}} \text{Smooth}_{l_1}(t_i - \hat{t}_{i,j}) \tag{5}$$

where the smooth term is defined by,

$$\text{Smooth}_{l_1}(a) = \begin{cases} 0.5a^2 & \text{if } |a| < 1 \\ |a| - 0.5 & \text{otherwise.} \end{cases} \tag{6}$$

Faceness Score. The faceness score of a face proposal in our ConvNet is computed by the sum of log probabilities of the predicted key-points,

$$\text{Score}(\hat{\mathbf{x}}_i, \hat{\ell}_i) = \sum_{i=1}^{10} \log(p_{\hat{\ell}_i}^{\hat{\mathbf{x}}_i}) \tag{7}$$

where for simplicity we do not account for the invisibilities of certain key-points. So the current faceness score has the issue of potential double-counting, especially for low-resolution faces. We observed that it hurts the quantitative performance in our experiments. We will address this issue in future work. See some heat maps of key-points in Fig. 1.

The Smooth l_1 Loss of Bounding Boxes. For each face bounding box proposal $\hat{B}$ (after NMS), our ConvNet computes its bounding box regression offsets, $t = (t_x, t_y, t_w, t_h)$, where t specifies a scale-invariant translation and log-space height/width shift relative to a proposal, as done in [14,32]. For the ground-truth bounding box B, we do the same parameterization and have $v = (v_x, v_y, v_w, v_h)$. Assuming that there are K bounding box proposals, we have,

$$\mathcal{L}_{loc}^{box}(\omega) = \frac{1}{K} \sum_{k=1}^{K} \sum_{i \in \{x,y,w,h\}} \text{Smooth}_{l_1}(t_i - v_i) \tag{8}$$

So, the overall loss function is defined by,

$$\mathcal{L}(\omega) = \mathcal{L}_{cls}(\omega) + \mathcal{L}_{loc}^{pt}(\omega) + \mathcal{L}_{loc}^{box}(\omega), \tag{9}$$

where the third term depends on the output of the first two terms, which makes the loss minimization more challenging. We adopt a method to implement the differentiable bounding box warping layer, similar to [6].

4   Experiments

In this section, we present the training procedure and implementation details and then show evaluation results on the FDDB [19] and AFW [41] benchmarks.

4.1   Experimental Settings

The Training Dataset. The only dataset we used for training our model is the AFLW dataset [20], which contains 25,993 annotated faces in real-world images. The facial key-points are annotated upon visibility w.r.t. a 3D mean face model with 21 landmarks. Of the images 70 % are used for training while the remaining is reserved as a validation set.

Training process. For convenience, the short edge of every image is resized to 600 pixels while preserving the aspect ratio (as done in the faster RCNN [32]), thus our model learns how to handle faces under various scale. To handle faces of different resolution, we randomly blur images using Gaussian filters in pre-processing. Apart from the rescaling and blurring, no other preprocessing mechanisms (e.g., random crop or left-right flipping) are used.

We adopt the method of image-centric sampling [14,32] which uses one image at a time in training. Under the consideration that grids around the labeled position share almost the same context information, thus the 3×3 grids around every labeled key-point's position are also regarded as the same positive examples, and we randomly choose the same amount of background examples outside the bounding boxes. The convolution filters are initialized by the VGG-16 [4] pretrained on the ImageNet [8]. We train the network for 13 epoch, and during the process, the learning rate is modified from 0.01 to 0.0001.

4.2   Evaluation of the Intermediate Results

Key-points classification in the validation dataset. As are shown by the heat maps in Fig. 1, our model is capable of detecting facial key-points with rough face configurations preserved, which shows the effectiveness of exploiting the 3D mean face model. Table 1 shows the key-point classification accuracy on the validation set in the last epoch in training.

Face proposals. To evaluate the quality of our face proposals, we first show some qualitative results on the FDDB dataset in Fig. 3. These ellipses are directly

Table 1. Classification accuracy of the key-points in the AFLW validation set at the end training.

Category	Accuracy	Category	Accuracy
Background	97.94 %	LeftEyeLeftCorner	99.12 %
RightEyeRightCorner	94.57 %	LeftEar	95.50 %
NoseLeft	98.48 %	NoseRight	97.78 %
RightEar	91.44 %	MouthLeftCorner	97.97 %
MouthRightCorner	98.64 %	ChinCenter	98.65 %
CenterBetweenEyes	96.04 %	AverageDetectionRate	97.50 %

Fig. 3. Examples of face proposals computed using predicted 3D transformation parameters without non-maximum suppression. For clarity, we randomly sample 1/30 of the original number of proposals.

calculated from the predicted 3D transformation parameters, forming several clusters around face instances. We also evaluate the quantitative results of face proposals. After a non-maximum suppression of IoU 0.7, the recall rate of 93.67 % is obtained with average 34.4 proposals per image.

4.3   Face Detection Results

To show the effectiveness of our method, we test our model on two popular face detection benchmarks: FDDB [19] and AFW [41].

Results on FDDB. FDDB is a challenge benchmark for face detection in unconstrained environment, which contains the annotations for 5171 faces in a set of 2845 images. We evaluate our results by using the evaluation code provided by the FDDB authors. The results on the FDDB dataset are shown in Fig. 4. Our result is represented by "Ours-Conv3D", which surpasses the recall rate of 90 % when encountering 2000 false positives and is competitive to the state-of-the-art methods. We compare with published methods only. Only DP2MFD [30] is slightly better than our model on discrete scores. It's worth noting that we beat all other methods on continuous scores. This is partly caused by the predefined 3D face model helps us better describe the pose and part locations of faces.

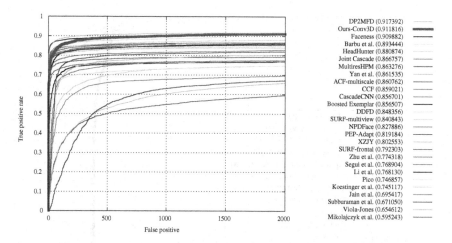

Fig. 4. FDDB results based on discrete scores using face bounding boxes in evaluation. The recall rates are computed against 2000 false positives.

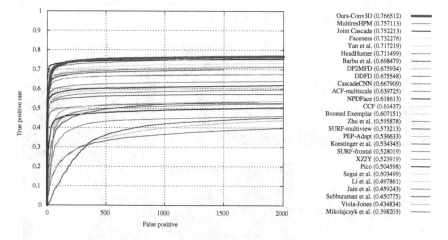

Fig. 5. FDDB results based on continuous scores using face ellipses in evaluation. The recall rates are computed against 2000 false positives.

We refer to the FDDB result webpage[2] for details of the published methods evaluated on it (Figs. 4 and 5).

When comparing with recent work Faceness [39], we both recognize that one of the central issues to alleviate the problems of the occlusion and pose variation is to introduce facial part detector. However, our mechanism of computing face bounding box candidates is more straight forward since we explicitly integrate the structural information of a 3D mean face model instead of using a heuristic way of assuming the facial part distribution over a bounding box.

---

[2] http://vis-www.cs.umass.edu/fddb/results.html.

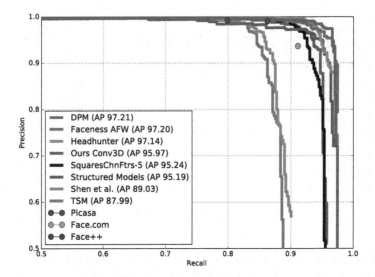

Fig. 6. Precision-recall curves on the AFW dataset (AP = average precision) without configuration pool and face bounding box regression used.

Fig. 7. Some qualitative results on the FDDB dataset

Results on AFW. AFW dataset contains 205 images with faces in various poses and view points. We use the evaluation toolbox provided by [27], which contains updated annotations for the AFW dataset where the original annotations are not comprehensive enough. Since the method of labeling face bounding boxes in AFW is different from that of in FDDB, we only use face proposals without configuration pooling and bounding box regression. The results on AFW are shown in Fig. 6.

Fig. 8. Some qualitative results on the AFW dataset

In our current implementation, there is one major limitation that prevents us from achieving better results. We do not explicitly handle invisible facial parts, which would be harmful when calculating the faceness score according to Eq. 7, we will refine the method and introduce mechanisms of handling the invisible problem in future work. More detection results on both datasets are shown in Figs. 7 and 8.

5   Conclusion and Discussion

We have presented a method of end-to-end integration of a ConvNet and a 3D model for face detection in the wild. Our method is a clean and straightforward solution when taking into account a 3D model in face detection. It also addresses two issues in state-of-the-art generic object detection ConvNets: eliminating heuristic design of anchor boxes by leveraging a 3D model, and overcoming generic and predefined RoI pooling by configuration pooling which exploits underlying object configurations. In experiments, we tested our method on two benchmarks, the FDDB dataset and the AFW dataset, with very compatible state-of-the-art performance obtained. We analyzed the experimental results and pointed out some current limitations.

In our on-going work, we are working on addressing the doubling-counting issue of the faceness score in the current implementation. We are also working on extending the proposed method for other types of rigid/semi-rigid object classes (e.g., cars). We expect that we will have a unified model for cars and faces which can achieve state-of-the-art performance, which will be very useful in a lot of practical applications such as surveillance and driveless cars.

Acknowledgement. Y. Li, B. Sun and Y. Wang were supported in part by China 973 Program under Grant no. 2015CB351800, and NSFC-61231010, 61527804, 61421062, 61210005. T. Wu was supported by the ECE startup fund 201473-02119 at NCSU.

References

1. Ahonen, T., Hadid, A., Pietikäinen, M.: Face description with local binary patterns: application to face recognition. IEEE Trans. Pattern Anal. Mach. Intell. **28**(12), 2037–2041 (2006)
2. Barbu, A., Gramajo, G.: Face detection using a 3D model on face keypoints. CoRR abs/1404.3596 (2014)
3. Bay, H., Ess, A., Tuytelaars, T., Gool, L.J.V.: Speeded-up robust features (SURF). Comput. Vis. Image Underst. **110**(3), 346–359 (2008)
4. Chatfield, K., Simonyan, K., Vedaldi, A., Zisserman, A.: Return of the devil in the details: delving deep into convolutional nets. In: British Machine Vision Conference (2014)
5. Chen, T., Li, M., Li, Y., Lin, M., Wang, N., Wang, M., Xiao, T., Xu, B., Zhang, C., Zhang, Z.: MXNet: a flexible and efficient machine learning library for heterogeneous distributed systems. CoRR abs/1512.01274 (2015)
6. Dai, J., He, K., Sun, J.: Instance-aware semantic segmentation via multi-task network cascades. In: CVPR (2016)
7. Dalal, N., Triggs, B.: Histograms of oriented gradients for human detection. In: CVPR (2005)
8. Deng, J., Dong, W., Socher, R., Li, L., Li, K., Li, F.: Imagenet: a large-scale hierarchical image database. In: CVPR, pp. 248–255 (2009)
9. Dollár, P., Appel, R., Belongie, S.J., Perona, P.: Fast feature pyramids for object detection. IEEE Trans. Pattern Anal. Mach. Intell. **36**(8), 1532–1545 (2014)
10. Felzenszwalb, P.F., Girshick, R.B., McAllester, D.A., Ramanan, D.: Object detection with discriminatively trained part-based models. IEEE Trans. Pattern Anal. Mach. Intell. **32**(9), 1627–1645 (2010)
11. Fleuret, F., Geman, D.: Coarse-to-fine face detection. Int. J. Comput. Vis. **41**(1/2), 85–107 (2001)
12. Freiwald, W.A., Tsao, D.Y.: Functional compartmentalization and viewpoint generalization within the macaque face-processing system. Science **330**(6005), 845–851 (2010)
13. Friedman, J., Hastie, T., Tibshirani, R.: Additive logistic regression: a statistical view of boosting. Ann. Stat. **28**, 2000 (1998)
14. Girshick, R.: Fast R-CNN. In: ICCV (2015)
15. Girshick, R.B., Donahue, J., Darrell, T., Malik, J.: Region-based convolutional networks for accurate object detection and segmentation. IEEE Trans. Pattern Anal. Mach. Intell. **38**(1), 142–158 (2016)

16. He, K., Zhang, X., Ren, S., Sun, J.: Deep residual learning for image recognition. In: CVPR (2016)
17. Hu, W., Zhu, S.: Learning 3D object templates by quantizing geometry and appearance spaces. IEEE Trans. Pattern Anal. Mach. Intell. **37**(6), 1190–1205 (2015)
18. Huang, C., Ai, H., Li, Y., Lao, S.: High-performance rotation invariant multiview face detection. IEEE Trans. Pattern Anal. Mach. Intell. **29**(4), 671–686 (2007)
19. Jain, V., Learned-Miller, E.: FDDB: a benchmark for face detection in unconstrained settings. Technical report UM-CS-2010-009, University of Massachusetts, Amherst (2010)
20. Koestinger, M., Wohlhart, P., Roth, P.M., Bischof, H.: Annotated facial landmarks in the wild: a large-scale, real-world database for facial landmark localization. In: First IEEE International Workshop on Benchmarking Facial Image Analysis Technologies (2011)
21. Krizhevsky, A., Sutskever, I., Hinton, G.E.: Imagenet classification with deep convolutional neural networks. In: NIPS (2012)
22. LeCun, Y., Bottou, L., Bengio, Y., Haffner, P.: Gradient-based learning applied to document recognition. Proc. IEEE **86**(11), 2278–2324 (1998)
23. Li, H., Lin, Z., Shen, X., Brandt, J., Hua, G.: A convolutional neural network cascade for face detection. In: CVPR (2015)
24. Liebelt, J., Schmid, C.: Multi-view object class detection with a 3D geometric model. In: CVPR (2010)
25. Liu, C., Shum, H.: Kullback-Leibler boosting. In: CVPR (2003)
26. Liu, W., Anguelov, D., Erhan, D., Szegedy, C., Reed, S., Fu, C.Y., Berg, A.C.: SSD: single shot multibox detector. arXiv preprint (2015). arXiv:1512.02325
27. Mathias, M., Benenson, R., Pedersoli, M., Gool, L.: Face detection without bells and whistles. In: Fleet, D., Pajdla, T., Schiele, B., Tuytelaars, T. (eds.) ECCV 2014. LNCS, vol. 8692, pp. 720–735. Springer, Heidelberg (2014). doi:10.1007/978-3-319-10593-2_47
28. Mita, T., Kaneko, T., Hori, O.: Joint Haar-like features for face detection. In: ICCV (2005)
29. Payet, N., Todorovic, S.: From contours to 3D object detection and pose estimation. In: ICCV (2011)
30. Ranjan, R., Patel, V.M., Chellappa, R.: A deep pyramid deformable part model for face detection. In: IEEE 7th International Conference on Biometrics Theory, Applications and Systems (2015)
31. Redmon, J., Divvala, S., Girshick, R., Farhadi, A.: You only look once: unified, real-time object detection. In: CVPR (2016)
32. Ren, S., He, K., Girshick, R., Sun, J.: Faster R-CNN: towards real-time object detection with region proposal networks. In: NIPS (2015)
33. Schapire, R.E., Singer, Y.: Improved boosting algorithms using confidence-rated predictions. Mach. Learn. **37**(3), 297–336 (1999)
34. Sinha, P., Balas, B., Ostrovsky, Y., Russell, R.: Face recognition by humans: 19 results all computer vision researchers should know about. Proc. IEEE **94**(11), 1948–1962 (2006)
35. Su, H., Sun, M., Li, F., Savarese, S.: Learning a dense multi-view representation for detection, viewpoint classification and synthesis of object categories. In: ICCV (2009)
36. Taigman, Y., Yang, M., Ranzato, M., Wolf, L.: Deepface: closing the gap to human-level performance in face verification. In: CVPR (2014)
37. Uijlings, J.R.R., van de Sande, K.E.A., Gevers, T., Smeulders, A.W.M.: Selective search for object recognition. Int. J. Comput. Vis. **104**(2), 154–171 (2013)

38. Viola, P.A., Jones, M.J.: Robust real-time face detection. Int. J. Comput. Vis. **57**(2), 137–154 (2004)
39. Yang, S., Luo, P., Loy, C.C., Tang, X.: From facial parts responses to face detection: a deep learning approach. In: ICCV (2015)
40. Zafeiriou, S., Zhang, C., Zhang, Z.: A survey on face detection in the wild. Comput. Vis. Image Underst. **138**(C), 1–24 (2015)
41. Zhu, X., Ramanan, D.: Face detection, pose estimation, and landmark localization in the wild. In: CVPR (2012)

Large Scale Asset Extraction for Urban Images

Lama Affara[✉], Liangliang Nan, Bernard Ghanem, and Peter Wonka

King Abdullah University of Science and Technology (KAUST),
Thuwal, Saudi Arabia
{lama.affara,bernard.ghanem}@kaust.edu.sa,
liangliang.nan@gmail.com, pwonka@gmail.com

Abstract. Object proposals are currently used for increasing the computational efficiency of object detection. We propose a novel adaptive pipeline for interleaving object proposals with object classification and use it as a formulation for asset detection. We first preprocess the images using a novel and efficient rectification technique. We then employ a particle filter approach to keep track of three priors, which guide proposed samples and get updated using classifier output. Tests performed on over 1000 urban images demonstrate that our rectification method is faster than existing methods without loss in quality, and that our interleaved proposal method outperforms current state-of-the-art. We further demonstrate that other methods can be improved by incorporating our interleaved proposals.

1 Introduction

The goal of our work is to efficiently extract high-quality assets of architectural elements from a large set of urban images. We define an asset as a rectangular image region depicting an architectural element, such as a window, door, ledge, ornament, or even a complete facade. Because these assets might be captured from different viewpoints, their corresponding image regions should be rectified and stored as textures, so they can be subsequently incorporated into applications such as urban modeling or architectural analysis.

We formulate asset extraction as an object detection problem with the following focus. First, we require a fast overall processing time, where we expect each urban image to require at most 1 s to be processed by our end-to-end pipeline. We believe that longer processing times are not feasible for practical scenarios where the image dataset is large nor for interactive applications. Second, small low-resolution assets are not interesting for most applications, so we make sure to ignore regions covering only a few pixels. Third, while the fundamental principles of our work are applicable in a wider context, we build a framework best suited for extracting architectural assets.

Electronic supplementary material The online version of this chapter (doi:10.1007/978-3-319-46487-9_27) contains supplementary material, which is available to authorized users.

© Springer International Publishing AG 2016
B. Leibe et al. (Eds.): ECCV 2016, Part III, LNCS 9907, pp. 437–452, 2016.
DOI: 10.1007/978-3-319-46487-9_27

To tackle this problem, we build on recent work in the area of object proposals. Since processing time is crucial in our application, we assume that a
state-of-the-art asset classifier can be learned from a given training set and that
it would take more than 1 s to exhaustively apply this classifier on all possible
image regions to retrieve high-quality assets. In this case, we pose the question: which image regions are good candidates for the classifier? Recent work
on object proposals, namely EdgeBoxes [33] and Geodesic proposals [14], have
shown great promise in the field of object detection. In fact, they have become
standard methods in many state-of-the-art detection pipelines. Also, we found
these two methods to be the most competitive on our urban asset datasets and
we therefore use them in our comparisons.

The basic idea of these two approaches (as well as most other object proposal
methods) is to find a simple scoring function that can quickly determine whether
a candidate region is likely to contain an object or not, thus, reducing the number
of negative instances that an object classifier is applied. We would like to extend
this idea to interleave object proposals with the classification. In doing so, the
proposal method evolves and adapts to the streaming image data. By analyzing
the classification result in a previous image or in a particular image region of the
current image, we can build insight on what image regions should be considered
next as proposals. We realize this idea using a probabilistic sampling strategy
akin to a particle filter, where the posterior distribution of the next proposal
state (e.g. scale, location, and aspect ratio) is updated with more observations
(outputs from the classifier).

Contributions. This work makes three main contributions. **(1)** For the task
of urban asset detection, we improve upon state-of-the-art object proposals by
using the concept of interleaved proposing and classification. **(2)** We propose a
novel rectification algorithm for images with a dominant plane, in general, and
urban images, in particular. This method is 18 times faster than previous work.
(3) We compile and manually annotate a large-scale dataset of urban images,
where each facade and window asset are precisely labelled. Our extensive experiments will show that our interleaved proposal technique can outperform state-
of-the-art proposal methods on over 1000 facades, as well as, be incorporated
into these methods to improve their performance on the same facade scenes.

2   Related Work

Asset extraction relates to techniques ranging from low-level image segmentation
to high-level semantic modeling. In this section, we mainly review the work that
is closely related to ours, in particular, facade parsing and object proposals.

Facade Parsing. This task aims to decompose facade images into semantically meaningful parts. One key ingredient to facade parsing is the detection of
translational symmetry, e.g. Müller et al. [19]. To classify facade elements, many
recent papers [4,17,20] employ machine learning techniques. By combining random forests with shape grammars, Teboul et al. [25] incorporate reinforcement

learning for parsing facades. Cech and Sara [1] define it as a maximum aposteriori probability labeling task. By assuming s structured facade can be represented as a rank-one matrix, Yang et al. [30] formulate the problem as a matrix decomposition problem. Riemenschneider et al. [20] utilize low-level classifiers combined with middle-level object detection for parsing irregular facades. They adapt a variation of the Cocke-Younger-Kasami (CYK) algorithm [22] for the split grammars, and the complexity of the CYK algorithm is significantly reduced by representing the facade as irregular lattices. By combining split grammar and shape priors, Kolinsky et al. [13] enable parsing of occluded facade parts.

In practice, shape grammars are usually manually constructed by experts for style-specific facade structures. To avoid this, Martinović et al. [18] propose a three-layered facade parsing approach that combines supervised learning with object detection and knowledge of the architecture. Borrowing ideas from natural language processing, authors in [17,28] propose to learn context-free grammars based on Bayesian Model Merging [23]. For efficiency, they exploit the similar idea of representing the facade structures as 2D lattices as in [20]. While some of these facade parsing methods can generate very good results, the computation time is too high for our application.

Object Proposals. In order to extract meaningful facade elements, an alternative approach is to use object detection techniques. However, traditional techniques usually apply sliding window search [9,10,15], which is computationally inefficient. In recent years, researchers proposed generic objectness proposals to reduce the large number of candidate windows [2,7,21,27,31].

By encoding the likelihood of neighboring superpixels into a connectivity graph, Manen et al. [16] generate object proposals as bounding boxes of randomized partial spanning trees. Krähenbühl and Koltun [14] also use superpixels where critical level sets in geodesic distance transforms are computed. Cheng et al. [2] resize the image windows to a small fixed size and use the norm of the gradients as features to detect object boundaries. This method can generate object proposals at a very high frame rate but at the cost of low recall. Zhao et al. [32] further reduce the number of candidate windows by analyzing the distributions of the locations and sizes of object rectangles. Similar to the work of [2], EdgeBoxes [33] relies on edge information. Specifically, the more the edges contained by a box, the more likely there is an object bounded by this box. For a comprehensive evaluation and an in-depth analysis of object proposal methods, please refer to the recent survey [11].

In this work, we follow the idea of object proposals and extend it to interleave object proposals with the task of classification. We compare our performance to the best state-of-the-art methods in Sect. 4.2.

3   Our Approach

Our asset extraction framework detects bounding boxes around urban assets using four major components visualized in Fig. 1.

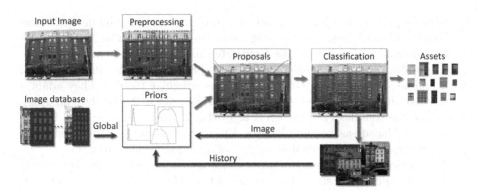

Fig. 1. Overall pipeline. Given an input image, rectification and rectangular superpixels are calculated. Proposals are generated using the estimated global priors as well as the adaptively updated history and image priors using the particle filter strategy. The output of our pipeline is urban assets stored as textures.

1. **Preprocessing:** Given an input image, we first detect line segments and rectify the image based on the detected most dominant facade. We then extract rectangular superpixels to restrict the search space for assets. (See Sect. 3.1)
2. **Prior Estimation:** We employ a particle filter to estimate prior distribution functions (pdf) for the four bounding box parameters. For each parameter, three pdfs are estimated and updated during detection: global prior, history prior, and image prior. (See Sect. 3.2)
3. **Object Proposals:** Object proposals are sampled as the evolving particle states and guided by the search space induced by estimated rectangular superpixels. (See Sect. 3.3)
4. **Asset Extraction:** The proposed objects are classified, and the classifier scores are used to update the priors, thus, guiding the sampling of object proposals. (See Sect. 3.4)

3.1   Preprocessing

Rectification. The first step in our framework is image rectification. Existing work handles this problem by calculating a homography starting from vanishing points (VP) or using relative scale changes constraints [3]. Such approaches have several drawbacks. First, they only transform vanishing lines to parallel, thus only resolving affine transformations, and more constraints need to be added to recover orthogonality and adequate aspect ratio. Second, slight discrepancies in VP locations significantly affect the final rectification. Wu et al. [29] handle this by a VP refinement technique. This brings us to the third disadvantage: the computational cost of finding the VPs and the added cost of their refinement.

Our approach uses line segments without requiring VP detection. We seek the best homography that vertically aligns the line segments vanishing to top/bottom, and horizontally aligns those vanishing to right/left. To achieve

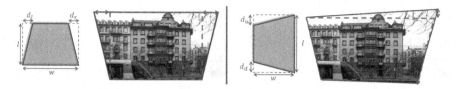

Fig. 2. Vertical perspective (left) and horizontal perspective (right) image transformations with an example horizontal and vertical perspective transformation applied to an urban image (see original image in Fig. 3-left).

this, we decompose the full transformation $\mathbf{H}$ into a concatenation of two simpler transformations: vertical perspective $\mathbf{H_v}$ and horizontal perspective $\mathbf{H_h}$ depicted in Fig. 2.

$$\mathbf{H} = \mathbf{H_v}\mathbf{H_h} \tag{1}$$

We use the following parameters to define the matrices $\mathbf{H_v}$ and $\mathbf{H_h}$: horizontal (d_l, d_r) and vertical (d_u, d_d) shifts of the image corners, as well as, image width w and length l. With these parameters, we can completely model matrices $\mathbf{H_v}$ (refer to Eq. 2) and $\mathbf{H_h}$ (refer to Eq. 3) shown below.

$$\mathbf{H_v} = \begin{bmatrix} 1 + \frac{d_r - d_l}{w} & \frac{-d_l}{l} & d_l \\ 0 & 1 + \frac{d_r - d_l}{w} & 0 \\ 0 & \frac{d_l - d_r}{wl} & 1 \end{bmatrix} \tag{2}$$

$$\mathbf{H_h} = \begin{bmatrix} 1 + \frac{d_d - d_u}{l} & 0 & 0 \\ \frac{-d_u}{w} & 1 + \frac{d_d - d_u}{l} & d_u \\ \frac{d_d - d_u}{wl} & 0 & 1 \end{bmatrix} \tag{3}$$

For vertical perspective, we use the following constraint to detect the line segments vanishing to the top/bottom: *Under perspective transformation, the orientations of the originally vertical segments changes linearly with their horizontal position in the image.* Figure 3, shows a scatter plot of the segment orientations as a function of the position of their midpoints. Using RANSAC line fitting, we filter the lines that agree with this vertical linearity constraint. Now, given a set of k line segments $\{\delta_i\}_{i=1}^{k}$, we find the best parameters that transform these line segments into vertical by minimizing the objective function below.

$$\underset{d_l, d_r}{\text{minimize}} \sum_{i=1}^{k} \left| \frac{h_1 a_i}{h_3 a_i} - \frac{h_1 b_i}{h_3 b_i} \right| \tag{4}$$

where a_i and b_i are the homogeneous coordinates of line segment δ_i's end points. Here, h_1 is the first row of $\mathbf{H_v}$, since we want the x-coordinates of the transformed line segments to be equal, and we divide by h_3, the third row of $\mathbf{H_v}$, since we are dealing with homogeneous coordinates.

For horizontal perspective, we first apply the vertical transformation $\mathbf{H_v}$ to the original line segments and image corners resulting in new line segments δ_i',

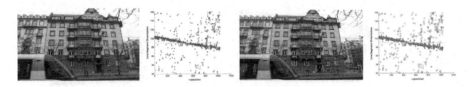

Fig. 3. Segment orientations as a function of the x-position of their midpoints. The line segment orientations vary slightly above $100°$ to slightly below $90°$. Outliers that are discarded by RANSAC are shown in red on the right. (Color figure online)

image width w' and length l'. Then similarly, we filter the transformed line segments that agree with the horizontal linearity constraint and minimize for (d_u, d_d). To solve either optimization problem, we use sequential quadratic programming. Once the four shift parameters are found, the homography is calculated using Eqs. 1–3. Figure 2 shows the result after applying the vertical and then the horizontal transformation for the original image shown in Fig. 3.

Rectangular Superpixels. Once images are rectified, the most prevalent assets are rectangular elements structured repetitively along horizontal and vertical directions. In fact, currently available urban parsing datasets are based on rectangular boxes of various assets. Based on this observation, we extract superpixels using a rectangular grid at locations where image gradients are large in magnitude. Our goal is a reduced search space $B_s = \{(x_j, y_j, s_j, a_j)\}$ for asset bounding box parameters where (x_j, y_j) is the location, s_j is the scale, and a_j is the aspect ratio. We first sum the image gradient magnitudes along horizontal and vertical directions and use the maxima to form a grid spanning the image. The grid oversegments the image into dense rectangular regions. We then merge color consistent regions to form the final superpixels. The top left corners of these superpixels are used as candidate locations for assets as shown in Fig. 4. We only consider bounding boxes that can be partitioned into superpixels. Finally, loose thresholds on window sizes and aspect ratios are used to eliminate extremely elongated and/or enlarged windows. We constrain scale to be between 0.05 and 0.2 and the aspect ratio to be between 0.25 and 4 in our implementation.

3.2 Prior Incorporation

The extracted search space comprises a large set of object proposals, a subset of which needs to be evaluated by the classifier. We determine this subset adaptively by a particle filter sampling technique. Our approach is adapted to the dataset at hand by estimating the prior probabilities of the parameters and sampling using the joint probabilities as weights. During our framework, we keep track of 12 prior distributions: 3 distributions for each of the 4 parameters.

1. **Global Prior** p^g is estimated from the training database. This prior gives us general information about the parameters. Window assets for example have mean aspect ratio of less than 1 while for balconies it is greater than 1.

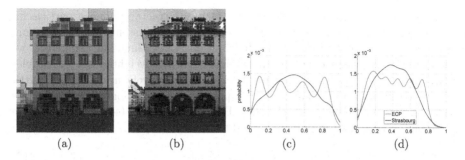

Fig. 4. A visualization of superpixels as regions (a) and superpixels' top left corners (b). Estimated history priors for x-locations (c) and y-locations (d) in the ECP and Strasbourg datasets. By looking at the distributions, one can note the difference in the structure of the two datasets.

2. **History Prior** p^h is updated by the detection history within an image dataset. Facade structures differ from city to city, and learning dataset-specific parameters helps in sampling based on the learned structure. Figure 4 shows the difference in the learned history prior for locations of window assets in the ECP (taken in Paris) and the Strasbourg datasets.
3. **Image Prior** p^i is updated by the detection scores in the current image. This prior guides the parameters according to the detected windows in the same image. As soon as new positive detections arise, the prior increases the weights for its parameters. This suits the problem of asset detection very well, since assets are usually repeated along aligned locations in the same image and with similar sizes.

Prior Update as a Particle Filter. We estimate and update the global, history, and image prior distributions used in generating the object proposals from a set of given bounding box samples. The global prior is estimated only once from the ground truth bounding boxes in the training set using kernel density estimation. The history prior is also estimated using kernel density estimation, but from the classified bounding boxes in the dataset. As for the image prior, we update it by casting it in a particle filter framework.

Particle filtering is a general Monte Carlo (sampling) technique used to estimate the state of a system that evolves over time. The general filtering problem involves the estimation of the posterior distribution of state variables $\mathbf{x}_t$ at time t given all observations $\mathbf{z}_{1:t}$ up to time t. The computation of the distribution $p(\mathbf{x}_t|\mathbf{z}_{1:t})$ can be done recursively in two major steps: (1) the prediction step which is computed using the previous state and all previous observations, and (2) the update step in which the distribution is updated with the new observation $\mathbf{z}_t$ using Bayes' rule.

$$p(\mathbf{x}_t|\mathbf{z}_{1:t-1}) = \int p(\mathbf{x}_t|\mathbf{x}_{t-1})p(\mathbf{x}_{t-1}|\mathbf{z}_{1:t-1})d\mathbf{x}_{t-1} \tag{5}$$

$$p(\mathbf{x}_t|\mathbf{z}_{1:t}) \propto p(\mathbf{z}_t|\mathbf{x}_t)p(\mathbf{x}_t|\mathbf{z}_{1:t-1}) \tag{6}$$

In general, Eqs. 5 and 6 are computationally intractable, hence particle filtering can be viewed as an approximate method for system state estimation, especially when the posterior state distribution is not Gaussian. Therefore, we estimate the posterior distribution at time t with a weighted set of samples $\{(\mathbf{x}_t^i, w_t^i), i = 1...N\}$, also called particles, and recursively update these particles to obtain an approximation to the posterior distribution at the next time step. The particle filter prediction (see Eq. 7) and update (see Eq. 8) steps are combined to assign an importance weight for each sample.

$$\mathbf{x}_t^i \sim p(\mathbf{x}_t | \mathbf{x}_{t-1}^i) \tag{7}$$

$$w_t^i = w_{t-1}^i p(\mathbf{z}_t | \mathbf{x}_t^i) \tag{8}$$

In our case, the state $\mathbf{x}_t \in \mathbb{R}^4$ represents the four parameters defining an object proposal (i.e. location, size, and aspect ratio). In other words, the particles are sampled bounding boxes in the image, while the observations are manifestations of particles in an image, namely image patches enclosed inside the particle's bounding box. The prediction step gives rise to the transition model of the particle filter and defines how the particles evolve in each iteration. Unlike many other use cases of particle filtering where the transition model is simplistic and assumed to be zero-mean Gaussian, we exploit the horizontally and vertically repeating patterns, which govern the spatial distribution of urban assets in facade images, to define this spatial transition model. This probabilistic model is shown in Eq. 9, where $\mathbf{r} = (r_x, r_y, 0, 0)$ denotes the estimated horizontal and vertical repetition intervals, $\mathbf{k} = (k_x, k_y, 0, 0)$ is a random variable which denotes the sampled number of repetitions, $\odot$ is the element-wise multiplication operator, and $\nu \sim N(\mathbf{0}, \Sigma)$ is additive Gaussian noise. Moreover, the update step gives rise to the observation model $p(\mathbf{z}_t | \mathbf{x}_t^i)$ and is taken to be the normalized score of the asset classifier when it is applied to the observed image patch $\mathbf{z}_t$.

$$\mathbf{x}_t = \mathbf{x}_{t-1} + \mathbf{k}_{t-1} \odot \mathbf{r}_{t-1} + \nu \tag{9}$$

By iterating through the aforementioned prediction and update steps, particles that manifest themselves as assets in an image maintain a higher weight than those that are not, which in turn biases the sampling strategy to focus more on the former particles in the next prediction iteration. As such, we use the asset content of an image to guide the particle sampling and, in turn, gradually evolve the image prior. In Fig. 5, we show the evolution of three particle filters on an example facade image. We first initialize the system state by probabilistically sampling bounding boxes using the learned priors. Starting from the initial state in the first iteration, horizontal and vertical repetitions are estimated and the particles evolve according to the previously described prediction step to produce the bounding boxes shown in Iteration 2. The particles keep evolving until particle discovery converges (i.e. when previously covered states are repeated).

| Iteration 1 | Iteration 2 | Iteration 4 | Iteration 7 | Iteration 12 |

Fig. 5. The evolution of the particle filter across an image. At the first iteration, particles are sampled around three initial states. The bounding boxes show the sampled particles with the weights represented by the color map on the left. Particles with higher weights are used more often in subsequent iterations. (Color figure online)

3.3 Guided Object Proposals

The particle filtering method can be viewed as an interleaving process between object proposals and classification. The output of the classification at each time step is fed back as weights to the particles, which are sampled based on the updated weights. The sampled N particles (bounding boxes) are output as object proposals and they are guided by the image and history priors. To guarantee sample diversity at each time step, we combine the three priors using a user-defined weighted sum as shown in Eq. 10 where we use $w_g = 0.3$, $w_h = 0.3$ and $w_i = 0.4$ in our implementation and we start with $N = 60$ particles.

$$p = w_g p^g + w_h p^h + w_i p^i \tag{10}$$

The repetition intervals are estimated at each time step by a voting scheme using the absolute horizontal and vertical weighted distances calculated from the sampled particles. The number of horizontal k_x and vertical repetitions k_y for each particle are sampled from a range $[k_{min}, k_{max}]$, using the prior probability of the x-location and y-location generated by shifting the particle by a $(r_x k_x, r_y k_y)$ translation. In our implementation, we use the range $[-2,2]$. Since we use multiple iterations, it is still possible to sample very large grids.

The image and history priors characterize different time scales of the observation history, and thus need to be updated at different time steps. We update the image prior k_i times in the same image. The history prior however is updated every k_h images. Small k_i and k_h means we are getting more feedback from the classifier, but at the cost of higher computation time. Increasing k_i and k_h however decreases classifier feedback which takes us back to traditional proposal methods. In our implementation, we choose $k_i = \frac{\#proposals}{20}$ and $k_h = 24$.

3.4 Asset Classification

Given a set of object proposals, a linear SVM classifier is used to classify which asset class each proposal belongs to, if any. We use aggregate channel features

Algorithm 1. Guided Asset Extraction

1: Train Classifier	11: Resample Particles
2: Estimate Global Prior	12: #proposals $+ = $ #particles
3: **for** each image $I_0 \in Dataset$ **do**	13: **if** processed k_i proposals **then**
4: $I =$Rectify(I_0)	14: Update Image Prior
5: $B_s =$Rectangular Superpixels(I)	15: **end if**
6: Sample Particles $x_1^1, ..., x_1^N$	16: **end for**
7: Compute Weights $w_1^1, ..., w_1^N$	17: **if** processed k_h images **then**
8: **for** $t = 2$ to T **do**	18: Update History Prior
9: Predict States $x_t^1, ..., x_t^N$	19: **end if**
10: Update Weights $w_t^1, ..., w_t^N$	20: **end for**

Fig. 6. Final detections on random images from the eTrims, CMP, ECP, Graz, London, and Strasbourg datasets (from left to right) with corresponding ground truth (bottom). Both our algorithm and ground truth are configured to ignore small windows.

[6] formed of 6 gradient orientations, 1 gradient magnitude, and 3 L-ab color channels to compute the feature descriptors. Inspired by the work of [6], instead of computing the exact features after resizing each object proposal patch to the classifier model size, we compute the channels on the full image and resize the channels. This leads to 3× speedup without much loss in final precision.

The classifier is applied at each update step on all the sampled object proposals. Its output is taken as final detection score for the currently classified proposals and is used in the particle filtering weight assignment step. The overall pipeline of our framework is described in Algorithm 1.

4 Results

We implement the algorithms described in the paper in MATLAB using the Parallel Computing Toolbox when possible and we use an Intel 3.1 GHz processor machine for testing. We used the Piotr toolbox [5] for superpixel estimation and feature extraction and the LibLinear package [8] for the SVM classifier.

Datasets. We use the following datasets for evaluation: GRAZ50 [20], ECP [24], eTrims [12], CMP [26] and two new datasets for *London* and *Strasbourg* that we

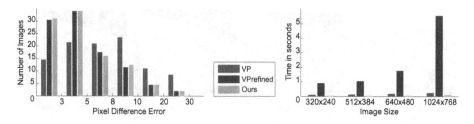

Fig. 7. The rectification accuracy for a dataset of 100 images (left). For each image we compute the pixel error compared to ground truth and report the results as a histogram. On the right we show computation time for images of different sizes.

manually compiled comprising 800 images taken in the wild. The total dataset size is 1392 images. We developed a user interface for rectifying and labeling facade images to obtain asset bounding boxes (e.g. for windows). The labeling of ECP is pixel based, and does not label window parts that are occluded by balconies as windows. Thus, we relabeled it to include the complete windows. We also annotated the ground truth for London and Strasbourg, by marking bounding boxes around urban assets (See Fig. 6 bottom).

We give an overview of the results below and more details in the **supplementary material**. We show an evaluation of the homography estimation, the object proposal recall rates, and PR curves for the final detection output. The goal of our asset extraction pipeline is to extract as many useful assets per time unit as possible, while maintaining a reasonable precision. Our results will show that our framework is better suited to serve this goal than previous work.

4.1   Homography Estimation

We compare our homography estimation method against two variants of the method by Wu et al. [29]: *VP*, a faster version using calculated VPs before refinement, and *VP-refined*, which uses the extracted VPs after refinement. To quantitatively evaluate the accuracy, we manually annotate a dataset of 100 images. Ground truth is depicted as lines that should be transformed to horizontal/vertical after rectification. The inconsistency of applied rectification is calculated as the average pixel difference error of transformed lines compared to the average correct line. Figure 7-left shows that the VP method is significantly less accurate than the other two approaches, and that our approach is comparable to that of VP-refined. We also evaluate the average rectification speed. Figure 7-right shows that our rectification method is faster than both approaches especially as the images grow in size. For 640×480 images, our method is 2 times faster than VP and 18 times faster when VP refinement is applied. Figure 8 shows a comparison of the final output of the three methods on a sample image.

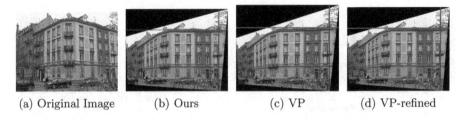

(a) Original Image   (b) Ours   (c) VP   (d) VP-refined

Fig. 8. Rectification applied on original image in (a) using three different methods. Notice in the output of the VP method (c), alignment artifacts are present in the right side of the image, which are fixed after refinement in (d).

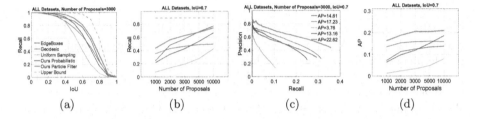

(a)   (b)   (c)   (d)

Fig. 9. Object proposals recall and detection results.

4.2   Object Proposals

We follow common practice to evaluate the quality of object proposals based on recall of ground truth annotations. The recall rate defines the fraction of ground truth retrieved with respect to an intersection over union (IoU) threshold. We use two metrics to evaluate the quality of proposal methods: (1) recall as the IoU threshold is varied for a fixed number of proposals, and (2) recall as the number of proposals is varied for a fixed IoU threshold. We evaluate the recall rates on the urban dataset described earlier. We compare against two existing proposal methods EdgeBoxes [33] and Geodesic [14]. We also evaluate the following proposal strategies (1) *Uniform Sampling* where we sample uniformly from the reduced search space, (2) *Ours Probabilistic* where we sample based on global prior only, (3) *Ours Particle Filter* where we sample using our particle filter approach with interleaving object proposals and classification, and (4) *Upper Bound* which shows the recall upper bound due to the reduced search space induced by our superpixel pre-process. Based on visual inspection, we choose an IoU threshold of 0.7 as the most reasonable in practice and fix number of proposals to 3000. For EdgeBoxes and Geodesic, we use the default parameters and models provided in the authors' implementations.

As shown in Fig. 9a and b, our approach provides the highest overall recall, competing with EdgeBoxes for more than 5000 proposals. The particle filter transition model together with the interleaving strategy give rise to an adaptive search space and thus high recall rates. In addition, the structure of urban assets agrees well with the EdgeBoxes scoring function which uses object boundaries estimates as features. Geodesic uses a segmentation scheme for proposing objects, and increasing the number of proposals doesn't improve their recall much. Figure 10a also shows the recall rate of our method compared to EdgeBoxes and Geodesic on the ECP and CMP datasets using balconies assets.

These recall rates evaluate the quantity rather than the quality of object proposals as they do not include precision or accuracy of returned bounding boxes. Our main concern in this pipeline is the final detection output and an evaluation of the precision of retrieved detections after applying the classifier on top of proposed bounding boxes. EdgeBoxes has high recall for ground truth windows, but at the cost of an increase in the number of false positives as we will show in the next section.

4.3   Asset Classification

We trained a Linear SVM classifier on a separate urban images dataset consisting of 3000 positive window examples from different architectural types, and randomly sampled negative examples making sure they have low overlap with the ground truth. We use two metrics to evaluate the detection quality of the proposals: (1) PR curves which show the precision of the classifier at different recall rates for a fixed number of proposals and IoU threshold, and (2) average precision (AP) as the number of proposals vary for a fixed IoU threshold. We apply the same classifier on all shown proposal methods.

As shown in Fig. 9c and d, our method has the highest AP, while that of EdgeBoxes gets lower than Geodesic after applying the classifier on top of the proposals. The AP scores of the probabilistic method increases with the increase in number of proposals but is still below our particle filter approach. This shows that our interleaving strategy performs well by capturing the good proposals earlier. We also show in Fig. 10b the AP scores for balconies assets.

To further show how the priors help get better proposals, we apply the prior weights as a scoring function for the exhaustive space of proposals retrieved by EdgeBoxes. Figure 10 shows how adding the priors improves the recall and thus AP of EdgeBoxes. In general, adding our adaptive priors to EdgeBoxes consistently extends the recall of EdgeBoxes, while not affecting the precision much. This means that the priors are reordering the proposals in such a way that better proposals are getting higher score.

4.4   Computational Cost

In this section, we evaluate the full pipeline comparing existing work for object proposals with ours. Table 1 shows the average running time to generate 3000 proposals from 640×480 resolution images in the urban dataset, described earlier. For our adaptive method, separating the computation time for object proposals and classification is difficult as they are interleaved steps, while for the other methods, the two steps are applied separately. As shown in Table 1, our probabilistic method gives the highest computation speed while the adaptive method comes next. The primary cause for increase in computation time is the prior

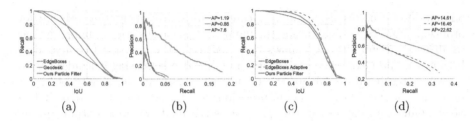

Fig. 10. Recall and PR curves using 3000 proposals on the balconies dataset (left) and for our prior combined with EdgeBoxes (right).

Table 1. Running time (in seconds) to generate 3000 proposals.

Method	Finding proposals	Asset classification	Total
Geodesic	0.18	4.32	4.5
EdgeBoxes	0.1	1.26	1.36
Ours probabilistic	**0.09**	**0.24**	**0.33**
Ours adaptive	-	-	**1.1**

update step. Since our MATLAB implementation is not optimized for speed, we would expect a significant speedup from a C++ implementation. Note that the running time for asset classification using Geodesic and EdgeBoxes proposals is larger. This is related to the quality of proposals returned by these methods (i.e. when providing more proposals that differ much in size/aspect ratio from that of the model, the feature extraction step gets slower because the proposals needs to be resized to fit the classification model). Our guided priors however make sure that we get consistent window sizes and aspect ratios, which give us the advantage of higher speeds. Figure 6 shows final detection results using our adaptive method on example images from each dataset.

5   Conclusion and Future Work

In this paper, we propose an efficient and effective framework for asset extraction in an urban image dataset. Our main contributions are the interleaving of object proposals with classification to improve overall retrieval results and a new and fast image rectification method. Extensive experiments show that using such an adaptive approach to detect urban assets helps build insight into how to guide proposed image regions, especially in the presence of multiple similar objects in the same image or across images. In future work, we would like to extend our framework to the task of asset extraction in urban videos.

Acknowledgement. This work was supported by the KAUST Office of Sponsored Research (OSR) under Award No. OCRF-2014-CGR3-62140401, and the Visual Computing Center at KAUST.

References

1. Cech, J., Sara, R.: Windowpane detection based on maximum aposteriori probability labeling. In: IWCIA Special Track on Applications, pp. 3–11 (2008)
2. Cheng, M.M., Zhang, Z., Lin, W.Y., Torr, P.: Bing: binarized normed gradients for objectness estimation at 300fps. In: Proceedings of IEEE Conference on Computer Vision and Pattern Recognition. IEEE (2014)
3. Chum, O., Matas, J.: Planar affine rectification from change of scale. In: Kimmel, R., Klette, R., Sugimoto, A. (eds.) ACCV 2010, Part IV. LNCS, vol. 6495, pp. 347–360. Springer, Heidelberg (2011)
4. Dai, D., Prasad, M., Schmitt, G., Van Gool, L.: Learning domain knowledge for Façade labelling. In: Fitzgibbon, A., Lazebnik, S., Perona, P., Sato, Y., Schmid, C. (eds.) ECCV 2012, Part I. LNCS, vol. 7572, pp. 710–723. Springer, Heidelberg (2012)
5. Dollár, P.: Piotr's Computer Vision Matlab Toolbox (PMT). http://vision.ucsd.edu/pdollar/toolbox/doc/index.html
6. Dollár, P., Appel, R., Belongie, S., Perona, P.: Fast feature pyramids for object detection. IEEE Trans. Pattern Anal. Mach. Intell. **36**(8), 1532–1545 (2014)
7. Endres, I., Hoiem, D.: Category-independent object proposals with diverse ranking. IEEE Trans. Pattern Anal. Mach. Intell. **36**(2), 222–234 (2014)
8. Fan, R.E., Chang, K.W., Hsieh, C.J., Wang, X.R., Lin, C.J.: Liblinear: a library for large linear classification. J. Mach. Learn. Res. **9**, 1871–1874 (2008)
9. Felzenszwalb, P.F., Girshick, R.B., McAllester, D., Ramanan, D.: Object detection with discriminatively trained part-based models. IEEE Trans. Pattern Anal. Mach. Intell. **32**(9), 1627–1645 (2010)
10. Gao, D., Mahadevan, V., Vasconcelos, N.: On the plausibility of the discriminant center-surround hypothesis for visual saliency. J. Vis. **8**(7), 13–13 (2008)
11. Hosang, J., Benenson, R., Dollár, P., Schiele, B.: What makes for effective detection proposals? IEEE Trans. Pattern Anal. Mach. Intell. **38**(4), 814–830 (2016)
12. Korc, F., Förstner, W.: eTRIMS image database for interpreting images of manmade scenes. Department of Photogrammetry, University of Bonn, Technical report (2009)
13. Kozinski, M., Gadde, R., Zagoruyko, S., Obozinski, G., Marlet, R.: A MRF shape prior for facade parsing with occlusions. In: Proceedings of IEEE Conference on Computer Vision and Pattern Recognition (2015)
14. Krähenbühl, P., Koltun, V.: Geodesic object proposals. In: Fleet, D., Pajdla, T., Schiele, B., Tuytelaars, T. (eds.) ECCV 2014, Part V. LNCS, vol. 8693, pp. 725–739. Springer, Heidelberg (2014)
15. Lampert, C.H., Blaschko, M.B., Hofmann, T.: Beyond sliding windows: object localization by efficient subwindow search. In: Proceedings of IEEE Conference on Computer Vision and Pattern Recognition. IEEE (2008)
16. Manen, S., Guillaumin, M., Van Gool, L.: Prime object proposals with randomized prim's algorithm. In: Proceedings of the IEEE International Conference on Computer Vision. IEEE (2013)
17. Martinović, A., Van Gool, L.: Bayesian grammar learning for inverse procedural modeling. In: Proceedings of IEEE Conference on Computer Vision and Pattern Recognition (2013)
18. Martinović, A., Mathias, M., Weissenberg, J., Van Gool, L.: A three-layered approach to facade parsing. In: Fitzgibbon, A., Lazebnik, S., Perona, P., Sato, Y., Schmid, C. (eds.) ECCV 2012, Part VII. LNCS, vol. 7578, pp. 416–429. Springer, Heidelberg (2012)

19. Müller, P., Zeng, G., Wonka, P., Van Gool, L.: Image-based procedural modeling of facades, vol. 26. ACM (2007)
20. Riemenschneider, H., Krispel, U., Thaller, W., Donoser, M., Havemann, S., Fellner, D., Bischof, H.: Irregular lattices for complex shape grammar facade parsing. In: Proceedings of IEEE Conference on Computer Vision and Pattern Recognition. IEEE (2012)
21. Van de Sande, K.E., Uijlings, J.R., Gevers, T., Smeulders, A.W.: Segmentation as selective search for object recognition. In: Proceedings of the IEEE International Conference on Computer Vision. IEEE (2011)
22. Schlesinger, M.I., Hlavac, V.: Ten Lectures on Statistical and Structural Pattern Recognition, vol. 24. Springer Science & Business Media, Berlin (2002)
23. Stolcke, A.: Bayesian learning of probabilistic language models. Ph.D. thesis, University of California, Berkeley (1994)
24. Teboul, O.: Ecole centrale paris facades database. http://vision.mas.ecp.fr/Personnel/teboul/data.php
25. Teboul, O., Kokkinos, I., Simon, L., Koutsourakis, P., Paragios, N.: Parsing facades with shape grammars and reinforcement learning. IEEE Trans. Pattern Anal. Mach. Intell. **35**(7), 1744–1756 (2013)
26. Tyleček, R., Šára, R.: Spatial pattern templates for recognition of objects with regular structure. In: Weickert, J., Hein, M., Schiele, B. (eds.) GCPR 2013. LNCS, vol. 8142, pp. 364–374. Springer, Heidelberg (2013)
27. Uijlings, J.R., van de Sande, K.E., Gevers, T., Smeulders, A.W.: Selective search for object recognition. Int. J. Comput. Vis. **104**(2), 154–171 (2013)
28. Weissenberg, J., Riemenschneider, H., Prasad, M., Van Gool, L.: Is there a procedural logic to architecture? In: Proceedings of IEEE Conference on Computer Vision and Pattern Recognition (2013)
29. Wu, C., Frahm, J.-M., Pollefeys, M.: Detecting large repetitive structures with salient boundaries. In: Maragos, P., Paragios, N., Daniilidis, K. (eds.) ECCV 2010, Part II. LNCS, vol. 6312, pp. 142–155. Springer, Heidelberg (2010)
30. Yang, C., Han, T., Quan, L., Tai, C.L.: Parsing facade with rank-one approximation. In: Proceedings of IEEE Conference on Computer Vision and Pattern Recognition (2012)
31. Zhang, Z., Warrell, J., Torr, P.H.: Proposal generation for object detection using cascaded ranking SVMs. In: Proceedings of IEEE Conference on Computer Vision and Pattern Recognition. IEEE (2011)
32. Zhao, Q., Liu, Z., Yin, B.: Cracking BING and Beyond. In: Proceedings of British Machine Vision Conference (2014)
33. Zitnick, C.L., Dollár, P.: Edge boxes: locating object proposals from edges. In: Fleet, D., Pajdla, T., Schiele, B., Tuytelaars, T. (eds.) ECCV 2014, Part V. LNCS, vol. 8693, pp. 391–405. Springer, Heidelberg (2014)

Multi-label Active Learning Based on Maximum Correntropy Criterion: Towards Robust and Discriminative Labeling

Zengmao Wang[1], Bo Du[1(✉)], Lefei Zhang[1], Liangpei Zhang[2], Meng Fang[3], and Dacheng Tao[4]

[1] State Key Laboratory of Software Engineering, School of Computer, Wuhan University, Wuhan, China
{kingmao,remoteking,zhanglefei}@whu.edu.cn
[2] State Key Laboratory of Information Engineering in Surveying, Mapping and Remote Sensing, Wuhan University, Wuhan, China
zlp62@whu.edu.cn
[3] Department of Computing and Information Systems, University of Melbourne, Parkville, Australia
meng.fang@unimelb.edu.au
[4] QCIS and FEIT, University of Technology Sydney, Sydney, NSW 2007, Australia
dacheng.tao@uts.edu.au

Abstract. Multi-label learning is a challenging problem in computer vision field. In this paper, we propose a novel active learning approach to reduce the annotation costs greatly for multi-label classification. State-of-the-art active learning methods either annotate all the relevant samples without diagnosing discriminative information in the labels or annotate only limited discriminative samples manually, that has weak immunity for the outlier labels. To overcome these problems, we propose a multi-label active learning method based on Maximum Correntropy Criterion (MCC) by merging uncertainty and representativeness. We use the the labels of labeled data and the prediction labels of unknown data to enhance the uncertainty and representativeness measurement by merging strategy, and use the MCC to alleviate the influence of outlier labels for discriminative labeling. Experiments on several challenging benchmark multi-label datasets show the superior performance of our proposed method to the state-of-the-art methods.

Keywords: Multi-label learning · Active learning · Correntropy · Robust

1 Introduction

Active learning has been widely used in computer visions to address the samples imbalance problem that the available labeled data is much less than the unlabeled data [18,35]. It is an iterative loop to find the most valuable samples for the oracle to label, and gradually improves the model generalization ability until the convergence condition is satisfied [39]. There are two motivations behind the design of

© Springer International Publishing AG 2016
B. Leibe et al. (Eds.): ECCV 2016, Part III, LNCS 9907, pp. 453–468, 2016.
DOI: 10.1007/978-3-319-46487-9_28

a practical active learning algorithm, namely, uncertainty and representativeness [8,15]. Uncertainty is to improve the models' generalization ability and representativeness is to prevent the bias of the models.

Among all the active learning based tasks, multi-label classification, which aims to assign each object with multiple labels, may be the most difficult and costly one [10,17,42]. In current research, active learning for multi-label learning has become even more important, reducing the costs of the various multi-label tasks [6,7,38,41]. State-of-the-art multi-label active learning can be classified into three categories based on the query function used to select the valuable samples. The first category relies on the labeled data to design a query function with uncertainty [25,28]. In such methods, the design of the query function ignores the latent structural information in the large-scale unlabeled data, leading to a serious sample bias and an undesirable performance. To eliminate this problem, the second category, which depends on the representativeness, has been developed [26]. In these approaches, the structural information of the unlabeled data is elaborately considered, but the discriminative (uncertain) information is discarded. Therefore, a large number of samples would be required before an optimal boundary is found. Since utilizing either the uncertainty criterion or the representativeness criterion may not achieve a desirable performance, the third category which combines both criteria borns naturally and it can effectively solve these problems [8,15]. However, the approaches in the third category are either heuristic in designing the specific query criterion or ad hoc in measuring the uncertainty and representativeness of the samples. The uncertainty still just relies on the limited labeled data. Most importantly, previous works ignore the outlier labels that exist in multi-label classification when designing a query model for active learning.

However, the outlier labels have significant influence on the measurement of uncertainty and representativeness in multi-label learning. In the following, we will discuss the outlier label and its negative influence on the measurement of uncertainty and representativeness in details.

Figure 1 shows a simple example about the influence of outlier labels. As the input, we annotate the image with three labels, namely tree, elephant and lion. Hence, the feature of image is combined with three parts, the feature of tree,

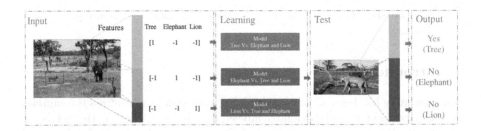

Fig. 1. The influence of outlier label in the learning process.

the feature of elephant and the feature of lion. Intuitively, in the image feature, the feature of tree is much more than elephant and lion, and the feature of lion is the least. If we use the image with the three labels to learn a lion/ non-lion binary classification model, the model would actually depend on the trees and elephants features rather than the lions. Thus it would be a biased model for classifying the lion and the non-lions. Given the test image where a lion covers the most regions in the image, the trained model would not recognize it. If we use such a model to measure the uncertainty in active learning, it may cause error measurement for images with lion label. We name the lion label in the input image as an outlier label.

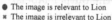

● The image is relevant to Lion   ● Lion is less relevant than Elephant
✻ The image is irrelevant to Lion   ● Elephant is less relevant than Tree
                                     ● Tree is less relevant than Grass

Fig. 2. The interface of two properties for outlier labels. Left: The outlier label (Lion) is relevant to the image; right: the outlier (Lion) is much less relevant to the image than the most relevant label (Tree) is.

Furthermore, we present the formal definition of the outlier label. Denote x, y_1 and y_2 as the selected instance and two relevant labels, respectively. Define y_1 as the outlier label, if it has two properties. The first one is that y_1 is a relevant label to the instance x, and the second is that y_1 is much less relevant to x than y_2 is. If the trained model could determine whether y_1 or y_2 is the outlier label to x, it would be very useful to build a promising model for a better query. Figure 2 shows the two properties. The definition of the outlier label is consistent with the fact that, given an image, some labels relevance to it is apparent, which can be recognized at first glance by the oracle, and some labels relevance is veiled, which may need much effort for the oracle to label. The definition of outlier label is also consistent with the query types proposed in [14]. For two multi-label images, if they have the same labels, but the outlier label is different in their labels, this may lead to the features of the two image have a large difference, therefore, it is very hard to diagnose the similarity between two instances with outlier labels. In Fig. 3, we provide a simple example to show such a problem, and we present the similarity between the sift features with Gaussian kernel [1,22,30,32], and the labels similarity based on MCC. Intuitively, the similarity between image 1 and image 2 should be larger than the similarity between image 2 and image 3, since the labels in image 1 and image 2 are exactly the same. However, the result is opposite when the similarity is measured with their sift features. This because

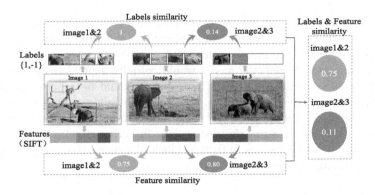

Fig. 3. The influence of the outlier labels for the measurement of similarity

the outlier label is lion in image 1, tree trunk and lion are two outlier labels in image 2, and the different outlier labels largely increase the difference between the features of the two images. In summary, the measurement of uncertainty and representativeness would be deteriorated with the outlier labels.

To address the above problems, in this paper, we propose the robust multi-label active learning (RMLAL) algorithm, which effectively combines the uncertainty and representativeness based on the MCC [40].

As to robustness, the correntropy has proved promising in information theoretic learning (ITL) and can efficiently handle the large outliers [40]. In traditional active learning algorithms, the mean square error (MSE) cannot easily control the large errors caused by the outliers [12,19,23,27,29,36]. We therefore replace the MSE criterion with the MCC in the proposed formulation with a minimum margin model. In this way, the proposed method is able to eliminate the outlier samples, making the query function more robust.

As to discriminative labeling, we use the MCC to measure the loss between the true label and the prediction label. MCC can improve the most discriminative information and suppress the little useless information or unexpected information. Hence, with MCC in the proposed method, if the label is not an outlier label, it will play an important role in the query model construction. Otherwise, the model will decrease the influence of the outlier label to measure the uncertainty. Then the discriminative labels effects are improved and the outlier labels are suppressed, and the discriminative labeling can be achieved.

For representativeness, we mix the prediction labels of unlabeled data with the MCC as the representativeness. As is shown in Fig. 3, although the samples have the same labels, their outlier labels are different, making their features distinguishing. If we just use the corresponding features to measure the similarity, it will lead to a wrong diagnosis. Hence, we propose to use the combination of labels and sample similarity to define the consistency between the labels and samples. With different space measurement making up for each other [33,34,37], the combination makes the measurement of representativeness more general. To decrease the computational complexity of the proposed method, the half-quadratic optimization technique is adopted to optimize the MCC. The contributions of our work can be summarized as follows:

- To the best of our knowledge, it is the first work to focus on the outlier labels in multi-label active learning. We find a robust and effective query model for multi-label active learning.
- The prediction labels of unlabeled data and the labels of labeled data are utilized with MCC to merge the uncertain and representative information, deriving an approach to make the uncertain information more precise.
- The proposed representative measurement considers labels similarity by MCC. It can effectively handle the outlier labels and makes the similarity more accuracy for multi-label data, and also provides a way to merge representativeness into uncertainty.

The rest of the paper is organized as following: Sect. 2 briefly introduces the related works. Then Sect. 3 defines and discusses a new objective for robust multi-label active learning and proposes an algorithm based on half-quadratic optimization. Section 4 evaluates our method on several benchmark multi-label data sets. Finally, we summarize the paper in Sect. 5.

2   Related Works

Since multi-label problem is universal in the real world, it has drawn great interests in many fields. For a multi-label object, it needs an oracle to consider all the relevant labels, leading to the labeling of multi-label tasks is more costly than single label learning, however, the research of active learning on multi-label is still less.

In multi-label learning, one instance is corresponding to more than one labels. To solve a multi-label problem, it is a direct way to convert it to several binary problems [21,31]. In these approaches, the uncertainty is measured for each label, and then a combining strategy is adopted to measure the uncertainty of one instance. [21] trained a probabilistic binary logistic regression classifier with different levels, and combined them with level switching strategy for adaptive selection. [31] converted the SVM margin to a probability score to select the instance for query. Recently, [26] selected the valuable instances by minimizing the Expected Error Reduction. Other works have done by combining the informativeness and representativeness together for a better query [8,20]. [20] combined the label cardinality inconsistency and the separation margin with a tradeoff parameter. [8] incorporated the data distribution in the selection process by using the appropriate dissimilarity between pairs of samples with sparse modeling representative selection for query. All the above algorithms were designed to query all the labels of the query instances. Another approaches have been developed to query the label-instance pairs with relevant label and instance at each iteration [14,16]. [14] queried the instance with relevant labels based on the types. [16] selected label-instance pairs based on a label ranking model. In these approaches, some important labels may be lost. In this study, considering the combination of informativeness and representativeness is very effective in active learning, we adopt this strategy.

No matter selecting the instance by all the labels or by the label-instance pairs, most of the active learning algorithms only selected the uncertain instance based on very limited samples, and ignored the labels information. For example, given all the labels to one instance, if the outlier labels are too much in label ranking, such instance may decrease the performance of the task. Moreover, given the relevant labels to one instance, some relevant labels may be lose with the limited query labels. To address these problems, we use the prediction labels of unlabeled data to enhance the uncertain measurement and adopt the MCC to consider the much relevant labels as much as possible except the outlier labels. As far to our knowledge, it is the first time to adopt the MCC in multi-label active learning with data labels for query.

3   Methodology

Suppose we are given a multi-label data set $D = \{x_i, x_2, \ldots, x_n\}$ with n samples and C possible labels for each sample. Initially, we label l samples in D. Without loss of generality, we denote the l labeled samples as set $L = \{(x_1, y_1), (x_2, y_2), \ldots, (x_l, y_l)\}$, where $y_i = (y_{i1}, y_{i2}, \ldots, y_{iC})$ is the labels set for sample x_i, with $y_{ik} \in \{-1, 1\}$; and the remaining $u = n - l$ unlabeled samples are denoted as set $U = \{x_{l+1}, x_{l+2}, \ldots, x_{l+u}\}$. It is the candidate set for active learning. Moreover, we denote x_q as the query sample in the active learning process. In each iteration, we select $x_q \in U$. And we use the bold symbol to denote the matrix or vector. In the following discussion, the symbols are used as above.

3.1   Maximum Correntropy Criterion

In multi-label classification tasks, the outlier labels pose a great challenge to train a precise classifier, mainly due to the unpredictable nature of the errors (bias) caused by these outliers. In active learning, in particular, the limited labeled samples with outliers easily lead to great bias. Since in active learning the supervised information is limited, it is hard to avoid the influence of the outlier labels when building the supervised model. This directly leads to the bias of uncertain information, furthermore makes the query instances are undesirable or even leads to bad performance.

Recently, the concept of correntropy was firstly proposed in ITL and it had drawn much attention in the signal processing and machine learning community for robust analysis, which can effectively handle the outliers [13]. In fact, correntropy is a similarity measure between two arbitrary random variables a and b [13], defined by

$$\hat{V}_\sigma(a, b) = E[K_\sigma(a, b)] \tag{1}$$

where $K_\sigma(\cdot)$ is the kernel function and $E[\cdot]$ is the expectation operator. We can observe that the definition of correntropy bases the kernel method, so it also has the same advantages that the kernel technique owns. However, different from the conventional kernel based methods, correntropy works independently with pairwise samples and has a strong theoretical foundation. With such a definition, the properties of correntropy are symmetric, positive and bounded.

Since the joint probability density function of a and b in practice is unknown, and the available data $\{a_i, b_i\}_{i=1}^n$ are usually finite, the sample estimator of correntropy is usually adopted by

$$\hat{V}_\sigma(a, b) = E[K_\sigma(a, b)] \tag{2}$$

where $K_\sigma(x_1, x_2) = exp(-||x_1 - x_2||^2)/2\sigma^2)$. According to [13], the correntropy between a and b is given by

$$\max_{p'} \frac{1}{n} \sum_{i=1}^n K_\sigma(a_i, b_i) \tag{3}$$

The objective function (3) is called maximum correntropy criterion (MCC) [13], where p' is the auxiliary parameter to be specified in Proposition 1. Compared with mean square error (MSE), which is a global metric, the correntropy is a local metric. That means the correntropy value is mainly determined by the kernel function along the line A = B [11].

3.2 The Proposed Approach

Usually, the uncertainty is measured according to the labeled data whereas the representativeness according to the unlabeled data. In this paper, we propose a novel approach to merge the uncertainty and representativeness of instances in active learning. Minimum margin is the most popular and direct approach to measure the uncertainty, which chooses the unlabeled sample by its prediction uncertainty [15]. Let f^* be the classifier that is trained by the labeled samples, and the sample x_q that we want to query in the unlabeled data based on the margin can be found as follows:

$$x_q = \arg\min_{x_i \in U} |f^*(x_i)| \tag{4}$$

Generally, with the labeled samples, we can find a classification model f^* for a binary class problem in supervised approach with the following loss function:

$$f^* = \arg\min_{f \in \mathcal{H}} \sum_{x_i \in L} \ell(Y_i, f(x_i)) + \lambda \|f\|_{\mathcal{H}}^2 \tag{5}$$

where $\mathcal{H}$ is a reproducing kernel Hilbert space endowed with kernel function $K(\cdot)$, $\ell(\cdot)$ is the loss function and Y_i belongs to $\{1, -1\}$. Following the works of [15], the criterion of the minimum margin can be written as

$$x_q = \arg\min_{x_j \in U} \max_{Y_j \pm 1} \min_{f \in \mathcal{H}} \sum_{x_i \in L} \ell(Y_i, f(x_i)) + \lambda \|f\|_{\mathcal{H}}^2 + \ell(Y_j, f(x_j)) \tag{6}$$

Y_j is a pseudo label for the unlabeled sample x_j. Since it is a binary class problem, Y_j is 1 or -1. Hence, we define $Y_j = -sign(f(x_j))$. In previous works, the loss function is adopted with quadratic loss for MSE, but it is not robust for the occasion of outliers. To overcome this problem, considering the properties of MCC, we introduce the MCC as the loss function. Different from MSE by minimizing the loss to solve minimization problem, MCC solves the minimization problem by maximizing the loss, presented by

$$\underset{x_q \in U, Y_q = \pm 1, f \in \mathcal{H}}{\arg\max} \sum_{x_i \in L} \exp\left(-\frac{\|Y_i - f(x_i)\|^2}{2\sigma^2}\right) - \lambda \|f\|_{\mathcal{H}}^2 + \exp\left(-\frac{\|Y_q - f(x_q)\|^2}{2\sigma^2}\right) \tag{7}$$

where σ is the kernel width. Following the minimum margin approach, the objective function (7) is equal to (4). In our work, we extend multi-label classification as several binary classification problems with label correlation [15]. For simple, we assume the label correlation is independent by learning one classifier for each label independently. Then, we use the summation as minimum margin in multi-label learning and use f_i as the classifier between i^{th} label and the other labels. The multi-label active learning to query the sample with minimum margin approach based on MCC with the worst case is given by

$$\mathcal{L}(x_q, f, L) = \underset{x_j \in U, f_k \in \mathcal{H}:k=\{1,2,..C\}}{\arg\max} \sum_{x_i \in L} \sum_{k=1}^{C} \exp\left(-\frac{\|y_{ik} - f_k(x_i)\|^2}{2\sigma^2}\right)$$
$$-\lambda \sum_{k=1}^{C} \|f_k\|_{\mathcal{H}}^2 + \sum_{k=1}^{C} \exp\left(-\frac{\left(1 + 2|f_k(x_q)| + f_k(x_q)^2\right)}{2\sigma^2}\right) \tag{8}$$

The labeled samples in L are very limited, so that it is very important to utilize the unlabeled data to enhance the performance of active learning. Since the labels of the unlabeled data are unknown, it is hard to add the unlabeled data in the supervised model. For the purpose to enhance the uncertain information, we merge the representative information into the uncertain information by prediction labels of unlabeled data. However, the current similarity is difficult to use the unlabeled data to enhance the uncertain information just with features. To overcome this problem, and considering the outlier labels influence, we take the prediction labels of unlabeled data into consideration for similarity measurement. We define a novel consistency between labels and sample similarity with sample-label pairs based on MCC as

$$s((x_i, y_i), (x_j, y_j)) = \exp\left(-\frac{\|y_i - y_j\|_2^2}{2\sigma^2}\right) w_{ij} \tag{9}$$

where w_{ij} is the similarity between two samples with kernel function. Let $S = [s_{ij}]^{u \times u}$ denote the symmetric similarity matrix for the unlabeled data, and s_{ij} is the consistency between x_i and x_j sample-label pairs points. With such a consistency matrix, the representativeness is to find the sample that can well represent the unlabeled data set. To do so, [8] proposed a convex optimization framework by introducing variables $p_{ij} \in [0,1]$ which indicates the probability that x_i represents x_j. In our consistency measurement based on MCC, if x_i can represent the point x_j, and it cannot represent the point x_t, there will be $s_{ij} \gg s_{it}$. Such a consistency measurement has already made the difference between representatives and non-representatives large. Therefore, we define that if x_i is the representative one, the probabilities $p_{ij}, j = 1, 2, ..u$ between x_i and the other unlabeled samples are 1, otherwise $p_{ij}, j = 1, 2, ..u$ are 0. Equally, we define $\boldsymbol{d} = [d_{ij}]^{u \times l}$ and $\boldsymbol{z} = [z_{ij}]^{u \times l}$ as the consistency matrix and probability between the unlabeled data and the labeled data respectively. By querying a desirable sample, which can not only represent the unlabeled data and but also not overlap the information in labeled data, we maximize the expectation operator and use a tradeoff parameter β to measure and balance the representative information in unlabeled data and labeled data

$$E\left[x_q, U, L\right] = \max_{x_q} \sum_{x_q \in U} \left[\left(\frac{1}{u} \sum_{x_j \in U} s_{qj} p_{qj} \right) - \beta \left(\frac{1}{l} \sum_{x_j \in L} d_{qj} z_{qj} \right) \right] \qquad (10)$$

In current research, it has proved that the combination between uncertainty and representativeness is very effective in active learning [8,15]. In our approach, we also combine them with a tradeoff parameter, given by

$$\mathcal{L}(x_q, f, L) + \beta_0 E[x_q, U, L] \qquad (11)$$

To merge the representative part into uncertain part, we use the prediction labels of unlabeled data. For each classifier f_k, we define $f_k(x)$ with a linear regression model in the kernel space as $f_k(x) = \omega_k^T \Phi(x)$ for each label, where $\Phi(x)$ is the feature mapping to the kernel space. In (11), the specific point x_q can be queried from the unlabeled data, but exhaustive search is not feasible due to the exponential nature of the search space. To solve such a problem, we use the numerical optimization-based techniques. An indicator vector $\boldsymbol{\alpha}$ is introduced, which is a binary vector with u length. Each entry α_j denotes whether the corresponding sample x_j is queried as the query sample. If x_j is queried as x_q, α_j is 1, otherwise, α_j is 0. Then the objective function can be defined as

$$\arg\max_{\omega; \alpha^T 1=1, \alpha_i \in \{0,1\}} \sum_{x_i \in L} \sum_{k=1}^{C} \exp\left(-\frac{\left\| y_{ik} - \omega_k^T \Phi(x_i) \right\|^2}{2\sigma^2} \right) - \lambda \sum_{k=1}^{C} \|\omega_k\|^2$$

$$+ \sum_{x_j \in U} \alpha_j \sum_{k=1}^{C} \exp\left(-\frac{\left(1 + 2\left|\omega_k^T \Phi(x_j)\right| + \left(\omega_k^T \Phi(x_j)\right)^2\right)}{2\sigma^2} \right)$$

$$+\beta_1 \sum_{x_j \in U} \alpha_j \left(\frac{1}{u}\right) \sum_{x_i \in U} \exp\left(-\frac{\left\| \omega^T [\boldsymbol{I} \otimes \Phi(x_j)] - \omega^T [\boldsymbol{I} \otimes \Phi(x_i)] \right\|_2^2}{2\sigma^2} \right) w_{ji}$$

$$-\beta_2 \sum_{x_j \in U} \alpha_j \left(\frac{1}{l}\right) \sum_{x_i \in L} \exp\left(-\frac{\left\| \omega^T [\boldsymbol{I} \otimes \Phi(x_j)] - y_i \right\|_2^2}{2\sigma^2} \right) w_{ji}$$

$$(12)$$

where $\omega = \{\omega_1, \omega_2, \ldots, \omega_C\}$ is the multi-label classifier. I is the identify matrix of size $C \times C$, and $\otimes$ is the kronecker product between matrices. Although the objective function (12) is neither convex nor linear, we derive an iterative algorithm based on half-quadratic technique [11,13] with the alternating optimization strategy [2] to solve it efficiently. Based on the theory of convex conjugated functions [3], we can easily derive the following proposition [40].

Proposition 1. *A convex conjugate function φ is exiting to make sure*
$$g(x) = \exp\left(-\frac{x^2}{2\sigma^2}\right) = \max_{p'}\left(p'\frac{\|x\|^2}{\sigma^2} - \varphi(p')\right)$$
where p' is the auxiliary variable, and with a fixed x, $g(x)$ reaches the maximum value at $p' = -g(x)$.

According to the Proposition 1, the objective function (12) can be formulated as

$$
\begin{aligned}
\arg\min_{\omega;\alpha^T 1 = 1, \alpha_i \in \{0,1\}} &\sum_{x_i \in L} \sum_{k=1}^{C}\left[m_{ik}\left\|y_{ik} - \omega_k^T \Phi(x_i)\right\|^2\right] + \lambda \sum_{k=1}^{C}\|\omega_k\|^2 \\
&+ \sum_{x_j \in U} \alpha_j \sum_{k=1}^{C}\left[n_{jk}\left(1 + 2\left|\omega_k^T \Phi(x_j)\right| + \left(\omega_k^T \Phi(x_j)\right)^2\right)\right] \\
&- \beta_1 \sum_{x_j \in U} \alpha_j\left(\frac{1}{u}\right)\sum_{x_i \in U} h_{ji}\left\|\omega^T[I \otimes \Phi(x_j)] - \omega^T[I \otimes \Phi(x_i)]\right\|_2^2 w_{ji} \\
&+ \beta_2 \sum_{x_j \in U} \alpha_j\left(\frac{1}{l}\right)\sum_{x_i \in L} v_{ji}\left\|\omega^T[I \otimes \Phi(x_j)] - y_i\right\|_2^2 w_{ji}
\end{aligned}
\tag{13}
$$

where $m_{ik}, n_{jk}, h_{ji},$ and v_{ji} are the auxiliary variables, with

$$m_{ik} = \exp\left(-\frac{\left\|y_{ik} - \omega_k^T \Phi(x_i)\right\|^2}{2\sigma^2}\right), x_i \in L, y_{ik} \in y_i$$

$$n_{jk} = \exp\left(-\frac{\left(1 + 2\left|\omega_k^T \Phi(x_j)\right| + \left(\omega_k^T \Phi(x_j)\right)^2\right)}{2\sigma^2}\right), x_j \in U$$

$$h_{ji} = \exp\left(-\frac{\left\|\omega^T[I \otimes \Phi(x_j)] - \omega^T[I \otimes \Phi(x_i)]\right\|_2^2}{2\sigma^2}\right), x_i, x_j \in U$$

$$v_{ji} = \exp\left(-\frac{\left\|\omega^T[I \otimes \Phi(x_j)] - y_i\right\|_2^2}{2\sigma^2}\right), x_j \in U, y_i \in y$$

The objective function (13) can be solved by the alternating optimization strategy. Firstly, we fix α, and the objective function is to find the optimal classifier ω. It can be solved by the alternating direction method of multipliers (ADMM) [4,24]. Secondly, we fix ω that is obtained in the first step, the objective function becomes

$$\arg\max_{\alpha^T 1 = 1, \alpha_i \in \{0,1\}} \alpha^T a + \beta_1 \alpha^T b - \beta_2 \alpha^T c \tag{14}$$

$$a_j = \sum_{k=1}^{C} \exp\left(-\frac{\left(1 + 2\left|\omega_k^T \Phi\left(x_j\right)\right| + \left(\omega_k^T \Phi\left(x_j\right)\right)^2\right)}{2\sigma^2}\right)$$

$$where\ b_j = \frac{1}{u} \sum_{x_i \in U} \exp\left(-\frac{\left\|\omega^T\left[\boldsymbol{I} \otimes \Phi\left(x_j\right)\right] - \omega^T\left[\boldsymbol{I} \otimes \Phi\left(x_i\right)\right]\right\|_2^2}{2\sigma^2}\right) w_{ji}$$

$$c_j = \frac{1}{l} \sum_{x_i \in L} \exp\left(-\frac{\left\|\omega^T\left[\boldsymbol{I} \otimes \Phi\left(x_i\right)\right] - y_i\right\|_2^2}{2\sigma^2}\right) w_{ji}$$

To solve (14), as in [5], we relax α_j to a continuous range [0, 1]. Thus, the $\boldsymbol{\alpha}$ can be solved with a linear program. The sample corresponding to the largest value in α will be queried as x_q. The RMLAL algorithm is summarized in Algorithm 1.

Algorithm 1. Robust Multi-label Active Learning

Input: Labeled data set L and unlabeled data set U, the tradeoff parameters β_1
         and β_2, and initial variables and parameters.
1: **repeat**
2:     Fixed $\boldsymbol{\alpha}$, calculate the function (13) with ADMM strategy to obtain the values
         of ω in kernel space with $\omega_k = \sum_{x_i \in L} \theta_{ki} \Phi(x_i)$, where $\theta_k = [\theta_{k1}, \theta_{k2}, \ldots, \theta_{kl}]^T$
         are auxiliary variables.
3:     With the values of ω, calculate the indicator vector $\boldsymbol{\alpha}$ by solving(14), and select
         the sample that is corresponding to the largest value in $\boldsymbol{\alpha}$.
4: **until** the tolerance is satisfied
Output: The query index of unlabeled samples.

---

4   Experiments

4.1   Settings

In this section, we present the experimental results to validate the effectiveness of the proposed method that compares with the prior methods on 9 multi-label data sets from Mulan project[1]. The characteristics of data sets are described in Table 1. To demonstrate the superior of our method, several methods are listed as follows as competitors.

1. RANDOM is the baseline which randomly selects instance label pairs.
2. AUDI [16] combines label ranking with threshold learning, then exploits both uncertainty and diversity in the instance space as well as the label space.
3. Adaptive [20] combines the max-margin prediction uncertainty and the label cardinality inconsistency as the criterion for active selection.

---

[1] http://mulan.sourceforge.net/datasets-mlc.html.

4. QUIRE [15] provides a systematic way for measuring and combining the informativeness and representativeness of an unlabeled instance by incorporating the correlation among labels.
5. Batchrank [5] selects the best query with an NP-hard optimization problem based on the mutual information.
6. RMLAL: Robust Multi-label Active Learning is the proposed in this paper.

LC is the average number of label for each instance in the data set. For each data set, we randomly divide it into two equal parts. One is regarded as the testing data set. For the other part, we randomly select 4 % samples as the initial labeled set, and the remaining samples of this part are used as the unlabeled data set for active learning. In the compared methods, AUDI and QUIRE query the relevance of an instance-label pairs in each iteration. We can notice that querying all labels for one instance is equal to query C label-instance pairs. Hence, for fair comparison, we query C label-instance pairs as one query instance in AUDI and QUIRE. For the method Batchrank, in the original paper, the tradeoff parameter sets as 1. For a fair comparison, we choose the tradeoff parameter from a candidate set that is the same in the proposed method. The parameters of other methods are all set as the same in original papers. For the kernel parameters, we adopt the same value for all methods.

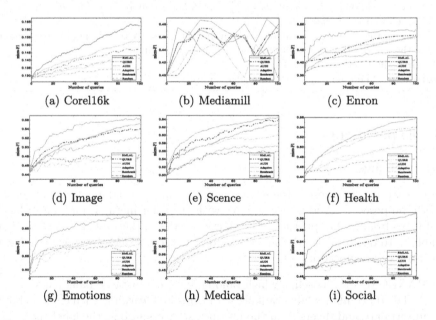

(a) Corel16k   (b) Mediamill   (c) Enron

(d) Image   (e) Scence   (f) Health

(g) Emotions   (h) Medical   (i) Social

Fig. 4. Comparison of different active learning methods on fifteen benchmark datasets. The curves show the micro-F1 accuracy over queries, and each curve represents the average result of 5 runs.

Without loss of generality, the liblinear[2] is adopted as the classifier for all methods [9], and micro-F1 is used to evaluate the performance [5], which is a commonly used performance measurement in multi-label learning. For each data set, we repeat each method for 5 times and report the average results. The querying process stops when 100 iterations are reached and one instance is queried at each iteration.

4.2 Results

For each data set, we reported the average results in Fig. 4. From all these results, we could observe that the proposed method performs the best on most of the data sets. It achieved the best results in almost the whole active learning process. In general, QUIRE and AUDI were two methods to query the label-instance pairs for labeling. They almost showed the superior performance to the Batchrank and Adaptive, which queried all labels for the instance. This demonstrated that querying the relevant labels was more efficient than querying all labels for one instance. But for our methods, it achieved the best performance with querying all labels for one instance than querying the relevant label-instance pairs. The reason may be that although the Batchrank and Adaptive queried all the labels, they could not avoid the influence of the outlier labels, leading to the query samples undesirable. For QUIRE and AUDI methods, some labels information lost when they just queried the limited relevant labels, and they need much samples to achieve a better performance. The results demonstrated the proposed method not only could achieve discriminative labeling but also could avoid the influence of the outlier labels. To put in nutshell, the proposed method merging the uncertainty and representativeness with MCC can solve the problems in multi-label active learning effectively as stated above.

4.3 Evaluation Parameters

In the proposed method, the kernel parameter σ is very important for the MCC. There are two tradeoff parameters on the uncertain part and representative part respectively. For conveniently, in our experiments, we defined kernel size $\gamma = 1/(2 * \sigma^2)$, and we fixed the kernel size as $1/C$ in the label space. For the feature space, we fixed the kernel size as $1/dim$ in feature space, where dim is the dimension of feature space. To discover the influence of the kernel size for the proposed method, we evaluated the kernel size for MCC in label space. We reported the average results when the kernel size was set as $\{\gamma, 2\gamma, 4\gamma\}$ respectively on two popular benchmark datasets emotions and scence [5], which had the same number of labels but with different LC. For the tradeoff parameters, we chose them from a fixed candidate set $\{1, 10, 100\}$ respectively, and we also reported the average results on the two data sets. The other settings were same to the previous experiments. Figure 5 showed the average results with the kernel size changing. We can observe that the results are not very sensitive to the kernel size. This may be that

---

[2] https://www.csie.ntu.edu.tw/~cjlin/liblinear/.

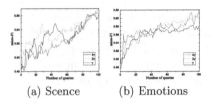 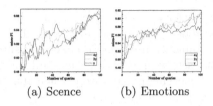

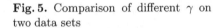

(a) Scence   (b) Emotions   (a) Scence   (b) Emotions

Fig. 5. Comparison of different γ on two data sets

Fig. 6. Comparison of different trade-off parameter pairs (β_1, β_2) on two data sets

the changing of the parameter γ just changes the relative value of the discriminative labels and outlier labels with MCC, but the value of discriminative labels with MCC are always larger than that of outlier labels. Relatively, we can set the kernel size as double of γ for a better selection. Figure 6 showed the results with different pairs of the tradeoff parameters. For these results, we can observe that uncertain information and representative information have a big influence on the results. However, the better results are obtained in contrast on the two data sets. The scence data obtains the good results when β_1 is small and β_2 is large, while the emotions data obtained the good results when β_1 is large and β_2 is small. This may be that the LC of scence is small than the emotions data, leading to the initial labeled information of scence is less. With so little supervised information, the labeled data become important to build a query model. When LC is large, the supervised information may be redundant, and the unlabeled data become important. Therefore, the tradeoff parameters can be adopted according to the different data sets adaptively with LC.

5   Conclusion

Outlier labels are very common in multi-label scenarios and may cause the supervised information bias. In this paper, we propose a robust multi-label active learning based on MCC to solve the problem. The proposed method queries the samples that can not only build training models with a good generalization ability but also represent the similarity well for multi-label data. With MCC, the supervised information of outlier labels will be suppressed, and that of discriminative labels will be expanded. It outperformed state-of-the-art methods in most of the experiments. The experimental analysis also reveals that it is beneficial to update the trade-off parameter that balances the uncertain and representative information during the query process. We plan to develop an adaptive mechanism to tune this parameter automatically to make our algorithm more practical.

Acknowledgements. This work was supported in part by the National Basic Research Program of China (973 Program) under Grant 2012CB719905, the National Natural Science Foundation of China under Grants 61471274, 41431175, 61401317, U1536204, 60473023, 61302111, and the Australian Research Council Projects DP-140102164, FT-130101457, and LE140100061.

References

1. Agrawal, P., Girshick, R., Malik, J.: Analyzing the performance of multilayer neural networks for object recognition. In: Fleet, D., Pajdla, T., Schiele, B., Tuytelaars, T. (eds.) ECCV 2014. LNCS, vol. 8695, pp. 329–344. Springer, Heidelberg (2014). doi:10.1007/978-3-319-10584-0_22

2. Bezdek, J.C., Hathaway, R.J.: Convergence of alternating optimization. Neural Parallel Sci. Comput. **11**(4), 351–368 (2003)

3. Boyd, S., Vandenberghe, L.: Convex optimization. Cambridge University Press, Cambridge (2004)

4. Boyd, S., Parikh, N., Chu, E., Peleato, B., Eckstein, J.: Distributed optimization and statistical learning via the alternating direction method of multipliers. Found. Trends Mach. Learn. **3**(1), 1–122 (2011)

5. Chakraborty, S., Balasubramanian, V., Sun, Q., Panchanathan, S., Ye, J.: Active batch selection via convex relaxations with guaranteed solution bounds. TPAMI **37**(10), 1945–1958 (2015)

6. Chen, X., Shrivastava, A., Gupta, A.: Neil: extracting visual knowledge from web data. In: CVPR, pp. 1409–1416 (2013)

7. Chen, Y., Krause, A.: Near-optimal batch mode active learning and adaptive submodular optimization. In: CVPR, pp. 160–168 (2013)

8. Elhamifar, E., Sapiro, G., Yang, A., Sasrty, S.: A convex optimization framework for active learning. In: ICCV, pp. 209–216 (2013)

9. Fan, R.E., Chang, K.W., Hsieh, C.J., Wang, X.R., Lin, C.J.: Liblinear: a library for large linear classification. JMLR **9**, 1871–1874 (2008)

10. Freytag, A., Rodner, E., Denzler, J.: Selecting influential examples: active learning with expected model output changes. In: Fleet, D., Pajdla, T., Schiele, B., Tuytelaars, T. (eds.) ECCV 2014. LNCS, vol. 8692, pp. 562–577. Springer, Heidelberg (2014). doi:10.1007/978-3-319-10593-2_37

11. He, R., Tan, T., Wang, L., Zheng, W.S.: $l_{2,1}$ regularized correntropy for robust feature selection. In: CVPR, pp. 2504–2511. IEEE (2012)

12. He, R., Zheng, W.S., Hu, B.G.: Maximum correntropy criterion for robust face recognition. CVPR **33**(8), 1561–1576 (2011)

13. He, R., Zheng, W.S., Tan, T., Sun, Z.: Half-quadratic-based iterative minimization for robust sparse representation. TPAMI **36**(2), 261–275 (2014)

14. Huang, S.J., Chen, S., Zhou, Z.H.: Multi-label active learning: query type matters. In: IJCAI, pp. 946–952. AAAI Press (2015)

15. Huang, S.J., Jin, R., Zhou, Z.H.: Active learning by querying informative and representative examples. TPAMI **36**(10), 1936–1949 (2014)

16. Huang, S.J., Zhou, Z.H.: Active query driven by uncertainty and diversity for incremental multi-label learning. In: ICDM, pp. 1079–1084. IEEE (2013)

17. Jing, L., Yang, L., Yu, J., Ng, M.K.: Semi-supervised low-rank mapping learning for multi-label classification. In: CVPR, June 2015

18. Kading, C., Freytag, A., Rodner, E., Bodesheim, P., Denzler, J.: Active learning and discovery of object categories in the presence of unnameable instances. In: CVPR, pp. 4343–4352. IEEE (2015)

19. Li, X.X., Dai, D.Q., Zhang, X.F., Ren, C.X.: Structured sparse error coding for face recognition with occlusion. TIP **22**(5), 1889–1900 (2013)

20. Li, X., Guo, Y.: Active learning with multi-label SVM classification. In: IJCAI. Citeseer (2013)

21. Li, X., Guo, Y.: Multi-level adaptive active learning for scene classification. In: Fleet, D., Pajdla, T., Schiele, B., Tuytelaars, T. (eds.) ECCV 2014. LNCS, vol. 8695, pp. 234–249. Springer, Heidelberg (2014). doi:10.1007/978-3-319-10584-0_16

22. Liu, C., Yuen, J., Torralba, A., Sivic, J., Freeman, W.T.: SIFT flow: dense correspondence across different scenes. In: Forsyth, D., Torr, P., Zisserman, A. (eds.) ECCV 2008. LNCS, vol. 5304, pp. 28–42. Springer, Heidelberg (2008). doi:10.1007/978-3-540-88690-7_3

23. Liu, T., Tao, D.: Classification with noisy labels by importance reweighting. TPAMI **38**(3), 447–461 (2016)

24. Liu, T., Tao, D., Song, M., Maybank, S.J.: Algorithm-dependent generalization bounds for multi-task learning. TPAMI (2016). doi:10.1109/TPAMI.2016.2544314

25. Long, C., Hua, G.: Multi-class multi-annotator active learning with robust gaussian process for visual recognition. In: ICCV, December 2015

26. Mac Aodha, O., Campbell, N., Kautz, J., Brostow, G.: Hierarchical subquery evaluation for active learning on a graph. In: CVPR, pp. 564–571 (2014)

27. Qian, J., Yang, J., Zhang, F., Lin, Z.: Robust low-rank regularized regression for face recognition with occlusion. In: CVPRW, pp. 21–26 (2014)

28. Settles, B.: Active learning literature survey. University of Wisconsin, Madison, vol. 52, no. 55–66, p. 11 (2010)

29. Settles, B.: Active learning. Synth. Lect. Artif. Intell. Mach. Learn. **6**(1), 1–114 (2012)

30. Singh, G., Kosecka, J.: Nonparametric scene parsing with adaptive feature relevance and semantic context. In: CVPR, pp. 3151–3157 (2013)

31. Singh, M., Curran, E., Cunningham, P.: Active learning for multi-label image annotation. In: ICAIC, pp. 173–182 (2009)

32. Tao, D., Li, X., Xindong, W., Maybank, S.: General tensor discriminant analysis and gabor features for gait recognition. TPAMI **29**(10), 1700–1715 (2007)

33. Tao, D., Li, X., Xindong, W., Maybank, S.: Geometric mean for subspace selection. TPAMI **31**(2), 260–274 (2009)

34. Tao, D., Tang, X., Li, X., Wu, X.: Asymmetric bagging and random subspace for support vector machines-based relevance feedback in image retrieval. TPAMI **28**(7), 1088–1099 (2006)

35. Vijayanarasimhan, S., Grauman, K.: Large-scale live active learning: training object detectors with crawled data and crowds. IJCV **108**(1–2), 97–114 (2014)

36. Xiong, X., Torre, F.: Supervised descent method and its applications to face alignment. In: CVPR, pp. 532–539 (2013)

37. Xu, C., Tao, D., Xu, C.: Multi-view intact space learning. TPAMI **37**(12), 2531–2544 (2015)

38. Yan, R., Yang, J., Hauptmann, A.: Automatically labeling video data using multiclass active learning. In: CVPR, pp. 516–523. IEEE (2003)

39. Yang, Y., Ma, Z., Nie, F., Chang, X., Hauptmann, A.G.: Multi-class active learning by uncertainty sampling with diversity maximization. IJCV **113**(2), 113–127 (2015)

40. Yuan, X.T., Hu, B.G.: Robust feature extraction via information theoretic learning. In: ICML. ACM (2009)

41. Zha, Z.J., Wang, M., Zheng, Y.T., Yang, Y., Hong, R., Chua, T.S.: Interactive video indexing with statistical active learning. TMM **14**(1), 17–27 (2012)

42. Zhao, F., Huang, Y., Wang, L., Tan, T.: Deep semantic ranking based hashing for multi-label image retrieval. In: CVPR, June 2015

Shading-Aware Multi-view Stereo

Fabian Langguth[1]([✉]), Kalyan Sunkavalli[2], Sunil Hadap[2], and Michael Goesele[1]

[1] TU Darmstadt, Darmstadt, Germany
[2] Adobe Research, San Francisco, USA

Abstract. We present a novel multi-view reconstruction approach that effectively combines stereo and shape-from-shading energies into a single optimization scheme. Our method uses image gradients to transition between stereo-matching (which is more accurate at large gradients) and Lambertian shape-from-shading (which is more robust in flat regions). In addition, we show that our formulation is invariant to spatially varying albedo without explicitly modeling it. We show that the resulting energy function can be optimized efficiently using a smooth surface representation based on bicubic patches, and demonstrate that this algorithm outperforms both previous multi-view stereo algorithms and shading based refinement approaches on a number of datasets.

1 Introduction

High-quality digitization of real world objects has been of great interest in recent years. The demand for effective and accurate digitization methods is increasing constantly to support applications such as 3D printing and visual effects. Passive reconstruction methods such as multi-view stereo [1] are able to achieve high quality results. However, stereo methods typically operate on image patches and/or use surface regularization in order to be robust to noise. As a result, they often cannot recover fine-scale surface details accurately. These details are often captured by shading variations, and recent work has focused on shading-based refinement of the geometry obtained from multi-view stereo (or in some cases using depth sensors or template models). Starting from the work of Wu et al. [2] that can only be used for objects with constant albedo, algorithms have evolved to operate on implicit surfaces [3] and real time settings [4]. All these methods treat the coarse input geometry as a fixed ground truth estimate of the shape and use it to regularize their optimization. Consequently, uncertainties in the inital reconstruction method are discarded and cannot be resolved reliably.

Another challenge for shading-based refinement techniques is that observed image intensities combine shading and surface albedo. Inferring fine-scale detail

---

Electronic supplementary material The online version of this chapter (doi:10.1007/978-3-319-46487-9_29) contains supplementary material, which is available to authorized users.

B. Leibe et al. (Eds.): ECCV 2016, Part III, LNCS 9907, pp. 469–485, 2016.
DOI: 10.1007/978-3-319-46487-9_29

from shading thus requires reasoning about surface albedo. This significantly increases the number of variables in the optimization. Most current techniques either assume constant albedo or apply strong regularization on the albedo, which can often fail on real-world surfaces.

In contrast to previous work, we propose a new multi-view surface reconstruction approach that combines stereo and shading-based data terms into a single optimization scheme. At the heart of our algorithm is the observation that stereo-matching and shape-from-shading have complementary strengths. While stereo correspondences are more accurate in regions with many large image gradients, shape-from-shading is typically more robust in flat regions with no albedo variations. The resulting algorithm provides three distinct advantages over previous work:

- It leads to a combined multi-view stereo and shading-based reconstruction that balances the two terms without committing, a priori, to either of them.
- It uses a simple image gradient-based trade-off between stereo and shading energies that maximizes their effectiveness.
- It treats spatially varying albedo implicitly, i.e. our optimization is robust against spatially varying albedo without explicitly modeling it.

We show that this combined energy can be optimized efficiently using a continuous surface representation [5]. We demonstrate the effectiveness of this technique on various datasets and show that it outperforms previous MVS and shading-based refinement techniques.

2   Related Work

High-quality surface reconstruction has been an active field of research over the past decade, and approaches have been developed for various forms of input data. Our technique uses an unstructured set of images (with camera parameters) of an approximately Lambertian scene and does not require any special hardware setup. We will review related methods that either operate on similar input data or use ideas similar to our approach.

Multi-view Stereo. Multi-view stereo algorithms [1] are arguably one of the most general passive reconstruction techniques. Approaches such as Goesele et al. [6] and Furukawa and Ponce [7] have shown that geometry can be recovered even for large scale and uncontrolled Internet data. Other approaches use more controlled settings or additional input such as object silhouettes [8]. Multi-view stereo approaches usually add a form of regularization to deal with structureless areas that are not well matched by classical stereo terms such as photo consistency. Similarly regularization is used in two-view stereo methods such as Hirschmueller [9], Bleyer et al. [10], and Galliani et al. [11], which can also be applied to multi-view scenarios by combining many two-view estimates into a robust multi-view estimate. In contrast, our goal is to avoid explicit regularization; instead, we use a new shading-based data term to handle sparsely textured regions where a traditional stereo term is not very effective. To do this we optimize both depth and normals of a continuous surface. In terms of surface representation, stereo algorithms usually recover a single depth per-pixel [6], a global point cloud [7], or an implicit surface model [8], all of which we found difficult to apply to our approach. Recently another surface representation was proposed inside a multi-view framework by Semerjian [5]. This approach uses bicubic patches to define a surface per view that has continuous depth and normals. We found this representation to be appropriate for our method and adopt it as described later.

Combining Multi-view and Photometric Cues. To recover more detail in regions where depth reconstruction is not very accurate, several methods have combined multi-view and photometric principles. Most of them, however, rely on a controlled and complex capture setup. The approach by Nehab et al. [12] combines two separate reconstructions. They capture depth using structured light, acquire surface normals using photometric stereo, and integrate both these estimates in a separate step. Other approaches such as Hernandez et al. [13] and Zhou et al. [14] combine photometric stereo information from multiple view points into a single framework. This requires a large amount of input data and a complex acquisition system as both light and camera positions need to be controlled. Beeler et al. [15] augment the geometry of captured faces with fine details using the assumption that small concavities in the skin appear darker than flat areas. They do not require a lot of input data but are still dependent on a calibrated capture setup as they do not have a variable lighting model.

Shading-Based Refinement for General Illumination. Most recently, a new line of work uses shading cues from images captured under uncontrolled illumination to improve a given geometry. Wu et al. [2] presented the first approach that uses a precomputed multi-view stereo reconstruction to estimate a spherical harmonics approximation of the lighting. They use this lighting and a shading model to improve the stereo reconstruction. Their approach is able to recover fine-scale details but is limited to objects with a single, constant albedo. Later, Yu et al. [16] and Han et al. [17] both presented algorithms that operate on a single RGB-D input image (e.g., from a Kinect sensor). These sensors usually generate very coarse geometry and shading-based refinement increases the quality and resolution of the output. Xu et al. [18] also extended the idea and developed a simultaneuos opimization of lighting and shape parameters. They do, however, require additional information about the visual hull of the object. Using GPU-based parallel solvers, Wu et al. [19] and Or-El et al. [4] were able to achieve real-time performance on similar input data. All these techniques are still limited to a single albedo [4,17,18], a fixed set of constant albedo clusters [16], or a coarse initial albedo estimate [19]. Other methods focus on more specific scenarios such as faces. Chai et al. [20] fit a parametric face model to an input image and use it for lighting estimation and shading-based refinement. The first technique to include a spatially varying albedo was proposed by Zollhoefer et al. [3]. They include the albedo in the optimization and constrain it using a chromaticity-based regularization scheme similar to Chen and Koltun [21].

Fig. 1. *Left*: An illustration of our Retinex-based assumption of separating albedo from shading. Large gradients in the image are usually caused by albedo changes; small gradients on the other hand are observed due to lighting. Based on this we compute a trade-off between stereo and shading energies. *Right*: Visualization of the trade-off for an input image. For every pixel we use mainly our stereo term (dark regions) or our shading term (bright regions) based on the magnitude of the image gradient.

While, this prevents shading from being absorbed into the albedo, it can fail in scenes where the albedo variation is not accurately predicted by chromaticities (e.g., albedos with the same chromaticity but different brightness).

Although shading-based refinement techniques have improved significantly in recent years, the basic principle of all existing methods remains the same: They use fixed input geometry, estimate lighting, and later refine the geometry using shading cues. While we also compute a lighting function on a coarse estimate of the geometry, we integrate the geometry refinement directly into the multi-view stereo reconstruction method. This allows us to balance stereo matching and shading cues as we can resolve ambiguities in the multi-view stereo energy, instead of treating the input geometry as fixed. This approach ultimately also enables us to optimize the geometry independent of the (potentially spatially-varying) albedo, i.e., without explicitly including albedo terms into our energy. This is a significant advantage because we do not have to rely on albedo regularization models that can often fail on real-world scenes.

3   Energy Formulation

Our energy balances geometric errors versus shading errors depending on the local image gradient. This is motivated by Land's Retinex theory [22], which assumes that shading introduces only small image gradients, changing the surface brightness gradually. Strong gradients on the other hand are usually caused by changes in surface materials and are thus independent of the illumination. Retinex theory has been commonly used to separate surface albedo and shading [23,24] (see Fig. 1).

In our context, this observation has two implications. First, in multi-view reconstruction the geometric stereo term is usually accurate and robust in regions with strong gradients but fails for small gradients. Many stereo methods therefore use surface regularization to keep textureless areas smooth. We instead utilize the fact that small gradients are most likely caused by lighting and define an additional data term based on a shading function that specifically constrains the direction in which the surface should change. Second, we show that, in regions of small gradients, we can factor the surface albedo out completely, resulting in an albedo-free shading term. Our error terms are based purely on point wise image gradients and do not involve image values or larger patches of pixels.

The input to our algorithm is an unstructured set of images as well as known camera parameters which can be either pre-calibrated or recovered by stucture from motion tools such as VisualSFM [25]. We aim to compute a depth map for evey view i using a set of neighbor views $j \in \mathcal{N}_i$.

3.1   Geometric Error

Our camera model follows standard definitions [26]. A 3D point $\mathbf{X}$ is transformed into an image location $\mathbf{x}$ in the camera coordinate system according to a camera calibration matrix K, rotation R, and translation $\mathbf{t}$ as

$$\mathbf{x} = \mathrm{K}\left(\mathrm{R}\mathbf{X} + \mathbf{t}\right). \tag{1}$$

For homogeneous coordinates the projection from a pixel coordinate $\mathbf{x}_i$ in camera i into another camera j can then be defined according to a depth value $d_i(\mathbf{x}_i)$ along the principal ray of view i:

$$P_j(\mathbf{x}_i, d_i(\mathbf{x}_i)) = \mathrm{K}_j\left(\mathrm{R}_j\mathrm{R}_i^{-1}\left(\mathrm{K}_i^{-1}\mathbf{x}_i \cdot d_i(\mathbf{x}_i) - \mathbf{t}_i\right) + \mathbf{t}_j\right) \tag{2}$$

The geometric error is now defined as a stereo term based on matching intensity gradients from the main view into neighboring views according to the current depth function. Traditional stereo methods often optimize using image values over a local patch of pixels. Even for illumination invariant measures such as normalized cross-correlation, this would be more difficult to integrate into our Retinex assumption as a patch of pixels is more likely to be affected by both albedo and shading changes. Instead, we specifically optimize this energy for local image gradients. A gradient-based stereo term was introduced by Scharstein [27] but has only been adapted in some specific scenarios like gradient domain rendering [28]. Semerjian [5] recently showed that a point-wise measure of gradients can be very effective for surface reconstruction if used correctly. We adopt this measure as it is well suited for our approach. For any two views i, j and their intensity functions I_i, I_j, and a pixel coordinate $\mathbf{x}_i$ it can be written as:

$$E_g^j(d_i, \mathbf{x}_i) = \nabla I_i(\mathbf{x}) - \nabla I_j(P_j(\mathbf{x}_i, d_i(\mathbf{x}_i))). \tag{3}$$

Here, and in further equations, ∇ denotes image gradients which are the derivatives computed with respect to image coordinates $\mathbf{x}_i$. Note that this also involves the derivative of the projection P_j which transforms the gradient into the correct coordinate system. In addition to constraints beween the main view and its neighbors, we also define pairwise terms between two neighbors as used by Semerjian [5]. Still using the depth of the main view d_i we get:

$$E_g^{j,k}(d_i, \mathbf{x}_i) = E_g^j(d_i, \mathbf{x}_i) - E_g^k(d_i, \mathbf{x}_i) = \nabla I_j(P_j(\mathbf{x}_i, d_i(\mathbf{x}_i)) - \nabla I_k(P_k(\mathbf{x}_i, d_i(\mathbf{x}_i)), \tag{4}$$

where $E_g^{i,j} = E_g^j$. This essentially measures the difference in error between neighbors and avoids overfitting to only one neighbor.

3.2   Shading Error

Lighting Model: Similar to previous work [2,3] we assume Lambertian reflectance. This allows us to define shading as a function of the surface normal **n**, and independent of the viewing direction. We also use third-order spherical harmonics basis functions B_h to approximate the incoming illumination. The outgoing radiance $R(\mathbf{x})$ at a point **x**, with albedo $a(\mathbf{x})$ and normal $\mathbf{n}(\mathbf{x})$, is a weighted sum of these bases, which we define as our shading function S:

$$R(\mathbf{x}) = a(\mathbf{x}) \cdot \sum_{h=1}^{16} B_h(\mathbf{n}(\mathbf{x})) \cdot \mathbf{l}_h = a(\mathbf{x}) \cdot S(\mathbf{n}(\mathbf{x}), \mathbf{l}) \tag{5}$$

The lighting parameters **l** are computed ahead of surface optimization using a coarse initial surface model derived from basic stereo. This optimization is identical to Zollhoefer et al. [3], i.e., we initialize the albedo as constant and simply solve a linear least squares system. In contrast to Zollhoefer et al., we optimize **l** using only our single main image. Using more images would make this estimation more robust, but we explicitly want to optimize for a separate lighting model per image to be invariant to changing light conditions, e.g., an object moving on a turn table or outdoor scenes with uncontrolled lighting. We also set our albedo to a constant value. As we will describe later, we are able to optimize the geometry without explicitly modeling the albedo. This has many advantages for the optimization procedure, but unlike Zollhoefer et al. [3] we cannot create an improved lighting model in further iterations. While there are obvious scenarios that will break this approach, the low number of lighting parameters causes the estimation to be robust enough for a variety of objects, as we will demonstrate in the results. In fact, we observed that in practical scenarios it is much more likely that errors appear due to specular surfaces, self shadowing and inter-reflections, which cannot be dealt with in either case.

Shading Error: Our shading term is also based on image gradients. Similar to [3], we assume that the observed image gradient, ∇I, should be identical to the gradient of the reflected intensity predicted by our model, ∇R, with:

$$\nabla R(\mathbf{x}) = \nabla a(\mathbf{x}) \cdot S(\mathbf{n}(\mathbf{x}), \mathbf{l}) + a(\mathbf{x}) \cdot \nabla S(\mathbf{n}(\mathbf{x}), \mathbf{l}). \tag{6}$$

However, at this point we do not have an accurate model of the albedo. Previous approaches therefore include the albedo in the optimization leading to a significantly bigger, under-constrained problem. This requires an explicit regularization on the albedo using approximate measures such as pairwise differences based on chromaticity. Instead, we use the Retinex assumption to create an albedo independent optimization that does not require any explicit regularization. A common approach for intrinsic images [21,23] is to operate in the log domain as this makes albedo and shading terms additive instead of multiplicative:

$$\log(R(\mathbf{x})) = \log(a(\mathbf{x})) + \log(S(\mathbf{n}(d_i(\mathbf{x})), \mathbf{l})). \tag{7}$$

If we take the gradient with respect to image coordinates we get:

$$\nabla \log(R(\mathbf{x})) = \frac{\nabla a(\mathbf{x})}{a(\mathbf{x})} + \frac{\nabla S(\mathbf{n}(d_i(\mathbf{x})), \mathbf{l})}{S(\mathbf{n}(d_i(\mathbf{x})), \mathbf{l})}. \tag{8}$$

If we now assume—according to the Retinex theory—that small gradients are caused solely by lighting, the albedo gradient vanishes and we can write:

$$\nabla \log(R(\mathbf{x})) = \frac{\nabla S(\mathbf{n}(d_i(\mathbf{x})), \mathbf{l})}{S(\mathbf{n}(d_i(\mathbf{x})), \mathbf{l})}. \tag{9}$$

This means that the difference, $\nabla \log(I(\mathbf{x})) - \nabla \log(R(\mathbf{x}))$, can in fact be minimized by solely optimizing over the shading function, $S(\mathbf{n}(\mathbf{x}), \mathbf{l})$. This indicates an albedo invariance which can also be thought of in the following way: If the albedo is locally constant, an intensity gradient is only caused by a change in surface normals, and given a lighting model, the surface normals have to change in a particular direction which does not depend on the actual value of the albedo. Our shading error is therefore defined as

$$E_s(d_i, \mathbf{x}) = \frac{\nabla I(\mathbf{x})}{I(\mathbf{x})} - \frac{\nabla S(\mathbf{n}(d_i(\mathbf{x})), \mathbf{l})}{S(\mathbf{n}(d_i(\mathbf{x})), \mathbf{l})}. \tag{10}$$

Note that this is a simple point-wise measure which matches the point-wise nature of our gradient-based stereo term and suggests a balanced optimization if both are combined.

3.3 Combined Energy

To formulate our final energy function we combine both data terms in a simple but effective way. For pixels with strong gradients, we rely on the geometric stereo term as it is very robust. For small gradients, we additionally use our shading error as it constrains the surface according to the given lighting model. As we want to do this on a per-pixel basis, we need a continuous trade-off to avoid artifacts. Our solution is to use the magnitude of the image gradient to compute a weight on the shading error term, see Fig. 1 for an example. For a set of neighbors, $\mathcal{N}_i$, including i itself, and a set of pixels, $\mathcal{V}_i$, that are visible in the corresponding neighbors, the final energy is defined as:

$$E(d_i) = \sum_{j,k \in \mathcal{N}_i}^{k>j} \sum_{\mathbf{x}_v \in \mathcal{V}_i} |E_g^{j,k}(d_i, \mathbf{x}_v)| + \frac{\alpha}{\|\nabla I(\mathbf{x}_v)\|_2} |E_s(d_i, \mathbf{x}_v)|, \tag{11}$$

where $\alpha = 0.01$ balances the scale of both terms as the shading error is measured in the log domain. We use the same value for all our datasets. We also experimented with normalizing the weight across pixels. The new weight β would then also affect the geometric error, i.e., $(1 - \beta)E_g + \beta E_s$, resulting in a total weight of 1 for each pixel. However, this led to worse results. Note that the final energy is constructed only with local measures and does not contain any explicit regularization terms. Instead it is implicitly regularized by the Retinex assumption

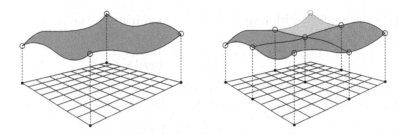

Fig. 2. Surface representation based on bicubic patches. Each patch is defined via 4 nodes (illustrated as circles) that are located at pixel corners (illustrated as dots on the pixel grid). When moving to a higher scale the patch is subdivided and some patches are removed if they have a high error.

and the lighting model. We also use the L1 norm for both our data terms as it is more robust to outliers that do not correspond to our Retinex assumption. It also avoids scale issues in the optimization that can be caused by the shading energy becoming very large in dark areas.

4   Surface Representation and Optimization

As discussed in Sect. 2, we use the framework of Semerjian [5] to optimize our energy function. It provides a surface representation with a continuous definition of depth values and surface normals which is very beneficial for our combined energy. Optimizing a depth map for each view allows us to handle datasets with varying lighting conditions and enables straight forward parallel processing. As this framework uses a different approach compared to simple pixel-wise depth values, we briefly summarize the main aspects.

4.1   Surface Representation

The surface is not represented as depth values per pixel but rather as a set of bicubic surface patches. Every patch is defined by bicubic interpolation between 4 nodes, and neighboring patches share two nodes (see Fig. 2). A node itself represents 4 optimization variables: the depth, the first derivatives of the depth and the mixed second derivative. The nodes are located at image coordinates of the main view and each bicubic patch covers a set of pixels. This also enables an easy formulation of scale, as patches can cover more pixels to represent a coarser scale and can be subdivived to move to a finer scale. At the finest scale the patches cover a 2×2 set of pixels.

4.2   Optimization

Given this representation, we can efficiently optimize the non-linear energy (Eq. 11) using a Gauss-Newton type solver. As our shading error is albedo-free, we do not need to introduce additional variables and can operate solely on the surface representation. Starting from an initial guess the current energy is linearized, and we solve for an update to the optimization variables. Let $\mathbf{d}$ be the vector of optimization parameters, $\hat{\mathbf{d}}$ the update, and $\mathbf{f}(\mathbf{d})$ the vector of residuals generated by our energy E. Linearizing the error function around the current solution using the Jacobian, $J_{\mathbf{f}}$, leads to the common linear system:

$$\mathbf{f}(\mathbf{d} + \hat{\mathbf{d}}) \approx \mathbf{f}(\mathbf{d}) + J_{\mathbf{f}}^T \hat{\mathbf{d}}, \qquad \left(J^T J\right) \hat{\mathbf{d}} = -J^T \mathbf{f} \qquad (12)$$

The approximate Hessian $J^T J$ consists of 4×4 blocks that correspond to the 4 optimization variables at each node. It is also very sparse due to the limited support of the bicubic patches; each node is used for a maximum of 4 patches. The linear system can therefore be solved efficiently using a conjugate gradient solver. The inverse of the block diagonal of $J^T J$ is a good preconditioner and can be computed quickly using Cholesky decompositions on the blocks.

4.3 Final Algorithm

We first create an initial geometry using the multi-scale formulation and surface operations of Semerjian [5] for coarse scales. Smaller patch sizes of 8×8 and lower are then optimized using our new energy. Applying our shading term for coarse scales would not improve the final result as geometry details are only revealed at finer scales. Another reason is efficiency; the shading error additionally involves the gradient of the shading function and is therefore more complicated to compute which increases the runtime compared to simple regularization. Finally, the reconstructed surfaces from all views are converted to a point set with normals and can be fused with any surface reconstruction algorithm [29–31]. Each view can also be represented as a depth or normal map.

5 Results

In the following, we evaluate our method using a variety of datasets. For all our results we used 6–9 neighbor images (except for the sparse Middlebury datasets) and fused them into a global model using Floating Scale Surface Reconstruction (FSSR) [30]. We chose this approach because it does not fill holes that may appear in the geometry due to large errors in our stereo and/or shading energy.

We first evaluate our approach on the well known Middlebury benchmark [1]. Comprehensive results are available on the website. The *Dino* dataset has many areas that are affected by self shadowing and interreflections. As Fig. 3 shows, our optimization can handle these effects in many cases if enough stereo information from multiple views is available. Note that our optimization handles cast shadows to some extent implicitly since the weight for the shading term is low at the shadow boundaries, and cast shadows can be matched well with stereo matching. The lighting model is, however, still wrong inside the shadowed

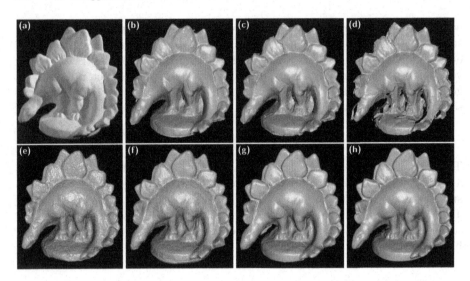

Fig. 3. Results on the *Dino* dataset of the Middlebury benchmark with decreasing number of input images. This dataset has strong shadowing which can be seen in the input image. However, in areas where our lighting model is correct we are able to recover a high amount of detail in the geometry even for sparse input data. *Top*: (a) Input image; (b) our reconstruction on full dataset, 363 images, using 9 neighbors; (c) ring dataset, 46 images, using 4 neighbors; and (d) sparse ring dataset, 16 images, using only 1 or 2 neighbors. *Bottom*: Results on full dataset submitted by (e) Furukawa et al. [7], (f) Galliani et al. [11], and (g) Semerjian [5]; and (h) ground truth.

areas since the incoming illumination is partially occluded. On the full dataset our result has an accuracy of 0.49 mm and a completeness of 96.9 %. For the sparse *Dino* dataset where stereo cues are not very strong, our shading term causes holes in the shadowed areas as we cannot find consistent normals in these areas. However, compared to other approaches, we are able to recover a significant amount of detail in areas that are not affected by shadows. In fact, we reconstruct the same amount of detail independent of the sparsity of the input data, which highlights another strength of our shading term. Even for the very sparse input data of 16 images and using only 2 neighbors we can reconstruct more detail than top scoring approaches on the full dataset. For the full *Temple* dataset (Fig. 4), we are able to achieve a high accuracy even though the back of the object has many concavities leading to strong interreflections that cannot be represented by our global lighting model. Compared to the results submitted by Semerjian [5] our shading term improves the accuracy on the full dataset by 0.15 mm to 0.47 mm and we achive a completeness of 98.7 %.

Figures 5 and 6 show *fountain-P11*, an outdoor dataset from the Strecha et al. [32] benchmark. The normal maps in Fig. 5 show the effect of different surface regularization weights on the original approach of Semerjian [5]. There is no globally correct weight as the reconstructed geometry is either too smooth or

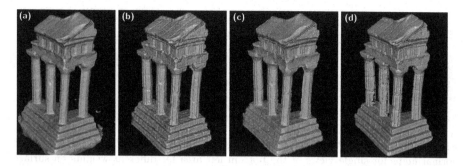

Fig. 4. Results on the *Temple* dataset of the Middlebury benchmark. *From left to right*: (a) Galliani et al. [11]; (b) Fuhrmann et al. [30] using the stereo from Goesele et al. [6]; (c) our reconstruction; and (d) ground truth. Our reconstruction achieves a good balance between capturing fine-scale detail without introducing noise.

too noisy. In contrast, our approach reconstructs smooth but detailed geometry due to the image gradient magnitude-based weight. Figure 6 demonstrates that this also translates to the fused geometry as integrating multiple views cannot remove the noise inherent in Semerjian's reconstruction effectively.

Next we present a multi-scale outdoor dataset included in the FSSR paper [30]. Figure 7 shows that our approach can recover detailed geometry in such a setting. The normal map captures even the finest details recovered in a single view. Our results from vastly different scales can be combined into a consistent model with FSSR. However, we can observe the boundaries between scales as the resolution and accuracy of the geometry changes drastically. This still illustrates an advantage compared to other systems that operate on a global model: our approach can scale to any amount of images and can easily reconstruct different levels of detail in a single dataset, whereas keeping a multi-scale global model in an efficient data structure is challenging and not arbitrarily scalable.

Figure 8 shows a dataset presented by Zollhoefer et al. [3]. This object already provides many gradients for stereo matching so we do not expect our shading term to result in a substantial improvement. Note, however, that our reconstruction has significantly better quality compared to the normal map reconstructed with Semerjian's approach, and compared to the Zollhoefer et al. [3] reconstruction provided on their project web page.

Finally, Fig. 9 presents results on a dataset captured under varying lighting conditions. The *Owl* was captured on a turn-table with fixed lights and a fixed camera, resulting in different lighting for each image (w.r.t. the image coordinates). The object is nearly diffuse apart from the dark specular areas where all the methods shown here fail. We compare against a patch based stereo method [6], which has no effective regularization as each pixel is optimized independently. This results in a very uneven surface and noise in (almost) textureless regions. Semerjian [5] uses a simple regularization term that keeps the surface variation low. This is effective in producing a continuous surface, but cannot recover

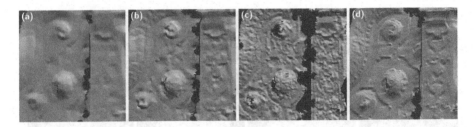

Fig. 5. The *fountain-P11* dataset from Strecha et al. [32]. *From left to right*: Closeup normal maps for single views of the bottom left area for different weights on surface regularization (a) high, (b) medium, and (c) low; and (d) normal map of our reconstruction. Basic regularization cannot find a good trade-off between overly smooth and noisy geometry. Our result reveals fine details without introducing noise.

Fig. 6. The *fountain-P11* dataset from Strecha et al. [32]. *From left to right*: Reconstruction by our implementation of Semerjian [5] using a low regularization weight to recover details; by our new optimization; and ground truth.

details in regions without strong gradients. In contrast, our combined method recovers a smooth surface and is able to relate small gradients to surface details.

5.1   Runtime

A C++ implementation of our technique is available as open source software[1]. This unoptimized prototype shows a roughly 20 % runtime increase compared to our implementation of Semerjian [5]. In practice, the full *Dino* and *Temple* datasets were computed in 75 and 63 min on a 32-core machine. The multi-scale outdoor dataset from Fuhrmann et al. [30] included 204 high resolution images and was computed in 115 min on the same machine, while the *Owl* dataset with 10 images took around 7 min. For a fair comparison to other stereo methods, we are reporting the run-times of our complete multi-view algorithm and not only the time required for solving our shading-based optimization.

---

[1] https://github.com/flanggut/smvs.

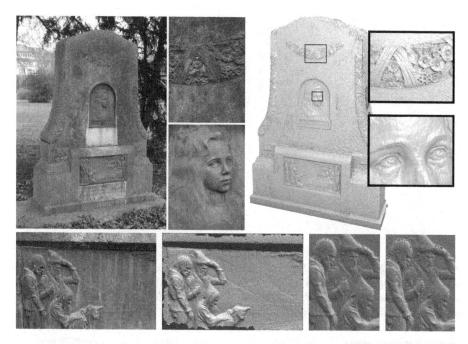

Fig. 7. Results on an outdoor dataset. *Top*: Input images at different scales, and our global model with details. Our method recovers more detail in regions that are imaged at higher-resolution. *Bottom*: A closeup input image; the reconstructed depth map shaded with the lighting; and close-up normals with regular (10^{-2}) and low (10^{-4}) value for α – decreasing the weight of the shading term results in more noise and less detail as the stereo term dominates the energy.

5.2 Limitations

We make two main assumptions in our method that can lead to errors in the final geometry if they are violated. First, we assume that the scene is Lambertian and a low frequency spherical harmonics lighting can accurately represent the illumination. As we show in the Middlebury *Dino* dataset, shadows and interreflections will cause errors in the reconstruction but we are still able to reconstruct details in areas where our lighting model is correct. A more sophisticated lighting model could solve the issues in future work, and would require only minor changes to our geometry optimization. Second, we assume that we can separate albedo and lighting according to the magnitude of the image gradient. While this holds for many datasets, there are objects where the albedo changes gradually, and this violation of Retinex can show up in our geometry if we relate these small gradients to shading and therefore changes in the surface normal. This suggests that some geometry regularization might still be needed in certain regions where we cannot easily decide between albedo and shading. As we rely solely on the stereo error for strong gradients, we are also limited by its accuracy. In certain configurations, e.g., observing horizontal lines under horizontal camera motion, or

Fig. 8. The *Figure* dataset. *Top from left to right*: An input image of the dataset; normal maps from the surface computed by our implementation of Semerjian [5], and our shading based approach. *Bottom*: Result presented by Zollhoefer et al. [3] (available at project website); and our fused model.

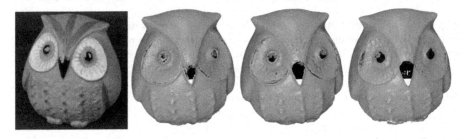

Fig. 9. Reconstruction of the *Owl* dataset with changing lighting in each image. *From left to right*: An input image; reconstruction by Goesele et al. [6]; by our implementation of Semerjian [5]; and using our new optimization. Our results capture more structural details (see the eyes for example) with less overall noise.

fine structures with aliasing effects, the stereo term might lead to wrong depth estimates that we cannot fix with our normal-based shading term.

6   Conclusion

In this paper, we have presented a novel multi-view surface optimization algorithm that efficiently combines a stereo energy term with a shading-based energy term in a single, combined approach, to create high quality reconstructions. Building on the Retinex assumption, we are able to completely remove the albedo from the shading-based error, which has not been done before. Our formulation relies solely on pixel-wise data terms and an implicit regularization via the shading function and surface representation. We present results that improve on previous multi-view stereo algorithms and shading based refinement systems. Our approach is limited by the basic lighting model and cannot account for self-shadowing, indirect illumination, and specular materials. In future work we will improve on this to create a more robust system that can be applied to more complex scenes. Overall, we believe that the idea of combining stereo and shading energies can be very powerful and will lead to more general approaches.

Acknowledgements. This work was supported in part by the European Commissions Seventh Framework Programme under grant agreements no. ICT-611089 (CR-PLAY).

References

1. Seitz, S., Curless, B., Diebel, J., Scharstein, D., Szeliski, R.: A comparison and evaluation of multi-view stereo reconstruction algorithms. In: IEEE Computer Society Conference on Computer Vision and Pattern Recognition (CVPR 2006), pp. 519–526. IEEE Computer Society (2006)
2. Wu, C., Wilburn, B., Matsushita, Y., Theobalt, C.: High-quality shape from multi-view stereo and shading under general illumination. In: Proceedings of the 2011 IEEE Conference on Computer Vision and Pattern Recognition, CVPR 2011 (2011)
3. Zollhöfer, M., Dai, A., Innmann, M., Wu, C., Stamminger, M., Theobalt, C., Nießner, M.: Shading-based refinement on volumetric signed distance functions. ACM Trans. Graph. **34**(4), 96:1–96:14 (2015). doi:10.1145/2766887. article no 96
4. Or-El, R., Rosman, G., Wetzler, A., Kimmel, R., Bruckstein, A.M.: RGBD-fusion: real-time high precision depth recovery. In: Computer Vision and Pattern Recognition (CVPR) (2015)
5. Semerjian, B.: A new variational framework for multiview surface reconstruction. In: Fleet, D., Pajdla, T., Schiele, B., Tuytelaars, T. (eds.) ECCV 2014. LNCS, vol. 8694, pp. 719–734. Springer, Heidelberg (2014). doi:10.1007/978-3-319-10599-4_46
6. Goesele, M., Snavely, N., Curless, B., Hoppe, H., Seitz, S.: Multi-view stereo for community photo collections. In: International Conference on Computer Vision (ICCV) (2007)
7. Furukawa, Y., Ponce, J.: Accurate, dense, and robust multi-view stereopsis. Trans. Pattern Anal. Mach. Intell. (PAMI) **32**(8), 1362–1376 (2010)
8. Heise, P., Jensen, B., Klose, S., Knoll, A.: Variational patchmatch multiview reconstruction and refinement. In: 2015 IEEE International Conference on Computer Vision (ICCV), pp. 882–890 (2015)
9. Hirschmüller, H.: Accurate and efficient stereo processing by semi-global matching and mutual information. In: Proceedings of the IEEE Conference on Computer Vision and Pattern Recognition. CVPR 2005, Washington, DC, USA, pp. 807–814. IEEE Computer Society (2005)
10. Bleyer, M., Rhemann, C., Rother, C.: Patchmatch stereo - stereo matching with slanted support windows. In: Proceedings of the British Machine Vision Conference, pp. 14.1-14.11 (2011)
11. Galliani, S., Lasinger, K., Schindler, K.: Massively parallel multiview stereopsis by surface normal diffusion. In: 2015 IEEE International Conference on Computer Vision (ICCV), pp. 873–881 (2015)

12. Nehab, D., Rusinkiewicz, S., Davis, J., Ramamoorthi, R.: Efficiently combining positions and normals for precise 3D geometry. In: ACM SIGGRAPH 2005 Papers (2005)

13. Hernandez Esteban, C., Vogiatzis, G., Cipolla, R.: Multiview photometric stereo. IEEE Trans. Pattern Anal. Mach. Intell. **30**(3), 548–554 (2008)

14. Zhou, Z., Wu, Z., Tan, P.: Multi-view photometric stereo with spatially varying isotropic materials. In: Computer Vision and Pattern Recognition (CVPR), pp. 1482–1489 (2013)

15. Beeler, T., Bickel, B., Beardsley, P., Sumner, B., Gross, M.: High-quality single-shot capture of facial geometry. ACM Trans. Graph. **29**(4), 40:1–40:9 (2010). doi:10. 1145/1778765.1778777. article no 40

16. Yu, L.F., Yeung, S.K., Tai, Y.W., Lin, S.: Shading-based shape refinement of RGB-D images. In: Computer Vision and Pattern Recognition (CVPR) (2013)

17. Han, Y., Lee, J.Y., Kweon, I.S.: High quality shape from a single RGB-D image under uncalibrated natural illumination. In: 2013 IEEE International Conference on Computer Vision (ICCV), pp. 1617–1624 (2013)

18. Xu, D., Duan, Q., Zheng, J., Zhang, J., Cai, J., Cham, T.J.: Recovering surface details under general unknown illumination using shading and coarse multi-view stereo. In: IEEE Conference on Computer Vision and Pattern Recognition, pp. 1526–1533 (2014)

19. Wu, C., Zollhöfer, M., Nießner, M., Stamminger, M., Izadi, S., Theobalt, C.: Real-time shading-based refinement for consumer depth cameras. ACM Trans. Graph. **33**(6), 200:1–200:10 (2014)

20. Chai, M., Luo, L., Sunkavalli, K., Carr, N., Hadap, S., Zhou, K.: High-quality hair modeling from a single portrait photo. ACM Trans. Graph. **34**(6), 204:1–204:10 (2015)

21. Chen, Q., Koltun, V.: A simple model for intrinsic image decomposition with depth cues. In: 2013 IEEE International Conference on Computer Vision (ICCV), pp. 241–248 (2013)

22. Land, E.H.: The retinex theory of color vision. Sci. Am. **237**(6), 108–128 (1977)

23. Horn, B.: Determining lightness from an image. Comput. Graph. Image Process. **3**(1), 277–299 (1974)

24. Grosse, R., Johnson, M.K., Adelson, E.H., Freeman, W.T.: Ground truth dataset and baseline evaluations for intrinsic image algorithms. In: Computer Vision, pp. 2335–2342. IEEE (2009)

25. Wu, C., Agarwal, S., Curless, B., Seitz, S.M.: Multicore bundle adjustment. In: 2011 IEEE Conference on Computer Vision and Pattern Recognition (CVPR), pp. 3057–3064 (2011)

26. Hartley, R.I., Zisserman, A.: Multiple View Geometry in Computer Vision, 2nd edn. Cambridge University Press, Cambridge (2004). ISBN: 0521540518

27. Scharstein, D.: Matching images by comparing their gradient fields. In: Proceedings of the 12th ICPR International Conference on Pattern Recognition, vol. 1, pp. 572–575 (1994)

28. Kopf, J., Langguth, F., Scharstein, D., Szeliski, R., Goesele, M.: Image-based rendering in the gradient domain. ACM Trans. Graph. **32**(6), 199:1–199:9 (2013). doi:10.1145/2508363.2508369. article no 199

29. Kazhdan, M., Hoppe, H.: Screened poisson surface reconstruction. ACM Trans. Graph. **32**(3), 29:1–29:13 (2013). doi:10.1145/2487228.2487237. article no 29

30. Fuhrmann, S., Goesele, M.: Floating scale surface reconstruction. In: Proceedings of ACM SIGGRAPH (2014)

31. Ummenhofer, B., Brox, T.: Global, dense multiscale reconstruction for a billion points. In: IEEE International Conference on Computer Vision (ICCV), December 2015
32. Strecha, C., von Hansen, W., Gool, L.V., Fua, P., Thoennessen, U.: On benchmarking camera calibration and multi-view stereo for high resolution imagery. In: IEEE Conference on Computer Vision and Pattern Recognition, CVPR 2008, pp. 1–8 (2008)

Fine-Scale Surface Normal Estimation
Using a Single NIR Image

Youngjin Yoon[1]([✉]), Gyeongmin Choe[1]([✉]), Namil Kim[1],
Joon-Young Lee[2], and In So Kweon[1]

[1] Korea Advanced Institute of Science and Technology (KAIST),
Daejeon, South Korea
{yjyoon,gmchoe,nikim}@rcv.kaist.ac.kr, iskweon@kaist.ac.kr
[2] Adobe Research, San jose, USA
jolee@adobe.com

Abstract. We present surface normal estimation using a single near
infrared (NIR) image. We are focusing on reconstructing fine-scale surface geometry using an image captured with an uncalibrated light source.
To tackle this ill-posed problem, we adopt a generative adversarial network, which is effective in recovering sharp outputs essential for fine-scale
surface normal estimation. We incorporate the angular error and an integrability constraint into the objective function of the network to make
the estimated normals incorporate physical characteristics. We train and
validate our network on a recent NIR dataset, and also evaluate the generality of our trained model by using new external datasets that are
captured with a different camera under different environments.

Keywords: Shape from shading · Near infrared image · Generative
adversarial network

1 Introduction

Estimating surface geometry is a fundamental problem in understanding the
properties of an object and reconstructing its 3D information. There are two
different approaches: geometric methods such as structure-from-motion and
multi-view stereo, and photometric methods such as photometric stereo and
shape-from-shading. The geometric methods are usually useful for metric reconstructions while the photometric methods are effective in estimating accurate
per-pixel surface geometry.

Recently, with the massive use of commercial depth sensors, *e.g.*, Kinect and
RealSense, many works have been proposed to enhance the depth quality of
the sensors by fusing the photometric cues of the color image [1,2] or the near
infrared (NIR) image [3,4]. Although these methods have proven their effectiveness in photometric shape estimation and have provided promising results, they
rely highly on the sensors and usually require heavy computational time.

Y. Yoon and G. Choe—provided equal contributions to this work.

© Springer International Publishing AG 2016
B. Leibe et al. (Eds.): ECCV 2016, Part III, LNCS 9907, pp. 486–500, 2016.
DOI: 10.1007/978-3-319-46487-9_30

On the other hand, deep convolutional neural networks (CNN) have been broadly used for various computer vision tasks such as image classification [5,6], object detection [7,8], segmentation [9,10], and depth estimation [11,12]. With its rich learning capability, deep CNN has shown state-of-the-art performances in many areas and has also made algorithms more practical with fast evaluation times. Lately, several works have also tried to solve depth or surface normal estimation using CNN [11,12]. However, they have largely been focused on scene-level estimation [12] or context-aware methods [13], which generate rough surface normals and therefore they cannot generate the fine-scale surface details of the target object.

The goal of this paper is to propose a practical system that estimates fine-scale surface normals, not a scene-level structure, from an image captured with an uncalibrated light source. We solve this shape-from-shading problem by training a deep CNN on a recent NIR dataset [14]. This dataset consists of 101 objects, captured by an NIR camera with 9 different viewing directions and 12 lighting directions. It allows us to train a variety of textures such as fabrics, leaves, and papers. As shown in [14], the major benefits of using NIR images for estimating fine-scale geometry are that the albedo variation in NIR images is less prevalent than in visible band images and undesired ambient indoor lightings are filtered out. Therefore, this setting can simplify a light model and makes building a practical system easier. The proposed model for training the mapping between NIR intensity distributions and normal maps is a generative adversarial network (GAN). We design the objective function of the GAN model to consider photometric characteristics of the surface geometry by incorporating angular error and an integrability constraint. Since we train various object images captured from different lighting directions, our method estimates fine-scale surface normals without the need for calibrating the lighting direction. We verify that deep CNN is effective in handling the ill-posed, uncalibrated shape-from-shading problem without complex heuristic assumptions. Also, we evaluate the generality of our trained model by testing our own datasets, which are captured using different configurations from that of the training dataset. One example result of our method is shown in Fig. 1.

The major contributions of our work are as follows:

• First work analyzing the relationship between an NIR image and its surface normal using a deep learning framework.

• Fine-scale surface normal estimation using a single NIR image where the light direction need not be calibrated.

• Suitable design of an objective function to reconstruct the fine details of a target object surface.

2   Related Work

Photometric Stereo and Shape from Shading. Photometric stereo [15] is one of the well-studied methods for estimating surface normals. By taking at least 3 images captured under different lighting directions, photometric stereo

Fig. 1. Comparison of reconstruction results, left: Input NIR image, middle: Our reconstruction from a single NIR image, right: ground-truth reconstruction using NIR images captured under 12 different lighting directions.

can determine a unique set of surface normals of an object. Also, the usage of more images makes the output increase in accuracy since it becomes an over-determined problem.

Shape from shading is a special case of photometric stereo, which predicts a shape from a single image. However, it is an ill-posed problem and needs to exploit many restrictions and constraints [16,17]. Beginning with numerical SfS methods [18], many works have shown results based on the Lambertian BRDF assumption. Tsai *et al.* [19] use discrete approximation of surface normals. Lee and Kuo [20] estimate shape by using a triangular element surface model. We refer readers to [21] for better understanding regarding comparisons and evaluations of the classical SfS methods.

Shape from a NIR image has been recently studied in several literatures [3,14]. They analyze the discriminative characteristics of NIR images and experimentally show the albedo (surface reflectance) simplicity in the NIR wavelength of various materials. In [3,4], they propose the shape refinement methods using the photometric cues in NIR images. They show the high-quality shape recovery results, however they need an additional depth camera to obtain the results.

Although many conventional photometric approaches can work on NIR images and the albedo simplicity in the NIR image actually help robust estimation, estimating the surface normal from a single NIR image still have many limitations for practical uses, such as heavy computation time, heuristic assumptions, special system configuration, and the calibration of a light direction. To overcome those limitations, we study the mapping from NIR intensity distributions to surface normal vectors via a deep CNN framework. We combine a GAN [22] with the specially designed objective function. Through the adversarial training process, our network naturally encodes the photometric cues of a scene and produces fine surface normals.

Data-Driven Shape Estimation. There have been various studies on estimating the shape information from images via data-driven approaches.

Saxena *et al.* [23] estimate depths using a discriminatively trained MRF model with multiple scales of monocular cues. Hoiem *et al.* [24] reconstruct rough surface orientations of a scene by statistically modeling categories of coarse structures (*e.g.*, ground, sky and vertical). Ladicky *et al.* [25] incorporate semantic labels of a scene to predict better depth outputs.

One of the emerging directions for shape estimation is using deep CNN. In [26], Fouhey *et al.* try to discover the right primitives in a scene. In [13], Wang *et al.* explore the effectiveness of CNNs for the tasks of surface normal estimation. Although this work infers the surface normals from a single color image, it outputs scene-level rough geometries and is not suitable for object-level detailed surface reconstruction. To estimate the object shape and the material property, Rematas *et al.* [27] use the two different CNN architectures which predict surface normals directly and indirectly. The direct architecture estimates a reflectance map from an input image while the indirect architecture estimates a surface orientation map as an intermediate step towards reflectance map estimation. In [28], Liu *et al.* estimate depths from a single image using a deep CNN framework by jointly learning the unary and pairwise potentials of the CRF loss. In [29], Eigen *et al.* use a multi-scale approach which uses coarse and fine networks to estimate a better depth map.

Compared to the existing works, we focus on estimating fine-scale surface normals suing a deep CNN framework, therefore we bear in mind to design a network to produce photometrically meaningful outputs.

3   Method

3.1   Generative Adversarial Network

Generative adversarial network (GAN) [22] is a framework for training generative models which consists of two different models; a generative network G for modeling the data distribution and a discriminative network D for estimating the state of a network input. For our setup, G tries to generate a realistic surface normal map for the input NIR image and D tries to determine whether the input surface normal map is from G or from the dataset. Therefore, the generative network learns to generate more realistic images to fool the latter, while the discriminative network learns to correctly classify its input as a real image or a generated image. The two networks are simultaneously trained through a minimax optimization.

Given an input image of the discriminative network, an initial discriminative parameter θ_D is stochastically updated to correctly predict whether the input comes from a training image I or a generated image F. After that, while keeping the discriminative parameter θ_D fixed, a generative parameter θ_G is trained to produce the better quality of images, which could be misclassified by the discriminative network as real images. These procedures are repeated until they converge. This minimax objective is denoted as:

$$\min_{\theta_G} \max_{\theta_D} \mathbb{E}_{F \sim D_{desire}}[logD(I)] + \mathbb{E}_{Z \sim D_{input}}[log(1 - D(F))] \tag{1}$$

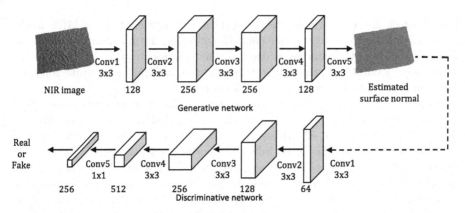

Fig. 2. Our network architecture. The proposed network produces surface normal map from a single NIR image. The generative model reconstructs surface normal map and the discriminative network predicts the probability whether the surface normal map comes from the training data or the generative model.

where D_{desire} is the distribution of images that we desired to estimate and D_{input} is that of the input domain. This objective function encourages D to be assigned to the correct label for both real and generated images and make G generate a realistic output F from an input Z. In our method, both the generative and the discriminative model are based on convolutional networks. The former takes a single NIR image as an input and results in a three-dimensional normal image as an output. The latter classifies an input by using the binary cross-entropy to make the probability high when an input comes from the training data.

3.2   Deep Shape from Shading

Based on the generative adversarial network explained in Sect. 3.1, we modified the GAN model to be suitable for the shape-from-shading problem. Since shape-from-shading is the ill-posed problem, it is important to incorporate proper constraints to uniquely determine the right solution. Therefore, we combine angular error and integrability loss, which are shown to be effective in many conventional SfS methods, into the objective function of the generative network. Also, the existing GAN approaches typically take a random noise vector [22], pre-encoded vector [30], or an image [31,32] as the input of their generative networks, and each generative model produces the output which lies in the same domain as its input. In this work, we apply the generative model to produce a three-dimensional normal map from a NIR image where both data lies in the different domains. Compared to the conventional SfS methods, we do not need to calibrate the lighting directions. To the best of our knowledge, our work is the first application of the adversarial training to estimate fine-scale geometry from a single NIR image.

Generative Networks. We use a fully convolutional network to construct the generative network. This type of a convolutional model was recently adopted in image restoration [33,34] and was verified to have superior performance in the task. To keep the image size of the input and output constant, we pad zeros before the convolution operations. Through our experiments, we found that this strategy works well in reconstructing the normal map.

Our network architecture is depicted in Fig. 2. We feed a 64×64 NIR patch to the generative network as an input. The network consists of 5 convolution layers (128-256-256-128-3 convolution filters at each of layers), each followed by ReLU except the last layer. Since the generative network is fully convolutional, the output of the network has same size as the input NIR image. We have empirically determined the number and sizes of filters for all networks.

Discriminative Networks. Given the output of the generative network, a typical choice of the objectives function is the averaged L_1 or L_2 distance between ground-truth and generated output. However, such a choice has some limitations to be applied to our problem. L_2 distance produces blurry predictions because it assumes that the errors follow the Gaussian distribution. In L_1 distance, this effect could be diminished, but the estimated images would be the median of the set of equally likely intensities. We propose to add the discriminative network as a loss function with the distance metric. Recently, [31] proved that the combination of the distance, gradient and discriminative networks as a loss function provides the realistic and accurate output. Our discriminative model has a binary cross-entropy loss to make the high probability when the input is real images, and vice versa.

3.3 Training

We will explain how we iteratively train the generative model G and the discriminative model D. Let us consider a single NIR image $Z \in \{Z_1, Z_2, \ldots, Z_j\}$ from a training dataset and the corresponding ground truth normal map $Y \in \{Y_1, Y_2, \ldots, Y_j\}$. The training dataset covers various objects captured from diverse lighting directions, and we uniformly sampled the image from the dataset in terms of the balance of lighting directions.

Basically, we followed the procedure of the paper [30]. Given N paired image set, we first train D to classify the real image pair (Z, Y) into the class 1 and the generated pair $(Z, G(Z))$ into the class 0. In this step, we fixed the parameters (θ_G) of the generative network G to solely update the parameters (θ_D) of D. The objective function of the discriminative model is denoted as:

$$\mathcal{L}_D(Z, Y) = \sum_{i=1}^{N} \mathcal{D}_{bce}(Y_i, 1) + \mathcal{D}_{bce}(G(Z_i), 0), \tag{2}$$

where $\mathcal{D}_{bce}$ is the binary cross-entropy, defined as

$$\mathcal{D}_{bce}(Y_i, C) = -C_i log(Y_i) + (1 - C_i) log(1 - Y_i), \tag{3}$$

where C_i is the binary class label. We minimize the objective function so that the network outputs high probability scores for real images Y_i and low probability scores for generated images $G(Z_i)$.

After that, we keep the parameters of D fixed and train the generative model G. Many previous deep learning based image restoration and generation methods [33, 35] used the mean square error(MSE) loss function to minimize between the ground-truth images and output images. However, as studied in the conventional SfS works, estimating accurate surface normal maps requires the minimization of angular errors and the output normals satisfy the integrability constraint. Therefore, we modified the objective function of the GAN model to incorporate those photometric objective functions. By taking the objective functions, we can effectively remove angular error and estimate physically meaningful surface normals.

Specifically, to evaluate surface normal properly, we defined the objective function of our generative network as:

$$\mathcal{L}_G(Z, Y) = \sum_{i=1}^{N} \mathcal{D}_{bce}(G(Z_i), 1) + \lambda_{l_p} L_p + \lambda_{ang} L_{ang} + \lambda_{curl} L_{curl}. \quad (4)$$

Following the conventional L_1 or L_2 loss, the estimated normal map difference $\mathcal{L}_p$ is denoted as:

$$\mathcal{L}_p(Y, G(Z)) = ||Y - G(Z)||_p^p \quad (5)$$

where $p = 1$ or $p = 2$

To estimate the accuracy of photometric stereo, the angular error is often used in conventional photometric approaches because it describes more physically meaningful error than direct normal map difference. To minimize the angular error, we normalize both the estimated normals $(G(Z))$ and the ground-truth normals (Y), then simply apply the dot product between them as:

$$\mathcal{L}_{ang}(Y, G(Z)) = 1 - \langle Y, G(Z) \rangle = 1 - \frac{Y^T G(Z)}{||Y||||G(Z)||} \quad (6)$$

The angular error provides physically meaningful measures, however it averaged entire surface normals. In order to encourage the generative network to estimate photometrically correct surface normals, we also add the integrability constraint in local neighbors into the objective function, which is denoted as:

$$\mathcal{L}_{curl} = || \bigtriangledown \times G(Z) \rangle ||. \quad (7)$$

The integrability constraint enforces that the integral of normal vectors in a local closed loop must sum up to zero, meaning that angles are returned to the same height. The integrability constraint prevents a drastic change and guarantees estimated normals lie on the same surface in a local region.

Fig. 3. Dataset [14] has various real-world object taken by 12 different lighting directions and 9 objects of view points. The leftmost is a normal map as the ground-truth and others are NIR images from different lighting directions. The Variety of lighting directions makes the same object appear vastly different.

4 Experiment

4.1 Dataset

To apply deep learning framework to our purpose, it is required to have a good quality dataset with numerous examples for training. However, most existing datasets are not large enough to train the network and are often inadequate for our tasks. Recently Choe *et al.* [14] opened a new NIR benchmark dataset, including 101 real-world objects such as fabrics, leaves and paper taken at 9 views and 12 lighting directions.

We used a pair of NIR as input and surface normal maps as target for ground truth. For fine-scale refinement, we augmented NIR images into 12 patches (64×64) within a single ground truth. For training, we used images from 91 objects and the remaining objects are for validation and test dataset. Note that we uniformly sampled validation and test samples according to the object category. When we trained the network, we normalized NIR images and normal maps to -1 and 1.

4.2 Training Parameters

We provide parameters used to train our proposed network. The configuration of the network is depicted in Table 1. Training used batches of size 32. For initializing weights, we assigned a Gaussian distribution with zero mean and a standard deviation of 0.02. We trained all experiments using the Adam optimizer [36] with momentum $\beta_1 = 0.5$. The learning rate started from 0.0002 and decreased by a factor of 0.95 every 5000 iterations. For balancing the scale of normalization, we set a hyperbolic tangent at the end of the generative network. Lastly, we used a 5×5 sliding window with 3 pixels overlap to compute the integrability. In the optimization procedure, we used a combined loss function including intensity(L_p), angular(L_{ang}), and integrability constraint(L_{curl}). Note that we did not tune the weighted parameters of each loss functions and set them with the same weights, $\lambda_p = \lambda_{ang} = \lambda_{curl} = 1$.

Table 1. Network configuration.

Layer	Number of filters	Filter size (w×h×ch)	Stride	Pad	Batch norm.	Activation function
Conv. 1	128	3×3×1	1	1	○	ReLU
Conv. 2	256	3×3×128	1	1	○	ReLU
Conv. 3	256	3×3×256	1	1	○	ReLU
Conv. 4	128	3×3×256	1	1	○	ReLU
Conv. 5	3	3×3×128	1	1	×	tanh

(a) Details of the Generative network.

Layer	Number of filters	Filter size (w×h×ch)	Stride	Pad	Batch norm.	Activation function
Conv. 1	64	3×3×3	2	0	×	L-ReLU
Conv. 2	128	3×3×64	2	0	○	L-ReLU
Conv. 3	256	3×3×128	2	0	○	L-ReLU
Conv. 4	512	3×3×256	2	0	○	L-ReLU
Conv. 5	256	1×1×512	1	0	×	sigmoid

(b) Details of the Discriminative network.

4.3   Experimental Result

We use Tensorflow[1] to implement and train the proposed network. The proposed network is a fully convolutional network, we apply the entire NIR image at evaluation. Computation time to estimate a surface normal is about 2 s with a Titan X, meanwhile the conventional shaped from shading method takes 10 min with Matlab implementation.

Quantitative Analysis. For the quantitative evaluation, firstly, we validate each terms of our cost functions. In this experiment, we tested our method using 3rd NIR direction among 12 lighting directions. To evaluate the performance of our method, we use three metrics; angular error, good pixel ratio and intensity error. In Table 2, all the quantitative errors are shown. Compared to case of using only intensity loss, when the angular cost function added, the performance is improved. This validates that our angular loss measures the physically meaningful error. The integrability term insures the continuity of the local normals. Although the integrability is satisfied for most of smooth surfaces, it does not guarantee performance improvement in some non-smooth surfaces. In our experiments, $L_2 + L_{ang}$ loss function shows the best performance for all views case, and $L_1 + L_{ang}$ achieves the lowest error for center view case. We compare our results with the conventional SfS method and we verified that our framework performs competitively. We also compare our method with the deep CNN-based surface normal estimation method [12]. Although this method estimates the surface normal, it is designed for reconstructing the scene-level low-frequency geometries and is not suitable for our purpose. We also measure errors for the

---

[1] https://www.tensorflow.org/.

Table 2. Quantitative evaluation. We validate each terms of our cost functions with various error measures.

View points	Methods	Angular error (°) (Lower Better)		Good pixels (%) (Higher Better)			Intensity error (Abs Error)	
		Mean	Median	10°	15°	20°	Mean	Median
All views	L_1	16.42	16.18	17.10	38.23	72.60	0.14	0.09
	L_2	16.72	16.68	17.49	36.13	69.80	0.14	0.10
	$L_1 + L_{ang}$	15.88	15.81	19.40	37.13	73.08	0.13	0.09
	$L_2 + L_{ang}$	**15.55**	**15.30**	**20.26**	**49.84**	**74.45**	0.13	0.08
	$L_1 + L_{ang} + L_{curl}$	16.27	15.89	17.90	38.34	73.70	0.13	0.09
	$L_2 + L_{ang} + L_{curl}$	16.20	15.54	18.65	41.77	73.04	0.13	0.09
Single view	L_1	10.02	9.19	58.17	82.82	93.47	0.08	0.05
	L_2	8.76	8.37	67.14	90.97	97.44	0.07	0.05
	$L_1 + L_{ang}$	**7.35**	6.74	77.07	**93.90**	**98.59**	0.06	0.04
	$L_2 + L_{ang}$	7.70	6.82	73.36	91.91	98.36	0.07	0.04
	$L_1 + L_{ang} + L_{curl}$	10.46	8.92	57.19	80.84	91.27	0.09	0.05
	$L_2 + L_{ang} + L_{curl}$	7.52	**6.43**	**77.28**	92.41	97.59	0.06	0.04
Single view	Eigen et al. [12]	77.87	80.78	0.48	0.96	1.52	0.61	0.75

Table 3. Quantitative evaluation on a detail map. In this evaluation, we subtract low-frequency geometry variations from the results to focus on fine-scale surface geometry.

View points	Methods	Angular error (°) (Lower Better)		Good pixels (%) (Higher Better)			Intensity error (Abs Error)	
		Mean	Median	10°	15°	20°	Mean	Median
All views	L_1	4.68	3.96	90.33	97.03	98.87	0.06	0.03
	L_2	**3.34**	2.88	96.57	99.40	99.80	0.05	0.02
	$L_1 + L_{ang}$	3.47	2.98	**96.73**	**99.42**	**99.81**	0.05	0.02
	$L_2 + L_{ang}$	3.61	2.99	95.98	99.09	99.61	0.06	0.02
	$L_1 + L_{ang} + L_{curl}$	3.95	3.39	94.30	98.83	99.66	0.06	0.02
	$L_2 + L_{ang} + L_{curl}$	3.83	**2.77**	95.56	98.25	98.86	0.06	0.02
Single view	L_1	4.53	3.70	90.13	96.32	98.43	0.07	0.03
	L_2	**2.91**	**2.35**	97.29	99.27	99.69	0.06	0.03
	$L_1 + L_{ang}$	3.06	2.57	**97.55**	**99.51**	**99.83**	0.05	0.02
	$L_2 + L_{ang}$	3.61	2.73	96.39	98.82	99.31	0.06	0.02
	$L_1 + L_{ang} + L_{curl}$	3.62	3.00	95.82	99.00	99.64	0.06	0.02
	$L_2 + L_{ang} + L_{curl}$	4.23	2.51	94.80	97.21	97.95	0.07	0.02
Single view	SfS	5.09	4.14	88.25	97.19	99.27	0.06	0.03

single view which provides the best performance. Since extreme viewing directions are saturated or under-exposed in some cases, measuring the error of the single view results in lower errors. We found that estimated normal maps are distorted in extreme view points (error in low-frequency geometry). To evaluate the fine-scale (high-frequency) geometry, we define a detail map (M) based on the measure in [37]. This measure is computed as: $M = f(Y) + G(Z) - f(G(Z))$, where function f is smoothing function. Table 3 shows the result.

Qualitative Analysis. Figures 4 and 5 show the qualitative results of our network. Our network is able to estimate fine-scale textures of objects. Comparing between L_2 and $L_2 + L_{ang}$, we figure out that the angular loss provides more fine-scale textures than intensity loss. By adding the integrability constraint, the result produces a smoother surface. This demonstrates, therefore, that our network is trained to follow physical properties relevant to SfS.

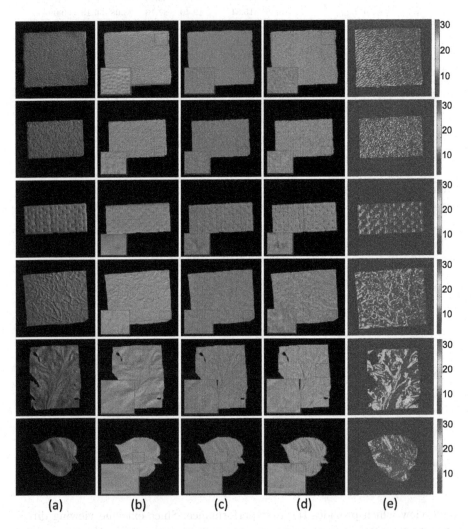

Fig. 4. Qualitative results of surface normal estimation using the proposed network. From left to right: (a) input NIR images, (b) ground-truth normal maps, (c) normal maps from L_2, (d) normal maps from $L_2 + L_{ang}$, (e) error maps of (d).

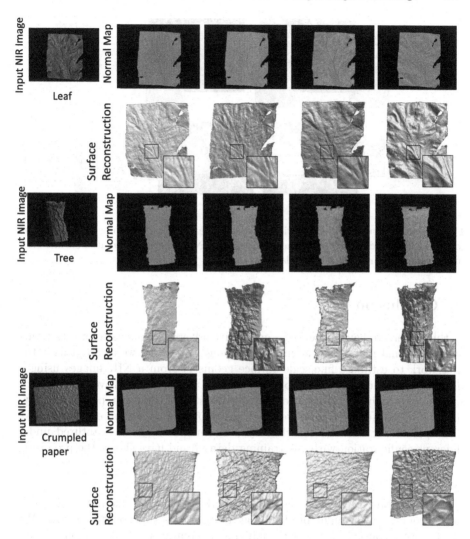

Fig. 5. Surface reconstruction results. From left to right: input, L_2, $L_2 + L_{ang}$, $L_2 + L_{ang} + L_{curl}$ and ground-truth. We compute a depth map from a surface normal map, then reconstruct a mesh. All three cases are visualized.

4.4 Shape Estimation at Arbitrary Lighting Direction

We evaluate our network for the surface estimation with an arbitrary lighting direction. Without prior knowledge of the lighting directions, SfS becomes a more challenging problem. As shown in Fig. 6, we captured several real-world objects. The glove has a complex surface geometry. Note that the bumpy surface and the stitches at the bottom are reconstructed. The cap has a 'C' letter on it and the geometry of this is reconstructed in mesh result.

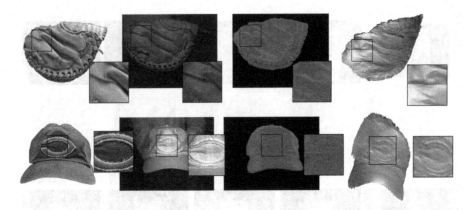

Fig. 6. Surface normal reconstruction results from an arbitrary lighting direction. From left to right, the columns show the RGB images, NIR images, estimated surface normals, and reconstructed 3D models.

5   Conclusion

In this paper, we have presented a generative adversarial network for estimating surface normal maps from a single NIR image. As far as we aware, this is the first work to estimate fine-scale surface geometry from a NIR images using a deep CNN framework. The proposed network shows competitive performance without any lighting information. We demonstrated that our photometically-inspired object function improves the quality of surface normal estimation. We also applied our network to arbitrary NIR images which are captured under different configuration with the training dataset and have shown the promising results.

Limitation and Future Work. In our work, we did not take inter-reflections into account, which might produce inaccurate normals at concave regions. We also observed convexity/concavity ambiguity at some examples analogous to conventional SfS methods. Further study should be conducted to resolve this problem. Our reconstruction might suffer from distortions of low-frequency geometry as stated in Sect. 4. This is because we have relatively small amount of training data and we restrict our goal as estimating fine-scale geometry to train our network without overfitting to the limited training data. Despite we aimed reconstructing fine-scale surface geometry, we believe this can be further combined with various scene-level depth estimation techniques. Moreover, our network can be extended to estimate a lighting direction as well as surface normals, which can be a strong prior for conventional SfS methods.

Acknowledgements. This research was supported by the Ministry of Trade, Industry & Energy and the Korea Evaluation Institute of Industrial Technology (KEIT) with the program number of 10060110.

References

1. Han, Y., Lee, J.Y., Kweon, I.: High quality shape from a single RGB-D image under uncalibrated natural illumination. In: Proceedings of the IEEE International Conference on Computer Vision, pp. 1617–1624 (2013)
2. Yu, L.F., Yeung, S.K., Tai, Y.W., Lin, S.: Shading-based shape refinement of RGB-D images. In: Proceedings of the IEEE International Conference on Computer Vision (2013)
3. Choe, G., Park, J., Tai, Y.W., Kweon, I.S.: Exploiting shading cues in Kinect IR images for geometry refinement. In: Proceedings of the IEEE Conference on Computer Vision and Pattern Recognition, pp. 3922–3929 (2014)
4. Haque, S., Chatterjee, A., Govindu, V.: High quality photometric reconstruction using a depth camera. In: Proceedings of the IEEE Conference on Computer Vision and Pattern Recognition, pp. 2275–2282 (2014)
5. He, K., Zhang, X., Ren, S., Sun, J.: Deep residual learning for image recognition (2015). arXiv:1512.03385
6. Krizhevsky, A., Sutskever, I., Hinton, G.E.: Imagenet classification with deep convolutional neural networks. In: Advances in Neural Information Processing Systems, pp. 1097–1105(2012)
7. Yoo, D., Park, S., Lee, J.Y., Paek, A.S., Kweon, I.S.: AttentionNet: aggregating weak directions for accurate object detection. In: Proceedings of the IEEE International Conference on Computer Vision, pp. 2659–2667 (2015)
8. Girshick, R., Donahue, J., Darrell, T., Malik, J.: Rich feature hierarchies for accurate object detection and semantic segmentation. In: Proceedings of the IEEE Conference on Computer Vision and Pattern Recognition, pp. 580–587 (2014)
9. Long, J., Shelhamer, E., Darrell, T.: Fully convolutional networks for semantic segmentation. In: Proceedings of the IEEE Conference on Computer Vision and Pattern Recognition, pp. 3431–3440 (2015)
10. Hong, S., Noh, H., Han, B.: Decoupled deep neural network for semi-supervised semantic segmentation. In: Advances in Neural Information Processing Systems, pp. 1495–1503 (2015)
11. Li, B., Shen, C., Dai, Y., van den Hengel, A., He, M.: Depth and surface normal estimation from monocular images using regression on deep features and hierarchical CRFS. In: Proceedings of the IEEE Conference on Computer Vision and Pattern Recognition, pp. 1119–1127 (2015)
12. Eigen, D., Fergus, R.: Predicting depth, surface normals and semantic labels with a common multi-scale convolutional architecture. In: Proceedings of the IEEE International Conference on Computer Vision, pp. 2650–2658 (2015)
13. Wang, X., Fouhey, D., Gupta, A.: Designing deep networks for surface normal estimation. In: Proceedings of the IEEE Conference on Computer Vision and Pattern Recognition, pp. 539–547 (2015)
14. Choe, G., Narasimhan, S.G., Kweon, I.S.: Simultaneous estimation of near IR BRDF and fine-scale surface geometry. In: Proceedings of the IEEE Conference on Computer Vision and Pattern Recognition (2016)
15. Woodham, R.J.: Photometric method for determining surface orientation from multiple images. Opt. Eng. **19**(1), 191139–191139 (1980)
16. Zheng, Q., Chellappa, R.: Estimation of illuminant direction, albedo, and shape from shading. In: Proceedings of the IEEE Computer Society Conference on Computer Vision and Pattern Recognition, CVPR 1991, 540–545. IEEE (1991)

17. Barron, J.T., Malik, J.: Shape, albedo, and illumination from a single image of an unknown object. In: 2012 IEEE Conference on Computer Vision and Pattern Recognition (CVPR), pp. 334–341. IEEE (2012)

18. Ikeuchi, K., Horn, B.K.: Numerical shape from shading and occluding boundaries. Artif. Intell. **17**(1–3), 141–184 (1981)

19. Ping-Sing, T., Shah, M.: Shape from shading using linear approximation. Image Vis. Comput. **12**(8), 487–498 (1994)

20. Lee, K.M., Kuo, C.: Shape from shading with a linear triangular element surface model. IEEE Trans. Pattern Anal. Mach. Intell. **15**(8), 815–822 (1993)

21. Zhang, R., Tsai, P.S., Cryer, J.E., Shah, M.: Shape-from-shading: a survey. IEEE Trans. Pattern Anal. Mach. Intell. **21**(8), 690–706 (1999)

22. Goodfellow, I., Pouget-Abadie, J., Mirza, M., Xu, B., Warde-Farley, D., Ozair, S., Courville, A., Bengio, Y.: Generative adversarial nets. In: Advances in Neural Information Processing Systems, pp. 2672–2680 (2014)

23. Saxena, A., Chung, S.H., Ng, A.Y.: Learning depth from single monocular images. In: Advances in Neural Information Processing Systems, pp. 1161–1168 (2005)

24. Hoiem, D., Efros, A.A., Hebert, M.: Automatic photo pop-up. ACM Trans. Graph. (TOG) **24**(3), 577–584 (2005)

25. Ladicky, L., Shi, J., Pollefeys, M.: Pulling things out of perspective. In: Proceedings of the IEEE Conference on Computer Vision and Pattern Recognition, pp. 89–96 (2014)

26. Fouhey, D., Gupta, A., Hebert, M.: Data-driven 3D primitives for single image understanding. In: Proceedings of the IEEE International Conference on Computer Vision, pp. 3392–3399 (2013)

27. Rematas, K., Ritschel, T., Fritz, M., Gavves, E., Tuytelaars, T.: Deep reflectance maps (2015). arXiv:1511.04384

28. Liu, F., Shen, C., Lin, G.: Deep convolutional neural fields for depth estimation from a single image. In: Proceedings of the IEEE Conference on Computer Vision and Pattern Recognition, pp. 5162–5170 (2015)

29. Eigen, D., Puhrsch, C., Fergus, R.: Depth map prediction from a single image using a multi-scale deep network. In: Advances in Neural Information Processing Systems, pp. 2366–2374 (2014)

30. Radford, A., Luke Metz, S.C.: Unsupervised representation learning with deep convolutional generative adversarial networks (2015). arXiv:1511.06434

31. Mathieu, M., Camille Couprie, Y.L.: Deep multi-scale video prediction beyond mean square error (2015). arXiv:1511.05440

32. Denton, E.L., Chintala, S., Fergus, R., et al.: Deep generative image models using a laplacian pyramid of adversarial networks. In: Advances in Neural Information Processing Systems, pp. 1486–1494 (2015)

33. Kim, J., Lee, J.K., Lee, K.M.: Accurate image super-resolution using very deep convolutional networks. (2015). arXiv:1511.04587

34. Dong, C., Loy, C.C., He, K., Tang, X.: Image super-resolution using deep convolutional networks (2015)

35. Flynn, J., Ivan Neulander, J.: Deepstereo: learning to predict new views from the world imagery. (2015). arXiv:1506.06825

36. Kingma, D., Ba, J.: Adam: a method for stochastic optimization (2014). arXiv:1412.6980

37. Nehab, D., Rusinkiewicz, S., Davis, J., Ramamoorthi, R.: Efficiently combining positions and normals for precise 3D geometry. ACM Trans. Graph. (TOG) **24**(3), 536–543 (2005)

Pixelwise View Selection for Unstructured Multi-View Stereo

Johannes L. Schönberger[1]([⊠]), Enliang Zheng[2], Jan-Michael Frahm[2], and Marc Pollefeys[1,3]

[1] ETH Zürich, Zürich, Switzerland
{jsch,pomarc}@inf.ethz.ch
[2] UNC Chapel Hill, Chapel Hill, USA
{ezheng,jmf}@cs.unc.edu
[3] Microsoft, Redmond, USA

Abstract. This work presents a Multi-View Stereo system for robust and efficient dense modeling from unstructured image collections. Our core contributions are the joint estimation of depth and normal information, pixelwise view selection using photometric and geometric priors, and a multi-view geometric consistency term for the simultaneous refinement and image-based depth and normal fusion. Experiments on benchmarks and large-scale Internet photo collections demonstrate state-of-the-art performance in terms of accuracy, completeness, and efficiency.

1 Introduction

Large-scale 3D reconstruction from Internet photos has seen a tremendous evolution in sparse modeling using Structure-from-Motion (SfM) [1–8] and in dense modeling using Multi-View Stereo (MVS) [9–15]. Many applications benefit from a dense scene representation, *e.g.*,, classification [16], image-based rendering [17], localization [18], *etc.* Despite the widespread use of MVS, the efficient and robust estimation of accurate, complete, and aesthetically pleasing dense models in uncontrolled environments remains a challenging task. Dense pixelwise correspondence search is the core problem of stereo methods. Recovering correct correspondence is challenging even in controlled environments with known viewing geometry and illumination. In uncontrolled settings, *e.g.*,, where the input consists of crowd-sourced images, it is crucial to account for various factors, such as heterogeneous resolution and illumination, scene variability, unstructured viewing geometry, and mis-registered views.

Our proposed approach improves the state of the art in dense reconstruction for unstructured images. This work leverages the optimization framework by Zheng *et al.* [14] to propose the following core contributions: (1) Pixelwise

Electronic supplementary material The online version of this chapter (doi:10.1007/978-3-319-46487-9_31) contains supplementary material, which is available to authorized users.

© Springer International Publishing AG 2016
B. Leibe et al. (Eds.): ECCV 2016, Part III, LNCS 9907, pp. 501–518, 2016.
DOI: 10.1007/978-3-319-46487-9_31

Fig. 1. Reconstructions for Louvre, Todai-ji, Paris Opera, and Astronomical Clock.

normal estimation embedded into an improved PatchMatch sampling scheme. (2) Pixelwise view selection using triangulation angle, incident angle, and image resolution-based *geometric priors*. (3) Integration of a "temporal" *view selection smoothness* term. (4) Adaptive window support through bilateral *photometric consistency* for improved occlusion boundary behavior. (5) Introduction of a multi-view *geometric consistency* term for simultaneous depth/normal estimation and image-based fusion. (6) Reliable depth/normal *filtering* and *fusion*. Outlier-free and accurate depth/normal estimates further allow for direct meshing of the resulting point cloud. We achieve state-of-the-art results on benchmarks (Middlebury [19], Strecha [20]). To demonstrate the advantages of our method in a more challenging setting, we process SfM models of a world-scale Internet dataset [5]. The entire algorithm is released to the public as an open-source implementation as part of [8] at https://github.com/colmap/colmap.

2   Related Work

Stereo methods have advanced in terms of accuracy, completeness, scalability, and benchmarking – from the minimal stereo setup with two views [21–24] to multi-view methods [9,10,14,15,25–28]. Furthermore, the joint estimation of semantics [29], dynamic scene reconstruction [30–34], and benchmarking [12,19,20,23]. Our method performs MVS with pixelwise view selection for depth/normal estimation and fusion. Here, we only review the most related approaches, within the large body of research in multi-view and two-view stereo.

MVS leverages multiple views to overcome the inherent occlusion problems of two-view approaches [35–37]. Accordingly, view selection plays a crucial role in the effectiveness of MVS. Kang *et al.* [38] heuristically select the best views with minimal cost (usually 50 %) for computing the depth of each pixel. Strecha *et al.* [39,40] probabilistically model scene visibility combined with a local depth smoothness assumption [39] in a Markov Random Field for pixelwise view selection. Different from our approach, their method is prohibitive in memory usage and does neither include normal estimation nor photometric and geometric priors for view selection. Gallup *et al.* [41] select different views and resolutions on a per-pixel basis to achieve a constant depth error. In contrast, our method simultaneously considers a variety of photometric and geometric priors improving upon the robustness and accuracy of the recently proposed depth estimation framework by Zheng *et al.* [14]. Their method is most closely related to our approach and is reviewed in more detail in Sect. 3.

MVS methods commonly use a fronto-parallel scene structure assumption. Gallup *et al.* [42] observed the distortion of the cost function caused by structure that deviates from this prior and combats it by using multiple sweeping directions deduced from the sparse reconstruction. Earlier approaches [43–45] similarly account for the surface normal in stereo matching. Recently, Bleyer *et al.* [46] use PatchMatch to estimate per-pixel normals to compensate for the distortion of the cost function. In contrast to these approaches, we propose to estimate normals not in isolation but also considering the photometric and geometric constraints guiding the matchabilty of surface texture and its accuracy. By probabilistically modeling the contribution of individual viewing rays towards reliable surface recovery, we achieve significantly improved depth and normal estimates.

Depth map fusion integrates multiple depth maps into a unified and augmented scene representation while mitigating any inconsistencies among individual estimates. Jancoseck and Pajdla [28] fuses multiple depth estimates into a surface and, by evaluating visibility in 3D space, they also attempt to reconstruct parts that are not directly supported by depth measurements. In contrast, our method aims at directly maximizing the estimated surface support in the depth maps and achieves higher completeness and accuracy (see Sect. 5). Goesele *et al.* [47] propose a method that explicitly targets at the reconstruction from crowd-sourced images. They first select camera clusters for each surface and adjust their resolution to the smallest common resolution. For depth estimation, they then use the four most suitable images for each pixel. As already noted in Zheng *et al.* [14], this early pre-selection of reduced camera clusters may lead to less complete results and is sensitive to noise. Our method avoids this restrictive selection scheme by allowing dataset-wide, pixelwise sampling for view selection. Zach [48] proposed a variational depth map formulation that enabled parallelized computation on the GPU. However, their volumetric approach imposes substantial memory requirements and is prohibitive for the large-scale scenes targeted by our method. Beyond these methods, there are several large-scale dense reconstruction and fusion methods for crowd-sourced images, *e.g.,*, Furukawa *et al.* [10] and Gallup *et al.* [49,50], who all perform heuristic pre-selection of views, which leads to reduced completeness and accuracy as compared to our method.

3   Review of Joint View Selection and Depth Estimation

This section reviews the framework by Zheng *et al.* [14] to introduce notation and context for our contributions. Since their method processes each row/column independently, we limit the description to a single image row with l as the column index. Their method estimates the depth θ_l for a pixel in the reference image X^{ref} from a set of unstructured source images $\boldsymbol{X}^{\mathrm{src}} = \{X^m \mid m = 1 \ldots M\}$. The estimate θ_l maximizes the color similarity between a patch X_l^{ref} in the reference image and homography-warped patches X_l^m in non-occluded source images. The binary indicator variable $Z_l^m \in \{0,1\}$ defines the set of non-occluded source images as $\bar{\boldsymbol{X}}_l^{\mathrm{src}} = \{X^m \mid Z_l^m = 1\}$. To sample $\bar{\boldsymbol{X}}_l^{\mathrm{src}}$, they infer the probability that the reference patch X_l^{ref} at depth θ_l is visible at the source patch X_l^m using

$$P(X_l^m|Z_l^m, \theta_l) = \begin{cases} \frac{1}{NA} \exp\left(-\frac{(1-\rho_l^m(\theta_l))^2}{2\sigma_\rho^2}\right) & \text{if } Z_l^m = 1 \\ \frac{1}{N}\mathcal{U} & \text{if } Z_l^m = 0, \end{cases} \tag{1}$$

where $A = \int_{-1}^{1} exp\{-\frac{(1-\rho)^2}{2\sigma_\rho^2}\} d\rho$ and N is a constant canceling out in the inference. In the case of occlusion, the color distributions of the two patches are unrelated and follow the uniform distribution $\mathcal{U}$ in the range $[-1, 1]$ with probability density 0.5. Otherwise, ρ_l^m describes the color similarity between the reference and source patch based on normalized cross-correlation (NCC) using fronto-parallel homography warping. The variable σ_ρ determines a soft threshold for ρ_l^m on the reference patch being visible in the source image. The state-transition matrix from the preceding pixel $l - 1$ to the current pixel l is $P(Z_l^m|Z_{l-1}^m) = \begin{pmatrix} \gamma & 1-\gamma \\ 1-\gamma & \gamma \end{pmatrix}$ and encourages spatially smooth occlusion indicators, where a larger γ enforces neighboring pixels to have more similar indicators. Given reference and source images $\boldsymbol{X} = \{X^{\text{ref}}, X^{\text{src}}\}$, the inference problem then boils down to recover, for all L pixels in the reference image, the depths $\boldsymbol{\theta} = \{\theta_l \mid l = 1 \ldots L\}$ and the occlusion indicators $\boldsymbol{Z} = \{Z_l^m \mid l = 1 \ldots L, m = 1 \ldots M\}$ from the posterior distribution $P(\boldsymbol{Z}, \boldsymbol{\theta}|\boldsymbol{X})$ with a uniform prior $P(\boldsymbol{\theta})$. To solve the computationally infeasible Bayesian approach of first computing the joint probability

$$P(\boldsymbol{X}, \boldsymbol{Z}, \boldsymbol{\theta}) = \prod_{l=1}^{L} \prod_{m=1}^{M} [P(Z_l^m|Z_{l-1}^m) P(X_l^m|Z_l^m, \theta_l)] \tag{2}$$

and then normalizing over $P(\boldsymbol{X})$, Zheng et al. use variational inference theory to develop a framework that is a variant of the generalized expectation-maximization (GEM) algorithm [51]. For the inference of $\boldsymbol{Z}$ in the hidden Markov-Chain, the forward-backward algorithm is used in the E step of GEM. PatchMatch-inspired [46] sampling serves as an efficient scheme for the inference of $\boldsymbol{\theta}$ in the M step of GEM. Their method iteratively solves for $\boldsymbol{Z}$ with fixed $\boldsymbol{\theta}$ and *vice versa* using interleaved row-/columnwise propagation. Full depth inference

$$\theta_l^{\text{opt}} = \underset{\theta_l^*}{\arg\min} \sum_{m=1}^{M} P_l(m)(1 - \rho_l^m(\theta_l^*)) \tag{3}$$

has high computational cost if M is large as PatchMatch requires the NCC to be computed many times. The value $P_l(m) = \frac{q(Z_l^m=1)}{\sum_{m=1}^{M} q(Z_l^m=1)}$ denotes the probability of the patch in source image m being similar to the reference patch, while $q(\boldsymbol{Z})$ is an approximation of the real posterior $P(\boldsymbol{Z})$. Source images with small $P_l(m)$ are non-informative for the depth inference, hence Zheng et al. propose a Monte Carlo based approximation of θ_l^{opt} for view selection

$$\hat{\theta}_l^{\text{opt}} = \underset{\theta_l^*}{\arg\min} \frac{1}{|S|} \sum_{m \in S} (1 - \rho_l^m(\theta_l^*)) \tag{4}$$

by sampling a subset of images $S \subset \{1 \ldots M\}$ from the distribution $P_l(m)$ and hence only computing the NCC for the most similar source images.

4   Algorithm

In this section, we describe our novel algorithm that leverages the optimization framework reviewed in the previous section. We first present the individual terms of the proposed likelihood function, while Sect. 4.6 explains their integration into the overall optimization framework.

4.1   Normal Estimation

Zheng *et al.* [14] map between the reference and source images using fronto-parallel homographies leading to artifacts for oblique structures [42]. In contrast, we estimate per-pixel depth θ_l and normals $n_l \in \mathbb{R}^3, \|n_l\| = 1$. A patch at $x_l \in \mathbb{P}^2$ in the reference image warps to a source patch at $x_l^m \in \mathbb{P}^2$ using $x_l^m = H_l x_l$ with $H_l = K^m(R^m - d_l^{-1}t^m n_l^T)K^{-1}$. Here, $R^m \in SO(3)$ and $t^m \in \mathbb{R}^3$ define the relative transformation from the reference to the source camera frame. K and K^m denote the calibration of the reference and source images, respectively, and $d_l = n_l^T p_l$ is the orthogonal distance from the reference image to the plane at the point $p_l = \theta_l K^{-1} x_l$.

Given no knowledge of the scene, we assume a uniform prior $P(N)$ in the inference of the normals $N = \{n_l \mid l = 1 \dots L\}$. Estimating N requires to change the terms $P(X_l^m | Z_l^m, \theta_l)$ and $P_l(m)$ from Eqs. (1) and (4) to also depend on N, as the color similarity ρ_l^m is now based on slanted rather than fronto-parallel homographies. Consequently, the optimal depth and normal are chosen as

$$(\hat{\theta}_l^{\text{opt}}, \hat{n}_l^{\text{opt}}) = \underset{\theta_l^*, n_l^*}{\operatorname{argmin}} \frac{1}{|S|} \sum_{m \in S} (1 - \rho_l^m(\theta_l^*, n_l^*)). \tag{5}$$

To sample unbiased random normals in PatchMatch, we follow the approach by Galliani *et al.* [15]. With the additional two unknown normal parameters, the number of unknowns per pixel in the M step of GEM increases from one to three. While this in theory requires PatchMatch to generate many more samples, we propose an efficient propagation scheme that maintains the convergence rate of depth-only inference. Since depth θ_l and normal n_l define a local planar surface in 3D, we propagate the depth $\theta_{l-1}^{\text{prp}}$ of the intersection of the ray of the current pixel x_l with the local surface of the previous pixel (θ_{l-1}, n_{l-1}). This exploits first-order smoothness of the surface (*cf.* [52]) and thereby drastically speeds up the optimization since correct depths propagate more quickly along the surface. Moreover, different from the typical iterative refinement of normals using bisection as an intermediate step between full sweeps of propagations (*cf.* [15,46]), we generate a small set of additional plane hypotheses at each propagation step. We observe that the current best depth and normal parameters can have the following states: neither of them, one of them, or both of them have the optimal solution or are close to it. By combining random and perturbed depths with current best normals and vice versa, we increase the chance of sampling the correct solution. More formally, at each step in PatchMatch, we choose the current best estimate for pixel l according to Eq. (4) from the set of hypotheses

$$\{(\theta_l, \boldsymbol{n}_l), (\theta_{l-1}^{\mathrm{prp}}, \boldsymbol{n}_{l-1}), (\theta_l^{\mathrm{rnd}}, \boldsymbol{n}_l), (\theta_l, \boldsymbol{n}_l^{\mathrm{rnd}}), (\theta_l^{\mathrm{rnd}}, \boldsymbol{n}_l^{\mathrm{rnd}}), (\theta_l^{\mathrm{prt}}, \boldsymbol{n}_l), (\theta_l, \boldsymbol{n}_l^{\mathrm{prt}})\}, \tag{6}$$

where θ_l^{rnd} and $\boldsymbol{n}_l^{\mathrm{rnd}}$ denote randomly generated samples. To refine the current parameters when they are close to the optimal solution, we perturb the current estimate as $\theta_l^{\mathrm{prt}} = (1 \pm \epsilon)\theta_l$ and $\boldsymbol{n}_l^{\mathrm{prt}} = \boldsymbol{R}_\epsilon \boldsymbol{n}_l$. The variable ϵ describes a small depth perturbation, and the rotation matrix $\boldsymbol{R}_\epsilon \in SO(3)$ perturbs the normal direction by a small angle subject to $\boldsymbol{p}_l^T \boldsymbol{n}_l^{\mathrm{prt}} < 0$. Normal estimation improves both the reconstruction completeness and accuracy, while the new sampling scheme leads to both fast convergence and more accurate estimates (Sect. 5).

4.2   Geometric Priors for View Selection

This section describes how to incorporate geometric priors in the pixelwise view selection for improved robustness in particular for unstructured imagery. On a high level, the proposed priors encourage the sampling of source images with sufficient baseline (*Triangulation Prior*), similar resolution (*Resolution Prior*), and non-oblique viewing direction (*Incident Prior*). In contrast to prior work (*e.g.*, [10,47,49]), which decouples inference and per-image geometric priors by pre-selecting source images, we integrate geometric priors on a per-pixel basis into the inference. The motivation for per-pixel geometric priors is similar to inferring per-pixel occlusion indicators $\boldsymbol{Z}$. Since the pre-selection of source images is based on a sparse and therefore incomplete scene representation, the selected source views are often sub-optimal. Occlusion boundaries, triangulation angles, relative image resolution, and incident angle can vary significantly between a single pair of reference and source images (Fig. 2). Incorporating geometric priors in addition to the photometric occlusion indicators $\boldsymbol{Z}$ leads to a more comprehensive and robust pixelwise view selection. In the following, we detail the proposed priors and explain their integration into the optimization framework.

Triangulation Prior. Zheng *et al.* [14] sample source images purely based on color similarity. Consequently, the more similar the reference patch is to the source patch, the higher the selection probability in the view sampling. Naturally, image pairs with small viewpoint change, which coincides with small baseline, have high color similarity. However, image pairs with zero baseline

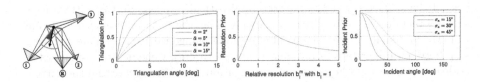

Fig. 2. Left: Illustration of geometric priors for reference view (R) and three source views (1–3). View 1 has similar resolution (red), and good triangulation (green) and incident angle (blue), while view 2 is oblique and has lower resolution. View 3 cannot see the patch. Right: Geometric prior likelihood functions with different parameters. (Color figure online)

do not carry information for depth inference, because reconstructed points can arbitrarily move along the viewing ray without changing the color similarity. Pure photometric view selection favors to sample these uninformative views. To eliminate this degenerate case, we calculate the triangulation angle $\alpha_l^m = \cos^{-1} \frac{(\boldsymbol{p}_l - \boldsymbol{c}^m)^T \boldsymbol{p}_l}{\|\boldsymbol{p}_l - \boldsymbol{c}^m\| \|\boldsymbol{p}_l\|}$ with $\boldsymbol{c}^m = -(\boldsymbol{R}^m)^T \boldsymbol{t}^m$ and $\alpha_l^m \in [0, \pi)$ between two intersecting viewing rays as a measure of the stability of the reconstructed point $\boldsymbol{p}_l$. Empirically, we choose the following likelihood function $P(\alpha_l^m) = 1 - \frac{(\min(\bar{\alpha}, \alpha_l^m) - \bar{\alpha})^2}{\bar{\alpha}^2}$ to describe how informative a source image is for reconstructing the correct point. Intuitively, this function assigns low likelihood to source images for which the triangulation angle is below an *a priori* threshold $\bar{\alpha}$. Otherwise, no additional view selection preference is imposed (see Fig. 2).

Resolution Prior. Unstructured datasets usually contain images captured by a multitude of camera types under diverse viewing geometry. As a consequence, images capture scene objects in a wide range of resolutions. To avoid under- and oversampling in computing ρ_l^m, the patches in the reference and source image should have similar size and shape [47]. Similar size is favorable as it avoids comparing images captured at vastly different resolutions, *e.g.*,, due to different zoom factors or distance to the object. Similar shape avoids significantly distorted source patches caused by different viewing directions. In the case of different shape, areas within the same source patch have different sampling rates. An approximate measure of the relative size and shape between the reference and source patch is $\beta_l^m = \frac{b_l}{b_l^m} \in \mathbb{R}^+$, where b_l and b_l^m denote the areas covered by the corresponding patches. In our implementation, the reference patch is always square. If the size and shape of the patches is similar, β_l^m is close to the value 1. To quantify the similarity in resolution between two images, we propose the likelihood function $P(\beta_l^m) = \min(\beta_l^m, (\beta_l^m)^{-1})$ and integrate it into $P_l(m)$. Note that, at increased computational cost, undersampling could alternatively be handled by adaptive resampling of the source image patch.

Incident Prior. The inferred per-pixel normals provide geometric constraints on the solution space that we encode in the form of a prior. The estimated plane restricts the possible space of source camera locations and orientations. By construction, the camera location can only lie in the positive half-space defined by the plane $(\theta_l, \boldsymbol{n}_l^m)$, while the camera viewing direction must face towards the opposite normal direction. Otherwise, it is geometrically impossible for the camera to observe the surface. To satisfy this geometric visibility constraint, the incident angle of the source camera $\kappa_l^m = \cos^{-1} \frac{(\boldsymbol{p}_l - \boldsymbol{c}^m)^T \boldsymbol{n}_l^m}{\|\boldsymbol{p}_l - \boldsymbol{c}^m\| \|\boldsymbol{n}_l^m\|}$ with $\kappa_l^m \in [0, \pi)$ must be in the interval $0 \le \kappa_l^m < \frac{\pi}{2}$. In our method, the likelihood function $P(\kappa_l^m) = \exp(-\frac{\kappa_l^{m2}}{2\sigma_\kappa^2})$ encodes the belief in whether this geometric constraint is satisfied. This associates some belief with a view even in the case where $\kappa_l^m \ge \frac{\pi}{2}$. The reason for this is, that in the initial inference stage, the variables θ_l and $\boldsymbol{n}_l^m$ are unknown and hence the geometric constraints are likely not yet correct.

Integration. Figure 2 visualizes the geometric priors, and Fig. 4 shows examples of specific priors over all reference image pixels. We integrate the priors into the inference as additional terms in the Monte-Carlo view sampling distribution

$$P_l(m) = \frac{q(Z_l^m = 1)q(\alpha_l^m)q(\beta_l^m)q(\kappa_l^m)}{\sum_{m=1}^{M} q(Z_l^m = 1)q(\alpha_l^m)q(\beta_l^m)q(\kappa_l^m)}, \tag{7}$$

where $q(\alpha_l^m), q(\beta_l^m), q(\kappa_l^m)$ are approximations during the variational inference, in the sense that they minimize the KL-divergence to the real posterior [53]. The distributions need no normalization in the inference because we solely use them as modulators for the sampling distribution $P_l(m)$. This formulation assumes statistical independence of the individual priors as a simplifying approximation, which makes the optimization feasible using relatively simple models for well-understood geometric relations. Intuitively, non-occluded images with sufficient baseline, similar resolution, and non-oblique viewing direction are favored in the view selection. Section 5 evaluates the priors in detail and shows how they improve the reconstruction robustness especially for unstructured datasets.

4.3   View Selection Smoothness

The graphical model associated with the likelihood function in Eq. (2) uses state-transition probabilities to model spatial view selection smoothness for neighboring pixels in the propagation direction. Due to the interleaved inference using alternating propagation directions, Z_l^m suffers from oscillation, leading to striping effects as shown in Fig. 5. To reduce the oscillation effect of $Z_{l,t}^m$ in iteration t, we insert an additional "temporal" smoothness factor into the graphical model. In this new model, the state of $Z_{l,t}^m$ depends not only on the state of its neighboring pixel $l-1$ but also on its own state in the previous iteration $t-1$. The temporal state-transition is defined as $P(Z_{l,t}^m | Z_{l,t-1}^m) = \begin{pmatrix} \lambda_t & 1-\lambda_t \\ 1-\lambda_t & \lambda_t \end{pmatrix}$, where a larger λ_t enforces greater temporal smoothness during the optimization. In fact, as the optimization progresses from $t = 1 \ldots T$, the value of the estimated Z_{t-1}^m should stabilize around the optimal solution. Therefore, we adaptively increase the state-transition probability as $\lambda_t = \frac{t}{2T} + 0.5$, $i.e.$,, the inferred $Z_{l,t}^m$ in iterations $t = 1$ and $t = T-1$ have maximal and minimal influence on the final value $Z_{l,T}^m$, respectively. The two state-transitions are jointly modeled as

$$P(Z_{l,t}^m | Z_{l-1,t}^m, Z_{l,t-1}^m) = P(Z_{l,t}^m | Z_{l-1,t}^m)P(Z_{l,t}^m | Z_{l,t-1}^m). \tag{8}$$

Figure 5 shows the evolution of $Z_{l,t}^m$ during the optimization and demonstrates the reduced oscillation, which effectively also leads to less noisy view sampling.

4.4   Photometric Consistency

Zheng et $al.$ [14] employ NCC to compute the color similarity ρ_l^m. NCC is statistically optimal for Gaussian noise but is especially vulnerable to producing blurred depth discontinuities [54]. Inspired by [46,55], we diminish these artifacts by using a bilaterally weighted adaption of NCC. We compute ρ_l^m between a reference patch $\boldsymbol{w}_l$ at $\boldsymbol{x}_l$ with a corresponding source patch $\boldsymbol{w}_l^m$ at $\boldsymbol{x}_l^m$ as

$$\rho_l^m = \frac{\mathrm{cov}_w(\boldsymbol{w}_l, \boldsymbol{w}_l^m)}{\sqrt{\mathrm{cov}_w(\boldsymbol{w}_l, \boldsymbol{w}_l) \, \mathrm{cov}_w(\boldsymbol{w}_l^m, \boldsymbol{w}_l^m)}} \tag{9}$$

where $\text{cov}_w(\boldsymbol{x}, \boldsymbol{y}) = E_w(\boldsymbol{x} - E_w(\boldsymbol{x})) \, E_w(\boldsymbol{y} - E_w(\boldsymbol{y}))$ is the weighted covariance and $E_w(\boldsymbol{x}) = \sum_i w_i x_i / \sum_i w_i$ is the weighted average. The per-pixel weight $w_i = \exp(-\frac{\Delta g_i}{2\sigma_g^2} - \frac{\Delta x_i}{2\sigma_x^2})$ indicates the likelihood that a pixel i in the local patch belongs to the same plane as its center pixel at l. It is a function of the grayscale color distance $\Delta g_i = |g_i - g_l|$ and the spatial distance $\Delta x_i = \|x_i - x_l\|$, whose importance is relatively scaled by the Gaussian dispersion σ_g and σ_x. By integrating the bilaterally weighted NCC into the term $P(X_l^m | Z_l^m, \theta_l, \boldsymbol{n}_l)$, our method achieves more accurate results at occlusion boundaries, as shown in Sect. 5.

4.5 Geometric Consistency

MVS typically suffers from gross outliers due to noise, ambiguities, occlusions, *etc.* In these cases, the photometric consistency for different hypotheses is ambiguous as large depth variations induce only small cost changes. Spatial smoothness constraints can often reduce but not fully eliminate the resulting artifacts. A popular approach to filter these outliers is to enforce multi-view depth coherence through left-right consistency checks as a post-processing step [15,46].

In contrast to most approaches, we integrate multi-view geometric consistency constraints into the inference to increase both the completeness and the accuracy. Similar to Zhang *et al.* [56], we infer the best depth and normal based on both photometric and geometric consistency in multiple views. Since photometric ambiguities are usually unique to individual views (except textureless surfaces), exploiting the information from multiple views can often help to pinpoint the right solution. We compute the geometric consistency between two views as the forward-backward reprojection error $\psi_l^m = \|x_l - H_l^m H_l x_l\|$, where H_l^m denotes the projective backward transformation from the source to the reference image. It is composed from the source image estimates $(\theta_l^m, \boldsymbol{n}_l^m)$ interpolated at the forward projection $x_l^m = H_l x_l$. Intuitively, the estimated depths and normals are consistent if the reprojection error ψ_l^m is small. Due to computational constraints, we cannot consider the occlusion indicators in the source image for the backward projection. Hence, to handle occlusion in the source image, we employ a robustified geometric cost in $\xi_l^m = 1 - \rho_l^m + \eta \min(\psi_l^m, \psi_{\max})$ using $\eta = 0.5$ as a constant regularizer and $\psi_{\max} = 3\text{px}$ as the maximum forward-backward reprojection error. Then, the optimal depth and normal is chosen as

$$(\hat{\theta}_l^{\text{opt}}, \hat{\boldsymbol{n}}_l^{\text{opt}}) = \underset{\theta_l^*, \boldsymbol{n}_l^*}{\text{argmin}} \frac{1}{|S|} \sum_{m \in S} \xi_l^m(\theta_l^*, \boldsymbol{n}_l^*). \tag{10}$$

The geometric consistency term is modeled as $P(\theta_l, \boldsymbol{n}_l | \theta_l^m, \boldsymbol{n}_l^m)$ in the likelihood function, and Sect. 4.6 shows how to integrate its inference into the overall optimization framework. Experiments in Sect. 5 demonstrate how this formulation improves both the accuracy and the completeness of the results.

4.6 Integration

This section contextualizes the individual terms of the proposed algorithm by explaining their integration into the overall optimization framework [14]. The joint likelihood function $P(X, Z, \theta, N)$ of our proposed algorithm is defined as

$$\prod_{l=1}^{L} \prod_{m=1}^{M} [P(Z_{l,t}^m | Z_{l-1,t}^m, Z_{l,t-1}^m) P(X_l^m | Z_l^m, \theta_l, n_l) P(\theta_l, n_l | \theta_l^m, n_l^m)]$$

over the input images X, the occlusion indicators Z, the depths θ, the normals N, and is composed of several individual terms. First, the spatial and temporal smoothness term $P(Z_{l,t}^m | Z_{l-1,t}^m, Z_{l,t-1}^m)$ (Sect. 4.3) enforces spatially smooth occlusion maps with reduced temporal oscillation during the optimization. Second, the photometric consistency term $P(X_l^m | Z_l^m, \theta_l, n_l)$ uses bilateral NCC (Sect. 4.4) and a slanted plane-induced homography (Sect. 4.1) to compute the color similarity ρ_l^m between the reference and source images. Third, the geometric consistency term $P(\theta_l, n_l | \theta_l^m, n_l^m)$ to enforce multi-view consistent depth and normal estimates. The photometric and geometric consistency terms are computed using Monte-Carlo view sampling from the distribution $P_l(m)$ in Eq. (7). The distribution encourages the sampling of non-occluded source images with informative and non-degenerate viewing geometry (Sect. 4.2).

Analog to Zheng *et al.* [14], we factorize the real posterior $P(Z, \theta, N | X)$ in its approximation $q(Z, \theta, N) = q(Z)q(\theta, N)$ [53]. Furthermore, for tractability, we constrain $q(\theta, N)$ to the family of Kronecker delta functions $q(\theta_l, n_l) = \delta(\theta_l = \theta_l^*, n_l = n_l^*)$. Variational inference then aims to infer the optimal member of the family of approximate posteriors to find the optimal Z, θ, N. The validity of using GEM for this type of problem has already been shown in [14,51]. To infer $q(Z_{l,t}^m)$ in iteration t of the E step of GEM, we employ the forward-backward algorithm as

$$q(Z_{l,t}^m) = \frac{1}{A} \overrightarrow{m}(Z_{l,t}^m) \overleftarrow{m}(Z_{l,t}^m) \tag{11}$$

with $\overrightarrow{m}(Z_{l,t}^m)$ and $\overleftarrow{m}(Z_{l,t}^m)$ being the recursive forward and backward messages

$$\overrightarrow{m}(Z_l^m) = P(X_l^m | Z_l^m, \theta_l, n_l) \sum_{Z_{l-1}^m} \overrightarrow{m}(Z_{l-1}^m) P(Z_{l,t}^m | Z_{l-1,t}^m, Z_{l,t-1}^m) \tag{12}$$

$$\overleftarrow{m}(Z_l^m) = \sum_{Z_{l+1}^m} \overleftarrow{m}(Z_{l+1}^m) P(X_{l+1}^m | Z_{l+1}^m, \theta_{l+1}, n_{l+1}) P(Z_{l,t}^m | Z_{l+1,t}^m, Z_{l,t-1}^m) \tag{13}$$

using an uninformative prior $\overrightarrow{m}(Z_0^m) = \overrightarrow{m}(Z_{L+1}^m) = 0.5$. The variable $q(Z_{l,t}^m)$ together with $q(\alpha_l^m), q(\beta_l^m), q(\kappa_l^m)$ determine the view sampling distribution $P_l(m)$ used in the M step of GEM as defined in Eq. (7). The M step uses PatchMatch propagation and sampling (Sect. 4.1) for choosing the optimal depth and normal parameters over $q(\theta_l, n_l)$. Since geometrically consistent depth and normal inference is not feasible for all images simultaneously due to memory constraints, we decompose the inference in two stages. In the first stage, we estimate initial depths and normals for each image in the input set X according to Eq. (5). In the second stage, we use coordinate descent optimization to infer geometrically consistent depths and normals according to Eq. (10) by keeping all images but the current reference image as constant. We interleave the E and M step in both stages using row- and column-wise propagation. Four propagations in all directions denote a sweep. In the second stage, a single sweep defines a coordinate descent step, *i.e.*,, we alternate between different reference images after propagating through the four directions. Typically, the first stage converges after $I_1 = 3$ sweeps, while the second stage requires another $I_2 = 2$ sweeps through the entire image collection to reach a stable state. We refer the reader to the supplementary material for an overview of the steps of our algorithm.

4.7 Filtering and Fusion

After describing the depth and normal inference, this section proposes a robust method to filter any remaining outliers, *e.g.*,, in textureless sky regions. In addition to the benefits described previously, the photometric and geometric consistency terms provide us with measures to robustly detect outliers at negligible computational cost. An inlier observation should be both photometrically and geometrically stable with support from multiple views. The sets

$$S_l^{\mathrm{pho}} = \{x_l^m \mid q(Z_l^m) > \bar{q}_Z\} \tag{14}$$
$$S_l^{\mathrm{geo}} = \{x_l^m \mid q(\alpha_l^m) \geq \bar{q}_\alpha, q(\beta_l^m) \geq \bar{q}_\beta, q(\kappa_l^m) > \bar{q}_\kappa, \psi_l^m < \psi_{\max}\} \tag{15}$$

determine the photometric and geometric support of a reference image pixel x_l. To satisfy both constraints, we define the effective support of an observation as $S_l = \{x_l^m \mid x_l^m \in S_l^{\mathrm{pho}}, x_l^m \in S_l^{\mathrm{geo}}\}$ and filter any observations with $|S_l| < s$. In all our experiments, we set $s = 3$, $\bar{q}_Z = 0.5$, $\bar{q}_\alpha = 1$, $\bar{q}_\beta = 0.5$, and $\bar{q}_\kappa = P(\kappa = 90°)$. Figures 3 and 6 show examples of filtered depth and normal maps.

The collection of support sets S over the observations in all input images defines a directed graph of consistent pixels. In this graph, pixels with sufficient support are nodes, and directed edges point from a reference to a source image pixel. Nodes are associated with depth and normal estimates and, together with

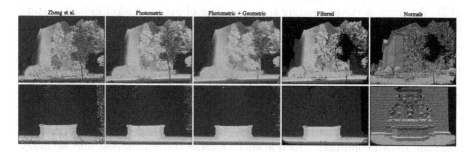

Fig. 3. Reconstruction results for *South Building* [29] and *Fountain* [20]. From left to right: Depth map by Zheng *et al.* [14], then ours only with the photometric term, with the photometric and geometric terms, and the final filtered depth and normal maps.

the intrinsic and extrinsic calibration, edges define a projective transformation from the reference to the source pixel. Our fusion finds clusters of consistent pixels in this graph by initializing a new cluster using the node with maximum support $|\mathcal{S}|$ and recursively collecting connected nodes that satisfy three constraints. Towards this goal, we project the first node into 3D to obtain the location $\boldsymbol{p}_0$ and normal $\boldsymbol{n}_0$. For the first constraint, the projected depth $\tilde{\theta}_0$ of the first node into the image of any other node in the cluster must be consistent with the estimated depth θ_i of the other node such that $\frac{|\tilde{\theta}_0 - \theta_i|}{\tilde{\theta}_0} < \epsilon_\theta$ (cf. [57]). Second, the normals of the two must be consistent such that $1 - \boldsymbol{n}_0^T \boldsymbol{n}_i < \epsilon_n$. Third, the reprojection error ψ_i of $\boldsymbol{p}_0$ w.r.t. the other node must be smaller than $\bar{\psi}$. Note that the graph can have loops, and therefore we only collect nodes once. In addition, multiple pixels in the same image can belong to the same cluster and, by choosing $\bar{\psi}$, we can control the resolution of the fused point cloud. When there is no remaining node that satisfies the three constraints, we fuse the cluster's elements, if it has at least three elements. The fused point has median location $\hat{\boldsymbol{p}}_j$ and mean normal $\boldsymbol{n}_j$ over all cluster elements. The median location is used to avoid artifacts when averaging over multiple neighboring pixels at large depth discontinuities. Finally, we remove the fused nodes from the graph and initialize a new cluster with maximum support $|\mathcal{S}|$ until the graph is empty. The resulting point cloud can then be colored (e.g., [58]) for visualization purposes and, since the points already have normals, we can directly apply meshing algorithms (e.g., Poisson reconstruction [59]) as an optional step.

5 Experiments

This section first demonstrates the benefits of the proposed contributions in isolation. Following that, we compare to other methods and show state-of-the-art results on both low- and high-resolution benchmark datasets. Finally, we evaluate the performance of our algorithm in the challenging setting of large-scale Internet photo collections. The algorithm lends itself for massive parallelization on the row- and column-wise propagation and the view level. In all our experiments, we use a CUDA implementation of our algorithm on a Nvidia Titan X GPU. We set $\gamma = 0.999$, leading to an average of one occlusion indicator state change per 1000 pixels. Empirically, we choose $\sigma_\rho = 0.6$, $\bar{\alpha} = 1°$, and $\sigma_k = 45°$.

Components. This paragraph shows the benefits of the individual components in isolation based on the *South Building* dataset [29], which consists of 128 unstructured images with a resolution of 7MP. We obtain sparse reconstructions using SfM [5]. For each reference view, we use all 127 images as source views with an average runtime of 50 s per sweep. *Normal Estimation*: Fig. 3 shows depth maps using fronto-parallel homographies (1st column) and with normal estimation (2nd to 5th columns), which leads to increased completeness and accuracy for depth inference of oblique scene elements, such as the ground. In addition, our method estimates more accurate normals than standard PatchMatch (Fig. 5(b)). Due to the proposed PatchMatch sampling scheme, our algorithm requires the

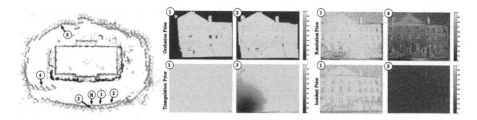

Fig. 4. Photometric and geometric priors for *South Building* dataset [29] between reference image (R) and each two selected source images (1–5).

same number sweeps to converge and only ≈25 % more runtime due to more hypotheses as compared to Zheng *et al.* [14], who only estimate per-pixel depths. *Geometric Priors*: Figure 4 demonstrates the benefit of each geometric prior. We show the likelihood functions for the reference view against one representative source image. For all priors, we observe varying likelihood within the same source image, underlining the benefit of pixel-wise view selection. The priors correctly downweigh the influence of source images with small triangulation angle, low resolution, or occluded views. *Selection Smoothness*: Figure 5(a) shows that our temporal smoothness term effectively mitigates the oscillation of the pure spatial smoothness term. While the occlusion variables in the formulation by Zheng *et al.* [14] oscillate depending on the propagation direction, in our method they quickly converge in a stable state leading to more stable view sampling. *Geometric Consistency*: Figure 3 demonstrates improved completeness when incorporating the geometric consistency term, and it also allows to reliably detect outliers for practically outlier-free filtered results. To measure the quantitative impact of our contributions, we obtain benchmark results by omitting a single component or combinations of components from the formulation (Table 1). We observe that each component is important to achieve the overall accuracy and completeness of our method. For further evaluations and impressions of the benefits of our method, we strongly encourage the reader to view the supplementary material.

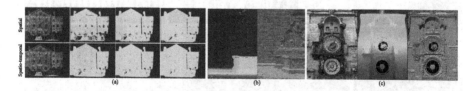

Fig. 5. (a) Comparison of spatial smoothness term [14] with our proposed spatial and temporal smoothness term for the occlusion variables $\boldsymbol{Z}$. Algorithm starts from the left with the first sweep and is followed by consecutive sweeps to the right. (b) Estimated depths and normals using standard PatchMatch propagation (*cf.* Fig. 3 for ours). (c) Reference image with filtered depths and normals for crowd-sourced images

Table 1. Strecha benchmark [20] with reported values from [60]. Ratio of pixels with error less than 2 cm and 10 cm. Ours w/o normals (\N), geom. priors (\P), temp. smoothness (\S), geom. consistency (\G), bilateral NCC (\B), and with all components.

		[14]	[60]	[9]	[62]	[61]	[28]	[15]	\N	\P	\S	\B	\PSB	\G	Ours
Fountain	2 cm	0.769	0.754	0.731	0.712	0.732	0.824	0.693	0.799	0.824	0.825	0.826	0.817	0.804	**0.827**
	10 cm	0.929	0.930	0.838	0.832	0.822	0.973	0.838	0.937	0.972	0.973	0.973	0.965	0.949	**0.975**
Herzjesu	2 cm	0.650	0.649	0.646	0.220	0.658	**0.739**	0.283	0.673	0.686	0.688	0.690	0.688	0.679	0.691
	10 cm	0.844	0.848	0.836	0.501	0.852	0.923	0.455	0.901	0.928	0.927	0.929	0.921	0.907	**0.931**

Benchmarks. The *Middlebury* benchmark [23] consists of the *Dino* and *Temple* models captured at 640×480 under varying settings (*Full, Ring, Sparse*). For each reference image, we use all views as source images at a runtime of ≈ 40 s per view for the *Full* models with ≈ 300 images. We achieve excellent accuracy and completeness on both models[1]. Specifically, using the standard settings, we rank 1st for *Dino Full* (tied) and *Dino Sparse*, while achieving competitive scores for the *Temple* (4th for *Full*, 8th for *Ring*). Note that our method performs best for higher resolutions, as normal estimation needs large patch sizes. Also, we use basic Poisson meshing [59], underlining the highly accurate and outlier-free depth/normal estimates produced by our method. The *Strecha* benchmark [20] consists of high-resolution images with ground-truth, and we follow the evaluation protocol of Hu and Mordohai [60]. Figure 3 shows outputs for the *Fountain* dataset and, Table 1 lists the results quantifying both the accuracy and completeness. To maintain comparability against Zheng *et al.* [14], we evaluate our raw depth maps against the ground-truth. We produce significantly more accurate and complete results than Zheng *et al.*, and we outperform the other methods in 3 of 4 categories, even though the results of [28,60,61] are evaluated based on the projection of a 3D surface obtained through depth map fusion.

Fig. 6. Reference image with filtered depths and normals for crowd-sourced images.

---

[1] Full results online at http://vision.middlebury.edu/mview/eval/.

Internet Photos. We densely reconstruct models of 100M Internet photos released by Heinly *et al.* [5,8] using a single machine with 4 Nvidia Titan X. We process the 41 K images at a rate of 70 s per view using 2 threads per GPU and finish after 4.2 days in addition to the 6 days needed for sparse modeling using SfM. Whenever we reach the GPU memory limits, we select the most connected source images ranked by the number of shared sparse points. Usually, this limit is reached for ≈ 200 images, while image sizes vary from 0.01MP to 9MP. The fusion and filtering steps consume negligible runtime. Figure 1 shows fused point clouds, Figs. 6 and 5(c) show depth/normal maps, and the supplementary material provides more results and comparisons against [9,10,47].

6 Conclusion

This work proposes a novel algorithm for robust and efficient dense reconstruction from unstructured image collections. Our method estimates accurate depth and normal information using photometric and geometric information for pixelwise view selection and for image-based fusion and filtering. We achieve state-of-the-art results on benchmarks and crowd-sourced data.

References

1. Schaffalitzky, F., Zisserman, A.: Multi-view matching for unordered image sets, or how do i organize my holiday snaps? In: Heyden, A., Sparr, G., Nielsen, M., Johansen, P. (eds.) ECCV 2002, Part I. LNCS, vol. 2350, pp. 414–431. Springer, Heidelberg (2002)
2. Snavely, N., Seitz, S., Szeliski, R.: Photo tourism: exploring photo collections in 3D. In: ACM Transactions on Graphics (2006)
3. Agarwal, S., Furukawa, Y., Snavely, N., Simon, I., Curless, B., Seitz, S., Szeliski, R.: Building Rome in a day. In: ICCV (2009)
4. Frahm, J.-M.: Building Rome on a cloudless day. In: Daniilidis, K., Maragos, P., Paragios, N. (eds.) ECCV 2010. LNCS, vol. 6314, pp. 368–381. Springer, Heidelberg (2010). doi:10.1007/978-3-642-15561-1_27
5. Heinly, J., Schönberger, J.L., Dunn, E., Frahm, J.M.: Reconstructing the world* in six days *(as captured by the Yahoo 100 million image dataset). In: CVPR (2015)
6. Zheng, E., Wu, C.: Structure from motion using structure-less resection. In: ICCV (2015)
7. Schönberger, J.L., Radenović, F., Chum, O., Frahm, J.M.: From single image query to detailed 3D reconstruction. In: CVPR (2015)
8. Schönberger, J.L., Frahm, J.M.: Structure-from-motion revisited. In: CVPR (2016)
9. Furukawa, Y., Ponce, J.: Accurate, dense, and robust multiview stereopsis. In: CVPR (2007)
10. Furukawa, Y., Curless, B., Seitz, S.M., Szeliski, R.: Towards internet-scale multiview stereo. In: CVPR (2010)
11. Bailer, C., Finckh, M., Lensch, H.P.A.: Scale robust multi view stereo. In: Fitzgibbon, A., Lazebnik, S., Perona, P., Sato, Y., Schmid, C. (eds.) ECCV 2012. LNCS, vol. 7574, pp. 398–411. Springer, Heidelberg (2012). doi:10.1007/978-3-642-33712-3_29

12. Shan, Q., Adams, R., Curless, B., Furukawa, Y., Seitz, S.M.: The visual turing test for scene reconstruction. In: 3DV (2013)
13. Shan, Q., Curless, B., Furukawa, Y., Hernandez, C., Seitz, S.M.: Occluding contours for multi-view stereo. In: CVPR (2014)
14. Zheng, E., Dunn, E., Jojic, V., Frahm, J.M.: Patchmatch based joint view selection and depthmap estimation. In: CVPR (2014)
15. Galliani, S., Lasinger, K., Schindler, K.: Massively parallel multiview stereopsis by surface normal diffusion. In: ICCV (2015)
16. Shotton, J., Sharp, T., Kipman, A., Fitzgibbon, A., Finocchio, M., Blake, A., Cook, M., Moore, R.: Real-time human pose recognition in parts from single depth images. Comm. ACM **56**(1), 116–124 (2013)
17. Chen, S.E., Williams, L.: View interpolation for image synthesis. In: Conference on Computer Graphics and Interactive Techniques (1993)
18. Forster, C., Pizzoli, M., Scaramuzza, D.: Air-ground localization and map augmentation using monocular dense reconstruction. In: IROS (2013)
19. Seitz, S.M., Curless, B., Diebel, J., Scharstein, D., Szeliski, R.: A comparison and evaluation of multi-view stereo reconstruction algorithms. In: CVPR (2006)
20. Strecha, C., von Hansen, W., Gool, L.V., Fua, P., Thoennessen, U.: On benchmarking camera calibration and multi-view stereo for high resolution imagery. In: CVPR (2008)
21. Intille, S.S., Bobick, A.F.: Disparity-space images and large occlusion stereo. In: Eklundh, J.-O. (ed.) ECCV 1994. LNCS, vol. 801, pp. 179–186. Springer, Heidelberg (1994)
22. Kanade, T., Okutomi, M.: A stereo matching algorithm with an adaptive window: theory and experiment. IEEE Trans. Pattern Anal. Mach. Intell. **16**(9), 920–932 (1994)
23. Scharstein, D., Szeliski, R.: A taxonomy and evaluation of dense two-frame stereo correspondence algorithms. IJCV **47**(1), 7–42 (2002)
24. Rhemann, C., Hosni, A., Bleyer, M., Rother, C., Gelautz, M.: Fast cost-volume filtering for visual correspondence and beyond. In: CVPR (2011)
25. Campbell, N.D.F., Vogiatzis, G., Hernández, C., Cipolla, R.: Using multiple hypotheses to improve depth-maps for multi-view stereo. In: Forsyth, D., Torr, P., Zisserman, A. (eds.) ECCV 2008. LNCS, vol. 5302, pp. 766–779. Springer, Heidelberg (2008). doi:10.1007/978-3-540-88682-2_58
26. Furukawa, Y., Curless, B., Seitz, S.M., Szeliski, R.: Manhattan-world stereo. In: CVPR (2009)
27. Furukawa, Y., Curless, B., Seitz, S.M., Szeliski, R.: Reconstructing building interiors from images. In: CVPR (2009)
28. Jancosek, M., Pajdla, T.: Multi-view reconstruction preserving weakly-supported surfaces. In: CVPR (2011)
29. Hane, C., Zach, C., Cohen, A., Angst, R., Pollefeys, M.: Joint 3D scene reconstruction and class segmentation. In: CVPR (2013)
30. Tung, T., Nobuhara, S., Matsuyama, T.: Complete multi-view reconstruction of dynamic scenes from probabilistic fusion of narrow and wide baseline stereo. In: ICCV (2009)
31. Ji, D., Dunn, E., Frahm, J.-M.: 3D reconstruction of dynamic textures in crowd sourced data. In: Fleet, D., Pajdla, T., Schiele, B., Tuytelaars, T. (eds.) ECCV 2014. LNCS, vol. 8689, pp. 143–158. Springer, Heidelberg (2014). doi:10.1007/978-3-319-10590-1_10
32. Oswald, M., Cremers, D.: A convex relaxation approach to space time multi-view 3D reconstruction. In: ICCV Workshops (2013)

33. Martin-Brualla, R., Gallup, D., Seitz, S.M.: 3D time-lapse reconstruction from internet photos. In: ICCV (2015)
34. Radenović, F., Schönberger, J.L., Ji, D., Frahm, J.M., Chum, O., Matas, J.: From dusk till dawn: modeling in the dark. In: CVPR (2016)
35. Yang, Q., Wang, L., Yang, R., Stewénius, H., Nistér, D.: Stereo matching with color-weighted correlation, hierarchical belief propagation, and occlusion handling. IEEE Trans. Pattern Anal. Mach. Intell. **31**(3), 492–504 (2009)
36. Sun, J., Li, Y., Kang, S.B., Shum, H.Y.: Symmetric stereo matching for occlusion handling. In: CVPR (2005)
37. Zitnick, C.L., Kanade, T.: A cooperative algorithm for stereo matching and occlusion detection. IEEE Trans. Pattern Anal. Mach. Intell. **22**(7), 675–684 (2000)
38. Kang, S.B., Szeliski, R., Chai, J.: Handling occlusions in dense multi-view stereo. In: CVPR (2001)
39. Strecha, C., Fransens, R., Van Gool, L.: Wide-baseline stereo from multiple views: a probabilistic account. In: CVPR (2004)
40. Strecha, C., Fransens, R., Van Gool, L.: Combined depth and outlier estimation in multi-view stereo. In: CVPR (2006)
41. Gallup, D., Frahm, J.M., Mordohai, P., Pollefeys, M.: Variable baseline/resolution stereo. In: CVPR (2008)
42. Gallup, D., Frahm, J.M., Mordohai, P., Yang, Q., Pollefeys, M.: Real-time plane-sweeping stereo with multiple sweeping directions. In: CVPR (2007)
43. Burt, P., Wixson, L., Salgian, G.: Electronically directed focal stereo. In: ICCV (1995)
44. Birchfield, S., Tomasi, C.: Multiway cut for stereo and motion with slanted surfaces. In: ICCV (1999)
45. Zabulis, X., Daniilidis, K.: Multi-camera reconstruction based on surface normal estimation and best viewpoint selection. In: 3DPVT (2004)
46. Bleyer, M., Rhemann, C., Rother, C.: Patchmatch stereo-stereo matching with slanted support windows. In: BMVC (2011)
47. Goesele, M., Snavely, N., Curless, B., Hoppe, H., Seitz, S.M.: Multi-view stereo for community photo collections. In: CVPR (2007)
48. Zach, C.: Fast and high quality fusion of depth maps. In: 3DPVT (2008)
49. Gallup, D., Pollefeys, M., Frahm, J.-M.: 3D reconstruction using an n-layer heightmap. In: Goesele, M., Roth, S., Kuijper, A., Schiele, B., Schindler, K. (eds.) Pattern Recognition. LNCS, vol. 6376, pp. 1–10. Springer, Heidelberg (2010)
50. Zheng, E., Dunn, E., Raguram, R., Frahm, J.M.: Efficient and scalable depthmap fusion. In: BMVC (2012)
51. Neal, R.M., Hinton, G.E.: A view of the EM algorithm that justifies incremental, sparse, and other variants. In: Jordan, M.I. (ed.) Learning in Graphical Models. Springer, Berlin (1998)
52. Heise, P., Jensen, B., Klose, S., Knoll, A.: Variational patchmatch multiview reconstruction and refinement. In: CVPR (2015)
53. Bishop, C.M.: Pattern Recognition and Machine Learning. Springer, Berlin (2006)
54. Hirschmüller, H., Scharstein, D.: Evaluation of stereo matching costs on images with radiometric differences. IEEE Trans. Pattern Anal. Mach. Intell. **31**(9), 1582–1599 (2009)
55. Yoon, K.J., Kweon, I.S.: Locally adaptive support-weight approach for visual correspondence search. In: CVPR (2005)
56. Zhang, G., Jia, J., Wong, T.T., Bao, H.: Recovering consistent video depth maps via bundle optimization. In: CVPR (2008)

57. Merrell, P., Akbarzadeh, A., Wang, L., Mordohai, P., Frahm, J.M., Yang, R., Nistér, D., Pollefeys, M.: Real-time visibility-based fusion of depth maps. In: CVPR (2007)

58. Waechter, M., Moehrle, N., Goesele, M.: Let there be color! Large-scale texturing of 3D reconstructions. In: Fleet, D., Pajdla, T., Schiele, B., Tuytelaars, T. (eds.) ECCV 2014. LNCS, vol. 8693, pp. 836–850. Springer, Heidelberg (2014). doi:10. 1007/978-3-319-10602-1_54

59. Kazhdan, M., Hoppe, H.: Screened poisson surface reconstruction. ACM Trans. Graph. (TOG) **32**(3), 29 (2013)

60. Hu, X., Mordohai, P.: Least commitment, viewpoint-based, multi-view stereo. In: 3DIMPVT (2012)

61. Tylecek, R., Sara, R.: Refinement of surface mesh for accurate multi-view reconstruction. IJVR **9**(1), 45–54 (2010)

62. Zaharescu, A., Boyer, E., Horaud, R.: Topology-adaptive mesh deformation for surface evolution, morphing, and multiview reconstruction. IEEE Trans. Pattern Anal. Mach. Intell. **33**(4), 823–837 (2011)

Laplacian Pyramid Reconstruction and Refinement for Semantic Segmentation

Golnaz Ghiasi[✉] and Charless C. Fowlkes

Department of Computer Science, University of California, Irvine, USA
{gghiasi,fowlkes}@ics.uci.edu

Abstract. CNN architectures have terrific recognition performance but rely on spatial pooling which makes it difficult to adapt them to tasks that require dense, pixel-accurate labeling. This paper makes two contributions: (1) We demonstrate that while the apparent spatial resolution of convolutional feature maps is low, the high-dimensional feature representation contains significant sub-pixel localization information. (2) We describe a multi-resolution reconstruction architecture based on a Laplacian pyramid that uses skip connections from higher resolution feature maps and multiplicative gating to successively refine segment boundaries reconstructed from lower-resolution maps. This approach yields state-of-the-art semantic segmentation results on the PASCAL VOC and Cityscapes segmentation benchmarks without resorting to more complex random-field inference or instance detection driven architectures.

Keywords: Semantic segmentation · Convolutional neural networks

1 Introduction

Deep convolutional neural networks (CNNs) have proven highly effective at semantic segmentation due to the capacity of discriminatively pre-trained feature hierarchies to robustly represent and recognize objects and materials. As a result, CNNs have significantly outperformed previous approaches (e.g., [2,3,28]) that relied on hand-designed features and recognizers trained from scratch. A key difficulty in the adaption of CNN features to segmentation is that feature pooling layers, which introduce invariance to spatial deformations required for robust recognition, result in high-level representations with reduced spatial resolution. In this paper, we investigate this *spatial-semantic uncertainty principle* for CNN hierarchies (see Fig. 1) and introduce two techniques that yield substantially improved segmentations.

First, we tackle the question of how much spatial information is represented at high levels of the feature hierarchy. A given spatial location in a convolutional feature map corresponds to a large block of input pixels (and an even larger "receptive field"). While max pooling in a single feature channel clearly destroys spatial information in that channel, spatial filtering prior to pooling introduces strong correlations across channels which could, in principle, encode

© Springer International Publishing AG 2016
B. Leibe et al. (Eds.): ECCV 2016, Part III, LNCS 9907, pp. 519–534, 2016.
DOI: 10.1007/978-3-319-46487-9_32

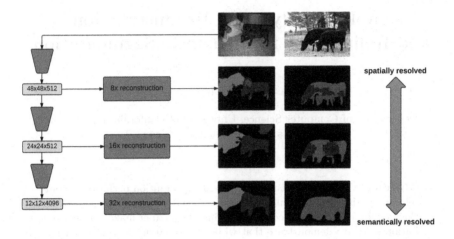

Fig. 1. In this paper, we explore the trade-off between spatial and semantic accuracy within CNN feature hierarchies. Such hierarchies generally follow a spatial-semantic uncertainty principle in which high levels of the hierarchy make accurate semantic predictions but are poorly localized in space while at low levels, boundaries are precise but labels are noisy. We develop reconstruction techniques for increasing spatial accuracy at a given level and refinement techniques for fusing multiple levels that limit these tradeoffs and produce improved semantic segmentations.

significant "sub-pixel" spatial information across the high-dimensional vector of sparse activations. We show that this is indeed the case and demonstrate a simple approach to spatial decoding using a small set of data-adapted basis functions that substantially improves over common upsampling schemes (see Fig. 2).

Second, having squeezed more spatial information from a given layer of the hierarchy, we turn to the question of fusing predictions across layers. A standard approach has been to either concatenate features (e.g., [15]) or linearly combine predictions (e.g., [24]). Concatenation is appealing but suffers from the high dimensionality of the resulting features. On the other hand, additive combinations of predictions from multiple layers does not make good use of the relative spatial-semantic content tradeoff. High-resolution layers are shallow with small receptive fields and hence yield inherently noisy predictions with high pixel-wise loss. As a result, we observe their contribution is significantly down-weighted relative to low-resolution layers during linear fusion and thus they have relatively little effect on final predictions.

Inspired in part by recent work on residual networks [16,17], we propose an architecture in which predictions derived from high-resolution layers are only required to correct residual errors in the low-resolution prediction. Importantly, we use multiplicative gating to avoid integrating (and hence penalizing) noisy high-resolution outputs in regions where the low-resolution predictions are confident about the semantic content. We call our method *Laplacian Pyramid Reconstruction and Refinement* (LRR) since the architecture uses a Laplacian reconstruction pyramid [1] to fuse predictions. Indeed, the class scores predicted at

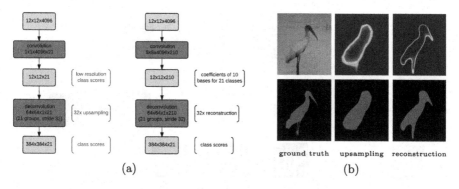

Fig. 2. (a) Upsampling architecture for FCN32s network (left) and our 32x reconstruction network (right). (b) Example of Class conditional probability maps and semantic segmentation predictions from FCN32s which performs upsampling (middle) and our 32x reconstruction network (right).

each level of our architecture typically look like bandpass decomposition of the full resolution segmentation mask (see Fig. 3).

2 Related Work

The inherent lack of spatial detail in CNN feature maps has been attacked using a variety of techniques. One insight is that spatial information lost during max-pooling can in part be recovered by unpooling and deconvolution [36] providing a useful way to visualize input dependency in feed-forward models [35]. This idea has been developed using learned deconvolution filters to perform semantic segmentation [26]. However, the deeply stacked deconvolutional output layers are difficult to train, requiring multi-stage training and more complicated object proposal aggregation.

A second key insight is that while activation maps at lower-levels of the CNN hierarchy lack object category specificity, they do contain higher spatial resolution information. Performing classification using a "jet" of feature map responses aggregated across multiple layers has been successfully leveraged for semantic segmentation [24], generic boundary detection [32], simultaneous detection and segmentation [15], and scene recognition [33]. Our architecture shares the basic skip connections of [24] but uses multiplicative, confidence-weighted gating when fusing predictions.

Our techniques are complementary to a range of other recent approaches that incorporate object proposals [10, 26], attentional scale selection mechanisms [7], and conditional random fields (CRF) [5, 21, 23]. CRF-based methods integrate CNN score-maps with pairwise features derived from superpixels [9, 25] or generic boundary detection [4, 19] to more precisely localize segment boundaries. We demonstrate that our architecture works well as a drop in unary potential in fully connected CRFs [20] and would likely further benefit from end-to-end training [37].

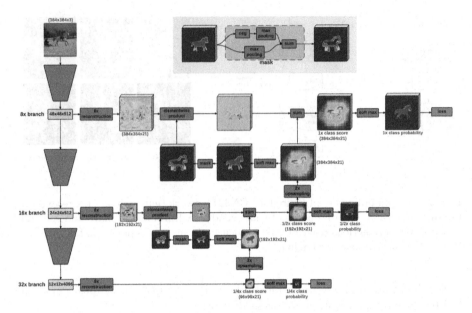

Fig. 3. Overview of our Laplacian pyramid reconstruction network architecture. We use low-resolution feature maps in the CNN hierarchy to reconstruct a coarse, low-frequency segmentation map and then refine this map by adding in higher frequency details derived from higher-resolution feature maps. Boundary masking (inset) suppresses the contribution of higher resolution layers in areas where the segmentation is confident, allowing the reconstruction to focus on predicting residual errors in uncertain areas (e.g., precisely localizing object boundaries). At each resolution layer, the reconstruction filters perform the same amount of upsampling which depends on the number of layers (e.g., our LRR-4x model utilizes 4x reconstruction on each of four branches). Standard 2x bilinear upsampling is applied to each class score map before combining it with higher resolution predictions.

3   Reconstruction with Learned Basis Functions

A standard approach to predicting pixel class labels is to use a linear convolution to compute a low-resolution class score from the feature map and then upsample the score map to the original image resolution. A bilinear kernel is a suitable choice for this upsampling and has been used as a fixed filter or an initialization for the upsampling filter [5,7,10,13,15,24,37]. However, upsampling low-resolution class scores necessarily limits the amount of detail in the resulting segmentation (see Fig. 2(a)) and discards any sub-pixel localization information that might be coded across the many channels of the low-resolution feature map. The simple fix of upsampling the feature map prior to classification poses computational difficulties due to the large number of feature channels (e.g. 4096). Furthermore, (bilinear) upsampling commutes with 1×1 convolutions used for class prediction so performing per-pixel linear classification on an upsampled feature map would yield equivalent results unless additional rounds of (non-linear) filtering were carried out on the high-resolution feature map.

To extract more detailed spatial information, we avoid immediately collapsing the high-dimensional feature map down to low-resolution class scores. Instead, we express the spatial pattern of high-resolution scores using a linear combination of high-resolution basis functions whose coefficients are predicted from the feature map (see Fig. 2(a)). We term this approach "reconstruction" to distinguish it from the standard upsampling (although bilinear upsampling can clearly be seen as special case with a single basis function).

Reconstruction by Deconvolution: In our implementation, we tile the high-resolution score map with overlapping basis functions (e.g., for 4x upsampled reconstruction we use basis functions with an 8×8 pixel support and a stride of 4). We use a convolutional layer to predict K basis coefficients for each of C classes from the high-dimensional, low-resolution feature map. The group of coefficients for each spatial location and class are then multiplied by the set of basis function for the class and summed using a standard deconvolution (convolution transpose) layer.

To write this explicitly, let s denote the stride, $q_s(i) = \lfloor \frac{i}{s} \rfloor$ denote the quotient, and $m_s(i) = i \bmod s$ the remainder of i by s. The reconstruction layer that maps basis coefficients $X \in \mathbb{R}^{H \times W \times K \times C}$ to class scores $Y \in \mathbb{R}^{sH \times sW \times C}$ using basis functions $B \in \mathbb{R}^{2s \times 2s \times K \times C}$ is given by:

$$Y_c[i,j] = \sum_{k=0}^{K-1} \sum_{(u,v) \in \{0,1\}^2} B_{k,c} \left[m_s(i) + s \cdot u, m_s(j) + s \cdot v \right] \cdot X_{k,c} \left[q_s(i) - u, q_s(j) - v \right]$$

where $B_{k,c}$ contains the k-th basis function for class c with corresponding spatial weights $X_{k,c}$. We assume $X_{k,c}$ is zero padded and Y_c is cropped appropriately.

Connection to Spline Interpolation: We note that a classic approach to improving on bilinear interpolation is to use a higher-order spline interpolant built from a standard set of non-overlapping polynomial basis functions where the weights are determined analytically to assure continuity between neighboring patches. Our approach using learned filters and basis functions makes minimal assumptions about mapping from high dimensional activations to the coefficients X but also offers no guarantees on the continuity of Y. We address this in part by using larger filter kernels (i.e., $5 \times 5 \times 4096$) for predicting the coefficients $X_{k,c}$ from the feature activations. This mimics the computation used in spline interpolation of introducing linear dependencies between neighboring basis weights and empirically improves continuity of the output predictions.

Learning Basis Functions: To leverage limited amounts of training data and speed up training, we initialize the deconvolution layers with a meaningful set of filters estimated by performing PCA on example segment patches. For this purpose, we extract 10000 patches for each class from training data where each patch is of size 32×32 and at least 2% of the patch pixels are members of the class. We apply PCA on the extracted patches to compute a class specific set of basis functions. Example bases for different categories of PASCAL VOC

Fig. 4. Category-specific basis functions for reconstruction are adapted to modeling the shape of a given object class. For example, airplane segments tend to be elongated in the horizontal direction while bottles are elongated in the vertical direction.

dataset are shown in Fig. 4. Interestingly, there is some significant variation among classes due to different segment shape statistics. We found it sufficient to initialize the reconstruction filters for different levels of the reconstruction pyramid with the same basis set (downsampled as needed). In both our model and the FCN bilinear upsampling model, we observed that end-to-end training resulted in insignificant ($<10^{-7}$) changes to the basis functions.

We experimented with varying the resolution and number of basis functions of our reconstruction layer built on top of the ImageNet-pretrained VGG-16 network. We found that 10 functions sampled at a resolution of 8×8 were sufficient for accurate reconstruction of class score maps. Models trained with more than 10 basis functions commonly predicted zero weight coefficients for the higher-frequency basis functions. This suggests some limit to how much spatial information can be extracted from the low-res feature map (i.e., roughly 3x more than bilinear). However, this estimate is only a lower-bound since there are obvious limitations to how well we can fit the model. Other generative architectures (e.g., using larger sparse dictionaries) or additional information (e.g., max pooling "switches" in deconvolution [36]) may do even better.

4   Laplacian Pyramid Refinement

The basic intuition for our multi-resolution architecture comes from Burt and Adelson's classic Laplacian Pyramid [1], which decomposes an image into disjoint frequency bands using an elegant recursive computation (analysis) that produces appropriately down-sampled sub-bands such that the sum of the resulting sub-bands (synthesis) perfectly reproduces the original image. While the notion of

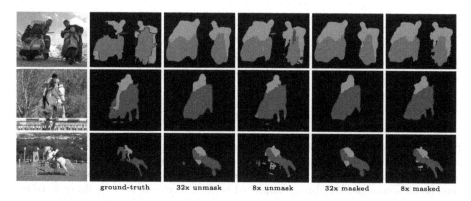

ground-truth   32x unmask   8x unmask   32x masked   8x masked

Fig. 5. Visualization of segmentation results produced by our model with and without boundary masking. For each row, we show the input image, ground-truth and the segmentation results of 32x and 8x layers of our model without masking (middle) and with masking (right). The segmentation results for 8x layer of the model without masking has some noise not present in the 32x output. Masking allows such noise to be repressed in regions where the 32x outputs have high confidence.

frequency sub-bands is not appropriate for the non-linear filtering performed by standard CNNs, casual inspection of the response of individual activations to shifted input images reveals a power spectral density whose high-frequency components decay with depth leaving primarily low-frequency components (with a few high-frequency artifacts due to disjoint bins used in pooling). This suggests the possibility that the standard CNN architecture could be trained to serve the role of the analysis pyramid (predicting sub-band coefficients) which could then be assembled using a synthesis pyramid to estimate segmentations.

Figure 3 shows the overall architecture of our model. Starting from the coarse scale "low-frequency" segmentation estimate, we carry out a sequence of successive refinements, adding in information from "higher-frequency" sub-bands to improve the spatial fidelity of the resulting segmentation masks. For example, since the 32x layer already captures the coarse-scale support of the object, prediction from the 16x layer does not need to include this information and can instead focus on adding finer scale refinements of the segment boundary.[1]

Boundary Masking: In practice, simply upsampling and summing the outputs of the analysis layers does not yield the desired effect. Unlike the Laplacian image analysis pyramid, the high resolution feature maps of the CNN do not have the "low-frequency" content subtracted out. As Fig. 1 shows, high-resolution layers still happily make "low-frequency" predictions (e.g., in the middle of a large segment) even though they are often incorrect. As a result, in an architecture that

---

[1] Closely related architectures were used in [11] for generative image synthesis where the output of a lower-resolution model was used as input for a CNN which predicted an additive refinement, and in [27], where fusing and refinement across levels was carried out via concatenation followed by several convolution+ReLU layers.

VOC 2011-val	pixel acc.	mean acc.	mean IoU
FCN-32s	89.1%	73.3%	59.4%
FCN-16s	90.0%	75.7%	62.4%
FCN-8s	90.3%	75.9%	62.7%
LRR-32x (w/o aug)	90.7%	78.9%	64.1%
LRR-32x	91.5%	81.6%	66.8%
LRR-16x	91.8%	81.6%	67.8%
LRR-8x	92.4%	83.2%	69.5%
LRR-4x	92.2%	83.7%	69.0%
LRR-4x-ms	92.8%	84.6%	71.4%

Fig. 6. Comparison of our segment reconstruction model, LRR (without boundary masking) and the baseline FCN model [24] which uses upsampling. We find consistent benefits from using a higher-dimensional reconstruction basis rather than upsampling class prediction maps. We also see improved performance from using multi-scale training augmentation, fusing multiple feature maps, and running on multiple scales at test time. Note that the performance benefit of fusing multiple resolution feature maps diminishes with no gain or even decrease performance from adding in the 4x layer. Boundary masking (cf. Fig. 7) allows for much better utilization of these fine scale features.

simply sums together predictions across layers, we found the learned parameters tend to down-weight the contribution of high-resolution predictions to the sum in order to limit the potentially disastrous effect of these noisy predictions. However, this hampers the ability of the high-resolution predictions to significantly refine the segmentation in areas containing high-frequency content (i.e., segment boundaries).

To remedy this, we introduce a masking step that serves to explicitly subtract out the "low-frequency" content from the high-resolution signal. This takes the form of a multiplicative gating that prevents the high-resolution predictions from contributing to the final response in regions where lower-resolution predictions are confident. The inset in Fig. 3 shows how this boundary mask is computed by using a max pooling operation to dilate the confident foreground and background predictions and taking their difference to isolate the boundary. The size of this dilation (pooling size) is tied to the amount of upsampling between successive layers of the pyramid, and hence fixed at 9 pixels in our implementation.

5   Experiments

We now describe a number of diagnostic experiments carried out using the PASCAL VOC [12] semantic segmentation dataset. In these experiments, models were trained on training/validation set split specified by [14] which includes 11287 training images and 736 held out validation images from the PASCAL 2011 val set. We focus primarily on the average Intersection-over-Union (IoU) metric which generally provides a more sensitive performance measure than per-pixel or per-class accuracy. We conduct diagnostic experiments on the model architecture using this validation data and test our final model via submission

VOC 2011-val	VOC			VOC+COCO			
	VGG-16			VGG-16			ResNet
	unmasked	masked	masked+DE	umasked	masked	masked+DE	masked+DE
LRR-4x(32x)	67.1%	67.0%	68.8%	71.3%	71.2%	72.9%	76.7%
LRR-4x(16x)	68.6%	69.2%	70.0%	72.1%	72.4%	73.9%	78.0%
LRR-4x(8x)	69.3%	70.3%	70.9%	72.9%	73.4%	74.9%	78.3%
LRR-4x	69.3%	70.5%	71.1%	72.9%	73.6%	75.1%	78.4%
LRR-4x-ms	71.9%	73.0%	73.6%	74.0%	75.0%	76.6%	79.2%
LRR-4x-ms-crf	73.2%	74.1%	74.6%	75.0%	76.1%	77.5%	79.9%

Fig. 7. Mean intersection-over-union (IoU) accuracy for intermediate outputs at different levels of our Laplacian reconstruction architecture trained with and without boundary masking (value in parentheses denotes an intermediate output of the full model). Masking allows us to squeeze additional gains out of high-resolution feature maps by focusing only on low-confidence areas near segment boundaries. Adding dilation and erosion losses (DE) to the 32x branch improves the accuracy of 32x predictions and as a result the overall performance. Running the model at multiple scales and performing post-processing using a CRF yielded further performance improvements.

to the PASCAL VOC 2012 test data server, which benchmarks on an additional set of 1456 images. We also report test benchmark performance on the recently released Cityscapes [8] dataset.

5.1 Parameter Optimization

We augment the layers of the ImageNet-pretrained VGG-16 network [29] or ResNet-101 [16] with our LRR architecture and fine-tune all layers via back-propagation. All models were trained and tested with Matconvnet [31] on a single NVIDIA GPU. We use standard stochastic gradient descent with batch size of 20, momentum of 0.9 and weight decay of 0.0005. The models and code are available at https://github.com/golnazghiasi/LRR.

Stage-Wise Training: Our 32x branch predicts a coarse semantic segmentation for the input image while the other branches add in details to the segmentation prediction. Thus 16x, 8x and 4x branches are dependent on 32x branch prediction and their task of adding details is meaningful only when 32x segmentation predictions are good. As a result we first optimize the model with only 32x loss and then add in connections to the other layers and continue to fine tune. At each layer we use a pixel-wise softmax log loss defined at a lower image resolution and use down-sampled ground-truth segmentations for training. For example, in LRR-4x the loss is defined at 1/8, 1/4, 1/2 and full image resolution for the 32x, 16x, 8x and 4x branches, respectively.

Dilation Erosion Objectives: We found that augmenting the model with branches to predict dilated and eroded class segments in addition of the original segments helps guide the model in predicting more accurate segmentation. For each training example and class, we compute a binary segmentation using the ground-truth and then compute its dilation and erosion using a disk with radius of 32 pixels. Since dilated segments of different classes are not mutually exclusive,

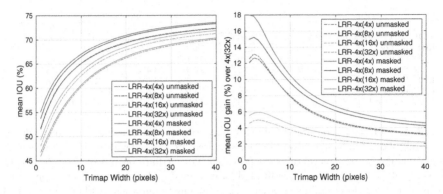

Fig. 8. The benefit of Laplacian pyramid boundary refinement becomes even more apparent when focusing on performance near object boundaries. Plots show segmentation performance within a thin band around the ground-truth object boundaries for intermediate predictions at different levels of our reconstruction pyramid. (right) Measuring accuracy or mean IoU relative to the baseline 32x output shows that the high-resolution feature maps are most valuable near object boundaries while masking improves performance both near and far from boundaries.

a k-way soft-max is not appropriate so we use logistic loss instead. We add these Dilation and Erosion (DE) losses to the 32x branch (at 1/8 resolution) when training LRR-4x. Adding these losses increased mean IoU of the 32x branch predictions from 71.2 % to 72.9 % and also the overall multi-scale accuracy from 75.0 % to 76.6 (see Fig. 7, built on VGG-16 and trained on VOC+COCO).

Multi-scale Data Augmentation: We augmented the training data with multiple scaled versions of each training examples. We randomly select an image size between 288 to 704 for each batch and then scale training examples of that batch to the selected size. When the selected size is larger than 384, we crop a window with size of 384 × 384 from the scaled image. This augmentation is helpful in improving the accuracy of the model and increased mean IoU of our 32x model from 64.07 % to 66.81 % on the validation data (see Fig. 6).

5.2   Reconstruction vs Upsampling

To isolate the effectiveness of our proposed reconstruction method relative to simple upsampling, we compare the performance of our model without masking to the fully convolutional net (FCN) of [24]. For this experiment, we trained our model without scale augmentation using exactly same training data used for training the FCN models. We observed significant improvement over upsampling using reconstruction with 10 basis filters. Our 32x reconstruction model (w/o aug) achieved a mean IoU of 64.1 % while FCN-32s and FCN-8s had a mean IoU of 59.4 % and 62.7 %, respectively (Fig. 6).

5.3 Multiplicative Masking and Boundary Refinement

We evaluated whether masking the contribution of high-resolution feature maps based on the confidence of the lower-resolution predictions resulted in better performance. We anticipated that this multiplicative masking would serve to remove noisy class predictions from high-resolution feature maps in high-confidence interior regions while allowing refinement of segment boundaries. Figure 5 demonstrates the qualitative effect of boundary masking. While the prediction from the 32x branch is similar for both models (relatively noise free), masking improves the 8x prediction noticeably by removing small, incorrectly labeled segments while preserving boundary fidelity. We compute mean IoU benchmarks for different intermediate outputs of our LRR-4x model trained with and without masking (Fig. 7). Boundary masking yields about 1 % overall improvement relative to the model without masking across all branches.

Evaluation Near Object Boundaries: Our proposed model uses the higher resolution feature maps to refine the segmentation in the regions close to the boundaries, resulting in a more detailed segmentation (see Fig. 11). However, boundaries constitute a relatively small fraction of the total image pixels, limiting the impact of these improvements on the overall IoU performance benchmark (see, e.g. Fig. 7). To better characterize performance differences between models, we also computed mean IoU restricted to a narrow band of pixels around the ground-truth boundaries. This partitioning into figure/boundary/background is sometimes referred to as a tri-map in the matting literature and has been previously utilized in analyzing semantic segmentation performance [5,18].

Figure 8 shows the mean IoU of our LRR-4x as a function of the width of the tri-map boundary zone. We plot both the absolute performance and performance relative to the low-resolution 32x output. As the curves confirm, adding in higher resolution feature maps results in the most performance gain near object boundaries. Masking improves performance both near and far from boundaries. Near boundaries masking allows for the higher-resolution layers to refine the boundary shape while far from boundaries the mask prevents those high-resolution layers from corrupting accurate low-resolution predictions.

5.4 CRF Post-Processing

To show our architecture can easily be integrated with CRF-based models, we evaluated the use of our LRR model predictions as a unary potential in a fully-connected CRF [4,20]. We resize each input image to three different scales (1,0.8,0.6), apply the LRR model and then compute the pixel-wise maximum of predicted class conditional probability maps. Post-processing with the CRF yields small additional gains in performance. Figure 7 reports the mean IoU for our LRR-4x model prediction when running at multiple scales and with the integration of the CRF. Fusing multiple scales yields a noticeable improvement (between 1.1 % to 2.5 %) while the CRF gives an additional gain (between 0.9 % to 1.4 %).

	mean	areo	bike	bird	boat	bottle	bus	car	cat	chair	cow	table	dog	horse	mbike	person	plant	sheep	sofa	train	tv
Only using VOC training data																					
FCN-8s[24]	62.2	76.8	34.2	68.9	49.4	60.3	75.3	74.7	77.6	21.4	62.5	46.8	71.8	63.9	76.5	73.9	45.2	72.4	37.4	70.9	55.1
Hypercol[15]	62.6	68.7	33.5	69.8	51.3	70.2	81.1	71.9	74.9	23.9	60.6	46.9	72.1	68.3	74.5	72.9	52.6	64.4	45.4	64.9	57.4
Zoom-out[25]	69.6	85.6	37.3	83.2	62.5	66.0	85.1	80.7	84.9	27.2	73.2	57.5	78.1	79.2	81.1	77.1	53.6	74.0	49.2	71.7	63.3
EdgeNet[4]	71.2	83.6	35.8	82.4	63.1	68.9	86.2	79.6	84.7	31.8	74.2	61.1	79.6	76.6	83.2	80.9	58.3	82.6	49.1	74.8	65.1
Attention[7]	71.5	86.0	38.8	78.2	63.1	70.2	89.6	84.1	82.9	29.4	75.2	58.7	79.3	78.4	83.9	80.3	53.5	82.6	51.5	79.2	64.2
DeepLab[5]	71.6	84.4	54.5	81.5	63.6	65.9	85.1	79.1	83.4	30.7	74.1	59.8	79.0	76.1	83.2	80.8	59.7	82.2	50.4	73.1	63.7
CRFRNN[37]	72.0	87.5	39.0	79.7	64.2	68.3	87.6	80.8	84.4	30.4	78.2	60.4	80.5	77.8	83.1	80.6	59.5	82.8	47.8	78.3	67.1
DeconvN[26]	72.5	89.9	39.3	79.7	63.9	68.2	87.4	81.2	86.1	28.5	77.0	62.0	79.0	80.3	83.6	80.2	58.8	83.4	54.3	80.7	65.0
DPN [23]	74.1	87.7	59.4	78.4	64.9	70.3	89.3	83.5	86.1	31.7	79.9	62.6	81.9	80.0	83.5	82.3	60.5	83.2	53.4	77.9	65.0
Adelaide[21]	75.3	90.6	37.6	80.0	67.8	74.4	92.0	85.2	86.2	39.1	81.2	58.9	83.8	83.9	84.3	84.8	62.1	83.2	58.2	80.8	72.3
LRR	74.7	89.2	40.3	81.2	63.9	73.1	91.7	86.2	87.2	35.4	80.1	62.4	82.6	84.4	84.8	81.7	59.5	83.6	54.3	83.7	69.3
LRR-CRF	75.9	91.8	41.0	83.0	62.3	74.3	93.0	86.8	88.7	36.6	81.8	63.4	84.7	85.9	85.1	83.1	62.0	84.6	55.6	84.9	70.0
Using VOC and COCO training data																					
EdgeNet[4]	73.6	88.3	37.0	89.8	63.6	70.3	87.3	82.0	87.6	31.1	79.0	61.9	81.6	80.4	84.5	83.3	58.4	86.1	55.9	78.2	65.4
CRFRNN[37]	74.7	90.4	55.3	88.7	68.4	69.8	88.3	82.4	85.1	32.6	78.5	64.4	79.6	81.9	86.4	81.8	58.6	82.4	53.5	77.4	70.1
BoxSup[10]	75.2	89.8	38.0	89.2	68.9	68.0	89.6	83.0	87.7	34.4	83.6	67.1	81.5	83.7	85.2	83.5	58.6	84.9	55.8	81.2	70.7
SBound[19]	75.7	90.3	37.9	89.6	67.8	74.6	89.3	84.1	89.1	35.8	83.6	66.2	82.9	81.7	85.6	84.6	60.3	84.8	60.7	78.3	68.3
Attention[7]	76.3	93.2	41.7	88.0	61.7	74.9	92.9	84.5	90.4	33.0	82.8	63.2	84.5	85.0	87.2	85.7	60.5	87.7	57.8	84.3	68.2
DPN [23]	77.5	89.0	61.6	87.7	66.8	74.7	91.2	84.3	87.6	36.5	86.3	66.1	84.4	87.8	85.6	85.4	63.6	87.3	61.3	79.4	66.4
Adelaide[21]	77.8	94.1	40.4	83.6	67.3	75.6	93.4	84.4	88.7	41.6	86.4	63.3	85.5	89.3	85.6	86.0	67.4	90.1	62.6	80.9	72.5
LRR	77.9	91.4	43.2	87.9	64.5	75.0	93.1	86.7	90.6	42.4	82.9	68.1	85.2	87.8	88.6	86.4	65.4	85.0	62.2	83.3	71.6
LRR-CRF	78.7	93.2	44.2	89.4	65.4	74.9	93.8	87.0	92.0	42.9	83.7	68.9	86.5	88.0	89.0	87.2	67.3	85.6	64.0	84.1	71.5
ResNet + Using VOC and COCO training data																					
DeepLab[6]	79.7	92.6	60.4	91.6	63.4	76.3	95.0	88.4	92.6	32.7	88.5	67.6	89.6	92.1	87.0	87.4	63.3	88.3	60.0	86.8	74.5
LRR	78.7	90.8	44.4	94.0	65.8	75.8	94.4	88.6	91.4	39.1	84.7	70.0	87.5	88.7	88.3	85.8	64.1	85.6	56.6	85.1	76.8
LRR-CRF	79.3	92.4	45.1	94.6	65.2	75.8	95.1	89.1	92.3	39.0	85.7	70.4	88.6	89.4	88.6	86.6	65.8	86.2	57.4	85.7	77.3

Fig. 9. Per-class mean intersection-over-union (IoU) performance on PASCAL VOC 2012 segmentation challenge test data. We evaluate models trained using only VOC training data as well as those trained with additional training data from COCO. We also separate out a high-performing variant built on the ResNet-101 architecture.

5.5   Benchmark Performance

PASCAL VOC Benchmark: As the Fig. 9 indicates, the current top performing models on PASCAL all use additional training data from the MS COCO dataset [22]. To compare our approach with these architectures, we also pre-trained versions of our model on MS COCO. We utilized the 20 categories in COCO that are also present in PASCAL VOC, treated annotated objects from other categories as background, and only used images where at least 0.02 % of the image contained PASCAL classes. This resulted in 97765 out of 123287 images of COCO training and validation set.

	unmasked+DE	masked+DE
LRR-4x(32x)	64.7%	64.7%
LRR-4x(16x)	66.7%	67.1%
LRR-4x(8x)	68.5%	69.3%
LRR-4x	68.9%	70.0%

(a)

	IoU class	iIoU class	IoU cat	iIoU cat
FCN-8s [24]	65.3%	41.7%	85.7%	70.1%
CRF-RNN [37]	62.5%	34.4%	82.7%	66.0%
Dilation10 [34]	67.1%	42.0%	86.5%	71.1%
DPN [23]	66.8%	39.1%	86.0%	69.1%
Pixel-level Encoding [30]	64.3%	41.6%	85.9%	73.9%
DeepLab(ResNet) [6]	70.4%	42.6%	86.4%	67.7%
Adelaide_Context [21]	71.6%	51.7%	87.3%	74.1%
LRR-4x(VGG16)	69.7%	48.0%	88.2%	74.7%

(b)

Fig. 10. (a) Mean intersection-over-union (IoU class) accuracy on Cityscapes validation set for intermediate outputs at different levels of our Laplacian reconstruction architecture trained with and without boundary masking. (b) Comparison of our model with state-of-the-art methods on the Cityscapes benchmark test set.

Fig. 11. Examples of semantic segmentation results on PASCAL VOC 2011 (top) and Cityscapes (bottom) validation images. For each row, we show the input image, ground-truth and the segmentation results of intermediate outputs of our LRR-4x model at the 32x, 16x and 8x layers. For the PASCAL dataset we also show segmentation results of FCN-8s [24].

Training was performed in two stages. In the first stage, we trained LRR-32x on VOC images and COCO images together. Since, COCO segmentation annotations are often coarser in comparison to VOC segmentation annotations, we did not use COCO images for training the LRR-4x. In the second stage, we used only PASCAL VOC images to further fine-tune the LRR-32x and then added in connections to the 16x, 8x and 4x layers and continue to fine-tune. We used the multi-scale data augmentation described in Sect. 5.1 for both stages. Training on this additional data improved the mean IoU of our model from 74.6 % to 77.5 % on PASCAL VOC 2011 validation set (see Fig. 7).

Cityscapes Benchmark: The Cityscapes dataset [8] contains high quality pixel-level annotations of images collected in street scenes from 50 different cities. The training, validation, and test sets contain 2975, 500, and 1525 images respectively (we did not use coarse annotations). This dataset contains labels for 19 semantic classes belonging to 7 categories of ground, construction, object, nature, sky, human, and vehicle.

The images of Cityscapes are high resolution (1024×2048) which makes training challenging due to limited GPU memory. We trained our model on a random crops of size 1024×512. At test time, we split each image to 2 overlapping windows and combined the predicted class probability maps. We did not use any CRF post-processing on this dataset. Figure 10 shows evaluation of our model built on VGG-16 on the validation and test data. It achieves competitive performance on the test data in comparison to the state-of-the-art methods, particularly on the category level benchmark. Examples of semantic segmentation results on the validation images are shown in Fig. 11.

6   Discussion and Conclusions

We have presented a system for semantic segmentation that utilizes two simple, extensible ideas: (1) sub-pixel upsampling using a class-specific reconstruction basis, (2) a multi-level Laplacian pyramid reconstruction architecture that uses multiplicative gating to more efficiently blend semantic-rich low-resolution feature map predictions with spatial detail from high-resolution feature maps. The resulting model is simple to train and achieves performance on PASCAL VOC 2012 test and Cityscapes that beats all but two recent models that involve considerably more elaborate architectures based on deep CRFs. We expect the relative simplicity and extensibility of our approach along with its strong performance will make it a ready candidate for further development or direct integration into more elaborate inference models.

Acknowledgements. This work was supported by NSF grants IIS-1253538 and DBI-1262547 and a hardware donation from NVIDIA.

References

1. Burt, P.J., Adelson, E.H.: The laplacian pyramid as a compact image code. IEEE Trans. Commun. **31**(4), 532–540 (1983)
2. Carreira, J., Li, F., Sminchisescu, C.: Object recognition by sequential figure-ground ranking. IJCV **98**(3), 243–262 (2012)
3. Carreira, J., Sminchisescu, C.: CPMC: automatic object segmentation using constrained parametric min-cuts. PAMI **34**(7), 1312–1328 (2012)
4. Chen, L.C., Barron, J.T., Papandreou, G., Murphy, K., Yuille, A.L.: Semantic image segmentation with task-specific edge detection using CNNs and a discriminatively trained domain transform. In: CVPR (2016)
5. Chen, L.C., Papandreou, G., Kokkinos, I., Murphy, K., Yuille, A.L.: Semantic image segmentation with deep convolutional nets and fully connected CRFs. In: ICLR (2015)
6. Chen, L.C., Papandreou, G., Kokkinos, I., Murphy, K., Yuille, A.L.: DeepLab: semantic image segmentation with deep convolutional nets, atrous convolution, and fully connectedCRFs (2016). arXiv preprint arXiv:1606.00915
7. Chen, L.C., Yang, Y., Wang, J., Xu, W., Yuille, A.L.: Attention to scale: scale-aware semantic image segmentation. In: CVPR (2015)
8. Cordts, M., Omran, M., Ramos, S., Rehfeld, T., Enzweiler, M., Benenson, R., Franke, U., Roth, S., Schiele, B.: The cityscapes dataset for semantic urban scene understanding. In: CVPR (2016)
9. Dai, J., He, K., Sun, J.: Convolutional feature masking for joint object and stuff segmentation (2014). arXiv preprint arXiv:1412.1283
10. Dai, J., He, K., Sun, J.: Boxsup: exploiting bounding boxes to supervise convolutional networks for semantic segmentation. In: ICCV, pp. 1635–1643 (2015)
11. Denton, E.L., Chintala, S., Fergus, R., et al.: Deep generative image models using a laplacian pyramid of adversarial networks. In: NIPS, pp. 1486–1494 (2015)
12. Everingham, M., Eslami, S.A., Van Gool, L., Williams, C.K., Winn, J., Zisserman, A.: The pascal visual object classes challenge: a retrospective. IJCV **111**, 98–136 (2015)
13. Gidaris, S., Komodakis, N.: Object detection via a multi-region and semantic segmentation-aware CNN model. In: ICCV, pp. 1134–1142 (2015)
14. Hariharan, B., Arbeláez, P., Bourdev, L., Maji, S., Malik, J.: Semantic contours from inverse detectors. In: ICCV, pp. 991–998 (2011)
15. Hariharan, B., Arbeláez, P., Girshick, R., Malik, J.: Hypercolumns for object segmentation and fine-grained localization. In: CVPR, pp. 447–456 (2015)
16. He, K., Zhang, X., Ren, S., Sun, J.: Deep residual learning for image recognition (2015). arXiv preprint arXiv:1512.03385
17. He, K., Zhang, X., Ren, S., Sun, J.: Identity mappings in deep residual networks. In: ECCV (2016)
18. Kohli, P., Ladick, L., Torr, P.H.: Robust higher order potentials for enforcing label consistency. IJCV **82**(3), 302–324 (2009)
19. Kokkinos, I.: Pushing the boundaries of boundary detection using deep learning. In: ICLR (2016)
20. Krähenbühl, P., Koltun, V.: Efficient inference in fully connected CRFs with gaussian edge potentials. In: NIPS (2011)
21. Lin, G., Shen, C., van den Hengel, A., Reid, I.: Efficient piecewise training of deep structured models for semantic segmentation. In: CVPR (2016)

22. Lin, T.-Y., Maire, M., Belongie, S., Hays, J., Perona, P., Ramanan, D., Dollár, P., Zitnick, C.L.: Microsoft COCO: common objects in context. In: Fleet, D., Pajdla, T., Schiele, B., Tuytelaars, T. (eds.) ECCV 2014. LNCS, vol. 8693, pp. 740–755. Springer, Heidelberg (2014). doi:10.1007/978-3-319-10602-1_48

23. Liu, Z., Li, X., Luo, P., Loy, C.C., Tang, X.: Semantic image segmentation via deep parsing network. In: ICCV, pp. 1377–1385 (2015)

24. Long, J., Shelhamer, E., Darrell, T.: Fully convolutional networks for semantic segmentation. In: CVPR, pp. 3431–3440 (2015)

25. Mostajabi, M., Yadollahpour, P., Shakhnarovich, G.: Feedforward semantic segmentation with zoom-out features. In: CVPR, pp. 3376–3385 (2015)

26. Noh, H., Hong, S., Han, B.: Learning deconvolution network for semantic segmentation. In: ICCV, pp. 1520–1528 (2015)

27. Pinheiro, P.O., Lin, T.Y., Collobert, R., Dollár, P.: Learning to refine object segments. In: ECCV (2016)

28. Shotton, J., Winn, J., Rother, C., Criminisi, A.: Textonboost for image understanding: multi-class object recognition and segmentation by jointly modeling texture, layout, and context. IJCV **81**(1), 2–23 (2009)

29. Simonyan, K., Zisserman, A.: Very deep convolutional networks for large-scale image recognition (2014). arXiv preprint arXiv:1409.1556

30. Uhrig, J., Cordts, M., Franke, U., Brox, T.: Pixel-level encoding and depth layering for instance-level semantic labeling (2016). arXiv preprint arXiv:1604.05096

31. Vedaldi, A., Lenc, K.: Matconvnet - convolutional neural networks for matlab. In: ICML (2015)

32. Xie, S., Tu, Z.: Holistically-nested edge detection. In: ICCV, pp. 1395–1403 (2015)

33. Yang, S., Ramanan, D.: Multi-scale recognition with dag-CNNs. In: ICCV, pp. 1215–1223 (2015)

34. Yu, F., Koltun, V.: Multi-scale context aggregation by dilated convolutions (2015). arXiv preprint arXiv:1511.07122

35. Zeiler, M.D., Fergus, R.: Visualizing and understanding convolutional networks. In: Fleet, D., Pajdla, T., Schiele, B., Tuytelaars, T. (eds.) ECCV 2014. LNCS, vol. 8689, pp. 818–833. Springer, Heidelberg (2014). doi:10.1007/978-3-319-10590-1_53

36. Zeiler, M.D., Taylor, G.W., Fergus, R.: Adaptive deconvolutional networks for mid and high level feature learning. In: ICCV, pp. 2018–2025 (2011)

37. Zheng, S., Jayasumana, S., Romera-Paredes, B., Vineet, V., Su, Z., Du, D., Huang, C., Torr, P.H.: Conditional random fields as recurrent neural networks. In: ICCV, pp. 1529–1537 (2015)

Generic 3D Representation
via Pose Estimation and Matching

Amir R. Zamir[1]([✉]), Tilman Wekel[1], Pulkit Agrawal[2],
Colin Wei[1], Jitendra Malik[2], and Silvio Savarese[1]

[1] Stanford University, Stanford, USA
zamir@cs.stanford.edu
[2] University of California, Berkeley, USA
http://3Drepresentation.stanford.edu/

Abstract. Though a large body of computer vision research has investigated developing generic semantic representations, efforts towards developing a similar representation for 3D has been limited. In this paper, we learn a generic 3D representation through solving a set of foundational proxy 3D tasks: object-centric camera pose estimation and wide baseline feature matching. Our method is based upon the premise that by providing supervision over a set of carefully selected foundational tasks, generalization to novel tasks and abstraction capabilities can be achieved. We empirically show that the internal representation of a multi-task ConvNet trained to solve the above core problems generalizes to novel 3D tasks (e.g., scene layout estimation, object pose estimation, surface normal estimation) without the need for fine-tuning and shows traits of abstraction abilities (e.g., cross modality pose estimation).

In the context of the core supervised tasks, we demonstrate our representation achieves state-of-the-art wide baseline feature matching results without requiring apriori rectification (unlike SIFT and the majority of learnt features). We also show 6DOF camera pose estimation given a pair local image patches. The accuracy of both supervised tasks come comparable to humans. Finally, we contribute a large-scale dataset composed of object-centric street view scenes along with point correspondences and camera pose information, and conclude with a discussion on the learned representation and open research questions.

Keywords: Generic vision · Representation · Descriptor learning · Pose estimation · Wide-baseline matching · Street view

1   Introduction

Supposed an image is given and we are interested in extracting some 3D information from it, such as, the scene layout or the pose of the visible objects. One

Electronic supplementary material The online version of this chapter (doi:10.1007/978-3-319-46487-9_33) contains supplementary material, which is available to authorized users.

© Springer International Publishing AG 2016
B. Leibe et al. (Eds.): ECCV 2016, Part III, LNCS 9907, pp. 535–553, 2016.
DOI: 10.1007/978-3-319-46487-9_33

potential approach would be to annotate a dataset for every single desired problem and train a fully supervised system for each (i.e., supervised learning). This is undesirable as an annotated dataset for each problem would be needed as well as the fact that the problems would be treated independently. In addition, unlike semantic annotations such as, object labels, certain annotations in 3D are cumbersome to collect and often require special sensors (imagine manually annotating exact pose of an object or surface normals). An alternative approach is to develop a system with a rather generic perception that can conveniently generalize to novel tasks. In this paper, we take a step towards developing a generic 3D perception system that (1) can solve novel 3D problems without fine-tuning, and (2) is capable of certain abstract generalizations in the 3D context (e.g., reason about pose similarity between two drastically different objects).

But, how could one learn such a generalizable system? Cognitive studies suggest living organisms can perform cognitive tasks for which they have not received supervision by supervised learning of other foundational tasks [28,45, 51]. Learning the relationship between visual appearance and changing the vantage point (self-motion) is among the first visual skills developed by infants and play a fundamental role in developing other skills, e.g., depth perception. A classic experiment [28] showed a kitten that was deprived from self-motion experienced fundamental issues in 3D perception, such as failing to understand depth when placed on the Visual Cliff [22]. Later works [45] argued this finding was not, at least fully, due to motion intentionality and the supervision signal of self-motion was indeed a crucial elements in learning basic visual skills. What these studies essentially suggest are: (1) by receiving supervision on a certain proxy task (in this case, self-motion), other tasks (depth understanding) can be solved sufficiently without requiring an explicit supervision, (2) some vision tasks are more foundational than others (e.g., self-motion perception vs depth understanding).

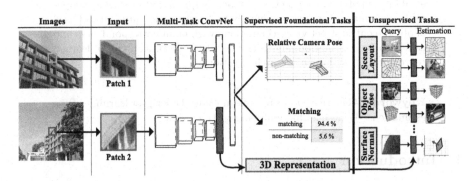

Fig. 1. Learning a generic 3D representation: we develop a supervised joint framework for camera pose estimation and wide baseline matching. We then show the internal representation of this framework can be used as a 3D representation generalizable to various 3D prediction tasks.

Inspired by the above discussion, we develop a supervised framework where a ConvNet is trained to perform 6DOF camera pose estimation. This basic task allows learning the relationship between an arbitrary change in the viewpoint and the appearance of an object/scene-point. One property of our approach is performing the camera pose estimation in a object/scene-centric manner: the training data is formed of image bundles that show the *same point of an object/scene* while the camera moves around (i.e., it fixates - see the Fig. 2(c)). This is different from existing video+metadata datasets [20], the problem of Visual Odometry [20,42], and recent works on ego-motion estimation [4,29], where in the training data, the camera moves independent of the scene. Our object/scene-centric approach is equivalent to allowing a learner to focus on a physical point while moving around and observing how the appearance of that particular point transforms according to viewpoint change. Therefore, the learner receives an additional piece of information that the observed pixels are indeed showing the same object, giving more information about how the element looks under different viewpoints and providing better grounds for learning visual encoding of an observation. Infants also explore object-motion relationships [51] in a similar way as they hold an object in hand and observe it from different views.

Our dataset also provides supervision for the task of wide baseline matching, defined as identifying if two images/patches are showing the same point regardless of the magnitude of viewpoint change. Wide baseline matching is also an important 3D problem and is closely related to object/scene-centric camera pose estimation: to identify whether two images could be showing the same point despite drastic changes in the appearance, an agent could learnt how viewpoint change impacts the appearance. Therefore, we perform our supervised training in a multi-task manner to simultaneously solve for both wide baseline matching and pose estimation. This has the advantage of learning a single representation that encodes both problems. In experiments Sect. 4.1, we show it is possible to have a single representation solving both problems without a performance drop compared to having two dedicate representations. This provides practical computational and storage advantages. Also, training ConvNets using multiple tasks/losses is desirable as it has been shown to be better regularized [23,58,63].[1]

We train the ConvNet (siamese structure with weight sharing) on patch pairs extracted from the training data and use the last FC vector of one siamese tower as the generic 3D representation (see Fig. 1). We will empirically investigate if this representation can be used for solving novel 3D problems (we evaluated on scene layout estimation, object pose estimation, surface normal estimation), and whether it can perform any 3D abstraction (we experimented on cross category pose estimation and relating the pose of synthetic geometric elements to images).

Dataset: We developed an object-centric dataset of street view scenes from the cities of Washington DC, NYC, San Francisco, Paris, Amsterdam, Las Vegas,

---

[1] Though visual matching/tracking is also one of early developed cognitive skills [10], we are unaware of any studies investigating its foundational role in developing visual perception. Therefore, we presume (and empirically observe) that the generality of our 3D representation is mostly attributed to the camera pose estimation component.

and Chicago, augmented with *camera pose* information and *point correspondences* (with >half a billion training data points). We release the dataset, trained models, and an online demo at http://3Drepresentation.stanford.edu/.

Novelty in the Supervised Tasks: Independent of providing a generic 3D representation, our approach to solving the two supervised tasks is novel in a few aspects. There is a large amount of previous work on detecting, describing, and matching image features, either through a handcrafting the feature [5,11,35,38–40] or learning it [9,19,25,49,50,65,66]. Unlike the majority of such features that utilize pre-rectification (within either the method or the training data), we argue that rectification prior to descriptor matching is not required; our representation can learn the impact of viewpoint change, rather than canceling it (by directly training on non-rectified data and supplying camera pose information during training). Therefore, it does not need an apriori rectification and is capable of performing wide baseline matching at the descriptor level. We report state-of-the-art results on feature matching. Wide baseline matching has been also the topic of many papers [24,44,54,62,67] with the majority of them focused on leveraging various geometric constraints for ruling out incorrect 'already-established' correspondences, as well as a number of methods that operate based on generating exhaustive warps [41] or assuming 3D information about the scene is given [61]. In contrast, we learn a descriptor that is supervised to internally handle a wide baseline in the first place.

In the context of pose estimation, we show estimating a 6DOF camera pose given only a pair of local image patches, and without the need for several point correspondences, is feasible. This is different from many previous works [3,8,14,20,26,52,59] from both visual odometry and SfM literature that perform the estimation through a two step process consisting of finding point correspondences between images followed by pose estimation. Koser and Koch [30] also demonstrate pose estimation from a local region, though the plane on which the region lies is assumed to be given. The recent works of [4,29] supervise a ConvNet on the camera pose from image batches but do not provide results on matching and pose estimation. We report a human-level accuracy on this task.

Existing Unsupervised Learning and ConvNet Initialization Works: The majority of previous unsupervised learning, transfer learning, and representation learning works have been targeted towards semantics [17,18,46,47,53]. It has been practically well observed [18,46] that the representation of a convnet trained on imagenet [32] can generalize to other, mostly semantic, tasks. A number of methods investigated initialization techniques for ConvNet training based on unsupervised/weakly supervised data to alleviate the need for a large training dataset for various tasks [17,57]. Very recently, the methods of [4,29] explored using motion metadata associated with videos (KITTI dataset [20]) as a form of supervision for training a ConvNet. However, they either do not investigate developing a 3D representation or intent to provide initialization strategies that are meant to be fine-tuned with supervised data for a desired task. In contrast, we investigate developing a generalizable 3D representation, perform the learning in an object-centric manner, and evaluate its unsupervised performance on various 3D tasks without any fine-tuning on the representation. We experimentally compare against the related recent works that made their models available [4,57].

Primary contributions of this paper are summarized as: (I) A generic 3D representation with empirically validated abstraction and generalization abilities. (II) A learned joint descriptor for wide baseline matching and camera pose estimation at the level of local image patches. (III) A large-scale object-centric dataset of street view scenes including camera pose and correspondence information.

2   Object-Centric Street View Dataset

The dataset for the formulated task needs to not only provide a large amount of training data, but also show a rich camera pose variety, while the scale of the aimed learning problem invalidates any manual procedure. We present a procedure that allows acquiring a large amount of training data in an automated manner, based on two sources of information: (1) Google street view [2] which is an almost inexhaustible source of geo-referenced and calibrated images, (2) 3D city models [1,2] that cover thousands of cities around the world.

The core idea of our approach is to form correspondences between the geo-referenced street view camera and physical 3D points that are given by the 3D models. More specifically, at any given street view location, we densely shoot rays into space in order to find intersections with nearby buildings. Each ray back projects one image pixel into the 3D space, as shown in Fig. 2-(a). By projecting the resulting intersection points onto adjacent street view panoramas (see Fig. 2-b), we can form image to image correspondences (see Fig. 2c). Each image is then associated with a (virtual) camera that fixates on the physical target point on a building by placing it on the optical center. To make the ray intersection procedure scalable, we perform occlusion reasoning on the 3D models to pre-identify from what GPS locations an arbitrary target would be visible and perform the ray intersection on those points only.

Pixel Alignment and Pruning: This system requires integration of multiple resources, including elevation maps, GPS from street view, and 3D models.

Fig. 2. Illustration of the object-centric data collection process. We use large-scale geo-registered 3D building models to register pixels in street view images on world coordinates system (see (a)) and use that for finding correspondences and their relative pose across multiple street view images (see (b)). Each ray represents one pixel-3D world coordinate correspondence. Each of the red, green, and blue colors represent one street view location. Each row in (c) shows a sample collected image bundle. The center pixel (marker) is expected to correspond to the same physical point. (Color figure online)

Though the quality of output exceeded our expectation (see samples in Fig. 2(c)), any slight inaccuracy in the metadata or 3D models can cause a pixel misalignment in the collected images (examples shown in the first and last rows of Fig. 2(c)). Also, there are undocumented objects such as trees or moving objects that cause occlusions. Thus, a content-based post alignment and pruning was necessary. We again used metadata in our alignment procedure to be able to handle image bundles with arbitrarily wide baselines (note that the collected image bundles can show large, often >100°, viewpoint changes). In the interest of space, we describe this procedure in supplementary material (Sect. 3).

This process forms our dataset composed of matching and non-matching patches as well as the relative camera pose for the matching pairs. We stopped collecting data when we reached the coverage of $>200 \, km^2$ from the 7 cities mentioned in Sect. 1. The collection procedure is currently done on Google street view, but can be performed using any geo-referenced calibrated imagery. We will experimentally show that the trained representation on this data does not manifest a clear bias towards street view scenes and outperforms existing feature learning methods on non-street view benchmarks.

Noise Statistics: We performed a user study through Amazon Mechanical Turk to quantify the amount of noise in the final dataset. Please see supplementary material (Sect. 3.2) for the complete discussion and results. Briefly, 68 % of the patch pairs were found to have at least 25 % of overlap in their content. The mean and standard deviation of pixel misalignment was 16.12 ($\approx$11 % of patch width) and 11.55 pixels, respectively. We did not perform any filtering or geo-fencing on top of the collected data as the amount of noise appeared to be within the robustness tolerance of ConvNet trainings and they converged.

3   Learning Using ConvNets

A joint feature descriptor was learnt by supervising a Convolutional Neural Network (ConvNet) to perform 6DOF camera pose estimation and wide baseline matching between pairs of image patches. For the purpose of training, any two image patches depicting the same physical target point in the street view dataset were labelled as matching and other pairs of images were labelled as non-matching. The training for camera pose estimation was performed using matching patches. The patches were always cropped from the center of the collected street view image to keep the optical center at the target point.

The camera pose between each pair of matching patches was represented by a 6D vector; the first three dimensions were Tait-Bryan angles (roll, yaw, pitch) and the last three dimensions were cartesian (x, y, z) translation coordinates expressed in meters. For the purpose of training, 6D pose vectors were preprocessed to be zero mean and unit standard deviation (i.e., z-scoring). The ground-truth and predicted pose vectors for the ith example are denoted by p_i^*, p_i respectively. The pose estimation loss $L_{pose}(p_i^*, p_i)$ was set to be the robust regression loss described in Eq. 1:

$$L_{pose}(p_i^*, p_i) = \begin{cases} e & \text{if } e \leq 1 \\ 1 + \log e & \text{if } e > 1 \end{cases} \text{ where } e = ||p_i^* - p_i||_{l_2}. \tag{1}$$

The loss function for patch matching $L_{match}(m_i^*, m_i)$ was set to be sigmoid cross entropy, where m_i^* is the ground-truth binary variable indicating matching/non-matching and m_i is the predicted probability of matching.

ConvNet training was performed to optimize the joint matching and pose estimation loss (L_{joint}) described in Eq. 2. The relative weighting between the pose (L_{pose}) and matching (L_{match}) losses was controlled by λ (we set $\lambda = 1$).

$$L_{joint}(p_i^*, m_i^*, p_i, m_i) = L_{pose}(p_i^*, p_i) + \lambda L_{match}(m_i, m_i^*). \tag{2}$$

Our training set consisted of patch pairs drawn from a wide distribution of baseline changes ranging from $0°$ to over $120°$. We consider patches of size 192×192 ($<15\%$ of the actual image size) and rescaled them to 101×101 before passing them into the ConvNet.

A ConvNet model with siamese architecture [15] containing two identical streams with identical set of weights was used for computing the relative pose and the matching score between the two input patches. A standard ConvNet architecture was used for each stream: C(20, 7, 1)-ReLU-P(2, 2)-C(40, 5, 1)-ReLU-P(2, 2)-C(80, 4, 1)-ReLU-P(2, 2)-C(160, 4, 2)-ReLU-P(2, 2)-F(500)-ReLU-F(500)-ReLU. The naming convention is as follows: C(n, k, s): convolutional layer n filters, spatial size $k \times k$, and stride s. P(k, s): max pooling layer of size $k \times k$ and stride s. ReLU: rectified linear unit. F(n): fully connected linear layer with n output units. The feature descriptors of both streams were concatenated and fed into a fully connected layer of 500 units which were then fed into the pose and matching losses. With this ConvNet configuration, the size of the image representation (i.e., the last FC vector of one siamese half - see Fig. 1) is 500. Our architecture is admittedly pretty common and standard. This allows us to evaluate if our good end performance is attributed to our hypothesis on learning on foundational tasks and the new dataset, rather than a novel architecture.

We trained the ConvNet model from scratch (i.e., randomly initialized weights) using SGD with momentum (initial learning rate of .001 divided by 10 per 60 K iterations), gradient clipping, and a batch size of 256. We found that the use of gradient clipping was essential for training as even robust regression losses produce unstable gradients at the starting of training. Our network converged after 210 K iterations. Training using Euler angles performed better than quaternions ($17.7°$ vs $29.8°$ median angular error), and the robust loss outperformed the non-robust l_2 loss ($17.7°$ vs $22.3°$ median angular error). Additional details about the training procedure can be found in the supplementary material.

4   Experimental Discussions and Results

We implemented our framework using data parallelism [31] on a cluster of 5–10 GPUs. At the test time, computing the representation is a feed-forward pass through a siamese half ConvNet and takes ~2.9 ms per image on a single processor. Sections 4.1 and 4.2 provide the evaluations of the learned representation on the supervised and novel 3D tasks, respectively.

4.1 Evaluations on the Supervised Tasks

Evaluations on the Street View Dataset. The test set of pose estimation is composed of 7725 pairs of matching patches from our dataset. The test set of matching includes 4223 matching and 18648 non-matching pairs. It is made sure that no data from those areas and their vicinity is used in training. Each patch pair in the test sets was verified by three Amazon Mechanical Turkers to verify the ground truth is indeed correct. For the matching pairs, the Turkers also ensured the center pixel of patches are no more than 25 pixels (~3 % of image width) apart. Visualizations of the test set can be seen on our website.

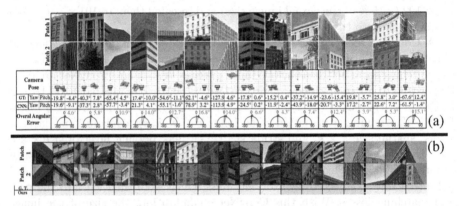

Fig. 3. (a) **Sample qualitative results of camera pose estimation.** 1st and 2nd rows show the patches. The 3rd row depicts the estimated relative camera poses on a unit sphere (black: patch 1's camera (reference), red: ground-truth pose of patch 2, blue: estimated pose of patch 2). Rightward and upward are the positive directions. (b) **Sample wide baseline matching results.** Green and red represent 'matching' and 'non-matching', respectively. Three failure cases are shown on the right. (Color figure online)

Pose Estimation. Figure 3-(a) provides qualitative results of pose estimation. The angular evaluation metric is the standard overall angular error [20,33], defined as the angle between the predicted pose vector and the ground truth vector in the plane defined by their cross product. The translational error metric is l_2 norm of the difference vector between the normalized predicted translation vector and ground truth [20,33]. The translation vector was normalized to enable comparing with up-to-scale SfM.

Figure 4-right provides the quantitative evaluations. The plots (a) and (c) illustrate the distribution of the test set with respect to pose estimation error for each method (the more skewed to the left, the better). The green curve shows pose estimation results by human subjects. Two users with computer vision

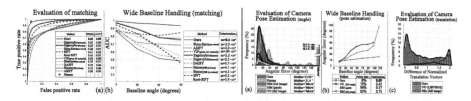

Fig. 4. Left: Quantitative evaluation of matching. ROC curves of each method and corresponding AUC and FPR@95 values are shown in (a). **Right: Quantitative evaluation of camera pose estimation.** VO and SfM denote Visual Odometery (LIBVISO2) and Structure-from-Motion (visualSfM), respectively. Evaluation of robustness to wide baseline camera shifts is shown in (b) plots. (Color figure online)

knowledge, but unaware of the particular use case, were asked to estimated the relative pitch and yaw between a random subset of 500 test pairs. They were allowed to train themselves with as many training sampled as they wished. ConvNet outperformed human on this task with a margin of 8° in median error.

Pose Estimation Baselines: We compared against Structure-from-Motion (visualSfM [59,60] with default components and tuned hyper-parameters for pairwise pose estimation on 192×192 patches and full images) and LIBVISO2 Visual Odometery [21] on full images. Both SfM and LIBVISO2 VO suffer from a large RANSAC failure rate mostly due to the wide baselines in test pairs.

Figure 4-right (b) shows how the median angular error (Y axis) changes as the baseline of the test pairs (X axis) increases. This is achieved through binning the test set into 8 bins based on their baseline size. This plot quantifies the ability of the evaluated methods in handling a wide baseline. We adopt the slope of the curves as the quantification of deterioration in accuracy as the baseline increases.

Wide Baseline Matching. Figure 3-(b) shows samples feature matching results using our approach, with three failure cases on the right. Figure 4-left provides the quantitative results. The standard metric [12] for descriptor matching is ROC curve acquired from sorting the test set pairs according to their matching score. For unsupervised methods, e.g., SIFT, the matching score is the l_2 distance. False Positive Rate at 95 % recall (FPR@95) and Area Under Curve (AUC) of ROC are standard scalar quantifications of descriptor matching [12,50].

Matching Baselines: We compared our results with the handcrafted features of SIFT [35], Root-SIFT [7], DAISY [55], VIP [61] (which requires the surface normals in the input for which we used the normals from the 3D models), and ASIFT [41]. The matching score of ASIFT was the number of found correspondences in the test pair given the *full images*. We also compared against the learning based features of Zagoruyko and Komodakis [65] (using the models of authors), Simonyan et al. [50] (with and without retraining), Simo-Serra et al. [49] (using authors' best pretrained model) as well as human subjects (the red dot on the

Table 1. Evaluations on Brown's Benchmark [12]. FPR@95 (↓) is the metric.

Train	Test	MatchNet [25]	Zagor. siam [65]	Simonyan [50]	Trzcinski [56]	Brown [12]	Root-SIFT [7]	Ours
Yos	ND	7.70	5.75	6.82	13.37	11.98	22.06	**4.17**
Yos	Lib	13.02	13.45	14.58	21.03	18.27	29.65	**11.66**
Lib	ND	4.75	4.33	7.22	14.15	N/A	22.06	**1.47**
ND	Lib	8.84	8.77	12.42	18.05	16.85	29.65	**7.39**
Lib	Yos	13.57	14.89	**11.18**	19.63	N/A	26.71	13.78
ND	Yos	11.00	13.23	**10.08**	15.86	13.55	26.71	12.30
mean		9.81	10.07	10.38	17.01	15.16	26.14	**8.46**

Table 2. Evaluation on Mikolajczyk and Schmid's [39]. The metric is mAP(↑).

Transf. magnitude	1	2	3	4	5
SIFT [35]	40.1	28.0	24.3	29.0	17.1
Zagor. [65]	43.2	37.5	29.2	28.0	16.8
Fischer et al. [19]	42.3	33.9	26.1	22.1	14.6
Ours-rectified	46.4	**41.3**	29.5	23.7	17.9
Ours-unrectified	**51.4**	37.8	**34.2**	**30.8**	**20.8**

ROC plot). Figure 4-left(b) provides the evaluations in terms of handling wide baselines, similar to Fig. 4-right(b).

Brown et al. Benchmark and Mikolajczyk's Benchmark. We performed evaluations on the *non-street view* benchmarks of Brown et al. [12] and Mikolajczyk and Schmid [39] to find if (1) if our representation was performing well only on street view scenery, and (2) if wide baseline handling capability was achieved at the expense of lower performance on small baselines (as these benchmarks have a narrower baseline compared to our dataset for the most part). Tables 1 and 2 provide the quantitative results. We include a thorough description of evaluation setup and detailed discussions in the supplementary material (Sect. 2).

Joint Feature Learning. We studied different aspects of joint learning the representation and information sharing among the core supervised tasks. In the interest of space, we provide quantitative results in supplementary material (Sect. 1). The conclusion of the tests was that: First, the problems of wide baseline matching and camera pose estimation have a great deal of shared information. Second, one descriptor can encode both problems with no performance drop.

4.2 Evaluating the 3D Representation on Novel Tasks

The results of evaluating our representation on novel 3D tasks are provided in this section. The tasks as well as the images (e.g., Airship images from ImageNet) used in these evaluations are significantly different from what our representation was trained for (i.e., camera pose estimation and matching on local patches of street view images). The fact that, despite such differences, our representation achieves best results among all unsupervised methods and gets close to supervised methods for each of the tasks empirically validates our hypothesis on learning on foundational tasks (see Sect. 1).

Our ways of evaluating and probing the representation in an unsupervised manner are (1) tSNE [36]: large-scale 2D embedding of the representation.

Fig. 5. 2D embedding of our representation on 3,000 unseen patches using tSNE. An organization based on the Manhattan pose of the patches can be seen. See comparable AlexNet's embedding in the supplementary material's Sect. 6. (best seen on screen)

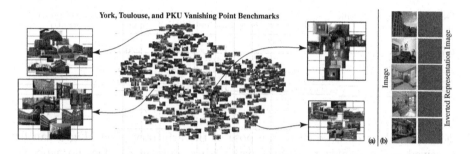

Fig. 6. (a) tSNE of a superset of various vanishing point benchmarks [6,16,34] (to battle the small size of datasets). (b) inversion [37] of our representation. Both plots shows traits of vanishing points.

This allows visualizing the space and getting a sense of similarity from the perspective of the representation, (2) Nearest Neighbors (NN) on the full dimensional representation, and (3) training a simple classifier (e.g., KNN or a linear classifier) on the *frozen* representation (i.e., no fine-tuning) to read out a desired variable. The latter enables quantifying if the required information for solving a novel task is encoded in the representation and can be extracted using a simple function. We compare against the representations of related methods that made their models available [4,57], various layers of AlexNet trained on ImageNet [32], and a number of supervised techniques for some of the tasks. Additional results are provided in the supplementary material and the website.

Surface Normals and Vanishing Points. Figure 5 shows tSNE embedding of 3,000 unseen patches showing that the organization of the representation space is based on geometry and not semantics/appearance. The ConvNet was trained to estimate the pose between *matching* patches only while in the embedding, the *non-matching* patches with a similar pose are placed nearby. This suggests the representation has generalized the concept of pose to non-matching patches. This indeed has relations to surface normals as the relative pose between an arbitrary

Fig. 7. **Scene layout NN search results between LSUN images and synthetic concave cubes defining abstract 3D layouts.** Images with yellow boundary show the ground truth layout. (Color figure online)

Table 3. Layout classification (LSUN)

Representation	Classification accuracy
AlexNet FC7	45.9%
AlexNet Pool5	47.7%
Ours	57.6%

Table 4. Layout estimation (LSUN)

Method	Corner error	Pixelwise error
UIUC (supervised)	0.11	0.17
Hedau et al. (supervised)	0.15	0.24
Ours (unsupervised)	0.16	0.29

Table 5. Object pose estimation (PASCAL3D)

Method	Av. pose error (°)
scratch	34°
AlexNet (ImaneNet)	23°
Ours	26°

and a frontal patch is equal to the pose of the arbitrary patch; Fig. 5 can be perceived as the organization of the patches based on their surface normals.

To better understand how this was achieved, we visualized the activations of the ConvNet at different layers. Similar to other ConvNets, the first few layers formed general gradient based filters while in higher layers, the edges parallel in the physical world seemed to persist and cluster together. This is similar to the concept of vanishing points, and from the theoretical perspective, would be intriguing and explain the pose estimation results, since three common vanishing points are theoretically enough for a full angular pose estimation [13,26]. To further investigate this, we generated the inversion of our representation using the method of [37] (see Fig. 6-(b)), which show patterns correlating with the vanishing points of the image. Figure 6-(a) also illustrates the tSNE of a superset of several vanishing point benchmarks showing that images with similar vanishing points are embedded nearby. Therefore, we speculate that the ConvNet has developed a representation based on the concept of vanishing points[2]. This would also explain the results shown in the following sections.

Surface Normal Estimation on NYUv2 [48]: Numerical evaluation on unsupervised surface normal estimation provided in supplementary material Sect. 4.

Scene Layout Estimation. We evaluated our representation on LSUN [64] layout benchmark using the standard protocol [64]. Table 4 provides the results

---

[2] We attempted to quantitatively evaluate this, but the largest vanishing point datasets (e.g., York [16] and PKU [34]) include only 102–200 images for both training and testing. Given a 500D descriptor, it was not feasible to provide a statistically significant evidence.

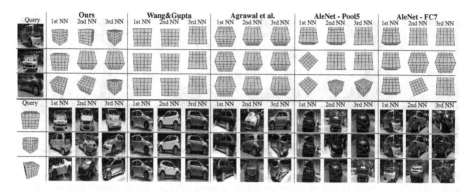

Fig. 8. NN search results between EPFL dataset images and a synthetic cube defining an abstract 3D pose. See the supplementary material (Sect. 5) for tSNE embedding of all cubes and car poses in a joint space. Note that the 3D poses defined by the cubes are 90° congruent.

of layout estimation using a simple NN classifier on our representation along with two supervised baselines, showing that our representation (with no fine-tuning) achieved a performance close to Hedau et al.'s [27] supervised method on this novel task. Table 3 provides the results of layout classification [64] using NN classifier on our representation compared to AlexNets FC7 and Pool5.

Abstraction: Cube⇆Layout: To evaluate the abstract generalization abilities of our representation, we generated a sparse set of 88 images showing the interior of a simple synthetic cube parametrized over different view angles. The rendered images can be seen as an abstract cubic layout of a room. We then performed NN search between these images and LSUN dataset using our representations and several baselines. As apparent in Fig. 7, our representation retrieves meaningful NNs while the baselines mostly overfit to appearance and retrieve either an incorrect or always the same NN. This suggests our representation could abstract away the irrelevant information and encode some information essential to the 3D of the image.

3D Object Pose Estimation.

Abstraction: Cube⇆Object: We performed a similar abstraction test between a set of 88 convex cubes and the images of EPFL Multi-View Car dataset [43], which includes a dense sampling of various viewpoints of cars in an exhibition. We picked this simple cube pattern as it is the simplest geometric element that defines three vanishing points. The same observation as the abstraction experiment on LSUN's is made here with our NNs being meaningful while baselines mostly overfit to appearance with no clear geometric abstraction trait (Fig. 8).

ImageNet: Figure 9 shows the tSNE embedding of several ImageNet categories based on our representation and the baselines. The embeddings of our representation are geometrically meaningful, while the baselines either perform a semantic organization or overfit to other aspects, such as color.

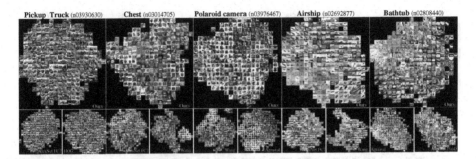

Fig. 9. tSNE of several ImageNet categories using our unsupervised representation along with several baselines. Our representation manifests a meaningful geometric organization of objects. tSNE of more categories in the supplementary material and the website. (best seen on screen) (Color figure online)

PASCAL3D: Figure 10 shows cross-category NN search results for our representation along with several baselines. This experiment also evaluates a certain level of abstraction as some of the object categories can be drastically different looking. We also quantitatively evaluated on 3D object pose estimation on PASCAL3D. For this experiment, we trained a ConvNet from scratch, fine-tuned AlexNet pre-trained on ImageNet, and fine-tuned our network; we read the pose out using a linear regressor layer.[3] Our results outperform scratch network and come close to AlexNet that has seen thousands of images from the same categories from ImageNet and other objects (Table 5). Note that certain aspects of object pose estimation, e.g., distinguishing between the front and back of a bus, are more of a semantic task rather than geometric/3D. This explains a considerable part of the failures of our representation which is object/semantic agnostic.

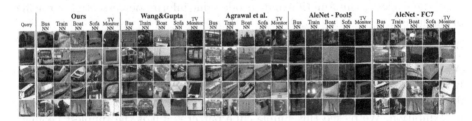

Fig. 10. Qualitative results of cross-category NN-search on PASCAL3D using our representation along with baselines.

---

[3] The classes of boat, sofa, and chair were showing a performance near statistical random for all methods and were removed from the evaluations.

5   Discussion and Conclusion

To summarize, we developed a generic 3D representation through solving a set of supervised foundational proxy tasks. We reported state-of-the-art results on the supervised tasks and showed the learned representation manifests generalization and abstraction traits. However, a number of questions remain open:

Though we were inspired by cognitive studies in defining the foundational supervised tasks leading to a generalizable representation, this remains at an inspiration level. Given that a 'taxonomy' among basic 3D tasks has not been developed, it is not concretely defined which tasks are foundational and which ones are secondary. Developing such a taxonomy (i.e., whether task A is inclusive of, overlapping with, or disjoint from task B) or generally efforts understanding the task space would be a rewarding step towards soundly developing the *3D complete* representation. Also, semantic and 3D aspects of the visual world are tangled together. So far, we have developed independent semantic and 3D representations, but investigating concrete techniques for integrating them (beyond simplistic late fusion or ConvNet fine-tuning) is a worthwhile future direction for research. Perhaps, inspirations from partitions of visual cortex could be insightful towards developing the ultimate *vision complete* representation.

Acknowledgement. MURI (1186514-1-TBCJE), Nissan (1188371-1-UDARQ).

References

1. http://opendata.dc.gov/
2. Google Street View. https://www.google.com/maps/streetview/
3. Agarwal, S., Furukawa, Y., Snavely, N., Simon, I., Curless, B., Seitz, S.M., Szeliski, R.: Building Rome in a day. Commun. ACM **54**(10), 105–112 (2011)
4. Agrawal, P., Carreira, J., Malik, J.: Learning to see by moving (2015)
5. Alahi, A., Ortiz, R., Vandergheynst, P.: FREAK: fast retina keypoint. In: 2012 IEEE Conference on Computer Vision and Pattern Recognition (CVPR), pp. 510–517. IEEE (2012)
6. Angladon, V., Gasparini, S., Charvillat, V.: The toulouse vanishing points dataset. In: Proceedings of the 6th ACM Multimedia Systems Conference (MMSys 2015) (2015)
7. Arandjelovic, R., Zisserman, A.: Three things everyone should know to improve object retrieval. In: 2012 IEEE Conference on Computer Vision and Pattern Recognition (CVPR), pp. 2911–2918. IEEE (2012)
8. Badino, H., Yamamoto, A., Kanade, T.: Visual odometry by multi-frame feature integration. In: 2013 IEEE International Conference on Computer Vision Workshops (ICCVW), pp. 222–229. IEEE (2013)
9. Balntas, V., Johns, E., Tang, L., Mikolajczyk, K.: PN-Net: conjoined triple deep network for learning local image descriptors. arXiv preprint arXiv:1601.05030 (2016)
10. Banks, M.S., Salapatek, P.: Infant visual perception. In: Mussen, P.H. (eds.) Handbook of Child Psychology: Formerly Carmichael's Manual of Child Psychology (1983)

11. Bay, H., Tuytelaars, T., Van Gool, L.: SURF: speeded up robust features. In: Leonardis, A., Bischof, H., Pinz, A. (eds.) ECCV 2006, Part I. LNCS, vol. 3951, pp. 404–417. Springer, Heidelberg (2006)

12. Brown, M., Hua, G., Winder, S.: Discriminative learning of local image descriptors. IEEE Trans. Pattern Anal. Mach. Intell. **33**(1), 43–57 (2011)

13. Caprile, B., Torre, V.: Using vanishing points for camera calibration. Int. J. Comput. Vis. **4**(2), 127–139 (1990)

14. Chen, D.M., Baatz, G., Köser, K., Tsai, S.S., Vedantham, R., Pylvä, T., Roimela, K., Chen, X., Bach, J., Pollefeys, M., et al.: City-scale landmark identification on mobile devices. In: 2011 IEEE Conference on Computer Vision and Pattern Recognition (CVPR), pp. 737–744. IEEE (2011)

15. Chopra, S., Hadsell, R., LeCun, Y.: Learning a similarity metric discriminatively, with application to face verification. In: IEEE Computer Society Conference on Computer Vision and Pattern Recognition, CVPR 2005, vol. 1, pp. 539–546. IEEE (2005)

16. Denis, P., Elder, J.H., Estrada, F.J.: Efficient edge-based methods for estimating manhattan frames in urban imagery. In: Forsyth, D., Torr, P., Zisserman, A. (eds.) ECCV 2008, Part II. LNCS, vol. 5303, pp. 197–210. Springer, Heidelberg (2008)

17. Doersch, C., Gupta, A., Efros, A.A.: Unsupervised visual representation learning by context prediction. In: Proceedings of the IEEE International Conference on Computer Vision, pp. 1422–1430 (2015)

18. Donahue, J., Jia, Y., Vinyals, O., Hoffman, J., Zhang, N., Tzeng, E., Darrell, T.: DeCAF: a deep convolutional activation feature for generic visual recognition. arXiv preprint arXiv:1310.1531 (2013)

19. Fischer, P., Dosovitskiy, A., Brox, T.: Descriptor matching with convolutional neural networks: a comparison to SIFT (2014). arXiv preprint arXiv:1405.5769

20. Geiger, A., Lenz, P., Urtasun, R.: Are we ready for autonomous driving? The KITTI vision benchmark suite. In: 2012 IEEE Conference on Computer Vision and Pattern Recognition (CVPR), pp. 3354–3361. IEEE (2012)

21. Geiger, A., Ziegler, J., Stiller, C.: StereoScan: dense 3d reconstruction in real-time. In: Intelligent Vehicles Symposium (IV) (2011)

22. Gibson, E.J., Walk, R.D.: The Visual Cliff, vol. 1. WH Freeman Company, New York (1960)

23. Girshick, R.: Fast R-CNN. In: Proceedings of the International Conference on Computer Vision (ICCV) (2015)

24. Goedemé, T., Tuytelaars, T., Van Gool, L.: Fast wide baseline matching for visual navigation. In: IEEE Computer Society Conference on Computer Vision and Pattern Recognition, vol. 1, pp. I–24 (2004)

25. Han, X., Leung, T., Jia, Y., Sukthankar, R., Berg, A.C.: MatchNet: unifying feature and metric learning for patch-based matching. In: Proceedings of the IEEE Conference on Computer Vision and Pattern Recognition, pp. 3279–3286 (2015)

26. Hartley, R., Zisserman, A.: Multiple View Geometry in Computer Vision. Cambridge University Press, Cambridge (2003)

27. Hedau, V., Hoiem, D., Forsyth, D.: Recovering the spatial layout of cluttered rooms. In: 2009 IEEE 12th International Conference on Computer Vision, pp. 1849–1856. IEEE (2009)

28. Held, R., Hein, A.: Movement-produced stimulation in the development of visually guided behavior. J. Comp. Physiol. Psychol. **56**(5), 872 (1963)

29. Jayaraman, D., Grauman, K.: Learning image representations tied to ego-motion. In: Proceedings of the IEEE International Conference on Computer Vision, pp. 1413–1421 (2015)
30. Köser, K., Koch, R.: Differential spatial resection - pose estimation using a single local image feature. In: Forsyth, D., Torr, P., Zisserman, A. (eds.) ECCV 2008, Part IV. LNCS, vol. 5305, pp. 312–325. Springer, Heidelberg (2008)
31. Krizhevsky, A.: One weird trick for parallelizing convolutional neural networks. arXiv preprint arXiv:1404.5997 (2014)
32. Krizhevsky, A., Sutskever, I., Hinton, G.E.: ImageNet classification with deep convolutional neural networks. In: Advances in Neural Information Processing Systems, pp. 1097–1105 (2012)
33. Kümmerle, R., Steder, B., Dornhege, C., Ruhnke, M., Grisetti, G., Stachniss, C., Kleiner, A.: On measuring the accuracy of SLAM algorithms. Auton. Robot. **27**(4), 387–407 (2009)
34. Li, B., Peng, K., Ying, X., Zha, H.: Simultaneous vanishing point detection and camera calibration from single images. In: Boyle, R., et al. (eds.) ISVC 2010, Part II. LNCS, vol. 6454, pp. 151–160. Springer, Heidelberg (2010)
35. Lowe, D.G.: Distinctive image features from scale-invariant keypoints. Int. J. Comput. Vis. **60**(2), 91–110 (2004)
36. Van der Maaten, L., Hinton, G.: Visualizing data using t-SNE. J. Mach. Learn. Res. **9**(2579–2605), 85 (2008)
37. Mahendran, A., Vedaldi, A.: Understanding deep image representations by inverting them. In: 2015 IEEE Conference on Computer Vision and Pattern Recognition (CVPR), pp. 5188–5196. IEEE (2015)
38. Matas, J., Chum, O., Urban, M., Pajdla, T.: Robust wide-baseline stereo from maximally stable extremal regions. Image Vis. Comput. **22**(10), 761–767 (2004)
39. Mikolajczyk, K., Schmid, C.: A performance evaluation of local descriptors. IEEE Trans. Pattern Anal. Mach. Intell. **27**(10), 1615–1630 (2005)
40. Moreels, P., Perona, P.: Evaluation of features detectors and descriptors based on 3D objects. Int. J. Comput. Vis. **73**(3), 263–284 (2007)
41. Morel, J.M., Yu, G.: ASIFT: a new framework for fully affine invariant image comparison. SIAM J. Imaging Sci. **2**(2), 438–469 (2009)
42. Nistér, D., Naroditsky, O., Bergen, J.: Visual odometry. In: Proceedings of the 2004 IEEE Computer Society Conference on Computer Vision and Pattern Recognition, CVPR 2004, vol. 1, pp. I-652. IEEE (2004)
43. Ozuysal, M., Lepetit, V., Fua, P.: Pose estimation for category specific multiview object localization. In: Conference on Computer Vision and Pattern Recognition, Miami, FL, June 2009
44. Pritchett, P., Zisserman, A.: Wide baseline stereo matching. In: Sixth International Conference on Computer Vision, 1998, pp. 754–760. IEEE (1998)
45. Rader, N., Bausano, M., Richards, J.E.: On the nature of the visual-cliff-avoidance response in human infants. Child Dev. 61–68 (1980)
46. Razavian, A., Azizpour, H., Sullivan, J., Carlsson, S.: CNN features off-the-shelf: an astounding baseline for recognition. In: Proceedings of the IEEE Conference on Computer Vision and Pattern Recognition Workshops, pp. 806–813 (2014)
47. Sermanet, P., Eigen, D., Zhang, X., Mathieu, M., Fergus, R., LeCun, Y.: OverFeat: integrated recognition, localization and detection using convolutional networks. arXiv preprint arXiv:1312.6229 (2013)

48. Silberman, N., Hoiem, D., Kohli, P., Fergus, R.: Indoor segmentation and support inference from RGBD images. In: Fitzgibbon, A., Lazebnik, S., Perona, P., Sato, Y., Schmid, C. (eds.) ECCV 2012, Part V. LNCS, vol. 7576, pp. 746–760. Springer, Heidelberg (2012)

49. Simo-Serra, E., Trulls, E., Ferraz, L., Kokkinos, I., Fua, P., Moreno-Noguer, F.: Discriminative learning of deep convolutional feature point descriptors. In: Proceedings of the IEEE International Conference on Computer Vision, pp. 118–126 (2015)

50. Simonyan, K., Vedaldi, A., Zisserman, A.: Learning local feature descriptors using convex optimisation. IEEE Trans. Pattern Anal. Mach. Intell. **36**(8) (2014)

51. Smith, L., Gasser, M.: The development of embodied cognition: six lessons from babies. Artif. Life **11**(1–2), 13–29 (2005)

52. Song, S., Chandraker, M., Guest, C.C.: Parallel, real-time monocular visual odometry. In: 2013 IEEE International Conference on Robotics and Automation (ICRA). IEEE (2013)

53. Tarr, M.J., Black, M.J.: A computational and evolutionary perspective on the role of representation in vision. CVGIP: Image Underst. **60**(1), 65–73 (1994)

54. Tell, D., Carlsson, S.: Combining appearance and topology for wide baseline matching. In: Heyden, A., Sparr, G., Nielsen, M., Johansen, P. (eds.) ECCV 2002, Part I. LNCS, vol. 2350, pp. 68–81. Springer, Heidelberg (2002)

55. Tola, E., Lepetit, V., Fua, P.: A fast local descriptor for dense matching. In: IEEE Conference on Computer Vision and Pattern Recognition, CVPR 2008, pp. 1–8. IEEE (2008)

56. Trzcinski, T., Christoudias, M., Lepetit, V., Fua, P.: Learning image descriptors with the boosting-trick. In: Advances in Neural Information Processing Systems, pp. 269–277 (2012)

57. Wang, X., Gupta, A.: Unsupervised learning of visual representations using videos. In: Proceedings of the IEEE International Conference on Computer Vision, pp. 2794–2802 (2015)

58. Weston, J., Ratle, F., Mobahi, H., Collobert, R.: Deep learning via semi-supervised embedding. In: Montavon, G., Orr, G.B., Müller, K.-R. (eds.) Neural Networks: Tricks of the Trade, 2nd edn. LNCS, vol. 7700, 2nd edn, pp. 639–655. Springer, Heidelberg (2012)

59. Wu, C.: VisualSFM: a visual structure from motion system (2011). http://ccwu. me/vsfm/

60. Wu, C., Agarwal, S., Curless, B., Seitz, S.M.: Multicore bundle adjustment. In: 2011 IEEE Conference on Computer Vision and Pattern Recognition (CVPR), pp. 3057–3064. IEEE (2011)

61. Wu, C., Clipp, B., Li, X., Frahm, J.M., Pollefeys, M.: 3D model matching with viewpoint-invariant patches (VIP). In: IEEE Conference on Computer Vision and Pattern Recognition, CVPR 2008, pp. 1–8. IEEE (2008)

62. Xiao, J., Shah, M.: Two-frame wide baseline matching. In: Proceedings of the Ninth IEEE International Conference on Computer Vision, 2003, pp. 603–609. IEEE (2003)

63. Xu, C., Lu, C., Liang, X., Gao, J., Zheng, W., Wang, T., Yan, S.: Multi-loss regularized deep neural network. IEEE Trans. Circuits Syst. Video Technol. **PP**(99), 1–1 (2015)

64. Yu, F., Zhang, Y., Song, S., Seff, A., Xiao, J.: Construction of a large-scale image dataset using deep learning with humans in the loop. arXiv preprint arXiv:1506.03365 (2015)
65. Zagoruyko, S., Komodakis, N.: Learning to compare image patches via convolutional neural networks (2015). arXiv preprint arXiv:1504.03641v1
66. Zbontar, J., LeCun, Y.: Computing the stereo matching cost with a convolutional neural network. In: Proceedings of the IEEE Conference on Computer Vision and Pattern Recognition, pp. 1592–1599 (2015)
67. Zhang, Z., Ganesh, A., Liang, X., Ma, Y.: TILT: transform invariant low-rank textures. Int. J. Comput. Vis. **99**(1), 1–24 (2012)

Hand Pose Estimation from Local Surface Normals

Chengde Wan[1]([⊠]), Angela Yao[2], and Luc Van Gool[1,3]

[1] Computer Vision Laboratory, D-ITET, ETH Zurich, Zürich, Switzerland
{wanc,vangool}@vision.ee.ethz.ch
[2] Department of Computer Science, University of Bonn, Bonn, Germany
yao@informatik.uni-bonn.de
[3] VISICS, ESAT, K.U. Leuven, Leuven, Belgium

Abstract. We present a hierarchical regression framework for estimating hand joint positions from single depth images based on local surface normals. The hierarchical regression follows the tree structured topology of hand from wrist to finger tips. We propose a conditional regression forest, *i.e.* the *Frame Conditioned Regression Forest* (FCRF) which uses a new normal difference feature. At each stage of the regression, the frame of reference is established from either the local surface normal or previously estimated hand joints. By making the regression with respect to the local frame, the pose estimation is more robust to rigid transformations. We also introduce a new efficient approximation to estimate surface normals. We verify the effectiveness of our method by conducting experiments on two challenging real-world datasets and show consistent improvements over previous discriminative pose estimation methods.

1 Introduction

We consider the problem of 3D hand pose estimation from single depth images. Hand pose estimation has important applications in human-computer interaction (HCI) and augmented reality (AR). Estimating the freely moving hand has several challenges including large viewpoint variance, finger similarity and self occlusion and versatile and rapid finger articulation.

Methods for hand pose estimation from depth generally fall into two camps. The first is frame-to-frame model based tracking [1–5]. Model-based tracking approaches can be highly accurate if given enough computational resources for the optimization. The second camp, where our work also falls, is single frame discriminative pose estimation [6–9]. These methods are less accurate than model-based trackers but much faster and are targeted towards real-time performance without GPUs. Model-based tracking and discriminative pose estimation are complementary to each other and there have been notable hybrid methods [10–14] which try to maintain the advantages of both camps.

Earlier methods for discriminative hand pose estimation tried to estimate all joints directly [15,16] though such approaches tend to fail with dramatic viewpoint changes and extreme articulations. Following the lead of several notable

© Springer International Publishing AG 2016
B. Leibe et al. (Eds.): ECCV 2016, Part III, LNCS 9907, pp. 554–569, 2016.
DOI: 10.1007/978-3-319-46487-9_34

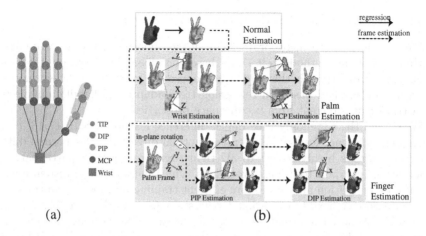

(a)   (b)

Fig. 1. Framework. (a) Shows the hand skeleton model used in our work. (b) Sketches our hierarchical regression framework, with each successive stage denoted by a shaded box. We first estimate a reference frame for every input point encoding all information from previous stages and use that reference frame as input to estimate the location of children joints. The sub-figure around the depth map amplifies a local region from the initial depth map and shows the corresponding frame for a specific point. To save space, only thumb and index finger cases are shown and finger tip points (TIP) estimation is omitted as it is identical to that of DIP **(best viewed in colour)** (Color figure online)

methods [6–8,10], we cast pose estimation as a hierarchical regression problem. The idea is to start with easier parent parts such as the wrist or palm, and then tackle subsequent and more difficult children parts such as the fingers. The assumption is that the children parts, once conditioned on the parents, will exhibit less variance and simplify the learning task. Furthermore, by constraining the underlying graphical model to follow the tree-structured topology of the hand, hierarchical regression implicitly captures the skeleton constraints and therefore shares some advantages of model-based tracking that are otherwise not present when directly estimating all joints independently.

Our framework starts with estimating the surface normals of given point clouds. The normal direction establishes the local reference frames used in later conditional regression and serves as features. We then apply our *Frame Conditioned Regression Forest* (FCRF) to hierarchically regress hand joints down from the wrist to the finger tips. At each stage, the frame of reference is established based on previously estimated local surface normal or joint positions. The regression forest considers offsets between input points and joints of interest with respect to the local reference frame and also conditions the feature with respect to these local frames. Our use of conditioned features is inspired by [6], though we consider angular differences between local surface normals, which is far more robust to rigid transformations than the original depth difference feature.

Our proposed method has the following contributions:

1. We are the first to incorporate local surface normals for pose estimation. Unlike previous methods [6,9,17,18] based on global geometry, ours is based on local geometry. To this end, we propose an extremely efficient normal estimation method based on regression trees adapted to handle unit vector distributions, different from vector space properties.
2. We extend the commonly used depth difference feature [6–8,10,17,18] to an angular difference feature between two normal directions. Our normal difference feature is highly robust to 3D rigid transformation. In particular, the feature is invariant to in-plane rotations, which means we can dispense with data augmentation and have more efficient training and testing routines.
3. We propose a flexible conditional regression framework, encoding all previously estimated information as a part of the local reference frame. This includes local point properties such as the normal direction and global properties such as the estimated joint position.

We validate our method on two real-world challenging hand pose estimation datasets, ICVL [7] and MSRA [6]. On ICVL, we achieve the state-of-art performance against all previous discriminative based methods [6–8] with a large margin. On MSRA, our method is on-par with the state-of-art methods [6,13] at the threshold of 40 mm, and with some minor modifications outperforms [6,13].

2   Related Works

We limit our discussion to the most relevant issues and works, and refer readers to [19,20] for more comprehensive reviews on hand pose estimation in general.

Hierarchical Regression. Several methods have adopted some form of hierarchical treatment of the pose estimation problem. For example, in [11,15,21], the hand is first classified into several classes according to posture or viewpoint; further pose estimation is then conditioned on such initial class. Obviously, such an approach cannot generalize to unseen postures and viewpoints.

Other works [6–10] hierarchically follow the tree-structured hand topology. In [7,8], data points are recursively partitioned into subsets and only corresponding subsets of points are considered for subsequent joint estimation. In [10], estimated parent joints are used as inputs for regressing children joints; a final energy minimization is applied to refine the estimation. In [6,9], predictions are made based on previously estimated reference frames. Our work is similar in spirit to [6,9], as we also make estimations based on reference frames. However, unlike [6,9], we utilize the normal direction to establish the reference frame and take local point properties into consideration. Further explanations on the differences between our work and [6,9] are given in Sects. 3.2 and 4.

Viewpoint Handling. The free moving hand can exhibit large viewpoint changes and a variety of techniques have been proposed to handle these. For example, [21, 22] discretize viewpoints into multiple classes and estimate pose in the view-specific classes. Unfortunately, these methods may introduce quantization errors and cannot generalize to unseen viewpoints. In [9], the regression for hand pose is conditioned on an estimated in-plane rotation angle. This is extended in [6], which regresses the pose residual iteratively, conditioned on the estimated 3D pose at each iteration. Such a method is highly sensitive to the pose initialization and may get trapped in local minima.

Point Cloud Features. Depth difference features are widely used together with random forests in body pose [17,18] and hand pose [6–10,15,21] estimation. Depth differences, however, ignore many local geometric properties of the point cloud, *e.g.* local surface normals and curvatures, and are not robust to rigid transformations and sensor noise.

In [3,4] geodesic extreme points such as finger tip candidates are used to guide later estimation. Rusu *et al.* [23] proposed a histogram feature describing different local properties. Inspired by [23], we establish local Darboux frames and using angular differences as feature values, but unlike [23], our features are based on random offsets and retain the efficiency of [17]. Most recently, convolutional neural networks (CNNs) have been used to automatically learn point cloud features [24,25]. Due to the heavy computational burden, CNNs can still not be used in real-time without a GPU.

3   Random Normal Difference Feature

3.1   Random Difference Features

One of the most commonly used features in depth-based pose estimation frameworks, for both body pose estimation [17,18] and hand pose estimation [6,9], is the random depth difference feature [17]. Formally, the random difference feature $f_{\mathcal{I}}$ for point $\mathbf{p}_i \in \mathcal{R}^3$ from depth map $\mathcal{I}$ is defined as follows,

$$f_{\mathcal{I}}(\mathbf{p}_i, \delta_1, \delta_2) = \Delta(\phi_{\mathcal{I}}(r(\mathbf{p}_i, \delta_1)), \phi_{\mathcal{I}}(r(\mathbf{p}_i, \delta_2))), \tag{1}$$

where $\delta_j \in \mathcal{R}^3, j = \{1, 2\}$ is a random offset, $r(\mathbf{p}_i, \delta_j) \in \mathcal{R}^3$ calculates a random position given point $\mathbf{p}_i$ and offset δ_j. $\phi_{\mathcal{I}}(\mathbf{q})$ is the local feature map for position $\mathbf{q} \in \mathcal{R}^3$ on the point cloud and $\Delta(\cdot, \cdot)$ returns the local feature difference. In the case of random depth difference features [6,9,17], ϕ_I is the recorded depth, though the same formalism applies for other features.

Random difference features are well suited for random forest frameworks; the many possible combinations of offsets perfectly utilize their feature selection and generalization power. In addition, every dimension of the feature is calculated independently, which gives rise to parallelization schemes and allows for both temporal and spatial efficiency in training and testing. One of the main drawbacks of the depth-difference feature, however, is its inability to cope with transformations. Since random offsets in $r(\mathbf{p}_i, \delta_1)$ are determined either *w.r.t.* the camera frame [17] or to a globally estimated frame [6,9], the depth difference for the same offset can vary widely under out of plane rotations.

3.2 Pose Conditioned Random Normal Difference Feature

Surface normals are an important local feature for many point-cloud based applications such as registration [23] and object detection [26–28]. Surface normals would seem a good cue for hand pose estimation too, since the direction of the surface helps to establish the local reference frame, as will be described in Sect. 4. For two given points, the angular difference between their normal directions remains unchanged after rigid transformations. Hence, we propose a pose-conditioned normal difference feature which is highly robust towards 3D rigid transformations.

To make random features invariant to 3D rigid transformations *i.e.*,

$$f_{\mathcal{I}}(\mathbf{p}_i, \delta_1, \delta_2) = f_{\mathcal{I}'}(\mathbf{p}'_i, \delta_1, \delta_2), \tag{2}$$

where $\mathcal{I}'$ and $\mathbf{p}'_i \in \mathcal{R}^3$ are the depth map and point position after transformation, it is necessary to satisfy the following two conditions:

i The random offset generator $r(\cdot, \cdot)$ should be invariant to rigid transformations, *i.e.*

$$T(r(\mathbf{p}_i, \delta_j)) = r(T(\mathbf{p}_i), T(\delta_j)), \tag{3}$$

where $T(\mathbf{q}) = \mathbf{R} \cdot \mathbf{q} + \mathbf{t}$ is the rigid transformation with $\mathbf{R} \in \mathrm{SO}(3)$[1] and $\mathbf{t}$ as its rotation and translation respectively. This condition is equivalent to guaranteeing that the relative position between $\mathbf{p}_i$ and $r(\mathbf{p}_i, \delta_j)$ remains unchanged after transformation, *i.e.*, $T(\mathbf{p}_i - r(\mathbf{p}_i, \delta_j)) = T(\mathbf{p}_i) - r(T(\mathbf{p}_i), T(\delta_j))$.

ii The feature difference $\Delta(\cdot, \cdot)$ should be invariant to rigid transformation, *i.e.*

$$\Delta(\phi_{\mathcal{I}}(\mathbf{q}_1), \phi_{\mathcal{I}}(\mathbf{q}_2)) = \Delta(\phi_{\mathcal{I}'}(\mathbf{q}'_1), \phi_{\mathcal{I}'}(\mathbf{q}'_2)), \tag{4}$$

where $\mathbf{q}'_j = T(\mathbf{q}_j), j \in \{1, 2\}$ is the transformed offset position.

To meet condition **i**, we extend the random position calculation $r(\mathbf{p}_i, \delta_j)$ as

$$r(\mathbf{p}_i, \delta_j, \mathbf{R}_i) = \mathbf{p}_i + \mathbf{R}_i \cdot \delta_j, \tag{5}$$

where $\mathbf{R}_i \in \mathrm{SO}(3)$ is a latent variable representing the pose of local reference frame Sect. 4. For any rigid transformation $\mathbf{T} = \begin{bmatrix} \mathbf{R} & \bar{\mathbf{p}} \\ 0 & 1 \end{bmatrix}$, Eq. 5 satisfies condition **i** *iff*

$$\mathbf{R}'_i = \bar{\mathbf{R}} \mathbf{R}_i, \tag{6}$$

---

[1] Readers unfamiliar with Lie group matrix notations may refer to http://ethaneade.com/lie.pdf for more details. In short, SO(3) represents a 3D rotation while SE(3) represents a 3D rigid transformation.

where $\mathbf{R}_i$ and $\mathbf{R}'_i$ are the estimated latent variable before and after rigid transformation respectively. In comparison to [6], which also uses a latent variable $\mathbf{R}$,
the $\mathbf{R}$ is estimated globally and therefore can be sensitive to the initialization.
For us, the local Darboux frame is established through the local surface normal
direction (see Sect. 5) and has no such sensitivity.

To meet condition **ii**, given the random positions $\mathbf{q}_1$ and $\mathbf{q}_2$, we use the
direction of the normal vector as our local feature map. The feature difference
is cast as the angle between two normals, *i.e.*

$$\Delta(\phi_\mathcal{I}(\widetilde{\mathbf{q}_1}), \phi_\mathcal{I}(\widetilde{\mathbf{q}_2})) = n(\widetilde{\mathbf{q}_1}) \cdot n(\widetilde{\mathbf{q}_2}), \tag{7}$$

where $\widetilde{q}$ denotes the 2D projection of the random position onto the image plane,
since the input 2.5D point cloud is indexed by the 2D projection coordinates.
$n(\cdot) \in \mathcal{R}^3$ denotes the corresponding normal vector. Since the angle between
two normal vectors remains unchanged under a rigid transformation for any two
given surface points, our feature also fulfills condition **ii**. In comparison, the
depth difference feature, as used in [6,9,17], does not fulfill this condition.

Our proposed normal difference feature can be computed based on any surface normal estimate. We describe a conventional method based on eigenvalue
decomposition in Sect. 3.3 and then propose an efficient approximation alternative in Sect. 3.4.

3.3 Surface Normal Estimation Based on Eigenvalue Decomposition

For an input 2.5D point cloud, we distinguish between inner points that lie inside
the point cloud and edge points on the silhouette of the point cloud. For edge
points, normal estimation degenerates to 2D curve normal estimation since the
normal direction is constrained to lie in the image plane.

For inner points, the local surface can be approximated by the k-
neighbourhood surface direction [26]. The eigenvector corresponding to the
smallest eigenvalue of the neighbourhood covariance matrix can be considered
the normal direction. The sign of the normal direction is further constrained to
be the same as the projection ray.

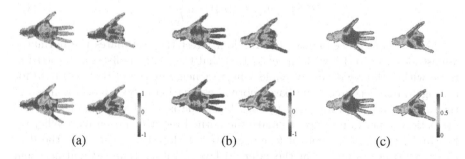

(a)   (b)   (c)

Fig. 2. Estimated surface normal. From (a) to (c) the x, y, z-axis coordinate of the
normal vector, resp. The first row is the regressed surface normal by the random forest
and the second row is estimated by PCA. (**Best viewed in colour**) (Color figure
online)

3.4   Surface Normal Regression with Random Forests

Estimating the normal at every inner point in the point cloud can become very computationally expensive, with an eigenvalue decomposition per point. Alternatively, we can take advantage of the efficiency of random forests and regress an approximate normal direction. Directly regressing the normal vectors in vector space does not maintain unit length so we parameterize the normal vector with spherical coordinates (θ, φ) where θ and φ are the polar and azimuth angles, resp. θ and φ are independent and can be regressed separately. We model the distribution of a set of angular values $\mathcal{S} = \{\theta_1, \cdots \theta_n\}$ as a Von Mises Distribution, which is the circular analogue of the normal distribution. The distribution is expressed as

$$p_{VM}(\theta_i|\mu, \kappa) = \frac{e^{\kappa \cos(\theta_i - \mu)}}{2\pi I_0(\kappa)}, \tag{8}$$

where μ is the mean of the angles, κ is inversely related to the variance of the approximated Gaussian and $I_0(\kappa)$ is the modified Bessel function of order 0. To estimate the mean and variance of the distribution, we first define

$$\overline{C} = \sum_i \cos(\theta_i), \quad \overline{S} = \sum_i \sin(\theta_i), \quad \overline{R} = (\overline{C}^2 + \overline{S}^2)^{\frac{1}{2}}. \tag{9}$$

Then the maximum likelihood estimates of μ and κ are

$$\mu = \operatorname{atan2}(\overline{S}, \overline{C}) \quad \text{and} \quad \overline{R} = \frac{I_1(\kappa)}{I_0(\kappa)}. \tag{10}$$

During training, each split node is set by maximizing the information gain as

$$I = H(\mathcal{S}) - \sum_{i \in \{L, R\}} \frac{|\mathcal{S}^i|}{|\mathcal{S}|} H(\mathcal{S}^i), \tag{11}$$

where the entropy of the Von Mises Distribution is defined as

$$H(\mathcal{S}) = \ln(2\pi I_0(\kappa)) - \kappa \frac{I_1(\kappa)}{I_0(\kappa)}. \tag{12}$$

The training procedure for the random forest that estimates the normal is almost identical to [17] with the exception that the random offsets are restricted to lie within the region of the same k-nearest neighbourhood that was used for the eigenvalue decomposition based normal estimation in Sect. 3.3. The mean of the angular values propagated to each leaf node is selected as the leaf node's prediction value. In practice, to make the normal regression even more efficient, we combine the estimation of θ and φ into one forest by regressing the θ in the first 10 layers and φ in the later 10 layers, rather than estimating them independently.

Since the random offset is limited to a small area, which restricts the randomness of the trees, we find that the average error between approximated and true normal directions only goes up from $\sim 12°$ to $\sim 14°$ when decreasing the number of trees from 10 to 1. As the normal difference feature is not sensitive to such minor errors, we use only 1 tree for all experiments in this paper. The proposed method is extremely efficient; normals for input point clouds can be estimated in ~ 4 ms on average, compared to ~ 14 ms based on eigenvalue decompositions on the same machine.

4   Frame Conditioned Regression Forest

We formulate hand joint estimation as a regression problem by regressing the 3D offsets between an input 3D point and a subset of hand joints. Directly regressing all joints of the hand at once, as has been done in previous works [15, 16] is difficult, given the highly articulated nature of the hand and the many ambiguities due to occlusions and local self-similarities of the fingers. Instead, we prefer to solve for the joints in a hierarchical manner, as state-of-the-art results [6,10] have demonstrated the benefits of solving the pose progressively down the kinematic chain.

In this section, we propose a conditional regression forest, namely the *Frame Conditioned Regression Forest* (FCRF) which performs regression conditioned on information estimated in the previous stages. The hand joints are regressed hierarchically by following the kinematic chain from wrist down to the finger joints. At each stage, we first estimate the reference frame based on results of previous stages and then regress the hand joints relevant to that stage with the FCRF.

There are three main benefits to using the FCRF. First of all, offsets between input points and finger joints are transformed into the local reference frame. This reduces the variance of the offsets and simplifies the training. It also implicitly incorporates skeleton constraints provided by the training data. Secondly, the related normal difference feature, as described in Sect. 3, is conditioned on the estimated reference frame and makes the joint regression highly robust to 3D rigid transformations. Finally, FCRF is in-plane rotation-invariant, and does not need manually generated in-plane rotated training samples for training as in [6–8], so the training time and resulting tree size can be reduced significantly.

Specifically, given input point $\mathbf{p}_i \in \mathcal{R}^3$ from the point cloud, the FCRF for the jth stage solves the following regression

$$\mathbf{O}_j^{(i)} = r_j(\mathcal{I}, \mathbf{C}_j^{(i)}), \tag{13}$$

where $\mathbf{O}_j^{(i)} \in \mathcal{R}^{3 \times n}$ is the offsets between input point $\mathbf{p}_i$ and the n joints to be estimated in j^{th} stage, $\mathcal{I}$ denotes the input depth map and $\mathbf{C}_j^{(i)} \in$ SE(3) is the corresponding local frame. We define the position of the input point $\mathbf{p}_i$ as the origin of the local reference frame, *i.e.*

$$\mathbf{C}_j^{(i)} = \left[\begin{array}{c|c} \mathbf{R}_j^{(i)} & \mathbf{p}_i \\ \hline 0 & 1 \end{array} \right], \tag{14}$$

where $\mathbf{R}_j^{(i)} = [\mathbf{x}, \mathbf{y}, \mathbf{z}] \in \mathrm{SO}(3)$ is a rotation matrix representing the frame pose, and $\mathbf{x}, \mathbf{y}, \mathbf{z} \in \mathcal{R}^3$ are the corresponding axis directions. Both $\mathbf{R}_i$ and $\mathbf{p}_i$ are defined with respect to the camera frame.

The regression $r_j(\mathcal{I}, \mathbf{C}_j^{(i)})$ is done by a random forest.

During training, $\mathbf{o}_{ik} \in \mathcal{R}^3$, the offset between point $\mathbf{p}_i$ and joint l_k to be estimated, is first rotated to the local reference frame $\mathbf{C}_j^{(i)}$ as $\widetilde{\mathbf{o}_{ik}}$, $i.e.$

$$\widetilde{\mathbf{o}_{ik}} = (\mathbf{R}_j^{(i)})^T \cdot \mathbf{o}_{ik}. \tag{15}$$

The distribution of offset samples are modeled as a uni-modal Gaussian as in [17]. For each split node of the tree, the normal difference feature which results in the maximum information gain from a random subset of features is selected. For each leaf node, mean-shift searching [29] is performed and the maximal density point is used as the leaf prediction value.

During testing, given the estimated local frame $\mathbf{C}_j^{(i)}$, the resulting offset $\mathbf{o}_{ik}$ can be re-projected to the camera frame as

$$\mathbf{o}_{ik} = (\mathbf{R}_j^{(i)}) \cdot \widetilde{\mathbf{o}_{ik}}. \tag{16}$$

5   Hierarchical Hand Joint Regression

In this section, we detail the design of reference frames used by FCRFs in every stage, given the estimated local surface normal and the parent joint positions from previous stages. Free moving hand pose estimation faces two major challenges, $i.e.$, large variations of viewpoints, and self-similarities of different fingers. We decompose hand pose estimation into two sub-problems that explicitly tackle these two challenges: first, we estimate the reference frame of the palm and second, we estimate the finger joints.

In Sects. 5.1 and 5.2 the palm estimation is introduced by first estimating the wrist joint (palm position) followed by MCP joints (Fig. 1(a)) for all 5 fingers (palm pose), in which the Darboux frame for every input point is established by taking the estimated wrist joint as reference point. In Sects. 5.3 and 5.4 the joints for each finger are estimated, progressively conditioned on the previously estimated joint position.

5.1   Wrist Estimation

We consider only edge points on the hand silhouette as inputs for estimating the wrist joint. Our rationale is that we cannot find unique reference frames for non-edge points, since knowing only the direction of the normal, $i.e.$ the z-axis, is insufficient to uniquely determine the x- and y-axis on the tangent plane. We assume orthographic projection for the point cloud, $i.e.$ the tangent plane of edge point is orthogonal to the image plane, then the local reference frame of edge point $\mathbf{p}_i$ can be defined uniquely as follows,

$$\mathbf{x}_{wrist}^{(i)} = \mathbf{n}, \mathbf{y}_{wrist}^{(i)} = \mathbf{z}_{wrist}^{(i)} \times \mathbf{x}_{wrist}^{(i)}, \mathbf{z}_{wrist}^{(i)} = \mathbf{n}_i, \tag{17}$$

where $\mathbf{n}$ is the image plane normal direction, $\mathbf{n}_i$ is the normal to the silhouette at point i. The resulting local reference frame is not only invariant to 2D rotations in the image plane but to some degree also robust to out-of-plane rotations, provided that the hand silhouette does not change too much.

5.2   Metacarpophalangeal (MCP) Joint Estimation

Given the estimated wrist point position as a reference point, we assume its relevant position under the local frame $C_{MCP}^{(i)}$ is unchanged then the local reference frame for point $\mathbf{p}_i$ is established as follows

$$\mathbf{x}_{MCP}^{(i)} = \mathbf{y}_{MCP}^{(i)} \times \mathbf{z}_{MCP}^{(i)}, \mathbf{y}_{MCP}^{(i)} = \frac{\mathbf{n}_i \times (\mathbf{p}_{wrist} - \mathbf{p}_i)}{\|\mathbf{n}_i \times (\mathbf{p}_{wrist} - \mathbf{p}_i)\|_2}, \mathbf{z}_{MCP}^{(i)} = \mathbf{n}_i, \quad (18)$$

where the z-axis of the local reference frame is defined as the normal direction $\mathbf{n}_i$, and the y-axis is defined by taking the wrist location $\mathbf{p}_{wrist}$ as a reference point. The MCP joints from all five fingers are then regressed simultaneously, i.e., $\mathbf{O}_{MCP}^{(i)} \in \mathcal{R}^{3 \times 5}$ using our previously defined FCRF.

The estimated MCP joints are then replaced by the transformed MCP position from a template palm to reduce the accumulated regression error. We first find a closed form solution of the palm pose using a variation of ICP [30]. The palm pose matrix $\mathbf{R}_{palm}$'s y-axis is defined as the direction from the wrist to the MCP joint of the middle finger, the z-axis is defined as the palm normal.

5.3   Proximal Interphalangeal (PIP) Joint Estimation

In the estimation of the PIP joint for finger k, all input reference frames share the same pose as the rotated palm reference frame as follows,

$$\mathbf{C}_{PIP_k}^{(i)} = \left[\begin{array}{c|c} \mathrm{Rot}_k(\mathbf{R}_{palm}) & \mathbf{p_i} \\ \hline 0 & 1 \end{array} \right], \quad (19)$$

where $\mathrm{Rot}_k(\cdot)$ is an in-plane rotation to align the reference frame's y-axis to the $k-^{\mathrm{th}}$ finger's empirical direction Fig. 1(a).

Given the local self-similarity between fingers, it can be easy to double-count evidence. To avoid this, we adopt two simple measures. First, we use points only from the neighbourhood of the parent MCP joint as input for regressing each PIP joint, since these points best describe the local surface distortion raised by the parent joint articulation [31]. Secondly we limit the offset of the FCRF to lie along the direction of the finger to maintain robustness to noisy observations from nearby fingers.

5.4   Distal Interphalangeal Joint (DIP) and Finger Tip (TIP) Estimation

The ways to estimate DIP and TIP joints are identical, since their parents are both 1-DoF joints. The local reference frame for each joint is defined as follows

$$\mathbf{x}_l = \mathbf{z}_{palm} \times \mathbf{y}_l, \mathbf{y}_l = \mathbf{p}(l) - \mathbf{g}(l), \mathbf{z}_l = \mathbf{x}_l \times \mathbf{y}_l, \quad (20)$$

where $\mathbf{z}_{palm}$ is the normal direction of palm, $\mathbf{p}(l)$ and $\mathbf{g}(l) \in \mathcal{R}^3$ denote the parent and grandparent joint of l respectively. To avoid double counting of local evidence, we adopt the same techniques as in Sect. 5.3.

6   Experiments

We apply our proposed hand estimation method to two publicly available real-world hand pose estimation datasets: ICVL [7] and MSRA [6]. The performance of our method is evaluated both quantitatively and qualitatively. For quantitative evaluation, two evaluation metrics, per-joint error (in mm) averaged over all frames and percentage of frames in which all joints are below a threshold [18], are used. We show qualitative results in Fig. 5.

All experiments are conducted on an Intel 3.40 GHz I7 machine and the *average run time* is 29.4 fps or 33.9 ms per image. The *maximum depth* of all the trees is set to 20. The *number of trees* for all joint regression forests are set to 5 and 1 for normal estimation (see Sect. 3.4).

To highlight the effectiveness of our proposed normal difference feature, we first apply our frame conditioned regression forests with the same hierarchical structure but based on the standard depth difference feature [17]. We denote this variation using the depth difference feature as our *baseline method*. It should be noted that the baseline does depend on normal estimation for the establishment of the local wrist frame. We also compare to methods directly regressing the wrist and MCP joint positions without establishing the frame [7,8] or based on an initial guess and the subsequent, iterative regression of the error [6].

6.1   ICVL Hand Dataset

The ICVL hand dataset [7] has 20 K images from 10 subjects and an additional 160K in-plane rotated images for training. Since our method is invariant to in-plane rotation, we train with only the initial 20 K. The test set is composed of 2 sequences with continuous finger movement but little viewpoint change.

We compare our method (both the baseline and the version with the normal difference feature) against the state-of-art methods Latent Regression Forest (LRF) [7], Segmentation Index Points (SIP) [8], and Cascaded Regression (Cascaded) [6]. Figure 3(a)–(c) shows that both variations of our proposed method outperform LRF [7] and SIP [8] by a large margin on both test sequences. In comparison to the Cascaded method of [6], shown in Fig. 3(c), our baseline is comparable or better at almost all allowed distances, while the variation with the normal difference feature boosts performance by another 5–10%. As shown in Fig. 3(d), our method significantly out-performs [7], and it outperforms [6] by $\sim$2 mm in terms of the mean error. These results confirm that conditioning finger localization on the wrist pose, as we have done and as is done in [6], can significantly boost accuracy. Furthermore, our proposed normal difference feature is able to better handle 3D rigid transformations.

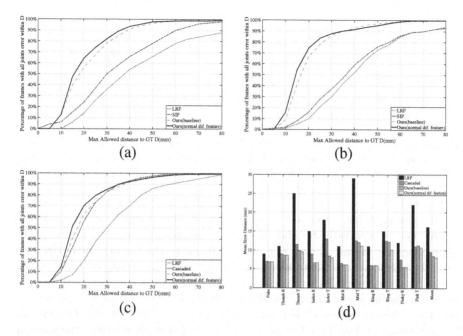

Fig. 3. Quantitative evaluation on ICVL dataset. From (a) to (c), success rates over different thresholds on sequence A, B and both respectively. (d) pre-joint average error on both sequences (R:root, T:tip)

6.2 MSRA Hand Dataset

The MSRA hand dataset [6] contains 76.5 K images from 9 subjects with 17 hand gestures. We use a leave-one-subject-out training/testing split and average the results over the 9 subjects. This dataset is complementary to the ICVL dataset since it has much larger viewpoint changes but limited finger movements. The sparse gesture set does not come close to reflecting the range of hand gestures in real-world HCI applications and as such, is not suitable for evaluating how well a method can generalize towards unseen hand gestures. Yet, this dataset is very good for evaluating the robustness of pose estimation methods to 3D rigid transformations; for HCI applications, this offers flexibility for mounting the camera in different locations.

As is shown in Fig. 4(a)–(b), using the normal difference exhibits less variance to viewpoint changes than using the depth difference. This is more prominent in the pitch angle due to the elongated hand shape. For a given pair of points, their depth difference exhibits larger variation *w.r.t.* pitch angle viewpoint changes. Nevertheless, the performance of the normal difference does decrease under large viewpoint changes. We attribute this to the errors in surface normal estimation due to point cloud noise and to the fact that a 2.5D point cloud only partially represents the full 3D surface.

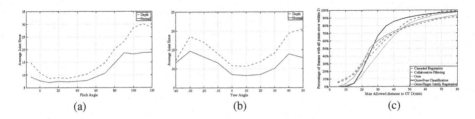

Fig. 4. Quantitative evaluation on MSRA dataset. (a) to (b): average joint error as a function of pitch and yaw angle of the palm pose with respect to camera frame; (c) success rates over different thresholds.

We compare our proposed method against the state-of-the-art Cascaded Regression (Cascaded) [6] and the Collaborative Filtering (Filtering) [13] approaches. Above an allowed distance of 40 mm to the ground truth, our approach is comparable to the others. Below the 40 mm threshold, our baseline and the normal difference feature version has around ~14 % less frames than competing methods. We attribute the difference to the fact that both the Cascaded and the Filtering approach consider the finger as a whole, in the former case for regression, and in the latter as a nearest neighbour search from the training data. While our method generalizes well to unseen finger poses by regressing each finger joint progressively, it is unable to utilize the sparse (albeit similar to testing) set of finger poses in the training. Nevertheless, in an HCI scenario, a user is often asked to first make calibration poses which are important to improve accuracy. As such, we propose two minor modifications to make more comparable evaluations.

For the first modification, we first regress the palm pose, normalize the hand, and then classify the hand pose as a whole. Based on the classification, we assign a corresponding pose sampled from the training set, transformed accordingly to the palm pose. This modification, which we denoted as *pose classification* is similar to Filtering [13] as both methods consider the hand as a whole. By classifying the 17 gesture classes as provided by the MSRA dataset we now outperform [13] over a large interval of thresholds larger than 22 mm. We attribute the increased performance to our accurate estimate of the palm pose.

For the second modification, we regress each finger (*i.e.* the 3 finger joints PIP, DIP, TIP) as a whole given the estimated palm pose. This is similar in spirit to the regression strategy in [6] which takes each finger as a whole. Our method outperforms [6] by ~5 % in the 25–30 mm threshold interval. We attribute this improvement to our palm pose estimation scheme which avoids sensitivity to initialization [6].

Despite our modifications, it should be noted that regressing the finger as a whole cannot generalize to unseen joint angle combinations for one finger, which is usually the case in real-world HCI scenarios, *e.g.* grasping a virtual object, where one finger may exhibit various joint angle combinations according to the shapes of different objects. However, the two strategies are complementary, *i.e.* regressing finger joints progressively can generalize to unseen finger poses while regressing the finger as a whole can capture finger joint correlations in training samples. Given enough computational resources, the two strategies can be performed in parallel, with the best estimation being selected according to an energy function as in model-based tracking. We leave this as our future work.

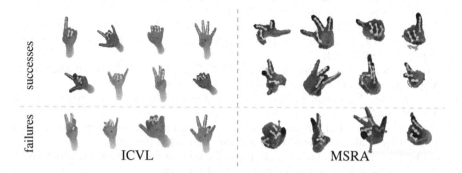

Fig. 5. Examples of successful and failed pose estimates on the ICVL [7] and the MSRA [6] dataset. Failures are due to extreme view point, wrongly estimated normal direction, etc. (best viewed in colour) (Color figure online)

7   Conclusion and Future Work

We have presented a hierarchical regression scheme conditioned on local reference frames. We utilize the local surface normal both as a feature map for regression and to establish the local reference frame. We also proposed an efficient surface normal estimation method based on random forests. Our system shows excellent results on two real-world, challenging datasets and is either comparable or outperforms state-of-the-art methods in hand pose estimation.

The surface normal serves as an important local property of the point cloud. While random forests are an efficient way of estimating the normal, they are only one way and other methods could be developed to be more accurate. Given the success of using surface normals in our work, we expect that there will be benefits for model-based tracking as well.

In our current work, we follow a tree-structured model of the hand. Given the flexibility of our proposed conditioned regression forest, one can also perform hierarchical regressions with other underlying graphical models. With different models, one could take into account the correlations and dependencies between fingers, especially with respect to grasping objects. We leave this as future work in improving the current system.

Acknowledgments. The authors gratefully acknowledge support by EU Framework Seven project ReMeDi (grant 610902) and Chinese Scholarship Council.

References

1. Oikonomidis, I., Kyriazis, N., Argyros, A.A.: Efficient model-based 3D tracking of hand articulations using kinect. In: BMVC (2011)
2. Oikonomidis, I., Lourakis, M., Argyros, A.: Evolutionary quasi-random search for hand articulations tracking. In: CVPR (2014)
3. Qian, C., Chen, Q., Xiao, S., Yichen, W., Xiaoou, T., Jian, S.: Realtime and robust hand tracking from depth. In: CVPR (2014)
4. Liang, H., Yuan, J., Thalmann, D., Zhang, Z.: Model-based hand pose estimation via spatial-temporal hand parsing and 3D fingertip localization. Vis. Comput. **29**(6), 837–848 (2013)
5. Stenger, B., Thayananthan, A., Torr, P.H.S., Cipolla, R.: Model-based hand tracking using a hierarchical Bayesian filter. TPAMI (2006)
6. Sun, X., Wei, Y., Liang, S., Tang, X., Sun, J.: Cascaded hand pose regression. In: CVPR (2015)
7. Tang, D., Chang, H.J., Tejani, A., Kim, T.K.: Latent regression forest: structured estimation of 3D articulated hand posture. In: CVPR (2014)
8. Li, P., Ling, H., Li, X., Liao, C.: 3D hand pose estimation using randomized decision forest with segmentation index points. In: ICCV (2015)
9. Xu, C., Cheng, L.: Efficient hand pose estimation from a single depth image. In: ICCV (2013)
10. Tang, D., Taylor, J., Kohli, P., Keskin, C., Kim, T.K., Shotton, J.: Opening the black box: hierarchical sampling optimization for estimating human hand pose. In: ICCV (2015)
11. Sharp, T., Keskin, C., Robertson, D., Taylor, J., Shotton, J., Kim, D., Rhemann, C., Leichter, I., Vinnikov, A., Wei, Y., et al.: Accurate, robust, and flexible real-time hand tracking. In: CHI (2015)
12. Sridhar, S., Mueller, F., Oulasvirta, A., Theobalt, C.: Fast and robust hand tracking using detection-guided optimization. In: CVPR (2015)
13. Choi, C., Sinha, A., Choi, J.H., Jang, S., Ramani, K.: A collaborative filtering approach to real-time hand pose estimation. In: ICCV (2015)
14. Ballan, L., Taneja, A., Gall, J., Van Gool, L., Pollefeys, M.: Motion capture of hands in action using discriminative salient points. In: Fitzgibbon, A., Lazebnik, S., Perona, P., Sato, Y., Schmid, C. (eds.) ECCV 2012, Part VI. LNCS, vol. 7577, pp. 640–653. Springer, Heidelberg (2012)
15. Keskin, C., Kıraç, F., Kara, Y.E., Akarun, L.: Hand pose estimation and hand shape classification using multi-layered randomized decision forests. In: Fitzgibbon, A., Lazebnik, S., Perona, P., Sato, Y., Schmid, C. (eds.) ECCV 2012, Part VI. LNCS, vol. 7577, pp. 852–863. Springer, Heidelberg (2012)
16. Poier, G., Roditakis, K., Schulter, S., Michel, D., Bischof, H., Argyros, A.A.: Hybrid one-shot 3D hand pose estimation by exploiting uncertainties. In: BMVC (2015)
17. Shotton, J., Girshick, R., Fitzgibbon, A., Sharp, T., Cook, M., Finocchio, M., Moore, R., Kohli, P., Criminisi, A., Kipman, A., Blake, A.: Efficient human pose estimation from single depth images. TPAMI (2013)
18. Taylor, J., Shotton, J., Sharp, T., Fitzgibbon, A.: The vitruvian manifold: inferring dense correspondences for one-shot human pose estimation. In: CVPR (2012)
19. Supancic, J.S., Rogez, G., Yang, Y., Shotton, J., Ramanan, D.: Depth-based hand pose estimation: data, methods, and challenges. In: ICCV (2015)
20. Erol, A., Bebis, G., Nicolescu, M., Boyle, R.D., Twombly, X.: Vision-based hand pose estimation: a review. CVIU (2007)

21. Tang, D., Yu, T.H., Kim, T.K.: Real-time articulated hand pose estimation using semi-supervised transductive regression forests. In: ICCV (2013)
22. Dantone, M., Gall, J., Fanelli, G., Van Gool, L.: Real-time facial feature detection using conditional regression forests. In: CVPR (2012)
23. Rusu, R.B., Blodow, N., Marton, Z.C., Beetz, M.: Aligning point cloud views using persistent feature histograms. In: IROS (2008)
24. Oberweger, M., Wohlhart, P., Lepetit, V.: Training a feedback loop for hand pose estimation. In: ICCV (2015)
25. Tompson, J., Stein, M., Lecun, Y., Perlin, K.: Real-time continuous pose recovery of human hands using convolutional networks. ACM Trans. Graph. (2014)
26. Rusu, R.B., Marton, Z.C., Blodow, N., Dolha, M., Beetz, M.: Towards 3D point cloud based object maps for household environments. TRAS (2008)
27. Hinterstoisser, S., Holzer, S., Cagniart, C., Ilic, S., Konolige, K., Navab, N., Lepetit, V.: Multimodal templates for real-time detection of texture-less objects in heavily cluttered scenes. In: ICCV (2011)
28. Gupta, S., Girshick, R., Arbeláez, P., Malik, J.: Learning rich features from RGB-D images for object detection and segmentation. In: Fleet, D., Pajdla, T., Schiele, B., Tuytelaars, T. (eds.) ECCV 2014, Part VII. LNCS, vol. 8695, pp. 345–360. Springer, Heidelberg (2014)
29. Comaniciu, D., Meer, P.: Mean shift: a robust approach toward feature space analysis. TPAMI (2002)
30. Pellegrini, S., Schindler, K., Nardi, D.: A generalisation of the ICP algorithm for articulated bodies. In: BMVC (2008)
31. Kovalsky, S., Basri, R., Jacobs, D.W.: Learning 3D articulation and deformation using 2D images. arXiv preprint (2015)

Abundant Inverse Regression Using Sufficient Reduction and Its Applications

Hyunwoo J. Kim[✉], Brandon M. Smith, Nagesh Adluru, Charles R. Dyer, Sterling C. Johnson, and Vikas Singh

University of Wisconsin-Madison, Madison, USA
hwkim@cs.wisc.edu
http://pages.cs.wisc.edu/~hwkim/projects/air

Abstract. Statistical models such as linear regression drive numerous applications in computer vision and machine learning. The landscape of practical deployments of these formulations is dominated by forward regression models that estimate the parameters of a function mapping a set of p covariates, x, to a response variable, y. The less known alternative, Inverse Regression, offers various benefits that are much less explored in vision problems. The goal of this paper is to show how Inverse Regression in the "abundant" feature setting (i.e., many subsets of features are associated with the target label or response, as is the case for images), together with a statistical construction called Sufficient Reduction, yields highly flexible models that are a natural fit for model estimation tasks in vision. Specifically, we obtain formulations that provide relevance of individual covariates used in prediction, at the level of specific examples/samples — in a sense, explaining why a particular prediction was made. With no compromise in performance relative to other methods, an ability to interpret why a learning algorithm is behaving in a specific way for each prediction, adds significant value in numerous applications. We illustrate these properties and the benefits of Abundant Inverse Regression on three distinct applications.

Keywords: Inverse regression · Kernel regression · Abundant regression · Temperature prediction · Alzheimer's disease · Age estimation

1 Introduction

Regression models are ubiquitous in computer vision applications (*e.g.*, medical imaging [1] and face alignment by shape regression [2]). In scientific data analysis, regression models are the default tool of choice for identifying the association between a set of input feature vectors (covariates) $\mathbf{x} \in \mathcal{X}$ and an output (dependent) variable $y \in \mathcal{Y}$. In most applications, the regressor is obtained by minimizing (or maximizing) the loss (or fidelity) function assuming the dependent variable y is corrupted with noise ϵ: $y = f(x) + \epsilon$. Consequently, solving for the regressor is,

---

Hyunwoo J. Kim and Brandon M. Smith are joint first authors.

© Springer International Publishing AG 2016
B. Leibe et al. (Eds.): ECCV 2016, Part III, LNCS 9907, pp. 570–584, 2016.
DOI: 10.1007/978-3-319-46487-9_35

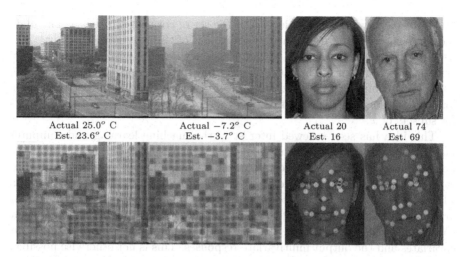

Actual 25.0° C   Actual −7.2° C   Actual 20   Actual 74
Est. 23.6° C   Est. −3.7° C   Est. 16   Est. 69

Fig. 1. Dynamic feature weights for two tasks: ambient temperature prediction (left) and age estimation (right). Our formulation provides a way to determine, at test time, which features are most important to the prediction. Our results are competitive, which demonstrates that we achieve this capability without sacrificing accuracy. (Color figure online)

in fact, equivalent to estimating the expectation $\mathbb{E}[y|\boldsymbol{x}]$; in statistics and machine learning, this construction is typically referred to as *forward (or standard) regression* [3]. The above formulation does not attempt to model noise in $\boldsymbol{x}$ directly. Even for linear forms of $f(\cdot)$, if the noise characteristics are not strictly additive and normally distributed (*i.e.*, so that $y = f(\boldsymbol{x} + \epsilon) \Leftrightarrow y = f(\boldsymbol{x}) + \epsilon'$), parameter estimates and consistency properties will not hold in general [4,5].

The above issues have long been identified in the statistics literature and a rich body of work has emerged. One form of these models (among several) is typically referred to as *inverse regression* [6]. Here, the main idea is to estimate $\mathbb{E}[\boldsymbol{x}|y]$ instead of $\mathbb{E}[y|\boldsymbol{x}]$, which offers asymptotic and practical benefits and is particularly suitable in high-dimensional settings. To see this, consider the simple setting in which we estimate a regressor for n samples of $\boldsymbol{x} \in \mathbf{R}^p$, $p \gg n$. The problem is ill-posed and regularization (*e.g.*, with ℓ_0 or ℓ_1 penalty) is required. Interestingly, for linear models in the inverse regression setting, the problem is still well specified since it is equivalent to a set of p univariate regression models going from y to a particular covariate x^j where $j \in \{1, \cdots, p\}$.

As an illustrative example, let us compare the forward and inverse regression models for $p > n$. For forward regression, we have $y = \mathbf{b}^\mathsf{T}\boldsymbol{x} + \epsilon$ and so $\mathbf{b}^* = (X^\mathsf{T}X)^{-1}X^\mathsf{T}\mathbf{y}$, where $X = [\boldsymbol{x}_1 \cdots \boldsymbol{x}_n]^\mathsf{T}$ and $\mathbf{y} = [y^1 \cdots y^n]^\mathsf{T}$. This is problematic due to a rank deficient $X^\mathsf{T}X$. But in the inverse regression case, we have $\boldsymbol{x} = \mathbf{b}y + \epsilon$ and so $\mathbf{b}^* = (\mathbf{y}^\mathsf{T}\mathbf{y})^{-1}\mathbf{y}^\mathsf{T}X$, which can be computed easily. In statistics, a widely used algorithm based on this observation is Sliced Inverse Regression (SIR) [3]. At a high level, SIR is a dimensionality reduction procedure that calculates $\mathbb{E}[\boldsymbol{x}|y]$ for each 'slice' (*i.e.*, bin) in the response variable y and finds subspaces where the projection of the set of covariates is dense. The main idea is that, instead of using the full covariance of the covariates x's or $[x^\top \ y]^\top$, we use the $\mathbb{E}[x|y]$ for each bin within y as a new feature with a weight proportional to the number of samples (or examples) within that specific bin. Then, a principal components-derived subspace for such a covariance matrix yields a lower-dimensional embedding that incorporates the proximity between the y's for subsets of x.

This idea has seen renewed interest in the machine learning and computer vision communities [7,8]. For example, consider the following simple example demonstrated in a relatively recent paper [9]: Their goal was to utilize an intrinsic low-dimensional (e.g., 2D or 3D) representation of the input image (or a silhouette) to predict body pose, which was parameterized as 3D joint angles at articulation points. Identifying the structure in the gram matrix of the output space enables identification of the conditional dependencies between the input covariates and the output multivariate responses. This is not otherwise possible. For example, we do not typically know which low-dimensional representation of the input images best predicts specific values of the output label.

The above discussion suggests that SIR models can effectively find a single global subspace for the input samples x considering the conditional distribution of $(x|y)$. However, there are a number of practical considerations that the SIR model is ill-equipped to handle. For example, in computer vision applications operating in the wild, such as the temperature prediction task shown in Fig. 1, we can rarely find a global embedding that fully explains the relationship between the covariates and the response. In fact, subsets of samples may be differently associated with slices of the output space. Further, many 'relevant' features may be systematically corrupted or unavailable in a non-trivial fraction of images. In practice, one finds that these issues strongly propagate as errors in the calculated embedding, making the downstream analysis unsatisfactory. Of course, in the forward regression setting, this problem is tackled by performing feature selection via sparsity-type penalties, which emphasize the reliable features in the estimation. The direct application of this idea in the inverse regression model is awkward since the 'predictor' y (which is the response in forward regression) for x is just one dimensional.

It turns out that the desirable properties we seek to incorporate within inverse regression actually fall out of an inherent characteristic in many vision datasets, namely an *abundance* of features. In other words, in associating a large set of features derived from an image to an output label (or response) y, it is often the case that different subsets of features/covariates predict the label *equally well*. In the inverse regression context, this property enables adapting associations between density windows of the output space with *different subsets of covariates* dynamically on a sample-by-sample basis. If a covariate is generally relevant but missing for a small subset of examples (e.g., due to occlusion, noise, or corruption), the formulation allows switching the hypothesis to a distinct 'support' of covariates for these samples alone.

In summary, exploiting abundance in inverse regression yields robust and highly flexible models. But perhaps more importantly, we obtain highly interpretable models (in an individual, sample-specific way), which is crucial in many applications. In a mammogram exam, for example, an explanation of why a patient was assigned a high probability of malignancy is critical for interpretability. With no compromise in performance, such functionality is valuable in applications but natively available in very few. Beyond Decision Trees and Inductive Logic Programming, regression models seldom yield such flexibility. Next, we give a few motivating examples and then list the main contributions of this paper.

1.1 Motivating Examples

Consider the two tasks in Fig. 1 where the relevance of features/covariates varies depending on the context and the specific samples under consideration. In facial age estimation, a feature from a local patch at a fiducial point (*e.g.*, lip, eye corners) carries a great deal of information for predicting age. But if the patch is occluded, this feature is not relevant for that particular image. Consider another example focused on ambient temperature estimation from outdoor scene images recently tackled in [10]. Here, we must deal not only with occlusion and corruption, but, depending on the context, the relevance of an otherwise predictive feature may also vary. For example, the appearance of a tree (*e.g.*, leaf color and density) may enable identifying subtle changes even within a specific season (*e.g.*, early or late spring). But in winter, after the trees have shed their leaves, this feature carries little useful information for predicting day-to-day temperature. In this case, the relevance of the feature varies with the specific values assigned to the response y. Importantly, being able to evaluate the different features driving a specific prediction can guide improvement of learning algorithms by enabling human interpretability.

1.2 Contributions

To summarize, *our contribution is a novel formulation using inverse regression and sufficient reduction that provides end-to-end statistical strategies for enabling (1) adaptive and dynamic associations between abundant input features and prediction outputs on an image-by-image basis, and (2) human interpretability of these associations.* Our model dynamically updates the relevance of each feature on a sample-by-sample basis and allows for missing or randomly corrupted covariates. Less formally, our algorithm explains *why* a specific decision was made for each example (based on feature-level dynamic weights). We analyze the statistical properties of our formulation and show experimental results in three different problem settings, which demonstrate its wide applicability.

2   Estimating the Conditional Confidence of Covariates

Given a supervised learning task, our overall workflow consists of two main modules. We will first derive a formulation to obtain the confidence associated with individual covariates x^j conditioned on the label y. Once the details of this procedure are derived, we will develop algorithms that exploit these conditional confidences for prediction while also providing information on *which* covariates were responsible for that specific prediction. We start by describing the details of the first module.

2.1   A Potential Solution Based on Sufficient Dimension Reduction

The ideal mechanism to assign a confidence score to individual covariates, x^j, should condition the estimate based on knowledge of all other (uncorrupted) covariates x^{-j} as well as the response variable y. This is a combinatorial problem that quickly becomes computationally intractable. For example, even when we consider only a single pair of covariates and a response, the number of terms will quadratically increase as $f(x^1|x^2, y), f(x^1|x^3, y), f(x^1|x^4, y), \ldots f(x^1|x^p, y)$. Another related issue is that, when considering dependencies between multiple variables $f(x^1|x^2, x^3, \ldots, y)$, estimation is challenging because the conditional distribution is high-dimensional and the number of samples may be small in comparison. Further, in the prediction phase, we do not have access to the true y, which makes conditioning somewhat problematic. An interesting starting point in formulating a solution is the concept of *sufficient dimension reduction* [11]. We provide a definition and subsequently describe our idea.

Definition 1. *Given a regression model* $h : X \to Y$*, a reduction* $\phi : \mathbf{R}^p \to \mathbf{R}^q, q \leq p$*, is sufficient for the regression task if it satisfies one of the following conditions:*

 (1) inverse reduction, $X|(Y, \phi(X)) \sim X|\phi(X)$*,*
 (2) forward reduction, $Y|X \sim Y|\phi(X)$*,*
 (3) joint reduction, $X \perp\!\!\!\perp Y|\phi(X)$*,*

where $\perp\!\!\!\perp$ *indicates independence,* $\sim$ *means identically distributed, and* $A|B$ *refers to the random vector A given the vector B[11,12].*

Example 1. Suppose we are interested in predicting obesity y of a subject using a regression model $h : x \to y$ with 10 covariates such as weight x^1, height x^2, education x^3, age x^4, gender x^5, ..., BMI x^{10}. Since obesity is highly correlated to weight and height, $(y|x^1, x^2, \ldots, x^{10}) \sim (y|\phi(x^1, \ldots, x^{10})) \sim (y|x^1, x^2)$. Here, we call $\phi : (x^1, \ldots, x^{10}) \to (x^1, x^2)$ a sufficient reduction for the given regression task. Also, for predicting BMI, *i.e.*, $h' : (x^1, \ldots, x^9, y) \to x^{10}$, $\phi' : (x^1, \cdots, x^9) \to (x^1, x^2)$ is a sufficient reduction since $(x^{10}|x^1, \ldots, x^9, y) \sim (x^{10}|x^1, x^2)$.

Our goal is to address the intractability problem by characterizing $(x^j|x^{-j}, y)$ in a simpler form based on the definition of sufficient reduction. Notice that sufficient reduction relies on specifying an appropriate regression model *and* we seek to derive identities for the expression $(x^j|x^{-j}, y)$. It therefore makes sense to structure our regression problem as $h : x^{-j}, y \to x^j$. The definition of forward reduction states that if $Y|X \sim Y|\phi(X)$ holds, $\phi(X)$ is a sufficient reduction for the regression problem h. In this definition, if we let $X = x^j$, $Y = (x^{-j}, y)$, and $\phi(X) = \phi(x^{-j}, y)$, we directly have $(x^j|x^{-j}, y) \sim (x^j|\phi(x^{-j}, y))$, as desired.

Why is this useful? The conditional distribution $f(x^j|x^1,\ldots,x^p) = f(x^j|\phi(x^{-j}))$ can be more efficiently estimated in a lower-dimensional space using sufficient reduction. In addition, once we make the assumption that the sufficient reduction function values coincide with y, *i.e.*, $\phi(x^{-j}) = y$, then estimating the conditional distribution simplifies to $f(x^j|x^1,\ldots,x^p) = f(x^j|\phi(x^{-j})) = f(x^j|y)$. Intuitively, this special case is closely related to the well-known conditional independence of features given a response used in a naïve Bayesian relationship:

$$f(y|x) \propto \frac{\prod f(x^j|y)f(y)}{f(x)}. \tag{1}$$

In other words, given a sufficient reduction, all covariates x^j are conditionally independent. The form in Eq. (1) is simply a special case where $\phi(\cdot)$ is y; the general form, on the other hand, allows significant flexibility in specifying other forms for $\phi(\cdot)$ (*e.g.*, any lower-dimensional map) as well as setting up the conditional dependence concretely in the context of conditional confidence. Note that sufficient reduction methods are related to generative models (including Naïve Bayes). It is tempting to think that generative models with lower-dimensional hidden variables play the same role as sufficient reduction. However, the distinction is that the sufficient reduction ϕ from SIR can be obtained independently for any downstream analysis (regression) whereas hidden variables in generative models need to be specified and learned for each regression model. Now, the remaining piece is to give an expression for the conditional confidence distribution. For simplicity, in this work, we will use a multivariate Gaussian, which facilitates evaluating $\mathbb{E}[x^i|y]$ and $\mathrm{VAR}[x^i|y]$ easily.

Remarks. Notice that x^j may not always correspond to a unique covariate. Instead, it may refer to a subset of covariates, *e.g.*, multiple features from a local patch in an image may constitute a specific x^j. In various practical situations it may turn out that one or more of these features may be irrelevant to the given regression problem. This situation requires special handling: briefly, we will consider the support of the regression coefficients for $\mathbb{E}[y|x^i]$ and measure the confidence of the feature by measuring the deviation from $\mathbb{E}[x|y]$ only along the related regression direction. These extensions will be described later.

2.2   A Simple Estimation Scheme Based on Abundant Features

The above description establishes the identity, $f(x^j|\phi(x^{-j})) = f(x^j|y)$, assuming $\phi(x^{-j}) = y$ and gives us a general expression to calculate the conditional confidence of individual covariates. What we have not addressed so far is a constructive scheme to actually calculate $\phi(x^{-j})$ so that it serves as a surrogate for y. We describe this procedure below based on sufficient reduction.

A natural strategy is to substitute y using predicted estimates, $\hat{y}$, derived from a subset of covariates, $\{1,\cdots,p\}\backslash j$. The difficulty, however, is that many of these subsets may be corrupted or unavailable. Fortunately, we find that in most situations (especially with image data), multiple exclusive subsets of the covariates can reliably predict the response. This corresponds to the *abundant* features assumption described earlier, and seems to be valid in many vision applications including the three examples studied in this paper. This means that we can define $\phi^I(x^I)$ for distinct subsets I of the covariate set, $\{1, \cdots, p\} \backslash j$. Intuitively, a potentially large number of I's will each index unique subsets and can eventually be used to obtain a reliable prediction for y, which makes the sufficient reduction condition, $\phi^I(x^I) = y$, sensible. Marginalizing over distinct I's, we can obtain $\mathbb{E}[x^j|\phi^I(x^I)]$ (described below). Then, by calculating the discrepancy between $\mathbb{E}[x^j|\phi^I(x^I)] = \mathbb{E}[x^j|\hat{y}^I]$ and x^j, we can evaluate the conditional confidence of each specific covariate x^j.

Marginalizing over I to calculate $\mathbb{E}[f(x^j|\phi^I(x^I))]$. To calculate $\mathbb{E}[f(x^j|\phi^I(x^I))]$, the only additional piece of information we need is the probability of the index set I. This can be accomplished by imposing a prior over each corresponding sufficient reduction, $\phi^I(\cdot)$, as $w_{\phi^I} := \mathbb{E}[(y - \phi^I(x^I))^2]^{-1}$ which expresses the belief that the reliability of distinct sufficient reductions $\phi^I(\cdot)$ will vary as a function of the subset of patches it indexes.[1] This means that the conditional confidence for a covariate is calculated by a weighted mean of $f(x^j|\phi^i(x^i)) = f(x^j|\hat{y}^i)$ using w_{ϕ^j} (see Line 4 in Algorithm 1). With these ingredients, we present the complete algorithm in Algorithm 1.

Algorithm 1. Conditional Confidence of Feature Aware Regression

---

1: **procedure** TRAINING
2:    Estimate a joint distribution for each covariate, $f(x^j, y)$
3:    Find sufficient reduction $\phi^I : x^I \to y$ for each subset of features x^I
4:    Estimate the prior/weight for $\phi_I(\cdot)$ as $w_{\phi^I} = \mathbb{E}[(y - \phi^I(x^I))^2]^{-1}$
5:    Estimate cond. confidence of feature $w_{x^j} := \sum_I w_{\phi^I} f(x^j|\hat{y}^I)/\sum_I w_{\phi^I}$
6:    Fit a feature confidence aware regressor $h : [\{x^j\}_{j=1}^K, \{w_{x^j}\}_{j=1}^K] \to y$
7: **procedure** PREDICTION
8:    Evaluate $w_{x^j} := \mathbb{E}f\left(x^j|\phi^I(x^I)\right)$ by lines 3 and 5, with learned w_{ϕ^I}.
9:    $\hat{y} = h(\{x^j\}_{j=1}^K, \{w_{x^j}\}_{j=1}^K)$

2.3 Deriving Priors for Sufficient Dimension Reduction

We now describe how to derive priors for sufficient dimension reduction using a convex combination of multiple sufficient reductions. We assume that each weak sufficient reduction $\Phi^I(\cdot)$ is an unbiased estimator for y. Since a convex combination of unbiased estimators (expectation over estimators) is also an unbiased estimator, our problem is to find the optimal weights for such a combination of the sufficient reductions. Note that such an estimator will satisfy a minimum variance property. Once calculated, we will directly use the estimates as a prior for $\phi^I(\cdot)$.

---

[1] Recall that individual patches correspond to covariates, which will be univariate or multivariate depending on the descriptor we choose for the patch. Here, I indexes different subsets of patches.

Let $\phi^1(x^1) \sim \mathcal{N}(y, \sigma_1^2), \ldots, \phi^K(x^K) \sim \mathcal{N}(y, \sigma_K^2)$ denote a set of sufficient reductions for different subsets I in $\{1, \cdots, p\} \backslash j$ where I indices belong in the set $\{1, \cdots, K\}$. This means that $y = \mathbb{E}(\phi^I(x^I))$ since each estimator is unbiased. Note that each estimator is independent given y, which means, roughly speaking, the prediction errors among the different sufficient reductions are not correlated. So, the problem of calculating the weights, w, reduces to the following optimization model,

$$\min_w \text{VAR}\left[\sum_{I=1}^K \phi^j(x^I)w^I\right] \text{ s.t. } \sum_I w^I = 1 \text{ and } w^I \geq 0, \text{ for all } I \in 1, \ldots, K. \quad (2)$$

Since we assume that the error is independent given y, Eq. (2) can be written as

$$\min_w \sum_{I=1}^K \sigma_I^2(w^I)^2 \text{ s.t. } \sum_I w^I = 1 \text{ and } w^I \geq 0, \text{ for all } I \in 1, \ldots, K \quad (3)$$

The optimal weights w have a closed form due to the following result.

Lemma 1. *Based on KKT optimality conditions, one can verify (see the extended paper) that the optimal weights for Eq. (3) are $w^I = \sigma_I^{-2}/\sum_{k=1}^K \sigma_k^{-2}$. This is a unique global optimum for Eq. (3) when $\sigma_I^2 > 0, \forall I \in \{1, \ldots, K\}$.*

This provides a weight for each subset $I \in \{1, \ldots, K\}$ for arbitrary constant K.

In the extended paper, we present a scheme to estimate the conditional confidence of specific features within a particular covariate by considering the sufficient reduction direction. This reduces the influence of irrelevant features within a multivariate covariate, given a regression task. Next, we introduce a variant of kernel regression when covariates (and their multivariate features) have an associated conditional confidence score.

3   Conditional Confidence Aware Kernel Regression

In this section we modify an existing kernel regressor formulation to exploit the conditional confidence of covariates. This final module is needed to leverage the conditional confidence towards constructions that can be applied to applications in machine learning and computer vision.

We start from the Nadaraya-Watson kernel regression with a Gaussian kernel. Since this estimator requires a dissimilarity measure between samples, we simply need to define a meaningful measure using the covariate confidences. To do so, we can use a simple adjustment such that the distance measure makes use of covariates (both univariate and multivariate) *differentially*, proportional to their confidence level. The expectation of distance of each pair of covariates weighted by confidence shown below is one such measure:

$$d_w(x_1, x_2, w_1, w_2) := \sqrt{\frac{\sum_j w_{x_1^j} w_{x_2^j} (x_1^j - x_2^j)^2}{\sum_j w_{x_1^j} w_{x_2^j}}}. \quad (4)$$

The expression in Eq. (4) can be interpreted as agnostic of the example-specific labels (even if they were available). Interestingly, the weights w_{x^j} are obtained via a surrogate to the unknown labels/responses via sufficient reduction. This scheme will still provide meaningful distances even when one or more covariates are corrupted or unavailable. Next, we modify Eq. (4) so we can guarantee that it is an unbiased estimator for distances between uncorrupted covariates under some conditions.

3.1 Unbiased Estimator for Distance Between Uncorrupted Covariates

This section covers a very important consequence of utilizing inverse regression. Notice that it is quite uncommon in the forward regression setting to derive proofs of unbiasedness for distance estimates in the presence of corrupted or missing covariates or features. This is primarily because few, if any, methods directly model the covariates x^j. Interestingly, inverse regression explicitly characterizes $f(x^j | \phi^I(x^I))$, which means that we have access to $\mathbb{E}[x^j | x^{-j}]$. Let us assume that the 'true' but unobserved value of the covariate is $z^j \approx \mathbb{E}[x^j | x^{-j}]$. Since our model assumes that x^j is observed with noise, we can model the variance of x^j given $\mathbb{E}[x^j | x^{-j}]$ using $\sigma^2_{x^j | z^j} = \mathbb{E}[(x^j - \mathbb{E}[x^j | x^{-j}])^2]$, i.e., $x^j \sim \mathcal{N}(z^j, \sigma^2_{x^j | z^j})$. This allows us to obtain a powerful "corrected" distance measure. We now have:

Proposition 1. *Assume that we observe covariates* x^1, x^2 *with Gaussian noise given ground truth feature values* z^1 *and* z^2, *i.e.,* $x_1^j \sim \mathcal{N}(\bar{z}_1^j, \sigma^2_{x^j | z^j})$ *and* $x_2^j \sim \mathcal{N}(\bar{x}_2^j, \sigma^2_{x^j | z^j})$. *Then, we have*

$$\mathbb{E}[(x_1 - x_2)^2] = \mathbb{E}[x_1]^2 + \mathbb{E}[x_2]^2 - 2\mathbb{E}[x_1]\mathbb{E}[x_2] - 2COV(x_1, x_2) + VAR[x_1] + VAR[x_2]$$
$$= \bar{x}_1^2 + \bar{x}_2^2 - 2\bar{x}_1\bar{x}_2 + 2\sigma^2_{x|z} = (\bar{x}_1 - \bar{x}_2)^2 + 2\sigma^2_{x|z} \qquad (5)$$

Thus, $(x_1 - x_2)^2 - 2\sigma^2_{x|z}$ *is an unbiased estimator for distances between true (but unobserved) covariate values, e.g.,* $(z_1 - z_2)^2 = \mathbb{E}[(x_1 - x_2)^2 - 2\sigma^2_{x|z}]$.

Once we have access to $2\sigma^2_{x|z}$, deriving the unbiased estimate simply involves a correction. So, we obtain the corrected distances:

$$d(x_1, x_2, w_1, w_2)^2 := \mathbb{E}_j \left[\left((x_1^j - x_2^j)^2 - 2\sigma_j^2 \right) \right] = \frac{\sum_j \left((x_1^j - x_2^j)^2 - 2\sigma_j^2 \right) w_{x_1^j} w_{x_2^j}}{\sum_j w_{x_1^j} w_{x_2^j}}. \qquad (6)$$

4 Results and Discussion

Our method is broadly applicable, and so we show results on three different computer vision datasets, each with an associated task: (1) outdoor photo archives for temperature prediction, (2) face images for age estimation, and (3) magnetic resonance imaging (MRI) of brains for Alzheimer's disease prediction. For temperature prediction on the *Hot or Not* dataset [10], we show that our algorithm can help explain *why* a specific prediction was made without sacrificing accuracy compared to the state-of-the-art. We use age estimation as a familiar example to demonstrate several properties of our approach, namely that our global (w_{ϕ^l}), and dynamic weights (w_{x^j}) are meaningful and intuitive. Finally, we show that our method can be used to pinpoint regions of the brain image that contribute most to Alzheimer's disease prediction, which is valuable to clinicians.

4.1   Temperature Prediction

Hot or Not [10] consists of geo-located image sequences from outdoor webcams (see supplement). The task is to predict ambient outdoor temperature using only an image of the scene. For fair comparison, we evaluated our method on the same 10 sequences selected by [10]. Like [10], we used the first-year images for training and the second-year images for testing.

We decompose temperature T into a low-frequency component T_{lo} and a high-frequency component T_{hi} as in [10]. We train our algorithm to predict T_{lo} and T_{hi} separately, and then estimate the final temperature as $T = T_{lo} + T_{hi}$. Intuitively, T_{lo} is correlated with seasonal variations (*e.g.*, the position of the sun in the sky at 11:00 am, the presence or absence of tree leaves) and T_{hi} is correlated with day-to-day variations (*e.g.*, atmospheric conditions).

Glasner *et al.* [10] demonstrated good performance using each pixel and color channel as a separate feature. Our approach assumes a set of consistent landmarks across the image set. In principle, we could treat each pixel and color channel as a 'landmark,' but doing so would result in impractically slow training. Therefore, we adopt a two-level (hierarchical) approach.

We first describe our lowest-level features. Let $z_t = I_{i,j,c,t}$ be the image intensity at pixel i, j, color channel $c \in \{\text{red}, \text{green}, \text{blue}, \text{gray}\}$, and time $t \in \mathcal{T}$. Let T_t be the ground truth temperature at time t. We omit the lo/hi subscript below. Each pixel produces a temperature estimate according to a simple linear model, $\hat{T}_{i,j,c,t} = a_{i,j,c}z_t + b_{i,j,c}$, where $\hat{T}_{i,j,c,t}$ is the estimated temperature at time t according to pixel i, j, c, t. We compute the regression coefficients $a^* = a^*_{i,j,c}$ and $b^* = b^*_{i,j,c}$ by solving $a^*, b^* = \min_{a,b} \sum_{t \in \mathcal{T}} \|az_t + b - T_t\|_2^2$. A straightforward way to produce a single prediction is to combine the pixel-wise predictions using a weighted average, $\hat{T}_t$. We form two feature vectors at each pixel, $\mathbf{t}_{i,j,t} = [\hat{T}_{\text{red}}, \hat{T}_{\text{green}}, \hat{T}_{\text{blue}}, \hat{T}_{\text{gray}}]$ corresponding to temperature estimates, and $\mathbf{v}_{i,j,t} = [z_{\text{gray}}, g_x, g_y]$, where z_{gray} is the grayscale pixel intensity and g_x and g_y are the x and y grayscale intensity gradients, respectively.

We divide the image into non-overlapping $h \times w$-pixel patches and assign a landmark to each patch (we empirically set $h = w = 15$). At each landmark k we construct a region covariance descriptor [13]. Specifically, for each patch $\mathcal{P}_{k,t}$ centered at k at time t we compute two covariance matrices, $\Sigma_\mathbf{v}$ and $\Sigma_\mathbf{t}$: The feature vector for landmark k is then $\mathbf{f}_k = [\sigma_\mathbf{v}, \sigma_\mathbf{t}]^\mathsf{T}$, where $\sigma_\mathbf{v}$ is a 1×6 vector of upper-right entries of $\Sigma_\mathbf{v}$ and $\sigma_\mathbf{t}$ is a 1×10 vector of upper-right entries of $\Sigma_\mathbf{t}$. We trained and tested our algorithm using the set of $\{\mathbf{f}_{k,t}\}$.

Figure 2 illustrates several interesting qualitative results of our approach on the *Hot or Not* dataset. Table 1 provides a quantitative comparison between the accuracy of variants of our proposed approach, and the accuracy of seven different estimation methods proposed by [10] on the *Hot or Not* dataset. The first seven rows are results reported by [10]. The bottom four rows are variants of our method. We note that, unlike Glasner *et al.* [10], our "Kernel Est. with $w_\phi w_x$" method is capable of producing *time-varying* (dynamic) landmark weights (see Fig. 2), which provides a meaningful and intuitive way to understand which parts of the image contribute most significantly to the temperature estimate. At the same time, the accuracy of "Kernel Est. with $w_\phi w_x$" is competitive, which shows that our method does not sacrifice accuracy to achieve this capability.

Table 1. Accuracy of Celsius temperature prediction on *Hot or Not* [10]. Each cell contains two values: R^2/RMSE, where $R^2 = 1 - \frac{\text{MSE}}{\sigma^2}$, MSE is the mean squared error of the temperature estimation, σ^2 is temperature variance, and RMSE is root MSE. The first seven rows are results from [10]. The bottom four rows are variants of our method. Our method produces a *time-varying* (dynamic) weight for each landmark, which provides a richer, more intuitive explanation of the estimation process.

	(a)	(b)	(c)	(d)	(e)	(f)	(g)	(h)	(i)	(j)
Last Year	0.42 / 9.14	0.56 / 8.16	0.54 / 7.53	0.41 / 5.44	0.61 / 7.35	0.00 / 4.30	0.67 / 6.20	0.59 / 6.77	0.00 / 4.84	0.61 / 7.64
Nearest Neighbor Image	0.47 / 8.72	0.59 / 7.83	0.51 / 7.73	0.15 / 6.51	0.13 /10.92	0.00 / 4.57	0.16 / 9.89	0.70 / 5.83	0.00 / 4.44	0.62 / 7.47
Local Regression	**0.67 / 6.85**	0.65 / 7.24	0.70 / 6.03	0.59 / 4.53	0.76 / 5.77	0.38 / 3.19	0.50 / 7.63	0.77 / 5.09	0.10 / 3.68	0.59 / 7.77
LR Temporal Window	0.61 / 7.52	0.69 / 6.86	0.72 / 5.82	**0.64 / 4.23**	0.79 / 5.39	**0.53 / 2.77**	0.54 / 7.35	0.76 / 5.22	0.11 / 3.67	0.58 / 7.85
Global Ridge Regression	0.00 /18.16	0.78 / 5.74	0.00 /35.02	0.00 /11.37	0.00 /43.51	0.10 / 3.84	**0.74 / 5.54**	0.00 /13.86	0.23 / 3.41	0.46 / 8.91
Convolutional NN	0.49 / 8.55	0.79 / 5.59	0.71 / 5.96	0.24 / 6.17	0.61 / 7.36	0.48 / 2.90	0.39 / 8.48	**0.79 / 4.88**	0.43 / 2.93	0.66 / 7.12
Transient Attributes	0.36 / 9.60	0.70 / 6.69	0.58 / 7.20	0.55 / 4.75	0.68 / 6.62	0.21 / 3.59	0.58 / 7.03	0.65 / 6.31	0.16 / 3.56	0.67 / 7.00
Weighted Avg. with w_ϕ	0.54 / 8.13	0.66 / 7.18	0.00 / 13.00	0.38 / 5.59	0.69 / 6.54	0.35 / 3.26	0.49 / 7.74	0.12 / 9.96	0.34 / 3.17	0.58 / 7.91
Kernel Est. (no weights)	0.55 / 8.01	0.81 / 5.38	0.75 / 5.54	0.56 / 4.69	0.82 / 4.92	0.00 / 4.23	0.33 / 8.89	0.71 / 5.68	0.45 / 2.88	**0.72 / 6.49**
Kernel Est. with w_ϕ	0.13 / 11.15	0.81 / 5.32	0.74 / 5.59	0.41 / 5.43	**0.83 / 4.82**	0.20 / 3.62	0.39 / 8.42	0.71 / 5.68	0.53 / 2.67	0.68 / 6.93
Kernel Est. with $w_\phi w_x$	0.28 / 10.16	**0.81 / 5.30**	**0.76 / 5.41**	0.32 / 5.82	0.83 / 4.87	0.22 / 3.56	0.38 / 8.52	0.72 / 5.59	**0.55 / 2.62**	0.68 / 6.93

4.2   Face Age Estimation

Face age estimation is a well-studied area in computer vision. For example, apparent age estimation [14] was a key topic in the 2015 Looking At People ICCV Challenge [15]. The top performers in that challenge all used a combination of deep convolutional neural networks and large training databases (*e.g.*, ~250k images). Given the significant engineering overhead required, we do not focus on achieving state-of-the-art accuracy using such large datasets. Instead, here we show qualitative results on a smaller age estimation dataset to illustrate several aspects of our approach. For experimentation, we used the Lifespan database [16], which has been previously used for age estimation [17] and modeling the evolution of facial landmark appearance [18].

The Lifespan database contains frontal face images with neutral and happy expressions, with ages ranging from 18 to 94 years. We used the 590 neutral expression faces with associated manually labeled landmarks from [17]. Following [17], we used five-fold cross-validation for our experiments.

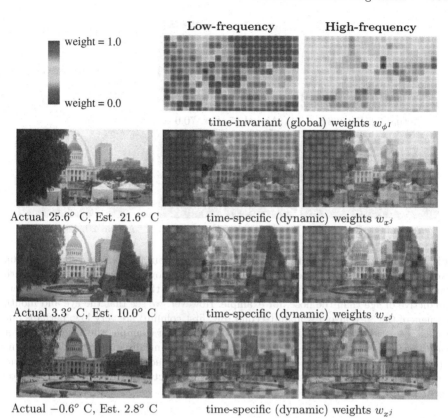

Fig. 2. Qualitative results on scene (a) from the *Hot or Not* dataset [10]: summer, late autumn, and winter. Notice that low-frequency global weights (row 1, middle column) tend to be larger around the background trees and at the edge of the foreground tree, which reflects that leaf appearance is well correlated with the season. Observe that high-frequency global weights (row 1, right column) tend to be larger on distant buildings, which reflects the intuition that daily weather variations (*e.g.*, fog, precipitation) can dramatically change the appearance of the atmosphere, which is especially noticeable against the backdrop of distant buildings. Note that our method correctly reduces the high-frequency weights on the crane (row 3, right column), which suggests that unpredictably occluded landmarks should not contribute to the estimate (appearance temporarily becomes uncorrelated with temperature). **Best viewed in color.** (Color figure online)

Figure 3 shows the age estimates and landmark weights produced by our method. We see that certain regions of the face (*e.g.*, eyes, mouth corners) generally received higher weights than others (*e.g.*, nose tip). However, this is not true for all faces. For example, cosmetics can alter appearance in ways that conceals apparent age, and landmarks can be occluded (*e.g.*, by hair or sunglasses). This implies that a globally consistent weight for each landmark is suboptimal.

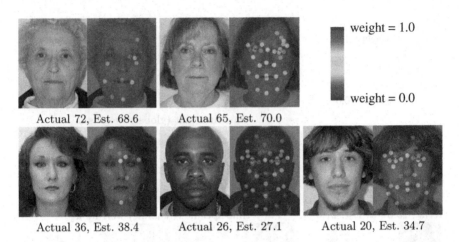

Actual 72, Est. 68.6   Actual 65, Est. 70.0

Actual 36, Est. 38.4   Actual 26, Est. 27.1   Actual 20, Est. 34.7

Fig. 3. Qualitative age estimation results on images from the *Lifespan* database [16]. Notice that landmarks occluded by hair are correctly down-weighted. Eye and mouth landmarks tend to have higher weight, which suggests that their appearance is more predictive of age than the nose, for example. However, we see that the eye and mouth corners of the 36-year-old woman (second row, first column) are very low, perhaps due to her cosmetics. Our method is not always accurate. For example, the age estimate for the 20-year-old man (second row, third column) is technically incorrect. However, his apparent age is arguably closer to the estimate than his actual age. See the supplementary material for additional results. **Best viewed electronically in color. (Color figure online)**

In contrast, our dynamic weights w_x adapt to each face instance to better handle such variations. See the supplementary material for additional results.

4.3   Alzheimer's Disease (AD) Classification

We further demonstrate the performance of our model on a clinically-relevant task of predicting disease status from neuroimaging data. For this set of experiments we used diffusion tensor imaging (DTI) data from an Alzheimer's disease (AD) dataset. We use the fractional anisotropy (FA) maps that are the normalized standard deviation maps of the eigenvalues of the DTI as a single channel image for deriving the feature vectors. We used standard image processing of DTI [19] to derive these measures in the entire white matter region of the brain from a total of 102 subjects. There were 44 subjects with AD diagnosis and 58 matched normal control (CN) subjects. We defined 186 regularly-placed landmarks on the lattice of the brain volume. At each of these landmarks we derived mean feature vector ($[I, Ix, Iy, Iz]$) using a local 3D patch of size $10 \times 10 \times 10$. I is the FA value, Ix, Iy, Iz are the differentiated FA values in the x, y and z directions, respectively. Since our algorithm performs regression, we used $\{0, 2\}$ for $\{CN, AD\}$ and thresholded the prediction results at 1. Using these features we obtained a classification accuracy of 86.17 % using 10-fold cross-validation.

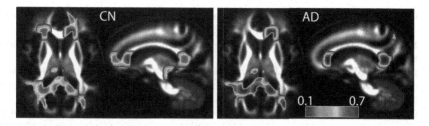

Fig. 4. Conditional confidence maps of two representative subjects from the normal control group (left) and the AD group (right). The maps are overlaid on the population mean FA map. Observe that different white matter regions play important roles in the prediction. For example, the frontal white matter is bilaterally important in the CN subject where as there is assymetry in the AD subject.

Even though our method is a regression model, this outperforms SVM with PCA on the same data set showing 80%–85% [20]. The resulting conditional confidence maps (computed using w_{x^j} in Algorithm 1) for the top 20 landmarks (of the 186) for two sample subjects are shown in Fig. 4.

5 Conclusions

This paper provided a statistical algorithm for identifying conditional confidence of covariates in a regression setting. We utilized the concept of Sufficient Reduction within an Inverse Regression (AIR) model to obtain formulations that offer individual-level relevance of covariates. On all three applications described here, we found that in addition to gross accuracy, the ability to explain a prediction for each test example can be valuable for many applications. Our approach comes with various properties such as optimal weights, unbiasedness, and procedures to calculate conditional densities along only relevant dimensions given a regression task; these are interesting side results. Our evaluations suggest that there is substantial value in further exploring how Abundant Inverse Regression can complement current regression approaches in computer vision, offer a viable tool for interpretation/feedback, and guide the design of new methods that exploit these conditional confidence capabilities directly.

Acknowledgements. This research was supported by NIH grants AG040396, and NSF CAREER award 1252725. Partial support was provided by UW ADRC AG033514, UW ICTR 1UL1RR025011, UW CPCP AI117924 and Waisman Core Grant P30 HD003352-45.

References

1. Friston, K.J., Holmes, A.P., Worsley, K.J., Poline, J.P., Frith, C.D., Frackowiak, R.S.: Statistical parametric maps in functional imaging: a general linear approach. Hum. Brain Mapp. **2**(4), 189–210 (1994)

2. Cao, X., Wei, Y., Wen, F., Sun, J.: Face alignment by explicit shape regression. Int. J. Comput. Vis. **107**(2), 177–190 (2014)
3. Li, K.C.: Sliced inverse regression for dimension reduction. J. Am. Stat. Assoc. **86**(414), 316–327 (1991)
4. Loh, P.L., Wainwright, M.J.: High-dimensional regression with noisy and missing data: provable guarantees with non-convexity. In: Proceedings of the Advances in Neural Information Processing Systems, pp. 2726–2734 (2011)
5. Chen, Y., Caramanis, C.: Noisy and missing data regression: distribution-oblivious support recovery. In: Proceedings of the 30th International Conference on Machine Learning, pp. 383–391 (2013)
6. Krutchkoff, R.: Classical and inverse regression methods of calibration. Technometrics **9**(3), 425–439 (1967)
7. Taddy, M.: Multinomial inverse regression for text analysis. J. Am. Stat. Assoc. **108**(503), 755–770 (2013)
8. Rabinovich, M., Blei, D.: The inverse regression topic model. In: Proceedings of the 31st International Conference on Machine Learning, pp. 199–207 (2014)
9. Kim, M., Pavlovic, V.: Dimensionality reduction using covariance operator inverse regression. In: Proceedings of the Computer Vision and Pattern Recognition, pp. 1–8. IEEE (2008)
10. Glasner, D., Fua, P., Zickler, T., Zelnik-Manor, L.: Hot or not: exploring correlations between appearance and temperature. In: Proceedings of the IEEE International Conference on Computer Vision, pp. 3997–4005 (2015)
11. Adragni, K.P., Cook, R.D.: Sufficient dimension reduction and prediction in regression. Philos. Trans. R. Soc. Lond. A: Math. Phys. Eng. Sci. **367**(1906), 4385–4405 (2009)
12. Cook, R.D.: Fisher lecture: dimension reduction in regression. Statist. Sci. **22**(1), 1–26 (2007). doi:10.1214/088342306000000682
13. Tuzel, O., Porikli, F., Meer, P.: Region covariance: a fast descriptor for detection and classification. In: Leonardis, A., Bischof, H., Pinz, A. (eds.) ECCV 2006. LNCS, vol. 3952, pp. 589–600. Springer, Heidelberg (2006)
14. Zhu, Y., Li, Y., Mu, G., Guo, G.: A study on apparent age estimation. In: Proceedings of the IEEE International Conference on Computer Vision Workshops, pp. 25–31 (2015)
15. Escalera, S., Fabian, J., Pardo, P., Baró, X., Gonzalez, J., Escalante, H.J., Misevic, D., Steiner, U., Guyon, I.: Chalearn looking at people 2015: apparent age and cultural event recognition datasets and results. In: Proceedings of the IEEE International Conference on Computer Vision Workshops, pp. 1–9 (2015)
16. Minear, M., Park, D.: A lifespan database of adult facial stimuli. Behav. Res. Methods **36**(4), 630–633 (2004)
17. Guo, G.D., Wang, X.: A study on human age estimation under facial expression changes. In: IEEE Conference on Computer Vision and Pattern Recognition (2012)
18. Kim, H.J., Xu, J., Vemuri, B.C., Singh, V.: Manifold-valued Dirichlet processes. In: Proceedings of the International Conference on Machine Learning, pp. 1199–1208 (2015)
19. Cook, P., Bai, Y., Nedjati-Gilani, S., Seunarine, K., Hall, M., Parker, G., Alexander, D.: Camino: open-source diffusion-MRI reconstruction and processing. In: Proceedings of the 14th Scientific Meeting of the International Society for Magnetic Resonance in Medicine, Seattle WA, USA (2006)
20. Hwang, S.J., Collins, M.D., Ravi, S.N., Ithapu, V.K., Adluru, N., Johnson, S.C., Singh, V.: A projection free method for generalized eigenvalue problem with a nonsmooth regularizer. In: Proceedings of the IEEE International Conference on Computer Vision, pp. 1841–1849 (2015)

Learning Diverse Models: The Coulomb Structured Support Vector Machine

Martin Schiegg[1,2], Ferran Diego[1], and Fred A. Hamprecht[1(✉)]

[1] University of Heidelberg, IWR/HCI, 69120 Heidelberg, Germany
{martin.schiegg,ferran.diego,fred.hamprecht}@iwr.uni-heidelberg.de
[2] Robert Bosch GmbH, 70465 Stuttgart, Germany

Abstract. In structured prediction, it is standard procedure to discriminatively train a single model that is then used to make a single prediction for each input. This practice is simple but risky in many ways. For instance, models are often designed with tractability rather than faithfulness in mind. To hedge against such model misspecification, it may be useful to train multiple models that all are a reasonable fit to the training data, but at least one of which may hopefully make more valid predictions than the single model in standard procedure. We propose the Coulomb Structured SVM (CSSVM) as a means to obtain at training time a full ensemble of different models. At test time, these models can run in parallel and independently to make diverse predictions. We demonstrate on challenging tasks from computer vision that some of these diverse predictions have significantly lower task loss than that of a single model, and improve over state-of-the-art diversity encouraging approaches.

Keywords: Structured output learning · Diverse predictions · Multiple output learning · Structured support vector machine

1 Introduction

The success of large margin methods for structured output learning, such as the structured support vector machine (SSVM) [1], is partly due to their good generalization performances achieved on test data, compared to, *e.g.* maximum likelihood learning on structured models [2]. Despite such regularization strategies, however, it is not guaranteed that the model which optimizes the learning objective function really generalizes well to unseen data. Reasons include wrong model assumptions, noisy data, ambiguities in the data, missing features, insufficient training data, or a task loss which is too complex to model directly.

To further decrease the generalization error, it is beneficial to either *(i)* generate multiple likely solutions from the model [3–5] or, *(ii)* learn *multiple* models which generate diverse predictions [6–8]. The different predictions for a given structured input may then be analyzed to compute robustness/uncertainty measures, or may be the input for a more complex model exploiting higher-order

© Springer International Publishing AG 2016
B. Leibe et al. (Eds.): ECCV 2016, Part III, LNCS 9907, pp. 585–599, 2016.
DOI: 10.1007/978-3-319-46487-9_36

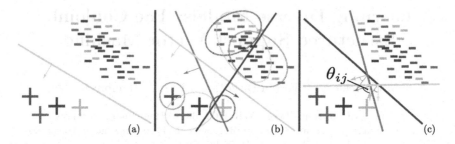

Fig. 1. Structured SVM learning. "+" indicates a structured training example whereas "−" in the same color are the corresponding structured outputs with task loss $\Delta(+, -) > 0$. (a) A standard linear SSVM maximizes the margin between positive and all "negative" examples (decision boundary with its normal vector in cyan). (b) Multiple choice learning [6] learns M SSVMs (here: 3) which cluster the space (clusters for positive and negative examples are depicted in the same color) to generate M outputs. (c) We propose the Coulomb Structured SVM which learns an ensemble of M SSVMs through a diversity term which maximizes the pairwise angles θ_{ij} between their (linear) decision boundaries, while seeking to best fit all training data. (Color figure online)

dependencies, as is done in re-ranking models, *e.g.* Yadollahpour *et al.* [9] augment their features with global ones for automatic re-ranking. Other successful applications include prediction of diverse hypotheses for machine translation [10], on-demand feature computation [11], or active learning methods [12,13]. Furthermore, an oracle may choose amongst all predictions that one which is closest to the ground truth. This becomes handy for proof-reading tasks in order to keep manual interactions at a minimum. It is particularly beneficial in structured output spaces to present to the user not only similarly likely, but also *diverse* proposal solutions. The set of diverse predictions may still contain a low-loss solution, even if the most likely prediction of the single model has a large loss. As a consequence, instead of minimizing the expected generalization error of a *single* model in structured learning, (cf. Fig. 1(a)), it is favorable to minimize the expected generalization error *amongst multiple* models, see Fig. 1(b, c).

Our main contribution is an algorithm termed the *Coulomb structured support vector machine* (CSSVM) which learns an ensemble of M models with different parameters, thanks to a corresponding diversity-encouraging prior. This is qualitatively different from previous work which requires that the *outputs* of the M models are diverse. In particular, we allow the M models in the ensemble to make identical predictions (and hence perfectly fit the data) at training time. Another benefit is that CSSVM can learn diverse models even if only a single structured training example is available. In Sect. 3.4, we generalize our algorithm to allow for structured clustering.

2   Related Work

One major research avenue is to generate at prediction time multiple (possibly diverse) solutions from a single previously trained structured model [3–5]. In order to find M similarly likely solutions, Yanover et al. [3] propose a message passing scheme to iteratively add constraints forbidding the previous solutions. Batra et al. [5] build on the same idea but incorporate these constraints directly into the objective function. This yields a deterministic framework which tries to find *diverse* solutions by requiring a minimum distance to the previous solutions. Their idea is extended in [14] to jointly infer diverse predictions at test time. Papandreou and Yuille [4], instead, perturb model parameters repeatedly with noise from a Gumbel distribution, and subsequently solve for the maximum-a-posteriori (MAP) solution to sample M plausible solutions. Their idea of perturbing the data term is natural when data is assumed to be noisy.

Sampling M solutions could of course also be achieved using Gibbs sampling or other MCMC techniques, however with very slow mixing time on general graphs; more efficient sampling strategies have been proposed recently [15]. Recent work aims at finding the M best modes of the probability distribution (local maxima) directly [16,17]. While promising, their algorithms are yet not applicable to general graphs. Another recently discussed approach to sample diverse predictions at test time are determinantal point processes [18].

Rather than learning one model and then sampling successively (possibly diverse) solutions from the model, recent developments [6–8] allow to *train* multiple diverse models, i.e. diversity is already considered at training time. Typically, only one ground truth solution is provided per training sample rather than a diverse set, and thus diversity amongst the models can not be directly measured by means of training data. There are multiple works which tackle this challenge successfully: Gane et al. [8] learn (multi-modal) distributions over the perturbations in Perturb-and-MAP models using latent variable models which include inverse convex programs to determine relations between the model parameters and the MAP solution. Most similar to our work is [6,7], where a set of M SSVMs is optimized while trading diversity versus data fit. In the former, diversity is encouraged through clustering: Each structured training example is assigned to the learner which achieves the lowest task loss for this sample in the current iteration. Their idea builds on the assumption that there are M clusters present in the training samples, thus requiring at least M (implicitly) diverse training samples. This requirement may be a crucial problem on small training sets. Our approach, in contrast, can learn M diverse models even if only one training example is present, as is often the case in CRF learning, e.g. co-segmentation (Sect. 4i), [19,20]. In their more recent work, Guzman-Rivera et al. [7] extend their idea by augmenting the learning objective directly with a convex term which explicitly rewards diversity in the *outputs* of different learners, as also done in [21]. In our approach, in contrast, the diversity prior is posed on the *parameters* of the M models, and thus, all learners might achieve the same loss on the training samples while still providing diverse predictions on test data, cf. Fig. 1(b, c).

3   Coulomb Structured Support Vector Machine

The goal of this work is to learn M mappings from one structured input to M possibly *diverse* structured outputs from a training set $\mathcal{D} = \{(\mathbf{x}_i, \mathbf{y}_i)\}_{i=1,\ldots,N}$.

3.1   Problem Description and Diversity Prior

For this purpose, we propose to learn an ensemble of M concurrent structured SVMs, which amounts to the following optimization problem:

$$\underset{\mathbf{w}_1,\ldots,\mathbf{w}_M}{\arg\min} \; \underbrace{\alpha\Gamma(W)}_{\text{diversity}} + \underbrace{\Omega(W)}_{\text{generalization}} + \underbrace{C \cdot R_M(W, \mathcal{D})}_{\text{data term}}, \tag{1}$$

where $R_M(W, \mathcal{D}) = \frac{1}{MN} \cdot \sum_{m=1}^{M} \left(\sum_{i=1}^{N} L(\mathbf{x}_i, \mathbf{y}_i; \mathbf{w}_m) \right)$ is the empirical risk with $L(\mathbf{x}_i, \mathbf{y}_i; \mathbf{w}_m)$ being the structured loss of the i-th training example evaluated by the m-th learner. $\Omega(W)$ is the regularization term on the parameters $W = [\mathbf{w}_1, \ldots, \mathbf{w}_M]$ (in SSVMs typically an L2 regularizer is used on each single $\mathbf{w}_i$), and a bias term is omitted since it does not have an influence on the optimization problem [22]. Diversity amongst the M learners is encouraged by the diversity prior $\Gamma(W)$ on the parameters W, where α regulates the degree of diversity. In this way, $\alpha = 0$ reveals the standard SSVM formulation, since all M weights converge to the same optimum.

For the ease of argument, let us now assume the training set is linearly separable[1] as in Fig. 1. Moreover, assume that feature selection yielded independent features. Our illustration of the structured learning problem in Fig. 1 is analogous to representations of flat classification problems where we regard the ground truth labeling of the structured training samples as the single positive examples and all other (exponentially many) labelings as corresponding negative examples. The objective in Fig. 1(a) is to find a weight vector $\mathbf{w}$ which separates the positive from the negative examples and maximizes the margin [1].

We define the *version space* $V(\mathcal{D})$ analogously as in flat classification [24,25], as

$$V(\mathcal{D}) = \{\mathbf{w} \in \mathcal{W} \mid R_1(\mathbf{w}, \mathcal{D}) = 0\}, \tag{2}$$

where R_1 is the empirical risk as in Eq. (1) with $M = 1$, and $\mathcal{W}$ is the space of feasible weight vectors. In other words, the version space is the set of all feasible weight vectors which yield zero loss on the training set $\mathcal{D}$. For linear classifiers, the weight vectors $\mathbf{w} \in \mathcal{W}$ are linear combinations of the training points $\mathbf{x}_i$ [25], *i.e.* $\mathbf{w} = \sum_{i=1}^{N} c_i \mathbf{x}_i$ for coefficients c_i, and the version space may be restricted appropriately. Note that the error of a structured model induced from a weight vector in version space may still be large for randomly chosen query points (*i.e.* high generalization error) in spite of achieving zero loss on the training set.

Typically, version space is only summarized by a single point such as the center of the largest inscribed sphere (the hard-margin SVM) or the center of

---

[1] Note that this is almost always true once we have a sufficient number of independent features, see the function counting theorem [23].

mass of the version space (the Bayes point machine [26]). To learn an ensemble of classifiers, our goal is to distribute M weight vectors $\mathbf{w}_m \in \mathcal{W}, m = 1, \dots, M$, in version space such that the most diverse predictions on unseen points are obtained. To this end, it is sufficient for structured models with energy functions linear in $\mathbf{w}$ – similar to flat linear classification [27] – to only investigate weight vectors on the unit sphere (*i.e.* $\|\mathbf{w}\|_2 = 1$): At prediction time, labelings are scored by the energy function of the structured model $E(\mathbf{x}, \mathbf{y}) = \mathbf{w}^\top f(\mathbf{x}, \mathbf{y})$, where $f(\mathbf{x}, \mathbf{y})$ is the joint feature function. Replacing $\mathbf{w}$ by $\lambda \mathbf{w}$, $\lambda > 0$, still yields the same ordering of the labelings.

We hence have to solve an experimental design problem on parts of the unit sphere to get an ensemble of *diverse* structured models, in other words – disregarding training data – we want to evenly distribute M points on the unit sphere. The goal of experimental design [28,29] is to select from a set of possible experiments/configurations/parameter settings the subset with greatest expected merit. In our case, the set of experiments to choose from is the sphere $\|\mathbf{w}\|_2 = 1$. In other words, rather than sample the sphere uniformly, we need to bias our experimental design towards parameters that produce low empirical loss. Hence, we next introduce the repulsive diversity energy term $\Gamma(W)$ which makes Eq. (1) a non-convex optimization problem, which we optimize approximately.

3.2 Diversity Through Coulomb Potential

Distributing M points evenly on the unit sphere is much studied in information theory and is known as a spherical code [30]: Different variants include *sphere packing* (maximize the minimal angle between any two parameter vectors) and *covering problems* (minimize the distance between any point on the sphere and the closest parameter vector). In three dimensions, the problem is known as the *Thomson problem*[2]: The goal is to minimize the energy configuration of M charges on a unit sphere while the charges repel each other with forces determined by Coulomb's law. While yet unsolved exactly, approximate solutions have been proposed in the literature, including spiral approximations [31], subdivisions of polyhedrons [32], or gradient descent methods [33–35] which correspond to electrostatic repulsion simulations exploiting Coulomb's law: Particles of equal charge repel each other with a force proportional to the square of their pairwise distance, the Coulomb force. More generally, in the equilibrium state of the M particles $\mathbf{p}_1, \dots, \mathbf{p}_M$ on the unit sphere, the Riesz energy,

$$E_s(\mathbf{p}_1, \dots, \mathbf{p}_M) = \sum_{i=1}^{M} \sum_{j=1, j \neq i}^{M} \frac{1}{\|\mathbf{p}_i - \mathbf{p}_j\|_2^s} \quad \text{s.t. } \|\mathbf{p}_i\|_2^2 = 1 \; \forall i \tag{3}$$

is minimal. In the following, we set $s = 1$ which yields the Coulomb energy $E_C = E_1$. The Coulomb force which affects particle $\mathbf{p}_i$ amounts to the negative gradient vector of Eq. (3) w.r.t. $\mathbf{p}_i$ [33,35,36] and is given by

---

[2] Note that we want to approximate this problem in a high dimensional space instead of only 3 dimensions.

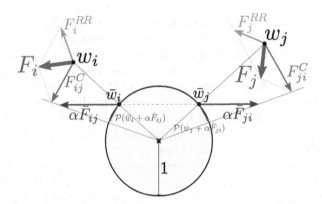

Fig. 2. Optimization. In each iteration of the subgradient algorithm, the current weights w of the competing M learners (here: 2) are projected to the unit sphere, $\bar{w}$, their Coulomb forces (green) are computed, and the resultant weight updates $\mathcal{P}(\bar{w}+\alpha\bar{F})$ are projected from the unit sphere to the original weight vectors w, yielding F^C (pink). Independently, the negative gradient of the regularized risk determines forces F^{RR} (blue). Added together, F^{RR} and F^C yield the update F of the weight vector (red). (Color figure online)

$$\bar{F}_i^C = -\frac{\partial E_C}{\partial \mathbf{p}_i}(\mathbf{p}_1,\dots,\mathbf{p}_M) = -\sum_{j=1,j\neq i}^{N}\frac{\mathbf{p}_j-\mathbf{p}_i}{\|\mathbf{p}_i-\mathbf{p}_j\|_2^3} = \sum_{j=1,j\neq i}^{N}\frac{\mathbf{e}_{ij}}{\|\mathbf{p}_i-\mathbf{p}_j\|_2^2}, \quad (4)$$

where $\mathbf{e}_{ij}$ is the unit vector from $\mathbf{p}_i$ to $\mathbf{p}_j$. Projecting the resultant of force $\bar{F}_i^C$ on $\mathbf{p}_i$ back to the unit sphere by the projection $\mathcal{P}(\mathbf{p}) = \frac{\mathbf{p}}{\|\mathbf{p}\|}$ yields the projected gradient descent update on $\mathbf{p}_i$, namely $\mathbf{p}_i' = \mathcal{P}(\mathbf{p}_i + \bar{F}_i^C)$.

3.3   Optimization by an Electrostatic Repulsion Model

In the following, we will specify the diversity term $\Gamma(W)$ in Eq. (1) and minimize it by utilizing the electrostatic repulsion simulation from the previous section. As derived in Sect. 3.1, the magnitudes of vectors $\mathbf{w}_m$ do not contribute to the diversity term $\Gamma(W)$. Thus, we project the weight vectors to the unit sphere, *i.e.* $\bar{\mathbf{w}}_m = \frac{\mathbf{w}_m}{\|\mathbf{w}_m\|}$, and use the Coulomb energy E_C as the diversity term[3] in Eq. (1),

$$\Gamma(\mathbf{w}_1,\dots\mathbf{w}_M) = E_C(\bar{\mathbf{w}}_1,\dots,\bar{\mathbf{w}}_M). \quad (5)$$

Note that the weights in both the regularizer $\Omega(W)$ and the risk $R_M(W,\mathcal{D})$ are *not* constrained to the unit sphere.

In Sect. 3.2, we derived the projected Coulomb forces which act on the point $\bar{\mathbf{w}}_m$ on the unit sphere. This update step can be projected to $\mathbf{w}_m$ utilizing the intercept theorem (*cf.* Fig. 2),

$$F_m^C = \|\mathbf{w}_m\|_2^2 \cdot \mathcal{P}(\bar{\mathbf{w}}_m + \alpha\bar{F}_m^C). \quad (6)$$

---

[3] Note that we assume electrostatic charges on the *parameters*, and not the *training samples* as done in [37].

Next, let us derive force F_m^{RR} which acts on particle $\mathbf{w}_m$ according to the regularized risk $\Omega(W) + C \cdot R_M(W, \mathcal{D})$ in Eq. (1). The regularized risk in a structured SVM can be minimized using subgradient methods [38] and the negative subgradient for the learner m amounts to the force F_m^{RR}, i.e. the direction to go in the next optimization step when only considering the regularized risk. The $L2$ regularized risk of *one* learner is given by $R_1(\mathbf{w}_m, \mathcal{D}) = \frac{1}{2}\|\mathbf{w}_m\|_2^2 + \frac{C}{N}\sum_{k=1}^{N} L(\mathbf{x}_k, \mathbf{y}_k; \mathbf{w}_m)$. When choosing the structured hinge loss $L(\mathbf{x}_k, \mathbf{y}_k; \mathbf{w}_m) = \max_{\mathbf{y} \in \mathcal{Y}} \left(\Delta(\mathbf{y}_k, \mathbf{y}) - \mathbf{w}_m^\top f(\mathbf{x}_k, \mathbf{y})\right) + \mathbf{w}_m^\top f(\mathbf{x}_k, \mathbf{y}_k)$, where $\Delta(\mathbf{y}_k, \mathbf{y})$ is the task loss, f the feature function, and $(\mathbf{x}_k, \mathbf{y}_k)$ are the training examples; then the subgradient $\mathbf{g}_k^m$ for training example k is given by

$$\hat{\mathbf{y}}^m = \max_{\mathbf{y} \in \mathcal{Y}} \left(\Delta(\mathbf{y}_k, \mathbf{y}) - \mathbf{w}_m^\top f(\mathbf{x}_k, \mathbf{y}))\right) + \mathbf{w}_m^\top f(\mathbf{x}_k, \mathbf{y}_k),$$

$$\mathbf{g}_k^m = f(\mathbf{x}_k, \mathbf{y}_k) - f(\mathbf{x}_k, \hat{\mathbf{y}}^m), \tag{7}$$

i.e. the regularized risk force on particle $\mathbf{w}_m$ is $F_m^{RR} = -\frac{1}{N}\sum_{k=1}^{N}\mathbf{g}_k^m$.

Finally, all forces acting on $\mathbf{w}_m$ can be summed to the total force F_m which determines the next update of $\mathbf{w}_m$: $F_m = F_m^{RR} + F_m^C$. In other words, defining η_t as the step size at iteration t and $\mathbf{g}_l^m$ as in Eq. (7), then the update of $\mathbf{w}_m$ is given by

$$\mathbf{w}_m' \leftarrow \mathbf{w}_m - \eta_t \Big(\mathbf{w}_m + \frac{C}{N}\sum_{k=1}^{N}\mathbf{g}_k^m - F_m^C\Big), \quad \text{or:} \tag{8}$$

$$\mathbf{w}_m' \leftarrow \mathbf{w}_m - \eta_t \left(\mathbf{w}_m + C\mathbf{g}_l^m - F_m^C\right), \tag{9}$$

where the latter is the update in the *stochastic* subgradient algorithm with a random $l \in \{1, \ldots, N\}$. Note that element $[\mathbf{w}_m']_i$ may be projected to zero to guarantee submodular energies during training as proved in [39]. For initialization of the CSSVM, we train one SSVM to get the optimum $\mathbf{w}_*$. Then M random perturbations of $\mathbf{w}_*$ give starting points for $\mathbf{w}_1, \ldots \mathbf{w}_M$.

3.4   Extension: Structured Clustering

Our model suggests a straightforward extension to structured clustering: In the stochastic subgradient update given in Eq. (8), a random training sample is chosen for each learner to update the weight vector. Instead of random selection, a steered selection of training samples for each individual learner would increase diversity. Similarly to the structured K-means block-coordinate descent algorithm proposed in [6], we assign training examples to individual learners: After each subgradient iteration in Sect. 3.3, the task losses $\Delta(\mathbf{y}^m, \mathbf{y}_i; \mathbf{w}_m)$ between prediction $\mathbf{y}^m$ and ground truth $\mathbf{y}_i$ are computed for each learner m, $m \in \{1, \ldots, M\}$, and normalized over all learners, i.e. $\pi_i^m = \frac{\Delta(y^m, y_i; \mathbf{w}_m)}{\sum_{k=1}^{M}\Delta(y^k, y_i; \mathbf{w}_k)}$, $\sum_m \pi_i^m = 1$.

Training example i is then assigned to any of the M learners according to some indicator vector $\sigma(\boldsymbol{\pi}_i)$, where $[\sigma(\boldsymbol{\pi}_i)]_m = 1$ if training sample i is assigned to learner m, 0 otherwise. In Table 1, we propose different alternatives for the mapping $\sigma(\cdot)$. The subgradient update step in Eq. (8) is then modified accordingly:

$$\mathbf{w}'_m \leftarrow \mathbf{w}_m - \eta_t \left(\mathbf{w}_m + \frac{C}{\sum_{j=1}^{N} [\sigma(\boldsymbol{\pi}_j)]_m} \sum_{j=1}^{N} [\sigma(\boldsymbol{\pi}_j)]_m \cdot \mathbf{g}_j^m - F_m^C \right). \tag{10}$$

4   Experiments and Results

To evaluate the performance of our approach, we run experiments on three challenging tasks from computer vision: *(i)* co-segmentation, *(ii)* foreground/background segmentation, and *(iii)* semantic segmentation. We use the iCoseg [40] database for *(i)* and *(ii)* and PASCAL VOC 2010 [41] for *(iii)*. Note that for clearer comparison with previous work, we focus on the evaluation of our first stage model usually used in a two stage pipeline. The proposed method can be combined with any second stage model [10–13, 42–44].

We implemented our algorithm in Python using the PyStruct [45] framework. The code is made available on https://github.com/martinsch/coulomb_ssvm. On all three tasks, we are comparing our results with the state-of-the-art diversity inducing methods Multiple Choice Learning [6] (MCL) and Diverse Multiple Choice Learning [7] (DivMCL), the Matlab implementations of which as well as their features/splitting criterions for the iCoseg dataset in task *(ii)* were kindly provided by the authors. The energies for tasks *(i)* and *(ii)* are submodular, and we thus use graph-cut as inference method; for the multi-label problem in *(iii)*, we utilize TRWS [46].

Generating M diverse outputs is particularly useful in early stages of cascaded approaches, where at a later stage, *e.g.* a human or a second complex model may choose the best of M predictions according to a higher-order loss function. The goal of our approach is, hence, to generate M diverse predictions some of which ought to achieve better task loss than the prediction of the single max-margin model. We therefore stick to the evaluation criterion as applied in prior works, where an oracle chooses the best out of M predictions. In this way, we can evaluate the usefulness of such an approach for cascade models. We relate to this loss as *pick best* error, *i.e.* the lowest task loss among the M predictions.

(i) Co-Segmentation. The design of the proposed CSSVM allows to learn an ensemble of diverse models on very small training sets, in fact, even on training sets which consist of one structured training example only. To demonstrate the usefulness of our approach on such tasks, we run experiments on a co-segmentation dataset. The goal in co-segmentation in general is the simultaneous segmentation of two images each containing similar objects [47]. In our experiments, we assume that a model can be learned on the annotations of one image to predict the segmentation of similar images. We choose six categories from the iCoseg database and use the superpixels and features from [7], their 12-dim. color features for the nodes and a contrast-sensitive and -insensitive Potts term for the edges.

The results for MCL, DivMCL, and our model are depicted in Fig. 3. For each category, we vary the number of models in the ensemble M from 1 to 10,

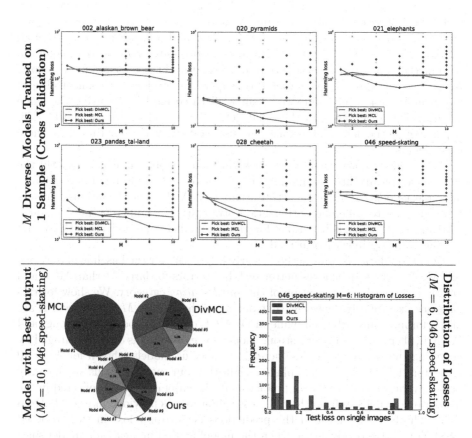

Fig. 3. Top: Hamming losses on the respective datasets of the iCoseg database averaged after cross-validation (lower is better): Each fold consists of exactly one image. We train our model, MCL [6], and DivMCL [7] on one fold, validate on three other folds, and take the remaining $N_c - 4$ folds as test folds, the errors of which we report. For each test example, we compute the M task losses of the predictions to the ground truth, report the minimum as the pick best error (line), and mark the averages of the second, third, etc. best errors in the graphs. In other words, the line represents the losses which an oracle achieves when selecting always the best out of the M predictions. Note that the average error when always selecting the prediction with highest task error (*i.e.* the worst prediction), is constantly lower in our model than in the competing MCL and DivMCL. Bottom left: Frequency of how often model #i, $i \in \{1, \ldots, M\}$, generates the best test prediction; here $M = 10$, speed-skating dataset. Note that in our algorithm, there is no dominant model and each of the M models achieves the pick-best error on a reasonable number of test samples, whereas in MCL and DivMCL the pick-best losses are attributed to only one or few models, respectively. Bottom right: Frequencies of task losses achieved among all test folds and models. All models in our CSSVM ensemble yield predominantly low losses whereas in Div-/MCL many predictions are useless.

where $M = 1$ may be viewed as the baseline and corresponds to the training of a standard SSVM. We perform a full N_c-fold crossvalidation on each category, where N_c is the number of images in category c, and report the test losses of all M models. We choose the regularization and diversity trade-off parameters of each method on a hold-out validation set consisting of three images per category. Note that these losses are computed on superpixel level rather than pixel level which makes for a fair comparison since all three models are using the same superpixels and features. In these datasets, N_c's are in the range of 10 to 33, dependent on the dataset. Obviously, we use strategy "all" from Table 1 for these experiments.

It should be noted that, if we took the same implementations, exactly the same losses for all three competing models for $M = 1$ would be obtained (since all three models are direct generalizations of SSVM). The deviations here are probably due to different optimization strategies, *e.g.* different minima on a plateau or not enough iterations for the subgradient method (Div-/MCL use cutting-plane optimization instead).

On all six datasets, our method clearly improves over the baseline of only one SSVM ($M = 1$) and achieves better pick-best errors for large M than MCL and DivMCL do, with the exception of the *speed-skating* category. We show for this category exemplarily, however, that our algorithm learns M models which are all performing similarly well while in DivMCL only few models are strong, and in MCL, there exists only one strong model since diversity is only encouraged by assigning the training samples (here: 1) to specific models (shown for $M = 10$ in bottom left of Fig. 3). The phenomenon that our method yields significantly better average errors across all predictors in the ensemble is also reflected in the histogram of all losses from the full cross validation, as provided in Fig. 3 bottom right. The fact that most of the predictions achieve low loss in the proposed CSSVM is a strong advantage when the model is used in a cascade model since *all* predictions are good candidates to be selected as the best solution.

Example images for $M = 10$ are presented in Fig. 5. Note that for CSSVM, all models in the ensemble achieve similar training performances while yielding high diversity on the test images. By design, diversity on the training samples is *not* rewarded but models are distributed diversely in version space as argued in Sect. 3.1 in order to achieve a low generalization error on unseen data when the predictions of all M models are considered jointly. This is in contrast to the competing methods, where diversity among the models is also enforced on the training set.

(ii) Foreground/Background Segmentation. In this experiment, we use all these categories together (166 images in total) and use the same split criterion for the 5-fold cross validation as in [7]. We train the models on one fold, select regularization and diversity trade off parameters on two validation folds and report the test error on the remaining two folds. Figure 4 presents the results for MCL, DivMCL, and our model with different sample assignment strategies as in Table 1. Since this dataset consists of different categories, it seems natural that the models which cluster the training data by assigning training instances to

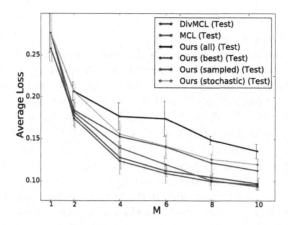

Fig. 4. Foreground/background Segmentation (iCoseg). Average pick-best error (Hamming distance, lower is better) on the set of all categories. Shown are the test errors with one standard deviation (error bars are slightly perturbed on the x-axis for illustration purposes). Our training sample assignment strategies are denoted as in Table 1.

Table 1. Possible mappings for the assignment of training samples to individual learners

$[\sigma(\boldsymbol{\pi}_i)]_m =$	Description	Abbrev.
1	Assign the sample i to every learner $m \in \{1, \ldots, M\}$, $i.e.$ Eq. (8)	**All**
$\mathbb{1}\left[m = \arg\min_{m'}\{\pi_i^{m'}\}\right]$	Assign the sample i to the learner m which achieves the best task loss	**Best**
$\mathbb{1}\left[m = \hat{m}(\pi_i^1, \ldots, \pi_i^M)\right]$	Sample a learner index $\hat{m}$ from the distribution defined by $q_i^1, \ldots q_i^M$ and assign the sample i to learner $\hat{m}$; here, $q_i^m = \frac{1-\pi_i^m}{\sum_j(1-\pi_j^m)}$, $\sum_m q_i^m = 1$	**Sampled**
$\mathbb{1}\left[i = \hat{j}_m\right]$	Sample one training example index $\hat{j}_m \in \{1, \ldots, N\}$ for each learner $m \in \{1, \ldots, M\}$, $i.e.$ Eq. (9)	**Stochastic**

distinct models (as in Div-/MCL, Ours-sampled, and Ours-best) perform better than the models which try to fit all M models to the *entire* dataset (Ours-all, Ours-stochastic). Our model achieves similar accuracies as the state-of-the-art method DivMCL in this experiment.

(iii) Semantic Segmentation. We also evaluate our algorithm on the PASCAL VOC 2010 benchmark dataset for object class segmentation (challenge 5). The dataset consists of an official training set and validation set comprising 964 images each, which contain 21 object classes. We use the SLIC superpixels and Textonboost potentials [48] publicly available from [45]. Due to the lack of a

publicly available test set, we are selecting the parameters of all three models on the official validation set and report these validation errors in Table 2 using the PASCAL VOC evaluation criterion, the Jaccard index. For structured learning, all models use a loss weighted by the inverse class frequency present in the training data. The baselines for this experiment are given by an arg max operation on our features ("unaries only"), a linear SVM on the unary features, and a structured SVM ($M = 1$). With these publicly available features, these baselines achieve average accuracies of 21.6 %, 27.4 %, and 29.1 % which is much lower than the current best results reported on this challenge. In this experiment, however, we want to focus on how much a baseline algorithm can be improved thanks to a diverse ensemble, and not indulge in feature and pipeline tuning.

By training $M = 6$ diverse models and selecting the best predictions amongst them according to the ground truth, all three competing methods yield significantly higher pick-best accuracies than a single SSVM. We can even improve the accuracy from 29.1 % to 37.6 % with the assignment strategy "best" (cf. Table 1). This massive relative improvement underlines the usefulness of a diverse ensemble approach. MCL (35.0 %) and DivMCL (34.5 %) yield inferior performance.

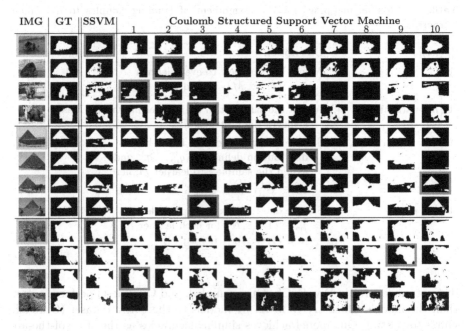

Fig. 5. Foreground/background Co-segmentation (white/black, respectively). The single training image in each dataset is marked in yellow, the best prediction is framed in green. Note that all $M = 10$ models of CSSVM fit the training images similarly well, whereas high diversity amongst the M models is present in the predictions of the test set. GT stands for ground truth.

Table 2. Pascal VOC 2010 Validation Accuracy (higher is better). We tune a popular conditional random field [45] as baseline structured models (top rows). We here focus on the relative improvement that different diversity strategies can achieve (bottom rows), rather than tweaking the baseline model itself.

Method	background	aeroplane	bicycle	bird	boat	bottle	bus	car	cat	chair	cow	diningtable	dog	horse	motorbike	person	plant	sheep	sofa	train	tvmonitor	Average Accuracy
Unaries only	80.2	25.0	0.1	10.6	14.3	13.8	32.1	44.0	30.0	4.9	9.5	4.4	11.9	15.4	27.5	35.5	10.5	19.8	12.0	28.6	22.3	21.6
Linear SVM	80.0	36.6	2.8	17.3	23.0	25.6	40.4	48.7	27.6	8.3	19.5	10.5	13.3	21.9	34.4	36.4	16.9	22.8	17.0	37.0	34.3	27.4
SSVM (M=1)	79.9	39.9	2.1	18.5	27.5	28.4	43.2	49.2	28.7	8.4	21.6	12.3	14.1	23.7	35.2	37.2	22.0	23.6	18.3	38.9	39.4	29.1
MCL (M=6)	82.0	49.1	1.0	31.5	21.2	31.4	55.3	57.7	37.0	12.0	33.0	27.9	28.0	28.8	40.9	39.4	15.1	32.1	23.2	42.4	46.5	35.0
DivMCL (M=6)	82.2	30.3	0.5	25.7	26.4	30.4	51.1	56.3	42.7	7.9	33.5	22.9	45.4	27.3	45.6	43.3	21.3	39.5	17.4	42.9	32.2	34.5
Ours (M=6, all)	83.4	44.4	1.7	37.4	34.1	34.2	47.7	54.9	42.8	8.9	34.4	22.8	40.4	24.7	33.2	44.5	25.7	29.1	20.3	40.1	41.3	35.5
Ours (M=6, stochastic)	83.5	40.1	2.4	25.1	23.0	28.5	57.4	51.8	35.3	8.4	33.7	18.9	31.3	24.9	37.9	42.0	22.7	37.8	24.3	44.4	51.3	34.5
Ours (M=6, best)	83.2	48.8	3.2	38.3	28.4	33.3	58.1	60.3	51.1	7.7	34.5	21.6	34.6	32.0	39.3	43.4	17.7	27.7	26.6	48.3	51.3	**37.6**
Ours (M=6, sampled)	83.9	42.4	1.7	27.6	27.5	33.1	55.9	53.0	46.6	7.6	34.1	25.6	34.6	26.1	41.6	45.6	27.4	32.6	25.8	46.5	48.4	36.6

5 Conclusion

We propose an algorithm termed the *Coulomb structured support vector machine* which learns an ensemble of multiple models in order to yield *diverse* predictions on *test data*. The diversity prior is imposed on the set of model weights rather than on the outputs of training samples as in previous approaches. This allows for the training of diverse models even on a single structured training example. The CSSVM trades off diversity, large margins, and a data term during training in order to optimize the minimum expected generalization error of the *entire* ensemble. The coupling between the M models is effective only at training but not at test time. As a consequence, predictions can be made in parallel without communication overhead in contrast to [5]. Our algorithm learns multiple *strong* predictors in an ensemble on the entire dataset, other than [6,7] where predictors 'focus' on the different clusters in the data, if present. We demonstrate on numerous real world datasets that the M diverse outputs of the proposed ensemble method include predictions with significantly lower task loss compared to only one model. Moreover, our approach of inducing diversity significantly improves over state-of-the-art methods on very small training sets while staying on par with the state-of-the-art methods on bigger training sets. The usefulness for machine learning tasks beyond computer vision is evident.

Acknowledgements. We would like to thank Abner Guzman-Rivera for making the (Div)MCL source code available.

References

1. Tsochantaridis, I., Joachims, T., Hofmann, T., Altun, Y.: Large margin methods for structured and interdependent output variables. JMLR **6**, 1453–1484 (2005)
2. Nowozin, S., Lampert, C.H.: Structured learning and prediction in computer vision. Found. Trends Comput. Graph. Vis. **6**(3–4), 185–365 (2011)
3. Yanover, C., Weiss, Y.: Finding the M most probable configurations in arbitrary graphical models. In: NIPS 2003, pp. 289–296 (2003)

4. Papandreou, G., Yuille, A.L.: Perturb-and-map random fields: using discrete optimization to learn and sample from energy models. In: ICCV (2011)

5. Batra, D., Yadollahpour, P., Guzman-Rivera, A., Shakhnarovich, G.: Diverse M-best solutions in Markov random fields. In: Fitzgibbon, A., Lazebnik, S., Perona, P., Sato, Y., Schmid, C. (eds.) ECCV 2012, Part V. LNCS, vol. 7576, pp. 1–16. Springer, Heidelberg (2012)

6. Guzman-Rivera, A., Batra, D., Kohli, P.: Multiple choice learning: learning to produce multiple structured outputs. In: NIPS, pp. 1808–1816 (2012)

7. Guzman-Rivera, A., Kohli, P., Batra, D., Rutenbar, R.A.: Efficiently enforcing diversity in multi-output structured prediction. In: AISTATS (2014)

8. Gane, A., Hazan, T., Jaakkola, T.: Learning with maximum a-posteriori perturbation models. In: AISTATS, pp. 247–256 (2014)

9. Yadollahpour, P., Batra, D., Shakhnarovich, G.: Discriminative re-ranking of diverse segmentations. In: CVPR (2013)

10. Gimpel, K., Batra, D., Dyer, C., Shakhnarovich, G.: A systematic exploration of diversity in machine translation. In: EMNLP (2013)

11. Roig, G., Boix, X., de Nijs, R., Ramos, S., Kühnlenz, K., Van Gool, L.: Active MAP inference in CRFs for efficient semantic segmentation. In: ICCV (2013)

12. Maji, S., Hazan, T., Jaakkola, T.: Active boundary annotation using random map perturbations. In: AISTATS (2014)

13. Premachandran, V., Tarlow, D., Batra, D.: Empirical minimum bayes risk prediction: how to extract an extra few % performance from vision models with just three more parameters. In: CVPR (2014)

14. Kirillov, A., Savchynskyy, B., Schlesinger, D., Vetrov, D., Rother, C.: Inferring m-best diverse labelings in a single one. In: ICCV, pp. 1814–1822 (2015)

15. Hazan, T., Maji, S., Jaakkola, T.: On sampling from the Gibbs distribution with random maximum a-posteriori perturbations. In: NIPS, pp. 1268–1276 (2013)

16. Chen, C., Kolmogorov, V., Zhu, Y., Metaxas, D., Lampert, C.: Computing the M most probable modes of a graphical model. In: AISTATS, pp. 161–169 (2013)

17. Chen, C., Liu, H., Metaxas, D., Zhao, T.: Mode estimation for high dimensional discrete tree graphical models. In: NIPS, pp. 1323–1331 (2014)

18. Kulesza, A., Taskar, B.: Determinantal point processes for machine learning. arXiv preprint arXiv:1207.6083 (2012)

19. Lucchi, A., Li, Y., Smith, K., Fua, P.: Structured image segmentation using kernelized features. In: Fitzgibbon, A., Lazebnik, S., Perona, P., Sato, Y., Schmid, C. (eds.) ECCV 2012, Part II. LNCS, vol. 7573, pp. 400–413. Springer, Heidelberg (2012)

20. Lou, X., Hamprecht, F.A.: Structured learning for cell tracking. In: NIPS (2011)

21. Li, Y.F., Zhou, Z.H.: Towards making unlabeled data never hurt. IEEE Trans. PAMI **37**(1), 175–188 (2015)

22. Lampert, C.H.: Maximum margin multi-label structured prediction. In: NIPS, pp. 289–297 (2011)

23. Cover, T.M.: Geometrical and statistical properties of systems of linear inequalities with applications in pattern recognition. IEEE Trans. Electron. Comput. **EC–14**(3), 326–334 (1965)

24. Mitchell, T.M.: Machine Learning, 1st edn. McGraw-Hill Inc., New York (1997)

25. Herbrich, R., Graepel, T., Williamson, R.C.: The structure of version space. Technical report MSR-TR-2004-63, Microsoft Research, July 2004

26. Herbrich, R., Graepel, T., Campbell, C.: Bayes point machines. JMLR **1**, 245–279 (2001)

27. Graepel, T., Herbrich, R.: The kernel Gibbs sampler. In: NIPS, pp. 514–520 (2001)
28. Sacks, J., Welch, W.J., Mitchell, T.J., Wynn, H.P.: Design and analysis of computer experiments. Stat. Sci. **4**, 409–423 (1989)
29. Hardin, R., Sloane, N.: A new approach to the construction of optimal designs. J. Stat. Plann. Infer. **37**(3), 339–369 (1993)
30. Conway, J.H., Sloane, N.J.A.: Sphere-packings, Lattices, and Groups. Springer, New York (1987)
31. Saff, E.B., Kuijlaars, A.B.: Distributing many points on a sphere. Math. Intell. **19**(1), 5–11 (1997)
32. Katanforoush, A., Shahshahani, M.: Distributing points on the sphere, I. Exp. Math. **12**(2), 199–209 (2003)
33. Claxton, T., Benson, G.: Stereochemistry and seven coordination. Can. J. Chem. **44**(2), 157–163 (1966)
34. Erber, T., Hockney, G.: Equilibrium configurations of n equal charges on a sphere. J. Phys. A: Math. Gen. **24**(23), L1369 (1991)
35. Lakhbab, H., EL Bernoussi, S., EL Harif, A.: Energy minimization of point charges on a sphere with a spectral projected gradient method. Int. J. Sci. Eng. Res. **3**(5) (2012)
36. Neubauer, S., Watkins, Z.: An algorithm for finding potential minimizing configurations of points on a sphere (1998). http://www.csun.edu/~hcmth007/electrons/algorithm.html. Accessed 30 Aug 2016
37. Hochreiter, S., Mozer, M.C., Obermayer, K.: Coulomb classifiers: generalizing support vector machines via an analogy to electrostatic systems. In: NIPS, pp. 561–568 (2003)
38. Ratliff, N.D., Bagnell, J.A., Zinkevich, M.A.: (Online) Subgradient methods for structured prediction. In: AISTATS (2007)
39. Prasad, A., Jegelka, S., Batra, D.: Submodular meets structured: finding diverse subsets in exponentially-large structured item sets. In: NIPS, pp. 2645–2653 (2014)
40. Batra, D., Kowdle, A., Parikh, D., Luo, J., Chen, T.: iCoseg: interactive co-segmentation with intelligent scribble guidance. In: CVPR (2010)
41. Everingham, M., Van Gool, L., Williams, C.K.I., Winn, J., Zisserman, A.: The PASCAL visual object classes challenge. Int. J. Comput. Vis. **88**, 303–338 (2010)
42. Tsai, Y.H., Yang, J., Yang, M.H.: Decomposed learning for joint object segmentation and categorization. In: BMVC (2013)
43. Lee, T., Fidler, S., Dickinson, S.: Learning to combine mid-level cues for object proposal generation. In: CVPR, pp. 1680–1688 (2015)
44. Wang, S., Fidler, S., Urtasun, R.: Lost shopping! monocular localization in large indoor spaces. In: ICCV (2015)
45. Müller, A.C., Behnke, S.: PyStruct - learning structured prediction in python. JMLR **15**, 2055–2060 (2014)
46. Kolmogorov, V.: Convergent tree-reweighted message passing for energy minimization. IEEE Trans. PAMI **28**(10), 1568–1583 (2006)
47. Rother, C., Minka, T., Blake, A., Kolmogorov, V.: Cosegmentation of image pairs by histogram matching-incorporating a global constraint into MRFs. In: CVPR, pp. 993–1000 (2006)
48. Koltun, V.: Efficient inference in fully connected CRFs with Gaussian edge potentials. In: NIPS (2011)

Pose Hashing with Microlens Arrays

Ian Schillebeeckx[✉] and Robert Pless

Department of Computer Science and Engineering,
Washington University in St. Louis, St. Louis, USA
{ischillebeeckx,pless}@wustl.edu

Abstract. We design and demonstrate a passive physical object whose appearance changes to give a discrete encoding of its pose. This object is created with a microlens array that is placed on top of a black and white pattern; when viewed from a particular viewpoint, the lenses appear black or white depending on the part of the pattern that each microlens projects towards that viewpoint. We analyze different design considerations that impact the information gained from the appearance of microlens array. In addition, we introduce the process through which the discrete microlens pattern can be turned into a viewpoint and a pose estimate. We empirically evaluate factors that impact viewpoint and pose estimation accuracy. Finally, we compare the pose estimation accuracy of the microlens array to other related fiducial markers.

Keywords: Microlens array · Fiducial marker · Pose estimation

1 Introduction

Fiducial markers are critical to many visual, augmented reality and robotic tasks. Most often, fiducial markers serve to create geometric constraints that relate the known position of the marker on the object to the observed position of the marker in the image. Multiple fiducial markers, or larger patterns with several observable points can be combined to constraint the relative pose of an object.

These approaches that relate the fiducial marker to the image suffer from two shortcomings. First, the geometric constraints from a set of points on a fronto-parallel plane are known to be sensitive to noise [1–3]. Second, for any viewpoint, patterns or sets of markers that are collinear or nearly collinear lead to poorly conditioned estimators for the pose estimation problem [4,5].

Some recent work attacks these limitations by designing fiducial markers whose appearance changes depending on the direction from which they are viewed. Images of these fiducial markers directly encode constraints on the object rotation and therefore require fewer markers and eliminate the need for non-collinear markers for pose estimation. Marker designs include lenticular arrays and microlens arrays that have a moire-pattern to encode the viewing angle and go by the name "Lentimark" [6,7] and "Arraymark" [8,9]. Other work uses lenticular arrays that change color depending on their viewing angle [10,11].

© Springer International Publishing AG 2016
B. Leibe et al. (Eds.): ECCV 2016, Part III, LNCS 9907, pp. 600–614, 2016.
DOI: 10.1007/978-3-319-46487-9_37

This paper expands this line of work. We propose the integration of a microlens array with a random black and white pattern adhered to the back. Because these microlenses focus parallel rays onto an approximately single point of their back-plane pattern, they will appear either black or white. Using different patterns behind different microlens dots means that a given viewing direction will cause some dots to be black, some to be white, and some to be in between because the viewpoint is on the boundary of black and white regions. The major contributions of this work are:

- the design of a microlens based fiducial marker with a random black and white back-plane pattern,
- a discrete, combinatorial approach to geometric inference based on images from this fiducial marker, and
- experimental evaluation of a physical instantiation of this marker design.

2   Related Work

Fiducial markers are widely used in computer vision and augmented reality. The most common current versions are AprilTags [12] and the ARTag [13], which are often used within augmented reality libraries such as ARtoolkit [14]. These tags are black and white patterns that are defined for easy detection, and which encode an index that can be used to differentiate multiple tags that are both visible at the same time. Larger scale calibration setups include the de-facto standard approach by Zhengyou Zhang [15]. This method requires the use of a large black-and-white checkerboard pattern to estimate the pose of the camera with respect to the pattern. In all cases, however, the fiducial marker is explicitly constructed to have a similar appearance for all possible viewing angles.

Both AprilTags and ARTags require matching a pattern, so the local orientation of the fiducial marker (and not just the position) is also available as a geometric cue. The derivation of geometric constraints that take advantage of this cue has been done for rigid body pose estimation [16], and in the context of geo-location where the correspondence of image points to a 3D scene model is unknown [17].

Most related to our work are approaches that explicitly make patterns that change their appearance depending on their viewing direction. The use of microlens arrays to both capture and render a complete lightfield was suggested by Nobel Prize winner Gabriel Lippmann in 1908 [18], in the context Integral Photography. Here "Integral" is used in the sense of complete, and the microlens arrays create a light field pattern that changes as the viewer moves so as to create the perspective effects that an array of microlenses captured on film by sampling the light field. In the context of fiducial marker design, Agam Fiducials were suggested in 2000 as drawings on corrugated paper where different orientations of the paper are painted different colors so that the visible color gives a constraint on the viewing direction [19]. Next, and more recently, the "Lentimark" [6,7] and "Arraymark" [8,9] fiducial markers use lenticular arrays or microlens arrays that change appearance for different viewpoints. Using a moire encoding pattern, this change in appearance is a bar or cross that translates relative to the rest of the marker. This beautiful approach gives both human and machine interpretable fiducial markers, but requires the fiducial to be imaged at relatively high resolution in order for the relative position of the dark spot to be measured accurately. Finally, a recent approach creates a lenticular pattern whose apparent color depends on its relative orientation to the camera [10,11]. This avoids the need for the fiducial marker to take up many pixels, but adds the challenge of using color as a good measurement in mixed lighting environments.

Several additional works also create markers that explicitly look differently from different orientations. The light-field probe is created with microlens arrays that each cover a color wheel, creating a color coded lightfield that was used to understand the shape of reflective and refractive objects [20–23]. Finally, the BoKodes work uses a very small projector in the scene to transmit into the scene a collection of QR-Codes [24]. For most camera settings this appears to be a small point, but when the camera is defocused the projector image that impinges on the camera lens is visible and the relative orientation of the BoKode is inferred from which QR code is visible.

This work is most inspired by the BoKode work which creates a discrete pattern that describes an orientation constraint. But because our signal is derived from the spatial layout of microlens patterns it is not necessary to defocus the camera and therefore the orientation encoding is available under standard use cases of a camera.

3   Discrete Encoding of Viewpoint with a Microlens Array

A microlens array is plastic sheet comprised of many small lenses, called lenslets, that are arranged in a regular grid. To create visual effects with the microlens array, the thickness of the sheet is set to be the same as the focal length of the lenslet so that parallel rays are focused onto a point on the back of the sheet. Parallel rays from different directions are focused onto different points. Because light is reversible, the lenslet can also be thought of as a (dim) projector, projecting the appearance of the pattern behind the lenslet out into the world. A schematic of this is shown in Fig. 1.

Thus, the appearance of the microlens array is defined by the pattern that is underneath each microlens. When that pattern is low frequency, the appearance of each lenslet will change slowly as the array is rotated. For patterns with higher frequency, the pattern will change more quickly, and if different lenslets have different patterns the microlens array has an apparent random flickering as each lenslet changes appearance independently of the others. Figure 1 shows two example viewpoints of a microlens array with a texture of many small, randomly placed black blocks. Because this texture is high contrast, the resulting microlens appearance changes quickly for different rotations.

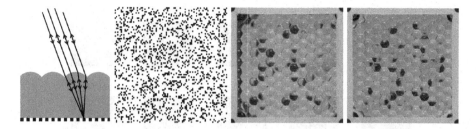

Fig. 1. A microlens array placed on top of a pattern creates an image where each lenslet magnifies a piece of the pattern below it. (Left) The microlens array is designed so that parallel rays focus at a point on the back of the array, so that point is magnified. (Left center) We show an example of a pattern with randomly placed black squares. For different viewpoints, each lenslet will focus at a different location on the pattern and thus produce the different sets of black and white appearances. (Right center and Right) We show the appearances for two different viewpoints after being transformed with a homography to make the images more easily comparable. The appearance of the array changes dramatically, and the discrete measurement of which lenslets are dark and light encodes its orientation.

By thresholding the appearance, one can limit a lenslet to 2 states to carry a bit of information. Considered together for a single viewpoint, all lenslets on the microlens array express a bit string that varies based on viewpoint. In an ideal case, a microlens array with n independent lenslets, could encode 2^n unique bit strings, and thus 2^n uniquely encoded appearances. With 12 lenslets giving binary measurements, this could suffice to encode viewpoints in the viewsphere up to 30 degrees from fronto-parallel to within 1 degree.

While this intuition of a discrete encoding of pose inspired us, random patterns may not give optimal encodings, and there is value in a non-binary classification of lenslet appearance. In the next section we consider practical approaches to choosing patterns that are most useful and consider what is the best discretization of the apparent lenslet brightness. After that we will derive a pose estimation approach and evaluate it with real images of a prototype.

4 Discretization and Entropy of Single Lenslet Measurements

A single lenslet will share the same appearance for a set of viewpoints because it is magnifying the black and white pattern directly beneath it. This magnified view constrains the orientation at which the lenslet is being viewed. To model this constraint, we consider a measurement of the intensity at the center of each lenslet, and experimentally measure the response across a set of viewpoints to create a response map. We explore thresholding the measured intensity at k intervals. The response map characterizes the apparent intensity of each lenslet when viewed from each orientation, and the state-map is the discretization of that response map in k states. Section 5 describes our measurement setup and Fig. 5 shows examples of the measured response map and discrete state maps.

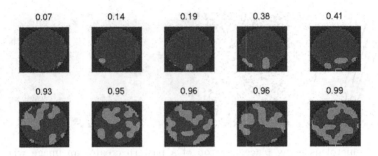

Fig. 2. The five lenslets whose discrete state map has the lowest (top row) and highest (bottom row) entropy. Green represents the views where the lenslet is in state 0, while red, state 1. The bottom lenslets are much more likely to be useful in estimating orientation; the median entropy of 90 lenslets in an array covering random dots is 0.8. (Color figure Online)

We characterize the value of a lenslet based on its entropy. The entropy H for a given lenslet and its map from viewpoint to state is:

$$H = -\sum_i^k p_i * log_2(p_i) \tag{1}$$

where p_i is the frequency in the range $(0, 1)$ of a lenslet being in state i for all viewpoints.

A lenslet which is in all states equiprobably has maximum entropy, and it should be easy to design a pattern to put underneath the microlens array which has this property. However, challenges in accurate printing, aligning a pattern to a lens array, and imperfectly manufactured microlenses that may be out of focus led us to use a random pattern. As a side effect, this lets us explore several questions. First, what is the entropy of a microlens array mounted on top of a random dot pattern?

Using the prototype array and texture patten shown in Fig. 1 we calculate the entropy of each lenslet. Figure 2 shows the binary response maps and entropy measures for lenslets that are thresholded at a intensity of 100 (out of 255). We show the 5 lenslets with the smallest entropy in the first row, and the 5 lenslets with the highest entropy in the 2nd row. The median entropy for all lenslets is about 0.8 indicating that most lenslets give substantial useful constraints.

On the left of Fig. 3, we show the distribution of entropies for all 90 lenslets for optimal discretizations of 2, 3, 4, 5, and 6 states. On the right of Fig. 3, we show these optimal thresholds. This shows two interesting features. First, measurements of the microlens intensity are not binary and discrete states can be selected to give a discrete encoding that maximizes the (per lenslet) entropy. Second, when more than 2 discrete states are used, the thresholds often clump, highlighting the value of noticing when a lenslet is changing between black and white.

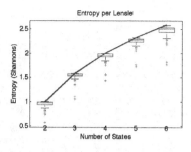
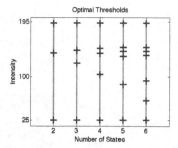

Fig. 3. We experimentally measure the entropy in discrete measurements from a microlens array covering a random pattern of small squares. Optimizing to choose discretization thresholds over all lenslets gives a distribution of the measured entropy that is close to the maximum entropy. On the right we show the optimized thresholds. This motivates the use of a random pattern as having nearly as much information as an optimal pattern.

5   Viewpoint Estimation with a Microlens Array

The state map can be used to characterize the discrete measurement for a lenslet viewed from a given viewpoint. We parameterize the viewpoint with the two-vector Θ which captures the direction of the camera rotated around the local x and y axes, and we define a_i to be the measured appearance of the lenslet. If a lenslet can exist in k states, then the lenslet appearance, a_i, is one of the first k positive integers.

We empirically determine the measurement a_i for each rotation Θ by imaging the microlens array for a grid of viewpoints with a DLSR camera. The microlens array is rotated with two programatically controlled motors which can change the orientation of the microlens array to any rotation around the x and y axis. We scanned over the dome of viewpoints that are $(30, -30)$ degrees from fronto parallel in 2 degree increments, yielding 677 images. We visualize the sampled viewing dome and show the motor setup in Fig. 4.

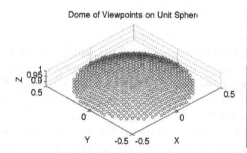
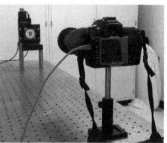

Fig. 4. The left shows the set of viewpoints from which we image the lenticular array, represented as points on a sphere. The right is a depiction of our image setup which includes a DSLR camera viewing the microlens array on a 2-axis motorized mount.

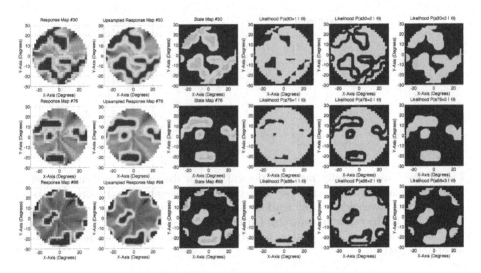

Fig. 5. For each lenslet, our calibration process characterizes the response as a function of viewpoint. Each row shows a different lenslet. From the left, the figure depicts first the raw, then the up-sampled response map. Third is the discrete state map where the response map is thresholded into one of three categories. The last three maps show the 0–1 likelihood function of the orientation as a function of each of the three possible discrete measurements.

For each image, four reference points on the corners of the microlens array are tracked and a homography is used to warp the image to a common coordinate system. Once warped, the center of each lenslet is sampled to create response maps for each lenslet. We show the response map and the responses thresholded into a trinary state map in Fig. 5.

We up-sample the response maps to have approximate measurements at every 0.5 degrees, using linear interpolation, then threshold to create the state map. The experimental section explores the performance gains for different amounts of up-sampling.

5.1   Inference

Using the microlens array, our task is to determine the 2D viewpoint orientation of camera in the reference of the microlens array. We seek to find the most probable viewpoint given the observed discrete appearance of all lenslets in the array. We employ a simple approach where black and white appearances at each lenslet vote for the most likely viewpoint.

Consider a lenslet at inference time with a state b_i. For all the Θs in that lenslet's statemap with state a_i that match b_i, we give one vote. Each lenslet will have a different statemap and will vote for a different set of Θs.

To estimate the viewpoint using the entire microlens array, we choose the Θ with the maximum number of votes. In the case of ties, which normally happen for similar Θs, we take the average. The next section describes how to combine this with measurements of the corner points of the microlens array to determine the full pose of the microlens array.

6   Pose Estimation with Microlens Array

The pose estimation problem seeks to estimate the 3×3 rotation matrix, R, and 3×1 translation vector T, needed to transform the camera reference frame into the microlens array reference frame. As a result, R represents the direction of the surface normal of the microlens array relative to the camera's direction and T is the vector from the camera to the origin of the microlens array.

We consider the pose estimation problem for images whose geometry is defined by a pinhole camera model. Using the standard geometric framework, we assume the origin of the camera coordinate system is centered at the pinhole, and the camera calibration is known and represented by a 3×3 calibration matrix K. According to this model, a point in the camera reference from P is thus projected to the image location p represented in homogeneous coordinates, via K:

$$p = KP \tag{2}$$

Therefore, a reference point Q in the reference frame of the microlens array is projected at the pixel location q' on the image according to the following linear projection:

$$q' = K\left(RQ + T\right) \tag{3}$$

Because the viewpoint estimate derived in the former section is in spherical coordinates, it only gives 2 of the 3 rotation parameters (because the appearance of a microlens is invariant to rotation around the line from it to the camera). Our approach is to use the θ and ϕ estimate of the rotation of the microlens around the x and y axis from before. We construct the complete 3×3 rotation matrix R parameterized by the unknown rotation around the z-axis ψ as:

$$R = R_z(\psi)R_x(\phi)R_z(\theta) \tag{4}$$

where $R_{x,z}(w)$ are the rotation matrices to rotate around the respective axes We denote the transformation to determine R from θ,ϕ, and ψ as $R(\theta, \phi, \psi)$.

We solve for the rotation parameter ψ and the translation vector T by using the known pixel and local locations of the 4 reference points used to rectify images of the microlens array and θ and ϕ estimated previously. Using a non-linear optimization, we solve for these four parameters via reprojection error:

$$\min_{\psi,T} \sum_i^4 \left\|q_i - K\left(R(\theta, \phi, \psi)Q_i + T\right)\right\|_2^2 \tag{5}$$

where q_i is the measured pixel location of a reference point, θ and ϕ are known and held constant, Q_i is the location of the reference point in the local reference frame, and $\|.\|_2$ denotes the euclidean norm. After optimizing for ψ, we can recover the full R matrix using $R(\theta, \phi, \psi)$.

The estimated R and T fully capture the orientation and position of the microlens array relative to the camera. In the next section, we explore the performance of using a microlens array to estimation viewpoint and pose.

7   Experimental Design and Evaluation

We explore the performance of using microlens arrays for viewpoint and full pose estimation. First, we explore how different design and environmental factors affect viewpoint estimation. Second, we explore how the number of lenslet states and the number of lenslets affect viewpoint estimation. Finally, we show pose estimation experimental results and compare these to other recent work with fiducial markers whose appearance depends on the viewpoint.

7.1   Experimental Setup

For the experiments evaluating viewpoint estimation, we test on 88 images randomly sampled from the dome of viewpoints 30 degrees from fronto parallel. These images are taken with the microlens array on the programmable motorized stage, but with Θ values that are randomly selected, and not at the same location as calibration images, but known so that there is ground-truth to compare to. We use a microlens array with a 9×10 regular grid of lenslets, and unless otherwise stated, we use all constraints from all 90 lenslets for viewpoint estimation.

In assessing the accuracy of our viewpoint estimations, we calculate the angular difference between a vector in the direction of the estimated viewpoint direction and a vector in the direction of the true viewpoint. We show summary statistics for all 88 random views as a boxplot. Each boxplot shows the median error in red, a box that shows the range from the 25 percentile to 75 percentile. Red crosses depict outliers, and have values more than 2.7 σ away from the mean, where σ is computed assuming that the data are normally distributed.

7.2   Design and Environmental Factors

We first characterize the effect of design and environmental factors on viewpoint estimation. These factors affect estimation regardless of the number of states the lenslets can occupy. Therefore, to simplify this first set of experimentation, we employ binary (2-state) measurements and threshold at an intensity value of 100. This threshold reflects general observations that that "white" lenslet have intensities above 120 and "black" lenslets had intensities below 50.

We first look at performance gains from up-sampling the response map. Second, we explore the effect of the number of lenslets on viewpoint estimation. Finally, we test the microlens arrays in varying lighting environments.

Response Map Precision. We build response maps for each lenslet by sampling rotations of the microlens array in 2 degree increments. How much can we improve our rotation estimates by up-sampling these response maps? We create increasingly more up-sampled response maps and assess their orientation estimation performance. Figure 6 shows that at the initial resolution, the microlens array constrains the orientation to a median error of 0.7 degrees. Increasing the precision of the response maps to 0.5 degrees (upsampling and interpolating the response maps by a factor of 4) gives a substantial improvement, and further upsampling the response maps has little additional benefit. We use this precision for the rest of the paper.

Number of Lenslets. Section 3 discusses the potential of combinatorial encodings of orientation, with the claim that in an ideal case 14 binary lenslets is sufficient to uniquely encode $\frac{1}{2}$ degree increments in a viewing dome of 30 degrees. This section gives an experimental evaluation of the correlation between estimation performance and number of lenslets. In this experiment, we randomly select k number of lenslets, and then perform orientation estimation. Figure 6 shows results using 20–90 lenslets in increments of 10 on the left, as well as a finer grain analysis with 10–20 lenslets in increments of 1 on the right. With 20 of the total 90 lenslets, we achieve orientation estimation accuracy with a median error below 1 degree. With fewer lenslets, the performance degrades. With less than 14 lenslets, the maximum error surpasses 10 degrees of error, anecdotally we see that sometimes in these cases there are far apart viewpoints that have very similar discrete encodings. To achieve a median viewpoint estimation error of 0.5 degrees, about 30 randomly chosen lenslets are necessary.

Light Environments. Related work uses hue to encode orientation with lenticular arrays [10], and one motivation of this work is use discrete measurements of black and white patterns to avoid problems that arise with varying lighting environments. We test the sensitivity of binary microlens arrays to different lighting environments and exposure settings by exploring 3 different lighting conditions. The first lighting environment is inside under overhead lights. This is the lighting environment used to generate the response maps for all lenslets and is used for all other of the experiments in this paper. The second lighting environment is similar to the first, but with an additional, strong white directional light. The third lighting environment has the scene lit entirely by 2 blue directional lights. In Fig. 7, we show the estimation results of these 3 different lighting environments. The common office environment with overhead lights achieves the lowest error with a median error of 0.3 degrees. However, even with the very extreme lighting environment of only blue directional light, the microlens array is able to estimation orientation with a median error of 0.6 degrees. This experiment suggests that even extreme lighting environments have a minimal effect on the binary encoding of orientation giving by the microlens arrays.

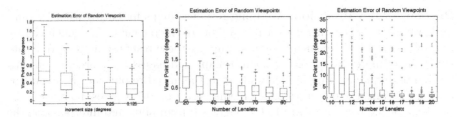

Fig. 6. (Left) Orientation estimation accuracy, as a function of the angular spacing of the response maps. The original measurements have an angular spacing of 2 degrees; all other data is based on up-sampling and interpolating this response map. (Center and Right) As fewer lenslet provide orientation cues, estimation accuracy goes down.

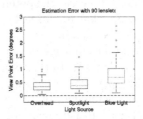

Fig. 7. Orientation estimation error as a function of lighting environment. Overhead lights match the calibration environment, and adding a spotlight light source has minimal impact. Lighting the scene with strong blue lights increases the median estimation error by about half a degree.

7.3 Measurement Discretization and Lenslet Selection

Here we explore choices driven by the entropy in the discrete state space for each lenslet. First we experiment with the number of discretized states using all lenslets, and then we determine the effect of using the most informative lenslets.

Number of States. In Sect. 4, we showed that individual lenslets with more states had a larger maximum entropy, and that by optimizing the threshold value allows a random texture to create appearances that have entropies approaching the maximum. In this section, we validate whether there is a corresponding improvement in viewpoint estimation by optimizing for high entropy. From the same response maps, we create state maps with 2,3,4,5, and 6 states. We use the same optimal thresholds for these state maps as described in Fig. 2. We also create a second binary statemap, but using a threshold of 100, as used in Sect. 7.2. To differentiate between the two binary conditions, we label one "2_opt" to indicate use of a threshold that maximizes entropy. With each choice of our discretization we get different state maps, and we use these to estimate the viewpoint. We report error versus the known true viewpoint.

The results of using all 90 lenslets are shown on the left in Fig. 8. In all cases, the median error is less than 0.5 degrees. There is no discernible trend, except

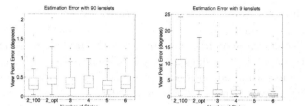 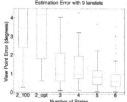

Fig. 8. The effect of the number and choice of lenslets on orientation estimation. Left, using all 90 lenslets, the median orientation error is less then 0.5 degrees across all discretization choices. The middle and right show the same plot at two scales. They highlight that using the 9 lenslets with highest entropy gives plausible results, and when using fewer lenslets it is especially important to go beyond a binary classification.

that a binary threshold at the entropy maximizing cutoff is worse than a default threshold of 100, perhaps because 100 was hand-chosen to be as far as possible from the appearance of completely white and completely black lenslets.

Using Minimal Lenslets. With 90 lenslets, there is a wealth of information. In order to test the limits of a the number of lenslets, we tested the viewpoint estimation with the same conditions of the previous section, but only using 9 lenslets. The 9 lenslets used were the lenslets with the highest entropy state maps. The middle of Fig. 8 shows these results. With fewer lenslets, and less information, the trend suggests that more states results in better estimates. In addition, using an optimal threshold with 2 states shows advantages with few lenslets. The left of Fig. 8 shows results that magnifies the y axis in order to better analyze estimation results for state maps with more than 2 states. Having more than 2 states results in median errors less than 1 degree. A statemap with 6 states results in the best performance, with 0.6 degrees of median error. These empirical results corroborate that, when a limited number of lenslets can be used, using more states results in better viewpoint estimation performance.

7.4   Pose Estimation

The unique appearance of a microlens array results in low error viewpoint estimations. It is therefore useful to use microlens arrays for pose estimation as well. In the next section, we determine the poses of a new set of images. In these images, we place the microlens array ≈ 1 m away and rotate it around the vertical axis from fronto-parallel to 30 degrees in 1 degree increments. We compare pose estimation to the standard fiducial marker, ARToolkit. After, we use these results to compare against other published results of a similar experiment.

Direct Comparison to ARToolkit. In Fig. 9, we show pose estimation results of using the microlens array. As a comparison, we also include results of using just the 4 reference points as used by ARToolkit [14] to estimate pose. In the left 2 plots of Fig. 9, we show the rotation estimation errors per axis using the microlens array (leftmost) and using just 4 reference points (left-center). The rotation error is defined as the angular difference between the unit axes using the true and estimated rotations. The translation error is defined as the euclidean distance between the true and estimated position. For each plot, the title shows the median errors over all frames for the axes in x, y, z order.

For all views, the microlens array is able to determine rotations accurately. In contrast, the standard "4 corner method" suffers from the well understood ambiguity of points on a fronto-parallel plane [1–3]. Since the microlens array gives orientation cues directly from the viewpoint estimation, our method does not suffer from this ambiguity.

In the right 2 plots of Fig. 9, we show the translation estimation errors per axis using the microlens array (right-center) and using just 4 reference points (rightmost). For both methods, there is some systematic error in the Z-axis while the X and Y axes have almost no error. For the ARToolkit method, the error could be a consequence of error in the rotation estimation. The images were taken at a long focal length ($\approx$300 mm), so the systematic errors may also be a consequence of errors in calibrating the K matrix.

Indirect Comparison Against Related Work. In the final experiment, we share a comparison of our rotation estimation results from above with the results reported in work that uses "Chromo-coded Markers" [10], the "Lentimark" [6], and the "Arraymark" [8]. All three papers perform a similar rotation estimation experiment that rotates the object around a single axis. In addition, all three papers also report the rotation error for the x,y, and z local axes. Table 1 summaries results reported for the "Chromo-coded Markers", "Lentimark", and "Arraymark" against our experiments done above in this section. The previous works and our method have comparably low rotation errors. However, our microlens array has slightly superior rotation estimation error for estimating the z axes.

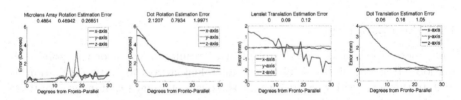

Fig. 9. We compare the rotation and translation estimation accuracy of our result with the method employed by the popular ARToolkit. In contrast to most position based fiducial markers like those used with the ARToolkit, our fiducial marker does not suffer from the well-known ambiguities of points that lie on a plane near fronto-normal

Table 1. The microlens array has similar or better accuracy than other work based on fiducial markers whose appearance is viewpoint dependent.

	Lentimark	Chromo-coded marker	Arraymark	Microlens array
x	0.372	0.910	0.63	0.488
y	1.359	0.703	0.47	0.469
z	0.324	1.222	0.61	0.269

8   Conclusion

We present a novel type of fiducial marker whose appearance is designed to give a combinatorial encoding of its orientation. This combinatorial encoding has the advantage over previous approaches that it can take on different form factors (including those where lenslets are disjointly spread across a plane), and it is insensitive to variations in the color of the scene lighting. We derive an approach to solve for the rotation of this new micro-lens based fiducial marker show that it improves pose estimation when combined with standard location based fiducials.

References

1. Uematsu, Y., Saito, H.: Improvement of accuracy for 2d marker-based tracking using particle filter. In: 17th International Conference on Artificial Reality and Telexistence, pp. 183–189. IEEE (2007)
2. Abawi, D.F., Bienwald, J., Dorner, R.: Accuracy in optical tracking with fiducial markers: an accuracy function for artoolkit. In: Proceedings of the 3rd IEEE/ACM International Symposium on Mixed and Augmented Reality, pp. 260–261. IEEE Computer Society (2004)
3. Pentenrieder, K., Meier, P., Klinker, G., et al.: Analysis of tracking accuracy for single-camera square-marker-based tracking. In: Proc. Dritter Workshop Virtuelle und Erweiterte Realitt der GIFachgruppe VR/AR, Koblenz, Germany (2006)
4. Haralick, R.M., Shapiro, L.G.: Computer and Robot Vision. Addison-Wesley Longman Publishing Co., Inc., Boston (1991)
5. Fitzpatrick, J.M., West, J.B.: The distribution of target registration error in rigid-body point-based registration. IEEE Trans. Med. Imaging **20**(9), 917–927 (2001)
6. Tanaka, H., Sumi, Y., Matsumoto, Y.: A visual marker for precise pose estimation based on lenticular lenses. In: IEEE International Conference on Robotics and Automation (2012)
7. Tanaka, H., Sumi, Y., Matsumoto, Y.: A solution to pose ambiguity of visual markers using moire patterns. In: IEEE/RSJ International Conference on Intelligent Robots and Systems (2014)
8. Tanaka, H., Sumi, Y., Matsumoto, Y.: A high-accuracy visual marker based on a microlens array. In: IEEE/RSJ International Conference on Intelligent Robotics and Systems (2012)
9. Tanaka, H., Sumi, Y., Matsumoto, Y.: Further stabilization of a microlens-array-based fiducial marker. In: IEEE International Symposium on Mixed and Augmented Reality (2013)

10. Schillebeeckx, I., Little, J., Kelly, B., Pless, R.: The geometry of colorful, lenticular fiducial markers. In: International Conference on 3D Vision (2015)

11. Schillebeeckx, I., Pless, R.: Structured light field design for correspondence free rotation estimation. In: International Conference on Computational Photography (ICCP) (2015)

12. Olson, E.: AprilTag: a robust and flexible visual fiducial system. In: 2011 IEEE International Conference on Robotics and Automation (ICRA), pp. 3400–3407. IEEE (2011)

13. Fiala, M.: Artag, a fiducial marker system using digital techniques. In: Proceedings of IEEE Conference on Computer Vision and Pattern Recognition (2005)

14. Kato, H., Billinghurst, M.: Marker tracking and hmd calibration for a video-based augmented reality conferencing system. In: IEEE and ACM International Workshop on Augmented Reality (1999)

15. Zhang, Z.: Flexible camera calibration by viewing a plane from unknown orientations. In: Proceedings of IEEE International Conference on Computer Vision, pp. 666–673 (1999)

16. Liu, X., Cevikalp, H., Fitzpatrick, J.M.: Marker orientation in fiducial registration. In: 2003 International Society for Optics and Photonics on Medical Imaging, pp. 1176–1185 (2003)

17. Bansal, M., Daniilidis, K.: Geometric urban geo-localization. In: 2014 IEEE Conference on Computer Vision and Pattern Recognition (CVPR), pp. 3978–3985. IEEE (2014)

18. Lippmann, G.: La photographie integrale. Comptes-Rendus (1908)

19. Bruckstein, A.M., Holt, R.J., Huang, T.S., Netravali, A.N.: New devices for 3d pose estimation: mantis eyes, agam paintings, sundials, and other space fiducials. Int. J. Comput. Vis. **39**(2), 131–139 (2000)

20. Wetzstein, G., Roodnick, D., Heidrich, W., Raskar, R.: Refractive shape from light field distortion. In: 2011 IEEE International Conference on Computer Vision (ICCV), pp. 1180–1186. IEEE (2011)

21. Wetzstein, G., Heidrich, W., Raskar, R.: Computational schlieren photography with light field probes. Int. J. Comput. Vis. **110**(2), 113–127 (2014)

22. Ji, Y., Ye, K., Yu, J.: Reconstructing gas flows using light-path approximation. In: International Conference on Computational Photography (ICCP) (2013)

23. Yang, W., Ji, Y., Lin, H., Yang, Y., Bing Kang, S., Yu, J.: Ambient occlusion via compressive visibility estimation. In: Proceedings of IEEE Conference on Computer Vision and Pattern Recognition, June 2015

24. Mohan, A., Woo, G., Hiura, S., Smithwick, Q., Raskar, R.: Bokode: imperceptible visual tags for camera based interaction from a distance. ACM Trans. Graph. (TOG) **28**(3), 98 (2009)

Image and Video Processing

The Fast Bilateral Solver

Jonathan T. Barron[1]([✉]) and Ben Poole[2]

[1] Google, Mountain View, USA
barron@google.com
[2] Stanford University, Stanford, USA
poole@cs.stanford.edu

Abstract. We present the bilateral solver, a novel algorithm for edge-aware smoothing that combines the flexibility and speed of simple filtering approaches with the accuracy of domain-specific optimization algorithms. Our technique is capable of matching or improving upon state-of-the-art results on several different computer vision tasks (stereo, depth superresolution, colorization, and semantic segmentation) while being 10–1000× faster than baseline techniques with comparable accuracy, and producing lower-error output than techniques with comparable runtimes. The bilateral solver is fast, robust, straightforward to generalize to new domains, and simple to integrate into deep learning pipelines.

1 Introduction

Images of the natural world exhibit a useful prior – many scene properties (depth, color, object category, etc.) are correlated within smooth regions of an image, while differing across discontinuities in the image. Edge-aware smoothing techniques exploit this relationship to propagate signals of interest within, but not across edges present in an image. Traditional approaches to edge-aware smoothing apply an image-dependent filter to a signal of interest. Examples of this include joint bilateral filtering [37,40] and upsampling [20], adaptive manifolds [12], the domain transform [11], the guided filter [16,17], MST-based filtering [41], and weighted median filtering [30,44]. These techniques are flexible and computationally efficient, but often insufficient for solving more challenging computer vision tasks. Difficult tasks often necessitate complex iterative inference or optimization procedures that encourage smoothness while maintaining fidelity with respect to some observation. Optimization algorithms of this nature have been used in global stereo [34], depth superresolution [10,19,24,26,29,32], colorization [25], and semantic segmentation [6,22,28,45]. These approaches are tailored to their specific task, and are generally computationally expensive. In this work we present an optimization algorithm that is 10–1000× faster than existing domain-specific approaches with comparable accuracy, and produces higher-quality output than lightweight filtering techniques with comparable runtimes.

Electronic supplementary material The online version of this chapter (doi:10. 1007/978-3-319-46487-9_38) contains supplementary material, which is available to authorized users.

© Springer International Publishing AG 2016
B. Leibe et al. (Eds.): ECCV 2016, Part III, LNCS 9907, pp. 617–632, 2016.
DOI: 10.1007/978-3-319-46487-9_38

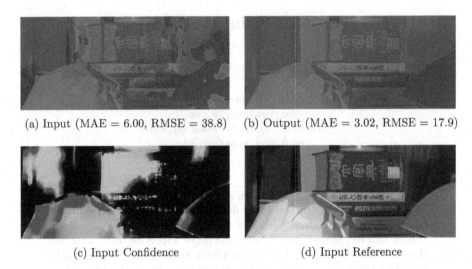

(a) Input (MAE = 6.00, RMSE = 38.8)   (b) Output (MAE = 3.02, RMSE = 17.9)

(c) Input Confidence   (d) Input Reference

Fig. 1. The bilateral solver can be used to improve depth maps. A depth map (a) from a state-of-the-art stereo method [43] is processed with our robust bilateral solver using a reference RGB image (d). Our output (b) is smooth with respect to the reference image, resulting in a 50 % reduction in error.

Our algorithm is based on the work of Barron *et al.* [2], who presented the idea of using fast bilateral filtering techniques to solve optimization problems in "bilateral-space". This allows for some optimization problems with bilateral affinity terms to be solved quickly, and also guarantees that the solutions to those problems are "bilateral-smooth" — smooth within objects, but not smooth across edges. In this paper we present a new form of bilateral-space optimization which we call *the bilateral solver*, which efficiently solves a regularized least-squares optimization problem to produce an output that is bilateral-smooth and close to the input. This approach has a number of benefits:

General. The bilateral solver is a single intuitive abstraction that can be applied to many different problems, while matching or beating the specialized state-of-the-art algorithms for each of these problems. It can be generalized to a variety of loss functions using standard techniques from M-estimation [14].

Differentiable. Unlike other approaches for edge-aware smoothness which require a complicated and expensive "unrolling" to perform backpropagation [45], the backward pass through our solver is as simple and fast as the forward pass, allowing it to be easily incorporated into deep learning architectures.

Fast. The bilateral solver is expressible as a linear least-squares optimization problem, unlike the non-linear optimization problem used in [2]. This enables a number of optimization improvements including a hierarchical preconditioner and initialization technique that hasten convergence, as well as efficient methods for solving multiple problems at once.

2   Problem Formulation

We begin by presenting the objective and optimization techniques that make up our bilateral solver. Let us assume that we have some per-pixel input quantities **t** (the "target" value, see Fig. 1a) and some per-pixel confidence of those quantities **c** (Fig. 1c), both represented as vectorized images. Let us also assume that we have some "reference" image (Fig. 1d), which is a normal RGB image. Our goal is to recover an "output" vector **x** (Fig. 1b), which will resemble the input target where the confidence is large while being smooth and tightly aligned to edges in the reference image. We will accomplish this by constructing an optimization problem consisting of an image-dependent smoothness term that encourages **x** to be bilateral-smooth, and a data-fidelity term that minimizes the squared residual between **x** and the target **t** weighted by our confidence **c**:

$$\underset{\mathbf{x}}{\text{minimize}} \ \frac{\lambda}{2} \sum_{i,j} \hat{W}_{i,j} \left(x_i - x_j \right)^2 + \sum_i c_i (x_i - t_i)^2 \tag{1}$$

The smoothness term in this optimization problem is built around an affinity matrix $\hat{W}$, which is a bistochastized version of a bilateral affinity matrix W. Each element of the bilateral affinity matrix $W_{i,j}$ reflects the affinity between pixels i and j in the reference image in the YUV colorspace:

$$W_{i,j} = \exp\left(-\frac{\|[p_i^x, p_i^y] - [p_j^x, p_j^y]\|^2}{2\sigma_{xy}^2} - \frac{(p_i^l - p_j^l)^2}{2\sigma_l^2} - \frac{\|[p_i^u, p_i^v] - [p_j^u, p_j^v]\|^2}{2\sigma_{uv}^2} \right) \tag{2}$$

Where p_i is a pixel in our reference image with a spatial position (p_i^x, p_i^y) and color (p_i^l, p_i^u, p_i^v)[1]. The σ_{xy}, σ_l, and σ_{uv} parameters control the extent of the spatial, luma, and chroma support of the filter, respectively.

This W matrix is commonly used in the bilateral filter [40], an edge-preserving filter that blurs within regions but not across edges by locally adapting the filter to the image content. There are techniques for speeding up bilateral filtering [1,5] which treat the filter as a "splat/blur/slice" procedure: pixel values are "splatted" onto a small set of vertices in a grid [2,5] or lattice [1] (a soft histogramming operation), then those vertex values are blurred, and then the filtered pixel values are produced via a "slice" (an interpolation) of the blurred vertex values. These splat/blur/slice filtering approaches all correspond to a compact and efficient factorization of W:

$$W = S^{\mathrm{T}} \bar{B} S \tag{3}$$

Barron *et al.* [2] built on this idea to allow for optimization problems to be "splatted" and solved in bilateral-space. They use a "simplified" bilateral grid and a technique for producing bistochastization matrices $D_\mathbf{n}$, $D_\mathbf{m}$ that together give the the following equivalences:

$$\hat{W} = S^{\mathrm{T}} D_\mathbf{m}^{-1} D_\mathbf{n} \bar{B} D_\mathbf{n} D_\mathbf{m}^{-1} S \qquad SS^{\mathrm{T}} = D_\mathbf{m} \tag{4}$$

---

[1] To reduce confusion between the Y's in "YUV" and "XY" we refer to luma as "l".

They also perform a variable substitution, which reformulates a high-dimensional pixel-space optimization problem in terms of the lower-dimensional bilateral-space vertices:

$$\mathbf{x} = S^{\mathrm{T}}\mathbf{y} \tag{5}$$

Where $\mathbf{y}$ is a small vector of values for each bilateral-space vertex, while $\mathbf{x}$ is a large vector of values for each pixel. With these tools we can not only reformulate our pixel-space loss function in Eq. 1 in bilateral-space, but we can rewrite that bilateral-space loss function in a quadratic form:

$$\underset{\mathbf{y}}{\text{minimize}} \quad \frac{1}{2}\mathbf{y}^{\mathrm{T}}A\mathbf{y} - \mathbf{b}^{\mathrm{T}}\mathbf{y} + c \tag{6}$$

$$A = \lambda(D_{\mathbf{m}} - D_{\mathbf{n}}\bar{B}D_{\mathbf{n}}) + \text{diag}(S\mathbf{c}) \qquad \mathbf{b} = S(\mathbf{c} \circ \mathbf{t}) \qquad c = \frac{1}{2}(\mathbf{c} \circ \mathbf{t})^{\mathrm{T}}\mathbf{t}$$

where $\circ$ is the Hadamard product. A derivation of this reformulation can be found in the supplement. While the optimization problem in Eq. 1 is intractably expensive to solve naively, in this bilateral-space formulation optimization can be performed quickly. Minimizing that quadratic form is equivalent to solving a sparse linear system:

$$A\mathbf{y} = \mathbf{b} \tag{7}$$

We can produce a pixel-space solution $\hat{\mathbf{x}}$ by simply slicing the solution to that linear system:

$$\hat{\mathbf{x}} = S^{\mathrm{T}}(A^{-1}\mathbf{b}) \tag{8}$$

With this we can describe our algorithm, which we will refer to as the "bilateral solver." The input to the solver is a reference RGB image, a target image that contains noisy observed quantities which we wish to improve, and a confidence image. We construct a simplified bilateral grid from the reference image, which is bistochastized as in [2] (see the supplement for details), and with that we construct the A matrix and $\mathbf{b}$ vector described in Eq. 6 which are used to solve the linear system in Eq. 8 to produce an output image. If we have multiple target images (with the same reference and confidence images) then we can construct a larger linear system in which $\mathbf{b}$ has many columns, and solve for each channel simultaneously using the same A matrix. In this many-target case, if $\mathbf{b}$ is low rank then that property can be exploited to accelerate optimization, as we show in the supplement.

Our pixel-space loss (Eq. 1) resembles that of weighted least squares filtering [8,9,31], with one critical difference being our use of bilateral-space optimization which allows for efficient optimization even when using a large spatial support in the bilateral affinity, thereby improving the quality of our output and the speed of our algorithm. Our algorithm is similar to the optimization problem that underlies the stereo technique of [2], but with several advantages: Our approach reduces to a simple least-squares problem, which allows us to optimize using standard techniques (we use the preconditioned conjugate gradient algorithm of [36], see the supplement for details). This simple least-squares formulation also allows us to efficiently backpropagate through the solver (Sect. 3), allowing it to be integrated into deep learning pipelines. This formulation also improves the rate of convergence during optimization, provides guarantees on correctness, allows us to use advanced techniques for preconditioning and initialization (Sect. 4), and enables robust and multivariate generalizations of our solver (see the supplement).

3   Backpropagation

Integrating any operation into a deep learning framework requires that it is possible to backpropagate through that operation. Backpropagating through global operators such as our bilateral solver is generally understood to be difficult, and is an active research area [18]. Unlike most global smoothing operators, our model is easy to backpropagate through by construction. Note that we do not mean backpropagating *through* a multiplication of a matrix inverse A^{-1}, which would simply be another multiplication by A^{-1}. Instead, we will backpropagate *onto* the A matrix used in the least-squares solve that underpins the bilateral solver, thereby allowing us to backpropagate through the bilateral solver itself.

Consider the general problem of solving a linear system:

$$A\mathbf{y} = \mathbf{b} \tag{9}$$

Where A is an invertible square matrix, and $\mathbf{y}$ and $\mathbf{b}$ are vectors. We can solve for $\hat{\mathbf{y}}$ as a simple least squares problem:

$$\hat{\mathbf{y}} = A^{-1}\mathbf{b} \tag{10}$$

Let us assume that A is symmetric in addition to being positive definite, which is true in our case. Now let us compute some loss with respect to our estimated vector $g(\hat{\mathbf{y}})$, whose gradient will be $\partial g/\partial \hat{\mathbf{y}}$. We would like to backpropagate that quantity onto A and $\mathbf{b}$:

$$\frac{\partial g}{\partial \mathbf{b}} = A^{-1}\frac{\partial g}{\partial \hat{\mathbf{y}}} \qquad \frac{\partial g}{\partial A} = \left(-A^{-1}\frac{\partial g}{\partial \hat{\mathbf{y}}}\right)\hat{\mathbf{y}}^{\mathrm{T}} = -\frac{\partial g}{\partial \mathbf{b}}\hat{\mathbf{y}}^{\mathrm{T}} \tag{11}$$

This can be derived using the implicit function theorem. We see that backpropagating a gradient through a linear system only requires a single least-squares solve. The gradient of the loss with respect to the diagonal of A can be computed more efficiently:

$$\frac{\partial g}{\partial \mathrm{diag}(A)} = -\frac{\partial g}{\partial \mathbf{b}} \circ \hat{\mathbf{y}} \tag{12}$$

We will use these observations to backpropagate through the bilateral solver. The bilateral solver takes some input target $\mathbf{t}$ and some input confidence $\mathbf{c}$, and then constructs a linear system that gives us a bilateral-space solution $\hat{\mathbf{y}}$, from which we can "slice" out a pixel-space solution $\hat{\mathbf{x}}$.

$$\hat{\mathbf{y}} = A^{-1}\mathbf{b} \qquad \hat{\mathbf{x}} = S^{\mathrm{T}}\hat{\mathbf{y}} \tag{13}$$

Note that A and $\mathbf{b}$ are both functions of $\mathbf{t}$ and $\mathbf{c}$, though they are not written as such. Let us assume that we have computed some loss $f(\hat{x})$ and its gradient $\partial f / \partial \hat{x}$. Remember that the A matrix and $\mathbf{b}$ vector in our linear system are functions of some input signal $\mathbf{t}$ and some input confidence $\mathbf{c}$. Using (11) we can compute the gradient of the loss with respect to the parameters of the linear system within the bilateral solver:

$$\frac{\partial f}{\partial \mathbf{b}} = A^{-1} \left(S \frac{\partial f}{\partial \hat{x}} \right) \qquad \frac{\partial f}{\partial \mathrm{diag}(A)} = -\frac{\partial f}{\partial \mathbf{b}} \circ \hat{\mathbf{y}} \tag{14}$$

We need only compute the gradient of the loss with respect to the diagonal of A as opposed to the entirety of A, because the off-diagonal elements of A do not depend on the input signal or confidence. We can now backpropagate the gradient of the loss $f(\hat{x})$ onto the inputs of the bilateral solver:

$$\frac{\partial f}{\partial \mathbf{t}} = \mathbf{c} \circ \left(S^{\mathrm{T}} \frac{\partial f}{\partial \mathbf{b}} \right) \qquad \frac{\partial f}{\partial \mathbf{c}} = \left(S^{\mathrm{T}} \frac{\partial f}{\partial \mathrm{diag}(A)} \right) + \left(S^{\mathrm{T}} \frac{\partial f}{\partial \mathbf{b}} \right) \circ \mathbf{t} \tag{15}$$

To review, the bilateral solver can be viewed as a function which takes in a reference image, some input signal and a per-pixel confidence in that input signal, and produces some smoothed output:

$$\text{output} \leftarrow \text{solver}_{\text{reference}}(\text{target}, \text{confidence}) \tag{16}$$

And we have shown how to backpropagate through the solver:

$$(\nabla \text{target}, \nabla \text{confidence}) \leftarrow \text{backprop}_{\text{reference}}(\nabla \text{output}) \tag{17}$$

Because the computational cost of the backwards pass is dominated by the least squares solve necessary to compute $\partial f / \partial \mathbf{b}$, computing the backward pass through the solver is no more costly than computing the forward pass. Contrast this with past approaches for using iterative optimization algorithms in deep learning architectures, which create a sequence of layers, one for each iteration in optimization [45]. The backward pass in these networks is a fixed function of the forward pass and so cannot adapt like the bilateral solver to the structure of the error gradient at the output. Furthermore, in these "unrolled" architectures, the output at each iteration (layer) must be stored during training, causing the memory requirement to grow linearly with the number of iterations. In the bilateral solver, the memory requirements are small and independent of the number of iterations, as we only need to store the bilateral-space output of the solver $\hat{\mathbf{y}}$ during training. These properties make the bilateral solver an attractive option for deep learning architectures where speed and memory usage are important.

4   Preconditioning and Initialization

Optimization of the quadratic objective of the bilateral solver can be sped up with improved initialization and preconditioning. In the previous work of [2], the non-linear optimization used a hierarchical technique which lifted optimization into a pyramid space, using a bilateral variant of the image pyramid optimization approach of [3]. This approach cannot be used by our solver, as most linear solvers require a preconditioner where the input is of the same dimensionality as the output. Regardless, the approach of [2] is also suboptimal for our use case, as the simple linear structure of our system allows us to construct more accurate and effective preconditioning and initialization techniques.

To best explain our preconditioning and initialization techniques we must first present baselines techniques for both. We can extract the diagonal of our A matrix to construct a Jacobi preconditioner:

$$\mathrm{diag}(A) = \lambda \left(\mathrm{diag}\left(D_{\mathbf{m}} \right) - \mathrm{diag}(D_{\mathbf{n}}) \, \bar{B}_{\mathrm{diag}} \mathrm{diag}(D_{\mathbf{n}}) \right) + S\mathbf{c}$$

This is straightforward to compute, as $D_{\mathbf{m}}$ and $D_{\mathbf{n}}$ are diagonal matrices and $\bar{B}$ has a constant value along the diagonal denoted here as $\bar{B}_{\mathrm{diag}}$. The Jacobi preconditioner is simply the inverse of the diagonal of A:

$$M_{jacobi}^{-1}(\mathbf{y}) = \mathrm{diag}(A)^{-1}\mathbf{y} \tag{18}$$

We can also initialize the state vector $\mathbf{y}$ in our optimization to the value which minimizes the data term in our loss, which has a closed form:

$$\mathbf{y}_{flat} = S(\mathbf{c} \circ \mathbf{t})/S(\mathbf{c}) \tag{19}$$

This preconditioner and initialization technique perform well, as can be seen in Fig. 2. But we can improve upon these baseline techniques by constructing hierarchical generalizations of each.

Hierarchical preconditioners have been studied extensively for image interpolation and optimization tasks. Unfortunately, techniques based on image pyramids [38] are not applicable to our task as our optimization occurs in a sparse 5-dimensional bilateral-space. More sophisticated image-dependent or graph based techniques [21,23,39] are effective preconditioners, but in our experiments the cost of constructing the preconditioner greatly outweighs the savings provided by the improved conditioning. We will present a novel preconditioner which is similar in spirit to hierarchical basis functions [38] or push-pull interpolation [13], but adapted to our task using the bilateral pyramid techniques presented in [2]. Because of its bilateral nature, our preconditioner is inherently locally adapted and so resembles image-adapted preconditioners [23,39].

We will use the multiscale representation of bilateral-space presented in [2] to implement our hierarchical preconditioner. This gives us $P(\mathbf{y})$ and $P^{\mathrm{T}}(\mathbf{z})$, which construct a pyramid-space vector $\mathbf{z}$ from a bilateral-space vector $\mathbf{y}$, and collapse $\mathbf{z}$ down to $\mathbf{y}$ respectively (see the supplement for details). To evaluate our preconditioner, we lift our bilateral-space vector into pyramid-space, apply an element-wise scaling of each pyramid coefficient, and then project back onto bilateral-space:

$$M_{hier}^{-1}(\mathbf{y}) = P^{\mathrm{T}}\left(\frac{\mathbf{z}_{weight} \circ P(\mathbf{1}) \circ P(\mathbf{y})}{P(\mathrm{diag}(A))} \right) \tag{20}$$

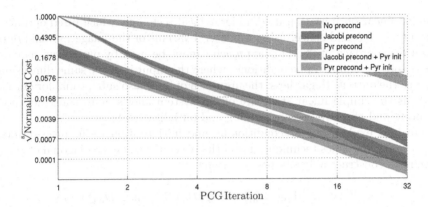

Fig. 2. Our loss during PCG for 20 4-megapixel images, with the loss for each image normalized to $[0, 1]$ and with the 25th-75th percentiles plotted. We see that preconditioning is critical, and that our hierarchical ("Pyr") preconditioning and initialization techniques significantly improve performance over the naive Jacobi preconditioner and "flat" initialization. Note the non-linear y-axis and logarithmic x-axis.

where the division is element-wise. $M_{hier}^{-1}(\cdot)$ includes an ad-hoc element-wise scaling:

$$\mathbf{z}_{weight} = \begin{cases} 1 & \text{if } k = 0 \\ \alpha^{-(\beta+k)} & \text{otherwise} \end{cases} \tag{21}$$

The pyramid-space scaling we use in Eq. 20 is proportional to: (1) the number of bilateral-space vertices assigned to each pyramid-space coefficient (computed by lifting a vector of ones), (2) the inverse of the diagonal of the A matrix, computed by lifting and inverting the diagonal of the A matrix, and (3) an exponential weighting of each pyramid-space coefficient according to its level in the pyramid. This per-level scaling $\mathbf{z}_{weight}$ is computed as a function of the level k of each coefficient, which allows us to prescribe the influence that each scale of the pyramid should have in the preconditioner. Note that as the coarser levels are weighed less (i.e., as α or β increases) our preconditioner degenerates naturally to the Jacobi preconditioner. In all experiments we use $(\alpha = 2, \beta = 5)$ for the preconditioner.

This same bilateral pyramid approach can be used to effectively initialize the state before optimization. Rather than simply taking the input target and using it as our initial state as was done in Eq. 19, we perform a push-pull filter of that initial state with the pyramid according to the input confidence:

$$\mathbf{y}_{hier} = P^{\mathrm{T}}\left(\frac{\mathbf{z}_{weight} \circ P(S(\mathbf{c} \circ \mathbf{t}))}{P(\mathbf{1})}\right) / P^{\mathrm{T}}\left(\frac{\mathbf{z}_{weight} \circ P(S(\mathbf{c}))}{P(\mathbf{1})}\right) \tag{22}$$

Like our hierarchical preconditioner, this initialization degrades naturally to our non-hierarchical initialization in Eq. 19 as α and β increase. In all experiments we use $(\alpha = 4, \beta = 0)$ for initialization.

Table 1. Our approach's runtime has a lower mean and variance than that of [2]. Runtimes are from the same workstation, averaged over the 20 4-megapixel images used in [2] for profiling.

Algorithm component	Time (ms)	
	Barron *et al.* [2]	This work
Problem construction	190 ± 167	35 ± 7
Optimization	460 ± 207	152 ± 36
Total	650 ± 266	187 ± 37

See Fig. 2 for a visualization of how our hierarchical preconditioning and initialization improve convergence during optimization, compared to the "flat" baseline algorithms. See Table 1 for a comparison of our runtime compared to [2], where we observe a substantial speedup with respect to the solver of [2]. Though the techniques presented here for efficient optimization and initialization are framed in terms of the forward pass through the solver, they all apply directly to the backward pass through the solver described in Sect. 3, and produce equivalent improvements in speed.

5   Applications

We evaluate our solver on a variety of applications: stereo, depth superresolution, image colorization, and semantic segmentation. Each of these tasks has been the focus of significant research, with specialized techniques having been developed for each problem. For some of these applications (semantic segmentation and stereo) our solver serves as a building block in a larger algorithm, while for others (colorization and depth superresolution) our solver is a complete algorithm. We will demonstrate that our bilateral solver produces results that are comparable to or better than the state-of-the-art for each problem, while being either 1–3 orders of magnitude faster. For those techniques with comparable runtimes, we will demonstrate that the bilateral solver produces higher quality output. Unless otherwise noted, all runtimes were benchmarked on a 2012 HP Z420 workstation (Intel Xeon CPU E5-1650, 3.20 GHz, 32 GB RAM), and our algorithm is implemented in standard, single-threaded C++. As was done in [2], the output of our bilateral solver is post-processed by the domain transform [11] to smooth out the blocky artifacts introduced by the simplified bilateral grid, and the domain transform is included in all runtimes. For all results of each application we use the same implementation of the same algorithm with different parameters, which are noted in each sub-section. Parameters are: the spatial bandwidths of the bilateral grid (σ_{xy}, σ_l, σ_{uv}), the smoothness multiplier (λ), the spatial and range bandwidths of the domain transform (σ'_{xy}, σ'_{rgb}). Unless otherwise stated, the bilateral solver is run for 25 iterations of PCG.

Table 2. Our robust bilateral solver significantly improves depth map quality the state-of-the-art MC-CNN [43] stereo algorithm on the Middlebury dataset V3 [33].

Method	All			NoOcc		
	bad 1%	MAE	RMSE	bad 1%	MAE	RMSE
Test Set						
MC − CNN[43]	28.1	17.9	55.0	18.0	3.82	21.3
MC − CNN[43]+RBS	28.2	8.19	29.9	18.9	2.67	15.0
Training Set						
MC-CNN[43]	20.07	5.93	18.36	10.42	1.94	9.07
MC-CNN[43] + TF[41]	29.15	5.67	16.18	20.15	2.17	7.71
MC-CNN[43] + FGF[16]	32.29	5.91	16.32	23.62	2.42	7.98
MC-CNN[43] + WMF[30]	33.37	5.30	15.62	26.29	2.32	8.22
MC-CNN[43] + DT[11]	25.17	5.69	16.53	15.53	2.01	7.72
MC-CNN[43] + RBS (Ours)	19.49	2.81	8.44	11.33	1.40	5.23

5.1 Stereo

We first demonstrate the utility of the bilateral solver as a post-processing procedure for stereo algorithms. Because depth maps produced by stereo algorithms tend to have heavy-tailed noise distributions, we use a variant of our technique called the robust bilateral solver (RBS) with the Geman-McClure loss (described in the supplement). We applied the RBS to the output of the top-performing MC-CNN [43] algorithm on the Middlebury Stereo Benchmark V3 [43]. For comparison, we also evaluated against four other techniques which can or have been used to post-process the output of stereo algorithms. In Table 2 we see that the RBS cuts test- and training-set absolute and RMS errors in half while having little negative effect on the "bad 1%" error metric (the percent of pixels which whose disparities are wrong by more than 1). This improvement is smaller when we only consider non-occluded (NoOcc) as most state-of-the-art stereo algorithms already perform well in the absence of occlusions. The improvement provided by the RBS is more dramatic when the depth maps are visualized, as can be seen in Fig. 1 and in the supplement. At submission time our technique achieved a lower test-set MAE and RMSE on the Middlebury benchmark than any published technique[2].

See the supplement for a discussion of how our baseline comparison results were produced, an evaluation of our RBS and our baseline techniques on three additional contemporary stereo algorithms, the parameters settings used in this experiment, how we compute the initial confidence **c** for the RBS, and many visualizations.

5.2 Depth Superresolution

With the advent of consumer depth sensors, techniques have been proposed for upsampling noisy depth maps produced by these sensors using a high-resolution

---

[2] http://vision.middlebury.edu/stereo/eval3/.

Table 3. Performance on the depth superresolution task of [10]. Runtimes in gray were not computed on our reference hardware, and algorithms which use external training data are indicated with a dagger.

Method	Err	Time (sec)
Nearest Neighbor	7.26	0.003
Bicubic	5.91	0.007
†Kiechle et al.[19]	5.86	450
Bilinear	5.16	0.004
Liu et al. [27]	5.10	16.60
Shen et al. [35]	4.24	31.48
Diebel & Thrun [7]	3.98	–
Chan et al.[4]	3.83	3.02
GuidedFilter[17, 10]	3.76	23.89
Min et al. [31]	3.74	0.383
†Lu & Forsyth[29]	3.69	20
Park et al.[32]	3.61	24.05

Method	Err	Time (sec)
Domain Transform [11]	3.56	0.021
Ma et al. [30]	3.49	18
GuidedFilter(Matlab)[17]	3.47	0.434
Zhang et al. [44]	3.45	1.346
FastGuidedFilter[16]	3.41	0.225
Yang 2015 [41]	3.41	0.304
Yang et al. 2007 [42]	3.25	–
Farbman et al. [9]	3.19	6.11
JBU [1, 20]	3.14	1.98
Ferstl et al.[10]	2.93	140
†Li et al.[26]	2.56	700
†Kwon et al.[24]	1.21	300
BS (Ours)	2.70	0.234

RGB reference image [4,10,19,24,26,27,29,31,32]. Other techniques have been developed for post-processing depth maps in other contexts [30,35,41], and many general edge-aware upsampling or filtering techniques can be used for this task [11,16,17,20,44]. We present an extensive evaluation of the bilateral solver against these approaches for the depth superresolution task. Given a noisy input depth map and an RGB reference image, we resize the depth map to be the size of the reference image with bicubic interpolation and then apply the bilateral solver or one of our baseline techniques. The hyperparameters used by the solver for all experiments are: $\sigma_{xy} = 8$, $\sigma_l = 4$, $\sigma_{uv} = 3$, $\sigma'_{xy} = \sigma'_{rgb} = 16$, $\lambda = 4^{f-1/2}$ (where f is the upsampling factor) and 15 iterations of PCG. Our confidence c is a Gaussian bump ($\sigma = f/4$) modeling the support of each low-resolution pixel in the upsampled image. To evaluate our model, we use the depth superreso-lution benchmark of [10] which is based on the Middlebury stereo dataset [34]. Our performance can be see in Table 3 and Fig. 3, with more detailed results in the supplement. The bilateral solver produces the third-lowest error rate for this task, though the two better-performing tasks [24,26] use large amounts of external training data and so have an advantage over our technique, which uses no learning for this experiment. Our approach is 600×, 1200×, and 3000× faster than the three most accurate techniques. The techniques with speeds compara-ble to or better than the bilateral solver [11,16,31,41] produce error rates that are 25–40% greater than our approach. The bilateral solver represents a effective combination of speed and accuracy, while requiring no training or learning. See the supplement for a more detailed table, a discussion of baselines and runtimes, and many visualizations.

5.3   Colorization

Colorization is the problem of introducing color to a grayscale image with a small amount of user input or outside information, for the purpose of improving

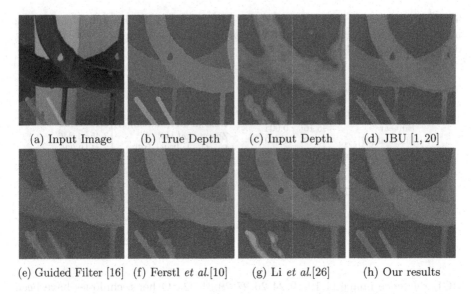

(a) Input Image   (b) True Depth   (c) Input Depth   (d) JBU [1, 20]

(e) Guided Filter [16] (f) Ferstl *et al.*[10]   (g) Li *et al.*[26]   (h) Our results

Fig. 3. Partial results for the depth superresolution task of [10], see the supplement for exhaustive visualizations.

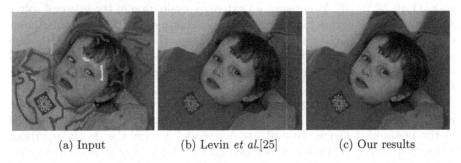

(a) Input   (b) Levin *et al.*[25]   (c) Our results

Fig. 4. Results for the user-assisted colorization task. Our bilateral solver produces comparable results to the technique of Levin *et al.* [25] while being 95× faster

black-and-white films or photographs. Levin *et al.* [25] presented an effective technique for this task by formulating and solving a specialized optimization problem. We can solve the same task using our bilateral solver: we use the grayscale image as the input reference image and the UV channels of the user-annotated scribbles as the input target images, with a confidence image that is 1 where the user has scribbled and 0 everywhere else. We then construct our final output by combining the grayscale image with our output UV images, and converting from YUV to RGB. Our results can be seen in Fig. 4, where we see that our output is nearly indistinguishable from that of [25]. The important distinction here is speed, as the approach of [25] take 80.99 s per megapixel while our approach takes 0.854 s per megapixel — a 95× speedup. For all results our parameters are $\sigma_{xy} = \sigma_l = \sigma_{uv} = 4$, $\lambda = 0.5$, $\sigma'_{xy} = 4$, $\sigma'_{rgb} = 8$. More results can be see in the supplement.

5.4   Semantic Segmentation

Semantic segmentation is the problem of assigning a category label to each pixel in an image. State-of-the-art approaches to semantic segmentation use large convolutional neural networks (CNNs) to map from pixels to labels [6,28]. The output of these CNNs is often smoothed across image boundaries, so recent approaches refine their output with a CRF [6,45]. These CRF-based approaches improve per-pixel labeling accuracy, but this accuracy comes at a computational cost: inference in a fully connected CRF on a 500×500 image can take up to a second (see Table 4). To evaluate whether the bilateral solver could improve the efficiency of semantic segmentation pipelines, we use it instead of the CRF component in two state-of-the-art models: DeepLab-LargeFOV [6] and CRF-RNN [45]. The DeepLab model consists of a CNN trained on Pascal VOC12 and then augmented with a fixed dense CRF. The CRF-RNN model generalizes the CRF with a recurrent neural network, and trains this component jointly with the CNN on Pascal and MSCOCO.

As the bilateral solver operates on real-valued inputs, it is not immediately clear how to map it onto the discrete optimization problem of the dense CRF. For each class, we compute the 21-channel class probability image from the CNN outputs of either the DeepLab or CRF-RNN model. As many class probability maps are zero across the entire image, the resulting **b** matrix in the bilateral solver is often low-rank, allowing us to solve a reduced linear system to recover the smoothed class probability maps (see the supplement). This approach produces nearly identical output, with a $5\times$ speedup on average.

We applied our bilateral solver to the class probability maps using uniform confidence. The resulting discrete segmentations are more accurate and qualitatively smoother than the CNN outputs, despite our per-channel smoothing pro-

Table 4. Semantic segmentation results and runtimes on Pascal VOC 2012 validation set. The bilateral solver improves performance over the CNN output while being substantially faster than the CRF-based approaches. "Post" is the time spent post-processing the CNN output, which is the dense CRF for DeepLab, and the generalized CRF-RNN component for CRF-RNN. FCN is the convolutional neural network component of the CRF-RNN model. *DeepLab-LargeFOV model from [6] trained on Pascal VOC 2012 training data augmented with data from [15]. †CRF-RNN model from [45] trained with additional MSCOCO data and evaluated on reduced Pascal validation set of 346 images.

Method	IOU(%)	Time (ms)		
		CNN	Post	Total
DeepLab	62.25*	58	0	58
DeepLab + CRF	67.64*	58	918	976
DeepLab + BS(Ours)	66.00*	58	111	169
CNN	69.60†	715	0	715
CRF – RNN	72.96†	715	2214	2929
CNN + BS(Ours)	70.68†	715	217	913

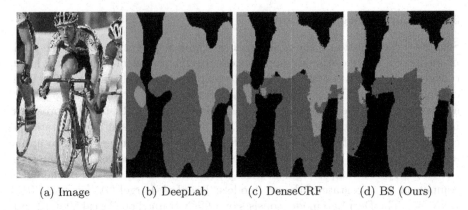

(a) Image   (b) DeepLab   (c) DenseCRF   (d) BS (Ours)

Fig. 5. Using the DeepLab CNN-based semantic segmentation algorithm [6] (5b) as input our bilateral solver can produce comparable edge-aware output (5d) to the Dense-CRF [22] used in [6] (5c), while being 8× faster.

viding no explicit smoothness guarantees on the argmax of the filtered per-class probabilities (Table. 4, Fig. 5). The bilateral solver is 8–10× faster than the CRF and CRF-RNN approaches when applied to the same inputs (Table 4). Although the bilateral solver performs slightly worse than the CRF-based approaches, its speed suggests that it may be a useful tool in contexts such as robotics and autonomous driving, where low latency is necessary.

6   Conclusion

We have presented the bilateral solver, a flexible and fast technique for inducing edge-aware smoothness. We have demonstrated that the solver can produce or improve state-of-the-art results on a variety of different computer vision tasks, while being faster or more accurate than other approaches. Its speed and generality suggests that the bilateral solver is a useful tool in the construction of computer vision algorithms and deep learning pipelines.

References

1. Adams, A., Baek, J., Davis, M.A.: Fast high-dimensional filtering using the permutohedral lattice. In: Eurographics (2010)
2. Barron, J.T., Adams, A., Shih, Y., Hernández, C.: Fast bilateral-space stereo for synthetic defocus. In: CVPR (2015)
3. Barron, J.T., Malik, J.: Shape, illumination, and reflectance from shading. In: TPAMI (2015)
4. Chan, D., Buisman, H., Theobalt, C., Thrun, S.: A noise-aware filter for real-time depth upsampling. In: ECCV Workshops (2008)
5. Chen, J., Paris, S., Durand, F.: Real-time edge-aware image processing with the bilateral grid. In: SIGGRAPH (2007)

6. Chen, L.C., Papandreou, G., Kokkinos, I., Murphy, K., Yuille, A.L.: Semantic image segmentation with deep convolutional nets and fully connected CRFs. In: ICLR (2015)

7. Diebel, J., Thrun, S.: An application of Markov random fields to range sensing. In: NIPS (2005)

8. Elad, M.: On the origin of the bilateral filter and ways to improve it. Trans. Image Process. **11**, 1141–1151 (2002)

9. Farbman, Z., Fattal, R., Lischinski, D., Szeliski, R.: Edge-preserving decompositions for multi-scale tone and detail manipulation. In: SIGGRAPH (2008)

10. Ferstl, D., Reinbacher, C., Ranftl, R., Ruether, M., Bischof, H.: Image guided depth upsampling using anisotropic total generalized variation. In: ICCV (2013)

11. Gastal, E.S.L., Oliveira, M.M.: Domain transform for edge-aware image and video processing. In: SIGGRAPH (2011)

12. Gastal, E.S.L., Oliveira, M.M.: Adaptive manifolds for real-time high-dimensional filtering. In: SIGGRAPH (2012)

13. Gortler, S.J., Grzeszczuk, R., Szeliski, R., Cohen, M.F.: The lumigraph. In: SIGGRAPH (1996)

14. Hampel, F.R., Ronchetti, E.M., Rousseeuw, P.J., Stahel, W.A.: Robust Statistics - The Approach Based on Influence Functions. Wiley, Hoboken (1986)

15. Hariharan, B., Arbelaez, P., Bourdev, L., Maji, S., Malik, J.: Semantic contours from inverse detectors. In: ICCV (2011)

16. He, K., Sun, J.: Fast guided filter. CoRR abs/1505.00996 (2015)

17. He, K., Sun, J., Tang, X.: Guided image filtering. In: Daniilidis, K., Maragos, P., Paragios, N. (eds.) ECCV 2010, Part I. LNCS, vol. 6311, pp. 1–14. Springer, Heidelberg (2010)

18. Ionescu, C., Vantzos, O., Sminchisescu, C.: Matrix backpropagation for deep networks with structured layers. In: ICCV (2015)

19. Kiechle, M., Hawe, S., Kleinsteuber, M.: A joint intensity and depth co-sparse analysis model for depth map super-resolution. In: ICCV (2013)

20. Kopf, J., Cohen, M.F., Lischinski, D., Uyttendaele, M.: Joint bilateral upsampling. In: SIGGRAPH (2007)

21. Koutis, I., Miller, G.L., Tolliver, D.: Combinatorial preconditioners and multilevel solvers for problems in computer vision and image processing. In: CVIU (2011)

22. Krähenbühl, P., Koltun, V.: Efficient inference in fully connected CRFs with Gaussian edge potentials. In: NIPS (2011)

23. Krishnan, D., Fattal, R., Szeliski, R.: Efficient preconditioning of Laplacian matrices for computer graphics. In: SIGGRAPH (2013)

24. Kwon, H., Tai, Y.W., Lin, S.: Data-driven depth map refinement via multi-scale sparse representation. In: CVPR (2015)

25. Levin, A., Lischinski, D., Weiss, Y.: Colorization using optimization. In: SIGGRAPH (2004)

26. Li, Y., Xue, T., Sun, L., Liu, J.: Joint example-based depth map super-resolution. In: ICME (2012)

27. Liu, M.Y., Tuzel, O., Taguchi, Y.: Joint geodesic upsampling of depth images. In: CVPR (2013)

28. Long, J., Shelhamer, E., Darrell, T.: Fully convolutional networks for semantic segmentation. In: CVPR (2015)

29. Lu, J., Forsyth, D.: Sparse depth super resolution. In: CVPR (2015)

30. Ma, Z., He, K., Wei, Y., Sun, J., Wu, E.: Constant time weighted median filtering for stereo matching and beyond. In: ICCV (2013)

31. Min, D., Choi, S., Lu, J., Ham, B., Sohn, K., Do, M.N.: Fast global image smoothing based on weighted least squares. Trans. Image Process. **23**, 5638–5653 (2014)
32. Park, J., Kim, H., Tai, Y.W., Brown, M.S., Kweon, I.: High quality depth map upsampling for 3D-TOF cameras. In: ICCV (2011)
33. Scharstein, D., Hirschmüller, H., Kitajima, Y., Krathwohl, G., Nešić, N., Wang, X., Westling, P.: High-resolution stereo datasets with subpixel-accurate ground truth. In: Jiang, X., Hornegger, J., Koch, R. (eds.) GCPR 2014. LNCS, vol. 8753, pp. 31–42. Springer, Heidelberg (2014)
34. Scharstein, D., Szeliski, R.: A taxonomy and evaluation of dense two-frame stereo correspondence algorithms. In: IJCV (2002)
35. Shen, X., Zhou, C., Xu, L., Jia, J.: Mutual-structure for joint filtering. In: ICCV (2015)
36. Shewchuk, J.R.: An introduction to the conjugate gradient method without the agonizing pain. Technical report, Carnegie Mellon University (1994)
37. Smith, S.M., Brady, J.M.: Susan - a new approach to low level image processing. In: IJCV (1997)
38. Szeliski, R.: Fast surface interpolation using hierarchical basis functions. In: TPAMI (1990)
39. Szeliski, R.: Locally adapted hierarchical basis preconditioning. In: SIGGRAPH (2006)
40. Tomasi, C., Manduchi, R.: Bilateral filtering for gray and color images. In: ICCV (1998)
41. Yang, Q.: Stereo matching using tree filtering. In: PAMI (2015)
42. Yang, Q., Yang, R., Davis, J., Nistér, D.: Spatial-depth super resolution for range images. In: CVPR (2007)
43. Zbontar, J., LeCun, Y.: Computing the stereo matching cost with a convolutional neural network. In: CVPR (2015)
44. Zhang, Q., Xu, L., Jia, J.: 100+ times faster weighted median filter (WMF). In: CVPR (2014)
45. Zheng, S., Jayasumana, S., Romera-Paredes, B., Vineet, V., Su, Z., Du, D., Huang, C., Torr, P.: Conditional random fields as recurrent neural networks. In: ICCV (2015)

Phase-Based Modification Transfer for Video

Simone Meyer[1,2](✉), Alexander Sorkine-Hornung[2], and Markus Gross[1,2]

[1] Department of Computer Science, ETH Zurich, Zurich, Switzerland
`simone.meyer@inf.ethz.ch`
[2] Disney Research, Zurich, Switzerland
`alex@disneyresearch.com`

Abstract. We present a novel phase-based method for propagating modifications of one video frame to an entire sequence. Instead of computing accurate pixel correspondences between frames, e.g. extracting sparse features or optical flow, we use the assumption that small motion can be represented as the phase shift of individual pixels. In order to successfully apply this idea to transferring image edits, we propose a correction algorithm, which adapts the phase shift as well as the amplitude of the modified images. As our algorithm avoids expensive global optimization and all computational steps are performed per-pixel, it allows for a simple and efficient implementation. We evaluate the flexibility of the approach by applying it to various types of image modifications, ranging from compositing and colorization to image filters.

Keywords: Phase-based method · Video processing · Edit propagation

1 Introduction

Many applications in video processing, e.g., frame interpolation or edit propagation, require some form of explicit correspondence mapping between pixels in consecutive frames. Common approaches are based on matching sparse feature points, or dense optical flow estimation. However, finding a pixel-accurate mapping is an inherently ill-posed problem, and existing dense approaches usually require computationally expensive regularization and optimization.

Recently, a number of novel phase-based video processing techniques have been proposed that are able to solve certain types of problems *without* the need for explicit correspondences. Examples include motion magnification [20], view synthesis for autostereoscopic displays [5], or frame interpolation for video [13]. The interesting advantage of such techniques over explicit methods is that they are based on efficient, local per-pixel operations, which do not require knowledge about the actual image-space motion of pixels between frames, and hence avoid the need for solving the above mentioned optimization problems. On the other

Electronic supplementary material The online version of this chapter (doi:10. 1007/978-3-319-46487-9_39) contains supplementary material, which is available to authorized users.

© Springer International Publishing AG 2016
B. Leibe et al. (Eds.): ECCV 2016, Part III, LNCS 9907, pp. 633–648, 2016.
DOI: 10.1007/978-3-319-46487-9_39

hand, the price is that phase-based methods are limited to much smaller motions between frames than, e.g., methods for sparse feature point matching. However, given today's steady increase in video resolution and frame rate, there is also an increasing need for computationally simple and efficient methods.

In this paper, we extend the range of possible applications for phase-based techniques. We introduce a method to propagate various types of image modifications over a sequence of video frames, without the need for explicit tracking or correspondences. As previous phase-based approaches, we decompose each frame of a video sequence using a complex-valued steerable pyramid into local phase and amplitude information. The key question we then address is how to adjust both phase and amplitude in this decomposition on subsequent frames in order to transfer edits made on the first frame of a sequence to all other frames. A particular feature of our method is that it works on textureless or homogeneous image regions, where explicit tracking approaches often struggle or require strong regularization. We present various applications of our algorithm, from adding novel image elements like a logo on a surface and video colorization to propagation of general image filters.

2   Related Work

Correspondence-Based Methods. Most methods for transferring modifications from one image to others require some form of explicit correspondences between the pixels. General approaches for such correspondence estimation techniques range from dense optical flow [1] to tracking of sparse features like SIFT [11]. Some early work using optical flow for propagation edits is proposed by Levin et al. [9]. Such methods often require expensive global optimization which is difficult to implement and parallelize.

Tracking particular image elements is a long-studied problem as well [12,17]. It has been used for propagating image edits in unordered image collections [7,23] as well as for video [16]. While methods for image collections can handle large displacements well, they are lacking temporal coherence to avoid artifacts such as flickering when applied to video. A further limitation of tracking-based approaches is that they usually require sufficiently well textured surfaces. More robust are template-based methods [14] for video editing, as they also work with minimal texture and deformable surfaces. However, the template image and the restshape needs to be known in advance, which is usually not the case for general videos.

Another area related to our work is appearance editing like color manipulation and colorization. In these methods, sparse user edits get propagated spatially and temporally throughout a video, usually by solving optimization problems proportional to resolution and number of frames. Recent works therefore focused in particular on reducing high computational costs and memory consumption [2,10,21]. Yatagawa et al.[22] propose a method independent of the total length of the video as it only processes two frames at the time. A general approach to ensure temporal consistency for various applications including optical flow and colorization has been proposed by Lang et al. [8]. Instead of optimizing directly for temporal consistency, Bonneel et al. [3] propose a method to restore temporal consistency after a filter operation has been applied to each frame of a video independently. This method also uses optical flow as guidance and assumes that the filter does not generate new content uncorrelated to its input. In contrast to such approaches, the advantage of our method is that it allows the propagation of global modifications without the knowledge of the particular used image filter.

Our correspondence-free, phase-based method is designed such that it can handle appearance editing, e.g. local recolorization and global changes by an image filter, as well as detailed edits such as adding novel image elements on a surface, given that image motion between video frames is small.

Phase-Based Methods. Recent works have shown that it is possible to use a phase representation of the motion between frames for various applications [5,20] that usually require explicit correspondences. Such a phase-based representation allows for efficient computation as only per-pixel modifications are required. As a drawback, they are limited to small motions between the frames. Effort has been put into extending the motion range, e.g., by combining it again with tracking or optical flow [6] or by computing a disparity map [24]. A purely phase-based approach to extend the range of admissible motion for video frame interpolation has been proposed by Meyer et al. [13].

All these methods have been used for applications that modify or interpolate the unmodified input frames. Complementary, we extend the set of phase-based applications by a method to propagate edits of modified frames, which can significantly differ from the input frames on which the phase information has been originally computed.

3   Motion as Phase Shift

Phase-based methods use the intuition that the motion of certain signals or functions can be represented as a shift of their phase. In this section we first explain the basic mathematical justification for the 1D case as well as derive the consequences and challenges when using it for propagating a *modified* signal.

1D Case. The Fourier Shift Theorem motivates the assumption that some small displacement motion can be encoded using phase differences. In the one dimensional case, a function $f(x)$ can be represented in the Fourier domain as a sum of complex sinusoids over all frequencies ω:

$$f(x) = \sum_{\omega=-\infty}^{\omega=+\infty} A_\omega e^{i\omega x} = \sum_{\omega=-\infty}^{\omega=+\infty} A_\omega e^{i\phi_\omega} , \qquad (1)$$

where A_ω and ϕ_ω represent the amplitude and the phase, respectively. The shifted version of $f(x)$ by a displacement function $\delta(t)$ is then defined as:

$$f(x - \delta(t)) = \sum_{\omega=-\infty}^{\omega=+\infty} A_\omega e^{i\omega(x-\delta(t))} . \qquad (2)$$

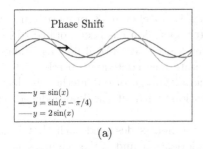
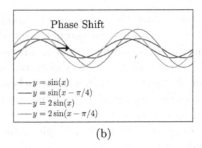

(a)   (b)

Fig. 1. Left: Given a simple sinusoidal input function (blue) and its translated version (red), a modification of the input (cyan) can be translated using the phase difference of the unmodified functions (Eq. 4) (orange, right). (Color figure online)

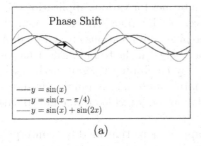
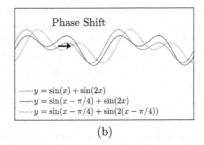

(a)   (b)

Fig. 2. For less trivial modifications of the input function, e.g., adding an additional frequency (left), transferring the modification using only the known phase difference (orange solid) does not correspond to the actually required, but generally unknown frequency dependent phase shift (orange dotted). (Color figure online)

The phase difference between the original and the shifted function

$$\phi_{diff}^{\omega} = \omega x - \omega(x - \delta(t)) = \omega\delta(t) \tag{3}$$

encodes the frequency-dependent version of the spatial displacement $\delta(t)$. In the context of phase-based methods $\delta(t)$ is also referred to as phase shift ϕ_{shift}.

For propagating modifications we are interested in using this phase difference to translate a modified input function $\hat{f}(x)$. Below we describe the challenges that arise from the fact that the modified function does not have the same frequency decomposition anymore as the original input function.

Challenges. Consider the example in Fig. 1a, where as an input we are given a function in the form of $f(x) = A\sin(\omega x - \phi)$ (blue). In our targeted application scenario this would correspond to a reference video frame. We also have a modification (cyan), and a translated version of the function (red), which corresponds to the following video frame that we want to propagate the modification to. In this simple example the translation is described by subtracting $\pi/4$ from the phase and the modification consists of replacing the old amplitude with a new amplitude $\hat{A} = 2$. We can compute the translation of the modified function

(Fig. 1b, orange) by subtracting the phase difference:

$$\hat{f}(x) = \hat{A}\sin(\omega x - \phi_{diff}) = \hat{A}\sin(\omega(x - \phi_{shift})). \qquad (4)$$

However, for handling less trivial modifications, e.g., adding new frequencies, we have to decompose the function according to the frequencies and estimate the necessary phase difference for each frequency separately. In our example in Fig. 2a this corresponds to the fact that we know the phase difference for the input frequency $\omega = 1$ but not for the added function with $\omega = 2$. This leads us to the main challenge of using phase differences to transfer modifications:

How can we transfer novel frequency content of a modified function that has not been present in the two unmodified input functions?

To solve this problem, we need an algorithm that detects which frequencies have been added in the modified function, and which frequencies in the original input functions represent the relevant motion. Besides addressing this central question, we also resolve some additional, less obvious issues that arise when performing phase-based modification transfer on video sequences.

4   Our Algorithm

4.1   Decomposition

For images rather than 1D functions, we first need to generalize the idea to two dimensions, where we can separate the sinusoids according to frequency ω and spatial orientation θ using, e.g., the complex-valued steerable pyramid [15,18,19]. This step is essentially identical to previous phase-based approaches [5,13,20] and we describe it only briefly for completeness. The steerable pyramid filters $\Psi_{\omega,\theta}$ resemble Gabor wavelets and decompose an input image I into oriented frequency bands $R_{\omega,\theta}$:

$$R_{\omega,\theta}(x,y) = (I * \Psi_{\omega,\theta})(x,y) \qquad (5)$$

$$= C_{\omega,\theta}(x,y) + i\,S_{\omega,\theta}(x,y) \qquad (6)$$

$$= A_{\omega,\theta}(x,y)\,e^{i\phi_{\omega,\theta}(x,y)}, \qquad (7)$$

where $C_{\omega,\theta}$ is the cosine part, representing the even-symmetric filter response, and $S_{\omega,\theta}$ is the sine part, representing the odd-symmetric filter response. By using such quadrature filter pairs we can compute the amplitude

$$A_{\omega,\theta}(x,y) = \sqrt{C_{\omega,\theta}(x,y)^2 + S_{\omega,\theta}(x,y)^2}, \qquad (8)$$

and the phase values

$$\phi_{\omega,\theta}(x,y) = \arctan(S_{\omega,\theta}(x,y)/C_{\omega,\theta}(x,y)). \qquad (9)$$

For our following algorithm it is important to note that this provides a decomposition with filter responses that are defined in the spatial domain and have local support, providing per-(multi-resolution)-pixel oriented phase and amplitude values. Please see [13,20] for a more detailed derivation. In general, this decomposition allows the computation of phase differences and amplitudes at various scales and orientations, which is the key element of phase-based methods. Establishing and appropriately using the relationships between different decompositions and across levels is the key element of our algorithm.

4.2   Overview

Given the above decomposition for two input images, I_{t-1} and I_t, as well as for a modified image $\hat{I}_{t-1}$, our algorithm allows us to recover the unknown, translated version of the modified input $\hat{I}_t$.

To reconstruct $\hat{I}_t$, we need to approximate its filter responses $\hat{A}^t_{\omega,\theta}$ and $\hat{\phi}^t_{\omega,\theta}$ based on the available information. The resulting image is then obtained by integrating the modified responses according to Eq. 1. Where clear from the context we omit the indices ω and θ in the equations for improved readability. In general, all computations are done for each pixel at each level and orientation.

Using again the assumption that small motion is encoded in the phase shift, we can use the phase difference ϕ_{diff} between the phases of the unmodified images I_{t-1} and I_t, i.e.,

$$\phi_{diff}^{t-1,t} = \operatorname{atan2}(\sin(\phi_{t-1} - \phi_t), \cos(\phi_{t-1} - \phi_t)), \tag{10}$$

as an initial approximation of the motion. Due to the circular property of the phase values we use the four-quadrant inverse tangent atan2 to get angular phase values between $[-\pi, \pi]$.

The phase of the modified input image can then be translated by subtracting the phase difference from its own phase. Assuming that the motion is small enough such that only the phase is affected, one could try to simply copy the amplitude values, i.e.:

$$\hat{\phi}_t = \hat{\phi}_{t-1} - \phi_{diff}^{t-1,t}, \tag{11}$$

$$\hat{A}_t = \hat{A}_{t-1}. \tag{12}$$

However, as explained in Sect. 3, and illustrated in Figs. 1 and 2, this only works when the modifications do not change the frequency content. Using this initial solution can lead to incomplete or even wrong propagation of some frequency levels. This is the case at locations where the amplitude of the modified image ($\hat{A}_{t-1}$) is large but not the amplitudes of the unmodified images (A_{t-1}, A_t). The smaller the amplitude (as a result of weak filter responses in smooth areas), the more noisy are usually the phase values. Artifacts arise in particular when noisy phase values are used for trying to propagate modifications from one image another, and get magnified due to larger corresponding amplitudes of the modified image. Locations with large amplitude values correspond to strong filter responses which have more influence on the final pixel value. Therefore it is important that the corresponding phase values are computed carefully.

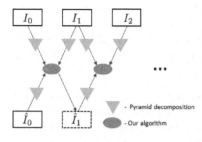

Fig. 3. Illustration of the general procedure. The pyramid decomposition of the input, two unmodified images, I_0 and I_1, as well as a modified image $\hat{I}_0$, are processed by our algorithm to generate the translated modified image $\hat{I}_1$. By repeating this to the next set of images, the whole sequence can be processed

Algorithm 1. The inputs are two unmodified images I_0 and I_1 and a modified image $\hat{I}_0$. The output is the modified image $\hat{I}_1$. P_i are the steerable pyramid decompositions consisting of A_i and ϕ_i.

$(P_0, P_1, \hat{P}_0) \leftarrow \text{decompose}(I_0, I_1, \hat{I}_0)$ $\triangleright$ [15]

$\phi_{diff} \leftarrow \text{phaseDifference}(\phi_0, \phi_1)$ $\triangleright$ Eq. 10
$(A_0, A_1, \hat{A}_0) \leftarrow \text{normalize}(A_0, A_1, \hat{A}_0)$
$\varphi_1 \leftarrow \text{significantMotion}(A_0, \hat{A}_0)$ $\triangleright$ Eq. 13
$\varrho_1 \leftarrow \text{relevantMotion}(A_0, A_1)$ $\triangleright$ Eq. 17
for all $l = L - 1 : 1$ **do**
    $\hat{\phi}_1^l \leftarrow \text{compute}(\hat{\phi}_0, \phi_{diff}, \varphi_1, \varrho_1)$ $\triangleright$ Eq. 20
end for

$\hat{I}_1 \leftarrow \text{reconstruct}(\hat{A}_0, \hat{\phi}_1)$
$\hat{P}_1 \leftarrow \text{decompose}(\hat{I}_1)$
$\hat{A}_1 \leftarrow \text{correctAmpl}(\hat{A}_0, A_1, \hat{\phi}_1)$ $\triangleright$ Sec. 4.5

$\hat{I}_1 \leftarrow \text{reconstruct}(\hat{P}_1)$ $\triangleright$ See [15]

We propose an extension to this initial solution in order to handle general modifications, which may alter the decomposition significantly. Furthermore, we are not only interested in propagating the modification to one additional frame but to a whole image sequence. Figure 3 provides an overview of our general procedure. Algorithm 1 provides a summary of the core steps of our algorithm. In order to solve the challenges stated above we have to solve two main tasks: First, determine the pixels per frequency band which contain information about the motion and those which have been changed due to the modification. Secondly, using this information to approximate the missing information in order to propagate the modifications to succeeding frames. As a guide we can use the amplitude information as larger amplitudes are the result of strong and reliable filter responses. In the following we explain the core algorithmic steps.

4.3 Detecting Missing Phase Information

Detecting the locations where we have new frequency content with unknown motion is the first central step in our algorithm. In principle we of course know exactly which pixels in the input image have been modified. However, it is important to consider which modifications result in actual frequency and phase changes, and on which decomposition level these changes happen.

Therefore we perform the detection process in two steps: We first detect pixels with significant modifications, and then decide whether the corresponding phase difference between the unmodified signals represent the motion. To guide this detection process we employ the available amplitude information, which indicates how strong the response at a specific pixel location is.

Amplitude Normalization. Before we can use the amplitude as a guide we need to normalize the values across the levels such that they are scale-independent and comparable. Because we are downsampling the image during the pyramid decomposition the amplitudes have to be rescaled by the scaling factor of the pyramid decomposition λ, i.e., $A(l, x, y) \leftarrow \frac{A(l,x,y)}{\lambda^{l-1}}$, with $l = 1$ being the topmost, i.e. finest, level of the pyramid.

Identification of Significant Modifications. In general, not all modifications result in a significant change on a specific frequency level. Significant means in our case that the modification results in large amplitude values compared to the amplitude values of the unmodified image. Without postprocessing (see next paragraph) possibly noisy phase values will be used. As a first idea to identify significant modifications one could use the difference between the amplitudes of the unmodified and modified image, i.e. $|\hat{A}_{t-1}(x, y) - A_{t-1}(x, y)|$ as a measurement on how much a pixel has changed. In order to get a relative measurement between all pixels and a definition of significance, we need to normalize the differences. Using the absolute difference and a fixed threshold, i.e. $|\hat{A}_{t-1}(x, y) - A_{t-1}(x, y)| > \vartheta$ would be feasible for a single image pair, but as we are interested in propagating the edits over a whole image sequence we need a more robust measurement.

Propagating phase information over several images results in diminishing response and therefore inevitably leads to smaller amplitudes and loss of information for the modified image. This reduction of the amplitude is shown for one time step in Fig. 4c (left). As a general solution we therefore propose to standardize the distribution of amplitude differences:

$$\varphi_t(A_{t-1}(x, y), \hat{A}_{t-1}(x, y)) = \frac{|\hat{A}_{t-1}(x, y) - A_{t-1}(x, y)| - \mu_t}{\sigma_t}, \qquad (13)$$

where μ_t represents the sample mean over all pixels, orientations and scales

$$\mu_t = \frac{1}{N} \sum_{x,y} |\hat{A}_{t-1}(x, y) - A_{t-1}(x, y)| \qquad (14)$$

and σ_t the sample standard deviation

$$\sigma_t = \sqrt{\frac{1}{N-1} \sum_{x,y} (|\hat{A}_{t-1}(x, y) - A_{t-1}(x, y)| - \mu_t)^2}. \qquad (15)$$

N is the number of all pixels over all orientations and scales. Although the amplitude differences are technically not normal distributed (only positive values, with a peak close to 0) experiments have shown that the concluded criterion together with a threshold τ_φ independent of t

$$\varphi_t(A_{t-1}(x, y), \hat{A}_{t-1}(x, y)) > \tau_\varphi \qquad (16)$$

allows for a robust identification of significant modifications.

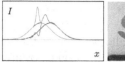  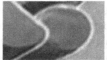 

(a) Propagation of edits without phase and amplitude correction introduces high frequency artifacts and decreases quality.

(b) Closeup left without, right with our proposed correction algorithm. Note the reduced low and high frequency artifacts.

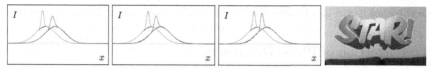

(c) The one dimensional signals illustrate the three intermediate steps of our algorithm improving the result (orange) from left to right: Correcting phase difference at all locations where significant modifications has been detected. Applying correction only where necessary, i.e. no relevant motion information is available. Postprocessing the amplitude to recover details. Our final result.

Fig. 4. Improvement of our algorithm for applications which changes the frequency content. The blue and red curve correspond to the unmodified input signals at two consecutive time steps. The cyan curve corresponds to the modification on the blue input curve, and the orange curve represents our result. (Color figure online)

Estimation of Relevant Motion. Until now we have only compared the unmodified image I_{t-1} with the modified one $\hat{I}_{t-1}$. In order to estimate how to use existing phase differences for edit propagation, we have to identify useful motion information between the two unmodified images I_{t-1} and I_t.

As a consequence of the downsampling, any modification affects the amplitude on the lower levels. On the other hand, the low frequency levels correspond to the general, more global image motion that we are interested in. We therefore distinguish pixels with significant modifications into two cases: either the corresponding phase difference already captures the relevant motion or not. Only in the second case we need to adjust the phase differences for better propagation.

For reliable motion (i.e., phase difference) estimation we require reliable phase information in both unmodified input images, which, in turn, depends on the relative strength of the respective amplitudes compared to other pyramid levels. We therefore measure pixels with relevant phase information using:

$$\varrho_t(A_{t-1}(x,y), A_t(x,y)) = \frac{min(A_{t-1}(x,y), A_t(x,y)) - \mu_t}{\sigma_t}, \qquad (17)$$

where μ_t and σ_t are the mean, respectively the standard deviation, of the $min(A_{t-1}(x,y), A_t(x,y))$ samples. Pixels with ϱ_t larger than some threshold τ_ϱ

$$\varrho_t(A_{t-1}(x,y), A_t(x,y)) > \tau_\varrho \qquad (18)$$

are defined to have a relevant motion.

The combination of these two criteria, Eqs. 16 and 18, define where we are missing relevant information, i.e., where we have significant change in amplitude information and no reliable motion information. This allows us to define an indicator function in which areas an adaption of the phase information is required in order to achieve phase-based edit propagation:

$$\mathbb{I}_A(x, y) = (\varphi_t > \tau_\varphi) \wedge (\varrho_t < \tau_\varrho). \tag{19}$$

The thresholds are independent of t and can be fixed for an image sequence.

4.4 Correction of Phase Differences

After having detected the locations where we are missing necessary phase difference information, we need to fill them in with values representing the required motion. Due to the change of frequency content this corresponds to inferring phase differences for frequencies which do not already exist in the input data. To approximate them we use the available information given by the pyramid decomposition. Due to the fact that the complex steerable pyramid is translation-invariant, we can assume that the frequency bands move in a similar way. In addition, we already know the relevant phase differences (Eq. 18), i.e. the relevant motion of the unmodified image pair. Therefore, in our correction algorithm, we substitute missing phase differences by a reliable phase difference from the closest lower level, denoted as k. To propagate the chosen phase difference ϕ^k_{diff} to the current level, we need to multiply it with the scale factor of the pyramid λ accordingly. At all other locations we can use the computed phase difference to translate the phase of the modified input image:

$$\hat{\phi}^l_t(x, y) = \begin{cases} \hat{\phi}^l_{t-1} - \lambda^{k-l}\phi^k_{diff} & \text{if } \mathbb{I}_A(x, y) = 1, \\ \hat{\phi}^l_{t-1} - \phi^l_{diff} & \text{otherwise.} \end{cases} \tag{20}$$

4.5 Correction of Amplitudes

Although the above algorithm improves the results there is still the problem of the diminishing response in the amplitude, see Fig. 4c, which manifests in images as increasing blur. One reason is the propagation of phase information from pyramid levels with lower resolution, which can result in a loss of sharpness of details. Secondly we assume that the motion is only captured in the phase, and the amplitude remains the same. The resulting artifacts such as ringing and blurriness are mainly visible at high frequency details such as edges. As we want to avoid the computation of any explicit correspondences which would allow to move the amplitude, we propose the following algorithm to recover some of the details by using only per pixel modifications.

By comparing the decomposition of the newly synthesized modified image $\hat{I}_t$ with the unmodified image I_t at the same time step we can detect how much the amplitudes have changed due to the modification. The idea is to increase the amplitude of the modified image where necessary using a specific transfer

(a) Input and modification, $t = 0$ (b) Input detail, $t = 20$ (unmodified)

(c) Blur without amplitude correction   (d) With correction of amplitudes

Fig. 5. Processing the amplitude helps to recover some of the details and reduces blur, but can also magnify artifacts such as ringing. In order to increase the visibility of the effect, the modification has been propagated over $t = 20$ frames.

function. At locations where the new amplitude is large, it is probably not as large as it should be. Because a linear transfer function unnecessarily enhances small amplitudes, we propose a sigmoid function. To get an estimation on how much energy in terms of the amplitudes has been lost, we use the amplitude of the previous modified image, i.e. $\max(\hat{A}_{t-1})/\max(\hat{A}_t)$. The proposed transfer function $\eta(\hat{A}_t(x, y))$ maps the input range of $[0, \max(\hat{A}_t)]$ to the range of the magnification factor $\left[1, \frac{\max(\hat{A}_{t-1})}{\max(\hat{A}_t)}\right]$:

$$
\eta(\hat{A}_t(x, y)) = \frac{\max\left(\frac{\max(\hat{A}_{t-1})}{\max(\hat{A}_t)} - 1, 0\right)}{1 + \left(\frac{\hat{A}_t(x,y)}{\alpha \max(\hat{A}_t) + \epsilon}\right)^{-\beta}} + 1 , \tag{21}
$$

where β defines the steepness of the curve, $\alpha \max(\hat{A}_t)$ the midpoint of the transition and $\epsilon = 10^{-4}$ is used to avoid division by 0. The maximal amplitude values are computed for each oriented frequency band separately. The advantages of this approach are demonstrated in Fig. 5.

5 Results

We demonstrate the flexibility of our method by applying it to various kinds of video editing operations, ranging from appearance changes to detailed edits including adding new image content. More detailed results can be found in the supplementary video on our project webpage.

Edit Image Appearance. The appearance of an image can be modified either locally or globally by changing its color or applying a filter. Modifications which only change the color of an image are easier to propagate as they do not change the frequency content significantly. In these cases we do not have to correct the

(a) Input and modification, $t = 0$ (b) Input detail, $t = 0$ (modi- (c) Our result,
                                         fied) and $t = 10$ (unmodified) $t = 10$

Fig. 6. Propagation result for local recolorization. A longer sequence of this example can be found in the supplementary video.

(a) Input and modification, $t = 0$ (b) Input detail, $t = 0$ (mod- (c) Our result,
                                         ified) and $t = 5$ (unmodified) $t = 5$

Fig. 7. Propagation result for applying a filter to the first image. In this case an artistic filter has been used, which adds an artistic blur to the image.

phase difference to adapt for changing frequencies. But our proposed correction of the amplitude is still a necessary step for the quality of the results as shown in Fig. 5. Figure 6 shows the result of a local recolorization, while Fig. 7 shows the propagation result of applying an artistic filter operation.

Adding Image Content. Due to our detection and correction algorithm we can also propagate image edits which significantly change the frequency content, see Fig. 8. Furthermore, our method is especially suitable to handle edits on homogeneous, textureless surfaces, see Fig. 9.

As the filter responses used in our method have local support, the method can also be applied to scenes with additional moving objects. Figure 9 shows such an example where a moving action has been captured while the hand-held camera was subject to small motion. Because in this case the motion between any frame and the first frame is sufficient small, we can apply our algorithm to process the current frame relatively to the first one. This avoids potential artifacts due to incremental propagation.

Furthermore, as the modifications only happen locally in a more or less static area, they can be localized easily, e.g. by using an approximate bounding box to the difference image of the unmodified/modified image pair. The propagation then only has to be applied to this area while the rest of the image can be substituted by the corresponding original frame of the input video sequence. This avoids potential artifacts in unmodified areas.

Qualitative Comparisons. The advantage of our method is that it is applicable to general modifications independent on whether they contain local or global modifications of the input image. The methods mentioned in the related work section are optimized for specific use cases. In order to compare our results

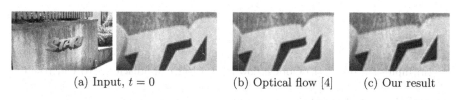

(a) Input, $t = 0$ (b) Optical flow [4]   (c) Our result

Fig. 8. Propagation result ($t = 10$) for adding image content on a wall and comparison to using optical flow based propagation.

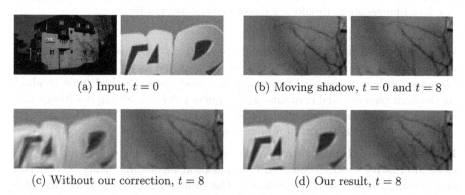

(a) Input, $t = 0$ (b) Moving shadow, $t = 0$ and $t = 8$

(c) Without our correction, $t = 8$ (d) Our result, $t = 8$

Fig. 9. Propagation result for a video with small camera motion while there is an additional motion happening, in this case a moving shadow on the wall. Due to the locality of the filter responses the camera motion and the additional motion can be processed separately.

visually to correspondence based methods we use a general approach consisting of computing the optical flow field [4] and using it to warp the modified image. Figure 8 shows that we obtain visually similar results. Because optical flow based approaches use explicit matching they introduce less blur and can naturally handle longer propagation sequences better, see Fig. 10.

Implementation Details. Our proposed phase-based approach has a few parameters. One set for controlling the pyramid decomposition, the other for the described phase and amplitude correction algorithm. The parameters for the pyramid decomposition are a tradeoff between separability and localization. Smaller frequency bands are better for separation but have a larger spatial support. Regarding the correction algorithm, experiments have shown that we obtain favorable results for a wide set of parameter choices. For the results in this paper we have used a fixed set of values: For constructing the pyramid we used $\#_\theta = 8$ number of orientations, a scale factor $\lambda = 1.2$, and the number of levels is determined such that the coarsest level has a minimal dimension of 10 pixels. For the correction of the phase difference we have used $\tau_\varphi = \tau_\varrho = 3$. The function for correcting the amplitude has been defined with $\beta = 8$ and $\alpha = 0.1$. Similar to previous phase-based methods, frequency content which has not been captured in the pyramid levels and is summarized in real valued high- and

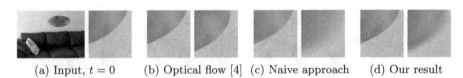

(a) Input, $t = 0$ (b) Optical flow [4] (c) Naive approach   (d) Our result

Fig. 10. The input image has been modified by adding a patch of Perlin noise to a flat, textureless wall. Our correction algorithm improves the propagation results, but propagation over several frames still lead to increased blur, see comparison with optical flow based propagation. Results are shown at $t = 1$ and $t = 10$.

low-pass residual needs to be treated specially. As we have no motion information available for these two residuals, we just use as an approximation the low-pass residual of the modified image $\hat{I}_{t-1}$ and ignore the high-pass residual. As the high-pass residual contains high frequency details, adding it without considering motion would potentially add artifacts. We share this open research question with previous works on phase-based methods.

Discussion and Limitations. While our method provides a novel and efficient alternative to traditional edit propagation algorithms using optical flow and tracking, it has some limitations. The difficulties lie in propagating high frequencies. As the phase-based encoding of the motion is only an approximation we lose sharpness in each propagation step. Additionally, the blurring gets increased by our multi-scale approach, as we are using the motion of lower levels which do not contain the same level of details as the higher levels to which the information gets propagated. Furthermore, sharp edges can cause ringing artifacts. Our current transfer function, used for correcting the amplitude and recovering details, can not distinguish between correct details and these artifacts. As a result, these get incorrectly amplified as well, see Fig. 5. In general, artifacts such as ringing and blurriness become more visible the further the edits get propagated resulting in a degeneration of quality. But our algorithm still enables an improved phase-based propagation, see Fig. 10.

6   Conclusions

We presented a novel approach for correspondence-free modification transfer for video, extending the existing range of video processing operations possible using purely phase-based approaches. We believe that, in particular in the context of the steady increase in video frame rate and resolution, phase-based approaches provide an interesting and efficient alternative to traditional approaches that require explicit frame-to-frame correspondences.

The recently regained interest in phase-based methods has opened up a number of surprising applications that were believed impossible before. We think that such methods bear potential for many more interesting research and applications, and hope that our work provides a new step in such a direction. For more immediate directions of future improvements and research the discussed limitations of our method provide various opportunities.

References

1. Baker, S., Scharstein, D., Lewis, J.P., Roth, S., Black, M.J., Szeliski, R.: A database and evaluation methodology for optical flow. IJCV **92**(1), 1–31 (2011)
2. Bie, X., Huang, H., Wang, W.: Real time edit propagation by efficient sampling. Comput. Graph. Forum **30**(7), 2041–2048 (2011)
3. Bonneel, N., Tompkin, J., Sunkavalli, K., Sun, D., Paris, S., Pfister, H.: Blind video temporal consistency. ACM Trans. Graph. **34**(6), 196 (2015)
4. Brox, T., Bruhn, A., Papenberg, N., Weickert, J.: High accuracy optical flow estimation based on a theory for warping. In: Pajdla, T., Matas, J.G. (eds.) ECCV 2004. LNCS, vol. 3024, pp. 25–36. Springer, Heidelberg (2004)
5. Didyk, P., Sitthi-amorn, P., Freeman, W.T., Durand, F., Matusik, W.: Joint view expansion and filtering for automultiscopic 3D displays. ACM Trans. Graph. **32**(6), 221 (2013)
6. Elgharib, M.A., Hefeeda, M., Durand, F., Freeman, W.T.: Video magnification in presence of large motions. In: CVPR, pp. 4119–4127 (2015)
7. Hasinoff, S.W., Jwiak, M., Durand, F., Freeman, W.T.: Search-and-replace editing for personal photo collections. In: ICCP, pp. 1–8 (2010)
8. Lang, M., Wang, O., Aydin, T.O., Smolic, A., Gross, M.H.: Practical temporal consistency for image-based graphics applications. ACM Trans. Graph. **31**(4), 34 (2012)
9. Levin, A., Lischinski, D., Weiss, Y.: Colorization using optimization. ACM Trans. Graph. **23**(3), 689–694 (2004)
10. Li, Y., Ju, T., Hu, S.: Instant propagation of sparse edits on images and videos. Comput. Graph. Forum **29**(7), 2049–2054 (2010)
11. Lowe, D.G.: Distinctive image features from scale-invariant keypoints. IJCV **60**(2), 91–110 (2004)
12. Lucas, B.D., Kanade, T.: An iterative image registration technique with an application to stereo vision. In: IJCAI, pp. 674–679 (1981)
13. Meyer, S., Wang, O., Zimmer, H., Grosse, M., Sorkine-Hornung, A.: Phase-based frame interpolation for video. In: CVPR, pp. 1410–1418 (2015)
14. Ngo, D.T., Park, S., Jorstad, A., Crivellaro, A., Yoo, C.D., Fua, P.: Dense image registration and deformable surface reconstruction in presence of occlusions and minimal texture. In: ICCV, pp. 2273–2281 (2015)
15. Portilla, J., Simoncelli, E.P.: A parametric texture model based on joint statistics of complex wavelet coefficients. IJCV **40**(1), 49–70 (2000)
16. Rav-acha, A., Kohli, P., Rother, C., Fitzgibbon, A.: Unwrap mosaics: a new representation for video editing. ACM Trans. Graph. **27**(3), 17 (2008)
17. Shi, J., Tomasi, C.: Good features to track. In: CVPR, pp. 593–600 (1994)
18. Simoncelli, E.P., Freeman, W.T.: The steerable pyramid: a flexible architecture for multi-scale derivative computation. In: ICIP, pp. 444–447 (1995)
19. Simoncelli, E.P., Freeman, W.T., Adelson, E.H., Heeger, D.J.: Shiftable multiscale transforms. IEEE Trans. Inf. Theor. **38**(2), 587–607 (1992)
20. Wadhwa, N., Rubinstein, M., Durand, F., Freeman, W.T.: Phase-based video motion processing. ACM Trans. Graph. **32**(4), 80 (2013)
21. Xu, K., Li, Y., Ju, T., Hu, S., Liu, T.: Efficient affinity-based edit propagation using K-D tree. ACM Trans. Graph. **28**(5), 118:1–118:6 (2009)
22. Yatagawa, T., Yamaguchi, Y.: Temporally coherent video editing using an edit propagation matrix. Comput. Graph. **43**, 1–10 (2014)

23. Yücer, K., Jacobson, A., Hornung, A., Sorkine, O.: Transfusive image manipulation. ACM Trans. Graph. **31**(6), 176 (2012)
24. Zhang, Z., Liu, Y., Dai, Q.: Light field from micro-baseline image pair. In: CVPR, pp. 3800–3809 (2015)

Colorful Image Colorization

Richard Zhang, Phillip Isola$^{(\boxtimes)}$, and Alexei A. Efros

University of California, Berkeley, USA
{rich.zhang,isola,efros}@eecs.berkeley.edu

Abstract. Given a grayscale photograph as input, this paper attacks the problem of hallucinating a *plausible* color version of the photograph. This problem is clearly underconstrained, so previous approaches have either relied on significant user interaction or resulted in desaturated colorizations. We propose a fully automatic approach that produces vibrant and realistic colorizations. We embrace the underlying uncertainty of the problem by posing it as a classification task and use class-rebalancing at training time to increase the diversity of colors in the result. The system is implemented as a feed-forward pass in a CNN at test time and is trained on over a million color images. We evaluate our algorithm using a "colorization Turing test," asking human participants to choose between a generated and ground truth color image. Our method successfully fools humans on 32 % of the trials, significantly higher than previous methods. Moreover, we show that colorization can be a powerful pretext task for self-supervised feature learning, acting as a *cross-channel encoder*. This approach results in state-of-the-art performance on several feature learning benchmarks.

Keywords: Colorization · Vision for graphics · CNNs · Self-supervised learning

1   Introduction

Consider the grayscale photographs in Fig. 1. At first glance, hallucinating their colors seems daunting, since so much of the information (two out of the three dimensions) has been lost. Looking more closely, however, one notices that in many cases, the semantics of the scene and its surface texture provide ample cues for many regions in each image: the grass is typically green, the sky is typically blue, and the ladybug is most definitely red. Of course, these kinds of semantic priors do not work for everything, e.g., the croquet balls on the grass might not, in reality, be red, yellow, and purple (though it's a pretty good guess). However, for this paper, our goal is not necessarily to recover the actual ground truth color, but rather to produce a *plausible* colorization that could potentially fool a human observer. Therefore, our task becomes much more achievable: to model enough of the statistical dependencies between the semantics and the textures of grayscale images and their color versions in order to produce visually compelling results.

© Springer International Publishing AG 2016
B. Leibe et al. (Eds.): ECCV 2016, Part III, LNCS 9907, pp. 649–666, 2016.
DOI: 10.1007/978-3-319-46487-9_40

Fig. 1. Example input grayscale photos and output colorizations from our algorithm. These examples are cases where our model works especially well. Please visit http:// richzhang.github.io/colorization/ to see the full range of results and to try our model and code. Best viewed in color (obviously). (Color figure online)

Given the lightness channel L, our system predicts the corresponding a and b color channels of the image in the CIE *Lab* colorspace. To solve this problem, we leverage large-scale data. Predicting color has the nice property that training data is practically free: any color photo can be used as a training example, simply by taking the image's L channel as input and its ab channels as the supervisory signal. Others have noted the easy availability of training data, and previous works have trained convolutional neural networks (CNNs) to predict color on large datasets [1,2]. However, the results from these previous attempts tend to look desaturated. One explanation is that [1,2] use loss functions that encourage conservative predictions. These losses are inherited from standard regression problems, where the goal is to minimize Euclidean error between an estimate and the ground truth.

We instead utilize a loss tailored to the colorization problem. As pointed out by [3], color prediction is inherently multimodal – many objects can take on several plausible colorizations. For example, an apple is typically red, green, or yellow, but unlikely to be blue or orange. To appropriately model the multimodal nature of the problem, we predict a distribution of possible colors for each pixel. Furthermore, we re-weight the loss at training time to emphasize rare colors. This encourages our model to exploit the full diversity of the large-scale data on which it is trained. Lastly, we produce a final colorization by taking the *annealed-mean* of the distribution. The end result is colorizations that are more vibrant and perceptually realistic than those of previous approaches.

Evaluating synthesized images is notoriously difficult [4]. Since our ultimate goal is to make results that are compelling to a human observer, we introduce a novel way of evaluating colorization results, directly testing their perceptual realism. We set up a "colorization Turing test," in which we show participants real and synthesized colors for an image, and ask them to identify the fake. In this quite difficult paradigm, we are able to fool participants on 32 % of the instances (ground truth colorizations would achieve 50 % on this metric), significantly higher than prior work [2]. This test demonstrates that in many cases, our algorithm is producing nearly photorealistic results (see Fig. 1 for selected successful examples from our algorithm). We also show that our system's colorizations are realistic enough to be useful for downstream tasks, in particular object classification, using an off-the-shelf VGG network [5].

We additionally explore colorization as a form of self-supervised representation learning, where raw data is used as its own source of supervision. The idea of learning feature representations in this way goes back at least to autoencoders [6]. More recent works have explored feature learning via data imputation, where a held-out subset of the complete data is predicted (e.g., [7–13]). Our method follows in this line, and can be termed a *cross-channel encoder*. We test how well our model performs in generalization tasks, compared to previous [8,10,14,15] and concurrent [16] self-supervision algorithms, and find that our method performs surprisingly well, achieving state-of-the-art performance on several metrics.

Our contributions in this paper are in two areas. First, we make progress on the graphics problem of automatic image colorization by (a) designing an appropriate objective function that handles the multimodal uncertainty of the colorization problem and captures a wide diversity of colors, (b) introducing a novel framework for testing colorization algorithms, potentially applicable to other image synthesis tasks, and (c) setting a new high-water mark on the task by training on a million color photos. Secondly, we introduce the colorization task as a competitive and straightforward method for self-supervised representation learning, achieving state-of-the-art results on several benchmarks.

Prior Work on Colorization. Colorization algorithms mostly differ in the ways they obtain and treat the data for modeling the correspondence between grayscale and color. Non-parametric methods, given an input grayscale image, first define one or more color reference images (provided by a user or retrieved automatically) to be used as source data. Then, following the Image Analogies framework [17], color is transferred onto the input image from analogous regions of the reference image(s) [18–21]. Parametric methods, on the other hand, learn prediction functions from large datasets of color images at training time, posing the problem as either regression onto continuous color space [1,2,22] or classification of quantized color values [3]. Our method also learns to classify colors, but does so with a larger model, trained on more data, and with several innovations in the loss function and mapping to a final continuous output.

Concurrent Work on Colorization. Concurrently with our paper, Larsson et al. [23] and Iizuka et al. [24] have developed similar systems, which leverage large-scale data and CNNs. The methods differ in their CNN architectures and loss functions. While we use a classification loss, with rebalanced rare classes, Larsson et al. use an un-rebalanced classification loss, and Iizuka et al. use a regression loss. In Sect. 3.1, we compare the effect of each of these types of loss function in conjunction with our architecture. The CNN architectures are also somewhat different: Larsson et al. use hypercolumns [25] on a VGG network [5], Iizuka et al. use a two-stream architecture in which they fuse global and local

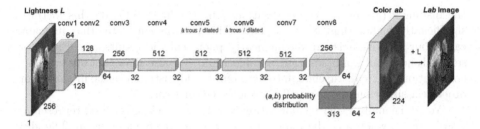

Fig. 2. Our network architecture. Each `conv` layer refers to a block of 2 or 3 repeated `conv` and `ReLU` layers, followed by a `BatchNorm` [30] layer. The net has no `pool` layers. All changes in resolution are achieved through spatial downsampling or upsampling between `conv` blocks. (Color figure online)

features, and we use a single-stream, VGG-styled network with added depth and dilated convolutions [26,27]. In addition, while we and Larsson et al. train our models on ImageNet [28], Iizuka et al. train their model on Places [29]. In Sect. 3.1, we provide quantitative comparisons to Larsson et al., and encourage interested readers to investigate both concurrent papers.

2 Approach

We train a CNN to map from a grayscale input to a distribution over quantized color value outputs using the architecture shown in Fig. 2. Architectural details are described in the supplementary materials on our project webpage[1], and the model is publicly available. In the following, we focus on the design of the objective function, and our technique for inferring point estimates of color from the predicted color distribution.

2.1 Objective Function

Given an input lightness channel $\mathbf{X} \in \mathbb{R}^{H \times W \times 1}$, our objective is to learn a mapping $\widehat{\mathbf{Y}} = \mathcal{F}(\mathbf{X})$ to the two associated color channels $\mathbf{Y} \in \mathbb{R}^{H \times W \times 2}$, where H, W are image dimensions. (We denote predictions with a $\widehat{\cdot}$ symbol and ground truth without.) We perform this task in CIE *Lab* color space. Because distances in this space model perceptual distance, a natural objective function, as used in [1,2], is the Euclidean loss $L_2(\cdot, \cdot)$ between predicted and ground truth colors:

$$L_2(\widehat{\mathbf{Y}}, \mathbf{Y}) = \frac{1}{2} \sum_{h,w} \| \mathbf{Y}_{h,w} - \widehat{\mathbf{Y}}_{h,w} \|_2^2 \tag{1}$$

However, this loss is not robust to the inherent ambiguity and multimodal nature of the colorization problem. If an object can take on a set of distinct *ab* values, the optimal solution to the Euclidean loss will be the mean of the set. In color prediction, this averaging effect favors grayish, desaturated results. Additionally, if the set of plausible colorizations is non-convex, the solution will in fact be out of the set, giving implausible results.

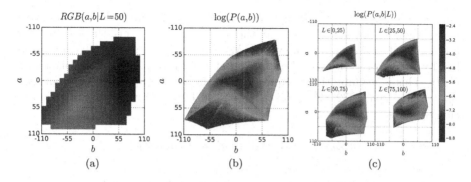

Fig. 3. (a) Quantized ab color space with a grid size of 10. A total of 313 ab pairs are in gamut. (b) Empirical probability distribution of ab values, shown in log scale. (c) Empirical probability distribution of ab values, conditioned on L, shown in log scale. (Color figure online)

Instead, we treat the problem as multinomial classification. We quantize the ab output space into bins with grid size 10 and keep the $Q = 313$ values which are in-gamut, as shown in Fig. 3(a). For a given input $\mathbf{X}$, we learn a mapping $\widehat{\mathbf{Z}} = \mathcal{G}(\mathbf{X})$ to a probability distribution over possible colors $\widehat{\mathbf{Z}} \in [0,1]^{H \times W \times Q}$, where Q is the number of quantized ab values.

To compare predicted $\widehat{\mathbf{Z}}$ against ground truth, we define function $\mathbf{Z} = \mathcal{H}_{gt}^{-1}(\mathbf{Y})$, which converts ground truth color $\mathbf{Y}$ to vector $\mathbf{Z}$, using a soft-encoding scheme[1]. We then use multinomial cross entropy loss $\mathrm{L}_{cl}(\cdot, \cdot)$, defined as:

$$\mathrm{L}_{cl}(\widehat{\mathbf{Z}}, \mathbf{Z}) = -\sum_{h,w} v(\mathbf{Z}_{h,w}) \sum_{q} \mathbf{Z}_{h,w,q} \log(\widehat{\mathbf{Z}}_{h,w,q}) \tag{2}$$

where $v(\cdot)$ is a weighting term that can be used to rebalance the loss based on color-class rarity, as defined in Sect. 2.2 below. Finally, we map probability distribution $\widehat{\mathbf{Z}}$ to color values $\widehat{\mathbf{Y}}$ with function $\widehat{\mathbf{Y}} = \mathcal{H}(\widehat{\mathbf{Z}})$, which will be further discussed in Sect. 2.3.

2.2 Class Rebalancing

The distribution of ab values in natural images is strongly biased towards values with low ab values, due to the appearance of backgrounds such as clouds, pavement, dirt, and walls. Figure 3(b) shows the empirical distribution of pixels in ab space, gathered from 1.3M training images in ImageNet [28]. Observe that the

---

[1] Each ground truth value $\mathbf{Y}_{h,w}$ can be encoded as a 1-hot vector $\mathbf{Z}_{h,w}$ by searching for the nearest quantized ab bin. However, we found that *soft*-encoding worked well for training, and allowed the network to quickly learn the relationship between elements in the output space [31]. We find the 5-nearest neighbors to $\mathbf{Y}_{h,w}$ in the output space and weight them proportionally to their distance from the ground truth using a Gaussian kernel with $\sigma = 5$.

number of pixels in natural images at desaturated values are orders of magnitude higher than for saturated values. Without accounting for this, the loss function is dominated by desaturated ab values. We account for the class-imbalance problem by reweighting the loss of each pixel at train time based on the pixel color rarity. This is asymptotically equivalent to the typical approach of resampling the training space [32]. Each pixel is weighed by factor $\mathbf{w} \in \mathbb{R}^Q$, based on its closest ab bin.

$$v(\mathbf{Z}_{h,w}) = \mathbf{w}_{q^*}, \quad \text{where } q^* = \arg\max_q \mathbf{Z}_{h,w,q} \tag{3}$$

$$\mathbf{w} \propto \left((1-\lambda)\widetilde{\mathbf{p}} + \frac{\lambda}{Q} \right)^{-1}, \quad \mathbb{E}[\mathbf{w}] = \sum_q \widetilde{\mathbf{p}}_q \mathbf{w}_q = 1 \tag{4}$$

To obtain smoothed empirical distribution $\widetilde{\mathbf{p}} \in \Delta^Q$, we estimate the empirical probability of colors in the quantized ab space $\mathbf{p} \in \Delta^Q$ from the full ImageNet training set and smooth the distribution with a Gaussian kernel $\mathbf{G}_\sigma$. We then mix the distribution with a uniform distribution with weight $\lambda \in [0,1]$, take the reciprocal, and normalize so the weighting factor is 1 on expectation. We found that values of $\lambda = \frac{1}{2}$ and $\sigma = 5$ worked well. We compare results with and without class rebalancing in Sect. 3.1.

2.3   Class Probabilities to Point Estimates

Finally, we define $\mathcal{H}$, which maps the predicted distribution $\widehat{\mathbf{Z}}$ to point estimate $\widehat{\mathbf{Y}}$ in ab space. One choice is to take the mode of the predicted distribution for each pixel, as shown in the right-most column of Fig. 4 for two example images. This provides a vibrant but sometimes spatially inconsistent result, e.g., the red splotches on the bus. On the other hand, taking the mean of the predicted distribution produces spatially consistent but desaturated results (left-most column of Fig. 4), exhibiting an unnatural sepia tone. This is unsurprising, as taking the mean after performing classification suffers from some of the same issues as optimizing for a Euclidean loss in a regression framework. To try to get the best of both worlds, we *interpolate* by re-adjusting the temperature T of the softmax distribution, and taking the mean of the result. We draw inspiration from the simulated annealing technique [33], and thus refer to the operation as taking the *annealed-mean* of the distribution:

$$\mathcal{H}(\mathbf{Z}_{h,w}) = \mathbb{E}\left[f_T(\mathbf{Z}_{h,w}) \right], \quad f_T(\mathbf{z}) = \frac{\exp(\log(\mathbf{z})/T)}{\sum_q \exp(\log(\mathbf{z}_q)/T)} \tag{5}$$

Setting $T = 1$ leaves the distribution unchanged, lowering the temperature T produces a more strongly peaked distribution, and setting $T \to 0$ results in a 1-hot encoding at the distribution mode. We found that temperature $T = 0.38$, shown in the middle column of Fig. 4, captures the vibrancy of the mode while maintaining the spatial coherence of the mean.

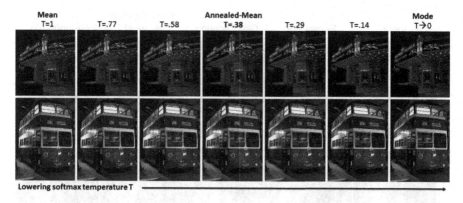

Fig. 4. The effect of temperature parameter T on the *annealed-mean* output (Eq. 5). The left-most images show the means of the predicted color distributions and the right-most show the modes. We use $T = 0.38$ in our system. (Color figure online)

Our final system $\mathcal{F}$ is the composition of CNN $\mathcal{G}$, which produces a predicted distribution over all pixels, and the annealed-mean operation $\mathcal{H}$, which produces a final prediction. The system is not quite end-to-end trainable, but note that the mapping $\mathcal{H}$ operates on each pixel independently, with a single parameter, and can be implemented as part of a feed-forward pass of the CNN.

3   Experiments

In Sect. 3.1, we assess the graphics aspect of our algorithm, evaluating the perceptual realism of our colorizations, along with other measures of accuracy. We compare our full algorithm to several variants, along with recent [2] and concurrent work [23]. In Sect. 3.2, we test colorization as a method for self-supervised representation learning. Finally, in Sect. 3.3, we show qualitative examples on legacy black and white images.

3.1   Evaluating Colorization Quality

We train our network on the 1.3 M images from the ImageNet training set [28], validate on the first 10 k images in the ImageNet validation set, and test on a separate 10 k images in the validation set, same as in [23]. We show quantitative results in Table 1 on three metrics. A qualitative comparison for selected success and failure cases is shown in Fig. 5. For a comparison on a full selection of random images, please see our project webpage.

To specifically test the effect of different loss functions, we train our CNN with various losses. We also compare to previous [2] and concurrent methods [23], which both use CNNs trained on ImageNet, along with naive baselines:

Fig. 5. Example results from our ImageNet test set. Our classification loss with rebalancing produces more accurate and vibrant results than a regression loss or a classification loss without rebalancing. Successful colorizations are above the dotted line. Common failures are below. These include failure to capture long-range consistency, frequent confusions between red and blue, and a default sepia tone on complex indoor scenes. Please visit http://richzhang.github.io/colorization/ to see the full range of results. (Color figure online)

1. **O**urs (full) Our full method, with classification loss, defined in Eq. 2, and class rebalancing, as described in Sect. 2.2. The network was trained from scratch with k-means initialization [36], using the ADAM solver for approximately 450 k iterations[2].
2. **O**urs (class) Our network on classification loss but no class rebalancing ($\lambda = 1$ in Eq. 4).
3. **O**urs (L2) Our network trained from scratch, with L2 regression loss, described in Eq. 1, following the same training protocol.
4. **O**urs (L2, ft) Our network trained with L2 regression loss, fine-tuned from our full classification with rebalancing network.
5. **L**arsson et al. [23] A CNN method that also appears in these proceedings.
6. **D**ahl[2] A previous model using a Laplacian pyramid on VGG features, trained with L2 regression loss.
7. **G**ray Colors every pixel gray, with $(a, b) = 0$.
8. **R**andom Copies the colors from a random image from the training set.

Evaluating the quality of synthesized images is well-known to be a difficult task, as simple quantitative metrics, like RMS error on pixel values, often fail to capture visual realism. To address the shortcomings of any individual evaluation, we test three that measure different senses of quality, shown in Table 1.

1. Perceptual Realism (AMT): For many applications, such as those in graphics, the ultimate test of colorization is how compelling the colors look to a human observer. To test this, we ran a *real vs. fake* two-alternative forced choice experiment on Amazon Mechanical Turk (AMT). Participants in the experiment were shown a series of pairs of images. Each pair consisted of a color photo next to a re-colorized version, produced by either our algorithm or a baseline. Participants were asked to click on the photo they believed contained *fake* colors generated by a computer program. Individual images of resolution 256×256 were shown for one second each, and after each pair, participants were given unlimited time to respond. Each experimental session consisted of 10 practice trials (excluded from subsequent analysis), followed by 40 test pairs. On the practice trials, participants were given feedback as to whether or not their answer was correct. No feedback was given during the 40 test pairs. Each session tested only a single algorithm at a time, and participants were only allowed to complete at most one session. A total of 40 participants evaluated each algorithm. To ensure that all algorithms were tested in equivalent conditions (i.e. time of day, demographics, etc.), all experiment sessions were posted simultaneously and distributed to Turkers in an i.i.d. fashion.

To check that participants were competent at this task, 10 % of the trials pitted the ground truth image against the Random baseline described above. Participants successfully identified these random colorizations as fake 87 % of the time, indicating that they understood the task and were paying attention.

---

[2] $\beta_1 = .9$, $\beta_2 = .99$, and weight decay $= 10^{-3}$. Initial learning rate was 3×10^{-5} and dropped to 10^{-5} and 3×10^{-6} when loss plateaued, at 200k and 375k iterations, respectively. Other models trained from scratch followed similar training protocol.

Table 1. Colorization results on 10k images in the ImageNet validation set [28], as used in [23]. AuC refers to the area under the curve of the cumulative error distribution over ab space [22]. Results column 2 shows the class-balanced variant of this metric. Column 3 is the classification accuracy after colorization using the VGG-16 [5] network. Column 4 shows results from our AMT *real vs. fake* test (with mean and standard error reported, estimated by bootstrap [34]). Note that an algorithm that produces ground truth images would achieve 50 % performance in expectation. Higher is better for all metrics. Rows refer to different algorithms; see text for a description of each. Parameter and feature memory, and runtime, were measured on a Titan X GPU using *Caffe* [35].

Colorization results on ImageNet

Method	Model			AuC		VGG Top-1 Class Acc (%)	AMT labeled real (%)
	Params (MB)	Feats (MB)	Runtime (ms)	non-rebal (%)	rebal (%)		
Ground truth	-	-	-	100	100	68.3	50
Gray	-	-	-	89.1	58.0	52.7	-
Random	-	-	-	84.2	57.3	41.0	13.0±4.4
Dahl [2]	-	-	-	90.4	58.9	48.7	18.3±2.8
Larsson et al. [23]	588	495	122.1	**91.7**	65.9	**59.4**	**27.2±2.7**
Ours (L2)	129	127	17.8	91.2	64.4	54.9	21.2±2.5
Ours (L2, ft)	129	127	17.8	91.5	66.2	56.5	23.9±2.8
Ours (class)	129	142	22.1	91.6	65.1	56.6	25.2±2.7
Ours (full)	129	142	22.1	89.5	**67.3**	56.0	**32.3±2.2**

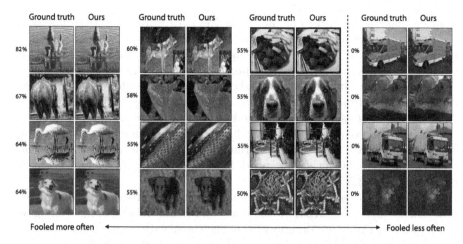

Fig. 6. Images sorted by how often AMT participants chose our algorithm's colorization over the ground truth. In all pairs to the left of the dotted line, participants believed our colorizations to be more real than the ground truth on $\geq 50\,\%$ of the trials. In some cases, this may be due to poor white balancing in the ground truth image, corrected by our algorithm, which predicts a more prototypical appearance. Right of the dotted line are examples where participants were never fooled.

Figure 6 gives a better sense of the participants' competency at detecting subtle errors made by our algorithm. The far right column shows example pairs where participants identified the fake image successfully in $100\,\%$ of the trials. Each of these pairs was scored by at least 10 participants. Close inspection reveals that on these images, our colorizations tend to have giveaway artifacts, such as the yellow blotches on the two trucks, which ruin otherwise decent results.

Nonetheless, our full algorithm fooled participants on $32\,\%$ of trials, as shown in Table 1. This number is significantly higher than all compared algorithms ($p < 0.05$ in each case) except for Larsson et al., against which the difference was not significant ($p = 0.10$; all statistics estimated by bootstrap [34]). These results validate the effectiveness of using both a classification loss and class-rebalancing.

Note that if our algorithm exactly reproduced the ground truth colors, the forced choice would be between two identical images, and participants would be fooled $50\,\%$ of the time on expectation. Interestingly, we can identify cases where participants were fooled *more* often than $50\,\%$ of the time, indicating our results were deemed more realistic than the ground truth. Some examples are shown in the first three columns of Fig. 6. In many case, the ground truth image is poorly white balanced or has unusual colors, whereas our system produces a more prototypical appearance.

2. Semantic Interpretability (VGG Classification): Does our method produce realistic enough colorizations to be interpretable to an off-the-shelf object classifier? We tested this by feeding our *fake* colorized images to a VGG network [5] that was trained to predict ImageNet classes from *real* color photos. If the classifier performs well, that means the colorizations are accurate enough to be informative about object class. Using an off-the-shelf classifier to assess the realism of synthesized data has been previously suggested by [12].

The results are shown in the second column from the right of Table 1. Classifier performance drops from 68.3 % to 52.7 % after ablating colors from the input. After re-colorizing using our full method, the performance is improved to 56.0 % (other variants of our method achieve slightly higher results). The Larsson et al. [23] method achieves the highest performance on this metric, reaching 59.4 %. For reference, a VGG classification network fine-tuned on grayscale inputs reaches a performance of 63.5 %.

In addition to serving as a perceptual metric, this analysis demonstrates a practical use for our algorithm: without any additional training or fine-tuning, we can improve performance on grayscale image classification, simply by colorizing images with our algorithm and passing them to an off-the-shelf classifier.

3. Raw Accuracy (AuC): As a low-level test, we compute the percentage of predicted pixel colors within a thresholded L2 distance of the ground truth in *ab* color space. We then sweep across thresholds from 0 to 150 to produce a cumulative mass function, as introduced in [22], integrate the area under the curve (AuC), and normalize. Note that this AuC metric measures *raw prediction accuracy*, whereas our method aims for *plausibility*.

Our network, trained on classification without rebalancing, outperforms our L2 variant (when trained from scratch). When the L2 net is instead fine-tuned from a color classification network, it matches the performance of the classification network. This indicates that the L2 metric can achieve accurate colorizations, but has difficulty in optimization from scratch. The Larsson et al. [23] method achieves slightly higher accuracy. Note that this metric is dominated by desaturated pixels, due to the distribution of *ab* values in natural images (Fig. 3(b)). As a result, even predicting gray for every pixel does quite well, and our full method with class rebalancing achieves approximately the same score.

Perceptually interesting regions of images, on the other hand, tend to have a distribution of *ab* values with higher values of saturation. As such, we compute a class-balanced variant of the AuC metric by re-weighting the pixels inversely by color class probability (Eq. 4, setting $\lambda = 0$). Under this metric, our full method outperforms all variants and compared algorithms, indicating that class-rebalancing in the training objective achieved its desired effect.

Figure 7. Task Generalization on ImageNet. We freeze pre-trained networks and learn linear classifiers on internal layers for ImageNet [28] classification. Features are average-pooled, with equal kernel and stride sizes, until feature dimensionality is below 10k. ImageNet [38], k-means [36], and Gaussian initializations were run with grayscale inputs, shown with dotted lines, as well as color inputs, shown with solid lines. Previous [10,14] and concurrent [16] self-supervision methods are shown.

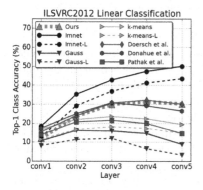

ILSVRC2012 Linear Classification

Fig. 7. ImageNet Linear Classification

Table 2. PASCAL Tests.

Dataset and task generalization on PASCAL				[37]
	Classification		Detection	Segmentation
	(% mAP)		(% mAP)	(% mIU)
Fine-tuned layers	fc8	fc6-fc8	All	All	All
ImageNet [38]	76.8	78.9	79.9	56.8	48.0
Gaussian	–	–	53.3	43.4	19.8
Autoencoder	24.8	16.0	53.8	41.9	25.2
k-means [38]	32.0	39.2	56.6	45.6	32.6
Agrawal et al. [8]	31.2	31.0	54.2	43.9	–
Wang & Gupta [15]	28.1	52.2	58.7	44.0	–
*Doersch et al. [14]	44.7	55.1	**65.3**	**51.1**	--
*Pathak et al. [10]	–	–	56.5	44.5	29.7
*Donahue et al. [16]	38.2	50.2	58.6	45.1	34.9
Ours (gray)	**52.4**	**61.5**	**65.9**	46.9	35.0
Ours (color)	**52.4**	**61.5**	65.6	47.9	**35.6**

Table 2. Task and Dataset Generalization on PASCAL. Classification and detection on PASCAL VOC 2007 [39] and segmentation on PASCAL VOC 2012 [40], using standard mean average precision (mAP) and mean intersection over union (mIU) metrics for each task. We fine-tune our network with grayscale inputs (gray) and color inputs (color). Methods noted with a * only pre-trained a subset of the AlexNet layers. The remaining layers were initialized with [36].

3.2   Cross-Channel Encoding as Self-supervised Feature Learning

In addition to making progress on the graphics task of colorization, we evaluate how colorization can serve as a pretext task for representation learning. Our model is akin to an autoencoder, except that the input and output are different image channels, suggesting the term *cross-channel encoder.*

To evaluate the feature representation learned through this kind of cross-channel encoding, we run two sets of tests on our network. First, we test the *task generalization* capability of the features by fixing the learned representation and training linear classifiers to perform object classification on already seen data (Fig. 7). Second, we fine-tune the network on the PASCAL dataset [37] for the tasks of classification, detection, and segmentation. Here, in addition to testing on held-out *tasks*, this group of experiments tests the learned representation on *dataset generalization*. To fairly compare to previous feature learning algorithms, we retrain an AlexNet [38] network on the colorization task, using our full method, for 450 k iterations. We find that the resulting learned representation achieves higher performance on object classification and segmentation tasks relative to previous methods tested (Table 2).

ImageNet Classification. The network was pre-trained to colorize images from the ImageNet dataset, without semantic label information. We test how well the learned features represent the object-level semantics. To do this, we freeze the weights of the network, provide semantic labels, and train linear classifiers on each convolutional layer. The results are shown in Fig. 7.

AlexNet directly trained on ImageNet classification achieves the highest performance, and serves as the ceiling for this test. Random initialization, with Gaussian weights or the k-means scheme implemented in [36], peak in the middle layers. Because our representation is learned on grayscale images, the network is handicapped at the input. To quantify the effect of this loss of information, we fine-tune AlexNet on grayscale image classification, and also run the random initialization schemes on grayscale images. Interestingly, for all three methods, there is a 6 % performance gap between color and grayscale inputs, which remains approximately constant throughout the network.

We compare our model to other recent self-supervised methods pre-trained on ImageNet [10,14,16]. To begin, our `conv1` representation results in worse linear classification performance than competing methods [14,16], but is comparable to other methods which have a grayscale input. However, this performance gap is immediately bridged at `conv2`, and our network achieves competitive performance to [14,16] throughout the remainder of the network. This indicates that despite the input handicap, solving the colorization task encourages representations that linearly separate semantic classes in the trained data distribution.

PASCAL Classification, Detection, and Segmentation. We test our model on the commonly used self-supervision benchmarks on PASCAL classification, detection, and segmentation, introduced in [10,14,36]. Results are shown in Table 2. Our network achieves strong performance across all three tasks, and state-of-the-art numbers in classification and segmentation. We use the method from [36], which rescales the layers so they "learn" at the same rate. We test our model in two modes: (1) keeping the input grayscale by disregarding color information (Ours (gray)) and (2) modifying `conv1` to receive a full 3-channel *Lab* input, initializing the weights on the *ab* channels to be zero (Ours (color)).

We first test the network on PASCAL VOC 2007 [39] classification, following the protocol in [16]. The network is trained by freezing the representation up to certain points, and fine-tuning the remainder. Note that when `conv1` is frozen, the network is effectively only able to interpret grayscale images. Across all three classification tests, we achieve state-of-the-art accuracy.

We also test detection on PASCAL VOC 2007, using Fast R-CNN [41], following the procedure in [36]. Doersch et al. [14] achieves 51.5 %, while we reach 46.9 % and 47.9 % with grayscale and color inputs, respectively. Our method is well above the strong k-means [36] baseline of 45.6 %, but all self-supervised methods still fall short of pre-training with ImageNet semantic supervision, which reaches 56.8 %.

Finally, we test semantic segmentation on PASCAL VOC 2012 [40], using the FCN architecture of [42], following the protocol in [10]. Our colorization task shares similarities to the semantic segmentation task, as both are per-pixel classification problems. Our grayscale fine-tuned network achieves performance of 35.0 %, approximately equal to Donahue et al. [16], and adding in color information increases performance to 35.6 %, above other tested algorithms.

Fig. 8. Applying our method to legacy black and white photos. Left to right: photo by David Fleay of a Thylacine, now extinct, 1936; photo by Ansel Adams of Yosemite; amateur family photo from 1956; *Migrant Mother* by Dorothea Lange, 1936

3.3   Legacy Black and White Photos

Since our model was trained using "fake" grayscale images generated by stripping ab channels from color photos, we also ran our method on real legacy black and white photographs, as shown in Fig. 8 (additional results can be viewed on our project webpage). One can see that our model is still able to produce good colorizations, even though the low-level image statistics of the legacy photographs are quite different from those of the modern-day photos on which it was trained.

4   Conclusion

While image colorization is a boutique computer graphics task, it is also an instance of a difficult pixel prediction problem in computer vision. Here we have shown that colorization with a deep CNN and a well-chosen objective function can come closer to producing results indistinguishable from real color photos. Our method not only provides a useful graphics output, but can also be viewed as a pretext task for representation learning. Although only trained to color, our network learns a representation that is surprisingly useful for object classification, detection, and segmentation, performing strongly compared to other self-supervised pre-training methods.

Acknowledgements. This research was supported, in part, by ONR MURI N000141010934, NSF SMA-1514512, an Intel research grant, and a hardware donation by NVIDIA Corp. We thank members of the Berkeley Vision Lab and Aditya Deshpande for helpful discussions, Philipp Krähenbühl and Jeff Donahue for help with self-supervision experiments, and Gustav Larsson for providing images for comparison to [23].

References

1. Cheng, Z., Yang, Q., Sheng, B.: Deep colorization. In: Proceedings of the IEEE International Conference on Computer Vision, pp. 415–423 (2015)
2. Dahl, R.: Automatic colorization (2016). http://tinyclouds.org/colorize/.
3. Charpiat, G., Hofmann, M., Schölkopf, B.: Automatic image colorization via multimodal predictions. In: Forsyth, D., Torr, P., Zisserman, A. (eds.) ECCV 2008, Part III. LNCS, vol. 5304, pp. 126–139. Springer, Heidelberg (2008)
4. Ramanarayanan, G., Ferwerda, J., Walter, B., Bala, K.: Visual equivalence: towards a new standard for image fidelity. ACM Trans. Graph. (TOG) 26(3), 76 (2007)
5. Simonyan, K., Zisserman, A.: Very deep convolutional networks for large-scale image recognition. arXiv preprint arXiv:1409.1556 (2014)
6. Bengio, Y., Courville, A., Vincent, P.: Representation learning: a review and new perspectives. IEEE Trans. Pattern Anal. Mach. Intell. 35(8), 1798–1828 (2013)
7. Ngiam, J., Khosla, A., Kim, M., Nam, J., Lee, H., Ng, A.Y.: Multimodal deep learning. In: Proceedings of the 28th International Conference on Machine Learning (ICML 2011), pp. 689–696 (2011)
8. Agrawal, P., Carreira, J., Malik, J.: Learning to see by moving. In: Proceedings of the IEEE International Conference on Computer Vision, pp. 37–45 (2015)
9. Jayaraman, D., Grauman, K.: Learning image representations tied to ego-motion. In: Proceedings of the IEEE International Conference on Computer Vision, pp. 1413–1421 (2015)
10. Pathak, D., Krähenbühl, P., Donahue, J., Darrell, T., Efros, A.: Context encoders: feature learning by inpainting. In: CVPR (2016)
11. Lotter, W., Kreiman, G., Cox, D.: Deep predictive coding networks for video prediction and unsupervised learning. arXiv preprint arXiv:1605.08104 (2016)
12. Owens, A., Isola, P., McDermott, J., Torralba, A., Adelson, E.H., Freeman, W.T.: Visually indicated sounds. In: CVPR (2016)
13. Owens, A., Wu, J., McDermott, J.H., Freeman, W.T., Torralba, A.: Ambient sound provides supervision for visual learning. In: ECCV (2016)
14. Doersch, C., Gupta, A., Efros, A.A.: Unsupervised visual representation learning by context prediction. In: Proceedings of the IEEE International Conference on Computer Vision, pp. 1422–1430 (2015)
15. Wang, X., Gupta, A.: Unsupervised learning of visual representations using videos. In: Proceedings of the IEEE International Conference on Computer Vision, pp. 2794–2802 (2015)
16. Donahue, J., Krähenbühl, P., Darrell, T.: Adversarial feature learning. arXiv preprint arXiv:1605.09782 (2016)
17. Hertzmann, A., Jacobs, C.E., Oliver, N., Curless, B., Salesin, D.H.: Image analogies. In: Proceedings of the 28th Annual Conference on Computer Graphics and Interactive Techniques, pp. 327–340. ACM (2001)
18. Welsh, T., Ashikhmin, M., Mueller, K.: Transferring color to greyscale images. ACM Trans. Graph. (TOG) 21(3), 277–280 (2002)
19. Gupta, R.K., Chia, A.Y.S., Rajan, D., Ng, E.S., Zhiyong, H.: Image colorization using similar images. In: Proceedings of the 20th ACM International Conference on Multimedia, pp. 369–378. ACM (2012)
20. Liu, X., Wan, L., Qu, Y., Wong, T.T., Lin, S., Leung, C.S., Heng, P.A.: Intrinsic colorization. ACM Trans. Graph. (TOG) 27, 152 (2008). ACM

21. Chia, A.Y.S., Zhuo, S., Gupta, R.K., Tai, Y.W., Cho, S.Y., Tan, P., Lin, S.: Semantic colorization with internet images. ACM Trans. Graph. (TOG) **30**, 156 (2011). ACM
22. Deshpande, A., Rock, J., Forsyth, D.: Learning large-scale automatic image colorization. In: Proceedings of the IEEE International Conference on Computer Vision, pp. 567–575 (2015)
23. Larsson, G., Maire, M., Shakhnarovich, G.: Learning representations for automatic colorization. In: European Conference on Computer Vision (2016)
24. Iizuka, S., Simo-Serra, E., Ishikawa, H.: Let there be color!: joint end-to-end learning of global and local image priors for automatic image colorization with simultaneous classification. ACM Trans. Graph. (Proc. SIGGRAPH 2016) **35**(4), 110 (2016). Kindly check and confirm if the inserted page range is correct for Ref. [24]
25. Hariharan, B., Arbeláez, P., Girshick, R., Malik, J.: Hypercolumns for object segmentation and fine-grained localization. In: Proceedings of the IEEE Conference on Computer Vision and Pattern Recognition, pp. 447–456 (2015)
26. Chen, L.C., Papandreou, G., Kokkinos, I., Murphy, K., Yuille, A.L.: Deeplab: semantic image segmentation with deep convolutional nets, atrous convolution, and fully connected CRFs. arXiv preprint arXiv:1606.00915 (2016)
27. Yu, F., Koltun, V.: Multi-scale context aggregation by dilated convolutions. In: International Conference on Learning Representations (2016)
28. Russakovsky, O., Deng, J., Su, H., Krause, J., Satheesh, S., Ma, S., Huang, Z., Karpathy, A., Khosla, A., Bernstein, M., et al.: Imagenet large scale visual recognition challenge. Int. J. Comput. Vis. **115**(3), 211–252 (2015)
29. Zhou, B., Lapedriza, A., Xiao, J., Torralba, A., Oliva, A.: Learning deep features for scene recognition using places database. In: Advances in Neural Information Processing Systems, pp. 487–495 (2014)
30. Ioffe, S., Szegedy, C.: Batch normalization: accelerating deep network training by reducing internal covariate shift. arXiv preprint arXiv:1502.03167 (2015)
31. Hinton, G., Vinyals, O., Dean, J.: Distilling the knowledge in a neural network. arXiv preprint arXiv:1503.02531 (2015)
32. Farabet, C., Couprie, C., Najman, L., LeCun, Y.: Learning hierarchical features for scene labeling. IEEE Trans. Pattern Anal. Mach. Intell. **35**(8), 1915–1929 (2013)
33. Kirkpatrick, S., Vecchi, M.P., et al.: Optimization by simmulated annealing. Science **220**(4598), 671–680 (1983)
34. Efron, B.: Bootstrap methods: another look at the jackknife. In: Kotz, S., Johnson, N.L. (eds.) Breakthroughs in Statistics, pp. 569–593. Springer, Heidelberg (1992)
35. Jia, Y., Shelhamer, E., Donahue, J., Karayev, S., Long, J., Girshick, R., Guadarrama, S., Darrell, T.: Caffe: convolutional architecture for fast feature embedding. In: Proceedings of the 22nd ACM International Conference on Multimedia, pp. 675–678. ACM (2014)
36. Krähenbühl, P., Doersch, C., Donahue, J., Darrell, T.: Data-dependent initializations of convolutional neural networks. In: International Conference on Learning Representations (2016)
37. Everingham, M., Van Gool, L., Williams, C.K., Winn, J., Zisserman, A.: The pascal visual object classes (VOC) challenge. Int. J. Comput. Vis. **88**(2), 303–338 (2010)
38. Krizhevsky, A., Sutskever, I., Hinton, G.E.: Imagenet classification with deep convolutional neural networks. In: Advances in Neural Information Processing Systems, pp. 1097–1105 (2012)
39. Everingham, M., Van Gool, L., Williams, C.K.I., Winn, J., Zisserman, A.: The PASCAL Visual Object Classes Challenge 2007 (VOC2007) Results. http://www.pascal-network.org/challenges/VOC/voc2007/workshop/index.html

40. Everingham, M., Van Gool, L., Williams, C.K.I., Winn, J., Zisserman, A.:The PASCAL Visual Object Classes Challenge 2012 (VOC2012) Results. http://www. pascal-network.org/challenges/VOC/voc2012/workshop/index.html
41. Girshick, R.: Fast R-CNN. In: Proceedings of the IEEE International Conference on Computer Vision, pp. 1440–1448 (2015)
42. Long, J., Shelhamer, E., Darrell, T.: Fully convolutional networks for semantic segmentation. In: Proceedings of the IEEE Conference on Computer Vision and Pattern Recognition, pp. 3431–3440 (2015)

Focal Flow: Measuring Distance and Velocity with Defocus and Differential Motion

Emma Alexander[1(✉)], Qi Guo[1], Sanjeev Koppal[2], Steven Gortler[1], and Todd Zickler[1]

[1] Harvard SEAS, Cambridge, USA
ealexander@seas.harvard.edu
[2] University of Florida, Gainesville, USA

Abstract. We present the focal flow sensor. It is an unactuated, monocular camera that simultaneously exploits defocus and differential motion to measure a depth map and a 3D scene velocity field. It does so using an optical-flow-like, per-pixel linear constraint that relates image derivatives to depth and velocity. We derive this constraint, prove its invariance to scene texture, and prove that it is exactly satisfied only when the sensor's blur kernels are Gaussian. We analyze the inherent sensitivity of the ideal focal flow sensor, and we build and test a prototype. Experiments produce useful depth and velocity information for a broader set of aperture configurations, including a simple lens with a pillbox aperture.

Computational sensors reduce the data processing burden of visual sensing tasks by physically manipulating light on its path to a photosensor. They analyze scenes using vision algorithms, optics, and post-capture computation that are jointly designed for a specific task or environment. By optimizing which light rays are sampled, and by moving some of the computation from electrical hardware into the optical domain, computational sensors promise to extend task-specific artificial vision to new extremes in size, autonomy, and power consumption [1–5].

We introduce the first computational sensor for depth and 3D scene velocity. It is called a *focal flow sensor*. It is passive and monocular, and it measures depth and velocity using a per-pixel linear constraint composed of spatial and temporal image derivatives. The sensor simultaneously exploits defocus and differential motion, and its underlying principle is depicted in Fig. 1. This figure shows the one-dimensional image values that would be measured from a front-parallel, Lambertian scene patch with a sinusoidal texture pattern, as it moves relative to a sensor. If the sensor is a pinhole camera, the patch is always in focus, and the images captured over time are variously stretched and shifted versions of the patch's texture pattern (Fig. 1A). The rates of stretching and shifting together resolve the time to contact and direction of motion (e.g., using [6]), but they are not sufficient to explicitly measure depth or velocity. The focal flow sensor is a real-aperture camera with a finite depth of field, so in addition to stretching and shifting, its images exhibit changes in contrast due to defocus (Fig. 1B). This additional piece of information resolves depth and velocity explicitly.

© Springer International Publishing AG 2016
B. Leibe et al. (Eds.): ECCV 2016, Part III, LNCS 9907, pp. 667–682, 2016.
DOI: 10.1007/978-3-319-46487-9_41

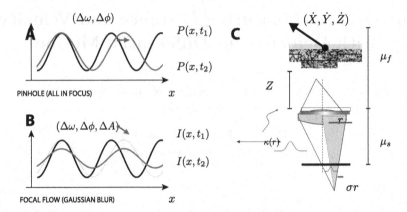

Fig. 1. The focal flow principle. A: When a 1D pinhole camera observes a world plane with sinusoidal texture, the image is also a sinusoid (black curve). Motion between camera and scene causes the sinusoidal image to change in frequency and phase (blue curve), and these two pieces of information reveal time to contact and direction of motion. **B**: When a finite-aperture camera images a similar moving scene, the motion additionally induces a change in image amplitude, because the scene moves in or out of focus. This third piece of information resolves depth and scene velocity. **C**: We show that, with an ideal thin lens and Gaussian blur $\kappa(r)$, depth and 3D velocity can be measured through a simple, per-pixel linear constraint, similar optical flow. The constraint applies to any generic scene texture. (Color figure online)

Our main contribution is the derivation of a per-pixel linear equation,

$$\left[I_x \ \ I_y \ \ (xI_x + yI_y) \ \ (I_{xx} + I_{yy}) \right] \cdot v + I_t = 0,$$

that relates spatial and temporal image derivatives to depth and 3D scene velocity, and that is valid *for any generic scene texture*. Over an image patch, depth and velocity are recovered simply by computing spatial and temporal derivatives, solving a 4×4 linear system for vector $v \in \mathbb{R}^4$, and then evaluating analytic expressions for depth $Z(v)$ and 3D velocity $(\dot{X}, \dot{Y}, \dot{Z})(v)$ determined by the physical characteristics of the calibrated sensor.

The focal flow cue is distinct from conventional passive depth cues like stereo and depth from defocus because it directly measures 3D velocity in addition to depth. It is also different because it does not require inferences about disparity or blur; instead, it provides per-pixel depth in closed form, using a relatively small number of multiply and add operations. The focal flow sensor might therefore be useful for applications, such as micro-robotics [3], that involve motion and that require visual sensing with low power consumption and small form factors.

We prove that this linear constraint is invariant to scene texture, that it exists analytically whenever the optical system's point spread functions are Gaussian, and that no other class of radially symmetric point spread functions—be they discs, binary codes, or continuous functions—provides the same capability. We also analyze the inherent sensitivity of the focal flow sensor, and show the effectiveness in practice of non-Gaussian aperture configurations including filter-free apertures. We demonstrate a working prototype that can measure depth within $\pm 5.5\,\mathrm{mm}$ over a range of more than $15\,\mathrm{cm}$ using an $f/4$ lens.

1   Related Work

Motion & Linear Constraints. Differential optical flow, which assumes that all images are in focus, is computable from a linear system of equations in a window [7]. A closely related linear system resolves time to contact [6,8]. The focal flow equation has a similar linear form, but it incorporates defocus blur and provides additional scene information in the form of depth and 3D velocity. Unlike previous work on time to contact [9], our focal flow analysis is restricted to front-parallel scene patches, though experimental results suggest that useful depth can be obtained for some slanted planes as well (see Fig. 5).

Defocus. When many images are collected under a variety of calibrated camera settings, a search for the most-in-focus image will yield depth [10]. This approach is called depth from focus, and it is reliable but expensive in terms of time and images captured. When restricted to a few images, none of which are guaranteed to be in focus, a depth from defocus algorithm must be used [11]. This method is more difficult because the underlying texture is unknown: we cannot tell if the scene is a blurry picture of an oil painting or the sharp image of a watercolor, and without natural image priors both solutions are equally valid. To reduce ambiguity, most depth from defocus techniques require at least two exposures with substantially different blur kernels, controlled by internal camera actuation that changes the focal length or aperture diaphragm to manipulate the blur kernel [11–14]. The complexity of recovering depth depends on the blur kernels and the statistical image model that is used for inference. Depth performance improves when well-designed binary attenuation patterns are included in the aperture plane [15–17], and with appropriate inference, binary codes can even provide useful depth from a single exposure [18–20].

Focal flow is similar to depth from defocus in that it relies on focus changes over a small set of defocused images to reveal depth, and that it requires a specific blur kernel. However, both the implied hardware and the computation are different. Unlike multi-shot depth from defocus, our sensor does not require internal actuation, and unlike binary aperture codes, it employs a continuous radially symmetric filter. Most importantly, by observing differential changes in defocus, it replaces costly inference with a much simpler measurement algorithm.

Differential defocus with Gaussian blur was previously considered by Farid and Simmoncelli [21], who used it to derive a two-aperture capture sequence. We build on this work by proving the uniqueness of the Gaussian filter, and by exploiting differential motion to avoid aperture actuation.

Cue Combination. Our use of relative motion between scene and sensor means that in many settings, such as robotics or motion-based interfaces, this cue comes without an additional power cost. Previous efforts to combine camera/scene motion and defocus cues [22–27] require intensive computations, though they often account for motion blur which we ignore. Even when motion is known, equivalent to combining defocus with stereo, measuring depth still requires inference [28,29]. The simplicity of focal flow provides an advantage in efficiency.

2   The Focal Flow Constraint

In differential optical flow, a pinhole camera views a Lambertian object with a temporally constant albedo pattern, here called texture and denoted $T : \mathbb{R}^2 \rightarrow [0, \infty)$. For now the texture is assumed to be differentiable, but this requirement will be relaxed later when deriving focal flow. For front-parallel planar objects, located at a time-varying offset (X, Y) and depth Z from the pinhole, the camera captures an all-in-focus image that varies in time t and pixel location (x, y) over a bounded patch S on a sensor located a distance μ_s from the pinhole. The intensity of this image $P : S \times \mathbb{R} \rightarrow [0, 1]$ is a magnified and translated version of the texture, scaled by an exposure-dependent constant γ:

$$P(x, y, t) = \gamma \, T \left(\frac{Z(t)}{-\mu_s} x - X(t), \, \frac{Z(t)}{-\mu_s} y - Y(t) \right). \tag{1}$$

It is well known that the ratios of the spatial and temporal derivatives of this image are independent of texture, and so can reveal information about the scene. A familiar formulation [7] provides optical flow $(\dot{x}, \dot{y})$ from image derivatives:

$$0 = \begin{bmatrix} P_x & P_y \end{bmatrix} \begin{bmatrix} \dot{x} \\ \dot{y} \end{bmatrix} + P_t, \tag{2}$$

while following [6] to split the translation and magnification terms:

$$0 = \begin{bmatrix} P_x & P_y & (xP_x + yP_y) \end{bmatrix} \boldsymbol{u} + P_t, \tag{3}$$

$$\boldsymbol{u} = [u_1, u_2, u_3]^T = \begin{bmatrix} -\frac{\dot{X}\mu_s}{Z}, & -\frac{\dot{Y}\mu_s}{Z}, & -\frac{\dot{Z}}{Z} \end{bmatrix}^T, \tag{4}$$

provides texture-independent time to contact $\frac{Z}{\dot{Z}} = \frac{-1}{u_3}$ and direction of motion $\left(\frac{\dot{X}}{Z}, \frac{\dot{Y}}{Z} \right) = \left(\frac{-u_1}{\mu_s u_3}, \frac{-u_2}{\mu_s u_3} \right)$.

For focal flow, we replace the pinhole camera with a finite-aperture camera having an ideal thin lens and an attenuating filter in the aperture plane. We represent the spatial transmittance profile of the filter with the function $\kappa : \mathbb{R}^2 \rightarrow [0, 1]$. We assume that this function is radially symmetric, so that this two-dimensional function of x and y can be written as a function of the single variable $r = \sqrt{x^2 + y^2}$. However, we do not require smoothness, which allows for pillboxes and binary codes as well as continuous filters. For a front-parallel world plane at depth Z, the filter induces a blur kernel k on the image that is a "stretched" version of the aperture filter:

$$k(r; Z) = \frac{1}{\sigma^2(Z)} \kappa \left(\frac{r}{\sigma(Z)} \right), \tag{5}$$

where the magnification factor σ, illustrated in Fig. 1C, is determined by object depth, sensor distance, and in-focus depth μ_f:

$$\sigma(Z) = \left(\frac{1}{Z} - \frac{1}{\mu_f} \right) \mu_s. \tag{6}$$

Denoting by $*$ a convolution in x and y, we can write the blurred image I as

$$I(x, y, t) = k \left(\sqrt{x^2 + y^2}; Z(t) \right) * P(x, y, t). \tag{7}$$

Unlike the pinhole image P, the ratios of the spatial and temporal derivatives of this defocus-blurred image I depend on texture. This is because the constant brightness constraint does not hold under defocus: pixel intensity changes both as image features move and also as patch contrast is reduced away from the focal plane. This difference, illustrated in Fig. 1, implies that any finite-aperture system for measuring optical flow will suffer a systematic error from defocus. Mathematically, this appears as an additive residual term on the time derivative, as shown in the following proposition.

Proposition. [1] *For an ideal thin lens camera and front-parallel planar scene,*

$$I_x = k_x * P, \tag{8}$$
$$I_y = k_y * P, \tag{9}$$
$$I_t = k_t * P + k * P_t \tag{10}$$
$$= -u_1 I_x - u_2 I_y - u_3(x I_x + y I_y) - R, \tag{11}$$

where, denoting by κ' the distributional derivative of κ,

$$R(x, y, t; P, \kappa, Z, \dot{Z}) = \frac{\dot{Z}}{Z - \mu_f} \frac{1}{\sigma^2(Z)} \left(2\kappa \left(\frac{r}{\sigma(Z)} \right) + \frac{r}{\sigma(Z)} \kappa' \left(\frac{r}{\sigma(Z)} \right) \right) * P. \tag{12}$$

The time-varying residual image $R(x, y, t)$ changes with depth, velocity, and camera design. It is troublesome because it also depends on the pinhole image P, which is not directly measured. Only the blurred image $I = k*P$ is available. This means that for almost all aperture filters, there is no way to express R using scene geometry and image information alone—it is inherently texture-dependent.

---

[1] *Proof.* From optical flow, $k * P_t = k * (-u_1 P_x - u_2 P_y - u_3(x P_x + y P_y))$. Because $k * x P_x = x(k * P_x) - (xk * P_x) = x(k * P_x) - (k + xk_x) * P$, then $k * P_t = -u_1 I_x - u_2 I_y - u_3(x I_x + y I_y) + u_3(2k + xk_x + yk_y) * P$. Likewise, $k_t * P = k_\sigma \dot{\sigma} * P \propto (2k + rk_r) * P$. $\square$

However, we observe that for a very specific aperture filter, this source of error can actually be transformed into a usable signal that resolves both depth and 3D velocity. For this to happen, the aperture filter must be paired with a particular linear image processing operation that, when combined with the filter, allows the decomposition of residual image R into a depth/velocity factor (analogous to u_1) and an accessible measurement (analogous to I_x). To formally identify such a filter and image operator, we seek triples (M, κ, v) of shift-invariant linear image operators M (like ∂_x and ∂_y), aperture filters κ, and scalar depth/velocity factors v (analogous to u_1 and u_2) that satisfy, for any texture,

$$v(t) \, M[I](x,y) = R(x,y,t). \tag{13}$$

We prove in the following theorem that there exists a unique family of such triples, comprised of Gaussian aperture filters and Laplacian image measurements. This leads directly to a simple sensor and algorithm that we prototype and evaluate in Sect. 4.

Theorem. *Let* $\kappa : \mathbb{R}^2 \to [0,1]$ *be radially symmetric, with* $\kappa(r)$ *and* $r\kappa(r)$ *Lebesgue integrable. For* $v : \mathbb{R} \to \mathbb{R}$ *and translation-invariant linear spatial operator* M *with finite support:*

$$v(t; Z, \dot{Z}) \, M \left[\frac{\kappa \left(\frac{\sqrt{x^2+y^2}}{\sigma(Z)} \right)}{\sigma^2(Z)} * P(x,y,t) \right] = R(x,y,t; P, \kappa, Z, \dot{Z}),$$

$$\forall P : S \times \mathbb{R} \to [0,1], \quad \forall Z \in \mathbb{R}^+, \quad \forall \dot{Z} \in \mathbb{R}, \quad \forall (x,y,t) \in \mathbb{R}^3 \tag{14}$$

if and only if, for aperture width and transmittance parameters $\Sigma, \alpha \in \mathbb{R}^+$ *and measurement scaling parameter* $\beta \in \{\mathbb{R} - 0\}$,

$$\kappa(r) = \alpha \, e^{-\frac{r^2}{2\Sigma^2}}, \tag{15}$$

$$M = \beta \, \nabla^2, \tag{16}$$

$$v(t; Z, \dot{Z}) = \frac{1}{\beta} \frac{\dot{Z}(t)}{Z(t)} \left(\frac{\mu_f}{Z(t)} - 1 \right) \left(\frac{\Sigma \mu_s}{\mu_f} \right)^2. \tag{17}$$

This theorem states that, when the filter $\kappa(r)$ is Gaussian, the residual R is proportional to the image Laplacian $M[I] = I_{xx} + I_{yy}$ and is therefore directly observable. Moreover, the Gaussian is the only radially-symmetric aperture filter—out of a broad class of possibilities including pillboxes, binary codes, and smooth functions—that permits observation by a depth-blind linear operator.

Combining the proposition and theorem leads to a per-pixel linear constraint, analogous to those used in measuring optical flow or time to contact.

Corollary. *For a camera with Gaussian point spread functions observing a front-parallel planar scene, the following constraint holds at each image pixel:*

$$0 = \begin{bmatrix} I_x & I_y & (xI_x + yI_y) & (I_{xx} + I_{yy}) \end{bmatrix} \boldsymbol{v} + I_t,$$

$$\boldsymbol{v} = [u_1, u_2, u_3, v]^T = \left[-\frac{\dot{X}\mu_s}{Z}, -\frac{\dot{Y}\mu_s}{Z}, -\frac{\dot{Z}}{Z}, -\frac{\dot{Z}}{Z}\left(1 - \frac{\mu_f}{Z}\right)\left(\frac{\Sigma\mu_s}{\mu_f}\right)^2 \right]^T. \quad (18)$$

Holding this constraint over a generic image patch yields a system of linear equations that can be solved for $\boldsymbol{u}$ and v. In the presence of axial motion ($\dot{Z} \neq 0$) the new scalar factor v provides enough additional information to directly recover complete depth and velocity:

$$Z = \frac{(\mu_s^2 \Sigma^2 \mu_f) u_3}{(\mu_s^2 \Sigma^2) u_3 - (\mu_f^2) v}, \quad (19)$$

$$(\dot{X}, \dot{Y}, \dot{Z}) = -(Zu_1/\mu_s, Zu_2/\mu_s, Zu_3). \quad (20)$$

This implies a simple patch-wise algorithm for measuring depth and velocity, about which we make a few notes. When an image patch is degenerate, meaning that the matrix having a row $[I_x, I_y, xI_x + yI_y, I_{xx} + I_{yy}]$ for each of the patch's pixels is not full rank, partial scene information can often still be obtained. For example, a patch that contains a single-orientation texture and is subject to the classical aperture problem gives rise to ambiguities in the lateral velocity $(\dot{X}, \dot{Y})$, but depth Z and axial velocity $\dot{Z}$ can still be determined. Separately, in the case of zero axial motion ($\dot{Z} = 0$) it follows that $u_3 = v = 0$, and the patch can only provide optical flow. Finally, note that unlike many depth from defocus methods, focal flow produces no side-of-focal-plane ambiguity.

The following proof draws heavily on the theory of distributions, for which we suggest [30] as a reference. Additional intuition may be gained from two alternate derivations of Eq. (18) that are provided in an associated technical report [31]. These alternate derivations are simpler because they begin by assuming a Gaussian filter instead of proving its uniqueness.

Proof. Because M is a translation-invariant linear operator with finite support, $M[I]$ can be written as a convolution

$$M[I] = m * I, \quad (21)$$

with a compactly-supported distribution m. This compactness, along with the compactness of P (which we relax later but need for uniqueness), guarantees that the convolution theorem applies to $m * \kappa * P$. Then, with 2D spatial Fourier transforms denoted by $\mathcal{F}[f(r)] = \hat{f}(\hat{r})$, Eq. (14) can be written as

$$\hat{m}(\hat{r})\hat{\kappa}(\sigma\hat{r})\hat{P} = -\frac{\hat{r}}{w}\hat{\kappa}'(\sigma\hat{r})\hat{P}, \quad (22)$$

$$w(t) = \frac{Z - \mu_f}{\dot{Z}}v(t), \quad (23)$$

which we require to hold for all textures by eliminating $\hat{P}$ terms. By assuming compactness of m and integrability of κ and $r\kappa$, $\hat{m}$ is smooth and $\hat{\kappa}$ has a continuous first derivative, so the resulting differential equation in $\hat{\kappa}$ has solution

$$\hat{\kappa}(\sigma\hat{r}) \propto e^{-w(t)\int_0^{\hat{r}} \frac{\hat{m}(\hat{s})}{\hat{s}} d\hat{s}}, \tag{24}$$

which restricts the class of possible $\hat{m}$ and w to the form[2]

$$\hat{m} \propto \hat{r}^{2n}, \quad w \propto \sigma^{2n}, \quad n \in \mathbb{R}. \tag{25}$$

These are Riesz kernels, with inverse Fourier transform

$$m(r; n) \propto \begin{cases} \text{undefined,} & n \leq -1 \\ (\delta''(x)\delta(y) + \delta(x)\delta''(y))^{*n}, & n \in \{0, 1, 2, ...\} \\ r^{-2(n-\lfloor |n| \rfloor)} * (\delta''(x)\delta(y) + \delta(x)\delta''(y))^{*\lfloor |n| \rfloor}, & n \in \mathbb{R}, \text{else,} \end{cases} \tag{26}$$

where starred exponents indicate repeated convolution. When n is not a non-negative integer, the corresponding m is undefined or has noncompact support. When $n = 0$, the aperture filter κ is a pinhole, violating the finite transmittance assumption. Thus, the complete set of image operators M that can satisfy condition (14) are powers of the Laplacian: $M \in \{\beta(\nabla^2)^n \mid n \in \mathbb{Z}^+, \beta \in \{\mathbb{R}-0\}\}$.

For the proportionality v between measurement $M[I]$ and residual R, note from Eq. (25) that w takes a constant value under unit magnification σ. Calling this constant Σ^2 so that $w = \Sigma^2\sigma^{2n}$, Eq. (23) produces v:

$$v(t; Z, \dot{Z}) = \dot{Z}\Sigma^2\sigma^{2n}/(\beta(Z - \mu_f)). \tag{27}$$

Since v/u_3 is monotonic in depth, it resolves complete scene information for any n. For aperture filter κ we take Eqs. (24, 25) under unit σ:

$$\kappa(r; n) = \mathcal{F}^{-1}\left[e^{-\Sigma^2\hat{r}^{2n}}\right], \tag{28}$$

which corresponds to a Gaussian filter for $n = 1$. For all $n \geq 2$, $\kappa(r; n)$ cannot describe a transmittance profile because it is negative for some r.[3] Thus $n = 1$,

---

[2] *Proof.* Because w is a function of time (and not spatial frequency), $\hat{m}$ a function of spatial frequency (and not time), and $\hat{\kappa}$ a function of the time-frequency product $\sigma\hat{r}$, this equation takes the form $h_0(xy) = e^{f(x)g(y)}$ or $h(xy) = \ln h_0 = f(x)g(y)$. Considering $x = 1$ and $y = 1$ in turn, we see that $g \propto h \propto f$, so that $f(x)f(y) \propto f(xy)$. Differentiating by x and considering the case $x = 1$ results in the differential equation $f(y) \propto yf'(y)$, with general solution $f(y) \propto y^n$, equivalently y^{2n}, $n \in \mathbb{C}$. Realness of v implies $n \in \mathbb{R}$. Differentiating $\int_0^{\hat{r}} \frac{\hat{m}(s')}{s'}ds' \propto \hat{r}^{2n}$ yields $\hat{m} \propto \hat{r}^{2n}$. □

[3] *Proof.* From the Fourier Slice Theorem [32,33], denoting by $\mathcal{F}_1$ the 1D Fourier transform, we have $\mathcal{F}_1\left[\int \kappa(x, y)dy\right] = \hat{\kappa}(\omega_x, 0) = e^{-|\omega_x|^{2n}}$. This function is not positive definite for $n \geq 2$ (which can be seen by taking $C(n) = \sum\sum z_i z_j e^{-|x_i - x_j|^{2n}}$ for $z = [1, -2, 1]$ and $x = [-.1^{2n}, 0, .1^{2n}]$, and noting that both $C(2)$ and $\frac{dC}{dn}$ are negative), so by Bochner's theorem it cannot be the (1D) Fourier transform of a finite positive Borel measure. The only property of such a measure that $\int \kappa$ could lack is non-negativity, so the existence of negative values of κ follows immediately. □

and $M[k]$ is a rapidly decreasing function, so $m * k * P$ is well-defined for any bounded locally-integrable P, and the focal flow constraint holds regardless of the compactness of the texture's support.   □

3   Inherent Sensitivity

Due to the loss of image contrast as an object moves away from the focal plane, we expect the focal flow depth signal to be strongest for scene patches that are in focus or nearly in focus. This is similar to the expected performance of stereo or depth from defocus, for which depth accuracy degrades at large distances. In those cases, accuracy is enhanced by increasing the baseline or aperture size. In focal flow, focal settings play the analogous role.

Following Schechner and Kiryati in [34], we can describe the inherent sensitivity of all three depth cues. Recall that for a stereo system with baseline b and an inference algorithm that estimates disparity Δx, depth is measured as

$$Z = \frac{b\mu_s}{\Delta x}, \tag{29}$$

with first-order sensitivity to the disparity estimate

$$\left| \frac{dZ}{d(\Delta x)} \right| = \left| \frac{b\mu_s}{-(\Delta x)^2} \right| = \frac{Z^2}{b\mu_s}. \tag{30}$$

Similarly, for a depth from defocus sensor with aperture radius A and an algorithm that estimates blur radius $\tilde{A}$, the sensitivity of depth to error in $\tilde{A}$ is

$$Z = \frac{\mu_f \mu_s A}{\mu_f \tilde{A} + \mu_s A}, \tag{31}$$

$$\left| \frac{dZ}{d\tilde{A}} \right| = \left| \frac{-\mu_f^2 \mu_s A}{(\mu_f \tilde{A} + \mu_s A)^2} \right| = \frac{Z^2}{A\mu_s}. \tag{32}$$

These equations show a fundamental similarity between stereo and depth from defocus, in which the baseline and aperture size are analogous.

For a toy model of focal flow, we consider images of a sinusoidal texture blurred by a normalized Gaussian. We assume the texture has frequency ω_0, unit amplitude, and arbitrary phase and orientation. Then, the image captured at time t has frequency ω and amplitude B, which are determined by depth:

$$\omega(t) = Z\omega_0/\mu_s, \tag{33}$$

$$B(t) = \iint \frac{e^{-\frac{x^2}{4\Sigma^2 \sigma^2}}}{4\pi \Sigma^2 \sigma^2} \cos(\omega(t)x) dx dy = e^{-\Sigma^2 \omega_0^2 \left(\frac{Z - \mu_f}{\mu_f} \right)^2}. \tag{34}$$

Depth can be measured from image amplitude, frequency, and their derivatives:

$$Z = \frac{\mu_f}{1 + \left(\frac{\mu_f}{\mu_s \Sigma} \right)^2 \frac{\dot{B}}{2B\omega\dot{\omega}}}. \tag{35}$$

When image quantities $(\omega, \dot{\omega}, B, \dot{B})$ are measured within error bounds $(\epsilon_\omega, \epsilon_{\dot{\omega}}, \epsilon_B, \epsilon_{\dot{B}})$, a simple propagation of uncertainty bounds the depth error ϵ_Z:

$$\epsilon_Z \leq \sqrt{\left(\frac{\partial Z}{\partial \omega}\right)^2 \epsilon_\omega^2 + \left(\frac{\partial Z}{\partial \dot{\omega}}\right)^2 \epsilon_{\dot{\omega}}^2 + \left(\frac{\partial Z}{\partial B}\right)^2 \epsilon_B + \left(\frac{\partial Z}{\partial B_1}\right)^2 \epsilon_{\dot{B}}^2} \tag{36}$$

$$= \frac{Z|Z - \mu_f|}{\mu_f} \sqrt{\frac{\epsilon_\omega^2}{\omega^2} + \frac{\epsilon_{\dot{\omega}}^2}{\dot{\omega}^2} + \frac{\epsilon_B^2}{B^2} + \frac{\epsilon_{\dot{B}}^2}{\dot{B}^2}}. \tag{37}$$

This combination of error terms suggests that accuracy in measuring either brightness or spatial frequency can be used to mitigate error in the other quantity. This presents a novel trade-off between bit depth and spatial resolution when selecting a photosensor.

Depending on the error model, the radicand in expression (37) could introduce additional scene dependencies, but in the simplest case, it is constant and focal flow is immediately comparable to stereo and depth from defocus. Just as the sensitivity of those measurements goes as depth squared, we see that focal flow measurements are sensitive to object distance from both the camera and the focal plane through the $Z|Z - \mu_f|$ term. The focal flow analogue to aperture size or baseline in this scenario is the ratio of focal depth to sensor distance.

4   Prototype and Evaluation of Non-idealities

In theory, when an ideal thin lens camera with an infinitely-wide Gaussian aperture filter observes a single moving, front-parallel, textured plane, there is a unique solution $v \in \mathbb{R}^4$ to the system of per-pixel linear focal flow constraints (Eq. (18)), and this uniquely resolves the scene depth $Z(v)$ and velocity $(\dot{X}, \dot{Y}, \dot{Z})(v)$ through Eqs. (19, 20). In practice, a physical instantiation of a focal flow sensor will deviate from the idealized model, and there will only be approximate solutions $\tilde{v} \in \mathbb{R}^4$ that can produce errors in depth and velocity.

We expect two main deviations from the idealized model. First, thick lenses have optical aberrations and a finite extent, making it impossible to create ideal Gaussian blur kernels that scale exactly with depth. Second, image derivatives must be approximated by finite differences between noisy photosensor values. We assess the impacts of both of these effects using the prototype in Fig. 2. Based on 1"-diameter optics, it includes an $f=100\,\mathrm{mm}$ planar-convex lens, a monochromatic camera (Grasshopper GS3-U3-23S6M-C, Point Grey Research), and an adjustable-length lens tube. The aperture side of the sensor supports various configurations, including an adjustable aperture diaphragm and the optional inclusion of a Gaussian apodizing filter (NDYR20B, Thorlabs) adjacent to the planar face of the lens. A complete list of parts can be found in [31].

Measurement Algorithm. For all results, we produce depth and velocity measurements using three frames from a temporal sequence, $I(x, y, t_i), i \in \{1, 2, 3\}$. To emulate a lower-noise sensor, each frame is created as the average of ten

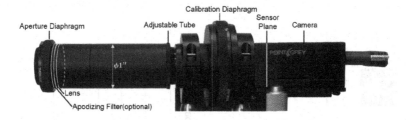

Fig. 2. Prototype focal flow sensor. The configurable aperture has a variable diaphragm the optional inclusion of a Gaussian apodizing filter. An adjustable lens tube enables varying pairs of focal and sensor distances (μ_s, μ_f).

shots from the camera, unless otherwise noted. We use temporal central differences, $I_t(x,y) \approx 1/2\,(I(x,y,t_3) - I(x,y,t_1))$, and spatial difference kernels $D_x = (-1/2, 0, 1/2)$, $D_{xx} = D_x * D_x$, and likewise in y, convolved with the middle frame $I(x,y,t_2)$. To densely estimate the scene vectors $v(x,y)$, we aggregate the per-pixel linear constraints over a square window into the matrix equation $Av = b$, and take the least-squares solution as the measurement for the central pixel. Similar to optical flow, this can be implemented efficiently by computing, storing, and inverting the normal equations $A^T Av = A^T b$ at all pixels in parallel. A reference implementation is included in [31].

This measurement process requires knowing the image sensor's principal point (the origin of the coordinate system for x and y in Eq. (18)). We set it to the central pixel during alignment. We also find that numerical stability is improved by pre-normalizing the spatial coordinates $x \leftarrow x/c, y \leftarrow y/c$ for some constant c (we use $c = 10^4$). This pre-normalization and the use finite differences lead to depth and velocity values that, if computed naively with Eqs. (19, 20), are scaled by an unknown constant. We accommodate these and other non-idealities through the following off-line calibration procedure.

Calibration. Mapping a scene vector v to depth and velocity requires only two calibrated values: the filter width parameter Σ, and sensor distance μ_s (which, along with the lens' focal length $f = 100$ mm, determines the object focal distance μ_f). Since blur kernels often deviate substantially from Gaussians, we optimize the calibration parameters directly with respect to depth accuracy. We mount a textured plane on a high-precision translation stage in front of the sensor, carefully align it to be normal to the optical axis, and use images of many translations to optimize the parameters μ_s and Σ. Details are included in [31]. To ensure that the system generalizes over texture patterns and focal depths, all reported results use textures and sensor distances μ_s that differ from those used in calibration.

Calibration must be repeated when the aperture is reconfigured, such as when inserting an apodizing filter or adjusting the diaphragm. When the effective blur kernels change, so does the optimal effective width Σ. But for a fixed aperture, we find that the sensor distance μ_s can be adjusted without re-calibrating Σ.

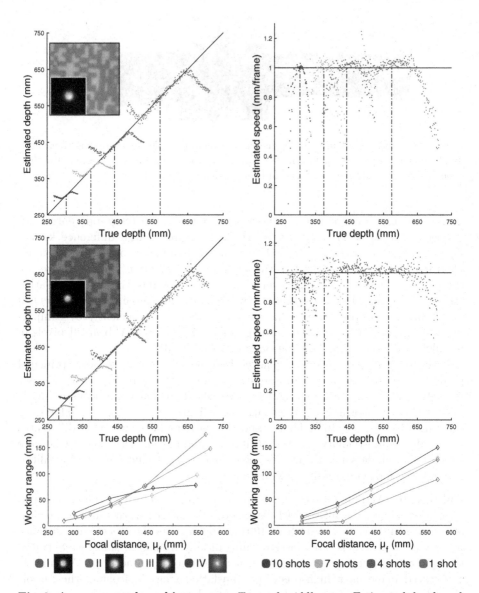

Fig. 3. Accuracy and working range. *Top and middle rows*: Estimated depth and speed versus true depth for two aperture settings: apodizing filter (*top*) and open diaphragm (*middle*). Solid black lines are true depth and speed. Insets are sample image and PSF. Colors are separate trials with different focal distances μ_f, marked by dashed vertical lines. Depth interval for which depth error is less than 1 % of μ_f defines the working range. *Bottom left*: Sample PSFs, and working range versus focal distance, for aperture settings: (I) diaphragm ⌀4.5 mm, no filter; (II) diaphragm open, with filter; (III) diaphragm ⌀8.5 mm, no filter; (IV) diaphragm ⌀25.4 mm, no filter. *Bottom right*: Working range for distinct noise levels, controlled by number of averaged shots.

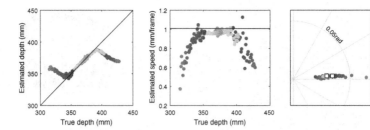

Fig. 4. Velocity. Measured depth, speed, and 3D direction $(\dot{X}, \dot{Y}, \dot{Z})/\|(\dot{X}, \dot{Y}, \dot{Z})\|$ versus true depth, with markers colored by true depth. Directions shown by orthographic projection to XY-plane, where the view direction is the origin. Ground truth is black lines for depth and speed, and white squares for direction. (Two ground truth directions result from remounting a translation stage to gain sufficient travel.)

Results. Figures 3 and 4 show performance for different apertures and noise levels. Accuracy is determined using a textured front-parallel plane whose ground truth position and velocity are precisely controlled by a translation stage. In each case, the measurement algorithm is applied to a 201×201 window around the image center. The top and middle rows of Fig. 3 compare the measured depth Z and speed $\|(\dot{X}, \dot{Y}, \dot{Z})\|$ to ground truth, indicated by solid black lines. Speed is measured in units of millimeter per video frame (mm/frame). Different colors in these plots represent experiments with different focus distances μ_f, corresponding to different lengths of the adjustable lens tube. We show measurements taken both with an apodizing filter (and open diaphragm) and without it (with diaphragm closed to about $\varnothing 4.5$ mm). In both cases, the inset point spread functions reveal a deviation from the Gaussian ideal, but the approximate solutions to the linear constraint equations still provide useful depth information over ranges that are roughly centered at, and proportional to, the focus distances.

The bottom of Fig. 3 shows the effects that aperture configuration and noise level have on the working range, defined as the range of depths for which the absolute difference between the measured depth and the true depth is less than 1% of the focus distance μ_f. The prototype achieves a working range of more than 15 cm. Figure 4 shows both the measured speed and the measured 3D direction of a moving texture. Comprehensive results for different textures, aperture configurations, and noise levels can be found in [31].

Figure 5 shows full-field depths maps measured by the system. Each is obtained by applying the reconstruction algorithm in parallel to overlapping windows. We used 71×71 windows for the top row and 241×241 windows for the bottom. We do not use multiple window sizes or any form of spatial regularization; we simply apply the reconstruction algorithm to every window independently. Even using this simple approach, the depths map are consistent with the scene's true shape, even when the shape is not front-parallel. The Matlab code used to generate these depth maps can be found in [31]. It executes in 6.5 s on a 2.93 GHz processor with Intel Xeon X5570 CPU.

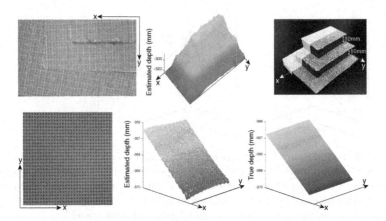

Fig. 5. Depth maps for two different scenes. From left to right: one frame from an input three-frame image sequence; per-pixel depth measured by independent focal flow reconstruction in overlapping square windows; and true scene shape for comparison.

5   Discussion

By combining blur and differential motion in a way that mitigates their individual weaknesses, focal flow enables a passive, monocular sensor that provides depth and 3D velocity from a simple, small-patch measurement algorithm. While the focal flow theory is developed using Gaussian blur kernels and front-parallel scene patches, we find in practice that it can provide useful scene information for a much broader class of aperture configurations, and some slanted scene planes.

The prototype described in this paper currently has some limitations. Its simple measurement algorithm uses naive derivative filters and performs independent measurement in every local patch. As such, it is overly sensitive to noise and requires high-contrast texture to be everywhere in the scene. Performance can likely be improved by including noise suppression and dynamical filtering that combines the available depth and velocity values. At the expense of additional computation, performance could also be improved by adapting techniques from optical flow and stereo, such as outlier-rejection, multi-scale reasoning, and spatial regularization that can interpolate depth in textureless regions.

Another way to extract depth with an unactuated, monocular sensor is single-shot depth from defocus with a binary coded aperture (e.g., [18,19,35]), where one explicitly deconvolves each image patch with a discrete set of per-depth blur kernels and selects the most "natural" result. Compared to focal flow, this provides a larger working range, but lower depth precision and a much greater computational burden. For example, a simulated comparison to [18] showed its working range to be at least four times larger, but its precision to be more than seven times lower and its computation time to be at least a hundred times greater [31]. The relative efficiency of focal flow suggests its suitability for small, low-power platforms, particularly those with well-defined working ranges and regular ambient motion, either from the platform or the scene.

Acknowledgments. We would like to thank J Zachary Gaslowitz and Ioannis Gkioulekas for helpful discussion. This work was supported by a gift from Texas Instruments Inc. and by the National Science Foundation under awards No. IIS-1212928 and 1514154 and Graduate Research Fellowship No. DGE1144152 to E.A.

References

1. Raghavendra, C.S., Sivalingam, K.M., Znati, T.: Wireless Sensor Networks. Springer, Heidelberg (2006)
2. Humber, J.S., Hyslop, A., Chinn, M.: Experimental validation of wide-field integration methods for autonomous navigation. In: Intelligent Robots and Systems (IROS) (2007)
3. Duhamel, P.E.J., Perez-Arancibia, C.O., Barrows, G.L., Wood, R.J.: Biologically inspired optical-flow sensing for altitude control of flapping-wing microrobots. IEEE/ASME Trans. Mechatron. **18**(2), 556–568 (2013)
4. Floreano, D., Zufferey, J.C., Srinivasan, M.V., Ellington, C.: Flying Insects and Robots. Springer, Heidelberg (2009)
5. Koppal, S.J., Gkioulekas, I., Zickler, T., Barrows, G.L.: Wide-angle micro sensors for vision on a tight budget. In: Computer Vision and Pattern Recognition (CVPR) (2011)
6. Horn, B.K., Fang, Y., Masaki, I.: Time to contact relative to a planar surface. In: Intelligent Vehicles Symposium (IV) (2007)
7. Horn, B.K., Schunck, B.G.: Determining optical flow. In: 1981 Technical Symposium East, International Society for Optics and Photonics (1981)
8. Lee, D.N.: A theory of visual control of braking based on information about time-to-collision. Perception **5**, 437–59 (1976)
9. Horn, B.K., Fang, Y., Masaki, I.: Hierarchical framework for direct gradient-based time-to-contact estimation. In: Intelligent Vehicles Symposium (IV) (2009)
10. Grossmann, P.: Depth from focus. Pattern Recogn. Lett. **5**(1), 63–69 (1987)
11. Pentland, A.P.: A new sense for depth of field. Pattern Anal. Mach. Intell. **9**(4), 523–531 (1987)
12. Subbarao, M., Surya, G.: Depth from defocus: a spatial domain approach. Int. J. Comput. Vis. **13**(3), 271–294 (1994)
13. Rajagopalan, A., Chaudhuri, S.: Optimal selection of camera parameters for recovery of depth from defocused images. In: Computer Vision and Pattern Recognition (CVPR) (1997)
14. Watanabe, M., Nayar, S.K.: Rational filters for passive depth from defocus. Int. J. Comput. Vis. **27**(3), 203–225 (1998)
15. Zhou, C., Lin, S., Nayar, S.: Coded aperture pairs for depth from defocus. In: International Conference on Computer Vision (ICCV) (2009)
16. Levin, A.: Analyzing depth from coded aperture sets. In: Daniilidis, K., Maragos, P., Paragios, N. (eds.) ECCV 2010, Part I. LNCS, vol. 6311, pp. 214–227. Springer, Heidelberg (2010)
17. Zhou, C., Lin, S., Nayar, S.K.: Coded aperture pairs for depth from defocus and defocus deblurring. Int. J. Comput. Vis. **93**(1), 53–72 (2011)
18. Levin, A., Fergus, R., Durand, F., Freeman, W.T.: Image and depth from a conventional camera with a coded aperture. In: ACM Transactions on Graphics (TOG) (2007)

19. Veeraraghavan, A., Raskar, R., Agrawal, A., Mohan, A., Tumblin, J.: Dappled photography: mask enhanced cameras for heterodyned light fields and coded aperture refocusing. In: ACM Transactions on Graphics (TOG) (2007)

20. Chakrabarti, A., Zickler, T.: Depth and deblurring from a spectrally-varying depth-of-field. In: Fitzgibbon, A., Lazebnik, S., Perona, P., Sato, Y., Schmid, C. (eds.) ECCV 2012, Part V. LNCS, vol. 7576, pp. 648–661. Springer, Heidelberg (2012)

21. Farid, H., Simoncelli, E.P.: Range estimation by optical differentiation. J. Opt. Soc. Am. A 15(7), 1777–1786 (1998)

22. Myles, Z., da Vitoria Lobo, N.: Recovering affine motion and defocus blur simultaneously. Pattern Anal. Mach. Intell. 20(6), 652–658 (1998)

23. Favaro, P., Burger, M., Soatto, S.: Scene and motion reconstruction from defocused and motion-blurred images via anisotropic diffusion. In: Pajdla, T., Matas, J.G. (eds.) ECCV 2004. LNCS, vol. 3021, pp. 257–269. Springer, Heidelberg (2004)

24. Lin, H.Y., Chang, C.H.: Depth from motion and defocus blur. Opt. Eng. 45(12), 127201–127201 (2006)

25. Seitz, S.M., Baker, S.: Filter flow. In: International Conference on Computer Vision (ICCV) (2009)

26. Paramanand, C., Rajagopalan, A.N.: Depth from motion and optical blur with an unscented Kalman filter. IEEE Trans. Image Process. 21(5), 2798–2811 (2012)

27. Sellent, A., Favaro, P.: Coded aperture flow. In: Jiang, X., Hornegger, J., Koch, R. (eds.) GCPR 2014. LNCS, vol. 8753, pp. 582–592. Springer, Heidelberg (2014)

28. Rajagopalan, A., Chaudhuri, S., Mudenagudi, U.: Depth estimation and image restoration using defocused stereo pairs. Pattern Anal. Mach. Intell. 26(11), 1521–1525 (2004)

29. Tao, M., Hadap, S., Malik, J., Ramamoorthi, R.: Depth from combining defocus and correspondence using light-field cameras. In: International Conference on Computer Vision (ICCV) (2013)

30. Rudin, W.: Functional Analysis. McGraw-Hill, New York (1991)

31. Alexander, E., Guo, Q., Koppal, S., Gortler, S., Zickler, T.: Focal flow: supporting material. Technical report TR-01-16, School of Engineering and Applied Science, Harvard University (2016)

32. Bracewell, R.N.: Strip integration in radio astronomy. Aust. J. Phys. 9(2), 198–217 (1956)

33. Ng, R.: Fourier slice photography. In: ACM Transactions on Graphics (TOG) (2005)

34. Schechner, Y.Y., Kiryati, N.: Depth from defocus vs. stereo: how different really are they? Int. J. Comput. Vis. 39(2), 141–162 (2000)

35. Tai, Y.W., Brown, M.S.: Single image defocus map estimation using local contrast prior. In: International Conference on Image Processing (ICIP) (2009)

Poster Session 4

An Evaluation of Computational Imaging Techniques for Heterogeneous Inverse Scattering

Ioannis Gkioulekas[1]([✉]), Anat Levin[2], and Todd Zickler[1]

[1] Harvard University, Cambridge, USA
igkiou@seas.harvard.edu
[2] Weizmann Institute of Science, Rehovot, Israel

Abstract. Inferring internal scattering parameters for general, heterogeneous materials, remains a challenging inverse problem. Its difficulty arises from the complex way in which scattering materials interact with light, as well as the very high dimensionality of the material space implied by heterogeneity. The recent emergence of diverse computational imaging techniques, together with the widespread availability of computing power, present a renewed opportunity for tackling this problem. We take first steps in this direction, by deriving theoretical results, developing an algorithmic framework, and performing quantitative evaluations for the problem of heterogeneous inverse scattering from simulated measurements of different computational imaging configurations.

Keywords: Inverse scattering · Computational imaging

1 Introduction

We consider the heterogeneous inverse scattering problem, where light can be controllably injected and measured at the boundary of a volume, and where we want to infer the scattering material parameters that vary internally. In the general form that we consider, this is an extreme multi-path problem. The volume can include parts of varying thickness, so that low-order scattering, mid-order scattering, and high-order scattering can all contribute substantially to the measurements; and the internal material varies spatially in terms of both absorption and angular scattering, so that the unknown variables number in the hundreds of thousands. Finding reliable solutions to this general problem would extend three-dimensional imaging to many types of turbid volumes (deep tissues, many gemstones, thick smoke and clouds) that cannot yet be accurately measured by any non-invasive, non-destructive means.

Despite decades of work on inverse scattering, the problem has yet to be considered at this level of generality and scale. But the growth of processing power and the accelerating development of computational imaging techniques, which allow unprecedented control and measurement of light at the boundary, are making this previously-intractable problem more interesting.

© Springer International Publishing AG 2016
B. Leibe et al. (Eds.): ECCV 2016, Part III, LNCS 9907, pp. 685–701, 2016.
DOI: 10.1007/978-3-319-46487-9_42

The most important questions to answer about the general heterogeneous inverse scattering problem are how to determine when a set of measurements is sufficient to reconstruct the internal volume; what internal ambiguities exist in the absence of sufficient measurements; and how to formulate and solve the massive optimization problem. While we do no provide definite answers to these questions in this paper, we make progress in several directions.

First, we describe a mathematical model of the problem that encompasses the types of measurements that are obtainable using almost any form of computational imaging, including structured lighting, spatial probing, and transient imaging. Second, we use this model to derive theoretical results about aspects of internal material information that are un-recoverable, and measurement configurations that can reduce internal ambiguities among the material parameters. Third, we generalize recent optimization frameworks [14,30], which are based on Monte Carlo rendering and stochastic gradient descent, to accommodate our more general material and measurement spaces. Fourth and finally, we use simulations to evaluate the utility of different computational imaging configurations for several heterogeneous inverse scattering problems. Our code and supplementary material are available at the project page [1].

2   Related Work

Inverse Scattering. Inverse radiative transport is studied in graphics, physics, chemistry, and biomedical sciences. A review can be found in [4]. Existing algorithms for volumetric reconstruction of scattering materials can be roughly classified into three categories. Methods based on the *diffusion* approximation consider optically thick media where high-order scattering is dominant. This allows for simpler inference and has been used for the acquisition of both homogeneous [9,28,39] and heterogemenous materials [46]. However, it also introduces ambiguities between different scattering parameters [49,51]. At the other extreme, methods based on the *single scattering* approximation assume that the unknown medium is so optically thin that all photons scatter only once. This allows directly measuring scattering parameters of media such as smoke and thin or dilutable liquids [12,17,20,34]. A third class of methods seek to use all orders of scattering when solving appearance matching objectives to infer scattering parameters [2,14,30,32,42]. Our method falls in this category, by extending the algorithms of [14,30] to apply to general heterogemenous media and different types of imaging techniques. Orthogonal to the above are techniques that, instead of volumetric reconstructions, recover surface-based descriptions of scattering materials (BSSRDF), which can be spatially-varying [8,10,15,41].

Computational Imaging. Different imaging techniques can be categorized as different ways to decompose photon contributions. *Pathlength decomposition* techniques, also referred to as *transient imaging*, separate photons in terms of the distance they travel from source to camera, and have been implemented using combinations of pulsed lasers with ultra-fast cameras [45,47,48], time-of-flight sensors [21,22,29,37], and optical coherence tomography [13,24].

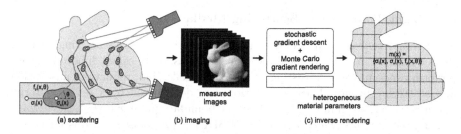

Fig. 1. (a) Photons traveling inside scattering materials perform random walks that depend on the material parameters. (b) Computational imaging techniques capture measurements of such materials by collecting different subsets of photons, depending on the paths they follow. (c) We present an inverse rendering algorithm that uses such measurements to recover the spatially-varying scattering material parameters.

Spatial probing techniques use camera-projector systems [36,38] or interferometry [13] to decompose photons in terms of the endpoints of their paths. Techniques from the two categories have been combined into imaging systems that simultaneously decompose photons in terms of both pathlength and endpoints [13,37]. Finally, structured light systems can be used to separate photons based on the number of times they bounce, into a direct (single bounce) and global (multiple bounces) component [18,35,43]. With respect to inverse scattering applications, pathlength decomposition has been used together with the diffusion approximation for measuring heterogeneous tissues [3,5]; whereas direct-global separation has been combined with single-scattering analysis to simplify appearance matching problems for scattering materials [33]. In our work, we describe all these types of decompositions in a unified theoretical framework that allows us to utilize them for heterogeneous inverse scattering, while accounting for all orders of scattering.

3   Theoretical Background

We begin with background on the *radiative transfer* framework for describing light in scattering materials. We use lower-case bold letters for points $\boldsymbol{x}$ in the Euclidean space $\mathbb{R}^3$ and directions $\boldsymbol{\omega}$ in the unit sphere $\mathbb{S}^2$. We use capital-case bold letters for position-direction pairs $\boldsymbol{X} = (\boldsymbol{x}, \boldsymbol{\omega})$, and the notation $\boldsymbol{x}\,(\boldsymbol{X})$ and $\boldsymbol{\omega}\,(\boldsymbol{X})$ to refer to the position or direction component of such pairs, respectively.

We assume that $\mathcal{M}$, a subset of $\mathbb{R}^3$, is occupied by a scattering medium with uniform index of refraction η, corresponding to speed of light $c = c_o/\eta$ inside the medium. We use $\partial\mathcal{M}$ for the boundary of $\mathcal{M}$, and at every boundary point $\boldsymbol{x} \in \partial\mathcal{M}$ we use $\hat{\boldsymbol{n}}\,(\boldsymbol{x})$ for the outward normal vector. We also define sets $\Gamma_i = \left\{(\boldsymbol{x}, \boldsymbol{\omega}) \in \partial\mathcal{M} \times \mathbb{S}^2 : \boldsymbol{\omega} \cdot \hat{\boldsymbol{n}}\,(\boldsymbol{x}) < 0\right\}$ and $\Gamma_o = \left\{(\boldsymbol{x}, \boldsymbol{\omega}) \in \partial\mathcal{M} \times \mathbb{S}^2 : \boldsymbol{\omega} \cdot \hat{\boldsymbol{n}}\,(\boldsymbol{x}) > 0\right\}$ of position-direction pairs on the boundary $\partial\mathcal{M}$ pointing in or out, respectively.

3.1 Light Transport in Scattering Media

In the radiative transfer framework, light propagation inside a scattering medium $\mathcal{M}$ is described in terms of idealized light particles, often called "photons", that perform random walks consisting of stochastic reflection, refraction, absorption and scattering events. These interactions are determined by a set of material parameters, as shown in Fig. 1(a): At every boundary point $x \in \partial\mathcal{M}$, the *bidirectional scattering distribution function* (BSDF) $f_s(x, \omega_o, \omega_i)$ controls refraction and reflection events. At every interior point $x \in \mathcal{M}$, the medium is characterized by the scattering parameters $m(x) = \{\sigma_a(x), \sigma_s(x), f_p(x, \cos\theta)\}$. The *scattering coefficient* $\sigma_s(x)$ and *absorption coefficient* $\sigma_a(x)$ determine the amount of light that is scattered or absorbed, respectively, at every scattering event. The *extinction coefficient* $\sigma_t(x) = \sigma_s(x) + \sigma_a(x)$ determines the spatial frequency of such events. The *phase function* $f_p(x, \cos\theta)$ determines the amount of light that scatters towards direction ω_o relative to the incident direction ω_i. As is usual, we make the assumption that the phase function is cylindrically-symmetric and invariant to rotations of ω_i, and is therefore a function of only $\cos\theta = \omega_i \cdot \omega_o$.

When a temporally-varying light source is applied at $\partial\mathcal{M}$, the photon random walks are described by the *time-dependent radiative transfer equation* (RTE),

$$\frac{1}{c}\frac{\partial L(x, \omega, t)}{\partial t} + \omega \cdot \nabla L(x, \omega, t) = -\sigma_t(x) L(x, \omega, t)$$
$$+ \sigma_s(x) \int_{\mathbb{S}^2} f_p(x, \omega \cdot \psi) L(x, \psi, t) \, d\psi, \quad (1)$$

subject to BSDF-dependent boundary conditions on Γ_i and Γ_o [7,25]. Note that more common in computer vision and graphics is the stationary form of the RTE, where radiance L is time-independent and there is no time derivative. We discuss the relationship between the two forms in the supplement [1].

The *time-dependent Green's function* $\mathcal{T}_m(X_o, X_i, t)$ is the solution of the RTE at $X_o \in \Gamma_o$ and time t, for an input pulse of infinitesimal duration $\delta(t)$ and unit radiance at $X_i \in \Gamma_i$. We use the subscript m to denote explicitly that $\mathcal{T}_m$ depends on the material parameters. The Green's function can also be defined inside the medium, but we restrict its point-direction arguments X_o, X_i to Γ_o, Γ_i, as we assume that we can only inject and measure light at the medium's boundary. For the same reason, we omit volumetric sources from Eq. (1).

The change of variables $\tau = ct$ converts time to (optical) pathlength. Then, the resulting *pathlength-resolved Green's function* $\mathcal{T}_m(X_o, X_i, \tau)$ is equal to the radiance produced by accumulating contributions only from photons that travel paths starting at boundary point $x(X_i)$ with direction $\omega(X_i)$, ending at boundary point $x(X_o)$ with direction $\omega(X_o)$, and having total length τ. The pathlength-resolved Green's function $\mathcal{T}_m(X_o, X_i, \tau)$ is the continuous equivalent of the pathlength-resolved *light transport matrix* [13,37]. In the sequel, we use the terms Green's function and light transport matrix interchangeably.

3.2 Imaging Scattering Media

The measurements produced using different imaging techniques can be described as different ways to sample the light transport matrix. Specifically, we can express them in terms of a *sampling function* $W : \Gamma_o \times \Gamma_i \times \mathbb{R}_{\geq 0} \to \mathbb{R}_{\geq 0}$, as,

$$\mathcal{S}\left(\mathcal{T}_m, W\right) \triangleq \int_{\Gamma_o} \int_{\Gamma_i} \int_0^\infty W\left(\mathbf{X}_o, \mathbf{X}_i, \tau\right) \mathcal{T}_m\left(\mathbf{X}_o, \mathbf{X}_i, \tau\right) \, \mathrm{d}\tau \, \mathrm{d}\mathbf{X}_i \, \mathrm{d}\mathbf{X}_o. \qquad (2)$$

In this equation, we assume that $\mathcal{T}_m$ and W are regular enough to allow changing the integration order. The sampling function W can typically be decomposed into three components: First, an *emittance function* $W_i : \Gamma_i \to \mathbb{R}_{\geq 0}$, which is non-zero on a subset of the inward boundary Γ_i and describes the incident illumination. Second, an *importance function* $W_o : \Gamma_o \to \mathbb{R}_{\geq 0}$, which is non-zero on a subset of the outward boundary Γ_o and corresponds to the rays accumulated by the sensor. Third, a *pathlength sampling function* $W_\tau : \mathbb{R}_{\geq 0} \to \mathbb{R}_{\geq 0}$, which is non-zero only for a subset of pathlength values. Then,

$$W\left(\mathbf{X}_o, \mathbf{X}_i, \tau\right) = W_o\left(\mathbf{X}_o\right) W_i\left(\mathbf{X}_i\right) W_\tau\left(\tau\right). \qquad (3)$$

Steady-State Imaging. Conventional imaging sensors measure all photons, regardless of the distance they have traveled inside the medium. This corresponds to using a pathlength sampling function $W_\tau\left(\tau\right) = 1$, for all values of τ.

Pathlength Decomposition. Pathlength decomposition discriminates between photons based on the pathlength they travel (Fig. 1(b): low-saturation, short paths versus high-saturation, long paths). Ideally, they sample pathlength slices of the light transport matrix, $W_\tau\left(\tau\right) = \delta\left(\tau - \tau_c\right)$, for some $\tau_c > 0$. Real systems instead have finite pathlength resolution, with $W_\tau\left(\tau\right)$ being, say, a Gaussian or a square function. Typically, pathlength decomposition techniques densely capture multiple such pathlength slices, each centered at a different τ_c.

Spatial Probing. Cameras typically have multiple sensor elements (pixels) that capture parallel sets of measurements $\{\mathcal{S}\left(\mathcal{T}_m, W_o^p \cdot W_i \cdot W_\tau\right), p = 1, \ldots, P\}$, with P the number of pixels. Conventionally, the measurements in such a set use different importance functions W_o^p and a common illumination W_i; but an alternative is to use spatial probing techniques that allow different pixels on the same sensor to capture measurements corresponding to different importance-emittance pairs, $\{\mathcal{S}\left(\mathcal{T}_m, W_o^p \cdot W_i^p \cdot W_\tau\right), p = 1, \ldots, P\}$. With reference to Fig. 1(b), this allows the orange and blue camera pixels to only measure photons that begin at the orange and blue source pixels, respectively. Note that equivalent measurements can be obtained by capturing multiple images sequentially, each time using a different source W_i^p and discarding unneeded pixels. Therefore, rather than providing a fundamentally different way to sample the light transport matrix, spatial probing allows reducing acquisition time through temporal multiplexing.

Types of sources. It is useful to define an *ideal source* that emits an ideally collimated and narrow beam, corresponding to emittance

$$W_i(\mathbf{X}_i) = \delta\left(\mathbf{x}\left(\mathbf{X}_i\right) - \mathbf{x}_l\right) \delta\left(\boldsymbol{\omega}\left(\mathbf{X}_i\right) - \boldsymbol{\omega}_l\right), \qquad (4)$$

for some $(\boldsymbol{x}_l, \boldsymbol{\omega}_l) \in \Gamma_i$. Note that such a source cannot be realized physically: The wave nature of light implies that a source cannot be perfectly concentrated in both the spatial and angular domains simultaneously [16]; and any source ideally concentrated in either domain would have zero etendue and power [6].

The utility of ideal sources lies in their convenience for analysis [4], and for synthesizing other, more realistic sources. For instance, a perfectly collimated area source can be created by combining ideal sources with different $\boldsymbol{x}_l$ but sharing the same $\boldsymbol{\omega}_l$. A diffuse point source is created by combining ideal sources that share the same $\boldsymbol{x}_l$, for each $\boldsymbol{\omega}_l \in \mathbb{S}^2$. Finally, a physical source with non-zero spatio-angular extent $E_i \subset \Gamma_i$ can be created as a weighted combination of ideal sources for each $(\boldsymbol{x}_l, \boldsymbol{\omega}_l) \in E_i$, with the weights depending on intrinsic (source power distribution) and extrinsic (geometry) factors.

Types of Cameras. Similar to the ideal source, we can define an *ideal sensor element* with an importance function

$$W_o(\boldsymbol{X}_o) = \delta\left(\boldsymbol{x}\left(\boldsymbol{X}_o\right) - \boldsymbol{x}_s\right) \delta\left(\boldsymbol{\omega}\left(\boldsymbol{X}_o\right) - \boldsymbol{\omega}_s\right), \tag{5}$$

for some $(\boldsymbol{x}_s, \boldsymbol{\omega}_s) \in \Gamma_o$. Arrays of such sensors can be used to construct different types of cameras. An *orthographic camera* has multiple ideal sensor elements, each with a different $\boldsymbol{x}_s$ but all sharing the same $\boldsymbol{\omega}_s$. As with sources, real sensors cannot be perfectly concentrated in either the spatial or angular domain, but can still be expressed as weighted combinations of ideal sensor elements. Simultaneously using an ideal sensor, source, and pathlength decomposition corresponds to sampling a single value $\mathcal{T}_m\left((\boldsymbol{x}_s, \boldsymbol{\omega}_s), (\boldsymbol{x}_l, \boldsymbol{\omega}_l), \tau_c\right)$ of the light transport matrix.

4 Imaging Design

Given the range of imaging options available, we discuss theoretical results and empirical observations that can be used to guide the design of imaging systems for inverse scattering applications. All proofs are shown in the supplement.

Local Ambiguities. In steady-state imaging, there exist *similarity relations* which, under certain conditions, allow changing the scattering parameters at a point $\boldsymbol{x} \in \mathcal{M}$ without changing the radiance at that point [49,51]. We prove that these similarity relations also hold for pathlength-decomposed measurements.

Lemma 1. *Let* $\{a_{n,l}(\boldsymbol{x}, \tau), n > 0, -n \le l \le n\}$ *be the coefficients of the spherical-harmonics expansion of the solution* $L(\boldsymbol{x}, \boldsymbol{\omega}, \tau)$ *of Eq.* (1) *at some point* $\boldsymbol{x} \in \mathcal{M}$, *and* $\{f_{p,n}(\boldsymbol{x}), n > 0\}$ *the coefficients of the Legendre expansion of* f_p *at that point. If there exists* $N > 0$ *such that* $a_{n,l}(\boldsymbol{x}, \tau) = 0$ *for all* $n > N$, *then two materials* m, m^* *will produce equal values* $L(\boldsymbol{x}, \boldsymbol{\omega}, \tau)$ *if, for* $1 \le n \le N$,

$$\sigma_a(\boldsymbol{x}) = \sigma_a^*(\boldsymbol{x}), \tag{6}$$

$$\sigma_s(\boldsymbol{x})\left(1 - f_{p,n}(\boldsymbol{x})\right) = \sigma_s^*(\boldsymbol{x})\left(1 - f_{p,n}^*(\boldsymbol{x})\right). \tag{7}$$

These similarity relations are *local*, as they describe ambiguities at one point $\boldsymbol{x} \in \mathcal{M}$. To reduce these ambiguities, Lemma 1 suggests maximizing the angular

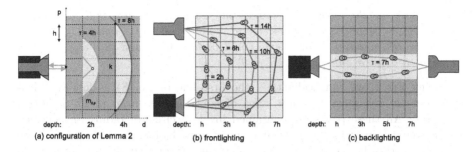

Fig. 2. (a) Configuration used for Lemma 2. (b) Frontlighting allows decomposing the inverse scattering problem into sub-problems for depth-wise layers, where at each layer the material parameters of lower-depth layers are known. (c) Backlighting allows measuring deep layers at shorter pathlengths τ, and thus higher SNR, than frontlighting.

frequency of $L(\boldsymbol{x}, \boldsymbol{\omega}, \tau)$ throughout the medium. For a given shape of $\mathcal{M}$, the only way to control this is through the incident illumination $W_i(\boldsymbol{X}_i)$, which provides a lower bound to the angular frequency of $L(\boldsymbol{x}, \boldsymbol{\omega}, \tau)$ by way of spherical convolution with the phase function in the RTE (1) acting as a low-pass filter. The best light sources will have high angular and spatial frequencies, such as the ideal sources of Eq. (4), or collimated area sources with high-frequency spatial profiles. These types of sources already feature prominently in previous theoretical and empirical work [14,15,33].

Non-local Ambiguities. On top of local ambiguities, a heterogeneous medium can exhibit *non-local* ambiguities involving material parameters at different points $\boldsymbol{x}$. In the following, we argue that pathlength decomposition combined with a specific input-output geometry can help reduce such non-local ambiguities. For this, we consider the scene in Fig. 2(a): A cubic volume is discretized into h-sized voxels indexed by coordinates $[d, p]$. We call the coordinate d the *depth* of a voxel, and we call the set of voxels with the same d the *layer* at depth d. We assume that material parameters $m[d, p]$ are constant within each voxel, and that h is also the spatial and pathlength resolution at which we can image.

We use an ideal source (Eq. (4)) co-located with an ideal sensor (Eq. (5)). Then, the following lemma states that, assuming all material parameters at layers $[h, 2h, \ldots, (n-1)h]$ are known from previous measurements, pathlength decomposed measurements at $\tau = 2nh$ and $\tau = (2n+1)h$ provide *linear* equations in the parameters of layer $d = nh$.

Lemma 2. *Using pathlength decomposition, the configuration of Fig. 2(a) provides measurements of the form*

$$
I_\tau =
\begin{cases}
Q_\tau + \sum\limits_{p \in k(n)} \sigma_s[nh, p] \int\limits_0^\pi f_p([nh, p], \theta) R_{\tau, p}(\theta) \, d\theta, & \tau = 2nh, \\[2mm]
S_\tau + \sum\limits_{p \in k(n)} \sigma_t[nh, p] T_{\tau, p}, & \tau = (2n+1)h,
\end{cases}
\tag{8}
$$

where $k(n)$ is the subset of voxels in layer $d = nh$ that are inter-sected by a source-centered circle of radius nh; Q_τ and $R_{\tau,p}(\theta)$ are functions of material parameters $\{m[d,p], d < nh\}$; and S_τ and $T_{\tau,p}$ of $\{m[d,p], d < nh; \sigma_s[nh,p]; f_p([nh,p], \theta)\}$.

Using Fig. 2, we can understand the first line of Eq. (8) as follows. Measurements of the form I_{2nh} are sums of contributions from paths of length $\tau = 2nh$. All these paths are contained inside a circle of radius nh centered at the source/sensor location. We can split the paths into two categories: those that stay within layers $[h, 2h, \ldots, (n-1)h]$, and those that reach layer $d = nh$. Most paths fall into the first category, and their contributions are included in the term Q. A fraction of the paths are in the second category, and when they reach layer $d = nh$, their interaction is limited to a single bounce somewhere within a particular subset of the voxels in that layer (denoted $k(n)$ and shaded orange in Fig. 2(a)). The parts of these paths that are contained in layers $d < nh$ correspond to the term R in Eq. (8), and their single-bounce interactions within layer $d = nh$ lead to linear dependence on parameters $\sigma_s f_p(\theta)$. Thus, when the materials in layers $d < nh$ are known, the terms Q and R can be computed; and we can build a system of linear equations in the parameters $\sigma_s f_p(\theta)$ for all voxels in layer $d = nh$ by changing the source/sensor location and, as discussed in the supplement, by shifting the sensor relative to the source.

Similarly, the second line of Eq. (8) refers to measurements $I_{(2n+1)h}$ of contributions from paths that have an odd number of steps, $\tau = (2n+1)h$. As explained in detail in the supplement, these paths may include up to two scattering events in layer $d = nh$, but only one that involves $\sigma_t[d,p]$. Therefore $I_{(2n+1)h}$ will depend linearly on $\sigma_t[d,p]$, and because the other parameters $\sigma_s[d,p]$ and $f_p([d,p], \theta)$ can be separately estimated from the even-step measurements, we can create a linear system of equations in σ_t for all voxels in layer $d = nh$ by combining odd-step measurements from different source and sensor locations.

Overall, Lemma 2 suggests a recursive, layer-wise procedure for inferring scattering parameters from pathlength-resolved measurements (Fig. 2(b)): Assuming parameters at layers $d < nh$ have been estimated from previous measurements, use measurements of the form of I_{2nh} and $I_{(2n+1)h}$ to estimate parameters at layer $d = nh$, through a linear system in $\sigma_s[d,p] f_p([d,p], \theta)$ and another linear system in $\sigma_t[d,p]$.

Noise Considerations. So far, we have shown that pathlength decomposed measurements in a *frontlighting* configuration, where there source and sensor are at the same side of the medium, helps reduce non-local ambiguities. To complete the picture, we must also consider the signal-to-noise ratio (SNR) of the measurements in Eq. (8) as pathlength τ increases. One observation is that their magnitude, and therefore SNR, decreases exponentially with τ due to volumetric attenuation (see Eq. (15)). Another is that, from Fig. 2(a), the ratio of the circle's area contained in layers $d < nh$ versus that in layer $d = nh$ increases with τ. This implies that the second terms in Eq. (8), which contain all information about parameters at depth $d = nh$, become smaller relative to the terms Q_τ, S_τ, which are independent of those parameters.

As a result of these two factors, the information available for inferring material parameters becomes progressively worse at greater depths. One way to ameliorate this noise is to use a supplementary *backlighting* configuration (Fig. 2(c)), where sources and sensors are on opposite sides of the medium. These backlighting measurements cannot be used in the recursive procedure described above, but they can provide cleaner measurements of deeper layers.

While these noise considerations also apply to the case of steady-state measurements from frontlighting and backlighting configurations, the preceding analysis of non-local ambiguities cannot be directly extended to that case. In place of theoretical analysis, we evaluate the relative utility of steady-state versus pathlength-resolved measurements quantitatively: We first introduce an inverse rendering algorithm for inferring heterogeneous scattering parameters from both types of measurements (Sect. 5), then we use this algorithm to perform inverse scattering experiments with simulated volumes and measurements (Sect. 6).

5   Inverse Rendering Algorithm

Measurements of the light transport matrix $\mathcal{T}_m$ provide information about internal scattering parameters. Given a measurement set $\{\bar{I}^n, n = 1, \ldots, N\}$ that is calibrated, meaning that sampling functions W^n are known, we can try to recover the parameters by solving an *appearance matching* optimization problem,

$$\min_{\boldsymbol{\pi}} \sum_{n=1}^{N} \frac{1}{2} \left(\bar{I}^n - \mathcal{S} \left(\mathcal{T}_{m(\boldsymbol{\pi})}, W^n \right) \right)^2, \tag{9}$$

where $\boldsymbol{\pi}$ is an appropriate K-dimensional parameterization of the material m (we will be omitting the dependence on $\boldsymbol{\pi}$ for notational simplicity). In the following, we introduce a framework for efficiently solving this inference problem. We do this by extending the inverse rendering algorithms introduced in [14,30], to apply to any possible set of measurements from the light transport matrix $\mathcal{T}_m$.

Path Formulation of Light Transport. Section 3 describes entries of the light transport matrix $\mathcal{T}_m$ and measurements $\mathcal{S}(\mathcal{T}_m, W)$ as different accumulations of photon contributions based on their paths. This intuition has been formalized in computer graphics and is the foundation of path-based rendering algorithms. We can also use it to derive our inverse rendering algorithm. For notation, we define a path $\bar{x}$ as an ordered sequence of points in the medium $\mathcal{M}$,

$$\bar{x} = x_0 \rightarrow x_1 \rightarrow \ldots \rightarrow x_B, \tag{10}$$

for any finite integer $B > 1$. We denote the space of all such paths as $\mathbb{P}$. For each path segment $x_b \rightarrow x_{b+1}$, we denote by $\omega(x_b \rightarrow x_{b+1})$ its direction. For each path $\bar{x}$, we denote by $o(\bar{x}) = x_0$ and $e(\bar{x}) = x_B$ its origin and end, by $\omega_o(\bar{x}) = \omega(x_0 \rightarrow x_1)$ and $\omega_e(\bar{x}) = -\omega(x_{B-1} \rightarrow x_B)$ its starting and ending directions, and by $\tau(\bar{x}) = \sum_{b=1}^{B} \|x_b - x_{b-1}\|_2$ its length.

Then, based on the path formulation of light transport [40, 44], every measurement of the light transport matrix can be written as,

$$S\left(\mathcal{T}_m, W\right) = \int_{\mathbb{P}} W\left(\bar{\boldsymbol{x}}\right) \bar{f}_m\left(\bar{\boldsymbol{x}}\right) \, \mathrm{d}\bar{\boldsymbol{x}}, \tag{11}$$

where we overload notation to make the sampling function of Eq. (2) apply to paths, based on their endpoints and length:

$$W\left(\bar{\boldsymbol{x}}\right) \triangleq W\left(\left(e\left(\bar{\boldsymbol{x}}\right), \boldsymbol{\omega}_e\left(\bar{\boldsymbol{x}}\right)\right), \left(o\left(\bar{\boldsymbol{x}}\right), \boldsymbol{\omega}_o\left(\bar{\boldsymbol{x}}\right)\right), \tau\left(\bar{\boldsymbol{x}}\right)\right). \tag{12}$$

The *throughput function* $\bar{f}_m$ determines the path's radiance contribution,

$$\bar{f}_m\left(\bar{\boldsymbol{x}}\right) = \prod_{b=1}^{B-1} f_m\left(\boldsymbol{x}_{b-1} \to \boldsymbol{x}_b \to \boldsymbol{x}_{b+1}\right), \tag{13}$$

$$f_m\left(\boldsymbol{x}_{b-1} \to \boldsymbol{x}_b \to \boldsymbol{x}_{b+1}\right) = a\left(\boldsymbol{x}_{b-1} \to \boldsymbol{x}_b\right) \sigma\left(\boldsymbol{x}_{b-1} \to \boldsymbol{x}_b \to \boldsymbol{x}_{b+1}\right), \tag{14}$$

$$a\left(\boldsymbol{x}_{b-1} \to \boldsymbol{x}_b\right) = \exp\left(-\int_{\boldsymbol{x}_{b-1}}^{\boldsymbol{x}_b} \sigma_t\left(\boldsymbol{x}\right) \, \mathrm{d}\boldsymbol{x}\right), \tag{15}$$

$$\sigma\left(\boldsymbol{x}_{b-1} \to \boldsymbol{x}_b \to \boldsymbol{x}_{b+1}\right) = \\ \begin{cases} f_s\left(\boldsymbol{x}_{b-1} \to \boldsymbol{x}_b \to \boldsymbol{x}_{b+1}\right), & \boldsymbol{x}_b \in \partial\mathcal{M}, \\ \sigma_s\left(\boldsymbol{x}_b\right) f_p\left(\boldsymbol{x}_b, \boldsymbol{\omega}\left(\boldsymbol{x}_{b-1} \to \boldsymbol{x}_b\right) \cdot \boldsymbol{\omega}\left(\boldsymbol{x}_b \to \boldsymbol{x}_{b+1}\right)\right), & \text{otherwise.} \end{cases} \tag{16}$$

Equation (15) is the volumetric attenuation along each path segment. Equation (16) corresponds to radiance transfer as direction changes at the end of a path segment. When $\boldsymbol{x}_b \in \partial\mathcal{M}$, the direction change is due to internal reflection at the medium boundary, and the amount of radiance transfered is determined by the material's BSDF. Otherwise, the direction change is due to scattering, and the radiance transfered is determined using the local phase function. If $\mathcal{M}$ is not convex, a path may exit and re-enter the medium before reaching the sensor, in which case the attenuation a for its corresponding segments equals 1.

Following [30], from Eq. (11), we can also formulate a path-based expression for the derivative of measurements of the light transport matrix with respect to any material parameter π_k. From the product form of $\bar{f}_m$ in Eq. (13), by applying the chain rule and re-arranging terms, we have that

$$\left.\frac{\partial S\left(\mathcal{T}_m, W\right)}{\partial \pi_k}\right|_{\boldsymbol{\pi}=\boldsymbol{\pi}_o} = \int_{\mathbb{P}} W\left(\bar{\boldsymbol{x}}\right) \left.\frac{\partial \bar{f}_m\left(\bar{\boldsymbol{x}}\right)}{\partial \pi_k}\right|_{\boldsymbol{\pi}=\boldsymbol{\pi}_o} \mathrm{d}\bar{\boldsymbol{x}} = \int_{\mathbb{P}} W\left(\bar{\boldsymbol{x}}\right) \bar{f}_m\left(\bar{\boldsymbol{x}}\right) \bar{S}_{m,k}\left(\bar{\boldsymbol{x}}\right) \mathrm{d}\bar{\boldsymbol{x}}, \tag{17}$$

$$\bar{S}_{m,k}\left(\bar{\boldsymbol{x}}\right) \triangleq \sum_{b=1}^{B-1} S_{m,k}\left(\boldsymbol{x}_{b-1} \to \boldsymbol{x}_b \to \boldsymbol{x}_{b+1}\right), \tag{18}$$

$$S_{m,k}\left(\boldsymbol{x}_{b-1} \to \boldsymbol{x}_b \to \boldsymbol{x}_{b+1}\right) \triangleq \frac{\left.\left(\partial f_m\left(\boldsymbol{x}_{b-1} \to \boldsymbol{x}_b \to \boldsymbol{x}_{b+1}\right) / \partial \pi_k\right)\right|_{\boldsymbol{\pi}=\boldsymbol{\pi}_o}}{f_m\left(\boldsymbol{x}_{b-1} \to \boldsymbol{x}_b \to \boldsymbol{x}_{b+1}\right)}. \tag{19}$$

In statistics, $S_{m,k}$ is known as the *score function* of f_m with respect to π_k.

Monte Carlo Integration. The integrals of Eqs. (11) and (17) can be estimated using Monte Carlo integration (Fig. 3): We first use any probability distribution μ on $\mathbb{P}$ to sample a set of paths $\{\bar{\boldsymbol{x}}_j, \quad j = 1, \ldots, J\}$; then we form the respective unbiased estimates,

$$I = \sum_{j=1}^{J} \frac{W(\bar{\boldsymbol{x}}_j)\,\bar{f}_m(\bar{\boldsymbol{x}}_j)}{\mu(\bar{\boldsymbol{x}}_j)}, \quad G_k = \sum_{j=1}^{J} \frac{W(\bar{\boldsymbol{x}}_j)\,\bar{f}_m(\bar{\boldsymbol{x}}_j)\,\bar{S}_{m,k}(\bar{\boldsymbol{x}}_j)}{\mu(\bar{\boldsymbol{x}}_j)}. \tag{20}$$

The paths $\{\bar{\boldsymbol{x}}_j, \quad j = 1, \ldots, J\}$ can be chosen using the sampling strategies developed for physically accurate rendering, such as (volumetric) path tracing, bidirectional path tracing, or Metropolis Light Transport [40,44]. Because of the need to render individual elements of the light transport matrix (corresponding to the infinitesimal emittance and importance functions of Eqs. (4) and (5)), we use bidirectional path tracing. When rendering pathlength-decomposed measurements, we also use the local sampling modifications of [27]. Finally, most rendering algorithms use the product form of Eq. (13) to efficiently compute the term $\bar{f}_m$ in Eq. (20) recursively while tracing a path. The same can be done for the term $\bar{S}_{m,k}$, using the sum form of Eq. (18).

Stochastic Optimization. We now consider the appearance matching problem of Eq. (9). Denoting by $E(\boldsymbol{\pi})$ its loss function, we have for its gradient,

$$\left.\frac{\partial E}{\partial \pi_k}\right|_{\boldsymbol{\pi}} = \sum_{n=1}^{N} \left(\bar{I}^n - \mathcal{S}(\mathcal{T}_m, W^n)\right) \left.\frac{\partial \mathcal{S}(\mathcal{T}_m, W^n)}{\partial \pi_k}\right|_{\boldsymbol{\pi}}. \tag{21}$$

We can estimate the gradient using the estimates of Eq. (20), as

$$g_k(\boldsymbol{\pi}) = \sum_{n=1}^{N} \left(\bar{I}^n - I^n\right) G_k^n. \tag{22}$$

This estimate g_k is unbiased if I^n and G_k^n are statistically independent, which can be achieved by rendering them using independently selected sets of paths. Following [14], we can combine these gradient estimates with stochastic gradient descent algorithms to solve the appearance matching problem of Eq. (9).

Standard SGD uses iterations $\boldsymbol{\pi}^{(t+1)} = \boldsymbol{\pi}^{(t)} - \beta^{(t)} \boldsymbol{g}^{(t)}$, with common step size $\beta^{(t)}$ for all unknown parameters. This converges slowly when gradient vectors are very sparse [11]. This applies to our problem because the gradient estimate g_k for some material voxel will be zero if, during the rendering operations of Eq. (20), no sampled paths travel through the voxel. We have experimented with a number of SGD variants that use separate, per-parameter step sizes, each decrementing adaptively based on the magnitudes of the per-parameter gradients in previous iterations [11,31,50]. We chose to use ADADELTA (Algorithm 1), which we found empirically to have the best performance for solving (9).

Initialization. We initialize Algorithm 1 using a multi-resolution procedure, that progressively increases the spatial resolution of material parameters. For pathlength-resolved measurements, we also use a layer-wise recursive procedure analogous to Fig. 2(b). We discuss both procedures in the supplement.

6   Experiments

Implementation. We implemented the inverse rendering framework of Sect. 5 on top of the Mitsuba physically based renderer [26]. We extended the bidirectional path tracing algorithm to support spatial probing and pathlength decomposition rendering, for both radiance and gradient estimation. The stochastic optimization layer distributes rendering tasks involved in gradient computation (multiple parameters and measurements) across a multi-CPU cluster. We ran all our experiments on 20-node Amazon EC2 clusters, with 36 cores per node.

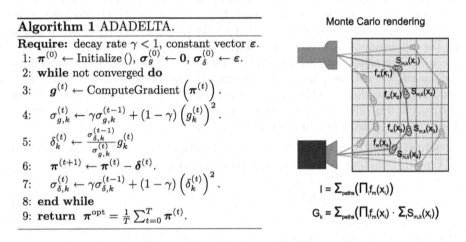

Algorithm 1 ADADELTA.

Require: decay rate $\gamma < 1$, constant vector $\boldsymbol{\varepsilon}$.
1: $\boldsymbol{\pi}^{(0)} \leftarrow$ Initialize (), $\boldsymbol{\sigma}_g^{(0)} \leftarrow \mathbf{0}$, $\boldsymbol{\sigma}_\delta^{(0)} \leftarrow \boldsymbol{\varepsilon}$.
2: **while** not converged **do**
3:    $\boldsymbol{g}^{(t)} \leftarrow$ ComputeGradient $\left(\boldsymbol{\pi}^{(t)}\right)$.
4:    $\sigma_{g,k}^{(t)} \leftarrow \gamma\sigma_{g,k}^{(t-1)} + (1-\gamma)\left(g_k^{(t)}\right)^2$.
5:    $\delta_k^{(t)} \leftarrow \dfrac{\sigma_{\delta,k}^{(t-1)}}{\sigma_{g,k}^{(t)}} g_k^{(t)}$
6:    $\boldsymbol{\pi}^{(t+1)} \leftarrow \boldsymbol{\pi}^{(t)} - \boldsymbol{\delta}^{(t)}$.
7:    $\sigma_{\delta,k}^{(t)} \leftarrow \gamma\sigma_{\delta,k}^{(t-1)} + (1-\gamma)\left(\delta_k^{(t)}\right)^2$.
8: **end while**
9: **return** $\boldsymbol{\pi}^{\text{opt}} = \frac{1}{T}\sum_{t=0}^{T}\boldsymbol{\pi}^{(t)}$.

Monte Carlo rendering

$I = \Sigma_{\text{paths}}\left(\Pi_i f_m(x_i)\right)$

$G_k = \Sigma_{\text{paths}}\left(\Pi_i f_m(x_i) \cdot \Sigma_i S_{m,k}(x_i)\right)$

Fig. 3. Inverse rendering algorithm. Left: We use the ADADELTA variant of stochastic gradient descent to minimize the appearance matching objective of Eq. (9). Right: We use a modified Monte Carlo rendering algorithm to compute stochastic gradient estimates. When shading a path, we compute for each segment both the usual throughput terms f_m and the score terms $S_{m,k}$. These are accumulated to determine the path's contribution to the image I and its derivative G_k (Eqs. (13) and (18)). We repeat this process over many paths that are sampled to satisfy the sampling function W corresponding to the input image measurement (Eq. (12)).

Comparison of Imaging Configurations. We perform inverse scattering experiments on synthetic volumes, to evaluate the performance of different imaging configurations. Following Fig. 2(a), we use a cubic medium of size $10 \times 10 \times 10\,\text{mm}^3$ discretized at resolution $0.4\,\text{mm}$, resulting in 15625 voxels. To reduce the space of possible imaging configurations, we assume that the material parameters are characterized by a cross-section of the cube along the $\{d,p\}$ plane, remaining constant across the third dimension, corresponding to $3 \times 625 = 1875$ unknowns. We use an imaging resolution four times that of the material grid, corresponding to pixel size $0.1 \times 0.1\,\text{mm}^2$ and pathlength resolution $0.1\,\text{mm}$.

We fix the medium refractive index to $\eta = 1.3$ and assume a smooth dielectric BSDF at its boundary. We adopt the single-parameter Henyey-Greenstein model

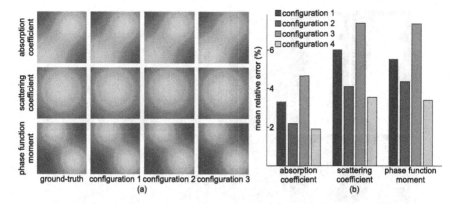

Fig. 4. Comparison of different imaging configurations. (a) Visualization of ground-truth and reconstructed material parameters as a function of location. (b) Mean relative reconstruction error for material parameters, averaged over multiple synthetic volumes.

for the phase function [23]; therefore, each material voxel is associated with corresponding unknown values for σ_a, σ_s, and the phase function parameter g (equal to the phase function's first moment). We constrain $\sigma_a, \sigma_s \in [1, 10]$ mm^{-1}, and $g \in [0, 0.6]$. We generate volumes by modeling each parameter inside the medium as a mixture of two Gaussians of random mean and variance.

We use these volumes to compare three imaging configurations: (1) Path-length decomposition where, for each ideal source, we measure the radiance exiting the volume at the opposite direction and from the same position, as well as its two spatial neighbors. We take measurements with the ideal source placed at every pixel on the medium boundary, including in sidelighting and backlighting positions. (2) Steady-state imaging where, for every ideal source, we use an orthographic camera to measure radiance exiting from all pixels in one surface of the cube. As before, we take measurements with the ideal source placed at every pixel on the medium boundary, and at every position at three different orientations. (3) Similar to (1), but instead of spatial shifts, we take measurements at multiple source orientations. Each of these configurations produces 120000 measurements, or 64 measurements per unknown. When rendering simulated measurements, we add sensor noise using [19].

In Fig. 4(a), we visualize the reconstructed parameters for one of the synthetic volumes. We observe that all three configurations are generally able to reconstruct all three spatially varying parameters, σ_a, σ_s, and g, within a mean relative error 7 % and maximum relative error 15 %, concentrated around areas of high absorption. In Fig. 4(b), we compare the RMS error in the estimation of each parameter by each configuration, averaged across five synthetic volumes. We see that, the configuration using only steady-state measurements has a lower RMS error. We expect that this is due to the very low SNR of pathlength-decomposition measurements corresponding to large pathlength values. We show in Fig. 4(b) the mean relative error obtained by a fourth configuration, created

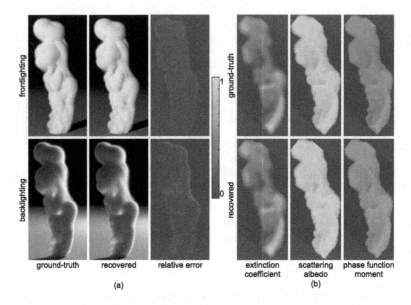

Fig. 5. (a) Renderings of a smoke volume using ground-truth and recovered material parameters under novel viewpoint and illumination conditions. (b) Ground-truth and recovered parameters for a vertical cross-section through the smoke volume.

by replacing measurements in configuration (1) of magnitude comparable to the additive sensor noise, with steady-state measurements from configuration (2) corresponding to large camera-sensor distances. We see that this combination produces the lowest RMS error among all imaging configurations.

3D Reconstruction. In Fig. 5, we show volumetric reconstructions of a dense heterogeneous smoke volume, with smoothly spatially-varying scattering parameters, and assuming index of refraction equal to 1. We generate our own parameters for the volume mesh provided by [26]. We use pathlength-resolved measurements in frontlighting, sidelighting, and backlighting configurations.

Figure 5(a) compares renderings of the smoke volume using the ground-truth and recovered material parameters under novel imaging configurations (not used as input to the inverse rendering algorithm). In Fig. 5(b), we compare ground-truth and recovered material parameters across a cross-section of the volume. Our algorithm accurately recovers all scattering parameters, with mean relative error 9.31 % and maximum relative error 19.73 %, and the recovered parameters can reproduce the appearance of the volume under new imaging conditions.

7   Conclusions

We have presented a theoretical and quantitative evaluation of various computational imaging techniques for the heterogeneous inverse scattering problem. Our theoretical results provide formal justification for the use of pathlength decomposition in applications requiring volumetric reconstruction of complex materials. Additionally, our experimental results suggest there are many different imaging configurations, including both steady-state and pathlength decomposition measurements, that can enable accurate recovery of heterogeneous scattering parameters. Our theoretical results and our optimization framework can be used to guide the design of new acquisition systems, such as when selecting from among various possible configurations, and when weighing practical considerations, such as hardware availability, exposure time, and geometry constraints.

Acknowledgments. This material is based upon work supported by: the US National Science Foundation under award IIS-1161564; the DARPA REVEAL program under Contract No. HR0011-16-C-0028; the European Research Council; the Israel Science Foundation; and research grants from Amazon Web Services.

References

1. Project page. http://vision.seas.harvard.edu/inverse_transient/
2. Antyufeev, V.: Monte Carlo Method for Solving Inverse Problems of Radiation Transfer. Inverse and Ill-Posed Problems Series, vol. 20. V.S.P. International Science, Utrecht (2000)
3. Arridge, S.R.: Optical tomography in medical imaging. Inverse Prob. **15**, R41–R93 (1999)
4. Bal, G.: Inverse transport theory and applications. Inverse Prob. **25**(5) (2009)
5. Boas, D.A., Brooks, D.H., Miller, E.L., DiMarzio, C.A., Kilmer, M., Gaudette, R.J., Zhang, Q.: Imaging the body with diffuse optical tomography. IEEE Signal Process. Mag. **18**, 57–75 (2001)
6. Boyd, R.W.: Radiometry and the Detection of Optical Radiation. Wiley, New York (1983)
7. Case, K.M., Zweifel, P.F.: Linear Transport Theory. Addison-Wesley Pub. Co., Boston (1967)
8. Debevec, P., Hawkins, T., Tchou, C., Duiker, H., Sarokin, W., Sagar, M.: Acquiring the reflectance field of a human face. In: Proceedings of SIGGRAPH 2000, Annual Conference Series (2000)
9. Donner, C., Jensen, H.: Light diffusion in multi-layered translucent materials. ACM Trans. Graph. **24**(3), 1032–1039 (2005)
10. Donner, C., Weyrich, T., d'Eon, E., Ramamoorthi, R., Rusinkiewicz, S.: A layered, heterogeneous reflectance model for acquiring and rendering human skin. ACM Trans. Graph. **27**(5) (2008)
11. Duchi, J., Hazan, E., Singer, Y.: Adaptive subgradient methods for online learning and stochastic optimization. J. Mach. Learn. Res. **12**, 2121–2159 (2011)
12. Fuchs, C., Chen, T., Goesele, M., Theisel, H., Seidel, H.: Density estimation for dynamic volumes. Comput. Graph. **31**(2), 205–211 (2007)
13. Gkioulekas, I., Levin, A., Durand, F., Zickler, T.: Micron-scale light transport decomposition using interferometry. ACM Trans. Graph. (2015)
14. Gkioulekas, I., Zhao, S., Bala, K., Zickler, T., Levin, A.: Inverse volume rendering with material dictionaries. ACM Trans. Graph. (2013)
15. Goesele, M., Lensch, H., Lang, J., Fuchs, C., Seidel, H.: Disco: acquisition of translucent objects. ACM Trans. Graph. **23**(3), 835–844 (2004)

16. Goodman, J.W.: Introduction to Fourier Optics. McGraw-Hill Book Company, New York (1968)
17. Gu, J., Nayar, S.K., Grinspun, E., Belhumeur, P.N., Ramamoorthi, R.: Compressive structured light for recovering inhomogeneous participating media. In: Forsyth, D., Torr, P., Zisserman, A. (eds.) ECCV 2008, Part IV. LNCS, vol. 5305, pp. 845–858. Springer, Heidelberg (2008)
18. Gupta, M., Agrawal, A., Veeraraghavan, A., Narasimhan, S.G.: Structured light 3D scanning in the presence of global illumination. In: 2011 IEEE Conference on Computer Vision and Pattern Recognition (CVPR), pp. 713–720, June 2011
19. Hasinoff, S., Durand, F., Freeman, W.: Noise-optimal capture for high dynamic range photography. In: IEEE CVPR (2010)
20. Hawkins, T., Einarsson, P., Debevec, P.: Acquisition of time-varying participating media. ACM Trans. Graph. 24(3), 812–815 (2005)
21. Heide, F., Hullin, M.B., Gregson, J., Heidrich, W.: Low-budget transient imaging using photonic mixer devices. ACM Trans. Graph. 32(4), 45:1–45:10 (2013)
22. Heide, F., Xiao, L., Kolb, A., Hullin, M.B., Heidrich, W.: Imaging in scattering media using correlation image sensors and sparse convolutional coding. Opt. Express 22(21), 26338–26350 (2014)
23. Henyey, L., Greenstein, J.: Diffuse radiation in the galaxy. Astrophys. J. 93, 70–83 (1941)
24. Huang, D., Swanson, E., Lin, C., Schuman, J., Stinson, W., Chang, W., Hee, M., Flotte, T., Gregory, K., Puliafito, C., Fujimoto, G.: Optical coherence tomography. Science 254(5035), 1178–1181 (1991)
25. Ishimaru, A.: Wave Propagation and Scattering in Random Media. Wiley-IEEE, New York (1978)
26. Jakob, W.: Mitsuba renderer (2010). http://www.mitsuba-renderer.org
27. Jarabo, A., Marco, J., Muñoz, A., Buisan, R., Jarosz, W., Gutierrez, D.: A framework for transient rendering. ACM Trans. Graph. 33(6), 177:1–177:10 (2014)
28. Jensen, H., Marschner, S., Levoy, M., Hanrahan, P.: A practical model for subsurface light transport. In: Proceedings of SIGGRAPH 2001, Annual Conference Series (2001)
29. Kadambi, A., Whyte, R., Bhandari, A., Streeter, L., Barsi, C., Dorrington, A., Raskar, R.: Coded time of flight cameras: sparse deconvolution to address multipath interference and recover time profiles. ACM Trans. Graph. 32(6), 167:1–167:10 (2013)
30. Khungurn, P., Schroeder, D., Zhao, S., Bala, K., Marschner, S.: Matching real fabrics with micro-appearance models. ACM Trans. Graph. 35(1), 1:1–1:26 (2015)
31. Kingma, D., Ba, J.: Adam: A method for stochastic optimization. In: ICLR (2015)
32. Levis, A., Schechner, Y., Aides, A., Davis, A.: Airborne three-dimensional cloud tomography. In: IEEE International Conference on Computer Vision (2015)
33. Mukaigawa, Y., Yagi, Y., Raskar, R.: Analysis of light transport in scattering media. In: IEEE CVPR (2010)
34. Narasimhan, S., Gupta, M., Donner, C., Ramamoorthi, R., Nayar, S., Jensen, H.: Acquiring scattering properties of participating media by dilution. ACM Trans. Graph. 25(3), 1003–1012 (2006)
35. Nayar, S.K., Krishnan, G., Grossberg, M.D., Raskar, R.: Fast separation of direct and global components of a scene using high frequency illumination. ACM Trans. Graph. 25(3), 935–944 (2006)
36. O'Toole, M., Mather, J., Kutulakos, K.: 3D Shape and indirect appearance by structured light transport. In: 2014 IEEE Conference on Computer Vision and Pattern Recognition (CVPR), pp. 3246–3253, June 2014

37. O'Toole, M., Heide, F., Xiao, L., Hullin, M.B., Heidrich, W., Kutulakos, K.N.: Temporal frequency probing for 5D transient analysis of global light transport. ACM Trans. Graph. **33**(4), 87:1–87:11 (2014)

38. O'Toole, M., Raskar, R., Kutulakos, K.N.: Primal-dual coding to probe light transport. ACM Trans. Graph. **31**(4), 39:1–39:11 (2012)

39. Papas, M., Regg, C., Jarosz, W., Bickel, B., Jackson, P., Matusik, W., Marschner, S., Gross, M.: Fabricating translucent materials using continuous pigment mixtures. ACM Trans. Graph. **32**(4), 146:1–146:12 (2013)

40. Pauly, M., Kollig, T., Keller, A.: Metropolis light transport for participating media. In: Péroche, B., Rushmeier, H. (eds.) Rendering Techniques 2000, pp. 11–22. Springer, Vienna (2000)

41. Peers, P., vom Berge, K., Matusik, W., Ramamoorthi, R., Lawrence, J., Rusinkiewicz, S., Dutré, P.: A compact factored representation of heterogeneous subsurface scattering. ACM Trans. Graph. **25**(3), 746–753 (2006)

42. Prahl, S., van Gemert, M., Welch, A.: Determining the optical properties of turbid media by using the adding-doubling method. Appl. Opt. **32**(4), 559–568 (1993)

43. Reddy, D., Ramamoorthi, R., Curless, B.: Frequency-space decomposition and acquisition of light transport under spatially varying illumination. In: Fitzgibbon, A., Lazebnik, S., Perona, P., Sato, Y., Schmid, C. (eds.) ECCV 2012, Part VI. LNCS, vol. 7577, pp. 596–610. Springer, Heidelberg (2012)

44. Veach, E.: Robust Monte Carlo methods for light transport simulation. Ph.D. thesis, Stanford University (1997)

45. Velten, A., Wu, D., Jarabo, A., Masia, B., Barsi, C., Joshi, C., Lawson, E., Bawendi, M., Gutierrez, D., Raskar, R.: Femto-photography: capturing and visualizing the propagation of light. ACM Trans. Graph. **32**(4), 44:1–44:8 (2013)

46. Wang, J., Zhao, S., Tong, X., Lin, S., Lin, Z., Dong, Y., Guo, B., Shum, H.: Modeling and rendering of heterogeneous translucent materials using the diffusion equation. ACM Trans. Graph. 27(1) (2008)

47. Wu, D., Velten, A., OToole, M., Masia, B., Agrawal, A., Dai, Q., Raskar, R.: Decomposing global light transport using time of flight imaging. ACM Trans. Graph. **107**(2), 123–138 (2014)

48. Wu, D., Wetzstein, G., Barsi, C., Willwacher, T., Dai, Q., Raskar, R.: Ultra-fast lensless computational imaging through 5D frequency analysis of time-resolved light transport. ACM Trans. Graph. **110**(2), 128–140 (2014)

49. Wyman, D., Patterson, M., Wilson, B.: Similarity relations for the interaction parameters in radiation transport. Appl. Opt. **28**(24), 5243–5249 (1989)

50. Zeiler, M.D.: Adadelta: an adaptive learning rate method. arXiv preprint arXiv:1212.5701 (2012)

51. Zhao, S., Ramamoorthi, R., Bala, K.: High-order similarity relations in radiative transfer. ACM Trans. Graph. (2014)

Precomputed Real-Time Texture Synthesis with Markovian Generative Adversarial Networks

Chuan Li[✉] and Michael Wand[✉]

Institut for Informatik, University of Mainz, Mainz, Germany
cl.chuanli@gmail.com, wandm@uni-mainz.de

Abstract. This paper proposes Markovian Generative Adversarial Networks (MGANs), a method for training generative networks for efficient texture synthesis. While deep neural network approaches have recently demonstrated remarkable results in terms of synthesis quality, they still come at considerable computational costs (minutes of run-time for low-res images). Our paper addresses this efficiency issue. Instead of a numerical deconvolution in previous work, we precompute a feed-forward, strided convolutional network that captures the feature statistics of *Markovian patches* and is able to directly generate outputs of arbitrary dimensions. Such network can directly decode brown noise to realistic texture, or photos to artistic paintings. With adversarial training, we obtain quality comparable to recent neural texture synthesis methods. As no optimization is required at generation time, our run-time performance (0.25 M pixel images at 25 Hz) surpasses previous neural texture synthesizers by a significant margin (at least 500 times faster). We apply this idea to texture synthesis, style transfer, and video stylization.

Keywords: Texture synthesis · Adversarial generative networks

1 Introduction

Image synthesis is a classical problem in computer graphics and vision [5]. The key challenges are to capture the structure of complex classes of images in a concise, learnable model, and to find efficient algorithms for learning such models and synthesizing new image data. Most traditional *"texture synthesis"* methods address the complexity constraints using Markov random field (MRF) models that characterize images by statistics of local patches of pixels.

Recently, generative models based on deep neural networks have shown exciting new perspectives for image synthesis [7,8]. Deep architectures capture appearance variations in object classes beyond the abilities of pixel-level approaches. However, there are still strong limitations of how much structure can

Electronic supplementary material The online version of this chapter (doi:10.1007/978-3-319-46487-9_43) contains supplementary material, which is available to authorized users.

© Springer International Publishing AG 2016
B. Leibe et al. (Eds.): ECCV 2016, Part III, LNCS 9907, pp. 702–716, 2016.
DOI: 10.1007/978-3-319-46487-9_43

be learned from limited training data. This currently leaves us with two main classes of "deep" generative models: (1) *full-image models* that generate whole images [3,8], and (2) *Markovian models* that also synthesize textures [7,15].

The first class, full-image models, are often designed as specially trained auto-encoders [12]. Results are impressive but limited to rather small images (typically around 64×64 pixels). The second class, the deep Markovian models, capture the statistics of local patches only and assemble them to high-resolution images. Consequently, the fidelity of details is good, but additional guidance is required if non-trivial global structure should be reproduced [1,5,7,9,15]. Our paper addresses this second approach of deep Markovian texture synthesis.

Previous neural methods of this type [7,15] are built upon a deconvolutional framework [18,25]. This naturally provides blending of patches and permits reusing the intricate, emergent multi-level feature representations of large, discriminatively trained neural networks like the VGG network [21], repurposing them for image synthesis. As a side note, we will later observe that this is actually crucial for high-quality result (Fig. 10). Gatys et al. [7] pioneer this approach by modeling patch statistics with a global Gaussian models of the higher-level feature vectors, and Li and Wand [15] utilize dictionaries of extended local patches of neural activation, trading-off flexibility for visual realism. Unfortunately, the run-time costs of the deconvolution approach are very high, requiring iterative back-propagation in order to estimate a pre-image (pixels) of the feature activations (higher network layer). In the case of [15], a high-end GPU needs several minutes to synthesize low-resolution images (such as a 512-by-512 pixels image).

The objective of our paper is therefore to improve the efficiency of deep Markovian texture synthesis. The key idea is to precompute the inversion of the network by fitting a strided convolutional network [20] to the inversion process, which operates purely in a feed-forward fashion. Despite being trained on patches of a fixed size, the resulting network can generate images of arbitrary dimension, yielding an efficient texture synthesizer of a specific style[1].

We train the convolutional network using adversarial training [20], which permits maintaining image quality similar to the original, expensive optimization approach. As result, we obtain significant speed-up: Our GPU implementation computes 512×512 images within 40 ms (on an nVidia TitanX). The key limitation, of course, is to precompute the feed-forward convolutional network for each texture style. Nonetheless, this is still an attractive trade-off for many potential applications, for example from the area of artistic image or video stylization.

2   Related Work

Deconvolutional neural networks have been introduced to visualize deep features and object classes. Zeiler and Fergus [25] back-project neural activations to highlight pixels. Mahendran and Vedaldi [17] reconstruct images from the neural encoding in intermediate layers. Recently, effort are made to improve the

---

[1] See supplementary material and code at: https://github.com/chuanli11/MGANs.

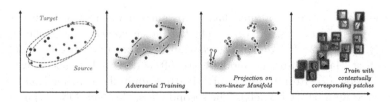

Fig. 1. Motivation: real world data does not always comply with a Gaussian distribution (first), but a complex nonlinear manifold (second). We adversarially learn a mapping to project contextually related patches to that manifold.

efficiency and accuracy of visualization [19,24]. Mordvintsev et al. have raised wide attention by showing how deconvolution of class-specific activations can create hallucinogenic imagery from discriminative networks [18]. The astonishing complexity of the obtained visual patterns has immediately spurred hope for new generative models: Gatys et al. [6,7] drove deconvolution by global covariance statistics of feature vectors on higher network layers, obtaining unprecedented results in artistic style transfer. However, enforcing per-feature-vector statistics permits a mixing of feature patterns that never appear in actual images and limit plausibility of the learned texture. This can be partially addressed by replacing point-wise feature statistics by statistics of spatial patches of feature activations [15]. This permits photo-realistic synthesis in some cases, but also reduces invariance because the simplistic dictionary of patches introduces rigidity.

Full image methods employ specially trained auto-encoders as generative networks [12]. For example, the Generative Adversarial Networks use two networks, one as the discriminator and other as the generator, to iteratively improve the model by playing a minimax game [8]. This model is extended to work with a Laplacian pyramid [3]. Very recently, Radford et al. [20] propose a set of architectural refinements[2] that stabilized the performance of this model, and show that the generators have vector arithmetic properties. One important strength of adversarial networks is that it offers perceptual metrics [4] that allows auto-encoders to be training more efficiently.

In very recent, two concurrent work, Ulyanov et al. [22] and Johnson et al. [10] propose fast implementations of Gatys et al.'s approach. Both of their methods employ precomputed decoders trained with a perceptual texture loss and obtain significant run-time benefits (higher decoder complexity reduces their speed-up a bit). The main difference in our paper is the use of Li and Wand's [15] feature-patch statistics as opposed to learning Gaussian distributions of individual feature vectors, which provides some benefits in reproducing textures more faithfully.

3   Model

Let us first conceptually motive our method. Statistics based methods [7,22] match the distributions of source (input photo or noise signal) and target

---

[2] Strided convolution, ReLUs, batch normalization, removing fully connected layers.

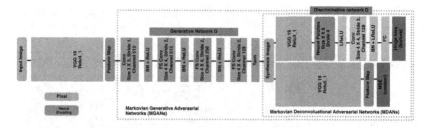

Fig. 2. Our model contains a generative network (blue blocks) and a discriminative network (green blocks). We apply the discriminative training on Markovian neural patches (purple block as the input of the discriminative network.). (Color figure online)

(texture) with a Gaussian model (Fig. 1, first). However, real world data does not always comply with a Gaussian distribution. Instead it can follow a complicated non-linear manifold. Adversarial training [8] recognizes such manifold (Fig. 1, second), and strengthens its generative power with projections (Fig. 1, third). We apply adversarial training on contextually corresponding Markovian patches (Fig. 1, fourth), so learning can focus on the mapping between different depictions of the same context, rather than the mixture of context and depictions.

Figure 2 visualizes our pipeline, which extends the patch-based synthesis algorithm of Li and Wand [15]. We first replace their patch dictionary (nearest-neighbor search) with a continuous discriminative network D (green blocks) that learns to distinguish actual feature patches (on VGG_19 layer Relu3_1, purple block) from inappropriately synthesized ones. A second comparison (pipeline below D) with a VGG_19 encoding of the same image on the higher, more abstract layer Relu5_1 can be optionally used for guidance. If we run deconvolution on the VGG networks (with the gradient from the discriminator and optionally from the guidance content), we obtain deconvolutional image synthesizer, which we call *Markovian Deconvolutional Adversarial Networks* (MDANs).

MDANs are very slow. Therefore we aim for an additional generative network G (blue blocks). It takes a VGG_19 layer Relu4_1 encoding of an image and decodes it to pixels. During training we do not change the *VGG_19* network (gray blocks), and only optimize D and G. We denote the overall architecture by *Markovian Generative Adversarial Networks* (MGANs).

3.1 Markovian Deconvolutional Adversarial Networks (MDANs)

MDANs synthesize textures with a deconvolutional process that is driven by adversarial training: a discriminative network D (green blocks in Fig. 2) is trained to distinguish between "neural patches" from the synthesis image and from the example image. We use regular sampling on layer *relu3_1* of *VGG_19* output (purple block). It outputs a classification score $s = \pm 1$ for each neural patch, indicating how "real" the patch is (with $s = 1$ being real). For each patch sampled

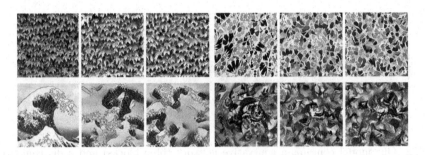

Fig. 3. Un-guided texture synthesis using MDANs. For each case the first image is the example texture, and the other two are the synthesis results. Image credits: [23]'s "Ivy", flickr user erwin brevis's "gell", Katsushika Hokusai's "The Great Wave off Kanagawa", Kandinsky's "Composition VII".

from the synthesized image, $1 - s$ is its texture loss to minimize. The deconvolution process back-propagates this loss to pixels. Like Radford et al. [20] we use batch normalization and leaky ReLU to improve the training of D.

Formally, we denote the example texture image by $\mathbf{x}_t \in \mathbb{R}^{w_t \times h_t}$, and the synthesized image by $\mathbf{x} \in \mathbb{R}^{w \times h}$. We initialize $\mathbf{x}$ with random noise for un-guided synthesis, or an content image $\mathbf{x}_c \in \mathbb{R}^{w \times h}$ for guided synthesis. The deconvolution iteratively updates $\mathbf{x}$ so the following energy is minimized:

$$\mathbf{x} = \arg \min_x E_t(\Phi(\mathbf{x}), \Phi(\mathbf{x}_t)) + \alpha_1 E_c(\Phi(\mathbf{x}), \Phi(\mathbf{x}_c)) + \alpha_2 \Upsilon(\mathbf{x}) \quad (1)$$

Here E_t denotes the texture loss, in which $\Phi(\mathbf{x})$ is $\mathbf{x}$'s feature map output from layer $relu3\_1$ of VGG_19. We sample patches from $\Phi(\mathbf{x})$, and compute E_t as the Hinge loss with their labels fixed to one:

$$E_t(\Phi(\mathbf{x}), \Phi(\mathbf{x}_t)) = \frac{1}{N} \sum_{i=1}^{N} \max(0, 1 - 1 \times s_i) \quad (2)$$

Here s_i denotes the classification score of i-th neural patch, and N is the total number of sampled patches in $\Phi(\mathbf{x})$. The discriminative network is trained on the fly: Its parameters are randomly initialized, and then updated after each deconvolution, so it becomes increasingly smarter as synthesis results improve.

The additional regularizer $\Upsilon(\mathbf{x})$ in Eq. 1 is a smoothness prior for pixels [17]. It is defined as $\sum_{i,j}((x_{i,j+1} - x_{i,j})^2 + (x_{i+1,j} - x_{i,j})^2)$, where $x_{i,j}$ is the color value of pixel at i-th row and j-th column. This term penalizes the color difference between adjacent pixels.

Using E_t and $\Upsilon(\mathbf{x})$ can synthesize random textures (Fig. 3). By minimizing an additional content loss E_c, the network can generate an image that is contextually related to a guidance image $\mathbf{x}_c$ (Fig. 4). This content loss is the Mean Squared Error between two feature maps $\Phi(\mathbf{x})$ and $\Phi(\mathbf{x}_c)$. We set the weights with $\alpha_1 = 1$ and $\alpha_2 = 0.0001$, and minimize Eq. 1 using back-propagation with ADAM [11] (learning rate 0.02, momentum 0.5). Notice each neural patch receives its own

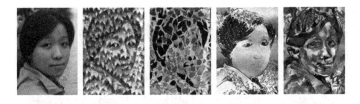

Fig. 4. Guided texture synthesis using MDANs. The reference textures are the same as in Fig. 3.

output gradient through the back-propagation of D. In order to have a coherent transition between adjacent patches, we blend their output gradient like texture optimization [13] did.

3.2 Markovian Generative Adversarial Networks (MGANs)

MDANs require many iterations and a separate run for each output image. We now train a variational auto-encoder (VAE) that decodes a feature map directly to pixels. The target examples (textured photos) are obtained from the MDANs. Our generator G (blue blocks in Fig. 2) takes the layer *relu4_1* of *VGG_19* as the input, and decodes a picture through a ordinary convolution followed by a cascade of fractional-strided convolutions (FS Conv). Although being trained with fixed size input, the generator naturally extends to arbitrary size images.

As Dosovitskiy and Brox [4] point out, it is crucially important to find a good metric for training an auto-encoder: Using the Euclidean distance between the synthesized image and the target image at the pixel level (Fig. 5, pixel VAE) yields an over-smoothed image. Comparing at the neural encoding level improves results (Fig. 5, neural VAE), and adversarial training improves the reproduction of the intended style further (Fig. 5, MGANs).

Our approach is similar to classical Generative Adversarial Networks (GANs) [8], with the key difference of not operating on full images, but neural patches from the *same* image. Doing so utilizes the contextual correspondence between the patches, and makes learning easier and more effective in contrast to learning the distribution of a object class [8] or a mapping between contextually irrelevant data [22]. In additional we also replace the Sigmoid function and the binary cross entropy criteria from [20] by a max margin criteria (Hinge loss). This avoids the vanishing gradient problem when learning D. This is more problematic in our case than in Radfort et al.'s [20] because of less diversity in our training data. Thus, the Sigmoid function can be easily saturated.

Figure 5 (MGANs) shows the results of a network that is trained to produce paintings in the style of Picasso's "Self-portrait 1907". For training, we randomly selected 75 faces photos from the CelebA data set [16], and in additional to it 25 non-celebrity photos from the public domain. We resize all photos so that the maximum dimension is 384 pixels. We augmented the training data by generating 9 copies of each photo with different rotations and scales. We regularly sample

Fig. 5. Our MGANs learn a mapping from *VGG_19* encoding of the input photo to the stylized example (MDANs). The reference style texture for MDANs is Pablo Picasso's "self portrait 1907". We compare the results of MGANs to Pixel VAE and Neural VAE in with both training and testing data.

subwindows of 128-by-128 croppings from them for batch processing. In total we have 24,506 training examples, each is treated as a training image where neural patches are sampled from its *relu3_1* encoding as the input of D.

Figure 5 (top row, MGANs) shows the decoding result of our generative network for a training photo. The bottom row shows the network generalizes well to test data. Notice the MDANs image for the test image is never used in the training. Nonetheless, direct decoding with G produces very good approximation of it. The main difference between MDANs and MGANs is: MDANs preserve the content of the input photo better and MGANs produce results that are more stylized. This is because MGANs was trained with many images, hence learned

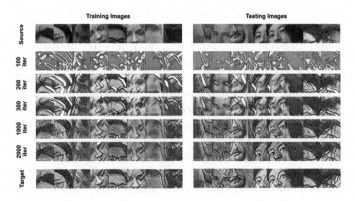

Fig. 6. Intermediate decoding results during the training of MGANs. The reference style texture for MDANs is Pablo Picasso's "self portrait 1907".

the most frequent features. Another noticeable difference is MDANs create more natural backgrounds (such as regions with flat color), due to its iterative refinement. Despite such flaws, the MGANs model produces comparable results with a speed that is 500 times faster.

Figure 6 shows some intermediate results MGANs. It is clear that the decoder gets better with more training. After 100 batches, the network is able to learn the overall color, and where the regions of strong contrast are. After 300 batches the network started to produce textures for brush strokes. After 1000 batches it learns how to paint eyes. Further training is able to remove some of the ghosting artifacts in the results. Notice the model generalizes well to testing data (right).

4 Experimental Analysis

We conduct empirical study with some hyper-parameters (layers for classification, patch size) and the complexity of the model (number of layers in the network, number of channels in each layer). While there may not be a universal optimal design for all textures, our study shed some light on how the model generally behaves. For fair comparison, the example textures in this study are fixed to 128-by-128 pixels, and synthesis output are fixed to 256-by-256 pixels.

Visualizing decoder features: We visualize the learned filters of decoder G in Fig. 7. These features are directly decoded from a one-hot input vector. Individual patches are similar to, but not very faithfully matching the example textures (due to the semi-distributed nature of the encoding). Nonetheless, the similarity seems to be strong enough for synthesizing new images.

Parameters: Here we experiment different input layers for the discriminative network. To do so we run unguided texture synthesis with discriminator D taking layer $relu2\_1$, $relu3\_1$, and $relu4\_1$ of VGG_19 as the input. We use patch sizes of 16, 8 and 4 respectively for the three options, so they have the same receptive field of 32 image pixels (ignoring padding). The first three results in Fig. 8 shows the results: Lower layers ($relu2\_1$) produce sharper appearances but at the cost of losing the structure. Higher layer ($relu4\_1$) preserves coarse structure better but at the risk of being too rigid for guided scenarios. Layer $relu3\_1$ offers a good balance between quality and flexibility. We then show the influence of

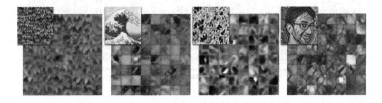

Fig. 7. Visualizing the learned features in the generative networks. Image credits: [23]'s "Ivy", flickr user erwin brevis's "gell", Katsushika Hokusai's "The Great Wave off Kanagawa", and Norman Jaklin.

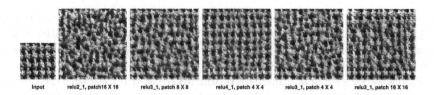

Input   relu2_1, patch16 X 16   relu3_1, patch 8 X 8   relu4_1, patch 4 X 4   relu3_1, patch 4 X 4   relu3_1, patch 16 X 16

Fig. 8. Different layers and patch sizes for training the discriminative network. Input image credit: "ropenet" from the project link of [14].

patch size: We fix the input layer of D to be *relu3_1*, and compare patch size of 4 and 16 to with the default setting of 8. The last two results in Fig. 8 shows that such changes also affect the rigidity of the model: smaller patches increase the flexibility and larger patches preserve better structure.

Complexity: We now study the influence of (1) the number of layers in the networks and (2) the number of channels in each layer. We first vary D by removing the convolutional layer. Doing so reduces the depth of the network and in consequence the synthesis quality (first column, Fig. 9). Bringing this convolutional layer back produces smoother synthesis (second column, Fig. 9). However, quality does not obviously improves with more additional layers (third column, Fig. 9). Testing D with 4, 64, and 128 channels for the convolutional layer, we observe that in general less channels leads to worse results (fourth column, Fig. 9), but there is no significance difference between 64 channels and 128 channels (second column v.s. fifth column). The optimal complexity also

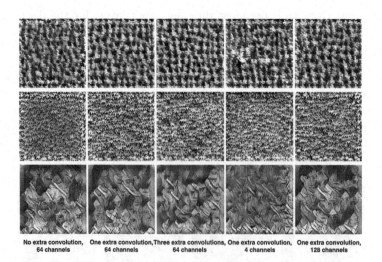

No extra convolution,   One extra convolution,   Three extra convolutions,   One extra convolution,   One extra convolution,
64 channels   64 channels   64 channels   4 channels   128 channels

Fig. 9. Different depths for training the discriminative netowrk. The input textures are "ropenet" from the project link of [14,23]'s "Ivy", and Pablo Picasso's "self portrait 1907".

depends on the actual texture. For example, the ivy texture is rather simple, so the difference between 4 channels and 64 channels are only marginal.

Next, we fix the discriminative network and vary G. We notice some quality loss when removing the first convolutional layer from G, or reducing the number of channels for all layers, and very limited improvement from a more complex design. However the difference is not very significant. This is likely because of all these networks are driven by the same D. The reluctance of further improvement indicates there might be non-trivial information from the deconvolutional process that can not be approximated by a feed forward process.

Initialization. Usually, networks are initialized with random values. However we found D has certain generalization ability. Thus, for transferring the same texture to different images with MDANs, a previously trained network can serve as initialization. Figure 10 shows initialization with pre-trained discriminative network (that has already transferred 50 face images) produces good result with only 50 iterations. In comparison, random initialization does not produce comparable quality even after the first 500 iterations. It is useful to initialize G with an auto-encoder that directly decodes the input feature to the original input photo. Doing so essentially approximates the process of inverting VGG_19, and let the whole adversarial network to be trained more stably.

The role of VGG: We also validate the importance of the pre-trained VGG_19 network. As the last two pictures in Fig. 10 show, training a discriminative network from scratch (from pixel to class label [20]) yields significantly worse results. This has also been observed by Ulyanov et al. [22]. Our explanation is that much

| Input | Pre-trained 50 iterations | Random initialization 50 iterations | Random initialization 500 iterations | no VGG 50 iterations | no VGG 500 iterations |

Fig. 10. Different initializations of the discriminative networks. The reference texture is Pablo Picasso's "self portrait 1907".

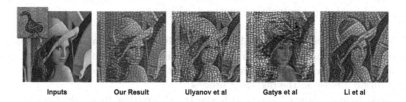

| Inputs | Our Result | Ulyanov et al | Gatys et al | Li et al |

Fig. 11. Comparisons with previous methods. Results of Ulyanov et al. [22], Gatys et al. [7] and input images are from [22].

of the statistical power of VGG_19 stems from building shared feature cascades for a diverse set of images, thereby approaching human visual perception more closely than a network trained with a limited example set.

5   Results

We train each model with 100 randomly selected ImageNet images and a single example texture. We first produce 100 transferred images using MDANs, then regularly sample 128-by-128 image croppings as training data for MGANs. In total we have around 16k samples. Each epoch min-batches through all samples in random order (about 12 min). We train each texture for upto five epochs.

Figure 11 compares our results with other methods. We observe that our method has a very different character in comparison to global statistics based models [7, 22]: It transfers texture more coherently, such as the hair and the eyes of Lena was consistently mapped to dark textures. In contrast, the Gaussian model [7, 22] failed to keep such consistency, in particular the eyes in [22]'s result and the entire face in [7]'s result are not textured. The patch based approach [15] produces the most coherent synthesis, due to the use of non-parametric sampling. However, their method requires patch matching so is significantly slower (generate this 384-by-384 picture in 110 s). Our method and Ulyanov et al. [22] run at the same level of speed; both bring significantly improvement of speed over Gatys et al. [7] (500 times faster) and Li and Wand [15] (5000 times faster).

Figure 12 further discuss the difference between the Gaussian based method [22] and our method[3]. In general [22] produces more faithful color distributions in respect to the style image. It also texture the background better (the starry night), whereas our method suffers due to the suppression from the VGG network. On the other hand, our method produces more coherent texture transfer for salient foreground objects, such as the facade in both examples. In comparison [22] produces either too much or too little textures in such complex regions.

MGANs can decode noise input into texture (Fig. 13): Perlin noise[4] images are forwarded through *VGG_19* to generate feature maps for the decoder. To our surprise, the model that was trained with ImageNet images is able to decode such features maps to plausible textures. This shows the generalization ability of our model. Figure 13 shows our video decoding result. As a feed-forward process our method is not only faster but also relatively more temporally coherent than per-frame based deconvolutional methods (Fig. 14).

---

[3] Since Ulyanov et al. [22] and Johnson et al. [10] are very similar approaches, here we only compare to one of them [22]. The main differences of [10] are: (1) using a residual architecture instead of concatenating the outputs from different layers; (2) no additional noise in the decoding process.

[4] We need to use "brown" noise with spectrum decaying to the higher frequencies because flat "white" noise creates an almost flat response in the encoding of the VGG network. Somer lower-frequency structure is required to trigger the feature detectors in the discriminative network.

Inputs   Our Results   Texture Networks   Inputs   Our Results   Texture Networks

Fig. 12. More comparisons with Texture Networks [22]. Results of [22] and input images are from [22].

Fig. 13. Generate random textures by decoding from Brown noise.

Last but not the least, we provide details for the time/memory usage of our method. The time measurement is based on a standard benchmark framework [2]: Our speed is at the same level as the concurrent work by Ulyanov et al. [22], who also use a feed-forward approach, perform significantly faster than previous deconvolution based approaches [7,15]. More precisely, both our method and Ulyanov et al. [22] are able to decode 512-by-512 images at 25 Hz, while [22] leads the race by a very small margin. The time cost of both methods scale linearly with the number of pixels in the image. For example, our method cost 10 ms for a 256-by-256 image, 40 ms for a 512-by-512 image, and 160 ms for a 1024-by-1024 image. Both methods show a very significant improvement in speed over previous deconvolutional methods such as Gatys et al. [7] and Li and Wand [15]: about 500 times faster than Gatys et al. [7], and 5000 times faster than Li and Wand [15]. In the meantime our method is also faster than most traditional pixel based texture synthesizers (which rely on expensive nearest-neighbor searching). A possible exceptions would be a GPU implementation of "Patch Match" [1], which could run at comparable speed. However, it provides the quality benefits (better blending, invariance) of a deep-neural-network method (as established in previous work [7,15]). Memory-wise, our generative model takes 70 Mb memory for its parameters(including the VGG network till layer Relu4_1). At runtime, the required memory to decode a image linearly depends on the image's size: for a 256-by-256 picture it takes about 600 Mb, and for a 512-by-512 picture it requires about 2.5 Gb memory. Notice memory usage can be reduced by subdividing the input photo into blocks and run the decoding in a scanline fashion. However, we do not further explore the optimization of memory usage in this paper.

Fig. 14. Decoding a 1080-by-810 video. We achieved the speed of 8 Hz. Input video is credited to flickr user macro antonio torres.

6   Limitation

Our current method works less well with non-texture data. For example, it failed to transfer facial features between two difference face photos. This is because facial features can not be treated as textures, and need semantic understanding (such as expression, pose, gender etc.). A possible solution is to couple our model with the learning of object class [20] so the local statistics is better conditioned. For synthesizing photo-realistic textures, Li and Wand [15] often produces better results due to its non-parametric sampling that prohibits data distortion. However, the rigidity of their model restricts its application domain. Our method works better with deformable textures, and runs significantly faster.

Our model has a very different character compared to Gaussian based models [7,22]. By capturing a global feature distribution, these other methods are able to better preserve the global "look and feels" of the example texture. In contrast, our model may deviate from the example's global color distribution.

Since our model learns the mapping between different depictions of the same content, it requires features highly invariant features. For this reason we use the pre-trained *VGG_19* network. This makes our method weaker in dealing with highly stationary backgrounds (sky, out of focus region etc.) due to their weak activation from *VGG_19*. We observed that in general statistics based methods [7,22] generate better textures for areas that has weak content, and our method works better for areas that consist of recognizable features. We believe it is valuable future work to combine the strength of both methods.

Finally, we discuss the noticeable difference between the results of MDANs and MGANs. The output of MGANs is often more consistent with the example texture, this shows MGANs' strength of learning from big data. MGANs has weakness in flat regions due to the lack of iterative optimization. More sophisticated architectures such as the recurrent neural networks can bring in state information that may improve the result.

7   Conclusion

The key insight of this paper is that adversarial generative networks can be applied in a Markovian setting to learn the mapping between different depictions of the same content. We develop a fully generative model that is trained from a single texture example and randomly selected images from ImageNet. Once trained, our model can decode brown noise to realistic texture, or photos into artworks. We show our model has certain advantages over the statistics based methods [7,22] in preserving coherent texture for complex image content.

Our method is only one step in the direction of learning generative models for images. For future work one can study the broader framework in a big-data scenario to learn not only Markovian models but also include coarse-scale structure models. This additional invariance to image layout could open up ways to also use more training data for the Markovian model, thus permitting more complex decoders with stronger generalization capability over larger classes.

Acknowledgments. This work has been partially supported by the Intel Visual Computing Institute and the Center for Computational Science Mainz. We like to thank Bertil Schmidt and Christian Hundt for providing additional computational resources; and Dmitry Ulyanov, Norman Jaklin for sharing results and input images.

References

1. Barnes, C., Shechtman, E., Finkelstein, A., Goldman, D.B.: PatchMatch: a randomized correspondence algorithm for structural image editing. In: SIGGRAH, pp. 24:1–24:11 (2009)
2. Chintala, S.: Easy benchmarking of all publicly accessible implementations of convnets (2015). https://github.com/soumith/convnet-benchmarks
3. Denton, E.L., Fergus, R., Szlam, A., Chintala, S.: Deep generative image models using a Laplacian pyramid of adversarial networks. In: NIPS (2015)
4. Dosovitskiy, A., Brox, T.: Generating images with perceptual similarity metrics based on deep networks. CoRR abs/1602.02644 (2016). http://arxiv.org/abs/1602.02644
5. Efros, A.A., Freeman, W.T.: Image quilting for texture synthesis and transfer. In: SIGGRAPH, pp. 341–346 (2001)
6. Gatys, L.A., Ecker, A.S., Bethge, M.: Texture synthesis and the controlled generation of natural stimuli using convolutional neural networks. In: NIPS, May 2015. http://arxiv.org/abs/1505.07376
7. Gatys, L.A., Ecker, A.S., Bethge, M.: A neural algorithm of artistic style (2015). arXiv preprint http://arxiv.org/abs/1508.06576
8. Goodfellow, I., Pouget-Abadie, J., Mirza, M., Xu, B., Warde-Farley, D., Ozair, S., Courville, A., Bengio, Y.: Generative adversarial nets. In: NIPS, pp. 2672–2680 (2014)
9. Hertzmann, A., Jacobs, C.E., Oliver, N., Curless, B., Salesin, D.H.: Image analogies. In: SIGGRAPH, pp. 327–340 (2001)
10. Johnson, J., Alahi, A., Li, F.F.: Perceptual losses for real-time style transfer and super-resolution. CoRR abs/1603.08155, March 2016. http://arxiv.org/abs/1603.08155v1
11. Kingma, D.P., Ba, J.: Adam: a method for stochastic optimization. CoRR abs/1412.6980 (2014). http://arxiv.org/abs/1412.6980
12. Kingma, D.P., Welling, M.: Auto-encoding variational bayes. CoRR abs/1312.6114 (2013). http://arxiv.org/abs/1312.6114
13. Kwatra, V., Essa, I., Bobick, A., Kwatra, N.: Texture optimization for example-based synthesis. SIGGRAPH **24**(3), 795–802 (2005)

14. Kwatra, V., Schödl, A., Essa, I., Turk, G., Bobick, A.: Graphcut textures: image and video synthesis using graph cuts. ACM Trans. Graph. **22**(3), 277–286 (2003)

15. Li, C., Wand, M.: Combining Markov random fields and convolutional neural networks for image synthesis. CoRR abs/1601.04589 (2016). http://arxiv.org/abs/1601.04589

16. Liu, Z., Luo, P., Wang, X., Tang, X.: Deep learning face attributes in the wild. In: ICCV (2015)

17. Mahendran, A., Vedaldi, A.: Understanding deep image representations by inverting them. In: CVPR (2015)

18. Mordvintsev, A., Olah, C., Tyka, M.: Inceptionism: going deeper into neural networks (2015). http://googleresearch.blogspot.com/2015/06/inceptionism-going-deeper-into-neural.html

19. Nguyen, A.M., Yosinski, J., Clune, J.: Multifaceted feature visualization: uncovering the different types of features learned by each neuron in deep neural networks. CoRR abs/1602.03616 (2016). http://arxiv.org/abs/1602.03616

20. Radford, A., Metz, L., Chintala, S.: Unsupervised representation learning with deep convolutional generative adversarial networks. CoRR abs/1511.06434 (2015). http://arxiv.org/abs/1511.06434

21. Simonyan, K., Zisserman, A.: Very deep convolutional networks for large-scale image recognition. CoRR (2014). http://arxiv.org/abs/1409.1556

22. Ulyanov, D., Lebedev, V., Vedaldi, A., Lempitsky, V.: Texture networks: feed-forward synthesis of textures and stylized images. CoRR abs/1603.03417, March 2016. http://arxiv.org/abs/1603.03417v1

23. Xie, J., Lu, Y., Zhu, S.C., Wu, Y.N.: A theory of generative convnet. CoRR arXiv:1602.03264 (2016). http://arxiv.org/abs/1602.03264

24. Yosinski, J., Clune, J., Nguyen, A.M., Fuchs, T., Lipson, H.: Understanding neural networks through deep visualization. CoRR abs/1506.06579 (2015). http://arxiv.org/abs/1506.06579

25. Zeiler, M.D., Fergus, R.: Visualizing and understanding convolutional networks. In: Fleet, D., Pajdla, T., Schiele, B., Tuytelaars, T. (eds.) ECCV 2014, Part I. LNCS, vol. 8689, pp. 818–833. Springer, Heidelberg (2014)

Fast Guided Global Interpolation for Depth and Motion

Yu Li[1], Dongbo Min[2], Minh N. Do[3], and Jiangbo Lu[1($\boxtimes$)]

[1] Advanced Digital Sciences Center, Singapore, Singapore
jiangbo.lu@adsc.com.sg
[2] Chungnam National University, Daejeon, Korea
[3] University of Illinois at Urbana-Champaign, Champaign, USA

Abstract. We study the problems of upsampling a low-resolution depth map and interpolating an initial set of sparse motion matches, with the guidance from a corresponding high-resolution color image. The common objective for both tasks is to densify a set of sparse data points, either regularly distributed or scattered, to a full image grid through a 2D guided interpolation process. We propose a unified approach that casts the fundamental guided interpolation problem into a hierarchical, global optimization framework. Built on a weighted least squares (WLS) formulation with its recent fast solver – fast global smoothing (FGS) technique, our method progressively densifies the input data set by efficiently performing the cascaded, global interpolation (or smoothing) with alternating guidances. Our cascaded scheme effectively addresses the potential structure inconsistency between the sparse input data and the guidance image, while preserving depth or motion boundaries. To prevent new data points of low confidence from contaminating the next interpolation process, we also prudently evaluate the consensus of the interpolated intermediate data. Experiments show that our general interpolation approach successfully tackles several notorious challenges. Our method achieves quantitatively competitive results on various benchmark evaluations, while running much faster than other competing methods designed specifically for either depth upsampling or motion interpolation.

Keywords: Image-guided interpolation · Depth upsampling · Optical flow

1 Introduction

Dense depth or optical flow maps often serve as a fundamental building block for many computer vision and computational photography applications, *e.g.*, 3D

Jiangbo Lu—This study is supported by the HCCS grant at the ADSC from Singapore's Agency for Science, Technology and Research (A*STAR).

Electronic supplementary material The online version of this chapter (doi:10.1007/978-3-319-46487-9_44) contains supplementary material, which is available to authorized users.

B. Leibe et al. (Eds.): ECCV 2016, Part III, LNCS 9907, pp. 717–733, 2016.
DOI: 10.1007/978-3-319-46487-9_44

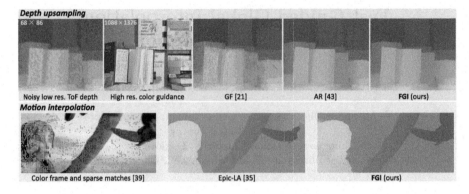

Fig. 1. Using the same guided interpolation pipeline, our technique gives strong results for two tasks: (top) depth upsampling and (bottom) optical flow field interpolation. Local or non-local methods (*e.g.* GF [21] and Epic-LA [35]) are usually efficient, but suffer from limitations like copying texture from the color guidance (green arrows) and inability to interpolate pixels in a distance (green rectangle). Methods using complicated models and global optimization (*e.g.* AR [43]) can obtain high quality results, but are often rather slow in computation. Our method, with a unified framework for both problems, is 1000× faster than AR [43] and even faster than local methods, while yielding competitive results when compared with state-of-the-art task-specific methods. (Color figure online)

scene reconstruction, object tracking, video editing, to name a few. An active range sensing technology such as time-of-flight (ToF) cameras has been recently advanced, emerging as an alternative to obtaining a depth map. It provides 2D depth maps at a video rate, but the quality of ToF depth maps is not as good as that of a high-quality color camera. The depth map is of low-resolution and noisy, and thus a post-processing for depth upsampling is usually required to enhance the quality of depth maps. Over the years, numerous approaches for optical flow estimation have also been developed, but several challenging issues still remain, including large displacements, non-rigid fine motion, large occlusion, and flow boundaries. To address these issues, modern optical flow approaches often use a discriminative descriptor (or patch) matching to estimate sparse or quasi-dense motion matches. These important anchor points are used to interpolate a dense flow map, which is then embedded into subsequent optimization procedures.

One prevailing strategy for both depth upsampling and motion field interpolation is via a guided interpolation that uses an associated high-quality color image, exploiting the correlation between the color guidance and the depth/motion data. For depth upsampling, many methods based on the guided interpolation have been proposed with either local or global formulations [10,12,17,21,22,28–30,32,34,43]. Similarly, the guided motion field interpolation has been actively adopted as a key element in state-of-the-art optical flow approaches [6,8,14,25,26,35,39]. Though both tasks share the same goal of densifying a set of sparse input data points to a full image grid, *most existing interpolation approaches have been developed in isolation, tailored to either the depth upsampling or motion densification tasks due to different characteristics of two data sets.* For instance, ToF depth observations are noisy but regularly distributed in the high-resolution image grid, while sparse motion matches after outlier removal are typically reliable but highly scattered with a varying density of valid motion data across an image. In addition, existing interpolation methods are usually complicated and computationally inefficient.

We propose a *unified* approach to cast the fundamental guided interpolation (or densification) problem for both depth and motion data into a hierarchical, global optimization framework. Leveraging a recent fast global smoothing (FGS) technique [31] based on a weighted least squares (WLS) formulation [16], our method progressively densifies the input data set by efficiently performing a cascaded, guided global interpolation (or smoothing). While most existing approaches for depth upsampling and motion interpolation primarily rely on the color guidance image, the proposed method alternates the color image and an interpolated intermediate depth or flow map as the guidance. As a result, our cascaded scheme effectively addresses the potential structure inconsistency between the sparse input data and the guidance image, while preserving depth or motion discontinuities. To prudently select reliable new data points to augment the input sparse data, we evaluate the consensus between the interpolated data points using guidances and the data points from a spatial interpolation. Figure 1 shows example results from our method. The contributions of this paper include:

– We propose a general fast guided interpolation (FGI) approach for both (1) noisy but regularly distributed depth maps and (2) typically reliable but highly scattered motion data.
– The proposed method successfully tackles several challenges such as texture-copy artifacts and loss of depth discontinuities in depth upsampling, and also large occlusions and motion boundaries in optical flow through a cascaded, guided global interpolation framework with alternating guidances.
– It achieves quantitatively competitive results on both tasks, while running much faster than state-of-the-art methods designed *specifically* for depth upsampling (over 600× faster) or motion interpolation (over 2× faster).
– Our technique is also generally applicable to other edge-aware filters such as the guided filter [21], and is shown to improve their interpolation quality.

1.1 Related Work

We review related work on depth upsampling and motion interpolation based on the guided interpolation. Other interpolation tasks (*e.g.*, spline fitting or single image super-resolution) without a guidance signal are beyond this paper's scope.

Depth Upsampling: In an early work, Diebel and Thrun [12] cast a depth upsampling problem into a MRF formulation and solved it using a conjugate gradient method, but it tends to generate oversmooth results and is also sensitive to noise. Lu *et al.* [29] proposed an improved MRF-based depth upsampling method, but it is computationally expensive due to a complex global optimization. In [34], a non-local means (NLM) regularization term was additionally used in the MRF optimization. Ferstl *et al.* [17] defined the depth upsampling as a convex optimization problem using a high-order regularization term, called total generalized variation (TGV), which enforces piecewise affine results. An adaptive color-guided auto-regressive (AR) model [43] was proposed by formulating the depth upsampling task into a minimization of AR prediction errors, producing satisfactory results on real depth data. As filtering-based approaches, the joint bilateral upsampling (JBU) [22] was proposed to upsample a low-resolution depth map by applying the bilateral filtering [38] with a guidance of a high-resolution color image. Afterwards, numerous filtering-based methods have been proposed using edge-aware filtering techniques, *e.g.* guided filter (GF) [21], cross-based local multipoint filter (CLMF) [30], and joint geodesic filter (JGF) [28]. The weighted mode filter (WMF) upsamples a low-resolution depth map by estimating a dominant mode from a joint histogram computed with an input depth data and a color guidance image [32]. One interesting work on devising a noise-aware filter [10] for depth upsampling took into account an inherent noisy nature of a depth map, preventing undesired texture-copy artifacts in the output depth map. Recently, Shen *et al.* [36] dealt with inconsistent structures existing in a pair of input signals *e.g.* NIR and RGB images with the concept of mutual-structure. But, this method focuses on the tasks such as joint restoration rather than tackling specific challenges in depth upsampling or motion interpolation, where the input data points are highly sparse.

Motion Field Interpolation: Modern optical flow algorithms have often used an interpolated motion data at an intermediate step for dealing with large displacement optical flow estimation. A set of sparse, reliable correspondences, first computed using a discriminative descriptor (or patch) matching, is interpolated and used as dense inputs for subsequent optimization steps. Using a non-local, approximated geodesic averaging or affine estimation, Revaud *et al.* [35] proposed an effective sparse-to-dense interpolation scheme termed 'EpicFlow', where sparse motion matches are computed from the deep matching method [39]. The interpolated output flow field was further refined through a variational energy minimization. The same interpolation and optimization pipeline was recently adopted in [6] to densify reliable flow fields after outlier filtering. However, EpicFlow solely counts on color edges detected with a structured edge detector (SED) [13] as the guidance for its interpolation, which are prone to the known issues of weak color boundaries or erroneous texture transferring in sparse data interpolation. Drayer and Brox proposed a combinatorial refinement of the initial matching [14], and then applied it to modern optical flow algorithms [8,35,39]. They utilized sparse motion matches as an input for motion interpolation and refinement. Though improving the flow accuracy, the whole process of [14] is still complex and slow. A sparse-to-dense interpolation approach was also used in [26], but a costly optimization process is involved in finding a set of initial matches and computing an affine model independently for each pixel.

2   Image Smoothing with WLS

Our pipeline is built on edge-aware image smoothing techniques, *e.g.* [7,15,16, 18,21,31,37,38]. In this paper, we choose the weighted least squares (WLS) formulation [16] as our fundamental engine based on the two considerations: (1) it uses a global optimization formulation that overcomes the limitation (*e.g.* halo artifacts) of edge-aware local filters [18,21,30] in the smoothing process; (2) the recent proposed fast WLS solver [31] shows comparable runtime to fast local filters. Such favorable properties allow us to exploit it with full extent in a hierarchical, multi-pass framework, meeting our requirements in terms of accuracy and efficiency, which would not be practical previously. Besides WLS, our framework is generally applicable to other edge-aware smoothing filters (Sect. 4).

In a WLS based smoothing approach, given an input image f and a guidance image g, an output image u is computed by minimizing the objective $\mathcal{E}$ as:

$$\mathcal{E}(u) = \sum_p (u_p - f_p)^2 + \lambda \sum_p \sum_{q \in \mathcal{N}_4(p)} w_{p,q}(g)(u_p - u_q)^2, \tag{1}$$

where $\mathcal{N}_4(p)$ consists of four neighbors for p. $w_{p,q}$ is a spatially varying weight function measuring how similar two pixels p and q are in the guidance image g. The weight λ balance the data term and the regularization term. This objective can also be written in a matrix/vector form:

$$\mathcal{E}(\mathbf{u}) = (\mathbf{u} - \mathbf{f})^\top(\mathbf{u} - \mathbf{f}) + \lambda \mathbf{u}^\top \mathbf{A} \mathbf{u}. \tag{2}$$

The matrix $\mathbf{A} = \mathbf{D} - \mathbf{W}$ is usually referred to as a Laplacian matrix. $\mathbf{D}$ is a degree matrix, where $\mathbf{D}(i,i) = \sum_{j \in N(i)} w_{i,j}(g)$, and $\mathbf{D}(i,j) = 0$ for $i \neq j$. $\mathbf{W}$ is an adjacency matrix defined with $\{w_{i,j|j \in N(i)}\}$. Equation (2) is strictly convex, and thus $\mathbf{u}$ is obtained by solving a linear system with a large sparse matrix as

$$(\mathbf{E} + \lambda \mathbf{A})\mathbf{u} = \mathbf{f}, \tag{3}$$

where $\mathbf{E}$ is an identity matrix. Though several methods [23,24] have been proposed for efficiently solving the linear system Eq. (3), they are an order of magnitude slower than the local filters [18,21]. Recently, a fast global smoothing (FGS) technique [31] was proposed as an efficient alternative to compute the solution of Eq. (2). The key idea is to approximate the large linear system by solving a series of 1D sub-systems in a separable way. The 1D sub-systems are defined with horizontal or vertical passes for an input 2D image. It has an efficient solution obtained by the Gaussian elimination algorithm. Specifically, its runtime for filtering a 1M pixel RGB image on a single CPU core is only **0.1 s** [31].

Limitations of WLS in Interpolation. The WLS based formulation was originally proposed for computational photography and image processing applications. We found that directly applying it to depth or motion interpolation, where an input data is highly sparse and/or noisy, does not yield an excellent result. Figure 2 shows the interpolation result based on the single scale WLS.

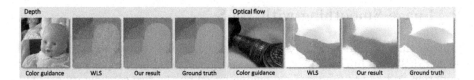

Fig. 2. Limitations of the WLS formulation [31] in depth upsampling (left) and motion match interpolation (right). Spurious structures mistakenly transferred from the color guidance are clearly visible in both cases, while our interpolator generates interpolation results that resemble the ground truth. (Best viewed in electronic version.)

It is because the one-pass optimization at a single scale is insufficient for interpolating highly sparse and noisy data with very low-density regions (*e.g.* 16× upsampling for depth data, namely only *one* raw depth value is available in a $16 \times 16 = 256$ region in the targeted full scale). This signal recovery instability caused by the highly deficient data observation matrix can also be understood from a theoretical perspective of the conditioning of linear systems [19,43]. In such a case, large gaps between observed sparse data points are forced to be filled by primarily counting on the structures in the color guidance. However, the color guidance is not always faithfully correlated with the data to be interpolated, thus often producing texture-copy artifacts or over-smoothing around weak edges.

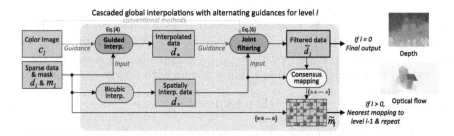

Fig. 3. Our fast guided interpolation (FGI) framework, taking sparse input data d_l, its mask m_l and a color guidance c_l as inputs for the level l. The guided interpolation/filtering with alternating guidances and consensus checking iterate a few times in a hierarchical way to get to the result at final resolution. In contrast, existing methods *e.g.* [43] directly take the bicubic estimation and the color guidance to infer the final results in a single pass joint filtering/optimization manner (denoted in dashed lines). (Color figure online)

3   Fast Guided Global Interpolation

As shown in Fig. 2, a single-pass WLS-based optimization often fails to generate high-quality interpolation results, when the input data is too sparse or scattered on a full image grid. To address these issues especially in depth upsampling and motion interpolation tasks in a unified manner, we propose a hierarchical, multi-pass guided interpolation framework. Specifically, we address the challenges in an iterative coarse-to-fine manner that divides the problems into a sequence of interpolation tasks with smaller scale factors, and gradually fills the large gap between the sparse measurement and the dense data.

Suppose the number of levels used in the hierarchical structure is L. We start the guided interpolation from the coarsest level $(l = L - 1)$, and progressively generates reliable data points to densify the sparse input data. This process is repeated until the finest level $(l = 0)$ is reached. Figure 3 illustrates the procedure of the proposed framework at the lth level. At each level, we first interpolate the sparse input d_l[1] by performing the WLS optimization using a corresponding color image c_l as the guidance and also a simple bicubic interpolation technique, respectively. Then, another WLS is applied with the interpolated dense data d_* from the first WLS interpolation output as the guidance and the bicubic interpolated map as the input signal. Finally, we select reliable points via consensus checking, and pass the augmented data points to the next level $l - 1$.

For a sparse data input, we use a mask m_l $(l = 0, ..., L-1)$ to denote the data observation or constraint map whose elements are 1 for pixels with valid data and 0 otherwise. At each level, we upsample the signal by a factor of 2. We also pre-compute a downsampled color image c_l for each level from a high resolution color image c such that $c_0 = c, c_l = c_{l-1} \downarrow (l = 1, 2, \ldots, L - 1)$, where $\downarrow$ denotes a downsampling operation by a factor of 2. A sparse input at the starting level $(l = L - 1)$ can be depth data from a low resolution depth map or irregular sparse motion matches mapped from descriptor matching methods (e.g. [39]).

3.1 Cascaded Filtering with Alternating Guidances

For a progressively densified input data d_l at a certain level l, our technique performs two cascaded WLS by alternating the color image c_l and an interme-diate interpolated depth or flow map d_* as the guidance (see Fig. 3). For the first WLS-based interpolation using the color guidance, the sparse input data d_l is quickly densified at the current scale. In this pass, the sparse data is inter-polated in accordance with the color structures. This process may introduce spurious structures to the interpolated data d_* (e.g. texture-copying effects) due to inconsistent structures between the color and sparse input depth/motion data, but d_* interpolated from the sparse input data d_l contains much weaker texture patterns than the original guidance signal c_l (see d_* in Fig. 4). Therefore, we pro-pose to append the second modified WLS smoothing step using the newly inter-polated data d_* as the guidance. During this second pass, the WLS optimization is solved with a more faithful guidance of the same modality (i.e. d_* rather than c_l), while being subject to dense data constraints from the bicubic-upsampled data d_o. We find this cascaded scheme effectively addresses the potential

---

[1] Hereinafter we denote the corresponding vectorized form of d as $\mathbf{d}$.

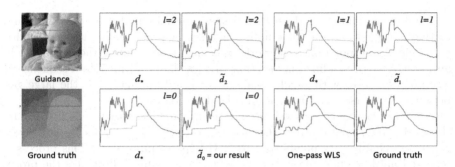

Fig. 4. Comparison of the 1D scanline results obtained by our cascaded WLS steps over three levels $l = 2, 1, 0$, and that obtained by the one-pass WLS. In all the subplots (right), the corresponding color signal is in *olive green*, while other kinds of signals are in different colors. The same is observed for optical flow interpolation. (Color figure online)

structure inconsistency between the sparse input data and the guidance image, while preserving true depth or motion discontinuities (see Figs. 2 and 4).

1st WLS Using c_l as the Guidance. When the sparse input data $\mathbf{d}_l$ and the guidance color image $\mathbf{c}_l$ are given at the lth level, the first WLS step, minimizing the following objective, is invoked to obtain an intermediate dense output $\mathbf{d}_*$:

$$\mathcal{E}(\mathbf{d}_*) = (\mathbf{d}_* - \mathbf{d}_l)^\top \mathbf{M}_l (\mathbf{d}_* - \mathbf{d}_l) + \lambda_1 \mathbf{d}_*^\top \mathbf{A}_{c_l} \mathbf{d}_* , \tag{4}$$

where $\mathbf{M}_l$ is a diagonal matrix with its elements given by the mask map m_l. $\mathbf{A}_{c_l}$ denotes the spatially varying Laplacian matrix defined by the guidance image c_l at the lth level. Unlike the image smoothing task using a dense input in (2), the input data $\mathbf{d}_l$ is sparse, and thus directly minimizing it in a separable manner leads to unstable results. Instead, as in [18,31], we compute the solution $\mathbf{d}_*$ with

$$\mathbf{d}_*(p) = \frac{((\mathbf{E} + \lambda \mathbf{A}_{c_l})^{-1} \mathbf{d}_l)(p)}{((\mathbf{E} + \lambda \mathbf{A}_{c_l})^{-1} \mathbf{m}_l)(p)} , \tag{5}$$

where $\mathbf{m}_l$ denotes the corresponding vectorized form of m_l. The WLS is applied twice to $\mathbf{d}_l$ and $\mathbf{m}_l$, respectively.

2nd WLS using d_* as the Guidance. Here, the input data $\mathbf{d}_o$ is obtained by a bicubic interpolation of $\mathbf{d}_l$ at the lth level, and the guidance signal is the intermediate interpolated data $\mathbf{d}_*$. A similar objective is minimized as:

$$\mathcal{E}(\tilde{\mathbf{d}}_l) = (\tilde{\mathbf{d}}_l - \mathbf{d}_o)^\top (\tilde{\mathbf{d}}_l - \mathbf{d}_o) + \lambda_2 \tilde{\mathbf{d}}_l^\top \mathbf{A}_{d_*} \tilde{\mathbf{d}}_l , \tag{6}$$

where $\mathbf{A}_{d_*}$ denotes the Laplacian matrix defined by d_*. Note that the input data $\mathbf{d}_o$ is dense in this pass, while $\mathbf{d}_l$ is sparse in the 1st WLS.

To give more intuitions of the proposed cascaded filtering process with alternating guidances, we show in Fig. 4 the processing results for one scanline (extracted from real images in Fig. 2): d_* and $\tilde{d}_l$ from the 1st and 2nd WLS steps, iterating from $l = 2$ down to $l = 0$. Over the iterations, both of our intermediate guidance signal d_* and the 2nd WLS output $\tilde{d}_l$ are progressively improved, with the final output $\tilde{d}_0$ close to the ground truth. In contrast, the result of applying the one-pass WLS contains spurious color structures (though attenuated), which are mistakenly transferred from highly-varying texture regions.

It is worth noting the difference from the rolling guidance filter (RGF) [44], though using progressively improved guidance signals appears somewhat related. First, they are developed for different objectives: RGF focuses on removing small structural details for image smoothing, but our FGI tackles notorious interpolation issues such as inconsistent structures between a color guidance image and a sparse depth or flow map. Second, RGF needs to carefully set the target scale parameter for its Gaussian prefiltering, but inconsistent structures across different signal modalities are often not small. Third, RGF has the limitation of blunting image corners, while FGI preserves important depth or motion structures.

3.2   Consensus-Based Data Point Augmentation

Thanks to the hierarchical interpolation framework, the proposed algorithm is not required to generate a fully dense data set for any intermediate level, which may propagate some unreliable data points to the next level otherwise. Therefore, we can be prudent in selecting reliable new data points to augment the input sparse data set d_l. As the last consistency checking in this current iteration l, we evaluate the consensus between the interpolated data points $\tilde{d}_l$ obtained from alternating guidance filtering and the data points d_o from a direct bicubic interpolation. In fact, without using the color guidance in the spatial interpolation process, d_o is free from color texture copying artifacts, though it has difficulties in restoring sharp edges/structures. Therefore, if we impose a consensus checking in the interpolated data between d_o and $\tilde{d}_l$, those unwanted color texture patterns in $\tilde{d}_l$ will not be chosen. This cautious design helps preventing those new data points of low confidence (e.g. undesired texture-copy patterns) from contaminating the next interpolation process.

Our consensus-based data point augmentation proceeds in a non-overlapping patch fashion. For each pixel q in the patch we check the consistency between the interpolated data points $\tilde{d}_l$ and the bicubic upsampled data points d_o as $\delta(q) = \|\tilde{d}_l(q) - d_o(q)\|$. After the consensus checking we pick the most consistent data location in the current patch (i.e. with the smallest $\delta(q)$ and also smaller than a preset threshold τ) and add this location to the data mask map $\tilde{m}_l$. Figure 3 illustrates this data augmentation process by denoting new data points in m_l^a as green triangles and initial sparse data points m_l as red dots. By selecting at most one new data point in each patch, we intend to avoid propagating the interpolation error to the next level. We use 2×2 patches in this paper.

3.3   Computational Complexity

The computational cost is mainly from solving the WLS objective in (3), as other parts have marginal computational overhead. To compare the complexity of our method with a single scale WLS based interpolation, we first count how many times the linear system is solved in both methods. In each level, the WLS based guided interpolation of (4) requires solving the linear system twice as in (5)– one for the input signal and one for the binary index signal, after which the final solution is obtained by an element-wise division. The WLS of (6) needs to solve the linear system once as its input $\mathbf{d}_o$ is dense. Thus, the linear system solver is applied 3 times at each level of our method. Since the interpolation grid is progressively rescaled with a factor of 2, our hierarchical framework increases the total computational complexity at most by $1/(1 - 1/4) = 4/3$. One can expect our hierarchical approach to have $(2+1) \times 4/3 = 4$ passes of executing the linear system solver, while the single scale WLS based interpolation needs **2** passes.

4   Experiments

We perform our experiments on a PC with Intel Xeon CPU (3.50 GHz) and 16 GB RAM. The implementation was in C++. For minimizing the WLS objective function, we use the FGS [31] solver provided on its project site [1] (also possible to use its OpenCV 3.1 function [2]). We will make our code publicly available. In all the experiments, we fix the smooth weights $\lambda_1 = 30.0^2, \lambda_2 = 10.0^2$, and the consensus checking threshold $\tau = 15(\text{depth})/1(\text{motion})$. For the affinity weight $w_{p,q}(g)$ in (1), we follow [31] to set $w_{p,q}(g) = \exp(-\|g_p - g_q\|/\sigma)$ with $\sigma = 0.005$.

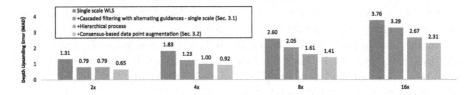

Fig. 5. The effect of each component of our pipeline evaluated on depth upsampling.

Table 1. Quantitative comparison (MAD) on ToF-like synthetic datasets [43]. Best results are in **bold**, and the second best are <u>underlined</u>.

Method	Art				Book				Moebius				Reindeer				Laundry				Dolls				Average			
	2x	4x	8x	16x	2x	4x	8x	16x	2x	4x	8x	16x	2x	4x	8x	16x	2x	4x	8x	16x	2x	4x	8x	16x	2x	4x	8x	16x
Bicubic	3.52	3.84	4.47	5.72	3.30	3.37	3.51	3.82	3.28	3.36	3.50	3.80	3.39	3.52	3.82	4.45	3.35	3.49	3.77	4.35	3.28	3.34	3.47	3.72	3.35	3.49	3.76	4.31
JGF [28]	2.36	2.74	3.64	5.46	2.12	2.25	2.49	3.25	2.09	2.24	2.56	3.28	2.18	2.40	2.89	3.94	2.16	2.37	2.85	3.90	2.09	2.22	2.49	3.25	2.17	2.37	2.82	3.85
GF [21]	1.49	1.97	3.00	4.91	0.8	1.22	1.95	3.04	1.18	1.90	2.77	3.55	1.29	1.99	2.99	4.14	1.28	2.05	3.04	4.10	1.19	1.94	2.80	3.50	1.21	1.85	2.76	3.87
CLMF0[30]	1.19	1.77	2.95	4.91	0.90	1.48	2.38	3.36	0.87	1.44	2.32	3.3	0.96	1.56	2.54	3.85	0.94	1.55	2.50	3.81	0.96	1.54	2.37	3.25	0.97	1.56	2.51	3.75
MRF+nlm[34]	1.69	2.40	3.60	5.75	1.12	1.44	1.81	2.59	1.13	1.45	1.95	2.91	1.20	1.60	2.40	3.97	1.28	1.63	2.20	3.34	1.14	1.54	2.07	3.02	1.26	1.68	2.34	3.60
TGV[17]	0.82	1.26	2.76	6.87	<u>0.50</u>	<u>0.74</u>	1.49	2.74	<u>0.56</u>	0.89	1.72	3.99	<u>0.59</u>	<u>0.84</u>	1.75	4.40	<u>0.61</u>	1.59	1.89	4.16	<u>0.66</u>	1.63	1.75	3.71	<u>0.62</u>	1.16	1.89	4.31
AR [43]	**0.76**	**1.01**	**1.70**	3.05	**0.47**	**0.70**	<u>1.15</u>	**1.81**	**0.46**	**0.72**	1.15	<u>1.92</u>	**0.48**	**0.80**	**1.29**	2.02	**0.51**	**0.85**	**1.30**	2.24	**0.59**	**0.91**	<u>1.32</u>	**2.08**	**0.55**	**0.83**	1.32	2.19
WLS [31]	1.34	1.90	2.95	4.63	1.25	1.70	2.39	3.29	1.34	1.92	2.66	3.56	1.47	2.05	2.82	4.09	1.11	1.55	2.24	3.49	1.34	1.85	2.55	3.50	1.31	1.83	2.60	3.76
FGI (ours)	<u>0.79</u>	<u>1.17</u>	<u>2.01</u>	**3.65**	0.58	0.80	**1.13**	<u>1.75</u>	0.58	<u>0.80</u>	**1.15**	**1.71**	0.65	0.89	<u>1.36</u>	**2.37**	0.65	<u>0.97</u>	<u>1.49</u>	<u>2.43</u>	0.67	<u>0.91</u>	**1.31**	<u>1.95</u>	0.65	<u>0.92</u>	**1.41**	**2.31**

4.1   Depth Upsampling Results

Pipeline Validation. First, we present a quick study on our pipeline design given in Sect. 3 on the depth upsampling task with the dataset provided by [43]. Starting from the single pass WLS based interpolation, we gradually add in new features until getting to our full pipeline. The comparison of the average error in the upsampled depth maps is plotted in Fig. 5. As can be seen, adding the cascaded filtering with one more WLS using alternating guidance in the single scale leads to lower errors in depth upsampling. Note, however, the gain from this step is almost fixed for all upsampling factors. To handle more challenging cases with high upsampling rates (*e.g.* 8 or 16), employing the hierarchical process yields better results, which meets our expectation. The last module tested is the consensus-based data point augmentation. This strategy further reduces the upsampling errors. Overall, our whole pipeline obtains much better depth upsampling results than the direct single pass WLS interpolation (see also Fig. 2).

We now evaluate the performance of depth upsampling with different edge-aware smoothing filters. We take the popular GF [21] for this test. The average error of a single pass interpolation with GF are 1.31/1.54/2.04/3.12 for upscaling rate 2/4/8/16. When using our pipeline with GF (*i.e.* replacing all the WLS steps with GF), the results are 1.06/1.21/1.63/2.59. The improvements confirm that our framework is generic to other edge-aware filtering techniques. We choose FGS [31] as our fundamental block for its best efficiency and accuracy.

Results on ToF-like Synthetic Datasets [43]. We evaluate the proposed FGI method on a ToF depth upsampling task using the synthetic datasets provided by [43]. They used six datasets from Middlebury benchmarks [3] to simulate ToF-like depth degradation by adding noise and performing downsampling with four different scales, *i.e.* 2, 4, 8, 16. Our FGI uses $L = 1, 2, 3, 4$ levels architecture for four different upsampling scales. Table 1 reports the Mean Absolute Difference (MAD) between ground truth depth maps and the results by various depth upsampling methods including ours. The proposed method clearly outperforms several existing methods like CLMF0 [30], JGF [28], MRF+nlm [34] and TGV [17] that used different color-guided upsampling or optimization techniques. Our method also yields much smaller error rates than the single-pass WLS interpolation, validating the effectiveness of our hierarchical structure. Finally, when compared with the state-of-the-art AR method [43] over all test image sets for challenging higher upsampling rates (8, 16), our FGI actually yields more accurate depth maps on half of them, *i.e. Book, Moebius,* and *Dolls.* Though slightly worse than AR [43] in terms of the MAD, our FGI is the second best among all leading methods, and runs over **1000×** faster than AR [43].

Table 2. Average runtime (in sec) to upsample by 4× an input depth map 272 × 344.

Method	MRF+nlm [34]	TGV [17]	AR [43]	GF [21]	CLMF0 [30]	WLS [31]	FGI (ours)
Runtime(s)	170	420	900	1.26	2.4	0.32	0.65

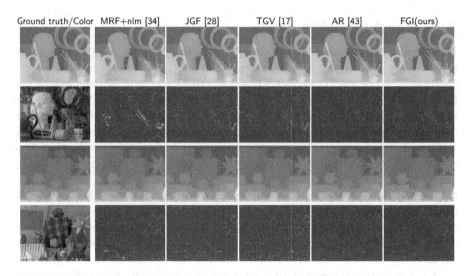

Fig. 6. Visual comparison on 8× upsampling results and error maps of *Art* and *Moebius* from the ToF-like synthetic dataset [43]. (Best viewed in electronic version.)

Table 2 summarizes the runtime of various methods whose source codes are available and timed on our PC. Generally, the methods using global optimizations *e.g.* MRF+nlm [34], TGV [17] and AR [43] come with much higher computational costs. GF [21] and CLMF0 [30], as local filtering methods, take less time to upsample a depth map, but they are still slower than our fast optimization-based method. The single-pass WLS with the FGS solver [31] takes only 0.32 s. Our FGI also takes advantage of the FGS solver [31] and is fast. Since we use different numbers of levels for different upsample rates, its runtimes vary slightly for them, *i.e.* 0.51/0.65/0.69/0.73 s for upscaling rate 2/4/8/16. The runtime results of the single-scale WLS and our FGI are also consistent with the complexity analysis in Sect. 3.3. Another efficient method JGF [28] reports 0.33 s in upsampling 8× to 0.4 M depth images, but FGI takes 0.19 s on the same size.

Figure 6 shows two visual comparisons of depth maps upsampled by different methods on this synthetic dataset. The results of MRF+nlm [34] fail to recover the depth for the thin structures in the *Art* case and show texture-copy artifacts in the *Moebius* case. The depth maps by JGF [28] contain noticeable noise as it is designed without any consideration of the noise issue from depth sensors. A separate noise removal process may be applied before JGF to solve the noise problem while our method (like most leading depth upsampling methods) does not require such a separate pre-processing. It is clearly observed that among all methods compared, AR [43] and our FGI recover accurate depths in homogeneous regions and along depth boundaries, and preserve thin structures better than other methods. More visual results are given in the supplemental materials.

Table 3. Quantitative results (MAD in millimeter) on the real ToFMark datasets [4].

	Bicubic	JBU [22]	GF [21]	JGF [28]	TGV [17]	FGI (ours)
Books	16.23	16.03	15.74	17.39	12.36	13.03
Devil	16.66	27.57	27.04	19.02	14.68	15.09
Shark	17.78	18.79	18.21	18.17	15.29	15.82

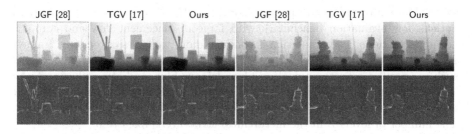

Fig. 7. Depth upsampling results and error maps of *Books* and *Devil* in ToFMark [4].

Results on the ToFMark Datasets [4]. We further test on the ToFMark datasets [4] provided in the TGV paper [17] that contain three real ToF depth and intensity image pairs *i.e. Books, Devil, Shark*. The ToF depth maps of spatial resolution 120 × 160 are real depth values in millimeter (mm), while the intensity images are of size 610 × 810. Table 3 presents the quantitative results measured by MAD in mm. Our method outperforms prevailing methods like

Table 4. Performance comparison (EPE) on the Sintel training set [9].

Method	Clean	Final	Runtime	Method	Clean	Final	Runtime
Epic-NW [35]	3.17	4.55	0.80 s	WLS [31]	3.23	4.68	0.21 s
Epic-LA [35]	2.65	4.10	0.94 s	**FGI (ours)**	2.75	4.14	0.39 s

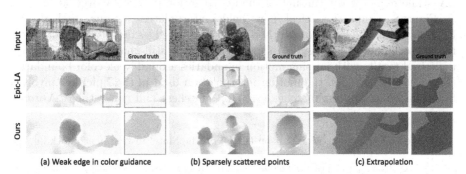

Fig. 8. Optical flow fields interpolated by our method and Epic-LA [35] on the Sintel datasets on three challenging cases. Please refer to Sect. 4.2 for more analysis.

JBU [22], GF [21], JGF [28], and obtains performance quite close to TGV [17]. Figure 7 shows the visual comparison of different methods. The depth recovered by JGF [28] again exhibits noticeable noise, while the results of TGV [17] and ours are much sharper and cleaner, but our FGI runs about **650×** faster than TGV [17].

4.2 Motion Field Interpolation for Optical Flow

We evaluate our motion interpolator using the MPI Sintel dataset [9], a modern optical flow evaluation benchmark with large displacement flow and complex non-rigid motions. The evaluation is conducted on two types of rendered frames, *i.e. clean* pass and *final* pass, where the final pass includes more complex effects such as specular reflections, motion blur, defocus blur, and atmospheric effects. We evenly sampled 331 frames from the whole training set and used them for evaluation and the rest of the frames were used to choose the best parameters. The number of levels L in the hierarchical structure is fixed to 3.

To generate a set of sparse matches, we adopt a leading descriptor-based matching algorithm – DeepMatching [39], one of the top methods on the Sintel benchmark. We perform the same match pruning step as EpicFlow [35] to remove unreliable matches, so the set of sparse matches used in our method and EpicFlow are exactly the same. After the pruning step, we usually can get 5000~6000 reliable matches on 436×1024 color frames. This motion interpolation task from sparse data with about 1 % density is challenging, especially considering the data points are not uniformly distributed. Note that besides [39], our framework is flexible to take in other choices of reliable motion matches *e.g.* [6].

For performance comparison on the 331 frames, we test with the single pass WLS [31], and also with both the locally-weighted affine (LA) and Nadaraya-Watson (NW) interpolators of EpicFlow [35], denoted as Epic-LA and Epic-NW. Table 4 reports the performance of these methods. Compared with the single pass WLS, our FGI shows improvements in the sparse-to-dense interpolation results, again demonstrating the effectiveness of our pipeline. Our method achieves a quantitative performance better than EpicFlow-NW and very close to EpicFlow-LA, while reducing the runtime of the interpolation process by over 50 %.

Figure 8 compares optical flow fields interpolated by our method and EpicFlow-LA. The EpicFlow method uses the color edges detected by a state-of-the-art technique [13] as a guidance signal, but it is still unavoidable to produce undesired results with missing motion boundaries around weak color boundaries (Fig. 8a). Furthermore, the motion interpolation used in the EpicFlow involves finding a set of nearest matches (*e.g.* 100 matches) and generating a Voronoi

Table 5. Performance comparison (EPE) on the Sintel testing benchmark [9].

	FlowFields[6]	EpicFlow[35]	PH-Flow[42]	FGI (ours)	Deep+R[14]	SPM-BP[27]	DeepFlow[39]	PCA-Layers[40]	MDP-Flow2[41]
Clean	3.748	4.115	4.388	4.664	5.041	5.202	5.377	5.730	5.837
Final	5.810	6.285	7.423	6.607	6.769	7.325	7.212	7.886	8.445

diagram, and such hard decisions or assignments often tend to produce patch-wise discretization artifacts (Fig. 8b). To address these issues, a variational energy minimization is applied as a post-processing, but such problems are not fully resolved due to the local minima of the variational approach. More seriously, in extremely low density regions, it often fails to densify the flow map prop-erly due to its essentially localized, approximated geodesic propagation strategy (Fig. 8c). In contrast, our approach does not detect color edges to directly guide the interpolation process, and also does not need an extra variational post-processing[2] thanks to the global optimization formulation using a hierarchical strategy.

Table 5 reports the quantitative evaluation on the Sintel test set [5]. On the benchmark, our FGI ranks the 8th for both clean and final passes among all 63 methods listed at the time of submission (Mar. 2016). Recent optical flow algo-rithms [6,14,35,40] use sparse matching or dense approximate nearest neighbor fields to handle large displacement and usually perform better than conventional methods [41]. The full version of EpicFlow in this table takes the advantage of local-weighted affine (LA) fitting and a variational energy minimization, per-forming slightly better than our FGI. However, unlike these optical flow specific methods [6,14,35,40], our proposed FGI is a generic, fast interpolator and does not need an extra post processing like variational optimization [6,35].

5   Conclusion

This paper presented a hierarchical, cascaded WLS-optimization based tech-nique that handles low-resolution and noisy depth upsampling and sparse motion match densification in a unified manner. Compared with the existing methods tailored specifically for one of these different tasks, our FGI achieves leading functional quality on benchmark evaluations as well as a highly efficient runtime over those top performers on each task. We used a basic WLS formulation as our key engine here to demonstrate its strength, but more robust sparse norms or an adaptively aggregated data term [31] can also be employed. Moreover, our technique has a potential advantage for further acceleration on GPUs and FPGA [11,20,33], offering a common engine for guided interpolation.

References

1. https://sites.google.com/site/globalsmoothing/
2. http://docs.opencv.org/master/da/d17/group__ximgproc__filters.html
3. http://vision.middlebury.edu/stereo/
4. http://rvlab.icg.tugraz.at/tofmark/
5. http://sintel.is.tue.mpg.de/results
6. Bailer, C., Taetz, B., Stricker, D.: Flow fields: dense correspondence fields for highly accurate large displacement optical flow estimation. In: ICCV (2015)

---

[2] We find adding it in FGI gives only marginal accuracy gain, unlike in EpicFlow [35].

7. Bao, L., Song, Y., Yang, Q., Yuan, H., Wang, G.: Tree filtering: efficient structure-preserving smoothing with a minimum spanning tree. IEEE Trans. Image Process. **23**(2), 555–569 (2014)

8. Brox, T., Bregler, C., Malik, J.: Large displacement optical flow. In: CVPR (2009)

9. Butler, D.J., Wulff, J., Stanley, G.B., Black, M.J.: A naturalistic open source movie for optical flow evaluation. In: Fitzgibbon, A., Lazebnik, S., Perona, P., Sato, Y., Schmid, C. (eds.) ECCV 2012, Part VI. LNCS, vol. 7577, pp. 611–625. Springer, Heidelberg (2012)

10. Chan, D., Buisman, H., Theobalt, C., Thrun, S.: A noise-aware filter for real-time depth upsampling. In: ECCV Workshop (2008)

11. Chaurasia, G., Ragan-Kelley, J., Paris, S., Drettakis, G., Durand, F.: Compiling high performance recursive filters. In: High Performance Graphics (2015)

12. Diebel, J., Thrun, S.: An application of markov random fields to range sensing. In: NIPS (2005)

13. Dollár, P., Zitnick, C.L.: Structured forests for fast edge detection. In: ICCV. IEEE (2013)

14. Drayer, B., Brox., T.: Combinatorial regularization of descriptor matching for optical flow estimation. In: BMVC (2015)

15. Elad, M.: On the origin of the bilateral filter and ways to improve it. IEEE Trans. Image Process. **11**(10), 1141–1151 (2002)

16. Farbman, Z., Fattal, R., Lischinski, D., Szeliski, R.: Edge-preserving decompositions for multi-scale tone and detail manipulation. ACM Trans. Graph. **27**(3), 67:1–67:10 (2008)

17. Ferstl, D., Reinbacher, C., Ranftl, R., Rüther, M., Bischof, H.: Image guided depth upsampling using anisotropic total generalized variation. In: ICCV (2013)

18. Gastal, E.S.L., Oliveira, M.M.: Domain transform for edge-aware image and video processing. ACM Trans. Graph. **30**(4), 69:1–69:12 (2011)

19. Golub, G.H., Loan, C.F.V.: Matrix Computations. Johns Hopkins University Press, Baltimore (1996)

20. Greisen, P., Runo, M., Guillet, P., Heinzle, S., Smolic, A., Kaeslin, H., Gross, M.: Evaluation and FPGA implementation of sparse linear solvers for video processing applications. IEEE Trans. Circuits Syst. Video Technol. **23**(8), 1402–1407 (2013)

21. He, K., Sun, J., Tang, X.: Guided image filtering. In: Daniilidis, K., Maragos, P., Paragios, N. (eds.) ECCV 2010, Part I. LNCS, vol. 6311, pp. 1–14. Springer, Heidelberg (2010)

22. Kopf, J., Cohen, M.F., Lischinski, D., Uyttendaele, M.: Joint bilateral upsampling. ACM Trans. Graph. **26**(3) (2007)

23. Koutis, I., Miller, G.L., Tolliver, D.: Combinatorial preconditioners and multilevel solvers for problems in computer vision and image processing. CVIU **115**(12), 1638–1646 (2011)

24. Krishnan, D., Fattal, R., Szeliski, R.: Efficient preconditioning of laplacian matrices for computer graphics. ACM Trans. Graph. **32**(4), 142:1–142:15 (2013)

25. Lang, M., Wang, O., Aydin, T., Smolic, A., Gross, M.: Practical temporal consistency for image-based graphics applications. ACM Trans. Graph. **31**(4), 34:1–34:8 (2012). doi:10.1145/2185520.2185530

26. Leordeanu, M., Zanfir, A., Sminchisescu, C.: Locally affine sparse-to-dense matching for motion and occlusion estimation. In: ICCV (2013)

27. Li, Y., Min, D., Brown, M.S., Do, M.N., Lu, J.: SPM-BP: sped-up patchmatch belief propagation for continuous MRFs. In: ICCV (2015)

28. Liu, M.Y., Tuzel, O., Taguchi, Y.: Joint geodesic upsampling of depth images. In: CVPR (2013)

29. Lu, J., Min, D., Pahwa, R.S., Do, M.N.: A revisit to MRF-based depth map super-resolution and enhancement. In: ICASSP (2011)
30. Lu, J., Shi, K., Min, D., Lin, L., Do, M.N.: Cross-based local multipoint filtering. In: CVPR (2012)
31. Min, D., Choi, S., Lu, J., Ham, B., Sohn, K., Do, M.N.: Fast global image smoothing based on weighted least squares. IEEE Trans. Image Process. **23**(12), 5638–5653 (2014)
32. Min, D., Lu, J., Do, M.N.: Depth video enhancement based on weighted mode filtering. IEEE Trans. Image Process. **21**(3), 1176–1190 (2012)
33. Nehab, D., Maximo, A., Lima, R.S., Hoppe, H.: GPU-efficient recursive filtering and summed-area tables. ACM Trans. Graph. **30**(6), 176:1–176:12 (2011)
34. Park, J., Kim, H., Tai, Y.W., Brown, M.S., Kweon, I.: High quality depth map upsampling for 3D-ToF cameras. In: ICCV (2011)
35. Revaud, J., Weinzaepfel, P., Harchaoui, Z., Schmid, C.: EpicFlow: edge-preserving interpolation of correspondences for optical flow. In: CVPR (2015)
36. Shen, X., Zhou, C., Xu, L., Jia, J.: Mutual-structure for joint filtering. In: ICCV (2015)
37. Talebi, H., Milanfar, P.: Nonlocal image editing. IEEE Trans. Image Process. **23**(10), 4460–4473 (2014)
38. Tomasi, C., Manduchi, R.: Bilateral filtering for gray and color images. In: IEEE International Conference on Computer Vision, pp. 839–846 (1998)
39. Weinzaepfel, P., Revaud, J., Harchaoui, Z., Schmid, C.: DeepFlow: large displacement optical flow with deep matching. In: ICCV (2013)
40. Wulff, J., Black, M.J.: Efficient sparse-to-dense optical flow estimation using a learned basis and layers. In: CVPR (2015)
41. Xu, L., Jia, J., Matsushita, Y.: Motion detail preserving optical flow estimation. TPAMI **34**(9), 1744–1757 (2012)
42. Yang, J., Li, H.: Dense, accurate optical flow estimation with piecewise parametric model. In: CVPR (2015)
43. Yang, J., Ye, X., Li, K., Hou, C., Wang, Y.: Color-guided depth recovery from RGB-D data using an adaptive autoregressive model. IEEE Trans. Image Process. **23**(8), 3443–3458 (2014)
44. Zhang, Q., Shen, X., Xu, L., Jia, J.: Rolling guidance filter. In: Fleet, D., Pajdla, T., Schiele, B., Tuytelaars, T. (eds.) ECCV 2014, Part III. LNCS, vol. 8691, pp. 815–830. Springer, Heidelberg (2014)

Learning High-Order Filters for Efficient Blind Deconvolution of Document Photographs

Lei Xiao[2,1]([✉]), Jue Wang[3], Wolfgang Heidrich[1,2], and Michael Hirsch[4]

[1] KAUST, Thuwal, Saudi Arabia
[2] University of British Columbia, Vancouver, Canada
leixiao@cs.ubc.ca
[3] Adobe Research, Seattle, USA
[4] MPI for Intelligent Systems, Tübingen, Germany

Abstract. Photographs of text documents taken by hand-held cameras can be easily degraded by camera motion during exposure. In this paper, we propose a new method for blind deconvolution of document images. Observing that document images are usually dominated by small-scale high-order structures, we propose to learn a multi-scale, interleaved cascade of shrinkage fields model, which contains a series of high-order filters to facilitate joint recovery of blur kernel and latent image. With extensive experiments, we show that our method produces high quality results and is highly efficient at the same time, making it a practical choice for deblurring high resolution text images captured by modern mobile devices.

Keywords: Text document · Camera motion · Blind deblurring · High-order filters

1 Introduction

Taking photographs of text documents (printed articles, receipts, newspapers, books, etc.) instead of scanning them has become increasingly common due to the popularity of mobile cameras. However, photos taken by hand-held cameras are likely to suffer from blur caused by camera shake during exposure. This is critical for document images, as slight blur can prevent existing optical-character-recognition (OCR) techniques from extracting correct text from them. Removing blur and recovering sharp, eligible document images is thus highly desirable. As in many previous work, we assume a simple image formation model for each local text region as

$$\mathbf{y} = \mathbf{Kx} + \mathbf{n}, \tag{1}$$

where $\mathbf{y}$ represents the degraded image, $\mathbf{x}$ the sharp latent image, matrix $\mathbf{K}$ the corresponding 2D convolution with blur kernel $\mathbf{k}$, and $\mathbf{n}$ white Gaussian noise.

Electronic supplementary material The online version of this chapter (doi:10.1007/978-3-319-46487-9_45) contains supplementary material, which is available to authorized users.

B. Leibe et al. (Eds.): ECCV 2016, Part III, LNCS 9907, pp. 734–749, 2016.
DOI: 10.1007/978-3-319-46487-9_45

The goal of the post-processing is to recover **x** and **k** from single input **y**, which is known as blind deconvolution or blind deblurring. This problem is highly ill-posed and non-convex. As shown in many previous work, good prior knowledge of both **x** and **k** is crucial for constraining the solution space and robust optimization. Specifically, most previous methods focus on designing effective priors for **x**, while **k** is usually restricted to be smooth.

Recent text image deblurring methods use sparse gradient priors (e.g., total variation [3], ℓ_0 gradient [5,14]) and text-specific priors (e.g., text classifier [5], ℓ_0 intensity [14]) for sharp latent image estimation. These methods can produce high-quality results in many cases, however their practical adaptation is hampered by several drawbacks. Firstly, their use of sparse gradient priors usually forces the recovered image to be piece-wise constant. Although these priors are effective for images with large-font text (i.e., high pixel-per-inch (PPI)), they do not work well for photographs of common text documents such as printed articles and newspapers where the font sizes are typically small [10]. Furthermore, these methods employ iterative sparse optimization techniques that are usually time-consuming for high resolution images taken by modern cameras (e.g., up to a few megapixels).

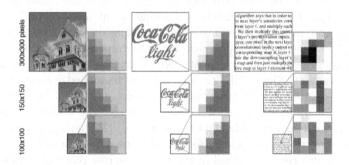

Fig. 1. Visual comparison between a natural image (left), a large-font text image (middle) and a common text document image at 150 PPI (right) at various scales.

In this paper, we propose a new algorithm for practical document deblurring that achieves both high quality and high efficiency. In contrast to previous works relying on low-order filter statistics, our algorithm aims to capture the domain-specific property of document images by learning a series of scale- and iteration-wise high-order filters. A motivational example is shown in Fig. 1, where we compare small patches extracted from a natural image, a large-font text image and a common text document image. Since most deblurring methods adopt a multi-scale framework in order to avoid bad local optima, we compare patches extracted from multiple scales. Evidently, the natural image and large-font text image both contain long, clear edges at all scales, making the use of sparse gradient priors effective. In contrast, patches from the document image with a small font size are mostly composed of small-scale high-order structures, especially at coarse scales, which makes sparse gradient priors to be inaccurate.

This observation motivates us to use high-order filter statistics as effective regularization for deblurring document images. We use a discriminative approach and learn such regularization terms by training a multi-scale, interleaved cascade of shrinkage field models [18], which was recently proposed as an effective tool for image restoration.

Our main contributions include:

- We demonstrate the importance of using high-order filters in text document image restoration.
- We propose a new algorithm for fast and high-quality deblurring of document photographs, suitable for processing high resolution images captured by modern mobile devices.
- Unlike the recent convolutional-neural-network (CNN) based document deblurring method [10], our approach is robust to page orientation, font style and text language, even though such variants are not included at our training.

2   Related Work

Blind Deblurring of Natural Images. Most deblurring methods solve the non-convex problem by alternately estimating latent image $\mathbf{x}$ and blur kernel $\mathbf{k}$, with an emphasis on designing effective priors on $\mathbf{x}$. Krishnan et al. [11] introduced a scale-invariant ℓ_1/ℓ_2 prior, which compensates for the attenuation of high frequencies in the blurry image. Xu et al. [24] used the ℓ_0 regularizer on the image gradient. Xiao et al. [22] used a color-channel edge-concurrence prior to facilitate chromatic kernel recovery. Goldstein and Fattal [8] estimated the kernel from the power spectrum of the blurred image. Yue et al. [25] improved [8] by fusing it with sparse gradient prior. Sun et al. [21] imposed patch priors to recover good partial latent images for kernel estimation. Michaeli and Irani [13] exploited the recurrence of small image patches across different scales of single natural images. Anwar et al. [2] learned a class-specific prior of image frequency spectrum for the restoration of frequencies that cannot be recovered with generic priors. Zuo et al. [26] learned iteration-wise parameters of the ℓ_p regularizer on image gradients. Schelten et al. [16] trained cascaded interleaved regression tree field (RTF) [19] to *post*-improve the result of other blind deblurring methods for natural images.

Another type of methods use explicit nonlinear filters to extract large-scale image edges from which kernels can be estimated rapidly. Cho and Lee [6] adopted a combination of shock and bilateral filters to predict sharp edges. Xu and Jia [23] improved [6] by neglecting edges with small spatial support as they impede kernel estimation. Schuler et al. [20] learned such nonlinear filters with a multi-layer convolutional neural network.

Blind Deblurring of Document Images. Most recent methods of text deblurring use the same sparse gradient assumption developed for natural images, and augment it with additional text-specific regularization. Chen et al. [3] and Cho et al. [5] applied explicit text pixel segmentation and enforced the text pixels to be dark or have similar colors. Pan et al. [14] used ℓ_0-regularized intensity and gradient priors for text deblurring. As discussed in Sect. 1 and as we will show in our experiments in Sect. 4, the use of sparse gradient priors makes such methods work well for large-font text images, but fail on common document images that have smaller fonts.

Hradiš et al. [10] trained a convolutional neural network to directly predict the sharp patch from a small blurry one, without considering the image formation model and explicit blur kernel estimation. With a large enough model and training dataset, this method produces good results on English documents with severe noise, large defocus blurs or simple motion blur. However, this method fails on more complicated motion trajectories, and is sensitive to page orientation, font style and text languages. Furthermore, this method often produces "hallucinated" characters or words which appears to be sharp and natural in the output image, but are completely wrong semantically. This undesirable side-effect severely limits its application range as most users do not expect the text to be changed in the deblurring process.

Discriminative Learning Methods for Image Restoration. Recently several methods were proposed to use trainable random field models for image restoration (denoising and *non-blind* deconvolution where the blur kernel is known a priori). These methods have achieved high-quality results with attractive run-times [4,18,19]. One representative technique is the shrinkage fields method [18], which reduces the optimization problem of random field models into cascaded quadratic minimization problems that can be efficiently solved in Fourier domain. In this paper, we extend this idea to the more challenging *blind* deconvolution problem, and employ the cascaded shrinkage fields model to capture high-order statistics of text document images.

3 Our Algorithm

The shrinkage fields (SF) model has been recently proposed as an effective and efficient tool for image restoration [18]. It has been successfully applied to both image denoising and non-blind image deconvolution, producing state-of-the-art results while maintaining high computational efficiency. Motivated by this success, we adopt the shrinkage field model for the challenging problem of *blind* deblurring of document images. In particular, we propose a multi-scale, interleaved cascade of shrinkage fields (CSF) which estimates the unknown blur kernel while progressively refining the estimation of the latent image. This is also partly inspired by [16], which proposes an interleaved cascade of regression tree fields (RTF) to *post*-improve the results of state-of-the-art natural image deblurring methods. However, in contrast to [16], our method *does not* depend on an initial kernel estimation from an auxiliary method. Instead, we estimate both the unknown blur kernel and latent sharp image from a single blurry input image.

3.1 Cascade of Shrinkage Fields (CSF)

The shrinkage field model can be derived from the field of experts (FoE) model [15]:

$$\operatorname*{argmin}_{\mathbf{x}} \mathcal{D}(\mathbf{x}, \mathbf{y}) + \sum_{i=1}^{N} \rho_i(\mathbf{F}_i \mathbf{x}), \tag{2}$$

where $\mathcal{D}$ represents the data fidelity given measurement $\mathbf{y}$, matrix $\mathbf{F}_i$ represents the corresponding 2D convolution with filter $\mathbf{f}_i$, and ρ_i is the penalty on the filter response. Half-quadratic optimization [7], a popular approach for the optimization of common random field models, introduces auxiliary variables $\mathbf{u}_i$ for all filter responses $\mathbf{F}_i \mathbf{x}$ and replaces the energy optimization problem Eq. 2 with a quadratic relaxation:

$$\operatorname*{argmin}_{\mathbf{x}, \mathbf{u}} \mathcal{D}(\mathbf{x}, \mathbf{y}) + \sum_{i=1}^{N} \left(\beta \|\mathbf{F}_i \mathbf{x} - \mathbf{u}_i\|_2^2 + \rho_i(\mathbf{u}_i) \right), \tag{3}$$

which for $\beta \to \infty$ converges to the original problem in Eq. 2. The key insight of [18] is that the minimizer of the second term w.r.t. $\mathbf{u}_i$ can be replaced by a flexible 1D shrinkage function ψ_i of filter response $\mathbf{F}_i \mathbf{x}$. Different from standard random fields which are parameterized through potential functions, SF models the shrinkage functions associated with the potential directly. Given data formation model as in Eq. 1, this reduces the original optimization problem Eq. 2 to a single quadratic minimization problem in each iteration, which can be solved efficiently as

$$\mathbf{x}^t = \mathcal{F}^{-1} \left[\frac{\mathcal{F}(\mathbf{K}_{t-1}^{\mathsf{T}} \mathbf{y} + \lambda^t \sum_{i=1}^{N} \mathbf{F}_i^{t \mathsf{T}} \psi_i^t(\mathbf{F}_i^t \mathbf{x}^{t-1}))}{\mathcal{F}(\mathbf{K}_{t-1}^{\mathsf{T}}) \cdot \mathcal{F}(\mathbf{K}_{t-1}) + \lambda^t \sum_{i=1}^{N} \mathcal{F}(\mathbf{F}_i^{t \mathsf{T}}) \cdot \mathcal{F}(\mathbf{F}_i^t)} \right], \tag{4}$$

where t is iteration index, $\mathbf{K}$ is the blur kernel matrix, $\mathcal{F}$ and $\mathcal{F}^{-1}$ indicate Fourier transform and its inverse, and ψ_i the shrinkage function. The model parameters $\Theta^t = (\mathbf{f}_i^t, \psi_i^t, \lambda^t)$ are trained by loss-minimization, e.g. by minimizing the ℓ_2 error between estimated images $\mathbf{x}^t$ and the ground truth. Performing multiple predictions of Eq. 4 is known as a cascade of shrinkage fields. For more details on the shrinkage fields model we refer readers to the supplemental material and [18].

3.2 Multi-scale Interleaved CSF for Blind Deconvolution

We do not follow the commonly used two-step deblurring procedure where kernel estimation and final latent image recovery are separated. Instead, we learn an interleaved CSF that directly produces both the estimated blur kernel and the predicted latent image. Our interleaved CSF is obtained by stacking multiple SFs into a cascade that is intermitted by kernel refinement steps. This cascade generates a sequence of iteratively refined blur kernel and latent image estimates, i.e. $\{\mathbf{k}^t\}_{t=1,..,T}$ and $\{\mathbf{x}^t\}_{t=1,..,T}$ respectively. At each stage of the cascade, we employ

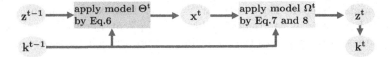

Fig. 2. Algorithm architecture.

a separately trained SF model for sharp image restoration. In addition, we learn an auxiliary SF model which generates a latent image $\mathbf{z}^t$ that is used to facilitate blur kernel estimation. The reason of including this extra SF model at each stage is to allow for selecting features that might benefit kernel estimation and eliminating other features and artifacts. Note that the idea of introducing such a latent feature image for improving kernel estimation is not new, and is a rather common practice in recent state-of-the-art blind deconvolution methods [6,23]. Figure 2 depicts a schematic illustration of a single stage of our interleaved CSF approach.

More specifically, given the input image $\mathbf{y}$, our method recovers $\mathbf{k}$ and $\mathbf{x}$ simultaneously by solving the following optimization problem:

$$(\mathbf{x}, \mathbf{k}) = \underset{\mathbf{x}, \mathbf{k}}{\operatorname{argmin}} \, ||\mathbf{y} - \mathbf{k} \otimes \mathbf{x}||_2^2 + \sum_{i=1}^{N} \rho_i(\mathbf{F}_i \mathbf{x}) + \tau ||\mathbf{k}||_2^2, \tag{5}$$

$$s.t. \quad \mathbf{k} \geq 0, ||\mathbf{k}||_1 = 1$$

To this end, our proposed interleaved CSF alternates between the following blur kernel and latent image estimation steps:

Update $\mathbf{x}^t$. For sharp image update we train a SF model with parameters $\Theta^t = (\mathbf{f}_i^t, \psi_i^t, \lambda^t)$. Analogously to Eq. 4 we obtain the following update for $\mathbf{x}^t$ at iteration t:

$$\mathbf{x}^t = \mathcal{F}^{-1} \left[\frac{\mathcal{F}(\mathbf{K}_{t-1}^{\mathsf{T}} \mathbf{y} + \lambda^t \sum_{i=1}^{N} \mathbf{F}_i^{t\mathsf{T}} \psi_i^t (\mathbf{F}_i^t \mathbf{z}^{t-1}))}{\mathcal{F}(\mathbf{K}_{t-1}^{\mathsf{T}}) \cdot \mathcal{F}(\mathbf{K}_{t-1}) + \lambda^t \sum_{i=1}^{N} \mathcal{F}(\mathbf{F}_i^{t\mathsf{T}}) \cdot \mathcal{F}(\mathbf{F}_i^t)} \right] \tag{6}$$

Update $\mathbf{z}^t$ and $\mathbf{k}^t$. For kernel estimation we first update the latent image $\mathbf{z}^t$ from $\mathbf{x}^t$ by learning a separate SF model. Denoting convolution with filter $\mathbf{g}_i^t$ by matrix $\mathbf{G}_i^t$, we have:

$$\mathbf{z}^t = \mathcal{F}^{-1} \left[\frac{\mathcal{F}(\mathbf{K}_{t-1}^{\mathsf{T}} \mathbf{y} + \eta^t \sum_{i=1}^{N} \mathbf{G}_i^{t\mathsf{T}} \phi_i^t (\mathbf{G}_i^t \mathbf{x}^t))}{\mathcal{F}(\mathbf{K}_{t-1}^{\mathsf{T}}) \cdot \mathcal{F}(\mathbf{K}_{t-1}) + \eta^t \sum_{i=1}^{N} \mathcal{F}(\mathbf{G}_i^{t\mathsf{T}}) \cdot \mathcal{F}(\mathbf{G}_i^t)} \right] \tag{7}$$

For kernel estimation we employ a simple Thikonov prior. Given the estimated latent image $\mathbf{z}^t$ and the blurry input image $\mathbf{y}$, the update for $\mathbf{k}^t$ reads:

$$\mathbf{k}^t = \mathcal{F}^{-1} \left[\frac{\mathcal{F}(\mathbf{z}^t)^* \cdot \mathcal{F}(\mathbf{y})}{\mathcal{F}(\mathbf{z}^t)^* \cdot \mathcal{F}(\mathbf{z}^t) + \tau^t} \right], \tag{8}$$

where $*$ indicates complex conjugate. The model parameters learned at this step are denoted as $\Omega^t = (\mathbf{g}_i^t, \phi_i^t, \eta^t, \tau^t)$. Note that Ω^t are trained to facilitate the update of both kernel $\mathbf{k}^t$ and image $\mathbf{z}^t$.

The $\mathbf{x}^t$ update step in Eq. 6 takes $\mathbf{z}^{t-1}$ rather than $\mathbf{x}^{t-1}$ as input, as $\mathbf{z}^{t-1}$ improves from $\mathbf{x}^{t-1}$ w.r.t. removing blur by Eq. 7 at iteration $t-1$. $\mathbf{x}^t$ and $\mathbf{z}^t$ is observed to converge as the latent image and kernel are recovered.

Algorithm 1. Blind deblurring at one scale

Input: blurry image $\mathbf{y}$
Output: estimated image $\mathbf{x}$ and kernel $\mathbf{k}$.
1: **for** $t = 1$ to 5 **do**
2:     Update $\mathbf{x}^t$ by Eq. 6.
3:     Update $\mathbf{z}^t$ by Eq. 7.
4:     Update $\mathbf{k}^t$ by Eq. 8.
5:     $\mathbf{k}^t = \max(0, \mathbf{k}^t), \mathbf{k}^t = \mathbf{k}^t / ||\mathbf{k}^t||_1$.
6: **end for**

Algorithm 1 summarizes the proposed approach for blind deblurring of document images. Note that there is translation and scaling ambiguity between the sharp image and blur kernel at blind deconvolution. The estimated kernel is normalized such that all its pixel values sum up to one. In Algorithm 2 for training, $\mathbf{x}^t$ is shifted to better align with the ground truth image $\bar{\mathbf{x}}$, before updating $\mathbf{k}$. We find that our algorithm usually converges in 5 iterations per scale.

3.3   Learning

Our interleaved CSF has two sets of model parameters at every stage $t = 1, .., 5$, one for sharp image restoration, $\Theta^t = (\mathbf{f}_i^t, \psi_i^t, \lambda^t)$, and the other for blur kernel estimation, $\Omega^t = (\mathbf{g}_i^t, \phi_i^t, \eta^t, \tau^t)$. All model parameters are learned through loss-minimization.

Algorithm 2. Learning at one scale

Input: blurry image $\mathbf{y}$; true image $\bar{\mathbf{x}}$; true kernel $\bar{\mathbf{k}}$.
Output: model parameters $(\mathbf{f}_i^t, \psi_i^t, \lambda^t, \mathbf{g}_i^t, \phi_i^t, \eta^t, \tau^t)$
1: **for** $t = 1$ to 5 **do**
2:     Train model parameters: $(\mathbf{f}_i^t, \psi_i^t, \lambda^t)$ to minimize $||\mathbf{x}^t - \bar{\mathbf{x}}||_2^2$ with gradient given in Eq. 9.
3:     Update $\mathbf{x}^t$ by Eq. 6.
4:     Shift $\mathbf{x}^t$ to better align with $\bar{\mathbf{x}}$.
5:     Train model parameters: $(\mathbf{g}_i^t, \phi_i^t, \eta^t, \tau^t)$ to minimize $||\mathbf{k}^t - \bar{\mathbf{k}}||_2^2 + \alpha||\mathbf{z}^t - \bar{\mathbf{x}}||_2^2$ with gradient given in Eq. 10.
6:     Update $\mathbf{z}^t$ by Eq. 7.
7:     Update $\mathbf{k}^t$ by Eq. 8.
8:     $\mathbf{k}^t = \max(0, \mathbf{k}^t), \mathbf{k}^t = \mathbf{k}^t / ||\mathbf{k}^t||_1$.
9: **end for**

Note that in addition to the blurry input image, each model receives also the previous image and blur kernel predictions as input, which are progressively refined at each iteration. This is in contrast to the non-blind deconvolution setting of [18], where the blur kernel is known and is kept fixed throughout all stages. Our interleaved CSF model is trained in a greedy fashion, i.e. stage by stage such that the learned SF models at one stage are able to adapt to the kernel and latent image estimated at the previous stage.

More specifically, at each stage we update our model parameters by iterating between the following two steps:

Update $\mathbf{x}^t$. To learn the model parameters Θ^t, we minimize the ℓ_2 error between the current image estimate and the ground truth image $\bar{\mathbf{x}}$, i.e. $\ell = ||\mathbf{x}^t - \bar{\mathbf{x}}||_2^2$. Its gradient w.r.t. the model parameters $\Theta^t = (\mathbf{f}_i^t, \psi_i^t, \lambda^t)$ can be readily computed as

$$\frac{\partial \ell}{\Theta^t} = \frac{\partial \mathbf{x}^t}{\partial \Theta^t} \frac{\partial \ell}{\mathbf{x}^t} \qquad (9)$$

The derivatives for specific model parameters are omitted here for brevity, but can be found in the supplemental material.

Update $\mathbf{z}^t$ and $\mathbf{k}^t$. The model parameters Ω^t of the SF models for kernel estimation at stage t are learned by minimizing the loss function $\ell = ||\mathbf{k}^t - \bar{\mathbf{k}}||_2^2 + \alpha ||\mathbf{z}^t - \bar{\mathbf{x}}||_2^2$, where $\bar{\mathbf{k}}$ denotes the ground truth blur kernel and α is a coupling constant. This loss accounts for errors in the kernel but also prevents the latent image used in Eq. (8) to diverge. Its gradient w.r.t. the model parameters $\Omega^t = (\mathbf{g}_i^t, \phi_i^t, \eta^t, \tau^t)$ reads

$$\frac{\partial \ell}{\partial \Omega^t} = \frac{\partial \mathbf{z}^t}{\partial \Omega^t} \frac{\partial \mathbf{k}^t}{\partial \mathbf{z}^t} \frac{\partial \ell}{\partial \mathbf{k}^t} + \frac{\partial \mathbf{k}^t}{\partial \Omega^t} \frac{\partial \ell}{\partial \mathbf{k}^t} + \frac{\partial \mathbf{z}^t}{\partial \Omega^t} \frac{\partial \ell}{\partial \mathbf{z}^t} \qquad (10)$$

Again, details for the computation of the derivatives w.r.t. to specific model parameters are included in the supplemental material. We want to point out that the kernel estimation error $||\mathbf{k}^t - \bar{\mathbf{k}}||_2^2$ is back-propagated to the model parameters $(\mathbf{g}_i^t, \phi_i^t, \eta^t)$ in the SF for $\mathbf{z}^t$. Hence, the latent image $\mathbf{z}^t$ is tailored for accurate kernel estimation and predicted such that the refinement in $\mathbf{k}^t$ in each iteration is optimal. This differs from related work in [16,26].

Multi-scale Approach. Our algorithm uses a multi-scale approach to prevent bad local optima. The kernel widths that are used at different scales are 5, 9, 17, 25 pixels. At each scale s, the blurry image $\mathbf{y}^s$, the true latent image $\bar{\mathbf{x}}^s$ and $\bar{\mathbf{k}}^s$ are downsampled (and normalized for $\bar{\mathbf{k}}^s$) from their original resolution. The scale index s is omitted for convenience. At the beginning of each scale $s > 1$, the estimated image $\mathbf{x}$ is initialized by bicubic upsampling its estimation at the previous scale, and the blur kernel $\mathbf{k}$ is initialized by nearest-neighbor upsampling, followed by re-normalization. At the coarsest scale $s = 1$, $\mathbf{x}$ is initialized as $\mathbf{y}$ and $\mathbf{k}$ is initialized as a delta peak. The coupling constant α in kernel estimation loss is defined as $\alpha = r \cdot \eta$, where r is the ratio between pixel numbers in kernel $\mathbf{k}^t$ and image $\mathbf{z}^t$ at current scale, η is initialized with 1 at the coarsest scale and at each subsequent scale it is multiplied by a factor of 0.25. Algorithm 2 summarizes our learning procedure for a single scale of our CSF model.

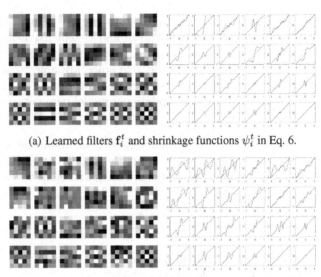

(a) Learned filters $\mathbf{f}_i^t$ and shrinkage functions ψ_i^t in Eq. 6.

(b) Learned filters $\mathbf{g}_i^t$ and shrinkage functions ϕ_i^t in Eq. 7.

Fig. 3. Learned filters and shrinkage functions (at 3rd scale, 1st iteration) for updating $\mathbf{x}^t$ (Eq. 6) and $\mathbf{z}^t$, $\mathbf{k}^t$ (Eq. 7), respectively. Other parameters learned at this iteration: $\lambda^t = 0.5757$, $\eta^t = 0.0218$, $\tau^t = 0.0018$.

Model Complexity. In both the model Θ^t for $\mathbf{x}^t$ and model Ω^t for $(\mathbf{z}^t, \mathbf{k}^t)$, we choose to use 24 filters $\mathbf{f}_i^t$ of size 5×5 for trade-off between result quality, model complexity and time efficiency. As in [18], we initialize the filters with a DCT filter bank. Each shrinkage function ψ_i^t and ϕ_i^t are composed of 51 equidistant-positioned radial basis functions (RBFs) and are initialized as identity function. We further enforce central symmetry to the shrinkage functions, so that the number of trainable RBFs reduces by half to 25. Figure 3 visualizes some learned models.

Training Datasets. We have found that that our method works well with a relatively small training dataset without over-fitting. We collected 20 motion blur kernels from [18], and randomly rotated them to generate 60 different kernels. We collected 60 sharp patches of 250×250 pixels cropped from documents rendered around 175 PPI, and rotated each with a random angle between -4 and 4 degrees. We then generated 60 blurry images by convolving each pair of sharp image and kernel, followed by adding white Gaussian noise and quantizing to 8 bits. We used the L-BFGS solver [17] in Matlab for training, which took about 12 h on a desktop with an Intel Xeon CPU.

4   Results

In this section we evaluate the proposed algorithm on both synthetic and real-world images. We compare with Pan et al. [14] and Hradiš et al. [10],

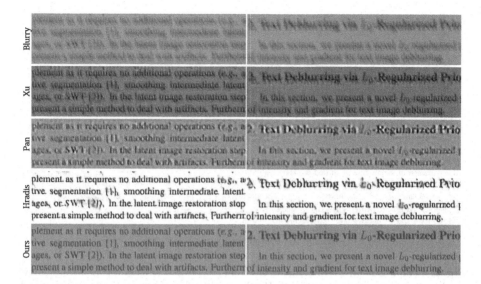

Fig. 4. Comparison on a real image taken from [10]. Row 1–5 from top to bottom show the blurry image, result of Xu [1], Pan [14], Hradiš et al. [10] and our method. Two cropped regions are shown here, the full resolution results along with more examples can be found in the supplemental.

the state-of-the-art methods for text image blind deblurring, and the natural image deblurring software produced by Xu [1], which are based on recently proposed state-of-the-art techniques [23, 24]. We used the code and binaries provided by the authors and tuned the parameters to generate the best possible results.

Real-World Images. In Figs. 4 and 5 we show comparisons on real images. The result images of Xu [1] and Pan [14] contain obvious artifacts due to ineffective image priors that lead to inaccurate kernel estimation. Hradiš et al. [10] fails to recover many characters and distorted the font type and illumination. Our method produces the best results in these cases, and our results are both visually pleasing and highly legible. The full resolution images and more results are included in the supplemental material.

Quantitative Comparisons. For quantitative evaluation, we test all methods on a synthetic dataset and compare results in terms of the peak-signal-to-noise-ratio (PSNR). We collect 8 sharp document images with 250×250 pixels cropped from documents rendered at 150 PPI (similar PPI as used for training in [10]). Each image is blurred with 8 kernels at 25×25 collected from [12], followed by adding 1 % Gaussian noise and 8-bit quantization. In Fig. 6, we show the average PSNR values of all 8 test images synthesized with the same blur kernel. Our method outperforms other methods in all cases by 0.5–6.0 dB. Hradiš et al. [10] has close performance to ours on kernel #3, which is close to defocus blur. It also performs reasonably well on kernel #6 which features a simple motion path,

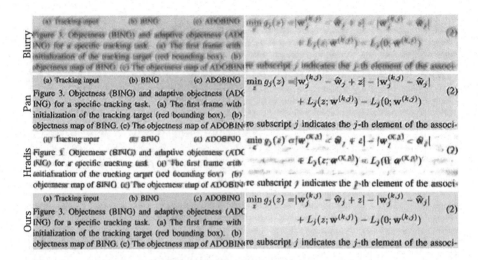

Fig. 5. Comparison on a real image taken from [10]. Row 1–4 from top to bottom show the blurry image, result of Pan [14], Hradiš et al. [10] and our method. Two cropped regions are shown, the full resolution results along with more results can be found in the supplemental.

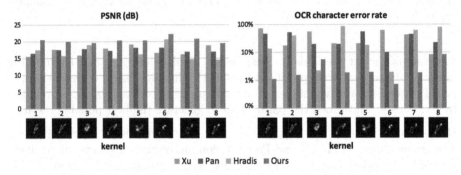

Fig. 6. PSNR and OCR comparison on a synthetic test dataset with 8 blur kernels.

but fails on other more challenging kernels. Some results along with the estimated kernels are shown in Fig. 7 for visual comparison.

An interesting question one may ask is whether improved deblur can directly lead to better optical-character-recognition (OCR) accuracy. To answer this question we evaluate OCR accuracy using the software ABBYY FineReader 12. We collected 8 sharp document images from the OCR test dataset in [10]. Each document image contains a continuous paragraph. We synthesized 64 blurry images with the 8 kernels and 1% Gaussian noise similarly as in the PSNR comparison. We run the OCR software and used the script provided by [10] to compute the average character error rate for all 8 test images synthesized with

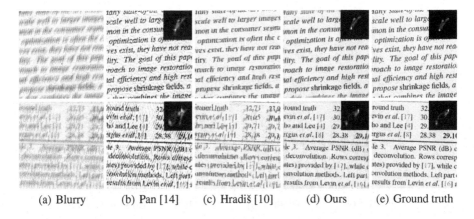

| (a) Blurry | (b) Pan [14] | (c) Hradiš [10] | (d) Ours | (e) Ground truth |

Fig. 7. Comparison on synthetic images from the PSNR experiments in Fig. 6. Note that the original results of [10] break the illumination of the images. We clamp the intensity of their results to match the ground truth image before computing the PSNR values.

Table 1. Run-time comparison (in seconds).

Image size	256^2	512^2	1024^2
Xu [1] (C++)	14.8	33.4	-
Pan [14] (Matlab)	19.6	84.3	271.9
Hradiš et al. [10] (C++)	48.5	193.7	594.9
Hradiš et al. [10] (GPU)	0.3	1.0	3.1
Ours (Matlab)	2.0	3.9	11.4
Pre-computation (Matlab)	1.8	4.6	15.3

the same kernel[1]. The results are shown in Fig. 6. They are consistent with the PSNR results also in Fig. 6. Hradiš et al. [10] performs well on kernel #3 and #6 but fails on other challenging kernels, while our method is consistently better than others. All the test images and results for PSNR and OCR comparisons are included in the supplemental material.

Run-Time Comparison. Table 1 provides a comparison on computational efficiency, using images blurred by a 17×17 kernel at three different resolutions. The experiments were done on an Intel i7 CPU with 16 GB RAM and a GeForce GTX TITAN GPU. Assuming the image sensor resolution is a known priori[2], we pre-compute the FFTs of the trained filters $\mathbf{f}_i$ and $\mathbf{g}_i$ for maximal efficiency. We report the timing of our Matlab implementation on CPU. A GPU implementation should significantly reduce the time as our method only

---

[1] We used the script 'eval.py' downloaded from the author webpage [10] to compute the error rate (after a bug was fixed).

[2] This is a common assumption especially for batch processing of document images.

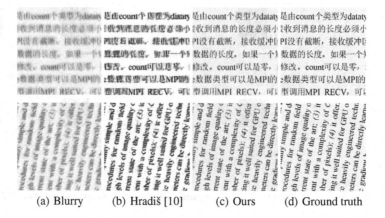

(a) Blurry   (b) Hradiš [10]   (c) Ours   (d) Ground truth

Fig. 8. Comparison on non-English text and severely rotated images. Note that such non-English text and large rotation were not included in our training dataset.

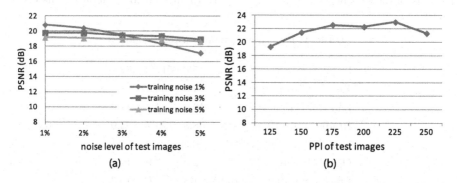

(a)   (b)

Fig. 9. Robustness test on noise level and image PPI (pixel-per-inch).

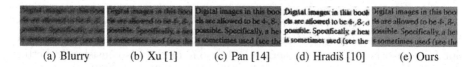

(a) Blurry   (b) Xu [1]   (c) Pan [14]   (d) Hradiš [10]   (e) Ours

Fig. 10. Comparison on a real image with large-font text. The reference results are from [10]. Following [10], the input of (d) Hradiš' and (e) our method was downsampled by factor of 3.

requires FFT, 2D convolution and 1D look-up-table (LUT) operations, which is our future work.

Robustness. In Fig. 8, we show results on non-English text and severely rotated image. Although both Hradiš et al. [10] and our method are only trained on English text data, our method can be applied to non-English text as well. This is a great benefit of our method as we do not need to train on every different language, or increase the model complexity to handle them as [10] would need to do.

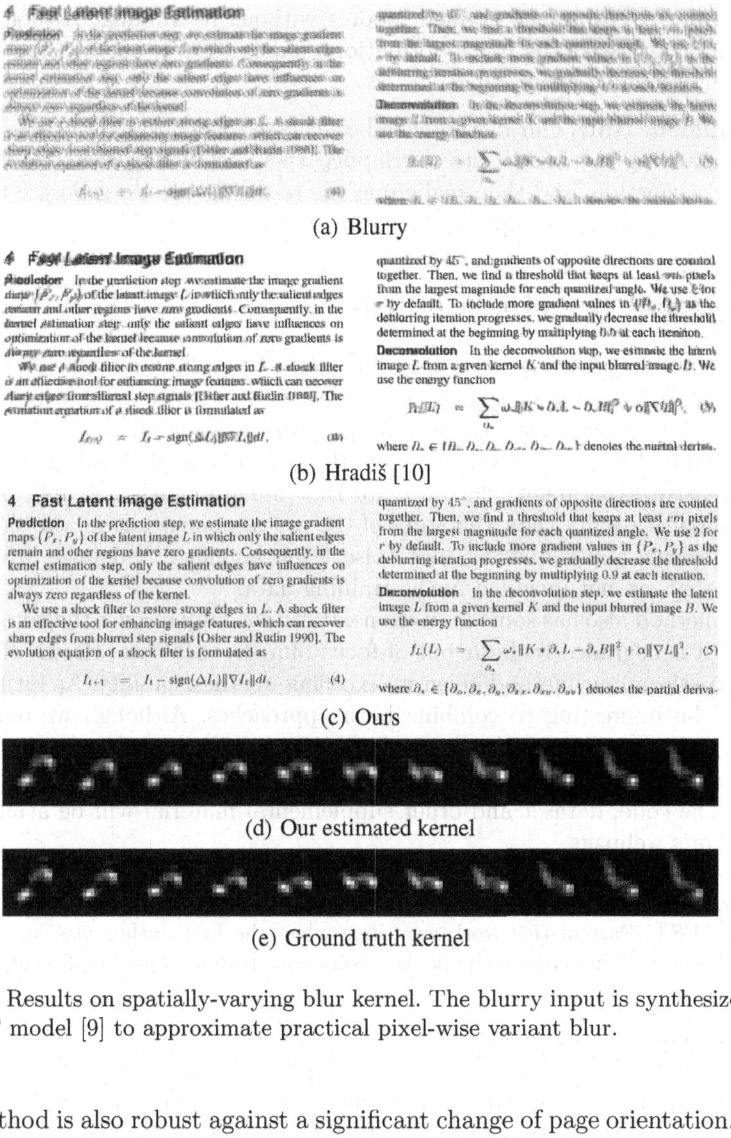

4 Fast Latent Image Estimation

Prediction In the prediction step, we estimate the image gradient maps $\{P_x, P_y\}$ of the latent image L in which only the salient edges remain and other regions have zero gradients. Consequently, in the kernel estimation step, only the salient edges have influences on optimization of the kernel because convolution of zero gradients is always zero regardless of the kernel.

We use a shock filter to restore strong edges in L. A shock filter is an effective tool for enhancing image features, which can recover sharp edges from blurred step signals [Osher and Rudin 1990]. The evolution equation of a shock filter is formulated as

$$I_{t+1} = I_t - \text{sign}(\Delta I_t)\|\nabla I_t\|dt, \quad (4)$$

quantized by $45°$, and gradients of opposite directions are counted together. Then, we find a threshold that keeps at least rn pixels from the largest magnitude for each quantized angle. We use 2 for r by default. To include more gradient values in $\{P_x, P_y\}$ as the deblurring iteration progresses, we gradually decrease the threshold determined at the beginning by multiplying 0.9 at each iteration.

Deconvolution In the deconvolution step, we estimate the latent image L from a given kernel K and the input blurred image B. We use the energy function

$$f_L(L) = \sum_{\partial_*} \omega_*\|K * \partial_* L - \partial_* B\|^2 + \alpha\|\nabla L\|^2, \quad (5)$$

where $\partial_* \in \{\partial_o, \partial_x, \partial_y, \partial_{xx}, \partial_{xy}, \partial_{yy}\}$ denotes the partial deriva-

(a) Blurry

(b) Hradiš [10]

(c) Ours

(d) Our estimated kernel

(e) Ground truth kernel

Fig. 11. Results on spatially-varying blur kernel. The blurry input is synthesized with the EFF model [9] to approximate practical pixel-wise variant blur.

Our method is also robust against a significant change of page orientation, which cannot be handled well by [10].

In Fig. 9, we show the results of our method when the noise level and PPI of the test data differs from the training data. Figure 9(a) shows that the performance of our method is fairly steady when the noise level in the test images is not too much higher than that of the training data, meaning that the models trained at sparse noise levels are sufficient for practical use. Figure 9(b) shows that our method works well in a fairly broad range of image PPIs given the training data are around 175 PPI.

In Fig. 10, we show a comparison on a real image with large-font text. Following [10], the input of Hradiš' and our method was downsampled by factor of 3 in order to apply the trained models without re-training. Although such downsampling breaks the image formation model in Eq. 1, our method can still generate reasonable result.

Non-uniform Blur. Our method can be easily extended to handle non-uniform blur by dividing the image into overlapped tiles, deblurring each tile with our proposed algorithm, and then realigning the resulting tiles to generate the final estimated image. An example is shown in Fig. 11.

5   Conclusion and Discussion

In this paper we present a new algorithm for fast and high-quality blind deconvolution of document photographs. Our key idea is to to use high-order filters for document image regularization, and propose to learn such filters and influences from training data using multi-scale, interleaved cascade of shrinkage field models. Extensive experiments demonstrate that our approach not only produces higher quality results than the state-of-the-art methods, but is also computational efficient, and robust against noise level, language and page orientation changes that are not included in the training data.

Our method also has some limitations. It cannot fully recover the details of an image if it is degraded by large out-of-focus blur. In such case, Hradiš et al. [10] may outperform our method given its excellent synthesis ability. As future work it would be interesting to combine both approaches. Although we only show learning our model on document photographs, we believe such a framework can also be applied to other domain-specific images, which we plan to explore in the future. The code, dataset and other supplemental material will be available on the author's webpage.

Acknowledgement. This work was supported in part by Adobe and Baseline Funding of KAUST. Part of this work was done when the first author was an intern at Adobe Research. The authors thank the anonymous reviewers for helpful suggestions.

References

1. Robust deblurring software. www.cse.cuhk.edu.hk/~leojia/deblurring.htm
2. Anwar, S., Phuoc Huynh, C., Porikli, F.: Class-specific image deblurring. In: ICCV (2015)
3. Chen, X., He, X., Yang, J., Wu, Q.: An effective document image deblurring algorithm. In: CVPR (2011)
4. Chen, Y., Yu, W., Pock, T.: On learning optimized reaction diffusion processes for effective image restoration. In: CVPR (2015)
5. Cho, H., Wang, J., Lee, S.: Text image deblurring using text-specific properties. In: Fitzgibbon, A., Lazebnik, S., Perona, P., Sato, Y., Schmid, C. (eds.) ECCV 2012, Part V. LNCS, vol. 7576, pp. 524–537. Springer, Heidelberg (2012)
6. Cho, S., Lee, S.: Fast motion deblurring. ACM Trans. Graph. **28**(5) (2009)
7. Geman, D., Yang, C.: Nonlinear image recovery with half-quadratic regularization. IEEE Trans. Image Process. **4**(7), 932–946 (1995)

8. Goldstein, A., Fattal, R.: Blur-Kernel estimation from spectral irregularities. In: Fitzgibbon, A., Lazebnik, S., Perona, P., Sato, Y., Schmid, C. (eds.) ECCV 2012, Part V. LNCS, vol. 7576, pp. 622–635. Springer, Heidelberg (2012)
9. Hirsch, M., Sra, S., Scholkopf, B., Harmeling, S.: Efficient filter flow for space-variant multiframe blind deconvolution. In: CVPR (2010)
10. Hradiš, M., Kotera, J., Zemcík, P., Šroubek, F.: Convolutional neural networks for direct text deblurring. In: BMVC (2015)
11. Krishnan, D., Tay, T., Fergus, R.: Blind deconvolution using a normalized sparsity measure. In: CVPR (2011)
12. Levin, A., Weiss, Y., Durand, F., Freeman, W.T.: Understanding and evaluating blind deconvolution algorithms. In: CVPR (2009)
13. Michaeli, T., Irani, M.: Blind deblurring using internal patch recurrence. In: Fleet, D., Pajdla, T., Schiele, B., Tuytelaars, T. (eds.) ECCV 2014, Part III. LNCS, vol. 8691, pp. 783–798. Springer, Heidelberg (2014)
14. Pan, J., Hu, Z., Su, Z., Yang, M.H.: Deblurring text images via. l0-regularized intensity and gradient prior. In: CVPR (2014)
15. Roth, S., Black, M.J.: Fields of experts: a framework for learning image priors. In: CVPR (2005)
16. Schelten, K., Nowozin, S., Jancsary, J., Rother, C., Roth, S.: Interleaved regression tree field cascades for blind image deconvolution. In: WACV (2015)
17. Schmidt, M.: minfunc: unconstrained differentiable multivariate optimization in matlab. http://www.cs.ubc.ca/~schmidtm/Software/minFunc.html
18. Schmidt, U., Roth, S.: Shrinkage fields for effective image restoration. In: CVPR (2014)
19. Schmidt, U., Rother, C., Nowozin, S., Jancsary, J., Roth, S.: Discriminative non-blind deblurring. In: CVPR (2013)
20. Schuler, C.J., Hirsch, M., Harmeling, S., Schölkopf, B.: Learning to deblur (2014). arXiv preprint arXiv:1406.7444
21. Sun, L., Cho, S., Wang, J., Hays, J.: Edge-based blur kernel estimation using patch priors. In: ICCP (2013)
22. Xiao, L., Gregson, J., Heide, F., Heidrich, W.: Stochastic blind motion deblurring. IEEE Trans. Image Process. **24**(10), 3071–3085 (2015)
23. Xu, L., Jia, J.: Two-Phase Kernel estimation for robust motion deblurring. In: Daniilidis, K., Maragos, P., Paragios, N. (eds.) ECCV 2010, Part I. LNCS, vol. 6311, pp. 157–170. Springer, Heidelberg (2010)
24. Xu, L., Zheng, S., Jia, J.: Unnatural l0 sparse representation for natural image deblurring. In: CVPR (2013)
25. Yue, T., Cho, S., Wang, J., Dai, Q.: Hybrid image deblurring by fusing edge and power spectrum information. In: Fleet, D., Pajdla, T., Schiele, B., Tuytelaars, T. (eds.) ECCV 2014, Part VII. LNCS, vol. 8695, pp. 79–93. Springer, Heidelberg (2014)
26. Zuo, W., Ren, D., Gu, S., Lin, L., Zhang, L.: Discriminative learning of iteration-wise priors for blind deconvolution. In: CVPR (2015)

Multi-view Inverse Rendering Under Arbitrary Illumination and Albedo

Kichang Kim$^{(\boxtimes)}$, Akihiko Torii, and Masatoshi Okutomi

Tokyo Institute of Technology, Tokyo, Japan
kichang.k@ok.ctrl.titech.ac.jp,
{torii,mxo}@ctrl.titech.ac.jp

Abstract. 3D shape reconstruction with multi-view stereo (MVS) relies on a robust evaluation of photo consistencies across images. The robustness is ensured by isolating surface albedo and scene illumination from the shape recovery, i.e. shading and colour variation are regarded as a nuisance in MVS. This yields a gap in the qualities between the recovered shape and the images used. We present a method to address it by jointly estimating detailed shape, illumination and albedo using the initial shape robustly recovered by MVS. This is achieved by solving the multi-view inverse rendering problem using the geometric and photometric smoothness terms and the normalized spherical harmonics illumination model. Our method allows spatially-varying albedo and per image illumination without any prerequisites such as training data or image segmentation. We demonstrate that our method can clearly improve the 3D shape and recover illumination and albedo on real world scenes.

Keywords: Multi-view stereo · Shape from shading · Inverse rendering

1 Introduction

3D reconstruction from multiple images is becoming a basic tool in various applications, *e.g.* CAD model creation [1] and 3D mapping [2] thanks to softwares based on structure-from-motion (SfM) [3–5] followed by multi-view stereo (MVS) [6–8]. 3D reconstruction typically begins with SfM from imagery. MVS is then used to reconstruct surface while finding more correspondences via pixel/feature matching. Since this is a non-trivial task as real images are taken under a variety of conditions, photo consistencies among images are robustly computed [9,10] in order to suppress the appearance changes among images. Such matching schemes work well for recovering distinctive objects but often fail with weakly textured objects.

In contrast to MVS, Shape from Shading (SfS) [11] recovers surface normals from a single image by solving the inverse problem of image rendering formed as a function of surface normal, albedo and shading. Since shading directly represents (high frequency) shape information under the smooth illumination, SfS can extract fine and detailed surface normal from shading variation. Although SfS

© Springer International Publishing AG 2016
B. Leibe et al. (Eds.): ECCV 2016, Part III, LNCS 9907, pp. 750–767, 2016.
DOI: 10.1007/978-3-319-46487-9_46

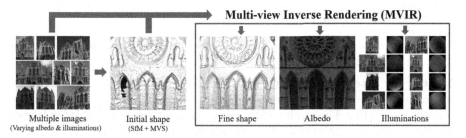

Fig. 1. Multi-view inverse rendering. We present a multi-view inverse rendering method for joint estimating of complex shape, spatially-varying albedo and per image illuminations.

Table 1. Comparison with closely related methods. Our method can recover detailed shape from images taken with both spatially-varying albedo and per image (temporally-varying) illumination without any prerequisite.

Method	Albedo	Illumination
Wu *et al.* [20]	Uniform	Constant among images
Shan *et al.* [21]	Spatially varying	Cloudy images ($\rightarrow$ temporally-varying)
Zollhöfer *et al.* [22]	Spatially varying	Constant among images
Proposed	Spatially varying	Per image (temporally varying)

requires surface albedo and/or shading information, recent approach solves this by using additional prerequisite [12] or multiple images captured under different illuminations, *i.e.* Photometric Stereo (PS) [13,14].

For these reasons, MVS and SfS are complementary to each other and several methods that fuse MVS and SfS have been proposed [15–19]. The main idea is to use MVS (or RGBD images) as an initial shape (depth and normal) and refine it by applying SfS techniques. Table 1 summarizes the relationships of the closely related methods based on multiple-view images. Previous methods can estimate albedo and illumination under limited conditions such as uniform albedo [20], the existence of known illumination images [21] and constant illumination among images [22].

Contribution. In this paper, we propose a method to reconstruct detailed shape only from images via multi-view inverse rendering (MVIR). To achieve this, we design cost function based on rendering term and regularization terms on shape and albedo (Sect. 3). The cost function consists of the rendering term that can handle temporally varying illumination, the geometric smoothness term that refines shape while preserving sharp edges and the photometric smoothness term (Sect. 3.2) that constrains albedo among multiple images. The proposed method is able to jointly estimate shape, albedo and illumination without any prerequisites and can be applied to images which capture complex objects under different illumination conditions (such as day/night images).

2 Related Work

In this section, we describe fundamental works on MVS, photometric methods (SfS and PS) and their combinations.

Multi-view Stereo. MVS in principle recovers depth by robustly measuring photo consistencies among images, *e.g.* SSD, NCC [9] and descriptor distances [10]. The typical MVS approach recovers depth for reference images [23,24] by optimizing the cost function that consists of a data term (photo consistencies) and smoothness (regularization) terms [25,26]. The scene is recovered by merging depth maps and determining surfaces that impact the final quality of surface [27–30].

Other popular approaches directly reconstruct points or patches in 3D space [7,31] by locally evaluating photo consistencies and conservatively expanding the reconstruction. This approach is robust for recovering complex objects as it suffers less from depth discontinuity or occlusions but will not work on weakly-textured objects. Jancosek and Pajdla [8] improves on this by introducing a modified graph-cut based surface reconstruction. Bao *et al.* [32] on the other hand solves this by fusing pre-trained semantic shape information. All-in-one MVS softwares [7,8,33] were, indeed, a breakthrough as they can provide 3D models with impressive quality when many photographs are taken in good conditions, *e.g.* using many images taken by DSLR cameras under a consistent lighting [9,34].

Although up-to-date MVS methods are well-balanced in accuracy, robustness and computational costs, the surface quality (accuracy and completeness) can be further improved by taking into account illumination and albedo encoded in the images.

Photometric Methods. Horn [11] introduced Shape from Shading that estimates the surface normal by decomposing shading information encoded in the image. This is achieved by solving the inverse rendering function formulated in a simplified form. Since SfS is an ill-posed problem, early SfS algorithms assume uniform albedo and known illumination [35,36]. Recently proposed methods loosen these conditions by extending the rendering model [37] and relaxing the albedo restriction under general illumination [38].

Using multiple images taken under different lighting conditions can also relax the conditions in SfS: Photometric Stereo (PS). Woodham [14] demonstrated that surface normal can be recovered from images captured at a fixed viewpoint under varying calibrated illuminations. Basri and Jacobs [39] extended this to more natural (uncalibrated) illumination by representing the illumination as low order spherical harmonics. Hernandez *et al.* [40] further relaxed the fixed view point condition by using visual hull information. This method used surface normals on object silhouettes to estimate direction of illumination for multi-view images.

Combination. Photometric methods in general prefer less-textured surface captured under different illuminations whereas MVS requires well-textured surfaces. Combining these two complementary approaches can produce higher quality 3D shape.

Wu *et al.* [20] presented a method to refine the initial shape obtained from MVS while taking care of ambient occlusion artifacts. They achieved this by modelling the inverse image rendering function using low order spherical harmonics. As summarized in Table 1, this method requires uniform surface albedo and constant (global) illumination among images in order to separate shading and albedo.

Shan *et al.* [21] showed that cloudy images can be a clue to decompose albedo and shading from images, *i.e.* using multiple cloudy images captured under ambient illumination as the source of albedo. They used an initial shape from MVS, decomposed surface albedo, and recovered other images with varying illumination on top of the estimated albedo. Shi *et al.* [41] introduced a method based on PS: it first recovers the initial shape by MVS, transfer images for "a reference camera" and apply uncalibrated PS using internet photos. This method refines shape and recovers temporally-varying illumination by altering the estimation procedures from the reference view point.

With the advent of low cost RGB-D sensors, several photometric-based techniques are introduced to fill the quality gap between the RGB image and depth map [42–45]. Barron and Malik [42] showed that a single RGB-D image can be used to compute a refined shape, albedo and scene illumination by using pre-trained mixtures of gaussians. Other works refine the depth by assuming uniform albedo [43,44] or multiple albedo (with image segmentation) [45] under a low order spherical harmonics model.

Most recently, Zollhöfer *et al.* [22] proposed a novel shape refinement technique by formulating the inverse rendering function including color and surface normals under the volumetric representation. In [22], surface refinement is performed in a voxel space in the form of optimizing TSDF that has a significant advantage on its memory efficiency and computational cost. Note that depths of each view are mapped into the voxel space and color values are cast to the voxels. As each voxel can have only a single color value, the method [22] is (so-far) incapable to deal with per-image illumination (Table 1).

Our Method. Our method jointly estimates the detailed shape, illumination and albedo using multiple images with no additional requirement such as cloudy images [21], pre-trained GM [42] or image segmentation [45]. Our formulation also enables to estimate spatially-varying albedo and temporally-varying (per image) illumination in contrast to [20,22]. The refined high quality shape, albedo and illumination can be also used for various applications, *e.g.* visualization of textured models and re-lighting images in high quality (Sect. 4).

3   MVIR Under Arbitrary Illumination and Albedo

In this section, we describe the proposed method for jointly estimating shape, albedo and illumination. We describe the pre-processing steps (Sect. 3.1) followed by our cost formulation of multi-view inverse rendering (Sect. 3.2) with the details of each regularization term and conclude with discussions. Figure 1 shows an overview of our method.

3.1 Pre-processing

Camera Poses and Initial Shape Estimation. The camera poses of input images and initial shape were estimated using structure from motion and multi-view stereo. In our experiment, we used VisualSFM [5,46] followed by CMP-MVS [8] or MVE [6] but other methods can also be used, *e.g.* Theia [47].

Visibility Calculation. The visibility of every mesh vertex in the initial shape is computed from ray-triangle intersections between the sight rays and all the surface meshes. A sight ray is a ray that starts from a vertex to each camera. If a vertex is located in the view frustum of a camera and its sight ray is not occluded by any other mesh, we regard the camera as visible from the vertex. We adopt octree space partitioning to reduce calculation cost [48].

Surface Subdivision. The surface mesh model must have sufficiently high resolution in order to recover the fine and detailed shape. We subdivide the surface meshes until the maximum size of each triangular face observed in the visible images becomes smaller than a threshold (we set 2 for images of VGA size, then proportionally increase to 9 for the images of 3072×2048 pixels). We used the state-of-the-art adaptive subdivision method [49].

3.2 Joint Estimation of Surface, Illumination and Albedo

Using the pre-processed information described above, we build the cost function for joint estimation of shape, albedo and scene illumination.

$$\arg \min_{D,R,L} E_{ren}(D, R, L) + \alpha E_{gsm}(D) + \beta E_{psm}(R) \tag{1}$$

The following is a list of variables to be estimated:

- $D \in \mathbb{R}^n$ is the 3D vertex displacement where n is the total number of vertices. To stabilize our optimization process, the displacement of each vertex i is constrained to the initial normal direction, *i.e.* $D^i \in \mathbb{R}^1$.
- $R \in \mathbb{R}^{n \times 3}$ is the vertex albedo. For each vertex, we express the components in RGB color space ($R^i \in \mathbb{R}^3 = (R_R, R_G, R_B)$).
- $L \in \mathbb{R}^{p \times 12}$ is the scene illumination matrix where p is the total number of cameras. $L^c \in \mathbb{R}^{12} = (L_0, \ldots, L_8, L_R, L_G, L_B)$ is the illumination basis of c-th camera. To simplify the optimization process, we represent scene illumination as a combination of a single spherical harmonics basis and RGB color scales. $L_0, \ldots, L_8$ are the coefficients of the 2nd-order spherical harmonics basis while L_R, L_G and L_B are the scales of red, green and blue channels (details are given below).

We next describe the cost terms E_{ren}, E_{gsm} and E_{psm}.

Rendering Term. The first term E_{ren} is the rendering term that measures image pixel errors between input and rendered images.

$$E_{ren}(R,D,L) = \sum_i^n \sum_{c\in V(i)} \frac{\|\hat{I}^{i,c}(D) - I^{i,c}(R,D,L)\|^2}{|V(i)|} \tag{2}$$

$\hat{I}^{i,c} \in \mathbb{R}^3$ is the RGB values of pixel i in the input image c and $I^{i,c} \in \mathbb{R}^3$ is the rendered values. $V(i)$ indicates the visible camera set for i-th vertex which is pre-computed in Sect. 3.1. The rendering function $I^{i,c}$ is defined as multiplication of albedo (R_R, R_G, R_B) and shading $S \in \mathbb{R}^1$ which is a function of the scene illumination L and the vertex displacement D:

$$I^{i,c}(R,D,L) = (R_R S L_R, R_G S L_G, R_B S L_B) \tag{3}$$

This rendering function assumes a simple Lambertian and ignore any other complex reflection component. Similar assumptions were also made in other works [20, 22].

The shading S is computed by using spherical harmonics illumination model [50],

$$S(N^i(D), L_0, \ldots, L_8) = L_0 + L_1 N_y + L_2 N_z + L_3 N_x + L_4 N_x N_y + L_5 N_y N_z$$
$$+ L_6(N_z^2 - \frac{1}{3}) + L_7 N_x N_z + L_8(N_x^2 - N_y^2) \tag{4}$$

where $N^i \in \mathbb{R}^3 = (N_x, N_y, N_z)$ is the normal vector computed using D by averaging normals of adjacent faces at the i-th vertex. The spherical harmonics illumination model assumes that light sources are located at infinity (environmental lights) [20]. This illumination model is particularly suitable for compactly representing complex illumination and is commonly used in the state-of-the-art shape refinement methods [12, 17, 22, 42].

In order to suppress the number of parameters in the optimization, we assume that illumination distribution is common among the RGB channels. This enables us to estimate the spherical harmonics basis $(L_0, \ldots, L_8)$ and the relative scales L_R and L_B only when setting $L_G = 1$. We chose the green channel to be 1 because it is known as most sensitive in the RGB color representation [51, 52].

Notice that our formulation allows the estimation of both per image illumination and spatially varying albedo which clearly differs from [20, 22]. The limitation is that our rendering function does not model shadow, ambient occlusion or other reflection components explicitly (see also Sect. 4). Their effects are absorbed as albedo variation.

Geometric Smoothness Term. We apply the geometric smoothness term E_{gsm}:

$$E_{gsm}(D) = \sum_i^n \{\frac{K(D^i, P^i(D, w_1))}{l^i}\}^2 \tag{5}$$

This term computes an approximated local surface curvature at each vertex using its neighboring vertices. In detail, l^i is the average edge length between adjacent vertices and its centroid. $K(D^i, P^i)$ is a distance between the vertex and the local plane P computed by weighted least squares [53] using adjacent vertices of the i-th vertex. The distance K is normalized with l^i so that this smoothness cost is independent of the scene scale. The weight w_1 for the local plane P is computed from the pixel value differences:

$$w_1 = \frac{\sum_{j \in A(i)} \sum_{c \in V(i)} e^{-k_1 \| \hat{I}^{i,c} - \hat{I}^{j,c} \|^2}}{|V(i)|} \tag{6}$$

$A(i)$ is a set of adjacent vertices of i-th vertex. This smoothness term with the weighted plane fitting encourages the surface to be flat while preserving sharp edges detected on images.

Photometric Smoothness Term. As our cost function allows for spatially-varying albedo on the surface mesh vertices, there are ambiguities when separating albedo from shading and illumination in the image rendering function, *i.e.* $R \cdot SL$. To regularize this ambiguity, we follow the approach often used in intrinsic decomposition [42,54,55], *i.e.* vertices having similar albedo should have similar color values in each input image. We establish the photometric smoothness term E_{psm} on albedo as:

$$E_{psm}(R) = \sum_i^n \sum_{j \in A(i)} \| w_{i,j}(R^i - R^j) \|^2 \tag{7}$$

$w_{i,j}$ is a weight controlling the balance between texture and shading:

$$w_{i,j} = \frac{\sum_{c \in V(i)} \min(w_2, w_3)}{|V(i)|} \tag{8}$$

The weight w_2 is computed using chromaticities between the input and rendered images:

$$w_2 = e^{-k_2 \left(1 - \frac{\hat{I}^{i,c}}{\|\hat{I}^{i,c}\|} \cdot \frac{\hat{I}^{i,c}}{\|\hat{I}^{i,c}\|}\right)} \tag{9}$$

We measure the differences by the angles of L2 normalized RGB vectors, similar to [22,55]. However, using this weight alone cannot resolve non-chromatic textures such as checker-board patterns. To suppress the effect of non-chromatic textures, we use an additional weight w_3 based on pixel intensities (L2 norm of RGB vector):

$$w_3 = e^{-k_3 (\| \hat{I}^{i,c} \| - \| \hat{I}^{j,c} \|)^2} \tag{10}$$

Setting a large value for k_3 makes w_3 sensitive to the non-chromatic (intensity) changes. Since this prevents the refinement using shading information, we set k_3 to be smaller than k_2 in the weight $w_{i,j}$. The weight $w_{i,j}$ then effectively

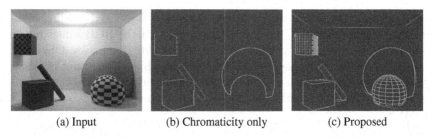

(a) Input   (b) Chromaticity only   (c) Proposed

Fig. 2. Effect of our photometric smoothness term. We render a typical CG model that includes a few objects with both sharp and smooth albedo variations as a toy example (a). (b) and (c) shows the weights as heat maps. The photometric smoothness contributes for shape recovery (large weight, blue) and does not contribute (small weight, red). The weight using chromaticity difference only (b) cannot detect non-chromatic changes, *e.g.* checker board like patterns on the top-left cube and bottom-right ball. Our weight using both chromaticity and intensity differences (c) successfully detects those sharp albedo changes while recognizing the smooth variation as it is induced by shading (change of surface normals). (Color figure online)

recognizes that the smooth variation is induced by shading (changes of surface normals) on the same material and the photometric smoothness positively contributes to recover it. In contrast, the sharp variation is detected as material change and the photometric smoothness does not influence on the shape recovery. It is important to note that the multi-view constraints appear on the regularization terms (Eqs. 5 and 7) because their weights are computed using the visible camera set $V(i)$ (Eqs. 6 and 8). Figure 2 visualizes the effect of our photometric smoothness term on a toy example.

Illumination Scale Ambiguity. MVIR has uncertainty to the illumination scale ambiguity. This is a similar phenomenon to the scale ambiguity found in SfM. To fix this in the optimization, we select a dominant camera which has the largest view frustum and constrain its illumination basis L^d to $\|L_0, \ldots, L_8\| = 1$ and $L_R = L_B = 1$. The resulted illuminations are relative to the illumination of the dominant camera. Notice that the choice of the dominant camera does not change property of cost function (the cost is simply biased) apart from numerical computation issue (same as bundle adjustment).

3.3 Discussions

Why Can We Deal both Spatially-Varying Albedo and Per-Image Illumination? It is interesting to note the following physical conditions that exist in the MVIR problem. According to the per image illumination model, a surface point (vertex) appears to have different RGB values on each image. However, the shape and albedo at this surface point should be unique [56]. This phenomenon is implemented in such a way that mesh vertices share variables for shape and albedo among the multiple views in the rendering term (Eq. 2). Furthermore, the rendering term, indeed, contributes to decompose albedo and shading because the wrong shape (shading) induces inconsistencies for the RGB values rendered across multiple views and, accordingly, the cost (error) increases. Obviously, a standard MVS does not take into account the smoothness constraint in this way. Although our cost function is non-convex, our experience shows the optimization is highly feasible thanks to stable initial shapes provided by recent SfM and MVS.

Benefit of Combining SfS and MVS. MVIR naturally takes into account photo consistencies among multiple views. It is beneficial, for example, to resolve bas-relief ambiguity. Figure 3 shows a toy example of demonstrating it. Starting from a uniform initial value, our MVIR without multi-view constraint which is similar to a single-view SfS method fails to recover shape correctly due to the bas-relief ambiguity (Fig. 3(a)). Our MVIR using only multi-view constraint (21 images) without photometric smoothness term which is close to MVS also fails to recover the details because the surface texture is not distinctive (Fig. 3(a)). Our MVIR recovers the shape successfully (Fig. 3(c)). This is a simple and classic example but clearly shows advantage w.r.t. the single-view based technique [42] and the per-view refinement [41].

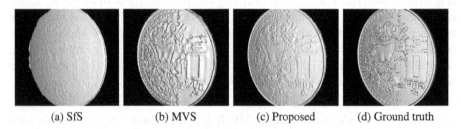

(a) SfS   (b) MVS   (c) Proposed   (d) Ground truth

Fig. 3. Benefit of combining SfS and MVS. This toy example shows that bas-relief ambiguity is a nuisance in a single-view SfS but is not when combining with multi-view stereo. A single-view SfS recovered the relief reversely (a) due to depth uncertainty. MVS without the photometric smoothness recovered the distorted surface (b) due to the lack of distinctive features. Thanks to the multiple-view constraint, our MVIR using multiple images is able to recover the shape (c) similar to ground truth shape (d).

4   Experiments

In this section, we first describe the implementation details and show experiments on both synthetic and real-world datasets in comparison with baseline approaches.

4.1 Implementation Details

The proposed MVIR was implemented using C# with external dependencies: Ceres Solver [57], OpenCV [58] and Armadillo [59]. We tested our method on a standard Windows 10 desktop PC consisted of Intel i7 CPU and 64 GB of memory. We conducted with no GPU optimization. Our software is online at [60].

Throughout the experiments, we used the same values for the parameters $\beta = 2$, $k_1 = 10$, $k_2 = 10$ and $k_3 = 100$. Only the geometric smoothness weight α is modified.

When visualizing our estimated albedo, we re-compute their values that firmly satisfy our rendering function (Eq. 3) and we take the median of re-computed values when the vertex is seen from multiple images. This post-processing results sharper albedo. Notice that this is necessary for visualization and does not influence in the optimization process.

4.2 Qualitative and Quantitative Evaluation Using Synthetic Dataset

To evaluate the performance of the proposed method numerically, we used a publicly available CG model: The Joyful Yell (Fig. 4). As the original shape has a constant albedo, we colored it by using the CG software [61]. To simulate various illumination conditions, the illumination is generated such that each image has a single color but randomly generated light sources. The object is assumed to have complete Lambertian surface. We generated 37 input images of 2048×1536 pixels by using CG rendering software [61]. For this dataset, we set $\alpha = 0.1$.

Figures 5 and 6 show the results for qualitative evaluation. The resulted shapes (Fig. 6(c) show that our method recovers both fine structures (hairs, ears and clothes) and smooth bodies. In contrast, CMPMVS [8] (Fig. 6(b)) is unsuccessful at especially recovering textureless parts (forehead and cheeks).

The resulted illumination map (Fig. 5(a)) shows that our method success-fully recovered the relative color variation and distribution of scene illuminations among the images. Furthermore, the albedo (Fig. 5(b)) is overall estimated suc-

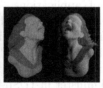

(a) Shape   (b) Albedo   (c) Rendered

Fig. 4. The synthetic dataset: Joyful Yell. As the original shape of CG data (a) has a constant albedo, we colored (b) and rendered (c) using the CG software [61].

Table 2. Quantitative evaluation on the Joyful Yell

Method	Depth (RMSE)	Normal (degree)
CMPMVS [8]	0.168	18.6
Proposed	**0.153**	**14.1**

cessfully but not identical to the ground truth colors. This is because the ambient occlusions and inter-reflections are represented as albedo variations [21,22].

Although the estimated albedo has some errors due to the simplified rendering function, the proposed joint estimation is beneficial for shape refinement. This is demonstrated in the quantitative evaluation w.r.t. the ground truth values in Table 2. We evaluate the average of depth errors (RMSE) and the average of angular errors computed on every image. This evaluation shows a clear improvement when compared with the input shape by CMPMVS [8].

Despite of feasible initial shape from MVS, our cost function may be failed to converge to the global minimum because the cost function is non-convex. In that case, we can re-compute surface mesh [33] with smoothing and then apply our MVIR again. This simple method already gives additional improvement.

4.3   Evaluation on the Internet Photo Dataset

We demonstrated the performance of the proposed MVIR using internet photos which have significantly different illuminations across images. We used the internet photos[1] at a specific landmark: Trevi Fountain [62]. We used the 57 images of various sizes and set $\alpha = 0.3$.

Figure 7 shows examples of input images, illuminations and albedo estimated by our MVIR. Notice that the input images were taken under various illumination conditions and our formulation (which allows per image illumination) successfully recovered relative illuminations and detailed shape (Fig. 8(c)) when compared with CMPMVS (a) and MVE (b).

We also compared the proposed MVIR with the MVS method that uses many images. We performed MVE using 414 images which are obtained by retrieving similar images from Rome16K dataset [63] by matching compact image descriptors [64]. The resulted shape by MVE using 414 images (Fig. 9(a)) gives some improvement when compared to MVE with 57 images (Fig. 8(b)) but the proposed MVIR using 57 images (Fig. 9(b)) is yet more detailed, *e.g.* arch, cornice. Notice that our MVIR shines more when estimation of high quality shape is required only using a limited number of images, *e.g.* photos from a place that can be rarely visiting (*e.g.* Mars) or already lost by natural damages/desasters.

Using the results of MVIR, we generated synthesized images under arbitrary illuminations as an example of applications. The effect of the light source/position change is clearly visible as shading (Fig. 10(b)), *e.g.* the half dome behind the statue. As the synthesized images (Fig. 10(b and c)) are very realistic, they can be potentially beneficial for machine learning approaches that require many images, *e.g.* deep learning.

We also experimented on the Yorkminster in 1DSfM dataset [65]. In similar manner as the DiTrevi experiments, using 9 images, we estimated initial mesh

---

[1]   The gamma calibration using a fixed value (2.2 as in [56]) on the internet photos gave no additional improvement in our preliminary experiments. However, the calibration of nonlinearity will be beneficial when it is performed precisely.

by CMPMVS and performed the MVIR. Figure 11 shows the input images, illuminations and albedo estimated by the proposed MVIR. Figure 12 shows the refined shape by the MVIR (c) in comparison with CMPMVS (a) and MVE (b). Notice that the MVIR (c) recovers a flat facade without losing the fine and sharp structures.

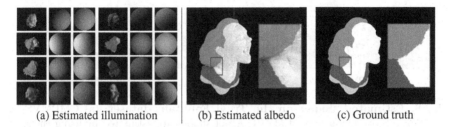

(a) Estimated illumination   (b) Estimated albedo   (c) Ground truth

Fig. 5. Examples of estimated illumination and albedo on the Joyful Yell. (a) Each triplet shows the input image (left), ground-truth illumination (middle) and the estimated illumination (right). We set the global scale of illumination to 0.4 for visualizing the estimated illuminations. (b) Albedo estimated by the proposed method. (c) Ground-truth albedo from the same viewpoint.

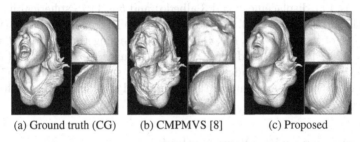

(a) Ground truth (CG)   (b) CMPMVS [8]   (c) Proposed

Fig. 6. Estimated shapes on the Joyful Yell. Our MVIR recovers fine details (clothes and hairs) as well as smooth body (forehead and cheeks) (c) when compared with CMPMVS [8] (b).

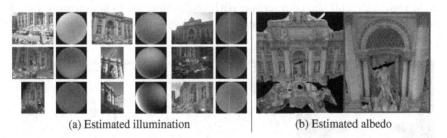

(a) Estimated illumination   (b) Estimated albedo

Fig. 7. Examples of estimated illumination and albedo on the Trevi Fountain dataset. (a) Each pair shows the input image (left) and the estimated illumination (right). (b) Albedo estimated by the proposed method.

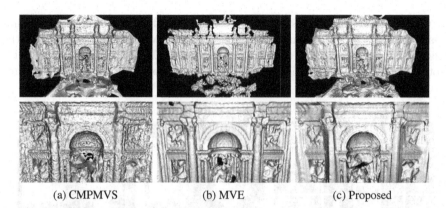

| (a) CMPMVS | (b) MVE | (c) Proposed |

Fig. 8. Estimated shapes on the Trevi Fountain dataset. (a) CMPMVS [8]. (b) MVE [6]. (c) The proposed MVIR. All of shapes are estimated by using the same 57 images.

4.4 Computational Complexity

The variables in the cost function (Eq. 1) are $aN_v + bN_c$ for N_v vertices and N_c images. a is 4 (1 displacement and 3 albedo) and b is 11 (9 spherical harmonics (SH) basis and 2 color scales). For example, in the DiTrevi experiment (Sect. 4), the number of variables is $4,130,417$. Total processing time of MVIR with 57 images is 12 h (Fig. 9(b)) and MVE with 414 images took 8 h (Fig. 9(a)). The cost is optimized using a standard non-linear least squares minimizer [57]. Computational efficiency can be improved by numerical approximation and hardware acceleration [22].

4.5 Comparison with Other Methods

We compared with a state-of-the-art method for joint estimation of shape, albedo and illumination using a single RGB-D image [42]. Although this method uses a single view only and the comparison with multi-view setup is not quite fair, we chose it because their code is the only one publicly available in this field of study.

| (a) MVE [6] with 414 images | (b) Proposed |

Fig. 9. Comparison with MVS using many images on the Trevi Fountain dataset. (a) MVE [6] with 414 images. (b) The proposed MVIR using 57 images (same with Fig. 8(c)).

For producing the RGB-D input, we selected an image from the Trevi Fountain dataset and computed its depth map using the initial shape of CMPMVS. Our result (Fig. 13(b)) clearly shows the advantage of recovering with multiple-view images when compared with (Fig. 13(b)).

We also compared our method with Wu *et al.* [20] which assumes a uniform albedo using their dataset. Figure 13(c and d) shows the qualitative result of shape refinement on the Angel dataset. Notice that our method (d) recovers more detailed shape when compared with (c) [20].

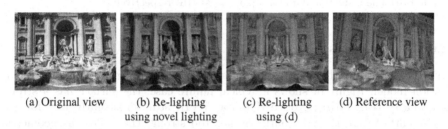

(a) Original view	(b) Re-lighting using novel lighting	(c) Re-lighting using (d)	(d) Reference view

Fig. 10. Examples of re-lighting on the Trevi Fountain dataset. We generated the synthesized image (b) at the target view point (a) by re-lighting using the estimated albedo and synthesized illumination. We also re-light (c) by using the illumination of reference view (d). Notice that our re-lighting can represent shading and shadow variation by using estimated high quality shape and albedo information.

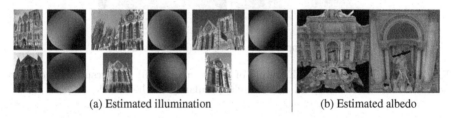

(a) Estimated illumination	(b) Estimated albedo

Fig. 11. Examples of estimated illumination and albedo on the Yorkminster dataset. (a) In each pair, the figures show the input image (left) and the estimated illumination (right). (b) Albedo estimated by the proposed method.

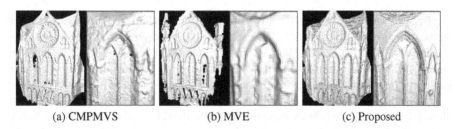

(a) CMPMVS	(b) MVE	(c) Proposed

Fig. 12. Estimated shapes on the Yorkminster dataset. (a) CMPMVS [8]. (b) MVE [6]. (c) The proposed MVIR. All of shapes are estimated by using the same 9 images.

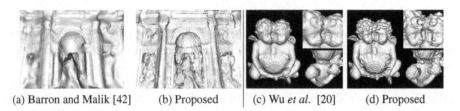

| (a) Barron and Malik [42] | (b) Proposed | (c) Wu *et al.* [20] | (d) Proposed |

Fig. 13. Qualitative evaluation with other methods. (a) and (b) The results of the single-view refinement by Barron and Malik [42] and our MVIR, respectively. (c) and (d) The results of Wu *et al.* [20] our MVIR, respectively.

4.6 Failure Cases

Our method cannot handle non-lambertian reflection and more complex illumination model. Figure 14 shows a typical failure case: the surface has a strong specularity (Fig. 14(b)). Notice that the MVIR still works fairly well for the other parts where the specularity is not too strong, thanks to the geometric smoothness term.

(a) Input   (b) Proposed

Fig. 14. Failure case. (a) Example of input images. (b) Our result (failed). The estimated surface is corrupted due to high specularity on the marble stairs.

5 Conclusion

We have presented a multi-view inverse rendering method for joint estimation of shape, albedo and illumination. We used the shape obtained from MVS as an initial input and incorporated shape-from-shading in our formulation. The detailed shape, albedo and illumination can be obtained by solving multi-view inverse rendering problem using the geometric and photometric smoothness terms and normalized spherical harmonics illumination model. Experimental results show that our method successfully recovers on not only the synthetic dataset but also real-world dataset under various albedo and illumination conditions.

Acknowledgments. This work was partly supported by JSPS KAKENHI Grant Number 25240025 and 15H05313.

References

1. Biehler, J., Fane, B.: 3D Printing with Autodesk: Create and Print 3D Objects with 123D, AutoCAD and Inventor, 1st edn. Que Publishing Company, Seattle (2014)
2. Anguelov, D., Dulong, C., Filip, D., Frueh, C., Lafon, S., Lyon, R., Ogale, A., Vincent, L., Weaver, J.: Google street view: capturing the world at street level. Computer **6**, 32–38 (2010)
3. Moulon, P., Monasse, P., Marlet, R., et al.: Openmvg. an open multiple view geometry library. https://github.com/openMVG/openMVG
4. Snavely, N., Seitz, S., Szeliski, R.: Modeling the world from internet photo collections. IJCV **80**(2), 189–210 (2008)
5. Wu, C., Agarwal, S., Curless, B., Seitz, S.M.: Multicore bundle adjustment. In: CVPR, pp. 3057–3064. IEEE (2011)
6. Fuhrmann, S., Langguth, F., Goesele, M.: MVE - a multi-view reconstruction environment. In: EG GCH (2014)
7. Furukawa, Y., Ponce, J.: Accurate, dense, and robust multiview stereopsis. PAMI **32**(8), 1362–1376 (2010)
8. Jancosek, M., Pajdla, T.: Multi-view reconstruction preserving weakly-supported surfaces. In: CVPR, pp. 3121–3128. IEEE (2011)
9. Furukawa, Y., Hernndez, C.: Multi-view stereo: a tutorial. Found. Trends Comput. Graph. Vis. **9**(1–2), 1–148 (2013)
10. Tola, E., Lepetit, V., Fua, P.: Daisy: an efficient dense descriptor applied to wide-baseline stereo. PAMI **32**(5), 815–830 (2010)
11. Horn, B.K.P.: Obtaining shape from shading information. In: Shape from Shading, pp. 123–171. MIT Press, Cambridge (1989)
12. Barron, J.T., Malik, J.: Shape, albedo, and illumination from a single image of an unknown object. In: CVPR, pp. 334–341. IEEE (2012)
13. Ikehata, S., Wipf, D., Matsushita, Y., Aizawa, K.: Photometric stereo using sparse bayesian regression for general diffuse surfaces. PAMI **36**(9), 1816–1831 (2014)
14. Woodham, R.J.: Photometric method for determining surface orientation from multiple images. Opt. Eng. **19**(1), 121–171 (1980)
15. Blake, A., Zisserman, A., Knowles, G.: Surface descriptions from stereo and shading. Image Vis. Comput. **3**(4), 183–191 (1985)
16. Jin, H., Cremers, D., Wang, D., Prados, E., Yezzi, A., Soatto, S.: 3-d reconstruction of shaded objects from multiple images under unknown illumination. IJCV **76**(3), 245–256 (2008)
17. Park, J., Sinha, S.N., Matsushita, Y., Tai, Y.W., Kweon, I.S.: Multiview photometric stereo using planar mesh parameterization. In: ICCV, pp. 1161–1168. IEEE (2013)
18. Samaras, D., Metaxas, D., Fua, P., Leclerc, Y.G.: Variable albedo surface reconstruction from stereo and shape from shading. In: CVPR, vol. 1, pp. 480–487. IEEE (2000)
19. Wu, C., Liu, Y., Dai, Q., Wilburn, B.: Fusing multiview and photometric stereo for 3d reconstruction under uncalibrated illumination. IEEE Trans. Visual Comput. Graphics **17**(8), 1082–1095 (2011)
20. Wu, C., Wilburn, B., Matsushita, Y., Theobalt, C.: High-quality shape from multiview stereo and shading under general illumination. In: CVPR, pp. 969–976. IEEE (2011)

21. Shan, Q., Adams, R., Curless, B., Furukawa, Y., Seitz, S.M.: The visual turing test for scene reconstruction. In: 3DV, pp. 25–32. IEEE (2013)
22. Zollhöfer, M., Dai, A., Innman, M., Wu, C., Stamminger, M., Theobalt, C., Nießner, M.: Shading-based refinement on volumetric signed distance functions. ACM Trans. Graph. **34**(4), 96:1–96:14 (2015)
23. Okutomi, M., Kanade, T.: A multiple-baseline stereo. PAMI **15**(4), 353–363 (1993)
24. Goesele, M., Curless, B., Seitz, S.M.: Multi-view stereo revisited. In: CVPR, vol. 2, pp. 2402–2409. IEEE (2006)
25. Kolmogorov, V., Zabih, R.: Multi-camera scene reconstruction via graph cuts. In: Heyden, A., Sparr, G., Nielsen, M., Johansen, P. (eds.) ECCV 2002, Part III. LNCS, vol. 2352, pp. 82–96. Springer, Heidelberg (2002)
26. Campbell, N.D.F., Vogiatzis, G., Hernández, C., Cipolla, R.: Using multiple hypotheses to improve depth-maps for multi-view stereo. In: Forsyth, D., Torr, P., Zisserman, A. (eds.) ECCV 2008, Part I. LNCS, vol. 5302, pp. 766–779. Springer, Heidelberg (2008)
27. Fuhrmann, S., Goesele, M.: Floating scale surface reconstruction. ACM Trans. Graph. **33**(4), 46:1–46:11 (2014)
28. Kutulakos, K.N., Seitz, S.M.: A theory of shape by space carving. IJCV **38**(3), 199–218 (2000)
29. Labatut, P., Pons, J.P., Keriven, R.: Efficient multi-view reconstruction of large-scale scenes using interest points, delaunay triangulation and graph cuts. In: ICCV, pp. 1–8. IEEE (2007)
30. Vogiatzis, G., Hernández, C., Torr, P.H., Cipolla, R.: Multiview stereo via volumetric graph-cuts and occlusion robust photo-consistency. PAMI **29**(12), 2241–2246 (2007)
31. Bleyer, M., Rhemann, C., Rother, C.: Patchmatch stereo-stereo matching with slanted support windows. BMVC **11**, 1–11 (2011)
32. Bao, S.Y., Chandraker, M., Lin, Y., Savarese, S.: Dense object reconstruction with semantic priors. In: CVPR, pp. 1264–1271. IEEE (2013)
33. Kazhdan, M., Bolitho, M., Hoppe, H.: Poisson surface reconstruction. In: Proceedings of the Fourth Eurographics Symposium on Geometry Processing, vol. 7 (2006)
34. Vu, H.H., Labatut, P., Pons, J.P., Keriven, R.: High accuracy and visibility-consistent dense multiview stereo. PAMI **34**(5), 889–901 (2012)
35. Ikeuchi, K., Horn, B.K.: Numerical shape from shading and occluding boundaries. Artif. Intell. **17**(13), 141–184 (1981)
36. Zhang, R., Tsai, P.S., Cryer, J.E., Shah, M.: Shape-from-shading: a survey. PAMI **21**(8), 690–706 (1999)
37. Forsyth, D.A.: Variable-source shading analysis. IJCV **91**(3), 280–302 (2011)
38. Johnson, M.K., Adelson, E.H.: Shape estimation in natural illumination. In: CVPR, pp. 2553–2560. IEEE (2011)
39. Basri, R., Jacobs, D.: Photometric stereo with general, unknown lighting. In: CVPR, vol. 2, pp. 374–381. IEEE (2001)
40. Hernandez, C., Vogiatzis, G., Cipolla, R.: Multiview photometric stereo. PAMI **30**(3), 548–554 (2008)
41. Shi, B., Inose, K., Matsushita, Y., Tan, P., Yeung, S.K., Ikeuchi, K.: Photometric stereo using internet images. In: 3DV, vol. 1, pp. 361–368. IEEE (2014)
42. Barron, J.T., Malik, J.: Intrinsic scene properties from a single rgb-d image. In: CVPR, pp. 17–24. IEEE (2013)
43. Han, Y., Lee, J.Y., Kweon, I.S.: High quality shape from a single rgb-d image under uncalibrated natural illumination. In: ICCV, pp. 1617–1624. IEEE (2013)

44. Wu, C., Zollhfer, M., Niener, M., Stamminger, M., Izadi, S., Theobalt, C.: Real-time shading-based refinement for consumer depth cameras. In: SIGGRAPH Asia (2014)
45. Yu, L.F., Yeung, S.K., Tai, Y.W., Lin, S.: Shading-based shape refinement of rgb-d images. In: CVPR, pp. 1415–1422. IEEE (2013)
46. Wu, C.: VisualSFM: a visual structure from motion system (2011). http://homes.cs.washington.edu/~ccwu/vsfm
47. Sweeney, C.: Theia Multiview Geometry Library: Tutorial & Reference. University of California, Santa Barbara
48. Meagher, D.: Geometric modeling using octree encoding. Comput. Graph. Image Process. **19**(2), 129–147 (1982)
49. Kobbelt, L.: $\sqrt{3}$-subdivision. In: SIGGRAPH, pp. 103–112. ACM (2000)
50. Ramamoorthi, R., Hanrahan, P.: An efficient representation for irradiance environment maps. In: SIGGRAPH, pp. 497–500. ACM (2001)
51. Bayer, B.E.: Color imaging array (20 1976) US Patent 3,971,065
52. Kang, H.R.: Computational Color Technology. Spie Press, Bellingham (2006)
53. Eberly, D.: Least Squares Fitting of Data. Magic Software, Chapel Hill (2000)
54. Horn, B.K.P.: Determining lightness from an image. Comput. Graph. Image Process. **3**(4), 277–299 (1974)
55. Jeon, J., Cho, S., Tong, X., Lee, S.: Intrinsic image decomposition using structure-texture separation and surface normals. In: Fleet, D., Pajdla, T., Schiele, B., Tuytelaars, T. (eds.) ECCV 2014, Part VII. LNCS, vol. 8695, pp. 218–233. Springer, Heidelberg (2014)
56. Laffont, P.Y., Bousseau, A., Paris, S., Durand, F., Drettakis, G.: Coherent intrinsic images from photo collections. ACM Trans. Graphics **31**(6), 202:1–202:11 (2012)
57. Agarwal, S., Mierle, K., et al.: Ceres solver. http://ceres-solver.org
58. Bradski, G., et al.: The openCV library. Doct. Dobbs J. **25**(11), 120–126 (2000)
59. Sanderson, C.: Armadillo: an open source C++ linear algebra library for fast prototyping and computationally intensive experiments. Technical report, NICTA (2010)
60. Project webpage (software, dataset). http://www.ok.ctrl.titech.ac.jp/~torii/project/mvir/
61. Blender - A 3D Modelling and Rendering Package. Blender Foundation, Blender Institute, Amsterdam (2015)
62. Havlena, M., Torii, A., Pajdla, T.: Efficient structure from motion by graph optimization. In: Daniilidis, K., Maragos, P., Paragios, N. (eds.) ECCV 2010, Part II. LNCS, vol. 6312, pp. 100–113. Springer, Heidelberg (2010)
63. Li, Y., Snavely, N., Huttenlocher, D.P.: Location recognition using prioritized feature matching. In: Daniilidis, K., Maragos, P., Paragios, N. (eds.) ECCV 2010, Part II. LNCS, vol. 6312, pp. 791–804. Springer, Heidelberg (2010)
64. Jégou, H., Douze, M., Schmid, C., Pérez, P.: Aggregating local descriptors into a compact image representation. In: CVPR, pp. 3304–3311. IEEE (2010)
65. Wilson, K., Snavely, N.: Robust global translations with 1DSfM. In: Fleet, D., Pajdla, T., Schiele, B., Tuytelaars, T. (eds.) ECCV 2014, Part III. LNCS, vol. 8691, pp. 61–75. Springer, Heidelberg (2014)

DAPs: Deep Action Proposals for Action Understanding

Victor Escorcia[1]([✉]), Fabian Caba Heilbron[1], Juan Carlos Niebles[2,3], and Bernard Ghanem[1]

[1] King Abdullah University of Science and Technology (KAUST),
Thuwal, Saudi Arabia
{victor.escorcia,fabian.caba,bernard.ghanem}@kaust.edu.sa
[2] Stanford University, Stanford, USA
jniebles@cs.stanford.edu
[3] Universidad del Norte, Barranquilla, Colombia

Abstract. Object proposals have contributed significantly to recent advances in object understanding in images. Inspired by the success of this approach, we introduce *Deep Action Proposals* (DAPs), an effective and efficient algorithm for generating temporal action proposals from long videos. We show how to take advantage of the vast capacity of deep learning models and memory cells to retrieve from untrimmed videos temporal segments, which are likely to contain actions. A comprehensive evaluation indicates that our approach outperforms previous work on a large scale action benchmark, runs at 134 FPS making it practical for large-scale scenarios, and exhibits an appealing ability to generalize, i.e. to retrieve good quality temporal proposals of actions unseen in training.

Keywords: Action proposals · Action detection · Long-short term memory

1 Introduction

Nowadays, the ubiquity of digital cameras and social networks has increased the amount of visual media content (especially videos) generated and shared by people. In the face of this data deluge, it becomes crucial to develop efficient and scalable algorithms that can intelligently parse/browse visual data to discover semantic information. In this paper, we focus on the task of quickly localizing temporal chunks in untrimmed videos that are likely to contain human activities of interest. This is the well-known task of temporal action proposal generation. The detected temporal proposals can facilitate and speedup activity detection, indexing, and retrieval in long videos. For example, a "good" action proposal method can retrieve video snippets of a home-run being scored within a large

Electronic supplementary material The online version of this chapter (doi:10. 1007/978-3-319-46487-9_47) contains supplementary material, which is available to authorized users.

© Springer International Publishing AG 2016
B. Leibe et al. (Eds.): ECCV 2016, Part III, LNCS 9907, pp. 768–784, 2016.
DOI: 10.1007/978-3-319-46487-9_47

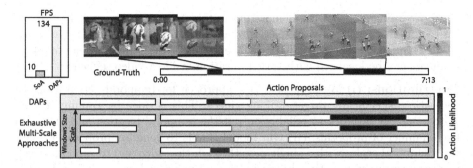

Fig. 1. An effective and efficient action proposal algorithm can localize segments of varied duration around actions occurring along a video without exhaustively exploring multiple temporal scales. This work shows how to produce high-quality temporal proposals likely to contain actions and to be 10x faster that the state of the art approach.

corpus of baseball games or extract important moments during the construction of a new skyscraper. Motivated by the large-scale nature of the problem, we develop a temporal proposal algorithm that retrieves high fidelity proposals with a much smaller computational cost than previous methods (refer to Fig. 1).

The idea of extracting regions with semantic content is not new in the computer vision community. Object proposals have proven to be one of the key elements in the current success of object detection at large scales, both in terms of efficiency and high detection rates [28,29]. Efficient object proposal modules have also enabled a boost in performance of other high-level visual tasks, such as simultaneous detection and segmentation, object tracking, and image captioning [13,14,16,20]. In order to push forward on high-level analysis of untrimmed videos, we argue that the development of action proposal methods should be put in the forefront of human activity understanding research.

Jain et al. [17] introduced the concept of action proposals by taking inspiration from object proposal methods in the image domain. Most previous action proposal approaches focused on producing spatio-temporal object proposals *i.e.* retrieving cuboids or tubelets containing actions [1,6,10,11,24,39]. It is tempting to think that keeping the temporal part of these tubelets would result in good temporal segments confining actions. However, it was recently shown that the temporal footprint of some methods can be as accurate as sampling temporal proposals uniformly in the video [4]. Moreover, these methods evaluate their performance on simple or repetitive actions in short video clips, which makes it difficult to gauge their scalability to large collections of video sequences containing more challenging activities [3,18]. Given the current state-of-the-art of spatio-temporal action proposals, it is worth exploring how only temporal action proposals can contribute to the semantic analysis of videos.

In fact, very recent work has explored the generation of temporal action proposals directly from videos [4,22,30]. Most of these approaches focus on exploring a large number of regions in the video at multiple scales (i.e. temporal lengths) and selecting among them proposals through an efficient feature extraction and classification pipeline. Unlike these methods and as illustrated in Fig. 1, we propose an effective and efficient approach that leverages the capacity of deep learning models with memory blocks to extract action proposals at different temporal scales in only one pass through the video. This is done by encoding a video sequence as a discriminative sequence of states, from which action likely segments can be localized with varied duration inside a video sequence.

Contributions: (i) We propose a new approach for temporal action proposal generation, specifically targeting long videos. This is done by training a well-suited memory network to reliably output the temporal location and scale of a fixed number of proposals. (ii) Our model is able to generate proposals of multiple temporal scales with a single pass through the video and to generalize well to new unseen actions. (iii) Extensive experiments on large-scale benchmarks show that our method achieves a better recall than other proposal methods. (iv) Our approach is computationally efficient and runs at 134 FPS.

1.1 Related Work

We summarize the most recent work on topics related to the task of action proposal generation and our proposed methodology.

Object Proposals: Exhaustively running computationally intensive object classifiers with a sliding window approach is not as common as it was eight years ago. Instead, the use of generic or class-specific object proposals is now a cornerstone in the object detection pipeline. These proposal algorithms retrieve high-quality candidate regions that are likely to contain an object (high recall), before classification is performed [8,15,29]. This approach has proven to be an effective and scalable way to find possible locations of an object in an image.

The latest trend in this area is designing algorithms with high ranking quality *i.e.* achieving high object recall with less number of bounding boxes, preferably with a small computational overhead and the potential to scale to hundreds of object categories [35,37,40]. Here, discriminative methods based on deep learning models have helped improve the ranking quality of proposal approaches [7,28, 32,37]. Inspired by this work, we extend the use of deep and recurrent networks to temporal action proposal generation by introducing a new architecture.

Action Detection: In contrast to object detection methods, the dominant approach for action detection is still to use a sliding window approach [12,18,26] combined with action classifiers trained on multiple features [2,9,33]. Previous approaches have reduced the computational overhead of sliding window search by using branch-and-bound techniques [5,27] and exploiting some characteristics of the visual descriptors. In contrast, our model efficiently reduces the number of evaluated windows by encoding a sequence of visual descriptors.

Spatio-Temporal Action Proposals: Recently, ideas from the area of object proposals have been extrapolated to action recognition in the video domain [6,10,11,17,21,24,39]. Most of these methods produce spatio-temporal object segments to perform spatio-temporal detection of simple or cyclic actions on short video sequences, hence their scalability to real-world scenarios is uncertain. These methods rely on straddling of voxels [6,17], reasoning over dense trajectories [24,39], or non real-time object proposals [11], which increase their computational cost and reduce their competitiveness at large scales.

Temporal Action Proposals: Very recently, work emerged that focused on temporal segments which are likely to contain human actions [4,22,30]. Similar to grouping techniques for retrieving object proposals, Mettes *et al.* create a hierarchy of fragments by hierarchical clustering based on semantic visual similarity of contiguous frames [22]. The main disadvantages of this approach are its strong dependence on an unsupervised grouping method that diminishes its repeatability [15] and the absence of an *actioness* score for each fragment in the hierarchy. In comparison, we use a supervised method that learns to generate segments on a video and predict their action likelihood. Most closely related with our approach are methods that use category-independent classifiers to explore many segments in video and exhaustively evaluate segments of multiple temporal scales [4,30]. Our method improves over previous ones by using a powerful deep learning model that allows for less windows to be scanned and multiple temporal scales to be considered simultaneously in a single pass through the video. We leverage long-short term memory cells to learn an appropriate encoding of the video sequence as a set of discriminative states. We experimentally show that this representation is able to regress the temporal location and duration of relevant segments on the original sequence, while running at 134 FPS.

2   Our Approach: Deep Action Proposals

We propose a new *Deep Action Proposals* (DAPs) network for the task of temporal action proposal generation. From a long input video sequence, we aim to retrieve temporal segments that likely contain actions of interest. Figure 2 summarizes our model architecture, which is described in detail in Sect. 2.1. Section 2.2 describes the training and inference procedures.

2.1   Architecture

Our DAPs network encodes a stream of visual observations of length T frames into discriminative states, from which we infer the temporal location and duration $\{s_i\}_{i=1}^{K}$ of K action proposals inside the stream. Each proposal s_i is associated with a confidence score c_i. Our network integrates the following modules:

Visual encoder: It encodes a small video volume into a meaningful low dimensional feature vector. In practice, we use activations from the top layer of a 3D convolutional network trained for action classification (C3D network [34]).

Sequence encoder: It encodes the sequence of visual codes as a discriminative sequence of hidden states. Here, we use a long-short term memory (LSTM) network. In contrast to traditional feed-forward layers, it directly models the sequential information in a principled and effective manner [23,31].

Localization module: It predicts the location of K proposals inside the stream based on a linear combination of the last state in the *sequence encoder*. In this

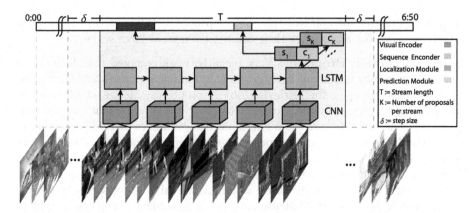

Fig. 2. Our Deep Action Proposals (DAPs) architecture effectively encodes a stream of visual observations (of length T frames) into discriminative states from which it is possible to localize K proposals $\{s_i\}_{i=1}^{K}$ with confidences $\{c_i\}_{i=1}^{K}$ inside the stream. We generate several segments where it is possible to find actions along a video sequence by sliding it with step size δ.

way, our model can output segments of different lengths in one pass instead of the traditional way of scanning over overlapping segments with multiple window sizes. Each proposal s_i is predicted by the localization module.

Prediction module: It predicts the confidence c_i that proposal s_i contains an action within its temporal extent. In practice, c_i is the output of a sigmoid function over a linear combination of the last state of the sequence encoder.

2.2   Inference and Learning

Inference: In order to produce several candidate segments where actions are likely within a long video sequence, we slide our DAPs network over it with step size δ. Every time our model scans a video stream of length T frames, it places K segments of varied duration inside it with their respective action likelihoods. In contrast with previous approaches that scan the same clip of video with multiple sized windows, we encode the information of the clip in order to improve efficiency at inference time. In that way, our algorithm scans the whole video sequence in *only* one pass with one stream (or window) size T, while still producing segments of different duration.

Learning: Another way to interpret our DAPs network is in the form of a function f that maps a video stream v (of length T frames) onto a set of K segments inside the stream with their respective action likelihood. Formally, we have $(S, C) = f_{K,T}(v; \theta)$ where $S = \{s_i\}_{i=1}^{K}$ and $C = \{c_i\}_{i=1}^{K}$ represent the set of all predicted segments and their action likelihoods, respectively. Here, θ represents the parameters of our model.

We are interested in learning an appropriate function f such that: (i) segments produced by our model match the locations of actions $A = \{a_i\}_{i=1}^{M}$ in the sequence (the number of these actions in stream v is assumed less than K); and (ii) confidence values associated with segments that match an action are higher than other segments. This is done by formulating an assignment problem, which solves for an optimal matching between predictions from our DAPs function and ground truth action annotations in the video stream. Without loss of generality, for each training segment, we solve the following problem:

$$(\mathbf{x}^*, \theta^*) = \underset{\mathbf{x},\theta}{\operatorname{argmin}} \quad \alpha \mathcal{L}_{\text{match}}(\mathbf{x}, S(\theta), A) + \mathcal{L}_{\text{conf}}(\mathbf{x}, C(\theta))$$
$$\text{s.t.} \quad x_{ij} \in \{0, 1\}, \quad \sum_i x_{ij} = 1 \tag{1}$$

where $x_{ij} = 1$ means that the i-th prediction s_i is assigned to the j-th ground truth annotation a_j. Here, we define $\mathcal{L}_{\text{match}}(\mathbf{x}, S(\theta), A)$ to be a function that penalizes (in the form of a Euclidean distance) matched segments that are distant from action annotations. Also, we take $\mathcal{L}_{\text{conf}}(\mathbf{x}, C(\theta))$ to enforce (in the form of binary cross-entropy) that the likelihood of matched segments be as high as possible, while simultaneously penalizing non-matched segments that occur with high likelihood. Finally, α is a tradeoff constant that combines both terms. This problem can be solved by alternating between solving the assignment problem for a given θ^k and back-propagating errors given an optimal assignment $\mathbf{x}^k$.

For simplicity we rely on a heuristic similar to [7] to relax the assignment problem by introducing K anchor segments $L = \{l_i\}_{i=1}^K$. In this way, we guide the localization module of the network towards K anchor segments summarizing the statistics of the annotations. This approach speeds up the optimization by: (i) guiding the learning towards statistically relevant locations; and (ii) solving the assignment problem up-front $i.e.$ for every instance v we compare the predictions of our function (S, C) with (L, Y), where $Y = \{y_i\}_{i=1}^K, y_i \in \{0, 1\}$ defining that the i-th anchor segment matches a ground-truth annotation of the instance.

In practice, we obtain the location and duration of each anchor proposal by clustering the ground-truth annotations with k-means which gives rise to a diverse set of anchors throughout the stream. More details about the optimization problem are provided in the supplementary material.

Implementation Details: for our visual encoder, we use the publicly available pre-trained C3D model [34] which has a temporal resolution of 16 frames. To shorten the training time of our implementation, we reduce the dimensionality of the activations from the second fully-connected layer ($fc7$) of our visual encoder from 4096 to 500 dimensions using PCA. By cross-validation, we find that one layer and 256 output units achieves a good trade-off between accuracy and run-time. We use back-propagation through time with ADAGRAD update rule to find the parameters θ of our sequence encoder and output modules. By hyper-parameter search, a learning rate of 10^{-4} and $\alpha = 1.0$ provide good results. In practice, we predict locations (s) as duration of the action and the frame index of its center (normalized by T).

The DAPs network is trained on video streams of length T frames from long untrimmed videos. From a labeled dataset like *THUMOS-14* with 11 h of video and more than 3000 annotations, we are able to generate a large corpus of video streams (over 500 thousands) that might contain multiple actions. In practice, we densely extract video streams and cluster them according to their $tIoU$ with annotations of the video. We sample streams from each cluster, so they are equally represented.

3 Experiments and Discussion

3.1 Experimental Setup

We validate the quality of our approach on labeled untrimmed videos from the challenging *THUMOS-14* benchmark, which contains over 24 h of video from about 20 sport action categories. This part comprises 413 videos divided into 200 validation videos and 213 test videos. We train our DAPs model using 180 out of 200 videos from the validation set and hold out 20 videos for validation. We report results on the 213 test videos with temporal annotations. To study the generalization capability of our model across datasets, we also test on the validation set of the *ActivityNet* benchmark (release 1.2) [3], which comprises 76 h of video and 100 action classes. No fine tuning is done on this benchmark.

Metrics. We assess the quality of our temporal proposals with the metrics from [15]. Specifically, we use *Average Recall* (AR) to measure the temporal proposal quality for a limited number of proposals. We compute AR for a $tIOU$ between 0.5 to 1, as a function of the number of proposals. We expect the best proposal approach to achieve the best recall by generating tight temporal proposals at a fixed number of proposals. We also measure the recall at a fixed number of proposals, as a function of $tIoU$. This metric measures the localization quality of temporal proposals. We consider 1000 proposals for this.

In Sect. 3.3, we investigate the impact of applying action proposals in the context of action detection. Following the standard evaluation protocol, we measure the *mean Average Precision* (mAP) at 50 % $tIoU$. We use the official toolkit provided by *THUMOS-14* [18].

3.2 Recall Analysis

In this section, we analyze recall performance of our method. Specifically, we study (i) the performance of variants of our approach, (ii) the performance competing temporal proposal methods, and (iii) the ability of our approach to generalize to actions that are unseen during training.

Variants of our approach. We evaluate the effect of hyper-parameters on our DAPs model on 20 videos from the *THUMOS-14* validation set. Figure 3 plots AR (first and third columns) and Recall at 1000 proposals (second and fourth columns) of our algorithm for different numbers of proposals per stream (K) and four different stream lengths (T).

As Fig. 3 shows (two leftmost columns), our model is not very sensitive to the number of anchor proposals K for a stream length $T = 512$ frames. Our experiments show that larger K does not necessarily translate into better performance. We hypothesize that this behavior is a result of using k-means to

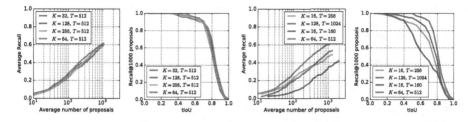

Fig. 3. We evaluate the effect of the hyper-parameters of our approach on a held-out portion of the validation set of *THUMOS-14*. We find that the performance of our model is stable with respect to the number of proposals per stream K (leftmost columns). On the other hand, we find that the choice of the stream length T is more critical (rightmost columns).

select the anchors. This result suggests that the difference between selecting multiple anchors per segment might not be predictable, so we resort to choose this hyper-parameter by cross-validation. We choose $K = 64$ for the rest of our experiments, as a reasonable tradeoff between capacity and AR. In fact, our DAPs model with $K = 64$ achieves the highest average recall rate for more than 100 proposals and about 100 % recall at a 50 % *tIoU* with 1000 proposals, as shown in Fig. 3 (second columns).

Next, we assess the impact of the stream length T on the performance of our architecture. We evaluate with $T \in \{160, 256, 512, 1024\}$ frames which covers $\{75, 92, 98, 99\}\%$ of the annotations in the validation set respectively. The results suggest that T is a crucial hyper-parameter for achieving high recall. From Fig. 3 (rightmost column), we find that for *tIoU* of 50 % at 1000 proposals the recall correlates with statistics of annotations. Therefore, we conclude that our model learns correctly to retrieve actions inside the range of T. Based on this analysis, we choose a value of $T = 512$ frames for other experiments.

In the experiments to follow, we report the results of our DAPs algorithm with $K = 64$, $T = 512$ which offers a good trade-off between accuracy, scalability, and run-time performance.

Comparison with other approaches. We compare the performance of our algorithm against recent approaches designed to retrieve temporal proposals, namely *Sparse-prop* [4], *BoFrag* [22], and *SCNN-prop* [30]. For completeness, we also compare to a representative spatio-temporal proposal method, *APT* [10]. For a fair comparison, we project *APT* spatio-temporal proposals to the temporal dimension only. We obtain *APT* results by running the public implementation provided by the authors. For all other methods, temporal proposals were kindly provided by the authors.

Figure 4 illustrates the AR and recall of 1000 proposals of all five methods on the *THUMOS-14* benchmark. Clearly, our DAPs significantly outperforms all other methods in both metrics. We hypothesize that it improves upon them by effectively encoding the sequence of visual codes as a discriminative set of states from where it is plausible to regress proposals with multiple durations.

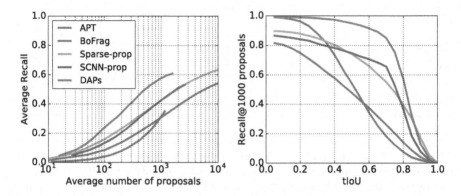

Fig. 4. Our DAPs network outperforms previous temporal and spatio-temporal approaches on *THUMOS-14* in terms of Average Recall as well as in terms of recall of 1000 proposals for a wide range of *tIoU*. This result evidences the importance of effectively encoding the visual sequence as a discriminative sequence of states in relation with previous approaches.

Notably, our DAPs algorithm boosts AR at 1000 proposals and recall of 1000 proposals at 50 % *tIoU* to 58.1 % and 95.7 %, respectively. The later represents a relative improvement in recall of 27.2 % over the *SCNN-prop* [30], which also trains a network to match temporal segmentation (based on *tIoU*) with ground truth annotations. Note that our approach achieves a better performance without exhaustively exploring multiple rigid temporal window sizes which suggests that our network is effectively encoding multiple action durations instead of sticking to a fixed length. It is worth to notice that the AR of DAPs with 1.6k proposals is better or comparable to the AR of *APT* and *SparseProp* for 10k proposals. We envision clever innovations of DAPs architecture to increase the number of proposals maintaining the same quality. Figure 4 (right) shows that our approach is the best to generate segments tightly localized around the actions up to 85 % *tIoU*. From this point, it is interesting that algorithms like DAPs and *SCNN-prop* exhibit a greater decreasing slope than other algorithms. We guess that this effect is partly due to the use of *tIoU* to define the supervisory signals.

On the other hand, we find that all supervised methods outperform the unsupervised ones (*BoFrag* [22] and *APT* [10]) by a considerable margin, especially at high *tIoU* values. This suggests that supervised methods are not over-fitting over their training set and they learn a good function to measure action likelihood. We believe that such *actioness* function may help to boost the performance of unsupervised approaches, especially on methods that do not provide an action likelihood score for each segment, like *BoFrag* and *APT*.

Is the network able to generalize the concept of an action? Proposal approaches are similar to classifier cascades in the sense that they reduce the computational cost of evaluating powerful classifiers on regions that can be "easily" rejected [36]. According to Hosang *et al.* [15], the main difference between these methods is that classifier cascades do not necessarily exhibit an

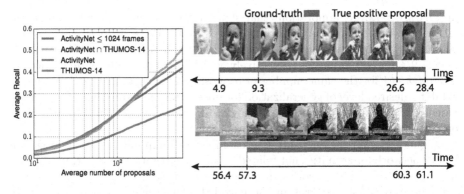

Fig. 5. We measure the generalization power of our DAPs network across dataset for unseen actions by evaluating its performance on *ActivityNet*. Interestingly, the AR performance of our network does not decrease significantly, at 600 proposals, on videos where action durations comes from a similar distribution, *ActivityNet ≤ 1024 frames* line. This suggests that discriminative sequence of states learned by our model capture common patterns that allows it to localize and score segments of unseen actions. On the right, we appreciate segments retrieved by our method focus on *brushing teeth* and *shoveling snow* actions, clearly not related with any sport.

ability to generalize beyond the categories they are trained on. Along these lines, we study the generalization capabilities of our DAPs network to validate that it is a proper proposal approach. We do that by applying our model, trained on 20 sports categories from *THUMOS-14*, on *ActivityNet*, a rich and diverse dataset in terms of actions. For example, just nine actions from *THUMOS-14* have a reasonable correspondence with the hundred activities in *ActivityNet*. Moreover, this dataset includes many categories unrelated with sports, such as *Preparing pasta*, *Playing saxophone*, *Shoveling snow*, to name a few.

Figure 5 (left) quantitatively summarizes the generalization capability of our approach. We show average recall results of our method on four datasets: *ActivityNet* (all 100 categories), *ActivityNet ∩ THUMOS-14* (on 9 categories shared between both benchmarks), *ActivityNet ≤ 512 frames* (videos of unseen categories with annotations up to 1024 frames), and *THUMOS-14*. By comparing the performance on *ActivityNet* and *THUMOS-14*, the generalization power of DAPs might not seem encouraging. However, we find that 42 % of the activity annotations in *ActivityNet* span more than 1024 frames (i.e. twice the size of our temporal stream T), hence it will be difficult for our model to achieve a high AR in this scenario. Since the distribution of activity durations in *ActivityNet* is very different to the one in *THUMOS-14*, a drop in recall performance is not surprising. In fact, Hosang *et al.* make a very similar observation in the context of generalizing 2D object proposals in images across datasets [15].

Following up on this observation, we study the performance of our approach on *ActivityNet ∩ THUMOS-14*, where we only consider annotations from common classes seen in training; and *ActivityNet ≤ 512 frames*, where we only consider annotations of unseen classes that have similar duration statistics observed in *THUMOS-14*, *i.e.* annotations that span up to 512 frames. When evaluating on these two datasets, DAPs performance is quite similar in both cases, especially when more proposals are retrieved. In fact, it achieves an AR of 50.9 % and 41.9 % for 600 proposals respectively, which are close to our performance on *THUMOS-14* for the same number of proposals. This suggests that DAPs does exhibit a desired level of generalization for unseen actions. Note that, *ActivityNet* videos are 50 % shorter than *THUMOS-14* videos on average so it is natural that our method produces less number of proposals.

Figure 5 (right) shows qualitative examples of temporal proposals retrieved by our network for activities not related to action categories used in training. We hypothesize that the network can generalize to these activities by discovering common underlying patterns in the encoded visual sequence that helps it to localize a proposal, as well as, score its likelihood.

3.3   DAPs for Action Detection

Inspired by the success of object detection approaches in combining object proposal methods with object classifiers, we study the benefit of applying our temporal action proposals in an action detection pipeline. To this end, we classify the action proposals generated by our approach and competing proposal methods using the same state-of-the-art action classifier trained on *THUMOS-14* [38]. In this section, we describe the action classifier, assess the impact of the number of proposals on detection performance, and compare our method against state-of-the-art approaches.

Action Classifier. Here, we adopt the recent approach of Xu *et al.* [38], which encodes features learned by a conv-net model using *VLAD*. Here, we use the activations from the *fc7* layer from a 3D conv-net [34] as our features. We first learn a codebook using k-means with $k = 256$. Then, we encode the *fc7* features that belong to each temporal segment using *VLAD* with power and L_2-normalization. Finally, we train a *one-vs-all* linear SVM classifier with $C = 100$. At test time, we run our activity classifier over all the generated action proposals and obtain an action confidence score for each of them. We apply non-maximum suppression with a 30 % *tIoU* to eliminate near-duplicate detections. As in common detection procedures, we generate a final prediction score by multiplying the classifier and proposal scores.

Detection results. Table 1 shows quantitative detection results comparing our proposal approach against competing methods. Following action detection convention, we report the mAP (mean AP) score at 50 % *tIoU*. We consistently outperform the competing methods by a significant margin. This substantiates our claim that our method produces high-quality proposals with a budgeted number of proposals.

Interestingly, *BoFrag* generates good localization results despite its modest recall performance. This suggests that *BoFrag* is producing proposals with a small number of hard negatives, which allows the activity classifier to keep the number of false positives low. We also observe that all methods tend to saturate

Table 1. Results for action detection experiments on *THUMOS-14*. We evaluate the performance of different proposal methods using mAP at P (mAP@P) number of proposals. The *tIoU* threshold for a correct detection is fixed to 50 % and "-" is used when a method is not able to produce the P number of proposals. Our method outperform competing methods by a significant margin for all number of proposals.

Method	mAP@50	mAP@100	mAP@200	mAP@500	mAP@1000
APT	4.1	5.2	6.2	6.8	6.4
BoFrag	5.3	6.6	7.0	8.5	8.3
SCNN-prop	5.3	5.6	7.8	-	-
Sparse-prop	5.7	6.3	7.6	8.2	8.0
DAPs	**8.4**	**12.1**	**13.9**	**12.5**	**12.0**

Table 2. Action detection state-of-the-art on *THUMOS-14*. We report the detection performance of our method at 200 proposals. Our method is able to achieve a competitive performance using a very limited number of proposals.

Method	Karaman *et al.* [19]	Caba Heilbron *et al.* [4]	Oneata *et al.* [25]	Shou *et al.* [30]	**Ours**
mAP	2.0	13.5	15.0	19.0	13.9

after using more than 500 proposals. This is in part due to the fact that all proposal methods are decoupled with the final action classifier. Therefore, it is plausible to fluster the action classifier when the ratio of true positives starts to decrease.

State-of-the-art comparison. Table 2 summarizes the action detection state-of-the-art on *THUMOS-14*. Our method achieves a significantly higher performance than Karaman *et al.* [19] which uses sliding window with a unique fixed temporal length. We attribute this improvement to the fact that our approach scans the video in a much more efficient way. We obtain a similar performance to Caba Heilbron *et al.* [4] and Oneata *et al.* [25]. This result is encouraging given that our detection pipeline operates at a much faster rate of 134 FPS. As compared to Shou *et al.* [30] (*SCNN-prop*), our results are promising considering that less number of windows are scanned to produce the final detection. In future work, we plan to combine directly our proposal network with the classification stage, as well as, fine tune the parameters of the C3D network to achieve further improvement in our detection results.

3.4   Run-Time Performance

By definition, action proposals should reduce the effort of applying an accurate and computationally expensive classifier on a large number of windows in a video. This means that a good action proposal method is expected to achieve a high

Table 3. Our DAPs network is the fastest action proposal method. We report the average time needed to apply DAPs to an average length video from *THUMOS-14* (3 min). Methods that we could not benchmark appear with "-", while N.A. refers to methods that do not require a specific stage (see text for more details).

Algorithm	Time [seconds]			Speedup	FPS
	Feature	Proposal	Total		
APT	2828.5	5120.3	7948.8	1.0	0.68
BoFrag	**90**	<u>5.5</u>	95.5	<u>83.23</u>	1.88
Sparse-prop	191.1	342.5	533.6	14.9	10.2
SCNN-prop	N.A	-	-	-	<u>60</u>
DAPs	N.A	**1.34**	**1.34**	**5931.9**	**134.1**

recall rate in the shortest amount of time possible. Table 3 summarizes the run-time performance of different proposal methods. Specifically, we compute the average run-time over all testing videos on a Titan-X GPU and report the time in terms of the average length of videos in *THUMOS-14* (3 min). The authors of other methods kindly provided the run-time of their approach.

Table 2 shows that our algorithm is the fastest method to generate temporal action proposals. This is due to: (i) an effective and efficient window scanning approach; and (ii) the use of hardware acceleration units (GPUs) to speed-up computation. A preliminary comparison with *SCNN-prop*, which also benefits from GPUs, shows a relative improvement of 123.5 %. Disregarding implementation details that can increase the performance of both approaches, the improvement on speed-up is a consequence of an effective encoding that reduces the exploration of multiple temporal scales on overlapping regions.

3.5 Qualitative Results

Figure 6 shows the top ranked proposal retrieved from videos of *THUMOS-14* as well as two sample videos with the best-matched proposals out of 100. We include examples where our method succeeds (True positive proposals) and fails (False positive proposals) to match the ground truth with a *tIoU* of 50 %. We observe that our method can produce tight segments around actions. We detect several failure cases in actions like *Shot put* where either the annotation is ambiguous or is hard to establish the temporal boundaries of the action. Interestingly, our method can retrieve segments semantically relevant around miss-labeled or incomplete actions in *THUMOS-14*. For example, the fourth row in Fig. 6 shows a proposal that matches an action where a woman is trying to perform *Pole vault* but fails.

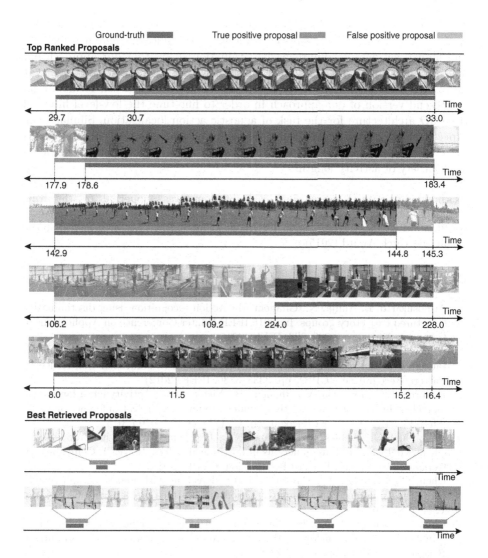

Fig. 6. Qualitative examples of retrieved segments by DAPs algorithm on sample videos from *THUMOS-14*. The first five rows show the top ranked proposal, its nearest ground truth action and the corresponding mapping to time (seconds). The first three rows show examples where our approach generates tightly segments around action instances. On the other hand, the next two rows correspond to failures modes of our model such as an unlabeled occurrence of an incomplete action (fourth row). The last two row visualize the best-matched segments retrieved in two different videos by DAPs out of 100 proposals.

4 Conclusion and Future Work

We present Deep Action Proposals (DAPs), an effective and efficient network that produces temporal segments over a long video sequence where it is likely to find human actions. A comprehensive evaluation shows that our approach not only produces high-quality segments in relationship to the state of the art, it also is the fastest method. A follow-up version of this work will formulate an end-to-end version of our approach in order to fine-tune the low-level filters of the *C3D* architecture for the task of agnostic action localization. Similarly, we expect to design novel architectures that reduce the computational footprint of the current approach and increase the quality of the segments retrieved for a large variety of activity lengths.

Acknowledgments. Research in this publication was supported by the King Abdullah University of Science and Technology (KAUST) Office of Sponsored Research, the Stanford AI Lab-Toyota Center for Artificial Intelligence Research and a Google Faculty Research Award (2015).

References

1. Atmosukarto, I., Ahuja, N., Ghanem, B.: Action recognition using discriminative structured trajectory groups. In: 2015 IEEE Winter Conference on Applications of Computer Vision, pp. 899–906. IEEE (2015)
2. Atmosukarto, I., Ghanem, B., Ahuja, N.: Trajectory-based fisher kernel representation for action recognition in videos. In: 2012 21st International Conference on Pattern Recognition (ICPR), pp. 3333–3336. IEEE (2012)
3. Heilbron, F.C., Escorcia, V., Ghanem, B., Niebles, J.C.: Activitynet: a large-scale video benchmark for human activity understanding. In: IEEE Conference on Computer Vision and Pattern Recognition, CVPR, pp. 961–970 (2015)
4. Heilbron, F.C., Niebles, J.C., Ghanem, B.: Fast temporal activity proposals for efficient detection of human actions in untrimmed videos. In: IEEE Conference on Computer Vision and Pattern Recognition, CVPR (2016)
5. Chen, C., Grauman, K.: Efficient activity detection with max-subgraph search. In: IEEE Conference on Computer Vision and Pattern Recognition, CVPR, pp. 1274–1281 (2012)
6. Chen, W., Xiong, C., Xu, R., Corso, J.J.: Actionness ranking with lattice conditional ordinal random fields. In: IEEE Conference on Computer Vision and Pattern Recognition CVPR, pp. 748–755 (2014)
7. Erhan, D., Szegedy, C., Toshev, A., Anguelov, D.: Scalable object detection using deep neural networks. In: IEEE Conference on Computer Vision and Pattern Recognition, CVPR, pp. 2147–2154 (2014)
8. Everingham, M., Eslami, S.M.A., Gool, L., Williams, C.K.I., Winn, J., Zisserman, A.: The pascal visual object classes challenge: a retrospective. Int. J. Comput. Vis. (IJCV) **111**(1), 98–136 (2015)
9. Gaidon, A., Harchaoui, Z., Schmid, C.: Temporal localization of actions with actoms. IEEE Trans. Pattern Anal. Mach. Intell. **35**(11), 2782–2795 (2013)
10. van Gemert, J.C., Jain, M., Gati, E., Snoek, C.G.: Apt: action localization proposals from dense trajectories. In: British Machine Vision Conference (BMVC) (2015)

11. Gkioxari, G., Malik, J.: Finding action tubes. In: IEEE Conference on Computer Vision and Pattern Recognition, CVPR, pp. 759–768 (2015)
12. Gorban, A., Idrees, H., Jiang, Y.G., Zamir, A.R., Laptev, I., Shah, M., Sukthankar, R.: THUMOS challenge: action recognition with a large number of classes (2015). http://www.thumos.info/
13. Gupta, S., Girshick, R., Arbeláez, P., Malik, J.: Learning rich features from RGB-D images for object detection and segmentation. In: Fleet, D., Pajdla, T., Schiele, B., Tuytelaars, T. (eds.) ECCV 2014, Part VII. LNCS, vol. 8695, pp. 345–360. Springer, Heidelberg (2014)
14. Hariharan, B., Arbeláez, P., Girshick, R., Malik, J.: Simultaneous detection and segmentation. In: Fleet, D., Pajdla, T., Schiele, B., Tuytelaars, T. (eds.) ECCV 2014, Part VII. LNCS, vol. 8695, pp. 297–312. Springer, Heidelberg (2014)
15. Hosang, J., Benenson, R., Dollár, P., Schiele, B.: What makes for effective detection proposals? IEEE Trans. Pattern Anal. Mach. Intell. **38**(4), 814–830 (2016). doi:10.1109/TPAMI.2015.2465908
16. Hua, Y., Alahari, K., Schmid, C.: Online object tracking with proposal selection. In: IEEE International Conference on Computer Vision (ICCV) (2015)
17. Jain, M., van Gemert, J.C., Jégou, H., Bouthemy, P., Snoek, C.G.M.: Action localization with tubelets from motion. In: IEEE Conference on Computer Vision and Pattern Recognition, pp. 740–747 (2014)
18. Jiang, Y.G., Liu, J., Zamir, A.R., Toderici, G., Laptev, I., Shah, M., Sukthankar, R.: THUMOS challenge: action recognition with a large number of classes (2014). http://crcv.ucf.edu/THUMOS14/
19. Karaman, S., Seidenari, L., Del Bimbo, A.: Fast saliency based pooling of fisher encoded dense trajectories (2014)
20. Karpathy, A., Fei-Fei, L.: Deep visual-semantic alignments for generating image descriptions. In: Advances in Neural Information Processing Systems (NIPS), pp. 3128–3137 (2014)
21. Lillo, I., Niebles, J.C., Soto, A.: A hierarchical pose-based approach to complex action understanding using dictionaries of actionlets and motion poselets. In: The IEEE Conference on Computer Vision and Pattern Recognition (CVPR) (June 2016)
22. Mettes, P., van Gemert, J., Cappallo, S., Mensink, T., Snoek, C.: Bag-of-fragments: selecting and encoding video fragments for event detection and recounting. In: ACM International Conference on Multimedia Retrieval (ICMR) (2015)
23. Ng, J.Y., Hausknecht, M.J., Vijayanarasimhan, S., Vinyals, O., Monga, R., Toderici, G.: Beyond short snippets: deep networks for video classification. In: IEEE Conference on Computer Vision and Pattern Recognition, CVPR, pp. 4694–4702 (2015)
24. Oneata, D., Revaud, J., Verbeek, J., Schmid, C.: Spatio-temporal object detection proposals. In: Fleet, D., Pajdla, T., Schiele, B., Tuytelaars, T. (eds.) ECCV 2014, Part III. LNCS, vol. 8691, pp. 737–752. Springer, Heidelberg (2014)
25. Oneata, D., Verbeek, J., Schmid, C.: The lear submission at thumos 2014 (2014)
26. Oneata, D., Verbeek, J.J., Schmid, C.: Action and event recognition with fisher vectors on a compact feature set. In: IEEE International Conference on Computer Vision, ICCV, pp. 1817–1824(2013)
27. Oneata, D., Verbeek, J.J., Schmid, C.: Efficient action localization with approximately normalized fisher vectors. In: IEEE Conference on Computer Vision and Pattern Recognition, CVPR, pp. 2545–2552 (2014)

28. Ren, S., He, K., Girshick, R., Sun, J.: Faster R-CNN: towards real-time object detection with region proposal networks. In: Advances in Neural Information Processing Systems (NIPS) (2015)

29. Russakovsky, O., Deng, J., Su, H., Krause, J., Satheesh, S., Ma, S., Huang, Z., Karpathy, A., Khosla, A., Bernstein, M., Berg, A.C., Fei-Fei, L.: Imagenet large scale visual recognition challenge. Int. J. Comput. Vis. (IJCV) **115**(3), 211–252 (2015)

30. Shou, Z., Wang, D., Chang, S.: Action temporal localization in untrimmed videos via multi-stage cnns. In: IEEE Conference on Computer Vision and Pattern Recognition, CVPR (2016)

31. Sutskever, I., Vinyals, O., Le, Q.V.: Sequence to sequence learning with neural networks. In: Advances in Neural Information Processing Systems (NIPS), pp. 3104–3112 (2014). http://papers.nips.cc/paper/5346-sequence-to-sequence-learning-with-neural-networks

32. Szegedy, C., Reed, S., Erhan, D., Anguelov, D.: Scalable, high-quality object detection. CoRR abs/1412.1441 (2014). http://arxiv.org/abs/1412.1441

33. Tang, K., Yao, B., Fei-Fei, L., Koller, D.: Combining the right features for complex event recognition. In: The IEEE International Conference on Computer Vision (ICCV), December 2013

34. Tran, D., Bourdev, L., Fergus, R., Torresani, L., Paluri, M.: Learning spatiotemporal features with 3d convolutional networks. In: IEEE International Conference on Computer Vision, ICCV, pp. 4489–4497 (2015)

35. Uijlings, J.R.R., van de Sande, K.E.A., Gevers, T., Smeulders, A.W.M.: Selective search for object recognition. Int. J. Comput. Vis. **104**(2), 154–171 (2013). http://dx.doi.org/10.1007/s11263-013-0620-5

36. Viola, P., Jones, M.: Rapid object detection using a boosted cascade of simple features. In: IEEE Conference on Computer Vision and Pattern Recognition, CVPRn, vol. 1, pp. I-511 (2001)

37. Kuo, W., Hariharan, J.M.B.: Deepbox:learning objectness with convolutional networks. In: IEEE International Conference on Computer Vision (ICCV) (2015)

38. Xu, Z., Yang, Y., Hauptmann, A.G.: A discriminative cnn video representation for event detection. In: IEEE Conference on Computer Vision and Pattern Recognition, CVPR (2015)

39. Yu, G., Yuan, J.: Fast action proposals for human action detection and search. In: IEEE Conference on Computer Vision and Pattern Recognition, CVPR, pp. 1302–1311 (2015)

40. Zitnick, C.L., Dollár, P.: Edge boxes: locating object proposals from edges. In: Fleet, D., Pajdla, T., Schiele, B., Tuytelaars, T. (eds.) ECCV 2014, Part V. LNCS, vol. 8693, pp. 391–405. Springer, Heidelberg (2014)

A Large Contextual Dataset for Classification, Detection and Counting of Cars with Deep Learning

T. Nathan Mundhenk[(✉)], Goran Konjevod,
Wesam A. Sakla, and Kofi Boakye

Computational Engineering Division,
Lawrence Livermore National Laboratory, Livermore, USA
{mundhenk1,konjevod1,sakla1}@llnl.gov,
kaboakye@gmail.com

Abstract. We have created a large diverse set of cars from overhead images (Data sets, annotations, networks and scripts are available from http://gdo-datasci.ucllnl.org/cowc/), which are useful for training a deep learner to binary classify, detect and count them. The dataset and all related material will be made *publically available*. The set contains contextual matter to aid in identification of difficult targets. We demonstrate classification and detection on this dataset using a neural network we call *ResCeption*. This network combines residual learning with Inception-style layers and is used to *count cars in one look*. This is a new way to count objects rather than by localization or density estimation. It is fairly accurate, fast and easy to implement. Additionally, the counting method is not car or scene specific. It would be easy to train this method to count other kinds of objects and counting over new scenes requires no extra set up or assumptions about object locations.

Keywords: Deep · Learning · CNN · COWC · Context · Cars · Automobile · Classification · Detection · Counting

1 Introduction

Automated analytics involving detection, tracking and counting of automobiles from satellite or aerial platform are useful for both commercial and government purposes. For instance, [1] have developed a product to count cars in parking lots for investment customers who wish to monitor the business volume of retailers. Governments can also use tracking and counting data to monitor volume and pattern of traffic as well as volume of parking. If satellite data is cheap and plentiful enough, then it can be more cost effective than embedding sensors in the road.

A problem encountered when trying to create automated systems for these purposes is a *lack of large standardized public datasets*. For instance *OIRDS* [2] has only 180 unique cars. A newer set *VEDAI* [3] has 2950 cars. However, both of these datasets are limited by not only the number of unique objects, but they

© Springer International Publishing AG 2016
B. Leibe et al. (Eds.): ECCV 2016, Part III, LNCS 9907, pp. 785–800, 2016.
DOI: 10.1007/978-3-319-46487-9_48

also tend to cover the same region or use the same sensors. For instance, all images in the VEDAI set come from the *AGRC* Utah image collection [4].

We have created a new large dataset of *Cars Overhead with Context* (COWC). Our set contains a large number of *unique cars* (32,716) from six different image sets each covering a different geographical location and produced by different imagers. The images cover regions from *Toronto Canada* [5], *Selwyn New Zealand* [6], *Potsdam* [7] and *Vaihingen Germany* [8], *Columbus* [9] and *Utah* [4] *United States*. The set is also designed to be difficult. It contains 58,247 usable negative targets. Many of these have been hand picked from items easy to mistake for cars. Examples of these are boats, trailers, bushes and A/C units. To compensate for the added difficulty, context is included around targets. Context can help tell us something may not be a car (is sitting in a pond?) or confirm it is a car (between other cars, on a road). In general, the idea is to allow a deep learner to determine the weight between context and appearance such that something that looks very much like a car is detected even if it's in an unusual place.

2   Related Work

We will focus on *three tasks* with our data set. The first task is a *two-class classifier*. To some extent, this is becoming trivial. For instance, [10] reports near 100 % classification on their set. This is part of the reason for trying to increase the difficulty of targets. Our contribution in this task is to demonstrate good classification on an intentionally difficult dataset. Also, we show that context does help with this task, but probably mostly on special difficult cases.

A more difficult problem is *detection and localization*. A very large number of detectors start with a trained classifier and some method for testing spatial locations to determine if a target is present. Many approaches use less contemporary SVM and Boosting based methods, but apply contextual assistance such as road patch detection or motion to reduce false positives [3,11–13]. Some methods use a deep learning network with strided locations [1,10] that generate a heat map. Our method for detection is similar to these, but we include context by expanding the region to be inspected in each stride. We also use a more recent neural network which can in theory handle said context better.

By far our most interesting contribution that uses our new data set is vehicle counting. Most contemporary counting methods can be broadly categorized as a *density estimator* [14–16] or, *detection instance counter* [11,13,17]. Density estimators try to create an estimation of the density of a countable object and then integrate over that density. They tend not to require many training samples, but are usually constrained to the same scene on which it was trained. Detection counters work in the more intuitive fashion of localizing each car uniquely and then counting the localizations. This can have the downside that the entire image needs to be inspected pixel by pixel to create the localizations. Also, occlusions and overlapping objects can create a special challenge since a detector may merge overlapping objects. Another approach tries to count large crowds of people by taking a fusion over many kinds of feature counts using a Markov random field constraint [18] and seems like a synthesis of the density and detection approaches. However, it uses object-specific localizers such as a head detector so it is unclear how well it would generalize to other objects.

Our method uses another approach. We teach a deep learning neural network to recognize the number of cars in an extended patch. It is trained only to count the number of objects *as a class* and is *not* given information about location or expected features. Then we count all the cars in a scene using a *very large stride* by counting them in groups at each stride location. This allows us to take one look at a large location and count by appearance. It has recently been demonstrated that *one-look* methods can excel at both speed and accuracy [19] for recognition and localization. The idea of using a one-look network counter to learn to count has recently been demonstrated on synthetic data patches [20] and by regression on subsampled crowd patches [21]. Here we utilize a more robust network, and demonstrate that a large strided scan can be used to *quickly count* a very large scene with reasonable accuracy. Additionally, we are not constrained by scene or location. Cars can be automatically counted *anywhere* in the world, even if they are not on roads or moving.

3   Data Set Details

Overhead imagery from the six sources is standardized to 15 cm per pixel at ground level from their original resolutions. This makes cars range in size from 24 to 48 pixels. Two of the sets (Vaihingen, Columbus) are grayscale. The other four are in RGB color. Typically, we can determine the approximate scale at ground level from imagery in the field (given metadata from camera and GPS, IMU calibrated SFM [22] or *a priori* known position for satellites). So we do not need to deal with scale invariance. However, we cannot assume as much in terms of quality, appearance or rotation. Many sets can still be in grayscale or have a variety of artifacts. Most of our data have some sort of *orthorectification artifacts* in places. These are common enough in most overhead data sets that they should be addressed here.

The image set is *annotated by single pixel points*. All cars in the annotated images have a dot placed on their center. Cars that have occlusions are included so long as the annotator is reasonably sure the item is a car. Large trucks are completely omitted since it can be unclear when something stops being a light vehicle and starts to become a truck. Vans and pickups are included as cars even if they are large. All boats, trailers and construction vehicles are always added as negatives. Each annotated image is methodically searched for any item that might at least slightly look like a car. These are then added. It is critical to try and include as many possible confounders as we can. If we do not, a trained system will underperform when introduced to new data.

Occasionally, some cars are highly ambiguous or may be distorted in the original image. Whether to include these in the patch sets depends on the task. For the *classification task*, if it was unclear if an item was or was not a car, it was left out. Distorted cars were included so long as the distortion was not too grave.

In both cases, this is a judgment call. For the *counting task*, one is forced to deal with these items since they appear incidentally in many training patches. For that, a best guess is made. If a car was highly distorted, it was counted as a car so long as it appeared to be a car.

To extract training and testing patches from large overhead images, they were subdivided into grids of size 1024×1024 (see Fig. 1). These grid regions were automatically assigned as training or testing regions. This keeps training and testing patches separate. The two types of patches cannot overlap. However, testing image patches may overlap other testing image patches and training patches overlap other training patches. In places like crowded parking lots, patches necessarily overlap. Every fourth grid location was used for testing. This creates an approximate ratio of more than three training patches for each testing patch. The patches are extracted in slightly different ways for different tasks. We do not include a validation set because we use a *held out set* of 2048×2048 scene images for final testing in the wild for each given task.

Fig. 1. The locations from which testing and training patches were extracted from an overhead image of Toronto. Blue areas are training patch areas while red areas are testing patch areas. (Color figure online)

Each held out scene is 2048×2048 (see Fig. 2). This is approximately 307×307 meters in size at ground level. Held out scenes are designed to be varied and *non-trivial*. For instance, one contains an auto reclamation junkyard filled with banged up cars. We have 10 labeled held out scene images, and 10 more where cars have been counted but not labeled. An additional 2048×2048 validation scene was used to adjust parameters before running on the held out scene data. The held out data is taken from the Utah set since there is an abundance of free data. They are also taken from locations far from where the patch data was taken. Essentially, all patch data was taken from *Salt Lake City* and all held out data was taken from *outside* of that metropolitan area. The held out data also contains mountainous wooded areas and a water park not found anywhere in the patch data. Other unique areas such as the aforementioned auto junkyard and a utility plant are included, but there are analogs to these in the patch data.

Fig. 2. Three examples of 2048 × 2048 held out scenes we used. These include a mixed commercial industrial area, a water park and a mountain forest area.

4   Classification and Detection

We created a contextual set of patches for classification training. These are sized 256 × 256. We created rotational variants with 15 degree aligned offsets of each unique car and each unique negative. This yielded a set of 308,988 *training patches* and 79,447 *testing patches*. A patch was considered to contain a car if it appeared in a central 48 × 48 region (The largest expected car length). Any car outside this central region was considered context. So, negative patches frequently had cars in them, so long as the car did not fall inside the 48 × 48 pixel region. An edge margin of 32 pixels was grayed out in each patch. This was determined to provide the optimal context (see Sect. 4.1 "Does Context Help?").

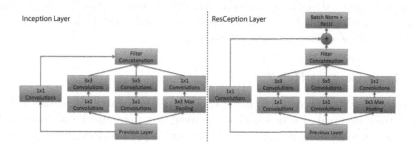

Fig. 3. *left* A standard Inception layer. *right* A ResCeption layer. The primary difference between it and Inception is that the 1 × 1 convolutions are used as a residual shortcut with projection.

We trained a few different networks for comparison. Since we want to include contextual information, larger more state-of-the-art networks are used. We used *AlexNet* [23] as our smaller baseline and *GoogLeNet/Inception* with *batch normalization* [24,25]. We created a third network to synthesize *Residual Learning* [26] with Inception. We called this one *ResCeption* (Fig. 3). The ResCeption network is created by removing the 1×1 convolutions in each Inception layer and replacing them with a residual "projection shortcut". In section five, the advantage of doing this will become more apparent. [27] published to *arXiv* at the time of this writing, is similar, but keeps the 1×1 convolution layers. These seem redundant with the residual shortcut which is why we removed them. The ResCeption version of GoogLeNet has about 5 % more operations than the Inception version, but interestingly runs about 5 % faster on our benchmark machine. All three networks were trained using *Caffe* [28] and stochastic gradient descent for 240 k iterations with a mini batch size of 64. A polynomial rate decay policy was used with initial learning rate of 0.01 and power of 0.5. Momentum was 0.9 and weight decay 0.0002. The network input size was 224×224, so training images were randomly cropped to move the target a little around inside the 48×48 central region. Testing images were center-cropped.

Table 1. The percentage of test patches correctly classified for each deep model. The Non-Utah model was trained with non-Utah data (the other five sets) and then tested with Utah data to observe generalization to new datasets.

Model	Correct
AlexNet	97.62 %
Inception	99.12 %
ResCeption	99.14 %
ResCeption non-utah	98.89 %

Table 1 shows that Inception and ResCeption work noticeably better than AlexNet. However, all three seem to do pretty well. Figure 4 shows examples of patches the ResCeption network got correct.

4.1   Does Context Help?

We were interested to determining if context really helps classification results. To do this, we created sets where we masked out margins of the patches. By adjusting the size of the margin, we can determine performance changes as more or less of each patch is visible. We did this in increments of 32 pixels starting from the smallest possible region with only 32×32 pixels visible. Each training was done on GoogLeNet by fine-tuning the default version from Caffe. Figure 5 shows the results. Even the version with a small amount of context does well, but performance does increase monotonically until 192×192 pixels are visible. This suggests that most of the time, context is not all that important. Cars seem easy to classify. Context might only help in the 1 % or 2 % of difficult cases where strong occlusions and poor visibility make a determination difficult. That we can have too much context might be a result of too much irrelevant information or bad hints from objects that are too far from a car.

Fig. 4. (*top row*) Test patches which the ResCeption network correctly classified as containing a car in the central region. Occlusions and visibility issues are commonly handled, but we note that they still appear to account for much of the error. (*bottom row*) Patches that were correctly classified as not containing a car in the central region. The leftmost image is not a mistake. It has a tree in the center while the shifted version above it has a car concealed slightly underneath the tree.

4.2 Detection

Next we wanted to ascertain how well our trained network might perform on a real world task. One task of interest, is *target verification*. In this, another item such an *object tracker* [29] would have been assigned to track a target car. Our network would then be used to verify each frame to tell if the tracker was still tracking a car or if it had drifted to another target. A second more difficult task would involve localization and detection. This is the ability to find cars and determine where they are in a natural scene. The two tasks are almost equivalent in how we will test them. The biggest difference is how we score the results.

For this task we used the trained ResCeption network since it had a slightly better result than Inception. Each of the 10 labeled 2048×2048 scene image were scanned with a stride of eight. At each stride location, 192×192 pixels were extracted and a 32 pixel margin was added to create a 224×224 patch.

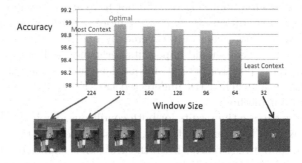

Fig. 5. The percentage of correct patches versus the amount of context present. As more context is included, accuracy improves. It appears optimal to cut out a small amount of context.

The softmax output was computed and taken to the power of 16 to create a wider gradient for the output around the extremes:

$$p = (o_1 - o_2 + 1)^{16} / 2^{16} \tag{1}$$

Fig. 6. (*left*) A held out scene super imposed with the derived heat map colored in red. (*right*) A close up of one of the sections (highlighted in yellow on left) showing examples of detections and misses. The lower left car is considered detected since it is mostly inside the box. The false positive appears to be a shed. (Color figure online)

This yielded a *heat map* with pixels p created from softmax outputs *car* o_1 and *not car* o_2. The value ranged from 0 to 1 with a strong upper skew. Location was determined using basic non-maximal suppression on the heat map (keeping it simple to establish a baseline). Bounding boxes were fixed at size 48 pixels which is the maximum length of a car. Boxes could overlap by as much as 20 pixels. Maximal locations were thresholded at 0.75 to avoid weak detections. These values were established on a special *validation scene*, not the hold out scenes. A car was labeled as a *detection* if at least half of its area was inside a bounding box. A car was a *false negative* if it was not at least half inside a box. A *false positive* occurred when a bounding box did not have at least half a car inside it. For the verification condition, *splits* (two or more detections on the same car) and *mergers* (two or more cars only covered by one box) did not count since these are not an effect that should impact its performance. For *detection*, a split yielded an extra false positive per extraneous detection. A merger was counted as a false negative for each extra undetected car. Figure 6 shows examples of detections from our method.

In Table 2, we can see the results for both conditions. Typically for car detections without explicit location constraints, precision/recall statistics range from 75 % to 85 % [3,10] but may reach 91 % if the problem is explicitly constrained to cars on pavement only [11–13]. This is not an exact comparison, but an F-score of 94.37 % over an unconstrained area of approximately 1 km^2 suggests we are doing relatively well.

Table 2. Verification and detection performance is shown for the ResCeption model. Count is the number of cars in the whole set. TP, FP and FN are true positive, false positive and false negative counts. F is the precision/recall related F-Score. Ideally the verification score should be similar to the patch correctness which was 99.14 %. So, we do incur some extra error. Detection error is higher since it includes splits and mergers.

Condition	Count	TP	FP	FN	Precision	Recall	F
Verification	260	253	9	7	96.56 %	97.31 %	96.93 %
Detection	260	250	20	10	92.59 %	96.15 %	94.34 %

5   Counting

The goal here was to create a one-look [19] counting network that would learn the combinatorial properties of cars in a scene. This is an idea that was previously described in [20] who counted objects in synthetic MNIST [30] scenes using a smaller five-layer network. The overhead scenes we wish to count from are too large for a single look since they can potentially span trillions of pixels. However, we may be able to use a very large stride and *count large patches at a time*. Thus, the counting task is broken into two parts. The *first part* is learning to count by one-look over a large patch. The *second part* is creating a stride that counts objects in a scene one patch at a time.

Training patches are sampled the same as for the classification task. However, the class for each patch is the number of cars in that patch. Very frequently, cars are split in half at the border of the patch. These cars are counted if the point annotation is at least 8 pixels into the visible region of the image. Thus, *a car must be mostly in the patch* in order to be counted. If a highly ambiguous object was in a patch, we did our best to determine whether it was or was not a car. This is different from the classification task were ambiguous objects could be left out. Here, they were too common as member objects that would incidentally appear in a patch even if not labeled.

We trained AlexNet [23], Inception [24,25] and ResCeption networks which only differed from the classification problem in the number of outputs. Here, we used a softmax with 64 outputs. A regression output may also be reasonable, but the maximum number of cars in a scene is sufficiently small that a softmax is feasible. Also, we cover the entire countable interval. So there are no gaps that would necessitate using regression. In all the training patches, we never observed more than 61 cars. We rounded up to 64 in case we ever came upon a set that large and wanted to fine tune over it.

We also trained a few new networks. The main idea for creating the ResCeption network was to allow us to stack Inception like layers much higher. This could give us the *lightweight* properties of GoogLeNet, but the ability to *go big* like with ResNet [26]. Here we have created a *double tall* GoogLeNet like network. This is done by repeating each ResCeption layer twice giving us 22 ResCeption layers rather than 11. It was unclear if we needed three error outputs like GoogLeNet, so we created two versions of our taller network. One double tall network has only one error output (o1) while another has three in the same fashion as GoogLeNet (o3).

Fig. 7. Examples of patches which were correctly counted by the ResCeption Taller o3 network. From left to right the correct number is 9, 3, 6, 13 and 47. Note that cars which are not mostly inside a patch are not counted. The center of the car must be at least 8 pixels inside the visible region.

For the non-tall networks, training parameters were the same as with classification. For the double tall networks, the mini batch size was reduced to 43 to fit in memory and the training was extended to 360 k iterations so that the same number of training exposures are used for both tall and non-tall networks. Table 3 shows the results of error in counting on patch data. Examples of correct patch counts can be seen in Fig. 7. It's interesting to note that we can train a very tall GoogLeNet like network with only one error output. This suggests that *the residual component is doing its job.*

Table 3. The patch based counting error statistics. The first data column is the percentage of test patches the network gets exactly correct. The next two columns show the percentage counted within 1 or 2 cars. MAE is the mean absolute error of count. RMSE is the root mean square error. The last column is the accuracy if we used the counting network as a proposal method. Thus, if we count zero cars, the region would be proposed to contain no cars. If the region contains at least one car, we propose that region has at least one car. The Taller ResCeption network with just one error output has the best metrics in three of the six columns. However, the improvement is somewhat modest.

Model	Correct	is $+/-1$	is $+/-2$	MAE	RMSE	Proposal Acc
AlexNet	67.97 %	95.69 %	98.82 %	0.527	1.192	95.32 %
Inception	80.35 %	95.89 %	98.87 %	0.257	0.665	97.79 %
ResCeption	80.34 %	95.95 %	98.86 %	0.255	**0.657**	97.69 %
ResCeption taller o1	**81.07**%	**96.11 %**	98.89 %	**0.248**	0.676	**97.84 %**
ResCeption taller o3	80.82 %	96.08 %	**98.95 %**	0.250	0.665	97.83 %

5.1   Counting Scenes

One of the primary difficulties in moving from counting cars in patches to counting cars in a scene using a large stride is that if we do not have overlap between strides, cars may be cut in half and counted twice or not at all. Since cars have to be mostly inside a patch, some overlap would be ideal. Thus, by requiring that cars are mostly inside the patch, we have created a remedy to the splitting and counting twice problem, but have increased the likelihood of not counting a split car at all. In this case, since we never mark the location of cars, there is no perfect solution for this source of error. We cannot eliminate cars as we count because we do not localize them. However, *we can adjust the stride to minimize the likelihood of this error.* We used the special validation scene with 628 cars and adjusted the stride until error was as low as possible. This resulted in a stride of 167. We would then use this stride in any other counting scene. An example of a strided count can be seen in Fig. 8. To allow any stride and make sure each section was counted, we padded the scene with zeros so that the center of the first patch starts at (0,0) in the image.

Fig. 8. A subsection of one of the held out scenes. It shows the stride used by the network as well as the number of cars it counted in each stride. Blue and green borders are used to help differentiate the region for each stride. One can see the overlapping region where the strides cross. 74 cars are counted among the six strides seen. The sub-scene contains 77 complete cars. Note that cars on their side are not counted since we are only concerned with cars that are mobile. (Color figure online)

We tested counting on a held out set of 20 2048 × 2048 scenes. The number of cars in each scene varied between 881 and 10 with a mean of 173. Each held out scene was from the Utah AGRC image set. However, we selected geolocations which were unique. All Utah patch data came from the Salt Lake City metropolitan area. The held out data came from locations outside of that metro. These included some unusual and difficult locations such as *mountain forest*, a *water park* and an *auto junkyard*. Many of the scenes have dense parking lots, but many do not. We included industrial, commercial and residential zones of different densities. The error results can be seen in Table 4. It is interesting to note that while the double tall ResCeption network with one output dominates the patch results, *the double tall ResCeption network with three outputs dominates the scene results*. This may be related to the lower RMSE and $+/-2$ error for the three-output network. The network may be less prone to outlier errors. The two extra error inputs may act to regulate it.

Table 4. Error for counting over all 20 held out scenes. Mean absolute error is expressed as a *percentage of cars* over or under counted. This is taken as a percentage since the mean absolute error (MAE) by count highly correlates with the number of cars in a scene (r > 0.80 for all models). RMSE is the root mean square of the percent errors. The maximum error shows what the largest error was on any of the 20 scenes. Cars in ME is how many cars were in the scene with the highest error. Scenes with smaller numbers of cars can bump error up strongly since missing one or two cars is a larger proportion of the count. Finally, we count how many cars are in the entire set of 20 scenes. The total error shows us how far off from the total count we are when we sum up all the results. So for instance, there are a total of 3456 cars in all 20 scenes. The taller ResCeption network with three outputs counts 3472 cars over all the scenes. Its total error is 0.46 %. A low total error suggests that error between scenes is more random and less biased since it centers around zero. This seems to contradict the correlation between error and size mentioned earlier. This may come about if there is a bias within scenes, but not between scenes (i.e. some types of scenes tend to be over counted and others tend to be under counted and this cancels out when we sum the scene counts).

Model	MAE	RMSE	Max error	Cars in ME	Total error
AlexNet	8.46 %	11.64 %	27.27 %	22	3.30 %
Inception	6.50 %	8.05 %	17.65 %	51	0.84 %
ResCeption	**5.78 %**	8.09 %	18.18 %	22	1.22 %
ResCeption taller o1	6.44 %	8.09 %	18.18 %	22	1.19 %
ResCeption taller o3	6.14 %	**7.57 %**	**15.69 %**	51	**0.46 %**

As a second experiment, we attempted to reduce the error caused by double counting or splitting by *averaging different counts* over the same scene. Each count has a different offset. So we have the original stride which starts at (0,0) and three new ones which start at (0,4), (4,0) and (4,4). Ideally, these slight offsets should not split or double count the same cars. The results can be seen in Table 5. Of the twenty scene error metrics we consider, 19 are reduced by averaging over several strides.

A comparison with other car counting methods with available data can be seen in Table 6. Mean accuracy is comparable to interactive density estimation [15]. However, our method is completely automatic. Scenes do not need any special interactive configuration. Another item of interest is that we make no explicit assumption about car location. [13] uses a pavement locator to help

Table 5. This is similar to Table 4 but here we show the mean result from four different slightly offset strides. In 19 of the 20 error statistics, this method improves results over Table 4. With some random error due to double counting removed, the three output taller ResCeption model is clearly superior.

Model	MAE	RMSE	Max error	Cars in ME	Total error
AlexNet	8.40 %	10.53 %	21.59 %	22	3.02 %
Inception	6.46 %	7.86 %	15.69 %	51	0.75 %
ResCeption	5.35 %	7.17 %	14.77 %	22	1.12 %
ResCeption taller o1	5.85 %	6.95 %	13.24 %	51	1.22 %
ResCeption taller o3	**5.15 %**	**6.70 %**	**12.75 %**	51	**0.20 %**

reduce false positives. In our case, cars are counted even if they are on someone's lawn. The deep learner may potentially ingest and understand context, so it is conceivable that it may be biased against counting a car in water or on a building top.

Table 6. Reported errors for two recent car counting methods are shown compared with the error from our best model's results. The first column indicates if the method is completely automatic. The second column tells us if we do not have any location restrictions such as only counting cars on roads or scenes that have been corrected. The Images column is how many scene images are in the test set. Total cars over all scenes is shown after that as well as how many cars were counted in total. The mean absolute error is given over all the test scenes. For the SIFT/SVM method, one single scene accounts for much of the error. This is not an apples-to-apples comparison, but it does give a general idea of performance given the strengths of our approach.

Method	Auto.	No Loc.	Images	Tot. cars	Counted	MAE	Tot. error
Density [15]	No	No	1	230	220	4.35 %	4.35 %
SIFT/SVM [11]	Yes	No	5	119	132	36.74 %	9.85 %
Deep learn	Yes	Yes	20	3456	3463	5.15 %	0.19 %

5.2 Counting Efficiency

In addition to accuracy, we wanted to measure the efficiency of our solution. We are using larger networks, but we are also using a very large stride. The cost of running GoogLeNet is 30 k ops per pixel at 224×224. With a stride of 167 on a scene, the cost increases to 54 k ops per pixel over the scene. By modern standards, this is not an outrageous cost. By comparison, a very small, single-pixel strided CNN would require at least a million ops per pixel over a scene. Table 7 shows the time of running the different counting network over a scene.

The AlexNet version will count cars at a rate of 1 km^2 per second. A company such as *Digital Globe* which produced satellite data at the rate of 680,000 km^2 per

Table 7. Performance results taken for our models running on *Caffe* on a single *Nvidia GeForce Titan X* based GPU. The number of batches required to run a full scene gives us an idea of the extra overhead from running larger models. The time is how many seconds it takes to run a single 2048×2048 scene. This yields a rate in *fps*. Finally we can see how many km^2 we can scan per second using the method.

Model	Batches	Time	FPS	km^2 PS
AlexNet	1	0.087	11.486	1.084
Inception	2	0.366	2.731	0.258
ResCeption	2	0.344	2.906	0.274
ResCeption taller o1	4	0.748	1.337	0.126
ResCeption taller o3	4	0.773	1.294	0.122

day in 2014 would theoretically be able to count the cars in all that data *online* with 8 GPUs. Indeed, another comparison would be to [1]. As their solution is proprietary, comparison data is difficult to come by. They have claimed that they can count cars in *4 trillion pixels worth of images in 48 h* using a cloud-based solution. Their approach is to label each pixel using a deep network [31] for the pixel's "car-ness". Assuming image data is supplied to the GPU just in time, our AlexNet based solution would be able to count that many pixels in *23 h using one single GPU*. AlexNet has 8.46 % mean absolute error, but if one is just analyzing trends such as number of customers at a shopping center, this is probably accurate enough.

6 Conclusion

We have created a large and difficult dataset of cars overhead that we have used to classify, detect and count cars. Our classification results are quite excellent and our detection results appear to be better than even those of methods that constrain the location of cars. Out counting method appears to be very efficient and yields results similar to methods which are scene constrained or need to be fine tuned to process scenes other than the ones used in training.

Acknowledgments. This work was funded from the NA-22 project at Lawrence Livermore National Laboratory's Global Security directorate. Thanks to ISPRS, DGPF and BSF Swissphoto for permission to use their data.

References

1. Crawford, J.: Beyond supply and demand: making the invisible hand visible. In: Re-Work Deep Learning Summit, San Francisco, January 2016
2. Tanner, F., Colder, B., Pullen, C., Heagy, D., Eppolito, M., Carlan, V., Oertel, C., Sallee, P.: Overhead imagery research data set: an annotated data library and tools to aid in the developement of computer vision algorithms. In: IEEE Applied Imagery Pattern Recognition Workshop (2009)

3. Razakarivony, S., Jurie, F.: Vehicle detection in aerial imegery: A small target detection benchmark. Journal of Visual Communication and Image Representation, December 2015. <hal-01122605v2>
4. Utah Automated Geographic Reference Center (AGRC): Utah 2012 HRO 6 inch orthophotography data. http://gis.utah.gov/data/aerial-photography/
5. International Society for Photogrammetry and Remote Sensing (ISPRS): WG3 Toronto overhead data. http://www2.isprs.org/commissions/comm3/wg4/tests.html
6. Land Information New Zealand (LINZ): Selwyn 0.125m urban aerial photos index tiles (2012–2013). https://data.linz.govt.nz/layer/1926-selwyn-0125m-urban-aerial-photos-2012-13/
7. International Society for Photogrammetry and Remote Sensing (ISPRS) and BSF Swissphoto: WG3 Potsdam overhead data. http://www2.isprs.org/commissions/comm3/wg4/tests.html
8. International Society for Photogrammetry and Remote Sensing (ISPRS) and the German Society of Photogrammetry, Remote Sensing and Geoinformation (DGPF): WG3 Vaihingen overhead data. http://www2.isprs.org/commissions/comm3/wg4/tests.html
9. United States Air Force Research Lab (AFRL): Columbus surrogate unmanned aerial vehicle (CSUAV) dataset. https://www.sdms.afrl.af.mil/index.php?collection=csuav
10. Chen, X., Xiang, S., Liu, C.L., Pan, C.H.: Vehicle detection in satellite images by parallel deep convolutional neural networks. In: Second IAPR Asian Conference on Pattern Recognition (2013)
11. Moranduzzo, T., Melgani, F.: Automatic car counting method for unmanned aerial vehicle images. IEEE Trans. Geosci. Remote Sens. **52**(3), 1635–1647 (2014)
12. Holt, A.C., Seto, E.Y.W., Rivard, T., Gong, P.: Object-based detection and classification of vehicles from high-resolution aerial photography. Photogram. Eng. Remote Sens. **75**(7), 871–880 (2009)
13. Kamenetsky, D., Sherrah, J.: Aerial car detection and urban understanding. In: IEEE Conference on Digital Image Computing: Techniques and Applications (DICTA) (2015)
14. Zhang, C., Li, H., Wang, X., Yang, X.: Cross-scene crowd counting via deep convolutional neural networks. In: CVPR (2015)
15. Arteta, C., Lempitsky, V., Noble, J.A., Zisserman, A.: Interactive object counting. In: Fleet, D., Pajdla, T., Schiele, B., Tuytelaars, T. (eds.) ECCV 2014, Part III. LNCS, vol. 8691, pp. 504–518. Springer, Heidelberg (2014)
16. Lempitsky, V., Zisserman, A.: Learning to count objects in images. In: NIPS (2010)
17. French, G., Fisher, M.H., Mackiewicz, M., Needle, C.L.: Convolutional neural network for counting fish in fisheries surveillance video. In: BMVC (2015)
18. Idrees, H., Saleemi, I., Seibert, C., Shah, M.: Multi-source multi-scale counting in extremely dense crowd images. In: CVPR (2013)
19. Redmon, J., Divvala, S., Girshick, R., Farhadi, A.: You only look once: Unified, real-time object detection. arXiv preprint arXiv:1506.02640 (2015)
20. Segue, S., Pujol, O., Vitria, J.: Learning to count with deep object features. In: CVPR (2015)
21. Wang, C., Zhang, H., Yang, L., Liu, S., Cao, X.: Deep people counting in extremely dense crowds. In: Proceedings of the 23rd Annual ACM Conference on Multimedia (2015)
22. Kelly, J., Sukhatme, G.S.: Visual-inertial simultaneous localization, mapping and sensor-to-sensor self-calibration. In: CIRA (2009)

23. Krizhevsky, A., Sutskever, I., Hinton, G.E.: Imagenet classification with deep convolutional neural networks. In: NIPS (2013)
24. Szegedy, C., Liu, W., Jia, Y., Sermanet, P., Reed, S., Anguelov, D., Erhan, D., Vanhoucke, V., Rabinovich, A.: Going deeper with convolutions. In: CVPR (2015)
25. Ioffe, S., Szegedy, C.: Batch normalization: accelerating deep network training by reducing internal covariate shift. In: ICML (2015)
26. He, K., Zhang, X., Ren, S., Sun, J.: Deep residual learning for image recognition. arXiv preprint arXiv:1512.03385 (2015)
27. Szegedy, C., Sergey Ioffe, V.V.: Inception-v4, inception-resnet and the impact of residual connections on learning. arXiv:1602.07261 (2016)
28. Jia, Y., Shelhamer, E., Donahue, J., Karayev, S., Long, J., Girshick, R., Guadarrama, S., Darrell, T.: Caffe: convolutional architecture for fast feature embedding. arXiv preprint arXiv:1408.5093 (2014)
29. Wu, Y., Yang, M.H., Lim, J.: Online object tracking: a benchmark. In: CVPR (2013)
30. LeCun, Y., Cortes, C., Burges, C.J.: The MNIST database of handwritten digits. http://yann.lecun.com/exdb/mnist/
31. Brust, C.A., Sickert, S., Simon, M., Rodner, E., Denzler, J.: Efficient convolutional patch networks for scene understanding. In: CVPR Scene Understanding Workshop (2015)

Reliable Attribute-Based Object Recognition Using High Predictive Value Classifiers

Wentao Luan[1(✉)], Yezhou Yang[2], Cornelia Fermüller[2], and John S. Baras[1]

[1] Institute for Systems Research, University of Maryland, College Park, USA
{wluan,baras}@umd.edu
[2] Computer Vision Lab, University of Maryland, College Park, USA
yzyang@cs.umd.edu, fer@umiacs.umd.edu

Abstract. We consider the problem of object recognition in 3D using an ensemble of attribute-based classifiers. We propose two new concepts to improve classification in practical situations, and show their implementation in an approach implemented for recognition from point-cloud data. First, the viewing conditions can have a strong influence on classification performance. We study the impact of the distance between the camera and the object and propose an approach to fusing multiple attribute classifiers, which incorporates distance into the decision making. Second, lack of representative training samples often makes it difficult to learn the optimal threshold value for best positive and negative detection rate. We address this issue, by setting in our attribute classifiers instead of just one threshold value, two threshold values to distinguish a positive, a negative and an uncertainty class, and we prove the theoretical correctness of this approach. Empirical studies demonstrate the effectiveness and feasibility of the proposed concepts.

1 Introduction

Reliable object recognition from 3D data is a fundamental task for active agents and a prerequisite for many cognitive robotic applications, such as assistive robotics or smart manufacturing. The viewing conditions, such as the distance of the sensor to the object, the illumination, and the viewing angle, have a strong influence on the accuracy of estimating simple as well as complex features, and thus on the accuracy of the classifiers. A common approach to tackle the problem of robust recognition is to employ attribute based classifiers, and combine the individual attribute estimates by fusing their information [1–3].

This work introduces two concepts to robustify the recognition by addressing common issues in the processing of 3D data, namely the problem of classifier dependence on viewing conditions, and the problem of insufficient training data.

We first study the influence of distance between the camera and the object on the performance of attribute classifiers. Unlike 2D image processing techniques, which usually scale the image to address the impact of distance, depth based object recognition procedures using input from 3D cameras tend to be affected by distance-dependent noise, and this effect cannot easily be overcome [4].

© Springer International Publishing AG 2016
B. Leibe et al. (Eds.): ECCV 2016, Part III, LNCS 9907, pp. 801–815, 2016.
DOI: 10.1007/978-3-319-46487-9_49

We propose an approach that addresses effects of distance on object recognition. It considers the response of individual attribute classifiers' depending on distance and incorporates it into the decision making. Though, the main factor studied here is distance, our mathematical approach is general, and can be applied to handle other factors affected by viewing conditions, such as lighting, viewing angle, motion blur, etc.

To implement the attribute classifiers, usually, the standard threshold method is used to determine the boundary between positive and negative examples. Using this threshold the existence of binary attributes is determined, which in turn controls the overall attribute space. However, there may not be enough training samples to accurately represent the underlying distributions, which makes it more difficult to learn one good classification threshold that minimizes the number of incorrect predictions (or maximizes the number of correct predictions).

Here we present an alternative approach which applies two thresholds with one aiming for a positive predictive value (PPV), giving high precision for positive classes, and the other aiming for a negative predictive value (NPV), giving high precision for negative classes. Each classifier can then have three types of output: "positive" when above the high PPV threshold, "negative" when below the high NPV threshold and "uncertain" when falling into the interval between the two thresholds. Recognition decisions, when fusing the classifiers, are then made based on the positive and negative results. More observations thereby are needed for drawing a conclusion, but we consider this trade-off affordable, since we assume that our active agent can control the number of observations. Note that two threshold approaches have previously been used for the purpose of achieving results of high confidence, for example in [5], and in probability ratio tests.

The underlying intuition here is that it should be easier to obtain the high PPV and NPV thresholds than the classical Bayes threshold (minimizing the classification error), when the number of training samples is too small to represent well the underlying distribution. Figure 1a illustrates the intuition. The top figure shows the ground truth distributions (of the classification score) of the positive and negative class. The lower figure depicts the estimated distributions from training samples, which are biased due to an insufficient amount of data. Furthermore, as our experiment revealed, even the ground truth distribution could be dependent on viewing conditions, which makes it more challenging to learn a single optimal threshold. In such a case, the system may end up with an inaccurate Bayes threshold. However, it is still possible to select high PPV (NPV) thresholds by setting these thresholds (at a safe distance) away from the negative (positive) distribution.

For each basic (attribute) classifier, we can also define a reliable working region indicating a fair separation of the distributions of positive and negative classes. Hence our approach can actively select "safe" samples and discard "unsafe" ones in unreliable regions. We prove the asymptotic correctness of this approach in Sect. 3.3.

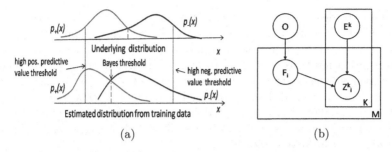

Fig. 1. (a): Illustration of common conditional probability density functions of the positive and negative class. Top: ground truth distribution of the two classes; bottom: a possible distribution represented by the training data. Blue line: positive class; red line: negative class. dashed line: (estimated) Bayes threshold; solid line: high PPV and NPV thresholds. (b): The relationship of Objects (O), attributes (F_i), environmental variables (E_k) and observations (Z_i^k) in our model. (Color figure online)

Integrating both concepts, our complete approach to 3D object recognition works as follows: Offline we learn attribute classifiers, which are distance dependent. In practice, we discretize the space into n distance intervals, and for each interval we learn classifiers with two thresholds. Also, we decide for each attribute classifier a reliable range of distance intervals. During the online process our active system takes RGBD images as it moves around the space. For each input image, it first decides the distance interval in order to use the classifiers tuned to that interval. Classifier measurements from multiple images are then combined via maximum a posteriori probability (MAP) estimation.

Our work has three main contributions: (1) We put forward a practical framework for fusing component classifiers' results by taking into account the distance, to accomplish reliable object recognition. (2) We prove our fusion framework's asymptotic correctness under certain assumptions on the attribute classifier and sufficient randomness of the input data. (3) The benefits of introducing simple attributes, which are more robust to viewing conditions, but less discriminative, are demonstrated in the experiment.

2   Related Work

Creating practical object recognition systems that can work reliably under different viewing conditions, including varying distance, viewing angle, illumination and occlusions, is still a challenging problem in Computer Vision. Current single source based recognition methods have robustness to some extent: features like SIFT [6] or the multifractal spectrum vector (MFS) [7] in practice are invariant to a certain degree to deformations of the scene and viewpoint changes; geometric-based matching algorithms like BOR3D [8] and LINEMOD [9] can recognize objects under large changes in illumination, where color based algorithms tend to fail. But in complicated working environments, these systems have difficulties to achieve robust performance.

One way to deal with variations in viewing conditions is to incorporate different sources of information (or cues) into the recognition process. However, how to fuse the information from multiple sources, is still an open problem.

Early fusion methods have tried to build more descriptive features by combining features from sources like texture, color and depth before classification. For example, Asako et al. builds voxelized shape and color histogram descriptors [1] and classifies objects using SVM, while in [10] information from color, depth, SIFT and shape distributions is described by histograms and objects are recognized using K-Nearest Neighbors.

Besides early fusion, late fusion also has gained much attention and achieves good results. Lutz et al. [3] proposes a probabilistic fusion approach, called MOPED [11], to combine a 3D model matcher, color histograms and feature based detection algorithm, where a quality factor, representing each method's discriminative capability, is integrated in the final classification score. Meta information [12] can also be added to create a new feature. Ziang et al. [2] blends classification scores from SIFT, shape, and color models with meta features providing information about each model's fitness from the input scene, which results in high precision and recall on the Challenge and Willow datasets. Considering influences due to viewing conditions, Ahmed [13] applies an AND/OR graph representation of different features and updates a Bayes conditional probability table based on measurements of the environment, such as intensity, distance and occlusions. However, these methods may suffer from inaccurate estimation of the conditional probabilities involved, because of insufficient training data.

In our work, we propose a framework for object recognition using multiple attribute classifiers, which considers both, effects due to viewing conditions and effects due to biased training data that systems face in practice. We implement our approach for an active agent that takes advantage of multiple inputs at various distances.

3   Assumptions and Formulation

Before going into the details and introducing the notation, let us summarize this section. Section 3.1 defines the data fusion of the different classification results through MAP estimation. Section 3.2 proves that MAP estimation will classify correctly under certain requirements and assumptions. The requirements are restrictions on the values of the PPV and NPV. The assumptions are that our attribute classifiers perform correctly in the following sense: A ground truth positive value should be classified as positive or uncertain and a ground truth negative value should be classified as negative or uncertain. Finally Sect. 3.3 proves asymptotic correctness of MAP estimation. The estimation will converge, even if the classifiers don't perform correctly, under stronger requirements on the values of the PPV and NPV.

Let the objects in the database be described by the set $\mathbb{O} = \{o_j\}$ ($j = 1, 2, ..., |\mathbb{O}|$). Each object $o_j \in \mathbb{O}$ is represented by a attribute vector $F^j = [f_{1j}, f_{2j}, ..., f_{Mj}]^T$, where M is the number of attributes. For the i-th attribute F_i, there is a corresponding component classifier to identify it. Denote its observation as Z_i^k, where i is the index for the classifier and k is the observation number. Here we consider binary attributes $f_{ij} \in Range(F_i) = \{0, 1\}$, $\forall i \in \{1, 2, ..., M\}$, and there are three possible values for the observation: $Z_i^k = \{0, 1, u\}$ $k \in 1, 2, ,,, K$, where u represents uncertainty for the case that the classification score falls in the interval between the high PPV and NPV thresholds.

The model also encodes effects due to viewing conditions (or environmental factors). In this work, we study the effect of distance. Thus, E is the distance between the object and the camera. However, in future work, other environmental factors can be encoded as additional components. Figure 1b illustrates the relationship between objects, attributes, environmental factors and observations in a graphical model.

In our notation $\mathbb{E}^K = \{E^1, E^2, ..., E^K\}$ represents the environmental variable at each observation, and $\mathbb{Z}_i^K = \{Z_i^1, Z_i^2, ..., Z_i^K\}$ is the set of observation results from the i-th classifier. We assume that an observation of an attribute Z_i^k only depends on the ground truth attribute variable F_i and the environmental variable E^k. Because we assume that each object o_j can be represented by an M-dimension attribute vector F^j, we have $P(F|O = o_j) = \begin{cases} 1 \text{ if } F = F^j, \\ 0 \text{ o.w.} \end{cases}$

3.1   Inference

With K observation results $\mathbb{Z}^K = \{\mathbb{Z}_1^K, ..., \mathbb{Z}_M^K\}$ and corresponding environmental conditions $\mathbb{E}^K$, we want to obtain the posterior probability of the target object being object $o_j \in \mathbb{O}$. i.e. $P(O = o_j | \mathbb{Z}^K, \mathbb{E}^K)$. Based on our graphical model we have:

$$P(O = o_j | \mathbb{Z}^K, \mathbb{E}^K) = \frac{P(O = o_j, \mathbb{Z}^K, \mathbb{E}^K)}{P(\mathbb{Z}^K, \mathbb{E}^K)} = \frac{P(O = o_j)P(\mathbb{Z}^K | F = F^j, \mathbb{E}^K)P(\mathbb{E}^K)}{P(\mathbb{Z}^K, \mathbb{E}^K)}$$

$$= \frac{P(\mathbb{E}^K)P(O = o_j)}{P(\mathbb{Z}^K, \mathbb{E}^K)} \prod_{k=1}^{K} \prod_{i=1}^{M} P(Z_i^k | F_i = f_{ij}, E^k) \tag{1}$$

$$= \lambda P(O = o_j) \prod_{k=1}^{K} \prod_{i=1}^{M} \frac{P(F_i = f_{ij} | Z_i^k, E^k)}{P(F_i = f_{ij})}$$

where $\lambda \triangleq \frac{P(\mathbb{E}^K) \prod_{k=1}^{K} \prod_{i=1}^{M} P(Z_i^k, E^k)}{P(\mathbb{Z}^K, \mathbb{E}^K) \prod_{k=1}^{K} \prod_{i=1}^{M} P(E^k)}$. Because

$$P(F_i = f_{ij}) = \sum_t P(O = o_t)P(F_i = f_{ij} | O = o_t) = \sum_{\{t | f_{it} = f_{ij}\}} P(O = o_t) \tag{2}$$

Finally, we have

$$P(O = o_j | \mathbb{Z}^K, \mathbb{E}^K) = \lambda P(O = o_j) \prod_{k=1}^{K} \prod_{i=1}^{M} \frac{P(F_i = f_{ij} | Z_i^k, E^k)}{\sum_{\{t | f_{it} = f_{ij}\}} P(O = o_t)}. \tag{3}$$

The recognition $\mathbb{A}$ then is derived using MAP estimation as:

$$\mathbb{A} \triangleq \underset{o_j}{\arg\max} \; P(O = o_j | \mathbb{Z}^K, \mathbb{E}^K). \tag{4}$$

In our framework, we use the high positive and negative predictive value observations ($Z = 0, 1$) to determine the posterior probability.

We also take into account the influence of environmental factors. That is, only observations from a reliable working region are adopted in the probability calculation. When the environmental factor is distance, the reliable working region is defined as a range of depth values where the attribute classifier work reasonably well. We treat a range of distance values as a reliable working region for a classifier, if the detection rate for this range is larger than a certain threshold, and the PPV meets the system requirement.

This requirement for the component classifiers is achievable if the positive conditional probability density function of the classification score has a non-overlapping area with the negative one. Then we can tune the classifier's PPV threshold towards the positive direction (towards left in Fig. 1a) to achieve a high precision with a guarantee of minimum detection rate.

Formally speaking, our $P(F_i = f_{ij}|Z_i^k, E^k)$ is defined as:

$$P(F_i = 1|Z_i^k, E^k) = \begin{cases} p_i^+ & \text{if } e_k \in \mathbb{R}_i \; \& \; z_i^k = 1, \\ 1 - p_i^- & \text{if } e_k \in \mathbb{R}_i \; \& \; z_i^k = 0, \\ \sum_{t|f_{it}=f_{ij}} P(O = o_t) & \text{o.w.} \end{cases} \tag{5}$$

where $\mathbb{R}_i$ is the set of environmental values for which the i-th classifier can achieve a PPV p_i^+ with a detection rate lower bound. As before, k denotes the k-th observation. If the above condition is not met, either the recognition is done in an unreliable region or the answer is uncertain. Now equation (3) can be rewritten as:

$$P(O = o_j | \mathbb{Z}^K, \mathbb{E}^K) = \lambda P(O = o_j) \prod_{k=1}^{K} \prod_{i \in \mathbb{I}^k} \frac{P(F_i = f_{ij} | Z_i^k, E^k)}{\sum_{\{t|f_{it}=f_{ij}\}} P(O = o_t)}, \tag{6}$$

where $\mathbb{I}^k = \mathbb{I}^{k+} \cup \mathbb{I}^{k-}$ is the index set of recognized attributes at the k-th observation with $\mathbb{I}^{k+} = \{i|e^k \in \mathbb{R}_i \; \& \; z_i^k = 1\}$ and $\mathbb{I}^{k-} = \{i|e^k \in \mathbb{R}_i \; \& \; z_i^k = 0\}$.

Intuitively, it means that we only use a component classifier's recognition result when 1) it works in its reliable range; 2) the result satisfies high PPV or NPV thresholds. In Sect. 3.2, we introduce the predictive value requirements for the component classifiers.

3.2 System Requirement for the Predictive Value

Here we put forward a predictive value requirement for each component classifier to have correct MAP estimations assuming there do not exist false positives or false negatives from observations.

To simplify our notation, we define the prior probability of object $\pi_j \triangleq P(O = o_j), j = (1, 2, ..., N_o)$ and the prior probability of attribute F_i being positive as $w_i \triangleq \sum_{\{t|f_{it}=1\}} \pi_t, (i = 1, 2, ..., M)$. For each attribute, the following ratios are calculated: $r_i^+ \triangleq \max(1, \frac{\max_{\{t|f_{it}=0\}} \pi_t}{\min_{\{t|f_{it}=1\}} \pi_t})$, $r_i^- \triangleq \max(1, \frac{\max_{\{t|f_{it}=1\}} \pi_t}{\min_{\{t|f_{it}=0\}} \pi_t})$. $\mathbb{I}_{F_j}^+$ and $\mathbb{I}_{F_j}^-$ are the index sets of positive and negative attributes in F^j, and the reliably recognized attributes' indexes at the k-th observation are denoted as $\mathbb{I} = \{\mathbb{I}^1, \mathbb{I}^2, ..., \mathbb{I}^K\}$ ($\mathbb{I}^k$ as defined in Sect. 3.1). We next state the conditions for correct MAP estimation.

Theorem 1. *If the currently recognized attributes $\bigcup_k \mathbb{I}^k$ can uniquely identify object o_j, i.e. $\bigcup_k \mathbb{I}^{k+} \subseteq \mathbb{I}_{F_j}^+$, $\bigcup_k \mathbb{I}^{k-} \subseteq \mathbb{I}_{F_j}^-$, $\forall t \neq j, \bigcup_k \mathbb{I}^{k+} \not\subseteq \mathbb{I}_{F_t}^+$ or $\bigcup_k \mathbb{I}^{k-} \not\subseteq \mathbb{I}_{F_t}^-$, and if $\forall i \in \{1, 2, ..., M\}$ the classifiers' predictive values satisfy $p_i^+ \geq \frac{r_i^+ w_i}{1+(r_i-1)w_i}$ and $p_i^- \geq \frac{r_i^-(1-w_i)}{w_i+r_i^-(1-w_i)}$, then the MAP estimation result $\mathbb{A} = \{o_j\}$.*

This requirement means that if 1) the attributes can differentiate an object from others, and 2) the component classifiers' predictive values satisfy the requirement, then for the correct observation input, the system is guaranteed to have a correct recognition result.

Proof. Based on (6) and the definition above, the posterior probability of o_j is,

$$P(O = o_j | \mathbb{Z}^K, \mathbb{E}^K) = \lambda \pi_j \prod_{k=1}^{K} \left(\prod_{i \in \mathbb{I}^{k+}} \frac{p_i^+}{w_i} \prod_{i \in \mathbb{I}^{k-}} \frac{p_i^-}{1-w_i} \right). \tag{7}$$

Because the current observed attributes $\bigcup_k \mathbb{I}^k$ can uniquely identify o_j, we will have $\forall o_g \in \mathbb{O}/\{o_j\}, \exists \mathbb{I}_g \subseteq \bigcup_k \mathbb{I}^k$ and $\mathbb{I}_g \neq \emptyset$, s.t. $\forall i \in \mathbb{I}_g, f_{gi} = 0$ if $i \in \mathbb{I}^{k+}$ or $f_{gi} = 1$ if $i \in \mathbb{I}^{k-}$. Thus, $\forall o_g \in \mathbb{O}/\{o_j\}$,

$$P(O = o_g | \mathbb{Z}^K, \mathbb{E}^K) = \lambda \pi_g \prod_{k=1}^{K} \left(\prod_{i \in \mathbb{I}^{k+}/\mathbb{I}_g} \frac{p_i^+}{w_i} \prod_{i \in \mathbb{I}^{k+} \cap \mathbb{I}_g} \frac{1-p_i^+}{1-w_i} \right.$$

$$\left. \prod_{i \in \mathbb{I}^{k-}/\mathbb{I}_g} \frac{p_i^-}{1-w_i} \prod_{i \in \mathbb{I}^{k-} \cap \mathbb{I}_g} \frac{1-p_i^-}{w_i} \right). \tag{8}$$

Since for each classifier, $p_i^+ \geq \frac{r_i^+ w_i}{1+(r_i^+ -1)w_i}$ and $r_i^+ = \max(1, \frac{\max_{\{t|f_{it}=0\}} \pi_t}{\min_{\{t|f_{it}=1\}} \pi_t})$, we have $\pi_j \frac{p_i^+}{w_i} \geq \pi_g \frac{1-p_i^+}{1-w_j}$ and $\frac{p_i^+}{w_i} \geq 1 \geq \frac{1-p_i^+}{1-w_i}$. For similar reasons, we have $\pi_j \frac{p_i^-}{1-w_i} \geq \pi_g \frac{1-p_i^-}{w_j}$ and $\frac{p_i^-}{1-w_i} \geq 1 \geq \frac{1-p_i^-}{w_i}$. Also since $\mathbb{I}_g \neq \emptyset$, we can have (7) > (8), an thus the conclusion is reached.

From the proof, we can extend the result to a more general case: if the currently recognized attributes cannot uniquely determine an object, i.e. there exists a non-empty set $\mathbb{O}' = \{o_j | o_j \in \mathbb{O}, \mathbb{I}_{F_j}^+ \supseteq \bigcup_k \mathbb{I}^{k+} \& \mathbb{I}_{F_j}^- \supseteq \bigcup_k \mathbb{I}^{k-}\}$, the final recognition result $\mathbb{A} = \underset{o_j \in \mathbb{O}'}{\operatorname{argmax}} \pi_j$. Furthermore, if an equal prior probability is assumed, then $\mathbb{A} = \mathbb{O}'$.

Theorem 1 proves the system's correctness under correct observations. Next, for the general case Sect. 3.3 proves that MAP estimation asymptotically converges to the actual result under certain assumptions.

3.3   Asymptotic Correctness of the MAP Estimation

Now we are going to prove that MAP estimation will converge to the correct result when 1) the attribute classifiers' PPV and NPV are high enough in their reliable working region, where a lower bound of detection rate exists, and 2) the inputs are sampled randomly.

Denote d_i as the detection rate and q_i as the false-positive rate of the i-th attribute classifier when applying the high PPV threshold in its reliable working region. Similarly, for the high NPV threshold, s_i denotes the true negative rate and v_i denotes the false negative rate.

Theorem 2. *We assume that the inputs are sampled sufficiently random such that each attribute classifier gets the same chance to work in its reliable region where a lower bound exists for its detection rate, $0 < A < d_i \le 1$ and all the objects have different positive attributes, i.e. $\forall i, j, \ i \ne j$ s.t. $\mathbb{I}_{F_i^+} \not\subseteq \mathbb{I}_{F_j^+}$. If the component classifiers' predictive values p_i^+ and p_i^- are high enough, MAP estimation will converge to the correct result asymptotically with an increasing number of observations.*

Proof. Consider the worst case, where only two candidates $\mathbb{O} = \{o_1, o_2\}$ exist. Without loss of generality, assume o_1 has positive attributes $\mathbb{I}_{F_1^+} = \{1, 2, ..., M_1\}$ and o_2 has all the remaining positive attribute $\mathbb{I}_{F_2^+} = \{M_1+1, M_1+2, ..., M\}$, where $M_1 \ge 1$. Also assume o_1 is the ground truth object. In this case all the false-positive and false-negatives will drive the estimation toward o_2.

Based on (6), the posterior probability distributions of o_1 and o_2 can be written as:

$$P(O = o_1 | \mathbb{Z}^K, \mathbb{E}^K) = \lambda \pi_1 \prod_{i=1}^{M_1} \left(\frac{p_i^+}{w_i}\right)^{n_i^+} \left(\frac{1 - p_i^-}{w_i}\right)^{n_i^-} \prod_{i=M_1+1}^{M} \left(\frac{1 - p_i^+}{1 - w_i}\right)^{n_i^+} \left(\frac{p_i^-}{1 - w_i}\right)^{n_i^-} \quad (9)$$

$$P(O = o_2 | \mathbb{Z}^K, \mathbb{E}^K) = \lambda \pi_2 \prod_{i=1}^{M_1} \left(\frac{1 - p_i^+}{1 - w_i}\right)^{n_i^+} \left(\frac{p_i^-}{1 - w_i}\right)^{n_i^-} \prod_{i=M_1+1}^{M} \left(\frac{p_i^+}{w_i}\right)^{n_i^+} \left(\frac{1 - p_i^-}{w_i}\right)^{n_i^-}, \quad (10)$$

where n_i^+ and n_i^- are the number of positive and negative recognition results of the i-th attribute. Denote n as the number of times the i-th classifier works in its reliable region $\mathbb{E}^i$. Based on the central limit theorem, we have $P(n_i^+ > n\frac{d_i}{\alpha}) = 1$ and $P(n_i^- < n\alpha v_i) = 1$ for $i = 1, 2, ..., M_1$ when n goes to infinity and α can be any positive constant larger than 1.

For the same reason, we have $P(n_i^+ < n\alpha q_i) = 1$ for $i = M_1 + 1, ..., M$ when n goes to infinity. We use the same n here assuming same likelihood of reliable working regions for each classifier. Actually it does not matter if there is a constant positive factor on n, which means that the chances for the classifiers' reliably working region may be proportional.

Dividing (9) by (10), we obtain:

$$\frac{P(O = o_1 | \mathbb{Z}^K, \mathbb{E}^K)}{P(O = o_2 | \mathbb{Z}^K, \mathbb{E}^K)} = \frac{\pi_1}{\pi_2} \frac{\prod_{i=1}^{M_1} (\frac{p_i^+/w_i}{(1-p_i^+)/(1-w_i)})^{n_i^+} (\frac{(1-p_i^-)/(w_i)}{p_i^-/(1-w_i)})^{n_i^-}}{\prod_{i=M_1+1}^{M} (\frac{p_i^+/w_i}{(1-p^+i)/(1-w_i)})^{n_i^+} (\frac{(1-p_i^-)/w_i}{p_i^-/(1-w_i)})^{n_i^-}}$$

$$\geq \frac{\pi_1}{\pi_2} \frac{\prod_{i=1}^{M_1} (\frac{p_i^+/w_i}{(1-p_i^+)/(1-w_i)})^{n\frac{d_i}{\alpha}} (\frac{(1-p_i^-)/(w_i)}{p_i^-/(1-w_i)})^{n\alpha v_i}}{\prod_{i=M_1+1}^{M} (\frac{p_i^+/w_i}{(1-p^+i)/(1-w_i)})^{n\alpha q_i}}$$

(p_i^+, p_i^- larger than the threshold in theorem 1)

$$= c_1 \left(c_2 \frac{\prod_{i=1}^{M_1} (\frac{p_i^+}{1-p_i^+})^{\frac{d_i}{\alpha}} (\frac{1-p_i^-}{p_i^-})^{\alpha v_i}}{\prod_{i=M_1+1}^{M} (\frac{p_i^+}{1-p_i^+})^{\alpha q_i}} \right)^n \geq c_1 \left(c_2 \frac{\prod_{i=1}^{M_1} (\frac{p_i^+}{1-p_i^+})^{\frac{A}{\alpha}} (\frac{1-p_i^-}{p_i^-})^{\alpha \frac{1-p_i^-}{w_i}}}{\prod_{i=M_1+1}^{M} (\frac{p_i^+}{1-p_i^+})^{\alpha \frac{(1-p_i^+)}{1-w_i}}} \right)^n$$

(for the upper bound of q_i and v_i see (Eq. 12))

$$(11)$$

Because $\lim_{p \to 1} \frac{p}{1-p} = \infty$ and $\lim_{p \to 1} (\frac{p}{1-p})^{1-p} = 1$, the division will be larger than 1 when the predictive value of each classifier is high enough, which means the MAP estimation will yield o_1 asymptotically.

The proof of upper bound of q_i and v_i:

$$q_i = P(Z_i = 1 | F_i = 0) = \frac{P(Z_i = 1)(1 - p_i^+)}{1 - w_i} \leq \frac{1 - p_i^+}{1 - w_i} \qquad (12)$$

$$v_i = P(Z_i = 0 | F_i = 1) = \frac{P(Z_i = 0)(1 - p_i^-)}{w_i} \leq \frac{1 - p_i^-}{w_i} \qquad (13)$$

Beyond providing theoretical background, in the next section we perform experiments on a real object recognition task to first demonstrate the influence of the environment, and then to validate our framework's performance.

4   Experiments

In this section, we demonstrate our framework on the task of recognizing objects on a table top. We first build a pipeline to collect our own data[1]. The reason for collecting our own data is that other available RGBD datasets [14,15] focus

---

[1] The dataset is available from http://ece.umd.edu/~wluan/ECCV2016.html.

on different aspects, usually pose or multiview recognition, and do not contain a sufficient amount of samples from varying observation distances.

Three experiments are conducted to show (1) the necessity of incorporating environmental factors (the recognition distance in our case) for object recognition; (2) the performance of the high predictive value threshold classifier in comparison to the single threshold one; and (3) the benefits of incorporating less discriminative attributes for extending the working range of classifiers.

4.1 Experimental Settings

The preprocessing pipeline is illustrated in Fig. 2a. After a point cloud is grabbed from a 3D camera such as Kinect or Xtion PRO LIVE, we first apply a passthrough filter to remove points that are too close or too far away from the camera. Then the table surface is located by matching the point could to a 3D plane model using random sample consensus (RANSAC), and only points above the table are kept. Finally, on the remaining points, Euclidean clustering is employed to generate object candidates, and point clouds with less than 600 points are discarded.

(a)   (b)

Fig. 2. (a) Illustration of the preprocessing pipeline. Left: input; Middle: point cloud after passthrough filtering; Right: segmented candidate object and removed table surface. (b) The objects we use in the task and their IDs.

For the segmented point clouds, three categories of classifiers are applied, which are tuned to attributes of fine shape, coarse shape, and color.

Fine shape is recognized by the Viewpoint Feature Histogram (VFH) descriptor, which encodes a point cloud into a 308 dimensional vector. Radu [16] provides a pipeline of computing VFH features and retrieving the minimum feature distance matching by fast approximate K-Nearest Neighbors, implemented in the Fast Library for Approximate Nearest Neighbors (FLANN) [17]. However, this approach tends to generate false positives when matching different point clouds with very different distances to the camera. Thus, we adapt the original recognition pipeline to a two step matching. We first pick up model point clouds from our database with similar distance to test input point cloud. Among the nearby template point clouds, we use the minimum VFH feature matching distance as the classification score. Both steps use FLANN to accelerate neighbor retrieval, where the former step uses the Euclidean distance and the latter the Chi-Square distance.

As another type of attribute, we use coarse shape, which is less selective than the fine shape attribute. Our experiments later on demonstrate its advantage of having a larger working region, thence it can help increase the system's recognition accuracy over a broader range of distance. Two coarse shapes, cylinders and planar surfaces, are recognized by fitting a cylindrical and a plane model, whose coefficients are estimated by RANSAC. The percentage of outlying points is counted as the classification score for the shape. Thus, a lower score indicates better coarse attribute fitting in our experiment.

The last type of attribute in our system is color, which is used to augment the system's recognition capability. To control the influence of illumination, all samples are collected under one stable lighting condition. The color histogram is calculated on point clouds after Euclidean clustering, where few background or irrelevant pixels are involved. The Hue and Saturation channels of color are discretized into 30 bins (5×6), which works well for differentiating the major colors.

As shown in Fig. 2b, there are 9 candidate objects in our dataset. To recognize them, we use 5 fine shape attributes: shape of cup, bottle, gable top carton, wide mouse bottle, and box; 2 coarse shape attributes: cylinder and plane surface; 3 major colors: red, blue and yellow. The attributes for all objects are listed in Table 1. In the following experiments, we fix the pose of objects, and set the recognition distance as the only changing factor.

Table 1. Object IDs and their list of attributes

Object ID	plane surface	cylinder	gable top carton shape	box shape	wide mouth bottle shape	cup shape	bottle shape	red color	blue color	yellow color
1	✓	-	✓	-	-	-	-	-	✓	-
2	✓	-	✓	-	-	-	-	✓	-	-
3	✓	-	✓	-	-	-	-	-	-	✓
4	✓	-	-	✓	-	-	-	✓	-	-
5	-	✓	-	-	✓	-	-	-	-	-
6	-	✓	-	-	-	✓	-	-	✓	-
7	-	✓	-	-	-	-	✓	-	-	✓
8	-	✓	-	-	-	-	✓	✓	-	-
9	-	✓	-	-	-	-	✓	-	✓	-

4.2 Experimental Results

EXPERIMENT ONE: The first experiment is designed to validate our claim that the classifiers' response score distributions are indeed distance variant. Therefore, it is necessary to integrate distance in a robust recognition system.

Taking the fine shape classifier of bottle shapes as example, we divide the distance range between 60 cm and 140 cm into 4 equally separated intervals and collect positive samples (object id 7, 8, 9) and negative samples from the remaining 9 objects in each distance interval. The number of positive samples in each interval is 120 with 40 objects from each positive instance, while the number of negative samples is 210 with 35 from each instance. The distribution of the bottle classifier's response score is approximated by Gaussian kernel density estimation with a standard deviation of 3, and plotted in Fig. 3.

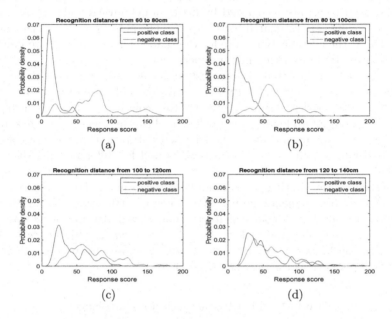

Fig. 3. Estimated distribution of bottle shape classifier's response score under 4 recognition distance intervals.

We observe that the output score distribution depends on the recognition distance interval. Therefore, relying on one single classification threshold across all the distance intervals would introduce additional error. More importantly, we observe that with a larger distance, the area of overlap between the positive and negative distributions, becomes wider, which makes classification more difficult.

EXPERIMENT TWO: Experiment one demonstrated the difficulty of learning a distance-variant ground truth distribution and corresponding classification thresholds. Therefore, we propose to use two high predicative value thresholds when multiple inputs are available. The second experiment is designed to validate this idea by comparing the classification accuracy of an estimator that (1) uses two high predicative value thresholds, with an estimator that uses (2) one optimal Bayes threshold minimizing the error in the training data.

To have a fair comparison, we set our task as recognizing 5 objects (id 1, 4, 5, 6, 9) with 5 fine shape attributes such that each object contains one positive attribute that uniquely identifies it. Both training and testing point clouds are collected at a distance of 100 cm to 120 cm. To learn the classification threshold, we sample 26 point clouds for each object and uniformly select 20 for training. The testing data for each object consists of 22 point clouds that we can randomly choose from to simulate the scenario of an active moving observer gathering multiple inputs. Here we want to mention a special case. When our framework is uncertain based on the current input, it randomly select (with equal probability) one of the possible objects. The classification accuracy between using a single threshold and using two high predicative value thresholds are shown in Fig. 4a respectively.

We can see that both methods' error rates decrease when the number of observations increases. The approach using two thresholds (the red line) has lower error rate than the one using a single threshold (the blue line). The green line shows the error introduced by random selection, when our framework cannot make a sole decision. The major part of the error in the two thresholds method is due to this error. It is worth mentioning that under theoretical conditions, the classical Bayes single threshold should still be the best in minimizing the classification error. Our method provides an alternative for cases when the training data in real world scenarios does not represent well the underlying distribution.

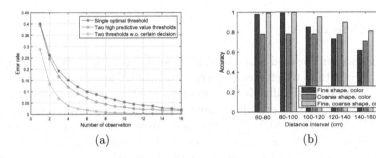

(a)   (b)

Fig. 4. (a): Error rate using classification with a single threshold (blue) and two high predictive value thresholds (red). The green line depicts the error component due to the cases where the two thresholds method has to randomly select. (b) Three systems' recognition accuracy for different working distance intervals. (Color figure online)

EXPERIMENT THREE: The third experiment demonstrates the benefits of using less discriminative attributes for extending the system's working range. To recognize the 9 objects in Fig. 2b, we build three recognition systems utilizing attributes of fine shape and color, coarse shape and color, and all of the three attributes, respectively. Considering the influence of the recognition distance on the response score distribution, the complete range of distances from 60 cm to 160 cm is split into 5 equal intervals. We then learn the classification thresholds and predictive values accordingly. Both, the training and the testing data, consist of around 100 samples from each object across recognition distances from 60 cm to 160 cm. We learn the PPV and NPV by counting the training data w.r.t. the thresholds and select thresholds satisfying a predictive value larger than 0.96. The minimum detection rate for the reliable working distance interval is 0.09. This means if (1) an attribute classifier cannot find a threshold with PPV larger than 0.96, and (2) detection rate larger than 0.09 in a certain distance interval, the output of this attribute classier in this interval will not be adopted for decision making. During the testing phase, for fair comparison, we constrain the number of input point clouds collected from the same distance interval in each working region. Around 120 point clouds are collected for each object. Once more, random selection is applied when multiple objects are found as possible candidates.

Figure 4b displays the systems' recognition accuracy after observing three times in each distance interval. As expected, the classification performance starts to decrease for larger distances. At 120 cm to 160 cm, the system using fine shape attributes (blue) performs even worse than the system using less selective coarse attributes (green). This validates that the coarse shape based classifier has a larger working region, though its simple mechanisms allows for less discrimination than the fine grain attribute based classifier. Finally, due to the complementary properties, the system using all attributes (yellow) achieves the best performance at each working region.

5   Conclusions

In this work we put forward a practical framework for using multiple attributes for object recognition, which incorporates recognition distance into the decision making. Considering the difficulties of finding a single best classification threshold and the availability of multiple inputs at testing time, we propose to learn a high PPV and a high NPV threshold and discard uncertain values during decision making. The framework's correctness was proven and a fundamental experiment was conducted to demonstrate our approach's feasibility and benefits. Additionally, we showed that less selective shape attributes (compared to the sophisticated ones) can have advantages, because their simple mechanism can lead to high reliability when the system is working at a large range of distances.

In future work, we plan to extend the approach to a variety of environmental factors such as lighting conditions, blur, and occlusions. Furthemore, additional attribute classifiers will be incorporated to improve the system's recognition performance.

Acknowledgment. This work was funded by the support of DARPA (through ARO) grant W911NF1410384, by NSF through grants CNS-1544787 and SMA-1540917 and Samsung under the GRO program (N020477, 355022).

References

1. Kanezaki, A., Marton, Z.C., Pangercic, D., Harada, T., Kuniyoshi, Y., Beetz, M.: Voxelized shape and color histograms for RGB-D. In: IEEE/RSJ International Conference on Intelligent Robots and Systems (IROS), Workshop on Active Semantic Perception and Object Search in the Real World, San Francisco, CA, USA, 25–30 September 2011

2. Xie, Z., Singh, A., Uang, J., Narayan, K.S., Abbeel, P.: Multimodal blending for high-accuracy instance recognition. In: Proceedings of the 26th IEEE/RSJ International Conference on Intelligent Robots and Systems (IROS) (2013)

3. Lutz, M., Stampfer, D., Schlegel, C.: Probabilistic object recognition and pose estimation by fusing multiple algorithms. In: 2013 IEEE International Conference on Robotics and Automation (ICRA), pp. 4244–4249, May 2013

4. Salih, Y., Malik, A.S., Walter, N., Sidibé, D., Saad, N., Meriaudeau, F.: Noise robustness analysis of point cloud descriptors. In: Blanc-Talon, J., Kasinski, A., Philips, W., Popescu, D., Scheunders, P. (eds.) ACIVS 2013. LNCS, vol. 8192, pp. 68–79. Springer, Heidelberg (2013)

5. Wu, T., Zhu, S.C.: Learning near-optimal cost-sensitive decision policy for object detection. In: IEEE International Conference of Computer Vision (2013)

6. Lowe, D.G.: Distinctive image features from scale-invariant keypoints. Int. J. Comput. Vis. **60**, 91–110 (2004)

7. Xu, Y., Ji, H., Fermüller, C.: A projective invariant for textures. In: 2006 IEEE Computer Society Conference on Computer Vision and Pattern Recognition, vol. 2, pp. 1932–1939 (2006)

8. Bertsche, M., Fromm, T., Ertel, W.: BOR3D: a use-case-oriented software framework for 3-d object recognition. In: 2012 IEEE International Conference on Technologies for Practical Robot Applications (TePRA), pp. 67–72, April 2012

9. Hinterstoisser, S., Lepetit, V., Ilic, S., Holzer, S., Bradski, G., Konolige, K., Navab, N.: Model based training, detection and pose estimation of texture-less 3d objects in heavily cluttered scenes. In: Lee, K.M., Matsushita, Y., Rehg, J.M., Hu, Z. (eds.) ACCV 2012, Part I. LNCS, vol. 7724, pp. 548–562. Springer, Heidelberg (2013)

10. Attamimi, M., Mizutani, A., Nakamura, T., Nagai, T., Funakoshi, K., Nakano, M.: Real-time 3d visual sensor for robust object recognition. In: 2010 IEEE/RSJ International Conference on Intelligent Robots and Systems (IROS), pp. 4560–4565, October 2010

11. Romea, C.A., Martinez Torres, M., Srinivasa, S.: The MOPED framework: object recognition and pose estimation for manipulation. Int. J. Robot. Res. **30**(10), 1284–1306 (2011)

12. Fromm, T., Staehle, B., Ertel, W.: Robust multi-algorithm object recognition using machine learning methods. In: IEEE Conference on Multisensor Fusion and Integration for Intelligent Systems (MFI), pp. 490–497, September 2012

13. Naguib, A., Lee, S.: Adaptive bayesian recognition with multiple evidences. In: 2014 International Conference on Multimedia Computing and Systems (ICMCS), pp. 337–344 (2014)

14. Lai, K., Bo, L., Ren, X., Fox, D.: A large-scale hierarchical multi-view RGB-D object dataset. In: 2011 IEEE International Conference on Robotics and Automation (ICRA), pp. 1817–1824, May 2011

15. Singh, A., Sha, J., Narayan, K.S., Achim, T., Abbeel, P.: BigBIRD: a large-scale 3d database of object instances. In: 2014 IEEE International Conference on Robotics and Automation (ICRA), pp. 509–516, May 2014

16. Rusu, R.B., Bradski, G., Thibaux, R., Hsu, J.: Fast 3d recognition and pose using the viewpoint feature histogram. In: Proceedings of the 23rd IEEE/RSJ International Conference on Intelligent Robots and Systems (IROS), Taipei, Taiwan (2010)

17. Muja, M., Lowe, D.G.: Scalable nearest neighbor algorithms for high dimensional data. IEEE Trans. Pattern Anal. Mach. Intell. **36**, 2227–2240 (2014)

Spatio-Temporal LSTM with Trust Gates for 3D Human Action Recognition

Jun Liu[1], Amir Shahroudy[1], Dong Xu[2], and Gang Wang[1(✉)]

[1] School of Electrical and Electronic Engineering, Nanyang Technological University,
Singapore, Singapore
{jliu029,amir3,wanggang}@ntu.edu.sg
[2] School of Electrical and Information Engineering, University of Sydney,
Sydney, Australia
dong.xu@sydney.edu.au

Abstract. 3D action recognition – analysis of human actions based on 3D skeleton data – becomes popular recently due to its succinctness, robustness, and view-invariant representation. Recent attempts on this problem suggested to develop RNN-based learning methods to model the contextual dependency in the temporal domain. In this paper, we extend this idea to spatio-temporal domains to analyze the hidden sources of action-related information within the input data over both domains concurrently. Inspired by the graphical structure of the human skeleton, we further propose a more powerful tree-structure based traversal method. To handle the noise and occlusion in 3D skeleton data, we introduce new gating mechanism within LSTM to learn the reliability of the sequential input data and accordingly adjust its effect on updating the long-term context information stored in the memory cell. Our method achieves state-of-the-art performance on 4 challenging benchmark datasets for 3D human action analysis.

Keywords: 3D action recognition · Recurrent neural networks · Long short-term memory · Trust gate · Spatio-temporal analysis

1 Introduction

In recent years, action recognition based on the locations of major joints of the body in 3D space has attracted a lot of attention. Different feature extraction and classifier learning approaches are studied for 3D action recognition [1–3]. For example, Yang and Tian [4] represented the static postures and the dynamics of the motion patterns via eigenjoints and utilized a Naïve-Bayes-Nearest-Neighbor classifier learning. A HMM was applied by [5] for modeling the temporal dynamics of the actions over a histogram-based representation of 3D joint locations. Evangelidis *et al.* [6] learned a GMM over the Fisher kernel representation of a succinct skeletal feature, called skeletal quads. Vemulapalli *et al.* [7] represented the skeleton configurations and actions as points and curves in a Lie group

© Springer International Publishing AG 2016
B. Leibe et al. (Eds.): ECCV 2016, Part III, LNCS 9907, pp. 816–833, 2016.
DOI: 10.1007/978-3-319-46487-9_50

respectively, and utilized a SVM classifier to classify the actions. A skeleton-based dictionary learning utilizing group sparsity and geometry constraint was also proposed by [8]. An angular skeletal representation over the tree-structured set of joints was introduced in [9], which calculated the similarity of these features over temporal dimension to build the global representation of the action samples and fed them to SVM for final classification.

Recurrent neural networks (RNNs) which are a variant of neural nets for handling sequential data with variable length, have been successfully applied to language modeling [10–12], image captioning [13,14], video analysis [15–24], human re-identification [25,26], and RGB-based action recognition [27–29]. They also have achieved promising performance in 3D action recognition [30–32].

Existing RNN-based 3D action recognition methods mainly model the long-term contextual information in the temporal domain to represent motion-based dynamics. However, there is also strong dependency between joints in the spatial domain. And the spatial configuration of joints in video frames can be highly discriminative for 3D action recognition task.

In this paper, we propose a spatio-temporal long short-term memory (ST-LSTM) network which extends the traditional LSTM-based learning to two concurrent domains (temporal and spatial domains). Each joint receives contextual information from neighboring joints and also from previous frames to encode the spatio-temporal context. Human body joints are not naturally arranged in a chain, therefore feeding a simple chain of joints to a sequence learner cannot perform well. Instead, a tree-like graph can better represent the adjacency properties between the joints in the skeletal data. Hence, we also propose a tree structure based skeleton traversal method to explore the kinematic relationship between the joints for better spatial dependency modeling.

In addition, since the acquisition of depth sensors is not always accurate, we further improve the design of the ST-LSTM by adding a new gating function, so called "trust gate", to analyze the reliability of the input data at each spatio-temporal step and give better insight to the network about when to update, forget, or remember the contents of the internal memory cell as the representation of long-term context information.

The contributions of this paper are: (1) spatio-temporal design of LSTM networks for 3D action recognition, (2) a skeleton-based tree traversal technique to feed the structure of the skeleton data into a sequential LSTM, (3) improving the design of the ST-LSTM by adding the trust gate, and (4) achieving state-of-the-art performance on all the evaluated datasets.

2   Related Work

Human action recognition using 3D skeleton information is explored in different aspects during recent years [33–50]. In this section, we limit our review to more recent RNN-based and LSTM-based approaches.

HBRNN [30] applied bidirectional RNNs in a novel hierarchical fashion. They divided the entire skeleton to five major groups of joints and each group was fed into a separated bidirectional RNN. The output of these RNNs were concatenated to represent upper-body and lower-body, then each was fed into another set of RNNs. The global body representation was obtained by concatenating the output of these two RNNs and it was fed to the next layer of RNN. The hidden representation of the final RNN was fed to a softmax classifier layer for action classification.

Zhu *et al.* [51] added a mixed-norm regularization term to a deep LSTM network's cost function in order to push the network towards learning co-occurrence of discriminative joints for action classification. They further introduced an internal dropout [52] technique within the LSTM unit, which was applied on all the gate activations.

Differential LSTM [31] added a new gating inside LSTM to keep track of the derivatives of the memory states in order to discover patterns within salient motion patterns. All the input features for each frame were concatenated and fed to the differential LSTM.

Part-aware LSTM [32] separated the memory cell to part-based sub-cells and pushed the network towards learning the long-term context representations individually for each part. The output of the network was learned over the concatenated part-based memory cells followed by the common output gate.

Unlike the above mentioned works, the framework proposed in this paper does not concatenate the joint-based input features, instead it explicitly models the dependencies between the joints and applies recurrent analysis over spatial and temporal domains concurrently. Besides, a novel trust gate is developed to make LSTM robust to noisy input data.

3   Spatio-Temporal Recurrent Networks

Human actions can be characterized by the motion of body parts over time. In 3D human action recognition, we have three dimensional locations of the major body joints in each frame. Recently, recurrent neural networks have been successfully employed for skeleton-based 3D action recognition [30,32,51].

Long Short-Term Memory (LSTM) networks [53] are very successful extensions of the recurrent neural networks (RNNs). They utilize the gating mechanism over an internal memory cell to learn and represent a better and more complex representation of the long-term dependencies among the input sequential data, thus they are suitable for feature learning over a sequence of temporal data.

In this section, first we will briefly review the standard LSTM networks, then describe the proposed spatio-temporal LSTM model and the skeleton-based tree traversal. Next we will introduce an effective gating scheme for LSTM to deal with the measurement noise in the input data (body joint locations) for the task of 3D human action recognition.

3.1   Temporal Modeling with LSTM

A typical LSTM unit contains an input gate i_t, a forget gate f_t, an output gate o_t, and an output state h_t, together with an internal memory cell state c_t. The LSTM transition equations are formulated as:

$$\begin{pmatrix} i_t \\ f_t \\ o_t \\ u_t \end{pmatrix} = \begin{pmatrix} \sigma \\ \sigma \\ \sigma \\ \tanh \end{pmatrix} \left(M \begin{pmatrix} x_t \\ h_{t-1} \end{pmatrix} \right) \tag{1}$$

$$c_t = i_t \odot u_t + f_t \odot c_{t-1} \tag{2}$$

$$h_t = o_t \odot \tanh(c_t) \tag{3}$$

where $\odot$ indicates element-wise product, x_t denotes the input to the network at time step t, and u_t denotes the modulated input. σ is the sigmoid activation function. $M : \Re^{D+d} \rightarrow \Re^{4d}$ is an affine transformation consisting of model parameters, where D is the dimensionality of input x_t and d is the number of LSTM cell state units.

Intuitively, the input gate i_t determines the extent to which the modulated input information (u_t) is supposed to update the memory cell at time t. The forget gate f_t determines the effectiveness of the previous state of the memory cell (c_{t-1}) on its current state (c_t). Finally, the output gate o_t governs the amount of information output from the memory cell. Readers are referred to [54] for more details about the mechanism of LSTM.

3.2 Spatio-Temporal LSTM

Very recent attempts on applying RNNs for 3D human action recognition [30–32, 51] show outstanding performance and prove the strengths of RNNs in modeling the complex dynamics of the human actions in temporal space.

The main focus of these existing methods was on utilizing RNNs over temporal domain for discovering the discriminative dynamics and body motion patterns for 3D action recognition. However, there is also discriminative information in static postures encoded within the joints' 3D locations in each individual frame and the sequential nature of skeleton data makes it possible to adopt RNN-based learning in spatial domain as well. Unlike other existing methods, which concatenated the joints information, we extend the recurrent analysis towards spatial domain to discover the spatial dependency patterns between different joints at each frame.

In this fashion, we propose a spatio-temporal LSTM (ST-LSTM) model which simultaneously models the spatial dependencies of the joints and the temporal dependencies among the frames. As shown in Fig. 1, every ST-LSTM unit corresponds to one of the skeletal joints. Each of the units receives the hidden representation of the previous joint and also the hidden representation of its own joint from the previous frame. In this section we assume joints are arranged in a chain-like sequence with the order shown in Fig. 2(a). In Sect. 3.3, we will show a more advanced method to take advantage of the adjacency information of the body joints as a tree structure.

We use $j \in \{1, ..., J\}$ and $t \in \{1, ..., T\}$ to denote the indices of joints and frames respectively. Each ST-LSTM unit is fed with its input ($x_{j,t}$, location of the corresponding joint at current frame), its own hidden representation at the

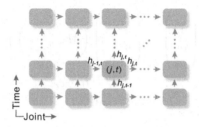

Fig. 1. The illustration of the proposed spatio-temporal LSTM network. In the spatial direction, body joints in a frame are fed in a sequence. In the temporal direction, the locations of the corresponding joints are fed over time. Each unit receives the hidden representation of previous joints and previous frames of the same joint as contextual information.

previous time step $(h_{j,t-1})$, and the hidden representation of the previous joint at current frame $(h_{j-1,t})$. Each unit is also equipped with two different forget gates corresponding to the two incoming channels of context information: $f^S_{j,t}$ for the spatial domain, and $f^T_{j,t}$ for the temporal domain. The proposed ST-LSTM is formulated as:

$$\begin{pmatrix} i_{j,t} \\ f^S_{j,t} \\ f^T_{j,t} \\ o_{j,t} \\ u_{j,t} \end{pmatrix} = \begin{pmatrix} \sigma \\ \sigma \\ \sigma \\ \sigma \\ \tanh \end{pmatrix} \left(M \begin{pmatrix} x_{j,t} \\ h_{j-1,t} \\ h_{j,t-1} \end{pmatrix} \right) \tag{4}$$

$$c_{j,t} = i_{j,t} \odot u_{j,t} + f^S_{j,t} \odot c_{j-1,t} + f^T_{j,t} \odot c_{j,t-1} \tag{5}$$

$$h_{j,t} = o_{j,t} \odot \tanh(c_{j,t}) \tag{6}$$

3.3   Tree-Structure Based Traversal

Arranging joints in a simple chain ignores the kinematic dependency relations between the joints and adds false connections between body joints which are not strongly related. In human parsing, skeletal joints are popularly modeled as a tree-based pictorial structure [55,56], as illustrated in Fig. 2(b). In our ST-LSTM framework, it is also beneficial to model the spatial dependency of the joints based on their adjacency tree structure. For example, hidden representation of the neck joint (number 2 in Fig. 2(a)) is expected to be more informative for the right hand joints (7, 8, 9) than the joint number 6.

However, trees cannot be directly fed into the ST-LSTM framework. To mitigate this issue, we propose a bidirectional tree traversal method to visit joints in a sequence which maintains the adjacency information of the skeletal tree structure.

As illustrated in Fig. 2(c), at the first spatial step, the root node (central spine joint) is fed to the network, then the network follows a depth-first traversal in the

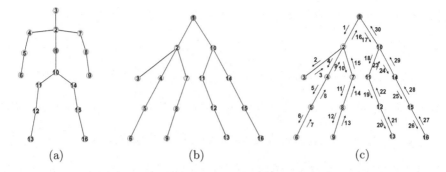

Fig. 2. (a) Skeletal joints of a human body. In the simple joint chain model, the joint visiting order is 1-2-3-...-16. (b) Skeleton is transformed to a tree structure. (c) Tree traversal over the spatial steps. The tree can be unfolded to a chain with the traversal, and the joint visiting order is 1-2-3-2-4-5-6-5-4-2-7-8-9-8-7-2-1-10-11-12-13-12-11-10-14-15-16-15-14-10-1.

spatial domain. When it reaches a leaf node, it goes back. In this fashion, each connection of the tree structure will be passed twice and the context information is fed along both directions. Upon the end of the traversal, it gets back to the root node.

This traversal strategy guarantees the transmission of the data in both directions (top-down and bottom-up) inside the adjacency tree structure. Therefore each node will have the contextual information from both its descendants and ancestors. Compared to the simple chain model described in Sect. 3.2, this tree traversal technique can discover stronger long-term spatial dependency patterns based on the joints' adjacency structure.

In addition, the input to the ST-LSTM network at each step is limited to a single joint in a specific frame, which is much smaller in size compared to the concatenated input features of other existing methods. As a result, we have much fewer model parameters and this can be considered as a weight sharing regularization inside our learning framework, which leads to better generalization in the scenarios with limited training samples. This is an advantage in 3D action recognition, because most of the current datasets have a small number of training samples.

Similar to other LSTM implementations [57,58], the representation capacity of our network can be improved by stacking multiple layers of the tree structured ST-LSTMs and constructing a deep yet completely tractable network, as illustrated in Fig. 3.

3.4   Spatio-Temporal LSTM with Trust Gates

The inputs of the proposed tree-structured ST-LSTM are the 3D positions of skeletal joints collected by sensors like Microsoft Kinect, which are not always reliable due to noise and occlusion. This limits the performance of the network. To address this issue, we propose to add a new gate to the LSTM unit which

Joints   ST-LSTM units (Layer 1)   ST-LSTM units (Layer 2)   Softmax classifier

Fig. 3. A graphical model of the deep tree-structured ST-LSTM network. For clarity, some arrows are omitted in the stacked network (better viewed in color). In this figure, the output of the first ST-LSTM layer is fed to the second ST-LSTM layer as its input. The second ST-LSTM layer's output is fed to softmax layer. (Color figure online)

analyzes the reliability of the input at each spatio-temporal step, based on the estimation of the input from the available contextual information.

Our novel gating method is inspired by the works in natural language processing [58] which predict next word based on LSTM representation of previous words. This idea worked well because of the high dependency among the words in a sentence. Similarly, since the skeletal joints often move together and this articulated motion follows common yet complex patterns at each spatio-temporal step, the input data $x_{j,t}$ is supposed to be predictable from the contextual representations $h_{j,t-1}$ and $h_{j-1,t}$.

This predictability inspired us to add new mechanism to ST-LSTM to predict the input and compare it with the actual incoming input. The amount of the estimation error is used as input to a new "trust gate". The derived trust value provides information to the long-term memory mechanism to learn better decisions about when and how to remember and forget the contents of the memory cell. For example, when the trust gate finds out the current joint has wrong 3D measurements, it can block the input gate and prevent the memory cell from updating based on current unreliable input.

Mathematically, for an input at step (j, t), we develop a function to generate its prediction, based on the available contextual information:

$$p_{j,t} = \tanh \left(M_p \begin{pmatrix} h_{j-1,t} \\ h_{j,t-1} \end{pmatrix} \right) \tag{7}$$

where the affine transformation M_p maps the data from $\Re^{2d}$ to $\Re^d$, so the dimensionality of $p_{j,t}$ is d. It is worth noting that the contextual information at each step is not limited to the hidden states of the previous spatial step but it also includes the previous temporal step, i.e., the long-term memory information of the same joint in previous frames and the contextual information of other visited joints in the same frame are seamlessly incorporated. Therefore, we can expect this function to be able to produce good predictions.

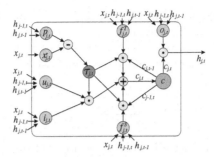

Fig. 4. Schema of the proposed ST-LSTM with trust gate.

The activation of the proposed trust gate τ is a vector in $\Re^d$, which is similar to the activation of the input gate and the forget gate, and it will be calculated as:

$$x'_{j,t} = \tanh\left(M_x\left(x_{j,t}\right)\right) \tag{8}$$

$$\tau_{j,t} = G(x'_{j,t} - p_{j,t}) \tag{9}$$

where $M_x : \Re^D \to \Re^d$ is an affine transformation, and the new activation function $G(\cdot)$ is an element-wise operation formulated as:

$$G(z) = \exp(-\lambda z^2) \tag{10}$$

In this equation, $\lambda > 0$ is a parameter to control the spread of the Gaussian function. $G(z)$ produces a large response if z is close to origin, and small response when z has a large absolute value.

Utilizing the proposed trust gate, the cell state of the ST-LSTM neuron can be updated as:

$$c_{j,t} = \tau_{j,t} \odot i_{j,t} \odot u_{j,t} + (1 - \tau_{j,t}) \odot f^S_{j,t} \odot c_{j-1,t} + (1 - \tau_{j,t}) \odot f^T_{j,t} \odot c_{j,t-1} \tag{11}$$

If the new input $x_{j,t}$ cannot be trusted (because of noise or occlusion), then we need to take advantage of more history information and try to block the new input. In contrast, if the input is reliable, we can let the learning algorithm update the memory cell by importing input information.

Figure 4 depicts the scheme of the new ST-LSTM unit empowered with the trust gate. This can be learned similar to other gates by back-propagation. The proposed trust gate technique is theoretically general and can be applied to other applications to deal with unreliable input data.

3.5   Learning the Classifier

Since the action labels are always given at the video level, we feed them as the training outputs of the ST-LSTM at each spatio-temporal step. The network learns to predict the action class $\hat{y}$ among a discrete set of classes Y using a softmax layer. The overall prediction of a video is computed by averaging the predictions of all the steps. Empirically, this method provides better performance compared to the minimization of the loss at the last step only.

The objective function of our model is formulated as:

$$L = \sum_{j=1}^{J} \sum_{t=1}^{T} l(\hat{y}_{j,t}, y) \tag{12}$$

where $l(\hat{y}_{j,t}, y)$ is the negative log-likelihood loss [54] measuring the difference between the true label y and the predicted result $\hat{y}_{j,t}$ at step (j, t). The objective function can be minimized using back-propagation through time (BPTT) algorithm [54].

4   Experiments

The proposed model is evaluated on four datasets: NTU RGB+D dataset, SBU Interaction dataset, UT-Kinect dataset, and Berkeley MHAD dataset. We conduct extensive experiments with different configurations as follows:

(1) "ST-LSTM (Joint Chain)": In this configuration, the joints are visited one by one in a simple chain order (see Fig. 2(a)).
(2) "ST-LSTM (Tree Traversal)": The proposed tree traversal strategy (Fig. 2(c)) is adopted in this configuration to fully exploit the tree-based spatial structure of human joints.
(3) "ST-LSTM (Tree Traversal) + Trust Gate": This configuration involves the trust gate to deal with noisy input.

4.1   Evaluation Datasets

NTU RGB+D Dataset [32]. To the best of our knowledge, this dataset is currently the largest depth-based action recognition dataset. It is collected by Kincet v2 and contains more than 56 thousand sequences and 4 million frames. A total of 60 different action classes including daily actions, pair actions, and medical conditions are performed by 40 subjects aged between 10 and 35. The 3D coordinates of 25 joints are provided in this dataset. The large intra-class and view point variations make this dataset very challenging. Due to the large amount of samples, this dataset is highly suitable for deep learning based action recognition.

SBU Interaction Dataset [59]. This dataset is captured with Kinect and contains 8 classes of two-person interactions. It includes 282 skeleton sequences in 6822 frames. Each skeleton has 15 joints. The challenges of this dataset include: (1) in most interactions, one person is acting and the other one is reacting; and (2) the joint coordinates in many sequences are of low accuracy.

UT-Kinect Dataset [5]. This dataset contains 10 action classes performed by 10 subjects, captured with a stationary Kinect. Each action was performed twice by every subject. The locations of 20 joints are provided in this dataset. The high intra-class variation and viewpoint diversity makes it challenging.

Berkeley MHAD [60]. The MHAD dataset is captured by a motion capture system. It consists of 659 sequences and about 82 min of recording. Eleven different action classes were performed by 7 male and 5 female subjects. The 3D locations of 35 joints are provided in this dataset.

4.2   Implementation Details

In our experiments, each video sequence is divided to T sub-sequences with the same length, and one frame was randomly selected from each sub-sequence. Such a method adds randomness into the process of data generation and improves the generalization capability. We observe this strategy achieves better performance in contrast to uniformly sampled frames. We cross-validated the performance based on leave-one-subject-out protocol on NTU RGB+D dataset, and found $T = 20$ as the optimum value.

We use Torch toolbox as the deep learning platform and an NVIDIA Tesla K40 GPU to run our experiments. We train the network using stochastic gradient descent, and set learning rate, momentum and decay rate as 2×10^{-3}, 0.9 and 0.95, respectively. For our network, we set the neuron size d to 128, and the parameter λ used in $G(\cdot)$ to 0.5. We use two ST-LSTM layers in the stacked network, and the applied probability of dropout is 0.5. Though there are variations in terms of sequence length, joint number, and data acquisition equipment for different datasets, we use the same parameter settings mentioned above. This indicates the insensitiveness of our method to the parameter settings, as it achieves promising results on all the datasets with the same configuration.

4.3   Experimental Results

NTU RGB+D Dataset. This dataset has two standard evaluation protocols [32]. One is cross-subject evaluation, for which half of the subjects are used for training and the remaining are for testing. The second is cross-view evaluation, for which two viewpoints are used for training and one is left out for testing.

The results are shown in Table 1. Deep RNN and deep LSTM models concatenate the joints features at each frame and then feed them to the network to model the temporal dynamics and ignore the spatial dynamics. As can be seen, both "ST-LSTM (Joint Chain)" and "ST-LSTM (Tree Traversal)" models outperform these methods by a notable margin.

It can also be observed that the trust gate brings significant performance improvement, because the data acquired by Kinect is noisy and some joints are frequently occluded in this dataset.

A notable portion of samples of this dataset are captured from side view, as shown in Fig. 5. Based on the design of Kinect's body tracking mechanism,

Fig. 5. Example images with noisy skeletons from NTU RGB+D dataset.

side view skeletal data is less accurate than the front view. To further show the effectiveness of trust gate, we analyze the performance using only the samples in side views. When using "ST-LSTM (Tree Traversal)", the accuracy is 76.5 %, while "ST-LSTM (Tree Traversal) + Trust Gate" achieves 81.6 %. This indicates the proposed trust gate can effectively handle severely noisy data.

To verify the effectiveness of layer stacking, we decrease the network size by using only one ST-LSTM layer, and the accuracies drop to 65.5 % (cross-subject) and 77.0 % (cross-view). It indicates our two-layer stacked model has better representation strengths than a single-layer model.

The sensitivity of the proposed model to neural unit sizes and λ values are also evaluated and the results are depicted in Fig. 6. When trust gate is used, our model achieves better performance for all the λ values tested compared to the model without trust gate.

Finally, we evaluate the classification performance on early stopping conditions by feeding the first p $(0 < p < 1)$ portion of the testing video to the trained network on cross-subject protocol. When setting p as $0.1, 0.2, ..., 1.0$, the corresponding accuracies are 13.4 %, 21.6 %, 33.9 %, 46.6 %, 55.5 %, 61.1 %, 64.6 %, 66.7 %, 68.2 %, 69.2 %, respectively. We can find that the results improve when a larger portion of video is fed.

Table 1. Experimental results (accuracies) on NTU RGB+D Dataset

Method	Cross subject	Cross view
Lie group [7]	50.1 %	52.8 %
Skeletal quads [6]	38.6 %	41.4 %
Dynamic skeletons [61]	60.2 %	65.2 %
HBRNN [30]	59.1 %	64.0 %
Part-aware LSTM [32]	62.9 %	70.3 %
Deep RNN [32]	56.3 %	64.1 %
Deep LSTM [32]	60.7 %	67.3 %
ST-LSTM (Joint Chain)	61.7 %	75.5 %
ST-LSTM (Tree Traversal)	65.2 %	76.1 %
ST-LSTM (Tree Traversal) + Trust Gate	**69.2 %**	**77.7 %**

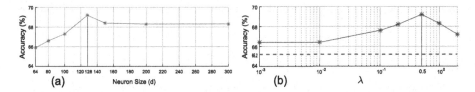

Fig. 6. (a) Comparison of the performance for different neuron size (*d*) values on NTU RGB+D dataset (cross-subject). (b) Comparison of different λ values on NTU RGB+D dataset (cross-subject). The blue line indicates the results when different λ values are used for trust gate, and the red dashed line indicates the performance when trust gate is not added. (Color figure online)

SBU Interaction Dataset. We follow the standard experimental protocol of [59] and perform 5-fold cross validation on SBU Interaction Dataset. In this dataset, two human skeletons are provided in each frame, so our traversal visits the joints throughout the two skeletons over the spatial steps. We summarize the results in terms of average classification accuracy in Table 2. In the table, [51] and [30] are both LSTM-based methods, which are more relevant to our model.

As can be seen, the proposed "ST-LSTM (Tree Traversal) + Trust Gate" model outperforms all other skeleton-based methods. "ST-LSTM (Tree Traversal)" yields higher accuracy than "ST-LSTM (Joint Chain)", as the latter adds some unreasonable links between the less related joints.

It is worth noting that deep LSTM [51], Co-occurrence LSTM [51], and HBRNN [30] all use the Svaitzky-Golay filter in temporal domain to smooth the skeleton joint positions to reduce the influence of the noise in the data captured by Kinect. However, even without trust gate (which aims at handling noisy input), the "ST-LSTM (Tree Traversal)" model outperforms HBRNN and deep LSTM, and achieves comparable result (88.6 %) to Co-occurrence LSTM. Once the trust gate is utilized, the accuracy jumps to 93.3 %. We do not adopt any skeleton normalization operation, such as translation or rotation of the skeleton [7], and achieve state-of-the-art performance. We notice that [62] obtained very similar result (93.4 %) on SBU dataset. However, their method utilized both RGB and depth images, while our method just uses the skeleton data.

UT-Kinect Dataset. There are two popular protocols on this dataset. First is the leave-one-out-cross-validation protocol [5]. Second is proposed in [63], for which half of the subjects are used for training and the remaining are used for testing. We use both protocols to evaluate the proposed method more extensively.

On the first protocol, our model achieves superior performance over other skeleton-based methods by a large margin, as shown in Table 3. On the second evaluation protocol (Table 4), our model achieves competitive result (95.0 %) to Elastic functional coding [68] (94.9 %).

Berkeley MHAD. We follow the protocol in [30] on MHAD dataset, in which 384 sequences corresponding to the first 7 subjects are used for training and the 275 sequences of the remaining 5 subjects are used for testing. The results are

Table 2. Experimental results on SBU interaction dataset

Method	Acc
Yun et al., [59]	80.3 %
Ji et al., [64]	86.9 %
CHARM [65]	83.9 %
HBRNN [30] (reported by [51])	80.4 %
Co-occurrence LSTM [51]	90.4 %
Deep LSTM (reported by [51])	86.0 %
ST-LSTM (Joint Chain)	84.7 %
ST-LSTM (Tree)	88.6 %
ST-LSTM (Tree) + Trust Gate	**93.3 %**

Table 3. Results on UT-kinect dataset (leave-one-out-cross-validation protocol [5])

Method	Acc
Histogram of 3D Joints [5]	90.9 %
Grassmann Manifold [66]	88.5 %
Riemannian Manifold [67]	91.5 %
ST-LSTM (Joint Chain)	91.0 %
ST-LSTM (Tree)	92.4 %
ST-LSTM (Tree) + Trust Gate	**97.0 %**

shown in Table 5. Our method achieves the accuracy of 100 % without preliminary smoothing operations, which are adopted in [30].

Besides, we have tested our model on **MSR Action3D dataset** [69] following the protocol in [30], and achieved an accuracy of 94.8 %, which is slightly superior to 94.5 % achieved by HBRNN [30].

4.4 Effectiveness of Trust Gate

To better study the effectiveness of the trust gate in the proposed network model, we specifically evaluate noisy samples from MSR Action3D dataset. We manually rectify some noisy joints of these samples by referring to the corresponding depth maps, and compared the activations of the trust gates on noisy and rectified inputs. As shown in Fig. 7(a), the activation of the trust gate is smaller when a noisy joint is fed, compared to the corresponding rectified joint. This shows how the network reduces the impact of the noisy input data.

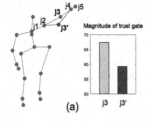 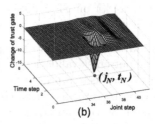

Fig. 7. Behavior of trust gate when inputting noisy data. (a) $j_{3'}$ is a noisy joint location, and j_3 is the corresponding rectified joint position. In the histogram, the blue bar is the magnitude of the trust gate when inputting the noisy joint $j_{3'}$. The red bar is the magnitude of the corresponding trust gate when $j_{3'}$ is rectified to j_3. (b) The difference between the trust gate calculated when inputting the original data and that calculated when the noise is imposed at the j_N-th spatial step and t_N-th time step. (Color figure online)

Table 4. Experimental results on UT-Kinect Dataset (half-vs-half protocol [63])

Method	Acc
Skeleton Joint Features [63]	87.9 %
Lie Group [7] (reported by [68])	93.6 %
Elastic functional coding [68]	94.9 %
ST-LSTM (Tree) + Trust Gate	**95.0 %**

Table 5. Experimental results on MHAD Dataset

Method	Acc
Vantigodi et al. [70]	96.1 %
Ofli et al. [71]	95.4 %
Vantigodi et al. [72]	97.6 %
Kapsouras et al. [73]	98.2 %
HBRNN [30]	**100 %**
ST-LSTM (Tree) + Trust Gate	**100 %**

To comprehensively evaluate the trust gate, we also manually add noise to one joint for all testing samples on MHAD dataset. Note that MHAD dataset was captured with motion capture system, thus the skeletal joints are much more accurate than those collected by Kinect. We add noise to the right foot joint by moving the joint away from the original position. The direction of the translation vector is randomly chosen and the norm is also a random value around 30 cm (this is a significant noise in the scale of human bodies). For each video, we add noise to the same joint at the same time step, and then analyze the effect in average.

We measure the difference in the magnitude of the trust gate activations between the original data and the noisy ones. For all the testing samples, we perform the same procedure, then calculate the average difference. The result is depicted in Fig. 7(b). We can see when the noisy data is fed to the network, the magnitude of the trust gate is reduced. This shows how the network ignores the noisy input, and tries to prevent it from affecting the network. In this experiment, we observe the overall accuracy does not drop after adding the noise.

5 Conclusion

In this paper we propose to extend the RNN-based 3D action recognition to spatio-temporal domain. A new ST-LSTM network is introduced which analyses the 3D location of each individual joint in each video frame, at each processing step. For better representation of the structured input to the network, a skeleton tree traversal algorithm is proposed which takes the adjacency graph of body joints into account and improves the performance of the network by arranging the most related joints together in the input sequence. Due to the unreliability of the 3D input data, a new gating mechanism is also proposed to improve the robustness of the network against noise and occlusion. The provided experimental results validate the proposed contributions and prove the effectiveness of our method by achieving superior performance over the existing state-of-the-art methods on four evaluated datasets.

Acknowledgement. The research is supported by Singapore Ministry of Education (MOE) Tier 2 ARC28/14, and Singapore A*STAR Science and Engineering Research Council PSF1321202099. This research was carried out at the Rapid-Rich Object Search (ROSE) Lab at Nanyang Technological University. The ROSE Lab is supported by the National Research Foundation, Singapore, under its Interactive Digital Media (IDM) Strategic Research Programme. We also would like to thank NVIDIA for the GPU donation.

References

1. Presti, L.L., La Cascia, M.: 3d skeleton-based human action classification: a survey. PR **53**, 130–147 (2016)
2. Han, F., Reily, B., Hoff, W., Zhang, H.: Space-time representation of people based on 3d skeletal data: a review. arXiv (2016)
3. Zhu, F., Shao, L., Xie, J., Fang, Y.: From handcrafted to learned representations for human action recognition: a survey. IVC (2016, in press)
4. Yang, X., Tian, Y.: Effective 3d action recognition using eigenjoints. JVCIR **25**, 2–11 (2014)
5. Xia, L., Chen, C., Aggarwal, J.: View invariant human action recognition using histograms of 3d joints. In: CVPRW (2012)
6. Evangelidis, G., Singh, G., Horaud, R.: Skeletal quads: Human action recognition using joint quadruples. In: ICPR (2014)
7. Vemulapalli, R., Arrate, F., Chellappa, R.: Human action recognition by representing 3d skeletons as points in a lie group. In: CVPR (2014)
8. Luo, J., Wang, W., Qi, H.: Group sparsity and geometry constrained dictionary learning for action recognition from depth maps. In: ICCV (2013)
9. Ohn-Bar, E., Trivedi, M.: Joint angles similarities and hog^2 for action recognition. In: CVPRW (2013)
10. Mikolov, T., Kombrink, S., Burget, L., Černocký, J.H., Khudanpur, S.: Extensions of recurrent neural network language model. In: ICASSP (2011)
11. Sundermeyer, M., Schlüter, R., Ney, H.: LSTM neural networks for language modeling. In: INTERSPEECH (2012)
12. Mesnil, G., He, X., Deng, L., Bengio, Y.: Investigation of recurrent-neural-network architectures and learning methods for spoken language understanding. In: INTERSPEECH (2013)
13. Vinyals, O., Toshev, A., Bengio, S., Erhan, D.: Show and tell: a neural image caption generator. In: CVPR (2015)
14. Xu, K., Ba, J., Kiros, R., Cho, K., Courville, A., Salakhudinov, R., Zemel, R., Bengio, Y.: Show, attend and tell: neural image caption generation with visual attention. In: ICML (2015)
15. Yue-Hei Ng, J., Hausknecht, M., Vijayanarasimhan, S., Vinyals, O., Monga, R., Toderici, G.: Beyond short snippets: deep networks for video classification. In: CVPR (2015)
16. Srivastava, N., Mansimov, E., Salakhudinov, R.: Unsupervised learning of video representations using LSTMS. In: ICML (2015)
17. Singh, B., Marks, T.K., Jones, M., Tuzel, O., Shao, M.: A multi-stream bi-directional recurrent neural network for fine-grained action detection. In: CVPR (2016)
18. Jain, A., Zamir, A.R., Savarese, S., Saxena, A.: Structural-RNN: deep learning on spatio-temporal graphs. In: CVPR (2016)

19. Alahi, A., Goel, K., Ramanathan, V., Robicquet, A., Fei-Fei, L., Savarese, S.: Social LSTM: Human trajectory prediction in crowded spaces. In: CVPR (2016)
20. Deng, Z., Vahdat, A., Hu, H., Mori, G.: Structure inference machines: Recurrent neural networks for analyzing relations in group activity recognition. In: CVPR (2016)
21. Ibrahim, M.S., Muralidharan, S., Deng, Z., Vahdat, A., Mori, G.: A hierarchical deep temporal model for group activity recognition. In: CVPR (2016)
22. Ma, S., Sigal, L., Sclaroff, S.: Learning activity progression in LSTMS for activity detection and early detection. In: CVPR (2016)
23. Ni, B., Yang, X., Gao, S.: Progressively parsing interactional objects for fine grained action detection. In: CVPR (2016)
24. Li, Y., Lan, C., Xing, J., Zeng, W., Yuan, C., Liu, J.: Online human action detection using joint classification-regression recurrent neural networks. arXiv (2016)
25. Varior, R.R., Shuai, B., Lu, J., Xu, D., Wang, G.: A siamese long short-term memory architecture for human re-identification. In: ECCV (2016)
26. Varior, R.R., Haloi, M., Wang, G.: Gated siamese convolutional neural network architecture for human re-identification. In: ECCV (2016)
27. Donahue, J., Anne Hendricks, L., Guadarrama, S., Rohrbach, M., Venugopalan, S., Saenko, K., Darrell, T.: Long-term recurrent convolutional networks for visual recognition and description. In: CVPR (2015)
28. Li, Q., Qiu, Z., Yao, T., Mei, T., Rui, Y., Luo, J.: Action recognition by learning deep multi-granular spatio-temporal video representation. In: ICMR (2016)
29. Wu, Z., Wang, X., Jiang, Y.G., Ye, H., Xue, X.: Modeling spatial-temporal clues in a hybrid deep learning framework for video classification. In: ACM MM (2015)
30. Du, Y., Wang, W., Wang, L.: Hierarchical recurrent neural network for skeleton based action recognition. In: CVPR (2015)
31. Veeriah, V., Zhuang, N., Qi, G.J.: Differential recurrent neural networks for action recognition. In: ICCV (2015)
32. Shahroudy, A., Liu, J., Ng, T.T., Wang, G.: NTU RGB+D: A large scale dataset for 3d human activity analysis. In: CVPR (2016)
33. Wang, J., Liu, Z., Wu, Y., Yuan, J.: Learning actionlet ensemble for 3d human action recognition. In: TPAMI (2014)
34. Meng, M., Drira, H., Daoudi, M., Boonaert, J.: Human-object interaction recognition by learning the distances between the object and the skeleton joints. In: FG (2015)
35. Shahroudy, A., Ng, T.T., Yang, Q., Wang, G.: Multimodal multipart learning for action recognition in depth videos. In: TPAMI (2016)
36. Wang, J., Wu, Y.: Learning maximum margin temporal warping for action recognition. In: ICCV (2013)
37. Rahmani, H., Mahmood, A., Huynh, D.Q., Mian, A.: Real time action recognition using histograms of depth gradients and random decision forests. In: WACV (2014)
38. Shahroudy, A., Wang, G., Ng, T.T.: Multi-modal feature fusion for action recognition in RGB-D sequences. In: ISCCSP (2014)
39. Wang, C., Wang, Y., Yuille, A.L.: Mining 3d key-pose-motifs for action recognition. In: CVPR (2016)
40. Rahmani, H., Mian, A.: Learning a non-linear knowledge transfer model for cross-view action recognition. In: CVPR (2015)
41. Lillo, I., Carlos Niebles, J., Soto, A.: A hierarchical pose-based approach to complex action understanding using dictionaries of actionlets and motion poselets. In: CVPR (2016)

42. Hu, J.F., Zheng, W.S., Ma, L., Wang, G., Lai, J.: Real-time RGB-D activity prediction by soft regression. In: ECCV (2016)
43. Chen, C., Jafari, R., Kehtarnavaz, N.: Fusion of depth, skeleton, and inertial data for human action recognition. In: ICASSP (2016)
44. Rahmani, H., Mian, A.: 3d action recognition from novel viewpoints. In: CVPR (2016)
45. Liu, Z., Zhang, C., Tian, Y.: 3d-based deep convolutional neural network for action recognition with depth sequences. IVC (2016, in press)
46. Cai, X., Zhou, W., Wu, L., Luo, J., Li, H.: Effective active skeleton representation for low latency human action recognition. TMM **18**, 141–154 (2016)
47. Al Alwani, A.S., Chahir, Y.: Spatiotemporal representation of 3d skeleton joints-based action recognition using modified spherical harmonics. PR Lett. (2016, in press)
48. Tao, L., Vidal, R.: Moving poselets: A discriminative and interpretable skeletal motion representation for action recognition. In: ICCVW (2015)
49. Shahroudy, A., Ng, T.T., Gong, Y., Wang, G.: Deep multimodal feature analysis for action recognition in RGB+D videos. arXiv (2016)
50. Du, Y., Fu, Y., Wang, L.: Representation learning of temporal dynamics for skeleton-based action recognition. TIP **25**, 3010–3022 (2016)
51. Zhu, W., Lan, C., Xing, J., Zeng, W., Li, Y., Shen, L., Xie, X.: Co-occurrence feature learning for skeleton based action recognition using regularized deep LSTM networks. In: AAAI (2016)
52. Srivastava, N., Hinton, G., Krizhevsky, A., Sutskever, I., Salakhutdinov, R.: Dropout: a simple way to prevent neural networks from overfitting. JMLR **15**, 1929–1958 (2014)
53. Hochreiter, S., Schmidhuber, J.: Long short-term memory. Neural Comput. **9**, 1735–1780 (1997)
54. Graves, A.: Supervised sequence labelling. In: Graves, A. (ed.) Supervised Sequence Labelling with Recurrent Neural Networks. SCI, vol. 385, pp. 5–13. Springer, Heidelberg (2012)
55. Zou, B., Chen, S., Shi, C., Providence, U.M.: Automatic reconstruction of 3d human motion pose from uncalibrated monocular video sequences based on markerless human motion tracking. PR **42**, 1559–1571 (2009)
56. Yang, Y., Ramanan, D.: Articulated pose estimation with flexible mixtures-of-parts. In: CVPR (2011)
57. Graves, A., Mohamed, A.r., Hinton, G.: Speech recognition with deep recurrent neural networks. In: ICASSP (2013)
58. Sutskever, I., Vinyals, O., Le, Q.V.: Sequence to sequence learning with neural networks. In: NIPS (2014)
59. Yun, K., Honorio, J., Chattopadhyay, D., Berg, T.L., Samaras, D.: Two-person interaction detection using body-pose features and multiple instance learning. In: CVPRW (2012)
60. Ofli, F., Chaudhry, R., Kurillo, G., Vidal, R., Bajcsy, R.: Berkeley MHAD: a comprehensive multimodal human action database. In: WACV (2013)
61. Hu, J.F., Zheng, W.S., Lai, J., Zhang, J.: Jointly learning heterogeneous features for RGB-D activity recognition. In: CVPR (2015)
62. Lin, L., Wang, K., Zuo, W., Wang, M., Luo, J., Zhang, L.: A deep structured model with radius-margin bound for 3d human activity recognition. IJCV **118**, 256–273 (2015)
63. Zhu, Y., Chen, W., Guo, G.: Fusing spatiotemporal features and joints for 3d action recognition. In: CVPRW (2013)

64. Ji, Y., Ye, G., Cheng, H.: Interactive body part contrast mining for human inter-action recognition. In: ICMEW (2014)
65. Li, W., Wen, L., Choo Chuah, M., Lyu, S.: Category-blind human action recognition: a practical recognition system. In: ICCV (2015)
66. Slama, R., Wannous, H., Daoudi, M., Srivastava, A.: Accurate 3d action recognition using learning on the grassmann manifold. PR **48**, 556–567 (2015)
67. Devanne, M., Wannous, H., Berretti, S., Pala, P., Daoudi, M., Del Bimbo, A.: 3-d human action recognition by shape analysis of motion trajectories on riemannian manifold. IEEE Trans. Cybern. **45**, 1340–1352 (2015)
68. Anirudh, R., Turaga, P., Su, J., Srivastava, A.: Elastic functional coding of human actions: from vector-fields to latent variables. In: CVPR (2015)
69. Li, W., Zhang, Z., Liu, Z.: Action recognition based on a bag of 3d points. In: CVPRW (2010)
70. Vantigodi, S., Babu, R.V.: Real-time human action recognition from motion capture data. In: NCVPRIPG (2013)
71. Ofli, F., Chaudhry, R., Kurillo, G., Vidal, R., Bajcsy, R.: Sequence of the most informative joints (SMIJ): a new representation for human skeletal action recognition. JVCIR **25**, 24–38 (2014)
72. Vantigodi, S., Radhakrishnan, V.B.: Action recognition from motion capture data using meta-cognitive RBF network classifier. In: ISSNIP (2014)
73. Kapsouras, I., Nikolaidis, N.: Action recognition on motion capture data using a dynemes and forward differences representation. JVCIR **25**, 1432–1445 (2014)

Going Further with Point Pair Features

Stefan Hinterstoisser[1]([✉]), Vincent Lepetit[2], Naresh Rajkumar[1],
and Kurt Konolige[1]

[1] Google, Mountain View, USA
hinterst@google.com, nareshkumar@google.com,
konolige@google.com
[2] TU-Graz, Graz, Austria
lepetit@icg.tugraz.at

Abstract. Point Pair Features is a widely used method to detect 3D
objects in point clouds, however they are prone to fail in presence of
sensor noise and background clutter. We introduce novel sampling and
voting schemes that significantly reduces the influence of clutter and
sensor noise. Our experiments show that with our improvements, PPFs
become competitive against state-of-the-art methods as it outperforms
them on several objects from challenging benchmarks, at a low computational cost.

1 Introduction

Object instance recognition and 3D pose estimation have received a lot of
attention recently, probably because of their importance in robotics applications [2,4,7,8,11,15,20,25]. For grasping and manipulation tasks, efficiency, reliability, and accuracy are all desirable properties that are still very challenging
in general environments.

While many approaches have been developed over the last years, we focus here
on the approach from Drost et al. [8], which relies on a depth camera. Since its
publication, it has been improved and extended by many authors [2,5,6,14,22].
However, we believe it has not delivered its full potential yet: Drost's technique
and its variants are based on votes from pairs of 3D points, but the sampling of
these pairs has been overlooked so far. As a result, these techniques are very inefficient, and it usually still takes several seconds to run them.

Moreover, this approach is also very sensitive to sensor noise and 3D background clutter—especially if it is close to the target object: Sensor noise can
disturb the quantization on which the approach relies heavily for fast accesses.
Background clutter casts spurious votes that can mask the effects of correct
ones. As a result, several other approaches [4,11,15,20] have shown significantly
better performance on recent datasets [11,15].

Electronic supplementary material The online version of this chapter (doi:10.
1007/978-3-319-46487-9_51) contains supplementary material, which is available to
authorized users.

© Springer International Publishing AG 2016
B. Leibe et al. (Eds.): ECCV 2016, Part III, LNCS 9907, pp. 834–848, 2016.
DOI: 10.1007/978-3-319-46487-9_51

Fig. 1. Several 3D objects are simultaneously detected with our method under different poses on cluttered background with partial occlusion and illumination changes. Each detected object is augmented with its 3D model, its 3D bounding box and its coordinate systems. For better visibility, the background is kept in gray and only detected objects are in color. (Color figure online)

In this paper, we propose a much better and efficient sampling strategy that, together with small modifications to the pre- and post-processing steps, makes our approach competitive against state-of-the-art methods: It beats them on several objects on recent challenging datasets, at a low computational cost.

In the remainder of this paper, we review related work, and describe in detail the method of Drost et al. [8]. We then introduce our contributions, which we compare against state-of-the-art methods in the last section (Fig. 1).

2   Related Work

The literature on object detection and 3D pose estimation is very broad. We focus here on recent work only and split them in several categories.

Sparse Feature-Based Methods. While popular for 3D object detection in color or intensity images several years ago, these methods are less popular now as practical robotics applications often consider objects that do not exhibit many stable feature points due to the lack of texture.

Template-Based Methods. Several methods are based on templates [11,20,26], where the templates capture the different appearances of objects under different viewpoints. An object is detected when a template matches the image and its 3D pose is given by the template. [11] uses synthetic renderings of a 3D object model to generate a large number of templates covering the full view hemisphere.

It employs an edge-based distance metric which works well for textureless objects, and refines the pose estimates using ICP to achieve an accurate 6D pose. Such template-based approaches can work accurately and quickly in practice. However, they show typical problems such as not being robust to clutter and occlusions.

Local Patch-Based Methods. [4,23] use forest-based voting schemes on local patches to detect and estimate 3D poses. While the former regresses object coordinates and conducts a subsequent energy-based pose estimation, the latter bases its voting on a scale-invariant patch representation and returns location and pose simultaneously. [3] also uses Random Forests to infer object and pose, but via a sliding window through a depth volume. In the experiment section, we compare our method against the recent approach of [4], which performs very well.

Point-Cloud-Based Methods. Detection of 3D objects in point cloud data has a very long history. A review can be found in [17]. One of the standard approaches for object pose estimation is ICP [16], which however requires an initial estimate and is not suited for object detection. Approaches based on 3D features are more suitable and are usually followed by ICP for the pose refinement. These methods include point pairs [8,16], spin-images [13], and point-pair histograms [21,24]. These methods are usually computationally expensive, and have difficulty in scenes with heavy clutter. However, we show in this paper that these drawbacks can be avoided.

The point cloud-based method proposed in [8] is the starting point of our own method, and we detail it in the next section.

3   "Drost-PPF" [8]

One of the most promising algorithms based on point clouds for matching 3D models to 3D scenes was proposed by Drost et al. [8]—in the rest of the paper, we will refer to it as *Drost-PPF*. Since our approach is based on it, we will describe it here in detail.

The authors of Drost-PPF coupled the existing idea of Point Pair Features (PPF) with a voting scheme to solve for the object pose and location simultaneously. More specifically, the goal of Drost-PPF is to establish for each scene point a correspondence to a model point and solve for the remaining degree of freedom to align the scene with the model data. This is done by using the relations between the corresponding points and all their neighboring points in model and scene space to vote in a Hough transform fashion for both unknowns.

Drost-PPF begins by extracting pairs of 3D points and their normals from the object's 3D model, to compute Point Pair Features (PPF) defined as a 4-vector:

$$\mathbf{F}(\mathbf{m}_1, \mathbf{m}_2, \mathbf{n}_1, \mathbf{n}_2) = [\|\mathbf{d}\|_2, \angle(\mathbf{n}_1, \mathbf{d}), \angle(\mathbf{n}_2, \mathbf{d}), \angle(\mathbf{n}_1, \mathbf{n}_2)]^\top , \qquad (1)$$

where $\mathbf{m}_1$ and $\mathbf{m}_2$ are two 3D points and $\mathbf{n}_1$ and $\mathbf{n}_2$ their normals, $\mathbf{d} = \mathbf{m}_2 - \mathbf{m}_1$, and $\angle(\mathbf{a}, \mathbf{b})$ the angle between vectors $\mathbf{a}$ and $\mathbf{b}$. This feature vector is invariant to rigid motions, which allows the method to detect the objects under these transformations.

The PPFs are discretized and used as indices of a lookup table. Each bin of this lookup table stores the list of first model points $\mathbf{m}_i$ and the corresponding rotation angles $\alpha_i{}^{model}$ of all the PPFs that are discretized to the bin's index. In this context, $\alpha_i{}^{model}$ describes the rotation angle around the normal of the first model point $\mathbf{m}_i$ that aligns the corresponding point pair that is descretized to the bin's index to a fixed canonical frame—as described in [8]. The stored data will be used during the voting stage.

At run-time, Drost-PPF tries to establish for each scene point a correspondence to a model point. This is achieved by pairing each scene point with all other scene points, compute the corresponding PPFs and match them with similar PPFs computed from 3D points on the target objects. The latter step can be performed efficiently using the lookup table: The content of the bins of the lookup table indexed by the discretzed PPFs are used to vote for pairs made of model points and discretized rotation angles $\alpha_i = \alpha_i{}^{model} - \alpha^{scene}$ in a Hough transform fashion. In this context, α^{scene} is the rotation around the normal of the first scene point that aligns the current scene point pair with the fixed canonical frame. Once a peak in the Hough space is extracted, the 3D pose of the object can be easily estimated from the extracted scene and model point correspondence and its corresponding rotation α_i.

[22] used this method to constrain a SLAM system by detecting multiple repetitive object models. They devised a strategy towards an efficient GPU implementation. Another immediate industrial application is bin picking, where multiple instances of the CAD model is sought in a pile of objects [12]. The approach has also been used in robotic applications [1,19].

In addition, several extensions to [8] have been proposed. A majority of these works focused on augmenting the feature description to incorporate color [5] or visibility context [14]. [6] proposed using points or boundaries to exploit the same framework in order to match planar industrial objects. [7] modified the pair description to include image gradient information. There are also attempts to boost the accuracy and performance of the matching, without modifying the features. [9] made use of the special symmetric object properties to speed up the detection by reducing the hash-table size. [25] proposed a scene specific weighted voting method by learning the distinctiveness of the features as well as the model points using a structured SVM.

Drost-PPF has often been criticized for the high dimensionality of the search space [4], for its inefficiency [11], for being sensitive to 3D background clutter and sensor noise [18]. Furthermore, other approaches significantly outperform it on many datasets [11,15].

In the next section, we discuss in greater detail the shortcomings of [8] and propose several suitable feature sampling strategies that allow it to outperform all state-of-the-art methods [4,11,15,20] on the standard dataset of [11] and the very challenging occlusion dataset of [15], in terms of recognition rate. In addition, we show how we can speed up the approach to be significant faster than [8].

4   Method

We describe here our contributions to make PPFs more discriminative, and more robust to background clutter and sensor noise. We evaluate the improvement provided by each of these contributions, and compare their combinations against state-of-the-art methods in the next section.

4.1   Pre-processing of the 3D Models and the Input Scene

During a pre-processing stage, Drost-PPF subsamples the 3D points of the target objects and the input scene. The advantage is two-fold: This speeds up the further computations and avoids considering too many ambiguous point pairs: Points that are close to each other tend to have similar normals, and generate many non-discriminative PPFs. Drost-PPF therefore subsamples the points so that two 3D points have at least a chosen minimal distance to each other.

This however can lead to a loss of useful information when normals are actually different. We therefore keep pairs even with a distance smaller than the minimal distance if the angle between the normals is larger than 30 degrees, as these pairs are likely to be discriminative. Subsampling is then done as in Drost-PPF, but with this additional constraint.

4.2   Smart Sampling of Point Pairs

After sub-sampling, in Drost-PPF, every scene point is paired with every other scene point during runtime. The complexity is therefore quadratic in the number of points in the 3D scene. In order to reduce computation time, [8] suggests using only every m-th scene point as the first point, where m is often set to 5 in practice. While this improves runtime, the complexity remains quadratic and matching performance suffers because we remove information from the already sampled scene point cloud.

We propose a better way to speed up the computations without discarding scene points: Given a first point from the scene it should be only paired with other scene points that can belong to the same object. For example, if the distance between the two points is larger than the size of the object, we know that these two points cannot possibly belong to the same object and therefore should not be paired. We show below that this leads to a method that can be implemented much more efficiently.

A conservative way to do so would be to ignore any point that is farther away than d_{obj} from the first point of a pair, where d_{obj} be the diameter of the enclosing sphere of the target object, which defines a voting ball.

However, a spherical region can be a very bad approximation for some objects. In particular, with narrow elongated objects, sampling from a sphere with radius d_{obj} will generate many points on the background clutter if the object is observed in a viewing direction parallel to its longest dimension, as depicted in Fig. 2.

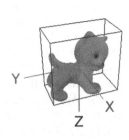

Fig. 2. Different voting spheres for a given first point projected into 2D. The yellow circle corresponds to a voting sphere with the smallest dimension of the object's bounding box as diameter. The blue circle corresponds to the voting sphere with the same diameter as the enclosing sphere. Points sampled in the yellow sphere are much more likely to lie on the object than points sampled in the blue sphere. (Color figure online)

In these cases we would like to use a smaller sampling volume where the ratio of scene points lying on the object compared to all other scene points is larger. However, we do not have any prior information on the pose of the object and the first scene point of the pair can lie anywhere on the object. It is therefore impossible to define a single volume that is smaller than the ball of radius d_{obj} without discarding pairs of scene points under certain object configurations that both lie on the target object.

We therefore opted for using consecutively two voting balls with different radiuses: A small one with radius $R_{\min} = \sqrt{d_{\min}^2 + d_{\text{med}}^2}$, where $d_{\min}$ is the smallest dimension of the object's bounding box and d_{med} is the median of its three dimensions, and the large conservative one with radius $R_{\max} = d_{\text{obj}}$. It can be easily seen that R_{min} is the smallest observable expansion of the object. We will say that a point pair is accepted by a voting ball if the first point is at the center of the ball and its distance to the second point is smaller than the radius of the ball.

We first populate the accumulator with votes from pairs that are accepted by the small ball. We extract the peaks from the accumulator, which each corresponds to a hypothesis on the object's 3D pose and correspondence between a model and scene point, as in Drost-PPF. We then continue populating the accumulator with votes from pairs accepted by the large ball but were rejected by the small one. We proceed as before and extract the peaks to generate pose and point correspondence hypotheses. This way, under poses such as the one illustrated by Fig. 2, we can get peaks that are less polluted by background clutter during the first pass, and still get peaks for the other configurations during the second pass.

To efficiently look for pairs accepted by a ball of radius d, we use a spatial lookup table: For a given scene, we build a voxel grid filled with the scene points.

The number of voxels in each dimension is adapted to the scene points and can differ in x, y, and z dimensions. Each voxel in this grid has size d, and stores the indices of the scene points that lie in it. Reciprocally, for each scene point we also store the voxel index to which it belongs. Building up this voxel grid is a $O(n)$ operation. In order to extract for a given first point all other scene points that are maximally d away, we first look up the voxel the scene reference point belongs to and extract all the scene point indices stored in this voxel and in all adjacent voxels. We check each of these scene points if its distance to the scene reference point is actually smaller or equal than d.

The complexity of this method is therefore $O(nk)$ where k is usually at least one magnitude smaller than n, compared to the quadratic complexity of Drost-PPF, while guaranteeing that all relevant point pairs are considered.

4.3   Accounting for Sensor Noise When Voting

For fast access, the PPFs are discretized. However, sensor noise can change the discretization bin, preventing some PPFs from being correctly matched. We overcome this problem by spreading the content of the look-up table during the pre-processing of the model. Instead of storing the first model point and the rotation angles only in the bin indexed by the discretized PPF vector, we also store them in the (80) neighborhood bins indexed by the adjacent discretized PPFs (there are $3^4 = 81 - 1$ adjacent bins).

We face a similar problem at run-time during voting for the quantized rotation angles around the point normals. To overcome this, we use the same strategy as above and vote not only for the original quantized rotation angle but also for its adjacent neighbors.

However, as shown in Fig. 3, spreading also has a drawback: Because of discretization and spreading in the feature+rotation space, it is very likely that pairs made of close scene points have the same quantized rotation angle and are mapped to the same look-up table bin. They will thus vote for the same bin in the accumulator space, introducing a bias in the votes.

A direct method to avoid multiple votes would be to use a 3D binary array $(a_{i,j,k})$ for each scene point to "flag" if a vote with the i-th model point, j-th model point as first and second point respectively, and k-th quantized rotation angle around the normal has already been cast, and prevent additional votes for this combination.

Unfortunately, such an array would be very large as its size is quadratic with the number of model points, and we would need to create one for each of the scene point. We propose a much more tractable solution.

Instead of indexing a flag array by the pair of model points and corresponding rotation, we use an array b indexed by the quantized PPFs the point pairs generate. Each element of b is a 32-bit integer initialized to 0, and each bit corresponds to a discretized rotation angle α^{scene}. We simply set the bit corresponding to a quantized PPF and scene rotation to 1 the first time it votes, and to prevent further voting for the same combination of quantized PPF and scene rotation, even if it is generated again by discretization and spreading. Spreading

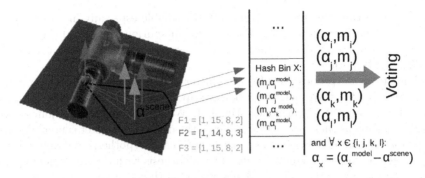

Fig. 3. A first scene point, in red, and three other scene points (green, blue and purple) build three point pair features. Because of discretization and spreading, all three point pair features correspond to the same scene rotation angle α^{scene}. Furthermore, feature discretization of F1 and F3 and spreading of F2 might lead to all three features being mapped to the same hash bin X which results in voting for the same combinations of model reference points and rotation angles (m_i, α_i), (m_j, α_j), (m_k, α_k), (m_l, α_l) several times. This artificially increases the voting for these specific combinations of model points and rotation angles and deteriorates the performance, especially in cases as shown in this figure where votes come from background. (Color figure online)

is achieved by generating for each discretized PPF created at run-time from the scene points the adjacent discretized PPFs, and treating them as the original discretized PPFs.

Note that we use here the scene rotations around the normals since it is only dependent on the scene point pair and not on the model points as shown in [8]. Thus, it is the same for all elements stored in one bin in the look-up table which allows us to leverage it to perform flagging in b.

This solution is more efficient than the direct method discussed above, as the number of possible entries is smaller in practice, thanks to the quantization of the PPFs. b is constant in size for all objects and scales linearly with the number of all possible quantizations of the PPFs. In practice, we quantize each angle and the distance of Eq. (1) into 22 and 40 bins respectively, yielding to $22^3 \times 40$ possible quantized PPFs. In our implementation, when the number of model points exceeds 650, the direct method takes significantly more time, with a typical slow-down of factor 3 for 1000 model points.

4.4 Generating Object Pose and Postprocessing

To extract object poses from the accumulator, Drost-PPF uses a greedy clustering approach. They extract the peaks from the accumulator, each corresponding to a hypothesis on the object's 3D pose and correspondence between a model and scene point, and process them in the same order as their numbers of votes, and assign them to the closest cluster if it is close enough, or otherwise create another cluster.

We found that this method is not always reliable especially in case of noisy sensors and background clutter. These result in spurious votes and the number of votes in the accumulator space is not necessarily a reliable indicator for the quality of a hypothesis.

Therefore, we propose a different cluster strategy that takes into account our voting strategy. We perform a bottom-up clustering of the pose hypotheses generated during voting with one voting ball. We allow hypotheses to join several clusters as long as their poses are similar to the one of the cluster center. We also keep track of the model points associated with each hypothesis and only allow a hypothesis to vote for a cluster if no other hypothesis with the same model point has voted for this cluster before. Thus, we avoid that ambiguous and repetitive geometric structures such as planar surfaces introduce biases.

For each of the few first clusters with the largest weights, we refine the estimated pose using projective ICP [10]. In practice, we consider the four first clusters for each of the two voting balls.

To reject the clusters that do not actually correspond to an object, we render the object according to the corresponding 3D pose, and count how many pixels have a depth close to the one of the rendering, how many are further away from the camera—and could be occluded, and how many are closer—and are therefore not consistent with the rendering. If the number of pixels that are closer is too large compared to the total number of pixels, we reject the cluster.

In practice, this threshold is set to 10 %. We also discard objects which are too much occluded. As a last check, we compute areas with significant depth or normal change in the scene, and compare them to the silhouette of the projected object: If the silhouette is not covered enough by depth or normal change, we discard the match. In practice, we use the same threshold that we use for occlusion check. We finally rank all remaining clusters according to how well they fit the scene points and return the pose of the best one only, or in case of multi-instance detection, the whole list of poses from all remaining clusters.

5   Experimental Results

We compare here our method against Drost-PPF, Linemod [11], DTTs [20], Birdal and Ilic [2], Bachmann et al. [4], and Krull et al. [15] on the ACCV dataset of [11] and on the Occlusion Dataset of [15].

For our method, we use the same parameters for all the experiments and objects, except for the post processing thresholds to account for the specificities of the occlusion dataset.

5.1   ACCV Dataset of [11]

We first tested our method on the standard benchmark from [11]. This dataset contains 16 objects with over 1100 depth and color images each, and provides the ground truth 3D poses for each object. We only evaluate our method for the non-ambiguous objects —we removed the bowl and the cup— because state-of-the-art approaches considered only these objects.

Table 1. Recognition rates according to the evaluation metric of [11] for different methods. We perform best for eight out of thirteen objects, while [4,11,20] use color data in addition to depth, and we only use depth data.

Approach	Our Appr	Linemod [11]	Drost et al. [8]	DTT [20]	Brachmann et al. [4]	Birdal and Ilic [2]
Sequence (#pics)			Matching score			
Ape (1235)	**98.5 %**	95.8 %	86.5 %	95.0 %	85.4 %	81.95 %
Bench V. (1214)	**99.8 %**	98.7 %	70.7 %	98.9 %	98.9 %	–
Cam (1200)	**99.3 %**	97.5 %	78.6 %	98.2 %	92.1 %	91.00 %
Can (1195)	**98.7 %**	95.4 %	80.2 %	96.3 %	84.4 %	–
Cat (1178)	**99.9 %**	99.3 %	85.4 %	99.1 %	90.6 %	95.76 %
Driller (1187)	93.4 %	93.6 %	87.3 %	94.3 %	**99.7 %**	81.22 %
Duck (1253)	**98.2 %**	95.9 %	46.0 %	94.2 %	92.7 %	–
Box (1253)	98.8 %	**99.8 %**	97.0 %	**99.8 %**	91.1 %	–
Glue (1219)	75.4 %	91.8 %	57.2 %	**96.3 %**	87.9 %	–
Hole P. (1236)	**98.1 %**	95.9 %	77.4 %	97.5 %	97.9 %	–
Iron (1151)	98.3 %	97.5 %	84.9 %	98.4 %	**98.8 %**	93.92 %
Lamp (1226)	96.0 %	97.7 %	93.3 %	**97.9 %**	97.6 %	–
Phone (1224)	**98.6 %**	93.3 %	80.7 %	88.3 %	86.1 %	–

[2] does not evaluate all objects and does not use refinement with ICP. For the approach of Bachmann et al. [4], we use the numbers reported for synthetic training without a ground plane, since adding a ground plane during training artificially adds additional knowledge about the test set.

Like [4,11,20] we only use features that are visible from the upper hemisphere of the object. However, differently to these methods and similarly to [2,8] we still allow the object to be detected in any arbitrary pose. Thus, we are solving for a much larger search space than [4,11,20].

In addition, as in [2,8], we only use the depth information and do not make use of the color information as [4,11,20]. However, as shown in Table 1, we perform best on eight objects out of thirteen.

5.2 Occlusion Dataset of [15]

The dataset of [11] is almost free of occlusion. Hence, to demonstrate robustness with respect to occlusions, we tested our method on the occlusion dataset of [15]. It is much more noisy and includes more background clutter than previous occlusion datasets [16]. It includes over 1200 real depth and color images with 8 objects and their ground truth 3D poses.

As Table 2 shows, our approach performs better for five objects while the method of Krull et al. [15] performs better on three objects. On average we perform 3.3 % better than Krull that was the state-of-the-art on this dataset.

Table 2. Recognition rates on the occlusion dataset [15] according to the evaluation metric of [15]. Our approach performs better for five objects out of eight. On average we perform 3.3 % better than Krull et al. [15], while Krull et al. [15] uses color data in addition to depth and a ground plane during training. We only use depth data.

Approach	Our approach	Linemod [11]	Brachmann et al. [4]	Krull et al. [15]
Sequence (#pics)		Matching score		
Ape (952)	**81.4 %**	49.8 %	62.6 %	77.9 %
Can (1143)	**94.7 %**	51.2 %	80.2 %	86.6 %
Cat (655)	55.2 %	34.9 %	50.0 %	**55.6 %**
Driller (1044)	86.0 %	59.6 %	84.3 %	**93.6 %**
Duck (911)	**79.7 %**	65.1 %	67.6 %	71.9 %
Box (770)	**65.6 %**	39.6 %	8.5 %	35.6 %
Glue (462)	52.1 %	23.3 %	62.8 %	**67.9 %**
Hole Puncher (1156)	**95.5 %**	67.2 %	63.2 %	94.8 %
Average	**76.3 %**	54.4 %	67.3 %	73.0 %

While we only use depth data, [15] also uses color data. Moreover, the method in [15] was trained with an added a ground plane during training[1], which gives an extra advantage.

5.3   Computation Times

Our approach takes between $0.1s$ and $0.8s$ to process a 640×480 depth map. Like Drost-PPF, the sub-sampling during pre-processing depends on the object diameter; denser sampling is used for smaller objects, which increases the processing time.

On average it is about 6 times faster than Drost-PPF, while being significantly more accurate. Moreover, our method could be implemented on GPU, as [22] did, for further acceleration.

5.4   Worst Case Runtime Discussion

In this section we discuss the worst case runtime behavior. Despite our smart sampling strategy presented in Sect. 4.2, the worst case runtime behavior is still $O(n^2)$ where n is the number of subsampled points in a scene. However, this is not a problem in practice as this happens only if all observed scene points lie in a sphere with radius $\sqrt{3} \times d_{obj}$ ($\sqrt{3}$ comes from taking the diagonal of voxels of width d_{obj} into account). This is because our spatial look-up table only gives back points that fall into the same voxel or adjacent voxels of the spatial look-up table as our candidate point falls into. When there are points outside

---

[1] Private email exchange with the authors.

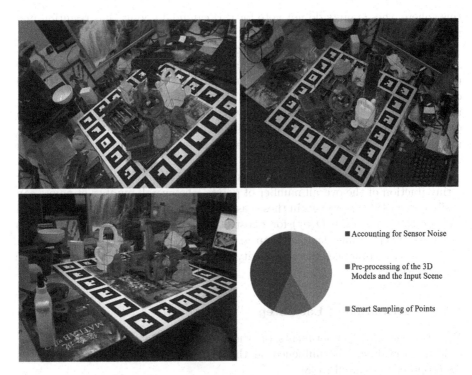

Fig. 4. Three images of the dataset of [15] with at least seven out of nine objects correctly detected. Note the strong background clutter and heavy occlusion. Lower Right: Contribution of each proposed step to the matching scores compared to [8]. Accounting for sensor noise and our sampling of points are almost equal, while our proposed pre-processing of the 3D model and the input scene has the smallest but still significant effect.

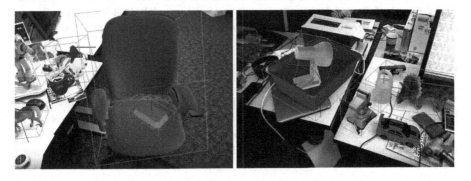

Fig. 5. Several 3D objects are simultaneously detected with our method under different poses on cluttered background with partial occlusion and illumination changes. Each detected object is augmented with its 3D model, its 3D bounding box and its coordinate systems. For better visibility, the background is kept in gray.

this sphere, these points do not vote for this candidate point thus resulting in a runtime $O(nk)$ with $k < n$.

Taking normals into account for subsampling increases the number of subsampled points by a factor typically smaller than two. Therefore the number of points falling into one voxel of the spatial look-up table is not very large and due to (self-) occlusion the overall number of visble points is fairly small, typically around 1000 or less. However, even 1000 points are easily handled in a $O(n^2)$ manner and in such a case matching is done quite quickly. For instance, matching for a close-up view of the chair seen in Fig. 5 is usually done in less than 200 ms.

More problematic are scenes where subsampled points on an object are only a tiny fraction of the overall number of points (the overall number of points can easily exceed $15k$). However, in these cases our spatial look-up table kicks in and the run-time goes from $O(n^2)$ for Drost et al. [8] to $O(kn)$ where $k \ll n$. k is often over twenty times smaller than n.

In short, in practice, the complexity of our approach is significantly better than Drost's [8].

5.5   Contribution of Each Step

We also performed experiments on the occlusion dataset [15] with all eight objects to evaluate the influence on the matching score of each of the steps we proposed compared to [8].

To do so, we first ran our implementation of the original Drost-PPF method, and computed the average matching score $\overline{S_{\text{Drost}}}$ for all eight objects on the dataset of [15]. We then turned on all our contributions and computed the new average matching score $\overline{S_{\text{Ours}}}$. The gain g_c from each contribution alone is computed by computing the average matching score $\overline{S_c}$ with only this contribution turned on, and taking $g_c = \overline{S_c}/(\overline{S_{\text{Ours}}} - \overline{S_{\text{Drost}}})$.

As Fig. 4 shows, accounting for sensor noise is with 43.1 % the most important part, directly followed by smart sampling of points with 41.3 % and finally our contribution to pre-processing of the 3D model and the input scene with 15.6 %.

6   Conclusion

We have shown that by cleverly sampling features and by adding feature spreading to account for sensor noise, we can boost the method from Drost et al. [8] to outperform state-of-the-art approaches in object instance detection and pose estimation, including those that use additional information such as color cues.

References

1. Beetz, M., Klank, U., Kresse, I., Maldonado, A., Mosenlechner, L., Pangercic, D., Ruhr, T., Tenorth, M.: Robotic roommates making pancakes. In: Humanoid Robots (2011)
2. Birdal, T., Ilic, S.: Point pair features based object detection and pose estimation revisited. In: IEEE International Conference on 3D Vision (2015)
3. Bonde, U., Badrinarayanan, V., Cipolla, R.: Robust instance recognition in presence of occlusion and clutter. In: European Conference on Computer Vision (2014)
4. Brachmann, E., Krull, A., Michel, F., Gumhold, S., Shotton, J., Rother, C.: Learning 6D object pose estimation using 3D object coordinates. In: Schiele, B., Tuytelaars, T., Fleet, D., Pajdla, T. (eds.) ECCV 2014, Part II. LNCS, vol. 8690, pp. 536–551. Springer, Heidelberg (2014)
5. Choi, C., Christensen, H.: 3D pose estimation of daily objects using an RGB-D camera. In: International Conference on Intelligent Robots and Systems (2012)
6. Choi, C., Taguchi, Y., Tuzel, O., Liu, M.L., Ramalingam, S.: Voting-based pose estimation for robotic assembly using a 3D sensor. In: International Conference on Robotics and Automation (2012)
7. Drost, B., Ilic, S.: 3D object detection and localization using multimodal point pair features. In: 3D Imaging, Modeling, Processing, Visualization and Transmission (2012)
8. Drost, B., Ulrich, M., Navab, N., Ilic, S.: Model globally, match locally: efficient and robust 3D object recognition. In: Conference on Computer Vision and Pattern Recognition (2010)
9. de Figueiredo, R.P., Moreno, P., Bernardino, A.: Fast 3D object recognition of rotationally symmetric objects. In: Sanches, J.M., Micó, L., Cardoso, J.S. (eds.) IbPRIA 2013. LNCS, vol. 7887, pp. 125–132. Springer, Heidelberg (2013)
10. Fisher, R.: Projective ICP and stabilizing architectural augmented reality overlays. In: International Symposium on Virtual and Augmented Architecture (2001)
11. Hinterstoisser, S., Lepetit, V., Ilic, S., Holzer, S., Bradski, G., Konolige, K., Navab, N.: Model based training, detection and pose estimation of texture-less 3D objects in heavily cluttered scenes. In: Matsushita, Y., Rehg, J.M., Hu, Z., Lee, K.M. (eds.) ACCV 2012, Part I. LNCS, vol. 7724, pp. 548–562. Springer, Heidelberg (2013)
12. Holz, D., Nieuwenhuisen, M., Droeschel, D., Stuckler, J., Berner, A., Li, J., Klein, R., Behnke, S.: Active recognition and manipulation for mobile robot bin picking. In: Röhrbein, F., Veiga, G., Natale, C. (eds.) Gearing Up and Accelerating Cross-fertilization Between Academic and Industrial Robotics Research in Europe. Springer, Berlin (2014)
13. Johnson, A., Hebert, M.: Using spin images for efficient object recognition in cluttered 3D scenes. IEEE Trans. Pattern Anal. Mach. Intell. (1999)
14. Kim, E., Medioni, G.: 3D object recognition in range images using visibility context. In: International Conference on Intelligent Robots and Systems (2011)
15. Krull, A., Brachmann, E., Michel, F., Yang, M.Y., Gumhold, S., Rother, C.: Learning analysis-by-synthesis for 6D pose estimation in RGB-D images. In: International Conference on Computer Vision (2015)
16. Mian, A., Bennamoun, M., Owens, R.: Three-dimensional model-based object recognition and segmentation in cluttered scenes. IEEE Trans. Pattern Anal. Mach. Intell. (2006)
17. Mian, A., Bennamoun, M., Owens, R.: Automatic correspondence for 3D modeling: an extensive review. Int. J. Shape Model. (2005)

18. Mohamad, M., Rappaport, D., Greenspan, M.: Generalized 4-points congruent sets for 3D registration. In: IEEE International Conference on 3D Vision (2014)
19. Nieuwenhuisen, M., Droeschel, D., Holz, D., Stuckler, J., Berner, A., Li, J., Klein, R., Behnke, S.: Mobile bin picking with an anthropomorphic service robot. In: International Conference on Robotics and Automation (2013)
20. Rios-Cabrera, R., Tuytelaars, T.: Discriminatively trained templates for 3D object detection: a real-time scalable approach. In: International Conference on Computer Vision (2013)
21. Rusu, R., Blodow, N., Beetz, M.: Fast point feature histograms (FPFH) for 3D registration. In: International Conference on Robotics and Automation (2009)
22. Salas-Moreno, R., Newcombe, R., Strasdat, H., Kelly, P., Davison, A.: SLAM++: simultaneous localisation and mapping at the level of objects. In: Conference on Computer Vision and Pattern Recognition (2013)
23. Tejani, A., Tang, D., Kouskouridas, R., Kim, T.-K.: Latent-class hough forests for 3D object detection and pose estimation. In: Fleet, D., Pajdla, T., Schiele, B., Tuytelaars, T. (eds.) ECCV 2014, Part VI. LNCS, vol. 8694, pp. 462–477. Springer, Heidelberg (2014)
24. Tombari, F., Salti, S., Di Stefano, L.: Unique signatures of histograms for local surface description. In: Maragos, P., Paragios, N., Daniilidis, K. (eds.) ECCV 2010, Part III. LNCS, vol. 6313, pp. 356–369. Springer, Heidelberg (2010)
25. Tuzel, O., Liu, M.-Y., Taguchi, Y., Raghunathan, A.: Learning to rank 3D features. In: Fleet, D., Pajdla, T., Schiele, B., Tuytelaars, T. (eds.) ECCV 2014, Part I. LNCS, vol. 8689, pp. 520–535. Springer, Heidelberg (2014)
26. Wohlhart, P., Lepetit, V.: Learning descriptors for object recognition and 3D pose estimation. In: Conference on Computer Vision and Pattern Recognition (2015)

Webly-Supervised Video Recognition by Mutually Voting for Relevant Web Images and Web Video Frames

Chuang Gan[1]($\boxtimes$), Chen Sun[2], Lixin Duan[3], and Boqing Gong[4]

[1] IIIS, Tsinghua University, Beijing, China
ganchuang1990@gmail.com
[2] Google Research, Mountain View, USA
[3] Amazon, Seattle, USA
[4] CRCV, University of Central Florida, Orlando, USA

Abstract. Video recognition usually requires a large amount of training samples, which are expensive to be collected. An alternative and cheap solution is to draw from the large-scale images and videos from the Web. With modern search engines, the top ranked images or videos are usually highly correlated to the query, implying the potential to harvest the labeling-free Web images and videos for video recognition. However, there are two key difficulties that prevent us from using the Web data directly. First, they are typically noisy and may be from a completely different domain from that of users' interest (e.g. cartoons). Second, Web videos are usually untrimmed and very lengthy, where some query-relevant frames are often hidden in between the irrelevant ones. A question thus naturally arises: to what extent can such noisy Web images and videos be utilized for labeling-free video recognition? In this paper, we propose a novel approach to mutually voting for relevant Web images and video frames, where two forces are balanced, i.e. aggressive matching and passive video frame selection. We validate our approach on three large-scale video recognition datasets.

1 Introduction

This paper aims to classify actions and events in user-captured videos without human labeling. The ubiquity of smart phones and surveillance cameras has created videos far surpassing what we can watch. Instead of "eyeballing" the videos for potential useful information, it is desirable to develop automatic video analysis and understanding algorithms. Video recognition in the wild is a very challenging task: videos from the same categories could vary greatly in lighting conditions, video resolutions, camera movements, etc. Meanwhile, those from different categories could be inherently similar (*e.g.* "apply eye makeup" and "apply lipstick"). To recognize actions and events, one commonly adopted framework is encoding hand-crafted features (*e.g.* improved dense trajectories [41]) into video-level representations with Fisher vectors [37]. There are also recent

© Springer International Publishing AG 2016
B. Leibe et al. (Eds.): ECCV 2016, Part III, LNCS 9907, pp. 849–866, 2016.
DOI: 10.1007/978-3-319-46487-9_52

Fig. 1. To utilize Web images and videos for video classification, our key observation is that the query-relevant images and frames typically appear in both domains with similar appearances, while the irrelevant images and videos have their own distinctiveness. Here we show Web images (top) and video frames (bottom) retrieved by keywords basketball dunk, bench press and pizza tossing from search engines. The relevant ones are marked in red. (Color figure online)

approaches based on deep convolutional neural networks [11,20,29,40] or recurrent networks [16,34]. All these approaches require and implicitly assume the existence of large-scale labeled training data.

Manually labeling large amount of video examples is time-consuming and difficult to scale up. On the other hand, there are abundant image and video examples on the Web that can be easily retrieved by querying action or event names from image/video search engines. These two observations motivate us to focus on Webly-supervised video recognition by exploiting Web images and Web videos. Using video frames in addition to images not only adds more diverse examples for training better appearance models, but also allows us to train better temporal models, as found in [12,38].

However, there are two key difficulties that prevent us from using Web data directly. First, the images and videos retrieved from Web search engines are typically noisy. They may contain irrelevant results, or relevant results from a completely different domain than users' interest (*e.g.* cartoons or closeup shots of objects). To make the problem worse, Web videos are usually untrimmed and could be several minutes to hours long. Even for a correctly tagged video, the majority of its frames could be irrelevant to the actual action or event. Our goal then becomes to identify query-relevant images and video frames from the Web data which are both noisily and weakly labeled, in order to train good machine learning models for action and event classification.

Our proposed method is based on the following observation: *the relevant images and video frames typically exhibit similar appearances, while the irrelevant images and videos have their own distinctiveness.* In Fig. 1, we show the Web images (top) and video frames (bottom) retrieved by keywords basketball dunk, bench press and pizza tossing. We can see that for the basketball dunk example, non-slam-dunk frames in the video are mostly about a basketball game. The irrelevant Web images are more likely to be cartoons. Similar observation also holds for bench press and pizza tossing, where the irrelevant images include cartoons and product shots. This observation indicates that selecting training examples from Web images and videos can be made easier, if they could be mutually filtered to keep those in common!

Our algorithm to mutually filtering Web images and video frames goes as follows: we first jointly choose images and video frames and try to match them *aggressively*. A good match between the subset of images and the subset of video frames occurs when both subsets are relevant to the action name, since "each irrelevant image or frame is irrelevant in its own way". We then impose a *passive* constraint over the video frames to be selected, such that they are collectively not too far from the original videos. We would like to be passive on the videos, in contrast to the images, because our ultimate goal is for video action recognition. Otherwise, the aggressive matching mechanism may end up with too few frames and causes a domain adaptation problem [28] between the training set and test videos. Once the Web images and video frames are selected for the actions or events of interest, they can be readily used to train action or event classifiers with a wide range of tools. Some examples include SVM, CNN and LSTM.

The remaining sections are organized as follows. Section 2 describes related work on video recognition, learning from the Web data and domain adaptation. Section 3 presents our approach to automatically selecting relevant examples from crawled images and videos to be used for Webly-supervised video recognition. Section 4 reports empirical results, followed by discussion and conclusion in Sect. 5.

2   Related Work

We discuss some related works to ours, including those on video recognition, learning from weakly-labeled Web data, and domain adaptation.

2.1   Video Recognition

Video recognition has been widely explored in Computer Vision and Multimedia communities. A survey can be found in [19]. Most of previous works use hand-designed features to extract motion and appearance information for video representation. So far, improved dense trajectories (iDT) [41] and its variants [22,42] show state-of-the-art performance on video recognition when combined with Fisher vector coding [25].

Motivated by the success of convolutional neural networks on image recognition tasks [21,30,39,45], there are also several attempts to apply deep learning techniques for video recognition. Karpathy *et al.* [20] compare several architectures for action recognition. Tran *et al.* [40] propose to learn generic spatial-temporal features with 3D convolutional filters. Simonyan and Zisserman [29] propose a two-stream architecture to capture both spatial and motion information with a pixel stream and an optical flow stream respectively. Wang *et al.* [43] further improve the results by using deeper neural networks. Instead of learning representation using video data, recent works [47] for complex event recognition have shown CNN features from models pre-trained from ImageNet [5] achieve promising results. More recently, Recurrent Neural Networks (RNNs) are shown effective to model temporal information in videos. Srivastava *et al.* [34] propose an LSTM encoder-decoder framework to learn video representations in an unsupervised manner [34]. Donahue *et al.* [7] train a two-layer LSTM network for action classification. Ng *et al.* [24] further demonstrate that a deeper LSTM network can further improve the performance. All these approaches require high-quality labeled training data. It remains unclear whether they can also obtain reasonable video recognition results using noisy Web data.

2.2   Learning from Weakly-Labeled Web Data

Web data is inherently noisy. To handle this problem, the NEIL system [4] iteratively refines its model using the discovered object relationships. LEVAN [6] clusters visual concepts into groups, and rejects those with low visual consistency. Chen and Gupta [3] propose a semi-supervised approach to learning CNN parameters with easier examples first and more complex examples later. Sun *et al.* [36] and Zhang *et al.* [48] propose to use multi-modal data to learn visual concepts. In the video domain, Duan *et al.* [9] describe a system that uses large amount of weakly labeled Web videos for visual event recognition with transfer learning techniques. Habibian *et al.* [15] obtain textual descriptions of videos from the Web and learn an embedding for few-example event recognition. Nevertheless, these approaches all require humans to annotate a few positive videos as "seeds". Sun *et al.* [38] and Gan *et al.* [12] propose domain transfer approaches from weakly-labeled Web images for action localization and event recognition tasks, where each video is guaranteed to contain relevant snippets. In contrast, our approach screens all the downloaded web videos (of a query) simultaneously and does not impose the assumption of existing relevant frames over any individual video. To alleviate the tedious human burden and achieve Webly-supervised action recognition, several researchers have attempted to learn video concept detectors by crawling images and videos [2,14,31,46] after querying the action/event name as well as associated queries. However, the quality of the obtained data is lower compared with the fully-supervised set, as the retrieved examples are not only noisy but also without spatiotemporal localization. The noisy and weak supervision is likely to confuse the training of video classifiers.

Recently, the studies in [35] and soon followed by [44] propose solutions to train deep convolutional networks (CNNs) when there exist mislabeled images in the training set; the idea is to introduce a label noise layer placed at the top of CNNs. This paper is different in that we focus on how to remove the noisy data before actually training any classifiers. Our work can thus benefit most generic classifiers in addition to CNNs.

2.3   Domain Adaptation

In order to mutually vote for video frames and images that are relevant to the action/event, we use maximum mean discrepancy (MMD) [17,33] to match them. MMD has been widely used in domain adaptation [27], e.g., for feature representation learning [26], data instance re-weighting [17], landmark selection [13], and classifier regularization [8]. Moreover, when it goes to the technical algorithm, our formulation shares some spirit with the work [13] on landmark selection. However, we emphasize that the goal of our work is not for domain adaptation at all; neither images nor videos we retrieved are our target domain for testing. Instead, we tackle Webly-supervised video recognition by learning classifiers from both relevant Web images and video frames.

3   Proposed Approach

In this section, we present the details of our approach to jointly selecting video frames and images from the Web data, for the purpose of Webly-supervised video recognition. Our algorithm is built upon the motivating observation that "all relevant images and frames to an action name are alike; each irrelevant image or frame is irrelevant in its own way." We firstly give the overall formulation, and then describe an alternative optimization procedure for solving the problem.

3.1   Joint Selection of Action/event Relevant Web Video Frames and Web Images

For the ease of presentation, we first define the following notations. For each class (of an action or event), we denote by $\mathcal{I} = \{\mathbf{x}_m\}_{m=1}^{M}$ the set of Web images, and by $\mathcal{V} = \{\mathbf{v}_n\}_{n=1}^{N}$ the set of video frames, both returned by some search engines in response to the query of the class name. The Web data are quite noisy; there are both relevant items and outliers for the class. In order to filter out the relevant items, we introduce M indicator variables $\boldsymbol{\alpha} = [\alpha_1, \ldots, \alpha_M]^{\top}$, where $\alpha_m \in \{0, 1\}$ for each image $\mathbf{x}_m$, and N indicator variables $\boldsymbol{\beta} = [\beta_1, \ldots, \beta_N]^{\top}$, where $\beta_n \in \{0, 1\}$ for each video frame $\mathbf{v}_n$. If $\alpha_m = 1$ (resp., $\beta_n = 1$), the corresponding image $\mathbf{x}_m$ (resp., video frame $\mathbf{v}_n$) will be identified as a relevant item to the class.

Aggressive Matching. If we conduct a pairwise comparison between a subset of the images $\mathcal{I}$ with a subset of the video frames $\mathcal{V}$, any class-irrelevant images or frames would decrease the similarity between the two subsets, because the irrelevant items are likely different from each other and also different from the relevant items. Therefore, we can let the images and video frames mutually vote for class-relevant items, by matching all possible pairwise subsets of them, respectively. Such a pair can be expressed by $(\{\alpha_m \mathbf{x}_m\}_{m=1}^{M}, \{\beta_n \mathbf{v}_n\}_{n=1}^{N})$. The pairs with high matching scores have lower chance of containing irrelevant images or video frames.

Because of the simplicity and effectiveness of the maximum mean discrepancy (MMD) criterion [17], we adopt it in this work to measure the degree of matching between any images and frames $(\{\alpha_m \mathbf{x}_m\}_{m=1}^{M}, \{\beta_n \mathbf{v}_n\}_{n=1}^{N})$. We propose to minimize the square of MMD such that the true negative images and video frames are expected to be *filtered out* (i.e., the corresponding α_m's or β_n's will tend to be zeros). In other words, the remaining images and video frames are expected to be the true positive items for the class. Formally, we formulate the following optimization problem:

$$\min_{\alpha_m, \beta_n \in \{0,1\}} \left\| \frac{1}{\sum_{m=1}^{M} \alpha_m} \sum_{m=1}^{M} \alpha_m \phi(\mathbf{x}_m) - \frac{1}{\sum_{n=1}^{N} \beta_n} \sum_{n=1}^{N} \beta_n \phi(\mathbf{v}_n) \right\|_{\mathcal{H}}^2, \quad (1)$$

where $\phi(\cdot)$ is a mapping function which maps a feature vector from its original space into a Reproducing Kernel Hilbert Space $\mathcal{H}$.

The above is an integer programming problem, which is very computationally expensive to solve. Following [13], we relax Eq. (1) by introducing $\hat{\alpha}_m = \frac{\alpha_m}{\sum_{m=1}^{M} \alpha_m}$ and $\hat{\beta}_n = \frac{\beta_n}{\sum_{n=1}^{N} \beta_n}$. Then, we arrive at the following optimization problem:

$$\min_{\hat{\alpha} \in [0,1]^M, \hat{\beta} \in [0,1]^N} \left(\hat{\alpha}^\top, \hat{\beta}^\top \right) \begin{pmatrix} K_I & -K_{IV} \\ -K_{VI}^\top & K_V \end{pmatrix} \begin{pmatrix} \hat{\alpha} \\ \hat{\beta} \end{pmatrix}, \quad (2)$$

where $\hat{\alpha} = [\alpha_1, \ldots, \alpha_M]^\top$, $\hat{\beta} = [\beta_1, \ldots, \beta_N]^\top$, $K_I \in \mathbb{R}^{M \times M}$ and $K_V \in \mathbb{R}^{N \times N}$ are the kernel matrices computed over the images and video frames respectively, and $K_{VI}^\top = K_{IV} \in \mathbb{R}^{M \times N}$ denotes the kernel matrix computed between the images and video frames, respectively. We use a Gaussian RBF kernel in our experiments.

Passive Video Frame Selection. Note that Eq. (1) matches a subset of images with a subset of video frames very aggressively. While there could be many pairs of subsets whose images and frames are all relevant to the class, Eq. (1) only choose the one with the best matching (in terms of the MMD measure). This strategy is effective in removing true negative images and frames. However, it may also abandon many relevant ones in order to reach the best matching. We thus introduce a passive term to balance the aggressive matching.

Since our eventual task is video recognition, we propose to impose a passive regularization over the selected video frames, such that they are collectively not too far from the original videos:

$$\min_{\hat{\boldsymbol{\beta}}\in[0,1]^M,W} \left\| V - V \cdot diag(\hat{\boldsymbol{\beta}}) \cdot W \right\|_F^2, \tag{3}$$

where $V = [\mathbf{v}_1,\ldots,\mathbf{v}_N]$, and the variable W is a linear transformation matrix which linearly reconstructs V from all the selected video frames, i.e., $V \cdot diag(\hat{\boldsymbol{\beta}})$. In order to have a low reconstruction error, one cannot keep too few video frames selected by the variables $\boldsymbol{\beta}$. On the other hand, it is fine to remove redundant frames from the candidate set $\mathcal{V}$. Our experiments show that removing the redundant frames incurs little loss on the overall performance, and even improves the performance of an LSTM-based classifier.

Combining Eqs. (2) and (3), we present our overall optimization problem as follows:

$$\min_{\substack{\hat{\boldsymbol{\alpha}}\in[0,1]^M, \\ \hat{\boldsymbol{\beta}}\in[0,1]^N,W}} \left(\hat{\boldsymbol{\alpha}}^\top,\hat{\boldsymbol{\beta}}^\top\right)\begin{pmatrix} K_I & -K_{IV} \\ -K_{IV}^\top & K_V \end{pmatrix}\begin{pmatrix} \hat{\boldsymbol{\alpha}} \\ \hat{\boldsymbol{\beta}} \end{pmatrix} + \lambda\|V - V \cdot diag(\hat{\boldsymbol{\beta}}) \cdot W\|_F^2, \tag{4}$$

where $\lambda > 0$ is a pre-defined tradeoff parameter to balance these two terms.

3.2 Optimization

To solve the optimization problem in Eq. (4), we develop a procedure to alternatively update $\{\hat{\boldsymbol{\alpha}},\hat{\boldsymbol{\beta}}\}$ and W until the value of the objective function in Eq. (4) converges.

Updating W: When we fix $\hat{\boldsymbol{\alpha}}$ and $\hat{\boldsymbol{\beta}}$, Eq. (4) reduces to

$$\min_{W} \|V - V \cdot diag(\hat{\boldsymbol{\beta}}) \cdot W\|_F^2, \tag{5}$$

whose closed-form solution can be derived to update W:

$$W_{\text{new}} = \left((V \cdot diag(\hat{\boldsymbol{\beta}}))^\top (V \cdot diag(\hat{\boldsymbol{\beta}}))\right)^\dagger (V \cdot diag(\hat{\boldsymbol{\beta}}))^\top, \tag{6}$$

where $\dagger$ denotes the pseudo-inverse of a matrix.

Updating $\hat{\boldsymbol{\alpha}}$ and $\hat{\boldsymbol{\beta}}$: We then fix W and solve for $\hat{\boldsymbol{\alpha}}$ and $\hat{\boldsymbol{\beta}}$. We first re-write Eq. (3) as:

$$\min_{\hat{\boldsymbol{\beta}}\in[0,1]^N} \sum_{n,n'} \hat{\beta}_n\hat{\beta}_{n'} \underbrace{V_{:n}^\top V_{:n'} W_{n':} W_{:n}^\top}_{A_{nn'}} -2\sum_n \hat{\beta}_n \underbrace{(V_{:n}^\top V W_{n:}^\top)}_{b_n}, \tag{7}$$

where $V_{:n}$ and $W_{:n}$ represent the nth columns of V and W respectively, and $V_{n:}$ and $W_{n:}$ denote the nth rows of V and W respectively. For simplicity, we define $A_{nn'} = V_{:n}^T V_{:n'} W_{n':} W_{:n}^\top$ and $b_n = V_{:n}^\top W_{n:}^\top$.

Substituting Eqs. (7) to (4), we arrive at the following:

$$\min_{\hat{\boldsymbol{\alpha}}\in[0,1]^M, \hat{\boldsymbol{\beta}}\in[0,1]^N} \left(\hat{\boldsymbol{\alpha}}^\top,\hat{\boldsymbol{\beta}}^\top\right)\begin{pmatrix} K_I & -K_{IV} \\ -K_{VI}^\top & K_V + \lambda A \end{pmatrix}\begin{pmatrix} \hat{\boldsymbol{\alpha}} \\ \hat{\boldsymbol{\beta}} \end{pmatrix} - 2\lambda\left(\hat{\boldsymbol{\alpha}}^\top,\hat{\boldsymbol{\beta}}^\top\right)\begin{pmatrix} \mathbf{0} \\ b \end{pmatrix}, \tag{8}$$

which can be efficiently solved by using off-the-shelf quadratic programming solvers.

3.3   Harvesting a Labeling-Free Training Set

After solving the optimization problem in Eq. (4), we have two ranking lists of the Web images and Web video frames, respectively, according to the values of $\hat{\alpha}$ and $\hat{\beta}$ at the last iteration of our alternative optimization procedure. We can thus keep some percentage of the top ranked images and videos as our labeling-free training set for video recognition. In our experiments, we examine different percentages from 95 % to 10 %. We will also test the effectiveness of this labeling-free training set for different classifiers, including SVM, fine-tuned deep neural networks, and an LSTM-based classifier.

4   Experiments

In this section, we evaluate the quality of our labeling-free training set under two fundamental tasks in video recognition: action recognition and event detection. We also contrast our algorithm to some competing baselines, and compare our results with those in the recent works on Webly-supervised video recognition.

4.1   Datasets

In the experiments, we collect our training data by downloading Web images and videos from the popular search engines with text queries. Specifically, given an action/event class name as the search query, we download about 600 top-ranked images from Google and 20 videos from YouTube. Duplicated images are removed by comparing color histogram features. To comply with the query format of Google image search, all occurrences of *without*, *non-* and *not* are replaced with the minus sign. For the downloaded Youtube videos, we limit the length of each video to be less than fifteen minutes for both memory and computational concerns. Most videos have the frame rate of 30 FPS.

For the test sets, we consider three well-labeled large-scale datasets.

UCF101   [32]. This is a large video dataset for action recognition collected from YouTube. It consists of 101 action classes, 13K clips, and 27 hours of video data. The task is generally considered challenging since many videos are captured under poor lighting, with cluttered background, or severe camera motion. As our framework requires no manually labeled training set, we only use the three provided test-splits to test and evaluate our framework. Each test-split has around 3,800 videos. The averaged classification accuracy over the three splits is used as the evaluation metric.

TRECVID MED 2013 [1] **and 2014**[2]. They are the two largest publicly available video datasets for high-level event detection, and are introduced by NIST for participants in the TRECVID competition. MED 2013 contains 20 events (E006 – E015 and E021 – E030), while MED 2014 has 20 events (E021 – E040).

---

[1] http://nist.gov/itl/iad/mig/med13.cfm.
[2] http://nist.gov/itl/iad/mig/med14.cfm.

Each dataset has three different partitions: *Background*, *100EX* and *MEDTest*. *Background* contains about 5000 background videos not belonging to any of the considered events; *100EX* contains 100 positive videos for each event that is used as the training set in TRECVID; *MEDTest* contains around 25,000 videos (over 960 hours of videos), with per-video ground truth annotations for 20 event categories. We evaluate our approach on *MEDTest* and apply the official average precision (AP) metric used in TRECVID contests.

Data Pre-processing. For both training and testing, the crawled videos from Web and testing videos in *MEDTest* are decomposed into a set of frames. Using all video frames would be computationally expensive and is not necessary, as there are lots of redundancy among the frames. Thus, we only use the key frames. To extract these, we start by detecting shot boundaries by calculating color histograms for all frames. For each frame, we then calculate the L_1 distance between the previous color histogram and the current one. If the distance is larger than a threshold (we set it as 0.2 in this paper), this frame is marked as a shot boundary. After detecting the shots, we define the key frames each as the one in the middle of a shot. By doing this, we extract around 150 key frames for a 5 min video.

Since some videos of the three large-scale datasets are also collected from Web, we check whether our crawled videos unintentionally include any videos in the testing set. Specifically, we extract the fc6 features using VGGNet19 for each key frame in our collected videos and the videos in testing set. Then we compute the pairwise distances. We find that there are no overlapped videos.

4.2 Action Classification Experiment

Experiment Setup. Here we use the UCF101 dataset for evaluation. Our framework automatically harvests a labeling-free training set. A high-quality training set is supposed to be able to produce all kinds of good action classifiers. We thus examine three types of classifiers in our experiments:

- **CNNs** [21]: CNNs pre-trained from ImageNet have been proven to generalize well to action recognition tasks with domain-specific fine-tuning [29]. We choose the VGGNet19 [30] released by Oxford to conduct experiments. To fine-tune the VGGNet19, we use the Caffe [18] toolbox, take selected Web images/video frames as inputs, and set the width of the last fully-connected layer and the softmax layer as the number of action categories. We initialize the network with pre-trained weights, except for the last fully-connected layer which is randomly initialized. Each key frame/image is resized with the shorter side to be 256 pixels which is compatible with the input requirement of VGGNet19. During training, all data are randomly shuffled, and organized as mini-batches with the size of 128 for VGGNet19 fine-tuning using stochastic gradient descend. The learning rate starts from 10^{-4} and decreases to 10^{-5} after 20K iterations, then to 10^{-6} after 40K iterations. The training is stopped after 50K iterations. For testing, to predict an action label for a video, we average the corresponding prediction scores of all the key frames of the video.

Table 1. Webly-supervised action recognition results on UCF101, by fine-tuning VGGNet19 using **both** Web images and Web video frames. (x%: percentage abandoned)

Method	# Number of training data	Acc (%)
All crawled data	426K	64.7
Validation	368K	66.5
One-class SVM (5 %)	405K	65.4
One-class SVM (10 %)	384k	65.9
One-class SVM (15 %)	363k	65.9
Unsupervised one-class SVM (5 %)	405K	66.6
Unsupervised one-class SVM (10 %)	384k	66.9
Unsupervised one-class SVM (15 %)	363k	66.4
Landmarks (5 %)	405K	67.9
Landmarks (10 %)	384k	68.3
Landmarks (15 %)	363k	67.7
Ours (5 %)	405K	**68.7**
Ours (10 %)	384k	**69.3**
Ours (15 %)	363k	**68.9**

- **LSTM** [16]: We feed the selected video frames into an LSTM with softmax classifier. We use the LSTM implemented by Caffe [18], and set the rolling time k as 25 and the number of hidden state as 256. The LSTM weights are learnt by using the BPTT algorithm. During training, we set the size of mini-batch as 10. And the learning rate starts from 10^{-3} and decreases to 10^{-4} after 50K iterations. The training is stopped after 80K iterations. For testing, the LSTM classifier directly gives a video-level prediction.
- **SVM**: we extract the fc6 features of pre-trained VGGNet19 for images or video frames, and train a multi-class SVM classifier using the LibLinear toolbox [10] by fixing soft margin cost as 1. Similarly to the CNN classifier, we use late fusion (average) of the frame-level scores to generate the video-level predictions.

Table 2. Webly-supervised action recognition results on UCF101, by fine-tuning VGGNet19 using **either** Web images or Web video frames. (x%: percentage abandoned)

Data	Method										
	All crawled data	Validation	One-class SVM			Landmarks			Ours		
			5 %	10 %	15 %	5 %	10 %	15 %	5 %	10 %	15 %
Images	61.2	61.7	61.2	62.1	61.7	63.9	64.1	64.3	64.7	64.9	**65.1**
Videos	57.6	58.1	58.2	58.4	**58.6**	58.0	58.2	58.1	58.2	58.3	58.5

For testing on the UCF101 dataset, we uniformly sample 25 frames per video as suggested in [29], and then utilize a CNN/LSTM/SVM classifier to make predictions.

Baseline Methods. To evaluate our framework, we compare against several state of the art noise removal approaches as baselines:

- **Validation:** For each action class, we split the crawled data U into K equal and disjoint subsets. Each subset is scored by a binary SVM classifier trained on the rest $K - 1$ subsets as positive and some random images of the other classes as negative. Every data point in U is predicted once. Negative-scored data are considered as noise and rejected. We use the implementation of LibSVM [1] with default hyper parameter $\lambda = 1$ to conduct experiments. In our experiment, we set K as 5.
- **One-class SVM:** We use LibSVM [1] to conduct the experiment.
- **Unsupervised one-class SVM:** We implemented Liu *et al.*' method [23] ourselves and followed the suggested details for tuning the hyper-parameters (*e.g.* using Gaussian kernels, soft labels and the number of neighbors).
- **Landmarks**: The concept of landmarks [13] is originally defined as a subset of data point from source domain that match the target domain. In our problem, we first treat Web images as the source domain (and Web video frames as

Table 3. Webly-supervised action recognition results on UCF101, by training a LSTM classifier using top 25 frames for each video.

Method	Acc (%)
Random	56.3
Validation	63.8
One-class SVM	64.6
Landmarks	64.2
Ours	**65.1**

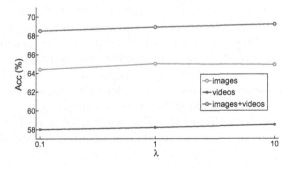

Fig. 2. Action recognition accuracies (Acc %) w.r.t the parameter λ on UCF101.

the target domain) to select "landmark" Web images. Then we reverse the source and target domains to select video frames. We use the code provided by authors for the experiments.

Results on UCF101. Table 1 reports the Webly-supervised action recognition results when our and the baseline approaches are used to select both Web images and video frames for fine-tuning CNNs. For one-class SVM, landmarks, and our own approach, we need to define the amount of data to be rejected. For fair comparison, we report the performances when rejecting 5 %, 10 %, and 15 % Web data for all the methods. To be noted, we take both Web images and video frames together as input for Validation and One-class SVM, and then keep the relevant training samples. For landmark and our own approach, we use Gaussian RBF kernels and fix the bandwidth parameter as 1 in all experiments. We solve the quadratic programming problem by using a Gurobi solver (http://www.gurobi.com). For our own approach, we fixed $\lambda = 10$ in Eq. (1) for all experiments, and we examine its effect when λ is set to 0.1, 1, and 10 with reject ratio of 10 % in Fig. 2. We also experiment with either of Web images or Web video frames for fine-tuning VGGNet19 in Table 2, with the top-ranked 25 frames per video for the LSTM classifier in Table 3, and with different percentages of Web images for the SVM classifier in Table 4.

Table 4. Webly-supervised action recognition results on UCF101, by a SVM classifier using only Web images. (x%: percentage abandoned).

Data	Method										
	All crawled data	Validation	One-class SVM			Landmarks			Ours		
			5 %	10 %	15 %	5 %	10 %	15 %	5 %	10 %	15 %
Images	53.2	54.1	54.2	54.9	54.6	55.1	55.4	55.6	56.0	56.4	**56.6**

From Table 1, we have two key observations. (1) The action recognition performance could be improved if some noisy data are removed by using one-class SVM, validation, landmarks, unsupervised one-class SVM and our proposed approach. These results validate the necessity of our study. (2) Our proposed approach to jointly selecting relevant images and video frames is more effective than the competing baselines, such as one-class SVM, unsupervised one-class SVM and Validation. In Table 2, we can find that the proposed framework can consistently achieve better results when using images only for fine-tuning CNN, with different ratios to reject the noise data. Under video frames only, the improvement of our approach compared with others is marginal, but ours still achieves better result compared with directly using the crawled data. Results in Table 4 shows that our approach is also a good companion for traditional SVM based classifications.

Table 5. Webly-supervised action recognition results on UCF101, by fine-tuning VGGNet19 using only 50 % and 10 % video frames (50 % and 90 % abandoned).

Method	# Number of training data	Acc (%)
All crawled data	360K	57.6
One-class SVM (50 %)	180K	55.7
One-class SVM (90 %)	36K	49.8
Landmarks (50 %)	180K	54.9
Landmarks (90 %)	36K	52.1
Ours (50 %)	180k	**58.8**
Ours (90 %)	36k	**58.2**

The Effectiveness of Removing Redundant Frames. In addition to removing noisy or outlier images and video frames, our approach also reduces redundant frames. The results in Table 3 show that frames selected by our proposed framework can achieve better performance than other approaches. We speculate that LSTM needs diverse sample to model the internal relationship in a sequence, and repetitively redundant frames would cripple its modeling capabilities. This requirement is a good match to our formulation.

Moreover, the redundant frames provide little extra information for the other classifiers either. To further evaluate whether our proposed framework can reduce the amount of training data to reach reasonable action classification performances when fine-tuning VGGNet19, we further conduct experiment by rejecting 50 % and 90 % frames during training. Experiment results are shown in Table 5. Surprisingly, the performance of our proposed approach has not dropped much from Table 2, even slightly better when rejecting 50 % video frames. However, one-class SVM and landmark-based approach decrease significantly. These results validate the effectiveness of our approach to reducing redundant video frames. The remaining video frames can maintain most of discriminative information and enjoy a lower computation cost.

Comparisons with State of the Arts that Use Fully Labeled Data. In Table 6, we add comparisons with the state-of-the-art results that are obtained by training classifiers from fully labeled training data. We directly quote the numbers from the published papers. Among the selected systems, LRCN [7], LSTM composite model [34], spatial stream network [29], and Karpathy et al. [20] are based on pure appearance features from static images. IDT+FV [41], C3D [40] include motion features from videos as well. We find that the performance of our Webly-supervsied approach is comparable to the spatial networks which use positive videos, but still has gaps when compared with motion features.

Table 6. Comparisons with state of the arts results using fully labeled data on UCF101.

Method	Acc (%)
LRCN [7]	71.1
LSTM composite model [34]	75.8
IDT + FV [41]	87.9
C3D [40]	82.3
Karpathy et al. [20]	65.4
Spatial stream network [29]	73.0
Ours (spatial)	69.3

4.3   Webly-Supervised Multimedia Event Detection

In order to have a better understanding of our approach, we also apply it to the large-scale TRECVID MED 2013 and 2014 datasets. There have been some systems on the MED tasks which learn event detectors from the Web data. While we only use the class names to download Web images and videos, the existing systems often employ additional queries like event related concepts. We contrast our work to the following: (1) Concept Discovery [2], (2) Bi-Concept [14], (3) Composite Concepts [14], (4) EventNet [46], and (5) Selected Concepts [31]. Approach (1) uses Web images to train event detectors, (2) – (4) use Web videos to train event detectors, and (5) firstly trains concept detectors using Web images, uses them to rank testing videos, and then re-trains event detectors with the top-ranked testing videos. We note that the strategy of (5) can be readily added as a post-processing component to other methods as well.

Table 7. Comparisons with other state-of-the-art zero-shot/webly-supervised event detection systems on MEDTest 2013.

Method	mAP (%)
Concept Discovery [2]	2.3
Bi-concept [14]	6.0
Composite Concept [14]	6.4
EventNet [46]	8.9
Selecting [31]	11.8
Ours	**16.1**

For a fair comparison, we report our results on MEDTest 2013 and directly compare them with state-of-the-art results quoted from original papers. The results in Table 7 show that our framework outperforms the other systems by a large margin. For additional analysis, we also provide per-event-class results in

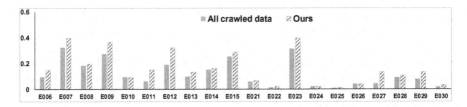

Fig. 3. Per-event detection result compared with All crawled data on MEDTest 2013 dataset.

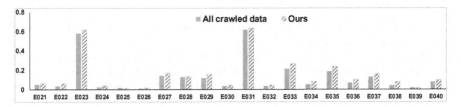

Fig. 4. Per-event detection result compared with All crawled data on MEDTest 2014 dataset.

Figs. 3 and 4, respectively on MEDTest 2013 and MEDTest 2014. The numbers are reported of using both all crawled data and our selected data (reject ratio 10 %) to fine-tune VGGNet19. We observe performance gains for 17 out of 20 classes on MEDTest 2013 and 18 of 20 classes on MEDTest 2014, verifying the effectiveness of our approach to removing noisy data from the Web images and Web video frames.

Implementation Details of Fine-Tuning. We use the Caffe [18] toolbox for fine-tuning CNNs, with a VGGNet19 model [30] that is pre-trained on ImageNet [5] by the authors. The learning rate starts from 10^{-4} and decreases to 10^{-5} after 25K iterations, then to 10^{-6} after 50K iterations. The training is stopped after 65K iterations. For testing, to predict an event label for a video, we average the corresponding prediction scores of all the key frames of the video. Momentum and weight decay coefficients are again set to 0.9 and 0.0005. All layers are fine-tuned, except the last fully-connected layer, which has to be changed to produce an output of event classes.

5 Conclusions

In this paper, we investigated to what extent the Web images and Web videos could be leveraged to conduct Webly-supervised video recognition. To distill useful data from the noisy Web ones, we proposed a unified approach to jointly removing irrelevant Web images and (also redundant) video frames. We developed an efficient alternative optimization procedure to solve our proposed formulation. Extensive experiments, for both action recognition and event detection, validate that our framework not only outperforms competing baselines, but also beats existing systems which also exploit Web data for event detection. We expect this work to benefit future research on large-scale video recognition tasks.

Acknowledgments. This work was supported in part by NSF IIS-1566511. Chuang Gan was partially supported by the National Basic Research Program of China Grant 2011CBA00300, 2011CBA00301, the National Natural Science Foundation of China Grant 61033001, 61361136003.

References

1. Chang, C.C., Lin, C.J.: LIBSVM: a library for support vector machines. ACM Trans. Intell. Syst. Technol. (2011)
2. Chen, J., Cui, Y., Ye, G., Liu, D., Chang, S.: Event-driven semantic concept discovery by exploiting weakly tagged internet images. In: ICMR (2014)
3. Chen, X., Gupta, A.: Webly supervised learning of convolutional networks. In: ICCV (2015)
4. Chen, X., Shrivastava, A., Gupta, A.: NEIL: extracting visual knowledge from web data. In: ICCV, pp. 1409–1416 (2013)
5. Deng, J., Dong, W., Socher, R., Li, L.J., Li, K., Fei-Fei, L.: Imagenet: a large-scale hierarchical image database. In: CVPR (2009)
6. Divvala, S.K., Farhadi, A., Guestrin, C.: Learning everything about anything: webly-supervised visual concept learning. In: CVPR, pp. 3270–3277 (2014)
7. Donahue, J., Hendricks, L.A., Guadarrama, S., Rohrbach, M., Venugopalan, S., Saenko, K., Darrell, T.: Long-term recurrent convolutional networks for visual recognition and description. In: CVPR (2015)
8. Duan, L., Tsang, I.W., Xu, D., Chua, T.S.: Domain adaptation from multiple sources via auxiliary classifiers. In: Proceedings of the 26th Annual International Conference on Machine Learning, pp. 289–296. ACM (2009)
9. Duan, L., Xu, D., Tsang, I.H., Luo, J.: Visual event recognition in videos by learning from web data. IEEE Trans. Pattern Anal. Mach. Intell. **34**(9), 1667–1680 (2012)
10. Fan, R.E., Chang, K.W., Hsieh, C.J., Wang, X.R., Lin, C.J.: Liblinear: a library for large linear classification. J. Mach. Learn. Res. **9**, 1871–1874 (2008)
11. Gan, C., Wang, N., Yang, Y., Yeung, D.Y., Hauptmann, A.G.: Devnet: a deep event network for multimedia event detection and evidence recounting. In: CVPR, pp. 2568–2577 (2015)
12. Gan, C., Yao, T., Yang, K., Yang, Y., Mei, T.: You lead, we exceed: labor-free video concept learning by jointly exploiting web videos and images. In: CVPR (2016)
13. Gong, B., Grauman, K., Sha, F.: Connecting the dots with landmarks: discriminatively learning domain-invariant features for unsupervised domain adaptation. In: ICML, pp. 222–230 (2013)
14. Habibian, A., Mensink, T., Snoek, C.G.: Composite concept discovery for zero-shot video event detection. In: ICMR, p. 17 (2014)
15. Habibian, A., Mensink, T., Snoek, C.G.: Videostory: a new multimedia embedding for few-example recognition and translation of events. In: ACM Multimedia, pp. 17–26 (2014)
16. Hochreiter, S., Schmidhuber, J.: Long short-term memory. Neural Comput. **9**(8), 1735–1780 (1997)

17. Huang, J., Gretton, A., Borgwardt, K.M., Schölkopf, B., Smola, A.J.: Correcting sample selection bias by unlabeled data. In: NIPS, pp. 601–608 (2006)
18. Jia, Y., Shelhamer, E., Donahue, J., Karayev, S., Long, J., Girshick, R.B., Guadarrama, S., Darrell, T.: Caffe: convolutional architecture for fast feature embedding. In: ACM Multimedia, vol. 2, p. 4 (2014)
19. Jiang, Y.G., Bhattacharya, S., Chang, S.F., Shah, M.: High-level event recognition in unconstrained videos. Int. J. Multimedia Inf. Retrieval 2(2), 73–101 (2013)
20. Karpathy, A., Toderici, G., Shetty, S., Leung, T., Sukthankar, R., Fei-Fei, L.: Large-scale video classification with convolutional neural networks. In: CVPR (2014)
21. Krizhevsky, A., Sutskever, I., Hinton, G.E.: Imagenet classification with deep convolutional neural networks. In: NIPS (2012)
22. Lan, Z., Lin, M., Li, X., Hauptmann, A.G., Raj, B.: Beyond gaussian pyramid: multi-skip feature stacking for action recognition. In: CVPR (2015)
23. Liu, W., Hua, G., Smith, J.R.: Unsupervised one-class learning for automatic outlier removal. In: CVPR, pp. 3826–3833 (2014)
24. Ng, J.Y.H., Hausknecht, M., Vijayanarasimhan, S., Vinyals, O., Monga, R., Toderici, G.: Beyond short snippets: deep networks for video classification. In: CVPR (2015)
25. Oneata, D., Verbeek, J., Schmid, C., et al.: Action and event recognition with fisher vectors on a compact feature set. In: ICCV (2013)
26. Pan, S.J., Tsang, I.W., Kwok, J.T., Yang, Q.: Domain adaptation via transfer component analysis. IEEE Trans. Neural Netw. 22(2), 199–210 (2011)
27. Pan, S.J., Yang, Q.: A survey on transfer learning. IEEE Trans. Knowl. Data Eng. 22(10), 1345–1359 (2010)
28. Saenko, K., Kulis, B., Fritz, M., Darrell, T.: Adapting visual category models to new domains. In: Maragos, P., Paragios, N., Daniilidis, K. (eds.) ECCV 2010, Part IV. LNCS, vol. 6314, pp. 213–226. Springer, Heidelberg (2010)
29. Simonyan, K., Zisserman, A.: Two-stream convolutional networks for action recognition in videos. In: NIPS (2014)
30. Simonyan, K., Zisserman, A.: Very deep convolutional networks for large-scale image recognition. In: ICLR (2015)
31. Singh, B., Han, X., Wu, Z., Morariu, V.I., Davis, L.S.: Selecting relevant web trained concepts for automated event retrieval. In: ICCV (2015)
32. Soomro, K., Zamir, A.R., Shah, M.: UCF101: a dataset of 101 human actions classes from videos in the wild. arXiv preprint arXiv:1212.0402 (2012)
33. Sriperumbudur, B.K., Gretton, A., Fukumizu, K., Schölkopf, B., Lanckriet, G.R.: Hilbert space embeddings and metrics on probability measures. J. Mach. Learn. Res. 11, 1517–1561 (2010)
34. Srivastava, N., Mansimov, E., Salakhutdinov, R.: Unsupervised learning of video representations using lstms. In: ICML (2015)
35. Sukhbaatar, S., Fergus, R.: Learning from noisy labels with deep neural networks. 2(3), 4 (2014). arXiv preprint arXiv:1406.2080
36. Sun, C., Gan, C., Nevatia, R.: Automatic concept discovery from parallel text and visual corpora. In: ICCV, pp. 2596–2604 (2015)
37. Sun, C., Nevatia, R.: Large-scale web video event classification by use of fisher vectors. In: WACV (2013)
38. Sun, C., Shetty, S., Sukthankar, R., Nevatia, R.: Temporal localization of fine-grained actions in videos by domain transfer from web images. In: ACM Multimedia, pp. 371–380 (2015)
39. Szegedy, C., Liu, W., Jia, Y., Sermanet, P., Reed, S., Anguelov, D., Erhan, D., Vanhoucke, V., Rabinovich, A.: Going deeper with convolutions. In: CVPR (2015)

40. Tran, D., Bourdev, L., Fergus, R., Torresani, L., Paluri, M.: C3D: generic features for video analysis. In: ICCV (2015)
41. Wang, H., Schmid, C.: Action recognition with improved trajectories. In: ICCV (2013)
42. Wang, L., Qiao, Y., Tang, X.: Action recognition with trajectory-pooled deep-convolutional descriptors. In: CVPR, pp. 4305–4314 (2015)
43. Wang, L., Xiong, Y., Wang, Z., Qiao, Y., Lin, D., Tang, X., Gool, L.V.: Temporal segment networks: towards good practices for deep action recognition. In: ECCV (2016)
44. Xiao, T., Xia, T., Yang, Y., Huang, C., Wang, X.: Learning from massive noisy labeled data for image classification. In: Proceedings of the IEEE Conference on Computer Vision and Pattern Recognition, pp. 2691–2699 (2015)
45. Yan, Z., Zhang, H., Piramuthu, R., Jagadeesh, V., DeCoste, D., Di, W., Yu, Y.: HD-CNN: Hierarchical deep convolutional neural networks for large scale visual recognition. In: ICCV, pp. 2740–2748 (2015)
46. Ye, G., Li, Y., Xu, H., Liu, D., Chang, S.F.: Eventnet: a large scale structured concept library for complex event detection in video. In: ACM Multimedia, pp. 471–480 (2015)
47. Zha, S., Luisier, F., Andrews, W., Srivastava, N., Salakhutdinov, R.: Exploiting image-trained CNN architectures for unconstrained video classification. In: BMVC (2015)
48. Zhang, H., Hu, Z., Deng, Y., Sachan, M., Yan, Z., Xing, E.P.: Learning concept taxonomies from multi-modal data. In: ACL (2016)

HFS: Hierarchical Feature Selection for Efficient Image Segmentation

Ming-Ming Cheng[1(✉)], Yun Liu[1(✉)], Qibin Hou[1], Jiawang Bian[1], Philip Torr[3], Shi-Min Hu[2], and Zhuowen Tu[4]

[1] CCCE & CS, Nankai University, Tianjin, China
cmm@nankai.edu.cn
[2] Tsinghua University, Beijing, China
[3] Oxford University, Oxford, UK
[4] UCSD, San Diego, USA

Abstract. In this paper, we propose a real-time system, Hierarchical Feature Selection (HFS), that performs image segmentation at a speed of 50 frames-per-second. We make an attempt to improve the performance of previous image segmentation systems by focusing on two aspects: (1) a careful system implementation on modern GPUs for efficient feature computation; and (2) an effective hierarchical feature selection and fusion strategy with learning. Compared with classic segmentation algorithms, our system demonstrates its particular advantage in speed, with comparable results in segmentation quality. Adopting HFS in applications like salient object detection and object proposal generation results in a significant performance boost. Our proposed HFS system (will be open-sourced) can be used in a variety computer vision tasks that are built on top of image segmentation and superpixel extraction.

Keywords: Image segmentation · Superpixel · Grouping

1 Introduction

Image segmentation is considered as a main challenge in computer vision that has been extensively studied in the past. After decades of research, a consensus nonetheless exists among researchers in the field that accurate segments, either as large regions or as small superpixels, serve as an effective input representation for middle-level and high-level vision tasks, albeit intrinsically ambiguous. Some typical tasks that have greatly benefited from building on good segmentations include object detection/recognition [24,25], tracking [44], saliency estimation [10,22], objectness proposal generation [2,8,43], and 3D inference [20]. The reason for this to happen is threefold: (i) extracted segments are meaningful units that carry informative features such as shapes, textures, *etc* [21,26,39]; (ii) the number of segments is often significantly lower than the number pixels in the

---

M.-M. Cheng and Y. Liu—Two joint first authors have made equal contribution to this paper.

© Springer International Publishing AG 2016
B. Leibe et al. (Eds.): ECCV 2016, Part III, LNCS 9907, pp. 867–882, 2016.
DOI: 10.1007/978-3-319-46487-9_53

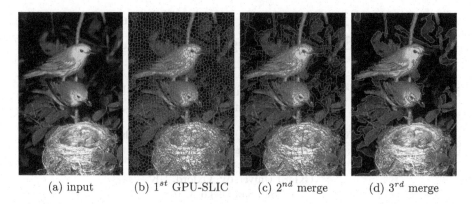

(a) input   (b) 1st GPU-SLIC   (c) 2nd merge   (d) 3rd merge

Fig. 1. Sample results from different steps of our methods. The original image is from BSDS500 [4] dataset. These image segmentation results are generated at 50 fps on GPU.

original image, resulting in a more compact representation with a great speed benefit [10]; (iii) the superpixel representation often has an improved coherency and robustness than the raw pixels [37].

In the past, several seminal works have emerged as the state-of-the-art systems that have been widely adopted in the field: spectral clustering based normalized cuts approach [38]; efficient feature (color) space mode seeking method, mean-shift algorithm [13]; efficient graph-based image segmentation method [17]; hierarchical region tree with transform contours [4]; and multi-scale normalized cuts algorithm [5]. Among these choices, efficient graph based image segmentation (EGB) and SLIC [1] methods are particularly popular in computer vision and computer graphics [2,7,8,10,20,22,24,25,43,44], due to their great speed advantage.

In this paper, we aim at developing a rapid image segmentation system that produces high quality image segments for real-time computer vision tasks. We propose a hierarchical feature selection framework that learns feature combination in individual stages of a hierarchical structure. Our effort starts with a GPU version of the SLIC method [1,34], to quickly obtain initial seed regions (superpixels) by performing oversegmentation. Image features are then extracted from the individual seed regions, followed by a feature combination process with a distance metric learnt from the training data. Note that to maintain the efficiency of our system, we only consider those image features that are appropriate for parallel computing, *i.e.* via GPUs. A region merging process is then performed based on the learned distance metric to output a new set of regions for the next level in the hierarchy. Our system then repeats for a few iterations.

The method developed in this paper has its practical importance to a variety of real-time applications by generating high quality image segments (see also Fig. 1) at 50 fps. The performance of our method is quantitatively evaluated in the well-known BSDS500 [4] dataset (see also Sect. 4). As demonstrated in the evaluation results (see also Table 2), our method strikes a favorable balance between segmentation quality and computational efficiency when compared with alternative approaches [1,4,5,17,40]. We will open-source our system to make it publicly available.

2   Related Work

Image segmentation is a fundamental problem in computer vision [30]. We refer readers to the popular BSDS500 [4] benchmark and other recent studies [3,5,28,42] for a comprehensive background discussion. Next, we highlight a few representative methods that are relevant and important to the method proposed here.

A certain degree of attention in the past was given to grouping algorithms that efficiently compute and implement the normalized-cuts algorithm [38]. A multigrid eigenvectors producer is designed [28], enabling substantial speed-up for eigenvector computation. In [42], Taylor *et al.* attempt to reduce the size of eigenvectors using a watershed oversegmentation to achieve the speed of computing eigenvectors in less than half a second. Pont-Tuset *et al.* [5] present an approach to downsample the eigenvectors first, solving them at a reduced size, followed by upsampling the solution to retrieve the structure of the image. Although satisfying segmentation results can be obtained by the above methods, the computational time is still a bottleneck for these spectral clustering based approaches.

Along a different direction, SLIC [1] emerges as one of the most celebrated methods with a good balance between accuracy and speed, and it has been adopted in many applications [6,9,23,41,49]. In [1], a k-means clustering approach is proposed to initialize cluster centers by sampling pixels at regular grid steps, followed by a labeling procedure in which each pixel is labeled with the index of the cluster center whose search region overlaps with its location.

A graph-based clustering methods presented by Felzenszwalb and Huttenlocher [17] has also been widely used. For an undirected graph with edges measuring the dissimilarity between adjacent pixels, the goal of [17] is to perform a clustering operation such that each region is the minimum spanning tree of the involved pixels. Since it starts with a merging process directly from single pixels with weak color information, the algorithm of [17] is prone to noise. Compared with [17], we instead start our clustering method from oversegmentations that contains more informative features than single pixels. We will discuss in detail in Sect. 3 about our procedure.

Other popular methods for image segmentation include those based on feature learning [35]. These methods demonstrate a good representation power by fusing together features such as brightness, color, and texture properties using discriminative classifiers. Ren *et al.* [35] propose a hierarchical segmentation approach in which a cascade of boundary classifiers are applied to recursively combine regions starting from initial oversegmentations. In this spirit, our work bears certain similarity to [35] where a cascade of classifiers are used for region grouping. Here, we strike the importance of real-time execution by carefully studying regional features that are appropriate for GPU implementation when combined with [17]. The main contribution of our work is the development of a real-time image segmentation system that is of practical importance to be used in many high-level computer vision tasks.

3   Our Method

In this section, we first introduce the problem formulation and our hierarchical merging algorithm. We then explain the parameter learning and feature extraction procedure, followed by a discussion about design choices behind our method.

3.1   Problem Formulation

Given an image I, we partition it into L level segmentations $\mathcal{S} = \{\mathcal{S}_1, \mathcal{S}_2, \cdots, \mathcal{S}_L\}$. Each segmentation $\mathcal{S}_l$ is a decomposition of the image I with K_l regions

$$\mathcal{S}_l = \{R_1^{(l)}, R_2^{(l)}, \ldots, R_{K_l}^{(l)}\}, \tag{1}$$

where l denotes the level index in the hierarchy. We start with the finest segmentation $\mathcal{S}_1$ consisting of a large number of regions, and gradually merge regions from level $\mathcal{S}_l$ to a coarser level $\mathcal{S}_{l+1}$. The coarsest level segmentation thus is composed of fewest regions.

We adopt a graph based approach [17] for the implementation of the region merging process $\mathcal{S}_l \Rightarrow \mathcal{S}_{l+1}$ at each step. Let

$$G_l = (\mathcal{S}_l, \mathcal{A}_l) \tag{2}$$

be an undirected graph, with vertices being a set of regions $\mathcal{S}_l$ as defined above, and edges $(R_i^{(l)}, R_j^{(l)}) \in \mathcal{A}_l$ corresponding to pairs of neighboring vertices. Each edge $(R_i^{(l)}, R_j^{(l)}) \in \mathcal{A}_l$ has a feature vector $\boldsymbol{T}_{i,j}^{(l)}$ (see also in Sect. 3.4), and a corresponding predict score $s_{i,j}^{(l)}$, which is a non-negative measure of the distance between regions $R_i^{(l)}$ and $R_j^{(l)}$.

Based on the above problem definition, our task is then to quickly merge regions to produce coherent segments that best match human annotations, such as those in the BSDS500 [4] benchmark.

3.2   Hierarchical Merging

To achieve high quality and retain top efficiency, we propose to (i) iteratively learn how to combine features and update image features after region merging in each level; (ii) use fast parallel superpixel generation methods [1,34] to group image pixels to initial regions before further merging.

The pipeline of our method is shown in Fig. 2, with example results displayed in Fig. 1 and the algorithm listed in Algorithm 1. In the first step, the GPU-SLIC method [1,34] is exploited to over-segment an input image into superpixels,

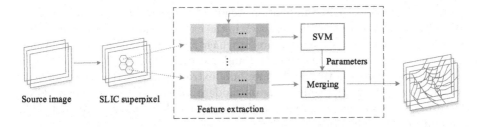

Fig. 2. Pipeline of our methods.

which serve as seed regions in the 1st level $\mathcal{S}_1 = \{R_1^{(1)}, R_2^{(1)}, \ldots, R_{K_l}^{(1)}\}$. In the subsequent steps, both internal and marginal features (see also Sect. 3.4) are extracted. Using support vector machine (SVM) regressors, we learn from training data (see also Sect. 3.3) how to map feature vectors $\boldsymbol{T}_{i,j}^{(l)}$ to suitable distance measure between regions $R_i^{(l)}$ and $R_j^{(l)}$. We progressively merge regions in $\mathcal{S}_l$ to arrive at a coarser segmentation $\mathcal{S}_{l+1}$, following the efficient graph based (EGB) image segmentation framework [17], with the graph defined in Eq. (2).

Our design principle is motivated by a recent trend of using discriminative learning approach to find proper feature combination for various vision tasks [4,22,30]. A number of psychophysics studies [36] suggest that humans use multi-cues to separate objects in natural scenes. Compared with an ad-hoc design, extracting image features and allowing the data to speak for themselves is proven to be an appropriate way of learning how to combine different visual cues [4,30]. Our system design is also motivated by an observation that image features play different roles at different scales, when deciding whether two regions should be merged. At a fine scale, *e.g.* pixel level, color similarity and spatial distance are important, which is observed in many state-of-the-art image segmentation methods [1,17]. With region merging/grouping progressing to a coarser level, texture similarity, edges between regions and other cues become more important deciding factors to judge whether two regions should be merged.

Instead of learning a single rule for cue/feature combination across all levels, [4,30], we experiment an alternative approach in which iteratively updating

---

Algorithm 1. HFS for region merging

Input: image I, weights $\mathbf{w}$, iteration L
Output: segmentation $\mathcal{S}_L$
Initialization: $\mathcal{S}_l = \{R_1^{(l)}, R_2^{(l)}, \ldots, R_{K_l}^{(l)}\} \Leftarrow$ GPU-SLIC(I) [1,34]
for $l = \{1, 2, \ldots, L-1\}$ **do**
   for each $(R_i^{(l)}, R_j^{(l)}) \in \mathcal{A}_l$ **do**
      $s_{i,j}^{(l)} \Leftarrow (\boldsymbol{T}_{i,j}^{(l)})^T \cdot \mathbf{w}^{(l)}$, see also Sect. 3.4 & 3.3 for $\boldsymbol{T}_{i,j}^{(l)}$ and $\mathbf{w}^{(l)}$ respectively
   end for
   $\mathcal{S}_{l+1} = \text{EGB}(\mathcal{A}_l, s_{i,j}^{(l)})$ [17]
end for

---

region features and their combination weights is implemented (see also Fig. 3). We see favorable aspect of our approach in the experiments. Based on this point, we design a hierarchical architecture in which multiple levels are engaged, followed by recursive region merging [17] and feature updating.

One thing worth noting is that we only extract features that are simplistic and suitable for parallel computing on modern GPUs. More informative CNN features can be engaged in an e.g. end-to-end edge detection system HED [46], to improve the segmentation results.

Our experimental results indicate that the F-measure [4]

$$F_\beta = \frac{2 \cdot Precision \times Recall}{Precision + Recall}, \tag{3}$$

can be increased by 6% when HED is used. However, because of the overhead of HED (0.4 s per-image), as opposed to 0.02 s in our vanilla version, we make using HED an optional choice.

3.3   Parameter Learning

As described above, given a set of initial regions, we learn an edge weight $w_{i,j}^{(l)} \in \mathbf{w}^{(l)}$ between every region pair $(R_i^{(l)}, R_j^{(l)}) \in \mathcal{A}_l$. Since every region pair is associated with a feature vector $\mathbf{T}_{i,j}^{(l)}$, our next step is to provide a label for each region pair at level l. Since the initial regions of each level may have irregular shapes, we use the F-measure to help determine the ground truth label of each region pair in $\mathcal{A}_l$.

We first calculate the F-measure of the initial segmentation at level l, denoted as $F_{init}^{(l)}$. Then, for each region pair $(R_i^{(l)}, R_j^{(l)})$ in $\mathcal{A}_l$, we compute the F-measure repeatedly after merging $(R_i^{(l)}, R_j^{(l)})$. If the F-measure after merging $(R_i^{(l)}, R_j^{(l)})$ is greater than $F_{init}^{(l)}$, the corresponding label $y_{i,j}^{(l)}$ of $(R_i^{(l)}, R_j^{(l)})$ will be assigned to 0. Otherwise, $y_{i,j}^{(l)}$ will be assigned to 1. We adopt support vector machine (SVM) regressor to learn feature weights $\mathbf{w}^{(l)}$.

3.4   Feature Extraction

Our system explores a group of simple features that can be efficiently calculated on modern GPUs. Both internal and marginal features are considered here. Table 1 lists the features we have considered. We discuss below the details of these features used in our system.

Brightness and Colors. The brightness and color cues in the CIELAB color space have been proved to be very useful [4,30]. We use mean L*a*b* values to represent the color of a segment. In order to tolerate variations in the relative weight of brightness and colors, we use both the Euler distance (d_c) and the distances in each channel (d_l, d_a, d_b) for two adjacent segments.

Table 1. Features for adjacent regions

Feature names	Dimension	Notation
Differences in each channel of CIELAB	3	d_l, d_a, d_b
Euler distance of CIELAB values	1	d_c
Average gradient maximum along boundary	1	d_g
χ^2 distance between RGB histograms	1	χ_h^2
χ^2 distance between gradient histograms	1	χ_H^2
Variances of RGB values	3	s_r, s_g, s_b
Variances of CIELAB values	3	s_l', s_a', s_b'
Average HED maximum along boundary	1	d_h

Average gradient maximum along boundary. Previous works have shown that gradient information is an important cue in boundary detection. Instead of using gradients directly, we use gradients after non-maxima suppression. For adjacent segments R_i and R_j, the computation starts by placing a small circular disc at the pixel $p_k \in \Gamma$, where Γ represents their boundaries. Then we calculate the maximum gradient $\delta'(p_k)$ in the disc. Thereby, the average $\delta'(p_k)$ is computed as the gradient difference $d_g(R_i, R_j)$.

χ^2 distance between RGB histograms. To make use of the details of color information, we employ the color histogram that has $8 \times 8 \times 8$ dimensions in the RGB color space. For histograms belonging to adjacent segments, we use χ^2 distance to measure their difference.

χ^2 distance between gradient histograms. The χ^2 distance of two segments when computing histograms of oriented gradient for each segment is also an attractive choice.

Variances. Variance is a good measure for the fluctuation of a piece of data. We apply variances in the RGB (s_r, s_g, s_b) and CIELAB (s_l', s_a', s_b') color spaces to $R_i \bigcup R_j$, where R_i and R_j are adjacent segments. The magnitude of the variances reflects the similarity between the two segments.

Average HED maximum along boundary. The HED feature is computed similarly to gradient feature above. However, because of the extra overhead of HED, we make this choice optional.

The above features play different roles in different levels. The weight comparison of features in the first and second level are shown in Fig. 3 (except for the HED features). To take computational complexity into account, we only choose a small set of features that are easy to calculate instead of using all of them. The top five features are d_l, d_a, d_b, d_c, and d_g. All the experimental results reported in this paper are based on these features.

3.5   Implementation Details

To design a practical system, we choose $L = 3$ as a default value in this paper. We do all experiments using a machine with an Intel Xeon CPU E5-2676 v3 @ 2.40 GHz and an NVIDIA GeForce GTX 980 Ti. All the running time is reported without data parallelism, except for the objectness proposal application part (Sect. 4.2) which is designed to adherence to the general practice.

4   Experiments

4.1   Evaluation

In this part, we evaluate our method on the BSDS500 [4] benchmark, which is widely used to evaluate segmentation and grouping methods. There are two choices of measures: *optimal dataset scale (ODS)* which is the optimization for the entire training dataset, and *optimal image scale (OIS)* which is the optimization for each test image. For boundary assessment, we use the F-measure of precision and recall on the ODS. The region-based measures contain:

- Variation of Information (VI), measuring the distance between *ground truth (GT)* and the proposed segmentation;
- Probabilistic Rand Index (PRI), measuring the pairwise compatibility of element assignment between GT and the proposed segmentation;
- Segmentation Covering (Covering), measuring the average overlap between GT and the proposed segmentation.

See [4] for more details. Figure 3 shows the weight comparison of the selected features. We can see clearly that the weight importance is different in different levels. To make our results more convincing, we compare our method with approaches [1,4,13,14,17,31,40], the MCG as well as SCG approaches in [5]. All the experiments are accomplished using publicly available source code.

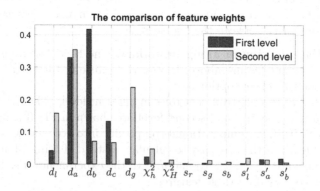

Fig. 3. The weight comparison of the features learned in the 1st and 2nd level.

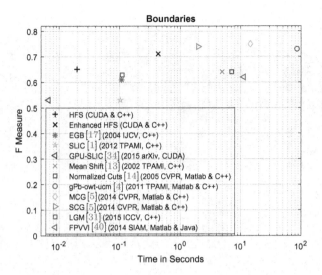

Fig. 4. Experimental evaluation for boundaries on BSDS500 [4] test set. The F-measure is computed by precision and recall at the Optimal Dataset Scale (ODS). And the execution time is tested without data parallel.

Table 2. Region Benchmarks on the BSDS500 [4]

Methods	GPU	Time (s)	Covering			PRI		VI	
			ODS	OIS	Best	ODS	OIS	ODS	OIS
Human	–	–	0.73	0.73	–	0.87	0.87	1.16	1.16
HFS	Y	0.02	0.56	0.61	0.70	0.81	0.84	1.87	1.68
Enhanced HFS	Y	0.43	0.58	0.65	0.72	0.82	0.86	1.80	1.64
EGB [17]	N	0.11	0.52	0.57	0.69	0.80	0.82	2.21	1.87
SLIC [1]	N	0.10	0.37	0.38	0.48	0.74	0.75	2.56	2.50
GPU-SLIC [34]	Y	0.007	0.34	0.37	0.47	0.73	0.75	2.95	2.81
Mean shift [13]	N	4.95	0.54	0.58	0.66	0.79	0.81	1.85	1.64
Normalized Cuts [14]	N	7.15	0.45	0.53	0.67	0.78	0.80	2.23	1.89
gPb-owt-ucm [4]	N	86.4	0.59	0.65	0.74	0.83	0.86	1.69	1.48
MCG [5]	N	14.5	0.61	0.66	0.76	0.83	0.86	1.57	1.40
SCG [5]	N	1.98	0.60	0.65	0.74	0.83	0.86	1.63	1.43
LGM [31]	N	0.11	0.52	0.56	0.63	0.78	0.81	1.93	1.79
FPVVI [40]	N	11.3	0.47	0.53	0.62	0.77	0.80	2.10	1.92

source image   SLIC [1]   EGB [17]   Ours

Fig. 5. Some examples of EGB, SLIC and our method. The reason why we only compare with these two algorithms is that they are the only two that is effcient enough to be used in applications. Left: Image. Middle left: SLIC. Middle right: EGB. Right: Ours. The regions are represented by their mean color. And all images are from the test set of BSDS500 [4].

We show the evaluation results on boundary benchmark in Fig. 4, in which all of the execution time is tested without data parallel. We can see that [5] achieves the best result comparing to others. However, its simplified version SCG still needs about 2 s to process an image. For this reason, it cannot be employed in nowadays applications in spite of its stroke of genius. Similarly, the accuracy of [4] is very competitive compared with other methods. However, the speed of this method is extremely slow taking about 86 s per image. Our approach is hundreds of times faster than [4,5], achieving 50 fps. When the data parallelism is enabled, the speed can be up to 200+ fps. In addition, our approach can be easily used in almost all the applications nowadays including some real-time systems. Comparing with some superpixel extraction methods, e.g. [1,17,31], Fig. 4 demonstrates that our method is much faster, and more importantly, the accuracy also has a significant improvement. When comparing with the rest three methods [13,14,40], our speed advantage is obvious, though the F-measure is only a little higher than them. Others, the F-measure of our enhanced version is very close to the best performance, with very fast speed.

Table 2 presents region benchmarks on the BSDS500 [4]. From Table 2, MCG performs best on all the metrics, but it needs about 15 s per image. SLIC achieves the worst results, although its GPU version can be very fast. It is not difficult to find that our approach is close to the best performance on all these criteria, especially the enhanced version. Thus, we can draw the conclusion that our approach can achieve better trade-off than others in both efficiency and quality. Figure 5 shows some examples of our method comparing with the other two fast algorithm [1,17].

The reason for not obtaining the best results on each criterion is two-fold. First, the initial superpixels produced by SLIC are not so desirable. For instance, when the step S is set to 8 pixels, intuitively 2200 superpixels would be produced for each image. However, the boundary recall of SLIC which measures the fraction of the ground truth contours that fall into the eight neighbourhoods of a superpixel boudary, is only 73 %. This fact may significantly affect the first-level results of our merging strategy. Second, since [17] is unable to control the compactness of generated superpixels, our merging strategy cannot get the desired regions. More specifically, in [17], only a constant parameter is used to prevent each region from being too large. In fact, this criterion is sometimes not reasonable because of the diversity of input pictures.

Nevertheless, because of our powerful architecture, our results still outperform most existing segmentation approaches. The following parts describe the applications of our approach in both saliency detection and objectness proposal, from which one can find the practicality of our approach.

4.2 Objectness

Generic object proposal generation has been a hot topic in recent years. As a preprocessing step in many applications such as object recognition and detection, it generates a number of bounding boxes that may contain objects. This type of algorithms have been used in many existing object detection methods [43,45].

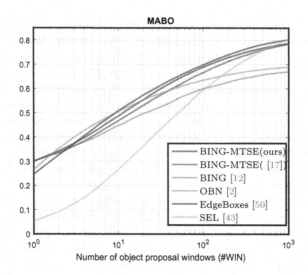

Fig. 6. Tradeoff between MABO and number of proposals using different methods on VOC2007 test set.

It has been shown that these object detection methods can perform better than the classical sliding-window-based paradigm [15, 16, 18].

As for metrics that measure the objectness approaches, we adopt mean average best overlap (MABO) across all the classes [43] and computational efficiency. Cheng *et al.* [12] recently propose a very fast method (BING), which generates box proposals at 300 fps, but this method cannot perform well on MABO benchmark. Chen *et al.* [8] propose a postprocessing approach (MTSE) to refine bounding boxes produced by objectness methods. In their algorithm, they use [17] to generate regions. In order to show the advantages of our segmentation method, we choose [8] as the postprocessing step of [12] and replace [17] with our method.

We extensively evaluate the new system on the challenging PASCAL VOC 2007 dataset [16]. To demonstrate the advantages of our system, we compare our results with some currently influential methods, including [2, 12, 43, 50]. From Fig. 6, one can find that our modified version performs better than the original one [8]. With our segmentation method, the speed has been significantly boosted. We can get competitive boxes at over 100 fps, comparing to 0.25 s per image as reported in [8]. And not only that, Fig. 6 indicates that the new system using our segmentation is one of the best objectness methods in terms of quality. As a result, our new system without doubt can make the best trade-off between efficiency and quality.

4.3 Saliency

In this part, we report the superiority of our method when it is used in another domain of computer vision. Visual saliency has been a fundamental problem in

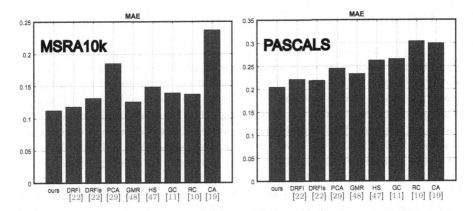

Fig. 7. Mean absolute errors of the state-of-the-art methods on MSRA10K [10] and PASCAL-S [27]. DRFIs is the single level version of DRFI, and note that our method is a single level. The proposed approach consistently achieves the lowest error rates on all datasets.

neuroscience, psychology, neural systems, and computer vision for a long time. In computer vision, detecting and segmenting salient objects in natural scenes, also known as salient object detection, has attracted a lot of focused research and has resulted in many applications. However, because most saliency detection methods are region-based, these exist two things as the bottleneck of salient object detection for a long period. First one is the segmentation quality [33] and the other is the computation efficiency. Recently, Jiang *et al.* [22] proposed a supervised learning method (DRFI) to predict a salient score of the regions produced by the popular segmentation method [17], which receives good performance on several popular datasets, such as MSRA10K [10] and PASCAL-S [27]. Here, we replace [17] with our segmentation method as a single level.

For a faithful comparison, we evaluate current popular detection methods [10, 11, 19, 22, 29, 47, 48] on several datasets mentioned above using mean absolute error(MAE) [32], which is introduced to reflect the negative saliency assignments. It is defined between a saliency map S and the binary groundtruth GT as:

$$MAE = \frac{1}{|I|} \sum_x |S(I_x) - GT(I_x)|, \tag{4}$$

where $|I|$ is the total number of pixels. The MAE results on these two datasets are shown in Fig. 7. Our method achieves the lowest MAE values on all datasets. Specifically speaking, it decreases by 0.57 % and 1.43 % over the second best algorithms in terms of MAE scores. This means that its predicted saliency pixels are closest to the ground truth.

5 Discussion

In this paper, we have proposed a hierarchical method for image segmentation. We design a hierarchical architecture to enjoy the benefits of engaging different feature setting in different scale levels. In addition, we explore the capability of modern GPUs to efficiently compute a set of simple but useful features. Our approach produces high quality hierarchical regions with substantial speed-up when compared with previous state-of-the-art works. Evaluation results on standard benchmark (BSDS500 [4]) show that our method achieves a favorable trade-off between efficiency and quality. When plugged into other computer vision tasks such as objectness and saliency detection, our method improves their performance. To encourage future works, we make the source code of this work publicly available at http://mmcheng.net/hfs/.

Acknowledgments. We would like to thank the anonymous reviewers for their useful feedbacks. This research was sponsored by NSFC (NO. 61572264), Huawei Innovation Research Program (HIRP), and CAST young talents plan.

References

1. Achanta, R., Shaji, A., Smith, K., Lucchi, A., Fua, P., Susstrunk, S.: SLIC superpixels compared to state-of-the-art superpixel methods. IEEE TPAMI **34**(11), 2274–2282 (2012)
2. Alexe, B., Deselaers, T., Ferrari, V.: Measuring the objectness of image windows. IEEE TPAMI **34**(11), 2189–2202 (2012)
3. Alpert, S., Galun, M., Brandt, A., Basri, R.: Image segmentation by probabilistic bottom-up aggregation and cue integration. IEEE TPAMI **34**(2), 315–327 (2012)
4. Arbelaez, P., Maire, M., Fowlkes, C., Malik, J.: Contour detection and hierarchical image segmentation. IEEE TPAMI **33**(5), 898–916 (2011)
5. Arbelaez, P., Pont-Tuset, J., Barron, J., Marques, F., Malik, J.: Multiscale combinatorial grouping. In: IEEE CVPR, pp. 328–335 (2014)
6. Chang, J., Wei, D., Fisher, J.W.: A video representation using temporal superpixels. In: IEEE CVPR, pp. 2051–2058 (2013)
7. Chen, T., Cheng, M.M., Tan, P., Shamir, A., Hu, S.M.: Sketch2Photo: internet image montage. ACM TOG **28**(5), 124 (2009)
8. Chen, X., Ma, H., Wang, X., Zhao, Z.: Improving object proposals with multi-thresholding straddling expansion. In: IEEE CVPR (2015)
9. Cheng, J., Liu, J., Xu, Y., Yin, F., Wong, D.W.K., Tan, N.M., Tao, D., Cheng, C.Y., Aung, T., Wong, T.Y.: Superpixel classification based optic disc and optic cup segmentation for glaucoma screening. IEEE Trans. Med. Imaging **32**(6), 1019–1032 (2013)
10. Cheng, M.M., Mitra, N.J., Huang, X., Torr, P.H., Hu, S.: Global contrast based salient region detection. IEEE TPAMI **37**(3), 569–582 (2015)
11. Cheng, M.M., Warrell, J., Lin, W.Y., Zheng, S., Vineet, V., Crook, N.: Efficient salient region detection with soft image abstraction. In: IEEE ICCV, pp. 1529–1536 (2013)
12. Cheng, M.M., Zhang, Z., Lin, W.Y., Torr, P.: Bing: binarized normed gradients for objectness estimation at 300fps. In: IEEE CVPR, pp. 3286–3293 (2014)

13. Comaniciu, D., Meer, P.: Mean shift: a robust approach toward feature space analysis. IEEE TPAMI **24**(5), 603–619 (2002)
14. Cour, T., Benezit, F., Shi, J.: Spectral segmentation with multiscale graph decomposition. In: IEEE CVPR, vol. 2, pp. 1124–1131 (2005)
15. Deng, J., Dong, W., Socher, R., Li, L.J., Li, K., Fei-Fei, L.: Imagenet: a large-scale hierarchical image database. In: IEEE CVPR, pp. 248–255 (2009)
16. Everingham, M., Van Gool, L., Williams, C.K., Winn, J., Zisserman, A.: The pascal visual object classes (VOC) challenge. IEEE ICCV **88**(2), 303–338 (2010)
17. Felzenszwalb, P.F., Huttenlocher, D.P.: Efficient graph-based image segmentation. IJCV **59**(2), 167–181 (2004)
18. Girshick, R., Donahue, J., Darrell, T., Malik, J.: Rich feature hierarchies for accurate object detection and semantic segmentation. In: IEEE CVPR, pp. 580–587 (2014)
19. Goferman, S., Zelnik-Manor, L., Tal, A.: Context-aware saliency detection. IEEE TPAMI **34**(10), 1915–1926 (2012)
20. Hoiem, D., Efros, A., Hebert, M., et al.: Geometric context from a single image. IEEE ICCV, vol. 1, pp. 654–661 (2005)
21. Hu, S.M., Zhang, F.L., Wang, M., Martin, R.R., Wang, J.: PatchNet: a patch-based image representation for interactive library-driven image editing. ACM TOG **32**(6), 196 (2013)
22. Jiang, H., Wang, J., Yuan, Z., Wu, Y., Zheng, N., Li, S.: Salient object detection: a discriminative regional feature integration approach. In: IEEE CVPR, pp. 2083–2090 (2013)
23. Jiang, Z., Davis, L.S.: Submodular salient region detection. In: IEEE CVPR, pp. 2043–2050 (2013)
24. Juneja, M., Vedaldi, A., Jawahar, C., Zisserman, A.: Blocks that shout: distinctive parts for scene classification. In: IEEE CVPR, pp. 923–930 (2013)
25. Kohli, P., Torr, P.H., et al.: Robust higher order potentials for enforcing label consistency. IJCV **82**(3), 302–324 (2009)
26. Li, K., Zhu, Y., Yang, J., Jiang, J.: Video super-resolution using an adaptive superpixel-guided auto-regressive model. Pattern Recogn. **51**, 59–71 (2016)
27. Li, Y., Hou, X., Koch, C., Rehg, J., Yuille, A.: The secrets of salient object segmentation. In: IEEE CVPR, pp. 280–287 (2014)
28. Maire, M., Yu, S.X.: Progressive multigrid eigensolvers for multiscale spectral segmentation. In: IEEE ICCV, pp. 2184–2191 (2013)
29. Margolin, R., Tal, A., Zelnik-Manor, L.: What makes a patch distinct? In: IEEE CVPR, pp. 1139–1146 (2013)
30. Martin, D.R., Fowlkes, C.C., Malik, J.: Learning to detect natural image boundaries using local brightness, color, and texture cues. IEEE TPAMI **26**(5), 530–549 (2004)
31. Nguyen, R.M., Brown, M.S.: Fast and effective l0 gradient minimization by region fusion. In: IEEE ICCV, pp. 208–216 (2015)
32. Perazzi, F., Krähenbühl, P., Pritch, Y., Hornung, A.: Saliency filters: contrast based filtering for salient region detection. In: IEEE CVPR, pp. 733–740 (2012)
33. Qi, W., Cheng, M.M., Borji, A., Lu, H., Bai, L.F.: SaliencyRank: two-stage manifold ranking for salient object detection. Comput. Vis. Media **1**(4), 309–320 (2015)
34. Ren, C.Y., Prisacariu, V.A., Reid, I.D.: gSLICr: SLIC superpixels at over 250Hz. arXiv preprint arXiv:1509.04232 (2015)
35. Ren, Z., Shakhnarovich, G.: Image segmentation by cascaded region agglomeration. In: IEEE CVPR, pp. 2011–2018 (2013)

36. Rivest, J., Cabanagh, P.: Localizing contours defined by more than one attribute. Vis. Res. **36**(1), 53–66 (1996)
37. Russell, C., Kohli, P., Torr, P.H., et al.: Associative hierarchical CRFs for object class image segmentation. In: IEEE ICCV, pp. 739–746 (2009)
38. Shi, J., Malik, J.: Normalized cuts and image segmentation. IEEE TPAMI **22**(8), 888–905 (2000)
39. Song, X., Zhang, J., Han, Y., Jiang, J.: Semi-supervised feature selection via hierarchical regression for web image classification. Multimedia Syst. **22**(1), 41–49 (2016)
40. Storath, M., Weinmann, A.: Fast partitioning of vector-valued images. SIAM J. Imaging Sci. **7**(3), 1826–1852 (2014)
41. Sun, J., Ponce, J.: Learning discriminative part detectors for image classification and cosegmentation. In: IEEE ICCV, pp. 3400–3407 (2013)
42. Taylor, C.J.: Towards fast and accurate segmentation. In: IEEE CVPR, pp. 1916–1922 (2013)
43. Uijlings, J.R., van de Sande, K.E., Gevers, T., Smeulders, A.W.: Selective search for object recognition. IJCV **104**(2), 154–171 (2013)
44. Wang, S., Lu, H., Yang, F., Yang, M.H.: Superpixel tracking. In: IEEE ICCV, pp. 1323–1330 (2011)
45. Wang, X., Yang, M., Zhu, S., Lin, Y.: Regionlets for generic object detection. In: IEEE ICCV, pp. 17–24 (2013)
46. Xie, S., Tu, Z.: Holistically-nested edge detection. In: IEEE ICCV, pp. 1395–1403 (2015)
47. Yan, Q., Xu, L., Shi, J., Jia, J.: Hierarchical saliency detection. In: IEEE CVPR, pp. 1155–1162 (2013)
48. Yang, C., Zhang, L., Lu, H., Ruan, X., Yang, M.H.: Saliency detection via graph-based manifold ranking. In: IEEE CVPR, pp. 3166–3173 (2013)
49. Zhang, L., Gao, Y., Xia, Y., Lu, K., Shen, J., Ji, R.: Representative discovery of structure cues for weakly-supervised image segmentation. IEEE Trans. Multimedia **16**(2), 470–479 (2014)
50. Zitnick, C.L., Dollár, P.: Edge boxes: locating object proposals from edges. In: Fleet, D., Pajdla, T., Schiele, B., Tuytelaars, T. (eds.) ECCV 2014, Part V. LNCS, vol. 8693, pp. 391–405. Springer, Heidelberg (2014)

Author Index